"The figure a poem makes. It begins in delight and ends in wisdom."
– Robert Frost

"The sonnet defends itself against the vicissitudes of fortune by its charmed structure, its beautiful bubble. All the while, though, chaos is lurking outside the gate."
– Rita Dove

"What is poetry? It is the human soul entire, squeezed like a lemon or a lime, drop by drop, into atomic words."
– Langston Hughes

"Poetry. . . makes immortal all that is best and most beautiful in the world."
– Percy Bysshe Shelley

"The poet's mission on earth is to inspire and to illuminate; and to leave behind to our glorious descendants an intricate and varied map of humanity."
– Marilyn Chin

"If I read a book and it makes my whole body so cold no fire can ever warm me, I know that it is poetry. If I feel physically as if the top of my head were taken off, I know that it is poetry. These are the only ways I know it. Is there any other way?"
– Emily Dickinson

poetry

drama

". . . the purpose of playing, whose end, both at the first and now, was and is to hold as 'twere the mirror up to nature, to show virtue her own feature, scorn her own image, and the very age and body of the time his form and pressure."
– William Shakespeare

"My task has been the description of humanity."
– Henrik Ibsen

"I believe, for myself, that the lasting appeal of tragedy is due to our need to face the fact of death in order to strengthen ourselves for life."
– Arthur Miller

"Man, as set down in the plays, is large. Enormous. Capable of anything at all. And yet fragile, too, this view of the human spirit; one feels it ought to be respected and protected and loved rather fiercely."
— Lorraine Hansberry

"Writing really helps you heal yourself. That is, if you write what you need to write, as opposed to what will make money, or what will make fame."
– Alice Walker

"Writers don't need tricks or gimmicks or even necessarily need to be the smartest fellows on the block. At the risk of appearing foolish, a writer sometimes needs to be able to just stand and gape at this or that thing — a sunset or an old shoe — in absolute and simple amazement."
– Raymond Carver

"One writes out of one thing only — one's own experience. Everything depends on how relentlessly one forces from this experience the last drop, sweet or bitter, it can possibly give. This is the only real concern of the artist, to recreate out of the disorder of life that order which is art."
– James Baldwin

"To learn to write is to learn to have ideas."
– Robert Frost

writing

Praise for Previous Editions of
LITERATURE AND ITS WRITERS

"Not only do I find *Literature and Its Writers* to be an excellent instructional text, but I also feel that my students are spending a semester with a literary gold mine. Many of them discover this and read far more selections than are assigned for the course."

–JANE WHORTON, *Pearl River Community College*

"I find everything about *Literature and Its Writers* appealing. No other introduction to literature text works so well to bring literature to life. The selection of literature in all three genres is dazzling. The emphasis on writer commentaries helps personalize selections for students, which in turn helps create enthusiasm. The Conversations units are a *great* feature. It's the best compact introduction to literature text available."

–JIM LYDDANE, *Mohave Community College*

"I find the selections tremendously stimulating—the variety is incredible."

–TOM ZANIELLO, *Northern Kentucky University*

"I love your commentaries. I've never seen that kind of commitment to hearing what the writers themselves have to say about writing and their own work in a student's text. It's a great idea and one I enjoy using with my classes!"

–ELIZABETH FLORES, *College of Lake County*

"I use the author commentaries to raise issues of intention versus other kinds of meaning, the critical commentaries to provide springboards for arguments, and other kinds of commentaries to provide social, historical, and intellectual contexts. These are wonderfully useful!"

–WES CHAPMAN, *Illinois Wesleyan University*

"Writing about literature is always the stumbling block in introductory classes, and the writing instruction here is among the best, most well written, and certainly the most student-friendly available."

–JONATHAN N. BARRON, *University of Southern Mississippi*

LITERATURE AND ITS WRITERS

An Introduction to Fiction, Poetry, and Drama

◆ Some Books Written or Edited by Ann Charters

The Story and Its Writer: An Introduction to Short Fiction
The American Short Story and Its Writer: An Anthology
Major Writers of Short Fiction: Stories and Commentaries
Beats & Company: Portrait of a Literary Generation
Kerouac: A Biography
The Portable Beat Reader
The Portable Jack Kerouac
The Portable Sixties Reader
Selected Letters of Jack Kerouac, 1940–1956
Selected Letters of Jack Kerouac, 1957–1969
Nobody: The Story of Bert Williams

◆ Some Books Written by Samuel Charters

Walking a Blues Road—Selected Prose
New Orleans: Playing a Jazz Chorus
A Trumpet Around the Corner: The Story of New Orleans Jazz
A Language of Song
Some Poems/Poets: Studies in American Underground Poetry
Elvis Presley Calls His Mother After the Ed Sullivan Show
Mr. Jabi and Mr. Smythe
Jelly Roll Morton's Last Night at the Jungle Inn: An Imaginary Memoir
Louisiana Black: A Novel
A Country Year: A Chronicle
From a Swedish Notebook
Robert Johnson
Sweet as the Showers of Rain
The Country Blues
The Day Is So Long and the Wages So Small: Music on a Summer Island
The Legacy of the Blues: A Glimpse into the Art and the Lives of Twelve Great Bluesmen
The Roots of the Blues: An African Search
The Bluesmen: The Story and the Music of the Men Who Made the Blues

◆ Books Written by Ann Charters and Samuel Charters

I Love: The Story of Vladimir Mayakovsky and Lili Brik
Blues Faces
Brother-Souls: John Clellon Holmes, Jack Kerouac, and the Beat Generation

◆ Collaborations by Ann Charters and Samuel Charters

Baltics by Tomas Tranströmer—translation by Samuel Charters and photographs by Ann Charters

Sixth Edition

LITERATURE AND ITS WRITERS

An Introduction to Fiction, Poetry, and Drama

Ann Charters
UNIVERSITY OF CONNECTICUT

Samuel Charters

BEDFORD / ST. MARTIN'S
Boston ◆ New York

For Bedford/St. Martin's

Senior Executive Editor: Stephen A. Scipione
Developmental Editor: Deja Earley
Senior Production Editor: Lori Chong Roncka
Assistant Production Manager: Joe Ford
Marketing Manager: Stacey Propps
Editorial Assistant: Regina Tavani
Production Assistants: Laura Winstead and Elise Keller
Copy Editor: Lisa Wehrle
Indexer: Anne Holmes, EdIndex
Photo Researcher: Connie Gardner
Permissions Manager: Kalina K. Ingham
Text Design: Anna Palchik, with additional design by Glenna Collett
Cover Design: Marine Miller
Composition: Jouve
Printing and Binding: Quad/Graphics

President, Bedford/St. Martin's: Denise B. Wydra
Presidents, Macmillan Higher Education: Joan E. Feinberg and Tom Scotty
Editor in Chief: Karen S. Henry
Director of Marketing: Karen R. Soeltz
Production Director: Susan W. Brown
Associate Production Director: Elise S. Kaiser
Managing Editor: Elizabeth M. Schaaf

Library of Congress Control Number: 2012935587

Manufactured in the United States of America.

7 6 5 4 3
f e d c b

For information, write: Bedford/St. Martin's, 75 Arlington Street, Boston, MA 02116 (617-399-4000)

ISBN 978-1-4576-0647-2

On the Cover: ZZ Packer uses her laptop in the Frank Conroy Reading Room during the Iowa Writers' Workshop 75th Anniversary Reunion at the University of Iowa on June 11, 2011. (*Photo by Tony Avelar/The Christian Science Monitor via Getty Images*)

Acknowledgments

Acknowledgments and copyrights appear at the back of the book on pages 1700–1714, which constitute an extension of the copyright page. It is a violation of the law to reproduce these selections by any means whatsoever without the written permission of the copyright holder.

Preface for Instructors

Introductory literature anthologies are designed to help students explore the many ways to read, think, and write about literature. This is what *Literature and Its Writers* does, but with an important difference: As much as possible, it lets the words of writers themselves—the storytellers, the poets, the dramatists whose works appear in the anthology—lead the exploration. Students are encouraged to recognize that the writers are in conversation about literature, its making and its meanings, its purpose and importance—and that they, too, can join the conversation through reading, discussing, and writing.

A DISTINCTIVE EMPHASIS ON WRITERS AND WRITING

Writers, we believe, provide invaluable perspectives on the literature they create. Accordingly, *Literature and Its Writers* is threaded with writer talk: with quotations that clarify, with examples that enlighten, and especially with *commentaries* that show how writers think and write about literature. We have found that students respond readily to these voices in the text. They are more willing to raise their own voices to enter the conversation. They listen more attentively to what is being said. They express themselves more confidently. Having before them examples of writers speaking plainly, or colorfully, or profoundly, or provokingly, they are better able to speak and write that way themselves. Through the weave of literary works and literary voices, students comprehend what a human enterprise literature is—the work of talented individuals like themselves. Not only do students explore *what* and *how* literature means—interpretation and analysis—but they also explore two fundamental questions about it: How is it made, and how is it related to us?

In our anthology, some sixty-five stories, three hundred poems, and ten full-length plays are complemented by more than one hundred commentaries that discuss specific literary works, literary form and influence, and the creative process. Students encounter not only "A Rose for Emily," but also what William Faulkner had to say about his famous story; not just the poetry of Emily Dickinson, but also Dickinson's remarks about her poetry in letters to Thomas Wentworth Higginson; not just Lorraine Hansberry's *A Raisin in the Sun*, but also Hansberry's tribute to William Shakespeare. The commentaries present countless opportunities for discussion and writing, as well as models of how writers think, read, and write about literature. But the focus on writers does not stop with the commentaries. Words of the writers themselves are interwoven throughout the uncommonly full biographical headnotes for individual authors, and in our definitions and discussions of the traditional elements of literary genres. Students hear from Flannery O'Connor on character, Robert Frost on rhyme, and Arthur Miller on playwriting.

HOW THE BOOK IS ORGANIZED

After a brief introduction that shows students connecting with literature, *Literature and Its Writers* is divided into four parts. Parts One, Two, and Three are devoted, respectively, to short fiction, to poetry, and to drama. Within each of these parts, introductory chapters discuss the genre, its elements, and how to read, think, and write about a work in a particular genre. Then comes the literature. Fiction is represented by the fullest selection available in a book of this scope, and is arranged alphabetically by author for teaching flexibility. A rich array of poems has been selected and organized to enable a variety of approaches to teaching poetry—through literary elements, themes, and individual poets. The chronologically arranged plays are some of the most widely taught works from the days of ancient Greece to contemporary America.

Within each of these three parts, the literary works are accompanied by commentaries which illuminate them. In every genre, important writers are discussed in depth through multiple commentaries. Although the commentaries mainly present the remarks of the writers themselves, they also include some examples of contemporary literary criticism, varieties of which are discussed in detail in Part Four, Writing about Literature. We've also identified teachable pairings of stories, poems, and plays within the table of contents and the book itself—look for the word "Connection," which identifies these tested and fruitful pairings.

Part Four is devoted to all aspects of reading and writing, and to understanding literary theory. Chapter 26 introduces students to important schools of literary theory and refers to commentaries throughout the book as examples of each critical approach. Chapters 27, 28, and 29 walk students through the process of writing an essay about literature, from journal keeping to revising; provide tips on writing basic types of literary papers with model student essays; and include an extensive up-to-date section on writing the research paper with step-by-step guidelines for finding a topic, evaluating online sources, drafting the paper, and documenting sources. Altogether, Part Four includes five student papers that provide realistic models for writing different types of essays.

NEW TO THIS EDITION

Over a third of the stories, poems, and plays are new. In choosing the literature, we have tried to balance the classic, the current, and the unusual. In the fiction section, twenty-two new selections include Lydia Davis's introspective "Blind Date," David Foster Wallace's brief, evocative "Everything Is Green," and Daniel Orozco's tale of workplace alienation, "Orientation." In the poetry section, the more than one hundred new poems include work by popular, classic, and contemporary poets from Ezra Pound and Christina Rossetti to Anne Sexton and Gwendolyn Brooks, side by side with less often anthologized but influential poets such as Amy Lowell, Jean Toomer, and Judith Ortiz Cofer, along with quirky, engaging outsider voices including Ann Menebroker and Gerald Locklin. New to the drama section are William Shakespeare's timeless *A Midsummer Night's Dream* and Edwin Sanchez's fresh monologue, *Pops*.

Enhanced coverage of reading and writing. In each genre, we've added more detailed instruction on literary elements, paired with brief and teachable literary examples, critical thinking questions, writing ideas, and useful terms to remember, all geared to help students read deeply and write meaningfully about what they read. While you'll still find most of our discussion questions and selection-specific writing suggestions in the instructor's manual, we're confident that the critical thinking questions and writing prompts, paired with effective literary examples, introduce students into the conversation and prepare them to model deep reading and thinking in the literature to follow. For example, the new instruction on plot includes Raymond Carver's brief and gritty "Popular Mechanics" and Alasdair Gray's compact and strange "Pillow Talk." By drawing on these two stories and equipping students with illuminating questions, the concept of plot is elucidated, offering students a way to seek out and articulate their own ideas about plot in other contexts and stories.

New unique casebook on 2011 Nobel laureate Tomas Tranströmer. A new conversation mixing poetry and commentary by poets and translators offers students the opportunity to go where no other introductory literature anthology has gone: into the world of the renowned and relevant work of the 2011 Nobel laureate, Tomas Tranströmer. As Tranströmer is a longtime friend of ours, we were able to draw on decades of conversation and collaboration in order to introduce students to this international literary conversation. We've included everything from a book review by Helen Vendler, which offers a psychological reading of his poetry, to a draft translation of one of Tranströmer's poems, complete with his own markings and corrections. You won't find a casebook like this—which explores Tranströmer's meditative, condensed poems with an insider's eye—in any other literature anthology.

A more convenient organization of the commentaries. Most commentaries now follow directly after the literature they discuss, allowing students to pursue their interest immediately into a deeper discussion of the work, and allowing for convenient access during class discussion. For each work followed by a commentary, we now include author photos in order to provide students with a more personal sense of the authors.

Literature and Its Writers *now comes with free videos.* Invite today's best writers into your class and let your students join the conversation. With *VideoCentral: Literature*, Bedford/St. Martin's growing collection of video interviews, your students can view conversations with Ha Jin, Chitra Banerjee Divakaruni, Anne Rice, and other important writers. Have your students watch Ha Jin talk about how he creates the inner life of characters, then tie it back to your discussion of his story, "Saboteur." By responding to the videos, your students truly enter conversations with contemporary writers. Please see page xiv for information about how to order the student edition of *Literature and Its Writers,* packaged with access to *VideoCentral: Literature*.

ACKNOWLEDGMENTS

In this sixth edition, we would like to acknowledge the steadfast support of the co-president of Macmillan Higher Education and former president of Bedford/St. Martin's, Joan Feinberg. We'd also like to thank president emeritus Charles Christensen, who originally came to us with the idea for this anthology, and the now-president of Bedford/St. Martin's, Denise Wydra. In shaping the direction of the book, we worked closely with senior executive editor Steve Scipione, who was assisted by developmental editor Deja Earley and editorial assistant Regina Tavani. Editor in chief Karen Henry and senior editor Maura Shea (who developed earlier editions of the book) were sources of ideas and inspiration. Our patient production editor Lori Chong Roncka attentively saw the book and the instructor's manual through the production process. We appreciate the enthusiasm and hard work of our marketing manager, Stacey Propps. We thank Caryn Burtt for her careful attention to the text permissions process, and Connie Gardner for her efficient and successful work with photo permissions. We are grateful to Herbert Lederer, Emeritus Professor of German at the University of Connecticut in Storrs, for serving as an experienced and knowledgeable consultant for the translation of the Kafka stories into American English, and to Kurt Fendt of MIT, for double-checking the translations and offering good advice. In the English Department at the University of Connecticut in Storrs, Professors Tom Roberts and Margaret Higonnet were kind enough to read a draft of the essay "Translating Kafka" and offer helpful suggestions for revision. Thanks to Henry Denander and Kamini Press for introducing us to today's chapbook poets. We thank Janet Gardner, formerly of the University of Massachusetts, Dartmouth, and Barbara Fister of Gustavus Adolphus College, who helped write the chapter on the research paper, and Barbara Flanagan, who updated the MLA citation information. For assistance with the instructor's manual, we are grateful to Susan Abbotson of the University of Connecticut, who wrote many of the entries in the drama section, and William Sheidley of the University of Southern Colorado, who wrote many of the entries in the fiction section.

In addition, professors who used the previous edition or editions of the anthology and generously took time to share their ideas about it include: Jessica Anthony, University of Southern Maine; Lawrence Barkley, Mt. San Jacinto College; Carolyn Barr, Broward Community College; Jonathan N. Barron, University of Southern Mississippi; Carole E. Barrowman, Alverno College;

Chris Beyers, Assumption College; William O. Boggs, Slippery Rock University of Pennsylvania; Deborah J. Brown, University of Central Oklahoma; Yvonne Bruce, The Citadel; Beth Brunk-Chavez, James Madison University; Mike Bove, Southern Maine Community College; Imogene Bunch, Newport University; Jennifer Campbell, Erie Community College North Campus; Kevin Cantwell, Macon State College; Evelyn Cartright, Barry University; Christine Caver, The University of Texas at San Antonio; Wes Chapman, Illinois Wesleyan University; Alice Church, Nashville State Technical Institute; Mary Coffman, Silver Creek High School; Laurie Coleman, San Antonio College; Robert Conklin, DeVry University; Keisha Cosand, Golden West College; Kelly Crawley, McDowell Technical Community College; Thomas Croak, William Rainey Harper College; Tracey Cummings, Lock Haven University; Marilynn Davis, Central Wyoming College–Jackson; Anne Dennis, Mohave Community College; Amy DiBello, College of the Desert; Jennifer Dorhauer, River Parishes Community College; Paul Edwards, Northwestern University; Sam Eisenstein, Los Angeles City College; Charlene Engleking, Lindenwood University; Patty Fairbanks, Northern Kentucky University; Michael Falter, Santa Fe Community College; Tyler Farrell, University of Wisconsin–Milwaukee; Philip Fishman, Barry University; Tracy Floreani, Baker University; Andy Fogle, George Mason University; John Christopher Frongillo, University of Central Florida; Scott D. Gilbert, Winthrop University; Billye Givens, Eastern Oklahoma State College; Lanell Gonzales, Tarleton State University; Beth Graham, Campbellsville University; Allen Grove, Alfred University; Paul Gustafson, George Mason University; Jean E. Hakes, Georgia Perimeter College; Thomas Harrison, Macon State College; Jennifer Ho, University of North Carolina–Chapel Hill; Tom Hooper, Bunker Hill Community College; Carol Johnson, Tulsa Community College; Linda A. Julian, Furman University; Robert Kelly, Macon State College; Pamela Kenley-Meschino, Portland State University; Lilian Klipsch, Vincennes University; Jeff Kosse, Iowa Western Community College; Marcela Kostihova, Hamline University; Keith Kroll, Kalamazoo Valley Community College; Cynthia Kuhn, Metro State; David C. Lowery, Jones County Junior College; Jim Lyddane, Mohave Community College; Judy Marnin, Iowa Western Community College; Daphne Matthews, Mississippi Delta Community College; Michael McAllister, Iowa Western Community College; Robert McIlvaine, Slippery Rock University of Pennsylvania; Agnetta Mendoza, Nashville State Community College; Nils Michals, Solano Community College and West Valley College; Lamont Missick, Barry University; Jacqueline Mohlman, Broward Community College; Sharon Morgan, Brigham Young University–Idaho; Joyce Morison, Miami University; John Morsellino, Niagara County Community College; Patrick Naick, University of Iowa; Jefferson Navicky, Southern Maine Community College; William Neal, Campbellsville University; Randy F. Nelson, Davidson College; Perry S. Nicholas, Erie Community College; Kelly M. Nims, Baruch College; Douglas A. Northrop, Ripon College; Maria Orban, Fayetteville State University; Donna Packer-Kinlaw, University of North Carolina–Wilmington; Ashley Paydo, San Antonio College; Robin Petrovic, University of Illinois Chicago; Jessica Powers, Skyline College; Janice Porth, Northern Kentucky University;

Donna Potratz, Miracosta College; Jessica Powers, Doña Ana Branch Community College; J. Andrew Prall, University of Denver; Dennis W. Radford, Assumption College; Steven J. Rayshick, Quinsigamond Community College; Catherine Rogers, Savannah State University; SueAnn Schatz, Lock Haven University; Linda Schmidt, Iowa Western Community College; Harsh Sharma, Niagara County Community College; Michele Sharp, East Carolina University; James Shea, Columbia College Chicago; Carolyn Sigler, University of Minnesota–Duluth; Michele Singletary, Nashville State Community College; David R. Stankiewicz, Southern Maine Community College; Virginia L. Stein, Community College of Allegheny County; Marva Stewart, Paine College; Lori A. Stoltz, Rochester Community College; Renee Swindle, Solano Community College; Alisa Thomas, Toccoa Falls College; Anthony Turner, George C. Wallace State Community College; Robert Vettese, Southern Maine Community College; Leanne Warshauer, Suffolk County Community College; Eleanor Whitaker, Fairfield University; Don T. Williamson, Baker University and Cowley College; Martha Willoughby, Pearl River Community College; Meredith Wilson, Solano Community College; Karen Wunsch, Queensborough Community College; Monica M. Young-Zook, Macon State College; and Ken Zahrt, Muskegon Community College.

Ann Charters
University of Connecticut

Samuel Charters

You Get More Resources for *Literature and Its Writers*

Literature and Its Writers doesn't stop with a book. Online, you'll find both free and affordable premium resources to help students get even more out of the book and your course. You'll also find convenient instructor resources. To learn more about or order any of the products below, contact your Bedford/St. Martin's sales representative, e-mail sales support (sales_support@bfwpub.com), or visit the Web site at **bedfordstmartins.com/charters/catalog**.

Literature and Its Writers Now Comes with Free Videos

Bring today's best writers into your classroom. *VideoCentral: Literature,* our growing library of more than fifty video interviews with today's writers, includes Ha Jin on how he uses humor, Chitra Banerjee Divakaruni on how she writes from experience, and T. C. Boyle on how he works with language and style. Biographical notes and questions make each video an assignable module. See **bedfordstmartins.com/videolit/catalog**.

This resource can be packaged for free with new student editions of this book. An activation code is required and must be purchased. To order *VideoCentral: Literature* with this print text, use **ISBN 978-1-4576-3117-7**.

Visit *Re:Writing for Literature*

bedfordstmartins.com/rewritinglit

Supplement your print text with our free and open resources for literature (no codes required) and flexible premium content.

Get free online help for your students. *Re:Writing for Literature* provides close reading help, reference materials, and support for working with sources.

- ***VirtuaLit*** tutorials for close reading (fiction, poetry, and drama)
- ***AuthorLinks*** and biographies for more than 800 authors
- **Glossary** of literary terms
- **MLA-style student papers**
- **Help for finding and citing sources**, including access to Diana Hacker's *Research and Documentation* online

Get teaching ideas you can use today. Are you looking for professional resources for teaching literature and writing? How about some help with planning classroom activities?

- **Instructor's Manual.** *Resources for Teaching Literature and Its Writers*, Sixth Edition, presents a wide range of teaching resources including essays that offer interpretations of individual works to explore in the classroom, selected bibliographies for many writers, questions to prompt student discussion, topics for writing, an extensive list of audiovisual resources, and a thematic table of contents. In addition to the print version, the manual is also available online from the catalog page: **bedfordstmartins.com/charters/catalog**.
- ***Teaching Central.*** We've gathered all of our print and online professional resources in one place. You'll find landmark reference works, sourcebooks on pedagogical issues, award-winning collections, and practical advice for the classroom—all free for instructors and available at **bedfordstmartins.com/teachingcentral**.
- ***LitBits* Blog: Ideas for Teaching Literature and Creative Writing.** Our new *LitBits* blog—hosted by a growing team of instructors, poets, novelists, and scholars—offers a fresh, regularly updated collection of ideas and assignments. You'll find simple ways to teach with new media, excite your students with activities, and join an ongoing conversation about teaching. Go to **bedfordstmartins.com/litbits/catalog** and **bedfordstmartins.com/litbits.**

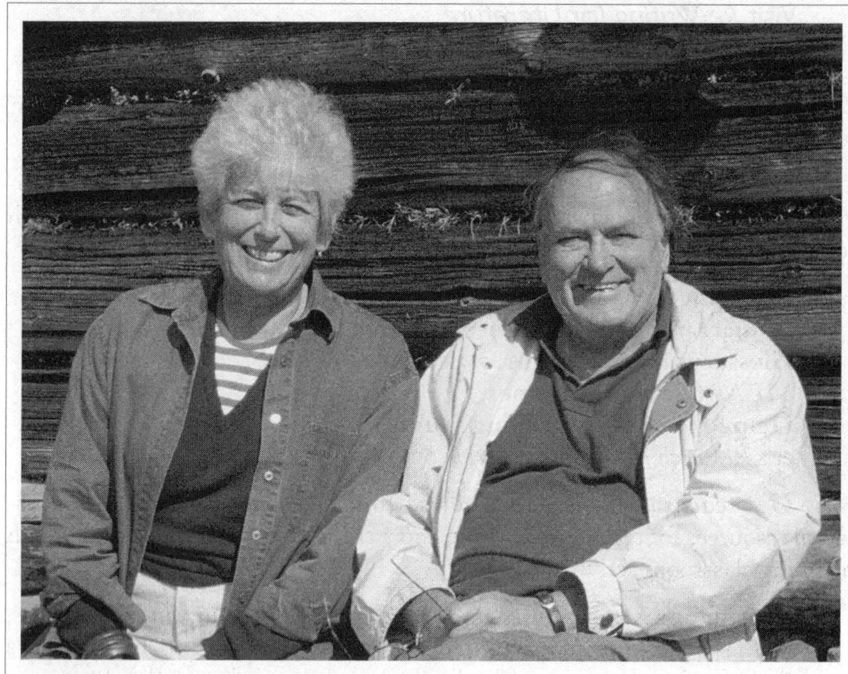
(Photo by Reenie Barrow)

ABOUT THE EDITORS

Ann Charters (Ph.D., Columbia University) is the editor of *The Story and Its Writer*, Eighth Edition (Bedford/St. Martin's, 2011), the best-selling introduction to fiction. She is a professor emeritus of English at the University of Connecticut and has taught introduction to literature courses for many years. A preeminent authority on the Beat writers, Charters has written a critically acclaimed biography of Jack Kerouac; compiled *Beats & Company*, a collection of her own photographs of Beat writers; and edited the best-selling *Portable Beat Reader*. Some recent books are *The Kerouac Reader*; *Selected Letters of Jack Kerouac, 1957–1969*; *Beat Down to Your Soul*; *The Portable Sixties Reader*; and *The American Short Story and Its Writer* (Bedford/St. Martin's, 2000).

Samuel Charters has taught creative writing and published widely in a variety of genres, including eleven books of poetry, four novels, a book of criticism on contemporary American poetry, two biographies (co-authored with Ann Charters), and translations of the poetry of Tomas Tranströmer and Edith Södergran. An ethnomusicologist, he produces blues and jazz recordings and has published many books about music, among them histories of New York and New Orleans jazz and a study of Robert Johnson.

Brief Contents

Preface for Instructors *ix*
Introduction: Connecting with Literature *1*

Part One ◆ FICTION *7*

1. What Is a Short Story? *9*
2. Reading, Thinking, and Writing about Short Fiction *14*
3. Plot and Point of View *25*
4. Character and Setting *40*
5. Style and Theme *57*
6. Stories and Storytellers *79*
7. Conversations on Stories and Storytellers: Flannery O'Connor and Edgar Allan Poe *636*

Part Two ◆ POETRY *667*

8. What Is a Poem? *669*
9. Reading, Thinking, and Writing about Poetry *681*
10. Rhyme *693*
11. Poetic Meter *713*
12. The Meaning of Words *726*

13. Traditional Forms *746*
14. Other Forms of Poetry *793*
15. Poets Respond to Other Poets *823*
16. Poets and Their Worlds: Emily Dickinson, Robert Frost, and Langston Hughes *836*
17. A Poet in the World Today: Tomas Tranströmer *908*
18. Poems and Poets *925*
19. Themes for Thinking and Writing about Poetry *1030*
20. Contemporary Movements in Poetry *1068*

Part Three ◆ DRAMA *1091*

21. What Is a Play? *1093*
22. Reading, Thinking, and Writing about Drama *1101*
23. The Elements of Drama *1110*
24. Plays and Playwrights *1126*
25. Conversation on *Hamlet* as Text and Performance *1592*

Part Four ◆ WRITING ABOUT LITERATURE *1611*

26. Critical Reading and Literary Theory *1613*
27. Using the Writing Process to Develop Your Paper *1623*
28. Basic Types of Literary Papers *1642*
29. Writing Research Papers *1654*

Glossary of Literary Terms *1685*
Index of First Lines *1715*
Index of Authors and Titles *1721*

For a list of resources on reading and writing about literature, see the inside back cover.

Contents

Preface for Instructors *ix*

Introduction: Connecting with Literature *1*

SAMPLE PAPER: *Raymond Carver's "Creative Writing 101"* *2*

Reading Literature *3*

Thinking and Writing about Literature *4*

Part One ◆ FICTION 7

1. What Is a Short Story? *9*

Old Testament, *The Judgment of King Solomon* *9*

Grace Paley, *Samuel* *11*

CONNECTIONS: Grace Paley, *A Conversation with My Father, 532*; Grace Paley, *A Conversation with Ann Charters, 536*

2. Reading, Thinking, and Writing about Short Fiction *14*

Close Reading Short Fiction *15*

◆ Guidelines for Reading Fiction *16*

Sample Close Reading: Grace Paley, *Samuel* *17*

Critical Thinking about Short Fiction *19*

Writing about Short Fiction *20*
SAMPLE PAPER: *Grace Paley's Commentary and "Samuel"* *21*
Other Resources to Help Your Writing *22*
SAMPLE PAPER: *Grace Paley's Point of View in "Samuel"* *23*

3. Plot and Point of View *25*

Plot *25*
Plot Summary *27*
Raymond Carver, *Popular Mechanics* *28*
◆ Questions for Critical Thinking about Plot *29*
◆ Topics for Writing about Plot *30*
Alasdair Gray, *Pillow Talk* *30*
Point of View *32*
Herta Müller, *Workday* *32*
First-Person Narration *33*
Third-Person Narration *34*
Dagoberto Gilb, *Love in L.A.* *35*
◆ Questions for Critical Thinking about Point of View *37*
◆ Topics for Writing about Point of View *37*
◆ Useful Terms to Remember *38*

4. Character and Setting *40*

Character *40*
Roberto Bolaño, *Jim* *42*
◆ Questions for Critical Thinking about Character *43*
◆ Topics for Writing about Character *43*
Jamaica Kincaid, *Girl* *44*
Setting *45*
Daniel Orozco, *Orientation* *46*
◆ Questions for Critical Thinking about Setting *50*
◆ Topics for Writing about Setting *50*
Gabriel García Márquez, *A Very Old Man with Enormous Wings* *51*
◆ Useful Terms to Remember *55*

5. Style and Theme *57*

Style *57*
David Foster Wallace, *Everything Is Green* *58*
Lydia Davis, *Blind Date* *59*

Voice 62

Tone 62

Irony 63

Symbol 63

Franz Kafka, *I Wish I Were a Red Indian* 64

Yasunari Kawabata, *The Grasshopper and the Bell Cricket* 65

◆ Questions for Critical Thinking about Style 68

◆ Topics for Writing about Style 68

Theme 68

Interpreting the Theme of a Story 70

Naguib Mahfouz, *Half a Day* 71

Rosario Morales, *The Day It Happened* 73

◆ Questions for Critical Thinking about Theme 76

◆ Topics for Writing about Theme 77

◆ Useful Terms to Remember 77

6. Stories and Storytellers 79

Sherman Alexie

The Lone Ranger and Tonto Fistfight in Heaven 80

COMMENTARY

Sherman Alexie, *Superman and Me* 85

Dorothy Allison

Jason Who Will Be Famous 88

Margaret Atwood

Happy Endings 95

James Baldwin

Sonny's Blues 99

COMMENTARY

James Baldwin, *Autobiographical Notes* 121

Toni Cade Bambara

The Lesson 126

José Antonio Burciaga

La Puerta 132

Raymond Carver

Cathedral 137

COMMENTARIES

Raymond Carver, *On Writing* 148

Raymond Carver, *Creative Writing 101* 151
CONNECTION: Raymond Carver, *Popular Mechanics, 28*

Anton Chekhov
The Lady with the Pet Dog 156
COMMENTARY
Anton Chekhov, *Technique in Writing the Short Story* 168
CONNECTION: Joyce Carol Oates, *The Lady with the Pet Dog, 439*

Kate Chopin
Désirée's Baby 170
The Story of an Hour 174
COMMENTARY
Kate Chopin, *How I Stumbled upon Maupassant* 176

Stephen Crane
The Open Boat 178
COMMENTARY
Stephen Crane, *The Sinking of the* Commodore 196

Junot Díaz
How to Date a Browngirl, Blackgirl, Whitegirl, or Halfie 200

Ralph Ellison
Battle Royal 204
COMMENTARY
Ralph Ellison, *The Influence of Folklore on "Battle Royal"* 214

William Faulkner
A Rose for Emily 217
COMMENTARY
William Faulkner, *The Meaning of "A Rose for Emily"* 224

Charlotte Perkins Gilman
The Yellow Wallpaper 226
COMMENTARIES
Charlotte Perkins Gilman, *Undergoing the Cure for Nervous Prostration* 238
Sandra M. Gilbert and Susan Gubar, *A Feminist Reading of Gilman's "The Yellow Wallpaper"* 240

Susan Glaspell
A Jury of Her Peers 243
COMMENTARY
Elaine Showalter, *On Glaspell's "A Jury of Her Peers"* 258

CONNECTIONS: Susan Glaspell, *Trifles, 1410*; Leonard Mustazza, *Generic Translation and Thematic Shifts in Glaspell's* Trifles *and "A Jury of Her Peers," 1420*; Lynn Nottage, *POOF!, 1582*

Nathaniel Hawthorne
Young Goodman Brown 261
COMMENTARY
Herman Melville, *Blackness in Hawthorne's "Young Goodman Brown"* 271
CONNECTION: Edgar Allan Poe, *The Importance of the Single Effect in a Prose Tale, 650*

Ernest Hemingway
Hills Like White Elephants 273

Zora Neale Hurston
Sweat 278
COMMENTARY
Zora Neale Hurston, *How It Feels to Be Colored Me* 286
CONNECTION: Alice Walker, *Zora Neale Hurston: A Cautionary Tale and a Partisan View, 616*

Shirley Jackson
The Lottery 290
COMMENTARY
Shirley Jackson, *The Morning of June 28, 1948, and "The Lottery"* 297

Sarah Orne Jewett
A White Heron 300

Ha Jin
Saboteur 308

James Joyce
Araby 317
CONNECTION: John Updike, *A & P, 599*

Franz Kafka
A Hunger Artist 322
COMMENTARY
R. Crumb and David Zane Mairowitz, *A Hunger Artist* 330
The Metamorphosis 340
COMMENTARY
Gustav Janouch, *Kafka's View of "The Metamorphosis"* 373
CONNECTION: Franz Kafka, *I Wish I Were a Red Indian, 64*

D. H. Lawrence
The Rocking-Horse Winner 375
CONNECTION: D. H. Lawrence, *On "The Fall of the House of Usher" and "The Cask of Amontillado," 653*

Jack London
To Build a Fire 387

Guy de Maupassant
The Necklace 399
CONNECTION: Kate Chopin, *How I Stumbled upon Maupassant, 176*

Herman Melville
Bartleby, the Scrivener 406
CONNECTION: Herman Melville, *Blackness in Hawthorne's "Young Goodman Brown," 271*

Lorrie Moore
How to Become a Writer 433

Joyce Carol Oates
The Lady with the Pet Dog 439
Where Are You Going, Where Have You Been? 452
COMMENTARY
Joyce Carol Oates, Smooth Talk: *Short Story into Film* 464
CONNECTION: Anton Chekhov, *The Lady with the Pet Dog, 156*

Tim O'Brien
The Things They Carried 468
COMMENTARY
Bobbie Ann Mason, *On Tim O'Brien's "The Things They Carried"* 481

Flannery O'Connor
Good Country People 483
A Good Man Is Hard to Find 497
CONNECTIONS: Flannery O'Connor, *From* Letters, 1954–55, *636; Writing Short Stories, 639; The Element of Suspense in "A Good Man Is Hard to Find," 644*; Sally Fitzgerald, *Southern Sources of "A Good Man Is Hard to Find," 647*

Tillie Olsen
I Stand Here Ironing 509

ZZ Packer
Brownies 516

Grace Paley
A Conversation with My Father 532

COMMENTARY
Grace Paley, *A Conversation with Ann Charters* 536
CONNECTION: Grace Paley, *Samuel, 11*

Luigi Pirandello
War 538

Edgar Allan Poe
The Cask of Amontillado 543
The Fall of the House of Usher 548
CONNECTIONS: Edgar Allan Poe, *The Importance of the Single Effect in a Prose Tale, 650*; D. H. Lawrence, *On "The Fall of the House of Usher" and "The Cask of Amontillado," 653*; Cleanth Brooks and Robert Penn Warren, *A New Critical Reading of "The Fall of the House of Usher," 656*; J. Gerald Kennedy, *On "The Fall of the House of Usher," 659*; David S. Reynolds, *Poe's Art of Transformation in "The Cask of Amontillado," 662*

Marjane Satrapi
From Persepolis: *"The Veil"* 563
COMMENTARY
Sydney Plum, *Reading "The Veil" by Marjane Satrapi* 570

Leslie Marmon Silko
Yellow Woman 572
COMMENTARY
Paula Gunn Allen, *Whirlwind Man Steals Yellow Woman* 579

John Steinbeck
The Chrysanthemums 581

Amy Tan
Two Kinds 590

John Updike
A & P 599
CONNECTION: James Joyce, *Araby, 317*

Kurt Vonnegut Jr.
Harrison Bergeron 604

Alice Walker
Everyday Use 610
COMMENTARY
Alice Walker, *Zora Neale Hurston: A Cautionary Tale and a Partisan View* 616
CONNECTION: Zora Neale Hurston, *Sweat, 278*

Eudora Welty
A Worn Path 619

COMMENTARY
Eudora Welty, *Is Phoenix Jackson's Grandson Really Dead?* 625

William Carlos Williams
The Use of Force 628

Tobias Wolff
Say Yes 632

7. Conversations on Stories and Storytellers: Flannery O'Connor and Edgar Allan Poe 636

On Flannery O'Connor's Fiction 636

COMMENTARIES
Flannery O'Connor, *From* Letters, 1954–55 636
Flannery O'Connor, *Writing Short Stories* 639
Flannery O'Connor, *The Element of Suspense in "A Good Man Is Hard to Find"* 644
Sally Fitzgerald, *Southern Sources of "A Good Man Is Hard to Find"* 647

On Critical Views of Edgar Allan Poe's Short Stories 648

COMMENTARIES
Edgar Allan Poe, *The Importance of the Single Effect in a Prose Tale* 650
D. H. Lawrence, *On "The Fall of the House of Usher" and "The Cask of Amontillado"* 653
Cleanth Brooks and Robert Penn Warren, *A New Critical Reading of "The Fall of the House of Usher"* 656
J. Gerald Kennedy, *On "The Fall of the House of Usher"* 659
David S. Reynolds, *Poe's Art of Transformation in "The Cask of Amontillado"* 662

◆ Topics for Writing about Flannery O'Connor and Edgar Allan Poe 665

Part Two ◆ POETRY 667

8. What Is a Poem? 669

Marianne Moore, *Poetry (1935 version)* 669
Pablo Neruda, *Poetry* 670
Archibald MacLeish, *Ars Poetica* 672
Ann Menebroker, *A Mere Glimpse* 675

Fred Voss, *How Many Times Can We Follow Dante Down Into Hell?* 676
Alice Walker, *I Said to Poetry* 677
Victor Hernández Cruz, *today is a day of great joy* 679
COMMENTARY
James Tate, *Like It or Not, We Are a Part of Our Time* 679

9. Reading, Thinking, and Writing about Poetry *681*

Reading Poetry *682*
Taniguchi Buson, *The nightingale is singing* 683
Anonymous, *Western wind, when wilt thou blow* 683
e. e. cummings, *since feeling is first* 684
Close Reading *684*
Paraphrase *685*
◆ Guidelines for Reading Poetry 686
Sample Close Reading: Linda Pastan, *To a Daughter Leaving Home* 686
Critical Thinking about Poetry *687*
Writing about Poetry *689*
SAMPLE PAPER: *A Moving Lyric: Pastan's "To a Daughter Leaving Home"* 690

10. Rhyme *693*

Emily Dickinson, *A word is dead* 693
Alliteration *694*
Assonance *694*
Walt Whitman, *A Farm Picture* 695
Onomatopoeia *695*
Rhyme *695*
A. E. Housman, *Loveliest of trees, the cherry now* 696
Georgia Douglas Johnson, *I Want to Die While You Love Me* 697
A Range of Rhyme *698*
Stevie Smith, *Not Waving but Drowning* 699
Rhymed Poems for Further Reading *701*
Sir Thomas Wyatt, *They Flee from Me* 702
Ben Jonson, *On My First Son* 703
Robert Herrick, *To the Virgins, to Make Much of Time* 703
Robert Browning, *A Woman's Last Word* 704

e. e. cummings, *when god lets my body be* 705
Theodore Roethke, *My Papa's Waltz* 706
Anne Sexton, *And One for My Dame* 706
Dana Gioia, *Summer Storm* 707
Rhyme and Popular Songs 708
Lou Reed, *Chelsea Girls* 708
Rhyme in Traditional Folk Blues 709
J. D. Short, *Slidin' Delta* 710
◆ Topics for Writing about Rhyme 711
◆ Useful Terms to Remember 712

11. Poetic Meter 713

Edgar Lee Masters, *Petit, the Poet* 714
Accent and Meter 714
Mary Coleridge, *A Clever Woman* 716
Ralph Waldo Emerson, *From "The Humble Bee"* 717
Henry Wadsworth Longfellow, *From* The Song of Hiawatha 718
Christina Rossetti, *What are heavy? sea-sand and sorrow* 719
Blank Verse 720
Elizabeth Barrett Browning, *I write. (from* Aurora Leigh*)* 720
The Stanza 721
Paul Laurence Dunbar, *Life* 721
Poems for Further Reading 722
Thomas Hood, *From* The Bridge of Sighs 722
Mary Coleridge, *Eyes* 723
Thomas Hardy, *I need not go* 723
◆ Topics for Writing about Poetic Meter 724
◆ Useful Terms to Remember 725

12. The Meaning of Words 726

Tone 726
Carl Sandburg, *Grass* 728
Edwin Arlington Robinson, *Miniver Cheevy* 728
Edwin Arlington Robinson, *Richard Cory* 729
Words and Their Meaning 730
Lewis Carroll, *Jabberwocky* 730
Denotative and Connotative Meaning 731
Diction 731
Syntax 732

Imagery *732*
Elizabeth Bishop, *The Bight* *733*
A Close Reading of "The Bight" *734*
Figurative and Literal Language *734*
Simile and Metaphor *734*
William Carlos Williams, *To Waken an Old Lady* *737*
Personification *737*
John Keats, *To Autumn* *738*
Rolf Aggestam, *Lightning Bolt* *739*
Les Murray, *The Cows on Killing Day* *740*
Other Figures of Speech: Symbol, Apostrophe, Metonymy, Synecdoche, Paradox, Oxymoron, Hyperbole, Understatement *741*
Poems for Further Reading *742*
Sylvia Plath, *Metaphors* *742*
Louise Glück, *The Wild Iris* *742*
Kate Gleason, *After Fighting for Hours* *743*
◆ Topics for Writing about Tone and Figurative Language *743*
◆ Useful Terms to Remember *744*

13. Traditional Forms *746*

The Structural Elements: Couplet, Stanza, Quatrain, Sestet, Octave, Tercet *746*
Narrative Poetry *748*
The Ballad *748*
Ballads for Further Reading *748*
Anonymous, *The Daemon Lover* *748*
Anonymous, *Barbara Allan* *750*
Amy Lowell, *Evelyn Ray* *751*
The Ode *753*
John Keats, *Ode on a Grecian Urn* *754*
Percy Bysshe Shelley, *Ode to the West Wind* *756*
The Elegy *758*
Thomas Gray, *Elegy Written in a Country Churchyard* *758*
Theodore Roethke, *Elegy for Jane* *762*
The Sonnet *763*
William Shakespeare, *That time of year thou mayst in me behold* *763*
Sonnets for Further Reading *764*
Francesco Petrarca, *Love's Inconsistency* *765*
Lady Mary Wroth, *When last I saw thee, I did not thee see,* *765*

John Donne, *Death, be not proud* 766
William Wordsworth, *Upon Westminster Bridge, Sept. 3, 1802* 766
Percy Bysshe Shelley, *Ozymandias* 767
Elizabeth Barrett Browning, *How Do I Love Thee?* 767
Countee Cullen, *Yet Do I Marvel* 768
Edna St. Vincent Millay, *What lips my lips have kissed, and where, and why,* 768
Gwendolyn Brooks, *The Rites for Cousin Vit* 769
June Jordan, *Something Like a Sonnet for Phillis Miracle Wheatley* 769

The Sestina and the Villanelle 769
Elizabeth Bishop, *Sestina* 770
Dylan Thomas, *Do Not Go Gentle into That Good Night* 771

Dramatic Poetry 772
William Shakespeare, *Tomorrow, and tomorrow, and tomorrow (from* Macbeth, *act V, scene V)* 772

The Dramatic Monologue 773
Robert Browning, *My Last Duchess* 773

The Pattern Poem 775
George Herbert, *Easter Wings* 775
Guillaume Apollinaire, *Hail World* 776
Guillaume Apollinaire, *It's Raining* 777

The Epigram, the Aphorism, and the Limerick 778
Dorothy Parker, *From* A Pig's-Eye View of Literature 778
James Richardson, *From* Vectors: Five Hundred Aphorisms and Ten-Second Essays 779
Dylan Thomas, *The last time I slept with the Queen* 779
Wendy Cope, *The fine English poet, John Donne* 780
J. Walker, *On T. S. Eliot's "Prufrock"* 780
Richard Leighton Greene, *Apropos Coleridge's "Kubla Khan"* 780
A. Cinna, *On* Hamlet 780

Poems for Further Reading 780
Andrew Marvell, *To His Coy Mistress* 780
William Wordsworth, *I Wandered Lonely as a Cloud* 782
Christina Rossetti, *A Birthday* 782
Alfred, Lord Tennyson, *Ulysses* 783

COMMENTARIES
Erica Jong, *Devouring Time: Shakespeare's Sonnets* 785
Percy Bysshe Shelley, *From* A Defence of Poetry 787

- Topics for Writing about Poetic Forms 791
- Useful Terms to Remember 791

14. Other Forms of Poetry *793*

H. D., *The Pool* *793*

Imagism *794*

Imagist Poems for Further Reading *795*

Ezra Pound, *In a Station of the Metro* *795*

T. E. Hulme, *Images* *795*

H. D., *Oread* *796*

D. H. Lawrence, *The White Horse* *796*

Amy Lowell, *Meeting-House Hill* *797*

William Carlos Williams, *The Red Wheelbarrow* *798*

Wallace Stevens, *Thirteen Ways of Looking at a Blackbird* *798*

Classical Chinese Verse and the Japanese Haiku *800*

Li T'ai Po, *A Song of Changgan* *801*

Ezra Pound, *The River-Merchant's Wife: A Letter* *802*

Charles Wright, *After Reading Tu Fu, I Go Outside to the Dwarf Orchard* *803*

An Introduction to Haiku *803*

Yone Noguchi, *Bits of song* *803*

Matsuo Bashō, *The summer grass* *805*

Matsuo Bashō, *Down this road* *805*

Matsuo Bashō, *It's spring* *805*

Matsuo Bashō, *Old pond* *805*

Lafcadio Hearn, *Old pond* *805*

Taniguchi Buson, *On the anniversary of Bashō's death* *805*

Taniguchi Buson, *The sparrow chirps* *806*

Kobayashi Issa, *Sitting with my father* *806*

Kobayashi Issa, *Children's imitations of cormorants* *806*

Masaoka Shiki, *A thawed pond* *806*

Masaoka Shiki, *Night and again* *806*

Some Contemporary Haiku *806*

Robert Spiess, *an aging willow* *806*

Ronald Baatz, *as though the whole earth* *807*

Matsuo Allard, *an icicle the moon* *807*

Alexis Rotella, *just friends* *807*

John Carley, *buoyed up on the rising tide* *807*

Cheryl Savageau, *Department of Labor Haiku* *807*

Poetry in Open Form and the Lyric Poem *808*

The Lyric Poem Today *808*

Philip Levine, *The Lost Angel* *809*

Confessional Mode *810*

Anne Sexton, *The Fortress* *810*

CONNECTIONS: See poems by Marilyn Chin, Audre Lorde, Sharon Olds, Alicia Suskin Ostriker, Sylvia Plath, and Anne Sexton.

The Prose Poem 812
Marcia Southwick, *A Star Is Born in the Eagle Nebula* 812
Eve Wood, *Recognition* 813
Claribel Alegría, *Carmen Bomba: Poet* 814

Poems for Further Study 814
Judith Ortiz Cofer, *Quinceañera* 814
Li-Young Lee, *Eating Alone* 815
Nick Carbó, *American Adobo* 815
Marisa de los Santos, *Because I Love You,* 817
Luis J. Rodríguez, *Carrying My Tools* 817

COMMENTARIES
Ezra Pound, *On the Principles of Imagism* 818
Amy Lowell, *On the Definition of Free Verse* 821

◆ Topics for Writing about Other Poetic Forms 822
◆ Useful Terms to Remember 822

15. Poets Respond to Other Poets 823

John Keats, *On First Looking into Chapman's Homer* 824

Quotation 826

Paraphrase 827

Allusion 828
Samuel Charters, *A Man Dancing Alone on an Island in Greece* 829

Imitation 830

Parody 830
Leigh Hunt, *Jenny Kiss'd Me* 831
T. S. Kerrigan, *Elvis Kissed Me* 831

Argument 831
Philip Larkin, *This Be the Verse* 832
Carol Rumens, *This Be the Verse (Philip Larkin)* 832

Address and Tribute 832
Allen Ginsberg, *A Supermarket in California* 833

COMMENTARY
Marilyn Chin, *On the Canon* 833

◆ Topics for Writing about Poets' Responses to Other Poets 834

16. Poets and Their Worlds: Emily Dickinson, Robert Frost, and Langston Hughes *836*

The World of Emily Dickinson *836*

DOCUMENT

Emily Dickinson (on Elizabeth Barrett Browning), *I think I was enchanted* *840*

Poems

Elizabeth Barrett Browning, *When our two souls stand up erect and strong,* *841*

Emily Brontë, *Last Lines* *841*

Christina Rossetti, *Remember* *842*

Christina Rossetti, *From* Sing-Song *842*

Emily Dickinson

Success is counted sweetest *844*

You love me—you are sure— *845*

I'm "wife"—I've finished that— *845*

I taste a liquor never brewed— *846*

Wild Nights—Wild Nights! *846*

"Hope" is the thing with feathers— *846*

There's a certain Slant of light, *847*

I'm Nobody! Who are you? *847*

After great pain, a formal feeling comes— *847*

Much Madness is divinest Sense— *848*

I died for Beauty—but was scarce *848*

I heard a Fly buzz—when I died— *848*

Because I could not stop for Death— *849*

A narrow Fellow in the Grass *850*

COMMENTARIES

Thomas Wentworth Higginson, *From "Emily Dickinson's Letters"* *851*

Thomas Bailey Aldrich, *In* Re Emily Dickinson *857*

Richard Wilbur, *On Emily Dickinson* *859*

The World of Robert Frost *861*

DOCUMENT

Louis Untermeyer, *A "book of people"* *866*

Poems

Thomas Hardy, *An August Midnight* *866*

Edwin Arlington Robinson, *Eros Tyrannos* *867*

Edgar Lee Masters, *Mabel Osborne* *868*

Edgar Lee Masters, *Lucinda Matlock* *869*

Edward Thomas, *Early One Morning* *869*

Robert Frost
In White 870
The Pasture 870
Mending Wall 870
Home Burial 872
After Apple-Picking 875
Birches 876
The Road Not Taken 877
To Earthward 878
Stopping by Woods on a Snowy Evening 879

COMMENTARIES
Rose C. Feld, *An Interview with Robert Frost* 879
Carol Frost, *From* Sincerity and Inventions: On Robert Frost 882
Philip L. Gerber, *On Frost's "After Apple-Picking"* 883
James Wright, *The Music of Robert Frost's "Stopping by Woods on a Snowy Evening"* 885

The World of Langston Hughes 886

DOCUMENTS FROM THE HARLEM RENAISSANCE
W. E. B. Du Bois, *From* The Souls of Black Folk 890
Alain Locke, *From* The New Negro 891

Poems
Langston Hughes, *The Negro Speaks of Rivers* 893
James Weldon Johnson, *The Creation* 893
Angelina Weld Grimké, *The Black Finger* 895
Angelina Weld Grimké, *Tenebris* 896
Claude McKay, *If We Must Die* 896
Claude McKay, *The Tropics in New York* 896
Jean Toomer, *Lyrics from* Cane 897
Countee Cullen, *From* Heritage 898
Countee Cullen, *Incident* 899

Langston Hughes
Negro 900
Mother to Son 901
I, Too 901
Song for a Dark Girl 902
House in the World 902
Love Again Blues 902

COMMENTARIES
Langston Hughes, *A Toast to Harlem* 903
Jessie Fauset, *Meeting Langston Hughes* 904
Arnold Rampersad, *Langston Hughes as Folk Poet* 906

17. A Poet in the World Today: Tomas Tranströmer 908

An Introduction to Tomas Tranströmer, by Samuel Charters 908

A Selected Bibliography of Works by Tomas Tranströmer in English 911

Tomas Tranströmer

Romanesque Arches 912

Allegro 912

Beginning of the Late Autumn Night's Novel 913

Schubertiana 913

March '79 915

COMMENTARIES

Tomas Tranströmer, *On Poetry* 915

Robert Bly, *On Tomas Tranströmer* 916

Robert Hass, *Tranströmer's Style* 917

Helen Vendler, *Tranströmer and the "Other Side" of Consciousness* 918

Samuel Charters, *On Translating Tomas Tranströmer* 919

Writing about Tomas Tranströmer 922

SAMPLE PAPER: *"Every Pane Stays Whole": The Sustaining Power of Art in Tranströmer's Poetry* 922

◆ Topics for Writing about Tomas Tranströmer 924

18. Poems and Poets 925

W. H. Auden

Musée des Beaux Arts 926

Stop All the Clocks 926

Lay your sleeping head, my love 927

Elizabeth Bishop

Manners 929

Sandpiper 929

The Fish 930

One Art 932

COMMENTARY

Brett C. Millier, *On Elizabeth Bishop's "One Art"* 932

William Blake

From Songs of Innocence: Introduction 934

The Lamb 935

Holy Thursday 935

The Little Boy Lost 936
The Little Boy Found 936
From Songs of Experience: Introduction 936
The Sick Rose 937
The Tyger 937
London 938
A Poison Tree 938
The Garden of Love 939

Anne Bradstreet
To My Dear and Loving Husband 940
Before the Birth of One of Her Children 940
In Memory of My Dear Grand-Child Elizabeth Bradstreet, Who Deceased August, 1665, Being a Year and a Half Old 941

Gwendolyn Brooks
We Real Cool 942
The Mother 942
The Bean Eaters 943
CONNECTION: Robert Hayden, *On Negro Poetry, 1043*

Marilyn Chin
How I Got That Name 944
Sad Guitar 946
CONNECTION: Marilyn Chin, *On the Canon, 834*

Samuel Taylor Coleridge
Kubla Khan: or, a Vision in a Dream 948
Frost at Midnight 949
CONNECTION: Richard Leighton Greene, *Apropos Coleridge's "Kubla Khan," 780*

Billy Collins
The Only Day in Existence 951
Memento Mori 952
Today 952

e. e. cummings
somewhere I have never travelled 953
Buffalo Bill 's 954
goodby Betty, don't remember me 954
in Just- 955

John Donne
A Valediction: Forbidding Mourning 956
The Sun Rising 957
The Flea 958

Batter my heart, three-personed God 959
CONNECTION: Wendy Cope, *The fine English poet, John Donne,* 780

Rita Dove
Singsong 960
The Pond, Porch-View: Six P.M., Early Spring 960

T. S. Eliot
The Love Song of J. Alfred Prufrock 961
COMMENTARY
Cleanth Brooks and Robert Penn Warren, *On Eliot's "The Love Song of J. Alfred Prufrock"* 965
CONNECTION: J. Walker, *On T. S. Eliot's "Prufrock,"* 780

Louise Glück
First Memory 969
Happiness 969

Seamus Heaney
Digging 970
Mid-Term Break 971

Gerard Manley Hopkins
The Windhover 972
Pied Beauty 973
God's Grandeur 973
Thou art indeed just, Lord 973
COMMENTARY
Bernard Bergonzi, *On Hopkins's "The Windhover"* 974

John Keats
Bright Star 976
Ode to a Nightingale 977
When I have fears 979

Robert Lowell
Skunk Hour 981
For the Union Dead 982
Epilogue 984
COMMENTARY
Robert Lowell, *An Explication of "Skunk Hour"* 984

Sharon Olds
Parents' Day 987
I Go Back to May 1937 988
Sex without Love 988

COMMENTARY

Ann Charters, *The Woman in the Long, Dark Raincoat: A Poetry Reading with Sharon Olds* 989

Sylvia Plath

Morning Song 991

Daddy 991

Adrienne Rich

Aunt Jennifer's Tigers 994

Diving into the Wreck 994

Anne Sexton

An Obsessive Combination of Ontological Inscape, Trickery and Love 998

To a Friend Whose Work Has Come to Triumph 998

Pain for a Daughter 998

CONNECTION: W. H. Auden, *Musée des Beaux Arts, 926*

Gary Soto

Mexicans Begin Jogging 1000

Oranges 1001

Waiting at the Curb: Lynwood, California, 1967 1002

Walt Whitman

From "Song of Myself," 1, 6, 50–52 1004

COMMENTARIES

Walt Whitman, *A Review of* Leaves of Grass 1006

Ezra Pound, *What I Feel about Walt Whitman* 1007

William Carlos Williams

Spring and All 1009

Danse Russe 1010

From "March" 1011

The Widow's Lament in Springtime 1011

COMMENTARY

William Carlos Williams, *Spirit of '76* 1012

William Wordsworth

Ode: Intimations of Immortality 1013

The world is too much with us 1019

COMMENTARY

William Wordsworth, *From the Introduction to* Lyrical Ballads 1019

James Wright

Evening 1023

A Blessing 1024
Lying in a Hammock at William Duffy's Farm in Pine Island, Minnesota 1025
COMMENTARY
Sven Birkerts, *James Wright's "Hammock": A Sounding* 1025
CONNECTION: James Wright, *The Music of Robert Frost's "Stopping by Woods on a Snowy Evening,"* 885

William Butler Yeats
The Lake Isle of Innisfree 1027
The Second Coming 1028
The Wild Swans at Coole 1028

19. Themes for Thinking and Writing about Poetry 1030

In Wonder at the Natural World 1030

DOCUMENT
Henry David Thoreau, *"It is difficult to begin without borrowing . . ." (from* Walden*)* 1031
Thomas Lovell Beddoes, *A Lake* 1032
John Clare, *The Sky Lark* 1032
Walt Whitman, *On the Beach at Night Alone* 1033
Edna St. Vincent Millay, *God's World* 1033
D. H. Lawrence, *A Doe at Evening* 1034
Mary Oliver, *Sleeping in the Forest* 1034
John Casteen, *Night Hunting* 1035

Women's Consciousness, Women's Voices 1035

DOCUMENT
Elizabeth Barrett Browning, *Books, books, books! (from* Aurora Leigh*)* 1036
Ruth Stone, *In an Iridescent Time* 1037
Alicia Suskin Ostriker, *The Change* 1038
Marilyn Hacker, *Rondeau after a Transatlantic Telephone Call* 1039
Anne Waldman, *stereo* 1039
Jenny Bornholdt, *The Boyfriends* 1040
Daisy Zamora, *Precisely* 1041

Black Consciousness, Black Voices 1042

DOCUMENT
Robert Hayden, *On Negro Poetry* 1043
Phillis Wheatley, *On Being Brought from Africa to America* 1045

Paul Laurence Dunbar, *Theology* 1045
Paul Laurence Dunbar, *Sympathy* 1046
James Weldon Johnson, *Sunset in the Tropics* 1046
Robert Hayden, *Those Winter Sundays* 1047
Etheridge Knight, *The Idea of Ancestry* 1047
Dudley Randall, *Ballad of Birmingham* 1048
Allen Polite, *Song* 1049
Audre Lorde, *Hanging Fire* 1050
Lucille Clifton, *to ms. ann* 1051

Poetry of Protest and Social Concern 1052

DOCUMENT
David Wojahn, *On Political Poetry* 1053
Nikki Giovanni, *Adulthood* 1053
Carolyn Forché, *The Colonel* 1055
Pat Mora, *Elena* 1056
Joan Jobe Smith, *Feminist Arm Candy for the Mafia and Sinatra* 1056
Fred Voss, *I Once Needed a Chance Too* 1057
Sara Holbrook, *Canvassing* 1058
Bob Dylan, *Blowin' in the Wind* 1059
Country Joe McDonald, *I-Feel-Like-I'm-Fixin'-to-Die Rag* 1059

The Faces of War 1061

DOCUMENT
Stephen Crane, *From* The Red Badge of Courage 1062
Herman Melville, *Shiloh* 1062
Stephen Crane, *War Is Kind* 1063
Thomas Hardy, *The Man He Killed* 1064
Wilfred Owen, *Dulce et Decorum Est* 1064
Randall Jarrell, *The Death of the Ball Turret Gunner* 1065
Ed Webster, *From* San Joaquin Valley Poems: 1969 1066
Forrest Hamer, *My Father's Viet Nam Tour Near Over* 1067

20. Contemporary Movements in Poetry 1068

Poetry of the Beat Generation 1068

DOCUMENT
John Clellon Holmes, *From* This Is the Beat Generation 1069
Bonnie Bremser, *A First Meeting with the Beats (from* Poets and Odd Fellows*)* 1071
Ray Bremser, *Blues for Bonnie—Take 1, January 1960* 1072
Allen Ginsberg, *Sunflower Sutra* 1073
Lawrence Ferlinghetti, *Dog* 1075

Frank O'Hara, *The Day Lady Died* 1077
Diane di Prima, *Revolutionary Letter #3* 1078
Gregory Corso, *I am 25* 1079
Edward Sanders, *After a Year of Isolation* 1080

Poetry of the Chaps and Zines 1081

DOCUMENT
Gerald Locklin, *The Small Presses and Little Magazines: A Few Reflections* 1082

Ann Menebroker, *Repossessed* 1083
Tom Kryss, *Things Thrown Away* 1084
d. a. levy, *perhaps (#5)* 1085
Robert E. McDonough, *Résumé* 1086
Susan Grimm, *Things I Can Know* 1086
Joan Jobe Smith, *The Carol Burnett Show* 1087
Ronald Baatz, *The Oldest Songs* 1088
Gerald Locklin, *So It Goes* 1089
Gerald Locklin, *Friday Night Lights* 1089

◆ Topics for Writing about Themes in Poetry 1090

Part Three ◆ DRAMA 1091

21. What Is a Play? 1093

August Strindberg, *The Stronger* 1096

22. Reading, Thinking, and Writing about Drama 1101

Reading Drama 1101
◆ Guidelines for Reading Drama 1102

Sample Close Reading: August Strindberg, *The Stronger* 1103

Critical Thinking about Drama 1104

Writing about Drama 1106

SAMPLE PAPER: *A Reader's Response to the Opening Lines of Strindberg's* The Stronger 1107

23. The Elements of Drama 1110

Anton Chekhov, *A Monologue* 1110

Plot 1112

Characters 1116

Dialogue 1117

Staging 1119

Theme 1121

Willy Russell, *From* Educating Rita 1122

- Questions for Critical Thinking about Drama 1124
- Topics for Writing about the Elements of Drama 1125
- Useful Terms to Remember 1125

24. Plays and Playwrights 1126

Sophocles

Oedipus the King 1129

COMMENTARIES

Aristotle, *On the Elements and General Principles of Tragedy* 1173

Sigmund Freud, *The Oedipus Complex* 1179

William Shakespeare

A Midsummer Night's Dream 1187

Hamlet, Prince of Denmark 1244

CONNECTIONS: Geoffrey Bullough, *Sources of Shakespeare's* Hamlet, *1594*; John Keats, *From a Letter to George and Thomas Keats, 21 December 1817, 1596*; Stephen Greenblatt, *On the Ghost in* Hamlet, *1597*; Tom Stoppard, Dogg's Hamlet: *The Encore, 1598*; Sir John Gielgud, *On Playing Hamlet, 1600*; John Lahr, *Review of* Hamlet, *1605*; Michael Pennington, *Hamlet's Madness, 1608*

Henrik Ibsen

A Doll House 1349

COMMENTARIES

Henrik Ibsen, *Notes for* A Doll House 1403

George Bernard Shaw, *On* A Doll House 1403

Joan Templeton, *Is* A Doll House *a Feminist Text?* 1405

Liv Ullmann, *On Performing Nora in Ibsen's* A Doll House 1407

Susan Glaspell

Trifles 1410

COMMENTARY

Leonard Mustazza, *Generic Translation and Thematic Shift in Glaspell's* Trifles *and "A Jury of Her Peers"* 1420

CONNECTIONS: Susan Glaspell, *A Jury of Her Peers, 243*; Lynn Nottage, *POOF!, 1582*

Arthur Miller

Death of a Salesman 1429

COMMENTARIES

Arthur Miller, *On* Death of a Salesman *as an American Tragedy* 1499

Helge Normann Nilsen, *Marxism and the Early Plays of Arthur Miller* 1502

Lorraine Hansberry

A Raisin in the Sun 1507

COMMENTARIES

Lorraine Hansberry, *An Author's Reflections: Willy Loman, Walter Younger, and He Who Must Live* 1575

Lorraine Hansberry, *My Shakespearean Experience* 1579

Lynn Nottage

POOF! 1582

COMMENTARY

Lynn Nottage, *On Writing* POOF! 1588

CONNECTION: Susan Glaspell, *Trifles, 1410*

Edwin Sanchez

Pops 1590

25. Conversation on *Hamlet* as Text and Performance 1592

COMMENTARIES

Geoffrey Bullough, *Sources of Shakespeare's* Hamlet 1594

John Keats, *From a Letter to George and Thomas Keats, 21 December 1817* 1596

Stephen Greenblatt, *On the Ghost in* Hamlet 1597

Tom Stoppard, Dogg's Hamlet: *The Encore* 1598

Sir John Gielgud, *On Playing Hamlet* 1600

John Lahr, *Review of* Hamlet 1605

Michael Pennington, *Hamlet's Madness* 1608

◆ Topics for Writing about Drama 1609

Part Four ◆ WRITING ABOUT LITERATURE 1611

26. Critical Reading and Literary Theory 1613

Formalist Criticism 1614

Biographical Criticism 1615

Psychological Criticism 1615
Mythological Criticism 1616
Historical Criticism 1617
Sociological Criticism 1617
Reader-Response Criticism 1618
Poststructuralist and Deconstructionist Criticism 1619
Gender Criticism 1619
Cultural Criticism 1620
Selected Bibliography 1620

27. Using the Writing Process to Develop Your Paper *1623*

Keeping a Journal or Notebook to Record Your Initial Responses to the Text 1624
Using the Commentaries to Ask New Questions about What You Have Read 1626
Generating Ideas by Brainstorming, Freewriting, and Listing 1626
Organizing Your Notes into a Preliminary Thesis Sentence and Outline 1629
Writing the First Draft 1631
Revising Your Paper 1633
SAMPLE REVISED DRAFT: *The Voice of the Storyteller in Eudora Welty's "A Worn Path"* 1634
Making a Final Check of Your Finished Paper 1636
Peer Review 1636
Common Problems in Writing about Literature 1637
◆ Guidelines for Writing a Paper about Literature 1640

28. Basic Types of Literary Papers *1642*

Explication 1642
SAMPLE PAPER: *An Interpretation of Langston Hughes's "The Negro Speaks of Rivers"* 1643
Analysis 1644
SAMPLE PAPER: *Nature and Neighbors in Robert Frost's "Mending Wall"* 1645
Comparison and Contrast 1647

SAMPLE PAPER: *On the Differences between Susan Glaspell's* Trifles *and "A Jury of Her Peers"* 1648

Writing about the Context of Literature 1652

29. Writing Research Papers 1654

Three Keys to Literary Research 1654

Finding and Focusing a Topic 1654

Assigned Topics 1655

Choosing Your Own Topic 1655

Finding and Using Sources 1656

Library Research 1657

Using the Web for Research 1658

Evaluating Print and Online Sources 1659

Your Working Bibliography 1660

Working with Sources and Taking Notes 1663

Drafting Your Research Paper 1665

Summarizing, Paraphrasing, and Quoting 1666

Documenting Your Sources 1669

MLA Format 1669

In-Text or Parenthetical Citations 1670

List of Works Cited 1671

Footnotes and Endnotes 1674

Revising Your Research Paper 1675

STUDENT RESEARCH PAPER: Jennifer Silva, *Emily Dickinson and Religion* 1676

Glossary of Literary Terms 1685

Index of First Lines 1715

Index of Authors and Titles 1721

Resources for Reading and Writing about Literature *inside back cover*

LITERATURE AND ITS WRITERS

An Introduction to Fiction, Poetry, and Drama

INTRODUCTION

Connecting with Literature

> Writing, for me, is an act of faith, a hope that I will discover what I mean by "truth." I also think of reading as an act of faith, a hope that I will discover something remarkable about ordinary life, about myself. And if the writer and the reader discover the same thing, if they have that connection, the act of faith has resulted in an act of magic. To me, that's the mystery and the wonder of both life and fiction—the connection between two individuals who discover in the end that they are more the same than they are different.
>
> – AMY TAN, "In the Canon, for All the Wrong Reasons"

Why study literature? You read stories, poems, and plays for many reasons. When you allow yourself to become fully immersed in an author's words and ideas, you can bring to life an imaginary world that can tell you something about your own everyday reality. As a student of literature, you will find that the stories, poems, and plays in this anthology will often enable you to view life with a new clarity and a deeper understanding as you relate what you have read to your own experience.

A good reader possesses an active imagination, a retentive memory, a college dictionary, and a rudimentary artistic sense. Furthermore, if you hope to become a great reader, you will also need to bring to the course—along with your imagination and memory—a strong desire to refine and develop your critical sense. This quality will evolve naturally from your close reading and your writing about literary texts.

Becoming a great reader always helps you to become a better writer. The American poet Robert Frost aptly described this process when he said, "To learn to write is to learn to have ideas." Reading closely and thinking critically about the literature in this anthology will suggest ideas that you can develop in class discussions and in your papers.

At first you may suppose that you have little in common with the distinguished authors gathered here, but bear in mind that each of them was once a beginner. The writer Raymond Carver described taking his first college course in "Creative Writing 101" (p. 151). After reading his commentary, one student recognized a connection with Carver's experience in this short paper.

SAMPLE PAPER

Raymond Carver's "Creative Writing 101"

We all have several turning points in our life. These turning points may include graduating from college, getting married, losing loved ones, having children, and changing jobs. However, we can have other turning points which exert more subtle effects on us and are no less significant.

The American writer Raymond Carver married young and had two children. He eked out a living to support his family, but he wanted to go to college because of his desire to be a writer. He felt in his bones that he had to get an education in order to learn more about being a writer. When he finally could enroll in a college writing course, he was fortunate to have John Gardner, a young novelist, as his instructor.

Studying with Gardner was a significant turning point in Carver's life. Gardner became aware of Carver's difficulty in finding a place to work on his fiction, so he offered his student the key to his office, where Carver could begin what he remembered as his "first serious attempts at writing." Just as important, Gardner read Carver's first stories seriously. Sometimes Carver had to revise a sentence several times to satisfy his teacher. Gardner insisted that a writer must be honest. He couldn't "fake it" by writing about something he didn't believe in.

Carver learned what he called "a writer's values and craft" from his first writing teacher. These were what Gardner taught him in Creative Writing 101, Carver's most important turning point as a writer.

Understanding Carver's experience in Creative Writing 101 as an important turning point is the connection the student made between her own knowledge of life and Carver's commentary. It helped her to begin the conversation about literature that she carried on in her paper. Going on to analyze the "values and craft" exemplified by works of literature will help you to develop your own skills as a reader and writer. For example, you can read American playwright Lorraine Hansberry's "My Shakespearean Experience" (p. 1579) and compare it in an essay with your own response to *Hamlet*. You can analyze the dazzling sparks of ideas about the themes of love and death in the works of

Emily Dickinson, or interpret the genius of Langston Hughes as he translates the pain of racism into poetry accessible to everyone.

In the essay "Good Readers and Good Writers," the novelist Vladimir Nabokov understood the complexity of our responses to literature. He believed that every author "may be considered as a storyteller, as a teacher, and as an enchanter. A major writer combines these three — storyteller, teacher, enchanter — but it is the enchanter in him that predominates and makes him a major writer."

Initially we all turn to storytellers for mental and emotional stimulation, the pleasure of entering an alternate universe to our own. This is evoked in our minds from our connection with the words of a literary text. Not only does great literature entertain us, it also provokes our thought. If we think about what we have read after we have finished a story, poem, or play, we realize that authors are often teachers — their words contribute to the development of our own sense of values and remind us of the inexorable brevity and essential mystery of our lives. Then we can return to the story, poem, or play for what many readers consider the most enchanting connection with literature: We can use our aesthetic sense to study what Nabokov called "the individual magic" of each writer's genius — the formal beauty resulting from the style, the imagery, and the pattern of the literary text.

READING LITERATURE

Regardless of where you start to read and write about literature — whether you begin with short stories, poems, or plays — the important thing to remember is that you should read your assignments slowly and carefully. When you become a student of literature, you do not read in the same casual way that you pick up a newspaper or a magazine, or scan material on the Internet. You even read differently from the way that you concentrate on assignments for your other courses. In those courses you look for textbook passages in which the author states the important ideas about a subject in words that you can underline to help you remember them for a quiz or an exam.

This way of reading so-called objective prose in science, accounting, or history textbooks, for example, can be described as linear, in that the objectivity of the concepts you are studying evokes a similar objectivity in your attention to the words on the page. You read along sentence by sentence, following the linear development of the author's thesis or argument. Works of literature, on the other hand, create meaning differently. Literary texts have an additional dimension of *significance* as well as meaning.

Significance is expressed through your personal response to the short story, poem, or play. It is how you connect with what the author as storyteller, teacher, and enchanter has created in the text — what *you* make of it. As you read, your understanding arises from your experience of life, which also includes your study of literature. Reading the author headnotes and commentaries in *Literature and Its Writers* will help you expand your literary background by addir to your knowledge of the writers' lives, historical times, and cultural traditior

Understanding the basic elements or means available to authors of works in each literary genre will also help you to connect with literature. The English critic Cyril Connolly observed that "literature is the art of writing something that will be read twice." Try to read your assignments twice, the first time enjoying the experience of *arriving* at the end of the text, seeing how the author resolves the plot of a short story or play or develops the subject of a poem. The second time you read a text, you can focus on *getting there,* becoming aware of how authors create the world evoked on the page by using the elements of their craft.

This is called **close reading.** It is essential for understanding what an author has created in the text. This process will assist you in interpreting accurately what you have read so that its significance for you is easier to grasp. Close reading will also evoke the pleasure you can take in revealing the writer's unique creation of design and pattern in the literary work, as distinctive to each author as his or her fingerprints. Through this process of close reading, you are taking the first steps toward thinking critically about the text and discovering its significance for you.

THINKING AND WRITING ABOUT LITERATURE

With literature, you help to create meaning. The way you interpret what you read determines the significance of a short story, poem, or play for you. Literature becomes meaningful when you read actively. Slow down. Take the time to think about the text. Relate the author's personal vision to your own experiences of life and literature. As Amy Tan urges at the start of this introduction, try to connect with the author through the words on the page.

Just as one student understood the parallel between Raymond Carver's commentary "Creative Writing 101" and her experience of life's "turning points," you create the significance that a short story, poem, or play has for you as you refine your thoughts about it. Expressing your ideas in a paper will help you to clarify your response for yourself and others. You write to discover what you know, hoping "to find truth at the end of a pencil," as Ernest Hemingway described it.

To facilitate your progress in *Literature and Its Writers,* you will find detailed suggestions throughout the book to help you think critically and write effectively about what you read. The first three parts of the anthology contain works of fiction, poetry, and drama. The introductory chapters to each section include examples of student papers showing you how to write about each genre. Part Four opens with a chapter on different critical perspectives and lit-
rary theory. It discusses ways of writing about literature with a specific critical
nt of view. Then follow two chapters that offer several strategies for devel-
your ideas as you write papers about literature. These include the differ-
rical techniques of explication, analysis, comparison and contrast, as
gestions for some ways to explore the cultural contexts of literature.
aches are all illustrated with student papers. The topic of the final
to write a longer research paper, with a sample paper as your

guide. Whatever your assignment, you will find that writing about literature will intensify your involvement in it and clarify its significance for you, as well as sharpen your ability to think critically.

WEB For study and discussion questions and further writing suggestions, visit bedfordstmartins.com/rewritinglit.

PART ONE

Fiction

A true work of fiction . . . strikes us, in the end, not simply as a thing done but as a shining performance.

–John Gardner

To plot is to move from asking the question *and then what happened?* to the question *why did it happen?*

–James Hillman

Surely every written story is, in the final analysis, a score for voice. These little black marks on the page mean nothing without their retranslation into sound.

–Margaret Atwood

1.

What Is a Short Story?

> Fiction is like the spider's web, attached ever so slightly perhaps, but still attached to life at all four corners.
>
> –VIRGINIA WOOLF, *A Room of One's Own*

Since the dawn of history people have told stories to entertain or to instruct one another. Sometimes the stories they told were about real events; other times the stories they told came from their imaginations. Their made-up stories became what we know now as myths, legends, fables, parables, and tales. Perhaps the most famous storyteller of all time was Sheherezade, who exemplifies the power of stories and our need to tell and hear them. Every night she stopped in the middle of the stories she was telling the Persian Sultan Shahryar so he would let her stay alive another night to finish them. She knew that he was a cruel tyrant so embittered about marriage after his previous wife had been unfaithful, that every night he took a new bride and had her killed in the morning. On the thousandth and one night, Sheherezade confessed that she couldn't remember any more stories. By then the power of her storytelling was so great that the Sultan had fallen in love with her. He spared her life, and she became his Queen.

The mythical Sheherezade is supposed to have lived in Persia a hundred years after the prophet Mohammed, though the oldest Arabic manuscript of the tales she supposedly told dates from the fourteenth century. You might have read an even earlier story in the Bible that became part of your literary heritage from the sea of stories that existed in ancient times. Found in the Old Testament, it's known today as the Judgment of King Solomon.

The Judgment of King Solomon

There came these two women, who were harlots, unto King Solomon, and stood before him.

The first woman said, "O my lord, this woman and I dwell in the same house, and I was delivered of a son with her in the house. Three days after the birth, she was delivered of a son also, and we were all alone in the house. After this woman's son died through her carelessness, she took my son out of my arms one night while I was sleeping and replaced him with her dead baby. When I woke up in the morning to nurse my son, I was holding a dead baby but it was not my child."

The second woman said, "No, the living child is my son, and the dead one is yours." The first woman replied, "No, the dead one is your son, and the living child is mine."

King Solomon commanded, "Bring me a sword and divide the living child in two, and give half to one mother and half to the other."

Then the woman whose son was the living child answered, "O my lord, give her the living child, and in no way kill it." But the second woman said, "Let it be neither mine nor yours, but divide it."

Then the king declared, "Give the first woman the living child, and do not slay it: she is the mother." And they all listened to King Solomon's judgment and feared him, for they saw that the wisdom of God was in his judgment. (1 Kings 3:16–28)

This story about King Solomon and the two women is a **parable**, a narrative that teaches a moral lesson, in this case that no mother would kill her own child. Its theme has come down to us in a memorable story with a dramatic plot involving a few characters in a biblical setting. In this English translation the parable is told by a narrator who relates the story in an almost casual tone. You recognize it as a story, but somehow you know that it isn't really a *short story*.

The terms *story* and *short story* do not necessarily mean the same thing, and actually the word *story* itself has two meanings. It can refer to a literary text like the biblical parable of King Solomon and the two women, or you could also say that the word *story* can refer to the events themselves that are depicted in a text. For example, Grace Paley tells a story about an accident on a New York subway and its consequences in her short story "Samuel."

The literary genre called the **short story** is much younger than the legends and myths that preceded it. The term *short story* always means that we're talking about the literary genre. It refers to a short fictional prose **narrative**, usually involving one unified episode, and it developed as a distinct literary form after the eighteenth century. The term is often applied to any work of narrative prose fiction shorter than a novel. Probably you've read many short stories, and you think you can recognize them. But what are the essential qualities of a short story such as Paley's "Samuel"?

GRACE PALEY
Samuel
1968

Some boys are very tough. They're afraid of nothing. They are the ones who climb a wall and take a bow at the top. Not only are they brave on the roof, but they make a lot of noise in the darkest part of the cellar where even the super hates to go. They also jiggle and hop on the platform between the locked doors of the subway cars.

Four boys are jiggling on the swaying platform. Their names are Alfred, Calvin, Samuel, and Tom. The men and the women in the cars on either side watch them. They don't like them to jiggle or jump but don't want to interfere. Of course some of the men in the cars were once brave boys like these. One of them had ridden the tail of a speeding truck from New York to Rockaway Beach without getting off, without his sore fingers losing hold. Nothing happened to him then or later. He had made a compact with other boys who preferred to watch: Starting at Eighth Avenue and Fifteenth Street, he would get to some specified place, maybe Twenty-third and the river, by hopping the tops of the moving trucks. This was hard to do when one truck turned a corner in the wrong direction and the nearest truck was a couple of feet too high. He made three or four starts before succeeding. He had gotten his idea from a film at school called *The Romance of Logging.* He had finished high school, married a good friend, was in a responsible job and going to night school.

These two men and others looked at the four boys jumping and jiggling on the platform and thought, It must be fun to ride that way, especially now the weather is nice and we're out of the tunnel and way high over the Bronx. Then they thought, These kids do seem to be acting sort of stupid. They *are* little. Then they thought of some of the brave things they had done when they were boys and jiggling didn't seem so risky.

The ladies in the car became very angry when they looked at the four boys. Most of them brought their brows together and hoped the boys could see their extreme disapproval. One of the ladies wanted to get up and say, Be careful, you dumb kids, get off that platform or I'll call a cop. But three of the boys were Negroes and the fourth was something else she couldn't tell for sure. She was afraid they'd be fresh and laugh at her and embarrass her. She wasn't afraid they'd hit her, but she was afraid of embarrassment. Another lady thought, Their mothers never know where they are. It wasn't true in this particular case. Their mothers all knew that they had gone to see the missile exhibit on Fourteenth Street.

Out on the platform, whenever the train accelerated, the boys would raise their hands and point them up to the sky to act like rockets going off, then they rat-tat-tatted the shatterproof glass pane like machine guns, although no machine guns had been exhibited.

For some reason known only to the motorman, the train began a sudden slowdown. The lady who was afraid of embarrassment saw the boys jerk forward and backward and grab the swinging guard chains. She had her own boy at home. She stood up with determination and went to the door. She slid it open and said, "You boys will be hurt. You'll be killed. I'm going to call the conductor if you don't just go into the next car and sit down and be quiet."

Two of the boys said, "Yes'm," and acted as though they were about to go. Two of them blinked their eyes a couple of times and pressed their lips together. The train resumed its speed. The door slid shut, parting the lady and the boys. She leaned against the side door because she had to get off at the next stop.

The boys opened their eyes wide at each other and laughed. The lady blushed. The boys looked at her and laughed harder. They began to pound each other's back. Samuel laughed the hardest and pounded Alfred's back until Alfred coughed and the tears came. Alfred held tight to the chain hook. Samuel pounded him even harder when he saw the tears. He said, "Why you bawling? You a baby, huh?" and laughed. One of the men whose boyhood had been more watchful than brave became angry. He stood up straight and looked at the boys for a couple of seconds. Then he walked in a citizenly way to the end of the car, where he pulled the emergency cord. Almost at once, with a terrible hiss, the pressure of air abandoned the brakes and the wheels were caught and held.

People standing in the most secure places fell forward, then backward. Samuel had let go of his hold on the chain so he could pound Tom as well as Alfred. All the passengers in the cars whipped back and forth, but he pitched only forward and fell head first to be crushed and killed between the cars.

The train had stopped hard, halfway into the station, and the conductor called at once for the trainmen who knew about this kind of death and how to take the body from the wheels and brakes. There was silence except for passengers from other cars who asked, What happened! What happened! The ladies waited around wondering if he might be an only child. The men recalled other afternoons with very bad endings. The little boys stayed close to each other, leaning and touching shoulders and arms and legs.

When the policeman knocked at the door and told her about it, Samuel's mother began to scream. She screamed all day and moaned all night, though the doctors tried to quiet her with pills.

Oh, oh, she hopelessly cried. She did not know how she could ever find another boy like that one. However, she was a young woman and she became pregnant. Then for a few months she was hopeful. The child born to her was a boy. They brought him to be seen and nursed. She smiled. But immediately she saw that this baby wasn't Samuel. She and her husband together have had other children, but never again will a boy exactly like Samuel be known.

When you finished reading "Samuel," you instinctively knew it was a short story, different from a biblical parable or a modern newspaper account, but how did you know this? For one thing, the story wasn't written primarily to teach a lesson or to report the facts of a recent subway accident. Paley begins and ends her narrative with her subjective response to the death of a young boy. Her first sentence, "Some boys are very tough," is not the way a newspaper reporter would open a story, unless perhaps it is meant for the editorial page. Also by the second paragraph of "Samuel," Paley is describing the antics of a group of boys on the swaying platform between two subway cars as they stunt for each other. As a short story writer, she is *showing* you their antics by giving you many specific details about them, not by *telling* you about their presumed toughness. She is making the events she describes come alive on the page.

The subtle way that Paley has used language to show her response to the events of a narrative, not merely tell about it, is the most important difference between a short story, a newspaper article, and a biblical parable. In an interview, Paley explained that her decision to write stories was her attempt to "get the world to explain itself to me, to speak to me." She regarded her decision to dramatize the events of her stories as an effort "to reach out to the world and get it to tell me what it was all about." To suggest a living world on the pages of a short story, authors of short fiction have various means at their disposal, including the elements of plot, point of view, characterization, setting, style, and theme.

With these elements of short fiction, skillful writers such as Paley can create entertaining stories that communicate their own unique sense of the mystery of life, the realization that "never again will a boy exactly like Samuel be known." Paley's story is very short because she chose to write in a literary style that was close to poetry. As she described it in her interview,

> I would say that stories are closer to poetry than they are to the novel because first they are shorter, and second they are more concentrated, more economical, and that kind of economy, the pulling together of all the information and making leaps across the information, is really close to poetry. By leaps I mean thought leaps and feeling leaps. Also, when short stories are working right, you pay more attention to language than most novelists do.

Paley believed that an author could have different intentions in telling a story. "It can be just telling a little tale, or writing a complicated philosophical story. It can be a song, almost." Paley chose her words carefully in "Samuel" to set you up for the shiver of recognition in her final sentence. All the elements of fiction were essential for her to create her short story, and when you understand the intricate way she used them, her story can have an even greater emotional impact. That's why we read literature much more attentively than the way we skim through a newspaper article or glance at an item on the Internet. Reading a short story will not only entertain you, but it will also help you, as Paley wrote, to "reach out to the world and get it to tell" you what our lives are about.

CONNECTION To read an interview with Grace Paley, see "A Conversation with Ann Charters," on page 536.

CONNECTION To read another story by Grace Paley, see "A Conversation with My Father," on page 532.

2.

Reading, Thinking, and Writing about Short Fiction

> General rules in art are useful chiefly as a lamp in a mine, or a handrail down a black stairway: they are necessary for the sake of the guidance they give, but it is a mistake, once they are formulated, to be too much in awe of them.
>
> –EDITH WHARTON, *The Writing of Fiction*

In your reading you will find that talented writers create short stories using six elements of fiction: plot, point of view, characters, setting, style, and theme. What makes their writing, the products of their skill and their creative imagination, stories that are considered works of art? What qualities must a story possess so that it lingers long in your memory, enchanting you as well as entertaining and instructing you?

For more than a century critics have tried to pin down the qualities that make some writers of stories literary artists and their works of short fiction works of art. Edgar Allan Poe was one of the first authors to try. In a magazine review in 1842 he argued ingeniously that the short story form had a theoretical claim to greatness as a "class of composition" since it could "best fulfill the demands of high genius." As an example, Poe cited the tales of Nathaniel Hawthorne, which Poe claimed "emphatically . . . belong to the highest region of Art." Poe listed what he considered the admirable qualities in Hawthorne's short stories or tales: "invention, creation, imagination, originality." The words he used are different from the terms that will help you to analyze and think critically about short stories, but you will learn that Poe's judgment is as valid today as it was in his time.

For example, when you imagine the vast wilderness of the Puritan world evoked by Hawthorne's words in the pages of "Young Goodman Brown" (p. 261), you may be struck by the detail of Faith's pink ribbon fluttering down from the silent night sky and seized by Goodman Brown in the dark forest with the compulsive cry, "My Faith is gone!" You understand that Goodman Brown is projecting his emotionally conflicted self onto the silence of the heavens to justify his loss of faith in God. The concrete image of his wife's floating pink ribbon as a symbol of his lost faith is a vivid illustration of Hawthorne's mastery of his allegorical style. The image may continue to haunt you long after you stop thinking about this particular fictional character's religious crisis. Hawthorne's creative genius in imagining memorable details like the pink ribbon is only one aspect of his artistry as a storyteller. Many authors of recently published short stories also possess the powerful attributes of invention, creation, imagination, and originality.

The contemporary short story author Lorrie Moore stated in her introduction to *The Best American Short Stories 2004* that the lasting impression of great works of art is due to "their distillation of emotion and circumstance." Moore felt that short stories were similar to song lyrics, both sharing an "interest in beautiful pain." A reader of Ernest Hemingway's story "Hills Like White Elephants" (p. 273), caught up in the intense conversation about life and death between the insistent young man and his troubled lover as they wait on a station platform for the arrival of the train to Madrid, will never forget the pain in the young woman's voice at the climax of the story. In a few pages Hemingway, a great short story writer, has created the impression we are hearing actual people talk to one another. As Moore understood, "that is how human life is best captured on the page: through its sound."

Like poems and plays, short stories are end-oriented. Their endings can shine a spotlight back to illuminate the meaning of what has gone before. The ending can also cast light on a character's epiphany or revelation of the true nature of his or her situation so clearly that it stays in your memory. Long after you have finished reading James Joyce's "Araby" (p. 317), for example, you will probably remember the scene at the end of the story where the author dramatizes the love-sick boy's painful consciousness of his folly.

In another story, "A Good Man Is Hard to Find" (p. 497), Flannery O'Connor imagines an ending that brilliantly suggests the random violence found in real life. When the author T. C. Boyle was a young college student, he first read "A Good Man Is Hard to Find" for a short story class, and he credits O'Connor's artistry as a storyteller with awakening in him the desire to be a writer.

> Here I was, enjoying a laugh-out-loud satiric piece about a conniving grandmother and the dreaded family vacation, when suddenly the story took the darkest turn possible. The work was ultimately tragic, shocking even, but I felt it and understood it in a way that forever reconfigured the way I felt about literature. There was a puzzle here—how was O'Connor able to pull it off?—and I was determined to take it apart and put it back together in order to find out.

As you become a more knowledgeable reader through your study of literature, your enjoyment of the art of the short story and your appreciation of good stories will stay with you for the rest of your life.

CLOSE READING SHORT FICTION

When you read a story for the first time, you may find it relatively easy to see how the elements of plot, character, and setting interact on the page. They stand out because they seem to make the story happen, and—at least for the casual reader—they appear to be what the story is about. Point of view, style, and theme, on the other hand, are less visible elements. Many insecure readers regard them with dread as part of what they call the "hidden meaning" of a story. While it is true that you may have to look for these particular elements deliberately, you will find that this hunt is worth the treasure. The more attentively you read, the easier it will be to appreciate how all the elements operate in short fiction. Your close reading will help you to understand more clearly that *how* a story is written is an essential part of *what* it is saying.

Close reading is reading works of literature analytically in order to understand the author's creation of design and pattern in the text. If you make the effort, you will find that reading literature is an activity that offers a worthy challenge. After finishing a short story for the first time, you may feel contradictory responses to it, uncertain how to interpret what you have read. A second reading may help clarify your impressions, or you may find you have to close your book and think about the story if it doesn't fit easily into your preconceptions about human behavior.

The effort is worthwhile. As the critic Ray Carey has explained, the different forms of storytelling can "point a way out of some of the traps of received forms of thinking and feeling. Every artist makes a fresh effort of awareness. . . . He [or she] can help us to new and potentially revolutionary understandings of our lives." Reading a good story can be an enlightening experience. You will discover that analyzing the means available to the storyteller will often help you to reach a deeper understanding of the text.

Stories are shorter than novels, but they're not necessarily easier to read. The editor Charles McGrath cautions that

> stories aren't just *brief,* they're *different,* and they require of the reader something like the degree of concentration they require of the writer. . . . You can't skim or coast or leap ahead, and if you have to put a story down, it's not always easy to pick up—emotionally, that is—where you left off. You have to backtrack a little, or even start over. It's not enough to read a story the way you read a book or a newspaper. Stories ask of us that we surrender ourselves to them.

GUIDELINES FOR READING FICTION

1. Read the story with a pen or pencil in hand, asking questions and making observations as you go. Don't be afraid to write in the margins of the text. (On the following pages you can see how you might annotate the opening of Paley's "Samuel.") Questions to consider as you read: What do you notice about the title? What's happening in the narrative? Are there words you should look up in a dictionary? Are there puzzling passages you'll want to reconsider once you've finished reading? How are the elements of fiction at work? Notice that simply highlighting sentences will not help you think as you go. Write your comments in the margins of this anthology or in your notebook.
2. Make an entry in your notebook for each story assigned in class, writing down the author's name and the story's title and date. As you begin to read your assignments, remember T. S. Eliot's advice in his

essay "Tradition and the Individual Talent." This important poet believed that "criticism is as inevitable as breathing, and that we should be none the worse for articulating what passes in our minds when we read a book and feel an emotion about it, for criticizing our own minds in their work of criticism."

3. Use a dictionary to look up any words in the story and its headnote that you do not understand.
4. After you have read the story, take notes about the way the author has used the elements of fiction; this will help you remember when you review the story later. Note, for example, the names of the characters, the geographical setting, the author's choice of a point of view, and the literary style in which it is written. Try summing up the story's theme in a sentence.
5. If you have difficulty understanding the story's meaning or how any of the elements of fiction work within it, write down your questions so you can ask them in class. The related commentaries may also throw light on the stories.
6. In class, take notes on the important material about the story that you learn from lectures and discussions, and ask any questions you have about the assignment. Later your notes may suggest new ideas to develop in your papers.
7. Review technical words about short fiction used in class in the glossary of literary terms (p. 1685). This will help you to understand them better and to use them more confidently in your writing.
8. If you have particularly enjoyed a story, go to the library to check out other works by its writer. Reading on your own will enrich the class assignments.

SAMPLE CLOSE READING

GRACE PALEY

Samuel

1968

Some boys are very tough. They're afraid of nothing. They are the ones who climb a wall and take a bow at the top. Not only are they brave on the roof, but they make a lot of noise in the darkest part of the cellar where even the super hates to go. They also jiggle and hop on the platform between the locked doors of the subway cars.

Four boys are jiggling on the swaying platform. Their names are Alfred, Calvin, Samuel, and Tom. The

In the title, Paley uses a full name, not nickname — serious tone

Introduction — Setting is a subway in New York City

Rising action — 4 boys are riding between the cars. Dangerous.

men and the women in the cars on either side watch them. They don't like them to jiggle or jump but don't want to interfere. Of course some of the men in the cars were once brave boys like these. One of them had ridden the tail of a speeding truck from New York to Rockaway Beach without getting off, without his sore fingers losing hold. Nothing happened to him then or later. He had made a compact with other boys who preferred to watch: Starting at Eighth Avenue and Fifteenth Street, he would get to some specified place, maybe Twenty-third and the river, by hopping the tops of the moving trucks. This was hard to do when one truck turned a corner in the wrong direction and the nearest truck was a couple of feet too high. He made three or four starts before succeeding. He had gotten his idea from a film at school called *The Romance of Logging.* He had finished high school, married a good friend, was in a responsible job and going to night school.

The men watching them are sympathetic.

Details about a minor character suggest that many young people take risks.

These two men and others looked at the four boys jumping and jiggling on the platform and thought, It must be fun to ride that way, especially now the weather is nice and we're out of the tunnel and way high over the Bronx. Then they thought, These kids do seem to be acting sort of stupid. They *are* little. Then they thought of some of the brave things they had done when they were boys and jiggling didn't seem so risky.

Hint of foreshadowing — they're really very young.

The ladies in the car became very angry when they looked at the four boys. Most of them brought their brows together and hoped the boys could see their extreme disapproval. One of the ladies wanted to get up and say, Be careful, you dumb kids, get off that platform or I'll call a cop. But three of the boys were Negroes and the fourth was something else she couldn't tell for sure. She was afraid they'd be fresh and laugh at her and embarrass her. She wasn't afraid they'd hit her, but she was afraid of embarrassment. Another lady thought, Their mothers never know where they are. It wasn't true in this particular case. Their mothers all knew that they had gone to see the missile exhibit on Fourteenth Street . . .

The women are angry and judgmental.

Actually the boys have responsible mothers.

CRITICAL THINKING ABOUT SHORT FICTION

You will find that reading a story carefully and discussing it in class are only part of the process of understanding it. Usually your thinking about a story begins with interpreting it, clarifying what the author is saying in the action of the plot, and making sure you understand the characters and have a clear idea of the theme of the story. Critical thinking goes a step beyond interpretation when you discuss how the form of the story is related to its content or when you analyze the story's significance, how it relates to your own experience.

Reading a commentary about a story for an essay assignment can help you to think critically. Ideas for writing can come from any number of sources. Sometimes your instructor will give you a specific assignment; other times you will be asked to generate the idea for the paper yourself. Whatever the case, your reading notes and the class discussions will help you prepare for writing about the story.

Before you can start thinking about writing your paper, you should feel that you thoroughly understand the story as a whole. When you read it again, notice the passages that strike you with particular force. Underline the words and sentences you consider significant—or, even better, make a list in your notebook of what seems important while you are rereading the story. These can be outstanding descriptions of the characters or settings, passages of meaningful dialogue, details showing the way the author builds toward the story's climax, or hints that foreshadow the conclusion. To stimulate ideas about topics, you may want to jot down answers to the following questions about the elements of the story as you reread it.

Plot. Does the plot depend on chance, or coincidence? Or does it grow out of the personalities of the characters? Are any later incidents foreshadowed early in the story? Are the events presented in chronological order? If not, why is this so? Does the climax indicate a change in a situation or a change in a character? How dramatic is this change? Or is there no change at all?

Point of View. How does the point of view shape the story? Would the story change if told from a different viewpoint? In first-person narration, can you trust the narrator?

Characterization. Are the characters believable? Are they stereotypes? Are they sympathetic or unsympathetic? Do they suggest real people or abstract qualities? Is there one protagonist, or are there several? Does the story have an antagonist? How does the author tell you about the main character: through description of physical appearance, actions, thoughts, and emotions, or through contrast with a minor character? Does the main character change in the course of the story? If so, how? Why?

Setting. How does the setting influence the plot and the characters? Does it help to suggest or develop the meaning of the story or to heighten the drama of the story?

Style. Is the story realistic or a fantasy? If dialect or colloquial speech is used, what is its effect? Does the author call attention to the way he or she uses words, or is the literary style inconspicuous? What is the tone of the story? Can you find evidence of any objects used as symbols in the narrative? If so, what do they symbolize?

Theme. Does the story's title help explain its meaning? Can you find a suggestion of the theme in specific passages of dialogue or description? Are certain symbols or repetitions of images important in revealing the author's intent in the story, what Edgar Allan Poe would call "the single effect"?

Now put the textbook aside and look over your notes. Can you see any pattern in them? You may find that you have written at length about the way the author developed characterizations, for example. Then you have a possible topic for your paper. Reading the related commentaries for a specific story may also generate ideas about its significance for you. Certainly if you have a choice, you should write about whatever most appeals to you in the story.

WRITING ABOUT SHORT FICTION

Your understanding of the elements of fiction can help you to interpret a story, but you can also appreciate that what you are reading is always much more than a self-contained, self-referential text. When writers create an imaginary world in a story, they are also referring to the world outside the text, what students often call "the real world." Literature's link to the events of human history is as real as the paper it is printed on or the screen on which it appears.

Literary critics point out that history penetrates literature in a variety of ways, and the closer a fictional work is to our own time, the more we take for granted its historical context. For example, the setting of Joyce Carol Oates's "Where Are You Going, Where Have You Been?" (p. 452) includes many details about teen culture in the early 1960s. When fifteen-year-old Connie hangs out with her friends at the drive-in restaurant across the street from the shopping plaza, they listen to "the music that made everything so good: the music was always in the background like music at a church service, it was something to depend on."

If you research the cultural context of this short story, you will learn that Connie is listening to such jukebox hits as "Kisses Sweeter Than Wine," "Chantilly Lace," "Do You Wanna Dance?" and "Ten Commandments of Love." The escapist lyrics of romantic songs like these echo in her mind when a menacing visitor, the psychopath Arnold Friend, turns up unexpectedly in her driveway. Oates dedicated the story to Bob Dylan, who redefined popular music in the mid-1960s when he wrote songs containing a tougher look at the reality of American society—songs like "It Ain't Me, Babe," "The Times They Are A-Changin'," and "Blowin' in the Wind" (p. 1059).

The historical background of some stories includes explicit statements of authorial intent that you might find helpful in writing about short fiction.

William Faulkner explained his thematic intentions in his comments on "A Rose for Emily" (p. 217). Flannery O'Connor did the same in her remarks about "A Good Man Is Hard to Find" (p. 497). For some stories you can investigate their origins by reading biographical material. At the end of the nineteenth century Charlotte Perkins Gilman dramatized her personal story to communicate how much she had suffered from mental illness, a subject not widely discussed when she wrote "The Yellow Wallpaper" (p. 226). The story emerged from Gilman's own experience of a "rest cure" prescribed by an eminent physician in Philadelphia who, like others of the time, refused to recognize a woman's need for intellectual stimulation.

Assignments for writing about short fiction may also involve the use of specific critical approaches to literature. If you take one of these approaches, you could analyze the symbolism in a story as a "reader-response" critic, or you may want to express your ideas about a story as a gender critic or a biographical critic. The headnotes and commentaries on the various authors and stories can suggest a range of approaches for you to take in an essay or a research paper.

For example, the biographical information in Grace Paley's commentary (p. 536) about how she began to write short stories after she had begun to experiment with poetry as a young writer may help you to write about her approach to storytelling in "Samuel" as a biographical critic. Paley explained that initially she wrote fiction because she was attracted to what she called "certain subject matter, women's lives specifically, and what was happening around me" (p. 537). The material in this commentary could focus your close reading of the text, stimulate your critical thinking, and help you get started on your paper. Notice that each quotation that the student uses to develop the paper is followed by a page number giving its source in *Literature and Its Writers.*

SAMPLE PAPER

Grace Paley's Commentary and "Samuel"

In an interview, Grace Paley said that she began to write poetry at an early age before she started to write short stories. When she was in her thirties she discovered that writing prose seemed to be more suited to what she called her developing interest in "certain subject matter, women's lives specifically, and what was happening around me" (p. 537).

"Samuel" is a short story that initially relies upon the author's familiarity with the subway system of New York City, where Paley was living in the 1960s when she wrote her story. She knew a lot about riding the subway when she described what happened after a passenger pulled the emergency cord, first on the train itself ("with a terrible hiss, the pressure of air abandoned the brakes and the wheels were caught and held"), and then on the passengers inside the cars ("People standing in the most secure places fell forward, then backward.") (p. 12).

In Paley's story she spent less time on her account of the accident than she did on her description of the people who happened to be in the car watching Samuel and his friends recklessly clowning around outside on the platform between the cars. The author wants the reader to care about the people in her story, rather than to dwell on the gory details of Samuel's sudden death. Paley was very restrained here. She mostly relied on action verbs, avoiding descriptive adverbs and adjectives, when she wrote her straight-forward, unflinching description of the young boy as we last see him: "he pitched only forward and fell head first to be crushed and killed between the cars" (p. 12). This brutal event prepares the reader for the introduction of Samuel's mother into the story, and her understandably hysterical response to the policeman's report of her son's death.

Paley's interest in what she called "women's lives specifically" (p. 537) is most evident in the conclusion of the story. The author's empathy for the mother's lasting sense of loss after the birth of another child is the strongest emotion in the story. Paley could have taken the death of a young boy in the subway accident as the subject of a poem, but she crafted her material into a successful prose short story as if she had tailor-made it for her readers.

OTHER RESOURCES TO HELP YOUR WRITING

Probably the best advice to give you as an aspiring writer is to tell you to write about what you know. The following chapters discuss in more detail the six elements of fiction, essential information to help you read closely and think critically about short stories. As the Russian author Isaac Babel's grandmother told him when he said he wanted to become a writer, "Then you must know everything." Understanding how different authors have used the elements of fiction to create short stories is essential to your analysis of them. To illustrate how much closer to the text these literary tools can take you, here is an example of a student paper analyzing the effect of Paley's use of point of view in "Samuel." You will find a discussion of point of view in the next chapter of this anthology.

SAMPLE PAPER

Grace Paley's Point of View in "Samuel"

As Paley's title suggests, this is a story about a particular boy named Samuel who becomes the young victim in a New York subway accident. Paley tells her story using the third-person point of view as an omniscient storyteller, knowing about events in the past and the future as well as the present. She has chosen this point of view because she believes that we are all part of one human family. We must be both cautious and compassionate when judging the actions of other people.

In the second paragraph of the story, Paley gives only the first names of the four boys: Alfred, Calvin, Samuel, and Tom. This makes you think that she knows them personally, unlike a journalist who would also use the third-person point of view reporting on a subway accident. A newspaper account would include the deceased boy's last name, but Paley is not interested in unnecessary particulars. She includes only the specific details that help you to visualize the situation so you can feel that you know her characters. Using the first names of the boys brings them closer. This sense of familiarity helps prepare you for the concluding paragraph of the story, when Paley focuses in on Samuel's mother's response to his death, something an omniscient storyteller would know.

Paley could have chosen to write "Samuel" using a first-person point of view, for example from the mother's point of view or from a spectator's point of view, but this choice would have limited the emotional impact of her story. As the omniscient storyteller she is at the scene of the accident. She is also sensitive to the gender differences in the responses to the four boys by the men and women riding in the subway car. She tells you that the men think mostly of themselves and how they did or did not take foolish chances when they were young. The women think about how the boys are putting themselves in danger by riding between the cars.

Paley also knows that judgments based on race are always present in New York City, as much today as when she published "Samuel." So as an omniscient storyteller, she takes pains to tell you that the boys came from caring homes, something that the adults on the subway don't know. The boys' mothers home in the Bronx are aware that their sons are riding the subway since "they had gone to see the missile exhibit on Fourteenth Street" (p. 11).

Paley stated in her commentary that she began writing stories because she was attracted to what she called "certain subject matter, women's lives specifically, and what was happening around me" (p. 537). To conclude her story, she tells us that "never again will a boy exactly like Samuel be known" (p. 12). Avoiding sentimentality, the omniscient author ends with a generalization reminding us that each human life is unique, and that the loss of a child is remembered by a family forever.

WEB For writing suggestions about authors in this anthology, visit bedfordstmartins.com/rewritinglit.

3.

Plot and Point of View

> A true work of fiction is a wonderfully simple thing—so simple that most so-called serious writers avoid trying it, feeling they ought to do something more important and ingenious, never guessing how incredibly difficult it is. A true work of fiction does all of the following things, and does them elegantly, efficiently: it creates a vivid and continuous dream in the reader's mind; it is implicitly philosophical; it fulfills or at least deals with all of the expectations it sets up; and it strikes us, in the end, not simply as a thing done but as a shining performance.
>
> –JOHN GARDNER, *"What Writers Do"*

Most of you will be familiar with short stories and can identify them as short fictional prose narratives, whether written by authors in the United States or in countries throughout the world, since all writers of short stories employ the same elements of fiction. In the imaginations of gifted storytellers, these components are set in motion and help to create the particular form each short story takes in the writing process. Literary critics generally agree that the basic means available to authors of short fiction comprise six different elements: plot, point of view, characterization, setting, style, and theme. Usually you begin a discussion of the elements of fiction with plot, since it is basic to this literary genre.

PLOT

The **short story** is defined as a prose narrative usually involving one unified episode or a sequence of related events. **Plot** is the sequence of events in a story and their relation to one another. Writers usually present the events of the plot in a coherent time frame that you can follow easily. As you read, you sense that the events are related by causation (or why something in the plot happened next), and their meaning lies in this relation. If you read the story casually, causation seems to result only from the writer's organization of the events into a chronological sequence. If you read it more carefully, however, you will understand that causation in the plot of a memorable short story also shows you something about the characters at the same time.

As the novelist E. M. Forster understood, plot not only answers the question *what* happened next, but it also suggests *why.* The psychologist James Hillman has explained in *Healing Fiction* that plot reveals "human intentions. Plot shows how it all hangs together and makes sense. Only when a narrative receives inner coherence in terms of the depths of human nature do we have fiction, and for this fiction we have to have plot. To plot is to move from asking the question *and then what happened?* to the question *why did it happen?*"

A short story can dramatize the events of a brief episode or compress a longer period of time. Analyzing why a short story is short, the critic Norman Friedman suggested that it "may be short not because its action is inherently small, but rather because the author has chosen—in working with an episode or plot—to omit certain of its parts. In other words, an action may be large in size and still be short in the telling because not all of it is there." A short story can describe something that happens in a few minutes or encompass action that takes years to conclude. The narrative possibilities are endless, as the writer may omit or condense complex episodes to intensify their dramatic effect or expand a single incident to make a relatively long story.

Regardless of length, the plot of a short story usually has what critics term an **end orientation**—the outcome of an action or the conclusion of the plot—inherent in its opening paragraphs. As Mark Twain humorously observed, "Fiction is obliged to stick to possibilities. Truth isn't." The novelist may conclude a single episode long before the end of a novel and then pick up the thread of another narrative, or interpret an event from another angle in a different character's point of view, linking episode to episode and character to character so that each illuminates the other. But a story stops earlier. As Edgar Allan Poe recognized in his review of Nathaniel Hawthorne's tales in 1842, its narrative dramatizes a single effect complete unto itself (p. 650).

The events in the plot of a short story usually involve a conflict or struggle between opposing forces. When you analyze a plot, you can often (but not always) see it develop in stages during the course of the narration. Typically you find that the first paragraphs of the story or **exposition** suggest the background or set the scene of the conflict. The **rising action** dramatizes the specific events that set the conflict in motion. Often there is a **turning point** in the story midway before further complications prolong the suspense of the conflict's resolution. The **climax** is the emotional high point of the narration. In the **falling action**, the events begin to wind down and prepare for the **conclusion** or **denouement** at the end of the story, which usually resolves the conflict to a greater or lesser degree. Sometimes the conclusion introduces an unexpected turn of events or a **surprise ending**. If the conflict dramatized in the story is not resolved in the conclusion, it is considered a story with an **open ending**. If the conflict is resolved, it is a **closed ending**. Stories concluding with the death of the main character are usually considered to have closed endings.

In successful stories the writer shapes these stages into a complex structure that may impress you with its balance and proportion. The beginning sets up the problem or conflict; the middle is where the author introduces various complications that prolong suspense and make the struggle more meaningful;

and the end resolves the conflict to a greater or lesser degree. Plots are satisfying because writers are free to imagine characters and actions that animate or bring to life a pattern that implies a meaning in its narrative "progress" toward resolution.

Plot Summary

Often you'll find that writing a summary of the plot or listing the story's important events as you analyze its narrative stages can help you to think critically about it. The plot of Paley's "Samuel," which you read in Chapter 1, is very simple since it is very short and describes only a brief episode on a New York City subway train. It dramatizes a sequence of events involving four young boys who are fooling around on the platform between two cars of a moving train. A woman watching them tells them they'll get hurt, but the boys only laugh at her. A man sees them laughing, gets angry, and pulls the emergency cord. The train lurches to a stop, causing one of the boys to fall and be crushed to death. The mother of the dead boy grieves, then becomes hopeful after she becomes pregnant again. After the birth of her baby, she realizes that the new child can never replace the son she has lost.

When you analyze the stages of the plot, you might say that the first part or *exposition* of "Samuel" is the opening paragraph. It introduces the idea that motivates the main characters of Paley's brief drama, the idea that boys have fun showing off for one another. The *rising action* dramatizes the conflict of interest between the young boys and the adults watching them in the subway car. Some of the men in the car sympathize with the kids, remembering the dangerous stunts they pulled when they were young. Most of the women in the car feel that the boys should behave more responsibly by taking seats and calming down. The *turning point* is when one of the women, with a son at home, summons her courage and admonishes the boys. They make fun of her, and this raises the tension of the story by adding a complicating factor of defiance to their behavior. The *climax* of "Samuel" occurs when an angry man pulls the emergency cord and Samuel is killed. In the *falling action,* Paley describes the result of the accident. Traffic on the subway line is stopped, the passengers who saw the accident are in shock, the others riding the train are curious, and a policeman notifies Samuel's mother of his death. The *conclusion* is the final paragraph of the story, more than a year later, when Samuel's parents understand the full dimension of their loss after the birth of another child.

Since Paley's story is so short, it is more of a sketch than a fully developed narrative. It has only a few sentences of **dialogue**. A woman warns the boys that they might get hurt, and the boys find her warning hilarious. Samuel pounds his buddy Alfred's back until tears come, saying "You a baby, huh?" Paley gives a hint of **foreshadowing** in the opening paragraphs, suggesting the accident to come, when some of the men watching the boys think, "These kids do seem to be acting sort of stupid. They *are* little." These words anticipate a turn of events that you may or may not expect as you read the story for the first time. When you reread the story, you see that Paley's plot runs along as solidly as a subway train. Not for her are the tricky surprise endings favored in stories by many earlier writers such as Guy de Maupassant and Kate Chopin, who often twisted the plots of their stories so they would take unexpected directions in their final sentences.

In "Samuel" you sense Paley's emotional involvement in her fictional characters as she chronicles the tragedy of a small boy's accidental death. With her choice of her main character's name as the title of the story, Paley sets up the expectation that her narrative will be about Samuel and that its "single effect" will be the shock of his death. Paley doesn't go on to tell us about the lives of the three boys who survive the accident or about the guilty feelings (and perhaps the subsequent breakdown?) of the angry man who pulls the emergency cord. That, after all, would be another story.

Regardless of the author's method of developing the plot, the goal is the same: The writer of short stories must *show* you something about human nature through the dramatic action of the plot and the other elements of the story, and not just *tell* you what to think. A good plot arouses your curiosity, engages your emotions, and keeps you in suspense. As the contemporary American writer Eudora Welty understood, "A narrative line is in its deeper sense, of course, the tracing out of a meaning, and the real continuity of a story lies in this probing forward." A storyteller must sustain the illusion of reality until the end of the story, unfolding events with the continuing revelation of an apparently endless silk handkerchief drawn from a skillful magician's coat sleeve.

Here is another contemporary short story, "Popular Mechanics" by Raymond Carver, for you to practice your skill at close reading as you analyze the various stages of a plot's development. Carver based his short story on the biblical parable about the judgment of King Solomon (p. 9), but the American author gave it a modern setting and a very different conclusion with his use of a surprise ending.

RAYMOND CARVER
Popular Mechanics

1977

Early that day the weather turned and the snow was melting into dirty water. Streaks of it ran down from the little shoulder-high window that faced the backyard. Cars slushed by on the street outside, where it was getting dark. But it was getting dark on the inside too.

He was in the bedroom pushing clothes into a suitcase when she came to the door.

I'm glad you're leaving! I'm glad you're leaving! she said. Do you hear?

He kept on putting his things into the suitcase.

Son of a bitch! I'm so glad you're leaving! She began to cry. You can't even look me in the face, can you?

Then she noticed the baby's picture on the bed and picked it up.

He looked at her and she wiped her eyes and stared at him before turning and going back to the living room.

Bring that back, he said.

Just get your things and get out, she said.

He did not answer. He fastened the suitcase, put on his coat, looked around the bedroom before turning off the light. Then he went out to the living room.

She stood in the doorway of the little kitchen, holding the baby.

I want the baby, he said.

Are you crazy?

No, but I want the baby. I'll get someone to come by for his things.

You're not touching this baby, she said.

The baby had begun to cry and she uncovered the blanket from around his head.

Oh, oh, she said, looking at the baby.

He moved toward her.

For God's sake! she said. She took a step back into the kitchen.

I want the baby.

Get out of here!

She turned and tried to hold the baby over in a corner behind the stove.

But he came up. He reached across the stove and tightened his hands on the baby.

Let go of him, he said.

Get away, get away! she cried.

The baby was red-faced and screaming. In the scuffle they knocked down a flowerpot that hung behind the stove.

He crowded her into the wall then, trying to break her grip. He held on to the baby and pushed with all his weight.

Let go of him, he said.

Don't, she said. You're hurting the baby, she said.

I'm not hurting the baby, he said.

The kitchen window gave no light. In the near-dark he worked on her fisted fingers with one hand and with the other hand he gripped the screaming baby up under an arm near the shoulder.

She felt her fingers being forced open. She felt the baby going from her.

No! she screamed just as her hands came loose.

She would have it, this baby. She grabbed for the baby's other arm. She caught the baby around the wrist and leaned back.

But he would not let go. He felt the baby slipping out of his hands and he pulled back very hard.

In this manner, the issue was decided.

◆ Questions for Critical Thinking about Plot ◆

1. How would you summarize the plot of "Popular Mechanics"?
2. Does the plot depend on chance or coincidence? Or does it grow out of the personalities of the characters?

3. Where is the exposition in the story? How does the foreshadowing in Carver's description of the weather heighten the dramatic situation of the quarreling couple?
4. How much of the interaction between the couple is the rising action of the plot?
5. What does this long rising action contribute to the sudden climax of the story?
6. Does the climax indicate a change in the situation or a change in the two characters?
7. Is there any falling action or conclusion in Carver's narrative?
8. What is the effect of the author's surprise ending?
9. What does Carver mean in the story's final sentence? How does this ending make this an open plotted story?
10. How does the title of the story relate to the plot?

◆ Topics for Writing about Plot ◆

1. Compare and contrast the plot of Carver's "Popular Mechanics" with the biblical story about the judgment of King Solomon (p. 9). You will find a discussion of how to use comparison and contrast, along with a sample student paper, on pages 1647–1651.
2. Create at least two additional paragraphs for "Popular Mechanics" after Carver's final words, "In this manner, the issue was decided." Then write a short paper analyzing what the story has gained or lost by the new ending you've created for the plot. You will find a discussion of how to use analysis, along with a sample paper, on pages 1644–1647.

Here is another recent story with a plot developed through an exchange of words or dialogue, Alasdair Gray's "Pillow Talk." This is a humorous story, and its plot doesn't have a disturbing surprise ending. It is an example of a closed ending since the particular quarrel dramatized in the story has been more or less resolved by the half hour of silence between the couple before the wife switches off her bedside lamp to go to sleep. As you read the story, notice how subtly the author divulges information to whet your curiosity about the unhappily married pair, instead of relying on sensational events to keep you interested in the plot. His artifice begins with the important first word of the story.

ALASDAIR GRAY

Pillow Talk

2003

Wakening he turned his head and saw she was still reading.

After a moment he said,

"About that e-mail you sent."

"I never sent you an e-mail," she said, eyes still on the book.

"Not before today, perhaps, but this afternoon you e-mailed me and said—"

"I repeat," she interrupted, looking hard at him, "I have never sent you or anyone else an e-mail in my life."

"But you did send one to the office this afternoon. I remember it perfectly—the heading stating it was from you to me and everyone else in the firm. Why did you have to tell *them*? You must have sent it from a friend's computer or one in the public library."

"You're still drunk."

"If you mean I was drunk when we came to bed you are wrong. We had only one bottle of wine with the evening meal and I drank only one more glass of it than you. I'm glad you're sorry you sent that message but you'll never persuade me you didn't."

"You're hallucinating. What am I supposed to have said?"

"That you want to leave me. Five words—*I want to leave you*—just that." She stared at him, shut the book and said bitterly, "Oh, very clever. Cruel, but clever."

"Do you want to leave me?"

"Yes, but I never told you so. I've never told anyone that—they think ours is such a *solid* marriage. You must have noticed it's a farce and this is your bloody cunning way of blaming me for something I never said and was never going to say."

"Blethers!" he cried, "I am *never* cunning, *never* cruel. I remember these words coming up very clear and distinct on the computer screen: *I want to leave you*."

"Then why didn't you mention it when you came home? Why didn't you mention it over dinner? Are you going to pretend you were brooding over it before we came to bed?" He thought hard for a while then said, "You're right. I must have dreamed it before I woke a moment ago."

"I'm glad you've sobered up," she said and resumed reading.

After a while he said, "But you want to leave me."

She sighed and said nothing.

"When will you do it?"

"I don't suppose I'll ever do it," she murmured, still appearing to read, "I haven't the courage to live alone. You're an alcoholic bore but not violent and I'm too old to find anyone better."

"I'm glad!" he said loudly. "I don't want you ever to leave because I love you. My life will be a misery if you leave me."

"Then you're luckier than I am. Go back to sleep."

He turned away from her and tried to sleep. About half an hour later he heard her shut the book and switch off the bedside lamp. He got up and went to a room next door where he had hidden

a bottle of whisky for this

sort of emergency.

POINT OF VIEW

Point of view refers to the author's choice of a **narrator** for the story. After you understand how the author developed the plot, it is helpful to consider the point of view taken in the story. Thinking critically about point of view often helps you to become more analytical about all the elements of fiction. Early in the writing process, the author must decide whether to employ **first-person narration**, using the pronoun *I*, or **third-person narration**, using the pronouns *he, she,* and *they.* **Second-person narration**, *you,* is less common, although the dramatic intimacy of second-person narrative address is often used in poetry and song lyrics.

First-person narration is usually the point of view you use when you tell stories about the events in your life. You might assume that your familiarity with it makes it easy to read and understand. Be aware that short story authors experiment with first-person narration just as often as they do with third-person narration. Telling a story in the first person is so commonplace that you may think that's the reason the 2009 Nobel Prize winner, Romanian-born German writer Herta Müller, reversed straightforward chronology instead of moving through time more or less sequentially in "Workday." This reversal begins in the third sentence of her brief story.

HERTA MÜLLER

Workday

1982

TRANSLATED BY SIEGLINDE LUG

Seven-thirty in the morning. The alarm rings.

I get up, take off my dress, put it on the pillow, put on my pajamas, go to the kitchen, get into the bathtub, take the towel, wash my face with it, take the comb, dry myself with it, take the toothbrush, comb my hair with it, take the sponge, brush my teeth with it. Then I go to the bathroom, eat a slice of tea, and drink a cup of bread.

I take off my wristwatch and my rings.

I take off my shoes.

I go out to the staircase, then I open the apartment door.

I take the elevator from the fifth to the first floor.

Then I walk up nine flights of stairs and find myself in the street.

In the food store I buy a newspaper, then I go to the streetcar stop and buy myself some rolls, and when I arrive at the newspaper stand I get into the streetcar.

Three stops before getting on I get off.

I answer the greeting of the doorman, then the doorman greets me and says, here it's Monday again and again a week is over.

I enter the office, say good-bye, hang my jacket on the desk, sit down at the coat rack, and start working. I work for eight hours.

In your close reading, after you understood Müller had deliberately organized the events of "Workday" into an incoherent time frame, did the story involve you on a deeper emotional level by engaging your curiosity and making you want to know more about the fictional character? Müller sacrificed more than temporal continuity in her story. You could argue that the author also sacrificed the plot in "Workday" since the character's actions seem to have no relation to one another and tell you very little about her.

"Workday" could be described as a simple **narrative**, a connected succession of events or happenings. Since Müller did not reveal the intentions or the feelings of the woman who performs the actions, you might not even consider it a story, though it is included in Müller's short story collections. Müller was experimenting with the point of view, and so can you. Try rewriting "Workday" as a third-person narration, using the pronoun "she" instead of "I." Then you might come closer to understanding the reason why Müller chose the first-person point of view.

A writer's choice of a point of view to narrate stories usually falls into two major categories:

FIRST-PERSON NARRATION (NARRATOR APPARENTLY A PARTICIPANT IN THE STORY)

1. A major character
2. A minor character

THIRD-PERSON NARRATION (NARRATOR A NONPARTICIPANT IN THE STORY)

1. Omniscient—seeing into the minds of all characters
2. Limited omniscient—seeing into one or, sometimes, two characters' minds
3. Objective—seeing into none of the characters' minds

First-Person Narration

When reading a story written in the first person, regardless of whether the narrator is a major or minor character, you should keep in mind that you are reading fiction and that the narrator is rarely the author. As a prize-winning writer, Müller is clearly not the fictional woman in "Workday" employed in an office job. Whether the first-person narrator is a major or a minor character, he or she can be an **unreliable narrator**. In many longer stories you may become aware that the account is skewed and that you can't trust the first-person narrator's point of view.

For example, at the beginning of Charlotte Perkins Gilman's "The Yellow Wallpaper" (p. 226), the first-person narrator, who is the major character in the story, says that she is trying to regain her health after a mental breakdown. As she tells her story, an attentive reader notices that her disorientation from the so-called real world becomes much more acute. She is an unreliable narrator, but this doesn't diminish the power of her story. In Herman Melville's "Bartleby, the Scrivener" (p. 406), a garrulous lawyer introduces himself as the first-person narrator. The name of his eccentric copier is the title of the story. As you read along you discover that the lawyer is concerned for his employees, but he is unreliable because he serves as a screen between you and the events he describes. This makes it impossible for you to come closer to Bartleby to gain your own impression of his enigmatic state of mind and heightens your frustration as you read about his actions "second hand." Both Melville and Gilman choose their first-person narrators carefully to heighten the emotional effect of their stories.

Third-Person Narration

Third-person narration means that the author tells the story using the pronouns *he* or *she* instead of the presumably more subjective *I*. Paley uses third-person narration in "Samuel." The narrator isn't a person who participates in the story, but she knows everything about it. She is an **omniscient narrator**, aware of everything about the characters, including important information that happened before the action of the story, such as that the boys' mothers gave them permission to take the subway downtown to see the missile exhibit in Manhattan. Paley gives you a sense of her authority so that you believe her story—or you suspend your disbelief while you read it—because she is so knowledgeable about the incident she describes. You trust her to get the story right. Most people like to read stories told by omniscient narrators, anticipating that they will usually find meaning in the events that they describe.

There can be significant differences in the way that authors handle third-person narration. Kate Chopin is a **limited-omniscient narrator** in "The Story of an Hour" (p. 174), confining herself to revealing the thoughts of only the central character, Mrs. Mallard. Chopin is making an effort to engage our sympathies for this character. Ernest Hemingway is an **objective narrator** in "Hills Like White Elephants" (p. 273). He relies almost entirely on the dialogue between the two characters to tell you about the crisis in their relationship. Hemingway attempts to create a totally detached point of view. He doesn't take sides in the battle between the two lovers over the important decision they must make. You don't have the narrator's comments or the characters' reflections. This heightens the emotion of the desperate struggle you sense reading between the lines of the story. Carver acknowledged his debt to Hemingway's earlier use of objective third-person narration. Müller experimented with the uncommon use of objective first-person narration in "Workday."

You can classify narration further into subcategories (for example, first- and third-person **stream-of-consciousness narration**). A writer's way of combining different points of view, if successful, always appears to be more flexible than the rigid categories imply. For example, Franz Kafka begins "The Metamorphosis" (p. 340) with a sentence of third-person objective omniscient narration, but in the second sentence he changes his focus to limit it to his protagonist Gregor Samsa's point of view. Kafka maintains this limited-omniscient narration until Gregor's death. Then, to heighten our sense of Gregor's alienation from his family, Kafka reverts back to his more distant, objective omniscient voice to finish the story.

Here's a short story by the California writer Dagoberto Gilb using a third-person point of view. In your first reading you may think that the story is narrated objectively, but you will find that the author gives you many clues about his attitude toward his main character.

DAGOBERTO GILB

Love in L.A.

1993

Jake slouched in a clot of near motionless traffic, in the peculiar gray of concrete, smog, and early morning beneath the overpass of the Hollywood Freeway on Alvarado Street. He didn't really mind because he knew how much worse it could be trying to make a left onto the onramp. He certainly didn't do that every day of his life, and he'd assure anyone who'd ask that he never would either. A steady occupation had its advantages and he couldn't deny thinking about that too. He needed an FM radio in something better than this '58 Buick he drove. It would have crushed velvet interior with electric controls for the L.A. summer, a nice warm heater and defroster for the winter drives at the beach, a cruise control for those longer trips, mellow speakers front and rear of course, windows that hum closed, snuffing out that nasty exterior noise of freeways. The fact was that he'd probably have to change his whole style. Exotic colognes, plush, dark nightclubs, maitais and daquiris, necklaced ladies in satin gowns, misty and sexy like in a tequila ad. Jake could imagine lots of possibilities when he let himself, but none that ended up with him pressed onto a stalled freeway.

Jake was thinking about this freedom of his so much that when he glimpsed its green light he just went ahead and stared bye bye to the steadily employed. When he turned his head the same direction his windshield faced, it was maybe one second too late. He pounced the brake pedal and steered the front wheels away from the tiny brakelights but the smack was unavoidable. Just one second sooner and it would only have been close. One second more and he'd be crawling up the Toyota's trunk. As it was, it seemed like only a harmless smack, much less solid than the one against his back bumper.

Jake considered driving past the Toyota but was afraid the traffic ahead would make it difficult. As he pulled up against the curb a few carlengths ahead, it occurred to him that the traffic might have helped him get away too.

He slammed the car door twice to make sure it was closed fully and to give himself another second more, then toured front and rear of his Buick for damage on or near the bumpers. Not an impressionable scratch even in the chrome. He perked up. Though the car's beauty was secondary to its ability to start and move, the body and paint were clean except for a few minor dings. This stood out as one of his few clearcut accomplishments over the years.

Before he spoke to the driver of the Toyota, whose looks he could see might present him with an added complication, he signaled to the driver of the car that hit him, still in his car and stopped behind the Toyota, and waved his hands and shook his head to let the man know there was no problem as far as he was concerned. The driver waved back and started his engine.

"It didn't even scratch my paint," Jake told her in that way of his. "So how you doin? Any damage to the car? I'm kinda hoping so, just so it takes a little more time and we can talk some. Or else you can give me your phone number now and I won't have to lay my regular b.s. on you to get it later."

He took her smile as a good sign and relaxed. He inhaled her scent like it was clean air and straightened out his less than new but not unhip clothes.

"You've got Florida plates. You look like you must be Cuban."

"My parents are from Venezuela."

"My name's Jake." He held out his hand.

"Mariana."

They shook hands like she'd never done it before in her life.

"I really am sorry about hitting you like that." He sounded genuine. He fondled the wide dimple near the cracked taillight. "It's amazing how easy it is to put a dent in these new cars. They're so soft they might replace waterbeds soon." Jake was confused about how to proceed with this. So much seemed so unlikely, but there was always possibility. "So maybe we should go out to breakfast somewhere and talk it over."

"I don't eat breakfast."

"Some coffee then."

"Thanks, but I really can't."

"You're not married, are you? Not that that would matter that much to me. I'm an openminded kinda guy."

She was smiling. "I have to get to work."

"That sounds boring."

"I better get your driver's license," she said.

Jake nodded, disappointed. "One little problem," he said. "I didn't bring it. I just forgot it this morning. I'm a musician," he exaggerated greatly, "and, well, I dunno, I left my wallet in the pants I was wearing last night. If you have some paper and a pen I'll give you my address and all that."

He followed her to the glove compartment side of her car.

"What if we don't report it to the insurance companies? I'll just get it fixed for you."

"I don't think my dad would let me do that."

"Your dad? It's not your car?"

"He bought it for me. And I live at home."

"Right." She was slipping away from him. He went back around to the back of her new Toyota and looked over the damage again. There was the trunk lid, the bumper, a rear panel, a taillight.

"You do have insurance?" she asked, suspicious, as she came around the back of the car.

"Oh yeah," he lied.

"I guess you better write the name of that down too."

He made up a last name and address and wrote down the name of an insurance company an old girlfriend once belonged to. He considered giving a real phone number but went against that idea and made one up.

"I act too," he lied to enhance the effect more. "Been in a couple of movies."

She smiled like a fan.

"So how about your phone number?" He was rebounding maturely.

She gave it to him.

"Mariana, you are beautiful," he said in his most sincere voice.

"Call me," she said timidly.

Jake beamed. "We'll see you, Mariana," he said holding out his hand. Her hand felt so warm and soft he felt like he'd been kissed.

Back in his car he took a moment or two to feel both proud and sad about his performance. Then he watched the rear view mirror as Mariana pulled up behind him. She was writing down the license plate numbers on his Buick, ones that he'd taken off a junk because the ones that belonged to his had expired so long ago. He turned the ignition key and revved the big engine and clicked into drive. His sense of freedom swelled as he drove into the now moving street traffic, though he couldn't stop the thought about that FM stereo radio and crushed velvet interior and the new car smell that would even make it better.

◆ Questions for Critical Thinking about Point of View ◆

1. How does the third-person point of view shape "Love in L.A."?
2. Is Gilb using an objective point of view in his story? Give some examples in the text where Gilb suggests his opinion of his main character.
3. What did Gilb gain by using third-person narration, instead of telling you about this minor traffic accident in Los Angeles from the first-person point of view of Jake or Mariana?
4. How does the point of view Gilb takes in narrating this story help you to understand the title of the story?

◆ Topics for Writing about Point of View ◆

1. Analyze the effect of the third-person, limited-omniscient point of view in "Love in L.A. " You will find a sample student paper analyzing the point of view in Paley's "Samuel" on page 23.
2. Rewrite "Love in L.A." from Mariana's point of view. Use the same plot, but expand the information about her in the narrative to emphasize her frame of mind, her family background, and her different interests as a young woman living in Southern California.

USEFUL TERMS TO REMEMBER

Climax The turning point or point of highest interest in a narrative, usually the point at which the most important part of the action takes place and the final outcome of the plot becomes inevitable.

Closed ending A story that concludes with a resolution of the conflict, even temporary. Stories that conclude with the death of the protagonist are considered to have closed endings.

Conclusion or denouement The end of the story in which the resolution of the climactic action is often presented.

Dialogue The exchange of words between characters in a story. Don't confuse it with DIALECT, which is a type of nonstandard English diction spoken by people from a particular geographic region, economic group, or social class.

End orientation The suggestion of the outcome of the action or the conclusion of the plot contained in the opening paragraphs of a short story.

Exposition The presentation of background information, usually early in a story, that a reader must be aware of, especially about situations that exist and events that have occurred before the plot begins.

Falling action The events of a narrative that follow the climax and bring the story to its conclusion or denouement.

Foreshadowing The introduction of specific words into a narrative to suggest or anticipate later events that are central to the action and its resolution.

Limited-omniscient narrator A way of telling a story in which the thoughts of only one character are revealed to the reader.

Narrative A connected succession of events or happenings.

Narrator The teller of the story, not necessarily the author.

Objective narrator A way of telling a story without revealing the thoughts or feelings of any character. The detached and impersonal narrator reports action and dialogue directly, without analysis or interpretation, relying on the dialogue, actions, and physical descriptions to reveal the meaning of the story to the reader.

Omniscient narrator Literally "all-knowingness"; the ability of an author or narrator (usually in third-person narration) to tell the reader directly about any events that have occurred, are occurring, or will occur in the plot of the story, and about the thoughts and feelings of any character.

Open ending A story that concludes without completing a resolution of the conflict.

Plot What happens in the action of a story.

Point of view The author's choice of a narrator for the story to shape what the reader knows and how the reader feels about the events of the story. See also FIRST-PERSON NARRATION, SECOND-PERSON NARRATION, and THIRD-PERSON NARRATION in the glossary.

Rising action The events of a narrative that precede the climax and heighten the tension or suspense of the story.

Short story A short fictional prose narrative, usually involving one unified episode or a sequence of significantly related events.

Stream-of-consciousness narration A way of telling a story that attempts to dramatize a preverbal level of consciousness in an interior monologue.

Surprise or twist ending A story that has an unexpected ending, often based on important information deliberately withheld from the earlier stages of the narrative.

Turning point A significant event in the rising action of the story that precipitates the climax.

Unreliable narrator A story narrator who cannot be trusted to describe the events or the other characters accurately.

4.

Character and Setting

CHARACTER

If you are like most readers, plot is what keeps you going when you first start a story, and character is what stays with you after you have finished reading it. **Characters** are usually the people who are involved in what happens in a story. Writers can use animals as characters, or giant insects such as Gregor Samsa, the protagonist of Franz Kafka's "The Metamorphosis" (p. 340), or even such inanimate objects as trees, chairs, and shoes. But by the term *character* we usually mean a human being with emotions whose mind works something like our own.

When we ask *Why did it happen?* about the plot of a story, we usually find the answer in the characters, who are convincing if we can understand their actions. You instinctively strive to connect the events of a story by more than their simple chronological sequence because assuming connections between the events and the lives of the characters makes the story seem coherent. In conventional stories most authors develop their fictional characters through description (what they do and what they think) and through dialogue (what they say and what they hear).

All of the characters in the stories you've read so far in these introductory chapters—King Solomon, Samuel, Jake and Mariana, as well as the unnamed characters—are considered to be **static**, not **dynamic**. The stories about them are so short that you don't see them change or develop by the conclusion of the plot. They are **flat**, not **round** characters. You don't get a chance to feel the play and pull of their responses to situations. They might even be considered **stock characters**, one-dimensional characters who exhibit only stereotypical features such as a wise biblical king. In the longer stories in this anthology you will meet many fictional characters, including Gregor Samsa, Bartleby, and the unnamed narrator of "The Yellow Wallpaper," who are so round and dynamic that they become unforgettable. When you think critically about a story, you will discover whether you feel that its fictional characters are **sympathetic** or **unsympathetic**, whether they arouse your sympathy or your negative judgment.

How are the characters in a short story to be understood? Any discussion of character tends to drift into a value judgment, as our principles of definition and evaluation for fictional characters are based on the ones used for real people, tentative and unfocused as they may be. You must remember that you are reading about *fictional* characters in a short story, not real ones. Sometimes the characters seem so vivid that they come to life on the page, and you feel sympathy for them even when you know that they are dishonest and deceitful. For example, Jack is so caught up in his dream life that you may have found him a sympathetic if weak character. Reading "Love in L.A.," you watch him swagger and lie as he tries unsuccessfully to impress Mariana. After he pulls away from her Toyota into the moving swirl of traffic, you may even feel a bit sorry for him as his attention drifts uncontrollably back to his voluptuous dream of what it would be like to drive an expensive new car.

The only evidence you have about characters is what the author puts into the story. The main character is often called the **protagonist**, and if the plot dramatizes a conflict, the secondary character is called the **antagonist**. Sometimes a group of people, such as Gregor Samsa's family members, can be considered antagonists since they seem to live in opposition to the protagonist.

Some authors, such as Edgar Allan Poe, create a fantasy world in their stories, imagining situations in which their characters have total control like Poe's protagonist Montresor in "The Cask of Amontillado" (p. 543). Pigeonholing his character does not bring you closer to understanding the sense of horror that Poe evokes in the story. You can appreciate it more readily by relishing the language Poe uses in dialogue and description to show us Montresor's thoughts and responses as he acts out his obsessive plan to avenge his honor by murdering Fortunato, the man he considers his enemy. As the literary critic David Reynolds has realized, the two characters in this classic short story, although limited, are not flat.

> They come swiftly alive before our eyes because Poe describes them with acute psychological realism. Montresor is a complex Machiavellian criminal, exhibiting a full range of traits from clever ingratiation to stark sadism. Fortunato, the dupe whose pride leads to his own downfall, nevertheless exhibits . . . admirable qualities. . . . The drama of the story lies in the carefully orchestrated interaction between the two. Poe directs our attention away from the merely sensational and toward the psychological.

Here's a recent story titled "Jim" by the Chilean writer Roberto Bolaño. It describes two characters who would have found themselves right at home in Poe's fictional world.

ROBERTO BOLAÑO

Jim

2003

TRANSLATED BY CHRIS ANDREWS

Many years ago I had a friend named Jim, and he was the saddest North American I've ever come across. I've seen a lot of desperate men. But never one as sad as Jim. Once he went to Peru—supposedly for more than six months, but it wasn't long before I saw him again. The Mexican street kids used to ask him, what's poetry made of, Jim? Listening to them, Jim would stare at the clouds and then he'd start throwing up. Vocabulary, eloquence, the search for truth. Epiphany. Like when you have a vision of the Virgin. He was mugged several times in Central America, which is surprising, because he'd been a Marine and fought in Vietnam. No more fighting, Jim used to say. I'm a poet now, searching for the extraordinary, trying to express it in ordinary, everyday words. So you think there are ordinary, everyday words? I think there are, Jim used to say. His wife was a Chicana poet: every so often she'd threaten to leave him. He showed me a photo of her. She wasn't especially pretty. Her face betrayed suffering, and under that suffering, simmering rage. I imagined her in an apartment in San Francisco or a house in Los Angeles, with the windows shut and the curtains open, sitting at a table, eating sliced bread and a bowl of green soup. Jim liked dark women, apparently, history's secret women, he would say, without elaborating. As for me, I liked blondes. Once I saw him watching fire-eaters on a street in Mexico City. I saw him from behind, and I didn't say hello, but it was obviously Jim. The badly cut hair, the dirty white shirt and the stoop, as if he were still weighed down by his pack. Somehow his neck, his red neck, summoned up the image of a lynching in the country—a landscape in black and white, without billboards or gas station lights—the country as it is or ought to be: one expanse of idle land blurring into the next, brick-walled rooms or bunkers from which we have escaped, standing there, awaiting our return. Jim had his hands in his pockets. The fire-eater was waving his torch and laughing fiercely. His blackened face was ageless: he could have been thirty-five or fifteen. He wasn't wearing a shirt and there was a vertical scar from his navel to his breastbone. Every so often he'd fill his mouth with flammable liquid and spit out a long snake of fire. The people in the street would watch him for a while, admire his skill, and continue on their way, except for Jim, who remained there on the edge of the sidewalk, stock-still, as if he expected something more from the fire-eater, a tenth signal (having deciphered the usual nine), or as if he'd seen in that discolored face the features of an old friend or of someone he'd killed. I watched him for a good long while. I was eighteen or nineteen at the time and believed I was immortal. If I'd realized that I wasn't, I would have turned around and walked away. After a while I got tired of looking at Jim's back and the fire-eater's grimaces. So I went over and called his name. Jim didn't seem to hear me. When he turned around I noticed that his face was covered with sweat. He seemed to be feverish, and it took him a while to work out who I was; he greeted me with a nod and then turned back to the fire-eater. Standing beside him, I noticed he was crying. He probably had a fever as well. I also discovered something that surprised me less at the time than it does now, writing this: the fire-eater was performing exclusively for Jim, as if all the other passersby on that corner in Mexico City simply didn't exist. Sometimes the flames came within a yard of where we were standing. What are you waiting for, I said, you want to get barbecued in the street? It was a stupid wisecrack, I said it without thinking, but then it hit me: that's exactly what Jim's waiting for. That year, I seem to remember, there was a song they kept playing in some of the funkier places with a refrain that went, *Chingado, hechizado (Fucked up, spellbound)*. That was Jim: fucked up and spellbound. Mexico's spell had bound him and now he was looking his demons right in the face. Let's get out of here, I said. I also asked him if he was high, or feeling ill. He shook his head. The fire-eater was staring at us. Then, with his cheeks puffed out like Aeolus, the god of the winds, he began to approach us. In a fraction of a second I realized that it wasn't a gust of wind we'd be getting. Let's go, I said, and yanked Jim away from the fatal edge of that sidewalk. We took ourselves off down the street toward Reforma, and after a while we went our separate ways. Jim didn't say a word in all that time. I never saw him again.

◆ Questions for Critical Thinking about Character ◆

1. Are the characters believable in "Jim"? How does Bolaño keep them from becoming stereotypes?
2. Do the characters suggest real people, or do they bring to mind abstract qualities?
3. Are there one or two protagonists in the story, or does Bolaño present one of the men as an antagonist? What is the difference between them, simmering below the surface but emerging in the insistent *I* of the first-person narrator? What do you think the narrator means when he says that he believed at the time he "was immortal"?
4. How does Bolaño show you the characters – through descriptions of physical appearance, actions, thoughts and emotions, or through contrast with the first-person narrator?
5. Do the characters change in the course of the story? If so, how?

◆ Topics for Writing about Character ◆

1. Analyze the roles played by the different characters in Bolaño's short story: Jim, the narrator, and the fire eater. For example, what does the reference to Jim's wife, the Chicana poet, add to the story? You will find a discussion of how to use analysis, along with a sample student paper, on pages 1644–1647.
2. Write a first-person narrative about a character – real or imaginary – whom you have saved from an accident.

"Girl" is an autobiographical story in which the author Jamaica Kincaid creates a dramatic character sketch. In "Jim" the narrator stood on the sidelines, while in "Girl" the narrator is positioned at the center of the story. Kincaid seems to be using multiple voices, as if suggesting her own complicated layers of memories about her girlhood in Antigua. The first sentences of the story appear to be an unusual second-person narration spoken in a monologue, but then a first-person voice in italics cuts through the nagging words. As you read them, you begin to realize that the girl is hearing the words of her overbearing mother. The different points of view add drama to the mother-daughter conflict.

JAMAICA KINCAID
Girl

1978

Wash the white clothes on Monday and put them on the stone heap; wash the color clothes on Tuesday and put them on the clothesline to dry; don't walk barehead in the hot sun; cook pumpkin fritters in very hot sweet oil; soak your little cloths right after you take them off; when buying cotton to make yourself a nice blouse, be sure that it doesn't have gum on it, because that way it won't hold up well after a wash; soak salt fish overnight before you cook it; is it true that you sing benna° in Sunday school?; always eat your food in such a way that it won't turn someone else's stomach; on Sundays try to walk like a lady and not like the slut you are so bent on becoming; don't sing benna in Sunday school; you mustn't speak to wharf-rat boys, not even to give directions; don't eat fruits on the street—flies will follow you; *but I don't sing benna on Sundays at all and never in Sunday school;* this is how to sew on a button; this is how to make a button-hole for the button you have just sewed on; this is how to hem a dress when you see the hem coming down and so to prevent yourself from looking like the slut I know you are so bent on becoming; this is how you iron your father's khaki shirt so that it doesn't have a crease; this is how you iron your father's khaki pants so that they don't have a crease; this is how you grow okra—far from the house, because okra tree harbors red ants; when you are growing dasheen, make sure it gets plenty of water or else it makes your throat itch when you are eating it; this is how you sweep a corner; this is how you sweep a whole house; this is how you sweep a yard; this is how you smile to someone you don't like too much; this is how you smile to someone you don't like at all; this is how you smile to someone you like completely; this is how you set a table for tea; this is how you set a table for dinner; this is how you set a table for dinner with an important guest; this is how you set a table for lunch; this is how you set a table for breakfast; this is how to behave in the presence of men who don't know you very well, and this way they won't recognize immediately the slut I have warned you against becoming; be sure to wash every day, even if it is with your own spit; don't squat down to play marbles—you are not a boy, you know; don't pick people's flowers—you might catch something; don't throw stones at blackbirds, because it might not be a blackbird at all; this is how to make a bread pudding; this is how to make doukona;° this is how to

benna: Calypso music. **doukona:** A spicy plantain pudding.

make pepper pot; this is how to make a good medicine for a cold; this is how to make a good medicine to throw away a child before it even becomes a child; this is how to catch a fish; this is how to throw back a fish you don't like, and that way something bad won't fall on you; this is how to bully a man; this is how a man bullies you; this is how to love a man, and if this doesn't work there are other ways, and if they don't work don't feel too bad about giving up; this is how to spit up in the air if you feel like it, and this is how to move quick so that it doesn't fall on you; this is how to make ends meet; always squeeze bread to make sure it's fresh; *but what if the baker won't let me feel the bread?*; you mean to say that after all you are really going to be the kind of woman who the baker won't let near the bread?

SETTING

Setting is the place and time of the story. To set the scene and suggest a mood or atmosphere for the events that follow, the writer attempts to create in your imagination the illusion of a solid world in which the story takes place as you read. Grace Paley uses only a few words to describe the New York City subway setting of her story "Samuel" (p. 11), but they create an image of power and danger. The doors are "locked." The platform is "swaying." The cars on either side are full of people, who watch the stunting boys uneasily. In the setting of "Jim" (p. 42), Roberto Bolaño also suggests a dangerous menace, this time lurking in Mexico City. The fire-eater giving the performance seems to be courting disaster when he recklessly throws flames that come so close to the bystanders that the narrator asks Jim if he wants "to get barbecued in the street."

When the writer locates the narrative in a physical setting, you are moved step by step toward acceptance of the fiction. The external reality of the writing is always an illusion, our mental images stimulated by the words that the writer has put on paper. Yet this invented setting is essential if we are to share the internal emotional life of the characters involved in the plot. A sense of place engages us in the fictional characters' situations.

In Nathanial Hawthorne's classic story "Young Goodman Brown" (p. 261), for example, when the protagonist Goodman Brown enters the dark, tangled world of the forest surrounding the colonial village of Salem to keep his appointment with the devil, you may perceive that Brown really enters the subjective world of his own mind. Exercising his own free will, he voluntarily exchanges the companionship of his pretty young wife for the attractions of Satan. "Young Goodman Brown" is an **allegory**, where Hawthorne intended every detail of the setting to represent abstract qualities or symbols. Sometimes the setting of an apparently realistic contemporary story can also be symbolic when it is described with such obsessive, close attention to details that you become conscious the writer is suggesting an idea or a theme that seems larger than the events of the story. This happens in Daniel Orozco's "Orientation" (see p. 46).

DANIEL OROZCO
Orientation

1994

Those are the offices and these are the cubicles. That's my cubicle there, and this is your cubicle. This is your phone. Never answer your phone. Let the Voicemail System answer it. This is your Voicemail System Manual. There are no personal phone calls allowed. We do, however, allow for emergencies. If you must make an emergency phone call, ask your supervisor first. If you can't find your supervisor, ask Phillip Spiers, who sits over there. He'll check with Clarissa Nicks, who sits over there. If you make an emergency phone call without asking, you may be let go.

These are your IN and OUT boxes. All the forms in your IN box must be logged in by the date shown in the upper left-hand corner, initialed by you in the upper right-hand corner, and distributed to the Processing Analyst whose name is numerically coded in the lower left-hand corner. The lower right-hand corner is left blank. Here's your Processing Analyst Numerical Code Index. And here's your Forms Processing Procedures Manual.

You must pace your work. What do I mean? I'm glad you asked that. We pace our work according to the eight-hour workday. If you have twelve hours of work in your IN box, for example, you must compress that work into the eight-hour day. If you have one hour of work in your IN box, you must expand that work to fill the eight-hour day. That was a good question. Feel free to ask questions. Ask too many questions, however, and you may be let go.

That is our receptionist. She is a temp. We go through receptionists here. They quit with alarming frequency. Be polite and civil to the temps. Learn their names, and invite them to lunch occasionally. But don't get close to them, as it only makes it more difficult when they leave. And they always leave. You can be sure of that.

The men's room is over there. The women's room is over there. John LaFountaine, who sits over there, uses the women's room occasionally. He says it is accidental. We know better, but we let it pass. John LaFountaine is harmless, his forays into the forbidden territory of the women's room simply a benign thrill, a faint blip on the dull flat line of his life.

Russell Nash, who sits in the cubicle to your left, is in love with Amanda Pierce, who sits in the cubicle to your right. They ride the same bus together after work. For Amanda Pierce, it is just a tedious bus ride made less tedious by the idle nattering of Russell Nash. But for Russell Nash, it is the highlight of his day. It is the highlight of his life. Russell Nash has put on forty pounds, and grows fatter with each passing month, nibbling on chips and cookies while peeking glumly over the partitions at Amanda Pierce, and gorging himself at home on cold pizza and ice cream while watching adult videos on TV.

Amanda Pierce, in the cubicle to your right, has a six-year-old son named Jamie, who is autistic. Her cubicle is plastered from top to bottom with the boy's crayon artwork—sheet after sheet of precisely drawn concentric circles and ellipses, in black and yellow. She rotates them every other Friday. Be sure to comment on them. Amanda Pierce also has a husband, who is a lawyer. He subjects her to an escalating array of painful and humiliating sex games, to which Amanda Pierce reluctantly submits. She comes to work exhausted and freshly wounded every morning, wincing from the abrasions on her breasts, or the bruises on her abdomen, or the second-degree burns on the backs of her thighs.

But we're not supposed to know any of this. Do not let on. If you let on, you may be let go.

Amanda Pierce, who tolerates Russell Nash, is in love with Albert Bosch, whose office is over there. Albert Bosch, who only dimly registers Amanda Pierce's existence, has eyes only for Ellie Tapper, who sits over there. Ellie Tapper, who hates Albert Bosch, would walk through fire for Curtis Lance. But Curtis Lance hates Ellie Tapper. Isn't the world a funny place? Not in the ha-ha sense, of course.

Anika Bloom sits in that cubicle. Last year, while reviewing quarterly reports in a meeting with Barry Hacker, Anika Bloom's left palm began to bleed. She fell into a trance, stared into her hand, and told Barry Hacker when and how his wife would die. We laughed it off. She was, after all, a new employee. But Barry Hacker's wife is dead. So unless you want to know exactly when and how you'll die, never talk to Anika Bloom.

Colin Heavey sits in that cubicle over there. He was new once, just like you. We warned him about Anika Bloom. But at last year's Christmas Potluck, he felt sorry for her when he saw that no one was talking to her. Colin Heavey brought her a drink. He hasn't been himself since. Colin Heavey is doomed. There's nothing he can do about it, and we are powerless to help him. Stay away from Colin Heavey. Never give any of your work to him. If he asks to do something, tell him you have to check with me. If he asks again, tell him I haven't gotten back to you.

This is the Fire Exit. There are several on this floor, and they are marked accordingly. We have a Floor Evacuation Review every three months, and an Escape Route Quiz once a month. We have our Biannual Fire Drill twice a year, and our Annual Earthquake Drill once a year. These are precautions only. These things never happen.

For your information, we have a comprehensive health plan. Any catastrophic illness, any unforeseen tragedy is completely covered. All dependents are completely covered. Larry Bagdikian, who sits over there, has six daughters. If anything were to happen to any of his girls, or to all of them, if all six were to simultaneously fall victim to illness or injury—stricken with a hideous degenerative muscle disease or some rare toxic blood disorder, sprayed with semiautomatic gunfire while on a class field trip, or attacked in their bunk beds by some prowling nocturnal lunatic—if any of this were to pass, Larry's girls would all be taken care of. Larry Bagdikian would not have to pay one dime. He would have nothing to worry about.

We also have a generous vacation and sick leave policy. We have an excellent disability insurance plan. We have a stable and profitable pension fund. We get group discounts for the symphony, and block seating at the ballpark. We get commuter ticket books for the bridge. We have Direct Deposit. We are all members of Costco.

This is our kitchenette. And this, this is our Mr. Coffee. We have a coffee pool, into which we each pay two dollars a week for coffee, filters, sugar, and CoffeeMate. If you prefer Cremora or half-and-half to CoffeeMate, there is a special pool for three dollars a week. If you prefer Sweet 'n Low to sugar, there is a special pool for two-fifty a week. We do not do decaf. You are allowed to join the coffee pool of your choice, but you are not allowed to touch the Mr. Coffee.

This is the microwave oven. You are allowed to *heat* food in the microwave oven. You are not, however, allowed to *cook* food in the microwave oven.

We get one hour for lunch. We also get one fifteen-minute break in the morning, and one fifteen-minute break in the afternoon. Always take your breaks. If you skip a break, it is gone forever. For your information, your break is a privilege, not a right. If you abuse the break policy, we are authorized to rescind your breaks. Lunch, however, is a right, not a privilege. If you abuse the lunch policy, our hands will be tied, and we will be forced to look the other way. We will not enjoy that.

This is the refrigerator. You may put your lunch in it. Barry Hacker, who sits over there, steals food from this refrigerator. His petty theft is an outlet for his grief. Last New Year's Eve, while kissing his wife, a blood vessel burst in her brain. Barry Hacker's wife was two months pregnant at the time, and lingered in a coma for a half a year before dying. It was a tragic loss for Barry Hacker. He hasn't been himself since. Barry Hacker's wife was a beautiful woman. She was also completely covered. Barry Hacker did not have to pay one dime. But his dead wife haunts him. She haunts all of us. We have seen her, reflected in the monitors of our computers, moving past our cubicles. We have seen the dim shadow of her face in our photocopies. She pencils herself in the receptionist's appointment book, with the notation: To see Barry Hacker. She has left messages in the receptionist's Voicemail box, messages garbled by the electronic chirrups and buzzes in the phone line, her voice echoing from an immense distance within the ambient hum. But the voice is hers. And beneath her voice, beneath the tidal *whoosh* of static and hiss, the gurgling and crying of a baby can be heard.

In any case, if you bring a lunch, put a little something extra in the bag for Barry Hacker. We have four Barrys in this office. Isn't that a coincidence?

This is Matthew Payne's office. He is our Unit Manager, and his door is always closed. We have never seen him, and you will never see him. But he is here. You can be sure of that. He is all around us.

This is the Custodian's Closet. You have no business in the Custodian's Closet.

And this, this is our Supplies Cabinet. If you need supplies, see Curtis Lance. He will log you in on the Supplies Cabinet Authorization Log, then give you a Supplies Authorization Slip. Present your pink copy of the Supplies Authorization Slip to Ellie Tapper. She will log you in on the Supplies Cabinet Key Log, then give you the key. Because the Supplies Cabinet is located outside the Unit Manager's office, you must be very quiet. Gather your supplies quietly. The Supplies Cabinet is divided into four sections. Section One contains letterhead stationery, blank paper and envelopes, memo and note pads, and so on. Section Two contains pens and pencils and typewriter and printer ribbons, and the like. In Section Three we have erasers, correction fluids, transparent tapes, glue sticks, et cetera. And in Section Four we have paper clips and push pins and scissors and razor blades. And here are the spare blades for the shredder. Do not touch the shredder, which is located over there. The shredder is of no concern to you.

Gwendolyn Stich sits in that office there. She is crazy about penguins, and collects penguin knickknacks: penguin posters and coffee mugs and stationery, penguin stuffed animals, penguin jewelry, penguin sweaters and T-shirts and socks. She has a pair of penguin fuzzy slippers she wears when working late at the office. She has a tape cassette of penguin sounds which she listens to for relaxation. Her favorite colors are black and white. She has personalized license plates that read PEN GWEN. Every morning, she passes through all the cubicles to wish each of us a *good* morning. She brings Danish on Wednesdays for Hump Day morning break, and doughnuts on Fridays for TGIF afternoon break. She organizes the Annual Christmas Potluck, and is in charge of the Birthday List. Gwendolyn Stich's door is always open to all of us. She will always lend an ear, and put in a good word for you; she will always give you a hand, or the shirt off her back, or a shoulder to cry on. Because her door is always open, she hides and cries in a stall in the women's room. And John LaFountaine—who, enthralled when a woman enters, sits quietly in his stall with his knees to his chest—John LaFountaine has heard her vomiting in there. We have come upon Gwendolyn Stich huddled in the stairwell, shivering in the updraft, sipping a Diet Mr. Pibb and hugging her knees. She does not let any of this interfere with her work. If it interfered with her work, she might have to be let go.

Kevin Howard sits in that cubicle over there. He is a serial killer, the one they call the Carpet Cutter, responsible for the mutilations across town. We're not supposed to know that, so do not let on. Don't worry. His compulsion inflicts itself on strangers only, and the routine established is elaborate and unwavering. The victim must be a white male, a young adult no older than thirty, heavyset, with dark hair and eyes, and the like. The victim must be chosen at random, before sunset, from a public place; the victim is followed home, and must put up a struggle; et cetera. The carnage inflicted is precise: the angle and direction of the incisions; the layering of skin and muscle tissue; the rearrangement of the visceral organs; and so on. Kevin Howard does not let any of this interfere with his work. He is, in fact, our fastest typist. He types as if he were on fire. He has a secret crush on Gwendolyn Stich, and leaves a red-foil-wrapped Hershey's Kiss on her desk every afternoon. But he hates Anika Bloom, and keeps well away from her. In his presence, she has uncontrollable fits of shaking and trembling. Her left palm does not stop bleeding.

In any case, when Kevin Howard gets caught, act surprised. Say that he seemed like a nice person, a bit of a loner, perhaps, but always quiet and polite.

This is the photocopier room. And this, this is our view. It faces southwest. West is down there, toward the water. North is back there. Because we are on the seventeenth floor, we are afforded a magnificent view. Isn't it beautiful? It overlooks the park, where the tops of those trees are. You can see a segment of the bay between those two buildings there. You can see the sun set in the gap between those two buildings over there. You can see this building reflected in the glass panels of that building across the way. There. See? That's you, waving. And look there. There's Anika Bloom in the kitchenette, waving back.

Enjoy this view while photocopying. If you have problems with the photocopier, see Russell Nash. If you have any questions, ask your supervisor. If you can't find your supervisor, ask Phillip Spiers. He sits over there. He'll check with Clarissa Nicks. She sits over there. If you can't find them, feel free to ask me. That's my cubicle. I sit in there.

◆ Questions for Critical Thinking about Setting ◆

1. How does the setting influence the plot of "Orientation"?
2. How does the setting influence the characters in the story?
3. The second-person point of view in the story assumes an intimacy with the reader that immediately conveys the impression that you are the "new hire" getting the orientation tour at your new job. How does this make you feel as you are taken through the office? What information about office routine puts you on your guard at the beginning of the tour?
4. At what point in your tour of the office do you begin to sense that perhaps the story is more than a satirical description of the rigidity of office protocol and that Orozco may be questioning our unquestioning acceptance of the practice of keeping workers in their place in today's corporate culture, with its authoritarian managerial style?

◆ Topics for Writing about Setting ◆

1. Compare and contrast the use of setting in Orozco's "Orientation" and Herta Müller's "Workday" (p. 32), based on your interpretation of how the two authors view the situation of low-wage workers and your own experience with part-time jobs. You will find a discussion of how to use comparison and contrast, along with a sample student paper, on pages 1647–1651.
2. Danger lurks everywhere on the job site in "Orientation." Analyze the different risks, both implicit and explicit, in the setting that create the ominous mood of Orozco's story. You will find a discussion of how to use analysis, along with a sample student paper, on pages 1644–1647.

Setting or a sense of place helps the characters seem real, but to be most effective, it must also have a dramatic use. It must be shown, or at least felt, to affect character or plot. For example, the emergency brake in the subway car precipitates the disaster of Samuel's death. The fire-eater recklessly performing on the dark street corner in Mexico City draws the narrator much too close when he stands beside his lost friend. Good writers try to make you see the fictional world that emerges on the printed page. They hold you fast in the illusion that while the story unfolds, it is the real world itself.

One of the masters at spinning words to create an illusion of setting is the Colombian writer Gabriel García Márquez. In "A Very Old Man with Enormous Wings" he imagines a hot, humid, stinking, remote village in a Catholic country in South America where the superstitions of the impoverished inhabitants are of little help when they are forced to deal with a miracle. This story is an example of **magical realist** fiction, where ordinary life and magical occurrences mix in an overall frame of realistic narrative. García Márquez uses an omniscient point of view to tell the story, which is amusingly appropriate to its celestial frame of reference. As you read, you might notice the ingenious ways that the setting motivates the plot and validates the responses of the various characters right up to the end of the story.

GABRIEL GARCÍA MÁRQUEZ
A Very Old Man with Enormous Wings 1955

TRANSLATED BY GREGORY RABASSA

On the third day of rain they had killed so many crabs inside the house that Pelayo had to cross his drenched courtyard and throw them into the sea, because the newborn child had a temperature all night and they thought it was due to the stench. The world had been sad since Tuesday. Sea and sky were a single ash-gray thing and the sands of the beach, which on March nights glimmered like powdered light, had become a stew of mud and rotten shellfish. The light was so weak at noon that when Pelayo was coming back to the house after throwing away the crabs, it was hard for him to see what it was that was moving and groaning in the rear of the courtyard. He had to go very close to see that it was an old man, a very old man, lying face down in the mud, who, in spite of his tremendous efforts, couldn't get up, impeded by his enormous wings.

Frightened by that nightmare, Pelayo ran to get Elisenda, his wife, who was putting compresses on the sick child, and he took her to the rear of the courtyard. They both looked at the fallen body with mute stupor. He was dressed like a ragpicker. There were only a few faded hairs left on his bald skull and very few teeth in his mouth, and his pitiful condition of a drenched great-grandfather had taken away any sense of grandeur he might have had. His huge buzzard wings, dirty and half-plucked, were forever entangled in the mud. They looked at him so long and so closely that Pelayo and Elisenda very soon overcame their surprise and in the end found him familiar. Then they dared speak to him, and he answered in an incomprehensible dialect with a strong sailor's voice. That was how they skipped over the inconvenience of the wings and quite intelligently concluded that he was a lonely castaway from some foreign ship wrecked by the storm. And yet, they called in a neighbor woman who knew everything about life and death to see him, and all she needed was one look to show them their mistake.

"He's an angel," she told them. "He must have been coming for the child, but the poor fellow is so old that the rain knocked him down."

On the following day everyone knew that a flesh-and-blood angel was held captive in Pelayo's house. Against the judgment of the wise neighbor woman, for whom angels in those times were the fugitive survivors of a celestial conspiracy, they did not have the heart to club him to death. Pelayo watched over him all afternoon from the kitchen, armed with his bailiff's club, and before going to bed he dragged him out of the mud and locked him up with the hens in the wire chicken coop. In the middle of the night, when the rain stopped, Pelayo and Elisenda were still killing crabs. A short time afterward the child woke up without a fever and with a desire to eat. Then they felt magnanimous and decided to put the angel on a raft with fresh water and provisions for three days and leave him to his fate on the high seas. But when they went out into the courtyard with the first light of dawn, they found the whole neighborhood in front of the chicken coop having fun with the angel, without the slightest reverence, tossing him things to eat through the openings in the wire as if he weren't a supernatural creature but a circus animal.

Father Gonzaga arrived before seven o'clock, alarmed at the strange news. By that time onlookers less frivolous than those at dawn had already arrived and they were making all kinds of conjectures concerning the captive's future. The simplest among them thought that he should be named mayor of the world. Others of sterner mind felt that he should be promoted to the rank of five-star general in order to win all wars. Some visionaries hoped that he could be put to stud in order to implant on earth a race of winged wise men who could take charge of the universe. But Father Gonzaga, before becoming a priest, had been a robust woodcutter. Standing by the wire, he reviewed his catechism in an instant and asked them to open the door so that he could take a close look at that pitiful man who looked more like a huge decrepit hen among the fascinated chickens. He was lying in a corner drying his open wings in the sunlight among the fruit peels and breakfast leftovers that the early risers had thrown him. Alien to the impertinences of the world, he only lifted his antiquarian eyes and murmured something in his dialect when Father Gonzaga went into the chicken coop and said good morning to him in Latin. The parish priest had his first suspicion of an imposter when he saw that he did not understand the language of God or know how to greet His ministers. Then he noticed that seen close up he was much too human: he had an unbearable smell of the outdoors, the back side of his wings was strewn with parasites and his main feathers had been mistreated by terrestrial winds, and nothing about him measured up to the proud dignity of angels. Then he came out of the chicken coop and in a brief sermon warned the curious against the risks of being ingenuous. He reminded them that the devil had the bad habit of making use of carnival tricks in order to confuse the unwary. He argued that if wings were not the essential element in determining the difference between a hawk and an airplane, they were even less so in the recognition of angels. Nevertheless, he promised to write a letter to his bishop so that the latter would write to his primate so that the latter would write to the Supreme Pontiff in order to get the final verdict from the highest courts.

His prudence fell on sterile hearts. The news of the captive angel spread with such rapidity that after a few hours the courtyard had the bustle of a marketplace and they had to call in troops with fixed bayonets to disperse the mob that was about to knock the house down. Elisenda, her spine all twisted from sweeping up so much marketplace trash, then got the idea of fencing in the yard and charging five cents admission to see the angel.

The curious came from far away. A traveling carnival arrived with a flying acrobat who buzzed over the crowd several times, but no one paid any attention to him because his wings were not those of an angel but, rather, those of a sidereal° bat. The most unfortunate invalids on earth came in search of health: a poor woman who since childhood had been counting her heartbeats and had run out of numbers; a Portuguese man who couldn't sleep because the noise of the stars disturbed him; a sleep-walker who got up at night to undo the things he had done while awake; and many others with less serious ailments. In the midst of that shipwreck disorder that made the earth tremble, Pelayo and Elisenda were happy with fatigue, for in less than a week they had crammed their rooms with money and the line of pilgrims waiting their turn to enter still reached beyond the horizon.

The angel was the only one who took no part in his own act. He spent his time trying to get comfortable in his borrowed nest, befuddled by the hellish heat of the oil lamps and sacramental candles that had been placed along the wire. At first they tried to make him eat some mothballs, which, according to the wisdom of the wise neighbor woman, were the food prescribed for angels. But he turned them down, just as he turned down the papal lunches that the penitents brought him, and they never found out whether it was because he was an angel or because he was an old man that in the end he ate nothing but eggplant mush. His only supernatural virtue seemed to be patience. Especially during the first days, when the hens pecked at him, searching for the stellar parasites that proliferated in his wings, and the cripples pulled out feathers to touch their defective parts with, and even the most merciful threw stones at him, trying to get him to rise so they could see him standing. The only time they succeeded in arousing him was when they burned his side with an iron for branding steers, for he had been motionless for so many hours that they thought he was dead. He awoke with a start, ranting in his hermetic language and with tears in his eyes, and he flapped his wings a couple of times, which brought on a whirlwind of chicken dung and lunar dust and a gale of panic that did not seem to be of this world. Although many thought that his reaction had been one not of rage but of pain, from then on they were careful not to annoy him, because the majority understood that his passivity was not that of a hero taking his ease but that of a cataclysm in repose.

Father Gonzaga held back the crowd's frivolity with formulas of maidservant inspiration while awaiting the arrival of a final judgment on the nature of the captive. But the mail from Rome showed no sense of urgency. They spent their time finding out if the prisoner had a navel, if his dialect had any connection with Aramaic, how many times he could fit on the head of a pin, or whether he wasn't just a Norwegian with wings. Those meager letters might have come and gone until the end of time if a providential event had not put an end to the priest's tribulations.

It so happened that during those days, among so many other carnival attractions, there arrived in town the traveling show of the woman who had been changed into a spider for having disobeyed her parents. The admission to see

---

sidereal: Coming from the stars.

her was not only less than the admission to see the angel, but people were permitted to ask her all manner of questions about her absurd state and to examine her up and down so that no one would ever doubt the truth of her horror. She was a frightful tarantula the size of a ram and with the head of a sad maiden. What was most heart-rending, however, was not her outlandish shape but the sincere affliction with which she recounted the details of her misfortune. While still practically a child she had sneaked out of her parents' house to go to a dance, and while she was coming back through the woods after having danced all night without permission, a fearful thunderclap rent the sky in two and through the crack came the lightning bolt of brimstone that changed her into a spider. Her only nourishment came from the meatballs that charitable souls chose to toss into her mouth. A spectacle like that, full of so much human truth and with such a fearful lesson, was bound to defeat without even trying that of a haughty angel who scarcely deigned to look at mortals. Besides, the few miracles attributed to the angel showed a certain mental disorder, like the blind man who didn't recover his sight but grew three new teeth, or the paralytic who didn't get to walk but almost won the lottery, and the leper whose sores sprouted sunflowers. Those consolation miracles, which were more like mocking fun, had already ruined the angel's reputation when the woman who had been changed into a spider finally crushed him completely. That was how Father Gonzaga was cured forever of his insomnia and Pelayo's courtyard went back to being as empty as during the time it had rained for three days and crabs walked through the bedrooms.

The owners of the house had no reason to lament. With the money they saved they built a two-story mansion with balconies and gardens and high netting so the crabs wouldn't get in during the winter, and with iron bars on the windows so that angels wouldn't get in. Pelayo also set up a rabbit warren close to town and gave up his job as bailiff for good, and Elisenda bought some satin pumps with high heels and many dresses of iridescent silk, the kind worn on Sunday by the most desirable women in those times. The chicken coop was the only thing that didn't receive any attention. If they washed it down with creolin and burned tears of myrrh inside it every so often, it was not in homage to the angel but to drive away the dungheap stench that still hung everywhere like a ghost and was turning the new house into an old one. At first, when the child learned to walk, they were careful that he not get too close to the chicken coop. But then they began to lose their fears and got used to the smell, and before the child got his second teeth he'd gone inside the chicken coop to play, where the wires were falling apart. The angel was no less standoffish with him than with other mortals, but he tolerated the most ingenious infamies with the patience of a dog who had no illusions. They both came down with chicken pox at the same time. The doctor who took care of the child couldn't resist the temptation to listen to the angel's heart, and he found so much whistling in the heart and so many sounds in his kidneys that it seemed impossible for him to be alive. What surprised him most, however, was the logic of his wings. They seemed so natural on that completely human organism that he couldn't understand why other men didn't have them too.

When the child began at school it had been some time since the sun and rain had caused the collapse of the chicken coop. The angel went dragging himself about here and there like a stray dying man. They would drive him out of the bedroom with a broom and a moment later find him in the kitchen. He seemed to be in so many places at the same time that they grew to think that he'd been duplicated, that he was reproducing himself all through the house, and the exasperated and unhinged Elisenda shouted that it was awful living in that hell full of angels. He could scarcely eat and his antiquarian eyes had also become so foggy that he went about bumping into posts. All he had left were the bare cannulae° of his last feathers. Pelayo threw a blanket over him and extended him the charity of letting him sleep in the shed, and only then did they notice that he had a temperature at night, and was delirious with the tongue twisters of an old Norwegian. That was one of the few times they became alarmed, for they thought he was going to die and not even the wise neighbor woman had been able to tell them what to do with dead angels.

And yet he not only survived his worst winter, but seemed improved with the first sunny days. He remained motionless for several days in the farthest corner of the courtyard, where no one would see him, and at the beginning of December some large, stiff feathers began to grow on his wings, the feathers of a scarecrow, which looked more like another misfortune of decrepitude. But he must have known the reason for those changes, for he was quite careful that no one should notice them, that no one should hear the sea chanteys that he sometimes sang under the stars. One morning Elisenda was cutting some bunches of onions for lunch when a wind that seemed to come from the high seas blew into the kitchen. Then she went to the window and caught the angel in his first attempts at flight. They were so clumsy that his fingernails opened a furrow in the vegetable patch and he was on the point of knocking the shed down with the ungainly flapping that slipped on the light and couldn't get a grip on the air. But he did manage to gain altitude. Elisenda let out a sigh of relief, for herself and for him, when she saw him pass over the last houses, holding himself up in some way with the risky flapping of a senile vulture. She kept watching him even when she was through cutting the onions and she kept on watching until it was no longer possible for her to see him, because then he was no longer an annoyance in her life but an imaginary dot on the horizon of the sea.

USEFUL TERMS TO REMEMBER

Allegory A story that has two levels of meaning, the literal and the symbolic. An allegory is usually restricted to a single meaning or general truth, in which characters, places, things, and events all represent abstract qualities.

Antagonist The character in a short story or play who is in real or imagined opposition to the protagonist.

---

cannulae: The tubular pieces by which feathers are attached to a body.

Character Any person who plays a part in a narrative work.

Dynamic character A character who is contradictory and changes in some way during the story.

Flat character A simple and one-dimensional character.

Magical realism Fiction in which ordinary life and magical occurrences mix in an overall frame of realistic narrative.

Protagonist The main character of a narrative, who engages the reader's interest and sympathy. The action of a story is usually the presentation and resolution of some internal or external conflict of the protagonist. If the conflict is with another major character, that character may be called the antagonist.

Round character A complex character described in detail.

Setting The physical details of the place, the time, and the social context that influence the actions of the characters. Often the setting also evokes a mood or an atmosphere in the story.

Static character An unsurprising and unchanging character.

Stock character A one-dimensional character who exhibits only stereotypical features.

Sympathetic character A character who arouses the reader's sympathy or with whom the reader identifies.

Unsympathetic character A character who arouses the reader's negative judgment or with whom the reader finds fault.

5.

Style and Theme

STYLE

Style is the characteristic way each author uses language to create literature. Style is the result of writers' habitual ways of choosing their words (**diction**) and ordering them into sentences (**syntax**). The linguistic means at the authors' disposal as they create their short stories consist of an infinite variety of rhetorical patterns involving word choice and placement, and sentence length and complexity. Writers can also use **figurative language**, or language that is literally inaccurate but helpful in creating a vivid effect. When the fictional characters speak, an author can put words in their mouths so that their dialogue suggests their different personalities and educational backgrounds. If the characters speak in **dialect** or nonstandard English diction, the author can suggest that they come from a particular geographic region, economic group, or social class.

For example, Grace Paley's prose style in "Samuel" (p. 11) is informal and friendly, even colloquial in her choice of language. In her story she uses mostly one-syllable words, even slang occasionally ("super" in the first paragraph refers to the superintendent or caretaker of an apartment building). On the other hand, Raymond Carver's style in "Popular Mechanics" (p. 28) is concise and impersonal. The third-person narrator keeps an emotional distance as he tells a brief story about a couple locked into a bitter quarrel that ends badly. Dagoberto Gilb's style is self-consciously stilted in "Love in L.A." (p. 35), as if he has chosen his words to reflect the awkward bumps in the life of his day-dreaming protagonist, "slouched in a clot" of traffic before he is forced to wake up and deal with the fender bender he has caused. Gabriel García Márquez's style in the translation from the Spanish by Gregory Rabassa is poetical, as in the use of personification in the second sentence of "A Very Old Man with Enormous Wings" (p. 51): "The world had been sad since Tuesday."

Here are two contemporary stories written in very different prose styles for you to analyze. David Foster Wallace's "Everything Is Green" is an example of an author writing in the style of an uneducated, first-person narrator named Mitch. His words are sometimes grammatically incorrect as he struggles to express his deepest feelings to the woman he loves.

DAVID FOSTER WALLACE

Everything Is Green

1989

She says I do not care if you believe me or not, it is the truth, go on and believe what you want to. So it is for sure that she is lying. When it is the truth she will go crazy trying to get you to believe her. So I feel like I know.

She lights up and looks off away from me, looking sly with her cigarette in light through a wet window, and I can not feel what to say.

I say Mayfly I can not feel what to do or say or believe you any more. But there is things I know. I know I am older and you are not. And I give to you all I got to give you, with my hands and my heart both. Every thing that is inside me I have gave you. I have been keeping it together and working steady every day. I have made you the reason I got for what I always do. I have tried to make a home to give to you, for you to be in, and for it to be nice.

I light up myself and I throw the match in the sink with other matches and dishes and a sponge and such things.

I say Mayfly my heart has been down the road and back for you but I am forty-eight years old. It is time I have got to not let things just carry me by any more. I got to use some time that is still mine to try to make everything feel right. I got to try to feel how I need to. In me there is needs which you can not even see any more, because there is too many needs in you that are in the way.

She does not say any thing and I look at her window and I can feel that she knows I know about it, and she shifts her self on my sofa lounger. She brings her legs up underneath her in some shorts.

I say it really does not matter what I seen or what I think I seen. That is not it any more. I know I am older and you are not. But now I am feeling like there is all of me going in to you and nothing of you is coming back any more.

Her hair is up with a barret and pins and her chin is in her hand, it's early, she looks like she is dreaming out at the clean light through the wet window over my sofa lounger.

Everything is green she says. Look how green it all is Mitch. How can you say the things you say you feel like when everything outside is green like it is.

The window over the sink of my kitchenet is cleaned off from the hard rain last night and it is a morning with a sun, it is still early, and there is a mess of green out. The trees are green and some grass out past the speed bumps is green and slicked down. But every thing is not green. The other trailers are not green and my card table out with puddles in lines and beer cans and butts floating in the ash trays is not green, or my truck, or the gravel of the lot, or the big wheel toy that is on its side under a clothes line without clothes on it by the next trailer, where the guy has got him some kids.

Everything is green she is saying. She is whispering it and the whisper is not to me no more I know.

I chuck my smoke and turn hard from the morning with the taste of something true in my mouth. I turn hard toward her in the light on the sofa lounger.

She is looking outside, from where she is sitting, and I look at her, and there is something in me that can not close up, in that looking. Mayfly has a body. And she is my morning. Say her name.

In Wallace's story his literary style is appropriate for his choice of point of view and his characterization of Mitch, who as the first-person narrator expresses himself in uneducated speech. Mitch is upset because he suspects his lover Mayfly has been unfaithful to him, though she denies it. She tries to evade his accusations by attempting to change the subject, trying to interest him in what she sees looking out of the window: "Look how green it all is Mitch." Her attempt doesn't work at first, but Mitch finds himself unable to continue their quarrel. When he looks at her, he realizes he doesn't want to lose her. "There is something in me that can not close up, in that looking." Mitch may be nearly inarticulate, but he isn't stupid. At forty-eight years old, he senses that life is passing him by. He is smart enough to listen to his feelings, which rise up within him and tell him that he would have less of a life if he were alone, without his Mayfly.

Just as the uneducated speech in "Everything Is Green" dramatizes the protagonist's emotional vulnerability in his challenging situation, the words spoken by educated, affluent fictional characters can suggest their comfortable social status and their customary self-esteem. Here, for example, is "Blind Date," a short story in standard English by another contemporary American writer, Lydia Davis.

LYDIA DAVIS
Blind Date 1999

"There isn't really much to tell," she said, but she would tell it if I liked. We were sitting in a midtown luncheonette. "I've only had one blind date in my life. And I didn't really have it. I can think of more interesting situations that are like a blind date—say when someone gives you a book as a present, when they fix you up with that book. I was once given a book of essays about reading, writing, book collecting. I felt it was a perfect match. I started reading it right away, in the back seat of the car. I stopped listening to the conversation in the front. I like to read about how other people read and collect books, even how they shelve their books. But by the time I was done with the book, I had taken a strong dislike to the author's personality. I won't have another date with *her*!" She laughed. Here we were interrupted by the waiter, and then a series of incidents followed that kept us from resuming our conversation that day.

The next time the subject came up, we were sitting in two Adirondack chairs looking out over a lake in, in fact, the Adirondacks. We were content to sit in silence at first. We were tired. We had been to the Adirondack Museum that day and seen many things of interest, including old guide boats and good examples of the original Adirondack chair. Now we watched the water and the edge of the woods, each thinking, I was sure, about James Fenimore Cooper. After some parties of canoers had gone by, older people in canvas boating hats, their quiet voices carrying far over the water to us, we went on talking. These were precious days of holiday together, and we were finishing many unfinished conversations.

"I was fifteen or sixteen, I guess," she said. "I was home from boarding school. Maybe it was summer. I don't know where my parents were. They were often away. They often left me alone there, sometimes for the evening, sometimes for weeks at a time. The phone rang. It was a boy I didn't know. He said he was a friend of a boy from school—I can't remember who. We talked a little and then he asked me if I wanted to have dinner with him. He sounded nice enough so I said I would, and we agreed on a day and a time and I told him where I lived.

"But after I got off the phone, I began thinking, worrying. What had this other boy said about me? What had the two of them said about me? Maybe I had some kind of a reputation. Even now I can't imagine that what they said was completely pure or innocent—for instance, that I was pretty and fun to be with. There had to be something nasty about it, two boys talking privately about a girl. The awful word that began to occur to me was *fast*. She's *fast*. I wasn't actually very fast. I was faster than some but not as fast as others. The more I imagined the two boys talking about me the worse I felt.

"I liked boys. I liked the boys I knew in a way that was much more innocent than they probably thought. I trusted them more than girls. Girls hurt my feelings, girls ganged up on me. I always had boys who were my friends, starting back when I was nine and ten and eleven. I didn't like this feeling that two boys were talking about me.

"Well, when the day came, I didn't want to go out to dinner with this boy. I just didn't want the difficulty of this date. It scared me—not because there was anything scary about the boy but because he was a stranger, I didn't know him. I didn't want to sit there face to face in some restaurant and start from the very beginning, knowing nothing. It didn't feel right. And there was the burden of that recommendation—'Give her a try.'

"Then again, maybe there were other reasons. Maybe I had been alone in that apartment so much by then that I had retreated into some kind of inner, unsociable space that was hard to come out of. Maybe I felt I had disappeared and I was comfortable that way and did not want to be forced back into existence. I don't know.

"At six o'clock, the buzzer rang. The boy was there, downstairs. I didn't answer it. It rang again. Still I did not answer it. I don't know how many times it rang or how long he leaned on it. I let it ring. At some point, I walked the length of the living room to the balcony. The apartment was four stories up. Across the street and down a flight of stone steps was a park. From the balcony on a clear day you could look out over the park and see all the way across town, maybe a mile, to the other river. At this point I think I ducked down or got down on my hands and knees and inched my way to the edge of the balcony. I think I looked over far enough to see him down there on the sidewalk below—looking up, as I remember it. Or he had gone across the street and was looking up. He didn't see me.

"I know that as I crouched there on the balcony or just back from it I had some impression of him being puzzled, disconcerted, disappointed, at a loss what to do now, not prepared for this—prepared for all sorts of other ways the date might go, other difficulties, but not for no date at all. Maybe he also felt angry or insulted, if it occurred to him then or later that maybe he hadn't made a mistake but that I had deliberately stood him up, and not the way I did it—alone up there in the apartment, uncomfortable and embarrassed, chickening out, hiding out—but, he would imagine, in collusion with someone else, a girlfriend or boyfriend, confiding in them, snickering over him.

"I don't know if he called me, or if I answered the phone if it rang. I could have given some excuse—I could have said I had gotten sick or had to go out suddenly. Or maybe I hung up when I heard his voice. In those days I did a lot of avoiding that I don't do now—avoiding confrontations, avoiding difficult encounters. And I did a fair amount of lying that I also don't do now.

"What was strange was how awful this felt. I was treating a person like a thing. And I was betraying not just him but something larger, some social contract. When you knew a decent person was waiting downstairs, someone you had made an appointment with, you did not just not answer the buzzer. What was even more surprising to me was what I felt about myself in that instant. I was behaving as though I had no responsibility to anyone or anything, and that made me feel as though I existed outside society, some kind of criminal, or didn't exist at all. I was annihilating myself even more than him. It was an awful violation."

She paused, thoughtful. We were sitting inside now, because it was raining. We had come inside to sit in a sort of lounge or recreation room provided for guests of that lakeside camp. The rain fell every afternoon there, sometimes for minutes, sometimes for hours. Across the water, the white pines and spruces were very still against the gray sky. The water was silver. We did not see any of the water birds we sometimes saw paddling around the edges of the lake—teals and loons. Inside, a fire burned in the fireplace. Over our heads hung a chandelier made of antlers. Between us stood a table constructed of a rough slab of wood resting on the legs of a deer, complete with hooves. On the table stood a lamp made from an old gun. She looked away from the lake and around the room. "In that book about the Adirondacks I was reading last night," she remarked, "he says this was what the Adirondacks was all about, I mean the Adirondacks style: things made from things."

A month or so later, when I was home again and she was back in the city, we were talking on the telephone and she said she had been hunting through one of the old diaries she had on her shelf there, that might say exactly what had happened—though of course, she said, she would just be filling in the details of something that did not actually happen. But she couldn't find this incident written down anywhere, which of course made her wonder if she had gotten the dates really wrong and she wasn't even in boarding school anymore by then. Maybe she was in college by then. But she decided to believe what she had told me. "But I'd forgotten how much I wrote about boys," she added. "Boys and books. What I wanted more than anything else at the age of sixteen was a great library."

VOICE

Other aspects of a writer's prose style are voice, tone, irony, and symbol. These are so important that some critics feel that they should be considered as separate elements of fiction. When you read a short story, you could think of the author's prose style as a projection of her or his **voice** as a writer, as if you were hearing the story instead of reading it. You encounter "Blind Date" as words on the page, but Davis handles standard English with such facility that as you read, you join the narrator in listening to words spoken by a close friend. You become part of an intimate conversation in which the speaker explores an embarrassing personal memory. Voice, as the Canadian writer Margaret Atwood described it, is "a speaking voice, like the singing voice in music, that moves not across a space, across the page, but through time. Surely every written story is, in the final analysis, a score for voice. These little black marks on the page mean nothing without their retranslation into sound."

We listen to stories even more often than we read them, and the voice of the storyteller can be very effective, as Sheherezade discovered long ago. Storytelling in human beings is so instinctive that it might even be part of our DNA. Nearly two centuries ago, when short stories first began to appear widely in print, they were usually meant to be read aloud by candlelight or gas lamps as the entire household gathered together for entertainment in the early evening hours.

TONE

Something else that helps you understand the author's attitude in a story is called **tone**. This is the emotional sound of the voice you hear in the narrative, the way the author conveys his or her unstated attitudes toward the story. You can sense that Wallace's tone is serious and respectful in "Everything Is Green" as he dramatizes his sympathy for Mitch's predicament. Davis's tone is cool and controlled in "Blind Date," almost deadpan, as if the woman telling her story still can't deal with the complex emotions she felt as a teenager after standing up the boy she was supposed to meet for a dinner date.

Be careful when you interpret the tone of stories that you read in an English translation from a foreign language. Unless you can also understand the original language, you can't be certain that the translator has caught the author's tone, even if the translation is verbally accurate. Perhaps in the progression of frank sentences in "Workday" (p. 32), Herta Müller was trying to say that the events of a workday are soul destroying. Since her sentences were translated from the German text, you can't be exactly sure what the author's attitude was toward the female character in the original story.

IRONY

Irony is another means by which writers tell stories. Irony makes you aware of a reality that differs from the reality the characters perceive (**dramatic irony**) or from the literal meaning of the author's words (**verbal irony**). It's dramatic irony in "Everything Is Green" when Mitch turns to look at Mayfly—signaling that he is ready to go ahead and end their quarrel—and she refuses to stop looking out the window and turn back to him, yet insists that everything is green. You'll find many examples of verbal irony in "A Very Old Man with Enormous Wings," as when García Márquez notes that Pelayo and Elisenda "quite intelligently" decide that their unexpected guest is a lonely castaway from a shipwreck.

You can read Gilb's title "Love in L.A." as an example of verbal irony if you think that he is referring to the two fictional characters whom he has presented sympathetically in his story. Their "love affair" quite literally doesn't go anywhere. If you want to argue that Gilb's primary intent as a narrator was to write a story about the horrendous traffic snarls in Los Angeles (though this would be an eccentric reading since he focused on Jake's behavior), then you could say that Gilb meant the title sarcastically. The difference between irony and sarcasm is that sarcasm is meant to hurt or denigrate a person or a place.

SYMBOL

The use of symbolism can also be an aspect of a writer's style. A literary **symbol** can be anything in a story's setting, plot, or characterization that suggests an abstract meaning to the reader in addition to its literal meaning. A symbol is usually a physical object or a description of an action that enables you to imagine something specific rather than abstract. In its compactness and specificity, it can suggest different abstract ideas to different readers. For example, in "Everything Is Green," the name *Mayfly* refers to the common housefly, and you could read it as a symbol of the flightiness of Mitch's unfaithful lover. Another reader who thinks about Mayfly's infidelity could see her name as a symbol of the brief duration of her love for Mitch, since the life of a mayfly is so short.

Some objects convey the idea of a **conventional symbol** whose meaning is accepted by everyone. For example, the red, white, and blue flag displayed everywhere on the Fourth of July in the United States is a symbol of the country. The "Red Indian" in Franz Kafka's whirlwind story is a conventional symbol of the freedom of the so-called natural man, free from the constraints of civilized life.

FRANZ KAFKA

I Wish I Were a Red Indian

1919

TRANSLATED BY ANN CHARTERS

If I were only an Indian, suddenly vigilant on a galloping horse, leaning into the wind, racing over the shaking ground, until I lost the spurs, because I didn't need spurs, dropped the reins, because I didn't need reins, and barely noticed that the land ahead was a smoothly cut meadow and the horse's neck and head had already vanished.

Writers can also create **personal symbols** when they depict ordinary objects so vividly in a story that they suggest powerful abstract ideas. You've already encountered this use of personal symbolism in Daniel Orozco's "Orientation" (p. 46), where the dehumanizing office routines suggest a larger, symbolic statement about work in our society. In "Blind Date," the table legs made out of "the legs of a deer, complete with hooves" could be read as Lydia Davis's eloquent personal symbol, brought into the story right after her friend relates her memory of acting like an animal "with no responsibility to anyone or anything." Another reader might interpret Davis's personal symbol to refer to an animal's instinct for self-preservation since the narrator also describes a lamp made out of an old gun. Then the symbol would also suggest dramatic irony since the deer was killed so that its legs could be used to construct an Adirondacks-style table.

Jamaica Kincaid told the interviewer Allan Vorda that years after writing "Girl" (p. 44) she began to see that her story was more than an autobiographical narrative. She explained that she could interpret it as a personal symbol. As a West Indian author, she meant that her depiction of the mother's relationship to her daughter in "Girl" was a statement about the relationship between the powerful and the powerless. With hindsight, Kincaid believed she was trying to show how colonial oppression and racism made native people feel inferior in their own country everywhere in the world, not only in Antigua and in the United States. Symbols are one of the most powerful means of any creative writer.

Usually an author is suggesting that something is to be read symbolically if it is emphasized in the text. If it seems to glow in your mind long after you come to the end of a story, illuminated by its suggestions of an important abstract meaning behind the literal image, it's probably a symbol. Symbols are more eloquent as specific images—visual ideas—than any paraphrase, suggesting infinitely more than they state. A long time ago St. Thomas Aquinas even argued that human beings "cannot understand without images." More recently the author Mary Gaitskill, writing about the form of the short story, observed that "writing is about words, but life is not about words. This is the transcendent potential of the form. Great writing uses words in such a way that they evoke images, feelings, associations and ideas that come together, line by black-and-white line, to create complex pictures that represent not just life, but something truer than what we think of as 'life' on a day-to-day basis."

You should be careful when you read a text closely, looking for symbols. Don't go out of your way to find them because most writers of short fiction use them sparingly. For example, Paley avoids any suggestion of symbolism or an abstract meaning in "Samuel" until her concluding sentence. Then Samuel, for all his foolish high spirits, becomes her personal symbol for the value of every individual human life in its precious uniqueness. Reading the story the first time, you might have wondered if the subway train where Samuel loses his life is a symbol of the inhuman forces that crush ordinary people in the crowded inner city. Re-reading the story, you realize it's more likely that Paley was presenting the train realistically as an ordinary uptown subway train about to be thrown off schedule while making its run to the Bronx. This train has no special significance in steering you toward Paley's transcendent theme, which is how effective symbols work in literature.

To practice recognizing how symbols can lead you to the theme of a short story, here is the Japanese author Yasunari Kawabata's well-known tale "The Grasshopper and the Bell Cricket."

YASUNARI KAWABATA

The Grasshopper and the Bell Cricket

1988

TRANSLATED BY LANE DUNLOP

Walking along the tile-roofed wall of the university, I turned aside and approached the upper school. Behind the white board fence of the school playground, from a dusky clump of bushes under the black cherry trees, an insect's voice could be heard. Walking more slowly and listening to that voice, and furthermore reluctant to part with it, I turned right so as not to leave the playground behind. When I turned to the left, the fence gave way to an embankment planted with orange trees. At the corner, I exclaimed with surprise. My eyes gleaming at what they saw up ahead, I hurried forward with short steps.

At the base of the embankment was a bobbing cluster of beautiful varicolored lanterns, such as one might see at a festival in a remote country village. Without going any farther, I knew that it was a group of children on an insect chase among the bushes of the embankment. There were about twenty lanterns.

Not only were there crimson, pink, indigo, green, purple, and yellow lanterns, but one lantern glowed with five colors at once. There were even some little red store-bought lanterns. But most of the lanterns were beautiful square ones which the children had made themselves with love and care. The bobbing lanterns, the coming together of children on this lonely slope—surely it was a scene from a fairy tale?

One of the neighborhood children had heard an insect sing on this slope one night. Buying a red lantern, he had come back the next night to find the insect. The night after that, there was another child. This new child could not buy a lantern. Cutting out the back and front of a small carton and papering it, he placed a candle on the bottom and fastened a string to the top. The number of children grew to five, and then to seven. They learned how to color the paper that they stretched over the windows of the cutout cartons, and to draw pictures on it. Then these wise child-artists, cutting out round, three-cornered, and lozenge leaf shapes in the cartons, coloring each little window a different color, with circles and diamonds, red and green, made a single and whole decorative pattern. The child with the red lantern discarded it as a tasteless object that could be bought at a store. The child who had made his own lantern threw it away because the design was too simple. The pattern of light that one had had in hand the night before was unsatisfying the morning after. Each day, with cardboard, paper, brush, scissors, penknife, and glue, the children made new lanterns out of their hearts and minds. Look at my lantern! Be the most unusually beautiful! And each night, they had gone out on their insect hunts. These were the twenty children and their beautiful lanterns that I now saw before me.

Wide-eyed, I loitered near them. Not only did the square lanterns have old-fashioned patterns and flower shapes, but the names of the children who had made them were cut out in squared letters of the syllabary. Different from the painted-over red lanterns, others (made of thick cutout cardboard) had their designs drawn onto the paper windows, so that the candle's light seemed to emanate from the form and color of the design itself. The lanterns brought out the shadows of the bushes like dark light. The children crouched eagerly on the slope wherever they heard an insect's voice.

"Does anyone want a grasshopper?" A boy, who had been peering into a bush about thirty feet away from the other children, suddenly straightened up and shouted.

"Yes! Give it to me!" Six or seven children came running up. Crowding behind the boy who had found the grasshopper, they peered into the bush. Brushing away their outstretched hands and spreading out his arms, the boy stood as if guarding the bush where the insect was. Waving the lantern in his right hand, he called again to the other children.

"Does anyone want a grasshopper? A grasshopper!"

"I do! I do!" Four or five more children came running up. It seemed you could not catch a more precious insect than a grasshopper. The boy called out a third time.

"Doesn't anyone want a grasshopper?"

Two or three more children came over.

"Yes. I want it."

It was a girl, who just now had come up behind the boy who'd discovered the insect. Lightly turning his body, the boy gracefully bent forward. Shifting the lantern to his left hand, he reached his right hand into the bush.

"It's a grasshopper."

"Yes. I'd like to have it."

The boy quickly stood up. As if to say "Here!" he thrust out his fist that held the insect at the girl. She, slipping her left wrist under the string of her lantern, enclosed the boy's fist with both hands. The boy quietly opened his fist. The insect was transferred to between the girl's thumb and index finger.

"Oh! It's not a grasshopper. It's a bell cricket." The girl's eyes shone as she looked at the small brown insect.

"It's a bell cricket! It's a bell cricket!" The children echoed in an envious chorus.

"It's a bell cricket. It's a bell cricket."

Glancing with her bright intelligent eyes at the boy who had given her the cricket, the girl opened the little insect cage hanging at her side and released the cricket in it.

"It's a bell cricket."

"Oh, it's a bell cricket," the boy who'd captured it muttered. Holding up the insect cage close to his eyes, he looked inside it. By the light of his beautiful many colored lantern, also held up at eye level, he glanced at the girl's face.

Oh, I thought. I felt slightly jealous of the boy, and sheepish. How silly of me not to have understood his actions until now! Then I caught my breath in surprise. Look! It was something on the girl's breast which neither the boy who had given her the cricket, nor she who had accepted it, nor the children who were looking at them noticed.

In the faint greenish light that fell on the girl's breast, wasn't the name "Fujio" clearly discernible? The boy's lantern, which he held up alongside the girl's insect cage, inscribed his name, cut out in the green papered aperture, onto her white cotton kimono. The girl's lantern, which dangled loosely from her wrist, did not project its pattern so clearly, but still one could make out, in a trembling patch of red on the boy's waist, the name "Kiyoko." This chance interplay of red and green—if it was chance or play—neither Fujio nor Kiyoko knew about.

Even if they remembered forever that Fujio had given her the cricket and that Kiyoko had accepted it, not even in dreams would Fujio ever know that his name had been written in green on Kiyoko's breast or that Kiyoko's name had been inscribed in red on his waist, nor would Kiyoko ever know that Fujio's name had been inscribed in green on her breast or that her own name had been written in red on Fujio's waist.

Fujio! Even when you have become a young man, laugh with pleasure at a girl's delight when, told that it's a grasshopper, she is given a bell cricket; laugh with affection at a girl's chagrin when, told that it's a bell cricket, she is given a grasshopper.

Even if you have the wit to look by yourself in a bush away from the other children, there are not many bell crickets in the world. Probably you will find a girl like a grasshopper whom you think is a bell cricket.

And finally, to your clouded, wounded heart, even a true bell cricket will seem like a grasshopper. Should that day come, when it seems to you that the world is only full of grasshoppers, I will think it a pity that you have no way to remember tonight's play of light, when your name was written in green by your beautiful lantern on a girl's breast.

◆ Questions for Critical Thinking about Style ◆

1. Is Kawabata's prose style primarily literal or figurative in "The Grasshopper and the Bell Cricket"?
2. Who is the narrator of the story? Why does the narrator describe the children's lanterns so elaborately?
3. What do the common grasshopper and the rare bell cricket symbolize in the final paragraphs of the story? Where else do you find symbolism? How do these symbols help you to state the story's theme or themes?
4. Is Kawabata's tale an allegory, a story that has two levels of meaning, the literal and the symbolic?
5. This modern story about insects may remind you of Aesop's fable "The Grasshopper and the Ant." How does Kawabata's literary style in this story differ from the style of a fable by Aesop?

◆ Topics for Writing about Style ◆

1. In the original German in which Kafka wrote "I Wish I Were a Red Indian," the author used third-person narration instead of first-person narration, using the pronoun *one* instead of the pronoun *I*. In a literal translation from German to English, the title would read "The Wish to Be a Red Indian," and the story would start "If one were only an Indian . . . until one lost one's spurs . . . and barely noticed that the land before one . . ." The result is a very formal prose style in the original German language. Write an essay in which you analyze the prose style of this English version of Kafka's story. How does the first-person narration affect the way you interpret its literary style?
2. Write an essay in which you analyze what the use of figurative language such as "my heart has been down this road and back for you" tells you about the narrator in David Foster Wallace's story "Everything Is Green."

THEME

Your close reading of a short story will help you state its **theme**, your generalization about the meaning of a story. Theme is often confused with the **subject** of the story, which is what the narrative is about. While the subject can be expressed in a few words ("The Grasshopper and the Bell Cricket" describes a children's game of catching grasshoppers), the theme requires a longer phrase or a sentence to do justice to the author's unifying vision. The theme of a story is also different from the plot, which is usually a summary of what happened in the action. (While the narrator watches a group of children with beautiful homemade paper lanterns collect insects, a boy catches what he thinks is a common grasshopper and gives it to a girl who tells him it's a rare bell cricket.) The theme of a short story is an abstract statement of the meaning of the story (finding true love is a rare experience, but it can happen to anyone open to it).

The theme of a story abstracts its meaning from the concrete details of its plot, point of view, characterization, setting, and style. If the author uses symbols, they can also lead you to the theme, as Kawabata implies in the final paragraphs of "The Grasshopper and the Bell Cricket." You can reread any story closely and let your interpretation of a symbol suggest the theme. In García Márquez's story, you may decide that he is playing with the symbol of an angel in order to explore the detrimental stronghold of religious superstition in an illiterate, underdeveloped community. On the other hand, you might believe that the very old man with enormous wings is a fallen angel and that the theme of the story is a biblical quotation from Hebrews 13:2: "Be not forgetful to entertain strangers, for thereby some have entertained angels unaware." In 1988, when García Márquez coauthored a screenplay of his story for Television Española, he used that quotation at the start of the film. Ironically, in the film version he simplified the story. There the old man is revealed as a trickster or confidence man who takes off his wings when he is alone.

Theme is a statement of the story's significance for you. You don't have to state it as a moral judgment. Of course the story's meaning can suggest principles of right and wrong behavior, as in "Blind Date," where Davis's theme could be the idea that an inconsiderate act that we do in haste can haunt us for a very long time. The impulse to tell a story can arise from several universal urges of the human spirit: to share experience, to communicate, to create, to raise ultimate questions and not only pragmatic ones—in short, to provide a personal expression in narrative form of our sense of what life is like. The writer Maya Angelou understood that "a bird doesn't sing because it has an answer. It sings because it has a song."

Most good writers don't intend to preach about specific moral values when they start working on a story. They create short fiction more like the way composers discover harmony, pattern, and aesthetic design in a piece of music. You will find that great short stories aren't simple moral parables in which good triumphs over evil. To create a complex fictional world reflecting actual human experience, writers often provide multiple moral viewpoints within the story through their dramatization of the conflicting perspectives of the various characters. They leave it to you to come up with your own moral judgment in the statement of the story's theme. A gifted storyteller says, "Let me tell you how it is," and our interest is always in what the whole story can show us about human experience.

The structure and theme of a story are fused like the body and soul of a reader. Their interaction creates a living pattern. Authors work hard to breathe life into their fiction. Most do not like to abstract the meaning of their stories to explain what they are "about." Sometimes it takes years for them to discover the significance of their stories, as in Kincaid's experience with the theme of "Girl." Even when they start writing with a specific idea, as the southern writer Flannery O'Connor did in her explanation of her theme in "A Good Man Is Hard to Find" (p. 497), some readers agree intellectually but not emotionally with the author's interpretation. O'Connor said she understood that her story might be read in different ways by different people, but she could have written it only with the one meaning she had in mind.

Interpreting the Theme of a Story

Different readers can find the same story significant in different ways, but to say that a story can have more than a single meaning doesn't imply that you can interpret it any way you choose. You have to be able to find enough important details that support your interpretation of the theme for it to be plausible. Often you find it difficult to formulate a single sentence that captures your sense of the significance of a story. In your first attempt to state the theme of "Blind Date," for example, you might have written "Don't stand up a blind date." On second thought, you might sense that you haven't done justice to the story. You've left out the woman's sense of guilt, which motivated her to tell her friend about the event that made her still feel ashamed many years later. You should try again to write a sentence that suggests the painful feelings at the heart of Davis's story.

After another close reading of "Blind Date," you might decide that it is most significant as an example of **metafiction**, a work of fiction that consciously explores its own nature as a literary creation. Davis was consciously creating what she calls "things from things" in "Blind Date." She might have imagined a friend telling a story about standing up a blind date, and then gone on to use the elements of fiction to transform the personal confession into a short story. If you are a budding short story writer, this could be the story's significance for you. After you've spent some time trying to reduce a story to its one-sentence essence, you may feel words coming irresistibly to mind from another context, as the American poet Archibald MacLeish wrote, "A poem should not mean / but be."

Good stories may suggest different themes to different readers, but the way the author creates the narrative by using all the elements of fiction to embody the theme is, of course, the most important achievement of the story. To appreciate the fact that the story itself is always more complex than its bare-bones meaning, try this experiment: Write a sentence stating the theme of any story you've read so far in this anthology. Then close your book and try to re-create that story. That should prove to you that all works of short fiction are much more than a combination of their elements. Their magic consists of *how* the elements work together in the story.

Though the summary of an author's theme is no substitute for the story in its entirety, your attempt to state it can help you to understand the story better. O'Connor insisted that a story is not its abstract meaning but rather what she called its "experienced" meaning. "A story is a way to say something that can't be said any other way, and it takes every word in the story to say what the meaning is. . . . When anybody asks what a story is about, the only proper thing is to tell him to read the story."

Here are two short stories that will give you the opportunity to practice your analysis of theme. One is a magic realism story by the Egyptian writer

Naguib Mahfouz, "Half a Day," in which dream and reality are blurred, and the narrator uses the images and metaphors of a poet. The other is a realistic story by the Hispanic writer Rosario Morales, "The Day It Happened." Both authors start with a young person telling the story in first-person narration before they take very different directions.

NAGUIB MAHFOUZ

Half a Day

1989

TRANSLATED BY DENYS JOHNSON-DAVIES

I proceeded alongside my father, clutching his right hand, running to keep up with the long strides he was taking. All my clothes were new: the black shoes, the green school uniform, and the red tarboosh.° My delight in my new clothes, however, was not altogether unmarred, for this was no feast day but the day on which I was to be cast into school for the first time.

My mother stood at the window watching our progress, and I would turn toward her from time to time, as though appealing for help. We walked along a street lined with gardens; on both sides were extensive fields planted with crops, prickly pears, henna trees, and a few date palms.

"Why school?" I challenged my father openly. "I shall never do anything to annoy you."

"I'm not punishing you," he said, laughing. "School's not a punishment. It's the factory that makes useful men out of boys. Don't you want to be like your father and brothers?"

I was not convinced. I did not believe there was really any good to be had in tearing me away from the intimacy of my home and throwing me into this building that stood at the end of the road like some huge, high-walled fortress, exceedingly stern and grim.

When we arrived at the gate we could see the courtyard, vast and crammed full of boys and girls. "Go in by yourself," said my father, "and join them. Put a smile on your face and be a good example to others."

I hesitated and clung to his hand, but he gently pushed me from him. "Be a man," he said. "Today you truly begin life. You will find me waiting for you when it's time to leave."

I took a few steps, then stopped and looked but saw nothing. Then the faces of boys and girls came into view. I did not know a single one of them, and none of them knew me. I felt I was a stranger who had lost his way. But glances of curiosity were directed toward me, and one boy approached and asked, "Who brought you?"

"My father," I whispered.

"My father's dead," he said quite simply.

---

tarboosh: A felt cap with a tassel, also known as a fez.

I did not know what to say. The gate was closed, letting out a pitiable screech. Some of the children burst into tears. The bell rang. A lady came along, followed by a group of men. The men began sorting us into ranks. We were formed into an intricate pattern in the great courtyard surrounded on three sides by high buildings of several floors; from each floor we were overlooked by a long balcony roofed in wood.

"This is your new home," said the woman. "Here too there are mothers and fathers. Here there is everything that is enjoyable and beneficial to knowledge and religion. Dry your tears and face life joyfully."

We submitted to the facts, and this submission brought a sort of contentment. Living beings were drawn to other living beings, and from the first moments my heart made friends with such boys as were to be my friends and fell in love with such girls as I was to be in love with, so that it seemed my misgivings had had no basis. I had never imagined school would have this rich variety. We played all sorts of different games: swings, the vaulting horse, ball games. In the music room we chanted our first songs. We also had our first introduction to language. We saw a globe of the Earth, which revolved and showed the various continents and countries. We started learning the numbers. The story of the Creator of the universe was read to us, we were told of His present world and of His Hereafter, and we heard examples of what He said. We ate delicious food, took a little nap, and woke up to go on with friendship and love, play and learning.

As our path revealed itself to us, however, we did not find it as totally sweet and unclouded as we had presumed. Dust-laden winds and unexpected accidents came about suddenly, so we had to be watchful, at the ready, and very patient. It was not all a matter of playing and fooling around. Rivalries could bring about pain and hatred or give rise to fighting. And while the lady would sometimes smile, she would often scowl and scold. Even more frequently she would resort to physical punishment.

In addition, the time for changing one's mind was over and gone and there was no question of ever returning to the paradise of home. Nothing lay ahead of us but exertion, struggle, and perseverance. Those who were able took advantage of the opportunities for success and happiness that presented themselves amid the worries.

The bell rang announcing the passing of the day and the end of work. The throngs of children rushed toward the gate, which was opened again. I bade farewell to friends and sweethearts and passed through the gate. I peered around but found no trace of my father, who had promised to be there. I stepped aside to wait. When I had waited for a long time without avail, I decided to return home on my own. After I had taken a few steps, a middle-aged man passed by, and I realized at once that I knew him. He came toward me, smiling, and shook me by the hand, saying, "It's a long time since we last met—how are you?"

With a nod of my head, I agreed with him and in turn asked, "And you, how are you?"

"As you can see, not all that good, the Almighty be praised!"

Again he shook me by the hand and went off. I proceeded a few steps, then came to a startled halt. Good Lord! Where was the street lined with gardens? Where had it disappeared to? When did all these vehicles invade it? And when did all these hordes of humanity come to rest upon its surface? How did these hills of refuse come to cover its sides? And where were the fields that bordered it? High buildings had taken over, the street surged with children, and disturbing noises shook the air. At various points stood conjurers showing off their tricks and making snakes appear from baskets. Then there was a band announcing the opening of a circus, with clowns and weight lifters walking in front. A line of trucks carrying central security troops crawled majestically by. The siren of a fire engine shrieked, and it was not clear how the vehicle would cleave its way to reach the blazing fire. A battle raged between a taxi driver and his passenger, while the passenger's wife called out for help and no one answered. Good God! I was in a daze. My head spun, I almost went crazy. How could all this have happened in half a day, between early morning and sunset? I would find the answer at home with my father. But where was my home? I could see only tall buildings and hordes of people. I hastened on to the crossroads between the gardens and Abu Khoda. I had to cross Abu Khoda to reach my house, but the stream of cars would not let up. The fire engine's siren was shrieking at full pitch as it moved at a snail's pace, and I said to myself, "Let the fire take its pleasure in what it consumes." Extremely irritated, I wondered when I would be able to cross. I stood there a long time, until the young lad employed at the ironing shop on the corner came up to me. He stretched out his arm and said gallantly, "Grandpa, let me take you across."

ROSARIO MORALES

The Day It Happened

1992

The day it happened I was washing my hair. I had long hair then that went halfway down my back and I washed it once a week and rinsed it with lemon juice "to bring out the blond highlights" Mami said. Then I'd set it into pin-curls that took an age to do because there was so much to wind around and around my finger. But if Mami was in a good mood, and she looked like she might be that day, she curled the back for me. I usually did all this on Saturday so I would look great for church on Sunday, and for a date Saturday night if I ever had one. ¡Ojalá!°

Naturally the moment when it all began I was rinsing the big soapy mess. Nosy Maria was leaning out the window drying her dark red fingernails in the breeze when Josie stepped out of our apartment house doorway with a suitcase in her hand. Maria sucked in her breath so hard the sound brought my mother, who took one look, crossed herself, or so Maria says, and started praying.

¡Ojalá!: Spanish for "God willing!"

Someone needed to pray for Josie. It was five o'clock and Ramón was due home any minute.

I wouldn't have known anything about any of this if Olga next door hadn't rung our doorbell and banged on the door just when Mami was too deep in prayer to hear and Maria was leaning out over the sill with her eyes bugging out. I cursed, very quietly of course, because if Mami or Papi heard me curse I'd get a slap across my face. I wrapped my sopping head in a towel and opened the door to Olga's "Oh my goodness, oh my dear. Oh honey, did you see? Look out the window this minute. I wouldn't have believed it if I hadn't seen it with my own two eyes. That poor little kid. I hate to think . . ." and on and on as we crossed the apartment to look out on the street.

Little Mikey from across the way was telling the rest of the kids how he'd found a taxi for Josie the minute he'd hit Southern Boulevard and how he'd hailed it and how the driver had let him ride back to Brook Street in the front seat—even though all of them had seen him arrive and step out with his back stiff with pride. Meantime Josie was back down in the street with Doña Toña from across the hall and Betty Murphy upstairs right behind her, all of them loaded down with two lamps, a typewriter and a big box of books. Doña Toña was muttering something we couldn't hear up here on the second story but it was probably either the prayer I was hearing on my right or the ". . . hurry oh hurry oh God he'll be here any minute are you mad girl, are you mad" that came at me from the left.

It was hard not to be scared as well as glad that Josie was packing up and leaving Ramón. They'd been married only six months but already they were in a pattern, like the Garcias down the block who did everything the same way on the same day, all year. Ramón worked late till seven every week day and five on Saturday. When he arrived he expected a good dinner to be on the table at the right temperature exactly five minutes after he walked in the door. He yelled if she didn't get it right and sometimes even if she did.

Saturday evening they went out to a party or the bar down the avenue, both of them dressed up and Ramón looking proud and cheerful for a change. Josie always looked great. She's so cute. Small and plump with long lashes on her dark eyes and, get this, naturally curly hair. She smiled a lot when she was happy but she hadn't been happy much lately and not at all since she got pregnant. I wasn't supposed to know this. God, I was almost thirteen! But Maria, who was fourteen and a half and thought she was twenty, listened in on conversations in the living room by opening the door a sliver and she told me all about it.

Saturday nights there was sure to be a fight. Either it was that Josie was "no fun, a man can't be a man with such a wet rag around." Or it was that Josie was "a tramp. Why else was that guy staring at you, eating you up with his eyes?" The first time it happened, soon after they moved in, it woke me up from a deep sleep and I was so scared I crept into Maria's bed. I'd never heard such yelling in my life. When my parents fight it's during the day and in angry whispers. It sounds like a snake convention in my parents' bedroom. That's bad enough. Maria and I get real nervous and nothing's right until they make up and talk in normal voices again. But Ramón could be heard right through the floor at two in the morning. And then he took to throwing things and then he started hitting her. The first time that happened Josie didn't go to morning mass at St. Francis and Mami went down to her apartment to see if she was sick or something. Josie came to the door with a big bruise on her face. After that Mami went to fetch her every Sunday and stayed with her if she was too ashamed to go to church.

After she found out she was pregnant Josie had talked it over with Doña Toña and Doña Toña had talked it over with Mami and by and by we all knew she was scared he would hurt the little baby growing inside of her and worried about the child growing up with Ramón for a father. He expected too much of everyone and little kids hurt so when a parent thinks whatever they do is all wrong. Ha! Tell that to Mami and Papi, will you.

I don't think there was anyone in the neighborhood on Ramón's side, not even Joe who liked to bully his wife and daughters but didn't realize he did or Tito who talked all the time about "wearing the pants in this family." Ramón was too much, even for them. Josie was so clearly a fine person, a quiet homebody, a sweetypie. Ramón was out of his mind, that's what most of us thought. I mean you had to be to be so regularly mean to a person who adored you. And she did, at least at first. You could see it in the way she looked at him, boasted about his strength, his good job, his brains. The way she excused his temper. "He can't help himself. He doesn't mean it."

And now she was packed up and sitting in the taxi. Waiting for him to come home, I guess. That was too much for Mami and she scooted out the door with Olga, Maria, Papi, no less, and me right behind her with that soaked blue towel wrapped sloppily around my head. "Ai Mamita! Jesus, Maria y José. Jesus Maria y José," came faintly up the stairs in the front of the hurrying line. I knew Mami and I knew she meant to stand in front of Josie to protect her from that bully and, sure as shooting, Papi was going to protect Mami who was going so fast in her house slippers she almost fell down except that Olga gripped her hard and kept her upright.

When we streamed out the door into the small crowd that had gathered by now it was to see Ramón coming down the street with a sour look on his face. He looked up once or twice but mostly just stared at his feet as he strode up the block. He swept past us and almost into the house the way he did when he came home weary from the shipyard and the long ride home. He would have missed seeing Josie for sure, as I was praying he would, except that she called to him.

"Ramón," she said in her soft voice, stepping out of the taxi. "Ramón." He looked up and around then, took in the crowd, the taxi with a tall lamp lying on the back seat and Josie in her good suit. He stood looking at all this and especially at Josie for a long time. When he spoke it was only to Josie, as if we weren't there at all. He had to clear his throat to say "Josie?"

I was totally surprised and confused. He sounded so small, you know. So uncertain. It was Josie looked tall now and hard. If I hadn't known what I knew I would've said Josie was the bully in the family. She looked him straight in the eye and said stiffly, as if they were lines someone had given her to memorize, "I warned you. I said I would leave if you ever hit me again. I am not safe with you. Our child is not safe with you. I'm going now. I left arroz con pollo° on the stove and the electric bill on the table." He didn't answer so she turned to hug Doña Toña and Mami before sitting herself back down. It was then that Ramón acted. Before I could blink he'd hurled himself at her, thrown himself on his knees and gripped her around her stockinged legs. "No! No te vayas. Tu no comprendes. Eres muy joven para comprender. Tu no puedes dejarme asi. Estamos casados para la vida. Te amo para siempre, para siempre. Josita, mi amor, no te vayas. Si te vas me mato. Te lo juro. No te puedes ir. No te puedes ir . . ." and on and on in a hoarse voice while Josie stood there frozen, fear on her face. There was no sound but Maria whispering occasional translations into Olga's impatient ear "Don't go." "You're too young to understand." "We're married for life." "I'll love you always." "I'll kill myself, I swear it."

It went on forever, Josie standing there, Ramón kneeling, all of us listening, tears running down my face, Josie's face, Mami's face. It was Olga who ended it, who walked up to Ramón, knelt down beside him, put an arm around him, and started talking, telling him Josie was a mother now and had to think about what was best for her baby, that it was his baby too, that he had to let her go now so she could bear a baby healthy in body and soul, that she knew he loved Josie, that his love would let him do what was best for them all. He was crying now, arguing with her while he slowly let go while he said he never could let her go, that she was his whole life, that he would die without her, while Josie kissed Toña quickly on the cheek and climbed in next to the taxi driver who sat there looking the way I probably looked, dazed, like he'd stumbled into a movie screen and couldn't get out. She had to tell him to drive off.

◆ Questions for Critical Thinking about Theme ◆

1. Do the titles of the two stories help to suggest their different themes?
2. Can you find a suggestion of the theme in specific passages of dialogue or description?
3. Are certain symbols or repetitions of images important in revealing the author's intent in each story?
4. In "Half a Day," at what point in the story does Mahfouz make you aware that he is not writing a realistic narrative?
5. How does the allegorical form of "Half a Day" contribute to Mahfouz's dramatization of his subject, the brevity of human life?
6. How does the realistic description in "The Day It Happened" contribute to Morales's depiction of spousal abuse?
7. Is it significant that the narrator of "Half a Day" is male and that the narrator of "The Day It Happened" is female? What does this difference in gender add to your understanding of the theme of each story?
8. Write a sentence summing up the theme of "Half a Day." Do the same for "The Day It Happened."

---

arroz con pollo: Rice with chicken.

◆ Topics for Writing about Theme ◆

1. Write an essay explicating either "Half a Day" or "The Day It Happened" to show how you have arrived at its theme. You will find a discussion of how to use explication, along with a sample student paper, on pages 1642–1644.
2. Discuss the specific symbols or repetitions of images in either "Half a Day" or "The Day It Happened" that suggest the theme of each story.

USEFUL TERMS TO REMEMBER

Conventional symbol A symbol that has so much meaning attached to it that you cannot see it without immediately thinking about something else at the same time.

Dialect A type of nonstandard English diction spoken by people from a particular geographic region, economic group, or social class. Don't confuse it with DIALOGUE, the exchange of words between characters in a story.

Diction A writer's choice of language, including words, phrases, and sentence structure.

Dramatic irony A figure of speech that occurs when the reader knows more about a situation than the imaginary characters.

Figurative language The use of a word or a group of words that is literally inaccurate but is used to describe or define a person, event, or thing more vividly by calling forth the sensations or responses that person, event, or thing evokes. Such language often takes the form of METAPHORS, in which one thing is equated with another, or SIMILES, in which one thing is compared to another by using *like*, *as*, or some other such connecting word.

Metafiction A work of fiction that consciously explores its own nature as a literary creation.

Personal symbol A symbol that has meaning that arises from the specific context of a story.

Style The distinctive and recognizable way an author uses language to create a work of literature. This can involve the author's use of diction, sentence length, syntax, tone, figures of speech, irony, and symbolism.

Subject The events of a story or what a narrative is about.

Symbol A word (or person, object, image, or event) that evokes a range of additional meanings that are usually more abstract than its literal significance.

Syntax A reference to the order of words. Syntax usually implies a word order that results in meaningful verbal patterns in the author's choice of words, phrases, and sentence structure. These verbal choices allow authors to emphasize any word of their choice as they manipulate syntax.

Theme An abstract statement of the meaning of a story.

Tone Authors' attitude to their material. Tone can be described as serious or comic, ironic or naive, angry or serene, or any other emotional state that human beings can experience and find words to express.

Verbal irony A figure of speech that occurs when a character says one thing but means the opposite. If the intention of the speaker is to hurt someone else, then this form of verbal irony verges on sarcasm.

Voice The specific manner chosen by the author to create a story. It is usually difficult to get a sense of the original author's voice or tone in a text that has been translated into English from a foreign language.

WEB Learn more about the elements of fiction with VirtuaLit Fiction at bedfordstmartins.com/virtualit/fiction.

6.

Stories and Storytellers

SHERMAN ALEXIE

Sherman Alexie (b. 1966) was born in Spokane, Washington. A registered member of the Spokane tribe through his mother, he attended grammar school on the Spokane reservation in Wellpinit, Washington. At Washington State University he found an anthology of Indian poetry in his first college literature class and discovered that women were paying more attention to him. "All these years I thought basketball would do it," he says humorously. "I should have been writing poems all along." After Alexie took a creative writing course with Alex Kuo, he began to publish in magazines such as *The Beloit Poetry Journal, The Journal of Ethnic Studies, New York Quarterly, Ploughshares,* and *Zyzzyva.* In 1991 he was awarded a poetry fellowship from the Washington State Arts Commission; the following year he received a poetry fellowship from the National Endowment for the Arts.

In 1992 Alexie published his first two books, *I Would Steal Horses* and *The Business of Fancydancing: Stories and Poems.* Several more titles followed in rapid order, including *The Lone Ranger and Tonto Fistfight in Heaven* (1993), which received a PEN/Hemingway Award for best first book of fiction. Alexie also won the American Book Award for his novel *Reservation Blues* (1995), in which he imagined what would happen if the legendary bluesman Robert Johnson were resurrected on the Spokane Indian Reservation. *Flight* (2007) is another recent novel. His film *Smoke Signals* won prizes at the Sundance Film Festival.

Alexie has stated, "I am a Spokane/Coeur d'Alene Indian from Wellpinit, Washington, where I live on the Spokane Indian Reservation. Everything I do now, writing and otherwise, has its origin in that." His short fiction, like "The Lone Ranger and Tonto Fistfight in Heaven," reflects his use of the icons of popular culture – radio and television programs, 7-Eleven stores, the neon promise of advertising – to facilitate a rapid crossover between storyteller and reader. As the critic Susan B. Brill has noticed, "Little ever changes in the lives of Alexie's characters. Commodity food, alcoholism, and desperation are constants in the stories." *The Toughest Indian in the World* (2000) and *War Dances* (2009) are two of his story collections.

WEB Research Sherman Alexie at bedfordstmartins.com/rewritinglit.

The Lone Ranger and Tonto Fistfight in Heaven 1993

Too hot to sleep so I walked down to the Third Avenue 7-11 for a Creamsicle and the company of a graveyard-shift cashier. I know that game. I worked graveyard for a Seattle 7-11 and got robbed once too often. The last time the bastard locked me in the cooler. He even took my money and basketball shoes.

The graveyard-shift worker in the Third Avenue 7-11 looked like they all do. Acne scars and a bad haircut, work pants that showed off his white socks, and those cheap black shoes that have no support. My arches still ache from my year at the Seattle 7-11.

"Hello," he asked when I walked into his store. "How you doing?"

I gave him a half-wave as I headed back to the freezer. He looked me over so he could describe me to the police later. I knew the look. One of my old girlfriends said I started to look at her that way, too. She left me not long after that. No, I left her and don't blame her for anything. That's how it happened. When one person starts to look at another like a criminal, then the love is over. It's logical.

"I don't trust you," she said to me. "You get too angry."

She was white and I lived with her in Seattle. Some nights we fought so bad that I would just get in my car and drive all night, only stop to fill up on gas. In fact, I worked the graveyard shift to spend as much time away from her as possible. But I learned all about Seattle that way, driving its back ways and dirty alleys.

Sometimes, though, I would forget where I was and get lost. I'd drive for hours, searching for something familiar. Seems like I'd spent my whole life that way, looking for anything I recognized. Once, I ended up in a nice residential neighborhood and somebody must have been worried because the police showed up and pulled me over.

"What are you doing out here?" the police officer asked me as he looked over my license and registration.

"I'm lost."

"Well, where are you supposed to be?" he asked me, and I knew there were plenty of places I wanted to be, but none where I was supposed to be.

"I got in a fight with my girlfriend," I said. "I was just driving around, blowing off steam, you know?"

"Well, you should be more careful where you drive," the officer said. "You're making people nervous. You don't fit the profile of the neighborhood."

I wanted to tell him that I didn't really fit the profile of the country but I knew it would just get me into trouble.

"Can I help you?" the 7-11 clerk asked me loudly, searching for some response that would reassure him that I wasn't an armed robber. He knew this dark skin and long, black hair of mine was dangerous. I had potential.

"Just getting a Creamsicle," I said after a long interval. It was a sick twist to pull on the guy, but it was late and I was bored. I grabbed my Creamsicle and walked back to the counter slowly, scanned the aisles for effect. I wanted to whistle low and menacingly but I never learned to whistle.

"Pretty hot out tonight?" he asked, that old rhetorical weather bullshit question designed to put us both at ease.

"Hot enough to make you go crazy," I said and smiled. He swallowed hard like a white man does in those situations. I looked him over. Same old green, red, and white 7-11 jacket and thick glasses. But he wasn't ugly, just misplaced and marked by loneliness. If he wasn't working there that night, he'd be at home alone, flipping through channels and wishing he could afford HBO or Showtime.

"Will this be all?" he asked me, in that company effort to make me do some impulse shopping. Like adding a clause onto a treaty. *We'll take Washington and Oregon, and you get six pine trees and a brand-new Chrysler Cordoba.* I knew how to make and break promises.

"No," I said and paused. "Give me a Cherry Slushie, too."

"What size?" he asked, relieved.

"Large," I said, and he turned his back to me to make the drink. He realized his mistake but it was too late. He stiffened, ready for the gunshot or the blow behind the ear. When it didn't come, he turned back to me.

"I'm sorry," he said. "What size did you say?"

"Small," I said and changed the story.

"But I thought you said large."

"If you knew I wanted a large, then why did you ask me again?" I asked him and laughed. He looked at me, couldn't decide if I was giving him serious shit or just goofing. There was something about him I liked, even if it was three in the morning and he was white.

"Hey," I said. "Forget the Slushie. What I want to know is if you know all the words to the theme from 'The Brady Bunch'?"

He looked at me, confused at first, then laughed.

"Shit," he said. "I was hoping you weren't crazy. You were scaring me."

"Well, I'm going to get crazy if you don't know the words."

He laughed loudly then, told me to take the Creamsicle for free. He was the graveyard-shift manager and those little demonstrations of power tickled him. All seventy-five cents of it. I knew how much everything cost.

"Thanks," I said to him and walked out the door. I took my time walking home, let the heat of the night melt the Creamsicle all over my hand. At three in the morning I could act just as young as I wanted to act. There was no one around to ask me to grow up.

In Seattle, I broke lamps. She and I would argue and I'd break a lamp, just pick it up and throw it down. At first she'd buy replacement lamps, expensive and beautiful. But after a while she'd buy lamps from Goodwill or garage sales. Then she just gave up the idea entirely and we'd argue in the dark.

"You're just like your brother," she'd yell. "Drunk all the time and stupid."

"My brother don't drink that much."

She and I never tried to hurt each other physically. I did love her, after all, and she loved me. But those arguments were just as damaging as a fist. Words can be like that, you know? Whenever I get into arguments now, I remember her and I also remember Muhammad Ali. He knew the power of his fists but, more importantly, he knew the power of his words, too. Even though he only had an IQ of 80 or so, Ali was a genius. And she was a genius, too. She knew exactly what to say to cause me the most pain.

But don't get me wrong. I walked through that relationship with an executioner's hood. Or more appropriately, with war paint and sharp arrows. She was a kindergarten teacher and I continually insulted her for that.

"Hey, schoolmarm," I asked. "Did your kids teach you anything new today?"

And I always had crazy dreams. I always have had them, but it seemed they became nightmares more often in Seattle.

In one dream, she was a missionary's wife and I was a minor war chief. We fell in love and tried to keep it secret. But the missionary caught us fucking in the barn and shot me. As I lay dying, my tribe learned of the shooting and attacked the whites all across the reservation. I died and my soul drifted above the reservation.

Disembodied, I could see everything that was happening. Whites killing Indians and Indians killing whites. At first it was small, just my tribe and the few whites who lived there. But my dream grew, intensified. Other tribes arrived on horseback to continue the slaughter of whites, and the United States Cavalry rode into battle.

The most vivid image of that dream stays with me. Three mounted soldiers played polo with a dead Indian woman's head. When I first dreamed it, I thought it was just a product of my anger and imagination. But since then, I've read similar accounts of that kind of evil in the old West. Even more terrifying, though, is the fact that those kinds of brutal things are happening today in places like El Salvador.

All I know for sure, though, is that I woke from that dream in terror, packed up all my possessions, and left Seattle in the middle of the night.

"I love you," she said as I left her. "And don't ever come back."

I drove through the night, over the Cascades, down into the plains of central Washington, and back home to the Spokane Indian Reservation.

When I finished the Creamsicle that the 7-11 clerk gave me, I held the wooden stick up into the air and shouted out very loudly. A couple lights flashed on in windows and a police car cruised by me a few minutes later. I waved to the men in blue and they waved back accidentally. When I got home it was still too hot to sleep so I picked up a week-old newspaper from the floor and read.

There was another civil war, another terrorist bomb exploded, and one more plane crashed and all aboard were presumed dead. The crime rate was rising in every city with populations larger than 100,000, and a farmer in Iowa shot his banker after foreclosure on his 1,000 acres.

A kid from Spokane won the local spelling bee by spelling the word *rhinoceros.*

When I got back to the reservation, my family wasn't surprised to see me. They'd been expecting me back since the day I left for Seattle. There's an old Indian poet who said that Indians can reside in the city, but they can never live there. That's as close to truth as any of us can get.

Mostly I watched television. For weeks I flipped through channels, searched for answers in the game shows and soap operas. My mother would circle the want ads in red and hand the paper to me.

"What are you going to do with the rest of your life?" she asked.

"Don't know," I said, and normally, for almost any other Indian in the country, that would have been a perfectly fine answer. But I was special, a former college student, a smart kid. I was one of those Indians who was supposed to make it, to rise above the rest of the reservation like a fucking eagle or something. I was the new kind of warrior.

For a few months I didn't even look at the want ads my mother circled, just left the newspaper where she had set it down. After a while, though, I got tired of television and started to play basketball again. I'd been a good player in high school, nearly great, and almost played at the college I attended for a couple years. But I'd been too out of shape from drinking and sadness to ever be good again. Still, I liked the way the ball felt in my hands and the way my feet felt inside my shoes.

At first I just shot baskets by myself. It was selfish, and I also wanted to learn the game again before I played against anybody else. Since I had been good before and embarrassed fellow tribal members, I knew they would want to take revenge on me. Forget about the cowboys versus Indians business. The most intense competition on any reservation is Indians versus Indians.

But on the night I was ready to play for real, there was this white guy at the gym, playing with all the Indians.

"Who is that?" I asked Jimmy Seyler.

"He's the new BIA° chief's kid."

"Can he play?"

"Oh, yeah."

And he could play. He played Indian ball, fast and loose, better than all the Indians there.

BIA: Bureau of Indian Affairs.

"How long's he been playing here?" I asked.

"Long enough."

I stretched my muscles, and everybody watched me. All these Indians watched one of their old and dusty heroes. Even though I had played most of my ball at the white high school I went to, I was still all Indian, you know? I was Indian when it counted, and this BIA kid needed to be beaten by an Indian, any Indian.

I jumped into the game and played well for a little while. It felt good. I hit a few shots, grabbed a rebound or two, played enough defense to keep the other team honest. Then that white kid took over the game. He was too good. Later, he'd play college ball back East and would nearly make the Knicks team a couple years on. But we didn't know any of that would happen. We just knew he was better that day and every other day.

The next morning I woke up tired and hungry, so I grabbed the want ads, found a job I wanted, and drove to Spokane to get it. I've been working at the high school exchange program ever since, typing and answering phones. Sometimes I wonder if the people on the other end of the line know that I'm Indian and if their voices would change if they did know.

One day I picked up the phone and it was her, calling from Seattle.

"I got your number from your mom," she said. "I'm glad you're working."

"Yeah, nothing like a regular paycheck."

"Are you drinking?"

"No, I've been on the wagon for almost a year."

"Good."

The connection was good. I could hear her breathing in the spaces between our words. How do you talk to the real person whose ghost has haunted you? How do you tell the difference between the two?

"Listen," I said. "I'm sorry for everything."

"Me, too."

"What's going to happen to us?" I asked her and wished I had the answer for myself.

"I don't know," she said. "I want to change the world."

These days, living alone in Spokane, I wish I lived closer to the river, to the falls where ghosts of salmon jump. I wish I could sleep. I put down my paper or book and turn off all the lights, lie quietly in the dark. It may take hours, even years, for me to sleep again. There's nothing surprising or disappointing in that.

I know how all my dreams end anyway.

COMMENTARY

SHERMAN ALEXIE

Sherman Alexie described his earliest response to books during his childhood on the Spokane Indian Reservation in eastern Washington state. His essay appeared in *The Most Wonderful Books* (1997), edited by Michael Dorris and Emilie Buchwald.

Superman and Me

1997

I learned to read with a *Superman* comic book. Simple enough, I suppose. I cannot recall which particular *Superman* comic book I read, nor can I remember which villain he fought in that issue. I cannot remember the plot, nor the means by which I obtained the comic book. What I can remember is this: I was three years old, a Spokane Indian boy living with his family on the Spokane Indian Reservation in eastern Washington state. We were poor by most standards, but one of my parents usually managed to find some minimum-wage job or another, which made us middle class by reservation standards. I had a brother and three sisters. We lived on a combination of irregular paychecks, hope, fear, and government-surplus food.

My father, who is one of the few Indians who went to Catholic school on purpose, was an avid reader of westerns, spy thrillers, murder mysteries, gangster epics, basketball-player biographies, and anything else he could find. He bought his books by the pound at Dutch's Pawn Shop, Goodwill, Salvation Army, and Value Village. When he had extra money, he bought new novels at supermarkets, convenience stores, and hospital gift shops. Our house was filled with books. They were stacked in crazy piles in the bathroom, bedrooms, and living room. In a fit of unemployment-inspired creative energy, my father built a set of bookshelves and soon filled them with a random assortment of books about the Kennedy assassination, Watergate, the Vietnam War, and the entire twenty-three-book series of the Apache westerns. My father loved books, and since I loved my father with an aching devotion, I decided to love books as well.

I can remember picking up my father's books before I could read. The words themselves were mostly foreign, but I still remember the exact moment when I first understood, with a sudden clarity, the purpose of a paragraph. I didn't have the vocabulary to say "paragraph," but I realized that a paragraph was a fence that held words. The words inside a paragraph worked together for a common purpose. They had some specific reason for being inside the same fence. This knowledge delighted me. I began to think of everything in terms of paragraphs. Our reservation was a small paragraph within the United States. My family's house was a paragraph, distinct from the other paragraphs of the LeBrets to the north, the Fords to our south, and the Tribal School to the west. Inside our house, each family member existed as a separate paragraph, but still had genetics and common experiences to link us. Now, using this logic, I can see my changed family as an essay of seven paragraphs: mother, father, older brother, the deceased sister, my younger twin sisters, and our adopted little brother.

At the same time I was seeing the world in paragraphs, I also picked up that *Superman* comic book. Each panel, complete with picture, dialogue, and narrative, was a three-dimensional paragraph. In one panel, Superman breaks through a door. His suit is red, blue, and yellow. The brown door shatters into many pieces. I look at the narrative above the picture. I cannot read the words, but I assume it tells me that Superman is breaking down the door. Aloud, I pretend to read the words and say "Superman is breaking down the door." Words, dialogue, also float out of Superman's mouth. Because he is breaking down the door, I assume he says, "I am breaking down the door." Once again, I pretend to read the words and say aloud, "I am breaking down the door." In this way, I learned to read.

This might be an interesting story all by itself. A little Indian boy teaches himself to read at an early age and advances quickly. He reads *Grapes of Wrath* in kindergarten when other children are struggling through Dick and Jane. If he'd been anything but an Indian boy living on the reservation, he might have been called a prodigy. But he is an Indian boy living on the reservation, and is simply an oddity. He grows into a man who often speaks of his childhood in the third-person, as if it will somehow dull the pain and make him sound more modest about his talents.

A smart Indian is a dangerous person, widely feared and ridiculed by Indians and non-Indians alike. I fought with my classmates on a daily basis. They wanted me to stay quiet when the non-Indian teacher asked for answers, for volunteers, for help. We were Indian children who were expected to be stupid. Most lived up to those expectations inside the classroom, but subverted them on the outside. They struggled with basic reading in school, but could remember how to sing a few dozen powwow songs. They were monosyllabic in front of their non-Indian teachers, but could tell complicated stories and jokes at the dinner table. They submissively ducked their heads when confronted by a non-Indian adult, but would slug it out with the Indian bully who was ten years older. As Indian children, we were expected to fail in the non-Indian world. Those who failed were ceremonially accepted by other Indians and appropriately pitied by non-Indians.

I refused to fail. I was smart. I was arrogant. I was lucky. I read books late into the night, until I could barely keep my eyes open. I read books at recess, then during lunch, and in the few minutes left after I had finished my classroom assignments. I read books in the car when my family traveled to powwows or basketball games. In shopping malls, I ran to the bookstores and read bits and pieces of as many books as I could. I read the books my father brought home from the pawnshops and secondhand stores. I read the books I borrowed from the library. I read the backs of cereal boxes. I read the newspaper. I read the bulletins posted on the walls of the school, the clinic, the tribal offices, the post office. I read junk mail. I read auto-repair manuals. I read magazines. I read anything that had words and paragraphs. I read with equal parts joy and desperation. I loved those books, but I also knew that love had only one purpose. I was trying to save my life.

Despite all the books I read, I am still surprised I became a writer. I was going to be a pediatrician. These days, I write novels, short stories, and poems. I visit schools and teach creative writing to Indian kids. In all my years in the reservation school system, I was never taught how to write poetry, short stories, or novels. I was certainly never taught that Indians wrote poetry, short stories, and novels. Writing was something beyond Indians. I cannot recall a single time that a guest teacher visited the reservation. There must have been visiting teachers. Who were they? Where are they now? Do they exist? I visit the schools as often as possible. The Indian kids crowd the classroom. Many are writing their own poems, short stories, and novels. They have read my books. They have read many other books. They look at me with bright eyes and arrogant wonder. They are trying to save their lives. Then there are the sullen and already defeated Indian kids who sit in the back rows and ignore me with theatrical precision. The pages of their notebooks are empty. They carry neither pencil nor pen. They stare out the window. They refuse and resist. "Books," I say to them. "Books," I say. I throw my weight against their locked doors. The door holds. I am smart. I am arrogant. I am lucky. I am trying to save our lives.

DOROTHY ALLISON

Dorothy Allison (b. 1949) was born in Greenville, South Carolina, the first child of a fifteen-year-old unwed mother who dropped out of the seventh grade to work as a waitress. Allison was raised in extreme poverty by her mother's family; she remembers "hiding out under the porch" so she could listen to her grandmother and aunt tell randy stories. In her childhood she was often beaten and raped by her abusive stepfather. Allison writes of her lasting sense of shame and guilt:

> Most of my life I have despised myself, the child who didn't tell her mother she was being raped. The one defense I ever found was sending my little sisters in to him, because I knew he wasn't as bad with them as he was with me. So I grew up convinced that I was an evil creature. Because I put people in harm's way to escape harm just a little bit.

After attending Florida Presbyterian College on a National Merit scholarship, Allison joined a feminist collective when the radical women's movement surfaced in the early 1970s. "Feminism saved my life. It was a substitute religion that made sense." She didn't try to see her family again until 1981. She felt that her first book of poetry, *The Women Who Hate Me* (1983), "wouldn't have happened if I hadn't started talking to my mother and my sisters again." Her second book, *Trash* (1988), a collection of short stories originally published by small lesbian presses and alternative magazines, won two Lambda Literary Awards. Four years later Allison received mainstream recognition with her autobiographical novel *Bastard Out of Carolina*, a finalist for the 1992 National Book Award. Allison's fourth book, *Two or Three Things I Know for Sure*, was published in 1994, followed by the novel *Cavedweller*. It won the 1998 Lambda Literary Award for Fiction and was made into a film in 2004. In recent years she has taught creative writing at several colleges and published short stories.

Allison has said that she got the idea for writing "Jason Who Will Be Famous" after watching a group of teenage boys hanging around the gas station in her small town. One of the boys left the group and walked off alone, "his backpack hanging over one shoulder and his muddy shoes almost coming off with every step." When he turned and made an insolent gesture, she thought, "Boy needs someone to shake him hard," but then – perhaps recalling her own past – she had the second thought, "He was no one I knew, a child in the world and for all I knew someone had already shaken him hard." She began to imagine what the boy might be thinking on his long walk home, and it became a story, "the one about living in hope if only."

Jason Who Will Be Famous 2009

Jason is going to be famous, and the best part is that he knows he will be good at it.

He has this real clear picture of himself, of him being interviewed—not of the place or even when it happens, but of the event itself. What he sees is him and the interviewer, a recording so clear and close up, he can see the reflections sparking off his own pupils. It's hi-def or Blu-ray or something past all that, a rendering that catches the way the soft hairs just forward of his earlobe lift and shine in the light reflecting off his pale cheeks. All he has to do is close his eyes and it begins to play, crisp and crackling with energy as the microphone bumps hollowly against the button on his open collar.

"A lot of it, I can't tell you," he says, and the interviewer nods.

Jason is sitting leaning forward. His features gleam in the bright light, his expression is carefully composed, focused on the interviewer. Jason nods his head and his hair swings down over his forehead. One auburn strand just brushes across the edges of his eyebrows. The interviewer is so close their elbows are almost touching. He is an older man with gray in his hair and an expression of watchful readiness—a man Jason has seen do this kind of thing on the news before, someone to be trusted, someone serious.

That is the word. Serious. The word echoes along Jason's nervous system. He is being taken seriously. Every time he imagines it again, the thought makes him take a deep breath. A little heat flares in his neck as the camera follows his eyes. He looks away from the interviewer, and his face goes still. He looks back and his eyes go dark and sad.

"I'm sorry to have to ask you about something so painful," the interviewer says to him.

"It's all right," Jason says. "I understand." He keeps his expression a mirror of the other man's, careful and composed. He can do this. Piece of cake.

Behind the cameraman, there are other people waiting to speak to Jason, others are standing close by to hear what he has to say. Everyone has questions, questions about what happened, of course, about the kidnapping and all the months in captivity. But they also want to ask him what he thinks about other things, about people, and events. In the interview as Jason sees it, he always has answers—surprising and complicated, wonderful answers.

"That boy is extraordinary," he hears the serious man tell another.

Extraordinary. The heat in his neck moves down into his chest, circles his diaphragm, and filters out to his arms and legs. He hopes it does not show on his face. Better to remain pale and impassive, pretend he does not hear what they say about him. How extraordinary he is, that everyone says so, some kind of genius. He half-smiles and then recomposes his expression. Genius. Jason is not sure what his genius is exactly, but he trusts it. He knows it will be revealed at the right time, in the right circumstances. It is simply that those events have not happened as of yet. But they will.

He opens his eyes. He has stopped at the edge of the road. Dust, white-grey and alkaline, has drifted up from his boots, and he can taste eucalyptus and piney resin. He looks up the road toward the next hill and the curve down into the shade of the redwood stand there. Should have brought a bottle of water, he thinks. Then, extraordinary. How would you know if you were extraordinary? Or a genius? He's pretty good at math, and music—though nothing that special. If he worked more, put more of himself into the work, no telling what he might not do. His dad told him that, once, when he was still living with them. His teachers have said something of the same thing. All of them though, his dad, teachers and his mom, they say it like it's a bad thing—his talents and his waste of them.

"If you worked more. If you worked harder."

They don't understand. No one does.

Jason wipes dust off his mouth and rocks his head from side to side. He knows the problem. It's not that he's lazy or stupid or even scared. No. The problem is that he never has had enough time or focus. There's just always so much that has to be done, and how does anyone do that kind of kung fu stuff anyway? How does anyone become extraordinary? Like Uma Thurman in the Tarantino movie?° Years going up and down staircases. It's like that. You do some stupid thing over and over and over, and sometime along in there, you discover you have achieved this enormous talent.

He glares up the road and resumes his pace, boots kicking dust and his hands gripping the straps of his backpack. He could do extraordinary stuff. Given the right circumstances, he has everything in him to do stuff that will startle everyone. It just takes the right circumstances—getting everything out of the way. He nods to himself. He can feel that coming toward him—the opportunity, the time, and the focus.

He has dreamed it so often, he knows it is coming—though he doesn't know all of how it will happen. That too, he sees like a movie, the movie of his life going on all the time. Step in and it is already in motion. Like that. He grins and speeds up slightly. Might be, he will be walking home along the river road from Connie's on a day just like this one. He'll have something in his backpack, after working for Connie all day, doing what he does so well, little baby buds his specialty. Connie always tells him how good he is. He knows exactly how to

Tarantino movie: In *Kill Bill: Vol. 2* (2004), which Quentin Tarantino directed and co-wrote, Thurman's character trains under a kung fu master.

clip and trim and harvest only what is ready to come away, leave what should be left behind. That shows talent. That shows aptitude. Bonsai killer weed work, he does that all the time. Connie knows she can trust him. Some people she strings along, but him she always pays with a ready smile and a touch along his arm or one quick knuckle push at his hip. Cash or buds, she pays him, and that's all good. Just as it is good no one knows what Jason has in his backpack. No one knows his business.

Still, he knows, the day is coming. Someone is going to snatch him up right off the road or outside the liquor store downtown—some old guy maybe, or even one of them scary old dykes from out the bay side of the Jenner beach. Those bitches are dangerous and he can barely imagine what they would do with a piece of work like him. Everyone knows they all got stuff, guns and money and stuff. Bitches like that stick together. But maybe it will be someone from nowhere nearby, some bunch of crazies with some plan he will never fully understand, that no one will understand.

He nods slowly, his hands gripping the straps tight as he imagines it—the snatch, the basement, the months alone and everything that comes after. He has been seeing it for a long time, the story in his head, the way it will happen. It was a dream the first time, a nightmare, grabby hands and the skin scraped off his knees—a nightmare of sweaty basement walls and dirt in his mouth. But by the third or fourth time he dreamed it, everything receded and it was not so nightmarish. He was fighting back and able to think. Then it was magical how he started thinking about it in the daytime, daydreaming it, planning what he would do, how he would handle things. Then what came after the snatch became more and more important. He had started imagining the person he would be afterward. He didn't think so much about the kidnapping then, or even the kidnappers. It was all about him and the basement and what he did down there, who he would become, who he was meant to become. It was set and in motion. It was coming, Jason was sure of it. Not that he thought he was psychic or anything, it was just that this big thing was coming, so big he could feel it, and he had thought it through and whatever happened, he was going to be ready.

He stumbles and stops. He is almost gasping, smelling the sweat on his neck, the dust on the road, the acrid breeze from the eucalyptus trees past the stand of old-growth stunted apple trees around the curve. He leans forward, stretching his back, and straightens to watch a turkey buzzard circling the hill to his left. No hurry. It is only half a mile to his mom's place, two twists in the road and an uphill grade. Jason shakes his head. He knows this road in its whole length, two and a half miles and every decrepit house along the way, every crumbling garage and leaning fence. Of course, everyone here also knows him, which is sometimes more than he can stand. But somewhere someone who does not know him is coming along, and they will change everything. He nods and resumes a steady pace. Everything will be made over—and he will never know when or why. It will be a mystery.

He thinks of the basement room, that dim space with the windows boarded over. Nothing much will be down there, but he won't need much. He would love a piano, of course, but a guitar is more the kind of thing you might find in a basement. Nothing fancy. Some dented old acoustic. Jason thinks about it, the throwaway object he will use. God knows what he will have to do to tune the thing. Not likely to be any help in the junk people keep in basements. But there will be paper or notebooks. The notebooks will have pages marked up, of course, but he can work around that, use the backs of pages or something. It is what he creates in the silence that will need to be written down, the songs or poems. Lyrics. He will write it all down—easy to imagine that—him singing to himself in the quiet. The pencil marks along the pages. Of course his music notation sucks. He's never been too good at that. He sighs and stops again.

Maybe there will be a recorder—some old thing probably. A little old tape recorder, not a good digital. But hey it will get the job done. He smiles and hears above him the turkey buzzard's awkward call. Ugly sound from an ugly bird. He watches a big white pickup truck drive slowly up and past him. Big metal locks clamp down on the storage bin at the front of the truck bed.

Connie's boyfriend, Grange, told Jason you could bust most of those locks with the right chisel and mallet. "It's all in the angle. Got to hit it right."

Jason has a chisel in his backpack but no mallet. He licks his lips and resumes his slow hike between the ditch and the road. You got to have the right stuff to get anything done. Unless you are lucky or have an edge.

Famous is the way to go, he thinks. You get stuff once you are famous.

Jason wipes sweat off his neck as he walks and imagines it again—the reporter, the camera, the intensity of the lights, the intensity of his genius. It will take time, but he will figure it out. Maybe it won't be music. Maybe it will be words. He's damn good with words, not like those assholes at school who talk all the time. He knows the value of words, keeps them in his head, not always spilling them out like they mean nothing. He doesn't have to tell what he knows. He just knows—lyrics and poetry and all that stuff. Good poetry, he tells himself. Not that crap they want him to read in school. Kind of stuff makes your neck go stiff, that kind of poetry, that's what he likes. He looks at the dust on his hand, sweat-darkened and spotted with little grey-green bits. Little nubbins of weeds and grass flung up with the dust as the trucks pass. He'll get on the computer tonight, look up all the words for grey-green. Emerald, olive-drab, unripe fruit, something or the other. Nothing too hard about getting the words right.

Jason wipes his hands on his jeans, enjoying the feel of the fabric under his palms. Truth is more important than how you tell it, he thinks. And he knows stuff, lots of stuff, secrets and stuff. He has stories.

Maybe that will be it, the stories he tells himself to pass the time. Movie scripts, plays, dialogues between characters that come and go when he is all gaunt and feverish. In the basement, they won't feed him much, so he will get all dramatic skinny and probably have lots of fever dreams. He'll write them down, everything. His hands will cramp and he'll go on writing, get up and pace back and forth and write some more. Pages on pages will pile up. He'll bathe his face in cool water and walk some more. He'll drink so much water his skin will clear up. His mom is always telling him that if he washed his face more, drank more water and yeah, and ate more vegetables, his skin would do that right away. Maybe she has a point. Maybe in the basement that's all they will give him. Vegetables and water—lots of water, 'cause you know they ain't gonna waste no greasy expensive stuff on no captive. No Coke, no potato chips, no Kentucky Fried Chicken.

Pure water and rivers of words. Jason grins and lengthens his stride. Maybe after a while he won't care what he eats, or he will learn to make an apple taste like a pie. That would be the kind of thing might happen. He could learn to eat imaginary meals and taste every bite—donuts and hot barbecue wings—and stay all skinny and pure. That would be something. He could teach people how to do that afterwards maybe. Some day he might run an ashram like the one his mama used to talk about.

The turkey buzzard swoops low and arcs downhill toward the river. Jason stops to watch its flight. A moment in time and the bird disappears. Things can change that fast. Anything could happen and you can't predict what might come along. But what he knows is that there won't be any distractions down in the basement, anything to get in the way. Cold walls and dim light and maybe just a shower. Might be it will only run cold water, but he can handle that. What he hates is tub baths, sitting in dirty water. No way there is not gonna be a shower in the basement, or, all right, maybe only a hose and a drain in the floor. But he knows he will bathe himself a lot 'cause what else will there be to do? 'Cept write what he knows and use the weights set. He laughs out loud. Maybe there won't be no weights, though every shed or garage he knows has some stacked in some corner or the other. If there's nothing like that in his basement, still there will be stuff, something he can use.

He grabs his backpack straps again and begins the uphill grade. His steps slow and he focuses on the notion of making do, figuring out what he will use. Stuff like old cans of paint or bundles of rebar or bricks left lying around. He'll Tarantino it all, laying on the concrete floor and pushing up and down over and over till his arms get all muscled, and his legs too. He'll push off against the wall or doorjamb or something. He's gonna be bored out of his mind. He'll get desperate. He'll be working out, running in place and lifting heavy things—whatever he finds. Yeah, he'll get pretty well muscled. He grins. That is how it will be. He's going to come out just amazing.

Jason looks up the road, quarter of a mile to his mom's turnoff. He's right at the spot where the old firebreak cuts uphill, right up to his dad's place. He can almost see around the redwoods along the hill up to the house. He won't be like his dad, he thinks, he won't waste his chances. He'll grab what comes and run with it. When he comes out of that basement, he'll be slick. That is what it is all gonna be. Slick and sure, and he will know how to manage it, not wind up house-sitting for some crappy old guy wants you to carry stuff and keep an eye on the dogs.

Fuck it. Jason says it out loud. "Fuck it!" He's gonna come out of that basement Brad-Pitt handsome and ready for anything. He'll be ready, all soulful and quirky like that guy from the White Stripes, only he won't take himself too seriously. Everyone else will do that for him. He'll know how to behave.

Jason laughs out loud again. "Yeah," he says. Yeah.

Serious. Yes. That's the word. He is going to be seriously famous.

That's when his mom will realize how shitty she has treated him. Then his dad will hear about it, for sure—and maybe let him come back up to the house and hang out. Of course that creep that owns the property will be around too, but Jason knows it won't be scary like last time. He'll have all those muscles, and he will have gotten past being scared of small shit like grabby old guys and dads that don't give a shit.

It will be different. It will all be different. His mom and his dad will work it all out. His dad will be his manager, his mom will take over the press stuff. You got to have someone handle that stuff, and if the creepy guy comes round to stake some kind of claim, it won't be no big deal. Everyone will know how to handle him—what to believe and what to laugh at. He can almost hear his dad talking out loud in his growly hoarse voice. He can hear him finally saying what he wanted him to say before.

"Jason didn't take nothing off you, old man. Look at him. What would he need off you?"

Yeah.

But maybe he will let the old guy hang around. Jason thinks about it, looking uphill and remembering. He gnaws at the nail on his left little finger.

Maybe not.

Why would he want that old bastard around?

He thinks about his dad, what he looks like now, all puffy and grey around the eyes with his hair so thin on top. His dad had this belly on him that he tries to hide under loose shirts, and he's always worried about money and stuff. That kind of old is embarrassing. After the basement though, his dad will be all different. He'll be old, but not so gross. He'll be more like Clint Eastwood old, craggy and wise. That's the notion, and his dad will have figured stuff out all that time worrying about Jason. Things will be different once he sees his son clear. Maybe he'll even own the property by then. The old guy can't live forever. Maybe he'll just give his dad the top of the hill as a kind of death tip. Might be it will turn out like that guy in Forestville a few years back, that black guy who got the thirty acres in the will of the man he worked for all that time.

That could happen. And then if his dad needs someone to help him with things, Jason will be there. That bad leg will hurt his dad a lot by then, even though he will try not to show it. Jason could do stuff—carry things for him and give him a hand. Maybe that is how they work it out—all the anger and guilt and shame and resentment. He can see that too, hear how it will go, them finally talking.

"You had no business running off like that, leaving Mom and me, I was just a little kid."

"You don't know how it was, how desperate I had gotten. I couldn't take care of you the way I wanted to, and you know your mom. She was always telling me I was lazy and the world wasn't gonna wait for me to get myself together."

That was just the kind of thing his mom said all the time. Jason nods. His mom can be a real pain in the ass. He sees himself looking at his dad and trying to imagine how he had felt when he had left. Maybe his dad had left in order to get himself together, to try and make something of himself so he could come back and take good care of them. After all that time cold and miserable and hungry in the basement, he will be able to feel stuff differently. Even standing in the dust of the road he can imagine his dad looking at him with an open face. Maybe they could talk finally, and it would shift all the anger around.

Maybe his dad will get to the point where he can look at him and see Jason clearly, see how he became so strong in that basement. Maybe he will finally see himself in his son. Of course, like everyone, his dad will know the story, how the kidnappers beat him, and starved him, and how Jason endured everything and stood up to them. It will make stuff in his dad shift around. He will get all wet-eyed and ashamed of himself. Jason can see that—the moment between them as real as the interviewer and the cameras, the moment burning him right through to his backbone. He almost sobs out loud, but then stops himself. His eyes are closed. The wind is picking up the way it always does as the afternoon settles toward evening. There is a birdcall somewhere up in the trees, but Jason is inside seeing into what is coming, what has to come.

They will touch each other like men do. Men. Yeah. Maybe his dad will embrace him, say his name. Jason can see that. It is as clear as anything. That is how it is in stories, how it is in his head, how it could be.

Jason sways a little there by the side of the road in the sun's heat. His ears are ringing with electric cricket sounds, the buzzard's cries, and the movement of the wind. Still, he hears a vehicle coming and the sound of its tires on the gritty tarmac. Rock and redwood debris grinding into dust and crackling as the wheels turn into the bend. Jason can see that, the wheels revolving and grinding forward. He imagines the kidnapper's truck, white and thick like one of those big Dodge Fat Boys, but one with a camper on the back—just the thing for snatching a guy off the road. Slowly Jason lets his face relax into a lazy smile. He doesn't look back. He keeps his eyes forward. His mom is always telling him to stop living in a dream, to be in the real world. But this is the real world, the road and the truck and everything that is coming toward him.

Anything can happen any time.

Everything can change, and it is going to, any time now.

Any time.

Any time.

Now.

MARGARET ATWOOD

Margaret Atwood (b. 1939) is a Canadian writer of poetry and fiction. Born in Ottawa, Ontario, she spent the first eleven years of her life in the sparsely settled "bush" country of northern Ontario and Quebec, where her father, an entomologist, did research. She remembers that

> I did not spend a full year in school until I was in Grade Eight. I began to write at the age of five–poems, "novels," comic books, and plays–but I had no thought of being a professional writer until I was sixteen. I entered Victoria

> College, University of Toronto, when I was seventeen and graduated in 1961. I won a Woodrow Wilson Fellowship to Harvard, where I studied Victorian Literature, and spent the next ten years in one place after another: Boston, Montreal, Edmonton, Toronto, Vancouver, England, and Italy, alternately teaching and writing.

Atwood's first poem was published when she was nineteen. To date she has published several collections of short stories, numerous novels – including the best-sellers *Surfacing* (1972), *Bodily Harm* (1982), *The Handmaid's Tale* (1986), *Cat's Eye* (1989), *The Robber Bride* (1993), *The Blind Assassin* (2000; Booker Prize winner), *Oryx and Crake* (2003), and *The Year of the Flood* (2009) – and more than a dozen books of poetry. She was encouraged to write as a young woman because Canadians of her generation felt a strong need to develop a national literature. She has described her early interest in science fiction in her recent book *In Other Worlds: SF and the Human Imagination* (2011).

Atwood has compared writing stories to telling riddles and jokes, all three requiring "the same mystifying buildup, the same surprising twist, the same impeccable sense of timing." She took pleasure in writing "Happy Endings," but she was puzzled by the form the story took. She has said,

> When I wrote "Happy Endings" – the year was, I think, 1982, and I was writing a number of short fictions then – I did not know what sort of creature it was. It was not a poem, a short story, or a prose poem. It was not quite a condensation, a commentary, a questionnaire, and it missed being a parable, a proverb, a paradox. It was a mutation. Writing it gave me a sense of furtive glee, like scribbling anonymously on a wall with no one looking.
>
> This summer I saw a white frog. It would not have been startling if I didn't know that this species of frog is normally green. This is the way such a mutant literary form unsettles us. We know what is expected, in a given arrangement of words; we know what is supposed to come next. And then it doesn't.
>
> It was a little disappointing to learn that other people had a name for such aberrations [metafiction], and had already made up rules.

WEB Research Margaret Atwood at bedfordstmartins.com/rewritinglit.

Happy Endings

1983

John and Mary meet.
What happens next?
If you want a happy ending, try A.

A

John and Mary fall in love and get married. They both have worthwhile and remunerative jobs which they find stimulating and challenging. They buy a charming house. Real estate values go up. Eventually, when they can afford live-in help, they have two children, to whom they are devoted. The children turn out well. John and Mary have a stimulating and challenging sex life and worthwhile friends. They go on fun vacations together. They retire. They both have hobbies which they find stimulating and challenging. Eventually they die. This is the end of the story.

B

Mary falls in love with John but John doesn't fall in love with Mary. He merely uses her body for selfish pleasure and ego gratification of a tepid kind. He comes to her apartment twice a week and she cooks him dinner, you'll notice that he doesn't even consider her worth the price of a dinner out, and after he's eaten the dinner he fucks her and after that he falls asleep, while she does the dishes so he won't think she's untidy, having all those dirty dishes lying around, and puts on fresh lipstick so she'll look good when he wakes up, but when he wakes up he doesn't even notice, he puts on his socks and his shorts and his pants and his shirt and his tie and his shoes, the reverse order from the one in which he took them off. He doesn't take off Mary's clothes, she takes them off herself, she acts as if she's dying for it every time, not because she likes sex exactly, she doesn't, but she wants John to think she does because if they do it often enough surely he'll get used to her, he'll come to depend on her and they will get married, but John goes out the door with hardly so much as a good-night and three days later he turns up at six o'clock and they do the whole thing over again.

Mary gets run-down. Crying is bad for your face, everyone knows that and so does Mary but she can't stop. People at work notice. Her friends tell her John is a rat, a pig, a dog, he isn't good enough for her, but she can't believe it. Inside John, she thinks, is another John, who is much nicer. This other John will emerge like a butterfly from a cocoon, a Jack from a box, a pit from a prune, if the first John is only squeezed enough.

One evening John complains about the food. He has never complained about the food before. Mary is hurt.

Her friends tell her they've seen him in a restaurant with another woman, whose name is Madge. It's not even Madge that finally gets to Mary: it's the restaurant. John has never taken Mary to a restaurant. Mary collects all the sleeping pills and aspirins she can find, and takes them and a half a bottle of sherry. You can see what kind of a woman she is by the fact that it's not even whiskey. She leaves a note for John. She hopes he'll discover her and get her to the hospital in time and repent and then they can get married, but this fails to happen and she dies.

John marries Madge and everything continues as in A.

C

John, who is an older man, falls in love with Mary, and Mary, who is only twenty-two, feels sorry for him because he's worried about his hair falling out. She sleeps with him even though she's not in love with him. She met him at work. She's in love with someone called James, who is twenty-two also and not yet ready to settle down.

John on the contrary settled down long ago: this is what is bothering him. John has a steady, respectable job and is getting ahead in his field, but Mary isn't impressed by him, she's impressed by James, who has a motorcycle and a fabulous record collection. But James is often away on his motorcycle, being free. Freedom isn't the same for girls, so in the meantime Mary spends Thursday evenings with John. Thursdays are the only days John can get away.

John is married to a woman called Madge and they have two children, a charming house which they bought just before the real estate values went up, and hobbies which they find stimulating and challenging, when they have the time. John tells Mary how important she is to him, but of course he can't leave his wife because a commitment is a commitment. He goes on about this more than is necessary and Mary finds it boring, but older men can keep it up longer so on the whole she has a fairly good time.

One day James breezes in on his motorcycle with some top-grade California hybrid and James and Mary get higher than you'd believe possible and they climb into bed. Everything becomes very underwater, but along comes John, who has a key to Mary's apartment. He finds them stoned and entwined. He's hardly in any position to be jealous, considering Madge, but nevertheless he's overcome with despair. Finally he's middle-aged, in two years he'll be bald as an egg and he can't stand it. He purchases a handgun, saying he needs it for target practice—this is the thin part of the plot, but it can be dealt with later—and shoots the two of them and himself.

Madge, after a suitable period of mourning, marries an understanding man called Fred and everything continues as in A, but under different names.

D

Fred and Madge have no problems. They get along exceptionally well and are good at working out any little difficulties that may arise. But their charming house is by the seashore and one day a giant tidal wave approaches. Real estate values go down. The rest of the story is about what caused the tidal wave and how they escape from it. They do, though thousands drown, but Fred and Madge are virtuous and lucky. Finally on high ground they clasp each other, wet and dripping and grateful, and continue as in A.

E

Yes, but Fred has a bad heart. The rest of the story is about how kind and understanding they both are until Fred dies. Then Madge devotes herself to charity work until the end of A. If you like, it can be "Madge," "cancer," "guilty and confused," and "bird watching."

F

If you think this is all too bourgeois, make John a revolutionary and Mary a counterespionage agent and see how far that gets you. Remember, this is Canada. You'll still end up with A, though in between you may get a lustful brawling saga of passionate involvement, a chronicle of our times, sort of.

You'll have to face it, the endings are the same however you slice it. Don't be deluded by any other endings, they're all fake, either deliberately fake, with malicious intent to deceive, or just motivated by excessive optimism if not by downright sentimentality.

The only authentic ending is the one provided here:

John and Mary die. John and Mary die. John and Mary die.

So much for endings. Beginnings are always more fun. True connoisseurs, however, are known to favor the stretch in between, since it's the hardest to do anything with.

That's about all that can be said for plots, which anyway are just one thing after another, a what and a what and a what.

Now try How and Why.

JAMES BALDWIN

James Baldwin (1924–1987) was born the son of a clergyman in Harlem, where he attended Public School 24, Frederick Douglass Junior High School, and DeWitt Clinton High School. While still a high school student he preached at the Fireside Pentecostal Assembly, but when he was seventeen he renounced the ministry. Two years later, living in Greenwich Village, he met Richard Wright, who encouraged him to be a writer and helped him win a Eugene Saxton Fellowship. Soon afterward Baldwin moved to France, as Wright had, to escape the stifling racial oppression he found in the United States. Although France was his more or less permanent residence until his death from cancer nearly forty years later, Baldwin regarded himself as a "commuter" rather than an expatriate. He said,

> Only white Americans can consider themselves to be expatriates. Once I found myself on the other side of the ocean, I could see where I came from very clearly, and I could see that I carried myself, which is my home, with me. You can never escape that. I am the grandson of a slave, and I am a writer. I must deal with both.

Baldwin began his career by publishing novels and short stories. *Go Tell It on the Mountain*, his first novel, was highly acclaimed when it appeared in 1953. It was based on his childhood in Harlem and his fear of his tyrannical father. Baldwin's frank depiction of homosexuality in the novels *Giovanni's Room* (1956) and *Another Country* (1962) drew criticism, but during the civil rights movement a few years later, he established himself as a brilliant essayist. In his lifetime Baldwin published several collections of essays, three more novels, and a book of five short stories, *Going to Meet the Man* (1965).

"Sonny's Blues," from that collection, is one of Baldwin's strongest psychological dramatizations of the frustrations of African American life in our time. Like Wright's autobiographical books, Baldwin's work is an inspiration to young writers struggling to express their experience of racism. The African writer Chinua Achebe has said that "as long as injustice exists . . . the words of James Baldwin will be there to bear witness and to inspire and elevate the struggle for human freedom."

WEB Research James Baldwin at bedfordstmartins.com/rewritinglit.

Sonny's Blues

1957

I read about it in the paper, in the subway, on my way to work. I read it, and I couldn't believe it, and I read it again. Then perhaps I just stared at it, at the newsprint spelling out his name, spelling out the story. I stared at it in the swinging lights of the subway car, and in the faces and bodies of the people, and in my own face, trapped in the darkness which roared outside.

It was not to be believed and I kept telling myself that, as I walked from the subway station to the high school. And at the same time I couldn't doubt it. I was scared, scared for Sonny. He became real to me again. A great block of ice got settled in my belly and kept melting there slowly all day long, while I taught my classes algebra. It was a special kind of ice. It kept melting, sending trickles of ice water all up and down my veins, but it never got less. Sometimes it hardened and seemed to expand until I felt my guts were going to come spilling out or that I was going to choke or scream. This would always be at a moment when I was remembering some specific thing Sonny had once said or done.

When he was about as old as the boys in my classes his face had been bright and open, there was a lot of copper in it; and he'd had wonderfully direct brown eyes, and great gentleness and privacy. I wondered what he looked like now. He had been picked up, the evening before, in a raid on an apartment downtown, for peddling and using heroin.

I couldn't believe it: but what I mean by that is that I couldn't find any room for it anywhere inside me. I had kept it outside me for a long time. I hadn't wanted to know. I had had suspicions, but I didn't name them, I kept putting them away. I told myself that Sonny was wild, but he wasn't crazy. And he'd always been a good boy, he hadn't ever turned hard or evil or disrespectful, the way kids can, so quick, so quick, especially in Harlem. I didn't want to believe that I'd ever see my brother going down, coming to nothing, all that light in his face gone out, in the condition I'd already seen so many others. Yet it had happened and here I was, talking about algebra to a lot of boys who might, every one of them for all I knew, be popping off needles every time they went to the head. Maybe it did more for them than algebra could.

I was sure that the first time Sonny had ever had horse, he couldn't have been much older than these boys were now. These boys, now, were living as we'd been living then, they were growing up with a rush and their heads bumped abruptly against the low ceiling of their actual possibilities. They were filled with rage. All they really knew were two darknesses, the darkness of their lives, which was now closing in on them, and the darkness of the movies, which had blinded them to that other darkness, and in which they now, vindictively, dreamed, at once more together than they were at any other time, and more alone.

When the last bell rang, the last class ended, I let out my breath. It seemed I'd been holding it for all that time. My clothes were wet—I may have looked as though I'd been sitting in a steam bath, all dressed up, all afternoon. I sat alone in the classroom a long time. I listened to the boys outside, downstairs, shouting and cursing and laughing. Their laughter struck me for perhaps the first time. It was not the joyous laughter which—God knows why—one associates with children. It was mocking and insular, its intent to denigrate. It was disenchanted, and in this, also, lay the authority of their curses. Perhaps I was listening to them because I was thinking about my brother and in them I heard my brother. And myself.

One boy was whistling a tune, at once very complicated and very simple, it seemed to be pouring out of him as though he were a bird, and it sounded very cool and moving through all that harsh, bright air, only just holding its own through all those other sounds.

I stood up and walked over to the window and looked down into the courtyard. It was the beginning of the spring and the sap was rising in the boys. A teacher passed through them every now and again, quickly, as though he or she couldn't wait to get out of that courtyard, to get those boys out of their sight and off their minds. I started collecting my stuff. I thought I'd better get home and talk to Isabel.

The courtyard was almost deserted by the time I got downstairs. I saw this boy standing in the shadow of a doorway, looking just like Sonny. I almost called his name. Then I saw that it wasn't Sonny, but somebody we used to know, a boy from around our block. He'd been Sonny's friend. He'd never been mine, having been too young for me, and, anyway, I'd never liked him. And now, even though he was a grown-up man, he still hung around that block, still spent hours on the street corners, was always high and raggy. I used to run into him from time to time and he'd often work around to asking me for a quarter or fifty cents. He always had some real good excuse, too, and I always gave it to him, I don't know why.

But now, abruptly, I hated him. I couldn't stand the way he looked at me, partly like a dog, partly like a cunning child. I wanted to ask him what the hell he was doing in the school courtyard.

He sort of shuffled over to me, and he said, "I see you got the papers. So you already know about it."

"You mean about Sonny? Yes, I already know about it. How come they didn't get you?"

He grinned. It made him repulsive and it also brought to mind what he'd looked like as a kid. "I wasn't there. I stay away from them people."

"Good for you." I offered him a cigarette and I watched him through the smoke. "You come all the way down here just to tell me about Sonny?"

"That's right." He was sort of shaking his head and his eyes looked strange, as though they were about to cross. The bright sun deadened his damp dark brown skin and it made his eyes look yellow and showed up the dirt in his kinked hair. He smelled funky. I moved a little away from him and I said, "Well, thanks. But I already know about it and I got to get home."

"I'll walk you a little ways," he said. We started walking. There were a couple of kids still loitering in the courtyard and one of them said goodnight to me and looked strangely at the boy beside me.

"What're you going to do?" he asked me. "I mean, about Sonny?"

"Look. I haven't seen Sonny for over a year. I'm not sure I'm going to do anything. Anyway, what the hell *can* I do?"

"That's right," he said quickly, "ain't nothing you can do. Can't much help old Sonny no more, I guess."

It was what I was thinking and so it seemed to me he had no right to say it.

"I'm surprised at Sonny, though," he went on—he had a funny way of talking, he looked straight ahead as though he were talking to himself—"I thought Sonny was a smart boy, I thought he was too smart to get hung."

"I guess he thought so too," I said sharply, "and that's how he got hung. And how about you? You're pretty goddamn smart, I bet."

Then he looked directly at me, just for a minute. "I ain't smart," he said. "If I was smart, I'd have reached for a pistol a long time ago."

"Look. Don't tell *me* your sad story, if it was up to me, I'd give you one." Then I felt guilty—guilty, probably, for never having supposed that the poor bastard *had* a story of his own, much less a sad one, and I asked, quickly, "What's going to happen to him now?"

He didn't answer this. He was off by himself some place. "Funny thing," he said, and from his tone we might have been discussing the quickest way to get to Brooklyn, "when I saw the papers this morning, the first thing I asked myself was if I had anything to do with it. I felt sort of responsible."

I began to listen more carefully. The subway station was on the corner, just before us, and I stopped. He stopped, too. We were in front of a bar and he ducked slightly, peering in, but whoever he was looking for didn't seem to be there. The juke box was blasting away with something black and bouncy and I half watched the barmaid as she danced her way from the juke box to her place behind the bar. And I watched her face as she laughingly responded to something someone said to her, still keeping time to the music. When she smiled one saw the little girl, one sensed the doomed, still-struggling woman beneath the battered face of the semi-whore.

"I never *give* Sonny nothing," the boy said finally, "but a long time ago I come to school high and Sonny asked me how it felt." He paused, I couldn't bear to watch him, I watched the barmaid, and I listened to the music which seemed to be causing the pavement to shake. "I told him it felt great." The music stopped, the barmaid paused and watched the juke box until the music began again. "It did."

All this was carrying me some place I didn't want to go. I certainly didn't want to know how it felt. It filled everything, the people, the houses, the music, the dark, quicksilver barmaid, with menace; and this menace was their reality.

"What's going to happen to him now?" I asked again.

"They'll send him away some place and they'll try to cure him." He shook his head. "Maybe he'll even think he's kicked the habit. Then they'll let him loose"—he gestured, throwing his cigarette into the gutter. "That's all."

"What do you mean, that's *all*?"

But I knew what he meant.

"I *mean*, that's *all*." He turned his head and looked at me, pulling down the corners of his mouth. "Don't you know what I mean?" he asked, softly.

"How the hell *would* I know what you mean?" I almost whispered it, I don't know why.

"That's right," he said to the air, "how would *he* know what I mean?" He turned toward me again, patient and calm, and yet I somehow felt him shaking, shaking as though he were going to fall apart. I felt that ice in my guts again, the dread I'd felt all afternoon; and again I watched the barmaid, moving about the bar, washing glasses, and singing. "Listen. They'll let him out and then it'll just start all over again. That's what I mean."

"You mean—they'll let him out. And then he'll just start working his way back in again. You mean he'll never kick the habit. Is that what you mean?"

"That's right," he said, cheerfully. "*You* see what I mean."

"Tell me," I said at last, "why does he want to die? He must want to die, he's killing himself, why does he want to die?"

He looked at me in surprise. He licked his lips. "He don't want to die. He wants to live. Don't nobody want to die, ever."

Then I wanted to ask him—too many things. He could not have answered, or if he had, I could not have borne the answers. I started walking. "Well, I guess it's none of my business."

"It's going to be rough on old Sonny," he said. We reached the subway station. "This is your station?" he asked. I nodded. I took one step down. "Damn!" he said, suddenly. I looked up at him. He grinned again. "Damn it if I didn't leave all my money home. You ain't got a dollar on you, have you? Just for a couple of days, is all."

All at once something inside gave and threatened to come pouring out of me. I didn't hate him any more. I felt that in another moment I'd start crying like a child.

"Sure," I said. "Don't sweat." I looked in my wallet and didn't have a dollar, I only had a five. "Here," I said. "That hold you?"

He didn't look at it—he didn't want to look at it. A terrible closed look came over his face, as though he were keeping the number on the bill a secret from him and me. "Thanks," he said, and now he was dying to see me go. "Don't worry about Sonny. Maybe I'll write him or something."

"Sure," I said. "You do that. So long."

"Be seeing you," he said. I went on down the steps.

And I didn't write Sonny or send him anything for a long time. When I finally did, it was just after my little girl died, he wrote me back a letter which made me feel like a bastard.

Here's what he said:

Dear brother,

You don't know how much I needed to hear from you. I wanted to write you many a time but I dug how much I must have hurt you and so I didn't write. But now I feel like a man who's been trying to climb up out

> of some deep, real deep and funky hole and just saw the sun up there, outside. I got to get outside.
>
> I can't tell you much about how I got here. I mean I don't know how to tell you. I guess I was afraid of something or I was trying to escape from something and you know I have never been very strong in the head (smile). I'm glad Mama and Daddy are dead and can't see what's happened to their son and I swear if I'd known what I was doing I would never have hurt you so, you and a lot of other fine people who were nice to me and who believed in me.
>
> I don't want you to think it had anything to do with me being a musician. It's more than that. Or maybe less than that. I can't get anything straight in my head down here and I try not to think about what's going to happen to me when I get outside again. Sometime I think I'm going to flip and *never* get outside and sometime I think I'll come straight back. I tell you one thing, though, I'd rather blow my brains out than go through this again. But that's what they all say, so they tell me. If I tell you when I'm coming to New York and if you could meet me, I sure would appreciate it. Give my love to Isabel and the kids and I was sure sorry to hear about little Gracie. I wish I could be like Mama and say the Lord's will be done, but I don't know it seems to me that trouble is the one thing that never does get stopped and I don't know what good it does to blame it on the Lord. But maybe it does some good if you believe it.
>
> Your brother,
> Sonny

Then I kept in constant touch with him and I sent him whatever I could and I went to meet him when he came back to New York. When I saw him many things I thought I had forgotten came flooding back to me. This was because I had begun, finally, to wonder about Sonny, about the life that Sonny lived inside. This life, whatever it was, had made him older and thinner and it had deepened the distant stillness in which he had always moved. He looked very unlike my baby brother. Yet, when he smiled, when we shook hands, the baby brother I'd never known looked out from the depths of his private life, like an animal waiting to be coaxed into the light.

"How you been keeping?" he asked me.

"All right. And you?"

"Just fine." He was smiling all over his face. "It's good to see you again."

"It's good to see you."

The seven years' difference in our ages lay between us like a chasm: I wondered if these years would ever operate between us as a bridge. I was remembering, and it made it hard to catch my breath, that I had been there when he was born; and I had heard the first words he had ever spoken. When he started to walk, he walked from our mother straight to me. I caught him just before he fell when he took the first steps he ever took in this world.

"How's Isabel?"

"Just fine. She's dying to see you."

"And the boys?"

"They're fine, too. They're anxious to see their uncle."

"Oh, come on. You know they don't remember me."

"Are you kidding? Of course they remember you."

He grinned again. We got into a taxi. We had a lot to say to each other, far too much to know how to begin.

As the taxi began to move, I asked, "You still want to go to India?"

He laughed. "You still remember that. Hell, no. This place is Indian enough for me."

"It used to belong to them," I said.

And he laughed again. "They damn sure knew what they were doing when they got rid of it."

Years ago, when he was around fourteen, he'd been all hipped on the idea of going to India. He read books about people sitting on rocks, naked, in all kinds of weather, but mostly bad, naturally, and walking barefoot through hot coals and arriving at wisdom. I used to say that it sounded to me as though they were getting away from wisdom as fast as they could. I think he sort of looked down on me for that.

"Do you mind," he asked, "if we have the driver drive alongside the park? On the west side—I haven't seen the city in so long."

"Of course not," I said. I was afraid that I might sound as though I were humoring him, but I hoped he wouldn't take it that way.

So we drove along, between the green of the park and the stony, lifeless elegance of hotels and apartment buildings, toward the vivid, killing streets of our childhood. These streets hadn't changed, though housing projects jutted up out of them now like rocks in the middle of a boiling sea. Most of the houses in which we had grown up had vanished, as had the stores from which we had stolen, the basements in which we had first tried sex, the rooftops from which we had hurled tin cans and bricks. But houses exactly like the houses of our past yet dominated the landscape, boys exactly like the boys we once had been found themselves smothering in these houses, came down into the streets for light and air and found themselves encircled by disaster. Some escaped the trap, most didn't. Those who got out always left something of themselves behind, as some animals amputate a leg and leave it in the trap. It might be said, perhaps, that I had escaped, after all, I was a school teacher; or that Sonny had, he hadn't lived in Harlem for years. Yet, as the cab moved uptown through streets which seemed, with a rush, to darken with dark people, and as I covertly studied Sonny's face, it came to me that what we both were seeking through our separate cab windows was that part of ourselves which had been left behind. It's always at the hour of trouble and confrontation that the missing member aches.

We hit 110th Street and started rolling up Lenox Avenue. And I'd known this avenue all my life, but it seemed to me again, as it had seemed on the day I'd first heard about Sonny's trouble, filled with a hidden menace which was its very breath of life.

"We almost there," said Sonny.

"Almost." We were both too nervous to say anything more.

We live in a housing project. It hasn't been up long. A few days after it was up it seemed uninhabitably new, now, of course, it's already rundown. It looks like a parody of the good, clean, faceless life—God knows the people who live in it do their best to make it a parody. The beat-looking grass lying around isn't enough to make their lives green, the hedges will never hold out the streets, and they know it. The big windows fool no one, they aren't big enough to make space out of no space. They don't bother with the windows, they watch the TV screen instead. The playground is most popular with the children who don't play at jacks, or skip rope, or roller skate, or swing, and they can be found in it after dark. We moved in partly because it's not too far from where I teach, and partly for the kids; but it's really just like the houses in which Sonny and I grew up. The same things happen, they'll have the same things to remember. The moment Sonny and I started into the house I had the feeling that I was simply bringing him back into the danger he had almost died trying to escape.

Sonny has never been talkative. So I don't know why I was sure he'd be dying to talk to me when supper was over the first night. Everything went fine, the oldest boy remembered him, and the youngest boy liked him, and Sonny had remembered to bring something for each of them; and Isabel, who is really much nicer than I am, more open and giving, had gone to a lot of trouble about dinner and was genuinely glad to see him. And she's always been able to tease Sonny in a way that I haven't. It was nice to see her face so vivid again and to hear her laugh and watch her make Sonny laugh. She wasn't, or, anyway, she didn't seem to be, at all uneasy or embarrassed. She chatted as though there were no subject which had to be avoided and she got Sonny past his first, faint stiffness. And thank God she was there, for I was filled with that icy dread again. Everything I did seemed awkward to me, and everything I said sounded freighted with hidden meaning. I was trying to remember everything I'd heard about dope addiction and I couldn't help watching Sonny for signs. I wasn't doing it out of malice. I was trying to find out something about my brother. I was dying to hear him tell me he was safe.

"Safe!" my father grunted, whenever Mama suggested trying to move to a neighborhood which might be safer for children. "Safe, hell! Ain't no place safe for kids, nor nobody."

He always went on like this, but he wasn't, ever, really as bad as he sounded, not even on weekends, when he got drunk. As a matter of fact, he was always on the lookout for "something a little better," but he died before he found it. He died suddenly, during a drunken weekend in the middle of the war, when Sonny was fifteen. He and Sonny hadn't ever got on too well. And this was partly because Sonny was the apple of his father's eye. It was because he loved Sonny so much and was frightened for him, that he was always fighting with him. It doesn't do any good to fight with Sonny. Sonny just moves back, inside himself, where he can't be reached. But the principal reason that they never hit it off is that they were so much alike. Daddy was big and rough and loud-talking, just the opposite of Sonny, but they both had—that same privacy.

Mama tried to tell me something about this, just after Daddy died. I was home on leave from the army.

This was the last time I ever saw my mother alive. Just the same, this picture gets all mixed up in my mind with pictures I had of her when she was younger. The way I always see her is the way she used to be on a Sunday afternoon, say, when the old folks were talking after the big Sunday dinner. I always see her wearing pale blue. She'd be sitting on the sofa. And my father would be sitting in the easy chair, not far from her. And the living room would be full of church folks and relatives. There they sit, in chairs all around the living room, and the night is creeping up outside, but nobody knows it yet. You can see the darkness growing against the windowpanes and you hear the street noises every now and again, or maybe the jangling beat of a tambourine from one of the churches close by, but it's real quiet in the room. For a moment nobody's talking, but every face looks darkening, like the sky outside. And my mother rocks a little from the waist, and my father's eyes are closed. Everyone is looking at something a child can't see. For a minute they've forgotten the children. Maybe a kid is lying on the rug, half asleep. Maybe somebody's got a kid in his lap and is absent-mindedly stroking the kid's head. Maybe there's a kid, quiet and big-eyed, curled up in a big chair in the corner. The silence, the darkness coming, and the darkness in the faces frightens the child obscurely. He hopes that the hand which strokes his forehead will never stop—will never die. He hopes that there will never come a time when the old folks won't be sitting around the living room, talking about where they've come from, and what they've seen, and what's happened to them and their kinfolk.

But something deep and watchful in the child knows that this is bound to end, is already ending. In a moment someone will get up and turn on the light. Then the old folks will remember the children and they won't talk any more that day. And when light fills the room, the child is filled with darkness. He knows that every time this happens he's moved just a little closer to that darkness outside. The darkness outside is what the old folks have been talking about. It's what they've come from. It's what they endure. The child knows that they won't talk any more because if he knows too much about what's happened to *them*, he'll know too much too soon, about what's going to happen to *him*.

The last time I talked to my mother, I remember I was restless. I wanted to get out and see Isabel. We weren't married then and we had a lot to straighten out between us.

There Mama sat, in black, by the window. She was humming an old church song, *Lord, you brought me from a long ways off*. Sonny was out somewhere. Mama kept watching the streets.

"I don't know," she said, "if I'll ever see you again, after you go off from here. But I hope you'll remember the things I tried to teach you."

"Don't talk like that," I said, and smiled. "You'll be here a long time yet."

She smiled, too, but she said nothing. She was quiet for a long time. And I said, "Mama, don't you worry about nothing. I'll be writing all the time, and you be getting the checks. . . ."

"I want to talk to you about your brother," she said, suddenly. "If anything happens to me he ain't going to have nobody to look out for him."

"Mama," I said, "ain't nothing going to happen to you *or* Sonny. Sonny's all right. He's a good boy and he's got good sense."

"It ain't a question of his being a good boy," Mama said, "nor of his having good sense. It ain't only the bad ones, nor yet the dumb ones that gets sucked under." She stopped, looking at me. "Your Daddy once had a brother," she said, and she smiled in a way that made me feel she was in pain. "You didn't never know that, did you?"

"No," I said, "I never knew that," and I watched her face.

"Oh, yes," she said, "your Daddy had a brother." She looked out of the window again. "I know you never saw your Daddy cry. But *I* did—many a time, through all these years."

I asked her, "What happened to his brother? How come nobody's ever talked about him?"

This was the first time I ever saw my mother look old.

"His brother got killed," she said, "when he was just a little younger than you are now. I knew him. He was a fine boy. He was maybe a little full of the devil, but he didn't mean nobody no harm."

Then she stopped and the room was silent, exactly as it had sometimes been on those Sunday afternoons. Mama kept looking out into the streets.

"He used to have a job in the mill," she said, "and, like all young folks, he just liked to perform on Saturday nights. Saturday nights, him and your father would drift around to different places, go to dances and things like that, or just sit around with people they knew, and your father's brother would sing, he had a fine voice, and play along with himself on his guitar. Well, this particular Saturday night, him and your father was coming home from some place, and they were both a little drunk and there was a moon that night, it was bright like day. Your father's brother was feeling kind of good, and he was whistling to himself, and he had his guitar slung over his shoulder. They was coming down a hill and beneath them was a road that turned off from the highway. Well, your father's brother, being always kind of frisky, decided to run down this hill, and he did, with that guitar banging and clanging behind him, and he ran across the road, and he was making water behind a tree. And your father was sort of amused at him and he was still coming down the hill, kind of slow. Then he heard a car motor and that same minute his brother stepped from behind the tree, into the road, in the moonlight. And he started to cross the road. And your father started to run down the hill, he says he don't know why. This car was full of white men. They was all drunk, and when they seen your father's brother they let out a great whoop and holler and they aimed the car straight at him. They was having fun, they just wanted to scare him, the way they do sometimes, you know. But they was drunk. And I guess the boy, being drunk, too, and scared, kind of lost his head. By the time he jumped it was too late. Your father says he heard his brother scream when the car rolled over him, and he heard the wood of that guitar when it give, and he heard them strings go flying, and he heard them white men shouting, and the car kept on a-going and it ain't stopped till this day. And, time your father got down the hill, his brother weren't nothing but blood and pulp."

Tears were gleaming on my mother's face. There wasn't anything I could say.

"He never mentioned it," she said, "because I never let him mention it before you children. Your Daddy was like a crazy man that night and for many a night thereafter. He says he never in his life seen anything as dark as that road after the lights of that car had gone away. Weren't nothing, weren't nobody on that road, just your Daddy and his brother and that busted guitar. Oh, yes. Your Daddy never did really get right again. Till the day he died he weren't sure but that every white man he saw was the man that killed his brother."

She stopped and took out her handkerchief and dried her eyes and looked at me.

"I ain't telling you all this," she said, "to make you scared or bitter or to make you hate nobody. I'm telling you this because you got a brother. And the world ain't changed."

I guess I didn't want to believe this. I guess she saw this in my face. She turned away from me, toward the window again, searching those streets.

"But I praise my Redeemer," she said at last, "that He called your Daddy home before me. I ain't saying it to throw no flowers at myself, but, I declare, it keeps me from feeling too cast down to know I helped your father get safely through this world. Your father always acted like he was the roughest, strongest man on earth. And everybody took him to be like that. But if he hadn't had *me* there—to see his tears!"

She was crying again. Still, I couldn't move. I said, "Lord, Lord, Mama, I didn't know it was like that."

"Oh, honey," she said, "there's a lot that you don't know. But you are going to find it out." She stood up from the window and came over to me. "You got to hold on to your brother," she said, "and don't let him fall, no matter what it looks like is happening to him and no matter how evil you gets with him. You going to be evil with him many a time. But don't you forget what I told you, you hear?"

"I won't forget," I said. "Don't you worry, I won't forget. I won't let nothing happen to Sonny."

My mother smiled as though she were amused at something she saw in my face. Then, "You may not be able to stop nothing from happening. But you got to let him know you's *there*."

Two days later I was married, and then I was gone. And I had a lot of things on my mind and I pretty well forgot my promise to Mama until I got shipped home on a special furlough for her funeral.

And, after the funeral, with just Sonny and me alone in the empty kitchen, I tried to find out something about him.

"What do you want to do?" I asked him.

"I'm going to be a musician," he said.

For he had graduated, in the time I had been away, from dancing to the juke box to finding out who was playing what, and what they were doing with it, and he had bought himself a set of drums.

"You mean, you want to be a drummer?" I somehow had the feeling that being a drummer might be all right for other people but not for my brother Sonny.

"I don't think," he said, looking at me very gravely, "that I'll ever be a good drummer. But I think I can play a piano."

I frowned. I'd never played the role of the older brother quite so seriously before, had scarcely ever, in fact, *asked* Sonny a damn thing. I sensed myself in the presence of something I didn't really know how to handle, didn't understand. So I made my frown a little deeper as I asked: "What kind of musician do you want to be?"

He grinned. "How many kinds do you think there are?"

"Be *serious*," I said.

He laughed, throwing his head back, and then looked at me. "I *am* serious."

"Well, then, for Christ's sake, stop kidding around and answer a serious question. I mean, do you want to be a concert pianist, you want to play classical music and all that, or—or what?" Long before I finished he was laughing again. "For Christ's *sake*, Sonny!"

He sobered, but with difficulty. "I'm sorry. But you sound so—*scared!*" and he was off again.

"Well, you may think it's funny now, baby, but it's not going to be so funny when you have to make your living at it, let me tell you *that*." I was furious because I knew he was laughing at me and I didn't know why.

"No," he said, very sober now, and afraid, perhaps, that he'd hurt me, "I don't want to be a classical pianist. That isn't what interests me. I mean"—he paused, looking hard at me, as though his eyes would help me to understand, and then gestured helplessly, as though perhaps his hand would help—"I mean, I'll have a lot of studying to do, and I'll have to study *everything*, but, I mean, I want to play *with*—jazz musicians." He stopped. "I want to play jazz," he said.

Well, the word had never before sounded as heavy, as real, as it sounded that afternoon in Sonny's mouth. I just looked at him and I was probably frowning a real frown by this time. I simply couldn't see why on earth he'd want to spend his time hanging around nightclubs, clowning around on bandstands, while people pushed each other around a dance floor. It seemed—beneath him, somehow. I had never thought about it before, had never been forced to, but I suppose I had always put jazz musicians in a class with what Daddy called "good-time people."

"Are you *serious*?"

"Hell, *yes*, I'm serious."

He looked more helpless than ever, and annoyed, and deeply hurt.

I suggested, helpfully: "You mean—like Louis Armstrong?"

His face closed as though I'd struck him. "No. I'm not talking about none of that old-time, down home crap."

"Well, look, Sonny, I'm sorry, don't get mad. I just don't altogether get it, that's all. Name somebody—you know, a jazz musician you admire."

"Bird."

"Who?"

"Bird! Charlie Parker! Don't they teach you nothing in the goddamn army?"

I lit a cigarette. I was surprised and then a little amused to discover that I was trembling. "I've been out of touch," I said. "You'll have to be patient with me. Now. Who's this Parker character?"

"He's just one of the greatest jazz musicians alive," said Sonny, sullenly, his hands in his pockets, his back to me. "Maybe *the* greatest," he added, bitterly, "that's probably why *you* never heard of him."

"All right," I said, "I'm ignorant. I'm sorry. I'll go out and buy all the cat's records right away, all right?"

"It don't," said Sonny, with dignity, "make any difference to me. I don't care what you listen to. Don't do me no favors."

I was beginning to realize that I'd never seen him so upset before. With another part of my mind I was thinking that this would probably turn out to be one of those things kids go through and that I shouldn't make it seem important by pushing it too hard. Still, I didn't think it would do any harm to ask: "Doesn't all this take a lot of time? Can you make a living at it?"

He turned back to me and half leaned, half sat, on the kitchen table. "Everything takes time," he said, "and—well, yes, sure, I can make a living at it. But what I don't seem to be able to make you understand is that it's the only thing I want to do."

"Well, Sonny," I said, gently, "you know people can't always do exactly what they *want* to do—"

"*No*, I don't know that," said Sonny, surprising me. "I think people *ought* to do what they want to do, what else are they alive for?"

"You getting to be a big boy," I said desperately, "it's time you started thinking about your future."

"I'm thinking about my future," said Sonny, grimly. "I think about it all the time."

I gave up. I decided, if he didn't change his mind, that we could always talk about it later. "In the meantime," I said, "you got to finish school." We had already decided that he'd have to move in with Isabel and her folks. I knew this wasn't the ideal arrangement because Isabel's folks are inclined to be dicty and they hadn't especially wanted Isabel to marry me. But I didn't know what else to do. "And we have to get you fixed up at Isabel's."

There was a long silence. He moved from the kitchen table to the window. "That's a terrible idea. You know it yourself."

"Do you have a *better* idea?"

He just walked up and down the kitchen for a minute. He was as tall as I was. He had started to shave. I suddenly had the feeling that I didn't know him at all.

He stopped at the kitchen table and picked up my cigarettes. Looking at me with a kind of mocking, amused defiance, he put one between his lips. "You mind?"

"You smoking already?"

He lit the cigarette and nodded, watching me through the smoke. "I just wanted to see if I'd have the courage to smoke in front of you." He grinned and blew a great cloud of smoke to the ceiling. "It was easy." He looked at my face. "Come on, now. I bet you was smoking at my age, tell the truth."

I didn't say anything but the truth was on my face, and he laughed. But now there was something very strained in his laugh. "Sure. And I bet that ain't all you was doing."

He was frightening me a little. "Cut the crap," I said. "We already decided that you was going to go and live at Isabel's. Now what's got into you all of a sudden?"

"*You* decided it," he pointed out. "*I* didn't decide nothing." He stopped in front of me, leaning against the stove, arms loosely folded. "Look, brother. I don't want to stay in Harlem no more, I really don't." He was very earnest. He looked at me, then over toward the kitchen window. There was something in his eyes I'd never seen before, some thoughtfulness, some worry all his own. He rubbed the muscle of one arm. "It's time I was getting out of here."

"Where do you want to *go*, Sonny?"

"I want to join the army. Or the navy, I don't care. If I say I'm old enough, they'll believe me."

Then I got mad. It was because I was so scared. "You must be crazy. You goddamn fool, what the hell do you want to go and join the *army* for?"

"I just told you. To get out of Harlem."

"Sonny, you haven't even finished *school*. And if you really want to be a musician, how do you expect to study if you're in the *army*?"

He looked at me, trapped, and in anguish. "There's ways. I might be able to work out some kind of deal. Anyway, I'll have the G.I. Bill when I come out."

"*If* you come out." We stared at each other. "Sonny, please. Be reasonable. I know the setup is far from perfect. But we got to do the best we can."

"I ain't learning nothing in school," he said. "Even when I go." He turned away from me and opened the window and threw his cigarette out into the narrow alley. I watched his back. "At least, I ain't learning nothing you'd want me to learn." He slammed the window so hard I thought the glass would fly out, and turned back to me. "And I'm sick of the stink of these garbage cans!"

"Sonny," I said, "I know how you feel. But if you don't finish school now, you're going to be sorry later that you didn't." I grabbed him by the shoulders. "And you only got another year. It ain't so bad. And I'll come back and I swear I'll help you do *whatever* you want to do. Just try to put up with it till I come back. Will you please do that? For me?"

He didn't answer and he wouldn't look at me.

"Sonny. You hear me?"

He pulled away. "I hear you. But you never hear anything *I* say."

I didn't know what to say to that. He looked out of the window and then back at me. "OK," he said, and sighed. "I'll try."

Then I said, trying to cheer him up a little, "They got a piano at Isabel's. You can practice on it."

And as a matter of fact, it did cheer him up for a minute. "That's right," he said to himself. "I forgot that." His face relaxed a little. But the worry, the thoughtfulness, played on it still, the way shadows play on a face which is staring into the fire.

But I thought I'd never hear the end of that piano. At first, Isabel would write me, saying how nice it was that Sonny was so serious about his music and how, as soon as he came in from school, or wherever he had been when he was supposed to be at school, he went straight to that piano and stayed there until suppertime. And, after supper, he went back to that piano and stayed there until everybody went to bed. He was at the piano all day Saturday and all day Sunday. Then he bought a record player and started playing records. He'd play one record over and over again, all day long sometimes, and he'd improvise along with it on the piano. Or he'd play one section of the record, one chord, one change, one progression, then he'd do it on the piano. Then back to the record. Then back to the piano.

Well, I really don't know how they stood it. Isabel finally confessed that it wasn't like living with a person at all, it was like living with sound. And the sound didn't make any sense to her, didn't make any sense to any of them—naturally. They began, in a way, to be afflicted by this presence that was living in their home. It was as though Sonny were some sort of god, or monster. He moved in an atmosphere which wasn't like theirs at all. They fed him and he ate, he washed himself, he walked in and out of their door; he certainly wasn't nasty or unpleasant or rude, Sonny isn't any of those things; but it was as though he were all wrapped up in some cloud, some fire, some vision all his own; and there wasn't any way to reach him.

At the same time, he wasn't really a man yet, he was still a child, and they had to watch out for him in all kinds of ways. They certainly couldn't throw him out. Neither did they dare to make a great scene about that piano because even they dimly sensed, as I sensed, from so many thousands of miles away, that Sonny was at that piano playing for his life.

But he hadn't been going to school. One day a letter came from the school board and Isabel's mother got it—there had, apparently, been other letters but Sonny had torn them up. This day, when Sonny came in, Isabel's mother showed him the letter and asked where he'd been spending his time. And she finally got it out of him that he'd been down in Greenwich Village, with musicians and other characters, in a white girl's apartment. And this scared her and she started to scream at him and what came up, once she began—though she denies it to this day—was what sacrifices they were making to give Sonny a decent home and how little he appreciated it.

Sonny didn't play the piano that day. By evening, Isabel's mother had calmed down but then there was the old man to deal with, and Isabel herself. Isabel says she did her best to be calm but she broke down and started crying. She says she just watched Sonny's face. She could tell, by watching him, what was happening with him. And what was happening was that they penetrated his cloud, they had reached him. Even if their fingers had been a thousand times more gentle than human fingers ever are, he could hardly help feeling that they had stripped him naked and were spitting on that nakedness. For he also had to see that his presence, that music, which was life or death to him, had been torture for them and that they had endured it, not at all for his sake, but only for mine. And Sonny couldn't take that. He can take it a little better today than he could then but he's still not very good at it and, frankly, I don't know anybody who is.

The silence of the next few days must have been louder than the sound of all the music ever played since time began. One morning, before she went to work, Isabel was in his room for something and she suddenly realized that all of his records were gone. And she knew for certain that he was gone. And he was. He went as far as the navy would carry him. He finally sent me a postcard from some place in Greece and that was the first I knew that Sonny was still alive. I didn't see him any more until we were both back in New York and the war had long been over.

He was a man by then, of course, but I wasn't willing to see it. He came by the house from time to time, but we fought almost every time we met. I didn't like the way he carried himself, loose and dreamlike all the time, and I didn't like his friends, and his music seemed to be merely an excuse for the life he led. It sounded just that weird and disordered.

Then we had a fight, a pretty awful fight, and I didn't see him for months. By and by I looked him up, where he was living, in a furnished room in the Village, and I tried to make it up. But there were lots of people in the room and Sonny just lay on his bed, and he wouldn't come downstairs with me, and he treated these other people as though they were his family and I weren't. So I got mad and then he got mad, and then I told him that he might just as well be dead as live the way he was living. Then he stood up and he told me not to worry about him any more in life, that he *was* dead as far as I was concerned. Then he pushed me to the door and the other people looked on as though nothing were happening, and he slammed the door behind me. I stood in the hallway, staring at the door. I heard somebody laugh in the room and then the tears came to my eyes. I started down the steps, whistling to keep from crying, I kept whistling to myself, *You going to need me, baby, one of these cold, rainy days.*

I read about Sonny's trouble in the spring. Little Grace died in the fall. She was a beautiful little girl. But she only lived a little over two years. She died of polio and she suffered. She had a slight fever for a couple of days, but it didn't seem like anything and we just kept her in bed. And we would certainly have called the doctor, but the fever dropped, she seemed to be all right. So we thought it had just been a cold. Then, one day, she was up, playing, Isabel was in the kitchen fixing lunch for the two boys when they'd come in from school, and she heard Grace fall down in the living room. When you have a lot of children you don't always start running when one of them falls, unless they start screaming or something. And, this time, Grace was quiet. Yet, Isabel says that when she heard that *thump* and then that silence, something happened in her to make her afraid. And she ran to the living room and there was little Grace on the floor, all twisted up, and the reason she hadn't screamed was that she couldn't get her breath. And when she did scream, it was the worst sound, Isabel says, that she'd ever heard in all her life, and she still hears it sometimes in her dreams. Isabel will sometimes wake me up with a low, moaning, strangled sound and I have to be quick to awaken her and hold her to me and where Isabel is weeping against me seems a mortal wound.

I think I may have written Sonny the very day that little Grace was buried. I was sitting in the living room in the dark, by myself, and I suddenly thought of Sonny. My trouble made his real.

One Saturday afternoon, when Sonny had been living with us, or, anyway, been in our house, for nearly two weeks, I found myself wandering aimlessly about the living room, drinking from a can of beer, and trying to work up the courage to search Sonny's room. He was out, he was usually out whenever I was home, and Isabel had taken the children to see their grandparents. Suddenly I was standing still in front of the living room window, watching Seventh Avenue. The idea of searching Sonny's room made me still. I scarcely dared to admit to myself what I'd be searching for. I didn't know what I'd do if I found it. Or if I didn't.

On the sidewalk across from me, near the entrance to a barbecue joint, some people were holding an old-fashioned revival meeting. The barbecue cook, wearing a dirty white apron, his conked hair reddish and metallic in the pale sun, and a cigarette between his lips, stood in the doorway, watching them. Kids and older people paused in their errands and stood there, along with some older men and a couple of very tough-looking women who watched everything that happened on the avenue, as though they owned it, or were maybe owned by it. Well, they were watching this, too. The revival was being carried on by three sisters in black, and a brother. All they had were their voices and their Bibles and a tambourine. The brother was testifying and while he testified two of the sisters stood together, seeming to say, amen, and the third sister walked around with the tambourine outstretched and a couple of people dropped coins into it. Then the brother's testimony ended and the sister who had been taking up the collection dumped the coins into her palm and transferred them to the pocket of her long black robe. Then she raised both hands, striking the tambourine against the air, and then against one hand, and she started to sing. And the two other sisters and the brother joined in.

It was strange, suddenly, to watch, though I had been seeing these street meetings all my life. So, of course, had everybody else down there. Yet, they paused and watched and listened and I stood still at the window. "*Tis the old ship of Zion,*" they sang, and the sister with the tambourine kept a steady, jangling beat, "*it has rescued many a thousand!*" Not a soul under the sound of their voices was hearing this song for the first time, not one of them had been rescued. Nor had they seen much in the way of rescue work being done around them. Neither did they especially believe in the holiness of the three sisters and the brother, they knew too much about them, knew where they lived, and how. The woman with the tambourine, whose voice dominated the air, whose face was bright with joy, was divided by very little from the woman who stood watching her, a cigarette between her heavy, chapped lips, her hair a cuckoo's nest, her face scarred and swollen from many beatings, and her black eyes glittering like coal. Perhaps they both knew this, which was why, when, as rarely, they addressed each other, they addressed each other as Sister. As the singing filled the air the watching, listening faces underwent a change, the eyes focusing on something within; the music seemed to soothe a poison out of them; and time seemed, nearly, to fall away from the sullen, belligerent, battered faces, as though they were fleeing back to their first condition, while dreaming of their last. The barbecue cook half shook his head and smiled, and dropped his cigarette and disappeared into his joint. A man fumbled in his pockets for change and stood holding it in his hand impatiently, as though he had just remembered a pressing appointment further up the avenue. He looked furious. Then I saw Sonny, standing on the edge of the crowd. He was carrying a wide, flat notebook with a green cover, and it made him look, from where I was standing, almost like a schoolboy. The coppery sun brought out the copper in his skin, he was very faintly smiling, standing very still. Then the singing stopped, the tambourine turned into a collection plate again. The furious man dropped in his coins and vanished, so did a couple of the women, and Sonny dropped some change in the plate, looking directly at the woman with a little smile. He started across the avenue, toward the house. He has a slow, loping walk, something like the way Harlem hipsters walk, only he's imposed on this his own half-beat. I had never really noticed it before.

I stayed at the window, both relieved and apprehensive. As Sonny disappeared from my sight, they began singing again. And they were still singing when his key turned in the lock.

"Hey," he said.

"Hey, yourself. You want some beer?"

"No. Well, maybe." But he came up to the window and stood beside me, looking out. "What a warm voice," he said.

They were singing *If I could only hear my mother pray again!*

"Yes," I said, "and she can sure beat that tambourine."

"But what a terrible song," he said, and laughed. He dropped his notebook on the sofa and disappeared into the kitchen. "Where's Isabel and the kids?"

"I think they went to see their grandparents. You hungry?"

"No." He came back into the living room with his can of beer. "You want to come some place with me tonight?"

I sensed, I don't know how, that I couldn't possibly say no. "Sure. Where?"

He sat down on the sofa and picked up his notebook and started leafing through it. "I'm going to sit in with some fellows in a joint in the Village."

"You mean, you're going to play, tonight?"

"That's right." He took a swallow of his beer and moved back to the window. He gave me a sidelong look. "If you can stand it."

"I'll try," I said.

He smiled to himself and we both watched as the meeting across the way broke up. The three sisters and the brother, heads bowed, were singing *God be with you till we meet again.* The faces around them were very quiet. Then the song ended. The small crowd dispersed. We watched the three women and the lone man walk slowly up the avenue.

"When she was singing before," said Sonny, abruptly, "her voice reminded me for a minute of what heroin feels like sometimes—when it's in your veins. It makes you feel sort of warm and cool at the same time. And distant. And—and sure." He sipped his beer, very deliberately not looking at me. I watched his face. "It makes you feel—in control. Sometimes you've got to have that feeling."

"Do you?" I sat down slowly in the easy chair.

"Sometimes." He went to the sofa and picked up his notebook again. "Some people do."

"In order," I asked, "to play?" And my voice was very ugly, full of contempt and anger.

"Well"—he looked at me with great, troubled eyes, as though, in fact, he hoped his eyes would tell me things he could never otherwise say—"they *think* so. And *if* they think so—!"

"And what do *you* think?" I asked.

He sat on the sofa and put his can of beer on the floor. "I don't know," he said, and I couldn't be sure if he were answering my question or pursuing his thoughts. His face didn't tell me. "It's not so much to *play.* It's to *stand* it, to be able to make it at all. On any level." He frowned and smiled: "In order to keep from shaking to pieces."

"But these friends of yours," I said, "they seem to shake themselves to pieces pretty goddamn fast."

"Maybe." He played with the notebook. And something told me that I should curb my tongue, that Sonny was doing his best to talk, that I should listen. "But of course you only know the ones that've gone to pieces. Some don't—or at least they haven't *yet* and that's just about all *any* of us can say." He paused. "And then there are some who just live, really, in hell, and they know it and they see what's happening and they go right on. I don't know." He sighed, dropped the notebook, folded his arms. "Some guys, you can tell from the way they play, they on something *all* the time. And you can see that, well, it makes something real for them. But of course," he picked up his beer from the floor and sipped it and put the can down again, "they *want* to, too, you've got to see that. Even some of them that say they don't—*some,* not all."

"And what about you?" I asked—I couldn't help it. "What about you? Do *you* want to?"

He stood up and walked to the window and remained silent for a long time. Then he sighed. "Me," he said. Then: "While I was downstairs before, on my way here, listening to that woman sing, it struck me all of a sudden how much suffering she must have had to go through—to sing like that. It's *repulsive* to think you have to suffer that much."

I said: "But there's no way not to suffer—is there, Sonny?"

"I believe not," he said and smiled, "but that's never stopped anyone from trying." He looked at me. "Has it?" I realized, with this mocking look, that there stood between us, forever, beyond the power of time or forgiveness, the fact that I had held silence—so long!—when he had needed human speech to help him. He turned back to the window. "No, there's no way not to suffer. But you try all kinds of ways to keep from drowning in it, to keep on top of it, and to make it seem—well, like *you.* Like you did something, all right, and now you're suffering for it. You know?" I said nothing. "Well you know," he said, impatiently, "why *do* people suffer? Maybe it's better to do something to give it a reason, *any* reason."

"But we just agreed," I said, "that there's no way not to suffer. Isn't it better, then, just to—take it?"

"But nobody just takes it," Sonny cried, "that's what I'm telling you! *Everybody* tries not to. You're just hung up on the *way* some people try—it's not *your* way!"

The hair on my face began to itch, my face felt wet. "That's not true," I said, "that's not true. I don't give a damn what other people do, I don't even care how they suffer. I just care how *you* suffer." And he looked at me. "Please believe me," I said, "I don't want to see you—die—trying not to suffer."

"I won't," he said, flatly, "die trying not to suffer. At least, not any faster than anybody else."

"But there's no need," I said, trying to laugh, "is there? in killing yourself."

I wanted to say more, but I couldn't. I wanted to talk about will power and how life could be—well, beautiful. I wanted to say that it was all within; but was it? or, rather, wasn't that exactly the trouble? And I wanted to promise that I would never fail him again. But it would all have sounded—empty words and lies.

So I made the promise to myself and prayed that I would keep it.

"It's terrible sometimes, inside," he said, "that's what's the trouble. You walk these streets, black and funky and cold, and there's not really a living ass to talk to, and there's nothing shaking, and there's no way of getting it out—that storm inside. You can't talk it and you can't make love with it, and when you finally try to get with it and play it, you realize *nobody's* listening. So *you've* got to listen. You got to find a way to listen."

And then he walked away from the window and sat on the sofa again, as though all the wind had suddenly been knocked out of him. "Sometimes you'll do *anything* to play, even cut your mother's throat." He laughed and looked at me. "Or your brother's." Then he sobered. "Or your own." Then: "Don't worry. I'm all right now and I think I'll *be* all right. But I can't forget—where I've been. I don't mean just the physical place I've been, I mean where I've *been*. And *what* I've been."

"What have you been, Sonny?" I asked.

He smiled—but sat sideways on the sofa, his elbow resting on the back, his fingers playing with his mouth and chin, not looking at me. "I've been something I didn't recognize, didn't know I could be. Didn't know anybody could be." He stopped, looking inward, looking helplessly young, looking old. "I'm not talking about it now because I feel *guilty* or anything like that—maybe it would be better if I did, I don't know. Anyway, I can't really talk about it. Not to you, not to anybody," and now he turned and faced me. "Sometimes, you know, and it was actually when I was most *out* of the world, I felt that I was in it, that I was *with* it, really, and I could play or I didn't really have to *play*, it just came out of me, it was there. And I don't know how I played, thinking about it now, but I know I did awful things, those times, sometimes, to people. Or it wasn't that I *did* anything to them—it was that they weren't real." He picked up the beer can; it was empty; he rolled it between his palms: "And other times—well, I needed a fix, I needed to find a place to lean, I needed to clear a space to *listen*—and I couldn't find it, and I—went crazy, I did terrible things to *me*, I was terrible *for* me." He began pressing the beer can between his hands, I watched the metal begin to give. It glittered, as he played with it, like a knife, and I was afraid he would cut himself, but I said nothing. "Oh well. I can never tell you. I was all by myself at the bottom of something, stinking and sweating and crying and shaking, and I smelled it, you know? *my* stink, and I thought I'd die if I couldn't get away from it and yet, all the same, I knew that everything I was doing was just locking me in with it. And I didn't know," he paused, still flattening the beer can, "I didn't know, I still *don't* know, something kept telling me that maybe it was good to smell your own stink, but I didn't think that *that* was what I'd been trying to do—and—who can stand it?" and he abruptly dropped the ruined beer can, looking at me with a small, still smile, and then rose, walking to the window as though it were the lodestone rock. I watched his face, he watched the avenue. "I couldn't tell you when Mama died—but the reason I wanted to leave Harlem so bad was to get away from drugs. And then, when I ran away, that's what I was running from—really. When I came back, nothing had changed, *I* hadn't changed, I was just—older." And he stopped, drumming with his fingers on the windowpane. The sun had vanished, soon darkness would fall. I watched his face. "It can come again," he said, almost as though speaking to himself. Then he turned to me. "It can come again," he repeated. "I just want you to know that."

"All right," I said, at last. "So it can come again, All right."

He smiled, but the smile was sorrowful. "I had to try to tell you," he said.

"Yes," I said. "I understand that."

"You're my brother," he said, looking straight at me, and not smiling at all.

"Yes," I repeated, "yes. I understand that."

He turned back to the window, looking out. "All that hatred down there," he said, "all that hatred and misery and love. It's a wonder it doesn't blow the avenue apart."

We went to the only nightclub on a short, dark street, downtown. We squeezed through the narrow, chattering, jam-packed bar to the entrance of the big room, where the bandstand was. And we stood there for a moment, for the lights were very dim in this room and we couldn't see. Then, "Hello, boy," said a voice and an enormous black man, much older than Sonny or myself, erupted out of all that atmospheric lighting and put an arm around Sonny's shoulder. "I been sitting right here," he said, "waiting for you."

He had a big voice, too, and heads in the darkness turned toward us.

Sonny grinned and pulled a little away, and said, "Creole, this is my brother. I told you about him."

Creole shook my hand. "I'm glad to meet you, son," he said, and it was clear that he was glad to meet me *there*, for Sonny's sake. And he smiled, "You got a real musician in *your* family," and he took his arm from Sonny's shoulder and slapped him, lightly, affectionately, with the back of his hand.

"Well. Now I've heard it all," said a voice behind us. This was another musician, and a friend of Sonny's, a coal-black, cheerful-looking man, built close to the ground. He immediately began confiding to me, at the top of his lungs, the most terrible things about Sonny, his teeth gleaming like a lighthouse and his laugh coming up out of him like the beginning of an earthquake. And it turned out that everyone at the bar knew Sonny, or almost everyone; some were musicians, working there, or nearby, or not working, some were simply hangers-on, and some were there to hear Sonny play. I was introduced to all of them and they were all very polite to me. Yet, it was clear that, for them,

I was only Sonny's brother. Here, I was in Sonny's world. Or, rather: his kingdom. Here, it was not even a question that his veins bore royal blood.

They were going to play soon and Creole installed me, by myself, at a table in a dark corner. Then I watched them, Creole, and the little black man, and Sonny, and the others, while they horsed around, standing just below the bandstand. The light from the bandstand spilled just a little short of them and, watching them laughing and gesturing and moving about, I had the feeling that they, nevertheless, were being most careful not to step into that circle of light too suddenly: that if they moved into the light too suddenly, without thinking, they would perish in flame. Then, while I watched, one of them, the small, black man, moved into the light and crossed the bandstand and started fooling around with his drums. Then—being funny and being, also, extremely ceremonious—Creole took Sonny by the arm and led him to the piano. A woman's voice called Sonny's name and a few hands started clapping. And Sonny, also being funny and being ceremonious, and so touched, I think, that he could have cried, but neither hiding it nor showing it, riding it like a man, grinned, and put both hands to his heart and bowed from the waist.

Creole then went to the bass fiddle and a lean, very bright-skinned brown man jumped up on the bandstand and picked up his horn. So there they were, and the atmosphere on the bandstand and in the room began to change and tighten. Someone stepped up to the microphone and announced them. Then there were all kinds of murmurs. Some people at the bar shushed others. The waitress ran around, frantically getting in the last orders, guys and chicks got closer to each other, and the lights on the bandstand, on the quartet, turned to a kind of indigo. Then they all looked different there. Creole looked about him for the last time, as though he were making certain that all his chickens were in the coop, and then he—jumped and struck the fiddle. And there they were.

All I know about music is that not many people ever really hear it. And even then, on the rare occasions when something opens within, and the music enters, what we mainly hear, or hear corroborated, are personal, private, vanishing evocations. But the man who creates the music is hearing something else, is dealing with the roar rising from the void and imposing order on it as it hits the air. What is evoked in him, then, is of another order, more terrible because it has no words, and triumphant, too, for that same reason. And his triumph, when he triumphs, is ours. I just watched Sonny's face. His face was troubled, he was working hard, but he wasn't with it. And I had the feeling that, in a way, everyone on the bandstand was waiting for him, both waiting for him and pushing him along. But as I began to watch Creole, I realized that it was Creole who held them all back. He had them on a short rein. Up there, keeping the beat with his whole body, wailing on the fiddle, with his eyes half closed, he was listening to everything, but he was listening to Sonny. He was having a dialogue with Sonny. He wanted Sonny to leave the shoreline and strike out for the deep water. He was Sonny's witness that deep water and drowning were not the same thing—he had been there, and he knew. And he wanted Sonny to know. He was waiting for Sonny to do the things on the keys which would let Creole know that Sonny was in the water.

And, while Creole listened, Sonny moved, deep within, exactly like someone in torment. I had never before thought of how awful the relationship must be between the musician and his instrument. He has to fill it, this instrument, with the breath of life, his own. He has to make it do what he wants it to do. And a piano is just a piano. It's made out of so much wood and wires and little hammers and big ones, and ivory. While there's only so much you can do with it, the only way to find this out is to try; to try and make it do everything.

And Sonny hadn't been near a piano for over a year. And he wasn't on much better terms with his life, not the life that stretched before him now. He and the piano stammered, started one way, got scared, stopped; started another way, panicked, marked time, started again; then seemed to have found a direction, panicked again, got stuck. And the face I saw on Sonny I'd never seen before. Everything had been burned out of it, and, at the same time, things usually hidden were being burned in, by the fire and fury of the battle which was occurring in him up there.

Yet, watching Creole's face as they neared the end of the first set, I had the feeling that something had happened, something I hadn't heard. Then they finished, there was scattered applause, and then, without an instant's warning, Creole started into something else, it was almost sardonic, it was *Am I Blue.* And, as though he commanded, Sonny began to play. Something began to happen. And Creole let out the reins. The dry, low, black man said something awful on the drums, Creole answered, and the drums talked back. Then the horn insisted, sweet and high, slightly detached perhaps, and Creole listened, commenting now and then, dry, and driving, beautiful and calm and old. Then they all came together again, and Sonny was part of the family again. I could tell this from his face. He seemed to have found, right there beneath his fingers, a damn brand-new piano. It seemed that he couldn't get over it. Then, for awhile, just being happy with Sonny, they seemed to be agreeing with him that brand-new pianos certainly were a gas.

Then Creole stepped forward to remind them that what they were playing was the blues. He hit something in all of them, he hit something in me, myself, and the music tightened and deepened, apprehension began to beat the air. Creole began to tell us what the blues were all about. They were not about anything very new. He and his boys up there were keeping it new, at the risk of ruin, destruction, madness, and death, in order to find new ways to make us listen. For, while the tale of how we suffer, and how we are delighted, and how we may triumph is never new, it always must be heard. There isn't any other tale to tell, it's the only light we've got in all this darkness.

And this tale, according to that face, that body, those strong hands on those strings, has another aspect in every country, and a new depth in every generation. Listen, Creole seemed to be saying, listen. Now these are Sonny's blues. He made the little black man on the drums know it, and the bright, brown man on the horn. Creole wasn't trying any longer to get Sonny in the water. He was wishing him Godspeed. Then he stepped back, very slowly, filling the air with the immense suggestion that Sonny speak for himself.

Then they all gathered around Sonny and Sonny played. Every now and again one of them seemed to say, amen. Sonny's fingers filled the air with life, his life. But that life contained so many others. And Sonny went all the way back, he really began with the spare, flat statement of the opening phrase of the song. Then he began to make it his. It was very beautiful because it wasn't hurried and it was no longer a lament. I seemed to hear with what burning he had made it his, with what burning we had yet to make it ours, how we could cease lamenting. Freedom lurked around us and I understood, at last, that he could help us to be free if we would listen, that he would never be free until we did. Yet, there was no battle in his face now. I heard what he had gone through, and would continue to go through until he came to rest in earth. He had made it his: that long line, of which we knew only Mama and Daddy. And he was giving it back, as everything must be given back, so that, passing through death, it can live forever. I saw my mother's face again, and felt, for the first time, how the stones of the road she had walked on must have bruised her feet. I saw the moonlit road where my father's brother died. And it brought something else back to me, and carried me past it. I saw my little girl again and felt Isabel's tears again, and I felt my own tears begin to rise. And I was yet aware that this was only a moment, that the world waited outside, as hungry as a tiger, and that trouble stretched above us, longer than the sky.

Then it was over. Creole and Sonny let out their breath, both soaking wet, and grinning. There was a lot of applause and some of it was real. In the dark, the girl came by and I asked her to take drinks to the bandstand. There was a long pause, while they talked up there in the indigo light and after awhile I saw the girl put a Scotch and milk on top of the piano for Sonny. He didn't seem to notice it, but just before they started playing again, he sipped from it and looked toward me, and nodded. Then he put it back on top of the piano. For me, then, as they began to play again, it glowed and shook above my brother's head like the very cup of trembling.

COMMENTARY

JAMES BALDWIN

James Baldwin wrote this account of how he became a writer in his book *Notes of a Native Son* (1955). He admitted that "the most difficult (and most rewarding) thing in my life has been the fact that I was born a Negro and was forced, therefore, to effect some kind of truce with this reality." As his biographer Louis H. Pratt has understood, this "truce" forced Baldwin "into an open confrontation with his experience, enabling him to make an honest assessment of his past. . . . Baldwin the artist has been liberated because he has found a way to use his past and to transform those experiences resulting therefrom into art."

Autobiographical Notes 1955

I was born in Harlem thirty-one years ago. I began plotting novels at about the time I learned to read. The story of my childhood is the usual bleak fantasy, and we can dismiss it with the unrestrained observation that I certainly would not consider living it again. In those days my mother was given to the exasperating and mysterious habit of having babies. As they were born, I took them over with one hand and held a book with the other. The children probably suffered, though they have since been kind enough to deny it, and in this way I read *Uncle Tom's Cabin* and *A Tale of Two Cities* over and over and over again; in this way, in fact, I read just about everything I could get my hands on—except the Bible, probably because it was the only book I was encouraged to read. I must also confess that I wrote—a great deal—and my first professional triumph, in any case, the first effort of mine to be seen in print, occurred at the age of twelve or thereabouts, when a short story I had written about the Spanish revolution won some sort of prize in an extremely short-lived church newspaper. I remember the story was censored by the lady editor, though I don't remember why, and I was outraged.

Also wrote plays, and songs, for one of which I received a letter of congratulations from Mayor La Guardia, and poetry, about which the less said, the better. My mother was delighted by all these goings-on, but my father wasn't; he wanted me to be a preacher. When I was fourteen I became a preacher, and when I was seventeen I stopped. Very shortly thereafter I left home. For God knows how long I struggled with the world of commerce and industry—I guess they would say they struggled with *me*—and when I was about twenty-one I had enough done of a novel to get a Saxton Fellowship. When I was twenty-two the fellowship was over, the novel turned out to be unsalable, and I started waiting on tables in a Village° restaurant and writing book reviews—mostly, as it turned out, about the Negro problem, concerning which the color of my skin made me automatically an expert. Did another book, in company with photographer Theodore Pelatowski, about the storefront churches in Harlem. This book met exactly the same fate as my first—fellowship, but no sale. (It was a Rosenwald Fellowship.) By the time I was twenty-four I had decided to stop reviewing books about the Negro problem—which, by this time, was only slightly less horrible in print than it was in life—and I packed my bags and went to France, where I finished, God knows how, *Go Tell It on the Mountain*.

Any writer, I suppose, feels that the world into which he was born is nothing less than a conspiracy against the cultivation of his talent—which attitude certainly has a great deal to support it. On the other hand, it is only because the world looks on his talent with such a frightening indifference that the artist is compelled to make his talent important. So that any writer, looking back over even so short a span of time as I am here forced to assess, finds that the things which hurt him and the things which helped him cannot be divorced from each other; he could be helped in a certain way only because he was hurt in a certain way; and his help is simply to be enabled to move from one conundrum to the next—one is tempted to say that he moves from one disaster to the next. When one begins looking for influences one finds them by the score. I haven't thought much about my own, not enough anyway; I hazard that the

---

Village: Greenwich Village, New York City.

King James Bible, the rhetoric of the store-front church, something ironic and violent and perpetually understated in Negro speech—and something of Dickens' love for bravura—have something to do with me today; but I wouldn't stake my life on it. Likewise, innumerable people have helped me in many ways; but finally, I suppose, the most difficult (and most rewarding) thing in my life has been the fact that I was born a Negro and was forced, therefore, to effect some kind of truce with this reality. (Truce, by the way, is the best one can hope for.)

One of the difficulties about being a Negro writer (and this is not special pleading, since I don't mean to suggest that he has it worse than anybody else) is that the Negro problem is written about so widely. The bookshelves groan under the weight of information, and everyone therefore considers himself informed. And this information, furthermore, operates usually (generally, popularly) to reinforce traditional attitudes. Of traditional attitudes there are only two—For or Against—and I, personally, find it difficult to say which attitude has caused me the most pain. I am perfectly aware that the change from ill-will to good-will, however motivated, however imperfect, however expressed, is better than no change at all.

But it is part of the business of the writer—as I see it—to examine attitudes, to go beneath the surface, to tap the source. From this point of view the Negro problem is nearly inaccessible. It is not only written about so widely; it is written about so badly. It is quite possible to say that the price a Negro pays for becoming articulate is to find himself, at length, with nothing to be articulate about. ("You taught me the language," says Caliban to Prospero,° "and my profit on't is I know how to curse.") Consider: The tremendous social activity that this problem generates imposes on whites and Negroes alike the necessity of looking forward, of working to bring about a better day. This is fine, it keeps the waters troubled; it is all, indeed, that has made possible the Negro's progress. Nevertheless, social affairs are not generally speaking the writer's prime concern, whether they ought to be or not; it is absolutely necessary that he establish between himself and these affairs a distance that will allow, at least, for clarity, so that before he can look forward in any meaningful sense, he must first be allowed to take a long look back. In the context of the Negro problem neither whites nor blacks, for excellent reasons of their own, have the faintest desire to look back; but I think that the past is all that makes the present coherent, and further, that the past will remain horrible for exactly as long as we refuse to assess it honestly.

I know, in any case, that the most crucial time in my own development came when I was forced to recognize that I was a kind of bastard of the West; when I followed the line of my past I did not find myself in Europe but in Africa. And this meant that in some subtle way, in a really profound way, I brought to Shakespeare, Bach, Rembrandt, to the stones of Paris, to the cathedral at Chartres, and to the Empire State Building, a special attitude. These

Caliban to Prospero: In Shakespeare's *The Tempest*, the monster Caliban is a servant of the magician Prospero.

were not really my creations, they did not contain my history; I might search in them in vain forever for any reflection of myself. I was an interloper; this was not my heritage. At the same time I had no other heritage which I could possibly hope to use—I had certainly been unfitted for the jungle or the tribe. I would have to appropriate these white centuries, I would have to make them mine—I would have to accept my special attitude, my special place in this scheme—otherwise I would have no place in *any* scheme. What was the most difficult was the fact that I was forced to admit something I had always hidden from myself, which the American Negro has had to hide from himself as the price of his public progress; that I hated and feared white people. This did not mean that I loved black people; on the contrary, I despised them, possibly because they failed to produce Rembrandt. In effect, I hated and feared the world. And this meant, not only that I thus gave the world an altogether murderous power over me, but also that in such a self-destroying limbo I could never hope to write.

One writes out of one thing only—one's own experience. Everything depends on how relentlessly one forces from this experience the last drop, sweet or bitter, it can possibly give. This is the only real concern of the artist, to recreate out of the disorder of life that order which is art. The difficulty then, for me, of being a Negro writer was the fact that I was, in effect, prohibited from examining my own experience too closely by the tremendous demands and the very real dangers of my social situation.

I don't think the dilemma outlined above is uncommon. I do think, since writers work in the disastrously explicit medium of language, that it goes a little way towards explaining why, out of the enormous resources of Negro speech and life, and despite the example of Negro music, prose written by Negroes has been generally speaking so pallid and so harsh. I have not written about being a Negro at such length because I expect that to be my only subject, but only because it was the gate I had to unlock before I could hope to write about anything else. I don't think that the Negro problem in America can be even discussed coherently without bearing in mind its context; its context being the history, traditions, customs, the moral assumptions and preoccupations of the country; in short, the general social fabric. Appearances to the contrary, no one in America escapes its effects and everyone in America bears some responsibility for it. I believe this the more firmly because it is the overwhelming tendency to speak of this problem as though it were a thing apart. But in the work of Faulkner, in the general attitude and certain specific passages in Robert Penn Warren,° and, most significantly, in the advent of Ralph Ellison, one sees the beginnings—at least—of a more genuinely penetrating search. Mr. Ellison, by the way, is the first Negro novelist I have ever read to utilize in language, and brilliantly, some of the ambiguity and irony of Negro life.

About my interests: I don't know if I have any, unless the morbid desire to own a sixteen-millimeter camera and make experimental movies can be so classified. Otherwise, I love to eat and drink—it's my melancholy conviction that

Robert Penn Warren: An American novelist, poet, and critic (1905–1989).

I've scarcely ever had enough to eat (this is because it's *impossible* to eat enough if you're worried about the next meal)—and I love to argue with people who do not disagree with me too profoundly, and I love to laugh. I do *not* like bohemia, or bohemians, I do not like people whose principal aim is pleasure, and I do not like people who are *earnest* about anything. I don't like people who like me because I'm a Negro; neither do I like people who find in the same accident grounds for contempt. I love America more than any other country in the world, and, exactly for this reason, I insist on the right to criticize her perpetually. I think all theories are suspect, that the finest principles may have to be modified, or may even be pulverized by the demands of life, and that one must find, therefore, one's own moral center and move through the world hoping that this center will guide one aright. I consider that I have many responsibilities, but none greater than this: to last, as Hemingway says, and get my work done.

I want to be an honest man and a good writer.

TONI CADE BAMBARA

Toni Cade Bambara (1939–1995) was born in New York City and grew up in Harlem and Bedford-Stuyvesant. As a child she began scribbling stories on the margins of her father's copies of the *New York Daily News* and the squares of thin white cardboard her mother's stockings came wrapped around. She has said of herself,

> I was raised by my family and community to be a combatant. Forays to the Apollo [Theater in Harlem] with my daddy and hanging tough on Speakers Corner with my mama taught me the power of the word, the importance of the resistance tradition, and the high standards our [black] community had regarding verbal performance. While my heart is a laughing gland and my favorite thing to be doing is laughing so hard I have to lower myself on the wall to keep from falling down, near that chamber is a blast furnace where a rifle pokes from the ribs.

In high school and at Queens College, Bambara remembered that she "hogged the lit journal." She took writing courses and wrote novels, stories, plays, film scripts, operas, "you-name-its." After graduating from Queens, she worked various jobs and studied for her M.A. at the City College of New York while she wrote fiction in "the predawn in-betweens." She began to publish her stories, and in 1972 she collected them in her first book, *Gorilla, My Love.* It wasn't until Bambara returned from a trip to Cuba in 1973 that she thought of herself as a writer: "There I learned what Langston Hughes and others, most especially my colleagues in the Neo-Black Arts Movement, had been teaching for years–that writing is a legitimate way, an important way, to participate in the empowerment of the community that names me." Her books of stories include *The Black Woman* (1970), *Tales and Stories for Black Folks* (1971), and *The Sea Birds Are Still Alive: Collected Stories* (1977). She also published two novels, *The Salt Eaters* (1980) and *If Blessing Comes* (1987).

Like Zora Neale Hurston, whom Bambara credited with giving her new ways to consider literary material (folkways as the basis of art) and new categories of perception (women's images), Bambara often used humor in her fiction. She said that "what I enjoy most in my work is the laughter and the outrage and the attention to language." Her stories, like "The Lesson," were often about children, but Bambara tried to avoid sentimentality. She attempted to keep her torrents of language and feeling under control by remembering the premises from which she proceeded as a black writer: "One, we are at war. Two, the natural response to oppression, ignorance, evil, and mystification is wide-awake resistance. Three, the natural response to stress and crisis is not breakdown and capitulation, but transformation and renewal."

WEB Research Toni Cade Bambara at bedfordstmartins.com/rewritinglit.

The Lesson

1972

Back in the days when everyone was old and stupid or young and foolish and me and Sugar were the only ones just right, this lady moved on our block with nappy hair and proper speech and no makeup. And quite naturally we laughed at her, laughed the way we did at the junk man who went about his business like he was some big-time president and his sorry-ass horse his secretary. And we kinda hated her too, hated the way we did the winos who cluttered up our parks and pissed on our handball walls and stank up our hallways and stairs so you couldn't halfway play hide-and-seek without a goddamn gas mask. Miss Moore was her name. The only woman on the block with no first name. And she was black as hell, cept for her feet, which were fish-white and spooky. And she was always planning these boring-ass things for us to do, us being my cousin, mostly, who lived on the block cause we all moved North the same time and to the same apartment then spread out gradual to breathe. And our parents would yank our heads into some kinda shape and crisp up our clothes so we'd be presentable for travel with Miss Moore, who always looked like she was going to church, though she never did. Which is just one of the things the grownups talked about when they talked behind her back like a dog. But when she came calling with some sachet she'd sewed up or some gingerbread she'd made or some book, why then they'd all be too embarrassed to turn her down and we'd get handed over all spruced up. She'd been to college and said it was only right that she should take responsibility for the young ones' education, and she not even related by marriage or blood. So they'd go for it. Specially Aunt Gretchen. She was the main gofer in the family. You got some ole dumb shit foolishness you want somebody to go for, you send for Aunt Gretchen. She been screwed into the go-along for so long, it's a blood-deep natural thing with her. Which is how she got saddled with me and Sugar and Junior in the first place while our mothers were in a la-de-da apartment up the block having a good ole time.

So this one day, Miss Moore rounds us all up at the mailbox and it's puredee hot and she's knockin herself out about arithmetic. And school suppose to let up in summer I heard, but she don't never let up. And the starch in my pinafore scratching the shit outta me and I'm really hating this nappy-head bitch and her goddamn college degree. I'd much rather go to the pool or to the show where it's cool. So me and Sugar leaning on the mailbox being surly, which is a Miss Moore word. And Flyboy checking out what everybody brought for lunch. And Fat Butt already wasting his peanut-butter-and-jelly sandwich like the pig he is. And Junebug punchin on Q.T.'s arm for potato chips. And Rosie Giraffe shifting from one hip to the other waiting for somebody to step on her foot or ask her if she from Georgia so she can kick ass, preferably Mercedes'. And Miss Moore asking us do we know what money is, like we a bunch of retards. I mean real money, she say, like it's only poker chips or monopoly papers we lay on the grocer. So right away I'm tired of this and say so. And would much rather snatch Sugar and go to the Sunset and terrorize the West Indian kids and take their hair ribbons and their money too. And Miss Moore files that remark away for next week's lesson on brotherhood, I can tell. And finally I say we oughta get to the subway cause it's cooler and besides we might meet some cute boys. Sugar done swiped her mama's lipstick, so we ready.

So we heading down the street and she's boring us silly about what things cost and what our parents make and how much goes for rent and how money ain't divided up right in this country. And then she gets to the part about we all poor and live in the slums, which I don't feature. And I'm ready to speak on that, but she steps out in the street and hails two cabs just like that. Then she hustles half the crew in with her and hands me a five-dollar bill and tells me to calculate 10 percent tip for the driver. And we're off. Me and Sugar and Junebug and Flyboy hangin out the window and hollering to everybody, putting lipstick on each other cause Flyboy a faggot anyway, and making farts with our sweaty armpits. But I'm mostly trying to figure how to spend this money. But they all fascinated with the meter ticking and Junebug starts laying bets as to how much it'll read when Flyboy can't hold his breath no more. Then Sugar lays bets as to how much it'll be when we get there. So I'm stuck. Don't nobody want to go for my plan, which is to jump out at the next light and run off to the first bar-b-que we can find. Then the driver tells us to get the hell out cause we there already. And the meter reads eighty-five cents. And I'm stalling to figure out the tip and Sugar say give him a dime. And I decide he don't need it bad as I do, so later for him. But then he tries to take off with Junebug foot still in the door so we talk about his mama something ferocious. Then we check out that we on Fifth Avenue and everybody dressed up in stockings. One lady in a fur coat, hot as it is. White folks crazy.

"This is the place," Miss Moore say, presenting it to us in the voice she uses at the museum. "Let's look in the windows before we go in."

"Can we steal?" Sugar asks very serious like she's getting the ground rules squared away before she plays. "I beg your pardon," say Miss Moore, and we fall out. So she leads us around the windows of the toy store and me and Sugar screamin, "This is mine, that's mine, I gotta have that, that was made for me, I was born for that," till Big Butt drowns us out.

"Hey, I'm going to buy that there."

"That there? You don't even know what it is, stupid."

"I do so," he say punchin on Rosie Giraffe. "It's a microscope."

"Whatcha gonna do with a microscope, fool?"

"Look at things."

"Like what, Ronald?" ask Miss Moore. And Big Butt ain't got the first notion. So here go Miss Moore gabbing about the thousands of bacteria in a drop of water and the somethinorother in a speck of blood and the million and one living things in the air around us is invisible to the naked eye. And what she say that for? Junebug go to town on that "naked" and we rolling. Then Miss Moore ask what it cost. So we all jam into the window smudgin it up and the price tag say $300. So then she ask how long'd take for Big Butt and Junebug to save up their allowances. "Too long," I say. "Yeh," adds Sugar, "outgrown it by that time." And Miss Moore say no, you never outgrow learning instruments. "Why, even medical students and interns and," blah, blah, blah. And we ready to choke Big Butt for bringing it up in the first damn place.

"This here costs four hundred eighty dollars," say Rosie Giraffe. So we pile up all over her to see what she pointin out. My eyes tell me it's a chunk of glass cracked with something heavy, and different-color inks dripped into the splits, then the whole thing put into a oven or something. But for $480 it don't make sense.

"That's a paperweight made of semi-precious stones fused together under tremendous pressure," she explains slowly, with her hands doing the mining and all the factory work.

"So what's a paperweight?" ask Rosie Giraffe.

"To weigh paper with, dumbbell," say Flyboy, the wise man from the East.

"Not exactly," say Miss Moore, which is what she say when you warm or way off too. "It's to weigh paper down so it won't scatter and make your desk untidy." So right away me and Sugar curtsy to each other and then to Mercedes who is more the tidy type.

"We don't keep paper on top of the desk in my class," say Junebug, figuring Miss Moore crazy or lyin one.

"At home, then," she say. "Don't you have a calendar and a pencil case and a blotter and a letter-opener on your desk at home where you do your homework?" And she know damn well what our homes look like cause she nosys around in them every chance she gets.

"I don't even have a desk," say Junebug. "Do we?"

"No. And I don't get no homework neither," says Big Butt.

"And I don't even have a home," says Flyboy like he do at school to keep the white folks off his back and sorry for him. Send this poor kid to camp posters, is his specialty.

"I do," says Mercedes. "I have a box of stationery on my desk and a picture of my cat. My godmother bought the stationery and the desk. There's a big rose on each sheet and the envelopes smell like roses."

"Who wants to know about your smelly-ass stationery," say Rosie Giraffe fore I can get my two cents in.

"It's important to have a work area all your own so that . . ."

"Will you look at this sailboat, please," say Flyboy, cutting her off and pointin to the thing like it was his. So once again we tumble all over each other to gaze at this magnificent thing in the toy store which is just big enough to maybe sail two kittens across the pond if you strap them to the posts tight. We all start reciting the price tag like we in assembly. "Handcrafted sailboat of fiberglass at one thousand one hundred ninety-five dollars."

"Unbelievable," I hear myself say and am really stunned. I read it again for myself just in case the group recitation put me in a trance. Same thing. For some reason this pisses me off. We look at Miss Moore and she lookin at us, waiting for I dunno what.

"Who'd pay all that when you can buy a sailboat set for a quarter at Pop's, a tube of glue for a dime, and a ball of string for eight cents? It must have a motor and a whole lot else besides," I say. "My sailboat cost me about fifty cents."

"But will it take water?" say Mercedes with her smart ass.

"Took mine to Alley Pond Park once," say Flyboy. "String broke. Lost it. Pity."

"Sailed mine in Central Park and it keeled over and sank. Had to ask my father for another dollar."

"And you got the strap," laugh Big Butt. "The jerk didn't even have a string on it. My old man wailed on his behind."

Little Q.T. was staring hard at the sailboat and you could see he wanted it bad. But he too little and somebody'd just take it from him. So what the hell. "This boat for kids, Miss Moore?"

"Parents silly to buy something like that just to get all broke up," say Rosie Giraffe.

"That much money it should last forever," I figure.

"My father'd buy it for me if I wanted it."

"Your father, my ass," say Rosie Giraffe getting a chance to finally push Mercedes.

"Must be rich people shop here," say Q.T.

"You are a very bright boy," say Flyboy. "What was your first clue?" And he rap him on the head with the back of his knuckles, since Q.T. the only one he could get away with. Though Q.T. liable to come up behind you years later and get his licks in when you half expect it.

"What I want to know is," I says to Miss Moore though I never talk to her, I wouldn't give the bitch that satisfaction, "is how much a real boat costs? I figure a thousand'd get you a yacht any day."

"Why don't you check that out," she says, "and report back to the group?" Which really pains my ass. If you gonna mess up a perfectly good swim day least you could do is have some answers. "Let's go in," she say like she got something up her sleeve. Only she don't lead the way. So me and Sugar turn the corner to where the entrance is, but when we get there I kinda hang back. Not that I'm scared, what's there to be afraid of, just a toy store. But I feel funny, shame. But what I got to be shamed about? Got as much right to go in as anybody. But somehow I can't seem to get hold of the door, so I step away from Sugar to lead. But she hangs back too. And I look at her and she looks at me and this is ridiculous. I mean, damn, I have never been shy about doing nothing or going nowhere. But then Mercedes steps up and then Rosie Giraffe and Big Butt crowd in behind and shove, and next thing we all stuffed into the doorway with only Mercedes squeezing past us, smoothing out her jumper and walking right down the aisle. Then the rest of us tumble in like a glued-together jigsaw done all wrong. And people lookin at us. And it's like the time me and Sugar crashed into the Catholic church on a dare. But once we got in there and everything so hushed and holy and the candles and the bowin and the handkerchiefs on all the drooping heads, I just couldn't go through with the plan. Which was for me to run up to the altar and do a tap dance while Sugar played the nose flute and messed around in the holy water. And Sugar kept givin me the elbow. Then later teased me so bad I tied her up in the shower and turned it on and locked her in. And she'd be there till this day if Aunt Gretchen hadn't finally figured I was lying about the boarder takin a shower.

Same thing in the store. We all walkin on tiptoe and hardly touchin the games and puzzles and things. And I watched Miss Moore who is steady watchin us like she waitin for a sign. Like Mama Drewery watches the sky and sniffs the air and takes note of just how much slant is in the bird formation. Then me and Sugar bump smack into each other, so busy gazing at the toys, 'specially the sailboat. But we don't laugh and go into our fat-lady bump-stomach routine. We just stare at that price tag. Then Sugar run a finger over the whole boat. And I'm jealous and want to hit her. Maybe not her, but I sure want to punch somebody in the mouth.

"Watcha bring us here for, Miss Moore?"

"You sound angry, Sylvia. Are you mad about something?" Givin me one of them grins like she tellin a grown-up joke that never turns out to be funny. And she's lookin very closely at me like maybe she plannin to do my portrait from memory. I'm mad, but I won't give her that satisfaction. So I slouch around the store being very bored and say, "Let's go."

Me and Sugar at the back of the train watchin the tracks whizzin by large then small then getting gobbled up in the dark. I'm thinkin about this tricky toy I saw in the store. A clown that somersaults on a bar then does chin-ups just cause you yank lightly at his leg. Cost $35. I could see me askin my mother for a $35 birthday clown. "You wanna who that costs what?" she'd say, cocking her head to the side to get a better view of the hole in my head. Thirty-five dollars could buy new bunk beds for Junior and Gretchen's boy. Thirty-five dollars and the whole household could go visit Granddaddy Nelson in the country. Thirty-five dollars would pay for the rent and the piano bill too. Who are these people that spend that much for performing clowns and $1000 for toy sailboats? What kinda work they do and how they live and how come we ain't in on it? Where we are is who we are, Miss Moore always pointin out. But it don't necessarily have to be that way, she always adds then waits for somebody to say that poor people have to wake up and demand their share of the pie and don't none of us know what kind of pie she talking about in the first damn place. But she ain't so smart cause I still got her four dollars from the taxi and she sure ain't gettin it. Messin up my day with this shit. Sugar nudges me in my pocket and winks.

Miss Moore lines us up in front of the mailbox where we started from, seem like years ago, and I got a headache for thinkin so hard. And we lean all over each other so we can hold up under the draggy-ass lecture she always finishes us off with at the end before we thank her for borin us to tears. But she just looks at us like she readin tea leaves. Finally she say, "Well, what did you think of F.A.O. Schwarz?"

Rosie Giraffe mumbles, "White folks crazy."

"I'd like to go there again when I get my birthday money," says Mercedes, and we shove her out the pack so she has to lean on the mailbox by herself.

"I'd like a shower. Tiring day," say Flyboy.

Then Sugar surprises me by sayin, "You know, Miss Moore, I don't think all of us here put together eat in a year what that sailboat costs." And Miss Moore lights up like somebody goosed her. "And?" she say, urging Sugar on. Only I'm standin on her foot so she don't continue.

"Imagine for a minute what kind of society it is in which some people can spend on a toy what it would cost to feed a family of six or seven. What do you think?"

"I think," say Sugar pushing me off her feet like she never done before, cause I whip her ass in a minute, "that this is not much of a democracy if you ask me. Equal chance to pursue happiness means an equal crack at the dough, don't it?" Miss Moore is besides herself and I am disgusted with Sugar's treachery. So I stand on her foot one more time to see if she'll shove me. She shuts up, and Miss Moore looks at me, sorrowfully I'm thinkin. And somethin weird is goin on, I can feel it in my chest.

"Anybody else learn anything today?" lookin dead at me. I walk away and Sugar has to run to catch up and don't even seem to notice when I shrug her arm off my shoulder.

"Well, we got four dollars anyway," she says.

"Uh, hunh."

"We could go to Hascombs and get half a chocolate layer and then go to the Sunset and still have plenty money for potato chips and ice cream sodas."

"Uh, hunh."

"Race you to Hascombs," she say.

We start down the block and she gets ahead which is O.K. by me cause I'm going to the West End and then over to the Drive to think this day through. She can run if she want to and even run faster. But ain't nobody gonna beat me at nuthin.

JOSÉ ANTONIO BURCIAGA

José Antonio Burciaga (1940–1996) was born in El Paso, Texas, into a Catholic Mexican family. He grew up living in the basement of a Jewish synagogue where his father worked as a janitor. His mother had been a teacher in Mexico, and Burciaga credited his parents for instilling in him at an early age a sense of humor and a determination never to compromise on what he felt was right.

After graduating from high school, Burciaga enlisted in the air force. He was stationed in Iceland and Spain, where he read the writing of Federico García Lorca, whom he later credited as helping him to conceptualize his Hispanic identity. In 1968 he earned a B.A. in fine arts at the University of Texas in El Paso. He worked as an illustrator for the air force in Texas and for the Central Intelligence Agency in Washington, D.C. In 1974 he married Cecilia Preciado, and they moved to California after she was offered a job as an administrator at Stanford University. There Burciaga began his career as a writer, publishing poetry and fiction as well as articles for newspapers and journals as a pioneer Chicano activist. In 1976 he published his novel *Restless Serpents*, followed in 1988 by a book of essays, *Weedee Peepo*. This title was a deliberate mispronunciation of "We the People," the opening words of the Constitution as spoken by his parents and other Hispanic immigrants who had to live with the social and cultural prejudices they found in the United States.

At Stanford, where Burciaga's wife worked as the Vice Provost for Chicano Affairs, the couple became active in the creation of a Chicano/Latino student center, and until 1994 they were also resident fellows at Casa Zapata, a Chicano dormitory. There with student help, Burciaga painted several murals, including "The Last Supper of Chicano Heroes," which became well known. It included the figures of César Chavez, Robert Kennedy, Che Guevara, and Martin Luther King Jr. In Burciaga's later prose and poetry he forged a unique Mexican American voice by writing in English, Spanish, Nahuatl, and Mexican American street dialect. He was also a standup comedian and a founding member of the theatrical comedy troupe Culture Clash. His story "La Puerta" was published in 1992, the year he won the National Book Award for *Undocumented Love*, a book of poetry. Its cover art was Burciaga's painting of a Mexican Christ figure attempting to cross a barbed-wire border while dripping blood onto an American flag. In 1995, after publishing the novel *Spilling the Beans: Loteria Chicana*, Burciaga received the National Hispanic Heritage Award for Literature. The following year he succumbed to cancer. *The Last Supper of Chicano Heroes: Selected Works of José Antonio Burciaga* was published in 2008.

La Puerta

1992

It had rained in thundering sheets every afternoon that summer. A dog-tired Sinesio returned home from his job in a mattress sweat shop. With a weary step from the *autobús*, Sinesio gathered the last of his strength and darted across the busy *avenida* into the ramshackle *colonia* where children played in the meandering pathways that would soon turn into a noisy *arroyo* of rushing water. The rain drops striking the *barrio's* tin, wooden and cardboard roofs would soon become a sheet of water from heaven.

Every afternoon Sinesio's muffled knock on their two-room shack was answered by Faustina, his wife. She would unlatch the door and return to iron more shirts and dresses of people who could afford the luxury. When thunder clapped, a frightened Faustina would quickly pull the electric cord, believing it would attract lightning. Then she would occupy herself with preparing dinner. Their three children would not arrive home for another hour.

On this day Sinesio laid down his tattered lunch bag, a lottery ticket and his week's wages on the oily tablecloth. Faustina threw a glance at the lottery ticket.

Sinesio's silent arrival always angered Faustina so she glared back at the lottery ticket, "Throwing money away! Buying paper dreams! We can't afford dreams, and you buy them!"

Sinesio ignored her anger. From the table, he picked up a letter, smelled it, studied the U.S. stamp, and with the emphatic opening of the envelope sat down at the table and slowly read aloud the letter from his brother Aurelio as the rain beat against the half tin, half wooden rooftop.

> Dear Sinesio,
>
> I write to you from this country of abundance, the first letter I write from los Estados Unidos. After two weeks of nerves and frustration I finally have a job at a canning factory. It took me that long only because I did not have the necessary social security number. It's amazing how much money one can make, but just as amazing how fast it goes. I had to pay for the social security number, two weeks of rent, food, and a pair of shoes. The good pair you gave me wore out on our journey across the border. From the border we crossed two mountains, and the desert in between.
>
> I will get ahead because I'm a better worker than the rest of my countrymen. I can see that already and so does the "boss." Coming here will be hard for you, leaving Faustina and the children. It was hard enough for me and I'm single without a worry in life. But at least you will have me here if you come and I'm sure I can get you a job. All you've heard about the crossing is true. Even the lies are true. "Saludos" from your "compadres" Silvio and Ramiro. They are doing fine. They're already bothering me for the bet you made against the Dodgers.
>
> Next time we get together I will relate my adventures and those of my "compañeros" . . . things to laugh and cry about.

Aurelio signed the letter *Saludos y abrazo.*° Sinesio looked off into space and imagined himself there already. But this dreaming was interrupted by the pelting rain and Faustina's knife dicing *nopal*, cactus, on the wooden board.

¿Qué crees?— "What do you think?" Faustina asked Sinesio.

¡No sé!— "I don't know," Sinesio responded with annoyance.

"But you do know, Sinesio. How could you not know? There's no choice. We have turned this over and around a thousand times. That miserable mattress factory will never pay you enough to eat with. We can't even afford the mattresses you make!"

Sinesio's heart sank as if he was being pushed out or had already left his home. She would join her *comadres* as another undocumented widow. Already he missed his three children, Celso, Jenaro, and Natasia his eldest, a joy every time he saw her. "An absence in the heart is an empty pain," he thought.

Faustina reminded Sinesio of the inevitable trip with subtle statements and proverbs that went straight to the heart of the matter. "Necessity knows no frontiers," she would say. The dicing of the *nopal* and onions took on the fast clip of the rain. Faustina looked up to momentarily study a trickle of water that

---

Saludos y abrazo: Regards.

had begun to run on the inside of a heavily patched glass on the door. It bothered her, but unable to fix it at the moment she went back to her cooking.

Sinesio accepted the answer to a question he wished he had never asked. The decision was made. There was no turning back. "I will leave for *el norte* in two weeks," he said gruffly and with authority.

Faustina's heart sank as she continued to make dinner. After the rain, Sinesio went out to help his *compadre* widen a ditch to keep the water from flooding in front of his door. The children came home, and it became Faustina's job to inform them that *Papá* would have to leave for a while. None of them said anything. Jenaro refused to eat. They had expected and accepted the news. From their friends, they knew exactly what it meant. Many of their friends' fathers had already left and many more would follow.

Throughout the following days, Sinesio continued the same drudgery at work but as his departure date approached he began to miss even that. He secured his family and home, made all the essential home repairs he had put off and asked his creditors for patience and trust. He asked his sisters, cousins and neighbors to check on his family. Another *compadre* lent him money for the trip and the coyote.° Sinesio did not know when he would return but told everyone "One year, no more. Save enough money, buy things to sell here and open up a *negocio*, a small business the family can help with."

The last trip home from work was no different except for the going-away gift, a bottle of *mezcal*, and the promise of his job when he returned. As usual, the *autobús* was packed. And as usual, the only ones to talk were two loud young men, *sinvergüenzas*—without shame.

The two young men talked about the *Lotería Nacional* and a lottery prize that had gone unclaimed for a week. "*¡Cien millones de pesos!*—One hundred million pesos! *¡Carajo!*" one of them kept repeating as he slapped the folded newspaper on his knees again and again. "Maybe the fool that bought it doesn't even know!"

"Or can't read!" answered the other. And they laughed with open mouths.

This caught Sinesio's attention. Two weeks earlier he had bought a lottery ticket. "Could . . . ? No!" he thought. But he felt a slight flush of blood rush to his face. Maybe this was his lucky day. The one day out of the thousands that he had lived in poverty.

The two jumped off the bus, and Sinesio reached for the newspaper they had left behind. There on the front page, was the winning number. At the end of the article was the deadline to claim the prize: 8 that night.

Sinesio did not have the faintest idea if his ticket matched the winning number. So he swung from the highest of hopes and dreams to resigned despair as he wondered if he had won one hundred million pesos.

Jumping off the bus, he ran home, at times slowing to a walk to catch his breath. The times he jogged, his heart pounded, the newspaper clutched in his hand, the heavy grey clouds ready to pour down.

---

coyote: A person who helps illegal immigrants enter the United States.

Faustina heard his desperate knock and swung the door open.

"*¿Dónde está?*" Sinesio pleaded. "Where is the lottery ticket I bought?" He said it slowly and clearly so he wouldn't have to repeat himself.

Faustina was confused, "What lottery ticket?"

Sinesio searched the table, under the green, oily cloth, on top of the dresser and through his papers, all the while with the jabbing question, "What did you do with the *boleto de lotería*?"

Thunder clapped. Faustina quit searching and unplugged the iron. Sinesio sounded off about no one respecting his papers and how no one could find anything in that house. *¿Dónde está el boleto de lotería?*—Where is the lottery ticket?

They both stopped to think. The rain splashed into a downpour against the door. Faustina looked at the door to see if she had fixed the hole in the glass.

¡La puerta!—"The door!" blurted Faustina, "I put it on the door to keep the rain from coming in!"

Sinesio turned to see the ticket glued on the broken window pane. It was light blue with red numbers and the letters *"Lotería Nacional."* Sinesio brought the newspaper up to the glued lottery ticket and with his wife compared the numbers off one by one—*Seis - tres - cuatro - uno - ocho - nueve - uno - ¡SIETE-DOS!*—Sinesio yelled.

"¡No!" trembled a disbelieving and frightened Sinesio, "One hundred million pesos!" His heart pounded afraid this was all a mistake, a bad joke. They checked it again and again only to confirm the matching numbers.

Sinesio then tried to peel the ticket off. His fingernail slid off the cold, glued lottery ticket. Faustina looked at Sinesio's stubby fingernails and moved in. But Faustina's thinner fingernails also slid off the lottery ticket. Sinesio walked around the kitchen table looking, thinking, trying to remain calm.

Then he grew frustrated and angry. "What time is it?"

"A quarter to seven," Faustina said looking at the alarm clock above the dresser. They tried hot water and a razor blade with no success. Sinesio then lashed out at Faustina in anger, "You! I never answered your mockery! Your lack of faith in me! I played the lottery because I knew this day would come! "*¡Por Dios Santo!*" and he swore and kissed his crossed thumb and forefinger. "And now? Look what you have done to me, to us, to your children!"

"We can get something at the *farmacia*! The doctor would surely have something to unglue the ticket."

"*¡Sí! ¡O sí!*" mocked Sinesio. "Sure! We have time to go there."

Time runs faster when there is a deadline. The last bus downtown was due in a few minutes. They tried to take the broken glass pane off the door but he was afraid the ticket would tear more. Sinesio's fear and anger mounted with each glance at the clock.

In frustration, he pushed the door out into the downpour and swung it back into the house, cracking the molding and the inside hinges. One more swing, pulling, twisting, splintering, and Sinesio broke the door completely off.

Faustina stood back with hands over her mouth as she recited a litany to all the *santos* and virgins in heaven as the rain blew into their home and splashed her face wet.

Sinesio's face was also drenched. But Faustina could not tell if it was from the rain or tears of anger, as he put the door over his head and ran down the streaming pathway to catch the *autobús*.

RAYMOND CARVER

Raymond Carver (1938–1988) grew up in a logging town in Oregon, where his father worked in a sawmill and his mother held odd jobs. After graduating from high school, Carver married at the age of nineteen and had two children. Working hard to support his wife and family, he managed to enroll briefly in 1958 as a student at Chico State College in California, where he took a creative writing course from a then nearly unknown young novelist named John Gardner. Carver remembered that he decided to try to become a writer because he liked to read pulp novels and magazines about hunting and fishing. He credited Gardner for giving him a strong sense of direction as a writer: "A writer's values and craft. This is what the man taught and what he stood for, and this is what I've kept by me in the years since that brief but all-important time."

In 1963 Carver received his B.A. from Humboldt State College in northern California. The following year he studied writing at the University of Iowa. But the 1960s, he said, were difficult for him and his wife:

> I learned a long time ago when my kids were little and we had no money, and we were working our hearts out and weren't getting anywhere, even though we were giving it our best, my wife and I, that there were more important things than writing a poem or a story. That was a very hard realization for me to come to. But it came to me, and I had to accept it or die. Getting milk and food on the table, getting the rent paid, if a choice had to be made, then I had to forgo writing.

Carver's desire to be a writer was so strong that he kept on writing long after the "cold facts" of his life told him he ought to quit. His first collection of stories, *Will You Please Be Quiet, Please?* was nominated for the National Book Award in 1976. Four more collections of stories followed, along with five books of poetry, before his death from lung cancer.

Critics have noted that the rapid evolution of Carver's style causes his fiction to fall into three distinct periods. The tentative writing in his first book of stories – many of which he subsequently revised and republished – was followed by a paring down of his prose. This resulted in the hard-edged and detached **minimalist style** of his middle period, exemplified by the stories in his collection *What We Talk About When We Talk About Love* (1981). In his final period, Carver developed a more expansive style, as in the collection *Cathedral* (1983) and the new stories in his last collection, *Where I'm Calling From: New and Selected Stories* (1988).

Influenced by the cadence of Ernest Hemingway's sentences, Carver also believed in simplicity. He wrote,

> It's possible, in a poem or a short story, to write about commonplace things and objects using commonplace but precise language, and to endow those things – a chair, a window curtain, a fork, a stone, a woman's earring – with immense, even startling power. . . . If the words are heavy with the writer's own unbridled emotions, or if they are imprecise and inaccurate for some other reason – if the words are in any way blurred – the reader's eyes will slide right over them and nothing will be achieved. The reader's own artistic sense will simply not be engaged.

CONNECTION Raymond Carver, "Popular Mechanics," page 28.

WEB Research Raymond Carver at bedfordstmartins.com/rewritinglit.

Cathedral

1981

This blind man, an old friend of my wife's, he was on his way to spend the night. His wife had died. So he was visiting the dead wife's relatives in Connecticut. He called my wife from his in-laws'. Arrangements were made. He would come by train, a five-hour trip, and my wife would meet him at the station. She hadn't seen him since she worked for him one summer in Seattle ten years ago. But she and the blind man had kept in touch. They made tapes and mailed them back and forth. I wasn't enthusiastic about his visit. He was no one I knew. And his being blind bothered me. My idea of blindness came from the movies. In the movies, the blind moved slowly and never laughed. Sometimes they were led by seeing-eye dogs. A blind man in my house was not something I looked forward to.

That summer in Seattle she had needed a job. She didn't have any money. The man she was going to marry at the end of the summer was in officers' training school. He didn't have any money, either. But she was in love with the guy, and he was in love with her, etc. She'd seen something in the paper: HELP WANTED—*Reading to Blind Man*, and a telephone number. She phoned and went over, was hired on the spot. She'd worked with this blind man all summer. She read stuff to him, case studies, reports, that sort of thing. She helped him organize his little office in the county social-service department. They'd become good friends, my wife and the blind man. How do I know these things? She told me. And she told me something else. On her last day in the office, the blind man asked if he could touch her face. She agreed to this. She told me he touched his fingers to every part of her face, her nose—even her neck! She never forgot it. She even tried to write a poem about it. She was always trying to write a poem. She wrote a poem or two every year, usually after something really important had happened to her.

When we first started going out together, she showed me the poem. In the poem, she recalled his fingers and the way they had moved around over her face. In the poem, she talked about what she had felt at the time, about what went through her mind when the blind man touched her nose and lips. I can remember I didn't think much of the poem. Of course, I didn't tell her that. Maybe I just don't understand poetry. I admit it's not the first thing I reach for when I pick up something to read.

Anyway, this man who'd first enjoyed her favors, the officer-to-be, he'd been her childhood sweetheart. So okay. I'm saying that at the end of the summer she let the blind man run his hands over her face, said goodbye to him, married her childhood etc., who was now a commissioned officer, and she moved away from Seattle. But they'd kept in touch, she and the blind man. She made the first contact after a year or so. She called him up one night from an Air Force base in Alabama. She wanted to talk. They talked. He asked her to send him a tape and tell him about her life. She did this. She sent the tape. On the tape, she told the blind man about her husband and about their life together in the military. She told the blind man she loved her husband but she didn't like it where they lived and she didn't like it that he was a part of the military-industrial thing. She told the blind man she'd written a poem and he was in it. She told him that she was writing a poem about what it was like to be an Air Force officer's wife. The poem wasn't finished yet. She was still writing it. The blind man made a tape. He sent her the tape. She made a tape. This went on for years. My wife's officer was posted to one base and then another. She sent tapes from Moody AFB, McGuire, McConnell, and finally Travis, near Sacramento, where one night she got to feeling lonely and cut off from people she kept losing in that moving-around life. She got to feeling she couldn't go it another step. She went in and swallowed all the pills and capsules in the medicine chest and washed them down with a bottle of gin. Then she got into a hot bath and passed out.

But instead of dying, she got sick. She threw up. Her officer—why should he have a name? he was the childhood sweetheart, and what more does he want?—came home from somewhere, found her, and called the ambulance. In time, she put it all on a tape and sent the tape to the blind man. Over the years, she put all kinds of stuff on tapes and sent the tapes off lickety-split. Next to writing a poem every year, I think it was her chief means of recreation. On one tape, she told the blind man she'd decided to live away from her officer for a time. On another tape, she told him about her divorce. She and I began going out, and of course she told her blind man about it. She told him everything, or so it seemed to me. Once she asked me if I'd like to hear the latest tape from the blind man. This was a year ago. I was on the tape, she said. So I said okay, I'd listen to it. I got us drinks and we settled down in the living room. We made ready to listen. First she inserted the tape into the player and adjusted a couple of dials. Then she pushed a lever. The tape squeaked and someone began to talk in this loud voice. She lowered the volume. After a few minutes of harmless chitchat, I heard my own name in the mouth of this stranger, this blind man I didn't even know! And then this: "From all you've said about him, I can only conclude—" But we were interrupted, a knock at the door, something, and we didn't ever get back to the tape. Maybe it was just as well. I'd heard all I wanted to.

Now this same blind man was coming to sleep in my house.

"Maybe I could take him bowling," I said to my wife. She was at the draining board doing scalloped potatoes. She put down the knife she was using and turned around.

"If you love me," she said, "you can do this for me. If you don't love me, okay. But if you had a friend, any friend, and the friend came to visit, I'd make him feel comfortable." She wiped her hands with the dish towel.

"I don't have any blind friends," I said.

"You don't have *any* friends," she said. "Period. Besides," she said, "goddamn it, his wife's just died! Don't you understand that? The man's lost his wife!"

I didn't answer. She'd told me a little about the blind man's wife. Her name was Beulah. Beulah! That's a name for a colored woman.

"Was his wife Negro?" I asked.

"Are you crazy?" my wife said. "Have you just flipped or something?" She picked up a potato. I saw it hit the floor, then roll under the stove. "What's wrong with you?" she said. "Are you drunk?"

"I'm just asking," I said.

Right then my wife filled me in with more detail than I cared to know. I made a drink and sat at the kitchen table to listen. Pieces of the story began to fall into place.

Beulah had gone to work for the blind man the summer after my wife had stopped working for him. Pretty soon Beulah and the blind man had themselves a church wedding. It was a little wedding—who'd want to go to such a wedding in the first place?—just the two of them, plus the minister and the minister's wife. But it was a church wedding just the same. It was what Beulah had wanted, he'd said. But even then Beulah must have been carrying the cancer in her glands. After they had been inseparable for eight years—my wife's word, *inseparable*—Beulah's health went into a rapid decline. She died in a Seattle hospital room, the blind man sitting beside the bed and holding on to her hand. They'd married, lived and worked together, slept together—had sex, sure—and then the blind man had to bury her. All this without his having ever seen what the goddamned woman looked like. It was beyond my understanding. Hearing this, I felt sorry for the blind man for a little bit. And then I found myself thinking what a pitiful life this woman must have led. Imagine a woman who could never see herself as she was seen in the eyes of her loved one. A woman who could go on day after day and never receive the smallest compliment from her beloved. A woman whose husband could never read the expression on her face, be it misery or something better. Someone who could wear makeup or not—what difference to him? She could, if she wanted, wear green eye-shadow around one eye, a straight pin in her nostril, yellow slacks and purple shoes, no matter. And then to slip off into death, the blind man's hand on her hand, his blind eyes streaming tears—I'm imagining now—her last thought maybe this: that he never even knew what she looked like, and she on an express to the grave. Robert was left with a small insurance policy and half of a twenty-peso Mexican coin. The other half of the coin went into the box with her. Pathetic.

So when the time rolled around, my wife went to the depot to pick him up. With nothing to do but wait—sure, I blamed him for that—I was having a drink and watching the TV when I heard the car pull into the drive. I got up from the sofa with my drink and went to the window to have a look.

I saw my wife laughing as she parked the car. I saw her get out of the car and shut the door. She was still wearing a smile. Just amazing. She went around to the other side of the car to where the blind man was already starting to get out. This blind man, feature this, he was wearing a full beard! A beard on a blind man! Too much, I say. The blind man reached into the back seat and dragged out a suitcase. My wife took his arm, shut the car door, and, talking all the way, moved him down the drive and then up the steps to the front porch. I turned off the TV. I finished my drink, rinsed the glass, dried my hands. Then I went to the door.

My wife said, "I want you to meet Robert. Robert, this is my husband. I've told you all about him." She was beaming. She had this blind man by his coat sleeve.

The blind man let go of his suitcase and up came his hand.

I took it. He squeezed hard, held my hand, and then he let it go.

"I feel like we've already met," he boomed.

"Likewise," I said. I didn't know what else to say. Then I said, "Welcome. I've heard a lot about you." We began to move then, a little group, from the porch into the living room, my wife guiding him by the arm. The blind man was carrying his suitcase in his other hand. My wife said things like, "To your left here, Robert. That's right. Now watch it, there's a chair. That's it. Sit down right here. This is the sofa. We just bought this sofa two weeks ago."

I started to say something about the old sofa. I'd liked that old sofa. But I didn't say anything. Then I wanted to say something else, small-talk, about the scenic ride along the Hudson. How going *to* New York, you should sit on the right-hand side of the train, and coming *from* New York, the left-hand side.

"Did you have a good train ride?" I said. "Which side of the train did you sit on, by the way?"

"What a question, which side!" my wife said. "What's it matter which side?" she said.

"I just asked," I said.

"Right side," the blind man said. "I hadn't been on a train in nearly forty years. Not since I was a kid. With my folks. That's been a long time. I'd nearly forgotten the sensation. I have winter in my beard now," he said. "So I've been told, anyway. Do I look distinguished, my dear?" the blind man said to my wife.

"You look distinguished, Robert," she said. "Robert," she said. "Robert, it's just so good to see you."

My wife finally took her eyes off the blind man and looked at me. I had the feeling she didn't like what she saw. I shrugged.

I've never met, or personally known, anyone who was blind. This blind man was late forties, a heavy-set, balding man with stooped shoulders, as if he carried a great weight there. He wore brown slacks, brown shoes, a light-brown shirt, a tie, a sports coat. Spiffy. He also had this full beard. But he didn't use a cane and he didn't wear dark glasses. I'd always thought dark glasses were a must for the blind. Fact was, I wished he had a pair. At first glance, his eyes looked like anyone else's eyes. But if you look close, there was something different about them. Too much white in the iris, for one thing, and the pupils seemed to move around in the sockets without his knowing it or being able to stop it. Creepy. As I stared at his face, I saw the left pupil turn in toward his nose while the other made an effort to keep in one place. But it was only an effort, for that eye was on the roam without his knowing it or wanting it to be.

I said, "Let me get you a drink. What's your pleasure? We have a little of everything. It's one of our pastimes."

"Bub, I'm a Scotch man myself," he said fast enough in this big voice.

"Right," I said. Bub! "Sure you are, I knew it."

He let his fingers touch his suitcase, which was sitting alongside the sofa. He was taking his bearings. I didn't blame him for that.

"I'll move that up to your room," my wife said.

"No, that's fine," the blind man said loudly. "It can go up when I go up."

"A little water with the Scotch?" I said.

"Very little," he said.

"I knew it," I said.

He said, "Just a tad. The Irish actor, Barry Fitzgerald? I'm like that fellow. When I drink water, Fitzgerald said, I drink water. When I drink whiskey, I drink whiskey." My wife laughed. The blind man brought his hand up under his beard. He lifted his beard slowly and let it drop.

I did the drinks, three big glasses of Scotch with a splash of water in each. Then we made ourselves comfortable and talked about Robert's travels. First the long flight from the West Coast to Connecticut, we covered that. Then from Connecticut up here by train. We had another drink concerning that leg of the trip.

I remembered having read somewhere that the blind didn't smoke because, as speculation had it, they couldn't see the smoke they exhaled. I thought I knew that much and that much only about blind people. But this blind man smoked his cigarette down to the nubbin and then lit another one. This blind man filled his ashtray and my wife emptied it.

When we sat down at the table for dinner, we had another drink. My wife heaped Robert's plate with cube steak, scalloped potatoes, green beans. I buttered him up two slices of bread. I said, "Here's bread and butter for you." I swallowed some of my drink. "Now let us pray," I said, and the blind man lowered his head. My wife looked at me, her mouth agape. "Pray the phone won't ring and the food doesn't get cold," I said.

We dug in. We ate everything there was to eat on the table. We ate like there was no tomorrow. We didn't talk. We ate. We scarfed. We grazed that table. We were into serious eating. The blind man had right away located his foods, he knew just where everything was on his plate. I watched with admiration as he used his knife and fork on the meat. He'd cut two pieces of meat, fork the meat into his mouth, and then go all out for the scalloped potatoes, the beans next, and then he'd tear off a hunk of buttered bread and eat that. He'd follow this up with a big drink of milk. It didn't seem to bother him to use his fingers once in a while, either.

We finished everything, including half a strawberry pie. For a few moments, we sat as if stunned. Sweat beaded on our faces. Finally, we got up from the table and left the dirty plates. We didn't look back. We took ourselves into the living room and sank into our places again. Robert and my wife sat on the sofa. I took the big chair. We had us two or three more drinks while they talked about the major things that had come to pass for them in the past ten years. For the most part, I just listened. Now and then I joined in. I didn't want him to think I'd left the room, and I didn't want her to think I was feeling left out. They talked of things that had happened to them — to them! — these past ten years. I waited in vain to hear my name on my wife's sweet lips: "And then my dear husband came into my life" — something like that. But I heard nothing of the sort. More talk of Robert. Robert had done a little of everything, it seemed, a regular blind jack-of-all-trades. But most recently he and his wife had had an Amway distributorship, from which, I gathered, they'd earned their living, such as it was. The blind man was also a ham radio operator. He talked in his loud voice about conversations he'd had with fellow operators in Guam, in the Philippines, in Alaska, and even in Tahiti. He said he'd have a lot of friends there if he ever wanted to go visit those places. From time to time, he'd turn his blind face toward me, put his hand under his beard, ask me something. How long had I been in my present position? (Three years.) Did I like my work? (I didn't.) Was I going to stay with it? (What were the options?) Finally, when I thought he was beginning to run down, I got up and turned on the TV.

My wife looked at me with irritation. She was heading toward a boil. Then she looked at the blind man and said, "Robert, do you have a TV?"

The blind man said, "My dear, I have two TVs. I have a color set and a black-and-white thing, an old relic. It's funny, but if I turn the TV on, and I'm always turning it on, I turn on the color set. It's funny, don't you think?"

I didn't know what to say to that. I had absolutely nothing to say to that. No opinions. So I watched the news program and tried to listen to what the announcer was saying.

"This is a color TV," the blind man said. "Don't ask me how, but I can tell."

"We traded up a while ago," I said.

The blind man had another taste of his drink. He lifted his beard, sniffed it, and let it fall. He leaned forward on the sofa. He positioned his ashtray on the coffee table, then put the lighter to his cigarette. He leaned back on the sofa and crossed his legs at the ankles.

My wife covered her mouth, and then she yawned. She stretched. She said, "I think I'll go upstairs and put on my robe. I think I'll change into something else. Robert, you make yourself comfortable," she said.

"I'm comfortable," the blind man said.

"I want you to feel comfortable in this house," she said.

"I am comfortable," the blind man said.

After she'd left the room, he and I listened to the weather report and then to the sports roundup. By that time, she'd been gone so long I didn't know if she was going to come back. I thought she might have gone to bed. I wished she'd come back downstairs. I didn't want to be left alone with a blind man. I asked him if he wanted another drink, and he said sure. Then I asked if he wanted to smoke some dope with me. I said I'd just rolled a number. I hadn't, but I planned to do so in about two shakes.

"I'll try some with you," he said.

"Damn right," I said. "That's the stuff."

I got our drinks and sat down on the sofa with him. Then I rolled us two fat numbers. I lit one and passed it. I brought it to his fingers. He took it and inhaled.

"Hold it as long as you can," I said. I could tell he didn't know the first thing.

My wife came back downstairs wearing her pink robe and her pink slippers.

"What do I smell?" she said.

"We thought we'd have us some cannabis," I said.

My wife gave me a savage look. Then she looked at the blind man and said, "Robert, I didn't know you smoked."

He said, "I do now, my dear. There's a first time for everything. But I don't feel anything yet."

"This stuff is pretty mellow," I said. "This stuff is mild. It's dope you can reason with," I said. "It doesn't mess you up."

"Not much it doesn't, bub," he said, and laughed.

My wife sat on the sofa between the blind man and me. I passed her the number. She took it and toked and then passed it back to me. "Which way is this going?" she said. Then she said, "I shouldn't be smoking this. I can hardly keep my eyes open as it is. That dinner did me in. I shouldn't have eaten so much."

"It was the strawberry pie," the blind man said. "That's what did it," he said, and he laughed his big laugh. Then he shook his head.

"There's more strawberry pie," I said.

"Do you want some more, Robert?" my wife said.

"Maybe in a little while," he said.

We gave our attention to the TV. My wife yawned again. She said, "Your bed is made up when you feel like going to bed, Robert. I know you must have had a long day. When you're ready to go to bed, say so." She pulled his arm. "Robert?"

He came to and said, "I've had a real nice time. This beats tapes, doesn't it?"

I said, "Coming at you," and I put the number between his fingers. He inhaled, held the smoke, and then let it go. It was like he'd been doing it since he was nine years old.

"Thanks, bub," he said. "But I think this is all for me. I think I'm beginning to feel it," he said. He held the burning roach out for my wife.

"Same here," she said. "Ditto. Me, too." She took the roach and passed it to me. "I may just sit here for a while between you two guys with my eyes closed. But don't let me bother you, okay? Either one of you. If it bothers you, say so. Otherwise, I may just sit here with my eyes closed until you're ready to go to bed," she said. "Your bed's made up, Robert, when you're ready. It's right next to our room at the top of the stairs. We'll show you up when you're ready.

You wake me up now, you guys, if I fall asleep." She said that and then she closed her eyes and went to sleep.

The news program ended. I got up and changed the channel. I sat back down on the sofa. I wished my wife hadn't pooped out. Her head lay across the back of the sofa, her mouth open. She'd turned so that her robe had slipped away from her legs, exposing a juicy thigh. I reached to draw her robe back over her, and it was then that I glanced at the blind man. What the hell! I flipped the robe open again.

"You say when you want some strawberry pie," I said.

"I will," he said.

I said, "Are you tired? Do you want me to take you up to your bed? Are you ready to hit the hay?"

"Not yet," he said. "No, I'll stay up with you, bub. If that's all right. I'll stay up until you're ready to turn in. We haven't had a chance to talk. Know what I mean? I feel like me and her monopolized the evening." He lifted his beard and he let it fall. He picked up his cigarettes and his lighter.

"That's all right," I said. Then I said, "I'm glad for the company."

And I guess I was. Every night I smoked dope and stayed up as long as I could before I fell asleep. My wife and I hardly ever went to bed at the same time. When I did go to sleep, I had these dreams. Sometimes I'd wake up from one of them, my heart going crazy.

Something about the church and the Middle Ages was on the TV. Not your run-of-the-mill TV fare. I wanted to watch something else. I turned to the other channels. But there was nothing on them, either. So I turned back to the first channel and apologized.

"Bub, it's all right," the blind man said. "It's fine with me. Whatever you want to watch is okay. I'm always learning something. Learning never ends. It won't hurt me to learn something tonight. I got ears," he said.

We didn't say anything for a time. He was leaning forward with his head turned at me, his right ear aimed in the direction of the set. Very disconcerting. Now and then his eyelids drooped and then they snapped open again. Now and then he put his fingers into his beard and tugged, like he was thinking about something he was hearing on the television.

On the screen, a group of men wearing cowls was being set upon and tormented by men dressed in skeleton costumes and men dressed as devils. The men dressed as devils wore devil masks, horns, and long tails. This pageant was part of a procession. The Englishman who was narrating the thing said it took place in Spain once a year. I tried to explain to the blind man what was happening.

"Skeletons," he said. "I know about skeletons," he said, and he nodded.

The TV showed this one cathedral. Then there was a long, slow look at another one. Finally, the picture switched to the famous one in Paris, with its flying buttresses and its spires reaching up to the clouds. The camera pulled away to show the whole of the cathedral rising above the skyline.

There were times when the Englishman who was telling the thing would shut up, would simply let the camera move around over the cathedrals. Or else the camera would tour the countryside, men in fields walking behind oxen. I waited as long as I could. Then I felt I had to say something. I said, "They're showing the outside of this cathedral now. Gargoyles. Little statues carved to look like monsters. Now I guess they're in Italy. Yeah, they're in Italy. There's paintings on the walls of this one church."

"Are those fresco paintings, bub?" he asked, and he sipped from his drink.

I reached for my glass. But it was empty. I tried to remember what I could remember. "You're asking me are those frescoes?" I said. "That's a good question. I don't know."

The camera moved to a cathedral outside Lisbon. The differences in the Portuguese cathedral compared with the French and Italian were not that great. But they were there. Mostly the interior stuff. Then something occurred to me, and I said, "Something has occurred to me. Do you have any idea what a cathedral is? What they look like, that is? Do you follow me? If somebody says cathedral to you, do you have any notion what they're talking about? Do you know the difference between that and a Baptist church, say?"

He let the smoke dribble from his mouth. "I know they took hundreds of workers fifty or a hundred years to build," he said. "I just heard the man say that, of course. I know generations of the same families worked on a cathedral. I heard him say that too. The men who began their life's work on them, they never lived to see the completion of their work. In that wise, bub, they're no different from the rest of us, right?" He laughed. Then his eyelids drooped again. His head nodded. He seemed to be snoozing. Maybe he was imagining himself in Portugal. The TV was showing another cathedral now. This one was in Germany. The Englishman's voice droned on. "Cathedrals," the blind man said. He sat up and rolled his head back and forth. "If you want the truth, bub, that's about all I know. What I just said. What I heard him say. But maybe you could describe one to me? I wish you'd do it. I'd like that. If you want to know, I really don't have a good idea."

I stared hard at the shot of the cathedral on the TV. How could I even begin to describe it? But say my life depended on it. Say my life was being threatened by an insane guy who said I had to do it or else.

I stared some more at the cathedral before the picture flipped off into the countryside. There was no use. I turned to the blind man and said, "To begin with, they're very tall." I was looking around the room for clues. "They reach way up. Up and up. Toward the sky. They're so big, some of them, they have to have these supports. To help hold them up, so to speak. These supports are called buttresses. They remind me of viaducts, for some reason. But maybe you don't know viaducts, either? Sometimes the cathedrals have devils and such carved into the front. Sometimes lords and ladies. Don't ask me why this is," I said.

He was nodding. The whole upper part of his body seemed to be moving back and forth.

"I'm not doing so good, am I?" I said.

He stopped nodding and leaned forward on the edge of the sofa. As he listened to me, he was running his fingers through his beard. I wasn't getting through to him, I could see that. But he waited for me to go on just the same. He nodded, like he was trying to encourage me. I tried to think what else to say. "They're really big," I said. "They're massive. They're built of stone. Marble, too, sometimes. In those olden days, when they built cathedrals, men wanted to be close to God. In those olden days, God was an important part of everyone's life. You could tell this from their cathedral-building. I'm sorry," I said, "but it looks like that's the best I can do for you. I'm just no good at it."

"That's all right, bub," the blind man said. "Hey, listen. I hope you don't mind my asking you. Can I ask you something? Let me ask you a simple question, yes or no. I'm just curious and there's no offense. You're my host. But let me ask if you are in any way religious? You don't mind my asking?"

I shook my head. He couldn't see that, though. A wink is the same as a nod to a blind man. "I guess I don't believe in it. In anything. Sometimes it's hard. You know what I'm saying?"

"Sure I do," he said.

"Right," I said.

The Englishman was still holding forth. My wife sighed in her sleep. She drew a long breath and went on with her sleeping.

"You'll have to forgive me," I said. "But I can't tell you what a cathedral looks like. It just isn't in me to do it. I can't do any more than I've done."

The blind man sat very still, his head down, as he listened to me.

I said, "The truth is, cathedrals don't mean anything special to me. Nothing. Cathedrals. They're something to look at on late-night TV. That's all they are."

It was then that the blind man cleared his throat. He brought something up. He took a handkerchief from his back pocket. Then he said, "I get it, bub. It's okay. It happens. Don't worry about it," he said. "Hey, listen to me. Will you do me a favor? I got an idea. Why don't you find us some heavy paper? And a pen. We'll do something. We'll draw one together. Get us a pen and some heavy paper. Go on, bub, get the stuff," he said.

So I went upstairs. My legs felt like they didn't have any strength in them. They felt like they did after I'd done some running. In my wife's room, I looked around. I found some ballpoints in a little basket on her table. And then I tried to think where to look for the kind of paper he was talking about.

Downstairs, in the kitchen, I found a shopping bag with onion skins in the bottom of the bag. I emptied the bag and shook it. I brought it into the living room and sat down with it near his legs. I moved some things, smoothed the wrinkles from the bag, spread it out on the coffee table.

The blind man got down from the sofa and sat next to me on the carpet.

He ran his fingers over the paper. He went up and down the sides of the paper. The edges, even the edges. He fingered the corners.

"All right," he said. "All right, let's do her."

He found my hand, the hand with the pen. He closed his hand over my hand. "Go ahead, bub, draw," he said. "Draw. You'll see. I'll follow along with you. It'll be okay. Just begin now like I'm telling you. You'll see. Draw," the blind man said.

So I began. First I drew a box that looked like a house. It could have been the house I lived in. Then I put a roof on it. At either end of the roof, I drew spires. Crazy.

"Swell," he said. "Terrific. You're doing fine," he said.

"Never thought anything like this could happen in your lifetime, did you, bub? Well, it's a strange life, we all know that. Go on now. Keep it up."

I put in windows with arches. I drew flying buttresses. I hung great doors. I couldn't stop. The TV station went off the air. I put down the pen and closed and opened my fingers. The blind man felt round over the paper. He moved the tips of his fingers over the paper, all over what I had drawn, and he nodded.

"Doing fine," the blind man said.

I took up the pen again, and he found my hand. I kept at it. I'm no artist. But I kept drawing just the same.

My wife opened up her eyes and gazed at us. She sat up on the sofa, her robe hanging open. She said, "What are you doing? Tell me, I want to know."

I didn't answer her.

The blind man said, "We're drawing a cathedral. Me and him are working on it. Press hard," he said to me. "That's right. That's good," he said. "Sure. You got it, bub. I can tell. You didn't think you could. But you can, can't you? You're cooking with gas now. You know what I'm saying? We're going to really have us something here in a minute. How's the old arm?" he said. "Put some people in there now. What's a cathedral without people?"

My wife said, "What's going on? Robert, what are you doing? What's going on?"

"It's all right," he said to her. "Close your eyes now," the blind man said to me.

I did it. I closed them just like he said.

"Are they closed? he said. "Don't fudge."

"They're closed," I said.

"Keep them that way," he said. He said, "Don't stop now. Draw."

So we kept on with it. His fingers rode my fingers as my hand went over the paper. It was like nothing else in my life up to now.

Then he said, "I think that's it. I think you got it," he said. "Take a look. What do you think?"

But I had my eyes closed. I thought I'd keep them that way for a little longer. I thought it was something I ought to do.

"Well?" he said. "Are you looking?"

My eyes were still closed. I was in my house. I knew that. But I didn't feel like I was inside anything.

"It's really something," I said.

COMMENTARIES

RAYMOND CARVER

Raymond Carver offers a clear example of how a contemporary author has responded to the work of earlier short story writers by following a line of thought that links him with his predecessors. Carver acknowledged the influence of Ernest Hemingway and Flannery O'Connor in his essay "On Writing." He also described his class with the young novelist John Gardner at Chico State College in California in "Creative Writing 101."

On Writing 1981

Back in the mid-1960s, I found I was having trouble concentrating my attention on long narrative fiction. For a time I experienced difficulty in trying to read it as well as in attempting to write it. My attention span had gone out on me; I no longer had the patience to try to write novels. It's an involved story, too tedious to talk about here. But I know it has much to do now with why I write poems and short stories. Get in, get out. Don't linger. Go on. It could be that I lost any great ambitions at about the same time, in my late twenties. If I did, I think it was good it happened. Ambition and a little luck are good things for a writer to have going for him. Too much ambition and bad luck, or no luck at all, can be killing. There has to be talent.

Some writers have a bunch of talent; I don't know any writers who are without it. But a unique and exact way of looking at things, and finding the right context for expressing that way of looking, that's something else. *The World According to Garp* is, of course, the marvelous world according to John Irving. There is another world according to Flannery O'Connor, and others according to William Faulkner and Ernest Hemingway. There are worlds according to Cheever, Updike, Singer, Stanley Elkin, Ann Beattie, Cynthia Ozick, Donald Barthelme, Mary Robison, William Kittredge, Barry Hannah, Ursula K. Le Guin. Every great or even every very good writer makes the world over according to his own specifications.

It's akin to style, what I'm talking about, but it isn't style alone. It is the writer's particular and unmistakable signature on everything he writes. It is his world and no other. This is one of the things that distinguishes one writer from another. Not talent. There's plenty of that around. But a writer who has some special way of looking at things and who gives artistic expression to that way of looking: that writer may be around for a time.

Isak Dinesen said that she wrote a little every day, without hope and without despair. Someday I'll put that on a three-by-five card and tape it to the wall beside my desk. I have some three-by-five cards on the wall now. "Fundamental accuracy of statement is the ONE sole morality of writing." Ezra Pound. It is not everything by ANY means, but if a writer has "fundamental accuracy of statement" going for him, he's at least on the right track.

I have a three-by-five up there with this fragment of a sentence from a story by Chekhov: ". . . and suddenly everything became clear to him." I find these words filled with wonder and possibility. I love their simple clarity, and the hint of revelation that's implied. There is mystery, too. What has been unclear before? Why is it just now becoming clear? What's happened? Most of all—what now? There are consequences as a result of such sudden awakenings. I feel a sharp sense of relief—and anticipation.

I overheard the writer Geoffrey Wolff say "No cheap tricks" to a group of writing students. That should go on a three-by-five card. I'd amend it a little to "No tricks." Period. I hate tricks. At the first sign of a trick or a gimmick in a piece of fiction, a cheap trick or even an elaborate trick, I tend to look for cover. Tricks are ultimately boring, and I get bored easily, which may go along with my not having much of an attention span. But extremely clever chi-chi writing, or just plain tomfoolery writing, puts me to sleep. Writers don't need tricks or gimmicks or even necessarily need to be the smartest fellows on the block. At the risk of appearing foolish, a writer sometimes needs to be able to just stand and gape at this or that thing—a sunset or an old shoe—in absolute and simple amazement.

Some months back, in the *New York Times Book Review*, John Barth said that ten years ago most of the students in his fiction writing seminar were interested in "formal innovation," and this no longer seems to be the case. He's a little worried that writers are going to start writing mom-and-pop novels in the 1980s. He worries that experimentation may be on the way out, along with liberalism. I get a little nervous if I find myself within earshot of somber discussions about "formal innovation" in fiction writing. Too often "experimentation" is a license to be careless, silly, or imitative in the writing. Even worse, a license to try to brutalize or alienate the reader. Too often such writing gives us no news of the world, or else describes a desert landscape and that's all—a few dunes and lizards here and there, but no people; a place uninhabited by anything recognizably human, a place of interest only to a few scientific specialists.

It should be noted that real experiment in fiction is original, hard-earned and cause for rejoicing. But someone else's way of looking at things—Barthelme's, for instance—should not be chased after by other writers. It won't work. There is only one Barthelme, and for another writer to try to appropriate Barthelme's peculiar sensibility or mise en scène under the rubric of innovation is for that writer to mess around with chaos and disaster and, worse, self-deception. The real experimenters have to Make It New, as Pound urged, and in the process have to find things out for themselves. But if writers haven't taken leave of their senses, they also want to stay in touch with us, they want to carry news from their world to ours.

It's possible, in a poem or a short story, to write about commonplace things and objects using commonplace but precise language, and to endow those things—a chair, a window curtain, a fork, a stone, a woman's earring—with immense, even startling power. It is possible to write a line of seemingly innocuous dialogue and have it send a chill along the reader's spine—the source of artistic delight, as Nabokov would have it. That's the kind of writing that most interests me. I hate sloppy or haphazard writing whether it flies under the banner of experimentation or else is just clumsily rendered realism. In Isaac Babel's wonderful short story, "Guy de Maupassant," the narrator has this to say about the writing of fiction: "No iron can pierce the heart with such force as a period put just at the right place." This too ought to go on a three-by-five.

Evan Connell said once that he knew he was finished with a short story when he found himself going through it and taking out commas and then going through the story again and putting commas back in the same places. I like that way of working on something. I respect that kind of care for what is being done. That's all we have, finally, the words, and they had better be the right ones, with the punctuation in the right places so that they can best say what they are meant to say. If the words are heavy with the writer's own unbridled emotions, or if they are imprecise and inaccurate for some other reason—if the words are in any way blurred—the reader's eyes will slide right over them and nothing will be achieved. The reader's own artistic sense will simply not be engaged. Henry James called this sort of hapless writing "weak specification."

I have friends who've told me they had to hurry a book because they needed the money, their editor or their wife was leaning on them or leaving them—something, some apology for the writing not being very good. "It would have been better if I'd taken the time." I was dumbfounded when I heard a novelist friend say this. I still am, if I think about it, which I don't. It's none of my business. But if the writing can't be made as good as it is within us to make it, then why do it? In the end, the satisfaction of having done our best, and the proof of that labor, is the one thing we can take into the grave. I wanted to say to my friend, for heaven's sake go do something else. There have to be easier and maybe more honest ways to try and earn a living. Or else just do it to the best of your abilities, your talents, and then don't justify or make excuses. Don't complain, don't explain.

In an essay called, simply enough, "Writing Short Stories," Flannery O'Connor talks about writing as an act of discovery. O'Connor says she most often did not know where she was going when she sat down to work on a short story. She says she doubts that many writers know where they are going when they begin something. She uses "Good Country People" as an example of how she put together a short story whose ending she could not even guess at until she was nearly there:

> When I started writing that story, I didn't know there was going to be a Ph.D. with a wooden leg in it. I merely found myself one morning writing a description of two women I knew something about, and before I realized it, I had equipped one of them with a daughter with a wooden leg. I brought in the Bible salesman, but I had no idea what I was going to do with him. I didn't know he was going to steal that wooden leg until ten or twelve lines before he did it, but when I found out that this was what was going to happen, I realized it was inevitable.

When I read this some years ago it came as a shock that she, or anyone for that matter, wrote stories in this fashion. I thought this was my uncomfortable secret, and I was a little uneasy with it. For sure I thought this way of working on a short story somehow revealed my own shortcomings. I remember being tremendously heartened by reading what she had to say on the subject.

I once sat down to write what turned out to be a pretty good story, though only the first sentence of the story had offered itself to me when I began it. For several days I'd been going around with this sentence in my head: "He was running the vacuum cleaner when the telephone rang." I knew a story was there and that it wanted telling. I felt it in my bones, that a story belonged with that beginning, if I could just have the time to write it. I found the time, an entire day—twelve, fifteen hours even—if I wanted to make use of it. I did, and I sat down in the morning and wrote the first sentence, and other sentences promptly began to attach themselves. I made the story just as I'd make a poem; one line and then the next, and the next. Pretty soon I could see a story, and I knew it was my story, the one I'd been wanting to write.

I like it when there is some feeling of threat or sense of menace in short stories. I think a little menace is fine to have in a story. For one thing, it's good for the circulation. There has to be tension, a sense that something is imminent, that certain things are in relentless motion, or else, most often, there simply won't be a story. What creates tension in a piece of fiction is partly the way the concrete words are linked together to make up the visible action of the story. But it's also the things that are left out, that are implied, the landscape just under the smooth (but sometimes broken and unsettled) surface of things.

V. S. Pritchett's° definition of a short story is "something glimpsed from the corner of the eye, in passing." Notice the "glimpse" part of this. First the glimpse. Then the glimpse given life, turned into something that illuminates the moment and may, if we're lucky—that word again—have even further-ranging consequences and meaning. The short story writer's task is to invest the glimpse with all that is in his power. He'll bring his intelligence and literary skill to bear (his talent), his sense of proportion and sense of the fitness of things: of how things out there really are and how he sees those things—like no one else sees them. And this is done through the use of clear and specific language, language used so as to bring to life the details that will light up the story for the reader. For the details to be concrete and convey meaning, the language must be accurate and precisely given. The words can be so precise they may even sound flat, but they can still carry; if used right, they can hit all the notes.

Creative Writing 101

1983

A long time ago—it was the summer of 1958—my wife and I and our two baby children moved from Yakima, Washington, to a little town outside of Chico, California. There we found an old house and paid twenty-five dollars a month rent. In order to finance this move, I'd had to borrow a hundred and twenty-five dollars from a druggist I'd delivered prescriptions for, a man named Bill Barton.

V. S. Pritchett: English master of the short story and literary critic (1900–1997).

This is by way of saying that in those days my wife and I were stone broke. We had to eke out a living, but the plan was that I would take classes at what was then called Chico State College. But for as far back as I can remember, long before we moved to California in search of a different life and our slice of the American pie, I'd wanted to be a writer. I wanted to write, and I wanted to write anything—fiction, of course, but also poetry, plays, scripts, articles for *Sports Afield, True, Argosy,* and *Rogue* (some of the magazines I was then reading), pieces for the local newspaper—anything that involved putting words together to make something coherent and of interest to someone besides myself. But at the time of our move, I felt in my bones I had to get some education in order to go along with being a writer. I put a very high premium on education then—much higher in those days than now, I'm sure, but that's because I'm older and have an education. Understand that nobody in my family had ever gone to college or for that matter had got beyond the mandatory eighth grade in high school. I didn't know *anything,* but I knew I didn't know anything.

So along with this desire to get an education, I had this very strong desire to write; it was a desire so strong that, with the encouragement I was given in college, and the insight acquired, I kept on writing long after "good sense" and the "cold facts"—the "realities" of my life told me, time and again, that I ought to quit, stop the dreaming, quietly go ahead and do something else.

That fall at Chico State I enrolled in classes that most freshman students have to take, but I enrolled as well for something called Creative Writing 101. This course was going to be taught by a new faculty member named John Gardner, who was already surrounded by a bit of mystery and romance. It was said that he'd taught previously at Oberlin College but had left there for some reason that wasn't made clear. One student said Gardner had been fired—students, like everyone else, thrive on rumor and intrigue—and another student said Gardner had simply quit after some kind of flap. Someone else said his teaching load at Oberlin, four or five classes of freshman English each semester, had been too heavy and that he couldn't find time to write. For it was said that Gardner was a real, that is to say a practicing, writer—someone who had written novels and short stories. In any case, he was going to teach CW 101 at Chico State, and I signed up.

I was excited about taking a course from a real writer. I'd never laid eyes on a writer before, and I was in awe. But where were these novels and short stories, I wanted to know. Well, nothing had been published yet. It was said that he couldn't get his work published and that he carried it around with him in boxes. (After I became his student, I was to see those boxes of manuscript. Gardner had become aware of my difficulty in finding a place to work. He knew I had a young family and cramped quarters at home. He offered me the key to his office. I see that gift now as a turning point. It was a gift not made casually, and I took it, I think, as a kind of mandate—for that's what it was. I spent part of every Saturday and Sunday in his office, which is where he kept the boxes of manuscript. The boxes were stacked up on the floor beside the desk. *Nickel Mountain,* grease-pencilled on one of the boxes, is the only title I recall. But it was in his office, within sight of his unpublished books, that I undertook my first serious attempts at writing.) . . .

For short story writers in his class, the requirement was one story, ten to fifteen pages in length. For people who wanted to write a novel—I think there must have been one or two of these souls—a chapter of around twenty pages, along with an outline of the rest. The kicker was that this one short story, or the chapter of the novel, might have to be revised ten times in the course of the semester for Gardner to be satisfied with it. It was a basic tenet of his that a writer found what he wanted to say in the ongoing process of seeing what he'd said. And this seeing, or seeing more clearly, came about through revision. He *believed* in revision, endless revision; it was something very close to his heart and something he felt was vital for writers, at whatever stage of their development. And he never seemed to lose patience rereading a student story, even though he might have seen it in five previous incarnations.

I think his idea of a short story in 1958 was still pretty much his idea of a short story in 1982; it was something that had a recognizable beginning, middle, and an end to it. Once in a while he'd go to the blackboard and draw a diagram to illustrate a point he wanted to make about rising or falling emotion in a story—peaks, valleys, plateaus, resolution, *denouement*, things like that. Try as I might, I couldn't muster a great deal of interest or really understand this side of things, the stuff he put on the blackboard. But what I did understand was the way he would comment on a student story that was undergoing class discussion. Gardner might wonder aloud about the author's reasons for writing a story about a crippled person, say, and leaving out the fact of the character's crippledness until the very end of the story. "So you think it's a good idea not to let the reader know this man is crippled until the last sentence?" His tone of voice conveyed his disapproval, and it didn't take more than an instant for everyone in class, including the author of the story, to see that it wasn't a good strategy to use. Any strategy that kept important and necessary information away from the reader in the hope of overcoming him by surprise at the end of the story was cheating.

In class he was always referring to writers whose names I was not familiar with. Or if I knew their names, I'd never read the work. . . . He talked about James Joyce and Flaubert and Isak Dinesen as if they lived just down the road, in Yuba City. He said, "I'm here to tell you who to read as well as teach you how to write." I'd leave class in a daze and make straight for the library to find books by these writers he was talking about.

Hemingway and Faulkner were the reigning authors in those days. But altogether I'd probably read at the most two or three books by these fellows. Anyway, they were so well-known and so much talked about, they couldn't be all that good, could they? I remember Gardner telling me, "Read all the Faulkner you can get your hands on, and then read all of Hemingway to clean the Faulkner out of your system."

He introduced us to the "little" or literary periodicals by bringing a box of these magazines to class one day and passing them around so that we could acquaint ourselves with their names, see what they looked like and what they felt like to hold in the hand. He told us that this was where most of the best fiction in the country and just about all of the poetry was appearing. Fiction, poetry, literary essays, book reviews of recent books, criticism of *living* authors *by* living authors. I felt wild with discovery in those days.

For the seven or eight of us who were in his class, he ordered heavy black binders and told us we should keep our written work in these. He kept his own work in such binders, he said, and of course that settled it for us. We carried our stories in those binders and felt we were special, exclusive, singled out from others. And so we were.

I don't know how Gardner might have been with other students when it came time to have conferences with them about their work. I suspect he gave everybody a good amount of attention. But it was and still is my impression that during that period he took my stories more seriously, read them closer and more carefully, than I had any right to expect. I was completely unprepared for the kind of criticism I received from him. Before our conference he would have marked up my story, crossing out unacceptable sentences, phrases, individual words, even some of the punctuation; and he gave me to understand that these deletions were not negotiable. In other cases he would bracket sentences, phrases, or individual words, and these were items we'd talk about, these cases were negotiable. And he wouldn't hesitate to add something to what I'd written—a word here and there, or else a few words, maybe a sentence that would make clear what I was trying to say. We'd discuss commas in my story as if nothing else in the world mattered more at that moment—and, indeed, it did not. He was always looking to find something to praise. When there was a sentence, a line of dialogue, or a narrative passage that he liked, something that he thought "worked" and moved the story along in some pleasant or unexpected way, he'd write "Nice" in the margin, or else "Good!" And seeing these comments, my heart would lift.

It was close, line-by-line criticism he was giving me, and the reasons behind the criticism, why something ought to be this way instead of that; and it was invaluable to me in my development as a writer. After this kind of detailed talk about the text, we'd talk about the larger concerns of the story, the "problem" it was trying to throw light on, the conflict it was trying to grapple with, and how the story might or might not fit into the grand scheme of story writing. It was his conviction that if the words in the story were blurred because of the author's insensitivity, carelessness, or sentimentality, then the story suffered from a tremendous handicap. But there was something even worse and something that must be avoided at all costs: if the words and the sentiments were dishonest, the author was faking it, writing about things he didn't care about or believe in, then nobody could ever care anything about it.

A writer's values and craft. This is what the man taught and what he stood for, and this is what I've kept by me in the years since that brief but all-important time.

ANTON CHEKHOV

Anton Chekhov (1860–1904), the Russian short story writer and playwright, wrote his first stories while he was a medical student at Moscow University, to help his family pay off debts. His grandfather had been a serf who had bought his freedom. His father was an unsuccessful grocer in Taganrog, in the southwestern part of the country. After completing medical school, Chekhov became an assistant to the district doctor in a provincial town. His early stories were mostly humorous sketches that he first published in newspapers under various pseudonyms, keeping his own name for his medical articles. But the popularity of these sketches made him decide to become a writer.

Chekhov's first two collections of short stories, published in 1886 and 1887, were acclaimed by readers, and from that time on he was able to devote all his time to writing. He bought a small estate near Moscow, where he lived with his family and treated sick peasants at no charge. Chekhov's kindness and good works were not a matter of any political program or religious impulse but, as Vladimir Nabokov put it, "the natural coloration of his talent." He was extremely modest about his extraordinary ability to empathize with his characters. Once he said to a visitor, "Do you know how I write my stories? Here's how!" And he glanced at his table, took up the first object that he saw – it was an ashtray – and said, "If you want it, you'll have a story tomorrow. It will be called 'The Ashtray.'" And it seemed to the visitor that Chekhov was conjuring up a story in front of his eyes: "Certain indefinite situations, adventures which had not yet found concrete form, were already beginning to crystallize about the ashtray."

Chekhov's story-writing technique appears disarmingly simple. Yet, as Virginia Woolf recognized, "as we read these little stories about nothing at all, the horizon widens; the soul gains an astonishing sense of freedom." Chekhov's remarkable absence of egotism can be seen in a masterpiece such as "The Lady with the Pet Dog," which he wrote toward the end of his life. He once sent a sketch describing himself to the editor who first encouraged him, giving a sense of the depth of his self-knowledge:

> Write a story, do, about a young man, the son of a serf, a former grocery boy, a choir singer, a high school pupil and university student, brought up to respect rank, to kiss the hands of priests, to truckle to the ideas of others – a young man who expressed thanks for every piece of bread, who was whipped many times, who went without galoshes to do his tutoring, who used his fists, tortured animals, was fond of dining with rich relatives, was a hypocrite in his dealings with God and men, needlessly, solely out of a realization of his own insignificance – write how this young man squeezes the slave out of himself, drop by drop, and how, on awaking one fine morning, he feels that the blood coursing through his veins is no longer that of a slave but that of a real human being.

Chekhov's more than 800 stories have immensely influenced writers of short fiction. Unconcerned with giving a social or ethical message in his work, he championed what he called "the holy of holies" – "love and absolute freedom – freedom from violence and lies, whatever their form."

CONNECTION To read a modern retelling of Chekhov's story, see Joyce Carol Oates's "The Lady with the Pet Dog" on page 439.

WEB Research Anton Chekhov at bedfordstmartins.com/rewritinglit.

The Lady with the Pet Dog 1899

TRANSLATED BY AVRAHM YARMOLINSKY

I

A new person, it was said, had appeared on the esplanade: a lady with a pet dog. Dmitry Dmitrich Gurov, who had spent a fortnight at Yalta and had got used to the place, had also begun to take an interest in new arrivals. As he sat in Vernet's confectionery shop, he saw, walking on the esplanade, a fair-haired young woman of medium height, wearing a beret; a white Pomeranian was trotting behind her.

And afterwards he met her in the public garden and in the square several times a day. She walked alone, always wearing the same beret and always with the white dog; no one knew who she was and everyone called her simply "the lady with the pet dog."

"If she is here alone without husband or friends," Gurov reflected, "it wouldn't be a bad thing to make her acquaintance."

He was under forty, but he already had a daughter twelve years old, and two sons at school. They had found a wife for him when he was very young, a student in his second year, and by now she seemed half as old again as he. She was a tall, erect woman with dark eyebrows, stately and dignified and, as she said of herself, intellectual. She read a great deal, used simplified spelling in her letters, called her husband, not Dmitry, but Dimitry, while he privately considered her of limited intelligence, narrow-minded, dowdy, was afraid of her, and did not like to be at home. He had begun being unfaithful to her long ago—had been unfaithful to her often and, probably for that reason, almost always spoke ill of women, and when they were talked of in his presence used to call them "the inferior race."

It seemed to him that he had been sufficiently tutored by bitter experience to call them what he pleased, and yet he could not have lived without "the inferior race" for two days together. In the company of men he was bored and ill at ease, he was chilly and uncommunicative with them; but when he was among women he felt free, and knew what to speak to them about and how to comport himself; and even to be silent with them was no strain on him. In his appearance, in his character, in his whole make-up there was something attractive and elusive that disposed women in his favor and allured them. He knew that, and some force seemed to draw him to them, too.

Oft-repeated and really bitter experience had taught him long ago that with decent people—particularly Moscow people—who are irresolute and slow to move, every affair which at first seems a light and charming adventure inevitably grows into a whole problem of extreme complexity, and in the end a painful situation is created. But at every new meeting with an interesting woman this lesson of experience seemed to slip from his memory, and he was eager for life, and everything seemed so simple and diverting.

One evening while he was dining in the public garden the lady in the beret walked up without haste to take the next table. Her expression, her gait, her dress, and the way she did her hair told him that she belonged to the upper class, that she was married, that she was in Yalta for the first time and alone, and that she was bored there. The stories told of the immorality in Yalta are to a great extent untrue; he despised them, and knew that such stories were made up for the most part by persons who would have been glad to sin themselves if they had had the chance; but when the lady sat down at the next table three paces from him, he recalled these stories of easy conquests, of trips to the mountains, and the tempting thought of a swift, fleeting liaison, a romance with an unknown woman of whose very name he was ignorant, suddenly took hold of him.

He beckoned invitingly to the Pomeranian, and when the dog approached him, shook his finger at it. The Pomeranian growled; Gurov threatened it again.

The lady glanced at him and at once dropped her eyes.

"He doesn't bite," she said and blushed.

"May I give him a bone?" he asked; and when she nodded he inquired affably, "Have you been in Yalta long?"

"About five days."

"And I am dragging out the second week here."

There was a short silence.

"Time passes quickly, and yet it is so dull here!" she said, not looking at him.

"It's only the fashion to say it's dull here. A provincial will live in Belyov or Zhizdra and not be bored, but when he comes here it's 'Oh, the dullness! Oh, the dust!' One would think he came from Granada."

She laughed. Then both continued eating in silence, like strangers, but after dinner they walked together and there sprang up between them the light banter of people who are free and contented, to whom it does not matter where they go or what they talk about. They walked and talked of the strange light on the sea: the water was a soft, warm, lilac color, and there was a golden band of moonlight upon it. They talked of how sultry it was after a hot day. Gurov told her that he was a native of Moscow, that he had studied languages and literature at the university, but had a post in a bank; that at one time he had trained to become an opera singer but had given it up, that he owned two houses in Moscow. And he learned from her that she had grown up in Petersburg, but had lived in S—— since her marriage two years previously, that she was going to stay in Yalta for about another month, and that her husband, who needed a rest, too, might perhaps come to fetch her. She was not certain whether her husband was a member of a Government Board or served on a Zemstvo Council,° and this amused her. And Gurov learned too that her name was Anna Sergeyevna.

Zemstvo Council: County council.

Afterwards in his room at the hotel he thought about her—and was certain that he would meet her the next day. It was bound to happen. Getting into bed he recalled that she had been a schoolgirl only recently, doing lessons like his own daughter; he thought how much timidity and angularity there was still in her laugh and her manner of talking with a stranger. It must have been the first time in her life that she was alone in a setting in which she was followed, looked at, and spoken to for one secret purpose alone, which she could hardly fail to guess. He thought of her slim, delicate throat, her lovely gray eyes.

"There's something pathetic about her, though," he thought, and dropped off.

II

A week had passed since they had struck up an acquaintance. It was a holiday. It was close indoors, while in the street the wind whirled the dust about and blew people's hats off. One was thirsty all day, and Gurov often went into the restaurant and offered Anna Sergeyevna a soft drink or ice cream. One did not know what to do with oneself.

In the evening when the wind had abated they went out on the pier to watch the steamer come in. There were a great many people walking about the dock; they had come to welcome someone and they were carrying bunches of flowers. And two peculiarities of a festive Yalta crowd stood out: the elderly ladies were dressed like young ones and there were many generals.

Owing to the choppy sea, the steamer arrived late, after sunset, and it was a long time tacking about before it put in at the pier. Anna Sergeyevna peered at the steamer and the passengers through her lorgnette as though looking for acquaintances, and whenever she turned to Gurov her eyes were shining. She talked a great deal and asked questions jerkily, forgetting the next moment what she had asked; then she lost her lorgnette in the crush.

The festive crowd began to disperse; it was now too dark to see people's faces; there was no wind anymore, but Gurov and Anna Sergeyevna still stood as though waiting to see someone else come off the steamer. Anna Sergeyevna was silent now, and sniffed her flowers without looking at Gurov.

"The weather has improved this evening," he said. "Where shall we go now? Shall we drive somewhere?"

She did not reply.

Then he looked at her intently, and suddenly embraced her and kissed her on the lips, and the moist fragrance of her flowers enveloped him; and at once he looked round him anxiously, wondering if anyone had seen them.

"Let us go to your place," he said softly. And they walked off together rapidly.

The air in her room was close and there was the smell of the perfume she had bought at the Japanese shop. Looking at her, Gurov thought: "What encounters life offers!" From the past he preserved the memory of carefree, good-natured women whom love made gay and who were grateful to him for the happiness he gave them, however brief it might be; and of women like his wife who loved without sincerity, with too many words, affectedly, hysterically, with an expression that it was not love or passion that engaged them but something more significant; and of two or three others, very beautiful, frigid women, across whose faces would suddenly flit a rapacious expression—an obstinate desire to take from life more than it could give, and these were women no longer young, capricious, unreflecting, domineering, unintelligent, and when Gurov grew cold to them their beauty aroused his hatred, and the lace on their lingerie seemed to him to resemble scales.

But here there was the timidity, the angularity of inexperienced youth, a feeling of awkwardness; and there was a sense of embarrassment, as though someone had suddenly knocked at the door. Anna Sergeyevna, "the lady with the pet dog," treated what had happened in a peculiar way, very seriously, as though it were her fall—so it seemed, and this was odd and inappropriate. Her features drooped and faded, and her long hair hung down sadly on either side of her face; she grew pensive and her dejected pose was that of a Magdalene in a picture by an old master.

"It's not right," she said. "You don't respect me now, you first of all."

There was a watermelon on the table. Gurov cut himself a slice and began eating it without haste. They were silent for at least half an hour.

There was something touching about Anna Sergeyevna; she had the purity of a well-bred, naive woman who has seen little of life. The single candle burning on the table barely illumined her face, yet it was clear that she was unhappy.

"Why should I stop respecting you, darling?" asked Gurov. "You don't know what you're saying."

"God forgive me," she said, and her eyes filled with tears. "It's terrible."

"It's as though you were trying to exonerate yourself."

"How can I exonerate myself? No. I am a bad, low woman; I despise myself and I have no thought of exonerating myself. It's not my husband but myself I have deceived. And not only just now; I have been deceiving myself for a long time. My husband may be a good, honest man, but he is a flunkey! I don't know what he does, what his work is, but I know he is a flunkey! I was twenty when I married him. I was tormented by curiosity; I wanted something better. 'There must be a different sort of life,' I said to myself. I wanted to live! To live, to live! Curiosity kept eating at me—you don't understand it, but I swear to God I could no longer control myself; something was going on in me; I could not be held back. I told my husband I was ill, and came here. And here I have been walking about as though in a daze, as though I were mad; and now I have become a vulgar, vile woman whom anyone may despise."

Gurov was already bored with her; he was irritated by her naive tone, by her repentance, so unexpected and so out of place, but for the tears in her eyes he might have thought she was joking or play-acting.

"I don't understand, my dear," he said softly. "What do you want?"

She hid her face on his breast and pressed close to him.

"Believe me, believe me, I beg you," she said, "I love honesty and purity, and sin is loathsome to me; I don't know what I'm doing. Simple people say, 'The Evil One has led me astray.' And I may say of myself now that the Evil One has led me astray."

"Quiet, quiet," he murmured.

He looked into her fixed, frightened eyes, kissed her, spoke to her softly and affectionately, and by degrees she calmed down, and her gaiety returned; both began laughing.

Afterwards when they went out there was not a soul on the esplanade. The town with its cypresses looked quite dead, but the sea was still sounding as it broke upon the beach; a single launch was rocking on the waves and on it a lantern was blinking sleepily.

They found a cab and drove to Oreanda.

"I found out your surname in the hall just now: it was written on the board—von Dideritz," said Gurov. "Is your husband German?"

"No; I believe his grandfather was German, but he is Greek Orthodox himself."

At Oreanda they sat on a bench not far from the church, looked down at the sea, and were silent. Yalta was barely visible through the morning mist; white clouds rested motionlessly on the mountaintops. The leaves did not stir on the trees, cicadas twanged, and the monotonous muffled sound of the sea that rose from below spoke of the peace, the eternal sleep awaiting us. So it rumbled below when there was no Yalta, no Oreanda here; so it rumbles now, and it will rumble as indifferently and as hollowly when we are no more. And in this constancy, in this complete indifference to the life and death of each of us, there lies, perhaps, a pledge of our eternal salvation, of the unceasing advance of life upon earth, of unceasing movement towards perfection. Sitting beside a young woman who in the dawn seemed so lovely, Gurov, soothed and spellbound by these magical surroundings—the sea, the mountains, the clouds, the wide sky—thought how everything is really beautiful in this world when one reflects: everything except what we think or do ourselves when we forget the higher aims of life and our own human dignity.

A man strolled up to them—probably a guard—looked at them, and walked away. And this detail, too, seemed so mysterious and beautiful. They saw a steamer arrive from Feodosia, its lights extinguished in the glow of dawn.

"There is dew on the grass," said Anna Sergeyevna, after a silence.

"Yes, it's time to go home."

They returned to the city.

Then they met every day at twelve o'clock on the esplanade, lunched and dined together, took walks, admired the sea. She complained that she slept badly, that she had palpitations, asked the same questions, troubled now by jealousy and now by the fear that he did not respect her sufficiently. And often in the square or the public garden, when there was no one near them, he suddenly drew her to him and kissed her passionately. Complete idleness, these kisses in broad daylight exchanged furtively in dread of someone's seeing them, the heat, the smell of the sea, and the continual flitting before his eyes of idle, well-dressed, well-fed people, worked a complete change in him; he kept telling Anna Sergeyevna how beautiful she was, how seductive, was urgently passionate; he would not move a step away from her, while she was often pensive and continually pressed him to confess that he did not respect her, did not love her in the least, and saw in her nothing but a common woman. Almost every evening rather late they drove somewhere out of town, to Oreanda or to the waterfall; and the excursion was always a success, the scenery invariably impressed them as beautiful and magnificent.

They were expecting her husband, but a letter came from him saying that he had eye-trouble, and begging his wife to return home as soon as possible. Anna Sergeyevna made haste to go.

"It's a good thing I am leaving," she said to Gurov. "It's the hand of Fate!"

She took a carriage to the railway station, and he went with her. They were driving the whole day. When she had taken her place in the express, and when the second bell had rung, she said, "Let me look at you once more—let me look at you again. Like this."

She was not crying but was so sad that she seemed ill and her face was quivering.

"I shall be thinking of you—remembering you," she said. "God bless you; be happy. Don't remember evil against me. We are parting forever—it has to be, for we ought never to have met. Well, God bless you."

The train moved off rapidly, its lights soon vanished, and a minute later there was no sound of it, as though everything had conspired to end as quickly as possible that sweet trance, that madness. Left alone on the platform, and gazing into the dark distance, Gurov listened to the twang of the grasshoppers and the hum of the telegraph wires, feeling as though he had just waked up. And he reflected, musing, that there had now been another episode or adventure in his life, and it, too, was at an end, and nothing was left of it but a memory. He was moved, sad, and slightly remorseful: this young woman whom he would never meet again had not been happy with him; he had been warm and affectionate with her, but yet in his manner, his tone, and his caresses there had been a shade of light irony, the slightly coarse arrogance of a happy male who was, besides, almost twice her age. She had constantly called him kind, exceptional, high-minded; obviously he had seemed to her different from what he really was, so he had involuntarily deceived her.

Here at the station there was already a scent of autumn in the air; it was a chilly evening.

"It is time for me to go north, too," thought Gurov as he left the platform. "High time!"

III

At home in Moscow the winter routine was already established; the stoves were heated, and in the morning it was still dark when the children were having breakfast and getting ready for school, and the nurse would light the lamp for a short time. There were frosts already. When the first snow falls, on the first day the sleighs are out, it is pleasant to see the white earth, the white roofs; one draws easy, delicious breaths, and the season brings back the days of one's youth. The old limes and birches, white with hoar-frost, have a good-natured look; they are closer to one's heart than cypresses and palms, and near them one no longer wants to think of mountains and the sea.

Gurov, a native of Moscow, arrived there on a fine frosty day, and when he put on his fur coat and warm gloves and took a walk along Petrovka, and when on Saturday night he heard the bells ringing, his recent trip and the places he had visited lost all charm for him. Little by little he became immersed in Moscow life, greedily read three newspapers a day, and declared that he did not read the Moscow papers on principle. He already felt a longing for restaurants, clubs, formal dinners, anniversary celebrations, and it flattered him to entertain distinguished lawyers and actors, and to play cards with a professor at the physicians' club. He could eat a whole portion of meat stewed with pickled cabbage and served in a pan, Moscow style.

A month or so would pass and the image of Anna Sergeyevna, it seemed to him, would become misty in his memory, and only from time to time he would dream of her with her touching smile as he dreamed of others. But more than a month went by, winter came into its own, and everything was still clear in his memory as though he had parted from Anna Sergeyevna only yesterday. And his memories glowed more and more vividly. When in the evening stillness the voices of his children preparing their lessons reached his study, or when he listened to a song or to an organ playing in a restaurant, or when the storm howled in the chimney, suddenly everything would rise up in his memory; what had happened on the pier and the early morning with the mist on the mountains, and the steamer coming from Feodosia, and the kisses. He would pace about his room a long time, remembering and smiling; then his memories passed into reveries, and in his imagination the past would mingle with what was to come. He did not dream of Anna Sergeyevna, but she followed him about everywhere and watched him. When he shut his eyes he saw her before him as though she were there in the flesh, and she seemed to him lovelier, younger, tenderer than she had been, and he imagined himself a finer man than he had been in Yalta. Of evenings she peered out at him from the bookcase, from the fireplace, from the corner—he heard her breathing, the caressing rustle of her clothes. In the street he followed the women with his eyes, looking for someone who resembled her.

Already he was tormented by a strong desire to share his memories with someone. But in his home it was impossible to talk of his love, and he had no one to talk to outside; certainly he could not confide in his tenants or in anyone at the bank. And what was there to talk about? He hadn't loved her then, had he? Had there been anything beautiful, poetical, edifying, or simply interesting in his relations with Anna Sergeyevna? And he was forced to talk vaguely of love, of women, and no one guessed what he meant; only his wife would twitch her black eyebrows and say, "The part of a philanderer does not suit you at all, Dimitry."

One evening, coming out of the physicians' club with an official with whom he had been playing cards, he could not resist saying:

"If you only knew what a fascinating woman I became acquainted with at Yalta!"

The official got into his sledge and was driving away, but turned suddenly and shouted:

"Dmitry Dmitrich!"

"What is it?"

"You were right this evening: the sturgeon was a bit high."

These words, so commonplace, for some reason moved Gurov to indignation, and struck him as degrading and unclean. What savage manners, what mugs! What stupid nights, what dull, humdrum days! Frenzied gambling, gluttony, drunkenness, continual talk always about the same thing! Futile pursuits and conversations always about the same topics take up the better part of one's time, the better part of one's strength, and in the end there is left a life clipped and wingless, an absurd mess, and there is no escaping or getting away from it—just as though one were in a madhouse or a prison.

Gurov, boiling with indignation, did not sleep all night. And he had a headache all the next day. And the following nights too he slept badly; he sat up in bed, thinking, or paced up and down his room. He was fed up with his children, fed up with the bank; he had no desire to go anywhere or to talk of anything.

In December during the holidays he prepared to take a trip and told his wife he was going to Petersburg to do what he could for a young friend—and he set off for S——. What for? He did not know, himself. He wanted to see Anna Sergeyevna and talk with her, to arrange a rendezvous if possible.

He arrived at S—— in the morning, and at the hotel took the best room, in which the floor was covered with gray army cloth, and on the table there was an inkstand, gray with dust and topped by a figure on horseback, its hat in its raised hand and its head broken off. The porter gave him the necessary information: von Dideritz lived in a house of his own on Staro-Goncharnaya Street, not far from the hotel: he was rich and lived well and kept his own horses; everyone in the town knew him. The porter pronounced the name: "Dridiritz."

Without haste Gurov made his way to Staro-Goncharnaya Street and found the house. Directly opposite the house stretched a long gray fence studded with nails.

"A fence like that would make one run away," thought Gurov, looking now at the fence, now at the windows of the house.

He reflected: this was a holiday, and the husband was apt to be at home. And in any case, it would be tactless to go into the house and disturb her. If he were to send her a note, it might fall into her husband's hands, and that might spoil everything. The best thing was to rely on chance. And he kept walking up and down the street and along the fence, waiting for the chance. He saw a beggar go in at the gate and heard the dogs attack him; then an hour later he heard a piano, and the sound came to him faintly and indistinctly. Probably it was Anna Sergeyevna playing. The front door opened suddenly, and an old woman came out, followed by the familiar white Pomeranian. Gurov was on the point of calling to the dog, but his heart began beating violently, and in his excitement he could not remember the Pomeranian's name.

He kept walking up and down, and hated the gray fence more and more, and by now he thought irritably that Anna Sergeyevna had forgotten him, and was perhaps already diverting herself with another man, and that that was very natural in a young woman who from morning till night had to look at that damn fence. He went back to his hotel room and sat on the couch for a long while, not knowing what to do, then he had dinner and a long nap.

"How stupid and annoying all this is!" he thought when he woke and looked at the dark windows: it was already evening. "Here I've had a good sleep for some reason. What am I going to do at night?"

He sat on the bed, which was covered with a cheap gray blanket of the kind seen in hospitals, and he twitted himself in his vexation:

"So there's your lady with the pet dog. There's your adventure. A nice place to cool your heels in."

That morning at the station a playbill in large letters had caught his eye. *The Geisha* was to be given for the first time. He thought of this and drove to the theater.

"It's quite possible that she goes to first nights," he thought.

The theater was full. As in all provincial theaters, there was a haze above the chandelier, the gallery was noisy and restless; in the front row, before the beginning of the performance the local dandies were standing with their hands clasped behind their backs; in the Governor's box the Governor's daughter, wearing a boa, occupied the front seat, while the Governor himself hid modestly behind the portiere and only his hands were visible; the curtain swayed; the orchestra was a long time tuning up. While the audience was coming in and taking their seats, Gurov scanned the faces eagerly.

Anna Sergeyevna, too, came in. She sat down in the third row, and when Gurov looked at her his heart contracted, and he understood clearly that in the whole world there was no human being so near, so precious, and so important to him; she, this little, undistinguished woman, lost in a provincial crowd, with a vulgar lorgnette in her hand, filled his whole life now, was his sorrow and his joy, the only happiness that he now desired for himself, and to the sounds of the bad orchestra, of the miserable local violins, he thought how lovely she was. He thought and dreamed.

A young man with small side-whiskers, very tall and stooped, came in with Anna Sergeyevna and sat down beside her; he nodded his head at every step and seemed to be bowing continually. Probably this was the husband whom at Yalta, in an access of bitter feeling, she had called a flunkey. And there really was in his lanky figure, his side-whiskers, his small bald patch, something of a flunkey's retiring manner; his smile was mawkish, and in his buttonhole there was an academic badge like a waiter's number.

During the first intermission the husband went out to have a smoke; she remained in her seat. Gurov, who was also sitting in the orchestra, went up to her and said in a shaky voice, with a forced smile:

"Good evening!"

She glanced at him and turned pale, then looked at him again in horror, unable to believe her eyes, and gripped the fan and the lorgnette tightly together in her hands, evidently trying to keep herself from fainting. Both were silent. She was sitting, he was standing, frightened by her distress and not daring to take a seat beside her. The violins and the flute that were being tuned up sang out. He suddenly felt frightened: it seemed as if all the people in the boxes were looking at them. She got up and went hurriedly to the exit; he followed her, and both of them walked blindly along the corridors and up and down stairs, and figures in the uniforms prescribed for magistrates, teachers, and officials of the Department of Crown Lands, all wearing badges, flitted before their eyes, as did also ladies, and fur coats on hangers; they were conscious of drafts and the smell of stale tobacco. And Gurov, whose heart was beating violently, thought:

"Oh, Lord! Why are these people here and this orchestra!"

And at that instant he suddenly recalled how when he had seen Anna Sergeyevna off at the station he had said to himself that all was over between them and that they would never meet again. But how distant the end still was!

On the narrow, gloomy staircase over which it said "To the Amphitheatre," she stopped.

"How you frightened me!" she said, breathing hard, still pale and stunned. "Oh, how you frightened me! I am barely alive. Why did you come? Why?"

"But do understand, Anna, do understand—" he said hurriedly, under his breath. "I implore you, do understand—"

She looked at him with fear, with entreaty, with love; she looked at him intently, to keep his features more distinctly in her memory.

"I suffer so," she went on, not listening to him. "All this time I have been thinking of nothing but you; I live only by the thought of you. And I wanted to forget, to forget; but why, oh, why have you come?"

On the landing above them two high school boys were looking down and smoking, but it was all the same to Gurov; he drew Anna Sergeyevna to him and began kissing her face and hands.

"What are you doing, what are you doing!" she was saying in horror, pushing him away. "We have lost our senses. Go away today; go away at once—I conjure you by all that is sacred, I implore you—People are coming this way!"

Someone was walking up the stairs.

"You must leave," Anna Sergeyevna went on in a whisper. "Do you hear, Dmitry Dmitrich? I will come and see you in Moscow. I have never been happy; I am unhappy now, and I never, never shall be happy, never! So don't make me suffer still more! I swear I'll come to Moscow. But now let us part. My dear, good, precious one, let us part!"

She pressed his hand and walked rapidly downstairs, turning to look round at him, and from her eyes he could see that she really was unhappy. Gurov stood for a while, listening, then when all grew quiet, he found his coat and left the theater.

IV

And Anna Sergeyevna began coming to see him in Moscow. Once every two or three months she left S—— telling her husband that she was going to consult a doctor about a woman's ailment from which she was suffering—and her husband did and did not believe her. When she arrived in Moscow she would stop at the Slavyansky Bazar Hotel, and at once send a man in a red cap to Gurov. Gurov came to see her, and no one in Moscow knew of it.

Once he was going to see her in this way on a winter morning (the messenger had come the evening before and not found him in). With him walked his daughter, whom he wanted to take to school; it was on the way. Snow was coming down in big wet flakes.

"It's three degrees above zero,° and yet it's snowing," Gurov was saying to his daughter. "But this temperature prevails only on the surface of the earth; in the upper layers of the atmosphere there is quite a different temperature."

"And why doesn't it thunder in winter, papa?"

He explained that, too. He talked, thinking all the while that he was on his way to a rendezvous, and no living soul knew of it, and probably no one would ever know. He had two lives, an open one, seen and known by all who needed to know it, full of conventional truth and conventional falsehood, exactly like the lives of his friends and acquaintances; and another life that went on in secret. And through some strange, perhaps accidental, combination of circumstances, everything that was of interest and importance to him, everything that was essential to him, everything about which he felt sincerely and did not deceive himself, everything that constituted the core of his life, was going on concealed from others; while all that was false, the shell in which he hid to cover the truth—his work at the bank, for instance, his discussions at the club, his references to the "inferior race," his appearances at anniversary celebrations with his wife—all that went on in the open. Judging others by himself, he did not believe what he saw, and always fancied that every man led his real, most interesting life under cover of secrecy as under cover of night. The personal life of every individual is based on secrecy, and perhaps it is partly for that reason that civilized man is so nervously anxious that personal privacy should be respected.

Having taken his daughter to school, Gurov went on to the Slavyansky Bazar Hotel. He took off his fur coat in the lobby, went upstairs, and knocked gently at the door. Anna Sergeyevna, wearing his favorite gray dress, exhausted by the journey and by waiting, had been expecting him since the previous evening. She was pale, and looked at him without a smile, and he had hardly entered when she flung herself on his breast. That kiss was a long, lingering one, as though they had not seen one another for two years.

"Well, darling, how are you getting on there?" he asked. "What news?"

"Wait; I'll tell you in a moment—I can't speak."

She could not speak; she was crying. She turned away from him, and pressed her handkerchief to her eyes.

"Let her have her cry; meanwhile I'll sit down," he thought, and he seated himself in an armchair.

Then he rang and ordered tea, and while he was having his tea she remained standing at the window with her back to him. She was crying out of sheer agitation, in the sorrowful consciousness that their life was so sad; that they could only see each other in secret and had to hide from people like thieves! Was it not a broken life?

---

three degrees above zero: On the Celsius scale—about thirty-seven degrees Fahrenheit.

"Come, stop now, dear!" he said.

It was plain to him that this love of theirs would not be over soon, that the end of it was not in sight. Anna Sergeyevna was growing more and more attached to him. She adored him, and it was unthinkable to tell her that their love was bound to come to an end some day; besides, she would not have believed it!

He went up to her and took her by the shoulders, to fondle her and say something diverting, and at that moment he caught sight of himself in the mirror.

His hair was already beginning to turn gray. And it seemed odd to him that he had grown so much older in the last few years, and lost his looks. The shoulders on which his hands rested were warm and heaving. He felt compassion for this life, still so warm and lovely, but probably already about to begin to fade and wither like his own. Why did she love him so much? He always seemed to women different from what he was, and they loved in him not himself, but the man whom their imagination created and whom they had been eagerly seeking all their lives; and afterwards, when they saw their mistake, they loved him nevertheless. And not one of them had been happy with him. In the past he had met women, come together with them, parted from them, but he had never once loved; it was anything you please, but not love. And only now when his head was gray he had fallen in love, really, truly—for the first time in his life.

Anna Sergeyevna and he loved each other as people do who are very close and intimate, like man and wife, like tender friends; it seemed to them that Fate itself had meant them for one another, and they could not understand why he had a wife and she a husband; and it was as though they were a pair of migratory birds, male and female, caught and forced to live in different cages. They forgave each other what they were ashamed of in their past, they forgave everything in the present, and felt that this love of theirs had altered them both.

Formerly in moments of sadness he had soothed himself with whatever logical arguments came into his head, but now he no longer cared for logic; he felt profound compassion, he wanted to be sincere and tender.

"Give it up now, my darling," he said. "You've had your cry; that's enough. Let us have a talk now, we'll think up something."

Then they spent a long time taking counsel together, they talked of how to avoid the necessity for secrecy, for deception, for living in different cities, and not seeing one another for long stretches of time. How could they free themselves from these intolerable fetters?

"How? How?" he asked, clutching his head. "How?"

And it seemed as though in a little while the solution would be found, and then a new and glorious life would begin; and it was clear to both of them that the end was still far off, and that what was to be most complicated and difficult for them was only just beginning.

COMMENTARY

ANTON CHEKHOV

Anton Chekhov described his theories of literature and his practice as a storyteller in countless letters to his family and friends. He was not a systematic critic, and he did not necessarily follow his own advice to other writers. Brevity and concentration on a few essentials of scene and character were the essence of his technique, but he was not always as drastically laconic in his stories as his letters suggest. What is consistently clear in his advice to other writers is his own untiring compassion and his desire to speak honestly in his efforts to help them. He wrote in his notebook, "It is not the function of art to solve problems but to present them clearly."

These letters are to his older brother, his publisher, and a younger author whose work he admired.

Technique in Writing the Short Story 1886–99

TRANSLATED BY CONSTANCE GARNETT

From a Letter to Alexander P. Chekhov, 1886

In my opinion a true description of Nature should be very brief and have a character of relevance. Commonplaces such as "the setting sun bathing in the waves of the darkening sea, poured its purple gold, etc." — "the swallows flying over the surface of the water twittered merrily" — such commonplaces one ought to abandon. In descriptions of Nature one ought to seize upon the little particulars, grouping them in such a way that, in reading, when you shut your eyes, you get a picture.

For instance, you will get the full effect of a moonlight night if you write that on the mill-dam a little glowing star-point flashed from the neck of a broken bottle, and the round, black shadow of a dog, or a wolf, emerged and ran, etc. Nature becomes animated if you are not squeamish about employing comparisons of her phenomena with ordinary human activities, etc.

In the sphere of psychology, details are also the thing. God preserve us from commonplaces. Best of all is it to avoid depicting the hero's state of mind; you ought to try to make it clear from the hero's actions. It is not necessary to portray many characters. The center of gravity should be in two persons: him and her.

From a Letter to Aleksey S. Suvorin, 1890

You abuse me for objectivity, calling it indifference to good and evil, lack of ideals and ideas, and so on. You would have me, when I describe horse-thieves, say: "Stealing horses is an evil." But that has been known for ages without my saying so. Let the jury judge them; it's my job simply to show what sort of people they are. I write: You are dealing with horse-thieves, so let me tell you that they are not beggars but well-fed people, that they are people of a special cult, and that horse-stealing is not simply theft but a passion. Of course it would be pleasant to combine art with a sermon, but for me personally it is extremely difficult and almost impossible, owing to the conditions of technique. You see, to depict horse-thieves in seven hundred lines I must all the time speak and think in their tone and feel in their spirit, otherwise, if I introduce subjectivity, the image becomes blurred and the story will not be as compact as all short stories ought to be. When I write, I reckon entirely upon the reader to add for himself the subjective elements that are lacking in the story.

From a Letter to Maxim Gorky, 1899

More advice: when reading the proofs, cross out a host of terms qualifying nouns and verbs. You have so many such terms that the reader's mind finds it a task to concentrate on them, and he soon grows tired. You understand it at once when I say, "The man sat on the grass"; you understand it because it is clear and makes no demands on the attention. On the other hand, it is not easily understood, and it is difficult for the mind, if I write, "A tall, narrow-chested, middle-sized man, with a red beard, sat on the green grass, already trampled by pedestrians, sat silently, shyly, and timidly looked about him." That is not immediately grasped by the mind, whereas good writing should be grasped at once—in a second.

KATE CHOPIN

Kate Chopin (1851–1904) was born in St. Louis. Her father died when she was four, and she was raised by her Creole mother's family. In 1870 she married Oscar Chopin, a cotton broker. They lived in Louisiana, first in New Orleans and then on a large plantation among the French-speaking Acadians. When her husband died in 1882, Chopin moved with her six children back to St. Louis. Friends encouraged her to write, and when she was nearly forty years old she published her first novel, *At Fault* (1890). Her stories began to appear in *Century* and *Harper's Magazine*, and two collections followed: *Bayou Folk* (1894) and *A Night in Arcadie* (1897). Working steadily from 1889 to 1901, she published two novels, thirteen essays, translations of Maupassant, poems, and over a hundred stories. Her last major work, the novel *The Awakening* (1899), is her masterpiece, but its sympathetic treatment of adultery shocked reviewers and readers throughout America. In St. Louis the novel was taken out of the libraries, and Chopin was denied membership in the St. Louis Fine Arts Club. When her third collection of stories was rejected by her publisher at the end of 1899, Chopin felt herself a literary outcast; she wrote very little in the last years of her life. She died at fifty-three of a brain hemorrhage.

What affronted the genteel readers of the 1890s was Chopin's attempt to write frankly about women's emotions in their relations with men, children, and their own sexuality. After her mother's death in 1885, she stopped being a practicing Catholic and accepted the Darwinian view of human evolution. Seeking God in nature rather than through the church, Chopin wrote freely on the subjects of sex and love, but she said she learned to her sorrow that for American authors, "the limitations imposed upon their art by their environment hamper a full and spontaneous expression." Magazine editors turned down her work if it challenged conventional social behavior, as does "The Story of an Hour," which feminist critics championed more than half a century after Chopin's death.

Chopin adopted Guy de Maupassant as a model after translating his stories from the French. She felt, "Here was life, not fiction; for where were the plots, the old fashioned mechanism and stage trappings that in a vague, unthinking way I had fancied were essential to the art of story making?" If her fiction is sometimes marred by stilted language or improbable coincidence, at her best, as in "Désirée's Baby," Chopin subtly emphasized character rather than plot in her dramatization of the tragic repercussions of racial prejudice and slavery.

WEB Research Kate Chopin at bedfordstmartins.com/rewritinglit.

Désirée's Baby

1892

As the day was pleasant, Madame Valmondé drove over to L'Abri to see Désirée and the baby.

It made her laugh to think of Désirée with a baby. Why, it seemed but yesterday that Désirée was little more than a baby herself; when Monsieur in riding through the gateway of Valmondé had found her lying asleep in the shadow of the big stone pillar.

The little one awoke in his arms and began to cry for "Dada." That was as much as she could do or say. Some people thought she might have strayed there of her own accord, for she was of the toddling age. The prevailing belief was that she had been purposely left by a party of Texans, whose canvas-covered wagon, late in the day, had crossed the ferry that Coton Maïs kept, just below the plantation. In time Madame Valmondé abandoned every speculation but the one that Désirée had been sent to her by a beneficent Providence to be the child of her affection, seeing that she was without child of the flesh. For the girl grew to be beautiful and gentle, affectionate and sincere,—the idol of Valmondé.

It was no wonder, when she stood one day against the stone pillar in whose shadow she had lain asleep, eighteen years before, that Armand Aubigny riding by and seeing her there, had fallen in love with her. That was the way all the Aubignys fell in love, as if struck by a pistol shot. The wonder was that he had not loved her before; for he had known her since his father brought him home from Paris, a boy of eight, after his mother died there. The passion that awoke in him that day, when he saw her at the gate, swept along like an avalanche, or like a prairie fire, or like anything that drives headlong over all obstacles.

Monsieur Valmondé grew practical and wanted things well considered: that is, the girl's obscure origin. Armand looked into her eyes and did not care. He was reminded that she was nameless. What did it matter about a name when he could give her one of the oldest and proudest in Louisiana? He ordered the *corbeille* from Paris, and contained himself with what patience he could until it arrived; then they were married.

Madame Valmondé had not seen Désirée and the baby for four weeks. When she reached L'Abri she shuddered at the first sight of it, as she always did. It was a sad looking place, which for many years had not known the gentle presence of a mistress, old Monsieur Aubigny having married and buried his wife in France, and she having loved her own land too well ever to leave it. The roof came down steep and black like a cowl, reaching out beyond the wide galleries that encircled the yellow stuccoed house. Big, solemn oaks grew close to it, and their thick-leaved, far-reaching branches shadowed it like a pall. Young Aubigny's rule was a strict one, too, and under it his negroes had forgotten how to be gay, as they had been during the old master's easy-going and indulgent lifetime.

The young mother was recovering slowly, and lay full length, in her soft white muslins and laces, upon a couch. The baby was beside her, upon her arm, where he had fallen asleep, at her breast. The yellow nurse woman sat beside a window fanning herself.

Madame Valmondé bent her portly figure over Désirée and kissed her, holding her an instant tenderly in her arms. Then she turned to the child.

"This is not the baby!" she exclaimed, in startled tones. French was the language spoken at Valmondé in those days.

"I knew you would be astonished," laughed Désirée, "at the way he has grown. The little *cochon de lait!*° Look at his legs, mamma, and his hands and fingernails,—real fingernails. Zandrine had to cut them this morning. Isn't it true, Zandrine?"

The woman bowed her turbaned head majestically, "Mais si, Madame."

"And the way he cries," went on Désirée, "is deafening. Armand heard him the other day as far away as La Blanche's cabin."

Madame Valmondé had never removed her eyes from the child. She lifted it and walked with it over to the window that was lightest. She scanned the baby narrowly, then looked as searchingly at Zandrine, whose face was turned to gaze across the fields.

"Yes, the child has grown, has changed," said Madame Valmondé, slowly, as she replaced it beside its mother. "What does Armand say?"

Désirée's face became suffused with a glow that was happiness itself.

"Oh, Armand is the proudest father in the parish, I believe, chiefly because it is a boy, to bear his name; though he says not,—that he would have loved a girl as well. But I know it isn't true. I know he says that to please me. And mamma," she added, drawing Madame Valmondé's head down to her and speaking in a whisper, "he hasn't punished one of them—not one of them—since baby is born. Even Négrillon, who pretended to have burnt his leg that he might rest from work—he only laughed, and said Négrillon was a great scamp. Oh, mamma, I'm so happy; it frightens me."

---

cochon de lait: An endearment (literally, "suckling pig" in French).

What Désirée said was true. Marriage, and later the birth of his son had softened Armand Aubigny's imperious and exacting nature greatly. This was what made the gentle Désirée so happy, for she loved him desperately. When he frowned she trembled, but loved him. When he smiled, she asked no greater blessing of God. But Armand's dark, handsome face had not often been disfigured by frowns since the day he fell in love with her.

When the baby was about three months old, Désirée awoke one day to the conviction that there was something in the air menacing her peace. It was at first too subtle to grasp. It had only been a disquieting suggestion; an air of mystery among the blacks; unexpected visits from far-off neighbors who could hardly account for their coming. Then a strange, an awful change in her husband's manner, which she dared not ask him to explain. When he spoke to her, it was with averted eyes, from which the old love-light seemed to have gone out. He absented himself from home; and when there, avoided her presence and that of her child, without excuse. And the very spirit of Satan seemed suddenly to take hold of him in his dealings with the slaves. Désirée was miserable enough to die.

She sat in her room, one hot afternoon, in her *peignoir*, listlessly drawing through her fingers the strands of her long, silky brown hair that hung about her shoulders. The baby, half naked, lay asleep upon her own great mahogany bed, that was like a sumptuous throne, with its satin-lined half-canopy. One of La Blanche's little quadroon boys—half naked too—stood fanning the child slowly with a fan of peacock feathers. Désirée's eyes had been fixed absently and sadly upon the baby, while she was striving to penetrate the threatening mist that she felt closing about her. She looked from her child to the boy who stood beside him, and back again; over and over. "Ah!" It was a cry that she could not help; which she was not conscious of having uttered. The blood turned like ice in her veins, and a clammy moisture gathered upon her face.

She tried to speak to the little quadroon boy; but no sound would come, at first. When he heard his name uttered, he looked up, and his mistress was pointing to the door. He laid aside the great, soft fan, and obediently stole away, over the polished floor, on his bare tiptoes.

She stayed motionless, with gaze riveted upon her child, and her face the picture of fright.

Presently her husband entered the room, and without noticing her, went to a table and began to search among some papers which covered it.

"Armand," she called to him, in a voice which must have stabbed him, if he was human. But he did not notice. "Armand," she said again. Then she rose and tottered towards him. "Armand," she panted once more, clutching his arm, "look at our child. What does it mean? Tell me."

He coldly but gently loosened her fingers from about his arm and thrust the hand away from him. "Tell me what it means!" she cried despairingly.

"It means," he answered lightly, "that the child is not white; it means that you are not white."

A quick conception of all that this accusation meant for her nerved her with unwonted courage to deny it. "It is a lie; it is not true, I am white! Look at my hair, it is brown; and my eyes are gray, Armand, you know they are gray. And my skin is fair," seizing his wrist. "Look at my hand; whiter than yours, Armand," she laughed hysterically.

"As white as La Blanche's," he returned cruelly; and went away leaving her alone with their child.

When she could hold a pen in her hand, she sent a despairing letter to Madame Valmondé.

"My mother, they tell me I am not white. Armand has told me I am not white. For God's sake tell them it is not true. You must know it is not true. I shall die. I must die. I cannot be so unhappy, and live."

The answer that came was as brief:

"My own Désirée: Come home to Valmondé; back to your mother who loves you. Come with your child."

When the letter reached Désirée she went with it to her husband's study, and laid it open upon the desk before which he sat. She was like a stone image: silent, white, motionless after she placed it there.

In silence he ran his cold eyes over the written words. He said nothing. "Shall I go, Armand?" she asked in tones sharp with agonized suspense.

"Yes, go."

"Do you want me to go?"

"Yes, I want you to go."

He thought Almighty God had dealt cruelly and unjustly with him; and felt, somehow, that he was paying Him back in kind when he stabbed thus into his wife's soul. Moreover he no longer loved her, because of the unconscious injury she had brought upon his home and his name.

She turned away like one stunned by a blow, and walked slowly towards the door, hoping he would call her back.

"Good-by, Armand," she moaned.

He did not answer her. That was his last blow at fate.

Désirée went in search of her child. Zandrine was pacing the sombre gallery with it. She took the little one from the nurse's arms with no word of explanation, and descending the steps, walked away, under the live-oak branches.

It was an October afternoon; the sun was just sinking. Out in the still fields the negroes were picking cotton.

Désirée had not changed the thin white garment nor the slippers which she wore. Her hair was uncovered and the sun's rays brought a golden gleam from its brown meshes. She did not take the broad, beaten road which led to the far-off plantation of Valmondé. She walked across a deserted field, where the stubble bruised her tender feet, so delicately shod, and tore her thin gown to shreds.

She disappeared among the reeds and willows that grew thick along the banks of the deep, sluggish bayou; and she did not come back again.

Some weeks later there was a curious scene enacted at L'Abri. In the centre of the smoothly swept back yard was a great bonfire. Armand Aubigny sat in the wide hallway that commanded a view of the spectacle; and it was he who dealt out to a half dozen negroes the material which kept this fire ablaze.

A graceful cradle of willow, with all its dainty furbishings, was laid upon the pyre, which had already been fed with the richness of a priceless *layette.* Then there were silk gowns, and velvet and satin ones added to these; laces, too, and embroideries; bonnets and gloves; for the *corbeille* had been of rare quality.

The last thing to go was a tiny bundle of letters; innocent little scribblings that Désirée had sent to him during the days of their espousal. There was the remnant of one back in the drawer from which he took them. But it was not Désirée's; it was part of an old letter from his mother to his father. He read it. She was thanking God for the blessing of her husband's love:—

"But, above all," she wrote, "night and day, I thank the good God for having so arranged our lives that our dear Armand will never know that his mother, who adores him, belongs to the race that is cursed with the brand of slavery."

The Story of an Hour 1894

Knowing that Mrs. Mallard was afflicted with a heart trouble, great care was taken to break to her as gently as possible the news of her husband's death.

It was her sister Josephine who told her, in broken sentences; veiled hints that revealed in half concealing. Her husband's friend Richards was there, too, near her. It was he who had been in the newspaper office when intelligence of the railroad disaster was received, with Brently Mallard's name leading the list of "killed." He had only taken the time to assure himself of its truth by a second telegram, and had hastened to forestall any less careful, less tender friend in bearing the sad message.

She did not hear the story as many women have heard the same, with a paralyzed inability to accept its significance. She wept at once, with sudden, wild abandonment, in her sister's arms. When the storm of grief had spent itself she went away to her room alone. She would have no one follow her.

There stood, facing the open window, a comfortable, roomy armchair. Into this she sank, pressed down by a physical exhaustion that haunted her body and seemed to reach into her soul.

She could see in the open square before her house the tops of trees that were all aquiver with the new spring life. The delicious breath of rain was in the air. In the street below a peddler was crying his wares. The notes of a distant song which some one was singing reached her faintly, and countless sparrows were twittering in the eaves.

There were patches of blue sky showing here and there through the clouds that had met and piled one above the other in the west facing her window.

She sat with her head thrown back upon the cushion of the chair, quite motionless, except when a sob came up into her throat and shook her, as a child who had cried itself to sleep continues to sob in its dreams.

She was young, with a fair, calm face, whose lines bespoke repression and even a certain strength. But now there was a dull stare in her eyes, whose gaze was fixed away off yonder on one of those patches of blue sky. It was not a glance of reflection, but rather indicated a suspension of intelligent thought.

There was something coming to her and she was waiting for it, fearfully. What was it? She did not know; it was too subtle and elusive to name. But she felt it, creeping out of the sky, reaching toward her through the sounds, the scents, the color that filled the air.

Now her bosom rose and fell tumultuously. She was beginning to recognize this thing that was approaching to possess her, and she was striving to beat it back with her will—as powerless as her two white slender hands would have been.

When she abandoned herself a little whispered word escaped her slightly parted lips. She said it over and over under her breath: "free, free, free!" The vacant stare and the look of terror that had followed it went from her eyes. They stayed keen and bright. Her pulses beat fast, and the coursing blood warmed and relaxed every inch of her body.

She did not stop to ask if it were or were not a monstrous joy that held her. A clear and exalted perception enabled her to dismiss the suggestion as trivial.

She knew that she would weep again when she saw the kind, tender hands folded in death; the face that had never looked save with love upon her, fixed and gray and dead. But she saw beyond that bitter moment a long procession of years to come that would belong to her absolutely. And she opened and spread her arms out to them in welcome.

There would be no one to live for her during those coming years: she would live for herself. There would be no powerful will bending hers in that blind persistence with which men and women believe they have a right to impose a private will upon a fellow-creature. A kind intention or a cruel intention made the act seem no less a crime as she looked upon it in that brief moment of illumination.

And yet she had loved him—sometimes. Often she had not. What did it matter! What could love, the unsolved mystery, count for in face of this possession of self-assertion which she suddenly recognized as the strongest impulse of her being!

"Free! Body and soul free!" she kept whispering.

Josephine was kneeling before the closed door with her lips to the keyhole, imploring for admission. "Louise, open the door! I beg; open the door—you will make yourself ill. What are you doing, Louise? For heaven's sake open the door."

"Go away. I am not making myself ill." No; she was drinking in a very elixir of life through that open window.

Her fancy was running riot along those days ahead of her. Spring days, and summer days, and all sorts of days that would be her own. She breathed a quick prayer that life might be long. It was only yesterday she had thought with a shudder that life might be long.

She arose at length and opened the door to her sister's importunities. There was a feverish triumph in her eyes, and she carried herself unwittingly like a goddess of Victory. She clasped her sister's waist, and together they descended the stairs. Richards stood waiting for them at the bottom.

Some one was opening the front door with a latchkey. It was Brently Mallard who entered, a little travel-stained, composedly carrying his gripsack and umbrella. He had been far from the scene of accident, and did not even know there had been one. He stood amazed at Josephine's piercing cry; at Richards' quick motion to screen him from the view of his wife.

But Richards was too late.

When the doctors came they said she had died of heart disease—of joy that kills.

COMMENTARY

KATE CHOPIN

Kate Chopin made a number of translations, mostly of stories by Guy de Maupassant, and she published several essays on literature in St. Louis periodicals. She wrote about the influence of Maupassant on her fiction in response to an invitation from the editor of the *Atlantic Monthly* in 1896. He returned her first version of the essay, however, advising her to "set forth the matter directly." Her revised version was later included in the magazine with the title "In the Confidence of a Story-Teller," but the section describing how she first encountered Maupassant's tales and the impression they made on her was dropped, perhaps because she spoke so enthusiastically about the French writer's escape "from tradition and authority." This portion of the essay is reprinted from the manuscript included in Volume 2 of *The Complete Works of Kate Chopin* (1969). To read a story by Maupassant, see page 399.

How I Stumbled upon Maupassant 1896

About eight years ago there fell accidentally into my hands a volume of Maupassant's tales. These were new to me. I had been in the woods, in the fields, groping around; looking for something big, satisfying, convincing, and finding nothing but—myself; a something neither big nor satisfying but wholly convincing. It was at this period of my emerging from the vast solitude in which I had been making my own acquaintance, that I stumbled upon Maupassant. I read his stories and marvelled at them. Here was life, not fiction; for where were the plots, the old fashioned mechanism and stage trapping that in a vague, unthinking way I had fancied were essential to the art of story making? Here was a man who had escaped from tradition and authority, who had entered into himself and looked out upon life through his own being and with his own eyes; and who, in a direct and simple way, told us what he saw. When a man does this, he gives us the best that he can; something valuable for it is genuine and spontaneous. He gives us his impressions. Someone told me the other day that Maupassant had gone out of fashion. I was not grieved to hear it. He has never seemed to me to belong to the multitude, but rather to the individual. He is not one whom we gather in crowds to listen to—whom we follow in procession—with beating of brass instruments. He does not move us to throw ourselves into the throng—having the integral of an unthinking whole to shout his praise. I even like to think that he appeals to me alone. You probably like to think that he reaches you exclusively. A whole multitude may be secretly nourishing the belief in regard to him for all I know. Someway I like to cherish the delusion that he has spoken to no one else so directly, so intimately as he does to me. He did not say, as another might have done, "do you see these are charming stories of mine? take them into your closet—study them closely—mark their combination—observe the method, the manner of their putting together—and if ever you are moved to write stories you can do no better than to imitate."

STEPHEN CRANE

Stephen Crane (1871–1900) wrote some of the most memorable fiction and poetry ever created by an American, publishing fourteen books in his short lifetime. The poet John Berryman, who wrote a biography of Crane, observed the essential truth about him: "Crane was a writer and nothing else: a man alone in a room with the English language, trying to get human feelings right." Crane's style in his short stories is as intensely personal as Edgar Allan Poe's or Nathaniel Hawthorne's, but he did not use the techniques of fantasy and allegory. "His eyes remained wide open on his world. He was almost illusionless, whether about his subjects or himself. Perhaps his sole illusion was the heroic one; and not even this, especially if he was concerned in it himself as a man, escaped his irony."

Crane was born in Newark, New Jersey, the youngest of fourteen children. His father, a Methodist minister, died when Crane was just a boy, and his mother supported the family by writing articles for Methodist papers and reporting for the *New York Tribune* and the *Philadelphia Press.* Crane briefly attended Lafayette College and Syracuse University before going to work in New York City as a freelance journalist. He became interested in life in the Bowery, one of the worst slums in New York, and he used this setting for his novel *Maggie: A Girl of the Streets*, a work so grimly naturalistic in its portrayal of slum life and so frank in its treatment of sex that Crane had to publish it at his own expense in 1893. Two years later he sold a long story about the Civil War to a syndicate for less than a hundred dollars. That work, *The Red Badge of Courage*, was such a vivid account of wartime experience – even though Crane had never been in a battle himself – that it established his literary reputation.

In the last five years of his life, before he died of tuberculosis in Germany, Crane traveled extensively as a reporter, first to the American West, then to Florida. He couldn't keep away from scenes of war or revolution, believing – as did Ernest Hemingway after him – that "the nearer a writer gets to life, the greater he becomes as an artist." Crane was en route to Florida on the steamship *Commodore* when the ship was wrecked on

New Year's Day 1897. He based one of his finest short stories, "The Open Boat," on what happened to him in a lifeboat with the other survivors. He had first reported the disaster in an article for his newspaper shortly after the shipwreck. Joseph Conrad admired Crane's writing and said of "The Open Boat" that "by the deep and simple humanity of its presentation [the story] seems somehow to illustrate the essentials of life itself, like a symbolic tale."

The Open Boat

1897

A Tale Intended to Be After the Fact. Being the Experience of Four Men from the Sunk Steamer *Commodore*

I

None of them knew the color of the sky. Their eyes glanced level, and were fastened upon the waves that swept toward them. These waves were of the hue of slate, save for the tops, which were of foaming white, and all of the men knew the colors of the sea. The horizon narrowed and widened, and dipped and rose, and at all times its edge was jagged with waves that seemed thrust up in points like rocks.

Many a man ought to have a bath-tub larger than the boat which here rode upon the sea. These waves were most wrongfully and barbarously abrupt and tall, and each froth-top was a problem in small boat navigation.

The cook squatted in the bottom and looked with both eyes at the six inches of gunwale which separated him from the ocean. His sleeves were rolled over his fat forearms, and the two flaps of his unbuttoned vest dangled as he bent to bail out the boat. Often he said: "Gawd! That was a narrow clip." As he remarked it he invariably gazed eastward over the broken sea.

The oiler,° steering with one of the two oars in the boat, sometimes raised himself suddenly to keep clear of water that swirled in over the stern. It was a thin little oar and it seemed often ready to snap.

The correspondent, pulling at the other oar, watched the waves and wondered why he was there.

The injured captain, lying in the bow, was at this time buried in that profound dejection and indifference which comes, temporarily at least, to even the bravest and most enduring when, willy nilly, the firm fails, the army loses, the ship goes down. The mind of the master of a vessel is rooted deep in the timbers of her, though he command for a day or a decade, and this captain had on him the stern impression of a scene in the grays of dawn of seven turned faces, and later a stump of a top-mast with a white ball on it that slashed to and fro at the waves, went low and lower, and down. Thereafter there was something strange in his voice. Although steady, it was deep with mourning, and of a quality beyond oration or tears.

"Keep'er a little more south, Billie," said he.

---

oiler: The person who oils machinery in the engine room of a ship.

"'A little more south,' sir," said the oiler in the stern.

A seat in this boat was not unlike a seat upon a bucking broncho, and, by the same token, a broncho is not much smaller. The craft pranced and reared, and plunged like an animal. As each wave came, and she rose for it, she seemed like a horse making at a fence outrageously high. The manner of her scramble over these walls of water is a mystic thing, and, moreover, at the top of them were ordinarily these problems in white water, the foam racing down from the summit of each wave, requiring a new leap, and a leap from the air. Then, after scornfully bumping a crest, she would slide, and race, and splash down a long incline and arrive bobbing and nodding in front of the next menace.

A singular disadvantage of the sea lies in the fact that after successfully surmounting one wave you discover that there is another behind it just as important and just as nervously anxious to do something effective in the way of swamping boats. In a ten-foot dingey one can get an idea of the resources of the sea in the line of waves that is not probable to the average experience, which is never at sea in a dingey. As each slaty wall of water approached, it shut all else from the view of the men in the boat, and it was not difficult to imagine that this particular wave was the final outburst of the ocean, the last effort of the grim water. There was a terrible grace in the move of the waves, and they came in silence, save for the snarling of the crests.

In the wan light, the faces of the men must have been gray. Their eyes must have glinted in strange ways as they gazed steadily astern. Viewed from a balcony, the whole thing would doubtlessly have been weirdly picturesque. But the men in the boat had no time to see it, and if they had had leisure there were other things to occupy their minds. The sun swung steadily up the sky, and they knew it was broad day because the color of the sea changed from slate to emerald-green, streaked with amber lights, and the foam was like tumbling snow. The process of the breaking day was unknown to them. They were aware only of this effect upon the color of the waves that rolled toward them.

In disjointed sentences the cook and the correspondent argued as to the difference between a life-saving station and a house of refuge. The cook had said: "There's a house of refuge just north of the Mosquito Inlet Light, and as soon as they see us, they'll come off in their boat and pick us up."

"As soon as who see us?" said the correspondent.

"The crew," said the cook.

"Houses of refuge don't have crews," said the correspondent. "As I understand them, they are only places where clothes and grub are stored for the benefit of shipwrecked people. They don't carry crews."

"Oh, yes, they do," said the cook.

"No, they don't," said the correspondent.

"Well, we're not there yet, anyhow," said the oiler, in the stern.

"Well," said the cook, "perhaps it's not a house of refuge that I'm thinking of as being near Mosquito Inlet Light. Perhaps it's a life-saving station."

"We're not there yet," said the oiler, in the stern.

II

As the boat bounced from the top of each wave, the wind tore through the hair of the hatless men, and as the craft plopped her stern down again the spray slashed past them. The crest of each of these waves was a hill, from the top of which the men surveyed, for a moment, a broad tumultuous expanse; shining and wind-riven. It was probably splendid. It was probably glorious, this play of the free sea, wild with lights of emerald and white and amber.

"Bully good thing it's an on-shore wind," said the cook. "If not, where would we be? Wouldn't have a show."

"That's right," said the correspondent.

The busy oiler nodded his assent.

Then the captain, in the bow, chuckled in a way that expressed humor, contempt, tragedy, all in one. "Do you think we've got much of a show, now, boys?" said he.

Whereupon the three were silent, save for a trifle of hemming and hawing. To express any particular optimism at this time they felt to be childish and stupid, but they all doubtless possessed this sense of the situation in their mind. A young man thinks doggedly at such times. On the other hand, the ethics of their condition was decidedly against any open suggestion of hopelessness. So they were silent.

"Oh, well," said the captain, soothing his children, "we'll get ashore all right."

But there was that in his tone which made them think, so the oiler quoth: "Yes! If this wind holds!"

The cook was bailing: "Yes! If we don't catch hell in the surf."

Canton flannel gulls° flew near and far. Sometimes they sat down on the sea, near patches of brown sea-weed that rolled over the waves with a movement like carpets on a line in a gale. The birds sat comfortably in groups, and they were envied by some in the dingey, for the wrath of the sea was no more to them than it was to a covey of prairie chickens a thousand miles inland. Often they came very close and stared at the men with black beadlike eyes. At these times they were uncanny and sinister in their unblinking scrutiny, and the men hooted angrily at them, telling them to be gone. One came, and evidently decided to alight on the top of the captain's head. The bird flew parallel to the boat and did not circle, but made short sidelong jumps in the air in chicken-fashion. His black eyes were wistfully fixed upon the captain's head. "Ugly brute," said the oiler to the bird. "You look as if you were made with a jackknife." The cook and the correspondent swore darkly at the creature. The captain naturally wished to knock it away with the end of the heavy painter,° but he did not dare do it, because anything resembling an emphatic gesture would have capsized this freighted boat, and so with his open hand, the captain gently and carefully waved the gull away. After it had been discouraged from the pursuit the captain

---

Canton flannel gulls: Canton flannel is a strong, warm cotton fabric, probably used here to suggest the imperviousness of the seagulls to the harsh elements.
painter: A rope attached to the bow of a boat for tying it to a dock.

breathed easier on account of his hair, and others breathed easier because the bird struck their minds at this time as being somehow grewsome and ominous.

In the meantime the oiler and the correspondent rowed. And also they rowed.

They sat together in the same seat, and each rowed an oar. Then the oiler took both oars; then the correspondent took both oars; then the oiler; then the correspondent. They rowed and they rowed. The very ticklish part of the business was when the time came for the reclining one in the stern to take his turn at the oars. By the very last star of truth, it is easier to steal eggs from under a hen than it was to change seats in the dingey. First the man in the stern slid his hand along the thwart and moved with care, as if he were of Sèvres.° Then the man in the rowing seat slid his hand along the other thwart. It was all done with the most extraordinary care. As the two sidled past each other, the whole party kept watchful eyes on the coming wave, and the captain cried: "Look out now! Steady there!"

The brown mats of sea-weed that appeared from time to time were like islands, bits of earth. They were travelling, apparently, neither one way nor the other. They were, to all intents, stationary. They informed the men in the boat that it was making progress slowly toward the land.

The captain, rearing cautiously in the bow, after the dingey soared on a great swell, said that he had seen the lighthouse at Mosquito Inlet. Presently the cook remarked that he had seen it. The correspondent was at the oars, then, and for some reason he too wished to look at the lighthouse, but his back was toward the far shore and the waves were important, and for some time he could not seize an opportunity to turn his head. But at last there came a wave more gentle than the others, and when at the crest of it he swiftly scoured the western horizon.

"See it?" said the captain.

"No," said the correspondent, slowly, "I didn't see anything."

"Look again," said the captain. He pointed. "It's exactly in that direction."

At the top of another wave, the correspondent did as he was bid, and this time his eyes chanced on a small still thing on the edge of the swaying horizon. It was precisely like the point of a pin. It took an anxious eye to find a lighthouse so tiny.

"Think we'll make it, captain?"

"If this wind holds and the boat don't swamp, we can't do much else," said the captain.

The little boat, lifted by each towering sea, and splashed viciously by the crests, made progress that in the absence of sea-weed was not apparent to those in her. She seemed just a wee thing wallowing, miraculously, top-up, at the mercy of five oceans. Occasionally, a great spread of water, like white flames, swarmed into her.

"Bail her, cook," said the captain, serenely.

"All right, captain," said the cheerful cook.

Sèvres: A delicate, ornately decorated French porcelain made near Paris.

III

It would be difficult to describe the subtle brotherhood of men that was here established on the seas. No one said that it was so. No one mentioned it. But it dwelt in the boat, and each man felt it warm him. They were a captain, an oiler, a cook, and a correspondent, and they were friends, friends in a more curiously iron-bound degree than may be common. The hurt captain, lying against the water-jar in the bow, spoke always in a low voice and calmly, but he could never command a more ready and swiftly obedient crew than the motley three of the dingey. It was more than a mere recognition of what was best for the common safety. There was surely in it a quality that was personal and heartfelt. And after this devotion to the commander of the boat there was this comradeship that the correspondent, for instance, who had been taught to be cynical of men, knew even at the time was the best experience of his life. But no one said that it was so. No one mentioned it.

"I wish we had a sail," remarked the captain. "We might try my overcoat on the end of an oar and give you two boys a chance to rest." So the cook and the correspondent held the mast and spread wide the overcoat. The oiler steered, and the little boat made good way with her new rig. Sometimes the oiler had to scull sharply to keep a sea from breaking into the boat, but otherwise sailing was a success.

Meanwhile the light-house had been growing slowly larger. It had now almost assumed color, and appeared like a little gray shadow on the sky. The man at the oars could not be prevented from turning his head rather often to try for a glimpse of this little gray shadow.

At last, from the top of each wave the men in the tossing boat could see land. Even as the light-house was an upright shadow on the sky, this land seemed but a long black shadow on the sea. It certainly was thinner than paper. "We must be about opposite New Smyrna,"° said the cook, who had coasted this shore often in schooners. "Captain, by the way, I believe they abandoned that life-saving station there about a year ago."

"Did they?" said the captain.

The wind slowly died away. The cook and the correspondent were not now obliged to slave in order to hold high the oar. But the waves continued their old impetuous swooping at the dingey, and the little craft, no longer under way, struggled woundily over them. The oiler or the correspondent took the oars again.

Shipwrecks are *apropos* of nothing. If men could only train for them and have them occur when the men had reached pink condition, there would be less drowning at sea. Of the four in the dingey none had slept any time worth mentioning for two days and two nights previous to embarking in the dingey, and in the excitement of clambering about the deck of a foundering ship they had also forgotten to eat heartily.

For these reasons, and for others, neither the oiler nor the correspondent was fond of rowing at this time. The correspondent wondered ingenuously

---

New Smyrna: A town on the Florida coast, south of Daytona Beach.

how in the name of all that was sane could there be people who thought it amusing to row a boat. It was not an amusement; it was a diabolical punishment, and even a genius of mental aberrations could never conclude that it was anything but a horror to the muscles and a crime against the back. He mentioned to the boat in general how the amusement of rowing struck him, and the weary-faced oiler smiled in full sympathy. Previously to the foundering, by the way, the oiler had worked double-watch in the engine-room of the ship.

"Take her easy, now, boys," said the captain. "Don't spend yourselves. If we have to run a surf you'll need all your strength, because we'll sure have to swim for it. Take your time."

Slowly the land arose from the sea. From a black line it became a line of black and a line of white, trees, and sand. Finally, the captain said that he could make out a house on the shore. "That's the house of refuge, sure," said the cook. "They'll see us before long, and come out after us."

The distant light-house reared high. "The keeper ought to be able to make us out now, if he's looking through a glass," said the captain. "He'll notify the life-saving people."

"None of those other boats could have got ashore to give word of the wreck," said the oiler, in a low voice. "Else the life-boat would be out hunting us."

Slowly and beautifully the land loomed out of the sea. The wind came again. It had veered from the northeast to the southeast. Finally, a new sound struck the ears of the men in the boat. It was the low thunder of the surf on the shore. "We'll never be able to make the light-house now," said the captain. "Swing her head a little more north, Billie," said the captain.

"'A little more north,' sir," said the oiler.

Whereupon the little boat turned her nose once more down the wind, and all but the oarsman watched the shore grow. Under the influence of this expansion doubt and direful apprehension was leaving the minds of the men. The management of the boat was still most absorbing, but it could not prevent a quiet cheerfulness. In an hour perhaps, they would be ashore.

Their back-bones had become thoroughly used to balancing in the boat and they now rode this wild colt of a dingey like circus men. The correspondent thought that he had been drenched to the skin, but happening to feel in the top pocket of his coat, he found therein eight cigars. Four of them were soaked with sea-water; four were perfectly scatheless. After a search, somebody produced three dry matches, and thereupon the four waifs rode in their little boat, and with an assurance of an impending rescue shining in their eyes, puffed at the big cigars and judged well and ill of all men. Everybody took a drink of water.

IV

"Cook," remarked the captain, "there don't seem to be any signs of life about your house of refuge."

"No," replied the cook. "Funny they don't see us!"

A broad stretch of lowly coast lay before the eyes of the men. It was of low dunes topped with dark vegetation. The roar of the surf was plain, and sometimes they could see the white lip of a wave as it spun up the beach. A tiny house was blocked out black upon the sky. Southward, the slim light-house lifted its little gray length.

Tide, wind, and waves were swinging the dingey northward. "Funny they don't see us," said the men.

The surf's roar was here dulled, but its tone was, nevertheless, thunderous and mighty. As the boat swam over the great rollers, the men sat listening to this roar.

"We'll swamp sure," said everybody.

It is fair to say here that there was not a life-saving station within twenty miles in either direction, but the men did not know this fact and in consequence they made dark and opprobrious remarks concerning the eyesight of the nation's life-savers. Four scowling men sat in the dingey and surpassed records in the invention of epithets.

"Funny they don't see us."

The light-heartedness of a former time had completely faded. To their sharpened minds it was easy to conjure pictures of all kinds of incompetency and blindness and, indeed, cowardice. There was the shore of the populous land, and it was bitter and bitter to them that from it came no sign.

"Well," said the captain, ultimately, "I suppose we'll have to make a try ourselves. If we stay out here too long we'll none of us have strength left to swim after the boat swamps."

And so the oiler, who was at the oars, turned the boat straight for the shore. There was a sudden tightening of muscles. There was some thinking.

"If we don't all get ashore—" said the captain. "If we don't all get ashore, I suppose you fellows know where to send news of my finish?"

They then briefly exchanged some addresses and admonitions. As for the reflections of the men, there was a great deal of rage in them. Perchance they might be formulated thus: "If I am going to be drowned—if I am going to be drowned—if I am going to be drowned, why, in the name of the seven mad gods who rule the sea, was I allowed to come thus far and contemplate sand and trees? Was I brought here merely to have my nose dragged away as I was about to nibble the sacred cheese of life? It is preposterous. If this old ninny-woman, Fate, cannot do better than this, she should be deprived of the management of men's fortunes. She is an old hen who knows not her intention. If she has decided to drown me, why did she not do it in the beginning and save me all this trouble. The whole affair is absurd. . . . But, no, she cannot mean to drown me. She dare not drown me. She cannot drown me. Not after all this work." Afterward the man might have had an impulse to shake his fist at the clouds: "Just you drown me, now, and then hear what I call you!"

The billows that came at this time were more formidable. They seemed always just about to break and roll over the little boat in a turmoil of foam. There was a preparatory and long growl in the speech of them. No mind unused to the sea would have concluded that the dingey could ascend these sheer heights in time. The shore was still afar. The oiler was a wily surfman. "Boys," he said, swiftly, "she won't live three minutes more and we're too far out to swim. Shall I take her to sea again, captain?"

"Yes! Go ahead!" said the captain.

This oiler, by a series of quick miracles, and fast and steady oarsmanship, turned the boat in the middle of the surf and took her safely to sea again.

There was a considerable silence as the boat bumped over the furrowed sea to deeper water. Then somebody in gloom spoke. "Well, anyhow, they must have seen us from the shore by now."

The gulls went in slanting flight up the wind toward the gray desolate east. A squall, marked by dingy clouds, and clouds brick-red, like smoke from a burning building, appeared from the southeast.

"What do you think of those life-saving people? Ain't they peaches?"

"Funny they haven't seen us."

"Maybe they think we're out here for sport! Maybe they think were fishin'. Maybe they think we're damned fools."

It was a long afternoon. A changed tide tried to force them southward, but wind and wave said northward. Far ahead, where coast-line, sea, and sky formed their mighty angle, there were little dots which seemed to indicate a city on the shore.

"St. Augustine?"

The captain shook his head. "Too near Mosquito Inlet."

And the oiler rowed, and then the correspondent rowed. Then the oiler rowed. It was a weary business. The human back can become the seat of more aches and pains than are registered in books for the composite anatomy of a regiment. It is a limited area, but it can become the theatre of innumerable muscular conflicts, tangles, wrenches, knots, and other comforts.

"Did you ever like to row, Billie?" asked the correspondent.

"No," said the oiler. "Hang it."

When one exchanged the rowing-seat for a place in the bottom of the boat, he suffered a bodily depression that caused him to be careless of everything save an obligation to wiggle one finger. There was cold sea-water swashing to and fro in the boat, and he lay in it. His head, pillowed on a thwart, was within an inch of the swirl of a wave crest, and sometimes a particularly obstreperous sea came in-board and drenched him once more. But these matters did not annoy him. It is almost certain that if the boat had capsized he would have tumbled comfortably out upon the ocean as if he felt sure that it was a great soft mattress.

"Look! There's a man on the shore!"

"Where?"

"There! See 'im? See 'im?"

"Yes, sure! He's walking along."

"Now he's stopped. Look! He's facing us!"

"He's waving at us!"

"So he is! By thunder!"

"Ah, now, we're all right! Now we're all right! There'll be a boat out here for us half an hour."

"He's going on. He's running. He's going up to that house there."

The remote beach seemed lower than the sea, and it required a searching glance to discern the little black figure. The captain saw a floating stick and they rowed to it. A bath-towel was by some weird chance in the boat, and, tying this on the stick, the captain waved it. The oarsman did not dare turn his head, so he was obliged to ask questions.

"What's he doing now?"

"He's standing still again. He's looking, I think. . . . There he goes again. Toward the house. . . . Now he's stopped again."

"Is he waving at us?"

"No, not now! he was, though."

"Look! There comes another man!"

"He's running."

"Look at him go, would you."

"Why, he's on a bicycle. Now he's met the other man. They're both waving at us. Look!"

"There comes something up the beach."

"What the devil is that thing?"

"Why, it looks like a boat."

"Why, certainly it's a boat."

"No, it's on wheels."

"Yes, so it is. Well, that must be the life-boat. They drag them along shore on a wagon."

"That's the life-boat, sure."

"No, by ——, it's—it's an omnibus."

"I tell you it's a life-boat."

"It is not! It's an omnibus. I can see it plain. See? One of these big hotel omnibuses."

"By thunder, you're right. It's an omnibus, sure as fate. What do you suppose they are doing with an omnibus? Maybe they are going around collecting the life-crew, hey?"

"That's it, likely. Look! There's a fellow waving a little black flag. He's standing on the steps of the omnibus. There come those other two fellows. Now they're all talking together. Look at the fellow with the flag. Maybe he ain't waving it."

"That ain't a flag, is it? That's his coat. Why, certainly, that's his coat."

"So it is. It's his coat. He's taken it off and is waving it around his head. But would you look at him swing it."

"Oh, say, there isn't any life-saving station there. That's just a winter resort hotel omnibus that has brought over some of the boarders to see us drown."

"What's that idiot with the coat mean? What's he signaling, anyhow?"

"It looks as if he were trying to tell us to go north. There must be a life-saving station up there."

"No! He thinks we're fishing. Just giving us a merry hand. See? Ah, there, Willie."

"Well, I wish I could make something out of those signals. What do you suppose he means?"

"He don't mean anything. He's just playing."

"Well, if he'd just signal us to try the surf again, or to go to sea and wait, or go north, or go south, or go to hell—there would be some reason in it. But look at him. He just stands there and keeps his coat revolving like a wheel. The ass!"

"There come more people."

"Now there's quite a mob. Look! Isn't that a boat?"

"Where? Oh, I see where you mean. No, that's no boat."

"That fellow is still waving his coat."

"He must think we like to see him do that. Why don't he quit it. It don't mean anything."

"I don't know. I think he is trying to make us go north. It must be that there's a life-saving station there somewhere."

"Say, he ain't tired yet. Look at 'im wave."

"Wonder how long he can keep that up. He's been revolving his coat ever since he caught sight of us. He's an idiot. Why aren't they getting men to bring a boat out. A fishing boat—one of those big yawls—could come out here all right. Why don't he do something?"

"Oh, it's all right, now."

"They'll have a boat out here for us in less than no time, now that they've seen us."

A faint yellow tone came into the sky over the low land. The shadows on the sea slowly deepened. The wind bore coldness with it, and the men began to shiver.

"Holy smoke!" said one, allowing his voice to express his impious mood, "if we keep on monkeying out here! If we've got to flounder out here all night!"

"Oh, we'll never have to stay here all night! Don't you worry. They've seen us now, and it won't be long before they'll come chasing out after us."

The shore grew dusky. The man waving a coat blended gradually into this gloom, and it swallowed in the same manner the omnibus and the group of people. The spray, when it dashed uproariously over the side, made the voyagers shrink and swear like men who were being branded.

"I'd like to catch the chump who waved the coat. I feel like soaking him one, just for luck."

"Why? What did he do?"

"Oh, nothing, but then he seemed so damned cheerful."

In the meantime the oiler rowed, and then the correspondent rowed, and then oiler rowed. Gray-faced and bowed forward, they mechanically, turn by turn, plied the leaden oars. The form of the light-house had vanished from the southern horizon, but finally a pale star appeared, just lifting from the sea. The streaked saffron in the west passed before the all-merging darkness, and the sea to the east was black. The land had vanished, and was expressed only by the low and drear thunder of the surf.

"If I am going to be drowned—if I am going to be drowned—if I am going to drowned, why, in the name of the seven mad gods, who rule the sea, was I allowed to come thus far and contemplate sand and trees? Was I brought here merely to have my nose dragged away as I was about to nibble the sacred cheese of life?"

The patient captain, drooped over the water-jar, was sometimes obliged to speak to the oarsman.

"Keep her head up! Keep her head up!"

" 'Keep her head up,' sir." The voices were weary and low.

This was surely a quiet evening. All save the oarsman lay heavily and listlessly in the boat's bottom. As for him, his eyes were just capable of noting the tall black waves that swept forward in a most sinister silence, save for an occasional subdued growl of a crest.

The cook's head was on a thwart, and he looked without interest at the water under his nose. He was deep in other scenes. Finally he spoke. "Billie," he murmured, dreamfully, "what kind of pie do you like best?"

V

"Pie," said the oiler and the correspondent, agitatedly. "Don't talk about those things, blast you!"

"Well," said the cook, "I was just thinking about ham sandwiches, and——"

A night on the sea in an open boat is a long night. As darkness settled finally, the shine of the light, lifting from the sea in the south, changed to full gold. On the northern horizon a new light appeared, a small bluish gleam on the edge of the waters. These two lights were the furniture of the world. Otherwise there was nothing but waves.

Two men huddled in the stern, and distances were so magnificent in the dingey that the rower was enabled to keep his feet partly warmed by thrusting them under his companions. Their legs indeed extended far under the rowing-seat until they touched the feet of the captain forward. Sometimes, despite the efforts of the tired oarsman, a wave came piling into the boat, an icy wave of the night, and the chilling water soaked them anew. They would twist their bodies for a moment and groan, and sleep the dead sleep once more, while the water in the boat gurgled about them as the craft rocked.

The plan of the oiler and the correspondent was for one to row until he lost the ability, and then arouse the other from his sea-water couch in the bottom of the boat.

The oiler plied the oars until his head drooped forward, and the overpowering sleep blinded him. And he rowed yet afterward. Then he touched a man in the bottom of the boat, and called his name. "Will you spell me for a little while?" he said, meekly.

"Sure, Billie," said the correspondent, awakening and dragging himself to a sitting position. They exchanged places carefully, and the oiler, cuddling down in the sea-water at the cook's side, seemed to go to sleep instantly.

The particular violence of the sea had ceased. The waves came without snarling. The obligation of the man at the oars was to keep the boat headed so that the tilt of the rollers would not capsize her, and to preserve her from filling when the crests rushed past. The black waves were silent and hard to be seen in the darkness. Often one was almost upon the boat before the oarsman was aware.

In a low voice the correspondent addressed the captain. He was not sure that the captain was awake, although this iron man seemed to be always awake. "Captain, shall I keep her making for that light north, sir?"

The same steady voice answered him. "Yes. Keep it about two points off the port bow."

The cook had tied a life-belt around himself in order to get even the warmth which this clumsy cork contrivance could donate, and he seemed almost stove-like when a rower, whose teeth invariably chattered wildly as soon as he ceased his labor, dropped down to sleep.

The correspondent, as he rowed, looked down at the two men sleeping under foot. The cook's arm was around the oiler's shoulders, and, with their fragmentary clothing and haggard faces, they were the babes of the sea, a grotesque rendering of the old babes in the wood.

Later he must have grown stupid at his work, for suddenly there was a growling of water, and a crest came with a roar and a swash into the boat, and it was a wonder that it did not set the cook afloat in his life-belt. The cook continued to sleep, but the oiler sat up, blinking his eyes and shaking with the new cold.

"Oh, I'm awful sorry, Billie," said the correspondent, contritely.

"That's all right, old boy," said the oiler, and lay down again and was asleep.

Presently it seemed that even the captain dozed, and the correspondent thought that he was the one man afloat on all the oceans. The wind had a voice as it came over the waves, and it was sadder than the end.

There was a long, loud swishing astern of the boat, and a gleaming trail of phosphorescence, like blue flame, was furrowed on the black waters. It might have been made by a monstrous knife.

Then there came a stillness, while the correspondent breathed with the open mouth and looked at the sea.

Suddenly there was another swish and another long flash of bluish light, and this time it was alongside the boat, and might almost have been reached with an oar. The correspondent saw an enormous fin speed like a shadow through the water, hurling the crystalline spray and leaving the long glowing trail.

The correspondent looked over his shoulder at the captain. His face was hidden, and he seemed to be asleep. He looked at the babes of the sea. They certainly were asleep. So, being bereft of sympathy, he leaned a little way to one side and swore softly into the sea.

But the thing did not then leave the vicinity of the boat. Ahead or astern, on one side or the other, at intervals long or short, fled the long sparkling streak, and there was to be heard the whiroo of the dark fin. The speed and power of the thing was greatly to be admired. It cut the water like a gigantic and keen projectile.

The presence of this biding thing did not affect the man with the same horror that it would if he had been a picnicker. He simply looked at the sea dully and swore in an undertone.

Nevertheless, it is true that he did not wish to be alone with the thing. He wished one of his companions to awaken by chance and keep him company with it. But the captain hung motionless over the water-jar and the oiler and the cook in the bottom of the boat were plunged in slumber.

VI

"If I am going to be drowned—if I am going to be drowned—if I am going to be drowned, why, in the name of the seven mad gods, who rule the sea, was I allowed to come thus far and contemplate sand and trees?"

During this dismal night, it may be remarked that a man would conclude that it was really the intention of the seven mad gods to drown him, despite the abominable injustice of it. For it was certainly an abominable injustice to drown a man who had worked so hard. The man felt it would be a crime most unnatural. Other people had drowned at sea since galleys swarmed with painted sails, but still——

When it occurs to a man that nature does not regard him as important, and that she feels she would not maim the universe by disposing of him, he at first wishes to throw bricks at the temple, and hates deeply the fact that there are no bricks and no temples. Any visible expression of nature would surely be pelleted with his jeers.

Then, if there be no tangible thing to hoot he feels, perhaps, the desire to confront a personification and indulge in pleas, bowed to one knee, and with hands supplicant, saying: "Yes, but I love myself."

A high cold star on a winter's night is the word he feels that she says to him. Thereafter he knows the pathos of his situation.

The men in the dingey had not discussed these matters, but each had, no doubt, reflected upon them in silence and according to his mind. There was seldom any expression upon their faces save the general one of complete weariness. Speech was devoted to the business of the boat.

To chime the notes of his emotion, a verse mysteriously entered the correspondent's head. He had even forgotten that he had forgotten this verse, but it suddenly was in his mind.

A soldier of the Legion lay dying in Algiers,
There was lack of woman's nursing, there was
dearth of woman's tears;
But a comrade stood beside him, and he took
that comrade's hand
And he said: "I shall never see my own, my
native land."°

In his childhood, the correspondent had been made acquainted with the fact that a soldier of the Legion lay dying in Algiers, but he had never regarded the fact as important. Myriads of his school-fellows had informed him of the soldier's plight, but the dinning had naturally ended by making him perfectly

A soldier . . . land: Crane is loosely quoting the first stanza of the popular poem about the death of a French legionnaire, "Bingen on the Rhine" (1883), by Caroline E. S. Norton (1808–1877): "A soldier of the Legion lay dying in Algiers, / There was a lack of woman's nursing, there was dearth of woman's tears; / But a comrade stood beside him, while his lifeblood ebbed away, / And bent with pitying glances, to hear what he might say. / The dying soldier faltered, and he took that comrade's hand, / And he said, "I nevermore shall see my own, my native land: / Take a message, and a token, to some distant friends of mine, / For I was born at Bingen,—at Bingen on the Rhine."

indifferent. He had never considered it his affair that a soldier of the Legion lay dying in Algiers, nor had it appeared to him as a matter for sorrow. It was less to him than breaking of a pencil's point.

Now, however, it quaintly came to him as a human, living thing. It was no longer merely a picture of a few throes in the breast of a poet, meanwhile drinking tea and warming his feet at the grate; it was an actuality—stern, mournful, and fine.

The correspondent plainly saw the soldier. He lay on the sand with his feet out straight and still. While his pale left hand was upon his chest in an attempt to thwart the going of his life, the blood came between his fingers. In the far Algerian distance, a city of low square forms was set against a sky that was faint with the last sunset hues. The correspondent, plying the oars and dreaming of the slow and slower movements of the lips of the soldier, was moved by a profound and perfectly impersonal comprehension. He was sorry for the soldier of the Legion who lay dying in Algiers.

The thing which had followed the boat and waited had evidently grown bored at the delay. There was no longer to be heard the slash of the cut-water, and there was no longer the flame of the long trail. The light in the north still glimmered, but it was apparently no nearer to the boat. Sometimes the boom of the surf rang in the correspondent's ears, and he turned the craft seaward then and rowed harder. Southward, someone had evidently built a watch-fire on the beach. It was too low and too far to be seen, but it made a shimmering, roseate reflection upon the bluff back of it, and this could be discerned from the boat. The wind came stronger, and sometimes a wave suddenly raged out like a mountain-cat and there was to be seen the sheen and sparkle of a broken crest.

The captain, in the bow, moved on his water-jar and sat erect. "Pretty long night," he observed to the correspondent. He looked at the shore. "Those life-saving people take their time."

"Did you see that shark playing around?"

"Yes, I saw him. He was a big fellow, all right."

"Wish I had known you were awake."

Later the correspondent spoke into the bottom of the boat.

"Billie!" There was a slow and gradual disentanglement. "Billie, will you spell me?"

"Sure," said the oiler.

As soon as the correspondent touched the cold comfortable sea-water in the bottom of the boat, and had huddled close to the cook's life-belt he was deep in sleep, despite the fact that his teeth played all the popular airs. This sleep was so good to him that it was but a moment before he heard a voice call his name in a tone that demonstrated the last stages of exhaustion. "Will you spell me?"

"Sure, Billie."

The light in the north had mysteriously vanished, but the correspondent took his course from the wide-awake captain.

Later in the night they took the boat farther out to sea, and the captain directed the cook to take one oar at the stern and keep the boat facing the seas. He was to call out if he should hear the thunder of the surf. This plan enabled the oiler and the correspondent to get respite together. "We'll give those boys a chance to get into shape again," said the captain. They curled down and, after a few preliminary chatterings and trembles, slept once more the dead sleep. Neither knew they had bequeathed to the cook the company of another shark, or perhaps the same shark.

As the boat caroused on the waves, spray occasionally bumped over the side and gave them a fresh soaking, but this had no power to break their repose. The ominous slash of the wind and the water affected them as it would have affected mummies.

"Boys," said the cook, with the notes of every reluctance in his voice, "she's drifted in pretty close. I guess one of you had better take her to sea again." The correspondent, aroused, heard the crash of the toppled crests.

As he was rowing, the captain gave him some whiskey and water, and this steadied the chills out of him. "If I ever get ashore and anybody shows me even a photograph of an oar——"

At last there was a short conversation.

"Billie. . . . Billie, will you spell me?"

"Sure," said the oiler.

VII

When the correspondent again opened his eyes, the sea and the sky were each of the gray hue of the dawning. Later, carmine and gold was painted upon the waters. The morning appeared finally, in its splendor, with a sky of pure blue, and the sunlight flamed on the tips of the waves.

On the distant dunes were set many little black cottages, and a tall white wind-mill reared above them. No man, nor dog, nor bicycle appeared on the beach. The cottages might have formed a deserted village.

The voyagers scanned the shore. A conference was held in the boat. "Well," said the captain, "if no help is coming, we might better try a run through the surf right away. If we stay out here much longer we will be too weak to do anything for ourselves at all." The others silently acquiesced in this reasoning. The boat was headed for the beach. The correspondent wondered if none ever ascended the tall wind-tower, and if then they never looked seaward. This tower was a giant, standing with its back to the plight of the ants. It represented in a degree, to the correspondent, the serenity of nature amid the struggles of the individual—nature in the wind, and nature in the vision of men. She did not seem cruel to him then, nor beneficent, nor treacherous, nor wise. But she was indifferent, flatly indifferent. It is, perhaps, plausible that a man in this situation pressed with the unconcern of the universe, should see the innumerable flaws of his life and have them taste wickedly in his mind and wish for another chance. A distinction between right and wrong seems absurdly clear to him, then, in this new ignorance of the grave-edge, and he understands that if he were given another opportunity he would mend his conduct and his words, and be better and brighter during an introduction, or at a tea.

"Now, boys," said the captain, "she is going to swamp sure. All we can do is to work her in as far as possible, and then when she swamps, pile out and scramble for the beach. Keep cool now and don't jump until she swamps sure."

The oiler took the oars. Over his shoulders he scanned the surf. "Captain," he said, "I think I'd better bring her about, and keep her head-on to the seas and back her in."

"All right, Billie," said the captain. "Back her in." The oiler swung the boat then and, seated in the stern, the cook and the correspondent were obliged to look over their shoulders to contemplate the lonely and indifferent shore.

The monstrous inshore rollers heaved the boat high until the men were again enabled to see the white sheets of water scudding up the slanted beach. "We won't get in very close," said the captain. Each time a man could wrest his attention from the rollers, he turned his glance toward the shore, and in the expression of the eyes during this contemplation there was a singular quality. The correspondent, observing the others, knew that they were not afraid, but the full meaning of their glances was shrouded.

As for himself, he was too tired to grapple fundamentally with the fact. He tried to coerce his mind into thinking of it, but the mind was dominated at this time by the muscles, and the muscles said they did not care. It merely occurred to him that if he should drown it would be a shame.

There were no hurried words, no pallor, no plain agitation. The men simply looked at the shore. "Now, remember to get well clear of the boat when you jump," said the captain.

Seaward the crest of a roller suddenly fell with a thunderous crash, and the long white comber came roaring down upon the boat.

"Steady now," said the captain. The men were silent. They turned their eyes from the shore to the comber and waited. The boat slid up the incline, leaped at the furious top, bounced over it, and swung down the long back of the waves. Some water had been shipped and the cook bailed it out.

But the next crest crashed also. The tumbling boiling flood of white water caught the boat and whirled it almost perpendicular. Water swarmed in from all sides. The correspondent had his hands on the gunwale° at this time, and when the water entered at that place he swiftly withdrew his fingers, as if he objected to wetting them.

The little boat, drunken with this weight of water, reeled and snuggled deeper into the sea.

"Bail her out, cook! Bail her out," said the captain.

"All right, captain," said the cook.

"Now, boys, the next one will do for sure," said the oiler. "Mind to jump clear of the boat."

The third wave moved forward, huge, furious, implacable. It fairly swallowed the dingey, and almost simultaneously the men tumbled into the sea. A piece of life-belt had lain in the bottom of the boat, and as the correspondent went overboard he held this to his chest with his left hand.

---

gunwale: The upper edge of the side of the boat.

The January water was icy, and he reflected immediately that it was colder than he had expected to find it off the coast of Florida. This appeared to his dazed mind as a fact important enough to be noted at the time. The coldness of the water was sad; it was tragic. This fact was somehow mixed and confused with his opinion of his own situation that it seemed almost a proper reason for tears. The water was cold.

When he came to the surface he was conscious of little but the noisy water. Afterward he saw his companions in the sea. The oiler was ahead in the race. He was swimming strongly and rapidly. Off to correspondent's left, the cook's great white and corked back bulged out of the water, and in the rear the captain was hanging with his one good hand to the keel of the overturned dingey.

There is a certain immovable quality to a shore, and the correspondent wondered at it amid the confusion of the sea.

It seemed also very attractive, but the correspondent knew that it was a long journey, and he paddled leisurely. The piece of life-preserver lay under him, and sometimes he whirled down the incline of a wave as if he were on a hand-sled.

But finally he arrived at a place in the sea where travel was beset with difficulty. He did not pause swimming to inquire what manner of current had caught him, but there his progress ceased. The shore was set before him like a bit of scenery on a stage, and he looked at it and understood with his eyes each detail of it.

As the cook passed, much farther to the left, the captain was calling to him, "Turn over on your back, cook! Turn over on your back and use the oar."

"All right, sir." The cook turned on his back, and, paddling with an oar, went ahead as if he were a canoe.

Presently the boat also passed to the left of the correspondent with the captain clinging with one hand to the keel. He would have appeared like a man raising himself to look over a board fence, if it were not for the extraordinary gymnastics of the boat. The correspondent marvelled that the captain could still hold it.

They passed on, nearer to shore—the oiler, the cook, the captain—and following them went the water-jar, bouncing gayly over the seas.

The correspondent remained in the grip of this strange new enemy—a current. The shore, with its white slope of sand and its green bluff, topped with little silent cottages, was spread like a picture before him. It was very near to him then, but he was impressed as one who in a gallery looks at a scene from Brittany or Algiers.

He thought: "I am going to drown? Can it be possible? Can it be possible? Can it be possible?" Perhaps an individual must consider his own death to be the final phenomenon of nature.

But later a wave perhaps whirled him out of this small deadly current, for he found suddenly that he could again make progress toward the shore. Later still, he was aware that the captain, clinging with one hand to the keel of the dingey, had his face turned away from the shore and toward him, and was calling his name. "Come to the boat! Come to the boat!"

In his struggle to reach the captain and the boat, he reflected that when one gets properly wearied, drowning must really be a comfortable arrangement, a cessation of hostilities accompanied by a large degree of relief, and he was glad of it, for the main thing in his mind for some moments had been horror of the temporary agony. He did not wish to be hurt.

Presently he saw a man running along the shore. He was undressing with most remarkable speed. Coat, trousers, shirt, everything flew magically off him.

"Come to the boat," called the captain.

"All right, captain." As the correspondent paddled, he saw the captain let himself down to bottom and leave the boat. Then the correspondent performed his one little marvel of the voyage. A large wave caught him and flung him with ease and supreme speed completely over the boat and far beyond it. It struck him even then as an event in gymnastics, and a true miracle of the sea. An overturned boat in the surf is not a plaything to a swimming man.

The correspondent arrived in water that reached only to his waist, but his condition did not enable him to stand for more than a moment. Each wave knocked him into a heap, and the under-tow pulled at him.

Then he saw the man who had been running and undressing, and undressing and running, come bounding into the water. He dragged ashore the cook, and then waded toward the captain, but the captain waved him away, and sent him to the correspondent. He was naked, naked as a tree in winter, but a halo was about his head, and he shone like a saint. He gave a strong pull, and a long drag, and a bully heave at the correspondent's hand. The correspondent, schooled in the minor formulae, said: "Thanks, old man." But suddenly the man cried: "What's that?" He pointed a swift finger. The correspondent said: "Go."

In the shallows, face downward, lay the oiler. His forehead touched sand that was periodically, between each wave, clear of the sea.

The correspondent did not know all that transpired afterward. When he achieved safe ground he fell, striking the sand with each particular part of his body. It was as if he had dropped from a roof, but the thud was grateful to him.

It seems that instantly the beach was populated with men with blankets, clothes, and flasks, and women with coffee-pots and all the remedies sacred to their minds. The welcome of the land to the men from the sea was warm and generous, but a still and dripping shape was carried slowly up the beach, and the land's welcome for it could only be the different and sinister hospitality of the grave.

When it came night, the white waves paced to and fro in the moonlight, and the wind brought the sound of the great sea's voice to the men on shore, and they felt that they could then be interpreters.

COMMENTARY

STEPHEN CRANE

Stephen Crane wrote about the wreck of the *Commodore* in the article "Stephen Crane's Own Story" in the *New York Press* on January 7, 1897. At that time arms and provisions were being smuggled from Florida to Cuba to aid the insurrection against Spanish rule. Crane boarded the *Commodore* in Jacksonville on December 31, 1896. The ship was loaded with a cargo of rifles and ammunition. As the scholar Olov W. Fryckstedt explained, Crane "looked forward to a long period of unknown adventures and exciting dangers in the Cuban mountains. But during the night of January 1 the ship foundered fifteen miles off the coast of Florida after a mysterious explosion in the engine room." The first part of Crane's newspaper story describes the loading of the ship, the peril of sandbars, the explosion in the engine room, and the lowering of the lifeboats. Then, with the ship's "whistle of despair," it became clear to everyone on board that the situation was hopeless. The bustling action before the shipwreck is the substance of Crane's newspaper report; his thirty desperate hours afterward in the ten-foot dinghy became the story of "The Open Boat."

The Sinking of the *Commodore* 1897

A Whistle of Despair

Now the whistle of the *Commodore* had been turned loose, and if there ever was a voice of despair and death, it was in the voice of this whistle. It had gained a new tone. It was as if its throat was already choked by the water, and this cry on the sea at night, with a wind blowing the spray over the ship, and the waves roaring over the bow, and swirling white along the decks, was to each of us probably a song of man's end.

It was now that the first mate showed a sign of losing his grip. To us who were trying in all stages of competence and experience to launch the lifeboat he raged in all terms of fiery satire and hammerlike abuse. But the boat moved at last and swung down toward the water.

Afterward, when I went aft, I saw the captain standing, with his arm in a sling, holding on to a stay with his one good hand and directing the launching of the boat. He gave me a five-gallon jug of water to hold, and asked me what I was going to do. I told him what I thought was about the proper thing, and he told me then that the cook had the same idea, and ordered me to go forward and be ready to launch the ten-foot dinghy.

In the Ten-Foot Dinghy

I remember well that he turned then to swear at a colored stoker who was prowling around, done up in life preservers until he looked like a feather bed. I went forward with my five-gallon jug of water, and when the captain came we launched the dinghy, and they put me over the side to fend her off from the ship with an oar.

They handed me down the water jug, and then the cook came into the boat, and we sat there in the darkness, wondering why, by all our hopes of future happiness, the captain was so long in coming over to the side and ordering us away from the doomed ship.

The captain was waiting for the other boat to go. Finally he hailed in the darkness: "Are you all right, Mr. Graines?"

The first mate answered: "All right, sir."

"Shove off, then," cried the captain.

The captain was just about to swing over the rail when a dark form came forward and a voice said, "Captain, I go with you."

The captain answered: "Yes, Billy; get in."

Higgins Last to Leave Ship

It was Billy Higgins, the oiler. Billy dropped into the boat and a moment later the captain followed, bringing with him an end of about forty yards of lead line. The other end was attached to the rail of the ship.

As we swung back to leeward the captain said: "Boys, we will stay right near the ship till she goes down."

This cheerful information, of course, filled us all with glee. The line kept us headed properly into the wind, and as we rode over the monstrous waves we saw upon each rise the swaying lights of the dying *Commodore.*

When came the gray shade of dawn, the form of the *Commodore* grew slowly clear to us as our little ten-foot boat rose over each swell. She was floating with such an air of buoyancy that we laughed when we had time, and said, "What a gag it would be on those other fellows if she didn't sink at all."

But later we saw men aboard of her, and later still they began to hail us.

Helping Their Mates

I had forgot to mention that previously we had loosened the end of the lead line and dropped much further to leeward. The men on board were a mystery to us, of course, as we had seen all the boats leave the ship. We rowed back to the ship, but did not approach too near, because we were four men in a ten-foot boat, and we knew that the touch of a hand on our gunwale would assuredly swamp us.

The first mate cried out from the ship that the third boat had foundered alongside. He cried that they had made rafts, and wished us to tow them.

The captain said, "All right."

Their rafts were floating astern. "Jump in!" cried the captain, but there was a singular and most harrowing hesitation. There were five white men and two negroes. This scene in the gray light of morning impressed one as would a view into some place where ghosts move slowly. These seven men on the stern of the sinking *Commodore* were silent. Save the words of the mate to the captain there was no talk. Here was death, but here also was a most singular and indefinable kind of fortitude.

Four men, I remember, clambered over the railing and stood there watching the cold, steely sheen of the sweeping waves.

"Jump," cried the captain again.

The old chief engineer first obeyed the order. He landed on the outside raft and the captain told him how to grip the raft and he obeyed as promptly and as docilely as a scholar in riding school.

The Mate's Mad Plunge

A stoker followed him, and then the first mate threw his hands over his head and plunged into the sea. He had no life belt and for my part, even when he did this horrible thing, I somehow felt that I could see in the expression of his hands, and in the very toss of his head, as he leaped thus to death, that it was rage, rage, rage unspeakable that was in his heart at the time.

And then I saw Tom Smith, the man who was going to quit filibustering after this expedition, jump to a raft and turn his face toward us. On board the *Commodore* three men strode, still in silence and with their faces turned toward us. One man had his arms folded and was leaning against the deckhouse. His feet were crossed, so that the toe of his left foot pointed downward. There they stood gazing at us, and neither from the deck nor from the rafts was a voice raised. Still was there this silence.

Tried to Tow the Rafts

The colored stoker on the first raft threw us a line and we began to tow. Of course, we perfectly understood the absolute impossibility of any such thing; our dinghy was within six inches of the water's edge, there was an enormous sea running, and I knew that under the circumstances a tugboat would have no light task in moving these rafts.

But we tried it, and would have continued to try it indefinitely, but that something critical came to pass. I was at an oar and so faced the rafts. The cook controlled the line. Suddenly the boat began to go backward and then we saw this negro on the first raft pulling on the line hand over hand and drawing us to him.

He had turned into a demon. He was wild—wild as a tiger. He was crouched on this raft and ready to spring. Every muscle of him seemed to be turned into an elastic spring. His eyes were almost white. His face was the face of a lost man reaching upward, and we knew that the weight of his hand on our gunwale doomed us.

The *Commodore* Sinks

The cook let go of the line. We rowed around to see if we could not get a line from the chief engineer, and all this time, mind you, there were no shrieks, no groans, but silence, silence and silence, and then the *Commodore* sank.

She lurched to windward, then swung afar back, righted and dove into the sea, and the rafts were suddenly swallowed by this frightful maw of the ocean. And then by the men on the ten-foot dinghy were words said that were still not words—something far beyond words.

The lighthouse of Mosquito Inlet stuck up above the horizon like the point of a pin. We turned our dinghy toward the shore.

The history of life in an open boat for thirty hours would no doubt be instructive for the young, but none is to be told here and now. For my part I would prefer to tell the story at once, because from it would shine the splendid manhood of Captain Edward Murphy and of William Higgins, the oiler, but let it suffice at this time to say that when we were swamped in the surf and making the best of our way toward the shore the captain gave orders amid the wildness of the breakers as clearly as if he had been on the quarter deck of a battleship.

John Kitchell of Daytona came running down the beach, and as he ran the air was filled with clothes. If he had pulled a single lever and undressed, even as the fire horses harness, he could not seem to me to have stripped with more speed. He dashed into the water and dragged the cook. Then he went after the captain, but the captain sent him to me, and then it was that he saw Billy Higgins lying with his forehead on sand that was clear of the water, and he was dead.

JUNOT DÍAZ

Junot Díaz (b. 1968) was born in Santo Domingo, Dominican Republic. At the age of seven he immigrated with his mother, brother, and sister to the United States and grew up in a black and Hispanic neighborhood in New Jersey. After graduating from Rutgers University, he earned his M.F.A. studying fiction at Cornell University and began to write stories about immigrants from the Dominican Republic who were redefining their American identity. In 1996 Díaz published his first book, *Drown*, a collection of ten stories, to great critical acclaim. The reviewer Francine Prose admired his "spare, tense, powerful" depiction of the "rocky, dangerous road that leads his characters to adulthood – from the barrios and villages of the Dominican Republic to the crowded apartments and crack dens of New Jersey's inner cities." *Drown* became an alternate selection of the Book-of-the-Month Club and the Quality Paperback Book Club, and *Newsweek* named Díaz as one of the "New Faces of 1996."

In contrast to the media's fanfare, Díaz quietly expressed his thanks on the last page of *Drown* to the many people who had helped him to develop his voice as a writer. He began with a general acknowledgment of his debt to the Hispanic community in Barrio XXI and to his family and continued with a list of thirty-two people who had supported and mentored him over the years, including the Hispanic writer Helena María Viramontes and his agent Nicole Aragi: "You believed and people listened."

Díaz has said that, when he was seven, what he wanted most out of his family's move to the United States was McDonald's fast food and television. Looking back, he now sees that "the moment my family set foot in Kennedy Airport a world ended for me. You'd think that sort of cataclysm would make itself apparent quickly and with umbrage, but in actuality it took me years to notice. The end was not so much an apocalypse as it was a fading, a merging, and, ultimately, a metamorphosis." Díaz didn't return to the Dominican Republic until he was in college because

> that world which was almost but not entirely lost has always haunted me. When I write I try to remember it well. . . . A lot of my fiction concerns itself with

> the lives of Dominicans in the United States, but I don't think I would perceive the landscape of those experiences as well without another lens through which to view it.

Currently Díaz lives and writes in Brooklyn, New York. "How to Date a Browngirl, Blackgirl, Whitegirl, or Halfie" is from *Drown. The Brief, Wondrous Life of Oscar Wao* (2007), his first novel, won the National Book Critics Circle Award and the Pulitzer Prize for Fiction.

WEB Research Junot Díaz at bedfordstmartins.com/rewritinglit.

How to Date a Browngirl, Blackgirl, Whitegirl, or Halfie 1996

Wait for your brother and your mother to leave the apartment. You've already told them that you're feeling too sick to go to Union City to visit that tía° who likes to squeeze your nuts. (He's gotten big, she'll say.) And even though your moms knows you ain't sick you stuck to your story until finally she said, Go ahead and stay, malcriado.°

Clear the government cheese from the refrigerator. If the girl's from the Terrace stack the boxes behind the milk. If she's from the Park or Society Hill hide the cheese in the cabinet above the oven, way up where she'll never see. Leave yourself a reminder to get it out before morning or your moms will kick your ass. Take down any embarrassing photos of your family in the campo, especially the one with the half-naked kids dragging a goat on a rope leash. The kids are your cousins and by now they're old enough to understand why you're doing what you're doing. Hide the pictures of yourself with an Afro. Make sure the bathroom is presentable. Put the basket with all the crapped-on toilet paper under the sink. Spray the bucket with Lysol, then close the cabinet.

Shower, comb, dress. Sit on the couch and watch TV. If she's an outsider her father will be bringing her, maybe her mother. Neither of them want her seeing any boys from the Terrace—people get stabbed in the Terrace—but she's strong-headed and this time will get her way. If she's a whitegirl you know you'll at least get a hand job.

The directions were in your best handwriting, so her parents won't think you're an idiot. Get up from the couch and check the parking lot. Nothing. If the girl's local, don't sweat it. She'll flow over when she's good and ready. Sometimes she'll run into her other friends and a whole crowd will show up at your apartment and even though that means you ain't getting shit it will be fun anyway and you'll wish these people would come over more often. Sometimes the girl won't flow over at all and the next day in school she'll say sorry, smile and you'll be stupid enough to believe her and ask her out again.

Wait and after an hour go out to your corner. The neighborhood is full of traffic. Give one of your boys a shout and when he says, Are you still waiting on that bitch? say, Hell yeah.

---

tía: Aunt.
malcriado: A spoiled or ill-mannered child.

Get back inside. Call her house and when her father picks up ask if she's there. He'll ask, Who is this? Hang up. He sounds like a principal or a police chief, the sort of dude with a big neck, who never has to watch his back. Sit and wait. By the time your stomach's ready to give out on you, a Honda or maybe a Jeep pulls in and out she comes.

Hey, you'll say.

Look, she'll say. My mom wants to meet you. She's got herself all worried about nothing.

Don't panic. Say, Hey, no problem. Run a hand through your hair like the whiteboys do even though the only thing that runs easily through your hair is Africa. She will look good. The white ones are the ones you want the most, aren't they, but usually the out-of-towners are black, blackgirls who grew up with ballet and Girl Scouts, who have three cars in their driveways. If she's a halfie don't be surprised that her mother is white. Say, Hi. Her moms will say hi and you'll see that you don't scare her, not really. She will say that she needs easier directions to get out and even though she has the best directions in her lap give her new ones. Make her happy.

You have choices. If the girl's from around the way, take her to El Cibao for dinner. Order everything in your busted-up Spanish. Let her correct you if she's Latina and amaze her if she's black. If she's not from around the way, Wendy's will do. As you walk to the restaurant talk about school. A local girl won't need stories about the neighborhood but the other ones might. Supply the story about the loco who'd been storing canisters of tear gas in his basement for years, how one day the canisters cracked and the whole neighborhood got a dose of the military strength stuff. Don't tell her that your moms knew right away what it was, that she recognized its smell from the year the United States invaded your island.

Hope that you don't run into your nemesis, Howie, the Puerto Rican kid with the two killer mutts. He walks them all over the neighborhood and every now and then the mutts corner themselves a cat and tear it to shreds, Howie laughing as the cat flips up in the air, its neck twisted around like an owl, red meat showing through the soft fur. If his dogs haven't cornered a cat, he will walk behind you and ask, Hey, Yunior, is that your new fuckbuddy?

Let him talk. Howie weighs about two hundred pounds and could eat you if he wanted. At the field he will turn away. He has new sneakers, and doesn't want them muddy. If the girl's an outsider she will hiss now and say, What a fucking asshole. A homegirl would have been yelling back at him the whole time, unless she was shy. Either way don't feel bad that you didn't do anything. Never lose a fight on a first date or that will be the end of it.

Dinner will be tense. You are not good at talking to people you don't know. A halfie will tell you that her parents met in the Movement, will say, Back then people thought it a radical thing to do. It will sound like something her parents made her memorize. Your brother once heard that one and said, Man, that sounds like a whole lot of Uncle Tomming to me. Don't repeat this.

Put down your hamburger and say, It must have been hard.

She will appreciate your interest. She will tell you more. Black people, she will say, treat me real bad. That's why I don't like them. You'll wonder how she feels about Dominicans. Don't ask. Let her speak on it and when you're both finished eating walk back into the neighborhood. The skies will be magnificent. Pollutants have made Jersey sunsets one of the wonders of the world. Point it out. Touch her shoulder and say, That's nice, right?

Get serious. Watch TV but stay alert. Sip some of the Bermúdez your father left in the cabinet, which nobody touches. A local girl may have hips and a thick ass but she won't be quick about letting you touch. She has to live in the same neighborhood you do, has to deal with you being all up in her business. She might just chill with you and then go home. She might kiss you and then go, or she might, if she's reckless, give it up, but that's rare. Kissing will suffice. A whitegirl might just give it up right then. Don't stop her. She'll take her gum out of her mouth, stick it to the plastic sofa covers and then will move close to you. You have nice eyes, she might say.

Tell her that you love her hair, that you love her skin, her lips, because, in truth, you love them more than you love your own.

She'll say, I like Spanish guys, and even though you've never been to Spain, say, I like you. You'll sound smooth.

You'll be with her until about eight-thirty and then she will want to wash up. In the bathroom she will hum a song from the radio and her waist will keep the beat against the lip of the sink. Imagine her old lady coming to get her, what she would say if she knew her daughter had just lain under you and blown your name, pronounced with her eighth-grade Spanish, into your ear. While she's in the bathroom call one of your boys and say, Lo hice, loco. Or just sit back on the couch and smile.

But usually it won't work this way. Be prepared. She will not want to kiss you. Just cool it, she'll say. The halfie might lean back, breaking away from you. She will cross her arms, say, I hate my tits. Stroke her hair but she will pull away. I don't like anybody touching my hair, she will say. She will act like somebody you don't know. In school she is known for her attention-grabbing laugh, as high and far-ranging as a gull, but here she will worry you. You will not know what to say.

You're the only kind of guy who asks me out, she will say. Your neighbors will start their hyena calls, now that the alcohol is in them. You and the blackboys.

Say nothing. Let her button her shirt, let her comb her hair, the sound of it stretching like a sheet of fire between you. When her father pulls in and beeps, let her go without too much of a good-bye. She won't want it. During the next hour the phone will ring. You will be tempted to pick it up. Don't. Watch the shows you want to watch, without a family around to debate you. Don't go downstairs. Don't fall asleep. It won't help. Put the government cheese back in its place before your moms kills you.

RALPH ELLISON

Ralph Ellison (1914–1994) was born in Oklahoma City. His father, a small-time vendor of ice and coal, died when Ellison was three, and thereafter his mother worked as a domestic servant to support herself and her son. Ellison later credited his mother, who recruited black votes for the Socialist Party, for turning him into an activist. She also brought home discarded books and phonograph records from the white households where she worked, and as a boy Ellison developed an interest in literature and music. He played trumpet in his high school band, and it was at this time that he began to relate the works of fiction he was reading to real life. "I began to look at my own life through the lives of fictional characters," he observed. "When I read Stendhal, I would search until I began to find patterns of a Stendhalian novel within the Negro communities in which I grew up. I began, in other words, quite early to connect the worlds projected in literature . . . with the life in which I found myself."

In 1933 Ellison entered Tuskegee Institute in Alabama, where he studied music for three years. Then he went to New York City and met the black writers Langston Hughes and Richard Wright, whose encouragement helped him to become a writer. Wright turned Ellison's attention to writing short stories and reading "those works in which writing was discussed as a craft . . . to Henry James's prefaces, to Conrad," and to other authors. In 1939 Ellison's short stories, essays, and reviews began to appear in periodicals. After World War II, he settled down to work on the novel *Invisible Man.* Published in 1952, it received the National Book Award for fiction and was listed in a 1965 *Book Week* poll as the most distinguished American novel of the preceding twenty years. As the critic Richard D. Lyons recognized, the novel was "a chronicle of a young black man's awakening to racial discrimination and his battle against the refusal of Americans to see him apart from his ethnic background, which in turn leads to humiliation and disillusionment." "Battle Royal," an excerpt from *Invisible Man,* is often anthologized. It appears after the prologue describing the underground chamber in which the nameless protagonist has retreated from the chaos of life aboveground.

Insisting that "art by its nature is social," Ellison began *Invisible Man* with the words "I am an invisible man. No, I am not a spook like those who haunted Edgar Allan Poe; nor am I one of your Hollywood-movie ectoplasms. I am a man of substance, of flesh and bone, fiber and liquids—and I might even be said to possess a mind. I am invisible, understand, simply because people refuse to see me." At the time of his death from cancer, Ellison left an unfinished second novel started in the late 1950s. His initial work on the manuscript was destroyed in a fire, and he never completed the book, which he called his "forty-year work in progress (*very* long in progress)." Titled *Juneteenth* (1999), it was edited posthumously by his widow, Fanny, and John Callahan. In addition to *Invisible Man,* Ellison published a few short stories and two collections of essays, *Shadow and Act* (1964) and *Going to the Territory* (1986). He was also the Albert Schweitzer Professor of Contemporary Literature and Culture at New York University.

WEB Research Ralph Ellison at bedfordstmartins.com/rewritinglit.

Battle Royal

1952

It goes a long way back, some twenty years. All my life I had been looking for something, and everywhere I turned someone tried to tell me what it was. I accepted their answers too, though they were often in contradiction and even self-contradictory. I was naïve. I was looking for myself and asking everyone except myself questions which I, and only I, could answer. It took me a long time and much painful boomeranging of my expectations to achieve a realization everyone else appears to have been born with: That I am nobody but myself. But first I had to discover that I am an invisible man!

And yet I am no freak of nature, nor of history. I was in the cards, other things having been equal (or unequal) eighty-five years ago. I am not ashamed of my grandparents for having been slaves. I am only ashamed of myself for having at one time been ashamed. About eighty-five years ago they were told that they were free, united with others of our country in everything pertaining to the common good, and, in everything social, separate like the fingers of the hand. And they believed it. They exulted in it. They stayed in their place, worked hard, and brought up my father to do the same. But my grandfather is the one. He was an odd old guy, my grandfather, and I am told I take after him. It was he who caused the trouble. On his deathbed he called my father to him and said, "Son, after I'm gone I want you to keep up the good fight. I never told you, but our life is a war and I have been a traitor all my born days, a spy in the enemy's country ever since I give up my gun back in the Reconstruction. Live with your head in the lion's mouth. I want you to overcome 'em with yeses, undermine 'em with grins, agree 'em to death and destruction, let 'em swoller you till they vomit or bust wide open." They thought the old man had gone out of his mind. He had been the meekest of men. The younger children were rushed from the room, the shades drawn, and the flame of the lamp turned so low that it sputtered on the wick like the old man's breathing. "Learn it to the younguns," he whispered fiercely; then he died.

But my folks were more alarmed over his last words than over his dying. It was as though he had not died at all, his words caused so much anxiety. I was warned emphatically to forget what he had said and, indeed, this is the first time it has been mentioned outside the family circle. It had a tremendous effect upon me, however. I could never be sure of what he meant. Grandfather had been a quiet old man who never made any trouble, yet on his deathbed he had called himself a traitor and a spy, and he had spoken of his meekness as a dangerous activity. It became a constant puzzle which lay unanswered in the back of my mind. And whenever things went well for me I remembered my grandfather and felt guilty and uncomfortable. It was as though I was carrying out his advice in spite of myself. And to make it worse, everyone loved me for it.

I was praised by the most lily-white men of the town. I was considered an example of desirable conduct—just as my grandfather had been. And what puzzled me was that the old man had defined it as *treachery.* When I was praised for my conduct I felt a guilt that in some way I was doing something that was really against the wishes of the white folks, that if they had understood they would have desired me to act just the opposite, that I should have been sulky and mean, and that that really would have been what they wanted, even though they were fooled and thought they wanted me to act as I did. It made me afraid that some day they would look upon me as a traitor and I would be lost. Still I was more afraid to act any other way because they didn't like that at all. The old man's words were like a curse. On my graduation day I delivered an oration in which I showed that humility was the secret, indeed, the very essence of progress. (Not that I believed this—how could I, remembering my grandfather?—I only believed that it worked.) It was a great success. Everyone praised me and I was invited to give the speech at a gathering of the town's leading white citizens. It was a triumph for our whole community.

It was in the main ballroom of the leading hotel. When I got there I discovered that it was on the occasion of a smoker, and I was told that since I was to be there anyway I might as well take part in the battle royal to be fought by some of my schoolmates as part of the entertainment. The battle royal came first.

All of the town's big shots were there in their tuxedoes, wolfing down the buffet foods, drinking beer and whiskey and smoking black cigars. It was a large room with a high ceiling. Chairs were arranged in neat rows around three sides of a portable boxing ring. The fourth side was clear, revealing a gleaming space of polished floor. I had some misgivings over the battle royal, by the way. Not from a distaste for fighting, but because I didn't care too much for the other fellows who were to take part. They were tough guys who seemed to have no grandfather's curse worrying their minds. No one could mistake their toughness. And besides, I suspected that fighting a battle royal might detract from the dignity of my speech. In those pre-invisible days I visualized myself as a potential Booker T. Washington. But the other fellows didn't care too much for me either, and there were nine of them. I felt superior to them in my way, and I didn't like the manner in which we were all crowded together into the servants' elevator. Nor did they like my being there. In fact, as the warmly lighted floors flashed past the elevator we had words over the fact that I, by taking part in the fight, had knocked one of their friends out of a night's work.

We were led out of the elevator through a rococo hall into an anteroom and told to get into our fighting togs. Each of us was issued a pair of boxing gloves and ushered out into the big mirrored hall, which we entered looking cautiously about us and whispering, lest we might accidentally be heard above the noise of the room. It was foggy with cigar smoke. And already the whiskey was taking effect. I was shocked to see some of the most important men of the town quite tipsy. They were all there—bankers, lawyers, judges, doctors, fire chiefs, teachers, merchants. Even one of the more fashionable pastors. Something we could not see was going on up front. A clarinet was vibrating sensuously and the men were standing up and moving eagerly forward. We were a small tight group, clustered together, our bare upper bodies touching and shining with anticipatory sweat; while up front the big shots were becoming increasingly excited over something we still could not see. Suddenly I heard the school superintendent, who had told me to come, yell, "Bring up the shines, gentlemen! Bring up the little shines!"

We were rushed up to the front of the ballroom, where it smelled even more strongly of tobacco and whiskey. Then we were pushed into place. I almost wet my pants. A sea of faces, some hostile, some amused, ringed around us, and in the center, facing us, stood a magnificent blonde—stark naked. There was dead silence. I felt a blast of cold air chill me. I tried to back away, but they were behind me and around me. Some of the boys stood with lowered heads, trembling. I felt a wave of irrational guilt and fear. My teeth chattered, my skin turned to goose flesh, my knees knocked. Yet I was strongly attracted and looked in spite of myself. Had the price of looking been blindness, I would have looked. The hair was yellow like that of a circus kewpie doll, the face heavily powdered and rouged, as though to form an abstract mask, the eyes hollow and smeared a cool blue, the color of a baboon's butt. I felt a desire to spit upon her as my eyes brushed slowly over her body. Her breasts were firm and round as the domes of East Indian temples, and I stood so close as to see the fine skin texture and beads of pearly perspiration glistening like dew around the pink and erected buds of her nipples. I wanted at one and the same time to run from the room, to sink through the floor, or go to her and cover her from my eyes and the eyes of the others with my body; to feel the soft thighs, to caress her and destroy her, to love her and murder her, to hide from her, and yet to stroke where below the small American flag tattooed upon her belly her thighs formed a capital V. I had a notion that of all in the room she saw only me with her impersonal eyes.

And then she began to dance, a slow sensuous movement; the smoke of a hundred cigars clinging to her like the thinnest of veils. She seemed like a fair bird-girl girdled in veils calling to me from the angry surface of some gray and threatening sea. I was transported. Then I became aware of the clarinet playing and the big shots yelling at us. Some threatened us if we looked and others if we did not. On my right I saw one boy faint. And now a man grabbed a silver pitcher from a table and stepped close as he dashed ice water upon him and stood him up and forced two of us to support him as his head hung and moans issued from his thick bluish lips. Another boy began to plead to go home. He was the largest of the group, wearing dark red fighting trunks much too small to conceal the erection which projected from him as though in answer to the insinuating low-registered moaning of the clarinet. He tried to hide himself with his boxing gloves.

And all the while the blonde continued dancing, smiling faintly at the big shots who watched her with fascination, and faintly smiling at our fear. I noticed a certain merchant who followed her hungrily, his lips loose and drooling. He was a large man who wore diamond studs in a shirtfront which swelled with the ample paunch underneath, and each time the blonde swayed her undulating hips he ran his hand through the thin hair of his bald head and, with his arms upheld, his posture clumsy like that of an intoxicated panda, wound his belly in a slow and obscene grind. This creature was completely hypnotized. The music had quickened. As the dancer flung herself about with a detached expression on her face, the men began reaching out to touch her. I could see their beefy fingers sink into her soft flesh. Some of the others tried to stop them and she began to move around the floor in graceful circles, as they gave chase, slipping and sliding over the polished floor. It was mad. Chairs went crashing, drinks were spilt, as they ran laughing and howling after her. They caught her just as she reached a door, raised her from the floor, and tossed her as college boys are tossed at a hazing, and above her red fixed-smiling lips I saw the terror and disgust in her eyes, almost like my own terror and that which I saw in some of the other boys. As I watched, they tossed her twice and her soft breasts seemed to flatten against the air and her legs flung wildly as she spun. Some of the more sober ones helped her to escape. And I started off the floor, heading for the anteroom with the rest of the boys.

Some were still crying and in hysteria. But as we tried to leave we were stopped and ordered to get into the ring. There was nothing to do but what we were told. All ten of us climbed under the ropes and allowed ourselves to be blindfolded with broad bands of white cloth. One of the men seemed to feel a bit sympathetic and tried to cheer us up as we stood with our backs against the ropes. Some of us tried to grin. "See that boy over there?" one of the men said. "I want you to run across at the bell and give it to him right in the belly. If you don't get him, I'm going to get you. I don't like his looks." Each of us was told the same. The blindfolds were put on. Yet even then I had been going over my speech. In my mind each word was as bright as flame. I felt the cloth pressed into place, and frowned so that it would be loosened when I relaxed.

But now I felt a sudden fit of blind terror. I was unused to darkness. It was as though I had suddenly found myself in a dark room filled with poisonous cottonmouths. I could hear the bleary voices yelling insistently for the battle royal to begin.

"Get going in there!"

"Let me at that big nigger!"

I strained to pick up the school superintendent's voice, as though to squeeze some security out of that slightly more familiar sound.

"Let me at those black sonsabitches!" someone yelled.

"No, Jackson, no!" another voice yelled. "Here, somebody, help me hold Jack."

"I want to get at that ginger-colored nigger. Tear him limb from limb," the first voice yelled.

I stood against the ropes trembling. For in those days I was what they called ginger-colored, and he sounded as though he might crunch me between his teeth like a crisp ginger cookie.

Quite a struggle was going on. Chairs were being kicked about and I could hear voices grunting as with a terrific effort. I wanted to see, to see more desperately than ever before. But the blindfold was as tight as a thick skin-puckering scab and when I raised my gloved hands to push the layers of white aside a voice yelled, "Oh, no you don't, black bastard! Leave that alone!"

"Ring the bell before Jackson kills him a coon!" someone boomed in the sudden silence. And I heard the bell clang and the sound of the feet scuffling forward.

A glove smacked against my head. I pivoted, striking out stiffly as someone went past, and felt the jar ripple along the length of my arm to my shoulder. Then it seemed as though all nine of the boys had turned upon me at once. Blows pounded me from all sides while I struck out as best I could. So many blows landed upon me that I wondered if I were not the only blindfolded fighter in the ring, or if the man called Jackson hadn't succeeded in getting me after all.

Blindfolded, I could no longer control my motions. I had no dignity. I stumbled about like a baby or a drunken man. The smoke had become thicker and with each new blow it seemed to sear and further restrict my lungs. My saliva became like hot bitter glue. A glove connected with my head, filling my mouth with warm blood. It was everywhere. I could not tell if the moisture I felt upon my body was sweat or blood. A blow landed hard against the nape of my neck. I felt myself going over, my head hitting the floor. Streaks of blue light filled the black world behind the blindfold. I lay prone, pretending that I was knocked out, but felt myself seized by hands and yanked to my feet. "Get going, black boy! Mix it up!" My arms were like lead, my head smarting from blows. I managed to feel my way to the ropes and held on, trying to catch my breath. A glove landed in my mid-section and I went over again, feeling as though the smoke had become a knife jabbed into my guts. Pushed this way and that by the legs milling around me, I finally pulled erect and discovered that I could see the black, sweat-washed forms weaving in the smoky-blue atmosphere like drunken dancers weaving to the rapid drum-like thuds of blows.

Everyone fought hysterically. It was complete anarchy. Everybody fought everybody else. No group fought together for long. Two, three, four, fought one, then turned to fight each other, were themselves attacked. Blows landed below the belt and in the kidney, with the gloves open as well as closed, and with my eye partly opened now there was not so much terror. I moved carefully, avoiding blows, although not too many to attract attention, fighting from group to group. The boys groped about like blind, cautious crabs crouching to protect their mid-sections, their heads pulled in short against their shoulders, their arms stretched nervously before them, with their fists testing the smoke-filled air like the knobbed feelers of hypersensitive snails. In one corner I glimpsed a boy violently punching the air and heard him scream in pain as he smashed his hand against a ring post. For a second I saw him bent over holding his hand, then going down as a blow caught his unprotected head. I played one group against the other, slipping in and throwing a punch then stepping out of range while pushing the others into the melee to take the blows blindly aimed at me. The smoke was agonizing and there were no rounds, no bells at three minute intervals to relieve our exhaustion. The room spun round me, a swirl of lights, smoke, sweating bodies surrounded by tense white faces. I bled from both nose and mouth, the blood spattering upon my chest.

The men kept yelling, "Slug him, black boy! Knock his guts out!"

"Uppercut him! Kill him! Kill that big boy!"

Taking a fake fall, I saw a boy going down heavily beside me as though we were felled by a single blow, saw a sneaker-clad foot shoot into his groin as the two who had knocked him down stumbled upon him. I rolled out of range, feeling a twinge of nausea.

The harder we fought the more threatening the men became. And yet, I had begun to worry about my speech again. How would it go? Would they recognize my ability? What would they give me?

I was fighting automatically and suddenly I noticed that one after another of the boys was leaving the ring. I was surprised, filled with panic, as though I had been left alone with an unknown danger. Then I understood. The boys had arranged it among themselves. It was the custom for the two men left in the ring to slug it out for the winner's prize. I discovered this too late. When the bell sounded two men in tuxedoes leaped into the ring and removed the blindfold. I found myself facing Tatlock, the biggest of the gang. I felt sick at my stomach. Hardly had the bell stopped ringing in my ears than it clanged again and I saw him moving swiftly toward me. Thinking of nothing else to do I hit him smash on the nose. He kept coming, bringing the rank sharp violence of stale sweat. His face was a black blank of a face, only his eyes alive—with hate of me and aglow with a feverish terror from what had happened to us all. I became anxious. I wanted to deliver my speech and he came at me as though he meant to beat it out of me. I smashed him again and again, taking his blows as they came. Then on a sudden impulse I struck him lightly and as we clinched, I whispered, "Fake like I knocked you out, you can have the prize."

"I'll break your behind," he whispered hoarsely.

"For *them*?"

"For *me*, sonofabitch!"

They were yelling for us to break it up and Tatlock spun me half around with a blow, and as a joggled camera sweeps in a reeling scene, I saw the howling red faces crouching tense beneath the cloud of blue-gray smoke. For a moment the world wavered, unraveled, flowed, then my head cleared and Tatlock bounced before me. That fluttering shadow before my eyes was his jabbing left hand. Then falling forward, my head against his damp shoulder, I whispered, "I'll make it five dollars more."

"Go to hell!"

But his muscles relaxed a trifle beneath my pressure and I breathed, "Seven!"

"Give it to your ma," he said, ripping me beneath the heart.

And while I still held him I butted him and moved away. I felt myself bombarded with punches. I fought back with hopeless desperation. I wanted to deliver my speech more than anything else in the world, because I felt that only these men could judge truly my ability, and now this stupid clown was ruining my chances. I began fighting carefully now, moving in to punch him and out again with my greater speed. A lucky blow to his chin and I had him going too—until I heard a loud voice yell, "I got my money on the big boy."

Hearing this, I almost dropped my guard. I was confused: Should I try to win against the voice out there? Would not this go against my speech, and was not this a moment for humility, for nonresistance? A blow to my head as I danced about sent my right eye popping like a jack-in-the-box and settled my dilemma. The room went red as I fell. It was a dream fall, my body languid and fastidious as to where to land, until the floor became impatient and smashed up to meet me. A moment later I came to. An hypnotic voice said FIVE emphatically.

And I lay there, hazily watching a dark red spot of my own blood shaping itself into a butterfly, glistening and soaking into the soiled gray world of the canvas.

When the voice drawled TEN I was lifted up and dragged to a chair. I sat dazed. My eye pained and swelled with each throb of my pounding heart and I wondered if now I would be allowed to speak. I was wringing wet, my mouth still bleeding. We were grouped along the wall now. The other boys ignored me as they congratulated Tatlock and speculated as to how much they would be paid. One boy whimpered over his smashed hand. Looking up front, I saw attendants in white jackets rolling the portable ring away and placing a small square rug in the vacant space surrounded by chairs. Perhaps, I thought, I will stand on the rug to deliver my speech.

Then the M.C. called to us, "Come on up here boys and get your money."

We ran forward to where the men laughed and talked in their chairs, waiting. Everyone seemed friendly now.

"There it is on the rug," the man said. I saw the rug covered with coins of all dimensions and a few crumpled bills. But what excited me, scattered here and there, were the gold pieces.

"Boys, it's all yours," the man said. "You get all you grab."

"That's right, Sambo," a blond man said, winking at me confidentially.

I trembled with excitement, forgetting my pain. I would get the gold and the bills, I thought. I would use both hands. I would throw my body against the boys nearest me to block them from the gold.

"Get down around the rug now," the man commanded, "and don't anyone touch it until I give the signal."

"This ought to be good," I heard.

As told, we got around the square rug on our knees. Slowly the man raised his freckled hand as we followed it upward with our eyes.

I heard, "These niggers look like they're about to pray!"

Then, "Ready," the man said. "Go!"

I lunged for a yellow coin lying on the blue design of the carpet, touching it and sending a surprised shriek to join those rising around me. I tried frantically to remove my hand but could not let go. A hot, violent force tore through my body, shaking me like a wet rat. The rug was electrified. The hair bristled up on my head as I shook myself free. My muscles jumped, my nerves jangled, writhed. But I saw that this was not stopping the other boys. Laughing in fear and embarrassment, some were holding back and scooping up the coins knocked off by the painful contortions of the others. The men roared above us as we struggled.

"Pick it up, goddamnit, pick it up!" someone called like a bass-voiced parrot. "Go on, get it!"

I crawled rapidly around the floor, picking up the coins, trying to avoid the coppers and to get greenbacks and the gold. Ignoring the shock by laughing, as I brushed the coins off quickly, I discovered that I could contain the electricity—a contradiction, but it works. Then the men began to push us onto the rug. Laughing embarrassedly, we struggled out of their hands and kept after the coins. We were all wet and slippery and hard to hold. Suddenly I saw a boy lifted into the air, glistening with sweat like a circus seal, and dropped, his wet back landing flush upon the charged rug, heard him yell and saw him literally dance upon his back, his elbows beating a frenzied tattoo upon the floor, his muscles twitching like the flesh of a horse stung by many flies. When he finally rolled off, his face was gray and no one stopped him when he ran from the floor amid booming laughter.

"Get the money," the M.C. called. "That's good hard American cash!"

And we snatched and grabbed, snatched and grabbed. I was careful not to come too close to the rug now, and when I felt the hot whiskey breath descend upon me like a cloud of foul air I reached out and grabbed the leg of a chair. It was occupied and I held on desperately.

"Leggo, nigger! Leggo!"

The huge face wavered down to mine as he tried to push me free. But my body was slippery and he was too drunk. It was Mr. Colcord, who owned a chain of movie houses and "entertainment palaces." Each time he grabbed me I slipped out of his hands. It became a real struggle. I feared the rug more than I did the drunk, so I held on, surprising myself for a moment by trying to topple *him* upon the rug. It was such an enormous idea that I found myself actually carrying it out. I tried not to be obvious, yet when I grabbed his leg, trying to tumble him out of the chair, he raised up roaring with laughter, and, looking at me with soberness dead in the eye, kicked me viciously in the chest. The chair leg flew out of my hand. I felt myself going and rolled. It was as though I had rolled through a bed of hot coals. It seemed a whole century would pass before I would roll free, a century in which I was seared through the deepest levels of my body to the fearful breath within me and the breath seared and heated to the point of explosion. It'll all be over in a flash, I thought as I rolled clear. It'll all be over in a flash.

But not yet, the men on the other side were waiting, red faces swollen as though from apoplexy as they bent forward in their chairs. Seeing their fingers coming toward me I rolled away as a fumbled football rolls off the receiver's fingertips, back into the coals. That time I luckily sent the rug sliding out of place and heard the coins ringing against the floor and the boys scuffling to pick them up and the M.C. calling, "All right, boys, that's all. Go get dressed and get your money."

I was limp as a dish rag. My back felt as though it had been beaten with wires.

When we had dressed the M.C. came in and gave us each five dollars, except Tatlock, who got ten for being last in the ring. Then he told us to leave. I was not to get a chance to deliver my speech, I thought. I was going out into the dim alley in despair when I was stopped and told to go back. I returned to the ballroom, where the men were pushing back their chairs and gathering in groups to talk.

The M.C. knocked on a table for quiet. "Gentlemen," he said, "we almost forgot an important part of the program. A most serious part, gentlemen. This boy was brought here to deliver a speech which he made at his graduation yesterday. . . ."

"Bravo!"

"I'm told that he is the smartest boy we've got out there in Greenwood. I'm told that he knows more big words than a pocket-sized dictionary."

Much applause and laughter.

"So now, gentlemen, I want you to give him your attention."

There was still laughter as I faced them, my mouth dry, my eye throbbing. I began slowly, but evidently my throat was tense, because they began shouting, "Louder! Louder!"

"We of the younger generation extol the wisdom of that great leader and educator," I shouted, "who first spoke these flaming words of wisdom: 'A ship lost at sea for many days suddenly sighted a friendly vessel. From the mast of the unfortunate vessel was seen a signal: "Water, water; we die of thirst!" The answer from the friendly vessel came back: "Cast down your bucket where you are." The captain of the distressed vessel, at last heeding the injunction, cast down his bucket, and it came up full of fresh sparkling water from the mouth of the Amazon River.' And like him I say, and in his words, 'To those of my race who depend upon bettering their condition in a foreign land, or who underestimate the importance of cultivating friendly relations with the Southern white man, who is his next-door neighbor, I would say: "Cast down your bucket where you are"—cast it down in making friends in every manly way of the people of all races by whom we are surrounded. . . .'"

I spoke automatically and with such fervor that I did not realize that the men were still talking and laughing until my dry mouth, filling up with blood from the cut, almost strangled me. I coughed, wanting to stop and go to one of the tall brass, sand-filled spittoons to relieve myself, but a few of the men, especially the superintendent, were listening and I was afraid. So I gulped it down, blood, saliva, and all, and continued. (What powers of endurance I had during those days! What enthusiasm! What a belief in the rightness of things!) I spoke even louder in spite of the pain. But still they talked and still they laughed, as though deaf with cotton in dirty ears. So I spoke with greater emotional emphasis. I closed my ears and swallowed blood until I was nauseated. The speech seemed a hundred times as long as before, but I could not leave out a single word. All had to be said, each memorized nuance considered, rendered. Nor was that all. Whenever I uttered a word of three or more syllables a group of voices would yell for me to repeat it. I used the phrase "social responsibility" and they yelled:

"What's the word you say, boy?"

"Social responsibility," I said.

"What?"

"Social . . ."

"Louder."

". . . responsibility."

"More!"

"Respon—"

"Repeat!"

"—sibility."

The room filled with the uproar of laughter until, no doubt, distracted by having to gulp down my blood, I made a mistake and yelled a phrase I had often seen denounced in newspaper editorials, heard debated in private.

"Social . . ."

"What?" they yelled.

". . . equality—"

The laughter hung smokelike in the sudden stillness. I opened my eyes, puzzled. Sounds of displeasure filled the room. The M.C. rushed forward. They shouted hostile phrases at me. But I did not understand.

A small dry mustached man in the front row blared out, "Say that slowly, son!"

"What sir?"

"What you just said!"

"Social responsibility, sir," I said.

"You weren't being smart, were you, boy?" he said, not unkindly.

"No, sir!"

"You sure that about 'equality' was a mistake?"

"Oh, yes, sir," I said. "I was swallowing blood."

"Well, you had better speak more slowly so we can understand. We mean to do right by you, but you've got to know your place at all times. All right, now, go on with your speech."

I was afraid. I wanted to leave but I wanted also to speak and I was afraid they'd snatch me down.

"Thank you, sir," I said, beginning where I had left off, and having them ignore me as before.

Yet when I finished there was a thunderous applause. I was surprised to see the superintendent come forth with a package wrapped in white tissue paper, and, gesturing for quiet, address the men.

"Gentlemen, you see that I did not overpraise this boy. He makes a good speech and some day he'll lead his people in the proper paths. And I don't have to tell you that that is important in these days and times. This is a good, smart boy, and so to encourage him in the right direction, in the name of the Board of Education I wish to present him a prize in the form of this . . ."

He paused, removing the tissue paper and revealing a gleaming calfskin brief case.

". . . in the form of this first-class article from Shad Whitmore's shop."

"Boy," he said, addressing me, "take this prize and keep it well. Consider it a badge of office. Prize it. Keep developing as you are and some day it will be filled with important papers that will help shape the destiny of your people."

I was so moved that I could hardly express my thanks. A rope of bloody saliva forming a shape like an undiscovered continent drooled upon the leather and I wiped it quickly away. I felt an importance that I had never dreamed.

"Open it and see what's inside," I was told.

My fingers a-tremble, I complied, smelling the fresh leather and finding an official-looking document inside. It was a scholarship to the state college for Negroes. My eyes filled with tears and I ran awkwardly off the floor.

I was overjoyed; I did not even mind when I discovered that the gold pieces I had scrambled for were brass pocket tokens advertising a certain make of automobile.

When I reached home everyone was excited. Next day the neighbors came to congratulate me. I even felt safe from grandfather, whose deathbed curse usually spoiled my triumphs. I stood beneath his photograph with my brief case in hand and smiled triumphantly into his stolid black peasant's face. It was a face that fascinated me. The eyes seemed to follow everywhere I went.

That night I dreamed I was at a circus with him and that he refused to laugh at the clowns no matter what they did. Then later he told me to open my brief case and read what was inside and I did, finding an official envelope stamped with the state seal; and inside the envelope I found another and another, endlessly, and I thought I would fall of weariness. "Them's years," he said. "Now open that one." And I did and in it I found an engraved document containing a short message in letters of gold. "Read it," my grandfather said. "Out loud."

"To Whom It May Concern," I intoned. "Keep This Nigger-Boy Running."

I awoke with the old man's laughter ringing in my ears.

(It was a dream I was to remember and dream again for many years after. But at the time I had no insight into its meaning. First I had to attend college.)

COMMENTARY

RALPH ELLISON

Ralph Ellison gave an interview for the "Art of Fiction" series of the *Paris Review* that was reprinted in his volume of essays, *Shadow and Act* (1964). In the introduction to that book he said that what is basic to the fiction writer's confrontation with the world is "converting experience into symbolic action. Good fiction is made of that which is real, and reality is difficult to come by. So much of it depends upon the individual's willingness to discover his true self, upon his defining himself – for the time being at least – against his background."

The Influence of Folklore on "Battle Royal" 1964

Interviewer: Can you give us an example of the use of folklore in your own novel?

Ellison: Well, there are certain themes, symbols, and images which are based on folk material. For example, there is the old saying amongst Negroes: If you're black, stay back; if you're brown, stick around; if you're white, you're right. And there is the joke Negroes tell on themselves about their being so black they can't be seen in the dark. In my book this sort of thing was merged with the meanings which blackness and light have long had in Western mythology: evil and goodness, ignorance and knowledge, and so on. In my novel the narrator's development is one through blackness to light; that is, from ignorance to enlightenment: invisibility to visibility. He leaves the South and goes North; this, as you will notice in reading Negro folktales, is always the road to freedom — the movement upward. You have the same thing again when he leaves his underground cave for the open.

It took me a long time to learn how to adapt such examples of myth into my work — also ritual. The use of ritual is equally a vital part of the creative process. I learned a few things from Eliot, Joyce, and Hemingway, but not how to adapt them. When I started writing, I knew that in both *The Waste Land*° and *Ulysses*° ancient myth and ritual were used to give form and significance to the material; but it took me a few years to realize that the myths and rites which we find functioning in our everyday lives could be used in the same way. In my first attempt at a novel — which I was unable to complete — I began by trying to manipulate the simple structural unities of *beginning, middle,* and *end,* but when I attempted to deal with the psychological strata — the images, symbols, and emotional configurations — of the experience at hand, I discovered that the unities were simply cool points of stability on which one could suspend the narrative line — but beneath the surface of apparently rational human relationships there seethed a chaos before which I was helpless. People rationalize what they shun or are incapable of dealing with; these superstitions and their rationalizations become ritual as they govern behavior. The rituals become social forms, and it is one of the functions of the artist to recognize them and raise them to the level of art.

I don't know whether I'm getting this over or not. Let's put it this way: Take the "Battle Royal" passage in my novel, where the boys are blindfolded and forced to fight each other for the amusement of the white observers. This is a vital part of behavior pattern in the South, which both Negroes and whites thoughtlessly accept. It is a ritual in preservation of caste lines, a keeping of taboo to appease the gods and ward off bad luck. It is also the initiation ritual to which all greenhorns are subjected. This passage which states what Negroes will see I did not have to invent; the patterns were already there in society, so that all I had to do was present them in a broader context of meaning. In any society there are many rituals of situation which, for the most part, go unquestioned. They can be simple or elaborate, but they are the connective tissue between the work of art and the audience.

Interviewer: Do you think a reader unacquainted with this folklore can properly understand your work?

Ellison: Yes, I think so. It's like jazz; there's no inherent problem which prohibits understanding but the assumptions brought to it. We don't all dig Shakespeare uniformly, or even *Little Red Riding Hood.* The understanding of art depends finally upon one's willingness to extend one's humanity and one's knowledge of human life. I noticed, incidentally, that the Germans, having no special caste assumptions concerning American Negroes, dealt with my work simply as a novel. I think Americans will come to view it that way in twenty years — if it's around that long.

Interviewer: Don't you think it will be?

Ellison: I doubt it. It's not an important novel. I failed of eloquence, and

---

The Waste Land: A long, extremely influential poem (1922) by T. S. Eliot (1888–1965).
Ulysses: An experimental novel (1922) by James Joyce (1882–1941).

many of the immediate issues are rapidly fading away. If it does last, it will be simply because there are things going on in its depth that are of more permanent interest than on its surface. I hope so, anyway.

WILLIAM FAULKNER

William Faulkner (1897–1962) was born in New Albany, Mississippi, into an old southern family. When he was a child, his parents moved to the isolated town of Oxford, Mississippi, and except for his service in World War I and some time in New Orleans and Hollywood, he spent the rest of his life there. "I discovered my own little postage stamp of native soil was worth writing about, and that I would never live long enough to exhaust it." His literary career began in New Orleans, where he lived for six months and wrote newspaper sketches and stories for the *Times-Picayune.* He met Sherwood Anderson in New Orleans, and Anderson helped him publish his first novel, *Soldier's Pay,* in 1926. Faulkner's major work was written in the late 1920s and the 1930s, when he created an imaginary county adjacent to Oxford, calling it Yoknapatawpha County and chronicling its history in a series of experimental novels. In *The Sound and the Fury* (1929), *As I Lay Dying* (1930), *Sanctuary* (1931), *Light in August* (1932), *Absalom, Absalom!* (1936), and *The Hamlet* (1940), he showed himself to be a writer of genius, although "a willfully and perversely chaotic one," as Jorge Luis Borges noted, whose "labyrinthine world" required a no less labyrinthine prose technique to describe in epic manner the disintegration of the South through many generations. Faulkner was awarded the Nobel Prize for literature in 1952.

Faulkner rarely included poetic imagery or stream-of-consciousness narration in his stories, which he wrote, he often said, to help him pay his rent. His biographer Frederick Karl has noted that he used short fiction "as a means of working through, or toward, larger ideas." He wrote nearly a hundred stories, often revising them later to fit as sections into a novel. Four books of his stories were published in his lifetime.

Although some readers found symbolism in "A Rose for Emily" that suggested that in the pair of white lovers he was implying a battle between the North (the character Homer Barron) and the South (Miss Emily herself), Faulkner denied a schematic interpretation. He said he had intended to write a ghost story, and "I think that the writer is too busy trying to create flesh-and-blood people that will stand up and cast a shadow to have time to be conscious of all the symbolism that he may put into what he does or what people may read into it."

WEB Research William Faulkner at bedfordstmartins.com/rewritinglit.

A Rose for Emily

1931

I

When Miss Emily Grierson died, our whole town went to her funeral: the men through a sort of respectful affection for a fallen monument, the women mostly out of curiosity to see the inside of her house, which no one save an old manservant—a combined gardener and cook—had seen in at least ten years.

It was a big, squarish frame house that had once been white, decorated with cupolas and spires and scrolled balconies in the heavily lightsome style of the seventies, set on what had once been our most select street. But garages and cotton gins had encroached and obliterated even the august names of that neighborhood; only Miss Emily's house was left, lifting its stubborn and coquettish decay above the cotton wagons and the gasoline pumps—an eyesore among eyesores. And now Miss Emily had gone to join the representatives of those august names where they lay in the cedar-bemused cemetery among the ranked and anonymous graves of Union and Confederate soldiers who fell at the battle of Jefferson.

Alive, Miss Emily had been a tradition, a duty, and a care; a sort of hereditary obligation upon the town, dating from that day in 1894 when Colonel Sartoris, the mayor—he who fathered the edict that no Negro woman should appear on the streets without an apron—remitted her taxes, the dispensation dating from the death of her father on into perpetuity. Not that Miss Emily would have accepted charity. Colonel Sartoris invented an involved tale to the effect that Miss Emily's father had loaned money to the town, which the town, as a matter of business, preferred this way of repaying. Only a man of Colonel Sartoris' generation and thought could have invented it, and only a woman could have believed it.

When the next generation, with its more modern ideas, became mayors and aldermen, this arrangement created some little dissatisfaction. On the first of the year they mailed her a tax notice. February came, and there was no reply. They wrote her a formal letter, asking her to call at the sheriff's office at her convenience. A week later the mayor wrote her himself, offering to call or to send his car for her, and received in reply a note on paper of an archaic shape, in a thin, flowing calligraphy in faded ink, to the effect that she no longer went out at all. The tax notice was also enclosed, without comment.

They called a special meeting of the Board of Aldermen. A deputation waited upon her, knocked at the door through which no visitor had passed since she ceased giving china-painting lessons eight or ten years earlier. They were admitted by the old Negro into a dim hall from which a stairway mounted into still more shadow. It smelled of dust and disuse—a close, dank smell. The Negro led them into the parlor. It was furnished in heavy, leather-covered furniture. When the Negro opened the blinds of one window, they could see that the leather was cracked; and when they sat down, a faint dust rose sluggishly about their thighs, spinning with slow motes in the single sun-ray. On a tarnished gilt easel before the fireplace stood a crayon portrait of Miss Emily's father.

They rose when she entered—a small, fat woman in black, with a thin gold chain descending to her waist and vanishing into her belt, leaning on an ebony cane with a tarnished gold head. Her skeleton was small and spare; perhaps that was why what would have been merely plumpness in another was obesity in her. She looked bloated, like a body long submerged in motionless water, and of that pallid hue. Her eyes, lost in the fatty ridges of her face, looked like two small pieces of coal pressed into a lump of dough as they moved from one face to another while the visitors stated their errand.

She did not ask them to sit. She just stood in the door and listened quietly until the spokesman came to a stumbling halt. Then they could hear the invisible watch ticking at the end of the gold chain.

Her voice was dry and cold. "I have no taxes in Jefferson. Colonel Sartoris explained it to me. Perhaps one of you can gain access to the city records and satisfy yourselves."

"But we have. We are the city authorities, Miss Emily. Didn't you get a notice from the sheriff, signed by him?"

"I received a paper, yes," Miss Emily said. "Perhaps he considers himself the sheriff. . . . I have no taxes in Jefferson."

"But there is nothing on the books to show that, you see. We must go by the—"

"See Colonel Sartoris. I have no taxes in Jefferson."

"But, Miss Emily—"

"See Colonel Sartoris." (Colonel Sartoris had been dead almost ten years.) "I have no taxes in Jefferson. Tobe!" The Negro appeared. "Show these gentlemen out."

II

So she vanquished them, horse and foot, just as she had vanquished their fathers thirty years before about the smell. That was two years after her father's death and a short time after her sweetheart—the one we believed would marry her—had deserted her. After her father's death she went out very little; after her sweetheart went away, people hardly saw her at all. A few of the ladies had the temerity to call, but were not received, and the only sign of life about the place was the Negro man—a young man then—going in and out with a market basket.

"Just as if a man—any man—could keep a kitchen properly," the ladies said; so they were not surprised when the smell developed. It was another link between the gross, teeming world and the high and mighty Griersons.

A neighbor, a woman, complained to the mayor, Judge Stevens, eighty years old.

"But what will you have me do about it, madam?" he said.

"Why, send her word to stop it," the woman said. "Isn't there a law?"

"I'm sure that won't be necessary," Judge Stevens said. "It's probably just a snake or a rat that nigger of hers killed in the yard. I'll speak to him about it."

The next day he received two more complaints, one from a man who came in diffident deprecation. "We really must do something about it, Judge. I'd be the last one in the world to bother Miss Emily, but we've got to do something." That night the Board of Aldermen met—three graybeards and one younger man, a member of the rising generation.

"It's simple enough," he said. "Send her word to have her place cleaned up. Give her a certain time to do it in, and if she don't. . . ."

"Dammit, sir," Judge Stevens said, "will you accuse a lady to her face of smelling bad?"

So the next night, after midnight, four men crossed Miss Emily's lawn and slunk about the house like burglars, sniffing along the base of the brickwork and at the cellar openings while one of them performed a regular sowing motion with his hand out of a sack slung from his shoulder. They broke open the cellar door and sprinkled lime there, and in all the outbuildings. As they recrossed the lawn, a window that had been dark was lighted and Miss Emily sat in it, the light behind her, and her upright torso motionless as that of an idol. They crept quietly across the lawn and into the shadow of the locusts that lined the street. After a week or two the smell went away.

That was when people had begun to feel really sorry for her. People in our town, remembering how old lady Wyatt, her great-aunt, had gone completely crazy at last, believed that the Griersons held themselves a little too high for what they really were. None of the young men were quite good enough for Miss Emily and such. We had long thought of them as a tableau, Miss Emily a slender figure in white in the background, her father a spraddled silhouette in the foreground, his back to her and clutching a horsewhip, the two of them framed by the backflung front door. So when she got to be thirty and was still single, we were not pleased exactly, but vindicated; even with insanity in the family she wouldn't have turned down all of her chances if they had really materialized.

When her father died, it got about that the house was all that was left to her; and in a way, people were glad. At last they could pity Miss Emily. Being left alone, and a pauper, she had become humanized. Now she too would know the old thrill and the old despair of a penny more or less.

The day after his death all the ladies prepared to call at the house and offer condolence and aid, as is our custom. Miss Emily met them at the door, dressed as usual and with no trace of grief on her face. She told them that her father was not dead. She did that for three days, with the ministers calling on her, and the doctors, trying to persuade her to let them dispose of the body. Just as they were about to resort to law and force, she broke down, and they buried her father quickly.

We did not say she was crazy then. We believed she had to do that. We remembered all the young men her father had driven away, and we knew that with nothing left, she would have to cling to that which had robbed her, as people will.

III

She was sick for a long time. When we saw her again, her hair was cut short, making her look like a girl, with a vague resemblance to those angels in colored church windows—sort of tragic and serene.

The town had just let the contracts for paving the sidewalks, and in the summer after her father's death they began the work. The construction company came with niggers and mules and machinery, and a foreman named Homer Barron, a Yankee—a big, dark, ready man, with a big voice and eyes lighter than his face. The little boys would follow in groups to hear him cuss the niggers, and the niggers singing in time to the rise and fall of picks. Pretty soon he knew everybody in town. Whenever you heard a lot of laughing anywhere about the square, Homer Barron would be in the center of the group. Presently, we began to see him and Miss Emily on Sunday afternoons driving in the yellow-wheeled buggy and the matched team of bays from the livery stable.

At first we were glad that Miss Emily would have an interest, because the ladies all said, "Of course a Grierson would not think seriously of a Northerner, a day laborer." But there were still others, older people, who said that even grief could not cause a real lady to forget *noblesse oblige*—without calling it *noblesse oblige.* They just said, "Poor Emily. Her kinsfolk should come to her." She had some kin in Alabama; but years ago her father had fallen out with them over the estate of old lady Wyatt, the crazy woman, and there was no communication between the two families. They had not even been represented at the funeral.

And as soon as the old people said, "Poor Emily," the whispering began. "Do you suppose it's really so?" they said to one another. "Of course it is. What else could. . . ." This behind their hands; rustling of craned silk and satin behind jalousies closed upon the sun of Sunday afternoon as the thin, swift clop-clop-clop of the matched team passed: "Poor Emily."

She carried her head high enough—even when we believed that she was fallen. It was as if she demanded more than ever the recognition of her dignity as the last Grierson; as if it had wanted that touch of earthiness to reaffirm her imperviousness. Like when she bought the rat poison, the arsenic. That was over a year after they had begun to say "Poor Emily," and while the two female cousins were visiting her.

"I want some poison," she said to the druggist. She was over thirty then, still a slight woman, though thinner than usual, with cold, haughty black eyes in a face the flesh of which was strained across the temples and about the eye-sockets as you imagine a lighthouse-keeper's face ought to look. "I want some poison," she said.

"Yes, Miss Emily. What kind? For rats and such? I'd recom——"

"I want the best you have. I don't care what kind."

The druggist named several. "They'll kill anything up to an elephant. But what you want is——"

"Arsenic," Miss Emily said. "Is that a good one?"

"Is . . . arsenic? Yes, ma'am. But what you want——"

"I want arsenic."

The druggist looked down at her. She looked back at him, erect, her face like a strained flag. "Why, of course," the druggist said. "If that's what you want. But the law requires you to tell what you are going to use it for."

Miss Emily just stared at him, her head tilted back in order to look him eye for eye, until he looked away and went and got the arsenic and wrapped it up. The Negro delivery boy brought her the package; the druggist didn't come back. When she opened the package at home there was written on the box, under the skull and bones: "For rats."

IV

So the next day we all said, "She will kill herself"; and we said it would be the best thing. When she had first begun to be seen with Homer Barron, we had said, "She will marry him." Then we said, "She will persuade him yet," because Homer himself had remarked—he liked men, and it was known that he drank with the younger men in the Elks' Club—that he was not a marrying man. Later we said, "Poor Emily" behind the jalousies as they passed on Sunday afternoon in the glittering buggy, Miss Emily with her head high and Homer Barron with his hat cocked and a cigar in his teeth, reins and whip in a yellow glove.

Then some of the ladies began to say that it was a disgrace to the town and a bad example to the young people. The men did not want to interfere, but at last the ladies forced the Baptist minister—Miss Emily's people were Episcopal—to call upon her. He would never divulge what happened during that interview, but he refused to go back again. The next Sunday they again drove about the streets, and the following day the minister's wife wrote to Miss Emily's relations in Alabama.

So she had blood-kin under her roof again and we sat back to watch developments. At first nothing happened. Then we were sure that they were to be married. We learned that Miss Emily had been to the jeweler's and ordered a man's toilet set in silver, with the letters H.B. on each piece. Two days later we learned that she had bought a complete outfit of men's clothing, including a nightshirt, and we said, "They are married." We were really glad. We were glad because the two female cousins were even more Grierson than Miss Emily had ever been.

So we were not surprised when Homer Barron—the streets had been finished some time since—was gone. We were a little disappointed that there was not a public blowing-off, but we believed that he had gone on to prepare for Miss Emily's coming, or to give her a chance to get rid of the cousins. (By that time it was a cabal, and we were all Miss Emily's allies to help circumvent the cousins.) Sure enough, after another week they departed. And, as we had expected all along, within three days Homer Barron was back in town. A neighbor saw the Negro man admit him at the kitchen door at dusk one evening.

And that was the last we saw of Homer Barron. And of Miss Emily for some time. The Negro man went in and out with the market basket, but the front door remained closed. Now and then we would see her at the window for a moment, as the men did that night when they sprinkled the lime, but for almost six months she did not appear on the streets. Then we knew that this was to be expected too; as if that quality of her father which had thwarted her woman's life so many times had been too virulent and too furious to die.

When we next saw Miss Emily, she had grown fat and her hair was turning gray. During the next few years it grew grayer and grayer until it attained an even pepper-and-salt iron-gray, when it ceased turning. Up to the day of her death at seventy-four it was still that vigorous iron-gray, like the hair of an active man.

From that time on her front door remained closed, save during a period of six or seven years, when she was about forty, during which she gave lessons in china-painting. She fitted up a studio in one of the downstairs rooms, where the daughters and granddaughters of Colonel Sartoris' contemporaries were sent to her with the same regularity and in the same spirit that they were sent to church on Sundays with a twenty-five-cent piece for the collection plate. Meanwhile her taxes had been remitted.

Then the newer generation became the backbone and the spirit of the town, and the painting pupils grew up and fell away and did not send their children to her with boxes of color and tedious brushes and pictures cut from the ladies' magazines. The front door closed upon the last one and remained closed for good. When the town got free postal delivery, Miss Emily alone refused to let them fasten the metal numbers above her door and attach a mailbox to it. She would not listen to them.

Daily, monthly, yearly we watched the Negro grow grayer and more stooped, going in and out with the market basket. Each December we sent her a tax notice, which would be returned by the post office a week later, unclaimed. Now and then we would see her in one of the downstairs windows—she had evidently shut up the top floor of the house—like the carven torso of an idol in a niche, looking or not looking at us, we could never tell which. Thus she passed from generation to generation—dear, inescapable, impervious, tranquil, and perverse.

And so she died. Fell ill in the house filled with dust and shadows, with only a doddering Negro man to wait on her. We did not even know she was sick; we had long since given up trying to get any information from the Negro. He talked to no one, probably not even to her, for his voice had grown harsh and rusty, as if from disuse.

She died in one of the downstairs rooms, in a heavy walnut bed with a curtain, her gray head propped on a pillow yellow and moldy with age and lack of sunlight.

V

The Negro met the first of the ladies at the front door and let them in, with their hushed, sibilant voices and their quick, curious glances, and then he disappeared. He walked right through the house and out the back and was not seen again.

The two female cousins came at once. They held the funeral on the second day, with the town coming to look at Miss Emily beneath a mass of bought flowers, with the crayon face of her father musing profoundly above the bier and the ladies sibilant and macabre; and the very old men—some in their brushed Confederate uniforms—on the porch and the lawn, talking of Miss Emily as if she had been a contemporary of theirs, believing that they had danced with her and courted her perhaps, confusing time with its mathematical progression, as the old do, to whom all the past is not a diminishing road but, instead, a huge meadow which no winter ever quite touches, divided from them now by the narrow bottleneck of the most recent decade of years.

Already we knew that there was one room in that region above stairs which no one had seen in forty years, and which would have to be forced. They waited until Miss Emily was decently in the ground before they opened it.

The violence of breaking down the door seemed to fill this room with pervading dust. A thin, acrid pall as of the tomb seemed to lie everywhere upon this room decked and furnished as for a bridal: upon the valance curtains of faded rose color, upon the rose-shaded lights, upon the dressing table, upon the delicate array of crystal and the man's toilet things backed with tarnished silver, silver so tarnished that the monogram was obscured. Among them lay a collar and tie, as if they had just been removed, which, lifted, left upon the surface a pale crescent in the dust. Upon a chair hung the suit, carefully folded; beneath it the two mute shoes and the discarded socks.

The man himself lay in the bed.

For a long while we just stood there, looking down at the profound and fleshless grin. The body had apparently once lain in the attitude of an embrace, but now the long sleep that outlasts love, that conquers even the grimace of love, had cuckolded him. What was left of him, rotted beneath what was left of the nightshirt, had become inextricable from the bed in which he lay; and upon him and upon the pillow beside him lay that even coating of the patient and biding dust.

Then we noticed that in the second pillow was the indentation of a head. One of us lifted something from it, and leaning forward, that faint and invisible dust dry and acrid in the nostrils, we saw a long strand of iron-gray hair.

COMMENTARY

WILLIAM FAULKNER

William Faulkner was writer-in-residence at the University of Virginia in 1957 and 1958. During that time he encouraged students to ask questions about his writing. He answered more than 2,000 queries on everything from spelling to the nature of man, including a series of questions about "A Rose for Emily" addressed to him at different interviews by students of Frederick Gwynn and Joseph Blotner. These professors later edited the book *Faulkner in the University* (1959), in which the following excerpt first appeared.

The Meaning of "A Rose for Emily" 1959

Interviewer: What is the meaning of the title "A Rose for Emily"?

Faulkner: Oh, it's simply the poor woman had had no life at all. Her father had kept her more or less locked up and then she had a lover who was about to quit her, she had to murder him. It was just "A Rose for Emily"—that's all.

Interviewer: I was wondering, one of your short stories, "A Rose for Emily," what ever inspired you to write this story . . . ?

Faulkner: That to me was another sad and tragic manifestation of man's condition in which he dreams and hopes, in which he is in conflict with himself or with his environment or with others. In this case there was the young girl with a young girl's normal aspirations to find love and then a husband and a family, who was brow-beaten and kept down by her father, a selfish man who didn't want her to leave home because he wanted a housekeeper, and it was a natural instinct of—repressed which—you can't repress it—you can mash it down but it comes up somewhere else and very likely in a tragic form, and that was simply another manifestation of man's injustice to man, of the poor tragic human being struggling with its own heart, with others, with its environment, for the simple things which all human beings want. In that case it was a young girl that just wanted to be loved and to love and to have a husband and a family.

Interviewer: And that purely came from your imagination?

Faulkner: Well, the story did but the condition is there. It exists. I didn't invent that condition, I didn't invent the fact that young girls dream of someone to love and children and a home, but the story of what her own particular tragedy was was invented, yes. . . .

Interviewer: Sir, it has been argued that "A Rose for Emily" is a criticism of the North, and others have argued saying that it is a criticism of the South. Now, could this story, shall we say, be more properly classified as a criticism of the times?

Faulkner: Now that I don't know, because I was simply trying to write about people. The writer uses environment—what he knows—and if there's a symbolism in which the lover represented the North and the woman who murdered him represents the South, I don't say that's not valid and not there, but it was no intention of the writer to say, Now let's see, I'm going to write a piece in which I will use a symbolism for the North and another symbol for the South, that he was simply writing about people, a story which he thought was tragic and true, because it came out of the human heart, the human aspiration, the human—the conflict of conscience with glands, with the Old Adam. It was a conflict not between the North and the South so much as between, well you might say, God and Satan.

Interviewer: Sir, just a little more on that thing. You say it's a conflict between God and Satan. Well, I don't quite understand what you mean. Who is—did one represent the—

Faulkner: The conflict was in Miss Emily, that she knew that you do not murder people. She had been trained that you do not take a lover. You marry, you don't take a lover. She had broken all the laws of her tradition, her background, and she had finally broken the law of God too, which says you do not take human life. And she knew she was doing wrong, and that's why her own life was wrecked. Instead of murdering one lover, and then to go and take another and when she used him up to murder him, she was expiating her crime.

Interviewer: Was the "Rose for Emily" an idea or a character? Just how did you go about it?

Faulkner: That came from a picture of the strand of hair on the pillow. It was a ghost story. Simply a picture of a strand of hair on the pillow in the abandoned house.

CHARLOTTE PERKINS GILMAN

Charlotte Perkins Gilman (1860–1935) was born in Hartford, Connecticut. Her father deserted the family shortly after she was born and provided her mother with only meager support. As a teenager Gilman attended the Rhode Island School of Design for a brief period and worked as a commercial artist and teacher. Like her great-aunt Harriet Beecher Stowe, she was concerned at an early age with social injustice and wrote poetry about the hardship of women's lives.

In 1884 she married the artist Charles Walter Stetson. Suffering extreme depression after the birth of a daughter, she left her husband and moved to California in 1888. They were divorced, and she later married George Houghton Gilman, with whom she lived for thirty-four years. In the 1890s Gilman established her reputation as a lecturer and writer of feminist tracts. Her book *Women and Economics* (1898) is considered one of the most important works of the early years of the women's movement in the United States. Gilman's later books – *Concerning Children* (1900), *The Home* (1904), and *Human Work* (1904) – argue that women should be educated to become financially independent; then they could contribute more to the amelioration of systems of justice and the improvement of society. From 1909 to 1917 Gilman published her own journal, *The Forerunner*, for which she wrote voluminously. At the end of her life, suffering from cancer, she committed suicide with chloroform.

Today Gilman's best-known work is "The Yellow Wallpaper," written around 1890, shortly after her own mental breakdown. A landmark story in its frank depiction of mental illness, it is part fantasy and part autobiography, an imaginative account of her suffering and treatment by the physician S. Weir Mitchell, who forbade her any activity, especially writing, the thing she most wanted to do. In setting the story Gilman used elements of the conventional gothic romances that were a staple in women's popular fiction – an isolated mansion, a distant but dominating male figure, and a mysterious household – all of which force the heroine into the role of passive victim of circumstances. But Gilman gave her own twist to the form. Using the brief paragraphs and simple sentences of popular fiction, she narrated her story with a clinical precision that avoided the trite language of typical romances.

WEB Research Charlotte Perkins Gilman at bedfordstmartins.com/rewritinglit.

The Yellow Wallpaper

1892

It is very seldom that mere ordinary people like John and myself secure ancestral halls for the summer.

A colonial mansion, a hereditary estate, I would say a haunted house and reach the height of romantic felicity—but that would be asking too much of fate!

Still I will proudly declare that there is something queer about it.

Else, why should it be let so cheaply? And why have stood so long untenanted?

John laughs at me, of course, but one expects that in marriage.

John is practical in the extreme. He has no patience with faith, an intense horror of superstition, and he scoffs openly at any talk of things not to be felt and seen and put down in figures.

John is a physician, and *perhaps*—(I would not say it to a living soul, of course, but this is dead paper and a great relief to my mind)—*perhaps* that is one reason I do not get well faster.

You see, he does not believe I am sick!

And what can one do?

If a physician of high standing, and one's own husband, assures friends and relatives that there is really nothing the matter with one but temporary nervous depression—a slight hysterical tendency—what is one to do?

My brother is also a physician, and also of high standing, and he says the same thing.

So I take phosphates or phosphites—whichever it is, and tonics, and journeys, and air, and exercise, and am absolutely forbidden to "work" until I am well again.

Personally, I disagree with their ideas.

Personally, I believe that congenial work, with excitement and change, would do me good.

But what is one to do?

I did write for a while in spite of them; but it *does* exhaust me a good deal—having to be so sly about it, or else meet with heavy opposition.

I sometimes fancy that in my condition if I had less opposition and more society and stimulus—but John says the very worst thing I can do is to think about my condition, and I confess it always makes me feel bad.

So I will let it alone and talk about the house.

The most beautiful place! It is quite alone, standing well back from the road, quite three miles from the village. It makes me think of English places that you read about, for there are hedges and walls and gates that lock, and lots of separate little houses for the gardeners and people.

There is a *delicious* garden! I never saw such a garden—large and shady, full of box-bordered paths, and lined with long grape-covered arbors with seats under them.

There were greenhouses, too, but they are all broken now.

There was some legal trouble, I believe, something about the heirs and co-heirs; anyhow, the place has been empty for years.

That spoils my ghostliness, I am afraid, but I don't care—there is something strange about the house—I can feel it.

I even said so to John one moonlight evening, but he said what I felt was a *draught*, and shut the window.

I get unreasonably angry with John sometimes. I'm sure I never used to be so sensitive. I think it is due to this nervous condition.

But John says if I feel so, I shall neglect proper self-control; so I take pains to control myself—before him, at least, and that makes me very tired.

I don't like our room a bit. I wanted one downstairs that opened on the piazza and had roses all over the window, and such pretty old-fashioned chintz hangings! but John would not hear of it.

He said there was only one window and not room for two beds, and no near room for him if he took another.

He is very careful and loving, and hardly lets me stir without special direction.

I have a schedule prescription for each hour in the day; he takes all care from me, and so I feel basely ungrateful not to value it more.

He said we came here solely on my account, that I was to have perfect rest and all the air I could get. "Your exercise depends on your strength, my dear," said he, "and your food somewhat on your appetite; but air you can absorb all the time." So we took the nursery at the top of the house.

It is a big, airy room, the whole floor nearly, with windows that look all ways, and air and sunshine galore. It was nursery first and then playroom and gymnasium, I should judge; for the windows are barred for little children, and there are rings and things in the walls.

The paint and paper look as if a boys' school had used it. It is stripped off—the paper—in great patches all around the head of my bed, about as far as I can reach, and in a great place on the other side of the room low down. I never saw a worse paper in my life.

One of those sprawling flamboyant patterns committing every artistic sin.

It is dull enough to confuse the eye in following, pronounced enough to constantly irritate and provoke study, and when you follow the lame uncertain curves for a little distance they suddenly commit suicide—plunge off at outrageous angles, destroy themselves in unheard of contradictions.

The color is repellant, almost revolting; a smouldering unclean yellow, strangely faded by the slow-turning sunlight.

It is a dull yet lurid orange in some places, a sickly sulphur tint in others.

No wonder the children hated it! I should hate it myself if I had to live in this room long.

There comes John, and I must put this away,—he hates to have me write a word.

We have been here two weeks, and I haven't felt like writing before, since that first day.

I am sitting by the window now, up in this atrocious nursery, and there is nothing to hinder my writing as much as I please, save lack of strength.

John is away all day, and even some nights when his cases are serious.

I am glad my case is not serious!

But these nervous troubles are dreadfully depressing.

John does not know how much I really suffer. He knows there is no *reason* to suffer, and that satisfies him.

Of course it is only nervousness. It does weigh on me so not to do my duty in any way!

I meant to be such a help to John, such a real rest and comfort, and here I am a comparative burden already!

Nobody would believe what an effort it is to do what little I am able,—to dress and entertain, and order things.

It is fortunate Mary is so good with the baby. Such a dear baby!

And yet I *cannot* be with him, it makes me so nervous.

I suppose John never was nervous in his life. He laughs at me so about this wall-paper!

At first he meant to repaper the room, but afterward he said that I was letting it get the better of me, and that nothing was worse for a nervous patient than to give way to such fancies.

He said that after the wall-paper was changed it would be the heavy bedstead, and then the barred windows, and then that gate at the head of the stairs, and so on.

"You know the place is doing you good," he said, "and really, dear, I don't care to renovate the house just for a three months' rental."

"Then do let us go downstairs," I said, "there are such pretty rooms there."

Then he took me in his arms and called me a blessed little goose, and said he would go down cellar, if I wished, and have it whitewashed into the bargain.

But he is right enough about the beds and windows and things.

It is an airy and comfortable room as anyone need wish, and, of course, I would not be so silly as to make him uncomfortable just for a whim.

I'm really getting quite fond of the big room, all but that horrid paper.

Out of one window I can see the garden, those mysterious deep-shaded arbors, the riotous old-fashioned flowers, and bushes and gnarly trees.

Out of another I get a lovely view of the bay and a little private wharf belonging to the estate. There is a beautiful shaded lane that runs down there from the house. I always fancy I see people walking in these numerous paths and arbors, but John has cautioned me not to give way to fancy in the least. He says that with my imaginative power and habit of story-making, a nervous weakness like mine is sure to lead to all manner of excited fancies, and that I ought to use my will and good sense to check the tendency. So I try.

I think sometimes that if I were only well enough to write a little it would relieve the press of ideas and rest me.

But I find I get pretty tired when I try.

It is so discouraging not to have any advice and companionship about my work. When I get really well, John says we will ask Cousin Henry and Julia down for a long visit; but he says he would as soon put fireworks in my pillow-case as to let me have those stimulating people about now.

I wish I could get well faster.

But I must not think about that. This paper looks to me as if it *knew* what a vicious influence it had!

There is a recurrent spot where the pattern lolls like a broken neck and two bulbous eyes stare at you upside down.

I get positively angry with the impertinence of it and the everlastingness. Up and down and sideways they crawl, and those absurd, unblinking eyes are everywhere. There is one place where two breadths didn't match, and the eyes go all up and down the line, one a little higher than the other.

I never saw so much expression in an inanimate thing before, and we all know how much expression they have! I used to lie awake as a child and get more entertainment and terror out of blank walls and plain furniture than most children could find in a toy-store.

I remember what a kindly wink the knobs of our big, old bureau used to have, and there was one chair that always seemed like a strong friend.

I used to feel that if any of the other things looked too fierce I could always hop into that chair and be safe.

The furniture in this room is no worse than inharmonious, however, for we had to bring it all from downstairs. I suppose when this was used as a playroom they had to take the nursery things out, and no wonder! I never saw such ravages as the children have made here.

The wall-paper, as I said before, is torn off in spots, and it sticketh closer than a brother—they must have had perseverance as well as hatred.

Then the floor is scratched and gouged and splintered, the plaster itself is dug out here and there, and this great heavy bed, which is all we found in the room, looks as if it had been through the wars.

But I don't mind it a bit—only the paper.

There comes John's sister. Such a dear girl as she is, and so careful of me! I must not let her find me writing.

She is a perfect and enthusiastic housekeeper, and hopes for no better profession. I verily believe she thinks it is the writing which made me sick!

But I can write when she is out, and see her a long way off from these windows.

There is one that commands the road, a lovely shaded winding road, and one that just looks off over the country. A lovely country, too, full of great elms and velvet meadows.

This wallpaper has a kind of sub-pattern in a different shade, a particularly irritating one, for you can only see it in certain lights, and not clearly then.

But in the places where it isn't faded and where the sun is just so—I can see a strange, provoking, formless sort of figure, that seems to skulk about behind that silly and conspicuous front design.

There's sister on the stairs!

Well, the Fourth of July is over! The people are all gone and I am tired out. John thought it might do me good to see a little company, so we just had mother and Nellie and the children down for a week.

Of course I didn't do a thing. Jennie sees to everything now.

But it tired me all the same.

John says if I don't pick up faster he shall send me to Weir Mitchell° in the fall.

But I don't want to go there at all. I had a friend who was in his hands once, and she says he is just like John and my brother, only more so!

Besides, it is such an undertaking to go so far.

I don't feel as if it was worthwhile to turn my hand over for anything, and I'm getting dreadfully fretful and querulous.

I cry at nothing, and cry most of the time.

Of course I don't when John is here, or anybody else, but when I am alone.

And I am alone a good deal just now. John is kept in town very often by serious cases, and Jennie is good and lets me alone when I want her to.

So I walk a little in the garden or down that lovely lane, sit on the porch under the roses, and lie down up here a good deal.

I'm getting really fond of the room in spite of the wallpaper. Perhaps *because* of the wallpaper.

It dwells in my mind so!

I lie here on this great immovable bed—it is nailed down, I believe—and follow that pattern about by the hour. It is as good as gymnastics, I assure you. I start, we'll say, at the bottom, down in the corner over there where it has not been touched, and I determine for the thousandth time that I *will* follow that pointless pattern to some sort of a conclusion.

I know a little of the principle of design, and I know this thing was not arranged on any laws of radiation, or alternation, or repetition, or symmetry, or anything else that I ever heard of.

It is repeated, of course, by the breadths, but not otherwise.

Looked at in one way each breadth stands alone, the bloated curves and flourishes—a kind of "debased Romanesque" with *delirium tremens*—go waddling up and down in isolated columns of fatuity.

But, on the other hand, they connect diagonally, and the sprawling outlines run off in great slanting waves of optic horror, like a lot of wallowing seaweeds in full chase.

The whole thing goes horizontally, too, at least it seems so, and I exhaust myself in trying to distinguish the order of its going in that direction.

Weir Mitchell: Dr. S. Weir Mitchell (1829–1914) was an eminent Philadelphia neurologist who advocated "rest cures" for nervous disorders. He was the author of *Diseases of the Nervous System, Especially of Women* (1881).

They have used a horizontal breadth for a frieze, and that adds wonderfully to the confusion.

There is one end of the room where it is almost intact, and there, when the crosslights fade and the low sun shines directly upon it, I can almost fancy radiation after all,—the interminable grotesques seem to form around a common centre and rush off in headlong plunges of equal distraction.

It makes me tired to follow it. I will take a nap I guess.

I don't know why I should write this.

I don't want to.

I don't feel able.

And I know John would think it absurd. But I *must* say what I feel and think in some way—it is such a relief!

But the effort is getting to be greater than the relief.

Half the time now I am awfully lazy, and lie down ever so much.

John says I mustn't lose my strength, and has me take cod liver oil and lots of tonics and things, to say nothing of ale and wine and rare meat.

Dear John! He loves me very dearly, and hates to have me sick. I tried to have a real earnest reasonable talk with him the other day, and tell him how I wish he would let me go and make a visit to Cousin Henry and Julia.

But he said I wasn't able to go, nor able to stand it after I got there; and I did not make out a very good case for myself, for I was crying before I had finished.

It is getting to be a great effort for me to think straight. Just this nervous weakness I suppose.

And dear John gathered me up in his arms, and just carried me upstairs and laid me on the bed, and sat by me and read to me till it tired my head.

He said I was his darling and his comfort and all he had, and that I must take care of myself for his sake, and keep well.

He says no one but myself can help me out of it, that I must use my will and self-control and not let any silly fancies run away with me.

There's one comfort, the baby is well and happy, and does not have to occupy this nursery with the horrid wallpaper.

If we had not used it, that blessed child would have! What a fortunate escape! Why, I wouldn't have a child of mine, an impressionable little thing, live in such a room for worlds.

I never thought of it before, but it is lucky that John kept me here after all, I can stand it so much easier than a baby, you see.

Of course I never mention it to them any more—I am too wise, but I keep watch of it all the same.

There are things in the wallpaper that nobody knows but me, or ever will.

Behind that outside pattern the dim shapes get clearer every day.

It is always the same shape, only very numerous.

And it is like a woman stooping down and creeping about behind that pattern. I don't like it a bit. I wonder—I begin to think—I wish John would take me away from here!

•

It is so hard to talk with John about my case, because he is so wise, and because he loves me so.

But I tried it last night.

It was moonlight. The moon shines in all around just as the sun does.

I hate to see it sometimes, it creeps so slowly, and always comes in by one window or another.

John was asleep and I hated to waken him, so I kept still and watched the moonlight on that undulating wallpaper till I felt creepy.

The faint figure behind seemed to shake the pattern, just as if she wanted to get out.

I got up softly and went to feel and see if the paper *did* move, and when I came back John was awake.

"What is it, little girl?" he said. "Don't go walking about like that—you'll get cold."

I thought it was a good time to talk, so I told him that I really was not gaining here, and that I wished he would take me away.

"Why, darling!" said he, "our lease will be up in three weeks, and I can't see how to leave before.

"The repairs are not done at home, and I cannot possibly leave town just now. Of course if you were in any danger, I could and would, but you really are better, dear, whether you can see it or not. I am a doctor, dear, and I know. You are gaining flesh and color, your appetite is better, I feel really much easier about you."

"I don't weigh a bit more," said I, "nor as much; and my appetite may be better in the evening when you are here but it is worse in the morning when you are away!"

"Bless her little heart!" said he with a big hug, "she shall be as sick as she pleases! But now let's improve the shining hours by going to sleep, and talk about it in the morning!"

"And you won't go away?" I asked gloomily.

"Why, how can I, dear? It is only three weeks more and then we will take a nice little trip of a few days while Jennie is getting the house ready. Really dear you are better!"

"Better in body perhaps—" I began, and stopped short, for he sat up straight and looked at me with such a stern, reproachful look that I could not say another word.

"My darling," said he, "I beg you, for my sake and for our child's sake, as well as for your own, that you will never for one instant let that idea enter your mind! There is nothing so dangerous, so fascinating, to a temperament like yours. It is a false and foolish fancy. Can you trust me as a physician when I tell you so?"

So of course I said no more on that score, and we went to sleep before long. He thought I was asleep first, but I wasn't, and lay there for hours trying to decide whether that front pattern and the back pattern really did move together or separately.

On a pattern like this, by daylight, there is a lack of sequence, a defiance of law, that is a constant irritant to a normal mind.

The color is hideous enough, and unreliable enough, and infuriating enough, but the pattern is torturing.

You think you have mastered it, but just as you get well underway in following, it turns a back-somersault and there you are. It slaps you in the face, knocks you down, and tramples upon you. It is like a bad dream.

The outside pattern is a florid arabesque, reminding one of a fungus. If you can imagine a toadstool in joints, an interminable string of toadstools, budding and sprouting in endless convolutions—why, that is something like it.

That is, sometimes!

There is one marked peculiarity about this paper, a thing nobody seems to notice but myself, and that is that it changes as the light changes.

When the sun shoots in through the east window—I always watch for that first long, straight ray—it changes so quickly that I never can quite believe it.

That is why I watch it always.

By moonlight—the moon shines in all night when there is a moon—I wouldn't know it was the same paper.

At night in any kind of light, in twilight, candlelight, lamplight, and worst of all by moonlight, it becomes bars! The outside pattern I mean, and the woman behind it is as plain as can be.

I didn't realize for a long time what the thing was that showed behind, that dim sub-pattern, but now I am quite sure it is a woman.

By daylight she is subdued, quiet. I fancy it is the pattern that keeps her so still. It is so puzzling. It keeps me quiet by the hour.

I lie down ever so much now. John says it is good for me, and to sleep all I can.

Indeed he started the habit by making me lie down for an hour after each meal.

It is a very bad habit I am convinced, for you see I don't sleep.

And that cultivates deceit, for I don't tell them I'm awake—O, no!

The fact is I am getting a little afraid of John.

He seems very queer sometimes, and even Jennie has an inexplicable look.

It strikes me occasionally, just as a scientific hypothesis,—that perhaps it is the paper!

I have watched John when he did not know I was looking, and come into the room suddenly on the most innocent excuses, and I've caught him several times *looking at the paper!* And Jennie too. I caught Jennie with her hand on it once.

She didn't know I was in the room, and when I asked her in a quiet, a very quiet voice, with the most restrained manner possible, what she was doing with the paper—she turned around as if she had been caught stealing, and looked quite angry—asked me why I should frighten her so!

Then she said that the paper stained everything it touched, that she had found yellow smooches on all my clothes and John's, and she wished we would be more careful!

Did not that sound innocent? But I know she was studying that pattern, and I am determined that nobody shall find it out but myself!

•

Life is very much more exciting now than it used to be. You see I have something more to expect, to look forward to, to watch. I really do eat better, and am more quiet than I was.

John is so pleased to see me improve! He laughed a little the other day, and said I seemed to be flourishing in spite of my wall-paper.

I turned it off with a laugh. I had no intention of telling him it was *because* of the wall-paper—he would make fun of me. He might even want to take me away.

I don't want to leave now until I have found it out. There is a week more, and I think that will be enough.

I'm feeling ever so much better! I don't sleep much at night, for it is so interesting to watch developments; but I sleep a good deal in the daytime.

In the daytime it is tiresome and perplexing.

There are always new shoots on the fungus, and new shades of yellow all over it. I cannot keep count of them, though I have tried conscientiously.

It is the strangest yellow, that wall-paper! It makes me think of all the yellow things I ever saw—not beautiful ones like buttercups, but old foul, bad yellow things.

But there is something else about that paper—the smell! I noticed it the moment we came into the room, but with so much air and sun it was not bad. Now we have had a week of fog and rain, and whether the windows are open or not, the smell is here.

It creeps all over the house.

I find it hovering in the dining-room, skulking in the parlor, hiding in the hall, lying in wait for me on the stairs.

It gets into my hair.

Even when I go to ride, if I turn my head suddenly and surprise it—there is that smell!

Such a peculiar odor, too! I have spent hours in trying to analyze it, to find what it smelled like.

It is not bad—at first, and very gentle, but quite the subtlest, most enduring odor I ever met.

In this damp weather it is awful, I wake up in the night and find it hanging over me.

It used to disturb me at first. I thought seriously of burning the house—to reach the smell.

But now I am used to it. The only thing I can think of that it is like is the *color* of the paper! A yellow smell.

There is a very funny mark on this wall, low down, near the mopboard. A streak that runs round the room. It goes behind every piece of furniture, except the bed, a long, straight, even *smooch*, as if it had been rubbed over and over.

I wonder how it was done and who did it, and what they did it for. Round and round and round—round and round and round—it makes me dizzy!

I really have discovered something at last.

Through watching so much at night, when it changes so, I have finally found out.

The front pattern *does* move—and no wonder! The woman behind shakes it!

Sometimes I think there are a great many women behind, and sometimes only one, and she crawls around fast, and her crawling shakes it all over.

Then in the very bright spots she keeps still, and in the very shady spots she just takes hold of the bars and shakes them hard.

And she is all the time trying to climb through. But nobody could climb through that pattern—it strangles so; I think that is why it has so many heads.

They get through, and then the pattern strangles them off and turns them upside down, and makes their eyes white!

If those heads were covered or taken off it would not be half so bad.

I think that woman gets out in the daytime!

And I'll tell you why—privately—I've seen her!

I can see her out of every one of my windows!

It is the same woman, I know, for she is always creeping, and most women do not creep by daylight.

I see her in that long shaded lane, creeping up and down. I see her in those dark grape arbors, creeping all around the garden.

I see her on that long road under the trees, creeping along, and when a carriage comes she hides under the blackberry vines.

I don't blame her a bit. It must be very humiliating to be caught creeping by daylight!

I always lock the door when I creep by daylight. I can't do it at night, for I know John would suspect something at once.

And John is so queer now, that I don't want to irritate him. I wish he would take another room! Besides, I don't want anybody to get that woman out at night but myself.

I often wonder if I could see her out of all the windows at once.

But, turn as fast as I can, I can only see out of one at one time.

And though I always see her, she *may* be able to creep faster than I can turn!

I have watched her sometimes away off in the open country, creeping as fast as a cloud shadow in a high wind.

If only that top pattern could be gotten off from the under one! I mean to try it, little by little.

I have found out another funny thing, but I shan't tell it this time! It does not do to trust people too much.

There are only two more days to get this paper off, and I believe John is beginning to notice. I don't like the look in his eyes.

And I heard him ask Jennie a lot of professional questions, about me. She had a very good report to give.

She said I slept a good deal in the daytime.

John knows I don't sleep very well at night, for all I'm so quiet!

He asked me all sorts of questions too, and pretended to be very loving and kind.

As if I couldn't see through him!

Still, I don't wonder he acts so, sleeping under this paper for three months.

It only interests me, but I feel sure John and Jennie are secretly affected by it.

Hurrah! This is the last day, but it is enough. John to stay in town over night, and won't be out until this evening.

Jennie wanted to sleep with me—the sly thing! But I told her I should undoubtedly rest better for a night all alone.

That was clever, for really I wasn't alone a bit! As soon as it was moonlight and that poor thing began to crawl and shake the pattern, I got up and ran to help her.

I pulled and she shook, I shook and she pulled, and before morning we had peeled off yards of that paper.

A strip about as high as my head and half around the room.

And then when the sun came and that awful pattern began to laugh at me, I declared I would finish it to-day!

We go away to-morrow, and they are moving all my furniture down again to leave things as they were before.

Jennie looked at the wall in amazement, but I told her merrily that I did it out of pure spite at the vicious thing.

She laughed and said she wouldn't mind doing it herself, but I must not get tired.

How she betrayed herself that time!

But I am here, and no person touches this paper but me,—not *alive!*

She tried to get me out of the room—it was too patent! But I said it was so quiet and empty and clean now that I believed I would lie down again and sleep all I could, and not to wake me even for dinner—I would call when I woke.

So now she is gone, and the servants are gone, and the things are gone, and there is nothing left but that great bedstead nailed down, with the canvas mattress we found on it.

We shall sleep downstairs to-night, and take the boat home to-morrow.

I quite enjoy the room, now it is bare again.

How those children did tear about here!

This bedstead is fairly gnawed!

But I must get to work.

I have locked the door and thrown the key down into the front path.

I don't want to go out, and I don't want to have anybody come in, till John comes.

I want to astonish him.

I've got a rope up here that even Jennie did not find. If that woman does get out, and tries to get away, I can tie her!

But I forgot I could not reach far without anything to stand on!

This bed will *not* move!

I tried to lift and push it until I was lame, and then I got so angry I bit off a little piece at one corner—but it hurt my teeth.

Then I peeled off all the paper I could reach standing on the floor. It sticks horribly and the pattern just enjoys it! All those strangled heads and bulbous eyes and waddling fungus growths just shriek with derision!

I am getting angry enough to do something desperate. To jump out of the window would be admirable exercise, but the bars are too strong even to try.

Besides I wouldn't do it. Of course not. I know well enough that a step like that is improper and might be misconstrued.

I don't like to *look* out of the windows even — there are so many of those creeping women, and they creep so fast.

I wonder if they all come out of that wall-paper as I did?

But I am securely fastened now by my well-hidden rope — you don't get *me* out in the road there!

I suppose I shall have to get back behind the pattern when it comes night, and that is hard!

It is so pleasant to be out in this great room and creep around as I please!

I don't want to go outside. I won't, even if Jennie asks me to.

For outside you have to creep on the ground, and everything is green instead of yellow.

But here I can creep smoothly on the floor, and my shoulder just fits in that long smooch around the wall, so I cannot lose my way.

Why, there's John at the door!

It is no use, young man, you can't open it!

How he does call and pound!

Now he's crying for an axe.

It would be a shame to break down that beautiful door!

"John dear!" said I in the gentlest voice, "the key is down by the front steps, under a plantain leaf!"

That silenced him for a few moments.

Then he said — very quietly indeed, "Open the door, my darling!"

"I can't," said I. "The key is down by the front door under a plantain leaf!"

And then I said it again, several times, very gently and slowly, and said it so often that he had to go and see, and he got it of course, and came in. He stopped short by the door.

"What is the matter?" he cried. "For God's sake, what are you doing!"

I kept on creeping just the same, but I looked at him over my shoulder.

"I've got out at last," said I, "in spite of you and Jane. And I've pulled off most of the paper, so you can't put me back!"

Now why should that man have fainted? But he did, and right across my path by the wall, so that I had to creep over him every time!

COMMENTARIES

CHARLOTTE PERKINS GILMAN

Charlotte Perkins Gilman wrote her autobiography, *The Living of Charlotte Perkins Gilman* (1935), in the last years of her life. Her intelligence and strength of character are evident in this work, as is her modesty after a long career as an eminent American feminist. Her straightforward description of her mental breakdown nearly fifty years earlier is in marked contrast to the obsessive fantasy of her story "The Yellow Wallpaper," written shortly after her illness.

Undergoing the Cure for Nervous Prostration 1935

This was a worse horror than before, for now I saw the stark fact—that I was well while away and sick while at home—a heartening prospect! Soon ensued the same utter prostration, the unbearable inner misery, the ceaseless tears. A new tonic had been invented, Essence of Oats, which was given me, and did some good for a time. I pulled up enough to do a little painting that fall, but soon slipped down again and stayed down. An old friend of my mother's, dear Mrs. Diman, was so grieved at this condition that she gave me a hundred dollars and urged me to go away somewhere and get cured.

At that time the greatest nerve specialist in the country was Dr. S. W. Mitchell of Philadelphia. Through the kindness of a friend of Mr. Stetson's living in that city, I went to him and took "the rest cure"; went with the utmost confidence, prefacing the visit with a long letter giving "the history of the case" in a way a modern psychologist would have appreciated. Dr. Mitchell only thought it proved self-conceit. He had a prejudice against the Beechers. "I've had two women of your blood here already," he told me scornfully. This eminent physician was well versed in two kinds of nervous prostration; that of the business man exhausted from too much work, and the society woman exhausted from too much play. The kind I had was evidently behind him. But he did reassure me on one point—there was no dementia, he said, only hysteria.

I was put to bed and kept there. I was fed, bathed, rubbed, and responded with the vigorous body of twenty-six. As far as he could see there was nothing the matter with me, so after a month of this agreeable treatment he sent me home, with this prescription:

> Live as domestic a life as possible. Have your child with you all the time. (Be it remarked that if I did but dress the baby it left me shaking and crying—certainly far from a healthy companionship for her, to say nothing of the effect on me.) Lie down an hour after each meal. Have but two hours' intellectual life a day. And never touch pen, brush, or pencil as long as you live.

I went home, followed those directions rigidly for months, and came perilously near to losing my mind. The mental agony grew so unbearable that I would sit blankly moving my head from side to side—to get out from under the pain. Not physical pain, not the least "headache" even, just mental torment, and so heavy in its nightmare gloom that it seemed real enough to dodge.

I made a rag baby, hung it on a doorknob, and played with it. I would crawl into remote closets and under beds—to hide from the grinding pressure of that profound distress. . . .

Finally, in the fall of '87, in a moment of clear vision, we agreed to separate, to get a divorce. There was no quarrel, no blame for either one, never an unkind word between us, unbroken mutual affection—but it seemed plain that if I went crazy, it would do my husband no good, and be a deadly injury to my child.

What this meant to the young artist, the devoted husband, the loving father, was so bitter a grief and loss that nothing would have justified breaking the marriage save this worse loss which threatened. It was not a choice between going and staying, but between going, sane, and staying, insane. If I had been of the slightest use to him or to the child, I would have "stuck it," as the English say. But this progressive weakening of the mind made a horror unnecessary to face; better for that dear child to have separated parents than a lunatic mother.

We had been married four years and more. This miserable condition of mind, this darkness, feebleness, and gloom, had begun in those difficult years of courtship, had grown rapidly worse after marriage, and was now threatening utter loss; whereas I had repeated proof that the moment I left home I began to recover. It seemed right to give up a mistaken marriage.

Our mistake was mutual. If I had been stronger and wiser I should never have been persuaded into it. Our suffering was mutual too, his unbroken devotion, his manifold cares and labors in tending a sick wife, his adoring pride in the best of babies, all coming to naught, ending in utter failure—we sympathized with each other but faced a bitter necessity. The separation must come as soon as possible, the divorce must wait for conditions.

If this decision could have been reached sooner it would have been much better for me, the lasting mental injury would have been less. Such recovery as I have made in forty years, and the work accomplished, seem to show that the fear of insanity was not fulfilled, but the effects of nerve bankruptcy remain to this day. So much of my many failures, of misplay and misunderstanding and "queerness" is due to this lasting weakness, and kind friends so unfailingly refuse to allow for it, to believe it, that I am now going to some length in stating the case.

SANDRA M. GILBERT AND SUSAN GUBAR

Sandra M. Gilbert and Susan Gubar presented a feminist reading of Charlotte Perkins Gilman's "The Yellow Wallpaper" in *The Madwoman in the Attic: The Woman Writer and the Nineteenth-Century Literary Imagination* (1979). In this book they argued that a recognizable literary tradition existed in English and American literature in which the female imagination had demonstrated "the anxiety of authorship." According to Gilbert and Gubar, "Images of enclosure and escape, fantasies in which maddened doubles functioned as asocial surrogates for docile selves . . . such patterns reoccurred throughout this tradition, along with obsessive depictions of diseases like anorexia, agoraphobia, and claustrophobia." Gilman's story is securely within this tradition of the "literature of confinement," in which a woman writer, trapped by the patriarchal society, tries to struggle free "through strategic redefinitions of self, art, and society."

A Feminist Reading of Gilman's "The Yellow Wallpaper"

1979

As if to comment on the unity of all these points—on, that is, the anxiety-inducing connections between what women writers tend to see as their parallel confinements in texts, houses, and maternal female bodies—Charlotte Perkins Gilman brought them all together in 1890 in a striking story of female confinement and escape, a paradigmatic tale which (like *Jane Eyre*°) seems to tell *the* story that all literary women would tell if they could speak their "speechless woe." "The Yellow Wallpaper," which Gilman herself called "a description of a case of nervous breakdown," recounts in the first person the experiences of a woman who is evidently suffering from a severe post-partum psychosis. Her husband, a censorious and paternalistic physician, is treating her according to methods by which S. Weir Mitchell, a famous "nerve specialist," treated Gilman herself for a similar problem. He has confined her to a large garret room in an "ancestral hall" he has rented, and he has forbidden her to touch pen to paper until she is well again, for he feels, says the narrator, "that with my imaginative power and habit of story-making, a nervous weakness like mine is sure to lead to all manner of excited fancies, and that I ought to use my will and good sense to check the tendency."

The cure, of course, is worse than the disease, for the sick woman's mental condition deteriorates rapidly. "I think sometimes that if I were only well enough to write a little it would relieve the press of ideas and rest me," she remarks, but literally confined in a room she thinks is a one-time nursery because it has "rings and things" in the walls, she is literally locked away from creativity. The "rings and things," although reminiscent of children's gymnastic equipment, are really the paraphernalia of confinement, like the gate at the head of the stairs, instruments that definitively indicate her imprisonment. Even more tormenting, however, is the room's wallpaper: a sulphurous yellow paper, torn off in spots, and patterned with "lame uncertain curves" that "plunge off at outrageous angles" and "destroy themselves in unheard of contradictions." Ancient, smoldering, "unclean" as the oppressive structures of the society in which she finds herself, this paper surrounds the narrator like an inexplicable text, censorious and overwhelming as her physician husband, haunting as the "hereditary estate" in which she is trying to survive. Inevitably she studies its suicidal implications—and inevitably, because of her "imaginative power and habit of story-making," she revises it, projecting her own passion for escape into its otherwise incomprehensible hieroglyphics. "This wallpaper," she decides, at a key point in her story,

> has a kind of subpattern in a different shade, a particularly irritating one, for you can only see it in certain lights, and not clearly then.
>
> But in the places where it isn't faded and where the sun is just so—I can see a strange, provoking, formless sort of figure, that seems to skulk about behind that silly and conspicuous front design.

***Jane Eyre*:** The classic Victorian novel (1847) by Charlotte Brontë (1816–1855) is considered an important feminist work.

As time passes, this figure concealed behind what corresponds (in terms of what we have been discussing) to the facade of the patriarchal text becomes clearer and clearer. By moonlight the pattern of the wallpaper "becomes bars! The outside pattern I mean, and the woman behind it is as plain as can be." And eventually, as the narrator sinks more deeply into what the world calls madness, the terrifying implications of both the paper and the figure imprisoned behind the paper begin to permeate—that is, to *haunt*—the rented ancestral mansion in which she and her husband are immured. The "yellow smell" of the paper "creeps all over the house," drenching every room in its subtle aroma of decay. And the woman creeps too—through the house, in the house, and out of the house, in the garden and "on that long road under the trees." Sometimes, indeed, the narrator confesses, "I think there are a great many women" both behind the paper and creeping in the garden, "and sometimes only one, and she crawls around fast, and her crawling shakes [the paper] all over. . . . And she is all the time trying to climb through. But nobody could climb through that pattern—it strangles so; I think that is why it has so many heads."

Eventually it becomes obvious to both reader and narrator that the figure creeping through and behind the wallpaper is both the narrator and the narrator's double. By the end of the story, moreover, the narrator has enabled this double to escape from her textual/architectural confinement: "I pulled and she shook, I shook and she pulled, and before morning we had peeled off yards of that paper." Is the message of the tale's conclusion mere madness? Certainly the righteous Doctor John—whose name links him to the anti-hero of Charlotte Brontë's *Villette*—has been temporarily defeated, or at least momentarily stunned. "Now why should that man have fainted?" the narrator ironically asks as she creeps around her attic. But John's unmasculine swoon of surprise is the least of the triumphs Gilman imagines for her madwoman. More significant are the madwoman's own imaginings and creations, mirages of health and freedom with which her author endows her like a fairy godmother showering gold on a sleeping heroine. The woman from behind the wallpaper creeps away, for instance, creeps fast and far on the long road, in broad daylight. "I have watched her sometimes away off in the open country," says the narrator, "creeping as fast as a cloud shadow in a high wind."

Indistinct and yet rapid, barely perceptible but inexorable, the progress of that cloud shadow is not unlike the progress of nineteenth-century literary women out of the texts defined by patriarchal poetics into the open spaces of their own authority. That such an escape from the numb world behind the patterned walls of the text was a flight from disease into health was quite clear to Gilman herself. When "The Yellow Wallpaper" was published she sent it to Weir Mitchell whose strictures had kept her from attempting the pen during her own breakdown, thereby aggravating her illness, and she was delighted to learn, years later, that "he had changed his treatment of nervous prostration since reading" her story. "If that is a fact," she declared, "I have not lived in vain." Because she was a rebellious feminist besides being a medical iconoclast, we can be sure that Gilman did not think of this triumph of hers in narrowly therapeutic terms. Because she knew, with Emily Dickinson, that "Infection in the sentence breeds," she knew that the cure for female despair must be spiritual as well as physical, aesthetic as well as social. What "The Yellow Wallpaper" shows she knew, too, is that even when a supposedly "mad" woman has been sentenced to imprisonment in the "infected" house of her own body, she may discover that, as Sylvia Plath° was to put it seventy years later, she has "a self to recover, a queen."

SUSAN GLASPELL

Susan Glaspell (1876–1948) was born in Davenport, Iowa, into a family that had been among the state's first settlers a generation before. After her graduation from high school, she worked as a reporter and society editor for various newspapers before enrolling at Drake University in Des Moines. There she studied literature, philosophy, and history; edited the college newspaper; and began to write short stories. In 1899 she took a job as statehouse reporter for the Des Moines *Daily News*. Years later she claimed that the discipline of newspaper work helped her to become a creative writer.

At the age of twenty-five, Glaspell returned to Davenport to live with her family, determined, as she said, to "boldly" quit journalism and "give all my time to my own writing. I say 'boldly,' because I had to earn my living." Slowly she began to publish her fiction, mostly sentimental magazine pieces and an undistinguished first novel – work that, as her biographer C. W. E. Bigsby noted, "suggested little of the originality and power which were to mark her work in the theater." In 1909 Glaspell met George Cram Cook, a novelist and utopian socialist from a wealthy family who divorced his second wife and left his two children to marry her. They moved to Greenwich Village and collaborated on a play for the Washington Square Players in 1915, *Suppressed Desires*. The following year, after the Players had moved to Provincetown on Cape Cod, Cook urged Glaspell to write a new play for the theater company, renamed the Provincetown Players. Her memory of a murder trial in Iowa that she had covered as a newspaper reporter served as the inspiration for the short play *Trifles* (1916). Glaspell recalled that she "had meant to do it as a short story, but the stage took it for its own."

Trifles was so successful as an experimental play that Glaspell turned it into a short story a year later, retitling it "A Jury of Her Peers." Her choice of a third-person, limited-omniscient point of view (via the character Martha Hale's perspective) and her description of the harsh realities of the rural setting in "A Jury of Her Peers" suggest the local-color tradition of such earlier writers as Sarah Orne Jewett, although Glaspell's suffragist sympathies were more radical than the views of nineteenth-century women writers. In 1912 Glaspell published her first book of stories, *Lifted Masks*, and she continued to write fiction as well as plays for most of her life. In her forty-seven-year career, she published fifty short stories, nine novels, and thirteen plays, including the Pulitzer Prize–winning play *Alison's House* (1931), based on Genevieve Taggard's biography of Emily Dickinson.

Sylvia Plath: American poet (1932–1963). See page 990.

CONNECTIONS To read Susan Glaspell's play *Trifles*, the precursor to this story, see page 1410. To read a short play that echoes Glaspell's, see *POOF!* by Lynn Nottage on page 1582. To read a commentary on Glaspell's story and play, see Leonard Mustazza, "Generic Translation and Thematic Shift in Glaspell's *Trifles* and "A Jury of Her Peers," on page 1420.

WEB Research Susan Glaspell at bedfordstmartins.com/rewritinglit.

A Jury of Her Peers

1917

When Martha Hale opened the storm-door and got a cut of the north wind, she ran back for her big woolen scarf. As she hurriedly wound that round her head her eye made a scandalized sweep of her kitchen. It was no ordinary thing that called her away—it was probably further from ordinary than anything that had ever happened in Dickson County. But what her eye took in was that her kitchen was in no shape for leaving: her bread all ready for mixing, half the flour sifted and half unsifted.

She hated to see things half done; but she had been at that when the team from town stopped to get Mr. Hale, and then the sheriff came running in to say his wife wished Mrs. Hale would come too—adding, with a grin, that he guessed she was getting scary and wanted another woman along. So she had dropped everything right where it was.

"Martha!" now came her husband's impatient voice. "Don't keep folks waiting out here in the cold."

She again opened the storm-door, and this time joined the three men and the one woman waiting for her in the big two-seated buggy.

After she had the robes tucked around her she took another look at the woman who sat beside her on the back seat. She had met Mrs. Peters the year before at the county fair, and the thing she remembered about her was that she didn't seem like a sheriff's wife. She was small and thin and didn't have a strong voice. Mrs. Gorman, sheriff's wife before Gorman went out and Peters came in, had a voice that somehow seemed to be backing up the law with every word. But if Mrs. Peters didn't look like a sheriff's wife, Peters made it up in looking like a sheriff. He was to a dot the kind of man who could get himself elected sheriff—a heavy man with a big voice, who was particularly genial with the law-abiding, as if to make it plain that he knew the difference between criminals and non-criminals. And right there it came into Mrs. Hale's mind, with a stab, that this man who was so pleasant and lively with all of them was going to the Wrights' now as a sheriff.

"The country's not very pleasant this time of year," Mrs. Peters at last ventured, as if she felt they ought to be talking as well as the men.

Mrs. Hale scarcely finished her reply, for they had gone up a little hill and could see the Wright place now, and seeing it did not make her feel like talking. It looked very lonesome this cold March morning. It had always been a lonesome-looking place. It was down in a hollow, and the poplar trees around it were lonesome-looking trees. The men were looking at it and talking about what had happened. The county attorney was bending to one side of the buggy, and kept looking steadily at the place as they drew up to it.

"I'm glad you came with me," Mrs. Peters said nervously, as the two women were about to follow the men in through the kitchen door.

Even after she had her foot on the door-step, her hand on the knob, Martha Hale had a moment of feeling she could not cross that threshold. And the reason it seemed she couldn't cross it now was simply because she hadn't crossed it before. Time and time again it had been in her mind, "I ought to go over and see Minnie Foster"—she still thought of her as Minnie Foster, though for twenty years she had been Mrs. Wright. And then there was always something to do and Minnie Foster would go from her mind. But *now* she could come.

The men went over to the stove. The women stood close together by the door. Young Henderson, the county attorney, turned around and said, "Come up to the fire, ladies."

Mrs. Peters took a step forward, then stopped. "I'm not—cold," she said.

And so the two women stood by the door, at first not even so much as looking around the kitchen.

The men talked for a minute about what a good thing it was the sheriff had sent his deputy out that morning to make a fire for them, and then Sheriff Peters stepped back from the stove, unbuttoned his outer coat, and leaned his hands on the kitchen table in a way that seemed to mark the beginning of official business. "Now, Mr. Hale," he said in a sort of semi-official voice, "before we move things about, you tell Mr. Henderson just what it was you saw when you came here yesterday morning."

The county attorney was looking around the kitchen.

"By the way," he said, "has anything been moved?" He turned to the sheriff. "Are things just as you left them yesterday?"

Peters looked from cupboard to sink; from that to a small worn rocker a little to one side of the kitchen table.

"It's just the same."

"Somebody should have been left here yesterday," said the county attorney.

"Oh—yesterday," returned the sheriff, with a little gesture as of yesterday having been more than he could bear to think of. "When I had to send Frank to Morris Center for that man who went crazy—let me tell you. I had my hands full *yesterday*. I knew you could get back from Omaha by today, George, and as long as I went over everything here myself—"

"Well, Mr. Hale," said the county attorney, in a way of letting what was past and gone go, "tell just what happened when you came here yesterday morning."

Mrs. Hale, still leaning against the door, had that sinking feeling of the mother whose child is about to speak a piece. Lewis often wandered along and got things mixed up in a story. She hoped he would tell this straight and plain, and not say unnecessary things that would just make things harder for Minnie Foster. He didn't begin at once, and she noticed that he looked queer—as if standing in that kitchen and having to tell what he had seen there yesterday morning made him almost sick.

"Yes, Mr. Hale?" the county attorney reminded.

"Harry and I had started to town with a load of potatoes," Mrs. Hale's husband began.

Harry was Mrs. Hale's oldest boy. He wasn't with them now, for the very good reason that those potatoes never got to town yesterday and he was taking them this morning, so he hadn't been home when the sheriff stopped to say he wanted Mr. Hale to come over to the Wright place and tell the county attorney his story there, where he could point it all out. With all Mrs. Hale's other emotions came the fear now that maybe Harry wasn't dressed warm enough—they hadn't any of them realized how that north wind did bite.

"We come along this road," Hale was going on, with a motion of his hand to the road over which they had just come, "and as we got in sight of the house I says to Harry, 'I'm goin' to see if I can't get John Wright to take a telephone.' You see," he explained to Henderson, "unless I can get somebody to go in with me they won't come out this branch road except for a price *I* can't pay. I'd spoke to Wright about it once before; but he put me off, saying folks talked too much anyway, and all he asked was peace and quiet—guess you know about how much he talked himself. But I thought maybe if I went to the house and talked about it before his wife, and said all the women-folks liked the telephones, and that in this lonesome stretch of road it would be a good thing—well, I said to Harry that that was what I was going to say—though I said at the same time that I didn't know as what his wife wanted made much difference to John—"

Now there he was!—saying things he didn't need to say. Mrs. Hale tried to catch her husband's eye, but fortunately the county attorney interrupted with:

"Let's talk about that a little later, Mr. Hale. I do want to talk about that, but I'm anxious now to get along to just what happened when you got here."

When he began this time, it was very deliberately and carefully:

"I didn't see or hear anything. I knocked at the door. And still it was all quiet inside. I knew they must be up—it was past eight o'clock. So I knocked again, louder, and I thought I heard somebody say, 'Come in.' I wasn't sure—I'm not sure yet. But I opened the door—this door," jerking a hand toward the door by which the two women stood, "and there, in that rocker"—pointing to it—"sat Mrs. Wright."

Everyone in the kitchen looked at the rocker. It came into Mrs. Hale's mind that that rocker didn't look in the least like Minnie Foster—the Minnie Foster of twenty years before. It was a dingy red, with wooden rungs up the back, and the middle rung was gone, and the chair sagged to one side.

"How did she—look?" the county attorney was inquiring.

"Well," said Hale, "she looked—queer."

"How do you mean—queer?"

As he asked it he took out a note-book and pencil. Mrs. Hale did not like the sight of that pencil. She kept her eye fixed on her husband, as if to keep him from saying unnecessary things that would go into that note-book and make trouble.

Hale did speak guardedly, as if the pencil had affected him too.

"Well, as if she didn't know what she was going to do next. And kind of—done up."

"How did she seem to feel about your coming?"

"Why, I don't think she minded—one way or other. She didn't pay much attention. I said, 'Ho' do, Mrs. Wright? It's cold, ain't it?' And she said, 'Is it?'—and went on pleatin' at her apron.

"Well, I was surprised. She didn't ask me to come up to the stove, or to sit down, but just set there, not even lookin' at me. And so I said: 'I want to see John.'

"And then she—laughed. I guess you would call it a laugh.

"I thought of Harry and the team outside, so I said, a little sharp, 'Can I see John?' 'No,' says she—kind of dull like. 'Ain't he home?' says I. Then she looked at me. 'Yes,' says she, 'he's home.' 'Then why can't I see him?' I asked her, out of patience with her now. 'Cause he's dead' says she, just as quiet and dull—and fell to pleatin' her apron. 'Dead?' says I, like you do when you can't take in what you've heard.

"She just nodded her head, not getting a bit excited, but rockin' back and forth.

"'Why—where is he?' says I, not knowing *what* to say.

"She just pointed upstairs—like this"—pointing to the room above.

"I got up, with the idea of going up there myself. By this time I—didn't know what to do. I walked from there to here; then I says: 'Why, what did he die of?'

"'He died of a rope around his neck,' says she; and just went on pleatin' at her apron."

Hale stopped speaking, and stood staring at the rocker, as if he were still seeing the woman who had sat there the morning before. Nobody spoke; it was as if every one were seeing the woman who had sat there the morning before.

"And what did you do then?" the county attorney at last broke the silence.

"I went out and called Harry. I thought I might—need help. I got Harry in, and we went upstairs." His voice fell almost to a whisper. "There he was—lying over the—"

"I think I'd rather have you go into that upstairs," the county attorney interrupted, "where you can point it all out. Just go on now with the rest of the story."

"Well, my first thought was to get that rope off. It looked—"

He stopped, his face twitching.

"But Harry, he went up to him, and he said, 'No, he's dead all right, and we'd better not touch anything.' So we went downstairs.

"She was still sitting that same way. 'Has anybody been notified?' I asked. 'No,' says she, unconcerned.

"'Who did this, Mrs. Wright?' said Harry. He said it businesslike, and she stopped pleatin' at her apron. 'I don't know,' she says. 'You don't *know*?' says Harry. 'Weren't you sleepin' in the bed with him?' 'Yes,' says she, 'but I was on the inside.' 'Somebody slipped a rope round his neck and strangled him, and you didn't wake up?' says Harry. 'I didn't wake up,' she said after him.

"We may have looked as if we didn't see how that could be, for after a minute she said, 'I sleep sound.'

"Harry was going to ask her more questions, but I said maybe that weren't our business; maybe we ought to let her tell her story first to the coroner or the sheriff. So Harry went fast as he could over to High Road—the Rivers' place, where there's a telephone."

"And what did she do when she knew you had gone for the coroner?" The attorney got his pencil in his hand all ready for writing.

"She moved from that chair to this one over here"—Hale pointed to a small chair in the corner—"and just sat there with her hands held together and looking down. I got a feeling that I ought to make some conversation, so I said I had come in to see if John wanted to put in a telephone; and at that she started to laugh, and then she stopped and looked at me—scared."

At the sound of a moving pencil the man who was telling the story looked up.

"I dunno—maybe it wasn't scared," he hastened: "I wouldn't like to say it was. Soon Harry got back, and then Dr. Lloyd came, and you, Mr. Peters, and so I guess that's all I know that you don't."

He said that last with relief, and moved a little, as if relaxing. Everyone moved a little. The county attorney walked toward the stair door.

"I guess we'll go upstairs first—then out to the barn and around there."

He paused and looked around the kitchen.

"You're convinced there was nothing important here?" he asked the sheriff. "Nothing that would—point to any motive?"

The sheriff too looked all around, as if to re-convince himself.

"Nothing here but kitchen things," he said, with a little laugh for the insignificance of kitchen things.

The county attorney was looking at the cupboard—a peculiar, ungainly structure, half closet and half cupboard, the upper part of it being built in the wall, and the lower part just the old-fashioned kitchen cupboard. As if its queerness attracted him, he got a chair and opened the upper part and looked in. After a moment he drew his hand away sticky.

"Here's a nice mess," he said resentfully.

The two women had drawn nearer, and now the sheriff's wife spoke.

"Oh—her fruit," she said, looking to Mrs. Hale for sympathetic understanding. She turned back to the county attorney and explained: "She worried about that when it turned so cold last night. She said the fire would go out and her jars might burst."

Mrs. Peters's husband broke into a laugh.

"Well, can you beat the women! Held for murder, and worrying about her preserves!"

The young attorney set his lips.

"I guess before we're through with her she may have something more serious than preserves to worry about."

"Oh, well," said Mrs. Hale's husband, with good-natured superiority, "women are used to worrying over trifles."

The two women moved a little closer together. Neither of them spoke. The county attorney seemed suddenly to remember his manners—and think of his future.

"And yet," said he, with the gallantry of a young politician, "for all their worries, what would we do without the ladies?"

The women did not speak, did not unbend. He went to the sink and began washing his hands. He turned to wipe them on the roller towel—whirled it for a cleaner place.

"Dirty towels! Not much of a housekeeper, would you say, ladies?"

He kicked his foot against some dirty pans under the sink.

"There's a great deal of work to be done on a farm," said Mrs. Hale stiffly.

"To be sure. And yet"—with a little bow to her—"I know there are some Dickson County farm-houses that do not have such roller towels." He gave it a pull to expose its full length again.

"Those towels get dirty awful quick. Men's hands aren't always as clean as they might be."

"Ah, loyal to your sex, I see," he laughed. He stopped and gave her a keen look. "But you and Mrs. Wright were neighbors. I suppose you were friends, too."

Martha Hale shook her head.

"I've seen little enough of her of late years. I've not been in this house—it's more than a year."

"And why was that? You didn't like her?"

"I liked her well enough," she replied with spirit. "Farmers' wives have their hands full, Mr. Henderson. And then—" She looked around the kitchen.

"Yes?" he encouraged.

"It never seemed a very cheerful place," said she, more to herself than to him.

"No," he agreed; "I don't think anyone would call it cheerful. I shouldn't say she had the home-making instinct."

"Well, I don't know as Wright had, either," she muttered.

"You mean they didn't get on very well?" he was quick to ask.

"No; I don't mean anything," she answered, with decision. As she turned a little away from him, she added: "But I don't think a place would be any the cheerfuller for John Wright's bein' in it."

"I'd like to talk to you about that a little later, Mrs. Hale," he said. "I'm anxious to get the lay of things upstairs now."

He moved toward the stair door, followed by the two men.

"I suppose anything Mrs. Peters does'll be all right?" the sheriff inquired. "She was to take in some clothes for her, you know—and a few little things. We left in such a hurry yesterday."

The county attorney looked at the two women whom they were leaving alone there among the kitchen things.

"Yes—Mrs. Peters," he said, his glance resting on the woman who was not Mrs. Peters, the big farmer woman who stood behind the sheriff's wife.

"Of course Mrs. Peters is one of us," he said, in a manner of entrusting responsibility. "And keep your eye out, Mrs. Peters, for anything that might be of use. No telling; you women might come upon a clue to the motive—and that's the thing we need."

Mr. Hale rubbed his face after the fashion of a showman getting ready for a pleasantry.

"But would the women know a clue if they did come upon it?" he said; and, having delivered himself of this, he followed the others through the stair door.

The women stood motionless and silent, listening to the footsteps, first upon the stairs, then in the room above them.

Then, as if releasing herself from something strange, Mrs. Hale began to arrange the dirty pans under the sink, which the county attorney's disdainful push of the foot had deranged.

"I'd hate to have men comin' into my kitchen," she said testily—"snoopin' round and criticizin'."

"Of course it's no more than their duty," said the sheriff's wife, in her manner of timid acquiescence.

"Duty's all right," replied Mrs. Hale bluffly; "but I guess that deputy sheriff that come out to make the fire might have got a little of this on." She gave the roller towel a pull. "Wish I'd thought of that sooner! Seems mean to talk about her for not having things slicked up, when she had to come away in such a hurry."

She looked around the kitchen. Certainly it was not "slicked up." Her eye was held by a bucket of sugar on a low shelf. The cover was off the wooden bucket, and beside it was a paper bag—half full.

Mrs. Hale moved toward it.

"She was putting this in there," she said to herself—slowly.

She thought of the flour in her kitchen at home—half sifted, half not sifted. She had been interrupted, and had left things half done. What had interrupted Minnie Foster? Why had that work been left half done? She made a move as if to finish it,—unfinished things always bothered her,—and then she glanced around and saw that Mrs. Peters was watching her—and she didn't want Mrs. Peters to get that feeling she had got of work begun and then—for some reason—not finished.

"It's a shame about her fruit," she said, and walked toward the cupboard that the county attorney had opened, and got on the chair, murmuring: "I wonder if it's all gone."

It was a sorry enough looking sight, but "Here's one that's all right," she said at last. She held it toward the light. "This is cherries, too." She looked again. "I declare I believe that's the only one."

With a sigh, she got down from the chair, went to the sink, and wiped off the bottle.

"She'll feel awful bad, after all her hard work in the hot weather. I remember the afternoon I put up my cherries last summer."

She set the bottle on the table, and, with another sigh, started to sit down in the rocker. But she did not sit down. Something kept her from sitting down in that chair. She straightened—stepped back, and, half turned away, stood looking at it, seeing the woman who had sat there "pleatin' at her apron."

The thin voice of the sheriff's wife broke in upon her: "I must be getting those things from the front-room closet." She opened the door into the other room, started in, stepped back. "You coming with me, Mrs. Hale?" she asked nervously. "You—you could help me get them."

They were soon back—the stark coldness of that shut-up room was not a thing to linger in.

"My!" said Mrs. Peters, dropping the things on the table and hurrying to the stove.

Mrs. Hale stood examining the clothes the woman who was being detained in town had said she wanted.

"Wright was close!"° she exclaimed, holding up a shabby black skirt that bore the marks of much making over. "I think maybe that's why she kept so much to herself. I s'pose she felt she couldn't do her part; and then, you don't enjoy things when you feel shabby. She used to wear pretty clothes and be lively—when she was Minnie Foster, one of the town girls, singing in the choir. But that—oh, that was twenty years ago."

With a carefulness in which there was something tender, she folded the shabby clothes and piled them at one corner of the table. She looked up at Mrs. Peters, and there was something in the other woman's look that irritated her.

"She don't care," she said to herself. "Much difference it makes to her whether Minnie Foster had pretty clothes when she was a girl."

Then she looked again, and she wasn't so sure; in fact, she hadn't at any time been perfectly sure about Mrs. Peters. She had that shrinking manner, and yet her eyes looked as if they could see a long way into things.

"This all you was to take in?" asked Mrs. Hale.

"No," said the sheriff's wife; "she said she wanted an apron. Funny thing to want," she ventured in her nervous little way, "for there's not much to get you dirty in jail, goodness knows. But I suppose just to make her feel more natural. If you're used to wearing an apron—. She said they were in the bottom drawer of this cupboard. Yes—here they are. And then her little shawl that always hung on the stair door."

She took the small gray shawl from behind the door leading upstairs, and stood a minute looking at it.

Suddenly Mrs. Hale took a quick step toward the other woman.

"Mrs. Peters!"

"Yes, Mrs. Hale?"

"Do you think she—did it?"

A frightened look blurred the other thing in Mrs. Peters's eyes.

"Oh, I don't know," she said, in a voice that seemed to shrink away from the subject.

"Well, I don't think she did," affirmed Mrs. Hale stoutly. "Asking for an apron, and her little shawl. Worryin' about her fruit."

---

close: Frugal, tightfisted.

"Mr. Peters says—." Footsteps were heard in the room above; she stopped, looked up, then went on in a lowered voice: "Mr. Peters says—it looks bad for her. Mr. Henderson is awful sarcastic in a speech, and he's going to make fun of her saying she didn't—wake up."

For a moment Mrs. Hale had no answer. Then, "Well, I guess John Wright didn't wake up—when they was slippin' that rope under his neck," she muttered.

"No, it's *strange*," breathed Mrs. Peters. "They think it was such a—funny way to kill a man."

She began to laugh; at the sound of the laugh, abruptly stopped.

"That's just what Mr. Hale said," said Mrs. Hale, in a resolutely natural voice. "There was a gun in the house. He says that's what he can't understand."

"Mr. Henderson said, coming out, that what was needed for the case was a motive. Something to show anger—or sudden feeling."

"Well, I don't see any signs of anger around here," said Mrs. Hale, "I don't—" She stopped. It was as if her mind tripped on something. Her eye was caught by a dishtowel in the middle of the kitchen table. Slowly she moved toward the table. One half of it was wiped clean, the other half messy. Her eyes made a slow, almost unwilling turn to the bucket of sugar and the half empty bag beside it. Things begun—and not finished.

After a moment she stepped back, and said, in that manner of releasing herself:

"Wonder how they're finding things upstairs? I hope she had it a little more redd up° up there. You know,"—she paused, and feeling gathered,—"it seems kind of *sneaking:* locking her up in town and coming out here to get her own house to turn against her!"

"But, Mrs. Hale," said the sheriff's wife, "the law is the law."

"I s'pose 'tis," answered Mrs. Hale shortly.

She turned to the stove, saying something about that fire not being much to brag of. She worked with it a minute, and when she straightened up she said aggressively:

"The law is the law—and a bad stove is a bad stove. How'd you like to cook on this?"—pointing with the poker to the broken lining. She opened the oven door and started to express her opinion of the oven; but she was swept into her own thoughts, thinking of what it would mean, year after year, to have that stove to wrestle with. The thought of Minnie Foster trying to bake in that oven—and the thought of her never going over to see Minnie Foster—.

She was startled by hearing Mrs. Peters say: "A person gets discouraged—and loses heart."

The sheriff's wife had looked from the stove to the sink—to the pail of water which had been carried in from outside. The two women stood there silent, above them the footsteps of the men who were looking for evidence against the woman who had worked in that kitchen. That look of seeing into things, of

---

redd up: Neat.

seeing through a thing to something else, was in the eyes of the sheriff's wife now. When Mrs. Hale next spoke to her, it was gently:

"Better loosen up your things, Mrs. Peters. We'll not feel them when we go out."

Mrs. Peters went to the back of the room to hang up the fur tippet she was wearing. A moment later she exclaimed, "Why, she was piecing a quilt," and held up a large sewing basket piled high with quilt pieces.

Mrs. Hale spread some of the blocks on the table.

"It's log-cabin pattern," she said, putting several of them together. "Pretty, isn't it?"

They were so engaged with the quilt that they did not hear the footsteps on the stairs. Just as the stair door opened Mrs. Hale was saying:

"Do you suppose she was going to quilt it or just knot it?"

The sheriff threw up his hands.

"They wonder whether she was going to quilt it or just knot it!"

There was a laugh for the ways of women, a warming of hands over the stove, and then the county attorney said briskly:

"Well, let's go right out to the barn and get that cleared up."

"I don't see as there's anything so strange," Mrs. Hale said resentfully, after the outside door had closed on the three men—"our taking up our time with little things while we're waiting for them to get the evidence. I don't see as it's anything to laugh about."

"Of course they've got awful important things on their minds," said the sheriff's wife apologetically.

They returned to an inspection of the block for the quilt. Mrs. Hale was looking at the fine, even sewing, and preoccupied with thoughts of the woman who had done that sewing, when she heard the sheriff's wife say, in a queer tone:

"Why, look at this one."

She turned to take the block held out to her.

"The sewing," said Mrs. Peters, in a troubled way. "All the rest of them have been so nice and even—but—this one. Why, it looks as if she didn't know what she was about!"

Their eyes met—something flashed to life, passed between them; then, as if with an effort, they seemed to pull away from each other. A moment Mrs. Hale sat there, her hands folded over that sewing which was so unlike all the rest of the sewing. Then she had pulled a knot and drawn the threads.

"Oh, what are you doing, Mrs. Hale?" asked the sheriff's wife, startled.

"Just pulling out a stitch or two that's not sewed very good," said Mrs. Hale mildly.

"I don't think we ought to touch things," Mrs. Peters said, a little helplessly.

"I'll just finish up this end," answered Mrs. Hale, still in that mild, matter-of-fact fashion.

She threaded a needle and started to replace bad sewing with good. For a little while she sewed in silence. Then, in that thin, timid voice, she heard:

"Mrs. Hale!"

"Yes, Mrs. Peters?"

"What do you suppose she was so—nervous about?"

"Oh, *I* don't know," said Mrs. Hale, as if dismissing a thing not important enough to spend much time on. "I don't know as she was—nervous. I sew awful queer sometimes when I'm just tired."

She cut a thread, and out of the corner of her eye looked up at Mrs. Peters. The small, lean face of the sheriff's wife seemed to have tightened up. Her eyes had that look of peering into something. But next moment she moved, and said in her thin, indecisive way:

"Well, I must get those clothes wrapped. They may be through sooner than we think. I wonder where I could find a piece of paper—and string."

"In that cupboard, maybe," suggested Mrs. Hale, after a glance around.

One piece of the crazy sewing remained unripped. Mrs. Peters's back turned, Martha Hale now scrutinized that piece, compared it with the dainty, accurate sewing of the other blocks. The difference was startling. Holding this block made her feel queer, as if the distracted thoughts of the woman who had perhaps turned to it to try and quiet herself were communicating themselves to her.

Mrs. Peters's voice roused her.

"Here's a bird-cage," she said. "Did she have a bird, Mrs. Hale?"

"Why, I don't know whether she did or not." She turned to look at the cage Mrs. Peters was holding up. "I've not been here in so long." She sighed. "There was a man round last year selling canaries cheap—but I don't know as she took one. Maybe she did. She used to sing real pretty herself."

Mrs. Peters looked around the kitchen.

"Seems kind of funny to think of a bird here." She half laughed—an attempt to put up a barrier. "But she must have had one—or why would she have a cage? I wonder what happened to it."

"I suppose maybe the cat got it," suggested Mrs. Hale, resuming her sewing.

"No; she didn't have a cat. She's got that feeling some people have about cats—being afraid of them. When they brought her to our house yesterday, my cat got in the room, and she was real upset and asked me to take it out."

"My sister Bessie was like that," laughed Mrs. Hale.

The sheriff's wife did not reply. The silence made Mrs. Hale turn round. Mrs. Peters was examining the bird-cage.

"Look at this door," she said slowly. "It's broke. One hinge has been pulled apart."

Mrs. Hale came nearer.

"Looks as if someone must have been—rough with it."

Again their eyes met—startled, questioning, apprehensive. For a moment neither spoke nor stirred. Then Mrs. Hale, turning away, said brusquely:

"If they're going to find any evidence, I wish they'd be about it. I don't like this place."

"But I'm awful glad you came with me, Mrs. Hale." Mrs. Peters put the bird-cage on the table and sat down. "It would be lonesome for me—sitting here alone."

"Yes, it would, wouldn't it?" agreed Mrs. Hale, a certain determined naturalness in her voice. She had picked up the sewing, but now it dropped in her lap, and she murmured in a different voice: "But I tell you what I *do* wish, Mrs. Peters. I wish I had come over sometimes when she was here. I wish—I had."

"But of course you were awful busy, Mrs. Hale. Your house—and your children."

"I could've come," retorted Mrs. Hale shortly. "I stayed away because it weren't cheerful—and that's why I ought to have come. I"—she looked around—"I've never liked this place. Maybe because it's down in a hollow and you don't see the road. I don't know what it is, but it's a lonesome place, and always was. I wish I had come over to see Minnie Foster sometimes. I can see now—" She did not put it into words.

"Well, you mustn't reproach yourself," counseled Mrs. Peters. "Somehow, we just don't see how it is with other folks till—something comes up."

"Not having children makes less work," mused Mrs. Hale, after a silence, "but it makes a quiet house—and Wright out to work all day—and no company when he did come in. Did you know John Wright, Mrs. Peters?"

"Not to know him. I've seen him in town. They say he was a good man."

"Yes—good," conceded John Wright's neighbor grimly. "He didn't drink, and kept his word as well as most, I guess, and paid his debts. But he was a hard man, Mrs. Peters. Just to pass the time of day with him—." She stopped, shivered a little. "Like a raw wind that gets to the bone." Her eye fell upon the cage on the table before her, and she added, almost bitterly: "I should think she would've wanted a bird!"

Suddenly she leaned forward, looking intently at the cage. "But what do you s'pose went wrong with it?"

"I don't know," returned Mrs. Peters; "unless it got sick and died."

But after she said it she reached over and swung the broken door. Both women watched it as if somehow held by it.

"You didn't know—her?" Mrs. Hale asked, a gentler note in her voice.

"Not till they brought her yesterday," said the sheriff's wife.

"She—come to think of it, she was kind of like a bird herself. Real sweet and pretty, but kind of timid and—fluttery. How—she—did—change."

That held her for a long time. Finally, as if struck with a happy thought and relieved to get back to everyday things, she exclaimed:

"Tell you what, Mrs. Peters, why don't you take the quilt in with you? It might take up her mind."

"Why, I think that's a real nice idea, Mrs. Hale," agreed the sheriff's wife, as if she too were glad to come into the atmosphere of a simple kindness. "There couldn't possibly be any objection to that, could there? Now, just what will I take? I wonder if her patches are in here—and her things?"

They turned to the sewing basket.

"Here's some red," said Mrs. Hale, bringing out a roll of cloth. Underneath that was a box. "Here, maybe her scissors are in here—and her things." She held it up. "What a pretty box! I'll warrant that was something she had a long time ago—when she was a girl."

She held it in her hand a moment; then, with a little sigh, opened it.

Instantly her hand went to her nose.

"Why—!"

Mrs. Peters drew nearer—then turned away.

"There's something wrapped up in this piece of silk," faltered Mrs. Hale.

"This isn't her scissors," said Mrs. Peters, in a shrinking voice.

Her hand not steady, Mrs. Hale raised the piece of silk. "Oh, Mrs. Peters!" she cried. "It's—"

Mrs. Peters bent closer.

"It's the bird," she whispered.

"But, Mrs. Peters!" cried Mrs. Hale. "*Look* at it! Its *neck*—look at its neck! It's all—other side *to*."

She held the box away from her.

The sheriff's wife again bent closer.

"Somebody wrung its neck," said she, in a voice that was slow and deep.

And then again the eyes of the two women met—this time clung together in a look of dawning comprehension, of growing horror. Mrs. Peters looked from the dead bird to the broken door of the cage. Again their eyes met. And just then there was a sound at the outside door.

Mrs. Hale slipped the box under the quilt pieces in the basket, and sank into the chair before it. Mrs. Peters stood holding to the table. The county attorney and the sheriff came in from outside.

"Well, ladies," said the county attorney, as one turning from serious things to little pleasantries, "have you decided whether she was going to quilt it or knot it?"

"We think," began the sheriff's wife in a flurried voice, "that she was going to—knot it."

He was too preoccupied to notice the change that came in her voice on that last.

"Well, that's very interesting, I'm sure," he said tolerantly. He caught sight of the bird-cage. "Has the bird flown?"

"We think the cat got it," said Mrs. Hale in a voice curiously even.

He was walking up and down, as if thinking something out.

"Is there a cat?" he asked absently.

Mrs. Hale shot a look up at the sheriff's wife.

"Well, not *now*," said Mrs. Peters. "They're superstitious, you know; they leave."

She sank into her chair.

The county attorney did not heed her. "No sign at all of anyone having come in from the outside," he said to Peters, in the manner of continuing an interrupted conversation. "Their own rope. Now let's go upstairs again and go over it, piece by piece. It would have to have been someone who knew just the—"

The stair door closed behind them and their voices were lost.

The two women sat motionless, not looking at each other, but as if peering into something and at the same time holding back. When they spoke now it was as if they were afraid of what they were saying, but as if they could not help saying it.

"She liked the bird," said Martha Hale, low and slowly. "She was going to bury it."

"When I was a girl," said Mrs. Peters, under her breath, "my kitten—

there was a boy took a hatchet, and before my eyes—before I could get there—" She covered her face an instant. "If they hadn't held me back I would have"—she caught herself, looked upstairs where footsteps were heard, and finished weakly—"hurt him."

Then they sat without speaking or moving.

"I wonder how it would seem," Mrs. Hale at last began, as if feeling her way over strange ground—"never to have had any children around?" Her eyes made a slow sweep of the kitchen, as if seeing what that kitchen had meant through all the years. "No, Wright wouldn't like the bird," she said after that—"a thing that sang. She used to sing. He killed that too." Her voice tightened.

Mrs. Peters moved uneasily.

"Of course we don't know who killed the bird."

"I knew John Wright," was Mrs. Hale's answer.

"It was an awful thing was done in this house that night, Mrs. Hale," said the sheriff's wife. "Killing a man while he slept—slipping a thing round his neck that choked the life out of him."

Mrs. Hale's hand went out to the bird-cage.

"His neck. Choked the life out of him."

"We don't *know* who killed him," whispered Mrs. Peters wildly. "We don't *know*."

Mrs. Hale had not moved. "If there had been years and years of—nothing, then a bird to sing to you, it would be awful—still—after the bird was still."

It was as if something within her not herself had spoken, and it found in Mrs. Peters something she did not know as herself.

"I know what stillness is," she said, in a queer, monotonous voice. "When we homesteaded in Dakota, and my first baby died—after he was two years old—and me with no other then—"

Mrs. Hale stirred.

"How soon do you suppose they'll be through looking for the evidence?"

"I know what stillness is," repeated Mrs. Peters, in just the same way. Then she too pulled back. "The law has got to punish crime, Mrs. Hale," she said in her tight little way.

"I wish you'd seen Minnie Foster," was the answer, "when she wore a white dress with blue ribbons, and stood up there in the choir and sang."

The picture of that girl, the fact that she had lived neighbor to that girl for twenty years, and had let her die for lack of life, was suddenly more than she could bear.

"Oh, I *wish* I'd come over here once in a while!" she cried. "That was a crime! Who's going to punish that?"

"We mustn't take on," said Mrs. Peters, with a frightened look toward the stairs.

"I might 'a' *known* she needed help! I tell you, it's *queer*, Mrs. Peters. We live close together, and we live far apart. We all go through the same things—it's all just a different kind of the same thing! If it weren't—why do you and I *understand*? Why do we *know*—what we know this minute?"

She dashed her hand across her eyes. Then, seeing the jar of fruit on the table, she reached for it and choked out:

"If I was you I wouldn't *tell* her her fruit was gone! Tell her it *ain't*. Tell her it's all right—all of it. Here—take this in to prove it to her! She—she may never know whether it was broke or not."

She turned away.

Mrs. Peters reached out for the bottle of fruit as if she were glad to take it—as if touching a familiar thing, having something to do, could keep her from something else. She got up, looked about for something to wrap the fruit in, took a petticoat from the pile of clothes she had brought from the front room, and nervously started winding that round the bottle.

"My!" she began, in a high, false voice, "it's a good thing the men couldn't hear us! Getting all stirred up over a little thing like a—dead canary." She hurried over that. "As if that could have anything to do with—with—My, wouldn't they *laugh?*"

Footsteps were heard on the stairs.

"Maybe they would," muttered Mrs. Hale—"maybe they wouldn't."

"No, Peters," said the county attorney incisively; "it's all perfectly clear, except the reason for doing it. But you know juries when it comes to women. If there was some definite thing—something to show. Something to make a story about. A thing that would connect up with this clumsy way of doing it."

In a covert way Mrs. Hale looked at Mrs. Peters. Mrs. Peters was looking at her. Quickly they looked away from each other. The outer door opened and Mr. Hale came in.

"I've got the team round now," he said. "Pretty cold out there."

"I'm going to stay here awhile by myself," the county attorney suddenly announced. "You can send Frank out for me, can't you?" he asked the sheriff. "I want to go over everything. I'm not satisfied we can't do better."

Again, for one brief moment, the two women's eyes found one another.

The sheriff came up to the table.

"Did you want to see what Mrs. Peters was going to take in?"

The county attorney picked up the apron. He laughed.

"Oh, I guess they're not very dangerous things the ladies have picked out."

Mrs. Hale's hand was on the sewing basket in which the box was concealed. She felt that she ought to take her hand off the basket. She did not seem able to. He picked up one of the quilt blocks which she had piled on to cover the box. Her eyes felt like fire. She had a feeling that if he took up the basket she would snatch it from him.

But he did not take it up. With another little laugh, he turned away, saying:

"No; Mrs. Peters doesn't need supervising. For that matter, a sheriff's wife is married to the law. Ever think of it that way, Mrs. Peters?"

Mrs. Peters was standing beside the table. Mrs. Hale shot a look up at her; but she could not see her face. Mrs. Peters had turned away. When she spoke, her voice was muffled.

"Not—just that way," she said.

"Married to the law!" chuckled Mrs. Peters's husband. He moved toward the door into the front room, and said to the county attorney:

"I just want you to come in here a minute, George. We ought to take a look at these windows."

"Oh—windows," said the county attorney scoffingly.

"We'll be right out, Mr. Hale," said the sheriff to the farmer, who was still waiting by the door.

Hale went to look after the horses. The sheriff followed the county attorney into the other room. Again—for one final moment—the two women were alone in that kitchen.

Martha Hale sprang up, her hands tight together, looking at that other woman, with whom it rested. At first she could not see her eyes, for the sheriff's wife had not turned back since she turned away at that suggestion of being married to the law. But now Mrs. Hale made her turn back. Her eyes made her turn back. Slowly, unwillingly, Mrs. Peters turned her head until her eyes met the eyes of the other woman. There was a moment when they held each other in a steady, burning look in which there was no evasion nor flinching. Then Martha Hale's eyes pointed the way to the basket in which was hidden the thing that would make certain the conviction of the other woman—that woman who was not there and yet who had been there with them all through that hour.

For a moment Mrs. Peters did not move. And then she did it. With a rush forward, she threw back the quilt pieces, got the box, tried to put it in her handbag. It was too big. Desperately she opened it, started to take the bird out. But there she broke—she could not touch the bird. She stood there helpless, foolish.

There was the sound of a knob turning in the inner door. Martha Hale snatched the box from the sheriff's wife, and got it in the pocket of her big coat just as the sheriff and the county attorney came back into the kitchen.

"Well, Henry," said the county attorney facetiously, "at least we found out that she was not going to quilt it. She was going to—what is it you call it, ladies?"

Mrs. Hale's hand was against the pocket of her coat.

"We call it—knot it, Mr. Henderson."

COMMENTARY

ELAINE SHOWALTER

Elaine Showalter, the eminent American feminist literary historian, discussed some legal aspects of Susan Glaspell's "A Jury of Her Peers" in Showalter's introduction to her book *A Jury of Her Peers: American Women Writers from Anne Bradstreet to Annie Proulx* (2009).

On Glaspell's "A Jury of Her Peers" 2009

In 1900, while she was a fledgling newspaper reporter in Des Moines, Iowa, Susan Glaspell covered a sensational murder case in which a farm woman was accused of murdering her husband. Glaspell was so haunted by the trial that she turned it into a one-act play, *Trifles*, in 1916, and then into a short story, "A Jury of Her Peers," in 1917. In both versions, two other farm women,

Mrs. Hale and Mrs. Peters, are summoned away from their household chores to accompany their husbands, the county attorney and the sheriff, to an isolated house where the miserly and reclusive John Wright has been found strangled in his own bed with a rope around his neck. His wife, Minnie, has been arrested for the crime, which she denies committing; and the sheriff and his party have come to the farmhouse to search for clues, while their wives pack some clothes to take to Minnie in the county jail where she awaits trial.

Minnie herself, in fact, never appears in either the story or the play, which are less about her innocence or guilt than about the ways the men and the women who are thinking about the murder reach conclusions and judgments. What's needed for a conviction, the men explain, is a motive, "something to show anger or sudden feeling." But as hard as they search the chilly farmhouse, they are unable to find the sort of clear physical evidence they need. Their wives, however, notice domestic details and the "trifles" that signify Minnie's mental distress—a half-filled sack of sugar from the bin; a half-cleaned kitchen table; a piece of patchwork sewn with wild stitches. Taking in the desolation of the childless house, the women haltingly begin to express their own remorse at having failed in friendship to Minnie and perhaps colluded in the isolation that finally drove her mad. Their mounting identification with Minnie's hard life is intensified by the men's loud laughter and mockery of women's trivial concerns as they come through the kitchen on their way to search the barn. When Mrs. Hale and Mrs. Peters discover a strangled canary in Minnie's sewing box, and see the twisted door of its cage, they arrive at a mutual but unspoken conclusion: that John Wright wrung the bird's neck, that he violently silenced the one source of pleasure, music, and joy in his wife's bleak life, and that with the strength of madness, she retaliated by strangling him with a rope, as if executing him by hanging. Wordlessly, the women conspire to conceal or destroy the evidence they have found, and to protect Minnie from the patriarchal system of the Law. In effect, they constitute themselves as a jury of her peers, and they acquit her of the crime of murder.

Since it was rediscovered and reprinted in the 1970s, "A Jury of Her Peers" has been widely discussed in law school courses, law review articles, and symposia on civil procedure and criminal law. It is often cited in discussions of jury selection and analyses of the meaning of the term "peer." Legally and politically, women were not the peers of men in 1917, when feminists were engaged in the final years of effort to secure the vote. In 1893, the suffrage activist Lucy Stone had demanded a "jury of her peers" for the accused murderer Lizzie Borden, contending that only women could understand Borden's actions and motivations. No state in 1893, however, and few in 1917, permitted women to serve on juries. Utah was the first to grant the right in 1898, but not until 1968 did Congress pass legislation guaranteeing it to women in the entire United States. As law professor Patricia L. Bryan has commented, many legal experts have come to recognize "what Susan Glaspell suggests . . . that the patriarchal norms and expectations of those who stood in judgment, both as jury members and as members of the community, prevented the legal system from doing justice." . . .

Glaspell's story asks us to consider what we mean by a peer. Is it someone of the same sex? The same race? The same age or class or region? Someone who shares a common language or cultural code? Nothing in U.S. law or in the

Constitution defines or guarantees such fine-tuned rights, although an elaborate "science" of jury selection has developed to find jurors likely to agree with a lawyer's case. Women are not always sympathetic to a woman defendant, and nothing prevents men from understanding women's stories when they are taught how to read them. Clearly the sheriff and the county attorney in Glaspell's story could be taught to recognize Minnie's clues and to interpret them as motives; otherwise Mrs. Hale and Mrs. Peters would not need to conceal and destroy the evidence. My experience in teaching "A Jury of Her Peers" is that men understand the story, and women's writing in general, perfectly well. When I have taught the story to federal judges, they have asked whether Mrs. Hale and Mrs. Peters genuinely do justice to Minnie Wright by destroying evidence that sheds light on her motives. Or do they actually suppress her chance to have a public hearing and bring out the details of domestic abuse that might sway the verdict in her favor? Are they her saviors or her accomplices? Legal experts who study Glaspell's story point out that all-male juries in 1900 were very reluctant to convict a woman of a serious crime, because of their chivalrous ideas about gentle womanhood. Indeed, in the real murder case upon which Glaspell based "A Jury of Her Peers," the defendant was ultimately set free. Is the best defense and the fairest trial a full airing of the evidence to an informed public? For the broader benefit of society, might a trial even lead to changes in public attitudes and laws?

I believe that American women writers no longer need specially constituted juries, softened judgment, unspoken agreements, or suppression of evidence in order to stand alongside the greatest artists in our literary heritage. Indeed, we need the vigorous public debate of a critical trial, with witnesses for the prosecution as well as the defense, to ensure that American women writers take their place in our literary heritage. What keeps literature alive, meaningful to read, and exciting to teach isn't unstinting approval or unanimous admiration, but rousing argument and robust dispute. . . .

NATHANIEL HAWTHORNE

Nathaniel Hawthorne (1804–1864), writer of short stories and novels, was born in Salem, Massachusetts, into an eminent family who traced their lineage back to the Puritans. After his graduation from Bowdoin College in 1825, Hawthorne lived at home while he wrote short fiction he called "tales" or "articles" that he tried to sell to periodicals. American magazines of the time were mostly interested in publishing ghost stories, Indian legends, and "village tales" based on historical anecdotes. Hawthorne (like his contemporary Edgar Allan Poe) created stories that transcended the limitations of these conventions; his imagination was stirred by what he called "an inveterate love of allegory."

Hawthorne published his first collection of stories, *Twice-Told Tales*, in 1837; a second book of stories, *Mosses from an Old Manse*, appeared in 1846. That year he stopped writing to earn a better living for his family as surveyor of customs for the port of Salem. This was a political appointment, and after the Whigs won the presidency three years later, Hawthorne—a Democrat—was out of a job. He returned to writing fiction, sketching his "official life" at the Custom House in the introduction to his novel *The Scarlet Letter* in 1850. During the last decade of his career as a writer he published three other novels, several books for children, and another collection of tales. In "The Custom House," Hawthorne humorously suggested that his profession would not have impressed his Puritan ancestors:

> "What is he?" murmurs one grey shadow of my forefathers to the other. "A writer of story-books! What kind of business in life, what manner of glorifying God, or being serviceable to mankind in his day and generation, may that be? Why, the degenerate fellow might as well have been a fiddler!" Such are the compliments bandied between my great-grandsires and myself across the gulf of time! And yet, let them scorn me as they will, strong traits of their nature have intertwined themselves with mine.

Despite Hawthorne's portrait of himself as an unappreciated artist, he was recognized by contemporaries such as Herman Melville and Edgar Allan Poe as a "genius of a very lofty order." Hawthorne wrote about 120 short tales and sketches in addition to his novels. His notebooks are filled with ideas for stories, more often jottings of abstract ideas than detailed observations of "real" individuals. "Young Goodman Brown" is one of his moral tales set in colonial New England.

CONNECTION Edgar Allan Poe discusses Hawthorne's tale in "The Importance of the Single Effect in a Prose Tale," page 650.

WEB Research Nathaniel Hawthorne at bedfordstmartins.com/rewritinglit.

Young Goodman Brown 1835

Young Goodman Brown came forth at sunset into the street at Salem village; but put his head back, after crossing the threshold, to exchange a parting kiss with his young wife. And Faith, as the wife was aptly named, thrust her own pretty head into the street, letting the wind play with the pink ribbons of her cap while she called to Goodman Brown.

"Dearest heart," whispered she, softly and rather sadly, when her lips were close to his ear, "prithee put off your journey until sunrise and sleep in your own bed to-night. A lone woman is troubled with such dreams and such thoughts that she's afeared of herself sometimes. Pray tarry with me this night, dear husband, of all nights in the year."

"My love and my Faith," replied young Goodman Brown, "of all nights in the year, this one night must I tarry away from thee. My journey, as thou callest it, forth and back again, must needs be done 'twixt now and sunrise. What, my sweet, pretty wife, dost thou doubt me already, and we but three months married?"

"Then God bless you!" said Faith, with the pink ribbons; "and may you find all well when you come back."

"Amen!" cried Goodman Brown. "Say thy prayers, dear Faith, and go to bed at dusk, and no harm will come to thee."

So they parted; and the young man pursued his way until, being about to turn the corner by the meeting-house, he looked back and saw the head of Faith still peeping after him with a melancholy air, in spite of her pink ribbons.

"Poor little Faith!" thought he, for his heart smote him. "What a wretch am I to leave her on such an errand! She talks of dreams, too. Methought as she spoke there was trouble in her face, as if a dream had warned her what work is to be done to-night. But no, no; 't would kill her to think it. Well, she's a blessed angel on earth, and after this one night I'll cling to her skirts and follow her to heaven."

With this excellent resolve for the future, Goodman Brown felt himself justified in making more haste on his present evil purpose. He had taken a dreary road, darkened by all the gloomiest trees of the forest, which barely stood aside to let the narrow path creep through, and closed immediately behind. It was all as lonely as could be; and there is this peculiarity in such a solitude, that the traveller knows not who may be concealed by the innumerable trunks and the thick boughs overhead; so that with lonely footsteps he may yet be passing through an unseen multitude.

"There may be a devilish Indian behind every tree," said Goodman Brown to himself; and he glanced fearfully behind him as he added, "What if the devil himself should be at my very elbow!"

His head being turned back, he passed a crook of the road, and, looking forward again, beheld the figure of a man, in grave and decent attire, seated at the foot of an old tree. He arose at Goodman Brown's approach and walked onward side by side with him.

"You are late, Goodman Brown," said he. "The clock of the Old South was striking as I came through Boston, and that is full fifteen minutes agone."

"Faith kept me back a while," replied the young man, with a tremor in his voice, caused by the sudden appearance of his companion, though not wholly unexpected.

It was now deep dusk in the forest, and deepest in that part of it where these two were journeying. As nearly as could be discerned, the second traveller was about fifty years old, apparently in the same rank of life as Goodman Brown, and bearing a considerable resemblance to him, though perhaps more in expression than features. Still they might have been taken for father and son. And yet, though the elder person was as simply clad as the younger, and as simple in manner too, he had an indescribable air of one who knew the world, and who would not have felt abashed at the governor's dinner table or in King William's court, were it possible that his affairs should call him thither. But the only thing about him that could be fixed upon as remarkable was his staff, which bore the likeness of a great black snake, so curiously wrought that it might almost be seen to twist and wriggle itself like a living serpent. This, of course, must have been an ocular deception, assisted by the uncertain light.

"Come, Goodman Brown," cried his fellow-traveller, "this is a dull pace for the beginning of a journey. Take my staff, if you are so soon weary."

"Friend," said the other, exchanging his slow pace for a full stop, "having kept covenant by meeting thee here, it is my purpose now to return whence I came. I have scruples touching the matter thou wot'st of."

"Sayest thou so?" replied he of the serpent, smiling apart. "Let us walk on, nevertheless, reasoning as we go; and if I convince thee not thou shalt turn back. We are but a little way in the forest yet."

"Too far! too far!" exclaimed the goodman, unconsciously resuming his walk. "My father never went into the woods on such an errand, nor his father before him. We have been a race of honest men and good Christians since the days of the martyrs; and shall I be the first of the name of Brown that ever took this path and kept"—

"Such company, thou wouldst say," observed the elder person, interpreting his pause. "Well said, Goodman Brown! I have been as well acquainted with your family as with ever a one among the Puritans; and that's no trifle to say. I helped your grandfather, the constable, when he lashed the Quaker woman so smartly through the streets of Salem; and it was I that brought your father a pitch-pine knot, kindled at my own hearth, to set fire to an Indian village, in King Philip's war.° They were my good friends, both; and many a pleasant walk have we had along this path, and returned merrily after midnight. I would fain be friends with you for their sake."

"If it be as thou sayest," replied Goodman Brown, "I marvel they never spoke of these matters; or, verily, I marvel not, seeing that the least rumor of the sort would have driven them from New England. We are a people of prayer, and good works to boot, and abide no such wickedness."

"Wickedness or not," said the traveller with the twisted staff, "I have a very general acquaintance here in New England. The deacons of many a church have drunk the communion wine with me; the selectmen of divers towns make me their chairman; and a majority of the Great and General Court are firm supporters of my interest. The governor and I, too—But these are state secrets."

"Can this be so?" cried Goodman Brown, with a stare of amazement at his undisturbed companion. "Howbeit, I have nothing to do with the governor and council; they have their own ways, and are no rule for a simple husbandman like me. But, were I to go on with thee, how should I meet the eye of that good old man, our minister, at Salem village? Oh, his voice would make me tremble both Sabbath day and lecture day."

Thus far the elder traveller had listened with due gravity; but now burst into a fit of irrepressible mirth, shaking himself so violently that his snake-like staff actually seemed to wriggle in sympathy.

"Ha! ha! ha!" shouted he again and again; then composing himself, "Well, go on, Goodman Brown, go on; but, prithee, don't kill me with laughing."

King Philip's war: King Philip, a Wampanoag chief, spearheaded the most destructive Indian war ever waged against the New England colonists (1675–76).

"Well, then, to end the matter at once," said Goodman Brown, considerably nettled, "there is my wife, Faith. It would break her dear little heart; and I'd rather break my own."

"Nay, if that be the case," answered the other, "e'en go thy ways, Goodman Brown. I would not for twenty old women like the one hobbling before us that Faith should come to any harm."

As he spoke he pointed his staff at a female figure on the path, in whom Goodman Brown recognized a very pious and exemplary dame, who had taught him his catechism in youth, and was still his moral and spiritual adviser, jointly with the minister and Deacon Gookin.

"A marvel, truly that Goody Cloyse should be so far in the wilderness at nightfall," said he. "But with your leave, friend, I shall take a cut through the woods until we have left this Christian woman behind. Being a stranger to you, she might ask whom I was consorting with and whither I was going."

"Be it so," said his fellow-traveller. "Betake you to the woods, and let me keep the path."

Accordingly the young man turned aside, but took care to watch his companion, who advanced softly along the road until he had come within a staff's length of the old dame. She, meanwhile, was making the best of her way, with singular speed for so aged a woman, and mumbling some indistinct words—a prayer, doubtless—as she went. The traveller put forth his staff and touched her withered neck with what seemed the serpent's tail.

"The devil!" screamed the pious old lady.

"Then Goody Cloyse knows her old friend?" observed the traveller, confronting her and leaning on his writhing stick.

"Ah, forsooth, and is it your worship indeed?" cried the good dame. "Yea, truly is it, and in the very image of my old gossip, Goodman Brown, the grandfather of the silly fellow that now is. But—would your worship believe it?—my broomstick hath strangely disappeared, stolen, as I suspect, by that unhanged witch, Goody Cory, and that, too, when I was all anointed with the juice of smallage, and cinquefoil, and wolf's bane"—

"Mingled with fine wheat and the fat of a new-born babe," said the shape of old Goodman Brown.

"Ah, your worship knows the recipe," cried the old lady, cackling aloud. "So, as I was saying, being all ready for the meeting, and no horse to ride on, I made up my mind to foot it; for they tell me there is a nice young man to be taken into communion to-night. But now your good worship will lend me your arm, and we shall be there in a twinkling."

"That can hardly be," answered her friend. "I may not spare you my arm, Goody Cloyse; but here is my staff, if you will."

So saying, he threw it down at her feet, where, perhaps, it assumed life, being one of the rods which its owner had formerly lent to the Egyptian magi. Of this fact, however, Goodman Brown could not take cognizance. He had cast up his eyes in astonishment, and, looking down again, beheld neither Goody Cloyse nor the serpentine staff, but his fellow-traveller alone, who waited for him as calmly as if nothing had happened.

"That old woman taught me my catechism," said the young man; and there was a world of meaning in this simple comment.

They continued to walk onward, while the elder traveller exhorted his companion to make good speed and persevere in the path, discoursing so aptly that his arguments seemed rather to spring up in the bosom of his auditor than to be suggested by himself. As they went, he plucked a branch of maple to serve for a walking stick, and began to strip it of the twigs and little boughs, which were wet with evening dew. The moment his fingers touched them they became strangely withered and dried up as with a week's sunshine. Thus the pair proceeded, at a good free pace, until suddenly, in a gloomy hollow of the road, Goodman Brown sat himself down on the stump of a tree and refused to go any farther.

"Friend," he said, stubbornly, "my mind is made up. Not another step will I budge on this errand. What if a wretched old woman do choose to go to the devil when I thought she was going to heaven: is that any reason why I should quit my dear Faith and go after her?"

"You will think better of this by and by," said his acquaintance, composedly. "Sit here and rest yourself a while; and when you feel like moving again, there is my staff to help you along."

Without more words, he threw his companion the maple stick, and was as speedily out of sight as if he had vanished into the deepening gloom. The young man sat a few moments by the roadside, applauding himself greatly, and thinking with how clear a conscience he should meet the minister in his morning walk, nor shrink from the eye of good old Deacon Gookin. And what calm sleep would be his that very night, which was to have been spent so wickedly, but so purely and sweetly now, in the arms of Faith! Amidst these pleasant and praiseworthy meditations, Goodman Brown heard the tramp of horses along the road, and deemed it advisable to conceal himself within the verge of the forest, conscious of the guilty purpose that had brought him thither, though now so happily turned from it.

On came the hoof tramps and the voices of the riders, two grave old voices, conversing soberly as they drew near. These mingled sounds appeared to pass along the road, within a few yards of the young man's hiding-place; but, owing doubtless to the depth of the gloom at that particular spot, neither the travellers nor their steeds were visible. Though their figures brushed the small boughs by the wayside, it could not be seen that they intercepted, even for a moment, the faint gleam from the strip of bright sky athwart which they must have passed. Goodman Brown alternately crouched and stood on tiptoe, pulling aside the branches and thrusting forth his head as far as he durst without discerning so much as a shadow. It vexed him the more, because he could have sworn, were such a thing possible, that he recognized the voices of the minister and Deacon Gookin, jogging along quietly, as they were wont to do, when bound to some ordination or ecclesiastical council. While yet within hearing, one of the riders stopped to pluck a switch.

"Of the two, reverend sir," said the voice like the deacon's, "I had rather miss an ordination dinner than to-night's meeting. They tell me that some of our community are to be here from Falmouth and beyond, and others from Connecticut and Rhode Island, besides several of the Indian powwows, who, after their fashion, know almost as much deviltry as the best of us. Moreover, there is a goodly young woman to be taken into communion."

"Mighty well, Deacon Gookin!" replied the solemn old tones of the minister. "Spur up, or we shall be late. Nothing can be done, you know, until I get on the ground."

The hoofs clattered again; and the voices, talking so strangely in the empty air, passed on through the forest, where no church had ever been gathered or solitary Christian prayed. Whither, then, could these holy men be journeying so deep into the heathen wilderness? Young Goodman Brown caught hold of a tree for support, being ready to sink down on the ground, faint and overburdened with the heavy sickness of his heart. He looked up to the sky, doubting whether there really was a heaven above him. Yet there was the blue arch, and the stars brightening in it.

"With heaven above and Faith below, I will yet stand firm against the devil!" cried Goodman Brown.

While he still gazed upward into the deep arch of the firmament and had lifted his hands to pray, a cloud, though no wind was stirring, hurried across the zenith and hid the brightening stars. The blue sky was still visible, except directly overhead, where this black mass of cloud was sweeping swiftly northward. Aloft in the air, as if from the depths of the cloud, came a confused and doubtful sound of voices. Once the listener fancied that he could distinguish the accents of towns-people of his own, men and women, both pious and ungodly, many of whom he had met at the communion table, and had seen others rioting at the tavern. The next moment, so indistinct were the sounds, he doubted whether he had heard aught but the murmur of the old forest, whispering without a wind. Then came a stronger swell of those familiar tones, heard daily in the sunshine at Salem village, but never until now from a cloud of night. There was one voice, of a young woman, uttering lamentations, yet with an uncertain sorrow, and entreating for some favor, which, perhaps, it would grieve her to obtain; and all the unseen multitude, both saints and sinners, seemed to encourage her onward.

"Faith!" shouted Goodman Brown, in a voice of agony and desperation; and the echoes of the forest mocked him, crying, "Faith! Faith!" as if bewildered wretches were seeking her all through the wilderness.

The cry of grief, rage, and terror was yet piercing the night, when the unhappy husband held his breath for a response. There was a scream, drowned immediately in a louder murmur of voices, fading into far-off laughter, as the dark cloud swept away, leaving the clear and silent sky above Goodman Brown. But something fluttered lightly down through the air and caught on the branch of a tree. The young man seized it, and beheld a pink ribbon.

"My Faith is gone!" cried he after one stupefied moment. "There is no good on earth; and sin is but a name. Come, devil; for to thee is this world given."

And, maddened with despair, so that he laughed loud and long, did Goodman Brown grasp his staff and set forth again, at such a rate that he seemed to fly along the forest path rather than to walk or run. The road grew wilder and drearier and more faintly traced, and vanished at length, leaving him in the heart of the dark wilderness, still rushing onward with the instinct that guides mortal man to evil. The whole forest was peopled with frightful sounds—the creaking of the trees, the howling of wild beasts, and the yell of Indians; while sometimes the wind tolled like a distant church bell, and sometimes gave a broad roar around the traveller, as if all Nature were laughing him to scorn. But he was himself the chief horror of the scene, and shrank not from its other horrors.

"Ha! ha! ha!" roared Goodman Brown when the wind laughed at him. "Let us hear which will laugh loudest. Think not to frighten me with your deviltry. Come witch, come wizard, come Indian powwow, come devil himself, and here comes Goodman Brown. You may as well fear him as he fear you."

In truth, all through the haunted forest there could be nothing more frightful than the figure of Goodman Brown. On he flew among the black pines, brandishing his staff with frenzied gestures, now giving vent to an inspiration of horrid blasphemy, and now shouting forth such laughter as set all the echoes of the forest laughing like demons around him. The fiend in his own shape is less hideous than when he rages in the breast of man. Thus sped the demoniac on his course, until, quivering among the trees, he saw a red light before him, as when the felled trunks and branches of a clearing have been set on fire, and throw up their lurid blaze against the sky, at the hour of midnight. He paused, in a lull of the tempest that had driven him onward, and heard the swell of what seemed a hymn, rolling solemnly from a distance with the weight of many voices. He knew the tune; it was a familiar one in the choir of the village meeting-house. The verse died heavily away, and was lengthened by a chorus, not of human voices, but of all the sounds of the benighted wilderness pealing in awful harmony together. Goodman Brown cried out, and his cry was lost to his own ear by its unison with the cry of the desert.

In the interval of silence he stole forward until the light glared full upon his eyes. At one extremity of an open space, hemmed in by the dark wall of the forest, arose a rock, bearing some rude, natural resemblance either to an altar or a pulpit, and surrounded by four blazing pines, their tops aflame, their stems untouched, like candles at an evening meeting. The mass of foliage that had overgrown the summit of the rock was all on fire, blazing high into the night and fitfully illuminating the whole field. Each pendent twig and leafy festoon was in a blaze. As the red light arose and fell, a numerous congregation alternately shone forth, then disappeared in shadow, and again grew, as it were, out of the darkness, peopling the heart of the solitary woods at once.

"A grave and dark-clad company," quoth Goodman Brown.

In truth they were such. Among them, quivering to and fro between gloom and splendor, appeared faces that would be seen next day at the council board of the province, and others which, Sabbath after Sabbath, looked devoutly heavenward, and benignantly over the crowded pews, from the holiest pulpits in the land. Some affirm that the lady of the governor was there. At least there were high dames well known to her, and wives of honored husbands, and widows, a great multitude, and ancient maidens, all of excellent repute, and fair young girls, who trembled lest their mothers should espy them. Either the sudden gleams of light flashing over the obscure field bedazzled Goodman Brown, or he recognized a score of the church members of Salem village famous for their especial sanctity. Good old Deacon Gookin had arrived, and waited at the skirts of that venerable saint, his revered pastor. But, irreverently consorting with these grave, reputable, and pious people, these elders of the church, these chaste dames and dewy virgins, there were men of dissolute lives and women of spotted fame, wretches given over to all mean and filthy vice, and suspected even of horrid crimes. It was strange to see that the good shrank not from the wicked, nor were the sinners abashed by the saints. Scattered also among their pale-faced enemies were the Indian priests, or powwows, who had often scared their native forest with more hideous incantations than any known to English witchcraft.

"But where is Faith?" thought Goodman Brown; and, as hope came into his heart, he trembled.

Another verse of the hymn arose, a slow and mournful strain, such as the pious love, but joined to words which expressed all that our nature can conceive of sin, and darkly hinted at far more. Unfathomable to mere mortals is the lore of fiends. Verse after verse was sung; and still the chorus of the desert swelled between like the deepest tone of a mighty organ; and with the final peal of that dreadful anthem there came a sound, as if the roaring wind, the rushing streams, the howling beasts, and every other voice of the unconverted wilderness were mingling and according with the voice of guilty man in homage to the prince of all. The four blazing pines threw up a loftier flame, and obscurely discovered shapes and visages of horror on the smoke wreaths above the impious assembly. At the same moment the fire on the rock shot redly forth and formed a flowing arch above its base, where now appeared a figure. With reverence be it spoken, the figure bore no slight similitude, both in garb and manner, to some grave divine of the New England churches.

"Bring forth the converts!" cried a voice that echoed through the field and rolled into the forest.

At the word, Goodman Brown stepped forth from the shadow of the trees and approached the congregation, with whom he felt a loathful brotherhood by the sympathy of all that was wicked in his heart. He could have well-nigh sworn that the shape of his own dead father beckoned him to advance, looking downward from a smoke wreath, while a woman, with dim features of despair, threw out her hand to warn him back. Was it his mother? But he had no power to retreat one step, nor to resist, even in thought, when the minister and good old Deacon Gookin seized his arms and led him to the blazing rock. Thither came also the slender form of a veiled female, led between Goody Cloyse, that pious teacher of the catechism, and Martha Carrier, who had received the devil's promise to be queen of hell. A rampant hag was she. And there stood the proselytes beneath the canopy of fire.

"Welcome, my children," said the dark figure, "to the communion of your race. Ye have found thus young your nature and your destiny. My children, look behind you!"

They turned; and flashing forth, as it were, in a sheet of flame, the fiend worshippers were seen; the smile of welcome gleamed darkly on every visage.

"There," resumed the sable form, "are all whom ye have reverenced from youth. Ye deemed them holier than yourselves and shrank from your own sin, contrasting it with their lives of righteousness and prayerful aspirations heavenward. Yet here are they all in my worshipping assembly. This night it shall be granted you to know their secret deeds: how hoary-bearded elders of the church have whispered wanton words to the young maids of their households; how many a woman, eager for widows' weeds, has given her husband a drink at bedtime and let him sleep his last sleep in her bosom; how beardless youths have made haste to inherit their fathers' wealth; and how fair damsels—blush not, sweet ones—have dug little graves in the garden, and bidden me, the sole guest, to an infant's funeral. By the sympathy of your human hearts for sin ye shall scent out all the places—whether in church, bedchamber, street, field, or forest—where crime has been committed, and shall exult to behold the whole earth one stain of guilt, one mighty blood spot. Far more than this. It shall be yours to penetrate, in every bosom, the deep mystery of sin, the fountain of all wicked arts, and which inexhaustibly supplies more evil impulses than human power—than my power at its utmost—can make manifest in deeds. And now, my children, look upon each other."

They did so; and, by the blaze of the hell-kindled torches, the wretched man beheld his Faith, and the wife her husband, trembling before that unhallowed altar.

"Lo, there ye stand, my children," said the figure, in a deep and solemn tone, almost sad with its despairing awfulness, as if his once angelic nature could yet mourn for our miserable race. "Depending upon one another's hearts, ye had still hoped that virtue were not all a dream. Now are ye undeceived. Evil is the nature of mankind. Evil must be your only happiness. Welcome again, my children, to the communion of your race."

"Welcome," repeated the fiend worshippers, in one cry of despair and triumph.

And there they stood, the only pair, as it seemed, who were yet hesitating on the verge of wickedness in this dark world. A basin was hollowed, naturally, in the rock. Did it contain water, reddened by the lurid light? or was it blood? or, perchance, a liquid flame? Herein did the shape of evil dip his hand and prepare to lay the mark of baptism upon their foreheads, that they might be partakers of the mystery of sin, more conscious of the secret guilt of others, both in deed and thought, than they could now be of their own. The husband cast one look at his pale wife, and Faith at him. What polluted wretches would the next glance show them to each other, shuddering alike at what they disclosed and what they saw!

"Faith! Faith!" cried the husband, "look up to heaven, and resist the wicked one."

Whether Faith obeyed he knew not. Hardly had he spoken when he found himself amid calm night and solitude, listening to a roar of the wind which died heavily away through the forest. He staggered against the rock, and felt it chill and damp; while a hanging twig, that had been all on fire, besprinkled his cheek with the coldest dew.

The next morning young Goodman Brown came slowly into the street of Salem village, staring around him like a bewildered man. The good old minister was taking a walk along the graveyard to get an appetite for breakfast and meditate his sermon, and bestowed a blessing, as he passed, on Goodman Brown. He shrank from the venerable saint as if to avoid an anathema. Old Deacon Gookin was at domestic worship, and the holy words of his prayer were heard through the open window. "What God doth the wizard pray to?" quoth Goodman Brown. Goody Cloyse, that excellent old Christian, stood in the early sunshine at her own lattice, catechizing a little girl who had brought her a pint of morning's milk. Goodman Brown snatched away the child as from the grasp of the fiend himself. Turning the corner by the meeting-house, he spied the head of Faith, with the pink ribbons, gazing anxiously forth, and bursting into such joy at sight of him that she skipped along the street and almost kissed her husband before the whole village. But Goodman Brown looked sternly and sadly into her face, and passed on without a greeting.

Had Goodman Brown fallen asleep in the forest and only dreamed a wild dream of a witch-meeting?

Be it so if you will; but, alas! it was a dream of evil omen for young Goodman Brown. A stern, a sad, a darkly meditative, a distrustful, if not a desperate man did he become from the night of that fearful dream. On the Sabbath day, when the congregation were singing a holy psalm, he could not listen because an anthem of sin rushed loudly upon his ear and drowned all the blessed strain. When the minister spoke from the pulpit with power and fervid eloquence, and, with his hand on the open Bible, of the sacred truths of our religion, and of saint-like lives and triumphant deaths, and of future bliss or misery unutterable, then did Goodman Brown turn pale, dreading lest the roof should thunder down upon the gray blasphemer and his hearers. Often, awaking suddenly at midnight, he shrank from the bosom of Faith; and at morning or eventide, when the family knelt down at prayer, he scowled and muttered to himself, and gazed sternly at his wife, and turned away. And when he had lived long, and was borne to his grave a hoary corpse, followed by Faith, an aged woman, and children and grandchildren, a goodly procession, besides neighbors not a few, they carved no hopeful verse upon his tombstone, for his dying hour was gloom.

COMMENTARY

HERMAN MELVILLE

Herman Melville wrote an eloquent essay on Nathaniel Hawthorne's volume of short stories, *Mosses from an Old Manse*, for the New York periodical the *Literary World* in August 1850. Unlike Edgar Allan Poe in his review of Hawthorne's short fiction, Melville did not use the opportunity to theorize about the form of the short story. Instead, he conveyed his enthusiasm for Hawthorne's tragic vision, what Melville saw as the "great power of blackness" in Hawthorne's writing that derived "its force from its appeals to that Calvinistic sense of Innate Depravity and Original Sin." This was the aspect of Hawthorne's tales that seemed most congenial to Melville's own genius while he continued work that summer on his novel-in-progress, *Moby-Dick*.

Blackness in Hawthorne's "Young Goodman Brown" 1850

It is curious, how a man may travel along a country road, and yet miss the grandest or sweetest of prospects, by reason of an intervening hedge so like all other hedges as in no way to hint of the wide landscape beyond. So has it been with me concerning the enchanting landscape in the soul of this Hawthorne, this most excellent Man of Mosses. His Old Manse has been written now four years, but I never read it till a day or two since. I had seen it in the bookstores—heard of it often—even had it recommended to me by a tasteful friend, as a rare, quiet book, perhaps too deserving of popularity to be popular. But there are so many books called "excellent" and so much unpopular merit, that amid the thick stir of other things, the hint of my tasteful friend was disregarded; and for four years the Mosses on the Old Manse never refreshed me with their perennial green. It may be, however, that all this while, the book, like wine, was only improving in flavor and body. . . .

But it is the least part of genius that attracts admiration. Where Hawthorne is known, he seems to be deemed a pleasant writer, with a pleasant style—a sequestered, harmless man, from whom any deep and weighty thing would hardly be anticipated: a man who means no meanings. But there is no man, in whom humor and love, like mountain peaks, soar to such a rapt height, as to receive the irradiations of the upper skies; there is no man in whom humor and love are developed in that high form called genius—no such man can exist without also possessing, as the indispensable complement of these, a great, deep intellect, which drops down into the universe like a plummet. Or, love and humor are only the eyes, through which such an intellect views this world. The great beauty in such a mind is but the product of its strength. . . .

For spite of all the Indian-summer sunlight on the hither side of Hawthorne's soul, the other side—like the dark half of the physical sphere—is shrouded in a blackness, ten times black. But this darkness but gives more effect to the ever-moving dawn, that forever advances through it, and circumnavigates his world. Whether Hawthorne has simply availed himself of this mystical blackness as a means to the wondrous effects he makes it to produce in his lights and shades; or whether there really lurks in him, perhaps unknown to himself, a touch of Puritanic gloom—this I cannot altogether tell. Certain it is, however, that this great power of blackness in him derives its force from its appeals to that Calvinistic sense of Innate Depravity and Original Sin, from whose visitations, in some shape or other, no deeply thinking mind is always and wholly free. For, in certain moods, no man can weigh this world, without throwing in something, somehow like Original Sin, to strike the uneven balance. . . .

But with whatever motive, playful or profound, Nathaniel Hawthorne has chosen to entitle his pieces in the manner he has, it is certain that some of them are directly calculated to deceive—egregiously deceive—the superficial skimmer of pages. To be downright and candid once more, let me cheerfully say that two of these titles did dolefully dupe no less an eagle-eyed reader than myself; and that, too, after I had been impressed with a sense of the great depth and breadth of this American man. "Who in the name of thunder" (as the country people say in this neighborhood), "who in the name of thunder," would anticipate any marvel in a piece entitled "Young Goodman Brown"? You would of course suppose that it was a simple little tale, intended as a supplement to "Goody Two-Shoes." Whereas it is deep as Dante; nor can you finish it, without addressing the author in his own words: "It is yours to penetrate, in every bosom, the deep mystery of sin." And with Young Goodman, too, in allegorical pursuit of his Puritan wife, you cry out in your anguish,

> "Faith!" shouted Goodman Brown, in a voice of agony and desperation; and the echoes of the forest mocked him, crying—"Faith! Faith!" as if bewildered wretches were seeking her, all through the wilderness.

Now this same piece, entitled "Young Goodman Brown," is one of the two that I had not at all read yesterday; and I allude to it now, because it is, in itself, such a strong positive illustration of that blackness in Hawthorne which I had assumed from the mere occasional shadows of it, as revealed in several of the other sketches. But had I previously perused "Young Goodman Brown," I should have been at no pains to draw the conclusion which I came to at a time when I was ignorant that the book contained one such direct and unqualified manifestation of it.

ERNEST HEMINGWAY

Ernest Hemingway (1899–1961) was born in Oak Park, Illinois, but he spent most of his boyhood in Michigan, where his father, a doctor, encouraged his enthusiasm for camping and hunting. Active as a reporter for his high school newspaper, Hemingway decided not to go on to college. Instead he worked as a reporter on the *Kansas City Star* for a few months before volunteering to serve in an American ambulance unit in France during World War I. Then he went to Italy, served at the front, and was severely wounded in action just before his nineteenth birthday. After the war he was too restless to settle down in the United States, so he lived in Paris and supported himself and his wife as a newspaper correspondent. He worked hard at learning how to write fiction; as he later said, "I found the greatest difficulty, aside from knowing what you really felt, rather than what you were supposed to feel, or had been taught to feel, was to put down what really happened in action: what the actual things were which produced the emotion that you experienced."

In America Hemingway had admired the work of Sherwood Anderson, especially the colloquial, "unliterary" tone of his stories, and in Paris he came under the influence of Gertrude Stein, telling Anderson in a letter of 1922 that "Gertrude Stein and me are just like brothers." As the critic A. Walton Litz and many others have recognized, Hemingway was receptive to several diverse influences as a young writer forging his literary style, including the work of the experimental poet Ezra Pound, whose advice in essays written in 1913 on the composition of imagist poetry is suggested in the style developed in Hemingway's early fiction:

1. Direct treatment of the "thing," without evasion or cliché.
2. The use of absolutely no word that does not contribute to the general design.
3. Fidelity to the rhythms of natural speech.
4. The natural object is always the adequate symbol.

Hemingway's first book, *In Our Time* (1925), is a collection of stories and sketches. His early novels, *The Sun Also Rises* (1926) and *A Farewell to Arms* (1929), established him as a master stylist, probably the most influential writer of American prose in the first half of the twentieth century. In 1938 he collected what he considered his best short fiction in *The Fifth Column and the First Forty-Nine Stories.* After publication of *The Old Man and the Sea,* he was awarded the Nobel Prize for literature in 1954. Seven years later, in poor health and haunted by the memory of the suicide of his father, who had shot himself with a Civil War pistol in 1929, Hemingway killed himself with a shotgun in his Idaho hunting lodge.

Hemingway's concise way of developing a plot through dialogue, as in "Hills Like White Elephants," attracted many imitators. He once explained how he achieved an intense compression by comparing his method to the principle of the iceberg: "There is seven-eighths of it under water for every part that shows. Anything you know you can eliminate and it only strengthens your iceberg. It is the part that doesn't show. If a writer omits something because he does not know it then there is a hole in the story." The most authoritative collection of Hemingway's stories, *The Complete Short Stories of Ernest Hemingway: The Finca-Vigia Edition,* was published in 1991.

WEB Research Ernest Hemingway at bedfordstmartins.com/rewritinglit.

Hills Like White Elephants

1927

The hills across the valley of the Ebro were long and white. On this side there was no shade and no trees and the station was between two lines of rails in the sun. Close against the side of the station there was the warm shadow of the building and a curtain, made of strings of bamboo beads, hung across the open door into the bar, to keep out flies. The American and the girl with him sat at a table in the shade, outside the building. It was very hot and the express from Barcelona would come in forty minutes. It stopped at this junction for two minutes and went on to Madrid.

"What should we drink?" the girl asked. She had taken off her hat and put it on the table.

"It's pretty hot," the man said.

"Let's drink beer."

"*Dos cervezas,*" the man said into the curtain.

"Big ones?" a woman asked from the doorway.

"Yes. Two big ones."

The woman brought two glasses of beer and two felt pads. She put the felt pads and the beer glasses on the table and looked at the man and the girl.

The girl was looking off at the line of hills. They were white in the sun and the country was brown and dry.

"They look like white elephants," she said.

"I've never seen one," the man drank his beer.

"No, you wouldn't have."

"I might have," the man said. "Just because you say I wouldn't have doesn't prove anything."

The girl looked at the bead curtain. "They've painted something on it," she said. "What does it say?"

"Anis del Toro. It's a drink."

"Could we try it?"

The man called "Listen" through the curtain. The woman came out from the bar.

"Four reales."

"We want two Anis del Toro."

"With water?"

"Do you want it with water?"

"I don't know," the girl said. "Is it good with water?"

"It's all right."

"You want them with water?" asked the woman.

"Yes, with water."

"It tastes like licorice," the girl said and put the glass down.

"That's the way with everything."

"Yes," said the girl. "Everything tastes of licorice. Especially all the things you've waited so long for, like absinthe."

"Oh, cut it out."

"You started it," the girl said. "I was being amused. I was having a fine time."

"Well, let's try and have a fine time."

"All right. I was trying. I said the mountains looked like white elephants. Wasn't that bright?"

"That was bright."

"I wanted to try this new drink: That's all we do, isn't it—look at things and try new drinks?"

"I guess so."

The girl looked across at the hills.

"They're lovely hills," she said. "They don't really look like white elephants. I just meant the coloring of their skin through the trees."

"Should we have another drink?"

"All right."

The warm wind blew the bead curtain against the table.

"The beer's nice and cool," the man said.

"It's lovely," the girl said.

"It's really an awfully simple operation, Jig," the man said. "It's not really an operation at all."

The girl looked at the ground the table legs rested on.

"I know you wouldn't mind it, Jig. It's really not anything. It's just to let the air in."

The girl did not say anything.

"I'll go with you and I'll stay with you all the time. They just let the air in and then it's all perfectly natural."

"Then what will we do afterward?"

"We'll be fine afterward. Just like we were before."

"What makes you think so?"

"That's the only thing that bothers us. It's the only thing that's made us unhappy."

The girl looked at the bead curtain, put her hand out, and took hold of two of the strings of beads.

"And you think then we'll be all right and be happy."

"I know we will. You don't have to be afraid. I've known lots of people that have done it."

"So have I," said the girl. "And afterward they were all so happy."

"Well," the man said, "if you don't want to you don't have to. I wouldn't have you do it if you didn't want to. But I know it's perfectly simple."

"And you really want to?"

"I think it's the best thing to do. But I don't want you to do it if you don't really want to."

"And if I do it you'll be happy and things will be like they were and you'll love me?"

"I love you now. You know I love you."

"I know. But if I do it, then it will be nice again if I say things are like white elephants, and you'll like it?"

"I'll love it. I love it now but I just can't think about it. You know how I get when I worry."

"If I do it you won't ever worry?"

"I won't worry about that because it's perfectly simple."

"Then I'll do it. Because I don't care about me."

"What do you mean?"

"I don't care about me."

"Well, I care about you."

"Oh, yes. But I don't care about me. And I'll do it and then everything will be fine."

"I don't want you to do it if you feel that way."

The girl stood up and walked to the end of the station. Across, on the other side, were fields of grain and trees along the banks of the Ebro. Far away, beyond the river, were mountains. The shadow of a cloud moved across the field of grain and she saw the river through the trees.

"And we could have all this," she said. "And we could have everything and every day we make it more impossible."

"What did you say?"

"I said we could have everything."

"We can have everything."

"No, we can't."

"We can have the whole world."

"No, we can't."

"We can go everywhere."

"No, we can't. It isn't ours any more."

"It's ours."

"No, it isn't. And once they take it away, you never get it back."

"But they haven't taken it away."

"We'll wait and see."

"Come on back in the shade," he said. "You mustn't feel that way."

"I don't feel any way," the girl said. "I just know things."

"I don't want you to do anything that you don't want to do——"

"Nor that isn't good for me," she said. "I know. Could we have another beer?"

"All right. But you've got to realize——"

"I realize," the girl said. "Can't we maybe stop talking?"

They sat down at the table and the girl looked across at the hills on the dry side of the valley and the man looked at her and at the table.

"You've got to realize," he said, "that I don't want you to do it if you don't want to. I'm perfectly willing to go through with it if it means anything to you."

"Doesn't it mean anything to you? We could get along."

"Of course it does. But I don't want anybody but you. I don't want any one else. And I know it's perfectly simple."

"Yes, you know it's perfectly simple."

"It's all right for you to say that, but I do know it."

"Would you do something for me now?"

"I'd do anything for you."

"Would you please please please please please please please stop talking?"

He did not say anything but looked at the bags against the wall of the station. There were labels on them from all the hotels where they had spent nights.

"But I don't want you to," he said, "I don't care anything about it."

"I'll scream," the girl said.

The woman came out through the curtains with two glasses of beer and put them down on the damp felt pads. "The train comes in five minutes," she said.

"What did she say?" asked the girl.

"That the train is coming in five minutes."

The girl smiled brightly at the woman, to thank her.

"I'd better take the bags over to the other side of the station," the man said. She smiled at him.

"All right. Then come back and we'll finish the beer."

He picked up the two heavy bags and carried them around the station to the other tracks. He looked up the tracks but could not see the train. Coming back, he walked through the barroom, where people waiting for the train were drinking. He drank an Anis at the bar and looked at the people. They were all waiting reasonably for the train. He went out through the bead curtain. She was sitting at the table and smiled at him.

"Do you feel better?" he asked.

"I feel fine," she said. "There's nothing wrong with me. I feel fine."

ZORA NEALE HURSTON

Zora Neale Hurston (1891–1960) was born to a family of sharecroppers in Notasulga, Alabama. When she was very young she moved to Eatonville, Florida, a town founded by African Americans. After her mother died in 1904, her father, a Baptist minister, could not raise their eight children, so Hurston was forced to move from one relative's home to another. She never finished grade school, but when she was old enough to support herself, she attended Howard University in Washington, D.C. In 1921 she published her first story, "John Redding Goes to Sea," in the student literary magazine.

In 1925 Hurston went to New York City and became active in the cultural renaissance in Harlem, collaborating with Langston Hughes on a folk comedy, *Mule Bone*. Like Hughes, she was deeply interested in the abiding folk spirit inherent in southern life. With several other writers of that time, she tried to express her cultural heritage by writing short stories. *The Eatonville Anthology* (1927) was the collection that first brought Hurston's work to national attention. After Hurston studied with the famous anthropologist Franz Boas at Barnard College, she returned to Florida to record the oral traditions of her native community. As critics have noted, from this time to the end of her life she tried to achieve a balance in her literary work expressing the folk culture of her racial background and her individuality as a developing artist. Realizing that many white people used stereotypes to keep African Americans, Asian Americans, Hispanic Americans, and Native Americans in their "place," Hurston insisted it was

> urgent to realize that minorities do think, and think about something other than the race problem. That they are very human and internally, according to natural endowment, are just like everybody else. So long as this is not conceived, there must remain that feeling of unsurmountable difference, and difference to the average man means something bad. If people were made right, they would be just like him.

During the Great Depression of the 1930s, Hurston turned all her energies to writing. She published *Mules and Men* (1935), based on material from her field trips to Florida, and *Their Eyes Were Watching God* (1937), a novel about a woman's search for love and personal identity, in addition to several other books, including an autobiography. Although she published more than any other African American woman writer of her time, in the last two decades of her life she earned very little from her writing, and she died penniless in Florida. Fifteen years after Hurston's death, stories such as "Sweat" were rediscovered, and she is now regarded as one of our most important American writers.

CONNECTION To read Alice Walker's tribute to Zora Neale Hurston, see "Zora Neale Hurston: A Cautionary Tale and a Partisan View" on page 616.

WEB Research Zora Neale Hurston at bedfordstmartins.com/rewritinglit.

Sweat 1926

I

It was eleven o'clock of a Spring night in Florida. It was Sunday. Any other night, Delia Jones would have been in bed for two hours by this time. But she was a washwoman, and Monday morning meant a great deal to her. So she collected the soiled clothes on Saturday when she returned the clean things. Sunday night after church, she sorted and put the white things to soak. It saved her almost a half-day's start. A great hamper in the bedroom held the clothes that she brought home. It was so much neater than a number of bundles lying around.

She squatted on the kitchen floor beside the great pile of clothes, sorting them into small heaps according to color, and humming a song in a mournful key, but wondering through it all where Sykes, her husband, had gone with her horse and buckboard.

Just then something long, round, limp, and black fell upon her shoulders and slithered to the floor beside her. A great terror took hold of her. It softened her knees and dried her mouth so that it was a full minute before she could cry out or move. Then she saw that it was the big bull whip her husband liked to carry when he drove.

She lifted her eyes to the door and saw him standing there bent over with laughter at her fright. She screamed at him.

"Sykes, what you throw dat whip on me like dat? You know it would skeer me—looks just like a snake, an' you knows how skeered Ah is of snakes."

"Course Ah knowed it! That's how come Ah done it." He slapped his leg with his hand and almost rolled on the ground in his mirth. "If you such a big fool dat you got to have a fit over a earth worm or a string, Ah don't keer how bad Ah skeer you."

"You ain't got no business doing it. Gawd knows it's a sin. Some day Ah'm gointuh drop dead from some of yo' foolishness. 'Nother thing, where you been wid mah rig? Ah feeds dat pony. He ain't fuh you to be drivin' wid no bull whip."

"You sho' is one aggravatin' nigger woman!" he declared and stepped into the room. She resumed her work and did not answer him at once. "Ah done tole you time and again to keep them white folks' clothes outa dis house."

He picked up the whip and glared at her. Delia went on with her work. She went out into the yard and returned with a galvanized tub and set it on the washbench. She saw that Sykes had kicked all of the clothes together again, and now stood in her way truculently, his whole manner hoping, *praying,* for an argument. But she walked calmly around him and commenced to re-sort the things.

"Next time, Ah'm gointer kick 'em outdoors," he threatened as he struck a match along the leg of his corduroy breeches.

Delia never looked up from her work, and her thin, stooped shoulders sagged further.

"Ah ain't for no fuss t'night, Sykes. Ah just come from taking sacrament at the church house."

He snorted scornfully. "Yeah, you just come from de church house on a Sunday night, but heah you is gone to work on them clothes. You ain't nothing but a hypocrite. One of them amen-corner Christians—sing, whoop, and shout, then come home and wash white folks' clothes on the Sabbath."

He stepped roughly upon the whitest pile of things, kicking them helter-skelter as he crossed the room. His wife gave a little scream of dismay, and quickly gathered them together again.

"Sykes, you quit grindin' dirt into these clothes! How can Ah git through by Sat'day if Ah don't start on Sunday?"

"Ah don't keer if you never git through. Anyhow, Ah done promised Gawd and a couple of other men, Ah ain't gointer have it in mah house. Don't gimme no lip neither, else Ah'll throw 'em out and put mah fist up side yo' head to boot."

Delia's habitual meekness seemed to slip from her shoulders like a blown scarf. She was on her feet; her poor little body, her bare knuckly hands bravely defying the strapping hulk before her.

"Looka heah, Sykes, you done gone too fur. Ah been married to you fur fifteen years, and Ah been takin' in washin' fur fifteen years. Sweat, sweat, sweat! Work and sweat, cry and sweat, pray and sweat!"

"What's that got to do with me?" he asked brutally.

"What's it got to do with you, Sykes? Mah tub of suds is filled yo' belly with vittles more times than yo' hands is filled it. Mah sweat is done paid for this house and Ah reckon Ah kin keep on sweatin' in it."

She seized the iron skillet from the stove and struck a defensive pose, which act surprised him greatly, coming from her. It cowed him and he did not strike her as he usually did.

"Naw you won't," she panted, "that ole snaggle-toothed black woman you runnin' with ain't comin' heah to pile up on *mah* sweat and blood. You ain't paid for nothin' on this place, and Ah'm gointer stay right heah till Ah'm toted out foot foremost."

"Well, you better quit gittin' me riled up, else they'll be totin' you out sooner than you expect. Ah'm so tired of you Ah don't know whut to do. Gawd! How Ah hates skinny wimmen!"

A little awed by this new Delia, he sidled out of the door and slammed the back gate after him. He did not say where he had gone, but she knew too well. She knew very well that he would not return until nearly daybreak also. Her work over, she went on to bed but not to sleep at once. Things had come to a pretty pass!

She lay awake, gazing upon the debris that cluttered their matrimonial trail. Not an image left standing along the way. Anything like flowers had long ago been drowned in the salty stream that had been pressed from her heart. Her tears, her sweat, her blood. She had brought love to the union and he had brought a longing after the flesh. Two months after the wedding, he had given her the first brutal beating. She had the memory of his numerous trips to Orlando with all of his wages when he had returned to her penniless, even before the first year had passed. She was young and soft then, but now she thought of her knotty, muscled limbs, her harsh knuckly hands, and drew herself up into an unhappy little ball in the middle of the big feather bed. Too late now to hope for love, even if it were not Bertha it would be someone else. This case differed from the others only in that she was bolder than the others. Too late for everything except her little home. She had built it for her old days, and planted one by one the trees and flowers there. It was lovely to her, lovely.

Somehow, before sleep came, she found herself saying aloud: "Oh well, whatever goes over the Devil's back, is got to come under his belly. Sometime or ruther, Sykes, like everybody else, is gointer reap his sowing." After that she was able to build a spiritual earthworks against her husband. His shells could no longer reach her. AMEN. She went to sleep and slept until he announced his presence in bed by kicking her feet and rudely snatching the covers away.

"Gimme some kivah heah, an' git yo' damn foots over on yo' own side! Ah oughter mash you in yo' mouf fuh drawing dat skillet on me."

Delia went clear to the rail without answering him. A triumphant indifference to all that he was or did.

II

The week was full of work for Delia as all other weeks, and Saturday found her behind her little pony, collecting and delivering clothes.

It was a hot, hot day near the end of July. The village men on Joe Clarke's porch even chewed cane listlessly. They did not hurl the cane-knots as usual. They let them dribble over the edge of the porch. Even conversation had collapsed under the heat.

"Heah come Delia Jones," Jim Merchant said, as the shaggy pony came 'round the bend of the road toward them. The rusty buckboard was heaped with baskets of crisp, clean laundry.

"Yep," Joe Lindsay agreed. "Hot or col', rain or shine, jes' ez reg'lar ez de weeks roll roun' Delia carries 'em an' fetches 'em on Sat'day."

"She better if she wanter eat," said Moss. "Syke Jones ain't wuth de shot an' powder hit would tek tuh kill 'em. Not to *huh* he ain't."

"He sho' ain't," Walter Thomas chimed in. "It's too bad, too, cause she wuz a right pretty li'l trick when he got huh. Ah'd uh mah'ied huh mahseff if he hadnter beat me to it."

Delia nodded briefly at the men as she drove past.

"Too much knockin' will ruin *any* 'oman. He done beat huh 'nough tuh kill three women, let 'lone change they looks," said Elijah Moseley. "How Syke kin stommuck dat big black greasy Mogul he's layin' roun' wid, gits me. Ah swear dat eight-rock couldn't kiss a sardine can Ah done thowed out de back do' 'way las' yeah."

"Aw, she's fat, thass how come. He's allus been crazy 'bout fat women," put in Merchant. "He'd a' been tied up wid one long time ago if he could a' found one tuh have him. Did Ah tell yuh 'bout him come sidlin' roun' *mah* wife—bringin' her a basket uh peecans outa his yard fuh a present? Yessir, mah wife! She tol' him tuh take 'em right straight back home, 'cause Delia works so hard ovah dat washtub she reckon everything on de place taste lak sweat an' soapsuds. Ah jus' wisht Ah'd a' caught 'im 'roun' dere! Ah'd a' made his hips ketch on fiah down dat shell road."

"Ah know he done it, too. Ah sees 'im grinnin' at every 'oman dat passes," Walter Thomas said. "But even so, he useter eat some mighty big hunks uh humble pie tuh git dat li'l 'oman he got. She wuz ez pritty ez a speckled pup! Dat wuz fifteen years ago. He useter be so skeered uh losin' huh, she could make him do some parts of a husband's duty. Dey never wuz de same in de mind."

"There oughter be a law about him," said Lindsay. "He ain't fit tuh carry guts tuh a bear."

Clarke spoke for the first time. "Tain't no law on earth dat kin make a man be decent if it ain't in 'im. There's plenty men dat takes a wife lak dey do a joint uh sugar-cane. It's round, juicy, an' sweet when dey gits it. But dey squeeze an' grind, squeeze an' grind an' wring tell dey wring every drop uh pleasure dat's in 'em out. When dey's satisfied dat dey is wrung dry, dey treats 'em jes' lak dey do a cane-chew. Dey thows 'em away. Dey knows whut dey is doin' while dey is at it, an' hates theirselves fuh it but they keeps on hangin' after huh tell she's empty. Den dey hates huh fuh bein' a cane-chew an' in de way."

"We oughter take Syke an' dat stray 'oman uh his'n down in Lake Howell swamp an' lay on de rawhide till they cain't say 'Lawd a' mussy.' He allus wuz uh ovahbearin' niggah, but since dat white 'oman from up north done teached 'im how to run a automobile, he done got too biggety to live—an' we oughter kill 'im," Old Man Anderson advised.

A grunt of approval went around the porch. But the heat was melting their civic virtue and Elijah Moseley began to bait Joe Clarke.

"Come on, Joe, git a melon outa dere an' slice it up for yo' customers. We'se all sufferin' wid de heat. De bear's done got *me!*"

"Thass right, Joe, a watermelon is jes' whut Ah needs tuh cure de eppizudicks," Walter Thomas joined forces with Moseley. "Come on dere, Joe. We all is steady customers an' you ain't set us up in a long time. Ah chooses dat long, bowlegged Floridy favorite."

"A god, an' be dough. You all gimme twenty cents and slice away," Clarke retorted. "Ah needs a col' slice m'self. Heah, everybody chip in. Ah'll lend y'all mah meat knife."

The money was all quickly subscribed and the huge melon brought forth. At that moment, Sykes and Bertha arrived. A determined silence fell on the porch and the melon was put away again.

Merchant snapped down the blade of his jackknife and moved toward the store door.

"Come on in, Joe, an' gimme a slab uh sow belly an' uh pound uh coffee—almost fuhgot 'twas Sat'day. Got to git on home." Most of the men left also.

Just then Delia drove past on her way home, as Sykes was ordering magnificently for Bertha. It pleased him for Delia to see.

"Git whutsoever yo' heart desires, Honey. Wait a minute, Joe. Give huh two bottles uh strawberry soda-water, uh quart parched ground-peas, an' a block uh chewin' gum."

With all this they left the store, with Sykes reminding Bertha that this was his town and she could have it if she wanted it.

The men returned soon after they left, and held their watermelon feast.

"Where did Syke Jones git dat 'oman from nohow?" Lindsay asked.

"Ovah Apopka. Guess dey musta been cleanin' out de town when she lef.' She don't look lak a thing but a hunk uh liver wid hair on it."

"Well, she sho' kin squall," Dave Carter contributed. "When she gits ready tuh laff, she jes' opens huh mouf an' latches it back tuh de las' notch. No ole granpa alligator down in Lake Bell ain't got nothin' on huh."

III

Bertha had been in town three months now. Sykes was still paying her room-rent at Della Lewis'—the only house in town that would have taken her in. Sykes took her frequently to Winter Park to "stomps." He still assured her that he was the swellest man in the state.

"Sho' you kin have dat li'l ole house soon's Ah git dat 'oman outa dere. Everything b'longs tuh me an' you sho' kin have it. Ah sho' 'bominates uh skinny 'oman. Lawdy, you sho' is got one portly shape on you! You kin git *anything* you wants. Dis is *mah* town an' you sho' kin have it."

Delia's work-worn knees crawled over the earth in Gethsemane° and up the rocks of Calvary many, many times during these months. She avoided the villagers and meeting places in her efforts to be blind and deaf. But Bertha nullified this to a degree, by coming to Delia's house to call Sykes out to her at the gate.

Delia and Sykes fought all the time now with no peaceful interludes. They slept and ate in silence. Two or three times Delia had attempted a timid friendliness, but she was repulsed each time. It was plain that the breaches must remain agape.

The sun had burned July to August. The heat streamed down like a million hot arrows, smiting all things living upon the earth. Grass withered, leaves browned, snakes went blind in shedding, and men and dogs went mad. Dog days!

Delia came home one day and found Sykes there before her. She wondered, but started to go on into the house without speaking, even though he was standing in the kitchen door and she must either stoop under his arm or ask

---

Gethsemane: A reference to the garden where Jesus was betrayed (in the Gospels) before being tried and crucified on Calvary or Golgotha, the "hill of skulls."

him to move. He made no room for her. She noticed a soap box beside the steps, but paid no particular attention to it, knowing that he must have brought it there. As she was stooping to pass under his outstretched arm, he suddenly pushed her backward, laughingly.

"Look in de box dere Delia, Ah done brung yuh somethin'!"

She nearly fell upon the box in her stumbling, and when she saw what it held, she all but fainted outright.

"Syke! Syke, mah Gawd! You take dat rattlesnake 'way from heah! You *gottuh.* Oh, Jesus, have mussy!"

"Ah ain't got tuh do nuthin' uh de kin'—fact is Ah ain't got tuh do nothin' but die. Tain't no use uh you puttin' on airs makin' out lak you skeered uh dat snake—he's gointer stay right heah tell he die. He wouldn't bite me cause Ah knows how tuh handle 'im. Nohow he wouldn't risk breakin' out his fangs 'gin *yo* skinny laigs."

"Naw, now Syke, don't keep dat thing 'round tryin' tuh skeer me tuh death. You knows Ah'm even feared uh earth worms. Thass de biggest snake Ah evah did see. Kill 'im Syke, please."

"Doan ast me tuh do nothin' fuh yuh. Goin' 'round tryin' tuh be so damn asterperious. Naw, Ah ain't gonna kill it. Ah think uh damn sight mo' uh him dan you! Dat's a nice snake an' anybody doan lak 'im kin jes' hit de grit."

The village soon heard that Sykes had the snake, and came to see and ask questions.

"How de hen-fire did you ketch dat six-foot rattler, Syke?" Thomas asked.

"He's full uh frogs so he cain't hardly move, thass how Ah eased up on 'm. But Ah'm a snake charmer an' knows how tuh handle 'em. Shux, dat ain't nothin'. Ah could ketch one eve'y day if Ah so wanted tuh."

"Whut he needs is a heavy hick'ry club leaned real heavy on his head. Dat's de bes' way tuh charm a rattlesnake."

"Naw, Walt, y'all jes' don't understand dese diamon' backs lak Ah do," said Sykes in a superior tone of voice.

The village agreed with Walter, but the snake stayed on. His box remained by the kitchen door with its screen wire covering. Two or three days later it had digested its meal of frogs and literally came to life. It rattled at every movement in the kitchen or the yard. One day as Delia came down the kitchen steps she saw his chalky-white fangs curved like scimitars hung in the wire meshes. This time she did not run away with averted eyes as usual. She stood for a long time in the doorway in a red fury that grew bloodier for every second that she regarded the creature that was her torment.

That night she broached the subject as soon as Sykes sat down to the table.

"Syke, Ah wants you tuh take dat snake 'way fum heah. You done starved me an' Ah put up widcher, you done beat me an Ah took dat, but you done kilt all mah insides bringin' dat varmint heah."

Sykes poured out a saucer full of coffee and drank it deliberately before he answered her.

"A whole lot Ah keer 'bout how you feels inside uh out. Dat snake ain't goin' no damn wheah till Ah gits ready fuh 'im tuh go. So fur as beatin' is concerned, yuh ain't took near all dat you gointer take ef yuh stay 'round *me.*"

Delia pushed back her plate and got up from the table. "Ah hates you, Sykes," she said calmly. "Ah hates you tuh de same degree dat Ah useter love yuh. Ah done took an' took till mah belly is full up tuh mah neck. Dat's de reason Ah got mah letter fum de church an' moved mah membership tuh Woodbridge—so Ah don't haftuh take no sacrament wid yuh. Ah don't wantuh see yuh 'round me atall. Lay 'round wid dat 'oman all yuh wants tuh, but gwan 'way from me an' mah house. Ah hates yuh lak uh suck-egg dog."

Sykes almost let the huge wad of corn bread and collard greens he was chewing fall out of his mouth in amazement. He had a hard time whipping himself up to the proper fury to try to answer Delia.

"Well, Ah'm glad you does hate me. Ah'm sho' tiahed uh you hangin' ontuh me. Ah don't want yuh. Look at yuh stringey ole neck! Yo' rawbony laigs an' arms is enough tuh cut uh man tuh death. You looks jes' lak de devvul's doll-baby tuh *me.* You cain't hate me no worse dan Ah hates you. Ah been hatin' *you* fuh years."

"Yo' ole black hide don't look lak nothin' tuh me, but uh passle uh wrinkled up rubber, wid yo' big ole yeahs flappin' on each side lak uh paih uh buzzard wings. Don't think Ah'm gointuh be run 'way fum mah house neither. Ah'm goin' tuh de white folks 'bout *you,* mah young man, de very nex' time you lay yo' han's on me. Mah cup is done run ovah." Delia said this with no signs of fear and Sykes departed from the house, threatening her, but made not the slightest move to carry out any of them.

That night he did not return at all, and the next day being Sunday, Delia was glad she did not have to quarrel before she hitched up her pony and drove the four miles to Woodbridge.

She stayed to the night service—"love feast"—which was very warm and full of spirit. In the emotional winds her domestic trials were borne far and wide so that she sang as she drove homeward,

> Jurden water, black an' col
> Chills de body, not de soul
> An' Ah wantah cross Jurden in uh calm time.

She came from the barn to the kitchen door and stopped.

"Whut's de mattah, ol' Satan, you ain't kicken' up yo' racket?" She addressed the snake's box. Complete silence. She went on into the house with a new hope in its birth struggles. Perhaps her threat to go to the white folks had frightened Sykes! Perhaps he was sorry! Fifteen years of misery and suppression had brought Delia to the place where she would hope *anything* that looked towards a way over or through her wall of inhibitions.

She felt in the match-safe behind the stove at once for a match. There was only one there.

"Dat niggah wouldn't fetch nothin' heah tuh save his rotten neck, but he kin run thew whut Ah brings quick enough. Now he done toted off nigh on tuh haff uh box uh matches. He done had dat 'oman heah in mah house, too."

Nobody but a woman could tell how she knew this even before she struck the match. But she did and it put her into a new fury.

Presently she brought in the tubs to put the white things to soak. This time she decided she need not bring the hamper out of the bedroom; she would go in there and do the sorting. She picked up the pot-bellied lamp and went in. The room was small and the hamper stood hard by the foot of the white iron bed. She could sit and reach through the bedposts—resting as she worked.

"Ah wantah cross Jurden in uh calm time." She was singing again. The mood of the "love feast" had returned. She threw back the lid of the basket almost gaily. Then, moved by both horror and terror, she sprang back toward the door. *There lay the snake in the basket!* He moved sluggishly at first, but even as she turned round and round, jumped up and down in an insanity of fear, he began to stir vigorously. She saw him pouring his awful beauty from the basket upon the bed, then she seized the lamp and ran as fast as she could to the kitchen. The wind from the open door blew out the light and the darkness added to her terror. She sped to the darkness of the yard, slamming the door after her before she thought to set down the lamp. She did not feel safe even on the ground, so she climbed up in the hay barn.

There for an hour or more she lay sprawled upon the hay a gibbering wreck.

Finally she grew quiet, and after that came coherent thought. With this stalked through her a cold, bloody rage. Hours of this. A period of introspection, a space of retrospection, then a mixture of both. Out of this an awful calm.

"Well, Ah done de bes' Ah could. If things ain't right, Gawd knows tain't mah fault."

She went to sleep—a twitch sleep—and woke up to a faint gray sky. There was a loud hollow sound below. She peered out. Sykes was at the wood-pile, demolishing a wire-covered box.

He hurried to the kitchen door, but hung outside there some minutes before he entered, and stood some minutes more inside before he closed it after him.

The gray in the sky was spreading. Delia descended without fear now, and crouched beneath the low bedroom window. The drawn shade shut out the dawn, shut in the night. But the thin walls held back no sound.

"Dat ol' scratch is woke up now!" She mused at the tremendous whirr inside, which every woodsman knows, is one of the sound illusions. The rattler is a ventriloquist. His whirr sounds to the right, to the left, straight ahead, behind, close under foot—everywhere but where it is. Woe to him who guesses wrong unless he is prepared to hold up his end of the argument! Sometimes he strikes without rattling at all.

Inside, Sykes heard nothing until he knocked a pot lid off the stove while trying to reach the match-safe in the dark. He had emptied his pockets at Bertha's.

The snake seemed to wake up under the stove and Sykes made a quick leap into the bedroom. In spite of the gin he had had, his head was clearing now.

"Mah Gawd!" he chattered, "ef Ah could on'y strack uh light!"

The rattling ceased for a moment as he stood paralyzed. He waited. It seemed that the snake waited also.

"Oh, fuh de light! Ah thought he'd be too sick"—Sykes was muttering to himself when the whirr began again, closer, right underfoot this time. Long before this, Sykes' ability to think had been flattened down to primitive instinct and he leaped—onto the bed.

Outside Delia heard a cry that might have come from a maddened chimpanzee, a stricken gorilla. All the terror, all the horror, all the rage that man possibly could express, without a recognizable human sound.

A tremendous stir inside there, another series of animal screams, the intermittent whirr of the reptile. The shade torn violently down from the window, letting in the red dawn, a huge brown hand seizing the window stick, great dull blows upon the wooden floor punctuating the gibberish of sound long after the rattle of the snake had abruptly subsided. All this Delia could see and hear from her place beneath the window, and it made her ill. She crept over to the four o'clocks and stretched herself on the cool earth to recover.

She lay there. "Delia, Delia!" She could hear Sykes calling in a most despairing tone as one who expected no answer. The sun crept on up, and he called. Delia could not move—her legs had gone flabby. She never moved, he called, and the sun kept rising.

"Mah Gawd!" She heard him moan, "Mah Gawd fum Heben!" She heard him stumbling about and got up from her flower-bed. The sun was growing warm. As she approached the door she heard him call out hopefully, "Delia, is dat you Ah heah?"

She saw him on his hands and knees as soon as she reached the door. He crept an inch or two toward her—all that he was able, and she saw his horribly swollen neck and his one open eye shining with hope. A surge of pity too strong to support bore her away from that eye that must, could not, fail to see the tubs. He would see the lamp. Orlando with its doctors was too far. She could scarcely reach the chinaberry tree, where she waited in the growing heat while inside she knew the cold river was creeping up and up to extinguish that eye which must know by now that she knew.

COMMENTARY

ZORA NEALE HURSTON

Zora Neale Hurston continued throughout her life to make what the critic Mary Helen Washington called "unorthodox and paradoxical assertions on racial issues." Often conveyed with great wit and style, Hurston's views were always passionately held, as in her essay "How It Feels to Be Colored Me," first published in 1928.

How It Feels to Be Colored Me 1928

I am colored but I offer nothing in the way of extenuating circumstances except the fact that I am the only Negro in the United States whose grandfather on the mother's side was *not* an Indian chief.

I remember the very day that I became colored. Up to my thirteenth year I lived in the little Negro town of Eatonville, Florida. It is exclusively a colored town. The only white people I knew passed through the town going to or coming from Orlando. The native whites rode dusty horses, the Northern tourists chugged down the sandy village road in automobiles. The town knew the Southerners and never stopped cane chewing when they passed. But the Northerners were something else again. They were peered at cautiously from behind curtains by the timid. The more venturesome would come out on the porch to watch them go past and got just as much pleasure out of the tourists as the tourists got out of the village.

The front porch might seem a daring place for the rest of the town, but it was a gallery seat for me. My favorite place was atop the gate-post. Proscenium box for a born first-nighter. Not only did I enjoy the show, but I didn't mind the actors knowing that I liked it. I usually spoke to them in passing. I'd wave at them and when they returned my salute, I would say something like this: "Howdy-do-well-I-thank-you-where-you-goin'?" Usually automobile or the horse paused at this, and after a queer exchange of compliments, I would probably "go a piece of the way" with them, as we say in farthest Florida. If one of my family happened to come to the front in time to see me, of course negotiations would be rudely broken off. But even so, it is clear that I was the first "welcome-to-our-state" Floridian, and I hope the Miami Chamber of Commerce will please take notice.

During this period, white people differed from colored to me only in that they rode through town and never lived there. They liked to hear me "speak pieces" and sing and wanted to see me dance the parse-me-la, and gave me generously of their small silver for doing these things, which seemed strange to me for I wanted to do them so much that I needed bribing to stop. Only they didn't know it. The colored people gave no dimes. They deplored any joyful tendencies in me, but I was their Zora nevertheless. I belonged to them, to the nearby hotels, to the county—everybody's Zora.

But changes came in the family when I was thirteen, and I was sent to school in Jacksonville. I left Eatonville, the town of the oleanders, as Zora. When I disembarked from the river-boat at Jacksonville, she was no more. It seemed that I had suffered a sea change. I was not Zora of Orange County any more, I was now a little colored girl. I found it out in certain ways. In my heart as well as in the mirror, I became a fast brown—warranted not to rub nor run.

But I am not tragically colored. There is no great sorrow dammed up in my soul, nor lurking behind my eyes. I do not mind at all. I do not belong to the sobbing school of Negrohood who hold that nature somehow has given them a lowdown dirty deal and whose feelings are all hurt about it. Even in the helter-skelter skirmish that is my life, I have seen that the world is to the strong regardless of a little pigmentation more or less. No, I do not weep at the world—I am too busy sharpening my oyster knife.

Someone is always at my elbow reminding me that I am the granddaughter of slaves. It fails to register depression with me. Slavery is sixty years in the past. The operation was successful and the patient is doing well, thank you. The terrible struggle that made me an American out of a potential slave said "On the line!" The Reconstruction said "Get set!"; and the generation before said "Go!" I am off to a flying start and I must not halt in the stretch to look behind and weep. Slavery is the price I paid for civilization, and the choice was not with me. It is a bully adventure and worth all that I have paid through my ancestors for it. No one on earth ever had a greater chance for glory. The world to be won and nothing to be lost. It is thrilling to think—to know that for any act of mine, I shall get twice as much praise or twice as much blame. It is quite exciting to hold the center of the national stage, with the spectators not knowing whether to laugh or to weep.

The position of my white neighbor is much more difficult. No brown specter pulls up a chair beside me when I sit down to eat. No dark ghost thrusts its leg against mine in bed. The game of keeping what one has is never so exciting as the game of getting.

I do not always feel colored. Even now I often achieve the unconscious Zora of Eatonville before the Hegira. I feel most colored when I am thrown against a sharp white background.

For instance at Barnard. "Beside the waters of the Hudson" I feel my race. Among the thousand white persons, I am a dark rock surged upon, and overswept, but through it all, I remain myself. When covered by the waters, I am; and the ebb but reveals me again.

Sometimes it is the other way around. A white person is set down in our midst, but the contrast is just as sharp for me. For instance, when I sit in the drafty basement that is The New World Cabaret with a white person, my color comes. We enter chatting about any little nothing that we have in common and are seated by the jazz waiters. In the abrupt way that jazz orchestras have, this one plunges into a number. It loses no time in circumlocutions, but gets right down to business. It constricts the thorax and splits the heart with its tempo and narcotic harmonies. This orchestra grows rambunctious, rears on its hind legs and attacks the tonal veil with primitive fury, rending it, clawing it until it breaks through to the jungle beyond. I follow those heathen—follow them exultingly. I dance wildly inside myself; I yell within, I whoop; I shake my assegai above my head, I hurl it true to the mark *yeeeeooww!* I am in the jungle and living in the jungle way. My face is painted red and yellow and my body is painted blue. My pulse is throbbing like a war drum. I want to slaughter something—give pain, give death to what, I do not know. But the piece ends. The men of the orchestra wipe their lips and rest their fingers. I creep back slowly to the veneer we call civilization with the last tone and find the white friend sitting motionless in his seat, smoking calmly.

"Good music they have here," he remarks, drumming the table with his fingertips.

Music. The great blobs of purple and red emotion have not touched him. He has only heard what I felt. He is far away and I see him but dimly across the ocean and the continent that have fallen between us. He is so pale with his whiteness then and I am *so* colored.

At certain times I have no race, I am *me.* When I set my hat at a certain angle and saunter down Seventh Avenue, Harlem City, feeling as snooty as the lions in front of the Forty-Second Street Library, for instance. So far as my feelings are concerned, Peggy Hopkins Joyce on the Boule Mich with her gorgeous raiment, stately carriage, knees knocking together in a most aristocratic manner, has nothing on me. The cosmic Zora emerges. I belong to no race nor time. I am the eternal feminine with its string of beads.

I have no separate feeling about being an American citizen and colored. I am merely a fragment of the Great Soul that surges within the boundaries. My country, right or wrong.

Sometimes, I feel discriminated against, but it does not make me angry. It merely astonishes me. How *can* any deny themselves the pleasure of my company? It's beyond me.

But in the main, I feel like a brown bag of miscellany propped against a wall. Against a wall in company with other bags, white, red and yellow. Pour out the contents, and there is discovered a jumble of small things priceless and worthless. A first-water diamond, an empty spool, bits of broken glass, lengths of string, a key to a door long since crumbled away, a rusty knife-blade, old shoes saved for a road that never was and never will be, a nail bent under the weight of things too heavy for any nail, a dried flower or two still a little fragrant. In your hand is the brown bag. On the ground before you is the jumble it held—so much like the jumble in the bags, could they be emptied, that all might be dumped in a single heap and the bags refilled without altering the content of any greatly. A bit of colored glass more or less would not matter. Perhaps that is how the Great Stuffer of Bags filled them in the first place—who knows?

SHIRLEY JACKSON

Shirley Jackson (1919–1965) was born in San Francisco, her mother a housewife and her father an employee of a lithographing company. Most of her early life was spent in Burlingame, California, which she later used as the setting for her first novel, *The Road through the Wall* (1948). As a child she was interested in writing; she won a poetry prize at age twelve, and in high school she began keeping a diary to record her writing progress. After high school she briefly attended the University of Rochester but left because of an attack of the mental depression that was to recur periodically in her later years. She recovered her health by living quietly at home and writing, conscientiously turning out 1,000 words of prose a day. In 1937 she entered Syracuse University, where she published stories in the student literary magazine. There she met Stanley Edgar Hyman, who was to become a noted literary critic. They were married in 1940, the year she received her degree. They had four children while both continued active literary careers, settling to raise their family in a large Victorian house in Vermont, where Hyman taught literature at Bennington College.

Jackson's first national publication was a humorous story written after a job at a department store during the Christmas rush: "My Life with R. H. Macy" appeared in *The New Republic* in 1941. Her first child was born the next year, but she wrote every day on a disciplined schedule, selling her stories to magazines and publishing three novels. She refused to take herself too seriously as a writer: "I can't persuade myself that writing is honest work. It is a very personal reaction, but 50 percent of my life is spent washing and dressing the children, cooking, washing dishes and clothes, and mending. After I get it all to bed, I turn around to my typewriter and try to – well, to create concrete things again. It's great fun, and I love it. But it doesn't tie any shoes."

Jackson's best-known work, "The Lottery," is often anthologized, dramatized, and televised. She regarded it as a *tale* in the sense that Nathaniel Hawthorne used the term – a moral allegory revealing the hidden evil of the human soul. She wrote later that "explaining just what I had hoped the story to say is very difficult. I supposed, I hoped, by setting a particularly brutal ancient rite in the present and in my own village, to shock the story's readers with a graphic dramatization of the pointless violence and general inhumanity in their own lives."

WEB Research Shirley Jackson at bedfordstmartins.com/rewritinglit.

The Lottery

1948

The morning of June 27th was clear and sunny, with the fresh warmth of a full-summer day; the flowers were blossoming profusely and the grass was richly green. The people of the village began to gather in the square, between the post office and the bank, around ten o'clock; in some towns there were so many people that the lottery took two days and had to be started on June 26th, but in this village, where there were only about three hundred people, the whole lottery took less than two hours, so it could begin at ten o'clock in the morning and still be through in time to allow the villagers to get home for noon dinner.

The children assembled first, of course. School was recently over for the summer, and the feeling of liberty sat uneasily on most of them; they tended to gather together quietly for a while before they broke into boisterous play, and their talk was still of the classroom and teacher, of books and reprimands. Bobby Martin had already stuffed his pockets full of stones, and the other boys soon followed his example, selecting the smoothest and roundest stones; Bobby and Harry Jones and Dickie Delacroix—the villagers pronounced this name "Dellacroy"—eventually made a great pile of stones in one corner of the square and guarded it against the raids of the other boys. The girls stood aside, talking among themselves, looking over their shoulders at the boys, and the very small children rolled in the dust or clung to the hands of their older brothers or sisters.

Soon the men began to gather, surveying their own children, speaking of planting and rain, tractors and taxes. They stood together, away from the pile of stones in the corner, and their jokes were quiet and they smiled rather than laughed. The women, wearing faded house dresses and sweaters, came shortly after their menfolk. They greeted one another and exchanged bits of gossip as they went to join their husbands. Soon the women, standing by their husbands, began to call to their children, and the children came reluctantly, having to be called four or five times. Bobby Martin ducked under his mother's grasping hand and ran, laughing, back to the pile of stones. His father spoke up sharply, and Bobby came quickly and took his place between his father and his oldest brother.

The lottery was conducted—as were the square dances, the teen-age club, the Halloween program—by Mr. Summers, who had time and energy to devote to civic activities. He was a round-faced, jovial man and he ran the coal business, and people were sorry for him, because he had no children and his wife was a scold. When he arrived in the square, carrying the black wooden box, there was a murmur of conversation among the villagers, and he waved and called, "Little late today, folks." The postmaster, Mr. Graves, followed him, carrying a three-legged stool, and the stool was put in the center of the square and Mr. Summers set the black box down on it. The villagers kept their distance, leaving a space between themselves and the stool, and when Mr. Summers said, "Some of you fellows want to give me a hand?" there was a hesitation before two men, Mr. Martin and his oldest son, Baxter, came forward to hold the box steady on the stool while Mr. Summers stirred up the papers inside it.

The original paraphernalia for the lottery had been lost long ago, and the black box now resting on the stool had been put into use even before Old Man Warner, the oldest man in town, was born. Mr. Summers spoke frequently to the villagers about making a new box, but no one liked to upset even as much tradition as was represented by the black box. There was a story that the present box had been made with some pieces of the box that had preceded it, the one that had been constructed when the first people settled down to make a village here. Every year, after the lottery, Mr. Summers began talking again about a new box, but every year the subject was allowed to fade off without anything's being done. The black box grew shabbier each year; by now it was no longer completely black but splintered badly along one side to show the original wood color, and in some places faded or stained.

Mr. Martin and his oldest son, Baxter, held the black box securely on the stool until Mr. Summers had stirred the papers thoroughly with his hand. Because so much of the ritual had been forgotten or discarded, Mr. Summers had been successful in having slips of paper substituted for the chips of wood that had been used for generations. Chips of wood, Mr. Summers had argued, had been all very well when the village was tiny, but now that the population was more than three hundred and likely to keep on growing, it was necessary to use something that would fit more easily into the black box. The night before the lottery, Mr. Summers and Mr. Graves made up the slips of paper and put them in the box, and it was then taken to the safe of Mr. Summers's coal company and locked up until Mr. Summers was ready to take it to the square next morning. The rest of the year, the box was put away, sometimes one place, sometimes another; it had spent one year in Mr. Graves's barn and another year underfoot in the post office, and sometimes it was set on a shelf in the Martin grocery and left there.

There was a great deal of fussing to be done before Mr. Summers declared the lottery open. There were the lists to make up—of heads of families, heads of households in each family, members of each household in each family. There was the proper swearing-in of Mr. Summers by the postmaster, as the official of the lottery; at one time, some people remembered, there had been a recital of some sort, performed by the official of the lottery, a perfunctory, tuneless chant that had been rattled off duly each year; some people believed that the official of the lottery used to stand just so when he said or sang it, others believed that he was supposed to walk among the people, but years and years ago this part of the ritual had been allowed to lapse. There had been, also, a ritual salute, which the official of the lottery had had to use in addressing each person who came up to draw from the box, but this also had changed with time, until now it was felt necessary only for the official to speak to each person approaching. Mr. Summers was very good at all this; in his clean white shirt and blue jeans, with one hand resting carelessly on the black box, he seemed very proper and important as he talked interminably to Mr. Graves and the Martins.

Just as Mr. Summers finally left off talking and turned to the assembled villagers, Mrs. Hutchinson came hurriedly along the path to the square, her sweater thrown over her shoulders, and slid into place in the back of the crowd. "Clean forgot what day it was," she said to Mrs. Delacroix, who stood next to her, and they both laughed softly. "Thought my old man was out back stacking wood," Mrs. Hutchinson went on, "and then I looked out the window and the kids was gone, and then I remembered it was the twenty-seventh and came a-running." She dried her hands on her apron, and Mrs. Delacroix said, "You're in time, though. They're still talking away up there."

Mrs. Hutchinson craned her neck to see through the crowd and found her husband and children standing near the front. She tapped Mrs. Delacroix on the arm as a farewell and began to make her way through the crowd. The people separated good-humoredly to let her through; two or three people said, in voices just loud enough to be heard across the crowd, "Here comes your Missus, Hutchinson," and "Bill, she made it after all." Mrs. Hutchinson reached her husband, and Mr. Summers, who had been waiting, said cheerfully, "Thought we were going to have to get on without you, Tessie." Mrs. Hutchinson said, grinning, "Wouldn't have me leave m'dishes in the sink, now, would you, Joe?" and soft laughter ran through the crowd as the people stirred back into position after Mrs. Hutchinson's arrival.

"Well, now," Mr. Summers said soberly, "guess we better get started, get this over with, so's we can go back to work. Anybody ain't here?"

"Dunbar," several people said. "Dunbar, Dunbar."

Mr. Summers consulted his list. "Clyde Dunbar," he said. "That's right. He's broke his leg, hasn't he? Who's drawing for him?"

"Me, I guess," a woman said, and Mr. Summers turned to look at her. "Wife draws for her husband," Mr. Summers said. "Don't you have a grown boy to do it for you, Janey?" Although Mr. Summers and everyone else in the village knew the answer perfectly well, it was the business of the official of the lottery to ask such questions formally. Mr. Summers waited with an expression of polite interest while Mrs. Dunbar answered.

"Horace's not but sixteen yet," Mrs. Dunbar said regretfully. "Guess I gotta fill in for the old man this year."

"Right," Mr. Summers said. He made a note on the list he was holding. Then he asked, "Watson boy drawing this year?"

A tall boy in the crowd raised his hand. "Here," he said. "I'm drawing for m'mother and me." He blinked his eyes nervously and ducked his head as several voices in the crowd said things like "Good fellow, Jack," and "Glad to see your mother's got a man to do it."

"Well," Mr. Summers said, "guess that's everyone. Old Man Warner make it?"

"Here," a voice said, and Mr. Summers nodded.

A sudden hush fell on the crowd as Mr. Summers cleared his throat and looked at the list. "All ready?" he called. "Now, I'll read the names—heads of families first—and the men come up and take a paper out of the box. Keep the paper folded in your hand without looking at it until everyone has had a turn. Everything clear?"

The people had done it so many times that they only half listened to the directions; most of them were quiet, wetting their lips, not looking around. Then Mr. Summers raised one hand high and said, "Adams." A man disengaged himself from the crowd and came forward. "Hi, Steve," Mr. Summers said, and Mr. Adams said, "Hi, Joe." They grinned at one another humorlessly and nervously. Then Mr. Adams reached into the black box and took out a folded paper. He held it firmly by one corner as he turned and went hastily back to his place in the crowd, where he stood a little apart from his family, not looking down at his hand.

"Allen," Mr. Summers said, "Anderson. . . . Bentham."

"Seems like there's no time at all between lotteries any more," Mrs. Delacroix said to Mrs. Graves in the back row. "Seems like we got through with the last one only last week."

"Time sure goes fast," Mrs. Graves said.

"Clark. . . . Delacroix."

"There goes my old man," Mrs. Delacroix said. She held her breath while her husband went forward.

"Dunbar," Mr. Summers said, and Mrs. Dunbar went steadily to the box while one of the women said, "Go on, Janey," and another said, "There she goes."

"We're next," Mrs. Graves said. She watched while Mr. Graves came around from the side of the box, greeted Mr. Summers gravely, and selected a slip of paper from the box. By now, all through the crowd there were men holding the small folded papers in their large hands, turning them over and over nervously. Mrs. Dunbar and her two sons stood together, Mrs. Dunbar holding the slip of paper.

"Harburt. . . . Hutchinson."

"Get up there, Bill," Mrs. Hutchinson said, and the people near her laughed.

"Jones."

"They do say," Mr. Adams said to Old Man Warner, who stood next to him, "that over in the north village they're talking of giving up the lottery."

Old Man Warner snorted. "Pack of crazy fools," he said. "Listening to the young folks, nothing's good enough for *them*. Next thing you know, they'll be wanting to go back to living in caves, nobody work any more, live *that* way for a while. Used to be a saying about 'Lottery in June, corn be heavy soon.' First thing you know, we'd all be eating stewed chickweed and acorns. There's *always* been a lottery," he added petulantly. "Bad enough to see young Joe Summers up there joking with everybody."

"Some places have already quit lotteries," Mrs. Adams said.

"Nothing but trouble in *that*," Old Man Warner said stoutly. "Pack of young fools."

"Martin." And Bobby Martin watched his father go forward. "Overdyke. . . . Percy."

"I wish they'd hurry," Mrs. Dunbar said to her older son. "I wish they'd hurry."

"They're almost through," her son said.

"You get ready to run tell Dad," Mrs. Dunbar said.

Mr. Summers called his own name and then stepped forward precisely and selected a slip from the box. Then he called, "Warner."

"Seventy-seventh year I been in the lottery," Old Man Warner said as he went through the crowd. "Seventy-seventh time."

"Watson." The tall boy came awkwardly through the crowd. Someone said, "Don't be nervous, Jack," and Mr. Summers said, "Take your time, son."

"Zanini."

After that, there was a long pause, a breathless pause, until Mr. Summers, holding his slip of paper in the air, said, "All right, fellows." For a minute, no one moved, and then all the slips of paper were opened. Suddenly, all the women began to speak at once, saying, "Who is it?" "Who's got it?" "Is it the Dunbars?" "Is it the Watsons?" Then the voices began to say, "It's Hutchinson. It's Bill," "Bill Hutchinson's got it."

"Go tell your father," Mrs. Dunbar said to her older son.

People began to look around to see the Hutchinsons. Bill Hutchinson was standing quiet, staring down at the paper in his hand. Suddenly, Tessie Hutchinson shouted to Mr. Summers, "You didn't give him time enough to take any paper he wanted. I saw you. It wasn't fair!"

"Be a good sport, Tessie," Mrs. Delacroix called, and Mrs. Graves said, "All of us took the same chance."

"Shut up, Tessie," Bill Hutchinson said.

"Well, everyone," Mr. Summers said, "that was done pretty fast, and now we've got to be hurrying a little more to get done in time." He consulted his next list. "Bill," he said, "you draw for the Hutchinson family. You got any other households in the Hutchinsons?"

"There's Don and Eva," Mrs. Hutchinson yelled. "Make *them* take their chance!"

"Daughters drew with their husbands' families, Tessie," Mr. Summers said gently. "You know that as well as anyone else."

"It wasn't *fair*," Tessie said.

"I guess not, Joe," Bill Hutchinson said regretfully. "My daughter draws with her husband's family, that's only fair. And I've got no other family except the kids."

"Then, as far as drawing for families is concerned, it's you," Mr. Summers said in explanation, "and as far as drawing for households is concerned, that's you, too. Right?"

"Right," Bill Hutchinson said.

"How many kids, Bill?" Mr. Summers asked formally.

"Three," Bill Hutchinson said. "There's Bill, Jr., and Nancy, and little Dave. And Tessie and me."

"All right, then," Mr. Summers said. "Harry, you got their tickets back?"

Mr. Graves nodded and held up the slips of paper. "Put them in the box, then," Mr. Summers directed. "Take Bill's and put it in."

"I think we ought to start over," Mrs. Hutchinson said, as quietly as she could. "I tell you it wasn't *fair*. You didn't give him time enough to choose. *Every*body saw that."

Mr. Graves had selected the five slips and put them in the box, and he dropped all the papers but those onto the ground, where the breeze caught them and lifted them off.

"Listen, everybody," Mrs. Hutchinson was saying to the people around her.

"Ready, Bill?" Mr. Summers asked, and Bill Hutchinson, with one quick glance around at his wife and children, nodded.

"Remember," Mr. Summers said, "take the slips and keep them folded until each person has taken one. Harry, you help little Dave." Mr. Graves took the hand of the little boy, who came willingly with him up to the box. "Take a paper out of the box, Davy," Mr. Summers said. Davy put his hand into the box and laughed. "Take just *one* paper," Mr. Summers said. "Harry, you hold it for him." Mr. Graves took the child's hand and removed the folded paper from the tight fist and held it while little Dave stood next to him and looked up at him wonderingly.

"Nancy next," Mr. Summers said. Nancy was twelve, and her school friends breathed heavily as she went forward, switching her skirt, and took a slip daintily from the box. "Bill, Jr.," Mr. Summers said, and Billy, his face red and his feet overlarge, nearly knocked the box over as he got a paper out. "Tessie," Mr. Summers said. She hesitated for a minute, looking around defiantly, and then set her lips and went up to the box. She snatched a paper out and held it behind her.

"Bill," Mr. Summers said, and Bill Hutchinson reached into the box and felt around, bringing his hand out at last with the slip of paper in it.

The crowd was quiet. A girl whispered, "I hope it's not Nancy," and the sound of the whisper reached the edges of the crowd.

"It's not the way it used to be," Old Man Warner said clearly. "People ain't the way they used to be."

"All right," Mr. Summers said. "Open the papers. Harry, you open little Dave's."

Mr. Graves opened the slip of paper and there was a general sigh through the crowd as he held it up and everyone could see that it was blank. Nancy and Bill, Jr., opened theirs at the same time, and both beamed and laughed, turning around to the crowd and holding their slips of paper above their heads.

"Tessie," Mr. Summers said. There was a pause, and then Mr. Summers looked at Bill Hutchinson, and Bill unfolded his paper and showed it. It was blank.

"It's Tessie," Mr. Summers said, and his voice was hushed. "Show us her paper, Bill."

Bill Hutchinson went over to his wife and forced the slip of paper out of her hand. It had a black spot on it, the black spot Mr. Summers had made the night before with the heavy pencil in the coal-company office. Bill Hutchinson held it up and there was a stir in the crowd.

"All right, folks," Mr. Summers said. "Let's finish quickly."

Although the villagers had forgotten the ritual and lost the original black box, they still remembered to use stones. The pile of stones the boys had made earlier was ready; there were stones on the ground with the blowing scraps of paper that had come out of the box. Mrs. Delacroix selected a stone so large she had to pick it up with both hands and turned to Mrs. Dunbar. "Come on," she said. "Hurry up."

Mrs. Dunbar had small stones in both hands, and she said, gasping for breath, "I can't run at all. You'll have to go ahead and I'll catch up with you."

The children had stones already, and someone gave little Davy Hutchinson a few pebbles.

Tessie Hutchinson was in the center of a cleared space by now, and she held her hands out desperately as the villagers moved in on her. "It isn't fair," she said. A stone hit her on the side of the head.

Old Man Warner was saying, "Come on, come on, everyone." Steve Adams was in the front of the crowd of villagers, with Mrs. Graves beside him.

"It isn't fair, it isn't right," Mrs. Hutchinson screamed and then they were upon her.

COMMENTARY

SHIRLEY JACKSON

Shirley Jackson wrote this "biography of a story" in 1960 as a lecture to be delivered before reading "The Lottery" to college audiences. After her death it was included in *Come Along with Me* (1968), edited by her husband, Stanley Edgar Hyman. The lecture also contained extensive quotations from letters she had received from readers who took the story literally. These so disgusted Jackson that she promised her listeners at the conclusion of her talk, "I am out of the lottery business for good."

The Morning of June 28, 1948, and "The Lottery" 1968

On the morning of June 28, 1948, I walked down to the post office in our little Vermont town to pick up the mail. I was quite casual about it, as I recall—I opened the box, took out a couple of bills and a letter or two, talked to the postmaster for a few minutes, and left, never supposing that it was the last time for months that I was to pick up the mail without an active feeling of panic. By the next week I had had to change my mailbox to the largest one in the post office, and casual conversation with the postmaster was out of the question, because he wasn't speaking to me. June 28, 1948, was the day *The New Yorker* came out with a story of mine in it. It was not my first published story, nor my last, but I have been assured over and over that if it had been the only story I ever wrote or published, there would be people who would not forget my name.

I had written the story three weeks before, on a bright June morning when summer seemed to have come at last, with blue skies and warm sun and no heavenly signs to warn me that my morning's work was anything but just another story. The idea had come to me while I was pushing my daughter up the hill in her stroller—it was, as I say, a warm morning, and the hill was steep, and beside my daughter the stroller held the day's groceries—and perhaps the effort of that last fifty yards up the hill put an edge to the story; at any rate, I had the idea fairly clearly in my mind when I put my daughter in her playpen and the frozen vegetables in the refrigerator, and, writing the story, I found that it went quickly and easily, moving from beginning to end without pause. As a matter of fact, when I read it over later I decided that except for one or two minor corrections, it needed no changes, and the story I finally typed up and sent off to my agent the next day was almost word for word the original draft. This, as any writer of stories can tell you, is not a usual thing. All I know is that when I came to read the story over I felt strongly that I didn't want to fuss with it. I didn't think it was perfect, but I didn't want to fuss with it. It was, I thought, a serious, straightforward story, and I was pleased and a little surprised at the ease with which it had been written; I was reasonably proud of it, and hoped that my agent would sell it to some magazine and I would have the gratification of seeing it in print.

My agent did not care for the story, but—as she said in her note at the time—her job was to sell it, not to like it. She sent it at once to *The New Yorker*, and about a week after the story had been written I received a telephone call from the fiction editor of *The New Yorker;* it was quite clear that he did not really care for the story, either, but *The New Yorker* was going to buy it. He asked for one change—that the date mentioned in the story be changed to coincide with the date of the issue of the magazine in which the story would appear, and I said of course. He then asked, hesitantly, if I had any particular interpretation of my own for the story; Mr. Harold Ross, then the editor of *The New Yorker*, was not altogether sure that he understood the story, and wondered if I cared to enlarge upon its meaning. I said no. Mr. Ross, he said, thought that the story might be puzzling to some people, and in case anyone telephoned the magazine, as sometimes happened, or wrote in asking about the story, was there anything in particular I wanted them to say? No, I said, nothing in particular; it was just a story I wrote.

I had no more preparation than that. I went on picking up the mail every morning, pushing my daughter up and down the hill in her stroller, anticipating pleasurably the check from *The New Yorker*, and shopping for groceries. The weather stayed nice and it looked as though it was going to be a good summer. Then, on June 28, *The New Yorker* came out with my story.

Things began mildly enough with a note from a friend at *The New Yorker:* "Your story has kicked up quite a fuss around the office," he wrote. I was flattered; it's nice to think that your friends notice what you write. Later that day there was a call from one of the magazine's editors; they had had a couple of people phone in about my story, he said, and was there anything I particularly wanted him to say if there were any more calls? No, I said, nothing particular; anything he chose to say was perfectly all right with me; it was just a story.

I was further puzzled by a cryptic note from another friend: "Heard a man talking about a story of yours on the bus this morning," she wrote. "Very exciting. I wanted to tell him I knew the author, but after I heard what he was saying I decided I'd better not."

One of the most terrifying aspects of publishing stories and books is the realization that they are going to be read, and read by strangers. I had never fully realized this before, although I had of course in my imagination dwelt lovingly upon the thought of the millions and millions of people who were going to be uplifted and enriched and delighted by the stories I wrote. It had simply never occurred to me that these millions and millions of people might be so far from being uplifted that they would sit down and write me letters I was downright scared to open; of the three-hundred-odd letters that I received that summer I can count only thirteen that spoke kindly to me, and they were mostly from friends. Even my mother scolded me: "Dad and I did not care at all for your story in *The New Yorker*," she wrote sternly, "it does seem, dear, that this gloomy kind of story is what all you young people think about these days. Why don't you write something to cheer people up?"

By mid-July I had begun to perceive that I was very lucky indeed to be safely in Vermont, where no one in our small town had ever heard of *The New Yorker*, much less read my story. Millions of people, and my mother, had taken a pronounced dislike to me.

The magazine kept no track of telephone calls, but all letters addressed to me care of the magazine were forwarded directly to me for answering, and all letters addressed to the magazine—some of them addressed to Harold Ross personally; these were the most vehement—were answered at the magazine and then the letters were sent me in great batches, along with carbons of the answers written at the magazine. I have all the letters still, and if they could be considered to give any accurate cross section of the reading public, or the reading public of *The New Yorker*, or even the reading public of one issue of *The New Yorker*, I would stop writing now.

Judging from these letters, people who read stories are gullible, rude, frequently illiterate, and horribly afraid of being laughed at. Many of the writers were positive that *The New Yorker* was going to ridicule them in print, and the most cautious letters were headed, in capital letters: NOT FOR PUBLICATION or PLEASE DO NOT PRINT THIS LETTER, or, at best, THIS LETTER MAY BE PUBLISHED AT YOUR USUAL RATES OF PAYMENT. Anonymous letters, of which there were a few, were destroyed. *The New Yorker* never published any comment of any kind about the story in the magazine, but did issue one publicity release saying that the story had received more mail than any piece of fiction they had ever published; this was after the newspapers had gotten into the act, in midsummer, with a front-page story in the San Francisco *Chronicle* begging to know what the story meant, and a series of columns in New York and Chicago papers pointing out that *New Yorker* subscriptions were being canceled right and left.

Curiously, there are three main themes which dominate the letters of that first summer—three themes which might be identified as bewilderment, speculation, and plain old-fashioned abuse. In the years since then, during which the story has been anthologized, dramatized, televised, and even—in one completely mystifying transformation—made into a ballet, the tenor of letters I receive has changed. I am addressed more politely, as a rule, and the letters largely confine themselves to questions like what does this story mean? The general tone of the early letters, however, was a kind of wide-eyed, shocked innocence. People at first were not so much concerned with what the story meant; what they wanted to know was where these lotteries were held, and whether they could go there and watch.

SARAH ORNE JEWETT

Sarah Orne Jewett (1849–1909) was born in South Berwick, Maine. Her father was a country doctor, and she often accompanied him on his horse-and-buggy rounds among sick people on the local farms. She later said that she got her real education from these trips, rather than from her classes at Miss Rayne's School and the Berwick Academy. She had a fine ear for local speech and the native idiom, which she used to good effect in her stories. Impressed as a girl by the sympathetic depiction of *local color* (the people and life of a particular geographical setting) in the fiction of Harriet Beecher Stowe, Jewett began to write stories herself, publishing her earliest one, "Jenny Garrow's Lovers," in a Boston weekly when she was eighteen years old. Shortly after her twentieth birthday, her work was accepted by the prestigious *Atlantic Monthly*, and her career was launched. Jewett published her first collection of stories, *Deephaven*, in 1877. She read the work of Gustave Flaubert, Émile Zola, Leo Tolstoy, and Henry James, and her style gradually matured, as is evident in the stories that make up the 1886 volume *A White Heron and Other Stories*.

Jewett took her favorite motto from Flaubert: "One should write of ordinary life as if one were writing history." Her masterpiece, *The Country of the Pointed Firs* (1896), is a book of scrupulously observed short sketches linked by the narrator's account of her stay in a Maine seacoast village and her growing involvement in the quiet lives of its people. Many stories were written about New England in Jewett's time, but hers have a unique quality stemming from her deep sympathy for the native characters and her ear for local speech. Once she laughingly told the younger writer Willa Cather that her head was full of dear old houses and dear old women, and when an old house and an old woman came together in her brain with a click, she knew a story was under way.

Although it is true that Jewett's realism heightens the attractive aspects of the rural New England character at the same time that it diminishes the harsher qualities, her literary technique is so candid and true to the larger aspects of human nature that the darker undercurrents of deprivation, both physical and psychological, are evident beneath the surface of her descriptions. Henry James recognized that Jewett was "surpassed only by Hawthorne as producer of the most finished and penetrating of the numerous 'short stories' that have the domestic life of New England for their general and their doubtless somewhat lean subject." In her time she was lauded for possessing an exquisitely simple, natural, and graceful style; now she is regarded as our most distinguished American regionalist writer, as evidenced by "A White Heron."

A White Heron 1886

I

The woods were already filled with shadows one June evening, just before eight o'clock, though a bright sunset still glimmered faintly among the trunks of the trees. A little girl was driving home her cow, a plodding, dilatory, provoking creature in her behavior, but a valued companion for all that. They were going away from whatever light there was, and striking deep into the woods, but their feet were familiar with the path, and it was no matter whether their eyes could see it or not.

There was hardly a night the summer through when the old cow could be found waiting at the pasture bars; on the contrary, it was her greatest pleasure to hide herself away among the huckleberry bushes, and though she wore a loud bell she had made the discovery that if one stood perfectly still it would not ring. So Sylvia had to hunt for her until she found her, and call Co'! Co'! with never an answering Moo, until her childish patience was quite spent. If the creature had not given good milk and plenty of it, the case would have seemed very different to her owners. Besides, Sylvia had all the time there was, and very little use to make of it. Sometimes in pleasant weather it was a consolation to look upon the cow's pranks as an intelligent attempt to play hide and seek, and as the child had no playmates she lent herself to this amusement with a good deal of zest. Though this chase had been so long that the wary animal herself had given an unusual signal of her whereabouts, Sylvia had only laughed when she came upon Mistress Moolly at the swampside, and urged her affectionately homeward with a twig of birch leaves. The old cow was not inclined to wander farther, she even turned in the right direction for once as they left the pasture, and stepped along the road at a good pace. She was quite ready to be milked now, and seldom stopped to browse. Sylvia wondered what her grandmother would say because they were so late. It was a great while since she had left home at half-past five o'clock, but everybody knew the difficulty of making this errand a short one. Mrs. Tilley had chased the hornéd torment too many summer evenings herself to blame any one else for lingering, and was only thankful as she waited that she had Sylvia, nowadays, to give such valuable assistance. The good woman suspected that Sylvia loitered occasionally on her own account; there never was such a child for straying about out-of-doors since the world was made! Everybody said that it was a good change for a little maid who had tried to grow for eight years in a crowded manufacturing town, but, as for Sylvia herself, it seemed as if she never had been alive at all before she came to live at the farm. She thought often with wistful compassion of a wretched geranium that belonged to a town neighbor.

"'Afraid of folks,'" old Mrs. Tilley said to herself, with a smile, after she had made the unlikely choice of Sylvia from her daughter's houseful of children, and was returning to the farm. "'Afraid of folks,' they said! I guess she won't be troubled no great with 'em up to the old place!" When they reached the door of the lonely house and stopped to unlock it, and the cat came to purr loudly, and rub against them, a deserted pussy, indeed, but fat with young robins, Sylvia whispered that this was a beautiful place to live in, and she never should wish to go home.

The companions followed the shady wood-road, the cow taking slow steps and the child very fast ones. The cow stopped long at the brook to drink, as if the pasture were not half a swamp, and Sylvia stood still and waited, letting her bare feet cool themselves in the shoal water, while the great twilight moths struck softly against her. She waded on through the brook as the cow moved away, and listened to the thrushes with a heart that beat fast with pleasure. There was a stirring in the great boughs overhead. They were full of little birds and beasts that seemed to be wide awake, and going about their world, or else saying good-night to each other in sleepy twitters. Sylvia herself felt sleepy as she walked along. However, it was not much farther to the house, and the air was soft and sweet. She was not often in the woods so late as this, and it made her feel as if she were a part of the gray shadows and the moving leaves. She was just thinking how long it seemed since she first came to the farm a year ago, and wondering if everything went on in the noisy town just the same as when she was there; the thought of the great red-faced boy who used to chase and frighten her made her hurry along the path to escape from the shadow of the trees.

Suddenly this little woods-girl is horror-stricken to hear a clear whistle not very far away. Not a bird's-whistle, which would have a sort of friendliness, but a boy's whistle, determined, and somewhat aggressive. Sylvia left the cow to whatever sad fate might await her, and stepped discreetly aside into the bushes, but she was just too late. The enemy had discovered her, and called out in a very cheerful and persuasive tone, "Halloa, little girl, how far is it to the road?" and trembling Sylvia answered almost inaudibly, "A good ways."

She did not dare to look boldly at the tall young man, who carried a gun over his shoulder, but she came out of her bush and again followed the cow, while he walked alongside.

"I have been hunting for some birds," the stranger said kindly, "and I have lost my way, and need a friend very much. Don't be afraid," he added gallantly. "Speak up and tell me what your name is, and whether you think I can spend the night at your house, and go out gunning early in the morning."

Sylvia was more alarmed than before. Would not her grandmother consider her much to blame? But who could have foreseen such an accident as this? It did not seem to be her fault, and she hung her head as if the stem of it were broken, but managed to answer "Sylvy," with much effort when her companion again asked her name.

Mrs. Tilley was standing in the doorway when the trio came into view. The cow gave a loud moo by way of explanation.

"Yes, you'd better speak up for yourself, you old trial! Where'd she tucked herself away this time, Sylvy?" But Sylvia kept an awed silence; she knew by instinct that her grandmother did not comprehend the gravity of the situation. She must be mistaking the stranger for one of the farmer-lads of the region.

The young man stood his gun beside the door, and dropped a lumpy game-bag beside it; then he bade Mrs. Tilley good-evening, and repeated his wayfarer's story, and asked if he could have a night's lodging.

"Put me anywhere you like," he said. "I must be off early in the morning, before day; but I am very hungry, indeed. You can give me some milk at any rate, that's plain."

"Dear sakes, yes," responded the hostess, whose long slumbering hospitality seemed to be easily awakened. "You might fare better if you went out to the main road a mile or so, but you're welcome to what we've got. I'll milk right off, and you make yourself at home. You can sleep on husks or feathers," she proffered graciously. "I raised them all myself. There's good pasturing for geese just below here towards the ma'sh. Now step round and set a plate for the gentleman, Sylvy!" And Sylvia promptly stepped. She was glad to have something to do, and she was hungry herself.

It was a surprise to find so clean and comfortable a little dwelling in this New England wilderness. The young man had known the horrors of its most primitive housekeeping, and the dreary squalor of that level of society which does not rebel at the companionship of hens. This was the best thrift of an old-fashioned farmstead, though on such a small scale that it seemed like a hermitage. He listened eagerly to the old woman's quaint talk, he watched Sylvia's pale face and shining gray eyes with ever growing enthusiasm, and insisted that this was the best supper he had eaten for a month, and afterward the new-made friends sat down in the door-way together while the moon came up.

Soon it would be berry-time, and Sylvia was a great help at picking. The cow was a good milker, though a plaguy thing to keep track of, the hostess gossiped frankly, adding presently that she had buried four children, so Sylvia's mother, and a son (who might be dead) in California were all the children she had left. "Dan, my boy, was a great hand to go gunning," she explained sadly. "I never wanted for pa'tridges or gray squer'ls while he was to home. He's been a great wand'rer, I expect, and he's no hand to write letters. There, I don't blame him, I'd ha' seen the world myself if it had been so I could."

"Sylvy takes after him," the grandmother continued affectionately, after a minute's pause. "There ain't a foot o' ground she don't know her way over, and the wild creaturs counts her one o' themselves. Squer'ls she'll tame to come an' feed right out o' her hands, and all sorts o' birds. Last winter she got the jay-birds to bangeing° here, and I believe she'd 'a' scanted herself of her own meals to have plenty to throw out amongst 'em, if I hadn't kep' watch. Anything but crows, I tell her, I'm willin' to help support—though Dan he had a tamed one o' them that did seem to have reason same as folks. It was round here a good spell after he went away. Dan an' his father they didn't hitch,—but he never held up his head ag'in after Dan had dared him an' gone off."

The guest did not notice this hint of family sorrows in his eager interest in something else.

"So Sylvy knows all about birds, does she?" he exclaimed, as he looked round at the little girl who sat, very demure but increasingly sleepy, in the moonlight. "I am making a collection of birds myself. I have been at it ever since I was a boy." (Mrs. Tilley smiled.) "There are two or three very rare ones I have been hunting for these five years. I mean to get them on my own ground if they can be found."

"Do you cage 'em up?" asked Mrs. Tilley doubtfully, in response to this enthusiastic announcement.

"Oh no, they're stuffed and preserved, dozens and dozens of them," said the ornithologist, "and I have shot or snared every one myself. I caught a glimpse of a white heron a few miles from here on Saturday, and I have followed it in this direction. They have never been found in this district at all. The little white heron, it is," and he turned again to look at Sylvia with the hope of discovering that the rare bird was one of her acquaintances.

But Sylvia was watching a hop-toad in the narrow footpath.

"You would know the heron if you saw it," the stranger continued eagerly. "A queer tall white bird with soft feathers and long thin legs. And it would have a nest perhaps in the top of a high tree, made of sticks, something like a hawk's nest."

Sylvia's heart gave a wild beat; she knew that strange white bird, and had once stolen softly near where it stood in some bright green swamp grass, away

---

bangeing: Maine dialect word for hanging about.

over at the other side of the woods. There was an open place where the sunshine always seemed strangely yellow and hot, where tall, nodding rushes grew, and her grandmother had warned her that she might sink in the soft black mud underneath and never be heard of more. Not far beyond were the salt marshes just this side the sea itself, which Sylvia wondered and dreamed much about, but never had seen, whose great voice could sometimes be heard above the noise of the woods on stormy nights.

"I can't think of anything I should like so much as to find that heron's nest," the handsome stranger was saying. "I would give ten dollars to anybody who could show it to me," he added desperately, "and I mean to spend my whole vacation hunting for it if need be. Perhaps it was only migrating, or had been chased out of its own region by some bird of prey."

Mrs. Tilley gave amazed attention to all this, but Sylvia still watched the toad, not divining, as she might have done at some calmer time, that the creature wished to get to its hole under the door-step, and was much hindered by the unusual spectators at that hour of the evening. No amount of thought, that night, could decide how many wished-for treasures the ten dollars, so lightly spoken of, would buy.

The next day the young sportsman hovered about the woods, and Sylvia kept him company, having lost her first fear of the friendly lad, who proved to be most kind and sympathetic. He told her many things about the birds and what they knew and where they lived and what they did with themselves. And he gave her a jack-knife, which she thought as great a treasure as if she were a desert-islander. All day long he did not once make her troubled or afraid except when he brought down some unsuspecting singing creature from its bough. Sylvia would have liked him vastly better without his gun; she could not understand why he killed the very birds he seemed to like so much. But as the day waned, Sylvia still watched the young man with loving admiration. She had never seen anybody so charming and delightful; the woman's heart, asleep in the child, was vaguely thrilled by a dream of love. Some premonition of that great power stirred and swayed these young creatures who traversed the solemn woodlands with soft-footed silent care. They stopped to listen to a bird's song; they pressed forward again eagerly, parting the branches—speaking to each other rarely and in whispers; the young man going first and Sylvia following, fascinated, a few steps behind, with her gray eyes dark with excitement.

She grieved because the longed-for white heron was elusive, but she did not lead the guest, she only followed, and there was no such thing as speaking first. The sound of her own unquestioned voice would have terrified her—it was hard enough to answer yes or no when there was need of that. At last evening began to fall, and they drove the cow home together, and Sylvia smiled with pleasure when they came to the place where she heard the whistle and was afraid only the night before.

II

Half a mile from home, at the farther edge of the woods, where the land was highest, a great pine-tree stood, the last of its generation. Whether it was left for a boundary mark, or for what reason, no one could say; the wood-choppers who had felled its mates were dead and gone long ago, and a whole forest of sturdy trees, pines and oaks and maples, had grown again. But the stately head of this old pine towered above them all and made a landmark for sea and shore miles and miles away. Sylvia knew it well. She had always believed that whoever climbed to the top of it could see the ocean; and the little girl had often laid her hand on the great rough trunk and looked up wistfully at those dark boughs that the wind always stirred, no matter how hot and still the air might be below. Now she thought of the tree with a new excitement, for why, if one climbed it at break of day could not one see all the world, and easily discover from whence the white heron flew, and mark the place, and find the hidden nest?

What a spirit of adventure, what wild ambition! What fancied triumph and delight and glory for the later morning when she could make known the secret! It was almost too real and too great for the childish heart to bear.

All night the door of the little house stood open and the whippoorwills came and sang upon the very step. The young sportsman and his old hostess were sound asleep, but Sylvia's great design kept her broad awake and watching. She forgot to think of sleep. The short summer night seemed as long as the winter darkness, and at last when the whippoorwills ceased, and she was afraid the morning would after all come too soon, she stole out of the house and followed the pasture path through the woods, hastening toward the open ground beyond, listening with a sense of comfort and companionship to the drowsy twitter of a half-awakened bird, whose perch she had jarred in passing. Alas, if the great wave of human interest which flooded for the first time this dull little life should sweep away the satisfactions of an existence heart to heart with nature and the dumb life of the forest!

There was the huge tree asleep yet in the paling moonlight, and small and silly Sylvia began with utmost bravery to mount to the top of it, with tingling, eager blood coursing the channels of her whole frame, with her bare feet and fingers, that pinched and held like bird's claws to the monstrous ladder reaching up, up, almost to the sky itself. First she must mount the white oak tree that grew alongside, where she was almost lost among the dark branches and the green leaves heavy and wet with dew; a bird fluttered off its nest, and a red squirrel ran to and fro and scolded pettishly at the harmless housebreaker. Sylvia felt her way easily. She had often climbed there, and knew that higher still one of the oak's upper branches chafed against the pine trunk, just where its lower boughs were set close together. There, when she made the dangerous pass from one tree to the other, the great enterprise would really begin.

She crept out along the swaying oak limb at last, and took the daring step across into the old pine-tree. The way was harder than she thought; she must reach far and hold fast, the sharp dry twigs caught and held her and scratched her like angry talons, the pitch made her thin little fingers clumsy and stiff as she went round and round the tree's great stem, higher and higher upward. The sparrows and robins in the woods below were beginning to wake and twitter to the dawn, yet it seemed much lighter there aloft in the pine-tree, and the child knew she must hurry if her project were to be of any use.

The tree seemed to lengthen itself out as she went up, and to reach farther and farther upward. It was like a great main-mast to the voyaging earth; it must truly have been amazed that morning through all its ponderous frame as it felt this determined spark of human spirit wending its way from higher branch to branch. Who knows how steadily the least twigs held themselves to advantage this light, weak creature on her way! The old pine must have loved his new dependent. More than all the hawks, and bats, and moths, and even the sweet voiced thrushes, was the brave, beating heart of the solitary gray-eyed child. And the tree stood still and frowned away the winds that June morning while the dawn grew bright in the east.

Sylvia's face was like a pale star, if one had seen it from the ground, when the last thorny bough was past, and she stood trembling and tired but wholly triumphant, high in the tree-top. Yes, there was the sea with the dawning sun making a golden dazzle over it, and toward that glorious east flew two hawks with slow-moving pinions. How low they looked in the air from that height when one had only seen them before far up, and dark against the blue sky. Their gray feathers were as soft as moths; they seemed only a little way from the tree, and Sylvia felt as if she too could go flying away among the clouds. Westward, the woodlands and farms reached miles and miles into the distance; here and there were church steeples, and white villages, truly it was a vast and awesome world!

The birds sang louder and louder. At last the sun came up bewilderingly bright. Sylvia could see the white sails of ships out at sea, and the clouds that were purple and rose-colored and yellow at first began to fade away. Where was the white heron's nest in the sea of green branches, and was this wonderful sight and pageant of the world the only reward for having climbed to such a giddy height? Now look down again, Sylvia, where the green marsh is set among the shining birches and dark hemlocks; there where you saw the white heron once you will see him again; look, look! a white spot of him like a single floating feather comes up from the dead hemlock and grows larger, and rises, and comes close at last, and goes by the landmark pine with steady sweep of wing and outstretched slender neck and crested head. And wait! wait! do not move a foot or a finger, little girl, do not send an arrow of light and consciousness from your two eager eyes, for the heron has perched on a pine bough not far beyond yours, and cries back to his mate on the nest and plumes his feathers for the new day!

The child gives a long sigh a minute later when a company of shouting cat-birds comes also to the tree, and vexed by their fluttering and lawlessness the solemn heron goes away. She knows his secret now, the wild, light, slender bird that floats and wavers, and goes back like an arrow presently to his home in the green world beneath. Then Sylvia, well satisfied, makes her perilous way down again, not daring to look far below the branch she stands on, ready to cry sometimes because her fingers ache and her lamed feet slip. Wondering over and over again what the stranger would say to her, and what he would think when she told him how to find his way straight to the heron's nest.

"Sylvy, Sylvy!" called the busy old grandmother again and again, but nobody answered, and the small husk bed was empty and Sylvia had disappeared.

The guest waked from a dream, and remembering his day's pleasure hurried to dress himself that might it sooner begin. He was sure from the way the shy little girl looked once or twice yesterday that she had at least seen the white heron, and now she must really be made to tell. Here she comes now, paler than ever, and her worn old frock is torn and tattered, and smeared with pine pitch. The grandmother and the sportsman stand in the door together and question her, and the splendid moment has come to speak of the dead hemlock-tree by the green marsh.

But Sylvia does not speak after all, though the old grandmother fretfully rebukes her, and the young man's kind, appealing eyes are looking straight in her own. He can make them rich with money; he has promised it, and they are poor now. He is so well worth making happy, and he waits to hear the story she can tell.

No, she must keep silence! What is it that suddenly forbids her and makes her dumb? Has she been nine years growing and now, when the great world for the first time puts out a hand to her, must she thrust it aside for a bird's sake? The murmur of the pine's green branches is in her ears, she remembers how the white heron came flying through the golden air and how they watched the sea and the morning together, and Sylvia cannot speak; she cannot tell the heron's secret and give its life away.

Dear loyalty, that suffered a sharp pang as the guest went away disappointed later in the day, that could have served and followed him and loved him as a dog loves! Many a night Sylvia heard the echo of his whistle haunting the pasture path as she came home with the loitering cow. She forgot even her sorrow at the sharp report of his gun and the sight of thrushes and sparrows dropping silent to the ground, their songs hushed and their pretty feathers stained and wet with blood. Were the birds better friends than their hunter might have been—who can tell? Whatever treasures were lost to her, woodlands and summer-time, remember! Bring your gifts and graces and tell your secrets to this lonely country child!

HA JIN

Ha Jin (b. 1956) was born Xuefei Jin in mainland China shortly before the start of the Cultural Revolution, which closed schools and colleges throughout the country. The son of an army officer, he volunteered at age fourteen for the army and served for nearly five years on the Russian border. He recalls that "In the beginning, I was basically illiterate. I couldn't read. Then in the second year, the border calmed down. We knew there would be no war, we would live in peace, and I began to think of education." Working as a telegrapher at a railroad company, he taught himself English from a radio course of study. In 1977, when colleges reopened in China, he left the army and enrolled as an English major at a university in Harbin. Jin earned a B.A. in English in 1981 and an M.A. in 1984. The next year he left China to become a doctoral student at Brandeis

University, intending to return to China as an English teacher and translator. The atrocity of the June 4, 1989, massacre at Tiananmen Square, where Chinese soldiers killed dissident students and civilians demonstrating against the repressive government, convinced him that he should stay in America with his Chinese wife and son. Jin said he became an American citizen because he felt he could never write honestly in China.

Accepting permanent exile, Jin began writing poetry and fiction in English at Brandeis, where he completed his doctorate in 1993. Under the pen name Ha Jin, he published his first book of poetry, *Between Silences*, in 1990. Working as a busboy, waiter, and night watchman because he couldn't find a job teaching Chinese literature, Jin supported his family while writing short stories. *Ocean of Words* (1996), his first story collection, won the PEN/Hemingway Award, while *Under the Red Flag* (1997) received the Flannery O'Connor Award for Short Fiction. Jin's novella *In the Pond* (1998) was selected as the best fiction book of that year by the *Chicago Tribune*. His short stories were included in *The Best American Short Stories* (1997 and 1999) and three Pushcart Prize anthologies. His novel *Waiting* won both the 1999 National Book Award for Fiction and the 2000 PEN/Faulkner Award. His novel *War Trash* was published in 2004. In 2008 he published an essay collection, *The Writer as Migrant. A Good Fall* (2009) is a recent collection of short stories.

Jin has told the interviewer Rich Rennicks that he feels "more at home" writing short fiction than poetry or novels.

> Poetry largely depends on luck. You never know when you can write the next poem. As for a novel, you need time and leisure – which I don't often have. You have to let yourself live in the novel for a long time, possessed by the characters. When I am teaching, this is difficult. But short fiction is possible. You can work on a story intensely for two or three hours a day, then go to teach your class.

Jin currently teaches at Boston University. In stories such as "Saboteur," he has stated that he is not attempting to explain Chinese culture to his Western readers. He believes that "at heart we are all the same. Literature operates on the principle of similarity and identity, not on difference." This story is from Jin's collection *The Bridegroom* and was included in the 2000 edition of *The Best American Short Stories.*

Saboteur

2000

Mr. Chiu and his bride were having lunch in the square before Muji Train Station. On the table between them were two bottles of soda spewing out brown foam and two paper boxes of rice and sautéed cucumber and pork. "Let's eat," he said to her, and broke the connected ends of the chopsticks. He picked up a slice of streaky pork and put it into his mouth. As he was chewing, a few crinkles appeared on his thin jaw.

To his right, at another table, two railroad policemen were drinking tea and laughing; it seemed that the stout, middle-aged man was telling a joke to his young comrade, who was tall and of athletic build. Now and again they would steal a glance at Mr. Chiu's table.

The air smelled of rotten melon. A few flies kept buzzing above the couple's lunch. Hundreds of people were rushing around to get on the platform or to catch buses to downtown. Food and fruit vendors were crying for customers in lazy voices. About a dozen young women, representing the local hotels, held up placards which displayed the daily prices and words as large as a palm, like FREE MEALS, AIR-CONDITIONING, and ON THE RIVER. In the center of the square stood a concrete statue of Chairman Mao, at whose feet peasants were napping, their backs on the warm granite and their faces toward the sunny sky. A flock of pigeons perched on the Chairman's raised hand and forearm.

The rice and cucumber tasted good, and Mr. Chiu was eating unhurriedly. His sallow face showed exhaustion. He was glad that the honeymoon was finally over and that he and his bride were heading back for Harbin. During the two weeks' vacation, he had been worried about his liver, because three months ago he had suffered from acute hepatitis; he was afraid he might have a relapse. But he had had no severe symptoms, despite his liver being still big and tender. On the whole he was pleased with his health, which could endure even the strain of a honeymoon; indeed, he was on the course of recovery. He looked at his bride, who took off her wire glasses, kneading the root of her nose with her fingertips. Beads of sweat coated her pale cheeks.

"Are you all right, sweetheart?" he asked.

"I have a headache. I didn't sleep well last night."

"Take an aspirin, will you?"

"It's not that serious. Tomorrow is Sunday and I can sleep in. Don't worry."

As they were talking, the stout policeman at the next table stood up and threw a bowl of tea in their direction. Both Mr. Chiu's and his bride's sandals were wet instantly.

"Hooligan!" she said in a low voice.

Mr. Chiu got to his feet and said out loud, "Comrade Policeman, why did you do this?" He stretched out his right foot to show the wet sandal.

"Do what?" the stout man asked huskily, glaring at Mr. Chiu while the young fellow was whistling.

"See, you dumped tea on our feet."

"You're lying. You wet your shoes yourself."

"Comrade Policemen, your duty is to keep order, but you purposely tortured us common citizens. Why violate the law you are supposed to enforce?" As Mr. Chiu was speaking, dozens of people began gathering around.

With a wave of his hand, the man said to the young fellow, "Let's get hold of him!"

They grabbed Mr. Chiu and clamped handcuffs around his wrists. He cried, "You can't do this to me. This is utterly unreasonable."

"Shut up!" The man pulled out his pistol. "You can use your tongue at our headquarters."

The young fellow added, "You're a saboteur, you know that? You're disrupting public order."

The bride was too petrified to say anything coherent. She was a recent college graduate, had majored in fine arts, and had never seen the police make an arrest. All she could say was, "Oh, please, please!"

The policemen were pulling Mr. Chiu, but he refused to go with them, holding the corner of the table and shouting, "We have a train to catch. We already bought the tickets."

The stout man punched him in the chest. "Shut up. Let your ticket expire." With the pistol butt he chopped Mr. Chiu's hands, which at once released the table. Together the two men were dragging him away to the police station.

Realizing he had to go with them, Mr. Chiu turned his head and shouted to his bride, "Don't wait for me here. Take the train. If I'm not back by tomorrow morning, send someone over to get me out."

She nodded, covering her sobbing mouth with her palm.

After removing his belt, they locked Mr. Chiu into a cell in the back of the Railroad Police Station. The single window in the room was blocked by six steel bars; it faced a spacious yard, in which stood a few pines. Beyond the trees, two swings hung from an iron frame, swaying gently in the breeze. Somewhere in the building a cleaver was chopping rhythmically. There must be a kitchen upstairs, Mr. Chiu thought.

He was too exhausted to worry about what they would do to him, so he lay down on the narrow bed and shut his eyes. He wasn't afraid. The Cultural Revolution was over already, and recently the Party had been propagating the idea that all citizens were equal before the law. The police ought to be a law-abiding model for common people. As long as he remained coolheaded and reasoned with them, they probably wouldn't harm him.

Late in the afternoon he was taken to the Interrogation Bureau on the second floor. On his way there, in the stairwell, he ran into the middle-aged policeman who had manhandled him. The man grinned, rolling his bulgy eyes and pointing his fingers at him as if firing a pistol. Egg of a tortoise! Mr. Chiu cursed mentally.

The moment he sat down in the office, he burped, his palm shielding his mouth. In front of him, across a long desk, sat the chief of the bureau and a donkey-faced man. On the glass desktop was a folder containing information on his case. He felt it bizarre that in just a matter of hours they had accumulated a small pile of writing about him. On second thought he began to wonder whether they had kept a file on him all the time. How could this have happened? He lived and worked in Harbin, more than three hundred miles away, and this was his first time in Muji City.

The chief of the bureau was a thin, bald man who looked serene and intelligent. His slim hands handled the written pages in the folder in the manner of a lecturing scholar. To Mr. Chiu's left sat a young scribe, with a clipboard on his knee and a black fountain pen in his hand.

"Your name?" the chief asked, apparently reading out the question from a form.

"Chiu Maguang."

"Age?"

"Thirty-four."

"Profession?"

"Lecturer."

"Work unit?"

"Harbin University."

"Political status?"

"Communist Party member."

The chief put down the paper and began to speak. "Your crime is sabotage, although it hasn't induced serious consequences yet. Because you are a Party member, you should be punished more. You have failed to be a model for the masses and you—"

"Excuse me, sir," Mr. Chiu cut him off.

"What?"

"I didn't do anything. Your men are the saboteurs of our social order. They threw hot tea on my feet and on my wife's feet. Logically speaking, you should criticize them, if not punish them."

"That statement is groundless. You have no witness. Why should I believe you?" the chief said matter-of-factly.

"This is my evidence." He raised his right hand. "Your man hit my fingers with a pistol."

"That doesn't prove how your feet got wet. Besides, you could have hurt your fingers yourself."

"But I am telling the truth!" Anger flared up in Mr. Chiu. "Your police station owes me an apology. My train ticket has expired, my new leather sandals are ruined, and I am late for a conference in the provincial capital. You must compensate me for the damage and losses. Don't mistake me for a common citizen who would tremble when you sneeze. I'm a scholar, a philosopher, and an expert in dialectical materialism. If necessary, we will argue about this in *The Northeastern Daily,* or we will go to the highest People's Court in Beijing. Tell me, what's your name?" He got carried away with his harangue, which was by no means trivial and had worked to his advantage on numerous occasions.

"Stop bluffing us," the donkey-faced man broke in. "We have seen a lot of your kind. We can easily prove you are guilty. Here are some of the statements given by eyewitnesses." He pushed a few sheets of paper toward Mr. Chiu.

Mr. Chiu was dazed to see the different handwritings, which all stated that he had shouted in the square to attract attention and refused to obey the police. One of the witnesses had identified herself as a purchasing agent from a shipyard in Shanghai. Something stirred in Mr. Chiu's stomach, a pain rising to his rib. He gave out a faint moan.

"Now you have to admit you are guilty," the chief said. "Although it's a serious crime, we won't punish you severely, provided you write out a self-criticism and promise that you won't disrupt the public order again. In other words, your release will depend on your attitude toward this crime."

"You're daydreaming!" Mr. Chiu cried. "I won't write a word, because I'm innocent. I demand that you provide me with a letter of apology so I can explain to my university why I'm late."

Both the interrogators smiled contemptuously. "Well, we've never done that," said the chief, taking a puff of his cigarette.

"Then make this a precedent."

"That's unnecessary. We are pretty certain that you will comply with our wishes." The chief blew a column of smoke toward Mr. Chiu's face.

At the tilt of the chief's head, two guards stepped forward and grabbed the criminal by the arms. Mr. Chiu meanwhile went on saying, "I shall report you to the Provincial Administration. You'll have to pay for this! You are worse than the Japanese military police."

They dragged him out of the room.

After dinner, which consisted of a bowl of millet porridge, a corn bun, and a piece of pickled turnip, Mr. Chiu began to have a fever, shaking with a chill and sweating profusely. He knew that the fire of anger had gotten into his liver and that he was probably having a relapse. No medicine was available, because his briefcase had been left with his bride. At home it would have been time for him to sit in front of their color TV, drinking jasmine tea and watching the evening news. It was so lonesome in here. The orange bulb above the single bed was the only source of light, which enabled the guards to keep him under surveillance at night. A moment ago he had asked them for a newspaper or a magazine to read, but they turned him down.

Through the small opening on the door noises came in. It seemed that the police on duty were playing cards or chess in a nearby office; shouts and laughter could be heard now and then. Meanwhile, an accordion kept coughing from a remote corner in the building. Looking at the ballpoint and the letter paper left for him by the guards when they took him back from the Interrogation Bureau, Mr. Chiu remembered the old saying, "When a scholar runs into soldiers, the more he argues, the muddier his point becomes." How ridiculous this whole thing was. He ruffled his thick hair with his fingers.

He felt miserable, massaging his stomach continually. To tell the truth, he was more upset than frightened, because he would have to catch up with his work once he was back home—a paper that was due at the printers next week, and two dozen books he ought to read for the courses he was going to teach in the fall.

A human shadow flitted across the opening. Mr. Chiu rushed to the door and shouted through the hole, "Comrade Guard, Comrade Guard!"

"What do you want?" a voice rasped.

"I want you to inform your leaders that I'm very sick. I have heart disease and hepatitis. I may die here if you keep me like this without medication."

"No leader is on duty on the weekend. You have to wait till Monday."

"What? You mean I'll stay in here tomorrow?"

"Yes."

"Your station will be held responsible if anything happens to me."

"We know that. Take it easy, you won't die."

It seemed illogical that Mr. Chiu slept quite well that night, though the light above his head had been on all the time and the straw mattress was hard and infested with fleas. He was afraid of ticks, mosquitoes, cockroaches—any kind of insect but fleas and bedbugs. Once, in the countryside, where his school's faculty and staff had helped the peasants harvest crops for a week, his colleagues had joked about his flesh, which they said must have tasted nonhuman to fleas. Except for him, they were all afflicted with hundreds of bites.

More amazing now, he didn't miss his bride a lot. He even enjoyed sleeping alone, perhaps because the honeymoon had tired him out and he needed more rest.

The backyard was quiet on Sunday morning. Pale sunlight streamed through the pine branches. A few sparrows were jumping on the ground, catching caterpillars and ladybugs. Holding the steel bars, Mr. Chiu inhaled the morning air, which smelled meaty. There must have been an eatery or a cooked-meat stand nearby. He reminded himself that he should take this detention with ease. A sentence that Chairman Mao had written to a hospitalized friend rose in his mind: "Since you are already in here, you may as well stay and make the best of it."

His desire for peace of mind originated in his fear that his hepatitis might get worse. He tried to remain unperturbed. However, he was sure that his liver was swelling up, since the fever still persisted. For a whole day he lay in bed, thinking about his paper on the nature of contradictions. Time and again he was overwhelmed by anger, cursing aloud, "A bunch of thugs!" He swore that once he was out, he would write an article about this experience. He had better find out some of the policemen's names.

It turned out to be a restful day for the most part; he was certain that his university would send somebody to his rescue. All he should do now was remain calm and wait patiently. Sooner or later the police would have to release him, although they had no idea that he might refuse to leave unless they wrote him an apology. Damn those hoodlums, they had ordered more than they could eat!

When he woke up on Monday morning, it was already light. Somewhere a man was moaning; the sound came from the backyard. After a long yawn, and kicking off the tattered blanket, Mr. Chiu climbed out of bed and went to the window. In the middle of the yard, a young man was fastened to a pine, his wrists handcuffed around the trunk from behind. He was wriggling and swearing loudly, but there was no sight of anyone else in the yard. He looked familiar to Mr. Chiu.

Mr. Chiu squinted his eyes to see who it was. To his astonishment, he recognized the man, who was Fenjin, a recent graduate from the Law Department at Harbin University. Two years ago Mr. Chiu had taught a course in Marxist materialism, in which Fenjin had enrolled. Now, how on earth had this young devil landed here?

Then it dawned on him that Fenjin must have been sent over by his bride. What a stupid woman! A bookworm, who only knew how to read foreign novels! He had expected that she would contact the school's Security Section, which would for sure send a cadre here. Fenjin held no official position; he merely worked in a private law firm that had just two lawyers; in fact, they had little business except for some detective work for men and women who suspected their spouses of having extramarital affairs. Mr. Chiu was overcome with a wave of nausea.

Should he call out to let his student know he was nearby? He decided not to because he didn't know what had happened. Fenjin must have quarreled with the police to incur such a punishment. Yet this could never have occurred if Fenjin hadn't come to his rescue. So no matter what, Mr. Chiu had to do something. But what could he do?

It was going to be a scorcher. He could see purple steam shimmering and rising from the ground among the pines. Poor devil, he thought, as he raised a bowl of corn glue to his mouth, sipped, and took a bite of a piece of salted celery.

When a guard came to collect the bowl and the chopsticks, Mr. Chiu asked him what had happened to the man in the backyard. "He called our boss 'bandit,'" the guard said. "He claimed he was a lawyer or something. An arrogant son of a rabbit."

Now it was obvious to Mr. Chiu that he had to do something to help his rescuer. Before he could figure out a way, a scream broke out in the backyard. He rushed to the window and saw a tall policeman standing before Fenjin, an iron bucket on the ground. It was the same young fellow who had arrested Mr. Chiu in the square two days before. The man pinched Fenjin's nose, then raised his hand, which stayed in the air for a few seconds, then slapped the lawyer across the face. As Fenjin was groaning, the man lifted up the bucket and poured water on his head.

"This will keep you from getting sunstroke, boy. I'll give you some more every hour," the man said loudly.

Fenjin kept his eyes shut, yet his wry face showed that he was struggling to hold back from cursing the policeman, or, more likely, that he was sobbing in silence. He sneezed, then raised his face and shouted, "Let me go take a piss."

"Oh, yeah?" the man bawled. "Pee in your pants."

Still Mr. Chiu didn't make any noise, gripping the steel bars with both hands, his fingers white. The policeman turned and glanced at the cell's window; his pistol, partly holstered, glittered in the sun. With a snort he spat his cigarette butt to the ground and stamped it into the dust.

Then the door opened and the guards motioned Mr. Chiu to come out. Again they took him upstairs to the Interrogation Bureau.

The same men were in the office, though this time the scribe was sitting there empty-handed. At the sight of Mr. Chiu the chief said, "Ah, here you are. Please be seated."

After Mr. Chiu sat down, the chief waved a white silk fan and said to him, "You may have seen your lawyer. He's a young man without manners, so our director had him taught a crash course in the backyard."

"It's illegal to do that. Aren't you afraid to appear in a newspaper?"

"No, we are not, not even on TV. What else can you do? We are not afraid of any story you make up. We call it fiction. What we do care about is that you cooperate with us. That is to say, you must admit your crime."

"What if I refuse to cooperate?"

"Then your lawyer will continue his education in the sunshine."

A swoon swayed Mr. Chiu, and he held the arms of the chair to steady himself. A numb pain stung him in the upper stomach and nauseated him, and his head was throbbing. He was sure that the hepatitis was finally attacking him. Anger was flaming up in his chest; his throat was tight and clogged.

The chief resumed, "As a matter of fact, you don't even have to write out your self-criticism. We have your crime described clearly here. All we need is your signature."

Holding back his rage, Mr. Chiu said, "Let me look at that."

With a smirk the donkey-faced man handed him a sheet, which carried these words:

> I hereby admit that on July 13 I disrupted public order at Muji Train Station, and that I refused to listen to reason when the railroad police issued their warning. Thus I myself am responsible for my arrest. After two days' detention, I have realized the reactionary nature of my crime. From now on, I shall continue to educate myself with all my effort and shall never commit this kind of crime again.

A voice started screaming in Mr. Chiu's ears, "Lie, lie!" But he shook his head and forced the voice away. He asked the chief, "If I sign this, will you release both my lawyer and me?"

"Of course, we'll do that." The chief was drumming his fingers on the blue folder—their file on him.

Mr. Chiu signed his name and put his thumbprint under his signature.

"Now you are free to go," the chief said with a smile, and handed him a piece of paper to wipe his thumb with.

Mr. Chiu was so sick that he couldn't stand up from the chair at first try. Then he doubled his effort and rose to his feet. He staggered out of the building to meet his lawyer in the backyard, having forgotten to ask for his belt back. In his chest he felt as though there were a bomb. If he were able to, he would have razed the entire police station and eliminated all their families. Though he knew he could do nothing like that, he made up his mind to do something.

"I'm sorry about this torture, Fenjin," Mr. Chiu said when they met.

"It doesn't matter. They are savages." The lawyer brushed a patch of dirt off his jacket with trembling fingers. Water was still dribbling from the bottoms of his trouser legs.

"Let's go now," the teacher said.

The moment they came out of the police station, Mr. Chiu caught sight of a tea stand. He grabbed Fenjin's arm and walked over to the old woman at the table. "Two bowls of black tea," he said and handed her a one-yuan note.

After the first bowl, they each had another one. Then they set out for the train station. But before they walked fifty yards, Mr. Chiu insisted on eating a bowl of tree-ear soup at a food stand. Fenjin agreed. He told his teacher, "You mustn't treat me like a guest."

"No, I want to eat something myself."

As if dying of hunger, Mr. Chiu dragged his lawyer from restaurant to restaurant near the police station, but at each place he ordered no more than two bowls of food. Fenjin wondered why his teacher wouldn't stay at one place and eat his fill.

Mr. Chiu bought noodles, wonton, eight-grain porridge, and chicken soup, respectively, at four restaurants. While eating, he kept saying through his teeth, "If only I could kill all the bastards!" At the last place he merely took a few sips of the soup without tasting the chicken cubes and mushrooms.

Fenjin was baffled by his teacher, who looked ferocious and muttered to himself mysteriously, and whose jaundiced face was covered with dark puckers. For the first time Fenjin thought of Mr. Chiu as an ugly man.

Within a month over eight hundred people contracted acute hepatitis in Muji. Six died of the disease, including two children. Nobody knew how the epidemic had started.

JAMES JOYCE

James Joyce (1882–1941) was born James Augustine Aloysius Joyce in Rathgar, a suburb of Dublin, during a turbulent era of political change in Ireland. His parents sent him at the age of six to the best Jesuit school, Clongowes Wood College, where he spent three years; but in 1891 his father was no longer able to afford the tuition, and he was withdrawn. During the period of his parents' financial decline, Joyce – a brilliant student – was educated at home and then given free tuition at Belvedere College, where he won prizes for his essays. Shortly after taking his bachelor's degree in 1902 from University College, Dublin, he left Ireland for Paris, where he attended one class at the Collège de Médecine but dropped out because he could not afford the fees. Nearly starving, he remained in Paris and wrote what he called "Epiphanies." These were notebook jottings of overheard conversations or passing observations that he later incorporated into his fiction, thinking that they illuminated in a flash the meaning of a group of apparently unrelated phenomena. In April 1903 Joyce returned to Dublin because his mother was dying. He remained in Ireland for a short time as a teacher, but the following year he went to live abroad again, disillusioned by his home country's political corruption and religious hypocrisy.

Dubliners (1914), a group of fifteen short stories begun in 1904, was Joyce's attempt to "write a chapter of the moral history" of Ireland. He chose Dublin for the setting because that city seemed to him "the center of paralysis," but he also thought of following the book with another titled "Provincials." As if to prove his perception of the extent of stifling moral repression in his country, he had great difficulties getting the book published – a struggle lasting nine years. This so angered and frustrated Joyce that he never again lived in Ireland; he settled in Trieste, Zurich, and Paris and wrote the novels that established him as one of the greatest authors of modern times: *A Portrait of the Artist as a Young Man* (1916), *Ulysses* (1922), and *Finnegans Wake* (1939).

Joyce's stories about the lives of young people, servants, politicians, and the complacent middle class were intended to represent a broad spectrum of Dublin life—not "a collection of tourist impressions" but a penetrating account of the spiritual waste of his times. Today's reader finds it difficult to believe that some stories in *Dubliners* could have appeared so scandalous to Joyce's publishers that at one point the plates were destroyed at the printers. As a stylist, Joyce blended a detached sympathy for his subject with a "scrupulous meanness" of observed detail. Instead of dramatic plots, he structured stories such as "Araby" around epiphanies—evanescent moments that reveal "a sudden spiritual manifestation, whether in the vulgarity of speech or of gesture or in a memorable expression of the mind itself."

WEB Research James Joyce at bedfordstmartins.com/rewritinglit.

Araby

1914

North Richmond Street, being blind, was a quiet street except at the hour when the Christian Brothers' School set the boys free. An uninhabited house of two storeys stood at the blind end, detached from its neighbours in a square ground. The other houses of the street, conscious of decent lives within them, gazed at one another with brown imperturbable faces.

The former tenant of our house, a priest, had died in the back drawing-room. Air, musty from having been long enclosed, hung in all the rooms, and the waste room behind the kitchen was littered with old useless papers. Among these I found a few paper-covered books, the pages of which were curled and damp: *The Abbot*, by Walter Scott, *The Devout Communicant*, and *The Memoirs of Vidocq*. I liked the last best because its leaves were yellow. The wild garden behind the house contained a central apple-tree and a few straggling bushes under one of which I found the late tenant's rusty bicycle-pump. He had been a very charitable priest; in his will he had left all his money to institutions and the furniture of his house to his sister.

When the short days of winter came dusk fell before we had well eaten our dinners. When we met in the street the houses had grown sombre. The space of sky above us was the colour of ever-changing violet and towards it the lamps of the street lifted their feeble lanterns. The cold air stung us and we played till our bodies glowed. Our shouts echoed in the silent street. The career of our play brought us through the dark muddy lanes behind the houses where we ran the gauntlet of the rough tribes from the cottages, to the back doors of the dark dripping gardens where odours arose from the ashpits, to the dark odorous stables where a coachman smoothed and combed the horse or shook music from the buckled harness. When we returned to the street light from the kitchen windows had filled the areas. If my uncle was seen turning the corner we hid in the shadow until we had seen him safely housed. Or if Mangan's sister came out on the doorstep to call her brother in to his tea we watched her from our shadow peer up and down the street. We waited to see whether she would remain or go in and, if she remained, we left our shadow and walked up to Mangan's steps resignedly. She was waiting for us, her figure defined by the light from the half-opened door. Her brother always teased her before he obeyed and I stood by the railings looking at her. Her dress swung as she moved her body and the soft rope of her hair tossed from side to side.

Every morning I lay on the floor in the front parlour watching her door. The blind was pulled down to within an inch of the sash so that I could not be seen. When she came out on the doorstep my heart leaped. I ran to the hall, seized my books, and followed her. I kept her brown figure always in my eye and, when we came near the point at which our ways diverged, I quickened my pace and passed her. This happened morning after morning. I had never spoken to her, except for a few casual words, and yet her name was like a summons to all my foolish blood.

Her image accompanied me even in places the most hostile to romance. On Saturday evenings when my aunt went marketing I had to go to carry some of the parcels. We walked through the flaring streets, jostled by drunken men and bargaining women, amid the curses of labourers, the shrill litanies of shop-boys who stood on guard by the barrel of pigs' cheeks, the nasal chanting of street-singers, who sang a *come-all-you* about O'Donovan Rossa,° or a ballad about the troubles in our native land. These noises converged in a single sensation of life for me: I imagined that I bore my chalice safely through a throng of foes. Her name sprang to my lips at moments in strange prayers and praises which I myself did not understand. My eyes were often full of tears (I could not tell why) and at times a flood from my heart seemed to pour itself out into my bosom. I thought little of the future. I did not know whether I would ever speak to her or not or, if I spoke to her, how I could tell her of my confused adoration. But my body was like a harp and her words and gestures were like fingers running upon the wires.

One evening I went into the back drawing-room in which the priest had died. It was a dark rainy evening and there was no sound in the house. Through one of the broken panes I heard the rain impinge upon the earth, the fine incessant needles of water playing in the sodden beds. Some distant lamp or lighted window gleamed below me. I was thankful that I could see so little. All my senses seemed to desire to veil themselves and, feeling that I was about to slip from them, I pressed the palms of my hands together until they trembled, murmuring: "*O love! O love!*" many times.

At last she spoke to me. When she addressed the first words to me I was so confused that I did not know what to answer. She asked me was I going to *Araby*. I forgot whether I answered yes or no. It would be a splendid bazaar, she said she would love to go.

"And why can't you?" I asked.

While she spoke she turned a silver bracelet round and round her wrist.

O'Donovan Rossa: Jeremiah O'Donovan (1831–1915), born in Ross Carberry of County Cork, was nicknamed "Dynamite Rossa" for championing violent means to achieve Irish independence.

She could not go, she said, because there would be a retreat that week in her convent. Her brother and two other boys were fighting for their caps and I was alone at the railings. She held one of the spikes, bowing her head towards me. The light from the lamp opposite our door caught the white curve of her neck, lit up her hair that rested there and, falling, lit up the hand upon the railing. It fell over one side of her dress and caught the white border of a petticoat, just visible as she stood at ease.

"It's well for you," she said.

"If I go," I said, "I will bring you something."

What innumerable follies laid waste my waking and sleeping thoughts after that evening! I wished to annihilate the tedious intervening days. I chafed against the work of school. At night in my bedroom and by day in the classroom her image came between me and the page I strove to read. The syllables of the word *Araby* were called to me through the silence in which my soul luxuriated and cast an Eastern enchantment over me. I asked for leave to go to the bazaar on Saturday night. My aunt was surprised and hoped it was not some Freemason affair. I answered few questions in class. I watched my master's face pass from amiability to sternness; he hoped I was not beginning to idle. I could not call my wandering thoughts together. I had hardly any patience with the serious work of life which, now that it stood between me and my desire, seemed to me child's play, ugly monotonous child's play.

On Saturday morning I reminded my uncle that I wished to go to the bazaar in the evening. He was fussing at the hallstand, looking for the hat-brush, and answered me curtly:

"Yes, boy, I know."

As he was in the hall I could not go into the front parlour and lie at the window. I left the house in bad humour and walked slowly towards the school. The air was pitilessly raw and already my heart misgave me.

When I came home to dinner my uncle had not yet been home. Still it was early. I sat staring at the clock for some time and, when its ticking began to irritate me, I left the room. I mounted the staircase and gained the upper part of the house. The high cold empty gloomy rooms liberated me and I went from room to room singing. From the front window I saw my companions playing below in the street. Their cries reached me weakened and indistinct and, leaning my forehead against the cool glass, I looked over at the dark house where she lived. I may have stood there for an hour, seeing nothing but the brown-clad figure cast by my imagination, touched discreetly by the lamplight at the curved neck, at the hand upon the railings and at the border below the dress.

When I came downstairs again I found Mrs. Mercer sitting at the fire. She was an old garrulous woman, a pawnbroker's widow, who collected used stamps for some pious purpose. I had to endure the gossip of the tea-table. The meal was prolonged beyond an hour and still my uncle did not come. Mrs. Mercer stood up to go: she was sorry she couldn't wait any longer, but it was after eight o'clock and she did not like to be out late, as the night air was bad for her. When she had gone I began to walk up and down the room, clenching my fists. My aunt said:

"I'm afraid you may put off your bazaar for this night of Our Lord."

At nine o'clock I heard my uncle's latchkey in the halldoor. I heard him talking to himself and heard the hallstand rocking when it had received the weight of his overcoat. I could interpret these signs. When he was midway through his dinner I asked him to give me the money to go to the bazaar. He had forgotten.

"The people are in bed and after their first sleep now," he said.

I did not smile. My aunt said to him energetically:

"Can't you give him the money and let him go? You've kept him late enough as it is."

My uncle said he was very sorry he had forgotten. He said he believed in the old saying: "All work and no play makes Jack a dull boy." He asked me where I was going and, when I had told him a second time he asked me did I know *The Arab's Farewell to his Steed.* When I left the kitchen he was about to recite the opening lines of the piece to my aunt.

I held a florin° tightly in my hand as I strode down Buckingham Street towards the station. The sight of the streets thronged with buyers and glaring with gas recalled to me the purpose of my journey. I took my seat in a third-class carriage of a deserted train. After an intolerable delay the train moved out of the station slowly. It crept onward among ruinous houses and over the twinkling river. At Westland Row Station a crowd of people pressed to the carriage doors; but the porters moved them back, saying that it was a special train for the bazaar. I remained alone in the bare carriage. In a few minutes the train drew up beside an improvised wooden platform. I passed out on to the road and saw by the lighted dial of a clock that it was ten minutes to ten. In front of me was a large building which displayed the magical name.

I could not find any sixpenny entrance and, fearing that the bazaar would be closed, I passed in quickly through a turnstile, handing a shilling to a weary-looking man. I found myself in a big hall girdled at half its height by a gallery. Nearly all the stalls were closed and the greater part of the hall was in darkness. I recognised a silence like that which pervades a church after a service. I walked into the centre of the bazaar timidly. A few people were gathered about the stalls which were still open. Before a curtain, over which the words *Café Chantant* were written in coloured lamps, two men were counting money on a salver. I listened to the fall of the coins.

Remembering with difficulty why I had come I went over to one of the stalls and examined porcelain vases and flowered tea-sets. At the door of the stall a young lady was talking and laughing with two young gentlemen. I remarked their English accents and listened vaguely to their conversation.

"O, I never said such a thing!"

"O, but you did!"

"O, but I didn't!"

"Didn't she say that?"

---

florin: A silver coin worth two shillings.

"Yes. I heard her."

"O, there's a . . . fib!"

Observing me the young lady came over and asked me did I wish to buy anything. The tone of her voice was not encouraging; she seemed to have spoken to me out of a sense of duty. I looked humbly at the great jars that stood like eastern guards at either side of the dark entrance to the stall and murmured:

"No, thank you."

The young lady changed the position of one of the vases and went back to the two young men. They began to talk of the same subject. Once or twice the young lady glanced at me over her shoulder.

I lingered before her stall, though I knew my stay was useless, to make my interest in her wares seem the more real. Then I turned away slowly and walked down the middle of the bazaar. I allowed the two pennies to fall against the sixpence in my pocket. I heard a voice call from one end of the gallery that the light was out. The upper part of the hall was now completely dark.

Gazing up into the darkness I saw myself as a creature driven and derided by vanity; and my eyes burned with anguish and anger.

FRANZ KAFKA

Franz Kafka (1883–1924), who said that a book should serve as "an axe to break up the frozen sea within us," led a life whose events are simple and sad. He was born into a Jewish family in Prague, and from youth onward he feared his authoritarian father so much that he stuttered in his presence, although he spoke easily with others. In 1906 he received a doctorate in jurisprudence, and for many years he worked a tedious job as a civil service lawyer investigating claims at the state Worker's Accident Insurance Institute. He never married and lived for the most part with his parents, writing fiction at night (he was an insomniac) and publishing only a few slim volumes of stories during his lifetime. *Meditation*, a collection of sketches, appeared in 1912; *The Stoker: A Fragment* in 1913; *The Metamorphosis* in 1915; *The Judgment* in 1916; *In the Penal Colony* in 1919; and *A Country Doctor* in 1920. Only a few of his friends knew that Kafka was also at work on the great novels that were published after his death from tuberculosis: *The Trial* (1925), *The Castle* (1926), and *Amerika* (1927). (He asked his literary executor, Max Brod, to burn these works in manuscript, but Brod refused.)

Kafka's despair with his writing, his job, his father, and his life was complete. Like Gustave Flaubert—whom he admired—he used his fiction as a "rock" to which he clung in order not to be drowned in the waves of the world around him. With typical irony, however, he saw the effort as futile: "By scribbling I run ahead of myself in order to catch myself up at the finishing post. I cannot run away from myself." He was driven to express "the tremendous world I have in my head. But how to free myself and free it without being torn to pieces. And a thousand times rather be torn to pieces than retain it in me or bury it."

In his diaries Kafka recorded his obsession with literature. "What will be my fate as a writer is very simple. My talent for portraying my dreamlike inner life has thrust all other matters into the background." The translator Joachim Neugroschel noted that in Kafka's more than seventy stories, he tested "certain expressionist and even surrealist innovations, shredding syntax, short-circuiting imagery, condensing emotions and tableaux into brief, sometimes even tiny shards and prose poems to evoke a moody and sometimes wistful lyricism." The late story "A Hunger Artist" is one of Kafka's most striking "parables of alienation," as his biographer Ernst Pawel has noted. The "dreamlike" quality of his imagination is apparent in all of Kafka's work.

Kafka is perhaps best known as the author of the waking nightmare "The Metamorphosis," whose remarkable first sentence is one of the most famous in short story literature. The hero of "The Metamorphosis," Gregor Samsa (pronounced *Zamza*), is the son of philistine, middle-class parents in Prague, as was Kafka, and literary critics have tended to interpret the story as an autobiographical fiction, in which Kafka projected his sense of inadequacy before his demanding father. Probably Kafka took Fyodor Dostoevsky's novella "The Double" (1846) as the inspiration for the plot, the mood, and the pace of his story. Vladimir Nabokov has suggested that the greatest literary influence on Kafka was Flaubert, who also used language with ironic precision. The visionary, nightmarish quality of Kafka's fiction is in striking contrast to its precise and formal style, the clarity of which intensifies the dark richness of the fantasy.

CONNECTION Franz Kafka, "I Wish I Were a Red Indian," page 64.

WEB Research Franz Kafka at bedfordstmartins.com/rewritinglit.

A Hunger Artist 1924

TRANSLATED BY ANN CHARTERS

In recent decades the public's interest in the art of fasting has suffered a marked decline. While formerly it used to pay very well to stage large exhibitions of this kind under private management, today this is quite impossible. Those were different times. Back then the whole town was engaged with the hunger artist; during his fast, the audience's involvement grew from day to day; everyone wanted to see the hunger artist at least once a day; during the later stages subscribers used to sit in specially reserved seats in front of the small barred cage all day long; there were even exhibitions at night by torchlight to heighten the effect; on fine days his cage was carried out into the open, and that was particularly the time when the hunger artist was shown to children; while for the adults he was often just an entertainment in which they took part because it happened to be in fashion, for the children, who stood openmouthed, holding each other's hands for safety's sake, watching him as he sat there on the straw spread out for him, even spurning a chair, he was a pale figure in a black leotard with enormously protruding ribs, sometimes nodding politely, answering questions with a forced smile, occasionally even stretching his arm through the bars to let them feel how skinny he was, but then again withdrawing completely into himself, paying attention to no one, not even noticing the striking of the clock, so important for him, the only piece of furniture in his cage, but merely staring into space with his eyes almost shut, taking a sip now and then from a tiny glass of water to moisten his lips.

Besides the changing spectators there were also permanent guards selected by the public—strangely enough, usually butchers—who had the job of watching the hunger artist day and night always three at a time to make sure that he didn't consume any nourishment in some secret manner. But this was no more than a formality introduced to reassure the public, because insiders knew well enough that during his fast, the hunger artist would never, under any circumstances, not even under duress, swallow the smallest crumb; his code of honor as an artist forbade it. Not every watchman, of course, was capable of understanding this; often there were groups of night guards who were very lax in carrying out their duties and deliberately congregated in a far corner and absorbed themselves in a game of cards, obviously intending to give the hunger artist the chance to take a little refreshment, which they assumed he could produce from some secret stash. Nothing was more tormenting to the hunger artist than such watchmen; they made him miserable; they made his fasting seem terribly difficult; sometimes he would overcome his physical weakness and sing for as long as he could keep it up during their watch, to show how unfair their suspicions were. But that was of little use; they only marveled at his skill in being able to eat even while singing. He much preferred the guards who sat right up against the bars and who weren't satisfied with the dim night lighting in the hall and so trained on him the beams of the flashlights supplied to them by his manager. The harsh light didn't disturb him at all, since he wasn't able to sleep deeply anyway, whereas he could always doze off a little whatever the light or the hour, even in the overcrowded, noisy hall. He was quite prepared to spend the whole night entirely without sleep with such watchmen; he was prepared to swap jokes with them, to tell them stories about his nomadic life and listen to their stories in turn, anything just to keep them awake, to be able to show them again and again that he had nothing to eat in his cage and that he was fasting like no one of them could fast. But he was happiest when morning came and a lavish breakfast was served to them at his expense, on which they threw themselves with the appetites of healthy men after a weary night's vigil. Of course there were even people who would see this breakfast as an attempt to bribe the guards, but that was really going too far, and when these people were asked if they would be willing to take over the night watch without breakfast, just for the sake of the cause, they slunk away, though they stuck to their suspicions all the same.

But suspicions of this nature were really inseparable from fasting. No one, after all, was capable of spending all his days and nights continuously watching the hunger artist, so no one could be absolutely certain from firsthand knowledge that his fasting had truly been an unbroken and faultless performance; only the hunger artist himself could know that, and only he, therefore, could be at the same time both the performer and the satisfied spectator of his own fasting. Yet there was another reason why he was never satisfied; perhaps it wasn't only his fasting that made him so emaciated that many people, much to their regret, couldn't attend his performances because they couldn't bear the sight of him; perhaps he had become so emaciated from dissatisfaction with himself. For he alone knew something that not even other insiders knew: how easy it was to fast. It was the easiest thing in the world. He made no secret of this, either, though no one believed him; at best some thought him modest, but mostly they regarded him as a publicity seeker or even took him for a fraud, a person for whom fasting was easy because he knew how to make it easy and then also even had the audacity more or less to admit it. He was forced to endure all of this, he'd even grown accustomed to it all in the course of time, but inwardly his own dissatisfaction gnawed at him, yet never after a single fasting period—you had to grant him this much—had he voluntarily left his cage. The manager had set forty days as the maximum period of the fasting; he would never allow a fast to run beyond this limit, not even in the major cities, and for good reason. Experience had shown that the public's interest in any town could be stimulated for about forty days by increasing the advertisements, but then the public lost interest, and a substantial drop in attendance was noted; naturally there were small variations in this matter between the different towns and regions, but as a rule forty days was the limit. So then on the fortieth day the gate of the flower-decorated cage was opened, an enthusiastic crowd of spectators filled the hall, a military band played, two doctors entered the cage to take the hunger artist's vital measurements, the results were announced to the audience through a megaphone, and finally two young ladies came forward, pleased that they had won the lottery for the honor of leading the hunger artist out of the cage and down a few steps toward a small table where a carefully prepared invalid's meal was served. And at this point, the hunger artist always resisted. True, he willingly surrendered his bony arms to the outstretched hands of these solicitous ladies as they bent down to him, but he refused to stand up. Why stop now, after just forty days? He could have kept going for much longer, infinitely longer; why stop now when he was at his best—indeed, when he had not yet even reached his best fasting form? Why did they want to rob him of the glory of fasting longer, not only of being the greatest hunger artist of all time, which he probably already was—but also of surpassing himself to achieve the unimaginable, because he felt that his capacity to fast was limitless. Why had this audience, which pretended to admire him so much, had so little patience with him; if he could endure fasting longer, why couldn't they endure it? Besides, he was tired, he was comfortable sitting in straw, and now he was supposed to stand upright and go to a meal; the thought alone nauseated him to such a point that he was prevented from expressing it with great difficulty, only out of regard for the ladies. And he gazed up into the eyes of the ladies, who appeared so friendly but were actually so cruel, and shook his head, which weighed heavily on his feeble neck. But then what happened was always what happened. The manager came forward, silently raised his arms over the hunger artist—the band music made speech impossible—as if he were calling upon heaven to look down on its handiwork there in the straw; on this pathetic martyr, which the hunger artist certainly was, only in an entirely different sense; he grasped the hunger artist around his emaciated waist with exaggerated care as if to suggest what a feeble object he had to deal with here; and giving him a secret shake or two, so that the hunger artist's legs and upper body wobbled to and fro, he handed him over to the care of the ladies, who had turned deathly pale in the meantime. Now the hunger artist submitted to everything; his head lay on his chest, as if it had rolled there by chance and stopped itself inexplicably; his body was hollowed out; his legs were squeezed tightly together at the knees in some instinct of self-preservation, but his feet were scraping at the ground, as if it weren't the real ground—they were still seeking the real ground; and the entire weight of his body, admittedly very modest, lay on one of the ladies, who—looking around for help, with panting breath—this wasn't how she had pictured her position of honor—first craned her neck back as far as possible, at least to keep her face from touching the hunger artist, then finding this impossible, when her more fortunate companion didn't come to her aid, instead contenting herself with carrying before her the small bundle of bones that was the hunger artist's hand, the first lady burst into tears amid the audience's delighted laughter and had to be replaced by an attendant who had been standing by in readiness. Then came the meal, a little of which the manager spooned into the nearly unconscious, comatose hunger artist to the accompaniment of cheerful patter designed to divert attention away from the hunger artist's condition; then came the toast drunk to the audience, which the hunger artist allegedly whispered to the manager; the band concluded everything with a great fanfare; the crowd melted away, and nobody had any cause to feel dissatisfied with the show, no one, only the hunger artist, always just him alone.

So he lived for many years with regular short periods of rest, in apparent glory honored by the world, yet in spite of that mostly in a dark mood that became even darker because no one took it seriously. And indeed, how could anyone have comforted him? What more could he wish for? And if once in awhile some good natured soul came along and felt sorry for him and tried to explain to him that his depression was probably caused by his fasting, it sometimes happened, especially if his fast were well advanced, that the hunger artist responded with a burst of rage and to everyone's alarm began to shake the bars of his cage like a wild beast. But the manager had a method of punishment that he was fond of using in such cases. He would apologize publicly to the assembled audience for the hunger artist, admitting that his behavior could only be excused as an irritable condition brought on by his fasting, something that well-fed people by no means could easily understand; in this connection, he would go on to speak of the hunger artist's claim that he was able to fast for a much longer time than he did fast; the manager praised the high aspirations, the good will, the great measure of self-denial undoubtedly implicit in this claim; but then he would seek to refute this claim simply enough by producing photographs, which were at the same time offered for sale to the public; for these pictures showed the hunger artist on his fortieth day of fasting, in bed, almost dead from exhaustion. This perversion of the truth, which assuredly was familiar to the hunger artist, always unnerved him anew and was too much for him. Here the result of the premature ending of his fast was presented as its cause! To fight against this lack of understanding, against this world of ignorance, was impossible. Up to that point he always stood clinging to the bars of his cage, listening eagerly to the manager in good faith, but as soon as the photographs appeared he would let go and sink back with a groan onto his straw, and the reassured public could come close again and inspect him.

When the witnesses to such scenes recalled them a few years later, they often failed to understand them at all. For in the meantime, the previously mentioned decline of the public's interest in fasting had occurred; it seemed to happen almost overnight; there may have been deeper reasons for it, but who cared about digging them up; in any case, the day came when the hunger artist found himself deserted by the pleasure-seeking crowds, who went streaming past him toward other exhibitions. For one last time his manager dragged him across half Europe to see if the old interest might be revived here and there; all in vain, it was as if a repulsion for exhibition fasting had set in everywhere by secret pact. In reality it couldn't have come about so suddenly, of course, and people now belatedly recalled a number of warning signs that had neither been adequately noted nor adequately dealt with in the flush of success, but now it was too late for countermeasures. Of course fasting would surely make a comeback some day, but that was no comfort to the living. What should the hunger artist do now? He who had been applauded by thousands couldn't appear as a sideshow in village fairs, and as for starting a new profession, the hunger artist was not merely too old, but he was also, above all, too fanatically devoted to his fasting. So he took leave of his manager, his companion throughout an unparalleled career, and found an engagement for himself with a large circus; in order to spare his own feelings, he avoided reading the terms of his contract.

A large circus, with its immense number of personnel and animals and apparatus, all constantly replacing and supplementing one another, can always find a use for anyone at any time, even a hunger artist, provided, of course, that his demands are sufficiently modest, and furthermore in this particular case it wasn't just the hunger artist himself who was being booked, but also his long-famous name; indeed, considering the peculiar nature of his art, which doesn't decrease with advancing age, one couldn't even say that he was a superannuated artist, past his prime, and seeking refuge in a quiet circus job; on the contrary, the hunger artist pledged that he could fast just as well as ever, which was clearly believable; in fact, he even claimed that if they let him have his way, as they readily promised him, he would truly astound the world by setting a new record, a claim that only provoked a smile from the experts, considering the public's current mood, which the hunger artist, in his enthusiasm, was apt to forget.

Basically, however, the hunger artist hadn't lost his sense of the real situation, and he accepted it as self-evident that he and his cage would not be placed as a star attraction in the center ring, but rather would be offered as a sideshow in a readily accessible site near the animal cages. Large, brightly colored posters made a frame for his cage and proclaimed what was to be seen there. When the audience came pouring out during the intermission to look at the animals, they almost inevitably had to pass the hunger artist's cage and stop there for a moment; they would perhaps have stayed longer, if those pressing them from behind in the narrow passageway, who couldn't understand the delay on the path to the animals they were so eager to see, hadn't made a longer, more leisurely contemplation impossible. This was also the reason why the hunger artist, who naturally looked forward to these visiting periods as his purpose in life, trembled at their prospect as well. At first he could hardly wait for the intermissions; he had been delighted watching the crowds come surging toward him, until it was made clear to him only too soon—not even the most obstinate, almost deliberate self-deception could obscure the fact—that most of these people, to judge from their actions, were again and again without exception on their way to the wild animals. And that first sight of them from a distance always remained the best. For as soon as they had reached him, he was immediately deafened by the shouting and cursing from the two contending factions which kept continuously forming—those who wanted to stop and stare at him (and the hunger artist soon found them the more distasteful) out of no real interest but only just as a whim or out of defiance, and those others who only wanted to go straight to the animal cages. Once the first rush was over, then came the stragglers, and these, who had nothing to prevent them from stopping as long as they liked, hurried by with long strides, without hardly even a side glance at him, as they rushed to see the animals in the remaining time. And it was an all too rare stroke of luck when the father of a family came along with his children, pointed to the hunger artist, explained in detail what was happening, told stories about earlier years when he himself had witnessed similar but incomparably more splendid performances, but then the children, since they hadn't been sufficiently prepared by either school or life, remained rather uncomprehending—what was fasting to them?—yet the gleam of their inquisitive eyes suggested something new to come, better and more merciful times. Perhaps, the hunger artist sometimes said to himself, things could become a little better if his cage were located not so close to the animal cages. That made the choice of destination too easy for people, to say nothing of how the stench of the stables, the restlessness of the animals at night, the serving of raw meat to the beasts of prey, and the roars at feeding time constantly offended and depressed him. But he did not dare to complain to the management; after all, he had the animals to thank for the throng of visitors, among them here and there even someone who was there just to see him; and who could tell where they might hide him if he called attention to his existence and thereby to the fact that, strictly speaking, he was no more than an obstacle in the path to the animals.

A small obstacle, to be sure, an obstacle growing smaller all the time. It has become customary nowadays to want to find it strange to call attention to a hunger artist, and in accordance with this custom his fate was sealed. He might fast as much as he could, and indeed he did, but nothing could save him now, people passed him by. Just try to explain the art of fasting to someone! Someone who doesn't feel it cannot be made to understand it. The colorful posters became dirty and illegible, they were torn down and no one thought to replace them; the little signboard tallying the number of days fasted, which at first had been carefully changed every day, had long remained the same, for after the first few weeks the staff had grown tired of even this small task; and so the hunger artist just went on fasting as he had once dreamed of doing, and it was indeed no trouble for him to do so, as he had always predicted, but no one counted the days; no one, not even the hunger artist himself, knew how great his achievement was, and his heart grew heavy. And once in a while, when some casual passer-by stopped, ridiculed the outdated number on the board, and talked about a hoax, that was in its way the stupidest lie ever invented by indifference and inherent malice, since the hunger artist didn't cheat, he was working honestly, but the world was cheating him of his reward.

So again many more days passed and there came an end to that as well. One day a supervisor happened to notice the cage, and he asked the attendants why this perfectly useful cage with the rotten straw in it was left unoccupied; no one knew, until somebody with the help of the signboard remembered the hunger artist. They poked into the straw with sticks and found the hunger artist underneath. "Are you still fasting?" asked the supervisor. "When on earth do you mean to stop?" "Forgive me, everybody," whispered the hunger artist; only the supervisor, who pressed his ear against the bars, understood him. "Certainly," said the supervisor, tapping his finger at the side of his forehead to suggest the hunger artist's condition to the staff, "we forgive you." "I always wanted you to admire my fasting," said the hunger artist. "We do admire it," said the supervisor obligingly. "But you shouldn't admire it," said the hunger artist. "All right, then, we don't admire it," said the supervisor, "but why shouldn't we admire it?" "Because I have to fast, I can't help it," said the hunger artist. "How about that," said the supervisor. "Why can't you help it?" "Because," said the hunger artist, lifting his shriveled head a little, and puckering his lips as if for a kiss, he spoke right into the supervisor's ear, so that nothing would be missed, "because I couldn't find the food I liked. If I had found it, believe me, I shouldn't have made any fuss and stuffed myself just like you and everyone else." These were his last words, but in his dying eyes there remained the firm, if no longer proud, conviction that he was still continuing to fast.

"Now clear this out!" said the supervisor, and they buried the hunger artist, straw and all. Then they put a young panther into the cage. Even the most insensitive felt it was refreshing to see this wild creature leaping about in a cage that had been neglected for so long. He lacked for nothing. The food that he liked was brought to him by his keepers without hesitation; he didn't even appear to miss his freedom; that noble body, full to almost bursting with all he needed, seemed to carry freedom itself around with it; it appeared to be placed somewhere in his jaws; and the joy of life streamed with such ardent passion from his throat, that it wasn't easy for the onlookers to withstand it. But they braced themselves, surrounded the cage, and never wanted to move on.

COMMENTARY

R. CRUMB AND DAVID ZANE MAIROWITZ

R. (Robert Dennis) Crumb is considered one of the founders of the underground "comix" movement of the 1960s. The graphic work that made him famous is politically and sexually radical, but he also drew versions of several of Franz Kafka's tales and passages from his life for *Introducing Kafka* (1993), written and with translations by David Zane Mairowitz. *Introducing Kafka* was popular enough to be reissued in 2004 as *R. Crumb's Kafka,* from which this version of "A Hunger Artist" is reprinted.

A Hunger Artist 1993

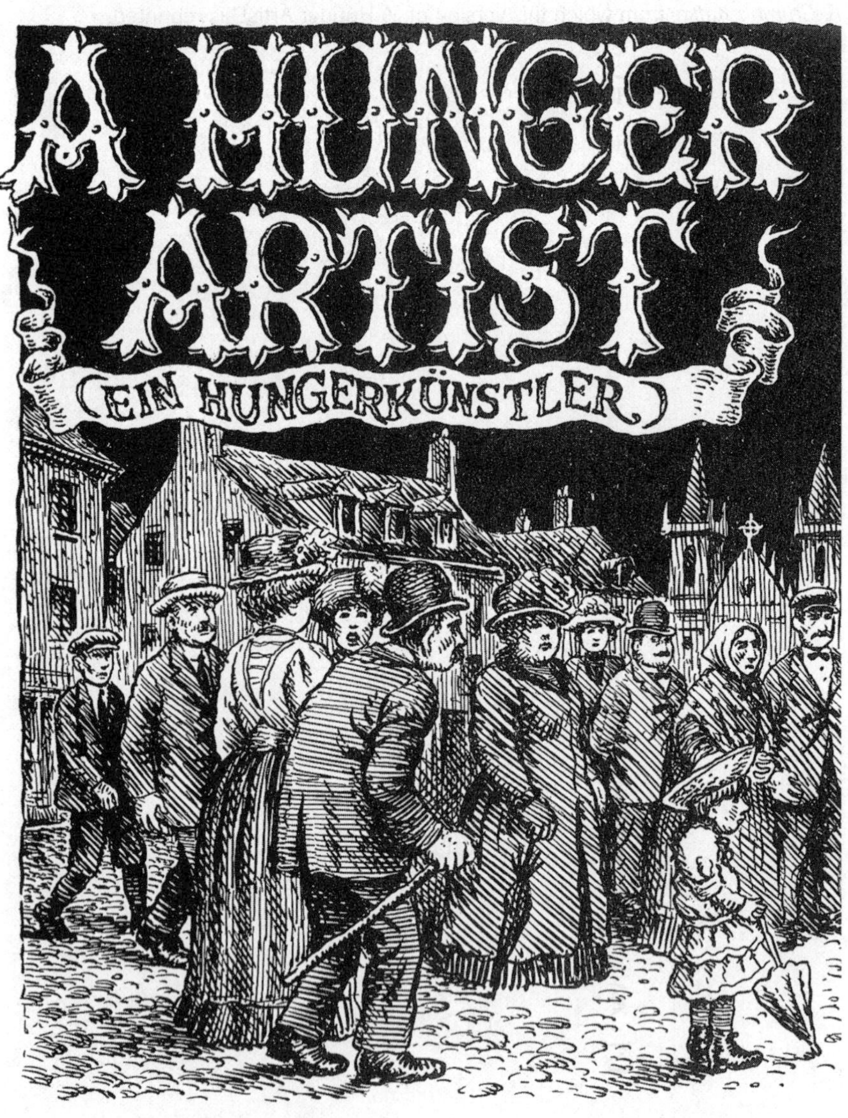

IN THE LAST FEW DECADES, THE INTEREST IN PROFESSIONAL HUNGER-ARTISTRY HAS GREATLY DIMINISHED. ONCE THE WHOLE TOWN CAME OUT TO SEE THE HUNGER-ARTIST. SOME EVEN BOUGHT SEASON TICKETS, AND AT NIGHT THE SCENE WAS BATHED IN THE LIGHT OF TORCHES.
GROUPS OF PROFESSIONAL WATCHERS, USUALLY BUTCHERS, WERE SENT TO WATCH HIM, IN CASE HE HAD SOME SECRET CACHE OF NOURISHMENT. BUT, DURING HIS FAST THE ARTISTE WOULD NEVER, EVEN UNDER COMPULSION, SWALLOW THE SMALLEST BIT OF FOOD; HIS PROFESSIONAL HONOR FORBADE IT. HE ALONE KNEW WHAT THE OTHERS DIDN'T: FASTING WAS THE EASIEST THING IN THE WORLD.
TICKETS
SEE THE HUNGER ARTIST

THE PERIOD OF FASTING WAS SET BY HIS IMPRESARIO AT FORTY DAYS MAXIMUM, BECAUSE AFTER THAT TIME THE PUB-LIC BEGAN TO LOSE INTEREST. SO, ON THE FORTIETH DAY, WITH AN EXCITED CROWD FILLING THE ARENA AND A MILITARY BAND PLAYING, TWO YOUNG LADIES CAME TO LEAD THE HUNGER-ARTIST OUT OF HIS CAGE. WHEN THIS HAPPENED HE ALWAYS PUT UP SOME RESISTANCE...WHY STOP AFTER ONLY FORTY DAYS?!? WHY SHOULD THEY TAKE FROM HIM THE GLORY OF FASTING EVEN LONGER, OF SURPASSING EVEN HIMSELF TO REACH UNIMAGINABLE HEIGHTS, FOR HE SAW HIS ABILITY TO GO ON FASTING AS UNLIMITED!

THEN CAME THE FEAST, WITH THE IMPRESARIO TRYING TO SPOONFEED THE NEARLY COMATOSE HUNGER-ARTIST, ALL THE WHILE CHATTING CHEER-FULLY IN ORDER TO DISTRACT AT-TENTION FROM HIS CONDITION.
AFTER THAT THERE WAS EVEN A TOAST TO THE AUDIENCE, SUPPOS-EDLY SUGGESTED BY THE HUNGER-ARTIST HIMSELF IN A WHISPER TO THE IMPRESARIO.

HE LIVED THIS WAY FOR MANY YEARS, HONORED BY ALL THE WORLD, YET TROUBLED IN HIS SOUL, DEEPLY FRUSTRATED THAT THEY WOULD NOT ALLOW HIS FASTING TO EXCEED FORTY DAYS. HE SPENT MOST OF HIS TIME IN A GLOOMY MOOD, AND WHEN SOME KIND-HEARTED PERSON WOULD TRY TO EXPLAIN THAT HIS DEPRESSION WAS THE RESULT OF THE FASTING, HE WOULD SOMETIMES FLY INTO A RAGE AND BEGIN RATTLING THE BARS OF HIS CAGE LIKE AN ANIMAL.

AS TIME WENT BY PEOPLE BECAME INTERESTED IN OTHER AMUSEMENTS, AND WERE REVOLTED BY PROFESSIONAL FASTING. THE HUNGER-ARTIST COULD NOT CHANGE JOBS, FANATICALLY DEVOTED TO FASTING AS HE WAS. SO, DISCHARGING THE IMPRESARIO, HE HIRED HIMSELF OUT TO A LARGE CIRCUS, WHERE HIS CAGE WAS PUT OUTSIDE, NEAR THOSE OF THE ANIMALS.
WORLD'S GREATEST HUNGER ARTIST
ASTOUNDING REVELATION OF HUMAN ENDURANCE
GAZE UPON THE MAN WHO DOES NOT EAT
DO NOT ATTEMPT TO
★ NO ★ FOOD IN 32 DAYS! HOW LONG CAN HE GO ON?
DAZZLED THE SCIENTISTS PUZZLED
PUBLIC
GO AS
WITHOUT

THE LITTLE SIGN SHOWING THE NUMBER OF DAYS FASTED HAD NOT BEEN CHANGED FOR SOME TIME. THE STAFF COULD NO LONGER BE BOTHERED WITH EVEN THIS SMALL TASK.
NO ONE, NOT EVEN THE HUNGER ARTIST HIMSELF, KNEW HOW GREAT HIS ACHIEVEMENT WAS, AND HIS HEART GREW HEAVY. AND WHEN, FROM TIME TO TIME, A PASSERBY STOPPED TO MAKE FUN OF THE OLD FIGURE, ACCUSING HIM OF FRAUD, IT WAS THE CRUELEST LIE THAT INDIFFERENCE AND MALICE COULD CONTRIVE...
WORLD'S GREATEST HUNGER ARTIST
NO FOOD IN
DAYS
THEN ONE DAY...
WHY IS THIS PERFECTLY GOOD CAGE ALLOWED TO STAND AROUND UNUSED, FULL OF ROTTEN STRAW ??

HE'S STILL IN THERE!
YOU STILL FASTING? AREN'T YOU EVER GOING TO STOP??
FORGIVE ME...
OF COURSE WE FORGIVE YOU!
I ALWAYS WANTED PEOPLE TO ADMIRE MY FASTING...
WE DO ADMIRE IT!
YOU SHOULDN'T...
WELL, ALRIGHT, WE DON'T ADMIRE IT, BUT WHY SHOULD-N'T WE ADMIRE IT?
...BECAUSE I HAVE NO CHOICE... I HAVE TO FAST...
YOU HAVE NO CHOICE? WHY DON'T YOU HAVE ANY CHOICE?

BECAUSE...BECAUSE I COULD NEVER FIND ANY FOOD I LIKED... IF I HAD FOUND ANY, BELIEVE ME, I WOULDN'T HAVE MADE ALL THIS FUSS! I'D HAVE STUFFED MYSELF THE SAME AS YOU OR ANYBODY ELSE!
THESE WERE HIS LAST WORDS, BUT IN HIS BROKEN EYES ONE COULD SEE THE FIRM, IF NO LONGER PROUD, CONVICTION THAT HE WAS FASTING STILL....
ALRIGHT, CLEAN UP THIS MESS...
THEY BURIED THE HUNGER-ARTIST TOGETHER WITH THE STRAW. INTO HIS CAGE THEY NOW PUT A YOUNG PANTHER...

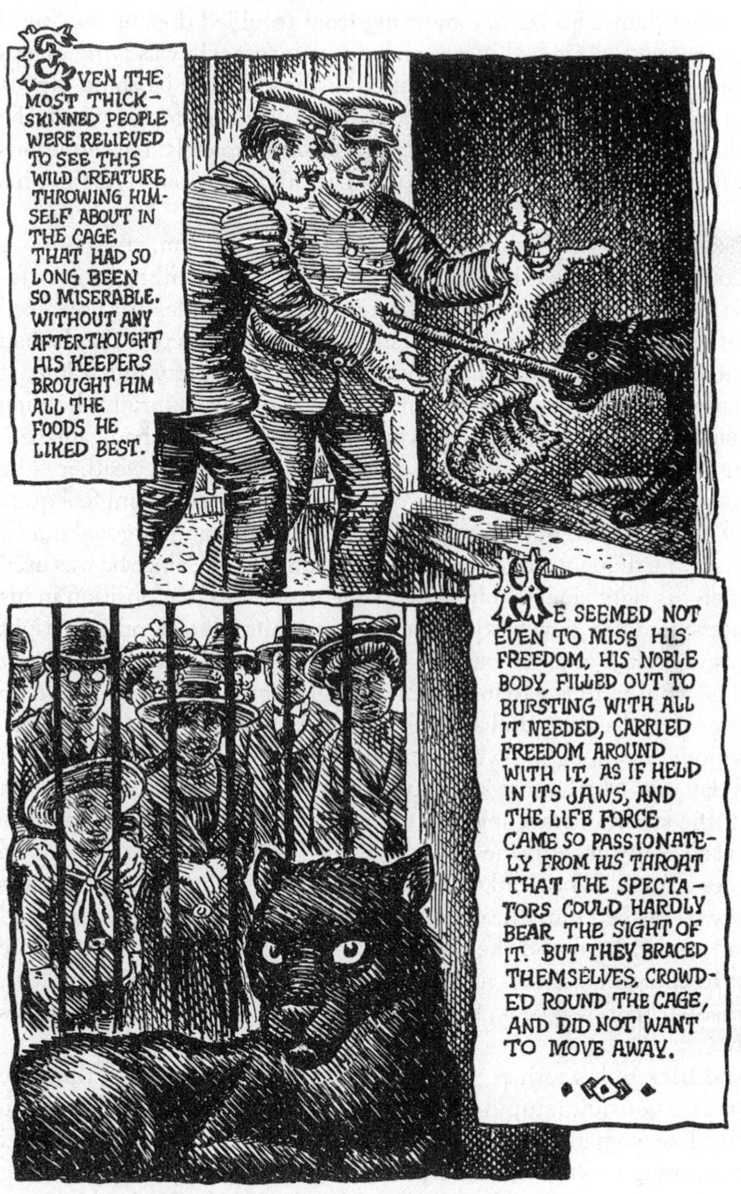
EVEN THE MOST THICK-SKINNED PEOPLE WERE RELIEVED TO SEE THIS WILD CREATURE THROWING HIMSELF ABOUT IN THE CAGE THAT HAD SO LONG BEEN SO MISERABLE. WITHOUT ANY AFTERTHOUGHT HIS KEEPERS BROUGHT HIM ALL THE FOODS HE LIKED BEST.
HE SEEMED NOT EVEN TO MISS HIS FREEDOM, HIS NOBLE BODY, FILLED OUT TO BURSTING WITH ALL IT NEEDED, CARRIED FREEDOM AROUND WITH IT, AS IF HELD IN ITS JAWS, AND THE LIFE FORCE CAME SO PASSIONATELY FROM HIS THROAT THAT THE SPECTATORS COULD HARDLY BEAR THE SIGHT OF IT. BUT THEY BRACED THEMSELVES, CROWDED ROUND THE CAGE, AND DID NOT WANT TO MOVE AWAY.

The Metamorphosis 1915

TRANSLATED BY ANN CHARTERS

I

As Gregor Samsa awoke one morning from troubled dreams, he found himself transformed in his bed into a monstrous insect. He was lying on his hard, armor-plated back, and when he lifted his head a little he could see his dome-like brown belly divided into bow-shaped ridges, on top of which the precariously perched bed quilt was about to slide off completely. His numerous legs, pitiably thin compared to the rest of him, fluttered helplessly before his eyes.

"What has happened to me?" he thought. It was no dream. His room—a normal, though rather small, human bedroom—lay quiet within its four familiar walls. Above the table, where a collection of cloth samples was unpacked and laid out—Samsa was a traveling salesman—hung the picture that he had recently cut from an illustrated magazine and put in a pretty gilt frame. It showed a lady wearing a small fur hat and a fur stole, sitting upright, holding out to the viewer a heavy fur muff into which her entire forearm had vanished.

Then Gregor looked toward the window, and the dreary weather—he heard the rain falling on the metal ledge of the window—made him feel quite melancholy. "What if I went back to sleep again for awhile and forgot about all this nonsense?" he thought, but it was absolutely impossible, since he was used to sleeping on his right side, and he was unable to get into that position in his present state. No matter how hard he tried to heave himself over onto his right side, he always rocked onto his back again. He tried a hundred times, closing his eyes so he wouldn't have to look at his wriggly legs, and he didn't give up until he began to feel a faint, dull ache in his side that he had never felt before.

"Oh God," he thought, "what a hard job I picked for myself! Traveling day in and day out. Much more stressful than working in the home office; on top of that, the strain of traveling, the worry about making connections, the bad meals at all hours, meeting new people, no real human contact, no one who ever becomes a friend. The devil take it all!" He felt a slight itch on top of his belly; slowly he pushed himself on his back closer to the bedpost, so he could lift his head better; he found the itchy place, which was covered with little white spots he couldn't identify; he tried to touch the place with one of his legs, but he immediately drew it back, for the contact sent icy shudders through his entire body.

He slid back to his former position. "Getting up so early like this," he thought, "makes you quite stupid. A man has to have his sleep. Other traveling salesmen live like women in a harem. For instance, when I return to the hotel during the morning to write up my orders, I find these gentlemen just sitting down to breakfast. I should try that with my boss; I would be fired on the spot. Anyway, who knows if that wouldn't be a good thing for me after all. If it weren't for my parents, I would have quit long ago, I would have gone to the boss and told him off. That would knock him off his desk! It's a strange thing, too, the way he sits on top of his desk and talks down to his employees from this height, especially since he's hard of hearing and we have to come so close to him. Now, I haven't totally given up hope; as soon as I've saved the money to pay back what my parents owe him—that should take another five or six years—I'll certainly do it. Then I'll take the big step. Right now, though, I have to get up, because my train leaves at five."

He looked over at the alarm clock, which was ticking on the chest of drawers. "Heavenly Father," he thought. It was half past six, and the hands of the clock were quietly moving forward; in fact, it was after half past, it was nearly quarter to seven. Was it possible the alarm hadn't rung? He saw from the bed that it was correctly set at four o'clock; surely it had rung. Yes, but was it possible to sleep peacefully right through that furniture-rattling noise? Well, he hadn't exactly slept peacefully, but probably all the more soundly. What should he do now? The next train left at seven o'clock; to catch it, he would have to rush like mad, and his samples weren't even packed yet, and he definitely didn't feel particularly fresh and rested. And even if he did catch the train, he wouldn't escape a scene with his boss, since the firm's office boy would have been waiting at the five o'clock train and would have reported back to the office long ago that he hadn't turned up. The office boy was the boss's own creature, without backbone or brains. Now, what if he called in sick? But that would be embarrassing, and it would look suspicious, because in the five years he'd been with the company, he'd never been sick before. His boss would be sure to show up with the doctor from the Health Insurance; he'd reproach his parents for their son's laziness, and he'd cut short any excuses by repeating the doctor's argument that people don't get sick, they're just lazy. And in this case, would he be so wrong? The fact was that except for being drowsy, which was certainly unnecessary after his long sleep, Gregor felt quite well, and he was even hungrier than usual.

As he was hurriedly turning all these thoughts over in his mind, still not able to decide to get out of bed—the alarm clock was just striking a quarter to seven—he heard a cautious tap on the door, close by the head of his bed. "Gregor"—someone called—it was his mother—"it's a quarter to seven. Didn't you want to leave?" That gentle voice! Gregor was shocked when he heard his own voice reply; it was unmistakably his old familiar voice, but mixed with it could be heard an irrepressible undertone of painful squeaking, which left the words clear for only a moment, immediately distorting their sound so that you didn't know if you had really heard them right. Gregor would have liked to answer fully and explain everything, but under the circumstances, he contented himself by saying, "Yes, yes, thank you, mother. I'm just getting up." No doubt the wooden door between them must have kept her from noticing the change in Gregor's voice, for his mother was reassured with his announcement and shuffled off. But because of this brief conversation, the other family members had become aware that Gregor unexpectedly was still at home, and soon his father began knocking on a side door softly, but with his fist. "Gregor, Gregor," he called, "what's the matter with you?" And after a little while, in a deeper, warning tone, "Gregor! Gregor!" At the other side door, his sister was asking plaintively, "Gregor, aren't you feeling well? Do you need anything?" To both sides of the room, Gregor answered, "I'm getting ready," and he forced himself to pronounce each syllable carefully and to separate his words by inserting long pauses, so his voice sounded normal. His father went back to his breakfast, but his sister whispered, "Gregor, open the door, please do." But Gregor had no intention of opening the door, and he congratulated himself on having developed the prudent habit during his travels of always locking all doors during the night, even at home.

As a start, he would get up quietly and undisturbed, get dressed, and—what was most important—eat breakfast, and then he would consider what to do next, since he realized that he would never come to a sensible conclusion about the situation if he stayed in bed. He remembered how many times before, perhaps when he was lying in bed in an unusual position, he had felt slight pains that turned out to be imaginary when he got up, and he was looking forward to finding out how this morning's fantasy would fade away. As for the change in his voice, he didn't doubt at all that it was nothing more than the first warning of a serious cold, a traveling salesman's occupational hazard.

It was easy to push off the quilt; all he had to do was to take a deep breath and it fell off by itself. But things got difficult with the next step, especially since he was now much broader. He could have used hands and arms to prop himself up, but all he had were his numerous little legs that never stopped moving in all directions and that he couldn't control at all. Whenever he tried to bend one of his legs, that was the first one to straighten itself out; and when it was finally doing what he wanted it to do, then all the other legs waved uncontrollably, in very painful agitation. "There's simply no use staying idle in bed," said Gregor to himself.

The first thing he meant to do was get the lower part of his body out of bed, but this lower part, which he still hadn't seen, and couldn't imagine either, proved to be too difficult to move, it shifted so slowly; and when finally, growing almost frantic, he gathered his strength and lurched forward, he miscalculated the direction, and banged himself violently into the bottom bedpost, and from the burning pain he felt, he realized that for the moment, it was the lower part of his body that was the most sensitive.

Next he tried to get the upper part of his body out first, and cautiously brought his head to the edge of the bed. This he managed easily, and eventually the rest of his body, despite its width and weight, slowly followed the direction of his head. But when he finally had moved his head off the bed into open space, he became afraid of continuing any further, because if he were to fall in this position, it would be a miracle if he didn't injure his head. And no matter what happened, he must not lose consciousness just now; he would be better off staying in bed.

But when he repeated his efforts and, sighing, found himself stretched out just as before, and again he saw his little legs struggling if possible even more wildly than ever, despairing of finding a way to bring discipline and order to this random movement, he once again realized that it was impossible to stay in bed, and that the wisest course was to make every sacrifice, if there was even the slightest hope of freeing himself from the bed. But at the same time, he continued to remind himself that it was always better to think calmly and coolly than make desperate decisions. In such stressful moments he usually turned his eyes toward the window, but unfortunately the view of the morning fog didn't inspire confidence or comfort; it was so thick that it obscured the other side of the narrow street. "Already seven o'clock," he said as the alarm clock rang again, "already seven o'clock and still such a heavy fog." And for a little while longer he lay quietly, breathing very gently as if expecting perhaps that the silence would restore real and normal circumstances.

But then he told himself, "Before it reaches quarter past seven, I must absolutely be out of bed without fail. Besides, by then someone from the office will be sent here to ask about me, since it opens at seven." And he began to rock the entire length of his body in a steady rhythm to swing it out of bed. If he maneuvered out of bed in this way, then his head, which he intended to lift up as he fell, would presumably escape injury. His back seemed to be hard; it wouldn't be harmed if he fell on the carpet. His biggest worry was the loud crash he was bound to make, which would certainly cause anxiety, perhaps even alarm, behind all the doors. Still, he had to take the risk.

When Gregor was already jutting halfway out of bed—his new approach was more a game than an exertion, for all he needed was to seesaw himself on his back—it occurred to him how easy his task would become if only he had help. Two strong people—he thought of his father and the maid—would have been enough; all they had to do was to slide their arms under his round back, lift him out of bed, bend down with their burden, and then wait patiently while he swung himself onto the ground, where he hoped that his little legs would find some purpose. Well, quite aside from the fact that the doors were locked, should he really have called for help? Despite his misery, he couldn't help smiling at the very thought of it.

By now he had pushed himself so far off the bed with his steady rocking that he could feel himself losing his balance, and he would finally have to decide what he was going to do, because in five minutes it would be quarter after seven—when the front doorbell rang. "That's somebody from the office," he said to himself, and his body became rigid, while his little legs danced in the air even faster. For a moment everything was quiet. "They won't open the door," Gregor told himself, with a surge of irrational hope. But then, as usual, the maid walked to the door with her firm step and opened it. Gregor needed only to hear the first words of greeting from the visitor to know who it was—the office manager himself. Why on earth was Gregor condemned to work for a company where the slightest sign of negligence was seized upon with the gravest suspicion? Were the employees, without exception, all scoundrels? Was no one among them a loyal and dedicated man, who, if he did happen to miss a few hours of work one morning, might drive himself so crazy with remorse that he couldn't get out of bed? Wouldn't it have been enough to send an apprentice to inquire—if inquiries were really necessary—did the manager himself have to come, and make it clear to the whole innocent family that any investigation into this suspicious matter could only be entrusted to a manager? And responding to these irritating thoughts more than to any conscious decision, Gregor swung himself out of bed with all his strength. There was a loud thud, but not really a crash. The carpet softened his fall, and his back was more resilient than Gregor had thought, so the resulting thud wasn't so noticeable. Only he hadn't held his head carefully enough and had banged it; he twisted it and rubbed it against the carpet in pain and annoyance.

"Something fell in there," said the manager in the adjoining room on the left. Gregor tried to imagine whether something similar to what had happened to him today might happen one day to the office manager; one really had to admit this possibility. But, as if in brusque reply, the manager took a few decisive steps in the next room, which made his patent leather boots creak. And in the adjoining room to the right, Gregor's sister whispered, as if warning him, "Gregor, the office manager is here." "I know," said Gregor to himself; but he didn't dare to raise his voice high enough so that his sister could hear.

"Gregor," said his father from the room to his left, "the office manager has come and wants to know why you didn't catch the early train. We don't know what to tell him. Besides, he wants to talk to you in person. So, please, open the door. Surely he will be kind enough to excuse the disorder in your room." "Good morning, Mr. Samsa," the manager was calling in a friendly tone. "He's not well," said his mother to the manager, while his father continued talking through the door. "He's not well, believe me, sir. Why else would Gregor miss a train! That boy doesn't have anything in his head but business. I'm almost upset, as it is, that he never goes out at night; he's been in town for the past week, but he's stayed home every evening. He just sits here with us at the table, quietly reading the newspaper or studying the railroad timetables. His only recreation is when he occupies himself with his fretsaw. For instance, during the past two or three evenings, he's made a small picture frame; you'd be surprised how pretty it is; it's hanging in his room; you'll see it as soon as Gregor opens up. I'm really glad you've come, sir, we haven't been able to persuade Gregor to open the door; he's so obstinate; and he must definitely be feeling unwell, although he denied it earlier this morning." "I'll be right there," said Gregor slowly and deliberately, but he didn't move, so as not to miss a word of the conversation. "Dear madam, I can think of no other explanation, either," said the office manager. "Let us only hope it's nothing serious. Though, on the other hand, I must say, that we business people—fortunately or unfortunately—often very simply must overlook a slight indisposition in order to get on with business." "Well, can the office manager come in now?" asked father impatiently and knocked again on the door. "No," said Gregor. In the room to the left, there was an embarrassed silence; in the room to the right, his sister began sobbing.

Why hadn't she joined the others? Probably she had just gotten out of bed and hadn't yet begun dressing. And why was she crying? Because he hadn't gotten up and let the office manager in, because he was in danger of losing his job, and because his boss would pester his parents again about their old debts? But surely for the moment these were unnecessary worries. Gregor was still here and would never consider abandoning the family. True, at this very moment he was lying on the carpet, and no one who could have seen his condition, could seriously expect him to open his door for the office manager. But Gregor could hardly be fired for this small discourtesy, for which he could easily find a plausible excuse later on. And it seemed to Gregor that it would be much more sensible just to leave him in peace for now, instead of pestering him with tears and speeches. But it was just this uncertainty about him that upset the others and excused their behavior.

"Mr. Samsa," the office manager now called out, raising his voice, "what is the matter with you? You are barricading yourself in your room, answering with only Yes and No, causing your parents serious and needless worries, and—I mention this only in passing—now suddenly you neglect your duties to the firm in an absolutely shocking manner. I'm speaking here in the name of your parents and your employer, and I must ask you to give an immediate and satisfactory explanation. I'm amazed, amazed! I took you for a quiet, sensible person, and now suddenly you seem intent on behaving in an absolutely strange manner. Early this morning, the head of the firm did suggest to me a possible explanation for your absence—it concerned the cash payment for sales that you received recently—but I practically gave him my word of honor that this couldn't be true. But now that I'm witness to your unbelievable obstinacy here, I haven't the slightest desire to defend you in any way whatsoever. And your job is by no means secure. I'd originally intended to confide this to you privately, but since you force me to waste my time here needlessly, I see no reason why your parents shouldn't hear it as well. For some time your sales have been quite unsatisfactory; to be sure, it's not the best season for business, we recognize that, but a season for doing no business at all just doesn't exist, Mr. Samsa, it *must* not exist."

"But, sir," Gregor called out, beside himself and forgetting everything in his agitation, "I'll open the door immediately, this very minute. A slight indisposition, a dizzy spell, kept me from getting up. I'm still lying in bed. But I feel completely well again. I'm just climbing out of bed. Please be patient for a moment. It's not going quite so well as I thought. But I'm really all right. How suddenly a thing like this can happen to a person! Just last night I felt fine, my parents know that, or rather last night I already had a slight foreboding. It must have been noticeable. Why didn't I let them know at the office! But you always think that you can recover from an illness without having to stay at home. Please, sir, please spare my parents! Because there are no grounds for all the accusations you just made; no one has ever said a word to me about them. Perhaps you haven't seen the last orders that I sent in. Anyway, I can still catch the eight o'clock train; the last couple hours of rest have made me feel much stronger. Don't delay here any longer, sir; I'll soon be back at work, and please be kind enough to report that to the office, and put in a good word for me with the head of the firm."

And while Gregor was hastily blurting all this out, hardly aware of what he was saying, he had easily reached the chest of drawers, perhaps as a result of his practice in bed, and he was trying to raise himself up against it. He really wanted to open his door, he actually looked forward to showing himself and speaking with the manager; he was eager to find out what the others, who so wanted to see him, would say when they caught sight of him. If they were frightened, then Gregor was no longer responsible and he could rest in peace. But if they took everything calmly, then he, too, had no grounds for alarm, and could still get to the station in time for the eight o'clock train—if he hurried. At first he kept sliding a few times down the side of the polished chest, but finally, giving one last heave, he stood upright; he no longer paid attention to the pain in his lower abdomen, though it hurt a lot. Then he let himself fall against the back of a nearby chair, clinging to its edges with his little legs. By doing this, he gained control over himself, and he stayed very quiet so he could listen to the office manager.

"Did you understand even a single word?" the manager asked the parents. "Surely he can't be trying to make fools of us?" "For Heaven's sake," cried his mother, already in tears, "perhaps he's seriously ill, and we're torturing him. Grete! Grete!" she then called. "Mother?" answered his sister from the other side—they were communicating across Gregor's room. "You must get the doctor immediately. Gregor is sick. Hurry, run for the doctor. Didn't you hear Gregor talking just now?" "That was an animal voice," said the office manager, in a tone much lower than the mother's shouting. "Anna! Anna!" yelled the father through the hallway into the kitchen, clapping his hands. "Get the locksmith at once!" And already the two young girls were running through the hallway with a rustling of skirts—how had his sister gotten dressed so quickly?—and tearing open the front door to the apartment. There was no sound of the door closing; they must have just left it open, as you sometimes do in homes where a great misfortune had occurred.

But Gregor had grown calmer. Apparently no one understood his words any longer, though they were sufficiently clear to himself, even clearer than before; perhaps his ears were getting adjusted to the sound. But at least people knew now that something was wrong with him and were ready to help him. His parents' first orders had been given with such confidence and dispatch that he already felt comforted. Once more he'd been drawn back into the circle of humanity, and he expected miraculous results from both the doctor and the locksmith, without distinguishing precisely between them. In order to make his voice as clear as possible for the conversations he anticipated in the future, he coughed a little, but as quietly as he could, because it might not sound like a human cough, and he could no longer trust his judgment. Meanwhile, it had become completely quiet in the next room. Perhaps his parents sat at the table whispering with the office manager; perhaps they were all leaning against his door and listening.

Gregor pushed himself along slowly to the door holding onto the chair, then he let go of it and fell against the door, holding himself upright—the balls of his little feet secreted a sticky substance—and rested there a moment from his efforts. Then he attempted to use his mouth to turn the key in the lock. It seemed, unfortunately, that he had no real teeth—then how was he to hold onto the key?—but to compensate for that, his jaws were certainly very powerful; with their help, he succeeded in getting the key to turn, ignoring the fact that he was undoubtedly somehow injuring himself, since a brown fluid was streaming out of his mouth, oozing over the lock and dripping onto the floor. "Listen to that," said the office manager in the next room, "he's turning the key." Gregor felt greatly encouraged; but he felt that all of them, mother and father too, should have been cheering him on. "Keep it up, Gregor," they should have shouted, "Keep going, keep working on that lock!" And imagining that everyone was eagerly following his efforts, he bit down on the key with all the strength he had in his jaws. As the key began to turn, he danced around the lock; hanging on with only his mouth, he used the full weight of his body to either push up on the key or press down on it. The clear click of the lock as it finally snapped open, broke Gregor's concentration. With a sigh of relief, he said to himself, "I didn't need the locksmith after all," and he laid his head down on the handle so the door could open wide.

Since he had to open the door in this manner, it could open out fairly widely while he himself wasn't yet visible. Next he had to turn his body slowly around one half of the double door, moving very carefully so he wouldn't fall flat on his back while crossing over the threshold. He was concentrating on this difficult maneuver, not thinking of anything else, when he heard the manager exclaim a loud "Oh"—it sounded like the wind howling—and then he could see him too, standing closest to the door, pressing his hand against his open mouth and slowly staggering back, as if driven by some invisible and intensely powerful force. His mother—despite the presence of the manager, she was standing in the room with untidy hair sticking out in all directions from the night before—first looked toward his father with her hands clasped; then she took two steps toward Gregor and collapsed on the floor, her skirts billowing out around her and her face hidden on her breast. His father clenched his fist with a menacing air, as if he wanted to knock Gregor back into his room; then he looked uncertainly around the living room, covered his eyes with his hands, and sobbed so hard that his powerful chest heaved.

Now Gregor decided not to enter the room after all; instead he leaned against his side of the firmly bolted wing of the double door, so that only half of his body was visible, his head tilting above it while he peered at the others. Meanwhile, it had become much brighter; across the street a section of an endlessly long, dark gray building was clearly visible—it was a hospital—with its facade starkly broken by regularly placed windows; it was still raining, but now large individual drops were falling, striking the ground one at a time. On the table, the breakfast dishes were set out in a lavish display, since his father considered breakfast the most important meal of the day; he lingered over it for hours, reading various newspapers. Directly on the opposite wall hung a photograph of Gregor, taken during his military service, wearing a lieutenant's uniform, his hand on his sword, with a carefree smile, demanding respect for his bearing and his rank. The door to the entrance hall was open, and since the apartment door also stood open, you could see out to the landing and the top of the descending stairs.

"Well, now," said Gregor, and he was quite aware that he was the only one who had remained calm. "I'll get dressed at once, pack my samples, and be on my way. Will you, will you all let me go catch my train? Now you see, sir, I'm not obstinate, and I'm glad to work; traveling is a hard job, but I couldn't live without it. Where are you going, sir? Back to the office? Yes? Will you give a true account of everything? A man may temporarily seem incapable of working, but that is precisely the moment to remember his past accomplishments and to consider that later on, after overcoming his obstacles, he's sure to work all the harder and more diligently. As you know very well, I'm deeply obligated to the head of the firm. And then I have to take care of my parents and my sister. I'm in a tight spot, but I'll work myself out of it again. Please don't make it harder for me than it already is. I beg you to put in a good word for me at the office. Traveling salesmen aren't regarded highly there, I know. They think we make lots of money and lead easy lives. They have no particular reason to think differently. But you, sir, you have a better idea of what's really going on than the rest of the office, why—speaking just between ourselves—you have an even better idea than the head of the firm himself, who, in his role as our employer, lets his judgment be swayed against his employees. You know very well that a traveling salesman, who's out of the office most of the year, can easily become a victim of gossip, coincidences, and unfounded complaints, against which he can't possibly defend himself, since he almost never hears about them, except perhaps after he returns exhausted from a trip, and then he himself personally suffers the grim consequences without understanding the reasons for them. Sir, please don't leave without having told me that you think I'm at least partly right!"

But at Gregor's very first words the office manager had already turned away, and now with open mouth, he simply stared back at him over a twitching shoulder. And during Gregor's speech, he never stood still for a moment, but—without taking his eyes off Gregor—he kept moving very gradually toward the door, as if there were a secret ban on leaving the room. He was already in the front hall, and from the abrupt way that he pulled his leg out of the living room, you might have thought that he had just scorched the sole of his foot. In the hall, however, he stretched out his right hand as far as he could toward the stairs, as if some supernatural deliverance were awaiting him there.

Gregor realized that he must not let the office manager leave in this frame of mind, or his position in the firm would be seriously compromised. His parents didn't quite understand the situation; over the years they'd convinced themselves that Gregor was set up for life in this firm, and besides, they were now so preoccupied by their immediate worries that they'd lost any sense of the future. But Gregor had more foresight. The office manager must be stopped, calmed down, persuaded, and finally won over; Gregor's future and that of his family depended on it! If only his sister had been here! She had understood, she had even started to cry when Gregor was still lying quietly on his back. And the office manager, a ladies' man, would certainly have listened to her; she would have shut the front door and talked him out of his fright in the hall. But she wasn't there; Gregor would have to handle the situation by himself. And forgetting that he was still completely unfamiliar with his present powers of movement, and also that very possibly, indeed probably once again his words hadn't been understood, he let go of the wing of the door, shoved himself through the opening, and tried to move toward the office manager, who was already on the landing, foolishly clutching the banister with both hands; but instead, groping for support, Gregor fell down with a small cry upon his many little legs. The instant that happened he felt a sense of physical well-being for the first time that morning; his little legs had solid ground under them; he was delighted to discover that they obeyed him perfectly; they even seemed eager to carry him off in whatever direction he chose; and now he felt sure that the end to all his suffering was at hand. But at that same moment, as he lay on the floor rocking with suppressed motion, not far away from his mother, directly opposite her, she—who had seemed so completely self-absorbed—suddenly jumped up, stretched out her arms, spread her fingers out wide, crying "Help, for Heaven's sake, help!" She craned her head forward, as if she wanted to get a better look at Gregor, but then inconsistently, she backed away instead; forgetting that the table laden with breakfast dishes was right behind her, she sat down on it hastily, as if distracted, and then failed to notice that next to her, the coffee was pouring out of the big, overturned pot in a steady stream onto the carpet.

"Mother, mother," Gregor said softly and looked up at her. For a moment, the office manager had completely slipped from his mind; on the other hand, at the sight of the flowing coffee, he couldn't help snapping his jaws a few times. That made his mother scream again; she fled from the table and collapsed into his father's arms as he was rushing towards her. But Gregor had no time now for his parents; the office manager was already on the stairs; his chin on the banister, he was taking a final look back. Gregor leaped forward, moving as fast as he could to catch him; the office manager must have anticipated this, for he jumped down several steps and vanished; but he was still yelling "Aaah!" and the sound echoed through the entire staircase. Unfortunately, the manager's flight seemed to confuse Gregor's father, who had remained relatively calm until now; for instead of running after the office manager himself, or at least not preventing Gregor from going after him, his father seized with his right hand the manager's cane—it had been left behind on a chair along with his hat and overcoat—and with his left hand, he picked up a large newspaper from the table, and stamping his feet, he began to brandish the cane and the newspaper to drive Gregor back to his room. No plea of Gregor's helped; indeed, no plea was understood; no matter how humbly he bent his head, his father only stamped his feet harder. Across the room, his mother had flung open a window despite the cold weather, and she was leaning far out of it with her face buried in her hands. A strong draft was created between the street and the staircase, so that the window curtains billowed up, the newspapers rustled on the table, and a few pages flew across the floor. Relentlessly, his father charged, making hissing noises like a savage. Since Gregor had as yet no practice in moving backwards, it was really slow going. If Gregor had only been able to turn around, he would have returned to his room right away, but he was afraid of making his father impatient by his slow rotation, while at any moment now the cane in his father's hand threatened a deadly blow to his back or his head. Finally, however, Gregor had no other choice when he realized with dismay that while moving backwards he had no control over his direction; and so with constant, fearful glances at his father, he began to turn himself around as quickly as he could, which was in reality very slowly. Perhaps his father sensed Gregor's good intentions, since he didn't interfere—occasionally he even steered the movement from a distance with the tip of the cane. If only his father would stop that unbearable hissing! It made Gregor lose his head completely. He had almost turned totally around, when distracted by the hissing, he made a mistake and briefly shifted the wrong way back again. But when at last he successfully brought his head around to the doorway, he discovered that his body was too wide to squeeze through. Naturally, in his father's present mood it didn't occur to him to open the other wing of the double door and create a passage wide enough for Gregor. He was simply obsessed with the idea that Gregor must return to his room as fast as possible. And he would never have allowed the intricate maneuvers that Gregor needed, in order to pull himself upright and try to fit through the door this way. Instead, as if there were no obstacles, he drove Gregor forward, making a lot of noise; the noise behind Gregor didn't sound any longer like the voice of a single father; now this was really getting serious, and Gregor—regardless of what would happen—jammed into the doorway. One side of his body lifted up, he lay lopsided in the opening, one of his sides was scraped raw, ugly blotches appeared on the white door, soon he was wedged in tightly and unable to move any further by himself; on one side his little legs were trembling in midair, while on the other side they were painfully crushed against the floor—when his father gave him a strong shove from behind that was truly his deliverance, so that he flew far into his room, bleeding profusely. The door was slammed shut with the cane, and at last there was silence.

II

Not until dusk did Gregor awaken from his heavy, torpid sleep. He would certainly have awakened by himself before long, even without being disturbed, for he felt that he had rested and slept long enough, but it seemed to him that a furtive step and a cautious closing of the hall door had aroused him. The light of the electric street lamps was reflected in pale patches here and there on the ceiling and on the upper parts of the furniture, but down below where Gregor lay, it was dark. Slowly, still groping awkwardly with his antennae, which he was just beginning to appreciate, he dragged himself toward the door to see what had been going on there. His left side felt like a single long, unpleasantly tightening scab, and he actually had to limp on his two rows of legs. One little leg, moreover, had been badly hurt during the morning's events—it seemed almost a miracle that only one had been injured—and it dragged along lifelessly.

Only when he reached the door did he discover what had really attracted him: it was the smell of something edible. For there stood a bowl filled with fresh milk in which floated small slices of white bread. He practically laughed with joy, since he was even hungrier now than in the morning, and he immediately plunged his head into the milk almost over his eyes. But he soon pulled it out again in disappointment; not only did he find eating difficult on account of his tender left side—and he could only eat if his whole heaving body joined in—but he also didn't care at all for the milk, which used to be his favorite drink, and that was surely why his sister had placed it there for him; in fact, he turned away from the bowl almost with disgust and crawled back into the middle of the room.

Through the crack in the double door, Gregor could look into the living room where the gas was lit, but while during this time his father was usually in the habit of reading the afternoon newspaper in a loud voice to his mother and sometimes to his sister as well, there wasn't a sound at present. Well, perhaps this practice of reading aloud that his sister was always telling him about and often mentioned in her letters, had recently been dropped altogether. But it was silent in all the other rooms too, though the apartment was certainly not empty. "What a quiet life the family's been leading," Gregor said to himself, and while he sat there staring into the darkness, he felt a great sense of pride that he had been able to provide such a life in so beautiful an apartment for his parents and sister. But what if all the peace, all the comfort, all the contentment were now to come to a terrible end? Rather than lose himself in such thoughts, Gregor decided to start moving and crawled up and down the room.

Once during the long evening, first one of the side doors and then the other was opened a tiny crack and quickly closed again; probably someone had felt the need to come in and then decided against it. Gregor now settled himself directly in front of the living room door, determined to persuade the hesitating visitor to come in or else at least to discover who it might be; but the door wasn't opened again, and Gregor waited in vain. That morning, when the doors had been locked, they all had wanted to come in to see him; now after he had opened one of the doors himself and the others had obviously been unlocked during the day, no one came in, and the keys were even put into the locks on the other side of the doors.

It wasn't until late at night that the light in the living room was turned off, and Gregor could easily tell that his parents and sister had stayed awake until then, because as he could clearly hear, all three of them were tiptoeing away. Certainly now no one would come into Gregor's room until morning; so he had ample time to reflect in peace and quiet about how he should restructure his life. But the high-ceilinged, spacious room in which he had to lie flat on the floor filled him with an anxiety he couldn't explain, since it was his own room and he had lived in it for the past five years; and with a half-unconscious movement—and not without a slight feeling of shame—he scurried under the sofa, where even though his back was slightly squeezed and he couldn't raise his head, he immediately felt quite comfortable, regretting only that his body was too wide to fit completely under the sofa.

There he stayed the entire night, which he spent either dozing and waking up from hunger with a start, or else fretting with vague hopes, but it all led him to the same conclusion, that for now he would have to stay calm and, by exercising patience and trying to be as considerate as possible, help the family to endure the inconveniences he was bound to cause them in his present condition.

Very early in the morning—it was still almost night—Gregor had the opportunity to test the strength of his new resolutions, because his sister, nearly fully dressed, opened the door from the hall and peered in uncertainly. She couldn't locate him immediately, but when she caught sight of him under the sofa—God, he had to be somewhere, he couldn't have flown away, could he?—she was so startled that, unable to control herself, she slammed the door shut again from the outside. But, apparently regretting her behavior, she immediately opened the door again and came in on tiptoe as if she were visiting someone seriously ill or even a complete stranger. Gregor had pushed his head forward just to the edge of the sofa and was watching her. Would she notice that he had left the milk standing, certainly not because he wasn't hungry, and would she bring in some other kind of food he liked better? If she didn't do it on her own, he would rather starve than bring it to her attention, though he felt a tremendous urge to dart out from under the sofa, throw himself at her feet and beg for something good to eat. But, to Gregor's surprise, his sister noticed at once that his bowl was still full, except for a little milk that had spilled around the edges; she immediately picked it up, to be sure not with her bare hands but with an old rag, and carried it out. Gregor was wildly curious to know what she would bring in its place, and he made various guesses about it. But he could never have guessed what his sister, in the goodness of her heart, actually did. To find out what he liked, she brought him a wide selection that she spread out on an old newspaper. There were old, half-rotten vegetables, bones left over from the evening meal covered with a congealed white sauce, a few raisins and almonds, some cheese that Gregor had considered inedible two days ago, a slice of dry bread, a slice of bread and butter, and a slice of bread and butter with some salt. In addition, she set down the bowl, now presumably reserved for Gregor's exclusive use, into which she had poured some water. And from a sense of delicacy, since she understood that Gregor was unlikely to eat in her presence, she quickly left the room and even turned the key in the lock outside so that Gregor would understand that he could indulge himself as freely as he liked. Gregor's little legs whirled as he hurried toward the food. His injuries must have fully healed already; he no longer felt any handicap, which amazed him, and made him think that over a month ago he had nicked his finger with a knife, and that this injury had still been hurting him the day before yesterday. "Could I have become less sensitive?" he wondered, sucking greedily at the cheese, which he was drawn to immediately, more than the other foods. Quickly, one after another, with tears of contentment streaming from his eyes, he devoured the cheese, the vegetables, and the white sauce; on the other hand, the fresh food didn't appeal to him; he couldn't stand the smell, and he even dragged the things he wanted to eat a little distance away. He had finished with everything long ago and was just resting lazily in the same spot, when his sister slowly turned the key in the lock as a signal that he should withdraw. That startled him at once, even though he was almost dozing off, and he scuttled back under the sofa again. But it took a lot of self-control to stay there, even for the brief time that his sister was in the room, because his body was bloated after his heavy meal, and he could hardly breathe in that cramped space. In between brief bouts of near suffocation, he watched with somewhat bulging eyes as his unsuspecting sister swept up with a broom not only the scraps he hadn't eaten, but also the foods that he hadn't touched, as if they were also no longer fit to eat, and then she hastily dumped everything into a bucket which she covered with a wooden lid, and carried it out. She had scarcely turned her back when Gregor came out from under the sofa to stretch himself and let his belly expand.

In this way Gregor was fed each day, once in the morning while his parents and the maid were still sleeping, and the second time in the afternoon after the family's meal, while his parents took a short nap and his sister sent the maid on some errand or other. Certainly they didn't want Gregor to starve either, but perhaps they couldn't stand to know about his feeding arrangements except by hearsay; or perhaps his sister also wished to spare them anything even mildly distressing, since they were already suffering enough as it was.

Gregor couldn't discover what excuses had been made that first morning to get rid of the doctor and the locksmith, for since the others couldn't understand him, no one thought that he could understand them—including his sister—and so whenever she was in his room, he had to content himself with hearing her occasional sighs and appeals to the saints. Not until later on, when she had become a little more used to it all—of course her complete adjustment was out of the question—Gregor sometimes caught a remark that was meant to be friendly or could be interpreted that way. "Today he really liked it," she said, when Gregor had gobbled up his food, or when he hadn't eaten much, as was gradually happening more and more frequently, she would say almost sadly, "Now he hasn't touched anything again."

But while Gregor couldn't get any news directly, he overheard many things from the adjoining rooms, and as soon as he heard the sound of voices, he would immediately run to the corresponding door and press his entire body against it. Especially in the early days, there was no conversation that didn't refer to him somehow, if only indirectly. For two whole days, there were family discussions at every meal about what they should do now; but they also talked about the same subject between meals, because now there were always at least two family members at home, since probably no one wanted to stay alone in the apartment. And yet, on no account could they leave it empty. Besides, on the very first day, the cook—it wasn't entirely clear what or how much she knew of the situation—had begged his mother on bended knees to let her leave at once, and when she departed fifteen minutes later, she thanked them tearfully for her dismissal as if it were the greatest favor they had ever bestowed on her in this house, and without being asked, she swore a solemn oath, promising not to say a word about what had happened to anyone.

So now his sister, together with his mother, had to do the cooking as well; this wasn't much trouble, of course, since they ate almost nothing. Again and again Gregor would hear how one encouraged another to eat, always getting the answer, "Thanks, I've had enough" or something similar. They didn't seem to drink anything either. Often his sister asked his father if he wanted some beer, and she kindly offered to get it herself; and then when his father didn't answer, she suggested that if he didn't want her to bother, she could send the janitor's wife for it, but in the end his father answered with a firm "No," and there wasn't any further discussion.

In the course of the very first day his father explained the family's financial situation and prospects to both the mother and sister. Every now and then he stood up from the table to get some receipt or account book from the small safe that he'd managed to salvage from the collapse of his business five years earlier. He could be heard opening the complicated lock, taking out what he was looking for, and closing it again. The father's explanations, to some extent, were the first encouraging news that Gregor had heard since his captivity. He had always supposed that his father had nothing at all left from his old business, at least his father had never told him anything to the contrary, though Gregor had never actually asked him about it. In those days Gregor's only concern had been to do all that he could to help the family forget as quickly as possible the business catastrophe that had plunged them all into complete despair. And so he had begun to work with exceptional zeal and was promoted almost overnight from a junior clerk to a traveling salesman, who naturally had a much greater earning potential, and his successes were immediately converted by way of commissions into cash that he could bring home and lay on the table for the astonished and delighted family. Those had been happy times, and they had never been repeated, at least not with such splendor, even though Gregor was eventually earning so much money that he was capable of meeting the expenses of the entire family, and in fact did so. They had simply grown used to it, the family as well as Gregor; they accepted the money gratefully and he gave it gladly, but it didn't arouse any especially warm feelings any longer. Only Gregor's sister had stayed close to him, and it was his secret plan that she, who—unlike Gregor—loved music and could play the violin very movingly, should be sent to the conservatory next year despite the considerable expense involved, and which he would certainly have to meet somehow. During Gregor's brief visits home, the conservatory was often mentioned in his conversations with his sister, but it was always only as a beautiful dream that could never come true, and his parents even disliked hearing those innocent allusions; but Gregor had definitely set his mind on it and had intended to announce his plan solemnly on Christmas Eve.

Such were the thoughts, quite futile in his present condition, that passed through his mind as he stood upright, glued to the door, eavesdropping. Sometimes he grew so weary that he could no longer listen and let his head bump carelessly against the door, but then he held it up again immediately, because even the slightest noise that he inadvertently made was enough to be heard next door and to reduce everyone to silence. "Just what's he up to now?" his father would say after a pause, obviously turning toward the door, and only then would the interrupted conversation gradually resume.

Gregor now had ample opportunity to discover—since his father would often repeat his explanations, partly because he hadn't concerned himself with these matters for a long time, and also partly because his mother couldn't always grasp everything the first time—that despite all their misfortune, a sum of money, to be sure a very small one, still remained from the old days and had even increased slightly in the meantime since the interest had never been touched. And besides that, the money Gregor had been bringing home every month—he'd only kept a little for himself—had not been entirely spent and had accumulated into a modest capital. Behind his door, Gregor nodded his head eagerly, delighted at this unexpected foresight and thrift. In fact, he could have used this surplus money to pay off more of his father's debt to the head of the firm, so the day when he could have quit his job would have been a lot closer, but now things were doubtless better the way his father had arranged them.

However, this money was by no means sufficient to allow the family to live off the interest; it might be enough to support them for a year, or for two at the most, but no more than that. It was really just a sum that shouldn't be touched, but instead saved for an emergency; money to live on would have to be earned. Now his father was still certainly healthy, but he was an old man who hadn't done any work for the past five years and couldn't be expected to take on very much; in those five years, which was his first vacation in his hard-working if unsuccessful life, he had put on weight and as a result, had become very sluggish. And as for his old mother, should she really start trying to earn money, when she suffered from asthma and found it a strain just to walk through the apartment, and spent every second day gasping for breath on the couch by the open window? And should his sister go out to work, she who was still a child at seventeen and whose life it would be a pity to disturb, since it consisted of wearing nice clothes, sleeping late, helping out with the house-work, enjoying a few modest amusements, and most of all, playing the violin? At first, whenever the conversation turned to the necessity of earning money, Gregor would always let go of the door immediately and then throw himself down on the cool leather sofa beside it, because he felt so flushed with shame and grief.

Often he lay there throughout the long nights, not sleeping a wink and just scrabbling on the leather for hours. Or else, undaunted by the great effort of shoving an armchair to the window, he would crawl to the sill and, propping himself up on the chair, lean against the panes, evidently inspired by some memory of the sense of freedom that he used to experience looking out the window. Because, in fact, from day to day he saw objects only a short distance away becoming more indistinct; the hospital across the street, which he used to curse because he saw it all too often, he now couldn't see at all, and if he weren't certain that he lived on the quiet but decidedly urban Charlotte Street, he might have believed that he was gazing out of his window into a barren waste-land where the gray sky and the gray earth merged indistinguishably. Only twice had his attentive sister needed to see the armchair standing by the win-dow; from then on whenever she cleaned the room, she carefully pushed the chair back to the window, and now she even left the inside windowpane open.

If Gregor had only been able to speak to his sister and thank her for all she had to do for him, he could have endured her services more easily, but as it was, they oppressed him. To be sure, she tried to ease the embarrassment of the situation as much as possible, and the longer time went on, the better she be-came at it, but in time Gregor too became more keenly aware of everything. Even the way she came in was terrible for him. Hardly had she entered the room when—not even taking time to close the door, though she was usually so careful to spare everyone the sight of Gregor's room—she'd run straight to the window and tear it open with impatient fingers, almost as if she were suffocat-ing, and then she stayed there for a while, taking deep breaths no matter how cold it was. With this hustle and bustle, she scared Gregor twice a day; he lay quaking under the sofa the entire time, and yet he knew perfectly well that she would surely have spared him if she had only found it possible to stand being in a room with him with the windows closed.

One time—it must have been a month since Gregor's transformation, so there was no particular reason for his sister to be surprised by his appearance any more—she came a little earlier than usual and caught Gregor as he was looking out the window, motionless and terrifyingly upright. It wouldn't have surprised Gregor if she hadn't come in, since his position prevented her from opening the window immediately, but not only did she not enter, she also actually jumped back and shut the door; a stranger might easily have thought that Gregor had been lying in wait for her and meant to bite her. Gregor naturally hid at once under the sofa, but he had to wait until noon before she came back, and she seemed much more uneasy than usual. From this he concluded that the sight of him was still unbearable to her and was bound to remain unbearable in the future, and that she probably was exercising great self-control not to run away at the sight of even the small portion of his body that protruded from under the sofa. To spare her even this sight, he draped the sheet on his back and dragged it over to the sofa one day—he needed four hours for this task—and placed it in such a way so as to conceal himself completely, so that she couldn't see him even if she stooped down. If she considered this sheet unnecessary, then of course she could remove it, because it was clear enough that Gregor was hardly shutting himself off so completely for his own sake; but she left the sheet the way it was, and Gregor believed he caught a grateful look when he once cautiously raised the sheet a little with his head to see how she was reacting to the new arrangement.

During the first two weeks his parents couldn't bring themselves to come in to him, and often he heard them say how much they appreciated his sister's work, whereas previously they'd been annoyed with her because she'd appeared to be a little useless. But often now, both his father and mother waited outside of Gregor's room while his sister was cleaning up inside, and as soon as she emerged, she had to give a detailed report about how the room looked, what Gregor had eaten, how he had behaved this time, and whether perhaps some slight improvement was noticeable. Gregor's mother, incidentally, wanted to visit him relatively soon, but at first his father and sister put her off with sensible arguments, which Gregor listened to most attentively and fully endorsed. But later his mother had to be held back by force, and when she cried out, "Let me go to Gregor; after all, he's my unfortunate son! Don't you understand that I must go to him?" then Gregor thought that perhaps it would be a good idea after all if she did come in; not every day, of course, but perhaps once a week; she surely understood everything much better than his sister, who for all her courage, was still only a child, and had perhaps, in the final analysis, merely taken on this demanding task out of childish recklessness.

Gregor's wish to see his mother was soon fulfilled. During the daytime Gregor didn't want to show himself at the window, if only out of consideration for his parents, but he couldn't crawl very far on his few square yards of floor space, either, nor could he bear to lie still during the night; eating had soon ceased to give him the slightest pleasure, and so as a distraction he got into the habit of crawling crisscross over the walls and ceiling. He especially enjoyed hanging from the ceiling; it was quite different from lying on the floor; he could breathe more freely, and a mild tingle ran through his body; and in the almost blissful oblivion in which Gregor found himself up there, it could happen that, to his surprise, he let himself go and crashed onto the floor. But now of course he had much greater control over his body than before, and he never hurt himself by even this great fall. Gregor's sister immediately noticed the new pastime that he had found for himself—after all, he left some traces of the sticky tracks of his crawling here and there—and she then took it into her head to enable Gregor to crawl around to the greatest possible extent, so she decided to remove the furniture that stood in his way, first of all, the chest of drawers and the desk. But she couldn't do this alone; she didn't dare ask her father for help; and the maid would most certainly not help her, because this girl (about sixteen years old) was bravely staying on since the previous cook had quit, but she'd asked permission to keep the kitchen locked at all times and to open it only when expressly called; so his sister had no other choice than to get her mother one day when her father was out. And indeed, with cries of eager delight, Gregor's mother approached his room, but she fell silent at the door. Of course his sister first looked in to check that everything in the room was in order; only then did she let her mother enter. Gregor had hastily pulled the sheet even lower down in tighter folds; the whole thing really looked like a sheet casually tossed over the sofa. This time Gregor also refrained from peering out from under the sheet; he denied himself the sight of his mother, and was only pleased to know that she had finally come. "Come on in, you can't see him," said his sister, and evidently she was leading her mother by the hand. Now Gregor heard the two weak women shifting the really heavy old chest of drawers from its place, and how his sister obstinately took on the hardest part of the work for herself, ignoring the warnings of her mother, who was afraid she'd strain herself. It took a very long time. After about a quarter of an hour's work, Gregor's mother said that it would be better to leave the chest where it was, because for one thing, it was just too heavy, they would not be finished before the father arrived, and with the chest in the middle of the room, Gregor's path would be blocked; and for the second, it wasn't at all certain that they were doing Gregor a favor to move the furniture. It seemed to her that the opposite was true; the sight of the bare walls made her heart ache; and why shouldn't Gregor also feel the same way, since after all he'd been accustomed to the furniture for so long and might feel abandoned in an empty room. "And doesn't it really look," concluded his mother very softly, in fact she'd been almost whispering the whole time, as if she were anxious that Gregor, whose exact whereabouts she didn't know, couldn't hear even the sound of her voice, for of course she was convinced that he couldn't understand her words, "and doesn't it look as if by moving the furniture we were showing that we'd given up all hope for improvement and were callously abandoning him to his own resources? I think it would be best if we tried to keep the room just as it was, so that when Gregor comes back to us again, everything will be unchanged and it can be easier to forget what happened in the meantime."

Hearing his mother's words, Gregor realized that the lack of all direct human exchange, together with his monotonous life in the midst of the family, must have confused his mind during these past two months, because otherwise he couldn't explain to himself how he could seriously have wanted his room cleared out. Had he really wanted his warm room, with its comfortable old family furniture, to be transformed into a cave in which he could crawl freely around in all directions, no doubt, but only at the cost of swiftly and totally losing his human past? Indeed, he was already on the verge of forgetting it, and only his mother's voice, which he hadn't heard for so long, had brought him to his senses. Nothing should be removed; everything must stay; he couldn't do without the beneficial effects of the furniture on his state of mind; and if the furniture interfered with his mindless crawling about, then it was not a loss but a great gain.

But unfortunately his sister thought differently; she had grown accustomed, to be sure not entirely without reason, to being the great expert on Gregor in any discussion with her parents, and so now her mother's proposal was cause enough for the sister to insist on removing not only the chest of drawers and the desk, as she had originally planned, but also the rest of the furniture in the room except for the indispensable sofa. It was, of course, not only her childish defiance and the self-confidence she had recently and so unexpectedly gained at such cost that led to this determination; but she had also in fact observed that Gregor needed more space to crawl around in, while on the other hand, as far as she could see, he never used the furniture. But, perhaps, what also played some part was the romantic spirit of girls of her age, which seeks satisfaction at every opportunity and tempted Grete to make Gregor's predicament even more frightening so that she might then be able to do even more for him than before. For most likely no one but Grete would ever dare to enter into a room where Gregor ruled the bare walls all by himself.

And so she refused to be dissuaded from her resolve by her mother, who in any case seemed unsure of herself in that room and who soon fell silent out of sheer nervousness, and helped the sister as best she could to move the chest of drawers out of the room. Well, Gregor could do without the chest, if necessary, but the desk had to stay. And no sooner had the two women, groaning and shoving the chest, left the room, when Gregor poked his head out from under the sofa to see how he could intervene as cautiously and tactfully as possible. Unfortunately, it was his mother who returned first, while Grete kept her arms around the chest in the next room, rocking it back and forth, and naturally unable to move it by herself from its spot. Gregor's mother, however, was not used to the sight of him; it might make her sick, and so Gregor scurried backwards in alarm to the other end of the sofa, though not in time to prevent the front of the sheet from stirring a little. That was enough to catch his mother's attention. She stopped short, stood still a moment, and then went back to Grete.

Although Gregor kept telling himself that nothing out of the ordinary was happening, that just a couple of pieces of furniture were being moved around, all the same he soon had to admit to himself that this walking back and forth by the women, their little cries to each other, the scraping of the furniture along the floor, were affecting him on all sides like a tremendous uproar, and no matter how tightly he tucked in his head and legs and pressed his body against the floor, he was forced to admit that he couldn't endure the fuss much longer. They were emptying out his room, stripping him of everything he loved; they had already removed the chest, which contained his fretsaw and other tools; and now they were prying loose the desk, which was almost embedded in the floor, and at which he'd done his homework when he was in business school, high school, and even as far back as elementary school—at this point he really had no more time to consider the good intentions of the two women, whose existence he had indeed almost forgotten, because by now they were working away in silence from sheer exhaustion, and he heard only the heavy shuffling of their feet.

And so he broke out—just at the moment the women were in the next room, leaning against the desk to catch their breath—and he changed direction four times, not really knowing what he should rescue first, and then he spotted the picture of the lady dressed in nothing but furs, hanging conspicuously on what was otherwise a bare wall opposite him; he crawled rapidly up to it and pressed himself against the glass, which held him fast and soothed his hot belly. At least this picture, which Gregor now completely covered, was definitely not going to be removed by anyone. He twisted his head around toward the door of the living room to observe the women on their return.

They had not given themselves much of a rest and were already coming back; Grete had put her arm around her mother and was almost carrying her. "Well, what should we take now?" said Grete and looked around. Then her eyes met Gregor's on the wall. No doubt it was only due to the presence of her mother that she kept her composure, lowered her head to keep her mother from looking about, and said, although rather shakily and without thinking, "Come on, why don't we go back to the living room for a moment?" Grete's intention was clear to Gregor; she wanted to get her mother to safety and then chase him down from the wall. Well, just let her try! He clung to his picture and wouldn't give it up. He would rather fly in Grete's face.

But Grete's words had made her mother even more anxious; she stepped to one side, caught sight of the huge brown splotch on the flowered wallpaper, and before realizing that what she saw was Gregor, she cried out in a hoarse, shrieking voice, "Oh God, oh God," and collapsed across the sofa with outstretched arms, as if giving up completely, and didn't move. "You, Gregor," cried the sister, raising her fist and glaring at him. These were the first words that she had addressed directly to him since his transformation. She ran into the next room to get some sort of medicine to revive her mother from her fainting fit; Gregor also wanted to help—there was time enough to save his picture later on—but he was stuck fast to the glass and had to wrench himself free; then he also ran into the next room, as if he could give some advice to his sister as in the old days; but once there he had to stand uselessly behind her while she was rummaging among various little bottles; she got frightened when she turned around; one of the bottles fell to the floor and shattered; a splinter of glass sliced Gregor's face, and some kind of burning medicine splashed around him; then without further delay, Grete grabbed as many bottles as she could hold and ran back to her mother with them; she slammed the door closed with her foot. Gregor was now cut off from his mother, who was perhaps nearly dying because of him; he dared not open the door for fear of frightening away his sister, who had to stay with his mother; now he had nothing to do but wait; and so, in an agony of self-reproach and anxiety, he began to crawl, to crawl over everything, walls, furniture, and ceiling; until finally when the entire room was spinning, he dropped in despair onto the middle of the big table.

A little while passed. Gregor lay worn out, all was quiet, perhaps that was a good sign. Then the doorbell rang. The maid, of course, was locked in the kitchen, and Grete had to open the door. Father was back. "What's happened?" were his first words; Grete's face must have told him everything. Grete replied in a muffled voice, evidently with her face pressing against her father's chest. "Mother fainted. But she's better now. Gregor's broken loose." "Just what I expected," said his father. "Just what I've always told you, but you women wouldn't listen." It was clear to Gregor that his father had misinterpreted Grete's all too brief statement and assumed that Gregor was guilty of some act of violence. That meant that he must now try to pacify his father, for he had neither the time nor the means to explain things to him. And so Gregor fled to the door of his room and pressed himself against it, so that as soon as his father came in from the hall, he should see that Gregor had the best intention of returning to his room immediately, and that it was unnecessary to drive him back; but that someone only had to open the door, and he would immediately disappear.

But his father was in no mood to observe such subtlety; "Ah ha!" he cried as soon as he entered, in a tone both furious and elated. Gregor drew his head back from the door and raised it toward his father. He hadn't really pictured his father at all, standing that way; admittedly he had been too preoccupied by the new sensation of crawling around to concern himself with what was going on in the rest of the household as before, and he really ought to have been prepared for some changes. And yet, and yet, was this really his father? The same man who used to lie wearily in bed when Gregor left early on one of his business trips; who always greeted him on his return in the evening wearing a robe and sitting in an armchair; who was actually hardly capable of standing up, but had merely raised his arms to show his pleasure; and who, during the rare family walks on a few Sundays a year and on the high holidays, would always shuffle laboriously along between Gregor and his mother, who walked slowly anyway, walking even a little slower than they walked, bundled in his old overcoat, planting his cane before him for each step he took, and when he wanted to say something, nearly always standing still and gathering his escorts around him? Now, however, he held himself erect, dressed in a tight blue uniform with gold buttons, like that worn by bank messengers; his heavy double chin bulged over the high stiff collar of his jacket; from under his bushy eyebrows, his black eyes flashed alert and observant glances; his previously tousled white hair was combed flat, meticulously parted and gleaming. He tossed his cap, on which was a gold monogram, probably that of some bank, right across the room in a wide arc onto the couch, and started toward Gregor with a grimly set face, the ends of his long uniform jacket thrown back, and his hands in his pockets. Probably he didn't know himself what he intended; nevertheless, he lifted his feet unusually high, and Gregor was astonished at the gigantic size of his boot soles. But Gregor didn't dwell on his reflections; he had known from the very first day of his new life that his father considered only the strictest measures appropriate for dealing with him. And so he fled from his father, pausing only when his father stood still, and immediately hurrying on again when he made any kind of a move. In that way they circled the room several times, without anything decisive happening; in fact, they proceeded in such a slow tempo that it didn't have the appearance of a chase. For this reason, Gregor stayed on the floor for the time being, especially since he feared his father might regard any escape onto the walls or ceiling as a particularly wicked act. At the same time, Gregor had to admit that he couldn't keep up with this kind of running for long; for while his father took a single step, he had to carry out a countless number of movements. Shortness of breath was beginning to appear, and even in his earlier days his lungs had never been entirely reliable. As he went staggering along, saving all his energy for running, hardly keeping his eyes open, in his stupor not even thinking of any other refuge than running, and having almost forgotten that the walls were available, though admittedly here these walls were blocked by elaborately carved furniture full of sharp points and corners—suddenly something came sailing past him, lightly tossed; it landed next to him and rolled away in front of him. It was an apple; immediately a second one came flying after it; Gregor stopped dead in fright; any further running was useless, because his father was determined to bombard him. He had filled his pockets from the fruit bowl on the sideboard and now, without taking careful aim, he was throwing one apple after another. These small red apples rolled around on the floor as if electrified, colliding with one another. One weakly thrown apple grazed Gregor's back and glanced off harmlessly. But another one thrown directly afterwards actually penetrated into Gregor's back; Gregor wanted to drag himself further, as if the surprising and unbelievable pain might pass if he changed his position; but he felt as if nailed to the spot and stretched himself flat out, all his senses in complete confusion. Now with his last conscious sight he saw how the door of his room was flung open, and his mother rushed out in her chemise, ahead of his screaming sister, for his sister had undressed her when she had fainted to make it easier for her to breathe; he saw his mother running to his father, shedding her loosened petticoats one by one on the floor behind her, and stumbling over her petticoats to fling herself upon his father, and embracing him, in complete union with him—but now Gregor's vision failed him—begging him, with her hands clasped around his father's neck, to spare Gregor's life.

III

Gregor suffered from his serious injury for over a month—the apple remained embedded in his flesh as a visible reminder since no one dared to remove it—and it even seemed to bring home to his father that despite Gregor's present deplorable and repulsive shape, he was still a member of the family who ought not to be treated as an enemy, but that on the contrary, family duty required them to swallow their disgust and put up with him, simply put up with him.

And now, although Gregor had probably suffered some permanent loss of mobility as a result of his injury and for the present needed long, long minutes to cross his room like an old invalid—crawling up the walls was out of the question—yet he thought he was granted entirely satisfactory compensation for this deterioration of his condition, since every day toward evening the living room door, which he used to watch intently for an hour or two beforehand, would be opened, so that lying in the darkness of his room and not visible from the living room, he could see the entire family at the lamp-lit table and could listen to the conversation as if by general consent, not at all as he had been obliged earlier to eavesdrop.

Of course, there were no longer the lively discussions of earlier days that Gregor used to recall wistfully in small hotel rooms whenever he had to sink down wearily into the damp bedding. Now it was mostly very quiet. The father fell asleep in his armchair shortly after supper; the mother and sister would caution each other to keep quiet; the mother, hunched forward under the light, stitched away at fine lingerie for a fashion boutique; the sister, who had taken a job as a salesgirl, studied shorthand and French every evening, in the hope of getting a better job some day. Occasionally the father woke up, and as if he didn't know he'd been sleeping, he said to the mother, "How long you've been sewing again today!" and instantly he'd doze off again, while the mother and sister smiled wearily at each other.

With a kind of perverse obstinacy, the father refused to take off his messenger's uniform even in the house, and while his robe hung uselessly on the clothes hook, he slept fully dressed in his chair, as if he were ever ready for duty and waiting for his superior's call even here. As a result, his uniform—not new to begin with—started to look less clean despite all the efforts of the mother and sister, and Gregor would often spend whole evenings staring at the soiled and spotted uniform, with its gleaming, constantly polished gold buttons, in which the old man slept in great discomfort and yet very peacefully.

As soon as the clock struck ten, the mother tried to wake up the father with a few gentle words, trying to persuade him to go to bed, because here he couldn't get any proper rest, which the father sorely needed, since he had to go on duty at six. But with the obstinacy that had possessed him since he'd become a bank messenger, he always insisted on staying at the table a little longer, though he regularly fell asleep, and it was then only with the greatest effort that he could be coaxed into exchanging his armchair for his bed. No matter how much the mother and sister cajoled and admonished him, he would go on shaking his head slowly for a quarter of an hour, keeping his eyes shut and refusing to get up. The mother plucked at his sleeve, whispering sweet words into his ear; the sister would leave her homework to help her mother, but none of this had any effect on the father. He merely sank deeper into his chair. He would open his eyes only when the two women took hold of him under his arms, look back and forth at the mother and sister, and usually say, "What a life. Such is the peace of my old age." And supported by both women, he rose to his feet laboriously, as if he himself were his greatest burden, and allowed the women to lead him to the door, where he waved them away and went on by himself, while the mother hastily dropped her sewing and the sister her pen, to run after the father and provide further assistance.

Who in this overworked and exhausted family had time to worry about Gregor any more than was absolutely necessary? The household was neglected even more; the maid was dismissed after all; a gigantic, bony cleaning woman with white hair fluttering around her head now came every morning and evening to do the heaviest chores; everything else was taken care of by the mother, along with all her sewing. It even came to pass that various pieces of family jewelry, which the mother and sister used to wear with great pleasure at parties and on great occasions, had to be sold, as Gregor learned in the evenings from the family's discussion of the prices they had fetched. But always their greatest complaint was that they couldn't leave this apartment, which was much too large for their present circumstances, since no one could imagine how to move Gregor. But Gregor fully understood that it was not only concern for him that prevented a move, for he could easily have been shipped in a suitable crate with a few air holes; what mostly stopped them was the complete hopelessness of their situation and their sense that they had been struck by a misfortune unlike anyone else in their entire circle of friends and relations. They were suffering to the limit what the world requires of poor people: the father brought in breakfast for junior bank clerks; the mother sacrificed herself sewing underwear for strangers; the sister ran to and fro behind a counter at the bidding of customers, but the family had no more strength beyond that. And the wound in Gregor's back began to hurt again whenever the mother and sister returned after putting the father to bed, dropped their work, drew close together, and sat cheek to cheek; then the mother, pointing to Gregor's room, said: "Close the door, Grete," so that Gregor was again left in darkness while in the next room, the women mingled their tears or stared dry-eyed at the table.

Gregor spent his nights and days almost entirely without sleep. Sometimes he fancied that the next time the door opened, he would once again take charge of the family affairs just as he had done in the past; in his thoughts there reappeared, as after a long absence, the director and the office manager, the clerks and the trainees, the slow-witted office boy, two or three friends from other firms, a maid in a country hotel (a charming, fleeting memory), a cashier in a hat shop whom he'd courted earnestly but too slowly—they all appeared mixed up with strangers or people he'd forgotten, but instead of helping him and his family, they were all inaccessible, and he was glad when they disappeared. But at other times he was in no mood to worry about his family; he was filled with rage over how badly he was looked after; and even though he couldn't imagine having an appetite for anything, he still invented plans for getting into the pantry so he could help himself to the food that was coming to him, even if he wasn't hungry. No longer considering what might give Gregor some special pleasure, the sister now quickly pushed any old food into Gregor's room with her foot before she rushed off to work both in the morning and at noon; then in the evening, not caring whether the food had only been nibbled at or—most frequently—left completely untouched, she swept it out with a swing of her broom. The cleaning of his room, which she now always took care of in the evening, couldn't have been more perfunctory. Grimy dirt streaked the walls, and balls of dust and filth lay here and there. At first Gregor would stand in particularly offensive corners when the sister came in, as if intending to reproach her. But he could have waited there for weeks without the sister making any improvement; she could see the dirt just as well as he could, of course, but she had simply made up her mind to leave it there. At the same time, with a touchiness that was new to her, and that indeed was felt in the entire family, she made certain that the cleaning of Gregor's room remained her exclusive responsibility. Once Gregor's mother subjected his room to a thorough cleaning, which she managed only by using several buckets of water—the resulting dampness made Gregor sick, of course, and he lay stretched out on the sofa, embittered and immobile—but the mother didn't escape her punishment. Because that evening, the moment Gregor's sister noticed the change in his room, she ran into the living room, deeply insulted, and although the mother raised her hands imploringly, the sister broke out in a fit of weeping, while the parents—the father had of course been frightened out of his armchair—gaped in helpless astonishment, until they too started in; the father reproached the mother on his right for not leaving the cleaning of Gregor's room to the sister, and he shouted at the sister on his left, warning her that she would never again be allowed to clean Gregor's room; meanwhile the mother tried to drag the father, who was beside himself with rage, into the bedroom; the sister, shaking with sobs, beat the table with her small fists; and Gregor hissed loudly in his fury because no one thought of closing the door and sparing him this spectacle and commotion.

But even if Gregor's sister, exhausted by her work at the shop, was fed up with taking care of him as before, it was by no means necessary for the mother to take her place to make sure that Gregor wouldn't be neglected. For now the cleaning woman was there. This old widow, who in her long life must have weathered the worst thanks to her sturdy constitution, wasn't really repelled by Gregor. Without being in the least nosy, she happened one day to open the door to Gregor's room, and at the sight of Gregor, who was completely taken by surprise and began scrambling back and forth though no one was chasing him, she had merely stood still in amazement, her hands folded on her stomach. Since then, she never failed to open his door a crack every morning and night to peep in at Gregor. Initially she would even call him over with words she probably considered friendly, such as "Come on over here, you old dung beetle," or "Just look at that old dung beetle!" Gregor never responded to such calls, but remained motionless where he stood, as if the door had never been opened. If only they had ordered this woman to clean out his room every day, instead of letting her disturb him whenever she pleased! Once, early in the morning—a heavy rain, perhaps a sign of the coming spring, was pelting the windowpanes—Gregor was so annoyed when the cleaning woman again launched into her phrases that he charged toward her as if to attack, but slowly and feebly. Instead of being frightened, the cleaning woman simply raised a chair placed near the door and stood there with her mouth wide open, obviously not intending to close it again until the chair in her hand came crashing down on Gregor's back. "So you're not coming any closer?" she asked, when Gregor turned around again, and she calmly put the chair back in the corner.

By this time Gregor was eating next to nothing. Only when he happened by chance to pass by the food spread out for him, would he take a bite in his mouth just for pleasure, hold it there for hours, and then mostly spit it back out again. At first he thought it was distress at the condition of his room that kept him from eating, but he soon became adjusted to these very changes. The family had gotten into the habit of putting things that had no other place into his room, and now there were plenty of such things, because they had rented a bedroom in the apartment to three boarders. These serious gentlemen—all three had full beards, as Gregor once observed through a crack in the door—were obsessed with order, not only in their room, but also, since they were paying rent there, throughout the apartment, particularly the kitchen. They couldn't stand any kind of useless odds and ends, let alone dirty ones. Furthermore, they had for the most part brought along their own furnishings. For this reason, many things had become superfluous that couldn't be sold but also couldn't be thrown away. All these things ended up in Gregor's room. As did the ash bucket and the garbage pail from the kitchen. Whatever was not being used at the moment was simply flung into Gregor's room by the cleaning woman, who was always in a hurry; Gregor was usually fortunate enough to see only the object in question and the hand that held it. Perhaps the cleaning woman intended to retrieve these objects when she had time and opportunity to do so, or else to throw out everything at once, but in fact they lay wherever they happened to land, unless Gregor waded through the junk pile and set it in motion, at first out of necessity because there was no free space to crawl; but later on with growing pleasure, though after such excursions he would lie still for hours, dead tired and miserable.

Since the boarders also sometimes took their evening meal at home in the common living room, Gregor's door stayed shut on many evenings, but he found it very easy to give up the open door, for when it was left open on many earlier evenings he had already not taken advantage of it, but without the family's notice, he had lain in the darkest corner of his room. Once, however, the cleaning woman had left the door to the living room open a small crack; and it stayed open, even when the boarders entered in the evening and the lamp was lit. They sat at the head of the table where the father, mother, and Gregor had sat in the old days, unfolded their napkins and picked up their knives and forks. Immediately the mother appeared in the doorway with a platter of meat, and right behind her was the sister with a platter piled high with potatoes. The food gave off thick clouds of steam. The boarders bent over the platters placed in front of them as if to examine them before eating, and in fact the man sitting in the middle (whom the other two seemed to regard as an authority) cut up a piece of meat on the platter, obviously in order to determine whether it was tender enough or should perhaps need to be sent back to the kitchen. He was satisfied, and so the mother and sister, who had been watching anxiously, breathed freely again and began to smile.

The family itself ate in the kitchen. Nevertheless, before the father headed for the kitchen, he came into the living room, bowed once, his cap in hand, and walked around the table. The boarders all rose simultaneously and muttered something into their beards. When they were alone again, they ate in almost complete silence. It seemed strange to Gregor that out of the various noises of eating, he could always distinguish the sound of their chomping teeth, as if to demonstrate to Gregor that teeth were necessary for eating, and that even the most wonderful toothless jaws could accomplish nothing. "I do have an appetite," said Gregor mournfully to himself, "but not for these things. How those boarders gorge themselves, and I'm starving to death."

On that very evening—Gregor couldn't remember having once heard the violin during all this time—it was heard from the kitchen. The boarders had already finished their supper, the middle one had taken out a newspaper, handing over a sheet apiece to the two others, and they were now leaning back, reading and smoking. When the violin began to play, they noticed it, stood up, and tiptoed to the hall, where they paused, huddled together. They must have been heard from the kitchen, because the father called, "Are the gentlemen disturbed by the music, perhaps? It can be stopped at once." "On the contrary," said the middle boarder, "wouldn't the young lady like to come in here with us and play in the living room, which is more spacious and comfortable?" "Oh, with pleasure," cried the father, as if he were the violinist. The boarders went back into the living room and waited. Soon the father came with the music stand, the mother with the sheet music, and the sister with the violin. The sister calmly got everything ready to play; the parents, who'd never rented rooms before and therefore were excessively polite to the boarders, didn't dare to sit on their own chairs; the father leaned against the door, his right hand thrust between two buttons of his closed uniform jacket; the mother, however, was offered a chair by one of the boarders and sat down on it just where he happened to put it, off to the side in a corner.

The sister began to play; the father and mother on either side of her followed the movements of her hands attentively. Gregor, attracted by her playing, had ventured out a little further, and his head was already in the living room. He was hardly surprised that he had recently begun to show so little concern for others; previously such thoughtfulness had been his pride. And yet right now he would have had even more reason than ever to stay hidden, because he was completely covered with dust as a result of the particles that lay everywhere in his room and flew about with his slightest movement; bits of fluff, hair, and food remnants also stuck to his back and trailed from his sides; his indifference to everything was much too great for him to lie on his back and rub himself against the carpet, as he had once done several times a day. And in spite of his condition, he felt no shame in edging forward a little onto the immaculate floor of the living room.

To be sure, no one paid any attention to him. The family was completely absorbed by the violin playing; on the other hand, the boarders, with their hands in their pockets, stood at first much too closely behind the sister's music stand so that they all would have been able to read the music, which surely must have distracted the sister, but they soon retreated to the window and stayed there with lowered heads, softly talking with each other, while the father watched them anxiously. Indeed it now appeared all too clearly that they seemed disappointed in their hopes of hearing beautiful or entertaining violin playing, as if they had had enough of the recital and were merely suffering this disturbance of their peace out of politeness. In particular, the way in which they all blew their cigar smoke through their nose and mouth into the air suggested their high degree of irritability. And yet the sister was playing so beautifully. Her face was inclined to one side, her eyes followed the notes of the music with a searching and sorrowful look. Gregor crawled a little bit further forward and kept his head close to the floor so that it might be possible for their eyes to meet. Was he an animal, that music could move him so? It seemed as if he were being shown the way to the unknown nourishment he longed for. He was determined to push his way up to his sister and tug at her skirt, and thus suggest that she should come into his room with her violin, for nobody here was worthy of her playing as he would be worthy of it. He would never let her out of his room again, at least not so long as he lived; his terrible shape would be useful to him for the first time; he would stand guard at all the doors of his room simultaneously, hissing at the intruders; his sister, however, wouldn't be forced to stay with him but should remain of her own free will; she should sit next to him on the sofa, bending her ear down to him, and then he would confide to her that he had made a firm resolve to send her to the Conservatory, and that if misfortune hadn't intervened, he would have announced this to everyone at Christmas—had Christmas passed already?—without listening to any objections. After this declaration his sister would burst into tears of emotion, and Gregor would raise himself up to her shoulder and kiss her on the neck, which—now that she went out to work—she kept free of ribbon or collar.

"Mr. Samsa!" cried the middle boarder to the father, and without wasting another word, he pointed with his forefinger at Gregor, who was slowly crawling forward. The violin fell silent, the middle boarder first smiled at his friends with a shake of his head and then looked at Gregor again. The father seemed to think that it was more urgent to pacify the boarders than to drive Gregor out, though they weren't at all upset, and Gregor seemed to entertain them more than the violin playing. With outstretched arms, the father rushed to them and tried to herd them back to their room, while simultaneously blocking their view of Gregor with his body. Now they really became a bit angry; it wasn't clear whether the father's behavior was to blame or whether the realization was dawning on them that they had unknowingly had a next door neighbor like Gregor. They demanded explanations from the father, waving their arms at him, nervously plucking their beards, and then they backed toward their room very reluctantly. In the meantime, the sister had recovered from the bewildered state she had fallen into with the sudden interruption of her music; after having dangled her violin and bow listlessly for awhile in her slack hands, continuing to gaze at the music as if she were still playing, she had suddenly pulled herself together, placed her instrument in her mother's lap (her mother was still sitting in her chair, gasping for breath with heaving lungs) and run into the next room, which the boarders were approaching more rapidly now under pressure from the father. One could see the blankets and pillows on the beds obeying the sister's skillful hands and arranging themselves neatly. Before the boarders had even reached their room, she finished making the beds and slipped out. Once again the father seemed so overcome by his obstinacy that he was forgetting any respect he still owed his boarders. He kept crowding them and crowding them until, just at the doorway to their room, the middle boarder thunderously stamped his foot and brought the father to a halt. "I hereby declare," he said, raising his hand and looking around for the mother and sister too, "that in view of the disgusting conditions prevailing in this household and family"—here he promptly spit on the floor—"I give immediate notice. I will of course not pay a cent for the days that I have been living here, either; on the contrary, I will think seriously about taking some sort of legal action against you, with claims—believe me—that would be very easy to substantiate." He was silent and looked straight ahead of him, as if he were expecting something. And in fact his two friends immediately chimed in with the words, "We're also leaving tomorrow." Thereupon he seized the door handle and banged the door shut.

Gregor's father staggered with groping hands to his armchair and let himself fall into it; he looked as if he were stretching out for his usual evening nap, but the rapid nodding of his head, as if it were out of control, showed that he was anything but asleep. All this time Gregor had been lying still in the same place where the boarders had caught sight of him. His disappointment over the failure of his plan, and perhaps also the weakness caused by his great hunger, made it impossible for him to move. With a fair degree of certainty, he feared that in the very next moment everything would collapse over him, and he was waiting. He was not even startled when the violin slipped through the mother's trembling fingers, fell off her lap, and gave off a reverberating clang.

"My dear parents," the sister said, striking the table with her hand by way of introduction, "things can't go on like this. Perhaps you don't realize that, but I do. I refuse to utter my brother's name in the presence of this monster, and so I say: we have to try to get rid of it. We've done everything humanly possible to take care of it and put up with it; I think no one could reproach us in the slightest."

"She's right a thousand times over," the father said to himself. Still struggling to catch her breath, a wild look in her eyes, the mother began to cough hollowly into her hand.

The sister rushed to the mother and held her forehead. The father's thoughts seemed to have become clearer as a result of the sister's words; he had sat up straight and was playing with his uniform cap among the dishes that still lay on the table from the boarders' supper, and from time to time he glanced over at Gregor, who remained motionless.

"We must try to get rid of it," said the sister, now only addressing the father, since the mother couldn't hear anything over her coughing. "It'll kill both of you, I can see that coming. When we all have to work as hard as we do, how can we stand this constant torment at home? At least I can't stand it anymore." And she burst out into such violent weeping that her tears flowed down onto her mother's face, where she mechanically wiped them away.

"My child," said the father compassionately and with remarkable comprehension, "but what are we supposed to do?"

The sister just shrugged her shoulders to show the helplessness that had now come over her during her crying fit, in contrast to her former self-confidence.

"If he understood us," said the father, half-questioningly; the sister, still sobbing, waved her hand vehemently to show how unthinkable it was.

"If he understood us," repeated the father, closing his eyes to absorb the sister's conviction that this was impossible, "then perhaps we might be able to come to some sort of agreement with him. But as it is—"

"He's got to go," cried the sister, "that's the only answer, father. You must just try to stop thinking that this is Gregor. The fact that we've believed it for so long is actually our true misfortune. But how can it be Gregor? If it were Gregor, he would long since have understood that it's impossible for people to live together with such a creature, and he would have gone away of his own free will. Then we wouldn't have a brother, but we could go on living and honor his memory. But instead this creature persecutes us, drives away the boarders, obviously wants to take over the entire apartment and let us sleep out in the street. Just look, father," she suddenly shrieked, "he's at it again!" And—in a state of panic that was totally incomprehensible to Gregor—the sister even abandoned her mother, literally bolting away from her chair as if she would rather sacrifice her mother than stay near Gregor, and she rushed behind her father, who got to his feet as well, alarmed at her behavior, and half raised his arms as if to protect her.

But Gregor hadn't the slightest intention of frightening anyone, least of all his sister. He had merely begun to turn himself around so as to return to his room, and that admittedly did attract attention, since in his feeble condition he had to use his head to achieve these difficult turns, raising it and bumping it against the floor several times. He paused and looked around. His good intentions seemed to have been recognized; it had only been a momentary alarm. Now they all watched him, silent and sad. His mother lay back in her chair, her legs stretched out and pressed together, her eyes almost shut from exhaustion; his father and sister were sitting side by side, his sister had placed her hand around her father's neck.

"Perhaps I'm allowed to turn around now," Gregor thought, and he resumed his work. He couldn't suppress his panting from the exertion and also had to stop and rest every once in a while. Otherwise no one hurried him, it was all left entirely to him. When he had completed the turn, he started to crawl back in a straight line. He was astonished at the great distance separating him from his room and couldn't comprehend how in his weak condition he could have covered the same ground a short time ago almost without noticing it. So intent was he on crawling rapidly, he scarcely noticed that no word or outcry from the family was disturbing his progress. Only when he was already in the doorway did he turn his head, not completely, for he felt his neck stiffening, but enough to see that nothing had changed behind him, except that his sister had stood up. His final gaze fell on his mother, who was now sound asleep.

No sooner was he inside his room than the door was hurriedly slammed shut, firmly bolted, and locked. The sudden noise behind him frightened Gregor so much that his little legs buckled. It was his sister who had been in such a hurry. She had been standing there ready and waiting, then she had swiftly leaped forward, Gregor hadn't even heard her coming, and she had cried "At last!" to her parents as she turned the key in the lock.

"And now?" Gregor asked himself, and peered around in the darkness. He soon made the discovery that he couldn't move at all. It didn't surprise him; rather it seemed unnatural to him that until now he had actually been able to get around on those thin little legs. Otherwise he felt relatively comfortable. He had pains throughout his body, of course, but it seemed to him that they were gradually getting weaker and weaker and would eventually disappear completely. The rotten apple in his back and the inflamed area around it, completely covered over by soft dust, scarcely bothered him. His thoughts went back to his family with tenderness and love. His conviction that he must disappear was, if possible, even stronger than his sister's. He remained in this state of empty, peaceful meditation until the tower clock struck three in the morning. He was just conscious of the beginning of the dawn outside his window. Then his head sank down completely, involuntarily, and his last breath issued faintly from his nostrils.

Early in the morning when the cleaning woman arrived—from sheer energy and impatience she would slam all the doors so loudly, no matter how many times she'd been asked not to do so, that it was impossible to sleep peacefully anywhere in the apartment—she found nothing unusual at first during her customary brief visit to Gregor. She thought that he was deliberately lying motionless like that, acting insulted; she credited him with unlimited intelligence. Since she happened to be holding the long broom in her hand, she tried to tickle Gregor with it from the doorway. When this produced no response, she became annoyed and jabbed Gregor a little, and it was only when she had moved him from his place without his resistance that she began to take notice. When she quickly grasped the fact of the matter, she opened her eyes wide and gave a low whistle, but she didn't stay there long; instead she tore open the bedroom door and shouted at the top of her voice into the darkness, "Come and take a look; it's croaked; it's lying there, completely and totally croaked!"

The Samsa parents sat up in their marriage bed and had to overcome the shock that the cleaning woman had given them before they could finally grasp her message. Then Mr. and Mrs. Samsa quickly climbed out of bed, one from each side; Mr. Samsa wrapped the blanket around his shoulders, Mrs. Samsa came out only in her nightgown; in this way they entered Gregor's room. Meanwhile the living room door had also opened; Grete had been sleeping there since the boarders had moved in; she was fully dressed, as if she'd not slept at all, and her pale face seemed to confirm this. "Dead?" asked Mrs. Samsa, and looked up inquiringly at the cleaning woman, though she could have examined everything herself, and the situation was plain enough without her doing so. "I'll say!" replied the cleaning woman, and to prove it she pushed Gregor's corpse with her broom off to one side. Mrs. Samsa made a movement as if she wanted to hold back the broom, but she didn't do it. "Well," said Mr. Samsa, "now we can thank God." He crossed himself, and the three women followed his example. Grete, who never took her eyes off the corpse, said, "Just look how thin he was. After all, he hadn't been eating anything for so long. The food came out of his room again just the way it went in." As a matter of fact, Gregor's body was completely flat and dry; this was really evident now for the first time when he was no longer lifted up by his little legs and also when nothing else diverted their gaze.

"Come in with us, Grete, for a little while," said Mrs. Samsa with a melancholy smile, and Grete followed her parents into their bedroom, not without looking back at the corpse. The cleaning woman shut Gregor's door and opened his window wide. Although it was early in the morning, the fresh air held a touch of mildness. By now it was nearly the end of March.

The three boarders emerged from their room and looked around in astonishment for their breakfast; they had been forgotten. "Where is breakfast?" the middle one gruffly asked the cleaning woman. But she put her finger to her lips and hastily and silently beckoned them to come into Gregor's room. In they went and stood with their hands in the pockets of their somewhat shabby jackets in a circle around Gregor's corpse in the room that by now was filled with light.

Just then the bedroom door opened, and Mr. Samsa appeared in his uniform with his wife on one arm and his daughter on the other. They all looked as if they had been crying; from time to time Grete pressed her face against her father's sleeve.

"Leave my apartment at once!" said Mr. Samsa and pointed to the door without letting go of the women. "What do you mean?" asked the middle boarder, somewhat dismayed and with a sugary smile. The two others held their hands behind their backs and rubbed them together incessantly, as if in gleeful anticipation of a major quarrel that could only turn out in their favor. "I mean exactly what I say," answered Mr. Samsa, and he marched in a line with his two women companions toward the boarder. At first the boarder quietly stood still and looked at the floor, as if he were rearranging matters in his head. "Well, then, we'll go," he said, and suddenly overcome with humility he looked up at Mr. Samsa as if he were seeking new approval for this decision. Mr. Samsa merely nodded several times, staring at him hard. At that the boarder immediately took long strides into the hall; his two friends, who had been listening for awhile, their hands entirely still, now practically went hopping right after him, as if afraid that Mr. Samsa would reach the hall ahead of them and cut them off from their leader. In the hall, all three took their hats from the coat rack, drew their canes out of the umbrella stand, bowed silently and left the apartment. Impelled by a mistrust that proved to be entirely unfounded, Mr. Samsa and the two women stepped out onto the landing and, leaning over the banister, they watched the three boarders slowly but surely descend the long staircase, disappearing on each floor at a certain turn and then reappearing a few moments later; the lower they got, the more the Samsa family's interest in them dwindled, and when a butcher's boy proudly carrying a tray on his head swung past them on up the stairs, Mr. Samsa and the women left the banister and, as if relieved, all went back to the apartment.

They decided to spend this day resting and going for a walk; they not only deserved a break from their work, they also desperately needed it. And so they sat down at the table to write their letters of excuse, Mr. Samsa to the bank manager, Mrs. Samsa to her employer, and Grete to the store owner. While they were writing, the cleaning woman came in to announce that she was going because her morning work was finished. The three letter writers merely nodded at first without looking up, but as the cleaning woman still kept lingering, they all looked up irritably. "Well?" asked Mr. Samsa. The cleaning woman stood smiling in the doorway as if she had some great news for the family but would only tell it if they questioned her properly. The little ostrich feather sticking up almost straight on her hat, which had annoyed Mr. Samsa during all the time she had been working for them, was fluttering in all directions. "Well, what is it you really want?" asked Mrs. Samsa, for whom the cleaning woman still had the most respect. "Well," answered the cleaning woman, and she couldn't go on immediately for her own good natured chuckling, "well, you don't have to worry about getting rid of the thing next door. It's already been taken care of." Mrs. Samsa and Grete bent their heads down over their letters, as if they intended to resume writing; Mr. Samsa, who realized that the cleaning woman was now eager to start describing everything in detail, cut her short with an outstretched hand. But since she couldn't tell her story, she remembered that she was in a great hurry and cried out, obviously offended, "Goodbye, everyone," then whirled around wildly and left the apartment with a thunderous slamming of the door.

"She'll be fired tonight," said Mr. Samsa, but he received no reply from either his wife or his daughter, because the cleaning woman seemed to have disturbed the peace of mind they had just recently acquired. They got up, went over to the window, and stayed there, their arms around each other. Mr. Samsa turned toward them in his chair and watched them quietly for awhile. Then he called, "Oh, come on over here. Stop brooding over the past. And have a little consideration for me, too." The women obeyed him at once, rushed over to him, caressed him, and hurriedly finished their letters.

Then they all three left the apartment together, which they hadn't done in months, and took the trolley out to the open country on the outskirts of the city. The car, in which they were the only passengers, was flooded with warm sunshine. Leaning back comfortably in their seats, they discussed their prospects for the future and it turned out that, on closer inspection, these weren't bad at all, because all three had positions which—though they hadn't ever really asked one another about them in any detail—were thoroughly advantageous and especially promising for the future. The greatest immediate improvement in their situation would easily result, of course, from a change in apartments; now they would move to a smaller and cheaper apartment, but one better located and in general more practical than their present one, which Gregor had chosen. While they were talking in this way, it occurred almost simultaneously to both Mr. and Mrs. Samsa, as they watched their daughter's increasing liveliness, that despite all the recent cares that had made her cheeks pale, she had blossomed into a good-looking and well-developed girl. Growing quieter and almost unconsciously communicating through glances, they thought it would soon be time, too, to find a good husband for her. And it was like a confirmation of their new dreams and good intentions when at the end of their ride, their daughter stood up first and stretched her young body.

COMMENTARY

GUSTAV JANOUCH

Gustav Janouch published his recollections of Franz Kafka in *Conversations with Kafka* (1953). Janouch's father was employed by the Workers' Accident Insurance Institute with Kafka, and he introduced his son to Kafka in 1920 because they were both "scribblers." Janouch was only seventeen at the time and very impressionable. Having read "The Metamorphosis," he was disappointed by his first sight of Kafka: "'So this is the creator of the mysterious bug, Samsa,' I said to myself, disillusioned to see before me a simple, well-mannered man." But when their conversation was over that day—after Kafka had told Janouch that he wrote at night because daytime was a "great enchantment . . . it distracts from the darkness within"—Janouch asked himself, "Is he not himself the unfortunate bug in 'The Metamorphosis'?" Their acquaintance ripened into a friendship, which lasted until Kafka's death in 1924.

Kafka's View of "The Metamorphosis" 1953

TRANSLATED BY GORONWY REES

I spent my first week's wages on having Kafka's three stories—*The Metamorphosis, The Judgement*, and *The Stoker*—bound in a dark brown leather volume, with the name *Franz Kafka* elegantly tooled in gold lettering.

The book lay in the brief-case on my knee as I told Kafka about the warehouse-cinema. [Janouch was a pianist at the cinema.] Then I proudly took the volume out of the case and gave it across the desk to Kafka.

"What is this?" he asked in astonishment.

"It's my first week's wages."

"Isn't that a waste?"

Kafka's eyelids fluttered. His lips were sharply drawn in. For a few seconds he contemplated the name in the gold lettering, hastily thumbed through the pages of the book and—with obvious embarrassment—placed it before me on the desk. I was about to ask why the book offended him, when he began to cough. He took a handkerchief from his pocket, held it to his mouth, replaced it when the attack was over, stood up and went to the small washstand behind his desk and washed his hands, then said as he dried them: "You overrate me. Your trust oppresses me."

He sat himself at his desk and said, with his hands to his temples: "I am no burning bush. I am not a flame."

I interrupted him. "You shouldn't say that. It's not just. To me, for example, you are fire, warmth, and light."

"No, no!" he contradicted me, shaking his head. "You are wrong. My scribbling does not deserve a leather binding. It's only my own personal spectre of horror. It oughtn't to be printed at all. It should be burned and destroyed. It is without meaning."

I became furious. "Who told you that?" I was forced to contradict him—"How can you say such a thing? Can you see into the future? What you are saying to me is entirely your subjective feeling. Perhaps your scribbling, as you call it, will tomorrow represent a significant voice in the world. Who can tell today?"

I drew a deep breath.

Kafka stared at the desk. At the corners of his mouth were two short, sharp lines of shadow.

I was ashamed of my outburst, so I said quietly, in a low, explanatory tone: "Do you remember what you said to me about the Picasso exhibition?"

Kafka looked at me without understanding.

I continued: "You said that art is a mirror which—like a clock running fast—foretells the future. Perhaps your writing is, in today's *Cinema of the Blind*, only a mirror of tomorrow."

"Please, don't go on," said Kafka fretfully, and covered his eyes with both hands.

I apologized. "Please forgive me, I didn't mean to upset you. I'm stupid."

"No, no—you're not that!" Without removing his hands, he rocked his whole body to and fro. "You are right. You are certainly right. Probably that's why I can't finish anything. I am afraid of the truth. But can one do otherwise?" He took his hands away from his eyes, placed his clenched fists on the table, and said in a low, suppressed voice: "One must be silent, if one can't give any help. No one, through his own lack of hope, should make the condition of the patient worse. For that reason, all my scribbling is to be destroyed. I am no light. I have merely lost my way among my own thorns. I'm a dead end."

Kafka leaned backwards. His hands slipped lifelessly from the table. He closed his eyes.

"I don't believe it," I said with utter conviction, yet added appeasingly: "And even if it were true, it would be worthwhile to display the dead end to people."

Kafka merely shook his head slowly. "No, no . . . I am weak and tired."

"You should give up your work here," I said gently, to relax the tension which I felt between us.

Kafka nodded. "Yes, I should. I wanted to creep away behind this office desk, but it only increased my weakness. It's become—," Kafka looked at me with an indescribably painful smile, "— a cinema of the blind."

Then he closed his eyes again.

I was glad at this moment there was a knock on the door behind me.

D. H. LAWRENCE

David Herbert Lawrence (1885–1930) was born the son of a coal miner in the industrial town of Eastwood, in Nottinghamshire, England. His mother had been a schoolteacher, and she was frustrated by the hard existence of a coal miner's wife. Through her financial sacrifices, Lawrence was able to complete high school; then he studied to become a teacher. He finished his university studies and was licensed as a teacher at the age of twenty-three. Moving to South London, he allied himself with the young literary rebels there, and his first novel, *The White Peacock*, was published in 1910. In 1912 Lawrence fell in love with an older married woman, Frieda von Richthofen, who abandoned her husband and children to run off with him to her native Germany. English society never forgave either of them, although the pair eventually married in 1914 and maintained their exceedingly stormy union, punctuated with frequent affairs, until Lawrence's death. In 1913, Lawrence was established as a major literary figure with the publication of *Sons and Lovers*.

Much of his fiction is about characters caught between their unsatisfactory relationships with others and their struggle to break free. Lawrence sought an ideal balance or, as he wrote in the novel *Women in Love* (1920), a "star equilibrium," in which two beings are attracted to each other but never lose their individuality. He felt that "no emotion is supreme, or exclusively worth living for. All emotions go to the achieving of a living relationship between a human being and the other human being or creature or thing he becomes purely related to."

A prolific writer, Lawrence suffered from tuberculosis and spent years wandering in Italy, Australia, Mexico, New Mexico, and southern France, seeking a warm, sunny climate. He also fled to primitive societies to escape the industrialization and commercialism of Western life. A virulent social critic, he was frequently harassed by censorship because his short stories, novels, and poetry were often explicitly sexual and he always challenged conventional moral attitudes. Literature, for Lawrence, had two great functions: providing an emotional experience, and then, if the reader had the courage of his or her own feelings and could live imaginatively, becoming "a mine of practical truth."

Lawrence wrote stories all his life, publishing a first collection, *The Prussian Officer*, in 1914; it was followed by four other collections. In 1961 his stories were compiled in a three-volume paperback edition that has gone through numerous reprintings. The style of the early stories is harshly realistic, but Lawrence's depiction of his characters' emotional situations changed in his later work, where he created fantasies like his famous and chilling story "The Rocking-Horse Winner."

CONNECTION To read D. H. Lawrence's take on two of Edgar Allan Poe's stories, see "On 'The Fall of the House of Usher' and 'The Cask of Amontillado,'" page 652.

WEB Research D. H. Lawrence at bedfordstmartins.com/rewritinglit.

The Rocking-Horse Winner 1926

There was a woman who was beautiful, who started with all the advantages, yet she had no luck. She married for love, and the love turned to dust. She had bonny children, yet she felt they had been thrust upon her, and she could not love them. They looked at her coldly, as if they were finding fault with her. And hurriedly she felt she must cover up some fault in herself. Yet what it was that she must cover up she never knew. Nevertheless, when her children were present, she always felt the center of her heart go hard. This troubled her, and in her manner she was all the more gentle and anxious for her children, as if she loved them very much. Only she herself knew that at the center of her heart was a hard little place that could not feel love, no, not for anybody. Everybody else said of her: "She is such a good mother. She adores her children." Only she herself, and her children themselves, knew it was not so. They read it in each other's eyes.

There were a boy and two little girls. They lived in a pleasant house, with a garden, and they had discreet servants, and felt themselves superior to anyone in the neighborhood.

Although they lived in style, they felt always an anxiety in the house. There was never enough money. The mother had a small income, and the father had a small income, but not nearly enough for the social position which they had to keep up. The father went into town to some office. But though he had good prospects, these prospects never materialized. There was always the grinding sense of the shortage of money, though the style was always kept up.

At last the mother said: "I will see if *I* can't make something." But she did not know where to begin. She racked her brains, and tried this thing and the other, but could not find anything successful. The failure made deep lines come into her face. Her children were growing up, they would have to go to school. There must be more money, there must be more money. The father, who was always very handsome and expensive in his tastes, seemed as if he never *would* be able to do anything worth doing. And the mother, who had a great belief in herself, did not succeed any better, and her tastes were just as expensive.

And so the house came to be haunted by the unspoken phrase: *There must be more money! There must be more money!* The children could hear it all the time though nobody said it aloud. They heard it at Christmas, when the expensive and splendid toys filled the nursery. Behind the shining modern rocking horse, behind the smart doll's house, a voice would start whispering: "There *must* be more money! There *must* be more money!" And the children would stop playing, to listen for a moment. They would look into each other's eyes, to see if they had all heard. And each one saw in the eyes of the other two that they too had heard. "There *must* be more money! There *must* be more money!"

It came whispering from the springs of the still-swaying rocking horse, and even the horse, bending his wooden, champing head, heard it. The big doll, sitting so pink and smirking in her new pram, could hear it quite plainly, and seemed to be smirking all the more self-consciously because of it. The foolish puppy, too, that took the place of the teddy bear, he was looking so extraordinarily foolish for no other reason but that he heard the secret whisper all over the house: "There *must* be more money!"

Yet nobody ever said it aloud. The whisper was everywhere, and therefore no one spoke it. Just as no one ever says: "We are breathing!" in spite of the fact that breath is coming and going all the time.

"Mother," said the boy Paul one day, "why don't we keep a car of our own? Why do we always use Uncle's, or else a taxi?"

"Because we're the poor members of the family," said the mother.

"But why *are* we, Mother?"

"Well—I suppose," she said slowly and bitterly, "it's because your father has no luck."

The boy was silent for some time.

"Is luck money, Mother?" he asked rather timidly.

"No, Paul. Not quite. It's what causes you to have money."

"Oh!" said Paul vaguely. "I thought when Uncle Oscar said *filthy lucker*, it meant money."

"*Filthy lucre* does mean money," said the mother. "But it's lucre, not luck."

"Oh!" said the boy. "Then what *is* luck, Mother?"

"It's what causes you to have money. If you're lucky you have money. That's why it's better to be born lucky than rich. If you're rich, you may lose your money. But if you're lucky, you will always get more money."

"Oh! Will you? And is Father not lucky?"

"Very unlucky, I should say," she said bitterly.

The boy watched her with unsure eyes.

"Why?" he asked.

"I don't know. Nobody ever knows why one person is lucky and another unlucky."

"Don't they? Nobody at all? Does *nobody* know?"

"Perhaps God. But He never tells."

"He ought to, then. And aren't you lucky either, Mother?"

"I can't be, if I married an unlucky husband."

"But by yourself, aren't you?"

"I used to think I was, before I married. Now I think I am very unlucky indeed."

"Why?"

"Well—never mind! Perhaps I'm not really," she said.

The child looked at her, to see if she meant it. But he saw, by the lines of her mouth, that she was only trying to hide something from him.

"Well, anyhow," he said stoutly, "I'm a lucky person."

"Why?" said his mother, with a sudden laugh.

He stared at her. He didn't even know why he had said it.

"God told me," he asserted, brazening it out.

"I hope He did, dear!" she said, again with a laugh, but rather bitter.

"He did, Mother!"

"Excellent!" said the mother.

The boy saw she did not believe him; or, rather, that she paid no attention to his assertion. This angered him somewhat, and made him want to compel her attention.

He went off by himself, vaguely, in a childish way, seeking for the clue to "luck." Absorbed, taking no heed of other people, he went about with a sort of stealth, seeking inwardly for luck. He wanted luck, he wanted it, he wanted it. When the two girls were playing dolls in the nursery, he would sit on his big rocking horse, charging madly into space, with a frenzy that made the little girls peer at him uneasily. Wildly the horse careered, the waving dark hair of the boy tossed, his eyes had a strange glare in them. The little girls dared not speak to him.

When he had ridden to the end of his mad little journey, he climbed down and stood in front of his rocking horse, staring fixedly into its lowered face. Its red mouth was slightly open, its big eye was wide and glassy-bright.

Now! he could silently command the snorting steed. Now, take me to where there is luck! Now take me!

And he would slash the horse on the neck with the little whip he had asked Uncle Oscar for. He *knew* the horse could take him to where there was luck, if only he forced it. So he would mount again, and start on his furious ride, hoping at last to get there. He knew he could get there.

"You'll break your horse, Paul!" said the nurse.

"He's always riding like that! I wish he'd leave off!" said his elder sister Joan.

But he only glared down on them in silence. Nurse gave him up. She could make nothing of him. Anyhow he was growing beyond her.

One day his mother and his uncle Oscar came in when he was on one of his furious rides. He did not speak to them.

"Hallo, you young jockey! Riding a winner?" said his uncle.

"Aren't you growing too big for a rocking horse? You're not a very little boy any longer, you know," said his mother.

But Paul only gave a blue glare from his big, rather close-set eyes. He would speak to nobody when he was in full tilt. His mother watched him with an anxious expression on her face.

At last he suddenly stopped forcing his horse into the mechanical gallop, and slid down.

"Well, I got there!" he announced fiercely, his blue eyes still flaring, and his sturdy long legs straddling apart.

"Where did you get to?" asked his mother.

"Where I wanted to go," he flared back at her.

"That's right, son!" said Uncle Oscar. "Don't you stop till you get there. What's the horse's name?"

"He doesn't have a name," said the boy.

"Gets on without all right?" asked the uncle.

"Well, he has different names. He was called Sansovino last week."

"Sansovino, eh? Won the Ascot. How did you know his name?"

"He always talks about horse races with Bassett," said Joan.

The uncle was delighted to find that his small nephew was posted with all the racing news. Bassett, the young gardener, who had been wounded in the left foot in the war and had got his present job through Oscar Cresswell, whose batman° he had been, was a perfect blade of the "turf." He lived in the racing events, and the small boy lived with him.

Oscar Cresswell got it all from Bassett.

"Master Paul comes and asks me, so I can't do more than tell him, sir," said Bassett, his face terribly serious, as if he were speaking of religious matters.

"And does he ever put anything on a horse he fancies?"

"Well—I don't want to give him away—he's a young sport, a fine sport, sir. Would you mind asking him himself? He sort of takes a pleasure in it, and perhaps he'd feel I was giving him away, sir, if you don't mind."

---

batman: An orderly assigned to serve a superior officer in the British military.

Bassett was serious as a church.

The uncle went back to his nephew and took him off for a ride in the car.

"Say, Paul, old man, do you ever put anything on a horse?" the uncle asked.

The boy watched the handsome man closely.

"Why, do you think I oughtn't to?" he parried.

"Not a bit of it! I thought perhaps you might give me a tip for the Lincoln."

The car sped on into the country, going down to Uncle Oscar's place in Hampshire.

"Honor bright?" said the nephew.

"Honor bright, son!" said the uncle.

"Well, then, Daffodil."

"Daffodil! I doubt it, sonny. What about Mirza?"

"I only know the winner," said the boy. "That's Daffodil."

"Daffodil, eh?"

There was a pause. Daffodil was an obscure horse comparatively.

"Uncle!"

"Yes, son?"

"You won't let it go any further, will you? I promised Bassett."

"Bassett be damned, old man! What's he got to do with it?"

"We're partners. We've been partners from the first. Uncle, he lent me my first five shillings, which I lost. I promised him, honor bright, it was only between me and him; only you gave me that ten-shilling note I started winning with, so I thought you were lucky. You won't let it go any further, will you?"

The boy gazed at his uncle from those big, hot, blue eyes, set rather close together. The uncle stirred and laughed uneasily.

"Right you are, son! I'll keep your tip private. Daffodil, eh? How much are you putting on him?"

"All except twenty pounds," said the boy. "I keep that in reserve."

The uncle thought it a good joke.

"You keep twenty pounds in reserve, do you, you young romancer? What are you betting, then?"

"I'm betting three hundred," said the boy gravely. "But it's between you and me, Uncle Oscar! Honor bright?"

The uncle burst into a roar of laughter.

"It's between you and me all right, you young Nat Gould,"° he said, laughing. "But where's your three hundred?"

"Bassett keeps it for me. We're partners."

"You are, are you! And what is Bassett putting on Daffodil?"

"He won't go quite as high as I do, I expect. Perhaps he'll go a hundred and fifty."

"What, pennies?" laughed the uncle.

Nat Gould: Nathaniel Gould (1857–1919) was a British novelist and sports columnist known best for a series of novels about horse racing.

"Pounds," said the child, with a surprised look at his uncle. "Bassett keeps a bigger reserve than I do."

Between wonder and amusement Uncle Oscar was silent. He pursued the matter no further, but he determined to take his nephew with him to the Lincoln races.

"Now, son," he said, "I'm putting twenty on Mirza, and I'll put five for you on any horse you fancy. What's your pick?"

"Daffodil, Uncle."

"No, not the fiver on Daffodil!"

"I should if it was my own fiver," said the child.

"Good! Good! Right you are! A fiver for me and a fiver for you on Daffodil."

The child had never been to a race meeting before, and his eyes were blue fire. He pursed his mouth tight, and watched. A Frenchman just in front had put his money on Lancelot. Wild with excitement, he flailed his arms up and down, yelling *"Lancelot! Lancelot!"* in his French accent.

Daffodil came in first, Lancelot second, Mirza third. The child, flushed and with eyes blazing, was curiously serene. His uncle brought him four five-pound notes, four to one.

"What am I to do with these?" he cried, waving them before the boy's eyes.

"I suppose we'll talk to Bassett," said the boy. "I expect I have fifteen hundred now; and twenty in reserve; and this twenty."

His uncle studied him for some moments.

"Look here, son!" he said. "You're not serious about Bassett and that fifteen hundred, are you?"

"Yes, I am. But it's between you and me, Uncle. Honor bright!"

"Honor bright all right, son! But I must talk to Bassett."

"If you'd like to be a partner, Uncle, with Bassett and me, we could all be partners. Only, you'd have to promise, honor bright, Uncle, not to let it go beyond us three. Bassett and I are lucky, and you must be lucky, because it was your ten shillings I started winning with. . . ."

Uncle Oscar took both Bassett and Paul into Richmond Park for an afternoon, and there they talked.

"It's like this, you see, sir," Bassett said. "Master Paul would get me talking about racing events, spinning yarns, you know, sir. And he was always keen on knowing if I'd made or if I'd lost. It's about a year since, now, that I put five shillings on Blush of Dawn for him—and we lost. Then the luck turned, with that ten shillings he had from you, that we put on Singhalese. And since then, it's been pretty steady, all things considering. What do you say, Master Paul?"

"We're all right when we're sure," said Paul. "It's when we're not quite sure that we go down."

"Oh, but we're careful then," said Bassett.

"But when are you *sure*?" Uncle Oscar smiled.

"It's Master Paul, sir," said Bassett, in a secret, religious voice. "It's as if he had it from heaven. Like Daffodil, now, for the Lincoln. That was as sure as eggs."

"Did you put anything on Daffodil?" asked Oscar Cresswell.

"Yes, sir. I made my bit."

"And my nephew?"

Bassett was obstinately silent, looking at Paul.

"I made twelve hundred, didn't I, Bassett? I told Uncle I was putting three hundred on Daffodil."

"That's right," said Bassett, nodding.

"But where's the money?" asked the uncle.

"I keep it safe locked up, sir. Master Paul he can have it any minute he likes to ask for it."

"What, fifteen hundred pounds?"

"And twenty! And *forty*, that is, with the twenty he made on the course."

"It's amazing!" said the uncle.

"If Master Paul offers you to be partners, sir, I would, if I were you; if you'll excuse me," said Bassett.

Oscar Cresswell thought about it.

"I'll see the money," he said.

They drove home again, and sure enough, Bassett came round to the garden house with fifteen hundred pounds in notes. The twenty pounds reserve was left with Joe Glee, in the Turf Commission deposit.

"You see, it's all right, Uncle, when I'm *sure*! Then we go strong, for all we're worth. Don't we, Bassett?"

"We do that, Master Paul."

"And when are you sure?" said the uncle, laughing.

"Oh, well, sometimes I'm *absolutely* sure, like about Daffodil," said the boy; "and sometimes I have an idea; and sometimes I haven't even an idea, have I, Bassett? Then we're careful, because we mostly go down."

"You do, do you! And when you're sure, like about Daffodil, what makes you sure, sonny?"

"Oh, well, I don't know," said the boy uneasily. "I'm sure, you know, Uncle; that's all."

"It's as if he had it from heaven, sir," Bassett reiterated.

"I should say so!" said the uncle.

But he became a partner. And when the Leger was coming on, Paul was "sure" about Lively Spark, which was a quite inconsiderable horse. The boy insisted on putting a thousand on the horse, Bassett went for five hundred, and Oscar Cresswell two hundred. Lively Spark came in first, and the betting had been ten to one against him. Paul had made ten thousand.

"You see," he said, "I was absolutely sure of him."

Even Oscar Cresswell had cleared two thousand.

"Look here, son," he said, "this sort of thing makes me nervous."

"It needn't, Uncle! Perhaps I shan't be sure again for a long time."

"But what are you going to do with your money?" asked the uncle.

"Of course," said the boy. "I started it for Mother. She said she had no luck, because Father is unlucky, so I thought if *I* was lucky, it might stop whispering."

"What might stop whispering?"

"Our house. I *hate* our house for whispering."

"What does it whisper?"

"Why—why"—the boy fidgeted—"why, I don't know. But it's always short of money, you know, Uncle."

"I know it, son, I know it."

"You know people send Mother writs, don't you, Uncle?"

"I'm afraid I do," said the uncle.

"And then the house whispers, like people laughing at you behind your back. It's awful, that is! I thought if I was lucky. . . ."

"You might stop it," added the uncle.

The boy watched him with big blue eyes, that had an uncanny cold fire in them, and he said never a word.

"Well, then!" said the uncle. "What are we doing?"

"I shouldn't like Mother to know I was lucky," said the boy.

"Why not, son?"

"She'd stop me."

"I don't think she would."

"Oh!"—and the boy writhed in an odd way—"I *don't* want her to know, Uncle."

"All right, son! We'll manage it without her knowing."

They managed it very easily. Paul, at the other's suggestion, handed over five thousand pounds to his uncle, who deposited it with the family lawyer, who was then to inform Paul's mother that a relative had put five thousand pounds into his hands, which sum was to be paid out a thousand pounds at a time, on the mother's birthday, for the next five years.

"So she'll have a birthday present of a thousand pounds for five successive years," said Uncle Oscar. "I hope it won't make it all the harder for her later."

Paul's mother had her birthday in November. The house had been "whispering" worse than ever lately, and, even in spite of his luck, Paul could not bear up against it. He was very anxious to see the effect of the birthday letter, telling his mother about the thousand pounds.

When there were no visitors, Paul now took his meals with his parents, as he was beyond the nursery control. His mother went into town nearly every day. She had discovered that she had an odd knack of sketching furs and dress materials, so she worked secretly in the studio of a friend who was the chief artist for the leading drapers. She drew the figures of ladies in furs and ladies in silk and sequins for the newspaper advertisements. This young woman artist earned several thousand pounds a year, but Paul's mother only made several hundreds, and she was again dissatisfied. She so wanted to be first in something, and she did not succeed, even in making sketches for drapery advertisements.

She was down to breakfast on the morning of her birthday. Paul watched her face as she read her letters. He knew the lawyer's letter. As his mother read it, her face hardened and became more expressionless. Then a cold, determined look came on her mouth. She hid the letter under the pile of others, and said not a word about it.

"Didn't you have anything nice in the post for your birthday, Mother?" said Paul.

"Quite moderately nice," she said, her voice cold and absent.

She went away to town without saying more.

But in the afternoon Uncle Oscar appeared. He said Paul's mother had had a long interview with the lawyer, asking if the whole five thousand could not be advanced at once, as she was in debt.

"What do you think, Uncle?" said the boy.

"I leave it to you, son."

"Oh, let her have it, then! We can get some more with the other," said the boy.

"A bird in the hand is worth two in the bush, laddie!" said Uncle Oscar.

"But I'm sure to *know* for the Grand National; or the Lincolnshire; or else the Derby. I'm sure to know for *one* of them," said Paul.

So Uncle Oscar signed the agreement, and Paul's mother touched the whole five thousand. Then something very curious happened. The voices in the house suddenly went mad, like a chorus of frogs on a spring evening. There were certain new furnishings, and Paul had a tutor. He was *really* going to Eton, his father's school, in the following autumn. There were flowers in the winter, and a blossoming of the luxury Paul's mother had been used to. And yet the voices in the house, behind the sprays of mimosa and almond blossom, and from under the piles of iridescent cushions, simply trilled and screamed in a sort of ecstasy: "There *must* be more money! Oh-h-h; there *must* be more money. Oh, now, now-w! Now-w-w—there *must* be more money!—more than ever! More than ever!"

It frightened Paul terribly. He studied away at his Latin and Greek. But his intense hours were spent with Bassett. The Grand National had gone by; he had not "known," and had lost a hundred pounds. Summer was at hand. He was in agony for the Lincoln. But even for the Lincoln he didn't "know," and he lost fifty pounds. He became wild-eyed and strange, as if something were going to explode in him.

"Let it alone, son! Don't you bother about it!" urged Uncle Oscar. But it was as if the boy couldn't really hear what his uncle was saying.

"I've got to know for the Derby! I've got to know for the Derby!" the child reiterated, his big blue eyes blazing with a sort of madness.

His mother noticed how overwrought he was.

"You'd better go to the seaside. Wouldn't you like to go now to the seaside, instead of waiting? I think you'd better," she said, looking down at him anxiously, her heart curiously heavy because of him.

But the child lifted his uncanny blue eyes. "I couldn't possibly go before the Derby, Mother!" he said. "I couldn't possibly!"

"Why not?" she said, her voice becoming heavy when she was opposed. "Why not? You can still go from the seaside to see the Derby with your uncle Oscar, if that's what you wish. No need for you to wait here. Besides, I think you care too much about these races. It's a bad sign. My family has been a gambling family, and you won't know till you grow up how much damage it has done. But it has done damage. I shall have to send Bassett away, and ask Uncle

Oscar not to talk racing to you, unless you promise to be reasonable about it; go away to the seaside and forget it. You're all nerves!"

"I'll do what you like, Mother, so long as you don't send me away till after the Derby," the boy said.

"Send you away from where? Just from this house?"

"Yes," he said, gazing at her.

"Why, you curious child, what makes you care about this house so much, suddenly? I never knew you loved it."

He gazed at her without speaking. He had a secret within a secret, something he had not divulged, even to Bassett or to his uncle Oscar.

But his mother, after standing undecided and a little bit sullen for some moments, said:

"Very well, then! Don't go to the seaside till after the Derby, if you don't wish it. But promise me you won't let your nerves go to pieces. Promise you won't think so much about horse racing and *events*, as you call them!"

"Oh, no," said the boy casually. "I won't think much about them, Mother. You needn't worry. I wouldn't worry, Mother, if I were you."

"If you were me and I were you," said his mother, "I wonder what we *should* do!"

"But you know you needn't worry, Mother, don't you?" the boy repeated.

"I should be awfully glad to know it," she said wearily.

"Oh, well you *can*, you know. I mean, you *ought* to know you needn't worry," he insisted.

"Ought I? Then I'll see about it," she said.

Paul's secret of secrets was his wooden horse, that which had no name. Since he was emancipated from a nurse and a nursery governess, he had had his rocking horse removed to his own bedroom at the top of the house.

"Surely, you're too big for a rocking horse!" his mother had remonstrated.

"Well, you see, Mother, till I can have a *real* horse, I like to have *some* sort of animal about," had been his quaint answer.

"Do you feel he keeps you company?" She laughed.

"Oh, yes! He's very good, he always keeps me company, when I'm there," said Paul.

So the horse, rather shabby, stood in an arrested prance in the boy's bedroom.

The Derby was drawing near, and the boy grew more and more tense. He hardly heard what was spoken to him, he was very frail, and his eyes were really uncanny. His mother had sudden strange seizures of uneasiness about him. Sometimes, for half an hour, she would feel a sudden anxiety about him that was almost anguish. She wanted to rush to him at once, and know he was safe.

Two nights before the Derby, she was at a big party in town, when one of her rushes of anxiety about her boy, her firstborn, gripped her heart till she could hardly speak. She fought with the feeling, might and main, for she believed in common sense. But it was too strong. She had to leave the dance and go downstairs to telephone to the country. The children's nursery governess was terribly surprised and startled at being rung up in the night.

"Are the children all right, Miss Wilmot?"

"Oh, yes, they are quite all right."

"Master Paul? Is he all right?"

"He went to bed as right as a trivet. Shall I run up and look at him?"

"No," said Paul's mother reluctantly. "No! Don't trouble. It's all right. Don't sit up. We shall be home fairly soon." She did not want her son's privacy intruded upon.

"Very good," said the governess.

It was about one o'clock when Paul's mother and father drove up to their house. All was still. Paul's mother went to her room and slipped off her white fur cloak. She had told her maid not to wait up for her. She heard her husband downstairs, mixing a whisky and soda.

And then, because of the strange anxiety at her heart, she stole upstairs to her son's room. Noiselessly she went along the upper corridor. Was there a faint noise? What was it?

She stood, with arrested muscles, outside his door, listening. There was a strange, heavy, and yet not loud noise. Her heart stood still. It was a soundless noise, yet rushing and powerful. Something huge, in violent, hushed motion. What was it? What in God's name was it? She ought to know. She felt that she knew the noise. She knew what it was.

Yet she could not place it. She couldn't say what it was. And on and on it went, like a madness.

Softly, frozen with anxiety and fear, she turned the door handle.

The room was dark. Yet in the space near the window, she heard and saw something plunging to and fro. She gazed in fear and amazement.

Then suddenly she switched on the light, and saw her son, in his green pajamas, madly surging on the rocking horse. The blaze of light suddenly lit him up, as he urged the wooden horse, and lit her up, as she stood, blonde, in her dress of pale green and crystal, in the doorway.

"Paul!" she cried. "Whatever are you doing?"

"It's Malabar!" he screamed, in a powerful, strange voice. "It's Malabar!"

His eyes blazed at her for one strange and senseless second, as he ceased urging his wooden horse. Then he fell with a crash to the ground, and she, all her tormented motherhood flooding upon her, rushed to gather him up.

But he was unconscious, and unconscious he remained, with some brain fever. He talked and tossed, and his mother sat stonily by his side.

"Malabar! It's Malabar! Bassett, Bassett, I *know!* It's Malabar!"

So the child cried, trying to get up and urge the rocking horse that gave him his inspiration.

"What does he mean by Malabar?" asked the heart-frozen mother.

"I don't know," said the father stonily.

"What does he mean by Malabar?" she asked her brother Oscar.

"It's one of the horses running for the Derby," was the answer.

And, in spite of himself, Oscar Cresswell spoke to Bassett, and himself put a thousand on Malabar: at fourteen to one.

The third day of the illness was critical: they were waiting for a change. The boy, with his rather long, curly hair, was tossing ceaselessly on the pillow.

He never slept nor regained consciousness, and his eyes were like blue stones. His mother sat, feeling her heart had gone, turned actually into a stone.

In the evening, Oscar Cresswell did not come, but Bassett sent a message, saying could he come up for one moment, just one moment? Paul's mother was very angry at the intrusion, but on second thought she agreed. The boy was the same. Perhaps Bassett might bring him to consciousness.

The gardener, a shortish fellow with a little brown mustache, and sharp little brown eyes, tiptoed into the room, touched his imaginary cap to Paul's mother, and stole to the bedside, staring with glittering, smallish eyes at the tossing, dying child.

"Master Paul!" he whispered. "Master Paul! Malabar came in first all right, a clean win. I did as you told me. You've made over seventy thousand pounds, you have; you've got over eighty thousand. Malabar came in all right, Master Paul."

"Malabar! Malabar! Did I say Malabar, Mother? Did I say Malabar? Do you think I'm lucky, Mother? I knew Malabar, didn't I? Over eighty thousand pounds! I call that lucky, don't you, Mother? Over eighty thousand pounds! I knew, didn't I know I knew? Malabar came in all right. If I ride my horse till I'm sure, then I tell you, Bassett, you can go as high as you like. Did you go for all you were worth, Bassett?"

"I went a thousand on it, Master Paul."

"I never told you, Mother, that if I can ride my horse, and *get there*, then I'm absolutely sure—oh, absolutely! Mother, did I ever tell you? I *am* lucky!"

"No, you never did," said the mother.

But the boy died in the night.

And even as he lay dead, his mother heard her brother's voice saying to her: "My God, Hester, you're eighty-odd thousand to the good, and a poor devil of a son to the bad. But, poor devil, poor devil, he's best gone out of a life where he rides his rocking horse to find a winner."

JACK LONDON

Jack London (1876–1916), unlike Bret Harte, Mark Twain, and most of the early American writers who wrote stories about the American West, was born in that region – in San Francisco. He had a hard childhood, forced to earn his own living by manual labor in a canning factory starting at age fifteen. Later he worked in a laundry, and still later he was a sailor. Descriptive writing came naturally to him, and two years before he graduated from Oakland High School he won first prize in a local newspaper's article contest for "Story of a Typhoon off the Coast of Japan." He attended the University of California at Berkeley for one semester, but he regarded himself as self-taught, reading Karl Marx and Friedrich Engels, Herbert Spencer, and Friedrich Nietzsche as a young man. He joined the Socialist Labor Party after he had become convinced that it was impossible for workers to secure better conditions without organizing to take over the means of production. In 1897 he joined the Klondike gold rush and spent the winter in the Yukon. Two years later, after his return from Alaska on a

2,000-mile boat trip down the Yukon River, he published his first professional story, "To the Man on the Trail," in the *Overland Monthly*, and began to write for his living. London's first collection of fiction, *Son of the Wolf*, appeared in 1900. His novel *The Call of the Wild* (1903) was his biggest success, selling 1.5 million copies, and he became the highest-paid author of his time. He regarded his adventure stories as inferior to his political writing, however; they were merely a means of making money to support his expanding interests in social reform as a Socialist speaker and political candidate. He covered the Russo-Japanese War as a correspondent, and wrote articles on the San Francisco earthquake of 1906 and the Mexican Revolution of 1914. Shortly before his death at the age of forty, he resigned from the Socialist Party "because of its lack of fire and fight, and its loss of emphasis on the class struggle." The circumstances of London's death strangely echoed the events of his semiautobiographical novel *Martin Eden* (1909), in which a writer achieves success, but after rejecting Socialist aims finds his life meaningless and commits suicide.

London produced almost fifty volumes of prose, including several collections of short stories such as *Son of the Wolf, South Sea Tales* (1911), and *The House of Pride and Other Tales of Hawaii* (1912). He learned to tell stories, he claimed, when he was bumming across the United States and had to decide exactly the right line to pitch between the moment the housewife opened the door and the moment she asked him what he wanted. He felt that poverty had made him hustle, but that only his good luck had prevented it from destroying him. Claiming "no mentor but myself" as a writer, he placed the highest value on original experience; the stamp of self on a writer's work was "a trademark of far greater value than copyright."

London's reputation as a storyteller has declined in the United States in recent times, but he remains one of our most translated authors. His literary style is simple, often journalistic, and his stories are known to countless readers around the world for championing social protest and dramatizing this country's rugged pioneer experience. As Jorge Luis Borges has observed, the vitality which permeated London's life is apparent in his best work. "To Build a Fire" tells the story of a man's struggle against nature, trying to survive against impossible odds in a universe indifferent to an individual's fate.

WEB Research Jack London at bedfordstmartins.com/rewritinglit.

To Build a Fire

1908

Day had broken cold and grey, exceedingly cold and grey, when the man turned aside from the main Yukon trail and climbed the high earth-bank, where a dim and little-travelled trail led eastward through the fat spruce timberland. It was a steep bank, and he paused for breath at the top, excusing the act to himself by looking at his watch. It was nine o'clock. There was no sun nor hint of sun, though there was not a cloud in the sky. It was a clear day, and yet there seemed an intangible pall over the face of things, a subtle gloom that made the day dark, and that was due to the absence of sun. This fact did not worry the man. He was used to the lack of sun. It had been days since he had seen the sun, and he knew that a few more days must pass before that cheerful orb, due south, would just peep above the skyline and dip immediately from view.

The man flung a look back along the way he had come. The Yukon lay a mile wide and hidden under three feet of ice. On top of this ice were as many feet of snow. It was all pure white, rolling in gentle undulations where the ice jams of the freeze-up had formed. North and south, as far as his eye could see, it was unbroken white, save for a dark hairline that curved and twisted from around the spruce-covered island to the south, and that curved and twisted away into the north, where it disappeared behind another spruce-covered island. This dark hairline was the trail—the main trail—that led south five hundred miles to the Chilcoot Pass, Dyea, and salt water; and that led north seventy miles to Dawson, and still on to the north a thousand miles to Nulato, and finally to St. Michael, on Bering Sea, a thousand miles and half a thousand more.

But all this—the mysterious, far-reaching hairline trail, the absence of sun from the sky, the tremendous cold, and the strangeness and weirdness of it all—made no impression on the man. It was not because he was long used to it. He was a newcomer in the land, a *chechaquo,* and this was his first winter. The trouble with him was that he was without imagination. He was quick and alert in the things of life, but only in the things, and not in the significances. Fifty degrees below zero meant eighty-odd degrees of frost. Such fact impressed him as being cold and uncomfortable, and that was all. It did not lead him to meditate upon his frailty as a creature of temperature, and upon man's frailty in general, able only to live within certain narrow limits of heat and cold; and from there on it did not lead him to the conjectural field of immortality and man's place in the universe. Fifty degrees below zero stood for a bite of frost that hurt and that must be guarded against by the use of mittens, ear flaps, warm moccasins, and thick socks. Fifty degrees below zero. That there should be anything more to it than that was a thought that never entered his head.

As he turned to go on, he spat speculatively. There was a sharp explosive crackle that startled him. He spat again. And again, in the air, before it could fall to the snow, the spittle crackled. He knew that at fifty below spittle crackled on the snow, but this spittle had crackled in the air. Undoubtedly it was colder than fifty below—how much colder he did not know. But the temperature did not matter. He was bound for the old claim on the left fork of Henderson Creek, where the boys were already. They had come over across the divide from the Indian Creek country, while he had come the roundabout way to take a look at the possibilities of getting out logs in the spring from the islands in the Yukon. He would be in to camp by six o'clock; a bit after dark, it was true, but the boys would be there, a fire would be going, and a hot supper would be ready. As for lunch, he pressed his hand against the protruding bundle under his jacket. It was also under his shirt, wrapped up in a handkerchief and lying against the naked skin. It was the only way to keep the biscuits from freezing. He smiled agreeably to himself as he thought of those biscuits, each cut open and sopped in bacon grease, and each enclosing a generous slice of fried bacon.

He plunged in among the big spruce trees. The trail was faint. A foot of snow had fallen since the last sled had passed over, and he was glad he was without a sled, travelling light. In fact, he carried nothing but the lunch wrapped in the handkerchief. He was surprised, however, at the cold. It certainly was cold, he concluded, as he rubbed his numb nose and cheekbones with his mittened hand. He was a warm-whiskered man, but the hair on his face did not protect the high cheekbones and the eager nose that thrust itself aggressively into the frosty air.

At the man's heels trotted a dog, a big native husky, the proper wolf-dog, grey-coated and without any visible or temperamental difference from its brother, the wild wolf. The animal was depressed by the tremendous cold. It knew that it was no time for travelling. Its instinct told it a truer tale than was told to the man by the man's judgment. In reality, it was not merely colder than fifty below zero; it was colder than sixty below, than seventy below. It was seventy-five below zero. Since the freezing point is thirty-two above zero, it meant that one hundred and seven degrees of frost obtained. The dog did not know anything about thermometers. Possibly in its brain there was no sharp consciousness of a condition of very cold such as was in the man's brain. But the brute had its instinct. It experienced a vague but menacing apprehension that subdued it and made it slink along at the man's heels, and that made it question eagerly every unwonted movement of the man as if expecting him to go into camp or to seek shelter somewhere and build a fire. The dog had learned fire, and it wanted fire, or else to burrow under the snow and cuddle its warmth away from the air.

The frozen moisture of its breathing had settled on its fur in a fine powder of frost, and especially were its jowls, muzzle, and eyelashes whitened by its crystal breath. The man's red beard and moustache were likewise frosted, but more solidly, the deposit taking the form of ice and increasing with every warm, moist breath he exhaled. Also, the man was chewing tobacco, and the muzzle of ice held his lips so rigidly that he was unable to clear his chin when he expelled the juice. The result was a crystal beard of the color and solidity of amber that was increasing its length on his chin. If he fell down it would shatter itself, like glass, into brittle fragments. But he did not mind the appendage. It was the penalty all tobacco chewers paid in that country, and he had been out before in two cold snaps. They had not been so cold as this, he knew, but by the spirit thermometer at Sixty Mile he knew they had been registered at fifty below and at fifty-five.

He held on through the level stretch of woods for several miles, crossed a wide flat of nigger heads, and dropped down a bank to the frozen bed of a small stream. This was Henderson Creek, and he knew he was ten miles from the forks. He looked at his watch. It was ten o'clock. He was making four miles an hour, and he calculated that he would arrive at the forks at half-past twelve. He decided to celebrate that event by eating his lunch there.

The dog dropped in again at his heels, with a tail drooping discouragement, as the man swung along the creek bed. The furrow of the old sled trail was plainly visible, but a dozen inches of snow covered up the marks of the last runners. In a month no man had come up or down that silent creek. The man held steadily on. He was not much given to thinking, and just then particularly he had nothing to think about save that he would eat lunch at the forks and that at six o'clock he would be in camp with the boys. There was nobody to talk to; and, had there been, speech would have been impossible because of the ice muzzle on his mouth. So he continued monotonously to chew tobacco and to increase the length of his amber beard.

Once in a while the thought reiterated itself that it was very cold and that he had never experienced such cold. As he walked along he rubbed his cheekbones and nose with the back of his mittened hand. He did this automatically, now and again changing hands. But, rub as he would, the instant he stopped his cheekbones went numb, and the following instant the end of his nose went numb. He was sure to frost his cheeks; he knew that, and experienced a pang of regret that he had not devised a nose strap of the sort Bud wore in cold snaps. Such a strap passed across the cheeks, as well, and saved them. But it didn't matter much, after all. What were frosted cheeks? A bit painful, that was all; they were never serious.

Empty as the man's mind was of thoughts, he was keenly observant, and he noticed the changes in the creeks, the curves and bends and timber jams, and always he sharply noted where he placed his feet. Once, coming round a bend, he shied abruptly, like a startled horse, curved away from the place where he had been walking, and retreated several paces back along the trail. The creek he knew was frozen clear to the bottom—no creek could contain water in that arctic winter—but he knew also that there were springs that bubbled out from the hillsides and ran along under the snow and on top of the ice of the creek. He knew that the coldest snaps never froze these springs, and he knew likewise their danger. They were traps. They hid pools of water under the snow that might be three inches deep, or three feet. Sometimes a skin of ice half an inch thick covered them, and in turn was covered by the snow. Sometimes there were alternate layers of water and ice skin, so that when one broke through he kept on breaking through for a while, sometimes wetting himself to the waist.

That was why he had shied in such a panic. He had felt the give under his feet and heard the crackle of a snow-hidden ice skin. And to get his feet wet in such a temperature meant trouble and danger. At the very least it meant delay, for he would be forced to stop and build a fire, and under its protection to bare his feet while he dried his socks and moccasins. He stood and studied the creek bed and its banks, and decided that the flow of water came from the right. He reflected awhile, rubbing his nose and cheeks, then skirted to the left, stepping gingerly and testing the footing for each step. Once clear of the danger, he took a fresh chew of tobacco and swung along at his four-mile gait.

In the course of the next two hours he came upon several similar traps. Usually the snow above the hidden pools had a sunken, candied appearance that advertised the danger. Once again, however, he had a close call; and once, suspecting danger, he compelled the dog to go on in front. The dog did not want to go. It hung back until the man shoved it forward, and then it went quickly across the white, unbroken surface. Suddenly it broke through, floundered to one side, and got away to firmer footing. It had wet its forefeet and legs, and almost immediately the water that clung to it turned to ice. It made quick efforts to lick the ice off its legs, then dropped down in the snow and began to bite out the ice that had formed between the toes. This was a matter of instinct. To permit the ice to remain would mean sore feet. It did not know this. It merely obeyed the mysterious prompting that arose from the deep crypts of its being. But the man knew, having achieved a judgment on the subject, and he removed the mitten from his right hand and helped to tear out the ice particles. He did not expose his fingers more than a minute, and was astonished at the swift numbness that smote them. It certainly was cold. He pulled on the mitten hastily, and beat the hand savagely across his chest.

At twelve o'clock the day was at its brightest. Yet the sun was too far south on its winter journey to clear the horizon. The bulge of the earth intervened between it and Henderson Creek, where the man walked under a clear sky at noon and cast no shadow. At half-past twelve, to the minute, he arrived at the forks of the creek. He was pleased at the speed he had made. If he kept it up, he would certainly be with the boys by six. He unbuttoned his jacket and shirt and drew forth his lunch. The action consumed no more than a quarter of a minute, yet in that brief moment the numbness laid hold of the exposed fingers. He did not put the mitten on, but, instead, struck the fingers a dozen sharp smashes against his leg. Then he sat down on a snow-covered log to eat. The sting that followed upon the striking of his fingers against his leg ceased so quickly that he was startled. He had had no chance to take a bite of biscuit. He struck the fingers repeatedly and returned them to the mitten, baring the other hand for the purpose of eating. He tried to take a mouthful, but the ice muzzle prevented. He had forgotten to build a fire and thaw out. He chuckled at his foolishness, and as he chuckled he noted the numbness creeping into the exposed fingers. Also, he noted that the stinging which had first come to his toes when he sat down was already passing away. He wondered whether the toes were warm or numb. He moved them inside the moccasins and decided that they were numb.

He pulled the mitten on hurriedly and stood up. He was a bit frightened. He stamped up and down until the stinging returned into the feet. It certainly was cold, was his thought. That man from Sulphur Creek had spoken the truth when telling how cold it sometimes got in the country. And he had laughed at him at the time! That showed one must not be too sure of things. There was no mistake about it, it *was* cold. He strode up and down, stamping his feet and threshing his arms, until reassured by the returning warmth. Then he got out matches and proceeded to make a fire. From the undergrowth, where high water of the previous spring had lodged a supply of seasoned twigs, he got his firewood. Working carefully from a small beginning, he soon had a roaring fire, over which he thawed the ice from his face and in the protection of which he ate his biscuits. For the moment the cold of space was outwitted. The dog took satisfaction in the fire, stretching out close enough for warmth and far enough away to escape being singed.

When the man had finished, he filled his pipe and took his comfortable time over a smoke. Then he pulled on his mittens, settled the ear flaps of his cap firmly about his ears, and took the creek trail up the left fork. The dog was disappointed and yearned back towards the fire. This man did not know cold. Possibly all the generations of his ancestry had been ignorant of cold, of real cold, of cold one hundred and seven degrees below freezing point. But the dog knew; all its ancestry knew, and it had inherited the knowledge. And it knew that it was not good to walk abroad in such fearful cold. It was the time to lie snug in a hole in the snow and wait for a curtain of cloud to be drawn across the face of outer space whence this cold came. On the other hand, there was no keen intimacy between the dog and the man. The one was the toil slave of the other, and the only caresses it had ever received were the caresses of the whip lash and of harsh and menacing throat sounds that threatened the whip lash. So the dog made no effort to communicate its apprehension to the man. It was not concerned in the welfare of the man; it was for its own sake that it yearned back towards the fire. But the man whistled, and spoke to it with the sound of whip lashes, and the dog swung in at the man's heels and followed after.

The man took a chew of tobacco and proceeded to start a new amber beard. Also, his moist breath quickly powdered with white his moustache, eyebrows, and lashes. There did not seem to be so many springs on the left fork of the Henderson, and for half an hour the man saw no signs of any. And then it happened. At a place where there were no signs, where the soft, unbroken snow seemed to advertise solidity beneath, the man broke through. It was not deep. He wet himself half-way to the knees before he floundered out of the firm crust.

He was angry, and cursed his luck aloud. He had hoped to get into camp with the boys at six o'clock, and this would delay him an hour, for he would have to build a fire and dry out his footgear. This was imperative at that low temperature—he knew that much; and he turned aside to the bank, which he climbed. On top, tangled in the underbrush about the trunks of several small spruce trees, was a high-water deposit of dry firewood—sticks and twigs, principally, but also larger portions of seasoned branches and fine, dry, last year's grasses. He threw down several large pieces on top of the snow. This served for a foundation and prevented the young flame from drowning itself in the snow it otherwise would melt. The flame he got by touching a match to a small shred of birch bark that he took from his pocket. This burned even more readily than paper. Placing it on the foundation, he fed the young flame with wisps of dry grass and with the tiniest dry twigs.

He worked slowly and carefully, keenly aware of his danger. Gradually, as the flame grew stronger, he increased the size of the twigs with which he fed it. He squatted in the snow pulling the twigs out from their entanglement in the brush and feeding directly to the flame. He knew there must be no failure. When it is seventy-five below zero, a man must not fail in his first attempt to build a fire—that is, if his feet are wet. If his feet are dry, and he fails, he can run along the trail for half a mile and restore his circulation. But the circulation of wet and freezing feet cannot be restored by running when it is seventy-five below. No matter how fast he runs, the wet feet will freeze the harder.

All this the man knew. The old-timer on Sulphur Creek had told him about it the previous fall, and now he was appreciating the advice. Already all sensation had gone out of his feet. To build the fire he had been forced to remove his mittens, and the fingers had quickly gone numb. His pace of four miles an hour had kept his heart pumping blood to the surface of his body and to all the extremities. But the instant he stopped, the action of the pump eased down. The cold of space smote the unprotected tip of the planet, and he, being on that unprotected tip, received the full force of the blow. The blood of his body recoiled before it. The blood was alive, like the dog, and like the dog it wanted to hide away and cover itself up from the fearful cold. So long as he walked four miles an hour, he pumped that blood, willy-nilly, to the surfaces; but now it ebbed away and sank down into the recesses of his body. The extremities were the first to feel its absence. His wet feet froze the faster, and his exposed fingers numbed the faster, though they had not yet begun to freeze. Nose and cheeks were already freezing, while the skin of all his body chilled as it lost its blood.

But he was safe. Toes and nose and cheeks would be only touched by the frost, for the fire was beginning to burn with strength. He was feeding it with twigs the size of his finger. In another minute he would be able to feed it with branches the size of his wrist, and then he could remove his wet footgear, and, while it dried, he could keep his naked feet warm by the fire, rubbing them at first, of course, with snow. The fire was a success. He was safe. He remembered the advice of the old-timer on Sulphur Creek, and smiled. The old-timer had been very serious in laying down the law that no man must travel alone in the Klondike after fifty below. Well, here he was; he had had the accident; he was alone; and he had saved himself. Those old-timers were rather womanish, some of them, he thought. All a man had to do was to keep his head, and he was all right. Any man who was a man could travel alone. But it was surprising, the rapidity with which his cheeks and nose were freezing. And he had not thought his fingers could go lifeless in so short a time. Lifeless they were, for he could scarcely make them move together to grip a twig, and they seemed remote from his body and from him. When he touched a twig, he had to look and see whether or not he had hold of it. The wires were pretty well down between him and his finger ends.

All of which counted for little. There was the fire, snapping and crackling and promising life with every dancing flame. He started to untie his moccasins. They were coated with ice; the thick German socks were like sheaths of iron halfway to the knees; and the moccasin strings were like rods of steel all twisted and knotted as by some conflagration. For a moment he tugged with his numb fingers, then, realizing the folly of it, he drew his sheath knife.

But before he could cut the strings, it happened. It was his own fault or, rather, his mistake. He should not have built the fire under the spruce tree. He should have built it in the open. But it had been easier to pull the twigs from the brush and drop them directly on the fire. Now the tree under which he had done this carried a weight of snow on its boughs. No wind had blown for weeks, and each bough was fully freighted. Each time he had pulled a twig he had communicated a slight agitation to the tree—an imperceptible agitation, so far as he was concerned, but an agitation sufficient to bring about the disaster. High up in the tree one bough capsized its load of snow. This fell on the boughs beneath, capsizing them. This process continued, spreading out and involving the whole tree. It grew like an avalanche, and it descended without warning upon the man and the fire, and the fire was blotted out! Where it had burned was a mantle of fresh and disordered snow.

The man was shocked. It was as though he had just heard his own sentence of death. For a moment he sat and stared at the spot where the fire had been. Then he grew very calm. Perhaps the old-timer on Sulphur Creek was right. If he had only had a trail mate he would have been in no danger now. The trail mate could have built the fire. Well, it was up to him to build the fire over again, and this second time there must be no failure. Even if he succeeded, he would most likely lose some toes. His feet must be badly frozen by now, and there would be some time before the second fire was ready.

Such were his thoughts, but he did not sit and think them. He was busy all the time they were passing through his mind. He made a new foundation for a fire, this time in the open, where no treacherous tree could blot it out. Next he gathered dry grasses and tiny twigs from the high-water flotsam. He could not bring his fingers together to pull them out, but he was able to gather them by the handful. In this way he got many rotten twigs and bits of green moss that were undesirable, but it was the best he could do. He worked methodically, even collecting an armful of the larger branches to be used later when the fire gathered strength. And all the while the dog sat and watched him, a certain yearning wistfulness in its eyes, for it looked upon him as the fire provider, and the fire was slow in coming.

When all was ready, the man reached in his pocket for a second piece of birch bark. He knew the bark was there, and, though he could not feel it with his fingers, he could hear its crisp rustling as he fumbled for it. Try as he would, he could not clutch hold of it. And all the time, in his consciousness, was the knowledge that each instant his feet were freezing. This thought tended to put him in a panic, but he fought against it and kept calm. He pulled on his mittens with his teeth, and threshed his arms back and forth, beating his hands with all his might against his sides. He did this sitting down, and he stood up to do it; and all the while the dog sat in the snow, its wolf brush of a tail curled around warmly over its forefront, its sharp wolf ears pricked forward intently as it watched the man. And the man, as he beat and threshed with his arms and hands, felt a great surge of envy as he regarded the creature that was warm and secure in its natural covering.

After a time he was aware of the first faraway signals of sensation in his beaten fingers. The faint tingling grew stronger till it evolved into a stinging ache that was excruciating, but which the man hailed with satisfaction. He stripped the mitten from his right hand and fetched forth the birch bark. The exposed fingers were quickly going numb again. Next he brought out his bunch of sulphur matches. But the tremendous cold had already driven the life out of his fingers. In his effort to separate one match from the others, the whole bunch fell in the snow. He tried to pick it out of the snow, but failed. The dead fingers could neither touch nor clutch. He was very careful. He drove the thought of his freezing feet, and nose, and cheeks, out of his mind, devoting his whole soul to the matches. He watched, using the sense of vision in place of that of touch, and when he saw his fingers on each side of the bunch, he closed them—that is, he willed to close them, for the wires were down, and the fingers did not obey. He pulled the mitten on the right hand, and beat it fiercely against his knee. Then with both mittened hands, he scooped the bunch of matches, along with much snow, into his lap. Yet he was no better off.

After some manipulation he managed to get the bunch between the heels of his mittened hands. In this fashion he carried it to his mouth. The ice crackled and snapped when by a violent effort he opened his mouth. He drew the lower jaw in, curled the upper lip out of the way, and scraped the bunch with his upper teeth in order to separate a match. He succeeded in getting one, which he dropped on his lap. He was no better off. He could not pick it up. Then he devised a way. He picked it up in his teeth and scratched it on his leg. Twenty times he scratched before he succeeded in lighting it. As it flamed he held it with his teeth to the birch bark. But the burning brimstone went up his nostrils and into his lungs, causing him to cough spasmodically. The match fell into the snow and went out.

The old-timer on Sulphur Creek was right, he thought in the moment of controlled despair that ensued: after fifty below, a man should travel with a partner. He beat his hands, but failed in exciting any sensation. Suddenly he bared both hands, removing the mittens with his teeth. He caught the whole bunch between the heels of his hands. His arm muscles not being frozen enabled him to press the hand heels tightly against the matches. Then he scratched the bunch along his leg. It flared into flame, seventy sulphur matches at once! There was no wind to blow them out. He kept his head to one side to escape the strangling fumes, and held the blazing bunch to the birch bark. As he so held it, he became aware of sensation in his hand. His flesh was burning. He could smell it. Deep down below the surface he could feel it. The sensation developed into pain that grew acute. And still he endured it, holding the flame of the matches clumsily to the bark that would not light readily because his own burning hands were in the way, absorbing most of the flame.

At last, when he could endure no more, he jerked his hands apart. The blazing matches fell sizzling into the snow, but the birch bark was alight. He began laying dry grasses and the tiniest twigs on the flame. He could not pick and choose, for he had to lift the fuel between the heels of his hands. Small pieces of rotten wood and green moss clung to the twigs, and he bit them off as well as he could with his teeth. He cherished the flame carefully and awkwardly. It meant life, and it must not perish. The withdrawal of blood from the surface of his body now made him begin to shiver, and he grew more awkward. A large piece of green moss fell squarely on the little fire. He tried to poke it out with his fingers, but his shivering frame made him poke too far, and he disrupted the nucleus of the little fire, the burning grasses and tiny twigs separating and scattering. He tried to poke them together again, but in spite of the tenseness of the effort, his shivering got away with him, and the twigs were hopelessly scattered. Each twig gushed a puff of smoke and went out. The fire provider had failed. As he looked apathetically about him, his eyes chanced on the dog, sitting across the ruins of the fire from him, in the snow, making restless, hunching movements, slightly lifting one forefoot and then the other, shifting its weight back and forth on them with wistful eagerness.

The sight of the dog put a wild idea into his head. He remembered the tale of the man, caught in a blizzard, who killed a steer and crawled inside the carcass, and so was saved. He would kill the dog and bury his hands in the warm body until the numbness went out of them. Then he could build another fire. He spoke to the dog, calling it to him; but in his voice was a strange note of fear that frightened the animal, who had never known the man to speak in such a way before. Something was the matter, and its suspicious nature sensed danger—it knew not what danger, but somewhere, somehow, in its brain arose an apprehension of the man. It flattened its ears down at the sound of the man's voice, and its restless, hunching movements and the liftings and shiftings of its forefeet became more pronounced; but it would not come to the man. He got on his hands and knees and crawled towards the dog. This unusual posture again excited suspicion, and the animal sidled mincingly away.

The man sat up in the snow for a moment and struggled for calmness. Then he pulled on his mittens, by means of his teeth, and got upon his feet. He glanced down at first in order to assure himself that he was really standing up, for the absence of sensation in his feet left him unrelated to the earth. His erect position in itself started to drive the webs of suspicion from the dog's mind; and when he spoke peremptorily, with the sound of whip lashes in his voice, the dog rendered its customary allegiance and came to him. As it came within reaching distance, the man lost his control. His arms flashed out to the dog, and he experienced genuine surprise when he discovered that his hands could not clutch, that there was neither bend nor feeling in the fingers. He had forgotten for the moment that they were frozen and that they were freezing more and more. All this happened quickly, and before the animal could get away, he encircled its body with his arms. He sat down in the snow, and in this fashion held the dog, while it snarled and whined and struggled.

But it was all he could do, hold its body encircled in his arms and sit there. He realized he could not kill the dog. There was no way to do it. With his helpless hands he could neither draw nor hold his sheath knife nor throttle the animal. He released it, and it plunged wildly away, with tail between its legs, and still snarling. It halted forty feet away and surveyed him curiously, with ears sharply pricked forward.

The man looked down at his hands in order to locate them, and found them hanging on the ends of his arms. It struck him as curious that one should have to use his eyes in order to find out where his hands were. He began threshing his arms back and forth, beating the mittened hands against his sides. He did this for five minutes, violently, and his heart pumped enough blood up to the surface to put a stop to his shivering. But no sensation was aroused in the hands. He had an impression that they hung like weights on the ends of his arms, but when he tried to run the impression down, he could not find it.

A certain fear of death, dull and oppressive, came to him. This fear quickly became poignant as he realized that it was no longer a mere matter of freezing his fingers and toes, or of losing his hands and feet, but that it was a matter of life and death with the chances against him. This threw him into a panic, and he turned and ran up the creek bed along the old, dim trail. The dog joined in behind him and kept up with him. He ran blindly, without intention, in fear such as he had never known in his life. Slowly, as he ploughed and floundered through the snow, he began to see things again—the banks of the creek, the old timber jams, the leafless aspens, and the sky. The running made him feel better. He did not shiver. Maybe, if he ran on, his feet would thaw out; and, anyway, if he ran far enough, he would reach camp and the boys. Without doubt he would lose some fingers and toes and some of his face; but the boys would take care of him, and save the rest of him when he got there. And at the same time there was another thought in his mind that said he would never get to the camp and the boys; that it was too many miles away, that the freezing had too great a start on him, and that he would soon be stiff and dead. This thought he kept in the background and refused to consider. Sometimes it pushed itself forward and demanded to be heard, but he thrust it back and strove to think of other things.

It struck him as curious that he could run at all on feet so frozen that he could not feel them when they struck the earth and took the weight of his body. He seemed to himself to skim along above the surface, and to have no connection with the earth. Somewhere he had once seen a winged Mercury, and he wondered if Mercury felt as he felt when skimming over the earth.

His theory of running until he reached camp and the boys had one flaw in it: he lacked the endurance. Several times he stumbled, and finally he tottered, crumpled up, and fell. When he tried to rise, he failed. He must sit and rest, he decided, and next time he would merely walk and keep on going. As he sat and regained his breath, he noted that he was feeling quite warm and comfortable. He was not shivering, and it even seemed that a warm glow had come to his chest and trunk. And yet, when he touched his nose or cheeks, there was no sensation. Running would not thaw them out. Nor would it thaw out his hands and feet. Then the thought came to him that the frozen portions of his body must be extending. He tried to keep this thought down, to forget it, to think of something else; he was aware of the panicky feeling that it caused, and he was afraid of the panic. But the thought asserted itself, and persisted, until it produced a vision of his body totally frozen. This was too much, and he made another wild run along the trail. Once he slowed down to a walk, but the thought of the freezing extending itself made him run again.

And all the time the dog ran with him, at his heels. When he fell down a second time, it curled its tail over its forefeet and sat in front of him, facing him, curiously eager and intent. The warmth and security of the animal angered him, and he cursed it till it flattened down its ears appeasingly. This time the shivering came more quickly upon the man. He was losing in his battle with the frost. It was creeping into his body from all sides. The thought of it drove him on, but he ran no more than a hundred feet, when he staggered and pitched headlong. It was his last panic. When he had recovered his breath and control, he sat up and entertained in his mind the conception of meeting death with dignity. However, the conception did not come to him in such terms. His idea of it was that he had been making a fool of himself, running around like a chicken with its head cut off—such was the simile that occurred to him. Well, he was bound to freeze anyway, and he might as well take it decently. With this new-found peace of mind came the first glimmerings of drowsiness. A good idea, he thought, to sleep off to death. It was like taking an anaesthetic. Freezing was not so bad as people thought. There were lots worse ways to die.

He pictured the boys finding his body next day. Suddenly he found himself with them, coming along the trail looking for himself. And, still with them, he came around a turn in the trail and found himself lying in the snow. He did not belong with himself any more, for even then he was out of himself, standing with the boys and looking at himself in the snow. It certainly was cold, was his thought. When he got back to the States he could tell the folks what real cold was. He drifted on from this to a vision of the old-timer on Sulphur Creek. He could see him quite clearly, warm and comfortable, and smoking a pipe.

"You were right, old hoss; you were right," the man mumbled to the old-timer of Sulphur Creek.

Then the man drowsed off into what seemed to him the most comfortable and satisfying sleep he had ever known. The dog sat facing him and waiting. The brief day drew to a close in a long, slow twilight. There were no signs of a fire to be made, and, besides, never in the dog's experience had it known a man to sit like that in the snow and make no fire. As the twilight drew on, its eager yearning for the fire mastered it, and with a great lifting and shifting of forefeet, it whined softly, then flattened its ears down in anticipation of being chidden by the man. But the man remained silent. Later the dog whined loudly. And still later it crept close to the man and caught the scent of death. This made the animal bristle and back away. A little longer it delayed, howling under the stars that leaped and danced and shone brightly in the cold sky. Then it turned and trotted up the trail in the direction of the camp it knew, where were the other food providers and fire providers.

GUY DE MAUPASSANT

Guy de Maupassant (1850–1893) was born in Normandy, the son of a wealthy stockbroker. Unable to accept discipline in school, he joined the army during the Franco-Prussian War of 1870–71. Then for seven years he apprenticed himself to Gustave Flaubert, a distant relative, who attempted to teach him to write. Maupassant remembered, "I wrote verses, short stories, longer stories, even a wretched play. Nothing survived. The master read everything. Then, the following Sunday at lunch, he developed his criticisms." Flaubert taught Maupassant that talent "is nothing other than a long patience. Work."

The essence of Flaubert's now famous teaching is that the writer must look at everything to find some aspect of it that no one has yet seen or expressed. "Everything contains some element of the unexplored because we are accustomed to use our eyes only with the memory of what other people before us have thought about the object we are looking at. The least thing has a bit of the unknown about it. Let us find this."

In 1880 Maupassant caused a sensation with the publication of his story "Boule de Suif" ("Ball of Fat"), a dramatic account of prostitution and bourgeois hypocrisy. During the next decade, before his gradual incapacitation and death from syphilis, he published nearly 300 stories. Characterized by compact and dramatic narrative lines, they read as modern short stories, eliminating the moral judgments and the long digressions used by many earlier writers. Along with his younger contemporary Anton Chekhov, Maupassant is responsible for technical advances that moved the short story toward an austerity that has marked it ever since. These two writers influenced nearly everyone who has written short fiction after them.

As Joseph Conrad recognized, "Facts, and again facts, are his [Maupassant's] unique concern. That is why he is not always properly understood." Maupassant's lack of sentimentality toward his characters, as in his depiction of the wife in "The Necklace," laid him open to charges of cynicism and hardness. Even if Maupassant's stories display a greater distance from his characters and a less sympathetic irony than Chekhov's, both writers were the most accomplished of narrators, equal in their powers of exact observation and independent judgment and in their supple, practiced knowledge of their craft.

CONNECTION To read Kate Chopin's tribute to Guy de Maupassant, see "How I Stumbled upon Maupassant" on page 176.

WEB Research Guy de Maupassant at bedfordstmartins.com/rewritinglit.

The Necklace

1884

TRANSLATED BY MARJORIE LAURIE

She was one of those pretty and charming girls who are sometimes, as if by a mistake of destiny, born in a family of clerks. She had no dowry, no expectations, no means of being known, understood, loved, wedded by any rich and distinguished man; and she let herself be married to a little clerk at the Ministry of Public Instructions.

She dressed plainly because she could not dress well, but she was as unhappy as though she had really fallen from her proper station, since with women there is neither caste nor rank: and beauty, grace, and charm act instead of family and birth. Natural fineness, instinct for what is elegant, suppleness of wit, are the sole hierarchy, and make from women of the people the equals of the very greatest ladies.

She suffered ceaselessly, feeling herself born for all the delicacies and all the luxuries. She suffered from the poverty of her dwelling, from the wretched look of the walls, from the worn-out chairs, from the ugliness of the curtains. All those things, of which another woman of her rank would never even have been conscious, tortured her and made her angry. The sight of the little Breton peasant who did her humble housework aroused in her regrets which were despairing and distracted dreams. She thought of the silent antechambers hung with Oriental tapestry, lit by tall bronze candelabra, and of the two great footmen in knee breeches who sleep in the big armchairs, made drowsy by the heavy warmth of the hot-air stove. She thought of the long *salons* fitted up with ancient silk, of the delicate furniture carrying priceless curiosities, and of the coquettish perfumed boudoirs made for talks at five o'clock with intimate friends, with men famous and sought after, whom all women envy and whose attention they all desire.

When she sat down to dinner, before the round table covered with a tablecloth three days old, opposite her husband, who uncovered the soup tureen and declared with an enchanted air, "Ah, the good *pot-au-feu*! I don't know anything better than that," she thought of dainty dinners, of shining silverware, of tapestry which peopled the walls with ancient personages and with strange birds flying in the midst of a fairy forest; and she thought of delicious dishes served on marvelous plates, and of the whispered gallantries which you listen to with a sphinxlike smile, while you are eating the pink flesh of a trout or the wings of a quail.

She had no dresses, no jewels, nothing. And she loved nothing but that; she felt made for that. She would so have liked to please, to be envied, to be charming, to be sought after.

She had a friend, a former schoolmate at the convent, who was rich, and whom she did not like to go and see any more, because she suffered so much when she came back.

But one evening, her husband returned home with a triumphant air, and holding a large envelope in his hand.

"There," said he. "Here is something for you."

She tore the paper sharply, and drew out a printed card which bore these words:

"The Minister of Public Instruction and Mme. Georges Ramponneau request the honor of M. and Mme. Loisel's company at the palace of the Ministry on Monday evening, January eighteenth."

Instead of being delighted, as her husband hoped, she threw the invitation on the table with disdain, murmuring:

"What do you want me to do with that?"

"But, my dear, I thought you would be glad. You never go out, and this is such a fine opportunity. I had awful trouble to get it. Everyone wants to go; it is very select, and they are not giving many invitations to clerks. The whole official world will be there."

She looked at him with an irritated glance, and said, impatiently:

"And what do you want me to put on my back?"

He had not thought of that; he stammered:

"Why, the dress you go to the theater in. It looks very well, to me."

He stopped, distracted, seeing his wife was crying. Two great tears descended slowly from the corners of her eyes toward the corners of her mouth. He stuttered:

"What's the matter? What's the matter?"

But, by violent effort, she had conquered her grief, and she replied, with a calm voice, while she wiped her wet cheeks:

"Nothing. Only I have no dress and therefore I can't go to this ball. Give your card to some colleague whose wife is better equipped than I."

He was in despair. He resumed:

"Come, let us see, Mathilde. How much would it cost, a suitable dress, which you could use on other occasions. Something very simple?"

She reflected several seconds, making her calculations and wondering also what sum she could ask without drawing on herself an immediate refusal and a frightened exclamation from the economical clerk.

Finally, she replied, hesitatingly:

"I don't know exactly, but I think I could manage it with four hundred francs."

He had grown a little pale, because he was laying aside just that amount to buy a gun and treat himself to a little shooting next summer on the plain of Nanterre, with several friends who went to shoot larks down there, of a Sunday.

But he said:

"All right. I will give you four hundred francs. And try to have a pretty dress."

The day of the ball drew near, and Mme. Loisel seemed sad, uneasy, anxious. Her dress was ready, however. Her husband said to her one evening:

"What is the matter? Come, you've been so queer these last three days."

And she answered:

"It annoys me not to have a single jewel, not a single stone, nothing to put on. I shall look like distress. I should almost rather not go at all."

He resumed:

"You might wear natural flowers. It's very stylish at this time of the year. For ten francs you can get two or three magnificent roses."

She was not convinced.

"No; there's nothing more humiliating than to look poor among other women who are rich."

But her husband cried:

"How stupid you are! Go look up your friend Mme. Forestier, and ask her to lend you some jewels. You're quite thick enough with her to do that."

She uttered a cry of joy:

"It's true. I never thought of it."

The next day she went to her friend and told of her distress.

Mme. Forestier went to a wardrobe with a glass door, took out a large jewelbox, brought it back, opened it, and said to Mme. Loisel:

"Choose, choose, my dear."

She saw first of all some bracelets, then a pearl necklace, then a Venetian cross, gold and precious stones of admirable workmanship. She tried on the ornaments before the glass, hesitated, could not make up her mind to part with them, to give them back. She kept asking:

"Haven't you any more?"

"Why, yes. Look. I don't know what you like."

All of a sudden she discovered, in a black satin box, a superb necklace of diamonds, and her heart began to beat with an immoderate desire. Her hands trembled as she took it. She fastened it around her throat, outside her high necked dress, and remained lost in ecstasy at the sight of herself.

Then she asked, hesitating, filled with anguish:

"Can you lend me that, only that?"

"Why, yes, certainly."

She sprang upon the neck of her friend, kissed her passionately, then fled with her treasure.

The day of the ball arrived. Mme. Loisel made a great success. She was prettier than them all, elegant, gracious, smiling, and crazy with joy. All the men looked at her, asked her name, endeavored to be introduced. All the attachés of the Cabinet wanted to waltz with her. She was remarked by the minister himself.

She danced with intoxication, with passion, made drunk by pleasure, forgetting all, in the triumph of her beauty, in the glory of her success, in a sort of cloud of happiness composed of all this homage, of all this admiration, of all these awakened desires, and of that sense of complete victory which is so sweet to a woman's heart.

She went away about four o'clock in the morning. Her husband had been sleeping since midnight, in a little deserted anteroom, with three other gentlemen whose wives were having a good time. He threw over her shoulders the wraps which he had brought, modest wraps of common life, whose poverty contrasted with the elegance of the ball dress. She felt this, and wanted to escape so as not to be remarked by the other women, who were enveloping themselves in costly furs.

Loisel held her back.

"Wait a bit. You will catch cold outside. I will go and call a cab."

But she did not listen to him, and rapidly descended the stairs. When they were in the street they did not find a carriage; and they began to look for one, shouting after the cabmen whom they saw passing by at a distance.

They went down toward the Seine, in despair, shivering with cold. At last they found on the quay one of those ancient noctambulant coupés° which, exactly as if they were ashamed to show their misery during the day, are never seen round Paris until after nightfall.

It took them to their door in the Rue des Martyrs, and once more, sadly, they climbed up homeward. All was ended, for her. And as to him, he reflected that he must be at the Ministry at ten o'clock.

She removed the wraps which covered her shoulders before the glass, so as once more to see herself in all her glory. But suddenly she uttered a cry. She no longer had the necklace around her neck!

Her husband, already half undressed, demanded:

"What is the matter with you?"

She turned madly toward him:

"I have—I have—I've lost Mme. Forestier's necklace."

He stood up, distracted.

"What!—how?—impossible!"

And they looked in the folds of her dress, in the folds of her cloak, in her pockets, everywhere. They did not find it.

He asked:

"You're sure you had it on when you left the ball?"

"Yes, I felt it in the vestibule of the palace."

"But if you had lost it in the street we should have heard it fall. It must be in the cab."

"Yes. Probably. Did you take his number?"

"No. And you, didn't you notice it?"

"No."

---

coupés: Enclosed four-wheeled carriages.

They looked, thunderstruck, at one another. At last Loisel put on his clothes.

"I shall go back on foot," said he, "over the whole route which we have taken to see if I can find it."

And he went out. She sat waiting on a chair in her ball dress, without strength to go to bed, overwhelmed, without fire, without a thought.

Her husband came back about seven o'clock. He had found nothing.

He went to Police Headquarters, to the newspaper offices, to offer a reward; he went to the cab companies—everywhere, in fact, whither he was urged by the least suspicion of hope.

She waited all day, in the same condition of mad fear before this terrible calamity.

Loisel returned at night with a hollow, pale face; he had discovered nothing.

"You must write to your friend," said he, "that you have broken the clasp of her necklace and that you are having it mended. That will give us time to turn round."

She wrote at his dictation.

At the end of a week they had lost all hope.

And Loisel, who had aged five years, declared:

"We must consider how to replace that ornament."

The next day they took the box which had contained it, and they went to the jeweler whose name was found within. He consulted his books.

"It was not I, madame, who sold that necklace; I must simply have furnished the case."

Then they went from jeweler to jeweler, searching for a necklace like the other, consulting their memories, sick both of them with chagrin and anguish.

They found, in a shop at the Palais Royal, a string of diamonds which seemed to them exactly like the one they looked for. It was worth forty thousand francs. They could have it for thirty-six.

So they begged the jeweler not to sell it for three days yet. And they made a bargain that he should buy it back for thirty-four thousand francs, in case they found the other one before the end of February.

Loisel possessed eighteen thousand francs which his father had left him. He would borrow the rest.

He did borrow, asking a thousand francs of one, five hundred of another, five louis here, three louis there. He gave notes, took up ruinous obligations, dealt with usurers and all the race of lenders. He compromised all the rest of his life, risked his signature without even knowing if he could meet it; and, frightened by the pains yet to come, by the black misery which was about to fall upon him, by the prospect of all the physical privation and of all the moral tortures which he was to suffer, he went to get the new necklace, putting down upon the merchant's counter thirty-six thousand francs.

When Mme. Loisel took back the necklace, Mme. Forestier said to her, with a chilly manner:

"You should have returned it sooner; I might have needed it."

She did not open the case, as her friend had so much feared. If she had detected the substitution, what would she have thought, what would she have said? Would she not have taken Mme. Loisel for a thief?

Mme. Loisel now knew the horrible existence of the needy. She took her part, moreover, all of a sudden, with heroism. That dreadful debt must be paid. She would pay it. They dismissed their servant; they changed their lodgings; they rented a garret under the roof.

She came to know what heavy housework meant and the odious cares of the kitchen. She washed the dishes, using her rosy nails on the greasy pots and pans. She washed the dirty linen, the shirts, and the dishcloths, which she dried upon a line; she carried the slops down to the street every morning, and carried up the water, stopping for breath at every landing. And, dressed like a woman of the people, she went to the fruiterer, the grocer, the butcher, her basket on her arm, bargaining, insulted, defending her miserable money sou by sou.

Each month they had to meet some notes, renew others, obtain more time.

Her husband worked in the evening making a fair copy of some tradesman's accounts, and late at night he often copied manuscript for five sous a page.

And this life lasted for ten years.

At the end of ten years, they had paid everything, everything, with the rates of usury, and the accumulations of the compound interest.

Mme. Loisel looked old now. She had become the woman of impoverished households—strong and hard and rough. With frowsy hair, skirts askew, and red hands, she talked loud while washing the floor with great swishes of water. But sometimes, when her husband was at the office, she sat down near the window, and she thought of that gay evening of long ago, of that ball where she had been so beautiful and so fêted.

What would have happened if she had not lost that necklace? Who knows? Who knows? How life is strange and changeful! How little a thing is needed for us to be lost or to be saved!

But, one Sunday, having gone to take a walk in the Champs Elysées to refresh herself from the labor of the week, she suddenly perceived a woman who was leading a child. It was Mme. Forestier, still young, still beautiful, still charming.

Mme. Loisel felt moved. Was she going to speak to her? Yes, certainly. And now that she had paid, she was going to tell her all about it. Why not?

She went up.

"Good-day, Jeanne."

The other, astonished to be familiarly addressed by this plain goodwife, did not recognize her at all, and stammered.

"But—madam!—I do not know—you must be mistaken."

"No. I am Mathilde Loisel."

Her friend uttered a cry.

"Oh, my poor Mathilde! How you are changed!"

"Yes, I have had days hard enough, since I have seen you, days wretched enough—and that because of you!"

"Of me! How so?"

"Do you remember that diamond necklace which you lent me to wear at the ministerial ball?"

"Yes. Well?"

"Well, I lost it."

"What do you mean? You brought it back."

"I brought you back another just like it. And for this we have been ten years paying. You can understand that it was not easy for us, who had nothing. At last it is ended, and I am very glad."

Mme. Forestier had stopped.

"You say that you bought a necklace of diamonds to replace mine?"

"Yes. You never noticed it, then! They were very like."

And she smiled with a joy which was proud and naïve at once.

Mme. Forestier, strongly moved, took her two hands.

"Oh, my poor Mathilde! Why, my necklace was paste. It was worth at most five hundred francs!"

HERMAN MELVILLE

Herman Melville (1819–1891) published his first short story in 1853 as "Bartleby, the Scrivener: A Story of Wall Street." Behind him were seven years of writing novels beginning with the burst of creative energy that produced his early books of sea adventure: *Typee* (1846), *Omoo* (1847), *Mardi* (1849), *Redburn* (1849), and *White-Jacket* (1850). All of these were based on his experiences onboard ship. Melville had been left in poverty at the age of fifteen when his father went bankrupt, and in 1839 he went to sea as a cabin boy. Two years later he sailed on a whaler bound for the Pacific, but he deserted in the Marquesas Islands and lived for a time with cannibals. Having little formal education, Melville later boasted that "a whale ship was my Yale College and my Harvard." His most ambitious book was *Moby-Dick* (1851), a work of great allegorical complexity heavily indebted to the influence of Nathaniel Hawthorne, Melville's neighbor in the Berkshires at the time he wrote it. *Moby-Dick* was not a commercial success, however, and the novel that followed it, *Pierre* (1852), was dismissed by critics as incomprehensible trash.

It was at this point that Melville turned to the short story. Between 1853 and 1856 he published fifteen sketches and stories and a serialized historical novel, promising the popular magazines that his stories would "contain nothing of any sort to shock the fastidious." But when this work and another novel (*The Confidence Man*, 1857) failed to restore his reputation, he ceased trying to support his family by his pen. He moved from his farm in the Berkshires to a house in New York City bought for him by his father-in-law, and worked for more than twenty years as an inspector of customs. He published a few books of poems and wrote a short novel, *Billy Budd*, which critics acclaimed as one of his greatest works when it was published – thirty years after his death.

Melville stood at the crossroads in the early history of American short fiction. When he began to publish in magazines, Hawthorne and Edgar Allan Poe had already done their best work in the romantic vein of tales and sketches, and the realistic local-color school of short stories had not yet been established. Melville created something new in "Bartleby, the Scrivener," a fully developed, if discursive, short story set in a contemporary social context. It baffled readers of *Putnam's Monthly Magazine* in 1853, when it was published in two installments. One reviewer called it "a Poeish tale with an infusion of more natural sentiment." For the rest of his stories, Melville used the conventional form of old-fashioned tales mostly set in remote times or places.

CONNECTION To read Herman Melville's tribute to Nathaniel Hawthorne, see "Blackness in Hawthorne's 'Young Goodman Brown,'" page 270.

WEB Research Herman Melville at bedfordstmartins.com/rewritinglit.

Bartleby, the Scrivener 1853

A Story of Wall Street

I am a rather elderly man. The nature of my avocations, for the last thirty years, has brought me into more than ordinary contact with what would seem an interesting and somewhat singular set of men, of whom, as yet, nothing, that I know of, has ever been written—I mean, the law-copyists, or scriveners. I have known very many of them, professionally and privately, and, if I pleased, could relate divers histories, at which good-natured gentlemen might smile, and sentimental souls might weep. But I waive the biographies of all other scriveners, for a few passages in the life of Bartleby, who was a scrivener, the strangest I ever saw, or heard of. While, of other law-copyists, I might write the complete life, of Bartleby nothing of that sort can be done. I believe that no materials exist, for a full and satisfactory biography of this man. It is an irreparable loss to literature. Bartleby was one of those beings of whom nothing is ascertainable, except from the original sources, and, in his case, those are very small. What my own astonished eyes saw of Bartleby, *that* is all I know of him, except, indeed, one vague report, which will appear in the sequel.

Ere introducing the scrivener, as he first appeared to me, it is fit I make some mention of myself, my *employés*, my business, my chambers, and general surroundings, because some such description is indispensable to an adequate understanding of the chief character about to be presented. Imprimis:° I am a man who, from his youth upwards, has been filled with a profound conviction that the easiest way of life is the best. Hence, though I belong to a profession proverbially energetic and nervous, even to turbulence, at times, yet nothing of that sort have I ever suffered to invade my peace. I am one of those unambitious lawyers who never address a jury, or in any way draw down public applause; but, in the cool tranquillity of a snug retreat, do a snug business among rich men's bonds, and mortgages, and title-deeds. All who know me, consider me an eminently *safe* man. The late John Jacob Astor, a personage little given to

Imprimis: In the first place (Latin).

poetic enthusiasm, had no hesitation in pronouncing my first grand point to be prudence; my next, method. I do not speak it in vanity, but simply record the fact, that I was not unemployed in my profession by the late John Jacob Astor; a name which, I admit, I love to repeat; for it hath a rounded and orbicular sound to it, and rings like unto bullion. I will freely add, that I was not insensible to the late John Jacob Astor's good opinion.

Some time prior to the period at which this little history begins, my avocations had been largely increased. The good old office, now extinct in the State of New York, of a Master in Chancery, had been conferred upon me. It was not a very arduous office, but very pleasantly remunerative. I seldom lose my temper; much more seldom indulge in dangerous indignation at wrongs and outrages; but I must be permitted to be rash here and declare, that I consider the sudden and violent abrogation of the office of Master in Chancery, by the new Constitution, as a —— premature act; inasmuch as I had counted upon a life-lease of the profits, whereas I only received those of a few short years. But this is by the way.

My chambers were up stairs, at No. — Wall Street. At one end, they looked upon the white wall of the interior of a spacious skylight shaft, penetrating the building from top to bottom.

This view might have been considered rather tame than otherwise, deficient in what landscape painters call "life." But, if so, the view from the other end of my chambers offered, at least, a contrast, if nothing more. In that direction, my windows commanded an unobstructed view of a lofty brick wall, black by age and everlasting shade; which wall required no spy-glass to bring out its lurking beauties, but, for the benefit of all near-sighted spectators, was pushed up to within ten feet of my window-panes. Owing to the great height of the surrounding buildings, and my chambers being on the second floor, the interval between this wall and mine not a little resembled a huge square cistern.

At the period just preceding the advent of Bartleby, I had two persons as copyists in my employment, and a promising lad as an office-boy. First, Turkey; second, Nippers; third, Ginger Nut. These may seem names, the like of which are not usually found in the Directory. In truth, they were nicknames, mutually conferred upon each other by my three clerks, and were deemed expressive of their respective persons or characters. Turkey was a short, pursy Englishman, of about my own age—that is, somewhere not far from sixty. In the morning, one might say, his face was of a fine florid hue, but after twelve o'clock, meridian—his dinner hour—it blazed like a grate full of Christmas coals; and continued blazing—but, as it were, with a gradual wane—till six o'clock, P.M., or thereabouts; after which, I saw no more of the proprietor of the face, which, gaining its meridian with the sun, seemed to set with it, to rise, culminate, and decline the following day, with the like regularity and undiminished glory. There are many singular coincidences I have known in the course of my life, not the least among which was the fact, that, exactly when Turkey displayed his fullest beams from his red and radiant countenance, just then, too, at that critical moment, began the daily period when I considered his business capacities as seriously disturbed for the remainder of the twenty-four hours. Not that he was absolutely idle, or averse to business then; far from it.

The difficulty was, he was apt to be altogether too energetic. There was a strange, inflamed, flurried, flighty recklessness of activity about him. He would be incautious in dipping his pen into his inkstand. All his blots upon my documents were dropped there after twelve o'clock, meridian. Indeed, not only would he be reckless, and sadly given to making blots in the afternoon, but, some days, he went further, and was rather noisy. At such times, too, his face flamed with augmented blazonry, as if cannel coal had been heaped on anthracite. He made an unpleasant racket with his chair; spilled his sand-box; in mending his pens, impatiently split them all to pieces, and threw them on the floor in a sudden passion; stood up, and leaned over his table, boxing his papers about in a most indecorous manner, very sad to behold in an elderly man like him. Nevertheless, as he was in many ways a most valuable person to me, and all the time before twelve o'clock, meridian, was the quickest, steadiest creature, too, accomplishing a great deal of work in a style not easily to be matched—for these reasons, I was willing to overlook his eccentricities, though, indeed, occasionally, I remonstrated with him. I did this very gently, however, because, though the civilest, nay, the blandest and most reverential of men in the morning, yet, in the afternoon, he was disposed, upon provocation, to be slightly rash with his tongue—in fact, insolent. Now, valuing his morning services as I did, and resolved not to lose them—yet, at the same time, made uncomfortable by his inflamed ways after twelve o'clock—and being a man of peace, unwilling by my admonitions to call forth unseemly retorts from him, I took upon me, one Saturday noon (he was always worse on Saturdays) to hint to him, very kindly, that, perhaps, now that he was growing old, it might be well to abridge his labors; in short, he need not come to my chambers after twelve o'clock, but, dinner over, had best go home to his lodgings, and rest himself till tea-time. But no; he insisted upon his afternoon devotions. His countenance became intolerably fervid, as he oratorically assured me—gesticulating with a long ruler at the other end of the room—that if his services in the morning were useful, how indispensable, then, in the afternoon?

"With submission, sir," said Turkey, on this occasion, "I consider myself your right-hand man. In the morning I but marshal and deploy my columns; but in the afternoon I put myself at their head, and gallantly charge the foe, thus"—and he made a violent thrust with the ruler.

"But the blots, Turkey," intimated I.

"True; but, with submission, sir, behold these hairs! I am getting old. Surely, sir, a blot or two of a warm afternoon is not to be severely urged against gray hairs. Old age—even if it blot the page—is honorable. With submission, sir, we *both* are getting old."

This appeal to my fellow-feeling was hardly to be resisted. At all events, I saw that go he would not. So, I made up my mind to let him stay, resolving, nevertheless, to see to it that, during the afternoon, he had to do with my less important papers.

Nippers, the second on my list, was a whiskered, sallow, and, upon the whole, rather piratical-looking young man, of about five-and-twenty. I always deemed him the victim of two evil powers—ambition and indigestion. The ambition was evinced by a certain impatience of the duties of a mere copyist, an unwarrantable usurpation of strictly professional affairs such as the original drawing up of legal documents. The indigestion seemed betokened in an occasional nervous testiness and grinning irritability, causing the teeth to audibly grind together over mistakes committed in copying; unnecessary maledictions, hissed, rather than spoken, in the heat of business; and especially by a continual discontent with the height of the table where he worked. Though of a very ingenious mechanical turn, Nippers could never get this table to suit him. He put chips under it, blocks of various sorts, bits of pasteboard, and at last went so far as to attempt an exquisite adjustment, by final pieces of folded blotting paper. But no invention would answer. If, for the sake of easing his back, he brought the table-lid at a sharp angle well up towards his chin, and wrote there like a man using the steep roof of a Dutch house for his desk, then he declared that it stopped the circulation in his arms. If now he lowered the table to his waistbands, and stooped over it in writing, then there was a sore aching in his back. In short, the truth of the matter was, Nippers knew not what he wanted. Or, if he wanted anything, it was to be rid of a scrivener's table altogether. Among the manifestations of his diseased ambition was a fondness he had for receiving visits from certain ambiguous-looking fellows in seedy coats, whom he called his clients. Indeed, I was aware that not only was he, at times, considerable of a ward-politician, but he occasionally did a little business at the justices' courts, and was not unknown on the steps of the Tombs.° I have good reason to believe, however, that one individual who called upon him at my chambers, and who, with a grand air, he insisted was his client, was no other than a dun, and the alleged title-deed, a bill. But, with all his failings, and the annoyances he caused me, Nippers, like his compatriot Turkey, was a very useful man to me; wrote a neat, swift hand; and, when he chose, was not deficient in a gentlemanly sort of deportment. Added to this, he always dressed in a gentlemanly sort of way; and so, incidentally, reflected credit upon my chambers. Whereas, with respect to Turkey, I had much ado to keep him from being a reproach to me. His clothes were apt to look oily, and smell of eating-houses. He wore his pantaloons very loose and baggy in summer. His coats were execrable, his hat not to be handled. But while the hat was a thing of indifference to me, inasmuch as his natural civility and deference, as a dependent Englishman, always led him to doff it the moment he entered the room, yet his coat was another matter. Concerning his coats, I reasoned with him; but with no effect. The truth was, I suppose, that a man with so small an income could not afford to sport such a lustrous face and a lustrous coat at one and the same time. As Nippers once observed, Turkey's money went chiefly for red ink. One winter day, I presented Turkey with a highly respectable-looking coat of my own—a padded gray coat, of a most comfortable warmth, and which buttoned straight up from the knee to the neck. I thought Turkey would appreciate the favor, and abate his rashness and obstreperousness of afternoons. But no; I verily believe that buttoning himself up in so downy and blanket-like a coat had a pernicious effect upon him upon the same principle that too much oats are bad

---

the Tombs: A prison in New York City.

for horses. In fact, precisely as a rash, restive horse is said to feel his oats, so Turkey felt his coat. It made him insolent. He was a man whom prosperity harmed.

Though, concerning the self-indulgent habits of Turkey, I had my own private surmises, yet, touching Nippers, I was well persuaded that, whatever might be his faults in other respects, he was, at least, a temperate young man. But, indeed, nature herself seemed to have been his vintner, and, at his birth, charged him so thoroughly with an irritable, brandy-like disposition, that all subsequent potations were needless. When I consider how, amid the stillness of my chambers, Nippers would sometimes impatiently rise from his seat, and stooping over his table, spread his arms wide apart, seize the whole desk, and move it, and jerk it, with a grim, grinding motion on the floor, as if the table were a perverse voluntary agent, intent on thwarting and vexing him, I plainly perceive that, for Nippers, brandy-and-water were altogether superfluous.

It was fortunate for me that, owing to its peculiar cause—indigestion—the irritability and consequent nervousness of Nippers were mainly observable in the morning, while in the afternoon he was comparatively mild. So that, Turkey's paroxysms only coming on about twelve o'clock, I never had to do with their eccentricities at one time. Their fits relieved each other, like guards. When Nippers' was on, Turkey's was off; and *vice versa*. This was a good natural arrangement, under the circumstances.

Ginger Nut, the third on my list, was a lad, some twelve years old. His father was a carman, ambitious of seeing his son on the bench instead of a cart, before he died. So he sent him to my office, as student at law, errand-boy, cleaner, and sweeper, at the rate of one dollar a week. He had a little desk to himself, but he did not use it much. Upon inspection, the drawer exhibited a great array of the shells of various sorts of nuts. Indeed, to this quick-witted youth, the whole noble science of the law was contained in a nutshell. Not the least among the employments of Ginger Nut, as well as one which he discharged with the most alacrity, was his duty as cake and apple purveyor for Turkey and Nippers. Copying lawpapers being proverbially a dry, husky sort of business, my two scriveners were fain to moisten their mouths very often with Spitzenbergs, to be had at the numerous stalls nigh the Custom House and Post Office. Also, they sent Ginger Nut very frequently for that peculiar cake—small, flat, round, and very spicy—after which he had been named by them. Of a cold morning, when business was but dull, Turkey would gobble up scores of these cakes, as if they were mere wafers—indeed, they sell them at the rate of six or eight for a penny—the scrape of his pen blending with the crunching of the crisp particles in his mouth. Of all the fiery afternoon blunders and flurried rashness of Turkey, was his once moistening a ginger-cake between his lips, and clapping it on to a mortgage, for a seal. I came within an ace of dismissing him then. But he mollified me by making an oriental bow, and saying—

"With submission, sir, it was generous of me to find you in stationery on my own account."

Now my original business—that of a conveyancer and title hunter, and drawer-up of recondite documents of all sorts—was considerably increased by receiving the Master's office. There was now great work for scriveners. Not only must I push the clerks already with me, but I must have additional help.

In answer to my advertisement, a motionless young man one morning stood upon my office threshold, the door being open, for it was summer. I can see that figure now—pallidly neat, pitiably respectable, incurably forlorn! It was Bartleby.

After a few words touching his qualifications, I engaged him, glad to have among my corps of copyists a man of so singularly sedate an aspect, which I thought might operate beneficially upon the flighty temper of Turkey, and the fiery one of Nippers.

I should have stated before that ground-glass folding-doors divided my premises into two parts, one of which was occupied by my scriveners, the other by myself. According to my humor, I threw open these doors, or closed them. I resolved to assign Bartleby a corner by the folding-doors, but on my side of them, so as to have this quiet man within easy call, in case any trifling thing was to be done. I placed his desk close up to a small side-window in that part of the room, a window which originally had afforded a lateral view of certain grimy brickyards and bricks, but which, owing to subsequent erections, commanded at present no view at all, though it gave some light. Within three feet of the panes was a wall, and the light came down from far above, between two lofty buildings, as from a very small opening in a dome. Still further to a satisfactory arrangement, I procured a high green folding screen, which might entirely isolate Bartleby from my sight, though not remove him from my voice. And thus, in a manner, privacy and society were conjoined.

At first, Bartleby did an extraordinary quantity of writing. As if long famishing for something to copy, he seemed to gorge himself on my documents. There was no pause for digestion. He ran a day and night line, copying by sunlight and by candle-light. I should have been quite delighted with his application, had he been cheerfully industrious. But he wrote on silently, palely, mechanically.

It is, of course, an indispensable part of a scrivener's business to verify the accuracy of his copy, word by word. Where there are two or more scriveners in an office, they assist each other in this examination, one reading from the copy, the other holding the original. It is a very dull, wearisome, and lethargic affair. I can readily imagine that, to some sanguine temperaments, it would be altogether intolerable. For example, I cannot credit that the mettlesome poet, Byron, would have contentedly sat down with Bartleby to examine a law document of, say five hundred pages, closely written in a crimpy hand.

Now and then, in the haste of business, it had been my habit to assist in comparing some brief document myself, calling Turkey or Nippers for this purpose. One object I had, in placing Bartleby so handy to me behind the screen, was to avail myself of his services on such trivial occasions. It was on the third day, I think, of his being with me, and before any necessity had arisen for having his own writing examined, that, being much hurried to complete a small affair I had in hand, I abruptly called to Bartleby. In my haste and natural expectancy of instant compliance, I sat with my head bent over the original on my desk, and my right hand sideways, and somewhat nervously extended with the copy, so that, immediately upon emerging from his retreat, Bartleby might snatch it and proceed to business without the least delay.

In this very attitude did I sit when I called to him, rapidly stating what it was I wanted him to do—namely, to examine a small paper with me. Imagine my surprise, nay, my consternation, when, without moving from his privacy, Bartleby, in a singularly mild, firm voice, replied, "I would prefer not to."

I sat awhile in perfect silence, rallying my stunned faculties. Immediately it occurred to me that my ears had deceived me, or Bartleby had entirely misunderstood my meaning. I repeated my request in the clearest tone I could assume; but in quite as clear a one came the previous reply, "I would prefer not to."

"Prefer not to," echoed I, rising in high excitement, and crossing the room with a stride. "What do you mean? Are you moonstruck? I want you to help me compare this sheet here—take it," and I thrust it towards him.

"I would prefer not to," said he.

I looked at him steadfastly. His face was leanly composed; his gray eye dimly calm. Not a wrinkle of agitation rippled him. Had there been the least uneasiness, anger, impatience, or impertinence in his manner; in other words, had there been anything ordinarily human about him, doubtless I should have violently dismissed him from the premises. But as it was, I should have as soon thought of turning my pale plaster-of-paris bust of Cicero out of doors. I stood gazing at him awhile, as he went on with his own writing, and then reseated myself at my desk. This is very strange, thought I. What had one best do? But my business hurried me. I concluded to forget the matter for the present, reserving it for my future leisure. So, calling Nippers from the other room, the paper was speedily examined.

A few days after this, Bartleby concluded four lengthy documents, being quadruplicates of a week's testimony taken before me in my High Court of Chancery. It became necessary to examine them. It was an important suit, and great accuracy was imperative. Having all things arranged, I called Turkey, Nippers, and Ginger Nut, from the next room, meaning to place the four copies in the hands of my four clerks, while I should read from the original. Accordingly, Turkey, Nippers, and Ginger Nut had taken their seats in a row, each with his document in his hand, when I called to Bartleby to join this interesting group.

"Bartleby! quick, I am waiting."

I heard a slow scrape of his chair legs on the uncarpeted floor, and soon he appeared standing at the entrance of his hermitage.

"What is wanted?" said he, mildly.

"The copies, the copies," said I, hurriedly. "We are going to examine them. There"—and I held towards him the fourth quadruplicate.

"I would prefer not to," he said, and gently disappeared behind the screen.

For a few moments I was turned into a pillar of salt, standing at the head of my seated column of clerks. Recovering myself, I advanced towards the screen, and demanded the reason for such extraordinary conduct.

"*Why* do you refuse?"

"I would prefer not to."

With any other man I should have flown outright into a dreadful passion, scorned all further words, and thrust him ignominiously from my presence. But there was something about Bartleby that not only strangely disarmed me, but, in a wonderful manner, touched and disconcerted me. I began to reason with him.

"These are your own copies we are about to examine. It is labor saving to you, because one examination will answer for your four papers. It is common usage. Every copyist is bound to help examine his copy. Is it not so? Will you not speak? Answer!"

"I prefer not to," he replied in a flute-like tone. It seemed to me that, while I had been addressing him, he carefully revolved every statement that I made; fully comprehended the meaning; could not gainsay the irresistible conclusion; but, at the same time, some paramount consideration prevailed with him to reply as he did.

"You are decided, then, not to comply with my request—a request made according to common usage and common sense?"

He briefly gave me to understand, that on that point my judgment was sound. Yes: his decision was irreversible.

It is not seldom the case that, when a man is browbeaten in some unprecedented and violently unreasonable way, he begins to stagger in his own plainest faith. He begins, as it were, vaguely to surmise that, wonderful as it may be, all the justice and all the reason is on the other side. Accordingly, if any disinterested persons are present, he turns to them for some reinforcement for his own faltering mind.

"Turkey," said I, "what do you think of this? Am I not right?"

"With submission, sir," said Turkey, in his blandest tone, "I think that you are."

"Nippers," said I, "what do *you* think of it?"

"I think I should kick him out of the office."

(The reader of nice perceptions will have perceived that, it being morning, Turkey's answer is couched in polite and tranquil terms, but Nippers replies in ill-tempered ones. Or, to repeat a previous sentence, Nippers' ugly mood was on duty, and Turkey's off.)

"Ginger Nut," said I, willing to enlist the smallest suffrage in my behalf, "what do *you* think of it?"

"I think, sir, he's a little *luny*," replied Ginger Nut, with a grin.

"You hear what they say," said I, turning towards the screen, "come forth and do your duty."

But he vouchsafed no reply. I pondered a moment in sore perplexity. But once more business hurried me. I determined again to postpone the consideration of this dilemma to my future leisure. With a little trouble we made out to examine the papers without Bartleby, though at every page or two Turkey deferentially dropped his opinion, that this proceeding was quite out of the common; while Nippers, twitching in his chair with a dyspeptic nervousness, ground out, between his set teeth, occasional hissing maledictions against the stubborn oaf behind the screen. And for his (Nippers') part, this was the first and the last time he would do another man's business without pay.

Meanwhile Bartleby sat in his hermitage, oblivious to everything but his own peculiar business there.

Some days passed, the scrivener being employed upon another lengthy work. His late remarkable conduct led me to regard his ways narrowly. I observed that he never went to dinner; indeed, that he never went anywhere. As yet I had never, of my personal knowledge, known him to be outside of my office. He was a perpetual sentry in the corner. At about eleven o'clock though, in the morning, I noticed that Ginger Nut would advance towards the opening in Bartleby's screen, as if silently beckoned thither by a gesture invisible to me where I sat. The boy would then leave the office, jingling a few pence, and reappear with a handful of ginger-nuts, which he delivered in the hermitage, receiving two of the cakes for his trouble.

He lives, then, on ginger-nuts, thought I; never eats a dinner, properly speaking; he must be a vegetarian, then, but no; he never eats even vegetables, he eats nothing but ginger-nuts. My mind then ran on in reveries concerning the probable effects upon the human constitution of living entirely on ginger-nuts. Ginger-nuts are so called, because they contain ginger as one of their peculiar constituents, and the final flavoring one. Now, what was ginger? A hot, spicy thing. Was Bartleby hot and spicy? Not at all. Ginger, then, had no effect upon Bartleby. Probably he preferred it should have none.

Nothing so aggravates an earnest person as a passive resistance. If the individual so resisted be of a not inhumane temper, and the resisting one perfectly harmless in his passivity, then, in the better moods of the former, he will endeavor charitably to construe to his imagination what proves impossible to be solved by his judgment. Even so, for the most part, I regarded Bartleby and his ways. Poor fellow! thought I, he means no mischief; it is plain he intends no insolence; his aspect sufficiently evinces that his eccentricities are involuntary. He is useful to me. I can get along with him. If I turn him away, the chances are he will fall in with some less indulgent employer, and then he will be rudely treated, and perhaps driven forth miserably to starve. Yes. Here I can cheaply purchase a delicious self-approval. To befriend Bartleby; to humor him in his strange wilfulness, will cost me little or nothing, while I lay up in my soul what will eventually prove a sweet morsel for my conscience. But this mood was not invariable with me. The passiveness of Bartleby sometimes irritated me. I felt strangely goaded on to encounter him in new opposition—to elicit some angry spark from him answerable to my own. But, indeed, I might as well have essayed to strike fire with my knuckles against a bit of Windsor soap. But one afternoon the evil impulse in me mastered me, and the following little scene ensued:

"Bartleby," said I, "when those papers are all copied, I will compare them with you."

"I would prefer not to."

"How? Surely you do not mean to persist in that mulish vagary?"

No answer.

I threw open the folding-doors nearby, and turning upon Turkey and Nippers, exclaimed:

"Bartleby a second time says, he won't examine his papers. What do you think of it, Turkey?"

It was afternoon, be it remembered. Turkey sat glowing like a brass boiler; his bald head steaming; his hands reeling among his blotted papers.

"Think of it?" roared Turkey. "I think I'll just step behind his screen, and black his eyes for him!"

So saying, Turkey rose to his feet and threw his arms into a pugilistic position. He was hurrying away to make good his promise, when I detained him, alarmed at the effect of incautiously rousing Turkey's combativeness after dinner.

"Sit down, Turkey," said I, "and hear what Nippers has to say. What do you think of it, Nippers? Would I not be justified in immediately dismissing Bartleby?"

"Excuse me, that is for you to decide, sir. I think his conduct quite unusual, and, indeed, unjust, as regards Turkey and myself. But it may only be a passing whim."

"Ah," exclaimed I, "you have strangely changed your mind, then—you speak very gently of him now."

"All beer," cried Turkey; "gentleness is effects of beer—Nippers and I dined together to-day. You see how gentle *I* am, sir. Shall I go and black his eyes?"

"You refer to Bartleby, I suppose. No, not to-day, Turkey," I replied; "pray, put up your fists."

I closed the doors, and again advanced towards Bartleby. I felt additional incentives tempting me to my fate. I burned to be rebelled against again. I remembered that Bartleby never left the office.

"Bartleby," said I, "Ginger Nut is away; just step around to the Post Office, won't you?" (it was but a three minutes' walk) "and see if there is anything for me."

"I would prefer not to."

"You *will* not?"

"I *prefer* not."

I staggered to my desk, and sat there in a deep study. My blind inveteracy returned. Was there any other thing in which I could procure myself to be ignominiously repulsed by this lean, penniless wight? my hired clerk? What added thing is there, perfectly reasonable, that he will be sure to refuse to do?

"Bartleby!"

No answer.

"Bartleby," in a louder tone.

No answer.

"Bartleby," I roared.

Like a very ghost, agreeably to the laws of magical invocation, at the third summons, he appeared at the entrance of his hermitage.

"Go to the next room, and tell Nippers to come to me."

"I would prefer not to," he respectfully and slowly said, and mildly disappeared.

"Very good, Bartleby," said I, in a quiet sort of serenely-severe self-possessed tone, intimating the unalterable purpose of some terrible retribution very close at hand. At the moment I half intended something of the kind. But upon the whole, as it was drawing towards my dinner-hour, I thought it best to put on my hat and walk home for the day, suffering much from perplexity and distress of mind.

Shall I acknowledge it? The conclusion of this whole business was, that it soon became a fixed fact of my chambers, that a pale young scrivener, by the name of Bartleby, had a desk there; that he copied for me at the usual rate of four cents a folio (one hundred words); but he was permanently exempt from examining the work done by him, that duty being transferred to Turkey and Nippers, out of compliment, doubtless, to their superior acuteness; moreover, said Bartleby was never, on any account, to be dispatched on the most trivial errand of any sort; and that even if entreated to take upon him such a matter, it was generally understood that he would "prefer not to"—in other words, that he would refuse point blank.

As days passed on, I became considerably reconciled to Bartleby. His steadiness, his freedom from all dissipation, his incessant industry (except when he chose to throw himself into a standing revery behind his screen), his great stillness, his unalterableness of demeanor under all circumstances, made him a valuable acquisition. One prime thing was this—*he was always there*—first in the morning, continually through the day, and the last at night. I had a singular confidence in his honesty. I felt my most precious papers perfectly safe in his hands. Sometimes, to be sure, I could not, for the very soul of me, avoid falling into sudden spasmodic passions with him. For it was exceeding difficult to bear in mind all the time those strange peculiarities, privileges, and unheard-of exemptions, forming the tacit stipulations on Bartleby's part under which he remained in my office. Now and then, in the eagerness of dispatching pressing business, I would inadvertently summon Bartleby, in a short, rapid tone, to put his finger, say, on the incipient tie of a bit of red tape with which I was about compressing some papers. Of course, from behind the screen the usual answer, "I prefer not to," was sure to come; and then, how could a human creature, with the common infirmities of our nature, refrain from bitterly exclaiming upon such perverseness—such unreasonableness? However, every added repulse of this sort which I received only tended to lessen the probability of my repeating the inadvertence.

Here it must be said, that, according to the custom of most legal gentlemen occupying chambers in densely populated law buildings, there were several keys to my door. One was kept by a woman residing in the attic, which person weekly scrubbed and daily swept and dusted my apartments. Another was kept by Turkey for convenience sake. The third I sometimes carried in my own pocket. The fourth I knew not who had.

Now, one Sunday morning I happened to go to Trinity Church, to hear a celebrated preacher, and finding myself rather early on the ground I thought I would walk round to my chambers for a while. Luckily I had my key with me; but upon applying it to the lock, I found it resisted by something inserted from the inside. Quite surprised, I called out; when to my consternation a key was turned from within; and thrusting his lean visage at me, and holding the door ajar, the apparition of Bartleby appeared, in his shirt-sleeves, and otherwise in a strangely tattered *deshabille*, saying quietly that he was sorry, but he was deeply engaged just then, and preferred not admitting me at present. In a brief word or two, he moreover added, that perhaps I had better walk round the block two or three times, and by that time he would probably have concluded his affairs.

Now, the utterly unsurmised appearance of Bartleby, tenanting my law-chambers of a Sunday morning, with his cadaverously gentlemanly *nonchalance,* yet withal firm and self-possessed, had such a strange effect upon me, that incontinently I slunk away from my own door, and did as desired. But not without sundry twinges of impotent rebellion against the mild effrontery of this unaccountable scrivener. Indeed, it was his wonderful mildness chiefly, which not only disarmed me, but unmanned me, as it were. For I consider that one, for the time, is sort of unmanned when he tranquilly permits his hired clerk to dictate to him, and order him away from his own premises. Furthermore, I was full of uneasiness as to what Bartleby could possibly be doing in my office in his shirt-sleeves, and in an otherwise dismantled condition on a Sunday morning. Was anything amiss going on? Nay, that was out of the question. It was not to be thought of for a moment that Bartleby was an immoral person. But what could he be doing there?—copying? Nay again, whatever might be his eccentricities, Bartleby was an eminently decorous person. He would be the last man to sit down to his desk in any state approaching to nudity. Besides, it was Sunday; and there was something about Bartleby that forbade the supposition that he would by any secular occupation violate the proprieties of the day.

Nevertheless, my mind was not pacified; and full of a restless curiosity, at last I returned to the door. Without hindrance I inserted my key, opened it, and entered. Bartleby was not to be seen. I looked round anxiously, peeped behind his screen; but it was very plain that he was gone. Upon more closely examining the place, I surmised that for an indefinite period Bartleby must have ate, dressed, and slept in my office, and that too without plate, mirror, or bed. The cushioned seat of a rickety old sofa in one corner bore the faint impress of a lean, reclining form. Rolled away under his desk, I found a blanket; under the empty grate, a blacking box and brush; on a chair, a tin basin, with soap and a ragged towel; in a newspaper a few crumbs of ginger-nuts and a morsel of cheese. Yes, thought I, it is evident enough that Bartleby has been making his home here, keeping bachelor's hall all by himself. Immediately then the thought came sweeping across me, what miserable friendlessness and loneliness are here revealed! His poverty is great; but his solitude, how horrible! Think of it. Of a Sunday, Wall Street is deserted as Petra;° and every night of every day it is an emptiness. This building, too, which of week-days hums with industry and life, at nightfall echoes with sheer vacancy, and all through Sunday is forlorn. And here Bartleby makes his home; sole spectator of a solitude which he has seen all populous—a sort of innocent and transformed Marius° brooding among the ruins of Carthage!

Petra: A city in what is now Jordan, once the center of an Arab kingdom. It was deserted for more than ten centuries, until its rediscovery by explorers in 1812.
Marius: Gaius Marius (157?–86 B.C.) was a Roman general, several times elected consul. Marius's greatest military successes came in the Jugurthine War, in Africa. Later, when his opponents gained power and he was banished, he fled to Africa. Carthage was a city in North Africa.

For the first time in my life a feeling of overpowering stinging melancholy seized me. Before, I had never experienced aught but a not unpleasing sadness. The bond of a common humanity now drew me irresistibly to gloom. A fraternal melancholy! For both I and Bartleby were sons of Adam. I remembered the bright silks and sparkling faces I had seen that day, in gala trim, swan-like sailing down the Mississippi of Broadway; and I contrasted them with the pallid copyist, and thought to myself, Ah, happiness courts the light, so we deem the world is gay; but misery hides aloof, so we deem that misery there is none. These sad fancyings—chimeras, doubtless, of a sick and silly brain—led on to other and more special thoughts, concerning the eccentricities of Bartleby. Presentiments of strange discoveries hovered round me. The scrivener's pale form appeared to me laid out, among uncaring strangers, in its shivering winding-sheet.

Suddenly I was attracted by Bartleby's closed desk, the key in open sight left in the lock.

I mean no mischief, seek the gratification of no heartless curiosity, thought I; besides, the desk is mine, and its contents, too, so I will make bold to look within. Everything was methodically arranged, the papers smoothly placed. The pigeon-holes were deep, and removing the files of documents, I groped into their recesses. Presently I felt something there, and dragged it out. It was an old bandanna handkerchief, heavy and knotted. I opened it, and saw it was a saving's bank.

I now recalled all the quiet mysteries which I had noted in the man. I remembered that he never spoke but to answer; that, though at intervals he had considerable time to himself, yet I had never seen him reading—no, not even a newspaper; that for long periods he would stand looking out, at his pale window behind the screen, upon the dead brick wall; I was quite sure he never visited any refectory or eating-house; while his pale face clearly indicated that he never drank beer like Turkey; or tea and coffee even, like other men; that he never went anywhere in particular that I could learn; never went out for a walk, unless, indeed, that was the case at present; that he had declined telling who he was, or whence he came, or whether he had any relatives in the world; that though so thin and pale, he never complained of ill-health. And more than all, I remembered a certain unconscious air of pallid—how shall I call it?—of pallid haughtiness, say, or rather an austere reserve about him, which has positively awed me into my tame compliance with his eccentricities, when I had feared to ask him to do the slightest incidental thing for me, even though I might know, from his long-continued motionlessness, that behind his screen he must be standing in one of those dead-wall reveries of his.

Revolving all these things, and coupling them with the recently discovered fact, that he made my office his constant abiding place and home, and not forgetful of his morbid moodiness; revolving all these things, a prudential feeling began to steal over me. My first emotions had been those of pure melancholy and sincerest pity; but just in proportion as the forlornness of Bartleby grew and grew to my imagination, did that same melancholy merge into fear, that pity into repulsion. So true it is, and so terrible, too, that up to a certain point the thought or sight of misery enlists our best affections; but, in certain special cases, beyond that point it does not. They err who would assert that invariably this is owing to the inherent selfishness of the human heart. It rather proceeds from a certain hopelessness of remedying excessive and organic ill. To a sensitive being, pity is not seldom pain. And when at last it is perceived that such pity cannot lead to effectual succor, common sense bids the soul be rid of it. What I saw that morning persuaded me that the scrivener was the victim of innate and incurable disorder. I might give alms to his body; but his body did not pain him; it was his soul that suffered, and his soul I could not reach.

I did not accomplish the purpose of going to Trinity Church that morning. Somehow, the things I had seen disqualified me for the time from church-going. I walked homeward, thinking what I would do with Bartleby. Finally, I resolved upon this — I would put certain calm questions to him the next morning, touching his history, etc., and if he declined to answer them openly and unreservedly (and I supposed he would prefer not), then to give him a twenty dollar bill over and above whatever I might owe him, and tell him his services were no longer required; but that if in any other way I could assist him, I would be happy to do so, especially if he desired to return to his native place, wherever that might be, I would willingly help to defray the expenses. Moreover, if, after reaching home, he found himself at any time in want of aid, a letter from him would be sure of a reply.

The next morning came.

"Bartleby," said I, gently calling to him behind his screen.

No reply.

"Bartleby," said I, in a still gentler tone, "come here; I am not going to ask you to do anything you would prefer not to do — I simply wish to speak to you."

Upon this he noiselessly slid into view.

"Will you tell me, Bartleby, where you were born?"

"I would prefer not to."

"Will you tell me *anything* about yourself?"

"I would prefer not to."

"But what reasonable objection can you have to speak to me? I feel friendly towards you."

He did not look at me while I spoke, but kept his glance fixed upon my bust of Cicero, which, as I then sat, was directly behind me, some six inches above my head.

"What is your answer, Bartleby?" said I, after waiting a considerable time for a reply, during which his countenance remained immovable, only there was the faintest conceivable tremor of the white attenuated mouth.

"At present I prefer to give no answer," he said, and retired into his hermitage.

It was rather weak in me I confess, but his manner, on this occasion, nettled me. Not only did there seem to lurk in it a certain calm disdain, but his perverseness seemed ungrateful, considering the undeniable good usage and indulgence he had received from me.

Again I sat ruminating what I should do. Mortified as I was at his behavior, and resolved as I had been to dismiss him when I entered my office, nevertheless I strangely felt something superstitious knocking at my heart, and forbidding me to carry out my purpose, and denouncing me for a villain if I dared to breathe one bitter word against this forlornest of mankind. At last, familiarly drawing my chair behind his screen, I sat down and said: "Bartleby, never mind, then, about revealing your history; but let me entreat you, as a friend, to comply as far as may be with the usages of this office. Say now, you will help to examine papers tomorrow or next day: in short, say now, that in a day or two you will begin to be a little reasonable:—say so, Bartleby."

"At present I would prefer not to be a little reasonable," was his mildly cadaverous reply.

Just then the folding-doors opened, and Nippers approached. He seemed suffering from an unusually bad night's rest, induced by severer indigestion than common. He overheard those final words of Bartleby.

"*Prefer not*, eh?" gritted Nippers—"I'd *prefer* him, if I were you, sir," addressing me—"I'd *prefer* him; I'd give him preferences, the stubborn mule! What is it, sir, pray, that he *prefers* not to do now?"

Bartleby moved not a limb.

"Mr. Nippers," said I, "I'd prefer that you would withdraw for the present."

Somehow, of late, I had got into the way of involuntarily using this word "prefer" upon all sorts of not exactly suitable occasions. And I trembled to think that my contact with the scrivener had already and seriously affected me in a mental way. And what further and deeper aberration might it not yet produce? This apprehension had not been without efficacy in determining me to summary measures.

As Nippers, looking very sour and sulky, was departing, Turkey blandly and deferentially approached.

"With submission, sir," said he, "yesterday I was thinking about Bartleby here, and I think that if he would but prefer to take a quart of good ale every day, it would do much towards mending him, and enabling him to assist in examining his papers."

"So you have got the word, too," said I, slightly excited.

"With submission, what word, sir?" asked Turkey, respectfully crowding himself into the contracted space behind the screen, and by so doing, making me jostle the scrivener. "What word, sir?"

"I would prefer to be left alone here," said Bartleby, as if offended at being mobbed in his privacy.

"*That's* the word, Turkey," said I—"*that's* it."

"Oh, *prefer*? oh yes—queer word. I never use it myself. But, sir, as I was saying, if he would but prefer—"

"Turkey," interrupted I, "you will please withdraw."

"Oh certainly, sir, if you prefer that I should."

As he opened the folding-door to retire, Nippers at his desk caught a glimpse of me, and asked whether I would prefer to have a certain paper copied on blue paper or white. He did not in the least roguishly accent the word "prefer." It was plain that it involuntarily rolled from his tongue. I thought to myself, surely I must get rid of a demented man, who already has in some degree turned the tongues, if not the heads of myself and clerks. But I thought it prudent not to break the dismission at once.

The next day I noticed that Bartleby did nothing but stand at his window in his dead-wall revery. Upon asking him why he did not write, he said that he had decided upon doing no more writing.

"Why, how now? what next?" exclaimed I, "do no more writing?"

"No more."

"And what is the reason?"

"Do you not see the reason for yourself?" he indifferently replied.

I looked steadfastly at him, and perceived that his eyes looked dull and glazed. Instantly it occurred to me, that his unexampled diligence in copying by his dim window for the first few weeks of his stay with me might have temporarily impaired his vision.

I was touched. I said something in condolence with him. I hinted that of course he did wisely in abstaining from writing for a while; and urged him to embrace that opportunity of taking wholesome exercise in the open air. This, however, he did not do. A few days after this, my other clerks being absent, and being in a great hurry to dispatch certain letters by the mail, I thought that, having nothing else earthly to do, Bartleby would surely be less inflexible than usual, and carry these letters to the Post Office. But he blankly declined. So, much to my inconvenience, I went myself.

Still added days went by. Whether Bartleby's eyes improved or not, I could not say. To all appearance, I thought they did. But when I asked him if they did he vouchsafed no answer. At all events, he would do no copying. At last, in replying to my urgings, he informed me that he had permanently given up copying.

"What!" exclaimed I; "suppose your eyes should get entirely well—better than ever before—would you not copy then?"

"I have given up copying," he answered, and slid aside.

He remained as ever, a fixture in my chamber. Nay—if that were possible—he became still more of a fixture than before. What was to be done? He would do nothing in the office; why should he stay there? In plain fact, he had now become a millstone to me, not only useless as a necklace, but afflictive to bear. Yet I was sorry for him. I speak less than truth when I say that, on his own account, he occasioned me uneasiness. If he would but have named a single relative or friend, I would instantly have written, and urged their taking the poor fellow away to some convenient retreat. But he seemed alone, absolutely alone in the universe. A bit of wreck in the mid-Atlantic. At length, necessities connected with my business tyrannized over all other considerations. Decently as I could, I told Bartleby that in six days' time he must unconditionally leave the office. I warned him to take measures, in the interval, for procuring some other abode. I offered to assist him in this endeavor, if he himself would but take the first step towards a removal. "And when you finally quit me, Bartleby," added I, "I shall see that you go not away entirely unprovided. Six days from this hour, remember."

At the expiration of that period, I peeped behind the screen, and lo! Bartleby was there.

I buttoned up my coat, balanced myself; advanced slowly towards him, touched his shoulder, and said, "The time has come; you must quit this place; I am sorry for you; here is money; but you must go."

"I would prefer not," he replied, with his back still towards me.

"You *must*."

He remained silent.

Now I had an unbounded confidence in this man's common honesty. He had frequently restored to me sixpences and shillings carelessly dropped upon the floor, for I am apt to be very reckless in such shirt-button affairs. The proceeding, then, which followed will not be deemed extraordinary.

"Bartleby," said I, "I owe you twelve dollars on account; here are thirty-two; the odd twenty are yours—Will you take it?" and I handed the bills towards him.

But he made no motion.

"I will leave them here, then," putting them under a weight on the table. Then taking my hat and cane and going to the door, I tranquilly turned and added—"After you have removed your things from these offices, Bartleby, you will of course lock the door—since every one is now gone for the day but you—and if you please, slip your key underneath the mat, so that I may have it in the morning. I shall not see you again; so good-bye to you. If, hereafter, in your new place of abode, I can be of any service to you, do not fail to advise me by letter. Good-bye, Bartleby, and fare you well."

But he answered not a word; like the last column of some ruined temple, he remained standing mute and solitary in the middle of the otherwise deserted room.

As I walked home in a pensive mood, my vanity got the better of my pity. I could not but highly plume myself on my masterly management in getting rid of Bartleby. Masterly I call it, and such it must appear to any dispassionate thinker. The beauty of my procedure seemed to consist in its perfect quietness. There was no vulgar bullying, no bravado of any sort, no choleric hectoring, and striding to and fro across the apartment, jerking out vehement commands for Bartleby to bundle himself off with his beggarly traps. Nothing of the kind. Without loudly bidding Bartleby depart—as an inferior genius might have done—I *assumed* the ground that depart he must; and upon that assumption built all I had to say. The more I thought over my procedure, the more I was charmed with it. Nevertheless, next morning, upon awakening, I had my doubts—I had somehow slept off the fumes of vanity. One of the coolest and wisest hours a man has, is just after he awakes in the morning. My procedure seemed as sagacious as ever—but only in theory. How it would prove in practice—there was the rub. It was truly a beautiful thought to have assumed Bartleby's departure; but, after all, that assumption was simply my own, and none of Bartleby's. The great point was, not whether I had assumed that he would quit me, but whether he would prefer to do so. He was more a man of preferences than assumptions.

After breakfast, I walked down town, arguing the probabilities *pro* and *con*. One moment I thought it would prove a miserable failure, and Bartleby would be found all alive at my office as usual; the next moment it seemed certain that I should find his chair empty. And so I kept veering about. At the corner of Broadway and Canal Street, I saw quite an excited group of people standing in earnest conversation.

"I'll take odds he doesn't," said a voice as I passed.

"Doesn't go?—done!" said I, "put up your money."

I was instinctively putting my hand in my pocket to produce my own, when I remembered that this was an election day. The words I had overheard bore no reference to Bartleby, but to the success or non-success of some candidate for the mayoralty. In my intent frame of mind, I had, as it were, imagined that all Broadway shared in my excitement, and were debating the same question with me. I passed on, very thankful that the uproar of the street screened my momentary absent-mindedness.

As I had intended, I was earlier than usual at my office door. I stood listening for a moment. All was still. He must be gone. I tried the knob. The door was locked. Yes, my procedure had worked to a charm; he indeed must be vanished. Yet a certain melancholy mixed with this: I was almost sorry for my brilliant success. I was fumbling under the door mat for the key, which Bartleby was to have left there for me, when accidentally my knee knocked against a panel, producing a summoning sound, and in response a voice came to me from within—"Not yet; I am occupied."

It was Bartleby.

I was thunderstruck. For an instant I stood like the man who, pipe in mouth, was killed one cloudless afternoon long ago in Virginia, by summer lightning; at his own warm open window he was killed, and remained leaning out there upon the dreamy afternoon, till someone touched him, when he fell.

"Not gone!" I murmured at last. But again obeying that wondrous ascendancy which the inscrutable scrivener had over me, and from which ascendancy, for all my chafing, I could not completely escape, I slowly went down stairs and out into the street, and while walking round the block, considered what I should next do in this unheard-of perplexity. Turn the man out by an actual thrusting I could not; to drive him away by calling him hard names would not do; calling in the police was an unpleasant idea; and yet, permit him to enjoy his cadaverous triumph over me—this, too, I could not think of. What was to be done? or, if nothing could be done, was there anything further that I could *assume* in the matter? Yes, as before I had prospectively assumed that Bartleby would depart, so now I might retrospectively assume that departed he was. In the legitimate carrying out of this assumption, I might enter my office in a great hurry, and pretending not to see Bartleby at all, walk straight against him as if he were air. Such a proceeding would in a singular degree have the appearance of a home-thrust. It was hardly possible that Bartleby could withstand such an application of the doctrine of assumption. But upon second thoughts the success of the plan seemed rather dubious. I resolved to argue the matter over with him again.

"Bartleby," said I, entering the office, with a quietly severe expression, "I am seriously displeased. I am pained, Bartleby. I had thought better of you. I had imagined you of such a gentlemanly organization, that in any delicate dilemma a slight hint would suffice—in short, an assumption. But it appears I am deceived. Why," I added, unaffectedly starting, "You have not even touched that money yet," pointing to it, just where I had left it the evening previous.

He answered nothing.

"Will you, or will you not, quit me?" I now demanded in a sudden passion, advancing close to him.

"I would prefer *not* to quit you," he replied, gently emphasizing the *not*.

"What earthly right have you to stay here? Do you pay any rent? Do you pay my taxes? Or is this property yours?"

He answered nothing.

"Are you ready to go on and write now? Are your eyes recovered? Could you copy a small paper for me this morning? or help examine a few lines? or step round to the Post Office? In a word, will you do anything at all, to give a coloring to your refusal to depart the premises?"

He silently retired into his hermitage.

I was now in such a state of nervous resentment that I thought it but prudent to check myself at present from further demonstrations. Bartleby and I were alone. I remembered the tragedy of the unfortunate Adams and the still more unfortunate Colt in the solitary office of the latter; and how poor Colt, being dreadfully incensed by Adams, and imprudently permitting himself to get wildly excited, was at unawares hurried into his fatal act—an act which certainly no man could possibly deplore more than the actor himself.° Often it had occurred to me in my ponderings upon the subject that had that altercation taken place in the public street, or at a private residence, it would not have terminated as it did. It was the circumstance of being alone in a solitary office, up stairs, of a building entirely unhallowed by humanizing domestic associations—an uncarpeted office, doubtless, of a dusty, haggard sort of appearance—this it must have been, which greatly helped to enhance the irritable desperation of the hapless Colt.

But when this old Adam of resentment rose in me and tempted me concerning Bartleby, I grappled him and threw him. How? Why, simply by recalling the divine injunction: "A new commandment give I unto you, that ye love one another." Yes, this it was that saved me. Aside from higher considerations, charity often operates as a vastly wise and prudent principle—a great safeguard to its possessor. Men have committed murder for jealousy's sake, and anger's sake, and hatred's sake, and selfishness' sake, and spiritual pride's sake; but no man, that ever I heard of, ever committed a diabolical murder for sweet charity's sake. Mere self-interest, then, if no better motive can be enlisted, should, especially with high-tempered men, prompt all beings to charity and philanthropy. At any rate, upon the occasion in question, I strove to drown my exasperated feelings towards the scrivener by benevolently construing his conduct. Poor fellow, poor fellow! thought I, he don't mean anything; and besides, he has seen hard times, and ought to be indulged.

---

the actor himself: John C. Colt murdered Samuel Adams in January 1842. Later that year, after his conviction, Colt committed suicide a half-hour before he was to be hanged. The case received wide and sensationalistic press coverage at the time.

I endeavored, also, immediately to occupy myself, and at the same time to comfort my despondency. I tried to fancy, that in the course of the morning, at such time as might prove agreeable to him, Bartleby, of his own free accord, would emerge from his hermitage and take up some decided line of march in the direction of the door. But no. Half-past twelve o'clock came; Turkey began to glow in the face, overturn his inkstand, and become generally obstreperous; Nippers abated down into quietude and courtesy; Ginger Nut munched his noon apple; and Bartleby remained standing at his window in one of his profoundest dead-wall reveries. Will it be credited? Ought I to acknowledge it? That afternoon I left the office without saying one further word to him.

Some days now passed, during which, at leisure intervals I looked a little into "Edwards on the Will,"° and "Priestley on Necessity."° Under the circumstances, those books induced a salutary feeling. Gradually I slid into the persuasion that these troubles of mine, touching the scrivener, had been all predestined from eternity, and Bartleby was billeted upon me for some mysterious purpose of an all-wise Providence, which it was not for a mere mortal like me to fathom. Yes, Bartleby, stay there behind your screen, thought I; I shall persecute you no more; you are harmless and noiseless as any of these old chairs; in short, I never feel so private as when I know you are here. At last I see it, I feel it; I penetrate to the predestined purpose of my life. I am content. Others may have loftier parts to enact; but my mission in this world, Bartleby, is to furnish you with office-room for such period as you may see fit to remain.

I believe that this wise and blessed frame of mind would have continued with me, had it not been for the unsolicited and uncharitable remarks obtruded upon me by my professional friends who visited the rooms. But thus it often is, that the constant friction of illiberal minds wears out at last the best resolves of the more generous. Though to be sure, when I reflected upon it, it was not strange that people entering my office should be struck by the peculiar aspect of the unaccountable Bartleby, and so be tempted to throw out some sinister observations concerning him. Sometimes an attorney, having business with me, and calling at my office, and finding no one but the scrivener there, would undertake to obtain some sort of precise information from him touching my whereabouts; but without heeding his idle talk, Bartleby would remain standing immovable in the middle of the room. So after contemplating him in that position for a time, the attorney would depart, no wiser than he came.

Also, when a reference was going on, and the room full of lawyers and witnesses, and business driving fast, some deeply-occupied legal gentleman

---

Edwards on the Will: Jonathan Edwards (1703–1758) was an important American theologian, a rigidly orthodox Calvinist who believed in the doctrine of predestination and a leader of the Great Awakening, the religious revival that swept the North American colonies in the 1740s. The work being alluded to here is *Freedom of the Will* (1754).

Priestley on Necessity: Joseph Priestley (1733–1803) was an English scientist and clergyman who began as a Unitarian but developed his own radical ideas on "natural determinism." As a scientist, he did early experiments with electricity and was one of the first to discover the existence of oxygen. As a political philosopher, he championed the French Revolution—a cause so unpopular in England that he had to flee that country and spend the last decade of his life in the United States.

present, seeing Bartleby wholly unemployed, would request him to run round to his (the legal gentleman's) office and fetch some papers for him. Thereupon, Bartleby would tranquilly decline, and yet remain idle as before. Then the lawyer would give a great stare, and turn to me. And what could I say? At last I was made aware that all through the circle of my professional acquaintance, a whisper of wonder was running round, having reference to the strange creature I kept at my office. This worried me very much. And as the idea came upon me of his possibly turning out a long-lived man, and keeping occupying my chambers, and denying my authority; and perplexing my visitors; and scandalizing my professional reputation; and casting a general gloom over the premises; keeping soul and body together to the last upon his savings (for doubtless he spent but half a dime a day), and in the end perhaps outlive me, and claim possession of my office by right of his perpetual occupancy: as all these dark anticipations crowded upon me more and more, and my friends continually intruded their relentless remarks upon the apparition in my room; a great change was wrought in me. I resolved to gather all my faculties together, and forever rid me of this intolerable incubus.

Ere revolving any complicated project, however, adapted to this end, I first simply suggested to Bartleby the propriety of his permanent departure. In a calm and serious tone, I commended the idea to his careful and mature consideration. But, having taken three days to meditate upon it, he apprised me, that his original determination remained the same; in short, that he still preferred to abide with me.

What shall I do? I now said to myself, buttoning up my coat to the last button. What shall I do? what ought I to do? what does conscience say I *should* do with this man, or, rather, ghost. Rid myself of him, I must; go, he shall. But how? You will not thrust him, the poor, pale, passive mortal you will not thrust such a helpless creature out of your door? you will not dishonor yourself by such cruelty? No, I will not, I cannot do that. Rather would I let him live and die here, and then mason up his remains in the wall. What, then, will you do? For all your coaxing, he will not budge. Bribes he leaves under your own paperweight on your table; in short, it is quite plain that he prefers to cling to you.

Then something severe, something unusual must be done. What! surely you will not have him collared by a constable, and commit his innocent pallor to the common jail? And upon what ground could you procure such a thing to be done?—a vagrant, is he? What! he a vagrant, a wanderer, who refuses to budge? It is because he will not be a vagrant, then, that you seek to count him *as* a vagrant. That is too absurd. No visible means of support: there I have him. Wrong again: for indubitably he *does* support himself, and that is the only unanswerable proof that any man can show of his possessing the means so to do. No more, then. Since he will not quit me, I must quit him. I will change my offices; I will move elsewhere, and give him fair notice, that if I find him on my new premises I will then proceed against him as a common trespasser.

Acting accordingly, next day I thus addressed him: "I find these chambers too far from the City Hall; the air is unwholesome. In a word, I propose to remove my offices next week, and shall no longer require your services. I tell you this now, in order that you may seek another place."

He made no reply, and nothing more was said.

On the appointed day I engaged carts and men, proceeded to my chambers, and, having but little furniture, everything was removed in a few hours. Throughout, the scrivener remained standing behind the screen, which I directed to be removed the last thing. It was withdrawn; and, being folded up like a huge folio, left him the motionless occupant of a naked room. I stood in the entry watching him a moment, while something from within me upbraided me.

I re-entered, with my hand in my pocket—and—and my heart in my mouth.

"Good-bye, Bartleby; I am going—good-bye, and God some way bless you; and take that," slipping something in his hand. But it dropped upon the floor, and then—strange to say—I tore myself from him whom I had so longed to be rid of.

Established in my new quarters, for a day or two I kept the door locked, started at every footfall in the passages. When I returned to my rooms, after any little absence, I would pause at the threshold for an instant, and attentively listen, ere applying my key. But these fears were needless. Bartleby never came nigh me.

I thought all was going well, when a perturbed-looking stranger visited me, inquiring whether I was the person who had recently occupied rooms at No.— Wall Street.

Full of forebodings, I replied that I was.

"Then, sir," said the stranger, who proved a lawyer, "you are responsible for the man you left there. He refuses to do any copying; he refuses to do anything; he says he prefers not to; and he refuses to quit the premises."

"I am very sorry, sir," said I, with assumed tranquillity, but an inward tremor, "but, really, the man you allude to is nothing to me—he is no relation or apprentice of mine, that you should hold me responsible for him."

"In mercy's name, who is he?"

"I certainly cannot inform you. I know nothing about him. Formerly I employed him as a copyist; but he has done nothing for me now for some time past."

"I shall settle him, then—good morning, sir."

Several days passed, and I heard nothing more; and, though I often felt a charitable prompting to call at the place and see poor Bartleby, yet a certain squeamishness, of I know not what, withheld me.

All is over with him, by this time, thought I, at last, when, through another week, no further intelligence reached me. But, coming to my room the day after, I found several persons waiting at my door in a high state of nervous excitement.

"That's the man here—he comes," cried the foremost one, whom I recognized as the lawyer who had previously called upon me alone.

"You must take him away, sir, at once," cried a portly person among them, advancing upon me, and whom I knew to be the landlord of No.— Wall Street. "These gentlemen, my tenants, cannot stand it any longer; Mr. B——" pointing to the lawyer, "has turned him out of his room, and he now persists in haunting the building generally, sitting upon the banisters of the stairs by day, and sleeping in the entry by night. Everybody is concerned; clients are leaving the offices; some fears are entertained of a mob; something you must do, and that without delay."

Aghast at this torrent, I fell back before it, and would fain have locked myself in my new quarters. In vain I persisted that Bartleby was nothing to me—no more than to any one else. In vain—I was the last person known to have anything to do with him, and they held me to the terrible account. Fearful, then, of being exposed in the papers (as one person present obscurely threatened), I considered the matter, and, at length, said, that if the lawyer would give me a confidential interview with the scrivener, in his (the lawyer's) own room, I would, that afternoon, strive my best to rid them of the nuisance they complained of.

Going up stairs to my old haunt, there was Bartleby silently sitting upon the banister at the landing.

"What are you doing here, Bartleby?" said I.

"Sitting upon the banister," he mildly replied.

I motioned him into the lawyer's room, who then left us.

"Bartleby," said I, "are you aware that you are the cause of great tribulation to me, by persisting in occupying the entry after being dismissed from the office?"

No answer.

"Now one of two things must take place. Either you must do something, or something must be done to you. Now what sort of business would you like to engage in? Would you like to re-engage in copying for some one?"

"No; I would prefer not to make any change."

"Would you like a clerkship in a dry-goods store?"

"There is too much confinement about that. No, I would not like a clerkship; but I am not particular."

"Too much confinement," I cried, "why, you keep yourself confined all the time!"

"I would prefer not to take a clerkship," he rejoined, as if to settle that little item at once.

"How would a bar-tender's business suit you? There is no trying of the eye-sight in that."

"I would not like it at all; though, as I said before, I am not particular."

His unwonted wordiness inspirited me. I returned to the charge.

"Well, then, would you like to travel through the country collecting bills for the merchants? That would improve your health."

"No, I would prefer to be doing something else."

"How, then, would going as a companion to Europe, to entertain some young gentleman with your conversation—how would that suit you?"

"Not at all. It does not strike me that there is anything definite about that. I like to be stationary. But I am not particular."

"Stationary you shall be, then," I cried, now losing all patience, and, for the first time in all my exasperating connections with him, fairly flying into a passion. "If you do not go away from these premises before night, I shall feel bound—indeed, I *am* bound—to—to—to quit the premises myself!" I rather absurdly concluded, knowing not with what possible threat to try to frighten his immobility into compliance. Despairing of all further efforts, I was precipitately leaving him, when a final thought occurred to me—one which had not been wholly unindulged before.

"Bartleby," said I, in the kindest tone I could assume under such exciting circumstances, "will you go home with me now not to my office, but my dwelling—and remain there till we can conclude upon some convenient arrangement for you at our leisure? Come, let us start now, right away."

"No: at present I would prefer not to make any change at all."

I answered nothing; but, effectually dodging every one by the suddenness and rapidity of my flight, rushed from the building, ran up Wall Street towards Broadway, and, jumping into the first omnibus, was soon removed from pursuit. As soon as tranquillity returned, I distinctly perceived that I had now done all that I possibly could, both in respect to the demands of the landlord and his tenants, and with regard to my own desire and sense of duty, to benefit Bartleby, and shield him from rude persecution. I now strove to be entirely care-free and quiescent; and my conscience justified me in the attempt; though, indeed, it was not so successful as I could have wished. So fearful was I of being again hunted out by the incensed landlord and his exasperated tenants, that, surrendering my business to Nippers, for a few days, I drove about the upper part of the town and through the suburbs, in my rockaway; crossed over to Jersey City and Hoboken, and paid fugitive visits to Manhattanville and Astoria. In fact, I almost lived in my rockaway for the time.

When again I entered my office, lo, a note from the landlord lay upon the desk. I opened it with trembling hands. It informed me that the writer had sent to the police, and had Bartleby removed to the Tombs as a vagrant. Moreover, since I knew more about him than any one else, he wished me to appear at that place, and make a suitable statement of the facts. These tidings had a conflicting effect upon me. At first I was indignant; but, at last, almost approved. The landlord's energetic, summary disposition, had led him to adopt a procedure which I do not think I would have decided upon myself; and yet, as a last resort, under such peculiar circumstances, it seemed the only plan.

As I afterwards learned, the poor scrivener, when told that he must be conducted to the Tombs, offered not the slightest obstacle, but, in his pale, unmoving way, silently acquiesced.

Some of the compassionate and curious by-standers joined the party; and headed by one of the constables arm-in-arm with Bartleby, the silent procession filed its way through all the noise, and heat, and joy of the roaring thoroughfares at noon.

The same day I received the note, I went to the Tombs, or, to speak more properly, the Halls of Justice. Seeking the right officer, I stated the purpose of my call, and was informed that the individual I described was, indeed, within. I then assured the functionary that Bartleby was a perfectly honest man, and greatly to be compassionated, however unaccountably eccentric. I narrated all I knew, and closed by suggesting the idea of letting him remain in as indulgent confinement as possible, till something less harsh might be done—though, indeed, I hardly knew what. At all events, if nothing else could be decided upon, the alms-house must receive him. I then begged to have an interview.

Being under no disgraceful charge, and quite serene and harmless in all his ways, they had permitted him freely to wander about the prison, and, especially, in the inclosed grass-platted yards thereof. And so I found him there, standing all alone in the quietest of the yards, his face towards a high wall, while all around, from the narrow slits of the jail windows, I thought I saw peering out upon him the eyes of murderers and thieves.

"Bartleby!"

"I know you," he said, without looking round—"and I want nothing to say to you."

"It was not I that brought you here, Bartleby," said I, keenly pained at his implied suspicion. "And to you, this should not be so vile a place. Nothing reproachful attaches to you by being here. And see, it is not so sad a place as one might think. Look, there is the sky, and here is the grass."

"I know where I am," he replied, but would say nothing more, and so I left him.

As I entered the corridor again, a broad meat-like man, in an apron, accosted me, and, jerking his thumb over my shoulder, said, "Is that your friend?"

"Yes."

"Does he want to starve? If he does, let him live on the prison fare, that's all."

"Who are you?" asked I, not knowing what to make of such an unofficially speaking person in such a place.

"I am the grub-man. Such gentlemen as have friends here, hire me to provide them with something good to eat."

"Is this so?" said I, turning to the turnkey.

He said it was.

"Well, then," said I, slipping some silver into the grub-man's hands (for so they called him), "I want you to give particular attention to my friend there; let him have the best dinner you can get. And you must be as polite to him as possible."

"Introduce me, will you?" said the grub-man, looking at me with an expression which seemed to say he was all impatience for an opportunity to give a specimen of his breeding.

Thinking it would prove of benefit to the scrivener, I acquiesced; and, asking the grub-man his name, went up with him to Bartleby.

"Bartleby, this is a friend; you will find him very useful to you."

"Your sarvant, sir, your sarvant," said the grub-man, making a low salutation behind his apron. "Hope you find it pleasant here, sir; nice grounds—cool apartments—hope you'll stay with us some time—try to make it agreeable. What will you have for dinner to-day?"

"I prefer not to dine to-day," said Bartleby, turning away. "It would disagree with me; I am unused to dinners." So saying, he slowly moved to the other side of the inclosure, and took up a position fronting the dead-wall.

"How's this?" said the grub-man, addressing me with a stare of astonishment. "He's odd, ain't he?"

"I think he is a little deranged," said I, sadly.

"Deranged? deranged is it? Well, now, upon my word, I thought that friend of yourn was a gentleman forger; they are always pale and genteel-like, them forgers. I can't help pity 'em—can't help it, sir. Did you know Monroe Edwards?" he added, touchingly, and paused. Then, laying his hand piteously on my shoulder, sighed, "he died of consumption at Sing-Sing. So you weren't acquainted with Monroe?"

"No, I was never socially acquainted with any forgers. But I cannot stop longer. Look to my friend yonder. You will not lose by it. I will see you again."

Some few days after this, I again obtained admission to the Tombs, and went through the corridors in quest of Bartleby; but without finding him.

"I saw him coming from his cell not long ago," said a turnkey, "may be he's gone to loiter in the yards."

So I went in that direction.

"Are you looking for the silent man?" said another turnkey, passing me. "Yonder he lies—sleeping in the yard there. 'Tis not twenty minutes since I saw him lie down."

The yard was entirely quiet. It was not accessible to the common prisoners. The surrounding walls, of amazing thickness, kept off all sounds behind them. The Egyptian character of the masonry weighed upon me with its gloom. But a soft imprisoned turf grew under foot. The heart of the eternal pyramids, it seemed, wherein, by some strange magic, through the clefts, grass-seed, dropped by birds, had sprung.

Strangely huddled at the base of the wall, his knees drawn up, and lying on his side, his head touching the cold stones, I saw the wasted Bartleby. But nothing stirred. I paused; then went close up to him; stooped over, and saw that his dim eyes were open; otherwise he seemed profoundly sleeping. Something prompted me to touch him. I felt his hand, when a tingling shiver ran up my arm and down my spine to my feet.

The round face of the grub-man peered upon me now. "His dinner is ready. Won't he dine to-day, either? Or does he live without dining?"

"Lives without dining," said I, and closed the eyes.

"Eh!—He's asleep, ain't he?"

"With kings and counselors,"° murmured I.

There would seem little need for proceeding further in this history. Imagination will readily supply the meagre recital of poor Bartleby's interment. But, ere parting with the reader, let me say, that if this little narrative has sufficiently interested him, to awaken curiosity as to who Bartleby was, and what manner of life he led prior to the present narrator's making his acquaintance, I can only reply, that in such curiosity I fully share, but am wholly unable to gratify it. Yet here I hardly know whether I should divulge one little item

---

With kings and counselors: A reference to Job 3:14. Job, who has lost his family and all his property and has been stricken by a terrible disease, wishes he had never been born: "then had I been at rest with kings and counselors of the earth, which built desolate places for themselves."

of rumor, which came to my ear a few months after the scrivener's decease. Upon what basis it rested, I could never ascertain; and hence, how true it is I cannot now tell. But, inasmuch as this vague report has not been without a certain suggestive interest to me, however sad, it may prove the same with some others; and so I will briefly mention it. The report was this: that Bartleby had been a subordinate clerk in the Dead Letter Office at Washington, from which he had been suddenly removed by a change in the administration. When I think over this rumor, hardly can I express the emotions which seize me. Dead letters! does it not sound like dead men? Conceive a man by nature and misfortune prone to a pallid hopelessness, can any business seem more fitted to heighten it than that of continually handling these dead letters, and assorting them for the flames? For by the cart-load they are annually burned. Sometimes from out the folded paper the pale clerk takes a ring the finger it was meant for, perhaps, moulders in the grave; a bank-note sent in swiftest charity he whom it would relieve, nor eats nor hungers any more; pardon for those who died despairing; hope for those who died unhoping; good tidings for those who died stifled by unrelieved calamities. On errands of life, these letters speed to death.

Ah, Bartleby! Ah, humanity!

LORRIE MOORE

Lorrie Moore (b. 1957) was born in Glen Falls, New York, daughter of an insurance executive and a housewife. After completing her studies at St. Lawrence University and Cornell University, where she earned an M.F.A. in 1982, Moore began teaching at the University of Wisconsin. As an undergraduate she won a *Seventeen* magazine short story contest in 1976, and she started publishing her fiction in magazines such as *Cosmopolitan, Ms.*, and *The New Yorker*. In 1987 her novel *Anagrams* was published.

Self-Help, Moore's first collection of short stories, appeared in 1985. As the title of the book suggests, several of the humorous stories, such as "How to Become a Writer," were narrated in what Moore calls "second person, mock-imperative" voices as she parodied the self-improvement manuals popular with American readers. In the book Moore included sketches to cover various situations—"The Kid's Guide to Divorce," "How to Talk to Your Mother," "How to Be an Other Woman."

Reviewers noted that typically the fictional characters narrating Moore's stories were intelligent people whose self-knowledge only contributed to their sense of distress, so they reacted by attempting to distance themselves from their dilemmas through humor. A character in Moore's second collection, *Like Life* (1990), is told, "Everything's a joke with you." She replies, "Nothing's a joke with me. It just all comes out like one." Moore has said that the stories in *Self-Help*, written between 1980 and 1983, were stylistic experiments. She thought,

> Let's see what happens when one eliminates the subject, leaves the verb shivering at the start of a clause; what happens when one appropriates the "how-to" form for a fiction, for an irony, for a "how-not-to" . . . the self-help proffered here, then, is perhaps only that of art itself, which, if you agree with Oscar Wilde, is quite useless.

Moore's books include *Who Will Run the Frog Hospital?* (1994), *Birds of America* (1998), *The Collected Stories* (2008), and the novel *A Gate at the Stairs* (2009).

WEB Research Lorrie Moore at bedfordstmartins.com/rewritinglit.

How to Become a Writer

1985

First, try to be something, anything, else. A movie star/astronaut. A movie star/missionary. A movie star/kindergarten teacher. President of the World. Fail miserably. It is best if you fail at an early age—say, fourteen. Early, critical disillusionment is necessary so that at fifteen you can write long haiku sequences about thwarted desire. It is a pond, a cherry blossom, a wind brushing against sparrow wing leaving for mountain. Count the syllables. Show it to your mom. She is tough and practical. She has a son in Vietnam and a husband who may be having an affair. She believes in wearing brown because it hides spots. She'll look briefly at your writing, then back up at you with a face blank as a donut. She'll say: "How about emptying the dishwasher?" Look away. Shove the forks in the fork drawer. Accidentally break one of the freebie gas station glasses. This is the required pain and suffering. This is only for starters.

In your high school English class look only at Mr. Killian's face. Decide faces are important. Write a villanelle about pores. Struggle. Write a sonnet. Count the syllables: nine, ten, eleven, thirteen. Decide to experiment with fiction. Here you don't have to count syllables. Write a short story about an elderly man and woman who accidentally shoot each other in the head, the result of an inexplicable malfunction of a shotgun which appears mysteriously in their living room one night. Give it to Mr. Killian as your final project. When you get it back, he has written on it: "Some of your images are quite nice, but you have no sense of plot." When you are home, in the privacy of your own room, faintly scrawl in pencil beneath his black-inked comments: "Plots are for dead people, pore-face."

Take all the babysitting jobs you can get. You are great with kids. They love you. You tell them stories about old people who die idiot deaths. You sing them songs like "Blue Bells of Scotland," which is their favorite. And when they are in their pajamas and have finally stopped pinching each other, when they are fast asleep, you read every sex manual in the house, and wonder how on earth anyone could ever do those things with someone they truly loved. Fall asleep in a chair reading Mr. McMurphy's *Playboy*. When the McMurphys come home, they will tap you on the shoulder, look at the magazine in your lap, and grin. You will want to die. They will ask you if Tracey took her medicine all right. Explain, yes, she did, that you promised her a story if she would take it like a big girl and that seemed to work out just fine. "Oh, marvelous," they will exclaim.

Try to smile proudly.

Apply to college as a child psychology major.

As a child psychology major, you have some electives. You've always liked birds. Sign up for something called "The Ornithological Field Trip." It meets Tuesdays and Thursdays at two. When you arrive at Room 134 on the first day of class, everyone is sitting around a seminar table talking about metaphors. You've heard of these. After a short, excruciating while, raise your hand and say diffidently, "Excuse me, isn't this Birdwatching One-oh-one?" The class stops and turns to look at you. They seem to all have one face—giant and blank as a vandalized clock. Someone with a beard booms out, "No, this is Creative Writing." Say: "Oh—right," as if perhaps you knew all along. Look down at your schedule. Wonder how the hell you ended up here. The computer, apparently, has made an error. You start to get up to leave and then don't. The lines at the registrar this week are huge. Perhaps you should stick with this mistake. Perhaps your creative writing isn't all that bad. Perhaps it is fate. Perhaps this is what your dad meant when he said, "It's the age of computers, Francie, it's the age of computers."

Decide that you like college life. In your dorm you meet many nice people. Some are smarter than you. And some, you notice, are dumber than you. You will continue, unfortunately, to view the world in exactly these terms for the rest of your life.

The assignment this week in creative writing is to narrate a violent happening. Turn in a story about driving with your Uncle Gordon and another one about two old people who are accidentally electrocuted when they go to turn on a badly wired desk lamp. The teacher will hand them back to you with comments: "Much of your writing is smooth and energetic. You have, however, a ludicrous notion of plot." Write another story about a man and a woman who, in the very first paragraph, have their lower torsos accidentally blitzed away by dynamite. In the second paragraph, with the insurance money, they buy a frozen yogurt stand together. There are six more paragraphs. You read the whole thing out loud in class. No one likes it. They say your sense of plot is outrageous and incompetent. After class someone asks you if you are crazy.

Decide that perhaps you should stick to comedies. Start dating someone who is funny, someone who has what in high school you called a "really great sense of humor" and what now your creative writing class calls "self-contempt giving rise to comic form." Write down all of his jokes, but don't tell him you are doing this. Make up anagrams of his old girlfriend's name and name all of your socially handicapped characters with them. Tell him his old girlfriend is in all of your stories and then watch how funny he can be, see what a really great sense of humor he can have.

Your child psychology advisor tells you you are neglecting courses in your major. What you spend the most time on should be what you're majoring in. Say yes, you understand.

In creative writing seminars over the next two years, everyone continues to smoke cigarettes and ask the same things: "But does it work?" "Why should we care about this character?" "Have you earned this cliché?" These seem like important questions.

On days when it is your turn, you look at the class hopefully as they scour your mimeographs for a plot. They look back up at you, drag deeply, and then smile in a sweet sort of way.

You spend too much time slouched and demoralized. Your boyfriend suggests bicycling. Your roommate suggests a new boyfriend. You are said to be self-mutilating and losing weight, but you continue writing. The only happiness you have is writing something new, in the middle of the night, armpits damp, heart pounding, something no one has yet seen. You have only those brief, fragile, untested moments of exhilaration when you know: you are a genius. Understand what you must do. Switch majors. The kids in your nursery project will be disappointed, but you have a calling, an urge, a delusion, an unfortunate habit. You have, as your mother would say, fallen in with a bad crowd.

Why write? Where does writing come from? These are questions to ask yourself. They are like: Where does dust come from? Or: Why is there war? Or: If there's a God, then why is my brother now a cripple?

These are questions that you keep in your wallet, like calling cards. These are questions, your creative writing teacher says, that are good to address in your journals but rarely in your fiction.

The writing professor this fall is stressing the Power of the Imagination. Which means he doesn't want long descriptive stories about your camping trip last July. He wants you to start in a realistic context but then to alter it. Like recombinant DNA. He wants you to let your imagination sail, to let it grow big-bellied in the wind. This is a quote from Shakespeare.

Tell your roommate your great idea, your great exercise of imaginative power: a transformation of Melville to contemporary life. It will be about monomania and the fish-eat-fish world of life insurance in Rochester, New York. The first line will be "Call me Fishmeal," and it will feature a menopausal suburban husband named Richard, who because he is so depressed all the time is called "Mopey Dick" by his witty wife Elaine. Say to your roommate: "Mopey Dick, get it?" Your roommate looks at you, her face blank as a large Kleenex. She comes up to you, like a buddy, and puts an arm around your burdened shoulders. "Listen, Francie," she says, slow as speech therapy. "Let's go out and get a big beer."

The seminar doesn't like this one either. You suspect they are beginning to feel sorry for you. They say: "You have to think about what is happening. Where is the story here?"

The next semester the writing professor is obsessed with writing from personal experience. You must write from what you know, from what has happened to you. He wants death, he wants camping trips. Think about what has happened to you. In three years there have been three things: you lost your virginity; your parents got divorced; and your brother came home from a forest ten miles from the Cambodian border with only half a thigh, a permanent smirk nestled into one corner of his mouth.

About the first you write: "It created a new space, which hurt and cried in a voice that wasn't mine, 'I'm not the same anymore, but I'll be okay.'"

About the second you write an elaborate story of an old married couple who stumble upon an unknown land mine in their kitchen and accidentally blow themselves up. You call it: "For Better or for Liverwurst."

About the last you write nothing. There are no words for this. Your typewriter hums. You can find no words.

At undergraduate cocktail parties, people say, "Oh, you write? What do you write about?" Your roommate, who has consumed too much wine, too little cheese, and no crackers at all, blurts: "Oh, my god, she always writes about her dumb boyfriend."

Later on in life you will learn that writers are merely open, helpless texts with no real understanding of what they have written and therefore must half-believe anything and everything that is said of them. You, however, have not yet reached this stage of literary criticism. You stiffen and say, "I do not," the same way you said it when someone in the fourth grade accused you of really liking oboe lessons and your parents really weren't just making you take them.

Insist you are not very interested in any one subject at all, that you are interested in the music of language, that you are interested in—in—syllables, because they are the atoms of poetry, the cells of the mind, the breath of the soul. Begin to feel woozy. Stare into your plastic wine cup.

"Syllables?" you will hear someone ask, voice trailing off, as they glide slowly toward the reassuring white of the dip.

Begin to wonder what you do write about. Or if you have anything to say. Or if there even is such a thing as a thing to say. Limit these thoughts to no more than ten minutes a day; like sit-ups, they can make you thin.

You will read somewhere that all writing has to do with one's genitals. Don't dwell on this. It will make you nervous.

Your mother will come visit you. She will look at the circles under your eyes and hand you a brown book with a brown briefcase on the cover. It is entitled: *How to Become a Business Executive.* She has also brought the *Names for Baby* encyclopedia you asked for; one of your characters, the aging clown-schoolteacher, needs a new name. Your mother will shake her head and say: "Francie, Francie, remember when you were going to be a child psychology major?"

Say: "Mom, I like to write."

She'll say: "Sure you like to write. Of course. Sure you like to write."

Write a story about a confused music student and title it: "Schubert Was the One with the Glasses, Right?" It's not a big hit, although your roommate likes the part where the two violinists accidentally blow themselves up in a recital room. "I went out with a violinist once," she says, snapping her gum.

•

Thank god you are taking other courses. You can find sanctuary in nineteenth-century ontological snags and invertebrate courting rituals. Certain globular mollusks have what is called "Sex by the Arm." The male octopus, for instance, loses the end of one arm when placing it inside the female body during intercourse. Marine biologists call it "Seven Heaven." Be glad you know these things. Be glad you are not just a writer. Apply to law school.

From here on in, many things can happen. But the main one will be this: you decide not to go to law school after all, and, instead, you spend a good, big chunk of your adult life telling people how you decided not to go to law school after all. Somehow you end up writing again. Perhaps you go to graduate school. Perhaps you work odd jobs and take writing courses at night. Perhaps you are working on a novel and writing down all the clever remarks and intimate personal confessions you hear during the day. Perhaps you are losing your pals, your acquaintances, your balance.

You have broken up with your boyfriend. You now go out with men who, instead of whispering "I love you," shout: "Do it to me, baby." This is good for your writing.

Sooner or later you have a finished manuscript more or less. People look at it in a vaguely troubled sort of way and say, "I'll bet becoming a writer was always a fantasy of yours, wasn't it?" Your lips dry to salt. Say that of all the fantasies possible in the world, you can't imagine being a writer even making the top twenty. Tell them you were going to be a child psychology major. "I bet," they always sigh, "you'd be great with kids." Scowl fiercely. Tell them you're a walking blade.

Quit classes. Quit jobs. Cash in old savings bonds. Now you have time like warts on your hands. Slowly copy all of your friends' addresses into a new address book.

Vacuum. Chew cough drops. Keep a folder full of fragments.

An eyelid darkening sideways.
World as conspiracy.
Possible plot? A woman gets on a bus.
Suppose you threw a love affair and nobody came?

At home drink a lot of coffee. At Howard Johnson's order the cole slaw. Consider how it looks like the soggy confetti of a map: where you've been, where you're going—"You Are Here," says the red star on the back of the menu.

Occasionally a date with a face blank as a sheet of paper asks you whether writers often become discouraged. Say that sometimes they do and sometimes they do. Say it's a lot like having polio.

"Interesting," smiles your date, and then he looks down at his arm hairs and starts to smooth them, all, always, in the same direction.

JOYCE CAROL OATES

Joyce Carol Oates (b. 1938) was born in Lockport, New York, one of three children in a Roman Catholic family. She began to put picture stories down on paper even before she could write, and she remembers that her parents "dutifully" supplied her with lined tablets and gave her a typewriter when she was fourteen. In 1956, after Oates graduated from high school, she went on a scholarship to major in English at Syracuse University, but she did not devote most of her time to writing until after she received her M.A. from the University of Wisconsin in 1961. Discovering by chance that one of her stories had been cited in the honor roll of Martha Foley's annual *The Best American Short Stories*, Oates assembled fourteen stories in her first book, *By the North Gate* (1963). Her career was launched, and as John Updike has speculated, she "was perhaps born a hundred years too late; she needs a lustier audience, a race of Victorian word-eaters to be worthy of her astounding productivity, her tireless gift of self-enthrallment."

One of our most prolific authors, Oates has published over seventy books and over a hundred stories, including her rewriting of Chekhov's story "The Lady with the Pet Dog." Notable collections of her stories are *Raven's Wing* (1986) and *The Assignation* (1988); the same year she published the essays in *(Woman) Writer: Occasions and Opportunities.* Oates also writes poetry and literary criticism. *New Heaven, New Earth* (1974) analyzes the "visionary experience in literature" as exemplified in the work of Henry James, Virginia Woolf, Franz Kafka, D. H. Lawrence, Flannery O'Connor, and others. As a writer, critic, and professor at Princeton University, she dedicates her life to "promoting and exploring literature. . . . I am not conscious of being in any particular literary tradition, though I share with my contemporaries an intense interest in the formal aspects of writing; each of my books is an experiment of a kind, an investigation of the relationship between a certain consciousness and its formal aesthetic expression."

The story "Where Are You Going, Where Have You Been?" was first published in *Epoch* in 1966; it was included in *The Best American Short Stories* of 1967 and *Prize Stories: The O. Henry Awards 1968* and was made into a film. Oates has said that this story, based on an article in *Life* magazine about a Tucson, Arizona, murderer, has been "constantly misunderstood by one generation, and intuitively understood by another." She sees the story as dealing with a human being "struggling heroically to define personal identity in the face of incredible opposition, even in the face of death itself." Some recent works are *High Lonesome: New and Collected Stories 1966–2006* (2006), *Wild Nights* (2008), and *A Widow's Story: A Memoir* (2011). In 1999 Oates was awarded the O. Henry Prize for Continued Achievement in the Short Story.

CONNECTION To read the story that inspired Joyce Carol Oates's "The Lady with the Pet Dog," see Anton Chekhov's story by the same title on page 156.

WEB Research Joyce Carol Oates at bedfordstmartins.com/rewritinglit.

The Lady with the Pet Dog

1972

I

Strangers parted as if to make way for him.

There he stood. He was there in the aisle, a few yards away, watching her.

She leaned forward at once in her seat, her hand jerked up to her face as if to ward off a blow—but then the crowd in the aisle hid him, he was gone. She pressed both hands against her cheeks. He was not here, she had imagined him.

"My God," she whispered.

She was alone. Her husband had gone out to the foyer to make a telephone call; it was intermission at the concert, a Thursday evening.

Now she saw him again, clearly. He was standing there. He was staring at her. Her blood rocked in her body, draining out of her head . . . she was going to faint . . . They stared at each other. They gave no sign of recognition. Only when he took a step forward did she shake her head *no—no—keep away.* It was not possible.

When her husband returned, she was staring at the place in the aisle where her lover had been standing. Her husband leaned forward to interrupt that stare.

"What's wrong?" he said. "Are you sick?"

Panic rose in her in long shuddering waves. She tried to get to her feet, panicked at the thought of fainting here, and her husband took hold of her. She stood like an aged woman, clutching the seat before her.

At home he helped her up the stairs and she lay down. Her head was like a large piece of crockery that had to be held still, it was so heavy. She was still panicked. She felt it in the shallows of her face, behind her knees, in the pit of her stomach. It sickened her, it made her think of mucus, of something thick and gray congested inside her, stuck to her, that was herself and yet not herself—a poison.

She lay with her knees drawn up toward her chest, her eyes hotly open, while her husband spoke to her. She imagined that other man saying, *Why did you run away from me?* Her husband was saying other words. She tried to listen to them. He was going to call the doctor, he said, and she tried to sit up. "No, I'm all right now," she said quickly. The panic was like lead inside her, so thickly congested. How slow love was to drain out of her, how fluid and sticky it was inside her head!

Her husband believed her. No doctor. No threat. Grateful, she drew her husband down to her. They embraced, not comfortably. For years now they had not been comfortable together, in their intimacy and at a distance, and now they struggled gently as if the paces of this dance were too rigorous for them. It was something they might have known once, but had now outgrown. The panic in her thickened at this double betrayal: she drew her husband to her, she caressed him wildly, she shut her eyes to think about that other man.

A crowd of men and women parting, unexpectedly, and there he stood—there he stood—she kept seeing him, and yet her vision blotched at the memory. It had been finished between them, six months before, but he had come out here . . . and she had escaped him, now she was lying in her husband's arms, in his embrace, her face pressed against his. It was a kind of sleep, this love-making. She felt herself falling asleep, her body falling from her. Her eyes shut.

"I love you," her husband said fiercely, angrily.

She shut her eyes and thought of that other man, as if betraying him would give her life a center.

"Did I hurt you? Are you—?" Her husband whispered.

Always this hot flashing of shame between them, the shame of her husband's near failure, the clumsiness of his love—

"You didn't hurt me," she said.

II

They had said good-by six months before. He drove her from Nantucket, where they had met, to Albany, New York, where she visited her sister. The hours of intimacy in the car had sealed something between them, a vow of silence and impersonality: she recalled the movement of the highways, the passing of other cars, the natural rhythms of the day hypnotizing her toward sleep while he drove. She trusted him, she could sleep in his presence. Yet she could not really fall asleep in spite of her exhaustion, and she kept jerking awake, frightened, to discover that nothing had changed—still the stranger who was driving her to Albany, still the highway, the sky, the antiseptic odor of the rented car, the sense of a rhythm behind the rhythm of the air that might unleash itself at any second. Everywhere on this highway, at this moment, there were men and women driving together, bonded together—what did that mean, to be together? What did it mean to enter into a bond with another person?

No, she did not really trust him; she did not really trust men. He would glance at her with his small cautious smile and she felt a declaration of shame between them.

Shame.

In her head she rehearsed conversations. She said bitterly, "You'll be relieved when we get to Albany. Relieved to get rid of me." They had spent so many days talking, confessing too much, driven to a pitch of childish excitement, laughing together on the beach, breaking into that pose of laughter that seems to eradicate the soul, so many days of this that the silence of the trip was like the silence of a hospital—all these surface noises, these rattles and hums, but an interior silence, a befuddlement. She said to him in her imagination, "One of us should die." Then she leaned over to touch him. She caressed the back of his neck. She said, aloud, "Would you like me to drive for a while?"

They stopped at a picnic area where other cars were stopped—couples, families—and walked together, smiling at their good luck. He put his arm around her shoulders and she sensed how they were in a posture together, a man and a woman forming a posture, a figure, that someone might sketch and show to them. She said slowly, "I don't want to go back. . . ."

Silence. She looked up at him. His face was heavy with her words, as if she had pulled at his skin with her fingers. Children ran nearby and distracted him—yes, he was a father too, his children ran like that, they tugged at his skin with their light, busy fingers.

"Are you so unhappy?" he said.

"I'm not unhappy, back there. I'm nothing. There's nothing to me," she said.

They stared at each other. The sensation between them was intense, exhausting. She thought that this man was her savior, that he had come to her at a time in her life when her life demanded completion, an end, a permanent fixing of all that was troubled and shifting and deadly. And yet it was absurd to think this. No person could save another. So she drew back from him and released him.

A few hours later they stopped at a gas station in a small city. She went to the women's rest room, having to ask the attendant for a key, and when she came back her eye jumped nervously onto the rented car—why? did she think he might have driven off without her?—onto the man, her friend, standing in conversation with the young attendant. Her friend was as old as her husband, over forty, with lanky, sloping shoulders, a full body, his hair thick, a dark, burnished brown, a festive color that made her eye twitch a little—and his hands were always moving, always those rapid conversational circles, going nowhere, gestures that were at once a little aggressive and apologetic.

She put her hand on his arm, a claim. He turned to her and smiled and she felt that she loved him, that everything in her life had forced her to this moment and that she had no choice about it.

They sat in the car for two hours, in Albany, in the parking lot of a Howard Johnson's restaurant, talking, trying to figure out their past. There was no future. They concentrated on the past, the several days behind them, lit up with a hot, dazzling August sun, like explosions that already belonged to other people, to strangers. Her face was faintly reflected in the green-tinted curve of the windshield, but she could not have recognized that face. She began to cry; she told herself: *I am not here, this will pass, this is nothing.* Still, she could not stop crying. The muscles of her face were springy, like a child's, unpredictable muscles. He stroked her arms, her shoulders, trying to comfort her. "This is so hard . . . this is impossible . . ." he said. She felt panic for the world outside this car, all that was not herself and this man, and at the same time she understood that she was free of him, as people are free of other people, she would leave him soon, safely, and within a few days he would have fallen into the past, the impersonal past. . . .

"I'm so ashamed of myself!" she said finally.

She returned to her husband and saw that another woman, a shadow-woman, had taken her place—noiseless and convincing, like a dancer performing certain difficult steps. Her husband folded her in his arms and talked to her of his own loneliness, his worries about his business, his health, his mother, kept tranquilized and mute in a nursing home, and her spirit detached itself from her and drifted about the rooms of the large house she lived in with her husband, a shadow-woman delicate and imprecise. There was no boundary to her, no edge. Alone, she took hot baths and sat exhausted in the steaming water, wondering at her perpetual exhaustion. All that winter she noticed the limp, languid weight of her arms, her veins bulging slightly with the pressure of her extreme weariness. *This is fate,* she thought, to be here and not there, to be one person and not another, a certain man's wife and not the wife of another man. The long, slow pain of this certainty rose in her, but it never became clear, it was baffling and imprecise. She could not be serious about it; she kept congratulating herself on her own good luck, to have escaped so easily, to have freed herself. So much love had gone into the first several years of her marriage that there wasn't much left, now, for another man. . . . She was certain of that. But the bath water made her dizzy, all that perpetual heat, and one day in January she drew a razor blade lightly across the inside of her arm, near the elbow, to see what would happen.

Afterward she wrapped a small towel around it, to stop the bleeding. The towel soaked through. She wrapped a bath towel around that and walked through the empty rooms of her home, lightheaded, hardly aware of the stubborn seeping of blood. There was no boundary to her in this house, no precise limit. She could flow out like her own blood and come to no end.

She sat for a while on a blue love seat, her mind empty. Her husband telephoned her when he would be staying late at the plant. He talked to her always about his plans, his problems, his business friends, his future. It was obvious that he had a future. As he spoke she nodded to encourage him, and her heartbeat quickened with the memory of her own, personal shame, the shame of this man's particular, private wife. One evening at dinner he leaned forward and put his head in his arms and fell asleep, like a child. She sat at the table with him for a while, watching him. His hair had gone gray, almost white, at the temples—no one would guess that he was so quick, so careful a man, still fairly young about the eyes. She put her hand on his head, lightly, as if to prove to herself that he was real. He slept, exhausted.

One evening they went to a concert and she looked up to see her lover there, in the crowded aisle, in this city, watching her. He was standing there, with his overcoat on, watching her. She went cold. That morning the telephone had rung while her husband was still home, and she had heard him answer it, heard him hang up—it must have been a wrong number—and when the telephone rang again, at 9:30, she had been afraid to answer it. She had left home to be out of the range of that ringing, but now, in this public place, in this busy auditorium, she found herself staring at that man, unable to make any sign to him, any gesture of recognition. . . .

He would have come to her but she shook her head. *No. Stay away.*

Her husband helped her out of the row of seats, saying, "Excuse us, please. Excuse us," so that strangers got to their feet, quickly, alarmed, to let them pass. Was that woman about to faint? What was wrong?

At home she felt the blood drain slowly back into her head. Her husband embraced her hips, pressing his face against her, in that silence that belonged to the earliest days of their marriage. She thought, *He will drive it out of me.* He made love to her and she was back in the auditorium again, sitting alone, now that the concert was over. The stage was empty; the heavy velvet curtains had not been drawn; the musicians' chairs were empty, everything was silent and expectant; in the aisle her lover stood and smiled at her—Her husband was impatient. He was apart from her, working on her, operating on her; and then, stricken, he whispered, "Did I hurt you?"

The telephone rang the next morning. Dully, sluggishly, she answered it. She recognized his voice at once—that "Anna?" with its lifting of the second syllable, questioning and apologetic and making its claim—"Yes, what do you want?" she said.

"Just to see you. Please—"

"I can't."

"Anna, I'm sorry, I didn't mean to upset you—"

"I can't see you."

"Just for a few minutes—I have to talk to you—"

"But why, why now? Why now?" she said.

She heard her voice rising, but she could not stop it. He began to talk again, drowning her out. She remembered his rapid conversation. She remembered his gestures, the witty energetic circling of his hands.

"Please don't hang up!" he cried.

"I can't—I don't want to go through it again—"

"I'm not going to hurt you. Just tell me how you are."

"Everything is the same."

"Everything is the same with me."

She looked up at the ceiling, shyly. "Your wife? Your children?"

"The same."

"Your son?"

"He's fine—"

"I'm so glad to hear that. I—"

"Is it still the same with you, your marriage? Tell me what you feel. What are you thinking?"

"I don't know. . . ."

She remembered his intense, eager words, the movement of his hands, that impatient precise fixing of the air by his hands, the jabbing of his fingers.

"Do you love me?" he said.

She could not answer.

"I'll come over to see you," he said.

"No," she said.

What will come next, what will happen?

Flesh hardening on his body, aging. Shrinking. He will grow old, but not soft like her husband. They are two different types: he is nervous, lean, energetic, wise. She will grow thinner, as the tension radiates out from her backbone, wearing down her flesh. Her collarbones will jut out of her skin. Her husband, caressing her in their bed, will discover that she is another woman—she is not there with him—instead she is rising in an elevator in a downtown hotel, carrying a book as a prop, or walking quickly away from that hotel, her head bent and filled with secrets. Love, what to do with it? . . . Useless as moths' wings, as moths' fluttering. . . . She feels the flutterings of silky, crazy wings in her chest.

He flew out to visit her every several weeks, staying at a different hotel each time. He telephoned her, and she drove down to park in an underground garage at the very center of the city.

She lay in his arms while her husband talked to her, miles away, one body fading into another. He will grow old, his body will change, she thought, pressing her cheek against the back of one of these men. If it was her lover, they were in a hotel room: always the propped-up little booklet describing the hotel's many services, with color photographs of its cocktail lounge and dining room and coffee shop. Grow old, leave me, die, go back to your neurotic wife and your sad, ordinary children, she thought, but still her eyes closed gratefully against his skin and she felt how complete their silence was, how they had come to rest in each other.

"Tell me about your life here. The people who love you," he said, as he always did.

One afternoon they lay together for four hours. It was her birthday and she was intoxicated with her good fortune, this prize of the afternoon, this man in her arms! She was a little giddy, she talked too much. She told him about her parents, about her husband. . . . "They were all people I believed in, but it turned out wrong. Now, I believe in you. . . ." He laughed as if shocked by her words. She did not understand. Then she understood. "But I believe truly in you. I can't think of myself without you," she said. . . . He spoke of his wife, her ambitions, her intelligence, her use of the children against him, her use of his younger son's blindness, all of his words gentle and hypnotic and convincing in the late afternoon peace of this hotel room . . . and she felt the terror of laughter, threatening laughter. Their words, like their bodies, were aging.

She dressed quickly in the bathroom, drawing her long hair up around the back of her head, fixing it as always, anxious that everything be the same. Her face was slightly raw, from his face. The rubbing of his skin. Her eyes were too bright, wearily bright. Her hair was blond but not so blond as it had been that summer in the white Nantucket air.

She ran water and splashed it on her face. She blinked at the water. Blind. Drowning. She thought with satisfaction that soon, soon, he would be back home, in that house on Long Island she had never seen, with that woman she had never seen, sitting on the edge of another bed, putting on his shoes. She wanted nothing except to be free of him. Why not be free? *Oh,* she thought suddenly, *I will follow you back and kill you. You and her and the little boy. What is there to stop me?*

She left him. Everyone on the street pitied her, that look of absolute zero.

III

A man and a child, approaching her. The sharp acrid smell of fish. The crashing of waves. Anna pretended not to notice the father with his son—there was something strange about them. That frank, silent intimacy, too gentle, the man's bare feet in the water and the boy a few feet away, leaning away from his father. He was about nine years old and still his father held his hand.

A small yipping dog, a golden dog, bounded near them.

Anna turned shyly back to her reading; she did not want to have to speak to these neighbors. She saw the man's shadow falling over her legs, then over the pages of her book, and she had the idea that he wanted to see what she was reading. The dog nuzzled her; the man called him away.

She watched them walk down the beach. She was relieved that the man had not spoken to her.

She saw them in town later that day, the two of them brown-haired and patient, now wearing sandals, walking with that same look of care. The man's white shorts were soiled and a little baggy. His pullover shirt was a faded green. His face was broad, the cheekbones wide, spaced widely apart, the eyes stark in their sockets, as if they fastened onto objects for no reason, ponderous and edgy. The little boy's face was pale and sharp; his lips were perpetually parted.

Anna realized that the child was blind.

The next morning, early, she caught sight of them again. For some reason she went to the back door of her cottage. She faced the sea breeze eagerly. Her heart hammered. . . . She had been here, in her family's old house, for three days, alone, bitterly satisfied at being alone, and now it was a puzzle to her how her soul strained to fly outward, to meet with another person. She watched the man with his son, his cautious, rather stooped shoulders above the child's small shoulders.

The man was carrying something, it looked like a notebook. He sat on the sand, not far from Anna's spot of the day before, and the dog rushed up to them. The child approached the edge of the ocean, timidly. He moved in short jerky steps, his legs stiff. The dog ran around him. Anna heard the child crying out a word that sounded like "Ty"—it must have been the dog's name—and then the man joined in, his voice heavy and firm.

"Ty—"

Anna tied her hair back with a yellow scarf and went down to the beach.

The man glanced around at her. He smiled. She stared past him at the waves. To talk to him or not to talk—she had the freedom of that choice. For a moment she felt that she had made a mistake, that the child and the dog would not protect her, that behind this man's ordinary, friendly face there was a certain arrogant maleness—then she relented, she smiled shyly.

"A nice house you've got there," the man said.

She nodded her thanks.

The man pushed his sunglasses up on his forehead. Yes, she recognized the eyes of the day before—intelligent and nervous, the sockets pale, untanned.

"Is that your telephone ringing?" he said.

She did not bother to listen. "It's a wrong number," she said.

Her husband calling: she had left home for a few days, to be alone.

But the man, settling himself on the sand, seemed to misinterpret this. He smiled in surprise, one corner of his mouth higher than the other. He said nothing. Anna wondered: *What is he thinking?* The dog was leaping about her, panting against her legs, and she laughed in embarrassment. She bent to pet it, grateful for its busyness. "Don't let him jump up on you," the man said. "He's a nuisance."

The dog was a small golden retriever, a young dog. The blind child, standing now in the water, turned to call the dog to him. His voice was shrill and impatient.

"Our house is the third one down—the white one," the man said.

She turned, startled. "Oh, did you buy it from Dr. Patrick? Did he die?"

"Yes, finally. . . ."

Her eyes wandered nervously over the child and the dog. She felt the nervous beat of her heart out to the very tips of her fingers, the fleshy tips of her fingers: little hearts were there, pulsing. *What is he thinking?* The man had opened his notebook. He had a piece of charcoal and he began to sketch something.

Anna looked down at him. She saw the top of his head, his thick brown hair, the freckles on his shoulders, the quick, deft movement of his hand. Upside down, Anna herself being drawn. She smiled in surprise.

"Let me draw you. Sit down," he said.

She knelt awkwardly a few yards away. He turned the page of the sketch pad. The dog ran to her and she sat, straightening out her skirt beneath her, flinching from the dog's tongue. "Ty!" cried the child. Anna sat, and slowly the pleasure of the moment began to glow in her; her skin flushed with gratitude.

She sat there for nearly an hour. The man did not talk much. Back and forth the dog bounded, shaking itself. The child came to sit near them, in silence. Anna felt that she was drifting into a kind of trance while the man sketched her, half a dozen rapid sketches, the surface of her face given up to him. "Where are you from?" the man asked.

"Ohio. My husband lives in Ohio."

She wore no wedding band.

"Your wife—" Anna began.

"Yes?"

"Is she here?"

"Not right now."

She was silent, ashamed. She had asked an improper question. But the man did not seem to notice. He continued drawing her, bent over the sketch pad. When Anna said she had to go, he showed her the drawings—one after another of her, Anna, recognizably Anna, a woman in her early thirties, her hair smooth and flat across the top of her head, tied behind by a scarf. "Take the one you like best," he said, and she picked one of her with the dog in her lap, sitting very straight, her brows and eyes clearly defined, her lips girlishly pursed, the dog and her dress suggested by a few quick irregular lines.

"Lady with pet dog," the man said.

She spent the rest of that day reading, nearer her cottage. It was not really a cottage—it was a two-story house, large and ungainly and weathered. It was mixed up in her mind with her family, her own childhood, and she glanced up from her book, perplexed, as if waiting for one of her parents or her sister to come up to her. Then she thought of that man, the man with the blind child, the man with the dog, and she could not concentrate on her reading. Someone—probably her father—had marked a passage that must be important, but she kept reading and rereading it: *We try to discover in things, endeared to us on that account, the spiritual glamour which we ourselves have cast upon them; we are disillusioned, and learn that they are in themselves barren and devoid of the charm that they owed, in our minds, to the association of certain ideas. . . .*

She thought again of the man on the beach. She lay the book aside and thought of him: his eyes, his aloneness, his drawings of her.

They began seeing each other after that. He came to her front door in the evening, without the child; he drove her into town for dinner. She was shy and extremely pleased. The darkness of the expensive restaurant released her; she heard herself chatter; she leaned forward and seemed to be offering her face up to him, listening to him. He talked about his work on a Long Island newspaper and she seemed to be listening to him, as she stared at his face, arranging her own face into the expression she had seen in that charcoal drawing. Did he see her like that, then?—girlish and withdrawn and patrician? She felt the weight of his interest in her, a force that fell upon her like a blow. A repeated blow. Of course he was married, he had children—of course she was married, permanently married. This flight from her husband was not important. She had left him before, to be alone, it was not important. Everything in her was slender and delicate and not important.

They walked for hours after dinner, looking at the other strollers, the weekend visitors, the tourists, the couples like themselves. Surely they were mistaken for a couple, a married couple. *This is the hour in which everything is decided,* Anna thought. They had both had several drinks and they talked a great deal. Anna found herself saying too much, stopping and starting giddily. She put her hand to her forehead, feeling faint.

"It's from the sun—you've had too much sun—" he said.

At the door to her cottage, on the front porch, she heard herself asking him if he would like to come in. She allowed him to lead her inside, to close the door. *This is not important,* she thought clearly, *he doesn't mean it, he doesn't love me, nothing will come of it.* She was frightened, yet it seemed to her necessary to give in; she had to leave Nantucket with that act completed, an act of adultery, an accomplishment she would take back to Ohio and to her marriage.

Later, incredibly, she heard herself asking: "Do you . . . do you love me?"

"You're so beautiful!" he said, amazed.

She felt this beauty, shy and glowing and centered in her eyes. He stared at her. In this large, drafty house, alone together, they were like accomplices, conspirators. She could not think: how old was she? which year was this? They had done something unforgivable together, and the knowledge of it was tugging at their faces. A cloud seemed to pass over her. She felt herself smiling shrilly.

Afterward, a peculiar raspiness, a dryness of breath. He was silent. She felt a strange, idle fear, a sense of the danger outside this room and this old comfortable bed—a danger that would not recognize her as the lady in that drawing, the lady with the pet dog. There was nothing to say to this man, this stranger. She felt the beauty draining out of her face, her eyes fading.

"I've got to be alone," she told him.

He left, and she understood that she would not see him again. She stood by the window of the room, watching the ocean. A sense of shame overpowered her: it was smeared everywhere on her body, the smell of it, the richness of it. She tried to recall him, and his face was confused in her memory: she would have to shout to him across a jumbled space, she would have to wave her arms wildly. *You love me! You must love me!* But she knew he did not love her, and she did not love him; he was a man who drew everything up into himself, like all men, walking away, free to walk away, free to have his own thoughts, free to envision her body, all the secrets of her body. . . . And she lay down again in the bed, feeling how heavy this body had become, her insides heavy with shame, the very backs of her eyelids coated with shame.

"This is the end of one part of my life," she thought.

But in the morning the telephone rang. She answered it. It was her lover: they talked brightly and happily. She could hear the eagerness in his voice, the love in his voice, that same still, sad amazement—she understood how simple life was, there were no problems.

They spent most of their time on the beach, with the child and the dog. He joked and was serious at the same time. He said, once, "You have defined my soul for me," and she laughed to hide her alarm. In a few days it was time for her to leave. He got a sitter for the boy and took the ferry with her to the mainland, then rented a car to drive her up to Albany. She kept thinking: *Now something will happen. It will come to an end.* But most of the drive was silent and hypnotic. She wanted him to joke with her, to say again that she had defined his soul for him, but he drove fast, he was serious, she distrusted the hawkish look of his profile—she did not know him at all. At a gas station she splashed her face with cold water. Alone in the grubby little rest room, shaky and very much alone. In such places are women totally alone with their bodies. The body grows heavier, more evil, in such silence. . . . On the beach everything had been noisy with sunlight and gulls and waves; here, as if run to earth, everything was cramped and silent and dead.

She went outside, squinting. There he was, talking with the station attendant. She could not think as she returned to him whether she wanted to live or not.

She stayed in Albany for a few days, then flew home to her husband. He met her at the airport, near the luggage counter, where her three pieces of pale-brown luggage were brought to him on a conveyer belt, to be claimed by him. He kissed her on the cheek. They shook hands, a little embarrassed. She had come home again.

"How will I live out the rest of my life?" she wondered.

In January her lover spied on her: she glanced up and saw him, in a public place, in the DeRoy Symphony Hall. She was paralyzed with fear. She nearly fainted. In this faint she felt her husband's body, loving her, working its love upon her, and she shut her eyes harder to keep out the certainty of his love—sometimes he failed at loving her, sometimes he succeeded, it had nothing to do with her or her pity or her ten years of love for him, it had nothing to do with a woman at all. It was a private act accomplished by a man, a husband, or a lover, in communion with his own soul, his manhood.

Her husband was forty-two years old now, growing slowly into middle age, getting heavier, softer. Her lover was about the same age, narrower in the shoulders, with a full, solid chest, yet lean, nervous. She thought, in her paralysis, of men and how they love freely and eagerly so long as their bodies are capable of love, love for a woman; and then, as love fades in their bodies, it fades from their souls and they become immune and immortal and ready to die.

Her husband was a little rough with her, as if impatient with himself. "I love you," he said fiercely, angrily. And then, ashamed, he said, "Did I hurt you? . . ."

"You didn't hurt me," she said.

Her voice was too shrill for their embrace.

While he was in the bathroom she went to her closet and took out that drawing of the summer before. There she was, on the beach at Nantucket, a lady with a pet dog, her eyes large and defined, the dog in her lap hardly more than a few snarls, a few coarse soft lines of charcoal . . . her dress smeared, her arms oddly limp . . . her hands not well drawn at all. . . . She tried to think: did she love the man who had drawn this? did he love her? The fever in her husband's body had touched her and driven her temperature up, and now she stared at the drawing with a kind of lust, fearful of seeing an ugly soul in that woman's face, fearful of seeing the face suddenly through her lover's eyes. She breathed quickly and harshly, staring at the drawing.

And so, the next day, she went to him at his hotel. She wept, pressing against him, demanding of him, "What do you want? Why are you here? Why don't you let me alone?" He told her that he wanted nothing. He expected nothing. He would not cause trouble.

"I want to talk about last August," he said.

"Don't—" she said.

She was hypnotized by his gesturing hands, his nervousness, his obvious agitation. He kept saying, "I understand. I'm making no claims upon you."

They became lovers again.

He called room service for something to drink and they sat side by side on his bed, looking through a copy of *The New Yorker*, laughing at the cartoons. It was so peaceful in this room, so complete. They were on a holiday. It was a secret holiday. Four-thirty in the afternoon, on a Friday, an ordinary Friday: a secret holiday.

"I won't bother you again," he said.

He flew back to see her again in March, and in late April. He telephoned her from his hotel—a different hotel each time—and she came down to him at once. She rose to him in various elevators, she knocked on the doors of various rooms, she stepped into his embrace, breathless and guilty and already angry with him, pleading with him. One morning in May, when he telephoned, she pressed her forehead against the doorframe and could not speak. He kept saying, "What's wrong? Can't you talk? Aren't you alone?" She felt that she was going insane. Her head would burst. Why, why did he love her, why did he pursue her? Why did he want her to die?

She went to him in the hotel room. A familiar room: had they been here before? "Everything is repeating itself. Everything is stuck," she said. He framed her face in his hands and said that she looked thinner—was she sick?—what was wrong? She shook herself free. He, her lover, looked about the same. There was a small, angry pimple on his neck. He stared at her, eagerly and suspiciously. Did she bring bad news?

"So you love me? You love me?" she asked.

"Why are you so angry?"

"I want to be free of you. The two of us free of each other."

"That isn't true—you don't want that—"

He embraced her. She was wild with that old, familiar passion for him, her body clinging to his, her arms not strong enough to hold him. Ah, what despair!—what bitter hatred she felt!—she needed this man for her salvation, he was all she had to live for, and yet she could not believe in him. He embraced her thighs, her hips, kissing her, pressing his warm face against her, and yet she could not believe in him, not really. She needed him in order to live, but he was not worth her love, he was not worth her dying. . . . She promised herself this: when she got back home, when she was alone, she would draw the razor more deeply across her arm.

The telephone rang and he answered it: a wrong number.

"Jesus," he said.

They lay together, still. She imagined their posture like this, the two of them one figure, one substance; and outside this room and this bed there was a universe of disjointed, separate things, blank things, that had nothing to do with them. She would not be Anna out there, the lady in the drawing. He would not be her lover.

"I love you so much . . ." she whispered.

"Please don't cry! We have only a few hours, please. . . ."

It was absurd, their clinging together like this. She saw them as a single figure in a drawing, their arms and legs entwined, their heads pressing mutely together. Helpless substance, so heavy and warm and doomed. It was absurd that any human being should be so important to another human being. She wanted to laugh: a laugh might free them both.

She could not laugh.

Sometime later he said, as if they had been arguing, "Look. It's you. You're the one who doesn't want to get married. You lie to me—"

"Lie to you?"

"You love me but you won't marry me, because you want something left over—Something not finished—All your life you can attribute your misery to me, to our not being married—you are using me—"

"Stop it! You'll make me hate you!" she cried.

"You can say to yourself that you're miserable because of *me.* We will never be married, you will never be happy, neither one of us will ever be happy—"

"I don't want to hear this!" she said.

She pressed her hands flatly against her face.

She went to the bathroom to get dressed. She washed her face and part of her body, quickly. The fever was in her, in the pit of her belly. She would rush home and strike a razor across the inside of her arm and free that pressure, that fever.

The impatient bulging of the veins: an ordeal over.

The demand of the telephone's ringing: that ordeal over.

The nuisance of getting the car and driving home in all that five o'clock traffic: an ordeal too much for a woman.

The movement of this stranger's body in hers: over, finished.

Now, dressed, a little calmer, they held hands and talked. They had to talk swiftly, to get all their news in: he did not trust the people who worked for him, he had faith in no one, his wife had moved to a textbook publishing company and was doing well, she had inherited a Ben Shahn painting from her father and wanted to "touch it up a little"—she was crazy!—his blind son was at another school, doing fairly well, in fact his children were all doing fairly well in spite of the stupid mistake of their parents' marriage—and what about her? what about her life? She told him in a rush the one thing he wanted to hear: that she lived with her husband lovelessly, the two of them polite strangers, sharing a bed, lying side by side in the night in that bed, bodies out of which souls had fled. There was no longer even any shame between them.

"And what about me? Do you feel shame with me still?" he asked.

She did not answer. She moved away from him and prepared to leave.

Then, a minute later, she happened to catch sight of his reflection in the bureau mirror—he was glancing down at himself, checking himself mechanically, impersonally, preparing also to leave. He too would leave this room: he too was headed somewhere else.

She stared at him. It seemed to her that in this instant he was breaking from her, the image of her lover fell free of her, breaking from her . . . and she realized that he existed in a dimension quite apart from her, a mysterious being. And suddenly, joyfully, she felt a miraculous calm. This man was her husband, truly—they were truly married, here in this room—they had been married haphazardly and accidentally for a long time. In another part of the city she had another husband, a "husband," but she had not betrayed that man, not really. This man, whom she loved above any other person in the world, above even her own self-pitying sorrow and her own life, was her truest lover, her destiny. And she did not hate him, she did not hate herself any longer; she did not wish to die; she was flooded with a strange certainty, a sense of gratitude, of pure selfless energy. It was obvious to her that she had, all along, been behaving correctly; out of instinct.

What triumph, to love like this in any room, anywhere, risking even the craziest of accidents!

"Why are you so happy? What's wrong?" he asked, startled. He stared at her. She felt the abrupt concentration in him, the focusing of his vision on her, almost a bitterness in his face, as if he feared her. What, was it beginning all over again? Their love beginning again, in spite of them? "How can you look so happy?" he asked. "We don't have any right to it. Is it because . . . ?"

"Yes," she said.

Where Are You Going, Where Have You Been? 1966

For Bob Dylan

Her name was Connie. She was fifteen and she had a quick nervous giggling habit of craning her neck to glance into mirrors, or checking other people's faces to make sure her own was all right. Her mother, who noticed everything and knew everything and who hadn't much reason any longer to look at her own face, always scolded Connie about it. "Stop gawking at yourself, who are you? You think you're so pretty?" she would say. Connie would raise her eyebrows at these familiar complaints and look right through her mother, into a shadowy vision of herself as she was right at that moment: she knew she was pretty and that was everything. Her mother had been pretty once too, if you could believe those old snapshots in the album, but now her looks were gone and that was why she was always after Connie.

"Why don't you keep your room clean like your sister? How've you got your hair fixed—what the hell stinks? Hair spray? You don't see your sister using that junk."

Her sister June was twenty-four and still lived at home. She was a secretary in the high school Connie attended, and if that wasn't bad enough—with her in the same building—she was so plain and chunky and steady that Connie had to hear her praised all the time by her mother and her mother's sisters. June did this, June did that, she saved money and helped clean the house and cooked and Connie couldn't do a thing, her mind was all filled with trashy daydreams. Their father was away at work most of the time and when he came home he wanted supper and he read the newspaper at supper and after supper he went to bed. He didn't bother talking much to them, but around his bent head Connie's mother kept picking at her until Connie wished her mother was dead and she herself was dead and it was all over. "She makes me want to throw up sometimes," she complained to her friends. She had a high, breathless, amused voice which made everything she said a little forced, whether it was sincere or not.

There was one good thing: June went places with girl friends of hers, girls who were just as plain and steady as she, and so when Connie wanted to do that her mother had no objections. The father of Connie's best girl friend drove the girls the three miles to town and left them off at a shopping plaza, so that they could walk through the stores or go to a movie, and when he came to pick them up again at eleven he never bothered to ask what they had done.

They must have been familiar sights, walking around that shopping plaza in their shorts and flat ballerina slippers that always scuffed the sidewalk, with charm bracelets jingling on their thin wrists; they would lean together to whisper and laugh secretly if someone passed by who amused or interested them. Connie had long dark blond hair that drew anyone's eye to it, and she wore part of it pulled up on her head and puffed out and the rest of it she let fall down her back. She wore a pullover jersey blouse that looked one way when she was at home and another way when she was away from home. Everything about her had two sides to it, one for home and one for anywhere that was not home: her walk that could be childlike and bobbing, or languid enough to make anyone think she was hearing music in her head, her mouth which was pale and smirking most of the time, but bright and pink on these evenings out, her laugh which was cynical and drawling at home—"Ha, ha, very funny"—but high-pitched and nervous anywhere else, like the jingling of the charms on her bracelet.

Sometimes they did go shopping or to a movie, but sometimes they went across the highway, ducking fast across the busy road, to a drive-in restaurant where older kids hung out. The restaurant was shaped like a big bottle, though squatter than a real bottle, and on its cap was a revolving figure of a grinning boy who held a hamburger aloft. One night in midsummer they ran across, breathless with daring, and right away someone leaned out a car window and invited them over, but it was just a boy from high school they didn't like. It made them feel good to be able to ignore him. They went up through the maze of parked and cruising cars to the bright-lit, fly-infested restaurant, their faces pleased and expectant as if they were entering a sacred building that loomed out of the night to give them what haven and what blessing they yearned for. They sat at the counter and crossed their legs at the ankles, their thin shoulders rigid with excitement and listened to the music that made everything so good: the music was always in the background like music at a church service, it was something to depend upon.

A boy named Eddie came in to talk with them. He sat backwards on his stool, turning himself jerkily around in semi-circles and then stopping and turning again, and after a while he asked Connie if she would like something to eat. She said she did and so she tapped her friend's arm on her way out—her friend pulled her face up into a brave droll look—and Connie said she would meet her at eleven, across the way. "I just hate to leave her like that," Connie said earnestly, but the boy said that she wouldn't be alone for long. So they went out to his car and on the way Connie couldn't help but let her eyes wander over the windshields and faces all around her, her face gleaming with the joy that had nothing to do with Eddie or even this place; it might have been the music. She drew her shoulders up and sucked in her breath with the pure pleasure of being alive, and just at that moment she happened to glance at a face just a few feet from hers. It was a boy with shaggy black hair, in a convertible jalopy painted gold. He stared at her and then his lips widened into a grin. Connie slit her eyes at him and turned away, but she couldn't help glancing back and there he was still watching her. He wagged a finger and laughed and said, "Gonna get you, baby," and Connie turned away again without Eddie noticing anything.

She spent three hours with him, at the restaurant where they ate hamburgers and drank Cokes in wax cups that were always sweating, and then down an alley a mile or so away, and when he left her off at five to eleven only the movie house was still open at the plaza. Her girl friend was there, talking with a boy. When Connie came up the two girls smiled at each other and Connie said, "How was the movie?" and the girl said, "*You* should know." They rode off with the girl's father, sleepy and pleased, and Connie couldn't help but look at the darkened shopping plaza with its big empty parking lot and its signs that were faded and ghostly now, and over at the drive-in restaurant where cars were still circling tirelessly. She couldn't hear the music at this distance.

Next morning June asked her how the movie was and Connie said, "So-so."

She and that girl and occasionally another girl went out several times a week that way, and the rest of the time Connie spent around the house—it was summer vacation—getting in her mother's way and thinking, dreaming, about the boys she met. But all the boys fell back and dissolved into a single face that was not even a face, but an idea, a feeling, mixed up with the urgent insistent pounding of the music and the humid night air of July. Connie's mother kept dragging her back to the daylight by finding things for her to do or saying suddenly, "What's this about the Pettinger girl?"

And Connie would say nervously, "Oh, her. That dope." She always drew thick clear lines between herself and such girls, and her mother was simple and kindly enough to believe her. Her mother was so simple, Connie thought, that it was maybe cruel to fool her so much. Her mother went scuffling around the house in old bedroom slippers and complained over the telephone to one sister about the other, then the other called up and the two of them complained about the third one. If June's name was mentioned her mother's tone was approving, and if Connie's name was mentioned it was disapproving. This did not really mean she disliked Connie and actually Connie thought that her mother preferred her to June because she was prettier, but the two of them kept up a pretense of exasperation, a sense that they were tugging and struggling over something of little value to either of them. Sometimes, over coffee, they were almost friends, but something would come up—some vexation that was like a fly buzzing suddenly around their heads—and their faces went hard with contempt.

One Sunday Connie got up at eleven—none of them bothered with church—and washed her hair so that it could dry all day long, in the sun. Her parents and sister were going to a barbecue at an aunt's house and Connie said no, she wasn't interested, rolling her eyes, to let mother know just what she thought of it. "Stay home alone then," her mother said sharply. Connie sat out back in a lawn chair and watched them drive away, her father quiet and bald, hunched around so that he could back the car out, her mother with a look that was still angry and not at all softened through the windshield, and in the back seat poor old June all dressed up as if she didn't know what a barbecue was, with all the running yelling kids and the flies. Connie sat with her eyes closed in the sun, dreaming and dazed with the warmth about her as if this were a kind of love, the caresses of love, and her mind slipped over onto thoughts of the boy she had been with the night before and how nice he had been, how sweet it always was, not the way someone like June would suppose but sweet, gentle, the way it was in movies and promised in songs; and when she opened her eyes she hardly knew where she was, the back yard ran off into weeds and a fenceline of trees and behind it the sky was perfectly blue and still. The asbestos "ranch house" that was now three years old startled her—it looked small. She shook her head as if to get awake.

It was too hot. She went inside the house and turned on the radio to drown out the quiet. She sat on the edge of her bed, barefoot, and listened for an hour and a half to a program called XYZ Sunday Jamboree, record after record of hard, fast, shrieking songs she sang along with, interspersed by exclamations from "Bobby King": "An' look here you girls at Napoleon's—Son and Charley want you to pay real close attention to this song coming up!"

And Connie paid close attention herself, bathed in a glow of slow-pulsed joy that seemed to rise mysteriously out of the music itself and lay languidly about the airless little room, breathed in and breathed out with each gentle rise and fall of her chest.

After a while she heard a car coming up the drive. She sat up at once, startled, because it couldn't be her father so soon. The gravel kept crunching all the way in from the road—the driveway was long—and Connie ran to the window. It was a car she didn't know. It was an open jalopy, painted a bright gold that caught the sun opaquely. Her heart began to pound and her fingers snatched at her hair, checking it, and she whispered, "Christ. Christ," wondering how bad she looked. The car came to a stop at the side door and the horn sounded four short taps as if this were a signal Connie knew.

She went into the kitchen and approached the door slowly, then hung out the screen door, her bare toes curling down off the step. There were two boys in the car and now she recognized the driver: he had shaggy, shabby black hair that looked crazy as a wig and he was grinning at her.

"I ain't late, am I?" he said.

"Who the hell do you think you are?" Connie said.

"Toldja I'd be out, didn't I?"

"I don't even know who you are."

She spoke sullenly, careful to show no interest or pleasure, and he spoke in a fast bright monotone. Connie looked past him to the other boy, taking her time. He had fair brown hair, with a lock that fell onto his forehead. His sideburns gave him a fierce, embarrassed look, but so far he hadn't even bothered to glance at her. Both boys wore sunglasses. The driver's glasses were metallic and mirrored everything in miniature.

"You wanta come for a ride?" he said.

Connie smirked and let her hair fall loose over one shoulder.

"Don'tcha like my car? New paint job," he said. "Hey."

"What?"

"You're cute."

She pretended to fidget, chasing flies away from the door.

"Don'tcha believe me, or what?" he said.

"Look, I don't even know who you are," Connie said in disgust.

"Hey, Ellie's got a radio, see. Mine's broke down." He lifted his friend's arm and showed her the little transistor the boy was holding, and now Connie began to hear the music. It was the same program that was playing inside the house.

"Bobby King?" she said.

"I listen to him all the time. I think he's great."

"He's kind of great," Connie said reluctantly.

"Listen, that guy's *great*. He knows where the action is."

Connie blushed a little, because the glasses made it impossible for her to see just what this boy was looking at. She couldn't decide if she liked him or if he was just a jerk, and so she dawdled in the doorway and wouldn't come down or go back inside. She said, "What's all that stuff painted on your car?"

"Can'tcha read it?" He opened the door very carefully, as if he was afraid it might fall off. He slid out just as carefully, planting his feet firmly on the ground, the tiny metallic world in his glasses slowing down like gelatine hardening and in the midst of it Connie's bright green blouse. "This here is my name, to begin with," he said. ARNOLD FRIEND was written in tar-like black letters on the side, with a drawing of a round grinning face that reminded Connie of a pumpkin, except it wore sunglasses. "I wanta introduce myself, I'm Arnold Friend and that's my real name and I'm gonna be your friend, honey, and inside the car's Ellie Oscar, he's kinda shy." Ellie brought his transistor up to his shoulder and balanced it there. "Now these numbers are a secret code, honey," Arnold Friend explained. He read off the numbers 33, 19, 17 and raised his eyebrows at her to see what she thought of that, but she didn't think much of it. The left rear fender had been smashed and around it was written, on the gleaming gold background: DONE BY CRAZY WOMAN DRIVER. Connie had to laugh at that. Arnold Friend was pleased at her laughter and looked up at her. "Around the other side's a lot more—you wanta come and see them?"

"No."

"Why not?"

"Why should I?"

"Don'tcha wanta see what's on the car? Don'tcha wanta go for a ride?"

"I don't know."

"Why not?"

"I got things to do."

"Like what?"

"Things."

He laughed as if she had said something funny. He slapped his thighs. He was standing in a strange way, leaning back against the car as if he were balancing himself. He wasn't tall, only an inch or so taller than she would be if she came down to him. Connie liked the way he was dressed, which was the way all of them dressed: tight faded jeans stuffed into black, scuffed boots, a belt that pulled his waist in and showed how lean he was, and a white pull-over shirt that was a little soiled and showed the hard small muscles of his arms and shoulders. He looked as if he probably did hard work, lifting and carrying things. Even his neck looked muscular. And his face was a familiar face, somehow: the jaw and chin and cheeks slightly darkened, because he hadn't shaved for a day or two, and the nose long and hawk-like, sniffing as if she were a treat he was going to gobble up and it was all a joke.

"Connie, you ain't telling the truth. This is your day set aside for a ride with me and you know it," he said, still laughing. The way he straightened and recovered from his fit of laughing showed that it had been all fake.

"How do you know what my name is?" she said suspiciously.

"It's Connie."

"Maybe and maybe not."

"I know my Connie," he said, wagging his finger. Now she remembered him even better, back at the restaurant, and her cheeks warmed at the thought of how she sucked in her breath just at the moment she passed him how she must have looked to him. And he had remembered her. "Ellie and I come out here especially for you," he said. "Ellie can sit in back. How about it?"

"Where?"

"Where what?"

"Where're we going?"

He looked at her. He took off the sunglasses and she saw how pale the skin around his eyes was, like holes that were not in shadow but instead in light. His eyes were like chips of broken glass that catch the light in an amiable way. He smiled. It was as if the idea of going for a ride somewhere, to some place, was a new idea to him.

"Just for a ride, Connie sweetheart."

"I never said my name was Connie," she said.

"But I know what it is. I know your name and all about you, lots of things," Arnold Friend said. He had not moved yet but stood still leaning back against the side of his jalopy. "I took a special interest in you, such a pretty girl, and found out all about you like I know your parents and sister are gone somewheres and I know where and how long they're going to be gone, and I know who you were with last night, and your best friend's name is Betty. Right?"

He spoke in a simple lilting voice, exactly as if he were reciting the words to a song. His smile assured her that everything was fine. In the car Ellie turned up the volume on his radio and did not bother to look around at them.

"Ellie can sit in the back seat," Arnold Friend said. He indicated his friend with a casual jerk of his chin, as if Ellie did not count and she could not bother with him.

"How'd you find out all that stuff?" Connie said.

"Listen? Betty Schultz and Tony Fitch and Jimmy Pettinger and Nancy Pettinger," he said, in a chant. "Raymond Stanley and Bob Hutter—"

"Do you know all those kids?"

"I know everybody."

"Look, you're kidding. You're not from around here."

"Sure."

"But—how come we never saw you before?"

"Sure you saw me before," he said. He looked down at his boots, as if he were a little offended. "You just don't remember."

"I guess I'd remember you," Connie said.

"Yeah?" He looked up at this, beaming. He was pleased. He began to mark time with the music from Ellie's radio, tapping his fists lightly together. Connie looked away from his smile to the car, which was painted so bright it almost hurt her eyes to look at it. She looked at that name, ARNOLD FRIEND. And up at the front fender was an expression that was familiar—MAN THE FLYING

SAUCERS. It was an expression kids had used the year before, but didn't use this year. She looked at it for a while as if the words meant something to her that she did not yet know.

"What're you thinking about? Huh?" Arnold Friend demanded. "Not worried about your hair blowing around in the car, are you?"

"No."

"Think I maybe can't drive good?"

"How do I know?"

"You're a hard girl to handle. How come?" he said. "Don't you know I'm your friend? Didn't you see me put my sign in the air when you walked by?"

"What sign?"

"My sign." And he drew an X in the air, leaning out toward her. They were maybe ten feet apart. After his hand fell back to his side the X was still in the air, almost visible. Connie let the screen door close and stood perfectly still inside it, listening to the music from her radio and the boy's blend together. She stared at Arnold Friend. He stood there so stiffly relaxed, pretending to be relaxed, with one hand idly on the door handle as if he were keeping himself up that way and had no intention of ever moving again. She recognized most things about him, the tight jeans that showed his thighs and buttocks and the greasy leather boots and the tight shirt, and even that slippery friendly smile of his, that sleepy dreamy smile that all the boys used to get across ideas they didn't want to put into words. She recognized all this and also the singsong way he talked, slightly mocking, kidding, but serious and a little melancholy, and she recognized the way he tapped one fist against the other in homage to the perpetual music behind him. But all these things did not come together.

She said suddenly, "Hey, how old are you?"

His smile faded. She could see then that he wasn't a kid, he was much older—thirty, maybe more. At this knowledge her heart began to pound faster.

"That's a crazy thing to ask. Can'tcha see I'm your own age?"

"Like hell you are."

"Or maybe a coupla years older, I'm eighteen."

"Eighteen?" she said doubtfully.

He grinned to reassure her and lines appeared at the corners of his mouth. His teeth were big and white. He grinned so broadly his eyes became slits and she saw how thick the lashes were, thick and black as if painted with a black tar-like material. Then he seemed to become embarrassed, abruptly, and looked over his shoulder at Ellie. "*Him,* he's crazy," he said. "Ain't he a riot, he's a nut, a real character." Ellie was still listening to the music. His sunglasses told nothing about what he was thinking. He wore a bright orange shirt unbuttoned halfway to show his chest, which was a pale, bluish chest and not muscular like Arnold Friend's. His shirt collar was turned up all around and the very tips of the collar pointed out past his chin as if they were protecting him. He was pressing the transistor radio up against his ear and sat there in a kind of daze, right in the sun.

"He's kinda strange," Connie said.

"Hey, she says you're kinda strange! Kinda strange!" Arnold Friend cried. He pounded on the car to get Ellie's attention. Ellie turned for the first time and Connie saw with shock that he wasn't a kid either—he had a fair, hairless face, cheeks reddened slightly as if the veins grew too close to the surface of his skin, the face of a forty-year-old baby. Connie felt a wave of dizziness rise in her at this sight and she stared at him as if waiting for something to change the shock of the moment, make it all right again. Ellie's lips kept shaping words, mumbling along with the words blasting his ear.

"Maybe you two better go away," Connie said faintly.

"What? How come?" Arnold Friend cried. "We come out here to take you for a ride. It's Sunday." He had the voice of the man on the radio now. It was the same voice, Connie thought. "Don'tcha know it's Sunday all day and honey, no matter who you were with last night today you're with Arnold Friend and don't you forget it!—Maybe you better step out here," he said, and this last was in a different voice. It was a little flatter, as if the heat was finally getting to him.

"No. I got things to do."

"Hey."

"You two better leave."

"We ain't leaving until you come with us."

"Like hell I am—"

"Connie, don't fool around with me. I mean, I mean, don't fool *around*," he said, shaking his head. He laughed incredulously. He placed his sunglasses on top of his head, carefully, as if he were indeed wearing a wig, and brought the stems down behind his ears. Connie stared at him, another wave of dizziness and fear rising in her so that for a moment he wasn't even in focus but was just a blur, standing there against his gold car, and she had the idea that he had driven up the driveway all right but had come from nowhere before that and belonged nowhere and that everything about him and even the music that was so familiar to her was only half real.

"If my father comes and sees you—"

"He ain't coming. He's at a barbecue."

"How do you know that?"

"Aunt Tillie's. Right now they're—uh—they're drinking. Sitting around," he said vaguely, squinting as if he were staring all the way to town and over to Aunt Tillie's back yard. Then the vision seemed to clear and he nodded energetically. "Yeah. Sitting around. There's your sister in a blue dress, huh? And high heels, the poor sad bitch—nothing like you, sweetheart! And your mother's helping some fat woman with the corn, they're cleaning the corn—husking the corn—"

"What fat woman?" Connie cried.

"How do I know what fat woman. I don't know every goddamn fat woman in the world!" Arnold Friend laughed.

"Oh, that's Mrs. Hornby. . . . Who invited her?" Connie said. She felt a little light-headed. Her breath was coming quickly.

"She's too fat. I don't like them fat. I like them the way you are, honey," he said, smiling sleepily at her. They stared at each other for a while, through the screen door. He said softly, "Now what you're going to do is this: you're going to come out that door. You're going to sit up front with me and Ellie's going to sit in the back, the hell with Ellie, right? This isn't Ellie's date. You're my date. I'm your lover, honey."

"What? You're crazy—"

"Yes, I'm your lover. You don't know what that is but you will," he said. "I know that too. I know all about you. But look: it's real nice and you couldn't ask for nobody better than me, or more polite. I always keep my word. I'll tell you how it is, I'm always nice at first, the first time. I'll hold you so tight you won't think you have to try to get away or pretend anything because you'll know you can't. And I'll come inside you where it's all secret and you'll give in to me and you'll love me—"

"Shut up! You're crazy!" Connie said. She backed away from the door. She put her hands against her ears as if she'd heard something terrible, something not meant for her. "People don't talk like that, you're crazy," she muttered. Her heart was almost too big now for her chest and its pumping made sweat break out all over her. She looked out to see Arnold Friend pause and then take a step toward the porch lurching. He almost fell. But, like a clever drunken man, he managed to catch his balance. He wobbled in his high boots and grabbed hold of one of the porch posts.

"Honey?" he said. "You still listening?"

"Get the hell out of here!"

"Be nice, honey. Listen."

"I'm going to call the police—"

He wobbled again and out of the side of his mouth came a fast spat curse, an aside not meant for her to hear. But even this "Christ!" sounded forced. Then he began to smile again. She watched this smile come, awkward as if he were smiling from inside a mask. His whole face was a mask, she thought wildly, tanned down onto his throat but then running out as if he had plastered make-up on his face but had forgotten about his throat.

"Honey—? Listen, here's how it is. I always tell the truth and I promise you this: I ain't coming in that house after you."

"You better not! I'm going to call the police if you—if you don't—"

"Honey," he said, talking right through her voice, "honey, I'm not coming in there but you are coming out here. You know why?"

She was panting. The kitchen looked like a place she had never seen before, some room she had run inside but which wasn't good enough, wasn't going to help her. The kitchen window had never had a curtain, after three years, and there were dishes in the sink for her to do—probably—and if you ran your hand across the table you'd probably feel something sticky there.

"You listening, honey? Hey?"

"—going to call the police—"

"Soon as you touch the phone I don't need to keep my promise and can come inside. You won't want that."

She rushed forward and tried to lock the door. Her fingers were shaking. "But why lock it," Arnold Friend said gently, talking right into her face. "It's just a screen door. It's just nothing." One of his boots was at a strange angle, as if his foot wasn't in it. It pointed out to the left, bent at the ankle. "I mean, anybody can break through a screen door and glass and wood and iron or anything else if he needs to, anybody at all and specially Arnold Friend. If the place got lit up with a fire, honey, you'd come running out into my arms, right into my arms and safe at home—like you knew I was your lover and'd stopped fooling around, I don't mind a nice shy girl but I don't like no fooling around." Part of those words were spoken with a slight rhythmic lilt, and Connie somehow recognized them—the echo of a song from last year, about a girl rushing into her boy friend's arms and coming home again—

Connie stood barefoot on the linoleum floor, staring at him. "What do you want?" she whispered.

"I want you," he said.

"What?"

"Seen you that night and thought, that's the one, yes sir. I never needed to look any more."

"But my father's coming back. He's coming to get me. I had to wash my hair first—" She spoke in a dry, rapid voice, hardly raising it for him to hear.

"No, your daddy is not coming and yes, you had to wash your hair and you washed it for me. It's nice and shining and all for me, I thank you, sweetheart," he said, with a mock bow, but again he almost lost his balance. He had to bend and adjust his boots. Evidently his feet did not go all the way down; the boots must have been stuffed with something so that he would seem taller. Connie stared out at him and behind him Ellie in the car, who seemed to be looking off toward Connie's right, into nothing. This Ellie said, pulling the words out of the air one after another as if he were just discovering them, "You want me to pull out the phone?"

"Shut your mouth and keep it shut," Arnold Friend said, his face red from bending over or maybe from embarrassment because Connie had seen his boots. "This ain't none of your business."

"What—what are you doing? What do you want?" Connie said. "If I call the police they'll get you, they'll arrest you—"

"Promise was not to come in unless you touch that phone, and I'll keep that promise," he said. He resumed his erect position and tried to force his shoulders back. He sounded like a hero in a movie, declaring something important. He spoke too loudly and it was as if he were speaking to someone behind Connie. "I ain't made plans for coming in that house where I don't belong but just for you to come out to me, the way you should. Don't you know who I am?"

"You're crazy," she whispered. She backed away from the door but did not want to go into another part of the house, as if this would give him permission to come through the door. "What do you. . . . You're crazy, you. . . ."

"Huh? What're you saying, honey?"

Her eyes darted everywhere in the kitchen. She could not remember what it was, this room.

"This is how it is, honey: you come out and we'll drive away, have a nice ride. But if you don't come out we're gonna wait till your people come home and then they're all going to get it."

"You want that telephone pulled out?" Ellie said. He held the radio away from his ear and grimaced, as if without the radio the air was too much for him.

"I toldja shut up, Ellie." Arnold Friend said, "You're deaf, get a hearing aid, right? Fix yourself up. This little girl's no trouble and's gonna be nice to me, so Ellie keep to yourself, this ain't your date—right? Don't hem in on me. Don't hog. Don't crush. Don't bird dog. Don't trail me," he said in a rapid meaningless voice, as if he were running through all the expressions he'd learned but was no longer sure which one of them was in style, then rushing on to new ones, making them up with his eyes closed, "Don't crawl under my fence, don't squeeze in my chipmunk hole, don't sniff my glue, suck my popsicle, keep your own greasy fingers on yourself!" He shaded his eyes and peered in at Connie, who was backed against the kitchen table. "Don't mind him, honey, he's just a creep. He's a dope. Right? I'm the boy for you and like I said you come out here nice like a lady and give me your hand, and nobody else gets hurt, I mean, your nice old bald-headed daddy and your mummy and your sister in her high heels. Because listen: why bring them in this?"

"Leave me alone," Connie whispered.

"Hey, you know that old woman down the road, the one with the chickens and stuff—you know her?"

"She's dead!"

"Dead? What? You know her?" Arnold Friend said.

"She's dead—"

"Don't you like her?"

"She's dead—she's—she isn't here any more—"

"But don't you like her, I mean, you got something against her? Some grudge or something?" Then his voice dipped as if he were conscious of rudeness. He touched the sunglasses on top of his head as if to make sure they were still there. "Now you be a good girl."

"What are you going to do?"

"Just two things, or maybe three," Arnold Friend said. "But I promise it won't last long and you'll like me that way you get to like people you're close to. You will. It's all over for you here, so come on out. You don't want your people in any trouble, do you?"

She turned and bumped against a chair or something, hurting her leg, but she ran into the back room and picked up the telephone. Something roared in her ear, a tiny roaring, and she was so sick with fear that she could do nothing but listen to it—the telephone was clammy and very heavy and her fingers groped down to the dial but were too weak to touch it. She began to scream into the phone, into the roaring. She cried out, she cried for her mother, she felt her breath start jerking back and forth in her lungs as if it were something Arnold Friend were stabbing her with again and again with no tenderness. A noisy sorrowful wailing rose all about her and she was locked inside it the way she was locked inside this house.

After a while she could hear again. She was sitting on the floor, with her wet back against the wall.

Arnold Friend was saying from the door, "That's a good girl. Put the phone back."

She kicked the phone away from her.

"No, honey. Pick it up. Put it back right."

She picked it up and put it back. The dial tone stopped.

"That's a good girl. Now you come outside."

She was hollow with what had been fear, but what was now just an emptiness. All that screaming had blasted it out of her. She sat, one leg cramped under her, and deep inside her brain was something like a pinpoint of light that kept going and would not let her relax. She thought, I'm not going to see my mother again. She thought, I'm not going to sleep in my bed again. Her bright green blouse was all wet.

Arnold Friend said, in a gentle-loud voice that was like a stage voice, "The place where you came from ain't there any more, and where you had in mind to go is cancelled out. This place you are now—inside your daddy's house—is nothing but a cardboard box I can knock down any time. You know that and always did know it. You hear me?"

She thought, I have got to think. I have to know what to do.

"We'll go out to a nice field, out in the country here where it smells so nice and it's sunny," Arnold Friend said. "I'll have my arms tight around you so you won't need to try to get away and I'll show you what love is like, what it does. The hell with this house! It looks solid all right," he said. He ran a fingernail down the screen and the noise did not make Connie shiver, as it would have the day before. "Now put your hand on your heart, honey. Feel that? That feels solid too but we know better, be nice to me, be sweet like you can because what else is there for a girl like you but to be sweet and pretty and give in?—and get away before her people come back?"

She felt her pounding heart. Her hands seemed to enclose it. She thought for the first time in her life that it was nothing that was hers, that belonged to her, but just a pounding, living thing inside this body that wasn't hers either.

"You don't want them to get hurt," Arnold Friend went on. "Now get up, honey. Get up all by yourself."

She stood.

"Now turn this way. That's right. Come over to me—Ellie, put that away, didn't I tell you? You dope. You miserable creepy dope," Arnold Friend said. His words were not angry but only part of an incantation. The incantation was kindly. "Now come out through the kitchen to me honey and let's see a smile, try it, you're a brave sweet little girl and now they're eating corn and hotdogs cooked to bursting over an outdoor fire, and they don't know one thing about you and never did and honey you're better than them because not one of them would have done this for you."

Connie felt the linoleum under her feet; it was cool. She brushed her hair back out of her eyes. Arnold Friend let go of the post tentatively and opened his arms for her, his elbows pointing up toward each other and his wrist limp, to show that this was an embarrassed embrace and a little mocking, he didn't want to make her self-conscious.

She put out her hand against the screen. She watched herself push the door slowly open as if she were safe back somewhere in the other doorway, watching this body and this head of long hair moving out into the sunlight where Arnold Friend waited.

"My sweet little blue-eyed girl," he said, in a half-sung sigh that had nothing to do with her brown eyes but was taken up just the same by the vast sunlit reaches of the land behind him and on all sides of him, so much land that Connie had never seen before and did not recognize except to know that she was going to it.

COMMENTARY

JOYCE CAROL OATES

Smooth Talk: Short Story into Film 1989

Some years ago in the American Southwest there surfaced a tabloid psychopath known as "The Pied Piper of Tucson." I have forgotten his name,[1] but his specialty was the seduction and occasional murder of teen-aged girls. He may or may not have had actual accomplices, but his bizarre activities were known among a circle of teenagers in the Tucson area; for some reason they kept his secret, deliberately did not inform parents or police. It was this fact, not the fact of the mass murderer himself, that struck me at the time. And this was a pre-Manson time, early or mid-1960s.

The Pied Piper mimicked teenagers in their talk, dress, and behavior, but he was not a teenager—he was a man in his early thirties. Rather short, he stuffed rags in his leather boots to give himself height. (And sometimes walked unsteadily as a consequence: did none among his admiring constituency notice?) He charmed his victims as charismatic psychopaths have always charmed their victims, to the bewilderment of others who fancy themselves free of all lunatic attractions. The Pied Piper of Tucson: a trashy dream, a tabloid archetype, sheer artifice, comedy, cartoon—surrounded, however improbably, and finally tragically, by real people. You think that, if you look twice, he won't be there. But there he is.

I don't remember any longer where I first read about this Pied Piper—very likely in *Life* Magazine. I do recall deliberately not reading the full article because I didn't want to be distracted by too much detail. It was not after all the mass murderer himself who intrigued me, but the disturbing fact that a number of teenagers—from "good" families—aided and abetted his crimes. This is the sort of thing authorities and responsible citizens invariably call "inexplicable" because they can't find explanations for it. *They* would not have fallen under this maniac's spell, after all.

An early draft of my short story "Where Are You Going, Where Have You Been?"—from which the film *Smooth Talk* was adapted by Joyce Chopra and Tom Cole—had the rather too explicit title "Death and the Maiden." It was cast in a mode of fiction to which I am still partial—indeed, every third or fourth story of mine is probably in this mode—"realistic allegory," it might be called. It is Hawthornean, romantic, shading into parable. Like the medieval German engraving from which my title was taken, the story was minutely detailed yet clearly an allegory of the fatal attractions of death (or the devil). An

[1]His name was Charles Schmid Jr.—Editors' note.

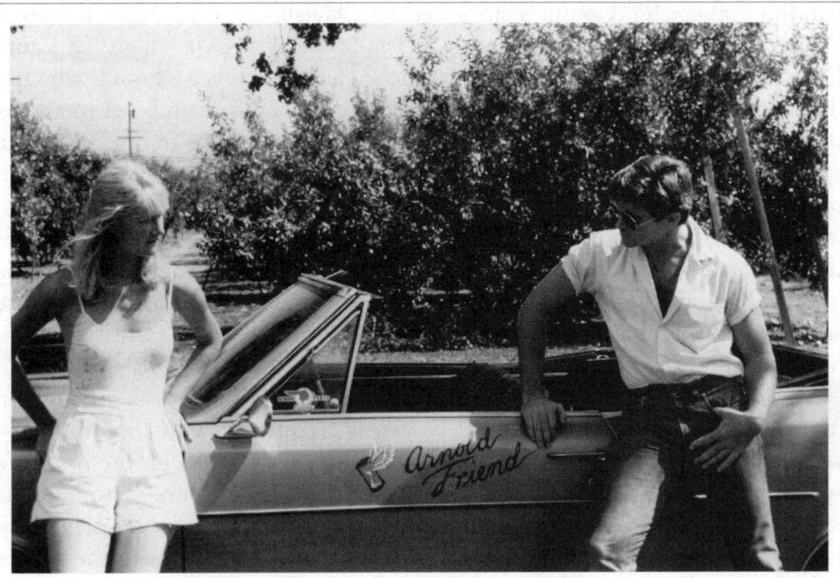

Laura Dern and Treat Williams in *Smooth Talk.* (Courtesy of the Kobal Collection/Ellison, Nancy/Goldcrest/Nepenthe.)

innocent young girl is seduced by way of her own vanity; she mistakes death for erotic romance of a particularly American/trashy sort.

In subsequent drafts the story changed its tone, its focus, its language, its title. It became "Where Are You Going, Where Have You Been?" Written at a time when the author was intrigued by the music of Bob Dylan, particularly the hauntingly elegiac song "It's All Over Now, Baby Blue," it was dedicated to Bob Dylan. The charismatic mass murderer drops into the background and his innocent victim, a fifteen-year-old, moves into the foreground. She becomes the true protagonist of the tale, courting and being courted by her fate, a self-styled 1950s pop figure, alternately absurd and winning. There is no suggestion in the published story that "Arnold Friend" has seduced and murdered other young girls, or even that he necessarily intends to murder Connie. Is his interest "merely" sexual? (Nor is there anything about the complicity of other teenagers. I saved that yet more provocative note for a current story, "Testimony.") Connie is shallow, vain, silly, hopeful, doomed—but capable nonetheless of an unexpected gesture of heroism at the story's end. Her smooth-talking seducer, who cannot lie, promises her that her family will be unharmed if she gives herself to him; and so she does. The story ends abruptly at the point of her "crossing over." We don't know the nature of her sacrifice, only that she is generous enough to make it.

In adapting a narrative so spare and thematically foreshortened as "Where Are You Going, Where Have You Been?" film director Joyce Chopra and screenwriter Tom Cole were required to do a good deal of filling in, expanding, inventing. Connie's story becomes lavishly, and lovingly, textured; she is not an allegorical figure so much as a "typical" teen-aged girl (if Laura Dern, spectacularly good-looking, can be so defined). Joyce Chopra, who has done documentary films on contemporary teenage culture and, yet more authoritatively, has an adolescent daughter of her own, creates in *Smooth Talk* a vivid and absolutely believable world for Connie to inhabit. Or worlds: as in the original story there is Connie-at-home, and there is Connie-with-her-friends. Two fifteen-year-old girls, two finely honed styles, two voices, sometimes but not often overlapping. It is one of the marvelous visual features of the film that we *see* Connie and her friends transform themselves, once they are safely free of parental observation. The girls claim their true identities in the neighborhood shopping mall. What freedom, what joy!

Smooth Talk is, in a way, as much Connie's mother's story as it is Connie's; its center of gravity, its emotional nexus, is frequently with the mother—warmly and convincingly played by Mary Kay Place. (Though the mother's sexual jealousy of her daughter is slighted in the film.) Connie's ambiguous relationship with her affable, somewhat mysterious father (well played by Levon Helm) is an excellent touch: I had thought, subsequent to the story's publication, that I should have built up the father, suggesting, as subtly as I could, an attraction there paralleling the attraction Connie feels for her seducer, Arnold Friend. And Arnold Friend himself—"A. Friend" as he says—is played with appropriately overdone sexual swagger by Treat Williams, who is perfect for the part; and just the right age. We see that Arnold Friend isn't a teenager even as Connie, mesmerized by his presumed charm, does not seem to *see* him at all. What is so difficult to accomplish in prose—nudging the reader to look over the protagonist's shoulder, so to speak—is accomplished with enviable ease in film.

Treat Williams as Arnold Friend is supreme in his very awfulness, as, surely, the original Pied Piper of Tucson must have been. (Though no one involved in the film knew about the original source.) Mr. Williams flawlessly impersonates Arnold Friend as Arnold Friend impersonates—is it James Dean? James Dean regarding himself in mirrors, doing James Dean impersonations? That Connie's fate is so trashy is in fact her fate.

What is outstanding in Joyce Chopra's *Smooth Talk* is its visual freshness, its sense of motion and life; the attentive intelligence the director has brought to the semi-secret world of the American adolescent—shopping mall flirtations, drive-in restaurant romances, highway hitchhiking, the fascination of rock music played very, very loud. (James Taylor's music for the film is wonderfully appropriate. We hear it as Connie hears it; it is the music of her spiritual being.) Also outstanding, as I have indicated, and numerous critics have noted, are the acting performances. Laura Dern is so dazzlingly right as "my" Connie that I may come to think I modeled the fictitious girl on her, in the way that writers frequently delude themselves about motions of causality.

My difficulties with *Smooth Talk* have primarily to do with my chronic hesitation—about seeing/hearing work of mine abstracted from its contexture of language. All writers know that language is their subject; quirky word choices, patterns of rhythm, enigmatic pauses, punctuation marks. Where the quick scanner sees "quick" writing, the writer conceals nine tenths of the iceberg. Of course we all have "real" subjects, and we will fight to the death to defend those subjects, but beneath the tale-telling it is the tale-telling that grips us so very fiercely. The writer works in a single dimension, the director works in three. I assume they are professionals to their fingertips; authorities in their medium as I am an authority (if I am) in mine. I would fiercely defend the placement of a semicolon in one of my novels but I would probably have deferred in the end to Joyce Chopra's decision to reverse the story's conclusion, turn it upside down, in a sense, so that the film ends not with death, not with a sleepwalker's crossing over to her fate, but upon a scene of reconciliation, rejuvenation.

A girl's loss of virginity, bittersweet but not necessarily tragic. Not today. A girl's coming-of-age that involves her succumbing to, but then rejecting, the "trashy dreams" of her pop teenage culture. "Where Are You Going, Where Have You Been?" defines itself as allegorical in its conclusion: Death and Death's chariot (a funky souped-up convertible) have come for the Maiden. Awakening is, in the story's final lines, moving out into the sunlight where Arnold Friend waits:

> "My sweet little blue-eyed girl," he said in a half-sung sigh that had nothing to do with [Connie's] brown eyes but was taken up just the same by the vast sunlit reaches of the land behind him and on all sides of him—so much land that Connie had never seen before and did not recognize except to know that she was going to it.

— a conclusion impossible to transfigure into film.

TIM O'BRIEN

Tim O'Brien (b. 1946) was born in Austin, Minnesota, and educated at Macalester College and Harvard University. Drafted into the army during the Vietnam War, he attained the rank of sergeant and received the Purple Heart.

O'Brien's first book, *If I Die in a Combat Zone, Box Me Up and Ship Me Home* (1973), is an account of his combat experience presented as "autofiction," a mixture of autobiography and fiction. His next book, *Northern Lights* (1974), depicts a conflict between two brothers. But O'Brien produced his finest novel to date in *Going after Cacciato* (1978), which won the National Book Award and was judged by many critics to be the best book by an American about the Vietnam War. This was followed by *The Nuclear Age* (1985), a novel set in 1995 about the ominous future of the human race, *In the Lake of the Woods* (1994), and *Tom Cat in Love* (1999). *July, July* (2003) is a recent novel.

"Soldiers are dreamers," a line by the English poet Siegfried Sassoon, who survived a sniper's bullet during World War I, is the epigraph for *Going after Cacciato.*

Dreams play an important role in all O'Brien's fiction, yet the note they sound in a story such as "The Things They Carried" is not surrealistic. The dream is always rooted so firmly in reality that it survives, paradoxically, as perhaps the most vital element in an O'Brien story. "The Things They Carried" first appeared in *Esquire* magazine and was included in *The Best American Short Stories* when Ann Beattie edited the volume in 1987. It is also included in O'Brien's collection *The Things They Carried* (1990).

WEB Research Tim O'Brien at bedfordstmartins.com/rewritinglit.

The Things They Carried 1986

First Lieutenant Jimmy Cross carried letters from a girl named Martha, a junior at Mount Sebastian College in New Jersey. They were not love letters, but Lieutenant Cross was hoping, so he kept them folded in plastic at the bottom of his rucksack. In the late afternoon, after a day's march, he would dig his foxhole, wash his hands under a canteen, unwrap the letters, hold them with the tips of his fingers, and spend the last hour of light pretending. He would imagine romantic camping trips into the White Mountains in New Hampshire. He would sometimes taste the envelope flaps, knowing her tongue had been there. More than anything, he wanted Martha to love him as he loved her, but the letters were mostly chatty, elusive on the matter of love. She was a virgin, he was almost sure. She was an English major at Mount Sebastian, and she wrote beautifully about her professors and roommates and midterm exams, about her respect for Chaucer and her great affection for Virginia Woolf. She often quoted lines of poetry; she never mentioned the war, except to say, Jimmy, take care of yourself. The letters weighed ten ounces. They were signed "Love, Martha," but Lieutenant Cross understood that "Love" was only a way of signing and did not mean what he sometimes pretended it meant. At dusk, he would carefully return the letters to his rucksack. Slowly, a bit distracted, he would get up and move among his men, checking the perimeter, then at full dark he would return to his hole and watch the night and wonder if Martha was a virgin.

The things they carried were largely determined by necessity. Among the necessities or near necessities were P-38 can openers, pocket knives, heat tabs, wrist watches, dog tags, mosquito repellant, chewing gum, candy, cigarettes, salt tablets, packets of Kool-Aid, lighters, matches, sewing kits, Military Payment Certificates, C rations, and two or three canteens of water. Together, these items weighed between fifteen and twenty pounds, depending upon a man's habits or rate of metabolism. Henry Dobbins, who was a big man, carried extra rations; he was especially fond of canned peaches in heavy syrup over pound cake. Dave Jensen, who practiced field hygiene, carried a toothbrush, dental floss, and several hotel-size bars of soap he'd stolen on R&R in Sydney, Australia. Ted Lavender, who was scared, carried tranquilizers until he was shot in the head outside the village of Than Khe in mid-April. By necessity, and because it was SOP,° they all carried steel helmets that weighed five pounds

SOP: Standard operating procedure.

including the liner and camouflage cover. They carried the standard fatigue jackets and trousers. Very few carried underwear. On their feet they carried jungle boots—2.1 pounds—and Dave Jensen carried three pairs of socks and a can of Dr. Scholl's foot powder as a precaution against trench foot. Until he was shot, Ted Lavender carried six or seven ounces of premium dope, which for him was a necessity. Mitchell Sanders, the RTO,° carried condoms. Norman Bowker carried a diary. Rat Kiley carried comic books. Kiowa, a devout Baptist, carried an illustrated New Testament that had been presented to him by his father, who taught Sunday school in Oklahoma City, Oklahoma. As a hedge against bad times, however, Kiowa also carried his grandmother's distrust of the white man, his grandfather's old hunting hatchet. Necessity dictated. Because the land was mined and booby-trapped, it was SOP for each man to carry a steel-centered, nylon-covered flak jacket, which weighed 6.7 pounds, but which on hot days seemed much heavier. Because you could die so quickly, each man carried at least one large compress bandage, usually in the helmet band for easy access. Because the nights were cold, and because the monsoons were wet, each carried a green plastic poncho that could be used as a raincoat or ground sheet or makeshift tent. With its quilted liner, the poncho weighed almost two pounds, but it was worth every ounce. In April, for instance, when Ted Lavender was shot, they used his poncho to wrap him up, then to carry him across the paddy, then to lift him into the chopper that took him away.

They were called legs or grunts.

To carry something was to "hump" it, as when Lieutenant Jimmy Cross humped his love for Martha up the hills and through the swamps. In its intransitive form, "to hump" meant "to walk," or "to march," but it implied burdens far beyond the intransitive.

Almost everyone humped photographs. In his wallet, Lieutenant Cross carried two photographs of Martha. The first was a Kodachrome snapshot signed "Love," though he knew better. She stood against a brick wall. Her eyes were gray and neutral, her lips slightly open as she stared straight-on at the camera. At night, sometimes, Lieutenant Cross wondered who had taken the picture, because he knew she had boyfriends, because he loved her so much, and because he could see the shadow of the picture taker spreading out against the brick wall. The second photograph had been clipped from the 1968 Mount Sebastian yearbook. It was an action shot—women's volleyball—and Martha was bent horizontal to the floor, reaching, the palms of her hands in sharp focus, the tongue taut, the expression frank and competitive. There was no visible sweat. She wore white gym shorts. Her legs, he thought, were almost certainly the legs of a virgin, dry and without hair, the left knee cocked and carrying her entire weight, which was just over one hundred pounds. Lieutenant Cross remembered touching that left knee. A dark theater, he remembered, and the movie was *Bonnie and Clyde*, and Martha wore a tweed skirt, and during the final scene, when he touched her knee, she turned and looked at him in

---

RTO: Radiotelephone operator.

a sad, sober way that made him pull his hand back, but he would always remember the feel of the tweed skirt and the knee beneath it and the sound of the gunfire that killed Bonnie and Clyde, how embarrassing it was, how slow and oppressive. He remembered kissing her good night at the dorm door. Right then, he thought, he should've done something brave. He should've carried her up the stairs to her room and tied her to the bed and touched that left knee all night long. He should've risked it. Whenever he looked at the photographs, he thought of new things he should've done.

What they carried was partly a function of rank, partly of field specialty.

As a first lieutenant and platoon leader, Jimmy Cross carried a compass, maps, code books, binoculars, and a .45-caliber pistol that weighed 2.9 pounds fully loaded. He carried a strobe light and the responsibility for the lives of his men.

As an RTO, Mitchell Sanders carried the PRC-25 radio, a killer, twenty-six pounds with its battery.

As a medic, Rat Kiley carried a canvas satchel filled with morphine and plasma and malaria tablets and surgical tape and comic books and all the things a medic must carry, including M&M's for especially bad wounds, for a total weight of nearly twenty pounds.

As a big man, therefore a machine gunner, Henry Dobbins carried the M-60, which weighed twenty-three pounds unloaded, but which was almost always loaded. In addition, Dobbins carried between ten and fifteen pounds of ammunition draped in belts across his chest and shoulders.

As PFCs or Spec 4s, most of them were common grunts and carried the standard M-16 gas-operated assault rifle. The weapon weighed 7.5 pounds unloaded, 8.2 pounds with its full twenty-round magazine. Depending on numerous factors, such as topography and psychology, the riflemen carried anywhere from twelve to twenty magazines, usually in cloth bandoliers, adding on another 8.4 pounds at minimum, fourteen pounds at maximum. When it was available, they also carried M-16 maintenance gear—rods and steel brushes and swabs and tubes of LSA oil—all of which weighed about a pound. Among the grunts, some carried the M-79 grenade launcher, 5.9 pounds unloaded, a reasonably light weapon except for the ammunition, which was heavy. A single round weighed ten ounces. The typical load was twenty-five rounds. But Ted Lavender, who was scared, carried thirty-four rounds when he was shot and killed outside Than Khe, and he went down under an exceptional burden, more than twenty pounds of ammunition, plus the flak jacket and helmet and rations and water and toilet paper and tranquilizers and all the rest, plus the unweighed fear. He was dead weight. There was no twitching or flopping. Kiowa, who saw it happen, said it was like watching a rock fall, or a big sandbag or something—just boom, then down—not like the movies where the dead guy rolls around and does fancy spins and goes ass over teakettle—not like that, Kiowa said, the poor bastard just flat-fuck fell. Boom. Down. Nothing else. It was a bright morning in mid-April. Lieutenant Cross felt the pain. He blamed himself. They stripped off Lavender's canteens and ammo, all the heavy things, and Rat Kiley said the obvious, the guy's dead, and Mitchell

Sanders used his radio to report one U.S. KIA° and to request a chopper. Then they wrapped Lavender in his poncho. They carried him out to a dry paddy, established security, and sat smoking the dead man's dope until the chopper came. Lieutenant Cross kept to himself. He pictured Martha's smooth young face, thinking he loved her more than anything, more than his men, and now Ted Lavender was dead because he loved her so much and could not stop thinking about her. When the dust-off arrived, they carried Lavender aboard. Afterward they burned Than Khe. They marched until dusk, then dug their holes, and that night Kiowa kept explaining how you had to be there, how fast it was, how the poor guy just dropped like so much concrete. Boom-down, he said. Like cement.

In addition to the three standard weapons—the M-60, M-16, and M-79—they carried whatever presented itself, or whatever seemed appropriate as a means of killing or staying alive. They carried catch-as-catch-can. At various times, in various situations, they carried M-14s and CAR-15s and Swedish Ks and grease guns and captured AK-47s and Chi-Coms and RPGs and Simonov carbines and black-market Uzis and .38-caliber Smith & Wesson handguns and 66 mm LAWs and shotguns and silencers and blackjacks and bayonets and C-4 plastic explosives. Lee Strunk carried a slingshot; a weapon of last resort, he called it. Mitchell Sanders carried brass knuckles. Kiowa carried his grandfather's feathered hatchet. Every third or fourth man carried a Claymore antipersonnel mine—3.5 pounds with its firing device. They all carried fragmentation grenades—fourteen ounces each. They all carried at least one M-18 colored smoke grenade—twenty-four ounces. Some carried CS or tear-gas grenades. Some carried white-phosphorus grenades. They carried all they could bear, and then some, including a silent awe for the terrible power of the things they carried.

In the first week of April, before Lavender died, Lieutenant Jimmy Cross received a good-luck charm from Martha. It was a simple pebble, an ounce at most. Smooth to the touch, it was a milky-white color with flecks of orange and violet, oval-shaped, like a miniature egg. In the accompanying letter, Martha wrote that she had found the pebble on the Jersey shoreline, precisely where the land touched water at high tide, where things came together but also separated. It was this separate-but-together quality, she wrote, that had inspired her to pick up the pebble and to carry it in her breast pocket for several days, where it seemed weightless, and then to send it through the mail, by air, as a token of her truest feelings for him. Lieutenant Cross found this romantic. But he wondered what her truest feelings were, exactly, and what she meant by separate-but-together. He wondered how the tides and waves had come into play on that afternoon along the Jersey shoreline when Martha saw the pebble and bent down to rescue it from geology. He imagined bare feet. Martha was a poet, with the poet's sensibilities, and her feet would be brown and bare, the toenails unpainted, the eyes chilly and somber like the ocean in March, and

KIA: Killed in action.

though it was painful, he wondered who had been with her that afternoon. He imagined a pair of shadows moving along the strip of sand where things came together but also separated. It was phantom jealousy, he knew, but he couldn't help himself. He loved her so much. On the march, through the hot days of early April, he carried the pebble in his mouth, turning it with his tongue, tasting sea salts and moisture. His mind wandered. He had difficulty keeping his attention on the war. On occasion he would yell at his men to spread out the column, to keep their eyes open, but then he would slip away into daydreams, just pretending, walking barefoot along the Jersey shore, with Martha, carrying nothing. He would feel himself rising. Sun and waves and gentle winds, all love and lightness.

What they carried varied by mission.

When a mission took them to the mountains, they carried mosquito netting, machetes, canvas tarps, and extra bug juice.

If a mission seemed especially hazardous, or if it involved a place they knew to be bad, they carried everything they could. In certain heavily mined AOs,° where the land was dense with Toe Poppers and Bouncing Betties, they took turns humping a twenty-eight-pound mine detector. With its headphones and big sensing plate, the equipment was a stress on the lower back and shoulders, awkward to handle, often useless because of the shrapnel in the earth, but they carried it anyway, partly for safety, partly for the illusion of safety.

On ambush, or other night missions, they carried peculiar little odds and ends. Kiowa always took along his New Testament and a pair of moccasins for silence. Dave Jensen carried night-sight vitamins high in carotin. Lee Strunk carried his slingshot; ammo, he claimed, would never be a problem. Rat Kiley carried brandy and M&M's. Until he was shot, Ted Lavender carried the starlight scope, which weighed 6.3 pounds with its aluminum carrying case. Henry Dobbins carried his girlfriend's pantyhose wrapped around his neck as a comforter. They all carried ghosts. When dark came, they would move out single file across the meadows and paddies to their ambush coordinates, where they would quietly set up the Claymores and lie down and spend the night waiting.

Other missions were more complicated and required special equipment. In mid-April, it was their mission to search out and destroy the elaborate tunnel complexes in the Than Khe area south of Chu Lai. To blow the tunnels, they carried one-pound blocks of pentrite high explosives, four blocks to a man, sixty-eight pounds in all. They carried wiring, detonators, and battery-powered clackers. Dave Jensen carried earplugs. Most often, before blowing the tunnels, they were ordered by higher command to search them, which was considered bad news, but by and large they just shrugged and carried out orders. Because he was a big man, Henry Dobbins was excused from tunnel duty. The others would draw numbers. Before Lavender died there were seventeen men in the platoon, and whoever drew the number seventeen would strip off his gear and crawl in head first with a flashlight and Lieutenant Cross's

---

AOs: Areas of operations.

.45-caliber pistol. The rest of them would fan out as security. They would sit down or kneel, not facing the hole, listening to the ground beneath them, imagining cobwebs and ghosts, whatever was down there—the tunnel walls squeezing in—how the flashlight seemed impossibly heavy in the hand and how it was tunnel vision in the very strictest sense, compression in all ways, even time, and how you had to wiggle in—ass and elbows—a swallowed-up feeling—and how you found yourself worrying about odd things—will your flashlight go dead? Do rats carry rabies? If you screamed, how far would the sound carry? Would your buddies hear it? Would they have the courage to drag you out? In some respects, though not many, the waiting was worse than the tunnel itself. Imagination was a killer.

On April 16, when Lee Strunk drew the number seventeen, he laughed and muttered something and went down quickly. The morning was hot and very still. Not good, Kiowa said. He looked at the tunnel opening, then out across a dry paddy toward the village of Than Khe. Nothing moved. No clouds or birds or people. As they waited, the men smoked and drank Kool-Aid, not talking much, feeling sympathy for Lee Strunk but also feeling the luck of the draw. You win some, you lose some, said Mitchell Sanders, and sometimes you settle for a rain check. It was a tired line and no one laughed.

Henry Dobbins ate a tropical chocolate bar. Ted Lavender popped a tranquilizer and went off to pee.

After five minutes, Lieutenant Jimmy Cross moved to the tunnel, leaned down, and examined the darkness. Trouble, he thought—a cave-in maybe. And then suddenly, without willing it, he was thinking about Martha. The stresses and fractures, the quick collapse, the two of them buried alive under all that weight. Dense, crushing love. Kneeling, watching the hole, he tried to concentrate on Lee Strunk and the war, all the dangers, but his love was too much for him, he felt paralyzed, he wanted to sleep inside her lungs and breathe her blood and be smothered. He wanted her to be a virgin and not a virgin, all at once. He wanted to know her. Intimate secrets—why poetry? Why so sad? Why the grayness in her eyes? Why so alone? Not lonely, just alone—riding her bike across campus or sitting off by herself in the cafeteria. Even dancing, she danced alone—and it was the aloneness that filled him with love. He remembered telling her that one evening. How she nodded and looked away. And how, later, when he kissed her, she received the kiss without returning it, her eyes wide open, not afraid, not a virgin's eyes, just flat and uninvolved.

Lieutenant Cross gazed at the tunnel. But he was not there. He was buried with Martha under the white sand at the Jersey shore. They were pressed together, and the pebble in his mouth was her tongue. He was smiling. Vaguely, he was aware of how quiet the day was, the sullen paddies, yet he could not bring himself to worry about matters of security. He was beyond that. He was just a kid at war, in love. He was twenty-two years old. He couldn't help it.

A few moments later Lee Strunk crawled out of the tunnel. He came up grinning, filthy but alive. Lieutenant Cross nodded and closed his eyes while the others clapped Strunk on the back and made jokes about rising from the dead.

Worms, Rat Kiley said. Right out of the grave. Fuckin' zombie.

The men laughed. They all felt great relief.

Spook City, said Mitchell Sanders.

Lee Strunk made a funny ghost sound, a kind of moaning, yet very happy, and right then, when Strunk made that high happy moaning sound, when he went *Ahhooooo*, right then Ted Lavender was shot in the head on his way back from peeing. He lay with his mouth open. The teeth were broken. There was a swollen black bruise under his left eye. The cheekbone was gone. Oh shit, Rat Kiley said, the guy's dead. The guy's dead, he kept saying, which seemed profound—the guy's dead. I mean really.

The things they carried were determined to some extent by superstition. Lieutenant Cross carried his good-luck pebble. Dave Jensen carried a rabbit's foot. Norman Bowker, otherwise a very gentle person, carried a thumb that had been presented to him as a gift by Mitchell Sanders. The thumb was dark brown, rubbery to the touch, and weighed four ounces at most. It had been cut from a VC corpse, a boy of fifteen or sixteen. They'd found him at the bottom of an irrigation ditch, badly burned, flies in his mouth and eyes. The boy wore black shorts and sandals. At the time of his death he had been carrying a pouch of rice, a rifle, and three magazines of ammunition.

You want my opinion, Mitchell Sanders said, there's a definite moral here.

He put his hand on the dead boy's wrist. He was quiet for a time, as if counting a pulse, then he patted the stomach, almost affectionately, and used Kiowa's hunting hatchet to remove the thumb.

Henry Dobbins asked what the moral was.

Moral?

You know. *Moral.*

Sanders wrapped the thumb in toilet paper and handed it across to Norman Bowker. There was no blood. Smiling, he kicked the boy's head, watched the flies scatter, and said, It's like with that old TV show—Paladin. Have gun, will travel.

Henry Dobbins thought about it.

Yeah, well, he finally said. I don't see no moral.

There it *is*, man.

Fuck off.

They carried USO stationery and pencils and pens. They carried Sterno, safety pins, trip flares, signal flares, spools of wire, razor blades, chewing tobacco, liberated joss sticks and statuettes of the smiling Buddha, candles, grease pencils, *The Stars and Stripes*, fingernail clippers, Psy Ops° leaflets, bush hats, bolos, and much more. Twice a week, when the resupply choppers came in, they carried hot chow in green Mermite cans and large canvas bags filled with iced beer and soda pop. They carried plastic water containers, each with a two-gallon capacity. Mitchell Sanders carried a set of starched tiger fatigues for special occasions. Henry Dobbins carried Black Flag insecticide. Dave Jensen carried empty sandbags that could be filled at night for added

---

Psy Ops: Psychological operations.

protection. Lee Strunk carried tanning lotion. Some things they carried in common. Taking turns, they carried the big PRC-77 scrambler radio, which weighed thirty pounds with its battery. They shared the weight of memory. They took up what others could no longer bear. Often, they carried each other, the wounded or weak. They carried infections. They carried chess sets, basketballs, Vietnamese-English dictionaries, insignia of rank, Bronze Stars and Purple Hearts, plastic cards imprinted with the Code of Conduct. They carried diseases, among them malaria and dysentery. They carried lice and ringworm and leeches and paddy algae and various rots and molds. They carried the land itself—Vietnam, the place, the soil—a powdery orange-red dust that covered their boots and fatigues and faces. They carried the sky. The whole atmosphere, they carried it, the humidity, the monsoons, the stink of fungus and decay, all of it, they carried gravity. They moved like mules. By daylight they took sniper fire, at night they were mortared, but it was not battle, it was just the endless march, village to village, without purpose, nothing won or lost. They marched for the sake of the march. They plodded along slowly, dumbly, leaning forward against the heat, unthinking, all blood and bone, simple grunts, soldiering with their legs, toiling up the hills and down into the paddies and across the rivers and up again and down, just humping, one step and then the next and then another, but no volition, no will, because it was automatic, it was anatomy, and the war was entirely a matter of posture and carriage, the hump was everything, a kind of inertia, a kind of emptiness, a dullness of desire and intellect and conscience and hope and human sensibility. Their principles were in their feet. Their calculations were biological. They had no sense of strategy or mission. They searched the villages without knowing what to look for, not caring, kicking over jars of rice, frisking children and old men, blowing tunnels, sometimes setting fires and sometimes not, then forming up and moving on to the next village, then other villages, where it would always be the same. They carried their own lives. The pressures were enormous. In the heat of early afternoon, they would remove their helmets and flak jackets, walking bare, which was dangerous but which helped ease the strain. They would often discard things along the route of march. Purely for comfort, they would throw away rations, blow their Claymores and grenades, no matter, because by nightfall the resupply choppers would arrive with more of the same, then a day or two later still more, fresh watermelons and crates of ammunition and sunglasses and woolen sweaters—the resources were stunning—sparklers for the Fourth of July, colored eggs for Easter. It was the great American war chest—the fruits of science, the smokestacks, the canneries, the arsenals at Hartford, the Minnesota forests, the machine shops, the vast fields of corn and wheat—they carried like freight trains; they carried it on their backs and shoulders—and for all the ambiguities of Vietnam, all the mysteries and unknowns, there was at least the single abiding certainty that they would never be at a loss for things to carry.

After the chopper took Lavender away, Lieutenant Jimmy Cross led his men into the village of Than Khe. They burned everything. They shot chickens and dogs, they trashed the village well, they called in artillery and watched the wreckage, then they marched for several hours through the hot afternoon, and then at dusk, while Kiowa explained how Lavender died, Lieutenant Cross found himself trembling.

He tried not to cry. With his entrenching tool, which weighed five pounds, he began digging a hole in the earth.

He felt shame. He hated himself. He had loved Martha more than his men, and as a consequence Lavender was now dead, and this was something he would have to carry like a stone in his stomach for the rest of the war.

All he could do was dig. He used his entrenching tool like an ax, slashing, feeling both love and hate, and then later, when it was full dark, he sat at the bottom of his foxhole and wept. It went on for a long while. In part, he was grieving for Ted Lavender, but mostly it was for Martha, and for himself, because she belonged to another world, which was not quite real, and because she was a junior at Mount Sebastian College in New Jersey, a poet and a virgin and uninvolved, and because he realized she did not love him and never would.

Like cement, Kiowa whispered in the dark. I swear to God—boom-down. Not a word.

I've heard this, said Norman Bowker.

A pisser, you know? Still zipping himself up. Zapped while zipping.

All right, fine. That's enough.

Yeah, but you had to see it, the guy just—

I *heard,* man. Cement. So why not shut the fuck *up*?

Kiowa shook his head sadly and glanced over at the hole where Lieutenant Jimmy Cross sat watching the night. The air was thick and wet. A warm, dense fog had settled over the paddies and there was the stillness that precedes rain.

After a time Kiowa sighed.

One thing for sure, he said. The Lieutenant's in some deep hurt. I mean that crying jag—the way he was carrying on—it wasn't fake or anything, it was real heavy-duty hurt. The man cares.

Sure, Norman Bowker said.

Say what you want, the man does care.

We all got problems.

Not Lavender.

No, I guess not, Bowker said. Do me a favor, though.

Shut up?

That's a smart Indian. Shut up.

Shrugging, Kiowa pulled off his boots. He wanted to say more, just to lighten up his sleep, but instead he opened his New Testament and arranged it beneath his head as a pillow. The fog made things seem hollow and unattached. He tried not to think about Ted Lavender, but then he was thinking how fast it was, no drama, down and dead, and how it was hard to feel anything except surprise. It seemed un-Christian. He wished he could find some great sadness, or even anger, but the emotion wasn't there and he couldn't make it happen. Mostly he felt pleased to be alive. He liked the smell of the New Testament under his cheek, the leather and ink and paper and glue, whatever the chemicals were. He liked hearing the sounds of night. Even his fatigue, it felt fine, the stiff muscles and the prickly awareness of his own body, a floating feeling. He enjoyed not being dead. Lying there, Kiowa admired Lieutenant Jimmy Cross's capacity for grief. He wanted to share the man's pain, he wanted to care as Jimmy Cross cared. And yet when he closed his eyes, all he could think was Boom-down, and all he could feel was the pleasure of having his boots off and the fog curling in around him and the damp soil and the Bible smells and the plush comfort of night.

After a moment Norman Bowker sat up in the dark.

What the hell, he said. You want to talk, *talk*. Tell it to me.

Forget it.

No, man, go on. One thing I hate, it's a silent Indian.

For the most part they carried themselves with poise, a kind of dignity. Now and then, however, there were times of panic, when they squealed or wanted to squeal but couldn't, when they twitched and made moaning sounds and covered their heads and said Dear Jesus and flopped around on the earth and fired their weapons blindly and cringed and sobbed and begged for the noise to stop and went wild and made stupid promises to themselves and to God and to their mothers and fathers, hoping not to die. In different ways, it happened to all of them. Afterward, when the firing ended, they would blink and peek up. They would touch their bodies, feeling shame, then quickly hiding it. They would force themselves to stand. As if in slow motion, frame by frame, the world would take on the old logic—absolute silence, then the wind, then sunlight, then voices. It was the burden of being alive. Awkwardly, the men would reassemble themselves, first in private, then in groups, becoming soldiers again. They would repair the leaks in their eyes. They would check for casualties, call in dust-offs, light cigarettes, try to smile, clear their throats and spit and begin cleaning their weapons. After a time someone would shake his head and say, No lie, I almost shit my pants, and someone else would laugh, which meant it was bad, yes, but the guy had obviously not shit his pants, it wasn't that bad, and in any case nobody would ever do such a thing and then go ahead and talk about it. They would squint into the dense, oppressive sunlight. For a few moments, perhaps, they would fall silent, lighting a joint and tracking its passage from man to man, inhaling, holding in the humiliation. Scary stuff, one of them might say. But then someone else would grin or flick his eyebrows and say, Roger-dodger, almost cut me a new asshole, *almost*.

There were numerous such poses. Some carried themselves with a sort of wistful resignation, others with pride or stiff soldierly discipline or good humor or macho zeal. They were afraid of dying but they were even more afraid to show it.

They found jokes to tell.

They used a hard vocabulary to contain the terrible softness. *Greased*, they'd say. *Offed, lit up, zapped while zipping*. It wasn't cruelty, just stage presence. They were actors and the war came at them in 3-D. When someone died, it wasn't quite dying, because in a curious way it seemed scripted, and because they had their lines mostly memorized, irony mixed with tragedy, and because they called it by other names, as if to encyst and destroy the reality of death itself. They kicked corpses. They cut off thumbs. They talked grunt lingo. They told stories about Ted Lavender's supply of tranquilizers, how the poor guy didn't feel a thing, how incredibly tranquil he was.

There's a moral here, said Mitchell Sanders.

They were waiting for Lavender's chopper, smoking the dead man's dope.

The moral's pretty obvious, Sanders said, and winked. Stay away from drugs. No joke, they'll ruin your day every time.

Cute, said Henry Dobbins.

Mind-blower, get it? Talk about wiggy—nothing left, just blood and brains.

They made themselves laugh.

There it is, they'd say, over and over, as if the repetition itself were an act of poise, a balance between crazy and almost crazy, knowing without going. There it is, which meant be cool, let it ride, because oh yeah, man, you can't change what can't be changed, there it is, there it absolutely and positively and fucking well *is*.

They were tough.

They carried all the emotional baggage of men who might die. Grief, terror, love, longing—these were intangibles, but the intangibles had their own mass and specific gravity, they had tangible weight. They carried shameful memories. They carried the common secret of cowardice barely restrained, the instinct to run or freeze or hide, and in many respects this was the heaviest burden of all, for it could never be put down, it required perfect balance and perfect posture. They carried their reputations. They carried the soldier's greatest fear, which was the fear of blushing. Men killed, and died, because they were embarrassed not to. It was what had brought them to the war in the first place, nothing positive, no dreams of glory or honor, just to avoid the blush of dishonor. They died so as not to die of embarrassment. They crawled into tunnels and walked point and advanced under fire. Each morning, despite the unknowns, they made their legs move. They endured. They kept humping. They did not submit to the obvious alternative, which was simply to close the eyes and fall. So easy, really. Go limp and tumble to the ground and let the muscles unwind and not speak and not budge until your buddies picked you up and lifted you into the chopper that would roar and dip its nose and carry you off to the world. A mere matter of falling, yet no one ever fell. It was not courage, exactly; the object was not valor. Rather, they were too frightened to be cowards.

By and large they carried these things inside, maintaining the masks of composure. They sneered at sick call. They spoke bitterly about guys who had found release by shooting off their own toes or fingers. Pussies, they'd say. Candyasses. It was fierce, mocking talk, with only a trace of envy or awe, but even so, the image played itself out behind their eyes.

They imagined the muzzle against flesh. They imagined the quick, sweet pain, then the evacuation to Japan, then a hospital with warm beds and cute geisha nurses.

They dreamed of freedom birds.

At night, on guard, staring into the dark, they were carried away by jumbo jets. They felt the rush of takeoff. *Gone!* they yelled. And then velocity, wings and engines, a smiling stewardess—but it was more than a plane, it was a real bird, a big sleek silver bird with feathers and talons and high screeching. They were flying. The weights fell off, there was nothing to bear. They laughed and held on tight, feeling the cold slap of wind and altitude, soaring, thinking *It's over, I'm gone!*—they were naked, they were light and free—it was all lightness, bright and fast and buoyant, light as light, a helium buzz in the brain, a giddy bubbling in the lungs as they were taken up over the clouds and the war, beyond duty, beyond gravity and mortification and global entanglements—*Sin loi!*° they yelled, *I'm sorry, motherfuckers, but I'm out of it, I'm goofed, I'm on a space cruise, I'm gone!*—and it was a restful, disencumbered sensation, just riding the light waves, sailing that big silver freedom bird over the mountains and oceans, over America, over the farms and great sleeping cities and cemeteries and highways and the golden arches of McDonald's. It was flight, a kind of fleeing, a kind of falling, falling higher and higher, spinning off the edge of the earth and beyond the sun and through the vast, silent vacuum where there were no burdens and where everything weighed exactly nothing. *Gone!* they screamed, *I'm sorry but I'm gone!* And so at night, not quite dreaming, they gave themselves over to lightness, they were carried, they were purely borne.

On the morning after Ted Lavender died, First Lieutenant Jimmy Cross crouched at the bottom of his foxhole and burned Martha's letters. Then he burned the two photographs. There was a steady rain falling, which made it difficult, but he used heat tabs and Sterno to build a small fire, screening it with his body, holding the photographs over the tight blue flame with the tips of his fingers.

He realized it was only a gesture. Stupid, he thought. Sentimental, too, but mostly just stupid.

Lavender was dead. You couldn't burn the blame.

Besides, the letters were in his head. And even now, without photographs, Lieutenant Cross could see Martha playing volleyball in her white gym shorts and yellow T-shirt. He could see her moving in the rain.

When the fire died out, Lieutenant Cross pulled his poncho over his shoulders and ate breakfast from a can.

There was no great mystery, he decided.

In those burned letters Martha had never mentioned the war, except to say, Jimmy, take care of yourself. She wasn't involved. She signed the letters "Love," but it wasn't love, and all the fine lines and technicalities did not matter.

The morning came up wet and blurry. Everything seemed part of everything else, the fog and Martha and the deepening rain.

Sin loi!: "Sorry about that!"

It was a war, after all.

Half smiling, Lieutenant Jimmy Cross took out his maps. He shook his head hard, as if to clear it, then bent forward and began planning the day's march. In ten minutes, or maybe twenty, he would rouse the men and they would pack up and head west, where the maps showed the country to be green and inviting. They would do what they had always done. The rain might add some weight, but otherwise it would be one more day layered upon all the other days.

He was realistic about it. There was that new hardness in his stomach.

No more fantasies, he told himself.

Henceforth, when he thought about Martha, it would be only to think that she belonged elsewhere. He would shut down the daydreams. This was not Mount Sebastian, it was another world, where there were no pretty poems or midterm exams, a place where men died because of carelessness and gross stupidity. Kiowa was right. Boom-down, and you were dead, never partly dead.

Briefly, in the rain, Lieutenant Cross saw Martha's gray eyes gazing back at him.

He understood.

It was very sad, he thought. The things men carried inside. The things men did or felt they had to do.

He almost nodded at her, but didn't.

Instead he went back to his maps. He was now determined to perform his duties firmly and without negligence. It wouldn't help Lavender, he knew that, but from this point on he would comport himself as a soldier. He would dispose of his good-luck pebble. Swallow it, maybe, or use Lee Strunk's slingshot, or just drop it along the trail. On the march he would impose strict field discipline. He would be careful to send out flank security, to prevent straggling or bunching up, to keep his troops moving at the proper pace and at the proper interval. He would insist on clean weapons. He would confiscate the remainder of Lavender's dope. Later in the day, perhaps, he would call the men together and speak to them plainly. He would accept the blame for what had happened to Ted Lavender. He would be a man about it. He would look them in the eyes, keeping his chin level, and he would issue the new SOPs in a calm, impersonal tone of voice, an officer's voice, leaving no room for argument or discussion. Commencing immediately, he'd tell them, they would no longer abandon equipment along the route of march. They would police up their acts. They would get their shit together, and keep it together, and maintain it neatly and in good working order.

He would not tolerate laxity. He would show strength, distancing himself.

Among the men there would be grumbling, of course, and maybe worse, because their days would seem longer and their loads heavier, but Lieutenant Cross reminded himself that his obligation was not to be loved but to lead. He would dispense with love; it was not now a factor. And if anyone quarreled or complained, he would simply tighten his lips and arrange his shoulders in the correct command posture. He might give a curt little nod. Or he might not. He might just shrug and say Carry on, then they would saddle up and form into a column and move out toward the villages of Than Khe.

COMMENTARY

BOBBIE ANN MASON

Bobbie Ann Mason described her response to Tim O'Brien's story "The Things They Carried" in Ron Hansen and Jim Shepard's collection *You've Got to Read This* (1994).

On Tim O'Brien's "The Things They Carried" 1994

Of all the stories I've read in the last decade, Tim O'Brien's "The Things They Carried" hit me hardest. It knocked me down, just as if a hundred-pound rucksack had been thrown right at me. The weight of the things the American soldiers carried on their interminable journey through the jungle in Vietnam sets the tone for this story. But the power of it is not just the poundage they were humping on their backs. The story's list of "things they carried" extends to the burden of memory and desire and confusion and grief. It's the weight of America's involvement in the war. You can hardly bear to contemplate all that this story evokes with its matter-of-fact yet electrifying details.

The way this story works makes me think of the Vietnam Veterans Memorial in Washington. The memorial is just a list of names, in a simple, dark—yet soaring—design. Its power is in the simplicity of presentation and in what lies behind each of those names.

In the story, there is a central incident, the company's first casualty on its march through the jungle. But the immediate drama is the effort—by the main character, by the narrator, by the writer himself—to contain the emotion, to carry it. When faced with a subject almost too great to manage or confront, the mind wants to organize, to categorize, to simplify. Restraint and matter-of-factness are appropriate deflective techniques for dealing with pain, and they work on several levels in the story. Sometimes it is more affecting to see someone dealing with pain than it is to know about the pain itself. That's what's happening here.

By using the simplicity of a list and trying to categorize the simple items the soldiers carried, O'Brien reveals the real terror of the war itself. And the categories go from the tangible—foot powder, photographs, chewing gum—to the intangible. They carried disease; memory. When it rained, they carried the sky. The weight of what they carried moves expansively, opens out, grows from the stuff in the rucksack to the whole weight of the American war chest, with its litter of ammo and packaging through the landscape of Vietnam. And then it moves back, away from the huge outer world, back into the interior of the self. The story details the way they carried themselves (dignity, laughter, words) as well as what they carried inside (fear, "emotional baggage").

And within the solemn effort to list and categorize, a story unfolds. PFC Ted Lavender, a grunt who carries tranquilizers, is on his way back from relieving himself in the jungle when he is shot by a sniper. The irony and horror of it are unbearable. Almost instantaneously, it seems, the central character, Lieutenant Cross, changes from a romantic youth to a man of action and duty. With his new, hard clarity, he is carried forward by his determination not to be caught unprepared again. And the way he prepares to lead his group is to list his resolves. He has to assert power over the event by detaching himself. It is a life-and-death matter.

So this effort to detach and control becomes both the drama and the technique of the story. For it is our impulse to deal with unspeakable horror and sadness by fashioning some kind of order, a story, to clarify and contain our emotions. As the writer, Tim O'Brien stands back far enough not to be seen but not so far that he isn't in charge.

"They carried all they could bear, and then some, including a silent awe for the terrible power of the things they carried."

FLANNERY O'CONNOR

Flannery O'Connor (1925–1964) was born in Savannah, Georgia, the only child of Roman Catholic parents. When she was thirteen her father was found to have disseminated lupus, an incurable disease in which antibodies in the immune system attack the body's own substances. After her father's death in 1941, O'Connor attended Georgia State College for Women in Milledgeville, where she also published stories and edited the literary magazine. On the strength of these stories, she was awarded a fellowship at the Writers Workshop at the University of Iowa and earned her M.F.A. degree there. Late in 1950 she became ill with what was diagnosed as lupus, and she returned to Milledgeville to start a series of treatments that temporarily arrested the disease. Living with her mother on the family's 500-acre dairy farm, O'Connor began to work again, writing from nine to twelve in the morning and spending the rest of the day resting, reading, writing letters, and raising peacocks.

O'Connor's first book, *Wise Blood*, a complex comic novel attacking the contemporary secularization of religion, was published in 1952. It was followed in 1955 by a collection of stories, *A Good Man Is Hard to Find.* O'Connor was able to see a second novel, *The Violent Bear It Away*, through to publication in 1960, but she died of lupus in 1964, having completed enough stories for a second collection, *Everything That Rises Must Converge* (1965). Her total output of just thirty-one stories, collected in her *Complete Stories*, won the National Book Award for fiction in 1972.

Despite her illness, O'Connor was never a recluse; she accepted as many lecture invitations as her health would permit. A volume of her lectures and occasional pieces was published in 1969 as *Mystery and Manners.* It is a valuable companion to her stories and novels, because she often reflected on her writing and interpreted her fiction. As a devout Roman Catholic, O'Connor was uncompromising in her religious views: "For I am no disbeliever in spiritual purpose and no vague believer. This means that for me the meaning of life is centered in our Redemption by Christ and what I see in the world I see in relation to that." As Joyce Carol Oates recognized in her essay "The Visionary Art of Flannery O'Connor," O'Connor is a great modern religious writer, thoroughly unique "in her celebration of the necessity of succumbing to the divine through violence that is immediate and irreparable. There is no mysticism in her work that is only spiritual; it is physical as well." O'Connor's stories, like the two included here, frequently involve family relationships but are not meant to be read as realistic fiction, despite her remarkable ear for dialogue. O'Connor said she wrote them as parables, as the epigraph to *A Good Man Is Hard to Find* attests.

CONNECTIONS See pages 636–648, including Flannery O'Connor, "From 'Letters, 1954–55,'" page 636, "Writing Short Stories," page 639, "The Element of Suspense in 'A Good Man Is Hard to Find,'" page 644; Sally Fitzgerald, "Southern Sources of 'A Good Man Is Hard to Find,'" page 647.

WEB Research Flannery O'Connor at bedfordstmartins.com/rewritinglit.

Good Country People 1955

Besides the neutral expression that she wore when she was alone, Mrs. Freeman had two others, forward and reverse, that she used for all her human dealings. Her forward expression was steady and driving like the advance of a heavy truck. Her eyes never swerved to left or right but turned as the story turned as if they followed a yellow line down the center of it. She seldom used the other expression because it was not often necessary for her to retract a statement, but when she did, her face came to a complete stop, there was an almost imperceptible movement of her black eyes, during which they seemed to be receding, and then the observer would see that Mrs. Freeman, though she might stand there as real as several grain sacks thrown on top of each other, was no longer there in spirit. As for getting anything across to her when this was the case, Mrs. Hopewell had given it up. She might talk her head off. Mrs. Freeman could never be brought to admit herself wrong on any point. She would stand there and if she could be brought to say anything, it was something like, "Well, I wouldn't of said it was and I wouldn't of said it wasn't," or letting her gaze range over the top kitchen shelf where there was an assortment of dusty bottles, she might remark, "I see you ain't ate many of them figs you put up last summer."

They carried on their most important business in the kitchen at breakfast. Every morning Mrs. Hopewell got up at seven o'clock and lit her gas heater and Joy's. Joy was her daughter, a large blonde girl who had an artificial leg. Mrs. Hopewell thought of her as a child though she was thirty-two years old and highly educated. Joy would get up while her mother was eating and lumber into the bathroom and slam the door, and before long, Mrs. Freeman would arrive at the back door. Joy would hear her mother call, "Come on in," and then they would talk a while in low voices that were indistinguishable in the bathroom. By the time Joy came in, they had usually finished the weather report and were on one or the other of Mrs. Freeman's daughters, Glynese or Carramae. Joy called them Glycerin and Caramel. Glynese, a redhead, was eighteen and had many admirers; Carramae, a blonde, was only fifteen but already married and pregnant. She could not keep anything on her stomach. Every morning Mrs. Freeman told Mrs. Hopewell how many times she had vomited since the last report.

Mrs. Hopewell liked to tell people that Glynese and Carramae were two of the finest girls she knew and that Mrs. Freeman was a *lady* and that she was never ashamed to take her anywhere or introduce her to anybody they might meet. Then she would tell how she had happened to hire the Freemans in the first place and how they were a godsend to her and how she had had them four years. The reason for her keeping them so long was that they were not trash. They were good country people. She had telephoned the man whose name they had given as a reference and he had told her that Mr. Freeman was a good farmer but that his wife was the nosiest woman ever to walk the earth. "She's got to be into everything," the man said. "If she don't get there before the dust settles, you can bet she's dead, that's all. She'll want to know all your business. I can stand him real good," he had said, "but me nor my wife neither could have stood that woman one more minute on this place." That had put Mrs. Hopewell off for a few days.

She had hired them in the end because there were no other applicants but she had made up her mind beforehand exactly how she would handle the woman. Since she was the type who had to be into everything, then, Mrs. Hopewell had decided, she would not only let her be into everything, she would *see to it* that she was into everything—she would give her the responsibility of everything, she would put her in charge. Mrs. Hopewell had no bad qualities of her own but she was able to use other people's in such a constructive way that she never felt the lack. She had hired the Freemans and she had kept them four years.

Nothing is perfect. This was one of Mrs. Hopewell's favorite sayings. Another was: that is life! And still another, the most important, was: well, other people have their opinions too. She would make these statements, usually at the table, in a tone of gentle insistence as if no one held them but her, and the large hulking Joy, whose constant outrage had obliterated every expression from her face, would stare just a little to the side of her, her eyes icy blue, with the look of someone who has achieved blindness by an act of will and means to keep it.

When Mrs. Hopewell said to Mrs. Freeman that life was like that, Mrs. Freeman would say, "I always said so myself." Nothing had been arrived at by anyone that had not first been arrived at by her. She was quicker than Mr. Freeman. When Mrs. Hopewell said to her after they had been on the place a while, "You know, you're the wheel behind the wheel," and winked, Mrs. Freeman had said, "I know it. I've always been quick. It's some that are quicker than others."

"Everybody is different," Mrs. Hopewell said.

"Yes, most people is," Mrs. Freeman said.

"It takes all kinds to make the world."

"I always said it did myself."

The girl was used to this kind of dialogue for breakfast and more of it for dinner; sometimes they had it for supper too. When they had no guest they ate in the kitchen because that was easier. Mrs. Freeman always managed to arrive at some point during the meal and to watch them finish it. She would stand in the doorway if it were summer but in the winter she would stand with one elbow on top of the refrigerator and look down on them, or she would stand by the gas heater, lifting the back of her skirt slightly. Occasionally she would stand against the wall and roll her head from side to side. At no time was she in any hurry to leave. All this was very trying on Mrs. Hopewell but she was a woman of great patience. She realized that nothing is perfect and that in the Freemans she had good country people and that if, in this day and age, you get good country people, you had better hang onto them.

She had had plenty of experience with trash. Before the Freemans she had averaged one tenant family a year. The wives of these farmers were not the kind you would want to be around you for very long. Mrs. Hopewell, who had divorced her husband long ago, needed someone to walk over the fields with her; and when Joy had to be impressed for these services, her remarks were usually so ugly and her face so glum that Mrs. Hopewell would say, "If you can't come pleasantly, I don't want you at all," to which the girl, standing square and rigid-shouldered with her neck thrust slightly forward, would reply, "If you want me, here I am—LIKE I AM."

Mrs. Hopewell excused this attitude because of the leg (which had been shot off in a hunting accident when Joy was ten). It was hard for Mrs. Hopewell to realize that her child was thirty-two now and that for more than twenty years she had had only one leg. She thought of her still as a child because it tore her heart to think instead of the poor stout girl in her thirties who had never danced a step or had any *normal* good times. Her name was really Joy but as soon as she was twenty-one and away from home, she had had it legally changed. Mrs. Hopewell was certain that she had thought and thought until she had hit upon the ugliest name in any language. Then she had gone and had the beautiful name, Joy, changed without telling her mother until after she had done it. Her legal name was Hulga.

When Mrs. Hopewell thought the name Hulga, she thought of the broad blank hull of a battleship. She would not use it. She continued to call her Joy to which the girl responded but in a purely mechanical way.

Hulga had learned to tolerate Mrs. Freeman who saved her from taking walks with her mother. Even Glynese and Carramae were useful when they occupied attention that might otherwise have been directed at her. At first she had thought she could not stand Mrs. Freeman for she had found that it was not possible to be rude to her. Mrs. Freeman would take on strange resentments and for days together she would be sullen but the source of her displeasure was always obscure; a direct attack, a positive leer, blatant ugliness to her face—these never touched her. And without warning one day, she began calling her Hulga.

She did not call her that in front of Mrs. Hopewell who would have been incensed but when she and the girl happened to be out of the house together, she would say something and add the name Hulga to the end of it, and the big spectacled Joy-Hulga would scowl and redden as if her privacy had been intruded upon. She considered the name her personal affair. She had arrived at it first purely on the basis of its ugly sound and then the full genius of its fitness had struck her. She had a vision of the name working like the ugly sweating Vulcan who stayed in the furnace and to whom, presumably, the goddess had to come when called. She saw it as the name of her highest creative act. One of her major triumphs was that her mother had not been able to turn her dust into Joy, but the greater one was that she had been able to turn it herself into Hulga. However, Mrs. Freeman's relish for using the name only irritated her. It was as if Mrs. Freeman's beady steel-pointed eyes had penetrated far enough behind her face to reach some secret fact. Something about her seemed to fascinate Mrs. Freeman and then one day Hulga realized that it was the artificial leg. Mrs. Freeman had a special fondness for the details of secret infections, hidden deformities, assaults upon children. Of diseases, she preferred the lingering or incurable. Hulga had heard Mrs. Hopewell give her the details of the hunting accident, how the leg had been literally blasted off, how she had never lost consciousness. Mrs. Freeman could listen to it any time as if it had happened an hour ago.

When Hulga stumped into the kitchen in the morning (she could walk without making the awful noise but she made it—Mrs. Hopewell was certain—because it was ugly-sounding), she glanced at them and did not speak. Mrs. Hopewell would be in her red kimono with her hair tied around her head in rags. She would be sitting at the table, finishing her breakfast and Mrs. Freeman would be hanging by her elbow outward from the refrigerator, looking down at the table. Hulga always put her eggs on the stove to boil and then stood over them with her arms folded, and Mrs. Hopewell would look at her—a kind of indirect gaze divided between her and Mrs. Freeman—and would think that if she would only keep herself up a little, she wouldn't be so bad looking. There was nothing wrong with her face that a pleasant expression wouldn't help. Mrs. Hopewell said that people who looked on the bright side of things would be beautiful even if they were not.

Whenever she looked at Joy this way, she could not help but feel that it would have been better if the child had not taken the Ph.D. It had certainly not brought her out any and now that she had it, there was no more excuse for her to go to school again. Mrs. Hopewell thought it was nice for girls to go to school to have a good time but Joy had "gone through." Anyhow, she would not have been strong enough to go again. The doctors had told Mrs. Hopewell that with the best of care, Joy might see forty-five. She had a weak heart. Joy had made it plain that if it had not been for this condition, she would be far from these red hills and good country people. She would be in a university lecturing to people who knew what she was talking about. And Mrs. Hopewell could very well picture her there, looking like a scarecrow and lecturing to more of the same. Here she went about all day in a six-year-old skirt and a yellow sweat shirt with a faded cowboy on a horse embossed on it. She thought this was funny; Mrs. Hopewell thought it was idiotic and showed simply that she was still a child. She was brilliant but she didn't have a grain of sense. It seemed to Mrs.

Hopewell that every year she grew less like other people and more like herself—bloated, rude, and squint-eyed. And she said such strange things! To her own mother she had said—without warning, without excuse, standing up in the middle of a meal with her face purple and her mouth half full—"Woman! do you ever look inside? Do you ever look inside and see what you are *not*? God!" she had cried sinking down again and staring at her plate, "Malebranche was right: we are not our own light. We are not our own light!" Mrs. Hopewell had no idea to this day what brought that on. She had only made the remark, hoping Joy would take it in, that a smile never hurt anyone.

The girl had taken the Ph.D. in philosophy and this left Mrs. Hopewell at a complete loss. You could say, "My daughter is a nurse," or "My daughter is a schoolteacher," or even, "My daughter is a chemical engineer." You could not say, "My daughter is a philosopher." That was something that had ended with the Greeks and Romans. All day Joy sat on her neck in a deep chair, reading. Sometimes she went for walks but she didn't like dogs or cats or birds or flowers or nature or nice young men. She looked at nice young men as if she could smell their stupidity.

One day Mrs. Hopewell had picked up one of the books the girl had just put down and opening it at random, she read, "Science, on the other hand, has to assert its soberness and seriousness afresh and declare that it is concerned solely with what-is. Nothing—how can it be for science anything but a horror and a phantasm? If science is right, then one thing stands firm: science wishes to know nothing of nothing. Such is after all the strictly scientific approach to Nothing. We know it by wishing to know nothing of Nothing." These words had been underlined with a blue pencil and they worked on Mrs. Hopewell like some evil incantation in gibberish. She shut the book quickly and went out of the room as if she were having a chill.

This morning when the girl came in, Mrs. Freeman was on Carramae. "She thrown up four times after supper," she said, "and was up twict in the night after three o'clock. Yesterday she didn't do nothing but ramble in the bureau drawer. All she did. Stand up there and see what she could run up on."

"She's got to eat," Mrs. Hopewell muttered, sipping her coffee, while she watched Joy's back at the stove. She was wondering what the child had said to the Bible salesman. She could not imagine what kind of a conversation she could possibly have had with him.

He was a tall gaunt hatless youth who had called yesterday to sell them a Bible. He had appeared at the door, carrying a large black suitcase that weighted him so heavily on one side that he had to brace himself against the door facing. He seemed on the point of collapse but he said in a cheerful voice, "Good morning, Mrs. Cedars!" and set the suitcase down on the mat. He was not a bad-looking young man though he had on a bright blue suit and yellow socks that were not pulled up far enough. He had prominent face bones and a streak of sticky-looking brown hair falling across his forehead.

"I'm Mrs. Hopewell," she said.

"Oh!" he said, pretending to look puzzled but with his eyes sparkling, "I saw it said 'The Cedars' on the mailbox so I thought you was Mrs. Cedars!" and he burst out in a pleasant laugh. He picked up the satchel and under cover of a pant, he fell forward into her hall. It was rather as if the suitcase had moved first, jerking him after it. "Mrs. Hopewell!" he said and grabbed her hand. "I hope you are well!" and he laughed again and then all at once his face sobered completely. He paused and gave her a straight earnest look and said, "Lady, I've come to speak of serious things."

"Well, come in," she muttered, none too pleased because her dinner was almost ready. He came into the parlor and sat down on the edge of a straight chair and put the suitcase between his feet and glanced around the room as if he were sizing her up by it. Her silver gleamed on the two sideboards; she decided he had never been in a room as elegant as this.

"Mrs. Hopewell," he began, using her name in a way that sounded almost intimate, "I know you believe in Chrustian service."

"Well yes," she murmured.

"I know," he said and paused, looking very wise with his head cocked on one side, "that you're a good woman. Friends have told me."

Mrs. Hopewell never liked to be taken for a fool. "What are you selling?" she asked.

"Bibles," the young man said and his eye raced around the room before he added, "I see you have no family Bible in your parlor, I see that is the one lack you got!"

Mrs. Hopewell could not say, "My daughter is an atheist and won't let me keep the Bible in the parlor." She said, stiffening slightly, "I keep my Bible by my bedside." This was not the truth. It was in the attic somewhere.

"Lady," he said, "the word of God ought to be in the parlor."

"Well, I think that's a matter of taste," she began. "I think . . ."

"Lady," he said, "for a Chrustian, the word of God ought to be in every room in the house besides in his heart. I know you're a Chrustian because I can see it in every line of your face."

She stood up and said, "Well, young man, I don't want to buy a Bible and I smell my dinner burning."

He didn't get up. He began to twist his hands and looking down at them he said softly, "Well lady, I'll tell you the truth—not many people want to buy one nowadays and besides, I know I'm real simple. I don't know how to say a thing but to say it. I'm just a country boy." He glanced up into her unfriendly face. "People like you don't like to fool with country people like me!"

"Why!" she cried, "good country people are the salt of the earth! Besides, we all have different ways of doing, it takes all kinds to make the world go 'round. That's life!"

"You said a mouthful," he said.

"Why, I think there aren't enough good country people in the world!" she said, stirred. "I think that's what's wrong with it!"

His face had brightened. "I didn't inraduce myself," he said. "I'm Manley Pointer from out in the country around Willohobie, not even from a place, just from near a place."

"You wait a minute," she said. "I have to see about my dinner." She went out to the kitchen and found Joy standing near the door where she had been listening.

"Get rid of the salt of the earth," she said, "and let's eat."

Mrs. Hopewell gave her a pained look and turned the heat down under the vegetables. "*I* can't be rude to anybody," she murmured and went back into the parlor.

He had opened the suitcase and was sitting with a Bible on each knee.

"You might as well put those up," she told him. "I don't want one."

"I appreciate your honesty," he said. "You don't see any more real honest people unless you go way out in the country."

"I know," she said, "real genuine folks!" Through the crack in the door she heard a groan.

"I guess a lot of boys come telling you they're working their way through college," he said, "but I'm not going to tell you that. Somehow," he said, "I don't want to go to college. I want to devote my life to Chrustian service. See," he said, lowering his voice, "I got this heart condition. I may not live long. When you know it's something wrong with you and you may not live long, well then, lady . . ." He paused, with his mouth open, and stared at her.

He and Joy had the same condition! She knew that her eyes were filling with tears but she collected herself quickly and murmured, "Won't you stay for dinner? We'd love to have you!" and was sorry the instant she heard herself say it.

"Yes mam," he said in an abashed voice, "I would sher love to do that!"

Joy had given him one look on being introduced to him and then throughout the meal had not glanced at him again. He had addressed several remarks to her, which she had pretended not to hear. Mrs. Hopewell could not understand deliberate rudeness, although she lived with it, and she felt she had always to overflow with hospitality to make up for Joy's lack of courtesy. She urged him to talk about himself and he did. He said he was the seventh child of twelve and that his father had been crushed under a tree when he himself was eight years old. He had been crushed very badly, in fact, almost cut in two and was practically not recognizable. His mother had got along the best she could by hard working and she had always seen that her children went to Sunday School and that they read the Bible every evening. He was now nineteen years old and he had been selling Bibles for four months. In that time he had sold seventy-seven Bibles and had the promise of two more sales. He wanted to become a missionary because he thought that was the way you could do most for people. "He who losest his life shall find it," he said simply and he was so sincere, so genuine and earnest that Mrs. Hopewell would not for the world have smiled. He prevented his peas from sliding onto the table by blocking them with a piece of bread which he later cleaned his plate with. She could see Joy observing sidewise how he handled his knife and fork and she saw too that every few minutes, the boy would dart a keen appraising glance at the girl as if he were trying to attract her attention.

After dinner Joy cleared the dishes off the table and disappeared and Mrs. Hopewell was left to talk with him. He told her again about his childhood and his father's accident and about various things that had happened to him. Every five minutes or so she would stifle a yawn. He sat for two hours until finally she told him she must go because she had an appointment in town. He packed his Bibles and thanked her and prepared to leave, but in the doorway he stopped and wrung her hand and said that not on any of his trips had he met a lady as nice as her and he asked if he could come again. She had said she would always be happy to see him.

Joy had been standing in the road, apparently looking at something in the distance, when he came down the steps toward her, bent to the side with his heavy valise. He stopped where she was standing and confronted her directly. Mrs. Hopewell could not hear what he said but she trembled to think what Joy would say to him. She could see that after a minute Joy said something and that then the boy began to speak again, making an excited gesture with his free hand. After a minute Joy said something else at which the boy began to speak once more. Then to her amazement, Mrs. Hopewell saw the two of them walk off together, toward the gate. Joy had walked all the way to the gate with him and Mrs. Hopewell could not imagine what they had said to each other, and she had not yet dared to ask.

Mrs. Freeman was insisting upon her attention. She had moved from the refrigerator to the heater so that Mrs. Hopewell had to turn and face her in order to seem to be listening. "Glynese gone out with Harvey Hill again last night," she said. "She had this sty."

"Hill," Mrs. Hopewell said absently, "is that the one who works in the garage?"

"Nome, he's the one that goes to chiropracter school," Mrs. Freeman said. "She had this sty. Been had it two days. So she says when he brought her in the other night he says, 'Lemme get rid of that sty for you,' and she says, 'How?' and he says, 'You just lay yourself down acrost the seat of that car and I'll show you.' So she done it and he popped her neck. Kept on a-popping it several times until she made him quit. This morning," Mrs. Freeman said, "she ain't got no sty. She ain't got no traces of a sty."

"I never heard of that before," Mrs. Hopewell said.

"He ast her to marry him before the Ordinary," Mrs. Freeman went on, "and she told him she wasn't going to be married in no *office*."

"Well, Glynese is a fine girl," Mrs. Hopewell said. "Glynese and Carramae are both fine girls."

"Carramae said when her and Lyman was married Lyman said it sure felt sacred to him. She said he said he wouldn't take five hundred dollars for being married by a preacher."

"How much would he take?" the girl asked from the stove.

"He said he wouldn't take five hundred dollars," Mrs. Freeman repeated.

"Well we all have work to do," Mrs. Hopewell said.

"Lyman said it just felt more sacred to him," Mrs. Freeman said. "The doctor wants Carramae to eat prunes. Says instead of medicine. Says them cramps is coming from pressure. You know where I think it is?"

"She'll be better in a few weeks," Mrs. Hopewell said.

"In the tube," Mrs. Freeman said. "Else she wouldn't be as sick as she is."

Hulga had cracked her two eggs into a saucer and was bringing them to the table along with a cup of coffee that she had filled too full. She sat down carefully and began to eat, meaning to keep Mrs. Freeman there by questions if for any reason she showed an inclination to leave. She could perceive her mother's eye on her. The first round-about question would be about the Bible salesman and she did not wish to bring it on. "How did he pop her neck?" she asked.

Mrs. Freeman went into a description of how he had popped her neck. She said he owned a '55 Mercury but that Glynese said she would rather marry a man with only a '36 Plymouth who would be married by a preacher. The girl asked what if he had a '32 Plymouth and Mrs. Freeman said what Glynese had said was a '36 Plymouth.

Mrs. Hopewell said there were not many girls with Glynese's common sense. She said what she admired in those girls was their common sense. She said that reminded her that they had had a nice visitor yesterday, a young man selling Bibles. "Lord," she said, "he bored me to death but he was so sincere and genuine I couldn't be rude to him. He was just good country people, you know," she said, "—just the salt of the earth."

"I seen him walk up," Mrs. Freeman said, "and then later—I seen him walk off," and Hulga could feel the slight shift in her voice, the slight insinuation, that he had not walked off alone, had he? Her face remained expressionless but the color rose into her neck and she seemed to swallow it down with the next spoonful of egg. Mrs. Freeman was looking at her as if they had a secret together.

"Well, it takes all kinds of people to make the world go 'round," Mrs. Hopewell said. "It's very good we aren't all alike."

"Some people are more alike than others," Mrs. Freeman said.

Hulga got up and stumped, with about twice the noise that was necessary, into her room and locked the door. She was to meet the Bible salesman at ten o'clock at the gate. She had thought about it half the night. She had started thinking of it as a great joke and then she had begun to see profound implications in it. She had lain in bed imagining dialogues for them that were insane on the surface but that reached below to depths that no Bible salesman would be aware of. Their conversation yesterday had been of this kind.

He had stopped in front of her and had simply stood there. His face was bony and sweaty and bright, with a little pointed nose in the center of it, and his look was different from what it had been at the dinner table. He was gazing at her with open curiosity, with fascination, like a child watching a new fantastic animal at the zoo, and he was breathing as if he had run a great distance to reach her. His gaze seemed somehow familiar but she could not think where she had been regarded with it before. For almost a minute he didn't say anything. Then on what seemed an insuck of breath, he whispered, "You ever ate a chicken that was two days old?"

The girl looked at him stonily. He might have just put this question up for consideration at the meeting of a philosophical association. "Yes," she presently replied as if she had considered it from all angles.

"It must have been mighty small!" he said triumphantly and shook all over with little nervous giggles, getting very red in the face, and subsiding finally into his gaze of complete admiration, while the girl's expression remained exactly the same.

"How old are you?" he asked softly.

She waited some time before she answered. Then in a flat voice she said, "Seventeen."

His smiles came in succession like waves breaking on the surface of a little lake. "I see you got a wooden leg," he said. "I think you're brave. I think you're real sweet."

The girl stood blank and solid and silent.

"Walk to the gate with me," he said. "You're a brave sweet little thing and I liked you the minute I seen you walk in the door."

Hulga began to move forward.

"What's your name?" he asked, smiling down on the top of her head.

"Hulga," she said.

"Hulga," he murmured, "Hulga. Hulga. I never heard of anybody name Hulga before. You're shy, aren't you, Hulga?" he asked.

She nodded, watching his large red hand on the handle of the giant valise.

"I like girls that wear glasses," he said. "I think a lot. I'm not like these people that a serious thought don't ever enter their heads. It's because I may die."

"I may die too," she said suddenly and looked up at him. His eyes were very small and brown, glittering feverishly.

"Listen," he said, "don't you think some people was meant to meet on account of what all they got in common and all? Like they both think serious thoughts and all?" He shifted the valise to his other hand so that the hand nearest her was free. He caught hold of her elbow and shook it a little. "I don't work on Saturday," he said. "I like to walk in the woods and see what Mother Nature is wearing. O'er the hills and far away. Pic-nics and things. Couldn't we go on a pic-nic tomorrow? Say yes, Hulga," he said and gave her a dying look as if he felt his insides about to drop out of him. He had even seemed to sway slightly toward her.

During the night she had imagined that she seduced him. She imagined that the two of them walked on the place until they came to the storage barn beyond the two back fields and there, she imagined, that things came to such a pass that she very easily seduced him and that then, of course, she had to reckon with his remorse. True genius can get an idea across even to an inferior mind. She imagined that she took his remorse in hand and changed it into a deeper understanding of life. She took all his shame away and turned it into something useful.

She set off for the gate at exactly ten o'clock, escaping without drawing Mrs. Hopewell's attention. She didn't take anything to eat, forgetting that food is usually taken on a pic-nic. She wore a pair of slacks and a dirty white shirt, and as an afterthought, she had put some Vapex on the collar of it since she did not own any perfume. When she reached the gate no one was there.

She looked up and down the empty highway and had the furious feeling that she had been tricked, that he had only meant to make her walk to the gate after the idea of him. Then suddenly he stood up, very tall, from behind a bush on the opposite embankment. Smiling, he lifted his hat which was new and wide-brimmed. He had not worn it yesterday and she wondered if he had bought it for the occasion. It was toast-colored with a red and white band around it and was slightly too large for him. He stepped from behind the bush still carrying the black valise. He had on the same suit and the same yellow socks sucked down in his shoes from walking. He crossed the highway and said, "I knew you'd come!"

The girl wondered acidly how he had known this. She pointed to the valise and asked, "Why did you bring your Bibles?"

He took her elbow, smiling down on her as if he could not stop. "You can never tell when you'll need the word of God, Hulga," he said. She had a moment in which she doubted that this was actually happening and then they began to climb the embankment. They went down into the pasture toward the woods. The boy walked lightly by her side, bouncing on his toes. The valise did not seem to be heavy today; he even swung it. They crossed half the pasture without saying anything and then, putting his hand easily on the small of her back, he asked softly, "Where does your wooden leg join on?"

She turned an ugly red and glared at him and for an instant the boy looked abashed. "I didn't mean you no harm," he said. "I only meant you're so brave and all. I guess God takes care of you."

"No," she said, looking forward and walking fast, "I don't even believe in God."

At this he stopped and whistled. "No!" he exclaimed as if he were too astonished to say anything else.

She walked on and in a second he was bouncing at her side, fanning with his hat. "That's very unusual for a girl," he remarked, watching her out of the corner of his eye. When they reached the edge of the wood, he put his hand on her back again and drew her against him without a word and kissed her heavily.

The kiss, which had more pressure than feeling behind it, produced that extra surge of adrenalin in the girl that enables one to carry a packed trunk out of a burning house, but in her, the power went at once to the brain. Even before he released her, her mind, clear and detached and ironic anyway, was regarding him from a great distance, with amusement but with pity. She had never been kissed before and she was pleased to discover that it was an unexceptional experience and all a matter of the mind's control. Some people might enjoy drain water if they were told it was vodka. When the boy, looking expectant but uncertain, pushed her gently away, she turned and walked on, saying nothing as if such business, for her, were common enough.

He came along panting at her side, trying to help her when he saw a root that she might trip over. He caught and held back the long swaying blades of thorn vine until she had passed beyond them. She led the way and he came breathing heavily behind her. Then they came out on a sunlit hillside, sloping softly into another one a little smaller. Beyond, they could see the rusted top of the old barn where the extra hay was stored.

The hill was sprinkled with small pink weeds. "Then you ain't saved?" he asked suddenly, stopping.

The girl smiled. It was the first time she had smiled at him at all. "In my economy," she said, "I'm saved and you are damned but I told you I didn't believe in God."

Nothing seemed to destroy the boy's look of admiration. He gazed at her now as if the fantastic animal at the zoo had put its paw through the bars and given him a loving poke. She thought he looked as if he wanted to kiss her again and she walked on before he had the chance.

"Ain't there somewheres we can sit down sometime?" he murmured, his voice softening toward the end of the sentence.

"In that barn," she said.

They made for it rapidly as if it might slide away like a train. It was a large two-story barn, cool and dark inside. The boy pointed up the ladder that led into the loft and said, "It's too bad we can't go up there."

"Why can't we?" she asked.

"Yer leg," he said reverently.

The girl gave him a contemptuous look and putting both hands on the ladder, she climbed it while he stood below, apparently awestruck. She pulled herself expertly through the opening and then looked down at him and said, "Well, come on if you're coming," and he began to climb the ladder, awkwardly bringing the suitcase with him.

"We won't need the Bible," she observed.

"You never can tell," he said, panting. After he had got into the loft, he was a few seconds catching his breath. She had sat down in a pile of straw. A wide sheath of sunlight, filled with dust particles, slanted over her. She lay back against a bale, her face turned away, looking out the front opening of the barn where hay was thrown from a wagon into the loft. The two pink-speckled hillsides lay back against a dark ridge of woods. The sky was cloudless and cold blue. The boy dropped down by her side and put one arm under her and the other over her and began methodically kissing her face, making little noises like a fish. He did not remove his hat but it was pushed far enough back not to interfere. When her glasses got in his way, he took them off of her and slipped them into his pocket.

The girl at first did not return any of the kisses but presently she began to and after she had put several on his cheek, she reached his lips and remained there, kissing him again and again as if she were trying to draw all the breath out of him. His breath was clear and sweet like a child's and the kisses were sticky like a child's. He mumbled about loving her and about knowing when he first seen her that he loved her, but the mumbling was like the sleepy fretting of a child being put to sleep by his mother. Her mind, throughout this, never stopped or lost itself for a second to her feelings. "You ain't said you loved me none," he whispered finally, pulling back from her. "You got to say that."

She looked away from him off into the hollow sky and then down at a black ridge and then down farther into what appeared to be two green swelling lakes. She didn't realize he had taken her glasses but this landscape could not seem exceptional to her for she seldom paid any close attention to her surroundings.

"You got to say it," he repeated. "You got to say you love me."

She was always careful how she committed herself. "In a sense," she began, "if you use the word loosely, you might say that. But it's not a word I use. I don't have illusions. I'm one of those people who see *through* to nothing."

The boy was frowning. "You got to say it. I said it and you got to say it," he said.

The girl looked at him almost tenderly. "You poor baby," she murmured. "It's just as well you don't understand," and she pulled him by the neck, face-down, against her. "We are all damned," she said, "but some of us have taken off our blindfolds and see that there's nothing to see. It's a kind of salvation."

The boy's astonished eyes looked blankly through the ends of her hair. "Okay," he almost whined, "but do you love me or don'tcher?"

"Yes," she said and added, "in a sense. But I must tell you something. There mustn't be anything dishonest between us." She lifted his head and looked him in the eye. "I am thirty years old," she said. "I have a number of degrees."

The boy's look was irritated but dogged. "I don't care," he said. "I don't care a thing about what all you done. I just want to know if you love me or don'tcher?" and he caught her to him and wildly planted her face with kisses until she said, "Yes, yes."

"Okay then," he said, letting her go. "Prove it."

She smiled, looking dreamily out on the shifty landscape. She had seduced him without even making up her mind to try. "How?" she asked, feeling that he should be delayed a little.

He leaned over and put his lips to her ear. "Show me where your wooden leg joins on," he whispered.

The girl uttered a sharp little cry and her face instantly drained of color. The obscenity of the suggestion was not what shocked her. As a child she had sometimes been subject to feelings of shame but education had removed the last traces of that as a good surgeon scrapes for cancer; she would no more have felt it over what he was asking than she would have believed in his Bible. But she was as sensitive about the artificial leg as a peacock about his tail. No one ever touched it but her. She took care of it as someone else would his soul, in private and almost with her own eyes turned away. "No," she said.

"I known it," he muttered, sitting up. "You're just playing me for a sucker."

"Oh no no!" she cried. "It joins on at the knee. Only at the knee. Why do you want to see it?"

The boy gave her a long penetrating look. "Because," he said, "it's what makes you different. You ain't like anybody else."

She sat staring at him. There was nothing about her face or her round freezing-blue eyes to indicate that this had moved her; but she felt as if her heart had stopped and left her mind to pump her blood. She decided that for the first time in her life she was face to face with real innocence. This boy, with an instinct that came from beyond wisdom, had touched the truth about her. When after a minute, she said in a hoarse high voice, "All right," it was like surrendering to him completely. It was like losing her own life and finding it again, miraculously, in his.

Very gently he began to roll the slack leg up. The artificial limb, in a white sock and brown flat shoe, was bound in a heavy material like canvas and ended in an ugly jointure where it was attached to the stump. The boy's face and his voice were entirely reverent as he uncovered it and said, "Now show me how to take it off and on."

She took it off for him and put it back on again and then he took it off himself, handling it as tenderly as if it were a real one. "See!" he said with a delighted child's face. "Now I can do it myself!"

"Put it back on," she said. She was thinking that she would run away with him and that every night he would take the leg off and every morning put it back on again. "Put it back on," she said.

"Not yet," he murmured, setting it on its foot out of her reach. "Leave it off for a while. You got me instead."

She gave a little cry of alarm but he pushed her down and began to kiss her again. Without the leg she felt entirely dependent on him. Her brain seemed to have stopped thinking altogether and to be about some other function that it was not very good at. Different expressions raced back and forth over her face. Every now and then the boy, his eyes like two steel spikes, would glance behind him where the leg stood. Finally she pushed him off and said, "Put it back on me now."

"Wait," he said. He leaned the other way and pulled the valise toward him and opened it. It had a pale blue spotted lining and there were only two Bibles in it. He took one of these out and opened the cover of it. It was hollow and contained a pocket flask of whiskey, a pack of cards, and a small blue box with printing on it. He laid these out in front of her one at a time in an evenly spaced row, like one presenting offerings at the shrine of a goddess. He put the blue box in her hand. THIS PRODUCT TO BE USED ONLY FOR THE PREVENTION OF DISEASE, she read, and dropped it. The boy was unscrewing the top of the flask. He stopped and pointed, with a smile, to the deck of cards. It was not an ordinary deck but one with an obscene picture on the back of each card. "Take a swig," he said, offering her the bottle first. He held it in front of her, but like one mesmerized, she did not move.

Her voice when she spoke had an almost pleading sound. "Aren't you," she murmured, "aren't you just good country people?"

The boy cocked his head. He looked as if he were just beginning to understand that she might be trying to insult him. "Yeah," he said, curling his lip slightly, "but it ain't held me back none. I'm as good as you any day in the week."

"Give me my leg," she said.

He pushed it farther away with his foot. "Come on now, let's begin to have us a good time," he said coaxingly. "We ain't got to know one another good yet."

"Give me my leg!" she screamed and tried to lunge for it but he pushed her down easily.

"What's the matter with you all of a sudden?" he asked, frowning as he screwed the top on the flask and put it quickly back inside the Bible. "You just a while ago said you didn't believe in nothing. I thought you was some girl!"

Her face was almost purple. "You're a Christian!" she hissed. "You're a fine Christian! You're just like them all — say one thing and do another. You're a perfect Christian, you're . . ."

The boy's mouth was set angrily. "I hope you don't think," he said in a lofty indignant tone, "that I believe in that crap! I may sell Bibles but I know which end is up and I wasn't born yesterday and I know where I'm going!"

"Give me my leg!" she screeched. He jumped up so quickly that she barely saw him sweep the cards and the blue box into the Bible and throw the Bible into the valise. She saw him grab the leg and then she saw it for an instant slanted forlornly across the inside of the suitcase with a Bible at either side of its opposite ends. He slammed the lid shut and snatched up the valise and swung it down the hole and then stepped through himself.

When all of him had passed but his head, he turned and regarded her with a look that no longer had any admiration in it. "I've gotten a lot of interesting things," he said. "One time I got a woman's glass eye this way. And you needn't to think you'll catch me because Pointer ain't really my name. I use a different name at every house I call at and don't stay nowhere long. And I'll tell you another thing, Hulga," he said, using the name as if he didn't think much of it, "you ain't so smart. I been believing in nothing ever since I was born!" and then the toast-colored hat disappeared down the hole and the girl was left, sitting on the straw in the dusty sunlight. When she turned her churning face toward the opening, she saw his blue figure struggling successfully over the green speckled lake.

Mrs. Hopewell and Mrs. Freeman, who were in the back pasture, digging up onions, saw him emerge a little later from the woods and head across the meadow toward the highway. "Why, that looks like that nice dull young man that tried to sell me a Bible yesterday," Mrs. Hopewell said, squinting. "He must have been selling them to the Negroes back in there. He was so simple," she said, "but I guess the world would be better off if we were all that simple."

Mrs. Freeman's gaze drove forward and just touched him before he disappeared under the hill. Then she returned her attention to the evil-smelling onion shoot she was lifting from the ground. "Some can't be that simple," she said. "I know I never could."

A Good Man Is Hard to Find 1955

The dragon is by the side of the road, watching those who pass. Beware lest he devour you. We go to the Father of Souls, but it is necessary to pass by the dragon.

—St. Cyril of Jerusalem

The grandmother didn't want to go to Florida. She wanted to visit some of her connections in east Tennessee and she was seizing at every chance to change Bailey's mind. Bailey was the son she lived with, her only boy. He was sitting on the edge of his chair at the table, bent over the orange sports section of the *Journal*. "Now look here, Bailey," she said, "see here, read this," and she stood with one hand on her thin hip and the other rattling the newspaper at his bald head. "Here this fellow that calls himself The Misfit is aloose from the Federal Pen and headed toward Florida and you read here what it says he did to these people. Just you read it. I wouldn't take my children in any direction with a criminal like that aloose in it. I couldn't answer to my conscience if I did."

Bailey didn't look up from his reading so she wheeled around then and faced the children's mother, a young woman in slacks, whose face was as broad and innocent as a cabbage and was tied around with a green headkerchief that had two points on the top like a rabbit's ears. She was sitting on the sofa, feeding the baby his apricots out of a jar. "The children have been to Florida before," the old lady said. "You all ought to take them somewhere else for a change so they would see different parts of the world and be broad. They never have been to east Tennessee."

The children's mother didn't seem to hear her but the eight-year-old boy, John Wesley, a stocky child with glasses, said, "If you don't want to go to Florida, why dontcha stay at home?" He and the little girl, June Star, were reading the funny papers on the floor.

"She wouldn't stay at home to be queen for a day," June Star said without raising her yellow head.

"Yes and what would you do if this fellow, The Misfit, caught you?" the grandmother asked.

"I'd smack his face," John Wesley said.

"She wouldn't stay at home for a million bucks," June Star said. "Afraid she'd miss something. She has to go everywhere we go."

"All right, Miss," the grandmother said. "Just remember that the next time you want me to curl your hair."

June Star said her hair was naturally curly.

The next morning the grandmother was the first one in the car, ready to go. She had her big black valise that looked like the head of a hippopotamus in one corner, and underneath it she was hiding a basket with Pitty Sing, the cat, in it. She didn't intend for the cat to be left alone in the house for three days because he would miss her too much and she was afraid he might brush against one of the gas burners and accidentally asphyxiate himself. Her son, Bailey, didn't like to arrive at a motel with a cat.

She sat in the middle of the back seat with John Wesley and June Star on either side of her. Bailey and the children's mother and the baby sat in front and they left Atlanta at eight forty-five with the mileage on the car at 55890. The grandmother wrote this down because she thought it would be interesting to say how many miles they had been when they got back. It took them twenty minutes to reach the outskirts of the city.

The old lady settled herself comfortably, removing her white cotton gloves and putting them up with her purse on the shelf in front of the back window. The children's mother still had on slacks and still had her head tied up in a green kerchief, but the grandmother had on a navy blue straw sailor hat with a bunch of white violets on the brim and a navy blue dress with a small white dot in the print. Her collars and cuffs were white organdy trimmed with lace and at her neckline she had pinned a purple spray of cloth violets containing a sachet. In case of an accident, anyone seeing her dead on the highway would know at once that she was a lady.

She said she thought it was going to be a good day for driving, neither too hot nor too cold, and she cautioned Bailey that the speed limit was fifty-five miles an hour and that the patrolmen hid themselves behind billboards and small clumps of trees and sped out after you before you had a chance to slow down. She pointed out interesting details of the scenery: Stone Mountain; the blue granite that in some places came up to both sides of the highway; the brilliant red clay banks slightly streaked with purple; and the various crops that made rows of green lace-work on the ground. The trees were full of silver-white sunlight and the meanest of them sparkled. The children were reading comic magazines and their mother had gone back to sleep.

"Let's go through Georgia fast so we won't have to look at it much," John Wesley said.

"If I were a little boy," said the grandmother, "I wouldn't talk about my native state that way. Tennessee has the mountains and Georgia has the hills."

"Tennessee is just a hillbilly dumping ground," John Wesley said, "and Georgia is a lousy state too."

"You said it," June Star said.

"In my time," said the grandmother, folding her thin veined fingers, "children were more respectful of their native states and their parents and everything else. People did right then. Oh look at the cute little pickaninny!" she said and pointed to a Negro child standing in the door of a shack. "Wouldn't that make a picture, now?" she asked and they all turned and looked at the little Negro out of the back window. He waved.

"He didn't have any britches on," June Star said.

"He probably didn't have any," the grandmother explained. "Little niggers in the country don't have things like we do. If I could paint, I'd paint that picture," she said.

The children exchanged comic books.

The grandmother offered to hold the baby and the children's mother passed him over the front seat to her. She set him on her knee and bounced him and told him about the things they were passing. She rolled her eyes and screwed up her mouth and stuck her leathery thin face into his smooth bland one. Occasionally he gave her a faraway smile. They passed a large cotton field with five or six graves fenced in the middle of it, like a small island. "Look at the graveyard!" the grandmother said, pointing it out. "That was the old family burying ground. That belonged to the plantation."

"Where's the plantation?" John Wesley asked.

"Gone with the Wind," said the grandmother. "Ha. Ha."

When the children finished all the comic books they had brought, they opened the lunch and ate it. The grandmother ate a peanut butter sandwich and an olive and would not let the children throw the box and the paper napkins out the window. When there was nothing else to do they played a game by choosing a cloud and making the other two guess what shape it suggested. John Wesley took one the shape of a cow and June Star guessed a cow and John Wesley said, no, an automobile, and June Star said he didn't play fair, and they began to slap each other over the grandmother.

The grandmother said she would tell them a story if they would keep quiet. When she told a story, she rolled her eyes and waved her head and was very dramatic. She said once when she was a maiden lady she had been courted by a Mr. Edgar Atkins Teagarden from Jasper, Georgia. She said he was a very good-looking man and a gentleman and that he brought her a watermelon every Saturday afternoon with his initials cut in it, E. A. T. Well, one Saturday, she said, Mr. Teagarden brought the watermelon and there was nobody at home and he left it on the front porch and returned in his buggy to Jasper, but she never got the watermelon, she said, because a nigger boy ate it when he saw the initials, E. A. T.! This story tickled John Wesley's funny bone and he giggled and giggled but June Star didn't think it was any good. She said she wouldn't marry a man that just brought her a watermelon on Saturday. The grandmother said she would have done well to marry Mr. Teagarden because he was a gentleman and had bought Coca-Cola stock when it first came out and that he had died only a few years ago, a very wealthy man.

They stopped at The Tower for barbecued sandwiches. The Tower was a part stucco and part wood filling station and dance hall set in a clearing outside of Timothy. A fat man named Red Sammy Butts ran it and there were signs stuck here and there on the building and for miles up and down the highway saying, TRY RED SAMMY'S FAMOUS BARBECUE. NONE LIKE FAMOUS RED SAMMY'S! RED SAM! THE FAT BOY WITH THE HAPPY LAUGH. A VETERAN! RED SAMMY'S YOUR MAN!

Red Sammy was lying on the bare ground outside The Tower with his head under a truck while a gray monkey about a foot high, chained to a small chinaberry tree, chattered nearby. The monkey sprang back into the tree and got on the highest limb as soon as he saw the children jump out of the car and run toward him.

Inside, The Tower was a long dark room with a counter at one end and tables at the other and dancing space in the middle. They all sat down at a board table next to the nickelodeon and Red Sam's wife, a tall burnt-brown woman with hair and eyes lighter than her skin, came and took their order. The children's mother put a dime in the machine and played "The Tennessee Waltz," and the grandmother said that tune always made her want to dance. She asked Bailey if he would like to dance but he only glared at her. He didn't have a naturally sunny disposition like she did and trips made him nervous. The grandmother's brown eyes were very bright. She swayed her head from side to side and pretended she was dancing in her chair. June Star said play something she could tap to so the children's mother put in another dime and played a fast number and June Star stepped out onto the dance floor and did her tap routine.

"Ain't she cute?" Red Sam's wife said, leaning over the counter. "Would you like to come be my little girl?"

"No I certainly wouldn't," June Star said. "I wouldn't live in a broken-down place like this for a million bucks!" and she ran back to the table.

"Ain't she cute?" the woman repeated, stretching her mouth politely.

"Aren't you ashamed?" hissed the grandmother.

Red Sam came in and told his wife to quit lounging on the counter and hurry up with these people's order. His khaki trousers reached just to his hip bones and his stomach hung over them like a sack of meal swaying under his shirt. He came over and sat down at a table nearby and let out a combination sigh and yodel. "You can't win," he said. "You can't win," and he wiped his sweating red face off with a gray handkerchief. "These days you don't know who to trust," he said. "Ain't that the truth?"

"People are certainly not nice like they used to be," said the grandmother.

"Two fellers come in here last week," Red Sammy said, "driving a Chrysler. It was a old beat-up car but it was a good one and these boys looked all right to me. Said they worked at the mill and you know I let them fellers charge the gas they bought? Now why did I do that?"

"Because you're a good man!" the grandmother said at once.

"Yes'm, I suppose so," Red Sam said as if he were struck with this answer.

His wife brought the orders, carrying the five plates all at once without a tray, two in each hand and one balanced on her arm. "It isn't a soul in this green world of God's that you can trust," she said. "And I don't count nobody out of that, not nobody," she repeated, looking at Red Sammy.

"Did you read about that criminal, The Misfit, that's escaped?" asked the grandmother.

"I wouldn't be a bit surprised if he didn't attack this place right here," said the woman. "If he hears about it being here, I wouldn't be none surprised to see him. If he hears it's two cent in the cash register, I wouldn't be a tall surprised if he. . . ."

"That'll do," Red Sam said. "Go bring these people their Co'-Colas," and the woman went off to get the rest of the order.

"A good man is hard to find," Red Sammy said. "Everything is getting terrible. I remember the day you could go off and leave your screen door unlatched. Not no more."

He and the grandmother discussed better times. The old lady said that in her opinion Europe was entirely to blame for the way things were now. She said the way Europe acted you would think we were made of money and Red Sam said it was no use talking about it, she was exactly right. The children ran outside into the white sunlight and looked at the monkey in the lacy chinaberry tree. He was busy catching fleas on himself and biting each one carefully between his teeth as if it were a delicacy.

They drove off again into the hot afternoon. The grandmother took cat naps and woke up every few minutes with her own snoring. Outside of Toombsboro she woke up and recalled an old plantation that she had visited in this neighborhood once when she was a young lady. She said the house had six white columns across the front and that there was an avenue of oaks leading up to it and two little wooden trellis arbors on either side in front where you sat down with your suitor after a stroll in the garden. She recalled exactly which road to turn off to get to it. She knew that Bailey would not be willing to lose any time looking at an old house, but the more she talked about it, the more she wanted to see it once again and find out if the little twin arbors were still standing. "There was a secret panel in this house," she said craftily, not telling the truth but wishing that she were, "and the story went that all the family silver was hidden in it when Sherman came through but it was never found. . . ."

"Hey!" John Wesley said. "Let's go see it! We'll find it! We'll poke all the woodwork and find it! Who lives there? Where do you turn off at? Hey Pop, can't we turn off there?"

"We never have seen a house with a secret panel!" June Star shrieked. "Let's go to the house with the secret panel! Hey Pop, can't we go see the house with the secret panel!"

"It's not far from here, I know," the grandmother said. "It won't take over twenty minutes."

Bailey was looking straight ahead. His jaw was as rigid as a horseshoe. "No," he said.

The children began to yell and scream that they wanted to see the house with the secret panel. John Wesley kicked the back of the front seat and June Star hung over her mother's shoulder and whined desperately into her ear that they never had any fun even on their vacation, that they could never do what THEY wanted to do. The baby began to scream and John Wesley kicked the back of the seat so hard that his father could feel the blows in his kidney.

"All right!" he shouted and drew the car to a stop at the side of the road. "Will you all shut up? Will you all just shut up for one second? If you don't shut up, we won't go anywhere."

"It would be very educational for them," the grandmother murmured.

"All right," Bailey said, "but get this: this is the only time we're going to stop for anything like this. This is the one and only time."

"The dirt road that you have to turn down is about a mile back," the grandmother directed. "I marked it when we passed."

"A dirt road," Bailey groaned.

After they had turned around and were headed toward the dirt road, the grandmother recalled other points about the house, the beautiful glass over the front doorway and the candle-lamp in the hall. John Wesley said that the secret panel was probably in the fireplace.

"You can't go inside this house," Bailey said. "You don't know who lives there."

"While you all talk to the people in front, I'll run around behind and get in a window," John Wesley suggested.

"We'll all stay in the car," his mother said.

They turned onto the dirt road and the car raced roughly along in a swirl of pink dust. The grandmother recalled the times when there were no paved roads and thirty miles was a day's journey. The dirt road was hilly and there were sudden washes in it and sharp curves on dangerous embankments. All at once they would be on a hill, looking down over the blue tops of trees for miles around, then the next minute, they would be in a red depression with the dust-coated trees looking down on them.

"This place had better turn up in a minute," Bailey said, "or I'm going to turn around."

The road looked as if no one had traveled on it for months.

"It's not much farther," the grandmother said and just as she said it, a horrible thought came to her. The thought was so embarrassing that she turned red in the face and her eyes dilated and her feet jumped up, upsetting her valise in the corner. The instant the valise moved, the newspaper top she had over the basket under it rose with a snarl and Pitty Sing, the cat, sprang onto Bailey's shoulder.

The children were thrown to the floor and their mother, clutching the baby, was thrown out the door onto the ground, the old lady was thrown into the front seat. The car turned over once and landed right-side-up in a gulch off the side of the road. Bailey remained in the driver's seat with the cat gray-striped with a broad white face and an orange nose clinging to his neck like a caterpillar.

As soon as the children saw they could move their arms and legs, they scrambled out of the car, shouting, "We've had an ACCIDENT!" The grandmother was curled up under the dashboard, hoping she was injured so that Bailey's wrath would not come down on her all at once. The horrible thought she had before the accident was that the house she had remembered so vividly was not in Georgia but in Tennessee.

Bailey removed the cat from his neck with both hands and flung it out the window against the side of a pine tree. Then he got out of the car and started looking for the children's mother. She was sitting against the side of the red gutted ditch, holding the screaming baby, but she only had a cut down her face and a broken shoulder. "We've had an ACCIDENT!" the children screamed in a frenzy of delight.

"But nobody's killed," June Star said with disappointment as the grandmother limped out of the car, her hat still pinned to her head but the broken front brim standing up at a jaunty angle and the violet spray hanging off the side. They all sat down in the ditch, except the children, to recover from the shock. They were all shaking.

"Maybe a car will come along," said the children's mother hoarsely.

"I believe I have injured an organ," said the grandmother, pressing her side, but no one answered her. Bailey's teeth were clattering. He had on a yellow sport shirt with bright blue parrots designed in it and his face was as yellow as the shirt. The grandmother decided that she would not mention that the house was in Tennessee.

The road was about ten feet above and they could only see the tops of the trees on the other side of it. Behind the ditch they were sitting in there were more woods, tall and dark and deep. In a few minutes they saw a car some distance away on top of a hill, coming slowly as if the occupants were watching them. The grandmother stood up and waved both arms dramatically to attract their attention. The car continued to come on slowly, disappeared around a bend and appeared again, moving even slower, on top of the hill they had gone over. It was a big black battered hearse-like automobile. There were three men in it.

It came to a stop just over them and for some minutes, the driver looked down with a steady expressionless gaze to where they were sitting, and didn't speak. Then he turned his head and muttered something to the other two and they got out. One was a fat boy in black trousers and a red sweat shirt with a silver stallion embossed on the front of it. He moved around on the right side of them and stood staring, his mouth partly open in a kind of loose grin. The other had on khaki pants and a blue striped coat and a gray hat pulled very low, hiding most of his face. He came around slowly on the left side. Neither spoke.

The driver got out of the car and stood by the side of it, looking down at them. He was an older man than the other two. His hair was just beginning to gray and he wore silver-rimmed spectacles that gave him a scholarly look. He had a long creased face and didn't have on any shirt or undershirt. He had on blue jeans that were too tight for him and was holding a black hat and a gun. The two boys also had guns.

"We've had an ACCIDENT!" the children screamed.

The grandmother had the peculiar feeling that the bespectacled man was someone she knew. His face was as familiar to her as if she had known him all her life but she could not recall who he was. He moved away from the car and began to come down the embankment, placing his feet carefully so that he wouldn't slip. He had on tan and white shoes and no socks, and his ankles were red and thin. "Good afternoon," he said. "I see you all had you a little spill."

"We turned over twice!" said the grandmother.

"Oncet," he corrected. "We seen it happen. Try their car and see will it run, Hiram," he said quietly to the boy with the gray hat.

"What you got that gun for?" John Wesley asked. "Whatcha gonna do with that gun?"

"Lady," the man said to the children's mother, "would you mind calling them children to sit down by you? Children make me nervous. I want all you all to sit down right together there where you're at."

"What are you telling US what to do for?" June Star asked.

Behind them the line of woods gaped like a dark open mouth. "Come here," said the mother.

"Look here now," Bailey said suddenly, "we're in a predicament! We're in . . ."

The grandmother shrieked. She scrambled to her feet and stood staring. "You're The Misfit!" she said. "I recognized you at once!"

"Yes'm," the man said, smiling slightly as if he were pleased in spite of himself to be known, "but it would have been better for all of you, lady, if you hadn't of reckernized me."

Bailey turned his head sharply and said something to his mother that shocked even the children. The old lady began to cry and The Misfit reddened.

"Lady," he said, "don't you get upset. Sometimes a man says things he don't mean. I don't reckon he meant to talk to you thataway."

"You wouldn't shoot a lady, would you?" the grandmother said and removed a clean handkerchief from her cuff and began to slap at her eyes with it.

The Misfit pointed the toe of his shoe into the ground and made a little hole and then covered it up again. "I would hate to have to," he said.

"Listen," the grandmother almost screamed, "I know you're a good man. You don't look a bit like you have common blood. I know you must come from nice people!"

"Yes mam," he said, "finest people in the world." When he smiled he showed a row of strong white teeth. "God never made a finer woman than my mother and my daddy's heart was pure gold," he said. The boy with the red sweat shirt had come around behind them and was standing with his gun at his hip. The Misfit squatted down on the ground. "Watch them children, Bobby Lee," he said. "You know they make me nervous." He looked at the six of them huddled together in front of him and he seemed to be embarrassed as if he couldn't think of anything to say. "Ain't a cloud in the sky," he remarked, looking up at it. "Don't see no sun but don't see no cloud neither."

"Yes, it's a beautiful day," said the grandmother. "Listen," she said, "you shouldn't call yourself The Misfit because I know you're a good man at heart. I can just look at you and tell."

"Hush!" Bailey yelled. "Hush! Everybody shut up and let me handle this!" He was squatting in the position of a runner about to sprint forward but he didn't move.

"I pre-chate that, lady," The Misfit said and drew a little circle in the ground with the butt of his gun.

"It'll take a half a hour to fix this here car," Hiram called, looking over the raised hood of it.

"Well, first you and Bobby Lee get him and that little boy to step over yonder with you," The Misfit said, pointing to Bailey and John Wesley. "The boys want to ast you something," he said to Bailey. "Would you mind stepping back in them woods there with them?"

"Listen," Bailey began, "we're in a terrible predicament! Nobody realizes what this is," and his voice cracked. His eyes were as blue and intense as the parrots in his shirt and he remained perfectly still.

The grandmother reached up to adjust her hat brim as if she were going to the woods with him but it came off in her hand. She stood staring at it and after a second she let it fall to the ground. Hiram pulled Bailey up by the arm as if he were assisting an old man. John Wesley caught hold of his father's hand and Bobby Lee followed. They went off toward the woods and just as they reached the dark edge, Bailey turned and supporting himself against a gray naked pine trunk, he shouted, "I'll be back in a minute, Mamma, wait on me!"

"Come back this instant!" his mother shrilled but they all disappeared into the woods.

"Bailey Boy!" the grandmother called in a tragic voice but she found she was looking at The Misfit squatting on the ground in front of her. "I just know you're a good man," she said desperately. "You're not a bit common!"

"Nome, I ain't a good man," The Misfit said after a second as if he had considered her statement carefully, "but I ain't the worst in the world neither. My daddy said I was a different breed of dog from my brothers and sisters. 'You know,' Daddy said, 'it's some that can live their whole life out without asking about it and it's others has to know why it is, and this boy is one of the latters. He's going to be into everything!' " He put on his black hat and looked up suddenly and then away deep into the woods as if he were embarrassed again. "I'm sorry I don't have on a shirt before you ladies," he said, hunching his shoulders slightly. "We buried our clothes that we had on when we escaped and we're just making do until we can get better. We borrowed these from some folks we met," he explained.

"That's perfectly all right," the grandmother said. "Maybe Bailey has an extra shirt in his suitcase."

"I'll look and see terrectly," The Misfit said.

"Where are they taking him?" the children's mother screamed.

"Daddy was a card himself," The Misfit said. "You couldn't put anything over on him. He never got in trouble with the Authorities though. Just had the knack of handling them."

"You could be honest too if you'd only try," said the grandmother. "Think how wonderful it would be to settle down and live a comfortable life and not have to think about somebody chasing you all the time."

The Misfit kept scratching in the ground with the butt of his gun as if he were thinking about it. "Yes'm, somebody is always after you," he murmured.

The grandmother noticed how thin his shoulder blades were just behind his hat because she was standing up looking down at him. "Do you ever pray?" she asked.

He shook his head. All she saw was the black hat wiggle between his shoulder blades. "Nome," he said.

There was a pistol shot from the woods, followed closely by another. Then silence. The old lady's head jerked around. She could hear the wind move through the tree tops like a long satisfied insuck of breath. "Bailey Boy!" she called.

"I was a gospel singer for a while," The Misfit said. "I been most everything. Been in the arm service, both land and sea, at home and abroad, been twict married, been an undertaker, been with the railroads, plowed Mother Earth, been in a tornado, seen a man burnt alive oncet," and he looked up at the children's mother and the little girl who were sitting close together, their faces white and their eyes glassy; "I even seen a woman flogged," he said.

"Pray, pray," the grandmother began, "pray, pray. . . ."

"I never was a bad boy that I remember of," The Misfit said in an almost dreamy voice, "but somewheres along the line I done something wrong and got sent to the penitentiary. I was buried alive," and he looked up and held her attention to him by a steady stare.

"That's when you should have started to pray," she said. "What did you do to get sent to the penitentiary, that first time?"

"Turn to the right, it was a wall," The Misfit said, looking up again at the cloudless sky. "Turn to the left, it was a wall. Look up it was a ceiling, look down it was a floor. I forgot what I done, lady. I set there and set there, trying to remember what it was I done and I ain't recalled it to this day. Oncet in a while, I would think it was coming to me, but it never come."

"Maybe they put you in by mistake," the old lady said vaguely.

"Nome," he said. "It wasn't no mistake. They had the papers on me."

"You must have stolen something," she said.

The Misfit sneered slightly. "Nobody had nothing I wanted," he said. "It was a head-doctor at the penitentiary said what I had done was kill my daddy but I known that for a lie. My daddy died in nineteen ought nineteen of the epidemic flu and I never had a thing to do with it. He was buried in the Mount Hopewell Baptist churchyard and you can see for yourself."

"If you would pray," the old lady said, "Jesus would help you."

"That's right," The Misfit said.

"Well then, why don't you pray?" she asked trembling with delight suddenly.

"I don't want no hep," he said. "I'm doing all right by myself."

Bobby Lee and Hiram came ambling back from the woods. Bobby Lee was dragging a yellow shirt with bright blue parrots in it.

"Throw me that shirt, Bobby Lee," The Misfit said. The shirt came flying at him and landed on his shoulder and he put it on. The grandmother couldn't name what the shirt reminded her of. "No, lady," The Misfit said while he was buttoning it up, "I found out the crime don't matter. You can do one thing or you can do another, kill a man or take a tire off his car, because sooner or later you're going to forget what it was you done and just be punished for it."

The children's mother had begun to make heaving noises as if she couldn't get her breath. "Lady," he asked, "would you and that little girl like to step off yonder with Bobby Lee and Hiram and join your husband?"

"Yes, thank you," the mother said faintly. Her left arm dangled helplessly and she was holding the baby, who had gone to sleep, in the other. "Hep that lady up, Hiram," The Misfit said as she struggled to climb out of the ditch, "and Bobby Lee, you hold onto that little girl's hand."

"I don't want to hold hands with him," June Star said. "He reminds me of a pig."

The fat boy blushed and laughed and caught her by the arm and pulled her off into the woods after Hiram and her mother.

Alone with The Misfit, the grandmother found that she had lost her voice. There was not a cloud in the sky nor any sun. There was nothing around her but woods. She wanted to tell him that he must pray. She opened and closed her mouth several times before anything came out. Finally she found herself saying, "Jesus, Jesus," meaning, Jesus will help you, but the way she was saying it, it sounded as if she might be cursing.

"Yes'm," The Misfit said as if he agreed. "Jesus thrown everything off balance. It was the same case with Him as with me except He hadn't committed any crime and they could prove I had committed one because they had the papers on me. Of course," he said, "they never shown me my papers. That's why I sign myself now. I said long ago, you get your signature and sign everything you do and keep a copy of it. Then you'll know what you done and you can hold up the crime to the punishment and see do they match and in the end you'll have something to prove you ain't been treated right. I call myself The Misfit," he said, "because I can't make what all I done wrong fit what all I gone through in punishment."

There was a piercing scream from the woods, followed closely by a pistol report. "Does it seem right to you, lady, that one is punished a heap and another ain't punished at all?"

"Jesus!" the old lady cried. "You've got good blood! I know you wouldn't shoot a lady! I know you come from nice people! Pray! Jesus, you ought not to shoot a lady. I'll give you all the money I've got!"

"Lady," The Misfit said, looking beyond her far into the woods, "there never was a body that give the undertaker a tip."

There were two more pistol reports and the grandmother raised her head like a parched old turkey hen crying for water and called, "Bailey Boy, Bailey Boy!" as if her heart would break.

"Jesus was the only One that ever raised the dead," The Misfit continued, "and He shouldn't have done it. He thrown everything off balance. If He did what He said, then it's nothing for you to do but throw away everything and follow Him, and if He didn't, then it's nothing for you to do but enjoy the few minutes you got left the best you can by killing somebody or burning down his house or doing some other meanness to him. No pleasure but meanness," he said and his voice had become almost a snarl.

"Maybe He didn't raise the dead," the old lady mumbled, not knowing what she was saying and feeling so dizzy that she sank down in the ditch with her legs twisted under her.

"I wasn't there so I can't say He didn't," The Misfit said. "I wisht I had of been there," he said, hitting the ground with his fist. "It ain't right I wasn't there because if I had of been there I would of known. Listen lady," he said in a high voice, "if I had of been there I would of known and I wouldn't be like I am now." His voice seemed about to crack and the grandmother's head cleared for an instant. She saw the man's face twisted close to her own as if he were going to cry and she murmured, "Why you're one of my babies. You're one of my own children!" She reached out and touched him on the shoulder. The Misfit sprang back as if a snake had bitten him and shot her three times through the chest. Then he put his gun down on the ground and took off his glasses and began to clean them.

Hiram and Bobby Lee returned from the woods and stood over the ditch, looking down at the grandmother who half sat and half lay in a puddle of blood with her legs crossed under her like a child's and her face smiling up at the cloudless sky.

Without his glasses, The Misfit's eyes were red-rimmed and pale and defenseless-looking. "Take her off and throw her where you thrown the others," he said, picking up the cat that was rubbing itself against his leg.

"She was a talker, wasn't she?" Bobby Lee said, sliding down the ditch with a yodel.

"She would of been a good woman," The Misfit said, "if it had been somebody there to shoot her every minute of her life."

"Some fun!" Bobby Lee said.

"Shut up, Bobby Lee," The Misfit said. "It's no real pleasure in life."

TILLIE OLSEN

Tillie Olsen (1913–2007) was born in Omaha, Nebraska, the daughter of political refugees from the Russian Czarist repression after the revolution of 1905. Her father was a farmer, packing-house worker, house painter, and jack-of-all-trades; her mother was a factory worker. At the age of sixteen Olsen dropped out of high school to help support her family during the Depression. She was a member of the Young Communist League, involved in the Warehouse Union's labor disputes in Kansas City. At age nineteen she began her first novel, *Yonnondio.* Four chapters of this book about a poverty-stricken working-class family were completed in the next four years, during which time she married, gave birth to her first child, and was left with the baby by her husband because, as she later wrote in her autobiographical story "I Stand Here Ironing," he "could no longer endure sharing want" with them. In 1934 a section of the first chapter of her novel was published in *Partisan Review,* but she abandoned the unfinished book in 1937. The year before she had married Jack Olsen, with whom she had three more children; raising the children and working for political causes took up all her time. In the 1940s she was a factory worker; in the 1950s, a secretary. It was not until 1953, when her youngest daughter started school, that she was able to begin writing again.

That year Olsen enrolled in a class in fiction writing at San Francisco State College. She was awarded a Stanford University creative writing fellowship for 1955 and 1956. During the 1950s she wrote the four stories collected in *Tell Me a Riddle,* which established her reputation when the book was published as a paperback in 1961. Identified as a champion of the reemerging feminist movement, Olsen wrote a biographical introduction to Rebecca Harding Davis's nineteenth-century proletarian story, *Life in the Iron Mills,* published by the Feminist Press in 1972. Two years later, after several grants and creative writing fellowships, she published the still-unfinished *Yonnondio. Silences,* a collection of essays exploring the different circumstances that obstruct or silence literary creation, appeared in 1978.

As the Canadian author Margaret Atwood has understood about Olsen,

> Few writers have gained such wide respect on such a small body of published work. . . . Among women writers in the United States, "respect" is too pale a word: "reverence" is more like it. This is presumably because women writers, even more than their male counterparts, recognize what a heroic feat it is to have held down a job, raised four children, and still somehow managed to become and to remain a writer.

A radical feminist, Olsen has said that she felt no personal guilt as a single parent over her daughter's predicament, as described in her confessional narrative "I Stand Here Ironing," since "guilt is a word used far too sloppily, to cover up harmful situations in society that must be changed." Her four stories have appeared in more than fifty anthologies and have been translated into many languages. In 1994 she received the Rea Award for the Short Story, a literary prize that honors a living American author who has made "a significant contribution to the short story as an art form."

WEB Research Tillie Olsen at bedfordstmartins.com/rewritinglit.

I Stand Here Ironing 1961

I stand here ironing, and what you asked me moves tormented back and forth with the iron.

"I wish you would manage the time to come in and talk with me about your daughter. I'm sure you can help me understand her. She's a youngster who needs help and whom I'm deeply interested in helping."

"Who needs help." . . . Even if I came, what good would it do? You think because I am her mother I have a key, or that in some way you could use me as a key? She has lived for nineteen years. There is all that life that has happened outside of me, beyond me.

And when is there time to remember, to sift, to weigh, to estimate, to total? I will start and there will be an interruption and I will have to gather it all together again. Or I will become engulfed with all I did or did not do, with what should have been and what cannot be helped.

She was a beautiful baby. The first and only one of our five that was beautiful at birth. You do not guess how new and uneasy her tenancy in her now-loveliness. You did not know her all those years she was thought homely, or see her poring over her baby pictures, making me tell her over and over how beautiful she had been—and would be, I would tell her—and was now, to the seeing eye. But the seeing eyes were few or nonexistent. Including mine.

I nursed her. They feel that's important nowadays, I nursed all the children, but with her, with all the fierce rigidity of first motherhood, I did like the books then said. Though her cries battered me to trembling and my breasts ached with swollenness, I waited till the clock decreed.

Why do I put that first? I do not even know if it matters, or if it explains anything.

She was a beautiful baby. She blew shining bubbles of sound. She loved motion, loved light, loved color and music and textures. She would lie on the floor in her blue overalls patting the surface so hard in ecstasy her hands and feet would blur. She was a miracle to me, but when she was eight months old I had to leave her daytimes with the woman downstairs to whom she was no miracle at all, for I worked or looked for work and for Emily's father, who "could no longer endure" (he wrote in his good-bye note) "sharing want with us."

I was nineteen. It was the pre-relief, pre-WPA world of the depression. I would start running as soon as I got off the streetcar, running up the stairs, the place smelling sour, and awake or asleep to startle awake, when she saw me she would break into a clogged weeping that could not be comforted, a weeping I can hear yet.

After a while I found a job hashing at night so I could be with her days, and it was better. But it came to where I had to bring her to his family and leave her.

It took a long time to raise the money for her fare back. Then she got chicken pox and I had to wait longer. When she finally came, I hardly knew her, walking quick and nervous like her father, looking like her father, thin, and dressed in a shoddy red that yellowed her skin and glared at the pockmarks. All the baby loveliness gone.

She was two. Old enough for nursery school they said, and I did not know then what I know now—the fatigue of the long day, and the lacerations of group life in the kinds of nurseries that are only parking places for children.

Except that it would have made no difference if I had known. It was the only place there was. It was the only way we could be together, the only way I could hold a job.

And even without knowing, I knew. I knew the teacher that was evil because all these years it has curdled into my memory, the little boy hunched in the corner, her rasp, "why aren't you outside, because Alvin hits you? that's no reason, go out, scaredy." I knew Emily hated it even if she did not clutch and implore "don't go Mommy" like the other children, mornings.

She always had a reason why we should stay home. Momma, you look sick. Momma, I feel sick. Momma, the teachers aren't there today, they're sick. Momma, we can't go, there was a fire there last night. Momma, it's a holiday today, no school, they told me.

But never a direct protest, never rebellion. I think of our others in their three-, four-year-oldness—the explosions, the tempers, the denunciations, the demands—and I feel suddenly ill. I put the iron down. What in me demanded that goodness in her? And what was the cost, the cost to her of such goodness?

The old man living in the back once said in his gentle way: "You should smile at Emily more when you look at her." What *was* in my face when I looked at her? I loved her. There were all the acts of love.

It was only with the others I remembered what he said, and it was the face of joy, and not of care or tightness or worry I turned to them—too late for Emily. She does not smile easily, let alone almost always as her brothers and sisters do. Her face is closed and sombre, but when she wants, how fluid. You must have seen it in her pantomimes, you spoke of her rare gift for comedy on the stage that rouses laughter out of the audience so dear they applaud and applaud and do not want to let her go.

Where does it come from, that comedy? There was none of it in her when she came back to me that second time, after I had to send her away again. She had a new daddy now to learn to love, and I think perhaps it was a better time.

Except when we left her alone nights, telling ourselves she was old enough.

"Can't you go some other time, Mommy, like tomorrow?" she would ask. "Will it be just a little while you'll be gone? Do you promise?"

The time we came back, the front door open, the clock on the floor in the hall. She rigid awake. "It wasn't just a little while. I didn't cry. Three times I called you, just three times, and then I ran downstairs to open the door so you could come faster. The clock talked loud. I threw it away, it scared me what it talked."

She said the clock talked loud again that night I went to the hospital to have Susan. She was delirious with the fever that comes before red measles, but she was fully conscious all the week I was gone and the week after we were home when she could not come near the new baby or me.

She did not get well. She stayed skeleton thin, not wanting to eat, and night after night she had nightmares. She would call for me, and I would rouse from exhaustion to sleepily call back: "You're all right, darling, go to sleep, it's just a dream," and if she still called, in a sterner voice, "now go to sleep, Emily, there's nothing to hurt you." Twice, only twice, when I had to get up for Susan anyhow, I went in to sit with her.

Now when it is too late (as if she would let me hold her and comfort her like I do the others) I get up and go to her at once at her moan or restless stirring. "Are you awake, Emily? Can I get you something?" And the answer is always the same: "No, I'm all right, go back to sleep, Mother."

They persuaded me at the clinic to send her away to a convalescent home in the country where "she can have the kind of food and care you can't manage for her, and you'll be free to concentrate on the new baby." They still send children to that place. I see pictures on the society page of sleek young women planning affairs to raise money for it, or dancing at the affairs, or decorating Easter eggs or filling Christmas stockings for the children.

They never have a picture of the children so I do not know if the girls still wear those gigantic red bows and the ravaged looks on the every other Sunday when parents can come to visit "unless otherwise notified"—as we were notified the first six weeks.

Oh it is a handsome place, green lawns and tall trees and fluted flower beds. High up on the balconies of each cottage the children stand, the girls in their red bows and white dresses, the boys in white suits and giant red ties. The parents stand below shrieking up to be heard and the children shriek down to be heard, and between them the invisible wall "Not To Be Contaminated by Parental Germs or Physical Affection."

There was a tiny girl who always stood hand in hand with Emily. Her parents never came. One visit she was gone. "They moved her to Rose Cottage," Emily shouted in explanation. "They don't like you to love anybody here."

She wrote once a week, the labored writing of a seven-year-old. "I am fine. How is the baby. If I write my leter nicly I will have a star. Love." There never was a star. We wrote every other day, letters she could never hold or keep but only hear read—once. "We simply do not have room for children to keep any personal possessions," they patiently explained when we pieced one Sunday's shrieking together to plead how much it would mean to Emily, who loved so to keep things, to be allowed to keep her letters and cards.

Each visit she looked frailer. "She isn't eating," they told us.

(They had runny eggs for breakfast or mush with lumps, Emily said later, I'd hold it in my mouth and not swallow. Nothing ever tasted good, just when they had chicken.)

It took us eight months to get her released home, and only the fact that she gained back so little of her seven lost pounds convinced the social worker.

I used to try to hold and love her after she came back, but her body would stay stiff, and after a while she'd push away. She ate little. Food sickened her, and I think much of life too. Oh she had physical lightness and brightness, twinkling by on skates, bouncing like a ball up and down up and down over the jump rope, skimming over the hill; but these were momentary.

She fretted about her appearance, thin and dark and foreign-looking at a time when every little girl was supposed to look or thought she should look a chubby blonde replica of Shirley Temple. The doorbell sometimes rang for her, but no one seemed to come and play in the house or to be a best friend. Maybe because we moved so much.

There was a boy she loved painfully through two school semesters. Months later she told me how she had taken pennies from my purse to buy him candy. "Licorice was his favorite and I brought him some every day, but he still liked Jennifer better'n me. Why, Mommy?" The kind of question for which there is no answer.

School was a worry for her. She was not glib or quick in a world where glibness and quickness were easily confused with ability to learn. To her overworked and exasperated teachers she was an overconscientious "slow learner" who kept trying to catch up and was absent entirely too often.

I let her be absent, though sometimes the illness was imaginary. How different from my now-strictness about attendance with the others. I wasn't working. We had a new baby. I was home anyhow. Sometimes, after Susan grew old enough, I would keep her home from school, too, to have them all together.

Mostly Emily had asthma, and her breathing, harsh and labored, would fill the house with a curiously tranquil sound. I would bring the two old dresser mirrors and her boxes of collections to her bed. She would select beads and single earrings, bottle tops and shells, dried flowers and pebbles, old postcards and scraps, all sorts of oddments; then she and Susan would play Kingdom, setting up landscapes and furniture, peopling them with action.

Those were the only times of peaceful companionship between her and Susan. I have edged away from it, that poisonous feeling between them, that terrible balancing of hurts and needs I had to do between the two, and did so badly, those earlier years.

Oh there were conflicts between the others too, each one human, needing, demanding, hurting, taking—but only between Emily and Susan, no, Emily toward Susan that corroding resentment. It seems so obvious on the surface, yet it is not obvious; Susan, the second child, Susan, golden- and curly-haired and chubby, quick and articulate and assured, everything in appearance and manner Emily was not; Susan, not able to resist Emily's precious things, losing or sometimes clumsily breaking them; Susan telling jokes and riddles to company for applause while Emily sat silent (to say to me later: that was *my* riddle, Mother, I told it to Susan); Susan, who for all the five years' difference in age was just a year behind Emily in developing physically.

I am glad for that slow physical development that widened the difference between her and her contemporaries, though she suffered over it. She was too vulnerable for that terrible world of youthful competition, of preening and parading, of constant measuring of yourself against every other, of envy, "If I had that copper hair," "If I had that skin. . . ." She tormented herself enough about not looking like the others, there was enough of unsureness, the having to be conscious of words before you speak, the constant caring—what are they thinking of me? without having it all magnified by the merciless physical drives.

Ronnie is calling. He is wet and I change him. It is rare there is such a cry now. That time of motherhood is almost behind me when the ear is not one's own but must always be racked and listening for the child cry, the child call. We sit for a while and I hold him, looking out over the city spread in charcoal with its soft aisles of light. "*Shoogily,*" he breathes and curls closer. I carry him back to bed, asleep. *Shoogily.* A funny word, a family word, inherited from Emily, invented by her to say: *comfort.*

In this and other ways she leaves her seal, I say aloud. And startle at my saying it. What do I mean? What did I start to gather together, to try and make coherent? I was at the terrible, growing years. War years. I do not remember them well. I was working, there were four smaller ones now, there was not time for her. She had to help be a mother, and housekeeper, and shopper. She had to get her seal. Mornings of crisis and near hysteria trying to get lunches packed, hair combed, coats and shoes found, everyone to school or Child Care on time, the baby ready for transportation. And always the paper scribbled on by a smaller one, the book looked at by Susan then mislaid, the homework not done. Running out to that huge school where she was one, she was lost, she was a drop; suffering over the unpreparedness, stammering and unsure in her classes.

There was so little time left at night after the kids were bedded down. She would struggle over books, always eating (it was in those years she developed her enormous appetite that is legendary in our family) and I would be ironing, or preparing food for the next day, or writing V-mail to Bill, or tending the baby. Sometimes, to make me laugh, or out of her despair, she would imitate happenings or types at school.

I think I said once: "Why don't you do something like this in the school amateur show?" One morning she phoned me at work, hardly understandable through the weeping: "Mother, I did it. I won, I won; they gave me first prize; they clapped and clapped and wouldn't let me go."

Now suddenly she was Somebody, and as imprisoned in her difference as she had been in anonymity.

She began to be asked to perform at other high schools, even in colleges, then at city and statewide affairs. The first one we went to, I only recognized her that first moment when thin, shy, she almost drowned herself into the curtains. Then: Was this Emily? The control, the command, the convulsing and deadly clowning, the spell, then the roaring, stamping audience, unwilling to let this rare and precious laughter out of their lives.

Afterwards: You ought to do something about her with a gift like that—but without money or knowing how, what does one do? We have left it all to her, and the gift has so often eddied inside, clogged and clotted, as been used and growing.

She is coming. She runs up the stairs two at a time with her light graceful step, and I know she is happy tonight. Whatever it was that occasioned your call did not happen today.

"Aren't you ever going to finish the ironing, Mother? Whistler painted his mother in a rocker. I'd have to paint mine standing over an ironing board." This is one of her communicative nights and she tells me everything and nothing as she fixes herself a plate of food out of the icebox.

She is so lovely. Why did you want me to come in at all? Why were you concerned? She will find her way.

She starts up the stairs to bed. "Don't get me up with the rest in the morning." "But I thought you were having midterms." "Oh, those," she comes back in, kisses me, and says quite lightly, "in a couple of years when we'll all be atom-dead they won't matter a bit."

She has said it before. She *believes* it. But because I have been dredging the past, and all that compounds a human being is so heavy and meaningful in me, I cannot endure it tonight.

I will never total it all. I will never come in to say: She was a child seldom smiled at. Her father left me before she was a year old. I had to work her first six years when there was work, or I sent her home and to his relatives. There were years she had care she hated. She was dark and thin and foreign-looking in a world where the prestige went to blondeness and curly hair and dimples, she was slow where glibness was prized. She was a child of anxious, not proud, love. We were poor and could not afford for her the soil of easy growth. I was a young mother, I was a distracted mother. There were other children pushing up, demanding. Her younger sister seemed all that she was not. There were years she did not want me to touch her. She kept too much in herself, her life was such she had to keep too much in herself. My wisdom came too late. She has much to her and probably little will come of it. She is a child of her age, of depression, of war, of fear.

Let her be. So all that is in her will not bloom—but in how many does it? There is still enough left to live by. Only help her to know—help make it so there is cause for her to know—that she is more than this dress on the ironing board, helpless before the iron.

ZZ PACKER

ZZ Packer (b. 1973) was named Zuwena, a Swahili name that means "good," before she became ZZ, a nickname given to her in childhood. Born in Chicago, she grew up in Atlanta and Louisville. She recalled in an interview with Robert Birnbaum that, while in high school,

> I was in this math and science program in the summers, and one of the things they did, which was amazing, was show us all these different colleges. There is no way in Louisville, Kentucky, that I would have been able to see these colleges. So we went on these trips and they were trying to get us to these Ivy League colleges.

When Packer began to attend Yale University, she was undecided about whether she wanted to major in the humanities or in the sciences, but after her graduation from Yale, she went on to a writing program at Johns Hopkins University. There, in a workshop with Francine Prose, she decided to become a writer.

To support herself, Packer taught public high school for two years. She stopped because the job didn't leave her sufficient time to continue writing. "Teaching, the students really need you. You can't just say, 'No, I am going to do this really selfish thing, scribble.'" A fellowship to the writers' program at the University of Iowa enabled Packer to continue working on her short fiction. She then moved on to the writing program at Stanford University on Wallace Stegner and Truman Capote fellowships, where she began to publish her stories in magazines such as *The New Yorker*, *Seventeen*, *Harper's*, and *Ploughshares*.

Packer's stories often contain what she calls "autobiographical elements, details and settings and that sort of thing." She chose the eight stories for her first collection, *Drinking Coffee Elsewhere* (2003), including "Brownies," from the fifty or so works of short fiction in her computer.

> I keep them on the hard drive and I keep long hand drafts and file them away. Every once in awhile, when I'm procrastinating while I'm supposed to be writing, I'll look through this very long list of the abandoned ones. I just keep them there to see. . . . I will sometimes cannibalize an old story. Nothing in here was good except this one line I could actually use.

In addition to teaching workshops at both Iowa and Stanford, Packer has been hailed by *Oprah Magazine* as a "thrilling new voice" and become the subject of photo spreads in *Vogue* and *Entertainment Weekly*. Despite the fanfare, she is currently teaching and working on a first novel, begun several years ago, about the adventures of the Buffalo Soldiers, an all-black military unit stationed in the West after the Civil War.

Brownies

2003

By our second day at Camp Crescendo, the girls in my Brownie troop had decided to kick the asses of each and every girl in Brownie Troop 909. Troop 909 was doomed from the first day of camp; they were white girls, their complexions a blend of ice cream: strawberry, vanilla. They turtled out from their bus in pairs, their rolled-up sleeping bags chromatized with Disney characters: Sleeping Beauty, Snow White, Mickey Mouse; or the generic ones cheap parents bought: washed-out rainbows, unicorns, curly-eyelashed frogs. Some clutched Igloo coolers and still others held on to stuffed toys like pacifiers, looking all around them like tourists determined to be dazzled.

Our troop was wending its way past their bus, past the ranger station, past the colorful trail guide drawn like a treasure map, locked behind glass.

"Man, did you smell them?" Arnetta said, giving the girls a slow once-over, "They smell like Chihuahuas. *Wet* Chihuahuas." Their troop was still at the entrance, and though we had passed them by yards, Arnetta raised her nose in the air and grimaced.

Arnetta said this from the very rear of the line, far away from Mrs. Margolin, who always strung our troop behind her like a brood of obedient ducklings. Mrs. Margolin even looked like a mother duck—she had hair cropped close to a small ball of a head, almost no neck, and huge, miraculous breasts. She wore enormous belts that looked like the kind that weightlifters wear, except hers would be cheap metallic gold or rabbit fur or covered with gigantic fake sunflowers, and often these belts would become nature lessons in and of themselves. "See," Mrs. Margolin once said to us, pointing to her belt, "this one's made entirely from the feathers of baby pigeons."

The belt layered with feathers was uncanny enough, but I was more disturbed by the realization that I had never actually *seen* a baby pigeon. I searched weeks for one, in vain—scampering after pigeons whenever I was downtown with my father.

But nature lessons were not Mrs. Margolin's top priority. She saw the position of troop leader as an evangelical post. Back at the A.M.E. church where our Brownie meetings were held, Mrs. Margolin was especially fond of imparting religious aphorisms by means of acrostics—"Satan" was the "Serpent Always Tempting and Noisome"; she'd refer to the "Bible" as "Basic Instructions Before Leaving Earth." Whenever she quizzed us on these, expecting to hear the acrostics parroted back to her, only Arnetta's correct replies soared over our vague mumblings. "Jesus?" Mrs. Margolin might ask expectantly, and Arnetta alone would dutifully answer, "Jehovah's Example, Saving Us Sinners."

Arnetta always made a point of listening to Mrs. Margolin's religious talk and giving her what she wanted to hear. Because of this, Arnetta could have blared through a megaphone that the white girls of Troop 909 were "wet Chihuahuas" without so much as a blink from Mrs. Margolin. Once, Arnetta killed the troop goldfish by feeding it a french fry covered in ketchup, and when Mrs. Margolin demanded that she explain what had happened, claimed the goldfish had been eyeing her meal for *hours,* then the fish—giving in to temptation—had leapt up and snatched a whole golden fry from her fingertips.

"*Serious* Chihuahua," Octavia added, and though neither Arnetta nor Octavia could *spell* "Chihuahua," had ever *seen* a Chihuahua, trisyllabic words had gained a sort of exoticism within our fourth-grade set at Woodrow Wilson Elementary. Arnetta and Octavia would flip through the dictionary, determined to work the vulgar-sounding ones like "Djibouti" and "asinine" into conversation.

"*Caucasian* Chihuahuas," Arnetta said.

That did it. The girls in my troop turned elastic: Drema and Elise doubled up on one another like inextricably entwined kites; Octavia slapped her belly; Janice jumped straight up in the air, then did it again, as if to slam-dunk her own head. They could not stop laughing. No one had laughed so hard since a boy named Martez had stuck a pencil in the electric socket and spent the whole day with a strange grin on his face.

"Girls, girls," said our parent helper, Mrs. Hedy. Mrs. Hedy was Octavia's mother, and she wagged her index finger perfunctorily, like a windshield wiper. "Stop it, now. Be good." She said this loud enough to be heard, but lazily, bereft of any feeling of indication that she meant to be obeyed, as though she could say these words again at the exact same pitch if a button somewhere on her were pressed.

But the rest of the girls didn't stop; they only laughed louder. It was the word "Caucasian" that got them all going. One day at school, about a month before the Brownie camping trip, Arnetta turned to a boy wearing impossibly high-ankled floodwater jeans and said, "What are you? *Caucasian?*" The word took off from there, and soon everything was Caucasian. If you ate too fast you ate like a Caucasian, if you ate too slow you ate like a Caucasian. The biggest feat anyone at Woodrow Wilson could do was to jump off the swing in midair, at the highest point in its arc, and if you fell (as I had, more than once) instead of landing on your feet, knees bent Olympic gymnast–style, Arnetta and

Octavia were prepared to comment. They'd look at each other with the silence of passengers who'd narrowly escaped an accident, then nod their heads, whispering with solemn horror, "*Caucasian.*"

Even the only white kid in our school, Dennis, got in on the Caucasian act. That time when Martez stuck a pencil in the socket, Dennis had pointed and yelled, "That was *so* Caucasian!"

When you lived in the south suburbs of Atlanta, it was easy to forget about whites. Whites were like those baby pigeons: real and existing, but rarely seen or thought about. Everyone had been to Rich's to go clothes shopping, everyone had seen white girls and their mothers coo-cooing over dresses; everyone had gone to the downtown library and seen white businessmen swish by importantly, wrists flexed in front of them to check the time as though they would change from Clark Kent into Superman at any second. But those images were as fleeting as cards shuffled in a deck, whereas the ten white girls behind us—*invaders*, Arnetta would later call them—were instantly real and memorable, with their long, shampoo-commercial hair, straight as spaghetti from the box. This alone was reason for envy and hatred. The only black girl most of us had ever seen with hair that long was Octavia, whose hair hung past her butt like a Hawaiian hula dancer's. The sight of Octavia's mane prompted other girls to listen to her reverentially, as though whatever she had to say would somehow activate their own follicles. For example, when, on the first day of camp, Octavia made as if to speak, and everyone fell silent. "Nobody," Octavia said, "calls us niggers."

At the end of that first day, when half of our troop made their way back to the cabin after tag-team restroom visits, Arnetta said she'd heard one of the Troop 909 girls call Daphne a nigger. The other half of the girls and I were helping Mrs. Margolin clean up the pots and pans from the campfire ravioli dinner. When we made our way to the restrooms to wash up and brush our teeth, we met up with Arnetta midway.

"Man, I completely heard the girl," Arnetta reported. "Right, Daphne?"

Daphne hardly ever spoke, but when she did, her voice was petite and tinkly, the voice one might expect from a shiny new earring. She'd written a poem once, for Langston Hughes Day, a poem brimming with all the teacher-winning ingredients—trees and oceans, sunsets and moons—but what cinched the poem for the grown-ups, snatching the win from Octavia's musical ode to Grandmaster Flash and the Furious Five, were Daphne's last lines:

You are my father, the veteran
When you cry in the dark
It rains and rains and rains in my heart

She'd always worn clean, though faded, jumpers and dresses when Chic jeans were the fashion, but when she went up to the dais to receive her prize journal, pages trimmed in gold, she wore a new dress with a velveteen bodice and a taffeta skirt as wide as an umbrella. All the kids clapped, though none of them understood the poem. I'd read encyclopedias the way others read comics, and I didn't get it. But those last lines pricked me, they were so eerie, and as my father and I ate cereal, I'd whisper over my Froot Loops, like a mantra, "*You are my father, the veteran. You are my father, the veteran, the veteran, the veteran,*" until my father, who acted in plays as Caliban and Othello and was not a veteran, marched me up to my teacher one morning and said, "Can you tell me what's wrong with this kid?"

I thought Daphne and I might become friends, but I think she grew spooked by me whispering those lines to her, begging her to tell me what they meant, and I soon understood that two quiet people like us were better off quiet alone.

"Daphne? Didn't you hear them call you a nigger?" Arnetta asked, giving Daphne a nudge.

The sun was setting behind the trees, and their leafy tops formed a canopy of black lace for the flame of the sun to pass through. Daphne shrugged her shoulders at first, then slowly nodded her head when Arnetta gave her a hard look.

Twenty minutes later, when my restroom group returned to the cabin, Arnetta was still talking about Troop 909. My restroom group had passed by some of the 909 girls. For the most part, they deferred to us, waving us into the restrooms, letting us go even though they'd gotten there first.

We'd seen them, but from afar, never within their orbit enough to see whether their faces were the way all white girls appeared on TV—ponytailed and full of energy, bubbling over with love and money. All I could see was that some of them rapidly fanned their faces with their hands, though the heat of the day had long passed. A few seemed to be lolling their heads in slow circles, half purposefully, as if exercising the muscles of their necks, half ecstatically, like Stevie Wonder.

"We can't let them get away with that," Arnetta said, dropping her voice to a laryngitic whisper. "We can't let them get away with calling us niggers. I say we teach them a lesson." She sat down cross-legged on a sleeping bag, an embittered Buddha, eyes glimmering acrylic-black. "We can't go telling Mrs. Margolin, either. Mrs. Margolin'll say something about doing unto others and the path of righteousness and all. Forget that shit." She let her eyes flutter irreverently till they half closed, as though ignoring an insult not worth returning. We could all hear Mrs. Margolin outside, gathering the last of the metal campware.

Nobody said anything for a while. Usually people were quiet after Arnetta spoke. Her tone had an upholstered confidence that was somehow both regal and vulgar at once. It demanded a few moments of silence in its wake, like the ringing of a church bell or the playing of taps. Sometimes Octavia would ditto or dissent to whatever Arnetta had said, and this was the signal that others could speak. But this time Octavia just swirled a long cord of hair into pretzel shapes.

"*Well?*" Arnetta said. She looked as if she had discerned the hidden severity of the situation and was waiting for the rest of us to catch up. Everyone looked from Arnetta to Daphne. It was, after all, Daphne who had supposedly been called the name, but Daphne sat on the bare cabin floor, flipping through the pages of the Girl Scout handbook, eyebrows arched in mock wonder, as if the handbook were a catalogue full of bright and startling foreign costumes. Janice broke the silence. She clapped her hands to broach her idea of a plan.

"They gone be sleeping," she whispered conspiratorially, "then we gone sneak into they cabin, then we'll put daddy longlegs in they sleeping bags. Then they'll wake up. Then we gone beat 'em up till they're as flat as frying pans!" She jammed her fist into the palm of her hand, then made a sizzling sound.

Janice's country accent was laughable, her looks homely, her jumpy acrobatics embarrassing to behold. Arnetta and Octavia volleyed amused, arrogant smiles whenever Janice opened her mouth, but Janice never caught the hint, spoke whenever she wanted, fluttered around Arnetta and Octavia futilely offering her opinions to their departing backs. Whenever Arnetta and Octavia shooed her away, Janice loitered until the two would finally sigh and ask, "What *is* it, Miss Caucasoid? What do you *want*?"

"Shut up, Janice," Octavia said, letting a fingered loop of hair fall to her waist as though just the sound of Janice's voice had ruined the fun of her hair twisting.

Janice obeyed, her mouth hung open in a loose grin, unflappable, unhurt.

"All right," Arnetta said, standing up. "We're going to have a secret meeting and talk about what we're going to do."

Everyone gravely nodded her head. The word "secret" had a built-in importance, the modifier form of the word carried more clout than the noun. A secret meant nothing; it was like gossip: just a bit of unpleasant knowledge about someone who happened to be someone other than yourself. A secret *meeting*, or a secret *club* was entirely different.

That was when Arnetta turned to me as though she knew that doing so was both a compliment and a charity.

"Snot, you're not going to be a bitch and tell Mrs. Margolin, are you?"

I had been called "Snot" ever since first grade, when I'd sneezed in class and two long ropes of mucus had splattered a nearby girl.

"Hey," I said. "Maybe you didn't hear them right—I mean—"

"Are you gonna tell on us or not?" was all Arnetta wanted to know, and by the time the question was asked, the rest of our Brownie troop looked at me as though they'd already decided their course of action, me being the only impediment.

Camp Crescendo used to double as a high-school-band and field hockey camp until an arcing field hockey ball landed on the clasp of a girl's metal barrette, knifing a skull nerve and paralyzing the right side of her body. The camp closed down for a few years and the girl's teammates built a memorial, filling the spot on which the girl fell with hockey balls, on which they had painted—all in nail polish—get-well tidings, flowers, and hearts. The balls were still stacked there, like a shrine of ostrich eggs embedded in the ground.

On the second day of camp, Troop 909 was dancing around the mound of hockey balls, their limbs jangling awkwardly, their cries like the constant summer squeal of an amusement park. There was a stream that bordered the field hockey lawn, and the girls from my troop settled next to it, scarfing down the last of lunch: sandwiches made from salami and slices of tomato that had gotten waterlogged from the melting ice in the cooler. From the stream bank, Arnetta eyed the Troop 909 girls, scrutinizing their movements to glean inspiration for battle.

"Man," Arnetta said, "we could bumrush them right now if that damn lady would *leave*."

The 909 troop leader was a white woman with the severe pageboy hairdo of an ancient Egyptian. She lay on a picnic blanket, sphinx-like, eating a banana, sometimes holding it out in front of her like a microphone. Beside her sat a girl slowly flapping one hand like a bird with a broken wing. Occasionally, the leader would call out the names of girls who'd attempted leapfrogs and flips, or of girls who yelled too loudly or strayed far from the circle.

"I'm just glad Big Fat Mama's not following us here," Octavia said. "At least we don't have to worry about her." Mrs. Margolin, Octavia assured us, was having her Afternoon Devotional, shrouded in mosquito netting, in a clearing she'd found. Mrs. Hedy was cleaning mud from her espadrilles in the cabin.

"I handled them." Arnetta sucked on her teeth and proudly grinned. "I told her we was going to gather leaves."

"Gather leaves," Octavia said, nodding respectfully. "That's a good one. Especially since they're so mad-crazy about this camping thing." She looked from ground to sky, sky to ground. Her hair hung down her back in two braids like a squaw's. "I mean, I really don't know why it's even called *camping*—all we ever do with Nature is find some twigs and say something like, 'Wow, this fell from a tree.'" She then studied her sandwich. With two disdainful fingers, she picked out a slice of dripping tomato, the sections congealed with red slime. She pitched it into the stream embrowned with dead leaves and the murky effigies of other dead things, but in the opaque water, a group of small silver-brown fish appeared. They surrounded the tomato and nibbled.

"Look!" Janice cried. "Fishes! Fishes!" As she scrambled to the edge of the stream to watch, a covey of insects threw up tantrums from the wheatgrass and nettle, a throng of tiny electric machines, all going at once. Octavia sneaked up behind Janice as if to push her in. Daphne and I exchanged terrified looks. It seemed as though only we knew that Octavia was close enough—and bold enough—to actually push Janice into the stream. Janice turned around quickly, but Octavia was already staring serenely into the still water as though she was gathering some sort of courage from it. "What's so funny?" Janice said, eyeing them all suspiciously.

Elise began humming the tune to "Karma Chameleon," all the girls joining in, their hums light and facile. Janice also began to hum, against everyone else, the high-octane opening chords of "Beat It."

"I love me some Michael Jackson," Janice said when she'd finished humming, smacking her lips as though Michael Jackson were a favorite meal. "I *will* marry Michael Jackson."

Before anyone had a chance to impress upon Janice the impossibility of this, Arnetta suddenly rose, made a sun visor of her hand, and watched Troop 909 leave the field hockey lawn.

"Dammit!" she said, "We've got to get them *alone*."

"They won't ever be alone." I said. All the rest of the girls looked at me, for I usually kept quiet. If I spoke even a word, I could count on someone calling me Snot. Everyone seemed to think that we could beat up these girls; no one entertained the thought that they might fight *back*. "The only time they'll be unsupervised is in the bathroom."

"Oh shut up, Snot," Octavia said.

But Arnetta slowly nodded her head. "The bathroom," she said. "The bathroom," she said, again and again. "The bathroom! The bathroom!"

According to Octavia's watch, it took us five minutes to hike to the restrooms, which were midway between our cabin and Troop 909's. Inside, the mirrors above the sinks returned only the vaguest of reflections, as though someone had taken a scouring pad to their surfaces to obscure the shine. Pine needles, leaves, and dirty, flattened wads of chewing gum covered the floor like a mosaic. Webs of hair matted the drain in the middle of the floor. Above the sinks and below the mirrors, stacks of folded white paper towels lay on a long metal counter. Shaggy white balls of paper towels sat on the sinktops in a line like corsages on display. A thread of floss snaked from a wad of tissues dotted with the faint red-pink of blood. One of those white girls, I thought, had just lost a tooth.

Though the restroom looked almost the same as it had the night before, it somehow seemed stranger now. We hadn't noticed the wooden rafters coming together in great V's. We were, it seemed, inside a whale, viewing the ribs of the roof of its mouth.

"Wow. It's a mess," Elise said.

"You can say that again."

Arnetta leaned against the doorjamb of a restroom stall. "This is where they'll be again," she said. Just seeing the place, just having a plan seemed to satisfy her. "We'll go in and talk to them. You know, 'How you doing? How long'll you be here?' That sort of thing. Then Octavia and I are gonna tell them what happens when they call any one of us a nigger."

"I'm going to say something, too," Janice said.

Arnetta considered this. "Sure," she said. "Of course. Whatever you want."

Janice pointed her finger like a gun at Octavia and rehearsed the line she'd thought up, " 'We're gonna teach you a *lesson*!' That's what I'm going to say." She narrowed her eyes like a TV mobster. " 'We're gonna teach you little girls a lesson!' "

With the back of her hand, Octavia brushed Janice's finger away. "You couldn't teach me to shit in a toilet."

"But," I said, "what if they say, 'We didn't say that? We didn't call anyone an N-I-G-G-E-R.' "

"Snot," Arnetta said, and then sighed. "Don't think. Just fight. If you even know how."

Everyone laughed except Daphne. Arnetta gently laid her hand on Daphne's shoulder. "Daphne. You don't have to fight. We're doing this for you."

Daphne walked to the counter, took a clean paper towel, and carefully unfolded it like a map. With it, she began to pick up the trash all around. Everyone watched.

"C'mon," Arnetta said to everyone. "Let's beat it." We all ambled toward the doorway, where the sunshine made one large white rectangle of light. We were immediately blinded, and we shielded our eyes with our hands and our forearms.

"Daphne?" Arnetta asked. "Are you coming?"

We all looked back at the bending girl, the thin of her back hunched like the back of a custodian sweeping a stage, caught in limelight. Stray strands of her hair were lit near-transparent, thin fiber-optic threads. She did not nod yes to the question, nor did she shake her head no. She abided, bent. Then she began again, picking up leaves, wads of paper, the cotton fluff innards from a torn stuffed toy. She did it so methodically, so exquisitely, so humbly, she must have been trained. I thought of those dresses she wore, faded and old, yet so pressed and clean. I then saw the poverty in them; I then could imagine her mother, cleaning the houses of others, returning home, weary.

"I guess she's not coming."

We left her and headed back to our cabin, over pine needles and leaves, taking the path full of shade.

"What about our secret meeting?" Elise asked.

Arnetta enunciated her words in a way that defied contradiction: "We just had it."

It was nearing our bedtime, but the sun had not yet set.

"Hey, your mama's coming," Arnetta said to Octavia when she saw Mrs. Hedy walk toward the cabin, sniffling. When Octavia's mother wasn't giving bored, parochial orders, she sniffled continuously, mourning an imminent divorce from her husband. She might begin a sentence, "I don't know what Robert will do when Octavia and I are gone. Who'll buy him cigarettes?" and Octavia would hotly whisper, "*Mama,*" in a way that meant: Please don't talk about our problems in front of everyone. Please shut up.

But when Mrs. Hedy began talking about her husband, thinking about her husband, seeing clouds shaped like the head of her husband, she couldn't be quiet, and no one could dislodge her from the comfort of her own woe. Only one thing could perk her up—Brownie songs. If the girls were quiet, and Mrs. Hedy was in her dopey, sorrowful mood, she would say, "Y'all know I like those songs, girls. Why don't you sing one?" Everyone would groan, except me and Daphne. I, for one, liked some of the songs.

"C'mon, everybody," Octavia said drearily, "She likes the Brownie song best."

We sang, loud enough to reach Mrs. Hedy:

"I've got something in my pocket;
It belongs across my face.
And I keep it very close at hand
  in a most convenient place.
I'm sure you couldn't guess it

If you guessed a long, long while.
So I'll take it out and put it on—
It's a great big Brownie smile!"

The Brownie song was supposed to be sung cheerfully, as though we were elves in a workshop, singing as we merrily cobbled shoes, but everyone except me hated the song so much that they sang it like a maudlin record, played on the most sluggish of rpms.

"That was good," Mrs. Hedy said, closing the cabin door behind her. "Wasn't that nice, Linda?"

"Praise God," Mrs. Margolin answered without raising her head from the chore of counting out Popsicle sticks for the next day's craft session.

"Sing another one," Mrs. Hedy said. She said it with a sort of joyful aggression, like a drunk I'd once seen who'd refused to leave a Korean grocery.

"God, Mama, get over it," Octavia whispered in a voice meant only for Arnetta, but Mrs. Hedy heard it and started to leave the cabin.

"Don't go," Arnetta said. She ran after Mrs. Hedy and held her by the arm. "We haven't finished singing." She nudged us with a single look. "Let's sing the 'Friends Song.' For Mrs. Hedy."

Although I liked some of the songs, I hated this one:

Make new friends
But keep the o-old,
One is silver
And the other gold.

If most of the girls in the troop could be any type of metal, they'd be bunched-up wads of tinfoil, maybe, or rusty iron nails you had to get tetanus shots for.

"No, no, no," Mrs. Margolin said before anyone could start in on the "Friends Song." "An uplifting song. Something to lift her up and take her mind off all these earthly burdens."

Arnetta and Octavia rolled their eyes. Everyone knew what song Mrs. Margolin was talking about, and no one, no one, wanted to sing it.

"Please, no," a voice called out. "Not 'The Doughnut Song.'"

"Please not 'The Doughnut Song,'" Octavia pleaded.

"I'll brush my teeth two times if I don't have to sing 'The Doughnut—'"

"Sing!" Mrs. Margolin demanded.

We sang:

"Life without Jesus is like a do-ough-nut!
Like a do-ooough-nut!
Like a do-ooough-nut!
Life without Jesus is like a do-ough-nut!
There's a hole in the middle of my soul!"

There were other verses, involving other pastries, but we stopped after the first one and cast glances toward Mrs. Margolin to see if we could gain a reprieve. Mrs. Margolin's eyes fluttered blissfully. She was half asleep.

"Awww," Mrs. Hedy said, as though giant Mrs. Margolin were a cute baby, "Mrs. Margolin's had a long day."

"Yes indeed," Mrs. Margolin answered. "If you don't mind, I might just go to the lodge where the beds are. I haven't been the same since the operation."

I had not heard of this operation, or when it had occurred, since Mrs. Margolin had never missed the once-a-week Brownie meetings, but I could see from Daphne's face that she was concerned, and I could see that the other girls had decided that Mrs. Margolin's operation must have happened long ago in some remote time unconnected to our own. Nevertheless, they put on sad faces. We had all been taught that adulthood was full of sorrow and pain, taxes and bills, dreaded work and dealings with whites, sickness and death. I tried to do what the others did. I tried to look silent.

"Go right ahead, Linda," Mrs. Hedy said, "I'll watch the girls." Mrs. Hedy seemed to forget about divorce for a moment; she looked at us with dewy eyes, as if we were mysterious, furry creatures. Meanwhile, Mrs. Margolin walked through the maze of sleeping bags until she found her own. She gathered a neat stack of clothes and pajamas slowly, as though doing so was almost painful. She took her toothbrush, her toothpaste, her pillow. "All right!" Mrs. Margolin said, addressing us all from the threshold of the cabin. "Be in bed by nine." She said it with a twinkle in her voice, letting us know she was allowing us to be naughty and stay up till nine-fifteen.

"C'mon everybody," Arnetta said after Mrs. Margolin left. "Time for us to wash up."

Everyone watched Mrs. Hedy closely, wondering whether she would insist on coming with us since it was night, making a fight with Troop 909 nearly impossible. Troop 909 would soon be in the bathroom, washing their faces, brushing their teeth—completely unsuspecting of our ambush.

"We won't be long," Arnetta said. "We're old enough to go to the restrooms by ourselves."

Ms. Hedy pursed her lips at this dilemma. "Well, I guess you Brownies are almost Girl Scouts, right?"

"Right!"

"Just one more badge," Drema said.

"And about," Octavia droned, "a million more cookies to sell." Octavia looked at all of us, *Now's our chance,* her face seemed to say, but our chance to do *what,* I didn't exactly know.

Finally, Mrs. Hedy walked to the doorway where Octavia stood dutifully waiting to say goodbye but looking bored doing it. Mrs. Hedy held Octavia's chin. "You'll be good?"

"Yes, Mama."

"And remember to pray for me and your father? If I'm asleep when you get back?"

"Yes, Mama."

When the other girls had finished getting their toothbrushes and washcloths and flashlights for the group restroom trip, I was drawing pictures of tiny birds with too many feathers. Daphne was sitting on her sleeping bag, reading.

"You're not going to come?" Octavia asked.

Daphne shook her head.

"I'm gonna stay, too," I said. "I'll go to the restroom when Daphne and Mrs. Hedy go."

Arnetta leaned down toward me and whispered so that Mrs. Hedy, who'd taken over Mrs. Margolin's task of counting Popsicle sticks, couldn't hear. "No, Snot. If we get in trouble, you're going to get in trouble with the rest of us."

We made our way through the darkness by flashlight. The tree branches that had shaded us just hours earlier, along the same path, now looked like arms sprouting menacing hands. The stars sprinkled the sky like spilled salt. They seemed fastened to the darkness, high up and holy, their places fixed and definite as we stirred beneath them.

Some, like me, were quiet because we were afraid of the dark; others were talking like crazy for the same reason.

"Wow!" Drema said, looking up. "Why are all the stars out here? I never see stars back on Oneida Street."

"It's a camping trip, that's why," Octavia said. "You're supposed to see stars on camping trips."

Janice said, "This place smells like my mother's air freshener."

"These woods are *pine*," Elise said. "Your mother probably uses *pine* air freshener."

Janice mouthed an exaggerated "Oh," nodding her head as though she just then understood one of the world's great secrets.

No one talked about fighting. Everyone was afraid enough just walking through the infinite deep of the woods. Even though I didn't fight to fight, was afraid of fighting, I felt I was part of the rest of the troop; like I was defending something. We trudged against the slight incline of the path, Arnetta leading the way.

"You know," I said, "their leader will be there. Or they won't even be there. It's dark already. Last night the sun was still in the sky. I'm sure they're already finished."

Arnetta acted as if she hadn't heard me. I followed her gaze with my flashlight, and that's when I saw the squares of light in the darkness. The bathroom was just ahead.

But the girls were there. We could hear them before we could see them.

"Octavia and I will go in first so they'll think there's just two of us, then wait till I say, 'We're gonna teach you a lesson,'" Arnetta said. "Then, bust in. That'll surprise them."

"That's what I was supposed to say," Janice said.

Arnetta went inside, Octavia next to her. Janice followed, and the rest of us waited outside.

They were in there for what seemed like whole minutes, but something was wrong. Arnetta hadn't given the signal yet. I was with the girls outside when I heard one of the Troop 909 girls say, "NO. That did NOT happen!"

That was to be expected, that they'd deny the whole thing. What I hadn't expected was *the voice* in which the denial was said. The girl sounded as though her tongue were caught in her mouth. "That's a BAD word!" the girl continued. "We don't say BAD words!"

"Let's go in," Elise said.

"No," Drema said, "I don't want to. What if we get beat up?"

"Snot?" Elise turned to me, her flashlight blinding. It was the first time anyone had asked my opinion, though I knew they were just asking because they were afraid.

"I say we go inside, just to see what's going on."

"But Arnetta didn't give us the signal," Drema said. "She's supposed to say, 'We're gonna teach you a lesson,' and I didn't hear her say it."

"C'mon," I said. "Let's just go in."

We went inside. There we found the white girls—about five girls huddled up next to one big girl. I instantly knew she was the owner of the voice we'd heard. Arnetta and Octavia inched toward us as soon as we entered.

"Where's Janice?" Elise asked, then we heard a flush. "Oh."

"I think," Octavia said, whispering to Elise, "they're retarded."

"We ARE NOT retarded!" the big girl said, though it was obvious that she was. That they all were. The girls around her began to whimper.

"They're just pretending," Arnetta said, trying to convince herself. "I know they are."

Octavia turned to Arnetta. "Arnetta. Let's just leave."

Janice came out of a stall, happy and relieved, then she suddenly remembered her line, pointed to the big girl, and said, "We're gonna teach you a lesson."

"Shut up, Janice," Octavia said, but her heart was not in it. Arnetta's face was set in a lost, deep scowl. Octavia turned to the big girl and said loudly, slowly, as if they were all deaf, "We're going to leave. It was nice meeting you, O.K.? You don't have to tell anyone that we were here. O.K.?"

"Why not?" said the big girl, like a taunt. When she spoke, her lips did not meet, her mouth did not close. Her tongue grazed the roof of her mouth, like a little pink fish. "You'll get in trouble. I know. *I* know."

Arnetta got back her old cunning. "If you said anything, then you'd be a tattletale."

The girl looked sad for a moment, then perked up quickly. A flash of genius crossed her face. "I *like* tattletale."

"It's all right, girls. It's gonna be all right!" the 909 troop leader said. All of Troop 909 burst into tears. It was as though someone had instructed them all to cry at once. The troop leader had girls under her arm, and all the rest of the girls crowded about her. It reminded me of a hog I'd seen on a field trip, where all the little hogs gathered about the mother at feeding time, latching onto her teats. The 909 troop leader had come into the bathroom, shortly after the big girl had threatened to tell. Then the ranger came, then, once the ranger had radioed the station, Mrs. Margolin arrived with Daphne in tow.

The ranger had left the restroom area, but everyone else was huddled just outside, swatting mosquitoes.

"Oh. They *will* apologize," Mrs. Margolin said to the 909 troop leader, but she said this so angrily, I knew she was speaking more to us than to the other troop leader. "When their parents find out, every one a them will be on punishment."

"It's all right, it's all right," the 909 troop leader reassured Mrs. Margolin. Her voice lilted in the same way it had when addressing the girls. She smiled the whole time she talked. She was like one of those TV-cooking-show women who talk and dice onions and smile all at the same time.

"See. It could have happened. I'm not calling your girls fibbers or anything." She shook her head ferociously from side to side, her Egyptian-style pageboy flapping against her cheeks like heavy drapes. "It *could* have happened. See. Our girls are *not* retarded. They are *delayed* learners." She said this in a syrupy instructional voice, as though our troop might be delayed learners as well, "We're from the Decatur Children's Academy. Many of them just have special needs."

"Now we won't be able to walk to the bathroom by ourselves!" the big girl said.

"Yes you will," the troop leader said, "but maybe we'll wait till we get back to Decatur—"

"I don't want to wait!" the girl said. "I want my Independence badge!"

The girls in my troop were entirely speechless. Arnetta looked stoic, as though she were soon to be tortured but was determined not to appear weak. Mrs. Margolin pursed her lips solemnly and said, "Bless them, Lord. Bless them."

In contrast, the Troop 909 leader was full of words and energy. "Some of our girls are echolalic—" She smiled and happily presented one of the girls hanging onto her, but the girl widened her eyes in horror, and violently withdrew herself from the center of attention, sensing she was being sacrificed for the village sins. "Echolalic," the troop leader continued. "That means they will say whatever they hear, like an echo—that's where the word comes from. It comes from 'echo.'" She ducked her head apologetically, "I mean, not all of them have the most *progressive* of parents, so if they heard a bad word, they might have repeated it. But I guarantee it would not have been *intentional*."

Arnetta spoke. "I saw her say the word. I heard her." She pointed to a small girl, smaller than any of us, wearing an oversized T-shirt that read: "Eat Bertha's Mussels."

The troop leader shook her head and smiled, "That's impossible. She doesn't speak. She can, but she doesn't."

Arnetta furrowed her brow. "No. It wasn't her. That's right. It was *her*."

The girl Arnetta pointed to grinned as though she'd been paid a compliment. She was the only one from either troop actually wearing a full uniform: the mocha-colored A-line shift, the orange ascot, the sash covered with badges, though all the same one—the Try-It patch. She took a few steps toward Arnetta and made a grand sweeping gesture toward the sash. "See," she said, full of self-importance, "I'm a Brownie." I had a hard time imagining this girl calling anyone a "nigger"; the girl looked perpetually delighted, as though she would have cuddled up with a grizzly if someone had let her.

On the fourth morning, we boarded the bus to go home.

The previous day had been spent building miniature churches from Popsicle sticks. We hardly left the cabin. Mrs. Margolin and Mrs. Hedy guarded us so closely, almost no one talked for the entire day.

Even on the day of departure from Camp Crescendo, all was serious and silent. The bus ride began quietly enough. Arnetta had to sit beside Mrs. Margolin; Octavia had to sit beside her mother. I sat beside Daphne, who gave me her prize journal without a word of explanation.

"You don't want it?"

She shook her head no. It was empty.

Then Mrs. Hedy began to weep. "Octavia," Mrs. Hedy said to her daughter without looking at her, "I'm going to sit with Mrs. Margolin. All right?"

Arnetta exchanged seats with Mrs. Hedy. With the two women up front, Elise felt it safe to speak. "Hey," she said, then she set her face into a placid, vacant stare, trying to imitate that of a Troop 909 girl. Emboldened, Arnetta made a gesture of mock pride toward an imaginary sash, the way the girl in full uniform had done. Then they all made a game of it, trying to do the most exaggerated imitations of the Troop 909 girls, all without speaking, all without laughing loud enough to catch the women's attention.

Daphne looked down at her shoes, white with sneaker polish. I opened the journal she'd given me. I looked out the window, trying to decide what to write, searching for lines, but nothing could compare with what Daphne had written, "*My father, the veteran,*" my favorite line of all time. It replayed itself in my head, and I gave up trying to write.

By then, it seemed that the rest of the troop had given up making fun of the girls in Troop 909. They were now quietly gossiping about who had passed notes to whom in school. For a moment the gossiping fell off, and all I heard was the hum of the bus as we sped down the road and the muffled sounds of Mrs. Hedy and Mrs. Margolin talking about serious things.

"You know," Octavia whispered, "why did *we* have to be stuck at a camp with retarded girls? You know?"

"*You* know why," Arnetta answered. She narrowed her eyes like a cat. "My mama and I were in the mall in Buckhead, and this white lady just kept looking at us. I mean, like we were foreign or something. Like we were from China."

"What did the woman say?" Elise asked.

"Nothing," Arnetta said. "She didn't say nothing."

A few girls quietly nodded their heads.

"There was this time," I said, "when my father and I were in the mall and—"

"Oh shut up, Snot," Octavia said.

I stared at Octavia, then rolled my eyes from her to the window. As I watched the trees blur, I wanted nothing more than to be through with it all:

the bus ride, the troop, school—all of it. But we were going home. I'd see the same girls in school the next day. We were on a bus, and there was nowhere else to go.

"Go on, Laurel," Daphne said to me. It seemed like the first time she'd spoken the whole trip, and she'd said my name. I turned to her and smiled weakly so as not to cry, hoping she'd remember when I'd tried to be her friend, thinking maybe that her gift of the journal was an invitation of friendship. But she didn't smile back. All she said was, "What happened?"

I studied the girls, waiting for Octavia to tell me to shut up again before I even had a chance to utter another word, but everyone was amazed that Daphne had spoken. The bus was silent. I gathered my voice. "Well," I said. "My father and I were in this mall, but *I* was the one doing the staring." I stopped and glanced from face to face. I continued. "There were these white people dressed like Puritans or something, but they weren't Puritans. They were Mennonites. They're these people who, if you ask them to do a favor, like paint your porch or something, they have to do it. It's in their rules."

"That sucks," someone said.

"C'mon," Arnetta said. "You're lying."

"I am not."

"How do you know that's not just some story someone made up?" Elise asked, her head cocked full of daring. "I mean, who's gonna do whatever you ask?"

"It's not made up. I know because when I was looking at them, my father said, 'See those people? If you ask them to do something, they'll do it. Anything you want.'"

No one would call anyone's father a liar—then they'd have to fight the person. But Drema parsed her words carefully. "How does your *father* know that's not just some story? Huh?"

"Because," I said, "he went up to the man and asked him would he paint our porch, and the man said yes. It's their religion."

"Man, I'm glad I'm a Baptist," Elise said, shaking her head in sympathy for the Mennonites.

"So did the guy do it?" Drema asked, scooting closer to hear if the story got juicy.

"Yeah," I said. "His whole family was with him. My dad drove them to our house. They all painted our porch. The woman and girl were in bonnets and long, long skirts with buttons up to their necks. The guy wore this weird hat and these huge suspenders."

"Why," Arnetta asked archly, as though she didn't believe a word, "would someone pick a *porch*? If they'll do anything, why not make them paint the whole *house*? Why not ask for a hundred bucks?"

I thought about it, and then remembered the words my father had said about them painting our porch, though I had never seemed to think about his words after he'd said them.

"He said," I began, only then understanding the words as they uncoiled from my mouth, "it was the only time he'd have a white man on his knees doing something for a black man for free."

I now understood what he meant, and why he did it, though I didn't like it. When you've been made to feel bad for so long, you jump at the chance to do it to others. I remembered the Mennonites bending the way Daphne had bent when she was cleaning the restroom. I remembered the dark blue of their bonnets, the black of their shoes. They painted the porch as though scrubbing a floor. I was already trembling before Daphne asked quietly, "Did he thank them?"

I looked out the window. I could not tell which were the thoughts and which were the trees. "No," I said, and suddenly knew there was something mean in the world that I could not stop.

Arnetta laughed. "If I asked them to take off their long skirts and bonnets and put on some jeans, would they do it?"

And Daphne's voice, quiet, steady: "Maybe they would. Just to be nice."

GRACE PALEY

Grace Paley (1922–2007) was born in New York City. She studied at Hunter College and New York University, and in 1942 she married for the first time. She had two children from that marriage. In the 1950s she turned from writing poetry to short fiction. Her first book of stories, *The Little Disturbances of Man* (1959), established her reputation as a writer with a remarkably supple gift for language. As Susan Sontag later said, "She is that rare kind of writer, a natural with a voice like no one else's – funny, sad, lean, modest, energetic, acute." When this book went out of print in 1965, its reputation survived, strengthened by the infrequent appearances of her new stories in magazines such as the *Atlantic Monthly*, *Esquire*, the *Noble Savage*, *Genesis West*, the *New American Review*, *Ararat*, and *Fiction*.

During the 1960s and 1970s Paley was prominent as a nonviolent activist protesting the Vietnam War. She was secretary of the Greenwich Village Peace Center, spent time in jail for her antiwar activities, and visited Hanoi and Moscow as a member of peace delegations, defining herself as a "somewhat combative pacifist and cooperative anarchist." During the World Peace Congress in Moscow in 1973, she condemned the Soviet Union for silencing political dissidents; the congress disassociated itself from her statement. Paley was a feminist and active in the antinuclear movement. In 1974 her second volume of stories, *Enormous Changes at the Last Minute*, was published. It is a quieter, more openly personal collection of seventeen stories, many of them, such as "A Conversation with My Father," autobiographical. Her third book of stories, *Later the Same Day*, which includes "Mother," appeared in 1985. In 1988 Paley was designated the first official New York State Author by an act of the state legislature.

Paley refused to blame her teaching jobs or her involvements as an activist for her relatively low productivity as a writer. As she put it, "There is a long time in me between knowing and telling." She said that she wrote "from distress." What she tried to get at in her stories was "a history of everyday life," and her subject matter and prose style are unmistakable. Dividing her time between a Vermont farm and a Manhattan apartment close to the Greenwich Village School (P.S. 41), Little Tony's Unisex Haircutters, the Famous Ray's Pizza, the H & H Fruit and Vegetable Market, and the Jefferson Market Branch of the New York Public Library, Paley observed her neighbors, friends, and family with compassion, humor, and hope. Her spare dissection of her characters was never performed at the expense of sympathy for the human condition. *The Collected Stories of Grace Paley* was published in 1994.

CONNECTION To read another story by Grace Paley, see "Samuel" on page 11.

A Conversation with My Father

1974

My father is eighty-six years old and in bed. His heart, that bloody motor, is equally old and will not do certain jobs any more. It still floods his head with brainy light. But it won't let his legs carry the weight of his body around the house. Despite my metaphors, this muscle failure is not due to his old heart, he says, but to a potassium shortage. Sitting on one pillow, leaning on three, he offers last-minute advice and makes a request.

"I would like you to write a simple story just once more," he says, "the kind de Maupassant wrote, or Chekhov, the kind you used to write. Just recognizable people and then write down what happened to them next."

I say, "Yes, why not? That's possible." I want to please him, though I don't remember writing that way. I *would* like to try to tell such a story, if he means the kind that begins: "There was a woman . . ." followed by plot, the absolute line between two points which I've always despised. Not for literary reasons, but because it takes all hope away. Everyone, real or invented, deserves the open destiny of life.

Finally I thought of a story that had been happening for a couple of years right across the street. I wrote it down, then read it aloud. "Pa," I said, "how about this? Do you mean something like this?"

> Once in my time there was a woman and she had a son. They lived nicely, in a small apartment in Manhattan. This boy at about fifteen became a junkie, which is not unusual in our neighborhood. In order to maintain her close friendship with him, she became a junkie too. She said it was part of the youth culture, with which she felt very much at home. After a while, for a number of reasons, the boy gave it all up and left the city and his mother in disgust. Hopeless and alone, she grieved. We all visit her.

"O.K., Pa, that's it," I said, "an unadorned and miserable tale."

"But that's not what I mean," my father said. "You misunderstood me on purpose. You know there's a lot more to it. You know that. You left everything out. Turgenev wouldn't do that. Chekhov wouldn't do that. There are in fact

Russian writers you never heard of, you don't have an inkling of, as good as anyone, who can write a plain ordinary story, who would not leave out what you have left out. I object not to facts but to people sitting in trees talking senselessly, voices from who knows where . . ."

"Forget that one, Pa, what have I left out now? In this one?"

"Her looks, for instance."

"Oh. Quite handsome, I think. Yes."

"Her hair?"

"Dark, with heavy braids, as though she were a girl or a foreigner."

"What were her parents like, her stock? That she became such a person. It's interesting, you know."

"From out of town. Professional people. The first to be divorced in their county. How's that? Enough?" I asked.

"With you, it's all a joke," he said. "What about the boy's father? Why didn't you mention him? Who was he? Or was the boy born out of wedlock?"

"Yes," I said. "He was born out of wedlock."

"For Godsakes, doesn't anyone in your stories get married? Doesn't anyone have the time to run down to City Hall before they jump into bed?"

"No," I said. "In real life, yes. But in my stories, no."

"Why do you answer me like that?"

"Oh, Pa, this is a simple story about a smart woman who came to N.Y.C. full of interest love trust excitement very up to date, and about her son, what a hard time she had in this world. Married or not, it's of small consequence."

"It is of great consequence," he said.

"O.K.," I said.

"O.K. O.K. yourself," he said, "but listen. I believe you that she's good-looking, but I don't think she was so smart."

"That's true," I said. "Actually that's the trouble with stories. People start out fantastic. You think they're extraordinary, but it turns out as the work goes along, they're just average with a good education. Sometimes the other way around, the person's a kind of dumb innocent, but he outwits you and you can't even think of an ending good enough."

"What do you do then?" he asked. He had been a doctor for a couple of decades and then an artist for a couple of decades and he's still interested in details, craft, technique.

"Well, you just have to let the story lie around till some agreement can be reached between you and the stubborn hero."

"Aren't you talking silly now?" he asked. "Start again," he said. "It so happens I'm not going out this evening. Tell the story again. See what you can do this time."

"O.K.," I said. "But it's not a five-minute job." Second attempt:

> Once, across the street from us, there was a fine handsome woman, our neighbor. She had a son whom she loved because she'd known him since birth (in helpless chubby infancy, and in the wrestling, hugging ages, seven to ten, as well as earlier and later). This boy, when he fell into the

fist of adolescence, became a junkie. He was not a hopeless one. He was in fact hopeful, an ideologue and successful converter. With his busy brilliance, he wrote persuasive articles for his high-school newspaper. Seeking a wider audience, using important connections, he drummed into Lower Manhattan newsstand distribution a periodical called *Oh! Golden Horse!*

In order to keep him from feeling guilty (because guilt is the stony heart of nine tenths of all clinically diagnosed cancers in America today, she said), and because she had always believed in giving bad habits room at home where one could keep an eye on them, she too became a junkie. Her kitchen was famous for a while—a center for intellectual addicts who knew what they were doing. A few felt artistic like Coleridge° and others were scientific and revolutionary like Leary.° Although she was often high herself, certain good mothering reflexes remained, and she saw to it that there was lots of orange juice around and honey and milk and vitamin pills. However, she never cooked anything but chili, and that no more than once a week. She explained, when we talked to her, seriously, with neighborly concern, that it was her part in the youth culture and she would rather be with the young, it was an honor, than with her own generation.

One week, while nodding through an Antonioni° film, this boy was severely jabbed by the elbow of a stern and proselytizing girl, sitting beside him. She offered immediate apricots and nuts for his sugar level, spoke to him sharply, and took him home.

She had heard of him and his work and she herself published, edited, and wrote a competitive journal called *Man Does Live by Bread Alone.* In the organic heat of her continuous presence he could not help but become interested once more in his muscles, his arteries, and nerve connections. In fact he began to love them, treasure them, praise them with funny little songs in *Man Does Live* . . .

the fingers of my flesh transcend
my transcendental soul
the tightness in my shoulders end
my teeth have made me whole

To the mouth of his head (that glory of will and determination) he brought hard apples, nuts, wheat germ, and soybean oil. He said to his old friends, From now on, I guess I'll keep my wits about me. I'm going on the natch. He said he was about to begin a spiritual deep-breathing journey. How about you too, Mom? he asked kindly.

His conversion was so radiant, splendid, that neighborhood kids his age began to say that he had never been a real addict at all, only a journalist along for the smell of the story. The mother tried several times

Coleridge: Samuel Taylor Coleridge (1772–1834), English Romantic poet, was an opium addict.
Leary: Timothy Leary (1920–1996), sometime Harvard professor of psychology and early advocate of the use of LSD.
Antonioni: Michelangelo Antonioni (1912–2007), an Italian modernist film director and writer.

to give up what had become without her son and his friends a lonely habit. This effort only brought it to supportable levels. The boy and his girl took their electronic mimeograph and moved to the bushy edge of another borough. They were very strict. They said they would not see her again until she had been off drugs for sixty days.

At home alone in the evening, weeping, the mother read and re-read the seven issues of *Oh! Golden Horse!* They seemed to her as truthful as ever. We often crossed the street to visit and console. But if we mentioned any of our children who were at college or in the hospital or dropouts at home, she would cry out, My baby! My baby! and burst into terrible, face-scarring, time-consuming tears. The End.

First my father was silent, then he said, "Number One: You have a nice sense of humor. Number Two: I see you can't tell a plain story. So don't waste time." Then he said sadly, "Number Three: I suppose that means she was alone, she was left like that, his mother. Alone. Probably sick?"

I said, "Yes."

"Poor woman. Poor girl, to be born in a time of fools, to live among fools. The end. The end. You were right to put that down. The end."

I didn't want to argue, but I had to say, "Well, it is not necessarily the end, Pa."

"Yes," he said, "what a tragedy. The end of a person."

"No, Pa," I begged him. "It doesn't have to be. She's only about forty. She could be a hundred different things in this world as time goes on. A teacher or a social worker. An ex-junkie! Sometimes it's better than having a master's in education."

"Jokes," he said. "As a writer that's your main trouble. You don't want to recognize it. Tragedy! Plain tragedy! Historical tragedy! No hope. The end."

"Oh, Pa," I said. "She could change."

"In your own life, too, you have to look it in the face." He took a couple of nitroglycerin. "Turn to five," he said, pointing to the dial on the oxygen tank. He inserted the tubes into his nostrils and breathed deep. He closed his eyes and said, "No."

I had promised the family to always let him have the last word when arguing, but in this case I had a different responsibility. That woman lives across the street. She's my knowledge and my invention. I'm sorry for her. I'm not going to leave her there in that house crying. (Actually neither would Life, which unlike me has no pity.)

Therefore: She did change. Of course her son never came home again. But right now, she's the receptionist in a storefront community clinic in the East Village. Most of the customers are young people, some old friends. The head doctor has said to her, "If we only had three people in this clinic with your experiences . . ."

"The doctor said that?" My father took the oxygen tubes out of his nostrils and said, "Jokes. Jokes again."

"No, Pa, it could really happen that way, it's a funny world nowadays."

"No," he said. "Truth first. She will slide back. A person must have character. She does not."

"No, Pa," I said. "That's it. She's got a job. Forget it. She's in that storefront working."

"How long will it be?" he asked. "Tragedy! You too. When will you look it in the face?"

COMMENTARY

GRACE PALEY

Grace Paley talked with Ann Charters about her experiences as a short story writer during lunch in her Greenwich Village apartment on a snowy day in February 1986. On the wall above the kitchen table hung an oil painting, a still life of vegetables painted by her father after his retirement from medicine. Paley mentions her father's interest in art in her story "A Conversation with My Father."

A Conversation with Ann Charters 1986

Charters: Some literary critics think that short stories are more closely related to poetry than to the novel. Would you agree?

Paley: I would say that stories are closer to poetry than they are to the novel because first they are shorter, and second they are more concentrated, more economical, and that kind of economy, the pulling together of all the information and making leaps across the information, is really close to poetry. By leaps I mean thought leaps and feeling leaps. Also, when short stories are working right, you pay more attention to language than most novelists do.

Charters: Poe said unity was an essential factor of short stories. Do you have any ideas about this in your own work?

Paley: I suppose there has to be some kind of unity, but that's true in a novel too. It seems to me that unity is form. Form is really the vessel in which the story or poem or novel exists. The reason I don't have an answer for you is that there's really no telling—sometimes I like to start a story with one thing and end it with another. I don't know where the unity is in that case. I see the word *unity* meaning that something has to be whole, even if it ends in an open way.

Charters: You mean, as you wrote in "A Conversation with My Father," that "everyone, real or invented, deserves the open destiny of life."

Paley: Yes.

Charters: You started writing poetry before short stories, and the language of your fiction is often as compressed and metaphorical as the language of poetry. Can you describe the process of how you learned to write?

Paley: Let me put it this way: I went to school to poetry—that was where I learned how to write. People learn to write by doing various things. I suppose I also wrote a lot of letters, since it was the time of the Second World War. But apart from that I wrote poems, that's what I wrote. I thought about language a lot. That was important to me. That was my teacher. My fiction teacher was poetry.

Charters: What poets did you read when you were learning how to write?

Paley: I just read all the poets. If there was an anthology of poets, I read every single one. I knew all the Victorians. I read the Imagists. At a certain point I fell in love with the Englishmen who came to America—Christopher Isherwood, Stephen Spender, and W. H. Auden. I thought Auden was the greatest. And I loved the poetry of Dylan Thomas. Yeats meant a lot to me. I paid attention to all of them and listened to all of them. Some of them must have gotten into my ear. That's not up to me to say. That's for the reader to say. The reader of my stories will tell me, "This is whom you're influenced by," but I can't say that. I feel I was influenced by everybody.

Charters: Why did you stop writing poetry and start writing stories? What did the form of the short story offer you that the poem didn't?

Paley: First of all, I began to think of certain subject matter, women's lives specifically, and what was happening around me. I was in my thirties, which I guess is the time people start to notice these things, women's and men's lives and what their relationship is. I knew lots of women with small kids, and I was developing very close relationships with a variety of women. All sorts of things began to worry me, and I began to think about them a lot. I couldn't deal with any of this subject matter in poetry; I just didn't know how. I didn't have the technique. Other people can, but I didn't want to write poems saying "I feel this" and "I feel that." That was the last thing I wanted to do.

I can give you a definition that can be proven wrong in many ways, but for me it was that in writing poetry I wanted to talk to the world, I wanted to address the world, so to speak. But writing stories, I wanted to get the world to explain itself to me, to speak to me. And for me that was the essential difference between writing poetry and stories, and it still is, in many ways. So I had to get that world to talk to me. I had to reach out to it, a very different thing than writing poems. I had to reach out to the world and get it to tell me what it was all about, because I didn't understand it. I just didn't understand. Also, I'd always been very interested in people and told funny stories, and I didn't have any room for doing that in poems, again because of my own self. My poems were too literary, that's the real reason.

LUIGI PIRANDELLO

Luigi Pirandello (1867–1936) was born into a wealthy family in southern Sicily the same year that his father was wounded in a fight against a Mafioso who had attempted to extort protection money for the sulfur mines the family owned and managed. Pirandello's father was the eighteenth of his parents' twenty-three children. As the translator John Linstrum understood, Pirandello's Sicilian background and inheritance included "an island of astonishing natural beauty and human degradation, inhabited by people of passion with a highly developed sense of formality. The social mores were extreme in their rigidity: hypocrisy, repression, and exploitation all went hand in hand with a powerful church regime, a strict morality, and a feudal society." Pirandello worked briefly in the mines and witnessed their harsh conditions, but at eighteen he left Sicily to attend the Universities of Rome and Bonn, where he studied law and literature. In 1891 he earned the degree of Doctor of Philosophy with a thesis on the phonetic development of the Sicilian dialect of his home region in Agrigento. Three years later he married the daughter of his father's business partner. She had a mental breakdown in 1903, after the mines flooded and the family business failed. To support his family, Pirandello taught Italian at a girls' school in Rome. One of his sons was wounded in World War I but survived, unlike the son in the story "War."

As a university student Pirandello had written plays and published his first volume of poetry in 1889. At first he was most successful at writing fiction, publishing several novels and fifteen volumes of short stories between 1894 and 1919. Then in 1918, after his wife was committed to a mental home, he began to write plays almost exclusively. Earlier Pirandello felt that writing for the conventional theater was less challenging than creating fiction, but he was able to fashion a radically new approach to drama in *The Rules of the Game*, his first success as a playwright. Two years later it was followed by his most famous play, *Six Characters in Search of an Author*, one of four plays published in 1921. The following year Pirandello briefly joined the Fascist party in Rome, supported by Benito Mussolini, the prime minister and dictator of Italy who was later allied with Adolf Hitler. From 1924 to 1928 Pirandello toured Europe and the United States with his own theatrical company. After a performance in Germany, the physicist Albert Einstein supposedly went up to him and confided that "we are kindred souls," sharing an interest in what Pirandello later described as the "conflict between life (which is always moving and changing) and form (which fixes it, immutable)." In 1930, while he was living in London, his innovative script *The Man with the Flower in His Mouth* was the first play ever to be presented on television, which he believed had the potential of developing into a showcase for serious drama. Four years later he was awarded the Nobel Prize for literature.

Like Anton Chekhov, Pirandello continued to write short stories after he became renowned as a playwright. Unfortunately he never fulfilled his ambition to write a story for every day in the year; he died in 1936 of a heart ailment with about a hundred stories left unwritten. His earliest fiction was full of Sicilian local color settings and dialect, but after World War I in later stories such as "War," his fictional world was modern Italy and his narratives became more philosophical, dramatizing the challenges that ordinary people had to meet in the course of their everyday lives.

War

1919

The passengers who had left Rome by the night express had had to stop until dawn at the small station of Fabriano in order to continue their journey by the small old-fashioned local joining the main line with Sulmona.

At dawn, in a stuffy and smoky second-class carriage in which five people had already spent the night, a bulky woman in deep mourning was hoisted in—almost like a shapeless bundle. Behind her, puffing and moaning, followed her husband—a tiny man, thin and weakly, his face death-white, his eyes small and bright and looking shy and uneasy.

Having at last taken a seat he politely thanked the passengers who had helped his wife and who had made room for her; then he turned round to the woman trying to pull down the collar of her coat, and politely inquired:

"Are you all right, dear?"

The wife, instead of answering, pulled up her collar again to her eyes, so as to hide her face.

"Nasty world," muttered the husband with a sad smile.

And he felt it his duty to explain to his traveling companions that the poor woman was to be pitied, for the war was taking away from her her only son, a boy of twenty to whom both had devoted their entire life, even breaking up their home at Sulmona to follow him to Rome, where he had to go as a student, then allowing him to volunteer for war with an assurance, however, that at least for six months he would not be sent to the front and now, all of a sudden, receiving a wire saying that he was due to leave in three days' time and asking them to go and see him off.

The woman under the big coat was twisting and wriggling, at times growling like a wild animal, feeling certain that all those explanations would not have aroused even a shadow of sympathy from those people who—most likely—were in the same plight as herself. One of them, who had been listening with particular attention, said:

"You should thank God that your son is only leaving now for the front. Mine has been sent there the first day of the war. He has already come back twice wounded and been sent back again to the front."

"What about me? I have two sons and three nephews at the front," said another passenger.

"Maybe, but in our case it is our only son," ventured the husband.

"What difference can it make? You may spoil your only son with excessive attentions, but you cannot love him more than you would all your other children if you had any. Paternal love is not like bread that can be broken into pieces and split amongst the children in equal shares. A father gives all his love to each one of his children without discrimination, whether it be one or ten, and if I am suffering now for my two sons, I am not suffering half for each of them but double."

"True . . . true . . ." sighed the embarrassed husband, "but suppose (of course we all hope it will never be your case) a father has two sons at the front and he loses one of them, there is still one left to console him . . . while . . ."

"Yes," answered the other, getting cross, "a son left to console him but also a son left for whom he must survive, while in the case of the father of an only son if the son dies the father can die too and put an end to his distress. Which of the two positions is the worse? Don't you see how my case would be worse than yours?"

"Nonsense," interrupted another traveler, a fat, red-faced man with bloodshot eyes of the palest gray.

He was panting. From his bulging eyes seemed to spurt inner violence of an uncontrolled vitality which his weakened body could hardly contain.

"Nonsense," he repeated, trying to cover his mouth with his hand so as to hide the two missing front teeth. "Nonsense. Do we give life to our children for our own benefit?"

The other travelers stared at him in distress. The one who had had his son at the front since the first day of the war sighed: "You are right. Our children do not belong to us, they belong to the Country. . . ."

"Bosh," retorted the fat traveler. "Do we think of the Country when we give life to our children? Our sons are born because . . . well, because they must be born and when they come to life they take our own life with them. This is the truth. We belong to them but they never belong to us. And when they reach twenty they are exactly what we were at their age. We too had a father and mother, but there were so many other things as well . . . girls, cigarettes, illusions, new ties . . . and the Country, of course, whose call we would have answered—when we were twenty—even if father and mother had said no. Now at our age, the love of our Country is still great, of course, but stronger than it is the love for our children. Is there any one of us here who wouldn't gladly take his son's place at the front if he could?"

There was a silence all round, everybody nodding as to approve.

"Why then," continued the fat man, "shouldn't we consider the feelings of our children when they are twenty? Isn't it natural that at their age they should consider the love for their Country (I am speaking of decent boys, of course) even greater than the love for us? Isn't it natural that it should be so, as after all they must look upon us as upon old boys who cannot move any more and must stay at home? If Country exists, if Country is a natural necessity, like bread, of which each of us must eat in order not to die of hunger, somebody must go to defend it. And our sons go, when they are twenty, and they don't want tears, because if they die, they die inflamed and happy (I am speaking, of course, of decent boys). Now, if one dies young and happy, without having the ugly sides of life, the boredom of it, the pettiness, the bitterness of disillusion . . . what more can we ask for him? Everyone should stop crying; everyone should laugh, as I do . . . or at least thank God—as I do—because my son, before dying, sent me a message saying that he was dying satisfied at having ended his life in the best way he could have wished. That is why, as you see, I do not even wear mourning. . . ."

He shook his light fawn coat as to show it; his livid lip over his missing teeth was trembling, his eyes were watery and motionless, and soon after he ended with a shrill laugh which might well have been a sob.

"Quite so . . . quite so . . ." agreed the others.

The woman who, bundled in a corner under her coat, had been sitting and listening had—for the last three months—tried to find in the words of her husband and her friends something to console her in her deep sorrow, something that might show her how a mother should resign herself to send her son not even to death but to a probably dangerous life. Yet not a word had she found amongst the many which had been said . . . and her grief had been greater in seeing that nobody—as she thought—could share her feelings.

But now the words of the traveler amazed and almost stunned her. She suddenly realized that it wasn't the others who were wrong and could not understand her, but herself who could not rise up to the same height of those fathers and mothers willing to resign themselves, without crying, not only to the departure of their sons but even to their death.

She lifted her head, she bent over from her corner trying to listen with great attention to the details which the fat man was giving to his companions about the way his son had fallen as a hero, for his King and his Country, happy and without regrets. It seemed to her that she had stumbled into a world she had never dreamt of, a world so far unknown to her and she was so pleased to hear everyone joining in congratulating that brave father who could so stoically speak of his child's death.

Then suddenly, just as if she had heard nothing of what had been said and almost as if waking up from a dream, she turned to the old man, asking him:

"Then . . . is your son really dead?"

Everybody stared at her. The old man, too, turned to look at her, fixing his great, bulging, horribly watery light gray eyes, deep in her face. For some little time he tried to answer, but words failed him. He looked and looked at her, almost as if only then—at that silly, incongruous question—he had suddenly realized at last that his son was really dead—gone forever—forever. His face contracted, became horribly distorted, then he snatched in haste a handkerchief from his pocket and, to the amazement of everyone, broke into harrowing, heart-rending, uncontrollable sobs.

EDGAR ALLAN POE

Edgar Allan Poe (1809–1849), the son of poor traveling actors, was adopted by the merchant John Allan of Richmond, Virginia, after the death of Poe's mother when Poe was three years old. He was educated in England and Virginia, enlisted and served two years in the army, then entered the military academy at West Point, from which he was expelled for absenteeism after a year. When John Allan disinherited him, Poe became a writer to earn his living.

In 1833 Poe's story "A MS. Found in a Bottle" won a fifty-dollar prize for the best story in a popular Baltimore periodical, and soon afterward he assumed editorship of the *Southern Literary Messenger.* In 1836 he married his cousin Virginia Clemm, shortly before her fourteenth birthday. Poe's brilliant reviews, poems, and stories attracted wide attention, but in 1837 he quarreled with the owner of the *Messenger* over his salary and the degree of his independence as an editor, and he resigned from the magazine.

In 1841 Poe became an editor of *Graham's Magazine*, and during his yearlong tenure he quadrupled subscriptions by publishing his own stories and articles. He left *Graham's* to start his own magazine, which failed. His remaining years as a freelance writer were a struggle with poverty, depression, poor health aggravated by addiction to drugs and alcohol, and – after 1847 – grief over the death of his wife. The writer Jorge Luis Borges observed that Poe's life "was short and unhappy, if unhappiness can be short."

Poe's first collection of twenty-five short stories appeared in two volumes in 1840, *Tales of the Grotesque and Arabesque.* His second collection of twelve stories, *Tales,* published in 1845, was so successful that it was followed by *The Raven and Other Poems* the same year. Poe was industrious, and his books of short fiction and poetry sold well, but his total income from them in his lifetime was less than three hundred dollars.

Most of Poe's best stories can be divided into two categories: melodramatic tales of gothic terror, symbolic psychological fiction that became the source of the modern horror story, such as "The Cask of Amontillado" and "The Fall of the House of Usher"; and stories of intellect or reason, analytic tales that were precursors of the modern detective story. After critics accused Poe of imitating the extravagant "mysticism" of German romantic writers in his monologues of inspired madness, Poe asserted his originality in the preface to his first story collection: "If in many of my productions terror has been the thesis, I maintain that terror is not of Germany, but of the soul."

Known as a literary critic as well as a poet and writer of short fiction, Poe published more than seventy tales. He is important as one of the earliest writers to attempt to formulate an aesthetic theory about the short story form, or "prose tale" as it was called in his time. Some of his most extensive comments on this subject are found in his reviews of Hawthorne's *Twice-Told Tales* for *Graham's Magazine* in 1842 and *Godey's Lady's Book* in 1847. In these essays he also described his own philosophy of composition. Poe believed that unity of a "single effect" was the most essential quality of all successful short fiction. He praised Hawthorne for his "invention, creation, imagination, originality"–qualities Poe himself possessed in abundance. In June 1846, Hawthorne returned the compliment by sending Poe a graceful letter with a copy of his second collection, *Mosses from an Old Manse*, saying that he would never fail to recognize Poe's "force and originality" as a writer of tales even if he sometimes disagreed with Poe's opinions as a critic.

Poe's stories were widely translated, and he became the first American writer of short fiction to be internationally celebrated. Interpretations of his creative work by writers living abroad usually focused on aspects of his genius that supported their views of America. The Russian novelist Fyodor Dostoevsky admired Poe's "strangely material" imagination and recognized that Poe, unlike the German romantic writers, did not give a large role to supernatural agents in his gothic tales. Instead, Dostoevsky felt that the "power of details" in Poe's descriptions was presented "with such stupendous plasticity that you cannot but believe in the reality or possibility of a fact which actually never has occurred."

The French poet Charles Baudelaire, who translated Poe's tales and championed his genius, regarded Poe from a completely different perspective when he identified him as an alienated artist–"le poète maudit"–a writer outside his society who reflected the derangement of a hypocritical country that professed individual freedom yet permitted slavery in the southern states and bigamy among the Mormons in Utah.

Other readers were more critical–for instance, the transcendentalist writer Margaret Fuller, who took Poe to task for what she considered his careless use of language. Perhaps the most sweeping dismissal of Poe's writing originated with Henry James, who–despite his interest in the psychological presentation of fictional characters–declared that "an enthusiasm for Poe is the mark of a decidedly primitive stage of reflection." Later critics are more appreciative and continue to engage in a lively conversation about Poe's work.

CONNECTIONS See pages 648–665, including Edgar Allan Poe, "The Importance of the Single Effect in a Prose Tale," page 650; D. H. Lawrence, "On 'The Fall of the House of Usher' and 'The Cask of Amontillado,'" page 652; Cleanth Brooks and Robert Penn Warren, "A New Critical Reading of 'The Fall of the House of Usher,'" page 656;

J. Gerald Kennedy, "On 'The Fall of the House of Usher,'" page 658; David S. Reynolds, "Poe's Art of Transformation in 'The Cask of Amontillado,'" page 661.

WEB Research Edgar Allan Poe at bedfordstmartins.com/rewritinglit.

The Cask of Amontillado

1846

The thousand injuries of Fortunato I had borne as I best could; but when he ventured upon insult, I vowed revenge. You, who so well know the nature of my soul, will not suppose, however, that I gave utterance to a threat. *At length* I would be avenged; this was a point definitely settled—but the very definitiveness with which it was resolved precluded the idea of risk. I must not only punish, but punish with impunity. A wrong is unredressed when retribution overtakes its redresser. It is equally unredressed when the avenger fails to make himself felt as such to him who has done the wrong.

It must be understood, that neither by word nor deed had I given Fortunato cause to doubt my good-will. I continued, as was my wont, to smile in his face, and he did not perceive that my smile *now* was at the thought of his immolation.

He had a weak point—this Fortunato—although in other regards he was a man to be respected and even feared. He prided himself on his connoisseurship in wine. Few Italians have the true virtuoso spirit. For the most part their enthusiasm is adopted to suit the time and opportunity—to practise imposture upon the British and Austrian *millionnaires.* In painting and gemmary Fortunato, like his countrymen, was a quack—but in the matter of old wines he was sincere. In this respect I did not differ from him materially: I was skilful in the Italian vintages myself, and bought largely whenever I could.

It was about dusk, one evening during the supreme madness of the carnival season, that I encountered my friend. He accosted me with excessive warmth, for he had been drinking much. The man wore motley. He had on a tight-fitting parti-striped dress, and his head was surmounted by the conical cap and bells. I was so pleased to see him, that I thought I should never have done wringing his hand.

I said to him: "My dear Fortunato, you are luckily met. How remarkably well you are looking to-day! But I have received a pipe° of what passes for Amontillado, and I have my doubts."

"How?" said he. "Amontillado? A pipe? Impossible! And in the middle of the carnival!"

"I have my doubts," I replied; "and I was silly enough to pay the full Amontillado price without consulting you in the matter. You were not to be found, and I was fearful of losing a bargain."

"Amontillado!"

"I have my doubts."

"Amontillado!"

"And I must satisfy them."

---

pipe: A large cask or keg.

"Amontillado!"

"As you are engaged, I am on my way to Luchesi. If any one has a critical turn, it is he. He will tell me——"

"Luchesi cannot tell Amontillado from Sherry."

"And yet some fools will have it that his taste is a match for your own."

"Come, let us go."

"Whither?"

"To your vaults."

"My friend, no; I will not impose upon your good nature. I perceive you have an engagement. Luchesi——"

"I have no engagement;—come."

"My friend, no. It is not the engagement, but the severe cold with which I perceive you are afflicted. The vaults are insufferably damp. They are encrusted with nitre."

"Let us go, nevertheless. The cold is merely nothing. Amontillado! You have been imposed upon. And as for Luchesi, he cannot distinguish Sherry from Amontillado."

Thus speaking, Fortunato possessed himself of my arm. Putting on a mask of black silk, and drawing a *roquelaire*° closely about my person, I suffered him to hurry me to my palazzo.

There were no attendants at home; they had absconded to make merry in honor of the time. I had told them that I should not return until the morning, and had given them explicit orders not to stir from the house. These orders were sufficient, I well knew, to insure their immediate disappearance, one and all, as soon as my back was turned.

I took from their sconces two flambeaux, and giving one to Fortunato, bowed him through several suites of rooms to the archway that led into the vaults. I passed down a long and winding staircase, requesting him to be cautious as he followed. We came at length to the foot of the descent, and stood together on the damp ground of the catacombs of the Montresors.

The gait of my friend was unsteady, and the bells upon his cap jingled as he strode.

"The pipe?" said he.

"It is farther on," said I; "but observe the white web-work which gleams from these cavern walls."

He turned toward me, and looked into my eyes with two filmy orbs that distilled the rheum of intoxication.

"Nitre?" he asked, at length.

"Nitre," I replied. "How long have you had that cough?"

"Ugh! ugh! ugh!—ugh! ugh! ugh!—ugh! ugh! ugh!—ugh! ugh! ugh!—ugh! ugh! ugh!"

My poor friend found it impossible to reply for many minutes.

"It is nothing," he said, at last.

---

roquelaire: A short cloak.

"Come," I said, with decision, "we will go back; your health is precious. You are rich, respected, admired, beloved; you are happy, as once I was. You are a man to be missed. For me it is no matter. We will go back; you will be ill, and I cannot be responsible. Besides, there is Luchesi——"

"Enough," he said; "the cough is a mere nothing; it will not kill me. I shall not die of a cough."

"True—true," I replied; "and, indeed, I had no intention of alarming you unnecessarily; but you should use all proper caution. A draught of this Medoc will defend us from the damps."

Here I knocked off the neck of a bottle which I drew from a long row of its fellows that lay upon the mould.

"Drink," I said, presenting him the wine.

He raised it to his lips with a leer. He paused and nodded to me familiarly, while his bells jingled.

"I drink," he said, "to the buried that repose around us."

"And I to your long life."

He again took my arm, and we proceeded.

"These vaults," he said, "are extensive."

"The Montresors," I replied, "were a great and numerous family."

"I forget your arms."

"A huge human foot d'or,° in a field azure; the foot crushes a serpent rampant whose fangs are imbedded in the heel."

"And the motto?"

"*Nemo me impune lacessit.*"°

"Good!" he said.

The wine sparkled in his eyes and the bells jingled. My own fancy grew warm with the Medoc. We had passed through walls of piled bones, with casks and puncheons intermingling into the inmost recesses of the catacombs. I paused again, and this time I made bold to seize Fortunato by an arm above the elbow.

"The nitre!" I said; "see, it increases. It hangs like moss upon the vaults. We are below the river's bed. The drops of moisture trickle among the bones. Come, we will go back ere it is too late. Your cough——"

"It is nothing," he said; "let us go on. But first, another draught of the Medoc."

I broke and reached him a flagon of De Grâve. He emptied it at a breath. His eyes flashed with a fierce light. He laughed and threw the bottle upward with a gesticulation I did not understand.

I looked at him in surprise. He repeated the movement—a grotesque one.

"You do not comprehend?" he said.

"Not I," I replied.

"Then you are not of the brotherhood."

---

d'or: Of gold.
Nemo me impune lacessit: "No one wounds me with impunity"; the motto of the royal arms of Scotland.

"How?"

"You are not of the masons."

"Yes, yes," I said; "yes, yes."

"You? Impossible! A mason?"

"A mason," I replied.

"A sign," he said.

"It is this," I answered, producing a trowel from beneath the folds of my *roquelaire.*

"You jest," he exclaimed, recoiling a few paces. "But let us proceed to the Amontillado."

"Be it so," I said, replacing the tool beneath the cloak, and again offering him my arm. He leaned upon it heavily. We continued our route in search of the Amontillado. We passed through a range of low arches, descended, passed on, and descending again, arrived at a deep crypt, in which the foulness of the air caused our flambeaux rather to glow than flame.

At the most remote end of the crypt there appeared another less spacious. Its walls had been lined with human remains, piled to the vault overhead, in the fashion of the great catacombs of Paris. Three sides of this interior crypt were still ornamented in this manner. From the fourth the bones had been thrown down, and lay promiscuously upon the earth, forming at one point a mound of some size. Within the wall thus exposed by the displacing of the bones, we perceived a still interior recess, in depth about four feet, in width three, in height six or seven. It seemed to have been constructed for no especial use within itself, but formed merely the interval between two of the colossal supports of the roof of the catacombs, and was backed by one of their circumscribing walls of solid granite.

It was in vain that Fortunato, uplifting his dull torch, endeavored to pry into the depth of the recess. Its termination the feeble light did not enable us to see.

"Proceed," I said; "herein is the Amontillado. As for Luchesi——"

"He is an ignoramus," interrupted my friend, as he stepped unsteadily forward, while I followed immediately at his heels. In an instant he had reached the extremity of the niche, and finding his progress arrested by the rock, stood stupidly bewildered. A moment more and I had fettered him to the granite. In its surface were two iron staples, distant from each other about two feet, horizontally. From one of these depended a short chain, from the other a padlock. Throwing the links about his waist, it was but the work of a few seconds to secure it. He was too much astounded to resist. Withdrawing the key I stepped back from the recess.

"Pass your hand," I said, "over the wall; you cannot help feeling the nitre. Indeed it is *very* damp. Once more let me *implore* you to return. No? Then I must positively leave you. But I must first render you all the little attentions in my power."

"The Amontillado!" ejaculated my friend, not yet recovered from his astonishment.

"True," I replied; "the Amontillado."

As I said these words I busied myself among the pile of bones of which I have before spoken. Throwing them aside, I soon uncovered a quantity of building stone and mortar. With these materials and with the aid of my trowel, I began vigorously to wall up the entrance of the niche.

I had scarcely laid the first tier of the masonry when I discovered that the intoxication of Fortunato had in a great measure worn off. The earliest indication I had of this was a low moaning cry from the depth of the recess. It was *not* the cry of a drunken man. There was then a long and obstinate silence. I laid the second tier, and the third, and the fourth; and then I heard the furious vibrations of the chain. The noise lasted for several minutes, during which, that I might hearken to it with the more satisfaction, I ceased my labors and sat down upon the bones. When at last the clanking subsided, I resumed the trowel, and finished without interruption the fifth, the sixth, and the seventh tier. The wall was now nearly upon a level with my breast. I again paused, and holding the flambeaux over the masonwork, threw a few feeble rays upon the figure within.

A succession of loud and shrill screams, bursting suddenly from the throat of the chained form, seemed to thrust me violently back. For a brief moment I hesitated—I trembled. Unsheathing my rapier, I began to grope with it about the recess; but the thought of an instant reassured me. I placed my hand upon the solid fabric of the catacombs, and felt satisfied. I reapproached the wall. I replied to the yells of him who clamored. I reechoed—I aided—I surpassed them in volume and in strength. I did this, and the clamorer grew still.

It was now midnight, and my task was drawing to a close. I had completed the eighth, the ninth, and the tenth tier. I had finished a portion of the last and the eleventh; there remained but a single stone to be fitted and plastered in. I struggled with its weight; I placed it partially in its destined position. But now there came from out the niche a low laugh that erected the hairs upon my head. It was succeeded by a sad voice, which I had difficulty in recognizing as that of the noble Fortunato. The voice said—

"Ha! ha! ha!—he! he!—a very good joke indeed—an excellent jest. We will have many a rich laugh about it at the palazzo—he! he! he!—over our wine—he! he! he!"

"The Amontillado!" I said.

"He! he! he!—he! he! he!—yes, the Amontillado. But is it not getting late? Will not they be awaiting us at the palazzo, the Lady Fortunato and the rest? Let us be gone."

"Yes," I said, "let us be gone."

"For the love of God, Montresor!"

"Yes," I said, "for the love of God!"

But to these words I hearkened in vain for a reply. I grew impatient. I called aloud:

"Fortunato!"

No answer. I called again:

"Fortunato!"

No answer still, I thrust a torch through the remaining aperture and let it fall within. There came forth in return only a jingling of the bells. My heart grew sick—on account of the dampness of the catacombs. I hastened to make an end of my labor. I forced the last stone into its position; I plastered it up. Against the new masonry I re-erected the old rampart of bones. For the half of a century no mortal has disturbed them. *In pace requiescat!*

The Fall of the House of Usher 1839

Son cœur est un luth suspendu;
Sitôt qu'on le touche il résonne.°

–DE BÉRANGER

During the whole of a dull, dark, and soundless day in the autumn of the year, when the clouds hung oppressively low in the heavens, I had been passing alone, on horseback, through a singularly dreary tract of country, and at length found myself, as the shades of the evening drew on, within view of the melancholy House of Usher. I know not how it was—but, with the first glimpse of the building, a sense of insufferable gloom pervaded my spirit. I say insufferable; for the feeling was unrelieved by any of that half-pleasurable, because poetic, sentiment, with which the mind usually receives even the sternest natural images of the desolate or terrible. I looked upon the scene before me—upon the mere house, and the simple landscape features of the domain—upon the bleak walls—upon the vacant eye-like windows—upon a few rank sedges—and upon a few white trunks of decayed trees—with an utter depression of soul which I can compare to no earthly sensation more properly than to the after-dream of the reveller upon opium—the bitter lapse into every-day life—the hideous dropping off of the veil. There was an iciness, a sinking, a sickening of the heart—an unredeemed dreariness of thought which no goading of the imagination could torture into aught of the sublime. What was it—I paused to think—what was it that so unnerved me in the contemplation of the House of Usher? It was a mystery all insoluble; nor could I grapple with the shadowy fancies that crowded upon me as I pondered. I was forced to fall back upon the unsatisfactory conclusion, that while, beyond doubt, there *are* combinations of very simple natural objects which have the power of thus affecting us, still the analysis of this power lies among considerations beyond our depth. It was possible, I reflected, that a mere different arrangement of the particulars of the scene, of the details of the picture, would be sufficient to modify, or perhaps to annihilate its capacity for sorrowful impression; and, acting upon this idea, I reined my horse to the precipitous brink of a black and lurid tarn that lay in unruffled lustre by the dwelling, and gazed down—but with a shudder even more thrilling than before—upon the remodelled and inverted images of the gray sedge, and the ghastly tree-stems, and the vacant and eye-like windows.

Epigraph: His heart is a suspended lute; / Which resonates as soon as touched.

Nevertheless, in this mansion of gloom I now proposed to myself a sojourn of some weeks. Its proprietor, Roderick Usher, had been one of my boon companions in boyhood; but many years had elapsed since our last meeting. A letter, however, had lately reached me in a distant part of the country—a letter from him—which, in its wildly importunate nature, had admitted of no other than a personal reply. The MS. gave evidence of nervous agitation. The writer spoke of acute bodily illness—of a mental disorder which oppressed him—and of an earnest desire to see me, as his best, and indeed his only personal friend, with a view of attempting, by the cheerfulness of my society, some alleviation of his malady. It was the manner in which all this, and much more, was said—it was the apparent *heart* that went with his request—which allowed me no room for hesitation; and I accordingly obeyed forthwith what I still considered a very singular summons.

Although, as boys, we had been even intimate associates, yet I really knew little of my friend. His reserve had been always excessive and habitual. I was aware, however, that his very ancient family had been noted, time out of mind, for a peculiar sensibility of temperament, displaying itself, through long ages, in many works of exalted art, and manifested, of late, in repeated deeds of munificent yet unobtrusive charity, as well as in a passionate devotion to the intricacies, perhaps even more than to the orthodox and easily recognizable beauties, of musical science. I had learned, too, the very remarkable fact, that the stem of the Usher race, all time-honoured as it was, had put forth, at no period, any enduring branch; in other words, that the entire family lay in the direct line of descent, and had always, with very trifling and very temporary variation, so lain. It was this deficiency, I considered, while running over in thought the perfect keeping of the character of the premises with the accredited character of the people, and while speculating upon the possible influence which the one, in the long lapse of centuries, might have exercised upon the other—it was this deficiency, perhaps of collateral issue, and the consequent undeviating transmission, from sire to son, of the patrimony with the name, which had, at length, so identified the two as to merge the original title of the estate in the quaint and equivocal appellation of the "House of Usher"—an appellation which seemed to include, in the minds of the peasantry who used it, both the family and the family mansion.

I have said that the sole effect of my somewhat childish experiment—that of looking down within the tarn—had been to deepen the first singular impression. There can be no doubt that the consciousness of the rapid increase of my superstition—for why should I not so term it?—served mainly to accelerate the increase itself. Such, I have long known, is the paradoxical law of all sentiments having terror as a basis. And it might have been for this reason only, that, when I again uplifted my eyes to the house itself, from its image in the pool, there grew in my mind a strange fancy—a fancy so ridiculous, indeed, that I but mention it to show the vivid force of the sensations which oppressed me. I had so worked upon my imagination as really to believe that about the whole mansion and domain there hung an atmosphere peculiar to themselves and their immediate vicinity—an atmosphere which had no affinity with the air of heaven, but which had reeked up from the decayed trees, and the gray wall, and the silent tarn—a pestilent and mystic vapour, dull, sluggish, faintly discernible, and leaden-hued.

Shaking off from my spirit what *must* have been a dream, I scanned more narrowly the real aspect of the building. Its principal feature seemed to be that of an excessive antiquity. The discoloration of ages had been great. Minute fungi overspread the whole exterior, hanging in a fine tangled web-work from the eaves. Yet all this was apart from an extraordinary dilapidation. No portion of the masonry had fallen; and there appeared to be a wild inconsistency between its still perfect adaptation of parts, and the crumbling condition of the individual stones. In this there was much that reminded me of the specious totality of the old woodwork which has rotted for long years in some neglected vault, with no disturbance from the breath of the external air. Beyond this indication of extensive decay, however, the fabric gave little token of instability. Perhaps the eye of a scrutinizing observer might have discovered a barely perceptible fissure, which, extending from the roof of the building in front, made its way down the wall in a zigzag direction, until it became lost in the sullen waters of the tarn.

Noticing these things, I rode over a short causeway to the house. A servant in waiting took my horse, and I entered the Gothic archway of the hall. A valet, of stealthy step, thence conducted me, in silence, through many dark and intricate passages in my progress to the *studio* of his master. Much that I encountered on the way contributed, I know not how, to heighten the vague sentiments of which I have already spoken. While the objects around me—while the carvings of the ceilings, the sombre tapestries of the walls, the ebon blackness of the floors, and the phantasmagoric armorial trophies which rattled as I strode, were but matters to which, or to such as which, I had been accustomed from my infancy—while I hesitated not to acknowledge how familiar was all this—I still wondered to find how unfamiliar were the fancies which ordinary images were stirring up. On one of the staircases, I met the physician of the family. His countenance, I thought, wore a mingled expression of low cunning and perplexity. He accosted me with trepidation and passed on. The valet now threw open a door and ushered me into the presence of his master.

The room in which I found myself was very large and lofty. The windows were long, narrow, and pointed, and at so vast a distance from the black oaken floor as to be altogether inaccessible from within. Feeble gleams of encrimsoned light made their way through the trellised panes, and served to render sufficiently distinct the more prominent objects around; the eye, however, struggled in vain to reach the remoter angles of the chamber, or the recesses of the vaulted and fretted ceiling. Dark draperies hung upon the walls. The general furniture was profuse, comfortless, antique, and tattered. Many books and musical instruments lay scattered about, but failed to give any vitality to the scene. I felt that I breathed an atmosphere of sorrow. An air of stern, deep, and irredeemable gloom hung over and pervaded all.

Upon my entrance, Usher arose from a sofa on which he had been lying at full length, and greeted me with a vivacious warmth which had much in it, I at first thought, of an overdone cordiality—of the constrained effort of the *ennuyé* man of the world. A glance, however, at his countenance convinced me of his perfect sincerity. We sat down; and for some moments, while he spoke not, I gazed upon him with a feeling half of pity, half of awe. Surely, man had never before so terribly altered, in so brief a period, as had Roderick Usher! It was with difficulty that I could bring myself to admit the identity of the wan being before me with the companion of my early boyhood. Yet the character of his face had been at all times remarkable. A cadaverousness of complexion; an eye large, liquid, and luminous beyond comparison; lips somewhat thin and very pallid, but of a surpassingly beautiful curve; a nose of a delicate Hebrew model, but with a breadth of nostril unusual in similar formations; a finely moulded chin, speaking, in its want of prominence, of a want of moral energy; hair of a more than web-like softness and tenuity; these features, with an inordinate expansion above the regions of the temple, made up altogether a countenance not easily to be forgotten. And now in the mere exaggeration of the prevailing character of these features, and of the expression they were wont to convey, lay so much of change that I doubted to whom I spoke. The now ghastly pallor of the skin, and the now miraculous lustre of the eye, above all things startled and even awed me. The silken hair, too, had been suffered to grow all unheeded, and as, in its wild gossamer texture, it floated rather than fell about the face, I could not, even with effort, connect its Arabesque expression with any idea of simple humanity.

In the manner of my friend I was at once struck with an incoherence—an inconsistency; and I soon found this to arise from a series of feeble and futile struggles to overcome an habitual trepidancy—an excessive nervous agitation. For something of this nature I had indeed been prepared, no less by his letter, than by reminiscences of certain boyish traits, and by conclusions deduced from his peculiar physical conformation and temperament. His action was alternately vivacious and sullen. His voice varied rapidly from a tremulous indecision (when the animal spirits seemed utterly in abeyance) to that species of energetic concision—that abrupt, weighty, unhurried, and hollow-sounding enunciation—that leaden, self-balanced, and perfectly modulated guttural utterance, which may be observed in the lost drunkard, or the irreclaimable eater of opium, during the periods of his most intense excitement.

It was thus that he spoke of the object of my visit, of his earnest desire to see me, and of the solace he expected me to afford him. He entered, at some length, into what he conceived to be the nature of his malady. It was, he said, a constitutional and a family evil, and one for which he despaired to find a remedy—a mere nervous affection, he immediately added, which would undoubtedly soon pass off. It displayed itself in a host of unnatural sensations. Some of these, as he detailed them, interested and bewildered me; although, perhaps, the terms and the general manner of their narration had their weight. He suffered much from a morbid acuteness of the senses; the most insipid food was alone endurable; he could wear only garments of certain texture; the odours of all flowers were oppressive; his eyes were tortured by even a faint light; and there were but peculiar sounds, and these from stringed instruments, which did not inspire him with horror.

To an anomalous species of terror I found him a bounden slave. "I shall perish," said he, "I *must* perish in this deplorable folly. Thus, thus, and not otherwise, shall I be lost. I dread the events of the future, not in themselves, but in their results. I shudder at the thought of any, even the most trivial, incident, which may operate upon this intolerable agitation of soul. I have, indeed, no abhorrence of danger, except in its absolute effect—in terror. In this unnerved—in this pitiable condition—I feel that the period will sooner or later arrive when I must abandon life and reason together, in some struggle with the grim phantasm, FEAR."

I learned, moreover, at intervals, and through broken and equivocal hints, another singular feature of his mental condition. He was enchained by certain superstitious impressions in regard to the dwelling which he tenanted, and whence, for many years, he had never ventured forth—in regard to an influence whose supposititious force was conveyed in terms too shadowy here to be re-stated—an influence which some peculiarities in the mere form and substance of his family mansion had, by dint of long sufferance, he said, obtained over his spirit—an effect which the *physique* of the gray wall and turrets, and of the dim tarn into which they all looked down, had, at length, brought about upon the *morale* of his existence.

He admitted, however, although with hesitation, that much of the peculiar gloom which thus afflicted him could be traced to a more natural and far more palpable origin—to the severe and long-continued illness—indeed to the evidently approaching dissolution—of a tenderly beloved sister, his sole companion for long years, his last and only relative on earth. "Her decease," he said, with a bitterness which I can never forget, "would leave him (him the hopeless and the frail) the last of the ancient race of the Ushers." While he spoke, the lady Madeline (for so was she called) passed slowly through a remote portion of the apartment, and, without having noticed my presence, disappeared. I regarded her with an utter astonishment not unmingled with dread—and yet I found it impossible to account for such feelings. A sensation of stupor oppressed me, as my eyes followed her retreating steps. When a door, at length, closed upon her, my glance sought instinctively and eagerly the countenance of the brother—but he had buried his face in his hands, and I could only perceive that a far more than ordinary wanness had overspread the emaciated fingers through which trickled many passionate tears.

The disease of the lady Madeline had long baffled the skill of her physicians. A settled apathy, a gradual wasting away of the person, and frequent although transient affections of a partially cataleptical character were the unusual diagnosis. Hitherto she had steadily borne up against the pressure of her malady, and had not betaken herself finally to bed; but on the closing in of the evening of my arrival at the house, she succumbed (as her brother told me at night with inexpressible agitation) to the prostrating power of the destroyer; and I learned that the glimpse I had obtained of her person would thus probably be the last I should obtain—that the lady, at least while living, would be seen by me no more.

For several days ensuing, her name was unmentioned by either Usher or myself: and during this period I was busied in earnest endeavours to alleviate the melancholy of my friend. We painted and read together, or I listened, as if in a dream, to the wild improvisations of his speaking guitar. And thus, as a closer and still closer intimacy admitted me more unreservedly into the recesses of his spirit, the more bitterly did I perceive the futility of all attempt at cheering a mind from which darkness, as if an inherent positive quality, poured forth upon all objects of the moral and physical universe in one unceasing radiation of gloom.

I shall ever bear about me a memory of the many solemn hours I thus spent alone with the master of the House of Usher. Yet I should fail in any attempt to convey an idea of the exact character of the studies, or of the occupations, in which he involved me, or led me the way. An excited and highly distempered ideality threw a sulphureous lustre over all. His long improvised dirges will ring forever in my ears. Among other things, I hold painfully in mind a certain singular perversion and amplification of the wild air of the last waltz of Von Weber. From the paintings over which his elaborate fancy brooded, and which grew, touch by touch, into vagueness at which I shuddered the more thrillingly, because I shuddered knowing not why;—from these paintings (vivid as their images now are before me) I would in vain endeavour to educe more than a small portion which should lie within the compass of merely written words. By the utter simplicity, by the nakedness of his designs, he arrested and overawed attention. If ever mortal painted an idea, that mortal was Roderick Usher. For me at least—in the circumstances then surrounding me—there arose out of the pure abstractions which the hypochondriac contrived to throw upon his canvas, an intensity of intolerable awe, no shadow of which I felt ever yet in the contemplation of the certainly glowing yet too concrete reveries of Fuseli.

One of the phantasmagoric conceptions of my friend, partaking not so rigidly of the spirit of abstraction, may be shadowed forth, although feebly, in words. A small picture presented the interior of an immensely long and rectangular vault or tunnel, with low walls, smooth, white, and without interruption or device. Certain accessory points of the design served well to convey the idea that this excavation lay at an exceeding depth below the surface of the earth. No outlet was observed in any portion of its vast extent, and no torch or other artificial source of light was discernible; yet a flood of intense rays rolled throughout, and bathed the whole in a ghastly and inappropriate splendour.

I have just spoken of that morbid condition of the auditory nerve which rendered all music intolerable to the sufferer, with the exception of certain effects of stringed instruments. It was, perhaps, the narrow limits to which he thus confined himself upon the guitar, which gave birth, in great measure, to the fantastic character of his performances. But the fervid *facility* of his *impromptus* could not be so accounted for. They must have been, and were, in the notes, as well as in the words of his wild fantasias (for he not unfrequently accompanied himself with rhymed verbal improvisations), the result of that intense mental collectedness and concentration to which I have previously alluded as observable only in particular moments of the highest artificial excitement. The words of one of these rhapsodies I have easily remembered. I was, perhaps, the more forcibly impressed with it, as he gave it, because, in the under or mystic current of its meaning, I fancied that I perceived, and for the first time, a full consciousness on the part of Usher, of the tottering of his lofty reason upon her throne. The verses, which were entitled "The Haunted Palace," ran very nearly, if not accurately, thus:

I

In the greenest of our valleys,
    By good angels tenanted,
Once a fair and stately palace—
    Radiant palace—reared its head.
In the monarch Thought's dominion—
    It stood there!
Never seraph spread a pinion
    Over fabric half so fair.

II

Banners yellow, glorious, golden,
    On its roof did float and flow;
(This—all this—was in the olden
    Time long ago)
And every gentle air that dallied,
    In that sweet day,
Along the ramparts plumed and pallid,
    A winged odour went away.

III

Wanderers in that happy valley
    Through two luminous windows saw
Spirits moving musically
    To a lute's well-tunèd law,
Round about a throne, where sitting
    (Porphyrogene!)
In state his glory well befitting,
    The ruler of the realm was seen.

IV

And all with pearl and ruby glowing
    Was the fair palace door,
Through which came flowing, flowing, flowing
    And sparkling evermore,
A troop of Echoes whose sweet duty
    Was but to sing,
In voices of surpassing beauty,
    The wit and wisdom of their king.

V

But evil things, in robes of sorrow,
    Assailed the monarch's high estate;
(Ah, let us mourn, for never morrow
    Shall dawn upon him, desolate!)
And, round about his home, the glory
    That blushed and bloomed
Is but a dim-remembered story
    Of the old time entombed.

VI

And travellers now within that valley,
    Through the red-litten windows see
Vast forms that move fantastically
    To a discordant melody;
While, like a rapid ghastly river,
    Through the pale door,
A hideous throng rush out forever,
    And laugh—but smile no more.

I well remember that suggestions arising from this ballad led us into a train of thought wherein there became manifest an opinion of Usher's which I mention not so much on account of its novelty (for other men° have thought thus), as on account of the pertinacity with which he maintained it. This opinion, in its general form, was that of the sentience of all vegetable things. But, in his disordered fancy, the idea had assumed a more daring character, and trespassed, under certain conditions, upon the kingdom of inorganization. I lack words to express the full extent, or the earnest *abandon* of his persuasion. The belief, however, was connected (as I have previously hinted) with the gray stones of the home of his forefathers. The conditions of the sentience had been here, he imagined, fulfilled in the method of collocation of these stones—in the order of their arrangement, as well as in that of the many *fungi* which overspread them, and of the decayed trees which stood around—above all, in the long undisturbed endurance of this arrangement, and in its reduplication in the still waters of the tarn. Its evidence—the evidence of the sentience—was to be seen, he said (and I here started as he spoke), in the gradual yet certain condensation of an atmosphere of their own about the waters and the walls. The result was discoverable, he added, in that silent yet importunate and terrible influence which for centuries had moulded the destinies of his family, and which made *him* what I now saw him—what he was. Such opinions need no comment, and I will make none.

Our books—the books which, for years, had formed no small portion of

---

other men: Watson, Dr. Percival, Spallanzani, and especially the Bishop of Landaff.—See *Chemical Essays*, vol. v. [Poe's note.]

the mental existence of the invalid—were, as might be supposed, in strict keeping with his character of phantasm. We pored together over such works as the Ververt et Chartreuse of Gresset; the Belphegor of Machiavelli; the Heaven and Hell of Swedenborg; the Subterranean Voyage of Nicholas Klimm of Holberg; the Chiromancy of Robert Flud, of Jean D'Indaginé, and of De la Chambre; the Journey into the Blue Distance of Tieck; and the City of the Sun of Campanella. One favourite volume was a small octavo edition of the *Directorium Inquisitorum*, by the Dominican Eymeric de Gironne; and there were passages in Pomponius Mela, about the old African Satyrs and Ægipans, over which Usher would sit dreaming for hours. His chief delight, however, was found in the perusal of an exceedingly rare and curious book in quarto Gothic—the manual of a forgotten church—the *Vigiliæ Mortuorum secundum Chorum Ecclesiæ Maguntinæ.*

I could not help thinking of the wild ritual of this work, and of its probable influence upon the hypochondriac, when, one evening, having informed me abruptly that the lady Madeline was no more, he stated his intention of preserving her corpse for a fortnight (previously to its final interment), in one of the numerous vaults within the main walls of the building. The worldly reason, however, assigned for this singular proceeding, was one which I did not feel at liberty to dispute. The brother had been led to his resolution (so he told me) by consideration of the unusual character of the malady of the deceased, of certain obtrusive and eager inquiries on the part of her medical men, and of the remote and exposed situation of the burial-ground of the family. I will not deny that when I called to mind the sinister countenance of the person whom I met upon the staircase, on the day of my arrival at the house, I had no desire to oppose what I regarded as at best but a harmless, and by no means an unnatural, precaution.

At the request of Usher, I personally aided him in the arrangements for the temporary entombment. The body having been encoffined, we two alone bore it to its rest. The vault in which we placed it (and which had been so long unopened that our torches, half smothered in its oppressive atmosphere, gave us little opportunity for investigation) was small, damp, and entirely without means of admission for light; lying, at great depth, immediately beneath that portion of the building in which was my own sleeping apartment. It had been used, apparently, in remote feudal times, for the worst purposes of a donjon-keep, and, in later days, as a place of deposit for powder, or some other highly combustible substance, as a portion of its floor, and the whole interior of a long archway through which we reached it, were carefully sheathed with copper. The door, of massive iron, had been, also, similarly protected. Its immense weight caused an unusually sharp grating sound, as it moved upon its hinges.

Having deposited our mournful burden upon tressels within this region of horror, we partially turned aside the yet unscrewed lid of the coffin, and looked upon the face of the tenant. A striking similitude between the brother and sister now first arrested my attention; and Usher, divining, perhaps, my thoughts, murmured out some few words from which I learned that the deceased and himself had been twins, and that sympathies of a scarcely intelligible nature had always existed between them. Our glances, however, rested not long upon the dead—for we could not regard her unawed. The disease which had thus entombed the lady in the maturity of youth, had left, as usual in all maladies of a strictly cataleptical character, the mockery of a faint blush upon the bosom and the face, and that suspiciously lingering smile upon the lip which is so terrible in death. We replaced and screwed down the lid, and, having secured the door of iron, made our way, with toil, into the scarcely less gloomy apartments of the upper portion of the house.

And now, some days of bitter grief having elapsed, an observable change came over the features of the mental disorder of my friend. His ordinary manner had vanished. His ordinary occupations were neglected or forgotten. He roamed from chamber to chamber with hurried, unequal, and objectless step. The pallor of his countenance had assumed, if possible, a more ghastly hue—but the luminousness of his eye had utterly gone out. The once occasional huskiness of his tone was heard no more; and a tremulous quaver, as if of extreme terror, habitually characterized his utterance. There were times, indeed, when I thought his unceasingly agitated mind was labouring with some oppressive secret, to divulge which he struggled for the necessary courage. At times, again, I was obliged to resolve all into the mere inexplicable vagaries of madness, for I beheld him gazing upon vacancy for long hours, in an attitude of the profoundest attention, as if listening to some imaginary sound. It was no wonder that his condition terrified—that it infected me. I felt creeping upon me, by slow yet certain degrees, the wild influences of his own fantastic yet impressive superstitions.

It was, especially, upon retiring to bed late in the night of the seventh or eighth day after the placing of the lady Madeline within the donjon, that I experienced the full power of such feelings. Sleep came not near my couch—while the hours waned and waned away. I struggled to reason off the nervousness which had dominion over me. I endeavoured to believe that much, if not all of what I felt, was due to the bewildering influence of the gloomy furniture of the room—of the dark and tattered draperies, which, tortured into motion by the breath of a rising tempest, swayed fitfully to and fro upon the walls, and rustled uneasily about the decorations of the bed. But my efforts were fruitless. An irrepressible tremour gradually pervaded my frame; and, at length, there sat upon my very heart an incubus of utterly causeless alarm. Shaking this off with a gasp and a struggle, I uplifted myself upon the pillows, and, peering earnestly within the intense darkness of the chamber, hearkened—I know not why, except that an instinctive spirit prompted me—to certain low and indefinite sounds which came, through the pauses of the storm, at long intervals, I knew not whence. Overpowered by an intense sentiment of horror, unaccountable yet unendurable, I threw on my clothes with haste (for I felt that I should sleep no more during the night), and endeavoured to arouse myself from the pitiable condition into which I had fallen, by pacing rapidly to and fro through the apartment.

I had taken but few turns in this manner, when a light step on an adjoining staircase arrested my attention. I presently recognised it as that of Usher. In an instant afterward he rapped, with a gentle touch, at my door, and entered, bearing a lamp. His countenance was, as usual, cadaverously wan—but, moreover, there was a species of mad hilarity in his eyes—an evidently restrained *hysteria* in his whole demeanour. His air appalled me—but anything was preferable to the solitude which I had so long endured, and I even welcomed his presence as a relief.

"And you have not seen it?" he said abruptly, after having stared about him for some moments in silence—"you have not then seen it?—but, stay! you shall." Thus speaking, and having carefully shaded his lamp, he hurried to one of the casements, and threw it freely open to the storm.

The impetuous fury of the entering gust nearly lifted us from our feet. It was, indeed, a tempestuous yet sternly beautiful night, and one wildly singular in its terror and its beauty. A whirlwind had apparently collected its force in our vicinity; for there were frequent and violent alterations in the direction of the wind; and the exceeding density of the clouds (which hung so low as to press upon the turrets of the house) did not prevent our perceiving the life-like velocity with which they flew careering from all points against each other, without passing away into the distance. I say that even their exceeding density did not prevent our perceiving this—yet we had no glimpse of the moon or stars—nor was there any flashing forth of the lightning. But the under surfaces of the huge masses of agitated vapour, as well as all terrestrial objects immediately around us, were glowing in the unnatural light of a faintly luminous and distinctly visible gaseous exhalation which hung about and enshrouded the mansion.

"You must not—you shall not behold this!" said I, shudderingly, to Usher, as I led him, with a gentle violence, from the window to a seat. "These appearances, which bewilder you, are merely electrical phenomena not uncommon—or it may be that they have their ghastly origin in the rank miasma of the tarn. Let us close this casement;—the air is chilling and dangerous to your frame. Here is one of your favourite romances. I will read, and you shall listen;—and so we will pass away this terrible night together."

The antique volume which I had taken up was the "Mad Trist" of Sir Launcelot Canning; but I had called it a favourite of Usher's more in sad jest than in earnest; for, in truth, there is little in its uncouth and unimaginative prolixity which could have had interest for the lofty and spiritual ideality of my friend. It was, however, the only book immediately at hand; and I indulged a vague hope that the excitement which now agitated the hypochondriac might find relief (for the history of mental disorder is full of similar anomalies) even in the extremeness of the folly which I could read. Could I have judged, indeed, by the wild overstrained air of vivacity with which he hearkened, or apparently hearkened, to the words of the tale, I might well have congratulated myself upon the success of my design.

I had arrived at that well-known portion of the story where Ethelred, the hero of the Trist, having sought in vain for peaceable admission into the dwelling of the hermit, proceeds to make good an entrance by force. Here, it will be remembered, the words of the narrative run thus:

"And Ethelred, who was by nature of a doughty heart, and who was now mighty withal, on account of the powerfulness of the wine which he had drunken, waited no longer to hold parley with the hermit, who, in sooth, was of an obstinate and maliceful turn, but, feeling the rain upon his shoulders, and fearing the rising of the tempest, uplifted his mace outright, and, with blows, made quickly room in the plankings of the door for his gauntleted hand; and now pulling therewith sturdily, he so cracked, and ripped, and tore all asunder, that the noise of the dry and hollow-sounding wood alarmed and reverberated throughout the forest."

At the termination of this sentence I started and, for a moment, paused; for it appeared to me (although I at once concluded that my excited fancy had deceived me)—it appeared to me that, from some very remote portion of the mansion, there came, indistinctly, to my ears, what might have been, in its exact similarity of character, the echo (but a stifled and dull one certainly) of the very cracking and ripping sound which Sir Launcelot had so particularly described. It was, beyond doubt, the coincidence alone which had arrested my attention; for, amid the rattling of the sashes of the casements, and the ordinary commingled noises of the still increasing storm, the sound, in itself, had nothing, surely, which should have interested or disturbed me. I continued the story:

"But the good champion Ethelred, now entering within the door, was sore enraged and amazed to perceive no signal of the maliceful hermit; but, in the stead thereof, a dragon of a scaly and prodigious demeanour, and of a fiery tongue, which sate in guard before a palace of gold, with a floor of silver; and upon the wall there hung a shield of shining brass with this legend enwritten—

> Who entereth herein, a conqueror hath bin;
> Who slayeth the dragon, the shield he shall win.

And Ethelred uplifted his mace, and struck upon the head of the dragon, which fell before him, and gave up his pesty breath, with a shriek so horrid and harsh, and withal so piercing, that Ethelred had fain to close his ears with his hands against the dreadful noise of it, the like whereof was never before heard."

Here again I paused abruptly, and now with a feeling of wild amazement—for there could be no doubt whatever that, in this instance, I did actually hear (although from what direction it proceeded I found it impossible to say) a low and apparently distant, but harsh, protracted, and most unusual screaming or grating sound—the exact counterpart of what my fancy had already conjured up for the dragon's unnatural shriek as described by the romancer.

Oppressed, as I certainly was, upon the occurrence of the second and most extraordinary coincidence, by a thousand conflicting sensations, in which wonder and extreme terror were predominant, I still retained sufficient presence of mind to avoid exciting, by any observation, the sensitive nervousness of my companion. I was by no means certain that he had noticed the sounds in question; although, assuredly, a strange alteration had, during the last few minutes, taken place in his demeanour. From a position fronting my own, he had gradually brought round his chair, so as to sit with his face to the door of the chamber; and thus I could but partially perceive his features, although I saw that his lips trembled as if he were murmuring inaudibly. His head had dropped upon his breast—yet I knew that he was not asleep, from the wide and rigid opening of the eye as I caught a glance of it in profile. The motion of his body, too, was at variance with this idea—for he rocked from side to side with a gentle yet constant and uniform sway. Having rapidly taken notice of all this, I resumed the narrative of Sir Launcelot, which thus proceeded:

"And now, the champion, having escaped from the terrible fury of the dragon, bethinking himself of the brazen shield, and of the breaking up of the enchantment which was upon it, removed the carcass from out of the way before him, and approached valorously over the silver pavement of the castle to where the shield was upon the wall; which in sooth tarried not for his full coming, but fell down at his feet upon the silver floor, with a mighty great and terrible ringing sound."

No sooner had these syllables passed my lips, than—as if a shield of brass had indeed, at the moment, fallen heavily upon a floor of silver—I became aware of a distinct, hollow, metallic, and clangorous, yet apparently muffled reverberation. Completely unnerved, I leaped to my feet; but the measured rocking movement of Usher was undisturbed. I rushed to the chair in which he sat. His eyes were bent fixedly before him, and throughout his whole countenance there reigned a stony rigidity. But, as I placed my hand upon his shoulder, there came a strong shudder over his whole person; a sickly smile quivered about his lips; and I saw that he spoke in a low, hurried, and gibbering murmur, as if unconscious of my presence. Bending closely over him, I at length drank in the hideous import of his words.

"Not hear it?—yes, I hear it, and *have* heard it. Long—long—long—many minutes, many hours, many days, have I heard it—yet I dared not—oh, pity me, miserable wretch that I am!—I dared not—I *dared* not speak! *We have put her living in the tomb!* Said I not that my senses were acute? I *now* tell you that I heard her first feeble movements in the hollow coffin. I heard them—many, many days ago—yet I dared not—I *dared not speak!* And now—tonight—Ethelred—ha! ha!—the breaking of the hermit's door, and the death-cry of the dragon, and the clangour of the shield!—say, rather, the rending of her coffin, and the grating of the iron hinges of her prison, and her struggles within the coppered archway of the vault! Oh whither shall I fly? Will she not be here anon? Is she not hurrying to upbraid me for my haste? Have I not heard her footsteps on the stair? Do I not distinguish that heavy and horrible beating of her heart? MADMAN!"—here he sprang furiously to his feet, and shrieked out his syllables, as if in the effort he were giving up his soul—"MADMAN! I TELL YOU THAT SHE NOW STANDS WITHOUT THE DOOR!"

As if in the superhuman energy of his utterance there had been found the potency of a spell—the huge antique panels to which the speaker pointed threw slowly back, upon the instant, their ponderous and ebony jaws. It was the work of the rushing gust — but then without those doors there *did* stand the lofty and enshrouded figure of the lady Madeline of Usher. There was blood upon her white robes, and the evidence of some bitter struggle upon every portion of her emaciated frame. For a moment she remained trembling and reeling to and fro upon the threshold, then, with a low moaning cry, fell heavily inward upon the person of her brother, and in her violent and now final death-agonies, bore him to the floor a corpse, and a victim to the terrors he had anticipated.

From that chamber, and from that mansion, I fled aghast. The storm was still abroad in all its wrath as I found myself crossing the old causeway. Suddenly there shot along the path a wild light, and I turned to see whence a gleam so unusual could have issued; for the vast house and its shadows were alone behind me. The radiance was that of the full, setting, and blood-red moon, which now shone vividly through that once barely discernible fissure, of which I have before spoken as extending from the roof of the building, in a zigzag direction, to the base. While I gazed, this fissure rapidly widened — there came a fierce breath of the whirlwind — the entire orb of the satellite burst at once upon my sight — my brain reeled as I saw the mighty walls rushing asunder — there was a long tumultuous shouting sound like the voice of a thousand waters — and the deep and dank tarn at my feet closed sullenly and silently over the fragments of the "HOUSE OF USHER."

MARJANE SATRAPI

Marjane Satrapi (b. 1969) was born in Rasht, Iran, and raised in Tehran. She is the only child of a father who was a successful architect and a mother who was a dress designer, and she is the granddaughter of the last Qadjar emperor of Persia. In 1984, five years after the Iranian Revolution, at the beginning of the war between Iran and Iraq that left a million dead, her parents sent her to live in Vienna, fearing that she would be arrested as an outspoken rebellious teenager in fundamentalist Tehran. Feeling exiled as an art student in Austria, Satrapi failed to fit in. Four years later she spent two winter months on the street, became suicidal, and was hospitalized. In 1989, when she returned home to the domestic repression of the totalitarian regime in Iran, she found that "everything was settled down. The revolution was far behind, ten years before. . . . We were so fed up with the eight years of war [with Iraq]; it was so good that the war was finished. People just wanted to live. . . . We didn't talk about politics because we were so scared. This new generation is different. They haven't lived what we have gone through. They don't have the same fears."

After a brief marriage Satrapi left Tehran for Paris in 1994, where she attended a comic book workshop called "The Association," which included Pierre-François Beauchard, whose black-and-white graphic novels, published under the name David B., dramatize family trauma. As a child Satrapi never dreamed that she would become a graphic artist, since she did not like to read comic books. While she was growing up, her cousins tried to interest her in the popular Tintin adventure series created by the Belgian artist Hergé, who incorporated actual news stories from 1929 to 1983 into his graphic narratives. Satrapi claims that Tintin – a peripatetic young journalist who traveled the world with his dog Snowy – didn't stop anywhere long enough to interact with young women characters, so she couldn't identify with him. It was encountering Art Spiegelman's Holocaust story *Maus* that captivated her. "When I read him I thought . . . it's possible to tell a story and make a point this way. It was amazing." She realized that she could express her ideas and feelings through pictures in a way that words alone could not communicate.

> Image is an international language. The first writing of the human being was drawing, not writing. That appeared much before the alphabet. And when you draw a situation – someone is scared or angry or happy – it means the same thing in all cultures. You cannot draw someone crying, and in one culture they think that he is happy. He would have the same expression. There's something direct about the image. Also, it is more accessible. People don't take it so seriously. And when you want to use a little bit of humor, it's much easier to use pictures.

"The Veil," a story told from the perspective of a ten-year-old girl, is from *Persepolis 1* (2003), subtitled "The Story of a Childhood," which describes Satrapi's life in Iran during the revolution and the first years of the war with Iraq. *Persepolis 2* (2004), called "The Story of a Return," begins with her arrival in Austria and ends with her return to her ravaged homeland. She wrote them after she moved to Paris, which has become her home. *Persepolis* is dedicated to her parents, but she didn't show them her first book based on their life together until just before it was published. She feels that

> maturity is knowing to say what to whom and when. Sometimes saying stuff is not a very good idea. You want to make yourself feel a little bit lighter, so you take your shit and you put it on somebody else's back. Well, that's extremely egoistic. One should know also how to hold things back and assume his or her own responsibility.

Describing her method, Satrapi, who writes in French, says she first decides how many frames she wants to put on each page and what she wants to say in each frame. Then she sketches a stick figure or the outline of a scene in each frame. "After that, I take a pencil and draw them. Once that is finished, I put my paper over the light box and ink it. It's a long process." Satrapi's other books include *Embroideries* (2005) and *Chicken with Plums* (2006). *Persepolis* is available as a film distributed by Sony Classics.

From *Persepolis*: "The Veil"

2003

THE VEIL

AND ALSO BECAUSE THE YEAR BEFORE, IN 1979, WE WERE IN A FRENCH NON-RELIGIOUS SCHOOL.

WHERE BOYS AND GIRLS WERE TOGETHER.

AND THEN SUDDENLY IN 1980...
ALL BILINGUAL SCHOOLS MUST BE CLOSED DOWN.

THEY ARE SYMBOLS OF CAPITALISM.
BRAVO!
WHAT WISDOM!

OF DECADENCE.
THIS IS CALLED A "CULTURAL REVOLUTION."

WE FOUND OURSELVES VEILED AND SEPARATED FROM OUR FRIENDS.

AND THAT WAS THAT...

EVERYWHERE IN THE STREETS THERE WERE DEMONSTRATIONS FOR AND AGAINST THE VEIL.
the veil!
the veil!
the veil!
freedom!
freedom!
freedom!
freedom!

AT ONE OF THE DEMONSTRATIONS, A GERMAN JOURNALIST TOOK A PHOTO OF MY MOTHER.

I WAS REALLY PROUD OF HER. HER PHOTO WAS PUBLISHED IN ALL THE EUROPEAN NEWSPAPERS.

AND EVEN IN ONE MAGAZINE IN IRAN. MY MOTHER WAS REALLY SCARED.
HAVE YOU SEEN THIS?
DON'T WORRY, DARLING.

SHE DYED HER HAIR,

AND WORE DARK GLASSES FOR A LONG TIME.

I REALLY DIDN'T KNOW WHAT TO THINK ABOUT THE VEIL. DEEP DOWN I WAS VERY RELIGIOUS BUT AS A FAMILY WE WERE VERY MODERN AND AVANT-GARDE.

I WAS BORN WITH RELIGION.

AT THE AGE OF SIX I WAS ALREADY SURE I WAS THE LAST PROPHET. THIS WAS A FEW YEARS BEFORE THE REVOLUTION.

BEFORE ME THERE HAD BEEN A FEW OTHERS.

I WANTED TO BE A PROPHET...

BECAUSE MY FATHER HAD A CADILLAC.

AND, ABOVE ALL, BECAUSE MY GRANDMOTHER'S KNEES ALWAYS ACHED.

LIKE ALL MY PREDECESSORS I HAD MY HOLY BOOK.

THE FIRST THREE RULES CAME FROM ZARATHUSTRA. HE WAS THE FIRST PROPHET IN MY COUNTRY BEFORE THE ARAB INVASION.
YOU MUST BASE EVERYTHING ON THESE THREE RULES: BEHAVE WELL, SPEAK WELL, ACT WELL.

I ALSO WANTED US TO CELEBRATE THE TRADITIONAL ZARATHUSTRIAN HOLIDAYS. LIKE THE FIRE CEREMONY,

BEFORE THE PERSIAN NEW YEAR, NOROUZ, ON MARCH 21ST, THE FIRST DAY OF SPRING.

ONLY MY GRANDMOTHER KNEW ABOUT MY BOOK.
RULE NUMBER SIX: EVERYBODY SHOULD HAVE A CAR.
RULE NUMBER SEVEN: ALL MAIDS SHOULD EAT AT THE TABLE WITH THE OTHERS.
RULE NUMBER EIGHT: NO OLD PERSON SHOULD HAVE TO SUFFER.
IN THAT CASE, I'LL BE YOUR FIRST DISCIPLE.
REALLY?
BUT TELL ME HOW YOU'LL ARRANGE FOR OLD PEOPLE NOT TO SUFFER?
IT WILL SIMPLY BE FORBIDDEN.

EVERY NIGHT I HAD A BIG DISCUSSION WITH GOD.
GOD, GIVE ME SOME MORE TIME. I AM NOT QUITE READY YET.

YES YOU ARE, CELESTIAL LIGHT, YOU ARE MY CHOICE, MY LAST AND MY BEST CHOICE.

EXCEPT FOR MY GRANDMOTHER I WAS OBVIOUSLY THE ONLY ONE WHO BELIEVED IN MYSELF.
WHAT DO YOU WANT TO BE WHEN YOU GROW UP?

I'LL BE A PROPHET.

HAHA! HAHA! HAHA!
SHE'S CRAZY.

MY PARENTS WERE CALLED IN BY THE TEACHER.
YOUR CHILD IS DISTURBED. SHE WANTS TO BECOME A PROPHET.

WHAT ABOUT IT?
DOESN'T THIS WORRY YOU?

NO ! NOT AT ALL !
?

NONETHELESS, MY PARENTS WERE PUZZLED.
SO TELL ME, MY CHILD, WHAT DO YOU WANT TO BE WHEN YOU GROW UP?
A PROPHET.

I WANT TO BE A DOCTOR.

THAT'S FINE MY LOVE. THAT'S FINE.

I FELT GUILTY TOWARDS GOD.
YOU WANT TO BE A DOCTOR? I THOUGHT THAT...

NO, NO, I WILL BE A PROPHET BUT THEY MUSTN'T KNOW.

I WANTED TO BE JUSTICE, LOVE AND THE WRATH OF GOD ALL IN ONE.

COMMENTARY

SYDNEY PLUM

Reading "The Veil" by Marjane Satrapi 2009

The opening chapter of Marjane Satrapi's graphic memoir *Persepolis*, "The Veil," begins a coming-of-age story in which conventions are redrawn to describe the impact of the Islamic Revolution on Satrapi's friends and family. *Persepolis* was first published in France in serial form—one reason why "The Veil" may be read as a self-contained short story. In language and iconography, it introduces a girl who is on the verge of a difficult, complicated journey into adulthood and has the story-telling ability, imagination, and humor to take us with her. It makes you want to turn the page.

"The Veil" introduces ten-year-old Marjane, who faces dramatic changes in her society that will leave her, as well as her friends and family, trying to come to terms with a disjuncture between their inner lives and the faces they now have to present. Satrapi uses graphic literature to expose the conflict between the veil she is required to wear and the individual hidden behind it. She uses humor to soften any antagonism. In the first panel of "The Veil" her solemn pose underscores her sincerity, but belies the humor of the second panel, which infuses her story.

Although practices vary about when a Muslim girl must begin wearing the veil, or hijab, as an expression of female modesty, the symbolism of passage into womanhood is clear. However, in this narrative, the veil is represented by the young Marjane as one aspect of the repression that closes down her bilingual school and separates the boys from the girls. It suppresses the individuality even of ten-year-olds, as shown by the difference between Golnaz, Mahshid, Narine, and Minna in the second panel of the story and the playful, individuated girls of the fifth panel. The Revolution causes her mother to change her appearance and attitude, confusing a young girl proud of her mother's stance and confused about female role models (suggested by the repetition of framed images). She must consider not only what it is to be a woman, but also what it is to be a woman veiled.

The precocious Marjane is also confused about the religious nature of this suppression of identity, as she has experienced religion as fostering her childlike sense of her own importance in her family and beyond. How could a religious belief require her to hide her light behind a veil?

This bemusement is the impetus for the second half of the chapter—a flashback to her younger life—in which she depicts herself as a prophet in the making, with her own holy book and a personal relationship with God. It might seem odd that a ten-year-old would need to look back on her life so far, yet isn't it the case that when we look back on our early childhood, we see ourselves as children in that lost world, rather than re-experiencing childhood subjectivity? In the forty-five panels of "The Veil," the narrative moves back and forth in time both subtly and abruptly. These movements are coherent because of the nature of graphic literature. As Scott McCloud explains in *Understanding Comics: The Invisible Art,* graphic literature is a sequential art that depends upon the reader/viewer's mind to complete what is missing, close gaps in time and space, and construct narratives, or at least relationships, from a static iconography enclosed in separate panels.

Consider the connections among the following images. An isolated Marjane in the first panel lets us know it is her story and that she sees herself set apart from her classmates. However, the solid, black tabletop of the first two panels joins her to her classmates in the next panel. A solid, black background unifies the sequence, in panels eight through eleven, embodying the Cultural Revolution in forbidding, apparently omniscient eyes set in a bearded face from an Assyrian relief. The same background is used toward the end of the chapter to signal nighttime, when Marjane has her conversations with God—as distinct from daytime confrontations with classmates and parents. The presence of these iconographically straightforward sequences makes it possible to take in slightly jarring synapses, which is as it should be—as Marjane's world has been severely fractured.

Throughout *Persepolis,* Satrapi's iconography shows us a figure struggling to find reason and meaning in a world captured in bold blocks of black and white. Sometimes the drawings seem to simplify Marjane's world into opposing forces, but much of the time the contrasts suggest connections between figures and ideas that complicate rather than simplify—as when Marjane's mother dyes her hair blond and wears dark glasses. Or when Marjane confesses to God that she has betrayed His choice of her as a prophet, and her white nightdress is suddenly figured with black and white flowers—and then she becomes a trinity.

All the sequences and asides are in the service of revealing to us the temperament, interests, and family background of a quite complicated protagonist. In the second panel, Satrapi draws the row of girls such that we can only see her elbow and fingers, describing the drawing as a class photo—from which she has been mysteriously cropped. She portrays herself as "the Last Prophet" looking like something from a kindergarten play, with a cardboard sunburst around her face. And the God with whom she converses from her bed looks amazingly like Albert Einstein. All of these images—some playful, others thought-provoking—lead us into a better understanding of and connection with this bright girl from another culture. Through the character of Marjane, we are drawn into a world that might otherwise not have interested us, eager to follow the engaging, amusing, often perplexed figure at its center.

LESLIE MARMON SILKO

Leslie Marmon Silko (b. 1948), a Laguna Pueblo Native American, was born and grew up in New Mexico. She was educated at Bureau of Indian Affairs schools in Laguna, a Catholic school in Albuquerque, and the University of New Mexico, where she received her B.A. in English in 1969. After teaching at various colleges, she became a professor of English at the University of Arizona at Tucson. Silko's first novel, *Ceremony* (1977), is regarded as one of the most important books in modern Native American literature. In it she forged a connection between the shared past of the tribe and the individual life of a Native American returning home after World War II. Silko has received a National Endowment for the Arts fellowship, a Pushcart Prize, and a three-year grant from the MacArthur Foundation, which enabled her to take time off from teaching and become "a little less beholden to the everyday world."

Storyteller (1981), a collection of tribal folktales, family anecdotes, photographs by her grandfather, and her own poems and stories, is Silko's personal anthology of the Laguna Pueblo culture. "Yellow Woman" is from that collection. It illustrates Silko's skill in retelling a traditional Native American legend in a realistic contemporary context that confirms its emotional truth and makes it accessible to a larger audience.

Tales about a "ka'tsina" mountain spirit who seduces the Yellow Woman away from her husband and family were first told to the fictional heroine by her grandfather. The Yellow Woman in the traditional captivity narratives can be interpreted in several ways—as a girl who runs off with a man outside the tribe, as a raped and kidnapped married woman, as a spirit, as a fertility archetype. In creating fiction, Silko works with all the implied meanings of the old legends; she has said that she writes "because I like seeing how I can translate [a] sort of feeling or flavor or sense of a story that's told and heard onto the page." Other books by Silko include *The Almanac of the Dead* (1991), *Sacred Water* (1993), *Yellow Woman and a Beauty of the Spirit: Essays on Native American Life* (1996), *Gardens in the Dunes* (1999), and *The Turquoise Ledge: A Memoir* (2010).

WEB Research Leslie Marmon Silko at bedfordstmartins.com/rewritinglit.

Yellow Woman 1974

I

My thigh clung to his with dampness, and I watched the sun rising up through the tamaracks and willows. The small brown water birds came to the river and hopped across the mud, leaving brown scratches in the alkali-white crust. They bathed in the river silently. I could hear the water, almost at our feet where the narrow fast channel bubbled and washed green ragged moss and fern leaves. I looked at him beside me, rolled in the red blanket on the white river sand. I cleaned the sand out of the cracks between my toes, squinting because the sun was above the willow trees. I looked at him for the last time, sleeping on the white river sand.

I felt hungry and followed the river south the way we had come the afternoon before, following our footprints that were already blurred by the lizard tracks and bug trails. The horses were still lying down, and the black one whinnied when he saw me but he did not get up—maybe it was because the corral was made out of thick cedar branches and the horses had not yet felt the sun like I had. I tried to look beyond the pale red mesas to the pueblo. I knew it was there, even if I could not see it, on the sand rock hill above the river, the same river that moved past me now and had reflected the moon last night.

The horse felt warm underneath me. He shook his head and pawed the sand. The bay whinnied and leaned against the gate trying to follow, and I remembered him asleep in the red blanket beside the river. I slid off the horse and tied him close to the other horse. I walked north with the river again, and the white sand broke loose in footprints over footprints.

"Wake up."

He moved in the blanket and turned his face to me with his eyes still closed. I knelt down to touch him.

"I'm leaving."

He smiled now, eyes still closed. "You are coming with me, remember?" He sat up now with his bare dark chest and belly in the sun.

"Where?"

"To my place."

"And will I come back?"

He pulled his pants on. I walked away from him, feeling him behind me and smelling the willows.

"Yellow Woman," he said.

I turned to face him. "Who are you?" I asked.

He laughed and knelt on the low, sandy bank, washing his face in the river. "Last night you guessed my name, and you knew why I had come."

I stared past him at the shallow moving water and tried to remember the night, but I could only see the moon in the water and remember his warmth around me.

"But I only said that you were him and that I was Yellow Woman—I'm not really her—I have my own name and I come from the pueblo on the other side of the mesa. Your name is Silva and you are a stranger I met by the river yesterday afternoon."

He laughed softly. "What happened yesterday has nothing to do with what you will do today, Yellow Woman."

"I know—that's what I'm saying—the old stories about the ka'tsina spirit° and Yellow Woman can't mean us."

My old grandpa liked to tell those stories best. There is one about Badger and Coyote who went hunting and were gone all day, and when the sun was going down they found a house. There was a girl living there alone, and she had

---

the ka'tsina spirit: A mountain spirit of the Pueblo Indians.

light hair and eyes and she told them that they could sleep with her. Coyote wanted to be with her all night so he sent Badger into a prairie-dog hole, telling him he thought he saw something in it. As soon as Badger crawled in, Coyote blocked up the entrance with rocks and hurried back to Yellow Woman.

"Come here," he said gently.

He touched my neck and I moved close to him to feel his breathing and to hear his heart. I was wondering if Yellow Woman had known who she was—if she knew that she would become part of the stories. Maybe she'd had another name that her husband and relatives called her so that only the ka'tsina from the north and the storytellers would know her as Yellow Woman. But I didn't go on; I felt him all around me, pushing me down into the white river sand.

Yellow Woman went away with the spirit from the north and lived with him and his relatives. She was gone for a long time, but then one day she came back and she brought twin boys.

"Do you know the story?"

"What story?" He smiled and pulled me close to him as he said this. I was afraid lying there on the red blanket. All I could know was the way he felt, warm, damp, his body beside me. This is the way it happens in the stories, I was thinking, with no thought beyond the moment she meets the ka'tsina spirit and they go.

"I don't have to go. What they tell in stories was real only then, back in time immemorial, like they say."

He stood up and pointed at my clothes tangled in the blanket. "Let's go," he said.

I walked beside him, breathing hard because he walked fast, his hand around my wrist. I had stopped trying to pull away from him, because his hand felt cool and the sun was high, drying the river bed into alkali. I will see someone, eventually I will see someone, and then I will be certain that he is only a man—some man from nearby—and I will be sure that I am not Yellow Woman. Because she is from out of time past and I live now and I've been to school and there are highways and pickup trucks that Yellow Woman never saw.

It was an easy ride north on horseback. I watched the change from the cottonwood trees along the river to the junipers that brushed past us in the foothills, and finally there were only piñons, and when I looked up at the rim of the mountain plateau I could see pine trees growing on the edge. Once I stopped to look down, but the pale sandstone had disappeared and the river was gone and the dark lava hills were all around. He touched my hand, not speaking, but always singing softly a mountain song and looking into my eyes.

I felt hungry and wondered what they were doing at home now—my mother, my grandmother, my husband, and the baby. Cooking breakfast, saying, "Where did she go?—maybe kidnapped," and Al going to the tribal police with the details: "She went walking along the river."

The house was made with black lava rock and red mud. It was high above the spreading miles of arroyos and long mesas. I smelled a mountain smell of pitch and buck brush. I stood there beside the black horse, looking down on the small, dim country we had passed, and I shivered.

"Yellow Woman, come inside where it's warm."

II

He lit a fire in the stove. It was an old stove with a round belly and an enamel coffeepot on top. There was only the stove, some faded Navajo blankets, and a bedroll and cardboard box. The floor was made of smooth adobe plaster, and there was one small window facing east. He pointed at the box.

"There's some potatoes and the frying pan." He sat on the floor with his arms around his knees pulling them close to his chest and he watched me fry the potatoes. I didn't mind him watching me because he was always watching me—he had been watching me since I came upon him sitting on the river bank trimming leaves from a willow twig with his knife. We ate from the pan and he wiped the grease from his fingers on his Levis.

"Have you brought women here before?" He smiled and kept chewing, so I said, "Do you always use the same tricks?"

"What tricks?" He looked at me like he didn't understand.

"The story about being a ka'tsina from the mountains. The story about Yellow Woman."

Silva was silent; his face was calm.

"I don't believe it. Those stories couldn't happen now," I said.

He shook his head and said softly, "But someday they will talk about us, and they will say, 'Those two lived long ago when things like that happened.'"

He stood up and went out. I ate the rest of the potatoes and thought about things—about the noise the stove was making and the sound of the mountain wind outside. I remembered yesterday and the day before, and then I went outside.

I walked past the corral to the edge where the narrow trail cut through the black rim rock. I was standing in the sky with nothing around me but the wind that came down from the blue mountain peak behind me. I could see faint mountain images in the distance miles across the vast spread of mesas and valleys and plains. I wondered who was over there to feel the mountain wind on those sheer blue edges—who walks on the pine needles in those blue mountains.

"Can you see the pueblo?" Silva was standing behind me.

I shook my head. "We're too far away."

"From here I can see the world." He stepped out on the edge. "The Navajo reservation begins over there." He pointed to the east. "The Pueblo boundaries are over here." He looked below us to the south, where the narrow trail seemed to come from. "The Texans have their ranches over there, starting with that valley, the Concho Valley. The Mexicans run some cattle over there too."

"Do you ever work for them?"

"I steal from them," Silva answered. The sun was dropping behind us and shadows were filling the land below. I turned away from the edge that dropped forever into the valleys below.

"I'm cold," I said; "I'm going inside." I started wondering about this man who could speak the Pueblo language so well but who lived on a mountain and rustled cattle. I decided that this man Silva must be Navajo, because Pueblo men didn't do things like that.

"You must be a Navajo."

Silva shook his head gently. "Little Yellow Woman," he said, "you never give up, do you? I have told you who I am. The Navajo people know me, too." He knelt down and unrolled the bedroll and spread the extra blankets out on a piece of canvas. The sun was down, and the only light in the house came from outside—the dim orange light from sundown.

I stood there and waited for him to crawl under the blankets.

"What are you waiting for?" he said, and I lay down beside him. He undressed me slowly like the night before beside the river—kissing my face gently and running his hands up and down my belly and legs. He took off my pants and then he laughed.

"Why are you laughing?"

"You are breathing so hard."

I pulled away from him and turned my back to him.

He pulled me around and pinned me down with his arms and chest. "You don't understand, do you, little Yellow Woman? You will do what I want."

And again he was all around me with his skin slippery against mine, and I was afraid because I understood that his strength could hurt me. I lay underneath him and I knew that he could destroy me. But later, while he slept beside me, I touched his face and I had a feeling—the kind of feeling for him that overcame me that morning along the river. I kissed him on the forehead and he reached out for me.

When I woke up in the morning he was gone. It gave me a strange feeling because for a long time I sat there on the blankets and looked around the little house for some object of his—some proof that he had been there or maybe that he was coming back. Only the blankets and the cardboard box remained. The .30–30° that had been leaning in the corner was gone, and so was the knife I had used the night before. He was gone, and I had my chance to go now. But first I had to eat, because I knew it would be a long walk home.

I found some dried apricots in the cardboard box, and I sat down on a rock at the edge of the plateau rim. There was no wind and the sun warmed me. I was surrounded by silence. I drowsed with apricots in my mouth, and I didn't believe that there were highways or railroads or cattle to steal.

When I woke up, I stared down at my feet in the black mountain dirt. Little black ants were swarming over the pine needles around my foot. They must have smelled the apricots. I thought about my family far below me. They would be wondering about me, because this had never happened to me before. The tribal police would file a report. But if old Grandpa weren't dead he would tell them what happened—he would laugh and say, "Stolen by a ka'tsina, a mountain spirit. She'll come home—they usually do." There are enough of them to handle things. My mother and grandmother will raise the baby like they raised me. Al will find someone else, and they will go on like before, except that there will be a story about the day I disappeared while I was walking along the river. Silva had come for me; he said he had. I did not decide to go. I just went. Moonflowers blossom in the sand hills before dawn, just as I followed

---

.30–30: A rifle.

him. That's what I was thinking as I wandered along the trail through the pine trees.

It was noon when I got back. When I saw the stone house I remembered that I had meant to go home. But that didn't seem important any more, maybe because there were little blue flowers growing in the meadow behind the stone house and the gray squirrels were playing in the pines next to the house. The horses were standing in the corral, and there was a beef carcass hanging on the shady side of a big pine in front of the house. Flies buzzed around the clotted blood that hung from the carcass. Silva was washing his hands in a bucket full of water. He must have heard me coming because he spoke to me without turning to face me.

"I've been waiting for you."

"I went walking in the big pine trees."

I looked into the bucket full of bloody water with brown-and-white animal hairs floating in it. Silva stood there letting his hand drip, examining me intently.

"Are you coming with me?"

"Where?" I asked him.

"To sell the meat in Marquez."

"If you're sure it's O.K."

"I wouldn't ask you if it wasn't," he answered.

He sloshed the water around in the bucket before he dumped it out and set the bucket upside down near the door. I followed him to the corral and watched him saddle the horses. Even beside the horses he looked tall, and I asked him again if he wasn't Navajo. He didn't say anything; he just shook his head and kept cinching up the saddle.

"But Navajos are tall."

"Get on the horse," he said, "and let's go."

The last thing he did before we started down the steep trail was to grab the .30–30 from the corner. He slid the rifle into the scabbard that hung from his saddle.

"Do they ever try to catch you?" I asked.

"They don't know who I am."

"Then why did you bring the rifle?"

"Because we are going to Marquez where the Mexicans live."

III

The trail leveled out on a narrow ridge that was steep on both sides like an animal spine. On one side I could see where the trail went around the rocky gray hills and disappeared into the southeast where the pale sandrock mesas stood in the distance near my home. On the other side was a trail that went west, and as I looked far into the distance I thought I saw the little town. But Silva said no, that I was looking in the wrong place, that I just thought I saw houses. After that I quit looking off into the distance; it was hot and the wildflowers were closing up their deep-yellow petals. Only the waxy cactus flowers bloomed in the bright sun, and I saw every color that a cactus blossom can be;

the white ones and the red ones were still buds, but the purple and the yellow were blossoms, open full and the most beautiful of all.

Silva saw him before I did. The white man was riding a big gray horse, coming up the trail toward us. He was traveling fast and the gray horse's feet sent rocks rolling off the trail into the dry tumbleweeds. Silva motioned for me to stop and we watched the white man. He didn't see us right away, but finally his horse whinnied at our horses and he stopped. He looked at us briefly before he loped the gray horse across the three hundred yards that separated us. He stopped his horse in front of Silva, and his young fat face was shadowed by the brim of his hat. He didn't look mad, but his small, pale eyes moved from the blood-soaked gunny sacks hanging from my saddle to Silva's face and then back to my face.

"Where did you get the fresh meat?" the white man asked.

"I've been hunting," Silva said, and when he shifted his weight in the saddle the leather creaked.

"The hell you have, Indian. You've been rustling cattle. We've been looking for the thief for a long time."

The rancher was fat, and sweat began to soak through his white cowboy shirt and the wet cloth stuck to the thick rolls of belly fat. He almost seemed to be panting from the exertion of talking, and he smelled rancid, maybe because Silva scared him.

Silva turned to me and smiled. "Go back up the mountain, Yellow Woman."

The white man got angry when he heard Silva speak in a language he couldn't understand. "Don't try anything, Indian. Just keep riding to Marquez. We'll call the state police from there."

The rancher must have been unarmed because he was very frightened and if he had a gun he would have pulled it out then. I turned my horse around and the rancher yelled, "Stop!" I looked at Silva for an instant and there was something ancient and dark—something I could feel in my stomach—in his eyes, and when I glanced at his hand I saw his finger on the trigger of the .30–30 that was still in the saddle scabbard. I slapped my horse across the flank and the sacks of raw meat swung against my knees as the horse leaped up the trail. It was hard to keep my balance, and once I thought I felt the saddle slipping backward; it was because of this that I could not look back.

I didn't stop until I reached the ridge where the trail forked. The horse was breathing deep gasps and there was a dark film of sweat on its neck. I looked down in the direction I had come from, but I couldn't see the place. I waited. The wind came up and pushed warm air past me. I looked up at the sky, pale blue and full of thin clouds and fading vapor trails left by jets.

I think four shots were fired—I remember hearing four hollow explosions that reminded me of deer hunting. There could have been more shots after that, but I couldn't have heard them because my horse was running again and the loose rocks were making too much noise as they scattered around his feet.

Horses have a hard time running downhill, but I went that way instead of uphill to the mountain because I thought it was safer. I felt better with the horse running southeast past the round gray hills that were covered with cedar trees and black lava rock. When I got to the plain in the distance I could see the dark green patches of tamaracks that grew along the river; and beyond the river I could see the beginning of the pale sandrock mesas. I stopped the horse and looked back to see if anyone was coming; then I got off the horse and turned the horse around, wondering if it would go back to its corral under the pines on the mountain. It looked back at me for a moment and then plucked a mouthful of green tumbleweeds before it trotted back up the trail with its ears pointed forward, carrying its head daintily to one side to avoid stepping on the dragging reins. When the horse disappeared over the last hill, the gunny sacks full of meat were still swinging and bouncing.

IV

I walked toward the river on a wood-hauler's road that I knew would eventually lead to the paved road. I was thinking about waiting beside the road for someone to drive by, but by the time I got to the pavement I had decided it wasn't very far to walk if I followed the river back the way Silva and I had come.

The river water tasted good, and I sat in the shade under a cluster of silvery willows. I thought about Silva, and I felt sad at leaving him; still, there was something strange about him, and I tried to figure it out all the way back home.

I came back to the place on the river bank where he had been sitting the first time I saw him. The green willow leaves that he had trimmed from the branch were still lying there, wilted in the sand. I saw the leaves and I wanted to go back to him—to kiss him and to touch him—but the mountains were too far away now. And I told myself, because I believe it, he will come back sometime and be waiting again by the river.

I followed the path up from the river into the village. The sun was getting low, and I could smell supper cooking when I got to the screen door of my house. I could hear their voices inside—my mother was telling my grandmother how to fix the Jell-O and my husband, Al, was playing with the baby. I decided to tell them that some Navajo had kidnapped me, but I was sorry that old Grandpa wasn't alive to hear my story because it was the Yellow Woman stories he liked to tell best.

COMMENTARY

PAULA GUNN ALLEN

Paula Gunn Allen was a poet and professor of literature. This story is from her book of Native American traditional tales, *Spider Woman's Granddaughters* (1989).

Whirlwind Man Steals Yellow Woman 1983

Kochinnenako, Yellow Woman, was grinding corn one day with her three sisters. They looked into the water jars and saw that they were empty. They said, "We need some water." Kochinnenako said she would go, and taking the jars made her way across the mesa and went down to the spring. She climbed the rockhewn stairs to the spring that lay in a deep pool of shade. As she knelt to dip the gourd dipper into the cool shadowed water, she heard someone coming down the steps. She looked up and saw Whirlwind Man. He said, "Gutwatzi, Kochinnenako. Are you here?"

"Da'waa'e," she said, dipping water calmly into the four jars beside her. She didn't look at him.

"Put down the dipper," he said. "I want you to come with me."

"I am filling these jars with water as you can see," she said. "My sisters and I are grinding corn, and they are waiting for me."

"No," Whirlwind Man said. "You must come and go with me. If you won't come, well, I'll have to kill you." He showed her his knife.

Kochinnenako put the dipper down carefully. "All right," she said. "I guess I'll go with you." She got up. She went with Whirlwind Man to the other side of the world where he lived with his mother, who greeted her like his wife.

The jars stayed, tall and fat and cool in the deep shade by the shadowed spring.

That was one story. She knew they laughed about Kochinnenako. Brought her up when some woman was missing for awhile. Said she ran off with a Navajo, or maybe with a mountain spirit, "Like Kochinnenako." Maybe the name had become synonymous with "whore" at Guadalupe. Ephanie knew that Yellow was the color of woman, ritual color of faces painted in death, or for some of the dances. But there was a tone of dismissal, or derision there that she couldn't quite pin down, there anyway. No one told how Kochinnenako went with Whirlwind Man because she was forced. Said, "Then Whirlwind Man raped Kochinnenako." Rather, the story was that his mother had greeted Yellow Woman, and made her at home in their way. And that when Kochinnenako wanted to return home, had agreed, asking only that she wait while the old woman prepared gifts for Kochinnenako's sisters.

Ephanie wondered if Yellow Woman so long ago had known what was happening to her. If she could remember it or if she thought maybe she had dreamed it. If they laughed at her, or threw her out when she returned. She wondered if Kochinnenako cried.

JOHN STEINBECK

John Steinbeck (1902–1968) was born in Salinas and raised near Monterey in the fertile farm country of the Salinas Valley in California, the locale for his story "The Chrysanthemums." His mother was a former schoolteacher; his father was the county treasurer. In high school Steinbeck wrote for the school newspaper and was president of his class. He enjoyed literature from an early age and read novels by Gustave Flaubert, Fyodor Dostoevsky, and Thomas Hardy in the family library. Enrolled at Stanford University as an English major, Steinbeck dropped out before graduating and worked at odd jobs—fruit picker, caretaker, laboratory assistant—while he practiced writing fiction. Several times he took short-term jobs with the Spreckels Sugar Company and gained a perspective on labor problems, which he would later describe in his novels.

In 1929 Steinbeck began his literary career by publishing *Cup of Gold*, a fictionalized biography of Henry Morgan, the seventeenth-century Welsh pirate. His next book, *The Pastures of Heaven* (1932), is a collection of short stories about the people in a farm community in California. The critic Brian Barbour has stated that Steinbeck realized early in his career that the short story form was not congenial to his talents. He needed the more expansive form of the novel to give his characters the room for what he considered real growth. In 1936 Steinbeck wrote *In Dubious Battle*, his first major political novel. He then published four more novels and another book of short fiction before his greatest work, *The Grapes of Wrath* (1939). This book, about a family from the Dust Bowl that emigrates to California and struggles to make a living despite agricultural exploitation, won Steinbeck the Pulitzer Prize. Among his many other successful novels are *East of Eden* (1952) and *The Winter of Our Discontent* (1961). He received the Nobel Prize for literature in 1962.

One of the most accomplished popular novelists in the United States, Steinbeck excelled—as did Ernest Hemingway—in the creation of exciting conflicts, convincing dialogue, and recognizable characters to dramatize his philosophy of life. Although his production of short stories was relatively slight, his work is often anthologized because of his clear, realistic treatment of social themes as his characters struggle to forge meaningful lives. "The Chrysanthemums" echoes the D. H. Lawrence story "Odour of Chrysanthemums" in its concerns with sexual roles and the difficulty of striking a balance between self-interest and the needs of others. Steinbeck's biographer, Jackson J. Benson, also commented that the excellence of "The Chrysanthemums" lies in "its delicate, indirect handling of a woman's emotions . . . [especially] the difficulty of the woman in finding a creative significant role in a male-dominated society."

WEB Research John Steinbeck at bedfordstmartins.com/rewritinglit.

The Chrysanthemums

1938

The high grey-flannel fog of winter closed off the Salinas Valley from the sky and from all the rest of the world. On every side it sat like a lid on the mountains and made of the great valley a closed pot. On the broad, level land floor the gang plows bit deep and left the black earth shining like metal where the shares had cut. On the foothill ranches across the Salinas River, the yellow stubble fields seemed to be bathed in pale cold sunshine, but there was no sunshine in the valley now in December. The thick willow scrub along the river flamed with sharp and positive yellow leaves.

It was a time of quiet and of waiting. The air was cold and tender. A light wind blew up from the southwest so that the farmers were mildly hopeful of a good rain before long; but fog and rain do not go together.

Across the river, on Henry Allen's foothill ranch there was little work to be done, for the hay was cut and stored and the orchards were plowed up to receive the rain deeply when it should come. The cattle on the higher slopes were becoming shaggy and rough-coated.

Elisa Allen, working in her flower garden, looked down across the yard and saw Henry, her husband, talking to two men in business suits. The three of them stood by the tractor shed, each man with one foot on the side of the little Fordson. They smoked cigarettes and studied the machine as they talked.

Elisa watched them for a moment and then went back to her work. She was thirty-five. Her face was lean and strong and her eyes were as clear as water. Her figure looked blocked and heavy in her gardening costume, a man's black hat pulled low down over her eyes, clod-hopper shoes, a figured print dress almost completely covered by a big corduroy apron with four big pockets to hold the snips, the trowel and scratcher, the seeds, and the knife she worked with. She wore heavy leather gloves to protect her hands while she worked.

She was cutting down the old year's chrysanthemum stalks with a pair of short and powerful scissors. She looked down toward the men by the tractor shed now and then. Her face was eager and mature and handsome; even her work with the scissors was overeager, overpowerful. The chrysanthemum stems seemed too small and easy for her energy.

She brushed a cloud of hair out of her eyes with the back of her glove, and left a smudge of earth on her cheek in doing it. Behind her stood the neat white farm house with red geraniums close-banked around it as high as the windows. It was a hard-swept looking little house with hard-polished windows, and a clean mud-mat on the front steps.

Elisa cast another glance toward the tractor shed. The strangers were getting into their Ford coupe. She took off a glove and put her strong fingers down into the forest of new green chrysanthemum sprouts that were growing around the old roots. She spread the leaves and looked down among the close-growing stems. No aphids were there, no sowbugs or snails or cutworms. Her terrier fingers destroyed such pests before they could get started.

Elisa started at the sound of her husband's voice. He had come near quietly, and he leaned over the wire fence that protected her flower garden from cattle and dogs and chickens.

"At it again," he said. "You've got a strong new crop coming."

Elisa straightened her back and pulled on the gardening glove again. "Yes. They'll be strong this coming year." In her tone and on her face there was a little smugness.

"You've got a gift with things," Henry observed. "Some of those yellow chrysanthemums you had this year were ten inches across. I wish you'd work out in the orchard and raise some apples that big."

Her eyes sharpened. "Maybe I could do it, too. I've a gift with things, all right. My mother had it. She could stick anything in the ground and make it grow. She said it was having planters' hands that knew how to do it."

"Well, it sure works with flowers," he said.

"Henry, who were those men you were talking to?"

"Why, sure, that's what I came to tell you. They were from the Western Meat Company. I sold thirty head of three-year-old steers. Got nearly my own price, too."

"Good," she said. "Good for you."

"And I thought," he continued, "I thought how it's Saturday afternoon, and we might go into Salinas for dinner at a restaurant, and then to a picture show—to celebrate, you see."

"Good," she repeated. "Oh, yes. That will be good."

Henry put on his joking tone. "There's fights tonight. How'd you like to go to the fights?"

"Oh, no," she said breathlessly. "No, I wouldn't like fights."

"Just fooling, Elisa. We'll go to a movie. Let's see. It's two now. I'm going to take Scotty and bring down those steers from the hill. It'll take us maybe two hours. We'll go in town about five and have dinner at the Cominos Hotel. Like that?"

"Of course I'll like it. It's good to eat away from home."

"All right, then. I'll go get up a couple of horses."

She said, "I'll have plenty of time to transplant some of these sets, I guess."

She heard her husband calling Scotty down by the barn. And a little later she saw the two men ride up the pale yellow hillside in search of the steers.

There was a little square sandy bed kept for rooting the chrysanthemums. With her trowel she turned the soil over and over, and smoothed it and patted it firm. Then she dug ten parallel trenches to receive the sets. Back at the chrysanthemum bed she pulled out the little crisp shoots, trimmed off the leaves at each one with her scissors, and laid it on a small orderly pile.

A squeak of wheels and plod of hoofs came from the road. Elisa looked up. The country road ran along the dense bank of willows and cottonwoods that bordered the river, and up this road came a curious vehicle, curiously drawn. It was an old spring-wagon, with a round canvas top on it like the corner of a prairie schooner. It was drawn by an old bay horse and a little grey-and-white burro. A big stubble-bearded man sat between the cover flaps and drove the crawling team. Underneath the wagon, between the hind wheels, a lean and rangy mongrel dog walked sedately. Words were painted on the canvas, in clumsy, crooked letters. "Pots, pans, knives, sisors, lawn mores, Fixed." Two rows of articles, and the triumphantly definitive "Fixed" below. The black paint had run down in little sharp points beneath each letter.

Elisa, squatting on the ground, watched to see the crazy, loose-jointed wagon pass by. But it didn't pass. It turned into the farm road in front of her house, crooked old wheels skirling and squeaking. The rangy dog darted from between the wheels and ran ahead. Instantly the two ranch shepherds flew out at him. Then all three stopped, and with stiff and quivering tails, with taut straight legs, with ambassadorial dignity, they slowly circled, sniffing daintily. The caravan pulled up to Elisa's wire fence and stopped. Now the newcomer dog, feeling outnumbered, lowered his tail and retired under the wagon with raised hackles and bared teeth.

The man on the seat called out, "That's a bad dog in a fight when he gets started."

Elisa laughed. "I see he is. How soon does he generally get started?"

The man caught up her laughter and echoed it heartily. "Sometimes not for weeks and weeks," he said. He climbed stiffly down, over the wheel. The horse and the donkey drooped like unwatered flowers.

Elisa saw that he was a very big man. Although his hair and beard were greying, he did not look old. His worn black suit was wrinkled and spotted with grease. The laughter had disappeared from his face and eyes the moment his laughing voice ceased. His eyes were dark, and they were full of the brooding that gets in the eyes of teamsters and of sailors. The calloused hands he rested on the wire fence were cracked, and every crack was a black line. He took off his battered hat.

"I'm off my general road, ma'am," he said. "Does this dirt road cut over across the river to the Los Angeles highway?"

Elisa stood up and shoved the thick scissors in her apron pocket. "Well, yes, it does, but it winds around and then fords the river. I don't think your team could pull through the sand."

He replied with some asperity, "It might surprise you what them beasts can pull through."

"When they get started?" she asked.

He smiled for a second. "Yes. When they get started."

"Well," said Elisa, "I think you'll save time if you go back to the Salinas road and pick up the highway there."

He drew a big finger down the chicken wire and made it sing. "I ain't in any hurry, ma'am. I go from Seattle to San Diego and back every year. Takes all my time. About six months each way. I aim to follow nice weather."

Elisa took off her gloves and stuffed them in the apron pocket with the scissors. She touched the under edge of her man's hat, searching for fugitive hairs. "That sounds like a nice kind of a way to live," she said.

He leaned confidentially over the fence. "Maybe you noticed the writing on my wagon. I mend pots and sharpen knives and scissors. You got any of them things to do?"

"Oh, no," she said, quickly. "Nothing like that." Her eyes hardened with resistance.

"Scissors is the worst thing," he explained. "Most people just ruin scissors trying to sharpen 'em, but I know how. I got a special tool. It's a little bobbit kind of thing, and patented. But it sure does the trick."

"No. My scissors are all sharp."

"All right, then. Take a pot," he continued earnestly, "a bent pot, or a pot with a hole. I can make it like new so you don't have to buy no new ones. That's a savings for you."

"No," she said shortly. "I tell you I have nothing like that for you to do."

His face fell to an exaggerated sadness. His voice took on a whining undertone. "I ain't had a thing to do today. Maybe I won't have no supper tonight. You see I'm off my regular road. I know folks on the highway clear from Seattle to San Diego. They save their things for me to sharpen up because they know I do it so good and save them money."

"I'm sorry," Elisa said irritably. "I haven't anything for you to do."

His eyes left her face and fell to searching the ground. They roamed about until they came to the chrysanthemum bed where she had been working. "What's them plants, ma'am?"

The irritation and resistance melted from Elisa's face. "Oh, those are chrysanthemums, giant whites and yellows. I raise them every year, bigger than anybody around here."

"Kind of a long-stemmed flower? Looks like a quick puff of colored smoke?" he asked.

"That's it. What a nice way to describe them."

"They smell kind of nasty till you get used to them," he said.

"It's a good bitter smell," she retorted, "not nasty at all."

He changed his tone quickly, "I like the smell myself."

"I had ten-inch-blooms this year," she said.

The man leaned farther over the fence. "Look, I know a lady down the road a piece, has got the nicest garden you ever seen. Got nearly every kind of flower but no chrysanthemums. Last time I was mending a copper-bottom washtub for her (that's a hard job but I do it good), she said to me, 'If you ever run acrost some nice chrysanthemums I wish you'd try to get me a few seeds.' That's what she told me."

Elisa's eyes grew alert and eager. "She couldn't have known much about chrysanthemums. You *can* raise them from seed, but it's much easier to root the little sprouts you see there."

"Oh," he said. "I s'pose I can't take none to her, then."

"Why yes you can," Elisa cried. "I can put some in damp sand, and you can carry them right along with you. They'll take root in the pot if you keep them damp. And then she can transplant them."

"She'd sure like to have some, ma'am. You say they're nice ones?"

"Beautiful," she said. "Oh, beautiful." Her eyes shone. She tore off the battered hat and shook out her dark pretty hair. "I'll put them in a flower pot, and you can take them right with you. Come into the yard."

While the man came through the picket gate Elisa ran excitedly along the geranium-bordered path to the back of the house. And she returned carrying a big red flower pot. The gloves were forgotten now. She kneeled on the ground by the starting bed and dug up the sandy soil with her fingers and scooped it into the bright new flower pot. Then she picked up the little pile of shoots she had prepared. With her strong fingers she pressed them into the sand and tamped around them with her knuckles. The man stood over her. "I'll tell you what to do," she said. "You remember so you can tell the lady."

"Yes, I'll try to remember."

"Well, look. These will take root in about a month. Then she must set them out, about a foot apart in good rich earth like this, see?" She lifted a handful of dark soil for him to look at. "They'll grow fast and tall. Now remember this: In July tell her to cut them down, about eight inches from the ground."

"Before they bloom?" he asked.

"Yes, before they bloom." Her face was tight with eagerness. "They'll grow right up again. About the last of September the buds will start."

She stopped and seemed perplexed. "It's the budding that takes the most care," she said hesitantly. "I don't know how to tell you." She looked deep into his eyes, searchingly. Her mouth opened a little, and she seemed to be listening. "I'll try to tell you," she said. "Did you ever hear of planting hands?"

"Can't say I have, ma'am."

"Well, I can only tell you what it feels like. It's when you're picking off the buds you don't want. Everything goes right down into your fingertips. You watch your fingers work. They do it themselves. You can feel how it is. They pick and pick the buds. They never make a mistake. They're with the plant. Do you see? Your fingers and the plant. You can feel that, right up your arm. They know. They never make a mistake. You can feel it. When you're like that you can't do anything wrong. Do you see that? Can you understand that?"

She was kneeling on the ground looking up at him. Her breast swelled passionately.

The man's eyes narrowed. He looked away self-consciously. "Maybe I know," he said. "Sometimes in the night in the wagon there—"

Elisa's voice grew husky. She broke in on him, "I've never lived as you do, but I know what you mean. When the night is dark—why, the stars are sharp-pointed, and there's quiet. Why, you rise up and up! Every pointed star gets driven into your body. It's like that. Hot and sharp and—lovely."

Kneeling there, her hand went out toward his legs in the greasy black trousers. Her hesitant fingers almost touched the cloth. Then her hand dropped to the ground. She crouched low like a fawning dog.

He said, "It's nice, just like you say. Only when you don't have no dinner, it ain't."

She stood up then, very straight, and her face was ashamed. She held the flower pot out to him and placed it gently in his arms. "Here. Put it in your wagon, on the seat, where you can watch it. Maybe I can find something for you to do."

At the back of the house she dug in the can pile and found two old and battered aluminum saucepans. She carried them back and gave them to him. "Here, maybe you can fix these."

His manner changed. He became professional. "Good as new I can fix them." At the back of his wagon he set a little anvil, and out of an oily tool box dug a small machine hammer. Elisa came through the gate to watch him while he pounded out the dents in the kettles. His mouth grew sure and knowing. At a difficult part of the work he sucked his underlip.

"You sleep right in the wagon?" Elisa asked.

"Right in the wagon, ma'am. Rain or shine I'm dry as a cow in there."

"It must be nice," she said. "It must be very nice. I wish women could do such things."

"It ain't the right kind of a life for a woman."

Her upper lip raised a little, showing her teeth. "How do you know? How can you tell?" she said.

"I don't know, ma'am," he protested. "Of course I don't know. Now here's your kettles, done. You don't have to buy no new ones."

"How much?"

"Oh, fifty cents'll do. I keep my prices down and my work good. That's why I have all them satisfied customers up and down the highway."

Elisa brought him a fifty-cent piece from the house and dropped it in his hand. "You might be surprised to have a rival some time. I can sharpen scissors, too. And I can beat the dents out of little pots. I could show you what a woman might do."

He put his hammer back in the oily box and shoved the little anvil out of sight. "It would be a lonely life for a woman, ma'am, and a scarey life, too, with animals creeping under the wagon all night." He climbed over the singletree, steadying himself with a hand on the burro's white rump. He settled himself in the seat, picked up the lines. "Thank you kindly, ma'am," he said. "I'll do like you told me; I'll go back and catch the Salinas road."

"Mind," she called, "if you're long in getting there, keep the sand damp."

"Sand, ma'am? . . . Sand? Oh, sure. You mean around the chrysanthemums. Sure I will." He clucked his tongue. The beasts leaned luxuriously into their collars. The mongrel dog took his place between the back wheels. The wagon turned and crawled out the entrance road and back the way it had come, along the river.

Elisa stood in front of her wire fence watching the slow progress of the caravan. Her shoulders were straight, her head thrown back, her eyes half-closed, so that the scene came vaguely into them. Her lips moved silently, forming the words "Good-bye—good-bye." Then she whispered, "That's a bright direction. There's a glowing there." The sound of her whisper startled her. She shook herself free and looked about to see whether anyone had been listening. Only the dogs had heard. They lifted their heads toward her from their sleeping in the dust, and then stretched out their chins and settled asleep again. Elisa turned and ran hurriedly into the house.

In the kitchen she reached behind the stove and felt the water tank. It was full of hot water from the noonday cooking. In the bathroom she tore off her soiled clothes and flung them into the corner. And then she scrubbed herself with a little block of pumice, legs and thighs, loins and chest and arms, until her skin was scratched and red. When she had dried herself she stood in front of a mirror in her bedroom and looked at her body. She tightened her stomach and threw out her chest. She turned and looked over her shoulder at her back.

After a while she began to dress, slowly. She put on her newest underclothing and her nicest stockings and the dress which was the symbol of her prettiness. She worked carefully on her hair, penciled her eyebrows and rouged her lips.

Before she was finished she heard the little thunder of hoofs and the shouts of Henry and his helper as they drove the red steers into the corral. She heard the gate bang shut and set herself for Henry's arrival.

His step sounded on the porch. He entered the house calling, "Elisa, where are you?"

"In my room, dressing. I'm not ready. There's hot water for your bath. Hurry up. It's getting late."

When she heard him splashing in the tub, Elisa laid his dark suit on the bed, and shirt and socks and tie beside it. She stood his polished shoes on the floor beside the bed. Then she went to the porch and sat primly and stiffly down. She looked toward the river road where the willow-line was still yellow with frosted leaves so that under the high grey fog they seemed a thin band of sunshine. This was the only color in the grey afternoon. She sat unmoving for a long time. Her eyes blinked rarely.

Henry came banging out of the door, shoving his tie inside his vest as he came. Elisa stiffened and her face grew tight. Henry stopped short and looked at her. "Why—why, Elisa. You look so nice!"

"Nice? You think I look nice? What do you mean by 'nice'?"

Henry blundered on. "I don't know. I mean you look different, strong and happy."

"I am strong? Yes, strong. What do you mean 'strong'?"

He looked bewildered. "You're playing some kind of a game," he said helplessly. "It's a kind of a play. You look strong enough to break a calf over your knee, happy enough to eat it like a watermelon."

For a second she lost her rigidity. "Henry! Don't talk like that. You didn't know what you said." She grew complete again. "I'm strong," she boasted, "I never knew before how strong."

Henry looked down toward the tractor shed, and when he brought his eyes back to her, they were his own again. "I'll get out the car. You can put on your coat while I'm starting."

Elisa went into the house. She heard him drive to the gate and idle down his motor, and then she took a long time to put on her hat. She pulled it here and pressed it there. When Henry turned the motor off she slipped into her coat and went out.

The little roadster bounced along on the dirt road by the river, raising the birds and driving the rabbits into the brush. Two cranes flapped heavily over the willow-line and dropped into the river-bed.

Far ahead on the road Elisa saw a dark speck. She knew.

She tried not to look as they passed it, but her eyes would not obey. She whispered to herself sadly, "He might have thrown them off the road. That wouldn't have been much trouble, not very much. But he kept the pot," she explained. "He had to keep the pot. That's why he couldn't get them off the road."

The roadster turned a bend and she saw the caravan ahead. She swung full around toward her husband so she could not see the little covered wagon and the mismatched team as the car passed them.

In a moment it was over. The thing was done. She did not look back.

She said loudly, to be heard above the motor. "It will be good, tonight, a good dinner."

"Now you're changed again," Henry complained. He took one hand from the wheel and patted her knee. "I ought to take you in to dinner oftener. It would be good for both of us. We get so heavy out on the ranch."

"Henry," she asked, "could we have wine at dinner?"

"Sure we could. Say! That will be fine."

She was silent for a while; then she said, "Henry, at those prize fights, do the men hurt each other very much?"

"Sometimes a little, not often. Why?"

"Well, I've read how they break noses, and blood runs down their chests. I've read how the fighting gloves get heavy and soggy with blood."

He looked around at her. "What's the matter, Elisa? I didn't know you read things like that." He brought the car to a stop, then turned to the right over the Salinas River bridge.

"Do any women ever go to the fights?" she asked.

"Oh, sure, some. What's the matter Elisa? Do you want to go? I don't think you'd like it, but I'll take you if you really want to go."

She relaxed limply in the seat. "Oh, no. No. I don't want to go. I'm sure I don't." Her face was turned away from him. "It will be enough if we can have wine. It will be plenty." She turned up her coat collar so he could not see that she was crying weakly—like an old woman.

AMY TAN

Amy Tan (b. 1952) was born in Oakland, California. Her father was educated as an engineer in Beijing; her mother left China in 1949, just before the Communist revolution. Tan remembers that as a child she felt like an American girl trapped in a Chinese body: "There was shame and self-hate. There is this myth that America is a melting pot, but what happens in assimilation is that we end up deliberately choosing the American things – hot dogs and apple pie – and ignoring the Chinese offerings."

After her father's death, Tan and her mother lived in Switzerland, where she attended high school. "I was a novelty," she recalls. "There were so few Asians in Europe that everywhere I went people stared. Europeans asked me out. I had never been asked out in America." After attending a small college in Oregon, she worked for IBM as a writer of computer manuals. In 1984 Tan and her mother visited China and met her relatives; there she made the important discovery, as she has said, that "I belonged to my family and my family belonged to China." A year later, back in San Francisco, Tan read Louise Erdrich's *Love Medicine* and was so impressed by the power of its interlocking stories about another cultural minority, Native Americans, that she began to write short stories herself. One of them was published in a little magazine read by a literary agent in San Diego, who urged Tan to outline a book about the conflicts between different cultures and generations of Chinese mothers and daughters in the United States. After her agent negotiated a $50,000 advance from Putnam, Tan worked full-time on the first draft of her book *The Joy Luck Club* (1989) and finished it in four months.

"Two Kinds" is an excerpt from that novel. At first Tan thought her book contract was "all a token minority thing. I thought they had to fill a quota since there weren't many Chinese Americans writing." But her book was a best-seller and was nominated for a National Book Award. As the novelist Valerie Miner has recognized, Tan's special gifts are her storytelling ability and her "remarkable ear for dialogue and dialect, representing the choppy English of the mother and the sloppy California vernacular of the daughter with a sensitive authenticity." At the heart of Tan's book is the tough bond between mother and daughter. "I'm my own person," the daughter says. "How can she be her own person," the mother answers, "When did I give her up?" Tan's other books include *The Kitchen God's Wife* (1991); a children's book, *The Moon Lady* (1992); *The*

Hundred Secret Senses (1995); *The Bonesetter's Daughter* (2001); *The Opposite of Fate* (2003); and *Saving Fish from Drowning* (2005).

WEB Research Amy Tan at bedfordstmartins.com/rewritinglit.

Two Kinds 1989

My mother believed you could be anything you wanted to be in America. You could open a restaurant. You could work for the government and get good retirement. You could buy a house with almost no money down. You could become rich. You could become instantly famous.

"Of course you can be prodigy, too," my mother told me when I was nine. "You can be best anything. What does Auntie Lindo know? Her daughter, she is only best tricky."

America was where all my mother's hopes lay. She had come here in 1949 after losing everything in China: her mother and father, her family home, her first husband, and two daughters, twin baby girls. But she never looked back with regret. There were so many ways for things to get better.

We didn't immediately pick the right kind of prodigy. At first my mother thought I could be a Chinese Shirley Temple. We'd watch Shirley's old movies on TV as though they were training films. My mother would poke my arm and say, *"Ni kan"*—You watch. And I would see Shirley tapping her feet, or singing a sailor song, or pursing her lips into a very round O while saying, "Oh my goodness."

"Ni kan," said my mother as Shirley's eyes flooded with tears. "You already know how. Don't need talent for crying!"

Soon after my mother got this idea about Shirley Temple, she took me to a beauty training school in the Mission district and put me in the hands of a student who could barely hold the scissors without shaking. Instead of getting big fat curls, I emerged with an uneven mass of crinkly black fuzz. My mother dragged me off to the bathroom and tried to wet down my hair.

"You look like Negro Chinese," she lamented, as if I had done this on purpose.

The instructor of the beauty training school had to lop off these soggy clumps to make my hair even again. "Peter Pan is very popular these days," the instructor assured my mother. I now had hair the length of a boy's, with straight-across bangs that hung at a slant two inches above my eyebrows. I liked the haircut and it made me actually look forward to my future fame.

In fact, in the beginning, I was just as excited as my mother, maybe even more so. I pictured this prodigy part of me as many different images, trying each one on for size. I was a dainty ballerina girl standing by the curtains, waiting to hear the right music that would send me floating on my tiptoes. I was like the Christ child lifted out of the straw manger, crying with holy indignity. I was Cinderella stepping from her pumpkin carriage with sparkly cartoon music filling the air.

In all of my imaginings, I was filled with a sense that I would soon become *perfect.* My mother and father would adore me. I would be beyond reproach. I would never feel the need to sulk for anything.

But sometimes the prodigy in me became impatient. "If you don't hurry up and get me out of here, I'm disappearing for good," it warned. "And then you'll always be nothing."

Every night after dinner, my mother and I would sit at the Formica kitchen table. She would present new tests, taking her examples from stories of amazing children she had read in *Ripley's Believe It or Not,* or *Good Housekeeping, Reader's Digest,* and a dozen other magazines she kept in a pile in our bathroom. My mother got these magazines from people whose houses she cleaned. And since she cleaned many houses each week, we had a great assortment. She would look through them all, searching for stories about remarkable children.

The first night she brought out a story about a three-year-old boy who knew the capitals of all the states and even most of the European countries. A teacher was quoted as saying the little boy could also pronounce the names of the foreign cities correctly.

"What's the capital of Finland?" my mother asked me, looking at the magazine story.

All I knew was the capital of California, because Sacramento was the name of the street we lived on in Chinatown. "Nairobi!" I guessed, saying the most foreign word I could think of. She checked to see if that was possibly one way to pronounce "Helsinki" before showing me the answer.

The tests got harder—multiplying numbers in my head, finding the queen of hearts in a deck of cards, trying to stand on my head without using my hands, predicting the daily temperatures in Los Angeles, New York, and London.

One night I had to look at a page from the Bible for three minutes and then report everything I could remember. "Now Jehoshaphat had riches and honor in abundance and . . . that's all I remember, Ma," I said.

And after seeing my mother's disappointed face once again, something inside of me began to die. I hated the tests, the raised hopes and failed expectations. Before going to bed that night, I looked in the mirror above the bathroom sink and when I saw only my face staring back—and that it would always be this ordinary face—I began to cry. Such a sad, ugly girl! I made high-pitched noises like a crazed animal, trying to scratch out the face in the mirror.

And then I saw what seemed to be the prodigy side of me—because I had never seen that face before. I looked at my reflection, blinking so I could see more clearly. The girl staring back at me was angry, powerful. This girl and I were the same. I had new thoughts, willful thoughts, or rather thoughts filled with lots of won'ts. I won't let her change me, I promised myself. I won't be what I'm not.

So now on nights when my mother presented her tests, I performed listlessly, my head propped on one arm. I pretended to be bored. And I was. I got so bored I started counting the bellows of the foghorns out on the bay while my mother drilled me in other areas. The sound was comforting and reminded me of the cow jumping over the moon. And the next day, I played a game with myself, seeing if my mother would give up on me before eight bellows. After a while I usually counted only one, maybe two bellows at most. At last she was beginning to give up hope.

Two or three months had gone by without any mention of my being a prodigy again. And then one day my mother was watching *The Ed Sullivan Show* on TV. The TV was old and the sound kept shorting out. Every time my mother got halfway up from the sofa to adjust the set, the sound would go back on and Ed would be talking. As soon as she sat down, Ed would go silent again. She got up, the TV broke into loud piano music. She sat down. Silence. Up and down, back and forth, quiet and loud. It was like a stiff embraceless dance between her and the TV set. Finally she stood by the set with her hand on the sound dial.

She seemed entranced by the music, a little frenzied piano piece with this mesmerizing quality, sort of quick passages and then teasing lilting ones before it returned to the quick playful parts.

"Ni kan," my mother said, calling me over with hurried hand gestures. "Look here."

I could see why my mother was fascinated by the music. It was being pounded out by a little Chinese girl, about nine years old, with a Peter Pan haircut. The girl had the sauciness of a Shirley Temple. She was proudly modest like a proper Chinese child. And she also did this fancy sweep of a curtsy, so that the fluffy skirt of her white dress cascaded slowly to the floor like the petals of a large carnation.

In spite of these warning signs, I wasn't worried. Our family had no piano and we couldn't afford to buy one, let alone reams of sheet music and piano lessons. So I could be generous in my comments when my mother bad-mouthed the little girl on TV.

"Play note right, but doesn't sound good! No singing sound," complained my mother.

"What are you picking on her for?" I said carelessly. "She's pretty good. Maybe she's not the best, but she's trying hard." I knew almost immediately I would be sorry I said that.

"Just like you," she said. "Not the best. Because you not trying." She gave a little huff as she let go of the sound dial and sat down on the sofa.

The little Chinese girl sat down also to play an encore of "Anitra's Dance" by Grieg. I remember the song, because later on I had to learn how to play it.

Three days after watching *The Ed Sullivan Show,* my mother told me what my schedule would be for piano lessons and piano practice. She had talked to Mr. Chong, who lived on the first floor of our apartment building. Mr. Chong was a retired piano teacher and my mother had traded housecleaning services for weekly lessons and a piano for me to practice on every day, two hours a day, from four until six.

When my mother told me this, I felt as though I had been sent to hell. I whined and then kicked my foot a little when I couldn't stand it anymore.

"Why don't you like me the way I am? I'm *not* a genius! I can't play the piano. And even if I could, I wouldn't go on TV if you paid me a million dollars!" I cried.

My mother slapped me. "Who ask you be genius?" she shouted. "Only ask you be your best. For you sake. You think I want you be genius? Hnnh! What for! Who ask you!"

"So ungrateful," I heard her mutter in Chinese. "If she had as much talent as she has temper, she would be famous now."

Mr. Chong, whom I secretly nicknamed Old Chong, was very strange, always tapping his fingers to the silent music of an invisible orchestra. He looked ancient in my eyes. He had lost most of the hair on top of his head and he wore thick glasses and had eyes that always looked tired and sleepy. But he must have been younger than I thought, since he lived with his mother and was not yet married.

I met Old Lady Chong once and that was enough. She had this peculiar smell like a baby that had done something in its pants. And her fingers felt like a dead person's, like an old peach I once found in the back of the refrigerator; the skin just slid off the meat when I picked it up.

I soon found out why Old Chong had retired from teaching piano. He was deaf. "Like Beethoven!" he shouted to me. "We're both listening only in our head!" And he would start to conduct his frantic silent sonatas.

Our lessons went like this. He would open the book and point to different things, explaining their purpose: "Key! Treble! Bass! No sharps or flats! So this is C major! Listen now and play after me!"

And then he would play the C scale a few times, a simple chord, and then, as if inspired by an old, unreachable itch, he gradually added more notes and running trills and a pounding bass until the music was really something quite grand.

I would play after him, the simple scale, the simple chord, and then I just played some nonsense that sounded like a cat running up and down on top of garbage cans. Old Chong smiled and applauded and then said, "Very good! But now you must learn to keep time!"

So that's how I discovered that Old Chong's eyes were too slow to keep up with the wrong notes I was playing. He went through the motions in half-time. To help me keep rhythm, he stood behind me, pushing down on my right shoulder for every beat. He balanced pennies on top of my wrists so I would keep them still as I slowly played scales and arpeggios. He had me curve my hand around an apple and keep that shape when playing chords. He marched stiffly to show me how to make each finger dance up and down, staccato like an obedient little soldier.

He taught me all these things, and that was how I also learned I could be lazy and get away with mistakes, lots of mistakes. If I hit the wrong notes because I hadn't practiced enough, I never corrected myself. I just kept playing in rhythm. And Old Chong kept conducting his own private reverie.

So maybe I never really gave myself a fair chance. I did pick up the basics pretty quickly, and I might have become a good pianist at that young age. But I was so determined not to try, not to be anybody different that I learned to play only the most ear-splitting preludes, the most discordant hymns.

Over the next year, I practiced like this, dutifully in my own way. And then one day I heard my mother and her friend Lindo Jong both talking in a loud bragging tone of voice so others could hear. It was after church, and I was leaning against the brick wall wearing a dress with stiff white petticoats. Auntie Lindo's daughter, Waverly, who was about my age, was standing farther down the wall about five feet away. We had grown up together and shared all the closeness of two sisters squabbling over crayons and dolls. In other words, for the most part, we hated each other. I thought she was snotty. Waverly Jong had gained a certain amount of fame as "Chinatown's Littlest Chinese Chess Champion."

"She bring home too many trophy," lamented Auntie Lindo that Sunday. "All day she play chess. All day I have no time do nothing but dust off her winnings." She threw a scolding look at Waverly, who pretended not to see her.

"You lucky you don't have this problem," said Auntie Lindo with a sigh to my mother.

And my mother squared her shoulders and bragged: "Our problem worser than yours. If we ask Jing-mei wash dish, she hear nothing but music. It's like you can't stop this natural talent."

And right then, I was determined to put a stop to her foolish pride.

A few weeks later, Old Chong and my mother conspired to have me play in a talent show which would be held in the church hall. By then, my parents had saved up enough to buy me a secondhand piano, a black Wurlitzer spinet with a scarred bench. It was the showpiece of our living room.

For the talent show, I was to play a piece called "Pleading Child" from Schumann's *Scenes from Childhood.* It was a simple, moody piece that sounded more difficult than it was. I was supposed to memorize the whole thing, playing the repeat parts twice to make the piece sound longer. But I dawdled over it, playing a few bars and then cheating, looking up to see what notes followed. I never really listened to what I was playing. I daydreamed about being somewhere else, about being someone else.

The part I liked to practice best was the fancy curtsy: right foot out, touch the rose on the carpet with a pointed foot, sweep to the side, left leg bends, look up and smile.

My parents invited all the couples from the Joy Luck Club to witness my debut. Auntie Lindo and Uncle Tin were there. Waverly and her two older brothers had also come. The first two rows were filled with children both younger and older than I was. The littlest ones got to go first. They recited simple nursery rhymes, squawked out tunes on miniature violins, twirled Hula Hoops, pranced in pink ballet tutus, and when they bowed or curtsied, the audience would sigh in unison, "Awww," and then clap enthusiastically.

When my turn came, I was very confident. I remember my childish excitement. It was as if I knew, without a doubt, that the prodigy side of me really did exist. I had no fear whatsoever, no nervousness. I remember thinking to myself, This is it! This is it! I looked out over the audience, at my mother's blank face, my father's yawn, Auntie Lindo's stiff-lipped smile, Waverly's sulky expression. I had on a white dress layered with sheets of lace, and a pink bow in my Peter Pan haircut. As I sat down I envisioned people jumping to their feet and Ed Sullivan rushing up to introduce me to everyone on TV.

And I started to play. It was so beautiful. I was so caught up in how lovely I looked that at first I didn't worry how I would sound. So it was a surprise to me when I hit the first wrong note and I realized something didn't sound quite right. And then I hit another and another followed that. A chill started at the top of my head and began to trickle down. Yet I couldn't stop playing, as though my hands were bewitched. I kept thinking my fingers would adjust themselves back, like a train switching to the right track. I played this strange jumble through two repeats, the sour notes staying with me all the way to the end.

When I stood up, I discovered my legs were shaking. Maybe I had just been nervous and the audience, like Old Chong, had seen me go through the right motions and had not heard anything wrong at all. I swept my right foot out, went down on my knee, looked up and smiled. The room was quiet, except for Old Chong, who was beaming and shouting, "Bravo! Bravo! Well done!" But then I saw my mother's face, her stricken face. The audience clapped weakly, and as I walked back to my chair, with my whole face quivering as I tried not to cry, I heard a little boy whisper loudly to his mother, "That was awful," and the mother whispered back, "Well, she certainly tried."

And now I realized how many people were in the audience, the whole world it seemed. I was aware of eyes burning into my back. I felt the shame of my mother and father as they sat stiffly throughout the rest of the show.

We could have escaped during intermission. Pride and some strange sense of honor must have anchored my parents to their chairs. And so we watched it all: the eighteen-year-old boy with a fake mustache who did a magic show and juggled flaming hoops while riding a unicycle. The breasted girl with white makeup who sang from *Madama Butterfly* and got honorable mention. And the eleven-year-old boy who won first prize playing a tricky violin song that sounded like a busy bee.

After the show, the Hsus, the Jongs, and the St. Clairs from the Joy Luck Club came up to my mother and father.

"Lots of talented kids," Auntie Lindo said vaguely, smiling broadly.

"That was somethin' else," said my father, and I wondered if he was referring to me in a humorous way, or whether he even remembered what I had done.

Waverly looked at me and shrugged her shoulders. "You aren't a genius like me," she said matter-of-factly. And if I hadn't felt so bad, I would have pulled her braids and punched her stomach.

But my mother's expression was what devastated me: a quiet, blank look that said she had lost everything. I felt the same way, and it seemed as if everybody were now coming up, like gawkers at the scene of an accident, to see what parts were actually missing. When we got on the bus to go home, my father was humming the busy-bee tune and my mother was silent. I kept thinking she wanted to wait until we got home before shouting at me. But when my father unlocked the door to our apartment, my mother walked in and then went to the back, into the bedroom. No accusations. No blame. And in a way, I felt disappointed. I had been waiting for her to start shouting, so I could shout back and cry and blame her for all my misery.

I assumed my talent-show fiasco meant I never had to play the piano again. But two days later, after school, my mother came out of the kitchen and saw me watching TV.

"Four clock," she reminded me as if it were any other day. I was stunned, as though she were asking me to go through the talent-show torture again. I wedged myself more tightly in front of the TV.

"Turn off TV," she called from the kitchen five minutes later.

I didn't budge. And then I decided. I didn't have to do what my mother said anymore. I wasn't her slave. This wasn't China. I had listened to her before and look what happened. She was the stupid one.

She came out from the kitchen and stood in the arched entryway of the living room. "Four clock," she said once again, louder.

"I'm not going to play anymore," I said nonchalantly. "Why should I? I'm not a genius."

She walked over and stood in front of the TV. I saw her chest was heaving up and down in an angry way.

"No!" I said, and I now felt stronger, as if my true self had finally emerged. So this was what had been inside me all along.

"No! I won't!" I screamed.

She yanked me by the arm, pulled me off the floor, snapped off the TV. She was frighteningly strong, half pulling, half carrying me toward the piano as I kicked the throw rugs under my feet. She lifted me up and onto the hard bench. I was sobbing by now, looking at her bitterly. Her chest was heaving even more and her mouth was open, smiling crazily as if she were pleased I was crying.

"You want me to be someone that I'm not!" I sobbed. "I'll never be the kind of daughter you want me to be!"

"Only two kinds of daughters," she shouted in Chinese. "Those who are obedient and those who follow their own mind! Only one kind of daughter can live in this house. Obedient daughter!"

"Then I wish I wasn't your daughter. I wish you weren't my mother," I shouted. As I said these things I got scared. I felt like worms and toads and slimy things were crawling out of my chest, but it also felt good, as if this awful side of me had surfaced, at last.

"Too late change this," said my mother shrilly.

And I could sense her anger rising to its breaking point. I wanted to see it spill over. And that's when I remembered the babies she had lost in China, the ones we never talked about. "Then I wish I'd never been born!" I shouted. "I wish I were dead! Like them."

It was as if I had said the magic words, Alakazam!—and her face went blank, her mouth closed, her arms went slack, and she backed out of the room, stunned, as if she were blowing away like a small brown leaf, thin, brittle, lifeless.

It was not the only disappointment my mother felt in me. In the years that followed, I failed her so many times, each time asserting my own will, my right to fall short of expectations. I didn't get straight As. I didn't become class president. I didn't get into Stanford. I dropped out of college.

For unlike my mother, I did not believe I could be anything I wanted to be. I could only be me.

And for all those years, we never talked about the disaster at the recital or my terrible accusations afterward at the piano bench. All that remained unchecked, like a betrayal that was now unspeakable. So I never found a way to ask her why she had hoped for something so large that failure was inevitable.

And even worse, I never asked her what frightened me the most: Why had she given up hope?

For after our struggle at the piano, she never mentioned my playing again. The lessons stopped, the lid to the piano was closed, shutting out the dust, my misery, and her dreams.

So she surprised me. A few years ago, she offered to give me the piano, for my thirtieth birthday. I had not played in all those years. I saw the offer as a sign of forgiveness, a tremendous burden removed.

"Are you sure?" I asked shyly. "I mean, won't you and Dad miss it?"

"No, this your piano," she said firmly. "Always your piano. You only one can play."

"Well, I probably can't play anymore," I said. "It's been years."

"You pick up fast," said my mother, as if she knew this was certain. "You have natural talent. You could been genius if you want to."

"No I couldn't."

"You just not trying," said my mother. And she was neither angry nor sad. She said it as if to announce a fact that could never be disproved. "Take it," she said.

But I didn't at first. It was enough that she had offered it to me. And after that, every time I saw it in my parents' living room, standing in front of the bay windows, it made me feel proud, as if it were a shiny trophy I had won back.

Last week I sent a tuner over to my parents' apartment and had the piano reconditioned, for purely sentimental reasons. My mother had died a few months before and I had been getting things in order for my father, a little bit at a time. I put the jewelry in special silk pouches. The sweaters she had knitted in yellow, pink, bright orange—all the colors I hated—I put those in mothproof boxes. I found some old Chinese silk dresses, the kind with little slits up the sides. I rubbed the old silk against my skin, then wrapped them in tissue and decided to take them home with me.

After I had the piano tuned, I opened the lid and touched the keys. It sounded even richer than I remembered. Really, it was a very good piano.

Inside the bench were the same exercise notes with handwritten scales, the same secondhand music books with their covers held together with yellow tape.

I opened up the Schumann book to the dark little piece I had played at the recital. It was on the left-hand side of the page, "Pleading Child." It looked more difficult than I remembered. I played a few bars, surprised at how easily the notes came back to me.

And for the first time, or so it seemed, I noticed the piece on the right-hand side. It was called "Perfectly Contented." I tried to play this one as well. It had a lighter melody but the same flowing rhythm and turned out to be quite easy. "Pleading Child" was shorter but slower; "Perfectly Contented" was longer but faster. And after I played them both a few times, I realized they were two halves of the same song.

JOHN UPDIKE

John Updike (1932–2009) was born in Shillington, Pennsylvania, an only child. His father taught algebra in a local high school, and his mother wrote short stories and novels. His mother's consciousness of a special destiny, combined with his family's meager income – they lived with his mother's parents for the first thirteen years of Updike's life – made him "both arrogant and shy" as a teenager. He wrote stories, drew cartoons, and clowned for the approval of his peers. After getting straight A's in high school, he went to Harvard University on a full scholarship, studying English and graduating summa cum laude in 1954. He spent a year at Oxford on a fellowship, then joined the staff of *The New Yorker.* In 1959 Updike published both his first book of short fiction, *The Same Door*, and his first novel, *The Poorhouse Fair.*

In the 1960s, 1970s, and early 1980s, Updike continued to alternate novels and collections of stories, adding occasional volumes of verse, collections of essays, and one play. His novels include *Rabbit, Run* (1960), *Couples* (1968), *Rabbit Redux* (1971), and *Marry Me* (1976). *Rabbit Is Rich* (1981), continuing the story of Harry "Rabbit" Angstrom, a suburban Pennsylvanian whom Updike has traced through adolescence, marriage, fatherhood, and middle age, won virtually every major American literary award for the year it appeared; Updike concluded the series with *Rabbit at Rest* (1991). Updike's collections of stories include *Pigeon Feathers* (1962), *Museums and Women* (1972), and *Problems and Other Stories* (1981). In 1983 Updike won the National Book Critics Circle Award for his collection of essays and criticism *Hugging the Shore.* In 1989 he published his memoir, *Self-Consciousness. The Early Stories* (2003) collects Updike's short fiction from 1953 to 1975. More recent collections are *My Father's Tears and Other Stories* (2009) and *The Maple Stories* (2009).

Updike has said he is indebted to Ernest Hemingway and J. D. Salinger's stories for the literary form he adopted to describe the painful experience of adolescence: "I learned a lot from Salinger's short stories; he did remove the short narrative from the wise-guy, slice-of-life stories of the thirties and forties. Like most innovative artists, he made new room for shapelessness, for life as it is lived." Updike writes realistic narrative, believing that "fiction is a tissue of lies that refreshes and informs our sense of actuality.

Reality is – chemically, atomically, biologically – a fabric of microscopic accuracies." His fiction, such as the story "A & P," concentrates on these "microscopic accuracies," tiny details of characterization and setting brilliantly described. The critic Louis Menand understood that Hemingway "would probably not have given" the boy in "A & P" his thought in the last sentence of the story, "or would not have permitted him to express it. But it is the sentence – in a story that somehow squeezes the whole pathos of Cold War life into a tiny, perfect anecdote – that produces the click," the effect of the story.

CONNECTION James Joyce, "Araby," page 317.

WEB Research John Updike at bedfordstmartins.com/rewritinglit.

A & P

1961

In walks these three girls in nothing but bathing suits. I'm in the third checkout slot, with my back to the door, so I don't see them until they're over by the bread. The one that caught my eye first was the one in the plaid green two-piece. She was a chunky kid, with a good tan and a sweet broad soft-looking can with those two crescents of white just under it, where the sun never seems to hit, at the top of the backs of her legs. I stood there with my hand on a box of HiHo crackers trying to remember if I rang it up or not. I ring it up again and the customer starts giving me hell. She's one of these cash-register-watchers, a witch about fifty with rouge on her cheekbones and no eyebrows, and I know it made her day to trip me up. She'd been watching cash registers for fifty years and probably never seen a mistake before.

By the time I got her feathers smoothed and her goodies into a bag—she gives me a little snort in passing, if she'd been born at the right time they would have burned her over in Salem—by the time I get her on her way the girls had circled around the bread and were coming back, without a pushcart, back my way along the counters, in the aisle between the checkouts and the Special bins. They didn't even have shoes on. There was this chunky one, with the two-piece—it was bright green and the seams on the bra were still sharp and her belly was still pretty pale so I guessed she just got it (the suit)—there was this one, with one of those chubby berry-faces, the lips all bunched together under her nose, this one, and a tall one, with black hair that hadn't quite frizzed right, and one of these sunburns right across under the eyes, and a chin that was too long—you know, the kind of girl other girls think is very "striking" and "attractive" but never quite makes it, as they very well know, which is why they like her so much—and then the third one, that wasn't quite so tall. She was the queen. She kind of led them, the other two peeking around and making their shoulders round. She didn't look around, not this queen, she just walked straight on slowly, on these long white prima-donna legs. She came down a little hard on her heels, as if she didn't walk in her bare feet that much, putting down her heels and then letting the weight move along to her toes as if she was testing the floor with every step, putting a little deliberate extra action into it. You never know for sure how girls' minds work (do you really think it's a mind in there or just a little buzz like a bee in a glass jar?) but you got the idea she had talked the other two into coming in here with her, and now she was showing them how to do it, walk slow and hold yourself straight.

She had on a kind of dirty-pink—beige maybe, I don't know—bathing suit with a little nubble all over it, and what got me, the straps were down. They were off her shoulders looped loose around the cool tops of her arms, and I guess as a result the suit had slipped a little on her, so all around the top of the cloth there was this shining rim. If it hadn't been there you wouldn't have known there could have been anything whiter than those shoulders. With the straps pushed off, there was nothing between the top of the suit and the top of her head except just *her*, this clean bare plane of the top of her chest down from the shoulder bones like a dented sheet of metal tilted in the light. I mean, it was more than pretty.

She had sort of oaky hair that the sun and salt had bleached, done up in a bun that was unravelling, and a kind of prim face. Walking into the A & P with your straps down, I suppose it's the only kind of face you *can* have. She held her head so high her neck, coming up out of those white shoulders, looked kind of stretched, but I didn't mind. The longer her neck was, the more of her there was.

She must have felt in the corner of her eye me and over my shoulder Stokesie in the second slot watching, but she didn't tip. Not this queen. She kept her eyes moving across the racks, and stopped, and turned so slow it made my stomach rub the inside of my apron, and buzzed to the other two, who kind of huddled against her for relief, and then they all three of them went up the cat-and-dog-food-breakfast-cereal-macaroni-rice-raisins-seasonings-spreads-spaghetti-soft-drinks-crackers-and-cookies aisle. From the third slot I look straight up this aisle to the meat counter, and I watched them all the way. The fat one with the tan sort of fumbled with the cookies, but on second thought she put the package back. The sheep pushing their carts down the aisle—the girls were walking against the usual traffic (not that we have one-way signs or anything)—were pretty hilarious. You could see them, when Queenie's white shoulders dawned on them, kind of jerk, or hop, or hiccup, but their eyes snapped back to their own baskets and on they pushed. I bet you could set off dynamite in an A & P and the people would by and large keep reaching and checking oatmeal off their lists and muttering "Let me see, there was a third thing, began with A, asparagus, no, ah, yes, applesauce!" or whatever it is they do mutter. But there was no doubt, this jiggled them. A few houseslaves in pin curlers even looked around after pushing their carts past to make sure what they had seen was correct.

You know, it's one thing to have a girl in a bathing suit down on the beach, where what with the glare nobody can look at each other much anyway, and another thing in the cool of the A & P, under the fluorescent lights, against all those stacked packages, with her feet paddling along naked over our checkerboard green-and-cream rubber-tile floor.

"Oh Daddy," Stokesie said beside me. "I feel so faint."

"Darling," I said. "Hold me tight." Stokesie's married, with two babies chalked up on his fuselage already, but as far as I can tell that's the only difference. He's twenty-two, and I was nineteen this April.

"Is it done?" he asks, the responsible married man finding his voice. I forgot to say he thinks he's going to be manager some sunny day, maybe in 1990 when it's called the Great Alexandrov and Petrooshki Tea Company or something.

What he meant was, our town is five miles from a beach, with a big summer colony out on the Point, but we're right in the middle of town, and the women generally put on a shirt or shorts or something before they get out of the car into the street. And anyway these are usually women with six children and varicose veins mapping their legs and nobody, including them, could care less. As I say, we're right in the middle of town, and if you stand at our front doors you can see two banks and the Congregational church and the newspaper store and three real-estate offices and about twenty-seven old freeloaders tearing up Central Street because the sewer broke again. It's not as if we're on the Cape; we're north of Boston and there's people in this town haven't seen the ocean for twenty years.

The girls had reached the meat counter and were asking McMahon something. He pointed, they pointed, and they shuffled out of sight behind a pyramid of Diet Delight peaches. All that was left for us to see was old McMahon patting his mouth and looking after them sizing up their joints. Poor kids, I began to feel sorry for them, they couldn't help it.

Now here comes the sad part of the story, at least my family says it's sad, but I don't think it's so sad myself. The store's pretty empty, it being Thursday afternoon, so there was nothing much to do except lean on the register and wait for the girls to show up again. The whole store was like a pinball machine and I didn't know which tunnel they'd come out of. After a while they come around out of the far aisle, around the light bulbs, records at discount of the Caribbean Six or Tony Martin Sings or some such gunk you wonder they waste the wax on, sixpacks of candy bars, and plastic toys done up in cellophane that fall apart when a kid looks at them anyway. Around they come, Queenie still leading the way, and holding a little gray jar in her hand. Slots Three through Seven are unmanned and I could see her wondering between Stokes and me, but Stokesie with his usual luck draws an old party in baggy gray pants who stumbles up with four giant cans of pineapple juice (what do these bums *do* with all that pineapple juice? I've often asked myself) so the girls come to me. Queenie puts down the jar and I take it into my fingers icy cold. Kingfish Fancy Herring Snacks in Pure Sour Cream: 49¢. Now her hands are empty, not a ring or a bracelet, bare as God made them, and I wonder where the money's coming from. Still with that prim look she lifts a folded dollar bill out of the hollow at the center of her nubbled pink top. The jar went heavy in my hand. Really, I thought that was so cute.

Then everybody's luck begins to run out. Lengel comes in from haggling with a truck full of cabbages on the lot and is about to scuttle into that door marked MANAGER behind which he hides all day when the girls touch his eye. Lengel's pretty dreary, teaches Sunday school and the rest, but he doesn't miss that much. He comes over and says, "Girls, this isn't the beach."

Queenie blushes, though maybe it's just a brush of sunburn I was noticing for the first time, now that she was so close. "My mother asked me to pick up a jar of herring snacks." Her voice kind of startled me, the way voices do when you see the people first, coming out so flat and dumb yet kind of tony, too, the way it ticked over "pick up" and "snacks." All of a sudden I slid right down her voice into her living room. Her father and the other men were standing around in ice-cream coats and bow ties and the women were in sandals picking up herring snacks on toothpicks off a big glass plate and they were all holding drinks the color of water with olives and sprigs of mint in them. When my parents have somebody over they get lemonade and if it's a real racy affair Schlitz in tall glasses with "They'll Do It Every Time" cartoons stencilled on.

"That's all right," Lengel said. "But this isn't the beach." His repeating this struck me as funny, as if it had just occurred to him, and he had been thinking all these years the A & P was a great big sand dune and he was the head lifeguard. He didn't like my smiling—as I say he doesn't miss much—but he concentrates on giving the girls that sad Sunday-school-superintendent stare.

Queenie's blush is no sunburn now, and the plump one in plaid, that I liked better from the back—a really sweet can—pipes up, "We weren't doing any shopping. We just came in for the one thing."

"That makes no difference," Lengel tells her, and I could see from the way his eyes went that he hadn't noticed she was wearing a two-piece before. "We want you decently dressed when you come in here."

"We *are* decent," Queenie says suddenly, her lower lip pushing, getting sore now that she remembers her place, a place from which the crowd that runs the A & P must look pretty crummy. Fancy Herring Snacks flashed in her very blue eyes.

"Girls, I don't want to argue with you. After this come in here with your shoulders covered. It's our policy." He turns his back. That's policy for you. Policy is what the kingpins want. What the others want is juvenile delinquency.

All this while, the customers had been showing up with their carts but, you know, sheep, seeing a scene, they had all bunched up on Stokesie, who shook open a paper bag as gently as peeling a peach, not wanting to miss a word. I could feel in the silence everybody getting nervous, most of all Lengel, who asks me, "Sammy, have you rung up their purchase?"

I thought and said "No" but it wasn't about that I was thinking. I go through the punches, 4, 9, GROC, TOT—it's more complicated than you think, and after you do it often enough, it begins to make a little song, that you hear words to, in my case "Hello (*bing*) there, you (*gung*) hap-py *pee*-pul (*splat*)!"—the *splat* being the drawer flying out. I uncrease the bill, tenderly as you may imagine, it just having come from between the two smoothest scoops of vanilla I had ever known were there, and pass a half and a penny into her narrow pink palm, and nestle the herrings in a bag and twist its neck and hand it over, all the time thinking.

The girls, and who'd blame them, are in a hurry to get out, so I say "I quit" to Lengel quick enough for them to hear, hoping they'll stop and watch me, their unsuspected hero. They keep right on going, into the electric eye; the door flies open and they flicker across the lot to their car, Queenie and Plaid and Big Tall Goony-Goony (not that as raw material she was so bad), leaving me with Lengel and a kink in his eyebrow.

"Did you say something, Sammy?"

"I said I quit."

"I thought you did."

"You didn't have to embarrass them."

"It was they who were embarrassing us."

I started to say something that came out "Fiddle-de-doo." It's a saying of my grandmother's, and I know she would have been pleased.

"I don't think you know what you're saying," Lengel said.

"I know you don't," I said. "But I do." I pull the bow at the back of my apron and start shrugging it off my shoulders. A couple customers that had been heading for my slot begin to knock against each other, like scared pigs in a chute.

Lengel sighs and begins to look very patient and old and gray. He's been a friend of my parents for years. "Sammy, you don't want to do this to your Mom and Dad," he tells me. It's true, I don't. But it seems to me that once you begin a gesture it's fatal not to go through with it. I fold the apron, "Sammy" stitched in red on the pocket, and put it on the counter, and drop the bow tie on top of it. The bow tie is theirs, if you've ever wondered. "You'll feel this for the rest of your life," Lengel says, and I know that's true, too, but remembering how he made that pretty girl blush makes me so scrunchy inside I punch the No Sale tab and the machine whirs "pee-pul" and the drawer splats out. One advantage to this scene taking place in summer, I can follow this up with a clean exit, there's no fumbling around getting your coat and galoshes, I just saunter into the electric eye in my white shirt that my mother ironed the night before, and the door heaves itself open, and outside the sunshine is skating around on the asphalt.

I look around for my girls, but they're gone, of course. There wasn't anybody but some young married screaming with her children about some candy they didn't get by the door of a powder-blue Falcon station wagon. Looking back in the big windows, over the bags of peat moss and aluminum lawn furniture stacked on the pavement, I could see Lengel in my place in the slot, checking the sheep through. His face was dark gray and his back stiff, as if he'd just had an injection of iron, and my stomach kind of fell as I felt how hard the world was going to be to me hereafter.

KURT VONNEGUT JR.

Kurt Vonnegut Jr. (1922–2007) was born on November 11 in Indianapolis, Indiana. The son of an architect and a homemaker, he attended Cornell University and Carnegie Mellon University before the outbreak of World War II, when he interrupted his studies to serve in the U.S. Army. As a prisoner of war in Dresden, Germany, he survived a devastating air raid on February 13, 1945, by staying in a meat locker under a slaughterhouse during the bombing. After World War II, Vonnegut worked in public relations at the General Electric Company in Schenectady, New York, before becoming a freelance writer. *Player Piano*, his first novel, appeared in 1952, followed by a second fantasy novel, *The Sirens of Titan,* in 1959. Two years later he published *Mother Night,* a first-person fictional narrative about World War II. In 1969 Vonnegut published another novel that has become a classic based on his own experience of the Allies' fire-bombing of Dresden. Vonnegut titled it *Slaughterhouse-Five; or, The Children's Crusade: A Duty-Dance with Death, by Kurt Vonnegut, Jr., a Fourth-Generation German-American Now Living in Easy Circumstances on Cape Cod (and Smoking Too Much) Who, as an American Infantry Scout Hors de Combat, as a Prisoner of War, Witnessed the Fire-Bombing of Dresden, Germany, the Florence of the Elbe, a Long Time Ago, and Survived to Tell the Tale; This Is a Novel Somewhat in the Telegraphic Schizophrenic Manner of Tales of the Planet Tralfamadore, Where the Flying Saucers Come From.*

After *Slaughterhouse-Five* was made into a film in 1972, Vonnegut's books achieved cult status. The critic Jerome Klinkowitz has observed that there was a "shift in taste" in the late 1960s and early 1970s that brought more serious appreciation to Vonnegut's fiction after a new generation of writers – Donald Barthelme, John Barth, Richard Brautigan, Jerzy Kosinski, Don DeLillo, Thomas Pynchon, and others – began publishing. "Ten years and several books their elder, Vonnegut by his long exile underground was well prepared to be the senior member of the new disruptive group."

Before Vonnegut's breakthrough as a novelist, he published short stories, like the fantasy tale "Harrison Bergeron," in *Canary in a Cathouse* (1961) and *Welcome to the Monkey House* (1968). John Updike understood that Vonnegut "began as a published writer with the so-called slick magazines" – *The Saturday Evening Post, Collier's,* and *The Ladies' Home Journal.* In the 1950s, slickness "was a verbal mechanism that raised the spectre of pain and then too easily delivered us from it. Yet the pain in Vonnegut was always real. Through the transpositions of science fiction, he found a way . . . to vaporize it, to scatter it on the plane of the cosmic and the comic." *Bagombo Snuff Box* (2002) and *While Mortals Sleep* (2011) are other collections of short narratives.

WEB Research Kurt Vonnegut Jr. at bedfordstmartins.com/rewritinglit.

Harrison Bergeron

1961

The year was 2081, and everybody was finally equal. They weren't only equal before God and the law. They were equal every which way. Nobody was smarter than anybody else. Nobody was better looking than anybody else. Nobody was stronger or quicker than anybody else. All this equality was due to the 211th, 212th, and 213th Amendments to the Constitution, and to the unceasing vigilance of agents of the United States Handicapper General.

Some things about living still weren't quite right, though. April, for instance, still drove people crazy by not being springtime. And it was in that clammy month that the H-G men took George and Hazel Bergeron's fourteen-year-old son, Harrison, away.

It was tragic, all right, but George and Hazel couldn't think about it very hard. Hazel had a perfectly average intelligence, which meant she couldn't think about anything except in short bursts. And George, while his intelligence was way above normal, had a little mental handicap radio in his ear. He was required by law to wear it at all times. It was tuned to a government transmitter. Every twenty seconds or so, the transmitter would send out some sharp noise to keep people like George from taking unfair advantage of their brains.

George and Hazel were watching television. There were tears on Hazel's cheeks, but she'd forgotten for the moment what they were about.

On the television screen were ballerinas.

A buzzer sounded in George's head. His thoughts fled in panic, like bandits from a burglar alarm.

"That was a real pretty dance, that dance they just did," said Hazel.

"Huh?" said George.

"That dance—it was nice," said Hazel.

"Yup," said George. He tried to think a little about the ballerinas. They weren't really very good—no better than anybody else would have been, anyway. They were burdened with sashweights and bags of birdshot, and their faces were masked, so that no one, seeing a free and graceful gesture or a pretty face, would feel like something the cat drug in. George was toying with the vague notion that maybe dancers shouldn't be handicapped. But he didn't get very far with it before another noise in his ear radio scattered his thoughts.

George winced. So did two out of the eight ballerinas.

Hazel saw him wince. Having no mental handicap herself, she had to ask George what the latest sound had been.

"Sounded like somebody hitting a milk bottle with a ball peen hammer," said George.

"I'd think it would be real interesting, hearing all the different sounds," said Hazel, a little envious. "All the things they think up."

"Um," said George.

"Only, if I was Handicapper General, you know what I would do?" said Hazel. Hazel, as a matter of fact, bore a strong resemblance to the Handicapper General, a woman named Diana Moon Glampers. "If I was Diana Moon Glampers," said Hazel, "I'd have chimes on Sunday—just chimes. Kind of in honor of religion."

"I could think, if it was just chimes," said George.

"Well—maybe make 'em real loud," said Hazel. "I think I'd make a good Handicapper General."

"Good as anybody else," said George.

"Who knows better'n I do what normal is?" said Hazel.

"Right," said George. He began to think glimmeringly about his abnormal son who was now in jail, about Harrison, but a twenty-one-gun salute in his head stopped that.

"Boy!" said Hazel, "that was a doozy, wasn't it?"

It was such a doozy that George was white and trembling, and tears stood on the rims of his red eyes. Two of the eight ballerinas had collapsed to the studio floor, were holding their temples.

"All of a sudden you look so tired," said Hazel. "Why don't you stretch out on the sofa, so's you can rest your handicap bag on the pillows, honeybunch." She was referring to the forty-seven pounds of birdshot in a canvas bag, which was padlocked around George's neck. "Go on and rest the bag for a little while," she said. "I don't care if you're not equal to me for a while."

George weighed the bag with his hands. "I don't mind it," he said. "I don't notice it any more. It's just a part of me."

"You been so tired lately—kind of wore out," said Hazel. "If there was just some way we could make a little hole in the bottom of the bag, and just take out a few of them lead balls. Just a few."

"Two years in prison and two thousand dollars fine for every ball I took out," said George. "I don't call that a bargain."

"If you could just take a few out when you came home from work," said Hazel. "I mean—you don't compete with anybody around here. You just set around."

"If I tried to get away with it," said George, "then other people'd get away with it—and pretty soon we'd be right back to the dark ages again, with everybody competing against everybody else. You wouldn't like that, would you?"

"I'd hate it," said Hazel.

"There you are," said George. "The minute people start cheating on laws, what do you think happens to society?"

If Hazel hadn't been able to come up with an answer to this question, George couldn't have supplied one. A siren was going off in his head.

"Reckon it'd fall all apart," said Hazel.

"What would?" said George blankly.

"Society," said Hazel uncertainly. "Wasn't that what you just said?"

"Who knows?" said George.

The television program was suddenly interrupted for a news bulletin. It wasn't clear at first as to what the bulletin was about, since the announcer, like all announcers, had a serious speech impediment. For about half a minute, and in a state of high excitement, the announcer tried to say, "Ladies and gentlemen—"

He finally gave up, handed the bulletin to a ballerina to read.

"That's all right—" Hazel said of the announcer, "he tried. That's the big thing. He tried to do the best he could with what God gave him. He should get a nice raise for trying so hard."

"Ladies and gentlemen—" said the ballerina, reading the bulletin. She must have been extraordinarily beautiful, because the mask she wore was hideous. And it was easy to see that she was the strongest and most graceful of all the dancers, for her handicap bags were as big as those worn by two-hundred-pound men.

And she had to apologize at once for her voice, which was a very unfair voice for a woman to use. Her voice was a warm, luminous, timeless melody. "Excuse me—" she said, and she began again, making her voice absolutely uncompetitive.

"Harrison Bergeron, age fourteen," she said in a grackle squawk, "has just escaped from jail, where he was held on suspicion of plotting to overthrow the government. He is a genius and an athlete, is under-handicapped, and should be regarded as extremely dangerous."

A police photograph of Harrison Bergeron was flashed on the screen—upside down, then sideways, upside down again, then right side up. The picture showed the full length of Harrison against a background calibrated in feet and inches. He was exactly seven feet tall.

The rest of Harrison's appearance was Halloween and hardware. Nobody had ever born heavier handicaps. He had outgrown hindrances faster than the H-G men could think them up. Instead of a little ear radio for a mental handicap, he wore a tremendous pair of earphones, and spectacles with thick wavy lenses. The spectacles were intended to make him not only half blind, but to give him whanging headaches besides.

Scrap metal was hung all over him. Ordinarily, there was a certain symmetry, a military neatness to the handicaps issued to strong people, but Harrison looked like a walking junkyard. In the race of life, Harrison carried three hundred pounds.

And to offset his good looks, the H-G men required that he wear at all times a red rubber ball for a nose, keep his eyebrows shaved off, and cover his even white teeth with black caps at snaggle-tooth random.

"If you see this boy," said the ballerina, "do not—I repeat, do not—try to reason with him."

There was the shriek of a door being torn from its hinges.

Screams and barking cries of consternation came from the television set. The photograph of Harrison Bergeron on the screen jumped again and again, as though dancing to the tune of an earthquake.

George Bergeron correctly identified the earthquake, and well he might have—for many was the time his own home had danced to the same crashing tune. "My God—" said George, "that must be Harrison!"

The realization was blasted from his mind instantly by the sound of an automobile collision in his head.

When George could open his eyes again, the photograph of Harrison was gone. A living, breathing Harrison filled the screen.

Clanking, clownish, and huge, Harrison stood in the center of the studio. The knob of the uprooted studio door was still in his hand. Ballerinas, technicians, musicians, and announcers cowered on their knees before him, expecting to die.

"I am the Emperor!" cried Harrison. "Do you hear? I am the Emperor! Everybody must do what I say at once!" He stamped his foot and the studio shook.

"Even as I stand here—" he bellowed, "crippled, hobbled, sickened—I am a greater ruler than any man who ever lived! Now watch me become what I *can* become!"

Harrison tore the straps of his handicap harness like wet tissue paper, tore straps guaranteed to support five thousand pounds.

Harrison's scrap-iron handicaps crashed to the floor.

Harrison thrust his thumbs under the bars of the padlock that secured his head harness. The bar snapped like celery. Harrison smashed his headphones and spectacles against the wall.

He flung away his rubber-ball nose, revealed a man that would have awed Thor, the god of thunder.

"I shall now select my Empress!" he said, looking down on the cowering people. "Let the first woman who dares rise to her feet claim her mate and her throne!"

A moment passed, and then a ballerina arose, swaying like a willow.

Harrison plucked the mental handicap from her ear, snapped off her physical handicaps with marvelous delicacy. Last of all, he removed her mask.

She was blindingly beautiful.

"Now—" said Harrison, taking her hand, "shall we show the people the meaning of the word dance? Music!" he commanded.

The musicians scrambled back into their chairs, and Harrison stripped them of their handicaps, too. "Play your best," he told them, "and I'll make you barons and dukes and earls."

The music began. It was normal at first—cheap, silly, false. But Harrison snatched two musicians from their chairs, waved them like batons as he sang the music as he wanted it played. He slammed them back into their chairs.

The music began again and was much improved.

Harrison and his Empress merely listened to the music for a while—listened gravely, as though synchronizing their heartbeats with it.

They shifted their weights to their toes.

Harrison placed his big hands on the girl's tiny waist, letting her sense the weightlessness that would soon be hers.

And then, in an explosion of joy and grace, into the air they sprang!

Not only were the laws of the land abandoned, but the law of gravity and the laws of motion as well.

They reeled, whirled, swiveled, flounced, capered, gamboled, and spun.

They leaped like deer on the moon.

The studio ceiling was thirty feet high, but each leap brought the dancers nearer to it.

It became their obvious intention to kiss the ceiling.

They kissed it.

And then, neutralizing gravity with love and pure will, they remained suspended in air inches below the ceiling, and they kissed each other for a long, long time.

It was then that Diana Moon Glampers, the Handicapper General, came into the studio with a double-barreled ten-gauge shotgun. She fired twice, and the Emperor and the Empress were dead before they hit the floor.

Diana Moon Glampers loaded the gun again. She aimed at the musicians and told them they had ten seconds to get their handicaps back on.

It was then that the Bergerons' television tube burned out.

Hazel turned to comment about the blackout to George. But George had gone out into the kitchen for a can of beer.

George came back in with the beer, paused while a handicap signal shook him up. And then he sat down again. "You been crying?" he said to Hazel.

"Yup," she said.

"What about?" he said.

"I forgot," she said. "Something real sad on television."

"What was it?" he said.

"It's all kind of mixed up in my mind," said Hazel.

"Forget sad things," said George.

"I always do," said Hazel.

"That's my girl," said George. He winced. There was the sound of a rivetting gun in his head.

"Gee—I could tell that one was a doozy," said Hazel.

"You can say that again," said George.

"Gee—" said Hazel, "I could tell that one was a doozy."

ALICE WALKER

Alice Walker (b. 1944) was the eighth and youngest child of Willie Lee and Minnie Lou Grant Walker, sharecroppers in Eatonton, Georgia. Walker did well in school, encouraged by her teachers and her mother, whose stories she loved as "a walking history of our community." For two years, Walker attended Spelman College in Atlanta, the oldest college for black women in the United States. Then she studied at Sarah Lawrence College in New York, where she began her writing career by publishing a book of poetry, *Once* (1968). Since that time Walker has published several collections of poetry, novels, volumes of short stories, and *Living by the Word* (1988), a book of essays. Her best-known novel, *The Color Purple* (1982), made her the first black woman to win the Pulitzer Prize. Some later books include *The Temple of My Familiar* (1989), *Possessing the Secret of Joy* (1992), *Anything We Love Can Be Saved: A Writer's Activism* (1997), *By the Light of My Father's Smile* (1999), *Now Is the Time to Open Your Heart* (2004), and *Devil's My Enemy* (2008).

Walker's works show her commitment to the idea of radical social change. She was active in the civil rights movement in Mississippi, where she met and married a civil rights lawyer from whom she separated after the birth of their daughter. In confronting the painful struggle of black people's history, Walker asserts that the creativity of black women—the extent to which they are permitted to express themselves—is a measure of the health of the entire American society. She calls herself a "womanist," her term for a black feminist. In her definition, "womanism" is preferable to "feminism" because, as she has said,

> part of our tradition as black women is that we are universalists. Black children, yellow children, red children, brown children, that is the black woman's normal, day-to-day relationship. In my family alone, we are about four different colors. When a black woman looks at the world, it is so different . . . when I look at the people in Iran they look like kinfolk. When I look at the people in Cuba, they look like my uncles and nieces.

Walker credits many writers for influencing her prose style in her short fiction. Virginia Woolf, Zora Neale Hurston, and Gabriel García Márquez seem to Walker to be "like musicians; at one with their cultures and their historical subconscious." Her two books of stories show a clear progression of theme. The women of *In Love and Trouble* (1973) struggle against injustice almost in spite of themselves, as does the protagonist in "Everyday Use" from that collection; the heroines of *You Can't Keep a Good Woman Down* (1981) consciously challenge conventions. Walker has said, "Writing really helps you heal yourself. I think if you write long enough, you will be a healthy person. That is, if you write what you need to write, as opposed to what will make money, or what will make fame." "Everyday Use" was first published in *Harper's* magazine in 1973.

CONNECTION Alice Walker, "I Said to Poetry," page 677.

WEB Research Alice Walker at bedfordstmartins.com/rewritinglit.

Everyday Use 1973

I will wait for her in the yard that Maggie and I made so clean and wavy yesterday afternoon. A yard like this is more comfortable than most people know. It is not just a yard. It is like an extended living room. When the hard clay is swept clean as a floor and the fine sand around the edges lined with tiny, irregular grooves, anyone can come and sit and look up into the elm tree and wait for the breezes that never come inside the house.

Maggie will be nervous until after her sister goes: she will stand hopelessly in corners, homely and ashamed of the burn scars down her arms and legs, eyeing her sister with a mixture of envy and awe. She thinks her sister has held life always in the palm of one hand, that "no" is a word the world never learned to say to her.

You've no doubt seen those TV shows where the child who has "made it" is confronted, as a surprise, by her own mother and father, tottering in weakly from backstage. (A pleasant surprise, of course: What would they do if parent and child came on the show only to curse out and insult each other?) On TV mother and child embrace and smile into each other's faces. Sometimes the mother and father weep, the child wraps them in her arms and leans across the table to tell how she would not have made it without their help. I have seen these programs.

Sometimes I dream a dream in which Dee and I are suddenly brought together on a TV program of this sort. Out of a dark and soft-seated limousine I am ushered into a bright room filled with many people. There I meet a smiling, gray, sporty man like Johnny Carson who shakes my hand and tells me what a fine girl I have. Then we are on the stage and Dee is embracing me with tears in her eyes. She pins on my dress a large orchid, even though she has told me once that she thinks orchids are tacky flowers.

In real life I am a large, big-boned woman with rough, man-working hands. In the winter I wear flannel nightgowns to bed and overalls during the day. I can kill and clean a hog as mercilessly as a man. My fat keeps me hot in zero weather. I can work outside all day, breaking ice to get water for washing; I can eat pork liver cooked over the open fire minutes after it comes steaming from the hog. One winter I knocked a bull calf straight in the brain between the eyes with a sledge hammer and had the meat hung up to chill before nightfall. But of course all this does not show on television. I am the way my daughter would want me to be: a hundred pounds lighter, my skin like an uncooked barley pancake. My hair glistens in the hot bright lights. Johnny Carson has much to do to keep up with my quick and witty tongue.

But that is a mistake. I know even before I wake up. Who ever knew a Johnson with a quick tongue? Who can even imagine me looking a strange white man in the eye? It seems to me I have talked to them always with one foot raised in flight, with my head turned in whichever way is farthest from them. Dee, though. She would always look anyone in the eye. Hesitation was no part of her nature.

"How do I look, Mama?" Maggie says, showing just enough of her thin body enveloped in pink skirt and red blouse for me to know she's there, almost hidden by the door.

"Come out into the yard," I say.

Have you ever seen a lame animal, perhaps a dog run over by some careless person rich enough to own a car, sidle up to someone who is ignorant enough to be kind to him? That is the way my Maggie walks. She has been like this, chin on chest, eyes on ground, feet in shuffle, ever since the fire that burned the other house to the ground.

Dee is lighter than Maggie, with nicer hair and a fuller figure. She's a woman now, though sometimes I forget. How long ago was it that the other house burned? Ten, twelve years? Sometimes I can still hear the flames and feel Maggie's arms sticking to me, her hair smoking and her dress falling off her in little black papery flakes. Her eyes seemed stretched open, blazed open by the flames reflected in them. And Dee. I see her standing off under the sweet gum tree she used to dig gum out of; a look of concentration on her face as she watched the last dingy gray board of the house fall in toward the red-hot brick chimney. Why don't you do a dance around the ashes? I'd wanted to ask her. She had hated the house that much.

I used to think she hated Maggie, too. But that was before we raised the money, the church and me, to send her to Augusta to school. She used to read to us without pity; forcing words, lies, other folks' habits, whole lives upon us two, sitting trapped and ignorant underneath her voice. She washed us in a river of make-believe, burned us with a lot of knowledge we didn't necessarily need to know. Pressed us to her with the serious way she read, to shove us away at just the moment, like dimwits, we seemed about to understand.

Dee wanted nice things. A yellow organdy dress to wear to her graduation from high school; black pumps to match a green suit she'd made from an old suit somebody gave me. She was determined to stare down any disaster in her efforts. Her eyelids would not flicker for minutes at a time. Often I fought off the temptation to shake her. At sixteen she had a style of her own: and knew what style was.

I never had an education myself. After second grade the school was closed down. Don't ask me why: in 1927 colored asked fewer questions than they do now. Sometimes Maggie reads to me. She stumbles along good-naturedly but can't see well. She knows she is not bright. Like good looks and money, quickness passed her by. She will marry John Thomas (who has mossy teeth in an earnest face) and then I'll be free to sit here and I guess just sing church songs to myself. Although I never was a good singer. Never could carry a tune. I was always better at a man's job. I used to love to milk till I was hooked in the side in '49. Cows are soothing and slow and don't bother you, unless you try to milk them the wrong way.

I have deliberately turned my back on the house. It is three rooms, just like the one that burned, except the roof is tin; they don't make shingle roofs any more. There are no real windows, just some holes cut in the sides, like the portholes in a ship, but not round and not square, with rawhide holding the shutters up on the outside. This house is in a pasture, too, like the other one. No doubt when Dee sees it she will want to tear it down. She wrote me once that no matter where we "choose" to live, she will manage to come see us. But she will never bring her friends. Maggie and I thought about this and Maggie asked me, "Mama, when did Dee ever *have* any friends?"

She had a few. Furtive boys in pink shirts hanging about on washday after school. Nervous girls who never laughed. Impressed with her they worshiped the well-turned phrase, the cute shape, the scalding humor that erupted like bubbles in lye. She read to them.

When she was courting Jimmy T she didn't have much time to pay to us, but turned all her faultfinding power on him. He *flew* to marry a cheap city gal from a family of ignorant flashy people. She hardly had time to recompose herself.

When she comes I will meet—but there they are!

Maggie attempts to make a dash for the house, in her shuffling way, but I stay her with my hand. "Come back here," I say. And she stops and tries to dig a well in the sand with her toe.

It is hard to see them clearly through the strong sun. But even the first glimpse of leg out of the car tells me it is Dee. Her feet were always neat-looking, as if God himself had shaped them with a certain style. From the other side of the car comes a short, stocky man. Hair is all over his head a foot long and hanging from his chin like a kinky mule tail. I hear Maggie suck in her breath. "Uhnnnh," is what it sounds like. Like when you see the wriggling end of a snake just in front of your foot on the road. "Uhnnnh."

Dee next. A dress down to the ground, in this hot weather. A dress so loud it hurts my eyes. There are yellows and oranges enough to throw back the light of the sun. I feel my whole face warming from the heat waves it throws out. Earrings gold, too, and hanging down to her shoulders. Bracelets dangling and making noises when she moves her arm up to shake the folds of the dress out of her armpits. The dress is loose and flows, and as she walks closer, I like it. I hear Maggie go "Uhnnnh" again. It is her sister's hair. It stands straight up like the wool on a sheep. It is black as night and around the edges are two long pigtails that rope about like small lizards disappearing behind her ears.

"Wa-su-zo-Tean-o!" she says, coming on in that gliding way the dress makes her move. The short stocky fellow with the hair to his navel is all grinning and he follows up with "Asalamalakim, my mother and sister!" He moves to hug Maggie but she falls back, right up against the back of my chair. I feel her trembling there and when I look up I see the perspiration falling off her chin.

"Don't get up," says Dee. Since I am stout it takes something of a push. You can see me trying to move a second or two before I make it. She turns, showing white heels through her sandals, and goes back to the car. Out she peeks next with a Polaroid. She stoops down quickly and lines up picture after picture of me sitting there in front of the house with Maggie cowering behind me. She never takes a shot without making sure the house is included. When a cow comes nibbling around the edge of the yard she snaps it and me *and* the house. Then she puts the Polaroid in the back seat of the car, and comes up and kisses me on the forehead.

Meanwhile Asalamalakim is going through the motions with Maggie's hand. Maggie's hand is as limp as a fish, and probably as cold, despite the sweat, and she keeps trying to pull it back. It looks like Asalamalakim wants to shake hands but wants to do it fancy. Or maybe he don't know how people shake hands. Anyhow, he soon gives up on Maggie.

"Well," I say. "Dee."

"No, Mama," she says. "Not 'Dee,' Wangero Leewanika Kemanjo!"

"What happened to 'Dee'?" I wanted to know.

"She's dead," Wangero said. "I couldn't bear it any longer being named after the people who oppress me."

"You know as well as me you was named after your aunt Dicie," I said. Dicie is my sister. She named Dee. We called her "Big Dee" after Dee was born.

"But who was *she* named after?" asked Wangero.

"I guess after Grandma Dee," I said.

"And who was she named after?" asked Wangero.

"Her mother," I said, and saw Wangero was getting tired. "That's about as far back as I can trace it," I said. Though, in fact, I probably could have carried it back beyond the Civil War through the branches.

"Well," said Asalamalakim, "there you are."

"Uhnnnh," I heard Maggie say.

"There I was not," I said, "before 'Dicie' cropped up in our family, so why should I try to trace it that far back?"

He just stood there grinning, looking down on me like somebody inspecting a Model A car. Every once in a while he and Wangero sent eye signals over my head.

"How do you pronounce this name?" I asked.

"You don't have to call me by it if you don't want to," said Wangero.

"Why shouldn't I?" I asked. "If that's what you want us to call you, we'll call you."

"I know it might sound awkward at first," said Wangero.

"I'll get used to it," I said. "Ream it out again."

Well, soon we got the name out of the way. Asalamalakim had a name twice as long and three times as hard. After I tripped over it two or three times he told me to just call him Hakim-a-barber. I wanted to ask him was he a barber, but I didn't really think he was, so I didn't ask.

"You must belong to those beef-cattle peoples down the road," I said. They said "Asalamalakim" when they met you, too, but they didn't shake hands. Always too busy: feeding the cattle, fixing the fences, putting up salt-lick shelters, throwing down hay. When the white folks poisoned some of the herd the men stayed up all night with rifles in their hands. I walked a mile and a half just to see the sight.

Hakim-a-barber said, "I accept some of their doctrines, but farming and raising cattle is not my style." (They didn't tell me, and I didn't ask, whether Wangero [Dee] had really gone and married him.)

We sat down to eat and right away he said he didn't eat collards and pork was unclean. Wangero, though, went on through the chitlins and corn bread, the greens and everything else. She talked a blue streak over the sweet potatoes. Everything delighted her. Even the fact that we still used the benches her daddy made for the table when we couldn't afford to buy chairs.

"Oh, Mama!" she cried. Then turned to Hakim-a-barber. "I never knew how lovely these benches are. You can feel the rump prints," she said, running her hands underneath her and along the bench. Then she gave a sigh and her hand closed over Grandma Dee's butter dish. "That's it!" she said. "I knew there was something I wanted to ask you if I could have." She jumped up from the table and went over in the corner where the churn stood, the milk in it clabber by now. She looked at the churn and looked at it.

"This churn top is what I need," she said. "Didn't Uncle Buddy whittle it out of a tree you all used to have?"

"Yes," I said.

"Uh-huh," she said happily. "And I want the dasher, too."

"Uncle Buddy whittle that, too?" asked the barber.

Dee (Wangero) looked up at me.

"Aunt Dee's first husband whittled the dash," said Maggie so low you almost couldn't hear her. "His name was Henry, but they called him Stash."

"Maggie's brain is like an elephant's," Wangero said, laughing. "I can use the churn top as a centerpiece for the alcove table," she said, sliding a plate over the churn, "and I'll think of something artistic to do with the dasher."

When she finished wrapping the dasher the handle stuck out. I took it for a moment in my hands. You didn't even have to look close to see where hands pushing the dasher up and down to make butter had left a kind of sink in the wood. In fact, there were a lot of small sinks; you could see where thumbs and fingers had sunk into the wood. It was beautiful light yellow wood, from a tree that grew in the yard where Big Dee and Stash had lived.

After dinner Dee (Wangero) went to the trunk at the foot of my bed and started rifling through it. Maggie hung back in the kitchen over the dishpan. Out came Wangero with two quilts. They had been pieced by Grandma Dee and then Big Dee and me had hung them on the quilt frames on the front porch and quilted them. One was in the Lone Star pattern. The other was Walk Around the Mountain. In both of them were scraps of dresses Grandma Dee had worn fifty and more years ago. Bits and pieces of Grandpa Jarrell's Paisley shirts. And one teeny faded blue piece, about the size of a penny matchbox, that was from Great Grandpa Ezra's uniform that he wore in the Civil War.

"Mama," Wangero said sweet as a bird. "Can I have these old quilts?"

I heard something fall in the kitchen, and a minute later the kitchen door slammed.

"Why don't you take one or two of the others?" I asked. "These old things was just done by me and Big Dee from some tops your grandma pieced before she died."

"No," said Wangero. "I don't want those. They are stitched around the borders by machine."

"That'll make them last better," I said.

"That's not the point," said Wangero. "These are all pieces of dresses Grandma used to wear. She did all this stitching by hand. Imagine!" She held the quilts securely in her arms, stroking them.

"Some of the pieces, like those lavender ones, come from old clothes her mother handed down to her," I said, moving up to touch the quilts. Dee (Wangero) moved back just enough so that I couldn't reach the quilts. They already belonged to her.

"Imagine!" she breathed again, clutching them closely to her bosom.

"The truth is," I said, "I promised to give them quilts to Maggie, for when she marries John Thomas."

She gasped like a bee had stung her.

"Maggie can't appreciate these quilts!" she said. "She'd probably be backward enough to put them to everyday use."

"I reckon she would," I said. "God knows I been saving 'em for long enough with nobody using 'em. I hope she will!" I didn't want to bring up how I had offered Dee (Wangero) a quilt when she went away to college. Then she had told me they were old-fashioned, out of style.

"But they're *priceless!*" she was saying now, furiously; for she has a temper. "Maggie would put them on the bed and in five years they'd be in rags. Less than that!"

"She can always make some more," I said. "Maggie knows how to quilt."

Dee (Wangero) looked at me with hatred. "You just will not understand. The point is these quilts, *these* quilts!"

"Well," I said, stumped. "What would *you* do with them?"

"Hang them," she said. As if that was the only thing you *could* do with quilts.

Maggie by now was standing in the door. I could almost hear the sound her feet made as they scraped over each other.

"She can have them, Mama," she said, like somebody used to never winning anything, or having anything reserved for her. "I can 'member Grandma Dee without the quilts."

I looked at her hard. She had filled her bottom lip with checkerberry snuff and it gave her face a kind of dopey, hangdog look. It was Grandma Dee and Big Dee who taught her how to quilt herself. She stood there with her scarred hands hidden in the folds of her skirt. She looked at her sister with something like fear but she wasn't mad at her. This was Maggie's portion. This was the way she knew God to work.

When I looked at her like that something hit me in the top of my head and ran down to the soles of my feet. Just like when I'm in church and the spirit of God touches me and I get happy and shout. I did something I never had done before: hugged Maggie to me, then dragged her on into the room, snatched the quilts out of Miss Wangero's hands and dumped them into Maggie's lap. Maggie just sat there on my bed with her mouth open.

"Take one or two of the others," I said to Dee.

But she turned without a word and went out to Hakim-a-barber.

"You just don't understand," she said, as Maggie and I came out to the car.

"What don't I understand?" I wanted to know.

"Your heritage," she said. And then she turned to Maggie, kissed her, and said, "You ought to try to make something of yourself, too, Maggie. It's really a new day for us. But from the way you and Mama still live you'd never know it."

She put on some sunglasses that hid everything above the tip of her nose and her chin.

Maggie smiled; maybe at the sunglasses. But a real smile, not scared. After we watched the car dust settle I asked Maggie to bring me a dip of snuff. And then the two of us sat there just enjoying, until it was time to go in the house and go to bed.

COMMENTARY

ALICE WALKER

Alice Walker wrote about Zora Neale Hurston in her collection *In Search of Our Mothers' Gardens: Womanist Prose* (1983). There she also looked at Flannery O'Connor, Langston Hughes, Jean Toomer, and other writers from what she called her "womanist" perspective as a radical black woman. To clarify the meaning of her term, Walker added that "womanist is to feminist as purple is to lavender."

CONNECTION To read a story by Zora Neale Hurston, see "Sweat" on page 278.

Zora Neale Hurston: A Cautionary Tale and a Partisan View

1979

During the early and middle years of her career Zora was a cultural revolutionary simply because she was always herself. Her work, so vigorous among the rather pallid productions of many of her contemporaries, comes from the essence of black folk life. During her later life she became frightened of the life she had always dared bravely before. Her work too became reactionary, static, shockingly misguided and timid. (This is especially true of her last novel, *Seraphs on the Sewannee*, which is not even about black people, which is no crime, but *is* about white people for whom it is impossible to care, which is.)

A series of misfortunes battered Zora's spirit and her health. And she was broke.

Being broke made all the difference.

Without money of one's own in a capitalist society, there is no such thing as independence. This is one of the clearest lessons of Zora's life, and why I consider the telling of her life "a cautionary tale." We must learn from it what we can.

Without money, an illness, even a simple one, can undermine the will. Without money, getting into a hospital is problematic and getting out without money to pay for the treatment is nearly impossible. Without money, one becomes dependent on other people, who are likely to be—even in their kindness—erratic in their support and despotic in their expectations of return. Zora was forced to rely, like Tennessee Williams's Blanche,° "on the kindness of strangers." Can anything be more dangerous, if the strangers are forever in control? Zora, who worked so hard, was never able to make a living from her work.

She did not complain about not having money. She was not the type. (Several months ago I received a long letter from one of Zora's nieces, a bright ten-year-old, who explained to me that her aunt was so proud that the only way the family could guess she was ill or without funds was by realizing they had no idea where she was. Therefore, none of the family attended either Zora's sickbed or her funeral.) Those of us who have had "grants and fellowships from 'white folks'" know this aid is extended in precisely the way welfare is extended in Mississippi. One is asked, *curtly*, more often than not: How much do you need *just to survive?* Then one is—if fortunate—given a third of that. What is amazing is that Zora, who became an orphan at nine, a runaway at fourteen, a maid and manicurist (because of necessity and not from love of the work) before she was twenty—with one dress—managed to become Zora Neale Hurston, author and anthropologist, at all.

For me, the most unfortunate thing Zora ever wrote is her autobiography. After the first several chapters, it rings false. One begins to hear the voice of someone whose life required the assistance of too many transitory "friends." A Taoist proverb states that *to act sincerely with the insincere is dangerous.* (A mistake blacks as a group have tended to make in America.) And so we have Zora sincerely offering gratitude and kind words to people one knows she could not have respected. But this unctuousness, so out of character for Zora, is also a result of dependency, a sign of her powerlessness, her inability to pay back her debts with anything but words. They must have been bitter ones for her. In her dependency, it should be remembered, Zora was not alone—because it is quite true that America does not support or honor us as human beings, let alone as

---

Tennessee Williams's Blanche: Main character in Williams's play *A Streetcar Named Desire* (1947).

blacks, women, and artists. We have taken help where it was offered because we are committed to what we do and to the survival of our work. Zora was committed to the survival of her people's cultural heritage as well.

In my mind, Zora Neale Hurston, Billie Holiday,° and Bessie Smith° form a sort of unholy trinity. Zora *belongs* in the tradition of black women singers, rather than among "the literati," at least to me. There were the extreme highs and lows of her life, her undaunted pursuit of adventure, passionate emotional and sexual experience, and her love of freedom. Like Billie and Bessie she followed her own road, believed in her own gods, pursued her own dreams, and refused to separate herself from "common" people. It would have been nice if the three of them had had one another to turn to, in times of need. I close my eyes and imagine them: Bessie would be in charge of all the money; Zora would keep Billie's masochistic tendencies in check and prevent her from singing embarrassing anything-for-a-man songs, thereby preventing Billie's heroin addiction. In return, Billie could be, along with Bessie, the family that Zora felt she never had.

We are a people. A people do not throw their geniuses away. And if they are thrown away, it is our duty *as artists and as witnesses for the future* to collect them again for the sake of our children, and, if necessary, bone by bone.

EUDORA WELTY

Eudora Welty (1909–2001) was born in Jackson, Mississippi, where she spent nearly her whole life. She had a predominately tranquil view of the South, so her stories and novels provide a strong contrast to the turbulent fiction of William Faulkner and Richard Wright, who also wrote about Mississippi. Welty grew up as one of three children in a close-knit family living two blocks from the state capitol. Her father was the president of an insurance company, and her mother was a thrifty housewife who kept a Jersey cow in a little pasture behind the backyard. An insatiable reader as a child, Welty began writing spontaneously and continued, without any particular encouragement or any plan to be a writer, during her years in college. In her mid-twenties she started to publish stories in the *Southern Review*, but she credited the persistence of her New York literary agent with helping her get a story published in the *Atlantic Monthly* in 1941. This event led directly to the publication of her first book of stories, *A Curtain of Green*, the same year.

Billie Holiday: African American jazz singer (1915–1959) known for her pioneering vocal style and tragic life.
Bessie Smith: Prominent African American blues singer and song writer (1898–1937), the highest paid black artist in the United States in the 1920s.

During World War II Welty was a staff member of the *New York Times Book Review* while she lived at home with her mother and continued to write short fiction. Another collection was published in 1943 as *The Wide Net and Other Stories.* After leaving her newspaper work, she turned a short story into her first novel, *Delta Wedding* (1946), on the advice of her agent. She produced several other story collections over the years. Her novel *The Optimist's Daughter* won the Pulitzer Prize in 1972. In 1980 *The Collected Stories of Eudora Welty* appeared, forty-one stories in all. Welty was also a fine critic of the short story. Her essays and reviews of the work of writers such as Anton Chekhov, Willa Cather, Katherine Anne Porter, and Virginia Woolf, as well as some comments on her own work, were collected in *The Eye of the Story* (1977). Eight years later the book *Conversations with Eudora Welty* was a best-seller.

In the preface to her collected stories, Welty stated,

> I have been told, both in approval and in accusation, that I seem to love all my characters. What I do in writing of any character is to try to enter into the mind, heart, and skin of a human being who is not myself. Whether this happens to be a man or a woman, old or young, with skin black or white, the primary challenge lies in making the jump itself. It is the act of a writer's imagination that I set most high.

Welty's usual manner was a calm celebration of her characters' minor victories, as in "A Worn Path." The e-mail software Eudora, used by millions of people, was named after her and her story "Why I Live at the P.O." According to inventor Steve Dorner, he felt as if he "lived at the post office" while developing it, so he transposed the short story title into his slogan, "Bringing the P.O. to Where You Live." Later Dorner publicly apologized for being "presumptuous" enough to name his e-mail program after a living person, but Welty's literary agent said the writer had been "pleased and amused" to hear of the tribute.

WEB Research Eudora Welty at bedfordstmartins.com/rewritinglit.

A Worn Path

1941

It was December—a bright frozen day in the early morning. Far out in the country there was an old Negro woman with her head tied in a red rag, coming along a path through the pinewoods. Her name was Phoenix Jackson. She was very old and small and she walked slowly in the dark pine shadows, moving a little from side to side in her steps, with the balanced heaviness and lightness of a pendulum in a grandfather clock. She carried a thin, small cane made from an umbrella, and with this she kept tapping the frozen earth in front of her. This made a grave and persistent noise in the still air, that seemed meditative like the chirping of a solitary little bird.

She wore a dark striped dress reaching down to her shoe tops, and an equally long apron of bleached sugar sacks, with a full pocket: all neat and tidy, but every time she took a step she might have fallen over her shoelaces, which dragged from her unlaced shoes. She looked straight ahead. Her eyes were blue with age. Her skin had a pattern all its own of numberless branching wrinkles and as though a whole little tree stood in the middle of her forehead, but a golden color ran underneath, and the two knobs of her cheeks were illumined by a yellow burning under the dark. Under the red rag her hair came down on her neck in the frailest of ringlets, still black, and with an odor like copper.

Now and then there was a quivering in the thicket. Old Phoenix said, "Out of my way, all you foxes, owls, beetles, jack rabbits, coons and wild animals! . . . Keep out from under these feet, little bobwhites. . . . Keep the big wild hogs out of my path. Don't let none of those come running my direction. I got a long way." Under her small black-freckled hand her cane, limber as a buggy whip, would switch at the brush as if to rouse up any hiding things.

On she went. The woods were deep and still. The sun made the pine needles almost too bright to look at, up where the wind rocked. The cones dropped as light as feathers. Down in the hollow was the mourning dove—it was not too late for him.

The path ran up a hill. "Seem like there is chains about my feet, time I get this far," she said, in the voice of argument old people keep to use with themselves. "Something always take a hold of me on this hill—pleads I should stay."

After she got to the top she turned and gave a full, severe look behind her where she had come. "Up through pines," she said at length. "Now down through oaks."

Her eyes opened their widest, and she started down gently. But before she got to the bottom of the hill a bush caught her dress.

Her fingers were busy and intent, but her skirts were full and long, so that before she could pull them free in one place they were caught in another. It was not possible to allow the dress to tear. "I in the thorny bush," she said. "Thorns, you doing your appointed work. Never want to let folks pass, no sir. Old eyes thought you was a pretty little *green* bush."

Finally, trembling all over, she stood free, and after a moment dared to stoop for her cane.

"Sun so high!" she cried, leaning back and looking, while the thick tears went over her eyes. "The time getting all gone here."

At the foot of this hill was a place where a log was laid across the creek.

"Now comes the trial," said Phoenix.

Putting her right foot out, she mounted the log and shut her eyes. Lifting her skirt, leveling her cane fiercely before her, like a festival figure in some parade, she began to march across. Then she opened her eyes and she was safe on the other side.

"I wasn't as old as I thought," she said.

But she sat down to rest. She spread her skirts on the bank around her and folded her hands over her knees. Up above her was a tree in a pearly cloud of mistletoe. She did not dare to close her eyes, and when a little boy brought her a plate with a slice of marble-cake on it she spoke to him. "That would be acceptable," she said. But when she went to take it there was just her own hand in the air.

So she left that tree, and had to go through a barbed-wire fence. There she had to creep and crawl, spreading her knees and stretching her fingers like a baby trying to climb the steps. But she talked loudly to herself: she could not let her dress be torn now, so late in the day, and she could not pay for having her arm or her leg sawed off if she got caught fast where she was.

At last she was safe through the fence and risen up out in the clearing. Big dead trees, like black men with one arm, were standing in the purple stalks of the withered cotton field. There sat a buzzard.

"Who you watching?"

In the furrow she made her way along.

"Glad this not the season for bulls," she said, looking sideways, "and the good Lord made his snakes to curl up and sleep in the winter. A pleasure I don't see no two-headed snake coming around that tree, where it come once. It took a while to get by him, back in the summer."

She passed through the old cotton and went into a field of dead corn. It whispered and shook and was taller than her head. "Through the maze now," she said, for there was no path.

Then there was something tall, black, and skinny there, moving before her.

At first she took it for a man. It could have been a man dancing in the field. But she stood still and listened, and it did not make a sound. It was as silent as a ghost.

"Ghost," she said sharply, "who be you the ghost of? For I have heard of nary death close by."

But there was no answer—only the ragged dancing in the wind.

She shut her eyes, reached out her hand, and touched a sleeve. She found a coat and inside that an emptiness, cold as ice.

"You scarecrow," she said. Her face lighted. "I ought to be shut up for good," she said with laughter. "My senses is gone. I too old. I the oldest people I ever know. Dance, old scarecrow," she said, "while I dancing with you."

She kicked her foot over the furrow, and with mouth drawn down, shook her head once or twice in a little strutting way. Some husks blew down and whirled in streamers about her skirts.

Then she went on, parting her way from side to side with the cane, through the whispering field. At last she came to the end, to a wagon track where the silver grass blew between the red ruts. The quail were walking around like pullets, seeming all dainty and unseen.

"Walk pretty," she said. "This the easy place. This the easy going."

She followed the track, swaying through the quiet bare fields, through the little strings of trees silver in their dead leaves, past cabins silver from weather, with the doors and windows boarded shut, all like old women under a spell sitting there. "I walking in their sleep," she said, nodding her head vigorously.

In a ravine she went where a spring was silently flowing through a hollow log. Old Phoenix bent and drank. "Sweet-gum makes the water sweet," she said, and drank more. "Nobody know who made this well, for it was here when I was born."

The track crossed a swampy part where the moss hung as white as lace from every limb. "Sleep on, alligators, and blow your bubbles." Then the track went into the road.

Deep, deep the road went down between the high green-colored banks. Overhead the live-oaks met, and it was as dark as a cave.

A black dog with a lolling tongue came up out of the weeds by the ditch. She was meditating, and not ready, and when he came at her she only hit him a little with her cane. Over she went in the ditch, like a little puff of milkweed.

Down there, her senses drifted away. A dream visited her, and she reached her hand up, but nothing reached down and gave her a pull. So she lay there and presently went to talking. "Old woman," she said to herself, "that black dog come up out of the weeds to stall you off, and now there he sitting on his fine tail, smiling at you."

A white man finally came along and found her—a hunter, a young man, with his dog on a chain.

"Well, Granny!" he laughed. "What are you doing there?"

"Lying on my back like a June-bug waiting to be turned over, mister," she said, reaching up her hand.

He lifted her up, gave her a swing in the air, and set her down. "Anything broken, Granny?"

"No sir, them old dead weeds is springy enough," said Phoenix, when she had got her breath. "I thank you for your trouble."

"Where do you live, Granny?" he asked, while the two dogs were growling at each other.

"Away back yonder, sir, behind the ridge. You can't even see it from here."

"On your way home?"

"No sir, I going to town."

"Why, that's too far! That's as far as I walk when I come out myself, and I get something for my trouble." He patted the stuffed bag he carried, and there hung down a little closed claw. It was one of the bobwhites, with its beak hooked bitterly to show it was dead. "Now you go on home, Granny!"

"I bound to go to town, mister," said Phoenix. "The time come around."

He gave another laugh, filling the whole landscape. "I know you old colored people! Wouldn't miss going to town to see Santa Claus!"

But something held old Phoenix very still. The deep lines in her face went into a fierce and different radiation. Without warning, she had seen with her own eyes a flashing nickel fall out of the man's pocket onto the ground.

"How old are you, Granny?" he was saying.

"There is no telling, mister," she said, "no telling."

Then she gave a little cry and clapped her hands and said, "Git on away from here, dog! Look! Look at that dog!" She laughed as if in admiration. "He ain't scared of nobody. He a big black dog." She whispered, "Sic him!"

"Watch me get rid of that cur," said the man. "Sic him, Pete! Sic him!"

Phoenix heard the dogs fighting, and heard the man running and throwing sticks. She even heard a gunshot. But she was slowly bending forward by that time, further and further forward, the lid stretched down over her eyes, as if she were doing this in her sleep. Her chin was lowered almost to her knees. The yellow palm of her hand came out from the fold of her apron. Her fingers slid down and along the ground under the piece of money with the grace and care they would have in lifting an egg from under a setting hen. Then she slowly straightened up, she stood erect, and the nickel was in her apron pocket. A bird flew by. Her lips moved. "God watching me the whole time. I come to stealing."

The man came back, and his own dog panted about them. "Well, I scared him off that time," he said, and then he laughed and lifted his gun and pointed it at Phoenix.

She stood straight and faced him.

"Doesn't the gun scare you?" he said, still pointing it.

"No, sir, I seen plenty go off closer by, in my day, and for less than what I done," she said, holding utterly still.

He smiled, and shouldered the gun. "Well, Granny," he said, "you must be a hundred years old, and scared of nothing. I'd give you a dime if I had any money with me. But you take my advice and stay home, and nothing will happen to you."

"I bound to go on my way, mister," said Phoenix. She inclined her head in the red rag. Then they went in different directions, but she could hear the gun shooting again and again over the hill.

She walked on. The shadows hung from the oak trees to the road like curtains. Then she smelled wood-smoke, and smelled the river, and she saw a steeple and the cabins on their steep steps. Dozens of little black children whirled around her. There ahead was Natchez shining. Bells were ringing. She walked on.

In the paved city it was Christmas time. There were red and green electric lights strung and crisscrossed everywhere, and all turned on in the daytime. Old Phoenix would have been lost if she had not distrusted her eyesight and depended on her feet to know where to take her.

She paused quietly on the sidewalk where people were passing by. A lady came along in the crowd, carrying an armful of red-, green-, and silver-wrapped presents; she gave off perfume like the red roses in hot summer, and Phoenix stopped her.

"Please, missy, will you lace up my shoe?" She held up her foot.

"What do you want, Grandma?"

"See my shoe," said Phoenix. "Do all right for out in the country, but wouldn't look right to go in a big building."

"Stand still then, Grandma," said the lady. She put her packages down on the sidewalk beside her and laced and tied both shoes tightly.

"Can't lace 'em with a cane," said Phoenix. "Thank you, missy. I doesn't mind asking a nice lady to tie up my shoe, when I gets out on the street."

Moving slowly and from side to side, she went into the big building, and into a tower of steps, where she walked up and around and around until her feet knew to stop.

She entered a door, and there she saw nailed up on the wall the document that had been stamped with the gold seal and framed in the gold frame, which matched the dream that was hung up in her head.

"Here I be," she said. There was a fixed and ceremonial stiffness over her body.

"A charity case, I suppose," said an attendant who sat at the desk before her.

But Phoenix only looked above her head. There was sweat on her face, the wrinkles in her skin shone like a bright net.

"Speak up, Grandma," the woman said. "What's your name? We must have your history, you know. Have you been here before? What seems to be the trouble with you?"

Old Phoenix only gave a twitch to her face as if a fly were bothering her.

"Are you deaf?" cried the attendant.

But then the nurse came in.

"Oh, that's just old Aunt Phoenix," she said. "She doesn't come for herself—she has a little grandson. She makes these trips just as regular as clockwork. She lives away back off the Old Natchez Trace." She bent down. "Well, Aunt Phoenix, why don't you just take a seat? We won't keep you standing after your long trip." She pointed.

The old woman sat down, bolt upright in the chair.

"Now, how is the boy?" asked the nurse.

Old Phoenix did not speak.

"I said, how is the boy?"

But Phoenix only waited and stared straight ahead, her face very solemn and withdrawn into rigidity.

"Is his throat any better?" asked the nurse. "Aunt Phoenix, don't you hear me? Is your grandson's throat any better since the last time you came for the medicine?"

With her hands on her knees, the old woman waited, silent, erect and motionless, just as if she were in armor.

"You mustn't take up our time this way, Aunt Phoenix," the nurse said. "Tell us quickly about your grandson, and get it over. He isn't dead, is he?"

At last there came a flicker and then a flame of comprehension across her face, and she spoke.

"My grandson. It was my memory had left me. There I sat and forgot why I made my long trip."

"Forgot?" The nurse frowned. "After you came so far?"

Then Phoenix was like an old woman begging a dignified forgiveness for waking up frightened in the night. "I never did go to school, I was too old at the Surrender," she said in a soft voice. "I'm an old woman without an education. It was my memory fail me. My little grandson, he is just the same, and I forgot it in the coming."

"Throat never heals, does it?" said the nurse, speaking in a loud, sure voice to old Phoenix. By now she had a card with something written on it, a little list. "Yes. Swallowed lye. When was it?—January—two, three years ago—"

Phoenix spoke unasked now. "No, missy, he not dead, he just the same. Every little while his throat began to close up again, and he not able to swallow. He not get his breath. He not able to help himself. So the time come around, and I go on another trip for the soothing medicine."

"All right. The doctor said as long as you came to get it, you could have it," said the nurse. "But it's an obstinate case."

"My little grandson, he sit up there in the house all wrapped up, waiting by himself," Phoenix went on. "We is the only two left in the world. He suffer and it don't seem to put him back at all. He got a sweet look. He going to last. He wear a little patch quilt and peep out holding his mouth open like a little bird. I remembers so plain now. I not going to forget him again, no, the whole enduring time. I could tell him from all the others in creation."

"All right." The nurse was trying to hush her now. She brought her a bottle of medicine. "Charity," she said, making a check mark in a book.

Old Phoenix held the bottle close to her eyes, and then carefully put it into her pocket.

"I thank you," she said.

"It's Christmas time, Grandma," said the attendant. "Could I give you a few pennies out of my purse?"

"Five pennies is a nickel," said Phoenix stiffly.

"Here's a nickel," said the attendant.

Phoenix rose carefully and held out her hand. She received the nickel and then fished the other nickel out of her pocket and laid it beside the new one. She stared at her palm closely, with her head on one side.

Then she gave a tap with her cane on the floor.

"This is what come to me to do," she said. "I going to the store and buy my child a little windmill they sells, made out of paper. He going to find it hard to believe there such a thing in the world. I'll march myself back where he waiting, holding it straight up in this hand."

She lifted her free hand, gave a little nod, turned around, and walked out of the doctor's office. Then her slow step began on the stairs, going down.

COMMENTARY

EUDORA WELTY

Eudora Welty included this discussion of her story "The Worn Path" in her book *The Eye of the Story* (1977). It appeared in the section "On Writing," along with her most extensive essays on the art of short fiction – essays that take up general topics such as place and time in fiction, and the art of reading and writing stories. Her reviews of the work of Ralph Ellison and William Faulkner are also included in this collection.

Is Phoenix Jackson's Grandson Really Dead? 1977

A story writer is more than happy to be read by students; the fact that these serious readers think and feel something in response to his work he finds life-giving. At the same time he may not always be able to reply to their specific questions in kind. I wondered if it might clarify something, for both the questioners and myself, if I set down a general reply to the question that comes to me most often in the mail, from both students and their teachers, after some classroom discussion. The unrivaled favorite is this: "Is Phoenix Jackson's grandson really *dead?*"

It refers to a short story I wrote years ago called "A Worn Path," which tells of a day's journey an old woman makes on foot from deep in the country into town and into a doctor's office on behalf of her little grandson; he is at home, periodically ill, and periodically she comes for his medicine; they give it to her as usual, she receives it and starts the journey back.

I had not meant to mystify readers by withholding any fact; it is not a writer's business to tease. The story is told through Phoenix's mind as she undertakes her errand. As the author at one with the character as I tell it, I must assume that the boy is alive. As the reader, you are free to think as you like, of course: The story invites you to believe that no matter what happens, Phoenix for as long as she is able to walk and can hold to her purpose will make her journey. The *possibility* that she would keep on even if he were dead is there in her devotion and its single-minded, single-track errand. Certainly the *artistic* truth, which should be good enough for the fact, lies in Phoenix's own answer to that question. When the nurse asks, "He isn't dead, is he?" she speaks for herself: "He still the same. He going to last."

The grandchild is the incentive. But it is the journey, the going of the errand, that is the story, and the question is not whether the grandchild is in reality alive or dead. It doesn't affect the outcome of the story or its meaning from start to finish. But it is not the question itself that has struck me as much as the idea, almost without exception implied in the asking, that for Phoenix's grandson to be dead would somehow make the story "better."

It's *all right*, I want to say to the students who write to me, for things to be what they appear to be, and for words to mean what they say. It's all right, too, for words and appearances to mean more than one thing—ambiguity is a fact of life. A fiction writer's responsibility covers not only what he presents as the facts of a given story but what he chooses to stir up as their implications; in the end, these implications, too, become facts, in the larger, fictional sense. But it is not all right, not in good faith, for things *not* to mean what they say.

The grandson's plight was real and it made the truth of the story, which is the story of an errand of love carried out. If the child no longer lived, the truth would persist in the "wornness" of the path. But his being dead can't increase the truth of the story, can't affect it one way or the other. I think I signal this, because the end of the story has been reached before old Phoenix gets home again: she simply starts back. To the question "Is the grandson really dead?" I could reply that it doesn't make any difference. I could also say that I did not make him up in order to let him play a trick on Phoenix. But my best answer would be: "*Phoenix* is alive."

The origin of a story is sometimes a trustworthy clue to the author—or can provide him with the clue—to its key image; maybe in this case it will do the same for the reader. One day I saw a solitary old woman like Phoenix. She was walking; I saw her, at middle distance, in a winter country landscape, and watched her slowly make her way across my line of vision. That sight of her made me write the story. I invented an errand for her, but that only seemed a living part of the figure she was herself: What errand other than for someone else could be making her go? And her going was the first thing, her persisting in her landscape was the real thing, and the first and the real were what I wanted and worked to keep. I brought her up close enough, by imagination, to describe her face, make her present to the eyes, but the full-length figure moving across the winter fields was the indelible one and the image to keep, and the perspective extending into the vanishing distance the true one to hold in mind.

I invented for my character, as I wrote, some passing adventures—some dreams and harassments and a small triumph or two, some jolts to her pride, some flights of fancy to console her, one or two encounters to scare her, a moment that gave her cause to feel ashamed, a moment to dance and preen—for it had to be a *journey*, and all these things belonged to that, parts of life's uncertainty.

A narrative line is in its deeper sense, of course, the tracing out of a meaning, and the real continuity of a story lies in this probing forward. The real dramatic force of a story depends on the strength of the emotion that has set it going. The emotional value is the measure of the reach of the story. What gives any such content to "A Worn Path" is not its circumstances but its *subject:* the deep-grained habit of love.

What I hoped would come clear was that in the whole surround of this story, the world it threads through, the only certain thing at all is the worn path. The habit of love cuts through confusion and stumbles or contrives its way out of difficulty, it remembers the way even when it forgets, for a dumfounded moment, its reason for being. The path is the thing that matters.

Her victory—old Phoenix's—is when she sees the diploma in the doctor's office, when she finds "nailed up on the wall the document that had been stamped with the gold seal and framed in the gold frame, which matched the dream that was hung up in her head." The return with the medicine is just a matter of retracing her own footsteps. It is the part of the journey, and of the story, that can now go without saying.

In the matter of function, old Phoenix's way might even do as a sort of parallel to your way of work if you are a writer of stories. The way to get there is the all-important, all-absorbing problem, and this problem is your reason for undertaking the story. Your only guide, too, is your sureness about your subject, about what this subject is. Like Phoenix, you work all your life to find your way, through all the obstructions and the false appearances and the upsets you may have brought on yourself, to reach a meaning—using inventions of your imagination, perhaps helped out by your dreams and bits of good luck. And finally too, like Phoenix, you have to assume that what you are working in aid of is life, not death.

But you would make the trip anyway—wouldn't you?—just on hope.

WILLIAM CARLOS WILLIAMS

William Carlos Williams (1883–1963), the poet, novelist, playwright, and short story writer, was born in Rutherford, New Jersey. After graduating from the University of Pennsylvania Medical School, he returned to Rutherford, where he practiced medicine as a pediatrician for the rest of his life. While still an undergraduate, he began to write poetry, influenced by his friends the poets Ezra Pound and Hilda Doolittle. Williams published his first book, *Poems*, in 1909. Initially he devoted himself to poetry, but his experimental writing in the 1920s led him to the novel and the short story. The story became for him a way to emphasize his social and humanitarian concerns, which influenced the gritty, down-to-earth realism of his literary style.

Williams wrote most of his stories during the Depression, when his patients in Rutherford were the poor people characterized by President Franklin Delano Roosevelt in 1933 as "ill-fed, ill-housed, and ill-clothed." Williams's patients were often down and out, but he saw them as splendidly vital people. When asked how he managed the two careers of medicine and writing, Williams answered, "It's no strain. In fact, the one [medicine] nourishes the other [writing], even if at times I've groaned to the contrary."

Like the doctor-writer Anton Chekhov before him, Williams understood the moral responsibility of his calling, and he was vigilant against his feelings of arrogance and self-importance. "There's nothing like a difficult patient to show us ourselves," he once told a medical student. "I would learn so much on my rounds, or making home visits. At times I felt like a thief because I heard words, lines, saw people and places—and used it all in my writing. I guess I've told people that, and no one's so surprised! There was something deeper going on, though—the *force* of all those encounters. I was put off guard again and again, and the result was—well, a descent into myself."

Williams collected his stories in four volumes: *The Knife of the Times* (1932), *Life along the Passaic River* (1938), *Make Light of It* (1950), and *The Farmers' Daughters* (1961). More recently Robert Coles compiled *The Doctor Stories* (1984). As Coles understands, in "The Use of Force," Williams "extends to us, really, moments of a doctor's self-recognition—rendered in such a way that the particular becomes the universal." Williams used vernacular American speech and direct observation in all his writing. His work includes twenty books of poetry, four novels, several books of nonfiction, a collection of plays, and an autobiography.

CONNECTIONS To read poems by William Carlos Williams, see "To Waken an Old Lady" on page 787, "The Red Wheelbarrow" on page 798, and pages 1009–1012 for "Spring and All," "Danse Russe," "From *March*," and "The Widow's Lament in Springtime."

WEB Research William Carlos Williams at bedfordstmartins.com/rewritinglit.

The Use of Force

1938

They were new patients to me, all I had was the name, Olson. Please come down as soon as you can, my daughter is very sick. When I arrived I was met by the mother, a big startled looking woman, very clean and apologetic who merely said, Is this the doctor? and let me in. In the back, she added. You must excuse us, doctor, we have her in the kitchen where it is warm. It is very damp here sometimes.

The child was fully dressed and sitting on her father's lap near the kitchen table. He tried to get up, but I motioned for him not to bother, took off my overcoat and started to look things over. I could see that they were all very nervous, eyeing me up and down distrustfully. As often, in such cases, they weren't telling me more than they had to, it was up to me to tell them; that's why they were spending three dollars on me.

The child was fairly eating me up with her cold, steady eyes, and no expression to her face whatever. She did not move and seemed, inwardly, quiet; an unusually attractive little thing, and as strong as a heifer in appearance. But her face was flushed, she was breathing rapidly, and I realized that she had a high fever. She had magnificent blonde hair, in profusion. One of those picture children often reproduced in advertising leaflets and the photogravure sections of the Sunday papers.

She's had a fever for three days, began the father and we don't know what it comes from. My wife has given her things, you know, like people do, but it don't do no good. And there's been a lot of sickness around. So we tho't you'd better look her over and tell us what is the matter.

As doctors often do I took a trial shot at it as a point of departure. Has she had a sore throat?

Both parents answered me together, No . . . No, she says her throat don't hurt her.

Does your throat hurt you? added the mother to the child. But the little girl's expression didn't change nor did she move her eyes from my face.

Have you looked?

I tried to, said the mother, but I couldn't see.

As it happens we had been having a number of cases of diphtheria in the school to which this child went during that month and we were all, quite apparently, thinking of that, though no one had as yet spoken of the thing.

Well, I said, suppose we take a look at the throat first. I smiled in my best professional manner and asking for the child's first name I said, come on, Mathilda, open your mouth and let's take a look at your throat.

Nothing doing.

Aw, come on, I coaxed, just open your mouth wide and let me take a look. Look, I said opening both hands wide, I haven't anything in my hands. Just open up and let me see.

Such a nice man, put in the mother. Look how kind he is to you. Come on, do what he tells you to. He won't hurt you.

At that I ground my teeth in disgust. If only they wouldn't use the word "hurt" I might be able to get somewhere. But I did not allow myself to be hurried or disturbed but speaking quietly and slowly I approached the child again.

As I moved my chair a little nearer suddenly with one catlike movement both her hands clawed instinctively for my eyes and she almost reached them too. In fact she knocked my glasses flying and they fell, though unbroken, several feet away from me on the kitchen floor.

Both the mother and father almost turned themselves inside out in embarrassment and apology. You bad girl, said the mother, taking her and shaking her by one arm. Look what you've done. The nice man . . .

For heaven's sake, I broke in. Don't call me a nice man to her. I'm here to look at her throat on the chance that she might have diphtheria and possibly die of it. But that's nothing to her. Look here, I said to the child, we're going to look at your throat. You're old enough to understand what I'm saying. Will you open it now by yourself or shall we have to open it for you?

Not a move. Even her expression hadn't changed. Her breaths however were coming faster and faster. Then the battle began. I had to do it. I had to have a throat culture for her own protection. But first I told the parents that it was entirely up to them. I explained the danger but said that I would not insist on a throat examination so long as they would take the responsibility.

If you don't do what the doctor says you'll have to go to the hospital, the mother admonished her severely.

Oh yeah? I had to smile to myself. After all, I had already fallen in love with the savage brat, the parents were contemptible to me. In the ensuing struggle they grew more and more abject, crushed, exhausted while she surely rose to magnificent heights of insane fury of effort bred of her terror of me.

The father tried his best, and he was a big man but the fact that she was his daughter, his shame at her behavior and his dread of hurting her made him release her just at the critical times when I had almost achieved success, till I wanted to kill him. But his dread also that she might have diphtheria made him tell me to go on, go on though he himself was almost fainting, while the mother moved back and forth behind us raising and lowering her hands in an agony of apprehension.

Put her in front of you on your lap, I ordered, and hold both her wrists.

But as soon as he did the child let out a scream. Don't, you're hurting me. Let go of my hands. Let them go I tell you. Then she shrieked terrifyingly, hysterically. Stop it! Stop it! You're killing me!

Do you think she can stand it, doctor! said the mother.

You get out, said the husband to his wife. Do you want her to die of diphtheria?

Come on now, hold her, I said.

Then I grasped the child's head with my left hand and tried to get the wooden tongue depressor between her teeth. She fought, with clenched teeth, desperately! But now I also had grown furious—at a child. I tried to hold myself down but I couldn't. I know how to expose a throat for inspection. And I did my best. When finally I got the wooden spatula behind the last teeth and just the point of it into the mouth cavity, she opened up for an instant but before I could see anything she came down again and gripped the wooden blade between her molars. She reduced it to splinters before I could get it out again.

Aren't you ashamed, the mother yelled at her. Aren't you ashamed to act like that in front of the doctor?

Get me a smooth-handled spoon of some sort, I told the mother. We're going through with this. The child's mouth was already bleeding. Her tongue was cut and she was screaming in wild hysterical shrieks. Perhaps I should have desisted and come back in an hour or more. No doubt it would have been better. But I have seen at least two children lying dead in bed of neglect in such cases, and feeling that I must get a diagnosis now or never I went at it again. But the worst of it was that I too had got beyond reason. I could have torn the child apart in my own fury and enjoyed it. It was a pleasure to attack her. My face was burning with it.

The damned little brat must be protected against her own idiocy, one says to one's self at such times. Others must be protected against her. It is a social necessity. And all these things are true. But a blind fury, a feeling of adult shame, bred of a longing for muscular release are the operatives. One goes on to the end.

In the final unreasoning assault I overpowered the child's neck and jaws. I forced the heavy silver spoon back of her teeth and down her throat till she gagged. And there it was—both tonsils covered with membrane. She had fought valiantly to keep me from knowing her secret. She had been hiding that sore throat for three days at least and lying to her parents in order to escape just such an outcome as this.

Now truly she was furious. She had been on the defensive before but now she attacked. Tried to get off her father's lap and fly at me while tears of defeat blinded her eyes.

TOBIAS WOLFF

Tobias Wolff (b. 1945) began *This Boy's Life*, his best-selling memoir, by writing, "My first stepfather used to say that what I didn't know would fill a book. Well, here it is." A compassionate sense of paradox and irony permeates his writing, as in "Say Yes," adding an emotional color to the transparently clear prose of his narratives.

Born in Birmingham, Alabama, Wolff followed his mother to the Pacific Northwest when his parents divorced. It is this period in his life that is the subject of *This Boy's Life* (1989), which was later made into a movie. After being expelled from prep school, he served in the U.S. Army in Vietnam from 1964 to 1968. Then he studied at Oxford University and Stanford University, where in 1975–76 he received a Wallace Stegner fellowship in creative writing. Two National Endowment for the Arts fellowships followed, along with a Mary Roberts Rinehart grant, an Arizona Council on the Arts fellowship, a Guggenheim fellowship, three O. Henry short story prizes, and the PEN/Faulkner Award for fiction for *The Barracks Thief* (1984), a novella about his army experience. Wolff's first book was a collection of short stories, *In the Garden of the North American Martyrs* (1981). *The Night in Question* (1997) is also a story collection, and a recent novel is *Old School* (2004). *Our Story Begins: New and Selected Stories* was published in 2008.

Wolff credits several writers as influences on his fiction: Ernest Hemingway, Anton Chekhov, Paul Bowles, Sherwood Anderson, John Cheever, Flannery O'Connor, and Raymond Carver—"the list has no end so I'd better stop here." He prefers writing short stories to novels because "when I write a short story, I feel like I'm somehow cooperating with the story; when I try to work in longer forms, I feel like I'm beating them into existence. I feel a kind of clumsiness that I don't feel when I'm writing short stories." Wolff regards writing as an "essentially optimistic art," because

> the very act of writing assumes, to begin with, that someone cares to hear what you have to say. It assumes that people share, that people can be reached, that people can be touched and even in some cases changed. . . . So

> many of the things in our world tend to lead us to despair. It seems to me that the final symptom of despair is silence, and that storytelling is one of the sustaining arts; it's one of the affirming arts. . . . A writer may have a certain pessimism in his outlook, but the very act of being a writer seems to me to be an optimistic act.

WEB Research Tobias Wolff at bedfordstmartins.com/rewritinglit.

Say Yes

1985

They were doing the dishes, his wife washing while he dried. He'd washed the night before. Unlike most men he knew, he really pitched in on the housework. A few months earlier he'd overheard a friend of his wife's congratulate her on having such a considerate husband, and he thought, *I try.* Helping out with the dishes was a way of showing how considerate he was.

They talked about different things and somehow got on the subject of whether white people should marry black people. He said that all things considered, he thought it was a bad idea.

"Why?" she asked.

Sometimes his wife got this look where she pinched her brows together and bit her lower lip and stared down at something. When he saw her like this he knew he should keep his mouth shut, but he never did. Actually it made him talk more. She had that look now.

"Why?" she asked again, and stood there with her hand inside a bowl, not washing it but just holding it above the water.

"Listen," he said, "I went to school with blacks, and I've worked with blacks and lived on the same street with blacks, and we've always gotten along just fine. I don't need you coming along now and implying that I'm a racist."

"I didn't imply anything," she said, and began washing the bowl again, turning it around in her hand as though she were shaping it. "I just don't see what's wrong with a white person marrying a black person, that's all."

"They don't come from the same culture as we do. Listen to them sometime—they even have their own language. That's okay with me, I *like* hearing them talk"—he did; for some reason it always made him feel happy—"but it's different. A person from their culture and a person from our culture could never really *know* each other."

"Like you know me?" his wife asked.

"Yes. Like I know you."

"But if they love each other," she said. She was washing faster now, not looking at him.

Oh boy, he thought. He said, "Don't take my word for it. Look at the statistics. Most of those marriages break up."

"Statistics." She was piling dishes on the drainboard at a terrific rate, just swiping at them with the cloth. Many of them were greasy, and there were flecks of food between the tines of the forks. "All right," she said, "what about foreigners? I suppose you think the same thing about two foreigners getting married."

"Yes," he said, "as a matter of fact I do. How can you understand someone who comes from a completely different background?"

"Different," said his wife. "Not the same, like us."

"Yes, different," he snapped, angry with her for resorting to this trick of repeating his words so that they sounded crass, or hypocritical. "These are dirty," he said, and dumped all the silverware back into the sink.

The water had gone flat and gray. She stared down at it, her lips pressed tight together, then plunged her hands under the surface. "Oh!" she cried, and jumped back. She took her right hand by the wrist and held it up. Her thumb was bleeding.

"Ann, don't move," he said. "Stay right there." He ran upstairs to the bathroom and rummaged in the medicine chest for alcohol, cotton, and a Band-Aid. When he came back down she was leaning against the refrigerator with her eyes closed, still holding her hand. He took the hand and dabbed at her thumb with the cotton. The bleeding had stopped. He squeezed it to see how deep the wound was and a single drop of blood welled up, trembling and bright, and fell to the floor. Over the thumb she stared at him accusingly. "It's shallow," he said. "Tomorrow you won't even know it's there." He hoped that she appreciated how quickly he had come to her aid. He'd acted out of concern for her, with no thought of getting anything in return, but now the thought occurred to him that it would be a nice gesture on her part not to start up that conversation again, as he was tired of it. "I'll finish up here," he said. "You go and relax."

"That's okay," she said. "I'll dry."

He began to wash the silverware again, giving a lot of attention to the forks.

"So," she said, "you wouldn't have married me if I'd been black."

"For Christ's sake, Ann!"

"Well, that's what you said, didn't you?"

"No, I did not. The whole question is ridiculous. If you had been black we probably wouldn't even have met. You would have had your friends and I would have had mine. The only black girl I ever really knew was my partner in the debating club, and I was already going out with you by then."

"But if we had met, and I'd been black?"

"Then you probably would have been going out with a black guy." He picked up the rinsing nozzle and sprayed the silverware. The water was so hot that the metal darkened to pale blue, then turned silver again.

"Let's say I wasn't," she said. "Let's say I am black and unattached and we meet and fall in love."

He glanced over at her. She was watching him and her eyes were bright. "Look," he said, taking a reasonable tone, "this is stupid. If you were black you wouldn't be you." As he said this he realized it was absolutely true. There was no possible way of arguing with the fact that she would not be herself if she were black. So he said it again: "If you were black you wouldn't be you."

"I know," she said, "but let's just say."

He took a deep breath. He had won the argument but he still felt cornered. "Say what?" he asked.

"That I'm black, but still me, and we fall in love. Will you marry me?"

He thought about it.

"Well?" she said, and stepped close to him. Her eyes were even brighter. "Will you marry me?"

"I'm thinking," he said.

"You won't, I can tell. You're going to say no."

"Let's not move too fast on this," he said. "There are lots of things to consider. We don't want to do something we would regret for the rest of our lives."

"No more considering. Yes or no."

"Since you put it that way—"

"Yes or no."

"Jesus, Ann. All right. No."

She said, "Thank you," and walked from the kitchen into the living room. A moment later he heard her turning the pages of a magazine. He knew that she was too angry to be actually reading it, but she didn't snap through the pages the way he would have done. She turned them slowly, as if she were studying every word. She was demonstrating her indifference to him, and it had the effect he knew she wanted it to have. It hurt him.

He had no choice but to demonstrate his indifference to her. Quietly, thoroughly, he washed the rest of the dishes. Then he dried them and put them away. He wiped the counters and the stove and scoured the linoleum where the drop of blood had fallen. While he was at it, he decided, he might as well mop the whole floor. When he was done the kitchen looked new, the way it looked when they were first shown the house, before they had ever lived here.

He picked up the garbage pail and went outside. The night was clear and he could see a few stars to the west, where the lights of the town didn't blur them out. On El Camino the traffic was steady and light, peaceful as a river. He felt ashamed that he had let his wife get him into a fight. In another thirty years or so they would both be dead. What would all that stuff matter then? He thought of the years they had spent together, and how close they were, and how well they knew each other, and his throat tightened so that he could hardly breathe. His face and neck began to tingle. Warmth flooded his chest. He stood there for a while, enjoying these sensations, then picked up the pail and went out the back gate.

The two mutts from down the street had pulled over the garbage can again. One of them was rolling around on his back and the other had something in her mouth. Growling, she tossed it into the air, leaped up and caught it, growled again and whipped her head from side to side. When they saw him coming they trotted away with short, mincing steps. Normally he would heave rocks at them, but this time he let them go.

The house was dark when he came back inside. She was in the bathroom. He stood outside the door and called her name. He heard bottles clinking, but she didn't answer him. "Ann, I'm really sorry," he said. "I'll make it up to you, I promise."

"How?" she asked.

He wasn't expecting this. But from a sound in her voice, a level and definite note that was strange to him, he knew that he had to come up with the right answer. He leaned against the door. "I'll marry you," he whispered.

"We'll see," she said. "Go on to bed. I'll be out in a minute."

He undressed and got under the covers. Finally he heard the bathroom door open and close.

"Turn off the light," she said from the hallway.

"What?"

"Turn off the light."

He reached over and pulled the chain on the bedside lamp. The room went dark. "All right," he said. He lay there, but nothing happened. "All right," he said again. Then he heard a movement across the room. He sat up, but he couldn't see a thing. The room was silent. His heart pounded the way it had on their first night together, the way it still did when he woke at a noise in the darkness and waited to hear it again—the sound of someone moving through the house, a stranger.

7. Conversations on Stories and Storytellers: Flannery O'Connor and Edgar Allan Poe

ON FLANNERY O'CONNOR'S FICTION

Flannery O'Connor is unusual among writers in that she shared with readers her own interpretations of her stories. In this section she comments particularly on "Good Country People" and "A Good Man Is Hard to Find." While acknowledging that there is usually more than one way to read a story, she also states that there was only one way that she could possibly have written it.

The correspondence below shows O'Connor gossiping about other contemporary writers and thinking aloud about her fiction with her editor, Robert Giroux, and her friends Robert and Sally Fitzgerald. Robert Fitzgerald, a poet and translator of Greek literature, would become O'Connor's literary executor. He and Sally, his second wife, would edit a posthumous collection of O'Connor's prose, *Mystery and Manners* (1969). On her own, Sally Fitzgerald edited *The Habit of Being: Letters of Flannery O'Connor* (1979).

COMMENTARIES

FLANNERY O'CONNOR

From *Letters, 1954–55* — 1955

To Sally Fitzgerald

26 Dec 54

. . . I have finally got off the ms. for my collection [*A Good Man Is Hard to Find*] and it is scheduled to appear in May. Without yr kind permission I have taken the liberty of dedicating (grand verb) it to you and Robert. This is because you all are my adopted kin and if I dedicated it to any of my blood kin they would think they had to go into hiding. Nine stories about original sin, with my compliments.

I have been invited to go to Greensboro to the Women's College in March to be on an arts panel. That is where Brother Randall Jarrell° holds forth. I accepted but I am not looking forward to it. Can you fancy me hung in conversation with the likes of him?

When I had lunch with Giroux [O'Connor's editor] in Atlanta he told me about Cal's° escapade in Cincinnati. It seems [Cal] convinced everybody it was Elizabeth who was going crazy. . . . Toward the end he gave a lecture at the university that was almost pure gibberish. I guess nobody noticed, thinking it was the new criticism. . . .

I just got a check for $200 for the 2nd prize in the O. Henry book° this year. My ex-mentor Paul Engle does the selecting. Jean Stafford° got the first one.

I am walking with a cane these days which gives me a great air of distinction. The scientist tells me this has nothing to do with the lupus but is rheumatism. I would not believe it except that the dose of ACTH has not been increased. Besides which I now feel it makes very little difference what you call it.

To Robert Giroux

22 January 55

Nothing has been said about a picture for the jacket of this collection *but if you have to have one*, I would be much obliged if you could use the enclosed so that I won't have to have a new picture made. This is a self-portrait with a pheasant cock, that I painted in 1953; however, I think it will do justice to the subject for some time to come.

26 February 55

I have just written a story called "Good Country People" that Allen and Caroline [Tate?] both say is the best thing I have written and should be in this collection. I told them I thought it was too late, but anyhow I am writing now to ask if it is. It is really a story that would set the whole collection on its feet. It is 27 pages and if you can eliminate the one called "A Stroke of Good Fortune," and the other called "An Afternoon in the Woods," this one would fit the available space nicely. Also I remember you said it would be good to have one that had never been published before. I could send it to you at once *on being wired*. Please let me know.

[Giroux wired O'Connor that every effort would be made to include the story. After he had read it, he wrote suggesting that an appearance by the mother and Mrs. Freeman at the end might improve it. Flannery recognized the value of the suggestion and added the sentences that are now a part of the story.]

Randall Jarrell: American poet and influential critic (1914–1965).
Cal: Robert Lowell, American poet (1917–1977).
O. Henry book: The O. Henry Prizes are awarded annually to outstanding American short stories, which are collected each year in a book. O. Henry was the pen name of the popular American short story writer William Sydney Porter (1862–1910).
Jean Stafford: American short story writer and novelist (1915–1979).

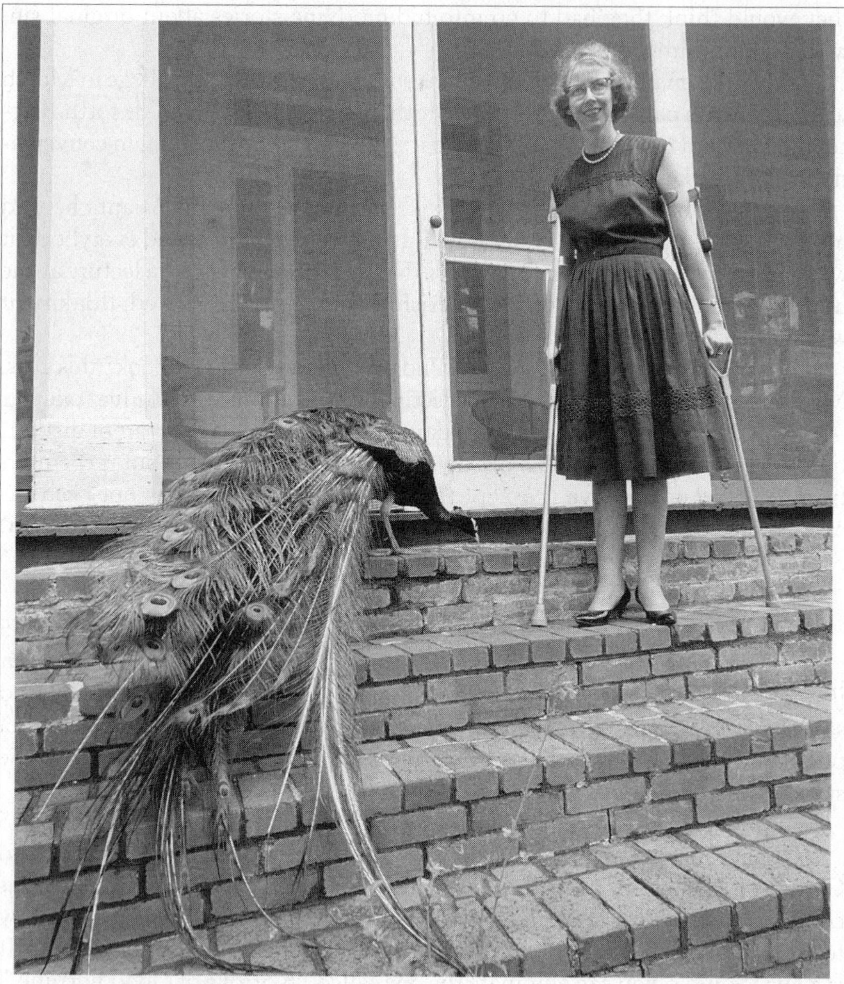

Flannery O'Connor in the summer of 1962 at Andalusia, her family farm and home outside Milledgeville, Georgia. (© Joe McTyre. Reprinted by permission of Joe McTyre Photo/ Atlanta Constitution.)

7 March 55

I like the suggestion about the ending of "Good Country People" and enclose a dozen or so lines that can be added on to *the present end.* I enclose them in case you can get them put on before I get the proofs. I am mighty wary of making changes on proofs. . . .

To Sally and Robert Fitzgerald

1 April 55

We are wondering if #6 is here yet or due to arrive momentarily. Let us hear and if you need any names, I'll be glad to cable you a rich collection. I have just got back from Greensboro where I said nothing intelligent the whole time, but enjoyed myself. Mr. Randall Jarrell, wife and stepdaughters I met and et dinner with. I must say I was shocked at what a very kind man he is—that is the last impression I expected to have of him. I also met Peter Taylor,° who is more like folks. Mrs. Jarrell is writing a novel. You get the impression the two stepdaughters may be at it too and maybe the dog. Mr. Jarrell has a beard and looks like Mephistopheles (sp?) only fatter. Mrs. Jarrell is very friendly & sunkist.

The Easter rabbit is bringing my mother a three-quarter ton truck.

I trust Giroux will be sending you a copy of the book soon. I wrote a very hot story at the last minute called "Good Country People": so now there are ten.

While I was in NC I heard somebody recite a barroom ballad. I don't remember anything but the end but beinst you all are poets I will give it to you as it is mighty deathless:

"They stacked the stiffs outside the door.
They made, I reckon, a cord or more."

I call that real poetry.

I have put the cane up and am walking on my own very well. Let us hear. Regards to children.

Writing Short Stories 1961

. . . Perhaps the central question to be considered in any discussion of the short story is what do we mean by short. Being short does not mean being slight. A short story should be long in depth and should give us an experience of meaning. I have an aunt who thinks that nothing happens in a story unless somebody gets married or shot at the end of it. I wrote a story about a tramp who marries an old woman's idiot daughter in order to acquire the old woman's automobile. After the marriage, he takes the daughter off on a wedding trip in the automobile and abandons her in an eating place and drives on by himself. Now that is a complete story. There is nothing more relating to the mystery of that man's personality that could be shown through that particular dramatization. But I've never been able to convince my aunt that it's a complete story. She wants to know what happened to the idiot daughter after that.

Not long ago that story was adapted for a television play, and the adapter, knowing his business, had the tramp have a change of heart and go back and pick up the idiot daughter and the two of them ride away, grinning madly. My aunt believes that the story is complete at last, but I have other sentiments about it—which are not suitable for public utterance. When you write a story, you only have to write one story, but there will always be people who will refuse to read the story you have written.

And this naturally brings up the awful question of what kind of a reader you are writing for when you write fiction. Perhaps we each think we have a

Peter Taylor: Tennessee-born-and-bred novelist and short story writer (1917–1994).

personal solution for this problem. For my own part, I have a very high opinion of the art of fiction and a very low opinion of what is called the "average" reader. I tell myself that I can't escape him, that this is the personality I am supposed to keep awake, but that at the same time, I am also supposed to provide the intelligent reader with the deeper experience that he looks for in fiction. Now actually, both of these readers are just aspects of the writer's own personality, and in the last analysis, the only reader he can know anything about is himself. We all write at our own level of understanding, but it is the peculiar characteristic of fiction that its literal surface can be made to yield entertainment on an obvious physical plane to one sort of reader while the selfsame surface can be made to yield meaning to the person equipped to experience it there.

Meaning is what keeps the short story from being short. I prefer to talk about the meaning in a story rather than the theme of a story. People talk about the theme of a story as if the theme were like the string that a sack of chicken feed is tied with. They think that if you can pick out the theme, the way you pick the right thread in the chicken-feed sack, you can rip the story open and feed the chickens. But this is not the way meaning works in fiction.

When you can state the theme of a story, when you can separate it from the story itself, then you can be sure the story is not a very good one. The meaning of a story has to be embodied in it, has to be made concrete in it. A story is a way to say something that can't be said any other way, and it takes every word in the story to say what the meaning is. You tell a story because a statement would be inadequate. When anybody asks what a story is about, the only proper thing is to tell him to read the story. The meaning of fiction is not abstract meaning but experienced meaning, and the purpose of making statements about the meaning of a story is only to help you to experience that meaning more fully.

Fiction is an art that calls for the strictest attention to the real—whether the writer is writing a naturalistic story or a fantasy. I mean that we always begin with what is or with what has an eminent possibility of truth about it. Even when one writes a fantasy, reality is the proper basis of it. A thing is fantastic because it is so real, so real that it is fantastic. Graham Greene° has said that he can't write, "I stood over a bottomless pit," because that couldn't be true, or "Running down the stairs I jumped into a taxi," because that couldn't be true either. But Elizabeth Bowen° can write about one of her characters that "she snatched at her hair as if she heard something in it," because that is eminently possible.

I would even go so far as to say that the person writing a fantasy has to be even more strictly attentive to the concrete detail than someone writing in a naturalistic vein—because the greater the story's strain on the credulity, the more convincing the properties in it have to be.

A good example of this is a story called "The Metamorphosis" by Franz Kafka. This is a story about a man who wakes up one morning to find that he

---

Graham Greene: English writer (1904–1991).
Elizabeth Bowen: Anglo-Irish novelist and short story writer (1899–1973).

has turned into a cockroach overnight, while not discarding his human nature. The rest of the story concerns his life and feelings and eventual death as an insect with human nature, and this situation is accepted by the reader because the concrete detail of the story is absolutely convincing. The fact is that this story describes the dual nature of man in such a realistic fashion that it is almost unbearable. The truth is not distorted here, but rather, a certain distortion is used to get at the truth. If we admit, as we must, that appearance is not the same thing as reality, then we must give the artist the liberty to make certain rearrangements of nature if these will lead to greater depths of vision. The artist himself always has to remember that what he is rearranging *is* nature, and that he has to know it and be able to describe it accurately in order to have the authority to rearrange it at all.

The peculiar problem of the short-story writer is how to make the action he describes reveal as much of the mystery of existence as possible. He has only a short space to do it in and he can't do it by statement. He has to do it by showing, not by saying, and by showing the concrete—so that his problem is really how to make the concrete work double time for him.

In good fiction, certain of the details will tend to accumulate meaning from the action of the story itself, and when this happens they become symbolic in the way they work. I once wrote a story called "Good Country People," in which a lady Ph.D. has her wooden leg stolen by a Bible salesman whom she has tried to seduce. Now I'll admit that, paraphrased in this way, the situation is simply a low joke. The average reader is pleased to observe anybody's wooden leg being stolen. But without ceasing to appeal to him and without making any statements of high intention, this story does manage to operate at another level of experience, by letting the wooden leg accumulate meaning. Early in the story, we're presented with the fact that the Ph.D. is spiritually as well as physically crippled. She believes in nothing but her own belief in nothing, and we perceive that there is a wooden part of her soul that corresponds to her wooden leg. Now of course this is never stated. The fiction writer states as little as possible. The reader makes this connection from things he is shown. He may not even know that he makes the connection, but the connection is there nevertheless and it has its effect on him. As the story goes on, the wooden leg continues to accumulate meaning. The reader learns how the girl feels about her leg, how her mother feels about it, and how the country woman on the place feels about it; and finally, by the time the Bible salesman comes along, the leg has accumulated so much meaning that it is, as the saying goes, loaded. And when the Bible salesman steals it, the reader realizes that he has taken away part of the girl's personality and has revealed her deeper affliction to her for the first time.

If you want to say that the wooden leg is a symbol, you can say that. But it is a wooden leg first, and as a wooden leg it is absolutely necessary to the story. It has its place on the literal level of the story, but it operates in depth as well as on the surface. It increases the story in every direction, and this is essentially the way a story escapes being short.

Now a little might be said about the way in which this happens. I wouldn't want you to think that in that story I sat down and said, "I am now going to write a story about a Ph.D. with a wooden leg, using the wooden leg as a symbol for another kind of affliction." I doubt myself if many writers know what they are going to do when they start out. When I started writing that story, I didn't know there was going to be a Ph.D. with a wooden leg in it. I merely found myself one morning writing a description of two women that I knew something about, and before I realized it, I had equipped one of them with a daughter with a wooden leg. As the story progressed, I brought in the Bible salesman, but I had no idea what I was going to do with him. I didn't know he was going to steal that wooden leg until ten or twelve lines before he did it, but when I found out that this was what was going to happen, I realized that it was inevitable. This is a story that produces a shock for the reader, and I think one reason for this is that it produced a shock for the writer.

Now despite the fact that this story came about in this seemingly mindless fashion, it is a story that almost no rewriting was done on. It is a story that was under control throughout the writing of it, and it might be asked how this kind of control comes about, since it is not entirely conscious.

I think the answer to this is what Maritain° calls "the habit of art." It is a fact that fiction writing is something in which the whole personality takes part—the conscious as well as the unconscious mind. Art is the habit of the artist; and habits have to be rooted deep in the whole personality. They have to be cultivated like any other habit, over a long period of time, by experience; and teaching any kind of writing is largely a matter of helping the student develop the habit of art. I think this is more than just a discipline, although it is that; I think it is a way of looking at the created world and of using the senses so as to make them find as much meaning as possible in things.

Now I am not so naïve as to suppose that most people come to writers' conferences in order to hear what kind of vision is necessary to write stories that will become a permanent part of our literature. Even if you do wish to hear this, your greatest concerns are immediately practical. You want to know how you can actually write a good story, and further, how you can tell when you've done it; and so you want to know what the form of a short story is, as if the form were something that existed outside of each story and could be applied or imposed on the material. Of course, the more you write, the more you will realize that the form is organic, that it is something that grows out of the material, that the form of each story is unique. A story that is any good can't be reduced, it can only be expanded. A story is good when you continue to see more and more in it, and when it continues to escape you. In fiction two and two is always more than four.

The only way, I think, to learn to write short stories is to write them, and then to try to discover what you have done. The time to think of technique is when you've actually got the story in front of you. The teacher can help the student by looking at his individual work and trying to help him decide if he has written a complete story, one in which the action fully illuminates the meaning.

Maritain: Jacques Maritain (1882–1973) was a French philosopher and critic.

Perhaps the most profitable thing I can do is to tell you about some of the general observations I made about these seven stories I read of yours. All of these observations will not fit any one of the stories exactly, but they are points nevertheless that it won't hurt anyone interested in writing to think about.

The first thing that any professional writer is conscious of in reading anything is, naturally, the use of language. Now the use of language in these stories was such that, with one exception, it would be difficult to distinguish one story from another. While I can recall running into several clichés, I can't remember one image or one metaphor from the seven stories. I don't mean there weren't images in them; I just mean that there weren't any that were effective enough to take away with you.

In connection with this, I made another observation that startled me considerably. With the exception of one story, there was practically no use made of the local idiom. Now this is a Southern Writers' Conference. All the addresses on these stories were from Georgia or Tennessee, yet there was no distinctive sense of Southern life in them. A few place-names were dropped, Savannah or Atlanta or Jacksonville, but these could just as easily have been changed to Pittsburgh or Passaic without calling for any other alteration in the story. The characters spoke as if they had never heard any kind of language except what came out of a television set. This indicates that something is way out of focus.

There are two qualities that make fiction. One is the sense of mystery and the other is the sense of manners. You get the manners from the texture of existence that surrounds you. The great advantage of being a Southern writer is that we don't have to go anywhere to look for manners; bad or good, we've got them in abundance. We in the South live in a society that is rich in contradiction, rich in irony, rich in contrast, and particularly rich in its speech. And yet here are six stories by Southerners in which almost no use is made of the gifts of the region.

Of course the reason for this may be that you have seen these gifts abused so often that you have become self-conscious about using them. There is nothing worse than the writer who doesn't *use* the gifts of the region, but wallows in them. Everything becomes so Southern that it's sickening, so local that it is unintelligible, so literally reproduced that it conveys nothing. The general gets lost in the particular instead of being shown through it.

However, when the life that actually surrounds us is totally ignored, when our patterns of speech are absolutely overlooked, then something is out of kilter. The writer should then ask himself if he is not reaching out for a kind of life that is artificial to him.

An idiom characterizes a society, and when you ignore the idiom, you are very likely ignoring the whole social fabric that could make a meaningful character. You can't cut characters off from their society and say much about them as individuals. You can't say anything meaningful about the mystery of a personality unless you put that personality in a believable and significant social context. And the best way to do this is through the character's own language. When the old lady in one of Andrew Lytle's stories says contemptuously that she has a mule that is older than Birmingham, we get in that one sentence a sense of a society and its history. A great deal of the Southern writers' work is done for him before he begins, because our history lives in our talk. In one of Eudora Welty's stories a character says, "Where I come from, we use fox for yard dogs and owls for chickens, but we sing true." Now there is a whole book in that one sentence; and when the people of your section can talk like that, and you ignore it, you're just not taking advantage of what's yours. The sound of our talk is too definite to be discarded with impunity, and if the writer tries to get rid of it, he is liable to destroy the better part of his creative power.

Another thing I observed about these stories is that most of them don't go very far inside a character, don't reveal very much of the character. I don't mean that they don't enter the character's mind, but they simply don't show that he has a personality. Again this goes back partly to speech. These characters have no distinctive speech to reveal themselves with; and sometimes they have no really distinctive features. You feel in the end that no personality is revealed because no personality is there. In most good stories it is the character's personality that creates the action of the story. In most of these stories, I feel that the writer has thought of some action and then scrounged up a character to perform it. You will usually be more successful if you start the other way around. If you start with a real personality, a real character, then something is bound to happen; and you don't have to know what before you begin. In fact it may be better if you don't know what before you begin. You ought to be able to discover something from your stories. If you don't, probably nobody else will.

The Element of Suspense in "A Good Man Is Hard to Find" 1969

A story really isn't any good unless it successfully resists paraphrase, unless it hangs on and expands in the mind. Properly, you analyze to enjoy, but it's equally true that to analyze with any discrimination, you have to have enjoyed already, and I think that the best reason to hear a story read is that it should stimulate that primary enjoyment.

I don't have any pretensions to being an Aeschylus or Sophocles and providing you in this story with a cathartic experience out of your mythic background, though this story I'm going to read certainly calls up a good deal of the South's mythic background, and it should elicit from you a degree of pity and terror, even though its way of being serious is a comic one. I do think, though, that like the Greeks you should know what is going to happen in this story so that any element of suspense in it will be transferred from its surface to its interior.

I would be most happy if you had already read it, happier still if you knew it well, but since experience has taught me to keep my expectations along these lines modest, I'll tell you that this is the story of a family of six which, on its way driving to Florida, gets wiped out by an escaped convict who calls himself the Misfit. The family is made up of the Grandmother and her son, Bailey, and his children, John Wesley and June Star and the baby, and there is also the cat and the children's mother. The cat is named Pitty Sing, and the Grandmother is taking him with them, hidden in a basket.

Now I think it behooves me to try to establish with you the basis on which reason operates in this story. Much of my fiction takes its character from a reasonable use of the unreasonable, though the reasonableness of my use of it may not always be apparent. The assumptions that underlie this use of it, however, are those of the central Christian mysteries. These are assumptions to which a large part of the modern audience takes exception. About this I can only say that there are perhaps other ways than my own in which this story could be read, but none other by which it could have been written. Belief, in my own case anyway, is the engine that makes perception operate.

The heroine of this story, the Grandmother, is in the most significant position life offers the Christian. She is facing death. And to all appearances she, like the rest of us, is not too well prepared for it. She would like to see the event postponed. Indefinitely.

I've talked to a number of teachers who use this story in class and who tell their students that the Grandmother is evil, that in fact, she's a witch, even down to the cat. One of these teachers told me that his students, and particularly his southern students, resisted this interpretation with a certain bemused vigor, and he didn't understand why. I had to tell him that they resisted it because they all had grandmothers or great-aunts just like her at home, and they knew, from personal experience, that the old lady lacked comprehension, but that she had a good heart. The southerner is usually tolerant of those weaknesses that proceed from innocence, and he knows that a taste for self-preservation can be readily combined with the missionary spirit.

This same teacher was telling his students that morally the Misfit was several cuts above the Grandmother. He had a really sentimental attachment to the Misfit. But then a prophet gone wrong is almost always more interesting than your grandmother, and you have to let people take their pleasures where they find them.

It is true that the old lady is a hypocritical old soul; her wits are no match for the Misfit's, nor is her capacity for grace equal to his; yet I think the unprejudiced reader will feel that the Grandmother has a special kind of triumph in this story which instinctively we do not allow to someone altogether bad.

I often ask myself what makes a story work, and what makes it hold up as a story, and I have decided that it is probably some action, some gesture of a character that is unlike any other in the story, one which indicates where the real heart of the story lies. This would have to be an action or a gesture which was both totally right and totally unexpected; it would have to be one that was both in character and beyond character; it would have to suggest both the world and eternity. The action or gesture I'm talking about would have to be in the anagogical level, that is, the level which has to do with the Divine life and our participation in it. It would be a gesture that transcended any neat allegory that might have been intended or any pat moral categories a reader could make. It would be a gesture which somehow made contact with mystery.

There is a point in this story where such a gesture occurs. The Grandmother is at last alone, facing the Misfit. Her head clears for an instant and she realizes, even in her limited way, that she is responsible for the man before her and joined to him by ties of kinship which have their roots deep in the mystery she has been merely prattling about so far. And at this point, she does the right thing, she makes the right gesture.

I find that students are often puzzled by what she says and does here, but I think myself that if I took out this gesture and what she says with it, I would have no story. What was left would not be worth your attention. Our age not only does not have a very sharp eye for the almost imperceptible intrusions of grace, it no longer has much feeling for the nature of the violences which precede and follow them. The devil's greatest wile, Baudelaire has said, is to convince us that he does not exist.

I suppose the reasons for the use of so much violence in modern fiction will differ with each writer who uses it, but in my own stories I have found that violence is strangely capable of returning my characters to reality and preparing them to accept their moment of grace. Their heads are so hard that almost nothing else will do the work. This idea, that reality is something to which we must be returned at considerable cost, is one which is seldom understood by the casual reader, but it is one which is implicit in the Christian view of the world.

I don't want to equate the Misfit with the devil. I prefer to think that, however unlikely this may seem, the old lady's gesture, like the mustard-seed, will grow to be a great crow-filled tree in the Misfit's heart, and will be enough of a pain to him there to turn him into the prophet he was meant to become. But that's another story.

This story has been called grotesque, but I prefer to call it literal. A good story is literal in the same sense that a child's drawing is literal. When a child draws, he doesn't intend to distort but to set down exactly what he sees, and as his gaze is direct, he sees the lines that create motion. Now the lines of motion that interest the writer are usually invisible. They are lines of spiritual motion. And in this story you should be on the lookout for such things as the action of grace in the Grandmother's soul, and not for the dead bodies.

We hear many complaints about the prevalence of violence in modern fiction, and it is always assumed that this violence is a bad thing and meant to be an end in itself. With the serious writer, violence is never an end in itself. It is the extreme situation that best reveals what we are essentially, and I believe these are times when writers are more interested in what we are essentially than in the tenor of our daily lives. Violence is a force which can be used for good or evil, and among other things taken by it is the kingdom of heaven. But regardless of what can be taken by it, the man in the violent situation reveals those qualities least dispensable in his personality, those qualities which are all he will have to take into eternity with him; and since the characters in this story are all on the verge of eternity, it is appropriate to think of what they take with them. In any case, I hope that if you consider these points in connection with the story, you will come to see it as something more than an account of a family murdered on the way to Florida.

SALLY FITZGERALD

Southern Sources of "A Good Man Is Hard to Find"

1997

The germ of the story, like a number of others, came from the newspapers close to home—in this instance from several newspaper accounts of unrelated matters shortly before she wrote the story, in 1953. The title she found in a local item—with photograph—concerning a prize-winning performance by a hideously painted-up little girl still in kitten teeth, decked out in ribbons and tutu and sausage curls, singing "A Good Man Is Hard to Find." Beyond the title, there is no connection between the photograph and the events of the short story, but possibly this child served to inspire the awful little granddaughter, June Star, who sasses her way through the action, and does her tap-routine at the barbecue stand of Red Sammy Butts, the fat veteran "with the happy laugh," who is so thoroughly nasty to his wife. Flannery thought well enough of this newspaper photograph and caption to pass them along for my delectation, together with various ads and testimonials for patent medicines and inspirational columns from the local press, and I remember the clipping very clearly. So did she, and she took the nectar from it to make her fictional honey.

About the same time, an article appeared in the Atlanta paper about a small-time robber who called himself "The Misfit," in a self-pitying explanation or excuse for his crimes. A clipping about him and his honorary title turned up among her papers. Obviously, the name he gave himself was the only thing about this man that much interested the author, and certainly he was no match for the towering figure she turned him into. Incidentally, his excuse for his peccadilloes was taken rather literally in the judicial system: he was judged to be of unsound mind and committed to the lunatic asylum—in Milledgeville, the town in which Flannery lived. This news cannot have escaped her notice. By the way, the mental hospital there was once the largest in the world under one roof. Flannery once described Milledgeville as a town of 8,000, of whom 4,000 were locked up.

There was a third element in the inspirational mix for the story, and this was also to be found in the newspapers, in a series of accounts of another criminal "aloose" in the region. The subject was the person of Mr. James Francis ("Three-Gun") Hill, who amassed a record of twenty-six kidnappings in four states, an equal number of robberies, ten car thefts, and a daring rescue of four Florida convicts from a prison gang—all brought off in two fun-filled weeks. The papers at the time were full of these accounts, and the lurid headlines of the day might well have excited a grandmother like the one who is shaking a newspaper at Bailey Boy's bald head and lecturing him on the dangers to be feared on the road to Florida, when the O'Connor story opens.

Mr. Hill was a far more formidable figure than the original self-styled Misfit, and a more vivid one. Newspaper photographs show him to have looked almost exactly as she described the character in her story, complete with metal-rimmed spectacles. There were other details evidently appropriated by

Flannery from life, or life as strained through the *Atlanta Journal* and the *Atlanta Constitution:* Mr. Hill was proud of his courtly manners, and in one press account called himself a "gentleman-bandit," explaining that he never cussed before ladies. (Readers will remember that Flannery's mass-murderer blushes when Bailey curses his mother for her incautious tongue.) In some accounts, "Three-Gun" Hill had two accomplices, although the fictional Hiram and Bobby Lee seem entirely imagined by O'Connor in their physical aspects and rather subhuman personalities.

The Misfit in O'Connor's story recounts a brush with a "head-doctor," which accords with the fate of both these actual criminals who initially inspired her. "Three-Gun" Hill, too, was committed to an insane asylum in the end, when he pled guilty to the charges against him. He was sent to a hospital in Tennessee, however, and not to Milledgeville, but the author no doubt read about the sentencing, and it may be that the eventual guilty plea suggested to her the beginnings of capitulation, the stirring of life in the Misfit, whom she conceived as a spoiled prophet, on which note her story ends.

ON CRITICAL VIEWS OF EDGAR ALLAN POE'S SHORT STORIES

Edgar Allan Poe offers a valuable opportunity to trace the evolution of some different methods that critics have used to read short stories over an extended period of time. In the essays that follow, you will find examples of early psychological criticism, New Criticism, deconstruction, and cultural criticism. These excerpts by various critics responding over the years to two of Poe's stories will suggest the wealth of different approaches available to the contemporary reader.

Poe himself was not a systematic critic, and his writing on the short story does not fall into any academic category. He was one of the earliest writers to discuss the aesthetic qualities of the short story—what he called "the prose tale"—in his two long reviews praising the tales of Nathaniel Hawthorne. These articles, published in *Graham's Magazine* in 1842 and *Godey's Lady's Book* in 1847, are pioneering examples of the analytic literary essay in America. This section begins with an excerpt from Poe's 1842 review, in which he introduces his theory of the short story and emphasizes the importance of unity of effect in a well-written tale.

In Poe's time, criticism of the short story, like the short story itself, was still a new field, but twentieth-century literary critics and scholars have developed many different approaches that enhance our understanding of short fiction, including Poe's mastery of this genre. Critics have been commenting on and analyzing Poe's tales for over a century. The field of literary theory investigating how authors tell their stories expanded greatly due to a variety of cultural changes following the disruptions of World War II, and although early critics in the United States were reluctant to recognize Poe's achievement, Poe's genius was widely recognized by the end of the 1950s. In a 1959 lecture on "The House of Poe" at the Library of Congress, the American poet Richard Wilbur concluded that "Poe is a great artist, and I would rest my case for him on his

Edgar Allan Poe, photographed in Lowell, Massachusetts, in the last year of his life. (© Hulton-Deutsch Collection/CORBIS.)

prose allegories of psychic conflict. In them, Poe broke new ground, and they remain the best things of their kind in our literature."

Most contemporary critics group the different ways of writing about literature into four broad categories: approaches that focus on either the author, the reader, the text, or the cultural and historical background of the text. Some critics combine two or more of these approaches when they develop their analyses of a short story. In this section, examples of some of the ways that critics have written about the texts and the backgrounds of "The Cask of Amontillado" (p. 543) and "The Fall of the House of Usher" (p. 548) follow Poe's pioneering 1842 review of Hawthorne's *Twice-Told Tales.* In addition to suggesting new ways to read Poe's short fiction, these essays show how different critics use different approaches to write about the same author, and how these approaches have developed in recent years. Since Poe is one of the most controversial American authors, these excerpts also suggest the continuing debate among academics over his place in the literary canon. An excellent overview of the major trends in Poe criticism is available in Scott Peeples' book *The Afterlife of Edgar Allan Poe* (2004).

COMMENTARIES

EDGAR ALLAN POE

The Importance of the Single Effect in a Prose Tale

1842

But it is of [Hawthorne's] tales that we desire principally to speak. The tale proper, in our opinion, affords unquestionably the fairest field for the exercise of the loftiest talent, which can be afforded by the wide domains of mere prose. Were we bidden to say how the highest genius could be most advantageously employed for the best display of its own powers, we should answer, without hesitation—in the composition of a rhymed poem, not to exceed in length what might be perused in an hour. Within this limit alone can the highest order of true poetry exist. We need only here say, upon this topic, that, in almost all classes of composition, the unity of effect or impression is a point of the greatest importance. It is clear, moreover, that this unity cannot be thoroughly preserved in productions whose perusal cannot be completed at one sitting. We may continue the reading of a prose composition, from the very nature of prose itself, much longer than we can persevere, to any good purpose, in the perusal of a poem. This latter, if truly fulfilling the demands of the poetic sentiment, induces an exaltation of the soul which cannot be long sustained. All high excitements are necessarily transient. Thus a long poem is a paradox. And, without unity of impression, the deepest effects cannot be brought about. Epics were the offspring of an imperfect sense of Art, and their reign is no more. A poem *too* brief may produce a vivid, but never an intense or enduring impression. Without a certain continuity of effort—without a certain duration or repetition of purpose—the soul is never deeply moved. There must be the dropping of the water upon the rock. . . .

Were we called upon, however, to designate that class of composition which, next to such a poem as we have suggested, should best fulfill the demands of high genius—should offer it the most advantageous field of exertion—we should unhesitatingly speak of the prose tale, as Mr. Hawthorne has here exemplified it. We allude to the short prose narrative, requiring from a half-hour to one or two hours in its perusal. The ordinary novel is objectionable, from its length, for reasons already stated in substance. As it cannot be read at one sitting, it deprives itself, of course, of the immense force derivable from *totality*. Worldly interests intervening during the pauses of perusal, modify, annul, or counteract, in a greater or less degree, the impressions of the book. But simple cessation in reading would, of itself, be sufficient to destroy the true unity. In the brief tale, however, the author is enabled to carry out the fullness of his intention, be it what it may. During the hour of perusal the soul of the reader is at the writer's control. There are no external or extrinsic influences—resulting from weariness or interruption.

A skillful literary artist has constructed a tale. If wise, he has not fashioned his thoughts to accommodate his incidents; but having conceived, with deliberate care, a certain unique or single *effect* to be wrought out, he then invents such incidents—he then combines such events as may best aid him in establishing this preconceived effect. If his very initial sentence tend not to the outbringing of this effect, then he has failed in his first step. In the whole composition there should be no word written, of which the tendency, direct or indirect, is not to the one pre-established design. And by such means, with such care and skill, a picture is at length painted which leaves in the mind of him who contemplates it with a kindred art, a sense of the fullest satisfaction. The idea of the tale has been presented unblemished, because undisturbed; and this is an end unattainable by the novel. Undue brevity is just as exceptionable here as in the poem; but undue length is yet more to be avoided.

We have said that the tale has a point of superiority even over the poem. In fact, while the *rhythm* of this latter is an essential aid in the development of the poem's highest idea—the idea of the Beautiful—the artificialities of this rhythm are an inseparable bar to the development of all points of thought or expression which have their basis in *Truth*. But Truth is often, and in very great degree, the aim of the tale. Some of the finest tales are tales of ratiocination. Thus the field of this species of composition, if not in so elevated a region of the mountain of Mind, is a tableland of far vaster extent than the domain of the mere poem. Its products are never so rich, but infinitely more numerous, and more appreciable by the mass of mankind. The writer of the prose tale, in short, may bring to his theme a vast variety of modes or reflections of thought and expression—(the ratiocinative, for example, the sarcastic, or the humorous) which are not only antagonistical to the nature of the poem, but absolutely forbidden by one of its most peculiar and indispensable adjuncts; we allude, of course, to rhythm. It may be added, here, *par parenthèse*, that the author who aims at the purely beautiful in a prose tale is laboring at a great disadvantage. For Beauty can be better treated in the poem. Not so with terror, or passion, or horror, or a multitude of such other points. . . .

Of Mr. Hawthorne's "Tales" we would say, emphatically, that they belong to the highest region of Art—an Art subservient to genius of a very lofty order. We have supposed, with good reason for so supposing, that he had been thrust into his present position by one of the impudent cliques which beset our literature, and whose pretensions it is our full purpose to expose at the earliest opportunity; but we have been most agreeably mistaken. We know of few compositions which the critic can more honestly commend than these "Twice-Told Tales." As Americans, we feel proud of the book.

Mr. Hawthorne's distinctive trait is invention, creation, imagination, originality—a trait which, in the literature of fiction, is positively worth all the rest. But the nature of the originality, so far as regards its manifestation in letters, is but imperfectly understood. The inventive or original mind as frequently displays itself in novelty of *tone* as in novelty of matter. Mr. Hawthorne is original in *all* points.

It would be a matter of some difficulty to designate the best of these tales; we repeat that, without exception, they are beautiful. . . . In the way of objection we have scarcely a word to say of these tales. There is, perhaps, a somewhat too general or prevalent *tone*—a tone of melancholy and mysticism. The subjects are insufficiently varied. There is not so much of *versatility* evinced as we might well be warranted in expecting from the high powers of Mr. Hawthorne. But beyond these trivial exceptions we have really none to make. The style is purity itself. Force abounds. High imagination gleams from every page. Mr. Hawthorne is a man of the truest genius.

D. H. LAWRENCE

D. H. Lawrence, the English novelist, poet, and critic, was fascinated by Poe's genius in his tales. Lawrence wrote an early form of psychological criticism of Poe's texts. Lawrence's approach was indebted to but often differed from the theories of the Austrian psychoanalyst Sigmund Freud (1856–1939). Freud's writing about human psychology, along with books by his disciples including Carl Jung, Marie Bonaparte, and Bruno Bettelheim, modified our understanding of human behavior, introducing such concepts as the unconscious forces of the id and the superego active within every individual.

Most literary criticism involves psychology to some degree, since we instinctively understand the human beings who are the creators or the subjects of short fiction in psychological terms. The way a text is interpreted also depends on the psychological assumptions of its reader. Lawrence, for example, projected his personal obsession about the potential of human relationships to become destructive into his interpretations of "The Fall of the House of Usher" and "The Cask of Amontillado."

Lawrence's chapter on Poe originally appeared in the *English Review* in 1919. It was later revised and reprinted in Lawrence's pioneering volume *Studies in Classic American Literature* (1923). In this book, Lawrence explored what he considered "the crisis of winterdeath," the disintegration of the soul of "the great white race in America." Lawrence believed that Poe's tales needed to be written "because old things need to die and disintegrate, because the old white psyche has to be gradually broken down before anything else can come to pass."

On "The Fall of the House of Usher" and "The Cask of Amontillado" 1919

[In "The Fall of the House of Usher,"] the love is between brother and sister. When the self is broken, and the mystery of the recognition of otherness fails, then the longing for identification with the beloved becomes a lust. And it is this longing for identification, utter merging, which is at the base of the incest problem. In psychoanalysis almost every trouble in the psyche is traced to an incest-desire. But this will not do. The incest-desire is only one of the manifestations of the self-less desire for merging. It is obvious that this desire for merging, or unification, or identification of the man with the woman, or the woman with the man, finds its gratification most readily in the merging of those things which are already near—mother with son, brother with sister, father with daughter. But it is not enough to say, as Jung does, that all life is a matter of lapsing towards, or struggling away from, mother-incest. It is necessary to see what lies at the back of this helpless craving for utter merging or identification with a beloved.

The motto to "The Fall of the House of Usher" is a couple of lines from De Béranger.

"Son coeur est un luth suspendu;
Sitôt qu'on le touche il résonne."

We have all the trappings of Poe's rather overdone vulgar fantasy. "I reined my horse to the precipitous brink of a black and lurid tarn that lay in unruffled lustre by the dwelling, and gazed down—but with a shudder even more thrilling than before—upon the remodelled and inverted images of the grey sedge, and the ghastly tree-stems, and the vacant and eye-like windows." The House of Usher, both dwelling and family, was very old. Minute fungi overspread the exterior of the house, hanging in festoons from the eaves. Gothic archways, a valet of stealthy step, sombre tapestries, ebon black floors, a profusion of tattered and antique furniture, feeble gleams of encrimsoned light through latticed panes, and over all "an air of stern, deep, irredeemable gloom"—this makes up the interior.

The inmates of the house, Roderick and Madeline Usher, are the last remnants of their incomparably ancient and decayed race. Roderick has the same large, luminous eye, the same slightly arched nose of delicate Hebrew model, as characterised Ligeia.° He is ill with the nervous malady of his family. It is he whose nerves are so strung that they vibrate to the unknown quiverings of the ether. He, too, has lost his self, his living soul, and become a sensitised instrument of the external influences; his nerves are verily like an aeolian harp which must vibrate. He lives in "some struggle with the grim phantasm, Fear," for he is only the physical, post-mortem reality of a living being.

It is a question how much, once the rich centrality of the self is broken, the instrumental consciousness of man can register. When man becomes

Ligeia: A reference to the heroine of Poe's short story "Ligeia."

self-less, wafting instrumental like a harp in an open window, how much can his elemental consciousness express? It is probable that even the blood as it runs has its own sympathies and responses to the material world, quite apart from seeing. And the nerves we know vibrate all the while to unseen presences, unseen forces. So Roderick Usher quivers on the edge of dissolution.

It is this mechanical consciousness which gives "the fervid facility of his impromptus." It is the same thing that gives Poe his extraordinary facility in versification. The absence of real central or impulsive being in himself leaves him inordinately mechanically sensitive to sounds and effects, associations of sounds, association of rhyme, for example—mechanical, facile, having no root in any passion. It is all a secondary, meretricious process. So we get Roderick Usher's poem, "The Haunted Palace," with its swift yet mechanical subtleties of rhyme and rhythm, its vulgarity of epithet. It is all a sort of dream-process, where the association between parts is mechanical, accidental as far as passional meaning goes.

Usher thought that all vegetable things had sentience. Surely all material things have a form of sentience, even the inorganic: surely they all exist in some subtle and complicated tension of vibration which makes them sensitive to external influence and causes them to have an influence on other external objects, irrespective of contact. It is of this vibrational or inorganic consciousness that Poe is master: the sleep-consciousness. Thus Roderick Usher was convinced that his whole surroundings, the stones of the house, the fungi, the water in the tarn, the very reflected image of the whole, was woven into a physical oneness with the family, condensed, as it were, into one atmosphere—the special atmosphere in which alone the Ushers could live. And it was this atmosphere which had moulded the destinies of his family.

In the human realm, Roderick had one connection: his sister Madeline. She, too, was dying of a mysterious disorder, nervous, cataleptic. The brother and sister loved each other passionately and exclusively. They were twins, almost identical in looks. It was the same absorbing love between them, where human creatures are absorbed away from themselves, into a unification in death. So Madeline was gradually absorbed into her brother; the one life absorbed the other in a long anguish of love.

Madeline died and was carried down by her brother into the deep vaults of the house. But she was not dead. Her brother roamed about in incipient madness—a madness of unspeakable terror and guilt. After eight days they were suddenly startled by a clash of metal, then a distinct, hollow, metallic, and clangorous, yet apparently muffled, reverberation. Then Roderick Usher, gibbering, began to express himself: "*We have put her living into the tomb!* Said I not that my senses were acute? *I now* tell you that I heard her first feeble movements in the hollow coffin. I heard them—many, many days ago—yet I dared not—*I dared not speak.*"

It is again the old theme of "each man kills the thing he loves." He knew his love had killed her. He knew she died at last, like Ligeia, unwilling and unappeased. So, she rose again upon him. "But then without those doors there *did* stand the lofty and enshrouded figure of the Lady Madeline of Usher. There was blood upon her white robes, and the evidence of some bitter struggle upon every portion of her emaciated frame. For a moment she remained trembling and reeling to and fro upon the threshold, then, with a low moaning cry, fell heavily inward upon the person of her brother, and in her violent and now final death-agonies bore him to the floor a corpse, and a victim to the terrors he had anticipated."

It is lurid and melodramatic, but it really is a symbolic truth of what happens in the last stages of this inordinate love, which can recognise none of the sacred mystery of *otherness,* but must unite into unspeakable identification, oneness in death. Brother and sister go down together, made one in the unspeakable mystery of death. It is the world-long incest problem, arising inevitably when man, through insistence of his will in one passion or aspiration, breaks the polarity of himself.

The best tales all have the same burden. Hate is as inordinate as love, and as slowly consuming, as secret, as underground, as subtle. All this underground vault business in Poe only symbolises that which takes place *beneath* the consciousness. On top, all is fair-spoken. Beneath, there is the awful murderous extremity of burying alive. Fortunato, in "The Cask of Amontillado," is buried alive out of perfect hatred, as the Lady Madeline of Usher is buried alive out of love. The lust of hate is the inordinate desire to consume and unspeakably possess the soul of the hated one, just as the lust of love is the desire to possess, or to be possessed by, the beloved, utterly. But in either case the result is the dissolution of both souls, each losing itself in transgressing its own bounds.

The lust of Montresor is to devour utterly the soul of Fortunato. It would be no use killing him outright. If a man is killed outright his soul remains integral, free to return into the bosom of some beloved, where it can enact itself. In walling-up his enemy in the vault, Montresor seeks to bring about the indescribable capitulation of the man's soul, so that he, the victor, can possess himself of the very being of the vanquished. Perhaps this can actually be done. Perhaps, in the attempt, the victor breaks the bounds of his own identity, and collapses into nothingness, or into the infinite.

What holds good for inordinate hate holds good for inordinate love. The motto, *Nemo me impune lacessit,*° might just as well be *Nemo me impune amat.*° . . .

As long as man lives he will be subject to the incalculable influence of love or of hate, which is only inverted love. The necessity to love is probably the source of all our unhappiness; but since it is the source of everything it is foolish to particularise. Probably even gravitation is only one of the lowest manifestations of the mystic force of love. But the triumph of love, which is the triumph of life and creation, does not lie in merging, mingling, in absolute identification of the lover with the beloved. It lies in the communion of beings, who, in the very perfection of communion, recognise and allow the mutual otherness. There is no desire to transgress the bounds of being. Each self remains

---

Nemo me impune lacessit: No one hates me with impunity.
Nemo me impune amat: No one loves me with impunity.

utterly itself—becomes, indeed, most burningly and transcendently itself in the uttermost embrace or communion with the other. One self may yield honourable precedence to the other, may pledge itself to undying service, and in so doing become fulfilled in its own nature. For the highest achievement of some souls lies in perfect service. But the giving and the taking of service does not obliterate the mystery of otherness, the being-in-singleness, either in master or servant. On the other hand, slavery is an avowed obliteration of the singleness of being.

CLEANTH BROOKS AND ROBERT PENN WARREN

Cleanth Brooks and Robert Penn Warren wrote what they termed New Criticism when they analyzed "The Fall of the House of Usher" in their book *Understanding Fiction* (1943). Their work influenced generations of academics who taught the New Critical method of analyzing texts in college literature classes.

In Brooks and Warren's analysis of "The Fall of the House of Usher," they practiced "close reading": They concentrated on showing how the various elements of the tale were integrated into a unique aesthetic structure. Avoiding biographical or psychological analysis, they examined the structure of the tale, concerned primarily with the text itself, not its author. As critics, they looked for qualities of textual complexity in works of literature, placing a high value on the presence of irony. With little imaginative sympathy for the protagonist Roderick Usher, Brooks and Warren were also unsympathetic to what they considered the excesses of Poe's romantic style. Later critics trained in the New Critical method admired Poe's tales and found much to praise in them by taking different approaches to the texts.

A New Critical Reading of "The Fall of the House of Usher" 1943

This is a story of horror, and the author has used nearly every kind of device at his disposal in order to stimulate a sense of horror in the reader: not only is the action itself horrible but the descriptions of the decayed house, the gloomy landscape in which it is located, the furnishings of its shadowy interior, the ghastly and unnatural storm—all of these are used to build up in the reader the sense of something mysterious and unnatural. Within its limits, the story is rather successful in inducing in the reader the sense of nightmare; that is, if the reader allows himself to enter into the mood of the story, the mood infects him rather successfully.

But one usually does not find nightmares pleasant, and though there is an element of horror in many of the great works of literature—Dante's *Inferno*, Shakespeare's tragedies—still, we do not value the sense of horror for its own sake. What is the meaning, the justification of the horror in this story? Does the story have a meaning, or is the horror essentially meaningless, horror aroused for its own sake?

In the beginning of the story, the narrator says of the House of Usher that he experienced "a sense of insufferable gloom," a feeling which had nothing of that "half-pleasurable, because poetic, sentiment with which the mind usually receives even the sternest natural images of the desolate or terrible. . . . It was a mystery all insoluble. . . ." Does the reader feel, with regard to the story as a whole, what the narrator in the story feels toward the house in the story?

One point to determine is the quality of the horror—whether it is merely vague and nameless, or an effect of a much more precise and special imaginative perception. Here, the description which fills the story will be helpful: the horror apparently springs from a perception of decay, a decay which constitutes a kind of life-in-death, monstrous because it represents death and yet pulsates with a special vitality of its own. For example, the house itself gets its peculiar *atmosphere* . . . from its ability apparently to defy reality: to remain intact and yet seem to be completely decayed in every detail. By the same token, Roderick Usher has a wild vitality, a preternatural acuteness and sensitiveness which itself springs from the fact that he is sick unto death. Indeed, Roderick Usher is more than once in the story compared to the house, and by more subtle hints, by implications of descriptive detail, throughout the story, the house is identified with its heir and owner. For example, the house is twice described as having "vacant eye-like windows"—the house, it is suggested, is like a man. Or, again, the mad song, which Roderick Usher sings with evident reference to himself, describes a man under the *allegory* . . . of a house. To repeat, the action of the story, the description, and the symbolism, consistently insist upon the horror as that which springs from the unnatural and monstrous. One might reasonably conclude that the "meaning" of the story lies in its perception of the dangers of divorcement from reality and the attempt to live in an unreal world of the past, or in any private and abstract world of thought. Certainly, elements of such a critique are to be found in the story. But their mere presence there does not in itself justify the pertinacious and almost loving care with which Poe conjures up for us the sense of the horrors of the dying House of Usher.

One may penetrate perhaps further into the question by considering the relation of the horror to Roderick Usher himself. The story is obviously his story. It is not Madeline's—in the story she hardly exists for us as a human being—nor is it the narrator's story, though his relation to the occupants of the doomed House of Usher becomes most important when we attempt to judge the ultimate success or failure of the story.

Roderick Usher, it is important to notice, recognizes the morbidity of the life which he is leading. Indeed, he even calls his persistence in carrying on his mode of living in the house a deplorable "folly." And yet one has little or no sense in the story that Roderick Usher is actually making any attempt to get away from the haunting and oppressive gloom of the place. Actually, there is abundant evidence that he is in love with "the morbid acuteness of the senses" which he has cultivated in the gloomy mansion, and that in choosing between this and the honest daylight of the outside world, there is but one choice for him. But, in stating what might be called the moral issue of the story in such terms as these, we have perhaps already overstated it. The reader gets no sense of struggle, no sense of real choice at all. Rather, Roderick Usher impresses the reader as being as thoroughly doomed as the decaying house in which he lives.

One may go further with this point: we hardly take Roderick Usher seriously as a real human being at all. Even on the part of the narrator who tells us that Usher has been one of his intimate companions in boyhood, there is little imaginative identification of his interests and feelings with those of Usher. At the beginning of the story, the narrator admits that he "really knew little" of his friend. Even his interest in Usher's character tends to be what may be called a "clinical" interest. Now, baffled by the vague terrors and superstitions that beset Roderick Usher, he is able to furnish us, not so much a reading of his friend's character as a list of symptoms and aberrations. Usher is a medical case, a fascinating case to be sure, a titillatingly horrible case, but merely another case after all.

In making these points, we are really raising questions that have to do with the limits of tragedy. The tragic protagonist must be a man who engages our own interests and hopes and fears as a Macbeth or a Lear, of superhuman stature though these be, engages them. We must not merely look on from without. . . .

In the case of Roderick Usher, then, there is on our part little imaginative sympathy and there is, on his own part, very little struggle. The story lacks tragic quality. One can go farther: the story lacks even pathos—that is, a feeling of pity, as for the misfortune of a weak person, or the death of a child. To sum up, Poe has narrowed the fate of his protagonist from a universal thing into something special and even peculiar, and he has played up the sense of gloom and monstrous derangement so heavily that free will and rational decision hardly exist in the nightmare world which he describes. The horror is relatively meaningless—it is generated for its own sake; and one is inclined to feel that Poe's own interest in the story was a morbid interest.

J. GERALD KENNEDY

J. Gerald Kennedy used deconstruction to analyze the function of the story of "the 'Mad Trist' of Sir Launcelot Canning" included in Poe's "The Fall of the House of Usher." *Deconstruction* emphasizes a close reading of literature guided not so much by a search for surface meaning as by an exploration of the text's internal contradictions, the places where meaning does not remain stable.

In his book *Poe, Death, and the Life of Writing*, published by Yale University Press in 1987, Kennedy attempted to show that "the 'Mad Trist'" was linked to what he called a "deep structure" in "The Fall of the House of Usher" that signified Poe's larger theme of his ultimate survival through his writing. Kennedy felt that "Poe's responsiveness to the problem of death led to self-conscious reflection upon writing and the power of words," and that "the rupture between word and world, signifier and signified, finds its origin in the semiotic impasse of mortality located by Poe."

On "The Fall of the House of Usher" 1987

What Poe reveals, in the succession of tales and poems which constitute his literary corpus, is the enormous complexity, the imaginative fecundity, of this elemental insight [—that by creating works of literature, he could defy his own physical death]. This is the problem to which he returns obsessively in his most striking enactments of the encounter with death. Hence, for example, the fatality of "The Fall of the House of Usher": at a crucial moment, the narrator attempts to calm his host by reading "the 'Mad Trist' of Sir Launcelot Canning" and in the correspondence between that narrative and underground noises, Poe suggests that the romance holds a clue to the curse upon the Ushers. At three separate points, events in the "Mad Trist" seem to evoke sounds within the mansion, as if the text possessed some preternatural agency which ultimately called forth Madeline from the burial vault. Although this "coincidence" may be dismissed as anticipatory anxiety—one can argue that the narrator unconsciously chooses a text which describes sounds like those he hears beneath the house—the details of the story indeed furnish a coded version of the problem of dread figured by Usher's relationship to his sister's corpse. And in a more important sense the "Mad Trist" exemplifies the way in which writing corresponds to the mortal condition which determines and authorizes it.

The episode supposedly read by the narrator (and then reproduced in the text of "Usher") depicts Ethelred's forcible entry into the dwelling of a "maliceful" hermit. Having battered down the door, the hero discovers no sign of the hermit; instead he confronts a scaly dragon which guards a golden palace ornamented by a brass shield bearing the inscription: "Who entereth herein, a conqueror hath bin; / Who slayeth the dragon, the shield he shall win." Ethelred promptly dispatches the dragon, which dies hideously, "[giving] up his pesty breath, with a shriek so horrid and harsh, and withal so piercing, that Ethelred had fain to close his ears with his hands against the dreadful noise of it, the like whereof was never before heard." Wishing to complete "the breaking up of the enchantment," Ethelred "[removes] the carcass from out of the way before him" and approaches the shield. But as if unfastened by the removal of the carcass, the shield falls to the silver floor with a "great and terrible ringing sound." At this juncture the reading of the "Mad Trist" is interrupted by a "clangorous" reverberation within the House of Usher, followed by Roderick's hysterical interpretation of the romance as a figuring of Madeline's return: "And now—tonight—Ethelred—ha! ha!—the breaking of the hermit's door, and the death-cry of the dragon, and the clangor of the shield!—say, rather, the rending of her coffin, and the grating of the iron hinges of her prison, and her struggles within the coppered archway of the vault." And indeed, the appearance of "the lofty and enshrouded figure of the lady Madeline of Usher" seems to validate this reading and imply an occult relationship between the "Mad Trist" and the fall of the Ushers.

But like the image of the house in the tarn, the analogy is reversed and inverted. For the ancient tale of Sir Launcelot Canning represents the dispelling of an enchantment, whereas the extinction of the Ushers marks the completion of a curse. And so the meaning of the last, horrific scene—the deadly embrace of Roderick by Madeline—becomes intelligible only through a consideration of the way in which it effects a reversal of the "Mad Trist." Reduced to constituent terms (the dragon, the palace, and the shield), the romance may be understood as a fantasy of psychic liberation; as such it corresponds closely to Poe's earlier insertion, "The Haunted Palace," and in some sense answers the despairing poem with a narrative of reclamation and recovery. Insofar as "The Haunted Palace" allegorizes the usurpation of reason by griefs and fears, the verses summarize the anxieties of Usher, who anticipates that he will "abandon life and reason together in some struggle with the grim phantasm, FEAR." Significantly, Ethelred too encounters a haunted palace and a frightening embodiment of that which holds the edifice in thrall; but he slays the monster, endures its dying shriek, disposes of the body, and shield, which signifies both victory over the beast and entitlement to the palace. If we understand the palace in both texts as a metaphor for mind, we must then construe both the "evil things, in robes of sorrow" and the scaly dragon as versions of that phantasm which threatens life and reason together—that is, as figurations of the fate which Roderick dreads, the fate prefigured by the transformation of his twin sister. Poe underscores the analogy through the "death-cry" of the dragon, which anticipates Madeline's "moaning cry" as she falls upon her brother "in her violent and now final death-agonies." But whereas Ethelred destroys the dragon and lifts the enchantment, Usher falls to the floor "a corpse, and a victim to the terrors he had anticipated."

In the difference between Ethelred's story and Usher's, Poe inscribes the dilemma of the new death within the metaphysical void of the modern age. One key distinction lies in the relation of the hero to the body of death: whereas the knight removes "the carcass from out of the way before him" and so figuratively confronts and resolves the fear of mortality, Usher experiences a paralysis of will, cannot bring himself to bury his sister's body, and is at last driven mad by the uncertainty signaled by her "temporary entombment." His indecision derives not simply from the ambiguity of her demise (with the attendant symptoms of catalepsy) but from the tension between that which bonds him to Madeline—the "striking similitude" of the twins and the "sympathies of a scarcely intelligible nature"—and that which horrifies him, the signs of her moribund condition. With the apparent death of Madeline (she is said to be "no more"), Usher is caught between the desire to preserve the possibly still-living body and the need to protect himself from the contagion of death. In the decline of Madeline, the cadaverous Usher has perceived the image of his own disintegration; but in his desolate world, it is a fate too ghastly to be contemplated. Ultimately, his anxiety about the physical condition of Madeline betrays an unarticulated despair about her spiritual destiny. By refusing to consign his sister to the earth, Usher simultaneously denies death and condemns himself to a life of horror.

For, as the story of Ethelred suggests, it is only by confronting the dragon and disposing of the carcass—that is, by recognizing that death is paradoxically the end of the monster of death—that one can liberate the palace and live one's life. What Usher fears—what we all fear—is not so much death itself but the experience of dying, the last agony. Though he claims to have heard his sister's "first feeble movements in the hollow coffin," Usher has been unable to summon the moral energy to face the possible image of decay; in psychic terms, his velleity is itself the product of a refusal to confront death. . . . And so when Usher deposits the body of Madeline in the vault beneath the house, figuratively pushing into the unconscious that overwhelming reality which she incarnates, he condemns himself to a death-in-life. He has not faced the shadow; he has evaded it. And so its eruption, in the form of Madeline's enshrouded figure, marks the inevitable—and fatal—return of the repressed.

In this complex metaphorizing of the problem of death, Poe articulates both the nature of the crisis and a figurative solution to the paralysis of death anxiety. But that solution seems as remote as the world of the romance; our spiritual contemporary, Usher dwells literally and figuratively on the brink of the abyss and cannot escape the fatality of his situation. Nor in fact does the putative narrator, who flees "aghast" from the crumbling mansion to record his tale and thus (like the Ancient Mariner) to signify the continuing hold of the experience upon his consciousness. But the writing of "Usher" may be construed as a modern effort to confront the dragon, to extract from the romance a principle of survival. In this sense the text of the "Mad Trist" presents a model of the complicity between inscription and mortality, for the surface action replicates the resistance to death which is the agony of writing. Poe attributes the romance to Canning, the same imaginary author to whom he later ascribed the motto for the *Stylus:* "—unbending that all men / Of thy firm TRUTH may say—'Lo! this is writ / With the antique *iron pen.*'" The idea of a writing whose truth outlasts death occurs in the "Mad Trist" as the legend "enwritten" on the magical brass shield: one who enters into writing "a conqueror hath bin." Ethelred's adventure enacts the ordeal undergone by both Canning and the narrator: that confrontation with death which impels writing by foreshadowing the silence of nonbeing.

To perceive "Usher" as a fable of dread and avoidance is to understand more clearly its centrality within the Poe canon. If the text signifies the survival of the writer, it also implies the impossibility of writing within the house of Usher—that is, in a condition of paralyzing denial. The narrator inscribes his account from an unspecified place on the opposite side of "the old causeway," at some geographical and psychic distance from the tarn into which the house disappears. Only elsewhere can he record Usher's struggle to preserve life and reason against the consciousness of impending annihilation. That struggle, objectified in the relationship of Usher to his dying sister, defines a fundamental opposition, a quintessential version of the deep structure which may be said to inform most of those texts Poe described as tales of effect.

DAVID S. REYNOLDS

David S. Reynolds practiced cultural criticism in his investigation of "Poe's Art of Transformation in 'The Cask of Amontillado.'" Culture critics analyze aspects of social forms such as religion and popular literature in a writer's background that might have influenced the creation of a specific literary work.

Reynolds's essay was commissioned for the volume *New Essays on Poe's Major Tales,* edited by Kenneth Silverman for Cambridge University Press in 1993. In the first half of the essay, Reynolds discussed Poe's ability to recycle materials from popular literature in his own tales, quoting Poe's statement that "the truest and surest test of originality is the manner of handling a hackneyed subject." In the second half, Reynolds focused on "The Cask of Amontillado" in an attempt to explain how the story transcended the specific cultural references of its time and place to attain its stature as an American masterpiece that continues to evoke emotions of pity and terror in new generations of readers.

Poe's Art of Transformation in "The Cask of Amontillado"

1993

Though grounded in nineteenth-century American culture, "The Cask of Amontillado" transcends its time-specific referents because it is crafted in such a way that it remains accessible to generations of readers unfamiliar with such sources as anti-Catholicism, temperance, and live-burial literature. The special power of the tale can be understood if we take into account Poe's theories about fiction writing, developed largely in response to emerging forms of popular literature that aroused both his interest and his concern. On the one hand, as a literary professional writing for popular periodicals ("Cask" appeared in the most popular of all, *Godey's Lady's Book*) Poe had to keep in mind the demands of an American public increasingly hungry for sensation. On the other hand, as a scrupulous craftsman he was profoundly dissatisfied with the way in which other writers handled sensational topics. John Neal's volcanic, intentionally disruptive fiction seemed energetic but formless to Poe, who saw in it "no precision, no finish . . . — always an excessive *force* but little of refined art."[1] Similarly, he wrote of the blackly humorous stories in Washington Irving's *Tales of a Traveller* that "the interest is subdivided and frittered away, and their conclusions are insufficiently *climacic* [sic]" (*ER*, 586–7). George Lippard's *The Ladye Annabel*, a dizzying novel involving medieval torture and necrophilic visions, struck him as indicative of genius yet chaotic. A serial novel by Edward Bulwer-Lytton wearied him with its "continual and vexatious shifting of scene," while N. P. Willis's sensational play *Tortesa* exhibited "the great error" of "*inconsequence*. Underplot is piled on underplot," as Willis gives us "vast designs that terminate in nothing" (*ER*, 153, 367).

In his own fiction Poe tried to correct the mistakes he saw in other writers. The good plot, he argued, was that from which nothing can be taken without detriment to the whole. If, as he rightly pointed out, much sensational fiction of the day was digressive and directionless, his best tales were tightly unified. Of them all, "The Cask of Amontillado" perhaps most clearly exemplifies the unity he aimed for.

[1]Poe, *Essays and Reviews* (New York: Library of America, 1984), p. 1151. This volume is hereafter cited parenthetically in the text as *ER*.

The tale's compactness becomes instantly apparent when we compare it with the popular live-burial works mentioned earlier. Headley's journalistic "A Man Built in a Wall" begins with a long passage about a lonely Italian inn and ends with an account of the countryside around Florence; the interpolated story about the entombed man dwells as much on the gruesome skeleton as on the vindictive crime. Balzac's "La Grande Bretêche" is a slowly developing tale in which the narrator gets mixed accounts about an old abandoned mansion near the Loire; only in the second half of the story does he learn from his landlady that the mansion had been the scene of a live burial involving a husband's jealous revenge. The entombment in "Apropos of Bores" is purely accidental (two unlucky men find themselves trapped in a wine vault) and is reduced to frivolous chatter when the narrator breaks off at the climactic moment and his listeners crack jokes and disperse to tea. Closest in spirit to Poe, perhaps, is the "dead-vault" scene in Lippard's *The Quaker City:* There is the same ritualistic descent into an immense cellar by a sadistic murderer intent on burying his victim alive. Lippard, however, constantly interrupts the scene with extraneous descriptions (he's especially fascinated by the skeletons and caskets strewn around the cellar). In addition, this is just one of countless bloodcurdling scenes in a meandering novel light-years distant, structurally, from Poe's carefully honed tale.

So tightly woven is "The Cask" that it may be seen as an effort at literary one-upsmanship on Poe's part, designed pointedly as a contrast to other, more casually constructed live-burial pieces. In his essays on popular literature, Poe expressed particular impatience with irrelevancies of plot or character. For instance, commenting on J. H. Ingraham's perfervid best-seller *Lafitte, the Pirate of the Gulf,* he wrote: "We are surfeited with unnecessary details. . . . Of outlines there are none. Not a dog yelps, unsung" (*ER*, 611).

There is absolutely no excess in "The Cask of Amontillado." Every sentence points inexorably to the horrifying climax. In the interest of achieving unity, Poe purposely leaves several questions unanswered. The tale is remarkable for what it leaves out. What are the "thousand injuries" Montresor has suffered at the hands of Fortunato? In particular, what was the "insult" that has driven Montresor to the grisly extreme of murder by live burial? What personal misfortune is he referring to when he tells his foe, "you are happy, as I once was"? Like a painter who leaves a lot of suggestive white canvas, Poe sketches character and setting lightly, excluding excess material. Even so simple a detail as the location of the action is unknown. Most assume the setting is Italy, but one commentator makes a good case for France.[2] What do we

[2]Pollin, *Discoveries in Poe,* pp. 29–33. Pollin points out that when Poe compares Montresor's crypts with "the great catacombs of Paris" he is revealing his awareness of contemporary accounts of the great necropolis under the Faubourg St. Jacques, in which the skeletal remains of some three million former denizens of Paris were piled along the walls. One such account had appeared in the "Editor's Table" of the *Knickerbocker Magazine* for March 1838. Pollin also develops parallels between "The Cask" and Victor Hugo's *Notre-Dame de Paris,* a novel Poe knew well.

know about the main characters? As discussed, both are bibulous and proud of their connoisseurship in wines. Fortunato, besides being a Mason, is "rich, respected, admired, beloved," and there is a Lady Fortunato who will miss him. Montresor is descended from "a great and numerous family" and is wealthy enough to sustain a palazzo, servants, and extensive wine vaults.

Other than that, Poe tells very little about the two. Both exist solely to fulfill the imperatives of the plot Poe has designed. Everything Montresor does and says furthers his strategy of luring his enemy to his death. Everything Fortunato does and says reveals the fatuous extremes his vanity about wines will lead him to. Though limited, these characters are not what E. M. Forster would call flat. They swiftly come alive before our eyes because Poe describes them with acute psychological realism. Montresor is a complex Machiavellian criminal, exhibiting a full range of traits from clever ingratiation to stark sadism. Fortunato, the dupe whose pride leads to his own downfall, nevertheless exhibits enough admirable qualities that one critic has seen him as a wronged man of courtesy and good will.[3] The drama of the story lies in the carefully orchestrated interaction between the two. Poe directs our attention away from the merely sensational and toward the psychological. . . .

Is "The Cask of Amontillado" intensely moralistic or frighteningly amoral? These questions, I would say, are finally unresolvable, and their very unresolvability reflects profound paradoxes within the antebellum cultural phenomena that lie behind the tale. A fundamental feature of anti-Catholic novels, dark temperance literature, and reform novels like Lippard's *The Quaker City* is that they invariably proclaimed themselves pure and moralistic but were criticized, with justification, for being violent and perverse. Many popular American writers of Poe's day wallowed in foul moral sewers with the announced intent of scouring them clean, but their seamy texts prove that they were more interested in wallowing than in cleaning. This paradox of immoral didacticism, as I have called it elsewhere,[4] helps account for the hermeneutic circularities of "The Cask of Amontillado." On the one hand, there is evidence

[3]Joy Rea, "In Defense of Fortunato's Courtesy," *Studies in Short Fiction*, 4 (1967): 57–69. I agree, however, with William S. Doxey, who in his rebuttal to Rea emphasizes Fortunato's vanity and doltishness; see Doxey, "Concerning Fortunato's 'Courtesy,'" *Studies in Short Fiction*, 4 (1967): 266. Others have pointed out that there may be an economic motive behind the revenge scheme. Montresor, who calls the wealthy Fortunato happy "as I once was," seems to feel as though he has fallen into social insignificance and to think delusively he can regain his "fortune" by the violent destruction of his supposed nemesis, who represents his former socially prominent self. See James Gargano, "'The Cask of Amontillado': A Masquerade of Motive and Identity," *Studies in Short Fiction*, 4 (1967): 119–26. That economic matters would be featured in this tale is not surprising, since Poe was impoverished and sickly during the period it was written. His preoccupation with money is reflected in the names Montresor, Fortunato, Luchesi ("Luchresi" in the original version)—"treasure," "fortune," and "lucre"—which, as David Ketterer points out, all add up to much the same thing (*The Rationale of Deception* [Baton Rouge: Louisiana State University Press], p. 110).

[4]David S. Reynolds, *Beneath the American Renaissance* (Boston: Harvard U.P., 1989), Chapter 2.

for a moral or even religious reading: The second sentence, "You, who know so well the nature of my soul," may be addressed to a priest to whom Montresor, now an old man, is confessing in an effort to gain deathbed expiation. On the other hand, there is no explicit moralizing, and the tale reveals an undeniable fascination with the details of cunning crime. Transforming the cultural phenomenon of immoral didacticism into a polyvalent dramatization of pathological behavior, Poe has it both ways: He satisfies the most fiendish fantasies of sensation lovers (including himself, at a time when revenge was on his mind), still retaining an aura of moral purpose. He thus serves two types of readers simultaneously: the sensationally inclined, curious about this cleverest of killers, and the religiously inclined, expectant that such a killer will eventually get his due. In the final analysis, he is pointing to the possibility that these ostensibly different kinds of readers are one and the same. Even the most devoutly religious reader, ready to grab at a moral lesson, could not help being intrigued by, and on some level moved by, this deftly told record of shrewd criminality.

Poe had famously objected to fiction that struck him as too allegorical, fiction in which imagery pointed too obviously to some exterior meaning, and had stressed that the province of literary art was not meaning but effect, not truth but pleasure. Effect is what a tale like "The Cask of Amontillado" is about. An overwhelming effect of terror is produced by this tightly knit tale that reverberates with psychological and moral implications. Curiosity and an odd kind of pleasure are stimulated by the interlocking images, by the puns and double meanings, and, surprisingly, by the ultimate humanity of the seemingly inhuman characters. Fortunato's emotional contortions as he is chained to the wall are truly frightening; they reveal depths in his character his previous cockiness had concealed. Montresor's moments of wavering suggest that Poe is delving beneath the surface of the stock revenge figure to reveal inchoate feelings of self-doubt and guilt. Unlike his many precursors in popular culture, Poe doesn't just entertain us with skeletons in the cellar. He makes us contemplate ghosts in the soul.

◆ Topics for Writing about Flannery O'Connor and Edgar Allan Poe ◆

1. On December 26, 1954, Flannery O'Connor described the subject of her collection *A Good Man Is Hard to Find* to Sally Fitzgerald as "nine stories about original sin." Write an essay in which you state the definition of original sin as you understand it, and then compare and contrast "A Good Man Is Hard to Find" and "Good Country People" to show how O'Connor used the elements of fiction to dramatize her subject.
2. In O'Connor's essay "Writing Short Stories," she said that she was "supposed to provide the intelligent reader with the deeper experience that he looks for in fiction." Taking the perspective of a reader-response critic, write an essay in which you analyze what you look for in fiction, using as your examples quotations from any of the stories you've read in this anthology.

3. Since Edgar Allan Poe published his review of Hawthorne's tales in 1842, literary critics have been discussing what he meant by the phrase "a certain unique or single effect" as the most important quality of a successful short story. Add your voice to the critical conversation by using Poe's definition in your own review of any story by an author included in this anthology.
4. Choose the critical perspective you found most helpful in your reading of the different commentaries on Poe's prose tales, and write an essay in which you analyze how this approach helped to deepen your understanding of Poe's short fiction, or the short fiction of any author in this anthology.

PART TWO

Poetry

> For the sake of a single poem, you must
> see many cities, many people and things,
> you must understand animals, must feel
> how birds fly, and know the gesture
> which small flowers make when they
> open in the morning.
>
> —Rainer Maria Rilke

8.

What Is a Poem?

> I, too, dislike it.
> Reading it, however, with a perfect contempt for it, one discovers in it, after all, a place for the genuine.
>
> —MARIANNE MOORE, "Poetry," 1935

What is a poem? Poets, who after all create poems, should be the best people to define what a poem is. If we ask them for a definition, we find that many poets leave this question to someone who creates definitions of literary terms or to someone who wants to explain to someone else what these terms mean. If asked what they think poetry *is*, a poet's answer can be as laconic as Robert Frost's statement, "Poetry is the kind of thing poets write."

Part of the difficulty with asking poets to define what they're doing is that poetry isn't written only with the mind as the poem's source of inspiration. The moment when a poem comes can involve feelings like the poet William Wordsworth described when he wrote of an emotion that was "too deep for words." Poems are written with the feelings and the emotions, with the intuition and the instincts, that make each of us who we are. Even reading a poem, for some writers, can have as strong an effect on them as writing itself. Emily Dickinson, in an answer to the question *What is poetry?*, said of her own way of experiencing poetry,

> If I read a book and it makes my whole body so cold no fire can ever warm me, I know that is poetry. If I feel physically as if the top of my head were taken off, I know that is poetry. These are the only ways I know it. Is there any other way?

Often poets can remember when they experienced this rush of emotion that came with their first encounter with poetry, this moment when poetry opened the door and walked into their lives. The Chilean poet Pablo Neruda, who received the Nobel Prize for literature, wrote of this moment that he felt as though he had been suddenly drawn into the universe in a way he'd never experienced before. Poetry simply arrived, and it made him feel as though he were being pulled out of his body. When this happened he had no idea who he had become. He was "without a face," but still poetry touched him. In the flood of excitement at what he was feeling, he "wheeled with the stars," and his heart was carried away from him on the wind.

PABLO NERUDA

Poetry

1924

TRANSLATED BY ALASTAIR REID

And it was at that age . . . Poetry arrived
in seach of me. I don't know, I don't know where
it came from, from winter or a river.
I don't know how or when,
no, they were not voices, they were not
words, nor silence,
but from a street I was summoned,
from the branches of night,
abruptly from the others,
among violent fires
or returning alone,
there I was without a face
and it touched me.

I did not know what to say, my mouth
had no way
with names,
my eyes were blind,
and something started in my soul.
fever or forgotten wings,
and I made my own way,
deciphering
that fire,
and I wrote the first faint line,
faint, without substance, pure
nonsense,
pure wisdom
of someone who knows nothing,
and suddenly I saw
the heavens
unfastened
and open,
planets,
palpitating plantations,
shadow perforated,
riddled
with arrows, fire and flowers,

the winding night, the universe.

And I, infinitesimal being,
drunk with the great starry
void,
likeness, image of
mystery,
felt myself a pure part
of the abyss,
I wheeled with the stars,
my heart broke loose on the wind.

One of the reasons it is difficult to define poetry is that there is so much of it. Poetry is the oldest of our language arts. Poems were written with sticks on clay tablets and painted on the walls of tombs before there was pen or paper. Only drama is nearly as old. It emerges, as closely as we can tell, two or three centuries after poetry, evolving from a long tradition of ceremony and performance. The novel, with its history of only three or four hundred years, and the short story, with its history of less than two hundred years, are newcomers in the world of literature, though storytelling has been part of our human experience since we learned to talk. With roots in Asia and in the cultures of the countries of the Middle East and Europe, poetry has had a continuous, unbroken line of tradition for almost three thousand years. If you look to the past, you will discover that poetry has changed as society has changed. Poets and their audiences have had continually new expectations of what poetry should express, and this adds to the complicated question of what a poem *is*.

One of the best-known poems in which a poet turns to defining what he creates is "Ars Poetica," written by the American poet Archibald MacLeish. He takes you through a series of comparisons to tell you what a poem *should* do. His comparisons, however, suggest again and again that what he wants you to know is that the poem finally defines itself. As he concludes, "A poem should not mean / But be." If you read the poem closely, you can follow the line of thought that MacLeish has presented. In the first lines he says that a poem should have a physical nature you can touch, that is "palpable," but that also it shouldn't speak. It should simply be present as a rounded pear or an apple is present. Like the pear or apple, the poem is simply *there*. Perhaps this comparison makes you think of the way fruit is portrayed in a still-life painting by an artist such as Henri Matisse, where the skin of the fruit seems real enough to touch.

In the lines that follow, MacLeish says that the poem should continue to be silent, as "old medallions to the thumb," but he is subtly reminding you that a poem, in its silence, is actually saying many things. From what is embossed on an old medallion, historians can decipher many things about a vanished culture. Each of MacLeish's comparisons has a meaning that you can trace, if you take the moment he asks for in your close reading of the poem. He is saying that in a description of an empty doorway and a maple leaf, a poem can tell us "the history of grief," which means that the poem can convey a feeling of loss through images of an empty doorway and a fallen leaf.

ARCHIBALD MacLEISH

Ars Poetica

1926

A poem should be palpable and mute
As a globed fruit

Dumb
As old medallions to the thumb

Silent as the sleeve-worn stone
Of casement ledges where the moss has grown—

•

A poem should be wordless
As the flight of birds

A poem should be motionless in time
As the moon climbs

Leaving, as the moon releases
Twig by twig the night-entangled trees,

Leaving, as the moon behind the winter leaves,
Memory by memory the mind—

A poem should be motionless in time
As the moon climbs

•

A poem should be equal to:
Not true

For all the history of grief
An empty doorway and a maple leaf

For love
The leaning grasses and two lights above the sea—

A poem should not mean
But be.

Many poets have defined poetry in terms that seem to tell you as much about the writers as about what they are defining. For Carl Sandburg, a poet with roots in the American heartland, poetry is "a series of explanations of life, fading off into horizons too swift for explanations." Robert Frost's well-known, no-nonsense description of poetry is "a momentary stay against confusion." For William Carlos Williams, who worked all his life as a small-town doctor, his concern was with the "things" in a poem, a poem is "a machine made out of words." For the contemporary poet Louise Glück, who turns again and again to her own family and the emotions of her childhood for her poems, "The poem may embody perception so luminous it seems truth, but what keeps it alive is not fixed discovery but the means of discovery; what keeps it alive is intelligence." For Wallace Stevens, who spent his life in an office as an insurance company executive, poetry was something almost unreal; his gruff dismissal was "poetry is the supreme fiction."

Sometimes poets tell you about what they do in phrases that are almost poems in themselves. The English poet Percy Bysshe Shelley suggested that "a poet is a nightingale, who sits in darkness and sings to cheer its own solitude with sweet sounds." William Wordsworth thought of what he did as "the spontaneous overflow of powerful feelings." Robert Frost, in a more eloquent description of his craft, said, "The figure a poem makes. It begins in delight and ends in wisdom." The San Francisco poet Lawrence Ferlinghetti declares, "A poem is a flower of an instant in eternity," and also suggests, "Poems are lifesavers when your boat capsizes." The American poet and novelist Erica Jong asks, "What is great poetry after all, but the continuation of the human voice after death?" Many poets would agree with these lines by Diane Ackerman, from her poem "The Work of the Poet Is to Name What Is Holy":

> The work of the poet
> is to name what is holy,
> a task for eternity
> or the small Eden of this hour. . . .

None of what you have read so far, however, gives you an answer to the question *What is a poem?* At this point it would be useful to turn to a dictionary. In *Webster's New Collegiate Dictionary*, you'll find that the word *poem* is derived from the Greek word *poiēma*, and it is given two meanings:

1. A composition in verse, characterized by imagination and poetic diction.
2. Any composition marked by qualities ascribed to poetry, as elevation or beauty.

Neither definition is very helpful since you now need to know the meaning of the terms *verse, poetic diction*, and *elevation*. An older dictionary's definition of *poetry* seems a little more helpful, though it turns to value judgments to make its point that poetry should be considered as on a higher plane than other kinds of writing.

> The art or work of poets; the embodiment in appropriate language of beautiful or high thought, imagination, or emotion, the language being rhythmical, usually metrical, and adapted to arouse the feelings and imagination; metrical composition; also poetical writings; poems collectively, verse.

What you can learn from these words is that poetry changes as society changes. This definition is from the 1949 edition of *Webster's Collegiate Dictionary*. It no longer expresses what we expect from poetry today. Visions of beauty expressed in rhythmical language are not what most poets have written in the last decades, since our expectations for the future have become more wary. Poetry does, however, continually present a conscious shaping of language and an awareness of form to set it apart from its sister *prose*. Also in the work of many contemporary poets is a consciousness, implied or expressed, of the long traditions behind the poetry they are writing.

However you define a poem, as you read you will understand it better if you can separate it into two parts. The first part is what the poem is telling you, the emotion or the thought present on the page. This is the poem's **theme**. At the same time, you should never forget that the theme of the poem is not necessarily the first thing you find on the page. What you find there is the poem's **subject**. As an example, the subject of the poem, what you first read there, might be the writer's pet cat, but you are also aware that the theme of the poem, the larger idea behind the lines themselves, is the writer's pleasure in the everyday things that the cat represents.

The second part of what you should consider when you read poetry is the **means** the writer has used to create the poem. A poem has a structure, a form, and often a special language called **poetic language** that includes unexpected words or ways of describing what the poem is about. The writer's means also include the sounds of the words the writer has chosen, the rhythms you feel as you read the lines, the allusions to other writers or other historical moments, and the references to music or to art. This grab bag of language, expression, and thought can be called the **elements** of poetry.

As you read, remember too that the poem's themes always come from within the writers themselves. They arise from the poets' thoughts, dreams, disappointments, or joys, or from their responses to someone else's dreams or disappointments. The themes you will find in the poems are our shared experience of life. They come from the human feelings that we all have known together. These themes will be continually renewed, and they will be always new.

The subject of a poem, however, is bound into the time and the place when it was written. What its language will mirror is the society in which the poets lived, the poetic traditions that they inherited, and their own needs, prejudices, and enthusiasms. Poems may tell you things you've known before, but they will be written in the language of their own time and place. Even though what they have to tell you might be something you've already read or heard, the ways they tell you will be different.

In this poem by a contemporary California writer, Ann Menebroker, she tells us how the poem "happened" for her, and she is describing what has happened to poets since they first began writing. For her it all begins with a glimpse. Try paraphrasing her poem, putting it into your own words, to get closer to it. As Menebroker explains in her first lines, the poem didn't come out of any idea that she had. Instead it was as though she had looked up in the night sky and seen "billions of stars" that reminded her of how much there is in the universe. Next she glimpsed a man out walking his dog, and she thought it was a moment of reality that she could use as the subject for a poem. "Write about it," she commanded. She knows that as a poet she can go on and on writing about what the man is doing out there on the street, and the process of writing will result in a poem, since she understands that "the vision we have / alters our perception / of what is." In her last lines, she is saying that though the stars are still there, the man and his dog are gone, and the street is empty. She has also found that in the final image of her poem, her theme suggests the brief span of human mortality.

ANN MENEBROKER
A Mere Glimpse

1985

The poem begins—
not with an idea
but with simple
physical action:
one word after
the other, as if
on a daily hike
letting the words come
as they will. It's like
looking up
at the night sky
trying to see
those billions of stars,
knowing there's
much more out there,
but the vision we have
alters our perception
of what is.
A man crosses the street
with his dog.
There! You have it—
reality.
Write about it.
But what about
this man's solitary
journey?
Where he has been.
Where he is headed.
The poem can go on
forever, or go
nowhere at all.
The stars are still
out there.
The street where the man
and the dog crossed
is empty.

You will find that the close reading you give to the lines of a poem will usually bring the poem to life for you. This kind of attention also helps when you approach poetry that is new or different in its presentation of everyday realities. Fred Voss, a poet who has worked most of his life in a California machine shop, insists that we think of "poetry" as something as real as sweat and clamor and noise. What he is telling us in the title of his poem, "How Many Times Can We Follow Dante Down Into Hell?," is that we can't just think of poetry as something left over from the past. The poet of the Italian Renaissance Dante Alighieri wrote his *Divine Comedy* in the fourteenth century, more than seven hundred years ago. As richly imagined as that poem is in its description of Dante's journey down into Hell, Voss wants us to know that there are other kinds of poetry for other places and times. In the machine shop where he works, he admits that he can't talk with the other machinists about the poems going through his head, but he sees old workers around him who still can dance in their excitement over completing a delicate job on their whirring, oil-slick machine lathes. Voss asks if their sweat "isn't / a poem." He wonders in the final lines if the workers' aching muscular pain isn't as "sacred" as poetry, since their hands "made / the world?"

FRED VOSS

How Many Times Can We Follow Dante Down Into Hell?

2006

I still have moments when I look around and wonder what I'm doing
in this machine shop
with these men
wearing steel-toed shoes
acting like I never read Shakespeare
Dostoyevsky Plato
I will never tape a poem to the side of my toolbox like
a drill chart
or a picture of a 1932 Ford
or a woman in a skimpy bathing suit
all
these poems forming inside my head secret behind my sparkling eyes
as my machine plunges smoking drills through slabs of steel
am I insane
between tin walls where never once in 100 years has a poem
been mentioned
where men would rather go to County Jail
than read a book of Keats
looking
for poems in tool steel worm gears
bloody knuckles
eyes
of old men who can still break out dancing
like 5-year-old boys
because they've made a tool bit shave through brass
like butter

there are enough poems about sunsets
about leaves
falling onto grass
how many times can we follow Dante down into Hell
admire
the ceiling of the Sistine Chapel
pretend
each drop of sweat that ever rolled down the skin of these men
    gripping machine handles
        isn't
a poem
each nut and bolt
tick of time clock
ache of bone
sacred
each hand
dripping with machine grease and cutting oil the one
that made
the world?

Another poet who described how poetry won't leave her alone is the American writer Alice Walker, author of the novel *The Color Purple* (1982). Her poem "I Said to Poetry" is a protest against the power that poetry has over her life. Here she has changed the abstract figure of "poetry" into an exasperating human presence who insists on waking her up in the middle of the night with lines that demand to be written and emotions that must be expressed. At the end of her long sleepless night she wryly admits it is poetry that has the upper hand.

ALICE WALKER

I Said to Poetry

1984

I said to Poetry: "I'm finished
with you."
Having to almost die
before some weird light
comes creeping through
is no fun.
"No thank you, Creation,
no muse need apply.
I'm out for good times—
at the very least,
some painless convention."
Poetry laid back

and played dead
until this morning.
I wasn't sad or anything,
only restless.

Poetry said: "You remember
the desert, and how glad you were
that you have an eye
to see it with? You remember
that, if ever so slightly?"
I said: "I didn't hear that.
Besides, it's five o'clock in the a.m.
I'm not getting up
in the dark
to talk to you."

Poetry said: "But think about the time
you saw the moon
over that small canyon
that you liked much better
than the grand one—and how surprised you were
that the moonlight was green
and you still had
one good eye
to see it with.

Think of that!"

"I'll join the church!" I said,
huffily, turning my face to the wall.
"I'll learn how to pray again!"

"Let me ask you," said Poetry.
"When you pray, what do you think
you'll see?"
Poetry had me.

"There's no paper
in this room," I said.
"And that new pen I bought
makes a funny noise."

"Bullshit," said Poetry.
"Bullshit," said I.

Even if poets don't give the same definitions of poetry, they share an excitement over poetry itself. In his poem "today is a day of great joy," Victor Hernández Cruz imagines a day when suddenly poems flood the streets, when poems come in the mail, when poems "knock down walls to / choke politicians." For once poems, which are mostly written and read in silence, fill the air with their noisy voices. Without taking any specific political stand, Hernández Cruz is celebrating the role of the poet as a revolutionary, someone who makes things change. For him this is the "true" poet, because if the poet brings just one day of joy, that is enough to celebrate. Hernández Cruz uses unadorned language, but his meaning is rich with his pleasure at what he has imagined and expressed in the poem.

VICTOR HERNÁNDEZ CRUZ

today is a day of great joy 2007

when they stop poems
in the mail & slap
their hands & dance to
them
when the women become pregnant
by the side of poems
the strongest sounds making
the river go along

it is a great day

as poems fall down to
movie crowds in restaurants
in bars

when poems start to
knock down walls to
choke politicians
when poems scream &
begin to break the air

that is the time of
true poets that is
the time of greatness

a true poet aiming
poems & watching things
fall to the ground

it is a great day

COMMENTARY

JAMES TATE

Like It or Not, We Are a Part of Our Time 1997

Like it or not, we are a part of our time. We speak the language of our time. For poets, it may be more rarefied; it may be more adorned or convoluted, but, nonetheless, in some way it is reflective of our culture. I, for instance, as a very young man, was relieved when I first read William Carlos Williams and I realized I could stop trying to write like Algernon Swinburne.

I know I am not alone when I confess that I have stared at a blank sheet of paper for hours, day after day. Why? Why is it so difficult? Because I want to travel to a new place. Not only do I want the language to be new, I also want the ideas to be new. I want the whole world to be new! We know that that is impossible, but desire is not rational.

Well, we know Columbus did not set sail for America. But what he got was not so bad. We concentrate all we know into the moment, with some fearful peeping into the near future. When I make the mistake of imagining how a whole poem should unfold, I immediately want to destroy that plan. Nothing should supplant the true act of discovery.

The poem is like a very demanding but beautiful pet. It says, "I want this. No, I don't want that. Now I need this, and more of that. But I don't want any of that," and so on. Corrective move. Wanting both truth and beauty, the beauty of language in pursuit of truth.

Some poems want to do their work in the quietest way, like a spider working in a corner. Others are very noisy, banging words against one another as if they were tin cans. One kind of poem is not inherently better than another.

Amazingly, year after year, surprising, subtle, profound, funny, and sad new poems are written and published. Poems we could not have imagined; poems we now know we needed. There is no end to our needing poetry. Without poetry our Culture and, more importantly, our collective Spirit, would be a tattered, wayward thing.

The daily routine of our lives can be good and even wonderful, but there is still a hunger in us for the mystery of the deep waters, and poetry can fulfill that hunger. It speaks to that place in us that seems incomplete. And it can assure us that we are not crazy or alone, and that is a tall order.

9.

Reading, Thinking, and Writing about Poetry

A poem should not mean
But be.
–ARCHIBALD MACLEISH, "Ars Poetica"

Sometimes if you're reading poetry for the first time you may be confused by someone saying this is a "good poem," or this is a good image or a good metaphor, a good line or verse. The question is, what do they mean by *good*, and how can you as a beginning reader learn to look for those elements of a poem that give it an enduring quality? Poets themselves often address these questions, and they judge each other's work by its qualities of originality and technical skill, the imaginative leap of its metaphors or the ingenuity of its rhymes. It is the poet's art—the art of the poem—that shapes the immediate response readers have to a poem, even if we don't consciously separate out the lines, or images, or other elements of the poet's technical skills that have moved us.

As you read the poems that have been gathered in the pages of this book you will find lines and phrases that exemplify this sudden discovery that a poem can bring. Certainly the imagination and the directness of the poem's language is one aspect that we respond to immediately. You will find images like Langston Hughes's poem of disappointed hope, in which hope is described as wrinkling up like "a raisin in the sun," which so captured the imagination of Lorraine Hansberry that it became the title of her popular play. The art—the skill—of the poet is in finding these words that give our experience a new perception, a new dimension. What could better describe the touch of someone in love than e. e. cummings's line, "nobody, not even the rain, has such small hands," or share with us the despair of losing a lover with more desolation than Anne Sexton, in her line "I am a watercolor / I wash off."

In the long experience we have had with poetry there have been lines and verses, shaped with the poet's art, that have expressed some of the deepest convictions of our society. In Percy Bysshe Shelley's "Ozymandias" (p. 767), it was false pride that was stripped bare:

> . . . on the pedestal these words appear:
> "My name is Ozymandias, king of kings:
> Look on my works, ye Mighty, and despair!"
> Nothing beside remains. Round the decay
> Of that colossal wreck, boundless and bare
> The lone and level sands stretch far away.

Part of the poet's art is also the power to express feelings so strongly that their words make it possible for us to share their emotion, and to bring it into ourselves. In this stanza from "Stop All the Clocks" (p. 926), W. H. Auden writes so powerfully about his grief at the death of a loved one that the verse can stand for our own grief if we find ourselves at this same tragic crossroad in our own lives:

> He was my North, my South, my East and West,
> My working week and my Sunday rest,
> My noon, my midnight, my talk, my song;
> I thought that love would last forever: I was wrong.

From today's poets we get the sense of questioning and exploration that is part of being young in a changing world. As Adrienne Su writes, when she confronts the questions she has to answer for herself as a woman and a writer:

> . . . she has to know from the gut whom to trust,
> Because what do her teachers know, living in books,
> And what does she know, starting from scratch?

In your reading you have probably come across many of the formal terms that we use to describe the art of the poem, terms such as *simile, rhyme, meter, iambic pentameter, tone, assonance, onomatopoeia, image, allusion*. These will help you as you go more deeply into your own responses to lines and verses that move you. At the same time, however, you should always have in your mind an awareness of the role that poetry can play in our lives, as Marilyn Chin expresses it in her description of the poet's mission: "The poet's mission on earth is to inspire and to illuminate; and to leave behind to our glorious descendants an intricate and varied map of humanity."

READING POETRY

With all of these elements of a poem that catch our eye, it is not surprising that for many readers the experience of reading a poem—even a poem that presents a familiar theme—can be an uneasy experience. Perhaps it is because poetry sometimes wears its heart on its sleeve, but for many readers the experience of reading a poem seems different from reading a short story or a play. It is easy to be put off by the formal arrangement of lines and verses, by writing that doesn't try to tell a story, or by language that seeks to describe private emotions or hidden dreams. Reading poetry, however, is an experience very similar to reading anything else. You read a poem for what you will find there, for what it will tell you about yourself and your world. Then you read it again for the pleasure you find in the way the poet has used the technical means you have studied.

In Chapter 8, "What Is a Poem?" you learned that it will help you to understand a poem if you can separate it into two parts as you read it over. First read the poem for what it is about, its subject and its theme; then read it to appreciate further the skill and imagination the poet has used in presenting this theme.

Even if you are not entirely sure that you understand everything in the poem in your first reading, you can be struck by the writer's skill. If we take a very short poem as an example, you can see that it is often the poet's ability to choose one thing out of the mass of small details that brings a poem to life. Here is a haiku by the Japanese poet Taniguchi Buson quoted by the American writer Jack Kerouac in his introduction to his own "Western Haikus":

> The nightingale is singing,
> Its small mouth
> open.

The description "Its small mouth / open" suggests the nightingale's song so simply and yet so vividly that the group of three short lines surrounded by the white space on the page seems to reverberate like the nightingale song itself in your imagination. Other poems can suggest an emotional situation so clearly and with such intensity that you find the words stay in your memory, even if you could not write them down exactly if you were asked. This short English medieval lyric has been part of our emotional storehouse for more than four hundred years.

> Western wind, when wilt thou blow,
> The small rain down can rain?
> Christ, if my love were in my arms,
> And I in my bed again!

You do not have to be told to read poems like these more than once. Their appeal to your feelings is immediate and unforgettable. The skill of the author has been in finding the small moment that suggests the poem's theme—the wonder of experiencing nature in Buson's haiku, and the joy of love in the medieval lyric.

Longer poems can be more difficult for the reader. Sometimes the language is unfamiliar; sometimes the theme is not clear at first reading. The general rule is to read the poem straight through to the end, even if you are unsure of the meaning of all the words or phrases the first time around. Inexperienced readers often stop after just a few lines if they begin to feel confused by what the poet appears to be saying.

If this happens, you should disregard your sense that you have lost your bearings in the poem and continue reading until you have finished it. Often the whole poem will clarify the meaning of the early images or lines. Unless you give yourself the opportunity to read the entire poem, you will not have a fair chance to find out what it is saying. For example, when you begin reading the poem "since feeling is first" (1926) by the American writer e. e. cummings, you might stumble on the word *syntax* or the phrase "syntax of things" in the third line of the poem. Do not stop reading to reach for a dictionary to help you puzzle out what the poem means by "syntax." Just continue on to the end of the poem. Reach for the dictionary, if necessary, *after* you have read it all the way through the first time.

since feeling is first
who pays any attention
to the syntax of things
will never wholly kiss you:
wholly to be a fool
while Spring is in the world
my blood approves,
and kisses are a better fate
than wisdom
lady i swear by all flowers. Don't cry
—the best gesture of my brain is less than
your eyelids' flutter which says
we are for each other:then
laugh, leaning back in my arms
for life's not a paragraph
And death i think is no parenthesis

CLOSE READING

When you go back to the beginning of the poem to give it a second reading, you will find that the last two lines illuminate the meaning of the word *syntax* that might have given you trouble on your first reading. The poet is using literary terms in a playful manner to write a love poem, making the point that life is different from literature and should be lived fully and instinctively while there is still time. The speaker in the poem is urging his lady to follow the impulse of her heart, which he tells her is worth more than his poem.

In your study of poetry, you can admire the skill with which cummings employs his technical means of alliteration, rhythm, and paradox. Aware that the poem was published in 1926, before the sexual revolution of the 1960s, you might also understand that the poet has written it to persuade his "lady" not to wait for a wedding ring but to abandon her caution, urging her to acknowledge the physical attraction between them and become his lover right away. Despite cummings's use of lowercase letters and the open form of his poem, you can recognize the traditional theme of *carpe diem*, the Latin words for "seize the day," in this modern poem.

The reason that you need to read more slowly when you read poetry is that your eyes and brain need more time to react to the words on the page. As the critic Sven Birkerts wrote in *The Electric Life* (1989),

> Poetry, through density, rhythm, and any number of concentrating devices, slows us down and, simultaneously, heightens our attentiveness. Words that we scarcely glance at in the morning paper become veritable combs of sensation. . . . Behind the sequential accounting of impressions

[of each word], like the forest we are constantly missing for the trees, is the timeless rustling of language.

PARAPHRASE

It is possible, of course, for you to pay close attention as you follow the words in a poem, read it carefully straight through to the end, reread it a second time, and still find its meaning elusive. Then you might find writing a *paraphrase* of the subject of the poem helps you to understand it as you attempt to put the poem into your own words. Your paraphrase of cummings's poem might look something like this:

> Feeling is more important than thinking. A person who thinks too much about the meaning of life will miss the pleasure of enjoying love. When you're young, you should throw caution to the winds and follow your heart. A love affair should take precedence over everything. Don't be sad thinking it won't work out. Letting yourself feel an attraction for someone is more important than any thought you can have. Relax and enjoy being with your lover, because life is short—it isn't as long as a paragraph, it's only a sentence. And death is a full stop—it isn't a parenthesis, it's a period.

Usually the effort of trying to find your own words to express the subject of a poem will help you to understand it. Writing a paraphrase will force you to spend more time focusing on the poem to clarify your thoughts. This is the first step in the process of thinking critically about poetry.

Poems are "meter-making arguments," so they usually represent an idea or develop a series of ideas in a coherent discourse. Poems are also "language charged with meaning to the utmost degree," so you may have to unravel the ideas behind the words as patiently as you would unravel a ball of string after your cat has played with it. When you write a paraphrase of a poem, you take the chance that you might be mistaken about all or part of its meaning. But you also have a method of clarifying the subject that usually brings you closer to the theme or the central idea that you sense behind the poem's words.

The more skilled you become as a reader of poetry, the more readily your intuition will help you grapple with the experience of the poem. At first your study of the poet's means will give you insight into the different writers' resources as they use language to create a poem. Your increased sensitivity to meter and rhyme, diction and symbolism, and the other means used by the poet should help you to understand and enjoy the work. At the beginning of your study of poetry, it may not be possible to paraphrase the entire poem successfully, but any effort you make should help to bring you closer to the poem.

GUIDELINES FOR READING POETRY

1. Make an entry in your notebook for each poem that is assigned in class, writing down the author's name, the title, and the date.
2. Read the poem through once in its entirety, regardless of whether you understand all the words.
3. When you read the poem a second time, use a dictionary to look up words you don't understand.
4. Copy the first lines of the poem into your notebook to scan the rhythm of the poem. Does it fall into any of the patterns you have studied?
5. Note what impresses you most about the way the poet uses language in the poem, in particular the poem's rhyme, its figurative language, and its diction.
6. Try to write a paraphrase of the subject of the poem, following the poet's argument closely as it develops throughout the lines of the poem. Does the poet use paradox, symbolism, allusion, or tribute? Summarize, if you can, the theme of the poem in a single sentence.
7. If you have difficulty understanding any parts of the poem, or the entire poem, write down specific questions about it so that you can ask them in class.
8. Review technical words about poetry that were used in class to be sure you understand them.

Now consider the following poem by the modern American poet Linda Pastan, and the annotations made by a close reader.

SAMPLE CLOSE READING

LINDA PASTAN

To a Daughter Leaving Home

1978

When I taught you — *Is "I" Pastan?*
at eight to ride
a bicycle, loping along
beside you
as you wobbled away — *All these o's and w's — alliteration, assonance*
on two round wheels,
my own mouth rounding

in surprise when you pulled
ahead down the curved
path of the park,
I kept waiting — *Why are these lines shorter?*
for the thud
of your crash as I
sprinted to catch up,
while you grew
smaller, more breakable
with distance,
pumping, pumping — *like a heart?*
for your life, screaming
with laughter,
the hair flapping
behind you like a — *simile*
handkerchief waving
goodbye.

CRITICAL THINKING ABOUT POETRY

Paraphrasing a poem will help you to understand its subject and its theme, a necessary step in the process of thinking critically about poetry. You will also find that identifying the various means the poet has used to create the poem will help you to analyze the creative strategies behind the author's choice of form and language. For example, you might ask yourself the following questions:

1. Who is the speaker of the poem? How does identifying the speaker contribute to your understanding of the poem?
2. How closely can you identify the speaker with the author of the poem?
3. What attitude toward the subject of the poem does the speaker convey? How does the tone of the poem help you understand this attitude?
4. What use has the poet made of technical means such as imagery, alliteration, allusion, and specific figures of speech?
5. How has the poet used metaphor and simile in the poem?
6. How would you describe the diction and the syntax of the poem?
7. What is the form of the poem? Why did the poet choose this form and not another?
8. Why do you feel the poet might have written this poem?
9. What does the language of the poem tell you about the reader for whom the poem was written? Is it addressed to a person close to the poet, or to a more general reader?
10. How might different readers interpret the poem from different critical perspectives – feminist, Marxist, historical, and so forth?

It might help clarify your thinking about poetry if you take a specific poem and read it closely with these questions in mind. The answers to the questions can generate additional ideas for writing about the poem. Applying the questions to Pastan's poem might generate some of the following responses:

1. The speaker of the poem is clearly the writer herself. We know from this that we are reading a lyric poem, which is concerned with a moment of everyday life. Knowing that the writer is speaking in her own voice helps us to understand the tone and the context of the poem.
2. In this poem the identity of the speaker and author of the poem are the same.
3. The subject of the poem is the poet's daughter, and the emotional attitude the poet expresses is her love for her child.
4. Although the poem is written in a casual, personal tone, there is a skillful ingenuity in the use of language. Instead of writing that her daughter rode away unsteadily, Pastan uses more striking imagery: "as you wobbled away / on two round wheels." It is also useful to notice that she has written "two . . . wheels." This is an allusion to the moment when a child grows from a tricycle or training wheels to a two-wheel bicycle, which is crucial in the child's development. Also notice the writer's use of alliteration in the phrases "loping along," with its repetition of *l* sounds; "wobbled away," with its *w* sounds; and "path of the park," with its *p*'s.

   There are several ways you could describe the image "my own mouth rounding / in surprise." The use of "rounding" to describe her mouth is certainly an allusion to the round wheels of the bicycle that she mentioned in the previous line. The denotative meaning of "rounding" is simply a description of the shape of her mouth, while the connotative meaning is, as she explains, that the round shape of her mouth is an expression of her surprise at what her daughter is doing.
5. The use of metaphor is very important in this poem, because the entire poem itself is a metaphor. What Pastan is describing is the moment when a daughter breaks away from her mother to become an adult. She has chosen to describe it in terms of a metaphor, that of her daughter riding away from her on the daughter's first excited trip on a two-wheel bicycle. The use of simile is very clear in the final lines, when she describes her daughter's hair "flapping . . . like a / handkerchief waving / goodbye." With the simile she has made the meaning of the poem clear. She sees her daughter's first moments on a bicycle and her wild, runaway ride along the path as the moment when her daughter leaves her.
6. The diction of the poem is contemporary and familiar; the syntax is the conversational word order of everyday speech.

7. Since the writer does not use rhyme and the lines don't follow a regular meter we would describe this as a poem in open form, and since it is a personal poem directed to a person close to the writer we would describe it as a lyric poem. The poet chose this form because it most closely matches the style of everyday speech. Since this is a personal poem to her daughter it would strike a modern reader as unconvincing if Pastan used a more elevated and consciously "literary" form.
8. The poet clearly wrote this poem as an expression of her love for her daughter. We know by the title that it was written when her daughter had grown up and become an adult. The poem was probably written both to express the poet's emotions and to soothe her pain at their separation by comparing this moment to her daughter's first bicycle ride.
9. We can tell by the familiar, tender tone of the poem that it was written for someone close to the writer. Since the experience she is describing is familiar to so many other people, however, the poem is also meaningful for a general reader.
10. It would perhaps be a feminist critic who would be most interested in writing about the poem, since the subject of mother-daughter relationships is crucial to feminist theory. A historical critic might want to compare the relative freedom of the mother-daughter relationship that is implied in the poem with the historical past, when women had less freedom to make any choices over their own lives.

WRITING ABOUT POETRY

An assignment to write a paper about a poem will help you to focus your ideas about it and sharpen your critical thinking about what you have read. Many students find that when asked to write a paper analyzing a poem they can work more easily with the poem if they type it on a computer and print it out double-spaced or simply write it out in longhand on a piece of paper. On your copy you can underline words that strike you as significant, and you can jot down your specific feelings and thoughts about the way the poet has used language and form. You can trace the development of the poet's theme, contrast this with the poem's subject, and try to verbalize your feelings about the theme. As you read the poem, are you intrigued, sympathetic, unsympathetic, or confused? Is the subject of the poem something you feel strongly about? Is the theme of the poem something that moves you emotionally? What is your overall reaction to the poem?

If the paper you are planning to write is intended to describe your own response to the poem, you could first concentrate on what it is about the poem that has triggered your response. Is it the subject, or the theme of the poem, or the various poetic means the author employed in creating the poem? Second, you could analyze what it is about you as a reader that caused this response.

Perhaps you had trouble with the poem because you were uncomfortable with the subject or theme. Did the poem's diction or syntax pose problems for you in understanding the lines? Was it the poem's use of language that caused you to respond favorably or unfavorably to it?

Here is a paper about Pastan's poem that draws on both the close reading annotations (pp. 686–687) and the responses to the critical thinking questions (pp. 688–689).

SAMPLE PAPER

A Moving Lyric: Pastan's "To a Daughter Leaving Home"

Lyric poems express personal feelings toward something or someone in particular. Nowadays, lyric poems have become rather common: in fact, we hear them daily on the radio. At their best, however, lyric poetry can tap directly into human emotions, reflecting shared experiences across time and space.

Linda Pastan's "To a Daughter Leaving Home" is an affecting example of a lyric poem, demonstrating how one poet's personal experience can be at once universalized and made unique through the skillful use of language and poetic devices.

Because Pastan's title declares that *her* daughter is the subject of the poem, it immediately suggests that the poem is lyric — an expression of personal feelings as the speaker watches her child leave home, presumably to become an adult. Yet what happens in the poem is not an actual home-leaving; it is instead a description of the moments when Pastan's daughter first learned to ride a bicycle. The distance between what the title says and what the poem describes opens a space for questions. Why is the daughter's learning to ride a two-wheeler like the momentous day she will leave home? How will the poet make the connection between the two?

Pastan's poetic use of language expresses her complex emotions and explores the space between the mundane actions she describes and the life-changing transition her title promises. She uses vivid imagery, made memorable by the use of poetic devices such as alliteration and assonance (note how many open-mouthed, anxious *o*'s recur in lines 3–7) to illustrate the shaky beginnings of her daughter's first attempts to ride a bike, penning phrases like "as you wobbled away / on two round wheels," rather than simply saying her daughter rode away unsteadily. Even here, within this sentence, Pastan uses alliteration to further enhance the image: note the *w* sound in "wobbled away."

Then lines 10–15 pick up speed; the shorter, quicker lines describe the daughter's pulling quickly away. They may also suggest the mother's growing short of breath, puffing out short sentences as she tries to keep up, or as she starts to feel a hint of panic. The phrase "more breakable with distance" reflects Pastan's fears that, as her daughter moves forward, she becomes more vulnerable to the dangers of the outside world. In particular, lines 16–20, while describing the daughter's pedaling, suggest a vulnerable heart "pumping, pumping" (a daughter's heart swelling with reckless excitement, or a mother's heart close to breaking?).

Pastan's use of metaphor is important as well, as the entire poem is a metaphor about growing up and letting go. The poet has chosen to use the moment her daughter first learned to ride a two-wheeler, capturing both her daughter's excitement and her own sadness, as she ties the two momentous occasions together. The poem's final lines — a simile in which Pastan describes her daughter's hair "flapping . . . like a / handkerchief waving / goodbye" — further clarify the poem's meaning: the poet views her daughter's first runaway bike ride as a rehearsal for her departure, a foreshadowing of the moment she truly leaves.

This moment is one with which many can identify. Because Pastan has chosen to write about an experience that is familiar to most people — children who leave home, parents who must let them go — the poem becomes meaningful to a general reader. Further, Pastan's skillful use of poetic devices only serves to strengthen her emotional message, lending to the lyric poem a vivid quality that renders the emotions in the piece all the more memorable and affecting.

When you are ready to begin your paper you can turn to the materials presented in the sections on reading and writing a literary essay. (See Part Four, "Writing about Literature," p. 1611.) You will find help there in planning your paper in stages, with whatever critical approach you take in writing it. You will also find suggestions about prewriting, first and final drafts, revision, and styling your paper.

All of these critical approaches depend on your close reading of the poem. The poem itself will always be the place where you begin your thinking. Recognizing the means that the poet employed in creating a poem will help you to reach deeper levels of response and will clarify your understanding of the poet's intentions.

WEB For writing suggestions on poets in this anthology, visit bedfordstmartins.com/rewritinglit.

10. Rhyme

Words are living fossils. The poet pieces the wild beast together.

–LAWRENCE FERLINGHETTI

Words are the material poets have to work with when they write. For them, the work of choosing the words—the essential *right* words—is one of the most important skills that poets rely on when they create poems. The meaning of the words has to express the thought or the description they are trying to get down on paper. For someone writing a story or a novel, this sense of what a word *means* will be what they think of first. Well-written prose has its own tone and its own rhythm, but for poets the *sound* of the lines can be as important in the poem as the meaning of the words that have gone into its composition.

Rhyme, which builds on the sound of words, was for many centuries considered the measure of a poet's literary skills. How good were the rhymes? How did the rhymes help with the effect of the poem? Were the rhymes new and imaginative? All of these questions were asking how skillfully the writer handled the sound of words. Here is a short poem by Emily Dickinson that can help you understand the effect that rhyme can have on your reading of a poem.

EMILY DICKINSON

A word is dead

c. 1872

A word is de
When it is sa
Some say.
I say it just
Begins to live
That day.

If you *say* the poem to yourself thoughtfully, pausing at the end of each of its short lines, what you will hear is the emphasis that Dickinson's simple rhyme scheme gives to "Some say" and "That day." If you read the lines to yourself again, you will probably find yourself subtly emphasizing those two brief phrases, since by *hearing* the poem its pattern has become clearer for you.

Before rhyme became a common attribute of poetry, poets began with simpler methods of organizing what they wanted to express into some kind of formal pattern. One of the methods that characterized some of the earliest verse in English is alliteration.

ALLITERATION

The dictionary we looked at in Chapter 8 wasn't much help in defining either *poem* or *poetry*, but it's very useful for a word that's more specific. This is the dictionary's concise definition of **alliteration**:

> Repetition of the same sound at the beginning of two or more consecutive words or of words near one another; *specifically* recurrence of the same consonant sound or of vowel sounds initially in accented syllables of verse.

Alliteration was a common effect in the earliest poetry written in English hundreds of years before the development of rhyme. *Beowulf*, from the beginning of the eighth century, is the first poem we know of to be composed in what became the English language, and its lines are structured through alliteration. The example of alliteration that the dictionary chooses is a line from the narrative poem *Piers Plowman*, composed sometime between 1361 and 1387. Even with the archaic spellings, you can hear the sounds of the letter *s* that come at the beginning of four of the line's nine words.

> In a somer seson whan soft was the sonne.

Alliteration still jumps out from unexpected places—an dd song title, "Ding-dong Daddy from Dumas," or a line from a humorous oem, "Round the room the rugged rascal ran." Nearly everyone at some po it in childhood hears alliteration used for comic effect, like the familiar tong-twister "Peter Piper picked a peck of pickled peppers." For practice you can y your own sentences using alliteration.

Another way poets found to organize their lines using e sound of words is called *assonance*.

ASSONANCE

Assonance is closely related to alliteration, but ises the repetition of vowel sounds within the poetic line or phrase. It can be elusive effect, something you feel rather than see immediately. A well-own example of assonance is this phrase from T. S. Eliot's poem "The Love g of J. Alfred Prufrock" (p. 961). It achieves its effect with the repetition of tound of the letter *o*.

In the room the women come and go
Talking of Michelangelo.

This small poem by Walt Whitman suggests an atmosphere of rural quiet with its flow of *a* and *o* sounds.

WALT WHITMAN

A Farm Picture

1865

Through the ample open door of the peaceful country barn,
A sun-lit pasture field, with cattle and horses feeding;
And haze, and vista, and the far horizon, fading away.

ONOMATOPOEIA

Another more obvious use of the sounds of words is the effect known as *onomatopoeia*. The word is derived from the Greek words for "to make names," which suggests that a word can make sounds itself. **Onomatopoeia** means that the word can "sound" like the noise it describes. From the world of nature we have words like *buzz* and *hiss* and *bang*. If you're thinking of bigger sound, *Boom!* Comic books are a treasure of words that imitate sounds. How about *Pow!*, *Splat!*, *Zap!*, *Ra Ta Tat!*, *Ping!*, and *Who-o-o-sh*? One American poet who used onomatopoeia extensively in his writing was Vachel Lindsay, a writer in the early twentieth century who performed his poetry for audiences across the United States. Read aloud the opening line of his poem about the founder of the Salvation Army, William S. Booth:

Booth led boldly with his big bass drum

Using the alliteration of the letter *b* and the near-alliteration of the letter *d*, Lindsay has caught the booming sound of the Salvation Army drums. In her free-blowing poem "a/coltrane/poem," the contemporary poet Sonia Sanchez used onomatopoeia to capture the furious sound of jazz tenor saxophonist John Coltrane in his epic solo "A Love Supreme."

scrEEEccCHHHHH screeeeEEECHHHHHHHHH
sCReeeEEECHHHHHH SCREEEECCCCHHHH
SCREEEEEEEECCCHHHHHHHHHHHH
a lovesupremealovesupremealovesupreme for our blk
people

RHYME

For hundreds of years rhyme was the most obvious characteristic of poetry that distinguished it from prose. It's easy to forget that during most of the long history of poetry, only a small number of people could read. Only the privileged classes and the clergy regarded reading as an essential skill. It wasn't considered necessary for women, servants, or laborers to waste their time learning. Poetry was written to be sung or to be read aloud, and that is the reason earlier poets gave so much of their attention to the sound of their words. Although writers employed other ways to shape what they were creating, rhyme became one of the poet's most admired skills. Rhyme leaves an imprint on a poem that goes beyond alliteration, assonance, or the sound of onomatopoeia. Rhyme by itself became a primary way that the poet could shape the poem.

You will find as you read rhymed poems that rhyme comes in many varieties. There is a form of rhyme that uses the spelling of words as a rhyme. The term for this is **eye rhyme**, which means that two words look as though they would sound alike, but when you say them out loud they have an entirely different tone. Some examples are *food* and *good* or *tough* and *though*. The essence of rhyme, however, is that the rhyming words should sound alike.

Two kinds of rhyme—**perfect rhyme** and **near** or **slant rhyme**—define most of what we mean when we use the term. The kind of rhyme you'll find in most of the traditional poetry you read will be perfect rhyme. Some of the pairs of rhyming words in perfect rhyme have been used so often that when you hear one of the words you can almost say the rhyming word to yourself, like *moon* and *soon* or *dream* and *seem*. Most often you will find the rhyming words at the end of a line, and the term for that is **end rhyme**.

One of the masters of rhymed verse in English was the Victorian poet A. E. Housman, and here is one of his most popular poems. If you say the last word of each line to yourself, you will hear that the rhyming sounds are a perfect match.

A. E. HOUSMAN

Loveliest of trees, the cherry now 1896

Loveliest of trees, the cherry now
Is hung with bloom along the bough,
And stands about the woodland ride
Wearing white for Eastertide.

Now, of my three score years and ten,
Twenty will not come again,
And take from seventy springs a score,
It only leaves me fifty more.

And since to look at things in bloom
Fifty springs are little room,
About the woodlands I will go
To see the cherry hung with snow.

For poets of this era, rhyme was the natural language for them to express their emotions. This fervent declaration of her love was written by African American poet Georgia Douglas Johnson, a woman associated with the writers of the Harlem Renaissance.

GEORGIA DOUGLAS JOHNSON
I Want to Die While You Love Me

1918

I want to die while you love me,
While yet you hold me fair,
While laughter lies upon my lips
And lights are in my hair.

I want to die while you love me.
I could not bear to see,
The glory of this perfect day,
Grow dim—or cease to be.

I want to die while you love me.
Oh! Who would care to live
Till love has nothing more to ask,
And nothing more to give.

I want to die while you love me,
And bear to that still bed
Your kisses, turbulent, unspent,
To warm me when I'm dead.

One of the reasons for the long popularity of rhyme was the seemingly endless variety of the kinds of rhymes poets discovered and the pleasure that readers found in the rhymes. As you read a rhymed poem, you begin to anticipate the sound of the rhymes. Hearing how the poem has been put together gives you a feeling that you and the poet are both thinking in the same way. Here is a gathering of rhymes from the last four hundred years of poetry by English and American writers. Rhyming involves not only imagination and vocabulary, but also the poet's patience and ingenuity to find the words that will both rhyme and make sense together. These two skills have always been considered essential items among the assortment of tools that poets bring to their trade as writers.

As you read the examples, it will help if you mark the rhyming words, asking yourself what kind of rhyme it is—a **perfect rhyme** or, as in the first poem with the words *his* and *miss*, a **near rhyme**, where the sound of the rhyming words is close but not exact. You should notice how the rhymes are placed in the poem. Also, notice in the final example that, as a show of textual virtuosity, Edna St. Vincent Millay used the same rhyming sound for all five lines without losing her poem's easy naturalness.

A Range of Rhyme

My true love hath my heart, and I have his,
By just exchange, one for the other given.
I hold his dear, and mine he cannot miss.
There never was a better bargain driven.

–Sir Philip Sidney, from "The Countess of Pembroke's Arcadia," 1590

Pavement slipp'ry, people sneezing,
Lords in ermine, beggars freezing;
Titled gluttons dainties carving,
Genius in a garret starving.

Lofty mansions, warm and spacious;
Courtiers cringing and voracious;
Misers scarce the wretched heeding;
Gallant soldiers fighting, bleeding.

–Mary Robinson, from "January, 1795," 1795

I am a parcel of vain strivings tied
By a chance bond together,
Dangling this way and that, their links
Were made so loose and wide,
Methinks,
For milder weather.

–Henry David Thoreau, from "I Am a Parcel of Vain Strivings Tied," 1841

Be still, sad heart! and cease repining;
Behind the clouds is the sun still shining;
Thy fate is the common fate of all,
Into each life some rain must fall . . .

–Henry Wadsworth Longfellow, from "The Rainy Day," 1849

To think that this meaningless thing was ever a rose,
Scentless, colourless, *this*!
Will it ever be thus (who knows?)
Thus with our bliss,
If we wait till the close?

–Christina Rossetti, from "Summer Is Ended," 1881

I have seen a lovely thing
Stark before a whip of weather:
The tree that was so wistful after spring
Beating barren twigs together.

–Arna Bontemps, from "Blight," 1926

White sky, over the hemlocks bowed with snow,
Saw you not at the beginning of evening the antlered buck and his doe
Standing in the apple-orchard? I saw them. I saw them suddenly go,
Tails up, with long leaps lovely and slow,
Over the stone-wall into the wood of hemlocks bowed with snow.

–Edna St. Vincent Millay, from "The Buck in the Snow," 1928

If rhyme was so much a part of the language of poetry for centuries, and most readers delighted in the anticipations and the surprises of rhymed poetry, why did rhyme lose its place in the popular conception of what poetry is? What did we gain—and what did we lose—in our new world of poems that don't rhyme? Part of the change has to do with what we want from poetry. What many readers expect from modern poems is a feeling of directness and authenticity, which means that the rules and the inhibitions of rhyme seem confining. How can we let our thoughts and our feelings express themselves freely if we have to stop what we're saying to think of a rhyme? Also, rhyme in itself has problems. When every line or a regular pattern of lines in the poem close with a rhyme, the repetition of the rhyming sounds can begin to get in the way. You sometimes feel that the rhyme is interrupting the poem's flow of ideas and imagery. Even worse, if perfect rhyme is used in a repetitive rhyme scheme without any variation, it can begin to sound monotonous.

In the past poets found many strategies to get around this problem. They quickly learned to work with subtle differences in the sound of the rhyming words. Words like *care* and *soar* don't make a perfect rhyme, but they both begin with a consonant and they end with the sound of the letter *r*. Other pairs of words like them are *read* and *red, seal* and *sail, ball* and *bell*. The sounds are close enough to give us a feeling that the poem is still rhyming. The term we use for this is **near rhyme** or, as it is also known, **half rhyme** or **slant rhyme**.

In her well-known poem "Not Waving but Drowning," Stevie Smith, a modern English poet, consciously used near rhyme to mirror the pathos of a drowning man whose waving people thought was only "larking," an English term for showing his high spirits. The truth was that his waving was a desperate signal for help.

STEVIE SMITH

Not Waving but Drowning

1957

Nobody heard him, the dead man,
But still he lay moaning:
I was much further out than you thought
And not waving but drowning.

Poor chap, he always loved larking
And now he's dead
It must have been too cold for him his heart gave way,
They said.

Oh, no, no, no, it was too cold always
(Still the dead one lay moaning)
I was much too far out all my life
And not waving but drowning.

Smith was a poet who was very conscious of her technical means, and she certainly could have found a perfect rhyme for the first and last stanzas of the poem. Instead she gives us "moaning" to rhyme with "drowning," a half rhyme that gives us a feeling of everything that was only half successful about the man's life.

Another problem with rhyme is that sometimes you have the feeling that the need to find a rhyme has forced the writer to use an awkward word order or clumsy expressions that can make the poem unclear or muddy. When you read the opening lines of the poem "In Tenebris" by the English poet Thomas Hardy, for example, you can hear that his need to find a rhyme has gotten in the way of the emotional effect of the poem. In the first verse, the unyielding discipline of the rhymes have caused Hardy to create a new word use and then alter the normal word order of the final phrase.

> Wintertime nighs;
> But my bereavement-pain
> It cannot come again;
> Twice no one dies.

What Hardy is saying to us is

> Wintertime grows nigh,
> But the pain of my bereavement
> cannot come again;
> No one dies twice.

For Hardy's readers in the nineteenth century, the rhyme was necessary, but for most readers today the more direct version feels closer to the emotional truth of what he has written.

Two other terms are also used in discussing rhyme: **masculine rhyme** and **feminine rhyme**. Words are pronounced in syllables, and some syllables are given more emphasis than others. The strong syllable is called an **accent**, and we will be talking more about accents when we discuss the rhythms of poetry. Masculine rhyme means that the accent on the rhyming words is on a final strong syllable. *Stay* and *away*, *bells* and *foretells*, *otherwise* and *guise* are masculine rhymes. In a feminine rhyme, the accent on the rhyming words is on a weak syllable. *Season* and *reason*, *tower* and *flower*, *thunder* and *wonder* are feminine rhymes.

You will sometimes notice that a poet uses rhyme in the middle of the line as well as the end. This is called **internal rhyme**. This example is from "Blow, Bugle, Blow" by the nineteenth-century English poet Alfred, Lord Tennyson. The internal rhyme occurs in the first and third lines:

> The splendor *falls* on castle *walls*
> And snowy summits old in story:
> The long light *shakes* across the *lakes*
> And the wild cataract leaps in glory.

There are two other terms that help describe what happens at the ends of the lines in a poem. If the meaning of the line comes to a definite end, it is called

end-stopped; if the meaning does not end but continues on to the next line, it is called **enjambed**. The noun for this running of one line into another line is **enjambment**. Here is an example of end-stopped lines:

I long to hear love's gentle tune.
I only mourn it ends so soon.

Here is an example of enjambed lines:

Oh, to feel the soft, soft touch of spring
again, and the April softness it will bring!

Usually the poet tries only for a rhyme with one syllable, but many multisyllabic words are also useful as rhymes, like *September* and *remember, despair* and *aware*. During the centuries when most poets were concerned with rhyme they often looked for complicated rhymes to show off their skill with language. A famous example is the two-line poem the English poet John Dryden sent to a patron whose family name was Cadwallader. His patron had promised to send him a rabbit for supper, and when it did not appear, Dryden sent him a note in rhyme:

Oh thou son of great Cadwallader
Hast thou my hare, or hast thou swallowed her?

Rhymed Poems for Further Reading

As you read this selection of poems that have been brought together for their use of rhyme, you might want to identify the pattern of the rhyme, or **rhyme scheme**. One customary way of doing this is by marking the rhyming words with letters. If you look at the poem that opens the selection, Sir Thomas Wyatt's "They Flee from Me," you notice that the first and third lines rhyme, so you can designate them as *A*. The second, fourth, and fifth lines rhyme—though the fourth and fifth lines are near rhymes—so they can be designated as *B*. Finally, the last two lines of the stanza are a new perfect rhyme. This was a popular rhyme scheme in Wyatt's time, and it was given the name **rhyme royal**. Here is how the stanza looks if you add the letters to show the rhyming pattern the poet has chosen.

They flee from me, that sometimes did me *seek*, A
With naked foot stalking in my *chamber*. B
I have seen them, gentle, tame, and *meek*, A
That now are wild, and do not *remember* B
That sometime they put themselves in *danger* B
To take bread at my hand; and now they *range*, C
Busily seeking with a continual *change*. C

Our shorthand note for this would be to write that the poem has an *ABABBCC* rhyme scheme. The rhyme scheme for the second poem, Ben Jonson's "On My First Son," would be notated as *AABBCCDDEEFF*, even though lines 5–6 and 9–10 form near rhymes. You can make the same shorthand notes for the other poems.

Once you have worked your way through the rhyme schemes of the poems, however, you should go back and read them again for what they are telling you. We have to remember that rhyme, after all, is only a technical means to give the lines of the poem a structure and form, adding at the same time a pleasure in the musicality of the paired words. If as you read "They Flee from Me" you only noted the rhyme scheme, you would be missing the tenderness and erotic memories that fill this great love poem as Wyatt recalls the moments when women, like shy deer, came to his room, risking the "danger" of making love with him, which he terms "to take bread at his hand." He writes that now they have grown wilder and they range more freely. One moment he remembers above all the others, since the woman gave herself to him with such honesty. Both of them have gone on to look for other loves, but he would like to know what she has found.

Like "They Flee from Me," each of these poems tells its own story. In your second reading, allow that story to hold your interest.

SIR THOMAS WYATT

They Flee from Me

1557

They flee from me, that sometime did me seek,
With naked foot stalking in my chamber.
I have seen them, gentle, tame, and meek,
That now are wild, and do not remember
That sometime they put themselves in danger
To take bread at my hand; and now they range,
Busily seeking with a continual change.

Thanked be Fortune it hath been otherwise,
Twenty times better; but once in special,
In thin array, after a pleasant guise,
When her loose gown from her shoulders did fall,
And she me caught in her arms long and small,
And therewith all sweetly did me kiss
And softly said, "Dear heart, how like you this?"

It was no dream, I lay broad waking.
But all is turned, thorough° my gentleness, *through*
Into a strange fashion of forsaking;
And I have leave to go, of her goodness,
And she also to use newfangleness.
But since that I so kindely am served,
I fain would know what she hath deserved.

BEN JONSON

On My First Son 1616

Farewell, thou child of my right hand,° and joy;
My sin was too much hope of thee, loved boy:
Seven years thou'wert lent to me, and I thee pay,
Exacted by thy fate, on the just day.°
Oh, could I lose all father now! for why
Will man lament the state he should envy,
To have so soon 'scaped world's and flesh's rage,
And, if no other misery, yet age?
Rest in soft peace, and asked, say, "Here doth lie
Ben Jonson his best piece of poetry."
For whose sake henceforth all his vows be such
As what he loves may never like too much.

ROBERT HERRICK

To the Virgins, to Make Much of Time 1648

Gather ye rosebuds while ye may,
  Old time is still a-flying;
And this same flower that smiles today
  Tomorrow will be dying.

The glorious lamp of heaven, the sun,
  The higher he's a-getting,
The sooner will his race be run,
  And nearer he's to setting.

That age is best which is the first,
  When youth and blood are warmer;
But being spent, the worse, and worst
  Times still succeed the former.

Then be not coy, but use your time,
  And, while ye may, go marry;
For, having lost but once your prime,
  You may forever tarry.

---

1. child of my right hand: The literal translation of the Hebrew name *Benjamin*; Jonson's first son. **4. the just day:** A reference to Benjamin's death on his seventh birthday.

ROBERT BROWNING

A Woman's Last Word

1855

I

Let's contend no more, Love,
Strive nor weep:
All be as before, Love
—Only sleep!

II

What so wild as words are?
I and thou
In debate, as birds are,
Hawk on bough!

III

See the creature stalking
While we speak!
Hush and hide the talking,
Cheek on cheek!

IV

What so false as truth is,
False to thee?
Where the serpent's tooth is
Shun the tree—

V

Where the apple reddens
Never pry—
Lest we lose our Edens,
Eve and I.

VI

Be a god and hold me
With a charm!
Be a man and fold me
With thine arm!

VII

Teach me, only teach, Love.
As I ought
I will speak thy speech, Love,
Think thy thought—

VIII

Meet, if thou require it,
    Both demands,
Laying flesh and spirit
    In thy hands.

IX

That shall be to-morrow
    Not to-night:
I must bury sorrow
    Out of sight:

X

—Must a little weep, Love,
    (Foolish me!)
And so fall asleep, Love,
    Loved by thee.

e. e. cummings

when god lets my body be

1922

when god lets my body be
From each brave eye shall sprout a tree
fruit that dangles therefrom
the purpled world will dance upon
Between my lips which did sing
a rose shall beget the spring
that maidens whom passion wastes
will lay between their little breasts
My strong fingers beneath the snow
Into strenuous birds shall go
my love walking in the grass
their wings will touch with her face
and all the while shall my heart be
with the bulge and nuzzle of the sea

THEODORE ROETHKE

My Papa's Waltz

1948

The whiskey on your breath
Could make a small boy dizzy;
But I hung on like death:
Such waltzing was not easy.

We romped until the pans
Slid from the kitchen shelf;
My mother's countenance
Could not unfrown itself.

The hand that held my wrist
Was battered on one knuckle;
At every step you missed
My right ear scraped a buckle.

You beat time on my head
With a palm caked hard by dirt,
Then waltzed me off to bed
Still clinging to your shirt.

ANNE SEXTON

And One for My Dame°

1966

A born salesman,
my father made all his dough
By selling wool to Fieldcrest, Woolrich and Faribo.

A born talker,
he could sell one hundred wet-down bales
of that white stuff. He could clock the miles and sales

And One for My Dame: The title of the poem is from the children's rhyme "Trot, trot to Boston," and it was certainly suggested by the trips Sexton's traveling salesman father made to many of these same towns. Here is the entire rhyme, usually recited as a parent or caregiver bounces a child on his or her knee.

Trot, trot to Boston,
Trot, trot to Lynn,
Trot, trot to Marblehead
And all fall in.
Here's one for my master,
And one for my dame,
And one for the little girl (boy)
Who lives in the lane.

and make it pay.
At home each sentence he would utter
had first pleased the buyer who'd paid him off in butter.

Each word
had been tried over and over, at any rate,
on the man who was sold by the man who filled my plate.

My father hovered
over the Yorkshire pudding and the beef:
a peddler, a hawker, a merchant and an Indian chief.

Roosevelt! Wilkie! and war!
How suddenly gauche I was
with my old-maid heart and my funny teenage applause.

Each night at home
my father was in love with maps
while the radio fought its battles with Nazis and Japs.

Except when he hid
in his bedroom on a three-day drunk,
he typed out complex itineraries, packed his trunk,

his matched luggage
and pocketed a confirmed reservation,
his heart already pushing over the red routes of the nation.

DANA GIOIA

Summer Storm

2000

We stood on the rented patio
While the party went on inside.
You knew the groom from college.
I was a friend of the bride.

We hugged the brownstone wall behind us
To keep our dress clothes dry
And watched the sudden summer storm
Floodlit against the sky.

The rain was like a waterfall
Of brilliant beaded light,
Cool and silent as the stars
The storm hid from the night.

To my surprise, you took my arm—
A gesture you didn't explain—
And we spoke in whispers, as if we two
Might imitate the rain.

Then suddenly the storm receded
As swiftly as it came.
The doors behind us opened up.
The hostess called your name.

I watched you merge into the group,
Aloof and yet polite.
We didn't speak another word
Except to say goodnight.

Why does that evening's memory
Return with this night's storm—
A party twenty years ago,
Its disappointments warm?

There are so many *might have beens,*
What ifs that won't stay buried,
Other cities, other jobs,
Strangers we might have married.

And memory insists on pining
For places it never went,
As if life would be happier
Just by being different.

Rhyme and Popular Songs

Rhyme may not be as important for poetry today as it was for poets in earlier centuries, but it has never yielded its place in song lyrics. Perhaps that's because when you listen to a song you don't have a chance to go back and re-read a line you missed. The song's rhymes can help you follow what you are hearing.

Lou Reed is one of the composers, such as Bob Dylan, Randy Newman, and Phil Ochs, who brought a commitment to social engagement to their lyrics in the 1960s. Reed's song "Chelsea Girls" describes the rock groupies who hung out in the corridors of New York's Chelsea Hotel, one of the popular places for bands to stay when they were in town for a gig or a recording. As in most song lyrics, Reed's internal rhymes and end rhymes are shaped by his musical accompaniment, and he often uses near rhymes or slant rhymes for their sound.

LOU REED

Chelsea Girls

1967

Here's Room 506
It's enough to make you sick
Bridget's all wrapped in foil
You wonder if she can uncoil

Here they come now
See them run now
Here they come now
Chelsea Girls
Here's Room 115
Filled with S & M queens
Magic marker row
You wonder just how high they go
Here's Pope dear Ondine
Rona's treated him so mean
She wants another scene
She wants to be a human being

Pepper she's having fun
She thinks she's some man's son
Her perfect loves don't last
Her future died in someone's past
Here they come now
See them run now
Here they come now
Chelsea Girls

Dear Ingrid's found her lick
She's turned another trick
Her treats and times revolve
She's got problems to be solved
Poor Mary, she's uptight
She can't turn out her light
She rolled Susan in a ball
and now she can't see her at all

Dropout, she's in a fix
amphetamine has made her sick
white powder in the air
She's got no bones and can't be scared

Here comes Johnny Bore
He collapsed on the floor
They shot him up with milk
And when he died sold him for silk
Here they come now
See them run now
Here they come now
Chelsea Girls

Rhyme in Traditional Folk Blues

It was their use of rhyme that gave the early folk blues their distinctive form and also helped the singers structure their verses. Fifty years ago J. D. Short, one of the first generation of Mississippi delta bluesmen, sat holding his guitar in his apartment above Delmar Avenue in St. Louis, his expression thoughtful as he went back in his memory to the traditional songs he remembered from his boyhood in Port Gibson, Mississippi.

> "Well, that song was—actually, I heard that song about 1907—'The Slidin' Delta.' That was an awful slow train down through Mississippi, they called it the Slidin' Delta. Now I just don't exactly know what towns it went through but the older people partially knowed. I didn't know because I was a small kid, but I heard them singin' about the Slidin' Delta."
>
> "Why was it called that?"
>
> A laugh, "Well, it means 'bout the train it's so slow until it almost slides, like a turtle!"

J. D. SHORT

Slidin' Delta

1907

Ohoo, Slidin' Delta done been here and gone,
        Hear me cryin' I ain't got no one.
Ohoo, Slidin' Delta done been here and gone,
That made me think about my baby, ohoo.

Oh, early this morning, creepin' through my door,
        Now don't you hear me cryin', pretty mama.
Early this morning, creepin' through my door,
I heard that whistle blow and she won't blow here no more.

Oh, slow down, train, now bring my baby back home,
        Now don't you hear me cryin', pretty mama.
Slow down, train, bring my baby back home,
Well, she been gone so long, ooh, make my poor heart burn.

One thing now I don't understand,
        Now don't you hear me cryin', pretty mama.
One thing now I don't understand,
I make nice to my baby, ooh, she gone with another man.

Ooh, thought I heard a freight train whistle blow,
        Now don't you hear me cryin', pretty mama.
Thought I heard a freight train whistle blow,
And she blowed back oo-hoo-yooho-yooho.

Oh run here, mama, sit down on my knees,
        Now don't you hear me cryin', pretty mama.
Run here, mama, and sit down on my knees,
I want to understand now, baby, how you treat poor me.

Now come home, baby, come to me,
        You know I'm your man to be.
Oh come on home, come on home to me,
You know I need your lovin' just like a man can be.

Topics for Writing about Rhyme

It might seem that rhyme would be an elusive subject to write about, but here are some ways to think about rhyme that can be helpful for planning a paper.

1. Write an essay on how rhyme works in a poem. Select a rhymed poem from the examples in the textbook and explain why the poem interests you. You can analyze the poem's rhyme scheme and list the rhymes with their alphabetical equivalents—*AABBCC*—or whatever is the rhyme scheme of the poem you selected. You will make it easier for yourself if you choose a poem of more than two or three stanzas, since you'll find interesting variations that you can comment on as you write your paper. Once you have worked out your general outline, go into some detail on the rhymes themselves. If they are near rhymes, illustrate the effect by commenting on the rhyming words. If enjambment helps create the poem's rhyme scheme, you should describe it.
2. Collect some interesting examples of alliteration and onomatopoeia from your reading and discuss how the sounds of words work in the poems you have selected.
3. If you'd like to take as a subject for your paper the still-continuing debate about the value of poetry that rhymes and of poetry that doesn't, look at the first stanza of a classic poem by Emily Dickinson that was published in the first edition of her poems with an irregular use of rhyme, just as she wrote it. The entire poem, "I taste a liquor never brewed," is on page 846 of your text. The original first stanza as it appeared in 1891 was

   I taste a liquor never brewed
   From tankards scooped in pearl.
   Not all the vats upon the Rhine
   Yield such an alcohol.

   If you read Thomas Bailey Aldrich's commentary on Dickinson and her poetry on page 857, you will see a "correction" that this conventional poet of the time wrote for his review of her book. To emphasize his point that Dickinson was lacking in poetical skills, Aldrich offered his own version of her stanza:

   I taste a liquor never brewed
   In vats upon the Rhine;
   No tankard ever held a draught
   Of alcohol like mine.

   For your paper you could describe the differences between the two versions and make a judgment yourself as to which version is more effective. A question you might also discuss is whether Dickinson would have considered "pearl" and "alcohol" a slant rhyme?
4. Although many poets don't use rhyme in their writing today, rhymed poetry will always play an important role in the history of literature in virtually every culture and language. Write an essay analyzing the perennial appeal of rhyme for readers of poetry.

USEFUL TERMS TO REMEMBER

Alliteration The repetition of the same consonant sounds beginning each word in a sequence of words.

Assonance The repetition of internal vowel sounds without the repetition of consonant sounds used as an alternative to rhyme in verse to create an aural unity within a poetic line or sequence of lines.

End rhyme Lines of a poem that end in words that rhyme.

Enjambment A poetic line whose meaning is not complete at the end but continues on without pause to the next line. This is also called a *run-on line.*

Exact rhyme or perfect rhyme Words that share the same stressed vowel sounds as well as the sounds that follow the vowel.

Eye rhyme Words that appear to be similarly spelled, but are differently pronounced.

Internal rhyme Words that rhyme within a line of poetry.

Near rhyme or slant rhyme The sound of the rhyming words is close but not exact.

Onomatopoeia A term referring to the use of a word that resembles the sound it denotes.

Rhyme The repetition of similar or identical terminal sounds of concluding syllables in different words, usually at the ends of lines.

Rhyme scheme The pattern of the rhymes in a poem.

11.

Poetic Meter

Tick, tick, tick, what little iambics,
While Homer and Whitman roared in the pines?
–EDGAR LEE MASTERS, from "Petit, the Poet," 1915

In the same way that writers heard the *sounds* of words and with these sounds created the kaleidoscopic, ever-changing world of rhyme, they also heard the *rhythms* of words and from these rhythms came the bulging storehouse of **poetic meter**, the term we use to describe the rhythms of poetry. If you can remember some of the rhymes that were sung to you when you were a child, can you still feel the rhythm of a phrase like "ba ba black sheep"? When you think of a crowd at a football game, how many times have you heard a chant like "De-Fense! De-Fense!" shouted over and over again? The rhythms of words are as much a part of the words as their sound.

As we begin our discussion of poetic meter, many of you will already be aware from your reading that the same turmoil we found in our study of rhyme also changed the story of meter. The storms of history that shook the world at the beginning of the twentieth century affected the rhythms of poetry in the same way as they did the venerable traditions of rhyme. Meter had been an integral part of the history of poetry for even longer periods than rhyme, though later it would be rhyme that was considered the sign that what you were reading was a poem. As the world changed, however, the barriers of privilege and tradition were falling, and in our Western societies it was the poets who were in the vanguard of the changes in literature and in our lives as well. Within only a few decades after their first challenges to rhyme and meter, the poets could proclaim that at last verse was free!

When a struggle of such decisive literary impact is lost, we don't often hear the loser's side, but you can sense the weary defeat in the lines from a poem published in 1915 that opens the chapter, "Tick, tick, tick, what little iambics / While Homer and Whitman roared in the pines?"

"What little iambics"—measures of formal poetic meter—the speaker of the poem ridicules as he thinks of the careful, orderly poems he has spent his life writing. As Petit looks back at his life, he realizes that he has wasted his chance to write the great poems of his dreams. As his name suggests, he was too cautious, too timid; he let the weight of tradition smother him. In his disappointment he names some of the most elegantly composed poetic forms, "Triolets, villanelles, rondels, rondeaus, / Ballades," only to dismiss them as more of the same outmoded conventions.

EDGAR LEE MASTERS

Petit, the Poet

1915

Seeds in a dry pod, tick, tick, tick,
Tick, tick, tick, like mites in a quarrel—
Faint iambics that the full breeze wakens—
But the pine tree makes a symphony thereof.
Triolets, villanelles, rondels, rondeaus,
Ballades by the score with the same old thought:
The snows and the roses of yesterday are vanished;
And what is love but a rose that fades?
Life all around me here in the village:
Tragedy, comedy, valor and truth,
Courage, constancy, heroism, failure—
All in the loom, and oh what patterns!
Woodlands, meadows, streams and rivers—
Blind to all of it all my life long.
Triolets, villanelles, rondels, rondeaus,
Seeds in a dry pod, tick, tick, tick,
Tick, tick, tick, what little iambics,
While Homer and Whitman roared in the pines?

If you only read poetry written in your own time, it might not seem meaningful to understand the imagination and the inventiveness that shaped the meters and rhythmic forms of traditional verse. In your study of the uses that poets have made of the rhythms of words, however, you will learn more about words themselves. What you are reading and discussing can be a resource for your own writing.

ACCENT AND METER

In the previous chapter, you learned the difference between masculine and feminine rhyme, which depends on where the **accent** comes on the strong syllable in a word when it is spoken. The accents of the words in each sentence or phrase give the poem its rhythm. All words with more than one syllable have at least one strong accent. The other syllables are called weak accents. Sometimes the terms used are **stressed** and **unstressed**, but they refer to the same pattern of accented and unaccented syllables.

A technical note: You should remember that one-syllable words like *a, the,* and *an,* which are called articles, generally are weak, unless we want to emphasize them. One of the most common of these effects is a phrase like "There was THE Elvis Presley, standing in our supermarket line!" This same rule applies to one-syllable prepositions like *at, from, by, with,* and *of,* and the conjunctions *and* and *but*.

One-syllable words like *I* and *me* are more complicated in their usage. You will find that all of these words can have strong or weak accents, depending on the words around them. Some short words have two strong accents: *uptight* is an example. Longer words can have complex patterns of strong and weak accents. Some, like *disenchanted,* stride briskly along alternating strong and weak accents; others, like *encyclopedia,* dance to a rhythm all their own.

´ ˘ ´ ˘
dis en chant ed

The pattern for *encyclopedia* would be

˘ ˘ ˘ ´ ˘ ˘
en cy clo pe di a

It will help you in your study of poetic meter if you mark the pattern of accents or stresses in a line of poetry that you are reading. Thinking through the meter will help you understand how the line achieves its effect, and it is a skill you should practice. You should practice it, however, by copying the poem into a notebook or into your computer. If you mark the poem on the page of your text, you will never be able to see the poem without its accent markings, and they will become small pricks that catch at your eye when you should be thinking about the meaning and the language of the poem. The term for this kind of analysis is **scansion**, and what you are doing is scanning the poem.

The pattern set up by a regular rhythm of words in a poem is called **meter**. To establish a pattern of meter, we need a line of more than one or two accents; so we will need to have at least three words to establish a meter. In some poems you will find you have to follow the pattern of accents all the way to the end of the poem to decide what the meter is.

The meters you will be studying all have names, based on what is called a **foot**. A foot is one unit of the rhythmic pattern that makes up the meter. This may sound as if you've just gone around in a circle, but it makes good sense if you write down a line of the poem and mark it with the symbols for stressed and unstressed (or accented and unaccented) syllables. Here is an example from a sonnet by William Shakespeare.

˘ ´ ˘ ´ ˘ ´ ˘ ´ ˘ ´
So oft | have I | invok'd | thee for | my muse

If you read the line aloud, the first syllable *So* is unaccented, so the pattern of weak and strong accents is weak-strong, weak-strong, weak-strong, weak-strong, weak-strong—and as you can see, the foot is marked off with the symbol |. A rhythm based on a foot of one weak and one strong syllable is called an **iamb**, and the rhythm is called **iambic meter**. It is close to the rhythms of our everyday speech, and it is one of the building blocks of poetry written in English.

What happens if you reverse the pattern of accents, and you have a line that shifts the initial stress on the first syllable?

Does he | ev er | won der | where I | am?

Here the pattern is strong-weak, strong-weak, strong-weak, strong-weak, strong. This metrical foot is called a **trochee**, and the name for its pattern of accents is **trochaic meter**.

Here are two examples by writers from the period when every poet was expected to be a skilled master of meter and rhyme. The first of the poems, written in iambic meter, is by Mary Coleridge, a great niece of the romantic poet Samuel Taylor Coleridge. To help you in understanding the meter, the accents of the first stanza are marked.

MARY COLERIDGE

A Clever Woman

1908

You thought I had the strength of men,
Because with men I dared to speak,
And courted Science now and then,
And studied Latin for a week;
But woman's woman, even when
She reads her Ethics in the Greek.

You thought me wiser than my kind;
You thought me "more than common tall";
You thought because I had a mind,
That I could have no heart at all;
But woman's woman you will find,
Whether she be great or small.

The second example is a vivid picture drawn from the nature of his native New England by the poet and philosopher Ralph Waldo Emerson. It was certainly the first word of the poem, *burly*, which is pronounced with the accent on the first syllable, that suggested to him that trochaic meter would best suit his description of an intrusive bee. The accents of the first stanza are marked as in the first example. The meter flows smoothly without a break, though you will be surprised by an old-fashioned way of spelling *Puerto Rico*.

RALPH WALDO EMERSON

From "The Humble Bee"

1839

Burly, dozing, humble-bee,
Where thou art is clime for me.
Let them sail for Porto Rique,
Far-off heats through seas to seek;
I will follow thee alone,
Thou animated torrid-zone!
Zigzag steerer, desert cheerer,
Let me chase thy waving lines;
Keep me nearer, me thy hearer,
Singing over shrubs and vines.

Insect lover of the sun,
Joy of thy dominion!
Sailor of the atmosphere;
Swimmer through the waves of air,
Voyager of light and noon;
Epicurean of June;
Wait, I prithee, till I come
Within earshot of thy hum,—
All without is martyrdom.

One of the best-known and universally loved American poets of the nineteenth century was Harvard professor Henry Wadsworth Longfellow. An important factor in his immense popularity was his use of distinctive poetic meters in long narratives that brought to life episodes in American history. His lines were meant to be declaimed aloud, and even reading them silently today you sometimes find your lips moving to the rhythmic cadences. One of his greatest successes was his tale of the Indian maid Hiawatha. To suggest the rhythm of Native American drumbeats, Longfellow employed insistent, drumming trochees.

He left his lines without rhyme, as though he intended to emphasize the effect of hearing the sound of the drumbeats through the echoes of the forest. His book-length poem, titled *The Song of Hiawatha,* was tightly structured, with each line composed with four strong accents, which is the meter known as trochaic tetrameter. The lines end with a feminine cadence. Here is a section from the poem's first pages, with the opening lines marked with the pattern of accents.

HENRY WADSWORTH LONGFELLOW

From *The Song of Hiawatha* 1855

Should you ask me, whence these stories?
Whence these legends and traditions,
With the odors of the forest,
With the dew and damp of meadows,
With the curling smoke of wigwams,
With the rushing of great rivers,
With their frequent repetitions,
And their wild reverberations,
As of thunder on the mountains?

I should answer, I should tell you,
"From the forests and the prairies,
From the great lakes of the Northland,
From the land of the Ojibways,
From the land of the Dacotahs,
From the mountains, moors, and fen-lands
Where the herons, the Shuh-shuh-gah°
Feeds among the reeds and rushes.
I repeat them as I heard them. . . ."

Two other rhythmic patterns are commonly found in poetry written during this period when the writer wanted to tell a story. The first is a rhythmic

Shuh-shuh-gah: The blue heron, from the Ojibway language.

foot of two unaccented syllables followed by a strong syllable. An example would be

˘ ˘ ´ ˘ ˘ ´ ˘ ˘ ´ ˘ ˘ ´
By the sea, | by the sea, | by the beau | ti ful sea.

The foot is called an **anapest**, and the line produces **anapestic meter**. The other foot reverses this pattern, and we have a strong syllable followed by two weak syllables:

´ ˘ ˘ ´ ˘ ˘ ´ ˘ ˘ ´
Down by the | sea, by the | beau ti ful | sea.

This foot is called a **dactyl** and its meter is **dactylic**.

As you begin using these terms for different meters, you should remember that poets usually do not follow the meters consistently through the entire poem. When the meter never varies, the poem may be considered too "sing-song." If you read through a poem and find that most of its lines are in one meter, then you will say that the poem is iambic or dactylic, trochaic or anapestic, depending on whichever rhythm is used most often in the poem. If you're scanning the poem, then you call any foot that is not part of the overall meter by its own name. You will also find that in some lines there is a break in the meter. It starts and stops somewhere within the line. This is called a **caesura**, and it is an important term to remember because it will help you sort through some of the meters of more complex lines. The symbol for a caesura is | |.

You will usually have some help in recognizing the caesura. There will often be punctuation—a period, a colon, or a semicolon. Even a comma can be enough to tell you that there is a break in the rhythm. In this poem by Christina Rossetti, the caesura is indicated by the question marks at the end the first phrase of each line.

CHRISTINA ROSSETTI

What are heavy? sea-sand and sorrow

before 1874

What are heavy? sea-sand and sorrow:
What are brief? to-day and to-morrow:
What are frail? Spring blossoms and youth:
What are deep? the ocean and truth.

Sometimes you will also find in your reading that there is an unstressed syllable at the beginning of a line that does not affect the overall meter. The term for this is an **anacrusis**. As an additional aid in describing poetic meter, you can use different terms for describing the length of the lines. These terms are derived from the Greek for almost all of the conceivable line lengths:

monometer is a line of one foot
dimeter, a line of two feet
trimeter, three feet

tetrameter, four feet
pentameter, five feet
hexameter, six feet
heptameter, seven feet
octameter, eight feet

Most of the poetry written in regular meter uses one of the shorter line lengths—three, four, or five strong syllables. Poems, however, have been written in all of these meters. One of the most famous poems from the nineteenth century, "The Raven" by Edgar Allan Poe, is an example of composition using an eight-syllable line. It is written with a strong-weak pattern of accents, which means that the technical term for the meter of the poem is *trochaic octameter*. Here is the poem's opening line.

Once up | on a | midnight | dreary, | while I | pondered | weak and | weary

There are two more variations in the meter of a line you may encounter in your reading. Two strong accents together are called a **spondee**, and two weak accents are called a **pyrrhus**. There are also some further refinements of the terms for poetic meter. We use the term **rising meter** for the two feet that begin with a weak syllable, iambic and anapestic, and the term **falling meter** for the two feet that begin with a strong syllable, trochaic and dactylic.

BLANK VERSE

Probably the most durable and richly varied meter in the English language is **iambic pentameter**, and if the lines are unrhymed, the term for them is **blank verse**. Shakespeare used this form of meter for the majestic language of his plays, but it was also a useful idiom for longer poetic narratives. Elizabeth Barrett Browning used blank verse for her novel-length feminist biography *Aurora Leigh*. Here are the opening lines.

ELIZABETH BARRETT BROWNING

I write. 1857

I write. My mother was a Florentine,
Whose rare blue eyes were shut from seeing me
When scarcely I was four years old, my life
A poor spark snatched up from a failing lamp
Which went out therefore. She was weak and frail;
She could not bear the joy of giving life,
The mother's rapture slew her. If her kiss
Had left a longer weight upon my lips
It might have steadied the uneasy breath,
And reconciled and fraternized my soul

With the new order. As it was, indeed,
I felt a mother-want about the world,
And still went seeking, like a bleating lamb
Left out at night in shutting up the fold,—
As restless as a nest-deserted bird
Grown chill through something being away, though what
It knows not. I, Aurora Leigh, was born
To make my father sadder, and myself
Not overjoyous, truly. Women know
The way to rear up children (to be just),
They know a simple, merry, tender knack
Of tying sashes, fitting baby-shoes,
And stringing pretty words that make no sense,
And kissing full sense into empty words,
Which things are corals to cut life upon,
Although such trifles: children learn by such,
Love's holy earnest in a pretty play. . . .

THE STANZA

As you review what you have studied about poetic meter and its role in structuring the words in a poem, you should also remember that meter is one of the important elements of the **stanza** in traditional poetry. As poets in the nineteenth century turned from lengthy epics and verse narratives to the intimacy of lyric poetry on personal themes, the use of meter continued to play an important role in their writing, even if the lines were written in a more conversational tone. It was meter that helped to give shape to the short stanzas that became the most popular forms of the new poetry. An example of the use of the metrical pattern repeated from stanza to stanza is the poem "Life" by the American poet Paul Laurence Dunbar. In his first stanza, he employs a conventional blend of metric forms to give a more relaxed tone to the poem, but each of the lines is composed with four accents and rhymed with a falling cadence. As a contrast, in an abrupt interjection in the stanza's final line, Dunbar answers his own description of his life's events with an interruption that is only two accents in length and ends on a rising cadence. You will notice that for the second stanza Dunbar repeats four accents of each line, but he has slightly altered the pattern of accents to achieve a more flexible conversational tone.

PAUL LAURENCE DUNBAR

Life

1896

˘ ´ ˘ ´ ˘ ˘ ´ ˘ ˘ ´ ˘
A crust of bread and a corner to sleep in,
˘ ´ ˘ ˘ ´ ˘ ˘ ´ ˘ ˘ ´ ˘
A minute to smile and an hour to weep in,

A pint of joy to a peck of trouble,
And never a laugh when moans come double:
  And that is life!

A crust and a corner that love makes precious,
With the smile to warm and the tears to refresh us:
And joy seems sweeter when care comes after,
And a moan is the finest of foils for laughter,
  And that is life!

Poems for Further Reading

THOMAS HOOD

From *The Bridge of Sighs* 1841

One more Unfortunate,
  Weary of breath,
Rashly importunate,
  Gone to her death!

Take her up tenderly
  Lift her with care;
Fashion'd so slenderly,
  Young, and so fair!

Look at her garments
Clinging like cerements;
Whilst the wave constantly
  Drips from her clothing;
Take her up instantly,
  Loving, not loathing.

Touch her not scornfully;
Think of her mournfully,
  Gently and humanly;
Not of the stains of her,
All that remains of her
  Now is pure womanly.

Make no deep scrutiny
Into her mutiny

Rash and undutiful:
Past all dishonor,
Death has left on her
Only the beautiful. . . .

Take her up tenderly,
Lift her with care;
Fashion'd so slenderly,
Young, and so fair! . . .

Owning° her weakness, *admitting*
Her evil behaviour,
And leaving, with meekness,
Her sins to her Saviour!

MARY COLERIDGE

Eyes 1908

Eyes, what are they? Coloured glass,
Where reflections come and pass.

Open windows — by them sit
Beauty, Learning, Love, and Wit.

Searching cross-examiners;
Comfort's holy ministers.

Starry silences of soul,
Music past the lips' control.

Fountains of unearthly light;
Prisons of the infinite.

THOMAS HARDY

I need not go 1901

I need not go
Through sleet and snow
To where I know
She waits for me;
She will tarry me there
Till I find it fair,
And have time to spare
From company.

When I've overgot
The world somewhat,
When things cost not
Such stress and strain,
Is soon enough
By cypress sough
To tell my Love
I am come again.

And if some day,
When none cries nay,
I still delay
To seek her side,
(Though ample measure
Of fitting leisure
Await my pleasure)
She will not chide.

What—not upbraid me
That I delay'd me,
Nor ask what stay'd me
So long? Ah, no!—
New cares may claim me.
New loves inflame me,
She will not blame me,
But suffer it so.

◆ Topics for Writing about Poetic Meter ◆

1. Choose one of the poems in this chapter and analyze its meter, noting whether the meter is irregular in any places. Once you have described the poem's meter, discuss how the meter helps the poem achieve its effect.
2. The poems for further study include examples of different meters. You can identify each of the meters represented and discuss how the author uses it in the poem.
3. Are there verses you remember from your childhood that have distinctive rhythms like "Trot, trot to Boston"? Do their rhythms help you remember the verses? In your discussion you can suggest how the rhythm of a poem helps keep it in your mind.
4. Although blank verse flourished as the language of the stage nearly five hundred years ago, there are actors and actresses today who still speak the lines of blank verse with artistry and conviction. Discuss why this theatrical language is still part of our tradition today, yet only rarely used by modern playwrights.

USEFUL TERMS TO REMEMBER

Accent The strong syllable, or syllables, in a word; the emphasis or stress given a syllable in pronunciation.

Anapest, anapestic meter Two weak accents followed by a strong accent.

Blank verse Unrhymed lines written in iambic pentameter.

Caesura A break in the meter in the middle of a line.

Dactyl, dactylic meter A strong accent followed by two weak accents.

Falling meter Meters that go from a strong to a weak accent: the trochee and the dactyl.

Foot A measure of a metric unit.

Iamb, iambic meter A weak accent followed by a strong accent.

Pyrrhus A foot of two weak syllables.

Rising meter Meters that go from a weak to a strong accent: the iamb and the anapest.

Scansion The process of examining a poem to determine its meter.

Spondee A foot of two strong syllables.

Stanza A series of lines whose pattern of rhyme and meter is followed by a similar series of lines.

Stressed syllables Syllables that have a strong emphasis when spoken.

Trochee, trochaic meter A strong accent followed by a weak accent.

Unstressed syllables Syllables that have a weak emphasis when spoken.

12.

The Meaning of Words

No tears for the writer, no tears for the reader. No surprise for the writer, no surprise for the reader.

–ROBERT FROST, from the introduction to *Collected Poems*, 1939

Most of the time you use words without thinking of the way they shape rhyme or meter, but you don't ever use words without being conscious of what they mean. Poets work with the meaning of words to enrich their writing in many ways. The general term for these adventures in language is figures of speech or **figurative language**. Some of them, like **simile** and **metaphor**, will be familiar to you; others, such as **personification** and **apostrophe** or **metonymy** and **synecdoche**, may not be so familiar. In your close reading of a poem, even before you begin to analyze the way the poet has used figurative language, you can't help noticing the overall tone of the language. It is used not only for describing the words of a poem but also for the language you encounter while close reading a short story or a longer prose work. **Tone** is the way that writers convey their unstated attitudes toward what they have written, attitudes that may not appear on the surface of the writing itself. These unstated attitudes may include the use of **irony**, when you become aware that the poet says one thing but means the opposite.

Tone

We are all familiar with the differences in tone in the things we say to each other in our everyday speech. The same words will mean entirely different things, depending on the tone of our voice when we say them. When a mother or father says admiringly to a young child, "You're so smart!" they will use an entirely different tone from the derisive cry of an angry classmate's voice when he or she says the same words, "You're so smart." So much of what we say to each other is shaded by our tone of voice and expression that we become accustomed to reading each other's intentions by responding to the tone of how something is said.

A poem presents us with a wide range of choices, but unless we are hearing the poem read aloud, we will have to look for the poem's meaning in the tone of its language. The words on the page will have to suggest enough for us to understand what the poet is trying to express. When we read these lines,

> What high, bright hopes
> her shining spirit brings!

we know from the words *high, bright,* and *shining* that the tone of the poem is positive and admiring. We would read the poem aloud with a strong, respectful tone. When we read these next lines, however, we immediately respond to a different tone.

> Whatever you thought you were doing,
> my love, it wasn't enough for me,
> Whatever you thought you were feeling,
> it wasn't, it wasn't,
> oh lord,
> it wasn't enough for me.

In the querulous phrase "whatever you thought you were doing," we hear a tone of exasperation and impatience, and if we read the lines aloud we find ourselves, almost without thinking, shaking our heads.

A poet's tone can convey complex emotions about world events as well as personal ones. Here is a poem written in 1918 by the American poet and folk singer Carl Sandburg. The Armistice in November of that year would finally bring to an end the most deadly war in human history up to that time, and the victims of the war were still being buried when Sandburg began to write his poem. There were many things he could have said about the slaughter that had left a generation of Europe's and America's young men and women dead on the battlefields and in the ruined cities, but the *tone* of his poem tells us immediately what he is feeling.

You will find no anger in Sandburg's lines and no patriotic sentiments describing the deaths as heroic or even necessary. What you read in his tone is a sad darkness, a resignation in the face of war's realities. Sandburg is saying that this all has happened before, and in the final lines he makes you aware that he knows it will happen again. The battles he names left their mark on history for their number of casualties. Two of the battles, Austerlitz and Waterloo, were waged in the Napoleonic wars in Europe. Gettysburg was a bitter, decisive struggle in the American Civil War. The campaigns in the trenches of Ypres and Verdun had raged in the First World War. What names of battles could you add to his list from the wars that have been fought since that first World War ended?

CARL SANDBURG
Grass 1918

Pile the bodies high at Austerlitz and Waterloo.
Shovel them under and let me work—
I am the grass; I cover all.

And pile them high at Gettysburg
And pile them high at Ypres and Verdun.
Shovel them under and let me work,
Two years, ten years, and passengers ask the conductor:
What place is this?
Where are we now?

I am the grass.
Let me work.

In the next two poems by the American poet Edwin Arlington Robinson, you will find an entirely different tone. Robinson has described the lives of two men, lives that seem familiar to us, but beneath their bland surface they are confused and defeated. One has become a drunkard because of his inability to accustom himself to a prosaic world so different from his vision of the noble pageantry and vivid colors of medieval chivalry. The other has hidden his depression under an unfailing gentlemanly appearance. The tone of both poems is mocking and ironic.

In "Miniver Cheevy," Robinson has employed a change in the meter of his lines to underline his comment about the character in the poem. To emphasize the contrast between Cheevy's dreams and his everyday reality, the poet has shortened the line, abruptly ending each stanza, almost as though he were dismissing Cheevy's fantasies with an impatient shrug. In the second poem, "Richard Cory," the shock of the unexpected ending sends us back to the beginning of the poem to read it again with new understanding.

EDWIN ARLINGTON ROBINSON
Miniver Cheevy 1910

Miniver Cheevy, child of scorn,
Grew lean while he assailed the seasons;
He wept that he was ever born,
And he had reasons.

Miniver loved the days of old
When swords were bright and steeds were prancing;
The vision of a warrior bold
Would set him dancing.

Miniver sighed for what was not,
And dreamed, and rested from his labors;
He dreamed of Thebes° and Camelot,°
And Priam's° neighbors.

Miniver mourned the ripe renown
That made so many a name so fragrant;
He mourned Romance, now on the town,
And Art, a vagrant.

Miniver loved the Medici,°
Albeit he had never seen one;
He would have sinned incessantly
Could he have been one.

Miniver cursed the commonplace
And eyed a khaki suit with loathing;
He missed the medieval grace
Of iron clothing.

Miniver scorned the gold he sought,
But sore annoyed was he without it;
Miniver thought, and thought, and thought,
And thought about it.

Miniver Cheevy, born too late,
Scratched his head and kept on thinking;
Miniver coughed, and called it fate,
And kept on drinking.

Richard Cory 1897

Whenever Richard Cory went down town,
We people on the pavement looked at him:
He was a gentleman from sole to crown,
Clean favored, and imperially slim.

And he was always quietly arrayed,
And he was always human when he talked;
But still he fluttered pulses when he said,
"Good-morning," and he glittered when he walked.

And he was rich—yes, richer than a king—
And admirably schooled in every grace:
In fine, we thought that he was everything
To make us wish that we were in his place.

---

11. Thebes: Ancient city of Greece; also, ancient city on the Nile River in Egypt. **Camelot:** The kingdom of King Arthur and legendary seat of the Knights of the Round Table in Britain. **12. Priam's:** Priam was the father of Hector and Paris and king of Troy during the Trojan War. **17. Medici:** The ruling family of Florence, Italy, from the fifteenth to the eighteenth century.

So on we worked, and waited for the light,
And went without the meat, and cursed the bread;
And Richard Cory, one calm summer night,
Went home and put a bullet through his head.

WORDS AND THEIR MEANING

All writers are conscious of their language, but since poets must think about the sound and the rhythm of every word they choose, they are even more conscious of the subtleties of meaning in what they write. Robinson deliberately created short, elegant, ironic poems to chronicle the wasted human potential of two ordinary men. Poets are also continually on the lookout for new and unexpected words to express their ideas. One of the most popular poems of the nineteenth century is "Jabberwocky" by Lewis Carroll. As though he were consciously making fun of this concern of poets to find something new, or simply mocking their despair at having continually to count meters and create rhyme, Carroll brilliantly invented words to create a nonsense poem. Readers ever since have been trying to decide what its meanings may be. It is ironic that one of the odd words Carroll invented, *chortle*, quickly became part of the language.

LEWIS CARROLL

Jabberwocky° 1871

'Twas brillig, and the slithy toves
  Did gyre and gimble in the wabe;
All mimsy were the borogoves,
  And the mome raths outgrabe.

"Beware the Jabberwock, my son!
  The jaws that bite, the claws that catch!
Beware the Jubjub bird, and shun
  The frumious Bandersnatch!"

He took his vorpal sword in hand;
  Long time the manxome foe he sought—
So rested he by the Tumtum tree,
  And stood awhile in thought.

And, as in uffish thought he stood,
  The Jabberwock, with eyes of flame,
Came whiffling through the tulgey wood,
  And burbled as it came!

Jabberwocky: Meaningless speech or writing. This poem is from the first chapter of Carroll's *Through the Looking Glass*.

One, two! One, two! And through and through
  The vorpal blade went snicker-snack!
He left it dead, and with its head
  He went galumphing back.

"And hast thou slain the Jabberwock?
  Come to my arms, my beamish boy!
O frabjous day! Callooh! Callay!"
  He chortled in his joy.

'Twas brillig, and the slithy toves
  Did gyre and gimble in the wabe;
All mimsy were the borogoves,
  And the mome raths outgrabe.

Denotative and Connotative Meaning

The meanings of many words may seem to be simple and direct, but other words have associations that affect the way we understand them. To describe them we use two terms. The first is **denotative**, or what a word denotes. By this we mean what the dictionary tells us the word means. The second term is **connotative**. By this we mean the associations that have built up around the word. As an example, we can take the word *sweat*.

> The *denotative* meaning, which we find in the dictionary: "Moisture exuded from the skin, perspiration."
>
> The *connotative* meaning, which we understand from hearing the word used around us: "hard work."

You have probably used the word with this meaning many times yourself. Someone asks you if you will do something for them, and you answer, "No sweat." What you have just said, though you have shortened it considerably, is "Doing what you have asked me to do will be so easy for me that I won't even perspire while I'm doing it." What you imply in the connotative meaning is that for you it will be an easy job. Why did you use the connotations of the word *sweat*? For the same reasons a writer uses connotations. These suggested or implied meanings make our language more varied and rich. In "Jabberwocky," Carroll often depends on your sensitivity to the connotation of the nonsense words he uses, such as the words "beamish boy" to suggest a boy beaming with happiness.

Diction

When we speak of **diction**, we are describing the language that a writer has chosen to use in the poem. As you read a poem, you can try to decide why one word was chosen and not another one that may have the same meaning. What you will have to consider is how the word sounds, how it fits into the poem's rhyme scheme, as well as the effect it has on the meter of the poem.

Another term was associated with the idea of diction in poetry for hundreds of years. When people discussed a poem's diction they meant a special kind of language that was called **poetic diction**. Poetry was considered such a refined art that you could only use refined words in writing it. Everyday language and slang were considered too raw for the lines of elegant verse. In the words of the poet and critic Samuel Johnson, who also compiled the first dictionary of the English language in the late eighteenth century, poetic diction was "a system of words refined from the grossness of domestic use." In the garbled diction of "Jabberwocky," Carroll could also have been poking fun at the elevated language in many poems written by his Victorian contemporaries.

Syntax

Syntax is derived from the Greek word "to arrange together." It refers to the order of the words in writing of any kind, not only poetry. A change in natural word order can affect the way we hear or read any kind of phrase or sentence. In poetry, where each word bears so much weight, any change becomes significant. Poets will sometimes spend as much time deciding the order of the words as they do deciding on what words to use in the first place. For anyone using the traditional poetic forms, which meant rhyme and meter, the most common decision about word order was often forced on the writer by the need to find a rhyme.

Imagery

We are all familiar with the familiar, denotative meaning of the word *image*. It means the physical appearance of something. If we say that someone is the image of her mother, we mean that she looks just like her. If you are talking about an image in a poem, however, the word has different connotations. You don't, in a literal sense, see something in a poem; you just read about it. What you call an image in poetry can be a concrete description of something that you can see, hear, or touch. There are terms to describe each of these three kinds of images: **visual images** (things you can see), **aural images** (things you can hear), and **tactile images** (things you can touch). If you were to write "an old, dark green convertible," that would be a visual image. If you went on to describe the convertible's "noisy, rattling roar," that would be an aural image. If you could imagine yourself sitting behind the wheel and feeling "the prickly upholstery" of the seat, that would be a tactile image.

Why have these images always been part of a writer's working tools? They are indispensible because they make us feel that what the poet is writing about is real. Our information about the world comes through our senses, which assemble what we see, hear, and touch as an explanation for what it is we are experiencing. Poems often include words like *beauty* and *truth*, but we don't consider them images. No matter how intensely we may feel about them, they have no concrete reality. The term we use for words like these is **abstractions**. If you are talking about the physical images in a poem, the word used to describe them is **imagery**.

In "The Bight," the American poet Elizabeth Bishop describes what she is seeing with vivid intensity, and her poem is constructed around concrete visual images. For your first reading of her poem, it will help you to know that a *bight* is a small bay or cove, usually by an ocean. *Marl* is the rich deposit of soil that streams have left on the bottom of the bay, and *claves* (pronounced *CLAW-vaze*) are sticks of wood used as percussion in Caribbean and South American dance orchestras. Baudelaire, who is named in line 7, was a nineteenth-century French poet who shocked his readers by the frank sensuality of his poetry. He also used drugs, which Bishop acknowledges by suggesting that he might hear the gas she sees in the waters of the bight as music from a marimba.

ELIZABETH BISHOP
The Bight

1955

(On My Birthday)

At low tide like this how sheer the water is.
White, crumbling ribs of marl protrude and glare
and the boats are dry, the pilings dry as matches.
Absorbing, rather than being absorbed,
the water in the bight doesn't wet anything,
the color of the gas flame turned as low as possible.
One can smell it turning to gas; if one were Baudelaire°
one could probably hear it turning into marimba music.
The little ochre dredge at work off the end of the dock
already plays the dry perfectly off-beat claves.
The birds are outsize. Pelicans crash
into this peculiar gas unnecessarily hard,
it seems to me, like pickaxes,
rarely coming up with anything to show for it,
and going off with humorous elbowings.
Black-and-white man-of-war birds soar
on impalpable drifts
and open their tails like scissors on the curves
or tense them like wishbones, till they tremble.
The frowsy sponge boats keep coming in
with the obliging air of retrievers,
bristling with jackstraw gaffs and hooks
and decorated with bobbles of sponges.
There is a fence of chicken wire along the dock
where, glinting like little plowshares,
the blue-gray shark tails are hung up to dry
for the Chinese-restaurant trade.
Some of the little white boats are still piled up
against each other, or lie on their sides, stove in,

7. Baudelaire: French poet Charles-Pierre Baudelaire (1821–1867).

and not yet salvaged, if they ever will be, from the last bad storm,
like torn-open, unanswered letters.
The bight is littered with old correspondences.
Click. Click. Goes the dredge,
and brings up a dripping jawful of marl.
All the untidy activity continues,
awful but cheerful.

A Close Reading of "The Bight"

It will help you in your own close reading if you go back to Bishop's poem a second time and take notes on her skillful use of tone, diction, imagery, and onomatopoeia, the sound of the words that she has chosen. In the first line she has changed the syntax, rearranging the order of the words, to tell us the most important thing about the scene at the beginning of the line. The words in a conventional order would read, "How sheer the water is like this at low tide." Instead, the first thing Bishop tells us is that it is low tide, so you'll see that as an immediate visual image.

Sheer is not an obvious choice to describe the gleam of the water on the mud flats, but Bishop has made a choice in the diction of the poem to use *sheer* instead of another possible word like *shiny*. *Sheer* has the connotations of something silky, and it also has an *r* sound, which relates to the *r* of *water,* which gives the line a subtle assonance. *Sheer* also has only one syllable, which smooths out the rhythm of the last half of the line to three iambic feet.

You can also see several other phrases in which Bishop has made choices in the poem's diction to create an even more vivid visual image: *ochre* instead of *yellow-brown* for the color of the dredge; *dry, perfectly off-beat* for the sound of the claves; the adjective *outsize* instead of *big* or *large* for the size of the birds; *frowsy* for the sponge boats instead of *tattered.* The poem is without rhyme or regular meter, but considering Bishop's brilliant skill with words, she probably intended to use the near rhyme of *marl* and *cheerful* to help bring the poem to a close.

Figurative and Literal Language

The term **figurative language** or **figures of speech** means that the poet has consciously chosen a word or a group of words that is literally inaccurate but used to describe or define a person, event, or thing more vividly by calling forth its connotative associations. The opposite term would be **literal language**, which means that each word is being used for its literal or denotative meaning. **Simile** and **metaphor** are the two most frequent types of figurative language you will encounter in reading poetry.

Simile and Metaphor

As we looked closely at Bishop's poem, we realized that she had other means of showing us the harbor. Several times she used comparisons—phrases that began with the word *like*. The term for this is **simile**. For an image of the pelicans flapping out of the water she used the phrase "humorous elbowing," which is an indirect comparison. The term for this is **metaphor**. Both of these terms are important in understanding how poems are written.

Writers have always used simile and metaphor because language without simile is as flat as chili without chili powder. If you have studied literature, you recognized that "as flat as chili without chili powder" is a simile. Simile and metaphor are both comparisons, but a simile tells us to watch out for the comparison with the words *like, as, as if,* or *as though,* while a metaphor does not.

Writers use comparisons for several reasons. It is often easier to describe something that is not familiar by comparing it to something that is, as in the sentence "The wing of a Morpha butterfly looks like a large blue leaf." Another use of a simile is to give a tangible reality to something that is intangible. An example: "Our love is like the shine of the sun on the sea."

The use of a metaphor has long been considered one of the measures of a poet's skill. The Greek philosopher Aristotle defined metaphor as "an intuitive perception of the similarity in dissimilars." A simple metaphor would be a phrase like "You are my sunshine." Most poets, however, try to find comparisons that are more unexpected, that make the reader think about what is similar in the two objects that are being drawn together in a comparison.

The Anglo-Saxon church historian the Venerable Bede included one of the first memorable extended similes in English literature (it was derived from Psalm 84) in his eighth-century *Ecclesiastical History of the English People*. Bede wrote that the brief span of our lifetime between birth and death is "as if a sparrow beaten with wind and weather" flies into a warm, lighted hall and then, after "a short space of this fair weather," departs back outside "to return from winter to winter again."

In Elizabeth Bishop's poem we identified both similes and a metaphor. The similes are strong word pictures. The pelicans crash into the water "like pickaxes," the man-of-war birds open their tails "like scissors," "glinting like little plowshares, / the blue-gray shark tails are hung up to dry," the little white boats lie damaged on the mud "like torn-open, unanswered letters." The metaphor is a description of pelicans struggling to fly up from the water. Bishop describes them as "going off with humorous elbowings," which compares them with people using their elbows to get through a crowd.

Here are some examples of similes:

Like as the waves make towards the pebbled shore,
So do our minutes hasten to their end.
—WILLIAM SHAKESPEARE, from "Sonnet 61"

Oh, my luve is like a red, red rose,
That's newly sprung in June.
—ROBERT BURNS, from "A Red, Red Rose"

I love smooth words, like gold-enameled fish
which circle slowly with a golden swish.
—ELINOR WYLIE, from "Pretty Words"

Let us go then, you and I
When the evening is spread out against the sky
Like a patient etherized upon a table.
–T. S. ELIOT, from "The Love Song of J. Alfred Prufrock"

I am scattered like
the hot shriveled seeds.
–H.D., from "Mid-day"

Love set you going like a fat gold watch.
–SYLVIA PLATH, from "Morning Song"

What happens to a dream deferred?
Does it dry up
like a raisin in the sun?
–LANGSTON HUGHES, from "Harlem"

I like small kindnesses.
In fact I actually prefer them to the more
substantial kindness that is always eyeing you,
like a large animal on a rug.
–LOUISE GLÜCK, from "Gratitude"

Here are some examples of metaphors:

My Rosalind, my Rosalind,
My frolic falcon, with bright eyes.
–ALFRED, LORD TENNYSON, from "Rosalind"

Your mind and you are our Sargasso Sea.
–EZRA POUND, from "Portrait d'une Femme"

Now that I have your voice by heart, I read
In the black chords upon a dulling page
Music that is not meant for music's cage,
Whose emblems mix with words that shake and bleed.
–LOUISE BOGAN, from "Song for the Last Act"

Often poets are drawn to a metaphor or a simile that is so strong that they write entire poems woven around the image. The poem "To Waken an Old Lady" by William Carlos Williams is an extended metaphor for old age that he imagines through an experience of waking an old woman and thinking about the life she has led. (Williams was very close to his mother, and the poem was probably written about her.) He describes her life as a flight of small birds, concluding in the poem's final lines that her life has been satisfying. Perhaps the snow outside her bedroom window was littered with seed husks, and the poet mentions them to suggest that she has led a comfortable life, since the winter wind, which is itself a metaphor for aging, is warmed with a "shrill / piping of plenty."

WILLIAM CARLOS WILLIAMS

To Waken an Old Lady

1921

Old age is
a flight of small
cheeping birds
skimming
bare trees
above a snow glaze.
Gaining and failing
they are buffeted
by a dark wind—
But what?
On harsh weedstalks
the flock has rested,
the snow
is covered with broken
seedhusks
and the wind tempered
by a shrill
piping of plenty.

Personification

Personification is a type of metaphor in which human characteristics are given to something inanimate, animal, or abstract. As you read the English Romantic poet John Keats's "To Autumn," you will find that he has filled his poem with concrete images of an autumn day in the English countryside, but he is also addressing the season of the harvest as if it were a mature woman. He had a specific imaginary woman in mind. She was named Demeter, the goddess of Earth, agriculture, and the autumn harvest in Greek mythology. Keats was so inspired by his subject that as you read his poem you may find yourself sniffing the heady smells he describes as well as hearing buzzing bees and slapping away clouds of insects. If you find the language of the poem old-fashioned, remember that Keats's readers regarded him as a revolutionary because he took his subject out of the classical realm of mythology and brought it into the tangible, physical world.

JOHN KEATS

To Autumn

1819

Season of mists and mellow fruitfulness,
Close bosom friend of the maturing sun:
Conspiring with him how to load and bless
With fruit the vines that round the thatch-eaves run;
To bend with apples the mossed cottage-trees,
And fill all fruit with ripeness to the core;
To swell the gourd, and plump the hazel shells
With a sweet kernel; to set budding more,
And still more, later flowers for the bees,
Until they think warm days will never cease,
For summer has o'er-brimmed their clammy cells.

Who hath not seen thee oft amid thy store?
Sometimes whoever seeks abroad may find
Thee sitting careless on a granary floor,
Thy hair soft-lifted by the winnowing wind;
Or on a half-reaped furrow sound asleep,
Drowsed with the fume of poppies, while thy hook
Spares the next swath and all its twined flowers:
And sometimes like a gleaner thou dost keep,
Steady thy laden head across a brook;
Or by a cider-press, with patient look,
Thou watchest the last oozings hours by hours.
Where are the songs of Spring? Ay, where are they?
Think not of them, thou hast thy music too,—
While barred clouds bloom the soft-dying day,
And touch the stubble-plains with rosy hue;
Then in a wailful choir the small gnats mourn
Among the river sallows, borne aloft
Or sinking as the light wind lives or dies;
And full-grown lambs loud bleat from hilly bourn;
Hedge-crickets sing: and now with treble soft
The red-breast whistles from a garden-croft;
and gathering swallows twitter in the skies.

In your second, close reading of "To Autumn," you might ask yourself some questions about his rich imagery. What is Keats describing in the lines, "Drowsed with the fume of poppies, while thy hook / Spares the next swath and all its twined flowers" or the line "in a wailful choir the small gnats mourn"? What is he telling you in the lines, "Where are the songs of Spring? Ay, where are they? / Think not of them, thou hast thy music too"?

You may have noticed that Keats is not only personifying autumn, but he is taking personification one step further when he also addresses autumn as "thee" in the second paragraph of his poem. He is using another figure of speech called **apostrophe**. This is when the poet addresses something that is inanimate or abstract as a personified thing. Here is a more recent poem, "Lightning Bolt," with a startling use of personification by the Swedish poet Rolf Aggestam. He personifies ordinary lightning when he describes it as a difficult and unpredictable barefoot companion.

ROLF AGGESTAM

Lightning Bolt

1997

TRANSLATED BY SAMUEL CHARTERS

A lightning bolt
is in heat most of the time and doesn't
believe in anything. Unfaithful to any
system. Doesn't measure things. Doesn't make
comparisons.
Doesn't have any hair.
A lightning bolt
is unsure of itself, incomprehensible and curious.
If you understand a lightning bolt it's too late.
You can stuff
a lightning bolt. Stand it up there staring from a
book shelf, seeing everything so clearly.
It hurls itself out of the bare sky and
immediately begins to look for earth.
Challenge the lightning bolt to perform
your deepest and most secret commission
and walk around it wearing heavy boots.
A lightning bolt wants earth under the soles of its feet.

Usually poets use personification to give the attributes of human sensibilities to one of Earth's other creatures or to an inanimate object. Instead, what if we allowed a nonhuman creature a chance to talk about us? "Cows on Killing Day" is an imaginative poem by the contemporary Australian writer Les Murray, in which he allows a cow to speak in its own language. Murray lives on a farm outside of Sydney, and he has imagined how one of the cows would describe a day in the life of the farm's small herd. In his poem the cows live a life so filled with their shared daily routines that the cow refers to the herd as "all me." A single cow becomes "one me." The people also are thought of in cow terms—the woman on the farm is the "heifer human," and the farmer himself is the "oldest bull human." The cow recognizes that the farm's dog is a little like them, "the dog me," but it is "our enemy / of the light loose tongue," and the cow dreams of goring it, "horning [it] dead." The cow thinks, "Me'd jam him in his squeals."

As you read Murray's poem, you may find yourself thinking about what your family's pet dog or cat would write, if they had the words to tell you their own thoughts.

LES MURRAY

The Cows on Killing Day

1998

All me are standing on feed. The sky is shining.

All me have just been milked. Teats all tingling still
from that dry toothless sucking by the chilly mouths
that gasp loudly in in in, and never breathe out.

All me standing on feed, move the feed inside me.
One me smells of needing the bull, that heavy urgent me,
the back-climber, who leaves me humped, straining, but light
and peaceful again, with crystalline moving inside me.

Standing on wet rock, being milked, assuages the calf-sorrow in me.
Now the me who needs mounts on me, hopping, to signal the bull.

The tractor comes trotting in its grumble; the heifer human
bounces on top of it, and cud comes with the tractor,
big rolls of tight dry feed: lucerne, clovers, buttercup, grass,
that's been bitten but never swallowed, yet is cud.
She walks up over the tractor and down it comes, roll on roll
and all me following, eating it, and dropping the good pats.

The heifer human smells of needing the bull human
and is angry. All me look nervously at her
as she chases the dog me dream of horning dead: our enemy
of the light loose tongue. Me'd jam him in his squeals.

Me, facing every way, spreading, out over feed.

One me is still in the yard, the place skinned of feed.
Me, old and sore-boned, little milk in that me now,
licks at the wood. The oldest bull human is coming.
Me in the peed yard. A stick goes out from the human
and cracks, like the whip. Me shivers and falls down
with the terrible, the blood of me, coming out behind an ear.
Me, that other me, down and dreaming in the bare yard.

All me come running. It's like the Hot Part of the sky
that's hard to look at, this that now happens behind wood
in the raw yard. A shining leaf, like off the bitter gum tree
is with the human. It works in the neck of me
and the terrible floods out, swamped and frothy. All me make the Roar,
some leaping stiff-kneed, trying to horn that worst horror.
The wolf-at-the-calves is the bull human. Horn the bull human!

But the dog and the heifer human drive away all me.

Looking back, the glistening leaf is still moving.
All of dry old me is crumpled, like the hills of feed,
and a slick me like a huge calf is coming out of me.

The carrion-stinking dog, who is calf of human and wolf,
is chasing and eating little blood things the humans scatter,
and all me run away, over smells, toward the sky.

Other Figures of Speech: Symbol, Apostrophe, Metonymy, Synecdoche, Paradox, Oxymoron, Hyperbole, Understatement

We've already seen how words and phrases have connotations and associations. A word becomes a **symbol** when it has so much meaning attached to it that we cannot hear it spoken or read it in a text without immediately thinking about what the word symbolizes. Mention of "the flag" brings up thoughts of patriotism and American values. Biblical language has supplied a wide range of words that have taken on a symbolic, rather than a literal, meaning. *Eden* suggests any innocent place, the *serpent* or the *snake* can symbolize any attempt to introduce evil into a happy situation. The *lamb* in both poetry and song represents Jesus Christ. In the 1920s, the poet T. S. Eliot became the center of a lengthy discussion about symbols and symbolism, since several of his most influential poems used words like *roses* or *yew trees* as symbols for his beliefs in tradition and religious faith. In our own period, poets more often write directly about what they mean, but words like *Hollywood* or *Barbie* come loaded with associations, and a term like *Wall Street* often is used as a symbol for American capitalism.

The term **apostrophe** means to address something intangible or someone not commonly spoken to. The opening line of this sonnet by John Donne (see p. 766) is an example of apostrophe, as the intangible presence he is crying out to is Death:

Death, be not proud, though some have callèd thee
Mighty and dreadful, for thou art not so;
For those whom thou think'st thou dost overthrow
Die not, poor Death. . . .

Metonymy and a type of figurative speech closely related to it, **synecdoche**, are similar to metaphor. In using metonymy the writer uses the name of one thing in place of the name of something closely related to it. Instead of saying "I knew him when he was young," the line could be "I knew him in his cradle." Synecdoche is the use of part of something to stand for the whole thing. If we say someone playing baseball or softball "has a heavy bat," we are using the bat as a substitute for the whole concept, which is that the batter hits the ball well.

There are other figures of speech that you will find in your reading, but most of these concepts are used by all writers, and you are probably already familiar with them. Some of these are *paradox, oxymoron, hyperbole,* and *understatement*. By **paradox** we mean a statement that on the surface seems that it cannot possibly be true but is true after all. In the last lines of the sonnet "Death, be not proud," John Donne uses a paradox when he suggests that because of the miracle of eternal life, it is Death itself that dies at the moment of mortality:

> One short sleep past, we wake eternally
> And death shall be no more; Death, thou shalt die.

An **oxymoron** is a statement that contradicts itself. Two of the best-known modern examples are the phrases "jumbo shrimp" and "plastic glass." A more literary example is "darkness visible," Milton's phrase describing hell in *Paradise Lost*. By **hyperbole** we mean exaggerated statements that we do not really intend to be taken for the truth. When the seventeenth-century American poet Anne Bradstreet writes, in "To My Dear and Loving Husband" (p. 940), "I prize thy love more than whole mines of gold / Or all the riches that the East doth hold," she is using hyperbole. **Understatement** is the opposite of hyperbole. Here something is deliberately described in terms that suggest it is much smaller or less important than we know it really is. The line "Life for me ain't been no crystal stair" from Langston Hughes's poem "Mother to Son" (p. 901) is an example of understatement.

Poems for Further Reading

SYLVIA PLATH

Metaphors 1960

I'm a riddle in nine syllables,
An elephant, a ponderous house,
A melon strolling on two tendrils.
O red fruit, ivory, fine timbers!
This loaf's big with its yeasty rising.
Money's new-minted in this fat purse.
I'm a means, a stage, a cow in calf.
I've eaten a bag of green apples,
Boarded the train there's no getting off.

LOUISE GLÜCK

The Wild Iris 1992

At the end of my suffering
there was a door.
Hear me out: that which you call death
I remember.

Overhead, noises, branches of the pine shifting.
Then nothing. The weak sun
flickered over the dry surface.

It is terrible to survive
as consciousness
buried in the dark earth.

Then it was over: that which you fear, being
a soul and unable
to speak, ending abruptly, the stiff earth
bending a little. And what I took to be
birds darting in low shrubs.

You who do not remember
passage from the other world
I tell you I could speak again: whatever
returns from oblivion returns
to find a voice:

from the center of my life came
a great fountain, deep blue
shadows on azure seawater.

KATE GLEASON

After Fighting for Hours

1997

When all else fails
we fall to making love,
our bodies like the pioneers
in rough covered wagons
whose oxen strained to cross the Rockies
until their hearts gave out trying,
those pioneers who had out-survived
fever, hunger, a run of broken luck,
those able-bodied men and women
who simply unlocked the animals
from their yokes, and taking
the hitches in their own hands, pulled
by the sheer desire of their bodies
their earthly goods over the divide.

◆ Topics for Writing about Tone and Figurative Language ◆

1. In "Grass" (p. 728), Carl Sandburg uses personification. Write an essay analyzing why personification is so effective in conveying his tone in the poem.

2. Choose three or four of your favorite made-up words in "Jabberwocky" (p. 730) and explicate the connotations of those words in an essay.
3. John Keats's ode "To Autumn" (p. 738) is one of the best-loved poems in the English language. Discuss what the poet achieved by using apostrophe. How did his lush natural imagery describing nature in the poem add to your impression of autumn as a living human being?
4. Compare and contrast the effect of the concrete imagery in Keats's "To Autumn" and Elizabeth Bishop's "The Bight" (p. 733).
5. Using Les Murray's "The Cows on Killing Day" (p. 740) as your example, write a poem in which you imagine a domestic animal facing a difficult situation.

USEFUL TERMS TO REMEMBER

Abstraction Language that describes ideas or qualities rather than tangible, observable people, places, and things that are described in *concrete* language.

Apostrophe A figure of speech in which the poet addresses something that is inanimate or abstract as a personified thing.

Connotative The associated meanings that have built up around a word.

Denotative The dictionary definition of a word.

Diction A writer's choice of language.

Figurative language (figures of speech) The use of a word or a group of words that is literally inaccurate but is used to describe or define a person, event, or thing more vividly by calling forth the sensations or responses that person, event, or thing evokes.

Hyperbole An exaggerated statement that is not intended to be taken for the truth.

Imagery A word, phrase, or figure of speech such as a SIMILE or a METAPHOR that suggests mental pictures of sensory impressions.

Literal language Words that are being used in their denotative sense.

Metaphor A figure of speech in which one thing is equated with another in an indirect comparison without using the word *like* or *as*.

Metonymy A type of metaphor in which the writer uses the name of one thing in place of the name of something closely related to it.

Oxymoron A statement that contradicts itself.

Paradox A statement that on the surface seems that it cannot possibly be true, but that turns out to be true after all.

Personification A type of metaphor in which human characteristics are given to something inanimate, animal, or abstract.

Poetic diction A use of language that is elevated in tone or employs a special vocabulary.

Simile A figure of speech that makes an explicit comparison between two things by using words such as *like* or *as*.

Symbol A word that evokes a range of additional meanings that are usually more abstract than its literal significance; the use of a part of something to stand for the whole.

Synecdoche A type of metaphor in which the writer uses part of something to stand for the whole thing.

Syntax The word order in the writing of any genre.

Tone Language that conveys the authors' unstated attitudes toward their subjects as revealed in their literary style.

Understatement The opposite of HYPERBOLE. A description that suggests something is smaller or less important than we know it is.

13.

Traditional Forms

> one loves only form
> and form only comes
> into existence when
> the thing is born
>
> —CHARLES OLSON

In our discussions of the different forms of rhyme and meter and the different uses poets have made of words and their meaning, we've also read examples of poetry in many different styles. The next step for you in your reading and understanding of poetry is to enter the world of poetic forms. As you've already seen, poems come in all shapes and sizes. In the long history of poetry there have been book-length poetic narratives that hold our interest in their tales of history or adventure. There have also been poems that in only a few words bring to life the magic of a single moment. Some of these poetic forms have been more popular at certain times of history, other forms are more closely tied to another historical period, but they all continue to hold our interest and they continue to offer examples of writing that can offer you help in your own work.

THE STRUCTURAL ELEMENTS: COUPLET, STANZA, QUATRAIN, SESTET, OCTAVE, TERCET

Although the variety of poetic forms sometimes seems as endless as the varieties of weeds that take over our gardens, when you look more closely at the poems you have been reading you become aware that there is a boundary that separates the poems into two distinct categories. Many of the poems you have read were written in traditional forms, with rhyme and meter as essential elements of their language. It has become popular in recent years to call this kind of poetry "**closed**," which can be taken as a short hand for the fact that the lines generally "close" with a rhyme. If you think a moment more about the term, however, you realize that it has other connotations. The term can also mean closed in, confined. When we think in terms of imagination, emotion, language, and skill, however, we realize that poems written in traditional forms are not closed at all. In the poems that linger in our minds, it is just as often those elements of rhyme and meter, the sound and the music of the lines, that we remember.

It will help you to think of poems like these as *traditional,* since most of the forms have passed from poet to poet for many generations, and part of their richness is this history that we sense is echoed in the forms of the poems themselves. The second category of poetry which will be familiar to you is written in **free verse** or **open form**, and we will discuss this widely used poetic style in the next chapter.

In your reading you also have seen that rhyme and meter and their complex interrelationship are at the core of all of the forms of traditional verse. For many of these poems, the basic building block is the **couplet**, a unit of two lines that end in perfect rhyme. In this poem, "Hymn to Godric," two couplets are joined together to make the basic unit of four lines called a **stanza** or a **verse**, which you have already encountered in your reading.

Sainte Marye, Christes bur° *shelter*
Maidenes clenhad,° moderes flur° *purity; flower*
Dilie° min sinne, rix° in min mod° *remove; merge; heart*
Bring me to winne° with the self God *joy*

You won't recognize all of the words since the language we speak is continually changing, but the four-line stanza, written in a line of four accents in iambic meter, was for hundreds of years one of the most widely used forms of traditional poetry. There are also infinite varieties of these basic verse forms, as you learned in the discussions of figures of speech. When you encounter them in your reading, you will find that they also have a name. The term that is used for the basic unit of four lines is a **quatrain**, especially when it is part of a larger unit within a poem. A group of six lines with a recurring rhyme scheme is called a **sestet**, and the term for an eight-line group is an **octave**.

Although the couplet is the basic unit for much of the traditional poetry you will read, occasionally a skilled writer will employ a unit of three lines, which is called a **tercet**. Tennyson, who was ingenious in his employment of rhyme, included a tercet in each stanza of his long ballad poem *The Lady of Shalott*.

A red-cross knight forever kneeled
To a lady in his shield,
That sparkled on a yellow field.

With these terms to give us a guideline, we can begin to look at some of the other forms of traditional poetry. The classic distinctions between the main poetic forms were *narrative, dramatic, lyric,* and *didactic*. When you read poetry today, the dominant form is the lyric, and didactic poetry, or poetry that is written to make a point or argue a political or religious position, has become what we call *poetry of commitment* or *political poetry*. Narrative and dramatic poetry still are part of our world, and they have a long, rich history.

NARRATIVE POETRY

A **narrative poem** is by definition a poem that tells a story, such as the familiar poem that begins "'Twas the night before Christmas and all through the house . . ." The oldest form of narrative poetry is the **epic**, which is best known today for the two great epic poems the *Iliad* and the *Odyssey*, composed almost three thousand years ago. The large scale of these narratives and their sweeping depiction of a moment in history have given us the familiar adjective *epic*. In many personal poems written in contemporary style today, the poet also describes a personal incident or tells an anecdote. These, however, usually are not considered narrative poems, which in contrast develop their themes or their characters at considerable length and end with the conclusion of the story.

The Ballad

A term that you are already familiar with from popular music today is the **ballad**. It tells you that the song will be in a slow tempo so you can follow the words and it will tell some kind of story. The same word was used for centuries to describe poems that told stories and usually were sung, either as a solo or with a **refrain** that allowed everyone in the audience to add their own voices to the performance. Ballads were generally written in four-line stanzas to give the solo singers a chance to catch their breath and present the story in smaller, more easily remembered sections that make it easier for the listeners to follow. It is probable that each of the ballads that have been passed to us from generation to generation had a balladeer whose name is lost who composed the earliest version, but later singers have freely used the story and its form to retell it to new audiences. The writer of these newer versions is generally titled *Anonymous*.

The theme of the woman tempted by the devil has its roots in antiquity, and in "The Daemon Lover," a cruel version of the tale from medieval Britain, the woman leaves not only home and husband, but also her two "small babes." She is tempted away by the appearance of the devil in the shape of a lover who left her to go to the sea seven years earlier, and the temptation the devil offers her is the promise of a fleet of ships and sailors to take her away with him and "music on every hand." As the story nears its sad ending, the devil taunts her with a vision of hell that appears as a mountain "dreary wi frost and snow." This contradicts the traditional view of hell as a region of fire and torment, and you should ask yourself what the anonymous composer of the ballad might have been suggesting by this seeming contradiction.

Ballads for Further Reading

The Daemon Lover

c. 1400

"O where have you been, my long, long love,
    This long seven years and mair?"
"O I'm come to seek my former vows
    Ye granted me before."

"O hold your tongue of your former vows,
For they will breed sad strife;
O hold your tongue of your former vows,
For I am become a wife."

He turned him right and round about,
And the tear blinded his ee:
"I wad never hae trodden on Irish ground
If it had not been for thee.

"I might hae had a king's daughter,
Far, far beyond the sea;
I might have had a king's daughter,
Had it not been for love o thee."

"If ye might have had a king's daughter,
Yersel ye had to blame;
Ye might have taken the king's daughter,
For ye kend° that I was nane.° *know; none*

"If I was to leave my husband dear,
And my two babes also,
O what have you to take me to,
If with you I should go?"

"I hae seven ships upon the sea—
The eighth brought me to land—
With four-and-twenty bold mariners,
And music on every hand."

She has taken up her two little babes,
Kissed them baith cheek and chin:
"O fair ye weel, my ain two babes,
For I'll never see you again."

She set her foot upon the ship,
No mariners could she behold;
But the sails were of the taffetie,° *silk fabric*
And the masts of the beaten gold.

She had not sailed a league, a league,
A league but barely three,
When dismal grew his countenance,
And drumlie° grew his ee. *gloomy*

They had not saild a league, league,
A league but barely three,
Until she espied his cloven foot,
And she wept right bitterlie.

"O hold your tongue of your weeping," says he,
"Of your weeping now let me be;
I will shew you how the lilies grow
On the banks of Italy."

"O what hills are yon, yon pleasant hills,
That the sun shines sweetly on?"
"O yon are the hills of heaven," he said,
"Where you will never win."

"O whaten a mountain is yon," she said,
"All so dreary wi frost and snow?"
"O yon is the mountain of hell," he cried,
"Where you and I will go."

He strack the tap-mast wi his hand,
The fore-mast wi his knee,
And he brake that gallant ship in twain,
And sank her in the sea.

One of the best-known ballads that has come down to us through the aural tradition is the folk ballad "Barbara Allan," still sung in the United States and the British Isles. It is composed in a verse form that uses alternating lines of three or four accents. As is common with ballads that are meant to be sung, there is considerable freedom in the metric beats. Another common characteristic of ballads is that rhyme is used only for the second and fourth lines of each verse.

Barbara Allan

It was in and about the Martinmas° time, *November 11*
When the green leaves were a-fallin',
That Sir John Graeme in the West Country
Fell in love with Barbara Allan.

He sent his man down through the town
To the place where she was dwellin':
"O haste and come to my master dear,
Gin° ye be Barbara Allan." *if*

O slowly, slowly rase° she up, *rose*
To the place where he was lyin',
And when she drew the curtain by:
"Young man, I think you're dyin'."

"O it's I'm sick, and very, very sick,
And 'tis a' for Barbara Allan."
"O the better for me ye sal° never be *shall*
Though your heart's blood were a-spillin'.

"O dinna ye mind, young man," said she,
"When ye the cups were fillin',
That ye made the healths gae round and round,
And slighted Barbara Allan?"

He turned his face unto the wall,
And death with him was dealin':
"Adieu, adieu, my dear friends all,
And be kind to Barbara Allan."

And slowly, slowly, rase she up,
And slowly, slowly left him;
And sighing said she could not stay,
Since death of life had reft him.

She had not gane a mile but twa,
When she heard the dead-bell knellin',
And every jow° that the dead-bell ga'ed *stroke*
It cried, "Woe to Barbara Allan."

"O mother, mother, make my bed,
O make it soft and narrow:
Since my love died for me today,
I'll die for him tomorrow."

The ballad may be one of our oldest forms, but many poets also turned to the ballad when they wanted to tell a story. These **literary ballads** are meant to be read quietly, so usually they don't have a refrain. In this modern ballad, the New England poet Amy Lowell tells the tragic story of a woman loved by two men, neither of whom would yield her to the other. The relentless progress of its narrative has the stark simplicity of a Greek drama.

AMY LOWELL

Evelyn Ray

1919

No decent man will cross a field
Laid down to hay, until its yield

Is cut and cocked, yet there was the track
Going in from the lane and none coming back.

But that was afterwards; before,
The field was smooth as a sea off shore

On a shimmering afternoon, waist-high
With bent, and red top, and timothy.

Lush with oat grass and tall fescue,
And the purple green of Kentucky blue;

A noble meadow, so broad each way
It took three good scythes to mow in a day.

Just where the field broke into a wood
A knotted old catalpa stood,

And in the old catalpa-tree
A cat-bird sang immoderately.

The sky above him was round and big
And its center seemed just over his twig.

The earth below him was fresh and fair,
With the sun's long fingers everywhere.

The cat-bird perched where a great leaf hung,
And the great leaf tilted, and flickered, and swung.

Of a windless wind in the daisy tops,
And the jar stalks make when a grasshopper hops.

Every now and then a bee boomed over
The black-eyed Susans in search of clover,

And crickets shrilled as crickets do:
One—two. One—two.

The cat-bird sang with his head in the air,
And the sun's bright fingers poked here and there,

Past leaf, and branch, and needle, and cone.
But the stone men stood like men of stone.

Each man lifted a dull stone hand
And his fingers felt like weaving sand,

And his feet seemed standing on a ball
Which tossed and turned in a waterfall.

Each man heard a shot somewhere
Dropping out of the distant air.

But the screaming saws no longer said
"Evelyn Ray," for the men were dead.

•

I often think of Evelyn Ray.
What did she do, what did she say?
Did she ever chance to pass that way?

I remember it as a lovely spot
Where a cat-bird sang. When he heard the shot,
Did he fly away? I have quite forgot.

When I went there last, he was singing again
Through a little fleeting, misty rain,
And pine-cones lay where they had lain.

This is the tale as I heard it when
I was young from a man who was threescore and ten.
A lady of clay and two stone men.

A pretty problem is here, no doubt,
If you have a fancy to work it out:
What happens to stone when clay is about?

Muse upon it as long as you will,
I think myself it will baffle your skill,
And your answer will be what is—nil,

But every sunny Summer's day
I am teased with the thought of Evelyn Ray,
Poor little image of painted clay.
And Heigh-o! I say.
What if there be a judgment day?

What if all religions be true,
And Gabriel's trumpet blow for you
And blow for them—what will you do?

Evelyn Ray, will you rise alone?
Or will your lovers of dull gray stone
Pace beside you through the wan

Twilight of that bitter day
To be judged as stone and judged as clay,
And no one to say the judgment nay?

Better be nothing, Evelyn Ray,
A handful of buttercups that sway
In the wind for a children's holiday.

For earth to earth is the best we know,
Where the good blind worms push to and fro
Turning us into the seeds which grow,

And lovers and ladies are dead indeed,
Lost in the sap of a flower seed.
Is this, think you, a sorry creed?

Well, be it so, for the world is wide
And opinions jostle on every side.
What has always been hidden will always hide.

And every year when the fields are high
With oat grass, and red top, and timothy,
I know that a creed is the shell of a lie.

Peace be with you, Evelyn Ray,
And to your lovers, if so it may,
For earth made stone and earth made clay.

The Ode

Among the oldest forms of lyric poetry is the **ode**. As a poem of praise, it is found in nearly every language and culture. For poets schooled in the European tradition, the style has a classical model, the odes written by the Greek poet Pindar to honor the victorious athletes of the Olympic Games of fifth-century Athens. His poems are sometimes called the Great Odes to separate them from the imitations that followed. Pindar intended them to be performed in public ceremonies by choruses that sang or chanted the lines. The emotions of the ceremonies could be compared to your feelings when you stand up with the cheering crowd in a sporting event and sing your school's song or the national anthem.

An ode is a long, usually serious, lyric poem addressed to a person or an object that presents philosophical ideas and moral concerns. Odes could be addressed to specific objects, like the antique Greek vase that John Keats chose for the subject of his "Ode on a Grecian Urn," or to an inanimate concept as in Percy Bysshe Shelley's "Ode to the West Wind." In Keats's ode, he looks at a half-imagined Greek vase or urn covered with painted scenes of a dance in the countryside. When he asks, in the first stanza, "What men or gods are these?" he is asking about the figures painted on the sides of the urn. In the turmoil and riot of life that he sees there, he imagines an eternal reality. The poem's closing lines,

> Beauty is truth, truth beauty—that is all
> Ye know on earth, and all ye need to know.

are among the best-known and most-often quoted lines in English poetry. They were read as a philosophical statement about what we find beautiful and what we consider to be true. As you read the poem, you can ask yourself if you agree with what those lines are telling you, and how you interpret the larger statement they are making.

JOHN KEATS

Ode on a Grecian Urn

1820

Thou still unravished bride of quietness,
Thou foster-child of silence and slow time,
Sylvan historian, who canst thus express
A flowery tale more sweetly than our rhyme:
What leaf-fringed legend haunts about thy shape
Of deities or mortals, or of both,
In Tempe or the dales of Arcady?°
What men or gods are these? What maidens loth?
What mad pursuit? What struggle to escape?
What pipes and timbrels? What wild ecstasy?

Heard melodies are sweet, but those unheard
Are sweeter; therefore, ye soft pipes, play on;
Not to the sensual° ear, but, more endeared, *physical*
Pipe to the spirit ditties of no tone:

7. Tempe . . . Arcady: Rural places in Greece.

Fair youth, beneath the trees, thou canst not leave
Thy song, nor ever can those trees be bare;
Bold Lover, never, never canst thou kiss,
Though winning near the goal—yet, do not grieve;
She cannot fade, though thou hast not thy bliss,
For ever wilt thou love, and she be fair!

Ah, happy, happy boughs! that cannot shed
Your leaves, nor ever bid the Spring adieu;
And, happy melodist, unwearièd,
For ever piping songs for ever new;
More happy love! more happy, happy love!
For ever warm and still to be enjoyed,
For ever panting, and for ever young;
All breathing human passion far above,
That leaves a heart high-sorrowful and cloyed,
A burning forehead, and a parching tongue.

Who are these coming to the sacrifice?
To what green altar, O mysterious priest,
Lead'st thou that heifer lowing at the skies,
And all her silken flanks with garlands drest?
What little town by river or sea shore,
Or mountain-built with peaceful citadel,
Is emptied of this folk, this pious morn?
And, little town, thy streets for evermore
Will silent be; and not a soul to tell
Why thou art desolate, can e'er return.

O Attic° shape! Fair attitude! with brede° *Greek; design*
Of marble men and maidens overwrought,
With forest branches and the trodden weed;
Thou, silent form, dost tease us out of thought
As doth Eternity: Cold Pastoral!
When old age shall this generation waste,
Thou shalt remain, in midst of other woe
Than ours, a friend to man, to whom thou say'st,
Beauty is truth, truth beauty,—that is all
Ye know on earth, and all ye need to know.

Shelley's "Ode to the West Wind" has none of the philosophic calm of Keats's ode. Shelley's poem is a tumultuous reflection of the personal difficulties that have almost overwhelmed him. He was in his mid-twenties when he wrote it, but he had already been forced to leave the university because of his views on religion. He had also married and abandoned a young wife for the sixteen-year-old daughter of a friend, and they were living a chaotic life in an isolated house in Italy in virtual exile from England. The autumn wind is an appropriate image for his emotions, driving before it the falling leaves that mark the approach of winter. Although it is a turbulent poem with many currents of feeling, it is written with great care and subtlety. Shelley allows himself more freedom with the meter than is usual in a formal poem, but each line has four stressed beats.

The complexity of the poem lies in the rhyme scheme. Shelley chose to write it in **terza rima**. The form is a tercet in iambic pentameter, with a sequence of rhymes that crosses from one stanza to the next, binding them together. The rhyme scheme is *ABA-BCB-CDC*, continuing with the same pattern. The final word of the middle line of each unit of the verse becomes the rhyme for the outer lines of the next tercet. Terza rima is especially effective for narrative poems and for poems, like this one, with a restless, unsettled mood. To strengthen the poem's overall structure, Shelley constructs the tercets in groups of four with an added couplet that rhymes with the middle line of the fourth tercet. This is the rhyme scheme for each of the poem's stanzas: *ABA-BCB-CDC-DED-EE.* As you read Shelley's ode, you can ask yourself what is the meaning of his famous metaphor "I fall upon the thorns of life! I bleed!" and decide whether what he has told us in the poem justifies this despairing cry. Does the poem also justify its positive conclusion: "O Wind, / If Winter comes, can Spring be far behind?"

PERCY BYSSHE SHELLEY

Ode to the West Wind

1819

I

O wild West Wind, thou breath of Autumn's being,
Thou, from whose unseen presence the leaves dead
Are driven, like ghosts from an enchanter fleeing,

Yellow, and black, and pale, and hectic red,
Pestilence-stricken multitudes: O Thou,
Who chariotest to their dark wintry bed

The winged seeds, where they lie cold and low,
Each like a corpse within its grave, until
Thine azure sister of the Spring shall blow

Her clarion° o'er the dreaming earth, and fill — *trumpet call*
(Driving sweet buds like flocks to feed in air)
With living hues and odours plain and hill:

Wild Spirit, which art moving everywhere;
Destroyer and Preserver; hear, O hear!

II

Thou on whose stream, 'mid the steep sky's commotion,
Loose clouds like Earth's decaying leaves are shed,
Shook from the tangled boughs of Heaven and Ocean,

Angels of rain and lightning: there are spread
On the blue surface of thine aery surge,
Like the bright hair uplifted from the head

Of some fierce Maenad,° even from the dim verge
Of the horizon to the zenith's height,
The locks of the approaching storm. Thou Dirge

Of the dying year, to which this closing night
Will be the dome of a vast sepulchre,
Vaulted with all thy congregated might

Of vapours, from whose solid atmosphere
Black rain and fire and hail will burst: O hear!

III

Thou who didst waken from his summer dreams
The blue Mediterranean, where he lay,
Lulled by the coil of his chrystalline streams,

Beside a pumice isle in Baiæ's bay,°
And saw in sleep old palaces and towers
Quivering within the wave's intenser day,

All overgown with azure moss and flowers
So sweet, the sense faints picturing them! Thou
For whose path the Atlantic's level powers

Cleave themselves into chasms, while far below
The sea-blooms and the oozy woods which wear
The sapless foliage of the ocean, know

Thy voice, and suddenly grow grey with fear,
And tremble and despoil themselves: O hear!

IV

If I were a dead leaf thou mightest bear;
If I were a swift cloud to fly with thee;
A wave to pant beneath thy power, and share

The impulse of thy strength, only less free
Than thou, O Uncontrollable! If even
I were as in my boyhood, and could be

The comrade of thy wanderings over Heaven,
As then, when to outstrip thy skiey speed
Scarce seemed a vision; I would ne'er have striven

As thus with thee in prayer in my sore need.
Oh! Lift me as a wave, a leaf, a cloud!
I fall upon the thorns of life! I bleed!

---

21. Maenad: Female worshiper of Bacchus, the Greek god of wine and revelry. **32. Baiæ's bay:** A bay near Naples, Italy.

A heavy weight of hours has chained and bowed
One too like thee: tameless, and swift, and proud.

V

Make me thy lyre, even as the forest is:
What if my leaves are falling like its own!
The tumult of thy mighty harmonies
Will take from both a deep, autumnal tone,
Sweet though in sadness. Be thou, Spirit fierce,
My spirit! Be thou me, impetuous one!
Drive my dead thoughts over the universe
Like withered leaves to quicken a new birth!
And, by the incantation of this verse,
Scatter, as from an unextinguished hearth
Ashes and sparks, my words among mankind!
Be through my lips to unawakened Earth
The trumpet of a prophecy! O Wind,
If Winter comes, can Spring be far behind?

The Elegy

The word **elegy** comes from the Greek word *elegos*, which means a song of mourning. In traditional poetry an elegy, however, was not a simple lament, a cry of grief at the death or loss of someone or something that was very dear to the writer. The elegy evolved into a formal poem that dealt at length not only with the death itself but with a philosophical statement of loss or despair as it memorialized its subject. As you read Thomas Gray's "Elegy Written in a Country Churchyard," probably the best-known elegy in the English language, you will find that an elegy can also address serious social and political issues.

THOMAS GRAY

Elegy Written in a Country Churchyard 1751

The curfew tolls the knell of parting day,
  The lowing herd wind slowly o'er the lea,° *pasture*
The plowman homeward plods his weary way,
  And leaves the world to darkness and to me.

Now fades the glimmering landscape on the sight,
  And all the air a solemn stillness holds,
Save where the beetle wheels his droning flight,
  And drowsy tinklings lull the distant folds;

Save that from yonder ivy-mantled tower
The moping owl does to the moon complain
Of such, as wand'ring near her secret bower,
Molest her ancient solitary reign.

Beneath those rugged elms, that yew tree's shade,
Where heaves the turf in many a mold'ring heap,
Each in his narrow cell forever laid,
The rude forefathers of the hamlet sleep.

The breezy call of incense-breathing morn,
The swallow twitt'ring from the straw-built shed,
The cock's shrill clarion, or the echoing horn,° *hunting horn*
No more shall rouse them from their lowly bed.

For them no more the blazing hearth shall burn,
Or busy housewife ply her evening care;
No children run to lisp their sire's return,
Or climb his knees the envied kiss to share.

Oft did the harvest to their sickle yield,
Their furrow oft the stubborn glebe° has broke; *turf*
How jocund did they drive their team afield!
How bowed the woods beneath their sturdy stroke!

Let not Ambition mock their useful toil,
Their homely joys, and destiny obscure;
Nor Grandeur hear with a disdainful smile
The short and simple annals of the poor.

The boast of heraldry, the pomp of pow'r,
And all that beauty, all that wealth e'er gave,
Awaits alike th' inevitable hour.
The paths of glory lead but to the grave.

Nor you, ye proud, impute to these the fault,
If Mem'ry o'er their tomb no trophies raise,
Where through the long-drawn aisle and fretted vault
The pealing anthem swells the note of praise.

Can storied urn or animated bust
Back to its mansion call the fleeting breath?
Can Honor's voice provoke the silent dust,
Or Flatt'ry soothe the dull cold ear of Death?

Perhaps in this neglected spot is laid
Some heart once pregnant with celestial fire;
Hands that the rod of empire might have swayed,
Or waked to ecstasy the living lyre.

But knowledge to their eyes her ample page
Rich with the spoils of time did ne'er unroll;
Chill Penury repressed their noble rage,
And froze the genial current of the soul.

Full many a gem of purest ray serene,
  The dark unfathomed caves of ocean bear:
Full many a flower is born to blush unseen,
  And waste its sweetness on the desert air.

Some village Hampden,° that with dauntless breast
  The little tyrant of his field withstood;
Some mute inglorious Milton° here may rest,
  Some Cromwell,° guiltless of his country's blood.

Th' applause of list'ning senates to command,
  The threats of pain and ruin to despise,
To scatter plenty o'er a smiling land,
  And read their hist'ry in a nation's eyes,

Their lot forbade; nor circumscribed alone
  Their growing virtues, but their crimes confined;
Forbade to wade through slaughter to a throne,
  And shut the gates of mercy on mankind,

The struggling pangs of conscious truth to hide,
  To quench the blushes of ingenuous shame,
Or heap the shrine of Luxury and Pride
  With incense kindled at the Muse's flame.°

Far from the madding crowd's ignoble strife,
  Their sober wishes never learned to stray;
Along the cool sequestered vale of life
  They kept the noiseless tenor° of their way. *continual movement*

Yet ev'n these bones from insult to protect
  Some frail memorial still erected nigh,
With uncouth rhymes and shapeless sculpture decked,
  Implores the passing tribute of a sigh.

Their name, their years, spelt by th' unlettered Muse,
  The place of fame and elegy supply:
And many a holy text around she strews,
  That teach the rustic moralist to die.

For who to dumb Forgetfulness a prey,
  This pleasing anxious being e'er resigned,
Left the warm precincts of the cheerful day,
  Nor cast one longing ling'ring look behind?

On some fond breast the parting soul relies,
  Some pious drops the closing eye requires;

57. Hampden: John Hampden (1594–1643) was a member of Parliament who resisted the illegal taxes on his lands that were imposed by Charles I. **59. Milton:** John Milton (1608–1674), the English poet. **60. Cromwell:** Oliver Cromwell (1599–1658) served as Lord Protector of England from 1653 until his death. **71–72: heap the shrine . . . Muse's flame:** Gray is criticizing poets who write to please wealthy patrons.

Ev'n from the tomb the voice of Nature cries,
  Ev'n in our ashes live their wonted fires.

For thee, who mindful of th' unhonored dead
  Dost in these lines their artless tale relate;
If chance, by lonely contemplation led,
  Some kindred spirit shall inquire thy fate,

Haply° some hoary-headed swain° may say, *perchance; shepherd*
  "Oft have we seen him at the peep of dawn
Brushing with hasty steps the dews away
  To meet the sun upon the upland lawn.

"There at the foot of yonder nodding beech
  That wreathes its old fantastic roots so high,
His listless length at noontide would he stretch,
  And pore upon the brook that babbles by.

"Hard by yon wood, now smiling as in scorn,
  Mutt'ring his wayward fancies he would rove,
Now drooping, woeful wan, like one forlorn,
  Or crazed with care, or crossed in hopeless love.

"One morn I missed him, on the customed hill,
  Along the heath and near his fav'rite tree;
Another came; nor yet beside the rill,
  Nor up the lawn, nor at the wood was he;

"The next with dirges due in sad array
  Slow through the churchway path we saw him borne.
Approach and read (for thou canst read) the lay,° *song or poem*
  Graved on the stone beneath yon aged thorn."

THE EPITAPH

Here rests his head upon the lap of Earth
  A youth to Fortune and to Fame unknown.
Fair Science frowned not on his humble birth,
  And Melancholy marked him for her own.

Large was his bounty, and his soul sincere,
  Heav'n did a recompense as largely send:
He gave to Mis'ry all he had, a tear,
  He gained from Heav'n ('twas all he wished) a friend.

No farther seek his merits to disclose,
  Or draw his frailties from their dread abode,
(There they alike in trembling hope repose),
  The bosom of His Father and his God.

The poem may seem to you to be placid and undramatic, but at the time it was written it was making a strong and disturbing political statement. The poem was unlike other elegies that had been written before it because the subject was an ordinary person. This young man was not a nobleman or a famed military leader; he was simply someone who had been buried in the village's churchyard. As Gray wrote in the epitaph that ends the poem,

Here rests his head upon the lap of Earth
    A youth to Fortune and to Fame unknown.

The person buried in the churchyard is never named. What Gray is insisting is that under other circumstances this ordinary person could have been the equal of any other person in their society. In the years leading up to the revolutions in the American colonies and in France—revolutions that overthrew the rigid class lines of the old social order—these were fiery sentiments. Another stanza from the poem, the twelfth, burned itself into the consciousness of the time, with its bold idea that in this humble grave might lie someone who could have ruled a nation or written immortal poetry. The phrases were echoed again and again by poets, orators, and politicians.

Perhaps in this neglected spot is laid
    Some heart once pregnant with celestial fire;
Hands that the rod of empire might have swayed,
    Or waked to ecstasy the living lyre.

The final line of the ninth stanza of his poem has been quoted in more speeches, books, sermons, and plays than Gray could ever have imagined: "The paths of glory lead but to the grave."

The elegy continued to be a poetic form that was adopted by many writers. This moving modern elegy was written by Theodore Roethke in memory of one of his students who was killed in a riding accident. In contrast to the larger themes of Gray's poem, Roethke has written a touching, personal portrait of a vivacious and mercurial girl who had died too young. As you read the poem, you might ask yourself what he is telling the reader in the final two lines: "I, with no rights in this matter, / Neither father nor lover."

THEODORE ROETHKE

Elegy for Jane

1953

(My student, Thrown by a Horse)

I remember the neckcurls, limp and damp as tendrils;
And her quick look, a sidelong pickerel smile;
And how, once startled into talk, the light syllables leaped for her,
And she balanced in the delight of her thought,
A wren, happy, tail into the wind,
Her song trembling the twigs and small branches.
The shade sang with her;
The leaves, their whispers turned to kissing;
And the mould sang in the bleached valleys under the rose.

Oh, when she was sad, she cast herself down into such a pure depth,
Even a father could not find her:
Scraping her cheek against straw;
Stirring the clearest water.

My sparrow, you are not here,
Waiting like a fern, making a spiny shadow.
The sides of wet stones cannot console me,
Nor the moss, wound with the last light.

If only I could nudge you from this sleep,
My maimed darling, my skittery pigeon.
Over this damp grave I speak the words of my love:
I, with no rights in this matter,
Neither father nor lover.

The Sonnet

Although the **sonnet** is now a venerable literary form with a five-hundred-year history behind it, you will still find poets today turning to the sonnet for its special qualities. The compactness of the form—usually fourteen lines, although sometimes more or less, with the lines of similar length—signal both to the writer and the reader that packed into its lines will be a presentation of a theme, a consideration of its implications, and a conclusion that summarizes the poet's response to the sonnet's theme. For centuries the sonnet conformed to strict rules of meter and rhyme, but writers today have found that the sonnet still has its own recognizable discipline and form even without the rules that formerly defined it. Poets have sometimes described the sonnet form as a "world in itself," and as you read the sonnets here you will be conscious that this poet's definition is a useful introduction to the form. A helpful beginning for your study of the sonnet is this example by perhaps the greatest of the "sonneteers"—as someone who writes sonnets is called—William Shakespeare.

WILLIAM SHAKESPEARE

That time of year thou mayst in me behold 1609

That time of year thou mayst in me behold
When yellow leaves, or none, or few, do hang
Upon those boughs which shake against the cold,
Bare ruined choirs, where late the sweet birds sang.
In me thou seest the twilight of such day
As after sunset fadeth in the west;
Which by and by black night doth take away,
Death's second self that seals up all in rest.
In me thou seest the glowing of such fire,

That on the ashes of his youth doth lie,
As the deathbed whereon it must expire,
Consumed with that which it was nourished by.
  This thou perceiv'st, which makes thy love more strong,
  To love that well, which thou must leave ere long.

If you look at the meter of Shakespeare's sonnet, you can see that it is written in iambic pentameter. The five-foot line, which is also the line of dramatic blank verse, has a feeling of weight and substance that the more commonly used four-foot line of much lyric poetry does not. The fourteen lines consist of three quatrains with a rhyme scheme of *ABAB-CDCD-EFEF* and a concluding couplet, *GG*. This way of structuring the rhyme is called the **English**, or **Shakespearean**, **sonnet**.

The other common form of rhyme that the English poets adopted from the translations of the Italian sonnets introduced into England is an octave of two quatrains with a rhyme scheme of *ABBA-ABBA*, followed by a sestet with a rhyme scheme that may have some variation but is usually either *CDECDE* or *CDCDCD*. The term for this is the **Italian sonnet**.

It will be helpful for you if you begin your study of a sonnet by writing your own **paraphrase** of the poem's theme and subject. A sonnet usually is making a philosophical statement, and its imagery is an extension of this basic theme. If you can make this clear in your own mind, it will help you in your writing about the sonnet. A paraphrase of the sonnet you have just read might be:

> Look at me, I look just like trees that lose their leaves in autumn. I'm just like the sun that's setting now, and in the darkness you can see the last of the glowing fire of my life. The sun made my life strong but its fire burned me. So you should understand this and let yourself love the things in your life even more since life ends so soon.

It will also help you to mark the rhyme scheme and determine whether it is an English or an Italian sonnet, or whether it is one of the almost infinite varieties of the modern sonnet form. With the thinking and writing you have done with your paraphrase of the theme and your close reading of the lines to understand the poem's rhyme scheme, you will come much closer to understanding the sonnet you have chosen to write about.

Sonnets for Further Reading

Because of the variety of subjects and influences in the sonnet, the best way to experience these poems is to read as many of them as you can. Try to follow their rhymes and the way each sonnet develops its themes. As you have already been told by the writers themselves, each sonnet is a world in itself.

As a help with your reading, although the sonnet by Gwendolyn Brooks may seem irregular, without a final rhyme, she has created a personal variation in the rhyme scheme, *ABBA-CDDC-EFGEFG*. With this rhyme pattern, she can end her poem with the word *Is,* setting it aside as its own sentence. As you read, you can ask yourself whether Brooks is telling you that her cousin Vit had so much life in her that, despite her "death," she still is very much alive.

FRANCESCO PETRARCA

Love's Inconsistency 1557

TRANSLATED BY SIR THOMAS WYATT

I find no peace, and all my war is done;
  I fear and hope, I burn and freeze likewise;
  I fly above the wind, yet cannot rise;
  And nought I have, yet all the world I seize on;
That looseth, nor locketh, holdeth me in prison,
  And holds me not, yet can I 'scape no wise;
  Nor lets me live, nor die, at my devise,
  And yet of death it giveth none occasion.
Without eyes I see, and without tongue I plain;
  I wish to perish, yet I ask for health;
  I love another, and yet I hate myself;
I feed in sorrow, and laugh in all my pain;
  Lo, thus displeaseth me both death and life,
  And my delight is causer of my grief.

LADY MARY WROTH

When last I saw thee, I did not thee see, 1621

When last I saw thee, I did not thee see,
  It was thine image, which in my thoughts lay
  So lively figured, as no time's delay
  Could suffer me in heart to parted be;

And sleep so favourable is to me,
  As not to let thy loved remembrance stray,
  Lest that I, waking, might have cause to say,
  There was one minute found to forget thee.

Then since my faith is such, so kind my sleep
  That gladly thee presents into my thought,
  And still true-lover-like thy face doth keep,
  So as some pleasure shadow-like is wrought:

Pity my loving, nay, of conscience, give
Reward to me, in whom thy self doth live.

JOHN DONNE
Death, be not proud

1633

Death, be not proud, though some have calléd thee
Mighty and dreadful, for thou art not so;
For those whom thou think'st thou dost overthrow
Die not, poor Death, nor yet canst thou kill me.
From rest and sleep, which but thy pictures be,
Much pleasure; then from thee much more must flow,
And soonest our best men with thee do go,
Rest of their bones, and soul's delivery.
Thou art slave to fate, chance, kings, and desperate men,
And dost with poison, war, and sickness dwell,
And poppy° or charms can make us sleep as well *opium*
And better than thy stroke; why swell'st thou then?
One short sleep past, we wake eternally
And death shall be no more; Death, thou shalt die.

WILLIAM WORDSWORTH
Upon Westminster Bridge, Sept. 3, 1802

1802

Earth has not anything to show more fair:
    Dull would he be of soul who could pass by
    A sight so touching in its majesty:
This City now doth, like a garment, wear
The beauty of the morning; silent, bare,
    Ships, towers, domes, theatres, and temples lie
    Open unto the fields, and to the sky;
All bright and glittering in the smokeless air.
Never did sun more beautifully steep
    In his first splendour, valley, rock, or hill;
Ne'er saw I, never felt, a calm so deep!
    The river glideth at his own sweet will:
Dear God! The very houses seem asleep;
    And all that mighty heart is lying still!

PERCY BYSSHE SHELLEY

Ozymandias° 1818

I met a traveler from an antique land
Who said: Two vast and trunkless legs of stone
Stand in the desert . . . Near them, on the sand,
Half sunk, a shattered visage lies, whose frown,
And wrinkled lip, and sneer of cold command,
Tell that its sculptor well those passions read
Which yet survive, stamped on these lifeless things,
The hand that mocked them, and the heart that fed:
And on the pedestal these words appear:
"My name is Ozymandias, king of kings:
Look on my works, ye Mighty, and despair!"
Nothing beside remains. Round the decay
Of that colossal wreck, boundless and bare
The lone and level sands stretch far away.

ELIZABETH BARRETT BROWNING

How Do I Love Thee? 1850

How do I love thee? Let me count the ways.
I love thee to the depth and breadth and height
My soul can reach, when feeling out of sight
For the ends of Being and ideal Grace.
I love thee to the level of every day's
Most quiet need, by sun and candlelight.
I love thee freely, as men strive for Right;
I love thee purely, as they turn from Praise;
I love thee with the passion put to use
In my old griefs, and with my childhood's faith.
I love thee with a love I seemed to lose
With my lost saints—I love thee with the breath,
Smiles, tears of all my life!—and, if God choose,
I shall but love thee better after death.

Ozymandias: Greek name for the thirteenth-century B.C. Egyptian pharaoh Ramses II.

COUNTEE CULLEN

Yet Do I Marvel

1925

I doubt not God is good, well-meaning, kind,
And did He stoop to quibble could tell why
The little buried mole continues blind,
Why flesh that mirrors Him must some day die,
Make plain the reason tortured Tantalus°
Is baited by the fickle fruit, declare
If merely brute caprice dooms Sisyphus°
To struggle up a never-ending stair.
Inscrutable His ways are, and immune
To catechism by a mind too strewn
With petty cares to slightly understand
What awful brain compels His awful hand.
Yet do I marvel at this curious thing:
To make a poet black, and bid him sing!

EDNA ST. VINCENT MILLAY

What lips my lips have kissed, and where, and why,

1923

What lips my lips have kissed, and where, and why,
I have forgotten, and what arms have lain
Under my head till morning; but the rain
Is full of ghosts tonight, that tap and sigh
Upon the glass and listen for reply,
And in my heart there stirs a quiet pain
For unremembered lads that not again
Will turn to me at midnight with a cry.
Thus in the winter stands the lonely tree,
Nor knows what birds have vanished one by one,
Yet knows its boughs more silent than before:
I cannot say what loves have come and gone;
I only know that summer sang in me
A little while, that in me sings no more.

---

5. Tantalus: In Hades, the Greek underworld, Tantalus was prevented from assuaging his hunger as he reached for fruit just beyond his grasp. **7. Sisyphus:** In Greek myth, Sisyphus was condemned to roll a huge stone uphill that always rolled back down just before he reached the top.

GWENDOLYN BROOKS

The Rites for Cousin Vit

1945

Carried her unprotesting out the door.
Kicked back the casket stand. But it can't hold her,
That stuff and satin aiming to enfold her,
The lid's contrition nor the bolts before.
Oh oh. Too much. Too much. Even now, surmise,
She rises in the sunshine. There she goes,
Back to the bars she knew and the repose
In love-rooms and the things in people's eyes.
Too vital and too squeaking. Must emerge.
Even now she does the snake-hips with a hiss,
Slops the bad wine across her shantung, talks
Of pregnancy, guitars and bridgework, walks
In parks or alleys, comes haply on the verge
Of happiness, haply hysterics. Is.

JUNE JORDAN

Something Like a Sonnet for Phillis Miracle Wheatley

1989

Girl from the realm of birds florid and fleet
flying full feather in far or near weather
Who fell to a dollar lust coffled like meat
Captured by avarice and hate spit together
Trembling asthmatic alone on the slave block
built by a savagery travelling by carriage
viewed like a species of flaw in the livestock
A child without safety of mother or marriage

Chosen by whimsy but born to surprise
They taught you to read but you learned how to write
Begging the universe into your eyes:
They dressed you in light but you dreamed with the night.
From Africa singing of justice and grace,
Your early verse sweetens the fame of our Race.

The Sestina and the Villanelle

Poets, like nearly everyone else, enjoy word games, and if you also like to play with words, you will find an absorbing challenge in two older poetic forms, the **sestina** and the **villanelle**. Many modern writers looking for a form of verse with the richness of the sonnet, but which also presents more of a technical challenge, have been drawn to these reminders of a more elegant period in poetry's history. The sestina is composed of six stanzas, each six lines long, with a concluding verse of three lines called the *envoy*. The form, which is called the "song of sixes," originated in France, where it is thought to have been introduced into Provençal love poetry in the thirteenth century. It is a complicated pattern of verse and rhyme. The last words of the first six lines are repeated as end words of the lines of the following five stanzas. The final three lines must include the words, but in any order. One of the best-known examples of a sestina is this poem by Elizabeth Bishop.

ELIZABETH BISHOP

Sestina

1965

September rain falls on the house.
In the failing light, the old grandmother
sits in the kitchen with the child
beside the Little Marvel Stove,
reading the jokes from the almanac,
laughing and talking to hide her tears.

She thinks that her equinoctial tears
and the rain that beats on the roof of the house
were both foretold by the almanac,
but only known to a grandmother.
The iron kettle sings on the stove.
She cuts some bread and says to the child,

It's time for tea now; but the child
is watching the teakettle's small hard tears
dance like mad on the hot black stove,
the way the rain must dance on the house.
Tidying up, the old grandmother
hangs up the clever almanac

on its string. Birdlike, the almanac
hovers half open above the child,
hovers above the old grandmother
and her teacup full of dark brown tears.
She shivers and says she thinks the house
feels chilly, and puts more wood in the stove.

It was to be, says the Marvel Stove.
I know what I know, says the almanac.
With crayons the child draws a rigid house
and a winding pathway. Then the child

puts in a man with buttons like tears
and shows it proudly to the grandmother.

But secretly, while the grandmother
busies herself about the stove,
the little moons fall down like tears
from between the pages of the almanac
into the flower bed the child
has carefully placed in the front of the house.

Time to plant tears, says the almanac.
The grandmother sings to the marvelous stove
and the child draws another inscrutable house.

The villanelle is composed of five tercets and a final quatrain, written in iambic pentameter. The rhyme scheme for the tercets is *ABA*, and the quatrain repeats the final rhyme, *ABAA*. Like the sestina, the poem is an elaborate game in which entire lines appear again and again. The first line becomes the final line of the second and fourth tercets, and it also becomes the next to last line of the quatrain. The last line of the first tercet becomes the last line of the third and fifth tercet and finally ends the poem. One of the best-loved examples of the modern villanelle is "Do Not Go Gentle into That Good Night," the Welsh poet Dylan Thomas's moving tribute to his father. In a note to his publisher when he sent the poem, Thomas wrote, "The only person I can't show the little enclosed poem to is my father, who doesn't know he is dying."

DYLAN THOMAS

Do Not Go Gentle into That Good Night 1951

Do not go gentle into that good night,
Old age should burn and rave at close of day;
Rage, rage against the dying of the light.

Though wise men at their end know dark is right,
Because their words had forked no lightning they
Do not go gentle into that good night.

Good men, the last wave by, crying how bright
Their frail deeds might have danced in a green bay,
Rage, rage against the dying of the light.

Wild men who caught and sang the sun in flight,
And learn, too late, they grieved it on its way,
Do not go gentle into that good night.

Grave men, near death, who see with blinding sight
Blind eyes could blaze like meteors and be gay,
Rage, rage against the dying of the light.

And you, my father, there on the sad height,
Curse, bless, me now with your fierce tears, I pray.
Do not go gentle into that good night.
Rage, rage against the dying of the light.

DRAMATIC POETRY

The term **dramatic poetry** doesn't mean, as you might think, someone exclaiming, "That was really a dramatic poem!" It means poetry used as the language of drama. Classical Greek drama was written in poetic forms, and in the great era of drama before the modern industrial age the plays of the theaters of England, France, Spain, and Germany were written in unrhymed verse. If we've grown up with English as our first language, when we think of dramatic dialogue declaimed on the stage, we probably are hearing, in our memory, the blank verse cadences of Shakespeare and the other writers for the Elizabethan theater. The monologues of Shakespeare's plays, moments when a character steps away from the action and tells his thoughts aloud to the audience, have long been popular as poems in themselves. The monologue "To be or not to be" from *Hamlet* is one of Shakespeare's most widely known works. Another monologue that has been recited almost as often occurs in *Macbeth*. At a dramatic moment when Macbeth is preparing for the play's decisive battle, he is brought the news that his wife, Lady Macbeth, is dead. He hesitates for a moment and speaks of his inner feelings.

WILLIAM SHAKESPEARE

Tomorrow, and tomorrow, and tomorrow° 1605

Tomorrow, and tomorrow, and tomorrow
Creeps in this petty pace from day to day,
To the last syllable of recorded time;
And all our yesterdays have lighted fools
The way to dusty death. Out, out, brief candle!
Life's but a walking shadow, a poor player
That struts and frets his hour upon the stage
And then is heard no more. It is a tale
Told by an idiot, full of sound and fury
Signifying nothing.

From *Macbeth* Act V, Scene V.

The Dramatic Monologue

The Victorian era in England, with its busy stages and its long tradition of theater and drama, was a period marked by excited interest in a new form called the **dramatic monologue**. It is usually defined as a poem written in the form of a speech or a long narrative that the person who is the subject of the poem is delivering to someone else. During its period of greatest popularity, when dramatic monologues were often delivered as theater spectacles, the monologue depicted a definite speaker who was talking to someone who was only imagined; there was some implied action; and the action took place in the present. Often the subject of the more lurid monologues was a woman who related in fearsome tones the tale of what had befallen her and then ended her story by hurling herself from an imagined cliff into the ocean.

The dramatic monologues written by the English poet Robert Browning, however, were insightful character studies, and the speakers reveal themselves to the audience as the poem unfolds. Browning's "My Last Duchess" is a classic of the form. If you read the poem aloud, you will hear the subtlety and ease of its language. The poem perfectly fits the nineteenth-century ideal of the dramatic monologue. It presents a definite speaker, a wealthy and powerful Duke, showing his art collection to a visitor who represents a new candidate for marriage, and the moment is the present as the Duke addresses the emissary.

Part of the fascination of "My Last Duchess" is the fate of the woman whose painting is on the wall. As you read Browning's poem, ask yourself, why is he speaking of her as his "last Duchess"? What has she done that caused him to be angry? What is the emissary doing there listening to the Duke's practiced, self-satisfied talk? Then you could ask yourself, what kind of society would regard a wife of so little value that her husband could put her to death for a trivial moment of annoyance without the fear of his retribution or punishment?

ROBERT BROWNING

My Last Duchess

1842

Ferrara

That's my last Duchess painted on the wall,
Looking as if she were alive. I call
That piece a wonder, now: Frà Pandolf's° hands
Worked busily a day, and there she stands.
Will't please you sit and look at her? I said
"Frà Pandolf" by design, for never read
Strangers like you that pictured countenance,
The depth and passion of its earnest glance,

3. Frà Pandolf's: Brother Pandolf, a fictional painter.

But to myself they turned (since none puts by
The curtain I have drawn for you, but I)
And seemed as they would ask me, if they durst,
How such a glance came there; so, not the first
Are you to turn and ask thus. Sir, 'twas not
Her husband's presence only, called that spot
Of joy into the Duchess' cheek: perhaps
Frà Pandolf chanced to say "Her mantle laps
Over my lady's wrist too much," or "Paint
Must never hope to reproduce the faint
Half-flush that dies along her throat": such stuff
Was courtesy, she thought, and cause enough
For calling up that spot of joy. She had
A heart—how shall I say?—too soon made glad,
Too easily impressed; she liked whate'er
She looked on, and her looks went everywhere.
Sir, 'twas all one! My favor at her breast,
The dropping of the daylight in the West,
The bough of cherries some officious fool
Broke in the orchard for her, the white mule
She rode with round the terrace—all and each
Would draw from her alike the approving speech,
Or blush, at least. She thanked men,—good! but thanked
Somehow—I know not how—as if she ranked
My gift of a nine-hundred-years-old name
With anybody's gift. Who'd stoop to blame
This sort of trifling? Even had you skill
In speech—which I have not—to make your will
Quite clear to such an one, and say, "Just this
Or that in you disgusts me; here you miss,
Or there exceed the mark"—and if she let
Herself be lessoned so, nor plainly set
Her wits to yours, forsooth, and made excuse,
—E'en then would be some stooping; and I choose
Never to stoop. Oh sir, she smiled, no doubt,
Whene'er I passed her; but who passed without
Much the same smile? This grew; I gave commands;
Then all smiles stopped together. There she stands
As if alive. Will't please you rise? We'll meet
The company below, then. I repeat,
The Count your master's known munificence
Is ample warrant that no just pretense
Of mine for dowry will be disallowed;
Though his fair daughter's self, as I avowed
At starting, is my object. Nay, we'll go
Together down, sir. Notice Neptune, though,

Taming a sea-horse, thought a rarity,
Which Claus of Innsbruck° cast in bronze for me!

The Pattern Poem

Perhaps the most exotic of the traditional poetic forms is the **pattern poem**. Pattern poems are usually unrhymed, they don't use any of the traditional meters, and in their use of words the only requirement is that the words tell us something about why the poem is the shape it is. Some of the earliest poetry by the classic Greek writers were sometimes composed as pattern poems, or **shaped poems**, as they are also called. One of the best-known pattern poems in English verse is "Easter Wings," by the seventeenth-century clergyman George Herbert. The pattern of the lines is intended to suggest the wings of a dove in flight.

GEORGE HERBERT

Easter Wings

1633

Lord, who createdst man in wealth and store,°
   Though foolishly he lost the same,
      Decaying more and more
         Till he became
            Most poor:
            With thee
         O let me rise
      As larks, harmoniously,
   And sing this day thy victories:
Then shall the fall further the flight in me.

My tender age in sorrow did begin:
   And still with sicknesses and shame
      Thou didst so punish sin,
         That I became
            Most thin.
            With thee
         Let me combine,
      And feel this day thy victory;
   For, if I imp° my wing on thine,
Affliction shall advance the flight in me.

56. Claus of Innsbruck: Unidentified; probably a fictional sculptor.
1. wealth and store: Abundance. **19. imp:** Graft, a term used in falconry.

Some of the most imaginative pattern poems of our modern era were written by the Polish-French modernist poet Guillaume Apollinaire. He fought in the French Army in the First World War and was seriously wounded in 1916. In the first poem, the shape is the famed Eiffel Tower in Paris. Apollinaire's poem delivers a sarcastic message to France's enemies who were threatening Paris as he was writing it.

GUILLAUME APOLLINAIRE

Hail World

1918

TRANSLATED BY ANNE HYDE GREET

H
A
I L
W O
R LD
WHOSE
ELOQUE
NT TON
GUE I A
M THAT ITS
M O U T H
OH PARIS
STICKS OUT AND
ALWAYS W I L L
A T THE
GER MANS

If you have some difficulty understanding what he has written, this is the text.

Hail World, whose eloquent tongue I am that its mouth
OH PARIS sticks out and always will AT THE GERMANS.

Apollinaire was the leader of a group of young rebellious writers, artists, and musicians called the **Surrealists**. They came together to challenge their society's conventional limits on behavior, belief, and tradition, which they found hypocritical and inhibiting. They were a major influence on the American Beat writers and artists of the 1950s, who considered them as their cultural forebears.

Apollinaire's most famous pattern poem is this picture of rain, as the sounds of the raindrops whisper the lines to him. The ancient music of the rain reminds him of women's voices and tells him of his life's marvelous encounters. He also sees the clouds whinnying and rearing like horses, and they tell him of the world and its multitude of cities. The last line seems to hint of the ties of ordinary life. This poem, despite the challenge of re-creating it using other words, has been translated into many languages.

GUILLAUME APOLLINAIRE

It's Raining

1915

TRANSLATED BY ANNE HYDE GREET

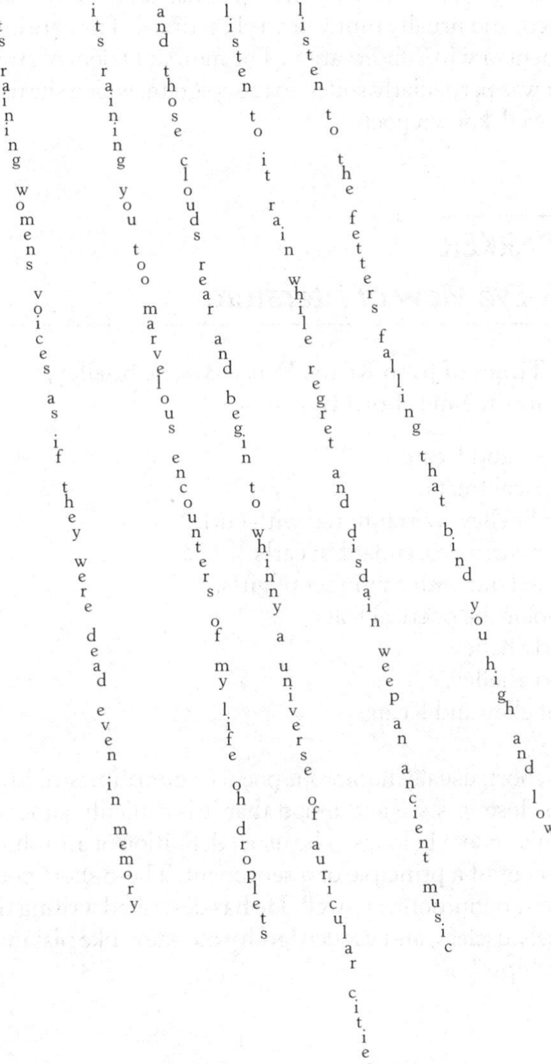
its raining womens voices as if they were dead even in memory
its raining you too marvelous encounters of my life o droplets
and those clouds rear and begin to whinny a universe of auricular cities
listen to it rain while regret and disdain weep an ancient music
listen to the fetters falling that bind you high and low

If you have difficulty following the lines, this is the text of the poem:

it's raining women's voices as if they were dead even in memory
it's raining you too marvelous encounters of my life, oh droplets
and those clouds rear and begin to whinny a universe of auricular cities
listen to it rain while regret and disdain weep an ancient music
listen to the fetters falling that bind you high and low

The Epigram, the Aphorism, and the Limerick

Lyric poetry, by its nature, has very loosely defined boundaries or limitations, and it also has room for many forms of humorous short poems. One of these is the **epigram**. Epigrams are usually short poems, never more than a few lines long, often rhymed, and usually funny or wryly satirical. They are intended to make a sharp comment or witty observation. The mordant talent of American writer Dorothy Parker was particularly suited to the epigram, which she uses here to comment on some well-known poets.

DOROTHY PARKER

From *A Pig's-Eye View of Literature* 1928

The Lives and Times of John Keats, Percy Bysshe Shelley, and George Gordon Noel, Lord Byron

Byron and Shelley and Keats
Were a trio of lyrical treats.
The forehead of Shelley was cluttered with curls,
And Keats never was a descendant of earls,
And Byron walked out with a number of girls,
But it didn't impair the poetical feats
    Of Byron and Shelley,
    Of Byron and Shelley,
Of Byron and Shelley and Keats.

Another kind of short, usually humorous poem is the **aphorism**. Epigrams and aphorisms are so close in style and mood that it is difficult sometimes to decide where a particular poem belongs. The usual definition of an aphorism is a short, concise statement of a principle or a sentiment. These short poems by James Richardson fit the definition very well. He has described writing them as "a distracting, obviously useless, and vaguely guilty pleasure, like playing video games or eating corn chips."

JAMES RICHARDSON

From *Vectors: Five Hundred Aphorisms and Ten-Second Essays* 2001

Of all the ways to avoid living perfect discipline is the most admired.

Who breaks the thread, the one who pulls, the one who holds on?

Despair says *I cannot lift that weight*. Happiness says, *I do not have to*.

Impatience is not wanting to understand that you don't understand.

Patience is not very different from courage. It just takes longer.

Every life is allocated one hundred seconds of true genius. They might be enough, if we could just be sure which ones they were.

They gave me most who took most gladly of my love.

The **limerick** is a short, humorous poem that is defined by its verse form. It has become one of the most widespread types of folk poetry, usually in the scatological and obscene forms that everyone has read or heard at some time in their lives. The form is a fixed five-line verse, and there is only a single stanza, rhyming *aabba*. It is the characteristic meter of limericks that makes them so easy to remember. Their rhythmic pattern is two rhyming lines of three strong accents, followed by two lines of two strong accents—with a different rhyme—then a final line that returns to the three accents of the first two lines and rhymes with them. The meter is an anapest, but the form allows for some variation.

Whatever a reader may think of limericks, there is no other kind of poetry quite like them. They are a good example of what we mean when we talk about freedom within limits. Often writers who are known for more serious work have used the form to write poems that are more lighthearted than their usual poetry.

DYLAN THOMAS

The last time I slept with the Queen

The last time I slept with the Queen
She said, as I whistled "Ich Dien":°
    "It's royalty's night out,
    But please put the light out,
The Queen may be had, but not seen."

Although it may seem a contradiction in terms, limericks are also very useful as literary criticism. Although these limericks, all by English writers, are

"Ich Dien": "I serve"—the official motto of the Prince of Wales.

meant to be laughed at, each of them is also a skillfully presented comment on the poem or the play that is the limerick's subject. It would be hard to think of a better short description of the central figure of T. S. Eliot's "The Love Song of J. Alfred Prufrock" (p. 961) than J. Walker's opening line, "An angst-ridden amorist, Fred . . ." A. Cinna, in a limerick's small dimensions, manages to present some of the questions that have often bothered students trying to make sense out of Shakespeare's *Hamlet*.

The fine English poet, John Donne,
Was wont to admonish the Sunne:
  "You busie old foole
  Lie still and keep coole,
For I am in bed having funne."
–WENDY COPE

ON T.S. ELIOT'S *PRUFROCK*

An angst-ridden amorist, Fred,
Saw sartorial changes ahead.
  His mind kept on ringing
  With fishy girls singing.
Soft fruit also filled him with dread.
–J. WALKER

APROPOS COLERIDGE'S *KUBLA KHAN*

When approached by a person from Porlock
It's best to take time by the forelock.
  Shout, "I'm not at home
  'Till I've finished this pome!"
And refuse to unfasten the door-lock.
–RICHARD LEIGHTON GREENE

ON *HAMLET*

Did Ophelia ask Hamlet to bed?
Was Gertrude incestuously wed?
  Is there anything certain?
  By the fall of the curtain
Almost everyone's certainly dead.
–A. CINNA

Poems for Further Reading

ANDREW MARVELL

To His Coy Mistress 1681

Had we but world enough, and time,
This coyness, lady, were no crime.
We would sit down, and think which way

To walk, and pass our long love's day.
Thou by the Indian Ganges' side
Shouldst rubies find; I by the tide
Of Humber would complain. I would
Love you ten years before the flood,
And you should, if you please, refuse
Till the conversion of the Jews.
My vegetable love should grow
Vaster than empires and more slow;
An hundred years should go to praise
Thine eyes, and on thy forehead gaze;
Two hundred to adore each breast,
But thirty thousand to the rest;
An age at least to every part,
And the last age should show your heart.
For, lady, you deserve this state,
Nor would I love at lower rate.

But at my back I always hear
Time's wingéd chariot hurrying near;
And yonder all before us lie
Deserts of vast eternity.
Thy beauty shall no more be found,
Nor, in thy marble vault, shall sound
My echoing song; then worms shall try
That long-preserved virginity,
And your quaint honor turn to dust,
And into ashes all my lust:
The grave's a fine and private place,
But none, I think, do there embrace.

Now therefore, while the youthful hue
Sits on thy skin like morning dew,
And while thy willing soul transpires° *breathes forth*
At every pore with instant fires,
Now let us sport us while we may,
And now, like amorous birds of prey,
Rather at once our time devour
Than languish in his slow-chapped° power. *slow-jawed*
Let us roll all our strength and all
Our sweetness up into one ball,
And tear our pleasures with rough strife
Thorough° the iron gates of life: *through*
Thus, though we cannot make our sun
Stand still, yet we will make him run.

WILLIAM WORDSWORTH

I Wandered Lonely as a Cloud

1804

I wandered lonely as a cloud
That floats on high o'er vales and hills,
When all at once I saw a crowd,
A host, of golden daffodils;
Beside the lake, beneath the trees,
Fluttering and dancing in the breeze.

Continuous as the stars that shine
And twinkle on the milky way,
They stretched in never-ending line
Along the margin of a bay:
Ten thousand saw I at a glance,
Tossing their heads in sprightly dance.

The waves beside them danced; but they
Outdid the sparkling waves in glee;
A poet could not but be gay,
In such a jocund company;
I gazed—and gazed—but little thought
What wealth the show to me had brought:

For oft, when on my couch I lie
In vacant or in pensive mood,
They flash upon that inward eye
Which is the bliss of solitude;
And then my heart with pleasure fills,
And dances with the daffodils.

CHRISTINA ROSSETTI

A Birthday

1848

My heart is like a singing bird
    Whose nest is in a watered shoot;
My heart is like an apple-tree
    Whose boughs are bent with thickset fruit;
My heart is like a rainbow shell
    That paddles in a halcyon sea;
My heart is gladder than all these
    Because my love is come to me.

Raise me a dais of silk and down;
    Hang it with vair and purple dyes;

Carve it in doves and pomegranates,
    And peacocks with a hundred eyes;
Work it in gold and silver grapes,
    In leaves and silver fleurs-de-lys;
Because the birthday of my life
    Is come, my love is come to me.

ALFRED, LORD TENNYSON

Ulysses

1833

It little profits that an idle king,
By this still hearth, among these barren crags,
Matched with an aged wife, I mete and dole
Unequal laws unto a savage race
That hoard, and sleep, and feed, and know not me.
I cannot rest from travel: I will drink
Life to the lees: all times I have enjoyed
Greatly, have suffered greatly, both with those
That loved me, and alone; on shore, and when
Through scudding drifts the rainy Hyades°
Vexed the dim sea: I am become a name;
For always roaming with a hungry heart
Much have I seen and known; cities of men
And manners, climates, councils, governments,
Myself not least, but honored of them all;
And drunk delight of battle with my peers,
Far on the ringing plains of windy Troy.
I am a part of all that I have met;
Yet all experience is an arch wherethrough
Gleams that untravelled world, whose margin fades
For ever and for ever when I move.
How dull it is to pause, to make an end,
To rust unburnished, not to shine in use!
As though to breathe were life. Life piled on life
Were all too little, and of one to me
Little remains: but every hour is saved
From that eternal silence, something more,
A bringer of new things; and vile it were
For some three suns to store and hoard myself,
And this gray spirit yearning in desire

10. Hyades: A cluster of stars whose rising was thought to be a sign of rain.

To follow knowledge like a sinking star,
Beyond the utmost bound of human thought.
  This is my son, mine own Telemachus,°
To whom I leave the scepter and the isle—
Well-loved of me, discerning to fulfil
This labor, by slow prudence to make mild
A rugged people, and through soft degrees
Subdue them to the useful and the good.
Most blameless is he, centered in the sphere
Of common duties, decent not to fail
In offices of tenderness, and pay
Meet° adoration to my household gods *proper*
When I am gone. He works his work, I mine.
  There lies the port: the vessel puffs her sail;
There gloom the dark broad seas. My mariners,
Souls that have toiled, and wrought, and thought with me—
That ever with a frolic welcome took
The thunder and the sunshine, and opposed
Free hearts, free foreheads—you and I are old;
Old age hath yet his honor and his toil;
Death closes all: but something ere the end,
Some work of noble note, may yet be done,
Not unbecoming men that strove with gods.
The lights begin to twinkle from the rocks:
The long day wanes: the slow moon climbs: the deep
Moans round with many voices. Come, my friends,
'Tis not too late to seek a newer world.
Push off, and sitting well in order smite
The sounding furrows; for my purpose holds
To sail beyond the sunset and the baths
Of all the western stars, until I die.
It may be that the gulfs will wash us down:
It may be we shall touch the Happy Isles°
And see the great Achilles, whom we knew.
Though much is taken, much abides; and though
We are not now that strength which in old days
Moved earth and heaven, that which we are, we are;
One equal temper of heroic hearts,
Made weak by time and fate but strong in will
To strive, to seek, to find, and not to yield.

33. Telemachus: The son of Odysseus and Penelope who plots with his father to murder his mother's suitors. **63. touch the Happy Isles:** In Greek mythology the Happy Isles were the home of dead warriors. In line 64, Ulysses speaks of his old comrade Achilles, who fought alongside him at Troy and was killed there.

COMMENTARIES

ERICA JONG

Erica Jong first became known for her feminist novel *Fear of Flying* (1973), but she has also published several collections of poetry and a memoir, *Any Woman's Blues* (1991). Her essay describes her discovery of Shakespeare's sonnets when she was a college student.

Devouring Time: Shakespeare's Sonnets 1996

My love affair with Shakespeare's sonnets began when I was in college. Looking back, it seems to me that at every stage of my adult life, the sonnets have meant something different to me—always deepening, always inexhaustible.

The most daunting challenge is to choose a favorite out of the 152 best poems in our language, since there are so many that move me deeply. I begin this impossible task by reading through the sonnets to myself silently, and then by listening to Sir John Gielgud's astonishing rendition of them, recorded in 1963, Shakespeare's quatercentenary. (I deliberately do not turn to my groaning bookshelves of Shakespeare criticism with their pointless, and ultimately snobbish, debates about the identity of "Mr. W. H." or whether or not our "Top Poet," as Auden called him, could really be a mere middle-class man of Stratford rather than the Earl of Oxford—or perhaps even the Virgin Queen herself. I want to return to the sonnets freshly—as a common reader, responding to them as a person first, a poet second.) As Gielgud's great actor's voice reawakens these dazzling poems for me, I hear again the toll of mortality in the sonnets, the elaboration of the themes of love and death and the stark repetition of their central word: "time."

Devouring time, the wastes of Time, Time's scythe, Wasteful time, in war with time, this bloody tyrant time, time's pencil, time's furrows, dear time's waste, Time's injurious hand, Time's spoils, Time's fool, a hell of time, Time's fickle glass. . . . It seems I cannot read or hear the sonnets without being reminded of how little time is left—which sends me to my desk to write with frenzied hand.

Time is the all-powerful, wrathful God of the sonnets. And to this awesome power, the poet opposes procreation, love, and poetry.

The first thirteen sonnets urge begetting a child to oppose death:

Th'ou art thy mother's glass, and she in thee
Calls back the lovely April of her prime.
(Sonnet 3)

Then the theme shifts, and by Sonnet 15 the poet is comparing his own craft to procreation as a way of winning the war with time:

And all in war with Time for love of you,
As he takes from you, I ingraft you new.

But poetry is fired by love, so these two forms of redemption are really the same. Children redeem us from time, poetry redeems us from time, and love is the force that drives them both. As the sonnets go on to tell their twisted tale of rival loves, rival poets, love, passion, parting, obsessional sexuality, wrath, reunion, forgiveness, self-love, self-loathing, and self-forgiveness, time never ceases to be the poet's alpha and omega, the deity he both worships and despises.

And so I find myself coming back again and again to Sonnet 19, a poet's credo if ever there were one.

Devouring Time, blunt thou the lion's paws,
And make the earth devour her own sweet brood;
Pluck the keen teeth from the fierce tiger's yaws,
And burn the long-liv'd phoenix in her blood;
Make glad and sorry seasons as thou fleet'st,
And do whate'er thou wilt, swift-footed Time,
To the wide world and all her fading sweets;
But I forbid thee one most heinous crime:
O, carve not with thy hours my love's fair brow,
Nor draw no lines there with thine antique pen;
Him in thy course untainted to do allow
For beauty's pattern to succeeding men.
    Yet do thy worst, old Time: despite thy wrong,
    My love shall in my verse ever live young.

Sonnet 19 is hardly the most complex of Shakespeare's sonnets, nor the most tortured. The sonnets that recount obsessional love, jealousy, and lust are far darker and more fretted. But Sonnet 19 calls me back again and again because it is one of the few in which the poet addresses time directly and takes him on—David against Goliath.

The simplicity of the sonnet's "statement" delights me: "Time, you big bully, you think you're so great. You can make people die and tigers lose their teeth and change the seasons so fast it makes us dizzy. But spare my love. Don't scribble on him with your antique pen. On second thought, do whatever the hell you like. You have the power to destroy, but I have an even greater power: I create. And by capturing my love in poetry, I can keep my love young forever, whatever you may do to destroy him!"

There is a fluidity to this sonnet that seems to me a triumph of this difficult form. The three quatrains flow into one another and become one exhortation. The couplet argues with them all, changing the direction swiftly and ironically. The poet is standing up to the bully. Suddenly "Devouring Time" becomes "old Time," as if in the course of fourteen lines he had withered like a vampire thrown into a raging inferno. The poem itself has subdued time, made him old before his time, vanquished him. The force of poetry alone defeats time.

This theme is elaborated often in the sonnets, but seldom with such simplicity, the simplicity of a person addressing a fearsome deity without fear: the poet speaking to the gods. Throughout the sonnets, the poet addresses his love, his siren, his lust, even himself, but only in this sonnet (and once more in Sonnet 123) does he address Time directly. He throws down the gauntlet and takes Time on as if one might defeat a powerful foe simply with the force of language.

And, of course, one *can*, as Shakespeare's sonnets prove. We go back to them again and again, discovering new depths in them as time carves new depths in our hearts.

In youth, we tend to love the love poems, the poems of obsessional lust, jealousy, and rage. "Th'expense of spirit in a waste of shame" (129) reminds us of our own struggles to master lust. "So are you to my thoughts as food to life" (75) reminds us of the yearning of first love. As we age, we increasingly see Time shadowing love and the bliss of creation as the only redemption. Shakespeare's sonnets are a fugue on the theme of time. They can be read together or separately, line by line, quatrain by quatrain, or as a narrative the power of art against decay. They prove the poet's point by their very durability.

Each time I go back to the sonnets, I find something that seemed not to be there before. Perhaps I have changed and my vision is less clouded, or else the sonnets metamorphose on the shelf. The sonnets I love best are those with sustained voices, those that sound like a person speaking. I think I hear Shakespeare's private voice in these sonnets, as if he were whispering directly in my ear.

That Shakespeare's sonnets have defeated death comforts me — for what is great poetry, after all, but the continuation of the human voice after death?

PERCY BYSSHE SHELLEY

Percy Bysshe Shelley's lyrical, impassioned defense of the poet and his art is an expression of the romantic attitude toward art and literature. In part, Shelley is defending poetry against Plato's idea that poets should be banished from the ideal city, but he is also presenting the poet and the artist as an individual who should be free of society's constrictions.

From *A Defence of Poetry* 1821

A poem is the very image of life expressed in its eternal truth. There is this difference between a story and a poem, that a story is a catalogue of detached facts, which have no other bond of connexion than time, place, circumstance, cause and effect; the other is the creation of actions according to the unchangeable forms of human nature, as existing in the mind of the creator, which is itself the image of all other minds. The one is partial, and applies only to a definite period of time, and a certain combination of events which can never again recur; the other is universal, and contains within itself the germ of a relation to whatever motives or actions have place in the possible varieties of human nature. Time, which destroys the beauty and the use of the story of particular facts, stript of the poetry which should invest them, augments that of Poetry, and for ever develops new and wonderful applications of the eternal truth which it contains. Hence epitomes have been called the moths of just history; they eat out the poetry of it. The story of particular facts is as a mirror which obscures and distorts that which should be beautiful: Poetry is a mirror which makes beautiful that which is distorted.

The parts of a composition may be poetical, without the composition as a whole being a poem. A single sentence may be considered as a whole though it be found in a series of unassimilated portions; a single word even may be a spark of inextinguishable thought. And thus all the great historians, Herodotus, Plutarch, Livy, were poets; and although the plan of these writers, especially that of Livy, restrained them from developing this faculty in its highest degree, they make copious and ample amends for their subjection, by filling all the interstices of their subjects with living images.

Having determined what is poetry, and who are poets, let us proceed to estimate its effects upon society.

Poetry is ever accompanied with pleasure: all spirits on which it falls, open themselves to receive the wisdom which is mingled with its delight. In the infancy of the world, neither poets themselves nor their auditors are fully aware of the excellence of poetry: for it acts in a divine and unapprehended manner, beyond and above consciousness; and it is reserved for future generations to contemplate and measure the mighty cause and effect in all the strength and splendour of their union. Even in modern times, no living poet ever arrived at the fullness of his fame; the jury which sits in judgement upon a poet, belonging as he does to all time, must be composed of his peers: it must be impaneled by Time from the selectest of the wise of many generations. A Poet is a nightingale, who sits in darkness and sings to cheer its own solitude with sweet sounds; his auditors are as men entranced by the melody of an unseen musician, who feel that they are moved and softened, yet know not whence or why. The poems of Homer and his contemporaries were the delight of infant Greece; they were the elements of that social system which is the column upon which all succeeding civilization has reposed. Homer embodied the ideal perfection of his age in human character; nor can we doubt that those who read his verses were awakened to an ambition of becoming like to Achilles, Hector and Ulysses: the truth and beauty of friendship, patriotism and persevering devotion to an object, were unveiled to the depths in these immortal creations: the sentiments of the auditors must have been refined and enlarged by a sympathy with such great and lovely impersonations, until from admiring they imitated, and from imitation they identified themselves with the objects of their admiration. Nor let it be objected, that these characters are remote from moral perfection, and that they can by no means be considered as edifying patterns for general imitation. Every epoch under names more or less specious has deified its peculiar errors; revenge is the naked Idol of the worship of a semi-barbarous age; and Self-deceit is the veiled Image of unknown evil before which luxury and satiety lie prostrate. But a poet considers the vices of his contemporaries as the temporary dress in which his creations must be arrayed, and which cover without concealing the eternal proportions of their beauty. An epic or dramatic personage is understood to wear them around his soul, as he may the antient armour or the modern uniform around his body; whilst it is easy to conceive a dress more graceful than either. The beauty of the internal nature cannot be so far concealed by its accidental vesture, but that the spirit of its form shall communicate itself to the very disguise, and indicate the shape it hides from the manner in which it is worn. A majestic form and graceful motions will express themselves through the most barbarous and tasteless costume. Few poets of the highest class have chosen to exhibit the beauty of their conceptions in its naked truth and splendour; and it is doubtful whether the alloy of costume, habit, etc., be not necessary to temper this planetary music for mortal ears. . . .

Poetry is indeed something divine. It is at once the centre and circumference of knowledge; it is that which comprehends all science, and that to which all science must be referred. It is at the same time the root and blossom of all other systems of thought; it is that from which all spring, and that which adorns all; and that which, if blighted, denies the fruit and the seed, and withholds from the barren world the nourishment and the succession of the scions of the tree of life. It is the perfect and consummate surface and bloom of things; it is as the odour and the colour of the rose to the texture of the elements which compose it, as the form and the splendor of unfaded beauty to the secrets of anatomy and corruption. What were Virtue, Love, Patriotism, Friendship etc.—what were the scenery of this beautiful Universe which we inhabit—what were our consolations on this side of the grave—and what were our aspirations beyond it—if Poetry did not ascend to bring light and fire from those eternal regions where the owl-winged faculty of calculation dare not ever soar? Poetry is not like reasoning, a power to be exerted according to the determination of the will. A man cannot say, "I will compose poetry." The greatest poet even cannot say it: for the mind in creation is as a fading coal which some invisible influence, like an inconstant wind, awakens to transitory brightness: this power arises from within, like the colour of a flower which fades and changes as it is developed, and the conscious portions of our natures are unprophetic either of its approach or its departure. Could this influence be durable in its original purity and force, it is impossible to predict the greatness of the results; but when composition begins, inspiration is already on the decline, and the most glorious poetry that has ever been communicated to the world is probably a feeble shadow of the original conception of the poet. I appeal to the greatest Poets of the present day, whether it be not an error to assert that the finest passages of poetry are produced by labour and study. The toil and the delay recommended by critics can be justly interpreted to mean no more than a careful observation of the inspired moments, and an artificial connexion of the spaces between their suggestions by the intertexture of conventional expressions; a necessity only imposed by the limitedness of the poetical faculty itself. For Milton conceived the Paradise Lost as a whole before he executed it in portions. We have his own authority also for the Muse having "dictated" to him the "unpremeditated song," and let this be an answer to those who would allege the fifty-six various readings of the first line of the Orlando Furioso. Compositions so produced are to poetry what mosaic is to painting. This instinct and intuition of the poetical faculty is still more observable in the plastic and pictorial arts: a great statue or picture grows under the power of the artist as a child in the mother's womb; and the very mind which directs the hands in formation is incapable of accounting to itself for the origin, the gradations, or the media of the process.

Poetry is the record of the best and happiest moments of the happiest and best minds. We are aware of evanescent visitations of thought and feeling sometimes associated with place or person, sometimes regarding our own mind alone, and always arising unforeseen and departing unbidden, but elevating and delightful beyond all expression: so that even in the desire and the regret they leave, there cannot but be pleasure, participating as it does in the nature of its object. It is as it were the interpenetration of a diviner nature through our own; but its footsteps are like those of a wind over a sea, where the coming calm erases, and whose traces remain only as on the wrinkled sand which paves it. These and corresponding conditions of being are experienced principally by those of the most delicate sensibility and the most enlarged imagination; and the state of mind produced by them is at war with every base desire. The enthusiasm of virtue, love, patriotism, and friendship is essentially linked with these emotions; and whilst they last, self appears as what it is, an atom to a Universe. Poets are not only subject to these experiences as spirits of the most refined organization, but they can colour all that they combine with the evanescent hues of this ethereal world; a word, or a trait in the representation of a sense or a passion, will touch the enchanted chord, and reanimate, in those who have ever experienced these emotions, the sleeping, the cold, the buried image of the past. Poetry thus makes immortal all that is best and most beautiful in the world; it arrests the vanishing apparitions which haunt the interlunations of life, and veiling them or in language or in form sends them forth among mankind, bearing sweet news of kindred joy to those with whom their sisters abide—abide, because there is no portal of expression from the caverns of the spirit which they inhabit into the universe of things. Poetry redeems from decay the visitations of the divinity in man.

Poetry turns all things to loveliness; it exalts the beauty of that which is most beautiful, and it adds beauty to that which is most deformed; it marries exultation and horror, grief and pleasure, eternity and change; it subdues to union under its light yoke all irreconcilable things. It transmutes all that it touches, and every form moving within the radiance of its presence is changed by wondrous sympathy to an incarnation of the spirit which it breathes; its secret alchemy turns to potable gold the poisonous waters which flow from death through life; it strips the veil of familiarity from the world, and lays bare the naked and sleeping beauty which is the spirit of its forms. . . .

. . . The most unfailing herald, companion, and follower of the awakening of a great people to work a beneficial change in opinion or institution, is Poetry. At such periods there is an accumulation of the power of communicating and receiving intense and impassioned conceptions respecting man and nature. The persons in whom this power resides, may often, as far as regards many portions of their nature, have little apparent correspondence with that spirit of good of which they are the ministers. But even whilst they deny and abjure, they are yet compelled to serve, the Power which is seated upon the throne of their own soul. It is impossible to read the compositions of the most celebrated writers of the present day without being startled with the electric life which burns within their words. They measure the circumference and sound the depths of human nature with a comprehensive and all-penetrating spirit, and they are themselves perhaps the most sincerely astonished at its manifestations, for it is less their spirit than the spirit of the age. Poets are the hierophants of an unapprehended inspiration, the mirrors of the gigantic shadows which futurity casts upon the present, the words which express what they understand not; the trumpets which sing to battle, and feel not what they inspire: the influence which is moved not, but moves. Poets are the unacknowledged legislators of the World.

◆ Topics for Writing about Poetic Forms ◆

1. Discuss the contrast between the vision of hell as a place of ice and snow in "The Daemon Lover" (p. 748) and the more usual depictions of hell as a place of fire and flame. The question you should consider is whether this might reflect the poet's own experience of winter or whether he is making a more complicated statement about the nature of spiritual punishment.
2. There are many contrasts between the two elegies in the text, "Elegy Written in a Country Churchyard" (p. 758) and "Elegy for Jane" (p. 762). Discuss these contrasts and analyze how they reflect the times in which the poems were written.
3. Choose a sonnet from those in the text or from your other reading and paraphrase its ideas. Using your paraphrase, analyze how the form of the sonnet shapes the concepts the poet has presented.
4. Discuss the idea that poets have defined the sonnet as a "world in itself."
5. Create a pattern poem of your own, choosing a theme with a visual idea and using the words to present a picture of the poem's theme.

USEFUL TERMS TO REMEMBER

Ballad A long narrative poem, generally rhymed and written in short stanzas.

Couplet Two rhyming lines in a poem.

Dramatic monologue A personal story, often tragic or tragicomic, written in the first person.

Dramatic poetry Poetry that is used for a stage performance.

Elegy Traditionally a long, serious poem describing a death or a tragic occurrence. In modern poetry, often used for personal statements.

Epic Lengthy narratives of historical events or strong figures written in verse.

Octave A stanza of eight lines.

Ode A poem presenting an important person or event written in verse.

Pattern poem A poem that uses words to create a visual picture of the poem's subject.

Quatrain A stanza of four rhyming lines.

Refrain A repeated line ending each verse of a poem, particularly used in ballads.

Sestet A six-line stanza.

Sestina A complex verse form from the Middle Ages with six stanzas, each of six lines, that repeat words in a carefully regulated pattern.

Sonnet A poem, generally of fourteen lines and with a traditional meter and rhyme scheme, that develops a central theme.

Stanza A unit of verse with a meter and rhyme scheme that is repeated in similar verse units in the poem.

Tercet Three lines of verse ending in the same rhyme.

Villanelle An older verse form still popular with modern poets composed of five tercets and a final quatrain. The lines of the poem alternate in a carefully established pattern.

14.

Other Forms of Poetry

I used to love Keats, Blake.
Now I try haiku
for its honed brevities,
its inclusive silences.
–JUDITH WRIGHT, from "Brevity"

In earlier chapters we discussed how the far-reaching social changes of the beginning of the twentieth century challenged many poets' assumptions of the need for rhyme and meter in their writing. Traditional form was also shaken, and a long period of argument and experiment finally led to the open form poetry we know today. Walt Whitman had already broken free of traditional forms in 1855 with the long, unrhymed lines of his *Leaves of Grass*, but many younger poets found his poems too verbose to be a model for their own writing. They felt that traditional verse wasn't suited to describe their new experiences and ideas, but there was no agreement on what form the new poetry should take. The argument was carried on in little magazines and newspaper articles and manifestos as poets searched for a new language.

One of the first steps toward a clearer perception of the writers' new direction was the new style of writing called **imagism**. In one sweep it did away with rhyme and meter and proposed writing in a succinct, clear style that was free of the excesses of the previous decades. One of the earliest imagist poets was the young American Hilda Doolittle, who published poetry using her initials H. D. As you read this imagist poem she wrote in 1914, you can sense the joy she is feeling at being able to write as she pleases.

H. D.

The Pool 1917

Are you alive?
I touch you.

You quiver like a sea-fish.
I cover you with my net.
What are you—banded one?

IMAGISM

You will find that the aims of the imagists—writing that is clear and precise, using a language that directly expresses the ideas of the writer—can also be a model for your work. Imagist poetry can suggest useful principles for everything you write, not only your essays about literature. The imagist credos and examples can serve as guides for your own choice of words, sentences, and paragraphs.

The first imagist poetry was published in England in the years just before the First World War. Two of the original group, H. D. and Ezra Pound, were Americans, while the others were the English poets T. E. Hulme and Richard Aldington, who was H. D.'s husband. The term itself was invented by Pound, who was living in London at the time. Their cause was taken up by the New England poet Amy Lowell, who came to London to meet Pound and published two anthologies in the United States in 1915 and 1916 introducing the new style. For Lowell what was important was freedom from poetic meter. Her commentary on "Vers libre" or "free verse" (p. 821) describes the point of controversy that involved many poets in that period. The French term for the new style was widely used since French poets had begun writing in what is now known as open form nearly thirty years before. The short poem of Stephen Crane, "War Is Kind" (p. 1063), published in 1896, is an early enigmatic example.

As a literary movement, imagism lasted only a few years, but it played an important role in the development of open form poetry. Even poets who did not think of themselves as imagists used the methods of the imagists for their own writing. The imagists were trying to create poetry that T. E. Hulme described as "a moment of discovery or awareness, created by effective metaphor which provides the sharp, intuitive insight that is the essence of life."

Often the debate about imagism was about language itself. Many poets found that the same phrases and words had been used so many times in traditional poetry that they had their own associations. The poets felt that the language they inherited gave them no way to say anything fresh about the turbulent world that seemed to be crashing around them. If you look at Pound's notes on language in his famous defense of imagism in 1918 (Commentary, p. 818), you will see that he warns against the kind of abstract language that was common in the lyric poetry of his day. Pound advised:

> Use no superfluous words, no adjective which does not reveal something. Don't use such an expression as "dim lands of *peace.*" It dulls the image. It mixes an abstraction with the concrete. It comes from the writer's not realizing that the natural object is always the adequate symbol.

The credo that opened the 1915 imagist anthology was specific about the changes needed to make the poetic language vital again. The first point of the credo was "to use the language of common speech, but the exact word, not the nearly exact, nor the mere decorative." The fourth point was that imagist poetry should "present an image. Poetry should render particulars exactly, and not deal in vague generalities, however magnificent and sonorous."

The lean, hard diction of the new imagist poetry was to have a lasting effect on modern poetry. Poets found that when writing in the new idiom they did not have to round every poem into generalities, and they could create poems in the new form that had no need for rhyme or meter. William Carlos Williams, who had been close to both Pound and H. D. in the United States, stayed at home in New Jersey, where he practiced medicine and wrote poetry in his own American voice, though he worked closely with the new style. He expressed the imagist ideal as "no ideas but in things."

Imagist Poems for Further Reading

It would help in your reading if you made notes about the poets' use of words and phrases that seem to you to represent the principles of imagism. What elements in the poems still continue to relate to the traditional forms of poetic language and form you have studied earlier?

The first poem by Ezra Pound is perhaps the best known of the early imagist poems. Pound wrote it as an example of what he meant by *imagism* in his introduction to a collection of his friends' poems. It is a description of people in the Paris subway on a rainy, dark night, but it is like a quick glance that leaves you with an unforgettable image, even if it takes a moment to visualize what the poet is describing.

EZRA POUND

In a Station of the Metro

1913

The apparition of these faces in the crowd
Petals on a wet, black bough.

T. E. Hulme's role in the early years of imagism is well known. He contributed several imagist poems in the same style as this description of a London scene to the movement's early anthologies. His poem, like Pound's, is a glimpse, a visual image.

T. E. HULME

Images

1914

Old houses were scaffolding once
                    and workmen whistling.

For a few months, when they both were students at the University of Pennsylvania, Pound and Hilda Doolittle had been engaged. When she came to London, she quickly became involved in his literary crusades, and he persuaded her to use her initials H. D. for her writing.

H.D.

Oread° 1914

Whirl up, sea—
whirl your pointed pines,
splash your great pines
on our rocks,
hurl your green over us,
cover us with your pools of fir.

D. H. Lawrence was a poet before he became a novelist, and he was closely associated with the early imagist group. Although this poem was written later it has all the characteristics of the classic imagist poem. It is a glimpse that leaves us with an image in our minds.

D. H. LAWRENCE

The White Horse 1928

The youth walks up to the white horse, to put its halter on
and the horse looks at him in silence.
They are so silent they are in another world.

The next three poems illustrate how the lessons of imagism—the precise imagery, the intense power of a glance, the terse language—were quickly absorbed into the new poetry that was written in response to the challenge of imagist principles. This poem by Amy Lowell, written in 1919, has the structure of a conventional poem, but between its opening and closing lines and their more familiar sentiments, the description of the hill and the meeting house has the sharp, hard clarity that the principles of imagism insist on.

Oread: Mountain nymph.

AMY LOWELL

Meeting-House Hill

1919

I must be mad, or very tired,
When the curve of a blue bay beyond a railroad track
Is shrill and sweet to me like the sudden springing of a tune,
And the sight of a white church above thin trees in a city square
Amazes my eyes as though it were the Parthenon.
Clear, reticent, superbly final,
With the pillars of its portico refined to a cautious elegance,
It dominates the weak trees,
And the shot of its spire
Is cool and candid,
Rising into an unresisting sky.
Strange meeting-house
Pausing a moment upon a squalid hill-top.
I watch the spire sweeping the sky,
I am dizzy with the movement of the sky;
I might be watching a mast
With its royals set full
Straining before a two-reef breeze.
I might be sighting a tea-clipper,
Tacking into the blue bay,
Just back from Canton
With her hold full of green and blue porcelain
And a Chinese coolie leaning over the rail
Gazing at the white spire
With dull, sea-spent eyes.

William Carlos Williams never considered himself an imagist, but the poetry he wrote after the group began to publish their anthologies reflected their aims. The best way to describe the effect of the imagist credo on his work is to say that he wrote poetry that was made possible by imagism. His poem "The Red Wheelbarrow" would be a classic imagist description of a wheelbarrow left out in the rain near some chickens, except for his enigmatic phrase, "so much depends upon." What Williams seems to be suggesting in his eight short lines is that he finds something very important in this image of rain and chickens and a wheelbarrow in a backyard. Although we know that the inspiration came for Dr. Williams as he stood looking out the window into the backyard of a patient's house, waiting, as he said, "for some news of her condition," the basic image of the poem has never given away all its secrets.

WILLIAM CARLOS WILLIAMS

The Red Wheelbarrow 1923

so much depends
upon

a red wheel
barrow

glazed with rain
water

beside the white
chickens

Although Wallace Stevens was an insurance executive who lived in Hartford, Connecticut, he was closely associated with Williams and other young poets who were experimenting with the new style. The first and last verses of his "Thirteen Ways of Looking at a Blackbird" have all the characteristics of an imagist poem. Other verses have a more didactic tone, like the seventh, with its admonition to the men of Haddam, a small town in Connecticut, to stop thinking about imagined exotic birds and see the blackbirds walking on the ground around their feet.

Like Williams's poem about the red wheelbarrow, this poem has also defied easy access to its meanings. Perhaps one way to understand it is to think of it as a series of imagist poems and short, enigmatic lyrics, with blackbirds suddenly flying through it. Despite its mysteries, it has been translated into many different languages. It is a poem that reminds us of the lines we read by Archibald MacLeish as we began our study of poetry. His conclusion in his "Ars Poetica" was "A poem should not mean / But be."

WALLACE STEVENS

Thirteen Ways of Looking at a Blackbird 1931

I

Among twenty snowy mountains
The only moving thing
Was the eye of the blackbird.

II

I was of three minds,
Like a tree
In which there are three blackbirds.

III

The blackbird whistled in the autumn winds.
It was a small part of the pantomime.

IV

A man and a woman
Are one.
A man and a woman and a blackbird
Are one.

V

I do not know which to prefer,
The beauty of inflections
Or the beauty of innuendoes,
The blackbird whistling
Or just after.

VI

Icicles filled the long window
With barbaric glass.
The shadow of the blackbird
Crossed it, to and fro.
The mood
Traced in the shadow
An indecipherable cause.

VII

O thin men of Haddam,
Why do you imagine golden birds?
Do you not see how the blackbird
Walks around the feet
Of the women about you?

VIII

I know noble accents
And lucid, inescapable rhythms;
But I know, too,
That the blackbird is involved
In what I know.

IX

When the blackbird flew out of sight,
It marked the edge
Of one of many circles.

X

At the sight of blackbirds
Flying in a green light,
Even the bawds of euphony
Would cry out sharply.

XI

He rode over Connecticut
In a glass coach.
Once, a fear pierced him,
In that he mistook
The shadow of his equipage
For blackbirds.

XII

The river is moving.
The blackbird must be flying.

XIII

It was evening all afternoon.
It was snowing
And it was going to snow.
The blackbird sat
In the cedar-limbs.

CLASSICAL CHINESE VERSE AND THE JAPANESE HAIKU

In the decades at the beginning of the last century when the new concepts of free verse and imagism were being tirelessly debated, other new influences added weight to the arguments for a new style of poetry. It was at this period that poets in Europe and the United States discovered the great classical traditions of poetry from China and Japan. The poems in free translations were presented as models for the new open form poetry that was slowly gaining ground against traditional poetic forms. The work of two of the greatest Chinese poets, Li T'ai Po, usually named Li Po in the West, and Du Fu, or Tu Fu as he is often known, became absorbed into the new poetic style.

It was from the longer forms of the Chinese poetry that most poets drew their inspiration, and also part of the force of the work of these poets was the awareness that it came from a much older tradition. Both Li T'ai Po and Du Fu lived in the eighth century A.D. Although the two poets were close friends and read each other's poetry, they were often separated by the turbulent political events that devastated China during this period. Their poems were written hundreds of years before poetry began to appear in the new languages developing in medieval Europe and nearly a thousand years before the development of the haiku in Japan. Here is an example of a freely translated version of a well-known poem by Li T'ai Po.

LI T'AI PO

A Song of Changgan

Eighth century A.D.

TRANSLATED BY WITTER BYNNER

My hair had hardly covered my forehead.
I was picking flowers, playing by my door,
When you, my lover, on a bamboo horse,
Came trotting in circles and throwing green plums.
We lived near together on a lane in Ch'ang-kan,
Both of us young and happy-hearted.

. . . At fourteen I became your wife,
So bashful that I dared not smile,
And I lowered my head toward a dark corner
And would not turn to your thousand calls;
But at fifteen I straightened my brows and laughed,
Learning that no dust could ever seal our love,
That even unto death I would await you by my post
And would never lose heart in the tower of silent watching.

. . . Then when I was sixteen, you left on a long journey
Through the Gorges of Ch'u-t'ang, of rock and whirling water.
And then came the Fifth-month, more than I could bear,
And I tried to hear the monkeys in your lofty far-off sky.
Your footprints by our door, where I had watched you go,
Were hidden, every one of them, under green moss,
Hidden under moss too deep to sweep away.
And the first autumn wind added fallen leaves.
And now, in the Eighth-month, yellowing butterflies
Hover, two by two, in our west-garden grasses
And, because of all this, my heart is breaking
And I fear for my bright cheeks, lest they fade.

. . . Oh, at last, when you return through the three Pa districts,
Send me a message home ahead!
And I will come and meet you and will never mind the distance,
All the way to Chang-feng Sha.

The poem is popular today in the following adaptation by Ezra Pound, though Pound published it with his own name as author. In Pound's version you can see the similarities between the Chinese original and the modern poem he created.

EZRA POUND

The River-Merchant's Wife: A Letter

1915

(after Rihaku)°

While my hair was still cut straight across my forehead
I played about the front gate, pulling flowers.
You came by on bamboo stilts, playing horse,
You walked about my seat, playing with blue plums.
And we went on living in the village of Chokan:
Two small people, without dislike or suspicion.

At fourteen I married My Lord you.
I never laughed, being bashful.
Lowering my head, I looked at the wall.
Called to, a thousand times, I never looked back.

At fifteen I stopped scowling,
I desired my dust to be mingled with yours
For ever and for ever and for ever.
Why should I climb the look out?

At sixteen you departed,
You went into far Ku-to-yen, by the river of swirling eddies,
And you have been gone five months.
The monkeys make sorrowful noise overhead.

You dragged your feet when you went out.
By the gate now, the moss is grown, the different mosses,
Too deep to clear them away!
The leaves fall early this autumn, in wind.
The paired butterflies are already yellow with August
Over the grass in the West garden;
They hurt me. I grow older.
If you are coming down through the narrows of the river Kiang,
Please let me know beforehand,
And I will come out to meet you
  As far as Cho-fu-Sa.

The contemporary American poet Charles Wright responded to the writing of Tu Fu after a reading of the Chinese poet that inspired Wright to create his own version of the poem.

Rihaku: Japanese name for Li T'ai Po.

CHARLES WRIGHT

After Reading Tu Fu, I Go Outside to the Dwarf Orchard

1995

East of me, west of me, full summer.
How deeper than elsewhere the dusk is in your own yard.
Birds fly back and forth across the lawn
                    looking for home
As night drifts up like a little boat.
Day after day, I become of less use to myself.
Like this mockingbird,
                    I flit from one thing to the next.
What do I have to look forward to at fifty-four?
Tomorrow is dark.
            Day-after-tomorrow is darker still.
The sky dogs are whimpering.
Fireflies are dragging the hush of evening
                    up from the damp grass.
Into the world's tumult, into the chaos of every day,
Go quietly, quietly.

AN INTRODUCTION TO HAIKU

European and American poets discovered the minimalist, concentrated poetry of the Japanese haiku at about the same time as they read the poetry of China. Haiku also had a strong effect on the development of imagism. Although Pound had presented his principles of imagism as entirely his own creation, he was influenced by the writings of Yone Noguchi, a Japanese writer and poet who had been educated in the United States. Noguchi sent Pound examples of his own haiku as well as his book *The Spirit of Japanese Poetry,* published in 1915. Here is an example of Noguchi's writing, which Pound described to friends as "beautiful."

YONE NOGUCHI

Bits of song

1908

Bits of song—what else?
I, a rider of the stream,
Lone between the clouds.

The great masters of haiku began writing in the seventeenth and eighteenth centuries, and their new style showed the influence of Zen Buddhism, with its philosophical ideals of stripping away excess and decoration. The version of haiku that has become popular in the West has some similarities to the Japanese forms, but it also reflects the Western taste for a more orderly structured poem.

In Japan, **haiku** were generally composed in seventeen characters, or ideograms, which are called *on*, and they were written in a single descending line. Most included a *kigo*, which is a reference to the season of the year, even if the reference was simply the word "mosquitoes," which in Japan come only in the summer. The essence of the poem was its abrupt juxtaposition of images, usually presented as two or three related thoughts, often tantalizing in the elusiveness of their connections, and usually with a bridging *on* to anticipate the unexpected change. Since an ideogram may be written in different ways, the style of calligraphy may also recall other thoughts. The writer can allude to other haiku or to another poet by the way in which the ideogram is set down on the paper. Specific places or certain seasons of the year were often identified with the classic writers.

With all of these possibilities, a haiku that can seem like a small, simple poem to someone reading it in English can present a Japanese reader with a world of allusion and response. This allusion and response are the essence of the spirit of haiku. The poem's brief words should waken in its readers a half-forgotten memory or open them to some moment of life itself. Haiku was originally the term for the opening poem of a series written by friends or family, which was called *hokku*. Some poets, however, began presenting these opening poems in their anthologies, and in the late eighteenth century these stand-alone poems were formally given the title of *haiku*.

The haiku popular with teachers in American schools present the Japanese characters as a three-line poem of seventeen syllables, arranged into lines of five-seven-five. The ideal of most American haiku is the simplicity and the directness of the poem's thought, with less emphasis on the Japanese poets' juxtaposition of images that often seem only distantly related. This simplified form is helpful as a beginning writing exercise, and there is an active world of writers of haiku who exchange their haiku and publish their own journals and anthologies. If you look again at the opening verse of Wallace Stevens's "Thirteen Ways of Looking at a Blackbird" you are aware that although it does not conform to the style of the haiku as taught in the United States, it can be read not only as an imagist stanza but as a classic haiku.

In the excerpt from the poem by Judith Wright that opened the chapter, she wrote about her new love for haiku poems. In the poem's following lines, she named the four writers whose writing meant the most to her.

> Issa. Shiki. Buson. Bashō.
> Few words and with no rhetoric.
> Enclosed by silence
> as is the thrush's call.

There have been thousands of writers of haiku since the discovery of the form in the seventeenth century, but it is these four poets whose work is generally considered to be the most important achievement in the form: Matsuo Bashō, Taniguchi Buson, Kobayashi Issa, and Masaoka Shiki.

Matsuo Bashō was born into a samurai family in 1644, but he chose a simple lifestyle as a wandering poet. He traveled by horseback and by foot over Japan's mountains and across the wide rivers and plains, stopping to meet other poets and exchange verses. He was contemplating further journeys at his death in 1694. The spare eloquence of his verses reflects his Zen Buddhist beliefs. Compare Bashō's "The summer grass" with the later poem "Grass" by Carl Sandburg (p. 728), which perhaps was influenced by Bashō's poem. Here are three of Bashō's haiku.[1]

The summer grass—
only that remains
of the warrior's dreams

•

Down this road
no one walking
this autumn evening

•

It's spring
this morning a hill without a name
is shrouded in mist

Another poem by Bashō is one of the best known of all haiku poems.

Old pond
Splash!
A frog leaps in

Bashō's words have been translated by many poets. Here is a version from 1898 by the American poet Lafcadio Hearn, an honored figure in Japanese cultural history, who spent much of his life in Japan translating and writing about the country's literature.

Old pond—frog jumped in—sound of water

Two generations after Bashō's death, his poetry was taken up by Taniguchi Buson, who was a well-educated writer and painter. Buson, who lived from 1716 to 1783, revered Bashō's poetry, and at the same time he brought his own sensitivity to the haiku form. Here are two examples of his haiku.

ON THE ANNIVERSARY OF BASHŌ'S DEATH

From the west, wind blowing
the fallen leaves gathering
in the east

•

[1]The versions of these three poems and the one that follows were translated by Samuel Charters.

The sparrow chirps—
small mouth
open

Kobayashi Issa lived at almost the same time as Buson, from 1763 to 1827. Issa's poetry had a distinctive tone that drew as much from his roots in the countryside as it did from his poetic studies, as in these two haiku.

Sitting with my father
I want to watch the dawn
over green fields

•

Children's imitations of cormorants
even more wonderful
than cormorants

Masaoka Shiki, who lived from 1872 to 1922, was responsible for bringing haiku into the modern world. The style was now considered old-fashioned, but in newspaper articles and in his own poetry collections he introduced a shortened haiku form. His poetry also turned to more contemporary subjects. Here are two haiku written after he adopted the practice of going out in nature and writing his poetry from the notes he made as he walked.

A thawed pond
a shrimp moving
through the algae

•

Night and again
while I'm waiting for you the wind
turns into rain

Some Contemporary Haiku

ROBERT SPIESS

an aging willow— 1996

an aging willow—
its image unsteady
in the flowing stream

RONALD BAATZ

as though the whole earth 2005

as though the whole earth
were ringing—
that's how many crickets

MATSUO ALLARD

an icicle the moon 1978

an icicle the moon drifting through it

ALEXIS ROTELLA

Just friends 1984

Just friends:
he watches my gauze dress
blowing on the line

JOHN CARLEY

buoyed up on the rising tide 2001

buoyed up on the rising tide
a fleet of head boards bang the wall

CHERYL SAVAGEAU

Department of Labor Haiku 2000

In the winter snow
the kitchens fill up with steam
and men out of work

POETRY IN OPEN FORM AND THE LYRIC POEM

At the beginning of the nineteenth century, a new style of writing poetry slowly took form under the influences of the free verse experiments, imagism, and the classical poetic traditions of China and Japan. Many writers believed that the struggle to free poetry from the confining strictures of traditional verse was over. Their mood is suggested by what the nineteenth-century inventor of photography, Louis Daguerre, was supposed to have cried out when he managed to capture an image on a silver-coated plate, "From this moment painting is dead!" Others feared that once poetry lost its centuries-old anchors of rhyme and meter, there would be no more poetry. As we know, poetry and painting are still very much part of our lives, even though we don't usually look for rhyme schemes or count the meter when we read a poem.

At first this new poetry was known as free verse, but by the 1980s it was usually called **open form** poetry. In the first years of the free verse movement, there was some feeling that poetry could be as "free" as the wind, and that a poem could take any form the writer chose. Though this was literally true, the writers found that even if the way they wrote had changed, many of the elements they had used to create a poem were unchanged. The new poetry had to show the concentration and the technical virtuosity of poetry written in traditional forms. Tone, denotation and connotation, simile and metaphor, personification, figurative and literal language still were rich, useful resources for every writer.

The Lyric Poem Today

Many of the contemporary poems you read and discussed were written in the traditions of the lyric poem, even though their writers had moved away from traditional rhyme and meter. You know the word *lyrics*, which is the term for the text of a popular song, and **lyric poetry** comes from this same source. The word itself is descended from *lyre*, the name of the small harp that the poets of ancient Greece used to accompany their songs. For many centuries lyric poems were written in stanza forms with the rhyme schemes already familiar from songs and ballads. The lyric poetry you read today is defined as a short poem that expresses the writer's thoughts and emotions. Often lyric poems are written in the first person, though the *I* of the poem may be a **persona**, which is another person through whom the poet is speaking. An example of a poet writing as though he were another person is already familiar to you if you have read the poems of Robert Frost (some of which appear in Chapter 16).

Lyric poetry is highly subjective, deeply personal, and usually intensely emotional. When you read these poems written in open form, it may seem that they are easy to write. As poet Charles Simic explains, however, they require the same resources of skill and imagination poets have always employed in their writing.

> Lyric poems require an exquisite ear on the part of the poet, an ability to weigh the exact amount of silence between words and images in order to make them rich with meaning. The shorter such poems are, the harder

> they are to write. We know from experience the impact a line of poetry can have, the miraculous ways in which two selves unknown to each other until that very moment come to share not only an understanding but a single imaginative space. . . . Despite infinite odds, somebody's private sentiments continue to enthrall generations of future readers. And yet, every time we read a poem, this is more or less what happens.[1]

At the same time, the older traditions didn't fade away in the rush of enthusiasm over writing in free verse or open form. When Walt Whitman wrote "I contain multitudes," he could have been speaking about poetry itself. We think of Whitman today as the person who first dared to write without regard for the conventions of verse, but in his lifetime his most-loved poem, "O Captain, My Captain," his grieving tribute to the murdered president Abraham Lincoln, was written in traditional rhymed stanzas. Many poets still use regular line lengths and conventional stanza formats to give their poems some of the sense of order and seriousness of the traditional forms. Philip Levine's poem "The Lost Angel" has the appearance of a Victorian lyric, with its three-line stanzas and its similar line lengths, even though it does not use rhyme and meter. The poem tells a simple story, though it has larger implications. As you read it, you can ask yourself if Levine's decision to shape his story into the form of an eight-stanza poem makes you read it with a different perception than if he had told it in a prose paragraph.

PHILIP LEVINE

The Lost Angel

1963

Four little children
in winged costumes—
it has something to do

with raising money.
Children are hungry
the one says, the one

who can talk.
And they go down the drive
in the driving rain, and there's

no car
to collect them, no
one waiting, and the bills

and coins spill
from his trailing hand
and float like pieces of light.

[1]Quoted in George Braziller, *The Renegade* (2009), p. 114.

Wait! Wait!
I yell, and run
to gather what I can,
and he turns,
the one who can talk,
holding his empty fists
as offerings,
two shaking hammers,
and gives me back my life.

Confessional Mode

During the twentieth century many poets began to use the new freedom to share with the reader details of their personal lives that had been considered too "private" to be published. For women writers it meant that for the first time they could express their own sexuality and their attitudes toward society and the restricted roles it assigned them. In his introduction to *Ariel* (1966), a collection of the last poems of Sylvia Plath, Robert Lowell used the word *confessional* to describe this new writing, and now the term **confessional poetry** is often used to describe these poems. In this poem by Anne Sexton, written about herself and her young daughter, the complex relationship between any mother and daughter is described with a candor and explicitness that is new to poetry. As you note, however, for her title "The Fortress" Sexton has chosen to use a metaphor, suggesting that her love for her child is a fortress protecting her daughter while she still is so young.

ANNE SEXTON

The Fortress

1962

while taking a nap with Linda

Under the pink quilted covers
I hold the pulse that counts your blood.
I think the woods outdoors
are half asleep,
left over from summer
like a stack of books after a flood,
left over like those promises I never keep.
On the right, the scrub pine tree
waits like a fruit store
holding up bunches of tufted broccoli.

We watch the wind from our square bed.
I press down my index finger—

half in jest, half in dread—
on the brown mole
under your left eye, inherited
from my right cheek: a spot of danger
where a bewitched worm ate its way through our soul
in search of beauty. My child, since July
the leaves have been fed
secretly from a pool of beet-red dye.

And sometimes they are battle green
with trunks as wet as hunters' boots,
smacked hard by the wind, clean
as oilskins. No,
the wind's not off the ocean.
Yes, it cried in your room like a wolf
and your pony tail hurt you. That was a long time ago.
The wind rolled the tide like a dying
woman. She wouldn't sleep,
she rolled there all night, grunting and sighing.
Darling, life is not in my hands;
life with its terrible changes
will take you, bombs or glands,
your own child at
your breast, your own house on your own land.
Outside the bittersweet turns orange.
Before she died, my mother and I picked those fat
branches, finding orange nipples
on the gray wire strands.
We weeded the forest, curing trees like cripples.

Your feet thump-thump against my back
and you whisper to yourself. Child,
what are you wishing? What pact
are you making?
What mouse runs between your eyes? What ark
can I fill for you when the world goes wild?
The woods are underwater, their weeds are shaking
in the tide; birches like zebra fish
flash by in a pack.
Child, I cannot promise that you will get your wish.

I cannot promise very much.
I give you the images I know.
Lie still with me and watch.
A pheasant moves
by like a seal, pulled through the mulch
by his thick white collar. He's on show
like a clown. He drags a beige feather that he removed,

one time, from an old lady's hat.
We laugh and we touch.
I promise you love. Time will not take away that.

CONNECTIONS To read other poems in the confessional mode, see works by Marilyn Chin, Audre Lorde, Sharon Olds, Alicia Suskin Ostriker, Sylvia Plath, and Anne Sexton.

The Prose Poem

As you continue with your reading, you will find the confessional mode is only one direction that open form has taken. Today poetry has a wide range of themes and subjects. A popular form is the **prose poem**, which as the name suggests shares qualities of both prose and poetry. A prose poem can have some kind of narrative, but the story will be only one of the means the poet uses to illustrate the theme of the poem. Some prose poems have the effect of a parable, a narrative used to point to a moral. Others have the effect of opening your mind to the possibilities of other ways of thinking. Even when a prose poem presents you with a single, condensed image, often what you have just read suggests some new thought or image. This kind of poetry is called **associative**. Here are three contemporary prose poems that demonstrate how form can summon up associations in the reader's mind. Note that Marcia Southwick's conversational, casual-seeming gathering of gossip is in reality a letter to her husband, who died when he was very young. With these shared jokes and concerns, Southwick returns to their life together, if only as a fantasy.

MARCIA SOUTHWICK

A Star Is Born in the Eagle Nebula 1999

to Larry Levis, 1946–1996

They've finally admitted that trying to save oil-soaked
seabirds doesn't work. You can wash them, rinse them
with a high-pressure nozzle, feed them activated charcoal
to absorb toxic chemicals, & test them for anemia, but the oil
still disrupts the microscopic alignment of feathers that creates
a kind of wet suit around the body. (Besides, it costs $600 to wash
the oil slick off a penguin & $32,000 to clean an Alaskan seabird.)
We now know that the caramel coloring in whiskey causes nightmares,
& an ingredient in beer produces hemorrhoids. Glycerol
in vodka causes anal seepage, & when girls enter puberty,
the growth of their left ventricles slows down for about a year.
Box-office receipts plummeted this week. Retail sales are sluggish.
The price of wheat rose. Soybeans sank. The Dow is up thirty points.
A man named Alan Gerry has bought Woodstock & plans
to build a theme park, a sort of combo Williamsburg-Disneyland

for graying hippies. The weather report predicts a batch of showers
preceding a cold front down on the Middle Atlantic Coast—
you aren't missing much. Day after day at the Ford research labs
in Dearborn, Michigan, an engineer in charge of hood latches
labors, measuring the weight of a hood, calculating the resistance
of the latch, coming up with the perfect closure, the perfect snapping
sound, while the shadow of Jupiter's moon, Io, races across cloud tops
at 10.5 miles a second, and a star is born in the Eagle Nebula.
Molecular hydrogen and dust condenses into lumps that contract
and ignite under their own gravity. In today's paper four girls
in a photo appear to be tied, as if by invisible threads, to five
soap bubbles floating along the street against the black wall
of the Park Avenue underpass. Nothing earthshattering. The girls
are simply *there*. They've blown the bubbles & are following them
up the street. That's the plot. *A life. Any life.* I turn the page
and there's Charlie Brown. He's saying, "Sometimes I lie awake
at night & ask, Does anyone remember me? Then a voice
comes to me out of the dark—'Sure, Frank, we remember you.'"

EVE WOOD

Recognition

1997

The woman on the subway touches my hand by mistake, and in that instant an autumn leaf presses flat against the wet window of the car. She is paler than a snow ferret, and I can see in her face the gentle eagerness of a woman admired all her life solely for her beauty. The leaf inches up the glass, and I feel the heat in her legs radiate out from her body which bumps against mine each time the train lunges forward. I would be so proud if she were my mother, small, blond token of my life, surely an example to follow, yet her mothering would not be enough to keep me. I would want more than is right. Rain leaks in through a crack in the window, and I wish she would look me in the face like the woman who trains dogs on television, who locks the red Doberman's snout between her thumb and forefinger, commanding his attention. I imagine she believes in ghosts and inexplicable passion, and I can do nothing but gnaw the inside of my lip to keep from moving closer. She could start a conversation. She could give herself over. We could hold hands in the rain and not care. The trees blur by, and the mist holds the windows together like a wide gray blanket we might lie down on in summer. Her yellow raincoat hurts my eyes as she leans against me in the wake of the train. She wears me out, and I am still so far from knowing anything.

CLARIBEL ALEGRÍA

Carmen Bomba: Poet

1987

TRANSLATED BY DARWIN J. FLAKOLL

Luisa always felt refreshed when she remembered Carmen Bomba, the porter and human beast of burden in the Santa Ana marketplace. Each afternoon when he finished work he'd get a bit drunk to arouse his courage, and he'd pause before each open window in the neighborhood to recite the verses he had composed that day.

Poems for Further Study

JUDITH ORTIZ COFER

Quinceañera°

1987

My dolls have been put away like dead
children in a chest I will carry
with me when I marry.
I reach under my skirt to feel
a satin slip bought for this day. It is soft
as the inside of my thighs. My hair
has been nailed back with my mother's
black hairpins to my skull. Her hands
stretched my eyes open as she twisted
braids into a tight circle at the nape
of my neck. I am to wash my own clothes
and sheets from this day on, as if
the fluids of my body were poison, as if
the little trickle of blood I believe
travels from my heart to the world were
shameful. Is not the blood of saints and
men in battle beautiful? Do Christ's hands
not bleed into your eyes from His cross?
At night I hear myself growing and wake
to find my hands drifting of their own will
to soothe skin stretched tight
over my bones.
I am wound like the guts of a clock,
waiting for each hour to release me.

Quinceañera: In Latino cultures, a party bringing a fifteen-year-old girl into the world.

LI-YOUNG LEE

Eating Alone

1986

I've pulled the last of the year's young onions.
The garden is bare now. The ground is cold,
brown and old. What is left of the day flames
in the maples at the corner of my
eye. I turn, a cardinal vanishes.
By the cellar door, I wash the onions,
then drink from the icy metal spigot.

Once, years back, I walked beside my father
among the windfall pears. I can't recall
our words. We may have strolled in silence. But
I still see him bend that way—left hand braced
on knee, creaky—to lift and hold to my
eye a rotten pear. In it, a hornet
spun crazily, glazed in slow, glistening juice.

It was my father I saw this morning
waving to me from the trees, I almost
called to him, until I came close enough
to see the shovel, leaning where I had
left it, in the flickering, deep green shade.

White rice steaming, almost done. Sweet green peas
fried in onions. Shrimp braised in sesame
oil and garlic. And my own loneliness.
What more could I, a young man, want.

NICK CARBÓ

American Adobo

1995

She showed up on the doorstep of my apartment
in Albuquerque just after the blizzard of '85
in a fluffy tan fake-fur coat, an elevated
I Love Lucy hairdo, and a twelve-year-old son.
I was honored to be given the front passenger seat
of her 1976 Datsun while her son aimed
his pink plastic water pistol from the back.
Her two bedroom duplex was nestled in the foothills
of the rust-covered Sandia mountains.

The hug back at the apartment was genuine—
my older cousin, Nancy, her son, Alfonso,
named after my father. This was a chance to ignite

memories from familiar names, to recuperate
the fallen leaves of our family tree, to run
back to our childhoods, separated
by two continents and an ocean.
She said she still believes
that "the Carbós are blue-blood,
a royalty from Spain." Nobody
could take that away from her—the promise
of gold crowns, swords forged
from Toledo steel with the Carbó name
glimmering on the blade. I didn't tell her
that the only title our grandfather carried
was that of *Perito Mercantil Colegiado*, a Certified
Public Accountant. I didn't tell her that the only
time he ruled the masses was as the Vice-Mayor
of the provincial town of Nueva Caceres.
"In 1956, when I was nine,
your mother and your father came to visit
our house on Losoya Street—they came out
of a black limousine, they looked so regal,
so elegant, they brought so many gifts."
She was standing by the microwave fluffing
a pot of Uncle Ben's Minute Rice
while I reviewed her family album on the couch
which was covered with a multi-colored
Mexican blanket. I understood the story
in black and white—
her American father left them in 1954,
my aunt Nana learned to change sheets
in motels on Central Avenue and serve coffee
at diners to earn enough money
for three children. When Nana died in 1982,
Nancy was the only child to sit by her bed.
"This was my mother's special recipe
for beef and pork Adobo. She cooked it
for us on Thanksgiving and Easter Sunday."
I didn't tell Nancy that her Adobo
was too watery, that it needed more soy sauce,
that it should have had more garlic.

MARISA DE LOS SANTOS

Because I Love You,

1998

I cannot tell you that last night in the exhaust-
fume impatience of nearly-stopped traffic
through which cars crept, linked
with short chains of light,
the driver at my front failed for whole minutes
to follow closely the blue Buick in front of him,
stopped, in fact, entirely, while a thousand
engines idled in molasses-sticky Virginia heat.

I caught the fine, still cut-out of his face
as he leaned a little out the window, looking,
so I turned, too, and saw what I had missed in long
minutes of waiting: a bank of cloud like descending
birds, a great, bright raspberry moon,
and I was surprised into loving this man as I
have loved others—ancient-eyed boys reading on benches,
crossing guards in white gloves,
businessmen sleeping on trains—easily,
as I have never loved you.

LUIS J. RODRÍGUEZ

Carrying My Tools

1994

Any good craftsman carries his tools.
Years ago, they were always at the ready.
In the car. In a knapsack.
Claw hammers, crisscrossed heads,
32 ouncers. Wrenches in all sizes,
sometimes with oil caked on the teeth.
Screwdrivers, with multicolored
plastic handles
(what needed screwing got screwed).
I had specialty types: Allen wrenches,
torpedo levels, taps and dies.
A trusty tape measure.
Maybe a chalk line.
Millwrights also carried dial indicators,
micrometers—the precision kind.
They were cherished like a fine car,
a bottle of rare wine,
or a moment of truth.

I believed that anyone could survive
without friends, without the comfort of blankets
or even a main squeeze
(for a short while anyway).
But without tools . . . now there was hard times.
Without tools, what kind of person could I be?
The tools were my ticket to new places.
I often met other travelers, their tools in tow,
and I'd say: "Go ahead, take my stereo and TV.
Take my car. Take my toys of leisure.
Just leave the tools."
Nowadays, I don't haul these mechanical implements.
But I still make sure to carry the tools
of my trade: Words and ideas,
the kind no one can take away.
So there may not be any work today,
but when there is, I'll be ready.
I got my tools.

COMMENTARIES

EZRA POUND

Ezra Pound was one of the founders of the short-lived but influential movement called imagism, which stressed clarity and economy of language. In this 1918 statement, which was later published under the title "A Retrospect" in a 1954 collection of his literary essays, Pound describes the imagists' aims.

On the Principles of Imagism 1918

There has been so much scribbling about a new fashion in poetry, that I may perhaps be pardoned this brief recapitulation and retrospect.

In the spring or early summer of 1912, "H.D.," Richard Aldington, and myself decided that we were agreed upon the three principles following:

1. Direct treatment of the "thing" whether subjective or objective.
2. To use absolutely no word that does not contribute to the presentation.
3. As regarding rhythm: to compose in the sequence of the musical phrase, not in sequence of a metronome.

Upon many points of taste and of predilection we differed, but agreeing upon these three positions we thought we had as much right to a group name, at least as much right, as a number of French "schools" proclaimed by Mr Flint in the August number of Harold Monro's magazine for 1911.

This school has since been "joined" or "followed" by numerous people who, whatever their merits, do not show any signs of agreeing with the second specification. Indeed *vers libre* has become as prolix and as verbose as any of the flaccid varieties that preceded it. It has brought faults of its own. The actual language and phrasing is often as bad as that of our elders without even the excuse that the words are shovelled in to fill a metric pattern or to complete the noise of a rhyme-sound. Whether or no the phrases followed by the followers are musical must be left to the reader's decision. At times I can find a marked metre in "vers libres," as stale and hackneyed as any pseudo-Swinburnian,° at times the writers seem to follow no musical structure whatever. But it is, on the whole, good that the field should be ploughed. Perhaps a few good poems have come from the new method, and if so it is justified.

Criticism is not a circumscription or a set of prohibitions. It provides fixed points of departure. It may startle a dull reader into alertness. That little of it which is good is mostly in stray phrases; or if it be an older artist helping a younger it is in great measure but rules of thumb, cautions gained by experience.

I set together a few phrases on practical working about the time the first remarks on imagism were published. The first use of the word "Imagiste" was in my note to T. E. Hulme's five poems, printed at the end of my "Ripostes" in the autumn of 1912. I reprint my cautions from *Poetry* for March, 1913.

A Few Don'ts

An "Image" is that which presents an intellectual and emotional complex in an instant of time. I use the term "complex" rather in the technical sense employed by the newer psychologists, such as Hart, though we might not agree absolutely in our application.

It is the presentation of such a "complex" instantaneously which gives that sense of sudden liberation; that sense of freedom from time limits and space limits; that sense of sudden growth, which we experience in the presence of the greatest works of art.

It is better to present one Image in a lifetime than to produce voluminous works.

All this, however, some may consider open to debate. The immediate necessity is to tabulate A LIST OF DON'TS for those beginning to write verses. I can not put all of them into Mosaic negative.

To begin with, consider the three propositions (demanding direct treatment, economy of words, and the sequence of the musical phrase), not as dogma—never consider anything as dogma—but as the result of long contemplation, which, even if it is some one else's contemplation, may be worth consideration.

Pay no attention to the criticism of men who have never themselves written a notable work. Consider the discrepancies between the actual writing of the Greek poets and dramatists, and the theories of the Graeco-Roman grammarians, concocted to explain their metres.

---

pseudo-Swinburnian: One who mimics the work of Algernon Charles Swinburne (1837–1909), the English poet whose poetry was noted for its romantic exaggeration.

Language

Use no superfluous word, no adjective which does not reveal something.

Don't use such an expression as "dim lands *of peace*." It dulls the image. It mixes an abstraction with the concrete. It comes from the writer's not realizing that the natural object is always the *adequate* symbol.

Go in fear of abstractions. Do not retell in mediocre verse what has already been done in good prose. Don't think any intelligent person is going to be deceived when you try to shirk all the difficulties of the unspeakably difficult art of good prose by chopping your composition into line lengths.

What the expert is tired of today the public will be tired of to-morrow.

Don't imagine that the art of poetry is any simpler than the art of music,or that you can please the expert before you have spent at least as much effort on the art of verse as the average piano teacher spends on the art of music.

Be influenced by as many great artists as you can, but have the decency either to acknowledge the debt outright, or to try to conceal it.

Don't allow "influence" to mean merely that you mop up the particular decorative vocabulary of some one or two poets whom you happen to admire. A Turkish war correspondent was recently caught red-handed babbling in his despatches of "dove-grey" hills, or else it was "pearl-pale," I cannot remember.

Use either no ornament or good ornament.

Rhythm and Rhyme

Let the candidate fill his mind with the finest cadences he can discover, preferably in a foreign language,[1] so that the meaning of the words may be less likely to divert his attention from the movement; e.g. Saxon charms, Hebridean Folk Songs, the verse of Dante, and the lyrics of Shakespeare—if he can dissociate the vocabulary from the cadence. Let him dissect the lyrics of Goethe coldly into their component sound values, syllables long and short, stressed and unstressed, into vowels and consonants.

It is not necessary that a poem should rely on its music, but if it does rely on its music that music must be such as will delight the expert.

Let the neophyte know assonance and alliteration, rhyme immediate and delayed, simple and polyphonic, as a musician would expect to know harmony and counterpoint and all the minutiae of his craft. No time is too great to give to these matters or to any one of them, even if the artist seldom have need of them.

Don't imagine that a thing will "go" in verse just because it's too dull to go in prose.

Don't be "viewy"—leave that to the writers of pretty little philosophic essays. Don't be descriptive; remember that the painter can describe a landscape much better than you can, and that he has to know a deal more about it.

When Shakespeare talks of the "Dawn in russet mantle clad" he presents something which the painter does not present. There is in this line of his nothing that one can call description; he presents.

---

[1]This is for rhythm, his vocabulary must of course be found in his native tongue. [Pound's note]

Consider the way of the scientists rather than the way of an advertising agent for a new soap.

The scientist does not expect to be acclaimed as a great scientist until he has *discovered* something. He begins by learning what has been discovered already. He goes from that point onward. He does not bank on being a charming fellow personally. He does not expect his friends to applaud the results of his freshman class work. Freshmen in poetry are unfortunately not confined to a definite and recognizable class room. They are "all over the shop." Is it any wonder "the public is indifferent to poetry"?

Don't chop your stuff into separate *iambs.* Don't make each line stop dead at the end, and then begin every next line with a heave. Let the beginning of the next line catch the rise of the rhythm wave, unless you want a definite longish pause.

In short, behave as a musician, a good musician, when dealing with that phase of your art which has exact parallels in music. The same laws govern, and you are bound by no others.

AMY LOWELL

On the Definition of Free Verse

1916

The definition of *vers libre* is a verse-form based upon cadence. Now cadence in music is one thing, cadence in poetry quite another, since we are not dealing with tone but with rhythm. It is the sense of perfect balance of flow and rhythm. Not only must the syllables so fall as to increase and continue the movement, but the whole poem must be as rounded and recurring as the circular swing of a balanced pendulum. It can be fast or slow, it may even jerk, but this perfect swing it must have, even its jerks must follow the central movement. To illustrate: Suppose a person were given the task of walking, or running, round a large circle, with two minutes given to do it in. Two minutes which he would just consume if he walked round the circle quietly. But in order to make the task easier for him, or harder, as the case might be, he was required to complete each half of the circle in exactly a minute. No other restrictions were placed upon him. He might dawdle in the beginning, and run madly to reach the half-circle mark on time, and then complete his task by walking steadily round the second half to goal. Or he might leap, and run, and skip, and linger in all sorts of ways, making up for slow going by fast, and for extra haste by pauses, and varying these movements on either lap of the circle as the humour seized him, only so that he were just one minute in traversing the first half-circle, and just one minute in traversing the second. Another illustration which may be employed is that of a Japanese wood-carving where a toad in one corner is balanced by a spray of blown flowers in the opposite upper one. The flowers are not the same shape as the toad, neither are they the same size, but the balance is preserved.

◆ Topics for Writing about Other Poetic Forms ◆

1. In a close reading of an imagist poem, show how the principles of imagism apply to the language used in the poem.
2. Discuss the importance of the classic poetry of China and Japan on the early forms of free verse.
3. Everyone has their own ideas about the haiku style. Choose three or four of the examples in the text and analyze what you see in the poems.
4. Discuss the question raised in the text about Philip Levine's poem "The Lost Angel." How much does the form of the poem affect the way we read it?

USEFUL TERMS TO REMEMBER

Associative poetry Poems that bring to our minds other ideas or images as we read them.

Confessional poetry Poetry that explores areas of sexuality and personal experience that had been denied to poets earlier.

Haiku A short Japanese verse form characterized by juxtaposed images and a minimalist language.

Imagism A style of poetry that advocated a precise language for writing that was shaped around physical images.

Open form Poetry written today that does not use rhyme, meter, or traditional poetic forms.

Persona A fictive person within a poem or story who is presented as the author.

Prose poem A poem that blends the appearance of prose with the imagery and associative power of poetry.

15.

Poets Respond to Other Poets

We're all writing the same poem.
— ROBERT DUNCAN

Have you ever asked yourself, "Why does anybody begin to write poetry?" If you ask poets themselves, they will invariably tell you that it was a poem that gave them the idea. Reading that first poem says to a would-be poet, "This is something I could do myself! I can see that writing this poem has helped this writer answer some of the questions everybody has. If I could write a poem, that could help me answer some of my own questions." If you asked the writers in the two other genres that are presented in your textbook, short fiction and drama, they would give you the same answer. As critic Harold Bloom described it, "Poems, stories, novels, plays come into being as a response to prior poems, stories, novels, and plays." Writers never lose this consciousness of each other's writing, and perhaps because poetry comes from emotions that lie so close to the surface of the skin, poets are very conscious of what other poets have created. Poets are their own best audience. Adrienne Rich has described her own experience of discovering poetry when she was still a child.

> I thought that the poets in the anthologies were the only real poets, that their being in the anthologies was proof of this, though some were classified as "great" and others as "minor." I owed much to these anthologies: *Silver Pennies*; the constant outflow of volumes edited by Louis Untermeyer; *The Cambridge Book of Poetry for Children*; Palgrave's *Golden Treasury*; the *Oxford Book of English Verse*. . . . I still believed that poets were inspired by some transcendental authority and spoke from some extraordinary height.

Margaret Atwood has described her emotions when she heard Rich read from her book *Diving into the Wreck* (1973): "When I first heard the author read from it, I felt as though the top of my head was being attacked, sometimes with an ice pick, sometimes with a blunter instrument: a hatchet or a hammer."

Atwood, in *her* turn, reminds the reader of Emily Dickinson's description of how she knew something she read was poetry: "If I feel physically as if the top of my head were taken off, I know that it is poetry."

You will find in your reading that it is not only modern poets who are so excited by the words of another poet. When a friend introduced John Keats to the translation of Homer by the Elizabethan poet George Chapman, they stayed up all night reading to each other. As Keats walked home at dawn he was already composing his sonnet "On First Looking into Chapman's Homer." The poem was finished and reached his friend by the first mail, only a few hours later.

JOHN KEATS

On First Looking into Chapman's Homer 1816

Much have I travell'd in the realms of gold,
  And many goodly states and kingdoms seen;
  Round many western islands have I been
Which bards in fealty to Apollo° hold.
Oft of one wide expanse had I been told
  That deep-browed Homer ruled as his demesne;°
  Yet never did I breathe its pure serene°
Till I heard Chapman° speak out loud and bold:
Then felt I like some watcher of the skies
  When a new planet swims into his ken;
Or like stout Cortez° when with eagle eyes
  He star'd at the Pacific—and all his men
Look'd at each other with a wild surmise—
  Silent upon a peak in Darien.

In his mood of exhilaration, Keats made a mistake in the name of the Spanish explorer who first saw the Pacific (it was Balboa and not Cortés), but critics have never felt that this diminishes the effect of his poem.

Many poets also have poets as friends, they translate one another's poems from other languages, they read their poems to each other, they send each other copies of new manuscripts, they publish magazines of each other's poetry. In the sense that living writers are part of a community, they also are an important

4. Apollo: Greek god of poetry. **6. demesne:** Domain. **7. serene:** Atmosphere. **8. Chapman:** George Chapman (c. 1560–1634), Elizabethan poet whose translations of Homer's Greek epics *Iliad* and *Odyssey* Keats found superior to the eighteenth-century translations with which he was familiar. **11. Cortez:** Keats mistakenly identifies Hernan Cortés, not Vasco Núñez de Balboa, as the first European to view the Pacific Ocean from Darien, a peak in Panama.

influence on each other. To speak of a poem from an earlier generation "influencing" a younger writer, however, is more complicated. In a discussion of young painters that applies equally well to young poets, art critic Michael Baxadall has pointed out that to say a writer or a text from an earlier generation "influences" a younger writer is misleading, since a poem written by a poet who is no longer living cannot "do" anything. It is the younger writer who *does* something. Baxadall drew up a list of the things that the younger writer can do. If the young writer is moved to respond to something by an older writer, the younger—in just the same way that a young painter responds to the work of an older artist—can

> draw on, resort to, avail oneself of, appropriate from, have recourse to, adapt, misunderstand, refer to, pick up, take on, engage with, react to, quote, differentiate oneself from, assimilate oneself to, assimilate, align oneself with, copy, address, paraphrase, absorb, make a variation on, revive, continue, remodel, ape, emulate, travesty, parody, extract from, distort, attend to, resist, simplify, reconstitute, elaborate on, develop, face up to, master, subvert, perpetuate, reduce, promote, respond to, transform, tackle. . . . [E]veryone will be able to think of others.

As we have seen in Keats's response to Homer, whichever way a young poet responds to the work of another poet, the result will be poetry.

For women readers today, the early centuries of poetry in English can present a difficult hurdle. Because of social attitudes, it is not until the nineteenth century that poetry written by women begins to play an important role in the poetic tradition. However, as critic Jan Montefiore shows us in her analysis of a sonnet by Edna St. Vincent Millay, an American poet of the 1920s, women poets did not feel that they were entirely excluded from this tradition, and they did not hesitate to take it and mold it for their own work. Montefiore writes,

> Millay's best-known sequence of love sonnets, *Fatal Interview*, depends on an individual voice speaking with a poetic vocabulary (thematic as well as lexical) which is drawn from Elizabethan poetry as reread by the Romantics, as in this excerpt from sonnet VIII:
>
> > Yet in an hour to come, disdainful dust,
> > You shall be bowed and brought to bed with me.
> > While the blood roars, or when the blood is rust
> > About a broken engine, this shall be.
> > If not today, then later; if not here,
> > On the green grass, with sighing and delight,
> > Then under it, all in good time, my dear,
> > We shall be laid together in the night.
>
> The poet's confidence and ease in handling the sonnet form are immediately apparent; she slides effortlessly from the twentieth-century image of "rust / About a broken engine" to the "timeless" line "On the green grass, with sighing and delight," using the associative rhymes "rust" and "dust" and the emphatic alliteration of "bowed and brought to bed" with an effect of relish, not cliché. Her appropriation of literary tradition is

> equally apparent in the way that the counterposing of love and death, the brevity of human life and the sleep of the grave, recalls Shakespeare, Marvell, and Catullus in a *cantabile* lyricism formed on Yeats. This is not an allusive poem; rather its themes are smoothed with poetic handling, and it is written in a style which assumes that poetry is timeless.

The term *allusive* that Montefiore uses, which means to allude or refer to some other writing, suggests one of the ways in which a poet responds to another poem. It is one of several ways that are part of the poet's means, the tools a poet uses to make a poem. Here are some of the most common you will find in your reading.

Quotation

Many poets quote directly or indirectly from other poems. Sometimes the use of someone else's words is indicated by quotation marks, but more often the quotation is left without any marks to indicate it. The writer wants to leave it to the reader, whether or not the different voice in the poem is heard. One of the uses of quotation that you will find is to give the poem a more general meaning or to present the poem in a clearer historical perspective. The California poet Robert Duncan used a quotation from the Greek poet Pindar as the title and the source of ideas for one of his major poems, *A Poem Beginning with a Line by Pindar*. The line from Pindar that begins the poem is "The light foot hears you and the brightness begins." In the poem, Duncan alludes to Walt Whitman's elegy on the death of Lincoln, *When Lilacs Last in the Dooryard Bloom'd*:

> What
> if lilacs last in *this* dooryard bloomd?

A few lines later he quotes directly from Whitman, using quotation marks:

> How sad "amid lanes and through old woods"
> echoes Whitman's love for Lincoln!

Marianne Moore used many quotations in her poetry. Often it was material from magazine articles or books she was reading, or phrases that she took from other poets or writers, sometimes slightly altering them. Consider these lines from the poem "The Student":

> . . . With us, a
> school—like the singing tree of which
> the leaves were mouths singing in concert
> is both a tree of knowledge
> and of liberty. . . .

Moore tells us in a note to the poem that she adapted the sentence "Each leaf was a mouth, and every leaf joined in concert" from the book *The Arabian Nights*.

A poet who was influenced by Moore, Amy Clampitt includes a note on the line in her poem "The Outer Bar" that describes the waves striking the sandbar:

chain-gang archangels that in their prismatic
frenzy fall, gall and gash the daylight. . . .

Clampitt's note points out that " 'fall, gall and gash the daylight' . . . derives, of course, from 'The Windhover' by Gerard Manley Hopkins." (Hopkins's poem appears on p. 972.)

Quotation is also used to "engage with," if we use another of the ways younger writers respond to other poems that we listed a few paragraphs ago. In the opening lines of her poem "the closing of the south park road," Tobey Hiller uses a quotation from Emily Dickinson:

the closing of the south park road

happens every year between Thanksgiving and Christmas
just when the light grows lucid, forgiving nothing and
disappearing *into beauty*,
as Emily says
on these days the air over the water opens into a hard wise body
lying low and immortal over everything it loves.

In the same way, Langston Hughes uses the last line from the song "Dixie" for a bitter, ironic comment on racism in "Song for a Dark Girl" (p. 902):

Way Down South in Dixie
(Break the heart of me)
They hung my black young lover
To a cross roads tree.

Way Down South in Dixie
(Bruised body high in air)
I asked the white Lord Jesus
What was the use of prayer.

As the critic Helen Vendler writes, "All cultural production comes about from constant interchanges of past works and ideas with current ones."

Paraphrase

Another way that a poet may use another poet's words is to **paraphrase** a line or a stanza. The denotative meaning of paraphrase is "to render freely, or amplify, a passage, or express its sense in other words." In his poem "Journey of the Magi," T. S. Eliot paraphrased a section from a sermon by the early English religious writer Lancelot Andrewes. This is the section from Andrewes's "Nativity Sermon" XV:

It was no summer progress. A cold coming they had of it at this time of the year, just the worst time of the year to take a journey, and specially a long journey in. The ways deep, the weather sharp, the days short, the sun furthest off, *in solstitio brumali*, "the very dead of winter."

This is Eliot's paraphrase, which he sets off with quotation marks to show that there is a source for the lines:

"A cold coming we had of it,
Just the worst time of the year
For a journey, and such a long journey:
The ways deep and the weather sharp,
The very dead of winter."

Eliot's poems were often a maze of unidentified paraphrases and translations. He felt that this was one way to respond to the traditions behind his poetry. As he wrote in an essay on Elizabethan drama, "One of the surest tests is the way in which a poet borrows. Immature poets imitate; mature poets steal; bad poets deface what they take; and good poets make it into something better, or at least something different."

Allusion

The denotative meaning of **allusion**—"to allude to"—means to "refer indirectly to something presumably known to the listener or reader." It is different from quotation because it is indirect. If you allude to something, you name it, or suggest it, and readers add their own understanding of the context. In his poem "The Love Song of J. Alfred Prufrock" (p. 961), T. S. Eliot alludes to Shakespeare with the line "I know the voices dying with a dying fall." Shakespeare's phrase, from *Twelfth Night*, is "If music be the food of love, play on. . . . That strain again! It had a dying fall." In act 2, scene 2 of *Hamlet* (p. 1285), Shakespeare alludes to the *Iliad* in Hamlet's soliloquy. After listening to one of the players begin to weep as he described the grief of Hecuba, Queen of Troy, at the death of her husband, Priam, Hamlet bursts out,

For Hecuba!
What's Hecuba to him, or he to Hecuba,
That he should weep for her?

Matthew Arnold, in his poem "Dover Beach," alludes to the Greek dramatist Sophocles when he describes the eternal note of sadness he hears in the sea:

Sophocles long ago
Heard it on the Aegean . . .

In the poem "A Man Dancing Alone on an Island in Greece," the writer alludes to John Keats's "Ode on a Grecian Urn" (p. 754) both in the theme of the poem, which describes a man dancing in a Greek *taverna* in the same way that Keats describes the dancers depicted on the side of the urn, and in the poem's conclusion, which echoes Keats's famous lines,

Beauty is truth, truth beauty,—that is all
Ye know on earth, and all ye need to know.

SAMUEL CHARTERS

A Man Dancing Alone on an Island in Greece

2007

for Henry Denander

His body moves to a solemn measure,
this man dancing alone,
arms extended as if they reached
into another space, then they turn
in as measured a sweep
to point down to his feet.
There is gray in his trimmed beard,
he wears a tan sweater over
a brown jersey, in dark rimmed
glasses, though his eyes are closed and he
isn't seeing with his glasses. He is seeing
something else, this man dancing alone
on an island in Greece.

He isn't alone, of course,
the rough restaurant tables in the darkness
under the trees are
filled with faces, shadowed
under umbrellas as a light rain falls.
But this man who is dancing alone
moves with sure steps over the
streaming flagstones that he sees
without seeing, without seeing us,
as he dances alone without us.

He is alone, this man dancing
who doesn't see with his eyes closed
the orchestra sitting behind him
under the roof overhang
out of the rain.
A violin, baglamas, sandouri, an accordian,
a dark haired man in a tee shirt with a guitar,
singing, a slim young woman
in a proper blouse who could tend a shop, singing,
but over the rude pulse of the orchestra,
the sound of voices at the tables,
the man goes on dancing alone.

I understand that the
solemn sweep of his movements
is telling me
that to move as his body is moving and
to see as he is not seeing is to

know the essence of dance,
and it isn't enough if I say
that in his measured movement
he has found beauty.
What I know is that in his dance,
in the stillness of his dance,
he has found truth.

For a moment I wonder—
could I find this essence within myself
if I stood up and despite my embarrassment
danced—alone?
For just a moment in the rain
could we all?

Imitation

At some point in their struggle to find their own voice, young writers usually try every form of traditional poetry. Sometimes in their mature work they will casually begin to imitate the work of another poet or another poetic style. The American poet James Merrill was very skillful at slipping in and out of a wide range of poetic voices. Often he used rhyme and near rhyme for groups of lines within his poems. As an example, in his long poem *Coda: The Higher Keys*, in addition to a crowd of allusions to other writers and other poems, his elegant diction and perfect rhyme in lines 120–28 suggest that the setting of the poem is an eighteenth-century English ballroom:

. . . A splendor
Across lawns meets, in Sandover's tall time—
Dappled mirrors, its own eye. Should rhyme
Calling to rhyme awaken the odd snore,
No harm done. I shall study to ignore
Looks that more boldly with each session yearn
Toward the buffet where steaming silver urn,
Cucumber sandwiches, rum punch, fudge laced
With hashish cater to whatever taste.

Parody

There is a saying that "imitation is the sincerest form of flattery," and **parody** achieves the same result, by paying an indirect tribute to the popularity of the poet whose work is the subject of the parody. The denotative meaning of parody is "a composition in which an author's characteristics are humorously imitated." Parodies have been written of almost every well-known writer, but the poem that is the subject of the parody has to be familiar enough for readers to get the point. Fledgling poets, who read everything, at some point usually encounter this classic example of light verse by the English nineteenth-century writer Leigh Hunt. Often, to their dismay, they find that the poem's inimitable rhymes and bright spirit linger in their memories long after their first readings. Here is Hunt's original and T. S. Kerrigan's modern parody.

LEIGH HUNT

Jenny Kiss'd Me

1838

Jenny kiss'd me when we met,
  Jumping from the chair she sat in;
Time, you thief, who love to get
  Sweets into your list, put that in!
Say I'm weary, say I'm sad,
  Say that health and wealth have miss'd me,
Say I'm growing old, but add,
  Jenny kiss'd me.

T. S. KERRIGAN

Elvis Kissed Me

1999

"Elvis kissed me once," she swears,
sitting in a neon dive
ordering her drinks in pairs.

Two stools down you nurse a beer,
sensing easy pickings here.

"Back in sixty-eight," she sighs,
smoothing back her yellow hair.
Teared mascara smears her eyes.

Drawing near, you claim you've met,
offer her a cigarette.

"Call me cheap," she sobs, "or bad,
say that decent men dismissed me,
say I've lost my looks, but add,
Elvis kissed me."

Argument

There are also times when poets disagree with each other, and without hesitation they turn to poetry to make their opinions known. In this pair of poems, English poet Carol Rumens responds to the sourly dismissive view of childhood and parenting by fellow poet Philip Larkin.

PHILIP LARKIN

This Be the Verse

1974

They fuck you up, your mum and dad.
They may not mean to, but they do.
They fill you with the faults they had
And add some extra, just for you.

But they were fucked up in their turn
By fools in old-style hats and coats,
Who half the time were soppy stern
And half at one another's throats,

Man hands on misery to man.
It deepens like a coastal shelf.
Get out as early as you can,
And don't have any kids yourself.

CAROL RUMENS

This Be the Verse (Philip Larkin)

2007

Not everybody's
        Childhood sucked:
There are some kiddies
        Not up-fucked.

They moan and shout,
        Won't take advice.
But—hang about—
        Most turn out nice—

If not better
        Than us, no worse.
Sad non-begetter,
        That bean't° the verse.

isn't

Address and Tribute

Another of the ways poets respond to other poets is to address them directly, and there is a long tradition of poetry written as a tribute from one writer to another. In his poem "A Supermarket in California," Allen Ginsberg addresses Walt Whitman, paying him an affectionate tribute. The García Lorca alluded to in the poem is the Spanish poet who was murdered by the Fascists during the Spanish Civil War.

ALLEN GINSBERG

A Supermarket in California

1956

What thoughts I have of you tonight, Walt Whitman, for I walked down the sidestreets under the trees with a headache self-conscious looking at the full moon.

In my hungry fatigue, and shopping for images, I went into the neon fruit supermarket, dreaming of your enumerations!

What peaches and what penumbras! Whole families shopping at night! Aisles full of husbands! Wives in the avocados, babies in the tomatoes! — and you, García Lorca, what were you doing down by the watermelons!

I saw you, Walt Whitman, childless, lonely old grubber, poking among the meats in the refrigerator and eyeing the grocery boys.

I heard you asking questions of each: Who killed the pork chops? What price bananas? Are you my Angel?

I wandered in and out of the brilliant stacks of cans following you, and followed in my imagination by the store detective.

We strode down the open corridors together in our solitary fancy tasting artichokes, possessing every frozen delicacy, and never passing the cashier.

Where are we going, Walt Whitman? The doors close in an hour. Which way does your beard point tonight?

(I touch your book and dream of our odyssey in the supermarket and feel absurd.)

Will we walk all night through solitary streets? The trees add shade to shade, lights out in the houses, we'll both be lonely.

Will we stroll dreaming of the lost America of love past blue automobiles in driveways, home to our silent cottage?

Ah, dear father, graybeard, lonely old courage-teacher, what America did you have when Charon° quit poling his ferry and you got out on a smoking bank and stood watching the boat disappear on the black waters of Lethe°?

Berkeley, 1955

COMMENTARY

MARILYN CHIN

Marilyn Chin, a Chinese American poet, responded to a question about "the canon" in a 1995 interview. In recent years much discussion has centered on the canon,

12. Charon: Greek mythological figure who ferries the souls of the dead over the Styx River. **Lethe:** River in Hades whose waters cause drinkers to forget their pasts.

the long tradition of literature that has served as the American educational standard. Some people believe the canon defines U.S. culture; others consider it a fence that has kept out writing by women and members of cultural minorities.

On the Canon

1995

My personal psychology regarding "the canon" is this: To the outer world I say in a devil-may-care manner "to hell with it." It's a fixed endgame: There will always be an imperialist, Eurocentric bias. The powers-that-be who lord over the selection process are and forevermore will be privileged white male critics. They will decide who will be validated along with Shakespeare and Milton and the latter-day saints of the like of Keats, Yeats, and Eliot. They will guard that "canon" jealously with their elaborate "critical" apparatus; and driven by their own Darwinian instinct to "survive," they will do the best they can to "exclude" us and to promote their own monolithic vision.

But deep inside me another voice rings resolute. I am a serious poet with a rich palette and important mission and I shall fight for the survival of my poetry. What I learned from my youth as a marginalized and isolated west coast Asian American poet is this: It's no fun to be "excluded" . . . as a matter of fact, it feels like hell. What is the purpose of spending most of your adult life hunched in a dark corner perfecting your poems, if your oeuvre will be buried and forgotten anyway? I don't believe any poet who tells me, "No, baby, I don't give a damn about the canon." I am certain that the very same poet has his little poems all dressed up, organized and alphabetized and locked in a vault to be opened in the next century.

The poet's mission on earth is to inspire and to illuminate; and to leave behind to our glorious descendents an intricate and varied map of humanity. One way to survive is to be like Milton, who sits aloft in the great pantheon in the sky and only a very few self-flagellating geeky scholar/poets could indulge into his knotty points. Another way to survive is to be like Gwendolyn Brooks; I predict that her poem "We Real Cool" will be warm on schoolchildren's lips forever. To survive is to be like Langston Hughes, whose poem "A Raisin in the Sun" inspired the young playwright Lorraine Hansberry to write a masterpiece bearing that same name. The true test of "validation" is when one's poems can serve as inspirational models and guiding spirits for a younger generation. We must survive! We must fight to be included in "the canon," so that our voices will sing through history and the global consciousness in eternal echoes. And I'll be damned if I'm going to miss out on THAT out-of-the-body experience!

◆ Topics for Writing about Poets' Responses to Other Poets ◆

1. After a close reading of John Keats's sonnet (p. 824), discuss the specific elements of his response to his discovery of John Chapman's translation of Homer.

2. Discuss the different categories of poets' responses in the chapter and give an example of each with an explanation of what the poet was saying about the poet whose work was selected.
3. One of the best-known categories of poets' response is the use of parody. Choose one of the poems in the text and write your own parody of it, explaining why you chose that poem for your writing.

16.

Poets and Their Worlds: Emily Dickinson, Robert Frost, and Langston Hughes

THE WORLD OF EMILY DICKINSON

DOCUMENT

Emily Dickinson (on Elizabeth Barrett Browning), *I think I was enchanted*

POEMS

Elizabeth Barrett Browning, *When our two souls stand up erect and strong,*
Emily Brontë, *Last Lines*
Christina Rossetti, *Remember*
Christina Rossetti, *From* Sing-Song

Emily Dickinson
Success is counted sweetest
You love me—you are sure—
I'm "wife"—I've finished that—
I taste a liquor never brewed—
Wild Nights—Wild Nights!
"Hope" is the thing with feathers—
There's a certain Slant of light
I'm Nobody! Who are you?
After great pain, a formal feeling comes—
Much Madness is divinest Sense—
I died for Beauty—but was scarce
I heard a Fly buzz—when I died—
Because I could not stop for Death—
A narrow Fellow in the Grass

COMMENTARIES

Thomas Wentworth Higginson, *From "Emily Dickinson's Letters"*
Thomas Bailey Aldrich, *In* Re Emily Dickinson
Richard Wilbur, *On Emily Dickinson*

In December 1859, in a letter to her cousin Louisa Norcross, Emily Dickinson asked her if she remembered a moment when

> you and I in the dining room decided to be distinguished. It's a great thing to be "great" Loo, and you and I might tug for a life, and never accomplish it, but no one can stop our looking on, and you know some

> cannot sing, but the orchard is full of birds and we all can listen. What if we learn ourselves some day!

Emily Dickinson did learn to "sing," as she termed writing poems, though she taught herself much of her art, as most poets do, by learning from other poets. As she found later, in her lines to her cousin about being "distinguished," she was not alone. She was one of a generation of women in England and the United States who had begun writing in ways women had not expressed themselves before, and who were insisting on being heard.

Dickinson is often thought of as living in isolation in her father's house in Amherst, Massachusetts, but for Dickinson it wasn't an isolation that shuttered her mind or her imagination. She had books, and many of the poems and novels she read insisted that women's lives could be freer, less bound by convention. For long periods her books were shared with her sister-in-law Sue Dickinson, the wife of her brother Austin, whose house was across the garden. One book they often exchanged was Sue's copy of Elizabeth Barrett Browning's novel in verse *Aurora Leigh*, published in 1857, when Dickinson was twenty-seven. Browning's book described her own struggle to learn for herself, despite the obstacles that women faced as they tried to free themselves from the restrictions placed on their lives. Both the Dickinson women, Sue and Emily, marked passages that struck them, most often sentences relating to a woman's need for self-fulfillment. As Emily characterized her own feelings about books in a poem,

> . . . this bequest of Wings
> was but a Book—what Liberty
> a loosened spirit brings—

As you read Emily Dickinson's poetry, you will instinctively try to place what you are reading within the quiet simplicities of her everyday life. Except for a school year at Mount Holyoke Female Seminary, only nine miles from her home, when she was sixteen, and short trips to Philadelphia and Boston to consult with medical specialists, she spent her life in her family's house. She lived with her retiring mother, her overpowering father, a faithful sister Lavinia, and her brother and his wife and children across the garden. The household included a hired woman who, with Dickinson's mother, did much of the housework. Because of problems with her health, Dickinson woke at three in the morning to write and to read in the isolation of her room or in a downstairs dining room where a small corner desk was set up for her. The work of the house went on without her until the afternoon. Emily's part in the domestic chores was baking, and she took pride in her puddings. For many years she never left the family house and its garden.

Whatever feelings the neighbors may have had about Dickinson's reclusive habits, her family never discussed their situation. She never married, though in one of her best-known poems she vividly proclaims her "marriage" and in another makes promises of the "Wild Nights" she would spend with a lover. There is no evidence that the poems were anything more than fantasies. She lived in a world of her books, of penciled notes to friends and neighbors, daily letters to women confidants that often contained her poems, and her personal diaries. For long periods of her life we know what she did on virtually every day, even those days and weeks when illness confined her to her bed.

What the family withheld from neighbors and friends was the nature of her illness. When Dickinson was twenty, she traveled to Boston to consult a specialist about the difficulties she had been experiencing for some time. The medication the physician advised, as noted in the surviving pharmaceutical records, was the most advanced treatment of that time for epilepsy. Although there was no cure for the disease, he could prescribe palliatives that provided some relief. She renewed the prescription for three years but had the medicine sent from Boston, probably so that the druggist in Amherst would not be aware of her illness. Epilepsy was known to occur within extended families, and Dickinson's nephew suffered from it, as did several cousins. Because of this danger some states passed laws prohibiting epileptics from marrying. There was also a popular misconception that epilepsy among women was caused by feminine hysteria. The attacks could occur without warning, and within moments the victim was helpless.

For Dickinson, among the causes precipitating her seizures seem to have been stressful excitement and close gatherings of people. Even the flash of sunlight through waving tree branches could have a disastrous effect on her. When she had to make a mandatory appearance at one of her father's official functions as part of his duties as treasurer of Amherst College, she would quickly walk through the gathering without speaking. When she writes about blinding lights or gathering darkness in her poetry, it could be her illness she is describing. In a letter she describes one attack that left her lying senseless for several hours, and then awaking to see the frightened faces of her sister and their servant leaning over her. In their fear of the possible social consequences, her family and their servant never spoke openly of the nature of her illness.

It seems now that it was the daunting possibility of an epileptic seizure that forced Dickinson to live in semi-seclusion, though the fantasies of her poetry reveal her strongly passionate nature. It wasn't until she was in her late forties that she considered that marriage might be possible. The man was Judge Otis Lord, an older family friend whose wife had died. He turned to Dickinson for comfort. She wrote him erotically charged letters, but before they could be married she experienced a severe seizure. Following her recovery some months later, Judge Lord suffered a heart attack and died.

The first poet whose influence can be traced in Dickinson's writing was the transcendentalist poet and philosopher Ralph Waldo Emerson, who lived not far from her in Concord, Massachusetts. Of his writing she wrote, "[He] has touched the secret spring." During her year at Mount Holyoke she studied the classic English poets, among them Alexander Pope, and she discovered the verse of Alfred, Lord Tennyson. In the next few years, back in her bedroom, she read works by William Wordsworth and the popular contemporary American poets Oliver Wendell Holmes and Henry Wadsworth Longfellow. She and her sister-in-law shared an enthusiasm for Longfellow's poem "The Rainy

Day." She read novels of every kind, and she loved Shakespeare. The two plays she returned to again and again were *Antony and Cleopatra* and *Othello*.

Already in her late teens she began to read the new books that were being published by the challenging women poets and novelists in England who were to change the course of Victorian literature. In 1846 the Brontë sisters, Charlotte, Emily, and Anne, self-published a small collection of their verse titled simply *Poems*, using the masculine pseudonyms Currer, Ellis, and Acton Bell. Dickinson owned a copy of this rare volume, and there were often echoes of the Brontës' lines and phrases in her writing. In 1847 Anne Brontë's novel *Agnes Gray* was published, followed within a few months by her sister Charlotte's *Jane Eyre*. The next year, Emily Brontë's *Wuthering Heights* appeared, in the same volume with Anne's second novel, *The Tenants of Wildfell Hall*. A decade later came Elizabeth Barrett Browning's *Aurora Leigh* in 1857, the book that Dickinson and her sister-in-law passed back and forth across the garden, each of them marking lines and passages. Also in that year George Eliot's first novel, *Scenes of Clerical Life*, appeared. They also read with great excitement *The Professor*, the posthumously published first novel of Charlotte Brontë.

In 1860, when Dickinson was thirty, George Eliot's *The Mill on the Floss* was published. Reading the novel had such a strong effect on Dickinson that she continued to regard it with great respect and affection for the rest of her life. In 1862 Christina Rossetti's brilliantly imagined long poem *Goblin Market* appeared, and Dickinson borrowed phrases from it for a poem she sent to a close friend, the newspaper publisher Samuel Bowles. During these same years there were also several losses for the two Amherst readers. Emily Brontë died in 1848, her sister Anne in 1849, and Charlotte in 1855. Elizabeth Barrett Browning died in 1861. Dickinson responded to their deaths in poems of her own, and she struggled with three versions of a lengthy poem honoring the poetry of Elizabeth Barrett Browning. She hung a portrait of Browning on the wall of her bedroom and changed her hair style to match that of the portrait.

It was these writers who were the world of Emily Dickinson when she sat at her writing table in her bedroom or at her small corner desk in the downstairs dining room. Only one of them lived long enough to become conscious of her American admirer. When the first collection of Dickinson's poems was published in 1891, five years after her death, an enthusiastic reader sent a copy to Christina Rossetti. Despite some misgivings about Dickinson's religious sentiments, Rossetti termed the book "a remarkable work of genius."

CONNECTIONS See also Emily Dickinson, "A word is dead," on page 693, and Ralph Waldo Emerson, "The Humble Bee," on page 717.

DOCUMENT

EMILY DICKINSON

I think I was enchanted

c. 1862

I think I was enchanted
When first a sombre Girl—
I read that Foreign Lady—
The Dark—felt beautiful—

And whether it was noon at night—
Or only Heaven—at Noon—
For very Lunacy of Light
I had not power to tell—

The Bees—became as Butterflies—
The Butterflies—as Swans—
Approached—and spurned the narrow Grass—
And just the meanest Tunes

That Nature murmured to herself
To keep herself in Cheer—
I took for Giants—practising
Titanic Opera—

The Days—to Mighty Metres stept—
The Homeliest—adorned
As if unto a Jubilee
'Twere suddenly confirmed—

I could not have defined the change—
Conversion of the Mind
Like Sanctifying in the Soul—
Is witnessed—not explained—

'Twas a Divine Insanity—
The Danger to be Sane
Should I again experience—
'Tis Antidote to turn—

To Tomes of solid Witchcraft—
Magicians be asleep—
But Magic—hath an Element
Like Deity—to keep—

---

3. Foreign Lady: The "Foreign Lady" of this emotional tribute is Elizabeth Barrett Browning. Dickinson wrote the poem shortly after learning of Browning's death.

Poems

ELIZABETH BARRETT BROWNING

When our two souls stand up erect and strong, 1850

When our two souls stand up erect and strong,
Face to face, silent, drawing nigh and nigher,
Until the lengthening wings break into fire
At either curvèd point,—what bitter wrong
Can the earth do to us, that we should not long
Be here contented? Think! In mounting higher,
The angels would press on us and aspire
To drop some golden orb of perfect song
Into our deep, dear silence. Let us stay
Rather on earth, Belovèd,—where the unfit
Contrarious moods of men recoil away
And isolate pure spirits, and permit
A place to stand and love in for a day,
With darkness and the death-hour rounding it.

EMILY BRONTË

Last Lines 1848

The following are the last lines my sister Emily ever wrote.
—CHARLOTTE BRONTË

No coward soul is mine,
No trembler in the world's storm-troubled sphere:
I see Heaven's glories shine,
And faith shines equal, arming me from fear.

O God within my breast,
Almighty, ever-present Deity!
Life—that in me has rest,
As I—undying Life—have power in thee!

Vain are the thousand creeds
That move men's hearts: unutterably vain;
Worthless as withered weeds,
Or idlest froth amid the boundless main,

To waken doubt in one
Holding so fast by thine infinity;
So surely anchored on
The steadfast rock of immortality.

With wide-embracing love
Thy spirit animates eternal years,
Pervades and broods above,
Changes, sustains, dissolves, creates, and rears.

Though earth and man were gone,
And suns and universes ceased to be,
And thou were left alone,
Every existence would exist in thee.

There is not room for Death,
Nor atom that his might could render void:
Thou — thou art Being and Breath,
And what thou art may never be destroyed.

CHRISTINA ROSSETTI

Remember

1849

Remember me when I am gone away,
Gone far away into the silent land;
When you can no more hold me by the hand,
Nor I half turn to go yet turning stay.
Remember me when no more day by day
You tell me of our future that you plann'd:
Only remember me; you understand
It will be late to counsel then or pray.
Yet if you should forget me for a while
And afterwards remember, do not grieve:
For if the darkness and corruption leave
A vestige of the thoughts that once I had,
Better by far you should forget and smile
Than that you should remember and be sad.

From *Sing-Song*

1872

I dug and dug amongst the snow,
And thought the flowers would never grow;
I dug and dug amongst the sand,
And still no green thing came to hand.

Melt, O Snow! the warm winds blow
To thaw the flowers and melt the snow;
But all the winds from every land
Will rear no blossom from the sand.

•

The days are clear,
Day after day,
When April's here
That leads to May,
And June:
Must flow soon:
Stay, June, stay!—
If only we could stop the moon
And June!

•

I planted a hand
And there came up a palm,
I planted a heart
And there came up a balm.

Then I planted a wish,
But there sprang up a thorn,
While heaven frowned with thunder
And earth sighed forlorn.

•

O sailor come ashore.
What have you brought for me?
Red coral, white coral,
Coral from the sea.
I did not dig it from the ground,
Nor pluck it from a tree;
Feeble insects made it
In the stormy sea.

•

The lily has a smooth stalk,
Will never hurt your hand;
But the rose upon the briar
Is lady of the land.

There's sweetness in the apple tree,
And profit in the corn;
But lady of all beauty
Is a rose upon a thorn.

When with moss and honey
She tips her bending briar,
And half unfolds her glowing heart,
She sets the world on fire.

A seventeen-year-old Emily Dickinson in a daguerreotype, the only authenticated likeness of her. (Reprinted by permission of the Robert Frost Library, Amherst College.)

EMILY DICKINSON

Success is counted sweetest

c. 1859

Success is counted sweetest
By those who ne'er succeed.
To comprehend a nectar
Requires sorest need.

Not one of all the purple Host
Who took the Flag today
Can tell the definition
So clear of Victory

As he defeated — dying —
On whose forbidden ear
The distant strains of triumph
Burst agonized and clear!

You love me — you are sure — c. 1860

You love me — you are sure —
I shall not fear mistake —
I shall not *cheated* wake —
Some grinning morn —
to find the Sunrise left —
And Orchards — unbereft —
And Dollie — gone!

I need not start — you're sure —
That night will never be —
When frightened — home to Thee I run —
To find the windows dark —
And no more Dollie — mark —
Quite none?

Be sure you're sure — you know —
I'll bear it better now —
If you'll just tell me so —
Than when — a little dull Balm grown —
Over this pain of mine —
You sting — again!

I'm "wife" — I've finished that — c. 1860

I'm "wife" — I've finished that —
That other state —
I'm Czar — I'm "Woman" now —
It's safer so —

How odd the Girl's life looks
Behind this soft Eclipse —
I think that Earth feels so
To folks in Heaven — now —

This being comfort — then
That other kind — was pain —
But why compare?
I'm "Wife"! Stop there!

I taste a liquor never brewed— c. 1860

I taste a liquor never brewed—
From Tankards scooped in Pearl—
Not all the Vats upon the Rhine
Yield such an Alcohol!

Inebriate of Air—am I—
And Debauchee of Dew—
Reeling—thro endless summer days—
From inns of Molten Blue—

When "Landlords" turn the drunken Bee
Out of the Foxglove's door—
When Butterflies—renounce their "drams"—
I shall but drink the more!

Till Seraphs swing their snowy Hats—
And Saints—to windows run—
To see the little Tippler
Leaning against the—Sun—

Wild Nights—Wild Nights! c. 1861

Wild Nights—Wild Nights!
Were I with thee
Wild Nights should be
Our luxury!

Futile—the Winds—
To a Heart in port—
Done with the Compass—
Done with the Chart!

Rowing in Eden—
Ah, the Sea!
Might I but moor—Tonight—
In Thee!

"Hope" is the thing with feathers— c. 1861

"Hope" is the thing with feathers—
That perches in the soul—
And sings the tune without the words—
And never stops—at all—

And sweetest—in the Gale—is heard—
And sore must be the storm—

That could abash the little Bird
That kept so many warm—

I've heard it in the chillest land—
And on the strangest Sea—
Yet, never, in Extremity,
It asked a crumb—of Me.

There's a certain Slant of light, c. 1861

There's a certain Slant of light,
Winter Afternoons—
That oppresses, like the Heft
Of Cathedral Tunes—

Heavenly Hurt, it gives us—
We can find no scar,
But internal difference,
Where the Meanings, are—

None may teach it—Any—
'Tis the Seal Despair—
An imperial affliction
Sent us of the Air—

When it comes, the Landscape listens—
Shadows—hold their breath—
When it goes, 'tis like the Distance
On the look of Death—

I'm Nobody! Who are you? c. 1861

I'm Nobody! Who are you?
Are you—Nobody—Too?
Then there's a pair of us!
Don't tell! they'd advertise—you know!

How dreary—to be—Somebody!
How public—like a Frog—
To tell one's name—the livelong June—
To an admiring Bog!

After great pain, a formal feeling comes— c. 1862

After great pain, a formal feeling comes—
The Nerves sit ceremonious, like Tombs—
The stiff Heart questions was it He, that bore,
And Yesterday, or Centuries before?

The Feet, mechanical, go round—
Of Ground, or Air, or Ought—
A Wooden way
Regardless grown,
A Quartz contentment, like a stone—

This is the Hour of Lead—
Remembered, if outlived,
As Freezing persons, recollect the Snow—
First—Chill—then Stupor—then the letting go—

Much Madness is divinest Sense— c. 1862

Much Madness is divinest Sense—
To a discerning Eye—
Much Sense—the starkest Madness—
'Tis the Majority
In this, as All, prevail—
Assent—and you are sane—
Demur—you're straightway dangerous—
And handled with a Chain—

I died for Beauty—but was scarce c. 1862

I died for Beauty—but was scarce
Adjusted in the Tomb
When One who died for Truth, was lain
In an adjoining Room—

He questioned softly "Why I failed"?
"For Beauty," I replied—
"And I—for Truth—Themself are One—
We Brethren, are," He said—

And so, as Kinsmen, met a Night—
We talked between the Rooms—
Until the Moss had reached our lips—
And covered up—our names—

I heard a Fly buzz—when I died— c. 1862

I heard a Fly buzz—when I died—
The Stillness in the Room
Was like the Stillness in the Air—
Between the Heaves of Storm—

The Eyes around—had wrung them dry—
And Breaths were gathering firm
For that last Onset—when the King
Be witnessed—in the Room—

I willed my Keepsakes—Signed away
What portion of me be
Assignable—and then it was
There interposed a Fly—

With Blue—uncertain stumbling Buzz—
Between the light—and me—
And then the Windows failed—and then
I could not see to see—

Because I could not stop for Death— c. 1863

Because I could not stop for Death—
He kindly stopped for me—
The Carriage held but just Ourselves—
And Immortality.

We slowly drove—He knew no haste
And I had put away
My labor and my leisure too,
For His Civility—

We passed the School, where Children strove
At Recess—in the Ring—
We passed the Fields of Gazing Grain—
We passed the Setting Sun—

Or rather—He passed Us—
The Dews drew quivering and chill—
For only Gossamer, my Gown—
My Tippet—only Tulle—

We paused before a House that seemed
A Swelling of the Ground—
The Roof was scarcely visible—
The Cornice—in the Ground—

Since then—'tis Centuries—and yet
Feels shorter than the Day
I first surmised the Horses' Heads
Were toward Eternity—

A narrow Fellow in the Grass

c. 1865

A narrow Fellow in the Grass
Occasionally rides—
You may have met Him—did you not
His notice sudden is—

The Grass divides as with a Comb—
A spotted shaft is seen—
And then it closes at your feet
And opens further on—

He likes a Boggy Acre
A Floor too cool for Corn—
Yet when a Boy, and Barefoot—
I more than once at Noon
Have passed, I thought, a Whip lash
Unbraiding in the Sun
When stooping to secure it
It wrinkled, and was gone—

Several of Nature's People
I know, and they know me—
I feel for them a transport
Of cordiality—

But never met this Fellow
Attended, or alone
Without a tighter breathing
And Zero at the Bone—

COMMENTARIES

In this section are three writers' commentaries on Emily Dickinson and her work. Thomas Wentworth Higginson was one of the most important literary figures in America at the time he met Dickinson and later was one of the editors of the first edition of her poems. Thomas Bailey Aldrich, at the time he wrote this slighting comment, was one of America's best-known poets. Although Aldrich suggests in his final sentence that Dickinson's work will soon be forgotten, the irony is that his own reputation has failed to survive into the present. Richard Wilbur is a distinguished contemporary American poet. Wilbur's comments on Emily Dickinson are excerpted from a speech he gave at the Town of Amherst's bicentennial celebration and later published under the title "'Sumptuous Destitution'" in *Responses: Prose Pieces, 1953–1976*.

THOMAS WENTWORTH HIGGINSON

From "Emily Dickinson's Letters" 1891

On April 16, 1862, I took from the post office in Worcester, Mass., where I was then living, the following letter:—

MR. HIGGINSON,—Are you too deeply occupied to say if my verse is alive?

The mind is so near itself it cannot see distinctly, and I have none to ask.

Should you think it breathed, and had you the leisure to tell me, I should feel quick gratitude.

If I make the mistake, that you dared to tell me would give me sincerer honor toward you.

I inclose my name, asking you, if you please, sir, to tell me what is true?

That you will not betray me it is needless to ask, since honor is its own pawn.

The letter was postmarked "Amherst," and it was in a handwriting so peculiar that it seemed as if the writer might have taken her first lessons by studying the famous fossil bird-tracks in the museum of that college town. Yet it was not in the slightest degree illiterate, but cultivated, quaint, and wholly unique. Of punctuation there was little; she used chiefly dashes, and it has been thought better, in printing these letters, as with her poems, to give them the benefit in this respect of the ordinary usages; and so with her habit as to capitalization, as the printers call it, in which she followed the Old English and present German method of thus distinguishing every noun substantive. But the most curious thing about the letter was the total absence of a signature. It proved, however, that she had written her name on a card, and put it under the shelter of a smaller envelope inclosed in the larger; and even this name was written—as if the shy writer wished to recede as far as possible from view—in pencil, not in ink. The name was Emily Dickinson. Inclosed with the letter were four poems, two of which have been already printed,—"Safe in their alabaster chambers" and "I'll tell you how the sun rose," together with the two that here follow. The first comprises in its eight lines a truth so searching that it seems a condensed summary of the whole experience of a long life:—

We play at paste
Till qualified for pearl;
Then drop the paste
And deem ourself a fool.

The shapes, though, were similar
And our new hands
Learned gem-tactics,
Practicing sands.

Then came one which I have always classed among the most exquisite of her productions, with a singular felicity of phrase and an aerial lift that bears the ear upward with the bee it traces:—

The nearest dream recedes unrealized.
    The heaven we chase,
    Like the June bee
    Before the schoolboy,
    Invites the race,
    Stoops to an easy clover,
Dips — evades — teases — deploys —
Then to the royal clouds
    Lifts his light pinnace,
    Heedless of the boy
Staring, bewildered, at the mocking sky
    Homesick for steadfast honey, —
    Ah! the bee flies not
Which brews that rare variety.

The impression of a wholly new and original poetic genius was as distinct on my mind at the first reading of these four poems as it is now, after thirty years of further knowledge; and with it came the problem never yet solved, what place ought to be assigned in literature to what is so remarkable, yet so elusive of criticism. The bee himself did not evade the schoolboy more than she evaded me; and even at this day I still stand somewhat bewildered, like the boy.

Circumstances, however, soon brought me in contact with an uncle of Emily Dickinson, a gentleman not now living; a prominent citizen of Worcester, a man of integrity and character, who shared her abruptness and impulsiveness but certainly not her poetic temperament, from which he was indeed singularly remote. He could tell but little of her, she being evidently an enigma to him, as to me. It is hard to tell what answer was made by me, under these circumstances, to this letter. It is probable that the adviser sought to gain time a little and find out with what strange creature he was dealing. I remember to have ventured on some criticism which she afterwards called "surgery," and on some questions, part of which she evaded, as will be seen, with a naïve skill such as the most experienced and worldly coquette might envy. Her second letter (received April 26, 1862), was as follows: —

MR. HIGGINSON, — Your kindness claimed earlier gratitude, but I was ill, and write to-day from my pillow.

Thank you for the surgery; it was not so painful as I supposed. I bring you others, as you ask, though they might not differ. While my thought is undressed, I can make the distinction; but when I put them in the gown, they look alike and numb.

You asked how old I was? I made no verse, but one or two, until this winter, sir.

I had a terror since September, I could tell to none; and so I sing, as the boy does of the burying ground, because I am afraid.

You inquire my books. For poets, I have Keats, and Mr. and Mrs. Browning. For prose, Mr. Ruskin, Sir Thomas Browne, and the Revelations. I went to school, but in your manner of the phrase had no education. When a little girl,

I had a friend who taught me Immortality; but venturing too near, himself, he never returned. Soon after my tutor died, and for several years my lexicon was my only companion. Then I found one more, but he was not contented I be his scholar, so he left the land.

You ask of my companions. Hills, sir, and the sundown, and a dog large as myself, that my father bought me. They are better than beings because they know, but do not tell; and the noise in the pool at noon excels my piano.

I have a brother and sister; my mother does not care for thought, and father, too busy with his briefs to notice what we do. He buys me many books, but begs me not to read them, because he fears they joggle the mind. They are religious, except me, and address an eclipse, every morning, whom they call their "Father."

But I fear my story fatigues you. I would like to learn. Could you tell me how to grow, or is it unconveyed, like melody or witchcraft?

You speak of Mr. Whitman. I never read his book, but was told that it was disgraceful.

I read Miss Prescott's Circumstance, but it followed me in the dark, so I avoided her.

Two editors of journals came to my father's house this winter, and asked me for my mind, and when I asked them "why" they said I was penurious, and they would use it for the world.

I could not weigh myself, myself. My size felt small to me. I read your chapters in the Atlantic, and experienced honor for you. I was sure you would not reject a confiding question.

Is this, sir, what you asked me to tell you? Your friend,

E. DICKINSON.

It will be seen that she had now drawn a step nearer, signing her name, and as my "friend." It will also be noticed that I had sounded her about certain American authors, then much read; and that she knew how to put her own criticisms in a very trenchant way. With this letter came some more verses, still in the same birdlike script, as for instance the following:—

Your riches taught me poverty,
  Myself a millionaire
In little wealths, as girls could boast,
  Till, broad as Buenos Ayre,
You drifted your dominions
  A different Peru,
And I esteemed all poverty
  For life's estate, with you.

Of mines, I little know, myself,
  But just the names of gems,
The colors of the commonest,
  And scarce of diadems
So much that, did I meet the queen
  Her glory I should know;

But this must be a different wealth,
    To miss it, beggars so.
I'm sure 't is India, all day,
    To those who look on you
Without a stint, without a blame,
    Might I but be the Jew!
I'm sure it is Golconda
    Beyond my power to deem,
To have a smile for mine, each day,
    How better than a gem!
At least, it solaces to know
    That there exists a gold
Although I prove it just in time
    Its distance to behold;
Its far, far treasure to surmise
    And estimate the pearl
That slipped my simple fingers through
    While just a girl at school!

Here was already manifest that defiance of form, never through carelessness, and never precisely from whimsy which so marked her. The slightest change in the order of words—the "While yet at school, a girl"—would have given her a rhyme for this last line but no; she was intent upon her thought and it would not have satisfied her to make the change. . . .

It is possible that in a second letter I gave more of distinct praise or encouragement, for her third is in a different mood. This was received June 8, 1862. There is something startling in its opening image: and in the yet stranger phrase that follows, where she apparently uses "mob" in the sense of chaos or bewilderment:—

Dear Friend,—Your letter gave no drunkenness, because I tasted rum before. Domingo comes but once; yet I have had few pleasures so deep as your opinion, and if I tried to thank you, my tears would block my tongue.

My dying tutor told me that he would like to live till I had been a poet, but Death was much of mob as I could master, then. And when, far afterward, a sudden light on orchards, or a new fashion in the wind troubled my attention, I felt a palsy, here, the verses just relieve.

Your second letter surprised me, and for a moment, swung. I had not supposed it. Your first gave no dishonor, because the true are not ashamed. I thanked you for your justice, but could not drop the bells whose jingling cooled my tramp. Perhaps the balm seemed better, because you bled me first. I smile when you suggest that I delay "to publish," that being foreign to my thought as firmament to fin.

If fame belonged to me, I could not escape her; if she did not, the longest day would pass me on the chase, and the approbation of my dog would forsake me then. My barefoot rank is better.

You think my gait "spasmodic." I am in danger, sir. You think me "uncontrolled." I have no tribunal.

Would you have time to be the "friend" you should think I need? I have a little shape: it would not crowd your desk, nor make much racket as the mouse that dents your galleries.

If I might bring you what I do—not so frequent to trouble you—and ask you if I told it clear, 't would be control to me. The sailor cannot see the North, but knows the needle can. The "hand you stretch me in the dark" I put mine in, and turn away. I have no Saxon now:—

As if I asked a common alms,
And in my wondering hand
A stranger pressed a kingdom,
And I, bewildered, stand;
As if I asked the Orient
Had it for me a morn,
And it should lift its purple dikes
And shatter me with dawn!

But, will you be my preceptor, Mr. Higginson?

With this came the poem already published in her volume and entitled Renunciation; and also that beginning "Of all the sounds dispatched abroad," thus fixing approximately the date of those two. I must soon have written to ask her for her picture, that I might form some impression of my enigmatical correspondent. To this came the following reply, in July, 1862:—

Could you believe me without? I had no portrait, now, but am small, like the wren; and my hair is bold, like the chestnut bur; and my eyes, like the sherry in the glass, that the guest leaves. Would this do just as well?

It often alarms father. He says death might occur, and he has moulds of all the rest, but has no mould of me; but I noticed the quick wore off those things, in a few days, and forestall the dishonor. You will think no caprice of me.

You said "Dark." I know the butterfly, and the lizard, and the orchis. Are not those *your* countrymen?

I am happy to be your scholar, and will deserve the kindness I cannot repay.

If you truly consent, I recite now. Will you tell me my fault, frankly as to yourself, for I had rather wince than die. Men do not call the surgeon to commend the bone, but to set it, sir, and fracture within is more critical. And for this, preceptor, I shall bring you obedience, the blossom from my garden, and every gratitude I know.

Perhaps you smile at me. I could not stop for that. My business is circumference. An ignorance, not of customs, but if caught with the dawn, or the sunset see me, myself the only kangaroo among the beauty, sir, if you please, it afflicts me, and I thought that instruction would take it away.

Because you have much business, beside the growth of me, you will appoint, yourself, how often I shall come, without your inconvenience.

And if at any time you regret you received me, or I prove a different fabric to that you supposed, you must banish me.

When I state myself, as the representative of the verse, it does not mean me, but a supposed person.

You are true about the "perfection." To-day makes Yesterday mean.

You spoke of Pippa Passes. I never heard anybody speak of Pippa Passes before. You see my posture is benighted.

To thank you baffles me. Are you perfectly powerful? Had I a pleasure you had not, I could delight to bring it.

YOUR SCHOLAR. . . .

At last, after many postponements, on August 16, 1870, I found myself face to face with my hitherto unseen correspondent. It was at her father's house, one of those large, square, brick mansions so familiar in our older New England towns, surrounded by trees and blossoming shrubs without, and within exquisitely neat, cool, spacious, and fragrant with flowers. After a little delay, I heard an extremely faint and pattering footstep like that of a child, in the hall, and in glided, almost noiselessly, a plain, shy little person, the face without a single good feature, but with eyes, as she herself said, "like the sherry the guest leaves in the glass," and with smooth bands of reddish chestnut hair. She had a quaint and nun-like look, as if she might be a German canoness of some religious order, whose prescribed garb was white piqué, with a blue net worsted shawl. She came toward me with two day-lilies, which she put in a childlike way into my hand, saying softly, under her breath, "These are my introduction," and adding, also under her breath, in childlike fashion, "Forgive me if I am frightened; I never see strangers, and hardly know what I say." But soon she began to talk, and thenceforward continued almost constantly; pausing sometimes to beg that I would talk instead, but readily recommencing when I evaded. There was not a trace of affectation in all this; she seemed to speak absolutely for her own relief, and wholly without watching its effect on her hearer. Led on by me, she told much about her early life, in which her father was always the chief figure,—evidently a man of the old type, *la vielle roche* of Puritanism—a man who, as she said, read on Sunday "lonely and rigorous books"; and who had from childhood inspired her with such awe, that she never learned to tell time by the clock till she was fifteen, simply because he had tried to explain it to her when she was a little child, and she had been afraid to tell him that she did not understand, and also afraid to ask any one else lest he should hear of it. Yet she had never heard him speak a harsh word, and it needed only a glance at his photograph to see how truly the Puritan tradition was preserved in him. He did not wish his children, when little, to read anything but the Bible; and when, one day, her brother brought her home Longfellow's Kavanagh, he put it secretly under the pianoforte cover, made signs to her, and they both afterwards read it. It may have been before this, however, that a student of her father's was amazed to find that she and her brother had never heard of Lydia Maria Child, then much read, and he brought Letters from New York, and hid it in the great bush of old-fashioned tree-box beside the front door. After the first book she thought in ecstasy, "This, then, is a book, and there are more of them." But she did not find so many as she expected, for she afterwards said to me, "When I lost the use of my eyes, it was a comfort to think that there were so few real books that I could easily find one to read me all of them." Afterwards, when she regained her eyes, she read Shakespeare, and thought to herself, "Why is any other book needed?"

She went on talking constantly and saying, in the midst of narrative, things quaint and aphoristic. "Is it oblivion or absorption when things pass from our minds?" "Truth is such a rare thing, it is delightful to tell it." "I find ecstacy in living; the mere sense of living is joy enough." When I asked her if she never felt any want of employment, not going off the grounds and rarely seeing a visitor, she answered, "I never thought of conceiving that I could ever have the slightest approach to such a want in all future time"; and then added, after a pause, "I feel that I have not expressed myself strongly enough," although it seemed to me that she had. She told me of her household occupations, that she made all their bread, because her father liked only hers; then saying shyly, "And people must have puddings," this very timidly and suggestively, as if they were meteors or comets. Interspersed with these confidences came phrases so emphasized as to seem the very wantonness of over-statement, as if she pleased herself with putting into words what the most extravagant might possibly think without saying, as thus: "How do most people live without any thoughts? There are many people in the world,—you must have noticed them in the street,—how do they live? How do they get strength to put on their clothes in the morning?" Or this crowning extravaganza: "If I read a book and it makes my whole body so cold no fire can ever warm me, I know that is poetry. If I feel physically as if the top of my head were taken off, I know that is poetry. These are the only ways I know it. Is there any other way?"

I have tried to describe her just as she was, with the aid of notes taken at the time; but this interview left our relation very much what it was before;—on my side an interest that was strong and even affectionate, but not based on any thorough comprehension; and on her side a hope, always rather baffled, that I should afford some aid in solving her abstruse problem of life. . . .

When I said, at parting, that I would come again some time, she replied, "Say, in a long time; that will be nearer. Some time is no time."

THOMAS BAILEY ALDRICH

In *Re Emily Dickinson* 1892

The English critic who said of Miss Emily Dickinson that she might have become a fifth-rate poet "if she had only mastered the rudiments of grammar and gone into metrical training for about fifteen years,"—the rather candid English critic who said this somewhat overstated his case. He had, however, a fairly good case. If Miss Dickinson had undergone the austere curriculum indicated, she would, I am sure, have become an admirable lyric poet of the second magnitude. In the first volume of her poetical chaos is a little poem which needs only slight revision in the initial stanza in order to make it worthy of ranking with some of the odd swallow flights in Heine's° lyrical *intermezzo*. I have ventured to desecrate this stanza by tossing a rhyme into it, as the other stanzas happened to rhyme, and here print the lyric, hoping the reader will not accuse me of overvaluing it:—

> I taste a liquor never brewed
> In vats upon the Rhine;
> No tankard ever held a draught
> Of alcohol like mine.
>
> Inebriate of air am I,
> And debauchee of dew,
> Reeling, through endless summer days,
> From inns of molten blue.
>
> When landlords turn the drunken bee
> Out of the Foxglove's door,
> When butterflies renounce their drams,
> I shall but drink the more!
>
> Till seraphs swing their snowy caps
> And saints to windows run,
> To see the little tippler
> Leaning against the sun!

Certainly those inns of molten blue, and that disreputable honey-gatherer who got himself turned out-of-doors at the sign of the Foxglove, are very taking matters. I know of more important things that interest me less. There are three or four bits in this kind in Miss Dickinson's book; but for the most part the ideas totter and toddle, not having learned to walk. In spite of this, several of the quatrains are curiously touching, they have such a pathetic air of yearning to be poems.

It is plain that Miss Dickinson possessed an extremely unconventional and grotesque fancy. She was deeply tinged by the mysticism of Blake, and strongly influenced by the mannerism of Emerson. The very way she tied her bonnet-strings, preparatory to one of her nunlike walks in her claustral garden, must have been Emersonian. She had much fancy of a queer sort, but only, as it appears to me, intermittent flashes of imagination. I fail to detect in her work any of that profound thought which her editor professes to discover in it. The phenomenal insight, I am inclined to believe, exists only in his partiality; for whenever a woman poet is in question Mr. Higginson always puts on his rose-colored spectacles. This is being chivalrous; but the invariable result is not clear vision. That Miss Dickinson's whimsical memoranda have a certain something which, for want of a more precise name, we term *quality* is not to be denied except by the unconvertible heathen who are not worth conversion. But the incoherence and formlessness of her—I don't know how to designate them—versicles are fatal. Sydney Smith, or some other humorist, mentions a

---

Heine's: Heinrich Heine (1797–1856), German poet and critic.

person whose bump of veneration was so inadequately developed as to permit him to damn the equator if he wanted to. This certainly established a precedent for independence; but an eccentric, dreamy, half-educated recluse in an out-of-the-way New England village (or anywhere else) cannot with impunity set at defiance the laws of gravitation and grammar. In his charming preface to Miss Dickinson's collection, Mr. Higginson insidiously remarks: "After all, when a thought takes one's breath away, a lesson on grammar seems an impertinence." But an ungrammatical thought does not, as a general thing, take one's breath away, except in a sense the reverse of flattering. Touching this matter of mere technique Mr. Ruskin° has a word to say (it appears that he said it "in his earlier and better days"), and Mr. Higginson quotes it: "No weight, nor mass, nor beauty of execution can outweigh one grain or fragment of thought." This is a proposition to which one would cordially subscribe, if it were not so intemperately stated. A suggestive commentary on Mr. Ruskin's impressive dictum is furnished by the fact that Mr. Ruskin has lately published a volume of the most tedious verse that has been printed in this century. The substance of it is weighty enough, but the workmanship lacks just that touch which distinguishes the artist from the bungler, — the touch which Mr. Ruskin seems not to have much regarded either in his later or "in his earlier and better days."

If Miss Dickinson's *disjecta membra* are poems, then Shakespeare's prolonged imposition should be exposed without further loss of time, and Lord Tennyson ought to be advised of the error of his ways before it is too late. But I do not hold the situation to be so desperate. Miss Dickinson's versicles have a queerness and a quaintness that have stirred a momentary curiosity in emotional bosoms. Oblivion lingers in the immediate neighborhood.

RICHARD WILBUR

On Emily Dickinson 1963

Emily Dickinson never lets us forget for very long that in some respects life gave her short measure; and indeed it is possible to see the greater part of her poetry as an effort to cope with her sense of privation. I think that for her there were three major privations: she was deprived of an orthodox and steady religious faith; she was deprived of love; she was deprived of literary recognition.

At the age of seventeen, after a series of revival meetings at Mount Holyoke Seminary, Emily Dickinson found that she must refuse to become a professing Christian. To some modern minds this may seem to have been a sensible and necessary step; and surely it was a step toward becoming such a poet as she became. But for her, no pleasure in her own integrity could then eradicate the feeling that she had betrayed a deficiency, a want of grace. In her letters to Abiah Root she tells of the enhancing effect of conversion on her fellow-students, and says of herself in a famous passage:

Ruskin: John Ruskin (1819–1900), English essayist, critic, and reformer.

> *I* am one of the lingering bad ones, and so do I slink away, and pause and ponder, and ponder and pause, and do work without knowing why, not surely, for this brief world, and more sure it is not for heaven, and I ask what this message *means* that they ask for so very eagerly: *you* know of this depth and fulness, will you try to tell me about it?

There is humor in that, and stubbornness, and a bit of characteristic lurking pride: but there is also an anguished sense of having separated herself, through some dry incapacity, from spiritual community, from purpose, and from magnitude of life. As a child of evangelical Amherst, she inevitably thought of purposive, heroic life as requiring a vigorous faith. Out of such a thought she later wrote:

> The abdication of Belief
> Makes the Behavior small—
> Better an ingis fatuus
> Than no illume at all—

That hers *was* a species of religious personality goes without saying; but by her refusal of such ideas as original sin, redemption, hell, and election, she made it impossible for herself—as Professor Whicher observed—"to share the religious life of her generation." She became an unsteady congregation of one.

Her second privation, the privation of love, is one with which her poems and her biographies have made us exceedingly familiar, though some biographical facts remain conjectural. She had the good fortune, at least once, to bestow her heart on another; but she seems to have found her life, in great part, a history of loneliness, separation, and bereavement.

As for literary fame, some will deny that Emily Dickinson ever greatly desired it, and certainly there is evidence, mostly from her latter years, to support such a view. She *did* write that "Publication is the auction / Of the mind of man." And she *did* say to Helen Hunt Jackson, "How can you print a piece of your soul?" But earlier, in 1861, she had frankly expressed to Sue Dickinson the hope that "sometime" she might make her kinfolk proud of her. The truth is, I think, that Emily Dickinson knew she was good, and began her career with a normal appetite for recognition. I think that she later came, with some reason, to despair of being understood or properly valued, and so directed against her hopes of fame what was by then a well-developed disposition to renounce. That she wrote a good number of poems about fame supports my view: the subjects to which a poet returns are those which vex him.

What did Emily Dickinson do, as a poet, with her sense of privation? One thing she quite often did was to pose as the laureate and attorney of the empty-handed, and question God about the economy of His creation. Why, she asked, is a fatherly God so sparing of His presence? Why is there never a sign that prayers are heard? Why does Nature tell us no comforting news of its Maker? Why do some receive a whole loaf, while others must starve on a crumb? Where is the benevolence in shipwreck and earthquake? By asking such questions as these, she turned complaint into critique, and used her own sufferings as experiential evidence about the nature of the deity. The God who emerges from these poems is a God who does not answer, an unrevealed God whom one cannot confidently approach through Nature or through doctrine.

But there was another way in which Emily Dickinson dealt with her sentiment of lack—another emotional strategy which was both more frequent and more fruitful. I refer to her repeated assertion of the paradox that privation is more plentiful than plenty; that to renounce is to possess the more; that "The Banquet of abstemiousness / Defaces that of wine." We all know how the poet illustrated this ascetic paradox in her behavior—how in her latter years she chose to live in relative retirement, keeping the world, even in its dearest aspects, at a physical remove. She would write her friends, telling them how she missed them, then flee upstairs when they came to see her; afterward, she might send a note of apology, offering the odd explanation that "We shun because we prize." Any reader of Dickinson biographies can furnish other examples, dramatic or homely, of this prizing and shunning, this yearning and renouncing: in my own mind's eye is a picture of Emily Dickinson watching a gay circus caravan from the distance of her chamber window.

THE WORLD OF ROBERT FROST

DOCUMENT

Louis Untermeyer, *A "book of people"*

POEMS

Thomas Hardy, *An August Midnight*
Edwin Arlington Robinson, *Eros Tyrannos*
Edgar Lee Masters, *Mabel Osborne*
Edgar Lee Masters, *Lucinda Matlock*
Edward Thomas, *Early One Morning*

Robert Frost
In White
The Pasture
Mending Wall
Home Burial
After Apple-Picking
Birches
The Road Not Taken
To Earthward
Stopping by Woods on a Snowy Evening

COMMENTARIES

Rose C. Feld, *An Interview with Robert Frost*
Carol Frost, *From* Sincerity and Inventions: On Robert Frost
Philip L. Gerber, *On Frost's "After Apple-Picking"*
James Wright, *The Music of Robert Frost's "Stopping by Woods on a Snowy Evening"*

As you read the poetry of Emily Dickinson or Langston Hughes, what you hear in their lines, despite Dickinson's shy evasions or Hughes's public stances, is the voice of the person who wrote the poetry. In their writings we meet the poets themselves: their loves, their disappointments, their beliefs, and their ambitions. When the poet writes "I" we expect that will be the person we encounter in the poetry. What you will find, however, as you study the poetry of Robert Frost, is that the "I" of his poems is not the person you might expect. With Robert Frost what we finally realize is that like a short story writer or a playwright, the stories he tells us in his poems are a kind of fiction. Should we think of this as simply another way of writing poetry? Or is it saying to us that the role of a poet is a costume to be put on and taken off when the poet leaves his work room and walks out the door into the ordinary world? As you read his poems this will be something for you to consider and answer for yourself.

Frost's poetry rings with the autumnal tones of New England, and the voice of his poetry suggests to you that he lived for much of his life in rural New Hampshire. His lines are filled with imagery and anecdotes that tie his experiences to the poor farms of the countryside. The reality, however, was that the life he led was very different. Frost was born in San Francisco in 1874 and lived there until the death of his father, when his mother moved with Robert and his younger sister Jeanie to Lawrence, Massachusetts. There she was able to find poorly paid work as a schoolteacher. For educated women at that time, teaching was one of the few jobs that were offered. For women without an education the only work they could find was in the mills of Lawrence or Lowell. Frost graduated from high school in Lawrence, and like Langston Hughes, who was the class poet of his Cleveland high school, Frost was selected as one of his class's valedictorians. Three years later, after a stormy and jealous courtship, he married the woman who had been the other valedictorian, Elinor White. It was a marriage with only brief moments of happiness, but Elinor gave birth to six children, two of whom died when still very young.

After high school Frost briefly attended Dartmouth College and Harvard University, and for the next twenty years he struggled to support his family with a series of poorly paid jobs, writing poems at night and sending them to local newspapers. One of his failed projects was an attempt to operate a chicken farm in New Hampshire. The farm was purchased for him by his grandfather, and when his grandfather died the poet was left free use of the farm for ten years. After that he could do what he wanted with it. He was also left a small annuity of $500 a year for ten years, and after that it would increase to $800. It wasn't enough to support Frost's family, but it was enough to keep them from the edge of poverty. What was most important about his unhappy experience on the New Hampshire chicken farm was that it would finally give him a setting for his poetry. The reality of his life was that in 1906 he began teaching school, and except for a stay in England that kept him away for three years, he taught school most of his life. As you read his poetry, this might be difficult to understand since there is not a single poem that directly describes his life as a schoolteacher, his family's struggles, the schools where he taught, his fellow teachers, or his students.

After Frost accepted his first teaching position at Pinkerton Academy in Derry, New Hampshire, he spent his nights writing poetry, but failed to place more than a handful of his poems with local newspapers. He was one of thousands of young writers who had learned from their reading what a poem should be like, but nothing in him told him how to set himself apart from the others. In 1911 the abandoned farm became his property, as in the terms of his grandfather's will, and his yearly stipend was increased. At this point in his life he was so discouraged by his failure as a writer and by the unhappiness of his marriage that he was near emotional collapse, deeply depressed, and suicidal. To break free from his situation, he sold the farm, and with the money from the sale and with his yearly annuity, he left the United States and settled with his family in England.

In your reading you found that some poets, like Dickinson, discovered their own path to their poetic language without having contact with other writers. Their books were enough. Others, like Hughes and the writers of the Harlem Renaissance, drew energy and encouragement from each other. In his rural teaching positions, Frost was almost completely without contact with anyone who shared his struggle to become a writer, and at this point in his life he needed other poets to show him new creative directions.

Frost went to England in 1912 as an unsuccessful author of mediocre newspaper verse. In the next three years, he found a new poetic language and new themes and directions for his poetry as he turned to his memories of his neighbors' lives in New Hampshire. Considering his later triumphant success, it is difficult to realize just how mediocre his poetry was in these years when he struggled to find his own style. The verses he was writing showed that he had read a great deal of poetry, but before he left for England his poems showed no sign of his individuality or of the fierce debate over free verse and imagism that engaged his contemporaries in the United States. These derivative, clumsily written stanzas are from Frost's early poem titled "Stars."

How countlessly they congregate
    O'er our tumultuous snow,
Which flows in shapes as tall as trees
    When wintry winds do blow!

As if with keenness for our fate,
    Our faltering few steps on
To white rest, and a place of rest
    Invisible at dawn. . . .

In London, Frost met Ezra Pound, who decided this was another American who needed his help, as he had already helped H. D. and later would help T. S. Eliot. A number of English writers had settled in the small village of Dymock in Gloucestershire, and Frost and his family rented a cottage and joined them. He met another writer who had moved from London with his wife and two children to a small village not far away. His name was Edward Thomas. He was introduced to Frost as a successful author of books about the English countryside, as well as the author of well-received biographies and a novel. He also had a steady position as a book reviewer for a major London newspaper. Thomas was four years younger than Frost and later Frost said of him, "I never had, I never shall have another such year of friendship." Thomas was, as Frost declared, "the nearest to a brother I would ever come."

Despite his long hours at his writing desk and his increasing reputation, however, Thomas, like Frost, continually struggled to earn enough money to support his family. He suffered from intermittent bouts of self-doubt and depression. His new life in the country village was at last giving him confidence to attempt writing that was more creative, and the two families soon became close. Frost and Thomas spent hours walking in the woods. Frost had become familiar with the wild flowers and plants of the New Hampshire woodlands, and Thomas helped his new friend with his knowledge of his own native landscape and its plants and birds. Thomas had always loved poetry, and he had begun publishing some of his first verses under a pseudonym, but with Frost's encouragement he began writing poetry more seriously. Frost also was going through the difficulties of abandoning his earlier way of writing and finding a language of his own. His problem was different from those faced by Dickinson and Hughes, who found a source for their way of writing when they were first searching for their poetic voice and never felt the need to change. Frost had been writing what he now saw as unsatisfactory poetry for nearly twenty years, and he had as much to unlearn as he had to learn.

The poetry that Frost and Thomas had begun writing found models in contemporary English verse, and there is a strong affinity in their new poetry to the poems of Thomas Hardy, who had turned his back on his successful career as a novelist and was living in the countryside in Dorset. Hardy's poems about rural life introduced themes and motives that would be an influence on the new style that Frost was creating. He and Thomas exchanged their poems, and as they walked in the woods, they talked about their poetry. In the evenings, they joined the other writers in the village and the talk continued into the night.

Ezra Pound had also been working on Frost's behalf, and at his urging a London publisher brought out Frost's first collection of poems in 1913, *A Boy's Will*, which included many of his early verses and didn't clearly reflect the new directions his work was taking. The next year, again with Pound as his supporter, Frost had a new book ready, *North of Boston*, which included his new poems—many of them the masterpieces for which he is best known. Thomas wrote a rave review of the book for his London newspaper, and with this review and Pound's support, *North of Boston* was taken by an American publisher. In 1915, when Frost returned to the United States, he was a celebrated poet, and he could create the life he had always dreamed of.

The First World War was now draining England of its young men, and when he'd settled with his family in New Hampshire again, Frost tried to convince Thomas to join them there. In their exchanges of letters was his poem "The Road Not Taken," which Frost intended as a joke about Thomas's continual inability to make up his mind about anything. Finally, Thomas's decision was to enlist in the British army. For some months he remained in England as a training instructor, and the young English poet Wilfred Owen was one of his new recruits. Over the next year and a half, Thomas wrote more than 140 poems, some about his experiences in the trenches in France where he had now been sent, but many of them reliving memories of his beloved English countryside and the people in his village. He was killed in April 1917 when a shell exploded close to him.

In the United States, Frost returned to a world that was ready for the dark tragedy of his longer poems, and also for his new skills writing in traditional poetic forms. As you read his poems, you will find him using blank verse, the sonnet, and a wide range of shorter lyric forms with a distinctive skill and intelligence. Before Frost's years in England, he had struggled with poorly paid teaching jobs and his unhappy domestic situation, and although his personal difficulties didn't enter into his writing as autobiography, their darkness hung over many of the poems. His readers in the United States had already been introduced to this struggling world of the small towns and the barren farms of rural America by the sardonic pessimism of the poetry of Edwin Arlington Robinson, whose poems like "Miniver Cheevy" (p. 728) and "Richard Cory" (p. 729) had attracted widespread attention when they were praised by the president of the United States, Theodore Roosevelt.

Another curtain was thrown back on this shadowed world with the publication in 1915 of Edgar Lee Masters's *Spoon River Anthology*, a chorus of the imagined voices of his townspeople talking about their lives from their graves in the small midwestern town of Spoon River. Masters's book was a major success. It sold widely, it became a busy topic of discussion, and its use of small-town life for its themes had an influence on other writing, like the collection of short stories by Sherwood Anderson, *Winesburg, Ohio*, published four years later. Masters's poems inspired plays and films, and its laconic speech and its unassuming use of free rhythm affected a generation of American poets. Frost's collection *North of Boston* presented a strong new poetic voice exploring some of these same themes, and, at the same time, his poems describing the land itself and his pleasure in his daily experiences walking alone in the forest sometimes had a joyousness that few American writers had achieved. His poetry ultimately became part of the American consciousness.

Frost continued teaching, but as a successful writer he was no longer employed at small academies in rural New Hampshire. He taught at Harvard University, then later at Amherst College, Middlebury College, and Dartmouth. He founded the Bread Loaf summer program for young writers and directed it until his death. He continued to write in traditional forms, and as he grew older his political views became increasingly conservative. Although he had become one of America's best-loved poets, he was rabidly jealous of other poets like Carl Sandburg and T. S. Eliot. His personal life still was shadowed with unhappiness. His son committed suicide, and one daughter had to be confined to a mental institution. After his retirement from teaching, he spent his winters in Key West, Florida, leaving the snow and the winds of New Hampshire behind. None of these things, however, were used as themes for his poetry, which became increasingly optimistic even through the long years of the Depression. As you read his poetry today, would you say, knowing his story, that Frost was a man who never dropped his mask? Or could it be that his mask, like Dickinson's withdrawal to the rooms of her family house, was finally his defense against a world that despite his rich success had caused him so much pain?

DOCUMENT

LOUIS UNTERMEYER

A "book of people"

1915

This review of Robert Frost's *North of Boston* (1915) appeared in critic Louis Untermeyer's *The New Era in American Poetry* (1919).

In *North of Boston* Frost found his own full utterance and himself. It is, as he calls it, a "book of people." And it is more than that. It is a book of a people, of the folk of New England, of New England itself with its hard hills and harder certainties, its repressions, its cold humor and inverted tenderness. Against this background, Frost has placed some of the most poignant and dramatic poems that the age has produced, perhaps the most authentic and powerful that have ever come out of America. These dramas, sometimes in dialog, sometimes in monolog, are the antithesis of the "arranged" and carefully planned pieces of stagecraft. There is a total absence of fine feathers and fustian, of red lights and rhetoric, of all the skillful literary mechanics we have been used to. Discarding these theatrical accessories Frost has taken the drama out into the air; he lets the sunlight play over his scenes and allows his actors to talk in a language that is rich and living, imaginative in its very adherence to reality. . . .

Another thing that gives these poems so potent an illusion of reality is the absence of the guiding hand of the creator; figures live and breathe and move of their own desire and necessity. And they are illumined by nothing so much as an intense sympathy that may easily be considered a brilliant psychology. This light does not merely set off his figures. It penetrates them. It reaches down through his people to their roots; it strikes the soil from which they grew. It even transforms the whole countryside and makes it something more than an effective background. It gives his setting the power of an immense and moving actor in the lives of the folk it overshadows.

Poems

THOMAS HARDY

An August Midnight

1899

I

A shaded lamp and a waving blind,
And the beat of a clock from a distant floor:
On this scene enter—winged, horned, and spined—
A longlegs, a moth, and a dumbledore;
While 'mid my page there idly stands
A sleepy fly, that rubs its hands . . .

II

Thus meet we five, in this still place,
At this point of time, at this point in space.
—My guests besmear my new-penned line,
Or bang at the lamp and fall supine.
'God's humblest, they!' I muse. Yet why?
They know Earth-secrets that know not I.

Max Gate,° 1899

EDWIN ARLINGTON ROBINSON

Eros Tyrannos

1916

She fears him, and will always ask
What fated her to choose him;
She meets in his engaging mask
All reasons to refuse him;
But what she meets and what she fears
Are less than are the downward years,
Drawn slowly to the foamless weirs
Of age, were she to lose him.

Between a blurred sagacity
That once had power to sound him,
And Love, that will not let him be
The Judas that she found him,
Her pride assuages her almost,
As if it were alone the cost.—
He sees that he will not be lost,
And waits and looks around him.

A sense of ocean and old trees
Envelops and allures him;
Tradition, touching all he sees,
Beguiles and reassures him;
And all her doubts of what he says
Are dimmed with what she knows of days—
Till even prejudice delays
And fades, and she secures him.

The falling leaf inaugurates
The reign of her confusion:
The pounding wave reverberates
The dirge of her illusion;

Max Gate: Hardy's country home.

And home, where passion lived and died,
Becomes a place where she can hide,
While all the town and harbor side
    Vibrate with her seclusion.

We tell you, tapping on our brows,
    The story as it should be—
As if the story of a house
    Were told, or ever could be;
We'll have no kindly veil between
Her visions and those we have seen,—
As if we guessed what hers have been,
    Or what they are or would be.

Meanwhile we do no harm; for they
    That with a god have striven,
Not hearing much of what we say,
    Take what the god has given;
Though like waves breaking it may be
Or like a changed familiar tree,
Or like a stairway to the sea
    Where down the blind are driven.

EDGAR LEE MASTERS

Mabel Osborne

1915

Your red blossoms amid green leaves
Are drooping, beautiful geranium!
But you do not ask for water.
You cannot speak! You do not need to speak—
Everyone knows that you are dying of thirst,
Yet they do not bring water!
They pass on, saying:
"The geranium wants water."
And I, who had happiness to share
And longed to share your happiness;
I who loved you, Spoon River,
And craved your love,
Withered before your eyes, Spoon River—
Thirsting, thirsting,
Voiceless from chasteness of soul to ask you for love,
You who knew and saw me perish before you,
Like this geranium which someone has planted over me,
And left to die.

Lucinda Matlock

1916

I went to the dances at Chandlerville,
And played snap-out at Winchester.
One time we changed partners,
Driving home in the moonlight of middle June,
And then I found Davis.
We were married and lived together for seventy years,
Enjoying, working, raising the twelve children,
Eight of whom we lost
Ere I had reached the age of sixty.
I spun, I wove, I kept the house, I nursed the sick,
I made the garden, and for holiday
Rambled over the fields where sang the larks,
And by Spoon River gathering many a shell,
And many a flower and medicinal weed—
Shouting to the wooded hills, singing to the green valleys.
At ninety-six I had lived enough, that is all,
And passed to a sweet repose.
What is this I hear of sorrow and weariness,
Anger, discontent and drooping hopes?
Degenerate sons and daughters,
Life is too strong for you—
It takes life to love Life.

EDWARD THOMAS

Early One Morning

1917

Early one morning in May I set out,
And nobody I knew was about.
I'm bound away for ever,
Away somewhere, away for ever.

There was no wind to trouble the weathercocks.
I had burnt my letters and darned my socks.

No one knew I was going away,
I thought myself I should come back some day.

I heard the brook through the town gardens run.
O sweet was the mud turned to dust by the sun.

A gate banged in a fence and banged in my head.
'A fine morning, sir,' a shepherd said.

I could not return from my liberty,
To my youth and my love and my misery.

The past is the only dead thing that smells sweet,
The only sweet thing that is not also fleet.
I'm bound away for ever,
Away somewhere, away for ever.

ROBERT FROST

In White

1913

A dented spider like a snow drop white
On a white Heal-all, holding up a moth
Like a white piece of lifeless satin cloth—
Saw ever curious eye so strange a sight?—
Portent in little, assorted death and blight
Like the ingredients of a witches' broth?—
The beady spider, the flower like a froth,
And the moth carried like a paper kite.

What had that flower to do with being white,
The blue prunella every child's delight.
What brought the kindred spider to that height?
(Make we no thesis of the miller's plight.)
What but design of darkness and of night?
Design, design! Do I use the word aright?

The Pasture

1913

I'm going out to clean the pasture spring;
I'll only stop to rake the leaves away
(And wait to watch the water clear, I may):
I shan't be gone long.—You come too.

I'm going out to fetch the little calf
That's standing by the mother. It's so young
It totters when she licks it with her tongue.
I shan't be gone long.—You come too.

Mending Wall

1914

Something there is that doesn't love a wall,
That sends the frozen-ground-swell under it,
And spills the upper boulders in the sun;
And makes gaps even two can pass abreast.
The work of hunters is another thing:

Robert Frost at his writing desk. (Reprinted by permission of Dartmouth College Library.)

I have come after them and made repair
Where they have left not one stone on a stone,
But they would have the rabbit out of hiding,
To please the yelping dogs. The gaps I mean,
No one has seen them made or heard them made,
But at spring mending-time we find them there.
I let my neighbor know beyond the hill;
And on a day we meet to walk the line
And set the wall between us once again.
We keep the wall between us as we go.
To each the boulders that have fallen to each.
And some are loaves and some so nearly balls
We have to use a spell to make them balance:
"Stay where you are until our backs are turned!"
We wear our fingers rough with handling them.
Oh, just another kind of outdoor game,
One on a side. It comes to little more:
There where it is we do not need the wall:

He is all pine and I am apple orchard.
My apple trees will never get across
And eat the cones under his pines, I tell him.
He only says, "Good fences make good neighbors."
Spring is the mischief in me, and I wonder
If I could put a notion in his head:
"*Why* do they make good neighbors? Isn't it
Where there are cows? But here there are no cows.
Before I built a wall I'd ask to know
What I was walling in or walling out,
And to whom I was like to give offense.
Something there is that doesn't love a wall,
That wants it down." I could say "Elves" to him,
But it's not elves exactly, and I'd rather
He said it for himself. I see him there
Bringing a stone grasped firmly by the top
In each hand, like an old-stone savage armed.
He moves in darkness as it seems to me,
Not of woods only and the shade of trees.
He will not go behind his father's saying,
And he likes having thought of it so well
He says again, "Good fences make good neighbors."

Home Burial

1914

He saw her from the bottom of the stairs
Before she saw him. She was starting down,
Looking back over her shoulder at some fear.
She took a doubtful step and then undid it
To raise herself and look again. He spoke
Advancing toward her: "What is it you see
From up there always—for I want to know."
She turned and sank upon her skirts at that,
And her face changed from terrified to dull.
He said to gain time: "What is it you see,"
Mounting until she cowered under him.
"I will find out now—you must tell me, dear."
She, in her place, refused him any help
With the least stiffening of her neck and silence.
She let him look, sure that he wouldn't see,
Blind creature; and a while he didn't see.
But at last he murmured, "Oh," and again, "Oh."

"What is it—what?" she said.

"Just that I see."

"You don't," she challenged. "Tell me what it is."

"The wonder is I didn't see at once.
I never noticed it from here before.
I must be wonted to it—that's the reason.
The little graveyard where my people are!
So small the window frames the whole of it.
Not so much larger than a bedroom, is it?
There are three stones of slate and one of marble,
Broad-shouldered little slabs there in the sunlight
On the sidehill. We haven't to mind *those*.
But I understand: it is not the stones,
But the child's mound——"

"Don't, don't, don't, don't," she cried.

She withdrew shrinking from beneath his arm
That rested on the banister, and slid downstairs;
And turned on him with such a daunting look,
He said twice over before he knew himself:
"Can't a man speak of his own child he's lost?"

"Not you! Oh, where's my hat? Oh, I don't need it!
I must get out of here. I must get air.
I don't know rightly whether any man can."
"Amy! Don't go to someone else this time.
Listen to me. I won't come down the stairs."
He sat and fixed his chin between his fists.
"There's something I should like to ask you, dear."

"You don't know how to ask it."

"Help me, then."
Her fingers moved the latch for all reply.

"My words are nearly always an offence.
I don't know how to speak of anything
So as to please you. But I might be taught
I should suppose. I can't say I see how.
A man must partly give up being a man
With women-folk. We could have some arrangement
By which I'd bind myself to keep hands off
Anything special you're a-mind to name.
Though I don't like such things 'twixt those that love.
Two that don't love can't live together without them.
But two that do can't live together with them."
She moved the latch a little. "Don't—don't go.
Don't carry it to someone else this time.
Tell me about it if it's something human.
Let me into your grief. I'm not so much
Unlike other folks as your standing there
Apart would make me out. Give me my chance.
I do think, though, you overdo it a little.

What was it brought you up to think it the thing
To take your mother-loss of a first child
So inconsolably—in the face of love.
You'd think his memory might be satisfied——"

"There you go sneering now!"

"I'm not, I'm not!
You make me angry. I'll come down to you.
God, what a woman! And it's come to this,
A man can't speak of his own child that's dead."

"You can't because you don't know how.
If you had any feelings, you that dug
With your own hand—how could you?—his little grave;
I saw you from that very window there,
Making the gravel leap and leap in air,
Leap up, like that, like that, and land so lightly
And roll back down the mound beside the hole.
I thought, Who is that man? I didn't know you.
And I crept down the stairs and up the stairs
To look again, and still your spade kept lifting.
Then you came in. I heard your rumbling voice
Out in the kitchen, and I don't know why,
But I went near to see with my own eyes.
You could sit there with the stains on your shoes
Of the fresh earth from your own baby's grave
And talk about your everyday concerns.
You had stood the spade up against the wall
Outside there in the entry, for I saw it."

"I shall laugh the worst laugh I ever laughed.
I'm cursed. God, if I don't believe I'm cursed."

"I can repeat the very words you were saying.
'Three foggy mornings and one rainy day
Will rot the best birch fence a man can build.'
Think of it, talk like that at such a time!
What had how long it takes a birch to rot
To do with what was in the darkened parlour.
You *couldn't* care! The nearest friends can go
With anyone to death, comes so far short
They might as well not try to go at all.
No, from the time when one is sick to death,
One is alone, and he dies more alone.
Friends make pretence of following to the grave,
But before one is in it, their minds are turned
And making the best of their way back to life
And living people, and things they understand.

But the world's evil. I won't have grief so
If I can change it. Oh, I won't, I won't!"

"There, you have said it all and you feel better.
You won't go now. You're crying. Close the door.
The heart's gone out of it: why keep it up.
Amy! There's someone coming down the road!"

"*You*—oh, you think the talk is all. I must go—
Somewhere out of this house. How can I make you——"

"If—you—do!" She was opening the door wider.
"Where do you mean to go? First tell me that.
I'll follow and bring you back by force. I *will!*—"

After Apple-Picking 1914

My long two-pointed ladder's sticking through a tree
Toward heaven still,
And there's a barrel that I didn't fill
Beside it, and there may be two or three
Apples I didn't pick upon some bough.
But I am done with apple-picking now.
Essence of winter sleep is on the night,
The scent of apples: I am drowsing off.
I cannot rub the strangeness from my sight
I got from looking through a pane of glass
I skimmed this morning from the drinking trough
And held against the world of hoary grass.
It melted, and I let it fall and break.
But I was well
Upon my way to sleep before it fell,
And I could tell
What form my dreaming was about to take.
Magnified apples appear and disappear,
Stem end and blossom end,
And every fleck of russet showing clear.
My instep arch not only keeps the ache,
It keeps the pressure of a ladder-round.
I feel the ladder sway as the boughs bend.
And I keep hearing from the cellar bin
The rumbling sound
Of load on load of apples coming in.
For I have had too much
Of apple-picking: I am overtired
Of the great harvest I myself desired.
There were ten thousand thousand fruit to touch,

Cherish in hand, lift down, and not let fall.
For all
That struck the earth,
No matter if not bruised or spiked with stubble,
Went surely to the cider-apple heap
As of no worth.
One can see what will trouble
This sleep of mine, whatever sleep it is.
Were he not gone,
The woodchuck could say whether it's like his
Long sleep, as I describe its coming on,
Or just some human sleep.

Birches 1916

When I see birches bend to left and right
Across the lines of straighter darker trees,
I like to think some boy's been swinging them.
But swinging doesn't bend them down to stay
As ice-storms do. Often you must have seen them
Loaded with ice a sunny winter morning
After a rain. They click upon themselves
As the breeze rises, and turn many-colored
As the stir cracks and crazes their enamel.
Soon the sun's warmth makes them shed crystal shells
Shattering and avalanching on the snow-crust—
Such heaps of broken glass to sweep away
You'd think the inner dome of heaven had fallen.
They are dragged to the withered bracken by the load,
And they seem not to break; though once they are bowed
So low for long, they never right themselves:
You may see their trunks arching in the woods
Years afterwards, trailing their leaves on the ground
Like girls on hands and knees that throw their hair
Before them over their heads to dry in the sun.
But I was going to say when Truth broke in
With all her matter-of-fact about the ice-storm,
I should prefer to have some boy bend them
As he went out and in to fetch the cows—
Some boy too far from town to learn baseball,
Whose only play was what he found himself,
Summer or winter, and could play alone.
One by one he subdued his father's trees
By riding them down over and over again
Until he took the stiffness out of them,

And not one but hung limp, not one was left
For him to conquer. He learned all there was
To learn about not launching out too soon
And so not carrying the tree away
Clear to the ground. He always kept his poise
To the top branches, climbing carefully
With the same pains you use to fill a cup
Up to the brim, and even above the brim.
Then he flung outward, feet first, with a swish,
Kicking his way down through the air to the ground.
So was I once myself a swinger of birches.
And so I dream of going back to be.
It's when I'm weary of considerations,
And life is too much like a pathless wood
Where your face burns and tickles with the cobwebs
Broken across it, and one eye is weeping
From a twig's having lashed across it open.
I'd like to get away from earth awhile
And then come back to it and begin over.
May no fate willfully misunderstand me
And half grant what I wish and snatch me away
Not to return. Earth's the right place for love:
I don't know where it's likely to go better.
I'd like to go by climbing a birch tree,
And climb black branches up a snow-white trunk,
Toward heaven, till the tree could bear no more,
But dipped its top and set me down again.
That would be good both going and coming back.
One could do worse than be a swinger of birches.

The Road Not Taken 1916

Two roads diverged in a yellow wood,
And sorry I could not travel both
And be one traveler, long I stood
And looked down one as far as I could
To where it bent in the undergrowth;

Then took the other, as just as fair,
And having perhaps the better claim,
Because it was grassy and wanted wear;
Though as for that the passing there
Had worn them really about the same,

And both that morning equally lay
In leaves no step had trodden black.

Oh, I kept the first for another day!
Yet knowing how way leads on to way,
I doubted if I should ever come back.

I shall be telling this with a sigh
Somewhere ages and ages hence:
Two roads diverged in a wood, and I—
I took the one less traveled by,
And that has made all the difference.

To Earthward

1923

Love at the lips was touch
As sweet as I could bear;
And once that seemed too much;
I lived on air

That crossed me from sweet things
The flow of—was it musk
From hidden grapevine springs
Down hill at dusk?

I had the swirl and ache
From sprays of honeysuckle
That when they're gathered shake
Dew on the knuckle.

I craved strong sweets, but those
Seemed strong when I was young;
The petal of the rose
It was that stung.

Now no joy but lacks salt
That is not dashed with pain
And weariness and fault;
I crave the stain

Of tears, the aftermark
Of almost too much love,
The sweet of bitter bark
And burning clove.

When stiff and sore and scarred
I take away my hand
From leaning on it hard
In grass and sand,

The hurt is not enough:
I long for weight and strength
To feel the earth as rough
To all my length.

Stopping by Woods on a Snowy Evening 1923

Whose woods these are I think I know.
His house is in the village, though;
He will not see me stopping here
To watch his woods fill up with snow.

My little horse must think it queer
To stop without a farmhouse near
Between the woods and frozen lake
The darkest evening of the year.

He gives his harness bells a shake
To ask if there is some mistake.
The only other sound's the sweep
Of easy wind and downy flake.

The woods are lovely, dark and deep,
But I have promises to keep,
And miles to go before I sleep,
And miles to go before I sleep.

COMMENTARIES

This section on Robert Frost begins with a perceptive interview with the poet by Rose C. Feld that appeared in the *New York Times Book Review* in 1923. The next commentary, from an essay by poet and English professor Carol Frost, considers the influence of Hardy and other writers on Frost's poems (the full essay is posted online at Poets.org, the Web site of the Academy of American Poets). Philip L. Gerber looks at Frost's "After Apple-Picking" (p. 875) as an example of the poet's "honest duplicity," a characteristic he finds essential to all poetry. The final commentary, by the poet James Wright (see p. 885), is an appreciation of Frost's famed "Stopping by Woods on a Snowy Evening" taken from *Master Poems* (1966), edited by Oscar Williams.

ROSE C. FELD

An Interview with Robert Frost 1923

Have you ever seen a sensitive child enter a dark room, fearful of the enveloping blackness, yet more than half ashamed of the fear? That is the way Robert Frost, poet, approached the interview arranged for him with the writer. He didn't want to come, he was half afraid of coming, and he was ashamed of the fear of meeting questions.

He was met at his publisher's office at the request of his friends there. "Come and get him, please," they said. "He is a shy person—a gentle and a sensitive person—and the idea of knocking at your doors, saying, 'Here I am, come to be interviewed,' will make him run and hide." The writer came and got him.

All the way down Fifth Avenue for ten or fifteen blocks he smiled often and talked rapidly to show that he was at ease and confident. But he was not. One could see the child telling itself not to be afraid.

Arrived at the house, he took the chair offered him and sat down rigidly. Still he smiled.

"Go ahead," he said. "Ask me the questions. Let's get at it."

"There are no questions—no specific questions. Suppose you just ramble on about American poetry, about poets, about men of the past and men of the present, about where we are drifting or where we are marching. Just talk."

He looked nonplused. The rigid smile gave way to one of relief and relaxation.

"You mean to say that you're not going to fire machine-gun questions at me and expect me to answer with skyrocketing repartee. Well, I wish I'd known. Well."

The brown hand opened up on the arms of the chair and the graying head leaned back. Robert Frost began to talk. He talked of some of the poets of the past, and in his quiet, gentle manner exploded the first bombshell. He exploded many others.

"One of the real American poets of yesterday," he said, "was Longfellow. No, I am not being sarcastic. I mean it. It is the fashion nowadays to make fun of him. I come across this pose and attitude with people I meet socially, with men and women I meet in the classrooms of colleges where I teach. They laugh at his gentleness, at his lack of worldliness, at his detachment from the world and the meaning thereof.

"When and where has it been written that a poet must be a club-swinging warrior, a teller of barroom tales, a participant of unspeakable experiences? That, today, apparently is the stamp of poetic integrity. I hear people speak of men who are writing today, and their eyes light up with a deep glow of satisfaction when they can mention some putrid bit of gossip about them. 'He writes such lovely things,' they say, and in the next breath add, half worshipfully, 'He lives such a terrible life.'

"I can't see it. I can't see that a man must needs have his feet plowing through unhealthy mud in order to appreciate more fully the glowing splendor of the clouds. I can't see that a man must fill his soul with sick and miserable experiences, self-imposed and self-inflicted, and greatly enjoyed, before he can sit down and write a lyric of strange and compelling beauty. Inspiration doesn't lie in the mud; it lies in the clean and wholesome life of the ordinary man.

"Maybe I am wrong. Maybe there is something wrong with me. Maybe I haven't the power to feel, to appreciate and live the extremes of dank living and beautiful inspiration.

"Men have told me, and perhaps they are right, that I have no 'straddle.' That is the term they use: I have no straddle. That means that I cannot spread out far enough to live in filth and write in the treetops. I can't. Perhaps it is because I am so ordinary. I like the middle way, as I like to talk to the man who walks the middle way with me.

"I have given thought to this business of straddling, and there's always seemed to me to be something wrong with it, something tricky. I see a man riding two horses, one foot on the back of one horse, one foot on the other. One horse pulls one way, the other a second. His straddle is wide, Heaven help him, but it seems to me that before long it's going to hurt him. It isn't the natural way, the normal way, the powerful way to ride. It's a trick." . . .

"People do me the honor to say that I am truly a poet of America. They point to my New England background, to the fact that my paternal ancestor came here some time in the sixteen hundreds. So much is true, but what they either do not know or do not say is that my mother was an immigrant. She came to these shores from Edinburgh in an old vessel that docked at Philadelphia. But she felt the spirit of America and became part of it before she even set her foot off the boat.

"She used to tell about it when I was a child. She was sitting on the deck of the boat waiting for orders to come ashore. Near her some workmen were loading Delaware peaches on to the ship. One of them picked out one of them and dropped it into her lap.

"'Here, take that,' he said. The way he said it and the spirit in which he gave it left an indelible impression on her mind.

"'It was a bonny peach,' she used to say, 'and I didn't eat it. I kept it to show my friends.'

"Looking back would I say that she was less the American than my father? No. America meant something live and real and virile to her. He took it for granted. He was a Fourth-of-July American, by which I mean that he rarely failed to celebrate in the way considered proper and appropriate. She, however, was a year-around American.

"I had an aunt in New England who used to talk long and loud about the foreigners who were taking over this country. Across the way from her house stood a French Catholic church which the new people of the village had put up. Every Sunday my aunt would stand at her window, behind the curtain, and watch the steady stream of men and women pouring into church. Her mouth would twist in the way that seems peculiar to dried-up New Englanders, and she would say, 'My soul!' Just that: 'My soul!'

"All the disapproval and indignation and disgust were concentrated in these two words. She never could see why I laughed at her, but it did strike me very funny for her to be calling upon her soul for help when this mass of industrious people were going to church to save theirs." . . .

"Today almost every man who writes poetry confesses his debt to Whitman. Many have gone very much further than Whitman would have traveled with them. They are the people who believe in wide straddling.

"I, myself, as I said before, don't like it for myself. I do not write free verse; I write blank verse. I must have the pulse beat of rhythm, I like to hear it beating under the things I write.

"That doesn't mean I do not like to read a bit of free verse occasionally. I do. It sometimes succeeds in painting a picture that is very clear and startling.

It's good as something created momentarily for its sudden startling effect; it hasn't the qualities, however, of something lastingly beautiful.

"And sometimes my objection to it is that it's a pose. It's not honest. When a man sets out consciously to tear up forms and rhythms and measures, then he is not interested in giving you poetry. He just wants to perform; he wants to show you his tricks. He will get an effect; nobody will deny that, but it is not a harmonious effect.

"Sometimes it strikes me that the free-verse people got their idea from incorrect proof sheets. I have had stuff come from the printers with lines half left out or positions changed about. I read the poems as they stood, distorted and half finished, and I confess I get a rather pleasant sensation from them. They make a sort of nightmarish half-sense."

As he rose to go, he said, "I am an ordinary man, I guess. That's what's the trouble with me. I like my school and I like my farm and I like people. Just ordinary, you see."

CAROL FROST

From *Sincerity and Inventions: On Robert Frost* 1997

The manner and situations and speech of New Englanders that Frost gives voice to originated, no doubt, in his daily interactions—walks and conversations, but there are other sources for the work. Frost read widely—almanacs, essays, and lots of other poetry, including the nineteenth-century poems collected in *Palgrave's Golden Treasury*—"the worn book of old-golden song," the young man in his poem "Waiting" carried with him on a walk. Frost read Poe, Homer, Untermeyer's *Modern American and British Poetry,* Henry James, Burroughs, Thoreau, Emerson, Browning, Virgil, Shelley, Wordsworth, Carlyle, Bryant, Keats, the Bible, and [Thomas] Hardy, all of which can be counted as influences. . . .

The ways that Frost's reading comes into his poetry can be seen in various poems. For instance, the scene in "Design" is quite similar to the scene in Hardy's "An August Midnight," in which he writes: "A shaded lamp and a waving blind / And the beat of a clock from a distant floor: / On this scene enter—winged, horned, and spined— / A longlegs, a moth, and a dumbledore." Hardy's influence can be seen in "Stars," which echoes the sentiment in "Hap" and "Nature's Questioning" that God is either hostile or at best indifferent to the fate of the helpless:

And yet with neither love or hate
Those stars like some snow-white
Minerva's snow-white marble eyes
Without the gift of sight.

The littleness of humanity in a vast cosmos implied by these lines also occurs in Hardy's "Waiting Both" by way of a star that "looks down on me, / and says 'Here I am and you / Stand, each in our degree: / What you mean to do.'"

Hardy echoes abound in Frost. . . .

PHILIP L. GERBER

On Frost's "After Apple-Picking"

1966

As an illustration of the "honest duplicity" of Frost's better verses, the early lyric "After Apple-Picking," although often analyzed, serves ideally. Some readers admire this poem because the deceptive simplicity of its surface picture has charmed them with a rich vision of idyllic New England harvest. Others treasure the poem as exemplifying the truth of John Ciardi's reminder that "a poem is never about what it seems to be about." . . .

Among the available interpretations of Frost's lyric, perhaps the most lucid and readily accessible is that based upon the Emersonian pattern of natural analogies: "things admit of being used as symbols because nature is a symbol, in the whole, and in every part." Emerson's doctrine of analogy between human life and the seasons, for instance, in which spring, summer, fall, and winter parallel the various ages of man, is seconded by Thoreau, who observed the same analogy operating within the span of the day: "The phenomena of the year take place every day in a pond on a small scale. Every morning, generally speaking, the shallow water is being warmed more rapidly than the deep, though it may not be made so warm after all, and every evening it is being cooled more rapidly until the morning. The day is an epitome of the year. The night is the winter, the morning and evening are the spring and fall, and the noon is summer." Building upon the suggestions of Emerson and Thoreau, and noting the centrality that Frost has afforded both to the yearly cycle and to the daily span, the reader begins to absorb the implications radiating from "After Apple-Picking."

On the surface of the poem, however, all seems serenely concrete and straightforward. An apple grower, eager for his awaited harvest of ripe red russets, has worked for days against the imminent arrival of autumn frost. Freezing temperatures, signs of which are already apparent, will close out his opportunities to profit fully from his year's labor. In tending his trees from springtime bud through summer growth, the man's toil has been buoyed by a tremendous stimulus of anticipation. But now the exertion of the harvest itself has wearied him. Tedium has set in. He knows he will not be allowed to pick every apple on his trees, nor does he expect to. Much more realistic now than in the spring and summer, he possibly no longer even desires to account for every piece of fruit.

The harvest has taught the apple-grower something of value. He has attempted to do more than one man can hope to do alone in a season. His excitement—as well as his weariness—has caused many apples to fall to earth. Bruised, ruined, spiked on stubble, these become relatively worthless. The energies of man and nature lavished upon bringing them to perfection seem to have been poured out for naught. Yet such accidents are to be expected in the normal course of any human scheme. It is natural also that some fruit will necessarily be left to freeze as winter closes in; for this is real, not ideal, harvest.

Sleepiness of late autumn pervades the air. All around the harvester nature is preparing herself for rest: trees are defoliating as the summer sap recedes; woodchucks are hibernating, snug in readied burrows. The harvester himself lies in bed after what he realizes may be the very last day of his harvest. He is tired to the bone, leaden-limbed; but ironically he is too fatigued to pass easily into his exhausted and well-earned slumber. His eyes swim. His feet ache from standing on the ladder rung for hours at a time. All ambition spent, he is ready to call a halt and take his rest, knowing that—like anyone totally committed to a task—he will continue the harvest of apples even in his sleep.

So accurately and so economically does Frost capture the essence of apple harvest that one cannot be faulted for finding adequate satisfaction within his portrayal of the apple-picking itself, needing no more. The sights and sounds are all there. Every sensation is recorded vigorously. No one who has used a ladder or labored long hours driven by desire, or nodded in the heady drowsiness of Indian summer, is likely to forget soon the achievement of this verse. As rural idyll, it gratifies.

Even so, the simple application of natural analogies to the poem discloses an entirely new dimension, and it does so without exertion or distortion. The explicit meaning of the poem communicates with the clarity of crystal. Just as clearly does the metaphor, camouflaged only slightly by the impressive veneer of sensory detail, make itself felt. Just as every line, detail, and word contributes to transmitting the essence of the harvest experience, so does every aspect of the poem fall into place as well within the analogies and press for their development.

One notes first that Frost selects as his setting both the night of the daily span and the winter of the yearly cycle. Either would guide the mind toward a prospect of death, but the conjunction of night and winter renders that prospect unmistakable. Numerous references to drowsiness and sleep, to strangeness of sight, and to the harvest itself all reinforce the parallel between the terminations of day, season, and existence. The span of life is embraced within the curve of season, spring to winter. But what completes the circle? Ordinarily spring again, returning after winter to bring rebirth. Hints emanate from at least two references and suggest that the resurrection of spring is probable. The first comes with an unobtrusive gesture in the poem's second line, its seemingly gratuitous reference to the ladder's pointing "toward heaven still." Without straining the issue, the word *heaven* elicits subconscious responses involving death and immortality. The second hint occurs at the finish, as the verse concludes with a whimsical contemplation of the woodchuck's sleep, the hibernation, the little imitation of death which also will terminate in springtime "resurrection." And obviously even "just some human sleep" implies a reawakening.

Snuggling within the curve of the natural cycles is another arc, that shaped by the harvest process fulfilling itself. The harvest is awaited expectantly, with nerves atingle for rosy signals of ripeness to appear on the fruit. With the "russet showing clear," the picker goes to work, heady with grandiose visions of a bumper crop gathered to the last plump apple. The elixir of enthusiasm is steadily diluted. First come endless hours of labor. Then a weariness engulfs what energy is yet unspent. Desire wanes. Then a realization grows that the original goal will not be reached without compromise forced by circumstance. Surprisingly, it no longer seems so very critical to finish. Finally comes the letting-go, first with the hands, then with the mind, but never with the heart. The apple-picker, a sadder but wiser man, relinquishes his task altogether. Now is the time to rest from toil, to accept the verdict on his performance, to listen to himself harshly judging himself.

This harvest action, complete in itself, slips so neatly into the convenient circle created by the natural symbolism, and the whole tallies so comfortably with the surface events of the poem, that the reader arrives at the final period in a euphoria of "rightness." Surface and symbol coincide neatly.

How fortunate that Frost resisted any impulse he may have felt to press his poem into the didactic mold. A phrase or two would have shaped the verse into a substantiation of the orthodox religious view—and would have done untold violence to the lyrical purity so far sustained. But he fortuitously elected instead to suggest, to hint. Whatever sleep it is, only a woodchuck, he says fancifully, could tell for sure. The poem thus ends in deliberate ambiguity. But if a reader chooses to see "After Apple-Picking" as an allegory of man's life ascending from the eager grasping of youth to the letting-go of age, Frost will not object. Nor will he frown upon his poem viewed as a moral tale of the world having its inevitable way with human ambition. Let there be no mistake; all poetry is hinting—is metaphor. Poetry is the legitimate means of saying one thing and meaning another, an "honest duplicity."

JAMES WRIGHT

The Music of Robert Frost's "Stopping by Woods on a Snowy Evening" 1966

Stanza by stanza, Frost's brief poem, so modest in its diction, so obvious in its setting and action, so unambitious in its pattern of sound, turns out to be a devastatingly rich combination of two great traditional lyrical devices: the stanza form of the *Rubáiyát* of Omar Khayyám and the *terza rima* of Dante combined into a new harmony. The fourth line of each stanza of the *Rubáiyát* rebels against the couplet pattern into which it is being forced, and, instead of meekly completing the imperious sound of its syntactical counterpart in the third line, abandons that sound to fend for itself, and becomes a pathetic echo flowing constantly back to repeat the fulfilled rhymes of the first couplet. The effect of the sound in the *Rubáiyát* is to make one's ear constantly aware of a gentle yet persistent tugging, almost a faint undertone of yearning toward what is already perfected, already fulfilled in pattern, and already past. The principle of rhyme in the *terza rima* is, of course, just the opposite: the ear of the reader, after hearing at least one completed pattern of rhyme at the beginning, naturally listens with specially alerted interest to the sound of a new word introduced at the end of any line that in itself does not fit into any already established pattern of rhyme, and concentrates its listening attention in the only direction from which the fulfillment of a rhyming pattern can possibly come. That is the direction of the future: the next line, perhaps, or the line after the next.

So Frost in his poem combines two irresistibly strong currents of sound, one toward what is past and fulfilled, the other toward what may yet come into its own fulfillment; the two undertones of time become a single current, and the listener's yearning back toward the one flows into his yearning forward toward the other. These movements of rhyme give lyrical embodiment to two inescapably serious kinds of human music: the music of pathos that sings of our yearning to return, and the music of present energy that sings of our need to waken and discover, or even to create, what is alive and new. Frost has fused the two distinct principles of the elegiac and the philosophical lyric into a new lyrical principle, which he sings in a voice unmistakably his own. His syntax is so colloquial, his tone of voice modulates itself so casually back and forth between the murmur of speech and the humming of a solitary sleigh driver poised—for an eternal, absent-minded instant—between snowfall and nightfall—that his poem seems to record that strange moment when time pauses, whispers, and miraculously renews itself.

THE WORLD OF LANGSTON HUGHES

DOCUMENTS FROM THE HARLEM RENAISSANCE
- W. E. B. Du Bois, *From* The Souls of Black Folk
- Alain Locke, *From* The New Negro

POEMS
- Langston Hughes, *The Negro Speaks of Rivers*
- James Weldon Johnson, *The Creation*
- Angelina Weld Grimké, *The Black Finger*
- Angelina Weld Grimké, *Tenebris*
- Claude McKay, *If We Must Die*
- Claude McKay, *The Tropics in New York*
- Jean Toomer, *Lyrics from Cane*
- Countee Cullen, *From* Heritage
- Countee Cullen, *Incident*

Langston Hughes
- *Negro*
- *Mother to Son*
- *I, Too*
- *Song for a Dark Girl*
- *House in the World*
- *Love Again Blues*

COMMENTARIES
- Langston Hughes, *A Toast to Harlem*
- Jessie Fauset, *Meeting Langston Hughes*
- Arnold Rampersad, *Langston Hughes as Folk Poet*

In your reading and discussions of poetry in the earlier chapters you learned that poetry has an almost limitless variety of speech, emotions, traditions, and styles. Even in the wide world of poetry, however, it would be difficult to find three poets who were more different than Emily Dickinson, Robert Frost, and Langston Hughes. Each of them created poetry that was unmistakably personal and individual, and each of them created a legacy of verse that made a lasting impression on the society in which they lived. Dickinson's poems often seemed to be shielding her against the world outside her parlor and her bedroom. Frost's writing created an indelible portrait of New England that for many Americans was almost entirely unknown. Hughes's poems invite in the whole world. While Dickinson wrote poems that circled endlessly around the only partially revealed events of her personal life and her emotions, Frost found a voice with which he could create an apparently simple mosaic of guarded memories and hopes. Hughes turned again and again to larger social issues, and he consciously used poetry as a weapon against discrimination and injustice. Dickinson introduced herself as a poet with shy notes to friends, while Frost achieved recognition with his first major book. In a half-serious reminiscence, Hughes recalled that he had become known as a poet when he was still in high school. He was elected class poet in an integrated school in Cleveland, where he had gone to live with his mother after the death of his grandmother, who had cared for him since childhood.

> My classmates, knowing that a poem had to have rhythm, elected me unanimously—thinking, no doubt, that I had some, being a Negro. . . . In the first half of the poem, I said that our school had the finest teachers there ever were. And in the latter half, I said our class was the greatest class ever graduated. Naturally everybody applauded loudly. That was the way I began to write poetry.

His anecdote in itself emphasizes the contrasting personalities of Dickinson, Frost, and Hughes. Dickinson was desperately homesick during her year at Mount Holyoke, Frost had to leave the country to find his voice, while Hughes was remembered by his teachers as one of the most popular pupils in his class. His life became more disruptive after his high school graduation. He went to live in Mexico with his father, who had left the United States as a protest against intolerance. He remained in Mexico for several months, learning to speak Spanish, and wrote his first successful poem, the now classic "The Negro Speaks of Rivers." It was published in the Harlem political/literary journal *The Crisis* in 1921. Hughes was only nineteen, but he had already written the poem that for the rest of his life would stand for his poetic art, for his political attitudes, and for a literary movement.

Perhaps the only point of similarity you can find between Dickinson and Hughes as poets is that at this point in their writing, each of them was influenced by a poet whose work left a deep impression on their writing. For Dickinson it was Concord transcendentalist Ralph Waldo Emerson; for Hughes it was the midwestern populist poet Carl Sandburg. If you read Hughes's poem, "The Negro Speaks of Rivers" included on page 893 with a selection of writing of the Harlem Renaissance, then turn to Sandburg's poem "Grass" (p. 728), you will immediately be struck by how skillfully Hughes has assimilated Sandburg's tone and his liberal social attitudes. Sandburg used free verse to take on subjects that no poet had considered suitable for verse before. His raw poem on Chicago in 1914, with its opening line "Hog Butcher for the World," attracted an audience he never lost. It was, though, the sympathy of Sandburg's finest images and his use of the new free poetic styles to catch the nuances of everyday speech that attracted Hughes to his writing. With lines like these from "Harrison Street Courts," written in 1915, Sandburg brought a new consciousness of daily realities to American poetry:

I heard a woman's lips
speaking to a companion
say these words:
"A woman what hustles
Never keeps nothin'
For all her hustlin'
Somebody always gets
What she goes on the street for."

Sandburg's open lines seemed to many writers to be the link between Whitman's freedom and the open form poetry of the new era. Hughes would continue his university studies and become widely versed in poetry's history and its rich variety, but his style of writing was essentially formed at this point, and the only distinctive change was when he also added the language of the blues to his poetic vocabulary a year or two later.

After Hughes found he wasn't able to live in Mexico with his father, he returned to the United States and moved to Harlem. Harlem and his modest apartment close to Lenox Avenue, Harlem's main street, would become his home for the rest of his life, though he traveled widely and lived abroad for long periods. When Hughes first arrived in New York City, he took odd jobs and worked on a freighter to travel to the west coast of Africa; then, with his father's reluctant support, he studied at Columbia University for a year, continuing his studies in literature. As his poetry steadily appeared in *The Crisis* and other journals, he soon became recognized as an essential figure in the emerging literary movement, the Harlem Renaissance. Arnold Rampersad, who wrote a definitive biography of Hughes, described the rise of the Harlem Renaissance writers, and also their ultimate triumph.

> The 1920s was a decade of extraordinary creativity for black Americans in the arts so that these years marked a glowing moment of achievement in the troubled history of blacks in America. . . . Most people would . . . agree that poetry, rather than fiction or drama, was either central to this literary movement or the foundation on which African American writers built as they attempted to establish themselves and their careers as part of the brave new world of African American culture in the 1920s.

Nineteen twenty-five was the great year of discovery of the Harlem poets by the major American publishing companies that had ignored black culture for nearly a century. Hughes's first collection of poems, *The Weary Blues*, was accepted for publication that same year. It appeared in January 1926, and despite a mixed outburst of praise and condemnation, it stayed in print through many subsequent printings into the 1940s. Many of his poems challenged other Harlem writers and the aspirations of the Harlem Renaissance. As you read the poems by writers of the movement like Claude McKay and Countee Cullen, you see that they were written as skillful examples of standard English verse. McKay had come to Harlem from Jamaica, where he'd published a collection of poems with many of them written in Jamaican patois, but he was a skillful sonneteer, and in Harlem even his most bitter poems like "If We Must Die" were composed in classic English verse forms.

Countee Cullen, who for the first years of the Renaissance was its most celebrated figure, also insisted on writing classical verse. As you read his poems like "Heritage" or "Incident," it might be difficult for you to relate their skillful rhymes and their sensitive imagery to this literary movement with black freedom of expression as its goal. The theme of "Heritage" is a romanticized view of the African past of Cullen's ancestors, but the poem itself is written in the same trochaic tetrameter that was employed by Emerson nearly a century before for his "The Humble Bee" (p. 717). You can ask yourself, however, whether these writers could have attracted the attention of a white world that was skeptical of any kind of achievement by African Americans with poems closer to the language of Harlem's streets. Their poems were intended to be a sign that black writers shared the same ideals and had the same talents as the poets of the white culture, and that finally they were insisting on being heard.

Hughes was personally modest and unassuming, slightly built, not tall, with an easy laughter that often disguised his inner thoughts. Like Dickinson and Frost, he was also certain of the importance of his own way of writing and he was courageous enough to challenge the accepted judgments. He responded to the accepted attitude that the writing of black poets should reflect the values of English and American literary traditions by calling his first volume of poems *The Weary Blues*. The title poem opened:

> Droning a drowsy syncopated tune,
> Rocking back and forth to a mellow croon,
>   I heard a Negro play.

Hughes describes an old musician sitting in a club on Lenox Avenue, playing on a worn-out piano.

> He made that poor piano moan with melody.
>   O Blues!

Hughes's challenge to other Harlem writers was to accept and to value African American everyday culture. The storm over the book by Harlem intellectuals that centered on the poems and their glorification of what they considered the worst aspects of African American culture had no effect on Hughes. He answered his critics in an essay titled "The Negro Artist and the Racial Mountain," and his answer could also be the answer of any of America's minority groups who have waged the same struggle to have their voices heard.

> The Negro artist works against an undertow of sharp criticism and misunderstanding from his own group. . . . "Oh, be respectable, write about nice people, show how good we are," say the Negroes. "Be stereotyped, don't go too far, don't shatter our illusions about you, don't amuse us too seriously. We will pay you," say the whites.

His own response was:

> I am as sincere as I know how to be in these poems and yet after every reading I answer questions like these from my own people: Do you think Negroes should always write about Negroes? I wish you wouldn't read some of your poems to white folks. How do you find anything interesting in a cabaret?

He would go on answering these questions in a lifetime of writing—poetry, novels, plays, and his wry parables of Harlem life, the "Simple" stories. He later summed up his own belief in the work that a poet can do in his life, as quoted in Rampersad's introduction to Hughes's *Collected Poems*.

"A poet is a human being," he declared. "Each human being must live within his time, with and for his people, and within the boundaries of his country." Hughes constantly called upon himself for the courage and the endurance necessary to write according to these beliefs. "Hang yourself, poet, in your own words," he urged. "Otherwise you are dead."

Three poets: one, Emily Dickinson, private, withdrawn, and secretive; another, Robert Frost, a public figure who created a persona he could present to the world; the third, Langston Hughes, a champion of his own society who never hesitated to speak freely. Had they met they probably would have had difficulty understanding one another, but they were all determined to write poetry that would express their unique views of their own lives. As you understand from your reading of their work, each of them is an essential voice in the chorus of voices that make up our world today.

DOCUMENTS FROM THE HARLEM RENAISSANCE

W. E. B. DU BOIS

From *The Souls of Black Folk* 1903

Between me and the other world there is ever an unasked question, unasked by some through feelings of delicacy; by others through the difficulty of rightly framing it. All, nevertheless, flutter around it. They approach me in a half-hesitant sort of way, eye me curiously or compassionately, and then, instead of saying directly, How does it feel to be a problem? they say, I know an excellent colored man in my town; or, I fought at Mechanicsville; or, Do not these Southern outrages make your blood boil? At these times I smile, or am interested, or reduce the boiling to a simmer, as the occasion may require. To the real question, How does it feel to be a problem? I answer seldom a word.

And yet, being a problem is a strange experience—peculiar even for me who has never been anything else, save perhaps in babyhood and in Europe. It is in the early days of rollicking boyhood that the revelation first bursts upon one, all in a day, as it were. I remember well when the shadow swept across me. I was a little thing, away up in the hills of New England, where the dark Housatonic winds between Hoosac and Taghkanic to the sea. In a wee wooden schoolhouse, something put it into the boys' and girls' heads to buy gorgeous visiting cards—ten cents a package—and exchange. The exchange was merry, until one girl, a tall newcomer refused my card—refused it peremptorily without a glance. Then it dawned on me with a certain suddenness that I was different from the others; or like, mayhap, in heart and life and longing, but shut out from their world by a vast veil. I had thereafter no desire to tear down that veil, to creep through it; I held all beyond it in common contempt, and lived above it in a region of blue sky and great wandering shadows. That sky was bluest when I could beat my mates at examination time, or beat them in a foot race, or even beat their stringy heads. Alas, with all the years this fine contempt began to fade; for the worlds I longed for; and all their dazzling opportunities were theirs, not mine. But they should not keep these prizes, I said, some, all, I would wrest from them. Just how I would do it I could never decide; by reading law, by healing the sick, by telling the wonderful tales that swam in my head,—some way. With other black boys the strife was not so fiercely sunny: their youth shrunk into tasteless sycophancy, or into silent hatred of the pale world above them and mocking distrust of everything white; or wasted itself in a bitter cry. Why did God make me an outcast and a stranger in mine own house? The shades of the prison-house closed round about us all: the walls strait and stubborn to the whitest, but relentlessly narrow, tall, and unscalable to sons of night who must plod darkly on in resignation, or beat unavailing palms against the stone, or steadily, half hopelessly, watch the streak of blue above.

ALAIN LOCKE

From *The New Negro* 1925

In the last decade something beyond the watch and guard of statistics has happened in the life of the American Negro and the three norns° who have traditionally presided over the Negro problem have a changeling in their laps. The Sociologist, the Philanthropist, the Race-leader are not unaware of the New Negro, but they are at a loss to account for him. He simply cannot be swathed in their formulæ. For the younger generation is vibrant with a new

---

three norns: In Norse mythology, the three fates.

psychology; the new spirit is awake in the masses, and under the very eyes of the professional observers is transforming what has been a perennial problem into the progressive phases of contemporary Negro life.

Could such a metamorphosis have taken place as suddenly as it has appeared to? The answer is no; not because the New Negro is not here, but because the Old Negro had long become more of a myth than a man. The Old Negro, we must remember, was a creature of moral debate and historical controversy. His has been a stock figure perpetuated as an historical fiction partly in innocent sentimentalism, partly in deliberate reactionism. The Negro himself has contributed his share to this through a sort of protective social mimicry forced upon him by the adverse circumstances of dependence. So for generations in the mind of America, the Negro has been more of a formula than a human being—a something to be argued about, condemned or defended, to be "kept down," or "in his place," or "helped up," to be worried with or worried over, harassed or patronized, a social bogey or a social burden. The thinking Negro even has been induced to share this same general attitude, to focus his attention on controversial issues, to see himself in the distorted perspective of a social problem. His shadow, so to speak, has been more real to him than his personality. Through having had to appeal from the unjust stereotypes of his oppressors and traducers to those of his liberators, friends and benefactors he has had to subscribe to the traditional positions from which his case has been viewed. Little true social or self-understanding has or could come from such a situation.

But while the minds of most of us, black and white, have thus burrowed in the trenches of the Civil War and Reconstruction, the actual march of development has simply flanked these positions, necessitating a sudden reorientation of view. We have not been watching in the right direction; set North and South on a sectional axis, we have not noticed the East till the sun has us blinking.

Recall how suddenly the Negro spirituals revealed themselves; suppressed for generations under the stereotypes of Wesleyan hymn harmony, secretive, half-ashamed, until the courage of being natural brought them out—and behold, there was folk-music. Similarly the mind of the Negro seems suddenly to have slipped from under the tyranny of social intimidation and to be shaking off the psychology of imitation and implied inferiority. By shedding the old chrysalis of the Negro problem we are achieving something like a spiritual emancipation. Until recently, lacking self-understanding, we have been almost as much of a problem to ourselves as we still are to others. But the decade that found us with a problem has left us with only a task. The multitude perhaps feels as yet only a strange relief and a new vague urge, but the thinking few know that in the reaction the vital inner gap of prejudice has been broken.

Poems

LANGSTON HUGHES

The Negro Speaks of Rivers 1921

I've known rivers:
I've known rivers ancient as the world and older than the
flow of human blood in human veins.

My soul has grown deep like the rivers.

I bathed in the Euphrates when dawns were young.
I built my hut near the Congo and it lulled me to sleep.
I looked upon the Nile and raised the Pyramids above it.
I heard the singing of the Mississippi when Abe Lincoln
went down to New Orleans, and I've seen its muddy
bosom turn all golden in the sunset.

I've known rivers:
Ancient, dusky rivers.

My soul has grown deep like the rivers.

JAMES WELDON JOHNSON

The Creation 1920

And God stepped out on space,
And he looked around and said:
I'm lonely—
I'll make me a world.

And far as the eye of God could see
Darkness covered everything,
Blacker than a hundred midnights
Down in a cypress swamp.

Then God smiled,
And the light broke,
And the darkness rolled up on one side,
And the light stood shining on the other,
And God said: That's good!

Then God reached out and took the light in his hands,
And God rolled the light around in his hands
Until he made the sun;
And he set that sun a-blazing in the heavens.
And the light that was left from making the sun

God gathered it up in a shining ball
And flung it against the darkness,
Spangling the night with the moon and stars.
Then down between
The darkness and the light
He hurled the world;
And God said: That's good!

Then God himself stepped down—
And the sun was on his right hand,
And the moon was on his left;
The stars were clustered about his head,
And the earth was under his feet.
And God walked, and where he trod
His footsteps hollowed the valleys out
And bulged the mountains up.

Then he stopped and looked and saw
That the earth was hot and barren.
So God stepped over to the edge of the world
And he spat out the seven seas—
He batted his eyes, and the lightnings flashed—
He clapped his hands, and the thunders rolled—
And the waters above the earth came down,
The cooling waters came down.

Then the green grass sprouted,
And the little red flowers blossomed,
The pine tree pointed his finger to the sky,
And the oak spread out his arms,
The lakes cuddled down in the hollows of the ground,
And the rivers ran down to the sea,
And God smiled again,
And the rainbow appeared,
And curled itself around his shoulder.

Then God raised his arm and he waved his hand
Over the sea and over the land,
And he said: Bring forth! Bring forth!
And quicker than God could drop his hand,
Fishes and fowls
And beasts and birds
Swam the rivers and the seas,
Roamed the forests and the woods,
And split the air with their wings.
And God said: That's good!

Then God walked around,
And God looked around
On all that he had made.

He looked at his sun,
And he looked at his moon,
And he looked at his little stars;
He looked on his world
With all its living things,
And God said: I'm lonely still.

Then God sat down—
On the side of a hill where he could think;
By a deep, wide river he sat down;
With his head in his hands,
God thought and thought,
Till he thought: I'll make me a man!

Up from the bed of the river
God scooped the clay;
And by the bank of the river
He kneeled him down;
And there the great God Almighty
Who lit the sun and fixed it in the sky,
Who flung the stars to the most far corner of the night,
Who rounded the earth in the middle of his hand;
This Great God,
Like a mammy bending over her baby,
Kneeled down in the dust
Toiling over a lump of clay
Till he shaped it in his own image;

Then into it he blew the breath of life,
And man became a living soul.
Amen. Amen.

ANGELINA WELD GRIMKÉ

The Black Finger 1927

I have just seen a beautiful thing
Slim and still,
Against a gold, gold sky,
A straight cypress,
Sensitive
Exquisite,
A black finger
Pointing upwards.
Why, beautiful, still finger are you black?
And why are you pointing upwards?

Tenebris

1927

There is a tree, by day,
That, at night,
Has a shadow,
A hand huge and black,
With fingers long and black.
  All through the dark,
Against the white man's house,
  In the little wind,
The black hand plucks and plucks
  At the bricks.
The bricks are the color of blood and very small.
  Is it a black hand,
  Or is it a shadow?

CLAUDE McKAY

If We Must Die

1919

If we must die, let it not be like hogs
Hunted and penned in an inglorious spot,
While round us bark the mad and hungry dogs,
Making their mock at our accursed lot.
If we must die, O let us nobly die,
So that our precious blood may not be shed
In vain; then even the monsters we defy
Shall be constrained to honor us though dead!
O kinsmen! we must meet the common foe!
Though far outnumbered let us show us brave,
And for their thousand blows deal one deathblow!
What though before us lies the open grave?
Like men we'll face the murderous, cowardly pack,
Pressed to the wall, dying, but fighting back!

The Tropics in New York

1920

Bananas ripe and green, and gingerroot,
  Cocoa in pods and alligator pears,
And tangerines and mangoes and grapefruit,
  Fit for the highest prize at parish fairs,
Set in the window, bringing memories
  Of fruit trees laden by low-singing rills,

And dewy dawns, and mystical blue skies
  In benediction over nunlike hills.

My eyes grew dim, and I could no more gaze;
  A wave of longing through my body swept,
And, hungry for the old, familiar ways,
  I turned aside and bowed my head and wept.

JEAN TOOMER

Lyrics from *Cane*

1923

Storm Ending

Thunder blossoms gorgeously above our heads,
Great, hollow, bell-like flowers,
Rumbling in the wind,
Stretching clappers to strike our ears . . .
Full-lipped flowers
Bitten by the sun
Bleeding Rain
Dripping rain like golden honey
And the sweet earth flying from the thunder

(Rock A-by Baby)

rock a-by baby . . .
Black mother sways, holding a white child on her bosom
when the bough bends
Her breath hums through pine-cones
cradle will fall . . .
Teat moon-children at your breasts,
down will come baby . . .
Black mother.

Reapers

Black reapers with the sound of steel on stones
Are sharpening scythes, I see them place the hones
In their hip-pockets as a thing that's done,
And start their silent swinging, one by one.
Black horses drive a mower through the weeds,
And there, a field rat, startled, squealing bleeds.
His belly close to ground, I see the blade,
Blood-stained, continue cutting weeds and shade.

COUNTEE CULLEN

From *Heritage* 1925

What is Africa to me:
Copper sun or scarlet sea,
Jungle star or jungle track,
Strong bronzed men, or regal black
Women from whose loins I sprang
When the birds of Eden sang?
One three centuries removed
From the scenes his fathers loved,
Spicy grove, cinnamon tree,
What is Africa to me?

So I lie, who all day long
Want no sound except the song
Sung by wild barbaric birds
Goading massive jungle herds,
Juggernauts of flesh that pass
Trampling tall defiant grass
Where young forest lovers lie,
Plighting troth beneath the sky.
So I lie, who always hear,
Though I cram against my ear
Both my thumbs, and keep them there,
Great drums throbbing through the air.
So I lie, whose fount of pride,
Dear distress, and joy allied,
Is my somber flesh and skin,
With the dark blood dammed within
Like great pulsing tides of wine
That, I fear, must burst the fine
Channels of the chafing net
Where they surge and foam and fret.

Africa? A book one thumbs
Listlessly, till slumber comes.
Unremembered are her bats
Circling through the night, her cats
Crouching in the river reeds,
Stalking gentle flesh that feeds
By the river brink; no more
Does the bugle-throated roar
Cry that monarch claws have leapt
From the scabbards where they slept.
Silver snakes that once a year
Doff the lovely coats you wear,

Seek no covert in your fear
Lest a mortal eye should see;
What's your nakedness to me?
Here no leprous flowers rear
Fierce corollas in the air;
Here no bodies sleek and wet,
Dripping mingled rain and sweat,
Tread the savage measures of
Jungle boys and girls in love.

What is last year's snow to me,
Last year's anything? The tree
Budding yearly must forget
How its past arose or set—
Bough and blossom, flower, fruit,
Even what shy bird with mute
Wonder at her travail there,
Meekly labored in its hair.
One three centuries removed
From the scenes his fathers loved,
Spicy grove, cinnamon tree
What is Africa to me?

Incident

1925

For Eric Walrond

Once riding in old Baltimore,
   Heart-filled, head-filled with glee,
I saw a Baltimorean
   Keep looking straight at me.

Now I was eight and very small,
   And he was no whit bigger,
And so I smiled, but he poked out
   His tongue, and called me, "Nigger."

I saw the whole of Baltimore
   From May until December;
Of all the things that happened there
   That's all that I remember.

Langston Hughes as photographed by photojournalist Gordon Parks in 1943. (Reproduced from the collections of the Library of Congress.)

LANGSTON HUGHES

Negro

1922

I am a Negro:
    Black as the night is black,
    Black like the depths of my Africa.

I've been a slave:
    Caesar told me to keep his door-steps clean.
    I brushed the boots of Washington.

I've been a worker:
    Under my hands the pyramids arose.
    I made mortar for the Woolworth Building.

I've been a singer:
    All the way from Africa to Georgia
    I carried my sorrow songs.
    I made ragtime.

I've been a victim:
  The Belgians cut off my hands in the Congo.
  They lynch me still in Mississippi.

I am a Negro:
  Black as the night is black,
  Black like the depths of my Africa.

Mother to Son

1926

Well, son, I'll tell you:
Life for me ain't been no crystal stair.
It's had tacks in it,
And splinters,
And boards torn up,
And places with no carpet on the floor—
Bare.
But all the time
I'se been a-climbin' on,
And reachin' landin's,
And turnin' corners,
And sometimes goin' in the dark
Where there ain't been no light.
So boy, don't you turn back.
Don't you set down on the steps
'Cause you finds it's kinder hard.
Don't you fall now—
For I'se still goin', honey,
I'se still climbin',
And life for me ain't been no crystal stair.

I, Too

1926

I, too, sing America.

I am the darker brother.
They send me to eat in the kitchen
When company comes,
But I laugh,
And eat well,
And grow strong.

Tomorrow,
I'll be at the table
When company comes.
Nobody'll dare
Say to me,

"Eat in the kitchen,"
Then.

Besides,
They'll see how beautiful I am
And be ashamed—

I, too, am America.

Song for a Dark Girl

1927

Way Down South in Dixie
(Break the heart of me)
They hung my black young lover
To a cross roads tree.

Way Down South in Dixie
(Bruised body high in air)
I asked the white Lord Jesus
What was the use of prayer.

Way Down South in Dixie
(Break the heart of me)
Love is a naked shadow
On a gnarled and naked tree.

House in the World

1931

I'm looking for a house
In the world
Where the white shadows
Will not fall.

There is no such house,
Dark brothers,
No such house
At all.

Love Again Blues

1940

My life ain't nothin'
But a lot o' Gawd-knows-what.
I say my life ain't nothin'
But a lot o' Gawd-knows-what.
Just one thing after 'nother
Added to de trouble that I got.

When I got you I
Thought I had an angel-chile.
When I got you
Thought I had an angel-chile.
You turned out to be a devil
That mighty nigh drove me wild!

Tell me, tell me,
What makes love such an ache and pain?
Tell me what makes
Love such an ache and pain?
It takes you and it breaks you—
But you got to love again.

COMMENTARIES

This section begins with a tribute by Hughes to his beloved Harlem. The excerpt is from one of the Simple stories Hughes wrote for a Harlem newspaper in which he used the character of a Harlem Everyman, Jessie Semple – nicknamed "Simple" – as a foil for his own attitudes and opinions. The next selection is a reminiscence published in *The Crisis*, an African American journal, in 1926 by the writer Jessie Fauset, a contemporary of Hughes and like him a member of the generation of writers, artists, musicians, and critics identified as the Harlem Renaissance. Next Arnold Rampersad, author of the first extended biography of Hughes, comments in his introduction to the collected poems about Hughes's role as a folk poet.

LANGSTON HUGHES

A Toast to Harlem 1950

Quiet can seem unduly loud at times. Since nobody at the bar was saying a word during a lull in the bright blues-blare of the Wishing Well's usually overworked juke box, I addressed my friend Simple.

"Since you told me last night you are an Indian, explain to me how it is you find yourself living in a furnished room in Harlem, my brave buck, instead of on a reservation?"

"I am a colored Indian," said Simple.

"In other words, a Negro."

"A Black Foot Indian, daddy-o, not a red one. Anyhow, Harlem is the place I always did want to be. And if it wasn't for landladies, I would be happy. That's a fact! I love Harlem."

"What is it you love about Harlem?"

"It's so full of Negroes," said Simple. "I feel like I got protection."

"From what?"

"From white folks," said Simple. "Furthermore, I like Harlem because it belongs to me."

"Harlem does not belong to you. You don't own the houses in Harlem. They belong to white folks."

"I might not own 'em," said Simple, "but I live in 'em. It would take an atom bomb to get me out."

"Or a depression," I said.

"I would not move for no depression. No, I would not go back down South, not even to Baltimore. I am in Harlem to stay! You say the houses ain't mine. Well, the sidewalk is—and don't nobody push me off. The cops don't even say, 'Move on,' hardly no more. They learned something from them Harlem riots. They used to beat your head right in public, but now they only beat it after they get you down to the stationhouse. And they don't beat it then if they think you know a colored congressman."

"Harlem has a few Negro leaders," I said.

"Elected by my *own* vote," said Simple. "Here I ain't scared to vote—that's another thing I like about Harlem. I also like it because we've got subways and it does not take all day to get downtown, neither are you Jim Crowed° on the way. Why, Negroes is running some of these subway trains. This morning I rode the A Train down to 34th Street. There were a Negro driving it, making ninety miles a hour. That cat *were really driving* that train! Every time he flew by one of them local stations looks like he was saying, 'Look at me! This train is mine!' That cat were gone, ole man. Which is another reason why I like Harlem! Sometimes I run into Duke Ellington on 125th Street and I say, 'What you know there, Duke?' Duke says, 'Solid, ole man.' He does not know me from Adam, but he speaks. One day I saw Lena Horne coming out of the Hotel Theresa and I said, 'Huba! Huba!' Lena smiled. Folks is friendly in Harlem. I feel like I got the world in a jug and the stopper in my hand! So drink a toast to Harlem!"

Simple lifted his glass of beer:

"Here's to Harlem!
They say Heaven is Paradise.
If Harlem ain't Heaven,
Then a mouse ain't mice!"

JESSIE FAUSET

Meeting Langston Hughes 1926

Very perfect is the memory of my first literary acquaintance with Langston Hughes. In the unforgettable days when we were publishing *The Brownies' Book* we had already appreciated a charming fragile conceit which read:

Jim Crowed: Jim Crow laws were the "legal" foundation for racial discrimination in the southern states.

Out of the dust of dreams,
Fairies weave their garments;
Out of the purple and rose of old memories,
They make purple wings.
No wonder we find them such marvelous things.

Then one day came "The Negro Speaks of Rivers." I took the beautiful dignified creation to Dr. Du Bois and said: "What colored person is there, do you suppose, in the United States who writes like that and yet is unknown to us?" And I wrote and found him to be a Cleveland high school graduate who had just gone to live in Mexico. Already he had begun to assume that remote, so elusive quality which permeates most of his work. Before long we had the pleasure of seeing the work of the boy, whom we had sponsored, copied, and recopied in journals far and wide. "The Negro Speaks of Rivers" even appeared in translation in a paper printed in Germany.

Not very long after Hughes came to New York and not long after that he began to travel and to set down the impressions, the pictures, which his sensitive mind had registered of new forms of life and living in Holland, in France, in Spain, in Italy, and in Africa.

His poems are warm, exotic, and shot through with color. Never is he preoccupied with form. But this fault, if it is one, has its corresponding virtue, for it gives his verse, which almost always is imbued with the essence of poetry, the perfection of spontaneity. And one characteristic which makes for this bubbling-like charm is the remarkable objectivity which he occasionally achieves, remarkable for one so young, and a first step toward philosophy. Hughes has seen a great deal of the world, and this has taught him that nothing matters much but life. Its forms and aspects may vary, but living is the essential thing. Therefore make no bones about it,—"make the most of what you may spend."

Some consciousness of this must have been in him even before he began to wander for he sent us as far back as 1921:

Shake your brown feet, honey,
Shake your brown feet, chile,
Shake your brown feet, honey,
Shake 'em swift and wil'— . . .
Sun's going down this evening—
Might never rise no mo'.
The sun's going down this very night—
Might never rise no mo'—
So dance with swift feet, honey,
(The banjo's sobbing low . . .
The sun's going down this very night—
Might never rise no mo'.

Now this is very significant, combining as it does the doctrine of the old Biblical exhortation, "eat, drink, and be merry for tomorrow ye die," Horace's "Carpe diem," the German "Freut euch des Lebens," and [Robert] Herrick's "Gather ye rosebuds while ye may." This is indeed a universal subject served

Negro-style and though I am no great lover of any dialect I hope heartily that Mr. Hughes will give us many more such combinations.

Mr. Hughes is not always the calm philosopher; he has feeling a-plenty and is not ashamed to show it. He "loved his friend" who left him and so taken up is he with the sorrow of it all that he has no room for anger or resentment. While I do not think of him as a protagonist of color,—he is too much the citizen of the world for that—, I doubt if any one will ever write more tenderly, more understandingly, more humorously of the life of Harlem shot through as it is with mirth, abandon and pain. Hughes comprehends this life, has studied it and loved it. In one poem he has epitomized its essence:

Does a jazz-band ever sob?
They say a jazz-band's gay.
Yet as the vulgar dancers whirled
And the wan night wore away,
One said she heard the jazz-band sob
When the little dawn was grey.

Harlem is undoubtedly one of his great loves; the sea is another. Indeed all life is his love and his work a brilliant, sensitive interpretation of its numerous facets.

ARNOLD RAMPERSAD

Langston Hughes as Folk Poet 1994

Hughes was often called, and sometimes called himself, a folk poet. To some people, this means that his work is almost artless and thus possibly beneath criticism. The truth indeed is that Hughes published many poems that are doggerel. To reach his primary audience—the black masses—he was prepared to write "down" to them. Some of the pieces in this volume were intended for public recitation mainly; some started as song lyrics. Like many democratic poets, such as William Carlos Williams, he believed that the full range of his poetry should reach print as soon as possible; poetry is a form of social action. However, for Hughes, as for all serious poets, the writing of poetry was virtually a sacred commitment. And while he wished to write no verse that was beyond the ability of the masses of people to understand, his poetry, in common with that of other committed writers, is replete with allusions that must be respected and understood if it is to be properly appreciated. To respect Hughes's work, above all one must respect the African American people and their culture, as well as the American people in general and their national culture.

If Hughes kept at the center of his art the hopes and dreams, as well as the actual lived conditions, of African Americans, he almost always saw these factors in the context of the eternally embattled but eternally inspiring American democratic tradition, even as changes in the world order, notably the collapse of colonialism in Africa, redefined the experiences of African peoples around the world. Almost always, too, Hughes attempted to preserve a sense of himself as a poet beyond race and other corrosive social pressures. By his absolute dedication to his art and to his social vision, as well as to his central audience, he fused his unique vision of himself as a poet to his production of art.

"What is poetry?" Langston Hughes asked near his death. He answered, "It is the human soul entire, squeezed like a lemon or a lime, drop by drop, into atomic words." He wanted no definition of the poet that divorced his art from the immediacy of life. "A poet is a human being," he declared. "Each human being must live within his time, with and for his people, and within the boundaries of his country." Hughes constantly called upon himself for the courage and the endurance necessary to write according to these beliefs. "Hang yourself, poet, in your own words," he urged all those who would take up the mantle of the poet and dare to speak to the world. "Otherwise, you are dead."

17.

A Poet in the World Today: Tomas Tranströmer

> If art is to nourish the roots of our culture, society must set the artist free to follow his vision wherever it takes him. We must never forget that art is not a form of propaganda; it is a form of truth. And as Archibald MacLeish once remarked of poets, there is nothing worse for our trade than to be in style. In a free society art is not a weapon and it does not belong in the sphere of polemics and ideology. Artists are not engineers of the soul.
>
> It may be different elsewhere. But democratic society—in it, the highest duty of the writer, the composer, the artist is to remain true to himself and let the chips fall where they may.
>
> –PRESIDENT JOHN F. KENNEDY speaking at Amherst College, October 26, 1963

AN INTRODUCTION TO TOMAS TRANSTRÖMER, BY SAMUEL CHARTERS

In the excitement that followed the announcement that Swedish poet Tomas Tranströmer had won the Nobel Prize for literature in 2011, a writer for the *New York Times* noted that for many American readers his name would be largely unknown. The writer, however, should also have added that among American poets he was a familiar friend, and readers everywhere in the world would have agreed with the headlines in the Swedish newspapers that proclaimed, "The Prize to Tranströmer is a Prize for Poetry Itself." The Nobel Prize is literature's highest award, just as the Nobel Peace Prize, awarded to Martin Luther King Jr. and President Barack Obama, is the highest recognition of an individual's service in the cause of world peace. American writers who have been honored with the literary prize include Ernest Hemingway, William Faulkner, T. S. Eliot, and Toni Morrison. The prize to Tranströmer was a prize for readers everywhere in the world since his poetry has been translated into more than sixty languages, and he has read his poems at poetry festivals and on extensive reading tours for more than half a century.

It was the poet Robert Bly, one of his American friends and enthusiastic translators, who introduced me to Tranströmer's poetry at a reading in the 1960s. Bly looked out over his audience and announced, "There's this great poet who's Swedish. His name's Tomas Tranströmer. Buy his books. He doesn't have any money. He needs to buy a new car." Bly then read the poem "Alle-

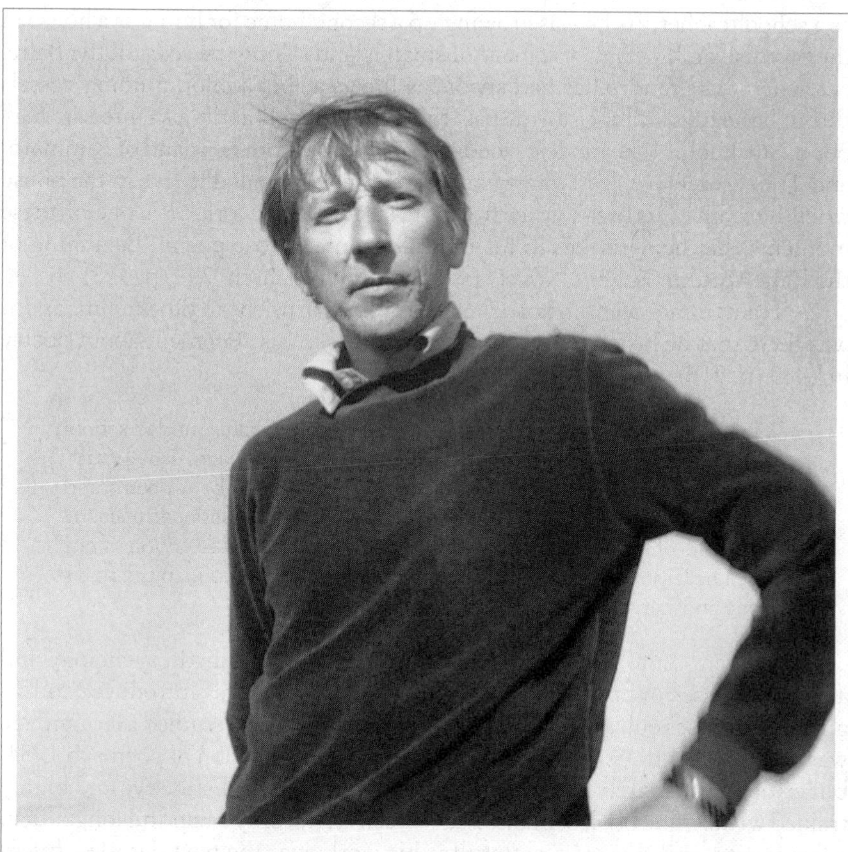

Tomas Tranströmer, 1973. (Photo by Ann Charters.)

gro," with its unforgettable imagery of the music of Haydn as a glass house that Tranströmer imagines as refuge against the world's compromises and deceits. In my translation:

> The music is a house of glass on the hillside
> where the stones fly, the stones roll.
>
> And the stones roll right on through
> but every pane stays whole.

When I met Tomas Tranströmer some years later, I found that although he was employed as a psychologist in the Swedish national employment service, as a father with young children he didn't have much money and he did need a new car. In all the years since then that our families have been friends, listening to music is something we have shared for many hours, and many times it has been Haydn that we listened to.

Tranströmer was born in Stockholm in April 1931 and grew up in a bustling neighborhood on Södermalm, one of the large islands that make up the city. His parents were divorced, and he was raised by his mother, who worked as a schoolteacher. As he was growing up a second home for him was a house in the Swedish archipelago, the maze of small islands along the coast of the Baltic Sea where his grandfather had spent his life as a ship's pilot, guiding vessels through the fogs and the storms past the hidden shoals and rocks into safe harbor in Stockholm. The modest wood-framed house is on the island of Runmarö, and Tranströmer spent his summers there, then continued to live in the house when he wanted to break away from the stress of his work. It is one of these moments that he describes in his richly imagined prose poem "Beginning of the Late Autumn Night's Novel" (p. 913) and in "March '79" (p. 915).

Tranströmer went to school close to the apartment in Stockholm, and it was there that he began to write, as he describes in his statement about poetry in 1989 (p. 915).

> When I started writing, at sixteen, I had a couple of like-minded school friends. Sometimes, when the lessons seemed more than usually trying, we would pass notes to each other between our desks—poems and aphorisms, which would come back with the more or less enthusiastic comments of the recipient. . . . *There* is the fundamental situation of poetry. The lesson of official life goes rumbling on. We send inspired notes to one another.

He went on to Stockholm University where he studied psychology and also took classes in history, religion, and literature. He was introduced to English in grade school, as all Swedish children are, and also studied German. He was only twenty-three when he published his first collection of poems in 1954, but critics immediately recognized that he was already a distinctive and highly trained writer. The book contained seventeen lyrics, only a handful longer than a few verses, and this set a pattern for his work over the next decades. Every four years a new small collection would appear, and with each collection his reputation grew.

He was married a few years after the appearance of his first book, and between 1960 and 1966 he and his wife and two small daughters lived in an isolated forest area where he was the director of a center for juvenile offenders. (At his readings years later in America, he was asked invariably, "How has your work as a psychologist affected your poetry?" His response was just as invariably, "My answer is how did my poetry affect my work as a psychologist?") Eventually Tranströmer left his director's position to take a half-time post as a staff psychologist at a government employment bureau in the small city of Västerås to have more time for his writing. By this time his poetry had found its way to the United States, and with Robert Bly taking the lead, Tranströmer was invited to appear at universities and literary festivals as often as he could take time from his work.

Sometimes when I joined him on later trips, I had the impression that he was friends with every American poet who was part of his generation's literary constellation, among them Robert Bly, Robert Hass, William Merwin, Toby Olson, Philip Levine, and Sharon Olds. Another close friend was the poet Richard Shelton, who wrote an arresting description of Tranströmer as a guest of Shelton and his family in their home in Tucson.

> Tomas Tranströmer is a tall, slender man with incredibly long, thin hands and feet. He moves with a quiet fluidity, as if even his bones could bend. Everything about him, including his voice, is relaxed and rhythmic, never hectic or static. He does not sit in a chair as much as drape himself over it, relaxing immediately and sliding down into an almost prone position, with his long legs extended and sometimes crossing each other at what seem to be impossible junctures. We have a tendency to call such men "lanky," but that is exactly the wrong word to describe him. I would have to say "sinuous."

When Ann Charters became a professor at the University of Connecticut, Tranströmer would often stay over at our home in Storrs on his reading trips, sometimes joined by his wife, Monica. When our family would visit Sweden in the summers, we would journey to the island where the Tranströmers lived, so our daughters could play with their daughters in the island's forests and beaches.

In 1990, Tranströmer suffered a severe stroke, and despite intensive therapy he never regained the use of his right hand and arm or his speech, except for a few words, and even walking became extremely difficult. He had always been an enthusiastic amateur pianist, however, and so discovered the extensive piano repertoire for the left hand alone. He taught himself to write slowly and painstakingly with his left hand. His publishers in Sweden have released two CDs of his piano playing, interwoven with readings from his poetry by actor friends. In recent years, many of his best-known poems have been presented in concert musical settings. On the night it was announced that he had won the Nobel Prize, a theater company premiered a dramatized performance of one of his early poetry collections.

For many years, Tranströmer had been a popular choice for the Nobel Prize, but perhaps thinking that it would look too much like favoritism the Swedish Academy, which presents the award, turned to other candidates. But in 2011, when the Academy's elaborate double doors were opened and the name of Tomas Tranströmer was at last announced, Sweden along with everyone in the world who knows and loves poetry joined the celebration.

A Selected Bibliography of Works by Tomas Tranströmer in English

Night Vision. Trans. Robert Bly. Chapel Hill: Lillabulero, 1971. Print.

Windows and Stones. Trans. May Swenson and Leif Sjoberg. Pittsburgh: U of Pittsburgh P, 1972. Print.

Baltics. Trans. Samuel Charters. 1975. Portland: Tavern Books, 2012. Print.

Selected Poems, 1954–1986. Ed. Robert Hass. New York: Ecco, 2000. Print.

The Half-Finished Heaven. Trans. Robert Bly. Minneapolis: Graywolf, 2001. Print.

The Great Enigma. Trans. Robin Fulton. New York: New Directions, 2006. Print.

The Deleted World. Trans. Robin Robertson. New York: Farrar, Straus and Giroux, 2011. Print.

For the Living and the Dead: Poems and a Memoir. 1995. New York: Ecco, 2011. Print.

TOMAS TRANSTRÖMER

Romanesque Arches 1995

TRANSLATED BY SAMUEL CHARTERS

The tourists are crowded into the enormous Romanesque church in the half darkness.
Vault gaping behind vault and no overview.
Some candle flames fluttered.
A faceless angel embraced me
and whispered through my whole body:
"Don't be ashamed that you're a human being, be proud!
Within you vaults open endlessly behind vaults.
You'll never be completed, and that's as it should be."
I was blind with tears
and I was driven out into the sun seething piazza
along with Mr. and Mrs. Jones, Herr Tanaka, and Signora Sabatini
and within each of them vaults opened endlessly behind vaults.

Allegro 1962

TRANSLATED BY SAMUEL CHARTERS

I play Haydn after a black day
and feel a simple warmth in my hands.

The keys are willing. Mild hammers strike.
The sound is green, lively, and calm.

The sound says that there is freedom
and that there is somebody who isn't paying taxes to the emperor.

I shove my hands down in my Haydnpockets
and act like I'm one of those people who regards the world calmly.

I hoist my Haydnflag—it means:
We don't give up. But want peace.

The music is a house of glass on the hillside
where the stones fly, the stones roll.

And the stones roll right on through
but every pane stays whole.

Beginning of the Late Autumn Night's Novel 1978

TRANSLATED BY SAMUEL CHARTERS

The passenger boat smells of oil and something rattles all the time like a compulsive thought. The lights are turned on. We're getting close to the dock. I'm the only one getting off here. "D'ya need the gangplank?" No. I take a long tottering stride right into the night and stand on the dock, on the island. I feel wet and clumsy, a butterfly that's just crept out of the cocoon. The plastic bags in each hand hang like malformed wings. I turn and see the boat glide away with its shining windows, then grope my way to the familiar house that's stood empty so long. All the houses in the neighborhood stand unoccupied. . . . It's pleasant to sleep in here. I lie on my back and don't know if I'm sleeping or awake. Some books I read pass by like old sailing ships on the way to the Bermuda Triangle, to disappear without trace. . . . A hollow sound is heard, an absent-minded drum. An object that the gale thumps again and again against something that the earth is holding still. If night isn't only the absence of light, if the night really *is* something, then it's this sound. The stethoscope sound from a slowing heart, it beats, is silent a moment, comes back. As if a person were moving in a zig-zag over the Frontier. Or someone beating in a wall, someone who belongs to the other world but was left here, beats, wants to go back. Too late. To get down there, to get up there, to get on board. . . . The other world's also this world. Next morning I see a hissing, golden brown leafy branch. A crawling root pile. Stones with faces. The forest is full of marooned monsters that I love.

Schubertiana 1978

TRANSLATED BY SAMUEL CHARTERS

I

In the evening darkness at a place outside New York, an outlook
where you can perceive eight million people's homes in a single glance.
The giant city there is a long flickering drift, a spiral galaxy from the side.
Within the galaxy coffee cups are pushed over the counter, the shop
windows beg from the passersby, a swarm of shoes that leave no tracks.
The clambering fire escapes, elevator doors that slip past, behind doors
with police locks a steady swell of voices.
Slouched bodies half asleep in the subway cars, the rushing catacombs.
I know too—without statistics—that Schubert's being played in
some room there and for someone the tones at this moment are more real than everything else.

II

The human brain's endless plains are crumpled up to the size of a clenched fist.
In April the swallow returns to her last year's nest under the gutter at just that barn in just that parish.
She flies from Transvaal, passes the Equator, flies for six weeks over two continents, steering towards that disappearing dot on the land mass.
And he who catches the signals from a whole life in some rather ordinary chords by a string quintet,
he who gets a river to flow through the eye of a needle
is a fat young gentleman from Vienna, called "the little mushroom" by his friends, who slept with his glasses on
and stood himself up punctually at his writing lectern in the morning.
At which the music script's wonderful centipedes set themselves in motion.

III

The string quintet is playing. I walk home through the humid woods with the ground springing under me,
huddle like one unborn, fall asleep, roll weightless into the future, know suddenly that the plants have thoughts.

IV

So much we have to trust to be able to live our daily day without sinking through the earth!
Trust the masses of snow that cling to the mountainsides above the village.
Trust promises to keep silent and the understanding smile, trust that the telegram about the accident doesn't refer to us and the sudden axe blow from within doesn't come.
Trust the axles that carry us on the highway in the middle of the three hundred times enlarged steel bee swarm.
But none of that is really worth our confidence.
The quintet says that we can trust something else. What else? Something else, and it follows us a little of the way there.
Like when the light goes out on the stairs and the hand follows—with confidence—the blind banister that finds its way in the darkness.

V

We crowd up to the piano and play with four hands in F-minor,° two drivers for the same carriage, it looks a little ridiculous.

---

four hands in F-minor: The piece is Schubert's "Fantasy in F-Minor for Piano, Four Hands." The two pianists are Tranströmer and Samuel Charters. "Annie" is Ann Charters.

Our hands seem to push ringing weights back and forth, as if we were moving counterweights
in an effort to shift the large scale's frightful balance: happiness and suffering weigh just the same.
Annie said: "This music is so heroic," and that's true.
But those who glance with furtive jealousy at men of action, those who secretly despise themselves for not being murderers, they don't recognize themselves here.
And the many who buy and sell people and believe that everybody can be bought, they don't recognize themselves here,
not their music. The long melody that is itself throughout all changes, sometimes sparkling and gentle, sometimes harsh and strong, snail track and steel wire.
The persistent humming that follows us this very moment
up
the depths.

March '79 1979

TRANSLATED BY SAMUEL CHARTERS

Tired of everyone who comes with words words but
no language
I went to the snow covered island.
The wild things have no words.
The unwritten pages stretch out in every direction!
I come across tracks of a deer's hooves in the snow.
Language but no words.

COMMENTARIES

TOMAS TRANSTRÖMER

Tranströmer was honored with a citation at the International Poetry Forum at the Carnegie Lecture Hall in New York City on April 15, 1989. The following is from his statement at that occasion.

On Poetry 1989

I think it is time to emphasize that poetry—in spite of all the bad poets and bad readers—starts from an advantageous position. A piece of paper, some words: it's simple and practical. It gives independence. Poetry requires no heavy, vulnerable apparatus that has to be lugged around, it isn't dependent on temperamental performers, dictatorial directors, bright producers with irresistible ideas. No big money is at stake. A poem doesn't come in one copy that somebody buys and locks up in a storeroom waiting for its market value to go up; it can't be stolen from a museum or become currency in the buying and selling of narcotics, or get burned up by a vandal.

When I started writing, at sixteen, I had a couple of like-minded school friends. Sometimes, when the lessons seemed more than usually trying, we would pass notes to each other between our desks—poems and aphorisms, which would come back with the more or less enthusiastic comments of the recipient. What an impression those scribblings would make! *There* is the fundamental situation of poetry. The lesson of official life goes rumbling on. We send inspired notes to one another.

ROBERT BLY

The poet and essayist Robert Bly was an early American admirer and translator of Tranströmer's poetry. The following comments are from his introduction to Tranströmer's *Night Vision.*

On Tomas Tranströmer 1972

Tomas Tranströmer seems to me the best poet to appear in Sweden for some years. He comes from a long line of ship-pilots who worked in and around the Stockholm Archipelago. He is at home on islands. His face is thin and angular, and the swift, spare face reminds one of Hans Christian Andersen's or the young Kierkegaard's. He has a strange genius for the image—images come up almost effortlessly. The images flow upward like water rising in some lonely place, in the swamps, or deep fir woods. . . .

Tranströmer, who was born in 1931, published his first book, *17 Poems,* in 1954. His next book, *Secrets on the Road,* contained fourteen poems, and he published that four years later. In 1962, after another gap of four years, he published *Half-Finished Heaven,* with twenty-one poems, fifty-two poems in all in about ten years. With many English and American poets, this number of poems is considered to be about six months' work. In 1968 he published a new book, *Resonance and Foot-Tracks.* The first seventeen poems were enough for him to be recognized by many critics as the finest poet of his generation.

Tomas Tranströmer's independence also shows itself in his choice of work. He does not teach, or edit for [his publisher] Bonniers. He was for some years a psychologist at the boy's prison in Linköping. He has recently moved to Västerås, where he does somewhat similar work. He is married, and has two daughters. The boys he counselled at Linköping evidently retain a lively impression of him. Someone sent me a clipping from Sweden recently, which recounted the adventures of a youth who had escaped a short time before from the Linköping reformatory. It transpired that he registered in various Swedish hotels and motels as "T. Tranströmer, psychologist." . . .

One of the most beautiful qualities in his poems is the space we feel in them. I think one reason for that is that the four or five main images which appear in each of his poems come from widely separated sources in the psyche.

His poems are a sort of railway station where trains that have come enormous distances stand briefly in the same building. One train may have some Russian snow still laying on the undercarriage, and another may have Mediterranean flowers still fresh in the compartments, and Ruhr soot on the roofs.

The poems are mysterious because of the distance the images have come to get there. Mallarmé believed there should by mystery in poetry, and urged poets to get it, if necessary, by removing the links that tie the poem to its occasion in the real world. In Tranströmer's poems, the link to the worldly occasion is stubbornly kept, and yet the poems have a mystery and surprise that never fade, even on many readings.

ROBERT HASS

Like Robert Bly, Robert Hass, who served as poet laureate of the United States in the 1990s, was an early advocate of Tranströmer's poetry. His comments here are from the 1993 program of the Nordic Poetry Festival in New York City.

Tranströmer's Style 1993

Tomas Tranströmer published his first book of poems—the stunning *17 Dikter* [*17 Poems*]—when he was twenty-three years old. Eight volumes have followed, each rather austere and beautifully made. The poems were, from the beginning, thick with the feel of life lived in a particular place: the dark, overpowering Swedish winters, the long thaws and brief paradisal summers in the Stockholm archipelago. But there were also piercing, inward poems, full of strange and intense accuracies of perception. . . . The brilliance of the metaphors, and their originality, was what most attracted the attention of other poets and made Tranströmer the most widely translated European poet of the post-war generation.

That brilliance is very difficult to separate from the terseness and almost classical restraint of a style that makes almost all other poets seem garrulous, sociable, eager—even in their most rebellious attitudes—to please. Tranströmer's metaphors suggest an uncannily alert imagination turned to an undeciphered, but not entirely undecipherable, world, whose meanings often come in hints, glimpses along the way. Sometimes the glimpses suggest a world brutal and ancient, sometimes one that is curiously innocent, unnervingly fresh. Almost always it is as peculiar, bald, and hermit as the opening of a hand when we cannot say whose it is or what purpose it intends.

And almost always in the poems, the everyday world, the one organized for the purposes of power, pleasure, transportation, is not the one we need to read. This also is conveyed in Tranströmer's darkly casual notations. This gives one a feeling, reading him, that one ought to wake up from whatever one's previous idea of being awake was.

The later poems often occur in the moments between sleeping and waking, between work and home, as a commuter on the outskirts of cities, as a tourist at the edge of cultures. They take place in the blurred seams of twentieth century life when the imagination has come unhinged a little and ceased to know what it thinks it knows about itself. These poems, more than any others I can think of, convey a sense of what it is like to be a private citizen—the phrase conveys the idea of a certain freedom, a certain level of comfort, and also some unease and isolation—anywhere this private citizenship exists—among the people who read and write books, for example—in the second half of the twentieth century.

HELEN VENDLER

In the September 7, 1975, issue of the *New York Times Book Review*, the critic Helen Vendler commented on a volume of Scandinavian poetry, *Friends You Drank Some Darkness*, in which a selection of Tranströmer's poetry appeared. She wrote that each of his poems "deserves quotation, meditation, and praise. He has an acute, almost pained sense of his own vocation, as he waits patiently . . . for the world and its people to manifest themselves through him, unable to act, only able to wait as the future gradually coalesces into the present." Vendler is perhaps anticipating a theory she proposes more than two decades later in the October 8, 1998, issue of the *New York Times Book Review*, where she suggests that Tranströmer became a poet after the "disorders" of a breakdown at the age of fifteen.

Tranströmer and the "Other Side" of Consciousness 1975

Tranströmer, a psychologist by profession, is a master of the underside of the psyche. He lives under obligation to the signs made from the other side of consciousness, which present themselves to him as knockings, voices, faces, memories, tirelessly soliciting him. Most of us keep a well-defended wall between the haunted night of the mind and its rational day. For some, however, the wall is breached, and without their consent. When Tranströmer was a boy of fifteen, in a year of great physical change ("At the beginning of that autumn term I was one of the smallest in the class, but by its end I was one of the tallest"), he experienced an involuntary convulsion caused by anxiety:

> Suddenly the atmosphere in the room was tense with dread. Something took total possession of me. Suddenly my body started shaking, especially my legs. I was a clockwork toy which had been wound up and now rattled and jumped helplessly. The cramps were quite beyond the control of my will, I had never experienced anything like this. I screamed for help and Mother came through. Gradually the cramps ebbed out. And did not return. But my dread intensified and from dusk to dawn would not leave me alone.

This experience, recalled in Tranströmer's fragmentary autobiography, "Memories Look at Me," was accompanied, in the subsequent weeks, by nightmares of horror at the unaesthetic:

> If the crisis had arisen a few years later . . . I would have managed to feel a little more sympathy for and a little less dread of the deformed and the sick who invaded my nocturnal consciousness.

Such a crisis might have been resolved in two different ways: the young sufferer could have built up defenses against the sources of dread and denied his own vulnerability; or he could have allowed into waking consciousness all the terrors of that time, and brought them under intellectual and imaginative scrutiny. It is clear from Tranströmer's poetry that it was the second of these that the poet (voluntarily or involuntarily) experienced. It is not that anxiety and depression and unwelcome images vanished: later writings testify to their continued presence in his life. It was rather that Tranströmer came to see such disorders as conferring a heightened aesthetic sense of peace and order.

SAMUEL CHARTERS

On Translating Tomas Tranströmer 2012

In his notes to his own translations of Tomas Tranströmer's poems, Keith Harrison began his discussion by emphasizing the difficulties for writers like Tranströmer of writing in their native languages.

> A poet in a minority culture in a world which is quickly becoming dominated by English will experience, at least from time to time, a certain unease, not to say anguish. Poets in English, even very good ones, have small enough audiences. Those in Sweden, or Norway or Wales have such a small public that they will feel a good deal of the time that they are talking to themselves. In a poet like Tranströmer, who knows English well, the temptation to write in English must be strong. Why does he resist? There are many answers to this, of course. Swedish is in his bones; English would always be a second language.[1]

Harrison understands the importance for these writers of their own landscape, which he calls their "region." Tranströmer's region, as Harrison recognizes,

> is an island in the archipelago off the east coast of Sweden. . . . That region, if you like, is his text. . . . It is a region which he cannot desert—not for long anyway.

In his discussion, Harrison also takes up the question of the difficulties of translating poetry in any language.

> If that sense of his own language is what holds Tranströmer it is also what attracts his readers—including his translators—to his work. Yet it is also that sense that makes his translators beat their brains. The old dilemma: good poetry cannot be translated, best to leave well alone.
>
> Well, at the risk of getting involved in endless argument, I want to say that I think a good deal of nonsense has been spoken about the translation of literature. Of course, it's impossible. But, having admitted that, we should also admit that it's absolutely necessary, and go on from there to talk about practical things.

[1]Keith Harrison, "Tomas Tranströmer in English: Some Notes," *Ironwood* 13, April 1979, p. 13.

The "practical things" about translation that Harrison names are a variety of factors. First, anyone translating a poem should have tried writing poetry themselves. The end result of your work will hopefully be a new poem in your own language, and it's helpful if you have that skill already there as a resource. You may have noticed translations where there are two names given. One is usually a person who for the other person named, generally a poet, has made a literal translation of the poem in a rough version that can be turned into a finished poem. It is always better, of course, if you have some familiarity with the language yourself since language carries along with it complex cultural baggage beyond the basic meanings of words.

Here are the opening lines from Tranströmer's poem "Schubertiana" in Swedish:

> I kvällsmörkret på en plats utanför New York, en utsiktspunkt där man
> med en enda blick kan omfatta åtta miljoner människör hem.
> Jättestaden där borta är en lång flimande driva, en spiralgalax från sidan.

Here are the same lines in a literal English translation:

> In the evening darkness at a place outside of New York, an outlook where
> someone in a single glance can see eight million people's homes.
> The giant city over there is a long flickering drift, a spiral galaxy from
> the side.

You will notice that although the words are different, the structure of the sentences themselves still remind you of an English sentence. This is another of the factors that Harrison mentioned in determining how a translation is made—the nature of the two languages you're working with. In this case, both Swedish and English have a common background in German, which at least gives you confidence that it will be possible to capture some of the feel of the poem in English. Other languages are much more difficult to work with. Russian, for example, is richer in linguistic elements than either Swedish or English, and to add to the translator's problems the basic language roots are so different that there are fewer words or phrases with a similar sound. As many translators have learned, if you are working with rhymed Russian poetry it is extremely difficult to convey both the meaning and the rhyme of the original poem. This similarity of sound between Swedish and English is basic to your work of translating Tranströmer's poetry. His poems also are unrhymed, which makes the work considerably less troublesome and time consuming. As you work with the poems, however, you realize that Swedish has a distinctive rhythmic quality, and it is important to try to get the feel of the rhythm in your new version.

Finally, an important factor in trying to create a new poem from the original is whether the poet also is familiar with your language. Tranströmer, as Harrison noted, speaks excellent English and he is there at your elbow, telling you exactly what he means with a line or phrase. As I wrote in an introduction to the translation of his long poem *Baltics*, if I wanted to know whether he meant a bay or a cove or an inlet with his Swedish word, we walked down to the beach together and he showed me what he was describing. He has been translated, however, into sixty languages, and he has to trust his translators, though

A summer morning the farmer's harrow catches
~~in~~ dead bones and ~~rags~~ of clothing. - ~~It~~
~~still was lying there when~~ the bog was drained
and in the light now stands and goes his way.

In every parish whirls the golden seed
around old guilts. The armour covered skull
in ~~tilled~~ fields. A hiker on ~~his way~~
and the mountain trails him with its glance.

In every parish murmurs the marksman's pipe
when ~~the wings break out at time of midnight~~
and ~~the past grows~~ in its ~~falling~~
and darker than the meteor of the heart.

A spirit's turn away makes the ~~script~~
voracious. A flag begins to snap. The wings
around the prey. This proud journey! where
the albatross is aged into a cloud
in Time's mouth. The culture is a whaling
station, where the stranger ~~takes~~ a walk
among the ~~white house gables and the children~~
~~playing conscious~~ still with every breath ~~of~~
the ~~covered~~ giant's presence.

A typed first draft of Samuel Charters's translation of a poem by Tomas Tranströmer, with his corrections added in ink. The poem titled "Elegy" originally appeared in *17 Poems* (1954).

he always is patient in his efforts to make his meanings clear. For the phrase "A crawling root pile" in the next to last line of his prose poem "Beginning of the Late Autumn Night's Novel," he turned over the page of the first version I'd done and drew a picture of tree roots to show me what he meant. The tone of all of the translations I have done of his poems reflects his concern with the precise clarity of his Swedish, even if sometimes a smoother English syntax would perhaps have sounded better to his American readers.

Obviously I think we can bring poetry across those invisible boundaries of language, but more important, I also feel that it is necessary that we try. Otherwise how could we learn what an essential poet like Tomas Tranströmer has to tell us about our world and its natural wonders and about ourselves?

(Note: On page 921 I have included a copy of a translation in progress. You can see Tranströmer's corrections on a rough draft of the translation of his poem "Elegy.")

WRITING ABOUT TOMAS TRANSTRÖMER

The following paper was written in response to an assigned topic: "Write a personal essay in which you discuss a theme that you find in at least two of Tomas Tranströmer's poems. Be sure to cite specific passages from the poems themselves to support your analysis and any claims you might make about the theme."

As you read the paper, consider how the main points are developed. Can you find further evidence in Tranströmer's poetry that supports the writer's argument? Would you modify the argument in any way using evidence you find in "Allegro," "Schubertiana," or any of the other poems in this chapter?

SAMPLE PAPER

"Every Pane Stays Whole": The Sustaining Power of Art in Tranströmer's Poetry

I've enjoyed playing music for a much longer time than I've enjoyed reading poetry, so I feel at home in the poetic world of Tomas Tranströmer. In poems such as "Allegro" and "Schubertiana" he describes sitting at a keyboard and feeling intense pleasure while he plays classical music. Actually what he feels is more than pleasure, since the compositions by Haydn and Schubert make him very thoughtful. These thoughts become the material he turns into poetry. Tranströmer expresses his thoughts in such consistent images that they come together to suggest a recurrent theme in his writing.

The theme uniting Tranströmer's work is that of the individual's struggle for identity and humanity in a world whose external events and mechanical forces threaten to pull him under. In this world, Nature is the only constant thing, and through her constancy she reminds the individual that art also has the power to transcend the moment. In society, on the other hand, recurrent wars, underhanded political power struggles, economic greed, and rapidly changing technology only increase a human being's sense of alienation.

In "Allegro," the final lines of the poem express this theme:

> The music is a house of glass on the hillside
> where the stones fly, the stones roll.
> And the stones roll right on through
> but every pane stays whole.

Earlier in this poem Tranströmer has suggested his alienation when he declares that "I hoist my Haydnflag—it means: / We don't give up. But want peace." Haydn's music has lasted while earlier wars and the taxes to pay for them have disappeared into the past. These are the "stones" that have failed to silence the music.

In "Schubertiana," a longer poem in five sections, Tranströmer makes the connection between the worlds of Nature and music, both with the power to sustain human trust. He ranges over a lot of territory in this poem, from the first section's description of his view of the "spiral galaxy" of heavily populated New York City, where somewhere someone is playing Schubert, to the solitary "humid woods" of his imagination in the poem's third section. Schubert, "a fat young gentleman from Vienna" in the second section, is still eternally alive everywhere in his music. In the fourth section, Tranströmer uses the image of our trust in a banister when we descend a flight of stairs in the darkness, a brilliant metaphor, to suggest how much we need to trust art "to be able to live our daily day without sinking / through the earth."

When Tranströmer was awarded the Nobel Prize, the judges stated that the clear images in his poetry had the power to remind us of the wonder of our everyday reality. The metaphors in "Allegro" and "Schubertiana" are powerful, but it is Tranströmer's theme that nature and art are essential to our survival as human beings that I find most important in his poetry.

◆ Topics for Writing about Tomas Tranströmer ◆

1. In your reading of Tomas Tranströmer's poems, you will encounter a wide range of figures of speech, including imagery, similes, metaphors, hyperbole, and paradox. Identify several figures of speech in the poems reprinted in these pages and discuss Tranströmer's use of them in his poems. Alternatively you may want to focus on his use of a specific figure of speech such as metaphor, of which he is considered a master by other poets and critics.
2. Tranströmer's poetry is presented here in translations from the original Swedish. Read the essay on translating poetry on page 919 and use it as a springboard to reflect on your own experiences with translations from other languages. You may want to focus on experiences faced in academic settings, such as high school or college language classes, where you had to read translations or compose them yourself. Or you may want to consider instances of language difference in your community or if you have lived in or traveled to other countries.
3. As you can see from the bibliography on page 911, numerous writers have tried their hand at translating Tranströmer's poetry. For a research project, track down a few of these volumes and browse through the poems. (In some cases, you will find that several poets have translated the same poem.) Then write an essay in which you compare your impressions. For example, does one translator's versions or interpretations of Tranströmer strike you as significantly different from another's? If so, try to characterize and explain the significant differences.
4. In 2011 Tranströmer was awarded the world's most prestigious literary honor, the Nobel Prize in literature. Research the history of the prize and its importance to our understanding of poetry today and suggest reasons why he was so honored.

18.

Poems and Poets

W. H. AUDEN

W. H. Auden (1907–1973) was born Wystan Hugh Auden in York, a large industrial city in northern England. He graduated from Oxford in 1930 and taught school for five years, but he was already publishing poetry and was considered one of the most exciting of a new, young group of English poets, which included Stephen Spender and C. Day Lewis.

In the 1930s Auden's poetry reflected his dismay at the effect of the world depression on England, and also his leftist views. In 1937 he went to Spain to take part in the civil war, but he was disturbed by the Loyalists' hostility to organized religion and returned to England without seeing active combat. In 1939 he moved to the United States, and in 1946 he became an American citizen. He returned to England as a professor of poetry at Oxford from 1956 to 1960, but in his last years he was part of the colorful cultural life of the Lower East Side in New York City.

Auden prided himself on his literary professionalism, and he wrote plays, the libretto for Igor Stravinsky's opera *The Rake's Progress*, and considerable literary commentary. For many years he toured U.S. universities as an excellent reader of his own poetry.

The well-known poem "Musée des Beaux Arts" was published in 1938, shortly before Auden moved to the United States. The poem "Stop All the Clocks," sometimes also called "Funeral Blues," was untitled when it was published in 1936. It was number XXXIV in his collection *Poems 1931–1936*. The poem was used in a moving funeral ceremony in the film *Four Weddings and a Funeral* (1994), and since then has been widely reprinted. The new title has been added since the film. "Lay your sleeping head, my love" expresses the complicated realities of the poet's emotional relationship before he left England for the United States.

WEB Research W. H. Auden at bedfordstmartins.com/rewritinglit.

Musée des Beaux Arts° 1938

About suffering they were never wrong,
The Old Masters: how well they understood
Its human position; how it takes place
While someone else is eating or opening a window or just walking
    dully along;
How, when the aged are reverently, passionately waiting
For the miraculous birth, there always must be
Children who did not specially want it to happen, skating
On a pond at the edge of the wood:
They never forgot
That even the dreadful martyrdom must run its course
Anyhow in a corner, some untidy spot
Where the dogs go on with their doggy life and the torturer's horse
Scratches its innocent behind on a tree.

In Brueghel's *Icarus,* ° for instance: how everything turns away
Quite leisurely from the disaster; the plowman may
Have heard the splash, the forsaken cry,
But for him it was not an important failure; the sun shown
As it had to on the white legs disappearing into the green
Water; and the expensive delicate ship that must have seen
Something amazing, a boy falling out of the sky,
Had somewhere to get to and sailed calmly on.

Stop All the Clocks 1936

Stop all the clocks, cut off the telephone,
Prevent the dog from barking with a juicy bone,
Silence the pianos and with muffled drum
Bring out the coffin, let the mourners come.
Let aeroplanes circle moaning overhead
Scribbling on the sky the message He Is Dead,
Put crêpe bows round the white necks of the public doves,
Let the traffic policemen wear black cotton gloves.

He was my North, my South, my East and West,
My working week and my Sunday rest,

Musée des Beaux Arts: The Museum of Fine Arts in Brussels.
14. Brueghel's *Icarus*: Refers to *Landscape with the Fall of Icarus,* by Pieter Brueghel the Elder (c. 1525–1569), in the Brussels museum. The painting represents the mythical Icarus as a tiny figure, dwarfed by other characters in the painting, as he falls into the sea.

My noon, my midnight, my talk, my song;
I thought that love would last for ever: I was wrong.

The stars are not wanted now; put out every one:
Pack up the moon and dismantle the sun;
Pour away the ocean and sweep up the woods:
For nothing now can ever come to any good.

Lay your sleeping head, my love 1937

Lay your sleeping head, my love,
Human on my faithless arm;
Time and fevers burn away
Individual beauty from
Thoughtful children, and the grave
Proves the child ephemeral:
But in my arms till break of day
Let the living creature lie,
Mortal, guilty, but to me
The entirely beautiful.

Soul and body have no bounds:
To lovers as they lie upon
Her tolerant enchanted slope
In their ordinary swoon,
Grave the vision Venus sends
Of supernatural sympathy,
Universal love and hope;
While an abstract insight wakes
Among the glaciers and the rocks
The hermit's sensual ecstasy.

Certainty, fidelity
On the stroke of midnight pass
Like vibrations of a bell,
And fashionable madmen raise
Their pedantic boring cry:
Every farthing of the cost,
All the dreaded cards foretell,
Shall be paid, but from this night
Not a whisper, not a thought,
Not a kiss nor look be lost.

Beauty, midnight, vision dies:
Let the winds of dawn that blow
Softly round your dreaming head
Such a day of sweetness show
Eye and knocking heart may bless,

Find the mortal world enough;
Noons of dryness see you fed
By the involuntary powers,
Nights of insult let you pass
Watched by every human love.

ELIZABETH BISHOP

Elizabeth Bishop (1911–1979) was the daughter of a successful Boston building contractor and his Canadian wife, but her father died when she was a baby, and when she was four her mother was placed in a mental institution. Bishop was raised by grandparents and relatives in Nova Scotia and Massachusetts. She suffered from severe asthma, and she was unable to attend school until she was sixteen. Among her friends, when she entered Vassar College in 1930, were the writers Muriel Rukeyser and Mary McCarthy.

Although Bishop grew up in a period in which talented women writers – among them Edna St. Vincent Millay, Elinor Wylie, and Louise Bogan – played a dominant role in American poetry, she found their work too traditional, and she took the modernist poet Marianne Moore as a mentor and friend. Another strong influence on her writing was her long friendship with poet Robert Lowell. A small trust fund made it possible for her to live as she wanted, and she spent several years in Key West, Florida. After reviving an old acquaintance with Lota de Macedo Soares, she moved with her to Brazil and remained there until Soares's suicide in 1977. Bishop then returned to the United States to teach at Harvard.

Bishop was a careful, selective poet, and she achieved considerable critical success. She won the Pulitzer Prize and the National Book Award, and her final collection was awarded the National Book Critics Circle Award. "Manners – For a Child of 1918" is a touching memory of her childhood in Nova Scotia when she was eight years old. "Sandpiper" is a small, perfectly shaped glimpse of the small, skittering birds at the sea's edge, where she often walked. "The Fish," one of her best-known poems, was included in her first collection *North and South,* published in 1946. "One Art" is one of Bishop's most anthologized poems, perhaps because of its wry acceptance of the everyday occurrences of our lives. (See also Bishop's "The Bight" on p. 733 and "Sestina" on p. 770.)

WEB Research Elizabeth Bishop at bedfordstmartins.com/rewritinglit.

Manners

1955

For a Child of 1918

My grandfather said to me
as we sat on the wagon seat,
"Be sure to remember to always
speak to everyone you meet."

We met a stranger on foot.
My grandfather's whip tapped his hat.
"Good day, sir. Good day. A fine day."
And I said it and bowed where I sat.

Then we overtook a boy we knew
with his big pet crow on his shoulder.
"Always offer everyone a ride;
don't forget that when you get older,"

my grandfather said. So Willy
climbed up with us, but the crow
gave a "Caw!" and flew off. I was worried.
How would he know where to go?

But he flew a little way at a time
from fence post to fence post, ahead;
and when Willy whistled he answered.
"A fine bird," my grandfather said,

"and he's well brought up. See, he answers
nicely when he's spoken to.
Man or beast, that's good manners.
Be sure that you both always do."

When automobiles went by,
the dust hid the people's faces,
but we shouted "Good day! Good day!
Fine day!" at the top of our voices.

When we came to Hustler Hill,
he said that the mare was tired,
so we all got down and walked,
as our good manners required.

Sandpiper

1965

The roaring alongside he takes for granted,
and that every so often the world is bound to shake.
He runs, he runs to the south, finical, awkward,
in a state of controlled panic, a student of Blake.

The beach hisses like fat. On his left, a sheet
of interrupting water comes and goes
and glazes over his dark and brittle feet.
He runs, he runs straight through it, watching his toes.

—Watching, rather, the spaces of sand between them,
where (no detail too small) the Atlantic drains
rapidly backwards and downwards. As he runs,
he stares at the dragging grains.

The world is a mist. And then the world is
minute and vast and clear. The tide
is higher or lower. He couldn't tell you which.
His beak is focused; he is preoccupied,

looking for something, something, something.
Poor bird, he is obsessed!
The millions of grains are black, white, tan, and gray,
mixed with quartz grains, rose and amethyst.

The Fish

1946

I caught a tremendous fish
and held him beside the boat
half out of water, with my hook
fast in a corner of his mouth.
He didn't fight.
He hadn't fought at all.
He hung a grunting weight,
battered and venerable
and homely. Here and there
his brown skin hung in strips
like ancient wallpaper,
and its pattern of darker brown
was like wallpaper:
shapes like full-blown roses
stained and lost through age.
He was speckled with barnacles,
fine rosettes of lime,
and infested
with tiny white sea-lice,
and underneath two or three
rags of green weed hung down.
While his gills were breathing in
the terrible oxygen
—the frightening gills,
fresh and crisp with blood,
that can cut so badly—

I thought of the coarse white flesh
packed in like feathers,
the big bones and the little bones,
the dramatic reds and blacks
of his shiny entrails,
and the pink swim-bladder
like a big peony.
I looked into his eyes
which were far larger than mine
but shallower, and yellowed,
the irises backed and packed
with tarnished tinfoil
seen through the lenses
of old scratched isinglass.
They shifted a little, but not
to return my stare.
—It was more like the tipping
of an object toward the light.
I admired his sullen face,
the mechanism of his jaw,
and then I saw
that from his lower lip
—if you could call it a lip—
grim, wet, and weaponlike,
hung five old pieces of fish-line,
or four and a wire leader
with the swivel still attached,
with all their five big hooks
grown firmly in his mouth.
A green line, frayed at the end
where he broke it, two heavier lines,
and a fine black thread
still crimped from the strain and snap
when it broke and he got away.
Like medals with their ribbons
frayed and wavering,
a five-haired beard of wisdom
trailing from his aching jaw.
I stared and stared
and victory filled up
the little rented boat,
from the pool of bilge
where oil had spread a rainbow
around the rusted engine
to the bailer rusted orange,
the sun-cracked thwarts,
the oarlocks on their strings,

the gunnels—until everything
was rainbow, rainbow, rainbow!
And I let the fish go.

One Art 1976

The art of losing isn't hard to master;
so many things seem filled with the intent
to be lost that their loss is no disaster.

Lose something every day. Accept the fluster
of lost door keys, the hour badly spent.
The art of losing isn't hard to master.

Then practice losing farther, losing faster:
places, and names, and where it was you meant
to travel. None of these will bring disaster.

I lost my mother's watch. And look! my last, or
next-to-last, of three loved houses went.
The art of losing isn't hard to master.

I lost two cities, lovely ones. And, vaster,
some realms I owned, two rivers, a continent.
I miss them, but it wasn't a disaster.

—Even losing you (the joking voice, a gesture
I love) I shan't have lied. It's evident
the art of losing's not too hard to master
though it may look like (*Write* it!) like disaster.

COMMENTARY

BRETT C. MILLIER

Brett C. Millier described the biographical context of the composition of the poem "One Art" in *Elizabeth Bishop: Life and the Memory of It.* This study was published by the University of California Press in 1993.

On Elizabeth Bishop's "One Art" 1993

Elizabeth Bishop left seventeen drafts of the poem "One Art" among her papers. In the first draft, she lists all the things she's lost in her life—keys, pens, glasses, cities—and then she writes "One might think this would have prepared me/for losing one average-sized not exceptionally/beautiful or dazzlingly intelligent person . . . /But it doesn't seem to have at all. . . ." By the seventeenth draft, nearly every word has been transformed, but most importantly, Bishop discovered along the way that there might be a way to master this loss.

One way to read Bishop's modulation between the first and last drafts from "the loss of you is impossible to master" to something like "I am still the master of losing even though losing you looks like a disaster" is that in the writing of such a disciplined, demanding poem as this villanelle ("[*Write* it!]") lies the potential mastery of the loss. Working through each of her losses—from the bold, painful catalog of the first draft to the finely honed and privately meaningful final version—is the way to overcome them or, if not to overcome them, then to see the way in which she might possibly master herself in the face of loss. It is all, perhaps, "one art"—writing elegy, mastering loss, mastering grief, self-mastery. Bishop had a precocious familiarity with loss. Her father died before her first birthday, and four years later her mother disappeared into a sanitarium, never to be seen by her daughter again. The losses in the poem are real: time in the form of the "hour badly spent" and, more tellingly for the orphaned Bishop "my mother's watch": the lost houses, in Key West, Petrópolis, and Ouro Prêto, Brazil. The city of Rio de Janeiro and the whole South American continent (where she had lived for nearly two decades) were lost to her with the suicide of her Brazilian companion. And currently, in the fall of 1975, she seemed to have lost her dearest friend and lover, who was trying to end their relationship. But each version of the poem distanced the pain a little more, depersonalized it, moved it away from the tawdry self-pity and "confession" that Bishop disliked in so many of her contemporaries.

Bishop's friends remained for a long time protective of her personal reputation, and unwilling to have her grouped among lesbian poets or even among the other great poets of her generation—Robert Lowell, John Berryman, Theodore Roethke—as they seemed to self-destruct before their readers' eyes. Bishop herself taught them this reticence by keeping her private life to herself, and by investing what "confession" there was in her poems deeply in objects and places, thus deflecting biographical inquiry. In the development of this poem, discretion is both a poetic method, and a part of a process of self-understanding, the seeing of a pattern in her own life.

WILLIAM BLAKE

William Blake (1757–1827) was born in London, one of several children of a London haberdasher. His family expected he would become a tradesman, and he was educated to be a commercial artist. He was sent to a drawing academy when he was ten, then he studied painting for a short time at the Royal Academy of Arts.

At the age of fourteen Blake was apprenticed to an engraver, and his seven-year apprenticeship provided him with enough knowledge and experience to set up his own small engraving business. At the same time he was reading on his own and beginning to write poetry. When he was twenty-four he married Catherine Boucher, whose father delivered produce to the London markets. The next year, 1783, his first book of poems, *Poetical Sketches*, was published.

Over the next ten years he produced his two most celebrated books. *Songs of Innocence* appeared in 1789, and *Songs of Innocence and of Experience* in 1794. He created the books with a method of engraving that combined the illustrations and the hand-lettered poetry on the page, then he and his wife hand-painted each page with watercolors. To do a single copy was so time-consuming that only a handful of editions were produced, but they were so unusual and so beautiful that Blake attracted the attention of a small group of connoisseurs and artists.

In 1800, with the financial assistance of a patron, the Blakes were able to move to the country, and he continued to draw and paint, to create illustrations for books by other writers and to create his own books of prophecy and mystical inspiration. To many of his contemporaries, Blake was an exasperating eccentric with radical opinions, who often described conversations he had just had with long-dead historical figures. As he said of his habit of seeing visions, "I do not distrust my corporeal or vegetative eye any more than I would distrust a window for its sight. I see through it, not with it." He died in 1827 at the age of seventy.

The selection of Blake's poetry is taken from *Songs of Innocence and Experience*.

WEB Research William Blake at bedfordstmartins.com/rewritinglit.

From *Songs of Innocence* 1789

Introduction

Piping down the valleys wild
Piping songs of pleasant glee
On a cloud I saw a child,
And he laughing said to me,
"Pipe a song about a Lamb";
So I piped with merry chear;
"Piper pipe that song again"—
So I piped, he wept to hear.

"Drop thy pipe thy happy pipe
Sing thy songs of happy chear";
So I sung the same again
While he wept with joy to hear.

"Piper sit thee down and write
In a book that all may read"—
So he vanish'd from my sight.
And I pluck'd a hollow reed,

And I made a rural pen,
And I stain'd the water clear,
And I wrote my happy songs
Every child may joy to hear.

The Lamb

1789

Little Lamb, who made thee?
Dost thou know who made thee?
Gave thee life, and bid thee feed
By the stream and o'er the mead;
Gave thee clothing of delight,
Softest clothing, wooly, bright;
Gave thee such a tender voice,
Making all the vales rejoice?
Little Lamb, who made thee?
Dost thou know who made thee?

Little Lamb, I'll tell thee,
Little Lamb, I'll tell thee:
He is callèd by thy name,
For he calls himself a Lamb.
He is meek, and he is mild;
He became a little child.
I a child, and thou a lamb,
We are callèd by his name.
Little Lamb, God bless thee!
Little Lamb, God bless thee!

Holy Thursday

1789

'Twas on a Holy Thursday, their innocent faces clean,
The children walking two & two, in red & blue & green;
Grey headed beadles walkd before with wands as white as snow,
Till into the high dome of Paul's° they like Thames' waters flow.

O what a multitude they seemd, these flowers of London town!
Seated in companies they sit with radiance all their own.
The hum of multitudes was there, but multitudes of lambs,
Thousands of little boys & girls raising their innocent hands.

Now like a mighty wind they raise to heaven the voice of song,
Or like harmonious thunderings the seats of heaven among.
Beneath them sit the agèd men, wise guardians of the poor;
Then cherish pity, lest you drive an angel from your door.

4. Paul's: St. Paul's Cathedral.

The Little Boy Lost 1789

"Father, father, where are you going?
O do not walk so fast.
Speak father, speak to your little boy
Or else I shall be lost."

The night was dark, no father was there,
The child was wet with dew.
The mire was deep, & the child did weep,
And away the vapour flew.

The Little Boy Found 1789

The little boy lost in the lonely fen,
Led by the wand'ring light,
Began to cry, but God ever nigh
Appeard like his father in white.

He kissed the child & by the hand led
And to his mother brought,
Who in sorrow pale, thro' the lonely dale,
Her little boy weeping sought.

From *Songs of Experience* 1794

Introduction

Hear the voice of the Bard!
Who Present, Past, & Future sees;
Whose ears have heard
The Holy Word
That walk'd among the ancient trees;

Calling the lapsèd Soul
And weeping in the evening dew,
That might controll
The starry pole,
And fallen, fallen light renew!

"O Earth, O Earth, return!
Arise from out the dewy grass;
Night is worn,
And the morn
Rises from the slumberous mass.

"Turn away no more;
Why wilt thou turn away?

The starry floor
The watry shore
Is giv'n thee till the break of day."

The Sick Rose 1794

O Rose, thou art sick!
The invisible worm
That flies in the night,
In the howling storm,

Has found out thy bed
Of crimson joy,
And his dark secret love
Does thy life destroy.

The Tyger 1794

Tyger! Tyger! burning bright
In the forests of the night,
What immortal hand or eye
Could frame thy fearful symmetry?

In what distant deeps or skies
Burnt the fire of thine eyes?
On what wings dare he aspire?
What the hand dare seize the fire?

And what shoulder, and what art,
Could twist the sinews of thy heart?
And when thy heart began to beat,
What dread hand? and what dread feet?

What the hammer? what the chain?
In what furnace was thy brain?
What the anvil? what dread grasp
Dare its deadly terrors clasp?

When the stars threw down their spears,
And watered heaven with their tears,
Did he smile his work to see?
Did he who made the Lamb make thee?

Tyger! Tyger! burning bright
In the forests of the night,
What immortal hand or eye
Dare frame thy fearful symmetry?

London

1794

I wander through each chartered° street *defined by law*
Near where the chartered Thames does flow,
And mark in every face I meet
Marks of weakness, marks of woe.

In every cry of every man,
In every Infant's cry of fear,
In every voice, in every ban,
The mind-forged manacles I hear.

How the Chimney-sweeper's cry
Every black'ning Church appalls;
And the hapless Soldier's sigh
Runs in blood down Palace walls.

But most through midnight streets I hear
How the youthful Harlot's curse° *syphilis*
Blasts the new-born Infant's tear,
And blights with plagues the Marriage hearse.

A Poison Tree

1794

I was angry with my friend:
I told my wrath, my wrath did end.
I was angry with my foe:
I told it not, my wrath did grow.

And I waterd it in fears,
Night & morning with my tears;
And I sunnèd it with smiles,
And with soft deceitful wiles.

And it grew both day and night,
Till it bore an apple bright.
And my foe beheld it shine,
And he knew that it was mine,

And into my garden stole,
When the night had veild the pole;
In the morning glad I see
My foe outstretched beneath the tree.

The Garden of Love

1794

I went to the Garden of Love,
And saw what I never had seen:
A Chapel was built in the midst,
Where I used to play on the green.

And the gates of this Chapel were shut,
And "Thou shalt not" writ over the door;
So I turn'd to the Garden of Love,
That so many sweet flowers bore,

And I saw it was filled with graves,
And tomb-stones where flowers should be;
And Priests in black gowns were walking their rounds,
And binding with briars my joys & desires.

ANNE BRADSTREET

Anne Bradstreet (c. 1612–1672) was born in England, the daughter of a "well borne woman" of modest wealth and a father who was the steward of the country estate of the Earl of Lincoln. Both the earl and Bradstreet's parents were Puritans, and she was given a much better education than most young women of her time. At sixteen she married Simon Bradstreet, also a Puritan, and two years later, in 1630, she, her husband, and her parents sailed to the Massachusetts Bay Colony. They lived first in Boston and in 1644 moved to North Andover, where Bradstreet lived for the rest of her life.

As a girl she had already begun writing poems that she and her father read with pleasure together. She continued to write, while she raised eight children and managed the household for her husband, who, as governor of the colony, was away for long periods.

In 1650, without her knowledge, her brother-in-law took a gathering of her poems to London. The collection was the first to be published by anyone living in the North American colonies, and the book attracted considerable attention. Because of the constraints placed on women's lives, her brother-in-law felt obliged to assure suspicious readers, in the introduction, that Bradstreet was respectable according to the standards of the time. The poems, he wrote, were "the work of a woman, honored and esteemed where she lives, for her gracious demeanor, her eminent parts, her pious conversation, her courteous disposition, her exact diligence in her place, and discreet managing of her family occasions."

"To My Dear and Loving Husband," "Before the Birth of One of Her Children," and "In Memory of My Dear Grand-Child Elizabeth Bradstreet, Who Deceased August, 1665, Being a Year and a Half Old" were all written during Bradstreet's years in North Andover.

WEB Research Anne Bradstreet at bedfordstmartins.com/rewritinglit.

To My Dear and Loving Husband 1678

If ever two were one, then surely we.
If ever man were loved by wife, then thee;
If ever wife was happy in a man,
Compare with me, ye women, if you can.
I prize thy love more than whole mines of gold
Or all the riches that the East doth hold.
My love is such that rivers cannot quench,
Nor ought but love from thee, give recompense.
Thy love is such I can no way repay,
The heavens reward thee manifold, I pray.
Then while we live, in love let's so persevere
That when we live no more, we may live ever.

Before the Birth of One of Her Children 1678

All things within this fading world hath end,
Adversity doth still our joys attend;
No ties so strong, no friends so dear and sweet,
But with death's parting blow is sure to meet.
The sentence past is most irrevocable,
A common thing, yet oh, inevitable.
How soon, my Dear, death may my steps attend,
How soon't may be thy lot to lose thy friend,
We both are ignorant, yet love bids me
These farewell lines to recommend to thee,
That when that knot's untied that made us one,
I may seem thine, who in effect am none.
And if I see not half my days that's due,
What nature would, God grant to yours and you;
The many faults that well you know I have
Let be interred in my oblivious grave;
If any worth or virtue were in me,
Let that live freshly in thy memory
And when thou feel'st no grief, as I no harms,
Yet love thy dead, who long lay in thine arms.
And when thy loss shall be repaid with gains
Look to my little babes, my dear remains.
And if thou love thyself, or loved'st me,
These O protect from step-dame's injury.
And if chance to thine eyes shall bring this verse,
With some sad sighs honour my absent hearse;
And kiss this paper for thy love's dear sake,
Who with salt tears this last farewell did take.

In Memory of My Dear Grand-Child Elizabeth Bradstreet, Who Deceased August, 1665, Being a Year and a Half Old

1665

1

Farewel dear babe, my hearts too much content,
Farewel sweet babe, the pleasure of mine eye,
Farewel fair flower that for a space was lent,
Then ta'en away unto Eternity.
Blest babe why should I once bewail thy fate,
Or sigh thy dayes so soon were terminate;
Sith thou art setled in an Everlasting state.

2

By nature Trees do rot when they are grown.
And Plumbs and Apples thoroughly ripe do fall,
And Corn and grass are in their season mown,
And time brings down what is both strong and tall.
But plants new set to be eradicate,
And buds new blown, to have so short a date,
Is by his hand alone that guides nature and fate.

GWENDOLYN BROOKS

Gwendolyn Brooks (1917–2000) was born in Topeka, Kansas, but her parents moved to Chicago's South Side soon after her birth. Her father worked as a janitor, and the family was poor, but her parents encouraged her to study in school and to write poetry. She wrote her first poems when she was seven. Her childhood was so contented that she wrote later in her autobiography, "I had always felt that to be black was good."

Brooks had almost immediate success as a writer. She was already publishing her poetry when she was seventeen. Her first book, *A Street in Bronzeville,* which appeared in 1945, won a series of prizes, and she was awarded a Guggenheim fellowship, which allowed her to spend a year devoted entirely to writing. In 1949 her second poetry collection, *Annie Allen,* won the Pulitzer Prize, the first time it had been given to an African American writer. She also published a novel, *Maud Martha,* in 1953, and taught at Chicago State University, where she was a Distinguished Professor.

In 1967 Brooks took part in the Second Black Writer's Conference at Fisk University, and she was swept up in the new militancy of the younger black poets like Amiri Baraka and don l. lee. Her poetry became more specifically political, and finally she turned to alternative publishing so she could have some control over the way her poetry was presented. From 1985 to 1986, Brooks served as consultant in poetry to the Library of Congress, a position now called poet laureate.

"We Real Cool" is one of her shortest poems, and it is also one of her most famous. "The Mother" is an early poem in which the woman speaker projects a scarring, personal unhappiness. Brooks herself was the mother of a son and a daughter. "The Bean Eaters," with its poignant suggestion of life's vagaries in the old couple's memories of "twinklings and twinges," first appeared in 1960.

CONNECTION Robert Hayden, "On Negro Poetry," page 1043.

WEB Research Gwendolyn Brooks at bedfordstmartins.com/rewritinglit.

We Real Cool 1960

The Pool Players.
Seven at the Golden Shovel.

We real cool. We
Left school. We

Lurk late. We
Strike straight. We

Sing sin. We
Thin gin. We

Jazz June. We
Die soon.

The Mother 1945

Abortions will not let you forget.
You remember the children you got that you did not get,
The damp small pulps with a little or with no hair,
The singers and workers that never handled the air.
You will never neglect or beat
Them, or silence or buy with a sweet.
You will never wind up the sucking-thumb
Or scuttle off ghosts that come.
You will never leave them, controlling your luscious sigh,
Return for a snack of them, with gobbling mother-eye.
I have heard in the voices of the wind the voices of my dim killed children.
I have contracted. I have eased
My dim dears at the breasts they could never suck.
I have said, Sweets, if I sinned, if I seized
Your luck
And your lives from your unfinished reach,
If I stole your births and your names,
Your straight baby tears and your games,
Your stilted or lovely loves, your tumults, your marriages, aches, and
your deaths,

If I poisoned the beginnings of your breaths,
Believe that even in my deliberateness I was not deliberate.
Though why should I whine,
Whine that the crime was other than mine?—
Since anyhow you are dead.
Or rather, or instead,
You were never made.
But that too, I am afraid,
Is faulty: oh, what shall I say, how is the truth to be said?
You were born, you had body, you died.
It is just that you never giggled or planned or cried.

Believe me, I loved you all.
Believe me, I knew you, though faintly, and I loved, I loved you
All.

The Bean Eaters 1960

They eat beans mostly, this old yellow pair.
Dinner is a casual affair.
Plain chipware on a plain and creaking wood,
Tin flatware.

Two who are Mostly Good.
Two who have lived their day,
But keep on putting on their clothes
And putting things away.

And remembering . . .
Remembering, with twinklings and twinges,
As they lean over the beans in their rented back room that is full of beads
and receipts and dolls and cloths, tobacco crumbs, vases and fringes.

MARILYN CHIN

Marilyn Mei Ling Chin (b. 1955) was born in Hong Kong, where her father operated a restaurant. He moved the family to Portland, Oregon, when she was a child, and changed his daughter's name from Mei Ling to Marilyn, in homage to the actress Marilyn Monroe. He also soon abandoned the family for a Caucasian woman, and this act has left a strong emotional imprint on Chin's poetry.

Chin graduated from the University of Massachusetts in 1977 and received her M.F.A. from the University of Iowa in 1981. Her first book, *Dwarf Bamboo*, was published in 1987. For several years she taught at San Diego State University, which she described as an "exile." Although she has assimilated into the mainstream American culture, she is concerned that she is losing her Chinese identity. As she told television interviewer Bill Moyers in 1995,

> I am afraid of losing my Chinese, losing my language, which would be like losing part of myself, losing part of my soul. Poetry seems a way to recapture that, but of course the truth is we can't recapture the past. The vector only goes one direction and that is toward the future. So the grandeur of China – the grandeur of that past of my grandfather's, of my grandmother's, of my mother's, and so forth – that will be all lost to me. I lose inches of it every day.

Chin's other books include two poetry collections, *The Phoenix Gone, The Terrace Empty* (1994) and *Rhapsody in Plain Yellow* (2002), and a novel, *Revenge of the Mooncake Vixen* (2009). She is co-director of the M.F.A. program at the University of San Diego.

"How I Got That Name" is an autobiographical poem and "Sad Guitar" continues the theme of autobiography, describing her isolation as an immigrant.

CONNECTION Marilyn Chin, "On the Canon," page 833.

How I Got That Name 1994

an essay on assimilation

I am Marilyn Mei Ling Chin.
Oh, how I love the resoluteness
of that first person singular
followed by that stalwart indicative
of "be," without the uncertain i-n-g
of "becoming." Of course,
the name had been changed
somewhere between Angel Island and the sea,
when my father the paperson
in the late 1950s
obsessed with a bombshell blonde
transliterated "Mei Ling" to "Marilyn."
And nobody dared question
his initial impulse—for we all know
lust drove men to greatness,
not goodness, not decency.
And there I was, a wayward pink baby,
named after some tragic white woman
swollen with gin and Nembutal.
My mother couldn't pronounce the "r."
She dubbed me "Numba one female offshoot"
for brevity: henceforth, she will live and die
in sublime ignorance, flanked
by loving children and the "kitchen deity."
While my father dithers,
a tomcat in Hong Kong trash—
a gambler, a petty thug,
who bought a chain of chopsuey joints
in Piss River, Oregon,

with bootlegged Gucci cash.
Nobody dared question his integrity given
his nice, devout daughters
and his bright, industrious sons
as if filial piety were the standard
by which all earthly men were measured.

Oh, how trustworthy our daughters,
how thrifty our sons!
How we've managed to fool the experts
in education, statistics and demography—
We're not very creative but not adverse to rote-learning.
Indeed, they can *use* us.
But the "Model Minority"° is a tease.
We know you are watching now,
so we refuse to give you any!
Oh, bamboo shoots, bamboo shoots!
The further west we go, we'll hit east;
the deeper down we dig, we'll find China.
History has turned its stomach
on a black polluted beach—
where life doesn't hinge
on that red, red wheelbarrow,°
but whether or not our new lover
in the final episode of "Santa Barbara"°
will lean over a scented candle
and call us a "bitch."
Oh God, where have we gone wrong?
We have no inner resources!

Then, one redolent spring morning
the Great Patriarch Chin
peered down from his kiosk in heaven
and saw that his descendants were ugly.
One had a squarish head and a nose without a bridge.
Another's profile—long and knobbed as a gourd.
A third, the sad, brutish one
may never, never marry.
And I, his least favorite—
"not quite boiled, not quite cooked,"
a plump pomfret° simmering in my juices—
too listless to fight for my people's destiny.
"To kill without resistance is not slaughter"

---

42. Model Minority: Asian Americans have been stereotyped as a well-behaved, industrious "model minority." **51. red, red wheelbarrow:** A reference to William Carlos Williams's brief modernist poem "The Red Wheelbarrow" (see p. 798 in this text). **53. "Santa Barbara":** Prime-time television "soap opera" about wealthy, glamorous characters living in the California seaside city. **68. pomfret:** A spiny, edible fish.

says the proverb. So, I wait for imminent death.
The fact that this death is also metaphorical
is testament to my lethargy.

So here lies Marilyn Mei Ling Chin,
married once, twice to so-and-so, a Lee and a Wong,
granddaughter of Jack "the patriarch"
and the brooding Suilin Fong,
daughter of the virtuous Yuet Kuen Wong
and G. G. Chin the infamous,
sister of a dozen, cousin of a million,
survived by everybody and forgotten by all.
She was neither black nor white,
neither cherished nor vanquished,
just another squatter in her own bamboo grove
minding her poetry—
when one day heaven was unmerciful,
and a chasm opened where she stood.
Like the jowls of a mighty white whale,
or the jaws of a metaphysical Godzilla,
it swallowed her whole.
She did not flinch nor writhe,
nor fret about the afterlife,
but stayed! Solid as wood, happily
a little gnawed, tattered, mesmerized
by all that was lavished upon her
and all that was taken away!

Sad Guitar

1994

(Sad Guitar series #3/3)

Blind immigrant,
do you understand this:
touch, wood,
this is wood
and not fire, this
earth and not wood.
This is elemental water.

Tea brews, rice boils,
ten days since your departure.
I stagger, stumble,
let old associations go.
What rhymes with flower,
bower, shower, power?

Stranger, have you ever loved
a Chinese woman?

Her heart is chrysanthemum.
And there are deeper chasms.

Oh, the goads, the rancor!
here I am within you, without you,
groping the fleshy dark,
conjuring the spirits and the furies.

I am a woman without rope
chasing a runaway horse
whose chariots neigh
and hoofbeats plunder.

I hear you, but I don't see you.
I touch you, but you seem far.
What I have learned about loneliness
is the three fingers that strum
the heart of the all-knowing—
the dark pith of the sad guitar.

SAMUEL TAYLOR COLERIDGE

Samuel Taylor Coleridge (1772–1834) was born in a small village in southern England, but after the death of his father he was sent to school in London. Despite his indolence, he could also be sporadically brilliant, and at nineteen he entered Cambridge University, where his lack of discipline overwhelmed him, and he was unable to complete his degree.

In 1794 Coleridge met the young poet Robert Southey and, filled with the fervor of the French Revolution, they decided to establish a utopian colony in Pennsylvania. Their plans fell apart, but Coleridge, as part of the plan, had married the sister of Southey's fiancée. The marriage was as unhappy as everything else Coleridge had attempted. The next year he met William Wordsworth and soon moved close to where the older poet and his sister Dorothy were living in England. Writing together, in a fever of excitement, he and Wordsworth completed the small collection titled *Lyrical Ballads*, which was published in 1798. With their book they attempted to write a new kind of poetry, closer to ordinary speech and drawing from everyday emotions. Coleridge's contribution was the long supernatural narrative "The Rime of the Ancient Mariner" and several shorter poems.

Coleridge by this time was addicted to opium, and his writing became chaotically uneven. "Kubla Khan" is the best known of his drug-influenced poems. When he later overcame his addiction he became one of the most important literary theorists and critics of the early nineteenth century. His lifelong friend, the writer Charles Lamb, described Coleridge as "an archangel, slightly damaged." "Frost at Midnight" is one of Coleridge's "conversation poems" in blank verse that moves back and forth between description of his surroundings and lofty meditation.

CONNECTION Richard Leighton Greene, "Apropos Coleridge's 'Kubla Khan,'" page 780.

WEB Research Samuel Taylor Coleridge at bedfordstmartins.com/rewritinglit.

Kubla Khan: or, a Vision in a Dream° 1798

In Xanadu did Kubla Khan°
A stately pleasure-dome decree:
Where Alph, the sacred river, ran
Through caverns measureless to man
Down to a sunless sea.
So twice five miles of fertile ground
With walls and towers were girdled round:
And here were gardens bright with sinuous rills
Where blossomed many an incense-bearing tree;
And there were forests ancient as the hills,
Enfolding sunny spots of greenery.

But oh! that deep romantic chasm which slanted
Down the green hill athwart a cedarn cover!°
A savage place! as holy and enchanted
As e'er beneath a waning moon was haunted
By woman wailing for her demon-lover!
And from this chasm, with ceaseless turmoil seething,
As if this earth in fast thick pants were breathing,
A mighty fountain momently was forced,
Amid whose swift half-intermitted burst
Huge fragments vaulted like rebounding hail,
Or chaffy grain beneath the thresher's flail:
And 'mid these dancing rocks at once and ever
It flung up momently the sacred river.
Five miles meandering with a mazy motion
Through wood and dale the sacred river ran,
Then reached the caverns measureless to man,
And sank in tumult to a lifeless ocean:
And 'mid this tumult Kubla heard from far
Ancestral voices prophesying war!
The shadow of the dome of pleasure
Floated midway on the waves;
Where was heard the mingled measure
From the fountain and the caves.
It was a miracle of rare device,
A sunny pleasure-dome with caves of ice!

A damsel with a dulcimer
In a vision once I saw:
It was an Abyssinian maid,

Vision in a Dream: Coleridge claimed this poem came to him in a dream, but when he woke and was transcribing it, he was interrupted by a visitor and was later unable to remember the rest of the poem. **1. Kubla Khan:** In Chinese history, Kublai Khan (1215–1294) founded the Mongol dynasty. **13. athwart . . . cover:** Encompassing a grove of cedar trees.

    And on her dulcimer she played,
    Singing of Mount Abora.
    Could I revive within me
    Her symphony and song,
    To such a deep delight 'twould win me,
That with music loud and long,
I would build that dome in air,
That sunny dome! those caves of ice!
And all who heard should see them there,
And all should cry, Beware! Beware!
His flashing eyes, his floating hair!
Weave a circle round him thrice,
And close your eyes with holy dread,
For he on honey-dew hath fed,
And drunk the milk of Paradise.

Frost at Midnight

1798

The Frost performs its secret ministry,
Unhelped by any wind. The owlet's cry
Came loud—and hark, again! loud as before.
The inmates of my cottage, all at rest,
Have left me to that solitude, which suits
Abstruser musings: save that at my side
My cradled infant slumbers peacefully.
'Tis calm indeed! so calm, that it disturbs
And vexes meditation with its strange
And extreme silentness. Sea, hill, and wood,
This populous village! Sea, and hill, and wood,
With all the numberless goings-on of life,
Inaudible as dreams! the thin blue flame
Lies on my low-burnt fire, and quivers not;
Only that film,° which fluttered on the grate, *soot*
Still flutters there, the sole unquiet thing.
Methinks its motion in this hush of nature
Gives it dim sympathies with me who live,
Making it a companionable form,
Whose puny flaps and freaks the idling Spirit
By its own moods interprets, everywhere
Echo or mirror seeking of itself,
And makes a toy of Thought.
                                        But O! how oft,
How oft, at school, with most believing mind,
Presageful, have I gazed upon the bars,
To watch that fluttering *stranger!* and as oft
With unclosed lids, already had I dreamt

Of my sweet birthplace, and the old church tower,
Whose bells, the poor man's only music, rang
From morn to evening, all the hot fair-day,
So sweetly, that they stirred and haunted me
With a wild pleasure, falling on mine ear
Most like articulate sounds of things to come!
So gazed I, till the soothing things, I dreamt,
Lulled me to sleep, and sleep prolonged my dreams!
And so I brooded all the following morn,
Awed by the stern preceptor's face, mine eye
Fixed with mock study on my swimming book:
Save if the door half opened, and I snatched
A hasty glance, and still my heart leaped up,
For still I hoped to see the *stranger's* face,
Townsman, or aunt, or sister more beloved,
My playmate when we both were clothed alike!

Dear Babe,° that sleepest cradled by my side, *Coleridge's infant son*
Whose gentle breathings, heard in this deep calm,
Fill up the interspersèd vacancies
And momentary pauses of the thought!
My babe so beautiful! it thrills my heart
With tender gladness, thus to look at thee,
And think that thou shalt learn far other lore,
And in far other scenes! For I was reared
In the great city, pent 'mid cloisters dim,
And saw nought lovely but the sky and stars.
But *thou*, my babe! shalt wander like a breeze
By lakes and sandy shores, beneath the crags
Of ancient mountain, and beneath the clouds,
Which image in their bulk both lakes and shores
And mountain crags: so shalt thou see and hear
The lovely shapes and sounds intelligible
Of that eternal language, which thy God
Utters, who from eternity doth teach
Himself in all, and all things in himself.
Great universal Teacher! he shall mold
Thy spirit, and by giving make it ask.

Therefore all seasons shall be sweet to thee,
Whether the summer clothe the general earth
With greenness, or the redbreast sit and sing
Betwixt the tufts of snow on the bare branch
Of mossy apple tree, while the nigh thatch
Smokes in the sun-thaw; whether the eave-drops fall
Heard only in the trances of the blast,
Or if the secret ministry of frost
Shall hang them up in silent icicles,
Quietly shining to the quiet Moon.

BILLY COLLINS

Billy Collins (b. 1941) was born in New York City. He studied at the College of the Holy Cross and at the University of California at Riverside. He returned to the East when his degree was completed, and for many years he has been a professor of English at Lehman College (City University of New York). From 2001 to 2003, he served as the poet laureate of the United States. Collins's most recent collection of poetry is *Ballistics* (2008). Collins has emerged only in recent years as one of the freshest and widely readable contemporary American poets, and behind his almost artless manner is a shrewd literary intelligence, which manages to be erudite and literary at the same time that his speech is as direct as something you might overhear on the street.

"The Only Day in Existence" is a brilliant sustained metaphor of the meaning of a single day in Collins's life. Its theme is suggested by the "ghost" he imagines he sees in the window, which he associates with the appearance of the ghost in Shakespeare's *Hamlet*. This suggests to him a classroom lecture, and it is this day itself that is the lecture, which he will study as he sits "in the wooden chair of his life."

"Memento Mori," with its image of the poet's reading lamp coming to his funeral, its cord dragging behind, is a startling example of Collins's use of personification. "To-day" captures the exuberance anyone feels at a perfect spring day, though most of us would probably not be tempted to smash a paperweight to let the small figures inside walk out into the sunlight.

WEB Research Billy Collins at bedfordstmartins.com/rewritinglit.

The Only Day in Existence 1998

The morning sun is so pale
I could be looking at a ghost
in the shape of a window,
a tall, rectangular spirit
peering down at me now in my bed,
about to demand that I avenge
the murder of my father.
But this light is only the first line
in the five-act play of this day—
the only day in existence—
or the opening chord of its long song,
or think of what is permeating
these thin bedroom curtains

as the beginning of a lecture
I must listen to until dark,
a curious student in a V-neck sweater,
angled into the wooden chair of his life,
ready with notebook and a chewed-up pencil,
quiet as a goldfish in winter,
serious as a compass at sea,
eager to absorb whatever lesson

this damp, overcast Tuesday
has to teach me,
here in the spacious classroom of the world
with its long walls of glass,
its heavy, low-hung ceiling.

Memento Mori

1991

There is no need for me to keep a skull on my desk,
to stand with one foot up on the ruins of Rome,
or to wear a locket with a sliver of a saint's bone.

It is enough to realize that every common object
in this small sunny room will outlive me—
the mirror, radio, bookstand and rocker.

Not one of these things will attend my burial,
not even this battered goosenecked lamp
with its steady, silent benediction of light,
though I could put worse things in my mind
than the image of it waddling across the cemetery
like an old servant, dragging the tail of its cord,
the small circle of mourners parting to make room.

Today

2002

If ever there were a spring day so perfect,
so uplifted by a warm intermittent breeze

that it made you want to throw
open all the windows in the house

and unlatch the door to the canary's cage,
indeed, rip the little door from its jamb,

a day when the cool brick paths
and the garden bursting with peonies

seemed so etched in sunlight
that you felt like taking

a hammer to the glass paperweight
on the living room end table,

releasing the inhabitants
from their snow-covered cottage

so they could walk out,
holding hands and squinting

into this larger dome of blue and white,
well, today is just that kind of day.

e. e. cummings

e. e. cummings (1894–1962) was born Edward Estlin Cummings in Cambridge, Massachusetts. His father was a Unitarian minister who taught sociology at Harvard. As a Harvard undergraduate, cummings wrote conventional verse, but under the influence of the poet and critic Ezra Pound, his poetry became less sentimental and more sharply satiric.

In 1917 he went to France with a friend to join the Red Cross Ambulance Corps, but he was careless in comments he made about the French army in letters home, forgetting that mail was censored. He was arrested by the French authorities and imprisoned for treason. His father, however, had important government connections and succeeded in getting cummings released after four months of detention. The experience became the subject of cummings's sardonic, exuberant book, *The Enormous Room*, which appeared in 1922.

When cummings's poetry began to appear in the mid-1920s, it incited considerable controversy, not only for his experimental techniques of breaking up words and punctuation, but also for his eroticism and his irreverence toward the heroism of World War I. He justified his poetic experiments by saying that he was searching for a way to express the ecstasy of life. As he described it in the introduction to his *Collected Poems* (1938), "We can never be born enough." In 1933 he traveled to the Soviet Union, and, characteristically, he was bored and disappointed with the Soviet social experiment.

Also a painter, cummings spent much of his life writing and painting in a small house in Greenwich Village. The love poem "somewhere i have never travelled" is a brilliantly free variation on the form of the sonnet. The elegy "Buffalo Bill 's" is one of his best-known poems. "goodby Betty, don't remember me" is a poem from his youthful years in Paris. "In Just-" is an example of his poetic technique at its freshest and most expressive.

WEB Research e. e. cummings at bedfordstmartins.com/rewritinglit.

somewhere i have never travelled 1931

somewhere i have never travelled,gladly beyond
any experience,your eyes have their silence:
in your most frail gesture are things which enclose me,
or which i cannot touch because they are too near

your slightest look easily will unclose me
though i have closed myself as fingers,
you open always petal by petal myself as Spring opens
(touching skilfully,mysteriously)her first rose

or if your wish be to close me,i and
my life will shut very beautifully,suddenly,
as when the heart of this flower imagines
the snow carefully everywhere descending;

nothing which we are to perceive in this world equals
the power of your intense fragility:whose texture
compels me with the colour of its countries,
rendering death and forever with each breathing
(i do not know what it is about you that closes
and opens;only something in me understands
the voice of your eyes is deeper than all roses)
nobody,not even the rain,has such small hands

Buffalo Bill 's° 1923

Buffalo Bill 's
defunct
                who used to
                ride a watersmooth-silver
                                                                stallion
and break onetwothreefourfive pigeonsjustlikethat
                                                                                                Jesus
he was a handsome man
                                                and what i want to know is
how do you like your blueeyed boy
Mister Death

goodby Betty, don't remember me 1922

goodby Betty, don't remember me
pencil your eyes dear and have a good time
with the tall tight boys at Tabari'
s, keep your teeth snowy, stick to beer and lime,
wear dark, and where your meeting breasts are round
have roses darling, it's all i ask of you—
but that when light fails and this sweet profound
Paris moves with lovers, two and two
bound for themselves, when passionately dusk
brings softly down the perfume of the world
(and just as smaller stars begin to husk
heaven) you, you exactly paled and curled
with mystic lips take twilight where i know:
proving to Death that Love is so and so.

Buffalo Bill 's: William Frederick Cody (1846–1917), known as Buffalo Bill, was a frontier scout who put together a "Wild West" show that was the most popular show in America for thirty years.

in Just- 1923

in Just-
spring   when the world is mud-
luscious the little
lame balloonman
whistles   far   and wee
and eddieandbill come
running from marbles and
piracies and it's
spring
when the world is puddle-wonderful
the queer
old balloonman whistles
far   and   wee
and bettyandisbel come dancing
from hop-scotch and jump-rope and
it's
spring
and
    the
        goat-footed
balloonMan   whistles
far
and
wee

JOHN DONNE

John Donne (1572–1631) was born a Roman Catholic during a period in English history when Roman Catholics were harassed by the Protestant government and were barred from advancement to most major positions of influence. His father died when he was four, and he was left with enough income to live well but not enough to purchase favor at the court of Queen Elizabeth. He studied at Oxford and Cambridge universities but earned no degrees.

In his early twenties, Donne lived like many other young, ambitious courtiers. He had many mistresses, traveled extensively in Europe, and took part in two raids against the Spanish at Cadiz and in the Azores. At the same time he read voraciously and wrote some of his most vivid erotic poetry. He had renounced his Catholicism but still hesitated to join the Church of England.

In 1598, when he was twenty-six, Donne became private secretary to Sir Thomas Egerton, one of the most powerful figures in the court of Queen Elizabeth. A brilliant future seemed certain, but three years later Donne fell deeply in love and secretly married Ann More, the seventeen-year-old niece of Lady Egerton. He was dismissed and thrown into prison, and for a dozen years he struggled against disappointment and financial difficulties. During this period his marriage was his only source of happiness.

Because of his brilliance and his early friendships, Donne was still welcome in the court, but King James, who succeeded Elizabeth, felt that Donne could be most useful to him in the church, and refused to consider granting Donne any other position. Donne finally surrendered and in 1615 became an Anglican priest. He was as talented in the church as he had been in court life, and in 1621 he became dean of St. Paul's Cathedral in London, where he delivered sermons and wrote devotional poetry and meditations until his death. His "Meditation XVII" includes this enduring passage:

> No man is an island, entire of itself; every man is a piece of the continent, a part of the main. If a clod be washed away by the sea, Europe is the less, as well as if a promontory were, as well as if a manor of thy friend's or of thine own were: any man's death diminishes me, because I am involved in mankind, and therefore never send to know for whom the bells tolls; it tolls for thee.

This selection of Donne's poetry includes one of his idiosyncratic love poems, "The Sun Rising." "A Valediction: Forbidding Mourning," written earlier, was composed for his wife before he left her on a trip to France. "The Flea" is a vivid erotic fantasy that has long intrigued its readers. "Batter my heart, three-personed God" is from his collection of "Holy Sonnets." (See also Donne's "Death, be not proud" on p. 766.)

CONNECTION Wendy Cope, "The fine English poet, John Donne," page 780.

WEB Research John Donne at bedfordstmartins.com/rewritinglit.

A Valediction:° Forbidding Mourning 1611

As virtuous men pass mildly away,
  And whisper to their souls to go,
Whilst some of their sad friends do say
  The breath goes now, and some say, no;

So let us melt, and make no noise,
  No tear-floods, nor sigh-tempests move,
'Twere profanation of our joys
  To tell the laity° our love.

Moving of th' earth brings harms and fears,
  Men reckon what it did and meant;
But trepidation of the spheres,°
  Though greater far, is innocent.

Valediction: A departure speech or discourse; a bidding of farewell. **8. laity:** Common people. **11. trepidation of the spheres:** A trembling of the celestial spheres, hypothesized by Ptolemaic astronomers to account for unpredicted variations in the paths of the heavenly bodies.

Dull sublunary° lovers' love
(Whose soul is sense) cannot admit
Absence, because it doth remove
Those things which elemented° it. *composed*

But we by a love so much refined
That our selves know not what it is,
Inter-assurèd of the mind,
Care less, eyes, lips, and hands to miss.

Our two souls therefore, which are one,
Though I must go, endure not yet
A breach, but an expansion,
Like gold to airy thinness beat.

If they be two, they are two so
As stiff twin compasses are two;
Thy soul, the fixed foot, makes no show
To move, but doth, if th' other do.

And though it in the center sit,
Yet when the other far doth roam,
It leans and hearkens after it,
And grows erect, as that comes home.

Such wilt thou be to me, who must
Like th' other foot, obliquely° run. *diagonally, aslant*
Thy firmness makes my circle° just,
And makes me end where I begun.

The Sun Rising 1633

Busy old fool, unruly sun,
Why dost thou thus
Through windows and through curtains call on us?
Must to thy motions lovers' seasons run
Saucy pedantic wretch, go chide
Late schoolboys and sour prentices,
Go tell court-huntsmen that the king will ride,
Call country ants to harvest offices;
Love, all alike, no season knows nor clime,
Nor hours, days, months, which are the rags of time.

Thy beams, so reverent and strong,
Why shouldst thou think?
I could eclipse and cloud them with a wink,
But that I would not lose her sight so long;

13. sublunary: Beneath the moon; earthly, hence, changeable. **35. circle:** The circle was a symbol of perfection; with a dot in the middle, it was also the alchemist's symbol for gold.

If her eyes have not blinded thine,
Look, and to-morrow late tell me
Whether both the Indias of spice and mine
Be where thou left'st them or lie here with me.
Ask for those kings whom thou saw'st yesterday,
And thou shalt hear all here in one bed lay.

She is all states and all princes I;
Nothing else is.
Princes do but play us; compared to this,
All honour's mimic; all wealth alchemy.
Thou sun art half as happy as we,
In that the world's contracted thus;
Thine age asks ease, and since thy duties be
To warm the world, that's done in warming us.
Shine here to us, and thou art everywhere;
This bed thy centre is, these walls thy sphere.

The Flea 1633

Mark but this flea, and mark in this,
How little that which thou deniest me is;
Me it sucked first, and now sucks thee,
And in this flea our two bloods mingled be;
Thou know'st that this cannot be said
A sin, or shame, or loss of maidenhead,
Yet this enjoys before it woo,
And pampered swells with one blood made of two,
And this, alas, is more than we would do.

Oh stay, three lives in one flea spare,
Where we almost, nay more than married are.
This flea is you and I, and this
Our mariage bed and mariage temple is;
Though parents grudge, and you, we are met,
And cloisterd in these living walls of jet.
Though use make you apt to kill me,
Let not to that, self-murder added be,
And sacrilege, three sins in killing three.

Cruel and sudden, hast thou since
Purpled thy nail in blood of innocence?
Wherein could this flea guilty be,
Except in that drop which it sucked from thee?
Yet thou triumph'st, and say'st that thou
Find'st not thy self, nor me the weaker now;
'Tis true; then learn how false, fears be:
Just so much honor, when thou yield'st to me,
Will waste, as this flea's death took life from thee.

Batter my heart, three-personed God

1633

Batter my heart, three-personed God; for You
As yet but knock, breathe, shine, and seek to mend;
That I may rise and stand, o'erthrow me,'and bend
Your force to break, blow, burn, and make me new.
I, like an usurped town, to'another due,
Labor to'admit You, but O, to no end;
Reason, Your viceroy'in me, me should defend,
But is captívcd, and proves weak or untrue.
Yet dearly'I love You,'and would be lovéd fain,
But am betrothed unto Your enemy.
Divorce me,'untie or break that knot again;
Take me to You, imprison me, for I,
Except You'enthrall me, never shall be free,
Nor ever chaste, except You ravish me.

RITA DOVE

Rita Dove (b. 1952) was born in Akron, Ohio, in an African American family who believed that the way out of the American racial dilemma was education. As Dove later wrote, "Education was the key: that much we knew, and so I was a good student. . . . I adored learning new things and looked forward to what intellectual adventures each school day would bring; some of the luckiest magic was to open a book and to come away the wiser after having been lost in the pages."

She graduated summa cum laude from Miami University in Ohio in 1973 and traveled abroad on a Fulbright/Hayes fellowship to study modern European literature at the University of Tübingen, in Germany. After two years in Germany, she returned to the United States and completed her M.F.A. at the University of Iowa in 1977. In Iowa she met and married German novelist Fred Viebahn. Her years in Europe and her marriage have given her writing an international flavor and a broad cultural outlook. Her first poetry collection, *Museum*, was published in 1983, when she was thirty-one. She was immediately recognized as an important new voice in American poetry and was awarded the Pulitzer Prize in 1986 for *Thomas and Beulah* (1986), a suite of biographical poems with her grandparents' lives as the central narrative. From 1993 to 1995, she was the poet laureate of the United States, the first African American, the first woman, and the youngest writer to be chosen for this honor. She is the Commonwealth Professor of English at the University of Virginia at Charlottesville, where she teaches creative writing.

The writers Michael S. Harper and Anthony Walton, in their *Vintage Book of African American Poetry* (2000), praised her work for its energy and elegance. "Her talent for disclosing vibrant inner images in elegant phrasing gives her lines their force and balance, ranking Dove's poems as among the finest of her era." "Singsong" and "The Pond, Porch-View: Six P.M., Early Spring" are from her collection *On the Bus with Rosa Parks* (1999).

WEB Research Rita Dove at bedfordstmartins.com/rewritinglit.

Singsong 1998

When I was young, the moon spoke in riddles
and the stars rhymed. I was a new toy
waiting for my owner to pick me up.

When I was young, I ran the day to its knees.
There were trees to swing on, crickets for capture.

I was narrowly sweet, infinitely cruel,
tongued in honey and coddled in milk,
sunburned and silvery and scabbed like a colt.

And the world was already old.
And I was older than I am today.

The Pond, Porch-View: Six P.M., Early Spring 1999

I sit, and sit, and will my thoughts
the way they used to wend
when thoughts were young
(i.e., accused of wandering).
The sunset ticks another notch
into the pressure treated rails
of the veranda. My heart, too,
has come down to earth;
I've missed the chance
to put things in reverse,
recapture childhood's backseat
universe. Where I'm at now
is more like riding on a bus
through unfamiliar neighborhoods—
chair in recline, the view chopped square
and dimming quick. I know
I vowed I'd get off
somewhere grand; like that dear goose
come honking down
from Canada, I tried to end up
anyplace but here.
Who am I kidding? Here I am.

T. S. ELIOT

T. S. Eliot (1888–1965) was born Thomas Stearns Eliot in St. Louis, Missouri. His mother was a schoolteacher who also wrote poetry, and his father was a successful businessman. Eliot was sent to finish his education at Milton Academy, south of Boston, and then attended Harvard College.

Following his graduation from Harvard in 1910, he spent a year in France studying at the Sorbonne and became intensely interested in the writing of a brilliant group of contemporary French poets who called themselves *symbolists.* When he returned to Harvard to earn his doctorate the next year, he began writing "The Love Song of J. Alfred Prufrock," a poem that included phrases and attitudes translated from the work of symbolist poets Jules Laforgue and Arthur Rimbaud. Conrad Aiken, a fellow student who was also a poet, encouraged him to publish it, but Eliot waited until he returned to Europe in 1914 and was studying at Oxford. He read the poem to Ezra Pound, who immediately sent it to an American magazine. It is considered by most critics to be the first modernist poem written in English.

In 1915 Eliot suddenly married Vivian Haigh-Wood, whom he had met in England, and had to find some kind of job to support them. He was first a schoolteacher, then a bank clerk, and finally a director in a London publishing house. With the publication in 1922 of his controversial long poem *The Wasteland*—a work begun during a stay in a sanatorium brought about by exhaustion, marital difficulties, and depression—he became one of the world's most widely read and discussed younger poets. His writing, both as a poet and a literary critic, had a decisive effect on nearly every poetic tradition before World War II. He became a British citizen in 1927. In 1948 he won the Nobel Prize for literature.

CONNECTION J. Walker, "On T. S. Eliot's 'Prufrock,'" page 780.

WEB Research T. S. Eliot at bedfordstmartins.com/rewritinglit.

The Love Song of J. Alfred Prufrock 1917

S'io credesse che mia risposta fosse
A persona che mai tornasse al mondo,
Questa fiamma staria senza piu scosse.
Ma perciocche giammai di questo fondo
Non torno vivo alcun, s'i'odo il vero,
Sensa tema d'infamia ti rispondo.°

S'io . . . rispondo: In Dante's *Inferno,* these lines are spoken by one of the "false counselors" whose soul is hidden within a flame that moves as it speaks: "If I believed my reply were given / to one who might ever return to the earth, this fire would cease further movement. / But as from this chasm / none has ever come back alive—if what I have heard is true— / without fearing infamy will I respond to you."

Let us go then, you and I,
When the evening is spread out against the sky
Like a patient etherized upon a table;
Let us go, through certain half-deserted streets,
The muttering retreats
Of restless nights in one-night cheap hotels
And sawdust restaurants with oyster-shells:
Streets that follow like a tedious argument
Of insidious intent
To lead you to an overwhelming question . . .
Oh, do not ask, "What is it?"
Let us go and make our visit.

In the room the women come and go
Talking of Michelangelo.

The yellow fog that rubs its back upon the window-panes
The yellow smoke that rubs its muzzle on the window-panes
Licked its tongue into the corners of the evening,
Lingered upon the pools that stand in drains,
Let fall upon its back the soot that falls from chimneys,
Slipped by the terrace, made a sudden leap,
And seeing that it was a soft October night,
Curled once about the house, and fell asleep.

And indeed there will be time
For the yellow smoke that slides along the street,
Rubbing its back upon the window-panes;
There will be time, there will be time
To prepare a face to meet the faces that you meet;
There will be time to murder and create,
And time for all the works and days of hands
That lift and drop a question on your plate;
Time for you and time for me,
And time yet for a hundred indecisions,
And for a hundred visions and revisions,
Before the taking of a toast and tea.

In the room the women come and go
Talking of Michelangelo.

And indeed there will be time
To wonder, "Do I dare?" and, "Do I dare?"
Time to turn back and descend the stair,
With a bald spot in the middle of my hair—
(They will say: "How his hair is growing thin!")
My morning coat, my collar mounting firmly to the chin,
My necktie rich and modest, but asserted by a simple pin—
(They will say: "But how his arms and legs are thin!")
Do I dare
Disturb the universe?

In a minute there is time
For decisions and revisions which a minute will reverse.

For I have known them all already, known them all:
Have known the evenings, mornings, afternoons,
I have measured out my life with coffee spoons;
I know the voices dying with a dying fall
Beneath the music from a farther room.
So how should I presume?

And I have known the eyes already, known them all—
The eyes that fix you in a formulated phrase,
And when I am formulated, sprawling on a pin,
When I am pinned and wriggling on the wall,
Then how should I begin
To spit out all the butt-ends of my days and ways?
And how should I presume?

And I have known the arms already, known them all—
Arms that are braceleted and white and bare
(But in the lamplight, downed with light brown hair!)
Is it perfume from a dress
That makes me so digress?
Arms that lie along a table, or wrap about a shawl.
And should I then presume?
And how should I begin?

Shall I say, I have gone at dusk through narrow streets
And watched the smoke that rises from the pipes
Of lonely men in shirt-sleeves, leaning out of windows? . . .

I should have been a pair of ragged claws
Scuttling across the floors of silent seas.

And the afternoon, the evening, sleeps so peacefully!
Smoothed by long fingers,
Asleep . . . tired . . . or it malingers,
Stretched on the floor, here beside you and me.
Should I, after tea and cakes and ices,
Have the strength to force the moment to its crisis?
But though I have wept and fasted, wept and prayed,
Though I have seen my head (grown slightly bald) brought in upon a
platter,°
I am no prophet—and here's no great matter;
I have seen the moment of my greatness flicker,
And I have seen the eternal Footman hold my coat, and snicker,
And in short, I was afraid.

82. upon a platter: A reference to the martyrdom of St. John the Baptist (Matthew 14:1–12).

And would it have been worth it, after all,
After the cups, the marmalade, the tea,
Among the porcelain, among some talk of you and me,
Would it have been worth while,
To have bitten off the matter with a smile,
To have squeezed the universe into a ball
To roll it toward some overwhelming question,
To say: "I am Lazarus,° come from the dead,
Come back to tell you all, I shall tell you all"—
If one, settling a pillow by her head,
    Should say: "That is not what I meant at all.
    That is not it, at all."

And would it have been worth it, after all,
Would it have been worth while,
After the sunsets and the dooryards and the sprinkled streets,
After the novels, after the teacups, after the skirts that trail along the
        floor—
And this, and so much more?—
It is impossible to say just what I mean!
But as if a magic lantern threw the nerves in patterns on a screen:
Would it have been worth while
If one, settling a pillow or throwing off a shawl,
And turning toward the window, should say:
    "That is not it at all,
    That is not what I meant, at all."

No! I am not Prince Hamlet, nor was meant to be;
Am an attendant lord, one that will do
To swell a progress, start a scene or two,
Advise the prince; no doubt, an easy tool,
Deferential, glad to be of use,
Politic, cautious, and meticulous;
Full of high sentence, but a bit obtuse;
At times, indeed, almost ridiculous—
Almost, at times, the Fool.

I grow old . . . I grow old . . .
I shall wear the bottoms of my trousers rolled.

Shall I part my hair behind? Do I dare to eat a peach?
I shall wear white flannel trousers, and walk upon the beach.
I have heard the mermaids singing, each to each.

I do not think that they will sing to me.

94. "I am Lazarus: A reference to the resurrected Lazarus (John II, 12:1–2).

I have seen them riding seaward on the waves
Combing the white hair of the waves blown back
When the wind blows the water white and black.

We have lingered in the chambers of the sea
By sea-girls wreathed with seaweed red and brown
Till human voices wake us, and we drown.

COMMENTARY

CLEANTH BROOKS AND ROBERT PENN WARREN

Cleanth Brooks and Robert Penn Warren (the literary critic and the American poet) discussed in their groundbreaking textbook *Understanding Poetry* (1938) T. S. Eliot's major early poem from the perspective of New Criticism, an approach that emphasizes close reading of the formal properties of literary works.

On Eliot's "The Love Song of J. Alfred Prufrock" 1938

The character of Prufrock, as we shall see, is really very much like that of Hamlet—a man who is apparently betrayed by his possession of such qualities as intellect and imagination. But it is particularly dangerous to attempt to portray, and make the audience believe in and take seriously, such a person as Prufrock. We are inclined to laugh at the person who is really so painfully self-conscious that he is inhibited from all action. Moreover, in so far as the poet is using Prufrock as a character typical of our age, he must in fairness to truth avoid treating him quite so heroically as a Hamlet. At the very beginning, therefore, the poet faces a difficult problem. In using the materials of the present, the desire to be accurate, to be thoroughly truthful, forces him to exhibit the character as not purely romantic or tragic. And yet there is in such a person as he describes a very real tragedy. How shall he treat him? To attempt to treat Prufrock in full seriousness is doomed to failure; on the other hand, to make him purely comic is to falsify matters too.

Faced with this problem, the poet resorts to irony, and by employing varying shades of irony he is able to do justice to the ludicrous elements in the situation and yet do justice to the serious ones also. The casual and careless reader will probably see only the comic aspects: he will be likely to fail to appreciate the underlying seriousness of the whole poem.

The title itself gives us the first clue to the fact that the poem is ironical. We think of a love song as simple and full of warm emotion. But this poem opens on a scene where the streets

. . . follow like a tedious argument
Of insidious intent
To lead you to an overwhelming question. . . .

One notices also that the character Prufrock is continually interested in stating that "there will be time" to make up his mind. But in saying that there will be time for this, he is so hopelessly unable to act that he continues in a sort of abstracted and unconscious patter to state that there will be time

> For the yellow smoke that slides along the street,
> Rubbing its back upon the window-panes;
> There will be time, there will be time
> To prepare a face to meet the faces that you meet;
> There will be time to murder and create,
> And time for all the works and days of hands
> That lift and drop a question on your plate.

Then, caught up by the irrelevance of his patter, he goes on to say that there will be time—not for decisions—but, ironically, for a "hundred indecisions," and for a "hundred visions and revisions."

The first part of the poem, then, can be imagined as the monologue of Prufrock himself as he finds his indecisiveness reflected in the apparently aimless streets of the city and in the fog which hangs over the city. It is filled with a rather bitter self-irony, a self-irony which is reflected in some of the abrupt transitions. But in observing this ironical monologue which illuminates the character, one has missed the point entirely if he has failed to see the psychological penetration in it. Take, for example, the tone and associations of the comparison of the evening to a "patient etherized upon a table." This comparison is "in character." It is an appropriate observation for Prufrock, being what he is, though it might not be very appropriate for an entirely different character or in a poem of entirely different tone. The evening—not any evening, but this particular evening, as seen by this particular observer—does seem to have the hushed quiet of the perfectly, and yet fatally relaxed, body of a person under ether.

Or notice also the psychological penetration of the remark, "To prepare a face to meet the faces that you meet." Again, the remark must be taken in character. Yet it is possible to observe, as a general truth, that we do prepare a face, an expression, a look, to meet the various "faces" that we meet—faces which have duly undergone a like preparation. A poorer poet would have written "To put on a mask to meet the people that you meet." Eliot's line with its concentration and its slight ironical shock is far superior. . . .

After the opening sections in which the character of the speaker is to some extent established for the reader, Prufrock describes a scene in which overcultured, bored women sip tea and discuss art. It is as though he had just stepped inside after wandering alone in the streets. Here are the people of whose criticism Prufrock is most afraid, and yet, as his characterization of them abundantly shows, he sees their shallowness. But Prufrock does not attempt to treat romantically or heroically his own character: he is able to see the ludicrous aspect of himself, his timid preciseness and vanity.

> With a bald spot in the middle of my hair—
> (They will say: "How his hair is growing thin!")
> My necktie rich and modest, but asserted by a simple pin.

But what is the function of a statement so abrupt as "I have measured out my life with coffee spoons"? Here again, the line must be taken in character. But if we are willing to take it in character, we shall be able to see that it is brilliantly ironical. It would mean literally, one supposes, that he has measured out his life in little driblets, coffee spoons being tiny in size. But it carries another and more concrete meaning: namely, that he has spent his life in just such an environment as this drawing room which he is describing. The comparison makes the same ironical point, therefore, as the lines

> And time yet for a hundred indecisions,
> And for a hundred visions and revisions,
> Before the taking of a toast and tea.

The poem's sense of fidelity to the whole situation—its willingness to take into account so many apparently discordant views and points of view—is shown in the lines

> Arms that are braceleted and white and bare
> (But in the lamplight, downed with light brown hair!)

These lines give us a contrast between what might be termed loosely the romantic and the realistic attitude. The ironical comment here parallels exactly the reference to his own bald head.

The structure of the poem is, as we have noticed, that of a sort of monologue in which the poet describes this scene or that and comments on them, and, by means of them, on himself. The irrelevance, or apparent irrelevance, is exactly the sort of irrelevance and abrupt transition which is often admired in a personal essay by a writer like Charles Lamb. The structure is essentially the same here (though of course with an entirely different tone and for a different effect). But having seen what the structure is—not a logical structure, or one following the lines of a narrative, or one based on the description of a scene, but the structure of the flow of ideas—the reader is not puzzled at the rather abrupt transition from the stanza about the arms to

> Shall I say, I have gone at dusk through narrow streets,

etc. It is a scene from the beginning of the poem—or perhaps it is a scene viewed earlier and brought back to memory by the statement about the streets and the smoke in the opening lines of the poem. It is the sort of scene which has a very real poignance about it. Prufrock feels that it meant something. But he is utterly incapable of stating the meaning before the bored and sophisticated audience of the world to which he belongs. He would be laughed at as a fool. And then comes the thought—apparently irrelevant, but the sort of thought which might easily occur in such a monologue:

> I should have been a pair of ragged claws
> Scuttling across the floors of silent seas.

A crab is about as vivid a symbol as one might find, for a person who is completely self-sufficing and cannot be, and does not need to be, sociable. And there is, moreover, a secondary implication of irony here growing out of Prufrock's disgust with these people about him and with himself: the crab is at least "alive" and has, as Prufrock does not have, a meaning and a place in its world. (Observe that the poet does not use the word *crab.* Why? Because in mentioning the most prominent feature of the crab, the claws, and with the vivid description of the effect of the crab's swimming, "scuttling," he makes the point more sharply.)

There are several literary allusions in the latter part of the poem, allusions which we must know in order to understand the poem. . . . Can they be justified? And if so, how? In the first place, they are fairly commonly known: an allusion to John the Baptist's head having been cut off at Herod's orders and brought in on a platter; an allusion to the raising of Lazarus from the dead; and a reference to Shakespeare's *Hamlet.* The poet has not imposed a very heavy burden on us, therefore, in expecting that we shall know these references. But what can be said by way of justification? In the first place, all the allusions are "in character." They are comparisons which would normally occur to such a person as Prufrock, and they would naturally occur in the sort of meditation in which he indulges in this poem. In the second place, they do a great deal to sharpen the irony in the poem. Prufrock is vividly conscious of the sorry figure which he cuts in comparison with the various great figures from the past or from literature whom, in a far-off sense, he resembles. He has seen his reputation picked to pieces—his head, a slightly bald head, brought in on a platter like that of John the Baptist. But *he* is no prophet—nothing is lost. Death itself in this society can be regarded as nothing more than a liveried footman, putting on the coats of the departing, and death, like the knowing and insolent footman, is quite capable, he believes, of snickering behind his back.

LOUISE GLÜCK

Louise Glück (b. 1943) was born in New York City, where her father was a business executive. She grew up on Long Island and later studied at Sarah Lawrence College and received her B.A. from Columbia University in 1965.

Glück's first book, *Firstborn,* was published in 1968, and it established her themes of family and her personal life. The critic Helen Vendler has said of Glück's poems,

> She sees experience from very far off, almost through the end of a telescope, transparently removed in space or time. It is this removal which gives such mythological power . . . to the account of her parents' lives and of her own childhood, and makes their family constellation into a universal one.

Glück"s book *Ararat* (1990), which was in part an emotional response to her father's death, won the Library of Congress's Rebekah Johnson Bobbitt National Prize for Poetry. Another collection of her poetry, *The Wild Iris* (1992), received the Pulitzer Prize. More recently, she has written *A Village Life: Poems* (2009) and served as the U.S. poet laureate from 2003 to 2004. She is currently a writer-in-residence at Yale University.

Although Glück's early poetry was often shadowed by an effort to understand her unhappy childhood, more recent poems suggest that she has come to accept the complexities of her own experience.

First Memory 1990

Long ago, I was wounded. I lived
to revenge myself
against my father, not
for what he was—
for what I was: from the beginning of time,
in childhood, I thought
that pain meant
I was not loved.
It meant I loved.

Happiness 1976

A man and woman lie on a white bed.
It is morning. I think
Soon they will waken.
On the bedside table is a vase
of lilies; sunlight
pools in their throats.
I watch him turn to her
as though to speak her name
but silently, deep in her mouth—
At the window ledge,
once, twice,
a bird calls.
And then she stirs; her body
fills with his breath.

I open my eyes; you are watching me.
Almost over this room
the sun is gliding.
Look at your face, you say,
holding your own close to me
to make a mirror.
How calm you are. And the burning wheel
passes gently over us.

SEAMUS HEANEY

Seamus Heaney (b. 1939) was born in Ireland, in Castledown in County Kerry. He grew up in a small farming community, and this has shaped his writing and his outlook on the world. He trained as a teacher and after teaching in a secondary school for a year he returned to the university and completed his studies in English at Queen's

College in Belfast. Belfast is the capital of Northern Ireland, and Heaney has spent his life in the midst of the violent struggle for political power between the province's Catholic minority and Protestant majority. He became a lecturer at Queen's College and in 1966 his first collection, *Death of a Naturalist*, appeared.

In the years since then, Heaney has continued to teach, to study the work of other poets, and to write. He has won nearly every major literary prize in England and Ireland and was awarded the Nobel Prize in 1995. For extended periods he has been a guest lecturer at Harvard University and Oxford University. As an Irish writer who is also a Catholic he has felt considerable pressure to become engaged in the effort of the Irish minority in the north to end the ties between the Protestant majority, which is largely of Scottish descent, and England, which maintains the status quo with a large military force. Although he is sympathetic to the Catholic minority's aims, he is deeply disturbed by the use of violence by the IRA, the underground Irish Republican Army. He has written poems that lament that situation, but he has also insisted that this is not the role of poetry. As he wrote in his essay "The Redress of Poetry," "Poetry cannot afford to lose its fundamentally self-delighting inventiveness, its joy in being a process of language as well as a representation of things in the world."

"Digging" and "Mid-Term Break" are two of his most frequently anthologized poems.

WEB Research Seamus Heaney at bedfordstmartins.com/rewritinglit.

Digging

1966

Between my finger and my thumb
The squat pen rests; snug as a gun.

Under my window, a clean rasping sound
When the spade sinks into gravelly ground:
My father, digging. I look down
Till his straining rump among the flowerbeds
Bends low, comes up twenty years away
Stooping in rhythm through potato drills°
Where he was digging.

The coarse boot nestled on the lug, the shaft
Against the inside knee was levered firmly.
He rooted out tall tops, buried the bright edge deep
To scatter new potatoes that we picked
Loving their cool hardness in our hands.

By god, the old man could handle a spade.
Just like his old man.

8. drills: Furrows in which seeds are sown.

My grandfather cut more turf° in a day
Than any other man on Toner's bog.
Once I carried him milk in a bottle
Corked sloppily with paper. He straightened up
To drink it, then fell to right away
Nicking and slicing neatly, heaving sods
Over his shoulder, going down and down
For the good turf. Digging.

The cold smell of potato mould, the squelch and slap
Of soggy peat, the curt cuts of an edge
Through living roots awaken in my head.
But I've no spade to follow men like them.

Between my finger and my thumb
The squat pen rests.
I'll dig with it.

Mid-Term Break 1966

I sat all morning in the college sick bay
Counting bells knelling classes to a close.
At two o'clock our neighbors drove me home.

In the porch I met my father crying—
He had always taken funerals in his stride—
And Big Jim Evans saying it was a hard blow.

The baby cooed and laughed and rocked the pram
When I came in, and I was embarrassed
By old men standing up to shake my hand

And tell me they were "sorry for my trouble."
Whispers informed strangers I was the eldest,
Away at school, as my mother held my hand

In hers and coughed out angry tearless sighs.
At ten o'clock the ambulance arrived
With the corpse, stanched and bandaged by the nurses.

Next morning I went up into the room. Snowdrops
And candles soothed the bedside; I saw him
For the first time in six weeks. Paler now,

Wearing a poppy bruise on his left temple,
He lay in the four foot box as in his cot.
No gaudy scars, the bumper knocked him clear.

A four foot box, a foot for every year.

---

17. turf: Bricks of peat used for fuel.

GERARD MANLEY HOPKINS

Gerard Manley Hopkins (1844–1889) was born in Essex, outside of London. As a student at Oxford he studied classic Greek and Roman literature and also was influenced by a religious revival movement that led him to convert from Protestantism to become a Roman Catholic, and eventually a Jesuit priest. His superiors were uncomfortable with his intellectual background, and he spent several years in working-class parishes until he was appointed a professor of Greek at University College in Dublin in 1877.

Hopkins was also a talented musician and painter, but he put aside his art and writing for the church. When he was ordained, he burned all the poems he had written. He found it impossible to give up poetry, however, and he began to write again when he was in his thirties. Hopkins never pursued publication, and his poems were left in their original manuscript form when he died. It was only after they were published some thirty years later that his genius was recognized.

Since Hopkins was not interested in publishing he could experiment with rhyme and diction in his writing, and his poems still startle readers more than a hundred years after they were written. As a musician he was interested in meter, and he developed a metric form he called "sprung rhythm," which counted the accents of each line by stress rather than syllable. As he described his poetic method in a letter to a friend, "No doubt my poetry errs on the side of oddness. . . . But as air, melody, is what strikes me most of all in music, and design in painting, so design, pattern, or what I am in the habit of calling *inscape* is what above all I aim at in poetry."

"The Windhover," "Pied Beauty," "God's Grandeur," and "Thou art indeed just, Lord" were published in 1918.

WEB Research Gerard Manley Hopkins at bedfordstmartins.com/rewritinglit.

The Windhover

1877

To Christ our Lord

I caught this morning morning's minion, king-
    dom of daylight's dauphin, dapple-dawn-drawn Falcon, in his riding
    Of the rolling level underneath him steady air, and striding
High there, how he rung upon the rein of a wimpling wing
In his ecstasy! then off, off forth on swing,
    As a skate's heel sweeps smooth on a bow-bend: the hurl and gliding
    Rebuffed the big wind. My heart in hiding
Stirred for a bird,—the achieve of, the mastery of the thing!
Brute beauty and valour and act, oh, air, pride, plume, here

Buckle! AND the fire that breaks from thee then, a billion
Times told lovelier, more dangerous, O my chevalier!

No wonder of it: shéer plód makes plough down sillion° *furrow*
Shine, and blue-bleak embers, ah my dear,
Fall, gall themselves, and gash gold-vermilion.

Pied Beauty
1877

Glory be to God for dappled things—
For skies of couple-colour as a brinded cow;
For rose-moles all in stipple upon trout that swim;
Fresh-firecoal chestnut-falls; finches' wings;
Landscape plotted and pieced—fold, fallow, and plough;
And áll trádes, their gear and tackle and trim.

All things counter, original, spare, strange;
Whatever is fickle, freckled (who knows how?)
With swift, slow; sweet, sour; adazzle, dim;
He fathers-forth whose beauty is past change:
Praise him.

God's Grandeur
1877

The world is charged with the grandeur of God.
It will flame out, like shining from shook foil;
It gathers to a greatness, like the ooze of oil
Crushed. Why do men then now not reck his rod?
Generations have trod, have trod, have trod;
And all is seared with trade; bleared, smeared with toil;
And wears man's smudge and shares man's smell: the soil
Is bare now, nor can foot feel, being shod.

And for all this, nature is never spent;
There lives the dearest freshness deep down things;
And though the last lights off the black West went
Oh, morning, at the brown brink eastwards, springs—
Because the Holy Ghost over the bent
World broods with warm breast and with ah! bright wings.

Thou art indeed just, Lord
1893

Thou art indeed just, Lord, if I contend
With thee; but, sir, so what I plead is just.
Why do sinners' ways prosper? and why must
Disappointment all I endeavour end?

Wert thou my enemy, O thou my friend,
How wouldst thou worse, I wonder, than thou dost
Defeat, thwart me? Oh, the sots and thralls of lust
Do in spare hours more thrive than I that spend,
Sir, life upon thy cause. See, banks and brakes
Now, leavèd how thick! lacèd they are again
With fretty chervil,° look, and fresh wind shakes *an herb*
Them; birds build—but not I build; no, but strain,
Time's eunuch, and not breed one work that wakes.
Mine, O thou lord of life, send my roots rain.

COMMENTARY

BERNARD BERGONZI

Bernard Bergonzi published this examination of Hopkins's poem in Paddy Kitchen's book *Gerard Manley Hopkins* (1977). It was included in a chapter aptly titled "Nearly Hard Poems' King," an anagram that poet Roy Fuller made of the letters of Hopkins's name.

On Hopkins's "The Windhover" 1977

Even the most selective remarks about the 1877 sonnets cannot ignore "The Windhover," which is probably the most famous, and certainly the most discussed and explicated. It is a magnificent poem, where Hopkins writes with unparallelled assurance and boldness, prosodically, lexically, and syntactically. The octet provides a superb mimetic sense of the bird's freedom and mastery on the wing. This much is generally recognized. Nevertheless, the poem has provoked a great deal of argument, not so much concerned with the refinements of interpretation as with establishing the basic sense of the words. This is largely because of the disabling ambiguity at a crucial point in the poem's development: "buckle" at the beginning of the twelfth line. As everyone knows, "buckle" has two senses, and they are opposed and irreconcilable, not mutually enriching. Hopkins, like other poets, enjoyed ambiguities and the multiple associations of words. But he also knew what he wanted to say, and I believe that he did not always realise the confusion he was causing by the insufficiently considered use of a simple noun with several meanings and no clue from the context. I have already referred to "World's strand, sway of the Sea" in the third line of "The Wreck of the *Deutschland*," and there is another example in "God's Grandeur," in the phrase "shining from shook foil." This could refer to a sword used in fencing, or to fine sheet metal, and either might be appropriate. In fact, we know what Hopkins intended because he told Bridges firmly enough: "I mean foil in its sense of leaf or tinsel, and no other word whatever will give the effect I want." Even the most unabashed anti-intentionalist cannot quite ignore such testimony. It is probable that, if asked,

Hopkins would have been equally sure which sense of "buckle" he intended, but in the lack of similar evidence speculation has continued. "Buckle" in the sense of "fasten together" gives the sestet, and hence the whole poem, a significantly different meaning from "buckle" in the sense of "give way under pressure." I now refer to the masterly and, I think, conclusive discussion of this crux in Professor [Elisabeth] Schneider's book. She sweeps aside the idea that both meanings can somehow be accommodated under the banner of "ambiguity":

> To observe that such-and-such a word—*buckle* it is in *The Windhover*—or this line or that image may mean either *x* or *y* and to conclude without more ado that it therefore means both is to ignore the requirement of *meaningful* reconciliation, which occurs only if something within the poem transforms *x* and *y* together into a *z*, or when a new enrichment of meaning *x* is produced by the presence of meaning *y*. Otherwise one is merely seeing double.[1]

Professor Schneider gives very convincing reasons for reading "buckle" as "collapse" or "give way under pressure." In her reading the sense of the sestet is that all the natural qualities associated with the falcon ("Brute beauty and valour and act . . ."), splendid and praiseworthy though they are, must give way ("buckle") in the face of the far lovelier fire that breaks from "my chevalier," Christ our Lord, who is directly addressed in line 11. Professor Schneider also persuades me to read "plough" as "plough-land," the sense in which it is used in "Pied Beauty," which clears up the other troublesome crux of the poem. One then reads the words, "sheer plod makes plough down sillion / Shine," as referring to the way in which the earth gleams when broken open in the act of ploughing, a phenomenon noticed in Hopkins's journal. In short, humble actions can produce a sudden unexpected beauty, just as dull embers can break open to reveal "gold-vermillion" fire. Such lowly achievements are characteristic of human endeavour, in contrast to the spectacular freedom of the brute creation exemplified by the bird. There is still room for subtleties of interpretation, but I follow Professor Schneider in believing that the sestet is a transformation of the experience of the octet, representing a movement from, or through, the physical to the spiritual; or from the natural to the human-and-divine.

JOHN KEATS

John Keats (1795–1821) was the oldest of five children. His mother was the wife of the head stableman in a London livery stable. In his brief school years, Keats, despite his small stature, was mostly distinguished for his numerous fist fights. He also developed

[1]Elisabeth W. Schneider, *The Dragon in the Gate* (Berkeley: University of California Press, 1968), p. 147.

a passion for reading, under the fortunate tutelage of Charles Cowden Clarke, but after the deaths of his parents he was apprenticed at age fifteen to an apothecary surgeon. When he completed a year of studies at Guy's College, he was licensed to continue his trade, but he quickly abandoned it to become a poet.

Little of the poetry Keats had written up to this time showed any sign of genius, although he received ample encouragement from a number of older writers, including Leigh Hunt, who introduced him to Percy Bysshe Shelley. The sonnet "On First Looking into Chapman's Homer" (p. 824), written when he was twenty-one, first hinted at what he would accomplish in the short time that was left to him. His language and ideas were an important influence on nineteenth-century English poetry.

His mother had died of tuberculosis, and Keats nursed a tubercular younger brother through his dying months in 1818. Keats contracted the disease and at the same time fell hopelessly in love with an eighteen-year-old girl named Fanny Brawne. Too poor and too ill to marry, he poured his emotions into poems and letters that were suffused with his despair, his love for Brawne, and his consciousness that his life was already running out. His sonnet "Bright Star" was the last poem he wrote and she was its subject.

Keats tried to fight his illness by traveling to Italy, but he was weakened by a series of hemorrhages and died in Rome at the age of twenty-six. In his last letter he apologized to a friend for writing such a clumsy good-bye. He wrote, "I always made an awkward bow."

"Ode to a Nightingale" was one of several poems Keats wrote in his remarkable year of 1819, when he composed several of his major works, including "To Autumn" (p. 738) and "Ode on a Grecian Urn" (p. 754). "When I have fears," with its tone of tragic prophecy, was written in January of the year before. (See also Keats's "On First Looking into Chapman's Homer" on p. 824.)

WEB Research John Keats at bedfordstmartins.com/rewritinglit.

Bright Star 1819

Bright star, would I were steadfast as thou art—
    Not in lone splendour hung aloft the night,
And watching, with eternal lids apart,
    Like Nature's patient sleepless Eremite,
The moving waters at their priest-like task
    Of pure ablution round earth's human shores,
Or gazing on the new soft-fallen mask
    Of snow upon the mountains and the moors—
No—yet still steadfast, still unchangeable,
    Pillowed upon my fair love's ripening breast,
To feel for ever its soft fall and swell,
    Awake for ever in a sweet unrest,
        Still, still to hear her tender-taken breath,
        And so live ever—or else swoon to death.

Ode to a Nightingale

1819

I

My heart aches, and a drowsy numbness pains
My sense, as though of hemlock° I had drunk, *a poison*
Or emptied some dull opiate to the drains
One minute past, and Lethe-wards° had sunk:
'Tis not through envy of thy happy lot,
But being too happy in thine happiness
That thou, light-wingèd Dryad° of the trees, *wood nymph*
In some melodious plot
Of beechen green, and shadows numberless,
Singest of summer in full-throated ease.

II

O, for a draught of vintage! that hath been
Cooled a long age in the deep-delved earth,
Tasting of Flora° and the country green, *goddess of flowers*
Dance, and Provençal song,° and sunburnt mirth!
O for a beaker full of the warm South,
Full of the true, the blushful Hippocrene,°
With beaded bubbles winking at the brim,
And purple-stainèd mouth;
That I might drink, and leave the world unseen,
And with thee fade away into the forest dim.

III

Fade far away, dissolve, and quite forget
What thou among the leaves hast never known,
The weariness, the fever, and the fret
Here, where men sit and hear each other groan;
Where palsy shakes a few, sad, last gray hairs,
Where youth grows pale, and specter-thin, and dies,
Where but to think is to be full of sorrow
And leaden-eyed despairs,
Where Beauty cannot keep her lustrous eyes;
Or new Love pine at them beyond tomorrow.

4. Lethe-wards: Lethe is the river of forgetfulness in Greek mythology. **14. Provençal song:** Provence, in medieval France, was famous for its troubadors. **16. Hippocrene:** Hippocrene is the fountain of the Muses, the goddesses of artistic inspiration.

IV

Away! away! for I will fly to thee,
Not charioted by Bacchus and his pards,°
But on the viewless wings of Poesy,
Though the dull brain perplexes and retards:
Already with thee! tender is the night,
And haply the Queen-Moon is on her throne,
Clustered around by all her starry Fays;° *fairies*
But here there is no light,
Save what from heaven is with the breezes blown
Through verdurous glooms and winding mossy ways.

V

I cannot see what flowers are at my feet,
Nor what soft incense hangs upon the boughs,
But, in embalmèd° darkness, guess each sweet *perfumed*
Wherewith the seasonable month endows
The grass, the thicket, and the fruit-tree wild;
What hawthorn, and the pastoral eglantine;
Fast fading violets covered up in leaves;
And mid-May's eldest child,
The coming musk-rose, full of dewy wine,
The murmurous haunt of flies on summer eves.

VI

Darkling° I listen; and for many a time *in the dark*
I have been half in love with easeful Death,
Called him soft names in many a musèd rhyme,
To take into the air my quiet breath;
Now more than ever seems it rich to die,
To cease upon the midnight with no pain,
While thou art pouring forth thy soul abroad
In such an ecstasy!
Still wouldst thou sing, and I have ears in vain—
To thy high requiem become a sod.

VII

Thou wast not born for death, immortal Bird!
No hungry generations tread thee down;
The voice I hear this passing night was heard
In ancient days by emperor and clown:

32. Bacchus and his pards: Bacchus, the god of wine, supposedly traveled in a chariot drawn by leopards.

Perhaps the selfsame song that found a path
Through the sad heart of Ruth,° when, sick for home,
She stood in tears amid the alien corn:
The same that oft-times hath
Charmed magic casements, opening on the foam
Of perilous seas, in faery lands forlorn.

VIII

Forlorn! the very word is like a bell
To toll me back from thee to my sole self!
Adieu! the fancy cannot cheat so well
As she is famed to do, deceiving elf.
Adieu! adieu! thy plaintive anthem fades
Past the near meadows, over the still stream,
Up the hill side; and now 'tis buried deep
In the next valley-glades:
Was it a vision, or a waking dream?
Fled is that music:—Do I wake or sleep?

When I have fears 1818

When I have fears that I may cease to be
Before my pen has gleaned my teeming brain,
Before high-pilèd books, in charact'ry,
Hold like rich garners the full-ripen'd grain;
When I behold, upon the night's starr'd face,
Huge cloudy symbols of a high romance,
And think that I may never live to trace
Their shadows, with the magic hand of chance;
And when I feel, fair creature of an hour!
That I shall never look upon thee more,
Never have relish in the faery power
Of unreflecting love!—then on the shore
Of the wide world I stand alone, and think,
Till Love and Fame to nothingness do sink.

66. the sad heart of Ruth: Reference to the young widow in the biblical Book of Ruth.

ROBERT LOWELL

Robert Lowell (1917–1977) was born in Boston to a distinguished New England family that had already produced two major poets, James Russell Lowell (1819–1891) and Amy Lowell (1874–1925), one of the leaders of the imagist movement (p. 797). After two years at Harvard University, Lowell left in 1937 for Kenyon College in Ohio to join a group of young poets who had gathered around teacher and poet John Crowe Ransom. Although his father had been a Navy officer, Lowell became a conscientious objector during World War II and was imprisoned for five months in 1943. He continued to write poetry through his personal crises, and his second book, *Lord Weary's Castle*, won the Pulitzer Prize in 1946.

Lowell published steadily, and his books were well received, but he was beginning to suffer from acute attacks of depression. Two of his three marriages were to novelists – first to Jean Stafford in 1940 and then to Elizabeth Hardwick in 1949. He was also drinking heavily and when he was drunk he was emotionally abusive. In the 1950s he visited San Francisco and experienced the excitement of the Beat Generation, the new literary movement that had sprung up there. After seeing the effect of Beat writer Allen Ginsberg's poetry on audiences and reading an emotional poem titled "Heart's Needle" by a former student named W. D. Snodgrass, he changed his way of writing. His poems became freer and more personal. His collection *Life Studies*, written in the new "confessional" style, was one of the most influential books published after the war, winning the National Book Award in 1959. At this same time he was teaching a poetry course at Boston University, and among his students were Sylvia Plath and Anne Sexton, who adopted the new style in their own writing.

Finally diagnosed as manic-depressive, Lowell was able to avoid with medication some of the psychotic episodes that had periodically caused him to be hospitalized. With novelist Norman Mailer, he was involved in the struggle against the Vietnam War, and in 1972 he married for the third time and settled in England. He had written plays and literary criticism and won the Bollingen Prize for his translations. In 1977 he returned to the United States planning to teach at Harvard, but he died of a heart attack a short time later.

One of his closest friends was poet Elizabeth Bishop – in emotional moments he asked her to marry him – and "Skunk Hour" is dedicated to her. His poem is a response to her "Armadillo." It reads almost like a letter, describing a scene that is familiar to both of them. "For the Union Dead" is also a description, this time of the Boston Common and the memorial statue by Augustus Saint-Gaudens to the Civil War regiment of African American soldiers that was destroyed with its young commander, Boston's Colonel Robert Shaw. In his late poem "Epilogue," Lowell compares the art of writing poetry to the art of painters like Vermeer, saying that the role of the poet is to inform, to name each figure in the picture.

WEB Research Robert Lowell at bedfordstmartins.com/rewritinglit.

Skunk Hour

1959

For Elizabeth Bishop

Nautilus Island's hermit
heiress still lives through winters in her Spartan cottage;
her sheep still graze above the sea.
Her son's a bishop. Her farmer
is first selectman in our village;
she's in her dotage.

Thirsting for
the hierarchic privacy
of Queen Victoria's century,
she buys up all
the eyesores facing her shore,
and lets them fall.

The season's ill—
we've lost our summer millionaire,
who seemed to leap from an L. L. Bean°
catalogue. His nine-knot yawl
was auctioned off to lobstermen.
A red fox stain covers Blue Hill.

And now our fairy
decorator brightens his shop for fall;
his fishnet's filled with orange cork,
orange, his cobbler's bench and awl;
there is no money in his work,
he'd rather marry.

One dark night,
my Tudor Ford climbed the hill's skull;
I watched for love-cars. Lights turned down,
they lay together, hull to hull,
where the graveyard shelves on the town. . . .
My mind's not right.

A car radio bleats,
"Love, O careless Love. . . ." I hear
my ill-spirit sob in each blood cell,
as if my hand were at its throat. . . .
I myself am hell;
nobody's here—

only skunks, that search
in the moonlight for a bite to eat.

15. L. L. Bean: A Maine mail-order store known for its sporting goods and outdoor equipment.

They march on their soles up Main Street:
white stripes, moonstruck eyes' red fire
under the chalk-dry and spar spire
of the Trinitarian Church.

I stand on top
of our back steps and breathe the rich air—
a mother skunk with her column of kittens swills the garbage pail.
She jabs her wedge-head in a cup
of sour cream, drops her ostrich tail,
and will not scare.

For the Union Dead

1964

"Relinquunt Omnia Servare Rem Publican."°

The old South Boston Aquarium stands
in a Sahara of snow now. Its broken windows are boarded.
The bronze weathervane cod has lost half its scales.
The airy tanks are dry.

Once my nose crawled like a snail on the glass;
my hand tingled
to burst the bubbles
drifting from the noses of the cowed, compliant fish.

My hand draws back. I often sigh still
for the dark downward and vegetating kingdom
of the fish and reptile. One morning last March,
I pressed against the new barbed and galvanized

fence on the Boston Common. Behind their cage,
yellow dinosaur steamshovels were grunting
as they cropped up tons of mush and grass
to gouge their underworld garage.

Parking spaces luxuriate like civic
sandpiles in the heart of Boston.
A girdle of orange, Puritan-pumpkin colored girders
braces the tingling Statehouse,

shaking over the excavations, as it faces Colonel Shaw
and his bell-cheeked Negro infantry
on St. Gaudens' shaking Civil War relief,
propped by a plank splint against the garage's earthquake.

Two months after marching through Boston,
half the regiment was dead;

Relinquunt . . . Publican: "They gave up all to serve the republic."

at the dedication,
William James° could almost hear the bronze Negroes breathe.

Their monument sticks like a fishbone
in the city's throat.
Its Colonel is as lean
as a compass-needle.

He has an angry wrenlike vigilance,
a greyhound's gentle tautness;
he seems to wince at pleasure,
and suffocate for privacy.

He is out of bounds now. He rejoices in man's lovely,
peculiar power to choose life and die—
when he leads his black soldiers to death,
he cannot bend his back.

On a thousand small town New England greens,
the old white churches hold their air
of sparse, sincere rebellion; frayed flags
quilt the graveyards of the Grand Army of the Republic.

The stone statues of the abstract Union Soldier
grow slimmer and younger each year—
wasp-waisted, they doze over muskets
and muse through their sideburns . . .

Shaw's father wanted no monument
except the ditch,
where his son's body was thrown
and lost with his "niggers."

The ditch is nearer.
There are no statues for the last war here;
on Boylston Street, a commercial photograph
shows Hiroshima boiling

over a Mosler Safe, the "Rock of Ages"
that survived the blast. Space is nearer.
When I crouch to my television set,
the drained faces of Negro school-children rise like balloons.

Colonel Shaw
is riding on his bubble,
he waits
for the blessèd break.

The Aquarium is gone. Everywhere,
giant finned cars nose forward like fish;
a savage servility
slides by on grease.

---

28. William James: Harvard psychologist and philosopher (1842–1910).

Epilogue

1977

Those blessèd structures, plot and rhyme—
why are they no help to me now
I want to make
something imagined, not recalled?
I hear the noise of my own voice:
The painter's vision is not a lens,
it trembles to caress the light.
But sometimes everything I write
with the threadbare art of my eye
seems a snapshot,
lurid, rapid, garish, grouped,
heightened from life,
yet paralyzed by fact.
All's misalliance.
Yet why not say what happened?
Pray for the grace of accuracy
Vermeer gave to the sun's illumination
stealing like the tide across a map
to his girl solid with yearning.
We are poor passing facts,
warned by that to give
each figure in the photograph
his living name.

COMMENTARY

ROBERT LOWELL

Robert Lowell's comments on "Skunk Hour" were a response to a discussion of the poem by fellow poets Richard Wilbur, John Frederick Nims, and John Berryman. The comments were included in the book *The Contemporary Artist as Artist and Critic* (1964), edited by Anthony Ostroff.

An Explication of "Skunk Hour"

1964

I. The Meaning

The author of a poem is not necessarily the ideal person to explain its meaning. He is as liable as anyone else to muddle, dishonesty, and reticence. Nor is it his purpose to provide a peg for a prose essay. Meaning varies in importance from poem to poem, and from style to style, but always it is only a strand and an element in the brute flow of composition. Other elements are pictures that please or thrill for themselves, phrases that ring for their music or carry some buried suggestion. For all this the author is an opportunist, throwing whatever comes to hand into his feeling for start, continuity, contrast, climax, and completion. It is imbecile for him not to know his intentions, and unsophisticated for him to know too explicitly and fully. . . .

I am not sure whether I can distinguish between intention and interpretation. I think this is what I more or less intended. The first four stanzas are meant to give a dawdling more or less amiable picture of a declining Maine sea town. I move from the ocean inland. Sterility howls through the scenery, but I try to give a tone of tolerance, humor, and randomness to the sad prospect. The composition drifts, its direction sinks out of sight into the casual, chancy arrangements of nature and decay. Then all comes alive in stanzas V and VI. This is the dark night. I hoped my readers would remember John of the Cross's° poem. My night is not gracious, but secular, puritan, and agnostical. An Existentialist night. Somewhere in my mind was a passage from Sartre or Camus° about reaching some point of final darkness where the one free act is suicide. Out of this comes the march and affirmation, an ambiguous one, of my skunks in the last two stanzas. The skunks are both quixotic and barbarously absurd, hence the tone of amusement and defiance. "Skunk Hour" is not entirely independent, but the anchor poem in its sequence. . . .

"Skunk Hour" was begun in mid-August 1957, and finished about a month later. In March of the same year, I had been giving readings on the West Coast, often reading six days a week and sometimes twice on a single day. I was in San Francisco, the era and setting of Allen Ginsberg, and all about very modest poets were waking up prophets. I became sorely aware of how few poems I had written, and that these few had been finished at the latest three or four years earlier. Their style seemed distant, symbol-ridden, and willfully difficult. I began to paraphrase my Latin quotations, and to add extra syllables to a line to make it clearer and more colloquial. I felt my old poems hid what they were really about, and many times offered a stiff, humorless, and even impenetrable surface. I am no convert to the "beats." I know well too that the best poems are not necessarily poems that read aloud. Many of the greatest poems can only be read to one's self, for inspiration is no substitute for humor, shock, narrative, and a hypnotic voice, the four musts for oral performance. Still, my own poems seemed like prehistoric monsters dragged down into the bog and death by their ponderous armor. I was reciting what I no longer felt. What influenced me more than San Francisco and reading aloud was that for some time I had been writing prose. I felt that the best style for poetry was none of the many poetic styles in English, but something like the prose of Chekhov or Flaubert.

When I returned to my home, I began writing lines in a new style. No poem, however, got finished and soon I left off and tried to forget the whole headache. Suddenly, in August, I was struck by the sadness of writing nothing, and having nothing to write, of having, at least, no language. When I began

---

John of the Cross's: Reference to Juan de Yepes y Alvarez (1542–1591), Spanish mystic and poet. **Sartre or Camus:** Jean-Paul Sartre (1905–1980) and Albert Camus (1913–1960) were important modern French writers.

writing "Skunk Hour," I felt that most of what I knew about writing was a hindrance.

The dedication is to Elizabeth Bishop, because rereading her suggested a way of breaking through the shell of my old manner. Her rhythms, idiom, images, and stanza structure seemed to belong to a later century. "Skunk Hour" is modeled on Miss Bishop's "The Armadillo," a much better poem and one I had heard her read and had later carried around with me. Both "Skunk Hour" and "The Armadillo" use short line stanzas, start with drifting description, and end with a single animal. . . .

"Skunk Hour" was written backwards, first the last two stanzas, I think, and then the next to last two. Anyway, there was a time when I had the last four stanzas much as they now are and nothing before them. I found the bleak personal violence repellent. All was too close, though watching the lovers was not mine, but from an anecdote about Walt Whitman in his old age. I began to feel that real poetry came, not from fierce confessions, but from something almost meaningless but imagined. I was haunted by an image of a blue china doorknob. I never used the doorknob, or knew what it meant, yet somehow it started the current of images in my opening stanzas. They were written in reverse order, and at last gave my poem an earth to stand on, and space to breathe.

SHARON OLDS

Sharon Olds (b. 1942) was born in San Francisco and grew up in Berkeley. She has consistently refused to answer questions about her family and her personal life, feeling that the people she describes in her poetry have a right to privacy. As she told an interviewer for the *New York Times*, "I promised I'd keep them out of this." She went on, "I never thought anyone would read anything I'd written. If I'd known the number of readers I would have, I would have used a pseudonym." Her critics and interviewers have generally respected her wishes, and there have been no published interviews or reminiscences by people who have been part of her life.

Olds was sent to the Dana Hall School in Wellesley, Massachusetts, but returned to California for her university years. She graduated from Stanford and moved to New York City to study for her Ph.D. at Columbia University. She married in the late 1960s and is the mother of a son and a daughter. The painful breakup of her marriage has also caused her to shield herself from personal questions.

Although Olds has preferred to present a low personal profile, her life in New York is a rush of public activity. She has taught creative writing at New York University since the mid-1980s, and from 1989 to 1991 she was director of the Graduate Creative Writing Program. In 1984 she founded a poetry workshop for the severely disabled in New York's Goldwater Hospital. From 1998 to 2000, Olds held the position of New York state poet, which involved presentations and appearances across the state. When one interviewer asked her about fitting all of these things into her life, she confessed that she had given up reading newspapers and watching television. She agreed that this has its disadvantages, but cheerfully defended herself by saying, "I try to look at the front page whenever I'm walking by a newsstand."

Olds also manages to fit a demanding line-up of readings into her schedule, and she is one of a handful of poets in the United States whose books sell in large quantities. *The Father* (1992) was reprinted several times within a few months of its publication, and her 1984 collection *The Dead and the Living*, which won the National Book Critics Circle Award, has sold more than 50,000 copies. The demands of her life, however, mean that each book is a gathering of work that was written years before. She writes continuously, and it is only after considerable time has passed that she feels the need to put together the poems that make up a book. Her poetry is composed in her head as she is busy with her other responsibilities, and the actual writing of a poem goes quickly. She joked with an interviewer that she could write a poem in half an hour. When the response to this was surprise, Olds laughed and agreed, "Forty-five minutes is much better."

In her poem "Parents' Day," Olds suggests the complex relation between a mother and her daughter, and in "I Go Back to May 1937," she responds to a photograph of her parents when they are a young and still happy couple. Perhaps no poem better reflects the uncertainty about sexual mores in our society today than her "Sex without Love."

WEB Research Sharon Olds at bedfordsmartins.com/rewritinglit.

Parents' Day 1995

I breathed shallow as I looked for her
in the crowd of oncoming parents, I strained
forward, like a gazehound held back on a leash,
then I raced toward her. I remember her being
much bigger than I, her smile of the highest
wattage, a little stiff, sparkling
with consciousness of her prettiness—I
pitied the other girls for having mothers
who looked like mothers, who did not blush.
Sometimes she would have braids around her head like a
goddess or an advertisement for California raisins—
I worshipped her cleanliness, her transfixing
irises, sometimes I thought she could
sense a few genes of hers
dotted here and there in my body
like bits of undissolved sugar
in a recipe that did not quite work out.
For years, when I thought of her, I thought
of the long souring of her life, but on Parents' Day

my heart would bang and my lungs swell so I could
feel the tucks and puckers of embroidered
smocking on my chest press into my ribs,
my washboard front vibrate like scraped
tin to see that woman arriving
and to know she was mine.

I Go Back to May 1937

1987

I see them standing at the formal gates of their colleges,
I see my father strolling out
under the ochre sandstone arch, the
red tiles glinting like bent
plates of blood behind his head, I
see my mother with a few light books at her hip
standing at the pillar made of tiny bricks,
the wrought-iron gate still open behind her, its
sword-tips aglow in the May air,
they are about to graduate, they are about to get married,
they are kids, they are dumb, all they know is they are
innocent, they would never hurt anybody.
I want to go up to them and say Stop,
don't do it—she's the wrong woman,
he's the wrong man, you are going to do things
you cannot imagine you would ever do,
you are going to do bad things to children,
you are going to suffer in ways you have not heard of,
you are going to want to die. I want to go
up to them there in the late May sunlight and say it,
her hungry pretty face turning to me,
her pitiful beautiful untouched body,
his arrogant handsome face turning to me,
his pitiful beautiful untouched body,
but I don't do it. I want to live. I
take them up like the male and female
paper dolls and bang them together
at the hips, like chips of flint, as if to
strike sparks from them, I say
Do what you are going to do, and I will tell about it.

Sex without Love

1983

How do they do it, the ones who make love
without love? Beautiful as dancers,
gliding over each other like ice-skaters

over the ice, fingers hooked
inside each other's bodies, faces
red as steak, wine, wet as the
children at birth whose mothers are going to
give them away. How do they come to the
come to the   come to the   God   come to the
still waters, and not love
the one who came there with them, light
rising slowly as steam off their joined
skin? These are the true religious,
the purists, the pros, the ones who will not
accept a false Messiah, love the
priest instead of the God. They do not
mistake the lover for their own pleasure,
they are like great runners: they know they are alone
with the road surface, the cold, the wind,
the fit of their shoes, their over-all cardio-
vascular health—just factors, like the partner
in the bed, and not the truth, which is the
single body alone in the universe
against its own best time.

COMMENTARY

ANN CHARTERS
The Woman in the Long, Dark Raincoat: A Poetry Reading with Sharon Olds
1999

Early one Saturday afternoon in November 1999, outside a large hotel in Miami, I noticed a slender woman in a dark, ankle-length, belted raincoat and black high heels, standing a few feet away as I waited for the shuttle van that would take me downtown to the Miami International Book Fair. The sky was overcast, rain misting the driveway as the cabs drew up and departed with their passengers. I was in Miami to appear on a panel of authors at the book fair later that afternoon, but I had decided to leave the hotel a couple of hours early so that I could hear the poet Sharon Olds, who was scheduled to read her poetry just before my panel.

Since all the writers I had met at the fair had been very gregarious, I decided that the slight, middle-aged woman standing near me in the long dark raincoat must be a librarian. Her blonde hair was braided close to her head in a very intricate, tight pattern. She appeared to be in her middle fifties, standing very still with her head averted, her eyes focused on something far away. We waited together in silence for nearly twenty minutes as the rain stopped and the clouds began to lighten. I decided not to try to begin a conversation. Clearly she liked the silence. When the van came, she got inside first, sitting in the farthest corner. I sat down in the empty front seat, beside the driver. She didn't speak during the short trip downtown, and she and I went our separate ways at the fair.

The auditorium was nearly full of people waiting for Sharon Olds to read her poetry. It took me awhile to find an empty chair, and when I'd settled I saw the woman who had ridden in the van with me already seated in the front row. There was a short introduction, and I watched her rise and take off her long, dark raincoat before she climbed the stairs to the stage. She was dressed in a jacket, a blouse, a very short skirt, and sheer white tights. At the podium she put down her papers and arranged her jacket carefully on a chair, revealing a low cut, sleeveless blouse, perfect for the muggy Miami weather. Finally she turned to the audience, a slim, pale, fully composed figure ready to begin her reading. The poet Sharon Olds was my silent "librarian."

As she read her poems, Olds was transformed into a skillful, passionately intense performer. Her clear voice uninhibitedly revealed her thoughts to a collection of strangers fascinated by her ability to spin elegant webs of allusion and insight from her reflections on her personal experiences. We were hushed in concentration listening to her rapt voice seemingly craft each poem anew as she made us hear the words on her pages. I especially remember one of the poems she read that afternoon, "At the Bay," from the book *Blood, Tin, Straw* (1999), about the wildlife she had observed in the water during a previous visit to Florida. The snowy egret, the pelicans, the great blue with its "snake neck and mallet beak," preceded the sight of a dolphin, and Olds concluded the last nine lines of the poem as if the earth were magically speaking to her, alerting her that what she had just seen was a poem of its own. Olds read these lines very slowly, with quiet deliberation, as if she had not been quite intelligent enough to see what was in front of her eyes without outside help. In turn, her voice was the help I needed for a deeper appreciation of the magic she had created in her poem.

SYLVIA PLATH

Sylvia Plath (1932–1963) was born in Boston. Her father, who had emigrated from a German area of Poland as a boy, taught entomology at Boston University. Their relationship, as she described it in her poetry, was complicated, but he died when she was eight, and her mother, a high-school language teacher, encouraged her to write. Plath attended Smith College and graduated summa cum laude, but between her junior and senior years she suffered a nervous breakdown and attempted suicide.

In 1955, after her graduation, she received a Fulbright grant to study at Cambridge University, where she met one of the most promising young English poets, Ted Hughes. They were married in 1956 and came to the United States, where Plath had a job teaching at Smith College and Hughes later took a job at Amherst College. After two years Hughes returned to England, and despite strains in their marriage Plath joined him there in December 1959. They had two children, a daughter born in 1960 and a son in 1962, and they settled in a cottage in Devon.

On the surface Plath's life seemed ideal, with a house in the English countryside, a husband who respected her writing, and the publication of her first book the same year her first child was born. The poems she was writing, however, depict her despair at her isolation and the tensions of marriage to someone who was also a gifted writer and who was attractive to other women. Hughes began a relationship with someone else and left the cottage in Devon in October 1962. Several weeks later Plath moved with her children into a bleak London flat. She had been writing at a frantic pace through the autumn months and, despite near poverty and a deepening sense of isolation, she continued to compose the poems that Hughes later collected in his edited version of the manuscript she had titled *Ariel*. By February she could no longer see any way out of her emotional turmoil and ended her life. As Robert Lowell wrote in an introduction to the poems, "Her art's immortality is life's disintegration."

"Morning Song" is the first poem in *Ariel*. It describes the birth of Plath's second child and their first night together. Plath completed "Daddy" on October 12, 1962, the day after Hughes left her, and she continued to write raging poems over the next weeks.

WEB Research Sylvia Plath at bedfordstmartins.com/rewritinglit.

Morning Song 1961

Love set you going like a fat gold watch.
The midwife slapped your footsoles, and your bald cry
Took its place among the elements.

Our voices echo, magnifying your arrival. New statue.
In a drafty museum, your nakedness
Shadows our safety. We stand round blankly as walls.

I'm no more your mother
Than the cloud that distils a mirror to reflect its own slow
Effacement at the wind's hand.

All night your moth-breath
Flickers among the flat pink roses. I wake to listen:
A far sea moves in my ear.

One cry, and I stumble from bed, cow-heavy and floral
In my Victorian nightgown.
Your mouth opens clean as a cat's. The window square

Whitens and swallows its dull stars. And now you try
Your handful of notes;
The clear vowels rise like balloons.

Daddy 1962

You do not do, you do not do
Any more, black shoe
In which I have lived like a foot

For thirty years, poor and white,
Barely daring to breathe or Achoo.

Daddy, I have had to kill you.
You died before I had time—
Marble-heavy, a bag full of God,
Ghastly statue with one gray toe
Big as a Frisco seal

And a head in the freakish Atlantic
Where it pours bean green over blue
In the waters off beautiful Nauset.
I used to pray to recover you.
Ach, du.° *Oh, you*

In the German tongue, in the Polish Town°
Scraped flat by the roller
Of wars, wars, wars.
But the name of the town is common.
My Polack friend

Says there are a dozen or two.
So I never could tell where you
Put your foot, your root,
I never could talk to you.
The tongue stuck in my jaw.

It stuck in a barb wire snare.
Ich, ich, ich, ich,° *I, I, I, I*
I could hardly speak.
I thought every German was you.
And the language obscene

An engine, an engine
Chuffing me off like a Jew.
A Jew to Dachau, Auschwitz, Belsen.°
I began to talk like a Jew.
I think I may well be a Jew.

The snows of the Tyrol, the clear beer of Vienna
Are not very pure or true.
With my gypsy-ancestress and my weird luck
And my Taroc° pack and my Taroc pack
I may be a bit of a Jew.

I have always been scared of *you*,
With your Luftwaffe,° your gobbledygoo.

---

16. Polish Town: Refers to Otto Plath's birthplace, Granbow. **33. Dachau . . . Belsen:** Nazi death camps in World War II. **39. Taroc:** Pack of fortune-telling (tarot) cards. **42. Luftwaffe:** World War II German aircorps.

And your neat mustache
And your Aryan eye, bright blue.
Panzer-man, panzer-man,° O You—
Not God but a swastika
So black no sky could squeak through.
Every woman adores a Fascist,
The boot in the face, the brute
Brute heart of a brute like you.

You stand at the blackboard, daddy,
In the picture I have of you,
A cleft in your chin instead of your foot
But no less a devil for that, no not
Any less the black man who

Bit my pretty red heart in two.
I was ten when they buried you.
At twenty I tried to die
And get back, back, back to you.
I thought even the bones would do

But they pulled me out of the sack,
And they stuck me together with glue.
And then I knew what to do.
I made a model of you,
A man in black with a Meinkampf° look

And a love of the rack and the screw.
And I said I do, I do.
So daddy, I'm finally through.
The black telephone's off at the root,
The voices just can't worm through.

If I've killed one man, I've killed two—
The vampire who said he was you
And drank my blood for a year,
Seven years, if you want to know.
Daddy, you can lie back now.

There's a stake in your fat black heart
And the villagers never liked you.
They are dancing and stamping on you.
They always *knew* it was you.
Daddy, daddy, you bastard, I'm through.

---

45. Panzer-man: In World War II, the German panzer division was that made up of armored vehicles. **65. Meinkampf:** Adolf Hitler's autobiography was titled *Mein kampf,* or "My Struggle."

ADRIENNE RICH

Adrienne Rich (1929–2012) was born in Baltimore. She graduated from Radcliffe College in 1951, the year her first book, *A Change of World*, was published as one of the Yale Series of Younger Poets, which immediately brought her to the attention of a large reading audience. While her early poetry was praised for its formal craftsmanship and a certain objectivity, it evolved away from these earlier qualities toward a more subjective, experimental, and exploratory style, giving voice to feminist and social concerns of the 1960s and 1970s. For many years she was one of many writers and intellectuals living in close contact on New York's Upper West Side. Her 1973 collection *Diving into the Wreck* won the National Book Award. In 1984 she moved to California, where she continued to write and publish until her death at age 82.

In a 1967 review, the poet Hayden Carruth wrote of her work:

> The dominating quality in Adrienne Rich's work, the quality which knits all, sound, syntax, and sense, into a marvelous unitary structure, is what she herself calls "fierce attention." . . . Other words have been used for it – compression, concern, concentration – and none is exactly right; but the poetry shows what it is: a need not simply to confront experience . . . but to solve it; to make it come right.

"Aunt Jennifer's Tigers" is one of the most popular poems from her early collections. "Diving into the Wreck" is now considered one of the most important feminist statements of its era.

WEB Research Adrienne Rich at bedfordstmartins.com/rewritinglit.

Aunt Jennifer's Tigers 1952

Aunt Jennifer's tigers prance across a screen,
Bright topaz denizens of a world of green.
They do not fear the men beneath the tree;
They pace in sleek chivalric certainty.

Aunt Jennifer's fingers fluttering through her wool
Find even the ivory needle hard to pull.
The massive weight of Uncle's wedding band
Sits heavily upon Aunt Jennifer's hand.

When Aunt is dead, her terrified hands will lie
Still ringed with ordeals she was mastered by.
The tigers in the panel that she made
Will go on prancing, proud and unafraid.

Diving into the Wreck 1971

First having read the book of myths,
and loaded the camera,
and checked the edge of the knife-blade,

I put on
the body-armor of black rubber
the absurd flippers
the grave and awkward mask.
I am having to do this
not like Cousteau° with his
assiduous team
aboard the sun-flooded schooner
but here alone.
There is a ladder.
The ladder is always there
hanging innocently
close to the side of the schooner.
We know what it is for,
we who have used it.
Otherwise
it is a piece of maritime floss
some sundry equipment.

I go down.
Rung after rung and still
the oxygen immerses me
the blue light
the clear atoms
of our human air.
I go down.
My flippers cripple me,
I crawl like an insect down the ladder
and there is no one
to tell me when the ocean
will begin.

First the air is blue and then
it is bluer and then green and then
black I am blacking out and yet
my mask is powerful
it pumps my blood with power
the sea is another story
the sea is not a question of power
I have to learn alone
to turn my body without force
in the deep element.

And now: it is easy to forget
what I came for

9. Cousteau: Jacques Cousteau (1910–1997), French underwater explorer, photographer, and author.

among so many who have always
lived here
swaying their crenellated° fans
between the reefs
and besides
you breathe differently down here.

I came to explore the wreck.
The words are purposes.
The words are maps.
I came to see the damage that was done
and the treasures that prevail.
I stroke the beam of my lamp
slowly along the flank
of something more permanent
than fish or weed

the thing I came for:
the wreck and not the story of the wreck
the thing itself and not the myth
the drowned face always staring
toward the sun
the evidence of damage
worn by salt and sway into this threadbare beauty
the ribs of the disaster
curving their assertion
among the tentative haunters.

This is the place.
And I am here, the mermaid whose dark hair
streams black, the merman in his armored body
We circle silently
about the wreck
we dive into the hold.
I am she: I am he

whose drowned face sleeps with open eyes
whose breasts still bear the stress
whose silver, copper, vermeil° cargo lies
obscurely inside barrels
half-wedged and left to rot
we are the half-destroyed instruments
that once held to a course
the water-eaten log
the fouled compass

48. crenellated: Notched with rounded or scalloped projections. **80. vermeil:** Gilded silver or bronze.

We are, I am, you are
by cowardice or courage
the one who find our way
back to this scene
carrying a knife, a camera
a book of myths
in which
our names do not appear.

ANNE SEXTON

Anne Sexton (1928–1974), the youngest of three daughters, was born in Newton, Massachusetts, a suburb of Boston, and grew up in Wellesley. She was from a well-off New England family, spending her winters in the city and her summers on Squirrel Island in Maine. When she was nineteen she eloped with a man who was, like her father, successful in the woolen industry.

Although outwardly she conformed to her family's expectations, Sexton was unable to resolve her inner conflicts. After the birth of each of her daughters, in 1953 and 1955, she was hospitalized for psychiatric treatment. When she first attempted suicide in 1956, her doctor suggested she begin writing poetry as therapy. She enrolled in her first writing workshop the next year, where she met the writer Maxine Kumin, who would become a close friend. The following year she enrolled in Robert Lowell's poetry class at Boston University. Another young poet, Sylvia Plath, was in the same class.

Sexton's first book, *To Bedlam and Part Way Back*, published in 1960, only a year after her class with Lowell, attracted considerable attention for its powerful confessional style. She received awards and grants, and in 1967 she won the Pulitzer Prize for her book *Live or Die*. She taught at Harvard and Colgate universities, and was appointed a professor at Boston University in 1972. Despite her recognition, however, she was unable to free herself from her emotional torment. She finally succeeded in a suicide attempt in 1974.

Sexton's "An Obsessive Combination of Ontological Inscape, Trickery and Love" is a high-spirited play on the endless intricacies of words, and ends with the exultant lines "a star / I touched and a miracle I really wrote." "To a Friend Whose Work Has Come to Triumph" is a reference to the legend of Icarus who made himself wings to fly to the sun, but as he came closer, the sun's heat melted the wax that held the wing's feathers together and he plunged to earth. Sexton's response was to write that he triumphed simply by so nearly achieving his goal. As she writes, "Who cares that he fell back to the sea?" Sexton wrote a series of tender, revealing poems for her daughter, and in "Pain for a Daughter" she watches helplessly as her daughter is painfully treated for a serious injury. (See also Sexton's "And One for My Dame" on p. 706 and "The Fortress" on p. 810.)

CONNECTION W. H. Auden, "Musée des Beaux Arts" (page 926).

WEB Research Anne Sexton at bedfordstmartins.com/rewritinglit.

An Obsessive Combination of Ontological Inscape, Trickery and Love 1959

Busy, with an idea for a code, I write
signals hurrying from left to right,
or right to left, by obscure routes,
for my own reasons; taking a word like "writes"
down tiers of tries until its secret rites
make sense; or until, suddenly, RATS
can amazingly and funnily become STAR
and right to left that small star
is mine, for my own liking, to stare
its five lucky pins inside out, to store
forever kindly, as if it were a star
I touched and a miracle I really wrote.

To a Friend Whose Work Has Come to Triumph 1962

Consider Icarus, pasting those sticky wings on,
testing that strange little tug at his shoulder blade,
and think of that first flawless moment over the lawn
of the labyrinth. Think of the difference it made!
There below are the trees, as awkward as camels;
and here are the shocked starlings pumping past
and think of innocent Icarus who is doing quite well:
larger than a sail, over the fog and the blast
of the plushy ocean, he goes. Admire his wings!
Feel the fire at his neck and see how casually
he glances up and is caught, wondrously tunneling
into that hot eye. Who cares that he fell back to the sea?
See him acclaiming the sun and come plunging down
while his sensible daddy goes straight into town.

Pain for a Daughter 1966

Blind with love, my daughter
has cried nightly for horses,
those long-necked marchers and churners
that she has mastered, any and all,
reigning them in like a circus hand—
the excitable muscles and the ripe neck;
tending this summer, a pony and a foal.
She who is too squeamish to pull

a thorn from the dog's paw,
watched her pony blossom with distemper,
the underside of the jaw swelling
like an enormous grape.
Gritting her teeth with love,
she drained the boil and scoured it
with hydrogen peroxide until pus
ran like milk on the barn floor.

Blind with loss all winter,
in dungarees, a ski jacket and a hard hat,
she visits the neighbors' stable,
our acreage not zoned for barns;
they who own the flaming horses
and the swan-whipped thoroughbred
that she tugs at and cajoles,
thinking it will burn like a furnace
under her small-hipped English seat.

Blind with pain she limps home.
The thoroughbred has stood on her foot.
He rested there like a building.
He grew into her foot until they were one.
The marks of the horseshoe printed
into her flesh, the tips of her toes
ripped off like pieces of leather,
three toenails swirled like shells
and left to float in blood in her riding boot.

Blind with fear, she sits on the toilet,
her foot balanced over the washbasin,
her father, hydrogen peroxide in hand,
performing the rites of the cleansing.
She bites on a towel, sucked in breath,
sucked in and arched against the pain,
her eyes glancing off me where
I stand at the door, eyes locked
on the ceiling, eyes of a stranger,
and then she cries . . .
Oh my God, help me!
Where a child would have cried *Mama!*
Where a child would have believed *Mama!*
she bit the towel and called on God
and I saw her life stretch out . . .
I saw her torn in childbirth,
and I saw her, at that moment,
in her own death and I knew that she
knew.

GARY SOTO

Gary Soto (b. 1952) was born to Mexican American parents in Fresno, an agricultural town in California's Central Valley. He worked in the fields in the summers and in the Fresno factories. After his graduation from high school, he entered California State University at Fresno, planning to study urban planning, but classes with poet Philip Levine turned his interest to literature and writing. After graduation he went on to the University of California at Irvine for an M.F.A.

Soto's first poems appeared when he was still a senior in college, and his first collection, *The Elements of San Joaquin*, was published in 1977. He began teaching literature and Chicano studies at the University of California campus at Berkeley the same year. His work has won many awards, and he has been granted a Guggenheim fellowship. Although Soto is perhaps the best known of the new Chicano poets, his writing has a personal identity that places it directly in the American mainstream.

"Mexicans Begin Jogging" is a wryly humorous memory from his youth. "Oranges" remembers when he was even younger and still new to the world's habits. In his poignant poem "Waiting at the Curb: Lynwood, California, 1967," he gives the reader a glimpse into the emotional difficulties that face all immigrant families, in any culture and in any moment of history.

WEB Research Gary Soto at bedfordstmartins.com/rewritinglit.

Mexicans Begin Jogging 1981

At the factory I worked
In the fleck of rubber, under the press
Of an oven yellow with flame,
Until the border patrol opened
Their vans and my boss waved for us to run.
"Over the fence, Soto," he shouted,
And I shouted that I was American.
"No time for lies," he said, and pressed
A dollar in my palm, hurrying me
Through the back door.

Since I was on his time, I ran
And became the wag to a short tail of Mexicans—
Ran past the amazed crowds that lined
The street and blurred like photographs, in rain.
I ran from that industrial road to the soft
Houses where people paled at the turn of an autumn sky.
What could I do but yell *vivas*
To baseball, milkshakes, and those sociologists
Who would clock me
As I jog into the next century
On the power of a great, silly grin.

Oranges

1985

The first time I walked
With a girl, I was twelve,
Cold, and weighted down
With two oranges in my jacket.
December. Frost cracking
Beneath my steps, my breath
Before me, then gone,
As I walked toward
Her house, the one whose
Porch light burned yellow
Night and day, in any weather.
A dog barked at me, until
She came out pulling
At her gloves, face bright
With rouge. I smiled,
Touched her shoulder, and led
Her down the street, across
A used car lot and a line
Of newly planted trees,
Until we were breathing
Before a drugstore. We
Entered, the tiny bell
Bringing a saleslady
Down a narrow aisle of goods.
I turned to the candies
Tiered like bleachers,
And asked what she wanted—
Light in her eyes, a smile
Starting at the corners
Of her mouth. I fingered
A nickel in my pocket,
And when she lifted a chocolate
That cost a dime,
I didn't say anything.
I took the nickel from
My pocket, then an orange,
And set them quietly on
The counter. When I looked up,
The lady's eyes met mine,
And held them, knowing
Very well what it was all
About.

Outside,
A few cars hissing past,

Fog hanging like old
Coats between the trees.
I took my girl's hand
In mine for two blocks,
Then released it to let
Her unwrap the chocolate.
I peeled my orange
That was so bright against
The gray of December
That, from some distance,
Someone might have thought
I was making a fire in my hands.

Waiting at the Curb: Lynwood, California, 1967 2005

for Deborah Escobedo

When the porch light snaps on,
Moths come alive around its orange glow.
Mother pushes open the screen door and calls,
"*Viejo*. It's Laugh-In." Father is watering
His lawn, the one green he can count on. He can't count
On money, or his Dodgers slipping on the green
Carpet of Chavez Ravine and into third place,
With nineteen games to go. "Be right there," Father says,
And then considers his daughter emerging in cut offs
Cut too short. And what's with the gypsy blouse
And those 45 records on her thumb?
Maybe he could speak his mind about decency,
Maybe he could lift his hose and spray off this girl child
Who has gone too far. But he rolls the garden hose
Onto the sling of his arm. "Debbie, where you going
With no clothes on?" he asks. The daughter spins
The records on her thumb, and answers,
"Dad, this is how it is." She steps off the porch,
Cuts across the wet lawn, and waits at the curb
For a friend in her own cut offs, for music that speaks to them,
For their cheeks collapsing from the pull on a paper straw.
She turns when the neighbor's screen door opens—
A woman in curlers yells to her own old man, "It's Laugh-In."
America is getting ready,
America is shoveling ice cream into Tupperware bowls,
America is setting up trays in front of snowy TVs.
This daughter wags a shaggy head of hair at the old folks,
Pulls at her cut offs creeping up. *I gotta get outta here,*
She thinks, and spins the music of her time
On what could be a hitchhiker's thumb.

WALT WHITMAN

Walt Whitman (1819–1892) was born on the eastern end of Long Island, New York. When he was three his father moved the family to Brooklyn. Whitman went to work as an errand boy when he was eleven and the next year took a job in a newspaper office. He educated himself by reading novels and soon was contributing poems to a Manhattan newspaper. For five years, beginning when he was sixteen, he worked mostly as a country schoolmaster on Long Island, boarding with the families of his students.

When Whitman gave up teaching, he went back to New York and Brooklyn, and for the next fifteen years he held a series of newspaper jobs, wrote a temperance novel, and published several short stories in a national magazine. By his mid-thirties he was living at home again, crowded into a shabby house in Brooklyn with his parents and his brothers and sisters. He had lost his newspaper job and was working – when he did work – as a carpenter. He spent his days walking the streets or sitting in local libraries. He was emotionally dependent on his mother, but he was careless about missing family meals, came and went as he pleased, and hid himself for hours writing poetry in the room he shared with his brother.

In the spring of 1855 Whitman arranged with a small Brooklyn print shop to bring out a book of the poems he had been writing. He titled it *Leaves of Grass*. He printed enough sheets for three hundred copies, had one hundred bound in green cloth with gold stamping, and sent copies to many important American writers. A few may have thrown their copies in the fire, but Ralph Waldo Emerson, then the leading American intellectual figure, recognized the book's genius and sent Whitman a letter that began, "I greet you at the beginning of a great career . . ."

Emerson's praise meant that the book received some attention, but Whitman's poetry confused most readers. It was unrhymed, the rhythms were so irregular that there was no way to determine the meter of the lines, and the language was as free and direct as someone shouting in the street. Readers were also confused because the only subject of the poems seemed to be Whitman himself. It was not only the form of his poems that opened the path to modern poetry. His use of himself as the persona of the poems was an important source for the tone of confession and self-examination of much twentieth-century American poetry.

Whitman spent the rest of his life trying to organize the writing that poured into his book. Each subsequent edition of *Leaves of Grass* contained new poems, and he also rewrote and retitled older poems. By the end of his life he was a revered literary figure whose work was read as enthusiastically in Europe as it was in the United States. Support from friends made it possible for him to buy a small house in Camden, New Jersey, where he died in 1892.

The first edition of *Leaves of Grass* opened with the poem "Song of Myself," though it was at that point still untitled. Through all the revisions of his book, Whitman continued to place "Song of Myself" close to the book's opening pages. Among the poem's sections, including 1 and 6, and the concluding sections, are some of his best-known and best-loved lines. "A Noiseless Patient Spider" is one of his most anthologized short poems. (See also Whitman's "A Farm Picture," p. 695.)

WEB Research Walt Whitman at bedfordstmartins.com/rewritinglit.

From "Song of Myself" 1855

1

I celebrate myself, and sing myself,
And what I assume you shall assume,
For every atom belonging to me as good belongs to you.

I loafe and invite my soul,
I lean and loafe at my ease observing a spear of summer grass.

My tongue, every atom of my blood, form'd from this soil, this air,
Born here of parents born here from parents the same, and their parents the same,
I, now thirty-seven years old in perfect health begin,
Hoping to cease not till death.

Creeds and schools in abeyance,
Retiring back a while sufficed at what they are, but never forgotten,
I harbor for good or bad, I permit to speak at every hazard,
Nature without check with original energy.

6

A child said *What is the grass?* fetching it to me with full hands;
How could I answer the child? I do not know what it is any more than he.

I guess it must be the flag of my disposition, out of hopeful green stuff woven.

Or I guess it is the handkerchief of the Lord,
A scented gift and remembrancer designedly dropt,
Bearing the owner's name someway in the corners, that we may see and remark, and say *Whose?*

Or I guess the grass is itself a child, the produced babe of the vegetation.

Or I guess it is a uniform hieroglyphic,
And it means, Sprouting alike in broad zones and narrow zones,
Growing among black folks as among white,
Kanuck, Tuckahoe, Congressman, Cuff, I give them the same, I receive them the same.

And now it seems to me the beautiful uncut hair of graves.

Tenderly will I use you curling grass,
It may be you transpire from the breasts of young men,
It may be if I had known them I would have loved them,

It may be you are from old people, or from offspring taken soon out of their mothers' laps,
And here you are the mothers' laps.

This grass is very dark to be from the white heads of old mothers,
Darker than the colorless beards of old men,
Dark to come from under the faint red roofs of mouths.

O I perceive after all so many uttering tongues,
And I perceive they do not come from the roofs of mouths for nothing.

I wish I could translate the hints about the dead young men and women,
And the hints about old men and mothers, and the offspring taken soon out of their laps.

What do you think has become of the young and old men?
And what do you think has become of the women and children?

They are alive and well somewhere,
The smallest sprout shows there is really no death,
And if ever there was it led forward life, and does not wait at the end to arrest it,
And ceas'd the moment life appear'd.

All goes onward and outward, nothing collapses,
And to die is different from what anyone supposed, and luckier.

50

There is that in me—I do not know what it is—but I know it is in me.

Wrench'd and sweaty—calm and cool then my body becomes,
I sleep—I sleep long.

I do not know it—it is without name—it is a word unsaid,
It is not in any dictionary, utterance, symbol.

Sometimes it swings on more than the earth I swing on,
To it the creation is the friend whose embracing awakes me.

Perhaps I might tell more. Outlines! I plead for my brothers and sisters.
Do you see O my brothers and sisters?
It is not chaos or death—it is form, union, plan—it is eternal life—it is Happiness.

51

The past and present wilt—I have fill'd them, emptied them.
And proceed to fill my next fold of the future.

Listener up there! what have you to confide to me?
Look in my face while I snuff the sidle of evening,
(Talk honestly, no one else hears you, and I stay only a minute longer.)

Do I contradict myself?
Very well then I contradict myself.
(I am large, I contain multitudes.)

I concentrate toward them that are nigh, I wait on the door-slab.
Who has done his day's work? who will soonest be through with his supper?
Who wishes to walk with me?
Will you speak before I am gone? will you prove already too late?

52

The spotted hawk swoops by and accuses me, he complains of my gab and my loitering.
I too am not a bit tamed, I too am untranslatable,
I sound my barbaric yawp over the roofs of the world.
The last scud of day holds back for me,
It flings my likeness after the rest and true as any on the shadowed wilds,
It coaxes me to the vapor and the dusk.
I depart as air, I shake my white locks at the runaway sun,
I effuse my flesh in eddies, and drift it in lacy jags.
I bequeath myself to the dirt to grow from the grass I love,
If you want me again look for me under your boot-soles.
You will hardly know who I am or what I mean,
But I shall be good health to you nevertheless,
And filter and fibre your blood.
Failing to fetch me at first keep encouraged,
Missing me one place search another,
I stop somewhere waiting for you.

COMMENTARIES

WALT WHITMAN

Walt Whitman worked for many years as a journalist and newspaper editor and he was keenly aware of the value of promotion for drawing the reading public's attention to new books. This is one of the anonymous reviews of his own *Leaves of Grass* he wrote to defend and explain his aims in his poetry. This eloquent statement appeared in New York City's *Saturday Post* for May 19, 1860.

A Review of *Leaves of Grass*

Some reflections may properly be submitted here, relative to the form in which Walt Whitman's poems are embodied and expressed. It is a form so rough and rugged—so careless, variable and peculiar—that perhaps it is very natural the poetry should sometimes degenerate into prose. Something is to be said, however in defence of this system of versification. It is at least original. The theory would seem to be, as Walt has variously indicated, that always the thought or passion of the poet should determine itself in natural, congenial expression. It is assumed in this theory, and indeed it is very true, that much of the verse ordinarily written, is written without a sincere motive, and has therefore neither power nor value. It is further assumed that the styles of versification generally accredited and employed are inadequate to the utterance of earnest thought and feeling. Consequently, Walt Whitman, who presents himself as the Poet of the American Republic in the Present Age, who *is* actuated by a sincere motive, and has earnest thought and feeling to express, refuses to confine and cripple himself within the laws of what to him is inefficient art. Reverencing the spirit of poetry above the form, he submits that the one shall determine the other. That his volume is poetic in spirit cannot rationally be denied; and, whatever the eccentricities of its form, no critical reader can fail to perceive that the expression seems always the suitable and natural result of the thought. It is indeed tame and prosy in the conveyance of any commonplace idea or feeling, but it rises and melts into sweet and thrilling music whenever impelled by the beautiful impulse of a grand thought or emotion.

EZRA POUND

Ezra Pound wrote this essay on Walt Whitman in 1909, only a year after he had left the United States to live permanently in Europe.

What I Feel about Walt Whitman 1909

From this side of the Atlantic I am for the first time able to read Whitman, and from the vantage of my education and—if it be permitted a man of my scant years—my world citizenship: I see him America's poet. The only Poet before the artists of the Carmen-Hovey° period, or better, the only one of the conventionally recognised "American Poets" who is worth reading.

He *is* America. His crudity is an exceeding great stench, but it *is* America. He is the hollow place in the rock that echoes with his time. He *does* "chant the crucial stage" and he is the "voice triumphant." He is disgusting. He is an exceedingly nauseating pill, but he accomplishes his mission.

Entirely free from the renaissance humanist ideal of the complete man or from the Greek idealism, he is content to be what he is, and he is his time and his people. He is a genius because he has vision of what he is and of his function. He knows that he is a beginning and not a classically finished work.

I honour him for he prophesied me while I can only recognise him as a forebear of whom I ought to be proud.

Carmen-Hovey: Canadian poet William Bliss Carman (1861–1929) and American poet Richard Hovey (1864–1900) collaborated on three books of verse in their *Songs of Vagabondia* series (1894, 1896, 1901).

In America there is much for the healing of the nations, but woe unto him of the cultured palate who attempts the dose.

As for Whitman, I read him (in many parts) with acute pain, but when I write of certain things I find myself using his rhythms. The expression of certain things related to cosmic consciousness seems tainted with this maramis.°

I am (in common with every educated man) an heir of the ages and I demand my birthright. Yet if Whitman represented his time in language acceptable to one accustomed to my standard of intellectual-artistic living he would belie his time and nation. And yet I am but one of his "ages and ages' encrustations" or to be exact an encrustation of the next age. The vital part of my message, taken from the sap and fibre of America, is the same as his.

Mentally I am a Walt Whitman who has learned to wear a collar and a dress shirt (although at times inimical to both). Personally I might be very glad to conceal my relationship to my spiritual father and brag about my more congenial ancestry—Dante, Shakespeare, Theocritus, Villon, but the descent is a bit difficult to establish. And, to be frank, Whitman is to my fatherland (*Patriam quam odi et amo*° for no uncertain reasons) what Dante is to Italy and I at my best can only be a strife for a renaissance in America of all the lost or temporarily mislaid beauty, truth, valour, glory of Greece, Italy, England, and all the rest of it.

And yet if a man has written lines like Whitman's to *Sunset Breeze* one has to love him. I think we have not yet paid enough attention to the deliberate artistry of the man, not in details but in the large.

I am immortal even as he is, yet with a lesser vitality as I am the more in love with beauty (If I really do love it more than he did). Like Dante he wrote in the "vulgar tongue," in a new metric. The first great man to write in the language of his people.

Et ego Petrarca in lingua vetera scribo,° and in a tongue my people understand not.

It seems to me I should like to drive Whitman into the old world. I sledge, he drill—and to scourge America with all the old beauty. (For Beauty *is* an accusation) and with a thousand thongs from Homer to Yeats, from Theocritus to Marcel Schwob. This desire is because I am young and impatient, were I old and wise I should content myself in seeing and saying that these things will come. But now, since I am by no means sure it would be true prophecy, I am fain set my own hand to the labour.

It is a great thing, reading a man to know, not "His Tricks are not as yet my Tricks, but I can easily make them mine" but "His message is my message. We will see that men hear it."

---

maramis: Likely "marasmus," wasting away. ***Patriam quam odi et amo*:** Latin for "Country that I hate and love. ***Et ego Petrarca in lingua vetera scribo*:** "And I, Petrarca, write in the old language." The Italian poet and scholar Francesco Petrarca (1304–1374) chose to write in Latin rather than Italian.

WILLIAM CARLOS WILLIAMS

William Carlos Williams (1883–1963) was born in Rutherford, New Jersey, where he lived and practiced medicine all his life. His mother was Puerto Rican; his father was English. Although he spent his life as a pediatrician, when he was a student at the University of Pennsylvania he was friends with Hilda Doolittle, who became the poet H.D., and the poet Ezra Pound. His encounter with them encouraged his own ambitions to be a poet, and he managed to lead a double life—as a doctor and a writer—until a series of strokes forced him to give up medicine in the 1950s.

Williams felt himself isolated in his small-town medical practice, but he was part of the avant-garde poetry movements of his time, and it was as an imagist (see imagism on pp. 794–800) that he was best known when he began publishing after World War I. During his long career he founded small magazines; contributed essays, poems, and stories to literary journals; and also found time to write novels, plays, and an autobiography.

Many of Williams's poems are short. In his autobiography he remembers that some of them were written on his office typewriter between patients, and some first versions of his poems were written on prescription blanks. He was the last of the modernist poets to achieve recognition, but his work became an important influence on younger poets like Allen Ginsberg, who brought Jack Kerouac, among others, to visit Williams in the 1950s.

"Spring and All" was published as an untitled entry in an experimental collection of writing with the title *Spring and All*, and the poem has assumed the book's name. "Danse Russe" is a joyous response to his sense of well-being, and its title refers to the Russian ballet company then appearing in New York, which Williams probably saw. He was responsive to the changes of the seasons, and "March" opens with the changing weather and goes on to assert that this eventful moment has led him to write poetry, "for the warmth there is in it." Spring is again the inspiration for the touching "The Widow's Lament in Springtime." (See also Williams's "The Red Wheelbarrow" on p. 798, and "To Waken an Old Lady" on p. 737.)

WEB Research William Carlos Williams at bedfordstmartins.com/rewritinglit.

Spring and All 1923

By the road to the contagious hospital,
under the surge of the blue
mottled clouds driven from the
northeast—cold wind. Beyond, the
waste of broad, muddy fields,
brown with dried weeds, standing and fallen,

patches of standing water,
the scattering of tall trees.

All along the road the reddish,
purplish, forked, upstanding, twiggy
stuff of brushes and small trees
with dead, brown leaves under them
leafless vines—

Lifeless in appearance, sluggish,
dazed spring approaches—
They enter the new world naked,
cold, uncertain of all
save that they enter. All about them
the cold, familiar wind—

Now the grass, tomorrow
the stiff curl of wild-carrot leaf.
One by one objects are defined—
It quickens: clarity, outline of leaf,

But now the stark dignity of
entrance—Still, the profound change
has come upon them; rooted, they
grip down and begin to awaken.

Danse Russe 1917

If I when my wife is sleeping
and the baby and Kathleen
are sleeping
and the sun is a flame-white disc
in silken mists
above shining trees,—
if I in my north room
dance naked, grotesquely
before my mirror
waving my shirt round my head
and singing softly to myself:
"I am lonely, lonely.
I was born to be lonely,
I am best so!"
If I admire my arms, my face,
my shoulders, flanks, buttocks
against the yellow drawn shades,—

Who shall say I am not
the happy genius of my household?

From "March" 1918

I

Winter is long in this climate
and spring—a matter of a few days
only—a flower or two picked
from mud or from among wet leaves
or at best against treacherous
bitterness of wind, and sky shining
teasingly, then closing in black
and sudden, with fierce jaws.

II

March,
you reminded me of
the pyramids, our pyramids—
stript of the polished stone
that used to guard them!
March,
you are like Fra Angelico
at Fiesole, painting on plaster!

March,
you are like a band of
young poets that have not learned
the blessedness of warmth
(or have forgotten it).
At any rate—
I am moved to write poetry
for the warmth there is in it
and for the loneliness—
a poem that shall have you
in it March.

The Widow's Lament in Springtime 1921

Sorrow is my own yard
where the new grass
flames as it has flamed
often before but not
with the cold fire
that closes round me this year.
Thirtyfive years
I lived with my husband.
The plumtree is white today

with masses of flowers.
Masses of flowers
load the cherry branches
and color some bushes
yellow and some red
but the grief in my heart
is stronger than they
for though they were my joy
formerly, today I notice them
and turn away forgetting.
Today my son told me
that in the meadows,
at the edge of the heavy woods
in the distance, he saw
trees of white flowers.
I feel that I would like
to go there
and fall into those flowers
and sink into the marsh near them.

COMMENTARY

WILLIAM CARLOS WILLIAMS

Spirit of '76

1920

Dear Miss Monroe:° Provided you will allow me to use small letters at the beginning of my lines, I submit the following excellent American poem to you for publication in your paying magazine:

Spirit of '76
Her father
built a bridge
over
the Chicago River
but she
built a bridge
over the moon.

This, as you will at once recognize, is an excellent poem and very American. I sincerely hope that no prehistoric prosodic rules will bar it from publication. Yours,

W. C. Williams

Monroe: Harriet Monroe was the editor of *Poetry Magazine*, which she founded in 1911. She was an early champion of the new "free" verse and poetic experiment.

WILLIAM WORDSWORTH

William Wordsworth (1770–1850) was born in the north of England, close to the Lake District. After the death of his mother when he was eight, he and his three brothers were raised in the countryside and often left free to roam. He also read hungrily and was encouraged to think of becoming a poet by his schoolmaster.

Wordsworth had a turbulent youth. In 1790, during his summer break from St. John's College in Cambridge, he went on a long walking trip through France and Switzerland, then returned to France after his graduation the next year, hoping to improve his French language skills enough to qualify as a teacher. He remained in France during the period of the wildest triumphs and fervors of the French Revolution. He fell in love with Annette Vallon, daughter of a family of Royalist sympathizers. She gave birth to Wordsworth's child, but the political turmoil forced him to return to England, and Annette was unable to follow him.

In England, Wordsworth was torn between the love he had left behind him and his disillusionment with the Revolution, which was becoming increasingly violent and despotic. At this moment, when he was struggling against a complete emotional collapse, a friend died and left Wordsworth enough money to enable the poet to devote himself entirely to his art. With his sister Dorothy, and a new friend, the young poet and critic Samuel Taylor Coleridge, Wordsworth began a new life.

Wordsworth and Coleridge set out to create a new style of poetry—poetry that would be closer to the language of ordinary people and would deal with genuine emotions. In 1798 they published a slim book, *Lyrical Ballads*, with poems by each of them. This book is considered the beginning of the **romantic movement** in English poetry.

In the course of his long life, Wordsworth lost the creative fire of his early years, but at his death he was hailed as one of the most significant literary figures England had ever produced. He began "Ode: Intimations of Immortality" in his mid-thirties, and it took him two years after he wrote the first four stanzas to complete the poem. He wrote to an admirer about its subject, "Nothing was more difficult for me in childhood than to admit the notion of death as a state applicable to my own being." The sonnet "The world is too much with us" was published the same year. (See also Wordsworth's "I Wandered Lonely as a Cloud" on p. 782.)

WEB Research William Wordsworth at bedfordstmartins.com/rewritinglit.

Ode

1807

Intimations of Immortality from Recollections of Early Childhood

The Child is Father of the Man;
And I could wish my days to be
Bound each to each by natural piety.

1

There was a time when meadow, grove, and stream,
The earth, and every common sight,
To me did seem
Apparelled in celestial light,
The glory and the freshness of a dream.
It is not now as it hath been of yore;—
Turn wheresoe'er I may,
By night or day,
The things which I have seen I now can see no more.

2

The Rainbow comes and goes,
And lovely is the Rose,
The Moon doth with delight
Look round her when the heavens are bare,
Waters on a starry night
Are beautiful and fair;
The sunshine is a glorious birth;
But yet I know, where'er I go,
That there hath past away a glory from the earth.

3

Now, while the birds thus sing a joyous song,
And while the young lambs bound
As to the tabor's sound,
To me alone there came a thought of grief:
A timely utterance gave that thought relief,
And I again am strong:
The cataracts blow their trumpets from the steep;
No more shall grief of mine the season wrong;
I hear the Echoes through the mountains throng,
The Winds come to me from the fields of sleep,
And all the earth is gay;
Land and sea
Give themselves up to jollity,
And with the heart of May
Doth every Beast keep holiday;—
Thou Child of Joy,
Shout round me, let me hear thy shouts, thou happy Shepherd-boy!

4

Ye blessed Creatures, I have heard the call
Ye to each other make; I see
The heavens laugh with you in your jubilee;
My heart is at your festival,

My head hath its coronal,°
The fulness of your bliss, I feel—I feel it all.
Oh evil day! if I were sullen
While Earth herself is adorning,
This sweet May-morning,
And the Children are culling
On every side,
In a thousand valleys far and wide,
Fresh flowers; while the sun shines warm,
And the Babe leaps up on his Mother's arm:—
I hear, I hear, with joy I hear!
—But there's a Tree, of many, one,
A single Field which I have looked upon,
Both of them speak of something that is gone:
The Pansy at my feet
Doth the same tale repeat:
Whither is fled the visionary gleam?
Where is it now, the glory and the dream?

5

Our birth is but a sleep and a forgetting:
The Soul that rises with us, our life's Star,
Hath had elsewhere its setting,
And cometh from afar:
Not in entire forgetfulness,
And not in utter nakedness,
But trailing clouds of glory do we come
From God, who is our home:
Heaven lies about us in our infancy!
Shades of the prison-house begin to close
Upon the growing Boy,
But He beholds the light, and whence it flows,
He sees it in his joy;
The Youth, who daily farther from the east
Must travel, still is Nature's Priest,
And by the vision splendid
Is on his way attended;
At length the Man perceives it die away,
And fade into the light of common day.

6

Earth fills her lap with pleasures of her own;
Yearnings she hath in her own natural kind,
And, even with something of a Mother's mind,

40. coronal: Crown of flowers worn by young shepherds in May.

And no unworthy aim,
The homely Nurse doth all she can
To make her Foster-child, her Inmate Man,
Forget the glories he hath known,
And that imperial palace whence he came.

7

Behold the Child among his new-born blisses,
A six years' Darling of a pigmy size!
See, where 'mid work of his own hand he lies,
Fretted by sallies of his mother's kisses,
With light upon him from his father's eyes!
See, at his feet, some little plan or chart,
Some fragment from his dream of human life,
Shaped by himself with newly-learnèd art;
A wedding or a festival,
A mourning or a funeral;
And this hath now his heart,
And unto this he frames his song:
Then will he fit his tongue
To dialogues of business, love, or strife;
But it will not be long
Ere this be thrown aside,
And with new joy and pride
The little Actor cons another part;
Filling from time to time his "humorous stage"°
With all the Persons, down to palsied Age,
That Life brings with her in her equipage;
As if his whole vocation
Were endless imitation.

8

Thou, whose exterior semblance doth belie
Thy Soul's immensity;
Thou best Philosopher, who yet dost keep
Thy heritage, thou Eye among the blind,
That, deaf and silent, read'st the eternal deep,
Haunted for ever by the eternal mind,—
Mighty Prophet! Seer blest!
On whom those truths do rest,
Which we are toiling all our lives to find,
In darkness lost, the darkness of the grave;

---

103. "humorous stage": Capriciousness, but also carries the sense of the classical temperaments ("humors").

Thou, over whom thy Immortality
Broods like the Day, a Master o'er a Slave,
A Presence which is not to be put by;
Thou little Child, yet glorious in the might
Of heaven-born freedom on thy being's height,
Why with such earnest pains dost thou provoke
The years to bring the inevitable yoke,
Thus blindly with thy blessedness at strife?
Full soon thy Soul shall have her earthly freight,
And custom lie upon thee with a weight,
Heavy as frost, and deep almost as life!

9

O joy! that in our embers
Is something that doth live,
That nature yet remembers
What was so fugitive!
The thought of our past years in me doth breed
Perpetual benediction: not indeed
For that which is most worthy to be blest;
Delight and liberty, the simple creed
Of Childhood, whether busy or at rest,
With new-fledged hope still fluttering in his breast—
Not for these I raise
The song of thanks and praise;
But for those obstinate questionings
Of sense and outward things,
Fallings from us, vanishings;
Blank misgivings of a Creature
Moving about in worlds not realised,
High instincts before which our mortal Nature
Did tremble like a guilty Thing surprised:
But for those first affections,
Those shadowy recollections,
Which, be they what they may,
Are yet the fountain light of all our day,
Are yet a master light of all our seeing;
Uphold us, cherish, and have power to make
Our noisy years seem moments in the being
Of the eternal Silence: truths that wake,
To perish never;
Which neither listlessness, nor mad endeavour,
Nor Man nor Boy,
Nor all that is at enmity with joy,
Can utterly abolish or destroy!
Hence in a season of calm weather

Though inland far we be,
Our Souls have sight of that immortal sea
Which brought us hither,
Can in a moment travel thither,
And see the Children sport upon the shore,
And hear the mighty waters rolling evermore.

10

Then sing, ye Birds, sing, sing a joyous song!
And let the young Lambs bound
As to the tabor's sound!
We in thought will join your throng,
Ye that pipe and ye that play,
Ye that through your hearts to-day
Feel the gladness of the May!
What though the radiance which was once so bright
Be now for ever taken from my sight,
Though nothing can bring back the hour
Of splendour in the grass, of glory in the flower;
We will grieve not, rather find
Strength in what remains behind;
In the primal sympathy
Which having been must ever be;
In the soothing thoughts that spring
Out of human suffering;
In the faith that looks through death,
In years that bring the philosophic mind.

11

And O, ye Fountains, Meadows, Hills, and Groves,
Forebode not any severing of our loves!
Yet in my heart of hearts I feel your might;
I only have relinquished one delight
To live beneath your more habitual sway.
I love the Brooks which down their channels fret,
Even more than when I tripped lightly as they;
The innocent brightness of a new-born Day
Is lovely yet;
The Clouds that gather round the setting sun
Do take a sober colouring from an eye
That hath kept watch o'er man's mortality;
Another race hath been, and other palms are won.
Thanks to the human heart by which we live,
Thanks to its tenderness, its joys, and fears,
To me the meanest flower that blows can give
Thoughts that do often lie too deep for tears.

The world is too much with us 1807

The world is too much with us; late and soon,
Getting and spending, we lay waste our powers:
Little we see in nature that is ours;
We have given our hearts away, a sordid boon!
This Sea that bares her bosom to the moon;
The Winds that will be howling at all hours
And are up-gathered now like sleeping flowers;
For this, for every thing, we are out of tune;
It moves us not—Great God! I'd rather be
A Pagan suckled in a creed outworn;
So might I, standing on this pleasant lea,
Have glimpses that would make me less forlorn;
Have sight of Proteus coming from the sea;
Or hear old Triton blow his wreathed horn.

COMMENTARY

WILLIAM WORDSWORTH

William Wordsworth wrote two introductions to the collection of poems titled *Lyrical Ballads*. This is the second introduction, to the edition of 1802, which expanded and explained ideas that he had presented in the introduction to the first edition of the work in 1798.

From the Introduction to *Lyrical Ballads* 1802

It is supposed, that by the act of writing in verse an author makes a formal engagement that he will gratify certain known habits of association; that he not only thus apprizes the reader that certain classes of ideas and expressions will be found in his book, but that others will be carefully excluded. This exponent or symbol held forth by metrical language must in different eras of literature have excited very different expectations: for example, in the age of Catullus, Terence, and Lucretius and that of Statius or Claudian,° and in our own country, in the age of Shakespeare and Beaumont and Fletcher, and that of Donne and Cowley, or Dryden, or Pope. I will not take upon me to determine the exact import of the promise which by the act of writing in verse an author, in the present day, makes to his reader; but I am certain, it will appear to many persons that I have not fulfilled the terms of an engagement thus voluntarily contracted.

Catullus . . . Claudian: Catullus (84–54 B.C.), Terence (186–159 B.C.), and Lucretius (96–55 B.C.) were Roman poets who wrote simply, in contrast to Statius (45–96) and Claudian (370?–410?), whose work was more elaborate.

They who have been accustomed to the gaudiness and inane phraseology of many modern writers, if they persist in reading this book to its conclusion, will, no doubt, frequently have to struggle with feelings of strangeness and awkwardness: they will look round for poetry, and will be induced to inquire by what species of courtesy these attempts can be permitted to assume that title. I hope therefore the reader will not censure me, if I attempt to state what I have proposed to myself to perform; and also (as far as the limits of a preface will permit) to explain some sort of the chief reasons which have determined me in the choice of my purpose: that at least he may be spared any unpleasant feeling of disappointment, and that I myself may be protected from the most dishonorable accusation which can be brought against an author, namely, that of an indolence which prevents him from endeavouring to ascertain what is his duty, or, when this duty is ascertained, prevents him from performing it.

The principal object, then, which I proposed to myself in these poems was to choose incidents and situations from common life, and to relate or describe them, throughout, as far as was possible, in a selection of language really used by men; and, at the same time, to throw over them a certain colouring of imagination, whereby ordinary things should be presented to the mind in an unusual way; and, further, and above all, to make these incidents and situations interesting by tracing in them, truly though not ostentatiously, the primary laws of our nature: chiefly, as far as regards the manner in which we associate ideas in a state of excitement. Low and rustic life was generally chosen, because in that condition, the essential passions of the heart find a better soil in which they can attain their maturity, are less under restraint, and speak a plainer and more emphatic language; because in that condition of life our elementary feelings co-exist in a state of greater simplicity, and, consequently, may be more accurately contemplated, and more forcibly communicated; because the manners of rural life germinate from those elementary feelings; and, from the necessary character of rural occupations, are more easily comprehended; and are more durable; and lastly, because in that condition the passions of men are incorporated with the beautiful and permanent forms of nature. The language, too, of these men is adopted (purified indeed from what appear to be its real defects, from all lasting and rational causes of dislike or disgust) because such men hourly communicate with the best objects from which the best part of language is originally derived; and because, from their rank in society and the sameness and narrow circle of their intercourse, being less under the influence of social vanity they convey their feelings and notions in simple and unelaborated expressions. Accordingly, such a language, arising out of repeated experience and regular feelings, is a more permanent, and a far more philosophical language, than that which is frequently substituted for it by poets, who think that they are conferring honour upon themselves and their art, in proportion as they separate themselves from the sympathies of men, and indulge in arbitrary and capricious habits of expression, in order to furnish food for fickle tastes, and fickle appetites, of their own creation.

I cannot, however, be insensible of the present outcry against the triviality and meanness both of thought and language, which some of my contemporaries have occasionally introduced into their metrical compositions; and

I acknowledge, that this defect, where it exists, is more dishonorable to the writer's own character than false refinement or arbitrary innovation, though I should contend at the same time that it is far less pernicious in the sum of its consequences. From such verses the poems in these volumes will be found distinguished at least by one mark of difference, that each of them has a worthy *purpose*. Not that I mean to say, that I always began to write with a distinct purpose formally conceived; but I believe that my habits of meditation have so formed my feelings, as that my descriptions of such objects as strongly excite those feelings, will be found to carry along with them a *purpose*. If in this opinion I am mistaken, I can have little right to the name of a poet. For all good poetry is the spontaneous overflow of powerful feelings: but though this be true, poems to which any value can be attached, were never produced on any variety of subjects but by a man who, being possessed of more than usual organic sensibility, had also thought long and deeply. For our continued influxes of feeling are modified and directed by our thoughts, which are indeed the representatives of all our past feelings; and, as by contemplating the relation of these general representatives to each other we discover what is really important to men, so, by the repetition and continuance of this act, our feelings will be connected with important subjects, till at length, if we be originally possessed of much sensibility, such habits of mind will be produced, that, by obeying blindly and mechanically the impulses of those habits, we shall describe objects, and utter sentiments, of such a nature and in such connection with each other, that the understanding of the being to whom we address ourselves, if he be in a healthful state of association, must necessarily be in some degree enlightened, and his affections ameliorated. . . .

I have said that poetry is the spontaneous overflow of powerful feelings: it takes its origin from emotion recollected in tranquillity: the emotion is contemplated till by a species of reaction the tranquillity gradually disappears, and an emotion, kindred to that which was before the subject of contemplation, is gradually produced, and does itself actually exist in the mind. In this mood successful composition generally begins, and in a mood similar to this it is carried on; but the emotion, of whatever kind and in whatever degree, from various causes is qualified by various pleasures, so that in describing any passions whatsoever, which are voluntarily described, the mind will upon the whole be in a state of enjoyment. Now, if nature be thus cautious in preserving in a state of enjoyment a being thus employed, the poet ought to profit by the lesson thus held forth to him, and ought especially to take care, that whatever passions he communicates to his reader, those passions, if his reader's mind be sound and vigorous, should always be accompanied with an overbalance of pleasure. Now the music of harmonious metrical language, the sense of difficulty overcome, and the blind association of pleasure which has been previously received from works of rhyme or metre of the same or similar construction, an indistinct perception perpetually renewed of language closely resembling that of real life, and yet, in the circumstance of metre, differing from it so widely, all these imperceptibly make up a complex feeling of delight, which is of the most important use in tempering the painful feeling which will always be found intermingled with powerful descriptions of the deeper passions. This effect is always produced in pathetic and impassioned poetry; while, in lighter compositions, the ease and gracefulness with which the poet manages his numbers are themselves confessedly a principal source of the gratification of the reader. I might perhaps include all which is *necessary* to say upon this subject by affirming, what few persons will deny, that, of two descriptions, either of passions, manners, or characters, each of them equally well executed, the one in prose and the other in verse, the verse will be read a hundred times where the prose is read once.

JAMES WRIGHT

James Wright (1927–1980) was born in Martin's Ferry, Ohio, and although he spent much of his life in New York City he returned again and again to images of his rural childhood for the inspiration for his poetry. He graduated from Kenyon College and completed his Ph.D. at the University of Washington. After he received his doctorate he lived for some time in Austria and then returned to the United States and a career as a teacher. He taught first at the University of Minnesota, then moved to Hunter College in New York City and remained there for the final years of his troubled life. In addition to his own poetry, he translated writing by important European and South American poets in conjunction with Robert Bly's *Fifties Press.* With Bly he translated George Trakl and Pablo Neruda, and he translated César Vallejo with Bly and John Knoeple.

In his introduction to the collection of essays he edited, *Clear Word: Essays on the Poetry of James Wright*, Dave Smith wrote,

> Wright continuously praised writers for telling the truth boldly and powerfully but shied away from such claims for himself. The irony . . . is that the more he brought his life into his poems, his emotional and ethical and biographical and mythical life, the more he made us feel in ourselves, the more courage he gave us.

"Evening," with its evocation of a father's search for his son in the garden when he's been called in to dinner, demonstrates Wright's sensitivity to the magic of ordinary moments. In the other poems, "A Blessing," and "Lying in a Hammock at William Duffy's Farm in Pine Island, Minnesota," each of them often anthologized, a simple country setting is again a cause for introspection and wonder.

CONNECTION James Wright, "The Music of Robert Frost's 'Stopping by Woods on a Snowy Evening,'" page 885.

WEB Research James Wright at bedfordstmartins.com/rewritinglit.

Evening

1959

I called him to come in,
The wide lawn darkened so.
Laughing, he held his chin
And hid beside a bush.
The light gave him a push,
Shadowy grass moved slow.
He crept on agile toes
Under a sheltering rose.

His mother, still beyond
The bare porch and the door,
Called faintly out of sound,
And vanished with her voice.
I caught his curious eyes
Measuring me, and more—
The light dancing behind
My shoulder in the wind.

Then, struck beyond belief
By the child's voice I heard,
I saw his hair turn leaf,
His dancing toes divide
To hooves on either side,
One hand become a bird.
Startled, I held my tongue
To hear what note he sang.

Where was the boy gone now?
I stood on the grass, alone.
Swung from the apple bough
The bees ignored my cry.
A dog roved past, and I
Turned up a sinking stone,
But found beneath no more
Than grasses dead last year.

Suddenly lost and cold,
I knew the yard lay bare.
I longed to touch and hold
My child, my talking child,
Laughing or tame or wild—
Solid in light and air,
The supple hands, the face
To fill that barren place.

Slowly, the leaves descended,
The birds resolved to hands;

Laugh, and the charm was ended,
The hungry boy stepped forth.
He stood on the hard earth,
Like one who understands
Fairy and ghost—but less
Our human loneliness.

Then, on the withering lawn,
He walked beside my arm.
Trees and the sun were gone,
Everything gone but us.
His mother sang in the house,
And kept our supper warm,
And loved us, God knows how,
The wide earth darkened so.

A Blessing

1963

Just off the highway to Rochester, Minnesota,
Twilight bounds softly forth on the grass.
And the eyes of those two Indian ponies
Darken with kindness.
They have come gladly out of the willows
To welcome my friend and me.
We step over the barbed wire into the pasture
Where they have been grazing all day, alone.
They ripple tensely, they can hardly contain their happiness
That we have come.
They bow shyly as wet swans. They love each other.
There is no loneliness like theirs.
At home once more,
They begin munching the young tufts of spring in the darkness.
I would like to hold the slenderer one in my arms,
For she has walked over to me
And nuzzled my left hand.
She is black and white,
Her mane falls wild on her forehead,
And the light breeze moves me to caress her long ear
That is delicate as the skin over a girl's wrist.
Suddenly I realize
That if I stepped out of my body I would break
Into blossom.

Lying in a Hammock at William Duffy's Farm in Pine Island, Minnesota

1963

Over my head, I see the bronze butterfly,
Asleep on the black trunk,
Blowing like a leaf in green shadow.
Down the ravine behind the empty house,
The cowbells follow one another
Into the distances of the afternoon.
To my right,
In a field of sunlight between two pines,
The droppings of last year's horses
Blaze up into golden stones.
I lean back, as the evening darkens and comes on.
A chicken hawk floats over, looking for home.
I have wasted my life.

COMMENTARY

SVEN BIRKERTS

Sven Birkerts is an American critic and essayist who now directs the Bennington College Writing Program. This essay appeared in his collection *The Electric Life: Essays on Modern Poetry* (1989).

James Wright's "Hammock": A Sounding

1984

Here is a poem that could fit snugly on the back of a postcard. It is a poem, though, and not a postcard. And we read it, and read it again, and again—for reading poetry is, in part, a process of clearing rubble. The postcard we would read once, for its sentiment or information; then, if its reverse appealed to us, we might fasten it to the bulletin board with a pin. But here is a poem, and something else is happening, something that, if we open our gates to it, pulls us in past sentiment, past information.

We read it through. "I have wasted my life," declares the poet, the speaker, the voice. We read it through again, more carefully. Something has happened and we are not sure what. There has been little, if indeed anything, to prepare us for that statement. When we move our eyes back up to the first line, it is with some of the wary watchfulness of a crack detective. Either we have overlooked something, or else the poet has tossed us a red herring. We go back through the lines, combing the language, rhythm, and syntax for evidence that will support the last declaration. The procedure is wrongheaded, ultimately—a poem is not the site of a murder, but of the most delicate nativity—but through such attentiveness we do, at least, engage it at the level of linguistic nuance that poetry depends upon.

A successful poem—or a great poem, or a "realized" poem—is an inexhaustible repository of sonic and semantic events/interactions. When we read such a poem we cannot err on the side of attentiveness; no discrimination is too fine. This is not to say that the poet has *consciously* located subtle resonance: If all effects were conscious we could pull them out just as he put them in, and after a while we would have come to the end of it. But the language web extends past the shifting boundary of the field of the conscious, and the poem-making process depends as much upon associative marriages sanctified by a feeling of "rightness" as it does upon rational choice. And there is no limiting the effects produced by the unconscious interactions. They cannot be invalidated through any appeal to the poet's intention. . . .

> Over my head, I see the bronze butterfly,
> Asleep on the black trunk,
> Blowing like a leaf in green shadow.

On the surface of it, these first three lines are straightforward enough—no oblique meanings or gnarled syntactic patches. The speaking voice has established a calm, descriptive tone. Repose is implicit, not least for the psychological reason that one does not remark details like the blowing of a butterfly when one is agitated or upset. A clear picture begins to emerge. Indeed, it is as though we were watching a painter at work. "Over my head"—the vertical axis is drawn; "the bronze butterfly" dabs in the first color, which, with the wide brushstroke of "black trunk" in the next line, is brightened by contrast. Nor is it only a contrast of colors; fragility and massive solidity are immediately put into opposition. "Green shadow" then softens the contrast of bronze and black through chromatic mediation. What's more, it brings dimension in, reminds us that we are not, in fact, looking at a simplified color composition. And as the impression of environment begins to take hold, we realize that it is by way of word-by-word widening of focus: A single butterfly is on a black trunk; the black trunk is bathed in green shadow. . . .

Color and scale apart, there are a few vital, though in some cases subliminal, linguistic effects to note. First, Wright is using the definite article, "the"—not "a"—with the butterfly. What we expect to, and perhaps do, read is the latter. The distinction seems minor, but it is not. With the definite article, as with the specificity of the title, the poet is preparing us for the "moment of truth." By saying "the," he has excerpted the moment of observation from temporal flow; he has weighted it. It is "the bronze butterfly" rather than "a bronze butterfly" because the perception represents the first step in what will be an unspoken internal movement—the beginning of a psychic dilation that will culminate in the words "I have wasted my life."

WILLIAM BUTLER YEATS

William Butler Yeats (1865–1939) was born in Dublin, but his parents were of English descent, and he spent much of his youth in London. His father, Jack Yeats, was a gifted but struggling artist. Yeats first decided to follow his father and become a painter. He changed his mind, however, after beginning his art studies. His first published poems appeared in the *Dublin University Review* when he was twenty.

For most of his life Yeats journeyed between England and Ireland, where he lived some of the time in Dublin and at other times with his mother's family in County Sligo, a rural area in northwest Ireland. All three of these very different environments had an effect on his writing. His early poetry often presented a soft mood of reverie, influenced by younger poets he met in London. He also drew from his Irish background in verse dramas based on Irish legends and myths. The rough countryside of County Sligo lent his poetry a sharper, less romantic tone than that of the London poets' verse.

In 1899 Yeats helped found the Irish National Theatre, but bitter struggles with the conservative middle-class audiences eventually drove him to London. The Irish Rebellion of 1916, however, when a group of Irish idealists attempted to seize power from the British occupying forces, brought him back, and when Ireland achieved partial independence in 1922 he was appointed a senator and served in the government for six years.

Yeats had a long and successful career as a writer, and he won the Nobel Prize for literature in 1923. "The Lake Isle of Innisfree" recalls a memory of his youth, and "The Second Coming" is one of his most impassioned visionary poems. In "The Wild Swans at Coole," he returns again to the past and his pain at the passage of time.

WEB Research William Butler Yeats at bedfordstmartins.com/rewritinglit.

The Lake Isle of Innisfree 1890

I will arise and go now, and go to Innisfree,
And a small cabin build there, of clay and wattles made;
Nine bean rows will I have there, a hive for the honey bee,
        And live alone in the bee-loud glade.

And I shall have some peace there, for peace comes dropping slow,
Dropping from the veils of the morning to where the cricket sings;
There midnight's all a glimmer, and noon a purple glow,
        And evening full of the linnet's wings.

I will arise and go now, for always night and day
I hear lake water lapping with low sounds by the shore;
While I stand on the roadway, or on the pavements gray,
        I hear it in the deep heart's core.

The Second Coming 1919

Turning and turning in the widening gyre
The falcon cannot hear the falconer;
Things fall apart; the centre cannot hold;
Mere anarchy is loosed upon the world,
The blood-dimmed tide is loosed, and everywhere
The ceremony of innocence is drowned;
The best lack all conviction, while the worst
Are full of passionate intensity.
Surely some revelation is at hand;
Surely the Second Coming is at hand.
The Second Coming! Hardly are those words out
When a vast image out of *Spiritus Mundi*°
Troubles my sight: somewhere in sands of the desert
A shape with lion body and the head of a man,
A gaze blank and pitiless as the sun,
Is moving its slow thighs, while all about it
Reel shadows of the indignant desert birds.
The darkness drops again; but now I know
That twenty centuries of stony sleep
Were vexed to nightmare by a rocking cradle,
And what rough beast, its hour come round at last,
Slouches towards Bethlehem to be born?

The Wild Swans at Coole 1917

The trees are in their autumn beauty,
The woodland paths are dry,
Under the October twilight the water
Mirrors a still sky;
Upon the brimming water among the stones
Are nine and fifty swans.
The nineteenth Autumn has come upon me
Since I first made my count;
I saw, before I had well finished,
All suddenly mount
And scatter, wheeling, in great broken rings
Upon their clamorous wings.
I have looked upon those brilliant creatures,
And now my heart is sore.
All's changed since I, hearing at twilight,

12. ***Spiritus Mundi*:** Spirit of the universe.

The first time on this shore,
The bell-beat of their wings above my head,
Trod with a lighter tread.

Unwearied still, lover by lover,
They paddle in the cold,
Companionable streams or climb the air;
Their hearts have not grown old;
Passion or conquest, wander where they will,
Attend upon them still.

But now they drift on the still water
Mysterious, beautiful;
Among what rushes will they build,
By what lake's edge or pool
Delight men's eyes, when I awake some day
To find they have flown away?

19.

Themes for Thinking and Writing about Poetry

In these next chapters you will have the opportunity to respond to poets writing about themes that are important in our world today. This time you can add your own voice to the discussion in your writing. You can decide for yourself if it is the poet who interests you, or perhaps you will choose to write about the theme of a particular poem, or the general subject of the discussion itself. You have an opportunity now to practice all the skills you have acquired in your study of poetry.

IN WONDER AT THE NATURAL WORLD

For the thousands of years that poetry has been part of our human expression, writers have taken the world of nature poetry as one of their subjects. As all of you have become aware, however, today there is a fierce debate that has spilled over onto television screens and into everyday conversations about what is happening to our natural environment and what we can we do about it. There is a new consciousness that the beauty and the bounty of our planet, which we have for so long taken for granted, is seriously threatened by exploitation and ever-expanding human populations. In recent poetry written in response to the wonder of the natural world, there is a growing conviction that what the poet sees today perhaps will be the last we will experience of this vision.

One of the most enduring documents of our relationship with this world of nature is the book *Walden,* written by Henry David Thoreau and published in 1855. It describes his sojourn in a cabin he built himself on the shore of Walden Pond in Massachusetts. He described himself as living in isolation; however, as he makes clear in this excerpt, he needed the assistance of his neighbors to begin his experiment. Thomas Lovell Beddoes and John Clare were both writing in early-nineteenth-century England, but Beddoes was middle class, and he used the classic poetic forms with comfortable ease. Clare was described in his own time as a "peasant poet," and his writing shows his intimate knowledge of the small creatures, the flowers, and the buzzing insects around his farm. For Walt Whitman and Edna St. Vincent Millay the breadth and the multiplicity of nature opens them to what Millay terms "God's Glory." The English novelist and poet D. H. Lawrence finds that a glimpse of young deer makes him conscious of the sense of mystery in the relationship between humankind and the Earth's other inhabitants. Mary Oliver's "Sleeping in the Forest" uses a rich blending of personification and metaphor to draw her readers into the sounds and the visionary dreams she experiences during the night she sleeps outdoors under the trees. John Casteen's "Night Hunting" presents the reader with some of the complex moral issues we face in our involvement with nature today.

DOCUMENT

HENRY DAVID THOREAU

"It is difficult to begin without borrowing . . ." 1855

Near the end of March, 1845, I borrowed an axe and went down to the woods by Walden Pond, nearest to where I intended to build my house, and began to cut down some tall arrowy white pines, still in their youth, for timber. It is difficult to begin without borrowing, but perhaps it is the most generous course thus to permit your fellow-men to have an interest in your enterprise. The owner of the axe, as he released his hold on it, said that it was the apple of his eye; but I returned it sharper than I received it. It was a pleasant hillside where I worked, covered with pine woods, through which I looked out on the pond, and a small open field in the woods where pines and hickories were springing up. The ice in the pond was not yet dissolved, though there were some open spaces, and it was all dark colored and saturated with water. There were some slight flurries of snow during the days that I worked there; but for the most part when I came out on to the railroad, on my way home, its yellow sand heap stretched away gleaming in the hazy atmosphere, and the rails shone in the spring sun, and I heard the lark and peewee and other birds already come to commence another year with us. They were pleasant spring days, in which the winter of man's discontent was thawing as well as the earth, and the life that had lain torpid began to stretch itself. One day, when my axe had come off and I had cut a green hickory for a wedge, driving it with a stone, and had placed the whole to soak in a pond hole in order to swell the wood, I saw a striped snake run into the water, and he lay on the bottom, apparently without inconvenience, as long as I staid there, or more than a quarter of an hour; perhaps because he had not yet fairly come out of the torpid state. It appeared to me that for a like reason men remain in their present low and primitive condition; but if they should feel the influence of the spring of springs arousing them, they would of necessity rise to a higher and more ethereal life.

THOMAS LOVELL BEDDOES

A Lake

1823

A lake
Is a river curled and asleep like a snake.

JOHN CLARE

The Sky Lark

1835

The rolls and harrows lie at rest beside
The battered road and spreading far and wide
Above the russet clods the corn is seen
Sprouting its spirey points of tender green
Where squats the hare to terrors wide awake
Like some brown clod the harrows failed to break
While neath the warm hedge boys stray far from home
To crop the early blossoms as they come
Where buttercups will make them eager run
Opening their golden caskets to the sun
To see who shall be first to pluck the prize
And from their hurry up the skylark flies
And oer her half formed nest with happy wings
Winnows the air—till in the clouds she sings
Then hangs a dust spot in the sunny skies
And drops and drops till in her nest she lies
Where boys unheeding past—neer dreaming then
That birds which flew so high—would drop agen
To nests upon the ground where any thing
May come at to destroy had they the wing
Like such a bird themselves would be too proud
And build on nothing but a passing cloud
As free from danger as the heavens are free
From pain and toil—there would they build and be
And sail about the world to scenes unheard
Of and unseen—O where they but a bird
So think they while they listen to its song
And smile and fancy and so pass along
While its low nest moist with the dews of morn
Lye safely with the leveret in the corn

WALT WHITMAN

On the Beach at Night Alone

1856

On the beach at night alone,
As the old mother sways her to and fro, singing her husky song,
As I watch the bright stars shining—I think a thought of the clef of the universes, and of the future.

A vast similitude interlocks all,
All spheres, grown, ungrown, small, large, suns, moons, planets, comets, asteroids,
All the substances of the same, and all that is spiritual upon the same,
All distances of place, however wide,
All distances of time—all inanimate forms,
All Souls—all living bodies, though they be ever so different, or in different worlds,
All gaseous, watery, vegetable, mineral processes—the fishes, the brutes,
All men and women—me also;
All nations, colors, barbarisms, civilizations, languages;
All identities that have existed, or may exist, on this globe, or any globe;
All lives and deaths—all of the past, present, future;
This vast similitude spans them, and always has spann'd, and shall forever span them, and compactly hold them, and enclose them.

EDNA ST. VINCENT MILLAY

God's World

1917

O world, I cannot hold thee close enough!
Thy winds, thy wide grey skies!
Thy mists, that roll and rise!
Thy woods, this autumn day, that ache and sag
And all but cry with colour! That gaunt crag
To crush! To lift the lean of that black bluff!
World, World, I cannot get thee close enough!

Long have I known a glory in it all,
But never knew I this:
Here such a passion is
As stretcheth me apart,—Lord, I do fear
Thou'st made the world too beautiful this year;
My soul is all but out of me,—let fall
No burning leaf; prithee, let no bird call.

D. H. LAWRENCE

A Doe at Evening

1917

As I went through the marshes
a doe sprang out of the corn
and flashed up the hill-side
leaving her fawn.

On the sky-line
she moved round to watch,
she pricked a fine black blotch
on the sky.

I looked at her
and felt her watching;
I became a strange being.
Still, I had my right to be there with her.

Her nimble shadow trotting
along the sky-line, she
put back her fine, level-balanced head.
And I knew her.

Ah yes, being male, is not my head hard-balanced, antlered?
Are not my haunches light?
Has she not fled on the same wind with me?
Does not my fear cover her fear?

MARY OLIVER

Sleeping in the Forest

1978

I thought the earth
remembered me, she
took me back so tenderly, arranging
her dark skirts, her pockets
full of lichens and seeds. I slept
as never before, a stone
on the riverbed, nothing
between me and the white fire of the stars
but my thoughts, and they floated
light as moths among the branches
of the perfect trees. All night
I heard the small kingdoms breathing
around me, the insects, and the birds
who do their work in the darkness. All night
I rose and fell, as if in water, grappling

with a luminous doom. By morning
I had vanished at least a dozen times
into something better.

JOHN CASTEEN

Night Hunting

2008

Because we wanted things the way they were
in our minds' black eyes we waited. The beaver
raising ripples in a vee behind his head
the thing we wanted. A weed is what might grow
where you don't want it; a dahlia could be a weed,
or love, or other notions. The heart can't choose
to find itself enchanted; the hand can't choose
to change the shape of water. How strange, to hope
to see the signs of motion, to make an end
to Peter's old refrain: *He'll be along, son of a bitch,*
and then you best be ready. So sure, and so sure
that when he shines the light the thing will show
along the other shore. What next? Well,
you've killed animals before. Invited here
for company in the cold night, and because
ever handy with rifles. What next is wait
and see, what next may be the lone report, the ever-
widening circles, blood-blossom, the spirit rising slow
like oily smoke above still waters. We wanted
a pond to look like a pond: standing poplars,
shallows unsullied, fish and frogs and salamanders.
The gleaming back of fur and fat may not belong,
or may: God of varmints, God of will, forgive us
our trespasses. We know precisely what we do.

WOMEN'S CONSCIOUSNESS, WOMEN'S VOICES

As all of you have known for most of your lives, throughout human history the roles of men and women, both in the family and in society, have been defined differently, and for centuries art and writing have been defined by gender. We are familiar with the negative designation of a story or a poem as "women's writing." In our modern period, women writers have reacted against this categorization, and at the same time they have examined women's writing more closely to celebrate its consciousness of the different experiences of men and women in many crucial aspects of our life.

This theme is documented in the writing of one of the most important poets of the nineteenth century, Elizabeth Barrett Browning, who introduces her reader to one of the ways women of her era found to explore life beyond the limited opportunities that were offered to them. As she described it in her feminist novel-in-verse *Aurora Leigh*, published in 1857, it was her discovery of books and the world of reading that was for her, as it was for so many women, the door that opened the way to a richer experience of her own life. Ruth Stone's "In an Iridescent Time" looks back to an earlier time in women's lives, when they turned a mundane task like doing the laundry into a shared moment, pinning "the fluttering intimacies of life" on a line stretched between the bushes and a tree in the garden. In Alicia Suskin Ostriker's "The Change," she allows the reader to glimpse the inner thoughts of a woman who understands that her young daughter is maturing quickly and soon will leave her. Marilyn Hacker divides her life between her teaching job in New York City and her house and garden in France, and as she makes clear in her poem describing one of her many phone calls between continents, she sometimes feels herself pulled between the two poles of her life.

For many women marriage is a central experience in their lives, and Anne Waldman offers an ironic view of the doubleness that marriage involves, where so many things have to be thought of, as she expresses it, in "stereo." New Zealand poet Jenny Bornholdt, with her resigned acceptance of the vagaries of boyfriends, makes it clear that this problem in women's lives is not restricted to any one country or society. For Daisy Zamora it is equally clear that for women it is often just as important to act on their wishes as it is simply to use words to express them.

DOCUMENT

ELIZABETH BARRETT BROWNING

Books, books, books!

1856

I had found the secret of a garret-room
Piled high with cases in my father's name,
Piled high, packed large,—where, creeping in and out
Among the giant fossils of my past,
Like some small nimble mouse between the ribs
Of a mastodon, I nibbled here and there
At this or that box, pulling through the gap,
In heats of terror, haste, victorious joy,
The first book first. And how I felt it beat
Under my pillow, in the morning's dark,
An hour before the sun would let me read!
My books!
　　　　At last because the time was ripe,

I chanced upon the poets.
As the earth
Plunges in fury, when the internal fires
Have reached and pricked her heart, and, throwing flat,
The marts and temples, the triumphal gates
And towers of observations, clears herself
To elemental freedom—thus, my soul,
At poetry's divine first finger touch,
Let go conventions and sprang up surprised,
Convicted of the great eternities
Before two worlds.
What's this, Aurora Leigh,
You write so of the poets, and not laugh?
Those virtuous liars, dreamers after dark,
Exaggerators of the sun and moon,
And soothsayers in a tea-cup?
I write so
Of the only truth-tellers now left to God—
The only speakers of essential truth. . . .

RUTH STONE

In an Iridescent Time° 1959

My mother, when young, scrubbed laundry in a tub,
She and her sisters on an old brick walk
Under the apple trees, sweet rub-a-dub.
The bees came round their heads, the wrens made talk.
Four young ladies, each with a rainbow board
Honed their knuckles, wrung their wrists to red,
Tossed back their braids and wiped their aprons wet.
The Jersey calf beyond the back fence roared;
and all the soft day, swarms around their pet
Buzzed at his big brown eyes and bullish head.
Four times they rinsed, they said. Sometimes they starched.
They shook them from the baskets two by two,
And pinned the fluttering intimacies of life
Between the lilac bushes and the yew:
Brown gingham, pink, and skirts of Alice Blue.

In an Iridescent Time: This poem's original title was "Laundry."

ALICIA SUSKIN OSTRIKER

The Change

1980

Happening now! it is happening
now! even while, after these
gray March weeks—
when every Saturday you drive
out of town into the country
to take your daughter to her riding lesson
and along the thin curving road you peer
into the brown stuff—
still tangled, bare, nothing
beginning

Nothing beginning, the mud,
the vines, the corpse-like trees
and their floor of sodden leaves unaltered,
oh, you would like to heave
the steering wheel from its socket
or tear your own heart out, exasperated—
that it should freeze and thaw,
then freeze again, and that
no buds have burst, sticky,
deep red, from their twigs—

You want to say it to your daughter.
You want to tell her also how the gray
beeches, ashes and oaks here on Cherry Hill Road
on the way to her riding school
feel the same, although they cannot
rip themselves up by the roots, or run about raving,
or take any action whatever, and are almost dead
with their wish to be alive,
to suck water, to send force through their fibers,
and to change! to change!

Your daughter, surly, unconversational,
a house locking its doors against you,
pulls away
when you touch her shoulder, looks out the window.

You are too old. You remind her of frozen mud.
Nevertheless it is happening, the planet
is swimming toward the sun
like a woman with naked breasts. She cannot help it.
Can you sense, under the ground, the great melting?

MARILYN HACKER

Rondeau° after a Transatlantic Telephone Call

1980

Love, it was good to talk to you tonight.
You lather me like summer though. I light
up, sip smoke. Insistent through walls comes
the downstairs neighbor's double-bass. It thrums
like toothache. I will shower away the sweat,

smoke, summer, sound. Slick, soapy, dripping wet,
I scrub the sharp edge off my appetite.
I want: crisp toast, cold wine prickling my gums,
love. It was good

imagining around your voice, you, late-
awake there. (It isn't midnight yet
here.) This last glass washes down the crumbs.
I wish that I could lie down in your arms
and, turned toward sleep there (later), say, "Goodnight,
love. It was good."

ANNE WALDMAN

stereo

2000

Marriage marriage is like you say everything everything in stereo stereo
fall fall on the bed bed at dawn dawn because you work work all night.
Night is an apartment. Meant to be marriage. Marriage is an apartment
& meant people people come in in because when when you marry marry
chances are there will be edibles edibles to eat at tables tables in the house.
House will be the apartment which is night night. There there will be a
bed bed & an extra bed bed a clean sheet sheet sheet or two two for guests
guests one extra towel. Extra towel. How will you be welcomed? There
will be drinks drinks galore galore brought by armies of guests guests
casks casks of liquors liquors & brandies brandies elixirs sweet & bitter
bitter bottle of Merlot Merlot Bustelo coffee. Will you have some when I
offer. When you are married married there will be handsome gifts for the
kitchen kitchen sometimes two of every thing. Everything is brand brand
new new. Espresso coffee cups, a Finnish plate, a clock, a doormat, pieces
of Art. And books of astonishing Medical Science with pictures. Even
richer lexicons. When you are married married there will be more sheets

Rondeau: A poem with two rhymes in three stanzas with the final line of the second and third stanza echoing the first line of the poem. Traditionally a rondeau has thirteen lines, though Hacker has written her poem in fifteen lines.

sheets & towels towels arriving arriving & often often a pet pet or two two. You definitely need a telephone & a cell phone when you are married married. Two two two two lines lines lines lines. You need need separate separate electronicmail electronicmail accounts accounts. When you are married married you will have sets sets of things things, of more sheets & towels matching, you will have duplicates of things, you will have just one tablecloth. When you are married married you will be responsible when neighbors neighbors greet you. You will smile smile in unison unison or you might say he is fine, she is fine, o she is just down with a cold, o he is consoling a weary traveler just now, arrived from across the Plains. She my husband is due home soon, he my wife is busy at the moment, my husband he is very very busy busy at the moment moment this very moment. Meant good-bye, good-bye. When you are married married sex sex will happen happen without delay delay. You will have a mailbox mailbox & a doorbell doorbell. Bell bell ring ring it rings rings again a double time. You do not have to answer. That's sure for when you are married people people understand understand you do not not have to answer answer a doorbell doorbell because sex sex may happen happen without delay delay. You will hear everything twice, through your ears & the ears of the other. Her or him as a case case may be be. He & he & she & she as a case case may be may be. When you are married married you can play play with names names & rename yourself if you like. You can add a name, have a double name with a hyphen if you like. You can open joint accounts when you are married. Marriage is no guarantee against depression. A shun is no guarantee against anything. Marriage is no guarantee against resolution. Revolution is a tricky word word. Here, you hear here? Marriage is sweeter sweeter than you think. Think.

JENNY BORNHOLDT

The Boyfriends

1989

The boyfriends all love you but they don't really know how.

They say it is tragic that you will not be together for the rest of
your lives. You will not be together for the rest of your lives
because they are lone spirits and you are a nice girl.

Because your father is a lawyer and because they like to think they
come from the wrong side of town, they say you will marry a
young lawyer. Someone nice, someone stable, someone able to
provide you with all the things you need and are accustomed to,
not a rogue, not an adventurous spirit like themselves. Not
someone who is destined to the lone life.

They say it will be all right for you. You will be very happy, they
can tell. It will all work out for you. You will find a young lawyer,

or a young lawyer will find you and you will get married and be
very happy.
This is what you want, of course.
They say you are made for happiness, anyone can see that.
You will be very happy, you'll see.

They imagine their own sorrow when the day finally comes.
They tell you about this. They imagine seeing you in town with
your new young lawyer. He will have his arm around your
shoulders. You will be looking happy. He will be looking happy.
You will both be looking very happy. They will look on and feel
tragic about it not working out, about the impossibility of the
great love. Because yours *is* the great love. The true love. Oh yes.
But it cannot work. The great love never works. The true love is
doomed to fail.

You suspect they have seen too many westerns with too many
cowboys riding off into too many sunsets.

In the end of course, you leave him. There isn't really much choice.
He is unhappy. Very unhappy. It is not all that romantic.

When you see him in the street you often cannot speak. You just
look at each other. You both cry a lot in public places. Other
people find this embarrassing and so do you.

He says please come back.
He says this is the worst thing that has ever happened. And it is.
Please he says. Please.

But you can't. Because it would be going back to leaving him.
You prepared yourself to leave him for years. It took such a
long time.

It took years of listening to him leaving you, knowing that
he wouldn't.
All that leaving.
All that is left is the leaving.

DAISY ZAMORA

Precisely

1993

TRANSLATED BY MARGARET RANDALL AND ELINOR RANDALL

Precisely because I do not have
the beautiful words I need
I call upon my acts
to speak to you.

BLACK CONSCIOUSNESS, BLACK VOICES

Although the writing of African Americans is now a vigorous and vital element of the American cultural mainstream, for many tragic years black Americans were the victims of widespread prejudice and legal discrimination. As you have seen, their writing, beginning with the early poetry of Phillis Wheatley, has reflected the racial oppression in the United States, and it has also reflected the obvious reality that there have emerged two Americas, one white and one black, with different, though intertwined, histories.

Paul Laurence Dunbar wrote sentimental dialect verse about black life which made him one of America's most widely read poets, but when he turned to express his thoughts about racial oppression he used classic English verse forms. His image of a "caged bird" symbolizes the thoughts of many of these poets about the racial barriers that surrounded them. James Weldon Johnson was celebrated for his great sermon-in-verse "The Creation" (p. 893), but in this short lyric he chose instead to create a description of a sunset in the tropics. Robert Hayden's haunting "Those Winter Sundays" can be read by anyone who has known the love of a father whom they misunderstood and often resented. In prison, where he is serving a sentence for drug abuse, Etheridge Knight turns to his family for solace. The gallery of their photos he has hung on the walls of his cell tells him of his roots and perhaps will trace for him a path back from where his life has taken him. Allen Polite found himself unable to accept any of the roles of racial identity he felt were assigned to him in the United States, so he emigrated to Sweden, where he lived with his new Swedish family as a member of a group of African American artists and writers who had made similar decisions in their own lives. His "Song" reflects his decision to be himself, wherever this would lead him. The story Dudley Randall's ballad tells is of one of the tragedies of our era as change was coming. For those children in their church and for their grieving families the change came too late. Audre Lorde and Lucille Clifton both return to early memories in their poems. Lorde turns back to her memories of her unhappy adolescence, memories which she shared with so many of the others of her generation. Clifton's poem reflects a lifetime of pain and insult as she resolves that she will no longer continue to accept these memories as a part of her life.

DOCUMENT

ROBERT HAYDEN

Robert Hayden's introduction to his anthology of African American poetry discusses the tradition of "Negro poetry," which, like American poetry generally, was concerned with developing a distinctive language and form.

On Negro Poetry

1967

The question whether we can speak with any real justification of "Negro poetry" arises often today. Some object to the term because it has been used disparagingly to indicate a kind of pseudo-poetry concerned with the race problem to the exclusion of almost everything else. Others hold that Negro poetry *per se* could only be produced in black Africa. Seen from this point of view, the poetry of the American Negro, its "specialized" content notwithstanding, is obviously not to be thought of as existing apart from the rest of our literature, but as having been shaped over some three centuries by social, moral, and literary forces essentially American.

Those who presently avow themselves "poets of the Negro revolution" argue that they do indeed constitute a separate group or school, since the purpose of their writing is to give Negroes a sense of human dignity and provide them with ideological weapons. A belligerent race pride moves these celebrants of Black Power to declare themselves not simply "poets," but "Negro poets." However, Countee Cullen, the brilliant lyricist of the Harlem Renaissance in the 1920s, insisted that he be considered a "poet," not a "Negro poet," for he did not want to be restricted to racial themes nor have his poetry judged solely on the basis of its relevance to the Negro struggle.

Cullen was aware of a peculiar risk Negro poets have had to face. The tendency of American critics has been to label the established Negro writer a "spokesman for his race." There are, as we have seen, poets who think of themselves in that role. But the effect of such labeling is to place any Negro author in a kind of literary ghetto where the standards applied to other writers are not likely to be applied to him, since he, being a "spokesman for his race," is not considered primarily a writer but a species of race-relations man, the leader of a cause, the voice of protest.

Protest has been a recurring element in the writing of American Negroes, a fact hardly to be wondered at, given the social conditions under which they have been forced to live. And the Negro poet's devotion to the cause of freedom is not in any way reprehensible, for throughout history poets have often been champions of human liberty. But bad poetry is another matter, and there is no denying that a great deal of "race poetry" is poor, because its content seems ready-made and art is displaced by argument.

Phillis Wheatley (c. 1750–1784), the first poet of African descent to win some measure of recognition, had almost nothing to say about the plight of her people. And if she resented her own ambiguous position in society, she did not express her resentment. One reason for her silence is that, although brought to Boston as a slave, she never lived as one. Another is that as a neoclassical poet she would scarcely have thought it proper to reveal much of herself in her poetry, although we do get brief glimpses of her in the poem addressed to the Earl of Dartmouth and in "On Being Brought from Africa to America." Neoclassicism emphasized reason rather than emotion and favored elegance and formality. The English poet Alexander Pope was the acknowledged master of this style, and in submitting to his influence Phillis Wheatley produced poetry that was as good as that of her American contemporaries. She actually wrote better than some of them.

But the poetry of Phillis Wheatley and her fellow poet, Jupiter Hammon, has historical and not literary interest for us now. The same can be said of much of eighteenth-century American poetry in general. Not until the nineteenth century did the United States begin to have literature of unqualified merit and originality. There were no Negro poets of stature in the period before the Civil War, but there were several with talent, among them George Moses Horton (1797–c. 1883) and Frances E. W. Harper (1825–1911). Didactic and sentimental, they wrote with competence and moral fervor in the manner of their times. Their poetry is remembered chiefly because it contributed to the antislavery struggle, and because it testifies to the creative efforts of Negroes under disheartening conditions. . . .

In the twentieth century Negro poets have abandoned dialect for an idiom truer to folk speech. The change has been due not only to differences in social outlook on their part but also to revolutionary developments in American poetry. The New Poetry movement, which began before the First World War and reached its definitive point in the 1920s, represented a break with the past. Free verse, diction close to everyday speech, a realistic approach to life, and the use of material once considered unpoetic—these were the goals of the movement. The Negro poet-critic, William Stanley Braithwaite, encouraged the "new" poetry through his articles in the *Boston Evening Transcript* and his yearly anthologies of magazine verse.

The New Negro movement or Negro Renaissance, resulting from the social, political, and artistic awakening of Negroes in the twenties, brought into prominence poets whose work showed the influence of the poetic revolution. Protest became more defiant, racial bitterness and racial pride more outspoken than ever before. Negro history and folklore were explored as new sources of inspiration. Spirituals, blues, and jazz suggested themes and verse patterns to young poets like Jean Toomer and Langston Hughes. Certain conventions, notably what has been called "literary Garveyism," grew out of a fervent Negro nationalism. Marcus Garvey, leader of the United Negro Improvement Association, advocated a "return" to Africa, the lost homeland, and nearly all the Renaissance poets wrote poems about their spiritual ties to Africa, about the dormant fires of African paganism in the Negro soul that the white man's civilization could never extingish. Countee Cullen's "Heritage" is one of the best of these poems, even though the Africa it presents is artificial, romanticized, and it reiterates exotic clichés in vogue during the period when it was written.

Harlem was the center of the Negro Renaissance, which for that reason is also referred to as the Harlem Renaissance. Two magazines, *The Crisis* and *Opportunity*, gave aid and encouragement to Negro writers by publishing their work and by awarding literary prizes.

In the decades since the New Negro movement, which ended with the twenties, protest and race consciousness have continued to find expression in the poetry of the American Negro. But other motivating forces are also in evidence. There are Negro poets who believe that any poet's most clearly defined task is to create with honesty and sincerity poems that will illuminate human experience—not exclusively "Negro experience." They reject the idea of poetry as racial propaganda, of poetry that functions as a kind of sociology. Their attitude is not wholly new, of course, being substantially that of Dunbar and Cullen. In counterpoise to it is the "Beat" or "nonacademic" view held by poets who are not only in rebellion against middle-class ideals and the older poetic traditions but who also advocate a militant racism in a definitely "Negro" poetry.

It has come to be expected of Negro poets that they will address themselves to the race question—and that they will all say nearly the same things about it. Such "group unity" is more apparent than real. Differences in vision and emphasis, fundamental differences in approach to the art of poetry itself, modify and give diversity to the writing of these poets, even when they employ similar themes. And certainly there is no agreement among them as to what the much debated role of the Negro poet should be.

PHILLIS WHEATLEY

On Being Brought from Africa to America 1773

'Twas mercy brought me from my *Pagan* land,
Taught my benighted soul to understand
That there's a God, that there's a *Saviour* too:
Once I redemption neither sought nor knew.
Some view our sable race with scornful eye,
"Their colour is a diabolic die."
Remember, *Christians, Negros*, black as *Cain*,°
May be refin'd, and join th'angelic train.

PAUL LAURENCE DUNBAR

Theology 1896

There is a heaven, for ever, day by day,
The upward longing of my soul doth tell me so.
There is a hell, I'm quite as sure; for pray,
If there were not, where would my neighbors go?

7. black as *Cain*: In Genesis 4:14, God puts a mark on Cain for having murdered his brother Abel. Some traditions hold that this "mark" is black skin.

Sympathy

1903

I know what the caged bird feels, alas!
When the sun is bright on the upland slopes;
When the wind stirs soft through the springing grass,
And the river flows like a stream of glass;
When the first bird sings and the first bud opes,
And the faint perfume from its chalice steals—
I know what the caged bird feels!

I know why the caged bird beats his wing
Till its blood is red on the cruel bars;
For he must fly back to his perch and cling
When he fain would be on the bough a-swing;
And a pain still throbs in the old, old scars
And they pulse again with a keener sting—
I know why he beats his wing!

I know why the caged bird sings, ah me,
When his wing is bruised and his bosom sore,
When he beats his bars and would be free;
It is not a carol of joy or glee,
But a prayer that he sends from his heart's deep core,
But a plea, that upward to Heaven he flings—
I know why the caged bird sings!

JAMES WELDON JOHNSON

Sunset in the Tropics

1917

A silver flash from the sinking sun,
Then a shot of crimson across the sky
That, bursting, lets a thousand colors fly
And riot among the clouds; they run,
Deepening in purple, flaming in gold,
Changing, and opening fold after fold,
Then fading through all of the tints of the rose into gray,
Till, taking quick fright at the coming night,
They rush out down the west,
In hurried quest
Of the fleeing day.

Now above where the tardiest color flares a moment yet,
One point of light, now two, now three are set
To form the starry stairs,—
And, in her fire-fly crown,
Queen Night, on velvet slippered feet, comes softly down.

ROBERT HAYDEN

Those Winter Sundays

1962

Sundays too my father got up early
and put his clothes on in the blueblack cold,
then with cracked hands that ached
from labor in the weekday weather made
banked fires blaze. No one ever thanked him.

I'd wake and hear the cold splintering, breaking.
When the rooms were warm, he'd call,
and slowly I would rise and dress,
fearing the chronic angers of that house,

Speaking indifferently to him,
who had driven out the cold
and polished my good shoes as well.
What did I know, what did I know
of love's austere and lonely offices?

ETHERIDGE KNIGHT

The Idea of Ancestry

1968

I

Taped to the wall of my cell are 47 pictures: 47 black
faces: my father, mother, grandmothers (1 dead), grand
fathers (both dead), brothers, sisters, uncles, aunts,
cousins (1st & 2nd), nieces, and nephews. They stare
across the space at me sprawling on my bunk. I know
their dark eyes, they know mine. I know their style,
they know mine. I am all of them, they are all of me;
they are farmers, I am a thief, I am me, they are thee.

I have at one time or another been in love with my mother,
1 grandmother, 2 sisters, 2 aunts (1 went to the asylum),
and 5 cousins. I am now in love with a 7 yr old niece
(she sends me letters written in large block print, and
her picture is the only one that smiles at me).

I have the same name as 1 grandfather, 3 cousins, 3 nephews,
and 1 uncle. The uncle disappeared when he was 15, just took
off and caught a freight (they say). He's discussed each year
when the family has a reunion, he causes uneasiness in
the clan, he is an empty space. My father's mother, who is 93
and who keeps the Family Bible with everybody's birth dates

(and death dates) in it, always mentions him. There is no
place in her Bible for "whereabouts unknown."

II

Each Fall the graves of my grandfathers call me, the brown
hills and red gullies of mississippi send out their electric
messages, galvanizing my genes. Last yr/ like a salmon quitting
the cold ocean—leaping and bucking up his birthstream/ I
hitchhiked my way from L.A. with 16 caps in my pocket and a
monkey on my back, and I almost kicked it with the kinfolks.
I walked barefoot in my grandmother's backyard/ I smelled the old
land and the woods /I sipped cornwhiskey from fruit jars with the men/
I flirted with the women/ I had a ball till the caps ran out
and my habit came down. That night I looked at my grandmother
and split/ my guts were screaming for junk/ but I was almost
contented/ I had almost caught up with me.
  The next day in Memphis I cracked a croaker's crib for a fix.

This yr there is a gray stone wall damming my stream, and when
the falling leaves stir my genes, I pace my cell or flop on my bunk
and stare at 47 black faces across the space. I am all of them,
they are all of me, I am me, they are thee, and I have no sons
to float in the space between.

DUDLEY RANDALL

Ballad of Birmingham° 1966

(On the bombing of a church in Birmingham, Alabama, 1963)

"Mother dear, may I go downtown
Instead of out to play,
And march the streets of Birmingham
In a Freedom March today?"

"No, baby, no, you may not go,
For the dogs are fierce and wild,
And clubs and hoses, guns and jails
Aren't good for a little child."

"But, mother, I won't be alone.
Other children will go with me,
And march the streets of Birmingham
To make our country free."

Birmingham: This poem was written in response to the 1963 bombing of the 16th Street Baptist Church in Birmingham, Alabama. Four black children perished in the explosion.

"No, baby, no, you may not go,
For I fear those guns will fire.
But you may go to church instead
And sing in the children's choir."

She has combed and brushed her night-dark hair,
And bathed rose petal sweet,
And drawn white gloves on her small brown hands,
And white shoes on her feet.

The mother smiled to know her child
Was in the sacred place,
But that smile was the last smile
To come upon her face.

For when she heard the explosion,
Her eyes grew wet and wild.
She raced through the streets of Birmingham
Calling for her child.

She clawed through bits of glass and brick,
Then lifted out a shoe
"Oh, here's the shoe my baby wore,
But, baby, where are you?"

ALLEN POLITE

Song

1958

When I sing this song without accompaniment
          I can hear the silence the emptiness
When I sing this song in which the only instrument
          is my voice
                    my voice which comes over the lips
          as a man comes out of a desert
                    just near death then near life

          I know why man sang before he talked
            Why he sings before he walks
            Why he hates to be a slave
            Why he is singing in the grave

I know what it is to long for
        that which we have never known

          I know why man sang before he talked
            Why he sings before he walks
            Why he hates to be a slave
            Why he is singing in the grave

When your voice joins mine, as something coming
    to meet the dead
See we then the genius of man? See him strike the first
instrument?
See him paint paradise as bird song?
See him paint wings on loaves of bread?

            I know why man sang before he talked
                Why he sings before he walks
                Why he hates to be a slave
                Why he is singing in the grave

And when we sing together without effort
    the stops in the greatest organ are like child's play
When we are singing into each others mouths and
hearing
        songs
Unison is night changing to day—

            I know why man sang before he talked
                Why he sings before he walks
                Why he hates to be a slave
                Why he is singing in the grave

AUDRE LORDE

Hanging Fire

1978

I am fourteen
and my skin has betrayed me
the boy I cannot live without
still sucks his thumb
in secret
how come my knees are
always so ashy
what if I die
before morning
and momma's in the bedroom
with the door closed.

I have to learn how to dance
in time for the next party
my room is too small for me
suppose I die before graduation
they will sing sad melodies
but finally
tell the truth about me
There is nothing I want to do

and too much
that has to be done
and momma's in the bedroom
with the door closed.
Nobody even stops to think
about my side of it
I should have been on Math Team
my marks were better than his
why do I have to be
the one
wearing braces
I have nothing to wear tomorrow
will I live long enough
to grow up
and momma's in the bedroom
with the door closed.

LUCILLE CLIFTON

to ms. ann

1994

i will have to forget
your face
when you watched me breaking
in the fields,
missing my children.
i will have to forget
your face
when you watched me carry
your husband's
stagnant water.
i will have to forget
your face
when you handed me
your house
to make a home,
and you never called me sister
then, you never called me sister
and it has only been forever and
i will have to forget your face.

POETRY OF PROTEST AND SOCIAL CONCERN

When you first began reading and discussing poetry, you might have shared a popular misconception of the role poetry plays in our society. Poetry is often thought of as a refined, elevated form of writing, removed from the struggles of everyday life. Poets, however, have been engaged in the social and political issues of their time from poetry's beginnings, and many of today's writers carry on the debates that challenged writers a generation ago. Although some of the strident rhetoric of the 1960s has been muted, today's writers still are deeply committed to the issues of their own moment of history. In the 1960s and 1970s, young African American poets like Nikki Giovanni raised their voices in anger at the racism they encountered in American society; at the same time, new women writers like Joan Jobe Smith began to give vent to their impatience with the sexual roles that society's customs were forcing on them. For this generation of writers, the voice of their protest was poetry. They wrote poems to convince us, shock us, or inform us, and they were more concerned with the message of their poetry than with the traditional poetic conventions of language, style, or form. Their poems continue to burn with their convictions. Poems like these have opened prayer meetings, they have been shouted on the streets, they have given relief in our moments of anger, and they have helped rally us in our moments of hesitation and doubt.

In Nikki Giovanni's "Adulthood" she describes with controlled anger the events and the emotions that led to her activist role in the 1960s and 1970s. Carolyn Forché, in "The Colonel," makes these themes specific with her account of a meeting with a South American military officer who boasts of the deaths he has caused. As Pat Mora's poem "Elena" shows her readers, the sense of exclusion can also affect someone whose life has been lived in quiet domesticity. Joan Jobe Smith and Fred Voss, who are husband and wife and live in Long Beach, California, bring a wry intelligence and sympathy to their accounts of their working lives. Smith's "Feminist Arm Candy for the Mafia and Sinatra" recounts the effort to bring social responsibility into a Playgal Club by one of the go-go dancers she works with. Voss, who has worked for many years as a lathe operator in a machine shop, shows in his "I Once Needed a Chance Too" that one person's sympathies can have a positive effect on the course of another life. Sara Holbrook, in her poignant poem "Canvassing," reminds us that social progress takes many small steps and that the obstacles to change can overwhelm many people caught in a cycle of despair.

The Sixties were a period of unrest and protest, and the new generation of popular singer-songwriters took up many of the same themes. Bob Dylan's "Blowin' in the Wind" became an anthem of the decade, expressing dissatisfaction at the society's problems. Country Joe McDonald's "I-Feel-Like-I'm-Fixin'-to-Die Rag," which he first recorded with his Berkeley band Country Joe and the Fish in 1966, became an international hit after his appearance singing it on the stage of the Woodstock Festival and was featured in the documentary film of the legendary festival from the summer of 1969.

DOCUMENT

DAVID WOJAHN

David Wojahn, whose poetry was collected in the award-winning volume *Interrogation Palace* (2006), contributed an essay on political verse to the *Writer's Chronicle* in 2007. This document is taken from that essay, whose title, "Maggie's Farm No More: The Fate of Political Poetry," alludes to a song by Bob Dylan.

On Political Poetry

2007

American poets seem to have lost the means to compellingly address political concerns in their work. We may read Milosz, Herbert, Hikmet, Ko Un, Vallejo, and other figures in Twentieth Century world poetry who have written about the intricate relationship between self and politics, but thanks to some general sense of inferiority before these greats, we have rarely permitted ourselves to be influenced by them in any but the most superficial of ways. Certain poets with political or topical concerns may enjoy a brief vogue—Carolyn Forché in the 1980s, for example, or more recently Iraq War veteran Brian Turner—but their writing as often as not soon passes into oblivion. Attempts are made to revive the reputations of unjustly forgotten poets of the left such as Thomas McGrath, Edgell Rickword, and Kenneth Fearing, but these writers are still not represented in the major anthologies. There are of course a few figures at work today who bring to their writing a compelling sense of political and historical import: Adrienne Rich again comes to mind, as well as Yusef Komunyakaa, but this pair is the exception rather than the rule. American poets may choose to look up from their laptop screens and out their windows long enough to add a couple of snide observations about their neighbors' SUVs or to bemoan the latest example of Bush administration hubris, but their efforts at combining the personal and the political remain for the most part failures, plagued by reductive thinking, a clumsy shuffling between anemic anecdote and simplistic rhetoric, and a pervasive sense of futility—we know how marginal we are, but don't know how to change our status.

NIKKI GIOVANNI

Adulthood

1969

(For Claudia)

i usta wonder who i'd be
when i was a little girl in indianapolis
sitting on doctors' porches with post-dawn pre-debs
(wondering would my aunt drag me to church sunday)

i was meaningless
and i wondered if life
would give me a chance to mean

i found a new life in the withdrawal from all things
not like my image

when i was a teen-ager i usta sit
on front steps conversing
the gym teacher's son with embryonic eyes
about the essential essence of the universe
(and other bullshit stuff)
recognizing the basic powerlessness of me

but then i went to college where i learned
that just because everything i was was unreal
i could be real and not just real through withdrawal
into emotional crosshairs or colored bourgeois
intellectual pretensions
but from involvement with things approaching reality
i could possibly have a life

so catatonic emotions and time wasting sex games
were replaced with functioning commitments to logic
and
necessity and the gray area was slowly darkened into
a Black thing

for a while progress was being made along with a certain
degree
of happiness cause i wrote a book and found a love
and organized a theatre and even gave some lectures on
Black history
and began to believe all good people could get
together and win without bloodshed
then
hammarskjöld was killed°

36–49. hammarskjöld . . . was killed: Giovanni names individuals whom she, along with many others, believed were targeted for championing human rights and peace in the turbulent decade of the 1960s. Swedish diplomat Dag Hammarskjöld was secretary-general of the United Nations when his plane crashed during his efforts to bring peace to the troubled Congo region in Africa. The cause of the 1961 crash has never been determined. Patrice Lumumba was prime minister of the Republic of the Congo, and following his requests for aid from the Soviet Union, he was jailed and murdered. Ngo Dinh Diem was the president of South Vietnam; Diem's killing was long considered to have been ordered by the U.S. government. President John F. Kennedy was assassinated in 1963. Michael Schwerner, James Chaney, Andrew Goodman, and Viola Liuzzo were civil rights workers murdered in the South in 1964 for promoting political equality for African Americans. Malcolm X was a dissident leader of the Black Muslim Church who was shot to death in 1965. Others, like Stokely Carmichael and Rap Brown, were members of the Student Nonviolent Coordinating Committee (SNCC or "Snick"), and some were killed in confrontations with the police. Martin Luther King Jr. and Robert Kennedy were both assassinated in 1968.

and lumumba was killed
and diem was killed
and kennedy was killed
and malcolm was killed
and evers was killed
and schwerner, chaney and goodman were killed
and liuzzo was killed
and stokely fled the country
and leroi was arrested
and rap was arrested
and pollard, thompson and cooper were killed
and king was killed
and kennedy was killed
and i sometimes wonder why i didn't become a
debutante
sitting on porches, going to church all the time,
wondering
is my eye make-up on straight
or a withdrawn discoursing on the stars and moon
instead of a for real Black person who must now feel
and inflict
pain

CAROLYN FORCHÉ

The Colonel

1978

What you have heard is true. I was in his house. His wife carried a tray of coffee and sugar. His daughter filed her nails, his son went out for the night. There were daily papers, pet dogs, a pistol on the cushion beside him. The moon swung bare on its black cord over the house. On the television was a cop show. It was in English. Broken bottles were embedded in the walls around the house to scoop the kneecaps from a man's legs or cut his hands to lace. On the windows there were gratings like those in liquor stores. We had dinner, rack of lamb, good wine, a gold bell was on the table for calling the maid. The maid brought green mangoes, salt, a type of bread. I was asked how I enjoyed the country. There was a brief commercial in Spanish. His wife took everything away. There was some talk then of how difficult it had become to govern. The parrot said hello on the terrace. The colonel told it to shut up, and pushed himself from the table. My friend said to me with his eyes: say nothing. The colonel returned with a sack used to bring groceries home. He spilled many human ears on the table. They were like dried peach halves. There is no other way to say this. He took one of them in his hands, shook it in our faces, dropped it into a water glass. It came alive there. I am tired of fooling around he said. As for the rights of anyone, tell your people they can go fuck themselves. He swept the ears to the floor with his arm and held the last of his wine in the air. Something for your poetry, no? he said. Some of the ears on the floor caught this scrap of his voice. Some of the ears on the floor were pressed to the ground.

PAT MORA

Elena

1984

My Spanish isn't enough.
I remember how I'd smile
listening to my little ones,
understanding every word they'd say,
their jokes, their songs, their plots.
Vamos a pedirle dulces a mamá. Vamos.°
But that was in Mexico.
Now my children go to American high schools.
They speak English. At night they sit around
the kitchen table, laugh with one another.
I stand by the stove and feel dumb, alone.
I bought a book to learn English.
My husband frowned, drank more beer.
My oldest said, "*Mamá*, he doesn't want you
to be smarter than he is." I'm forty,
embarrassed at mispronouncing words,
embarrassed at the laughter of my children,
the grocer, the mailman. Sometimes I take
my English book and lock myself in the bathroom,
say the thick words softly,
for if I stop trying, I will be deaf
when my children need my help.

JOAN JOBE SMITH

Feminist Arm Candy for the Mafia and Sinatra

1999

Go-go girl Sindy, who changed the first letter of her name
from "C" to "S" for obvious reasons, said us go-go girls
at the Playgal Club in 1968 were nothing but waitresses
in bikinis, dancing workhorses, indentured servitude
(forgetting how much money we made, more than tenured

6. Vamos . . . Vamos: Let's go ask Mama for sweets. Let's go.

Cal Tech profs, aerospace executive engineers, drove new
cars, dressed groovy as Cher, had cuter boyfriends, guys
in the band were *our* groupies) so Sindy tried to organize
a Go-go Girl Union, make the Playgal Club millionaire
owners give us vacation pay, sick leave, retirement funds,
overtime for that hour extra we worked cleaning up the place
while our mean boss Spike called us lazy tramps; Sindy went
to the California state labor board, ACLU, wrote letters to our
Congressman detailing us go-go girls's "UNendowment of
inalienable Rights" promised us in the U.S. Constitution and
when the bosses told her Shut up, get back to work, one night
she shing-a-linged, right in the middle of Dick Dale's famous
showstopper solo, Sindy jumped off the stage, pulled the plug
on Dick Dale's electric guitar as she went off to Las Vegas for
some fun in the sun to be a showgirl at the Tropicana or Flamingo,
marry a millionaire and six months later when she returned to say
hello-goodbye-again 20 pounds thinner, her hair bleached white
dried-up Monet haystack, eyes swollen from a week-ago beating,
nostrils cracked from snorting cocaine, bloodshot eyeballs from
smoking pot in the daytime and a slipped disc because they'd
made her wear 50-pound headpieces, work matinees and four
shows a night 7 days a week plus be arm candy after hours for
the Mafia and Sinatra, she warned us: "Stay the hell away from
Vegas, baby, all the men there are BAD." Then she walked out,
off again, this time for Chicago, her name changed to Windy as in
bad weather blowing in. What Windy was going to do there in the
Windy City of Chicago to set the world right for us women, find
Life, Liberty and the Pursuit of Happiness in 1969, God only knew.

FRED VOSS

I Once Needed a Chance Too 2006

19-year-old Hector
stands beside me at the machine
ready to learn.
He has never held a micrometer in his hands before,
doesn't know anything about what the thousandth-of-an-inch
calibration marks
on its barrel mean,
what tolerances on dimensions on blueprints
mean,
what a cutter is or rpm
or how to turn the handles
or punch the buttons
of a machine.

He looks up into my eyes eager to learn
and suddenly the big metal crucifix
hanging around his neck
and the blue tattoos covering his arms
and neck and all the fear and anger and shock
in his eyes from all the gang violence
and madness he has grown up with in the barrio
and my peaceful middle class on-the-way-to-college-and-a-lawyer-
or-doctor-future
upbringing
mean nothing
in the face of his desperate need of a chance
and we nod at each other
and put our hands on the tools he will need to do the job
and look into each other's eyes
and become father
and son.

SARA HOLBROOK

Canvassing

2008

These are the front doors made of steel
that open into throbbing bass apartments
of coffee table filing systems
for wrappers from burgers bought four for five bucks,
of wide-eyed children leg clinging scared of
white folks who knock on front doors.
Doors opened by parents whose crossed brows and weak smiles
take the literature hesitantly.
Nothing good never come from door knocks before.

These are not the front doors made of steel
that open into foyers of marble tile
and direct eye contact that demands explanations
accompanied by a wafting potpourri of lavender, violins and steak.
Not the doors anointed by well oiled brass knockers.
Not the focal point of brick walks and twin shrubs.
Not the doors that open onto down payment gifts
from parents who are downsizing,
of diplomas hanging on walls warmly illuminated by
glowing fires held safely behind glass,
reflecting on family rooms floors floored in hard wood.

These are the front doors
opened between shifts of minimum wage.
Doors accustomed to hard knocks and routine downsizing

that open off of hallways scented by a stewing of onions,
urine and crack cocaine, littered by broken toys.
These are the front doors made of steel
opened when the world wants more.

May I have your vote?

BOB DYLAN

Blowin' in the Wind

1963

How many roads must a man walk down
Before you call him a man?
Yes, 'n' how many seas must a white dove sail
Before she sleeps in the sand?
Yes, 'n' how many times must the cannonballs fly
Before they're forever banned?
The answer, my friend, is blowin' in the wind
The answer is blowin' in the wind

How many years can a mountain exist
Before it's washed to the sea?
Yes, 'n' how many years can some people exist
Before they're allowed to be free?
Yes, 'n' how many times can a man turn his head
Pretending he just doesn't see?
The answer, my friend, is blowin' in the wind
The answer is blowin' in the wind

How many times must a man look up
Before he can see the sky?
Yes, 'n' how many ears must one man have
Before he can hear people cry?
Yes, 'n' how many deaths will it take till he knows
That too many people have died?
The answer, my friend, is blowin' in the wind
The answer is blowin' in the wind

COUNTRY JOE McDONALD

I-Feel-Like-I'm-Fixin'-to-Die Rag

1968

1

Come on all of you big strong men,
Uncle Sam needs your help again.
He's got himself in a terrible jam

Way down yonder in Vietnam,
So put down your books and pick up a gun.
We're gonna have a whole lotta fun.

CHORUS:

And it's one, two, three, what are we fightin' for?
Don't ask me, I don't give a damn,
Next stop is Vietnam;
And it's five, six, seven, open up the pearly gates
Well, there ain't no time to wonder why,
Whoopee! We're all gonna die.

2

Come on Generals, let's move fast;
Your big chance has come at last.
Gotta go out and get those Reds—
The only good Commie is the one that's dead.
You know that peace can only be won,
When we've blown 'em all to kingdom come.

(CHORUS)

3

Come on Wall Street, don't move slow.
Why, Man, this is war Au-Go-Go
There's plenty good money to be made
by supplying the Army with the tools of the trade
Just hope and pray that if they drop the bomb,
They drop it on the Viet Cong.

(CHORUS)

4

Come on Mothers throughout the land,
Pack your boys off to Vietnam.
Come on Fathers, don't hesitate,
Send your sons off before it's too late.
You can be the first ones in your block
To have your boy come home in a box.

(CHORUS)

THE FACES OF WAR

A continuing subject in the story of poetry is one of the most common of human activities: war. Many of you may have read passages from one of the earliest of our literary classics, the *Iliad*, an epic poem written several hundred years before the Christian era by the blind Greek poet Homer. The poem narrates the story of the ten-year-long war between the Greeks and their enemies the Trojans in what is now eastern Turkey. The poems in this group take up the theme of war in our modern age, from the American Civil War to the First World War, the Second World War, and America's long agony in Vietnam.

Often poets who turned to the experience of battle and war were viewing their subject from a distance; mourning the dead, or recounting the glory. The novelist Herman Melville's sorrowing poem "Shiloh" laments the slaughter at the battle that swirled around Shiloh Church in western Tennessee in April 1862 during the Civil War, when 24,000 men were killed, wounded, or missing after two days of fighting that ended in no clear victory. Stephen Crane wrote a youthful celebration of war in his novel *The Red Badge of Courage,* but in his sardonic poem "War Is Kind," written later, his attitude toward war and its tragedy had changed. Two English poets, Thomas Hardy and Wilfred Owen, wrote their poems on war from different perspectives. Hardy's "The Man He Killed" is written as a reminiscence by a veteran of the Boer War in South Africa between the first Dutch settlers and British occupiers of their lands. The veteran looks back in sadness at the death he has caused. Owen's bitterness in "Dulce et Decorum Est" draws on his own daily experience. He wrote it while he still was serving on the Western Front in the First World War, and he was killed in action a few months later. The Latin phrase of the poem's title, which translates as "It is a sweet and beautiful thing to give one's life for one's country," was part of the education of young men everywhere in Europe. Randall Jarrell's "The Death of the Ball Turret Gunner" speaks in the resigned voice of one of the men who manned machine guns in the moving turrets of the B-19 bombers sent out on bombing missions over Germany in the Second World War. Ed Webster's "San Joaquin Valley Poems" and Forrest Hamer's "My Father's Viet Nam Tour Near Over" are both written by sons of men who were in combat in Vietnam. For Webster the war was a kind of adventure that his father was experiencing, an experience he could fantasize being part of himself. As Hamer tells us in the title of his poem, however, he understands that his father's life is still in danger, and he can talk only about what he has already seen of the effect of death on the families of men who have already died.

In his novel *The Red Badge of Courage,* a twenty-three-year-old Stephen Crane fantasized on the ideal of heroism on the battlefields of the Civil War, which had ended less than thirty years before. He was born too late to serve in the war himself, but he had grown up hearing the tales told by veterans and experienced the excitement of the parades and celebrations honoring their heroism. His novel vividly documents this youthful fascination with the roar and the tumult of battle.

DOCUMENT

STEPHEN CRANE

From *The Red Badge of Courage* 1895

There was a youthful private who listened with eager ears to the words of the tall soldier and the various comments of his comrades. After receiving a fill of discussions concerning marches and attacks, he went to his hut and crawled through an intricate hole that served as a door. He wished to be alone with some new thoughts that had lately come to him.

He lay down on a wide bunk that stretched across the end of the room. In the other end, cracker boxes were made to serve as furniture. They were grouped around the fireplace. A picture from an illustrated weekly was upon the log walls, and three rifles were paralleled on pegs. Equipment hung on handy projections, and some tin dishes lay upon a small pile of firewood. A folded tent was serving as a roof. The sunlight, without, beating upon it, made it glow a light yellow shade. A small window shot an oblique square of light upon the cluttered floor. The smoke from the fire at times neglected the clay chimney and wreathed into the room, and this flimsy chimney of clay and sticks made endless threats to set ablaze the entire establishment.

The youth was in a little trance of astonishment. So they were at last going to fight. On the morrow, perhaps, there would be a battle and he would be in it. For a time he was obliged to make himself believe. He could not accept with assurance an omen that he was about to mingle in one of the great affairs of the earth.

He had, of course, dreamed of battles all his life — of vague and bloody conflicts that had thrilled him with their sweep and fire. In visions he had seen himself in many struggles. He had imagined people secure in the shadow of his eagle eyed prowess. But awake he had regarded battles as crimson blotches on the pages of the past. He had put them as things of the bygone with his thought — images of heavy crowns and high castles. There was a portion of the world's history which he had regarded as the time of wars, but it, he thought, had been long gone over the horizon and had disappeared forever.

HERMAN MELVILLE

Shiloh 1866

A Requiem

(April, 1862)

Skimming lightly, wheeling still,
    The swallows fly low

Over the field in clouded days,
The forest-field of Shiloh—
Over the field where April rain
Solaced the parched ones stretched in pain
Through the pause of night
That followed the Sunday fight
Around the church of Shiloh—
The church so lone, the log-built one,
That echoed to many a parting groan
And natural prayer
Of dying foemen mingled there—
Foemen at morn, but friends at eve—
Fame or country least their care:
(What like a bullet can undeceive!)
But now they lie low,
While over them the swallows skim,
And all is hushed at Shiloh.

STEPHEN CRANE

War Is Kind

1896

Do not weep, maiden, for war is kind.
Because your lover threw wild hands toward the sky
And the affrighted steed ran on alone,
Do not weep.
War is kind.

Hoarse, booming drums of the regiment,
Little souls who thirst for fight,
These men were born to drill and die.
The unexplained glory flies above them,
Great is the battle-god, great, and his kingdom—
A field where a thousand corpses lie.

Do not weep, babe, for war is kind
Because your father tumbled in the yellow trenches,
Raged at his breast, gulped and died,
Do not weep.
War is kind.

Swift blazing flag of the regiment,
Eagle with crest of red and gold,
These men were born to drill and die.
Point for them the virtue of slaughter,
Make plain to them the excellence of killing
And a field where a thousand corpses lie.

Mother whose heart hung humble as a button
On the bright splendid shroud of your son,
Do not weep.
War is kind.

THOMAS HARDY

The Man He Killed

1902

"Had he and I but met
By some old ancient inn,
We should have sat us down to wet
Right many a nipperkin!°

"But ranged as infantry,
And staring face to face,
I shot at him as he at me,
And killed him in his place.

"I shot him dead because—
Because he was my foe,
Just so: my foe of course he was:
That's clear enough; although

"He thought he'd 'list, perhaps,
Off-hand-like—just as I—
Was out of work—had sold his traps—
No other reason why.

"Yes; quaint and curious war is!
You shoot a fellow down
You'd treat, if met where any bar is,
Or help to half-a-crown."

WILFRED OWEN

Dulce et Decorum Est°

1920

Bent double, like old beggars under sacks,
Knock-kneed, coughing like hags, we cursed through sludge,
Till on the haunting flares we turned our backs

4. nipperkin: A measure of alcohol less than a half pint. **Dulce et Decorum Est:** The Latin phrase in lines 27–28 reads, "It is sweet and proper to die for one's country" (from the Roman poet Horace).

And towards our distant rest began to trudge.
Men marched asleep. Many had lost their boots
But limped on, blood-shod. All went lame; all blind;
Drunk with fatigue; deaf even to the hoots
Of tired, outstripped Five-Nines° that dropped behind.

Gas! Gas! Quick, boys!—An ecstasy of fumbling
Fitting the clumsy helmets just in time;
But someone still was yelling out and stumbling
And flound'ring like a man in fire or lime . . .
Dim, through the misty panes and thick green light,°
As under a green sea, I saw him drowning.

In all my dreams, before my helpless sight,
He plunges at me, guttering, choking, drowning.

If in some smothering dreams you too could pace
Behind the wagon that we flung him in,
And watch the white eyes writhing in his face,
His hanging face, like a devil's sick of sin;
If you could hear, at every jolt, the blood
Come gargling from the froth-corrupted lungs,
Obscene as cancer, bitter as the cud
Of vile, incurable sores on innocent tongues,—
My friend,° you would not tell with such high zest
To children ardent for some desperate glory,
The old Lie: Dulce et decorum est
Pro patria mori.

RANDALL JARRELL

The Death of the Ball Turret Gunner

1945

From my mother's sleep I fell into the state
And I hunched in its belly till my wet fur froze.
Six miles from earth, loosed from its dream of life,
I woke to black flak and the nightmare fighters.
When I died they washed me out of the turret with a hose.

8. Five-Nines: German 59 mm artillery shells. **13. misty . . . light:** Through a gas mask. **25. My friend:** The poem is addressed to a poet known for patriotic verse, Jessie Pope (1868–1941).

ED WEBSTER

From *San Joaquin Valley Poems: 1969* 1995

i. After Mail Call

When my father wrote from the Tonkin Gulf about coyotes—
recollecting those he'd see on his way out
to the airfield, loping ahead on the quiet road
with their jokes of jackrabbit gristle—
my brother and I would wander, looking out
across soybean fields into tumbleweed and pogonip,
ignoring for a time the toads, to look
for bones, or anything telltale.
Finding nothing, we'd tally his *cat shots*
and pretend to fly, hurling ourselves into the air—
stock still to 130 in two seconds—
small warriors roaring over the flight deck,
ripping over rows of irrigation ditches
as we lost our father daily
to the Red River Delta.

ii. Juvenilia

I remember writing a poem
when I was 7 or 8. It was printed up
at the grade school and my father was proud.
War is a terrible thing.
A pilot's fear is a burning wing . . .
I catalogued everything I could remember
from movies. I rarely thought of it
later, even when a family friend
hurtled the length of the catapult
and exploded into the ocean. I never imagined
the great *Oriskany* fire, or later,
my father eyeing the tracer rounds drifting up
over Haiphong Harbor.
There were the distractions of summer.
It was life yet.

FORREST HAMER

My Father's Viet Nam Tour Near Over

2000

The young dead soldier was younger
than they thought: the 14-year-old passed
himself as seventeen, forged
a father's signature. In the army no more
than months, he was killed early
the week before a cease-fire.
The boy was someone-I-somewhat-knew's
older brother and someone-my-mother-
had-taught's son, and, lying
in the standard army casket, an American
flag draped over the unopened half,
the boy didn't look like anyone
anybody would know — a big kid his dark skin
peached pale, lips pouted. I was sure
I didn't recognize him.

When kids older than us
closed down one campus after another,
I thought they'd close all colleges down,
and there would be no place for me
when it was my time. It didn't seem fair.

Capt. Howell's wife answered
the door one day, and two men
in military dress asked to come in.
She had no choice, I suppose,
but once they came into her living room,
she no longer had a husband, and
the three boys and the girl no longer
had their father. *So this is how*
it happens, I thought: two men come
to your house in the middle of the day,
ringing a bell or rapping on the door.
And, afterwards, there's nothing left
to look forward to.

20. Contemporary Movements in Poetry

POETRY OF THE BEAT GENERATION

Probably all of you have had some brush with the Beat Generation, even if it was only to read Beat novelist Jack Kerouac's name in a rock review or see pictures of Beat poet Allen Ginsberg with Bob Dylan or John Lennon. From being a raw, chaotic movement without order or any plan, the Beat Generation is now seen as an essential ingredient in the mix of idealism, nostalgia, and uncertainty that is America today. In her introduction to the Beat poets in the 1993 volume *The Columbia History of American Poetry*, Ann Charters emphasized the values that lay behind the seeming disorder of the new rebellion.

> The Beat poets were determined to put the idealism of the American dream of individual freedom to the ultimate test. They rebelled against what they saw as their country's social conformity, political repression, and prevailing materialism by championing unconventional aesthetic, sexual, and spiritual values. They insisted that Americans could find an alternate life style despite the prevailing conformism of their time—and like Emerson and Whitman before them—they reaffirmed the sanctity of individual experience. . . . Emerging at a time of significant postwar cultural changes, the Beat literary movement was absorbed into the more turbulent counterculture movement of the late 1960s. It was both a social and literary movement. At its heart were its writers, who included some of the most widely read American poets of the last half century.

Bonnie Bremser's excerpt from her unpublished memoir *Poets and Odd Fellows* is a reminiscence of her first encounter with the new Beat lifestyle and it captures the confused response she shared with many other spectators at that same time. Ray Bremser's "Blues for Bonnie" is a spontaneous "riff" celebrating their meeting. Allen Ginsberg's "Sunflower Sutra" reflects the religious themes that were an important element of this early period of the Beat movement. "Dog" by poet, publisher, and bookstore owner Lawrence Ferlinghetti slyly describes his San Francisco neighborhood and the political climate of the period through the eyes of his dog Homer. "The Day Lady Died" by Frank O'Hara, a New York poet and friend of the Beat writers, is a lament for the death of one of the idols of the generation, singer Billie Holiday. Diane di Prima's "Revolutionary Letter #3" is an expression of the anxiety that hung over many people who were concerned about the threat of atomic attack. In Gregory Corso's "I am 25" and Edward Sanders's "After a Year of Isolation," the personal voices of the younger generation of writers influenced by the work of the original Beat Generation poets are heard.

DOCUMENT

JOHN CLELLON HOLMES

John Clellon Holmes's essay "This Is the Beat Generation" was written for the *New York Times* shortly after the publication of his first novel *Go* in 1952, which introduced the term "Beat Generation" in a conversation and also depicted the new lifestyle in its plot and characters. Holmes was a close friend of Jack Kerouac and influenced the writing of Kerouac's novel *On the Road.* Holmes's essay is a document of its time, evidence that a new literary movement was about to emerge in America that would reflect the turbulence of the social change that followed the Second World War.

From *This Is the Beat Generation* 1952

Any attempt to label an entire generation is unrewarding, and yet the generation which went through the last war, or at least could get a drink easily once it was over, seems to possess a uniform, general quality which demands an adjective. . . . The origins of the word "beat" are obscure, but the meaning is only too clear to most Americans. More than mere weariness, it implies the feeling of having been used, of being raw. It involves a sort of nakedness of mind, and, ultimately, of soul; a feeling of being reduced to the bedrock of consciousness. In short, it means being undramatically pushed up against the wall of oneself. A man is beat whenever he goes for broke and wagers the sum of his resources on a single number; and the young generation has done that continually from early youth.

Its members have an instinctive individuality, needing no bohemianism or imposed eccentricity to express it. Brought up during the collective bad circumstances of a dreary depression, weaned during the collective uprooting of a global war, they distrust collectivity. But they have never been able to keep the world out of their dreams. The fancies of their childhood inhabited the half-light of Munich, the Nazi-Soviet pact, and the eventual blackout. Their adolescence was spent in a topsy-turvy world of war bonds, swing shifts, and troop movements. They grew to independent mind on beachheads, in gin mills and

USOs, in past-midnight arrivals and pre-dawn departures. Their brothers, husbands, fathers, or boy friends turned up dead one day at the other end of a telegram. At the four trembling corners of the world, or in the home town invaded by factories or lonely servicemen, they had intimate experience with the nadir and the zenith of human conduct, and little time for much that came between. The peace they inherited was only as secure as the next headline. It was a cold peace. Their own lust for freedom, and the ability to live at a pace that kills (to which the war had adjusted them), led to black markets, bebop, narcotics, sexual promiscuity, hucksterism, and Jean-Paul Sartre.° The beatness set in later.

It is a postwar generation, and, in a world which seems to mark its cycles by its wars, it is already being compared to that other postwar generation, which dubbed itself "lost." The Roaring Twenties, and the generation that made them roar, are going through a sentimental revival, and the comparison is valuable. The Lost Generation was discovered in a roadster, laughing hysterically because nothing meant anything anymore. It migrated to Europe, unsure whether it was looking for the "orgiastic future" or escaping from the "puritanical past." Its symbols were the flapper, the flask of bootleg whiskey, and an attitude of desperate frivolity best expressed by the line: "Tennis, anyone?" It was caught up in the romance of disillusionment, until even that became an illusion. Every act in its drama of lostness was a tragic or ironic third act, and T. S. Eliot's *The Waste Land* was more than the dead-end statement of a perceptive poet. The pervading atmosphere of that poem was an almost objectless sense of loss, through which the reader felt immediately that the cohesion of things had disappeared. It was, for an entire generation, an image which expressed, with dreadful accuracy, its own spiritual condition.

But the wild boys of today are not lost. Their flushed, often scoffing, always intent faces elude the word, and it would sound phony to them. For this generation conspicuously lacks that eloquent air of bereavement which made so many of the exploits of the Lost Generation symbolic actions. Furthermore, the repeated inventory of shattered ideals, and the laments about the mud in moral currents, which so obsessed the Lost Generation, do not concern young people today. They take these things frighteningly for granted. They were brought up in these ruins and no longer notice them. They drink to "come down" or to "get high," not to illustrate anything. Their excursions into drugs or promiscuity come out of curiosity, not disillusionment.

Only the most bitter among them would call their reality a nightmare and protest that they have indeed lost something, the future. For ever since they were old enough to imagine one, that has been in jeopardy anyway. The absence of personal and social values is to them, not a revelation shaking the ground beneath them, but a problem demanding a day-to-day solution. *How* to live seems to them much more crucial than *why*. And it is precisely at this point that the copywriter and the hotrod driver meet and their identical beatness becomes significant, for, unlike the Lost Generation, which was occupied with the loss of faith, the Beat Generation is becoming more and more occupied

---

Jean-Paul Sartre: French existentialist philosopher (1905–1980).

with the need for it. As such, it is a disturbing illustration of Voltaire's reliable old joke: "If there were no God, it would be necessary to invent him." Not content to bemoan His absence, they are busily and haphazardly inventing totems for Him on all sides.

BONNIE BREMSER

A First Meeting with the Beats

2001

First there was me. Then there was Ray and me. It happened like this. I had dropped out of college and Ray was fresh out of jail, practically at the same time. I was living at 19th and F near Pennsylvania Avenue, just two blocks from the White House in D.C., my first apartment. It was 1959 and I was nineteen years old. Ray was twenty-five and came down to D.C. with a bunch of New York poets.

February was cold in D.C., the bare trees, wet with the winter rain, were close around the entrance of the Odd Fellows Hall as I got out of the cab. Kind of a surprise. The big glass doors, though pointed obliquely into the winter wind, were brightly lit, and winter stayed outside.

The lonely day fell away from me as I entered. The atmosphere was warm and I felt my face relax as I looked around to see if people were staring at me as I was them, amazed at the differences. But no one noticed me, for the poetry reading had already started. I was free to study the interesting faces there. What beautiful long hair and gentle expressions of countenance. Soft smiles, a little ecstatic. But even more, a sense of excitement, perhaps it was hope, shining from eyes. Maybe the poetry was doing it, opening emotions, lifting the spirit. Maybe it was communication making them all understand as one mind. It felt good to be there and yet the familiar discomfort in my own skin made me an outsider. Had I experienced any of that communication? Would someone teach me? I took a deep breath, trying to be ready for whatever came.

The crowd more than filled the hall and I leaned against the wall on the nearest side where many people were sitting on the floor. I could see well there and yet was somewhat removed. Down front was a stage on which were a grand piano and a small table with one chair. All of the lights were on in the hall, illuminating the audience as well as the stage. No artificial barrier between the crowd and the poets except the elevation of the stage. The poets stood around the stage. This small Negro guy apparently was in charge making introductions. He introduced the next poet, Peter Orlovsky, very blond and good-looking. I thought I would like to know someone like that. He laughed at himself while reading a very short poem. Then another poet stood and read in an excited voice about a lion in his bedroom closet. "Yeah, a lion, wow!" I thought, laughing with the people around me, catching the excitement of his reading. Who? Allen Ginsberg? But he was funny. "There goes my image of an English professor," I thought, glad that I had come.

The crowd was noisy and excited. "Thanks to the education of the New Jersey penal system, a jailhouse poet, Ray Bremser!" I heard the announcer say something about Poems of Madness. And then there was this tall guy with an army fatigue jacket and red sweatshirt underneath, the hood drooping down his back. He looked like a monk. He sat at the little table looking down at the audience, reading with a strong accent. A black binder full of poems was on his lap. The poem was about how his father always bet on the horses. The words came fast in a barrage and I couldn't catch it all. But the rhythm carried it and I found I could understand anyway.

Here one of my shy moods overtook me. What if someone spoke to me, or asked my opinion? Suppose I were expected to be friendly, spontaneous and free like these other people. I'd have to come out of my aloof, stuck-up shell, even admit that I was painfully scared of people. What if I had to turn my head and look directly at the person next to me? I was uncomfortable that way. I felt suddenly confused and wanted to get outside again, back to my apartment, and yet at the same time I wanted more than anything to be a part of this crowd for once, to fit in. I moved to the back of the hall on an impulse to leave. OK, so maybe I am a phony, so what, I swung my ass a little, in defiance of the human race.

RAY BREMSER

Blues for Bonnie—Take 1, January 1960 1960

"these blues broke out in a gallery,
on 9th street . . ."
"no."
"9th avenue . . . 43rd street."
"hell—it's hell's kitchen again."
funny blues . . .
bonnie in washington
waiting for march and
cummings coming
bringing glad tidings.
"of 9th avenue?"
zoo.
a dam-giraff.
whallop, a
lalapalooza floozie
on via flamina piazza

masticating a ruddy pizza
pie—
pie-pie.
bye-bye, baby.
off to Riker a foodery . . .
(i dig food—soup.)
(if i don't get straight quick
the fuzz'll bust me sure as
i reek o reefer.
Rio Rita—that's as far as i'm
taking it.)

. . . i would eat the food
instead, oney this stud
along side me pounces eyeball
gawks as if to say,
"high as rat-shit."
and 2 fried eggs in my plate
the same thing.

how do you eat
the accuser?
and which one first?

Rio Rita.

ALLEN GINSBERG
Sunflower Sutra

1955

I walked on the banks of the tincan banana dock and sat down under the huge shade of a Southern Pacific locomotive to look at the sunset over the box house hills and cry.
Jack Kerouac sat beside me on a busted rusty iron pole, companion, we thought the same thoughts of the soul, bleak and blue and sad-eyed, surrounded by the gnarled steel roots of trees of machinery.
The oily water on the river mirrored the red sky, sun sank on top of final Frisco peaks, no fish in that stream, no hermit in those mounts, just ourselves rheumy-eyed and hung-over like old bums on the riverbank, tired and wily.
Look at the Sunflower, he said, there was a dead gray shadow against the sky, big as a man, sitting dry on top of a pile of ancient sawdust—
—I rushed up enchanted—it was my first sunflower, memories of Blake—my visions—Harlem

and Hells of the Eastern rivers, bridges clanking Joes Greasy Sandwiches, dead baby carriages, black treadless tires forgotten and unretreaded, the poem of the riverbank, condoms & pots, steel knives, nothing stainless, only the dank muck and the razor-sharp artifacts passing into the past—
and the gray Sunflower poised against the sunset, crackly bleak and dusty with the smut and smog and smoke of olden locomotives in its eye—
corolla of bleary spikes pushed down and broken like a battered crown, seeds fallen out of its face, soon-to-be-toothless mouth of sunny air, sunrays obliterated on its hairy head like a dried wire spiderweb,
leaves stuck out like arms out of the stem, gestures from the sawdust root, broke pieces of plaster fallen out of the black twigs, a dead fly in its ear,
Unholy battered old thing you were, my sunflower O my soul, I loved you then!
The grime was no man's grime but death and human locomotives,
all that dress of dust, that veil of darkened railroad skin, that smog of cheek, that eyelid of black mis'ry, that sooty hand or phallus or protuberance of artificial worse-than-dirt—industrial—modern—all that civilization spotting your crazy golden crown—
and those blear thoughts of death and dusty loveless eyes and ends and withered roots below, in the home-pile of sand and sawdust, rubber dollar bills, skin of machinery, the guts and innards of the weeping coughing car, the empty lonely tin-cans with their rusty tongues alack, what more could I name, the smoked ashes of some cock cigar, the cunts of wheelbarrows and the milky breasts of cars, wornout asses out of chairs & sphincters of dynamos—all these
entangled in your mummied roots—and you there standing before me in the sunset, all your glory in your form!
A perfect beauty of a sunflower! a perfect excellent lovely sunflower existence! a sweet natural eye to the new hip moon, woke up alive and excited grasping in the sunset shadow sunrise golden monthly breeze!
How many flies buzzed round you innocent of your grime, while you cursed the heavens of the railroad and your flower soul?
Poor dead flower? when did you forget you were a flower? when did you look at your skin and decide you were an impotent dirty old locomotive? the ghost of a locomotive? the specter and shade of a once powerful mad American locomotive?
You were never no locomotive, Sunflower, you were a sunflower!
And you Locomotive, you are a locomotive, forget me not!
So I grabbed up the skeleton thick sunflower and stuck it at my side like a scepter,

and deliver my sermon to my soul, and Jack's soul too, and anyone who'll listen,
—We're not our skin of grime, we're not our dread bleak dusty imageless locomotive, we're all golden sunflowers inside, blessed by our own seed & hairy naked accomplishment-bodies growing into mad black formal sunflowers in the sunset, spied on by our eyes under the shadow of the mad locomotive riverbank sunset Frisco hilly tincan evening sit-down vision.

LAWRENCE FERLINGHETTI

Dog

1958

The dog trots freely in the street
and sees reality
and the things he sees
are bigger than himself
and the things he sees
are his reality
Drunks in doorways
Moons on trees
The dog trots freely thru the street
and the things he sees
are smaller than himself
Fish on newsprint
Ants in holes
Chickens in Chinatown windows
their heads a block away
The dog trots freely in the street
and the things he smells
smell something like himself
The dog trots freely in the street
past puddles and babies
cats and cigars
poolrooms and policemen
He doesn't hate cops
He merely has no use for them
and he goes past them
and past the dead cows hung up whole
in front of the San Francisco Meat Market
He would rather eat a tender cow
than a tough policeman
though either might do
And he goes past the Romeo Ravioli Factory

and past Colt's Tower
and past Congressman Doyle
He's afraid of Colt's Tower
but he's not afraid of Congressman Doyle
although what he hears is very discouraging
very depressing
very absurd
to a sad young dog like himself
to a serious dog like himself
But he has his own free world to live in
His own fleas to eat
He will not be muzzled
Congressman Doyle is just another
fire hydrant
to him
The dog trots freely in the street
and has his own dog's life to live
and to think about
and to reflect upon
touching and tasting and testing everything
investigating everything
without benefit of perjury
a real realist
with a real tale to tell
and a real tail to tell it with
a real live
barking
democratic dog
engaged in real
free enterprise
with something to say
about ontology
something to say
about reality
and how to see it
and how to hear it
with his head cocked sideways
at streetcorners
as if he is just about to have
his picture taken
for Victor Records
listening for
His Master's Voice
and looking
like a living questionmark
into the

great gramophone
of puzzling existence
with its wondrous hollow horn
which always seems
just about to spout forth
some Victorious answer
to everything

FRANK O'HARA

The Day Lady° Died

1964

It is 12:20 in New York a Friday
three days after Bastille day, yes
it is 1959 and I go get a shoeshine
because I will get off the 4:19 in Easthampton
at 7:15 and then go straight to dinner
and I don't know the people who will feed me

I walk up the muggy street beginning to sun
and have a hamburger and a malted and buy
an ugly NEW WORLD WRITING to see what the poets
in Ghana are doing these days
I go on to the bank
and Miss Stillwagon (first name Linda I once heard)
doesn't even look up my balance for once in her life
and in the GOLDEN GRIFFIN I get a little Verlaine
for Patsy with drawings by Bonnard° although I do
think of Hesiod,° trans. Richmond Lattimore or
Brendan Behan's new play° or *Le Balcon* or *Les Nègres*
of Genet,° but I don't, I stick with Verlaine
after practically going to sleep with quandariness

and for Mike I just stroll into the PARK LANE
Liquor Store and ask for a bottle of Strega and
then I go back where I came from to 6th Avenue
and the tobacconist in the Ziegfeld Theatre and

Lady: Billie Holiday (1915–1959), known as "Lady Day," a popular African American singer of the 1930s, who struggled at the end of her career against alcohol and drug abuse. **14–15. Verlaine . . . Bonnard:** Paul Verlaine (1844–1896), the French poet; the reference is to an edition of Verlaine's poems with illustrations by Pierre Bonnard (1867–1947). **16. Hesiod:** Greek poet (eighth century B.C.). **17. Brendan Behan's new play:** Possibly *The Quare Fellow* (1956) or *The Hostage* (1958). **18. Genet:** Jean Genet (1910–1986), French novelist and playwright whose plays included *The Balcony* (1956) and *The Blacks* (1958).

casually ask for a carton of Gauloises and a carton
of Picayunes, and a NEW YORK POST with her face on it
and I am sweating a lot by now and thinking of
leaning on the john door in the 5 SPOT
while she whispered a song along the keyboard
to Mal Waldron° and everyone and I stopped breathing

DIANE DI PRIMA

Revolutionary Letter #3

1971

store water; make a point of filling your bathtub
at the first news of trouble: they turned off the water
in the 4th ward for a whole day during the Newark riots;
or better yet make a habit
of keeping the tub clean and full when not in use
change this once a day, it should be good enough
for washing, flushing toilets when necessary
and cooking, in a pinch, but it's a good idea
to keep some bottled water handy too
get a couple of five gallon jugs and keep them full
for cooking

store food—dry stuff like rice and beans stores best
goes farthest. SALT VERY IMPORTANT: it's health and energy
healing too, keep a couple pounds
sea salt around, and, because we're spoiled, some tins
tuna, etc. to keep up morale—keep up the sense
of 'balanced diet' 'protein intake' remember
the stores may be closed for quite some time, the trucks
may not enter your section of the city for weeks, you can cool it
indefinitely
with 20 lb brown rice
20 lb whole wheat flour
10 lb cornmeal
10 lb good beans—kidney or soy
5 lb sea salt
2 qts good oil
dried fruit and nuts
add nutrients and a sense of luxury
to this diet, a squash or coconut
in a cool place in your pad will keep six months

29. Mal Waldron: A jazz pianist who sometimes accompanied Holiday in her club engagements.

remember we are all used to eating less
than the 'average American' and take it easy
before we
ever notice we're hungry the rest of the folk will be starving
used as they are to meat and fresh milk daily
and help will arrive, until the day no help arrives
and then you're on your own.

hoard matches, we aren't good
at rubbing sticks together any more
a tinder box is useful, if you can work it
don't count on gas stove, gas heater
electric light
keep hibachi and charcoal, CHARCOAL STARTER a help
kerosene lamp and candles, learn to keep warm
with breathing
remember the blessed American habit of bundling

GREGORY CORSO

I am 25

1955

with a love a madness for Shelley
Chatterton Rimbaud
and the needy-yap of my youth
has gone from ear to ear:
I HATE OLD POETMEN!
Especially old poetmen who retract
who consult other old poetmen
who speak their youth in whispers,
saying:—I did those then
but that was then—
that was then—
O I would quiet old men
say to them:—I am your friend
what you once were, thru me
you'll be again—
Then at night in the confidence of their homes
rip out their apology-tongues
and steal their poems.

EDWARD SANDERS

After a Year of Isolation

1995

I am hungering
to correspond with poets—
those forms
    that grow
        from the finest search
from the days
that leave dried blood
        on the calendar.

& I know
    that poets are bitter
& each line of type
        is an Ozymandias
but the quick chatter
    the Li Po toss-offs
        the laughs & chuckles
I crave it

•

The evening star
is high upon the maples
I say your name
I feel it pulling

In dreams and daydreams
        poems and paintings
I hear it calling
    I hear it calling

The earth is a creature
that loves to commingle
when the swirl of our wings
makes the hot winds kiss
    I believe, I believe
    in the hot, hot winds

They say don't waste time
Don't dare waste a minute
but even if we're perfect
Time wastes everything
        Time wastes everything

    I believe, I believe
    in the hot, hot winds

  I wanted so badly
  to believe in the soul

so that I could swirl with you
in those hot, hot winds

    I believe, I believe
    in the hot, hot winds

POETRY OF THE CHAPS AND ZINES

If you've heard friends talk about a *zine,* you know that what they mean is a magazine—usually a magazine that has something like music or sports or a hobby as its focus. A zine usually doesn't have much, if any, advertising, and the design and layout sometimes look as if they were done in a beginner's design class. The word *chap* might cause more of a problem since it isn't a term you hear as often. It refers to a *chapbook,* which is often a kind of literary collection—poetry, sometimes fiction, or an individual essay. Usually chapbooks are printed in small numbers of copies, and often they don't get widely distributed. Now most of them are produced on computers and copying machines, but earlier many of them were laboriously hand printed with old-fashioned hand-set type, and some were illustrated with work by major artists like Pablo Picasso, who contributed drawings to many chapbooks.

For hundreds of years these two worlds of poetry have existed comfortably side by side with mainstream publishers. The creators of chaps and zines have the advantage of being able to publish writing by new, unknown authors, to champion new styles of writing, and to advance ideas that the larger society still finds challenging or unacceptable. In 1956 Allen Ginsberg's *Howl* was first published as a chapbook by City Lights books in San Francisco, and both the publisher and the clerk in his bookshop who sold the book were quickly arrested. Once the poem had been vindicated by a San Francisco judge as having redeeming social significance, however, it heralded the opening of a new period of experimentation in American poetry. Ginsberg's chapbook itself, still in print, has gone on to sell nearly a million copies. It was the small literary zines of a century ago that fought the battle of free verse. Many well-known poets presented their early work in chapbooks or magazines often published by other poets or published by themselves. With today's Internet, poems from the zines and the chaps make their way around the world with the tap of a computer key, and there is certainly more poetry being written and published in the world now than ever before.

Although each of the poets in this section has been widely published, five of them were associated in the pages of the little magazine *Wormwood Review*: Ann Menebroker, Tom Kryss, Joan Jobe Smith, Ronald Baatz, and Gerald Locklin. Menebroker and Locklin are California writers. Menebroker grew up in Sacramento, where she still lives and writes, while Locklin taught for many years at the University of California at Long Beach. Menebroker's "Repossessed" turns to the theme of the new beginning that a new house represents. Locklin's "So It Goes" and "Friday Night Lights" remind his readers of the complications of parenting and aging. The title "Friday Night Lights" refers to the lights in the stadium where the games he's watching are being played, and for older readers it will also remind them of a popular television boxing program of the 1960s, "Friday Night Fights." In "The Carol Burnett Show," Joan Jobe Smith writes about her experience as a divorced mom earning money to pay for her college education by working long nights as a go-go girl. (See also her poem "Feminist Arm Candy for the Mafia and Sinatra" on p. 1056.)

Ronald Baatz was living on a quiet road in rural upstate New York when his poem "The Oldest Songs" was written, and the lines reflect the peacefulness of his surroundings. d.a. levy, whose poem "perhaps (#5)" describes a typically chaotic incident in the 1960s, was the dominant figure in the Cleveland underground poetry scene. As a publisher, poet, and artist he produced hundreds of mimeographed publications. Often in conflict with the law on issues of censorship, he was arrested twice by the Cleveland police and his mimeograph machine was confiscated after the second arrest. He committed suicide in 1968 at the age of twenty-six. Robert E. McDonough and Susan Grimm also were part of the Cleveland poetry scene. McDonough's "Résumé" considers his role in the larger society when he reflects on the use that his work might accomplish. Grimm's "Things I Can Know" sums up what any of us can know about our lives, for whatever comfort or hope the knowledge might give.

DOCUMENT

GERALD LOCKLIN

One of the most prolific of the poets using these new ways to reach their audiences is Gerald Locklin. He has published more than 3,000 poems that have been collected into more than 100 books. For him this new way of finding the audience for poetry has been an opening into an exciting world of communication.

The Small Presses and Little Magazines: A Few Reflections

2008

Forty years ago, on a Small Press/Little Magazine panel, I was asked what I thought was most important about them. Without hesitation, I replied, "That they publish my stuff."

That was a half-truth: they didn't always accept my poems and stories, and the university quarterlies did not always reject them. There has always been, however, a democratic, sometimes populist bent to the poetry underground: almost anyone can find a niche somewhere in the pages of *Poet's Market* or *The International Directory of Little Magazines and Small Presses*. That accessibility seems to me quite healthy. It guarantees a basic Freedom—that of Expression—which has been exponentially abetted by the Internet. To each his own.

I ask of those who would argue for strict standards of quality or propriety, Who appointed you the Poetry Police? And on what basis: Wealth? Politics?

Friends? A prestigious education? Geographic location? Diversity? Hell, we strive to uphold our own eclectic aesthetic taste at the *Chiron Review*, where Ray Zepeda, John Brantingham, my son Zachary, and I assist the founder/ editor, Michael Hathaway. We cannot accept everything, but our tabloid, newsprint format allows us to take chances, play hunches. We think it works. We were among the first to publish Sherman Alexie and Adrian Louis.

My personal taste runs more to the poetry I find in *The New York Quarterly* than what I encounter in *The New Yorker*. Frankly, I would rather read Edward Field than John Ashbery, although no one since Gertrude Stein has displayed a more seductive sleight-of-semantic-hand than the latter. Of course, all poetry mags have severely limited circulations. *The Wormwood Review*, edited by the legendary Marvin Malone, which I consider the best (or my favorite) poetry magazine of the second half of the Twentieth Century, faithfully and tastefully produced 700 copies per issue for 145 issues. How many copies were published of the first editions of James Joyce's books? The permanence of authors is seldom determined within their lifetimes. The term "famous poet" is virtually oxymoronic. How many customers in the Starbucks of America would be able to name a single work by Hopkins or Yeats, let alone Dryden or Donne? Shakespeare is a mandated exception, but for how much longer?

The divisions between the twin realms of the "establishment" and the "underground" are largely based on socioeconomic and political considerations, but the borders are regularly crossed in both directions. Nor are the little mags the minor leagues from which a few will graduate to "the bigs." William Carlos Williams died with one poem alone—the magnificent but atypical "Yachts"—included in most Intro to Lit anthologies, and yet he was already recognized by Allen Ginsberg as the godfather of postmodern poetry. *Poetry* (Chicago) squeezed two uncharacteristically tame poems by Charles Bukowski into its pages shortly before his death.

So let's write what we like, and read what we enjoy, and not take our publishing "credits" too seriously, and look neither up nor down upon our fellow scribblers: because all our works are destined for eventual inclusion only in that most voluminous but dusty of anthologies: the one in which the entire yellowing Table of Contents is attributed to "Anon."

ANN MENEBROKER

Repossessed

1969

We are moving to this house out in the country
with nothing on either side of it but dirt
and weeds and whatever small things can hide.
The poor people who originally lived there went
under. So the savings and loan said, "Sorry,

no money, no house, no two acres." And they
took it back.

We came along looking for something we could
afford and this had to be it. The place was filthy
from ceiling to floor, as if the original owners
had taken out their financial fury on the heart
of the house. But they wrecked it just enough
to lower the price to our level. God, I thought, is
this the capitalist in me?
But no one is in the house now. Only spiders are
there who have spun a million webs where
the mosquitoes and moths are caught. And outside, some
chickens running around, wild and frightened.

So I said, "Let's get it." And we did.
Tomorrow we're going out to mop the place and scrub
the walls and put our own paint on it. We
will get caught in our own webs, thank you.
Pray for us.

TOM KRYSS

Things Thrown Away

1994

A chair missing only two rungs.
a bicycle sans only seat, handlebars,
fenders, and wheels.
A bicycle pump.
Checkerboard without checkers.
Wait—there's a black one
under the beer cans,
mixed with the chicken bones.

A whole IBM typewriter—
no guarantees.
The one-thousand piece Mt. Shasta puzzle,
still in original box—
even less guarantee.

Seven cartons of books containing
at the bottom still readable
portions of *Wind, Sand, and Stars*
and *Letters to Theo.*

One half of a child's walkie-talkie set.
A single badminton racquet.
An Osmond LP with only one or two scratches;
just the empty, slightly beaten-up
Rubber Soul jacket.

What did you expect?
The lamp with the genie still sleeping in it?
The lost half of the stub at fifty to one?

Remember, these are only the things
people threw away—
there's a reason the pickings
are slim and slimmer than nothing.

d. a. levy

perhaps (#5)

1966

the sun was shining
but it was a rainy day
sumwher inside me
    OR chicken tracks at
    a one night CRYSTAL PALACE

unknown friends
stumble in from
being lost in New York
for a month
                thin pale
                streaked grey faces
                with stars in eyes

me & Mara
try to stuff soup
& steak into them
what are looking
as if just dug out
of a New Orleans
Cemetery for a voodoo
                        CERAMIC

them bringing in anxious arms
full of black velvet silk
screens posters poems
                            TIREDness

we finally put them to
bed like stuffed toys
              in the morning i
        find them shooting Speed
        in my living room & i
        get sick   sum
        freudian hangup on syringes
        & needles

they left carrying their Works
in an old army munitions case
& now my living rooms got
        A Grand Ole Memory
WATCHING men SHOOT death
INTO their ARMS in LONE
liness & despair
the stars in their eyes
as they flashed

perhaps they were dreaming
of frozen methedrine
advertised on tv
        someone in my head
        KEEPS YELLING
        Laugh or You'll Die

ROBERT E. McDONOUGH

Résumé

1988

  This is what I do: I teach
plain English, reading and writing
to men and women who hardly ever
become doctors, lawyers, or even
English teachers. I work to give them
language to handle their language.
"Introduction," I say,
"body, conclusion. Strong topic
sentences, transitions."
I show them outlines like ladders.
"Hard work," they answer; "anything's possible."
We succeed, or, often, we fail—
I teach failure, too.

SUSAN GRIMM

Things I Can Know

2004

The year my parents met, an earthquake rocked
Cleveland. Calvin Coolidge was President. Liquor
was smuggled across Lake Erie in boats. The average
worker earned $26 a week. Lindbergh had yet
to cross the Atlantic, Trotsky had not yet

been exiled, and the Taisho Dynasty was about to end.
My mother was fourteen, just in from the country.
She shrugs off this encounter. Before they date,
Gandhi will be imprisoned, the stock market will crash,
and Edward VIII will abdicate his throne;
the planet Pluto will be discovered, Donald Duck
will appear in his first movie, and the Cleveland
Bloomer Girls will become national softball champs.

How much did a gardenia cost in 1938? My father
might remember. On Schaaf Road someone pinched
back the plants for weeks to coax my parents'
signature flower, glassed in under Cleveland's
cool skies. They drank Brandy Alexanders
and Pink Ladies; they danced like young trees.
Were breezy Fred and Ginger their models? Bonnie
and Clyde had already been shot dead. Before
they marry, child labor will be outlawed, cave
paintings will be discovered in Lascaux,
and the Seventh World's Poultry Congress
will convene in Cleveland. Germany will invade
Austria, Bohemia, Norway, war spilling over the world
like a kitchen accident hardening out of reach.

In 1945 Roosevelt dies, Hitler shoots himself,
the atomic bomb is dropped on Hiroshima. Bread
is 16 cents a loaf, coffee is 39 cents a pound,
and a man's suit costs $42.50. 11,945
marriages are recorded in Cuyahoga County.
My parents toast with champagne in the backyard
under a sycamore tree. In their photo—framed,
in the bedroom—my mother holds a cascade
of flowers, one for each night of their nuptial
drive to the South. My father still keeps
these honeymoon receipts in the family Bible.

JOAN JOBE SMITH

The Carol Burnett Show

1989–1991

After my father died and I had to
drop out of college for the second time
to go back to being a go-go girl, my
mother came to live with me to take
care of my kids although she didn't
approve one bit of what I did for a

living, said I was just goofing off and
having a good time even though I told her
I wasn't, and so ashamed was she of me
she lied to my grandmothers, told them I
was a dancer on the Carol Burnett Show
and that's why I worked nights, wore mini
skirts, false hair and eyelashes, but my
mother told the truth about me to her sister
Vera, a divorcée like me, and when Vera came
to visit, the two of them came to see me
at the Playgal Club and Spike the manager
gave them a front row table and a free
pitcher of beer and potato chips and there
they sat, wearing white gloves and Jackie
Kennedy pillbox hats, Kleenexes from their
purses for napkins on their laps as they
watched us go-go girls dance, sling pitchers,
kegs, tanks of beer to the drunken aerospace
execs, construction workers, surfers, Nam-
bound marines, watched us empty ashtrays, dance,
wash glasses, dance, sweep up broken glass
after some pool hustlers got into a fight, and
dance and the next day at noon as I sat in the
kitchen, nibbling my bowl of Rice Krispies,
a somnolent zombie and achy from working till
3 a.m., I heard my mother outside yelling at
the trashmen not to make so much noise banging
trashcans, they might wake up her daughter who
worked nights and her daughter worked DAMNED HARD
to earn a living! It was the finest tribute my
mother ever gave me and now, years later,
finally I can appreciate it,
now that I'm all rested up.

RONALD BAATZ

The Oldest Songs

1994

the bright sunlight against the snows
of a long winter is almost blinding, so
there is no thought of going outdoors
without sunglasses. i sit on the front
steps peeling an orange, then eating
all the neat little sections until
only peels are left. these

i throw out onto the hard covering
of snow. but the steps
are too cold, and i cannot stay
out here any longer. this
sunlight, it is more intense
than the sunlight of july.
the july sunlight is taken
and soaked and darkened
into green. march sunlight
is primarily converted
into a blinding atmosphere.
the birds won't even fly
about that much, actually only
going from branch to branch
in the same tree, calling out
warnings to one another:
the earth's
oldest songs.

GERALD LOCKLIN

So It Goes 1978

"I wish," he says, "it was the opposite
And I was *your* father."

"And you'd make *me* go to museums?"
"Yeah!" he says.

"Well," I say, "one of these days
Perhaps you'll have your own kids
And you can make *them* go to museums."

"With my luck," he says,
"My kids will *like* museums."

Friday Night Lights 2010

What a great life I've had—
Kids, literature, California—
And yet just like these young men
Trying to play their way out of
Odessa, Texas,

I am still at times afflicted by
The what-might-have-beens
If that pass had not glanced off my fingertips;

If I'd grown a few more inches;
Been a little faster, tougher, springier,
Braver, or more reckless;
If I could have actualized my daydreams.

My friends have often also been frustrated jocks:
D., the near-Olympic swimmer;
B., the near-Olympic Water Polo player;
D., the high school pitching phenom;
R., the running back turned aspiring actor . . .

In fact we all saw enough of the world
Of athletic success to know how lucky we are
To have flunked out of it,

But try telling that to the little boys
That you give birth to,
Or the little boy inside of you
Whose voice will never cease to narrate
The bittersweet scenarios of heroism.

◆ Topics for Writing about Themes in Poetry ◆

1. Choose one of the nature poems and analyze the questions it raises about our responsibility to the natural world, or discuss the experience of nature that it presents and relate it to your own experience. (See pp. 1030–1035.)
2. Discuss the role that books and poetry readings have played in the new consciousness in women's writing today. (See pp. 1035–1041.)
3. Choose one of the poems and discuss its insights or responses to the questions of racial discrimination that it raises. (See pp. 1042–1051.)
4. One question is always asked about poetry that is politically motivated: does it make any difference in the world itself? Discuss the point of view of one of the poems in this section and relate it to what ways you think it might or might not have influenced public action. (See pp. 1052–1060.)
5. The poems and the document on pages 1061–1067 present several different views of war, from the wondering excitement of Stephen Crane's young soldier to the harsh realities described by Wilfred Owen. Compare the emotions in two of the poems and discuss their relationship to the experience of war as it is waged today.
6. The Beat Generation still is a controversial subject to many people. Analyze one of the poems on pages 1068–1081 and discuss how its descriptions of the Beat scene or its opinions could challenge accepted attitudes.
7. A characteristic of recent poems from the chaps and zines is that they are written in an informal, everyday language. (See pages 1081–1090.) Discuss whether this helps you to understand the poet and the theme of the writing, and contrast this informality to the traditional forms of poetry you have encountered in earlier chapters.

PART THREE

Drama

. . . the lasting appeal of tragedy is due to our need to face the fact of death in order to strengthen ourselves for life. . . .

—ARTHUR MILLER

I don't think you should frighten them [the audience], I think you should terrify them.

—EDWARD ALBEE

The great and only possible dignity of man lies in his power deliberately to choose certain moral values by which to live as steadfastly as if he, too, like a character in a play, were immured against the corrupting rush of time.

—TENNESSEE WILLIAMS

21. What Is a Play?

> Suit the action to the word, the word to the action; with this special observance, that you o'erstep not the modesty of nature: for any thing so o'erdone is from the purpose of playing, whose end, both at the first and now, was and is, to hold, as 't were, the mirror up to nature.
>
> —HAMLET TO THE PLAYERS

Drama is our second oldest literary form, after poetry. To say that this literary genre consists primarily of plays written to be performed in the theater is true only for the earliest plays. Later works known as "closet dramas," written in the nineteenth century by such poets as Percy Bysshe Shelley and such playwrights as Henrik Ibsen, were meant to be performed in the solitary theater of the reader's mind. A play can be defined as a story told in dialogue, but even here there are exceptions. The modern playwright Samuel Beckett wrote stories without dialogue for the stage intended to be mimed by a single performer. Today millions of viewers watch works of drama—movies, television sitcoms, prime-time soap operas, weekly network dramatic series—that were never intended to be performed in a theater. But for centuries *drama* meant a stage play, and it is this meaning of the word that we primarily have in mind when we speak of drama as a literary genre.

As Aristotle understood, action or conflict is the essence of drama. This is suggested in the origin of the word *drama,* which is the Greek verb *dran,* "to perform." A century after drama flourished in Greece, Aristotle wrote the *Poetics* (c. 340 B.C.), a work in which he analyzed the literary form used by Sophocles and other Greek dramatists. For Aristotle, a play was the process of imitating a significant action complete unto itself by means of language "made sensuously attractive" and spoken by the persons involved in the action, not presented through narrative. Aristotle's definition of tragedy contained six important elements: (1) plot or action, the basic principle of drama; (2) characterization, an almost equally important element; (3) the thought or theme of the play; (4) verbal expression or dialogue; (5) visual adornment or stage decoration and costumes and masks for the actors; and (6) song or music to accompany the performers' words and movement.

Because most modern plays are literary works meant to give an illusion of reality through their performance onstage, a playwright who has set actors in motion to tell a story cannot interrupt the action, as in a work of fiction, to offer background information about the characters or summarize events taking place over a period of time, unless he introduces a narrator at the beginning of the play. Usually, the playwright gives the audience information about the story through dialogue. Playwrights can also suggest the development of their story by the physical behavior of the actors onstage and by changes in their costumes, lighting, and sets.

When we think of the literary genre of drama, we have in mind plays created to give an illusion of reality invented for a striking effect when performed by actors. Plays are acts of make-believe—performances in which the author, actors, stage technicians, and audience are united in their participation in an imaginary world. This world onstage can mimic "real life" in such plays as Lorraine Hansberry's *A Raisin in the Sun* (1959) with actors and sets representing contemporary everyday reality, or it can project a view of our experience as in a dream, in such poetic plays as William Shakespeare's *Hamlet* (c. 1600).

As stories primarily told in dialogue, most plays in the classic repertoire fall into one of three conventional categories: tragedy, comedy, and tragicomedy. Broadly speaking, in **tragedy** the story ends unhappily, usually in the death of the main character, as in Sophocles' *Oedipus the King* (c. 430 B.C.). In **comedy** the story ends happily, often with a marriage symbolizing the continuation of life and the resolution of the conflict, as in Shakespeare's *A Midsummer Night's Dream* (c. 1594–95). **Tragicomedy** combines these two categories. These categories can be further divided in modern plays into dark comedy, where the playwright's sardonic humor offers a frightening glimpse of the futility of life, and farce, a short play that depends for its comic effect on exaggerated, improbable situations and slapstick action. In the hands of gifted playwrights, the categories can be stretched beyond these simple definitions. For example, in *Poof!* (1993), Lynn Nottage used the form of a farce to write a short play dramatizing her response to the serious subject of marital abuse against women (see p. 1582).

Drama has experienced many innovations in form and staging in the last several decades. Such noted practitioners as the contemporary English playwright Tom Stoppard have made fun of the increasing pace of our lives and the trivialization of our most cherished institutions, including the theater. In *Dogg's Hamlet* (1979), Stoppard created two short versions of Shakespeare's *Hamlet*—one that would take fifteen minutes to perform and a second, even briefer "encore" version of the play—streamlined for a production on a double-decker London bus.

As brief as it is, when you read the text of Stoppard's encore version of *Hamlet* (see "Conversation on *Hamlet* as Text and Performance," p. 1592), you will see that it still satisfies the standard definition of a play as a performance by actors of a story told in dialogue. Stoppard has edited Shakespeare's words so drastically that our familiarity with the original *Hamlet*—one of the most famous plays in the European tradition—is essential to our understanding of the cut version.

If the text of *Hamlet* were performed in its complete version, it would take almost six hours onstage. Every director makes some cuts in the script, but Stoppard's version is so short that he seems to be implying that contemporary audiences lack the time and the patience to sit still through the long classic plays. He also assumes that the tradition of European theater continues to be relevant today. The people who bought tickets when Stoppard's play was performed on the bus probably studied Shakespeare in school, where they might have become familiar with the complicated plot of *Hamlet* through reading the play or a summary of it for an English class.

If you are familiar with Shakespeare's play, Stoppard's collapsed (more than condensed) version will remind you of what has been cut. The encore version of *Hamlet* conveys none of the complexity of the young hero's passionate character, none of the poetry of his unforgettable soliloquies, and none of the tragedy of his dilemma. This bizarre version is meant to be only a faint, funny echo of the original.

Stoppard wrote his farcical version of *Hamlet* for a specific theater company in England, intending his play to be seen and heard as well as read. This adds another dimension to our experience of drama. When performed in front of an audience, the text of a play is transmitted by the theatrical director, the costume and set designers, the technical staff responsible for sound and lighting, and the actors who bring the play to life. All these people work together to shape a play's meaning for the audience.

Even on a red double-decker London bus, an actor interpreting the role of Hamlet as an aristocrat dressed in luxurious black velvet and silk ruffles will elicit a different response to the hero's personality and emotional situation than an actor who depicts Hamlet as a clown in a silly wig and circus tights, or as a scruffy, leather-jacketed, metal-studded biker, or as a pajama-clad patient recently escaped from a psychiatric hospital. Actors have performed the role in all these costumes, and they are all—at least in name—Hamlet. Every time an actor "plays" this role, or any other character in a drama, there is the potential for interpreting Hamlet differently. And when women take on the role of Hamlet, as they sometimes do, an even greater potential exists for fresh interpretations from the actors onstage and from the viewers in the audience.

Because drama is a collaborative effort that results in a work performed on a stage in front of an audience, a writer who creates a play is called a *playwright*, suggesting a highly skilled craftsperson or artisan who makes something tangible. But the basic text of a play—the author's creation of dialogue and stage action and the description on the page of the setting and the characters—has a special significance. The text is the only aspect of the theater in which the writer has the last word. When you read a play, following the dialogue and the stage directions make you conscious of how the story might take on another life when performed on a stage or in a film. You are also aware as you follow the text that reading a play puts you into a special relationship with the playwright. Between you and the lines of the play are no actors, costumes, or sets. You aren't a member of a theater audience whose reactions could influence your perception of the play. Alone with the text, you have only words to fire your imagination.

What endures is the play on the page, not the stage. As Aristotle wrote about the primacy of the text in the *Poetics*: "The visual adornment of the dramatic persons can have a strong emotional effect but is the least artistic element, the least connected with the poetic art; in fact the force of tragedy can be felt even without benefit of public performance and actors, while for the production of the visual effect the property man's art is even more decisive than that of the poet's."

For a play to survive beyond its ephemeral stage or film presentation, it needs a text. As literature, the printed words on the page offer you several advantages. When you read a play in addition to seeing it performed, you can understand the work better, especially if its language or meaning is difficult to follow in the action onstage.

From your seat in the theater or in front of a screen, you cannot stop a play in the middle of a scene to tell the actor, "Wait. I didn't understand that line. Please repeat it." As a reader, however, you have the luxury of being able to stop while you are reading to ponder the meaning of a line or to go over an entire scene that is not immediately clear to you. Then, in your own way, you can become a player, an active participant among the generations of readers responding to the play's action, characters, language, structure, and deeper meaning or theme.

Here is a short play, *The Stronger*, by the innovative Swedish playwright August Strindberg, written in 1888. It will come alive again as you allow the elements of plot, characterization, dialogue, setting, and theme to interact in the theater of your mind.

AUGUST STRINDBERG

The Stronger

1888–89

TRANSLATED BY ANN CHARTERS

THE CHARACTERS

MRS. X, an actress, married
MISS Y, an actress, unmarried
A WAITRESS

A corner of an upscale café popular with women. Two small metal tables, a red upholstered sofa, and a few chairs. Mrs. X enters, dressed for winter in a stylish hat and coat, carrying an expensive shopping bag on her arm. Miss Y is seated at a table before a bottle of imported beer and a half-empty glass. She is reading a magazine, which she exchanges during the play for another magazine from a pile in front of her. It is late afternoon.

MRS. X: Why, Amelia darling! It's the day before Christmas and you're sitting here all alone, like a poor old bachelor!

Miss Y looks up from her magazine, nods, and continues reading.

MRS. X: You know, I really feel sorry for you, here alone, all by yourself in a café—and on Christmas Eve! Somehow it reminds me of a time when I was in Paris and I saw a wedding party in a restaurant. The bride sat and read a joke book while the groom played billiards with the ushers. How strange, I thought. If they start like this, how will they go on and how will they end? I mean, he was playing billiards on his wedding day, and she was reading a joke book. Well, maybe it's not quite the same.

Waitress enters, places a cup of hot chocolate in front of Mrs. X, and exits.

MRS. X: You know what, Amelia? I *really* think you'd have been better off if you'd kept him! Don't you remember that I was the first one to tell you, "Forgive him!" Remember that? You could have been married by now and had your own home. Do you remember last Christmas, how happy you felt after you visited his parents in the country; how you raved on about a happy home life and said you longed to retire from the stage? Yes, dear Amelia, home is best—after the theater—and children, you know—but of course you don't.

Miss Y looks at her with contempt.

MRS. X (*takes a few sips of her hot chocolate; then opens her shopping bag and takes out Christmas presents*): Look what I've bought for my little darlings. (*She shows off a doll.*) Look at this—it's for little Lisa. Watch, she can blink her eyes and turn her head! See! And here's a toy gun for Teddy. (*She loads the popgun and shoots at Miss Y.*)

Miss Y makes a gesture of fear.

MRS. X: Were you frightened? Did you think I wanted to shoot you? Darling, I can't believe you thought that! If *you* had wanted to shoot me, I'd understand—because you think I've stood in your way—and I know you can never forget that—though I'm completely innocent. You still think that I persuaded them to drop your contract at the theater, but I didn't! I really didn't, though you believe I did.—Well, it's no use going on about it, because I can't change your mind! (*She takes out a pair of embroidered slippers.*) And these are for my dear husband. During rehearsals I embroidered the tulips. I hate tulips, of course, but he wants tulips on everything.

Miss Y looks up from the magazine with ironic curiosity.

MRS. X (*puts a hand in each slipper*): See what small feet Bob has, look! And you should see how elegantly he walks! But of course you've never seen him in slippers!

Miss Y laughs aloud.

MRS. X: Look, I'll show you! (*She pretends to walk the slippers on the table.*)

Miss Y laughs aloud again.

MRS. X: And darling, look—when he's angry, this is the way he stamps his foot: "What, our stupid maids will never learn how to make a decent cup of coffee! Damn them! Now those idiots haven't trimmed the lamp properly!" Or when he feels a draft and his bare feet get cold: "Ugh, it's freezing. Those damned morons can't even keep the stove hot!" (*She rubs the sole of one slipper against the top of the other.*)

Miss Y laughs even louder.

MRS. X: And then he comes home and can't find his slippers, because the maid has hidden them under the bureau. . . . Oh, it's a shame to sit here and make fun of my husband like this. He's a sweetheart, actually—a really good man—you should have a husband like him, Amelia! Why are you laughing? Why? Why?—I know that he's faithful to me, really. Oh yes, I'm sure. Because he told me himself—why are you laughing?—that while I was touring in Norway that bitch Frieda tried to seduce him—can you imagine?—she's shameless! (*pause*) Of course I'd have scratched her eyes out if she'd tried that when I was home! (*pause*) I'm glad that he told me about it himself, so I didn't have to hear about it later from some gossip! (*pause*) She wasn't the only one, you can be sure of that. I don't know why it is, but women are absolutely crazy about my husband. They must think he can get them a contract because he works in the theater office. Perhaps you've been running after him too! I've never really trusted you—but now I *know* that he wasn't interested in you. You bore a grudge against him, or so it always seemed to me.

Long pause while they look at each other uncertainly.

MRS. X: Come over tonight, Amelia, if you can, and let us see that you're not angry with us, not angry with me, anyway. I don't know why, but I feel terrible being on bad terms with anyone, especially you. Maybe it's because I stood in your way that time—(*gradually slowing down*)—or—I don't know—why—really? (*pause*)

Miss Y looks curiously at Mrs. X.

MRS. X (*thoughtfully*): Our friendship has always been so strange. When I saw you for the first time I was afraid of you, so scared that I didn't dare let you out of my sight. Wherever I went, I was careful to stay near you. I didn't dare to be your enemy, so I became your friend. But I always felt awkward when you visited us, because I saw that my husband couldn't stand you—and that made me feel uncomfortable, as though my clothes didn't fit. I did all I could to make him treat you nicely, but it was no good. Then you went off and got engaged! Afterwards you and he suddenly struck up a real friendship, as if you felt so secure that you could show your true feelings for the first time—and then—what happened next? I didn't become jealous—so strange. I remember when our first baby was christened—we made you the godmother, and I made Bob kiss you—and he did, but you got so upset—though I didn't worry about it at the time—I haven't thought of it since—at least not before—now! (*She stands up suddenly.*) Why are you so quiet? You haven't said a word all this time, you just let me keep on talking! You've sat there staring at me and pulling all my thoughts out of me like silk from a cocoon—thoughts—suspicions, perhaps—let me see! Why did you break off your engagement? Why didn't you ever come to our house after you broke it off? Why won't you come and visit us tonight?

Miss Y seems about to speak.

MRS. X: Quiet! You don't need to say anything because I understand it all now! So that's why—and why—and why! Aha, now everything makes sense. So that's it!—Ugh, I don't want to sit at the same table with you. (*She moves her things to the other table.*)

That's why I had to embroider his slippers with tulips, which I hate, because you liked tulips, that's why. (*She throws the slippers on the floor.*) Now I know why we had to vacation at the lake every summer—it's because you hated the ocean. That's why my son had to be named Edward, because that was your father's name. That's why I had to wear clothes in the colors you liked, read your favorite books, eat your favorite food, drink your favorite drinks—your hot chocolate, for example—that's why—oh, my God!—it's horrible when I think of it, horrible! Everything, everything comes from you to me, even making love! Your soul crept into mine like a worm into an apple, ate and ate, dug and dug, until nothing was left except the skin and a little black dust. I wanted to run away from you, but I couldn't. You lay there like a snake with your dark eyes and bewitched me—I tried to use my wings but they only dragged me down. I lay in the water with my feet bound, and the more I tried to swim with my hands, the deeper I sank, deeper and deeper to the bottom where you lay like a giant crab waiting to grab me with your sharp claws—and I'm still lying there.

Ugh, how I hate you, hate you, hate you! But you just sit there, silent, calm, removed from it all, not caring if it's up or down, Christmas or New Year, or if others are happy or sad. You're unable to hate or love, as patient as a stork at a rat hole; you can't go after your victim yourself so you have to wait for her! Here you sit in your corner—you're really what they call a rat trap—reading your magazines to see if anyone's in trouble—or been ruined, or lost her job at the theater. Here you sit, waiting for your victims, counting your chances like a pilot calculates a shipwreck or a goddess demands her sacrifices!

Poor Amelia! Do you know that I feel sorry for you anyway, because I know you're unhappy, unhappy because you've been hurt. You turned evil because you've been hurt. I can't hate you even though I want to, because you're the weaker one, not me. Yes, whatever happened between you and Bob doesn't bother me—why should it? If you taught me to drink hot chocolate or someone else did, what difference does it make now? (*She takes a sip from her cup, then continues sententiously.*) Anyway, chocolate is very good for you. And if you've taught me how to dress, well, thank you very much—it just made my husband love me even more. Your loss has been my gain. Yes, to judge by certain signs, I'd say you've already lost him. I suppose you expected me to run away—as you did—and now you sit here and regret it—but you can see I don't regret anything! We mustn't be petty, you know. If no one else wanted my husband, then why should I?

You know, perhaps when all is said and done, I really am the stronger person right now. You never took anything from me—you simply gave.

You might even call me a thief—because when you woke up, I had what you'd lost!

Let me ask you, why did everything become so worthless and sterile in your hands? You couldn't keep any man's love with your tulips and your passions—as I could. Your books couldn't teach you the art of living, but they taught me. You never had a child named Edward, just a father named Edward!

And why are you always so silent, silent? Yes, I used to think you were strong, but perhaps it was only that you didn't have anything to say! Because you couldn't think for yourself! (*She stands and picks up the slippers.*)

Now I'm going home. I'm taking the tulips with me—*your* tulips! You couldn't learn anything from others—you couldn't bend—and therefore you broke, like a dry reed. But I didn't!

Thank you, Amelia, for all the good lessons. Thanks for teaching my husband how to love! Now I'm going home to love him!

She exits.

22.

Reading, Thinking, and Writing about Drama

> If my tragedy makes a tragic impression on people, they have only themselves to blame.
>
> —AUGUST STRINDBERG, Preface to *Miss Julie*

READING DRAMA

Reading a play allows you to have it both ways: You can stop the action at any time to think about the words on the page, and you can envision what is happening in a make-believe performance in the theater of your mind. Whether you follow a play as a passive spectator or an imaginative reader, you understand that its author is engaged in more than an act of "let's pretend." Most playwrights are attempting to make a serious statement about how we live—both as individuals and as members of society. Like other forms of literature, drama takes us out of our lives and allows us access to a wider range of human thoughts, feelings, and experiences, showing us our vast potential as individuals for both good and evil.

Having drama available as a text has another advantage. Like other writers, playwrights are conscious of themselves as contributing to an ongoing tradition. It is possible to see many of the plays in this anthology produced onstage or as a film, but they are always accessible to you gathered together in the format of this textbook. Even in such short, relatively simple plays as Strindberg's *The Stronger*, you probably need two readings of the text to be able to discuss it in class. On your first reading, let your imagination expand and try to visualize the play enacted onstage. On your second reading, be more detached from the text and try to analyze it as a work of literature by thinking about how the playwright has used the elements of drama.

Sometimes you will still have questions about the meaning of a play even after your second reading. Give yourself some time to think about what you have read. Your effort to understand takes time, and it is a necessary part of the learning process. In noted director Peter Brook's *The Open Door* (1993), he understood that "in order for something of quality to take place, an empty space needs to be created. An empty space makes it possible for a new phenomenon to come to life, for anything that touches on content, meaning, expression, language, and music can exist only if the experience is fresh and new. However, no fresh and new experience is possible if there isn't a pure, virgin space ready to receive it." If you are still confused after you have thought about the play, write down your questions and bring them to the next class discussion.

In a sense, reading drama is easier than reading poetry and short fiction because playwrights introduce you in a more leisurely fashion to the imaginative world they create in the text. For one thing, plays begin with a description of the characters who perform the action. For example, opening to the first page of Sophocles' *Oedipus the King* (p. 1129), you encounter a list of characters right after the title of the play. The setting or "scene" of the play is also described before you start to read the dialogue between the various characters.

In *Oedipus the King* you are told that the Greek stage is meant to suggest the front of the royal house of Thebes. This is a neutral description, but then you learn that a small crowd of people have assembled onstage, bringing branches and olive leaves in supplication to King Oedipus. The editor of the text is giving you an important clue to prepare you for the serious mood in which the play begins. You do not know what has caused the people to become so upset, but when Oedipus begins to speak the opening lines of the play, you have more information to help you understand his words than you have when you begin to read a poem or a short story.

The opening dialogue between Oedipus and the Priest who speaks for the supplicants is an admirable illustration of the conflict at the heart of a great play. There is no physical action as such between the two characters—no brawny fisticuffs, no spectacular duel, no arm-waving display of histrionics. Standing side by side, the two actors exchange only words. But their dialogue allows you to create a personality for Oedipus and get a first sense of the conflict—or mystery—within his situation that will evoke a sense of pity and terror for him as the play unfolds.

GUIDELINES FOR READING DRAMA

1. Make an entry in your notebook for each play assigned in class, writing down the author's name and the title and date of the play.
2. Use a dictionary to look up words in the headnote or in the play that you do not understand.
3. Remember that the type of theater—Greek, Elizabethan, realistic, or modern—prevalent at the time the playwright is working can influence his or her plays.
4. When you start to read a play, note the list of characters and the playwright's description of them. Try to envision the set, if it is described at the beginning of the various scenes and acts.
5. As you read the dialogue, imagine the gestures and the costumes of the actors specified in the stage directions or suggested by what the characters say and do.

6. Notice what the characters *don't* say in the dialogue—their pauses and silences. Remember that their words, like those of real people, are not always to be trusted.
7. Annotate the text of the play with the thoughts that occur to you as you read it closely.

SAMPLE CLOSE READING

AUGUST STRINDBERG
The Stronger

1888–89

TRANSLATED BY ANN CHARTERS

The title suggests a duel or a serious conflict of interest.

THE CHARACTERS

MRS. X, an actress, married
MISS Y, an actress, unmarried
A WAITRESS

A corner of an upscale café popular with women. Two small metal tables, a red upholstered sofa, and a few chairs. Mrs. X enters, dressed for winter in a stylish hat and coat, carrying an expensive shopping bag on her arm. Miss Y is seated at a table before a bottle of imported beer and a half-empty glass. She is reading a magazine, which she exchanges during the play for another magazine from a pile in front of her. It is late afternoon.

This phrase suggests an intimate, nonthreatening location—later it will seem ironic that the two women are deadly rivals.

Mrs. X seems more prosperous and successful than Miss Y.

MRS. X: Why, Amelia darling! It's the day before Christmas and you're sitting here all alone, like a poor old bachelor!

An odd simile, as if being independent and unmarried are necessarily negative traits.

Miss Y looks up from her magazine, nods, and continues reading.

MRS. X: You know, I really feel sorry for you, here alone, all by yourself in a café—and on Christmas Eve! Somehow it reminds me of a time when I was in Paris and I saw a wedding party in a restaurant. The bride sat and read a joke book while the groom played billiards with the ushers. How strange, I thought. If they start

Mrs. X has a volatile imagination and has traveled a lot.

like this, how will they go on and how will they end? I mean, he was playing billiards on his wedding day, and she was reading a joke book. Well, maybe it's not quite the same.

Mrs. X is very talkative and has a weird sense of humor.

Waitress enters, places a cup of hot chocolate in front of Mrs. X, and exits.

MRS. X: You know what, Amelia? I *really* think you'd have been better off if you'd kept him! Don't you remember that I was the first one to tell you, "Forgive him!" Remember that? You could have been married by now and had your own home. . . .

Whom should Miss Y have "kept"? She must have broken her engagement. Mrs. X seems obsessed with marriage.

CRITICAL THINKING ABOUT DRAMA

As in your study of short fiction and poetry, your critical thinking about a play depends on your first having formulated an interpretation of it after reading and perhaps rereading the text. Then you can begin asking yourself questions about different aspects of the work's structure, depending on the topic you are writing about. The various elements of drama are often the focus of a critical inquiry. The questions to help you think critically about drama are similar to those asked of short fiction. You might consider the following topics as you read.

Plot. What is the conflict of the play? Is it developed in separate stages of rising action, complication, climax, falling action, and resolution? Can you find examples of foreshadowing? Does the play have a subplot or second plot? How is it related to the main plot? Is there any repetition of significant action? If so, what do you think the playwright intended?

Characters. Is there a protagonist and an antagonist in the play? Do you think that they are presented as round or flat, static or dynamic characters? Are they realistic or symbolic? Often in drama it helps you to think critically about characterization if you select one character for your analysis. How is this character described in stage directions? How do other characters in the play see him or her? How does the character view himself or herself? What words or actions given to this character help to define his or her personality?

Dialogue. Which is given more emphasis in the play, dialogue or physical action? Is the dialogue realistic or symbolic? To what effect does the author use poetic, colloquial, or dialect English? What is the tone of the speeches? Does the playwright use consistent patterns of imagery or metaphor in the speeches of different characters in order to suggest something important about them?

Stage Setting. How does the setting help establish the time and place of the play? Is the setting realistic or symbolic? What objects onstage are particularly important in suggesting the mood of the characters or their values? What does the setting suggest about the theme of the play? How would a different staging of the play affect your interpretation?

Irony and Symbolism. Can you find any instances of dramatic irony in the play when you (as a reader or spectator) know more about the situation than do the onstage characters? Does this make you more or less sympathetic toward the characters? What aspects of the play and its staging seem symbolic? What do they symbolize? Is the symbolism extensive enough to form an allegorical system? If so, what is the meaning implied by the allegory?

Theme. What ideas explored by the play seem most significant to you? Which of the preceding elements of the play conveys the theme most effectively? Does the playwright give a clear statement of the theme to any one of the characters? If there is no resolution of the theme in the action of the play, what emotional effect does this have on you? Is the conflict between the characters a struggle between moral good and moral evil? Is the playwright attempting to *explain* or to *explore* the issues?

It will also help you to understand drama if you remember that playwrights, like all other writers, create their plays within a tradition. The genius of Sophocles, Shakespeare, and Henrik Ibsen is inimitable, but their plays have inspired later playwrights to give their own interpretation of similar themes or develop their own approach based on an awareness of the earlier writers' dramatic techniques. Writing their plays during periods when the theater flourished in ancient Greece and Renaissance England, Sophocles and Shakespeare borrowed or appropriated the plots of *Oedipus the King* and *Hamlet* from legend, history, and earlier plays—a standard practice among playwrights in their historical periods. Appropriation, or creating a new work by taking something from a previous work, continues today as part of the legacy of our cultural heritage of literature, music, and art. As a technique or method of working, appropriation can become a new vehicle for playwrights to express their view of the human condition.

Sophocles' and Shakespeare's versions of earlier material survive because their dramatic works reveal the fullest dimensions of their sources. Their brilliant exploration of the characters of Oedipus and Hamlet have kept their plays alive in theater repertoires throughout the world, whereas the literature that gave them the ideas for their plays is now known only to specialists. The essay by Geoffrey Bullough on *Hamlet* in Chapter 25, "Conversations on *Hamlet* as Text and Performance" (p. 1594), will help you to understand how Shakespeare transformed his sources into a great work of literature.

The influence of Greek dramatists such as Sophocles has continued to the present day. When Arthur Miller was interviewed by Leonard Moss in 1980, Miller said that he "would have liked to live in Greece with the tragedies." He went on to explain the influence of earlier writers on him: "I attach myself to Ibsen because I saw him as a contemporary Greek, and I suppose it's because there was a terrific reliance in him as there was in the Greeks on the idea of the continuity between the distant past and the present. 'The birds come home to roost'—they always did; your character was your fate. I like that immensely."

Playwrights are often willing to discuss how they were influenced by earlier writers. A few years after the debut of *Death of a Salesman,* when Miller adapted Ibsen's play *An Enemy of the People* for American audiences in 1951, he wrote a preface to the published version of the play to explain the strong influence of Ibsen's work on him:

> There is one quality in Ibsen that no serious writer can afford to overlook. It lies at the very center of his force, and I found in it—as I hope others will—a profound source of strength. It is his insistence, his utter conviction, that he is going to say what he has to say, and that the audience, by God, is going to listen. It is the very same quality that makes a star actor, a great public speaker, and a lunatic. Every Ibsen play begins with the unwritten words: "Now listen here!" And these words have shown me a path through the wall of "entertainment," a path that leads beyond the formulas and dried-up precepts, the pretense and fraud, of the business of the stage. Whatever else Ibsen has to teach, this is his first and greatest contribution.

As the critic Seymour L. Flaxman observed, "The realistic drama reached the peak of its development with Ibsen, and in many ways this style continues to dominate the drama today." Ibsen extended the use of discussion and debate in the dialogues between his characters to probe their mental states, and his method of analytic exposition survives in the structure of later work by Miller, Lorraine Hansberry, and Lynn Nottage, to name only a few contemporary dramatists.

Reading widely in the history of drama, you become aware that talented writers often come of age in clusters or groups, sometimes influenced by specific theaters or directors. The cluster of playwrights in Athens who created the great tragedies for the stage during the Golden Age of Greece is well known and includes Aeschylus, Euripides, and Sophocles. The Provincetown Players, an experimental theater that flourished in the early years of the twentieth century in the bohemian enclaves of Provincetown, Massachusetts, and Greenwich Village in New York City, supported another group of writers whose plays have stood the test of time—Susan Glaspell, Eugene O'Neill, and Edna St. Vincent Millay, among scores of others. The creative work of these playwrights helped establish the modern American theater, preparing the way for the gifted playwrights of the next generation.

WRITING ABOUT DRAMA

An assignment to write an essay about a specific play or aspect of drama will give you the opportunity to bring your ideas about what you have read into focus. The process of writing about drama will sharpen your critical analysis of the text you have chosen to discuss and will clarify your understanding of the ideas dramatized by the playwright. Because every reader's background is different, your reading of the plays will reflect the life experiences that you bring to them. Using the vocabulary of the elements of drama to help you express your thoughts about the plays, you have the opportunity to articulate your interpretations clearly to another reader.

In Part One of this anthology, you can read the story by Susan Glaspell that has a counterpart in her play *Trifles* (p. 1410). Glaspell wrote her story "A Jury of Her Peers" (p. 243) after the success of *Trifles* at the Provincetown Playhouse. Comparing the short story with the play, you will gain a deeper appreciation of the differences in the two literary genres and the different resources available to playwrights and short story writers. In a Commentary, the critic Leonard Mustazza considers the similarities and differences between the story and the play (p. 1420). You can also appreciate the scope of William Shakespeare's extraordinary achievement as a playwright and as a poet by reading his selections in the different parts of this anthology.

Finally, remember that while you can always compare and contrast the literary texts in this anthology, you can also get additional ideas for your papers by seeing a play produced on film or in the theater. In your essay, you will be expected to analyze your impression beyond summarizing the plot. The questions about drama earlier in this chapter can help you think critically about the play.

Often, choosing a specific critical approach in your paper—biographical, historical, or reader-response, for example—can give you a perspective from which to take useful notes during your second close reading of the play. Taking such an approach will clarify your understanding of how the playwright has developed dialogue, recurrent images, and characterization. In the Commentaries on the various plays, you will find material that illustrates different critical perspectives and suggests helpful background information for your essays.

Here is a sample paper about Strindberg's *The Stronger* in which a student chose to write about the play from the perspective of a reader's response, discussing the way he read the first scene of the drama.

SAMPLE PAPER

A Reader's Response to the Opening Lines
of Strindberg's *The Stronger*

The first two comments by Mrs. X, reacted to silently by Miss Y, comprise the brief exposition or introduction to Strindberg's one-act play *The Stronger*. Mrs. X's comments were so startling that they captured my attention immediately. I wanted to continue reading the play so I could get to know more about this outspoken character, who seemed both brash and sensitive at the same time.

Mrs. X's first words seem friendly as she comes into the café and sees someone whom we later learn is her rival, sitting by herself at a table drinking beer. "Why, Amelia darling!" is her initial greeting, and it couldn't be friendlier. The two women are on a first-name basis, and the word *darling* is usually a sign of affection, though it also can sound insincere. Since I learned from the list of characters preceding the play that both women were actresses, I thought that the word *darling* could also be a conventional greeting in their profession.

Mrs. X follows "darling" with a description of her friend that startled me and suggested that appearances can be deceiving. She says, "It's the day before Christmas and you're sitting here all alone, like a poor old bachelor!" Mrs. X may have intended her comment as a joke, but I don't know enough yet about either of the women to assume that Mrs. X has a wicked sense of humor and enjoys insulting her friends. Obviously Mrs. X has focused on the fact that the other woman is not married, but her comment that she resembles a "poor old bachelor" who has no friends or family to keep her company on Christmas Eve hints that she really doesn't like Miss Y very much.

Miss Y's cool response says a lot about her. She "looks up from her magazine, nods, and continues reading." The fact that she doesn't answer is a surprise because good manners dictate that Miss Y should at least greet Mrs. X with a friendly word or two after being called "darling." Clearly the two women aren't close, especially since Miss Y continues to read her magazine while Mrs. X goes on talking to her, another and more serious breach of etiquette. On the other hand, Miss Y could do a number of other things besides just sitting there with her magazine. She could immediately get up and leave the café, for example, which would repay Mrs. X's insult. Of course if Miss Y exited, the play would be over, and I know that Strindberg is just beginning to develop the conflict between the two women.

Then Mrs. X continues her attack. First she makes explicit what she implied in her condescending opening statement, repeating the lie that she feels sorry to find her friend alone on Christmas Eve. She is rubbing salt in the wound, pretending that Miss

Y was too stupid to understand what she really meant the first time. Abruptly she rushes into a confusing and seemingly unrelated story about remembering the sight of a bridal couple in a Paris restaurant, when the groom was "playing billiards on his wedding day" with his ushers while his bride sat by herself "reading a joke book." This memory makes Mrs. X appear sensitive to the discomfort of other people, such as a newly married couple who don't want to be with each other on their wedding day. But why does she tell this story to Miss Y?

It isn't immediately apparent what this memory has to do with the sight of Miss Y sitting alone in the café, but it is actually a preparation for Mrs. X's emotional breakdown later in the play, when she describes Miss Y as being "as patient as a stork at a rat hole; you can't go after your victim yourself so you have to wait for her!" Unconsciously Mrs. X must be aware that her marriage to her husband Bob was in trouble from the start since Miss Y had her eye on him too. Mrs. X is like the bride who sat "reading a joke book." She will soon discover that her husband has conducted an extramarital affair with Miss Y. With hindsight it is possible to see the underlying reason why Mrs. X brings up the Parisian couple in Strindberg's *The Stronger.* After she unexpectedly comes face to face with her rival in the café, she will be forced to face the fact that as far as Miss Y is concerned, the sanctity of Mrs. X's relationship with her husband is a joke. She will have to be "the stronger" if she wants her marriage to survive.

WEB For more information on the playwrights in this anthology, visit bedfordstmartins.com/rewritinglit.

23. The Elements of Drama

INTERVIEWER: Which playwrights did you most admire when you were young?

ARTHUR MILLER: Well, first the Greeks, for their magnificent form, the symmetry. Half the time I couldn't really repeat the story because the characters in the mythology were completely blank to me. I had no background at that time to know really what was involved in these plays, but the architecture was clear. One looks at some building of the past whose use one is ignorant of, and yet it has a modernity. It had its own specific gravity. That form has never left me; I suppose it just got burned in.

—ARTHUR MILLER, *Paris Review* interview (1967)

Like short story writers and poets, playwrights have several important means or elements at their disposal in creating dramatic works for the stage. Familiarizing yourself with these elements will help you appreciate the artistry of these creations and understand them better. Some terms used to analyze drama (for instance, *plot, characterizations,* and *theme*) are also used in discussing short fiction; others (*dialogue* and *staging*) refer exclusively to theater.

Even the most basic form of drama, the **monologue**—words meant to be spoken by one actor—suggests the resources available to the playwright. Consider, for example, the following fragment by Anton Chekhov. Found in his handwriting among his papers after his death, it appears to be a page that survived from one of his early attempts to rewrite his play *Uncle Vanya* (1896):

SOLOMON (*alone*): Oh! how dark is life! No night, when I was a child, so terrified me by its darkness as does my invisible existence. Lord, to David my father thou gavest only the gift of harmonizing words and songs, to sing and praise thee on strings, to lament sweetly, to make people weep or admire beauty; but why hast thou given me a meditative, sleepless, hungry mind? Like an insect born of the dust, I hide in darkness; and in fear and despair, all shaking and shivering, I see and hear in everything an invisible mystery. Why this morning? Why does the sun come out from behind the temple and gild the palm tree? Why this beauty of women? Where does the bird hurry, what is the meaning of its flight, if it and its young and the place to which it hastens will like myself, turn to dust? It were better I had never been

> born or were a stone, to which God has given neither eyes nor thoughts. In order to tire out my body by nightfall, all day yesterday, like a mere workman, I carried marble to the temple; but now the night has come and I cannot sleep. . . . I'll go and lie down. Phorses told me that if one imagines a flock of sheep running and fixes one's attention upon it, the mind gets confused and one falls asleep. I'll do it. . . . (*Exit.*)

Chekhov suggests several elements of drama in this monologue. The first word gives us the name of the character speaking the lines, Solomon, the son of King David, the great Hebrew poet whose psalms are included in the Old Testament. Solomon himself is a judge, not a poet, renowned throughout his kingdom for his wisdom (see "The Judgment of King Solomon" in Ch. 1, p. 9). His first words ("Oh! how dark is life!") suggest the poetic language of his speech in his use of a metaphor. His next words ("No night, when I was a child, so terrified me by its darkness as does my invisible existence") suggest the subject or theme of his monologue, a philosophical contemplation of his own mortality. His words take on the element of dramatic irony, because the reader assumes that a man as wise as King Solomon would not be troubled by doubts or uncertainties.

Chekhov uses an elegant structure to present the progression of Solomon's thoughts, beginning with his statement or exposition of the theme. Solomon's situation is then developed in the rising action of the monologue, when he compares himself to his father and states the conflict within his personality: Unlike David, he is not content to praise the Lord; he has a "sleepless, hungry mind." Next, Solomon gives specific examples of his dilemma—first his awareness of the darkness and mystery in the world, then his observation of the same mystery in sunlight and beauty. Finally, at the climax of his thought, when he recognizes his own mortality and the evidence all around him of the futility of all existence ("turn to dust"), he admits, "It were better I had never been born or were a stone, to which God has given neither eyes nor thoughts." In the falling action he reminds himself about the advice he's heard from Phorses, about a method of counting sheep to put himself to sleep, and he leaves the stage determined to try it.

This monologue is a fragment, with no resolution other than Solomon's exit from the stage. It also lacks any physical action other than the speech itself, wherein Solomon meditates on mortality and attempts to fill the time before he tries to sleep. His words suggest a plot, telling us about what he did the previous day, trying to shake off his depression by carrying blocks of heavy marble in order to exhaust himself for sleep. Movement or staging of the monologue would depend on the actor saying the words onstage. We would not actually see Solomon pick up the marble slabs, but he could suggest his heavy labor—or his fatigue—by his physical stance and gestures. Each of us can imagine an appropriate staging for the monologue of a great Hebrew king, as ornate or as simple as we wish—a room in a realistic set that suggests a palace filled with silver and gold objects, or a symbolic bare stage furnished only with a classic plain-cloth backdrop. These choices, of course, affect how the viewer perceives the scene and the actor speaking his lines.

Plot, characterization, dialogue, and theme are the four main elements that you analyze when you think about plays as literary texts. Naturally, in plays with more than one character, playwrights can develop these elements in more complex ways.

PLOT

Plot is the structuring of the events in a play. Also called the story, plot is the essential element with which a dramatist works. As in a short story, plot is one unified episode or a sequence of related events usually involving a conflict between people. If "to play," according to the dictionary definition, is to engage in mimicry, acting, or make-believe, then "a play" is a literary work performed by actors who imitate a sequence of related events in order to tell a story that resolves or does not resolve the conflict.

The plot of *The Stronger* is the story of how two women confront each other unexpectedly in a café, where Mrs. X suddenly puts the pieces of her past together to discover that Miss Y has not only been a rival in her career as an actress but also a rival in her marriage as her husband's mistress. Far from being destroyed by this revelation, Mrs. X emerges the stronger, deciding that it is better to bend and accept the situation than to break and lose her husband. When she exits the stage at the end of the play, we sense she is confident that she is the winner in her duel with Miss Y. The conflict between her and her rival has been resolved, at least in her mind, and the action is complete.

Analyzing the structure of a play, just as you analyze the structure of a short story, will help you to discover how writers achieve the coherence and consistency, as well as the underlying aesthetic balance and harmony, of their plots. The terms are similar when you analyze the plots of plays and short stories. The **exposition** or introduction to the plot of *The Stronger* begins when Mrs. X enters the café and notices Miss Y sitting by herself at a table reading a magazine. Mrs. X addresses her as "Amelia darling" and wonders why she is alone on the afternoon before Christmas day. Setting down her shopping bag, Mrs. X is ready to chat, though Amelia's greeting is noticeably cool. She only nods to Mrs. X and continues reading her magazine.

Since Strindberg's play is very short, more of a sketch than a one-act play, written to be presented in a theater with other plays on the same program, the playwright loses no time in introducing the conflict between the two women. Actually he hints at their rivalry in the opening words of the exposition when Mrs. X describes her unmarried friend looking "like a poor old bachelor," choosing words that hardly flatter Miss Y. The dialogue that concludes the exposition is Mrs. X's startling statement that the sight of Amelia has triggered a distant memory of a seemingly ill-paired couple in a Parisian restaurant celebrating their wedding. This memory hints that something is definitely amiss between the two women, but by shrugging it off and sitting down with her friend, Mrs. X shows her willingness to risk a confrontation between them.

The entrance of the waitress with Mrs. X's cup of hot chocolate concludes the exposition and serves as a natural break before the beginning of the next section of the plot, the **rising action**. While the exposition is brief, the rising action is usually the longest part of the play since it must develop and deepen the conflict. As Mrs. X continues to talk to Amelia, she heightens the unspoken tension between them by her words and her actions as she gradually reveals their long-standing rivalry, first in the theater and then over Mrs. X's husband Bob. The **climax** of the rising action is when she suddenly understands that Amelia has been Bob's lover for a long time. Mrs. X is so disturbed by this revelation that she immediately gets up and moves to her own table. This physical action suggests a turning point in the plot.

As Mrs. X continues to speak in the **falling action** of the play, she expresses her hatred of Miss Y by pouring out her feelings. In this way Mrs. X purges herself of her sense of having been victimized as a result of her husband's infatuation for Amelia. This emotional catharsis leads to a **resolution** of the conflict. Since Mrs. X thinks that she has a reason to believe that the affair is long over—Amelia has never visited them again after breaking off her engagement—Mrs. X feels sorry for Miss Y and believes that she is the stronger of the two of them because she can accept the knowledge of her husband's infidelity. Her marriage has survived, and she has the satisfaction of leaving the café to return home to her husband and children while her rival remains alone on Christmas Eve. This is the **conclusion** of the plot.

The progression of events in a plot develops a story with a beginning, a middle, and an end. Watching and listening to the interchanges between the characters on the stage, an audience has the opportunity to develop empathy for their situation as the plot is resolved. What drives the plot is conflict, and drama can be defined most simply as a progression both of events on the stage and of words spoken by the actors that develop and usually resolve conflicts. Strindberg's play continues a tradition of drama begun in the fifth century B.C. by such Greek playwrights as Sophocles and analyzed by Aristotle in the *Poetics*. Aristotle emphasized that the plot or story of a play should be unified and complete, with all aspects of the conflict resolved by the end. Suspense is created for the audience as the playwright develops different aspects of the conflict. Despite its brevity, you can see both conflict and suspense in *The Stronger*.

We do not know that there is a problem when the two women initially greet each other in the café during the exposition of the play. All we know is that one of them enters and recognizes the other, but after the first words of greeting, the second woman merely nods in recognition of the presence of the newcomer, not uttering a word. The brevity and chilliness of the exchange immediately suggest a conflict. There's no effusive—and false—exchange of hearty holiday greetings. Strindberg was just beginning his career as a playwright when he wrote *The Stronger*, but he was already pioneering a new kind of drama with a compact form and concise dialogue, streamlining the wordy, conventionally diffuse, often elaborate plots of his predecessors. Right at the start he presents us with a terse dramatic situation that suggests the conflict between the two women.

During the events of the rising action, suspense begins to build while Strindberg keeps us in the dark about the nature of the two women's quarrel and whether they will be able to resolve their differences. After her initial greeting, Mrs. X immediately begins to challenge Miss Y by reminding her that she would be better off if she had married and not broken off her engagement: She would have had her own home, instead of sitting by herself in a café on Christmas Eve. Then she taunts Amelia by reminding her that she doesn't have children, and Amelia responds by looking at her "with contempt." Now their quarrel is in the open. Mrs. X tries to make Miss Y jealous by showing off the Christmas presents she's bought her children, an expensive doll for her small daughter and a popgun for her older son. She even pretends to shoot Miss Y, referring to an old quarrel between them while insisting she was "completely innocent" when Amelia lost her contract at the theater.

Finally Mrs. X flourishes her Christmas present for her husband Bob, a pair of slippers she's embroidered with tulips, his favorite flower. She demonstrates her skill as an actress by slipping her hands into the slippers and pretending to walk, giving an imitation of how Bob scolds the servants at home when he's angry. Her comical performance makes Amelia laugh, and Mrs. X is so encouraged that she goes too far. She feels such solidarity with the other woman, laughing as she makes fun of a man, that she tells Amelia that she should have a husband like Bob. This brings about another laugh, which instantly puts Mrs. X on the defensive. She claims that Bob is a faithful husband. When Miss Y laughs again, Mrs. X insists that Bob was faithful to her while she was away on tour, even though many actresses threw themselves at him.

Then for the first time, led by the unspoken association of ideas following the path of the logical syllogism that often underlies our thinking (many actresses wanted her husband, Amelia is an actress, therefore she also wanted Bob), Mrs. X admits she and Miss Y are rivals—"I've never really trusted you." At the midpoint of the play, Strindberg heightens the suspense by revealing that the two women are locked in a battle over the same man. Now Mrs. X drops her playful banter and becomes serious. The two women are heading for a painful confrontation.

Their conflict becomes more complicated when Mrs. X shows that she isn't as innocent as she seems. She indirectly admits that she was guilty of standing in Miss Y's way in the theater. In this mode of confession she pours out her doubts about her friend and describes the uneasy progression of their long friendship, which led to Amelia's becoming the godmother of Mrs. X's son Edward. Recalling the awkward circumstances of that event, when Miss Y became upset after Bob kissed her at the christening ceremony, Mrs. X finally begins to see the entire picture. She realizes that her friend and her husband have been lovers. She is so distressed that she has a visceral reaction to the news—she stands up and moves her things to another table—and her physical revulsion to Miss Y underscores our sense that the rising action has reached its climax.

In the falling action of the play, Strindberg heightens the dramatic consequences of the situation. At first Mrs. X is so disturbed at her discovery of her husband's adultery with her friend that she becomes very emotional. Impulsively she acts out her anger by throwing Bob's slippers on the floor, and she erupts into a tirade of accusations about Amelia's influence on her life, insinuating that her friend was a parasite who destroyed her. She portrays herself as being helplessly consumed by her enemy, imagining the conflict between them in an outburst of extravagant images of Miss Y as a worm, a snake, and a giant crab. Having released her feelings, Mrs. X returns to the attack on her rival. She finds her evil, "a rat trap," preying on other women's lives like "a goddess demands her sacrifices."

Another, quieter change of mood ushers in the resolution of the play, slowing the pace down a little. Now Mrs. X declares that she pities Miss Y and exults in being the victor in their competition over Bob. Piling insult upon injury, she concludes by saying that Amelia is stupid, even taunting her for never speaking during the play. In the final lines of dialogue, Mrs. X gathers up her possessions and goes home to her loving family. The conclusion of the plot is apparently her complete triumph over her rival. With Mrs. X's exit we return to our initial sense of stability onstage.

The action of Strindberg's one-act play is very tightly constructed, exhibiting what Aristotle would call the unity of time and place. Its action takes less than an hour, and it occurs in one place, the café. In defining the elements of classic drama, Aristotle stipulated that the action of a well-made play should be contained within a restricted period of time and a single physical place. In Sophocles' *Oedipus the King* (p. 1129), for example, the action occurs within one day, and the setting represents one place, the exterior of Oedipus's palace. For centuries theater critics judged playwrights according to their fidelity to Aristotle's rules about these unities, even though such brilliant writers as Shakespeare broke the rules constantly, writing plays like *Hamlet* (p. 1244) that have complicated **subplots** with action occurring in different locations over extended periods of time.

In the eighteenth century, the great English critic Samuel Johnson brought some common sense to the debate. In *The Preface to Shakespeare*, Johnson wrote that Aristotle's analysis was not "an unquestionable principle":

> The truth is that the spectators [of a play in the theater] are always in their senses, and know, from the first act to the last, that the stage is only a stage, and that the players are only players. They came to hear a certain number of lines recited with just gesture and elegant modulation. The lines related to some action, and an action must be in some place; but the different actions that complete a story may be in places very remote from each other. . . . [A] lapse of years is as easily conceived as a passage of hours. In contemplation we easily contract the time of real actions, and therefore willingly permit it to be contracted when we only see their imitation.

Johnson understood that all literature, including drama, is an imitation of life. The actions we watch onstage in *The Stronger* are only imitations of what could happen in a real-life conflict between a married woman and her husband's mistress. In the play, as Johnson would have put it, these "imitations produce pain or pleasure, not because they are mistaken for realities, but because they bring realities to mind."

CHARACTERS

Another important means of the playwright is characterization, which, as in a short story, can be the presentation of characters who play either major or minor roles in the action. In *The Stronger,* Mrs. X plays the major role and Miss Y has the minor role. Because Mrs. X is given the words to express her wide range of thoughts and feelings, she is a **round character**, a complex psychological being whose responses to the painful discovery of her husband's marital affair exhibit a range of emotions from her initial shock to her final acceptance and triumph over the situation. She works through her feelings step by step, resolving her conflict with Miss Y by the conclusion of the play.

In contrast, the waitress and her rival Miss Y are **flat characters**, simple and one-dimensional. The waitress has a walk-on role; her only function in the play is to carry in the cup of hot chocolate for Mrs. X in the exposition of the play. She comes on stage primarily to advance the action of the story. The character of Miss Y has more dimensions to her personality; she remains on stage throughout the play and takes part in the conversation with Mrs. X in her own way. She is a **static character** since her basic hostility to Mrs. X doesn't change, despite her three bursts of laughter during the rising action of *The Stronger.* Strindberg gives her no dialogue to say in the play, so we must depend on her facial gestures and laughter to clue us in to what she is feeling. While they imply a very expressive, consistent language of their own, they lack the range and subtlety of verbal dialogue. Yet her silence heightens the spectator's sense of mystery about her character, adding to the emotional effect of the play.

Since Miss Y has been both an adulteress and a false friend to Mrs. X, we regard her as the villain or **antagonist** in the play. Mrs. X is the **protagonist**, the hero or central character, who must resolve two imperative conflicts: first, with her rival for her husband's affection, and second, with herself until she can overcome her anger and decide what to do. She is presented as a complex character because we learn that she is a liar and has acted spitefully when she blocked Miss Y's contract at the theater.

In classic drama, where conflict between the characters is a confrontation between clearly delineated moral good and moral evil, playwrights create heroes and villains. But in actual fact, in 1888 Strindberg might have felt very differently about conventional morality when he created the roles for the two actresses in *The Stronger.* He wrote the character of Mrs. X for his wife, the Finnish actress Siri von Essen, who was living with him in Copenhagen and appearing on the stage of the Experimental Theatre there. As the biographer Michael Meyer noted in his introduction to *The Stronger,* all of Strindberg's plays were based on fact. Since his marriage, the playwright had several affairs with other women, and his wife had always accepted them, "possibly because they seemed the only means of diverting his own suspicions away from her; and after each affair, he came back to her."

As a husband Strindberg might have held unconventional ideas about adultery in his open marriage with Siri, but as a playwright in 1888 he understood that his theater audiences would have a different attitude toward actresses portraying a wife and a mistress, conventionally regarding one as a hero and the other as a villain. Mrs. X might have been capable of blocking her rival's contract at the theater, but her marital fidelity is never in question in *The Stronger*. She is also a virtuous hero for being merciful toward her rival by turning her cheek in the Christian manner at the conclusion of the play—which just happens to be Christmas Eve.

Strindberg portrays the intense rivalry between the two women so remorselessly that he later called his method of psychological realism "psychic murders." Since the actors playing the characters have the last word, they can also shape our responses. In the stage directions Strindberg doesn't tell us anything about Mrs. X and Miss Y, except that Mrs. X is expensively dressed and Miss Y is drinking beer. Actresses playing the two roles can interpret their roles differently to suggest sympathetic and unsympathetic characteristics for each woman, depending on the director's instructions.

At the end of the play Mrs. X believes that the affair is over between Miss Y and her husband, but this might not be true. Miss Y's posture and facial expression might imply that she feels amused, not defeated, when her rival triumphantly sweeps off the stage. Strindberg wrote *The Stronger* during a time when many women in Europe and the United States were insisting on equality with men. He has shown us that Mrs. X is capable of lying, so Miss Y's character also might not be so simple as she seems.

Aristotle maintained in the *Poetics* that characterization in a play was second to the element of plot or action, yet he emphasized the importance of the characters. In his ranking of the elements of drama, Aristotle was apparently as much a pragmatist as he was a theorist, judging the relative importance of plot, character, dialogue, theme, and the other elements on the basis of the literature he had actually seen and read.

As evidence for his belief that structuring a good plot was the most essential element in drama, Aristotle said he noticed that beginning writers "manage to hit the mark in verbal expression and character portrayal sooner than they do in plot construction." Other critics have argued that dialogue, not characterization or plot action, is the most important element in drama. You can reach your own conclusion in this matter after you have read more plays.

DIALOGUE

Dialogue is the exchange of words between the characters in a play. In short fiction and poetry, dialogue is often set emotionally for us by the descriptive words that authors use to introduce it. They write, "He shouted," to show strong emotion, for example, or "She wailed," to show extreme unhappiness. At a crucial point in *The Stronger* Strindberg tells us that Mrs. X speaks more slowly when she begins to admit to herself that Miss Y hasn't been a faithful friend. In the falling action, the playwright also describes Mrs. X's tone of voice as sententious, when she assures herself that chocolate is "very good for you." She is trying to console herself after the shock of discovering that her friend and her husband had been lovers.

The fact that Miss Y isn't given any dialogue and doesn't speak during the play doesn't necessarily imply that she is stupid, as Mrs. X maintains. In

The Stronger Miss Y's facial gestures express her reactions to what Mrs. X is saying. Strindberg also had Siri von Essen in mind for the role of Miss Y, and he deliberately might have made her silent so that his wife could play the role in Paris and in other cities outside Scandinavia, where her marked Finnish accent would have been a handicap for foreign audiences. Other major dramatists have been known to create silent roles for this reason. For example, in Stockholm in 1938 when the German playwright Bertolt Brecht wrote *Mother Courage,* he made the Daughter mute so that his wife, the gifted actress Helene Weigel, could play the part in Sweden, where he assumed his play would have its premier.

Most critics agree that dialogue has three main functions in a play: to advance the plot, to establish the setting, and to reveal character. When we say that plot is *dialogue-driven* in drama, we mean that the words of the actors advance the plot. In the exposition at the start of the play, the actors' words can also reveal important information about what has happened before the stage action commences; dialogue continues to introduce new complications throughout the development of the plot.

Mrs. X's opening words tell us a great deal: We learn that the setting is the day before Christmas, and that she is on familiar, first-name terms with the other woman sitting in the café. Her choice of words to describe Amelia as a "poor old bachelor" flash a warning light to the audience as her dialogue moves along rapidly to reveal the conflict between them. When Miss Y later tries to speak up for herself, Mrs. X tells her to be quiet, suggesting Mrs. X's need to dominate the situation and suggesting that she is much tougher than she looks.

When we say that Strindberg has written realistic dialogue in *The Stronger* we mean that the words Mrs. X speaks onstage strike us as the way people could actually have a conversation. With a little thought, we realize that this is not true. Where are the pauses, incomplete sentences, rushes of words, and fillers like "like," "uh," and "you know" that creep into our usual attempts at verbal communication with another human being? We may think we are having a dialogue when we exchange words with another person, but usually it is nothing like the dialogue we hear onstage. There every word has been chosen for its effect on the listener. This does not mean that Strindberg's dialogue strikes our ears as false or badly written. This new translation from his original Swedish to English tries to be as colloquial as possible, but it is a tribute to Strindberg's skill as a playwright in his use of Swedish more than a century ago that we believe that Mrs. X is speaking the way that people today *could* talk—if they were speaking their lines onstage.

Taking Chekhov's plays as an example, the director Peter Brook has described in *The Open Door* the way that playwrights must go beyond an imitation of life in order to create effective dialogue:

> Life in the theatre is more readable and intense because it is more concentrated. The act of reducing space and compressing time creates a concentrate.
>
> In life we speak in a chattering tumble of repetitive words, yet this quite natural way of expressing ourselves always takes a great deal of time in relation to the actual content of what one wants to say. . . . The

> [dramatist's] compression consists of removing everything that is not strictly necessary and intensifying what is there, such as putting a strong adjective in the place of a bland one, whilst preserving the impression of spontaneity. If this impression is maintained, we reach the point where if in life it takes two people three hours to say something, onstage it should take three minutes. . . .
>
> With Chekhov, the text gives the impression of having been recorded on tape, of taking its sentences from daily life. But there is not a phrase of Chekhov's that has not been chiseled, polished, modified, with great skill and artistry so as to give the impression that the actor is really speaking "like in daily life."
>
> However, if one tries to speak and behave just like in daily life, one cannot play Chekhov. The actor and director must follow the same process as the author, which is to be aware that each word, even if it appears to be innocent, is not so. It contains in itself, and in the silence that precedes and follows it, an entire unspoken complexity of energies between the characters. If one can manage to find that, and if, furthermore, one looks for the art needed to conceal it, then one succeeds in saying these simple words and giving the impression of life.

In *The Stronger*, Strindberg wrote a realistic play using realistic dialogue. He deliberately avoids the heights of poetic fancy expressed in Shakespearean dialogue. Even when Mrs. X is speaking emotionally about her hatred for Miss Y, describing her enemy as a worm in an apple and as a "giant crab waiting to grab me with your sharp claws," the words she uses in her images remain faithful to ordinary speech. It is light years away from the poetry of Hamlet's words pledging obedience to his father's ghost in act I, scene V, of *Hamlet*:

> Remember thee!
> Yes, from the table of my memory
> I'll wipe away all trivial fond records,
> All saws of books, all forms, all pressures past
> That youth and observation copied there,
> And thy commandment all alone shall live
> Within the book and volume of my brain,
> Unmix'd with baser matter. . . .

The poetic dialogues Shakespeare created in *Hamlet* are a treasury of words, not only in Hamlet's speeches to the other characters in the play but also in his **soliloquies** (speeches spoken when he is alone onstage). Strindberg has written Mrs. X's dialogue in *The Stronger* to mirror her flatter expectations. Describing her sense of discomfort when Miss Y visited her house, she says she felt "as though my clothes don't fit." Not for her is the poetry of the lines in *Hamlet*.

STAGING

The staging of a play refers to the physical spectacle it presents to the audience in a performance by the actors. It takes into account such elements as the stage set, the different props and costumes used by the actors, their movement onstage, and the lighting and sound effects. *The Stronger* is a one-set play, with its simple café setting contributing to the spectator's sense of listening in on an intimate quarrel. By entering the deserted café, Mrs. X becomes emotionally accessible to Miss Y in a way that she would not be if the place were a crowded public space. We can read the description of the setting at the beginning of the play to locate ourselves physically in the world of the drama between imaginary characters, even if the playwright gives only sparse directions to help us place ourselves in their story.

The transformation of a play from the page to the stage is usually a collaboration among the director, the actors, and the costume, light, and set designers. The designers' creativity can help the audience interpret what the dialogue reveals to them as the drama proceeds. The lighting of the sets (now often controlled by technicians with computers transmitting hundreds of cues during a performance) helps to give the stage composition a focus. Light also casts shadows, suggesting a mood and a sense of dimensionality to the actors. The designers' work enables the viewer to *feel* a scene rather than just see it.

The actors' movements onstage during their delivery of the dialogue is called **blocking**. Their nonverbal gestures are known as stage business. A director can suggest ways for the actors to move on the set and give them stage business to further the action of the plot or support the desired illusion. When the Swedish film director Ingmar Bergman staged Ibsen's *A Doll House* (p. 1349) in 1992, he began his production by raising the curtain to reveal the actress playing the main character Nora wearing a wine-red dress and seated on a red plush sofa. Surrounded by a clutter of toys, dolls, and doll furniture, she waited motionless for a few moments, staring out into empty space like a human doll.

Costumes are very important. They can signal aspects of character that the actors are trying to project. In one production, a Japanese company performed *The Stronger* with the actress playing the wife as a nervous chatterer dressed in a dowdy traditional costume and the mistress presented as an ironic femme fatale dressed in trendy Western clothes. When Siri von Essen premiered the role of Mrs. X in Copenhagen, Strindberg told her to buy a new dress if her old ones didn't look fashionable and expensive enough. She was also to buy a new fur hat, and if she needed a new winter coat, it should be a fancy one—"beware of plain surfaces, and plain pleats."

As his biographer Michael Meyer wrote, Strindberg also gave his wife a list of advice about how to play the role onstage, telling her to remember that Mrs. X was an actress, "not just an ordinary respectable housewife." She was the stronger character in the play, "i.e. the softer. What is hard and stiff breaks, what is elastic gives and returns to its shape." Strindberg advised her to play the role of Mrs. X "simply—but not too simply! Give it an undertone of 50% charlatanism (like Nora in *A Doll House*) . . . and suggest depths that do not exist." She was free to "change any phrases that don't come naturally, and work up to an exit that will bring applause, without making a meal of it."

Strindberg also advised his wife not to "squeak or rant" when she performed the role of Mrs. X, but her Finnish accent was so thick that many

Danes in the audience were unable to follow her dialogue when she premiered *The Stronger* in Copenhagen on March 8, 1889. The play was put away until 1902, when it was produced by the eminent director Max Reinhardt in Berlin. Throughout the twentieth century it was performed in English as one of Strindberg's most popular short plays, beginning in London at the Bloomsbury Hall in 1906 and continuing with a 1971 production on London Weekend Television featuring rock star Marianne Faithful as Miss Y.

THEME

As with short fiction and poetry, **theme** is the underlying meaning of a dramatic work, suggested through the dialogue spoken by the characters as they move through the action of the play. Theme must also take into account the overall effect of the different elements of drama, including the way we imagine the play staged in a theater. The theme of Strindberg's *The Stronger* could be that marriage is a struggle for survival, and at stake are the rewards of security in a family and a home.

Other interpretations of the theme are possible, of course, just as long as they do not contradict the facts in the play. The clash between the wife and the mistress is a brutal one since the deception in their friendship has gone on for years, with each of them guilty of perfidy, violating the trust of each other. It would be wrong to conclude that neither woman cares much about the outcome of the situation or takes the adultery lightly.

Strindberg's theme is so universal in *The Stronger* and his treatment is so brilliant that the play is frequently presented as a "curtain raiser" by theater companies. In a few pages he captures the essence of drama, a conflict that strips bare the human heart in all of us. As readers of a play we become the director, the set designer, and the actors all in one, sensing the thematic unity implicit in the dialogue and acting evoked in the theater of our minds as we follow the text.

Awareness of the genre of a play can also help you to express its theme. Reading early plays like Sophocles' *Oedipus the King* and Shakespeare's *Hamlet*, you might find it easier to summarize the theme if you remember that these are examples of *tragedy*. Both of the title characters have a tragic flaw, or defect of character, that brings about the end of their lives as if inevitably decreed by fate. In Tom Stoppard's play *Rosencrantz and Guildenstern Are Dead* (1967), which—like his farcical *Dogg's Hamlet* (p. 1598)—is based on Shakespeare's classic, the character of the Player gives this definition of tragedy: "We're tragedians, you see. We follow directions—there is no *choice* involved. The bad end unhappily, the good unluckily. That is what tragedy means."

Willy Russell, a contemporary of Stoppard, explored the definition of tragedy in a funny scene from his play *Educating Rita*. Here the title character, a young woman from a working-class background employed as a hairdresser who is taking classes at an English university, is so excited after seeing her first production of a Shakespeare play that she rushes back to the office of her tutor, Frank, to talk to him about it.

WILLY RUSSELL
From *Educating Rita*

1983

Frank enters carrying a briefcase and a pile of essays. He goes to the filing cabinet, takes his lecture notes from the briefcase and puts them in a drawer. He takes the sandwiches and apple from his briefcase and puts them on his desk and then goes to the window desk and dumps the essays and briefcase. He switches on the radio and then sits in the swivel chair. He opens the packet of sandwiches, takes a bite, and then picks up a book and starts reading.

Rita bursts through the door out of breath.

FRANK: What are you doing here? (*He looks at his watch.*) It's Thursday, you . . .

RITA (*moving over to the desk; quickly*): I know I shouldn't be here, it's me dinner hour, but listen, I've gotta tell someone, have y' git a few minutes, can y' spare. . . ?

FRANK (*alarmed*): My God, what is it?

RITA: I had to come an' tell y', Frank, last night, I went to the theatre! A proper one, a professional theatre.

Frank gets up and switches off the radio and then returns to the swivel chair.

FRANK (*sighing*): For God's sake, you had me worried, I thought it was something serious.

RITA: No, listen, it was. I went out an' got me ticket, it was Shakespeare, I thought it was gonna be dead borin' . . .

FRANK: Then why did you go in the first place?

RITA: I wanted to find out. But listen, it wasn't borin', it was bleedin' great, honest, ogh, it done me in, it was fantastic. I'm gonna do an essay on it.

FRANK (*smiling*): Come on, which one was it?

Rita moves upper right centre.

RITA: ". . . Out, out, brief candle!
Life's but a walking shadow, a poor player
That struts and frets his hour upon the stage
And then is heard no more. It is a tale
Told by an idiot, full of sound and fury
Signifying nothing."

FRANK (*deliberately*): Ah, *Romeo and Juliet*.

RITA (*moving towards Frank*): Tch. Frank! Be serious. I learnt that today from the book. (*She produces a copy of* Macbeth.) Look, I went out an' bought the book. Isn't it great? What I couldn't get over is how excitin' it was.

Frank puts his feet up on the desk.

RITA: Wasn't his wife a cow, eh? An' that fantastic bit where he meets Macduff an' he thinks he's all invincible. I was on the edge of me seat at that bit. I wanted to shout out an' tell Macbeth, warn him.

FRANK: You didn't, did you?

RITA: Nah. Y' can't do that in a theatre, can y'? It was dead good. It was like a thriller.

FRANK: Yes. You'll have to go and see more.
RITA: I'm goin' to. *Macbeth*'s a tragedy, isn't it?

Frank nods.

RITA: Right.

Rita smiles at Frank and he smiles back at her.

Well I just—I just had to tell someone who'd understand.
FRANK: I'm honoured that you chose me.
RITA (*moving towards the door*): Well, I better get back. I've left a customer with a perm lotion. If I don't get a move on there'll be another tragedy.
FRANK: No. There won't be a tragedy.
RITA: There will, y' know. I know this woman; she's dead fussy. If her perm doesn't come out right there'll be blood an' guts everywhere.
FRANK: Which might be quite tragic—(*He throws her the apple from his desk which she catches.*)—but it won't be a tragedy.
RITA: What?
FRANK: Well—erm—look; the tragedy of the drama has nothing to do with the sort of tragic event you're talking about. Macbeth is flawed by his ambition—yes?
RITA (*going and sitting in the chair by the desk*): Yeh. Go on. (*She starts to eat the apple.*)
FRANK: Erm—it's that flaw which forces him to take the inevitable steps towards his own doom. You see?

Rita offers him the can of soft drink. He takes it and looks at it.

FRANK (*putting the can down on the desk*): No thanks. Whereas, Rita, a woman's hair being reduced to an inch of stubble, or—or the sort of thing you read in the paper that's reported as being tragic, "Man Killed By Falling Tree," is not a tragedy.
RITA: It is for the poor sod under the tree.
FRANK: Yes, it's tragic, absolutely tragic. But it's not a tragedy in the way that *Macbeth* is a tragedy. Tragedy in dramatic terms is inevitable, pre-ordained. Look, now, even without ever having heard the story of *Macbeth* you wanted to shout out, to warn him and prevent him going on, didn't you? But you wouldn't have been able to stop him would you?
RITA: No.
FRANK: Why?
RITA: They would have thrown me out the theatre.
FRANK: But what I mean is that your warning would have been ignored. He's warned in the play. But he can't go back. He still treads the path to doom. But the poor old fellow under the tree hasn't arrived there by following any inevitable steps has he?
RITA: No.
FRANK: There's no particular flaw in his character that has dictated his end. If he'd been warned of the consequences of standing beneath that particular tree he wouldn't have done it, would he? Understand?
RITA: So—so Macbeth brings it on himself?

FRANK: Yes. You see he goes blindly on and on and with every step he's spinning one more piece of thread which will eventually make up the network of his own tragedy. Do you see?

RITA: I think so. I'm not used to thinkin' like this.

FRANK: It's quite easy, Rita.

RITA: It is for you. I just thought it was a dead excitin' story. But the way you tell it you make me see all sorts of things in it. (*After a pause.*) It's fun, tragedy, isn't it?

Frank's explanation of why the death of "the poor old sod under the tree" is not an example of tragedy suggests the difference between tragedy and pathos. Pathos, according to the playwright Arthur Miller, arouses our feelings of "sadness, sympathy, identification, and even fear," while tragedy "brings us knowledge or enlightenment" about the "right way of living in the world." As Miller observed, "The reason we confuse the tragic with the pathetic, as well as why we create so few [new] tragedies, is twofold: in the first place many of our writers have given up trying to search out the right way of living, and secondly, there is not among us any commonly accepted faith in a way of life that will give us not only material gain but satisfaction."

Another category of drama is the **didactic** play, which teaches a lesson. Although presented within the context of a comedy, Frank's explanation of tragedy in *Educating Rita* is a didactic scene. Didactic plays often teach a lesson about the best way to live or lecture the audience about serious matters.

Modern plays by such authors as Henrik Ibsen, Susan Glaspell, Arthur Miller, and Lorraine Hansberry are realistic dramas in which the characters seem to exhibit free will in regard to their choices for future action. They are usually a mixture of comic and tragic elements. There is no end to the ways in which plays can be classified (recall Hamlet's troupe of touring actors who are proficient in acting "tragedy, comedy, history, pastoral, pastoral-comical, historical-pastoral, tragical-historical, tragical-comical-historical-pastoral, scene individable, or poem unlimited"). In each case, the way you classify the play can help you to clarify the dramatist's underlying theme.

◆ Questions for Critical Thinking about Drama ◆

1. What is the conflict in *The Stronger*? How is it developed and resolved in the play's rising action, complication, climax, falling action, resolution, and conclusion?
2. Why did Strindberg need both a protagonist and an antagonist in *The Stronger*? How does he arouse your sympathy for both characters?
3. Mrs. X's speech about her hatred of Amelia, comparing her to a worm that dug into an apple "until nothing was left except the skin and a little black dust," is a passionate outcry against her rival's power over her husband. How does Mrs. X's emotional outburst prepare you for the resolution of the play?
4. How could an actress play the role of Amelia so that the audience could find her the stronger character in the play?

◆ Topics for Writing about the Elements of Drama ◆

1. Remember that Aristotle believed that the action of a play meant the physical sequence of morally and spiritually fraught events, rather than mere sensation. Write an essay in which you analyze the moral significance of the situation of the two women in *The Stronger*.
2. Write an essay in which you define *tragedy*, basing your definition on Willy Russell's definition in *Educating Rita*. Judging from this definition, is Amelia a tragic character in *The Stronger*?
3. Rewrite the ending of *The Stronger*, imagining a soliloquy for Amelia as she sits alone in the café after Mrs. X goes home to celebrate Christmas with her family.

USEFUL TERMS TO REMEMBER

Blocking The actors' movements onstage during their delivery of the dialogue.

Characters The people who come onstage to play a role in the drama. They can be ROUND CHARACTERS, FLAT CHARACTERS, or STATIC CHARACTERS. The hero or central character is called the *protagonist*; the villain or the character in conflict with the protagonist is known as the *antagonist*.

Dialogue The exchange of words between the characters in a play.

Monologue Words in a play meant to be spoken by one actor.

Plot The way the playwright structures the events in the play to present a sequence of related events usually involving a conflict between the characters. The plot often consists of *exposition, rising action, climax, falling action, resolution,* and *conclusion*.

Staging The physical spectacle the play presents to the audience in a performance by the actors.

Subplot A secondary or minor conflict in a play.

Theme The underlying meaning of a dramatic work.

Tragedy A drama typically describing the downfall of a human being, leading to a disastrous conclusion that excites pity or terror. A *tragic flaw* is a defect in the tragic hero that precipitates his or her downfall, such as ambition or pride.

24. Plays and Playwrights

SOPHOCLES

Sophocles (495–406 B.C.), along with Aeschylus and Euripides, was one of the three major authors of Greek tragedy. He lived for nearly ninety years through most of the turbulent events of his country during the fifth century B.C. He was only five when the Greek army turned back the invading Persians at Marathon, but he no doubt heard that after the battle a messenger brought word of the victory back to Athens, running the twenty-six miles between Marathon and Athens and dying of exhaustion while delivering the news. Ten years later, in 480 B.C., the Greeks won another major battle against the Persian navy at Salamis. At the victory celebration Sophocles, a teenager trained in dance, is said to have made his first public appearance dancing nude to his own lyre accompaniment.

The period in which the Greek playwrights flourished is known as the Golden Age. Athens became rich as the city's allies paid its statesmen tribute money, and statesmen honored the gifted poets, playwrights, philosophers, architects, and scientists who thrived in the city. This great period lasted barely to the last years of the century, starting its decline when the armed forces of the Greek city-state were defeated in Sicily in 413 B.C. Six years later, just before the death of Sophocles, the Spartans destroyed the Greek navy at Aegospotami and imposed their own government in Athens, bringing the Golden Age to an end.

The earliest extant Greek play for two actors, Aeschylus's *The Persians*, dates from 472 B.C. Thirty years younger than Aeschylus, Sophocles won his first prize for one of his plays in 468 B.C. at the Great Dionysia during the competition for playwrights in Athens. The Great Dionysia was the name given to the important holiday each year when the Greek plays were produced. Occurring just before the arrival of spring, the festival honored Dionysus, the god of fertility and growth, who was mysteriously linked to Hades, the lord of the underworld and death. The celebration began in Athens with a procession carrying a statue of Dionysus from his temple to the theater at the Acropolis. It included the ritual slaying of a sacrificial bull and much drunken revelry, as Dionysus was also the god of wine in Greece.

The high point of the annual festival was the three-day competition among the playwrights, each of whom submitted four plays: three tragedies (tragedy was considered the highest form of drama by the Greeks) and a brief satyr play, which combined slapstick and erotic comedy. A comic play was also included in the performances, so although the plays were relatively short, the audience was expected to have sufficient stamina and interest to sit through several plays each day. As the British playwright Tony Harrison has observed, the Greek dramatists were "open-eyed about suffering but with a heart still open to celebration and physical affirmation." Traditionally during the Great Dionysia, a comic play began the program each day, and the tragic plays were followed by a satyr play to maintain "a kind of celebratory route in the sensual and everyday to follow the tragedy."

The dramatic performances at the Acropolis were part of a religious celebration, a public holiday rather than a commercial theater, with the entire population of the city marching in the procession and thousands of people filling the amphitheater on the slopes of the Acropolis to watch the plays. Originally the audience sat on the ground, then on wooden seats. When the weight of the crowd caused the wooden seats to collapse, they were replaced with concentric tiers of stone seats designed on the hillside to surround the stage almost completely. The high priest of Dionysus sat at the place of honor at the center of the first tier of this theater-in-the-round in Athens.

To keep order among the huge crowd, there were strict laws – apparently even the penalty of death – against taking another person's seat or engaging in fights. Tickets were expensive (almost the price of a laborer's daily wage), but funds were available so that poor people and slaves could attend. To underscore the religious importance of the event, prisoners were released from jail so they could also participate. Evidence suggests that women weren't admitted into the audience to watch Greek plays, but this is a contentious point argued by archeologists and historians.

During the three days of theater in Athens each year, it was customary for playwrights to act in their own plays. Apparently Sophocles could dance better than he could project his voice onstage (contemporary viewers describe him as having a "small voice"), and this would explain why he did not perform the leading role in his plays. Sophocles originated the practice of giving parts to a third actor onstage and introduced such innovations as painted scenery and a larger tragic chorus (increasing it from twelve men to fifteen). Active as a playwright in Athens for over half a century, he wrote more than a hundred plays and won first prize at the Great Dionysia eighteen times, more than any other playwright. Today only seven complete Sophoclean tragedies survive (the Oedipus trilogy and the plays *Philoctetes, Ajax, Trachiniae*, and *Elektra*) as well as a satyr play about the childhood of the god Hermes and nearly a thousand fragments of his other plays.

Sophocles and other playwrights who introduced their work during the Great Dionysia sought to arouse pity and fear among the spectators with their tragic plays about death and suffering; they sought to instill a sense of religious awe at the mysterious power of the gods, whose perfect knowledge of events stands in contrast to the imperfect knowledge of mortal beings. In classical Greek theater, only men were actors. They wore shoes with high heels to increase their stature and masks to help amplify their voices and simulate their appearance as mythical heroes or gods. The masks and costumes also enabled them to assume the roles of women, who were often central characters in the plays that dramatized mythical stories and legends made famous by earlier poets and historians. Actors were trained in singing and dancing as well as speaking, but in the large amphitheaters they were judged by how effectively they projected their voices to suggest the emotional states of their characters. The design of the outdoor theater and the costuming and masks of the actors contributed to the audience's sense of participation in a religious ritual. The importance of respecting the oracles—and of accepting the gods' prophecy, which is often fulfilled in ways that humans do not expect—is frequently mentioned in *Oedipus the King*. At the end of the play Oedipus has learned to his sorrow that the gods are omnipotent and that he cannot escape his fate.

Audiences watching *Oedipus the King* would have known the legendary story before they came to the theater. At the beginning of the play they were aware of the tragic flaw of pride in Oedipus's character and understood the mysterious circumstances of his birth far better than he did. In the theater, the spectators' pleasure would derive from recognizing the dramatic irony in the poetic dialogue and the elegant way Sophocles structured the events of the story as Oedipus gradually uncovers the truth about his past. Unlike Aeschylian tragedy, which is essentially static, Sophocles unfolded the incidents of Oedipus's past like a detective story, linking events by cause and effect and motivating them plausibly. In the process Sophocles also revealed different dimensions of his protagonist's character, his strong as well as his weak points. Oedipus exhibits a high moral character as king. He is genuinely concerned about his subjects and eager to help them during the plague that has descended on the city. Yet he is quick to suspect his loyal brother-in-law Creon of a plot to usurp his power and ready to taunt his heartbroken wife, Jocasta, when he thinks she is glorying in her "noble blood."

Sophocles was nicknamed "the Attic Bee" because he relied on such earlier works as Homer's *Iliad* and *Odyssey* for material for his plays, but he always developed his characterizations far beyond his sources and created dialogue marked by eloquence and vigor. He also gave active roles to the chorus of citizens and the messenger, who function as important characters in the play. When Sophocles began *Oedipus the King* by having the king promise the chorus of citizens to help fight the plague, the playwright knew that this detail would arouse sympathy in the Athenian audience, because plague had ravaged their city only five years before. This addition also deepens our sense of foreboding at the beginning of the play, because Sophocles was suggesting a further irony about Oedipus's character. It was believed at the time that the well-being of the state was a reflection of the health of its ruler. The Greek audience would know that, according to legend, Oedipus was a descendent of Cadmus, the founder of Thebes. The city had a disputed leadership because of a fraternal rivalry that the gods had decreed would wipe out Cadmus's entire family. *Oedipus the King* is the first of the trilogy of plays Sophocles wrote about this tragic situation. When the three plays are produced together, they are usually presented in the order that follows the chronology of events in the plot: *Oedipus the King* (first produced between 430 and 427 B.C.), *Oedipus at Colonus* (posthumously produced in 401 B.C.), and *Antigone* (first produced in 441 B.C.).

Oedipus the King was considered such a masterpiece a century after its creation that the philosopher and critic Aristotle used it in the *Poetics* as the example on which to base his aesthetic theory of drama. Aristotle understood that Sophocles structured the story of *Oedipus the King* so that the rising action that revealed the complications of the plot led to Oedipus's moment of recognition in the second half of the play, precisely at the time the falling action began. In Aristotle's analysis, this combination of a serious character defect combined with the destiny ordained by the implacable gods constitutes a "tragic flaw." Sophocles structured his play so as to first arouse pity and fear in the spectators watching the proud and headstrong Oedipus gradually unravel the truth about his past, and then allow them to experience a purging or catharsis of their emotions at the sight of Oedipus broken by the gods' prophecy at the end of the play. Yet, paradoxically, the blinded figure of Oedipus remains heroic, because his determination to discover the truth about his own identity remains a moral victory despite the tragic outcome of his search. This dramatic illustration of the gods' power over human frailty must have been a transcendent religious experience for the audience during the festival of Dionysus.

WEB Research Sophocles at bedfordstmartins.com/rewritinglit.

Oedipus the King

C. 430 B.C.

TRANSLATED BY ROBERT FAGLES

CHARACTERS

OEDIPUS, king of Thebes
A PRIEST of Zeus
CREON, brother of Jocasta
A CHORUS of Theban citizens and their LEADER
TIRESIAS, a blind prophet
JOCASTA, the queen, wife of Oedipus
A MESSENGER from Corinth
A SHEPHERD
A MESSENGER from inside the palace
ANTIGONE, ISMENE, daughters of Oedipus and Jocasta
GUARDS AND ATTENDANTS
PRIESTS OF THEBES

TIME AND SCENE: *The royal house of Thebes. Double doors dominate the facade; a stone altar stands at the center of the stage.*

Many years have passed since Oedipus solved the riddle of the Sphinx° and ascended the throne of Thebes, and now a plague has struck the city. A procession of

s.d. the riddle of the Sphinx: The Sphinx asked, "What walks on four legs in the morning, two at noon, and three in the evening?" Oedipus replied, "Man."

priests enters; suppliants, broken and despondent, they carry branches wound in wool° and lay them on the altar.

The doors open. Guards assemble. Oedipus comes forward, majestic but for a telltale limp, and slowly views the condition of his people.

OEDIPUS: Oh my children, the new blood of ancient Thebes,
why are you here? Huddling at my altar,
praying before me, your branches wound in wool.
Our city reeks with the smoke of burning incense,
rings with cries for the Healer and wailing for the dead.
I thought it wrong, my children, to hear the truth
from others, messengers. Here I am myself—
you all know me, the world knows my fame:
I am Oedipus.

Helping a Priest to his feet.

Speak up, old man. Your years,
your dignity—you should speak for the others.
Why here and kneeling, what preys upon you so?
Some sudden fear? some strong desire?
You can trust me; I am ready to help,
I'll do anything. I would be blind to misery
not to pity my people kneeling at my feet.

PRIEST: Oh Oedipus, king of the land, our greatest power!
You see us before you, men of all ages
clinging to your altars. Here are boys,
still too weak to fly from the nest,
and here the old, bowed down with the years,
the holy ones—a priest of Zeus° myself—and here
the picked, unmarried men, the young hope of Thebes.
And all the rest, your great family gathers now,
branches wreathed, massing in the squares,
kneeling before the two temples of queen Athena°
or the river-shrine where the embers glow and die
and Apollo sees the future in the ashes.

Our city—
look around you, see with your own eyes—
our ship pitches wildly, cannot lift her head
from the depths, the red waves of death . . .
Thebes is dying. A blight on the fresh crops
and the rich pastures, cattle sicken and die,
and the women die in labor, children stillborn,
and the plague, the fiery god of fever hurls down
on the city, his lightning slashing through us—

---

s.d. wool: Wool was used in offerings to Apollo, the god of poetry, sun, prophecy, and healing. **21. Zeus:** The highest Olympian deity and father of Apollo. **25. Athena:** The goddess of wisdom and protector of Greek cities.

raging plague in all its vengeance, devastating
the house of Cadmus!° And Black Death luxuriates
in the raw, wailing miseries of Thebes.

Now we pray to you. You cannot equal the gods,
your children know that, bending at your altar.
But we do rate you first of men,
both in the common crises of our lives
and face-to-face encounters with the gods.
You freed us from the Sphinx; you came to Thebes
and cut us loose from the bloody tribute we had paid
that harsh, brutal singer. We taught you nothing,
no skill, no extra knowledge, still you triumphed.
A god was with you, so they say, and we believe it—
you lifted up our lives.
So now again,
Oedipus, king, we bend to you, your power—
we implore you, all of us on our knees:
find us strength, rescue! Perhaps you've heard
the voice of a god or something from other men,
Oedipus . . . what do you know?
The man of experience—you see it every day—
his plans will work in a crisis, his first of all.
Act now—we beg you, best of men, raise up our city!
Act, defend yourself, your former glory!
Your country calls you savior now
for your zeal, your action years ago.
Never let us remember of your reign:
you helped us stand, only to fall once more.
Oh raise up our city, set us on our feet.
The omens were good that day you brought us joy—
be the same man today!
Rule our land, you know you have the power,
but rule a land of the living, not a wasteland.
Ship and towered city are nothing, stripped of men
alive within it, living all as one.

OEDIPUS: My children,
I pity you. I see—how could I fail to see
what longings bring you here? Well I know
you are sick to death, all of you,
but sick as you are, not one is sick as I.
Your pain strikes each of you alone, each
in the confines of himself, no other. But my spirit
grieves for the city, for myself and all of you.
I wasn't asleep, dreaming. You haven't wakened me—

37. Cadmus: The legendary founder of Thebes.

I've wept through the nights, you must know that,
groping, laboring over many paths of thought.
After a painful search I found one cure:
I acted at once. I sent Creon,
my wife's own brother, to Delphi° —
Apollo the Prophet's oracle — to learn
what I might do or say to save our city.

Today's the day. When I count the days gone by
it torments me . . . what is he doing?
Strange, he's late, he's gone too long.
But once he returns, then, then I'll be a traitor
if I do not do all the god makes clear.

PRIEST: Timely words. The men over there
are signaling — Creon's just arriving.

OEDIPUS:

Sighting Creon, then turning to the altar.

Lord Apollo,
let him come with a lucky word of rescue,
shining like his eyes!

PRIEST: Welcome news, I think — he's crowned, look,
and the laurel wreath is bright with berries.

OEDIPUS: We'll soon see. He's close enough to hear —

Enter Creon from the side; his face is shaded with a wreath.

Creon, prince, my kinsman, what do you bring us?
What message from the god?

CREON: Good news.
I tell you even the hardest things to bear,
if they should turn out well, all would be well.

OEDIPUS: Of course, but what were the god's *words*? There's no hope
and nothing to fear in what you've said so far.

CREON: If you want my report in the presence of these . . .

Pointing to the priests while drawing Oedipus toward the palace.

I'm ready now, or we might go inside.

OEDIPUS: Speak out,
speak to us all. I grieve for these, my people,
far more than I fear for my own life.

CREON: Very well,
I will tell you what I heard from the god.
Apollo commands us — he was quite clear —
"Drive the corruption from the land,
don't harbor it any longer, past all cure,
don't nurse it in your soil — root it out!"

---

82. Delphi: The shrine where the oracle of Apollo held forth.

OEDIPUS: How can we cleanse ourselves—what rites?
What's the source of the trouble?
CREON: Banish the man, or pay back blood with blood.
Murder sets the plague-storm on the city.
OEDIPUS: Whose murder?
Whose fate does Apollo bring to light?
CREON: Our leader,
my lord, was once a man named Laius,
before you came and put us straight on course.
OEDIPUS: I know—
or so I've heard. I never saw the man myself.
CREON: Well, he was killed, and Apollo commands us now—
he could not be more clear,
"Pay the killers back—whoever is responsible."
OEDIPUS: Where on earth are they? Where to find it now,
the trail of the ancient guilt so hard to trace?
CREON: "Here in Thebes," he said.
Whatever is sought for can be caught, you know,
whatever is neglected slips away.
OEDIPUS: But where,
in the palace, the fields or foreign soil,
where did Laius meet his bloody death?
CREON: He went to consult an oracle, he said,
and he set out and never came home again.
OEDIPUS: No messenger, no fellow-traveler saw what happened?
Someone to cross-examine?
CREON: No,
they were all killed but one. He escaped,
terrified, he could tell us nothing clearly,
nothing of what he saw—just one thing.
OEDIPUS: What's that?
One thing could hold the key to it all,
a small beginning gives us grounds for hope.
CREON: He said thieves attacked them—a whole band,
not single-handed, cut King Laius down.
OEDIPUS: A thief,
so daring, wild, he'd kill a king? Impossible,
unless conspirators paid him off in Thebes.
CREON: We suspected as much. But with Laius dead
no leader appeared to help us in our troubles.
OEDIPUS: Trouble? Your *king* was murdered—royal blood!
What stopped you from tracking down the killer
then and there?
CREON: The singing, riddling Sphinx.
She . . . persuaded us to let the mystery go
and concentrate on what lay at our feet.

OEDIPUS: No,
I'll start again — I'll bring it all to light myself!
Apollo is right, and so are you, Creon,
to turn our attention back to the murdered man.
Now you have *me* to fight for you, you'll see:
I am the land's avenger by all rights
and Apollo's champion too.
But not to assist some distant kinsman, no,
for my own sake I'll rid us of this corruption.
Whoever killed the king may decide to kill me too,
with the same violent hand — by avenging Laius
I defend myself.

To the priests.

Quickly, my children.
Up from the steps, take up your branches now.

To the guards.

One of you summon the city here before us,
tell them I'll do everything. God help us,
we will see our triumph — or our fall.

Oedipus and Creon enter the palace, followed by the guards.

PRIEST: Rise, my sons. The kindness we came for
Oedipus volunteers himself.
Apollo has sent his word, his oracle —
Come down, Apollo, save us, stop the plague.

The priests rise, remove their branches, and exit to the side. Enter a Chorus, the citizens of Thebes, who have not heard the news that Creon brings. They march around the altar, chanting.

CHORUS: Zeus!
Great welcome voice of Zeus, what do you bring?
What word from the gold vaults of Delphi
comes to brilliant Thebes? I'm racked with terror —
terror shakes my heart
and I cry your wild cries, Apollo, Healer of Delos°
I worship you in dread . . . what now, what is your price?
some new sacrifice? some ancient rite from the past
come round again each spring? —
what will you bring to birth?
Tell me, child of golden Hope
warm voice that never dies!
You are the first I call, daughter of Zeus
deathless Athena — I call your sister Artemis,°
heart of the market place enthroned in glory,

---

173. Delos: Apollo was born on this sacred island. **181. Artemis:** Apollo's sister, the goddess of hunting, the moon, and chastity.

guardian of our earth—
I call Apollo astride the thunderheads of heaven—
O triple shield against death, shine before me now!
If ever, once in the past, you stopped some ruin
launched against our walls
you hurled the flame of pain
far, far from Thebes—you gods
come now, come down once more!
No, no
the miseries numberless, grief on grief, no end—
too much to bear, we are all dying
O my people . . .
Thebes like a great army dying
and there is no sword of thought to save us, no
and the fruits of our famous earth, they will not ripen
no and the women cannot scream their pangs to birth—
screams for the Healer, children dead in the womb
and life on life goes down
you can watch them go
like seabirds winging west, outracing the day's fire
down the horizon, irresistibly
streaking on to the shores of Evening
Death
so many deaths, numberless deaths on deaths, no end—
Thebes is dying, look, her children
stripped of pity . . .
generations strewn on the ground
unburied, unwept, the dead spreading death
and the young wives and gray-haired mothers with them
cling to the altars, trailing in from all over the city—
Thebes, city of death, one long cortege
and the suffering rises
wails for mercy rise
and the wild hymn for the Healer blazes out
clashing with our sobs our cries of mourning—
O golden daughter of god, send rescue
radiant as the kindness in your eyes!
Drive him back!—the fever, the god of death
that raging god of war
not armored in bronze, not shielded now, he burns me,
battle cries in the onslaught burning on—
O rout him from our borders!
Sail him, blast him out to the Sea-queen's chamber
the black Atlantic gulfs
or the northern harbor, death to all
where the Thracian surf comes crashing.
Now what the night spares he comes by day and kills—

the god of death.
O lord of the stormcloud,
you who twirl the lightning, Zeus, Father,
thunder Death to nothing!

Apollo, lord of the light, I beg you—
whip your longbow's golden cord
showering arrows on our enemies—shafts of power
champions strong before us rushing on!

Artemis, Huntress,
torches flaring over the eastern ridges—
ride Death down in pain!

God of the headdress gleaming gold, I cry to you—
your name and ours are one, Dionysus°—
come with your face aflame with wine
your raving women's cries°
your army on the march! Come with the lightning
come with torches blazing, eyes ablaze with glory!
Burn that god of death that all gods hate!

Oedipus enters from the palace to address the Chorus, as if addressing the entire city of Thebes.

OEDIPUS: You pray to the gods? Let me grant your prayers.
Come, listen to me—do what the plague demands:
you'll find relief and lift your head from the depths.

I will speak out now as a stranger to the story,
a stranger to the crime. If I'd been present then,
there would have been no mystery, no long hunt
without a clue in hand. So now, counted
a native Theban years after the murder,
to all of Thebes I make this proclamation:
if any one of you knows who murdered Laius,
the son of Labdacus, I order him to reveal
the whole truth to me. Nothing to fear,
even if he must denounce himself,
let him speak up
and so escape the brunt of the charge—
he will suffer no unbearable punishment,
nothing worse than exile, totally unharmed.

Oedipus pauses, waiting for a reply.

Next,
if anyone knows the murderer is a stranger,
a man from alien soil, come, speak up.

---

239. Dionysus: The god of fertility and wine. **241. your . . . cries:** Dionysus was attended by female celebrants.

I will give him a handsome reward, and lay up
gratitude in my heart for him besides.

Silence again, no reply.

But if you keep silent, if anyone panicking,
trying to shield himself or friend or kin,
rejects my offer, then hear what I will do.
I order you, every citizen of the state
where I hold throne and power: banish this man—
whoever he may be—never shelter him, never
speak a word to him, never make him partner
to your prayers, your victims burned to the gods.
Never let the holy water touch his hands.
Drive him out, each of you, from every home.
He is the plague, the heart of our corruption,
as Apollo's oracle has revealed to me
just now. So I honor my obligations:
I fight for the god and for the murdered man.

Now my curse on the murderer. Whoever he is,
a lone man unknown in his crime
or one among many, let that man drag out
his life in agony, step by painful step—
I curse myself as well . . . if by any chance
he proves to be an intimate of our house,
here at my hearth, with my full knowledge,
may the curse I just called down on him strike me!

These are your orders: perform them to the last.
I command you, for my sake, for Apollo's, for this country
blasted root and branch by the angry heavens.
Even if god had never urged you on to act,
how could you leave the crime uncleansed so long?
A man so noble—your king, brought down in blood—
you should have searched. But I am the king now,
I hold the throne that he held then, possess his bed
and a wife who shares our seed . . . why, our seed
might be the same, children born of the same mother
might have created blood-bonds between us
if his hope of offspring hadn't met disaster—
but fate swooped at his head and cut him short.
So I will fight for him as if he were my father,
stop at nothing, search the world
to lay my hands on the man who shed his blood,
the son of Labdacus descended of Polydorus,
Cadmus of old and Agenor, founder of the line:
their power and mine are one.
Oh dear gods,

my curse on those who disobey these orders!
Let no crops grow out of the earth for them—
shrivel their women, kill their sons,
burn them to nothing in this plague
that hits us now, or something even worse.
But you, loyal men of Thebes who approve my actions,
may our champion, Justice, may all the gods
be with us, fight beside us to the end!

LEADER: In the grip of your curse, my king, I swear
I'm not the murderer, cannot point him out.
As for the search, Apollo pressed it on us—
he should name the killer.

OEDIPUS: Quite right,
but to force the gods to act against their will—
no man has the power.

LEADER: Then if I might mention
the next best thing . . .

OEDIPUS: The third best too—
don't hold back, say it.

LEADER: I still believe . . .
Lord Tiresias sees with the eyes of Lord Apollo.
Anyone searching for the truth, my king,
might learn it from the prophet, clear as day.

OEDIPUS: I've not been slow with that. On Creon's cue
I sent the escorts, twice, within the hour.
I'm surprised he isn't here.

LEADER: We need him—
without him we have nothing but old, useless rumors.

OEDIPUS: Which rumors? I'll search out every word.

LEADER: Laius was killed, they say, by certain travelers.

OEDIPUS: I know—but no one can find the murderer.

LEADER: If the man has a trace of fear in him
he won't stay silent long,
not with your curses ringing in his ears.

OEDIPUS: He didn't flinch at murder,
he'll never flinch at words.

Enter Tiresias, the blind prophet, led by a boy with escorts in attendance. He remains at a distance.

LEADER: Here is the one who will convict him, look,
they bring him on at last, the seer, the man of god.
The truth lives inside him, him alone.

OEDIPUS: O Tiresias,
master of all the mysteries of our life,
all you teach and all you dare not tell,
signs in the heavens, signs that walk the earth!
Blind as you are, you can feel all the more

what sickness haunts our city. You, my lord,
are the one shield, the one savior we can find.

We asked Apollo—perhaps the messengers
haven't told you—he sent his answer back:
"Relief from the plague can only come one way.
Uncover the murderers of Laius,
put them to death or drive them into exile."
So I beg you, grudge us nothing now, no voice,
no message plucked from the birds, the embers
or the other mantic ways within your grasp.
Rescue yourself, your city, rescue me—
rescue everything infected by the dead.
We are in your hands. For a man to help others
with all his gifts and native strength:
that is the noblest work.

TIRESIAS: How terrible—to see the truth
when the truth is only pain to him who sees!
I knew it well, but I put it from my mind,
else I never would have come.

OEDIPUS: What's this? Why so grim, so dire?

TIRESIAS: Just send me home. You bear your burdens,
I'll bear mine. It's better that way,
please believe me.

OEDIPUS: Strange response—unlawful,
unfriendly too to the state that bred and raised you;
you're withholding the word of god.

TIRESIAS: I fail to see
that your own words are so well-timed.
I'd rather not have the same thing said of me . . .

OEDIPUS: For the love of god, don't turn away,
not if you know something. We beg you,
all of us on our knees.

TIRESIAS: None of you knows—
and I will never reveal my dreadful secrets,
not to say your own.

OEDIPUS: What? You know and you won't tell?
You're bent on betraying us, destroying Thebes?

TIRESIAS: I'd rather not cause pain for you or me.
So why this . . . useless interrogation?
You'll get nothing from me.

OEDIPUS: Nothing! You,
you scum of the earth, you'd enrage a heart of stone!
You won't talk? Nothing moves you?
Out with it, once and for all!

TIRESIAS: You criticize my temper . . . unaware
of the one *you* live with, you revile me.

OEDIPUS: Who could restrain his anger hearing you?
What outrage—you spurn the city!
TIRESIAS: What will come will come.
Even if I shroud it all in silence.
OEDIPUS: What will come? You're bound to *tell* me that.
TIRESIAS: I'll say no more. Do as you like, build your anger
to whatever pitch you please, rage your worst—
OEDIPUS: Oh I'll let loose, I have such fury in me—
now I see it all. You helped hatch the plot,
you did the work, yes, short of killing him
with your own hands—and given eyes I'd say
you did the killing single-handed!
TIRESIAS: Is that so!
I charge you, then, submit to that decree
you just laid down: from this day onward
speak to no one, not these citizens, not myself.
You are the curse, the corruption of the land!
OEDIPUS: You, shameless—
aren't you appalled to start up such a story?
You think you can get away with this?
TIRESIAS: I have already.
The truth with all its power lives inside me.
OEDIPUS: Who primed you for this? Not your prophet's trade.
TIRESIAS: You did, you forced me, twisted it out of me.
OEDIPUS: What? Say it again—I'll understand it better.
TIRESIAS: Didn't you understand, just now?
Or are you tempting me to talk?
OEDIPUS: No, I can't say I grasped your meaning.
Out with it, again!
TIRESIAS: I say you are the murderer you hunt.
OEDIPUS: That obscenity, twice—by god, you'll pay.
TIRESIAS: Shall I say more, so you can really rage?
OEDIPUS: Much as you want. Your words are nothing—
futile.
TIRESIAS: You cannot imagine . . . I tell you,
you and your loved ones live together in infamy,
you cannot see how far you've gone in guilt.
OEDIPUS: You think you can keep this up and never suffer?
TIRESIAS: Indeed, if the truth has any power.
OEDIPUS: It does
but not for you, old man. You've lost your power,
stone-blind, stone-deaf—senses, eyes blind as stone!
TIRESIAS: I pity you, flinging at me the very insults
each man here will fling at you so soon.
OEDIPUS: Blind,
lost in the night, endless night that nursed you!
You can't hurt me or anyone else who sees the light—

you can never touch me.
TIRESIAS: True, it is not your fate
to fall at my hands. Apollo is quite enough,
and he will take some pains to work this out.
OEDIPUS: Creon! Is this conspiracy his or yours?
TIRESIAS: Creon is not your downfall, no, you are your own.
OEDIPUS: O power—
wealth and empire, skill outstripping skill
in the heady rivalries of life,
what envy lurks inside you! Just for this,
the crown the city gave me—I never sought it,
they laid it in my hands—for this alone, Creon,
the soul of trust, my loyal friend from the start
steals against me . . . so hungry to overthrow me
he sets this wizard on me, this scheming quack,
this fortune-teller peddling lies, eyes peeled
for his own profit—seer blind in his craft!

Come here, you pious fraud. Tell me,
when did you ever prove yourself a prophet?
When the Sphinx, that chanting Fury kept her deathwatch here,
why silent then, not a word to set our people free?
There was a riddle, not for some passer-by to solve—
it cried out for a prophet. Where were you?
Did you rise to the crisis? Not a word,
you and your birds, your gods—nothing.
No, but I came by, Oedipus the ignorant,
I stopped the Sphinx! With no help from the birds,
the flight of my own intelligence hit the mark.
And this is the man you'd try to overthrow?
You think you'll stand by Creon when he's king?
You and the great mastermind—
you'll pay in tears, I promise you, for this,
this witch-hunt. If you didn't look so senile
the lash would teach you what your scheming means!
LEADER: I'd suggest his words were spoken in anger,
Oedipus . . . yours too, and it isn't what we need.
The best solution to the oracle, the riddle
posed by god—we should look for that.
TIRESIAS: You are the king no doubt, but in one respect,
at least, I am your equal: the right to reply.
I claim that privilege too.
I am not your slave. I serve Apollo.
I don't need Creon to speak for me in public.
So,
you mock my blindness? Let me tell you this.
You with your precious eyes,

you're blind to the corruption of your life,
to the house you live in, those you live with—
who *are* your parents? Do you know? All unknowing
you are the scourge of your own flesh and blood,
the dead below the earth and the living here above,
and the double lash of your mother and your father's curse
will whip you from this land one day, their footfall
treading you down in terror, darkness shrouding
your eyes that now can see the light!
Soon, soon
you'll scream aloud—what haven won't reverberate?
What rock of Cithaeron° won't scream back in echo?
That day you learn the truth about your marriage,
the wedding-march that sang you into your halls,
the lusty voyage home to the fatal harbor!
And a load of other horrors you'd never dream
will level you with yourself and all your children.

There. Now smear us with insults—Creon, myself
and every word I've said. No man will ever
be rooted from the earth as brutally as you.

OEDIPUS: Enough! Such filth from him? Insufferable—
what, still alive? Get out—
faster, back where you came from—vanish!
TIRESIAS: I'd never have come if you hadn't called me here.
OEDIPUS: If I thought you'd blurt out such absurdities,
you'd have died waiting before I'd had you summoned.
TIRESIAS: Absurd, am I? To you, not to your parents:
the ones who bore you found me sane enough.
OEDIPUS: Parents—who? Wait . . . who is my father?
TIRESIAS: This day will bring your birth and your destruction.
OEDIPUS: Riddles—all you can say are riddles, murk and darkness.
TIRESIAS: Ah, but aren't you the best man alive at solving riddles?
OEDIPUS: Mock me for that, go on, and you'll reveal my greatness.
TIRESIAS: Your great good fortune, true, it was your ruin.
OEDIPUS: Not if I saved the city—what do I care?
TIRESIAS: Well then, I'll be going.

To his attendant.

TIRESIAS: Take me home, boy.
OEDIPUS: Yes, take him away. You're a nuisance here.
Out of the way, the irritation's gone.

Turning his back on Tiresias, moving toward the palace.

TIRESIAS: I will go,

---

481. Cithaeron: The mountains where Oedipus was abandoned as an infant.

once I have said what I came here to say.
I'll never shrink from the anger in your eyes—
you can't destroy me. Listen to me closely:
the man you've sought so long, proclaiming,
cursing up and down, the murderer of Laius—
he is here. A stranger,
you may think, who lives among you,
he soon will be revealed a native Theban
but he will take no joy in the revelation.
Blind who now has eyes, beggar who now is rich,
he will grope his way toward a foreign soil,
a stick tapping before him step by step.

Oedipus enters the palace.

Revealed at last, brother and father both
to the children he embraces, to his mother
son and husband both—he sowed the loins
his father sowed, he spilled his father's blood!

Go in and reflect on that, solve that.
And if you find I've lied
from this day onward call the prophet blind.

Tiresias and the boy exit to the side.

CHORUS: Who—
who is the man the voice of god denounces
resounding out of the rocky gorge of Delphi?
The horror too dark to tell,
whose ruthless bloody hands have done the work?
His time has come to fly
to outrace the stallions of the storm
his feet a streak of speed—
Cased in armor, Apollo son of the Father
lunges on him, lightning-bolts afire!
And the grim unerring Furies°
closing for the kill.
Look,
the word of god has just come blazing
flashing off Parnassus'° snowy heights!
That man who left no trace—
after him, hunt him down with all our strength!
Now under bristling timber
up through rocks and caves he stalks
like the wild mountain bull—

536. Furies: Three spirits who avenged evildoers. **539. Parnassus:** A mountain in Greece associated with Apollo.

cut off from men, each step an agony, frenzied, racing blind
but he cannot outrace the dread voices of Delphi
ringing out of the heart of Earth,
the dark wings beating around him shrieking doom
the doom that never dies, the terror—

The skilled prophet scans the birds and shatters me with terror!
I can't accept him, can't deny him, don't know what to say,
I'm lost, and the wings of dark foreboding beating—
I cannot see what's come, what's still to come . . .
and what could breed a blood feud between
Laius' house and the son of Polybus?°
I know of nothing, not in the past and not now,
no charge to bring against our king, no cause
to attack his fame that rings throughout Thebes—
not without proof—not for the ghost of Laius,
not to avenge a murder gone without a trace.

Zeus and Apollo know, they know, the great masters
of all the dark and depth of human life.
But whether a mere man can know the truth,
whether a seer can fathom more than I—
there is no test, no certain proof
though matching skill for skill
a man can outstrip a rival. No, not till I see
these charges proved will I side with his accusers.
We saw him then, when the she-hawk° swept against him,
saw with our own eyes his skill, his brilliant triumph—
there was the test—he was the joy of Thebes!
Never will I convict my king, never in my heart.

Enter Creon from the side.

CREON: My fellow-citizens, I hear King Oedipus
levels terrible charges at me. I had to come.
I resent it deeply. If, in the present crisis,
he thinks he suffers any abuse from me,
anything I've done or said that offers him
the slightest injury, why, I've no desire
to linger out this life, my reputation a shambles.
The damage I'd face from such an accusation
is nothing simple. No, there's nothing worse:
branded a traitor in the city, a traitor
to all of you and my good friends.

LEADER: True,
but a slur might have been forced out of him,

555. Polybus: The King of Corinth, who is thought to be Oedipus's father.
569. she-hawk: The Sphinx.

by anger perhaps, not any firm conviction.
CREON: The charge was made in public, wasn't it?
I put the prophet up to spreading lies?
LEADER: Such things were said . . .
I don't know with what intent, if any.
CREON: Was his glance steady, his mind right
when the charge was brought against me?
LEADER: I really couldn't say. I never look
to judge the ones in power.

The doors open. Oedipus enters.

Wait,
here's Oedipus now.
OEDIPUS: You—here? You have the gall
to show your face before the palace gates?
You, plotting to kill me, kill the king—
I see it all, the marauding thief himself
scheming to steal my crown and power!
Tell me,
in god's name, what did you take me for,
coward or fool, when you spun out your plot?
Your treachery—you think I'd never detect it
creeping against me in the dark? Or sensing it,
not defend myself? Aren't you the fool,
you and your high adventure. Lacking numbers,
powerful friends, out for the big game of empire—
you need riches, armies to bring that quarry down!
CREON: Are you quite finished? It's your turn to listen
for just as long as you've . . . instructed me.
Hear me out, then judge me on the facts.
OEDIPUS: You've a wicked way with words, Creon,
but I'll be slow to learn—from you.
I find you a menace, a great burden to me.
CREON: Just one thing, hear me out in this.
OEDIPUS: Just one thing,
don't tell me you're not the enemy, the traitor.
CREON: Look, if you think crude, mindless stubbornness
such a gift, you've lost your sense of balance.
OEDIPUS: If you think you can abuse a kinsman,
then escape the penalty, you're insane.
CREON: Fair enough, I grant you. But this injury
you say I've done you, what is it?
OEDIPUS: Did you induce me, yes or no,
to send for that sanctimonious prophet?
CREON: I did. And I'd do the same again.
OEDIPUS: All right then, tell me, how long is it now
since Laius . . .

CREON: Laius—what did *he* do?
OEDIPUS: Vanished,
swept from sight, murdered in his tracks.
CREON: The count of the years would run you far back . . .
OEDIPUS: And that far back, was the prophet at his trade?
CREON: Skilled as he is today, and just as honored.
OEDIPUS: Did he ever refer to me then, at that time?
CREON: No,
never, at least, when I was in his presence.
OEDIPUS: But you did investigate the murder, didn't you?
CREON: We did our best, of course, discovered nothing.
OEDIPUS: But the great seer never accused me then—why not?
CREON: I don't know. And when I don't, *I* keep quiet.
OEDIPUS: You do know this, you'd tell it too—
if you had a shred of decency.
CREON: What?
If I know, I won't hold back.
OEDIPUS: Simply this:
if the two of you had never put heads together,
we'd never have heard about *my* killing Laius.
CREON: If that's what he says . . . well, you know best.
But now I have a right to learn from you
as you just learned from me.
OEDIPUS: Learn your fill,
you never will convict me of the murder.
CREON: Tell me, you're married to my sister, aren't you?
OEDIPUS: A genuine discovery—there's no denying that.
CREON: And you rule the land with her, with equal power?
OEDIPUS: She receives from me whatever she desires.
CREON: And I am the third, all of us are equals?
OEDIPUS: Yes, and it's there you show your stripes—
you betray a kinsman.
CREON: Not at all.
Not if you see things calmly, rationally,
as I do. Look at it this way first:
who in his right mind would rather rule
and live in anxiety than sleep in peace?
Particularly if he enjoys the same authority.
Not I, I'm not the man to yearn for kingship,
not with a king's power in my hands. Who would?
No one with any sense of self-control.
Now, as it is, you offer me all I need,
not a fear in the world. But if I wore the crown . . .
there'd be many painful duties to perform,
hardly to my taste.
How could kingship
please me more than influence, power

without a qualm? I'm not that deluded yet,
to reach for anything but privilege outright,
profit free and clear.
Now all men sing my praises, all salute me,
now all who request your favors curry mine.
I'm their best hope: success rests in me.
Why give up that, I ask you, and borrow trouble?
A man of sense, someone who sees things clearly
would never resort to treason.
No, I've no lust for conspiracy in me,
nor could I ever suffer one who does.

Do you want proof? Go to Delphi yourself,
examine the oracle and see if I've reported
the message word-for-word. This too:
if you detect that I and the clairvoyant
have plotted anything in common, arrest me,
execute me. Not on the strength of one vote,
two in this case, mine as well as yours.
But don't convict me on sheer unverified surmise.

How wrong it is to take the good for bad,
purely at random, or take the bad for good.
But reject a friend, a kinsman? I would as soon
tear out the life within us, priceless life itself.
You'll learn this well, without fail, in time.
Time alone can bring the just man to light;
the criminal you can spot in one short day.

LEADER: Good advice,
my lord, for anyone who wants to avoid disaster.
Those who jump to conclusions may be wrong.

OEDIPUS: When my enemy moves against me quickly,
plots in secret, I move quickly too, I must,
I plot and pay him back. Relax my guard a moment,
waiting his next move—he wins his objective,
I lose mine.

CREON: What do you want?
You want me banished?

OEDIPUS: No, I want you dead.

CREON: Just to show how ugly a grudge can . . .

OEDIPUS: So,
still stubborn? you don't think I'm serious?

CREON: I think you're insane.

OEDIPUS: Quite sane—in my behalf.

CREON: Not just as much in mine?

OEDIPUS: You—my mortal enemy?

CREON: What if you're wholly wrong?

OEDIPUS: No matter—I must rule.

CREON: Not if you rule unjustly.
OEDIPUS: Hear him, Thebes, my city!
CREON: My city too, not yours alone!
LEADER: Please, my lords.

Enter Jocasta from the palace.

Look, Jocasta's coming,
and just in time too. With her help
you must put this fighting of yours to rest.

JOCASTA: Have you no sense? Poor misguided men,
such shouting—why this public outburst?
Aren't you ashamed, with the land so sick,
to stir up private quarrels?

To Oedipus.

Into the palace now. And Creon, you go home.
Why make such a furor over nothing?

CREON: My sister, it's dreadful . . . Oedipus, your husband,
he's bent on a choice of punishments for me,
banishment from the fatherland or death.
OEDIPUS: Precisely. I caught him in the act, Jocasta,
plotting, about to stab me in the back.
CREON: Never—curse me, let me die and be damned
if I've done you any wrong you charge me with.
JOCASTA: Oh god, believe it, Oedipus,
honor the solemn oath he swears to heaven.
Do it for me, for the sake of all your people.

The Chorus begins to chant.

CHORUS: Believe it, be sensible
give way, my king, I beg you!
OEDIPUS: What do you want from me, concessions?
CHORUS: Respect him—he's been no fool in the past
and now he's strong with the oath he swears to god.
OEDIPUS: You know what you're asking?
CHORUS: I do.
OEDIPUS: Then out with it!
CHORUS: The man's your friend, your kin, he's under oath—
don't cast him out, disgraced
branded with guilt on the strength of hearsay only.
OEDIPUS: Know full well, if that's what you want
you want me dead or banished from the land.
CHORUS: Never—
no, by the blazing Sun, first god of the heavens!
Stripped of the gods, stripped of loved ones,
let me die by inches if that ever crossed my mind.
But the heart inside me sickens, dies as the land dies
and now on top of the old griefs you pile this,
your fury—both of you!

OEDIPUS: Then let him go,
even if it does lead to my ruin, my death
or my disgrace, driven from Thebes for life.
It's you, not him I pity—your words move me.
He, wherever he goes, my hate goes with him.
CREON: Look at you, sullen in yielding, brutal in your rage—
you'll go too far. It's perfect justice:
natures like yours are hardest on themselves.
OEDIPUS: Then leave me alone—get out!
CREON: I'm going.
You're wrong, so wrong. These men know I'm right.

Exit to the side. The Chorus turns to Jocasta.

CHORUS: Why do you hesitate, my lady
why not help him in?
JOCASTA: Tell me what's happened first.
CHORUS: Loose, ignorant talk started dark suspicions
and a sense of injustice cut deeply too.
JOCASTA: On both sides?
CHORUS: Oh yes.
JOCASTA: What did they say?
CHORUS: Enough, please, enough! The land's so racked already
or so it seems to me . . .
End the trouble here, just where they left it.
OEDIPUS: You see what comes of your good intentions now?
And all because you tried to blunt my anger.
CHORUS: My king,
I've said it once, I'll say it time and again—
I'd be insane, you know it,
senseless, ever to turn my back on you.
You who set our beloved land—storm-tossed, shattered—
straight on course. Now again, good helmsman,
steer us through the storm!

The Chorus draws away, leaving Oedipus and Jocasta side by side.

JOCASTA: For the love of god,
Oedipus, tell me too, what is it?
Why this rage? You're so unbending.
OEDIPUS: I will tell you. I respect you, Jocasta,
much more than these . . .

Glancing at the Chorus.

Creon's to blame, Creon schemes against me.
JOCASTA: Tell me clearly, how did the quarrel start?
OEDIPUS: He says *I* murdered Laius—I am guilty.
JOCASTA: How does he know? Some secret knowledge
or simple hearsay?
OEDIPUS: Oh, he sent his prophet in

to do his dirty work. You know Creon,
Creon keeps his own lips clean.

JOCASTA: A prophet?
Well then, free yourself of every charge!
Listen to me and learn some peace of mind:
no skill in the world,
nothing human can penetrate the future.
Here is proof, quick and to the point.
An oracle came to Laius one fine day
(I won't say from Apollo himself
but his underlings, his priests) and it said
that doom would strike him down at the hands of a son,
our son, to be born of our own flesh and blood. But Laius,
so the report goes at least, was killed by strangers,
thieves, at a place where three roads meet . . . my son—
he wasn't three days old and the boy's father
fastened his ankles, had a henchman fling him away
on a barren, trackless mountain.
There, you see?
Apollo brought neither thing to pass. My baby
no more murdered his father than Laius suffered—
his wildest fear—death at his own son's hands.
That's how the seers and their revelations
mapped out the future. Brush them from your mind.
Whatever the god needs and seeks
he'll bring to light himself, with ease.

OEDIPUS: Strange,
hearing you just now . . . my mind wandered,
my thoughts racing back and forth.

JOCASTA: What do you mean? Why so anxious, startled?

OEDIPUS: I thought I heard you say that Laius
was cut down at a place where three roads meet.

JOCASTA: That was the story. It hasn't died out yet.

OEDIPUS: Where did this thing happen? Be precise.

JOCASTA: A place called Phocis, where two branching roads,
one from Daulia, one from Delphi,
come together—a crossroads.

OEDIPUS: When? How long ago?

JOCASTA: The heralds no sooner reported Laius dead
than you appeared and they hailed you king of Thebes.

OEDIPUS: My god, my god—what have you planned to do to me?

JOCASTA: What, Oedipus? What haunts you so?

OEDIPUS: Not yet.
Laius—how did he look? Describe him.
Had he reached his prime?

JOCASTA: He was swarthy,
and the gray had just begun to streak his temples,

and his build . . . wasn't far from yours.

OEDIPUS: Oh no no,
I think I've just called down a dreadful curse
upon myself—I simply didn't know!

JOCASTA: What are you saying? I shudder to look at you.

OEDIPUS: I have a terrible fear the blind seer can see.
I'll know in a moment. One thing more—

JOCASTA: Anything,
afraid as I am—ask, I'll answer, all I can.

OEDIPUS: Did he go with a light or heavy escort,
several men-at-arms, like a lord, a king?

JOCASTA: There were five in the party, a herald among them,
and a single wagon carrying Laius.

OEDIPUS: Ai—
now I can see it all, clear as day.
Who told you all this at the time, Jocasta?

JOCASTA: A servant who reached home, the lone survivor.

OEDIPUS: So, could he still be in the palace—even now?

JOCASTA: No indeed. Soon as he returned from the scene
and saw you on the throne with Laius dead and gone,
he knelt and clutched my hand, pleading with me
to send him into the hinterlands, to pasture,
far as possible, out of sight of Thebes.
I sent him away. Slave though he was,
he'd earned that favor—and much more.

OEDIPUS: Can we bring him back, quickly?

JOCASTA: Easily. Why do you want him so?

OEDIPUS: I'm afraid,
Jocasta, I have said too much already.
That man—I've got to see him.

JOCASTA: Then he'll come.
But even I have a right, I'd like to think,
to know what's torturing you, my lord.

OEDIPUS: And so you shall—I can hold nothing back from you,
now I've reached this pitch of dark foreboding.
Who means more to me than you? Tell me,
whom would I turn toward but you
as I go through all this?
My father was Polybus, king of Corinth.
My mother, a Dorian, Merope. And I was held
the prince of the realm among the people there,
till something struck me out of nowhere,
something strange . . . worth remarking perhaps,
hardly worth the anxiety I gave it.
Some man at a banquet who had drunk too much
shouted out—he was far gone, mind you—
that I am not my father's son. Fighting words!

I barely restrained myself that day
but early the next I went to mother and father,
questioned them closely, and they were enraged
at the accusation and the fool who let it fly.
So as for my parents I was satisfied,
but still this thing kept gnawing at me,
the slander spread—I had to make my move.
And so,
unknown to mother and father I set out for Delphi,
and the god Apollo spurned me, sent me away
denied the facts I came for,
but first he flashed before my eyes a future
great with pain, terror, disaster—I can hear him cry,
"You are fated to couple with your mother, you will bring
a breed of children into the light no man can bear to see—
you will kill your father, the one who gave you life!"
I heard all that and ran. I abandoned Corinth,
from that day on I gauged its landfall only
by the stars, running, always running
toward some place where I would never see
the shame of all those oracles come true.
And as I fled I reached that very spot
where the great king, you say, met his death.
Now, Jocasta, I will tell you all.
Making my way toward this triple crossroad
I began to see a herald, then a brace of colts
drawing a wagon, and mounted on the bench . . . a man,
just as you've described him, coming face-to-face,
and the one in the lead and the old man himself
were about to thrust me off the road—brute force—
and the one shouldering me aside, the driver,
I strike him in anger!—and the old man, watching me
coming up along his wheels—he brings down
his prod, two prongs straight at my head!
I paid him back with interest!
Short work, by god—with one blow of the staff
in this right hand I knock him out of his high seat,
roll him out of the wagon, sprawling headlong—
I killed them all—every mother's son!

Oh, but if there is any blood-tie
between Laius and this stranger . . .
what man alive more miserable than I?
More hated by the gods? *I* am the man
no alien, no citizen welcomes to his house,
law forbids it—not a word to me in public,
driven out of every hearth and home.

And all these curses I—no one but I
brought down these piling curses on myself!
And you, his wife, I've touched your body with these,
the hands that killed your husband cover you with blood.

Wasn't I born for torment? Look me in the eyes!
I am abomination—heart and soul!
I must be exiled, and even in exile
never see my parents, never set foot
on native earth again. Else I'm doomed
to couple with my mother and cut my father down . . .
Polybus who reared me, gave me life.
But why, why?
Wouldn't a man of judgment say—and wouldn't he be right—
some savage power has brought this down upon my head?
Oh no, not that, you pure and awesome gods,
never let me see that day! Let me slip
from the world of men, vanish without a trace
before I see myself stained with such corruption,
stained to the heart.

LEADER: My lord, you fill our hearts with fear.
But at least until you question the witness,
do take hope.

OEDIPUS: Exactly. He is my last hope—
I'm waiting for the shepherd. He is crucial.

JOCASTA: And once he appears, what then? Why so urgent?

OEDIPUS: I'll tell you. If it turns out that his story
matches yours, I've escaped the worst.

JOCASTA: What did I say? What struck you so?

OEDIPUS: You said *thieves*—
he told you a whole band of them murdered Laius.
So, if he still holds to the same number,
I cannot be the killer. One can't equal many.
But if he refers to one man, one alone,
clearly the scales come down on me:
I am guilty.

JOCASTA: Impossible. Trust me,
I told you precisely what he said,
and he can't retract it now;
the whole city heard it, not just I.
And even if he should vary his first report
by one man more or less, still, my lord,
he could never make the murder of Laius
truly fit the prophecy. Apollo was explicit:
my son was doomed to kill my husband . . . my son,
poor defenseless thing, he never had a chance
to kill his father. They destroyed him first.

So much for prophecy. It's neither here nor there.
From this day on, I wouldn't look right or left.

OEDIPUS: True, true. Still, that shepherd,
someone fetch him — now!

JOCASTA: I'll send at once. But do let's go inside.
I'd never displease you, least of all in this.

Oedipus and Jocasta enter the palace.

CHORUS: Destiny guide me always
Destiny find me filled with reverence
pure in word and deed.
Great laws tower above us, reared on high
born for the brilliant vault of heaven —
Olympian sky their only father,
nothing mortal, no man gave them birth,
their memory deathless, never lost in sleep:
within them lives a mighty god, the god does not grow old.

Pride breeds the tyrant
violent pride, gorging, crammed to bursting
with all that is overripe and rich with ruin —
clawing up to the heights, headlong pride
crashes down the abyss — sheer doom!
No footing helps, all foothold lost and gone,
But the healthy strife that makes the city strong —
I pray that god will never end that wrestling:
god, my champion, I will never let you go.

But if any man comes striding, high and mighty
in all he says and does,
no fear of justice, no reverence
for the temples of the gods —
let a rough doom tear him down,
repay his pride, breakneck, ruinous pride!
If he cannot reap his profits fairly
cannot restrain himself from outrage —
mad, laying hands on the holy things untouchable!
Can such a man, so desperate, still boast
he can save his life from the flashing bolts of god?
If all such violence goes with honor now
why join the sacred dance?

Never again will I go reverent to Delphi,
the inviolate heart of Earth
or Apollo's ancient oracle at Abae
or Olympia of the fires —
unless these prophecies all come true
for all mankind to point toward in wonder.
King of kings, if you deserve your titles

Zeus, remember, never forget!
You and your deathless, everlasting reign.

They are dying, the old oracles sent to Laius,
now our masters strike them off the rolls.
Nowhere Apollo's golden glory now—
the gods, the gods go down.

Enter Jocasta from the palace, carrying a suppliant's branch wound in wool.

JOCASTA: Lords of the realm, it occurred to me,
just now, to visit the temples of the gods,
so I have my branch in hand and incense too.

Oedipus is beside himself. Racked with anguish,
no longer a man of sense, he won't admit
the latest prophecies are hollow as the old—
he's at the mercy of every passing voice
if the voice tells of terror.
I urge him gently, nothing seems to help,
so I turn to you, Apollo, you are nearest.

Placing her branch on the altar, while an old herdsman enters from the side, not the one just summoned by the king but an unexpected messenger from Corinth.

I come with prayers and offerings . . . I beg you,
cleanse us, set us free of defilement!
Look at us, passengers in the grip of fear,
watching the pilot of the vessel go to pieces.

MESSENGER:

Approaching Jocasta and the Chorus.

Strangers, please, I wonder if you could lead us
to the palace of the king . . . I think it's Oedipus.
Better, the man himself—you know where he is?

LEADER: This is his palace, stranger. He's inside.
But here is his queen, his wife and mother
of his children.

MESSENGER: Blessings on you, noble queen,
queen of Oedipus crowned with all your family—
blessings on you always!

JOCASTA: And the same to you, stranger, you deserve it . . .
such a greeting. But what have you come for?
Have you brought us news?

MESSENGER: Wonderful news—
for the house, my lady, for your husband too.

JOCASTA: Really, what? Who sent you?

MESSENGER: Corinth.
I'll give you the message in a moment.
You'll be glad of it—how could you help it?—
though it costs a little sorrow in the bargain.

JOCASTA: What can it be, with such a double edge?
MESSENGER: The people there, they want to make your Oedipus
king of Corinth, so they're saying now.
JOCASTA: Why? Isn't old Polybus still in power?
MESSENGER: No more. Death has got him in the tomb.
JOCASTA: What are you saying? Polybus, dead?—dead?
MESSENGER: If not,
if I'm not telling the truth, strike me dead too.
JOCASTA:

To a servant.

Quickly, go to your master, tell him this!

You prophecies of the gods, where are you now?
This is the man that Oedipus feared for years,
he fled him, not to kill him—and now he's dead,
quite by chance, a normal, natural death,
not murdered by his son.
OEDIPUS:

Emerging from the palace.

Dearest,
what now? Why call me from the palace?
JOCASTA:

Bringing the Messenger closer.

Listen to *him*, see for yourself what all
those awful prophecies of god have come to.
OEDIPUS: And who is he? What can he have for me?
JOCASTA: He's from Corinth, he's come to tell you
your father is no more—Polybus—he's dead!
OEDIPUS:

Wheeling on the Messenger.

What? Let me have it from your lips.
MESSENGER: Well,
if that's what you want first, then here it is:
make no mistake, Polybus is dead and gone.
OEDIPUS: How—murder? sickness?—what? what killed him?
MESSENGER: A light tip of the scales can put old bones to rest.
OEDIPUS: Sickness then—poor man, it wore him down.
MESSENGER: That,
and the long count of years he'd measured out.
OEDIPUS: So!
Jocasta, why, why look to the Prophet's hearth,
the fires of the future? Why scan the birds
that scream above our heads? They winged me on
to the murder of my father, did they? That was my doom?
Well look, he's dead and buried, hidden under the earth,

and here I am in Thebes, I never put hand to sword—
unless some longing for me wasted him away,
then in a sense you'd say I caused his death.
But now, all those prophecies I feared—Polybus
packs them off to sleep with him in hell!
They're nothing, worthless.

JOCASTA: There.
Didn't I tell you from the start?

OEDIPUS: So you did. I was lost in fear.

JOCASTA: No more, sweep it from your mind forever.

OEDIPUS: But my mother's bed, surely I must fear—

JOCASTA: Fear?
What should a man fear? It's all chance,
chance rules our lives. Not a man on earth
can see a day ahead, groping through the dark.
Better to live at random, best we can.
And as for this marriage with your mother—
have no fear. Many a man before you,
in his dreams, has shared his mother's bed.
Take such things for shadows, nothing at all—
Live, Oedipus,
as if there's no tomorrow!

OEDIPUS: Brave words,
and you'd persuade me if mother weren't alive.
But mother lives, so for all your reassurances
I live in fear, I must.

JOCASTA: But your father's death,
that, at least, is a great blessing, joy to the eyes!

OEDIPUS: Great, I know . . . but I fear *her*—she's still alive.

MESSENGER: Wait, who is this woman, makes you so afraid?

OEDIPUS: Merope, old man. The wife of Polybus.

MESSENGER: The queen? What's there to fear in her?

OEDIPUS: A dreadful prophecy, stranger, sent by the gods.

MESSENGER: Tell me, could you? Unless it's forbidden
other ears to hear.

OEDIPUS: Not at all.
Apollo told me once—it is my fate—
I must make love with my own mother,
shed my father's blood with my own hands.
So for years I've given Corinth a wide berth,
and it's been my good fortune too. But still,
to see one's parents and look into their eyes
is the greatest joy I know.

MESSENGER: You're afraid of that?
That kept you out of Corinth?

OEDIPUS: My *father*, old man—
so I wouldn't kill my father.

MESSENGER: So that's it.
Well then, seeing I came with such good will, my king,
why don't I rid you of that old worry now?
OEDIPUS: What a rich reward you'd have for that.
MESSENGER: What do you think I came for, majesty?
So you'd come home and I'd be better off.
OEDIPUS: Never, I will never go near my parents.
MESSENGER: My boy, it's clear, you don't know what you're doing.
OEDIPUS: What do you mean, old man? For god's sake, explain.
MESSENGER: If you ran from *them,* always dodging home . . .
OEDIPUS: Always, terrified Apollo's oracle might come true—
MESSENGER: And you'd be covered with guilt, from both your parents.
OEDIPUS: That's right, old man, that fear is always with me.
MESSENGER: Don't you know? You've really nothing to fear.
OEDIPUS: But why? If I'm their son—Merope, Polybus?
MESSENGER: Polybus was nothing to you, that's why, not in blood.
OEDIPUS: What are you saying—Polybus was not my father?
MESSENGER: No more than I am. He and I are equals.
OEDIPUS: My father—
how can my father equal nothing? You're nothing to me!
MESSENGER: Neither was he, no more your father than I am.
OEDIPUS: Then why did he call me his son?
MESSENGER: You were a gift,
years ago—know for a fact he took you
from my hands.
OEDIPUS: No, from another's hands?
Then how could he love me so? He loved me, deeply . . .
MESSENGER: True, and his early years without a child
made him love you all the more.
OEDIPUS: And you, did you . . .
buy me? find me by accident?
MESSENGER: I stumbled on you,
down the woody flanks of Mount Cithaeron.
OEDIPUS: So close,
what were you doing here, just passing through?
MESSENGER: Watching over my flocks, grazing them on the slopes.
OEDIPUS: A herdsman, were you? A vagabond, scraping for wages?
MESSENGER: Your savior too, my son, in your worst hour.
OEDIPUS: Oh—
when you picked me up, was I in pain? What exactly?
MESSENGER: Your ankles . . . they tell the story. Look at them.
OEDIPUS: Why remind me of that, that old affliction?
MESSENGER: Your ankles were pinned together; I set you free.
OEDIPUS: That dreadful mark—I've had it from the cradle.
MESSENGER: And you got your name from that misfortune too,
the name's still with you.
OEDIPUS: Dear god, who did it?—

mother? father? Tell me.

MESSENGER: I don't know.
The one who gave you to me, he'd know more.

OEDIPUS: What? You took me from someone else?
You didn't find me yourself?

MESSENGER: No sir,
another shepherd passed you on to me.

OEDIPUS: Who? Do you know? Describe him.

MESSENGER: He called himself a servant of . . .
if I remember rightly—Laius.

Jocasta turns sharply.

OEDIPUS: The king of the land who ruled here long ago?

MESSENGER: That's the one. That herdsman was *his* man.

OEDIPUS: Is he still alive? Can I see him?

MESSENGER: They'd know best, the people of these parts.

Oedipus and the Messenger turn to the Chorus.

OEDIPUS: Does anyone know that herdsman,
the one he mentioned? Anyone seen him
in the fields, in town? Out with it!
The time has come to reveal this once for all.

LEADER: I think he's the very shepherd you wanted to see,
a moment ago. But the queen, Jocasta,
she's the one to say.

OEDIPUS: Jocasta,
you remember the man we just sent for?
Is *that* the one he means?

JOCASTA: That man . . .
why ask? Old shepherd, talk, empty nonsense,
don't give it another thought, don't even think—

OEDIPUS: What—give up now, with a clue like this?
Fail to solve the mystery of my birth?
Not for all the world!

JOCASTA: Stop—in the name of god,
if you love your own life, call off this search!
My suffering is enough.

OEDIPUS: Courage!
Even if my mother turns out to be a slave,
and I a slave, three generations back,
you would not seem common.

JOCASTA: Oh no,
listen to me, I beg you, don't do this.

OEDIPUS: Listen to you? No more. I must know it all,
see the truth at last.

JOCASTA: No, please—
for your sake—I want the best for you!

OEDIPUS: Your best is more than I can bear.

JOCASTA: You're doomed—
may you never fathom who you are!
OEDIPUS:

To a servant.

Hurry, fetch me the herdsman, now!
Leave her to glory in her royal birth.
JOCASTA: Aieeeee—
man of agony—
that is the only name I have for you,
that, no other—ever, ever, ever!

Flinging [herself] through the palace doors. A long, tense silence follows.

LEADER: Where's she gone, Oedipus?
Rushing off, such wild grief . . .
I'm afraid that from this silence
something monstrous may come bursting forth.
OEDIPUS: Let it burst! Whatever will, whatever must!
I must know my birth, no matter how common
it may be—must see my origins face-to-face.
She perhaps, she with her woman's pride
may well be mortified by my birth,
but I, I count myself the son of Chance,
the great goddess, giver of all good things—
I'll never see myself disgraced. She is my mother!
And the moons have marked me out, my blood-brothers,
one moon on the wane, the next moon great with power.
That is my blood, my nature—I will never betray it,
never fail to search and learn my birth!
CHORUS: Yes—if I am a true prophet
if I can grasp the truth,
by the boundless skies of Olympus,
at the full moon of tomorrow, Mount Cithaeron
you will know how Oedipus glories in you—
you, his birthplace, nurse, his mountain-mother!
And we will sing you, dancing out your praise—
you lift our monarch's heart!
Apollo, Apollo, god of the wild cry
may our dancing please you!
Oedipus—
son, dear child, who bore you?
Who of the nymphs who seem to live forever
mated with Pan,° the mountain-striding Father?
Who was your mother? who, some bride of Apollo

1207. Pan: The god of shepherds, who was, like Hermes and Dionysus, associated with the wilderness.

the god who loves the pastures spreading toward the sun?
Or was it Hermes, king of the lightning ridges?
Or Dionysus, lord of frenzy, lord of the barren peaks—
did he seize you in his hands, dearest of all his lucky finds?—
found by the nymphs, their warm eyes dancing, gift
to the lord who loves them dancing out his joy!

Oedipus strains to see a figure coming from the distance. Attended by palace guards, an old Shepherd enters slowly, reluctant to approach the King.

OEDIPUS: I never met the man, my friends . . . still,
if I had to guess, I'd say that's the shepherd,
the very one we've looked for all along.
Brothers in old age, two of a kind,
he and our guest here. At any rate
the ones who bring him in are my own men,
I recognize them.

Turning to the Leader.

But you know more than I,
you should, you've seen the man before.

LEADER: I know him, definitely. One of Laius' men,
a trusty shepherd, if there ever was one.

OEDIPUS: You, I ask you first, stranger,
you from Corinth—is this the one you mean?

MESSENGER: You're looking at him. He's your man.

OEDIPUS:

To the Shepherd.

You, old man, come over here—
look at me. Answer all my questions.
Did you ever serve King Laius?

SHEPHERD: So I did . . .
a slave, not bought on the block though,
born and reared in the palace.

OEDIPUS: Your duties, your kind of work?

SHEPHERD: Herding the flocks, the better part of my life.

OEDIPUS: Where, mostly? Where did you do your grazing?

SHEPHERD: Well,
Cithaeron sometimes, or the foothills round about.

OEDIPUS: This man—you know him? ever see him there?

SHEPHERD:

Confused, glancing from the Messenger to the King.

Doing what—what man do you mean?

OEDIPUS:

Pointing to the Messenger.

This one here—ever have dealings with him?

SHEPHERD: Not so I could say, but give me a chance,
my memory's bad . . .

MESSENGER: No wonder he doesn't know me, master.
But let me refresh his memory for him.
I'm sure he recalls old times we had
on the slopes of Mount Cithaeron;
he and I, grazing our flocks, he with two
and I with one—we both struck up together,
three whole seasons, six months at a stretch
from spring to the rising of Arcturus° in the fall,
then with winter coming on I'd drive my herds
to my own pens, and back he'd go with his
to Laius' folds.

To the Shepherd.

Now that's how it was,
wasn't it—yes or no?
SHEPHERD: Yes, I suppose . . .
it's all so long ago.
MESSENGER: Come, tell me,
you gave me a child back then, a boy, remember?
A little fellow to rear, my very own.
SHEPHERD: What? Why rake up that again?
MESSENGER: Look, here he is, my fine old friend—
the same man who was just a baby then.
SHEPHERD: Damn you, shut your mouth—quiet!
OEDIPUS: Don't lash out at him, old man—
you need lashing more than he does.
SHEPHERD: Why,
master, majesty—what have I done wrong?
OEDIPUS: You won't answer his question about the boy.
SHEPHERD: He's talking nonsense, wasting his breath.
OEDIPUS: So, you won't talk willingly—
then you'll talk with pain.

The guards seize the Shepherd.

SHEPHERD: No, dear god, don't torture an old man!
OEDIPUS: Twist his arms back, quickly!
SHEPHERD: God help us, why?—
what more do you need to know?
OEDIPUS: Did you give him that child? He's asking.
SHEPHERD: I did . . . I wish to god I'd died that day.
OEDIPUS: You've got your wish if you don't tell the truth.
SHEPHERD: The more I tell, the worse the death I'll die.
OEDIPUS: Our friend here wants to stretch things out, does he?

Motioning to his men for torture.

SHEPHERD: No, no, I gave it to him—I just said so.

1249. Arcturus: A star whose rising marked the end of summer.

OEDIPUS: Where did you get it? Your house? Someone else's?
SHEPHERD: It wasn't mine, no, I got it from . . . someone.
OEDIPUS: Which one of them?

Looking at the citizens.

Whose house?
SHEPHERD: No—
god's sake, master, no more questions!
OEDIPUS: You're a dead man if I have to ask again.
SHEPHERD: Then—the child came from the house . . .
of Laius.
OEDIPUS: A slave? or born of his own blood?
SHEPHERD: Oh no,
I'm right at the edge, the horrible truth—I've got to say it!
OEDIPUS: And I'm at the edge of hearing horrors, yes, but I must hear!
SHEPHERD: All right! His son, they said it was—his son!
But the one inside, your wife,
she'd tell it best.
OEDIPUS: My wife—
she gave it to you?
SHEPHERD: Yes, yes, my king.
OEDIPUS: Why, what for?
SHEPHERD: To kill it.
OEDIPUS: Her own child,
how could she?
SHEPHERD: She was afraid—
frightening prophecies.
OEDIPUS: What?
SHEPHERD: They said—
he'd kill his parents.
OEDIPUS: But you gave him to this old man—why?
SHEPHERD: I pitied the little baby, master,
hoped he'd take him off to his own country,
far away, but he saved him for this, this fate.
If you are the man he says you are, believe me,
you were born for pain.
OEDIPUS: O god—
all come true, all burst to light!
O light—now let me look my last on you!
I stand revealed at last—
cursed in my birth, cursed in marriage,
cursed in the lives I cut down with these hands!

Rushing through the doors with a great cry. The Corinthian Messenger, the Shepherd, and attendants exit slowly to the side.

CHORUS: O the generations of men
the dying generations—adding the total
of all your lives I find they come to nothing . . .

does there exist, is there a man on earth
who seizes more joy than just a dream, a vision?
And the vision no sooner dawns than dies
blazing into oblivion.

You are my great example, you, your life,
your destiny, Oedipus, man of misery—
I count no man blest.

You outranged all men!
Bending your bow to the breaking-point
you captured priceless glory, O dear god,
and the Sphinx came crashing down,
the virgin, claws hooked
like a bird of omen singing, shrieking death—
like a fortress reared in the face of death
you rose and saved our land.

From that day on we called you king
we crowned you with honors, Oedipus, towering over all—
mighty king of the seven gates of Thebes.

But now to hear your story—is there a man more agonized?
More wed to pain and frenzy? Not a man on earth,
the joy of your life ground down to nothing
O Oedipus, name for the ages—
one and the same wide harbor served you
son and father both
son and father came to rest in the same bridal chamber.
How, how could the furrows your father plowed
bear you, your agony, harrowing on
in silence O so long?
But now for all your power
Time, all-seeing Time has dragged you to the light,
judged your marriage monstrous from the start—
the son and the father tangling, both one—
O child of Laius, would to god
I'd never seen you, never never!
Now I weep like a man who wails the dead
and the dirge comes pouring forth with all my heart!
I tell you the truth, you gave me life
my breath leapt up in you
and now you bring down night upon my eyes.

Enter a Messenger from the palace.

MESSENGER: Men of Thebes, always the first in honor,
what horrors you will hear, what you will see,
what a heavy weight of sorrow you will shoulder . . .
if you are true to your birth, if you still have

some feeling for the royal house of Thebes.
I tell you neither the waters of the Danube
nor the Nile can wash this palace clean.
Such things it hides, it soon will bring to light—
terrible things, and none done blindly now,
all done with a will. The pains
we inflict upon ourselves hurt most of all.

LEADER: God knows we have pains enough already.
What can you add to them?

MESSENGER: The queen is dead.

LEADER: Poor lady—how?

MESSENGER: By her own hand. But you are spared the worst,
you never had to watch . . . I saw it all,
and with all the memory that's in me
you will learn what that poor woman suffered.

Once she'd broken in through the gates,
dashing past us, frantic, whipped to fury,
ripping her hair out with both hands—
straight to her rooms she rushed, flinging herself
across the bridal-bed, doors slamming behind her—
once inside, she wailed for Laius, dead so long,
remembering how she bore his child long ago,
the life that rose up to destroy him, leaving
its mother to mother living creatures
with the very son she'd borne.
Oh how she wept, mourning the marriage-bed
where she let loose that double brood—monsters—
husband by her husband, children by her child.
And then—
but how she died is more than I can say. Suddenly
Oedipus burst in, screaming, he stunned us so
we couldn't watch her agony to the end,
our eyes were fixed on him. Circling
like a maddened beast, stalking, here, there
crying out to us—
Give him a sword! His wife,
no wife, his mother, where can he find the mother earth
that cropped two crops at once, himself and all his children?
He was raging—one of the dark powers pointing the way,
none of us mortals crowding around him, no,
with a great shattering cry—someone, something leading him on—
he hurled at the twin doors and bending the bolts back
out of their sockets, crashed through the chamber.
And there we saw the woman hanging by the neck,
cradled high in a woven noose, spinning,
swinging back and forth. And when he saw her,

giving a low, wrenching sob that broke our hearts,
slipping the halter from her throat, he eased her down,
in a slow embrace he laid her down, poor thing . . .
then, what came next, what horror we beheld!
He rips off her brooches, the long gold pins
holding her robes—and lifting them high,
looking straight up into the points,
he digs them down the sockets of his eyes, crying, "You,
you'll see no more the pain I suffered, all the pain I caused!
Too long you looked on the ones you never should have seen,
blind to the ones you longed to see, to know! Blind
from this hour on! Blind in the darkness—blind!"
His voice like a dirge, rising, over and over
raising the pins, raking them down his eyes.
And at each stroke blood spurts from the roots,
splashing his beard, a swirl of it, nerves and clots—
black hail of blood pulsing, gushing down.

These are the griefs that burst upon them both,
coupling man and woman. The joy they had so lately,
the fortune of their old ancestral house
was deep joy indeed. Now, in this one day,
wailing, madness and doom, death, disgrace,
all the griefs in the world that you can name,
all are theirs forever.

LEADER: Oh poor man, the misery—
has he any rest from pain now?

A voice within, in torment.

MESSENGER: He's shouting,
"Loose the bolts, someone, show me to all of Thebes!
My father's murderer, my mother's—"
No, I can't repeat it, it's unholy.
Now he'll tear himself from his native earth,
not linger, curse the house with his own curse.
But he needs strength, and a guide to lead him on.
This is sickness more than he can bear.

The palace doors open.

Look,
he'll show you himself. The great doors are opening—
you are about to see a sight, a horror
even his mortal enemy would pity.

Enter Oedipus, blinded, led by a boy. He stands at the palace steps, as if surveying his people once again.

CHORUS: O the terror—
the suffering, for all the world to see,
the worst terror that ever met my eyes.

What madness swept over you? What god,
what dark power leapt beyond all bounds,
beyond belief, to crush your wretched life?—
godforsaken, cursed by the gods!
I pity you but I can't bear to look.
I've much to ask, so much to learn,
so much fascinates my eyes,
but you . . . I shudder at the sight.

OEDIPUS: Oh, Ohhh—
the agony! I am agony—
where am I going? where on earth?
where does all this agony hurl me?
where's my voice?—
winging, swept away on a dark tide—
My destiny, my dark power, what a leap you made!

CHORUS: To the depths of terror, too dark to hear, to see.

OEDIPUS: Dark, horror of darkness
my darkness, drowning, swirling around me
crashing wave on wave—unspeakable, irresistible
headwind, fatal harbor! Oh again,
the misery, all at once, over and over
the stabbing daggers, stab of memory
making me insane.

CHORUS: No wonder you suffer
twice over, the pain of your wounds,
the lasting grief of pain.

OEDIPUS: Dear friend, still here?
Standing by me, still with a care for me,
the blind man? Such compassion,
loyal to the last. Oh it's you,
I know you're here, dark as it is
I'd know you anywhere, your voice—
it's yours, clearly yours.

CHORUS: Dreadful, what you've done . . .
how could you bear it, gouging out your eyes?
What superhuman power drove you on?

OEDIPUS: Apollo, friends, Apollo—
he ordained my agonies—these, my pains on pains!
But the hand that struck my eyes was mine,
mine alone—no one else—
I did it all myself!
What good were eyes to me?
Nothing I could see could bring me joy.

CHORUS: No, no, exactly as you say.

OEDIPUS: What can I ever see?
What love, what call of the heart
can touch my ears with joy? Nothing, friends.

Take me away, far, far from Thebes,
quickly, cast me away, my friends—
this great murderous ruin, this man cursed to heaven,
the man the deathless gods hate most of all!

CHORUS: Pitiful, you suffer so, you understand so much . . .
I wish you'd never known.

OEDIPUS: Die, die—
whoever he was that day in the wilds
who cut my ankles free of the ruthless pins,
he pulled me clear of death, he saved my life
for this, this kindness—
Curse him, kill him!
If I'd died then, I'd never have dragged myself,
my loved ones through such hell.

CHORUS: Oh if only . . . would to god.

OEDIPUS: I'd never have come to this,
my father's murderer—never been branded
mother's husband, all men see me now! Now,
loathed by the gods, son of the mother I defiled
coupling in my father's bed, spawning lives in the loins
that spawned my wretched life. What grief can crown this grief?
It's mine alone, my destiny—I am Oedipus!

CHORUS: How can I say you've chosen for the best?
Better to die than be alive and blind.

OEDIPUS: What I did was best—don't lecture me,
no more advice. I, with *my* eyes,
how could I look my father in the eyes
when I go down to death? Or mother, so abused . . .
I've done such things to the two of them,
crimes too huge for hanging.
Worse yet,
the sight of my children, born as they were born,
how could I long to look into their eyes?
No, not with these eyes of mine, never.
Not this city either, her high towers,
the sacred glittering images of her gods—
I am misery! I, her best son, reared
as no other son of Thebes was ever reared,
I've stripped myself, I gave the command myself.
All men must cast away the great blasphemer,
the curse now brought to light by the gods,
the son of Laius—I, my father's son!

Now I've exposed my guilt, horrendous guilt,
could I train a level glance on you, my countrymen?
Impossible! No, if I could just block off my ears,
the springs of hearing, I would stop at nothing—
I'd wall up my loathsome body like a prison,

blind to the sound of life, not just the sight.
Oblivion — what a blessing . . .
for the mind to dwell a world away from pain.
O Cithaeron, why did you give me shelter?
Why didn't you take me, crush my life out on the spot?
I'd never have revealed my birth to all mankind.

O Polybus, Corinth, the old house of my fathers,
so I believed — what a handsome prince you raised —
under the skin, what sickness to the core.
Look at me! Born of outrage, outrage to the core.

O triple roads — it all comes back, the secret,
dark ravine, and the oaks closing in
where the three roads join . . .
You drank my father's blood, my own blood
spilled by my own hands — you still remember me?
What things you saw me do? Then I came here
and did them all once more!
Marriages! O marriage,
you gave me birth, and once you brought me into the world
you brought my sperm rising back, springing to light
fathers, brothers, sons — one deadly breed —
brides, wives, mothers. The blackest things
a man can do, I have done them all!
No more —
it's wrong to name what's wrong to do. Quickly,
for the love of god, hide me somewhere,
kill me, hurl me into the sea
where you can never look on me again.

Beckoning to the Chorus as they shrink away.

Closer,
it's all right. Touch the man of sorrow.
Do. Don't be afraid. My troubles are mine
and I am the only man alive who can sustain them.

Enter Creon from the palace, attended by palace guards.

LEADER: Put your requests to Creon. Here he is,
just when we need him. He'll have a plan, he'll act.
Now that he's the sole defense of the country
in your place.
OEDIPUS: Oh no, what can I say to him?
How can I ever hope to win his trust?
I wronged him so, just now, in every way.
You must see that — I was so wrong, so wrong.
CREON: I haven't come to mock you, Oedipus,
or to criticize your former failings.

Turning to the guards.

You there,
have you lost all respect for human feeling?
At least revere the Sun, the holy fire
that keeps us all alive. Never expose a thing
of guilt and holy dread so great it appalls
the earth, the rain from heaven, the light of day!
Get him into the halls—quickly as you can.
Piety demands no less. Kindred alone
should see a kinsman's shame. This is obscene.

OEDIPUS: Please, in god's name . . . you wipe my fears away,
coming so generously to me, the worst of men.
Do one thing more, for your sake, not mine.

CREON: What do you want? Why so insistent?

OEDIPUS: Drive me out of the land at once, far from sight,
where I can never hear a human voice.

CREON: I'd have done that already, I promise you.
First I wanted the god to clarify my duties.

OEDIPUS: The god? His command was clear, every word:
death for the father-killer, the curse—
he said destroy me!

CREON: So he did. Still, in such a crisis
it's better to ask precisely what to do.

OEDIPUS: You'd ask the oracle about a man like me?

CREON: By all means. And this time, I assume,
even you will obey the god's decrees.

OEDIPUS: I will,
I will. And you, I command you—I beg you . . .
the woman inside, bury her as you see fit.
It's the only decent thing,
to give your own the last rites. As for me,
never condemn the city of my fathers
to house my body, not while I'm alive, no,
let me live on the mountains, on Cithaeron,
my favorite haunt, I have made it famous.
Mother and father marked out that rock
to be my everlasting tomb—buried alive.
Let me die there, where they tried to kill me.
Oh but this I know: no sickness can destroy me,
nothing can. I would never have been saved
from death—I have been saved
for something great and terrible, something strange.
Well let my destiny come and take me on its way!

About my children, Creon, the boys at least,
don't burden yourself. They're men;
wherever they go, they'll find the means to live.

But my two daughters, my poor helpless girls,
clustering at our table, never without me
hovering near them . . . whatever I touched,
they always had their share. Take care of them,
I beg you. Wait, better—permit me, would you?
Just to touch them with my hands and take
our fill of tears. Please . . . my king.
Grant it, with all your noble heart.
If I could hold them, just once, I'd think
I had them with me, like the early days
when I could see their eyes.

Antigone and Ismene, two small children, are led in from the palace by a nurse.

What's that?
O god! Do I really hear you sobbing?—
my two children. Creon, you've pitied me?
Sent me my darling girls, my own flesh and blood!
Am I right?

CREON: Yes, it's my doing.
I know the joy they gave you all these years,
the joy you must feel now.

OEDIPUS: Bless you, Creon!
May god watch over you for this kindness,
better than he ever guarded me.
Children, where are you?
Here, come quickly—

Groping for Antigone and Ismene, who approach their father cautiously, then embrace him.

Come to these hands of mine,
your brother's hands, your own father's hands
that served his once bright eyes so well—
that made them blind. Seeing nothing, children,
knowing nothing, I became your father,
I fathered you in the soil that gave me life.

How I weep for you—I cannot see you now . . .
just thinking of all your days to come, the bitterness,
the life that rough mankind will thrust upon you.
Where are the public gatherings you can join,
the banquets of the clans? Home you'll come,
in tears, cut off from the sight of it all,
the brilliant rites unfinished.
And when you reach perfection, ripe for marriage,
who will he be, my dear ones? Risking all
to shoulder the curse that weighs down my parents,
yes and you too—that wounds us all together.
What more misery could you want?

Your father killed his father, sowed his mother,
one, one and the selfsame womb sprang you—
he cropped the very roots of his existence.
Such disgrace, and you must bear it all!
Who will marry you then? Not a man on earth.
Your doom is clear: you'll wither away to nothing,
single, without a child.

Turning to Creon.

Oh Creon,
you are the only father they have now . . .
we who brought them into the world
are gone, both gone at a stroke—
Don't let them go begging, abandoned,
women without men. Your own flesh and blood!
Never bring them down to the level of my pains.
Pity them. Look at them, so young, so vulnerable,
shorn of everything—you're their only hope.
Promise me, noble Creon, touch my hand.

Reaching toward Creon, who draws back.

You, little ones, if you were old enough
to understand, there is much I'd tell you.
Now, as it is, I'd have you say a prayer.
Pray for life, my children,
live where you are free to grow and season.
Pray god you find a better life than mine,
the father who begot you.

CREON: Enough.
You've wept enough. Into the palace now.
OEDIPUS: I must, but I find it very hard.
CREON: Time is the great healer, you will see.
OEDIPUS: I am going—you know on what condition?
CREON: Tell me. I'm listening.
OEDIPUS: Drive me out of Thebes, in exile.
CREON: Not I. Only the gods can give you that.
OEDIPUS: Surely the gods hate me so much—
CREON: You'll get your wish at once.
OEDIPUS: You consent?
CREON: I try to say what I mean; it's my habit.
OEDIPUS: Then take me away. It's time.
CREON: Come along, let go of the children.
OEDIPUS: No—
don't take them away from me, not now! No no no!

Clutching his daughters as the guards wrench them loose and take them through the palace doors.

CREON: Still the king, the master of all things?

No more: here your power ends.
None of your power follows you through life.

Exit Oedipus and Creon to the palace. The Chorus comes forward to address the audience directly.

CHORUS: People of Thebes, my countrymen, look on Oedipus.
He solved the famous riddle with his brilliance,
he rose to power, a man beyond all power.
Who could behold his greatness without envy?
Now what a black sea of terror has overwhelmed him.
Now as we keep our watch and wait the final day,
count no man happy till he dies, free of pain at last.

Exit in procession.

COMMENTARIES

ARISTOTLE

Aristotle (384–322 B.C.), the Greek philosopher, included an analysis of tragedy in his *Poetics* a century after Sophocles' plays were performed during the Great Dionysia in Athens. A student of Plato, Aristotle founded his own school, called the Lyceum, where he lectured on philosophy, science, and the arts. His lectures or treatises were so insightful that they were preserved by his students, and nearly two thousand years later, they form the basis of literary criticism. As the critic Lee Jacobus points out, Aristotle's work not only provides insight into the theoretical basis of the work of the Greek playwrights, but it also "helps us see that the drama was significant enough in Greek intellectual life to warrant an examination by the most influential Greek minds."

On the Elements and General Principles of Tragedy

C. 340 B.C.

TRANSLATED BY GERALD F. ELSE

Tragedy and Its Six Constituent Elements

. . . At present let us deal with tragedy, recovering from what has been said so far the definition of its essential nature, as it was in development. Tragedy, then, is a process of imitating an action which has serious implications, is complete, and possesses magnitude; by means of language which has been made sensuously attractive, with each of its varieties found separately in the parts; enacted by the persons themselves and not presented through narrative; through a course of pity and fear completing the purification of tragic acts which have those emotional characteristics. By "language made sensuously attractive" I mean language that has rhythm and melody, and by "its varieties found separately" I mean the fact that certain parts of the play are carried on through spoken verses alone and others the other way around, through song.

Now first of all, since they perform the imitation through action (by acting it), the adornment of their visual appearance will perforce constitute some part of the making of tragedy; and song-composition and verbal expression also, for those are the media in which they perform the imitation. By "verbal expression" I mean the actual composition of the verses, and by "song-composition" something whose meaning is entirely clear.

Next, since it is an imitation of an action and is enacted by certain people who are performing the action, and since those people must necessarily have certain traits both of character and thought (for it is thanks to these two factors that we speak of people's actions also as having a defined character, and it is in accordance with their actions that all either succeed or fail); and since the imitation of the action is the plot, for by "plot" I mean here the structuring of the events, and by the "characters" that in accordance with which we say that the persons who are acting have a defined moral character, and by "thought" all the passages in which they attempt to prove some thesis or set forth an opinion—it follows of necessity, then, that tragedy as a whole has just six constituent elements, in relation to the essence that makes it a distinct species; and they are plot, characters, verbal expression, thought, visual adornment, and song-composition. For the elements by which they imitate are two (i.e., verbal expression and song-composition), the manner in which they imitate is one (visual adornment), the things they imitate are three (plot, characters, thought), and there is nothing more beyond these. These then are the constituent forms they use.

The Relative Importance of the Six Elements

The greatest of these elements is the structuring of the incidents. For tragedy is an imitation not of men but of a life, an action, and they have moral quality in accordance with their characters but are happy or unhappy in accordance with their actions; hence they are not active in order to imitate their characters, but they include the characters along with the actions for the sake of the latter. Thus the structure of events, the plot, is the goal of tragedy, and the goal is the greatest thing of all. . . .

Again: if one strings end to end speeches that are expressive of character and carefully worked in thought and expression, he still will not achieve the result which we said was the aim of tragedy; the job will be done much better by a tragedy that is more deficient in these other respects but has a plot, a structure of events. It is much the same case as with painting: the most beautiful pigments smeared on at random will not give as much pleasure as a black-and-white outline picture. Besides, the most powerful means tragedy has for swaying our feelings, namely the peripeties and recognitions,° are elements of plot.

Again: an indicative sign is that those who are beginning a poetic career manage to hit the mark in verbal expression and character portrayal sooner

---

peripeties and recognitions: The turning-about of fortune and the recognition on the part of the tragic hero of the truth. This is, for Aristotle, a critical moment in the drama, especially if both events happen simultaneously, as they do in *Oedipus the King*. It is quite possible for these moments to happen apart from one another. [All notes are the translator's.]

than they do in plot construction; and the same is true of practically all the earliest poets.

So plot is the basic principle, the heart and soul, as it were, of tragedy, and the characters come second: . . . it is the imitation of an action and imitates the persons primarily for the sake of their action.

Third in rank is thought. This is the ability to state the issues and appropriate points pertaining to a given topic, an ability which springs from the arts of politics and rhetoric; in fact the earliest poets made their characters talk "politically," the present-day poets rhetorically. But "character" is that kind of utterance which clearly reveals the bent of a man's moral choice (hence there is no character in that class of utterances in which there is nothing at all that the speaker is choosing or rejecting), while "thought" is the passages in which they try to prove that something is so or not so, or state some general principle.

Fourth is the verbal expression of the speeches. I mean by this the same thing that was said earlier, that the "verbal expression" is the conveyance of thought through language: a statement which has the same meaning whether one says "verses" or "speeches."

The song-composition of the remaining parts is the greatest of the sensuous attractions, and the visual adornment of the dramatic persons can have a strong emotional effect but is the least artistic element, the least connected with the poetic art; in fact the force of tragedy can be felt even without benefit of public performance and actors, while for the production of the visual effect the property man's art is even more decisive than that of the poets.

General Principles of the Tragic Plot

With these distinctions out of the way, let us next discuss what the structuring of the events should be like, since this is both the basic and the most important element in the tragic art. We have established, then, that tragedy is an imitation of an action which is complete and whole and has some magnitude (for there is also such a thing as a whole that has no magnitude). "Whole" is that which has beginning, middle, and end. "Beginning" is that which does not necessarily follow on something else, but after it something else naturally is or happens; "end," the other way around, is that which naturally follows on something else, either necessarily or for the most part, but nothing else after it; and "middle" that which naturally follows on something else and something else on it. So, then, well-constructed plots should neither begin nor end at any chance point but follow the guidelines just laid down.

Furthermore, since the beautiful, whether a living creature or anything that is composed of parts, should not only have these in a fixed order to one another but also possess a definite size which does not depend on chance—for beauty depends on size and order; hence neither can a very tiny creature turn out to be beautiful (since our perception of it grows blurred as it approaches the period of imperceptibility) nor an excessively huge one (for then it cannot all be perceived at once and so its unity and wholeness are lost), if for example there were a creature a thousand miles long—so, just as in the case of living creatures they must have some size, but one that can be taken in a single view, so with plots: they should have length, but such that they are easy to remember.

As to a limit of the length, the one is determined by the tragic competitions and the ordinary span of attention. (If they had to compete with a hundred tragedies they would compete by the water clock, as they say used to be done [?].) But the limit fixed by the very nature of the case is: the longer the plot, up to the point of still being perspicuous as a whole, the finer it is so far as size is concerned; or to put it in general terms, the length in which, with things happening in unbroken sequence, a shift takes place either probably or necessarily from bad to good fortune or from good to bad—that is an acceptable norm of length.

But a plot is not unified, as some people think, simply because it has to do with a single person. A large, indeed an indefinite number of things can happen to a given individual, some of which go to constitute no unified event; and in the same way there can be many acts of a given individual from which no single action emerges. Hence it seems clear that those poets are wrong who have composed *Heracleïds, Theseïds,* and the like. They think that since Heracles was a single person it follows that the plot will be single too. But Homer, superior as he is in all other respects, appears to have grasped this point well also, thanks either to art or nature, for in composing an *Odyssey* he did not incorporate into it everything that happened to the hero, for example how he was wounded on Mt. Parnassus° or how he feigned madness at the muster, neither of which events, by happening, made it at all necessary or probable that the other should happen. Instead, he composed the *Odyssey*—and the *Iliad* similarly—around a unified action of the kind we have been talking about.

A poetic imitation, then, ought to be unified in the same way as a single imitation in any other mimetic field, by having a single object: since the plot is an imitation of an action, the latter ought to be both unified and complete, and the component events ought to be so firmly compacted that if any one of them is shifted to another place, or removed, the whole is loosened up and dislocated; for an element whose addition or subtraction makes no perceptible extra difference is not really a part of the whole.

From what has been said it is also clear that the poet's job is not to report what has happened but what is likely to happen: that is, what is capable of happening according to the rule of probability or necessity. Thus the difference between the historian and the poet is not in their utterances being in verse or prose (it would be quite possible for Herodotus' work to be translated into verse, and it would not be any the less a history with verse than it is without it); the difference lies in the fact that the historian speaks of what has happened, the poet of the kind of thing that *can* happen. Hence also poetry is a more philosophical and serious business than history; for poetry speaks more of universals, history of particulars. "Universal" in this case is what kind of person is likely to do or say certain kinds of things, according to probability or necessity;

Mt. Parnassus: A mountain in central Greece traditionally sacred to Apollo. In legend, Odysseus was wounded there, but the point Aristotle is making is that the writer of epics need not include every detail of his hero's life in a given work. Homer, in writing the *Odyssey,* was working with a hero, Odysseus, whose story had been legendary long before he began writing.

that is what poetry aims at, although it gives its persons particular names afterward; while the "particular" is what Alcibiades did or what happened to him.

In the field of comedy this point has been grasped: our comic poets construct their plots on the basis of general probabilities and then assign names to the persons quite arbitrarily, instead of dealing with individuals as the old iambic poets° did. But in tragedy they still cling to the historically given names. The reason is that what is possible is persuasive; so what has not happened we are not yet ready to believe is possible, while what has happened is, we feel, obviously possible: for it would not have happened if it were impossible. Nevertheless, it is a fact that even in our tragedies, in some cases only one or two of the names are traditional, the rest being invented, and in some others none at all. It is so, for example, in Agathon's *Antheus*—the names in it are as fictional as the events—and it gives no less pleasure because of that. Hence the poets ought not to cling at all costs to the traditional plots, around which our tragedies are constructed. And in fact it is absurd to go searching for this kind of authentication, since even the familiar names are familiar to only a few in the audience and yet give the same kind of pleasure to all.

So from these considerations it is evident that the poet should be a maker of his plots more than of his verses, insofar as he is a poet by virtue of his imitations and what he imitates is actions. Hence even if it happens that he puts something that has actually taken place into poetry, he is none the less a poet; for there is nothing to prevent some of the things that have happened from being the kind of things that can happen, and that is the sense in which he is their maker.

Simple and Complex Plots

Among simple plots and actions the episodic are the worst. By "episodic" plot I mean one in which there is no probability or necessity for the order in which the episodes follow one another. Such structures are composed by the bad poets because they are bad poets, but by the good poets because of the actors: in composing contest pieces for them, and stretching out the plot beyond its capacity, they are forced frequently to dislocate the sequence.

Furthermore, since the tragic imitation is not only of a complete action but also of events that are fearful and pathetic,° and these come about best when they come about contrary to one's expectation yet logically, one following from the other; that way they will be more productive of wonder than if they

old iambic poets: Aristotle may be referring to Archilochus (fl. 650 B.C.) and the iambic style he developed. The iamb is a metrical foot of two syllables, a short and a long syllable, and was the most popular metrical style before the time of Aristotle. "Dealing with individuals" implies using figures already known to the audience rather than figures whose names can be arbitrarily assigned because no one knows who they are.

fearful and pathetic: Aristotle said that tragedy should evoke two emotions: terror and pity. The terror results from our realizing that what is happening to the hero might just as easily happen to us; the pity results from our human sympathy with a fellow sufferer. Therefore, the fearful and pathetic represent significant emotions appropriate to our witnessing drama.

happen merely at random, by chance—because even among chance occurrences the ones people consider most marvelous are those that seem to have come about as if on purpose: for example the way the statue of Mitys at Argos killed the man who had been the cause of Mitys' death, by falling on him while he was attending the festival; it stands to reason, people think, that such things don't happen by chance—so plots of that sort cannot fail to be artistically superior.

Some plots are simple, others are complex; indeed the actions of which the plots are imitations already fall into these two categories. By "simple" action I mean one the development of which being continuous and unified in the manner stated above, the reversal comes without peripety or recognition, and by "complex" action one in which the reversal is continuous but with recognition or peripety or both. And these developments must grow out of the very structure of the plot itself, in such a way that on the basis of what has happened previously this particular outcome follows either by necessity or in accordance with probability; for there is a greater difference in whether these events happen because of those or merely after them.

"Peripety" is a shift of what is being undertaken to the opposite in the way previously stated, and that in accordance with probability or necessity as we have just been saying; as for example in the *Oedipus* the man who has come, thinking that he will reassure Oedipus, that is, relieve him of his fear with respect to his mother, by revealing who he once was, brings about the opposite; and in the *Lynceus*, as he (Lynceus) is being led away with every prospect of being executed, and Danaus pursuing him with every prospect of doing the executing, it comes about as a result of the other things that have happened in the play that *he* is executed and Lynceus is saved. And "recognition" is, as indeed the name indicates, a shift from ignorance to awareness, pointing in the direction either of close blood ties or of hostility, of people who have previously been in a clearly marked state of happiness or unhappiness.

The finest recognition is one that happens at the same time as a peripety, as is the case with the one in the *Oedipus*. Naturally, there are also other kinds of recognition: it is possible for one to take place in the prescribed manner in relation to inanimate objects and chance occurrences, and it is possible to recognize whether a person has acted or not acted. But the form that is most integrally a part of the plot, the action, is the one aforesaid; for that kind of recognition combined with peripety will excite either pity or fear (and these are the kinds of action of which tragedy is an imitation according to our definition), because both good and bad fortune will also be most likely to follow that kind of event. Since, further, the recognition is a recognition of persons, some are of one person by the other one only (when it is already known who the "other one" is), but sometimes it is necessary for both persons to go through a recognition, as for example Iphigenia is recognized by her brother through the sending of the letter, but of him by Iphigenia another recognition is required.

These then are two elements of plot: peripety and recognition; third is the *pathos*. Of these, peripety and recognition have been discussed; a *pathos* is a destructive or painful act, such as deaths on stage, paroxysms of pain, woundings, and all that sort of thing.

SIGMUND FREUD

Sigmund Freud (1856–1939) used Sophocles' play in *The Interpretation of Dreams* (1900) to derive the term *Oedipus complex*, which is central to his explanation of neurosis in his theory of psychoanalysis. Freud sought to explain the drama's enduring psychological appeal for audiences despite its lack of a contemporary religious context. He hypothesized that audiences respond to Sophocles' tragedy because they recognize that Oedipus's relationship to his parents "might have been ours" as children. According to Freud's interpretation, the incest theme is dramatized so forcefully in *Oedipus the King* that it enables us to recognize our own "primeval wishes," suppressed in our later psychological development as individuals.

The Oedipus Complex

1900

In my experience, which is already extensive, the chief part in the mental lives of all children who later become psychoneurotics is played by their parents. Being in love with the one parent and hating the other are among the essential constituents of the stock of psychical impulses which is formed at that time and which is of such importance in determining the symptoms of the later neurosis. It is not my belief, however, that psychoneurotics differ sharply in this respect from other human beings who remain normal—that they are able, that is, to create something absolutely new and peculiar to themselves. It is far more probable—and this is confirmed by occasional observations on normal children—that they are only distinguished by exhibiting on a magnified scale feelings of love and hatred to their parents which occur less obviously and less intensely in the minds of most children.

This discovery is confirmed by a legend that has come down to us from classical antiquity: a legend whose profound and universal power to move can only be understood if the hypothesis I have put forward in regard to the psychology of children has an equally universal validity. What I have in mind is the legend of King Oedipus and Sophocles' drama which bears his name.

Oedipus, son of Laius, King of Thebes, and of Jocasta, was exposed as an infant because an oracle had warned Laius that the still unborn child would be his father's murderer. The child was rescued and grew up as a prince in an alien court, until, in doubts as to his origin, he too questioned the oracle and was warned to avoid his home since he was destined to murder his father and take his mother in marriage. On the road leading away from what he believed was his home, he met King Laius and slew him in a sudden quarrel. He came next to Thebes and solved the riddle set him by the Sphinx who barred his way. Out of gratitude the Thebans made him their king and gave him Jocasta's hand in marriage. He reigned long in peace and honor, and she who, unknown to him, was his mother bore him two sons and two daughters. Then at last a plague broke out and the Thebans made inquiry once more of the oracle. It is at this point that Sophocles' tragedy opens. The messengers bring back the reply that the plague will cease when the murderer of Laius has been driven from the land.

> But he, where is he? Where shall now be read
> The fading record of this ancient guilt?[1]

The action of the play consists in nothing other than the process of revealing, with cunning delays and ever-mounting excitement—a process that can be likened to the work of a psychoanalysis—that Oedipus himself is the murderer of Laius, but further that he is the son of the murdered man and of Jocasta. Appalled at the abomination which he has unwittingly perpetrated, Oedipus blinds himself and forsakes his home. The oracle has been fulfilled.

Oedipus Rex is what is known as a tragedy of destiny. Its tragic effect is said to lie in the contrast between the supreme will of the gods and the vain attempts of mankind to escape the evil that threatens them. The lesson which, it is said, the deeply moved spectator should learn from the tragedy is submission to the divine will and realization of his own impotence. Modern dramatists have accordingly tried to achieve a similar tragic effect by weaving the same contrast into a plot invented by themselves. But the spectators have looked on unmoved while a curse or an oracle was fulfilled in spite of all the efforts of some innocent man: later tragedies of destiny have failed in their effect.

If *Oedipus Rex* moves a modern audience no less than it did the contemporary Greek one, the explanation can only be that its effect does not lie in the contrast between destiny and human will, but is to be looked for in the particular nature of the material on which that contrast is exemplified. There must be something which makes a voice within us ready to recognize the compelling force of destiny in the *Oedipus*, while we can dismiss as merely arbitrary such dispositions as are laid down in [Grillparzer's] *Die Ahnfrau* or other modern tragedies of destiny. And a factor of this kind is in fact involved in the story of King Oedipus. His destiny moves us only because it might have been ours—because the oracle laid the same curse upon us before our birth as upon him. It is the fate of all of us, perhaps, to direct our first sexual impulse toward our mother and our first hatred and our first murderous wish against our father. Our dreams convince us that that is so. King Oedipus, who slew his father Laius and married his mother Jocasta, merely shows us the fulfillment of our own childhood wishes. But, more fortunate than he, we have meanwhile succeeded, in so far as we have not become psychoneurotics, in detaching our sexual impulses from our mothers and in forgetting our jealousy of our fathers. Here is one in whom these primeval wishes of our childhood have been fulfilled, and we shrink back from him with the whole force of the repression by which those wishes have since that time been held down within us. While the poet, as he unravels the past, brings to light the guilt of Oedipus, he is at the same time compelling us to recognize our own inner minds, in which those same impulses, though suppressed, are still to be found. The contrast with which the closing Chorus leaves us confronted—

---

[1]Lewis Campbell's translation (1883), lines 108ff. [Cf. lines 123–124 of the Fagles translation in this volume.—Editors' note]

. . . Fix on Oedipus your eyes,
Who resolved the dark enigma, noblest champion and most wise.
Like a star his envied fortune mounted beaming far and wide:
Now he sinks in seas of anguish, whelmed beneath a raging tide . . .[2]

—strikes as a warning at ourselves and our pride, at us who since our childhood have grown so wise and so mighty in our own eyes. Like Oedipus, we live in ignorance of these wishes, repugnant to morality, which have been forced upon us by Nature, and after their revelation we may all of us well seek to close our eyes to the scenes of our childhood.[3]

There is an unmistakable indication in the text of Sophocles' tragedy itself that the legend of Oedipus sprang from some primeval dream material which had as its content the distressing disturbance of a child's relation to his parents owing to the first stirrings of sexuality. At a point when Oedipus, though he is not yet enlightened, has begun to feel troubled by his recollection of the oracle, Jocasta consoles him by referring to a dream which many people dream, though, as she thinks, it has no meaning:

Many a man ere now in dreams hath lain
With her who bare him. He hath least annoy
Who with such omens troubleth not his mind.[4]

Today, just as then, many men dream of having sexual relations with their mothers, and speak of the fact with indignation and astonishment. It is clearly the key to the tragedy and the complement to the dream of the dreamer's father being dead. The story of Oedipus is the reaction of the imagination to these two typical dreams. And just as these dreams, when dreamt by adults, are accompanied by feelings of repulsion, so too the legend must include horror and self-punishment. Its further modification originates once again in a misconceived secondary revision of the material, which has sought to exploit it for theological purposes. . . . The attempt to harmonize divine omnipotence with human responsibility must naturally fail in connection with this subject matter just as with any other.

---

[2]Lewis Campbell's translation, lines 1524ff. [Cf. lines 1678–1682 in the Fagles translation in this volume.—Editors' note]

[3][*Footnote added by Freud in 1914 edition.*] None of the findings of psychoanalytic research has provoked such embittered denials, such fierce opposition—or such amusing contortions—on the part of critics as this indication of the childhood impulses toward incest which persist in the unconscious. An attempt has even been made recently to make out, in the face of all experience, that the incest should only be taken as "symbolic."—Ferenczi (1912) has proposed an ingenious "overinterpretation" of the Oedipus myth, based on a passage in one of Schopenhauer's letters. [*Added 1919.*] Later studies have shown that the "Oedipus complex," which was touched upon for the first time in the above paragraphs in the *Interpretation of Dreams,* throws a light of undreamt-of importance on the history of the human race and the evolution of religion and morality.

[4]Lewis Campbell's translation, lines 982ff. [Cf. lines 1074–1078 in the Fagles translation in this volume.—Editors' note]

WILLIAM SHAKESPEARE

William Shakespeare (1564–1616), the great English playwright and poet, was born in Stratford, the third of eight children of Mary Arden, daughter of a prosperous landowner, and John Shakespeare, a glovemaker. We know much more about Shakespeare's life than we know about Sophocles' life two thousand years earlier. Some forty documents of Shakespeare's time offer details about him, commensurate with his social status and professional activities. The register of the Stratford parish church documents Shakespeare's baptism and burial, along with the baptisms of his daughter Susanna and his twins, Judith and Hamnet. We also know that in 1582, at the age of eighteen, he married Anne Hathaway in Stratford (she was twenty-six), and that before his death he made a will leaving most of his considerable property to his two daughters (his son, Hamnet, had died at age eleven). Shakespeare willed only his "second best bed" to his wife, whom he apparently left in Stratford with his children when he went off to London to make his fortune in the theater.

As a young man in London, Shakespeare worked as an actor and playwright, but his first publications were two books of poetry. In 1593, after an outbreak of the plague had closed the London theaters, he published his first poem, *Venus and Adonis*, dedicated to his wealthy patron the Earl of Southampton. A year later he published another long narrative poem, *The Rape of Lucrece*. (A third book, his collection of sonnets, was published in 1609.) When the theaters reopened in London at the end of 1594, Shakespeare joined the new Lord Chamberlain's Company, for whom he continued to act and write plays until 1613. The literary historian François Laroque has described the astute way Shakespeare managed his career before his retirement as a wealthy man in Stratford:

> The Chamberlain's Men were organized in an unusual manner: the six main actors [including Shakespeare] formed an association in which each was a shareholder, directly receiving part of the takings from performances. The actors were financially independent, paying only rent to the theatre proprietor James Burbage. . . . Shakespeare never changed company, a fact rare enough to be worthy of note. From now on he worked to strengthen his position as both player and playwright. In addition to his acting he wrote an average of two plays a year until 1608, when the pace of theatrical production slackened. The decision early in his career to remain in one place, with one company, enabled him quickly to consolidate his first successes as a writer and to become in his lifetime the most highly sought after dramatist of the Elizabethan and Jacobean stage.

The exact number of plays written by Shakespeare is unknown, as the practice of his time was for playwrights to collaborate on scripts, often reworking and adapting older material, but thirty-seven plays currently make up the Shakespeare canon. Seven years after his death, thirty-six of his plays were collected by actors in his theater company desirous to honor his memory and to protect his work from unscrupulous publishers. The table of contents in this First Folio edition of 1623 reads, "A Catalogue of the several Comedies, Histories, and Tragedies contained in this Volume." This way of organizing the plays has continued to the present day.

The comedies included, among other plays, *The Tempest, The Comedy of Errors, A Midsummer Night's Dream, As You Like It, The Taming of the Shrew*, and *The Merchant of Venice*. The history plays—most of which Shakespeare wrote early in his career, between 1590 and 1597—included *Richard II; Henry IV, Parts 1 and 2; Henry V; Henry VI, Parts 1–3*; and *Richard III*. The tragedies included *Romeo and Juliet, Macbeth, King Lear, Othello*, and *Hamlet*. Although eighteen of Shakespeare's plays were published in his lifetime as small books called *quartos*, no play manuscript used by a printer in this time has survived, so we depend on the work of scholars for the editing of his texts.

The Elizabethan theater flourished during the reign of Elizabeth I and her successor, James I, having its origins in fifteenth-century religious pageants and plays such as *The Second Shepherd's Play* and *Everyman*, which were performed by actors who were part of traveling companies. The first permanent theater in England was not built until 1576, only about fifteen years before Shakespeare came to London to begin his career. Toward the end of the sixteenth century, playwrights began to glorify English history, turning to secular material for their subjects. National patriotism was stirred by the defeat of the Spanish Armada, which had failed spectacularly in its attempt to conquer England in 1588. When Shakespeare began to write plays, there were several professional acting companies in London, and we have a good idea of the design of their theaters from the foundations of the Rose Playhouse, excavated in 1988. A

Interior of the first Globe Playhouse. (Drawing by C. Walter Hodges. Reprinted by permission of the Folger Shakespeare Library.)

The reconstructed Globe Theatre. Southwark, London, 1999. (Photo © Nik Wheeler/CORBIS.)

reconstruction of the Globe Playhouse, in which Shakespeare once held a one-tenth interest as a partner in the company of the Chamberlain's Men, opened in London in 1997. The original structure's thatched roof sported a globe with the Latin inscription *totus mundus agit histrionem*—"All the world's a stage."

Elizabethan theaters such as the Rose and the Globe, the two largest public theaters in London, were tall buildings, usually round or octagonal, with three tiers of galleries for the spectators. The Globe was located south of the Thames River in a neighborhood famous for its bearbaiting pits, gambling houses, brothels, and theaters. The Globe was the finest playhouse in London, yet its raised, covered stage, which projected into the audience, was so small that no more than a dozen actors could appear at a time. The gallery directly behind the stage was used by musicians or actors (as for the balcony scene in *Romeo and Juliet*). In the front section of the stage was a trapdoor used for the entrance and disappearance of devils and ghosts, or for burial scenes, as in *Hamlet*. Actors could also stand under the stage, as in the mention in *Hamlet* that the "ghost cries under the stage."

Audiences of up to eight hundred people paid a penny each to stand in the uncovered pit to watch the play, with ticket prices increasing up to six pence for a seat in the galleries, which held an additional fifteen hundred spectators. Plays were performed in these public theaters only in daylight, without artificial illumination. As in Greek and classical Japanese Nō theater, only men were trained as actors, including boys who played women's roles until their voices broke. Shakespeare wrote complex parts for specific actors in his company, such as Richard Burbage, who first played the role of Hamlet. As an actor Shakespeare was not a star performer; probably he played the ghost of the murdered king in productions of *Hamlet*. In theater records he was designated a "principal comedian" in 1598, a "principle tragedian" in 1603, and one of the "man players" in 1608.

On June 29, 1613, soon after Shakespeare's retirement to Stratford, the Globe Playhouse burned to the ground during a performance of his play *Henry VIII.* A volley of blank shots fired by an actor onstage set fire to the thatched roof of the galleries. Everyone in the audience escaped unharmed, with the exception of a man whose trousers caught fire in the blaze; according to spectators, he doused the fire in his clothes with a bottle of ale. Thirty years later, all the theaters in England would be torn down by order of Parliament in 1642 and 1644 under Puritan rule.

While Shakespeare and his generation of gifted contemporaries – Christopher Marlowe, Thomas Kyd, and Ben Jonson, to name only a few – were creating their plays, audiences crammed into the theaters six days a week, eager to witness stage spectacles and listen to the players' grandiloquence. Plays such as *Hamlet,* which included a ghost, stabbings, suicide, and duels, in addition to rich and complex lines of poetry, were the regular fare of the patrons of the Globe Playhouse. Shakespeare and his company of actors were so successful that they enjoyed royal patronage. They performed for Queen Elizabeth I on the average of three times a year, and it is recorded that King James I was in attendance at the first performance of *Macbeth* in 1604.

A Midsummer Night's Dream was written in 1595 or early 1596, according to most Shakespeare authorities, about four years before *Hamlet.* The earlier play is a comedy, and it was probably commissioned to be performed at an aristocratic wedding, where its extensive use of music, dance, magical spectacles, and supernatural beings celebrating a royal marriage would be highly appropriate. While no known previous literary work is a source for *A Midsummer Night's Dream,* at least a dozen works provided general ideas for the play, including Chaucer's "The Knight's Tale" in *The Canterbury Tales,* which provided the characters Theseus and Hippolyta, and Ovid's *Metamorphosis* in a 1567 translation by Arthur Golding, which provided the legend of Pyramus and Thisbe.

Dramatizing the theme that love is a wholly irrational passion, where the lovers are victims of whim and illusion, the characters in *A Midsummer Night's Dream* are stylized and unrealistic, created to evoke the audience's wonder and surprise. The cast of nobles, paired lovers, elves, and fairies includes Robin Goodfellow or Puck, based on a character in an early tract against the persecution of witches, and his cohorts Peaseblossom, Cobweb, Moth, and Mustardseed, all creatures of Shakespeare's imagination. Bottom and his fellow artisans represent ordinary village people: Nick Bottom himself is a weaver, Francis Flute a bellows mender, Robin Starveling a tailor, Tom Snout a tinker, and Snug a joiner. Peter Quince could have been played by Shakespeare himself as a self-directed satire about a man who both writes a drama and then acts in it. The rustic play they perform ridicules the entertainments that were the staple fare in Elizabethan times. As the critic Wolfgang Clemen observed, "The exaggerated tragedy of Pyramus and Thisbe parodies not only the torments of love, but also the Senecan style of Elizabethan tragedy with its devices as apostrophe, alliteration, hyperbole, and rhetorical questions."

A Midsummer Night's Dream became one of Shakespeare's most popular comedies. By the nineteenth century it was described as "pure enchantment" in productions throughout Europe. In Berlin it inspired an overture and incidental music in 1827 by the composer Felix Mendelssohn that became one of his best-loved works. In the

United States in 1935 it was made into a film starring James Cagney as Bottom and Mickey Rooney as Puck. In 1939 it was produced in a jazz version titled *Swinging the Dream* featuring the Benny Goodman sextet with Louis Armstrong as Bottom. In 1960 it became the subject of an opera by the English composer Benjamin Britten.

While *A Midsummer Night's Dream* is one of Shakespeare's shortest plays, *Hamlet* is one of his longest. In the four years between them, Shakespeare matured as a dramatist, and *Hamlet* is probably his most famous play. Just as he depended on his contemporary historian Raphael Holinshed's chronicles for the material of his English history plays, Shakespeare used earlier sources as the basis for *Hamlet*. He was also influenced by Kyd's *Spanish Tragedy* (c. 1587), which set the standard for a new genre of English plays called "revenge tragedies." In addition, writings by Shakespeare's contemporaries indicate that a "lost play" of *Hamlet* was known to Shakespeare before he wrote his version of the play. In creating their **revenge tragedies** (plays in which the plot typically centers on a spectacular attempt to avenge the murder of a family member), Shakespeare and other popular English dramatists took the early Roman playwrights as their models. The Greek playwrights were not popular at the time, but a contemporary account credited Shakespeare with being as polished a writer of comedy and tragedy as the Romans Plautus and Seneca, respectively.

The extraordinary richness of Shakespeare's theatrical world is made evident in *Hamlet*. Unlike other avengers in the revenge tragedies of his time, Hamlet is a complex figure. He plays the multiple roles of son, lover, philosopher, actor, and prince. He questions the reality of his experience, procrastinates in carrying out his promise to avenge his father's death, considers his own failure of will and emotional paralysis, and contemplates suicide. Because most of us can sympathize with his difficult situation, *Hamlet* is the best known and most often performed of Shakespeare's plays. Actors have offered different interpretations of the role as diverse as Sir John Gielgud's aristocratic, disillusioned Hamlet in 1934 to the young actor Mark Rylance's performance of a psychotic Hamlet dressed in striped pajamas, inhabiting the Danish court as if it were a psychiatric hospital. As the critic Edward Hubler recognized, "Tragedy of the first order is a rare phenomenon. It came into being in Greece in the fifth century B.C., where it flourished for a while, and it did not appear again until some two thousand years later when Shakespeare wrote *Hamlet* in 1600."

CONNECTIONS See pages 1592–1609, including Geoffrey Bullough, "Sources of Shakespeare's *Hamlet*," page 1594; John Keats, "From a Letter to George and Thomas Keats, 21 December 1817," page 1596; Stephen Greenblatt, "On the Ghost in *Hamlet*," page 1597; Tom Stoppard, "*Dogg's Hamlet*: The Encore," page 1598; Sir John Gielgud, "On Playing Hamlet," page 1600; Photographs of *Hamlet* in performance, pages 1602–1604; John Lahr, "Review of *Hamlet*," page 1605; Michael Pennington, "Hamlet's Madness," page 1608.

WEB Research William Shakespeare at bedfordstmartins.com/rewritinglit.

A Midsummer Night's Dream c. 1596

[DRAMATIS PERSONAE

THESEUS, Duke of Athens
EGEUS, father to Hermia
LYSANDER, DEMETRIUS, } in love with Hermia
PHILOSTRATE, Master of the Revels to Theseus

QUINCE, a carpenter
SNUG, a joiner
BOTTOM, a weaver
FLUTE, a bellows-mender
SNOUT, a tinker
STARVELING, a tailor

HIPPOLYTA, Queen of the Amazons, betrothed to Theseus
HERMIA, daughter to Egeus, in love with Lysander
HELENA, in love with Demetrius
OBERON, King of the Fairies
TITANIA, Queen of the Fairies
PUCK, or Robin Goodfellow
PEASEBLOSSOM, COBWEB, MOTH, MUSTARDSEED, } fairies
Other FAIRIES attending their king and queen
ATTENDANTS on Theseus and Hippolyta

SCENE: *Athens, and a wood near it.*]

[ACT I]

[SCENE I: *The palace of Theseus.*]

Enter Theseus, Hippolyta, [*Philostrate,*] *with others.*

THESEUS: Now, fair Hippolyta, our nuptial hour
Draws on apace. Four happy days bring in
Another moon; but, O, methinks, how slow
This old moon wanes! She lingers° my desires
Like to a step-dame° or a dowager°
Long withering out a young man's revenue.

Note: The text of *A Midsummer Night's Dream* has come down to us in different versions—such as the first quarto, the second quarto, and the first Folio. The copy of the text used here is largely drawn from the first quarto. Passages enclosed in square brackets are taken from one of the other versions. ACT I, SCENE I. **4. lingers:** Lengthens, protects. **5. step-dame:** Stepmother. **dowager:** Widow with a jointure or dower [an estate or title from her deceased husband].

HIPPOLYTA: Four days will quickly steep themselves in night,
Four nights will quickly dream away the time;
And then the moon, like to a silver bow
New-bent in heaven, shall behold the night
Of our solemnities.

THESEUS: Go, Philostrate,
Stir up the Athenian youth to merriments,
Awake the pert and nimble spirit of mirth,
Turn melancholy forth to funerals;
The pale companion° is not for our pomp.°

[*Exit Philostrate.*]

Hippolyta, I woo'd thee with my sword,°
And won thy love doing thee injuries;
But I will wed thee in another key,
With pomp, with triumph,° and with reveling.

Enter Egeus and his daughter Hermia, and Lysander, and Demetrius.

EGEUS: Happy be Theseus, our renowned Duke!

THESEUS: Thanks, good Egeus. What's the news with thee?

EGEUS: Full of vexation come I, with complaint
Against my child, my daughter Hermia.
Stand forth, Demetrius. My noble lord,
This man hath my consent to marry her.
Stand forth, Lysander. And, my gracious Duke,
This man hath bewitch'd the bosom of my child.
Thou, thou, Lysander, thou hast given her rhymes
And interchang'd love tokens with my child.
Thou hast by moonlight at her window sung
With feigning voice verses of feigning° love,
And stol'n the impression of her fantasy,°
With bracelets of thy hair, rings, gauds,° conceits,°
Knacks,° trifles, nosegays, sweetmeats—messengers
Of strong prevailment in unhardened youth.
With cunning hast thou filch'd my daughter's heart,
Turn'd her obedience, which is due to me,
To stubborn harshness. And, my gracious Duke,
Be it so she will not here before your Grace
Consent to marry with Demetrius,
I beg the ancient privilege of Athens:
As she is mine, I may dispose of her,
Which shall be either to this gentleman

---

15. companion: Fellow. **pomp:** Ceremonial magnificence. **16. with my sword:** In a military engagement against the Amazons, when Hippolyta was taken captive. **19. triumph:** Public festivity. **31. feigning:** (1) Counterfeiting, (2) faining, desirous. **32. And . . . fantasy:** And made her fall in love with you (imprinting your image on her imagination) by stealthy and dishonest means. **33. gauds:** Playthings. **conceits:** Fanciful trifles. **34. Knacks:** Knickknacks.

Or to her death, according to our law
Immediately° provided in that case.
THESEUS: What say you, Hermia? Be advis'd, fair maid.
To you your father should be as a god—
One that compos'd your beauties, yea, and one
To whom you are but as a form in wax
By him imprinted and within his power
To leave° the figure or disfigure° it.
Demetrius is a worthy gentleman.
HERMIA: So is Lysander.
THESEUS: In himself he is;
But in this kind,° wanting° your father's voice,°
The other must be held the worthier.
HERMIA: I would my father look'd but with my eyes.
THESEUS: Rather your eyes must with his judgment look.
HERMIA: I do entreat your Grace to pardon me.
I know not by what power I am made bold,
Nor how it may concern° my modesty,
In such a presence here to plead my thoughts;
But I beseech your Grace that I may know
The worst that may befall me in this case,
If I refuse to wed Demetrius.
THESEUS: Either to die the death, or to abjure
Forever the society of men.
Therefore, fair Hermia, question your desires,
Know of your youth, examine well your blood,°
Whether, if you yield not to your father's choice,
You can endure the livery° of a nun,
For aye° to be in shady cloister mew'd,°
To live a barren sister all your life,
Chanting faint hymns to the cold fruitless moon.
Thrice blessed they that master so their blood
To undergo such maiden pilgrimage,
But earthlier happy° is the rose distill'd,
Than that which withering on the virgin thorn
Grows, lives, and dies in single blessedness.
HERMIA: So will I grow, so live, so die, my lord,
Ere I will yield my virgin patent° up
Unto his lordship, whose unwished yoke
My soul consents not to give sovereignty.
THESEUS: Take time to pause; and, by the next new moon—

---

45. Immediately: Expressly. **51. leave:** Leave unaltered. **disfigure:** Obliterate. **54. kind:** Respect. **wanting:** Lacking **voice:** Approval. **60. concern:** Befit. **68. blood:** Passions. **70. livery:** Habit. **71. aye:** Ever. **mew'd:** Shut in (said of a hawk, poultry, etc.). **76. earthlier happy:** Happier as respects this world. **80. patent:** Privilege.

The sealing-day betwixt my love and me
For everlasting bond of fellowship—
Upon that day either prepare to die
For disobedience to your father's will,
Or° else to wed Demetrius, as he would,
Or on Diana's altar° to protest°
For aye austerity and single life.

DEMETRIUS: Relent, sweet Hermia, and, Lysander, yield
Thy crazed° title to my certain right.

LYSANDER: You have her father's love, Demetrius;
Let me have Hermia's. Do you marry him.

EGEUS: Scornful Lysander! True, he hath my love,
And what is mine my love shall render him.
And she is mine, and all my right of her
I do estate unto° Demetrius.

LYSANDER: I am, my lord, as well deriv'd° as he,
As well possess'd;° my love is more than his;
My fortunes every way as fairly° rank'd,
If not with vantage,° as Demetrius';
And, which is more than all these boasts can be,
I am belov'd of beauteous Hermia.
Why should not I then prosecute my right?
Demetrius, I'll avouch it to his head,°
Made love to Nedar's daughter, Helena,
And won her soul; and she, sweet lady, dotes,
Devoutly dotes, dotes in idolatry,
Upon this spotted° and inconstant man.

THESEUS: I must confess that I have heard so much,
And with Demetrius thought to have spoke thereof;
But, being over-full of self-affairs,
My mind did lose it. But, Demetrius, come,
And come, Egeus, you shall go with me;
I have some private schooling for you both.
For you, fair Hermia, look you arm° yourself
To fit your fancies° to your father's will;
Or else the law of Athens yields you up—
Which by no means we may extenuate°—
To death, or to a vow of single life.
Come, my Hippolyta. What cheer, my love?
Demetrius and Egeus, go° along.

---

88. Or: Either. **89. Diana's altar:** Diana was a virgin goddess. **protest:** Vow. **92. crazed:** Cracked, unsound. **98. estate unto:** Settle or bestow upon. **99. deriv'd:** Descended, i.e., "as well born." **100. possess'd:** Endowed with wealth. **101. fairly:** Handsomely. **102. vantage:** Superiority. **106. head:** Face. **110. spotted:** Morally stained. **117. look you arm:** Take care you prepare. **118. fancies:** Likings, thoughts of love. **120. extenuate:** Mitigate. **123. go:** Come.

I must employ you in some business
Against° our nuptial, and confer with you
Of something nearly that° concerns yourselves.

EGEUS: With duty and desire we follow you.

Exeunt° [*all but Lysander and Hermia*].

LYSANDER: How now, my love, why is your cheek so pale?
How chance the roses there do fade so fast?

HERMIA: Belike° for want of rain, which I could well
Beteem° them from the tempest of my eyes.

LYSANDER: Ay me! For aught that I could ever read,
Could ever hear by tale or history,
The course of true love never did run smooth;
But either it was different in blood°—

HERMIA: O cross,° too high to be enthrall'd to low!

LYSANDER: Or else misgraffed° in respect of years—

HERMIA: O spite, too old to be engag'd to young!

LYSANDER: Or else it stood upon the choice of friends°—

HERMIA: O hell, to choose love by another's eyes!

LYSANDER: Or, if there were a sympathy in choice,
War, death, or sickness did lay siege to it,
Making it momentany° as a sound,
Swift as a shadow, short as any dream,
Brief as the lightning in the collied° night,
That, in a spleen,° unfolds° both heaven and earth,
And ere a man hath power to say "Behold!"
The jaws of darkness do devour it up.
So quick° bright things come to confusion.°

HERMIA: If then true lovers have been ever cross'd,°
It stands as an edict in destiny.
Then let us teach our trial patience,°
Because it is a customary cross,
As due to love as thoughts and dreams and sighs,
Wishes and tears, poor fancy's° followers.

LYSANDER: A good persuasion. Therefore, hear me, Hermia.
I have a widow aunt, a dowager
Of great revenue, and she hath no child.
From Athens is her house remote seven leagues;
And she respects° me as her only son.

---

125. Against: In preparation for. **126. nearly that:** That closely. **127. s.d. Exeunt:** Latin for "they go out." **130. Belike:** Very likely. **131. Beteem:** Grant, afford. **135. blood:** Hereditary station. **136. cross:** Vexation. **137. misgraffed:** Ill grafted, badly matched. **139. friends:** Relatives. **143. momentany:** Lasting but a moment. **145. collied:** Blackened (as with coal dust), darkened. **146. in a spleen:** In a swift impulse in a violent flash. **unfolds:** Discloses. **149. quick:** Quickly; or, perhaps, living, alive. **confusion:** Ruin. **150. ever cross'd:** Always thwarted. **152. teach . . . patience:** Teach ourselves patience in this trial. **155. fancy's:** Amorous passion's. **160. respects:** Regards.

There, gentle Hermia, may I marry thee,
And to that place the sharp Athenian law
Cannot pursue us. If thou lovest me, then,
Steal forth thy father's house tomorrow night;
And in the wood, a league without the town,
Where I did meet thee once with Helena
To do observance to a morn of May,°
There will I stay for thee.

HERMIA: My good Lysander!
I swear to thee, by Cupid's strongest bow,
By his best arrow with the golden head,°
By the simplicity° of Venus' doves,°
By that which knitteth souls and prospers loves,
And by that fire which burn'd the Carthage queen,
When the false Troyan° under sail was seen,
By all the vows that ever men have broke,
In number more than ever women spoke,
In that same place thou hast appointed me
Tomorrow truly will I meet with thee.

LYSANDER: Keep promise, love. Look, here comes Helena.

Enter Helena.

HERMIA: God speed fair° Helena, whither away?

HELENA: Call you me fair? That fair again unsay.
Demetrius loves your fair.° O happy fair!°
Your eyes are lodestars,° and your tongue's sweet air°
More tuneable° than lark to shepherd's ear
When wheat is green, when hawthorn buds appear.
Sickness is catching. O, were favor° so,
Yours would I catch, fair Hermia, ere I go;
My ear should catch your voice, my eye your eye,
My tongue should catch your tongue's sweet melody.
Were the world mine, Demetrius being bated,°
The rest I'd give to be to you translated.°
O, teach me how you look, and with what art
You sway the motion° of Demetrius' heart.

HERMIA: I frown upon him, yet he loves me still.

---

167. do . . . May: Perform the ceremonies of May Day. **170. best arrow . . . golden head:** Cupid's best gold-pointed arrows were supposed to induce love, his blunt leaden arrows aversion. **171. simplicity:** Innocence. **doves:** Those that drew Venus's chariot. **173–174. by that fire . . . false Troyan:** Dido, Queen of Carthage, immolated herself on a funeral pyre after having been deserted by the Trojan hero Aeneas. **180. fair:** Fair-complexioned (generally regarded by the Elizabethans as more beautiful than dark-complexioned). **182. your fair:** Your beauty (even though Hermia is dark-complexioned). **happy fair:** Lucky fair one. **183. lodestars:** Guiding stars. **air:** Music. **184. tuneable:** Tuneful, melodious. **186. favor:** Appearance, looks. **190. bated:** Excepted. **191. translated:** Transformed. **193. motion:** Impulse.

HELENA: O that your frowns would teach my smiles such skill!
HERMIA: I give him curses, yet he gives me love.
HELENA: O that my prayers could such affection° move!°
HERMIA: The more I hate, the more he follows me.
HELENA: The more I love, the more he hateth me.
HERMIA: His folly, Helena, is no fault of mine.
HELENA: None, but your beauty. Would that fault were mine!
HERMIA: Take comfort. He no more shall see my face.
Lysander and myself will fly this place.
Before the time I did Lysander see,
Seem'd Athens as a paradise to me.
O, then, what graces in my love do dwell,
That he hath turn'd a heaven unto a hell!
LYSANDER: Helen, to you our minds we will unfold.
Tomorrow night, when Phoebe° doth behold
Her silver visage in the wat'ry glass,°
Decking with liquid pearl the bladed grass,
A time that lovers' flights doth still° conceal,
Through Athens' gates have we devis'd to steal.
HERMIA: And in the wood, where often you and I
Upon faint° primrose beds were wont to lie,
Emptying our bosoms of their counsel° sweet,
There my Lysander and myself shall meet;
And thence from Athens turn away our eyes,
To seek new friends and stranger companies.
Farewell, sweet playfellow. Pray thou for us,
And good luck grant thee thy Demetrius!
Keep word, Lysander. We must starve our sight
From lovers' food till morrow deep midnight.
LYSANDER: I will, my Hermia. *Exit Hermia.*
Helena, adieu.
As you on him, Demetrius dote on you!
Exit Lysander.
HELENA: How happy some o'er other some can be!°
Through Athens I am thought as fair as she.
But what of that? Demetrius thinks not so;
He will not know what all but he do know.
And as he errs, doting on Hermia's eyes,
So I, admiring of° his qualities.
Things base and vile, holding no quantity,°
Love can transpose to form and dignity.
Love looks not with the eyes, but with the mind,

197. affection: Passion. **move:** Arouse. **209. Phoebe:** Diana, the moon. **210. glass:** Mirror. **212. still:** Always. **215. faint:** Pale. **216. counsel:** Secret thought. **226. o'er . . . can be:** Can be in comparison to some others. **231. admiring of:** Wondering at. **232. holding no quantity:** Unsubstantial, unshapely.

And therefore is wing'd Cupid painted blind.
Nor hath Love's mind of any judgment taste;°
Wings, and no eyes, figure° unheedy haste.
And therefore is Love said to be a child,
Because in choice he is so oft beguil'd.
As waggish boys in game° themselves forswear,
So the boy Love is perjur'd everywhere.
For ere Demetrius look'd on Hermia's eyne,°
He hail'd down oaths that he was only mine;
And when this hail some heat from Hermia felt,
So he dissolv'd, and show'rs of oaths did melt.
I will go tell him of fair Hermia's flight.
Then to the wood will he tomorrow night
Pursue her; and for this intelligence°
If I have thanks, it is a dear° expense.°
But herein mean I to enrich my pain,
To have his sight thither and back again. *Exit.*

[SCENE II: *Athens. Quince's house(?).*]

Enter Quince the Carpenter, and Snug the Joiner, and Bottom the Weaver, and Flute the Bellows-Mender, and Snout the Tinker, and Starveling the Tailor.

QUINCE: Is all our company here?

BOTTOM: You were best to call them generally,° man by man, according to the scrip.°

QUINCE: Here is the scroll of every man's name which is thought fit, through all Athens, to play in our interlude before the Duke and the Duchess on his wedding-day at night.

BOTTOM: First, good Peter Quince, say what the play treats on, then read the names of the actors, and so grow to° a point.

QUINCE: Marry,° our play is "The most lamentable comedy and most cruel death of Pyramus and Thisby."

BOTTOM: A very good piece of work, I assure you, and a merry. Now, good Peter Quince, call forth your actors by the scroll. Masters, spread yourselves.

QUINCE: Answer as I call you. Nick Bottom, the weaver.

BOTTOM: Ready. Name what part I am for, and proceed.

QUINCE: You, Nick Bottom, are set down for Pyramus.

BOTTOM: What is Pyramus? A lover, or a tyrant?

QUINCE: A lover, that kills himself most gallant for love.

BOTTOM: That will ask some tears in the true performing of it. If I do it, let the audience look to their eyes. I will move storms; I will condole° in some

---

236. Nor . . . taste: Nor has Love, which dwells in the fancy or imagination, any *taste* or least bit of judgment or reason. **237. figure:** Are a symbol of. **240. game:** Sport, jest. **242. eyne:** Eyes (old form of plural). **248. intelligence:** Information. **249. dear:** Costly. **a dear expense:** A trouble worth taking. ACT I, SCENE II. **2. generally:** Bottom's blunder for *individually.* **3. scrip:** Script, written list. **8. grow to:** Come to. **9. Marry:** A mild oath, originally the name of the Virgin Mary. **19. condole:** Lament, arouse pity.

measure. To the rest—yet my chief humor° is for a tyrant. I could play Ercles° rarely, or a part to tear a cat° in, to make all split.°
"The raging rocks
And shivering shocks
Shall break the locks
Of prison gates;
And Phibbus' car°
Shall shine from far
And make and mar
The foolish Fates."
This was lofty! Now name the rest of the players. This is Ercles' vein, a tyrant's vein. A lover is more condoling.

QUINCE: Francis Flute, the bellows-mender.

FLUTE: Here, Peter Quince.

QUINCE: Flute, you must take Thisby on you.

FLUTE: What is Thisby? A wand'ring knight?

QUINCE: It is the lady that Pyramus must love.

FLUTE: Nay, faith, let not me play a woman. I have a beard coming.

QUINCE: That's all one.° You shall play it in a mask, and you may speak as small° as you will.

BOTTOM: An° I may hide my face, let me play Thisby too. I'll speak in a monstrous little voice, "Thisne, Thisne!" "Ah Pyramus, my lover dear! Thy Thisby dear, and lady dear!"

QUINCE: No, no; you must play Pyramus; and, Flute, you Thisby.

BOTTOM: Well, proceed.

QUINCE: Robin Starveling, the tailor.

STARVELING: Here, Peter Quince.

QUINCE: Robin Starveling, you must play Thisby's mother. Tom Snout, the tinker.

SNOUT: Here, Peter Quince.

QUINCE: You, Pyramus' father; myself, Thisby's father; Snug, the joiner, you, the lion's part; and I hope here is a play fitted.

SNUG: Have you the lion's part written? Pray you, if it be, give it me, for I am slow of study.

QUINCE: You may do it extempore, for it is nothing but roaring.

BOTTOM: Let me play the lion too. I will roar that I will do any man's heart good to hear me. I will roar that I will make the Duke say, "Let him roar again, let him roar again."

QUINCE: An you should do it too terribly, you would fright the Duchess and the ladies, that they would shriek; and that were enough to hang us all.

ALL: That would hang us, every mother's son.

---

20. humor: Inclination, whim. **21. Ercles:** Hercules (the tradition of ranting came from Seneca's *Hercules Furens*). **tear a cat:** Rant. **make all split:** Cause a stir, bring the house down. **26. Phibbus' car:** Phoebus's, the sun-god's, chariot. **38. That's all one:** It makes no difference. **small:** High-pitched. **40. An:** If.

BOTTOM: I grant you, friends, if you should fright the ladies out of their wits, they would have no more discretion but to hang us; but I will aggravate° my voice so that I will roar you° as gently as any sucking dove; I will roar you an 'twere any nightingale.

QUINCE: You can play no part but Pyramus; for Pyramus is a sweet-fac'd man, a proper° man as one shall see in a summer's day, a most lovely gentleman-like man. Therefore you must needs play Pyramus.

BOTTOM: Well, I will undertake it. What beard were I best to play it in?

QUINCE: Why, what you will.

BOTTOM: I will discharge° it in either your° straw-color beard, your orange-tawny beard, your purple-in-grain° beard, or your French-crown-color° beard, your perfect yellow.

QUINCE: Some of your French crowns° have no hair at all, and then you will play barefac'd. But, masters, here are your parts. [*He distributes parts.*] And I am to entreat you, request you, and desire you, to con° them by tomorrow night; and meet me in the palace wood, a mile without the town, by moonlight. There will we rehearse; for if we meet in the city, we shall be dogg'd with company, and our devices° known. In the meantime I will draw a bill° of properties, such as our play wants. I pray you, fail me not.

BOTTOM: We will meet, and there we may rehearse most obscenely° and courageously. Take pains, be perfect;° adieu.

QUINCE: At the Duke's oak we meet.

BOTTOM: Enough. Hold, or cut bow-strings.°

Exeunt.

[ACT II]

[SCENE I: *A wood near Athens.*]

Enter a Fairy at one door, and Robin Goodfellow [*Puck*] *at another.*

PUCK: How now, spirit! Whither wander you?

FAIRY: Over hill, over dale,
Thorough° bush, thorough brier,
Over park, over pale,°
Thorough flood, thorough fire,
I do wander every where,
Swifter than the moon's sphere;
And I serve the Fairy Queen,
To dew her orbs° upon the green.

---

62. aggravate: Bottom's blunder for *diminish.* **63. roar you:** Roar for you. **66. proper:** Handsome. **70. discharge:** Perform. **your:** I.e., you know the kind I mean. **71. purple-in-grain:** Dyed a very deep red (from *grain*, the name applied to the dried insect used to make the dye). **French-crown-color:** Color of a French crown, a gold coin. **73. crowns:** Heads bald from syphilis, the "French disease." **75. con:** Learn by heart. **78. devices:** Plans. **79. bill:** List. **80. obscenely:** An unintentionally funny blunder, whatever Bottom meant to say. **81. perfect:** Letter-perfect in memorizing your parts. **83. Hold . . . bow-strings:** An archer's expression not definitely explained, but probably meaning here "keep your promises, or give up the play." ACT II, SCENE I: **3. Thorough:** Through. **4. pale:** Enclosure. **9. orbs:** Circles, i.e., fairy rings.

The cowslips tall her pensioners° be.
In their gold coats spots you see;
Those be rubies, fairy favors,°
In those freckles live their savors.°
I must go seek some dewdrops here
And hang a pearl in every cowslip's ear.
Farewell, thou lob° of spirits; I'll be gone.
Our Queen and all her elves come here anon.°

PUCK: The King doth keep his revels here tonight.
Take heed the Queen come not within his sight.
For Oberon is passing fell° and wrath,°
Because that she as her attendant hath
A lovely boy, stolen from an Indian king;
She never had so sweet a changeling.°
And jealous Oberon would have the child
Knight of his train, to trace° the forests wild.
But she perforce° withholds the loved boy,
Crowns him with flowers and makes him all her joy.
And now they never meet in grove or green,
By fountain° clear, or spangled starlight sheen,
But they do square,° that all their elves for fear
Creep into acorn-cups and hide them there.

FAIRY: Either I mistake your shape and making quite,
Or else you are that shrewd° and knavish sprite°
Call'd Robin Goodfellow. Are not you he
That frights the maidens of the villagery,
Skim milk, and sometimes labor in the quern,°
And bootless° make the breathless huswife churn,
And sometime make the drink to bear no barm,°
Mislead night-wanderers, laughing at their harm?
Those that Hobgoblin call you and sweet Puck,
You do their work, and they shall have good luck.
Are you not he?

PUCK: Thou speakest aright;
I am that merry wanderer of the night.
I jest to Oberon and make him smile
When I a fat and bean-fed horse beguile,
Neighing in likeness of a filly foal;
And sometime lurk I in a gossip's° bowl,
In very likeness of a roasted crab,°

---

10. pensioners: Retainers, members of the royal bodyguard. **12. favors:** Love tokens. **13. savors:** Sweet smells. **16. lob:** Country bumpkin. **17. anon:** At once. **20. passing fell:** Exceedingly angry. **wrath:** Wrathful. **23. changeling:** Child exchanged for another by the fairies. **25. trace:** Range through. **26. perforce:** Forcibly. **29. fountain:** Spring. **30. square:** Quarrel. **33. shrewd:** Mischievous. **sprite:** Spirit. **36. quern:** Handmill. **37. bootless:** In vain. **38. barm:** Yeast, head on the ale. **47. gossip's:** Old woman's. **48. crab:** Crab apple.

And when she drinks, against her lips I bob
And on her withered dewlap° pour the ale.
The wisest aunt,° telling the saddest° tale,
Sometime for three-foot stool mistaketh me;
Then slip I from her bum, down topples she,
And "tailor"° cries, and falls into a cough;
And then the whole quire° hold their hips and laugh,
And waxen° in their mirth and neeze° and swear
A merrier hour was never wasted there.
But, room, fairy! Here comes Oberon.

FAIRY: And here my mistress. Would that he were gone!

Enter [Oberon] the King of Fairies at one door, with his train; and [Titania] the Queen at another, with hers.

OBERON: Ill met by moonlight, proud Titania.

TITANIA: What, jealous Oberon? Fairies, skip hence.
I have forsworn his bed and company.

OBERON: Tarry, rash wanton.° Am not I thy lord?

TITANIA: Then I must be thy lady; but I know
When thou hast stolen away from fairy land,
And in the shape of Corin° sat all day,
Playing on pipes of corn° and versing love
To amorous Phillida.° Why art thou here,
Come from the farthest steep° of India,
But that, forsooth, the bouncing Amazon,
Your buskin'd° mistress and your warrior love,
To Theseus must be wedded, and you come
To give their bed joy and prosperity.

OBERON: How canst thou thus for shame, Titania,
Glance at my credit with Hippolyta,°
Knowing I know thy love to Theseus?
Didst not thou lead him through the glimmering night
From Perigenia,° whom he ravished?
And make him with fair Aegles° break his faith,
With Ariadne° and Antiopa?°

---

50. dewlap: Loose skin on neck. **51. aunt:** Old woman. **saddest:** Most serious. **54. tailor:** Possibly because she ends up sitting cross-legged on the floor, looking like a tailor. **55. quire:** Company. **56. waxen:** Increase. **neeze:** Sneeze. **63. wanton:** Headstrong creature. **66, 68. Corin, Phillida:** Conventional names of pastoral lovers. **67. corn:** Here, oat stalks. **69. steep:** Mountain range. **71. buskin'd:** Wearing half-boots called buskins. **75. Glance . . . Hippolyta:** Make insinuations about my favored relationship with Hippolyta. **78. Perigenia:** Perigouna, one of Theseus's conquests. (This and the following women are named in Thomas North's translation of Plutarch's *Life of Theseus.*) **79. Aegles:** Aegle, for whom Theseus deserted Ariadne according to some accounts. **80. Ariadne:** The daughter of Minos, King of Crete, who helped Theseus escape the labyrinth after killing the Minotaur; later she was abandoned by Theseus. **Antiopa:** Queen of the Amazons and wife of Theseus; elsewhere identified with Hippolyta, but here thought of as a separate woman.

TITANIA: These are the forgeries of jealousy;
And never, since the middle summer's spring,°
Met we on hill, in dale, forest, or mead,
By paved° fountain or by rushy° brook,
Or in° the beached margent° of the sea,
To dance our ringlets° to the whistling wind,
But with thy brawls thou hast disturb'd our sport.
Therefore the winds, piping to us in vain,
As in revenge, have suck'd up from the sea
Contagious° fogs; which falling in the land
Hath every pelting° river made so proud
That they have overborne their continents.°
The ox hath therefore stretch'd his yoke in vain,
The ploughman lost his sweat, and the green corn°
Hath rotted ere his youth attain'd a beard;
The fold° stands empty in the drowned field,
And crows are fatted with the murrion° flock;
The nine men's morris° is fill'd up with mud,
And the quaint mazes° in the wanton° green
For lack of tread are undistinguishable.
The human mortals want° their winter° here;
No night is now with hymn or carol bless'd.
Therefore° the moon, the governess of floods,
Pale in her anger, washes all the air,
That rheumatic diseases° do abound.
And thorough this distemperature° we see
The seasons alter: hoary-headed frosts
Fall in the fresh lap of the crimson rose,
And on old Hiems'° thin and icy crown
An odorous chaplet of sweet summer buds
Is, as in mockery, set. The spring, the summer,
The childing° autumn, angry winter, change
Their wonted liveries,° and the mazed° world,
By their increase,° now knows not which is which.

---

82. middle summer's spring: Beginning of midsummer. **84. paved:** With pebbled bottom. **rushy:** Bordered with rushes. **85. in:** On. **margent:** Edge, border. **86. ringlets:** Dances in a ring. (See *orbs* in line 9.) **90. Contagious:** Noxious. **91. pelting:** Paltry; or striking, moving forcefully. **92. continents:** Banks that contain them. **94. corn:** Grain of any kind. **96. fold:** Pen for sheep or cattle. **97. murrion:** Having died of the murrain, plague. **98. nine men's morris:** Portion of the village green marked out in a square for a game played with nine pebbles or pegs. **99. quaint mazes:** Intricate paths marked out on the village green to be followed rapidly on foot as a kind of contest. **wanton:** Luxuriant. **101. want:** Lack. **winter:** Regular winter season; or proper observances of winter, such as the *hymn or carol* in the next line (?). **103. Therefore:** I.e., as a result of our quarrel. **105. rheumatic diseases:** Colds, flu, and other respiratory infections. **106. distemperature:** Disturbance in nature. **109. Hiems:** The winter god. **112. childing:** Fruitful, pregnant. **113. wonted liveries:** Usual apparel. **mazed:** Bewildered. **114. their increase:** Their yield, what they produce.

And this same progeny of evils comes
From our debate,° from our dissension;
We are their parents and original.°

OBERON: Do you amend it then; it lies in you.
Why should Titania cross her Oberon?
I do but beg a little changeling boy,
To be my henchman.°

TITANIA: Set your heart at rest.
The fairy land buys not the child of me.
His mother was a vot'ress° of my order,
And, in the spiced Indian air, by night,
Full often hath she gossip'd by my side,
And sat with me on Neptune's yellow sands,
Marking th' embarked traders° on the flood,°
When we have laugh'd to see the sails conceive
And grow big-bellied with the wanton° wind;
Which she, with pretty and with swimming gait,
Following — her womb then rich with my young squire —
Would imitate, and sail upon the land
To fetch me trifles, and return again,
As from a voyage, rich with merchandise.
But she, being mortal, of that boy did die;
And for her sake do I rear up her boy,
And for her sake I will not part with him.

OBERON: How long within this wood intend you stay?

TITANIA: Perchance till after Theseus' wedding-day.
If you will patiently dance in our round°
And see our moonlight revels, go with us;
If not, shun me, and I will spare° your haunts.

OBERON: Give me that boy, and I will go with thee.

TITANIA: Not for thy fairy kingdom. Fairies, away!
We shall chide downright, if I longer stay.

Exeunt [Titania with her train].

OBERON: Well, go thy way. Thou shalt not from° this grove
Till I torment thee for this injury.
My gentle Puck, come hither. Thou remember'st
Since° once I sat upon a promontory,
And heard a mermaid on a dolphin's back
Uttering such dulcet and harmonious breath°
That the rude sea grew civil at her song
And certain stars shot madly from their spheres,
To hear the sea-maid's music.

---

116. debate: Quarrel. **117. original:** Origin. **121. henchman:** Attendant, page. **123. vot'ress:** Female votary; devotee, worshiper. **127. traders:** Trading vessels. **flood:** Flood tide. **129. wanton:** Sportive. **140. round:** Circular dance. **142. spare:** Shun. **146. from:** Go from. **149. Since:** When. **151. breath:** Voice, song.

PUCK: I remember.
OBERON: That very time I saw, but thou couldst not,
Flying between the cold moon and the earth,
Cupid all° arm'd. A certain aim he took
At a fair vestal° throned by the west,
And loos'd his love-shaft smartly from his bow,
As° it should pierce a hundred thousand hearts;
But I might° see young Cupid's fiery shaft
Quench'd in the chaste beams of the wat'ry moon,
And the imperial vot'ress passed on,
In maiden meditation, fancy-free.°
Yet mark'd I where the bolt of Cupid fell:
It fell upon a little western flower,
Before milk-white, now purple with love's wound,
And maidens call it love-in-idleness.°
Fetch me that flow'r; the herb I showed thee once.
The juice of it on sleeping eyelids laid
Will make or man or° woman madly dote
Upon the next live creature that it sees.
Fetch me this herb, and be thou here again
Ere the leviathan° can swim a league.
PUCK: I'll put a girdle round about the earth
In forty° minutes. [*Exit.*]
OBERON: Having once this juice,
I'll watch Titania when she is asleep,
And drop the liquor of it in her eyes.
The next thing then she waking looks upon,
Be it on lion, bear, or wolf, or bull,
On meddling monkey, or on busy ape,
She shall pursue it with the soul of love.
And ere I take this charm from off her sight,
As I can take it with another herb,
I'll make her render up her page to me.
But who comes here? I am invisible,
And I will overhear their conference.

Enter Demetrius, Helena following him.

DEMETRIUS: I love thee not, therefore pursue me not.
Where is Lysander and fair Hermia?
The one I'll slay, the other slayeth me.
Thou told'st me they were stol'n unto this wood;

---

157. all: Fully. **158. vestal:** Vestal virgin (contains a complimentary allusion to Queen Elizabeth as a votaress of Diana and probably refers to an actual entertainment in her honor at Elvetham in 1591). **160. As:** As if. **161. might:** Could. **164. fancy-free:** Free of love's spell. **168. love-in-idleness:** Pansy, heartsease. **171. or . . . or:** Either . . . or. **174. leviathan:** Sea monster, whale. **176. forty:** Used indefinitely.

And here am I, and wode° within this wood,
Because I cannot meet my Hermia.
Hence, get thee gone, and follow me no more.
HELENA: You draw me, you hard-hearted adamant;°
But yet you draw not iron, for my heart
Is true as steel. Leave° you your power to draw,
And I shall have no power to follow you.
DEMETRIUS: Do I entice you? Do I speak you fair?°
Or, rather, do I not in plainest truth
Tell you I do not nor I cannot love you?
HELENA: And even for that do I love you the more.
I am your spaniel; and, Demetrius,
The more you beat me, I will fawn on you.
Use me but as your spaniel, spurn me, strike me,
Neglect me, lose me; only give me leave,
Unworthy as I am, to follow you.
What worser place can I beg in your love—
And yet a place of high respect with me—
Than to be used as you use your dog?
DEMETRIUS: Tempt not too much the hatred of my spirit,
For I am sick when I do look on thee.
HELENA: And I am sick when I look not on you.
DEMETRIUS: You do impeach° your modesty too much
To leave the city and commit yourself
Into the hands of one that loves you not,
To trust the opportunity of night
And the ill counsel of a desert° place
With the rich worth of your virginity.
HELENA: Your virtue° is my privilege.° For that°
It is not night when I do see your face,
Therefore I think I am not in the night;
Nor doth this wood lack worlds of company,
For you in my respect° are all the world.
Then how can it be said I am alone,
When all the world is here to look on me?
DEMETRIUS: I'll run from thee and hide me in the brakes,°
And leave thee to the mercy of wild beasts.
HELENA: The wildest hath not such a heart as you.
Run when you will, the story shall be chang'd:

192. wode: Mad (pronounced "wood" and often spelled so). **195. adamant:** Lodestone, magnet (with pun on *hard-hearted,* since adamant was also thought to be the hardest of all stones and was confused with the diamond). **197. Leave:** Give up. **199. fair:** Courteously. **214. impeach:** Call into question. **218. desert:** Deserted. **220. virtue:** Goodness or power to attract. **privilege:** Safeguard, warrant. **For that:** Because. **224. in my respect:** As far as I am concerned. **227. brakes:** Thickets.

Apollo flies and Daphne holds the chase,°
The dove pursues the griffin,° the mild hind°
Makes speed to catch the tiger—bootless° speed,
When cowardice pursues and valor flies.

DEMETRIUS: I will not stay° thy questions.° Let me go!
Or if thou follow me, do not believe
But I shall do thee mischief in the wood.

HELENA: Ay, in the temple, in the town, the field,
You do me mischief. Fie, Demetrius!
Your wrongs do set a scandal on my sex.
We cannot fight for love, as men may do;
We should be woo'd and were not made to woo.
[*Exit Demetrius.*]
I'll follow thee and make a heaven of hell,
To die upon° the hand I love so well. [*Exit.*]

OBERON: Fare thee well, nymph. Ere he do leave this grove,
Thou shalt fly him and he shall seek thy love.

Enter Puck.

Hast thou the flower there? Welcome, wanderer.

PUCK: Ay, there it is. [*Offers the flower.*]

OBERON: I pray thee, give it me.
I know a bank where the wild thyme blows,°
Where oxlips° and the nodding violet grows,
Quite over-canopied with luscious woodbine,°
With sweet musk-roses° and with eglantine.°
There sleeps Titania sometime of the night
Lull'd in these flowers with dances and delight;
And there the snake throws° her enamel'd skin,
Weed° wide enough to wrap a fairy in.
And with the juice of this I'll streak° her eyes,
And make her full of hateful fantasies.
Take thou some of it, and seek through this grove.
[*Gives some love-juice.*]
A sweet Athenian lady is in love
With a disdainful youth. Anoint his eyes,
But do it when the next thing he espies
May be the lady. Thou shalt know the man

231. Apollo . . . chase: In the ancient myth, Daphne fled from Apollo and was saved from rape by being transformed into a laurel tree; here it is the female who *holds the chase,* or pursues, instead of the male. **232. griffin:** A fabulous monster with the head of an eagle and the body of a lion. **hind:** Female deer. **233. bootless:** Fruitless. **235. stay:** Wait for. **questions:** Talk or argument. **244. upon:** By. **249. blows:** Blooms. **250. oxlips:** Flowers resembling cow-slip and primrose. **251. woodbine:** Honeysuckle. **252. musk-roses:** A kind of large, sweet-scented rose. **eglantine:** Sweetbriar, another kind of rose. **255. throws:** Sloughs off, sheds. **256. Weed:** Garment. **257. streak:** Anoint, touch gently.

By the Athenian garments he hath on.
Effect it with some care, that he may prove
More fond on° her than she upon her love;
And look thou meet me ere the first cock crow.

PUCK: Fear not, my lord, your servant shall do so.

Exeunt.

[SCENE II: *The wood.*]

Enter Titania, Queen of Fairies, with her train.

TITANIA: Come, now a roundel° and a fairy song;
Then, for the third part of a minute, hence—
Some to kill cankers° in the musk-rose buds,
Some war with rere-mice° for their leathern wings,
To make my small elves coats, and some keep back
The clamorous owl, that nightly hoots and wonders
At our quaint° spirits. Sing me now asleep.
Then to your offices and let me rest.

Fairies sing.

FIRST FAIRY: You spotted snakes with double° tongue,
Thorny hedgehogs, be not seen;
Newts° and blindworms, do no wrong,
Come not near our fairy queen.
[*Chorus.*] Philomel,° with melody
Sing in our sweet lullaby;
Lulla, lulla, lullaby, lulla, lulla, lullaby.
Never harm,
Nor spell nor charm,
Come our lovely lady nigh.
So, good night, with lullaby.

FIRST FAIRY: Weaving spiders, come not here;
Hence, you long-legg'd spinners, hence!
Beetles black, approach not near;
Worm nor snail, do no offense.
[*Chorus.*] Philomel, with melody, etc.

SECOND FAIRY: Hence, away! Now all is well.
One aloof stand sentinel.

[*Exeunt Fairies. Titania sleeps.*]

Enter Oberon [*and squeezes the flower on Titania's eyelids*].

OBERON: What thou seest when thou dost wake,
Do it for thy true-love take;

266. fond on: Doting on. ACT II, SCENE II. **1. roundel:** Dance in a ring. **3. cankers:** Cankerworms. **4. rere-mice:** Bats. **7. quaint:** Dainty. **9. double:** Forked. **11. Newts:** water lizards (considered poisonous, as were blindworms—small snakes with tiny eyes—and spiders). **13. Philomel:** The nightingale. (Philomela, daughter of King Pandion, was transformed into a nightingale, according to Ovid's *Metamorphoses*, after she had been raped by her sister Procne's husband, Tereus.)

Love and languish for his sake.
Be it ounce,° or cat, or bear,
Pard,° or boar with bristled hair,
In thy eye that shall appear
When thou wak'st, it is thy dear
Wake when some vile thing is near. [*Exit.*]

Enter Lysander and Hermia.

LYSANDER: Fair love, you faint with wand'ring in the wood;
And to speak troth,° I have forgot our way.
We'll rest us, Hermia, if you think it good,
And tarry for the comfort of the day.
HERMIA: Be 't so, Lysander. Find you out a bed,
For I upon this bank will rest my head.
LYSANDER: One turf shall serve as pillow for us both,
One heart, one bed, two bosoms, and one troth.°
HERMIA: Nay, good Lysander; for my sake, my dear,
Lie further off yet, do not lie so near.
LYSANDER: O, take the sense, sweet, of my innocence!°
Love takes the meaning in love's conference.°
I mean, that my heart unto yours is knit
So that but one heart we can make of it;
Two bosoms interchained with an oath—
So then two bosoms and a single troth.
Then by your side no bed-room me deny,
For lying so, Hermia, I do not lie.°
HERMIA: Lysander riddles very prettily.
Now much beshrew° my manners and my pride
If Hermia meant to say Lysander lied.
But, gentle friend, for love and courtesy
Lie further off, in human° modesty;
Such separation as may well be said
Becomes a virtuous bachelor and a maid,
So far be distant; and, good night, sweet friend.
Thy love ne'er alter till thy sweet life end!
LYSANDER: Amen, amen, to that fair prayer, say I,
And then end life when I end loyalty!
Here is my bed. Sleep give thee all his rest!
HERMIA: With half that wish the wisher's eyes be press'd!°
[*They sleep, separated by a short distance.*]

30. ounce: Lynx. **31. Pard:** Leopard. **36. troth:** Truth. **42. troth:** Faith, troth-plight. **45. take . . . innocence:** Interpret my intention as innocent. **46. Love . . . conference:** When lovers confer, love teaches each lover to interpret the other's meaning lovingly. **52. lie:** Tell a falsehood (with a riddling pun on *lie*, recline). **54. beshrew:** Curse (but mildly meant). **57. human:** Courteous. **65. With . . . press'd:** May we share your wish, so that your eyes too are *press'd*, closed, in sleep.

Enter Puck.

PUCK: Through the forest have I gone,
But Athenian found I none
On whose eyes I might approve°
This flower's force in stirring love.
Night and silence.—Who is here?
Weeds of Athens he doth wear.
This is he, my master said,
Despised the Athenian maid;
And here the maiden, sleeping sound,
On the dank and dirty ground.
Pretty soul! She durst not lie
Near this lack-love, this kill-courtesy.
Churl, upon thy eyes I throw
All the power this charm doth owe.°
[*Applies the love-juice.*]
When thou wak'st, let love forbid
Sleep his seat on thy eyelid.
So awake when I am gone,
For I must now to Oberon. *Exit.*

Enter Demetrius and Helena, running.

HELENA: Stay, though thou kill me, sweet Demetrius.
DEMETRIUS: I charge thee, hence, and do not haunt me thus.
HELENA: O, wilt thou darkling° leave me? Do not so.
DEMETRIUS: Stay, on thy peril!° I alone will go.
[*Exit.*]
HELENA: O, I am out of breath in this fond° chase!
The more my prayer, the lesser is my grace.°
Happy is Hermia, wheresoe'er she lies,°
For she hath blessed and attractive eyes.
How came her eyes so bright? Not with salt tears;
If so, my eyes are oft'ner wash'd than hers.
No, no, I am as ugly as a bear;
For beasts that meet me run away for fear.
Therefore no marvel though Demetrius
Do, as a monster, fly my presence thus.
What wicked and dissembling glass of mine
Made me compare with Hermia's sphery eyne?°
But who is here? Lysander, on the ground?
Dead, or asleep? I see no blood, no wound.
Lysander, if you live, good sir, awake.

---

68. approve: Test. **79. owe:** Own. **86. darkling:** In the dark. **87. on thy peril:** On pain of danger to you if you don't obey me and stay. **88. fond:** Doting. **89. my grace:** The favor I obtain. **90. lies:** Dwells. **99. sphery eyne:** Eyes as bright as stars in their spheres.

LYSANDER [*awaking*]: And run through fire I will for thy sweet sake.
Transparent° Helena! Nature shows art,
That through thy bosom makes me see thy heart.
Where is Demetrius? O, how fit a word
Is that vile name to perish on my sword!

HELENA: Do not say so, Lysander, say not so.
What though he love your Hermia? Lord, what though?
Yet Hermia still loves you. Then be content.

LYSANDER: Content with Hermia? No! I do repent
The tedious minutes I with her have spent.
Not Hermia but Helena I love.
Who will not change a raven for a dove?
The will of man is by his reason sway'd,
And reason says you are the worthier maid.
Things growing are not ripe until their season;
So I, being young, till now ripe not° to reason.
And touching° now the point° of human skill,°
Reason becomes the marshal to my will
And leads me to your eyes, where I o'erlook°
Love's stories written in love's richest book.

HELENA: Wherefore was I to this keen mockery born?
When at your hands did I deserve this scorn?
Is 't not enough, is 't not enough, young man,
That I did never, no, nor never can,
Deserve a sweet look from Demetrius' eye,
But you must flout my insufficiency?
Good troth,° you do me wrong, good sooth,° you do,
In such disdainful manner me to woo.
But fare you well. Perforce I must confess
I thought you lord of° more true gentleness.
O, that a lady, of° one man refus'd,
Should of another therefore be abus'd!° *Exit.*

LYSANDER: She sees not Hermia. Hermia, sleep thou there,
And never mayst thou come Lysander near!
For as a surfeit of the sweetest things
The deepest loathing to the stomach brings,
Or as the heresies that men do leave
Are hated most of those they did deceive,
So thou, my surfeit and my heresy,
Of all be hated, but the most of me!
And, all my powers, address your love and might
To honor Helen and to be her knight! *Exit.*

---

104. Transparent: (1) Radiant; (2) able to be seen through. **118. ripe not:** (Am) not ripened. **119. touching:** Reaching. **point:** Summit. **skill:** Judgment. **121. o'erlook:** Read. **129. Good troth, good sooth:** Indeed, truly. **132. lord of:** Possessor of. **gentleness:** Courtesy. **133. of:** By. **134. abus'd:** Ill treated.

HERMIA [*awaking*]: Help me, Lysander, help me! Do thy best
To pluck this crawling serpent from my breast!
Ay me, for pity! What a dream was here!
Lysander, look how I do quake with fear.
Methought a serpent eat° my heart away,
And you sat smiling at his cruel prey.°
Lysander! What, remov'd? Lysander! Lord!
What, out of hearing? Gone? No sound, no word?
Alack, where are you? Speak, an if you hear,
Speak, of all loves!° I swoon almost with fear.
No? Then I well perceive you are not nigh.
Either death, or you, I'll find immediately.

Exit. [*Manet*° *Titania lying asleep.*]

[ACT III]

[SCENE I: *Scene continues.*]

Enter the Clowns [*Quince, Snug, Bottom, Flute, Snout, and Starveling*].

BOTTOM: Are we all met?

QUINCE: Pat, pat; and here's a marvailes° convenient place for our rehearsal. This green plot shall be our stage, this hawthorn brake° our tiring-house,° and we will do it in action as we will do it before the Duke.

BOTTOM: Peter Quince?

QUINCE: What sayest thou, bully° Bottom?

BOTTOM: There are things in this comedy of Pyramus and Thisby that will never please. First, Pyramus must draw a sword to kill himself, which the ladies cannot abide. How answer you that?

SNOUT: By 'r lakin,° a parlous° fear.

STARVELING: I believe we must leave the killing out, when all is done.°

BOTTOM: Not a whit. I have a device to make all well. Write me° a prologue; and let the prologue seem to say, we will do no harm with our swords and that Pyramus is not kill'd indeed; and, for the more better assurance, tell them that I Pyramus am not Pyramus, but Bottom the weaver. This will put them out of fear.

QUINCE: Well, we will have such a prologue, and it shall be written in eight and six.°

BOTTOM: No, make it two more; let it be written in eight and eight.

SNOUT: Will not the ladies be afeard of the lion?

STARVELING: I fear it, I promise you.

---

149. eat: Ate (pronounced "et"). **150. prey:** Act of preying. **154. of all loves:** For all love's sake. **156. s.d. Manet:** Latin for "she remains." ACT III, SCENE I. **2. marvailes:** Marvelous. **3. brake:** Thicket. **tiring-house:** Attiring area, hence backstage. **6. bully:** Worthy, jolly, fine fellow. **10. By 'r lakin:** By our ladykin, the Virgin Mary. **parlous:** Perilous. **11. when all is done:** When all is said and done. **12. Write me:** Write at my suggestion. **17–18. eight and six:** Alternate lines of eight and six syllables, a common ballad measure.

BOTTOM: Masters, you ought to consider with yourselves, to bring in—God shield us!—a lion among ladies,° is a most dreadful thing. For there is not a more fearful° wild-fowl than your lion living; and we ought to look to 't.

SNOUT: Therefore another prologue must tell he is not a lion.

BOTTOM: Nay, you must name his name, and half his face must be seen through the lion's neck, and he himself must speak through, saying thus, or to the same defect:° "Ladies"—or "Fair ladies—I would wish you"—or "I would request you"—or "I would entreat you—not to fear, not to tremble; my life for yours.° If you think I come hither as a lion, it were pity of my life.° No, I am no such thing, I am a man as other men are." And there indeed let him name his name, and tell them plainly he is Snug the joiner.

QUINCE: Well, it shall be so. But there is two hard things: that is, to bring the moonlight into a chamber; for, you know, Pyramus and Thisby meet by moonlight.

SNOUT: Doth the moon shine that night we play our play?

BOTTOM: A calendar, a calendar! Look in the almanac. Find out moonshine, find out moonshine.

[*They consult an almanac.*]

QUINCE: Yes, it doth shine that night.

BOTTOM: Why then may you leave a casement of the great chamber window, where we play, open, and the moon may shine in at the casement.

QUINCE: Ay; or else one must come in with a bush of thorns° and a lantern, and say he comes to disfigure,° or to present,° the person of Moonshine. Then there is another thing: we must have a wall in the great chamber; for Pyramus and Thisby, says the story, did talk through the chink of a wall.

SNOUT: You can never bring in a wall. What say you, Bottom?

BOTTOM: Some man or other must present Wall. And let him have some plaster, or some loam, or some rough-cast° about him, to signify wall; and let him hold his fingers thus, and through that cranny shall Pyramus and Thisby whisper.

QUINCE: If that may be, then all is well. Come, sit down, every mother's son, and rehearse your parts. Pyramus, you begin. When you have spoken your speech, enter into that brake, and so every one according to his cue.

Enter Robin [*Puck*].

---

23. lion among ladies: A contemporary pamphlet tells how at the christening in 1594 of Prince Henry, eldest son of King James VI of Scotland, later James I of England, a "blackmoor" instead of a lion drew the triumphal chariot, since the lion's presence might have "brought some fear to the nearest." **24. fearful:** Fear-inspiring. **29. defect:** Bottom's blunder for *effect*. **31. my life for yours:** I pledge my life to make your lives safe. **31–32. it were . . . life:** My life would be endangered. **44. bush of thorns:** Bundle of thornbush faggots (part of the accoutrements of the man in the moon, according to the popular notions of the time, along with his lantern and his dog). **45. disfigure:** Quince's blunder for *prefigure*. **present:** Represent. **50. rough-cast:** A mixture of lime and gravel used to plaster the outside of buildings.

PUCK: What hempen° home-spuns have we swagg'ring here,
So near the cradle of the Fairy Queen?
What, a play toward?° I'll be an auditor;°
An actor too perhaps, if I see cause.

QUINCE: Speak, Pyramus. Thisby, stand forth.

BOTTOM: "Thisby, the flowers of odious savors sweet,"—

QUINCE: Odors, odors.

BOTTOM: —"Odors savors sweet;
So hath thy breath, my dearest Thisby dear.
But hark, a voice! Stay thou but here awhile,
And by and by I will to thee appear." *Exit.*

PUCK: A stranger Pyramus than e'er played here.°

[*Exit.*]

FLUTE: Must I speak now?

QUINCE: Ay, marry, must you; for you must understand he goes but to see a noise that he heard, and is to come again.

FLUTE: "Most radiant Pyramus, most lily-white of hue,
Of color like the red rose on triumphant brier,
Most brisky juvenal° and eke° most lovely Jew,°
As true as truest horse that yet would never tire.
I'll meet thee, Pyramus, at Ninny's tomb."

QUINCE: "Ninus'° tomb," man. Why, you must not speak that yet. That you answer to Pyramus. You speak all your part at once, cues and all. Pyramus enter. Your cue is past; it is, "never tire."

FLUTE: O—"As true as truest horse, that yet would never tire."

[*Enter Puck, and Bottom as Pyramus with the ass head.*]°

BOTTOM: "If I were fair,° Thisby, I were° only thine."

QUINCE: O monstrous! O strange! We are haunted.
Pray, masters! Fly, masters! Help!

[*Exeunt Quince, Snug, Flute, Snout, and Starveling.*]

PUCK: I'll follow you, I'll lead you about a round,°
Through bog, through bush, through brake, through brier.
Sometime a horse I'll be, sometime a hound,
A hog, a headless bear, sometime a fire,°
And neigh, and bark, and grunt, and roar, and burn,
Like horse, hound, hog, bear, fire, at every turn.

Exit.

BOTTOM: Why do they run away? This is a knavery of them to make me afeard.

---

56. hempen: Made of hemp, a rough fiber. **58. toward:** About to take place. **auditor:** One who listens, i.e., part of the audience. **67. here:** In this theater (?). **73. brisky juvenal:** Brisk youth. **eke:** Also. **Jew:** Probably an absurd repetition of the first syllable of *juvenal*. **76. Ninus:** Mythical founder of Nineveh (whose wife, Semiramis, was supposed to have built the walls of Babylon where the story of Pyramus and Thisby takes place). **79. s.d. with the ass head:** This stage direction, taken from the Folio, presumably refers to a standard stage property. **80. fair:** Handsome. **were:** Would be. **83. about a round:** Roundabout. **86. fire:** Will-o'-the-wisp.

Enter Snout.

SNOUT: O Bottom, thou art chang'd! What do I see on thee?
BOTTOM: What do you see? You see an ass-head of your own, do you?
[*Exit Snout.*]

Enter Quince.

QUINCE: Bless thee, Bottom, bless thee! Thou art translated.° *Exit.*

BOTTOM: I see their knavery. This is to make an ass of me, to fright me, if they could. But I will not stir from this place, do what they can. I will walk up and down here, and I will sing, that they shall hear I am not afraid.
[*Sings.*]

The woosel cock° so black of hue,
With orange-tawny bill,
The throstle° with his note so true,
The wren with little quill° —

TITANIA [*awaking*]: What angel wakes me from my flow'ry bed?

BOTTOM [*sings*]: The finch, the sparrow, and the lark,
The plain-song° cuckoo grey,
Whose note full many a man doth mark,
And dares not answer nay° —
For, indeed, who would set his wit to so foolish a bird? Who would give a bird the lie,° though he cry "cuckoo" never so?°

TITANIA: I pray thee, gentle mortal, sing again.
Mine ear is much enamored of thy note;
So is mine eye enthralled to thy shape;
And thy fair virtue's force° perforce doth move me
On the first view to say, to swear, I love thee.

BOTTOM: Methinks, mistress, you should have little reason for that. And yet, to say the truth, reason and love keep little company together nowadays. The more the pity that some honest neighbors will not make them friends. Nay, I can gleek° upon occasion.

TITANIA: Thou art as wise as thou art beautiful.

BOTTOM: Not so, neither. But if I had wit enough to get out of this wood, I have enough to serve mine own turn.°

TITANIA: Out of this wood do not desire to go.
Thou shalt remain here, whether thou wilt or no.
I am a spirit of no common rate.°
The summer still° doth tend upon my state;°
And I do love thee. Therefore, go with me.
I'll give thee fairies to attend on thee,

---

92. translated: Transformed. **96. woosel cock:** Male ousel or ouzel, blackbird. **98. throstle:** Song thrush. **99. quill:** Literally, a reed pipe; hence, the bird's piping song. **102. plain-song:** Singing a melody without variations. **104. dares . . . nay:** Cannot deny that he is a cuckold. **105–106. give . . . lie:** Call the bird a liar. **106. never so:** Ever so much. **110. thy . . . force:** The power of your beauty. **115. gleek:** Scoff, jest. **118. serve . . . turn:** Answer my purpose. **121. rate:** Rank, value. **122. still:** Ever always. **doth . . . state:** Waits upon me as part of my royal retinue.

And they shall fetch thee jewels from the deep,
And sing while thou on pressed flowers dost sleep.
And I will purge thy mortal grossness so
That thou shalt like an airy spirit go.
Peaseblossom, Cobweb, Moth,° and Mustardseed!

Enter four Fairies [Peaseblossom, Cobweb, Moth, and Mustardseed].

PEASEBLOSSOM: Ready.
COBWEB: And I.
MOTH: And I
MUSTARDSEED: And I.
ALL: Where shall we go?
TITANIA: Be kind and courteous to this gentleman.
Hop in his walks and gambol in his eyes;
Feed him with apricocks and dewberries,
With purple grapes, green figs, and mulberries;
The honey-bags steal from the humble-bees,
And for night-tapers crop their waxen thighs
And light them at the fiery glow-worm's eyes,
To have my love to bed and to arise;
And pluck the wings from painted butterflies
To fan the moonbeams from his sleeping eyes.
Nod to him, elves, and do him courtesies.
PEASEBLOSSOM: Hail, mortal!
COBWEB: Hail!
MOTH: Hail!
MUSTARDSEED: Hail!

BOTTOM: I cry your worship's mercy, heartily. I beseech your worship's name.

COBWEB: Cobweb.

BOTTOM: I shall desire you of more acquaintance, good Master Cobweb. If I cut my finger, I shall make bold with you.° Your name, honest gentleman?

PEASEBLOSSOM: Peaseblossom.

BOTTOM: I pray you, commend me to Mistress Squash,° your mother, and to Master Peascod,° your father. Good Master Peaseblossom, I shall desire you of more acquaintance too. Your name, I beseech you, sir?

MUSTARDSEED: Mustardseed.

BOTTOM: Good Master Mustardseed, I know your patience° well. That same cowardly, giant-like ox-beef hath devour'd many a gentleman of your house. I promise you your kindred hath made my eyes water ere now. I desire you of more acquaintance, good Master Mustardseed.

TITANIA: Come wait upon him; lead him to my bower.
The moon methinks looks with a wat'ry eye;
And when she weeps,° weeps every little flower,

129. Moth: Mote, speck. (The two words *moth* and *mote* were pronounced alike.) **149–150. If . . . you:** Cobwebs were used to stanch bleeding. **152. Squash:** Unripe pea pod. **153. Peascod:** Ripe pea pod. **156. your patience:** What you have endured. **162. she weeps:** I.e., she causes dew.

Lamenting some enforced° chastity.
Tie up my lover's tongue, bring him silently.

Exeunt.

[SCENE II: *The wood.*]

Enter [*Oberon,*] *King of Fairies.*

OBERON: I wonder if Titania be awak'd;
Then, what it was that next came in her eye,
Which she must dote on in extremity.

[*Enter*] *Robin Goodfellow* [*Puck*].

Here comes my messenger. How now, mad spirit?
What night-rule° now about this haunted° grove?
PUCK: My mistress with a monster is in love.
Near to her close° and consecrated bower,
While she was in her dull° and sleeping hour,
A crew of patches,° rude mechanicals,°
That work for bread upon Athenian stalls,
Were met together to rehearse a play
Intended for great Theseus' nuptial day.
The shallowest thick-skin of that barren sort,°
Who Pyramus presented,° in their sport
Forsook his scene° and ent'red in a brake.
When I did him at this advantage take,
An ass's nole° I fixed on his head.
Anon his Thisby must be answered,
And forth my mimic° comes. When they him spy,
As wild geese that the creeping fowler eye,
Or russet-pated choughs,° many in sort,°
Rising and cawing at the gun's report,
Sever° themselves and madly sweep the sky,
So, at his sight, away his fellows fly;
And, at our stamp, here o'er and o'er one falls;
He murder cries and help from Athens calls.
Their sense thus weak, lost with their fears thus strong,
Made senseless things begin to do them wrong,
For briers and thorns at their apparel snatch;
Some, sleeves—some, hats; from yielders all things catch.
I led them on in this distracted fear
And left sweet Pyramus translated there,

---

163. enforced: Forced, violated; or, possibly, constrained (since Titania at this moment is hardly concerned about chastity). ACT III, SCENE II. **5. night-rule:** Diversion for the night. **haunted:** Much frequented. **7. close:** Secret, private. **8. dull:** Drowsy. **9. patches:** Clowns, fools. **rude mechanicals:** Ignorant artisans. **13. barren sort:** Stupid company or crew. **14. presented:** Acted. **15. scene:** Playing area. **17. nole:** Noddle, head. **19. mimic:** Burlesque actor. **21. russet-pated choughs:** Gray-headed jackdaws. **in sort:** In a flock. **23. Sever:** Scatter.

When in that moment, so it came to pass,
Titania wak'd and straightway lov'd an ass.
OBERON: This falls out better than I could devise.
But hast thou yet latch'd° the Athenian's eyes
With the love-juice, as I did bid thee do?
PUCK: I took him sleeping—that is finish'd too—
And the Athenian woman by his side,
That, when he wak'd, of force° she must be ey'd.

Enter Demetrius and Hermia.

OBERON: Stand close. This is the same Athenian.
PUCK: This is the woman, but not this the man.
[*They stand aside.*]
DEMETRIUS: O, why rebuke you him that loves you so?
Lay breath so bitter on your bitter foe.
HERMIA: Now I but chide; but I should use thee worse,
For thou, I fear, hast given me cause to curse.
If thou hast slain Lysander in his sleep,
Being o'er shoes in blood, plunge in the deep,
And kill me too.
The sun was not so true unto the day
As he to me. Would he have stolen away
From sleeping Hermia? I'll believe as soon
This whole° earth may be bor'd and that the moon
May through the center creep and so displease
Her brother's° noontide with th' Antipodes.°
It cannot be but thou has murd'red him;
So should a murderer look, so dead,° so grim.
DEMETRIUS: So should the murdered look, and so should I,
Pierc'd through the heart with your stern cruelty.
Yet you, the murderer, look as bright, as clear,
As yonder Venus in her glimmering sphere.
HERMIA: What's this to my Lysander? Where is he?
Ah, good Demetrius, wilt thou give him me?
DEMETRIUS: I had rather give his carcass to my hounds.
HERMIA: Out dog! Out cur! Thou driv'st me past the bounds
Of maiden's patience. Hast thou slain him, then?
Henceforth be never numb'red among men!
O, once tell true, tell true, even for my sake!
Durst thou have look'd upon him being awake,
And hast thou kill'd him sleeping? O brave touch!°
Could not a worm,° an adder, do so much?

---

36. latch'd: Moistened, anointed. **40. of force:** Perforce. **53. whole:** Solid. **55. Her brother's:** I.e., the sun's. **th' Antipodes:** The people on the opposite side of the earth. **57. dead:** Deadly, or deathly pale. **70. brave touch:** Noble exploit (said ironically). **71. worm:** Serpent.

An adder did it, for with doubler tongue
Than thine, thou serpent, never adder stung.
DEMETRIUS: You spend your passion° on a mispris'd mood.°
I am not guilty of Lysander's blood,
Nor is he dead, for aught that I can tell.
HERMIA: I pray thee, tell me then that he is well.
DEMETRIUS: An if I could, what should I get therefore?
HERMIA: A privilege never to see me more.
And from thy hated presence part I so.
See me no more, whether he be dead or no.

Exit.

DEMETRIUS: There is no following her in this fierce vein.
Here therefore for a while I will remain.
So sorrow's heaviness doth heavier° grow
For debt that bankrupt° sleep doth sorrow owe;
Which now in some slight measure it will pay,
If for his tender here I make some stay.°

Lie down [and sleep].

OBERON: What hast thou done? Thou hast mistaken quite
And laid the love-juice on some true-love's sight.
Of thy misprision° must perforce ensue
Some true love turn'd and not a false turn'd true.
PUCK: Then fate o'er-rules, that, one man holding troth,°
A million fail, confounding oath on oath.°
OBERON: About the wood go swifter than the wind,
And Helena of Athens look thou find.
All fancy-sick° she is and pale of cheer°
With sighs of love, that cost the fresh blood° dear.
By some illusion see thou bring her here.
I'll charm his eyes against she do appear.°
PUCK: I go, I go; look how I go
Swifter than arrow from the Tartar's bow.°

[Exit.]

OBERON: Flower of this purple dye,
Hit with Cupid's archery.
Sink in angle of his eye.

[Applies love-juice to Demetrius' eyes.]

---

74. passion: Violent feelings. **mispris'd mood:** Anger based on misconception. **84. heavier:** (1) Harder to bear, (2) drowsier. **85. bankrupt:** Demetrius is saying that his sleepiness adds to the weariness caused by sorrow. **86–87. Which . . . stay:** To a small extent I will be able to "pay back" and hence find some relief from sorrow, if I pause here a while (*make some stay*) while sleep "tenders" or offers itself by way of paying the debt owed to sorrow. **90. misprision:** Mistake. **92. troth:** Faith. **93. confounding . . . oath:** Invalidating one oath with another. **96. fancy-sick:** Lovesick. **cheer:** Face. **97. sighs . . . blood:** An allusion to the physiological theory that each sigh costs the heart a drop of blood. **99. against . . . appear:** In anticipation of her coming. **101. Tartar's bow:** Tartars were famed for their skill with the bow.

When his love he doth espy,
Let her shine as gloriously
As the Venus of the sky.
When thou wak'st, if she be by,
Beg of her for remedy.

Enter Puck.

PUCK: Captain of our fairy band,
Helena is here at hand,
And the youth, mistook by me,
Pleading for a lover's fee.°
Shall we their fond pageant° see?
Lord, what fools these mortals be!

OBERON: Stand aside. The noise they make
Will cause Demetrius to awake.

PUCK: Then will two at once woo one;
That must needs be sport alone;°
And those things do best please me
That befall prepost'rously.°

[*They stand aside.*]

Enter Lysander and Helena.

LYSANDER: Why should you think that I should woo in scorn?
Scorn and derision never come in tears.
Look when° I vow, I weep; and vows so born,
In their nativity all truth appears.°
How can these things in me seem scorn to you,
Bearing the badge° of faith, to prove them true?

HELENA: You do advance° your cunning more and more.
When truth kills truth,° O devilish-holy fray!
These vows are Hermia's. Will you give her o'er?
Weigh oath with oath, and you will nothing weigh.
Your vows to her and me, put in two scales
Will even weigh, and both as light as tales.°

LYSANDER: I had no judgment when to her I swore.

HELENA: Nor none, in my mind, now you give her o'er.

LYSANDER: Demetrius loves her, and he loves not you.

DEMETRIUS [*awaking*]: O Helen, goddess, nymph, perfect, divine!
To what, my love, shall I compare thine eyne?
Crystal is muddy. O, how ripe in show°
Thy lips, those kissing cherries, tempting grow!

---

113. fee: Privilege, reward. **114. fond pageant:** Foolish exhibition. **119. alone:** Unequaled. **121. prepost'rously:** Out of the natural order. **124. Look when:** Whenever. **124–125. vows . . . appears:** Vows made by one who is weeping give evidence thereby of their sincerity. **127. badge:** Identifying device such as that worn on servants' livery. **128. advance:** Carry forward, display. **129. truth kills truth:** One of Lysander's vows must invalidate the other. **133. tales:** Lies. **139. show:** Appearance.

That pure congealed white, high Taurus'° snow,
Fann'd with the eastern wind, turns to a crow°
When thou hold'st up thy hand. O, let me kiss
This princess of pure white, this seal° of bliss!

HELENA: O spite! O hell! I see you all are bent
To set against me for your merriment.
If you were civil and knew courtesy,
You would not do me thus much injury.
Can you not hate me, as I know you do,
But you must join in souls to mock me too?
If you were men, as men you are in show,
You would not use a gentle lady so—
To vow, and swear, and superpraise° my parts,°
When I am sure you hate me with your hearts.
You both are rivals, and love Hermia;
And now both rivals, to mock Helena.
A trim° exploit, a manly enterprise,
To conjure tears up in a poor maid's eyes
With your derision! None of noble sort
Would so offend a virgin and extort°
A poor soul's patience, all to make you sport.

LYSANDER: You are unkind, Demetrius. Be not so;
For you love Hermia; this you know I know.
And here, with all good will, with all my heart,
In Hermia's love I yield you up my part;
And yours of Helena to me bequeath,
Whom I do love and will do till my death.

HELENA: Never did mockers waste more idle breath.

DEMETRIUS: Lysander, keep thy Hermia; I will none.°
If e'er I lov'd her, all that love is gone.
My heart to her but as guest-wise sojourn'd,
And now to Helen is it home return'd,
There to remain.

LYSANDER: Helen, it is not so.

DEMETRIUS: Disparage not the faith thou dost not know,
Lest, to thy peril, thou aby° it dear.
Look where thy love comes; yonder is thy dear.

Enter Hermia.

HERMIA: Dark night, that from the eye his° function takes,
The ear more quick of apprehension makes;
Wherein it doth impair the seeing sense,
It pays the hearing double recompense.

---

141. Taurus: A lofty mountain range in Asia Minor. **142. turns to a crow:** Seems black by contrast. **144. seal:** Pledge. **153. superpraise:** Overpraise. **parts:** Qualities. **157. trim:** Pretty, fine (said ironically). **160. extort:** Twist, torture. **169. will none:** Wish none of her. **175. aby:** Pay for. **177. his:** Its.

Thou art not by mine eye, Lysander, found;
Mine ear, I thank it, brought me to thy sound.
But why unkindly didst thou leave me so?
LYSANDER: Why should he stay, whom love doth press to go?
HERMIA: What love could press Lysander from my side?
LYSANDER: Lysander's love, that would not let him bide,
Fair Helena, who more engilds the night
Than all yon fiery oes° and eyes of light.
Why seek'st thou me? Could not this make thee know,
The hate I bear thee made me leave thee so?
HERMIA: You speak not as you think. It cannot be.
HELENA: Lo, she is one of this confederacy!
Now I perceive they have conjoin'd all three
To fashion this false sport, in spite of me.°
Injurious Hermia, most ungrateful maid!
Have you conspir'd, have you with these contriv'd°
To bait° me with this foul derision?
Is all the counsel° that we two have shar'd,
The sisters' vows, the hours that we have spent,
When we have chid the hasty-footed time
For parting us—O, is all forgot?
All school-days friendship, childhood innocence?
We, Hermia, like two artificial° gods,
Have with our needles created both one flower,
Both on one sampler, sitting on one cushion,
Both warbling of one song, both in one key,
As if our hands, our sides, voices, and minds
Had been incorporate. So we grew together,
Like to a double cherry, seeming parted,
But yet an union in partition;
Two lovely° berries molded on one stem;
So, with two seeming bodies, but one heart;
Two of the first, like coats in heraldry,
Due but to one and crowned with one crest.°
And will you rent° our ancient love asunder,
To join with men in scorning your poor friend?
It is not friendly, 'tis not maidenly.
Our sex, as well as I, may chide you for it,
Though I alone do feel the injury.
HERMIA: I am amazed at your passionate words.
I scorn you not. It seems that you scorn me.

---

188. oes: Circles, orbs, stars. **194. in spite of me:** To vex me. **196. contriv'd:** Plotted. **197. bait:** Torment, as one sets on dogs to bait a bear. **198. counsel:** Confidential talk. **203. artificial:** Skilled in art or creation. **211. lovely:** Loving. **213–214. Two . . . crest:** We have two separate bodies, just as a coat of arms in heraldry can be represented twice on a shield but surmounted by a single crest. **215. rent:** Rend.

HELENA: Have you not set Lysander, as in scorn,
To follow me and praise my eyes and face?
And made your other love, Demetrius,
Who even but now did spurn me with his foot,
To call me goddess, nymph, divine and rare,
Precious, celestial? Wherefore speaks he this
To her he hates? And wherefore doth Lysander
Deny your love, so rich within his soul,
And tender° me, forsooth, affection,
But by your setting on, by your consent?
What though I be not so in grace° as you,
So hung upon with love, so fortunate,
But miserable most, to love unlov'd?
This you should pity rather than despise.
HERMIA: I understand not what you mean by this.
HELENA: Ay, do! Persever, counterfeit sad° looks,
Make mouths° upon° me when I turn my back,
Wink each at other, hold the sweet jest up.
This sport, well carried,° shall be chronicled.
If you have any pity, grace, or manners,
You would not make me such an argument.°
But fare ye well. 'Tis partly my own fault,
Which death, or absence, soon shall remedy.
LYSANDER: Stay, gentle Helena; hear my excuse,
My love, my life, my soul, fair Helena!
HELENA: O excellent!
HERMIA: Sweet, do not scorn her so.
DEMETRIUS: If she cannot entreat,° I can compel.
LYSANDER: Thou canst compel no more than she entreat.
Thy threats have no more strength than her weak prayers.
Helen, I love thee, by my life, I do!
I swear by that which I will lose for thee,
To prove him false that says I love thee not.
DEMETRIUS: I say I love thee more than he can do.
LYSANDER: If thou say so, withdraw, and prove it too.
DEMETRIUS: Quick, come!
HERMIA: Lysander, whereto tends all this?
LYSANDER: Away, you Ethiope!°
[*He tries to break away from Hermia.*]
DEMETRIUS: No, no; he'll
Seem to break loose; take on as you would follow,
But yet come not. You are a tame man, go!

---

230. tender: Offer. **232. grace:** Favor. **237. sad:** Grave, serious. **238. mouths:** Maws, faces, grimaces. **upon:** At. **240. carried:** Managed. **242. argument:** Subject for a jest. **248. entreat:** Succeed by entreaty. **257. Ethiope:** Referring to Hermia's relatively dark hair and complexion; see also *tawny Tartar* six lines later.

LYSANDER: Hang off,° thou cat, thou burr! Vile thing, let loose,
Or I will shake thee from me like a serpent!
HERMIA: Why are you grown so rude? What change is this,
Sweet love?
LYSANDER: Thy love? Out, tawny Tartar, out!
Out, loathed med'cine!° O hated potion, hence!
HERMIA: Do you not jest?
HELENA: Yes, sooth,° and so do you.
LYSANDER: Demetrius, I will keep my word with thee.
DEMETRIUS: I would I had your bond, for I perceive
A weak bond° holds you. I'll not trust your word.
LYSANDER: What, should I hurt her, strike her, kill her dead?
Although I hate her, I'll not harm her so.
HERMIA: What, can you do me greater harm than hate?
Hate me? Wherefore? O me, what news,° my love?
Am not I Hermia? Are not you Lysander?
I am as fair now as I was erewhile.°
Since night you lov'd me; yet since night you left me.
Why, then you left me—O, the gods forbid!—
In earnest, shall I say?
LYSANDER: Ay, by my life!
And never did desire to see thee more.
Therefore be out of hope, of question, of doubt;
Be certain, nothing truer. 'Tis no jest
That I do hate thee and love Helena.
HERMIA: O me! You juggler! You cankerblossom!°
You thief of love! What, have you come by night
And stol'n my love's heart from him?
HELENA: Fine, i' faith!
Have you no modesty, no maiden shame,
No touch of bashfulness? What, will you tear
Impatient answers from my gentle tongue?
Fie, fie! You counterfeit, you puppet,° you!
HERMIA: Puppet? Why so? Ay, that way goes the game.
Now I perceive that she hath made compare
Between our statures; she hath urg'd her height,
And with her personage, her tall personage,
Her height, forsooth, she hath prevail'd with him.
And are you grown so high in his esteem,
Because I am so dwarfish and so low?
How low am I, thou painted maypole? Speak!

---

260. Hang off: Let go. **264. med'cine:** Poison. **265. sooth:** Truly. **268. weak bond:** Hermia's arm (with a pun on *bond*, oath, in the previous line). **272. what news:** What is the matter. **274. erewhile:** Just now. **282. cankerblossom:** Worm that destroys the flower bud (?). **288. puppet:** (1) Counterfeit, (2) dwarfish woman (in reference to Hermia's smaller stature).

How low am I? I am not yet so low
But that my nails can reach unto thine eyes.
[*She flails at Helena but is restrained.*]

HELENA: I pray you, though you mock me, gentlemen,
Let her not hurt me. I was never curst;°
I have no gift at all in shrewishness;
I am a right° maid for my cowardice.
Let her not strike me. You perhaps may think,
Because she is something° lower than myself,
That I can match her.

HERMIA: Lower! Hark, again!

HELENA: Good Hermia, do not be so bitter with me.
I evermore did love you, Hermia,
Did ever keep your counsels, never wrong'd you;
Save that, in love unto Demetrius,
I told him of your stealth° unto this wood.
He followed you; for love I followed him.
But he hath chid me hence and threat'ned me
To strike me, spurn me, nay, to kill me too.
And now, so° you will let me quiet go,
To Athens will I bear my folly back
And follow you no further. Let me go.
You see how simple and how fond° I am.

HERMIA: Why, get you gone. Who is 't that hinders you?

HELENA: A foolish heart, that I leave here behind.

HERMIA: What, with Lysander?

HELENA: With Demetrius.

LYSANDER: Be not afraid; she shall not harm thee, Helena.

DEMETRIUS: No, sir, she shall not, though you take her part.

HELENA: O, when she is angry, she is keen and shrewd!°
She was a vixen when she went to school;
And though she be but little, she is fierce.

HERMIA: "Little" again! Nothing but "low" and "little"!
Why will you suffer her to flout me thus?
Let me come to her.

LYSANDER: Get you gone, you dwarf!
You minimus,° of hind'ring knot-grass° made!
You bead, you acorn!

DEMETRIUS: You are too officious
In her behalf that scorns your services.
Let her alone. Speak not of Helena;
Take not her part. For, if thou dost intend°

300. curst: Shrewish. **302. right:** True. **304. something:** Somewhat. **310. stealth:** Stealing away. **314. so:** If only. **317. fond:** Foolish. **323. shrewd:** Shrewish. **329. minimus:** Diminutive creature. **knot-grass:** A weed, an infusion of which was thought to stunt the growth. **333. intend:** Give sign of.

Never so little show of love to her,
Thou shalt aby° it.

LYSANDER: Now she holds me not;
Now follow, if thou dar'st, to try whose right,
Of thine or mine, is most in Helena. [*Exit.*]

DEMETRIUS: Follow? Nay, I'll go with thee, cheek by jowl.°
[*Exit, following Lysander.*]

HERMIA: You, mistress, all this coil° is 'long of° you.
Nay, go not back.°

HELENA: I will not trust you, I,
Nor longer stay in your curst company.
Your hands than mine are quicker for a fray;
My legs are longer, though, to run away. [*Exit.*]

HERMIA: I am amaz'd, and know not what to say.
Exit.

OBERON: This is thy negligence. Still thou mistak'st,
Or else committ'st thy knaveries willfully.

PUCK: Believe me, king of shadows, I mistook.
Did not you tell me I should know the man
By the Athenian garments he had on?
And so far blameless proves my enterprise
That I have 'nointed an Athenian's eyes;
And so far am I glad it so did sort°
As this their jangling I esteem a sport.

OBERON: Thou see'st these lovers seek a place to fight.
Hie therefore, Robin, overcast the night;
The starry welkin° cover thou anon
With drooping fog as black as Acheron,°
And lead these testy rivals so astray
As° one come not within another's way.
Like to Lysander sometime frame thy tongue,
Then stir Demetrius up with bitter wrong;°
And sometime rail thou like Demetrius.
And from each other look thou lead them thus,
Till o'er their brows death-counterfeiting sleep
With leaden legs and batty° wings doth creep.
Then crush this herb° into Lysander's eye,
[*Gives herb.*]
Whose liquor hath this virtuous° property,
To take from thence all error with his° might

335. aby: Pay for. **338. cheek by jowl:** Side by side. **339. coil:** Turmoil, dissension. **'long of:** On account of. **340. go not back:** Don't retreat. (Hermia is again proposing a fight.) **352. sort:** Turn out. **356. welkin:** Sky. **357. Acheron:** River of Hades (here representing Hades itself). **359. As:** That. **361. wrong:** Insults. **365. batty:** Batlike. **366. this herb:** The antidote (mentioned in II, 1, 184) to love-in-idleness. **367. virtuous:** Efficacious. **368. his:** Its.

And make his eyeballs roll with wonted° sight.
When they next wake, all this derision°
Shall seem a dream and fruitless vision,
And back to Athens shall the lovers wend
With league whose date° till death shall never end.
Whiles I in this affair do thee employ,
I'll to my queen and beg her Indian boy;
And then I will her charmed eye release
From monster's view, and all things shall be peace.

PUCK: My fairy lord, this must be done with haste,
For night's swift dragons° cut the clouds full fast,
And yonder shines Aurora's harbinger,°
At whose approach, ghosts, wand'ring here and there,
Troop home to churchyards. Damned spirits all,
That in crossways and floods have burial,°
Already to their wormy beds are gone.
For fear lest day should look their shames upon,
They willfully themselves exile from light
And must for aye° consort with black-brow'd night.

OBERON: But we are spirits of another sort.
I with the Morning's love° have oft made sport,
And, like a forester,° the groves may tread
Even till the eastern gate, all fiery-red,
Opening on Neptune with fair blessed beams,
Turns into yellow gold his salt green streams.
But, notwithstanding, haste; make no delay.
We may effect this business yet ere day. [*Exit.*]

PUCK: Up and down, up and down,
I will lead them up and down.
I am fear'd in field and town.
Goblin, lead them up and down.
Here comes one.

Enter Lysander.

LYSANDER: Where art thou, proud Demetrius? Speak thou now.

PUCK [*mimicking Demetrius*]: Here, villain, drawn° and ready. Where art thou?

LYSANDER: I will be with thee straight.°

PUCK: Follow me, then,
To plainer° ground.

---

369. wonted: Accustomed. **370. derision:** Laughable business. **373. date:** Term of existence. **379. dragons:** Supposed to be yoked to the car of the goddess of night. **380. Aurora's harbinger:** The morning star, precursor of dawn. **383. crossways . . . burial:** Those who had committed suicide were buried at crossways, with a stake driven through them; those drowned, i.e., buried in floods or great waters, were condemned to wander disconsolate for want of burial rites. **387. for aye:** Forever. **389. Morning's love:** Cephalus, a beautiful youth beloved by Aurora; or perhaps the goddess of the dawn herself. **390. forester:** Keeper of a royal forest. **402. drawn:** With drawn sword. **403. straight:** Immediately. **404. plainer:** Smoother.

[*Lysander wanders about, following the voice.*]°

Enter Demetrius.

DEMETRIUS: Lysander! Speak again!
Thou runaway, thou coward, art thou fled?
Speak! In some bush? Where dost thou hide thy head?

PUCK: [*mimicking Lysander*]: Thou coward, art thou bragging to the stars,
Telling the bushes that thou look'st for wars,
And wilt not come? Come, recreant;° come, thou child,
I'll whip thee with a rod. He is defil'd
That draws a sword on thee.

DEMETRIUS: Yea, art thou there?

PUCK: Follow my voice. We'll try° no manhood here.

Exeunt.

[*Lysander returns.*]

LYSANDER: He goes before me and still dares me on.
When I come where he calls, then he is gone.
The villain is much lighter-heel'd than I.
I followed fast, but faster he did fly,
That fallen am I in dark uneven way,
And here will rest me. [*Lies down.*] Come, thou gentle day!
For if but once thou show me thy gray light,
I'll find Demetrius and revenge this spite. [*Sleeps.*]

[*Enter*] *Robin* [*Puck*] *and Demetrius.*

PUCK: Ho, ho, ho! Coward, why com'st thou not?

DEMETRIUS: Abide me, if thou dar'st; for well I wot°
Thou runn'st before me, shifting every place,
And dar'st not stand nor look me in the face.
Where art thou now?

PUCK: Come hither. I am here.

DEMETRIUS: Nay, then, thou mock'st me. Thou shalt buy° this dear,°
If ever I thy face by daylight see.
Now, go thy way. Faintness constraineth me
To measure out my length on this cold bed.
By day's approach look to be visited.

[*Lies down and sleeps.*]

Enter Helena.

HELENA: O weary night, O long and tedious night,
Abate° thy hours! Shine, comforts, from the east,
That I may back to Athens by daylight,
From these that my poor company detest;

---

s.d. Lysander wanders about: It is not clearly necessary that Lysander exit at this point; neither exit nor reentrance is indicated in the early texts. **409. recreant:** Cowardly wretch. **412. try:** Test. **422. wot:** Know. **426. buy:** Pay for. **dear:** Dearly. **432. Abate:** Lessen, shorten.

And sleep, that sometimes shuts up sorrow's eye,
Steal me awhile from mine own company.

[*Lies down and*] *sleep*[*s*].

PUCK: Yet but three? Come one more;
Two of both kinds makes up four.
Here she comes, curst and sad.
Cupid is a knavish lad,
Thus to make poor females mad.

[*Enter Hermia.*]

HERMIA: Never so weary, never so in woe,
Bedabbled with the dew and torn with briers,
I can no further crawl, no further go;
My legs can keep no pace with my desires.
Here will I rest me till the break of day.
Heavens shield Lysander, if they mean a fray!

[*Lies down and sleeps.*]

PUCK: On the ground
Sleep sound.
I'll apply
To your eye,
Gentle lover, remedy.

[*Squeezing the juice on Lysander's eyes.*]

When thou wak'st,
Thou tak'st
True delight
In the sight
Of thy former lady's eye;
And the country proverb known,
That every man should take his own,
In your waking shall be shown:
Jack shall have Jill;
Nought shall go ill;
The man shall have his mare again, and all shall be well.

[*Exit. Manent the four lovers.*]

[ACT IV]

[SCENE I: *Scene continues. The four lovers are still asleep onstage.*]

Enter [*Titania,*] *Queen of Fairies, and* [*Bottom the*] *Clown, and Fairies; and* [*Oberon,*] *the King, behind them.*

TITANIA: Come, sit thee down upon this flow'ry bed,
While I thy amiable° cheeks do coy,°
And stick musk-roses in thy sleek smooth head,
And kiss thy fair large ears, my gentle joy.

ACT IV, SCENE I. **2. amiable:** Lovely. **coy:** Caress.

[*They recline.*]

BOTTOM: Where's Peaseblossom?

PEASEBLOSSOM: Ready.

BOTTOM: Scratch my head, Peaseblossom. Where's Mounsieur Cobweb?

COBWEB: Ready.

BOTTOM: Mounsieur Cobweb, good mounsieur, get you your weapons in your hand, and kill me a red-hipp'd humble-bee on the top of a thistle; and, good mounsieur, bring me the honey-bag. Do not fret yourself too much in the action, mounsieur; and, good mounsieur, have a care the honey-bag break not; I would be loath to have you overflown with a honey-bag, signior. Where's Mounsieur Mustardseed?

MUSTARDSEED: Ready.

BOTTOM: Give me your neaf,° Mounsieur Mustardseed.
Pray you, leave your curtsy,° good mounsieur.

MUSTARDSEED: What's your will?

BOTTOM: Nothing, good mounsieur, but to help Cavalery° Cobweb° to scratch. I must to the barber's, mounsieur; for methinks I am marvailes hairy about the face; and I am such a tender ass, if my hair do but tickle me, I must scratch.

TITANIA: What, wilt thou hear some music, my sweet love?

BOTTOM: I have a reasonable good ear in music. Let's have the tongs and the bones.°

[*Music: tongs, rural music.*]°

TITANIA: Or say, sweet love, what thou desirest to eat.

BOTTOM: Truly, a peck of provender. I could munch your good dry oats. Methinks I have a great desire to a bottle° of hay. Good hay, sweet hay, hath no fellow.°

TITANIA: I have a venturous fairy that shall seek
The squirrel's hoard, and fetch thee new nuts.

BOTTOM: I had rather have a handful or two of dried peas. But, I pray you, let none of your people stir me. I have an exposition° of sleep come upon me.

TITANIA: Sleep thou, and I will wind thee in my arms.
Fairies, be gone, and be all ways° away.

[*Exeunt fairies.*]

So doth the woodbine the sweet honeysuckle
Gently entwist; the female ivy so
Enrings the barky fingers of the elm.
Oh, how I love thee! How I dote on thee!

[*They sleep.*]

---

16. neaf: Fist. **17. leave your curtsy:** Put on your hat. **19. Cavalery:** Cavalier. Form of address for a gentleman. **Cobweb:** Seemingly an error, since Cobweb has been sent to bring honey, whereas Peaseblossom has been asked to scratch. **24–25. tongs . . . bones:** Instruments for rustic music. (The tongs were played like a triangle, whereas the bones were held between the fingers and used as clappers.) **s.d. Music . . . music:** This stage direction is added from the Folio. **28. bottle:** Bundle. **29. fellow:** Equal. **33. exposition:** Bottom's word for *disposition*. **35. all ways:** In all directions.

Enter Robin Goodfellow [*Puck*].

OBERON [*advancing*]: Welcome, good Robin. See'st thou this sweet sight?
Her dotage now I do begin to pity.
For, meeting her of late behind the wood,
Seeking sweet favors° for this hateful fool,
I did upbraid her and fall out with her.
For she his hairy temples then had rounded
With coronet of fresh and fragrant flowers;
And that same dew, which sometime° on the buds
Was wont to swell like round and orient pearls,°
Stood now within the pretty flouriets'° eyes
Like tears that did their own disgrace bewail.
When I had at my pleasure taunted her,
And she in mild terms begg'd my patience,
I then did ask of her her changeling child;
Which straight she gave me, and her fairy sent
To bear him to my bower in fairy land.
And, now I have the boy, I will undo
This hateful imperfection of her eyes.
And, gentle Puck, take this transformed scalp
From off the head of this Athenian swain,
That, he awaking when the other° do,
May all to Athens back again repair,
And think no more of this night's accidents
But as the fierce vexation of a dream.
But first I will release the Fairy Queen.

[*Squeezes juice in her eyes.*]

Be as thou wast wont to be;
See as thou wast wont to see.
Dian's bud° o'er Cupid's flower
Hath such force and blessed power.
Now, my Titania, wake you, my sweet queen.

TITANIA [*waking*]: My Oberon! What visions have I seen!
Methought I was enamor'd of an ass.

OBERON: There lies your love.

TITANIA: How came these things to pass?
O, how mine eyes do loathe his visage now!

OBERON: Silence awhile. Robin, take off this head.
Titania, music call, and strike more dead

43. favors: I.e., gifts of flowers. **47. sometime:** Formerly. **48. orient pearls:** The most beautiful of all pearls, those coming from the Orient. **49. flouriets':** Flowerets'. **60. other:** Others. **67. Dian's bud:** Perhaps the flower of the *agnus castus* or chaste-tree, supposed to preserve chastity; or perhaps referring simply to Oberon's herb by which he can undo the effects of "Cupid's flower," the love-in-idleness of II, i, 165–168.

Than common sleep of all these five° the sense.
TITANIA: Music, ho! Music, such as charmeth sleep!
[*Music.*]
PUCK [*removing the ass's head*]: Now, when thou wak'st, with thine own fool's eyes peep.
OBERON: Sound, music! Come, my queen, take hands with me,
And rock the ground whereon these sleepers be.
[*Dance.*]
Now thou and I are new in amity,
And will tomorrow midnight solemnly°
Dance in Duke Theseus' house triumphantly
And bless it to all fair prosperity.
There shall the pairs of faithful lovers be
Wedded, with Theseus, all in jollity.
PUCK: Fairy King, attend, and mark:
I do hear the morning lark.
OBERON: Then, my queen, in silence sad,°
Trip we after night's shade.
We the globe can compass soon,
Swifter than the wand'ring moon.
TITANIA: Come, my lord, and in our flight
Tell me how it came this night
That I sleeping here was found
With these mortals on the ground. *Exeunt.*
Wind horn [*within*].

Enter Theseus and all his train; [*Hippolyta, Egeus*].

THESEUS: Go, one of you, find out the forester,
For now our observation° is perform'd;
And since we have the vaward° of the day,
My love shall hear the music of my hounds.
Uncouple in the western valley; let them go.
Dispatch, I say, and find the forester.
[*Exit an Attendant.*]
We will, fair queen, up to the mountain's top
And mark the musical confusion
Of hounds and echo in conjunction.
HIPPOLYTA: I was with Hercules and Cadmus° once,
When in a wood of Crete they bay'd° the bear
With hounds of Sparta.° Never did I hear
Such gallant chiding; for, besides the groves,

76. these five: I.e., the four lovers and Bottom. **83. solemnly:** Ceremoniously. **90. sad:** Sober. **99. observation:** Observance to a morn of May (I, i, 167). **100. vaward:** Vanguard, i.e., earliest part. **107. Cadmus:** Mythical founder of Thebes. (This story about him is unknown.) **108. bay'd:** Brought to bay. **109. hounds of Sparta:** Breed famous in antiquity for their hunting skill.

The skies, the fountains, every region near
Seem'd all one mutual cry. I never heard
So musical a discord, such sweet thunder.

THESEUS: My hounds are bred out of the Spartan kind,
So flew'd,° so sanded;° and their heads are hung
With ears that sweep away the morning dew;
Crook-knee'd, and dewlapp'd° like Thessalian bulls;
Slow in pursuit, but match'd in mouth like bells,
Each under each.° A cry° more tuneable°
Was never holla'd to, nor cheer'd with horn,
In Crete, in Sparta, nor in Thessaly.
Judge when you hear. [*Sees the sleepers.*] But, soft! What nymphs are these?

EGEUS: My lord, this' my daughter here asleep;
And this, Lysander; this Demetrius is;
This Helena, old Nedar's Helena.
I wonder of their being here together.

THESEUS: No doubt they rose up early to observe
The rite of May, and, hearing our intent,
Came here in grace of our solemnity.°
But speak, Egeus. Is not this the day
That Hermia should give answer of her choice?

EGEUS: It is, my lord.

THESEUS: Go, bid the huntsmen wake them with their horns.

[*Exit an Attendant.*]

Shout within. Wind horns. They all start up.

Good morrow, friends. Saint Valentine° is past.
Begin these wood-birds but to couple now?

LYSANDER: Pardon, my lord. [*They kneel.*]

THESEUS: I pray you all, stand up.
I know you two are rival enemies;
How comes this gentle concord in the world,
That hatred is so far from jealousy
To sleep by hate and fear no enmity?

LYSANDER: My lord, I shall reply amazedly,
Half sleep, half waking; but as yet, I swear,
I cannot truly say how I came here.
But, as I think—for truly would I speak,
And now I do bethink me, so it is—

115. So flew'd: Similarly having large hanging chaps or fleshy covering of the jaw. **sanded:** Of sandy color. **117. dewlapp'd:** Having pendulous folds of skin under the neck. **118–119. match'd . . . under each:** Harmoniously matched in their various cries like a set of bells, from treble down to bass. **119. cry:** Pack of hounds. **tuneable:** Well tuned, melodious. **129. solemnity:** Observance of these same rites of May. **134. Saint Valentine:** Birds were supposed to choose their mates on St. Valentine's Day.

I came with Hermia hither. Our intent
Was to be gone from Athens, where° we might,
Without° the peril of the Athenian law—

EGEUS: Enough, enough, my lord; you have enough.
I beg the law, the law, upon his head.
They would have stol'n away; they would, Demetrius,
Thereby to have defeated you and me,
You of your wife and me of my consent,
Of my consent that she should be your wife.

DEMETRIUS: My lord, fair Helen told me of their stealth,
Of this their purpose hither to this wood,
And I in fury hither followed them,
Fair Helena in fancy following me.
But, my good lord, I wot not by what power—
But by some power it is—my love to Hermia,
Melted as the snow, seems to me now
As the remembrance of an idle gaud.°
Which in my childhood I did dote upon;
And all the faith, the virtue of my heart,
The object and the pleasure of mine eye,
Is only Helena. To her, my lord,
Was I betroth'd ere I saw Hermia,
But like a sickness did I loathe this food;
But, as in health, come to my natural taste,
Now I do wish it, love it, long for it,
And will for evermore be true to it.

THESEUS: Fair lovers, you are fortunately met.
Of this discourse we more will hear anon.
Egeus, I will overbear your will;
For in the temple, by and by, with us
These couples shall eternally be knit.
And, for° the morning now is something° worn,
Our purpos'd hunting shall be set aside.
Away with us to Athens. Three and three,
We'll hold a feast in great solemnity.
Come, Hippolyta.

[*Exeunt Theseus, Hippolyta, Egeus, and train.*]

DEMETRIUS: These things seem small and undistinguishable,
Like far-off mountains turned into clouds.

HERMIA: Methinks I see these things with parted° eye,
When every thing seems double.

---

147. where: Wherever; or to where. **148. Without:** Outside of, beyond. **162. idle gaud:** Worthless trinket. **177. for:** Since. **something:** Somewhat. **184. parted:** Improperly focused.

HELENA: So methinks;
And I have found Demetrius like a jewel,
Mine own, and not mine own.°
DEMETRIUS: Are you sure
That we are awake? It seems to me
That yet we sleep, we dream. Do not you think
The Duke was here, and bid us follow him?
HERMIA: Yea, and my father.
HELENA: And Hippolyta.
LYSANDER: And he did bid us follow to the temple.
DEMETRIUS: Why, then, we are awake. Let's follow him,
And by the way let us recount our dreams.
[*Exeunt.*]

BOTTOM [*awaking*]: When my cue comes, call me, and I will answer. My next is, "Most fair Pyramus." Heigh-ho! Peter Quince! Flute, the bellows-mender! Snout, the tinker! Starveling! God's my life, stol'n hence, and left me asleep! I have had a most rare vision. I have had a dream, past the wit of man to say what dream it was. Man is but an ass, if he go about° to expound this dream. Methought I was—there is no man can tell what. Methought I was—and me thought I had—but man is but a patch'd° fool, if he will offer° to say what me-thought I had. The eye of man hath not heard, the ear of man hath not seen, man's hand is not able to taste, his tongue to conceive, nor his heart to report, what my dream was. I will get Peter Quince to write a ballad of this dream. It shall be call'd "Bottom's Dream," because it hath no bottom; and I will sing it in the latter end of a play, before the Duke. Peradventure, to make it the more gracious, I shall sing it at her° death. [*Exit.*]

[SCENE II: *Athens. Quince's house (?).*]

Enter Quince, Flute, [*Snout, and Starveling*].

QUINCE: Have you sent to Bottom's house? Is he come home yet?
STARVELING: He cannot be heard of. Out of doubt he is transported.°
FLUTE: If he come not, then the play is marr'd. It goes not forward, doth it?
QUINCE: It is not possible. You have not a man in all Athens able to discharge° Pyramus but he.
FLUTE: No, he hath simply the best wit of any handicraft man in Athens.
QUINCE: Yea, and the best person too; and he is a very paramour for a sweet voice.
FLUTE: You must say "paragon." A paramour is, God bless us, a thing of naught.

Enter Snug the Joiner.

186–187. like . . . not mine own: Like a jewel that one finds by chance and therefore possesses but cannot certainly consider one's own property. **199. go about:** Attempt. **201. patch'd:** Wearing motley, i.e., a dress of various colors. **202. offer:** Venture. **208. her:** Thisby's (?). ACT IV, SCENE II. **2. transported:** Carried off by fairies; or, possibly, transformed. **4. discharge:** Perform.

SNUG: Masters, the Duke is coming from the temple, and there is two or three lords and ladies more married. If our sport had gone forward, we had all been made men.

FLUTE: O sweet bully Bottom! Thus hath he lost six-pence a day° during his life; he could not have scap'd sixpence a day. An the Duke had not given him sixpence a day for playing Pyramus, I'll be hang'd. He would have deserv'd it. Sixpence a day in Pyramus, or nothing.

Enter Bottom.

BOTTOM: Where are these lads? Where are these hearts?°

QUINCE: Bottom! O most courageous day! O most happy hour!

BOTTOM: Masters, I am to discourse wonders.° But ask me not what; for if I tell you, I am no true Athenian. I will tell you everything, right as it fell out.

QUINCE: Let us hear, sweet Bottom.

BOTTOM: Not a word of° me. All that I will tell you is, that the Duke hath din'd. Get your apparel together, good strings° to your beards, new ribands° to your pumps, meet presently° at the palace, every man look o'er his part; for the short and the long is, our play is preferr'd.° In any case, let Thisby have clean linen; and let not him that plays the lion pare his nails, for they shall hang out for the lion's claws. And, most dear actors, eat no onions nor garlic, for we are to utter sweet breath; and I do not doubt but to hear them say, it is a sweet comedy. No more words. Away! go, away!

[*Exeunt.*]

[ACT V]

[SCENE I: *Athens. The palace of Theseus.*]

Enter Theseus, Hippolyta, and Philostrate, [*Lords, and Attendants*].

HIPPOLYTA: 'Tis strange, my Theseus, that° these lovers speak of.

THESEUS: More strange than true. I never may° believe
These antic° fables, nor these fairy toys.°
Lovers and madmen have such seething brains
Such shaping fantasies,° that apprehend
More than cool reason ever comprehends.
The lunatic, the lover, and the poet
Are of imagination all compact.°
One sees more devils than vast hell can hold;
That is the madman. The lover, all as frantic,
Sees Helen's° beauty in a brow of Egypt.°
The poet's eye, in a fine frenzy rolling,

---

13. sixpence a day: As a royal pension. **17. hearts:** Good fellows. **19. am . . . wonders:** Have wonders to relate. **22. of:** Out of. **23. strings:** To attach the beards. **ribands:** Ribbons. **24. presently:** Immediately. **25. preferr'd:** Selected for consideration. ACT V, SCENE I. **1. that:** That which. **2. may:** Can. **3. antic:** Strange, grotesque (with additional punning sense of *antique,* ancient). **fairy toys:** Trifling stories about fairies. **5. fantasies:** Imaginations. **8. compact:** Formed, composed. **11. Helen's:** Of Helen of Troy, pattern of beauty. **brow of Egypt:** Face of a gypsy.

Doth glance from heaven to earth, from earth to heaven;
And as imagination bodies forth
The forms of things unknown, the poet's pen
Turns them to shapes and gives to airy nothing
A local habitation and a name.
Such tricks hath strong imagination
That, if it would but apprehend some joy,
It comprehends some bringer° of that joy;
Or in the night, imagining some fear,°
How easy is a bush suppos'd a bear!

HIPPOLYTA: But all the story of the night told over,
And all their minds transfigur'd so together,
More witnesseth than fancy's images°
And grows to something of great constancy;°
But, howsoever,° strange and admirable.°

Enter lovers: Lysander, Demetrius, Hermia, and Helena.

THESEUS: Here come the lovers, full of joy and mirth.
Joy, gentle friends! Joy and fresh days of love
Accompany your hearts!

LYSANDER: More than to us
Wait in your royal walks, your board, your bed!

THESEUS: Come now, what masques, what dances shall we have,
To wear away this long age of three hours
Between our after-supper and bed-time?
Where is our usual manager of mirth?
What revels are in hand? Is there no play,
To ease the anguish of a torturing hour?
Call Philostrate.

PHILOSTRATE: Here, mighty Theseus.

THESEUS: Say, what abridgement° have you for this evening?
What masque? What music? How shall we beguile
The lazy time, if not with some delight?

PHILOSTRATE: There is a brief° how many sports are ripe.
Make choice of which your Highness will see first.
[*Giving a paper.*]

THESEUS [*reads*]: "The battle with the Centaurs,° to be sung
By an Athenian eunuch to the harp."
We'll none of that. That have I told my love,

---

20. bringer: Source. **21. fear:** Object of fear. **25. More . . . images:** Testifies to something more substantial than mere imaginings. **26. constancy:** Certainty. **27. howsoever:** In any case. **admirable:** A source of wonder. **39. abridgement:** Pastime (to abridge or shorten the evening). **42. brief:** Short written statement, list. **44. "battle . . . Centaurs":** Probably refers to the battle of the Centaurs and the Lapithae, when the Centaurs attempted to carry off Hippodamia, bride of Theseus's friend Pirothous.

In glory of my kinsman° Hercules.
[*Reads.*] "The riot of the tipsy Bacchanals,
Tearing the Thracian singer in their rage."°
That is an old device; and it was play'd
When I from Thebes came last a conqueror.
[*Reads.*] "The thrice three Muses mourning for the death
Of Learning, late deceas'd in beggary."°
That is some satire, keen and critical,
Not sorting with° a nuptial ceremony.
[*Reads.*] "A tedious brief scene of young Pyramus
And his love Thisby; very tragical mirth."
Merry and tragical? Tedious and brief?
That is, hot ice and wondrous strange° snow.
How shall we find the concord of this discord?

PHILOSTRATE: A play there is, my lord, some ten words long,
Which is as brief as I have known a play;
But by ten words, my lord, it is too long,
Which makes it tedious. For in all the play
There is not one word apt, one player fitted.
And tragical, my noble lord, it is,
For Pyramus therein doth kill himself.
Which, when I saw rehears'd, I must confess,
Made mine eyes water, but more merry tears
The passion of loud laughter never shed.

THESEUS: What are they that do play it?

PHILOSTRATE: Hard-handed men that work in Athens here,
Which never labor'd in their minds till now,
And now have toil'd° their unbreathed° memories
With this same play, against° your nuptial.

THESEUS: And we will hear it.

PHILOSTRATE: No, my noble lord,
It is not for you. I have heard it over,
And it is nothing, nothing in the world;
Unless you can find sport in their intents,
Extremely stretch'd° and conn'd° with cruel pain,
To do you service.

---

47. kinsman: Plutarch's *Life of Theseus* states that Hercules and Theseus were near-kinsmen. Theseus is referring to a version of the battle of the Centaurs in which Hercules was said to be present. **48–49. "The riot . . . rage":** This was the story of the death of Orpheus, as told in *Metamorphoses.* **52–53. "The thrice . . . beggary":** Possibly an allusion to Spenser's *Teares of the Muses* (1591), though "satires" deploring the neglect of learning and the creative arts were common-place. **55. sorting with:** Befitting. **59. strange:** Seemingly an error for some adjective that would contrast with *snow,* just as *hot* contrasts with *ice.* **74. toil'd:** Taxed. **unbreathed:** Unexercised. **75. against:** In preparation for. **80. stretch'd:** Strained. **conn'd:** Memorized.

THESEUS: I will hear that play;
For never anything can be amiss'
When simpleness and duty tender it.
Go, bring them in; and take your places, ladies.
[Philostrate goes to summon the players.]

HIPPOLYTA: I love not to see wretchedness o'ercharg'd°
And duty in his service° perishing.
THESEUS: Why, gentle sweet, you shall see no such thing.
HIPPOLYTA: He says they can do nothing in this kind.°
THESEUS: The kinder we, to give them thanks for nothing.
Our sport shall be to take what they mistake;
And what poor duty cannot do, noble respect
Takes it in might, not merit.°
Where I have come, great clerks° have purposed
To greet me with premeditated welcomes;
Where I have seen them shiver and look pale,
Make periods in the midst of sentences,
Throttle their practic'd accent° in their fears,
And in conclusion dumbly have broke off,
Not paying me a welcome. Trust me, sweet,
Out of this silence yet I pick'd a welcome;
And in the modesty of fearful duty
I read as much as from the rattling tongue
Of saucy and audacious eloquence.
Love, therefore, and tongue-tied simplicity
In least° speak most, to my capacity.°

[Philostrate returns.]

PHILOSTRATE: So please your Grace, the Prologue° is address'd.°
THESEUS: Let him approach. *[Flourish of trumpets.]*

Enter the Prologue [Quince].

PROLOGUE: If we offend, it is with our good will.
That you should think, we come not to offend,
But with good will. To show our simple skill,
That is the true beginning of our end.
Consider, then, we come but in despite.
We do not come, as minding° to content you,
Our true intent is. All for your delight

---

85. wretchedness o'ercharg'd: Incompetence over-burdened. **86. his service:** Its attempt to serve. **88. kind:** Kind of thing. **92. Takes . . . merit:** Values it for the effort made rather than for the excellence achieved. **93. clerks:** Learned men. **97. practic'd accent:** Rehearsed speech; or usual way of speaking. **105. least:** Saying least. **to my capacity:** In my judgment and understanding. **106. Prologue:** Speaker of the prologue. **address'd:** Ready. **113. minding:** Intending.

We are not here. That you should here repent you,
The actors are at hand; and, by their show,
You shall know all that you are like to know.

THESEUS: This fellow doth not stand upon points.°

LYSANDER: He hath rid his prologue like a rough° colt; he knows not the stop.° A good moral, my lord: it is not enough to speak, but to speak true.

HIPPOLYTA: Indeed he hath play'd on his prologue like a child on a recorder;° a sound, but not in government.°

THESEUS: His speech was like a tangled chain, nothing° impair'd, but all disorder'd. Who is next?

Enter Pyramus and Thisby, and Wall, and Moonshine, and Lion.

PROLOGUE: Gentles, perchance you wonder at this show;
But wonder on, till truth make all things plain.
This man is Pyramus, if you would know;
This beauteous lady Thisby is certain.
This man, with lime and rough-cast, doth present
Wall, that vile Wall which did these lovers sunder;
And through Wall's chink, poor souls, they are content
To whisper. At the which let no man wonder.
This man, with lantern, dog, and bush of thorn,
Presenteth Moonshine; for, if you will know,
By moonshine did these lovers think no scorn°
To meet at Ninus' tomb, there, there to woo.
This grisly beast, which Lion hight° by name,
The trusty Thisby, coming first by night,
Did scare away, or rather did affright;
And, as she fled, her mantle she did fall,°
Which Lion vile with bloody mouth did stain.
Anon comes Pyramus, sweet youth and tall,°
And finds his trusty Thisby's mantle slain;
Whereat, with blade, with bloody blameful blade,
He bravely broach'd° his boiling bloody breast.
And Thisby, tarrying in mulberry shade,
His dagger drew, and died. For all the rest,
Let Lion, Moonshine, Wall, and lovers twain
At large° discourse, while here they do remain.

Exeunt Lion, Thisby, and Moonshine.

---

118. stand upon points: (1) Heed niceties or small points, (2) pay attention to punctuation in his reading. (The humor of Quince's speech is in the blunders of its punctuation.) **119. rough:** Unbroken. **stop:** (1) The stopping of a colt by reining it in, (2) punctuation mark. **121. recorder:** A wind instrument like a flute. **122. government:** Control. **123. nothing:** Not at all. **135. think no scorn:** Think it no disgraceful matter. **137. hight:** Is called. **140. fall:** Let fall. **142. tall:** Courageous. **145. broach'd:** Stabbed. **149. At large:** In full, at length.

THESEUS: I wonder if the lion be to speak.
DEMETRIUS: No wonder, my lord. One lion may, when many asses do.
WALL: In this same interlude it doth befall
That I, one Snout by name, present a wall;
And such a wall, as I would have you think,
That had in it a crannied hole or chink,
Through which the lovers, Pyramus and Thisby,
Did whisper often very secretly.
This loam, this rough-cast, and this stone doth show
That I am that same wall; the truth is so.
And this the cranny is, right and sinister,°
Through which the fearful lovers are to whisper.
THESEUS: Would you desire lime and hair to speak better?
DEMETRIUS: It is the wittiest partition° that ever I heard discourse, my lord.

[*Pyramus comes forward.*]

THESEUS: Pyramus draws near the wall. Silence!
PYRAMUS: O grim-look'd° night! O night with hue so black!
O night, which ever art when day is not!
O night, O night! Alack, alack, alack,
I fear my Thisby's promise is forgot.
And thou, O wall, O sweet, O lovely wall,
That stand'st between her father's ground and mine,
Thou wall, O wall, O sweet and lovely wall,
Show me thy chink, to blink through with mine eyne!

[*Wall holds up his fingers.*]

Thanks, courteous wall. Jove shield thee well for this!
But what see I? No Thisby do I see.
O wicked wall, through whom I see no bliss!
Curs'd be thy stones for thus deceiving me!
THESEUS: The wall, methinks, being sensible,° should curse again.
PYRAMUS: No, in truth, sir, he should not. "Deceiving me" is Thisby's cue: she is to enter now, and I am to spy her through the wall. You shall see, it will fall pat as I told you. Yonder she comes.

Enter Thisby.

THISBY: O wall, full often hast thou heard my moans,
For parting my fair Pyramus and me.
My cherry lips have often kiss'd thy stones,
Thy stones with lime and hair knit up in thee.
PYRAMUS: I see a voice. Now will I to the chink,
To spy an° I can hear my Thisby's face.
Thisby!

---

160. right and sinister: The right side of it and the left (sinister); or running from right to left, horizontally. **163. partition:** (1) Wall, (2) section of a learned treatise or oration. **165. grim-look'd:** Grim-looking. **177. sensible:** Capable of feeling. **186. an:** If.

THISBY: My love! Thou art my love, I think.
PYRAMUS: Think what thou wilt, I am thy lover's grace;°
And, like Limander° am I trusty still.
THISBY: And I like Helen,° till the Fates me kill.
PYRAMUS: Not Shafalus° to Procrus° was so true.
THISBY: As Shafalus to Procrus, I to you.
PYRAMUS: O, kiss me through the hole of this vile wall!
THISBY: I kiss the wall's hole, not your lips at all.
PYRAMUS: Wilt thou at Ninny's tomb meet me straightway?
THISBY: 'Tide° life, 'tide death, I come without delay.
[*Exeunt Pyramus and Thisby.*]

WALL: Thus have I, Wall, my part discharged so;
And, being done, thus Wall away doth go. [*Exit.*]
THESEUS: Now is the mural down between the two neighbors.
DEMETRIUS: No remedy, my lord, when walls are so willful to hear° without warning.°
HIPPOLYTA: This is the silliest stuff that ever I heard.
THESEUS: The best in this kind° are but shadows;° and the worst are no worse, if imagination amend them.
HIPPOLYTA: It must be your imagination then, and not theirs.
THESEUS: If we imagine no worse of them than they of themselves, they may pass for excellent men. Here come two noble beasts in, a man and a lion.

Enter Lion and Moonshine.

LION: You, ladies, you, whose gentle hearts do fear
The smallest monstrous mouse that creeps on floor,
May now perchance both quake and tremble here,
When lion rough in wildest rage doth roar.
Then know that I, as Snug the joiner, am
A lion fell,° nor else no lion's dam;
For, if I should as lion come in strife
Into this place, 'twere pity on my life.
THESEUS: A very gentle beast, and of a good conscience.
DEMETRIUS: The very best at a beast, my lord, that e'er I saw.
LYSANDER: This lion is a very fox for his valor.°
THESEUS: True; and a goose for his discretion.°
DEMETRIUS: Not so, my lord; for his valor cannot carry his discretion; and the fox carries the goose.

---

189. lover's grace: Gracious lover. **190. Limander:** Blunder for *Leander.* **191. Helen:** Blunder for *Hero.* **192. Shafalus, Procrus:** Blunders for *Cephalus* and *Procris,* also famous lovers. **197. 'Tide:** Betide, come. **201. to hear:** As to hear. **201–202. without warning:** Without warning the parents. **204. in this kind:** Of this sort. **shadows:** Likenesses, representations. **214. lion fell:** Fierce lion (with a play on the idea of *lion skin*). **219. is . . . valor:** His valor consists of craftiness and discretion. **220. goose . . . discretion:** As discreet as a goose, that is, more foolish than discreet.

THESEUS: His discretion, I am sure, cannot carry his valor, for the goose carries not the fox. It is well. Leave it to his discretion, and let us listen to the moon.

MOON: This lanthorn° doth the horned moon present—

DEMETRIUS: He should have worn the horns on his head.°

THESEUS: He is no crescent, and his horns are invisible within the circumference.

MOON: This lanthorn doth the horned moon present; Myself the man i' th' moon do seem to be.

THESEUS: This is the greatest error of all the rest. The man should be put into the lanthorn. How is it else the man i' th' moon?

DEMETRIUS: He dares not come there for the° candle; for, you see, it is already in snuff.°

HIPPOLYTA: I am aweary of this moon. Would he would change!

THESEUS: It appears, by his small light of discretion, that he is in the wane; but yet, in courtesy, in all reason, we must stay the time.

LYSANDER: Proceed, Moon.

MOON: All that I have to say is to tell you that the lanthorn is the moon, I, the man in the moon, this thorn-bush my thorn-bush, and this dog my dog.

DEMETRIUS: Why, all these should be in the lanthorn; for all these are in the moon. But silence! Here comes Thisby.

Enter Thisby.

THISBY: This is old Ninny's tomb. Where is my love?

LION [*roaring*]: *Oh*— [*Thisby runs off.*]

DEMETRIUS: Well roar'd, Lion.

THESEUS: Well run, Thisby.

HIPPOLYTA: Well shone, Moon. Truly, the moon shines with a good grace.

[*The Lion shakes Thisby's mantle, and exit.*]

THESEUS: Well mous'd,° Lion.

DEMETRIUS: And then came Pyramus.

LYSANDER: And so the lion vanish'd.

Enter Pyramus.

PYRAMUS: Sweet Moon, I thank thee for thy sunny beams;
I thank thee, Moon, for shining now so bright;
For, by thy gracious, golden, glittering gleams,
I trust to take of truest Thisby sight.
But stay, O spite!
But mark, poor knight,
What dreadful dole° is here!

---

226. lanthorn: This original spelling may suggest a play on the *horn* of which lanterns were made and also on a cuckold's horns; but the spelling *lanthorn* is not used consistently for comic effect in this play or elsewhere. In V, i, 135, for example, the word is *lantern* in the original. **227. on his head:** As a sign of cuckoldry. **233. for the:** Because of the. **234. in snuff:** (1) Offended, (2) in need of snuffing. **248. mous'd:** Shaken. **257. dole:** Grievous event.

Eyes, do you see?
How can it be?
O dainty duck! O dear!
Thy mantle good,
What, stain'd with blood!
Approach, ye Furies fell!°
O Fates, come, come,
Cut thread and thrum;°
Quail,° crush, conclude, and quell!°

THESEUS: This passion, and the death of a dear friend, would go near to make a man look sad.°

HIPPOLYTA: Beshrew my heart, but I pity the man.

PYRAMUS: O wherefore, Nature, didst thou lions frame?
Since lion vile hath here deflow'r'd my dear,
Which is—no, no—which was the fairest dame
That liv'd, that lov'd, that lik'd, that look'd with cheer.°
Come, tears, confound,
Out, sword, and wound
The pap of Pyramus;
Ay, that left pap,
Where heart doth hop. [*Stabs himself.*]
Thus die I, thus, thus, thus.
Now am I dead,
Now am I fled;
My soul is in the sky.
Tongue, lose thy light;
Moon, take thy flight. [*Exit Moonshine.*]
Now die, die, die, die, die. [*Dies.*]

DEMETRIUS: No die, but an ace,° for him; for he is but one.°

LYSANDER: Less than an ace, man; for he is dead, he is nothing.

THESEUS: With the help of a surgeon he might yet recover, and yet prove an ass.°

HIPPOLYTA: How chance Moonshine is gone before Thisby comes back and finds her lover?

THESEUS: She will find him by starlight. Here she comes; and her passion ends the play.

[*Enter Thisby.*]

HIPPOLYTA: Methinks she should not use a long one for such a Pyramus. I hope she will be brief.

---

263. fell: Fierce. **265. thread and thrum:** The warp in weaving and the loose end of the warp. **266. Quail:** Overpower. **quell:** Kill, destroy. **267–268. This . . . sad:** If one had other reason to grieve, one might be sad, but not from this absurd portrayal of passion. **273. cheer:** Countenance. **286. ace:** The side of the die featuring the single pip, or spot. (The pun is on *die* as a singular of *dice;* Bottom's performance is not worth a whole *die* but rather one single face of it, one small portion.) **one:** (1) An individual person, (2) unique. **288. ass:** With a pun on *ace.*

DEMETRIUS: A mote will turn the balance, which Pyramus, which° Thisby, is the better: he for a man God warr'nt us; she for a woman, God bless us.

LYSANDER: She hath spied him already with those sweet eyes.

DEMETRIUS: And thus she means,° videlicet:°

THISBY: Asleep, my love?
What, dead, my dove?
O Pyramus, arise!
Speak, speak. Quite dumb?
Dead, dead? A tomb
Must cover thy sweet eyes.
These lily lips,
This cherry nose,
These yellow cowslip cheeks,
Are gone, are gone!
Lovers, make moan.
His eyes were green as leeks.
O Sisters Three,°
Come, come to me,
With hands as pale as milk;
Lay them in gore,
Since you have shore°
With shears his thread of silk.
Tongue, not a word.
Come, trusty sword,
Come, blade, my breast imbrue!° [*Stabs herself.*]
And farewell, friends.
Thus Thisby ends.
Adieu, adieu, adieu. [*Dies.*]

THESEUS: Moonshine and Lion are left to bury the dead.

DEMETRIUS: Ay, and Wall too.

BOTTOM [*starting up*]: No, I assure you; the wall is down that parted their fathers. Will it please you to see the epilogue, or to hear a Bergomask dance° between two of our company?

THESEUS: No epilogue, I pray you; for your play needs no excuse. Never excuse; for when the players are all dead, there need none to be blam'd. Marry, if he that writ it had play'd Pyramus and hang'd himself in Thisby's garter, it would have been a fine tragedy; and so it is, truly, and very notably discharg'd. But, come, your Bergomask. Let your epilogue alone.
[*A dance.*]
The iron tongue of midnight hath told° twelve.
Lovers, to bed; 'tis almost fairy time.

---

295. which . . . which: Whether . . . or. **298. means:** Moans, laments. **videlicet:** To wit. **311. Sisters Three:** The Fates. **315. shore:** Shorn. **319. imbrue:** Stain with blood. **326. Bergomask dance:** A rustic dance named for Bergamo, a province in the state of Venice. **333. told:** Counted, struck ("tolled").

I fear we shall outsleep the coming morn
As much as we this night have overwatch'd.°
This palpable-gross° play hath well beguil'd
The heavy° gait of night. Sweet friends, to bed.
A fortnight hold we this solemnity,
In nightly revels and new jollity. *Exeunt.*

Enter Puck

PUCK: Now the hungry lion roars,
And the wolf behowls the moon;
Whilst the heavy ploughman snores,
All with weary task fordone.°
Now the wasted brands° do glow,
Whilst the screech-owl, screeching loud,
Puts the wretch that lies in woe
In remembrance of a shroud.
Now it is the time of night
That the graves, all gaping wide,
Every one lets forth his sprite,°
In the churchway paths to glide.
And we fairies, that do run
By the triple Hecate's° team
From the presence of the sun,
Following darkness like a dream,
Now are frolic.° Not a mouse
Shall disturb this hallowed house.
I am sent with broom before,
To sweep the dust behind° the door.

Enter [Oberon and Titania,] King and Queen of Fairies, with all their train.

OBERON: Through the house give glimmering light,
By the dead and drowsy fire;
Every elf and fairy sprite
Hop as light as bird from brier;
And this ditty, after me,
Sing, and dance it trippingly.

TITANIA: First, rehearse your song by rote,
To each word a warbling note.
Hand in hand, with fairy grace,
Will we sing, and bless this place.

[*Song and dance.*]

---

336. overwatch'd: Stayed up too late. **337. palpable-gross:** Obviously crude. **338. heavy:** Drowsy, dull. **344. fordone:** Exhausted. **345. wasted brands:** Burned-out logs. **351. Every . . . sprite:** Every grave lets forth its ghost. **354. triple Hecate's:** Hecate ruled in three capacities: as Luna or Cynthia in heaven, as Diana on earth, and as Proserpina in hell. **357. frolic:** Merry. **360. behind:** From behind. (Robin Goodfellow was a household spirit who helped good housemaids and punished lazy ones.)

OBERON: Now, until the break of day,
Through this house each fairy stray.
To the best bride-bed will we,
Which by us shall blessed be;
And the issue there create°
Ever shall be fortunate.
So shall all the couples three
Ever true in loving be;
And the blots of Nature's hand
Shall not in their issue stand;
Never mole, hare lip, nor scar,
Nor mark prodigious,° such as are
Despised in nativity,
Shall upon their children be.
With this field-dew consecrate,°
Every fairy take his gait,°
And each several° chamber bless,
Through this palace, with sweet peace;
And the owner of it blest
Ever shall in safety rest.
Trip away; make no stay;
Meet me all by break of day.

Exeunt [*Oberon, Titania, and train*].

PUCK: If we shadows have offended,
Think but this, and all is mended,
That you have but slumb'red here°
While these visions did appear.
And this weak and idle theme,
No more yielding but° a dream,
Gentles, do not reprehend.
If you pardon, we will mend.
And, as I am an honest Puck,
If we have unearned luck
Now to scape the serpent's tongue,°
We will make amends ere long;
Else the Puck a liar call.
So, good night unto you all.
Give me your hands,° if we be friends,
And Robin shall restore amends. [*Exit.*]

375. create: Created. **382. prodigious:** Monstrous, unnatural. **385. consecrate:** Consecrated. **386. take his gait:** Go his way. **387. several:** Separate. **395. That . . . here:** That it is a "midsummer night's dream." **398. No . . . but:** Yielding no more than. **403. serpent's tongue:** Hissing. **407. Give . . . hands:** Applaud.

Hamlet, Prince of Denmark

c. 1600

[DRAMATIS PERSONAE

CLAUDIUS, King of Denmark
HAMLET, son to the late and nephew to the present king
POLONIUS, lord chamberlain
HORATIO, friend to Hamlet
LAERTES, son to Polonius
VOLTIMAND, CORNELIUS, ROSENCRANTZ, GUILDENSTERN, OSRIC — courtiers
A GENTLEMAN
A PRIEST
MARCELLUS, BERNARDO — officers
FRANCISCO, a soldier
REYNALDO, servant to Polonius
PLAYERS
TWO CLOWNS, grave-diggers
FORTINBRAS, Prince of Norway
A CAPTAIN
ENGLISH AMBASSADORS
GERTRUDE, Queen of Denmark, and mother to Hamlet
OPHELIA, daughter to Polonius
LORDS, LADIES, OFFICERS, SOLDIERS, SAILORS, MESSENGERS, and other ATTENDANTS
GHOST of Hamlet's father

SCENE: *Denmark.*]

[ACT I

SCENE I: *Elsinore. A platform° before the castle.*]

Enter Bernardo and Francisco, two sentinels.

BERNARDO: Who's there?
FRANCISCO: Nay, answer me:° stand, and unfold yourself.
BERNARDO: Long live the king!°
FRANCISCO: Bernardo?
BERNARDO: He.
FRANCISCO: You come most carefully upon your hour.
BERNARDO: 'Tis now struck twelve; get thee to bed, Francisco.
FRANCISCO: For this relief much thanks: 'tis bitter cold,
And I am sick at heart.
BERNARDO: Have you had quiet guard?
FRANCISCO: Not a mouse stirring.
BERNARDO: Well, good night.
If you do meet Horatio and Marcellus,
The rivals° of my watch, bid them make haste.

Enter Horatio and Marcellus.

FRANCISCO: I think I hear them. Stand, ho! Who is there?
HORATIO: Friends to this ground.

ACT I, SCENE I. **s.d. platform:** A level space on the battlements of the royal castle at Elsinore, a Danish seaport; now Helsingör. **2. me:** This is emphatic, since Francisco is the sentry. **3. Long live the king:** Either a password or greeting; Horatio and Marcellus use a different one in line 15. **13. rivals:** Partners.

MARCELLUS: And liegemen to the Dane.
FRANCISCO: Give you° good night.
MARCELLUS: O, farewell, honest soldier:
Who hath reliev'd you?
FRANCISCO: Bernardo hath my place.
Give you good night. *Exit Francisco.*
MARCELLUS: Holla! Bernardo!
BERNARDO: Say,
What, is Horatio there?
HORATIO: A piece of him.
BERNARDO: Welcome, Horatio: welcome, good Marcellus.
MARCELLUS: What, has this thing appear'd again to-night?
BERNARDO: I have seen nothing.
MARCELLUS: Horatio says 'tis but our fantasy,
And will not let belief take hold of him
Touching this dreaded sight, twice seen of us:
Therefore I have entreated him along
With us to watch the minutes of this night;
That if again this apparition come,
He may approve° our eyes and speak to it.
HORATIO: Tush, tush, 'twill not appear.
BERNARDO: Sit down awhile;
And let us once again assail your ears,
That are so fortified against our story
What we have two nights seen.
HORATIO: Well, sit we down,
And let us hear Bernardo speak of this.
BERNARDO: Last night of all,
When yond same star that's westward from the pole°
Had made his course t' illume that part of heaven
Where now it burns, Marcellus and myself,
The bell then beating one, —

Enter Ghost.

MARCELLUS: Peace, break thee off; look, where it comes again!
BERNARDO: In the same figure, like the king that's dead.
MARCELLUS: Thou art a scholar;° speak to it, Horatio.
BERNARDO: Looks 'a° not like the king? mark it, Horatio.
HORATIO: Most like: it harrows° me with fear and wonder.
BERNARDO: It would be spoke to.°
MARCELLUS: Speak to it, Horatio.
HORATIO: What art thou that usurp'st this time of night,

---

16. Give you: God give you. **29. approve:** Corroborate. **36. pole:** Polestar. **42. scholar:** Exorcisms were performed in Latin, which Horatio, as an educated man, would be able to speak. **43. a:** He **44. harrows:** Lacerates the feelings. **45. It . . . to:** A ghost could not speak until spoken to.

Together with that fair and warlike form
In which the majesty of buried Denmark°
Did sometimes march? by heaven I charge thee, speak!
MARCELLUS: It is offended.
BERNARDO: See it stalks away!
HORATIO: Stay! speak, speak! I charge thee, speak! *Exit Ghost.*
MARCELLUS: 'Tis gone, and will not answer.
BERNARDO: How now, Horatio! you tremble and look pale:
Is not this something more than fantasy?
What think you on 't?
HORATIO: Before my God, I might not this believe
Without the sensible and true avouch
Of mine own eyes.
MARCELLUS: Is it not like the king?
HORATIO: As thou art to thyself:
Such was the very armour he had on
When he the ambitious Norway combated;
So frown'd he once, when, in an angry parle,
He smote° the sledded Polacks° on the ice.
'Tis strange.
MARCELLUS: Thus twice before, and jump° at this dead hour,
With martial stalk hath he gone by our watch.
HORATIO: In what particular thought to work I know not;
But in the gross and scope° of my opinion,
This bodes some strange eruption to our state.
MARCELLUS: Good now,° sit down, and tell me, he that knows,
Why this same strict and most observant watch
So nightly toils° the subject° of the land,
And why such daily cast° of brazen cannon,
And foreign mart° for implements of war;
Why such impress° of shipwrights, whose sore task
Does not divide the Sunday from the week;
What might be toward, that this sweaty haste
Doth make the night joint-labourer with the day:
Who is't that can inform me?
HORATIO: That can I;
At least, the whisper goes so. Our last king,
Whose image even but now appear'd to us,
Was, as you know, by Fortinbras of Norway,
Thereto prick'd on° by a most emulate° pride,

48. buried Denmark: The buried king of Denmark. **63. smote:** Defeated. **sledded Polacks:** Polish people using sledges. **65. jump:** Exactly. **68. gross and scope:** General drift. **70. Good now:** An expression denoting entreaty or expostulation. **72. toils:** Causes or makes to toil. **subject:** People, subjects. **73. cast:** Casting, founding. **74. mart:** Buying and selling, traffic. **75. impress:** Impressment. **83. prick'd on:** Incited. **emulate:** Rivaling.

Dar'd to the combat; in which our valiant Hamlet—
For so this side of our known world esteem'd him—
Did slay this Fortinbras; who, by a seal'd compact,
Well ratified by law and heraldry,°
Did forfeit, with his life, all those his lands
Which he stood seiz'd° of, to the conqueror:
Against the which, a moiety competent°
Was gaged by our king; which had return'd
To the inheritance of Fortinbras,
Had he been vanquisher; as, by the same comart,°
And carriage° of the article design'd,
His fell to Hamlet. Now, sir, young Fortinbras,
Of unimproved° mettle hot and full,°
Hath in the skirts of Norway here and there
Shark'd up° a list of lawless resolutes,°
For food and diet,° to some enterprise
That hath a stomach in't; which is no other—
As it doth well appear unto our state—
But to recover of us, by strong hand
And terms compulsatory, those foresaid lands
So by his father lost: and this, I take it,
Is the main motive of our preparations,
The source of this our watch and the chief head
Of this post-haste and romage° in the land.

BERNARDO: I think it be no other but e'en so:
Well may it sort° that this portentous figure
Comes armed through our watch; so like the king
That was and is the question of these wars.

HORATIO: A mote° it is to trouble the mind's eye.
In the most high and palmy state° of Rome,
A little ere the mightiest Julius fell,
The graves stood tenantless and the sheeted dead
Did squeak and gibber in the Roman streets:
As stars with trains of fire° and dews of blood,
Disasters° in the sun; and the moist star°
Upon whose influence Neptune's empire° stands
Was sick almost to doomsday with eclipse:
And even the like precurse° of fear'd events,

---

87. law and heraldry: Heraldic law, governing combat. **89. seiz'd:** Possessed. **90. moiety competent:** Adequate or sufficient portion. **93. comart:** Joint bargain. **94. carriage:** Import, bearing. **96. unimproved:** Not turned to account. **hot and full:** Full of fight. **98. Shark'd up:** Got together in haphazard fashion. **resolutes:** Desperadoes. **99. food and diet:** No pay but their keep. **107. romage:** Bustle, commotion. **109. sort:** Suit. **112. mote:** Speck of dust. **113. palmy state:** Triumphant sovereignty. **117. stars . . . fire:** I.e., comets. **118. Disasters:** Unfavorable aspects. **moist star:** The moon, governing tides. **119. Neptune's empire:** The sea. **121. precurse:** Heralding.

As harbingers preceding still the fates
And prologue to the omen coming on,
Have heaven and earth together demonstrated
Unto our climatures and countrymen.—

Enter Ghost.

But soft, behold! lo, where it comes again!
I'll cross° it, though it blast me. Stay, illusion!
If thou hast any sound, or use of voice,
Speak to me! *It° spreads his arms.*
If there be any good thing to be done,
That may to thee do ease and grace to me,
Speak to me!
If thou art privy to thy country's fate,
Which, happily, foreknowing may avoid,
O, speak!
Or if thou hast uphoarded in thy life
Extorted treasure in the womb of earth,
For which, they say, you spirits oft walk in death, *The cock crows.*
Speak of it:° stay, and speak! Stop it, Marcellus.

MARCELLUS: Shall I strike at it with my partisan?°

HORATIO: Do, if it will not stand.

BERNARDO: 'Tis here!

HORATIO: 'Tis here!

MARCELLUS: 'Tis gone! *[Exit Ghost.]*
We do it wrong, being so majestical,
To offer it the show of violence;
For it is, as the air, invulnerable,
And our vain blows malicious mockery.

BERNARDO: It was about to speak, when the cock crew.°

HORATIO: And then it started like a guilty thing
Upon a fearful summons. I have heard,
The cock, that is the trumpet to the morn,
Doth with his lofty and shrill-sounding throat
Awake the god of day; and, at his warning,
Whether in sea or fire, in earth or air,
Th' extravagant and erring° spirit hies
To his confine:° and of the truth herein
This present object made probation.°

MARCELLUS: It faded on the crowing of the cock.

---

127. cross: Meet, face, thus bringing down the evil influence on the person who crosses it. **129. It:** The Ghost, or perhaps Horatio. **133–139. If . . . it:** Horatio recites the traditional reasons why ghosts might walk. **140. partisan:** Long-handled spear with a blade having lateral projections. **147. cock crew:** According to traditional ghost lore, spirits returned to their confines at cockcrow. **154. extravagant and erring:** Wandering. Both words mean the same thing. **155. confine:** Place of confinement. **156. probation:** Proof, trial.

Some say that ever 'gainst° that season comes
Wherein our Saviour's birth is celebrated,
The bird of dawning singeth all night long:
And then, they say, no spirit dare stir abroad;
The nights are wholesome; then no planets strike,°
No fairy takes, nor witch hath power to charm,
So hallow'd and so gracious° is that time.

HORATIO: So have I heard and do in part believe it.
But, look, the morn, in russet mantle clad,
Walks o'er the dew of yon high eastward hill:
Break we our watch up; and by my advice,
Let us impart what we have seen to-night
Unto young Hamlet; for, upon my life,
This spirit, dumb to us, will speak to him.
Do you consent we shall acquaint him with it,
As needful in our loves, fitting our duty?

MARCELLUS: Let's do 't, I pray; and I this morning know
Where we shall find him most conveniently. *Exeunt.*

[SCENE II: *A room of state in the castle.*]

Flourish. Enter Claudius, King of Denmark, Gertrude the Queen, Councilors, Polonius and his Son Laertes, Hamlet, cum aliis° [*including Voltimand and Cornelius*].

KING: Though yet of Hamlet our dear brother's death
The memory be green, and that it us befitted
To bear our hearts in grief and our whole kingdom
To be contracted in one brow of woe,
Yet so far hath discretion fought with nature
That we with wisest sorrow think on him,
Together with remembrance of ourselves.
Therefore our sometime sister, now our queen,
Th' imperial jointress° to this warlike state,
Have we, as 'twere with a defeated joy, —
With an auspicious and a dropping eye,
With mirth in funeral and with dirge in marriage,
In equal scale weighing delight and dole, —
Taken to wife: nor have we herein barr'd
Your better wisdoms, which have freely gone
With this affair along. For all, our thanks.
Now follows, that° you know, young Fortinbras,
Holding a weak supposal° of our worth,
Or thinking by our late dear brother's death

158. 'gainst: Just before. **162. planets strike:** It was thought that planets were malignant and might strike travelers by night. **164. gracious:** Full of goodness. ACT I, SCENE II. **s.d. cum aliis:** With others. **9. jointress:** Woman possessed of a jointure, or joint tenancy of an estate. **17. that:** That which. **18. weak supposal:** Low estimate.

Our state to be disjoint° and out of frame,°
Colleagued° with this dream of his advantage,°
He hath not fail'd to pester us with message,
Importing° the surrender of those lands
Lost by his father, with all bands of law,
To our most valiant brother. So much for him.
Now for ourself and for this time of meeting:
Thus much the business is: we have here writ
To Norway, uncle of young Fortinbras,—
Who, impotent and bed-rid, scarcely hears
Of this his nephew's purpose,—to suppress
His further gait° herein; in that the levies,
The lists and full proportions, are all made
Out of his subject:° and we here dispatch
You, good Cornelius, and you, Voltimand,
For bearers of this greeting to old Norway;
Giving to you no further personal power
To business with the king, more than the scope
Of these delated° articles allow.
Farewell, and let your haste commend your duty.

CORNELIUS: / VOLTIMAND: In that and all things will we show our duty.

KING: We doubt it nothing: heartily farewell.

[*Exeunt Voltimand and Cornelius.*]

And now, Laertes, what's the news with you?
You told us of some suit; what is't, Laertes?
You cannot speak of reason to the Dane,°
And lose your voice:° what wouldst thou beg, Laertes,
That shall not be my offer, not thy asking?
The head is not more native° to the heart,
The hand more instrumental° to the mouth,
Than is the throne of Denmark to thy father.
What wouldst thou have, Laertes?

LAERTES: My dread lord,
Your leave and favour to return to France;
From whence though willingly I came to Denmark,
To show my duty in your coronation,
Yet now, I must confess, that duty done,
My thoughts and wishes bend again toward France
And bow them to your gracious leave and pardon.°

---

20. disjoint: Distracted, out of joint. **frame:** Order. **21. Colleagued:** added to. **dream . . . advantage:** Visionary hope of success. **23. Importing:** Purporting, pertaining to. **31. gait:** Proceeding. **33. Out of his subject:** At the expense of Norway's subjects (collectively). **38. delated:** Expressly stated. **44. the Dane:** Danish king. **45. lose your voice:** Speak in vain. **47. native:** Closely connected, related. **48. instrumental:** Serviceable. **56. leave and pardon:** Permission to depart.

KING: Have you your father's leave? What says Polonius?
POLONIUS: He hath, my lord, wrung from me my slow leave
By laboursome petition, and at last
Upon his will I seal'd my hard consent:
I do beseech you, give him leave to go.
KING: Take thy fair hour, Laertes; time be thine,
And thy best graces spend it at thy will!
But now, my cousin° Hamlet, and my son,—
HAMLET [*aside*]: A little more than kin, and less than kind!°
KING: How is it that the clouds still hang on you?
HAMLET: Not so, my lord; I am too much in the sun.°
QUEEN: Good Hamlet, cast thy nighted colour off,
And let thine eye look like a friend on Denmark.
Do not for ever with thy vailed lids
Seek for thy noble father in the dust:
Thou know'st 'tis common; all that lives must die,
Passing through nature to eternity.
HAMLET: Ay, madam, it is common.°
QUEEN: If it be,
Why seems it so particular with thee?
HAMLET: Seems, madam! nay, it is; I know not "seems."
'Tis not alone my inky cloak, good mother,
Nor customary suits° of solemn black,
Nor windy suspiration° of forc'd breath,
No, nor the fruitful river in the eye,
Nor the dejected 'haviour of the visage,
Together with all forms, moods, shapes of grief,
That can denote me truly: these indeed seem,
For they are actions that a man might play:
But I have that within which passeth show;
These but the trappings and the suits of woe.
KING: 'Tis sweet and commendable in your nature, Hamlet,
To give these mourning duties to your father:
But, you must know, your father lost a father;
That father lost, lost his, and the survivor bound
In filial obligation for some term
To do obsequious° sorrow: but to persever
In obstinate condolement° is a course

64. cousin: Any kin not of the immediate family. **65. A little . . . kind:** My relation to you has become more than kinship warrants; it has also become unnatural. **67. I am . . . sun:** The senses seem to be: I am too much out of doors, I am too much in the sun of your grace (ironical), I am too much of a son to you. Possibly an allusion to the proverb "Out of heaven's blessing into the warm sun"; i.e., Hamlet is out of house and home in being deprived of the kingship. **74. Ay . . . common:** It is common, but it hurts nevertheless; possibly a reference to the commonplace quality of the queen's remark. **78. customary suits:** Suits prescribed by custom for mourning. **79. windy suspiration:** Heavy sighing. **92. obsequious:** Dutiful. **93. condolement:** Sorrowing.

Of impious stubbornness; 'tis unmanly grief;
It shows a will most incorrect° to heaven,
A heart unfortified, a mind impatient,
An understanding simple and unschool'd:
For what we know must be and is as common
As any the most vulgar thing° to sense,
Why should we in our peevish opposition
Take it to heart? Fie! 'tis a fault to heaven,
A fault against the dead, a fault to nature,
To reason most absurd; whose common theme
Is death of fathers, and who still hath cried,
From the first corse till he that died to-day,
"This must be so." We pray you, throw to earth
This unprevailing° woe, and think of us
As of a father: for let the world take note,
You are the most immediate° to our throne;
And with no less nobility° of love
Than that which dearest father bears his son,
Do I impart° toward you. For your intent
In going back to school in Wittenberg,°
It is most retrograde° to our desire:
And we beseech you, bend you° to remain
Here, in the cheer and comfort of our eye,
Our chiefest courtier, cousin, and our son.

QUEEN: Let not thy mother lose her prayers, Hamlet:
I pray thee, stay with us; go not to Wittenberg.

HAMLET: I shall in all my best obey you, madam.

KING: Why, 'tis a loving and a fair reply:
Be as ourself in Denmark. Madam, come;
This gentle and unforc'd accord of Hamlet
Sits smiling to my heart: in grace whereof,
No jocund health that Denmark drinks to-day,
But the great cannon to the clouds shall tell,
And the king's rouse° the heaven shall bruit again,°
Re-speaking earthly thunder. Come away.

Flourish. Exeunt all but Hamlet.

HAMLET: O, that this too too sullied flesh would melt,
Thaw and resolve itself into a dew!
Or that the Everlasting had not fix'd
His canon 'gainst self-slaughter! O God! God!

---

95. incorrect: Untrained, uncorrected. **99. vulgar thing:** Common experience. **107. unprevailing:** Unavailing. **109. most immediate:** Next in succession. **110. nobility:** High degree. **112. impart:** The object is apparently love (line 110). **113. Wittenberg:** Famous German university founded in 1502. **114. retrograde:** Contrary. **115. bend you:** Incline yourself; imperative. **127. rouse:** Draft of liquor. **bruit again:** Echo.

How weary, stale, flat and unprofitable,
Seem to me all the uses of this world!
Fie on't! ah fie! 'tis an unweeded garden,
That grows to seed; things rank and gross in nature
Possess it merely.° That it should come to this!
But two months dead: nay, not so much, not two:
So excellent a king; that was, to this,
Hyperion° to a satyr; so loving to my mother
That he might not beteem° the winds of heaven
Visit her face too roughly. Heaven and earth!
Must I remember? why, she would hang on him,
As if increase of appetite had grown
By what it fed on: and yet, within a month—
Let me not think on't—Frailty, thy name is woman!—
A little month, or ere those shoes were old
With which she followed my poor father's body,
Like Niobe,° all tears:—why she, even she—
O God! a beast, that wants discourse of reason,°
Would have mourn'd longer—married with my uncle,
My father's brother, but no more like my father
Than I to Hercules: within a month:
Ere yet the salt of most unrighteous tears
Had left the flushing in her galled° eyes,
She married. O, most wicked speed, to post
With such dexterity° to incestuous sheets!
It is not nor it cannot come to good:
But break, my heart; for I must hold my tongue.

Enter Horatio, Marcellus, and Bernardo.

HORATIO: Hail to your lordship!
HAMLET: I am glad to see you well:
Horatio!—or I do forget myself.
HORATIO: The same, my lord, and your poor servant ever.
HAMLET: Sir, my good friend; I'll change that name with you:°
And what make you from Wittenberg, Horatio?
Marcellus?
MARCELLUS: My good lord—
HAMLET: I am very glad to see you. Good even, sir.
But what, in faith, make you from Wittenberg?

---

137. merely: Completely, entirely. **140. Hyperion:** God of the sun in the older regime of ancient gods. **141. beteem:** Allow. **149. Niobe:** Tantalus's daughter, who boasted that she had more sons and daughters than Leto; for this Apollo and Artemis slew her children. She was turned into stone by Zeus on Mount Sipylus. **150. discourse of reason:** Process or faculty of reason. **155. galled:** Irritated. **157. dexterity:** Facility. **163. I'll . . . you:** I'll be your servant; you shall be my friend; also explained as "I'll exchange the name of friend with you."

HORATIO: A truant disposition, good my lord.
HAMLET: I would not hear your enemy say so,
Nor shall you do my ear that violence,
To make it truster of your own report
Against yourself: I know you are no truant.
But what is your affair in Elsinore?
We'll teach you to drink deep ere you depart.
HORATIO: My lord, I came to see your father's funeral.
HAMLET: I prithee, do not mock me, fellow-student;
I think it was to see my mother's wedding.
HORATIO: Indeed, my lord, it follow'd hard° upon.
HAMLET: Thrift, thrift, Horatio! the funeral bak'd meats°
Did coldly furnish forth the marriage tables.
Would I had met my dearest° foe in heaven
Or ever I had seen that day, Horatio!
My father!—methinks I see my father.
HORATIO: Where, my lord!
HAMLET: In my mind's eye, Horatio.
HORATIO: I saw him once; 'a° was a goodly king.
HAMLET: 'A was a man, take him for all in all,
I shall not look upon his like again.
HORATIO: My lord, I think I saw him yesternight.
HAMLET: Saw? who?
HORATIO: My lord, the king your father.
HAMLET: The king my father!
HORATIO: Season your admiration° for a while
With an attent ear, till I may deliver,
Upon the witness of these gentlemen,
This marvel to you.
HAMLET: For God's love, let me hear.
HORATIO: Two nights together had these gentlemen,
Marcellus and Bernardo, on their watch,
In the dead waste and middle of the night,
Been thus encount'red. A figure like your father,
Armed at point exactly, cap-a-pe,°
Appears before them, and with solemn march
Goes slow and stately by them: thrice he walk'd
By their oppress'd° and fear-surprised eyes,
Within his truncheon's° length; whilst they, distill'd°
Almost to jelly with the act° of fear,

179. hard: Close. **180. bak'd meats:** Meat pies. **182. dearest:** Direst. The adjective *dear* in Shakespeare has two different origins: O.E. *deore,* "beloved," and O.E. *deor,* "fierce." *Dearest* is the superlative of the second. **186. 'a:** He. **192. Season your admiration:** Restrain your astonishment. **200. cap-a-pe:** From head to foot. **203. oppress'd:** Distressed. **204. truncheon:** Officer's staff. **distill'd:** Softened, weakened. **205. act:** Action.

Stand dumb and speak not to him. This to me
In dreadful secrecy impart they did;
And I with them the third night kept the watch:
Where, as they had deliver'd, both in time,
Form of the thing, each word made true and good,
The apparition comes: I knew your father;
These hands are not more like.
HAMLET: But where was this?
MARCELLUS: My lord, upon the platform where we watch'd.
HAMLET: Did you not speak to it?
HORATIO: My lord, I did;
But answer made it none: yet once methought
It lifted up it° head and did address
Itself to motion, like as it would speak;
But even then the morning cock crew loud,
And at the sound it shrunk in haste away,
And vanish'd from our sight.
HAMLET: 'Tis very strange.
HORATIO: As I do live, my honour'd lord, 'tis true;
And we did think it writ down in our duty
To let you know of it.
HAMLET: Indeed, indeed, sirs, but this troubles me.
Hold you the watch to-night?
MARCELLUS: }
BERNARDO: } We do, my lord.
HAMLET: Arm'd, say you?
MARCELLUS: }
BERNARDO: } Arm'd, my lord.
HAMLET: From top to toe?
MARCELLUS: }
BERNARDO: } My lord, from head to foot.
HAMLET: Then saw you not his face?
HORATIO: O, yes, my lord; he wore his beaver° up.
HAMLET: What, look'd he frowningly?
HORATIO: A countenance more
In sorrow than in anger.
HAMLET: Pale or red?
HORATIO: Nay, very pale.
HAMLET: And fix'd his eyes upon you?
HORATIO: Most constantly.
HAMLET: I would I had been there.
HORATIO: It would have much amaz'd you.
HAMLET: Very like, very like. Stay'd it long?
HORATIO: While one with moderate haste might tell a hundred.

216. it: Its. **230. beaver:** Visor on the helmet.

MARCELLUS: }
BERNARDO: } Longer, longer.
HORATIO: Not when I saw't.
HAMLET: His beard was grizzled, — no?
HORATIO: It was, as I have seen it in his life,
A sable° silver'd.
HAMLET: I will watch to-night;
Perchance 'twill walk again.
HORATIO: I warr'nt it will.
HAMLET: If it assume my noble father's person,
I'll speak to it, though hell itself should gape
And bid me hold my peace. I pray you all,
If you have hitherto conceal'd this sight,
Let it be tenable in your silence still;
And whatsoever else shall hap to-night,
Give it an understanding, but no tongue:
I will requite your loves. So, fare you well:
Upon the platform, 'twixt eleven and twelve,
I'll visit you.
ALL: Our duty to your honour.
HAMLET: Your loves, as mine to you: farewell. *Exeunt [all but Hamlet].*
My father's spirit in arms! all is not well;
I doubt° some foul play: would the night were come!
Till then sit still, my soul: foul deeds will rise,
Though all the earth o'erwhelm them, to men's eyes. *Exit.*

[SCENE III: *A room in Polonius's house.*]

Enter Laertes and Ophelia, his Sister.

LAERTES: My necessaries are embark'd: farewell:
And, sister, as the winds give benefit
And convoy is assistant,° do not sleep,
But let me hear from you.
OPHELIA: Do you doubt that?
LAERTES: For Hamlet and the trifling of his favour,
Hold it a fashion° and a toy in blood,°
A violet in the youth of primy° nature,
Forward,° not permanent, sweet, not lasting,
The perfume and suppliance of a minute;°
No more.
OPHELIA: No more but so?
LAERTES: Think it no more:
For nature, crescent,° does not grow alone

241. sable: Black color. **255. doubt:** Fear. ACT I, SCENE III. **3. convoy is assistant:** Means of conveyance are available. **6. fashion:** Custom, prevailing usage. **toy in blood:** Passing amorous fancy. **7. primy:** In its prime. **8. Forward:** Precocious. **9. suppliance of a minute:** Diversion to fill up a minute. **11. crescent:** Growing, waxing.

In thews° and bulk, but, as this temple° waxes,
The inward service of the mind and soul
Grows wide withal. Perhaps he loves you now,
And now no soil° nor cautel° doth besmirch
The virtue of his will: but you must fear,
His greatness weigh'd,° his will is not his own;
For he himself is subject to his birth:
He may not, as unvalued persons do,
Carve for himself; for on his choice depends
The safety and health of this whole state;
And therefore must his choice be circumscrib'd
Unto the voice and yielding° of that body
Whereof he is the head. Then if he says he loves you,
It fits your wisdom so far to believe it
As he in his particular act and place
May give his saying deed;° which is no further
Than the main voice of Denmark goes withal.
Then weigh what loss your honour may sustain,
If with too credent° ear you list his songs,
Or lose your heart, or your chaste treasure open
To his unmast'red° importunity.
Fear it, Ophelia, fear it, my dear sister,
And keep you in the rear of your affection,
Out of the shot and danger of desire.
The chariest° maid is prodigal enough,
If she unmask her beauty to the moon:
Virtue itself 'scapes not calumnious strokes:
The canker galls the infants of the spring,°
Too oft before their buttons° be disclos'd,°
And in the morn and liquid dew° of youth
Contagious blastments° are most imminent.
Be wary then; best safety lies in fear:
Youth to itself rebels, though none else near.

OPHELIA: I shall the effect of this good lesson keep,
As watchman to my heart. But, good my brother,
Do not, as some ungracious° pastors do,
Show me the steep and thorny way to heaven;
Whiles, like a puff'd° and reckless libertine,
Himself the primrose path of dalliance treads,
And recks° not his own rede.°

---

12. thews: Bodily strength. **temple:** Body. **15. soil:** blemish. **cautel:** Crafty device. **17. greatness weigh'd:** High position considered. **23. voice and yielding:** Assent, approval. **27. deed:** Effect. **30. credent:** Credulous. **32. unmast'red:** Unrestrained. **36. chariest:** Most scrupulously modest. **39. The canker . . . spring:** The canker-worm destroys the young plants of spring. **40. buttons:** Buds. **disclos'd:** Opened. **41. liquid dew:** I.e., time when dew is fresh. **42. blastments:** Blights. **47. ungracious:** Graceless. **49. puff'd:** Bloated. **51. recks:** Heeds. **rede:** Counsel.

Enter Polonius.

LAERTES: O, fear me not.
I stay too long: but here my father comes.
A double° blessing is a double grace;
Occasion° smiles upon a second leave.
POLONIUS: Yet here, Laertes? aboard, aboard, for shame!
The wind sits in the shoulder of your sail,
And you are stay'd for. There; my blessing with thee!
And these few precepts° in thy memory
Look thou character.° Give thy thoughts no tongue,
Nor any unproportion'd° thought his act.
Be thou familiar, but by no means vulgar.°
Those friends thou hast, and their adoption tried,
Grapple them to thy soul with hoops of steel;
But do not dull thy palm with entertainment
Of each new-hatch'd, unfledg'd° comrade. Beware
Of entrance to a quarrel, but being in,
Bear't that th' opposed may beware of thee.
Give every man thy ear, but few thy voice;
Take each man's censure, but reserve thy judgement.
Costly thy habit as thy purse can buy,
But not express'd in fancy;° rich, not gaudy;
For the apparel oft proclaims the man,
And they in France of the best rank and station
Are of a most select and generous chief in that.°
Neither a borrower nor a lender be;
For loan oft loses both itself and friend,
And borrowing dulleth edge of husbandry.°
This above all: to thine own self be true,
And it must follow, as the night the day,
Thou canst not then be false to any man.
Farewell: my blessing season° this in thee!
LAERTES: Most humbly do I take my leave, my lord.
POLONIUS: The time invites you; go; your servants tend.
LAERTES: Farewell, Ophelia; and remember well
What I have said to you.
OPHELIA: 'Tis in my memory lock'd,
And you yourself shall keep the key of it.
LAERTES: Farewell. *Exit Laertes.*

---

53. double: I.e., Laertes has already bade his father good-by. **54. Occasion:** Opportunity. **58. precepts:** Many parallels have been found to the series of maxims which follows, one of the closer being that in Lyly's *Euphues.* **59. character:** Inscribe. **60. unproportion'd:** Inordinate. **61. vulgar:** Common. **65. unfledg'd:** Immature. **71. express'd in fancy:** Fantastical in design. **74. Are . . . that:** *Chief* is usually taken as a substantive meaning "head," "eminence." **77. husbandry:** Thrift. **81. season:** Mature.

POLONIUS: What is 't, Ophelia, he hath said to you?
OPHELIA: So please you, something touching the Lord Hamlet.
POLONIUS: Marry, well bethought:
'Tis told me, he hath very oft of late
Given private time to you; and you yourself
Have of your audience been most free and bounteous:
If it be so, as so't is put on° me,
And that in way of caution, I must tell you,
You do not understand yourself so clearly
As it behooves my daughter and your honour.
What is between you? give me up the truth.
OPHELIA: He hath, my lord, of late made many tenders°
Of his affection to me.
POLONIUS: Affection! pooh! you speak like a green girl,
Unsifted° in such perilous circumstance.
Do you believe his tenders, as you call them?
OPHELIA: I do not know, my lord, what I should think.
POLONIUS: Marry, I will teach you: think yourself a baby;
That you have ta'en these tenders° for true pay,
Which are not sterling.° Tender° yourself more dearly;
Or—not to crack the wind° of the poor phrase,
Running it thus—you'll tender me a fool.°
OPHELIA: My lord, he hath importun'd me with love
In honourable fashion.
POLONIUS: Ay, fashion° you may call it; go to, go to.
OPHELIA: And hath given countenance° to his speech, my lord,
With almost all the holy vows of heaven.
POLONIUS: Ay, springes° to catch woodcocks.° I do know,
When the blood burns, how prodigal the soul
Lends the tongue vows: these blazes, daughter,
Giving more light than heat, extinct in both,
Even in their promise, as it is a-making,
You must not take for fire. From this time
Be somewhat scanter of your maiden presence;
Set your entreatments° at a higher rate
Than a command to parley.° For Lord Hamlet,
Believe so much in him,° that he is young,
And with a larger tether may he walk
Than may be given you: in few,° Ophelia,

---

94. put on: Impressed on. **99, 103. tenders:** Offers. **102. Unsifted:** Untried. **106. tenders:** Promises to pay. **107. sterling:** Legal currency. **Tender:** Hold. **108. crack the wind:** I.e., run it until it is broken-winded. **109. tender . . . fool:** Show me a fool (for a daughter). **112. fashion:** Mere form, pretense. **113. countenance:** Credit, support. **115. springes:** Snares. **woodcocks:** Birds easily caught, type of stupidity. **122. entreatments:** Conversations, interviews. **123. command to parley:** Mere invitation to talk. **124. so . . . him:** This much concerning him. **126. in few:** Briefly.

Do not believe his vows; for they are brokers;°
Not of that dye° which their investments° show,
But mere implorators of° unholy suits,
Breathing° like sanctified and pious bawds,
The better to beguile. This is for all:
I would not, in plain terms, from this time forth,
Have you so slander° any moment leisure,
As to give words or talk with the Lord Hamlet.
Look to 't, I charge you: come your ways.

OPHELIA: I shall obey, my lord. *Exeunt.*

[SCENE IV: *The platform.*]

Enter Hamlet, Horatio, and Marcellus.

HAMLET: The air bites shrewdly; it is very cold.
HORATIO: It is a nipping and an eager air.
HAMLET: What hour now?
HORATIO: I think it lacks of twelve.
MARCELLUS: No, it is struck.
HORATIO: Indeed? I heard it not: then it draws near the season
Wherein the spirit held his wont to walk.

A flourish of trumpets, and two pieces go off.

What does this mean, my lord?
HAMLET: The king doth wake° to-night and takes his rouse,°
Keeps wassail,° and the swagg'ring up-spring° reels;°
And, as he drains his draughts of Rhenish° down,
The kettle-drum and trumpet thus bray out
The triumph of his pledge.°
HORATIO: Is it a custom?
HAMLET: Ay, marry, is 't:
But to my mind, though I am native here
And to the manner born,° it is a custom
More honour'd in the breach than the observance.
This heavy-headed revel east and west
Makes us traduc'd and tax'd of other nations:
They clepe° us drunkards, and with swinish phrase°
Soil our addition;° and indeed it takes
From our achievements, though perform'd at height,
The pith and marrow of our attribute.°

---

127. brokers: Go-betweens, procurers. **128. dye:** Color or sort. **investments:** Clothes. **129. implorators of:** Solicitors of. **130. Breathing:** Speaking. **133. slander:** Bring disgrace or reproach upon. ACT I, SCENE IV. **8. wake:** Stay awake, hold revel. **rouse:** Carouse, drinking bout. **9. wassail:** Carousal. **up-spring:** Last and wildest dance at German merry-makings. **reels:** Reels through. **10. Rhenish:** Rhine wine. **12. triumph . . . pledge:** His glorious achievement as a drinker. **15. to . . . born:** Destined by birth to be subject to the custom in question. **19. clepe:** Call. **with swinish phrase:** By calling us swine. **20. addition:** Reputation. **22. attribute:** Reputation.

So, oft it chances in particular men,
That for some vicious mole of nature° in them,
As, in their birth—wherein they are not guilty,
Since nature cannot choose his origin—
By the o'ergrowth of some complexion,
Oft breaking down the pales° and forts of reason,
Or by some habit that too much o'er-leavens°
The form of plausive° manners, that these men,
Carrying, I say, the stamp of one defect,
Being nature's livery,° or fortune's star,°—
Their virtues else—be they as pure as grace,
As infinite as man may undergo—
Shall in the general censure take corruption
From that particular fault: the dram of eale
Doth all the noble substance of a doubt
To his own scandal.°

Enter Ghost.

HORATIO: Look, my lord, it comes!

HAMLET: Angels and ministers of grace° defend us!
Be thou a spirit of health or goblin damn'd,
Bring with thee airs from heaven or blasts from hell,
Be thy intents wicked or charitable,
Thou com'st in such a questionable° shape
That I will speak to thee: I'll call thee Hamlet,
King, father, royal Dane: O, answer me!
Let me not burst in ignorance; but tell
Why thy canoniz'd° bones, hearsed° in death,
Have burst their cerements;° why the sepulchre,
Wherein we saw thee quietly interr'd,
Hath op'd his ponderous and marble jaws,
To cast thee up again. What may this mean,
That thou, dead corse, again in complete steel
Revisits thus the glimpses of the moon,°
Making night hideous; and we fools of nature°
So horridly to shake our disposition
With thoughts beyond the reaches of our souls?
Say, why is this? wherefore? what should we do?

---

24. mole of nature: Natural blemish in one's constitution. **28. pales:** Palings (as of a fortification). **29. o'er-leavens:** Induces a change throughout (as yeast works in bread). **30. plausive:** Pleasing. **32. nature's livery:** Endowment from nature. **fortune's star:** The position in which one is placed by fortune, a reference to astrology. The two phrases are aspects of the same thing. **36–38. the dram . . . scandal:** A famous crux: dram of eale has had various interpretations, the preferred one being probably, "a dram of evil." **39. ministers of grace:** Messengers of God. **43. questionable:** Inviting question or conversation. **47. canoniz'd:** Buried according to the canons of the church. **hearsed:** Coffined. **48. cerements:** Grave-clothes. **53. glimpses of the moon:** The earth by night. **54. fools of nature:** Mere men, limited to natural knowledge.

[Ghost] beckons [Hamlet].

HORATIO: It beckons you to go away with it,
As if it some impartment° did desire
To you alone.

MARCELLUS: Look, with what courteous action
It waves you to a more removed° ground:
But do not go with it.

HORATIO: No, by no means.

HAMLET: It will not speak; then I will follow it.

HORATIO: Do not, my lord!

HAMLET: Why, what should be the fear?
I do not set my life at a pin's fee;
And for my soul, what can it do to that,
Being a thing immortal as itself?
It waves me forth again: I'll follow it.

HORATIO: What if it tempt you toward the flood, my lord,
Or to the dreadful summit of the cliff
That beetles o'er° his base into the sea,
And there assume some other horrible form,
Which might deprive your sovereignty of reason°
And draw you into madness? think of it:
The very place puts toys of desperation,°
Without more motive, into every brain
That looks so many fathoms to the sea
And hears it roar beneath.

HAMLET: It waves me still.
Go on; I'll follow thee.

MARCELLUS: You shall not go, my lord.

HAMLET: Hold off your hands!

HORATIO: Be rul'd; you shall not go.

HAMLET: My fate cries out,
And makes each petty artere° in this body
As hardy as the Nemean lion's° nerve.°
Still am I call'd. Unhand me, gentlemen.
By heaven, I'll make a ghost of him that lets° me!
I say, away! Go on; I'll follow thee. *Exeunt Ghost and Hamlet.*

HORATIO: He waxes desperate with imagination.

MARCELLUS: Let's follow; 'tis not fit thus to obey him.

HORATIO: Have after. To what issue° will this come?

---

59. impartment: Communication. **61. removed:** Remote. **71. beetles o'er:** Overhangs threateningly. **73. deprive . . . reason:** Take away the sovereignty of your reason. It was thought that evil spirits would sometimes assume the form of departed spirits in order to work madness in a human creature. **75. toys of desperation:** Freakish notions of suicide. **82. artere:** Artery. **83. Nemean lion's:** The Nemean lion was one of the monsters slain by Hercules. **nerve:** Sinew, tendon. The point is that the arteries which were carrying the spirits out into the body were functioning and were as stiff and hard as the sinews of the lion. **85. lets:** Hinders. **89. issue:** Outcome.

MARCELLUS: Something is rotten in the state of Denmark.
HORATIO: Heaven will direct it.°
MARCELLUS: Nay, let's follow him. *Exeunt.*

[SCENE V: *Another part of the platform.*]

Enter Ghost and Hamlet.

HAMLET: Whither wilt thou lead me? speak; I'll go no further.
GHOST: Mark me.
HAMLET: I will.
GHOST: My hour is almost come,
When I to sulphurous and tormenting flames
Must render up myself.
HAMLET: Alas, poor ghost!
GHOST: Pity me not, but lend thy serious hearing
To what I shall unfold.
HAMLET: Speak; I am bound to hear.
GHOST: So art thou to revenge, when thou shalt hear.
HAMLET: What?
GHOST: I am thy father's spirit,
Doom'd for a certain term to walk the night,
And for the day confin'd to fast° in fires,
Till the foul crimes done in my days of nature
Are burnt and purg'd away. But that I am forbid
To tell the secrets of my prison-house,
I could a tale unfold whose lightest word
Would harrow up thy soul, freeze thy young blood,
Make thy two eyes, like stars, start from their spheres,°
Thy knotted° and combined° locks to part
And each particular hair to stand an end,
Like quills upon the fretful porpentine:°
But this eternal blazon° must not be
To ears of flesh and blood. List, list, O, list!
If thou didst ever thy dear father love—
HAMLET: O God!
GHOST: Revenge his foul and most unnatural° murder.
HAMLET: Murder!
GHOST: Murder most foul, as in the best it is;
But this most foul, strange and unnatural.
HAMLET: Haste me to know't, that I, with wings as swift
As meditation or the thoughts of love,
May sweep to my revenge.

91. it: I.e., the outcome. ACT I, SCENE V. **11. fast:** Probably, do without food. It has been sometimes taken in the sense of doing general penance. **17. spheres:** Orbits. **18. knotted:** Perhaps intricately arranged. **combined:** Tied, bound. **20. porpentine:** Porcupine. **21. eternal blazon:** Promulgation or proclamation of eternity, revelation of the hereafter. **25. unnatural:** I.e., pertaining to fratricide.

GHOST: I find thee apt;
And duller shouldst thou be than the fat weed°
That roots itself in ease on Lethe wharf,°
Wouldst thou not stir in this. Now, Hamlet, hear:
'Tis given out that, sleeping in my orchard,
A serpent stung me; so the whole ear of Denmark
Is by a forged process of my death
Rankly abus'd: but know, thou noble youth,
The serpent that did sting thy father's life
Now wears his crown.
HAMLET: O my prophetic soul!
My uncle!
GHOST: Ay, that incestuous, that adulterate° beast,
With witchcraft of his wit, with traitorous gifts, —
O wicked wit and gifts, that have the power
So to seduce! — won to his shameful lust
The will of my most seeming-virtuous queen:
O Hamlet, what a falling-off was there!
From me, whose love was of that dignity
That it went hand in hand even with the vow
I made to her in marriage, and to decline
Upon a wretch whose natural gifts were poor
To those of mine!
But virtue, as it never will be moved,
Though lewdness court it in a shape of heaven,
So lust, though to a radiant angel link'd,
Will sate itself in a celestial bed,
And prey on garbage.
But, soft! methinks I scent the morning air;
Brief let me be. Sleeping within my orchard,
My custom always of the afternoon,
Upon my secure° hour thy uncle stole,
With juice of cursed hebona° in a vial,
And in the porches of my ears did pour
The leperous° distilment; whose effect
Holds such an enmity with blood of man
That swift as quicksilver it courses through
The natural gates and alleys of the body,
And with a sudden vigour it doth posset°
And curd, like eager° droppings into milk,

---

32. fat weed: Many suggestions have been offered as to the particular plant intended, including asphodel; probably a general figure for plants growing along rotting wharves and piles. **33. Lethe wharf:** Bank of the river of forgetfulness in Hades. **42. adulterate:** Adulterous. **61. secure:** Confident, unsuspicious. **62. hebona:** Generally supposed to mean henbane, conjectured hemlock; ebenus, meaning "yew." **64. leperous:** Causing leprosy. **68. posset:** Coagulate, curdle. **69. eager:** Sour, acid.

The thin and wholesome blood: so did it mine;
And a most instant tetter bark'd about,
Most lazar-like,° with vile and loathsome crust,
All my smooth body.
Thus was I, sleeping, by a brother's hand
Of life, of crown, of queen, at once dispatch'd:°
Cut off even in the blossoms of my sin,
Unhous'led,° disappointed,° unanel'd,°
No reck'ning made, but sent to my account
With all my imperfections on my head:
O, horrible! O, horrible! most horrible!°
If thou hast nature in thee, bear it not;
Let not the royal bed of Denmark be
A couch for luxury° and damned incest.
But, howsomever thou pursues this act,
Taint not thy mind,° nor let thy soul contrive
Against thy mother aught: leave her to heaven
And to those thorns that in her bosom lodge,
To prick and sting her. Fare thee well at once!
The glow-worm shows the matin° to be near,
And 'gins to pale his uneffectual fire:°
Adieu, adieu, adieu! remember me. [*Exit.*]

HAMLET: O all you host of heaven! O earth! what else?
And shall I couple° hell? O, fie! Hold, hold, my heart;
And you, my sinews, grow not instant old,
But bear me stiffly up. Remember thee!
Ay, thou poor ghost, whiles memory holds a seat
In this distracted globe.° Remember thee!
Yea, from the table of my memory
I'll wipe away all trivial fond records,
All saws° of books, all forms, all pressures° past,
That youth and observation copied there;
And thy commandment all alone shall live
Within the book and volume of my brain,
Unmix'd with baser matter: yes, by heaven!
O most pernicious woman!
O villain, villain, smiling, damned villain!
My tables,°—meet it is I set it down,

---

72. lazar-like: Leperlike. **75. dispatch'd:** Suddenly bereft. **77. Unhous'led:** Without having received the sacrament. **disappointed:** Unready, without equipment for the last journey. **unanel'd:** Without having received extreme unction. **80. O . . . horrible:** Many editors give this line to Hamlet; Garrick and Sir Henry Irving spoke it in that part. **83. luxury:** Lechery. **85. Taint . . . mind:** Probably, deprave not thy character, do nothing except in the pursuit of a natural revenge. **89. matin:** Morning. **90. uneffectual fire:** Cold light. **93. couple:** Add. **97. distracted globe:** Confused head. **100. saws:** Wise sayings. **pressures:** Impressions stamped. **107. tables:** Probably a small portable writing tablet carried at the belt.

That one may smile, and smile, and be a villain;
At least I am sure it may be so in Denmark: [*Writing.*]
So, uncle, there you are. Now to my word;°
It is "Adieu, adieu! remember me,"
I have sworn't.

Enter Horatio and Marcellus.

HORATIO: My lord, my lord—
MARCELLUS: Lord Hamlet,—
HORATIO: Heavens secure him!
HAMLET: So be it!
MARCELLUS: Hillo, ho, ho,° my lord!
HAMLET: Hillo, ho, ho, boy! come, bird, come.
MARCELLUS: How is't, my noble lord?
HORATIO: What news, my lord?
HAMLET: O, wonderful!
HORATIO: Good my lord, tell it.
HAMLET: No; you will reveal it.
HORATIO: Not I, my lord, by heaven.
MARCELLUS: Nor I, my lord.
HAMLET: How say you, then; would heart of man once think it?
But you'll be secret?
HORATIO: / MARCELLUS: Ay, by heaven, my lord.
HAMLET: There's ne'er a villain dwelling in all Denmark
But he's an arrant° knave.
HORATIO: There needs no ghost, my lord, come from the grave
To tell us this.
HAMLET: Why, right; you are in the right;
And so, without more circumstance at all,
I hold it fit that we shake hands and part:
You, as your business and desire shall point you;
For every man has business and desire,
Such as it is; and for my own poor part,
Look you, I'll go pray.
HORATIO: These are but wild and whirling words, my lord.
HAMLET: I am sorry they offend you, heartily;
Yes, 'faith, heartily.
HORATIO: There's no offence, my lord.
HAMLET: Yes, by Saint Patrick,° but there is, Horatio,
And much offence too. Touching this vision here,
It is an honest° ghost, that let me tell you:
For your desire to know what is between us,

---

110. word: Watchword. **115. Hillo, ho, ho:** A falconer's call to a hawk in air. **124. arrant:** Thoroughgoing. **136. Saint Patrick:** St. Patrick was keeper of Purgatory and patron saint of all blunders and confusion. **138. honest:** I.e., a real ghost and not an evil spirit.

O'ermaster 't as you may. And now, good friends,
As you are friends, scholars and soldiers,
Give me one poor request.

HORATIO: What is 't, my lord? we will.

HAMLET: Never make known what you have seen to-night.

HORATIO: }
MARCELLUS: } My lord, we will not.

HAMLET: Nay, but swear 't.

HORATIO: In faith,
My lord, not I.

MARCELLUS: Nor I, my lord, in faith.

HAMLET: Upon my sword.°

MARCELLUS: We have sworn, my lord, already.

HAMLET: Indeed, upon my sword, indeed. *Ghost cries under the stage.*

GHOST: Swear.

HAMLET: Ah, ha, boy! say'st thou so? art thou there, truepenny?°
Come on — you hear this fellow in the cellarage —
Consent to swear.

HORATIO: Propose the oath, my lord.

HAMLET: Never to speak of this that you have seen,
Swear by my sword.

GHOST [*beneath*]: Swear.

HAMLET: Hic et ubique?° then we'll shift our ground.
Come hither, gentlemen,
And lay your hands again upon my sword:
Swear by my sword,
Never to speak of this that you have heard.

GHOST [*beneath*]: Swear by his sword.

HAMLET: Well said, old mole! canst work i' th' earth so fast?
A worthy pioner!° Once more remove, good friends.

HORATIO: O day and night, but this is wondrous strange!

HAMLET: And therefore as a stranger give it welcome.
There are more things in heaven and earth, Horatio,
Than are dreamt of in your philosophy.
But come;
Here, as before, never, so help you mercy,
How strange or odd soe'er I bear myself,
As I perchance hereafter shall think meet
To put an antic° disposition on,
That you, at such times seeing me, never shall,
With arms encumb'red° thus, or this head-shake,
Or by pronouncing of some doubtful phrase,
As "Well, well, we know," or "We could, an if we would,"

---

147. sword: I.e., the hilt in the form of a cross. **150. truepenny:** Good old boy, or the like. **156. Hic et ubique?:** Here and everywhere? **163. pioner:** Digger, miner. **172. antic:** Fantastic. **174. encumb'red:** Folded or entwined.

Or "If we list to speak," or "There be, an if they might,"
Or such ambiguous giving out,° to note°
That you know aught of me: this not to do,
So grace and mercy at your most need help you,
Swear.

GHOST [*beneath*]: Swear.

HAMLET: Rest, rest, perturbed spirit! [*They swear.*] So, gentlemen,
With all my love I do commend me to you:
And what so poor a man as Hamlet is
May do, t' express his love and friending° to you,
God willing, shall not lack. Let us go in together;
And still your fingers on your lips, I pray.
The time is out of joint: O cursed spite,
That ever I was born to set it right!
Nay, come, let's go together. *Exeunt.*

[ACT II

SCENE I: *A room in Polonius's house.*]

Enter old Polonius with his man [*Reynaldo*].

POLONIUS: Give him this money and these notes, Reynaldo.

REYNALDO: I will, my lord.

POLONIUS: You shall do marvellous wisely, good Reynaldo,
Before you visit him, to make inquire
Of his behaviour.

REYNALDO: My lord, I did intend it.

POLONIUS: Marry, well said; very well said. Look you, sir,
Inquire me first what Danskers° are in Paris;
And how, and who, what means, and where they keep,°
What company, at what expense; and finding
By this encompassment° and drift° of question
That they do know my son, come you more nearer
Than your particular demands will touch it:°
Take° you as 'twere, some distant knowledge of him;
As thus, "I know his father and his friends,
And in part him": do you mark this, Reynaldo?

REYNALDO: Ay, very well, my lord.

POLONIUS: "And in part him; but" you may say "not well:
But, if 't be he I mean, he's very wild;
Addicted so and so": and there put on° him

---

178. giving out: Profession of knowledge. **to note:** To give a sign. **186. friending:** Friendliness. ACT II, SCENE I. **7. Danskers:** Danke was a common variant for "Denmark"; hence "Dane." **8. keep:** Dwell. **10. encompassment:** Roundabout talking. **drift:** Gradual approach or course. **11–12. come . . . it:** I.e., you will find out more this way than by asking pointed questions. **13. Take:** Assume, pretend. **19. put on:** Impute to.

What forgeries° you please; marry, none so rank
As may dishonour him; take heed of that;
But, sir, such wanton,° wild and usual slips
As are companions noted and most known
To youth and liberty.

REYNALDO: As gaming, my lord.

POLONIUS: Ay, or drinking, fencing,° swearing, quarrelling,
Drabbing;° you may go so far.

REYNALDO: My lord, that would dishonour him.

POLONIUS: 'Faith, no; as you may season it in the charge.
You must not put another scandal on him,
That he is open to incontinency;°
That's not my meaning: but breathe his faults so quaintly°
That they may seem the taints of liberty°
The flash and outbreak of a fiery mind,
A savageness in unreclaimed° blood,
Of general assault.°

REYNALDO: But, my good lord,—

POLONIUS: Wherefore should you do this?

REYNALDO: Ay, my lord,
I would know that.

POLONIUS: Marry, sir, here's my drift;
And, I believe, it is a fetch of wit:°
You laying these slight sullies on my son,
As 'twere a thing a little soil'd i' th' working,
Mark you,
Your party in converse, him you would sound,
Having ever° seen in the prenominate° crimes
The youth you breathe of guilty, be assur'd
He closes with you in this consequence;°
"Good sir," or so, or "friend," or "gentleman,"
According to the phrase or the addition
Of man and country.

REYNALDO: Very good, my lord.

POLONIUS: And then, sir, does 'a this—'a does—what was I about to say? By the mass, I was about to say something: where did I leave?

REYNALDO: At "closes in the consequence," at "friend or so," and "gentleman."

POLONIUS: At "closes in the consequence," ay, marry;
He closes thus: "I know the gentleman;

---

20. forgeries: Invented tales. **22. wanton:** Sportive, unrestrained. **25. fencing:** Indicative of the ill repute of professional fencers and fencing schools in Elizabethan times. **26. Drabbing:** Associating with immoral women. **30. incontinency:** Habitual loose behavior. **31. quaintly:** Delicately, ingeniously. **32. taints of liberty:** Blemishes due to freedom. **34. unreclaimed:** Untamed. **35. general assault:** Tendency that assails all untrained youth. **38. fetch of wit:** Clever trick. **43. ever:** At any time. **prenominate:** Before-mentioned. **45. closes . . . consequence:** Agrees with you in this conclusion.

I saw him yesterday, or t' other day,
Or then, or then; with such, or such; and, as you say,
There was 'a gaming; there o'ertook in 's rouse°
There falling out at tennis": or perchance,
"I saw him enter such a house of sale,"
Videlicet,° a brothel, or so forth.
See you now;
Your bait of falsehood takes this carp of truth:
And thus do we of wisdom and of reach,°
With windlasses° and with assays of bias,°
By indirections° find directions° out:
So by my former lecture° and advice,
Shall you my son. You have me, have you not?

REYNALDO: My lord, I have.

POLONIUS: God bye ye;° fare ye well.

REYNALDO: Good my lord!

POLONIUS: Observe his inclination in yourself.°

REYNALDO: I shall, my lord.

POLONIUS: And let him ply his music.°

REYNALDO: Well, my lord.

POLONIUS: Farewell! *Exit Reynaldo.*

Enter Ophelia.

How now, Ophelia! what's the matter?

OPHELIA: O, my lord, my lord, I have been so affrighted!

POLONIUS: With what, i' th' name of God?

OPHELIA: My lord, as I was sewing in my closet,°
Lord Hamlet, with his doublet° all unbrac'd;°
No hat upon his head; his stockings foul'd,
Ungart'red, and down-gyved° to his ankle;
Pale as his shirt; his knees knocking each other;
And with a look so piteous in purport
As if he had been loosed out of hell
To speak of horrors,—he comes before me.

POLONIUS: Mad for thy love?

OPHELIA: My lord, I do not know;
But truly, I do fear it.

POLONIUS: What said he?

---

56. o'ertook in 's rouse: Overcome by drink. **59. Videlicet:** Namely. **62. reach:** Capacity, ability. **63. windlasses:** I.e., circuitous paths. **assays of bias:** Attempts that resemble the course of the bowl, which, being weighted on one side, has a curving motion. **64. indirections:** Devious courses. **directions:** Straight courses, i.e., the truth. **65. lecture:** Admonition. **67. bye ye:** Be with you. **69. Observe . . . yourself:** In your own person, not by spies; or conform your own conduct to his inclination; or test him by studying yourself. **71. ply his music:** Probably to be taken literally. **75. closet:** Private chamber. **76. doublet:** Close-fitting coat. **unbrac'd:** Unfastened. **78. down-gyved:** Fallen to the ankles (like gyves or fetters).

OPHELIA: He took me by the wrist and held me hard;
Then goes he to the length of all his arm;
And, with his other hand thus o'er his brow,
He falls to such perusal of my face
As 'a would draw it. Long stay'd he so;
At last, a little shaking of mine arm
And thrice his head thus waving up and down,
He rais'd a sigh so piteous and profound
As it did seem to shatter all his bulk°
And end his being: that done, he lets me go:
And, with his head over his shoulder turn'd,
He seem'd to find his way without his eyes;
For out o' doors he went without their helps,
And, to the last, bended their light on me.

POLONIUS: Come, go with me: I will go seek the king.
This is the very ecstasy of love,
Whose violent property° fordoes° itself
And leads the will to desperate undertakings
As oft as any passion under heaven
That does afflict our natures. I am sorry.
What, have you given him any hard words of late?

OPHELIA: No, my good lord, but, as you did command,
I did repel his letters and denied
His access to me.

POLONIUS: That hath made him mad.
I am sorry that with better heed and judgement
I had not quoted° him: I fear'd he did but trifle,
And meant to wrack thee; but, beshrew my jealousy!°
By heaven, it is as proper to our age
To cast beyond° ourselves in our opinions
As it is common for the younger sort
To lack discretion. Come, go we to the king:
This must be known; which, being kept close, might move
More grief to hide than hate to utter love.°
Come. *Exeunt.*

[SCENE II: *A room in the castle.*]

Flourish. Enter King and Queen, Rosencrantz, and Guildenstern [*with others*].

KING: Welcome, dear Rosencrantz and Guildenstern!
Moreover that° we much did long to see you,
The need we have to use you did provoke

---

93. bulk: Body. **101. property:** Nature. **fordoes:** Destroys. **110. quoted:** Observed. **111. beshrew my jealousy:** Curse my suspicions. **113. cast beyond:** Overshoot, miscalculate. **116–117. might . . . love:** I.e., I might cause more grief to others by hiding the knowledge of Hamlet's love to Ophelia than hatred to me and mine by telling of it. ACT II, SCENE II. **2. Moreover that:** Besides the fact that.

Our hasty sending. Something have you heard
Of Hamlet's transformation; so call it,
Sith° nor th' exterior nor the inward man
Resembles that it was. What it should be,
More than his father's death, that thus hath put him
So much from th' understanding of himself,
I cannot dream of: I entreat you both,
That, being of so young days° brought up with him,
And sith so neighbour'd to his youth and haviour,
That you vouchsafe your rest° here in our court
Some little time: so by your companies
To draw him on to pleasures, and to gather,
So much as from occasion you may glean,
Whether aught, to us unknown, afflicts him thus,
That, open'd, lies within our remedy.

QUEEN: Good gentlemen, he hath much talk'd of you;
And sure I am two men there are not living
To whom he more adheres. If it will please you
To show us so much gentry° and good will
As to expend your time with us awhile,
For the supply and profit° of our hope,
Your visitation shall receive such thanks
As fits a king's remembrance.

ROSENCRANTZ: Both your majesties
Might, by the sovereign power you have of us,
Put your dread pleasures more into command
Than to entreaty.

GUILDENSTERN: But we both obey,
And here give up ourselves, in the full bent°
To lay our service freely at your feet,
To be commanded.

KING: Thanks, Rosencrantz and gentle Guildenstern.

QUEEN: Thanks, Guildenstern and gentle Rosencrantz:
And I beseech you instantly to visit
My too much changed son. Go, some of you,
And bring these gentlemen where Hamlet is.

GUILDENSTERN: Heavens make our presence and our practices
Pleasant and helpful to him!

QUEEN: Ay, amen!

Exeunt Rosencrantz and Guildenstern [*with some Attendants*].

Enter Polonius.

POLONIUS: Th' ambassadors from Norway, my good lord,
Are joyfully return'd.

---

6. Sith: Since. **11. of . . . days:** From such early youth. **13. vouchsafe your rest:** Please to stay. **22. gentry:** Courtesy. **24. supply and profit:** Aid and successful outcome. **30. in . . . bent:** To the utmost degree of our mental capacity.

KING: Thou still hast been the father of good news.
POLONIUS: Have I, my lord? I assure my good liege,
I hold my duty, as I hold my soul,
Both to my God and to my gracious king:
And I do think, or else this brain of mine
Hunts not the trail of policy so sure
As it hath us'd to do, that I have found
The very cause of Hamlet's lunacy.
KING: O, speak of that; that do I long to hear.
POLONIUS: Give first admittance to th' ambassadors;
My news shall be the fruit to that great feast.
KING: Thyself do grace to them, and bring them in. [*Exit Polonius.*]
He tells me, my dear Gertrude, he hath found
The head and source of all your son's distemper.
QUEEN: I doubt° it is no other but the main;°
His father's death, and our o'erhasty marriage.
KING: Well, we shall sift him.

Enter Ambassadors [*Voltimand and Cornelius, with Polonius.*]

Welcome, my good friends!
Say, Voltimand, what from our brother Norway?
VOLTIMAND: Most fair return of greetings and desires.
Upon our first, he sent out to suppress
His nephew's levies; which to him appear'd
To be a preparation 'gainst the Polack;
But, better look'd into, he truly found
It was against your highness: whereat griev'd,
That so his sickness, age and impotence
Was falsely borne in hand,° sends out arrests
On Fortinbras; which he, in brief, obeys;
Receives rebuke from Norway, and in fine°
Makes vow before his uncle never more
To give th' assay° of arms against your majesty.
Whereon old Norway, overcome with joy,
Gives him three score thousand crowns in annual fee,
And his commission to employ those soldiers,
So levied as before, against the Polack:
With an entreaty, herein further shown, [*giving a paper.*]
That it might please you to give quiet pass
Through your dominions for this enterprise,
On such regards of safety and allowance°
As therein are set down.

---

56. doubt: Fear. **main:** Chief point, principal concern. **67. borne in hand:** Deluded. **69. in fine:** In the end. **71. assay:** Assault, trial (of arms). **79. safety and allowance:** Pledges of safety to the country and terms of permission for the troops to pass.

KING: It likes° us well;
And at our more consider'd° time we'll read,
Answer, and think upon this business.
Meantime we thank you for your well-took labour:
Go to your rest; at night we'll feast together:
Most welcome home! *Exeunt Ambassadors.*

POLONIUS: This business is well ended.
My liege, and madam, to expostulate
What majesty should be, what duty is,
Why day is day, night night, and time is time,
Were nothing but to waste night, day and time.
Therefore, since brevity is the soul of wit,°
And tediousness the limbs and outward flourishes,°
I will be brief: your noble son is mad:
Mad call I it; for, to define true madness
What is 't but to be nothing else but mad?
But let that go.

QUEEN: More matter, with less art.

POLONIUS: Madam, I swear I use no art at all.
That he is mad, 'tis true: 'tis true 'tis pity;
And pity 'tis 'tis true: a foolish figure;°
But farewell it, for I will use no art.
Mad let us grant him, then: and now remains
That we find out the cause of this effect,
Or rather say, the cause of this defect,
For this effect defective comes by cause:
Thus it remains, and the remainder thus.
Perpend.°
I have a daughter—have while she is mine—
Who, in her duty and obedience, mark,
Hath given me this: now gather, and surmise. [*Reads the letter.*] "To the celestial and my soul's idol,
the most beautified Ophelia,"—
That's an ill phrase, a vile phrase; "beautified" is a vile phrase: but you shall hear. Thus: [*Reads.*]
"In her excellent white bosom, these, & c."

QUEEN: Came this from Hamlet to her?

POLONIUS: Good madam, stay awhile; I will be faithful. [*Reads.*]
"Doubt thou the stars are fire;
Doubt that the sun doth move;
Doubt truth to be a liar;
But never doubt I love.

---

80. likes: Pleases. **81. consider'd:** Suitable for deliberation. **90. wit:** Sound sense or judgment. **91. flourishes:** Ostentation, embellishments. **98. figure:** Figure of speech. **105. Perpend:** Consider.

"O dear Ophelia, I am ill at these numbers;° I have not art to reckon° my groans: but that I love thee best, O most best, believe it. Adieu.

"Thine evermore, most dear lady, whilst this machine° is to him,
HAMLET."

This, in obedience, hath my daughter shown me,
And more above,° hath his solicitings,
As they fell out° by time, by means° and place,
All given to mine ear.

KING: But how hath she
Receiv'd his love?

POLONIUS: What do you think of me?

KING: As of a man faithful and honourable.

POLONIUS: I would fain prove so. But what might you think,
When I had seen this hot love on the wing—
As I perceiv'd it, I must tell you that,
Before my daughter told me—what might you,
Or my dear majesty your queen here, think,
If I had play'd the desk or table-book,°
Or given my heart a winking,° mute and dumb,
Or look'd upon this love with idle sight;
What might you think? No, I went round to work,
And my young mistress thus I did bespeak:°
"Lord Hamlet is a prince, out of thy star;°
This must not be": and then I prescripts gave her,
That she should lock herself from his resort,
Admit no messengers, receive no tokens.
Which done, she took the fruits of my advice;
And he, repelled—a short tale to make—
Fell into a sadness, then into a fast,
Thence to a watch,° thence into a weakness,
Thence to a lightness,° and, by this declension,°
Into the madness wherein now he raves,
And all we mourn for.

KING: Do you think 'tis this?

QUEEN: It may be, very like.

POLONIUS: Hath there been such a time—I would fain know that—
That I have positively said " 'Tis so,"
When it prov'd otherwise?

KING: Not that I know.

---

120. ill . . . numbers: Unskilled at writing verses. **reckon:** Number metrically, scan. **122. machine:** Bodily frame. **125. more above:** Moreover. **126. fell out:** Occurred. **means:** Opportunities (of access). **135. play'd . . . table-book:** I.e., remained shut up, concealed this information. **136. given . . . winking:** Given my heart a signal to keep silent. **139. bespeak:** Address. **140. out . . . star:** Above thee in position. **147. watch:** State of sleeplessness. **148. lightness:** Lightheadedness. **declension:** Decline, deterioration.

POLONIUS [*pointing to his head and shoulder*]: Take this from this, if this be otherwise:
If circumstances lead me, I will find
Where truth is hid, though it were hid indeed
Within the centre.°

KING: How may we try it further?

POLONIUS: You know, sometimes he walks four hours together
Here in the lobby.

QUEEN: So he does indeed.

POLONIUS: At such a time I'll loose my daughter to him:
Be you and I behind an arras° then;
Mark the encounter: if he love her not
And be not from his reason fall'n thereon,°
Let me be no assistant for a state,
But keep a farm and carters.

KING: We will try it.

Enter Hamlet [*reading on a book*].

QUEEN: But, look, where sadly the poor wretch comes reading.

POLONIUS: Away, I do beseech you both, away:

Exeunt King and Queen [*with Attendants*].

I'll board° him presently. O, give me leave.
How does my good Lord Hamlet?

HAMLET: Well, God-a-mercy.

POLONIUS: Do you know me, my lord?

HAMLET: Excellent well; you are a fishmonger.°

POLONIUS: Not I, my lord.

HAMLET: Then I would you were so honest a man.

POLONIUS: Honest, my lord!

HAMLET: Ay, sir; to be honest, as this world goes, is to be one man picked out of ten thousand.

POLONIUS: That's very true, my lord.

HAMLET: For if the sun breed maggots in a dead dog, being a good kissing carrion,°—Have you a daughter?

POLONIUS: I have, my lord.

HAMLET: Let her not walk i' the sun:° conception° is a blessing: but as your daughter may conceive—Friend, look to 't.

POLONIUS [aside]: How say you by° that? Still harping on my daughter: yet he knew me not at first; 'a said I was a fishmonger: 'a is far gone, far gone: and truly in my youth I suffered much extremity for love; very near this. I'll speak to him again. What do you read, my lord?

---

158. centre: Middle point of the earth. **162. arras:** Hanging, tapestry. **164. thereon:** On that account. **169. board:** Accost. **173. fishmonger:** An opprobrious expression meaning "bawd," "procurer." **180–181. good kissing carrion:** I.e., a good piece of flesh for kissing (?). **183. i' the sun:** In the sunshine of princely favors. **conception:** Quibble on "understanding" and "pregnancy." **185. by:** Concerning.

HAMLET: Words, words, words.

POLONIUS: What is the matter,° my lord?

HAMLET: Between who?°

POLONIUS: I mean, the matter that you read, my lord.

HAMLET: Slanders, sir: for the satirical rogue says here that old men have grey beards, that their faces are wrinkled, their eyes purging° thick amber and plum-tree gum and that they have a plentiful lack of wit, together with most weak hams: all which, sir, though I most powerfully and potently believe, yet I hold it not honesty° to have it thus set down, for yourself, sir, should be old as I am, if like a crab you could go backward.

POLONIUS [*aside*]: Though this be madness, yet there is method in 't.—Will you walk out of the air, my lord?

HAMLET: Into my grave.

POLONIUS: Indeed, that's out of the air. (*Aside.*) How pregnant sometimes his replies are! a happiness° that often madness hits on, which reason and sanity could not so prosperously° be delivered of. I will leave him, and suddenly contrive the means of meeting between him and my daughter.— My honourable lord, I will most humbly take my leave of you.

HAMLET: You cannot, sir, take from me any thing that I will more willingly part withal: except my life, except my life, except my life.

Enter Guildenstern and Rosencrantz.

POLONIUS: Fare you well, my lord.

HAMLET: These tedious old fools!

POLONIUS: You go to seek the Lord Hamlet; there he is.

ROSENCRANTZ [*to Polonius*]: God save you, sir! [*Exit Polonius.*]

GUILDENSTERN: My honoured lord!

ROSENCRANTZ: My most dear lord!

HAMLET: My excellent good friends! How dost thou, Guildenstern? Ah, Rosencrantz! Good lads, how do ye both?

ROSENCRANTZ: As the indifferent° children of the earth.

GUILDENSTERN: Happy, in that we are not over-happy;
On Fortune's cap we are not the very button.

HAMLET: Nor the soles of her shoe?

ROSENCRANTZ: Neither, my lord.

HAMLET: Then you live about her waist, or in the middle of her favours?

GUILDENSTERN: 'Faith, her privates° we.

HAMLET: In the secret parts of Fortune? O, most true; she is a strumpet. What's the news?

ROSENCRANTZ: None, my lord, but that the world's grown honest.

HAMLET: Then is doomsday near: but your news is not true. Let me question more in particular: what have you, my good friends, deserved at the hands of Fortune, that she sends you to prison hither?

---

190. matter: Substance. **191. Between who:** Hamlet deliberately takes matter as meaning "basis of dispute." **194. purging:** discharging. **197. honesty:** Decency. **203. happiness:** Felicity of expression. **204. prosperously:** Successfully. **217. indifferent:** Ordinary. **223. privates:** I.e., ordinary men (sexual pun on *private parts*).

GUILDENSTERN: Prison, my lord!

HAMLET: Denmark's a prison.

ROSENCRANTZ: Then is the world one.

HAMLET: A goodly one; in which there are many confines,° wards and dungeons, Denmark being one o' the worst.

ROSENCRANTZ: We think not so, my lord.

HAMLET: Why, then, 'tis none to you; for there is nothing either good or bad, but thinking makes it so: to me it is a prison.

ROSENCRANTZ: Why then, your ambition makes it one; 'tis too narrow for your mind.

HAMLET: O God, I could be bounded in a nutshell and count myself a king of infinite space, were it not that I have bad dreams.

GUILDENSTERN: Which dreams indeed are ambition, for the very substance of the ambitious° is merely the shadow of a dream.

HAMLET: A dream itself is but a shadow.

ROSENCRANTZ: Truly, and I hold ambition of so airy and light a quality that it is but a shadow's shadow.

HAMLET: Then are our beggars bodies, and our monarchs and outstretched heroes the beggars' shadows. Shall we to the court? for, by my fay,° I cannot reason.°

ROSENCRANTZ: GUILDENSTERN: } We'll wait upon° you.

HAMLET: No such matter: I will not sort° you with the rest of my servants, for, to speak to you like an honest man, I am most dreadfully attended.° But, in the beaten way of friendship,° what make you at Elsinore?

ROSENCRANTZ: To visit you, my lord: no other occasion.

HAMLET: Beggar that I am, I am ever poor in thanks; but I thank you: and sure, dear friends, my thanks are too dear a° halfpenny. Were you not sent for? Is it your own inclining? Is it a free visitation? Come, come, deal justly with me: come, come; nay, speak.

GUILDENSTERN: What should we say, my lord?

HAMLET: Why, any thing, but to the purpose. You were sent for; and there is a kind of confession in your looks which your modesties have not craft enough to colour: I know the good king and queen have sent for you.

ROSENCRANTZ: To what end, my lord?

HAMLET: That you must teach me. But let me conjure° you, by the rights of our fellowship, by the consonancy of our youth,° by the obligation of our ever-preserved love, and by what more dear a better proposer° could charge you withal, be even and direct with me, whether you were sent for, or no?

---

233. confines: Places of confinement. **242–243. very . . . ambitious:** That seemingly most substantial thing which the ambitious pursue. **248. fay:** Faith. **249. reason:** Argue. **250. wait upon:** Accompany. **251. sort:** Class. **252. dreadfully attended:** Poorly provided with servants. **253. in the . . . friendship:** As a matter of course among friends. **256. a:** I.e., at a. **264. conjure:** Adjure, entreat. **265. consonancy of our youth:** The fact that we are of the same age. **266. better proposer:** One more skillful in finding proposals.

ROSENCRANTZ [*aside to Guildenstern*]: What say you?

HAMLET [*aside*]: Nay, then, I have an eye of you. — If you love me, hold not off.

GUILDENSTERN: My lord, we were sent for.

HAMLET: I will tell you why; so shall my anticipation prevent your discovery,° and your secrecy to the king and queen moult no feather. I have of late — but wherefore I know not — lost all my mirth, forgone all custom of exercises; and indeed it goes so heavily with my disposition that this goodly frame, the earth, seems to me a sterile promontory, this most excellent canopy, the air, look you, this brave o'erhanging firmament, this majestical roof fretted° with golden fire, why, it appeareth nothing to me but a foul and pestilent congregation of vapours. What a piece of work is a man! how noble in reason! how infinite in faculties° in form and moving how express° and admirable! in action how like an angel! in apprehension° how like a god! the beauty of the world! the paragon of animals! And yet, to me, what is this quintessence° of dust? man delights not me: no, nor woman neither, though by your smiling you seem to say so.

ROSENCRANTZ: My lord, there was no such stuff in my thoughts.

HAMLET: Why did you laugh then, when I said "man delights not me"?

ROSENCRANTZ: To think, my lord, if you delight not in man, what lenten° entertainment the players shall receive from you: we coted° them on the way; and hither are they coming, to offer you service.

HAMLET: He that plays the king shall be welcome; his majesty shall have tribute of me; the adventurous knight shall use his foil and target;° the lover shall not sigh gratis; the humorous man° shall end his part in peace; the clown shall make those laugh whose lungs are tickle o' the sere;° and the lady shall say her mind freely, or the blank verse shall halt for 't.° What players are they?

ROSENCRANTZ: Even those you were wont to take delight in, the tragedians of the city.

HAMLET: How chances it they travel? their residence,° both in reputation and profit, was better both ways.

ROSENCRANTZ: I think their inhibition° comes by the means of the late innovation.°

---

273. prevent your discovery: Forestall your disclosure. **279. fretted:** Adorned. **281. faculties:** Capacity. **282. express:** Well-framed (?), exact (?). **283. apprehension:** Understanding. **284. quintessence:** The fifth essence of ancient philosophy, supposed to be the substance of the heavenly bodies and to be latent in all things. **289. lenten:** Meager. **290. coted:** Overtook and passed beyond. **293. foil and target:** Sword and shield. **294. humorous man:** Actor who takes the part of the humor characters. **295. tickle o' the sere:** Easy on the trigger. **295–296. the lady . . . for 't:** The lady (fond of talking) shall have opportunity to talk, blank verse or no blank verse. **300. residence:** Remaining in one place. **302. inhibition:** Formal prohibition (from acting plays in the city or, possibly, at court). **302–303. innovation:** The new fashion in satirical plays performed by boy actors in the "private" theaters.

HAMLET: Do they hold the same estimation they did when I was in the city? are they so followed?

ROSENCRANTZ: No, indeed, are they not.

HAMLET: How° comes it? do they grow rusty?

ROSENCRANTZ: Nay, their endeavour keeps in the wonted pace: but there is, sir, an aery° of children, little eyases,° that cry out on the top of question,° and are most tyrannically° clapped for 't: these are now the fashion, and so berattle° the common stages°—so they call them—that many wearing rapiers° are afraid of goose-quills° and dare scarce come thither.

HAMLET: What, are they children? who maintains 'em? how are they escoted?° Will they pursue the quality° no longer than they can sing?° will they not say afterwards, if they should grow themselves to common° players—as it is most like, if their means are no better—their writers do them wrong, to make them exclaim against their own succession?°

ROSENCRANTZ: 'Faith, there has been much to do on both sides; and the nation holds it no sin to tarre° them to controversy: there was, for a while, no money bid for argument,° unless the poet and the player went to cuffs° in the question.°

HAMLET: Is't possible?

GUILDENSTERN: O, there has been much throwing about of brains.

HAMLET: Do the boys carry it away?°

ROSENCRANTZ: Ay, that they do, my lord; Hercules and his load° too.

HAMLET: It is not very strange; for my uncle is king of Denmark, and those that would make mows° at him while my father lived, give twenty, forty, fifty, a hundred ducats° a-piece for his picture in little.° 'Sblood, there is something in this more than natural, if philosophy could find it out.

A flourish [*of trumpets within*].

GUILDENSTERN: There are the players.

HAMLET: Gentlemen, you are welcome to Elsinore. Your hands, come then: the appurtenance of welcome is fashion and ceremony: let me comply° with you in this garb,° lest my extent° to the players, which, I tell you,

---

307–325. How . . . load too: The passage is the famous one dealing with the War of the Theatres (1599–1602); namely, the rivalry between the children's companies and the adult actors. **309. aery:** Nest. **eyases:** Young hawks. **cry . . . question:** Speak in a high key dominating conversation; clamor forth the height of controversy; probably "excel" (cf. line 462); perhaps intended to decry leaders of the dramatic profession. **310. tyrannically:** Outrageously. **311. berattle:** Berate. **common stages:** Public theaters. **311–312. many wearing rapiers:** Many men of fashion, who were afraid to patronize the common players for fear of being satirized by the poets who wrote for the children. **312. goose-quills:** I.e., pens of satirists. **313. escoted:** Maintained. **314. quality:** Acting profession. **no longer . . . sing:** I.e., until their voices change. **315. common:** Regular, adult. **317. succession:** future careers. **319. tarre:** Set on (as dogs). **320. argument:** Probably, plot for a play. **went to cuffs:** Came to blows. **321. question:** Controversy. **324. carry it away:** Win the day. **325. Hercules . . . load:** Regarded as an allusion to the sign of the Globe Theatre, which was Hercules bearing the world on his shoulder. **327. mows:** Grimaces. **328. ducats:** Gold coins worth 9s. 4d. **in little:** In miniature. **332. comply:** Observe the formalities of courtesy. **333. garb:** Manner. **extent:** Showing of kindness.

must show fairly outwards, should more appear like entertainment than yours. You are welcome: but my uncle-father and aunt-mother are deceived.

GUILDENSTERN: In what, my dear lord?

HAMLET: I am but mad north-north-west:° when the wind is southerly I know a hawk from a handsaw.°

Enter Polonius.

POLONIUS: Well be with you, gentlemen!

HAMLET: Hark you, Guildenstern; and you too: at each ear a hearer: that great baby you see there is not yet out of his swaddling-clouts.°

ROSENCRANTZ: Happily he is the second time come to them; for they say an old man is twice a child.

HAMLET: I will prophesy he comes to tell me of the players; mark it.—You say right, sir: o' Monday morning;° 'twas then indeed.

POLONIUS: My lord, I have news to tell you.

HAMLET: My lord, I have news to tell you. When Roscius° was an actor in Rome,—

POLONIUS: The actors are come hither, my lord.

HAMLET: Buz, buz!°

POLONIUS: Upon my honour,—

HAMLET: Then came each actor on his ass,—

POLONIUS: The best actors in the world, either for tragedy, comedy, history, pastoral, pastoral-comical, historical-pastoral, tragical-historical, tragical-comical-historical-pastoral, scene individable,° or poem unlimited:° Seneca° cannot be too heavy, nor Plautus° too light. For the law of writ and the liberty,° these are the only men.

HAMLET: O Jephthah, judge of Israel,° what a treasure hadst thou!

POLONIUS: What a treasure had he, my lord?

HAMLET: Why,

"One fair daughter, and no more,
The which he loved passing well."

POLONIUS [*aside*]: Still on my daughter.

HAMLET: Am I not i' the right, old Jephthah?

POLONIUS: If you call me Jephthah, my lord, I have a daughter that I love passing° well.

---

338. I am . . . north-north-west: I am only partly mad, i.e., in only one point of the compass. **339. handsaw:** A proposed reading of *hernshaw* would mean "heron"; *handsaw* may be an early corruption of *hernshaw.* Another view regards *hawk* as the variant of *hack,* a tool of the pickax type, and *handsaw* as a saw operated by hand. **342. swaddling-clouts:** Cloths in which to wrap a newborn baby. **346. o' Monday morning:** Said to mislead Polonius. **348. Roscius:** A famous Roman actor. **351. Buz, buz:** An interjection used at Oxford to denote stale news. **356. scene individable:** A play observing the unity of place. **poem unlimited:** A play disregarding the unities of time and place. **357. Seneca:** Writer of Latin tragedies, model of early Elizabethan writers of tragedy. **Plautus:** Writer of Latin comedy. **357–358. law . . . liberty:** Pieces written according to rules and without rules, i.e., "classical" and "romantic" dramas. **359. Jephthah . . . Israel:** Jephthah had to sacrifice his daughter; see Judges 11. **366–367. passing:** Surpassingly.

HAMLET: Nay, that follows not.
POLONIUS: What follows, then, my lord?
HAMLET: Why,
"As by lot, God wot,"
and then, you know,
"It came to pass, as most like° it was,"—
the first row° of the pious chanson° will show you more; for look, where my abridgement comes.°

Enter the Players.

You are welcome, masters; welcome, all. I am glad to see thee well. Welcome, good friends. O, old friend! why, thy face is valanced° since I saw thee last: comest thou to beard me in Denmark? What, my young lady and mistress! By'r lady, your ladyship is nearer to heaven than when I saw you last, by the altitude of a chopine.° Pray God, your voice, like a piece of uncurrent° gold, be not cracked within the ring.° Masters, you are all welcome. We'll e'en to 't like French falconers, fly at any thing we see: we'll have a speech straight: come, give us a taste of your quality; come, a passionate speech.

FIRST PLAYER: What speech, my good lord?

HAMLET: I heard thee speak me a speech once, but it was never acted; or, if it was, not above once; for the play, I remember, pleased not the million; 'twas caviary to the general:° but it was—as I received it, and others, whose judgements in such matters cried in the top of° mine—an excellent play, well digested in the scenes, set down with as much modesty as cunning.° I remember, one said there were no sallets° in the lines to make the matter savoury, nor no matter in the phrase that might indict° the author of affectation; but called it an honest method, as wholesome as sweet, and by very much more handsome than fine.° One speech in 't I chiefly loved: 'twas Æneas' tale to Dido;° and thereabout of it especially, where he speaks of Priam's slaughter: if it live in your memory, begin at this line: let me see, let me see—
"The rugged Pyrrhus,° like th' Hyrcanian beast,"°—
'tis not so:—it begins with Pyrrhus:—

---

373. like: Probable. **374. row:** Stanza. **chanson:** Ballad. **375. abridgement comes:** Opportunity comes for cutting short the conversation. **377. valanced:** Fringed (with a beard). **380. chopine:** Kind of shoe raised by the thickness of the heel; worn in Italy, particularly at Venice. **381. uncurrent:** Not passable as lawful coinage. **cracked within the ring:** In the center of coins were rings enclosing the sovereign's head; if the coin was cracked within this ring, it was unfit for currency. **388. caviary to the general:** Not relished by the multitude. **389. cried in the top of:** Spoke with greater authority than. **391. cunning:** Skill. **sallets:** Salads: here, spicy improprieties. **392. indict:** Convict. **393–394. as wholesome . . . fine:** Its beauty was not that of elaborate ornament, but that of order and proportion. **395. Æneas' tale to Dido:** The lines recited by the player are imitated from Marlowe and Nashe's *Dido Queen of Carthage* (II.i.214ff.). They are written in such a way that the conventionality of the play within a play is raised above that of ordinary drama. **398. Pyrrhus:** A Greek hero in the Trojan War. **Hyrcanian beast:** The tiger; see Virgil, *Aeneid*, IV.266.

"The rugged Pyrrhus, he whose sable arms,
Black as his purpose, did the night resemble
When he lay couched in the ominous horse,°
Hath now this dread and black complexion smear'd
With heraldry more dismal; head to foot
Now is he total gules;° horridly trick'd°
With blood of fathers, mothers, daughters, sons,
Bak'd and impasted° with the parching streets,
That lend a tyrannous and a damned light
To their lord's murder: roasted in wrath and fire,
And thus o'er-sized° with coagulate gore,
With eyes like carbuncles, the hellish Pyrrhus
Old grandsire Priam seeks."
So, proceed you.

POLONIUS: 'Fore God, my lord, well spoken, with good accent and good discretion.

FIRST PLAYER: "Anon he finds him
Striking too short at Greeks; his antique sword,
Rebellious to his arm, lies where it falls,
Repugnant° to command: unequal match'd,
Pyrrhus at Priam drives; in rage strikes wide;
But with the whiff and wind of his fell sword
Th' unnerved father falls. Then senseless Ilium,°
Seeming to feel this blow, with flaming top
Stoops to his base, and with a hideous crash
Takes prisoner Pyrrhus' ear: for, lo! his sword
Which was declining on the milky head
Of reverend Priam, seem'd i' th' air to stick:
So, as a painted tyrant,° Pyrrhus stood,
And like a neutral to his will and matter,°
Did nothing.
But, as we often see, against° some storm,
A silence in the heavens, the rack° stand still,
The bold winds speechless and the orb below
As hush as death, anon the dreadful thunder
Doth rend the region,° so, after Pyrrhus' pause,
Aroused vengeance sets him new a-work;
And never did the Cyclops' hammers fall
On Mars's armour forg'd for proof eterne°
With less remorse than Pyrrhus' bleeding sword

402. ominous horse: Trojan horse. **405. gules:** Red, a heraldic term. **trick'd:** Spotted, smeared. **407. impasted:** Made into a paste. **410. o'er-sized:** Covered as with size or glue. **419. Repugnant:** Disobedient. **422. Then senseless Ilium:** Insensate Troy. **428. painted tyrant:** Tyrant in a picture. **429. matter:** Task. **431. against:** Before. **432. rack:** Mass of clouds. **435. region:** Assembly. **438. proof eterne:** External resistance to assault.

Now falls on Priam.
Out, out, thou strumpet, Fortune! All you gods,
In general synod,° take away her power;
Break all the spokes and fellies° from her wheel,
And bowl the round nave° down the hill of heaven,
As low as to the fiends!"

POLONIUS: This is too long.

HAMLET: It shall to the barber's, with your beard. Prithee, say on: he's for a jig° or a tale of bawdry,° or he sleeps: say on: come to Hecuba.°

FIRST PLAYER: "But who, ah woe! had seen the mobled° queen—"

HAMLET: "The mobled queen?"

POLONIUS: That's good; "mobled queen" is good.

FIRST PLAYER: "Run barefoot up and down, threat'ning the flames
With bisson rheum;° a clout° upon that head
Where late the diadem stood, and for a robe,
About her lank and all o'er-teemed° loins,
A blanket, in the alarm of fear caught up;
Who this had seen, with tongue in venom steep'd,
'Gainst Fortune's state would treason have pronounc'd:°
But if the gods themselves did see her then
When she saw Pyrrhus make malicious sport
In mincing with his sword her husband's limbs,
The instant burst of clamour that she made,
Unless things mortal move them not at all,
Would have made milch° the burning eyes of heaven,
And passion in the gods."

POLONIUS: Look, whe'r he has not turned° his colour and has tears in 's eyes. Prithee, no more.

HAMLET: 'Tis well; I'll have thee speak out the rest soon. Good my lord, will you see the players well bestowed? Do you hear, let them be well used; for they are the abstract° and brief chronicles of the time: after your death you were better have a bad epitaph than their ill report while you live.

POLONIUS: My lord, I will use them according to their desert.

HAMLET: God's bodykins,° man, much better: use every man after his desert, and who shall 'scape whipping? Use them after your own honour and dignity: the less they deserve, the more merit is in your bounty. Take them in.

POLONIUS: Come, sirs.

HAMLET: Follow him, friends: we'll hear a play tomorrow. [*Aside to First Player.*] Dost thou hear me, old friend; can you play the Murder of Gonzago?

---

442. synod: Assembly. **443. fellies:** Pieces of wood forming the rim of a wheel. **444. nave:** Hub. **447. jig:** Comic performance given at the end or in an interval of a play. **448. bawdry:** Indecency. **Hecuba:** Wife of Priam, king of Troy. **449. mobled:** Muffled. **453. bisson rheum:** Blinding tears. **clout:** Piece of cloth. **455. o'er-teemed:** Worn out with bearing children. **458. pronounc'd:** Proclaimed. **464. milch:** Moist with tears. **466. turned:** Changed. **470. abstract:** Summary account. **473. bodykins:** Diminutive form of the oath "by God's body."

FIRST PLAYER: Ay, my lord.

HAMLET: We'll ha 't to-morrow night. You could, for a need, study a speech of some dozen or sixteen lines,° which I would set down and insert in 't, could you not?

FIRST PLAYER: Ay, my lord.

HAMLET: Very well. Follow that lord; and look you mock him not.—My good friends, I'll leave you till night: you are welcome to Elsinore.

Exeunt Polonius and Players.

ROSENCRANTZ: Good my lord! *Exeunt* [*Rosencrantz and Guildenstern.*]

HAMLET: Ay, so, God bye to you.—Now I am alone.
O, what a rogue and peasant° slave am I!
Is it not monstrous that this player here,
But in a fiction, in a dream of passion,
Could force his soul so to his own conceit
That from her working all his visage wann'd,°
Tears in his eyes, distraction in 's aspect,
A broken voice, and his whole function suiting
With forms to his conceit?° and all for nothing!
For Hecuba!
What's Hecuba to him, or he to Hecuba,
That he should weep for her? What would he do,
Had he the motive and the cue for passion
That I have? He would drown the stage with tears
And cleave the general ear with horrid speech,
Make mad the guilty and appall the free,
Confound the ignorant, and amaze indeed
The very faculties of eyes and ears.
Yet I,
A dull and muddy-mettled° rascal, peak,°
Like John-a-dreams,° unpregnant of° my cause,
And can say nothing; no, not for a king.
Upon whose property° and most dear life
A damn'd defeat was made. Am I a coward?
Who calls me villain? breaks my pate across?
Plucks off my beard, and blows it in my face?
Tweaks me by the nose? gives me the lie i' th' throat,
As deep as to the lungs? who does me this?
Ha!
'Swounds, I should take it: for it cannot be

---

482. dozen or sixteen lines: Critics have amused themselves by trying to locate Hamlet's lines. Lucianus's speech III.ii.226–231 is the best guess. **489. peasant:** Base. **493. wann'd:** Grew pale. **495–496. his whole . . . conceit:** His whole being responded with forms to suit his thought. **507. muddy-mettled:** Dull-spirited. **peak:** Mope, pine. **508. John-a-dreams:** An expression occurring elsewhere in Elizabethan literature to indicate a dreamer. **unpregnant of:** Not quickened by. **510. property:** Proprietorship (of crown and life).

But I am pigeon-liver'd° and lack gall
To make oppression bitter, or ere this
I should have fatted all the region kites°
With this slave's offal: bloody, bawdy villain!
Remorseless, treacherous, lecherous, kindless° villain!
O, vengeance!
Why, what an ass am I! This is most brave,
That I, the son of a dear father murder'd,
Prompted to my revenge by heaven and hell,
Must, like a whore, unpack my heart with words,
And fall a-cursing, like a very drab,°
A stallion!°
Fie upon 't! foh! About,° my brains! Hum, I have heard
That guilty creatures sitting at a play
Have by the very cunning of the scene
Been struck so to the soul that presently
They have proclaim'd their malefactions;
For murder, though it have no tongue, will speak
With most miraculous organ. I'll have these players
Play something like the murder of my father
Before mine uncle: I'll observe his looks:
I'll tent° him to the quick: if 'a do blench,°
I know my course. The spirit that I have seen
May be the devil:° and the devil hath power
T' assume a pleasing shape; yea, and perhaps
Out of my weakness and my melancholy,
As he is very potent with such spirits,°
Abuses me to damn me: I'll have grounds
More relative° than this:° the play's the thing
Wherein I'll catch the conscience of the king. *Exit.*

[ACT III

SCENE I: *A room in the castle.*]

Enter King, Queen, Polonius, Ophelia, Rosencrantz, Guildenstern, Lords.

KING: And can you, by no drift of conference,°
Get from him why he puts on this confusion,
Grating so harshly all his days of quiet
With turbulent and dangerous lunacy?

---

518. pigeon-liver'd: The pigeon was supposed to secrete no gall; if Hamlet, so he says, had had gall, he would have felt the bitterness of oppression, and avenged it. **520. region kites:** Kites of the air. **522. kindless:** Unnatural. **528. drab:** Prostitute. **529. stallion:** Prostitute (male or female). **530. About:** About it, or turn thou right about. **539. tent:** Probe. **blench:** Quail, flinch. **541. May be the devil:** Hamlet's suspicion is properly grounded in the belief of the time. **544. spirits:** Humors. **546. relative:** Closely related, definite. **this:** I.e., the ghost's story. ACT III, SCENE I. **1. drift of conference:** Device of conversation.

ROSENCRANTZ: He does confess he feels himself distracted;
But from what cause 'a will by no means speak.
GUILDENSTERN: Nor do we find him forward° to be sounded,
But, with a crafty madness, keeps aloof,
When we would bring him on to some confession
Of his true state.
QUEEN: Did he receive you well?
ROSENCRANTZ: Most like a gentleman.
GUILDENSTERN: But with much forcing of his disposition.°
ROSENCRANTZ: Niggard of question;° but, of our demands,
Most free in his reply.
QUEEN: Did you assay° him
To any pastime?
ROSENCRANTZ: Madam, it so fell out, that certain players
We o'er-raught° on the way: of these we told him;
And there did seem in him a kind of joy
To hear of it: they are here about the court,
And, as I think, they have already order
This night to play before him.
POLONIUS: 'Tis most true:
And he beseech'd me to entreat your majesties
To hear and see the matter.
KING: With all my heart; and it doth much content me
To hear him so inclin'd.
Good gentlemen, give him a further edge,°
And drive his purpose into these delights.
ROSENCRANTZ: We shall, my lord. *Exeunt Rosencrantz and Guildenstern.*
KING: Sweet Gertrude, leave us too;
For we have closely° sent for Hamlet hither,
That he, as 'twere by accident, may here
Affront° Ophelia:
Her father and myself, lawful espials,°
Will so bestow ourselves that, seeing, unseen,
We may of their encounter frankly judge,
And gather by him, as he is behav'd,
If 't be th' affliction of his love or no
That thus he suffers for.
QUEEN: I shall obey you.
And for your part, Ophelia, I do wish
That your good beauties be the happy cause
Of Hamlet's wildness:° so shall I hope your virtues

7. forward: Willing. **12. forcing of his disposition:** I.e., against his will. **13. Niggard of question:** Sparing of conversation. **14. assay:** Try to win. **17. o'er-raught:** Overtook. **26. edge:** Incitement. **29. closely:** Secretly. **31. Affront:** Confront. **32. lawful espials:** Legitimate spies. **40. wildness:** Madness.

Will bring him to his wonted way again,
To both your honours.

OPHELIA: Madam, I wish it may. [*Exit Queen.*]

POLONIUS: Ophelia, walk you here. Gracious,° so please you,
We will bestow ourselves. [*To Ophelia.*] Read on this book;
That show of such an exercise° may colour°
Your loneliness. We are oft to blame in this,—
'Tis too much prov'd—that with devotion's visage
And pious action we do sugar o'er
The devil himself.

KING: [*aside*] O, 'tis too true!
How smart a lash that speech doth give my conscience!
The harlot's cheek, beautied with plast'ring art,
Is not more ugly to° the thing° that helps it
Than is my deed to my most painted word:
O heavy burthen!

POLONIUS: I hear him coming: let's withdraw, my lord.
[*Exeunt King and Polonius.*]

Enter Hamlet.

HAMLET: To be, or not to be: that is the question:
Whether 'tis nobler in the mind to suffer
The slings and arrows of outrageous fortune,
Or to take arms against a sea° of troubles,
And by opposing end them? To die: to sleep;
No more; and by a sleep to say we end
The heart-ache and the thousand natural shocks
That flesh is heir to, 'tis a consummation
Devoutly to be wish'd. To die, to sleep;
To sleep: perchance to dream: ay, there's the rub;
For in that sleep of death what dreams may come
When we have shuffled° off this mortal coil,°
Must give us pause: there's the respect°
That makes calamity of so long life;°
For who would bear the whips and scorns of time,°
Th' oppressor's wrong, the proud man's contumely,
The pangs of despis'd° love, the law's delay,
The insolence of office° and the spurns°
That patient merit of th' unworthy takes,

43. Gracious: Your grace (addressed to the king). **45. exercise:** Act of devotion (the book she reads is one of devotion). **colour:** Give a plausible appearance to. **52. to:** Compared to. **thing:** I.e., the cosmetic. **59. sea:** The mixed metaphor of this speech has often been commented on; a later emendation *siege* has sometimes been spoken on the stage. **67. shuffled:** Sloughed, cast. **coil:** Usually means "turmoil"; here, possibly "body" (conceived of as wound about the soul like rope); *clay, soil, veil* have been suggested as emendations. **68. respect:** Consideration. **69. of . . . life:** So long-lived. **70. time:** The world. **72. despis'd:** Rejected. **73. office:** Office-holders. **spurns:** Insults.

When he himself might his quietus° make
With a bare bodkin?° who would fardels° bear,
To grunt and sweat under a weary life,
But that the dread of something after death,
The undiscover'd country from whose bourn°
No traveller returns, puzzles the will
And makes us rather bear those ills we have
Than fly to others that we know not of?
Thus conscience° does make cowards of us all;
And thus the native hue° of resolution
Is sicklied o'er° with the pale cast° of thought,
And enterprises of great pitch° and moment°
With this regard° their currents° turn awry,
And lose the name of action—Soft you now!
The fair Ophelia! Nymph, in thy orisons°
Be all my sins rememb'red.

OPHELIA: Good my lord,
How does your honour for this many a day?

HAMLET: I humbly thank you; well, well, well.

OPHELIA: My lord, I have remembrances of yours,
That I have longed long to re-deliver;
I pray you, now receive them.

HAMLET: No, not I;
I never gave you aught.

OPHELIA: My honour'd lord, you know right well you did;
And, with them, words of so sweet breath compos'd
As made the things more rich: their perfume lost,
Take these again; for to the noble mind
Rich gifts wax poor when givers prove unkind.
There, my lord.

HAMLET: Ha, ha! are you honest?°

OPHELIA: My lord?

HAMLET: Are you fair?

OPHELIA: What means your lordship?

HAMLET: That if you be honest and fair, your honesty° should admit no discourse to° your beauty.

OPHELIA: Could beauty, my lord, have better commerce° than with honesty?

---

75. quietus: Acquittance; here, death. **76. bare bodkin:** Mere dagger; bare is sometimes understood as "unsheathed." **fardels:** Burdens. **79. bourn:** Boundary. **83. conscience:** Probably, inhibition by the faculty of reason restraining the will from doing wrong. **84. native hue:** Natural color; metaphor derived from the color of the face. **85. sicklied o'er:** Given a sickly tinge. **cast:** Shade of color. **86. pitch:** Height (as of a falcon's flight). **moment:** Importance. **87. regard:** Respect, consideration. **currents:** Courses. **89. orisons:** Prayers. **103–108. are you honest . . . beauty:** *Honest* meaning "truthful" and "chaste" and *fair* meaning "just, honorable" (line 105) and "beautiful" (line 107) are not mere quibbles; the speech has the irony of a double entendre. **107. your honesty:** Your chastity. **107–108. discourse to:** Familiar intercourse with. **109. commerce:** Intercourse.

HAMLET: Ay, truly; for the power of beauty will sooner transform honesty from what it is to a bawd than the force of honesty can translate beauty into his likeness: this was sometime a paradox, but now the time° gives it proof. I did love you once.

OPHELIA: Indeed, my lord, you made me believe so.

HAMLET: You should not have believed me; for virtue cannot so inoculate° our old stock but we shall relish of it:° I loved you not.

OPHELIA: I was the more deceived.

HAMLET: Get thee to a nunnery: why wouldst thou be a breeder of sinners? I am myself indifferent honest;° but yet I could accuse me of such things that it were better my mother had not borne me: I am very proud, revengeful, ambitious, with more offences at my beck° than I have thoughts to put them in, imagination to give them shape, or time to act them in. What should such fellows as I do crawling between earth and heaven? We are arrant knaves, all; believe none of us. Go thy ways to a nunnery. Where's your father?

OPHELIA: At home, my lord.

HAMLET: Let the doors be shut upon him, that he may play the fool no where but in 's own house. Farewell.

OPHELIA: O, help him, you sweet heavens!

HAMLET: If thou dost marry, I'll give thee this plague for thy dowry: be thou as chaste as ice, as pure as snow, thou shalt not escape calumny. Get thee to a nunnery, go: farewell. Or, if thou wilt needs marry, marry a fool; for wise men know well enough what monsters° you make of them. To a nunnery, go, and quickly too. Farewell.

OPHELIA: O heavenly powers, restore him!

HAMLET: I have heard of your° paintings too, well enough; God hath given you one face, and you make yourselves another: you jig,° you amble, and you lisp; you nick-name God's creatures, and make your wantonness your ignorance.° Go to, I'll no more on 't; it hath made me mad. I say, we will have no moe marriage: those that are married already, all but one,° shall live; the rest shall keep as they are. To a nunnery, go. *Exit.*

OPHELIA: O, what a noble mind is here o'er-thrown!
The courtier's, soldier's, scholar's, eye, tongue, sword;
Th' expectancy and rose° of the fair state,
The glass of fashion and the mould of form,°
Th' observ'd of all observers,° quite, quite down!
And I, of ladies most deject and wretched,

---

112. the time: The present age. **115. inoculate:** Graft (metaphorical). **116. but . . . it:** I.e., that we do not still have about us a taste of the old stock; i.e., retain our sinfulness. **119. indifferent honest:** Moderately virtuous. **121. beck:** Command. **133. monsters:** An allusion to the horns of a cuckold. **136. your:** Indefinite use. **137. jig:** Move with jerky motion; probably allusion to the *jig*, or song and dance, of the current stage. **138–139. make . . . ignorance:** I.e., excuse your wantonness on the ground of your ignorance. **140. one:** I.e., the king. **144. expectancy and rose:** Source of hope. **145. The glass . . . form:** The mirror of fashion and the pattern of courtly behavior. **146. observ'd . . . observers:** I.e., the center of attention in the court.

That suck'd the honey of his music vows,
Now see that noble and most sovereign reason,
Like sweet bells jangled, out of time and harsh;
That unmatch'd form and feature of blown° youth
Blasted with ecstasy:° O, woe is me,
T' have seen what I have seen, see what I see!

Enter King and Polonius.

KING: Love! his affections do not that way tend;
Nor what he spake, though it lack'd form a little,
Was not like madness. There's something in his soul,
O'er which his melancholy sits on brood;
And I do doubt° the hatch and the disclose°
Will be some danger: which for to prevent,
I have in quick determination
Thus set it down: he shall with speed to England,
For the demand of our neglected tribute:
Haply the seas and countries different
With variable° objects shall expel
This something-settled° matter in his heart,
Whereon his brains still beating puts him thus
From fashion of himself.° What think you on 't?

POLONIUS: It shall do well: but yet do I believe
The origin and commencement of his grief
Sprung from neglected love. How now, Ophelia!
You need not tell us what Lord Hamlet said;
We heard it all. My lord, do as you please;
But, if you hold it fit, after the play
Let his queen mother all alone entreat him
To show his grief: let her be round° with him;
And I'll be plac'd, so please you, in the ear
Of all their conference. If she find him not,
To England send him, or confine him where
Your wisdom best shall think.

KING: It shall be so:
Madness in great ones must not unwatch'd go. *Exeunt.*

[SCENE II: *A hall in the castle.*]

Enter Hamlet and three of the Players.

HAMLET: Speak the speech, I pray you, as I pronounced it to you, trippingly on the tongue: but if you mouth it, as many of your° players do, I had as lief the town-crier spoke my lines. Nor do not saw the air too much with your

---

151. blown: Blooming. **152. ecstasy:** Madness. **158. doubt:** Fear. **disclose:** Disclosure or revelation (by chipping of the shell). **164. variable:** Various. **165. something-settled:** Somewhat settled. **167. From . . . himself:** Out of his natural manner. **175. round:** Blunt. ACT III, SCENE II. **2. your:** Indefinite use.

hand, thus, but use all gently; for in the very torrent, tempest, and, as I may say, whirlwind of your passion, you must acquire and beget a temperance that may give it smoothness. O, it offends me to the soul to hear a robustious° periwig-pated° fellow tear a passion to tatters, to very rags, to split the ears of the groundlings,° who for the most part are capable of° nothing but inexplicable° dumb-shows and noise: I would have such a fellow whipped for o'er-doing Termagant;° it out-herods Herod:° pray you, avoid it.

FIRST PLAYER: I warrant your honour.

HAMLET: Be not too tame neither, but let your own discretion be your tutor: suit the action to the word, the word to the action; with this special observance, that you o'er-step not the modesty of nature: for any thing so overdone is from the purpose of playing, whose end, both at the first and now, was and is, to hold, as 't were, the mirror up to nature; to show virtue her own feature, scorn her own image, and the very age and body of the time his form and pressure.° Now this overdone, or come tardy off,° though it make the unskilful laugh, cannot but make the judicious grieve; the censure of the which one° must in your allowance o'erweigh a whole theatre of others. O, there be players that I have seen play, and heard others praise, and that highly, not to speak it profanely, that, neither having the accent of Christians nor the gait of Christian, pagan, nor man, have so strutted and bellowed that I have thought some of nature's journeymen° had made men and not made them well, they imitated humanity so abominably.

FIRST PLAYER: I hope we have reformed that indifferently° with us, sir.

HAMLET: O, reform it altogether. And let those that play your clowns speak no more than is set down for them; for there be of° them that will themselves laugh, to set on some quantity of barren° spectators to laugh too; though, in the mean time, some necessary question of the play be then to be considered: that's villanous, and shows a most pitiful ambition in the fool that uses it. Go, make you ready. [*Exeunt Players.*]

Enter Polonius, Guildenstern, and Rosencrantz.

How now, my lord! will the king hear this piece of work?

POLONIUS: And the queen too, and that presently.

HAMLET: Bid the players make haste. [*Exit Polonius.*]

Will you two help to hasten them?

---

7. robustious: Violent, boisterous. **periwig-pated:** Wearing a wig. **8. groundlings:** Those who stood in the yard of the theater. **9. capable of:** Susceptible of being influenced by. **inexplicable:** Of no significance worth explaining. **10. Termagant:** A god of the Saracens; a character in the St. Nicholas play, where one of his worshipers, leaving him in charge of goods, returns to find them stolen; whereupon he beats the god (or idol), which howls vociferously. **11. Herod:** Herod of Jewry; a character in *The Slaughter of the Innocents* and other cycle plays. The part was played with great noise and fury. **19. pressure:** Stamp, impressed character. **come tardy off:** Inadequately done. **20–21. the censure . . . one:** The judgment of even one of whom. **26. journeymen:** Laborers not yet masters in their trade. **28. indifferently:** Fairly, tolerably. **30. of:** I.e., some among them. **31. barren:** I.e., of wit.

ROSENCRANTZ: }
GUILDENSTERN: } We will, my lord.
Exeunt they two.

HAMLET: What ho! Horatio!

Enter Horatio.

HORATIO: Here, sweet lord, at your service.
HAMLET: Horatio, thou art e'en as just° a man
As e'er my conversation cop'd withal.
HORATIO: O, my dear lord,—
HAMLET: Nay, do not think I flatter;
For what advancement may I hope from thee
That no revenue hast but thy good spirits,
To feed and clothe thee? Why should the poor be flatter'd?
No, let the candied tongue lick absurd pomp,
And crook the pregnant° hinges of the knee
Where thrift° may follow fawning. Dost thou hear?
Since my dear soul was mistress of her choice
And could of men distinguish her election,
S' hath seal'd thee for herself; for thou hast been
As one, in suff'ring all, that suffers nothing,
A man that fortune's buffets and rewards
Hast ta'en with equal thanks: and blest are those
Whose blood and judgement are so well commeddled,
That they are not a pipe for fortune's finger
To sound what stop° she please. Give me that man
That is not passion's slave, and I will wear him
In my heart's core, ay, in my heart of heart,
As I do thee.—Something too much of this.—
There is a play to-night before the king;
One scene of it comes near the circumstance
Which I have told thee of my father's death:
I prithee, when thou seest that act afoot,
Even with the very comment of thy soul°
Observe my uncle: if his occulted° guilt
Do not itself unkennel in one speech,
It is a damned° ghost that we have seen,
And my imaginations are as foul
As Vulcan's stithy.° Give him heedful note;
For I mine eyes will rivet to his face,
And after we will both our judgements join
In censure of his seeming.°

---

41. just: Honest, honorable. **48. pregnant:** Pliant. **49. thrift:** Profit. **58. stop:** Hole in a wind instrument for controlling the sound. **66. very . . . soul:** Inward and sagacious criticism. **67. occulted:** Hidden. **69. damned:** In league with Satan. **71. stithy:** Smithy, place of *stiths* (anvils). **74. censure . . . seeming:** Judgment of his appearance or behavior.

HORATIO: Well, my lord:
If 'a steal aught the whilst this play is playing,
And 'scape detecting, I will pay the theft.

Enter trumpets and kettledrums, King, Queen, Polonius, Ophelia, [Rosencrantz, Guildenstern, and others].

HAMLET: They are coming to the play; I must be idle:° Get you a place.

KING: How fares our cousin Hamlet?

HAMLET: Excellent, i' faith; of the chameleon's dish:° I eat the air, promise-crammed: you cannot feed capons so.

KING: I have nothing with° this answer, Hamlet; these words are not mine.°

HAMLET: No, nor mine now. [*To Polonius.*] My lord, you played once i' the university, you say?

POLONIUS: That did I, my lord; and was accounted a good actor.

HAMLET: What did you enact?

POLONIUS: I did enact Julius Cæsar: I was killed i' the Capitol; Brutus killed me.

HAMLET: It was a brute part of him to kill so capital a calf there. Be the players ready?

ROSENCRANTZ: Ay, my lord; they stay upon your patience.

QUEEN: Come hither, my dear Hamlet, sit by me.

HAMLET: No, good mother, here's metal more attractive.

POLONIUS [to the king]: O, ho! do you mark that?

HAMLET: Lady, shall I lie in your lap? [*Lying down at Ophelia's feet.*]

OPHELIA: No, my lord.

HAMLET: I mean, my head upon your lap?

OPHELIA: Ay, my lord.

HAMLET: Do you think I meant country° matters?

OPHELIA: I think nothing, my lord.

HAMLET: That's a fair thought to lie between maids' legs.

OPHELIA: What is, my lord?

HAMLET: Nothing.

OPHELIA: You are merry, my lord.

HAMLET: Who, I?

OPHELIA: Ay, my lord.

HAMLET: O God, your only° jig-maker.° What should a man do but be merry? for, look you, how cheerfully my mother looks, and my father died within's two hours.

OPHELIA: Nay, 'tis twice two months, my lord.

HAMLET: So long? Nay then, let the devil wear black, for I'll have a suit of sables.° O heavens! die two months ago, and not forgotten yet? Then

---

77. idle: Crazy, or not attending to anything serious. **79. chameleon's dish:** Chameleons were supposed to feed on air. (Hamlet deliberately misinterprets the king's "fares" as "feeds.") **81. have . . . with:** Make nothing of. **are not mine:** Do not respond to what I ask. **98. country:** With a bawdy pun. **106. your only:** Only your. **jig-maker:** Composer of jigs (song and dance). **110–111. suit of sables:** Garments trimmed with the fur of the sable, with a quibble on *sable* meaning "black."

there's hope a great man's memory may outlive his life half a year: but, by 'r lady, 'a must build churches, then; or else shall 'a suffer not thinking on,° with the hobbyhorse, whose epitaph is "For, O, for, O, the hobby-horse is forgot."°

The trumpets sound. Dumb show follows.

Enter a King and a Queen [very lovingly]; the Queen embracing him, and he her. [She kneels, and makes show of protestation unto him.] He takes her up, and declines his head upon her neck: he lies him down upon a bank of flowers: she, seeing him asleep, leaves him. Anon comes in another man, takes off his crown, kisses it, pours poison in the sleeper's ears, and leaves him. The Queen returns; finds the King dead, makes passionate action. The Poisoner, with some three or four come in again, seem to condole with her. The dead body is carried away. The Poisoner woos the Queen with gifts: she seems harsh awhile, but in the end accepts love. [*Exeunt.*]

OPHELIA: What means this, my lord?

HAMLET: Marry, this is miching mallecho;° it means mischief.

OPHELIA: Belike this show imports the argument of the play.

Enter Prologue.

HAMLET: We shall know by this fellow: the players cannot keep counsel; they'll tell all.

OPHELIA: Will 'a tell us what this show meant?

HAMLET: Ay, or any show that you'll show him: be not you ashamed to show, he'll not shame to tell you what it means.

OPHELIA: You are naught, you are naught:° I'll mark the play.

PROLOGUE: For us, and for our tragedy,
Here stooping° to your clemency,
We beg your hearing patiently. [*Exit.*]

HAMLET: Is this a prologue, or the posy° of a ring?

OPHELIA: 'Tis brief, my lord.

HAMLET: As woman's love.

Enter [two Players as] King and Queen.

PLAYER KING: Full thirty times hath Phoebus' cart gone round
Neptune's salt wash° and Tellus'° orbed ground,
And thirty dozen moons with borrowed° sheen
About the world have times twelve thirties been,
Since love our hearts and Hymen° did our hands
Unite commutual° in most sacred bands.

PLAYER QUEEN: So many journeys may the sun and moon
Make us again count o'er ere love be done!
But, woe is me, you are so sick of late,

113–114. suffer . . . on: Undergo oblivion. **114–115. "For . . . forgot":** Verse of a song occurring also in *Love's Labour's Lost,* III.i.30. The hobbyhorse was a character in the Morris Dance. **117. miching mallecho:** Sneaking mischief. **124. naught:** Indecent. **126. stooping:** Bowing. **128. posy:** Motto. **132. salt wash:** The sea. **Tellus:** Goddess of the earth (*orbed ground*). **133. borrowed:** I.e., reflected. **135. Hymen:** God of matrimony. **136. commutual:** Mutually.

So far from cheer and from your former state,
That I distrust° you. Yet, though I distrust,
Discomfort you, my lord, it nothing must:
For women's fear and love holds quantity;°
In neither aught, or in extremity.
Now, what my love is, proof hath made you know;
And as my love is siz'd, my fear is so:
Where love is great, the littlest doubts are fear;
Where little fears grow great, great love grows there.

PLAYER KING: 'Faith, I must leave thee, love, and shortly too;
My operant° powers their functions leave° to do:
And thou shalt live in this fair world behind,
Honour'd, belov'd; and haply one as kind
For husband shalt thou —

PLAYER QUEEN: O, confound the rest!
Such love must needs be treason in my breast:
In second husband let me be accurst!
None wed the second but who kill'd the first.

HAMLET (*aside*): Wormwood, wormwood.

PLAYER QUEEN: The instances that second marriage move
Are base respects of thrift, but none of love:
A second time I kill my husband dead,
When second husband kisses me in bed.

PLAYER KING: I do believe you think what now you speak;
But what we do determine oft we break.
Purpose is but the slave to memory,
Of violent birth, but poor validity:
Which now, like fruit unripe, sticks on the tree;
But fall, unshaken, when they mellow be.
Most necessary 'tis that we forget
To pay ourselves what to ourselves is debt:
What to ourselves in passion we propose,
The passion ending, doth the purpose lose.
The violence of either grief or joy
Their own enactures° with themselves destroy:
Where joy most revels, grief doth most lament;
Grief joys, joy grieves, on slender accident.
This world is not for aye,° nor 'tis not strange
That even our loves should with our fortunes change;
For 'tis a question left us yet to prove,
Whether love lead fortune, or else fortune love.
The great man down, you mark his favourite flies;
The poor advanc'd makes friends of enemies.
And hitherto doth love on fortune tend;

---

141. distrust: Am anxious about. **143. holds quantity:** Keeps proportion between. **150. operant:** Active. **leave:** Cease. **173. enactures:** Fulfillments. **176. aye:** Ever.

For who° not needs shall never lack a friend,
And who in want a hollow friend doth try,
Directly seasons° him his enemy.
But, orderly to end where I begun,
Our wills and fates do so contrary run
That our devices still are overthrown;
Our thoughts are ours, their ends° none of our own:
So think thou wilt no second husband wed;
But die thy thoughts when thy first lord is dead.

PLAYER QUEEN: Nor earth to me give food, nor heaven light!
Sport and repose lock from me day and night!
To desperation turn my trust and hope!
An anchor's° cheer° in prison be my scope!
Each opposite° that blanks° the face of joy
Meet what I would have well and it destroy!
Both here and hence pursue me lasting strife,
If, once a widow, ever I be wife!

HAMLET: If she should break it now!

PLAYER KING: 'Tis deeply sworn. Sweet, leave me here awhile;
My spirits grow dull, and fain I would beguile
The tedious day with sleep. [*Sleeps.*]

PLAYER QUEEN: Sleep rock thy brain;
And never come mischance between us twain! *Exit.*

HAMLET: Madam, how like you this play?

QUEEN: The lady doth protest too much, methinks.

HAMLET: O, but she'll keep her word.

KING: Have you heard the argument? Is there no offence in 't?

HAMLET: No, no, they do but jest, poison in jest; no offence i' the world.

KING: What do you call the play?

HAMLET: The Mouse-trap. Marry, how? Tropically.° This play is the image of a murder done in Vienna: Gonzago° is the duke's name; his wife, Baptista: you shall see anon; 't is a knavish piece of work: but what o' that? your majesty and we that have free souls, it touches us not: let the galled jade° winch,° our withers° are unwrung.°

Enter Lucianus.

This is one Lucianus, nephew to the king.

OPHELIA: You are as good as a chorus,° my lord.

---

183. who: Whoever. **185. seasons:** Matures, ripens. **189. ends:** Results. **195. An anchor's:** An anchorite's. **cheer:** Fare; sometimes printed as chair. **196. opposite:** Adverse thing. **blanks:** Causes to blanch or grow pale. **211. Tropically:** Figuratively, *trapically* suggests a pun on trap in *Mouse-trap* (line 211). **212. Gonzago:** In 1538 Luigi Gonzago murdered the Duke of Urbano by pouring poisoned lotion in his ears. **214. galled jade:** Horse whose hide is rubbed by saddle or harness. **215. winch:** Wince. **withers:** The part between the horse's shoulder blades. **unwrung:** Not wrung or twisted. **217. chorus:** In many Elizabethan plays the action was explained by an actor known as the "chorus"; at a puppet show the actor who explained the action was known as an "interpreter," as indicated by the lines following.

HAMLET: I could interpret between you and your love, if I could see the puppets dallying.°

OPHELIA: You are keen, my lord, you are keen.

HAMLET: It would cost you a groaning to take off my edge.

OPHELIA: Still better, and worse.°

HAMLET: So you mistake° your husbands. Begin, murderer; pox,° leave thy damnable faces, and begin. Come: the croaking raven doth bellow for revenge.

LUCIANUS: Thoughts black, hands apt, drugs fit, and time agreeing;
Confederate° season, else no creature seeing;
Thou mixture rank, of midnight weeds collected,
With Hecate's° ban° thrice blasted, thrice infected,
Thy natural magic and dire property,
On wholesome life usurp immediately.

[Pours the poison into the sleeper's ears.]

HAMLET: 'A poisons him i' the garden for his estate. His name's Gonzago: the story is extant, and written in very choice Italian: you shall see anon how the murderer gets the love of Gonzago's wife.

OPHELIA: The king rises.

HAMLET: What, frighted with false fire!°

QUEEN: How fares my lord?

POLONIUS: Give o'er the play.

KING: Give me some light: away!

POLONIUS: Lights, lights, lights! *Exeunt all but Hamlet and Horatio.*

HAMLET: Why, let the strucken deer go weep,
The hart ungalled play;
For some must watch, while some must sleep:
Thus runs the world away.°
Would not this,° sir, and a forest of feathers°—if the rest of my fortunes turn Turk with° me—with two Provincial roses° on my razed° shoes, get me a fellowship in a cry° of players,° sir?

HORATIO: Half a share.°

HAMLET: A whole one, I.
For thou dost know, O Damon dear,

---

219. dallying: With sexual suggestion, continued in *keen* (sexually aroused), *groaning* (i.e., in pregnancy), and *edge* (i.e., sexual desire or impetuosity). **222. Still . . . worse:** More keen, less decorous. **223. mistake:** Err in taking. **pox:** An imprecation. **227. Confederate:** Conspiring (to assist the murderer). **229. Hecate:** The goddess of witchcraft. **ban:** Curse. **236. false fire:** Fireworks, or a blank discharge. **241–244. Why . . . away:** Probably from an old ballad, with allusion to the popular belief that a wounded deer retires to weep and die. Cf. *As You Like It*, II.i.66. **245. this:** I.e., the play. **feathers:** Allusion to the plumes which Elizabethan actors were fond of wearing. **246. turn Turk with:** Go back on. **two Provincial roses:** Rosettes of ribbon like the roses of Provins near Paris, or else the roses of Provence. **razed:** Cut, slashed (by way of ornament). **247. cry:** Pack (as of hounds). **fellowship . . . players:** Partnership in a theatrical company. **248. Half a share:** Allusion to the custom in dramatic companies of dividing the ownership into a number of shares among the householders.

This realm dismantled° was
Of Jove himself; and now reigns here
A very, very°—pajock.°

HORATIO: You might have rhymed.

HAMLET: O good Horatio, I'll take the ghost's word for a thousand pound. Didst perceive?

HORATIO: Very well, my lord.

HAMLET: Upon the talk of the poisoning?

HORATIO: I did very well note him.

HAMLET: Ah, ha! Come, some music! come, the recorders!°
For if the king like not the comedy,
Why then, belike, he likes it not, perdy.°
Come, some music!

Enter Rosencrantz and Guildenstern.

GUILDENSTERN: Good my lord, vouchsafe me a word with you.

HAMLET: Sir, a whole history.

GUILDENSTERN: The king, sir,—

HAMLET: Ay, sir, what of him?

GUILDENSTERN: Is in his retirement marvellous distempered.

HAMLET: With drink, sir?

GUILDENSTERN: No, my lord, rather with choler.°

HAMLET: Your wisdom should show itself more richer to signify this to his doctor; for, for me to put him to his purgation would perhaps plunge him into far more choler.

GUILDENSTERN: Good my lord, put your discourse into some frame° and start not so wildly from my affair.

HAMLET: I am tame, sir: pronounce.

GUILDENSTERN: The queen, your mother, in most great affliction of spirit, hath sent me to you.

HAMLET: You are welcome.

GUILDENSTERN: Nay, good my lord, this courtesy is not of the right breed. If it shall please you to make me a wholesome° answer, I will do your mother's commandment; if not, your pardon and my return shall be the end of my business.

HAMLET: Sir, I cannot.

GUILDENSTERN: What, my lord?

HAMLET: Make you a wholesome answer; my wit's diseased: but, sir, such answer as I can make, you shall command; or, rather, as you say, my mother: therefore no more, but to the matter:° my mother, you say,—

---

251. dismantled: Stripped, divested. **250–253. For . . . very:** Probably from an old ballad having to do with Damon and Pythias. **253. pajock:** Peacock (a bird with a bad reputation). Possibly the word was *patchock,* diminutive of *patch,* clown. **260. recorders:** Wind instruments of the flute kind. **262. perdy:** Corruption of *par dieu.* **270. choler:** Bilious disorder, with quibble on the sense "anger." **274. frame:** Order. **281. wholesome:** Sensible. **288. matter:** Matter in hand.

ROSENCRANTZ: Then thus she says; your behaviour hath struck her into amazement and admiration.

HAMLET: O wonderful son, that can so 'stonish a mother! But is there no sequel at the heels of this mother's admiration? Impart.

ROSENCRANTZ: She desires to speak with you in her closet, ere you go to bed.

HAMLET: We shall obey, were she ten times our mother. Have you any further trade with us?

ROSENCRANTZ: My lord, you once did love me.

HAMLET: And do still, by these pickers and stealers.°

ROSENCRANTZ: Good my lord, what is your cause of distemper? you do, surely, bar the door upon your own liberty, if you deny your griefs to your friend.

HAMLET: Sir, I lack advancement.

ROSENCRANTZ: How can that be, when you have the voice° of the king himself for your succession in Denmark?

HAMLET: Ay, sir, but "While the grass grows,"°—the proverb is something musty.

Enter the Players with recorders.

O, the recorders! let me see one. To withdraw° with you:—why do you go about to recover the wind° of me, as if you would drive me into a toil?°

GUILDENSTERN: O, my lord, if my duty be too bold, my love is too unmannerly.°

HAMLET: I do not well understand that. Will you play upon this pipe?

GUILDENSTERN: My lord, I cannot.

HAMLET: I pray you.

GUILDENSTERN: Believe me, I cannot.

HAMLET: I beseech you.

GUILDENSTERN: I know no touch of it, my lord.

HAMLET: 'Tis as easy as lying: govern these ventages° with your fingers and thumb, give it breath with your mouth, and it will discourse most eloquent music. Look you, these are the stops.

GUILDENSTERN: But these cannot I command to any utterance of harmony; I have not the skill.

HAMLET: Why, look you now, how unworthy a thing you make of me! You would play upon me; you would seem to know my stops; you would pluck out the heart of my mystery; you would sound me from my lowest note to the top of my compass:° and there is much music, excellent voice, in this little organ;° yet cannot you make it speak. 'Sblood, do you think I am easier to be played on than a pipe? Call me what instrument you will, though you can fret° me, you cannot play upon me.

---

297. pickers and stealers: Hands, so called from the catechism "to keep my hands from picking and stealing." **301. voice:** Support. **303. "While . . . grows":** The rest of the proverb is "the silly horse starves." Hamlet may be destroyed while he is waiting for the succession to the kingdom. **305. withdraw:** Speak in private. **306. recover the wind:** Get to the windward side. **toil:** Snare. **307. if . . . unmannerly:** If I am using an unmannerly boldness, it is my love which occasions it. **314. ventages:** Stops of the recorders. **322. compass:** Range of voice. **323. organ:** Musical instrument, i.e., the pipe. **325. fret:** Quibble on meaning "irritate" and the piece of wood, gut, or metal which regulates the fingering.

Enter Polonius.

God bless you, sir!

POLONIUS: My lord, the queen would speak with you, and presently.

HAMLET: Do you see yonder cloud that 's almost in shape of a camel?

POLONIUS: By the mass, and 'tis like a camel, indeed.

HAMLET: Methinks it is like a weasel.

POLONIUS: It is backed like a weasel.

HAMLET: Or like a whale?

POLONIUS: Very like a whale.

HAMLET: Then I will come to my mother by and by. [*Aside.*] They fool me to the top of my bent.° — I will come by and by.°

POLONIUS: I will say so. [*Exit.*]

HAMLET: By and by is easily said.
Leave me, friends. [*Exeunt all but Hamlet.*]
'Tis now the very witching time° of night,
When churchyards yawn and hell itself breathes out
Contagion to this world: now could I drink hot blood,
And do such bitter business as the day
Would quake to look on. Soft! now to my mother.
O heart, lose not thy nature; let not ever
The soul of Nero° enter this firm bosom:
Let me be cruel, not unnatural:
I will speak daggers to her, but use none;
My tongue and soul in this be hypocrites;
How in my words somever she be shent,°
To give them seals° never, my soul, consent! *Exit.*

[SCENE III: *A room in the castle.*]

Enter King, Rosencrantz, and Guildenstern.

KING: I like him not, nor stands it safe with us
To let his madness range. Therefore prepare you;
I your commission will forthwith dispatch,°
And he to England shall along with you:
The terms° of our estate° may not endure
Hazard so near us as doth hourly grow
Out of his brows.°

GUILDENSTERN: We will ourselves provide:
Most holy and religious fear it is
To keep those many many bodies safe
That live and feed upon your majesty.

---

335. top of my bent: Limit of endurance, i.e., extent to which a bow may be bent. **by and by:** Immediately. **339. witching time:** I.e., time when spells are cast. **345. Nero:** Murderer of his mother, Agrippina. **349. shent:** Rebuked. **350. give them seals:** Confirm with deeds. ACT III, SCENE III. **3. dispatch:** Prepare. **5. terms:** Condition, circumstances. **estate:** State. **7. brows:** Effronteries.

ROSENCRANTZ: The single and peculiar° life is bound,
With all the strength and armour of the mind,
To keep itself from noyance;° but much more
That spirit upon whose weal depend and rest
The lives of many. The cess° of majesty
Dies not alone; but, like a gulf,° doth draw
What's near it with it: it is a massy wheel,
Fix'd on the summit of the highest mount,
To whose huge spokes ten thousand lesser things
Are mortis'd and adjoin'd; which, when it falls,
Each small annexment, petty consequence,
Attends° the boist'rous ruin. Never alone
Did the king sigh, but with a general groan.
KING: Arm° you, I pray you, to this speedy voyage;
For we will fetters put about this fear,
Which now goes too free-footed.
ROSENCRANTZ: We will haste us.
Exeunt Gentlemen [Rosencrantz and Guildenstern].

Enter Polonius.

POLONIUS: My lord, he's going to his mother's closet:
Behind the arras° I'll convey° myself,
To hear the process;° I'll warrant she'll tax him home:°
And, as you said, and wisely was it said,
'Tis meet that some more audience than a mother,
Since nature makes them partial, should o'erhear
The speech, of vantage.° Fare you well, my liege:
I'll call upon you ere you go to bed,
And tell you what I know.
KING: Thanks, dear my lord. *Exit [Polonius].*
O, my offence is rank, it smells to heaven;
It hath the primal eldest curse° upon't,
A brother's murder. Pray can I not,
Though inclination be as sharp as will:°
My stronger guilt defeats my strong intent;
And, like a man to double business bound,
I stand in pause where I shall first begin,
And both neglect. What if this cursed hand
Were thicker than itself with brother's blood,
Is there not rain enough in the sweet heavens

11. single and peculiar: Individual and private. **13. noyance:** Harm. **15. cess:** Decease. **16. gulf:** Whirlpool. **22. Attends:** Participates in. **24. Arm:** Prepare. **28. arras:** Screen of tapestry placed around the walls of household apartments. **convey:** Implication of secrecy, convey was often used to mean "steal." **29. process:** Proceedings. **tax him home:** Reprove him severely. **33. of vantage:** From an advantageous place. **37. primal eldest curse:** The curse of Cain, the first to kill his brother. **39. sharp as will:** I.e., his desire is as strong as his determination.

To wash it white as snow? Whereto serves mercy
But to confront° the visage of offence?
And what's in prayer but this two-fold force,
To be forestalled° ere we come to fall,
Or pardon'd being down? Then I'll look up;
My fault is past. But, O, what form of prayer
Can serve my turn? "Forgive me my foul murder"?
That cannot be: since I am still possess'd
Of those effects for which I did the murder,
My crown, mine own ambition° and my queen.
May one be pardon'd and retain th' offence?°
In the corrupted currents° of this world
Offence's gilded hand° may shove by justice,
And oft 'tis seen the wicked prize° itself
Buys out the law: but 'tis not so above;
There is no shuffling,° there the action lies°
In his true nature; and we ourselves compell'd,
Even to the teeth and forehead° of our faults,
To give in evidence. What then? what rests?°
Try what repentance can: what can it not?
Yet what can it when one can not repent?
O wretched state! O bosom black as death!
O limed° soul, that, struggling to be free,
Art more engag'd!° Help, angels! Make assay!°
Bow, stubborn knees; and, heart with strings of steel,
Be soft as sinews of the new-born babe!
All may be well. *[He kneels.]*

Enter Hamlet.

HAMLET: Now might I do it pat,° now he is praying;
And now I'll do't. And so 'a goes to heaven;
And so am I reveng'd. That would be scann'd:°
A villain kills my father; and for that,
I, his sole son, do this same villain send
To heaven.
Why, this is hire and salary, not revenge.
'A took my father grossly, full of bread;°
With all his crimes broad blown,° as flush° as May;
And how his audit stands who knows save heaven?

---

47. confront: Oppose directly. **49. forestalled:** Prevented. **55. ambition:** I.e., realization of ambition. **56. offence:** Benefit accruing from offense. **57. currents:** Courses. **58. gilded hand:** Hand offering gold as a bribe. **59. wicked prize:** Prize won by wickedness. **61. shuffling:** Escape by trickery. **lies:** Is sustainable. **63. teeth and forehead:** Very face. **64. rests:** Remains. **68. limed:** Caught as with birdlime. **69. engag'd:** Embedded. **assay:** Trial. **73. pat:** Opportunely. **75. would be scann'd:** Needs to be looked into. **80. full of bread:** Enjoying his worldly pleasures (see Ezekiel 16:49). **81. broad blown:** In full bloom. **flush:** Lusty.

But in our circumstance and course° of thought,
'Tis heavy with him: and am I then reveng'd,
To take him in the purging of his soul,
When he is fit and season'd for his passage?°
No!
Up, sword; and know thou a more horrid hent:°
When he is drunk asleep,° or in his rage,
Or in th' incestuous pleasure of his bed;
At game, a-swearing, or about some act
That has no relish of salvation in't;
Then trip him, that his heels may kick at heaven,
And that his soul may be as damn'd and black
As hell, whereto it goes. My mother stays:
This physic° but prolongs thy sickly days. *Exit.*
KING: [*Rising*] My words fly up, my thoughts remain below:
Words without thoughts never to heaven go. *Exit.*

[SCENE IV: *The Queen's closet.*]

Enter [*Queen*] *Gertrude and Polonius.*

POLONIUS: 'A will come straight. Look you lay° home to him:
Tell him his pranks have been too broad° to bear with,
And that your grace hath screen'd and stood between
Much heat° and him. I'll sconce° me even here.
Pray you, be round° with him.
HAMLET (*within*): Mother, mother, mother!
QUEEN: I'll warrant you,
Fear me not: withdraw, I hear him coming.

[*Polonius hides behind the arras.*]

Enter Hamlet.

HAMLET: Now, mother, what's the matter?
QUEEN: Hamlet, thou hast thy father much offended.
HAMLET: Mother, you have my father° much offended.
QUEEN: Come, come, you answer with an idle tongue.
HAMLET: Go, go, you question with a wicked tongue.
QUEEN: Why, how now, Hamlet!
HAMLET: What's the matter now?
QUEEN: Have you forgot me?
HAMLET: No, by the rood,° not so:
You are the queen, your husband's brother's wife;
And—would it were not so!—you are my mother.

83. in . . . course: As we see it in our mortal situation. **86. fit . . . passage:** I.e., reconciled to heaven by forgiveness of his sins. **88. hent:** Seizing; or more probably, occasion of seizure. **89. drunk asleep:** In a drunken sleep. **96. physic:** Purging (by prayer). ACT III, SCENE IV. **1. lay:** Thrust. **2. broad:** Unrestrained. **4. Much heat:** I.e., the king's anger. **sconce:** Hide. **5. round:** Blunt. **9–10. thy father, my father:** I.e., Claudius, the elder Hamlet. **14. rood:** Cross.

QUEEN: Nay, then, I'll set those to you that can speak.
HAMLET: Come, come, and sit you down; you shall not budge;
You go not till I set you up a glass
Where you may see the inmost part of you.
QUEEN: What wilt thou do? thou wilt not murder me?
Help, help, ho!
POLONIUS [*behind*] What, ho! help, help; help!
HAMLET [*drawing*] How now! a rat? Dead, for a ducat, dead!
[*Makes a pass through the arras.*]
POLONIUS [*behind*]: O, I am slain! [*Falls and dies.*]
QUEEN: O me, what hast thou done?
HAMLET: Nay, I know not:
Is it the king?
QUEEN: O, what a rash and bloody deed is this!
HAMLET: A bloody deed! almost as bad, good mother,
As kill a king, and marry with his brother.
QUEEN: As kill a king!
HAMLET: Ay, lady, it was my word.
[*Lifts up the arras and discovers Polonius.*]
Thou wretched, rash, intruding fool, farewell!
I took thee for thy better: take thy fortune;
Thou find'st to be too busy is some danger.
Leave wringing of your hands: peace! sit you down,
And let me wring your heart; for so I shall,
If it be made of penetrable stuff,
If damned custom have not braz'd° it so
That it be proof and bulwark against sense.
QUEEN: What have I done, that thou dar'st wag thy tongue
In noise so rude against me?
HAMLET: Such an act
That blurs the grace and blush of modesty,
Calls virtue hypocrite, takes off the rose
From the fair forehead of an innocent love
And sets a blister° there, makes marriage-vows
As false as dicers' oaths: O, such a deed
As from the body of contraction° plucks
The very soul, and sweet religion° makes
A rhapsody° of words: heaven's face does glow
O'er this solidity and compound mass
With heated visage, as against the doom
Is thought-sick at the act.°

---

38. braz'd: Brazened, hardened. **45. sets a blister:** Brands as a harlot. **47. contraction:** The marriage contract. **48. religion:** Religious vows. **49. rhapsody:** Senseless string. **49–52. heaven's . . . act:** Heaven's face blushes to look down upon this world, compounded of the four elements, with hot face as though the day of doom were near, and thought-sick at the deed (i.e., Gertrude's marriage).

QUEEN: Ay me, what act,
That roars so loud, and thunders in the index?°
HAMLET: Look here, upon this picture, and on this.
The counterfeit presentment° of two brothers.
See, what grace was seated on this brow;
Hyperion's° curls; the front° of Jove himself;
An eye like Mars, to threaten and command;
A station° like the herald Mercury
New-lighted on a heaven-kissing hill;
A combination and a form indeed,
Where every god did seem to set his seal,
To give the world assurance° of a man:
This was your husband. Look you now, what follows:
Here is your husband; like a mildew'd ear,°
Blasting his wholesome brother. Have you eyes?
Could you on this fair mountain leave to feed,
And batten° on this moor?° Ha! have you eyes?
You cannot call it love; for at your age
The hey-day° in the blood is tame, it's humble,
And waits upon the judgement: and what judgement
Would step from this to this? Sense, sure, you have,
Else could you not have motion;° but sure, that sense
Is apoplex'd;° for madness would not err,
Nor sense to ecstasy was ne'er so thrall'd°
But it reserv'd some quantity of choice,°
To serve in such a difference. What devil was't
That thus hath cozen'd° you at hoodman-blind?°
Eyes without feeling, feeling without sight,
Ears without hands or eyes, smelling sans° all,
Or but a sickly part of one true sense
Could not so mope.°
O shame! where is thy blush? Rebellious hell,
If thou canst mutine° in a matron's bones,
To flaming youth let virtue be as wax,
And melt in her own fire: proclaim no shame
When the compulsive ardour gives the charge,°

---

53. index: Prelude or preface. **55. counterfeit presentment:** Portrayed representation. **57. Hyperion's:** The sun god's. **front:** Brow. **59. station:** Manner of standing. **63. assurance:** Pledge, guarantee. **65. mildew'd ear:** See Genesis 41:5–7. **68. batten:** Grow fat. **moor:** Barren upland. **70. hey-day:** State of excitement. **72–73. Sense . . . motion:** Sense and motion are functions of the middle or sensible soul, the possession of sense being the basis of motion. **74. apoplex'd:** Paralyzed. Mental derangement was thus of three sorts: apoplexy, ecstasy, and diabolic possession. **75. thrall'd:** Enslaved. **76. quantity of choice:** Fragment of the power to choose. **78. cozen'd:** Tricked, cheated. **hoodman-blind:** Blindman's buff. **80. sans:** Without. **82. mope:** Be in a depressed, spiritless state, act aimlessly. **84. mutine:** Mutiny, rebel. **87. gives the charge:** Delivers the attack.

Since frost itself as actively doth burn
And reason pandars will.°

QUEEN: O Hamlet, speak no more:
Thou turn'st mine eyes into my very soul;
And there I see such black and grained° spots
As will not leave their tinct.

HAMLET: Nay, but to live
In the rank sweat of an enseamed° bed,
Stew'd in corruption, honeying and making love
Over the nasty sty, —

QUEEN: O, speak to me no more;
These words, like daggers, enter in mine ears;
No more, sweet Hamlet!

HAMLET: A murderer and a villain;
A slave that is not twentieth part the tithe
Of your precedent lord;° a vice of kings;°
A cutpurse of the empire and the rule,
That from a shelf the precious diadem stole,
And put it in his pocket!

QUEEN: No more!

Enter Ghost.

HAMLET: A king of shreds and patches, ° —
Save me, and hover o'er me with your wings,
You heavenly guards! What would your gracious figure?

QUEEN: Alas, he's mad!

HAMLET: Do you not come your tardy son to chide,
That, laps'd in time and passion, ° lets go by
Th' important° acting of your dread command?
O, say!

GHOST: Do not forget: this visitation
Is but to whet thy almost blunted purpose.
But, look, amazement° on thy mother sits:
O, step between her and her fighting soul:
Conceit in weakest bodies strongest works:
Speak to her, Hamlet.

HAMLET: How is it with you, lady?

QUEEN: Alas, how is 't with you,

---

89. reason pandars will: The normal and proper situation was one in which reason guided the will in the direction of good; here, reason is perverted and leads in the direction of evil. **91. grained:** Dyed in grain. **93. enseamed:** Loaded with grease, greased. **99. precedent lord:** I.e., the elder Hamlet. **vice of kings:** Buffoon of kings; a reference to the Vice, or clown, of the morality plays and interludes. **103. shreds and patches:** I.e., motley, the traditional costume of the Vice. **108. laps'd . . . passion:** Having suffered time to slip and passion to cool; also explained as "engrossed in casual events and lapsed into mere fruitless passion, so that he no longer entertains a rational purpose." **109. important:** Urgent. **113. amazement:** Frenzy, distraction.

That you do bend your eye on vacancy
And with th' incorporal° air do hold discourse?
Forth at your eyes your spirits wildly peep;
And, as the sleeping soldiers in th' alarm,
Your bedded° hair, like life in excrements,°
Start up, and stand an° end. O gentle son,
Upon the heat and flame of thy distemper
Sprinkle cool patience. Whereon do you look?

HAMLET: On him, on him! Look you, how pale he glares!
His form and cause conjoin'd,° preaching to stones,
Would make them capable.—Do not look upon me;
Lest with this piteous action you convert
My stern effects:° then what I have to do
Will want true colour;° tears perchance for blood.

QUEEN: To whom do you speak this?

HAMLET: Do you see nothing there?

QUEEN: Nothing at all; yet all that is I see.

HAMLET: Nor did you nothing hear?

QUEEN: No, nothing but ourselves.

HAMLET: Why, look you there! look, how it steals away!
My father, in his habit as he liv'd!
Look, where he goes, even now, out at the portal! *Exit Ghost.*

QUEEN: This is the very coinage of your brain:
This bodiless creation ecstasy
Is very cunning in.

HAMLET: Ecstasy!
My pulse, as yours, doth temperately keep time,
And makes as healthful music: it is not madness
That I have utt'red: bring me to the test,
And I the matter will re-word,° which madness
Would gambol° from. Mother, for love of grace,
Lay not that flattering unction° to your soul,
That not your trespass, but my madness speaks:
It will but skin and film the ulcerous place,
Whiles rank corruption, mining° all within,
Infects unseen. Confess yourself to heaven;
Repent what's past; avoid what is to come;°

---

119. incorporal: Immaterial. **122. bedded:** Laid in smooth layers. **excrements:** The hair was considered an excrement or voided part of the body. **123. an:** On. **127. conjoin'd:** United. **129–130. convert . . . effects:** Divert me from my stern duty. For *effects,* possibly *affects* (affections of the mind). **131. want true colour:** Lack good reason so that (with a play on the normal sense of *colour*) I shall shed tears instead of blood. **144. re-word:** Repeat in words. **145. gambol:** Skip away. **146. unction:** Ointment used medicinally or as a rite; suggestion that forgiveness for sin may not be so easily achieved. **149. mining:** Working under the surface. **151. what is to come:** I.e., the sins of the future.

And do not spread the compost° on the weeds,
To make them ranker. Forgive me this my virtue;°
For in the fatness° of these pursy° times
Virtue itself of vice must pardon beg,
Yea, curb° and woo for leave to do him good.

QUEEN: O Hamlet, thou hast cleft my heart in twain.

HAMLET: O, throw away the worser part of it,
And live the purer with the other half.
Good night: but go not to my uncle's bed;
Assume a virtue, if you have it not.
That monster, custom, who all sense doth eat,
Of habits devil, is angel yet in this,
That to the use of actions fair and good
He likewise gives a frock or livery,
That aptly is put on. Refrain to-night,
And that shall lend a kind of easiness
To the next abstinence: the next more easy;
For use almost can change the stamp of nature,
And either . . . the devil, or throw him out°
With wondrous potency. Once more, good night:
And when you are desirous to be bless'd,°
I'll blessing beg of you. For this same lord, [*Pointing to Polonius.*]
I do repent: but heaven hath pleas'd it so,
To punish me with this and this with me,
That I must be their scourge and minister.
I will bestow him, and will answer well
The death I gave him. So, again, good night.
I must be cruel, only to be kind:
Thus bad begins and worse remains behind.
One word more, good lady.

QUEEN: What shall I do?

HAMLET: Not this, by no means, that I bid you do:
Let the bloat° king tempt you again to bed;
Pinch wanton on your cheek; call you his mouse;
And let him, for a pair of reechy° kisses,
Or paddling in your neck with his damn'd fingers,
Make you to ravel all this matter out,
That I essentially° am not in madness,
But mad in craft. 'Twere good you let him know;
For who, that's but a queen, fair, sober, wise,

---

152. compost: Manure. **153. this my virtue:** My virtuous talk in reproving you. **154. fatness:** Grossness. **pursy:** Short-winded, corpulent. **156. curb:** Bow, bend the knee. **170.** Defective line usually emended by inserting *master* after *either.* **172. be bless'd:** Become blessed, i.e., repentant. **183. bloat:** Bloated. **185. reechy:** Dirty, filthy. **188. essentially:** In my essential nature.

Would from a paddock,° from a bat, a gib,°
Such dear concernings° hide? who would do so?
No, in despite of sense and secrecy,
Unpeg the basket on the house's top,
Let the birds fly, and, like the famous ape.°
To try conclusions,° in the basket creep,
And break your own neck down.

QUEEN: Be thou assur'd, if words be made of breath,
And breath of life, I have no life to breathe
What thou hast said to me.

HAMLET: I must to England; you know that?

QUEEN: Alack,
I had forgot: 'tis so concluded on.

HAMLET: There's letters seal'd: and my two schoolfellows,
Whom I will trust as I will adders fang'd,
They bear the mandate; they must sweep my way,°
And marshal me to knavery. Let it work;
For 'tis the sport to have the enginer°
Hoist° with his own petar:° and 't shall go hard
But I will delve one yard below their mines,
And blow them at the moon: O, 'tis most sweet,
When in one line two crafts° directly meet.
This man shall set me packing:°
I'll lug the guts into the neighbour room.
Mother, good night. Indeed this counsellor
Is now most still, most secret and most grave,
Who was in life a foolish prating knave.
Come, sir, to draw° toward an end with you.
Good night, mother. *Exeunt [severally; Hamlet dragging in Polonius.]*

[ACT IV

SCENE I: *A room in the castle.*]

Enter King and Queen, with Rosencrantz and Guildenstern.

KING: There's matter in these sighs, these profound heaves:
You must translate: 'tis fit we understand them.
Where is your son?

---

191. paddock: Toad. **gib:** Tomcat. **192. dear concernings:** Important affairs. **195. the famous ape:** A letter from Sir John Suckling seems to supply other details of the story, otherwise not identified: "It is the story of the jackanapes and the partridges; thou starest after a beauty till it be lost to thee, then let'st out another, and starest after that till it is gone too." **196. conclusions:** Experiments. **205. sweep my way:** Clear my path. **207. enginer:** Constructor of military works, or possibly, artilleryman. **208. Hoist:** Blown up. **petar:** Defined as a small engine of war used to blow in a door or make a breach, and as a case filled with explosive materials. **211. two crafts:** Two acts of guile, with quibble on the sense of "two ships." **212. set me packing:** Set me to making schemes, and set me to lugging (him), and, also, send me off in a hurry. **217. draw:** Come, with quibble on literal sense.

QUEEN: Bestow this place on us a little while.
[*Exeunt Rosencrantz and Guildenstern.*]
Ah, mine own lord, what have I seen to-night!
KING: What, Gertrude? How does Hamlet?
QUEEN: Mad as the sea and wind, when both contend
Which is the mightier: in his lawless fit,
Behind the arras hearing something stir,
Whips out his rapier, cries, "A rat, a rat!"
And, in this brainish° apprehension,° kills
The unseen good old man.
KING: O heavy deed!
It had been so with us, had we been there:
His liberty is full of threats to all;
To you yourself, to us, to every one.
Alas, how shall this bloody deed be answer'd?
It will be laid to us, whose providence°
Should have kept short,° restrain'd and out of haunt,°
This mad young man: but so much was our love,
We would not understand what was most fit;
But, like the owner of a foul disease,
To keep it from divulging,° let it feed
Even on the pith of life. Where is he gone?
QUEEN: To draw apart the body he hath kill'd:
O'er whom his very madness, like some ore
Among a mineral° of metals base,
Shows itself pure; 'a weeps for what is done.
KING: O Gertrude, come away!
The sun no sooner shall the mountains touch,
But we will ship him hence: and this vile deed
We must, with all our majesty and skill,
Both countenance and excuse. Ho, Guildenstern!

Enter Rosencrantz and Guildenstern.

Friends both, go join you with some further aid:
Hamlet in madness hath Polonius slain,
And from his mother's closet hath he dragg'd him:
Go seek him out; speak fair, and bring the body
Into the chapel. I pray you, haste in this.
[*Exeunt Rosencrantz and Guildenstern.*]
Come, Gertrude, we'll call up our wisest friends;
And let them know, both what we mean to do,
And what's untimely done . . .°

ACT IV, SCENE I. **11. brainish:** Headstrong, passionate. **apprehension:** Conception, imagination. **17. providence:** Foresight. **18. short:** I.e., on a short tether. **out of haunt:** Secluded. **22. divulging:** Becoming evident. **26. mineral:** Mine. **40.** Defective line; some editors add: *so, haply, slander*; others add: *for, haply, slander*; other conjectures.

Whose whisper o'er the world's diameter,°
As level° as the cannon to his blank,°
Transports his pois'ned shot, may miss our name,
And hit the woundless° air. O, come away!
My soul is full of discord and dismay. *Exeunt.*

[SCENE II: *Another room in the castle.*]

Enter Hamlet.

HAMLET: Safely stowed.

ROSENCRANTZ: }
GUILDENSTERN: } (*within*) Hamlet! Lord Hamlet!

HAMLET: But soft, what noise? who calls on Hamlet? O, here they come.

Enter Rosencrantz and Guildenstern.

ROSENCRANTZ: What have you done, my lord, with the dead body?

HAMLET: Compounded it with dust, whereto 'tis kin.

ROSENCRANTZ: Tell us where 'tis, that we may take it thence
And bear it to the chapel.

HAMLET: Do not believe it.

ROSENCRANTZ: Believe what?

HAMLET: That I can keep your counsel° and not mine own. Besides, to be demanded of a sponge! what replication° should be made by the son of a king?

ROSENCRANTZ: Take you me for a sponge, my lord?

HAMLET: Ay, sir, that soaks up the king's countenance, his rewards, his authorities.° But such officers do the king best service in the end: he keeps them, like an ape an apple, in the corner of his jaw; first mouthed, to be last swallowed: when he needs what you have gleaned, it is but squeezing you, and, sponge, you shall be dry again.

ROSENCRANTZ: I understand you not, my lord.

HAMLET: I am glad of it: a knavish speech sleeps in a foolish ear.

ROSENCRANTZ: My lord, you must tell us where the body is, and go with us to the king.

HAMLET: The body is with the king, but the king is not with the body.° The king is a thing—

GUILDENSTERN: A thing, my lord!

HAMLET: Of nothing: bring me to him. Hide fox, and all after.° *Exeunt.*

---

41. diameter: Extent from side to side. **42. level:** Straight. **blank:** White spot in the center of a target. **44. woundless:** Invulnerable. ACT IV, SCENE II. **9. keep your counsel:** Hamlet is aware of their treachery but says nothing about it. **10. replication:** Reply. **13–14. authorities:** Authoritative backing. **22. The body . . . body:** There are many interpretations; possibly, "The body lies in death with the king, my father; but my father walks disembodied"; or "Claudius has the bodily possession of kingship, but kingliness, or justice of inheritance, is not with him." **25. Hide . . . after:** An old signal cry in the game of hide-and-seek.

[SCENE III: *Another room in the castle.*]

Enter King, and two or three.

KING: I have sent to seek him, and to find the body.
How dangerous is it that this man goes loose!
Yet must not we put the strong law on him:
He's lov'd of the distracted° multitude,
Who like not in their judgement, but their eyes;
And where 'tis so, th' offender's scourge° is weigh'd,°
But never the offence. To bear all smooth and even,
This sudden sending him away must seem
Deliberate pause:° diseases desperate grown
By desperate appliance are reliev'd,
Or not at all.

Enter Rosencrantz, [Guildenstern,] and all the rest.

How now! what hath befall'n?

ROSENCRANTZ: Where the dead body is bestow'd, my lord,
We cannot get from him.

KING: But where is he?

ROSENCRANTZ: Without, my lord; guarded, to know your pleasure.

KING: Bring him before us.

ROSENCRANTZ: Ho! bring in the lord.

They enter [with Hamlet].

KING: Now, Hamlet, where's Polonius?

HAMLET: At supper.

KING: At supper! where?

HAMLET: Not where he eats, but where 'a is eaten: a certain convocation of politic° worms° are e'en at him. Your worm is your only emperor for diet: we fat all creatures else to fat us, and we fat ourselves for maggots: your fat king and your lean beggar is but variable service,° two dishes, but to one table: that's the end.

KING: Alas, alas!

HAMLET: A man may fish with the worm that hath eat of a king, and eat of the fish that hath fed of that worm.

KING: What dost thou mean by this?

HAMLET: Nothing but to show you how a king may go a progress° through the guts of a beggar.

KING: Where is Polonius?

HAMLET: In heaven; send thither to see: if your messenger find him not there, seek him i' the other place yourself. But if indeed you find him not within this month, you shall nose him as you go up the stairs into the lobby.

ACT IV, SCENE III. **4. distracted:** I.e., without power of forming logical judgments. **6. scourge:** Punishment. **weigh'd:** Taken into consideration. **9. Deliberate pause:** Considered action. **20–21. convocation . . . worms:** Allusion to the Diet of Worms (1521). **politic:** Crafty. **23. variable service:** A variety of dishes. **29. progress:** Royal journey of state.

KING [*to some Attendants*]: Go seek him there.
HAMLET: 'A will stay till you come. [*Exeunt Attendants.*]
KING: Hamlet, this deed, for thine especial safety,—
Which we do tender,° as we dearly grieve
For that which thou hast done,—must send thee hence
With fiery quickness: therefore prepare thyself;
The bark is ready, and the wind at help,
Th' associates tend, and everything is bent
For England.
HAMLET: For England!
KING: Ay, Hamlet.
HAMLET: Good.
KING: So is it, if thou knew'st our purposes.
HAMLET: I see a cherub° that sees them. But, come; for England! Farewell, dear mother.
KING: Thy loving father, Hamlet.
HAMLET: My mother: father and mother is man and wife; man and wife is one flesh; and so, my mother. Come, for England! *Exit.*
KING: Follow him at foot;° tempt him with speed aboard;
Delay it not; I'll have him hence to-night:
Away! for every thing is seal'd and done
That else leans on th' affair: pray you, make haste.
[*Exeunt all but the King.*]
And, England, if my love thou hold'st at aught—
As my great power thereof may give thee sense,
Since yet thy cicatrice° looks raw and red
After the Danish sword, and thy free awe°
Pays homage to us—thou mayst not coldly set
Our sovereign process; which imports at full,
By letters congruing to that effect,
The present death of Hamlet. Do it, England;
For like the hectic° in my blood he rages,
And thou must cure me: till I know 'tis done,
Howe'er my haps,° my joys were ne'er begun. *Exit.*

[SCENE IV: *A plain in Denmark.*]

Enter Fortinbras with his Army over the stage.

FORTINBRAS: Go, captain, from me greet the Danish king;
Tell him that, by his license,° Fortinbras
Craves the conveyance° of a promis'd march
Over his kingdom. You know the rendezvous.
If that his majesty would aught with us,

---

38. tender: Regard, hold dear. **45. cherub:** Cherubim are angels of knowledge. **50. at foot:** Close behind, at heel. **56. cicatrice:** Scar. **57. free awe:** Voluntary show of respect. **62. hectic:** Fever. **64. haps:** Fortunes. ACT IV, SCENE IV. **2. license:** Leave. **3. conveyance:** Escort, convoy.

We shall express our duty in his eye;°
And let him know so.

CAPTAIN: I will do't, my lord.

FORTINBRAS: Go softly° on. [*Exeunt all but Captain.*]

Enter Hamlet, Rosencrantz, [Guildenstern,] &c.

HAMLET: Good sir, whose powers are these?

CAPTAIN: They are of Norway, sir.

HAMLET: How purpos'd, sir, I pray you?

CAPTAIN: Against some part of Poland.

HAMLET: Who commands them, sir?

CAPTAIN: The nephew to old Norway, Fortinbras.

HAMLET: Goes it against the main° of Poland, sir,
Or for some frontier?

CAPTAIN: Truly to speak, and with no addition,
We go to gain a little patch of ground
That hath in it no profit but the name.
To pay five ducats, five, I would not farm it;°
Nor will it yield to Norway or the Pole
A ranker rate, should it be sold in fee.°

HAMLET: Why, then the Polack never will defend it.

CAPTAIN: Yes, it is already garrison'd.

HAMLET: Two thousand souls and twenty thousand ducats
Will not debate the question of this straw:°
This is th' imposthume° of much wealth and peace,
That inward breaks, and shows no cause without
Why the man dies. I humbly thank you, sir.

CAPTAIN: God be wi' you, sir. [*Exit.*]

ROSENCRANTZ: Will 't please you go, my lord?

HAMLET: I'll be with you straight. Go a little before.
[*Exeunt all except Hamlet.*]

How all occasions° do inform against° me,
And spur my dull revenge! What is a man,
If his chief good and market of his time°
Be but to sleep and feed? a beast, no more.
Sure, he that made us with such large discourse,
Looking before and after, gave us not
That capability and god-like reason
To fust° in us unus'd. Now, whether it be
Bestial oblivion, or some craven scruple
Of thinking too precisely on th' event,

---

6. in his eye: In his presence. **8. softly:** Slowly. **15. main:** Country itself. **20. farm it:** Take a lease of it. **22. fee:** Fee simple. **26. debate . . . straw:** Settle this trifling matter. **27. imposthume:** Purulent abscess or swelling. **32. occasions:** Incidents, events. **inform against:** Generally defined as "show," "betray" (i.e., his tardiness); more probably *inform* means "take shape," as in *Macbeth*, II.i.48. **34. market of his time:** The best use he makes of his time, or, that for which he sells his time. **39. fust:** Grow moldy.

A thought which, quarter'd, hath but one part wisdom
And ever three parts coward, I do not know
Why yet I live to say "This thing 's to do";
Sith I have cause and will and strength and means
To do 't. Examples gross as earth exhort me:
Witness this army of such mass and charge
Led by a delicate and tender prince,
Whose spirit with divine ambition puff'd
Makes mouths at the invisible event,
Exposing what is mortal and unsure
To all that fortune, death and danger dare,
Even for an egg-shell. Rightly to be great
Is not to stir without great argument,
But greatly to find quarrel in a straw
When honour's at the stake. How stand I then,
That have a father kill'd, a mother stain'd,
Excitements of° my reason and my blood,
And let all sleep? while, to my shame, I see
The imminent death of twenty thousand men,
That, for a fantasy and trick° of fame,
Go to their graves like beds, fight for a plot°
Whereon the numbers cannot try the cause,
Which is not tomb enough and continent
To hide the slain? O, from this time forth,
My thoughts be bloody, or be nothing worth! *Exit.*

[SCENE V: *Elsinore. A room in the castle.*]

Enter Horatio, [Queen] Gertrude, and a Gentleman.

QUEEN: I will not speak with her.
GENTLEMAN: She is importunate, indeed distract:
Her mood will needs be pitied.
QUEEN: What would she have?
GENTLEMAN: She speaks much of her father; says she hears
There's tricks° i' th' world; and hems, and beats her heart;°
Spurns enviously at straws;° speaks things in doubt,
That carry but half sense: her speech is nothing,
Yet the unshaped° use of it doth move
The hearers to collection;° they yawn° at it,
And botch° the words up fit to their own thoughts;
Which, as her winks, and nods, and gestures yield° them,

---

58. Excitements of: Incentives to. **61. trick:** Toy, trifle. **62. plot:** I.e., of ground. ACT IV, SCENE V. **5. tricks:** Deceptions. **heart:** I.e., breast. **6. Spurns . . . straws:** Kicks spitefully at small objects in her path. **8. unshaped:** Unformed, artless. **9. collection:** Inference, a guess at some sort of meaning. **yawn:** Wonder. **10. botch:** Patch. **11. yield:** Deliver, bring forth (her words).

Indeed would make one think there might be thought,
Though nothing sure, yet much unhappily.°
HORATIO: 'Twere good she were spoken with: for she may strew
Dangerous conjectures in ill-breeding minds.°
QUEEN: Let her come in. [*Exit Gentleman.*]
[*Aside.*] To my sick soul, as sin's true nature is,
Each toy seems prologue to some great amiss:°
So full of artless jealousy is guilt,
It spills itself in fearing to be spilt.°

Enter Ophelia [*distracted*].

OPHELIA: Where is the beauteous majesty of Denmark?
QUEEN: How now, Ophelia!
OPHELIA (*she sings*): How should I your true love know
From another one?
By his cockle hat° and staff,
And his sandal shoon.°
QUEEN: Alas, sweet lady, what imports this song?
OPHELIA: Say you? nay, pray you mark.
(*Song*) He is dead and gone, lady,
He is dead and gone;
At his head a grass-green turf,
At his heels a stone.
O, ho!
QUEEN: Nay, but, Ophelia—
OPHELIA: Pray you, mark
[*Sings.*] White his shroud as the mountain snow,—

Enter King.

QUEEN: Alas, look here, my lord.
OPHELIA (*Song*): Larded° all with flowers;
Which bewept to the grave did not go
With true-love showers.
KING: How do you, pretty lady?
OPHELIA: Well, God 'ild° you! They say the owl° was a baker's daughter. Lord, we know what we are, but know not what we may be. God be at your table!
KING: Conceit upon her father.

---

13. much unhappily: Expressive of much unhappiness. **15. ill-breeding minds:** Minds bent on mischief. **18. great amiss:** Calamity, disaster. **19–20. So . . . spilt:** Guilt is so full of suspicion that it unskillfully betrays itself in fearing to be betrayed. **25. cockle hat:** Hat with cockleshell stuck in it as a sign that the wearer has been a pilgrim to the shrine of St. James of Compostella. The pilgrim's garb was a conventional disguise for lovers. **26. shoon:** Shoes. **38. Larded:** Decorated. **42. God 'ild:** God yield or reward. **owl:** Reference to a monkish legend that a baker's daughter was turned into an owl for refusing bread to the Savior.

OPHELIA: Pray let's have no words of this; but when they ask you what it means, say you this:
(*Song*) To-morrow is Saint Valentine's day,
All in the morning betime,
And I a maid at your window,
To be your Valentine.°
Then up he rose, and donn'd his clothes,
And dupp'd° the chamber-door;
Let in the maid, that out a maid
Never departed more.

KING: Pretty Ophelia!

OPHELIA: Indeed, la, without an oath, I'll make an end on 't:
[*Sings.*] By Gis° and by Saint Charity,
Alack, and fie for shame!
Young men will do 't, if they come to 't;
By cock,° they are to blame.
Quoth she, before you tumbled me,
You promis'd me to wed.
So would I ha' done, by yonder sun,
An thou hadst not come to my bed.

KING: How long hath she been thus?

OPHELIA: I hope all will be well. We must be patient: but I cannot choose but weep, to think they would lay him i' the cold ground. My brother shall know of it: and so I thank you for your good counsel. Come, my coach! Good night, ladies; good night, sweet ladies; good night, good night.

[*Exit.*]

KING: Follow her close; give her good watch, I pray you. [*Exit Horatio.*]
O, this is the poison of deep grief; it springs
All from her father's death. O Gertrude, Gertrude,
When sorrows come, they come not single spies,
But in battalions. First, her father slain:
Next your son gone; and he most violent author
Of his own just remove: the people muddied,
Thick and unwholesome in their thoughts and whispers,
For good Polonius' death; and we have done but greenly,°
In hugger-mugger° to inter him: poor Ophelia
Divided from herself and her fair judgement,
Without the which we are pictures, or mere beasts:
Last, and as much containing as all these,
Her brother is in secret come from France;
Feeds on his wonder, keeps himself in clouds,°

---

51. Valentine: This song alludes to the belief that the first girl seen by a man on the morning of this day was his valentine or true love. **53. dupp'd:** Opened. **58. Gis:** Jesus. **61. cock:** Perversion of "God" in oaths. **79. greenly:** Foolishly. **80. hugger-mugger:** Secret haste. **85. in clouds:** Invisible.

And wants not buzzers° to infect his ear
With pestilent speeches of his father's death;
Wherein necessity, of matter beggar'd,°
Will nothing stick° our person to arraign
In ear and ear.° O my dear Gertrude, this,
Like to a murd'ring-piece,° in many places
Gives me superfluous death. *A noise within.*

QUEEN: Alack, what noise is this?

KING: Where are my Switzers?° Let them guard the door.

Enter a Messenger.

What is the matter?

MESSENGER: Save yourself, my lord:
The ocean, overpeering° of his list,°
Eats not the flats with more impiteous haste
Than young Laertes, in a riotous head,
O'erbears your officers. The rabble call him lord;
And, as the world were now but to begin,
Antiquity forgot, custom not known,
The ratifiers and props of every word,°
They cry "Choose we: Laertes shall be king":
Caps, hands, and tongues, applaud it to the clouds:
"Laertes shall be king, Laertes king!" *A noise within.*

QUEEN: How cheerfully on the false trail they cry!
O, this is counter,° you false Danish dogs!

KING: The doors are broke.

Enter Laertes with others.

LAERTES: Where is this king? Sirs, stand you all without.

DANES: No, let's come in.

LAERTES: I pray you, give me leave.

DANES: We will, we will. [*They retire without the door.*]

LAERTES: I thank you: keep the door. O thou vile king,
Give me my father!

QUEEN: Calmly, good Laertes.

LAERTES: That drop of blood that's calm proclaims me bastard,
Cries cuckold to my father, brands the harlot
Even here, between the chaste unsmirched brow
Of my true mother.

KING: What is the cause, Laertes,
That thy rebellion looks so giant-like?

---

86. buzzers: Gossipers. **88. of matter beggar'd:** Unprovided with facts. **89. nothing stick:** Not hesitate. **90. In ear and ear:** In everybody's ears. **91. murd'ring-piece:** Small cannon or mortar; suggestion of numerous missiles fired. **93. Switzers:** Swiss guards, mercenaries. **95. overpeering:** Overflowing. **list:** Shore. **101. word:** Promise. **106. counter:** A hunting term meaning to follow the trail in a direction opposite to that which the game has taken.

Let him go, Gertrude; do not fear our person:
There's such divinity doth hedge a king,
That treason can but peep to° what it would°
Acts little of his will. Tell me, Laertes,
Why thou art thus incens'd. Let him go, Gertrude.
Speak, man.

LAERTES: Where is my father?

KING: Dead.

QUEEN: But not by him.

KING: Let him demand his fill.

LAERTES: How came he dead? I'll not be juggled with:
To hell, allegiance! vows, to the blackest devil!
Conscience and grace, to the profoundest pit!
I dare damnation. To this point I stand,
That both the worlds I give to negligence,°
Let come what comes; only I'll be reveng'd
Most throughly° for my father.

KING: Who shall stay you?

LAERTES: My will,° not all the world's:
And for my means, I'll husband them so well,
They shall go far with little.

KING: Good Laertes,
If you desire to know the certainty
Of your dear father, is 't writ in your revenge,
That, swoopstake,° you will draw both friend and foe,
Winner and loser?

LAERTES: None but his enemies.

KING: Will you know them then?

LAERTES: To his good friends thus wide I'll ope my arms;
And like the kind life-rend'ring pelican,°
Repast° them with my blood.

KING: Why, now you speak
Like a good child and a true gentleman.
That I am guiltless of your father's death,
And am most sensibly in grief for it,
It shall as level to your judgement 'pear
As day does to your eye. *A noise within: "Let her come in."*

LAERTES: How now! what noise is that?

Enter Ophelia.

O heat,° dry up my brains! tears seven times salt,

---

120. peep to: I.e., look at from afar off. **would:** Wishes to do. **130. give to negligence:** He despises both the here and the hereafter. **132. throughly:** thoroughly. **133. My will:** He will not be stopped except by his own will. **138. swoopstake:** Literally, drawing the whole stake at once, i.e., indiscriminately. **142. pelican:** Reference to the belief that the pelican feeds its young with its own blood. **143. Repast:** Feed. **150. heat:** Probably the heat generated by the passion of grief.

Burn out the sense and virtue of mine eye!
By heaven, thy madness shall be paid with weight,
Till our scale turn the beam. O rose of May!
Dear maid, kind sister, sweet Ophelia!
O heavens! is 't possible, a young maid's wits
Should be as mortal as an old man's life?
Nature is fine in love, and where 'tis fine,
It sends some precious instance of itself
After the thing it loves.

OPHELIA (*Song*): They bore him barefac'd on the bier;
Hey non nonny, nonny, hey nonny;
And in his grave rain'd many a tear:—
Fare you well, my dove!

LAERTES: Hadst thou thy wits, and didst persuade revenge,
It could not move thus.

OPHELIA [*sings*]: You must sing a-down a-down,
An you call him a-down-a.
O, how the wheel° becomes it! It is the false steward,° that stole his master's daughter.

LAERTES: This nothing's more than matter.

OPHELIA: There's rosemary,° that's for remembrance; pray you, love, remember: and there is pansies,° that's for thoughts.

LAERTES: A document° in madness, thoughts and remembrance fitted.

OPHELIA: There's fennel° for you, and columbines:° there's rue° for you; and here's some for me: we may call it herb of grace o' Sundays: O, you must wear your rue with a difference. There's a daisy:° I would give you some violets,° but they withered all when my father died: they say 'a made a good end,—
[*Sings.*] For bonny sweet Robin is all my joy.°

LAERTES: Thought° and affliction, passion, hell itself,
She turns to favour and to prettiness.

OPHELIA (*Song*): And will 'a not come again?°
And will 'a not come again?
No, no, he is dead:
Go to thy death-bed:
He never will come again.

---

168. wheel: Spinning wheel as accompaniment to the song refrain. **false steward:** The story is unknown. **171. rosemary:** Used as a symbol of remembrance both at weddings and at funerals. **172. pansies:** Emblems of love and courtship. Cf. French *pensées.* **173. document:** Piece of instruction or lesson. **174. fennel:** Emblem of flattery. **columbines:** Emblem of unchastity (?) or ingratitude (?). **rue:** Emblem of repentance. It was usually mingled with holy water and then known as *herb of grace.* Ophelia is probably playing on the two meanings of *rue,* "repentant" and "even for ruth (pity)"; the former signification is for the queen, the latter for herself. **176. daisy:** Emblem of dissembling, faithlessness. **177. violets:** Emblems of faithfulness. **179. For . . . joy:** Probably a line from a Robin Hood ballad. **180. Thought:** Melancholy thought. **182. And . . . again:** This song appeared in the songbooks as "The Merry Milkmaids' Dumps."

His beard was as white as snow,
All flaxen was his poll:°
He is gone, he is gone,
And we cast away° moan:
God ha' mercy on his soul!
And of all Christian souls, I pray God. God be wi' you. [*Exit.*]

LAERTES: Do you see this, O God?

KING: Laertes, I must commune with your grief,
Or you deny me right.° Go but apart,
Make choice of whom your wisest friends you will,
And they shall hear and judge 'twixt you and me:
If by direct or by collateral° hand
They find us touch'd,° we will our kingdom give,
Our crown, our life, and all that we call ours,
To you in satisfaction; but if not,
Be you content to lend your patience to us,
And we shall jointly labour with your soul
To give it due content.

LAERTES: Let this be so;
His means of death, his obscure funeral—
No trophy, sword, nor hatchment° o'er his bones,
No noble rite nor formal ostentation—
Cry to be heard, as 'twere from heaven to earth,
That I must call 't in question.

KING: So you shall;
And where th' offence is let the great axe fall.
I pray you, go with me. *Exeunt.*

[SCENE VI: *Another room in the castle.*]

Enter Horatio and others.

HORATIO: What are they that would speak with me?

GENTLEMAN: Sea-faring men, sir: they say they have letters for you.

HORATIO: Let them come in. [*Exit Gentleman.*]
I do not know from what part of the world
I should be greeted, if not from lord Hamlet.

Enter Sailors.

FIRST SAILOR: God bless you, sir.

HORATIO: Let him bless thee too.

FIRST SAILOR: 'A shall sir, an 't please him. There's a letter for you, sir; it comes from the ambassador that was bound for England; if your name be Horatio, as I am let to know it is.

---

188. poll: Head. **190. cast away:** Shipwrecked. **195. right:** My rights. **198. collateral:** Indirect. **199. touch'd:** Implicated. **206. hatchment:** Tablet displaying the armorial bearings of a deceased person.

HORATIO [*reads*]: "Horatio, when thou shalt have overlooked this, give these fellows some means° to the king: they have letters for him. Ere we were two days old at sea, a pirate of very warlike appointment gave us chase. Finding ourselves too slow of sail, we put on a compelled valour, and in the grapple I boarded them: on the instant they got clear of our ship; so I alone became their prisoner. They have dealt with me like thieves of mercy:° but they knew what they did; I am to do a good turn for them. Let the king have the letters I have sent; and repair thou to me with as much speed as thou wouldest fly death. I have words to speak in thine ear will make thee dumb; yet are they much too light for the bore° of the matter. These good fellows will bring thee where I am. Rosencrantz and Guildenstern hold their course for England: of them I have much to tell thee. Farewell.

"He that thou knowest thine, HAMLET."

Come, I will give you way for these your letters;
And do 't the speedier, that you may direct me
To him from whom you brought them. *Exeunt.*

[SCENE VII: *Another room in the castle.*]

Enter King and Laertes.

KING: Now must your conscience° my acquittance seal,
And you must put me in your heart for friend,
Sith you have heard, and with a knowing ear,
That he which hath your noble father slain
Pursued my life.

LAERTES: It well appears: but tell me
Why you proceeded not against these feats,
So criminal and so capital° in nature,
As by your safety, wisdom, all things else,
You mainly° were stirr'd up.

KING: O, for two special reasons;
Which may to you, perhaps, seem much unsinew'd,°
But yet to me th' are strong. The queen his mother
Lives almost by his looks; and for myself—
My virtue or my plague, be it either which—
She's so conjunctive° to my life and soul,
That, as the star moves not but in his sphere,°
I could not but by her. The other motive,
Why to a public count° I might not go,

ACT IV, SCENE VI. **12. means:** Means of access. **16–17. thieves of mercy:** Merciful thieves. **20. bore:** Caliber, importance. ACT IV, SCENE VII. **1. conscience:** Knowledge that this is true. **7. capital:** Punishable by death. **9. mainly:** Greatly. **10. unsinew'd:** Weak. **14. conjunctive:** Conformable (the next line suggesting planetary conjunction). **15. sphere:** The hollow sphere in which, according to Ptolemaic astronomy, the planets were supposed to move. **17. count:** Account, reckoning.

Is the great love the general gender° bear him;
Who, dipping all his faults in their affection,
Would, like the spring° that turneth wood to stone,
Convert his gyves° to graces; so that my arrows,
Too slightly timber'd° for so loud° a wind,
Would have reverted to my bow again,
And not where I had aim'd them.

LAERTES: And so have I a noble father lost;
A sister driven into desp'rate terms,°
Whose worth, if praises may go back° again,
Stood challenger on mount° of all the age°
For her perfections: but my revenge will come.

KING: Break not your sleeps for that: you must not think
That we are made of stuff so flat and dull
That we can let our beard be shook with danger
And think it pastime. You shortly shall hear more:
I lov'd your father, and we love ourself;
And that, I hope, will teach you to imagine—

Enter a Messenger with letters.

How now! what news?

MESSENGER: Letters, my lord, from Hamlet:
These to your majesty; this to the queen.°

KING: From Hamlet! who brought them?

MESSENGER: Sailors, my lord, they say; I saw them not:
They were given me by Claudio;° he receiv'd them
Of him that brought them.

KING: Laertes, you shall hear them.
Leave us. [*Exit Messenger.*]
[*Reads.*] "High and mighty, You shall know I am set naked° on your kingdom. To-morrow shall I beg leave to see your kingly eyes: when I shall, first asking your pardon thereunto, recount the occasion of my sudden and more strange return. "HAMLET."
What should this mean? Are all the rest come back?
Or is it some abuse, and no such thing?

LAERTES: Know you the hand?

KING: 'Tis Hamlet's character. "Naked!"
And in a postscript here, he says "alone."
Can you devise° me?

---

18. general gender: Common people. **20. spring:** I.e., one heavily charged with lime. **21. gyves:** Fetters; here, faults, or possibly, punishments inflicted (on him). **22. slightly timber'd:** Light. **loud:** Strong. **26. terms:** State, condition. **27. go back:** I.e., to Ophelia's former virtues. **28. on mount:** Set up on high, *mounted* (on horseback). **of all the age:** Qualifies *challenger* and not *mount*. **37. to the queen:** One hears no more of the letter to the queen. **40. Claudio:** This character does not appear in the play. **43. naked:** Unprovided (with retinue). **51. devise:** Explain to.

LAERTES: I'm lost in it, my lord. But let him come;
It warms the very sickness in my heart,
That I shall live and tell him to his teeth,
"Thus didst thou."
KING: If it be so, Laertes—
As how should it be so? how otherwise?° —
Will you be rul'd by me?
LAERTES: Ay, my lord;
So you will not o'errule me to a peace.
KING: To thine own peace. If he be now return'd,
As checking at° his voyage, and that he means
No more to undertake it, I will work him
To an exploit, now ripe in my device,
Under the which he shall not choose but fall:
And for his death no wind of blame shall breathe,
But even his mother shall uncharge the practice°
And call it accident.
LAERTES: My lord, I will be rul'd;
The rather, if you could devise it so
That I might be the organ.°
KING: It falls right.
You have been talk'd of since your travel much,
And that in Hamlet's hearing, for a quality
Wherein, they say, you shine: your sum of parts
Did not together pluck such envy from him
As did that one, and that, in my regard,
Of the unworthiest siege.°
LAERTES: What part is that, my lord?
KING: A very riband in the cap of youth,
Yet needful too; for youth no less becomes
The light and careless livery that it wears
Than settled age his sables° and his weeds,
Importing health and graveness. Two months since,
Here was a gentleman of Normandy:—
I have seen myself, and serv'd against, the French,
And they can well° on horseback: but this gallant
Had witchcraft in 't; he grew unto his seat;
And to such wondrous doing brought his horse,
As had he been incorps'd and demi-natur'd°

---

56. As . . . otherwise? How can this (Hamlet's return) be true? (yet) how otherwise than true (since we have the evidence of his letter)? Some editors read *How should it not be so,* etc., making the words refer to Laertes' desire to meet with Hamlet. **60. checking at:** Used in falconry of a hawk's leaving the quarry to fly at a chance bird, turn aside. **65. uncharge the practice:** Acquit the stratagem of being a plot. **68. organ:** Agent, instrument. **74. siege:** Rank. **78. sables:** Rich garments. **82. can well:** Are skilled. **85. incorps'd and demi-natur'd:** Of one body and nearly of one nature (like the centaur).

With the brave beast: so far he topp'd° my thought,
That I, in forgery° of shapes and tricks,
Come short of what he did.

LAERTES: A Norman was 't?

KING: A Norman.

LAERTES: Upon my life, Lamord.°

KING: The very same.

LAERTES: I know him well: he is the brooch indeed
And gem of all the nation.

KING: He made confession° of you,
And gave you such a masterly report
For art and exercise° in your defence°
And for your rapier most especial,
That he cried out, 'twould be a sight indeed,
If one could match you: the scrimers° of their nation,
He swore, had neither motion, guard, nor eye,
If you oppos'd them. Sir, this report of his
Did Hamlet so envenom with his envy
That he could nothing do but wish and beg
Your sudden coming o'er, to play° with you.
Now, out of this,—

LAERTES: What out of this, my lord?

KING: Laertes, was your father dear to you?
Or are you like the painting of a sorrow,
A face without a heart?

LAERTES: Why ask you this?

KING: Not that I think you did not love your father;
But that I know love is begun by time;
And that I see, in passages of proof,°
Time qualifies the spark and fire of it.
There lives within the very flame of love
A kind of wick or snuff that will abate it;
And nothing is at a like goodness still;
For goodness, growing to a plurisy,°
Dies in his own too much:° that we would do,
We should do when we would; for this "would" changes
And hath abatements° and delays as many
As there are tongues, are hands, are accidents;°
And then this "should" is like a spendthrift° sigh,

86. topp'd: Surpassed. **87. forgery:** Invention. **90. Lamord:** This refers possibly to Pietro Monte, instructor to Louis XII's master of the horse. **93. confession:** Grudging admission of superiority. **95. art and exercise:** Skillful exercise. **defence:** Science of defense in sword practice. **98. scrimers:** Fencers. **103. play:** Fence. **110. passages of proof:** Proved instances. **115. plurisy:** Excess, plethora. **116. in his own too much:** Of its own excess. **118. abatements:** Diminutions. **119. accidents:** Occurrences, incidents. **120. spendthrift:** An allusion to the belief that each sigh cost the heart a drop of blood.

That hurts by easing. But, to the quick o' th' ulcer:° —
Hamlet comes back: what would you undertake,
To show yourself your father's son in deed
More than in words?

LAERTES: To cut his throat i' th' church.

KING: No place, indeed, should murder sanctuarize;°
Revenge should have no bounds. But, good Laertes,
Will you do this, keep close within your chamber.
Hamlet return'd shall know you are come home:
We'll put on those shall praise your excellence
And set a double varnish on the fame
The Frenchman gave you, bring you in fine together
And wager on your heads: he, being remiss,
Most generous and free from all contriving,
Will not peruse the foils; so that, with ease,
Or with a little shuffling, you may choose
A sword unbated,° and in a pass of practice°
Requite him for your father.

LAERTES: I will do 't:
And, for that purpose, I'll anoint my sword.
I bought an unction of a mountebank,°
So mortal that, but dip a knife in it,
Where it draws blood no cataplasm° so rare,
Collected from all simples° that have virtue
Under the moon,° can save the thing from death
That is but scratch'd withal: I'll touch my point
With this contagion, that, if I gall° him slightly,
It may be death.

KING: Let's further think of this;
Weigh what convenience both of time and means
May fit us to our shape:° if this should fail,
And that our drift look through our bad performance,°
'Twere better not assay'd: therefore this project
Should have a back or second, that might hold,
If this should blast in proof.° Soft! let me see:
We'll make a solemn wager on your cunnings:°
I ha 't:
When in your motion you are hot and dry—
As make your bouts more violent to that end—

121. quick o' th' ulcer: Heart of the difficulty. **125. sanctuarize:** Protect from punishment; allusion to the right of sanctuary with which certain religious places were invested. **136. unbated:** Not blunted, having no button. **pass of practice:** Treacherous thrust. **139. mountebank:** Quack doctor. **141. cataplasm:** Plaster or poultice. **142. simples:** Herbs. **143. Under the moon:** I.e., when collected by moonlight to add to their medicinal value. **145. gall:** Graze, wound. **148. shape:** Part we propose to act. **149. drift . . . performance:** Intention be disclosed by our bungling. **152. blast in proof:** Burst in the test (like a cannon). **153. cunnings:** Skills.

And that he calls for drink, I'll have prepar'd him
A chalice° for the nonce, whereon but sipping,
If he by chance escape your venom'd stuck,°
Our purpose may hold there. But stay, what noise?

Enter Queen.

QUEEN: One woe doth tread upon another's heel,
So fast they follow: your sister's drown'd, Laertes.
LAERTES: Drown'd! O, where?
QUEEN: There is a willow° grows askant° the brook,
That shows his hoar° leaves in the glassy stream;
There with fantastic garlands did she make
Of crow-flowers,° nettles, daisies, and long purples°
That liberal° shepherds give a grosser name,
But our cold maids do dead men's fingers call them:
There, on the pendent boughs her crownet° weeds
Clamb'ring to hang, an envious sliver° broke;
When down her weedy° trophies and herself
Fell in the weeping brook. Her clothes spread wide;
And, mermaid-like, awhile they bore her up:
Which time she chanted snatches of old lauds;°
As one incapable° of her own distress,
Or like a creature native and indued°
Upon that element: but long it could not be
Till that her garments, heavy with their drink,
Pull'd the poor wretch from her melodious lay
To muddy death.
LAERTES: Alas, then, she is drown'd?
QUEEN: Drown'd, drown'd.
LAERTES: Too much of water hast thou, poor Ophelia,
And therefore I forbid my tears: but yet
It is our trick;° nature her custom holds,
Let shame say what it will: when these are gone,
The woman will be out.° Adieu, my lord:
I have a speech of fire, that fain would blaze,
But that this folly drowns it. *Exit.*
KING: Let's follow, Gertrude:
How much I had to do to calm his rage!
Now fear I this will give it start again;
Therefore let 's follow. *Exeunt.*

---

158. chalice: Cup. **159. stuck:** Thrust (from *stoccado*). **164. willow:** For its significance of forsaken love. **askant:** Aslant. **165. hoar:** White (i.e., on the underside). **167. crow-flowers:** Buttercups. **long purples:** Early purple orchids. **168. liberal:** Probably, free-spoken. **170. crownet:** Coronet; made into a chaplet. **171. sliver:** Branch. **172. weedy:** I.e., of plants. **175. lauds:** Hymns. **176. incapable:** Lacking capacity to apprehend. **177. indued:** Endowed with qualities fitting her for living in water. **185. trick:** Way. **186–187. when . . . out:** When my tears are all shed, the woman in me will be satisfied.

[ACT V

SCENE I: *A churchyard.*]

Enter two Clowns° [*with spades, &c.*].

FIRST CLOWN: Is she to be buried in Christian burial when she wilfully seeks her own salvation?

SECOND CLOWN: I tell thee she is; therefore make her grave straight:° the crowner° hath sat on her, and finds it Christian burial.

FIRST CLOWN: How can that be, unless she drowned herself in her own defence?

SECOND CLOWN: Why, 'tis found so.

FIRST CLOWN: It must be "se offendendo";° it cannot be else. For here lies the point: if I drown myself wittingly,° it argues an act: and an act hath three branches;° it is, to act, to do, and to perform: argal,° she drowned herself wittingly.

SECOND CLOWN: Nay, but hear you, goodman delver,°—

FIRST CLOWN: Give me leave. Here lies the water; good: here stands the man; good: if the man go to this water, and drown himself, it is, will he, nill he, he goes,—mark you that; but if the water come to him and drown him, he drowns not himself: argal, he that is not guilty of his own death shortens not his own life.

SECOND CLOWN: But is this law?

FIRST CLOWN: Ay, marry, is 't; crowner's quest° law.

SECOND CLOWN: Will you ha' the truth on 't? If this had not been a gentlewoman, she should have been buried out o' Christian burial.

FIRST CLOWN: Why, there thou say'st:° and the more pity that great folk should have countenance° in this world to drown or hang themselves, more than their even° Christian. Come, my spade. There is no ancient gentlemen but gardeners, ditchers, and grave-makers: they hold up° Adam's profession.

SECOND CLOWN: Was he a gentleman?

FIRST CLOWN: 'A was the first that ever bore arms.

SECOND CLOWN: Why, he had none.

FIRST CLOWN: What, art a heathen? How dost thou understand the Scripture? The Scripture says "Adam digged": could he dig without arms? I'll put another question to thee: if thou answerest me not to the purpose, confess thyself°—

SECOND CLOWN: Go to.°

ACT V, SCENE I. **s.d. Clowns:** The word *clown* was used to denote peasants as well as humorous characters; here applied to the rustic type of clown. **3. straight:** Straightway, immediately; some interpret "from east to west in a direct line, parallel with the church." **4. crowner:** Coroner. **7. "se offendendo":** For *se defendendo,* term used in verdicts of justifiable homicide. **8. wittingly:** Intentionally. **8–9. three branches:** Parody of legal phraseology. **argal:** Corruption of *ergo,* therefore. **11. delver:** Digger. **18. quest:** Inquest. **21. there thou say'st:** That's right. **22. countenance:** Privilege. **23. even:** Fellow. **24. hold up:** Maintain, continue. **31–32. confess thyself:** "And be hanged" completes the proverb. **33. Go to:** Perhaps, "begin," or some other form of concession.

FIRST CLOWN: What is he that builds stronger than either the mason, the shipwright, or the carpenter?

SECOND CLOWN: The gallows-maker; for that frame outlives a thousand tenants.

FIRST CLOWN: I like thy wit well, in good faith: the gallows does well; but how does it well? it does well to those that do ill: now thou dost ill to say the gallows is built stronger than the church: argal, the gallows may do well to thee. To 't again, come.

SECOND CLOWN: "Who builds stronger than a mason, a shipwright, or a carpenter?"

FIRST CLOWN: Ay, tell me that, and unyoke.°

SECOND CLOWN: Marry, now I can tell.

FIRST CLOWN: To 't.

SECOND CLOWN: Mass,° I cannot tell.

Enter Hamlet and Horatio [at a distance].

FIRST CLOWN: Cudgel thy brains no more about it, for your dull ass will not mend his pace with beating; and, when you are asked this question next, say "a grave-maker": the houses he makes lasts till doomsday. Go, get thee in, and fetch me a stoup° of liquor.

[*Exit Second Clown.*] *Song.* [*He digs.*]

In youth, when I did love, did love,
Methought it was very sweet,
To contract—O—the time, for—a—my behove,°
O, methought, there—a—was nothing—a—meet.

HAMLET: Has this fellow no feeling of his business, that 'a sings at grave-making?

HORATIO: Custom hath made it in him a property of easiness.°

HAMLET: 'Tis e'en so: the hand of little employment hath the daintier sense.

FIRST CLOWN: (*Song.*) But age, with his stealing steps,
Hath claw'd me in his clutch,
And hath shipped me into the land
As if I had never been such. [*Throws up a skull.*]

HAMLET: That skull had a tongue in it, and could sing once: how the knave jowls° it to the ground, as if 'twere Cain's jaw-bone,° that did the first murder! This might be the pate of a politician,° which this ass now o'er-reaches;° one that would circumvent God, might it not?

HORATIO: It might, my lord.

HAMLET: Or of a courtier; which could say "Good morrow, sweet lord! How dost thou, sweet lord?" This might be my lord such-a-one, that praised my lord such-a-one's horse, when he meant to beg it; might it not?

44. unyoke: After this great effort you may unharness the team of your wits. **47. Mass:** By the Mass. **51. stoup:** Two-quart measure. **54. behove:** Benefit. **58. property of easiness:** A peculiarity that now is easy. **65. jowls:** Dashes. **Cain's jaw-bone:** Allusion to the old tradition that Cain slew Abel with the jawbone of an ass. **66. politician:** Schemer, plotter. **66–67. o'er-reaches:** Quibble on the literal sense and the sense "circumvent."

HORATIO: Ay, my lord.

HAMLET: Why, e'en so: and now my Lady Worm's; chapless,° and knocked about the mazzard° with a sexton's spade: here's fine revolution, an we had the trick to see 't. Did these bones cost no more the breeding, but to play at loggats° with 'em? mine ache to think on 't.

FIRST CLOWN: (*Song.*) A pick-axe, and a spade, a spade,
For and° a shrouding sheet:
O, a pit of clay for to be made
For such a guest is meet. [*Throws up another skull.*]

HAMLET: There's another: why may not that be the skull of a lawyer? Where be his quiddities° now, his quillities,° his cases, his tenures,° and his tricks? why does he suffer this mad knave now to knock him about the sconce° with a dirty shovel, and will not tell him of his action of battery? Hum! This fellow might be in 's time a great buyer of land, with his statutes, his recognizances,° his fines, his double vouchers,° his recoveries:° is this the fine° of his fines, and the recovery of his recoveries, to have his fine pate full of fine dirt? will his vouchers vouch him no more of his purchases, and double ones too, than the length and breadth of a pair of indentures?° The very conveyances of his lands will scarcely lie in this box; and must the inheritor° himself have no more, ha?

HORATIO: Not a jot more, my lord.

HAMLET: Is not parchment made of sheep-skins?

HORATIO: Ay, my lord, and of calf-skins° too.

HAMLET: They are sheep and calves which seek out assurance in that.° I will speak to this fellow. Whose grave's this, sirrah?

FIRST CLOWN: Mine, sir.
[*Sings.*] O, a pit of clay for to be made
For such a guest is meet.

HAMLET: I think it be thine, indeed; for thou liest in 't.

FIRST CLOWN: You lie out on 't, sir, and therefore 't is not yours: for my part, I do not lie in 't, yet it is mine.

HAMLET: Thou dost lie in 't, to be in 't and say it is thine: 'tis for the dead, not for the quick; therefore thou liest.

FIRST CLOWN: 'Tis a quick lie, sir; 'twill away again, from me to you.

HAMLET: What man dost thou dig it for?

FIRST CLOWN: For no man, sir.

---

73. chapless: Having no lower jaw. **74. mazzard:** Head. **76. loggats:** A game in which six sticks are thrown to lie as near as possible to a stake fixed in the ground, or block of wood on a floor. **78. For and:** And moreover. **82. quiddities:** Subtleties, quibbles. **quillities:** Verbal niceties, subtle distinctions. **tenures:** The holding of a piece of property or office or the conditions or period of such holding. **83. sconce:** Head. **85–86. statutes, recognizances:** Legal terms connected with the transfer of land. **vouchers:** Persons called on to warrant a tenant's title. **recoveries:** Process for transfer of entailed estate. **87. fine:** The four uses of this word are as follows: (1) end, (2) legal process, (3) elegant, (4) small. **90. indentures:** Conveyances or contracts. **91. inheritor:** Possessor, owner. **94. calf-skins:** Parchments. **95. assurance in that:** Safety in legal parchments.

HAMLET: What woman, then?

FIRST CLOWN: For none, neither.

HAMLET: Who is to be buried in 't?

FIRST CLOWN: One that was a woman, sir; but, rest her soul, she's dead.

HAMLET: How absolute° the knave is! we must speak by the card,° or equivocation° will undo us. By the Lord, Horatio, these three years I have taken note of it; the age is grown so picked° that the toe of the peasant comes so near the heel of the courtier, he galls° his kibe.° How long hast thou been a grave-maker?

FIRST CLOWN: Of all the day i' the year, I came to 't that day that our last king Hamlet overcame Fortinbras.

HAMLET: How long is that since?

FIRST CLOWN: Cannot you tell that? every fool can tell that: it was the very day that young Hamlet was born; he that is mad, and sent into England.

HAMLET: Ay, marry, why was he sent into England?

FIRST CLOWN: Why, because 'a was mad: 'a shall recover his wits there; or, if 'a do not, 'tis no great matter there.

HAMLET: Why?

FIRST CLOWN: 'Twill not be seen in him there; there the men are as mad as he.

HAMLET: How came he mad?

FIRST CLOWN: Very strangely, they say.

HAMLET: How strangely?

FIRST CLOWN: Faith, e'en with losing his wits.

HAMLET: Upon what ground?

FIRST CLOWN: Why, here in Denmark: I have been sexton here, man and boy, thirty years.°

HAMLET: How long will a man lie i' the earth ere he rot?

FIRST CLOWN: Faith, if 'a be not rotten before 'a die—as we have many pocky° corses now-a-days, that will scarce hold the laying in—'a will last you some eight year or nine year: a tanner will last you nine year.

HAMLET: Why he more than another?

FIRST CLOWN: Why, sir, his hide is so tanned with his trade, that 'a will keep out water a great while; and your water is a sore decayer of your whoreson dead body. Here's a skull now hath lain you i' th' earth three and twenty years.

HAMLET: Whose was it?

FIRST CLOWN: A whoreson mad fellow's it was: whose do you think it was?

HAMLET: Nay, I know not.

FIRST CLOWN: A pestilence on him for a mad rogue! 'a poured a flagon of Rhenish on my head once. This same skull, sir, was Yorick's skull, the king's jester.

---

112. absolute: Positive, decided. **by the card:** With precision, i.e., by the mariner's card on which the points of the compass were marked. **112–113. equivocation:** Ambiguity in the use of terms. **114. picked:** Refined, fastidious. **115. galls:** Chafes. **kibe:** Chilblain. **133. thirty years:** This statement with that in lines 120–121 shows Hamlet's age to be thirty years. **135. pocky:** Rotten, diseased.

HAMLET: This?

FIRST CLOWN: E'en that.

HAMLET: Let me see. [*Takes the skull.*] Alas, poor Yorick! I knew him, Horatio: a fellow of infinite jest, of most excellent fancy: he hath borne me on his back a thousand times; and now, how abhorred in my imagination it is! my gorge rises at it. Here hung those lips that I have kissed I know not how oft. Where be your gibes now? your gambols? your songs? your flashes of merriment, that were wont to set the table on a roar? Not one now, to mock your own grinning? quite chap-fallen? Now get you to my lady's chamber, and tell her, let her paint an inch thick, to this favour she must come; make her laugh at that. Prithee, Horatio, tell me one thing.

HORATIO: What's that, my lord?

HAMLET: Dost thou think Alexander looked o' this fashion i' the earth?

HORATIO: E'en so.

HAMLET: And smelt so? pah! [*Puts down the skull.*]

HORATIO: E'en so, my lord.

HAMLET: To what base uses we may return, Horatio! Why may not imagination trace the noble dust of Alexander, till 'a find it stopping a bunghole?

HORATIO: 'Twere to consider too curiously,° to consider so.

HAMLET: No, faith, not a jot; but to follow him thither with modesty enough, and likelihood to lead it: as thus: Alexander died, Alexander was buried, Alexander returneth into dust; the dust is earth; of earth we make loam;° and why of that loam, whereto he was converted, might they not stop a beer-barrel?

Imperious° Cæsar, dead and turn'd to clay,
Might stop a hole to keep the wind away:
O, that that earth, which kept the world in awe,
Should patch a wall t'expel the winter's flaw!°
But soft! but soft awhile! here comes the king,

Enter King, Queen, Laertes, and the Corse of [*Ophelia, in procession, with Priest, Lords, etc.*].

The queen, the courtiers: who is this they follow?
And with such maimed rites? This doth betoken
The corse they follow did with desp'rate hand
Fordo° it° own life: 'twas of some estate.
Couch° we awhile, and mark. [*Retiring with Horatio.*]

LAERTES: What ceremony else?

HAMLET: That is Laertes,
A very noble youth: mark.

LAERTES: What ceremony else?

FIRST PRIEST: Her obsequies have been as far enlarg'd°

---

167. curiously: Minutely. **170. loam:** Clay paste for brickmaking. **173. Imperious:** Imperial. **176. flaw:** Gust of wind. **181. Fordo:** Destroy. **it:** Its. **182. Couch:** Hide, lurk. **186. enlarg'd:** Extended, referring to the fact that suicides are not given full burial rites.

As we have warranty: her death was doubtful;
And, but that great command o'ersways the order,
She should in ground unsanctified have lodg'd
Till the last trumpet; for charitable prayers,
Shards,° flints and pebbles should be thrown on her:
Yet here she is allow'd her virgin crants,°
Her maiden strewments° and the bringing home
Of bell and burial.°

LAERTES: Must there no more be done?

FIRST PRIEST: No more be done:
We should profane the service of the dead
To sing a requiem and such rest to her
As to peace-parted° souls.

LAERTES: Lay her i' th' earth:
And from her fair and unpolluted flesh
May violets spring! I tell thee, churlish priest,
A minist'ring angel shall my sister be,
When thou liest howling.°

HAMLET: What, the fair Ophelia!

QUEEN: Sweets to the sweet: farewell! [*Scattering flowers.*]
I hop'd thou shouldst have been my Hamlet's wife;
I thought thy bride-bed to have deck'd, sweet maid,
And not have strew'd thy grave.

LAERTES: O, treble woe
Fall ten times treble on that cursed head,
Whose wicked deed thy most ingenious sense°
Depriv'd thee of! Hold off the earth awhile,
Till I have caught her once more in mine arms: [*Leaps into the grave.*]
Now pile your dust upon the quick and dead,
Till of this flat a mountain you have made,
T' o'ertop old Pelion,° or the skyish head
Of blue Olympus.

HAMLET: [*Advancing*] What is he whose grief
Bears such an emphasis? whose phrase of sorrow
Conjures the wand'ring stars,° and makes them stand
Like wonder-wounded hearers? This is I,
Hamlet the Dane. [*Leaps into the grave.*]

LAERTES: The devil take thy soul! [*Grappling with him.*]

---

191. Shards: Broken bits of pottery. **192. crants:** Garlands customarily hung upon the biers of unmarried women. **193. strewments:** Traditional strewing of flowers. **193–194. bringing . . . burial:** The laying to rest of the body, to the sound of the bell. **198. peace-parted:** Allusion to the text "Lord, now lettest thou thy servant depart in peace." **202. howling:** I.e., in hell. **208. ingenious sense:** Mind endowed with finest qualities. **213. Pelion:** Olympus, Pelion, and Ossa are mountains in the north of Thessaly. **216. wand'ring stars:** Planets.

HAMLET: Thou pray'st not well.
I prithee, take thy fingers from my throat;
For, though I am not splenitive° and rash,
Yet have I in me something dangerous,
Which let thy wisdom fear: hold off thy hand.
KING: Pluck them asunder.
QUEEN: Hamlet, Hamlet!
ALL: Gentlemen, —
HORATIO: Good my lord, be quiet.
[*The Attendants part them, and they come out of the grave.*]
HAMLET: Why, I will fight with him upon this theme
Until my eyelids will no longer wag.°
QUEEN: O my son, what theme?
HAMLET: I lov'd Ophelia: forty thousand brothers
Could not, with all their quantity° of love,
Make up my sum. What wilt thou do for her?
KING: O, he is mad, Laertes.
QUEEN: For love of God, forbear° him.
HAMLET: 'Swounds,° show me what thou 'lt do:
Woo 't° weep? woo 't fight? woo 't fast? woo 't tear thyself?
Woo 't drink up eisel?° eat a crocodile?
I'll do 't. Dost thou come here to whine?
To outface me with leaping in her grave?
Be buried quick with her, and so will I:
And, if thou prate of mountains, let them throw
Millions of acres on us, till our ground,
Singeing his pate against the burning zone,°
Make Ossa like a wart! Nay, an thou 'lt mouth,
I'll rant as well as thou.
QUEEN: This is mere madness:
And thus awhile the fit will work on him;
Anon, as patient as the female dove.
When that her golden couplets° are disclos'd,
His silence will sit drooping.
HAMLET: Hear you, sir;
What is the reason that you use me thus?
I lov'd you ever: but it is no matter;
Let Hercules himself do what he may,
The cat will mew and dog will have his day.

---

221. splenitive: Quick-tempered. **227. wag:** Move (not used ludicrously). **230. quantity:** Some suggest that the word is used in a deprecatory sense (little bits, fragments). **233. forbear:** Leave alone. **234. 'Swounds:** Oath, "God's wounds." **235. Woo 't:** Wilt thou. **236. eisel:** Vinegar. Some editors have taken this to be the name of a river, such as the Yssel, the Weissel, and the Nile. **242. burning zone:** Sun's orbit. **247. golden couplets:** The pigeon lays two eggs; the young when hatched are covered with golden down.

KING: I pray thee, good Horatio, wait upon him. *Exit Hamlet and Horatio.*
[*To Laertes.*] Strengthen your patience in° our last night's speech;
We'll put the matter to the present push.°
Good Gertrude, set some watch over your son.
This grave shall have a living° monument:
An hour of quiet shortly shall we see;
Till then, in patience our proceeding be. *Exeunt.*

[SCENE II: *A hall in the castle.*]

Enter Hamlet and Horatio.

HAMLET: So much for this, sir: now shall you see the other;
You do remember all the circumstance?
HORATIO: Remember it, my lord!
HAMLET: Sir, in my heart there was a kind of fighting,
That would not let me sleep: methought I lay
Worse than the mutines° in the bilboes.° Rashly°
And prais'd be rashness for it, let us know,
Our indiscretion sometime serves us well,
When our deep plots do pall:° and that should learn us
There's a divinity that shapes our ends,
Rough-hew° them how we will,—
HORATIO: That is most certain.
HAMLET: Up from my cabin,
My sea-gown° scarf'd about me, in the dark
Grop'd I to find out them; had my desire,
Finger'd° their packet, and in fine° withdrew
To mine own room again; making so bold,
My fears forgetting manners, to unseal
Their grand commission; where I found, Horatio,—
O royal knavery!—an exact command,
Larded° with many several sorts of reasons
Importing Denmark's health and England's too,
With, ho! such bugs° and goblins in my life,°
That, on the supervise,° no leisure bated,°
No, not to stay the grinding of the axe,
My head should be struck off.
HORATIO: Is 't possible?

---

254. in: By recalling. **255. present push:** Immediate test. **257. living:** Lasting; also refers (for Laertes' benefit) to the plot against Hamlet. ACT V, SCENE II. **6. mutines:** Mutineers. **bilboes:** Shackles. **Rashly:** Goes with line 12. **9. pall:** Fail. **11. Rough-hew:** Shape roughly; it may mean "bungle." **13. sea-gown:** "A sea-gown, or a coarse, high-collered, and short-sleeved gowne, reaching down to the mid-leg, and used most by seamen and saylors" (Cotgrave, quoted by Singer). **15. Finger'd:** Pilfered, filched. **in fine:** Finally. **20. Larded:** Enriched. **22. bugs:** Bugbears. **such . . . life:** Such imaginary dangers if I were allowed to live. **23. supervise:** Perusal. **leisure bated:** Delay allowed.

HAMLET: Here's the commission: read it at more leisure.
But wilt thou hear me how I did proceed?
HORATIO: I beseech you.
HAMLET: Being thus be-netted round with villanies,—
Ere I could make a prologue to my brains,
They had begun the play°—I sat me down,
Devis'd a new commission, wrote it fair:
I once did hold it, as our statists° do,
A baseness to write fair° and labour'd much
How to forget that learning, but, sir, now
It did me yeoman's° service: wilt thou know
Th' effect of what I wrote?
HORATIO: Ay, good my lord.
HAMLET: An earnest conjuration from the king,
As England was his faithful tributary,
As love between them like the palm might flourish,
As peace should still her wheaten garland° wear
And stand a comma° 'tween their amities,
And many such-like 'As'es° of great charge,°
That, on the view and knowing of these contents,
Without debatement further, more or less,
He should the bearers put to sudden death,
Not shriving-time° allow'd.
HORATIO: How was this seal'd?
HAMLET: Why, even in that was heaven ordinant.°
I had my father's signet in my purse,
Which was the model of that Danish seal;
Folded the writ up in the form of th' other,
Subscrib'd it, gave 't th' impression, plac'd it safely,
The changeling never known. Now, the next day
Was our sea-fight; and what to this was sequent°
Thou know'st already.
HORATIO: So Guildenstern and Rosencrantz go to 't.
HAMLET: Why, man, they did make love to this employment;
They are not near my conscience; their defeat
Does by their own insinuation° grow:
'Tis dangerous when the baser nature comes

30–31. prologue . . . play: I.e., before I could begin to think, my mind had made its decision. **33. statists:** Statesmen. **34. fair:** In a clear hand. **36. yeoman's:** I.e., faithful. **41. wheaten garland:** Symbol of peace. **42. comma:** Smallest break or separation. Here *amity* begins and *amity* ends the period, and *peace* stands between like a dependent clause. The comma indicates continuity, link. **43. 'As'es:** The "whereases" of a formal document, with play on the word *ass*. **charge:** Import, and burden. **47. shriving-time:** Time for absolution. **48. ordinant:** Directing. **54. sequent:** Subsequent. **59. insinuation:** Interference.

Between the pass° and fell incensed° points
Of mighty opposites.

HORATIO: Why, what a king is this!

HAMLET: Does it not, think thee, stand° me now upon—
He that hath kill'd my king and whor'd my mother,
Popp'd in between th' election° and my hopes,
Thrown out his angle° for my proper life,
And with such coz'nage°—is 't not perfect conscience,
To quit° him with this arm? and is 't not to be damn'd,
To let this canker° of our nature come
In further evil?

HORATIO: It must be shortly known to him from England
What is the issue of the business there.

HAMLET: It will be short: the interim is mine;
And a man's life's no more than to say "One."
But I am very sorry, good Horatio,
That to Laertes I forgot myself;
For, by the image of my cause, I see
The portraiture of his: I'll court his favours:
But, sure, the bravery° of his grief did put me
Into a tow'ring passion.

HORATIO: Peace! who comes here?

Enter a Courtier [*Osric*].

OSRIC: Your lordship is right welcome back to Denmark.

HAMLET: I humbly thank you, sir. [*To Horatio.*] Dost know this water-fly?°

HORATIO: No, my good lord.

HAMLET: Thy state is the more gracious; for 'tis a vice to know him. He hath much land, and fertile: let a beast be lord of beasts,° and his crib shall stand at the king's mess:° 'tis a chough;° but, as I say, spacious in the possession of dirt.

OSRIC: Sweet lord, if your lordship were at leisure, I should impart a thing to you from his majesty.

HAMLET: I will receive it, sir, with all diligence of spirit. Put your bonnet to his right use; 'tis for the head.

OSRIC: I thank you lordship, it is very hot.

HAMLET: No, believe me, 'tis very cold; the wind is northerly.

OSRIC: It is indifferent° cold, my lord, indeed.

---

61. pass: Thrust. **fell incensed:** Fiercely angered. **63. stand:** Become incumbent. **65. election:** The Danish throne was filled by election. **66. angle:** Fishing line. **67. coz'nage:** Trickery. **68. quit:** Repay. **69. canker:** Ulcer, or possibly the worm which destroys buds and leaves. **79. bravery:** Bravado. **82. water-fly:** Vain or busily idle person. **85. lord of beasts:** Cf. Genesis 1:26, 28. **85–86. his crib . . . mess:** He shall eat at the king's table, i.e., be one of the group of persons (usually four) constituting a *mess* at a banquet. **86. chough:** Probably, chattering jackdaw; also explained as *chuff*, provincial boor or churl. **94. indifferent:** Somewhat.

HAMLET: But yet methinks it is very sultry and hot for my complexion.

OSRIC: Exceedingly, my lord; it is very sultry, — as 'twere, — I cannot tell how. But, my lord, his majesty bade me signify to you that 'a has laid a great wager on your head: sir, this is the matter, —

HAMLET: I beseech you, remember° — [*Hamlet moves him to put on his hat.*]

OSRIC: Nay, good my lord; for mine ease,° in good faith. Sir, here is newly come to court Laertes; believe me, an absolute gentleman, full of most excellent differences, of very soft° society and great showing:° indeed, to speak feelingly° of him, he is the card° or calendar of gentry,° for you shall find in him the continent of what part a gentleman would see.

HAMLET: Sir, his definement° suffers no perdition° in you; though, I know, to divide him inventorially° would dozy° the arithmetic of memory, and yet but yaw° neither, in respect of his quick sail. But, in the verity of extolment, I take him to be a soul of great article;° and his infusion° of such dearth and rareness,° as, to make true diction of him, his semblable° is his mirror; and who else would trace° him, his umbrage,° nothing more.

OSRIC: Your lordship speaks most infallibly of him.

HAMLET: The concernancy,° sir? why do we wrap the gentleman in our more rawer breath?°

OSRIC: Sir?

HORATIO [*aside to Hamlet*]: Is 't not possible to understand in another tongue?° You will do 't, sir, really.

HAMLET: What imports the nomination° of this gentleman?

OSRIC: Of Laertes?

HORATIO [*aside to Hamlet*]: His purse is empty already; all 's golden words are spent.

HAMLET: Of him, sir.

OSRIC: I know you are not ignorant —

HAMLET: I would you did, sir; yet, in faith, if you did, it would not much approve° me. Well, sir?

OSRIC: You are not ignorant of what excellence Laertes is —

HAMLET: I dare not confess that, lest I should compare with him in excellence; but, to know a man well, were to know himself.°

---

99. remember: I.e., remember thy courtesy; conventional phrase for "Be covered." **100. mine ease:** Conventional reply declining the invitation of "Remember thy courtesy." **102. soft:** Gentle. **showing:** Distinguished appearance. **103. feelingly:** With just perception. **card:** Chart, map. **gentry:** Good breeding. **105. definement:** Definition. **perdition:** Loss, diminution. **106. divide him inventorially:** I.e., enumerate his graces. **dozy:** Dizzy. **107. yaw:** To move unsteadily (of a ship). **108. article:** Moment or importance. **infusion:** Infused temperament, character imparted by nature. **109. dearth and rareness:** Rarity. **semblable:** True likeness. **110. trace:** Follow. **umbrage:** Shadow. **113. concernancy:** Import. **114. breath:** Speech. **116. Is 't . . . tongue?:** I.e., can one converse with Osric only in this outlandish jargon? **118. nomination:** Naming. **125. approve:** Command. **128. but . . . himself:** But to know a man as excellent were to know Laertes.

OSRIC: I mean, sir, for his weapon; but in the imputation° laid on him by them, in his meed° he's unfellowed.

HAMLET: What's his weapon?

OSRIC: Rapier and dagger.

HAMLET: That's two of his weapons: but, well.

OSRIC: The king, sir, hath wagered with him six Barbary horses: against the which he has impawned,° as I take it, six French rapiers and poniards, with their assigns, as girdle, hangers,° and so: three of the carriages, in faith, are very dear to fancy,° very responsive° to the hilts, most delicate° carriages, and of very liberal conceit.°

HAMLET: What call you the carriages?

HORATIO [*aside to Hamlet*]: I knew you must be edified by the margent° ere you had done.

OSRIC: The carriages, sir, are the hangers.

HAMLET: The phrase would be more german° to the matter, if we could carry cannon by our sides: I would it might be hangers till then. But, on: six Barbary horses against six French swords, their assigns, and three liberal-conceited carriages; that's the French bet against the Danish. Why is this "impawned," as you call it?

OSRIC: The king, sir, hath laid, that in a dozen passes between yourself and him, he shall not exceed you three hits: he hath laid on twelve for nine; and it would come to immediate trial, if your lordship would vouchsafe the answer.

HAMLET: How if I answer "no"?

OSRIC: I mean, my lord, the opposition of your person in trial.

HAMLET: Sir, I will walk here in the hall: if it please his majesty, it is the breathing time° of day with me; let the foils be brought, the gentleman willing, and the king hold his purpose, I will win for him as I can; if not, I will gain nothing but my shame and the odd hits.

OSRIC: Shall I re-deliver you e'en so?

HAMLET: To this effect, sir; after what flourish your nature will.

OSRIC: I commend my duty to your lordship.

HAMLET: Yours, yours. [*Exit Osric.*] He does well to commend it himself; there are no tongues else for 's turn.

HORATIO: This lapwing° runs away with the shell on his head.

HAMLET: 'A did comply, sir, with his dug,° before 'a sucked it. Thus has he—and many more of the same breed that I know the drossy° age dotes on—

129. imputation: Reputation. **130. meed:** Merit. **135. he has impawned:** He has wagered. **136. hangers:** Straps on the sword belt from which the sword hung. **137. dear to fancy:** Fancifully made. **responsive:** Probably, well balanced, corresponding closely. **delicate:** I.e., in workmanship. **138. liberal conceit:** Elaborate design. **140. margent:** Margin of a book, place for explanatory notes. **143. german:** Germane, appropriate. **154–155. breathing time:** Exercise period. **163. lapwing:** Peewit; noted for its wiliness in drawing a visitor away from its nest and its supposed habit of running about when newly hatched with its head in the shell; possibly an allusion to Osric's hat. **164. did comply . . . dug:** Paid compliments to his mother's breast. **165. drossy:** Frivolous.

only got the tune° of the time and out of an habit of encounter;° a kind of yesty° collection, which carries them through and through the most fann'd and winnowed° opinions; and do but blow them to their trial, the bubbles are out.°

Enter a Lord.

LORD: My lord, his majesty commended him to you by young Osric, who brings back to him, that you attend him in the hall: he sends to know if your pleasure hold to play with Laertes, or that you will take longer time.

HAMLET: I am constant to my purposes; they follow the king's pleasure: if his fitness speaks, mine is ready; now or whensoever, provided I be so able as now.

LORD: The king and queen and all are coming down.

HAMLET: In happy time.°

LORD: The queen desires you to use some gentle entertainment to Laertes before you fall to play.

HAMLET: She well instructs me. [*Exit Lord.*]

HORATIO: You will lose this wager, my lord.

HAMLET: I do not think so; since he went into France, I have been in continual practice; I shall win at the odds. But thou wouldst not think how ill all 's here about my heart: but it is no matter.

HORATIO: Nay, good my lord,—

HAMLET: It is but foolery; but it is such a kind of gain-giving,° as would perhaps trouble a woman.

HORATIO: If your mind dislike any thing, obey it: I will forestall their repair hither, and say you are not fit.

HAMLET: Not a whit, we defy augury: there's a special providence in the fall of a sparrow. If it be now, 'tis not to come; if it be not to come, it will be now; if it be not now, yet it will come: the readiness is all:° since no man of aught he leaves knows, what is 't to leave betimes? Let be.

A table prepared. [*Enter*] *Trumpets, Drums, and Officers with cushions; King, Queen,* [*Osric,*] *and all the State; foils, daggers,* [*and wine borne in;*] *and Laertes.*

KING: Come, Hamlet, come, and take this hand from me.

[*The King puts Laertes' hand into Hamlet's.*]

HAMLET: Give me your pardon, sir: I have done you wrong;
But pardon 't as you are a gentleman.
This presence° knows,
And you must needs have heard, how I am punish'd
With a sore distraction. What I have done,
That might your nature, honour and exception°
Roughly awake, I here proclaim was madness.

---

166. tune: Temper, mood. **habit of encounter:** Demeanor of social intercourse. **167. yesty:** Frothy. **168. fann'd and winnowed:** Select and refined. **168–169. blow . . . out:** I.e., put them to the test, and their ignorance is exposed. **177. In happy time:** A phrase of courtesy. **186. gain-giving:** Misgiving. **192. all:** All that matters. **197. presence:** Royal assembly. **200. exception:** Disapproval.

Was 't Hamlet wrong'd Laertes? Never Hamlet:
If Hamlet from himself be ta'en away,
And when he's not himself does wrong Laertes,
Then Hamlet does it not, Hamlet denies it.
Who does it, then? His madness: if 't be so,
Hamlet is of the faction that is wrong'd;
His madness is poor Hamlet's enemy.
Sir, in this audience,
Let my disclaiming from a purpos'd evil
Free me so far in your most generous thoughts,
That I have shot mine arrow o'er the house,
And hurt my brother.

LAERTES: I am satisfied in nature,°
Whose motive, in this case, should stir me most
To my revenge: but in my terms of honour
I stand aloof; and will no reconcilement,
Till by some elder masters, of known honour,
I have a voice° and precedent of peace,
To keep my name ungor'd. But till that time,
I do receive your offer'd love like love,
And will not wrong it.

HAMLET: I embrace it freely;
And will this brother's wager frankly play.
Give us the foils. Come on.

LAERTES: Come, one for me.

HAMLET: I'll be your foil,° Laertes: in mine ignorance
Your skill shall, like a star i' th' darkest night,
Stick fiery off° indeed.

LAERTES: You mock me, sir.

HAMLET: No, by this hand.

KING: Give them the foils, young Osric. Cousin Hamlet,
You know the wager?

HAMLET: Very well, my lord;
Your grace has laid the odds o' th' weaker side.

KING: I do not fear it; I have seen you both:
But since he is better'd, we have therefore odds.

LAERTES: This is too heavy, let me see another.

HAMLET: This likes me well. These foils have all a length?
[*They prepare to play.*]

OSRIC: Ay, my good lord.

KING: Set me the stoups of wine upon that table.
If Hamlet give the first or second hit,

213. nature: I.e., he is personally satisfied, but his honor must be satisfied by the rules of the code of honor. **218. voice:** Authoritative pronouncement. **224. foil:** Quibble on the two senses: "background which sets something off," and "blunted rapier for fencing." **226. Stick fiery off:** Stand out brilliantly.

Or quit in answer of the third exchange,
Let all the battlements their ordnance fire;
The king shall drink to Hamlet's better breath;
And in the cup an union° shall he throw,
Richer than that which four successive kings
In Denmark's crown have worn. Give me the cups;
And let the kettle° to the trumpet speak,
The trumpet to the cannoneer without,
The cannons to the heavens, the heavens to earth,
"Now the king drinks to Hamlet." Come begin: *Trumpets the while.*
And you, the judges, bear a wary eye.

HAMLET: Come on, sir.
LAERTES: Come, my lord. [*They play.*]
HAMLET: One.
LAERTES: No.
HAMLET: Judgement.
OSRIC: A hit, a very palpable hit.
Drum, trumpets, and shot. Flourish. A piece goes off.
LAERTES: Well; again.
KING: Stay; give me drink. Hamlet, this pearl° is thine;
Here's to thy health. Give him the cup.
HAMLET: I'll play this bout first; set it by awhile.
Come. [*They play.*] Another hit; what say you?
LAERTES: A touch, a touch, I do confess 't.
KING: Our son shall win.
QUEEN: He's fat,° and scant of breath.
Here, Hamlet, take my napkin, rub thy brows:
The queen carouses° to thy fortune, Hamlet.
HAMLET: Good madam!
KING: Gertrude, do not drink.
QUEEN: I will, my lord; I pray you, pardon me. [*Drinks.*]
KING [*aside*]: It is the poison'd cup: it is too late.
HAMLET: I dare not drink yet, madam; by and by.
QUEEN: Come, let me wipe thy face.
LAERTES: My lord, I'll hit him now.
KING: I do not think 't.
LAERTES [*aside*]: And yet 'tis almost 'gainst my conscience.
HAMLET: Come, for the third, Laertes: you but dally;
I pray you, pass with your best violence;
I am afeard you make a wanton° of me.
LAERTES: Say you so? come on. [*They play.*]

---

241. union: Pearl. **244. kettle:** Kettledrum. **251. pearl:** I.e., the poison. **256. fat:** Not physically fit, out of training. Some earlier editors speculated that the term applied to the corpulence of Richard Burbage, who originally played the part, but the allusion now appears unlikely. *Fat* may also suggest "sweaty." **258. carouses:** Drinks a toast. **268. wanton:** Spoiled child.

OSRIC: Nothing, neither way.
LAERTES: Have at you now!
[*Laertes wounds Hamlet; then, in scuffling, they change rapiers*° *and Hamlet wounds Laertes.*]
KING: Part them; they are incens'd.
HAMLET: Nay, come again. [*The Queen falls.*]
OSRIC: Look to the queen there, ho!
HORATIO: They bleed on both sides. How is it, my lord?
OSRIC: How is 't, Laertes?
LAERTES: Why, as a woodcock° to mine own springe,° Osric;
I am justly kill'd with mine own treachery.
HAMLET: How does the queen?
KING: She swounds° to see them bleed.
QUEEN: No, no, the drink, the drink,—O my dear Hamlet,—
The drink, the drink! I am poison'd. [*Dies.*]
HAMLET: O villainy! Ho! let the door be lock'd:
Treachery! Seek it out. [*Laertes falls.*]
LAERTES: It is here, Hamlet: Hamlet, thou art slain;
No med'cine in the world can do thee good;
In thee there is not half an hour of life;
The treacherous instrument is in thy hand,
Unbated° and envenom'd: the foul practice
Hath turn'd itself on me; lo, here I lie,
Never to rise again: thy mother's poison'd:
I can no more: the king, the king's to blame.
HAMLET: The point envenom'd too!
Then, venom, to thy work. [*Stabs the King.*]
ALL: Treason! treason!
KING: O, yet defend me, friends; I am but hurt.
HAMLET: Here, thou incestuous, murd'rous, damned Dane,
Drink off this potion. Is thy union here?
Follow my mother. [*King dies.*]
LAERTES: He is justly serv'd;
It is a poison temper'd° by himself.
Exchange forgiveness with me, noble Hamlet:
Mine and my father's death come not upon thee,
Nor thine on me! [*Dies.*]
HAMLET: Heaven make thee free of it! I follow thee.
I am dead, Horatio. Wretched queen, adieu!
You that look pale and tremble at this chance,
That are but mutes° or audience to this act,

---

271. s.d. in scuffling, they change rapiers: According to a widespread stage tradition, Hamlet receives a scratch, realizes that Laertes' sword is unbated, and accordingly forces an exchange. **275. woodcock:** As type of stupidity or as decoy. **springe:** Trap, snare. **277. swounds:** Swoons. **286. Unbated:** Not blunted with a button. **297. temper'd:** Mixed. **304. mutes:** Performers in a play who speak no words.

Had I but time—as this fell sergeant,° Death,
Is strict in his arrest—O, I could tell you—
But let it be. Horatio, I am dead;
Thou livest; report me and my cause aright
To the unsatisfied.

HORATIO: Never believe it:
I am more an antique Roman° than a Dane:
Here 's yet some liquor left.

HAMLET: As th' art a man,
Give me the cup: let go, by heaven, I'll ha 't.
O God! Horatio, what a wounded name,
Things standing thus unknown, shall live behind me!
If thou didst ever hold me in thy heart,
Absent thee from felicity awhile,
And in this harsh world draw thy breath in pain,
To tell my story. *A march afar off.*
What warlike noise is this?

OSRIC: Young Fortinbras, with conquest come from Poland,
To the ambassadors of England gives
This warlike volley.

HAMLET: O, I die, Horatio;
The potent poison quite o'er-crows° my spirit:
I cannot live to hear the news from England;
But I do prophesy th' election lights
On Fortinbras: he has my dying voice;
So tell him, with th' occurrents,° more and less,
Which have solicited.° The rest is silence. [*Dies.*]

HORATIO: Now cracks a noble heart. Good night, sweet prince;
And flights of angels sing thee to thy rest!
Why does the drum come hither? [*March within.*]

Enter Fortinbras, with the [*English*] *Ambassadors* [*and others*].

FORTINBRAS: Where is this sight?

HORATIO: What is it you would see?
If aught of woe or wonder, cease your search.

FORTINBRAS: This quarry° cries on havoc.° O proud Death,
What feast is toward in thine eternal cell,
That thou so many princes at a shot
So bloodily hast struck?

FIRST AMBASSADOR: The sight is dismal;
And our affairs from England come too late:
The ears are senseless that should give us hearing,

---

305. sergeant: Sheriff's officer. **310. Roman:** It was the Roman custom to follow masters in death. **322. o'er-crows:** Triumphs over. **326. occurrents:** Events, incidents. **327. solicited:** Moved, urged. **333. quarry:** Heap of dead. **cries on havoc:** Proclaims a general slaughter.

To tell him his commandment is fulfill'd,
That Rosencrantz and Guildenstern are dead:
Where should we have our thanks?

HORATIO: Not from his mouth,°
Had it th' ability of life to thank you:
He never gave commandment for their death.
But since, so jump° upon this bloody question,°
You from the Polack wars, and you from England,
Are here arriv'd, give order that these bodies
High on a stage° be placed to the view;
And let me speak to th' yet unknowing world
How these things came about: so shall you hear
Of carnal, bloody, and unnatural acts,
Of accidental judgements, casual slaughters,
Of deaths put on by cunning and forc'd cause,
And, in this upshot, purposes mistook
Fall'n on th' inventors' heads: all this can I
Truly deliver.

FORTINBRAS: Let us haste to hear it,
And call the noblest to the audience.
For me, with sorrow I embrace my fortune:
I have some rights of memory° in this kingdom,
Which now to claim my vantage doth invite me.

HORATIO: Of that I shall have also cause to speak,
And from his mouth whose voice will draw on more:°
But let this same be presently perform'd,
Even while men's minds are wild; lest more mischance,
On° plots and errors, happen.

FORTINBRAS: Let four captains
Bear Hamlet, like a soldier, to the stage;
For he was likely, had he been put on,
To have prov'd most royal: and, for his passage,°
The soldiers' music and the rites of war
Speak loudly for him.
Take up the bodies: such a sight as this
Becomes the field,° but here shows much amiss.
Go, bid the soldiers shoot.

Exeunt [*marching, bearing off the dead bodies; after which a peal of ordnance is heard*].

---

341. his mouth: I.e., the king's. **344. jump:** Precisely. **question:** Dispute. **347. stage:** Platform. **358. of memory:** Traditional, remembered. **361. voice . . . more:** Vote will influence still others. **364. On:** On account of, or possibly, on top of, in addition to. **367. passage:** Death. **371. field:** I.e., of battle.

CONNECTION For a Conversation on *Hamlet* as Text and Performance, see page 1592.

HENRIK IBSEN

Henrik Ibsen (1828–1906), dramatist and poet, was born the second child of a merchant in a small town in southeast Norway. After the ruin of his father's business, Ibsen was raised in extreme poverty. His familiarity with economic hardship and his long struggle to make ends meet were later reflected in his realistic dramas. As a teenager Ibsen intended to study medicine, and he helped support his family by working for six years in an apothecary shop in the seaport town of Grimstad. Self-educated, he wrote his first play, *Catilina*, in verse when he was twenty-one. A year later he left Grimstad to become a student in Oslo, and then in 1851 he became active in the newly formed National Theatre at Bergen, the first theater in Norway to use Norwegian actors (Danish actors had previously dominated the stage). There Ibsen gained practical experience designing costumes, keeping the accounts, directing, and writing. After the theater went bankrupt, he left Norway with his wife and young son in 1864 and settled in Rome. Living abroad, he wrote the historical plays *Brand* (1866) and *Peer Gynt* (1867) as closet dramas, intended to be read, not acted. These plays' poetic vision of the human situation made Ibsen famous throughout Scandinavia when they were published, and Ibsen was awarded a government pension, although the plays were not staged for many years.

In 1875 Ibsen moved to Munich, where he began to experiment with a different kind of drama in *The Pillars of Society* (1877), the first of his twelve realistic prose plays addressing social issues. Four years later, living in Rome and Amalfi, he wrote *A Doll House*. Its portrayal of a marriage in crisis aroused so much controversy that the play caused an immediate sensation when it was performed. His next play, *Ghosts* (1881), was also attacked for its subject matter (syphilis passed on from father to son within a respected, upper-class family), although it was staged the following year by a small experimental theater company in Chicago. In the 1880s Ibsen's plays – *An Enemy of the People* (1882) and *The Wild Duck* (1884) among them – were regarded as obscure and unconventional. The earliest major English-language production of any of his plays was in 1889 when *A Doll House* was performed in London. In 1891, after writing *Hedda Gabler* in Munich, Ibsen returned to live for the remainder of his life in Norway, where he wrote his four last plays about spiritual conflicts in a new symbolic style.

Ibsen based the plot of *A Doll House* on a true story. In 1871 a young Norwegian woman named Laura Petersen sent him a sequel that she had written to his play *Brand*. Ibsen encouraged her to continue writing, calling her his "skylark." The following year she married a Danish schoolmaster who, suffering from tuberculosis, learned that he had to live in a warmer climate. The couple was poor, so Laura secretly arranged a loan to finance their trip to Italy. In 1878, after her creditor demanded repayment of the loan, she wrote a novel and sent it to Ibsen, asking him to recommend it to his publisher. Ibsen refused to endorse her book, and acting in panic, she forged a check to repay the debt. When the bank refused payment, Laura confessed to her husband what she had done. Instead of being sympathetic because she had been so concerned about his health, he accused her of being a criminal and an unfit mother for their children. Laura had a nervous breakdown, and her husband had her committed to a psychiatric hospital. After a month in the institution, she begged her husband to let her come back home for their children's sake, which he did, making it clear to her that it was against his higher moral principles. As Ibsen's biographer Michael Meyer understood, "The incident must have seemed to Ibsen to crystallize not merely woman's, but mankind's fight against conventional morality and prejudice."

Three months after hearing that Laura Petersen had been institutionalized, Ibsen composed his "Notes for a Modern Tragedy," in which he stated the germ of the idea that he developed in *A Doll House*: "There are two kinds of moral laws, two kinds of conscience, one for men and one, quite different, for women. They don't understand each other; but in practical life, woman is judged by masculine law, as though she weren't a woman but a man." Ibsen had been interested for some time in what was then called the problem of women's rights. His wife, Suzannah, championed the cause, and his friend the Norwegian novelist Camilla Collett had criticized what she considered his old-fashioned ideas about women's place in society.

The English writer John Stuart Mill's *The Subjection of Women* had been translated into Norwegian in 1869, the same year that Ibsen wrote his comedy *The League of Youth*. In this play one of the minor characters, a young wife, tells her husband, "You dressed me up like a doll; you played with me as one plays with a child." The Danish theater critic and champion of modernism Georg Brandes told Ibsen that a strong woman character like her might be a good subject for a play. In *The Pillars of Society*, which Ibsen completed just before *A Doll House*, he created two roles for women who rebel against the subordinate position dictated to them by their uncompromising patriarchal society. Yet he later insisted that in *A Doll House* he had not "worked for the Women's Rights movement. I am not even very sure what Women's Rights really are." What he really wanted to show in creating the character of Nora, he told Brandes, was a revolution of the human spirit.

By 1879, when *A Doll House* premiered at the Royal Theatre in Copenhagen, stage production had developed into the realistic theater familiar to us today. In his printed stage directions Ibsen had described the set in minute detail as a middle-class apartment, and the Danes followed his floor plan closely, adding flowering plants and a reproduction of Raphael's painting of the Madonna and child on the wall above the piano. The Royal Theatre even envisioned how to furnish Torvald's study offstage authentically with a paperweight and two candlesticks, although this view of his desk would be seen by very few people in the audience. Betty Hennings, the beautiful twenty-nine-year-old Danish actress playing Nora, was an accomplished dancer, and she was so attractive in the role that she became established as an international star. One reviewer who had come under Hennings's spell declared that in the first two acts she presented such a charming "picture of the young, inexperienced, naive, and carefree wife and mother that one truly envied" her husband for "the treasure which he possessed," thus completely missing the point of the play.

By the end of *A Doll House*, nineteenth-century audiences were nearly unanimous in their sympathy for Nora's husband, Torvald. Theater historians Frederick Marker and Lise-Lone Marker point out that in 1879, all the reviewers of this first production agreed that "the spiritual metamorphosis" that Nora undergoes in the third act of *A Doll House* from a naive wife and mother to a self-possessed independent woman was totally unconvincing. Attacked for being immoral, the play aroused so much controversy in Copenhagen that a placard reading *Her tales ikke Dukkehjem* ("No *Doll House* discussions here") was sold for Danes to put in their parlors to keep the peace at home.

Two months after the Danish premier, Ibsen rewrote the play for a German actress who refused to appear on stage unless there was a happy ending – an ending in which Nora (as a so-called normal mother) agrees to stay home to continue her marriage. This version of the play was not a success, and Ibsen restored the original ending. Later critics understood that in *A Doll House* Ibsen had gone beyond the conventional idea of a "well-made play" in realistic drama to create a new type of "discussion play." Where the carefully plotted well-made play ends in a denouement or a closed ending that resolves all the aspects of the conflict between the characters, Ibsen's discussion play culminates in an open ending without a clear resolution of the issues dramatized onstage, because the debate itself is intended to be an integral part of the dramatic action. Contemporary audiences accept Ibsen's open ending in the play, but a century ago most people were shocked by Nora's decision to leave her children and go off on her own. When she shut the door of her husband's house at the end of the play, the sound reverberated round the world.

WEB Research Henrik Ibsen at bedfordstmartins.com/rewritinglit.

A Doll House

TRANSLATED BY B. FARQUHARSON SHARP

DRAMATIS PERSONAE

TORVALD HELMER
NORA, his wife
DOCTOR RANK
MRS. LINDE
NILS KROGSTAD
Helmer's three young children
ANNE, their nurse
A Housemaid
A Porter

SCENE: *The action takes place in Helmer's house.*

ACT I

SCENE: *A room furnished comfortably and tastefully, but not extravagantly. At the back, a door to the right leads to the entrance-hall, another to the left leads to Helmer's study. Between the doors stands a piano. In the middle of the left-hand wall is a door, and beyond it a window. Near the window are a round table, armchairs and a small sofa. In the right-hand wall, at the farther end, another door; and on the same side, nearer the footlights, a stove, two easy chairs and a rocking-chair; between the stove and the door, a small table. Engravings on the walls; a cabinet with china and other small objects; a small book-case with well-bound books. The floors are carpeted, and a fire burns in the stove. It is winter.*

A bell rings in the hall; shortly afterwards the door is heard to open. Enter Nora, humming a tune and in high spirits. She is in outdoor dress and carries a number of parcels; these she lays on the table to the right. She leaves the outer door open after her, and through it is seen a Porter who is carrying a Christmas Tree and a basket, which he gives to the Maid who has opened the door.

NORA: Hide the Christmas Tree carefully, Helen. Be sure the children do not see it until this evening, when it is dressed. (*To the Porter, taking out her purse.*) How much?

PORTER: Sixpence.

NORA: There is a shilling. No, keep the change. (*The Porter thanks her, and goes out. Nora shuts the door. She is laughing to herself, as she takes off her hat and coat. She takes a packet of macaroons from her pocket and eats one or two; then goes cautiously to her husband's door and listens.*) Yes, he is in. (*Still humming, she goes to the table on the right.*)

HELMER (*calls out from his room*): Is that my little lark twittering out there?

NORA (*busy opening some of the parcels*): Yes, it is!

HELMER: Is it my little squirrel bustling about?

NORA: Yes!

HELMER: When did my squirrel come home?

NORA: Just now. (*Puts the bag of macaroons into her pocket and wipes her mouth.*) Come in here, Torvald, and see what I have bought.

HELMER: Don't disturb me. (*A little later, he opens the door and looks into the room, pen in hand.*) Bought, did you say? All these things? Has my little spendthrift been wasting money again?

NORA: Yes but, Torvald, this year we really can let ourselves go a little. This is the first Christmas that we have not needed to economise.

HELMER: Still, you know, we can't spend money recklessly.

NORA: Yes, Torvald, we may be a wee bit more reckless now, mayn't we? Just a tiny wee bit! You are going to have a big salary and earn lots and lots of money.

HELMER: Yes, after the New Year; but then it will be a whole quarter before the salary is due.

NORA: Pooh! we can borrow until then.

HELMER: Nora! (*Goes up to her and takes her playfully by the ear.*) The same little featherhead! Suppose, now, that I borrowed fifty pounds to-day, and you spent it all in the Christmas week, and then on New Year's Eve a slate fell on my head and killed me, and—

NORA (*putting her hands over his mouth*): Oh! don't say such horrid things.

HELMER: Still, suppose that happened,—what then?

NORA: If that were to happen, I don't suppose I should care whether I owed money or not.

HELMER: Yes, but what about the people who had lent it?

NORA: They? Who would bother about them? I should not know who they were.

HELMER: That is like a woman! But seriously, Nora, you know what I think about that. No debt, no borrowing. There can be no freedom or beauty about a home life that depends on borrowing and debt. We two have kept bravely on the straight road so far, and we will go on the same way for the short time longer that there need be any struggle.

NORA (*moving towards the stove*): As you please, Torvald.

HELMER (*following her*): Come, come, my little skylark must not droop her wings. What is this! Is my little squirrel out of temper? (*Taking out his purse.*) Nora, what do you think I have got here?

NORA (*turning round quickly*): Money!

HELMER: There you are. (*Gives her some money.*) Do you think I don't know what a lot is wanted for housekeeping at Christmas-time?

NORA (*counting*): Ten shillings—a pound—two pounds! Thank you, thank you, Torvald; that will keep me going for a long time.

HELMER: Indeed it must.

NORA: Yes, yes, it will. But come here and let me show you what I have bought. And all so cheap! Look, here is a new suit for Ivar, and a sword; and a horse and a trumpet for Bob; and a doll and dolly's bedstead for Emmy,—they are very plain, but anyway she will soon break them in pieces. And here are dress-lengths and handkerchiefs for the maids; old Anne ought really to have something better.

HELMER: And what is in this parcel?

NORA (*crying out*): No, no! you mustn't see that until this evening.

HELMER: Very well. But now tell me, you extravagant little person, what would you like for yourself?

NORA: For myself? Oh, I am sure I don't want anything.

HELMER: Yes, but you must. Tell me something reasonable that you would particularly like to have.

NORA: No, I really can't think of anything—unless, Torvald—

HELMER: Well?

NORA (*playing with his coat buttons, and without raising her eyes to his*): If you really want to give me something, you might—you might—

HELMER: Well, out with it!

NORA (*speaking quickly*): You might give me money, Torvald. Only just as much as you can afford; and then one of these days I will buy something with it.

HELMER: But, Nora—

NORA: Oh, do! dear Torvald; please, please do! Then I will wrap it up in beautiful gilt paper and hang it on the Christmas Tree. Wouldn't that be fun?

HELMER: What are little people called that are always wasting money?

NORA: Spendthrifts—I know. Let us do as you suggest, Torvald, and then I shall have time to think what I am most in want of. That is a very sensible plan, isn't it?

HELMER (*smiling*): Indeed it is—that is to say, if you were really to save out of the money I give you, and then really buy something for yourself. But if you spend it all on the housekeeping and any number of unnecessary things, then I merely have to pay up again.

NORA: Oh but, Torvald—

HELMER: You can't deny it, my dear little Nora. (*Puts his arm round her waist.*) It's a sweet little spendthrift, but she uses up a deal of money. One would hardly believe how expensive such little persons are!

NORA: It's a shame to say that. I do really save all I can.

HELMER (*laughing*): That's very true,—all you can. But you can't save anything!

NORA (*smiling quietly and happily*): You haven't any idea how many expenses we skylarks and squirrels have, Torvald.

HELMER: You are an odd little soul. Very like your father. You always find some new way of wheedling money out of me, and, as soon as you have got it, it seems to melt in your hands. You never know where it has gone. Still, one must take you as you are. It is in the blood; for indeed it is true that you can inherit these things, Nora.

NORA: Ah, I wish I had inherited many of papa's qualities.

HELMER: And I would not wish you to be anything but just what you are, my sweet little skylark. But, do you know, it strikes me that you are looking rather—what shall I say—rather uneasy today?

NORA: Do I?

HELMER: You do, really. Look straight at me.

NORA (*looks at him*): Well?

HELMER (*wagging his finger at her*): Hasn't Miss Sweet Tooth been breaking rules in town today?

NORA: No; what makes you think that?

HELMER: Hasn't she paid a visit to the confectioner's?

NORA: No, I assure you, Torvald—

HELMER: Not been nibbling sweets?

NORA: No, certainly not.

HELMER: Not even taken a bite at a macaroon or two?

NORA: No, Torvald, I assure you really—

HELMER: There, there, of course I was only joking.

NORA (*going to the table on the right*): I should not think of going against your wishes.

HELMER: No, I am sure of that; besides, you gave me your word—(*Going up to her.*) Keep your little Christmas secrets to yourself, my darling. They will all be revealed to-night when the Christmas Tree is lit, no doubt.

NORA: Did you remember to invite Doctor Rank?

HELMER: No. But there is no need; as a matter of course he will come to dinner with us. However, I will ask him when he comes in this morning. I have ordered some good wine. Nora, you can't think how I am looking forward to this evening.

NORA: So am I! And how the children will enjoy themselves, Torvald!

HELMER: It is splendid to feel that one has a perfectly safe appointment, and a big enough income. It's delightful to think of, isn't it?

NORA: It's wonderful!

HELMER: Do you remember last Christmas? For a full three weeks beforehand you shut yourself up every evening until long after midnight, making ornaments for the Christmas Tree, and all the other fine things that were to be a surprise to us. It was the dullest three weeks I ever spent!

NORA: I didn't find it dull.

HELMER (*smiling*): But there was precious little result, Nora.

NORA: Oh, you shouldn't tease me about that again. How could I help the cat's going in and tearing everything to pieces?

HELMER: Of course you couldn't, poor little girl. You had the best of intentions to please us all, and that's the main thing. But it is a good thing that our hard times are over.

NORA: Yes, it is really wonderful.

HELMER: This time I needn't sit here and be dull all alone, and you needn't ruin your dear eyes and your pretty little hands—

NORA (*clapping her hands*): No, Torvald, I needn't any longer, need I! It's wonderfully lovely to hear you say so! (*Taking his arm.*) Now I will tell you how I have been thinking we ought to arrange things, Torvald. As soon as Christmas is over—(*A bell rings in the hall.*) There's the bell. (*She tidies the room a little.*) There's some one at the door. What a nuisance!

HELMER: If it is a caller, remember I am not at home.

MAID (*in the doorway*): A lady to see you, ma'am,—a stranger.

NORA: Ask her to come in.

MAID (*to Helmer*): The doctor came at the same time, sir.

HELMER: Did he go straight into my room?

MAID: Yes, sir.

Helmer goes into his room. The Maid ushers in Mrs. Linde, who is in travelling dress, and shuts the door.

MRS. LINDE (*in a dejected and timid voice*): How do you do, Nora?

NORA (*doubtfully*): How do you do—

MRS. LINDE: You don't recognise me, I suppose.

NORA: No, I don't know—yes, to be sure, I seem to—(*Suddenly.*) Yes! Christine! Is it really you?

MRS. LINDE: Yes, it is I.

NORA: Christine! To think of my not recognising you! And yet how could I—(*In a gentle voice.*) How you have altered, Christine!

MRS. LINDE: Yes, I have indeed. In nine, ten long years—

NORA: Is it so long since we met? I suppose it is. The last eight years have been a happy time for me, I can tell you. And so now you have come into the town, and have taken this long journey in winter—that was plucky of you.

MRS. LINDE: I arrived by steamer this morning.

NORA: To have some fun at Christmas-time, of course. How delightful! We will have such fun together! But take off your things. You are not cold, I hope. (*Helps her.*) Now we will sit down by the stove, and be cosy. No, take this armchair; I will sit here in the rocking-chair. (*Takes her hands.*) Now you look like your old self again; it was only the first moment—You are a little paler, Christine, and perhaps a little thinner.

MRS. LINDE: And much, much older, Nora.

NORA: Perhaps a little older; very, very little; certainly not much. (*Stops suddenly and speaks seriously.*) What a thoughtless creature I am, chattering away like this. My poor, dear Christine, do forgive me.

MRS. LINDE: What do you mean, Nora?

NORA (*gently*): Poor Christine, you are a widow.

MRS. LINDE: Yes; it is three years ago now.

NORA: Yes, I knew; I saw it in the papers. I assure you, Christine, I meant ever so often to write to you at the time, but I always put it off and something always prevented me.

MRS. LINDE: I quite understand, dear.

NORA: It was very bad of me, Christine. Poor thing, how you must have suffered. And he left you nothing?

MRS. LINDE: No.

NORA: And no children?

MRS. LINDE: No.

NORA: Nothing at all, then.

MRS. LINDE: Not even any sorrow or grief to live upon.

NORA (*looking incredulously at her*): But, Christine, is that possible?

MRS. LINDE (*smiles sadly and strokes her hair*): It sometimes happens, Nora.

NORA: So you are quite alone. How dreadfully sad that must be. I have three lovely children. You can't see them just now, for they are out with their nurse. But now you must tell me all about it.

MRS. LINDE: No, no; I want to hear about you.

NORA: No, you must begin. I mustn't be selfish today; today I must only think of your affairs. But there is one thing I must tell you. Do you know we have just had a great piece of good luck?

MRS. LINDE: No, what is it?

NORA: Just fancy, my husband has been made manager of the Bank!

MRS. LINDE: Your husband? What good luck!

NORA: Yes, tremendous! A barrister's profession is such an uncertain thing, especially if he won't undertake unsavoury cases; and naturally Torvald has never been willing to do that, and I quite agree with him. You may imagine how pleased we are! He is to take up his work in the Bank at the New Year, and then he will have a big salary and lots of commissions. For the future we can live quite differently—we can do just as we like. I feel so relieved and so happy, Christine! It will be splendid to have heaps of money and not need to have any anxiety, won't it?

MRS. LINDE: Yes, anyhow I think it would be delightful to have what one needs.

NORA: No, not only what one needs, but heaps and heaps of money.

MRS. LINDE (*smiling*): Nora, Nora, haven't you learned sense yet? In our school-days you were a great spendthrift.

NORA (*laughing*): Yes, that is what Torvald says now. (*Wags her finger at her.*) But "Nora, Nora" is not so silly as you think. We have not been in a position for me to waste money. We have both had to work.

MRS. LINDE: You too?

NORA: Yes; odds and ends, needlework, crotchet-work, embroidery, and that kind of thing. (*Dropping her voice.*) And other things as well. You know Torvald left his office when we were married? There was no prospect of promotion there, and he had to try and earn more than before. But during the first year he over-worked himself dreadfully. You see, he had to make money every way he could, and he worked early and late; but he couldn't stand it, and fell dreadfully ill, and the doctors said it was necessary for him to go south.

MRS. LINDE: You spent a whole year in Italy, didn't you?

NORA: Yes. It was no easy matter to get away, I can tell you. It was just after Ivar was born; but naturally we had to go. It was a wonderfully beautiful journey, and it saved Torvald's life. But it cost a tremendous lot of money, Christine.

MRS. LINDE: So I should think.

NORA: It cost about two hundred and fifty pounds. That's a lot, isn't it?

MRS. LINDE: Yes, and in emergencies like that it is lucky to have the money.

NORA: I ought to tell you that we had it from papa.

MRS. LINDE: Oh, I see. It was just about that time that he died, wasn't it?

NORA: Yes; and, just think of it, I couldn't go and nurse him. I was expecting little Ivar's birth every day and I had my poor sick Torvald to look after. My dear, kind father—I never saw him again, Christine. That was the saddest time I have known since our marriage.

MRS. LINDE: I know how fond you were of him. And then you went off to Italy?

NORA: Yes; you see we had money then, and the doctors insisted on our going, so we started a month later.

MRS. LINDE: And your husband came back quite well?

NORA: As sound as a bell!

MRS. LINDE: But—the doctor?

NORA: What doctor?

MRS. LINDE: I thought your maid said the gentleman who arrived here just as I did, was the doctor?

NORA: Yes, that was Doctor Rank, but he doesn't come here professionally. He is our greatest friend, and comes in at least once everyday. No, Torvald has not had an hour's illness since then, and our children are strong and healthy and so am I. (*Jumps up and claps her hands.*) Christine! Christine! it's good to be alive and happy!—But how horrid of me; I am talking of nothing but my own affairs. (*Sits on a stool near her, and rests her arms on her knees.*) You mustn't be angry with me. Tell me, is it really true that you did not love your husband? Why did you marry him?

MRS. LINDE: My mother was alive then, and was bedridden and helpless, and I had to provide for my two younger brothers; so I did not think I was justified in refusing his offer.

NORA: No, perhaps you were quite right. He was rich at that time, then?

MRS. LINDE: I believe he was quite well off. But his business was a precarious one; and, when he died, it all went to pieces and there was nothing left.

NORA: And then?—

MRS. LINDE: Well, I had to turn my hand to anything I could find—first a small shop, then a small school, and so on. The last three years have seemed like one long working-day, with no rest. Now it is at an end, Nora. My poor mother needs me no more, for she is gone; and the boys do not need me either; they have got situations and can shift for themselves.

NORA: What a relief you must feel it—

MRS. LINDE: No, indeed; I only feel my life unspeakably empty. No one to live for anymore. (*Gets up restlessly.*) That was why I could not stand the life in my little backwater any longer. I hope it may be easier here to find something which will busy me and occupy my thoughts. If only I could have the good luck to get some regular work—office work of some kind—

NORA: But, Christine, that is so frightfully tiring, and you look tired out now. You had far better go away to some watering-place.

MRS. LINDE (*walking to the window*): I have no father to give me money for a journey, Nora.

NORA (*rising*): Oh, don't be angry with me!

MRS. LINDE (*going up to her*): It is you that must not be angry with me, dear. The worst of a position like mine is that it makes one so bitter. No one to work for, and yet obliged to be always on the lookout for chances. One must live, and so one becomes selfish. When you told me of the happy turn your fortunes have taken—you will hardly believe it—I was delighted not so much on your account as on my own.

NORA: How do you mean?—Oh, I understand. You mean that perhaps Torvald could get you something to do.

MRS. LINDE: Yes, that was what I was thinking of.

NORA: He must, Christine. Just leave it to me; I will broach the subject very cleverly—I will think of something that will please him very much. It will make me so happy to be of some use to you.

MRS. LINDE: How kind you are, Nora, to be so anxious to help me! It is doubly kind in you, for you know so little of the burdens and troubles of life.

NORA: I—? I know so little of them?

MRS. LINDE (*smiling*): My dear! Small household cares and that sort of thing!—You are a child, Nora.

NORA (*tosses her head and crosses the stage*): You ought not to be so superior.

MRS. LINDE: No?

NORA: You are just like the others. They all think that I am incapable of anything really serious—

MRS. LINDE: Come, come—

NORA: —that I have gone through nothing in this world of cares.

MRS. LINDE: But, my dear Nora, you have just told me all your troubles.

NORA: Pooh!—those were trifles. (*Lowering her voice.*) I have not told you the important thing.

MRS. LINDE: The important thing? What do you mean?

NORA: You look down upon me altogether, Christine—but you ought not to. You are proud, aren't you, of having worked so hard and so long for your mother?

MRS. LINDE: Indeed, I don't look down on anyone. But it is true that I am both proud and glad to think that I was privileged to make the end of my mother's life almost free from care.

NORA: And you are proud to think of what you have done for your brothers?

MRS. LINDE: I think I have the right to be.

NORA: I think so, too. But now, listen to this; I too have something to be proud and glad of.

MRS. LINDE: I have no doubt you have. But what do you refer to?

NORA: Speak low. Suppose Torvald were to hear! He mustn't on any account—no one in the world must know, Christine, except you.

MRS. LINDE: But what is it?

NORA: Come here. (*Pulls her down on the sofa beside her.*) Now I will show you that I too have something to be proud and glad of. It was I who saved Torvald's life.

MRS. LINDE: "Saved"? How?

NORA: I told you about our trip to Italy. Torvald would never have recovered if he had not gone there—

MRS. LINDE: Yes, but your father gave you the necessary funds.

NORA (*smiling*): Yes, that is what Torvald and all the others think, but—

MRS. LINDE: But—

NORA: Papa didn't give us a shilling. It was I who procured the money.

MRS. LINDE: You? All that large sum?

NORA: Two hundred and fifty pounds. What do you think of that?

MRS. LINDE: But, Nora, how could you possibly do it? Did you win a prize in the Lottery?

NORA (*contemptuously*): In the Lottery? There would have been no credit in that.

MRS. LINDE: But where did you get it from, then?

NORA (*humming and smiling with an air of mystery*): Hm, hm! Aha!

MRS. LINDE: Because you couldn't have borrowed it.

NORA: Couldn't I? Why not?

MRS. LINDE: No, a wife cannot borrow without her husband's consent.

NORA (*tossing her head*): Oh, if it is a wife who has any head for business—a wife who has the wit to be a little bit clever—

MRS. LINDE: I don't understand it at all, Nora.

NORA: There is no need you should. I never said I had borrowed the money. I may have got it some other way. (*Lies back on the sofa.*) Perhaps I got it from some other admirer. When anyone is as attractive as I am—

MRS. LINDE: You are a mad creature.

NORA: Now, you know you're full of curiosity, Christine.

MRS. LINDE: Listen to me, Nora dear. Haven't you been a little bit imprudent?

NORA (*sits up straight*): Is it imprudent to save your husband's life?

MRS. LINDE: It seems to me imprudent, without his knowledge, to—

NORA: But it was absolutely necessary that he should not know! My goodness, can't you understand that? It was necessary he should have no idea what a dangerous condition he was in. It was to me that the doctors came and said that his life was in danger, and that the only thing to save him was to live in the south. Do you suppose I didn't try, first of all, to get what I wanted as if it were for myself? I told him how much I should love to travel abroad like other young wives; I tried tears and entreaties with him; I told him that he ought to remember the condition I was in, and that he ought to be kind and indulgent to me; I even hinted that he might raise a loan. That nearly made him angry, Christine. He said I was thoughtless, and that it was his duty as my husband not to indulge me in my whims and caprices—as I believe he called them. Very well, I thought, you must be saved—and that was how I came to devise a way out of the difficulty—

MRS. LINDE: And did your husband never get to know from your father that the money had not come from him?

NORA: No, never. Papa died just at that time. I had meant to let him into the secret and beg him never to reveal it. But he was so ill then—alas, there never was any need to tell him.

MRS. LINDE: And since then have you never told your secret to your husband?

NORA: Good Heavens, no! How could you think so? A man who has such strong opinions about these things! And besides, how painful and humiliating it would be for Torvald, with his manly independence, to know that he owed me anything! It would upset our mutual relations altogether; our beautiful happy home would no longer be what it is now.

MRS. LINDE: Do you mean never to tell him about it?

NORA (*meditatively, and with a half smile*): Yes—someday, perhaps, after many years, when I am no longer as nice-looking as I am now. Don't laugh at me! I mean, of course, when Torvald is no longer as devoted to me as he is now; when my dancing and dressing-up and reciting have palled on him; then it may be a good thing to have something in reserve—(*Breaking off.*) What nonsense! That time will never come. Now, what do you think of my great secret, Christine? Do you still think I am of no use? I can tell you, too, that this affair has caused me a lot of worry. It has been by no means easy for me to meet my engagements punctually. I may tell you that there is something that is called, in business, quarterly interest, and another thing called payment in installments, and it is always so dreadfully difficult to manage them. I have had to save a little here and there, where I could, you understand. I have not been able to put aside much from my housekeeping money, for Torvald must have a good table. I couldn't let my children be shabbily dressed; I have felt obliged to use up all he gave me for them, the sweet little darlings!

MRS. LINDE: So it has all had to come out of your own necessaries of life, poor Nora?

NORA: Of course. Besides, I was the one responsible for it. Whenever Torvald has given me money for new dresses and such things, I have never spent more than half of it; I have always bought the simplest and cheapest things. Thank Heaven, any clothes look well on me, and so Torvald has never noticed it. But it was often very hard on me, Christine—because it is delightful to be really well dressed, isn't it?

MRS. LINDE: Quite so.

NORA: Well, then I have found other ways of earning money. Last winter I was lucky enough to get a lot of copying to do; so I locked myself up and sat writing every evening until quite late at night. Many a time I was desperately tired; but all the same it was a tremendous pleasure to sit there working and earning money. It was like being a man.

MRS. LINDE: How much have you been able to pay off in that way?

NORA: I can't tell you exactly. You see, it is very difficult to keep an account of a business matter of that kind. I only know that I have paid every penny that I could scrape together. Many a time I was at my wits' end. (*Smiles.*) Then I used to sit here and imagine that a rich old gentleman had fallen in love with me—

MRS. LINDE: What! Who was it?

NORA: Be quiet!—that he had died; and that when his will was opened it contained, written in big letters, the instruction: "The lovely Mrs. Nora Helmer is to have all I possess paid over to her at once in cash."

MRS. LINDE: But, my dear Nora—who could the man be?

NORA: Good gracious, can't you understand? There was no old gentleman at all; it was only something that I used to sit here and imagine, when I couldn't think of any way of procuring money. But it's all the same now; the tiresome old person can stay where he is, as far as I am concerned; I don't care about him or his will either, for I am free from care now. (*Jumps up.*) My goodness, it's delightful to think of, Christine! Free from care! To be able to be free from care, quite free from care; to be able to play and romp with the children; to be able to keep the house beautifully and have everything just as Torvald likes it! And, think of it, soon the spring will come and the big blue sky! Perhaps we shall be able to take a little trip—perhaps I shall see the sea again! Oh, it's a wonderful thing to be alive and be happy. (*A bell is heard in the hall.*)

MRS. LINDE (*rising*): There is the bell; perhaps I had better go.

NORA: No, don't go; no one will come in here; it is sure to be for Torvald.

SERVANT (*at the hall door*): Excuse me, ma'am—there is a gentleman to see the master, and as the doctor is with him—

NORA: Who is it?

KROGSTAD (*at the door*): It is I, Mrs. Helmer (*Mrs. Linde starts, trembles, and turns to the window.*)

NORA (*takes a step towards him, and speaks in a strained, low voice*): You? What is it? What do you want to see my husband about?

KROGSTAD: Bank business—in a way. I have a small post in the Bank, and I hear your husband is to be our chief now—

NORA: Then it is—

KROGSTAD: Nothing but dry business matters, Mrs. Helmer; absolutely nothing else.

NORA: Be so good as to go into the study, then. (*She bows indifferently to him and shuts the door into the hall; then comes back and makes up the fire in the stove.*)

MRS. LINDE: Nora—who was that man?

NORA: A lawyer, of the name of Krogstad.

MRS. LINDE: Then it really was he.

NORA: Do you know the man?

MRS. LINDE: I used to—many years ago. At one time he was a solicitor's clerk in our town.

NORA: Yes, he was.

MRS. LINDE: He is greatly altered.

NORA: He made a very unhappy marriage.

MRS. LINDE: He is a widower now, isn't he?

NORA: With several children. There now, it is burning up. (*Shuts the door of the stove and moves the rocking-chair aside.*)

MRS. LINDE: They say he carries on various kinds of business.

NORA: Really! Perhaps he does; I don't know anything about it. But don't let us think of business; it is so tiresome.

DOCTOR RANK (*comes out of Helmer's study. Before he shuts the door he calls to him*): No, my dear fellow, I won't disturb you; I would rather go in to your wife for a little while. (*Shuts the door and sees Mrs. Linde.*) I beg your pardon; I am afraid I am disturbing you too.

NORA: No, not at all. (*Introducing him.*) Doctor Rank, Mrs. Linde.

RANK: I have often heard Mrs. Linde's name mentioned here. I think I passed you on the stairs when I arrived, Mrs. Linde?

MRS. LINDE: Yes, I go up very slowly; I can't manage stairs well.

RANK: Ah! some slight internal weakness?

MRS. LINDE: No, the fact is I have been overworking myself.

RANK: Nothing more than that? Then I suppose you have come to town to amuse yourself with our entertainments?

MRS. LINDE: I have come to look for work.

RANK: Is that a good cure for overwork?

MRS. LINDE: One must live, Doctor Rank.

RANK: Yes, the general opinion seems to be that it is necessary.

NORA: Look here, Doctor Rank—you know you want to live.

RANK: Certainly. However wretched I may feel, I want to prolong the agony as long as possible. All my patients are like that. And so are those who are morally diseased; one of them, and a bad case too, is at this very moment with Helmer—

MRS. LINDE (*sadly*): Ah!

NORA: Whom do you mean?

RANK: A lawyer of the name of Krogstad, a fellow you don't know at all. He suffers from a diseased moral character, Mrs. Helmer; but even he began talking of its being highly important that he should live.

NORA: Did he? What did he want to speak to Torvald about?

RANK: I have no idea; I only heard that it was something about the Bank.

NORA: I didn't know this—what's his name—Krogstad had anything to do with the Bank.

RANK: Yes, he has some sort of appointment there. (*To Mrs. Linde.*) I don't know whether you find also in your part of the world that there are certain people who go zealously snuffing about to smell out moral corruption, and, as soon as they have found some, put the person concerned into some lucrative position where they can keep their eye on him. Healthy natures are left out in the cold.

MRS. LINDE: Still I think the sick are those who most need taking care of.

RANK (*shrugging his shoulders*): Yes, there you are. That is the sentiment that is turning Society into a sick-house.

Nora, who has been absorbed in her thoughts, breaks out into smothered laughter and claps her hands.

RANK: Why do you laugh at that? Have you any notion what Society really is?

NORA: What do I care about tiresome Society? I am laughing at something quite different, something extremely amusing. Tell me, Doctor Rank, are all the people who are employed in the Bank dependent on Torvald now?

RANK: Is that what you find so extremely amusing?

NORA (*smiling and humming*): That's my affair! (*Walking about the room.*) It's perfectly glorious to think that we have—that Torvald has so much power over so many people. (*Takes the packet from her pocket.*) Doctor Rank, what do you say to a macaroon?

RANK: What, macaroons? I thought they were forbidden here.

NORA: Yes, but these are some Christine gave me.

MRS. LINDE: What! I?—

NORA: Oh, well, don't be alarmed! You couldn't know that Torvald had forbidden them. I must tell you that he is afraid they will spoil my teeth. But, bah!—once in a way—That's so, isn't it, Doctor Rank? By your leave! (*Puts a macaroon into his mouth.*) You must have one too, Christine. And I shall have one, just a little one—or at most two. (*Walking about.*) I am tremendously happy. There is just one thing in the world now that I should dearly love to do.

RANK: Well, what is that?

NORA: It's something I should dearly love to say, if Torvald could hear me.

RANK: Well, why can't you say it?

NORA: No, I daren't; it's so shocking.

MRS. LINDE: Shocking?

RANK: Well, I should not advise you to say it. Still, with us you might. What is it you would so much like to say if Torvald could hear you?

NORA: I should just love to say—Well, I'm damned!

RANK: Are you mad?

MRS. LINDE: Nora, dear—!

RANK: Say it, here he is!

NORA (*hiding the packet*): Hush! Hush! Hush! (*Helmer comes out of his room, with his coat over his arm and his hat in his hand.*)

NORA: Well, Torvald dear, have you got rid of him?

HELMER: Yes, he has just gone.

NORA: Let me introduce you—this is Christine, who has come to town.

HELMER: Christine—? Excuse me, but I don't know—

NORA: Mrs. Linde, dear; Christine Linde.

HELMER: Of course. A school friend of my wife's, I presume?

MRS. LINDE: Yes, we have known each other since then.

NORA: And just think, she has taken a long journey in order to see you.

HELMER: What do you mean?

MRS. LINDE: No, really, I—

NORA: Christine is tremendously clever at book-keeping, and she is frightfully anxious to work under some clever man, so as to perfect herself—

HELMER: Very sensible, Mrs. Linde.

NORA: And when she heard you had been appointed manager of the Bank—the news was telegraphed, you know—she travelled here as quick as she could. Torvald, I am sure you will be able to do something for Christine, for my sake, won't you?

HELMER: Well, it is not altogether impossible. I presume you are a widow, Mrs. Linde?

MRS. LINDE: Yes.

HELMER: And have had some experience of book-keeping?

MRS. LINDE: Yes, a fair amount.

HELMER: Ah! well, it's very likely I may be able to find something for you—

NORA (*clapping her hands*): What did I tell you? What did I tell you?

HELMER: You have just come at a fortunate moment, Mrs. Linde.

MRS. LINDE: How am I to thank you?

HELMER: There is no need. (*Puts on his coat.*) But to-day you must excuse me—

RANK: Wait a minute; I will come with you. (*Brings his fur coat from the hall and warms it at the fire.*)

NORA: Don't be long away, Torvald dear.

HELMER: About an hour, not more.

NORA: Are you going too, Christine?

MRS. LINDE (*putting on her cloak*): Yes, I must go and look for a room.

HELMER: Oh, well then, we can walk down the street together.

NORA (*helping her*): What a pity it is we are so short of space here; I am afraid it is impossible for us—

MRS. LINDE: Please don't think of it! Good-bye, Nora dear, and many thanks.

NORA: Good-bye for the present. Of course you will come back this evening. And you too, Dr. Rank. What do you say? If you are well enough? Oh, you must be! Wrap yourself up well. (*They go to the door all talking together. Children's voices are heard on the staircase.*)

NORA: There they are! There they are! (*She runs to open the door. The Nurse comes in with the children.*) Come in! Come in! (*Stoops and kisses them.*) Oh, you sweet blessings! Look at them, Christine! Aren't they darlings?

RANK: Don't let us stand here in the draught.

HELMER: Come along, Mrs. Linde; the place will only be bearable for a mother now!

Rank, Helmer, and Mrs. Linde go downstairs. The Nurse comes forward with the children; Nora shuts the hall door.

NORA: How fresh and well you look! Such red cheeks like apples and roses. (*The children all talk at once while she speaks to them.*) Have you had great fun? That's splendid! What, you pulled both Emmy and Bob along on the sledge?—both at once?—that was good. You are a clever boy, Ivar. Let me take her for a little, Anne. My sweet little baby doll! (*Takes the baby from the Maid and dances it up and down.*) Yes, yes, mother will dance with Bob too. What! Have you been snowballing? I wish I had been there too! No, no, I will take their things off, Anne; please let me do it, it is such fun. Go in now, you look half frozen. There is some hot coffee for you on the stove.

The Nurse goes into the room on the left. Nora takes off the children's things and throws them about, while they all talk to her at once.

NORA: Really! Did a big dog run after you? But it didn't bite you? No, dogs don't bite nice little dolly children. You mustn't look at the parcels, Ivar. What are they? Ah, I daresay you would like to know. No, no—it's something nasty! Come, let us have a game! What shall we play at? Hide and Seek? Yes, we'll play Hide and Seek. Bob shall hide first. Must I hide? Very well, I'll hide first. (*She and the children laugh and shout, and romp in and out of the room; at last Nora hides under the table, the children rush in and out for her, but do not see her; they hear her smothered laughter, run to the table, lift up the cloth and find her. Shouts of laughter. She crawls forward and pretends to frighten them. Fresh laughter. Meanwhile there has been a knock at the hall door, but none of them has noticed it. The door is half opened, and Krogstad appears. He waits a little; the game goes on.*)

KROGSTAD: Excuse me, Mrs. Helmer.

NORA (*with a stifled cry, turns round and gets up on to her knees*): Ah! what do you want?

KROGSTAD: Excuse me, the outer door was ajar; I suppose someone forgot to shut it.

NORA (*rising*): My husband is out, Mr Krogstad.

KROGSTAD: I know that.

NORA: What do you want here, then?

KROGSTAD: A word with you.

NORA: With me?—(*To the children, gently.*) Go in to nurse. What? No, the strange man won't do mother any harm. When he has gone we will have another game. (*She takes the children into the room on the left, and shuts the door after them.*) You want to speak to me?

KROGSTAD: Yes, I do.

NORA: To-day? It is not the first of the month yet.

KROGSTAD: No, it is Christmas Eve, and it will depend on yourself what sort of a Christmas you will spend.

NORA: What do you mean? To-day it is absolutely impossible for me—

KROGSTAD: We won't talk about that until later on. This is something different. I presume you can give me a moment?

NORA: Yes—yes, I can—although—

KROGSTAD: Good. I was in Olsen's Restaurant and saw your husband going down the street—

NORA: Yes?

KROGSTAD: With a lady.

NORA: What then?

KROGSTAD: May I make so bold as to ask if it was a Mrs. Linde?

NORA: It was.

KROGSTAD: Just arrived in town?

NORA: Yes, to-day.

KROGSTAD: She is a great friend of yours, isn't she?

NORA: She is. But I don't see—

KROGSTAD: I knew her too, once upon a time.

NORA: I am aware of that.

KROGSTAD: Are you? So you know all about it; I thought as much. Then I can ask you, without beating about the bush—is Mrs. Linde to have an appointment in the Bank?

NORA: What right have you to question me, Mr. Krogstad?—You, one of my husband's subordinates! But since you ask, you shall know. Yes, Mrs. Linde *is* to have an appointment. And it was I who pleaded her cause, Mr. Krogstad, let me tell you that.

KROGSTAD: I was right in what I thought, then.

NORA (*walking up and down the stage*): Sometimes one has a tiny little bit of influence, I should hope. Because one is a woman, it does not necessarily follow that—. When anyone is in a subordinate position, Mr. Krogstad, they should really be careful to avoid offending anyone who—who—

KROGSTAD: Who has influence?

NORA: Exactly.

KROGSTAD (*changing his tone*): Mrs. Helmer, you will be so good as to use your influence on my behalf.

NORA: What? What do you mean?

KROGSTAD: You will be so kind as to see that I am allowed to keep my subordinate position in the Bank.

NORA: What do you mean by that? Who proposes to take your post away from you?

KROGSTAD: Oh, there is no necessity to keep up the pretence of ignorance. I can quite understand that your friend is not very anxious to expose herself to the chance of rubbing shoulders with me; and I quite understand, too, whom I have to thank for being turned off.

NORA: But I assure you—

KROGSTAD: Very likely; but, to come to the point, the time has come when I should advise you to use your influence to prevent that.

NORA: But, Mr. Krogstad, I *have* no influence.

KROGSTAD: Haven't you? I thought you said yourself just now—

NORA: Naturally I did not mean you to put that construction on it. What should make you think I have any influence of that kind with my husband?

KROGSTAD: Oh, I have known your husband from our student days. I don't suppose he is any more unassailable than other husbands.

NORA: If you speak slightingly of my husband, I shall turn you out of the house.

KROGSTAD: You are bold, Mrs. Helmer.

NORA: I am not afraid of you any longer. As soon as the New Year comes, I shall in a very short time be free of the whole thing.

KROGSTAD (*controlling himself*): Listen to me, Mrs. Helmer. If necessary, I am prepared to fight for my small post in the Bank as if I were fighting for my life.

NORA: So it seems.

KROGSTAD: It is not only for the sake of the money; indeed, that weighs least with me in the matter. There is another reason—well, I may as well tell you. My position is this. I daresay you know, like everybody else, that once, many years ago, I was guilty of an indiscretion.

NORA: I think I have heard something of the kind.

KROGSTAD: The matter never came into court; but every way seemed to be closed to me after that. So I took to the business that you know of. I had to do something; and, honestly, I don't think I've been one of the worst. But now I must cut myself free from all that. My sons are growing up; for their sake I must try and win back as much respect as I can in the town. This post in the Bank was like the first step up for me—and now your husband is going to kick me downstairs again into the mud.

NORA: But you must believe me, Mr. Krogstad; it is not in my power to help you at all.

KROGSTAD: Then it is because you haven't the will; but I have means to compel you.

NORA: You don't mean that you will tell my husband that I owe you money?

KROGSTAD: Hm!—suppose I were to tell him?

NORA: It would be perfectly infamous of you. (*Sobbing.*) To think of his learning my secret, which has been my joy and pride, in such an ugly, clumsy way—that he should learn it from you! And it would put me in a horribly disagreeable position—

KROGSTAD: Only disagreeable?

NORA (*impetuously*): Well, do it, then!—and it will be the worse for you. My husband will see for himself what a blackguard you are, and you certainly won't keep your post then.

KROGSTAD: I asked you if it was only a disagreeable scene at home that you were afraid of?

NORA: If my husband does get to know of it, of course he will at once pay you what is still owing, and we shall have nothing more to do with you.

KROGSTAD (*coming a step nearer*): Listen to me, Mrs. Helmer. Either you have a very bad memory or you know very little of business. I shall be obliged to remind you of a few details.

NORA: What do you mean?

KROGSTAD: When your husband was ill, you came to me to borrow two hundred and fifty pounds.

NORA: I didn't know anyone else to go to.

KROGSTAD: I promised to get you that amount—

NORA: Yes, and you did so.

KROGSTAD: I promised to get you that amount, on certain conditions. Your mind was so taken up with your husband's illness, and you were so anxious to get the money for your journey, that you seem to have paid no attention to the conditions of our bargain. Therefore it will not be amiss if I remind you of them. Now, I promised to get the money on the security of a bond which I drew up.

NORA: Yes, and which I signed.

KROGSTAD: Good. But below your signature there were a few lines constituting your father a surety for the money; those lines your father should have signed.

NORA: Should? He did sign them.

KROGSTAD: I had left the date blank; that is to say, your father should himself have inserted the date on which he signed the paper. Do you remember that?

NORA: Yes, I think I remember—

KROGSTAD: Then I gave you the bond to send by post to your father. Is that not so?

NORA: Yes.

KROGSTAD: And you naturally did so at once, because five or six days afterwards you brought me the bond with your father's signature. And then I gave you the money.

NORA: Well, haven't I been paying it off regularly?

KROGSTAD: Fairly so, yes. But—to come back to the matter in hand—that must have been a very trying time for you, Mrs. Helmer.

NORA: It was, indeed.

KROGSTAD: Your father was very ill, wasn't he?

NORA: He was very near his end.

KROGSTAD: And he died soon afterwards?

NORA: Yes.

KROGSTAD: Tell me, Mrs. Helmer, can you by any chance remember what day your father died?—on what day of the month, I mean.

NORA: Papa died on the 29th of September.

KROGSTAD: That is correct; I have ascertained it for myself. And, as that is so, there is a discrepancy (*taking a paper from his pocket*) which I cannot account for.

NORA: What discrepancy? I don't know—

KROGSTAD: The discrepancy consists, Mrs. Helmer, in the fact that your father signed this bond three days after his death.

NORA: What do you mean? I don't understand—

KROGSTAD: Your father died on the 29th of September. But, look here; your father has dated his signature the 2nd of October. It is a discrepancy, isn't it? (*Nora is silent.*) Can you explain it to me? (*Nora is still silent.*) It is a remarkable thing, too, that the words "2nd of October," as well as the year, are not written in your father's handwriting but in one that I think I know. Well, of course it can be explained; your father may have forgotten to date his signature, and someone else may have dated it haphazard before they knew of his death. There is no harm in that. It all depends on the signature of the name; and *that* is genuine, I suppose, Mrs. Helmer? It was your father himself who signed his name here?

NORA (*after a short pause, throws her head up and looks defiantly at him*): No, it was not. It was I that wrote papa's name.

KROGSTAD: Are you aware that is a dangerous confession?

NORA: In what way? You shall have your money soon.

KROGSTAD: Let me ask you a question; why did you not send the paper to your father?

NORA: It was impossible; papa was so ill. If I had asked him for his signature, I should have had to tell him what the money was to be used for; and when he was so ill himself I couldn't tell him that my husband's life was in danger—it was impossible.

KROGSTAD: It would have been better for you if you had given up your trip abroad.

NORA: No, that was impossible. That trip was to save my husband's life; I couldn't give that up.

KROGSTAD: But did it never occur to you that you were committing a fraud on me?

NORA: I couldn't take that into account; I didn't trouble myself about you at all. I couldn't bear you, because you put so many heartless difficulties in my way, although you knew what a dangerous condition my husband was in.

KROGSTAD: Mrs. Helmer, you evidently do not realise clearly what it is that you have been guilty of. But I can assure you that my one false step, which lost me all my reputation, was nothing more or nothing worse than what you have done.

NORA: You? Do you ask me to believe that you were brave enough to run a risk to save your wife's life?

KROGSTAD: The law cares nothing about motives.

NORA: Then it must be a very foolish law.

KROGSTAD: Foolish or not, it is the law by which you will be judged, if I produce this paper in court.

NORA: I don't believe it. Is a daughter not to be allowed to spare her dying father anxiety and care? Is a wife not to be allowed to save her husband's life? I don't know much about law; but I am certain that there must be laws permitting such things as that. Have you no knowledge of such laws—you who are a lawyer? You must be a very poor lawyer, Mr. Krogstad.

KROGSTAD: Maybe. But matters of business—such business as you and I have had together—do you think I don't understand that? Very well. Do as you please. But let me tell you this—if I lose my position a second time, you shall lose yours with me. (*He bows, and goes out through the hall.*)

NORA (*appears buried in thought for a short time, then tosses her head*): Nonsense! Trying to frighten me like that!—I am not so silly as he thinks. (*Begins to busy herself putting the children's things in order.*) And yet—? No, it's impossible! I did it for love's sake.

CHILDREN (*in the doorway on the left*): Mother, the stranger man has gone out through the gate.

NORA: Yes, dears, I know. But, don't tell anyone about the stranger man. Do you hear? Not even papa.

CHILDREN: No, mother; but will you come and play again?

NORA: No, no,—not now.

CHILDREN: But, mother, you promised us.

NORA: Yes, but I can't now. Run away in; I have such a lot to do. Run away in, my sweet little darlings. (*She gets them into the room by degrees and shuts the door on them; then sits down on the sofa, takes up a piece of needlework and sews a few stitches, but soon stops.*) No! (*Throws down the work, gets up, goes to the hall door and calls out.*) Helen! bring the Tree in. (*Goes to the table on the left, opens a drawer, and stops again.*) No, no! it is quite impossible!

MAID (*coming in with the Tree*): Where shall I put it, ma'am?

NORA: Here, in the middle of the floor.

MAID: Shall I get you anything else?

NORA: No, thank you. I have all I want. (*Exit Maid.*)

NORA (*begins dressing the tree*): A candle here—and flowers here—. The horrible man! It's all nonsense—there's nothing wrong. The Tree shall be splendid! I will do everything I can think of to please you, Torvald!—I will sing for you, dance for you—(*Helmer comes in with some papers under his arm.*) Oh! are you back already?

HELMER: Yes. Has anyone been here?

NORA: Here? No.

HELMER: That is strange. I saw Krogstad going out of the gate.

NORA: Did you? Oh yes, I forgot, Krogstad was here for a moment.

HELMER: Nora, I can see from your manner that he has been here begging you to say a good word for him.

NORA: Yes.

HELMER: And you were to appear to do it of your own accord; you were to conceal from me the fact of his having been here; didn't he beg that of you too?

NORA: Yes, Torvald, but—

HELMER: Nora, Nora, and you would be a party to that sort of thing? To have any talk with a man like that, and give him any sort of promise? And to tell me a lie into the bargain?

NORA: A lie—?

HELMER: Didn't you tell me no one had been here? (*Shakes his finger at her.*) My little song-bird must never do that again. A song-bird must have a clean beak to chirp with—no false notes! (*Puts his arm around her waist.*) That is so, isn't it? Yes, I am sure it is. (*Lets her go.*) We will say no more about it. (*Sits down by the stove.*) How warm and snug it is here! (*Turns over his papers.*)

NORA (*after a short pause, during which she busies herself with the Christmas Tree*): Torvald!

HELMER: Yes.

NORA: I am looking forward tremendously to the fancy-dress ball at the Stenborgs' the day after to-morrow.

HELMER: And I am tremendously curious to see what you are going to surprise me with.

NORA: It was very silly of me to want to do that.

HELMER: What do you mean?

NORA: I can't hit upon anything that will do; everything I think of seems so silly and insignificant.

HELMER: Does my little Nora acknowledge that at last?

NORA (*standing behind his chair with her arms on the back of it*): Are you very busy, Torvald?

HELMER: Well—

NORA: What are all those papers?

HELMER: Bank business.

NORA: Already?

HELMER: I have got authority from the retiring manager to undertake the necessary changes in the staff and in the rearrangement of the work; and I must make use of the Christmas week for that, so as to have everything in order for the new year.

NORA: Then that was why this poor Krogstad—

HELMER: Hm!

NORA (*leans against the back of his chair and strokes his hair*): If you hadn't been so busy I should have asked you a tremendously big favour, Torvald.

HELMER: What is that? Tell me.

NORA: There is no one has such good taste as you. And I do so want to look nice at the fancy-dress ball. Torvald, couldn't you take me in hand and decide what I shall go as, and what sort of a dress I shall wear?

HELMER: Aha! so my obstinate little woman is obliged to get someone to come to her rescue?

NORA: Yes, Torvald, I can't get along a bit without your help.

HELMER: Very well, I will think it over, we shall manage to hit upon something.

NORA: That is nice of you. (*Goes to the Christmas Tree. A short pause.*) How pretty the red flowers look—. But, tell me, was it really something very bad that this Krogstad was guilty of?

HELMER: He forged someone's name. Have you any idea what that means?

NORA: Isn't it possible that he was driven to do it by necessity?

HELMER: Yes; or, as in so many cases, by imprudence. I am not so heartless as to condemn a man altogether because of a single false step of that kind.

NORA: No, you wouldn't, would you, Torvald?

HELMER: Many a man has been able to retrieve his character, if he has openly confessed his fault and taken his punishment.

NORA: Punishment—?

HELMER: But Krogstad did nothing of that sort; he got himself out of it by a cunning trick, and that is why he has gone under altogether.

NORA: But do you think it would—?

HELMER: Just think how a guilty man like that has to lie and play the hypocrite with every one, how he has to wear a mask in the presence of those near and dear to him, even before his own wife and children. And about the children—that is the most terrible part of it all, Nora.

NORA: How?

HELMER: Because such an atmosphere of lies infects and poisons the whole life of a home. Each breath the children take in such a house is full of the germs of evil.

NORA (*coming nearer him*): Are you sure of that?

HELMER: My dear, I have often seen it in the course of my life as a lawyer. Almost everyone who has gone to the bad early in life has had a deceitful mother.

NORA: Why do you only say—mother?

HELMER: It seems most commonly to be the mother's influence, though naturally a bad father's would have the same result. Every lawyer is familiar with the fact. This Krogstad, now, has been persistently poisoning his own children with lies and dissimulation; that is why I say he has lost all moral character. (*Holds out his hands to her.*) That is why my sweet little

Nora must promise me not to plead his cause. Give me your hand on it. Come, come, what is this? Give me your hand. There now, that's settled. I assure you it would be quite impossible for me to work with him; I literally feel physically ill when I am in the company of such people.

NORA (*takes her hand out of his and goes to the opposite side of the Christmas Tree*): How hot it is in here; and I have such a lot to do.

HELMER (*getting up and putting his papers in order*): Yes, and I must try and read through some of these before dinner; and I must think about your costume, too. And it is just possible I may have something ready in gold paper to hang up on the Tree. (*Puts his hand on her head.*) My precious little singing-bird! (*He goes into his room and shuts the door after him.*)

NORA (*after a pause, whispers*): No, no—it isn't true. It's impossible; it must be impossible.

The Nurse opens the door on the left.

NURSE: The little ones are begging so hard to be allowed to come in to mamma.

NORA: No, no, no! Don't let them come in to me! You stay with them, Anne.

NURSE: Very well, ma'am. (*Shuts the door.*)

NORA (*pale with terror*): Deprave my little children? Poison my home? (*A short pause. Then she tosses her head.*) It's not true. It can't possibly be true.

ACT II

THE SAME SCENE: *The Christmas Tree is in the corner by the piano, stripped of its ornaments and with burnt-down candle-ends on its dishevelled branches. Nora's cloak and hat are lying on the sofa. She is alone in the room, walking about uneasily. She stops by the sofa and takes up her cloak.*

NORA (*drops her cloak*): Someone is coming now! (*Goes to the door and listens.*) No—it is no one. Of course, no one will come to-day, Christmas Day—nor to-morrow either. But, perhaps—(*opens the door and looks out*). No, nothing in the letter-box; it is quite empty. (*Comes forward.*) What rubbish! of course he can't be in earnest about it. Such a thing couldn't happen; it is impossible—I have three little children.

Enter the Nurse from the room on the left, carrying a big cardboard box.

NURSE: At last I have found the box with the fancy dress.

NORA: Thanks; put it on the table.

NURSE (*doing so*): But it is very much in want of mending.

NORA: I should like to tear it into a hundred thousand pieces.

NURSE: What an idea! It can easily be put in order—just a little patience.

NORA: Yes, I will go and get Mrs. Linde to come and help me with it.

NURSE: What, out again? In this horrible weather? You will catch cold, ma'am, and make yourself ill.

NORA: Well, worse than that might happen. How are the children?

NURSE: The poor little souls are playing with their Christmas presents, but—

NORA: Do they ask much for me?

NURSE: You see, they are so accustomed to have their mamma with them.

NORA: Yes, but, nurse, I shall not be able to be so much with them now as I was before.

NURSE: Oh well, young children easily get accustomed to anything.

NORA: Do you think so? Do you think they would forget their mother if she went away altogether?

NURSE: Good heavens!—went away altogether?

NORA: Nurse, I want you to tell me something I have often wondered about—how could you have the heart to put your own child out among strangers?

NURSE: I was obliged to, if I wanted to be little Nora's nurse.

NORA: Yes, but how could you be willing to do it?

NURSE: What, when I was going to get such a good place by it? A poor girl who has got into trouble should be glad to. Besides, that wicked man didn't do a single thing for me.

NORA: But I suppose your daughter has quite forgotten you.

NURSE: No, indeed she hasn't. She wrote to me when she was confirmed, and when she was married.

NORA (*putting her arms round her neck*): Dear old Anne, you were a good mother to me when I was little.

NURSE: Little Nora, poor dear, had no other mother but me.

NORA: And if my little ones had no other mother, I am sure you would—What nonsense I am talking! (*Opens the box.*) Go in to them. Now I must—. You will see to-morrow how charming I shall look.

NURSE: I am sure there will be no one at the ball so charming as you, ma'am. (*Goes into the room on the left.*)

NORA (*begins to unpack the box, but soon pushes it away from her*): If only I dared go out. If only no one would come. If only I could be sure nothing would happen here in the meantime. Stuff and nonsense! No one will come. Only I mustn't think about it. I will brush my muff. What lovely, lovely gloves! Out of my thoughts, out of my thoughts! One, two, three, four, five, six—(*Screams.*) Ah! there is someone coming—. (*Makes a movement towards the door, but stands irresolute.*)

Enter Mrs. Linde from the hall, where she has taken off her cloak and hat.

NORA: Oh, it's you, Christine. There is no one else out there, is there? How good of you to come!

MRS. LINDE: I heard you were up asking for me.

NORA: Yes, I was passing by. As a matter of fact, it is something you could help me with. Let us sit down here on the sofa. Look here. To-morrow evening there is to be a fancy-dress ball at the Stenborgs', who live above us; and Torvald wants me to go as a Neapolitan fisher-girl, and dance the Tarantella that I learned at Capri.

MRS. LINDE: I see; you are going to keep up the character.

NORA: Yes, Torvald wants me to. Look, here is the dress; Torvald had it made for me there, but now it is all so torn, and I haven't any idea—

MRS. LINDE: We will easily put that right. It is only some of the trimming come unsewn here and there. Needle and thread? Now then, that's all we want.

NORA: It *is* nice of you.

MRS. LINDE (*sewing*): So you are going to be dressed up to-morrow, Nora. I will tell you what — I shall come in for a moment and see you in your fine feathers. But I have completely forgotten to thank you for a delightful evening yesterday.

NORA (*gets up, and crosses the stage*): Well, I don't think yesterday was as pleasant as usual. You ought to have come to town a little earlier, Christine. Certainly Torvald does understand how to make a house dainty and attractive.

MRS. LINDE: And so do you, it seems to me; you are not your father's daughter for nothing. But tell me, is Doctor Rank always as depressed as he was yesterday?

NORA: No; yesterday it was very noticeable. I must tell you that he suffers from a very dangerous disease. He has consumption of the spine, poor creature. His father was a horrible man who committed all sorts of excesses; and that is why his son was sickly from childhood, do you understand?

MRS. LINDE (*dropping her sewing*): But, my dearest Nora, how do you know anything about such things?

NORA (*walking about*): Pooh! When you have three children, you get visits now and then from — from married women, who know something of medical matters, and they talk about one thing and another.

MRS. LINDE: (*goes on sewing. A short silence*) Does Doctor Rank come here everyday?

NORA: Everyday regularly. He is Torvald's most intimate friend, and a great friend of mine too. He is just like one of the family.

MRS. LINDE: But tell me this — is he perfectly sincere? I mean, isn't he the kind of man that is very anxious to make himself agreeable?

NORA: Not in the least. What makes you think that?

MRS. LINDE: When you introduced him to me yesterday, he declared he had often heard my name mentioned in this house; but afterwards I noticed that your husband hadn't the slightest idea who I was. So how could Doctor Rank — ?

NORA: That is quite right, Christine. Torvald is so absurdly fond of me that he wants me absolutely to himself, as he says. At first he used to seem almost jealous if I mentioned any of the dear folk at home, so naturally I gave up doing so. But I often talk about such things with Doctor Rank, because he likes hearing about them.

MRS. LINDE: Listen to me, Nora. You are still very like a child in many things, and I am older than you in many ways and have a little more experience. Let me tell you this — you ought to make an end of it with Doctor Rank.

NORA: What ought I to make an end of?

MRS. LINDE: Of two things, I think. Yesterday you talked some nonsense about a rich admirer who was to leave you money —

NORA: An admirer who doesn't exist, unfortunately! But what then?

MRS. LINDE: Is Doctor Rank a man of means?

NORA: Yes, he is.

MRS. LINDE: And has no one to provide for?

NORA: No, no one; but —

MRS. LINDE: And comes here everyday?

NORA: Yes, I told you so.

MRS. LINDE: But how can this well-bred man be so tactless?

NORA: I don't understand you at all.

MRS. LINDE: Don't prevaricate, Nora. Do you suppose I don't guess who lent you the two hundred and fifty pounds?

NORA: Are you out of your senses? How can you think of such a thing! A friend of ours, who comes here everyday! Do you realise what a horribly painful position that would be?

MRS. LINDE: Then it really isn't he?

NORA: No, certainly not. It would never have entered into my head for a moment. Besides, he had no money to lend then; he came into his money afterwards.

MRS. LINDE: Well, I think that was lucky for you, my dear Nora.

NORA: No, it would never have come into my head to ask Doctor Rank. Although I am quite sure that if I had asked him—

MRS. LINDE: But of course you won't.

NORA: Of course not. I have no reason to think it could possibly be necessary. But I am quite sure that if I told Doctor Rank—

MRS. LINDE: Behind your husband's back?

NORA: I must make an end of it with the other one, and that will be behind his back too. I *must* make an end of it with him.

MRS. LINDE: Yes, that is what I told you yesterday, but—

NORA (*walking up and down*): A man can put a thing like that straight much easier than a woman—

MRS. LINDE: One's husband, yes.

NORA: Nonsense! (*Standing still.*) When you pay off a debt you get your bond back, don't you?

MRS. LINDE: Yes, as a matter of course.

NORA: And can tear it into a hundred thousand pieces, and burn it up—the nasty dirty paper!

MRS. LINDE (*looks hard at her, lays down her sewing and gets up slowly*): Nora, you are concealing something from me.

NORA: Do I look as if I were?

MRS. LINDE: Something has happened to you since yesterday morning. Nora, what is it?

NORA (*going nearer to her*): Christine! (*Listens.*) Hush! there's Torvald come home. Do you mind going in to the children for the present? Torvald can't bear to see dressmaking going on. Let Anne help you.

MRS. LINDE (*gathering some of the things together*): Certainly—but I am not going away from here until we have had it out with one another. (*She goes into the room on the left, as Helmer comes in from the hall.*)

NORA (*going up to Helmer*): I have wanted you so much, Torvald dear.

HELMER: Was that the dressmaker?

NORA: No, it was Christine; she is helping me to put my dress in order. You will see I shall look quite smart.

HELMER: Wasn't that a happy thought of mine, now?

NORA: Splendid! But don't you think it is nice of me, too, to do as you wish?

HELMER: Nice?—because you do as your husband wishes? Well, well, you little rogue, I am sure you did not mean it in that way. But I am not going to disturb you; you will want to be trying on your dress, I expect.

NORA: I suppose you are going to work.

HELMER: Yes. (*Shows her a bundle of papers.*) Look at that. I have just been into the bank. (*Turns to go into his room.*)

NORA: Torvald.

HELMER: Yes.

NORA: If your little squirrel were to ask you for something very, very prettily—?

HELMER: What then?

NORA: Would you do it?

HELMER: I should like to hear what it is, first.

NORA: Your squirrel would run about and do all her tricks if you would be nice, and do what she wants.

HELMER: Speak plainly.

NORA: Your skylark would chirp about in every room, with her song rising and falling—

HELMER: Well, my skylark does that anyhow.

NORA: I would play the fairy and dance for you in the moonlight, Torvald.

HELMER: Nora—you surely don't mean that request you made to me this morning?

NORA (*going near him*): Yes, Torvald, I beg you so earnestly—

HELMER: Have you really the courage to open up that question again?

NORA: Yes, dear, you *must* do as I ask; you *must* let Krogstad keep his post in the bank.

HELMER: My dear Nora, it is his post that I have arranged Mrs. Linde shall have.

NORA: Yes, you have been awfully kind about that; but you could just as well dismiss some other clerk instead of Krogstad.

HELMER: This is simply incredible obstinacy! Because you chose to give him a thoughtless promise that you would speak for him, I am expected to—

NORA: That isn't the reason, Torvald. It is for your own sake. This fellow writes in the most scurrilous newspapers; you have told me so yourself. He can do you an unspeakable amount of harm. I am frightened to death of him—

HELMER: Ah, I understand; it is recollections of the past that scare you.

NORA: What do you mean?

HELMER: Naturally you are thinking of your father.

NORA: Yes—yes, of course. Just recall to your mind what these malicious creatures wrote in the papers about papa, and how horribly they slandered him. I believe they would have procured his dismissal if the Department had not sent you over to inquire into it, and if you had not been so kindly disposed and helpful to him.

HELMER: My little Nora, there is an important difference between your father and me. Your father's reputation as a public official was not above suspicion. Mine is, and I hope it will continue to be so, as long as I hold my office.

NORA: You never can tell what mischief these men may contrive. We ought to be so well off, so snug and happy here in our peaceful home, and have no cares—you and I and the children, Torvald! That is why I beg you so earnestly—

HELMER: And it is just by interceding for him that you make it impossible for me to keep him. It is already known at the Bank that I mean to dismiss Krogstad. Is it to get about now that the new manager has changed his mind at his wife's bidding—

NORA: And what if it did?

HELMER: Of course!—if only this obstinate little person can get her way! Do you suppose I am going to make myself ridiculous before my whole staff, to let people think that I am a man to be swayed by all sorts of outside influence? I should very soon feel the consequences of it, I can tell you! And besides, there is one thing that makes it quite impossible for me to have Krogstad in the Bank as long as I am manager.

NORA: Whatever is that?

HELMER: His moral failings I might perhaps have overlooked, if necessary—

NORA: Yes, you could—couldn't you?

HELMER: And I hear he is a good worker, too. But I knew him when we were boys. It was one of those rash friendships that so often prove an incubus in afterlife. I may as well tell you plainly, we were once on very intimate terms with one another. But this tactless fellow lays no restraint on himself when other people are present. On the contrary, he thinks it gives him the right to adopt a familiar tone with me, and every minute it is "I say, Helmer, old fellow!" and that sort of thing. I assure you it is extremely painful for me. He would make my position in the Bank intolerable.

NORA: Torvald, I don't believe you mean that.

HELMER: Don't you? Why not?

NORA: Because it is such a narrow-minded way of looking at things.

HELMER: What are you saying? Narrow-minded? Do you think I am narrow-minded?

NORA: No, just the opposite, dear—and it is exactly for that reason.

HELMER: It's the same thing. You say my point of view is narrow-minded, so I must be so too. Narrow-minded! Very well—I must put an end to this. (*Goes to the hall door and calls.*) Helen!

NORA: What are you going to do?

HELMER (*looking among his papers*): Settle it. (*Enter Maid.*) Look here; take this letter and go downstairs with it at once. Find a messenger and tell him to deliver it, and be quick. The address is on it, and here is the money.

MAID: Very well, sir. (*Exit with the letter.*)

HELMER (*putting his papers together*): Now then, little Miss Obstinate.

NORA (*breathlessly*): Torvald—what was that letter?

HELMER: Krogstad's dismissal.

NORA: Call her back, Torvald! There is still time. Oh Torvald, call her back! Do it for my sake—for your own sake—for the children's sake! Do you hear me, Torvald? Call her back! You don't know what that letter can bring upon us.

HELMER: It's too late.

NORA: Yes, it's too late.

HELMER: My dear Nora, I can forgive the anxiety you are in, although really it is an insult to me. It is, indeed. Isn't it an insult to think that I should be afraid of a starving quill-driver's vengeance? But I forgive you nevertheless, because it is such eloquent witness to your great love for me. (*Takes her in his arms.*) And that is as it should be, my own darling Nora. Come what will, you may be sure I shall have both courage and strength if they be needed. You will see I am man enough to take everything upon myself.

NORA (*in a horror-stricken voice*): What do you mean by that?

HELMER: Everything, I say—

NORA (*recovering herself*): You will never have to do that.

HELMER: That's right. Well, we will share it, Nora, as man and wife should. That is how it shall be. (*Caressing her.*) Are you content now? There! there!—not these frightened dove's eyes! The whole thing is only the wildest fancy!—Now, you must go and play through the Tarantella and practise with your tambourine. I shall go into the inner office and shut the door, and I shall hear nothing; you can make as much noise as you please. (*Turns back at the door.*) And when Rank comes, tell him where he will find me. (*Nods to her, takes his papers and goes into his room, and shuts the door after him.*)

NORA (*bewildered with anxiety, stands as if rooted to the spot, and whispers*): He was capable of doing it. He will do it. He will do it in spite of everything.—No, not that! Never, never! Anything rather than that! Oh, for some help, some way out of it! (*The door-bell rings.*) Doctor Rank! Anything rather than that—anything, whatever it is! (*She puts her hands over her face, pulls herself together, goes to the door and opens it. Rank is standing without, hanging up his coat. During the following dialogue it begins to grow dark.*)

NORA: Good-day, Doctor Rank. I knew your ring. But you mustn't go in to Torvald now; I think he is busy with something.

RANK: And you?

NORA (*brings him in and shuts the door after him*): Oh, you know very well I always have time for you.

RANK: Thank you. I shall make use of as much of it as I can.

NORA: What do you mean by that? As much of it as you can?

RANK: Well, does that alarm you?

NORA: It was such a strange way of putting it. Is anything likely to happen?

RANK: Nothing but what I have long been prepared for. But I certainly didn't expect it to happen so soon.

NORA (*gripping him by the arm*): What have you found out? Doctor Rank, you must tell me.

RANK (*sitting down by the stove*): It is all up with me. And it can't be helped.

NORA (*with a sigh of relief*): Is it about yourself?

RANK: Who else? It is no use lying to one's self. I am the most wretched of all my patients, Mrs. Helmer. Lately I have been taking stock of my internal economy. Bankrupt! Probably within a month I shall lie rotting in the churchyard.

NORA: What an ugly thing to say!

RANK: The thing itself is cursedly ugly, and the worst of it is that I shall have to face so much more that is ugly before that. I shall only make one more examination of myself; when I have done that, I shall know pretty certainly when it will be that the horrors of dissolution will begin. There is something I want to tell you. Helmer's refined nature gives him an unconquerable disgust at everything that is ugly; I won't have him in my sick-room.

NORA: Oh, but, Doctor Rank—

RANK: I won't have him there. Not on any account. I bar my door to him. As soon as I am quite certain that the worst has come, I shall send you my card with a black cross on it, and then you will know that the loathsome end has begun.

NORA: You are quite absurd to-day. And I wanted you so much to be in a really good humour.

RANK: With death stalking beside me?—To have to pay this penalty for another man's sin? Is there any justice in that? And in every single family, in one way or another, some such inexorable retribution is being exacted—

NORA (*putting her hands over her ears*): Rubbish! Do talk of something cheerful.

RANK: Oh, it's a mere laughing matter, the whole thing. My poor innocent spine has to suffer for my father's youthful amusements.

NORA (*sitting at the table on the left*): I suppose you mean that he was too partial to asparagus and pâté de foie gras, don't you?

RANK: Yes, and to truffles.

NORA: Truffles, yes. And oysters too, I suppose?

RANK: Oysters, of course, that goes without saying.

NORA: And heaps of port and champagne. It is sad that all these nice things should take their revenge on our bones.

RANK: Especially that they should revenge themselves on the unlucky bones of those who have not had the satisfaction of enjoying them.

NORA: Yes, that's the saddest part of it all.

RANK (*with a searching look at her*): Hm!—

NORA (*after a short pause*): Why did you smile?

RANK: No, it was you that laughed.

NORA: No, it was you that smiled, Doctor Rank!

RANK (*rising*): You are a greater rascal than I thought.

NORA: I am in a silly mood to-day.

RANK: So it seems.

NORA (*putting her hands on his shoulders*): Dear, dear Doctor Rank, death mustn't take you away from Torvald and me.

RANK: It is a loss you would easily recover from. Those who are gone are soon forgotten.

NORA (*looking at him anxiously*): Do you believe that?

RANK: People form new ties, and then—

NORA: Who will form new ties?

RANK: Both you and Helmer, when I am gone. You yourself are already on the high road to it, I think. What did that Mrs. Linde want here last night?

NORA: Oho!—you don't mean to say you are jealous of poor Christine?

RANK: Yes, I am. She will be my successor in this house. When I am done for, this woman will—

NORA: Hush! don't speak so loud. She is in that room.

RANK: To-day again. There, you see.

NORA: She has only come to sew my dress for me. Bless my soul, how unreasonable you are! (*Sits down on the sofa.*) Be nice now, Doctor Rank, and to-morrow you will see how beautifully I shall dance, and you can imagine I am doing it all for you—and for Torvald too, of course. (*Takes various things out of the box.*) Doctor Rank, come and sit down here, and I will show you something.

RANK (*sitting down*): What is it?

NORA: Just look at those!

RANK: Silk stockings.

NORA: Flesh-coloured. Aren't they lovely? It is so dark here now, but to-morrow—. No, no, no! you must only look at the feet. Oh well, you may have leave to look at the legs too.

RANK: Hm!—

NORA: Why are you looking so critical? Don't you think they will fit me?

RANK: I have no means of forming an opinion about that.

NORA (*looks at him for a moment*): For shame! (*Hits him lightly on the ear with the stockings.*) That's to punish you. (*Folds them up again.*)

RANK: And what other nice things am I to be allowed to see?

NORA: Not a single thing more, for being so naughty. (*She looks among the things, humming to herself.*)

RANK (*after a short silence*): When I am sitting here, talking to you as intimately as this, I cannot imagine for a moment what would have become of me if I had never come into this house.

NORA (*smiling*): I believe you do feel thoroughly at home with us.

RANK (*in a lower voice, looking straight in front of him*): And to be obliged to leave it all—

NORA: Nonsense, you are not going to leave it.

RANK (*as before*): And not be able to leave behind one the slightest token of one's gratitude, scarcely even a fleeting regret—nothing but an empty place which the first comer can fill as well as any other.

NORA: And if I asked you now for a—? No!

RANK: For what?

NORA: For a big proof of your friendship—

RANK: Yes, yes!

NORA: I mean a tremendously big favour.

RANK: Would you really make me so happy for once?

NORA: Ah, but you don't know what it is yet.

RANK: No—but tell me.

NORA: I really can't, Doctor Rank. It is something out of all reason; it means advice, and help, and a favour—

RANK: The bigger a thing it is the better. I can't conceive what it is you mean. Do tell me. Haven't I your confidence?

NORA: More than anyone else. I know you are my truest and best friend, and so I will tell you what it is. Well, Doctor Rank, it is something you must help me to prevent. You know how devotedly, how inexpressibly deeply Torvald loves me; he would never for a moment hesitate to give his life for me.

RANK (*leaning towards her*): Nora—do you think he is the only one—?

NORA (*with a slight start*): The only one—?

RANK: The only one who would gladly give his life for your sake.

NORA (*sadly*): Is that it?

RANK: I was determined you should know it before I went away, and there will never be a better opportunity than this. Now you know it, Nora. And now you know, too, that you can trust me as you would trust no one else.

NORA (*rises, deliberately and quietly*): Let me pass.

RANK (*makes room for her to pass him, but sits still*): Nora!

NORA (*at the hall door*): Helen, bring in the lamp. (*Goes over to the stove.*) Dear Doctor Rank, that was really horrid of you.

RANK: To have loved you as much as anyone else does? Was that horrid?

NORA: No, but to go and tell me so. There was really no need—

RANK: What do you mean? Did you know—? (*Maid enters with lamp, puts it down on the table, and goes out.*) Nora—Mrs. Helmer—tell me, had you any idea of this?

NORA: Oh, how do I know whether I had or whether I hadn't? I really can't tell you—To think you could be so clumsy, Doctor Rank! We were getting on so nicely.

RANK: Well, at all events you know now that you can command me, body and soul. So won't you speak out?

NORA (*looking at him*): After what happened?

RANK: I beg you to let me know what it is.

NORA: I can't tell you anything now.

RANK: Yes, yes. You mustn't punish me in that way. Let me have permission to do for you whatever a man may do.

NORA: You can do nothing for me now. Besides, I really don't need any help at all. You will find that the whole thing is merely fancy on my part. It really is so—of course it is! (*Sits down in the rocking-chair, and looks at him with a smile.*) You are a nice sort of man, Doctor Rank!—don't you feel ashamed of yourself, now the lamp has come?

RANK: Not a bit. But perhaps I had better go—for ever?

NORA: No, indeed, you shall not. Of course you must come here just as before. You know very well Torvald can't do without you.

RANK: Yes, but you?

NORA: Oh, I am always tremendously pleased when you come.

RANK: It is just that, that put me on the wrong track. You are a riddle to me. I have often thought that you would almost as soon be in my company as in Helmer's.

NORA: Yes—you see there are some people one loves best, and others whom one would almost always rather have as companions.

RANK: Yes, there is something in that.

NORA: When I was at home, of course I loved papa best. But I always thought it tremendous fun if I could steal down into the maids' room, because they never moralised at all, and talked to each other about such entertaining things.

RANK: I see—it is *their* place I have taken.

NORA (*jumping up and going to him*): Oh, dear, nice Doctor Rank, I never meant that at all. But surely you can understand that being with Torvald is a little like being with papa—

Enter Maid from the hall.

MAID: If you please, ma'am. (*Whispers and hands her a card.*)

NORA (*glancing at the card*): Oh! (*Puts it in her pocket.*)

RANK: Is there anything wrong?

NORA: No, no, not in the least. It is only something—it is my new dress—

RANK: What? Your dress is lying there.

NORA: Oh, yes, that one; but this is another. I ordered it. Torvald mustn't know about it—

RANK: Oho! Then that was the great secret.

NORA: Of course. Just go in to him; he is sitting in the inner room. Keep him as long as—

RANK: Make your mind easy; I won't let him escape. (*Goes into Helmer's room.*)

NORA (*to the Maid*): And he is standing waiting in the kitchen?

MAID: Yes; he came up the back stairs.

NORA: But didn't you tell him no one was in?

MAID: Yes, but it was no good.

NORA: He won't go away?

MAID: No; he says he won't until he has seen you, ma'am.

NORA: Well, let him come in—but quietly. Helen, you mustn't say anything about it to anyone. It is a surprise for my husband.

MAID: Yes, ma'am, I quite understand. (*Exit.*)

NORA: This dreadful thing is going to happen! It will happen in spite of me! No, no, no, it can't happen—it shan't happen! (*She bolts the door of Helmer's room. The Maid opens the hall door for Krogstad and shuts it after him. He is wearing a fur coat, high boots and a fur cap.*)

NORA (*advancing towards him*): Speak low—my husband is at home.

KROGSTAD: No matter about that.

NORA: What do you want of me?

KROGSTAD: An explanation of something.

NORA: Make haste then. What is it?

KROGSTAD: You know, I suppose, that I have got my dismissal.

NORA: I couldn't prevent it, Mr. Krogstad. I fought as hard as I could on your side, but it was no good.

KROGSTAD: Does your husband love you so little, then? He knows what I can expose you to, and yet he ventures—

NORA: How can you suppose that he has any knowledge of the sort?

KROGSTAD: I didn't suppose so at all. It would not be the least like our dear Torvald Helmer to show so much courage—

NORA: Mr. Krogstad, a little respect for my husband, please.

KROGSTAD: Certainly—all the respect he deserves. But since you have kept the matter so carefully to yourself, I make bold to suppose that you have a little clearer idea, than you had yesterday, of what it actually is that you have done?

NORA: More than you could ever teach me.

KROGSTAD: Yes, such a bad lawyer as I am.

NORA: What is it you want of me?

KROGSTAD: Only to see how you were, Mrs. Helmer. I have been thinking about you all day long. A mere cashier, a quill-driver, a—well, a man like me—even he has a little of what is called feeling, you know.

NORA: Show it, then; think of my little children.

KROGSTAD: Have you and your husband thought of mine? But never mind about that. I only wanted to tell you that you need not take this matter too seriously. In the first place there will be no accusation made on my part.

NORA: No, of course not; I was sure of that.

KROGSTAD: The whole thing can be arranged amicably; there is no reason why anyone should know anything about it. It will remain a secret between us three.

NORA: My husband must never get to know anything about it.

KROGSTAD: How will you be able to prevent it? Am I to understand that you can pay the balance that is owing?

NORA: No, not just at present.

KROGSTAD: Or perhaps that you have some expedient for raising the money soon?

NORA: No expedient that I mean to make use of.

KROGSTAD: Well, in any case, it would have been of no use to you now. If you stood there with ever so much money in your hand, I would never part with your bond.

NORA: Tell me what purpose you mean to put it to.

KROGSTAD: I shall only preserve it—keep it in my possession. No one who is not concerned in the matter shall have the slightest hint of it. So that if the thought of it has driven you to any desperate resolution—

NORA: It has.

KROGSTAD: If you had it in your mind to run away from your home—

NORA: I had.

KROGSTAD: Or even something worse—

NORA: How could you know that?

KROGSTAD: Give up the idea.

NORA: How did you know I had thought of *that*?

KROGSTAD: Most of us think of that at first. I did, too—but I hadn't the courage.

NORA (*faintly*): No more had I.

KROGSTAD (*in a tone of relief*): No, that's it, isn't it—you hadn't the courage either?

NORA: No, I haven't—I haven't.

KROGSTAD: Besides, it would have been a great piece of folly. Once the first storm at home is over—. I have a letter for your husband in my pocket.

NORA: Telling him everything?

KROGSTAD: In as lenient a manner as I possibly could.

NORA (*quickly*): He mustn't get the letter. Tear it up. I will find some means of getting money.

KROGSTAD: Excuse me, Mrs. Helmer, but I think I told you just now—

NORA: I am not speaking of what I owe you. Tell me what sum you are asking my husband for, and I will get the money.

KROGSTAD: I am not asking your husband for a penny.

NORA: What do you want, then?

KROGSTAD: I will tell you. I want to rehabilitate myself, Mrs. Helmer; I want to get on; and in that your husband must help me. For the last year and a half I have not had a hand in anything dishonourable, and all that time I have been struggling in most restricted circumstances. I was content to work my way up step by step. Now I am turned out, and I am not going to be satisfied with merely being taken into favour again. I want to get on, I tell you. I want to get into the Bank again, in a higher position. Your husband must make a place for me—

NORA: That he will never do!

KROGSTAD: He will; I know him; he dare not protest. And as soon as I am in there again with him, then you will see! Within a year I shall be the manager's right hand. It will be Nils Krogstad and not Torvald Helmer who manages the Bank.

NORA: That's a thing you will never see!

KROGSTAD: Do you mean that you will—?

NORA: I have courage enough for it now.

KROGSTAD: Oh, you can't frighten me. A fine, spoilt lady like you—

NORA: You will see, you will see.

KROGSTAD: Under the ice, perhaps? Down into the cold, coal-black water? And then, in the spring, to float up to the surface, all horrible and unrecognisable, with your hair fallen out—

NORA: You can't frighten me.

KROGSTAD: Nor you me. People don't do such things, Mrs. Helmer. Besides, what use would it be? I should have him completely in my power all the same.

NORA: Afterwards? When I am no longer—

KROGSTAD: Have you forgotten that it is I who have the keeping of your reputation? (*Nora stands speechlessly looking at him.*) Well, now, I have warned you. Do not do anything foolish. When Helmer has had my letter, I shall expect a message from him. And be sure you remember that it is your husband himself who has forced me into such ways as this again. I will never forgive him for that. Good-bye, Mrs. Helmer. (*Exit through the hall.*)

NORA (*goes to the hall door, opens it slightly and listens*): He is going. He is not putting the letter in the box. Oh no, no! that's impossible! (*Opens the door by degrees.*) What is that? He is standing outside. He is not going downstairs. Is he hesitating? Can he—? (*A letter drops into the box; then Krogstad's footsteps are heard, till they die away as he goes downstairs. Nora utters a stifled cry, and runs across the room to the table by the sofa. A short pause.*)

NORA: In the letter-box. (*Steals across to the hall door.*) There it lies—Torvald, Torvald, there is no hope for us now!

Mrs. Linde comes in from the room on the left, carrying the dress.

MRS. LINDE: There, I can't see anything more to mend now. Would you like to try it on—?

NORA (*in a hoarse whisper*): Christine, come here.

MRS. LINDE (*throwing the dress down on the sofa*): What is the matter with you? You look so agitated!

NORA: Come here. Do you see that letter? There, look—you can see it through the glass in the letter-box.

MRS. LINDE: Yes, I see it.

NORA: That letter is from Krogstad.

MRS. LINDE: Nora—it was Krogstad who lent you the money!

NORA: Yes, and now Torvald will know all about it.

MRS. LINDE: Believe me, Nora, that's the best thing for both of you.

NORA: You don't know all. I forged a name.

MRS. LINDE: Good heavens—!

NORA: I only want to say this to you, Christine—you must be my witness.

MRS. LINDE: Your witness? What do you mean? What am I to—?

NORA: If I should go out of my mind—and it might easily happen—

MRS. LINDE: Nora!

NORA: Or if anything else should happen to me—anything, for instance, that might prevent my being here—

MRS. LINDE: Nora! Nora! you are quite out of your mind.

NORA: And if it should happen that there were some one who wanted to take all the responsibility, all the blame, you understand—

MRS. LINDE: Yes, yes—but how can you suppose—?

NORA: Then you must be my witness, that it is not true, Christine. I am not out of my mind at all! I am in my right senses now, and I tell you no one else has known anything about it; I, and I alone, did the whole thing. Remember that.

MRS. LINDE: I will, indeed. But I don't understand all this.

NORA: How should you understand it? A wonderful thing is going to happen!

MRS. LINDE: A wonderful thing?

NORA: Yes, a wonderful thing!—But it is so terrible, Christine; it *mustn't* happen, not for all the world.

MRS. LINDE: I will go at once and see Krogstad.

NORA: Don't go to him; he will do you some harm.

MRS. LINDE: There was a time when he would gladly do anything for my sake.

NORA: He?

MRS. LINDE: Where does he live?

NORA: How should I know—? Yes (*feeling in her pocket*), here is his card. But the letter, the letter—!

HELMER (*calls from his room, knocking at the door*): Nora!

NORA (*cries out anxiously*): Oh, what's that? What do you want?

HELMER: Don't be so frightened. We are not coming in; you have locked the door. Are you trying on your dress?

NORA: Yes, that's it. I look so nice, Torvald.

MRS. LINDE (*who has read the card*): I see he lives at the corner here.

NORA: Yes, but it's no use. It is hopeless. The letter is lying there in the box.

MRS. LINDE: And your husband keeps the key?

NORA: Yes, always.

MRS. LINDE: Krogstad must ask for his letter back unread, he must find some pretence—

NORA: But it is just at this time that Torvald generally—

MRS. LINDE: You must delay him. Go in to him in the meantime. I will come back as soon as I can. (*She goes out hurriedly through the hall door.*)

NORA (*goes to Helmer's door, opens it and peeps in*): Torvald!

HELMER (*from the inner room*): Well? May I venture at last to come into my own room again? Come along, Rank, now you will see—(*Halting in the doorway.*) But what is this?

NORA: What is what, dear?

HELMER: Rank led me to expect a splendid transformation.

RANK (*in the doorway*): I understood so, but evidently I was mistaken.

NORA: Yes, nobody is to have the chance of admiring me in my dress until to-morrow.

HELMER: But, my dear Nora, you look so worn out. Have you been practising too much?

NORA: No, I have not practised at all.

HELMER: But you will need to—

NORA: Yes, indeed I shall, Torvald. But I can't get on a bit without you to help me; I have absolutely forgotten the whole thing.

HELMER: Oh, we will soon work it up again.

NORA: Yes, help me, Torvald. Promise that you will! I am so nervous about it—all the people—. You must give yourself up to me entirely this evening. Not the tiniest bit of business—you mustn't even take a pen in your hand. Will you promise, Torvald dear?

HELMER: I promise. This evening I will be wholly and absolutely at your service, you helpless little mortal. Ah, by the way, first of all I will just—(*Goes towards the hall door.*)

NORA: What are you going to do there?

HELMER: Only see if any letters have come.

NORA: No, no! don't do that, Torvald!

HELMER: Why not?

NORA: Torvald, please don't. There is nothing there.

HELMER: Well, let me look. (*Turns to go to the letter-box. Nora, at the piano, plays the first bars of the Tarantella. Helmer stops in the doorway.*) Aha!

NORA: I can't dance tomorrow if I don't practise with you.

HELMER (*going up to her*): Are you really so afraid of it, dear?

NORA: Yes, so dreadfully afraid of it. Let me practise at once; there is time now, before we go to dinner. Sit down and play for me, Torvald dear; criticise me, and correct me as you play.

HELMER: With great pleasure, if you wish me to. (*Sits down at the piano.*)

NORA (*takes out of the box a tambourine and a long variegated shawl. She hastily drapes the shawl round her. Then she springs to the front of the stage and calls out*): Now play for me! I am going to dance!

Helmer plays and Nora dances. Rank stands by the piano behind Helmer, and looks on.

HELMER (*as he plays*): Slower, slower!
NORA: I can't do it any other way.
HELMER: Not so violently, Nora!
NORA: This is the way.
HELMER (*stops playing*): No, no—that is not a bit right.
NORA (*laughing and swinging the tambourine*): Didn't I tell you so?
RANK: Let me play for her.
HELMER (*getting up*): Yes, do. I can correct her better then.

Rank sits down at the piano and plays. Nora dances more and more wildly. Helmer has taken up a position beside the stove, and during her dance gives her frequent instructions. She does not seem to hear him; her hair comes down and falls over her shoulders; she pays no attention to it, but goes on dancing. Enter Mrs. Linde.

MRS. LINDE (*standing as if spell-bound in the doorway*): Oh!—
NORA (*as she dances*): Such fun, Christine!
HELMER: My dear darling Nora, you are dancing as if your life depended on it.
NORA: So it does.
HELMER: Stop, Rank; this is sheer madness. Stop, I tell you! (*Rank stops playing, and Nora suddenly stands still. Helmer goes up to her.*) I could never have believed it. You have forgotten everything I taught you.
NORA (*throwing away the tambourine*): There, you see.
HELMER: You will want a lot of coaching.
NORA: Yes, you see how much I need it. You must coach me up to the last minute. Promise me that, Torvald!
HELMER: You can depend on me.
NORA: You must not think of anything but me, either to-day or to-morrow; you mustn't open a single letter—not even open the letter-box—
HELMER: Ah, you are still afraid of that fellow—
NORA: Yes, indeed I am.
HELMER: Nora, I can tell from your looks that there is a letter from him lying there.
NORA: I don't know; I think there is; but you must not read anything of that kind now. Nothing horrid must come between us until this is all over.
RANK (*whispers to Helmer*): You mustn't contradict her.
HELMER (*taking her in his arms*): The child shall have her way. But to-morrow night, after you have danced—
NORA: Then you will be free. (*The Maid appears in the doorway to the right.*)
MAID: Dinner is served, ma'am.
NORA: We will have champagne, Helen.
MAID: Very good, ma'am. [*Exit.*]
HELMER: Hullo!—are we going to have a banquet?

NORA: Yes, a champagne banquet until the small hours. (*Calls out.*) And a few macaroons, Helen—lots, just for once!

HELMER: Come, come, don't be so wild and nervous. Be my own little skylark, as you used.

NORA: Yes, dear, I will. But go in now and you too, Doctor Rank. Christine, you must help me to do up my hair.

RANK (*whispers to Helmer as they go out*): I suppose there is nothing—she is not expecting anything?

HELMER: Far from it, my dear fellow; it is simply nothing more than this childish nervousness I was telling you of. (*They go into the right-hand room.*)

NORA: Well!

MRS. LINDE: Gone out of town.

NORA: I could tell from your face.

MRS. LINDE: He is coming home to-morrow evening. I wrote a note for him.

NORA: You should have let it alone; you must prevent nothing. After all, it is splendid to be waiting for a wonderful thing to happen.

MRS. LINDE: What is it that you are waiting for?

NORA: Oh, you wouldn't understand. Go in to them, I will come in a moment. (*Mrs. Linde goes into the dining-room. Nora stands still for a little while, as if to compose herself. Then she looks at her watch.*) Five o'clock. Seven hours until midnight; and then four-and-twenty hours until the next midnight. Then the Tarantella will be over. Twenty-four and seven? Thirty-one hours to live.

HELMER (*from the doorway on the right*): Where's my little skylark?

NORA (*going to him with her arms outstretched*): Here she is!

ACT III

THE SAME SCENE: *The table has been placed in the middle of the stage, with chairs round it. A lamp is burning on the table. The door into the hall stands open. Dance music is heard in the room above. Mrs. Linde is sitting at the table idly turning over the leaves of a book; she tries to read, but does not seem able to collect her thoughts. Every now and then she listens intently for a sound at the outer door.*

MRS. LINDE (*looking at her watch*): Not yet—and the time is nearly up. If only he does not—. (*Listens again.*) Ah, there he is. (*Goes into the hall and opens the outer door carefully. Light footsteps are heard on the stairs. She whispers.*) Come in. There is no one here.

KROGSTAD (*in the doorway*): I found a note from you at home. What does this mean?

MRS. LINDE: It is absolutely necessary that I should have a talk with you.

KROGSTAD: Really? And is it absolutely necessary that it should be here?

MRS. LINDE: It is impossible where I live; there is no private entrance to my rooms. Come in; we are quite alone. The maid is asleep, and the Helmers are at the dance upstairs.

KROGSTAD (*coming into the room*): Are the Helmers really at a dance to-night?

MRS. LINDE: Yes, why not?

KROGSTAD: Certainly—why not?

MRS. LINDE: Now, Nils, let us have a talk.

KROGSTAD: Can we two have anything to talk about?

MRS. LINDE: We have a great deal to talk about.

KROGSTAD: I shouldn't have thought so.

MRS. LINDE: No, you have never properly understood me.

KROGSTAD: Was there anything else to understand except what was obvious to all the world — a heartless woman jilts a man when a more lucrative chance turns up?

MRS. LINDE: Do you believe I am as absolutely heartless as all that? And do you believe that I did it with a light heart?

KROGSTAD: Didn't you?

MRS. LINDE: Nils, did you really think that?

KROGSTAD: If it were as you say, why did you write to me as you did at the time?

MRS. LINDE: I could do nothing else. As I had to break with you, it was my duty also to put an end to all that you felt for me.

KROGSTAD (*wringing his hands*): So that was it. And all this — only for the sake of money!

MRS. LINDE: You must not forget that I had a helpless mother and two little brothers. We couldn't wait for you, Nils; your prospects seemed hopeless then.

KROGSTAD: That may be so, but you had no right to throw me over for anyone else's sake.

MRS. LINDE: Indeed I don't know. Many a time did I ask myself if I had the right to do it.

KROGSTAD (*more gently*): When I lost you, it was as if all the solid ground went from under my feet. Look at me now — I am a shipwrecked man clinging to a bit of wreckage.

MRS. LINDE: But help may be near.

KROGSTAD: It *was* near; but then you came and stood in my way.

MRS. LINDE: Unintentionally, Nils. It was only to-day that I learned it was your place I was going to take in the Bank.

KROGSTAD: I believe you, if you say so. But now that you know it, are you not going to give it up to me?

MRS. LINDE: No, because that would not benefit you in the least.

KROGSTAD: Oh, benefit, benefit — I would have done it whether or no.

MRS. LINDE: I have learned to act prudently. Life, and hard, bitter necessity have taught me that.

KROGSTAD: And life has taught me not to believe in fine speeches.

MRS. LINDE: Then life has taught you something very reasonable. But deeds you must believe in?

KROGSTAD: What do you mean by that?

MRS. LINDE: You said you were like a shipwrecked man clinging to some wreckage.

KROGSTAD: I had good reason to say so.

MRS. LINDE: Well, I am like a shipwrecked woman clinging to some wreckage — no one to mourn for, no one to care for.

KROGSTAD: It was your own choice.

MRS. LINDE: There was no other choice—then.

KROGSTAD: Well, what now?

MRS. LINDE: Nils, how would it be if we two shipwrecked people could join forces?

KROGSTAD: What are you saying?

MRS. LINDE: Two on the same piece of wreckage would stand a better chance than each on their own.

KROGSTAD: Christine!

MRS. LINDE: What do you suppose brought me to town?

KROGSTAD: Do you mean that you gave me a thought?

MRS. LINDE: I could not endure life without work. All my life, as long as I can remember, I have worked, and it has been my greatest and only pleasure. But now I am quite alone in the world—my life is so dreadfully empty and I feel so forsaken. There is not the least pleasure in working for one's self. Nils, give me someone and something to work for.

KROGSTAD: I don't trust that. It is nothing but a woman's overstrained sense of generosity that prompts you to make such an offer of yourself.

MRS. LINDE: Have you ever noticed anything of the sort in me?

KROGSTAD: Could you really do it? Tell me—do you know all about my past life?

MRS. LINDE: Yes.

KROGSTAD: And do you know what they think of me here?

MRS. LINDE: You seemed to me to imply that with me you might have been quite another man.

KROGSTAD: I am certain of it.

MRS. LINDE: Is it too late now?

KROGSTAD: Christine, are you saying this deliberately? Yes, I am sure you are. I see it in your face. Have you really the courage, then—?

MRS. LINDE: I want to be a mother to someone, and your children need a mother. We two need each other. Nils, I have faith in your real character—I can dare anything together with you.

KROGSTAD (*grasps her hands*): Thanks, thanks, Christine! Now I shall find a way to clear myself in the eyes of the world. Ah, but I forgot—

MRS. LINDE (*listening*): Hush! The Tarantella! Go, go!

KROGSTAD: Why? What is it?

MRS. LINDE: Do you hear them up there? When that is over, we may expect them back.

KROGSTAD: Yes, yes—I will go. But it is all no use. Of course you are not aware what steps I have taken in the matter of the Helmers.

MRS. LINDE: Yes, I know all about that.

KROGSTAD: And in spite of that have you the courage to—?

MRS. LINDE: I understand very well to what lengths a man like you might be driven by despair.

KROGSTAD: If I could only undo what I have done!

MRS. LINDE: You cannot. Your letter is lying in the letter-box now.

KROGSTAD: Are you sure of that?

MRS. LINDE: Quite sure, but—

KROGSTAD (*with a searching look at her*): Is that what it all means?—that you want to save your friend at any cost? Tell me frankly. Is that it?

MRS. LINDE: Nils, a woman who has once sold herself for another's sake, doesn't do it a second time.

KROGSTAD: I will ask for my letter back.

MRS. LINDE: No, no.

KROGSTAD: Yes, of course I will. I will wait here until Helmer comes; I will tell him he must give me my letter back—that it only concerns my dismissal—that he is not to read it—

MRS. LINDE: No, Nils, you must not recall your letter.

KROGSTAD: But, tell me, wasn't it for that very purpose that you asked me to meet you here?

MRS. LINDE: In my first moment of fright, it was. But twenty-four hours have elapsed since then, and in that time I have witnessed incredible things in this house. Helmer must know all about it. This unhappy secret must be disclosed; they must have a complete understanding between them, which is impossible with all this concealment and falsehood going on.

KROGSTAD: Very well, if you will take the responsibility. But there is one thing I can do in any case, and I shall do it at once.

MRS. LINDE (*listening*): You must be quick and go! The dance is over; we are not safe a moment longer.

KROGSTAD: I will wait for you below.

MRS. LINDE: Yes, do. You must see me back to my door.

KROGSTAD: I have never had such an amazing piece of good fortune in my life! (*Goes out through the outer door. The door between the room and the hall remains open.*)

MRS. LINDE (*tidying up the room and laying her hat and cloak ready*): What a difference! what a difference! Some-one to work for and live for—a home to bring comfort into. That I will do, indeed. I wish they would be quick and come—(*Listens.*) Ah, there they are now. I must put on my things. (*Takes up her hat and cloak. Helmer's and Nora's voices are heard outside; a key is turned, and Helmer brings Nora almost by force into the hall. She is in an Italian costume with a large black shawl around her; he is in evening dress, and a black domino which is flying open.*)

NORA (*hanging back in the doorway, and struggling with him*): No, no, no!—don't take me in. I want to go upstairs again; I don't want to leave so early.

HELMER: But, my dearest Nora—

NORA: Please, Torvald dear—please, *please*—only an hour more.

HELMER: Not a single minute, my sweet Nora. You know that was our agreement. Come along into the room; you are catching cold standing there. (*He brings her gently into the room, in spite of her resistance.*)

MRS. LINDE: Good-evening.

NORA: Christine!

HELMER: You here, so late, Mrs. Linde?

MRS. LINDE: Yes, you must excuse me; I was so anxious to see Nora in her dress.

NORA: Have you been sitting here waiting for me?

MRS. LINDE: Yes, unfortunately I came too late, you had already gone upstairs; and I thought I couldn't go away again without having seen you.

HELMER (*taking off Nora's shawl*): Yes, take a good look at her. I think she is worth looking at. Isn't she charming, Mrs. Linde?

MRS. LINDE: Yes, indeed she is.

HELMER: Doesn't she look remarkably pretty? Everyone thought so at the dance. But she is terribly self-willed, this sweet little person. What are we to do with her? You will hardly believe that I had almost to bring her away by force.

NORA: Torvald, you will repent not having let me stay, even if it were only for half an hour.

HELMER: Listen to her, Mrs. Linde! She had danced her Tarantella, and it had been a tremendous success, as it deserved—although possibly the performance was a trifle too realistic—a little more so, I mean, than was strictly compatible with the limitations of art. But never mind about that! The chief thing is, she had made a success—she had made a tremendous success. Do you think I was going to let her remain there after that, and spoil the effect? No, indeed! I took my charming little Capri maiden—my capricious little Capri maiden, I should say—on my arm; took one quick turn round the room; a curtsey on either side, and, as they say in novels, the beautiful apparition disappeared. An exit ought always to be effective, Mrs. Linde; but that is what I cannot make Nora understand. Pooh! this room is hot. (*Throws his domino on a chair, and opens the door of his room.*) Hullo! it's all dark in here. Oh, of course—excuse me—. (*He goes in, and lights some candles.*)

NORA (*in a hurried and breathless whisper*): Well?

MRS. LINDE (*in a low voice*): I have had a talk with him.

NORA: Yes, and—

MRS. LINDE: Nora, you must tell your husband all about it.

NORA (*in an expressionless voice*): I knew it.

MRS. LINDE: You have nothing to be afraid of as far as Krogstad is concerned; but you must tell him.

NORA: I won't tell him.

MRS. LINDE: Then the letter will.

NORA: Thank you, Christine. Now I know what I must do. Hush—!

HELMER (*coming in again*): Well, Mrs. Linde, have you admired her?

MRS. LINDE: Yes, and now I will say good-night.

HELMER: What, already? Is this yours, this knitting?

MRS. LINDE (*taking it*): Yes, thank you, I had very nearly forgotten it.

HELMER: So you knit?

MRS. LINDE: Of course.

HELMER: Do you know, you ought to embroider.

MRS. LINDE: Really? Why?

HELMER: Yes, it's far more becoming. Let me show you. You hold the embroidery thus in your left hand, and use the needle with the right—like this—with a long, easy sweep. Do you see?

MRS. LINDE: Yes, perhaps—

HELMER: But in the case of knitting—that can never be anything but ungraceful; look here—the arms close together, the knitting-needles going up and down—it has a sort of Chinese effect—. That was really excellent champagne they gave us.

MRS. LINDE: Well,—good-night, Nora, and don't be self-willed any more.

HELMER: That's right, Mrs. Linde.

MRS. LINDE: Good-night, Mr. Helmer.

HELMER (*accompanying her to the door*): Good-night, good-night. I hope you will get home all right. I should be very happy to—but you haven't any great distance to go. Good-night, good-night. (*She goes out; he shuts the door after her, and comes in again.*) Ah!—at last we have got rid of her. She is a frightful bore, that woman.

NORA: Aren't you very tired, Torvald?

HELMER: No, not in the least.

NORA: Nor sleepy?

HELMER: Not a bit. On the contrary, I feel extraordinarily lively. And you?—you really look both tired and sleepy.

NORA: Yes, I am very tired. I want to go to sleep at once.

HELMER: There, you see it was quite right of me not to let you stay there any longer.

NORA: Everything you do is quite right, Torvald.

HELMER (*kissing her on the forehead*): Now my little skylark is speaking reasonably. Did you notice what good spirits Rank was in this evening?

NORA: Really? Was he? I didn't speak to him at all.

HELMER: And I very little, but I have not for a long time seen him in such good form. (*Looks for a while at her and then goes nearer to her.*) It is delightful to be at home by ourselves again, to be all alone with you—you fascinating, charming little darling!

NORA: Don't look at me like that, Torvald.

HELMER: Why shouldn't I look at my dearest treasure?—at all the beauty that is mine, all my very own?

NORA (*going to the other side of the table*): You mustn't say things like that to me to-night.

HELMER (*following her*): You have still got the Tarantella in your blood, I see. And it makes you more captivating than ever. Listen—the guests are beginning to go now. (*In a lower voice.*) Nora—soon the whole house will be quiet.

NORA: Yes, I hope so.

HELMER: Yes, my own darling Nora. Do you know, when I am out at a party with you like this, why I speak so little to you, keep away from you, and only send a stolen glance in your direction now and then?—do you know why I do that? It is because I make believe to myself that we are secretly in love, and you are my secretly promised bride, and that no one suspects there is anything between us.

NORA: Yes, yes—I know very well your thoughts are with me all the time.

HELMER: And when we are leaving, and I am putting the shawl over your beautiful young shoulders—on your lovely neck—then I imagine that you are my young bride and that we have just come from the wedding, and I am bringing you for the first time into our home—to be alone with you for the first time—quite alone with my shy little darling! All this evening I have longed for nothing but you. When I watched the seductive figures of the Tarantella, my blood was on fire; I could endure it no longer, and that was why I brought you down so early—

NORA: Go away, Torvald! You must let me go. I won't—

HELMER: What's that? You're joking, my little Nora! You won't—you won't? Am I not your husband—? (*A knock is heard at the outer door.*)

NORA (*starting*): Did you hear—?

HELMER (*going into the hall*): Who is it?

RANK (*outside*): It is I. May I come in for a moment?

HELMER (*in a fretful whisper*): Oh, what does he want now? (*Aloud.*) Wait a minute! (*Unlocks the door.*) Come, that's kind of you not to pass by our door.

RANK: I thought I heard your voice, and felt as if I should like to look in. (*With a swift glance round.*) Ah, yes!—these dear familiar rooms. You are very happy and cosy in here, you two.

HELMER: It seems to me that you looked after yourself pretty well upstairs too.

RANK: Excellently. Why shouldn't I? Why shouldn't one enjoy everything in this world?—at any rate as much as one can, and as long as one can. The wine was capital—

HELMER: Especially the champagne.

RANK: So you noticed that too? It is almost incredible how much I managed to put away!

NORA: Torvald drank a great deal of champagne to-night too.

RANK: Did he?

NORA: Yes, and he is always in such good spirits afterwards.

RANK: Well, why should one not enjoy a merry evening after a well-spent day?

HELMER: Well spent? I am afraid I can't take credit for that.

RANK (*clapping him on the back*): But I can, you know!

NORA: Doctor Rank, you must have been occupied with some scientific investigation to-day.

RANK: Exactly.

HELMER: Just listen!—little Nora talking about scientific investigations!

NORA: And may I congratulate you on the result?

RANK: Indeed you may.

NORA: Was it favourable, then?

RANK: The best possible, for both doctor and patient—certainty.

NORA (*quickly and searchingly*): Certainty?

RANK: Absolute certainty. So wasn't I entitled to make a merry evening of it after that?

NORA: Yes, you certainly were, Doctor Rank.

HELMER: I think so too, so long as you don't have to pay for it in the morning.

RANK: Oh well, one can't have anything in this life without paying for it.

NORA: Doctor Rank—are you fond of fancy-dress balls?

RANK: Yes, if there is a fine lot of pretty costumes.

NORA: Tell me — what shall we two wear at the next?

HELMER: Little featherbrain! — are you thinking of the next already?

RANK: We two? Yes, I can tell you. You shall go as a good fairy —

HELMER: Yes, but what do you suggest as an appropriate costume for that?

RANK: Let your wife go dressed just as she is in everyday life.

HELMER: That was really very prettily turned. But can't you tell us what you will be?

RANK: Yes, my dear friend, I have quite made up my mind about that.

HELMER: Well?

RANK: At the next fancy-dress ball I shall be invisible.

HELMER: That's a good joke!

RANK: There is a big black hat — have you never heard of hats that make you invisible? If you put one on, no one can see you.

HELMER (*suppressing a smile*): Yes, you are quite right.

RANK: But I am clean forgetting what I came for. Helmer, give me a cigar — one of the dark Havanas.

HELMER: With the greatest pleasure. (*Offers him his case.*)

RANK (*takes a cigar and cuts off the end*): Thanks.

NORA (*striking a match*): Let me give you a light.

RANK: Thank you. (*She holds the match for him to light his cigar.*) And now good-bye!

HELMER: Good-bye, good-bye, dear old man!

NORA: Sleep well, Doctor Rank.

RANK: Thank you for that wish.

NORA: Wish me the same.

RANK: You? Well, if you want me to sleep well! And thanks for the light. (*He nods to them both and goes out.*)

HELMER (*in a subdued voice*): He has drunk more than he ought.

NORA (*absently*): Maybe. (*Helmer takes a bunch of keys out of his pocket and goes into the hall.*) Torvald! what are you going to do there?

HELMER: Empty the letter-box; it is quite full; there will be no room to put the newspaper in to-morrow morning.

NORA: Are you going to work to-night?

HELMER: You know quite well I'm not. What is this? Someone has been at the lock.

NORA: At the lock — ?

HELMER: Yes, someone has. What can it mean? I should never have thought the maid —. Here is a broken hairpin. Nora, it is one of yours.

NORA (*quickly*): Then it must have been the children —

HELMER: Then you must get them out of those ways. There, at last I have got it open. (*Takes out the contents of the letter-box, and calls to the kitchen.*) Helen! — Helen, put out the light over the front door. (*Goes back into the room and shuts the door into the hall. He holds out his hand full of letters.*) Look at that — look what a heap of them there are. (*Turning them over.*) What on earth is that?

NORA (*at the window*): The letter — No! Torvald, no!

HELMER: Two cards—of Rank's.

NORA: Of Doctor Rank's?

HELMER (*looking at them*): Doctor Rank. They were on the top. He must have put them in when he went out.

NORA: Is there anything written on them?

HELMER: There is a black cross over the name. Look there—what an uncomfortable idea! It looks as if he were announcing his own death.

NORA: It is just what he is doing.

HELMER: What? Do you know anything about it? Has he said anything to you?

NORA: Yes. He told me that when the cards came it would be his leave-taking from us. He means to shut himself up and die.

HELMER: My poor old friend! Certainly I knew we should not have him very long with us. But so soon! And so he hides himself away like a wounded animal.

NORA: If it has to happen, it is best it should be without a word—don't you think so, Torvald?

HELMER (*walking up and down*): He had so grown into our lives. I can't think of him as having gone out of them. He, with his sufferings and his loneliness, was like a cloudy background to our sunlit happiness. Well, perhaps it is best so. For him, anyway. (*Standing still.*) And perhaps for us too, Nora. We two are thrown quite upon each other now. (*Puts his arms round her.*) My darling wife, I don't feel as if I could hold you tight enough. Do you know, Nora, I have often wished that you might be threatened by some great danger, so that I might risk my life's blood, and everything, for your sake.

NORA (*disengages herself, and says firmly and decidedly*): Now you must read your letters, Torvald.

HELMER: No, no; not to-night. I want to be with you, my darling wife.

NORA: With the thought of your friend's death—

HELMER: You are right, it has affected us both. Something ugly has come between us—the thought of the horrors of death. We must try and rid our minds of that. Until then—we will each go to our own room.

NORA (*hanging on his neck*): Good-night, Torvald—Good-night!

HELMER (*kissing her on the forehead*): Good-night, my little singing-bird. Sleep sound, Nora. Now I will read my letters through. (*He takes his letters and goes into his room, shutting the door after him.*)

NORA (*gropes distractedly about, seizes Helmer's domino, throws it round her, while she says in quick, hoarse, spasmodic whispers*): Never to see him again. Never! Never! (*Puts her shawl over her head.*) Never to see my children again either—never again. Never! Never!—Ah! the icy, black water—the unfathomable depths—If only it were over! He has got it now—now he is reading it. Good-bye, Torvald and my children! (*She is about to rush out through the hall, when Helmer opens his door hurriedly and stands with an open letter in his hand.*)

HELMER: Nora!

NORA: Ah!—

HELMER: What is this? Do you know what is in this letter?

NORA: Yes, I know. Let me go! Let me get out!

HELMER (*holding her back*): Where are you going?

NORA (*trying to get free*): You shan't save me, Torvald!

HELMER (*reeling*): True? Is this true, that I read here? Horrible! No, no—it is impossible that it can be true.

NORA: It is true. I have loved you above everything else in the world.

HELMER: Oh, don't let us have any silly excuses.

NORA (*taking a step towards him*): Torvald—!

HELMER: Miserable creature—what have you done?

NORA: Let me go. You shall not suffer for my sake. You shall not take it upon yourself.

HELMER: No tragedy airs, please. (*Locks the hall door.*) Here you shall stay and give me an explanation. Do you understand what you have done? Answer me! Do you understand what you have done?

NORA (*looks steadily at him and says with a growing look of coldness in her face*): Yes, now I am beginning to understand thoroughly.

HELMER (*walking about the room*): What a horrible awakening! All these eight years—she who was my joy and pride—a hypocrite, a liar—worse, worse—a criminal! The unutterable ugliness of it all!—For shame! For shame! (*Nora is silent and looks steadily at him. He stops in front of her.*) I ought to have suspected that something of the sort would happen. I ought to have foreseen it. All your father's want of principle—be silent!—all your father's want of principle has come out in you. No religion, no morality, no sense of duty—. How I am punished for having winked at what he did! I did it for your sake, and this is how you repay me.

NORA: Yes, that's just it.

HELMER: Now you have destroyed all my happiness. You have ruined all my future. It is horrible to think of! I am in the power of an unscrupulous man; he can do what he likes with me, ask anything he likes of me, give me any orders he pleases—I dare not refuse. And I must sink to such miserable depths because of a thoughtless woman!

NORA: When I am out of the way, you will be free.

HELMER: No fine speeches, please. Your father had always plenty of those ready, too. What good would it be to me if you were out of the way, as you say? Not the slightest. He can make the affair known everywhere; and if he does, I may be falsely suspected of having been a party to your criminal action. Very likely people will think I was behind it all—that it was I who prompted you! And I have to thank you for all this—you whom I have cherished during the whole of our married life. Do you understand now what it is you have done for me?

NORA (*coldly and quietly*): Yes.

HELMER: It is so incredible that I can't take it in. But we must come to some understanding. Take off that shawl. Take it off, I tell you. I must try and appease him some way or another. The matter must be hushed up at any cost. And as for you and me, it must appear as if everything between us were just as before—but naturally only in the eyes of the world. You will still remain in my house, that is a matter of course. But I shall not allow you to bring up the children; I dare not trust them to you. To think that I should be obliged to say so to one whom I have loved so dearly, and whom I still—. No, that is all over. From this moment happiness is not the question; all that concerns us is to save the remains, the fragments, the appearance—

A ring is heard at the front-door bell.

HELMER (*with a start*): What is that? So late! Can the worst—? Can he—? Hide yourself, Nora. Say you are ill.

Nora stands motionless. Helmer goes and unlocks the hall door.

MAID (*half-dressed, comes to the door*): A letter for the mistress.

HELMER: Give it to me. (*Takes the letter, and shuts the door.*) Yes, it is from him. You shall not have it; I will read it myself.

NORA: Yes, read it.

HELMER (*standing by the lamp*): I scarcely have the courage to do it. It may mean ruin for both of us. No, I must know. (*Tears open the letter, runs his eye over a few lines, looks at a paper enclosed, and gives a shout of joy.*) Nora! (*She looks at him questioningly.*) Nora!—No, I must read it once again—. Yes, it is true! I am saved! Nora, I am saved!

NORA: And I?

HELMER: You too, of course; we are both saved, both you and I. Look, he sends you your bond back. He says he regrets and repents—that a happy change in his life—never mind what he says! We are saved, Nora! No one can do anything to you. Oh, Nora, Nora!—no, first I must destroy these hateful things. Let me see—. (*Takes a look at the bond.*) No, no, I won't look at it. The whole thing shall be nothing but a bad dream to me. (*Tears up the bond and both letters, throws them all into the stove, and watches them burn.*) There—now it doesn't exist any longer. He says that since Christmas Eve you—. These must have been three dreadful days for you, Nora.

NORA: I have fought a hard fight these three days.

HELMER: And suffered agonies, and seen no way out but—. No, we won't call any of the horrors to mind. We will only shout with joy, and keep saying, "It's all over! It's all over!" Listen to me, Nora. You don't seem to realise that it is all over. What is this?—such a cold, set face! My poor little Nora, I quite understand; you don't feel as if you could believe that I have forgiven you. But it is true, Nora, I swear it; I have forgiven you everything. I know that what you did, you did out of love for me.

NORA: That is true.

HELMER: You have loved me as a wife ought to love her husband. Only you had not sufficient knowledge to judge of the means you used. But do you suppose you are any the less dear to me, because you don't understand how to act on your own responsibility? No, no; only lean on me; I will advise you and direct you. I should not be a man if this womanly helplessness did not just give you a double attractiveness in my eyes. You must not think anymore about the hard things I said in my first moment of consternation, when I thought everything was going to overwhelm me. I have forgiven you, Nora; I swear to you I have forgiven you.

NORA: Thank you for your forgiveness. (*She goes out through the door to the right.*)

HELMER: No, don't go—. (*Looks in.*) What are you doing in there?

NORA (*from within*): Taking off my fancy dress.

HELMER (*standing at the open door*): Yes, do. Try and calm yourself, and make your mind easy again, my frightened little singing-bird. Be at rest, and feel secure; I have broad wings to shelter you under. (*Walks up and down by the door.*) How warm and cosy our home is, Nora. Here is shelter for you; here I will protect you like a hunted dove that I have saved from a hawk's claws; I will bring peace to your poor beating heart. It will come, little by little, Nora, believe me. To-morrow morning you will look upon it all quite differently; soon everything will be just as it was before. Very soon you won't need me to assure you that I have forgiven you; you will yourself feel the certainty that I have done so. Can you suppose I should ever think of such a thing as repudiating you, or even reproaching you? You have no idea what a true man's heart is like, Nora. There is something so indescribably sweet and satisfying, to a man, in the knowledge that he has forgiven his wife—forgiven her freely, and with all his heart. It seems as if that had made her, as it were, doubly his own; he has given her a new life, so to speak; and she has in a way become both wife and child to him. So you shall be for me after this, my little scared, helpless darling. Have no anxiety about anything, Nora; only be frank and open with me, and I will serve as will and conscience both to you—. What is this? Not gone to bed? Have you changed your things?

NORA (*in everyday dress*): Yes, Torvald, I have changed my things now.

HELMER: But what for?—so late as this.

NORA: I shall not sleep to-night.

HELMER: But, my dear Nora—

NORA (*looking at her watch*): It is not so very late. Sit down here, Torvald. You and I have much to say to one another. (*She sits down at one side of the table.*)

HELMER: Nora—what is this?—this cold, set face?

NORA: Sit down. It will take some time; I have a lot to talk over with you.

HELMER (*sits down at the opposite side of the table*): You alarm me, Nora!—and I don't understand you.

NORA: No, that is just it. You don't understand me, and I have never understood you either—before to-night. No, you mustn't interrupt me. You must simply listen to what I say. Torvald, this is a settling of accounts.

HELMER: What do you mean by that?

NORA (*after a short silence*): Isn't there one thing that strikes you as strange in our sitting here like this?

HELMER: What is that?

NORA: We have been married now eight years. Does it not occur to you that this is the first time we two, you and I, husband and wife, have had a serious conversation?

HELMER: What do you mean by serious?

NORA: In all these eight years — longer than that — from the very beginning of our acquaintance, we have never exchanged a word on any serious subject.

HELMER: Was it likely that I would be continually and forever telling you about worries that you could not help me to bear?

NORA: I am not speaking about business matters. I say that we have never sat down in earnest together to try and get at the bottom of anything.

HELMER: But, dearest Nora, would it have been any good to you?

NORA: That is just it; you have never understood me. I have been greatly wronged, Torvald — first by papa and then by you.

HELMER: What! By us two — by us two, who have loved you better than anyone else in the world?

NORA (*shaking her head*): You have never loved me. You have only thought it pleasant to be in love with me.

HELMER: Nora, what do I hear you saying?

NORA: It is perfectly true, Torvald. When I was at home with papa, he told me his opinion about everything, and so I had the same opinions; and if I differed from him I concealed the fact, because he would not have liked it. He called me his doll-child, and he played with me just as I used to play with my dolls. And when I came to live with you —

HELMER: What sort of an expression is that to use about our marriage?

NORA (*undisturbed*): I mean that I was simply transferred from papa's hands into yours. You arranged everything according to your own taste, and so I got the same tastes as you — or else I pretended to, I am really not quite sure which — I think sometimes the one and sometimes the other. When I look back on it, it seems to me as if I had been living here like a poor woman — just from hand to mouth. I have existed merely to perform tricks for you, Torvald. But you would have it so. You and papa have committed a great sin against me. It is your fault that I have made nothing of my life.

HELMER: How unreasonable and how ungrateful you are, Nora! Have you not been happy here?

NORA: No, I have never been happy. I thought I was, but it has never really been so.

HELMER: Not — not happy!

NORA: No, only merry. And you have always been so kind to me. But our home has been nothing but a playroom. I have been your doll-wife, just as at home I was papa's doll-child; and here the children have been my dolls. I thought it great fun when you played with me, just as they thought it great fun when I played with them. That is what our marriage has been, Torvald.

HELMER: There is some truth in what you say—exaggerated and strained as your view of it is. But for the future it shall be different. Playtime shall be over, and lesson-time shall begin.

NORA: Whose lessons? Mine, or the children's?

HELMER: Both yours and the children's, my darling Nora.

NORA: Alas, Torvald, you are not the man to educate me into being a proper wife for you.

HELMER: And you can say that!

NORA: And I—how am I fitted to bring up the children?

HELMER: Nora!

NORA: Didn't you say so yourself a little while ago—that you dare not trust me to bring them up?

HELMER: In a moment of anger! Why do you pay any heed to that?

NORA: Indeed, you were perfectly right. I am not fit for the task. There is another task I must undertake first. I must try and educate myself—you are not the man to help me in that. I must do that for myself. And that is why I am going to leave you now.

HELMER (*springing up*): What do you say?

NORA: I must stand quite alone, if I am to understand myself and everything about me. It is for that reason that I cannot remain with you any longer.

HELMER: Nora, Nora!

NORA: I am going away from here now, at once. I am sure Christine will take me in for the night—

HELMER: You are out of your mind! I won't allow it! I forbid you!

NORA: It is no use forbidding me anything any longer. I will take with me what belongs to myself. I will take nothing from you, either now or later.

HELMER: What sort of madness is this!

NORA: To-morrow I shall go home—I mean, to my old home. It will be easiest for me to find something to do there.

HELMER: You blind, foolish woman!

NORA: I must try and get some sense, Torvald.

HELMER: To desert your home, your husband and your children! And you don't consider what people will say!

NORA: I cannot consider that at all. I only know that it is necessary for me.

HELMER: It's shocking. This is how you would neglect your most sacred duties.

NORA: What do you consider my most sacred duties?

HELMER: Do I need to tell you that? Are they not your duties to your husband and your children?

NORA: I have other duties just as sacred.

HELMER: That you have not. What duties could those be?

NORA: Duties to myself.

HELMER: Before all else, you are a wife and a mother.

NORA: I don't believe that any longer. I believe that before all else I am a reasonable human being, just as you are—or, at all events, that I must try and become one. I know quite well, Torvald, that most people would think you right, and that views of that kind are to be found in books; but I can no longer content myself with what most people say, or with what is found in books. I must think over things for myself and get to understand them.

HELMER: Can you not understand your place in your own home? Have you not a reliable guide in such matters as that?—have you no religion?

NORA: I am afraid, Torvald, I do not exactly know what religion is.

HELMER: What are you saying?

NORA: I know nothing but what the clergyman said, when I went to be confirmed. He told us that religion was this, and that, and the other. When I am away from all this, and am alone, I will look into that matter too. I will see if what the clergyman said is true, or at all events if it is true for me.

HELMER: This is unheard of in a girl of your age! But if religion cannot lead you aright, let me try and awaken your conscience. I suppose you have some moral sense? Or—answer me—am I to think you have none?

NORA: I assure you, Torvald, that is not an easy question to answer. I really don't know. The thing perplexes me altogether. I only know that you and I look at it in quite a different light. I am learning, too, that the law is quite another thing from what I supposed; but I find it impossible to convince myself that the law is right. According to it a woman has no right to spare her old dying father, or to save her husband's life. I can't believe that.

HELMER: You talk like a child. You don't understand the conditions of the world in which you live.

NORA: No, I don't. But now I am going to try. I am going to see if I can make out who is right, the world or I.

HELMER: You are ill, Nora; you are delirious; I almost think you are out of your mind.

NORA: I have never felt my mind so clear and certain as to-night.

HELMER: And is it with a clear and certain mind that you forsake your husband and your children?

NORA: Yes, it is.

HELMER: Then there is only one possible explanation.

NORA: What is that?

HELMER: You do not love me anymore.

NORA: No, that is just it.

HELMER: Nora!—and you can say that?

NORA: It gives me great pain, Torvald, for you have always been so kind to me, but I cannot help it. I do not love you any more.

HELMER (*regaining his composure*): Is that a clear and certain conviction too?

NORA: Yes, absolutely clear and certain. That is the reason why I will not stay here any longer.

HELMER: And can you tell me what I have done to forfeit your love?

NORA: Yes, indeed I can. It was to-night, when the wonderful thing did not happen; then I saw you were not the man I had thought you.

HELMER: Explain yourself better. I don't understand you.

NORA: I have waited so patiently for eight years; for, goodness knows, I knew very well that wonderful things don't happen every day. Then this horrible misfortune came upon me; and then I felt quite certain that the wonderful thing was going to happen at last. When Krogstad's letter was lying out there, never for a moment did I imagine that you would consent to accept this man's conditions. I was so absolutely certain that you would say to him: Publish the thing to the whole world. And when that was done—

HELMER: Yes, what then?—when I had exposed my wife to shame and disgrace?

NORA: When that was done, I was so absolutely certain, you would come forward and take everything upon yourself, and say: I am the guilty one.

HELMER: Nora—!

NORA: You mean that I would never have accepted such a sacrifice on your part? No, of course not. But what would my assurances have been worth against yours? That was the wonderful thing which I hoped for and feared; and it was to prevent that, that I wanted to kill myself.

HELMER: I would gladly work night and day for you, Nora—bear sorrow and want for your sake. But no man would sacrifice his honour for the one he loves.

NORA: It is a thing hundreds of thousands of women have done.

HELMER: Oh, you think and talk like a heedless child.

NORA: Maybe. But you neither think nor talk like the man I could bind myself to. As soon as your fear was over—and it was not fear for what threatened me, but for what might happen to you—when the whole thing was past, as far as you were concerned it was exactly as if nothing at all had happened. Exactly as before, I was your little skylark, your doll, which you would in future treat with doubly gentle care, because it was so brittle and fragile. (*Getting up.*) Torvald—it was then it dawned upon me that for eight years I had been living here with a strange man, and had borne him three children—. Oh, I can't bear to think of it! I could tear myself into little bits!

HELMER (*sadly*): I see, I see. An abyss has opened between us—there is no denying it. But, Nora, would it not be possible to fill it up?

NORA: As I am now, I am no wife for you.

HELMER: I have it in me to become a different man.

NORA: Perhaps—if your doll is taken away from you.

HELMER: But to part!—to part from you! No, no, Nora, I can't understand that idea.

NORA (*going out to the right*): That makes it all the more certain that it must be done. (*She comes back with her cloak and hat and a small bag which she puts on a chair by the table.*)

HELMER: Nora, Nora, not now! Wait until to-morrow.

NORA (*putting on her cloak*): I cannot spend the night in a strange man's room.

HELMER: But can't we live here like brother and sister—?

NORA (*putting on her hat*): You know very well that would not last long. (*Puts the shawl round her.*) Good-bye, Torvald. I won't see the little ones. I know they are in better hands than mine. As I am now, I can be of no use to them.

HELMER: But some day, Nora—some day?

NORA: How can I tell? I have no idea what is going to become of me.

HELMER: But you are my wife, whatever becomes of you.

NORA: Listen, Torvald. I have heard that when a wife deserts her husband's house, as I am doing now, he is legally freed from all obligations towards her. In any case, I set you free from all your obligations. You are not to feel yourself bound in the slightest way, any more than I shall. There must be perfect freedom on both sides. See, here is your ring back. Give me mine.

HELMER: That too?

NORA: That too.

HELMER: Here it is.

NORA: That's right. Now it is all over. I have put the keys here. The maids know all about everything in the house — better than I do. To-morrow, after I have left her, Christine will come here and pack up my own things that I brought with me from home. I will have them sent after me.

HELMER: All over! All over! — Nora, shall you never think of me again?

NORA: I know I shall often think of you, the children, and this house.

HELMER: May I write to you, Nora?

NORA: No — never. You must not do that.

HELMER: But at least let me send you —

NORA: Nothing — nothing —

HELMER: Let me help you if you are in want.

NORA: No. I can receive nothing from a stranger.

HELMER: Nora — can I never be anything more than a stranger to you?

NORA (*taking her bag*): Ah, Torvald, the most wonderful thing of all would have to happen.

HELMER: Tell me what that would be!

NORA: Both you and I would have to be so changed that — . Oh, Torvald, I don't believe any longer in wonderful things happening.

HELMER: But I will believe in it. Tell me! So changed that — ?

NORA: That our life together would be a real wedlock. Good-bye. (*She goes out through the hall.*)

HELMER (*sinks down on a chair at the door and buries his face in his hands*): Nora! Nora! (*Looks round, and rises.*) Empty. She is gone. (*A hope flashes across his mind.*) The most wonderful thing of all — ?

The sound of a door shutting is heard from below.

COMMENTARIES

HENRIK IBSEN

Henrik Ibsen wrote his first notes for the play that would become *A Doll House* on October 19, 1878. At first he conceived of the drama essentially as a marital conflict that would lead to Nora's destruction because of what he saw as her entrapment in a patriarchal society. This excerpt from Ibsen's notes is from the translator A. G. Chater's *From Ibsen's Workshop* (1978).

Notes for *A Doll House* 1878

There are two kinds of spiritual law, two kinds of conscience, one in man and another, altogether different, in woman. They do not understand each other; but in practical life the woman is judged by man's law, as though she were not a woman but a man.

The wife in the play ends by having no idea of what is right or wrong; natural feeling on the one hand and belief in authority on the other have altogether bewildered her.

A woman cannot be herself in the society of the present day, which is an exclusively masculine society, with laws framed by men and with a judicial system that judges feminine conduct from a masculine point of view.

She has committed forgery, and she is proud of it; for she did it out of love for her husband, to save his life. But this husband with his commonplace principles of honor is on the side of the law and looks at the question from the masculine point of view.

Spiritual conflicts. Oppressed and bewildered by the belief in authority, she loses faith in her moral right and ability to bring up her children. Bitterness. A mother in modern society, like certain insects who go away and die when she has done her duty in the propagation of the race. Love of life, of home, of husband and children and family. Now and then a womanly shaking off of her thoughts. Sudden return of anxiety and terror. She must bear it all alone. The catastrophe approaches, inexorably, inevitably. Despair, conflict, and destruction.

GEORGE BERNARD SHAW

George Bernard Shaw (1856–1950), the British playwright, was one of the first authors to recognize the importance of Ibsen's work in the theater. In *The Quintessence of Ibsenism* (1891; rev. ed. 1913) Shaw summarized the plot of the play and analyzed Nora's character with great sensitivity to the social issues that Ibsen had raised in the drama.

On *A Doll House* 1891

In the famous [*Doll*] *House,* the pillar of society who owns the doll is a model husband, father, and citizen. In his little household, with the three darling children and the affectionate little wife, all on the most loving terms with one another, we have the sweet home, the womanly woman, the happy family life of the idealist's dream. Mrs. Nora Helmer is happy in the belief that she has attained a valid realization of all these illusions; that she is an ideal wife and mother; and that Helmer is an ideal husband who would, if the necessity arose, give his life to save her reputation. A few simply contrived incidents disabuse her effectually on all these points. One of her earliest acts of devotion to her husband has been the secret raising of a sum of money to enable him to make a tour which was necessary to restore his health. As he would have broken down sooner than go into debt, she has had to persuade him that the money was a gift from her father. It was really obtained from a moneylender, who refused to make her the loan unless she induced her father to endorse the promissory note. This being impossible, as her father was dying at the time, she took the shortest way out of the difficulty by writing the name herself, to the entire satisfaction of the moneylender, who, though not at all duped, knew that forged bills are often the surest to be paid. Since then she has slaved in secret at scrivener's work until she has nearly paid off the debt.

At this point Helmer is made manager of the bank in which he is employed; and the moneylender, wishing to obtain a post there, uses the forged bill to force Nora to exert her influence with Helmer on his behalf. But she, having a hearty contempt for the man, cannot be persuaded by him that there was any harm in putting her father's name on the bill, and ridicules the suggestion that the law would not recognize that she was right under the circumstances. It is her husband's own contemptuous denunciation of a forgery formerly committed by the moneylender himself that destroys her self-satisfaction and opens her eyes to her ignorance of the serious business of the world to which her husband belongs: the world outside the home he shares with her. When he goes on to tell her that commercial dishonesty is generally to be traced to the influence of bad mothers, she begins to perceive that the happy way in which she plays with the children, and the care she takes to dress them nicely, are not sufficient to constitute her a fit person to train them. To redeem the forged bill, she resolves to borrow the balance due upon it from an intimate friend of the family. She has learnt to coax her husband into giving her what she asks by appealing to his affection for her: that is, by playing all sorts of pretty tricks until he is wheedled into an amorous humor. This plan she has adopted without thinking about it, instinctively taking the line of least resistance with him. And now she naturally takes the same line with her husband's friend. An unexpected declaration of love from him is the result; and it at once explains to her the real nature of the domestic influence she has been so proud of.

All her illusions about herself are now shattered. She sees herself as an ignorant and silly woman, a dangerous mother, and a wife kept for her husband's pleasure merely; but she clings all the harder to her illusion about him: He is still the ideal husband who would make any sacrifice to rescue her from ruin. She resolves to kill herself rather than allow him to destroy his own career by taking the forgery on himself to save her reputation. The final disillusion comes when he, instead of at once proposing to pursue this ideal line of conduct when he hears of the forgery, naturally enough flies into a vulgar rage and heaps invective on her for disgracing him. Then she sees that their whole family life has been a fiction: their home a mere doll's house in which they have been playing at ideal husband and father, wife and mother. So she leaves him then and there and goes out into the real world to find out its reality for herself, and to gain some position not fundamentally false, refusing to see her children again until she is fit to be in charge of them, or to live with him until she and he become capable of a more honorable relation to one another. He at first cannot understand what has happened, and flourishes the shattered ideals over her as if they were as potent as ever. He presents the course most agreeable to him—that of her staying at home and avoiding a scandal—as her duty to her husband, to her children, and to her religion; but the magic of these disguises is gone; and at last even he understands what has really happened, and sits down alone to wonder whether that more honorable relation can ever come to pass between them.

JOAN TEMPLETON

Joan Templeton prepared her ironic summary of the responses of a dozen critics writing about Ibsen's theme in his famous play for the *Publication of the Modern Language Association.* After reading the critics, you may find Templeton's conclusion surprises you in its uncompromising statement of uncommon sense.

Is *A Doll House* a Feminist Text? 1989

> *A Doll House* is no more about women's rights than Shakespeare's *Richard II* is about the divine right of kings, or *Ghosts* about syphilis. . . . Its theme is the need of every individual to find out the kind of person he or she is and to strive to become that person.[1]

Ibsen has been resoundingly saved from feminism, or, as it was called in his day, "the woman question." His rescuers customarily cite a statement the dramatist made on 26 May 1898 at a seventieth-birthday banquet given in his honor by the Norwegian Women's Rights League:

> I thank you for the toast, but must disclaim the honor of having consciously worked for the women's rights movement. . . . True enough, it is desirable to solve the woman problem, along with all the others; but that has not been the whole purpose. My task has been the description of humanity.[2]

Ibsen's champions like to take this disavowal as a precise reference to his purpose in writing *A Doll House* twenty years earlier, his "original intention," according to Maurice Valency.[3] Ibsen's biographer Michael Meyer urges all reviewers of *Doll House* revivals to learn Ibsen's speech by heart,[4] and James McFarlane, editor of *The Oxford Ibsen,* includes it in his explanatory material on *A Doll House,* under "Some Pronouncements of the Author," as though Ibsen had been speaking of the play.[5] Whatever propaganda feminists may

---

[1]Michael Meyer, *Ibsen* (Garden City: Doubleday, 1971), 457.

[2]Henrik Ibsen, *Letters and Speeches,* ed. and trans. Evert Sprinchorn (New York: Hill, 1964), 337.

[3]Maurice Valency, *The Flower and the Castle: An Introduction to Modern Drama* (New York: Schocken, 1982), 151.

[4]Meyer, 774.

[5]James McFarlane, "A Doll's House: Commentary" in *The Oxford Ibsen,* ed. McFarlane (Oxford UP, 1961), V, 456.

have made of *A Doll House,* Ibsen, it is argued, never meant to write a play about the highly topical subject of women's rights; Nora's conflict represents something other than, or something more than, woman's. In an article commemorating the half century of Ibsen's death, R. M. Adams explains, "*A Doll House* represents a woman imbued with the idea of becoming a person, but it proposes nothing categorical about women becoming people; in fact, its real theme has nothing to do with the sexes."[6] Over twenty years later, after feminism had resurfaced as an international movement, Einar Haugen, the doyen of American Scandinavian studies, insisted that "Ibsen's Nora is not just a woman arguing for female liberation; she is much more. She embodies the comedy as well as the tragedy of modern life."[7] In the Modern Language Association's *Approaches to Teaching* A Doll House, the editor speaks disparagingly of "reductionist views of [*A Doll House*] as a feminist drama." Summarizing a "major theme" in the volume as "the need for a broad view of the play and a condemnation of a static approach," she warns that discussions of the play's "connection with feminism" have value only if they are monitored, "properly channeled and kept firmly linked to Ibsen's text."[8]

Removing the woman question from *A Doll House* is presented as part of a corrective effort to free Ibsen from his erroneous reputation as a writer of thesis plays, a wrongheaded notion usually blamed on Shaw, who, it is claimed, mistakenly saw Ibsen as the nineteenth century's greatest iconoclast and offered that misreading to the public as *The Quintessence of Ibsenism.* Ibsen, it is now de rigueur to explain, did not stoop to "issues." He was a poet of the truth of the human soul. That Nora's exit from her dollhouse has long been the principal international symbol for women's issues, including many that far exceed the confines of her small world, is irrelevant to the essential meaning of *A Doll House,* a play, in Richard Gilman's phrase, "pitched beyond sexual difference."[9] Ibsen, explains Robert Brustein, "was completely indifferent to (the woman question) except as a metaphor for individual freedom."[10] Discussing the relation of *A Doll House* to feminism, Halvdan Koht, author of the definitive Norwegian Ibsen life, says in summary, "Little by little the topical controversy died away; what remained was the work of art, with its demand for truth in every human relation."[11]

Thus, it turns out, the *Uncle Tom's Cabin* of the women's rights movement is not really about women at all. "Fiddle-faddle," pronounced R. M. Adams, dismissing feminist claims for the play.[12] Like angels, Nora has no sex. Ibsen meant her to be Everyman.

---

[6]R. M. Adams, "The Fifty-First Anniversary," *Hudson Review* 10 (1957), 416.
[7]Einar Haugen, *Ibsen's Drama: Author to Audience* (Minneapolis: U of Minnesota P, 1979), vii.
[8]Yvonne Shafer, ed., *Approaches to Teaching Ibsen's* A Doll House (New York: MLA, 1985), 32.
[9]Richard Gilman, *The Making of Modern Drama* (New York: Farrar, 1972), 65.
[10]Robert Brustein, *The Theatre of Revolt* (New York: Little, 1962), 105.
[11]Halvdan Koht, *Life of Ibsen* (New York: Blom, 1971), 323.
[12]Adams, 416.

LIV ULLMANN

Liv Ullmann, the Norwegian actress, writer, and film director, played Nora in Henrik Ibsen's *A Doll House* in New York City in 1975. In her journal she noted her interpretation of the character. She found that performing the role in English after having learned it in the original Norwegian was very difficult, and she made several changes in the translation. As she said, "Nora's words are so full of meaning for me. I know them so well, and I think the English translation has missed a lot of what is Nora's distinctive quality." Ullmann's comments appeared in her memoir *Changing* (1977).

On Performing Nora in Ibsen's *A Doll House* 1977

I love Nora. She is beautiful, and perfectly drawn by Ibsen.

Her need to be accepted. Her fear of presenting herself as she really is.

A woman who says one thing and means something quite different. Who wants to be friends with, and liked by, everyone. Who exclaims, "Don't be angry with me!" the moment she senses she might have said something that could offend. And who all the while lives her secret life, and with strength and determination conducts financial transactions (unusual for a woman in those days) in order to save her husband's life.

This woman, who uses and manipulates those around her while at the same time wanting to help and love them, refuses to do something she feels is morally repugnant to her when the decisive moment comes. It is beyond her imagination to conceive of exploiting the situation when Dr. Rank declares his love and begs to give her the money she so badly needs.

Like Helmer, Nora is one of society's victims. She behaves in a way one would expect of a woman, of a wife, of a doll child.

She plays her part just as Helmer plays his. Neither of them gives the other a chance, because they are always in service to the other's role.

When she finally *sees*, she also understands that the anger she feels over everything that is false between them is directed just as much against herself as against him. Her responsibility was as great as his. She hopes that the change will also take place in him—not for her sake, but for his own.

Not because he is threatened by a new Nora, who shows a strength he doesn't comprehend, and which frightens him, but because he has discovered a new human being whose motives he may learn to understand.

I believe that Nora's most beautiful declaration and act of love is leaving her husband.

She says goodbye to everything that is familiar and secure. She does not walk through the door to find somebody else to live with and for; she is leaving the house more insecure than she ever realized she could be. But she hopes to find out who she is and why she is.

In this there is a great freedom: the knowledge that I have to part with my present life. I don't know for what. For myself. To be something more than I am now.

About ten times Nora exclaims: "Oh, I am so happy!" I choose to have her say it without joy — and the last time with sorrow, anxiety and longing. A critic states that I am trying to help Ibsen, so that the farewell in the final act will not come as such a shock. But I am sure Ibsen was aware of what he was doing. Do we need to go around repeating constantly that we are so happy if we really are?

Nora is strong, even in the first act: think of the joy with which she tells her friend about the long nights when she locks herself in and works.

Nora is lonely. When the doorbell rings she says to Kristina: "It's no one for me."

In the first acts Nora is not just the songbird and the squirrel; neither is she pure wisdom and feminine strength in the last.

To me, Helmer's and Nora's last scene is not a bravura number for Nora. That would be too easy. This is not how we leave someone we have loved, and presumably still love. It is not with fanfare and the sound of drums that we walk away from the familiar and go out into a new and strange world. With so little knowledge.

It is a little girl who slams the door behind her. A little girl in the process of growing up.

SUSAN GLASPELL

Susan Glaspell (1876–1948) was born in Davenport, Iowa, into a family that had been among the state's first settlers a generation before. After her graduation from high school, she worked as a reporter and society editor for various newspapers before enrolling at Drake University in Des Moines, where she studied literature, philosophy, and history. She also edited the college newspaper and began to write short stories. In 1899 she took a job as statehouse reporter for the *Des Moines Daily News*. Years later she claimed that the discipline of newspaper work helped her to become a creative writer.

At the age of twenty-five, Glaspell returned to Davenport to live with her family, "boldly" determined, as she said, to quit journalism and "give all my time to my own writing. I say 'boldly,' because I had to earn my living." Slowly she began to publish her own work, mostly sentimental magazine stories and an undistinguished first novel – fiction that, as her biographer C. W. E. Bigsby has noted, "suggested little of the originality and power which were to mark her work in the theater." In 1909 Glaspell met George Cram Cook, a novelist and utopian socialist from a wealthy family who divorced his second wife and left his two children to marry her.

Glaspell and Cook moved to Greenwich Village in New York City and collaborated on a short play for the experimental Washington Square Players in 1915, *Suppressed Desires*, a comedy about psychoanalysis and its founder, Sigmund Freud, whom they sarcastically referred to as "the new Messiah." The simple sets and amateur performances in this off-Broadway theater company contrasted with the ostentation then prevailing on Broadway. There producers such as David Belasco went to extreme lengths in the lavishness of their sets and costumes, transferring to the stage every detail of an actual Child's Restaurant, for example, in the popular play *The Governor's Lady* in 1912. After the Players left Greenwich Village to relocate in Provincetown on Cape Cod in 1916, Cook urged Glaspell to write a new play for their fledgling theater company, renamed the Provincetown Players. When she protested that she did not know how to write plays, he told her, "Nonsense. You've got a stage, haven't you?"

Glaspell's memory of a murder trial in Iowa that she'd covered as a newspaper reporter served as the inspiration for the short play *Trifles* (1916). A decade later, in her biography of her husband, *The Road to the Temple* (1927), Glaspell recalled how she visualized the play while sitting in a ramshackle fish house at the end of a wharf in Provincetown:

> So I went out on the wharf, sat alone on one of our wooden benches without a back, and looked a long time at that bare little stage. After a time the stage became a kitchen – a kitchen there all by itself. I saw just where the stove was, the table, and the steps going upstairs. Then the door at the back opened, and people all bundled up came in – two or three men, I wasn't sure which, but sure enough about the two women, who hung back, reluctant to enter that kitchen. When I was a newspaper reporter out in Iowa, I was sent down-state to do a murder trial, and I never forgot going into the kitchen of a woman locked up in town. I had meant to do it as a short story, but the stage took it for its own, so I hurried in from the wharf to write down what I had seen. Whenever I got stuck, I would run across the street to the old wharf, sit in that leaning little theater under which the sea sounded, until the play was ready to continue. Sometimes things written in my room would not form on the stage, and I must go home and cross them out.

Glaspell finished *Trifles* in ten days. It opened on August 8, 1916, with Glaspell and Cook in the cast. Glaspell went on to write ten more plays for the Provincetown Players, but *Trifles* is the one play of hers that is continually reprinted. She also published a short story version of the play, titled "A Jury of Her Peers," in 1917. During the six years of Cook's visionary leadership, the Provincetown Players produced one hundred plays by fifty-two authors. The company's promotion of American playwrights was an important landmark in the history of theater in the United States. As the historian Barbara Ozieblo realized, the Provincetown Players "constituted a laboratory for their two stars, Eugene O'Neill and Susan Glaspell; they triumphed both in the United States and in England; they broke the hegemony of Broadway, proving the value of little theatres and their experimental work and so seeding the mature drama of America."

CONNECTIONS Susan Glaspell, "A Jury of Her Peers," page 243; Lynn Nottage, *POOF!* page 1582.

WEB Research Susan Glaspell at bedfordstmartins.com/rewritinglit.

Trifles

1916

CHARACTERS

GEORGE HENDERSON, county attorney

HENRY PETERS, sheriff

LEWIS HALE, a neighboring farmer

MRS. PETERS

MRS. HALE

SCENE: *The kitchen in the now abandoned farmhouse of John Wright, a gloomy kitchen, and left without having been put in order—the walls covered with a faded wall paper. Down right is a door leading to the parlor. On the right wall above this door is a built-in kitchen cupboard with shelves in the upper portion and drawers below. In the rear wall at right, up two steps is a door opening onto stairs leading to the second floor. In the rear wall at left is a door to the shed and from there to the outside. Between these two doors is an old-fashioned black iron stove. Running along the left wall from the shed door is an old iron sink and sink shelf, in which is set a hand pump. Downstage of the sink is an uncurtained window. Near the window is an old wooden rocker. Center stage is an unpainted wooden kitchen table with straight chairs on either side. There is a small chair down right. Unwashed pans under the sink, a loaf of bread outside the breadbox, a dish towel on the table—other signs of incompleted work. At the rear the shed door opens and the Sheriff comes in followed by the County Attorney and Hale. The Sheriff and Hale are men in middle life, the County Attorney is a young man; all are much bundled up and go at once to the stove. They are followed by the two women—the Sheriff's wife, Mrs. Peters, first; she is a slight wiry woman, a thin nervous face. Mrs. Hale is larger and would ordinarily be called more comfortable looking, but she is disturbed now and looks fearfully about as she enters. The women have come in slowly, and stand close together near the door.*

COUNTY ATTORNEY (*at stove rubbing his hands*): This feels good. Come up to the fire, ladies.

MRS. PETERS (*after taking a step forward*): I'm not—cold.

SHERIFF (*unbuttoning his overcoat and stepping away from the stove to right of table as if to mark the beginning of official business*): Now, Mr. Hale, before we move things about, you explain to Mr. Henderson just what you saw when you came here yesterday morning.

COUNTY ATTORNEY (*crossing down to left of the table*): By the way, has anything been moved? Are things just as you left them yesterday?

SHERIFF (*looking about*): It's just about the same. When it dropped below zero last night I thought I'd better send Frank out this morning to make a fire for us—(*sits right of center table*) no use getting pneumonia with a big case on, but I told him not to touch anything except the stove—and you know Frank.

COUNTY ATTORNEY: Somebody should have been left here yesterday.

SHERIFF: Oh—yesterday. When I had to send Frank to Morris Center for that man who went crazy—I want you to know I had my hands full yesterday. I knew you could get back from Omaha by today and as long as I went over everything here myself——

COUNTY ATTORNEY: Well, Mr. Hale, tell just what happened when you came here yesterday morning.

HALE (*crossing down to above table*): Harry and I had started to town with a load of potatoes. We came along the road from my place and as I got here I said, "I'm going to see if I can't get John Wright to go in with me on a party telephone." I spoke to Wright about it once before and he put me off, saying folks talked too much anyway, and all he asked was peace and quiet—I guess you know about how much he talked himself; but I thought maybe if I went to the house and talked about it before his wife, though I said to Harry that I didn't know as what his wife wanted made much difference to John——

COUNTY ATTORNEY: Let's talk about that later, Mr. Hale. I do want to talk about that, but tell now just what happened when you got to the house.

HALE: I didn't hear or see anything; I knocked at the door, and still it was all quiet inside. I knew they must be up, it was past eight o'clock. So I knocked again, and I thought I heard somebody say, "Come in." I wasn't sure, I'm not sure yet, but I opened the door—this door (*indicating the door by which the two women are still standing*) and there in that rocker—(*pointing to it*) sat Mrs. Wright. (*They all look at the rocker down left.*)

COUNTY ATTORNEY: What—was she doing?

HALE: She was rockin' back and forth. She had her apron in her hand and was kind of—pleating it.

COUNTY ATTORNEY: And how did she—look?

HALE: Well, she looked queer.

COUNTY ATTORNEY: How do you mean—queer?

HALE: Well, as if she didn't know what she was going to do next. And kind of done up.

COUNTY ATTORNEY (*takes out notebook and pencil and sits left of center table*): How did she seem to feel about your coming?

HALE: Why, I don't think she minded—one way or other. She didn't pay much attention. I said, "How do, Mrs. Wright, it's cold, ain't it?" And she said, "Is it?"—and went on kind of pleating at her apron. Well, I was surprised; she didn't ask me to come up to the stove, or to set down, but just sat there, not even looking at me, so I said, "I want to see John." And then she—laughed. I guess you would call it a laugh. I thought of Harry and the team outside, so I said a little sharp: "Can't I see John?" "No," she says, kind o' dull like. "Ain't he home?" says I. "Yes," says she, "he's home." "Then why can't I see him?" I asked her, out of patience. "'Cause he's dead," says she. "*Dead?*" says I. She just nodded her head, not getting a bit excited, but rockin' back and forth. "Why—where is he?" says I, not knowing what to say. She just pointed upstairs—like that. (*Himself pointing to the room above.*) I started for the stairs, with the idea of going up there. I walked from there to here—then I says, "Why, what did he die of?" "He died of a rope round his neck," says she, and just went on pleatin' at her apron. Well, I went out and called Harry. I thought I might—need help. We went upstairs and there he was lyin'——

COUNTY ATTORNEY: I think I'd rather have you go into that upstairs, where you can point it all out. Just go on now with the rest of the story.

HALE: Well, my first thought was to get that rope off. It looked . . . (*stops; his face twitches*) . . . but Harry, he went up to him, and he said, "No, he's dead all right, and we'd better not touch anything." So we went back downstairs. She was still sitting that same way. "Has anybody been notified?" I asked. "No," says she, unconcerned. "Who did this, Mrs. Wright?" said Harry. He said it businesslike—and she stopped pleatin' of her apron. "I don't know," she says. "You don't *know*?" says Harry. "No," says she. "Weren't you sleepin' in the bed with him?" says Harry. "Yes," says she, "but I was on the inside." "Somebody slipped a rope round his neck and strangled him and you didn't wake up?" says Harry. "I didn't wake up," she said after him. We must 'a' looked as if we didn't see how that could be, for after a minute she said, "I sleep sound." Harry was going to ask her more questions but I said maybe we ought to let her tell her story first to the coroner, or the sheriff, so Harry went fast as he could to Rivers' place, where there's a telephone.

COUNTY ATTORNEY: And what did Mrs. Wright do when she knew that you had gone for the coroner?

HALE: She moved from the rocker to that chair over there (*pointing to a small chair in the down right corner*) and just sat there with her hands held together and looking down. I got a feeling that I ought to make some conversation, so I said I had come in to see if John wanted to put in a telephone, and at that she started to laugh, and then she stopped and looked at me—scared. (*The County Attorney, who has had his notebook out, makes a note.*) I dunno, maybe it wasn't scared. I wouldn't like to say it was. Soon Harry got back, and then Dr. Lloyd came and you, Mr. Peters, and so I guess that's all I know that you don't.

COUNTY ATTORNEY (*rising and looking around*): I guess we'll go upstairs first—and then out to the barn and around there. (*To the Sheriff.*) You're convinced that there was nothing important here—nothing that would point to any motive?

SHERIFF: Nothing here but kitchen things. (*The County Attorney, after again looking around the kitchen, opens the door of a cupboard closet in right wall. He brings a small chair from right—gets on it and looks on a shelf. Pulls his hand away, sticky.*)

COUNTY ATTORNEY: Here's a nice mess. (*The women draw nearer up center.*)

MRS. PETERS (*to the other woman*): Oh, her fruit; it did freeze. (*To the Lawyer.*) She worried about that when it turned so cold. She said the fire'd go out and her jars would break.

SHERIFF (*rises*): Well, can you beat the woman! Held for murder and worryin' about her preserves.

COUNTY ATTORNEY (*getting down from chair*): I guess before we're through she may have something more serious than preserves to worry about. (*Crosses down right center.*)

HALE: Well, women are used to worrying over trifles. (*The two women move a little closer together.*)

COUNTY ATTORNEY (*with the gallantry of a young politician*): And yet, for all their worries, what would we do without the ladies? (*The women do not unbend. He goes below the center table to the sink, takes a dipperful of water from the pail, and pouring it into a basin, washes his hands. While he is doing this the Sheriff and Hale cross to cupboard, which they inspect. The County Attorney starts to wipe his hands on the roller towel, turns it for a cleaner place.*) Dirty towels! (*Kicks his foot against the pans under the sink.*) Not much of a housekeeper, would you say, ladies?

MRS. HALE (*stiffly*): There's a great deal of work to be done on a farm.

COUNTY ATTORNEY: To be sure. And yet (*with a little bow to her*) I know there are some Dickson County farmhouses which do not have such roller towels. (*He gives it a pull to expose its full-length again.*)

MRS. HALE: Those towels get dirty awful quick. Men's hands aren't always as clean as they might be.

COUNTY ATTORNEY: Ah, loyal to your sex, I see. But you and Mrs. Wright were neighbors. I suppose you were friends, too.

MRS. HALE (*shaking her head*): I've not seen much of her of late years. I've not been in this house—it's more than a year.

COUNTY ATTORNEY (*crossing to women up center*): And why was that? You didn't like her?

MRS. HALE: I liked her all well enough. Farmers' wives have their hands full, Mr. Henderson. And then ——

COUNTY ATTORNEY: Yes ——?

MRS. HALE (*looking about*): It never seemed a very cheerful place.

COUNTY ATTORNEY: No—it's not cheerful. I shouldn't say she had the home-making instinct.

MRS. HALE: Well, I don't know as Wright had, either.

COUNTY ATTORNEY: You mean that they didn't get on very well?

MRS. HALE: No, I don't mean anything. But I don't think a place'd be any cheerfuller for John Wright's being in it.

COUNTY ATTORNEY: I'd like to talk more of that a little later. I want to get the lay of things upstairs now. (*He goes past the women to up right where steps lead to a stair door.*)

SHERIFF: I suppose anything Mrs. Peters does'll be all right. She was to take in some clothes for her, you know, and a few little things. We left in such a hurry yesterday.

COUNTY ATTORNEY: Yes, but I would like to see what you take, Mrs. Peters, and keep an eye out for anything that might be of use to us.

MRS. PETERS: Yes, Mr. Henderson. (*The men leave by up right door to stairs. The women listen to the men's steps on the stairs, then look about the kitchen.*)

MRS. HALE (*crossing left to sink*): I'd hate to have men coming into my kitchen, snooping around and criticizing. (*She arranges the pans under sink which the lawyer had shoved out of place.*)

MRS. PETERS: Of course it's no more than their duty. (*Crosses to cupboard up right.*)

MRS. HALE: Duty's all right, but I guess that deputy sheriff that came out to make the fire might have got a little of this on. (*Gives the roller towel a pull.*) Wish I'd thought of that sooner. Seems mean to talk about her for not having things slicked up when she had to come away in such a hurry. (*Crosses right to Mrs. Peters at cupboard.*)

MRS. PETERS (*who has been looking through cupboard, lifts one end of towel that covers a pan*): She had bread set. (*Stands still.*)

MRS. HALE (*eyes fixed on a loaf of bread beside the breadbox, which is on a low shelf of the cupboard*): She was going to put this in there. (*Picks up loaf, abruptly drops it. In a manner of returning to familiar things.*) It's a shame about her fruit. I wonder if it's all gone. (*Gets up on the chair and looks.*) I think there's some here that's all right, Mrs. Peters. Yes—here; (*holding it toward the window*) this is cherries, too. (*Looking again.*) I declare I believe that's the only one. (*Gets down, jar in her hand. Goes to the sink and wipes it off on the outside.*) She'll feel awful bad after all her hard work in the hot weather. I remember the afternoon I put up my cherries last summer. (*She puts the jar on the big kitchen table, center of the room. With a sigh, is about to sit down in the rocking chair. Before she is seated realizes what chair it is; with a slow look at it, steps back. The chair which she has touched rocks back and forth. Mrs. Peters moves to center table and they both watch the chair rock for a moment or two.*)

MRS. PETERS (*shaking off the mood which the empty rocking chair has evoked. Now in a businesslike manner she speaks*): Well I must get those things from the front room closet. (*She goes to the door at the right but, after looking into the other room, steps back.*) You coming with me, Mrs. Hale? You could help me carry them. (*They go in the other room; reappear, Mrs. Peters carrying a dress, petticoat, and skirt, Mrs. Hale following with a pair of shoes.*) My, it's cold in there. (*She puts the clothes on the big table and hurries to the stove.*)

MRS. HALE (*right of center table examining the skirt*): Wright was close. I think maybe that's why she kept so much to herself. She didn't even belong to the Ladies' Aid. I suppose she felt she couldn't do her part, and then you don't enjoy things when you feel shabby. I heard she used to wear pretty clothes and be lively, when she was Minnie Foster, one of the town girls singing in the choir. But that—oh, that was thirty years ago. This all you want to take in?

MRS. PETERS: She said she wanted an apron. Funny thing to want, for there isn't much to get you dirty in jail, goodness knows. But I suppose just to make her feel more natural. (*Crosses to cupboard.*) She said they was in the top drawer in this cupboard. Yes, here. And then her little shawl that always hung behind the door. (*Opens stair door and looks.*) Yes, here it is. (*Quickly shuts door leading upstairs.*)

MRS. HALE (*abruptly moving toward her*): Mrs. Peters?

MRS. PETERS: Yes, Mrs. Hale? (*At up right door.*)

MRS. HALE: Do you think she did it?

MRS. PETERS (*in a frightened voice*): Oh, I don't know.

MRS. HALE: Well, I don't think she did. Asking for an apron and her little shawl. Worrying about her fruit.

MRS. PETERS (*starts to speak, glances up, where footsteps are heard in the room above. In a low voice*): Mr. Peters says it looks bad for her. Mr. Henderson is awful sarcastic in a speech and he'll make fun of her sayin' she didn't wake up.

MRS. HALE: Well, I guess John Wright didn't wake when they was slipping that rope under his neck.

MRS. PETERS (*crossing slowly to table and placing shawl and apron on table with other clothing*): No, it's strange. It must have been done awful crafty and still. They say it was such a—funny way to kill a man, rigging it all up like that.

MRS. HALE (*crossing to left of Mrs. Peters at table*): That's just what Mr. Hale said. There was a gun in the house. He says that's what he can't understand.

MRS. PETERS: Mr. Henderson said coming out that what was needed for the case was a motive; something to show anger, or—sudden feeling.

MRS. HALE (*who is standing by the table*): Well, I don't see any signs of anger around here. (*She puts her hand on the dish towel, which lies on the table, stands looking down at table, one-half of which is clean, the other half messy.*) It's wiped to here. (*Makes a move as if to finish work, then turns and looks at loaf of bread outside the breadbox. Drops towel. In that voice of coming back to familiar things.*) Wonder how they are finding things upstairs. (*Crossing below table to down right.*) I hope she had it a little more redd up° up there. You know, it seems kind of *sneaking*. Locking her up in town and then coming out here and trying to get her own house to turn against her!

MRS. PETERS: But, Mrs. Hale, the law is the law.

MRS. HALE: I s'pose 'tis. (*Unbuttoning her coat.*) Better loosen up your things, Mrs. Peters. You won't feel them when you go out. (*Mrs. Peters takes off her fur tippet, goes to hang it on chair back left of table, stands looking at the work basket on floor near down left window.*)

MRS. PETERS: She was piecing a quilt. (*She brings the large sewing basket to the center table and they look at the bright pieces, Mrs. Hale above the table and Mrs. Peters left of it.*)

MRS. HALE: It's a log cabin pattern. Pretty, isn't it? I wonder if she was goin' to quilt it or just knot it? (*Footsteps have been heard coming down the stairs. The Sheriff enters followed by Hale and the County Attorney.*)

SHERIFF: They wonder if she was going to quilt it or just knot it! (*The men laugh, the women look abashed.*)

COUNTY ATTORNEY (*rubbing his hands over the stove*): Frank's fire didn't do much up there, did it? Well, let's go out to the barn and get that cleared up. (*The men go outside by up left door.*)

MRS. HALE (*resentfully*): I don't know as there's anything so strange, our takin' up our time with little things while we're waiting for them to get the evidence. (*She sits in chair right of table smoothing out a block with decision.*) I don't see as it's anything to laugh about.

MRS. PETERS (*apologetically*): Of course they've got awful important things on their minds. (*Pulls up a chair and joins Mrs. Hale at the left of the table.*)

---

redd up: Neat.

MRS. HALE (*examining another block*): Mrs. Peters, look at this one. Here, this is the one she was working on, and look at the sewing! All the rest of it has been so nice and even. And look at this! It's all over the place! Why, it looks as if she didn't know what she was about! (*After she has said this they look at each other, then start to glance back at the door. After an instant Mrs. Hale has pulled at a knot and ripped the sewing.*)

MRS. PETERS: Oh, what are you doing, Mrs. Hale?

MRS. HALE (*mildly*): Just pulling out a stitch or two that's not sewed very good. (*Threading a needle.*) Bad sewing always made me fidgety.

MRS. PETERS (*with a glance at door, nervously*): I don't think we ought to touch things.

MRS. HALE: I'll just finish up this end. (*Suddenly stopping and leaning forward.*) Mrs. Peters?

MRS. PETERS: Yes, Mrs. Hale?

MRS. HALE: What do you suppose she was so nervous about?

MRS. PETERS: Oh—I don't know. I don't know as she was nervous. I sometimes sew awful queer when I'm just tired. (*Mrs. Hale starts to say something, looks at Mrs. Peters, then goes on sewing.*) Well, I must get these things wrapped up. They may be through sooner than we think. (*Putting apron and other things together.*) I wonder where I can find a piece of paper, and string. (*Rises.*)

MRS. HALE: In that cupboard, maybe.

MRS. PETERS (*crosses right looking in cupboard*): Why, here's a bird-cage. (*Holds it up.*) Did she have a bird, Mrs. Hale?

MRS. HALE: Why, I don't know whether she did or not—I've not been here for so long. There was a man around last year selling canaries cheap, but I don't know as she took one; maybe she did. She used to sing real pretty herself.

MRS. PETERS (*glancing around*): Seems funny to think of a bird here. But she must have had one, or why would she have a cage? I wonder what happened to it?

MRS. HALE: I s'pose maybe the cat got it.

MRS. PETERS: No, she didn't have a cat. She's got that feeling some people have about cats—being afraid of them. My cat got in her room and she was real upset and asked me to take it out.

MRS. HALE: My sister Bessie was like that. Queer, ain't it?

MRS. PETERS (*examining the cage*): Why, look at this door. It's broke. One hinge is pulled apart. (*Takes a step down to Mrs. Hale's right.*)

MRS. HALE (*looking too*): Looks as if someone must have been rough with it.

MRS. PETERS: Why, yes. (*She brings the cage forward and puts it on the table.*)

MRS. HALE (*glancing toward up left door*): I wish if they're going to find any evidence they'd be about it. I don't like this place.

MRS. PETERS: But I'm awful glad you came with me, Mrs. Hale. It would be lonesome for me sitting here alone.

MRS. HALE: It would, wouldn't it? (*Dropping her sewing.*) But I tell you what I do wish, Mrs. Peters. I wish I had come over sometimes when *she* was here. I—(*looking around the room*)—wish I had.

MRS. PETERS: But of course you were awful busy, Mrs. Hale—your house and your children.

MRS. HALE (*rises and crosses left*): I could've come. I stayed away because it weren't cheerful—and that's why I ought to have come. I—(*looking out left window*)—I've never liked this place. Maybe because it's down in a hollow and you don't see the road. I dunno what it is, but it's a lonesome place and always was. I wish I had come over to see Minnie Foster sometimes. I can see now—(*Shakes her head.*)

MRS. PETERS (*left of table and above it*): Well, you mustn't reproach yourself, Mrs. Hale. Somehow we just don't see how it is with other folks until—something turns up.

MRS. HALE: Not having children makes less work—but it makes a quiet house, and Wright out to work all day, and no company when he did come in. (*Turning from window.*) Did you know John Wright, Mrs. Peters?

MRS. PETERS: Not to know him; I've seen him in town. They say he was a good man.

MRS. HALE: Yes—good; he didn't drink, and kept his word as well as most, I guess, and paid his debts. But he was a hard man, Mrs. Peters. Just to pass the time of day with him—(*Shivers.*) Like a raw wind that gets to the bone. (*Pauses, her eye falling on the cage.*) I should think she would 'a' wanted a bird. But what do you suppose went with it?

MRS. PETERS: I don't know, unless it got sick and died. (*She reaches over and swings the broken door, swings it again, both women watch it.*)

MRS. HALE: You weren't raised round here, were you? (*Mrs. Peters shakes her head.*) You didn't know—her?

MRS. PETERS: Not till they brought her yesterday.

MRS. HALE: She—come to think of it, she was kind of like a bird herself—real sweet and pretty, but kind of timid and—fluttery. How—she—did—change. (*Silence: then as if struck by a happy thought and relieved to get back to everyday things. Crosses right above Mrs. Peters to cupboard, replaces small chair used to stand on to its original place down right.*) Tell you what, Mrs. Peters, why don't you take the quilt in with you? It might take up her mind.

MRS. PETERS: Why, I think that's a real nice idea, Mrs. Hale. There couldn't possibly be any objection to it could there? Now, just what would I take? I wonder if her patches are in here—and her things. (*They look in the sewing basket.*)

MRS. HALE (*crosses to right of table*): Here's some red. I expect this has got sewing things in it. (*Brings out a fancy box.*) What a pretty box. Looks like something somebody would give you. Maybe her scissors are in here. (*Opens box. Suddenly puts her hand to her nose.*) Why ——— (*Mrs. Peters bends nearer, then turns her face away.*) There's something wrapped up in this piece of silk.

MRS. PETERS: Why, this isn't her scissors.

MRS. HALE (*lifting the silk*): Oh, Mrs. Peters—it's ——— (*Mrs. Peters bends closer.*)

MRS. PETERS: It's the bird.

MRS. HALE: But, Mrs. Peters—look at it! Its neck! Look at its neck! It's all—other side *to*.

MRS. PETERS: Somebody—wrung—its—neck. (*Their eyes meet. A look of growing comprehension, of horror. Steps are heard outside. Mrs. Hale slips box under quilt pieces, and sinks into her chair. Enter Sheriff and County Attorney. Mrs. Peters steps down left and stands looking out of window.*)

COUNTY ATTORNEY (*as one turning from serious things to little pleasantries*): Well, ladies, have you decided whether she was going to quilt it or knot it? (*Crosses to center above table.*)

MRS. PETERS: We think she was going to—knot it. (*Sheriff crosses to right of stove, lifts stove lid, and glances at fire, then stands warming hands at stove.*)

COUNTY ATTORNEY: Well, that's interesting, I'm sure. (*Seeing the bird-cage.*) Has the bird flown?

MRS. HALE (*putting more quilt pieces over the box*): We think the—cat got it.

COUNTY ATTORNEY (*preoccupied*): Is there a cat? (*Mrs. Hale glances in a quick covert way at Mrs. Peters.*)

MRS. PETERS (*turning from window takes a step in*): Well, not *now*. They're superstitious, you know. They leave.

COUNTY ATTORNEY (*to Sheriff Peters, continuing an interrupted conversation*): No sign at all of anyone having come from the outside. Their own rope. Now let's go up again and go over it piece by piece. (*They start upstairs.*) It would have to have been someone who knew just the——(*Mrs. Peters sits down left of table. The two women sit there not looking at one another, but as if peering into something and at the same time holding back. When they talk now it is in the manner of feeling their way over strange ground, as if afraid of what they are saying, but as if they cannot help saying it.*)

MRS. HALE (*hesitantly and in hushed voice*): She liked the bird. She was going to bury it in that pretty box.

MRS. PETERS (*in a whisper*): When I was a girl—my kitten—there was a boy took a hatchet, and before my eyes—and before I could get there——(*Covers her face an instant.*) If they hadn't held me back I would have—(*catches herself, looks upstairs where steps are heard, falters weakly*)—hurt him.

MRS. HALE (*with a slow look around her*): I wonder how it would seem never to have had any children around. (*Pause.*) No, Wright wouldn't like the bird—a thing that sang. She used to sing. He killed that, too.

MRS. PETERS (*moving uneasily*): We don't know who killed the bird.

MRS. HALE: I knew John Wright.

MRS. PETERS: It was an awful thing was done in this house that night, Mrs. Hale. Killing a man while he slept, slipping a rope around his neck that choked the life out of him.

MRS. HALE: His neck. Choked the life out of him. (*Her hand goes out and rests on the bird-cage.*)

MRS. PETERS (*with rising voice*): We don't know who killed him. We don't *know*.

MRS. HALE (*her own feeling not interrupted*): If there'd been years and years of nothing, then a bird to sing to you, it would be awful—still, after the bird was still.

MRS. PETERS (*something within her speaking*): I know what stillness is. When we homesteaded in Dakota, and my first baby died—after he was two years old, and me with no other then ———

MRS. HALE (*moving*): How soon do you suppose they'll be through looking for the evidence?

MRS. PETERS: I know what stillness is. (*Pulling herself back.*) The law has got to punish crime, Mrs. Hale.

MRS. HALE (*not as if answering that*): I wish you'd seen Minnie Foster when she wore a white dress with blue ribbons and stood up there in the choir and sang. (*A look around the room.*) Oh, I *wish* I'd come over here once in a while! That was a crime! That was a crime! Who's going to punish that?

MRS. PETERS (*looking upstairs*): We mustn't—take on.

MRS. HALE: I might have known she needed help! I know how things can be—for women. I tell you, it's queer, Mrs. Peters. We live close together and we live far apart. We all go through the same things—it's all just a different kind of the same thing. (*Brushes her eyes, noticing the jar of fruit, reaches out for it.*) If I was you I wouldn't tell her her fruit was gone. Tell her it *ain't.* Tell her it's all right. Take this in to prove it to her. She—she may never know whether it was broke or not.

MRS. PETERS (*takes the jar, looks about for something to wrap it in; takes petticoat from the clothes brought from the other room, very nervously begins winding this around the jar. In a false voice*): My, it's a good thing the men couldn't hear us. Wouldn't they just laugh! Getting all stirred up over a little thing like a—dead canary. As if that could have anything to do with—with—wouldn't they *laugh*! (*The men are heard coming downstairs.*)

MRS. HALE (*under her breath*): Maybe they would—maybe they wouldn't.

COUNTY ATTORNEY: No, Peters, it's all perfectly clear except a reason for doing it. But you know juries when it comes to women. If there was some definite thing. (*Crosses slowly to above table. Sheriff crosses down right. Mrs. Hale and Mrs. Peters remain seated at either side of table.*) Something to show—something to make a story about—a thing that would connect up with this strange way of doing it ——— (*The women's eyes meet for an instant. Enter Hale from outer door.*)

HALE (*remaining by door*): Well, I've got the team around. Pretty cold out there.

COUNTY ATTORNEY: I'm going to stay awhile by myself. (*To the Sheriff.*) You can send Frank out for me, can't you? I want to go over everything. I'm not satisfied that we can't do better.

SHERIFF: Do you want to see what Mrs. Peters is going to take in? (*The Lawyer picks up the apron, laughs.*)

COUNTY ATTORNEY: Oh, I guess they're not very dangerous things the ladies have picked out. (*Moves a few things about, disturbing the quilt pieces which cover the box. Steps back.*) No, Mrs. Peters doesn't need supervising. For that matter a sheriff's wife is married to the law. Ever think of it that way, Mrs. Peters?

MRS. PETERS: Not—just that way.

SHERIFF (*chuckling*): Married to the law. (*Moves to down right door to the other room.*) I just want you to come in here a minute, George. We ought to take a look at these windows.

COUNTY ATTORNEY (*scoffingly*): Oh, windows!

SHERIFF: We'll be right out, Mr. Hale. (*Hale goes outside. The Sheriff follows the County Attorney into the room. Then Mrs. Hale rises, hands tight together, looking intensely at Mrs. Peters, whose eyes make a slow turn, finally meeting Mrs. Hale's. A moment Mrs. Hale holds her, then her own eyes point the way to where the box is concealed. Suddenly Mrs. Peters throws back quilt pieces and tries to put the box in the bag she is carrying. It is too big. She opens box, starts to take bird out, cannot touch it, goes to pieces, stands there helpless. Sound of a knob turning in the other room. Mrs. Hale snatches the box and puts it in the pocket of her big coat. Enter County Attorney and Sheriff, who remains down right.*)

COUNTY ATTORNEY (*crosses to up left door facetiously*): Well, Henry, at least we found out that she was not going to quilt it. She was going to—what is it you call it, ladies?

MRS. HALE (*standing center below table facing front, her hand against her pocket*): We call it—knot it, Mr. Henderson.

Curtain.

COMMENTARY

LEONARD MUSTAZZA

Leonard Mustazza considers the similarities and differences between Glaspell's play and short story. This essay was published in the literary journal *Studies in Short Fiction.*

Generic Translation and Thematic Shift in Glaspell's *Trifles* and "A Jury of Her Peers" 1989

Commentators on Susan Glaspell's classic feminist short story, "A Jury of Her Peers" (1917), and the one-act play from which it derives, *Trifles* (1916), have tended to regard the two works as essentially alike. And even those few who have noticed the changes that Glaspell made in the process of generic translation have done so only in passing. In his monograph on Glaspell, Arthur Waterman, who seems to have a higher regard for the story than for the play, suggests that the story is a "moving fictional experience" because of the progressive honing of the author's skills, the story's vivid realism owing to her work as a local-color writer for the *Des Moines Daily News*, and its unified plot due to its dramatic origin.[1] More specifically, Elaine Hedges appropriately

[1]Arthur E. Waterman, *Susan Glaspell* (New York: Twayne, 1966), pp. 29–30.

notes the significance of Glaspell's change in titles from *Trifles*, which emphasizes the supposedly trivial household items with which the women "acquit" their accused peer, to "A Jury of Her Peers," which emphasizes the question of legality. In 1917, Hedges observes, women were engaged in the final years of their fight for the vote, and Glaspell's change in titles thus "emphasizes the story's contemporaneity, by calling attention to its references to the issue of women's legal place in American society."[2] Apart from these and a few other passing remarks, however, critics have chosen to focus on one work or the other. Indeed, thematic criticisms of the respective pieces are virtually indistinguishable, most of these commentaries focusing on the question of assumed "roles" in the works.[3]

On one level, there is good reason for this lack of differentiation. Not only is the overall narrative movement of the works similar, but Glaspell incorporated in the short story virtually every single line of the dialogue from *Trifles*.[4] By the same token, though, she also added much to the short story,

[2]Elaine Hedges, "Small Things Reconsidered: Susan Glaspell's 'A Jury of Her Peers,'" *Women's Studies*, 12, No. 1 (1986), 106.

[3]Rachel France notes that *Trifles* reveals "the dichotomy between men and women in rural life," an important feature of that dichotomy being the men's "proclivity for the letter of the law" as opposed to the women's more humane understanding of justice ("Apropos of Women and the Folk Play," in *Women in American Theatre: Careers, Images, Movements*, ed. Helen Krich Chinoy and Linda Walsh Jenkins [New York: Crown, 1981], p. 151). Karen Alkalay-Gut observes three polarities in "Jury": the opposition between the large external male world and the women's more circumscribed place within the home; the attitudes of men and women generally; and the distinction between *law*, which is identified with "the imposition of abstractions on individual circumstances," and *justice*, "the extrapolation of judgment from individual circumstances" ("Jury of Her Peers: The Importance of *Trifles*," *Studies in Short Fiction*, 21 [Winter 1984], 2). Karen Stein calls the play "an anomaly in the murder mystery genre, which is predominantly a male tour de force." By bonding together, she goes on, the women act in a manner that is "diametrically opposed to the solo virtuosity usually displayed by male detectives" ("The Women's World of Glaspell's *Trifles*," in *Women in American Theatre*, ed. Helen Krich Chinoy and Linda Walsh Jenkins [New York: Crown, 1981], p. 254). Judith Fetterly also advances an interesting and imaginative interpretation. She sees the characters in "Jury" as readers and the trivial household items as their text. The men fail to read the same meanings in that text that the women do because they are committed to "the equation of textuality with masculine subject matter and masculine point of view" ("Reading about Reading: 'A Jury of Her Peers,' 'The Murders in the Rue Morgue,' and 'The Yellow Wallpaper,'" in *Gender and Reading: Essays on Readers, Texts and Contexts*, ed. Elizabeth A. Flynn and Patrocinio P. Schweickart [Baltimore: Johns Hopkins Univ. Press, 1986], pp. 147–48).

[4]Elaine Hedges notes that one reference included in the play but omitted from "Jury" is Mrs. Hale's lament that, because of Mr. Wright's parsimony, Minnie could not join the Ladies' Aid, a society in which women cooperated with the local church to make items like carpets and quilts. These items were then sold to support ministers' salaries and to aid foreign missions. Minnie is thus denied not only the company of other women but also one of the few public roles that farm women were allowed to play ("Small Things Reconsidered," p. 102). In this regard, the story reveals, as Jeannie McKnight suggests, "a kind of classic 'cabin fever' as motivation for the homicide . . ." ("American Dream, Nightmare Underside: Diaries, Letters, and Fiction of Women on the American Frontier," in *Women, Women Writers, and the West*, ed. L. L. Lee and Merrill Lewis [Troy, NY: Whitson, 1979], p. 31).

which is about twice as long as the play. The nature of these additions is twofold, the first and most obvious being her descriptions of locales, modes of utterance, characters, props, and so on—the kinds of descriptions that the prose writer's form will allow but the dramatist's will not. The other type of alteration is more subtle, and it involves the revisions, embellishments, and redirections that occur when an existent story is retold. When, for instance, a novel is turned into a film or a play, the best that can be said about the generic translation is that it is "faithful," but never is it identical. So it is with "Jury." It is certainly faithful to the play, but it is also different in a variety of ways, and it is these differences, which took place in the act of generic translation, that I would like to consider here.

In her article on *Trifles*, Beverly Smith makes an interesting observation. Noting that the women in the play, Mrs. Hale and Mrs. Peters, function as defense counsel for and jury of their accused peer, Minnie Foster Wright, she goes on to suggest that the men's role, their official capacities notwithstanding, are comparable to that of a Greek Chorus, "the voice of the community's conscience," entering at various points to reiterate their major themes—Minnie's guilt and the triviality of the women's occupations, avocations, and preoccupations.[5] This equation is, I think, quite useful, for the periodic entries, commentaries, and exits of the male characters in both Glaspell works do in fact mark the progressive stages of the narrative, which primarily concerns the women, including the absent Minnie Foster.[6] Though not on stage for the entire drama, as is the Greek Chorus, the men nevertheless function in much the same way, providing commentary and separating the major movements of the narrative. What is more, if we regard the men's exits from the stage as marking these movements, we will recognize the first principal difference between the play and the story—namely, that the latter contains twice as many movements as the former and is therefore necessarily a more developed and complex work.

Trifles opens with Mr. Hale's account of what he found when he arrived at the Wright farm the day before. Of the women themselves, we know almost nothing beyond their general appearances as described in the opening stage directions—that Mrs. Peters, the sheriff's wife, is "a slight wiry woman [with] a thin nervous face"; and that Mrs. Hale, the witness's wife, is larger than Mrs. Peters and "comfortable looking," though now appearing fearful and disturbed as she enters the scene of the crime. Standing close together as they enter the Wrights' home, the women remain almost completely undifferentiated until, some time later, they begin to speak. Thus, Glaspell underscores here the male/female polarities that she will explore in the course of the play.

---

[5]Beverly A. Smith, "Women's Work—Trifles? The Skill and Insight of Playwright Susan Glaspell," *International Journal of Women's Studies*, 5 (March–April 1982), 175.

[6]Cynthia Sutherland aptly observes that the story's effect depends to a large extent upon the removal of Minnie from the sight of the audience, thus focusing our attention on the facts of her plight rather than on her appearance and mannerisms ("American Women Playwrights as Mediators of the 'Woman Problem,'" *Modern Drama*, 21 [September 1978], 323).

Her entire narrative technique is different in the prose version. That story begins in Mrs. Hale's disordered kitchen, which will later serve as a point of comparison with the major scene of the story, Mrs. Wright's kitchen. Annoyed at being called away from her housework, she nevertheless agrees to Sheriff Peters's request that she come along to accompany Mrs. Peters, who is there to fetch some personal effects for the jailed woman. Quite unlike the play's opening, which emphasizes the physical closeness of and the attitudinal similarities between the women, "Jury," taking us as it does into Mrs. Hale's thoughts, emphasizes the women's apartness:

> She had met Mrs. Peters the year before at the county fair, and the thing she remembered about her was that *she didn't seem to like the sheriff's wife*. She was small and thin and didn't have a strong voice. Mrs. Gorman, the sheriff's wife before Gorman went out and Peters came in, had a voice that somehow seemed to be backing up the law with every word. But if Mrs. Peters didn't look like a sheriff's wife, Peters made up for it in looking like a sheriff. . . . a heavy man with a big voice, who was particularly genial with the law-abiding, as if to make it plain that he knew the difference between criminals and non-criminals. (emphasis added)

Interestingly, for all the added material here, Glaspell omits mention of what the women look like. In fact, we will get no explicit statements on their appearance.

On the other hand, what we do get in this revised opening is much that sharply differentiates the story from the play. In the latter, we are provided with no indication of Mrs. Hale's bad feelings about the sheriff's wife, and, if anything, their close physical proximity leads us to conclude the opposite. Although the women in the story will later assume this same protective stance when they enter the accused's kitchen and then again when the county attorney criticizes Mrs. Wright's kitchen, the movement together there is little more than reflexive. Elaine Hedges has argued that the latter movement together begins the process of establishing "their common bonds with each other and with Minnie."[7] This may be so of their physical proximity in the play, where no distance is established between the women at the outset, but the story presents a different situation altogether, for any emotional closeness we might infer from their act is undercut by our knowledge of Mrs. Hale's lack of respect for Mrs. Peters, particularly by comparison with her predecessor, Mrs. Gorman.

Ironically, however, despite her seeming mismatch with her husband, her lack of corporal "presence," Mrs. Peters turns out to be more suited to her assumed public role than Mrs. Hale had suspected—all too suited, in fact, since she perfectly assumes her male-approved role. "Of course Mrs. Peters is one of us," the county attorney asserts prior to getting on with his investigation of the house, and that statement turns out to be laden with meaning in the story. In *Trifles*, when the men leave to go about their investigative business, the women, we are told, "listen to the men's steps, then look about the kitchen."

---

[7] "Small Things Reconsidered," p. 98.

In "Jury," however, we get much more. Again here, the women stand motionless, listening to the men's footsteps, but this momentary stasis is followed by a significant gesture: "Then, *as if releasing herself from something strange*, Mrs. Hale began to arrange the dirty pans under the sink, which the county attorney's disdainful push of the foot had deranged" (emphasis added). One is prompted here to ask: what is this "something strange" from which she releases herself? Though the actions described in the play and the story are the same, why does Glaspell not include in the stage directions to the play an indication of Mrs. Hale's facial expression?

The answer, I think, lies again in the expanded and altered context of "Jury," where the author continually stresses the distance between the women. If Mrs. Peters is, as the county attorney has suggested, one of "them," Mrs. Hale certainly is not, and she distances herself from her male-approved peer in word and deed. The something strange from which she releases herself is, in this context, her reflexive movement towards Mrs. Peters. Mrs. Hale is, in fact, both extricating herself from the male strictures placed upon all of the women and asserting her intellectual independence. Karen Alkalay-Gut has correctly observed that, to the men, the disorder of Mrs. Wright's kitchen implies her "potential homicidal tendencies, inconceivable in a good wife."[8] For her part, Mrs. Hale is rejecting the men's specious reasoning, complaining about the lawyer's disdainful treatment of the kitchen things and asserting, "I'd hate to have men comin' into my kitchen, snoopin' round and criticizin'," obviously recalling the disorder in her kitchen and resenting the conclusions about her that could be drawn. Lacking that opening scene, the play simply does not resonate so profoundly.

Even more telling is a subtle but important change that Glaspell made following Mrs. Hale's testy assertion. In both the play and the story, Mrs. Peters offers the meek defense, "Of course it's no more than their duty," and then the two works diverge. In *Trifles*, Mrs. Peters manages to change the subject. Noticing some dough that Mrs. Wright had been preparing the day before, she says flatly, "she had set bread," and that statement directs Mrs. Hale's attention to the half-done and ruined kitchen chores. In effect, the flow of conversation is mutually directed in the play, and the distance between the women is thus minimized. When she wrote the play, however, Glaspell omitted mention of the bread and instead took us into Mrs. Hale's thoughts, as she does at the beginning of the story:

> She thought of the flour in her kitchen at home—half sifted, half not sifted. She had been interrupted, and had left things half done. What had interrupted Minnie Foster? Why had that work been left half done? She made a move as if to finish it,—unfinished things always bothered her,—and then she glanced around and saw that Mrs. Peters was watching her—and she didn't want Mrs. Peters to get that feeling she got of work begun and then—for some reason—not finished.
>
> "It's a shame about her fruit," she said. . . .

[8]"Jury of Her Peers: The Importance of *Trifles*," p. 3.

Although mention of the ruined fruit preserves is included in the play as well, two significant additions are made in the above passage. First, there is the continual comparison between Mrs. Hale's life and Mrs. Wright's. Second, and more important, we get the clear sense here of Mrs. Hale's suspicion of Mrs. Peters, her not wanting to call attention to the unfinished job for fear that the sheriff's wife will get the wrong idea—or, in this case, the right idea, for the evidence of disturbance, however circumstantial, is something the men may be able to use against Mrs. Wright. In other words, unlike the play, the story posits a different set of polarities, with Mrs. Peters presumably occupying a place within the official party and Mrs. Hale taking the side of the accused against all of them.

We come at this point to a crossroads in the story. Mrs. Hale can leave things as they are and keep information to herself, or she can recruit Mrs. Peters as a fellow "juror" in the case, moving the sheriff's wife away from her sympathy for her husband's position and towards identification with the accused woman. Mrs. Hale chooses the latter course and sets about persuading Mrs. Peters to emerge, in Alkalay-Gut's words, "as an individual distinct from her role as sheriff's wife." Once that happens, "her identification with Minnie is rapid and becomes complete."[9]

The persuasive process begins easily but effectively, with Mrs. Hale reflecting upon the change in Minnie Foster Wright over the thirty or so years she has known her—the change, to use the metaphor that Glaspell will develop, from singing bird to muted caged bird. She follows this reminiscence with a direct question to Mrs. Peters about whether the latter thinks that Minnie killed her husband. "Oh, I don't know," is the frightened response in both works, but, as always, the story provides more insight and tension than does the drama. Still emphasizing in her revision the distance between the women, Glaspell has Mrs. Hale believe that her talk of the youthful Minnie has fallen on deaf ears: "Much difference it makes to her whether Minnie Foster had pretty clothes when she was a girl." This sense of the other woman's indifference to such irrelevant trivialities is occasioned not only by Mrs. Hale's persistent belief in the other woman's official role but also by an odd look that crosses Mrs. Peters's face. At second glance, however, Mrs. Hale notices something else that melts her annoyance and undercuts her suspicions about the sheriff's wife: "Then she looked again, and she wasn't so sure; in fact, she hadn't at any time been perfectly sure about Mrs. Peters. She had that shrinking manner, and yet her eyes looked as if they could see a long way into things." Whereas the play shows the women meandering towards concurrence, the short story is here seen to evolve—and part of that evolution, we must conclude, is due to Mrs. Hale's ability to persuade her peer to regard the case from her perspective. The look that she sees in Mrs. Peters's eyes suggests to her that she might be able to persuade her, that the potential for identification is there. Hence, when she asks whether Mrs. Peters thinks Minnie is guilty, the question resonates here in ways the play does not.

---

[9]"Jury of Her Peers: The Importance of *Trifles*," p. 6.

Accordingly, Mrs. Hale will become much more aggressive in her arguments hereafter, taking on something of the persuader's hopeful hostility, which, in the case of the story, stands in marked contrast to the hostility she felt for Mrs. Peters's official role earlier. Thus, when Mrs. Peters tries to retreat into a male argument, weakly asserting that "the law is the law," the Mrs. Hale of the short story does not let the remark pass, as the one in *Trifles* does: "the law is the law—and a bad stove is a bad stove. How'd you like to cook on this?" Even she, however, is startled by Mrs. Peters's immediate response to her homey analogy and *ad hominem* attack: "A person gets discouraged—and loses heart," Mrs. Peters says—"That look of seeing . . . through a thing to something else" back on her face.

As far as I am concerned, the addition of this passage is the most important change that Glaspell made in her generic translation. Having used this direct personal attack and having noted the ambivalence that Mrs. Peters feels for her role as sheriff's wife, Mrs. Hale will now proceed to effect closure of the gap between them—again, a gap that is never this widely opened in *Trifles*. Now Mrs. Hale will change her entire mode of attack, pushing the limits, doing things she hesitated doing earlier, assailing Mrs. Peters whenever she lapses into her easy conventional attitudes. For instance, when Mrs. Peters objects to Mrs. Hale's repair of a badly knitted quilt block—in effect, tampering with circumstantial evidence of Minnie's mental disturbance of the day before—Mrs. Hale proceeds to do it anyway. As a measure of how much she has changed, we have only to compare this act with her earlier hesitation to finish another chore for fear of what Mrs. Peters might think. She has no reason to be distrustful of Mrs. Peters any longer, for the process of identification is now well underway.

That identification becomes quite evident by the time the women find the most compelling piece of circumstantial evidence against Mrs. Wright—the broken bird cage and the dead bird, its neck wrung and its body placed in a pretty box in Mrs. Wright's sewing basket. When the men notice the cage and Mrs. Hale misleadingly speculates that a cat may have been at it, it is Mrs. Peters who confirms the matter. Asked by the county attorney whether a cat was on the premises, Mrs. Peters—fully aware that there is no cat and never has been—quickly and evasively replies, "Well, not *now*. . . . They're superstitious, you know; they leave." Not only is Mrs. Peters deliberately lying here, but, more important, she is assuming quite another role from the one she played earlier. Uttering a banality, she plays at being the shallow woman who believes in superstitions, thus consciously playing one of the roles the men expect her to assume and concealing her keen intellect from them, her ability to extrapolate facts from small details.

From this point forward, the play and the short story are essentially the same. Mrs. Hale will continue her persuasive assault, and Mrs. Peters will continue to struggle inwardly. The culmination of this struggle occurs when, late in the story, the county attorney says that "a sheriff's wife is married to the law," and she responds, "Not—just that way." In "Jury," however, this protest carries much greater force than it does in *Trifles* for the simple reason that it is a measure of how far Mrs. Peters has come in the course of the short story.

Appropriately enough, too, Mrs. Hale has the final word in both narratives. Asked derisively by the county attorney what stitch Mrs. Wright had been using to make her quilt, Mrs. Hale responds with false sincerity, "We call it—knot it, Mr. Henderson." Most critics have read this line as an ironic reference to the women's solidarity at this point.[10] That is quite true, but, as I have been suggesting here, the progress towards this solidarity varies subtly but unmistakably in the two narratives. Whereas *Trifles*, opening as it does with the women's close physical proximity, reveals the dichotomy between male and female concepts of justice and social roles, "A Jury of Her Peers" is much more concerned with the separateness of the women themselves and their self-injurious acquiescence in male-defined roles. Hence, in her reworking of the narrative, Glaspell did much more than translate the material from one genre to another. Rather, she subtly changed its theme, and, in so doing, she wrote a story that is much more interesting, resonant, and disturbing than the slighter drama from which it derives.

ARTHUR MILLER

Arthur Miller (1915–2005), the son of a clothing manufacturer, was born in Manhattan but moved to Brooklyn as a teenager when his father's business collapsed during the Depression. After high school he worked for two years in an automobile parts warehouse to save money for his college tuition. He wrote his first play in 1935 as a journalism student at the University of Michigan, later recalling for a *Paris Review* interviewer that

> it was written on a spring vacation in six days. I was so young that I dared do such things, begin it and finish it in a week. I'd seen about two plays in my life, so I didn't know how long an act was supposed to be, but across the hall there was a fellow who did the costumes for the University theater and he said, "Well, it's roughly forty minutes." I had written an enormous amount of material and I got an alarm clock. It was all a lark to me, and not to be taken too seriously . . . that's what I told myself. As it turned out, the acts were longer than that, but the sense of timing was in me even from the beginning, and the play had a form right from the start.

[10]Beverly Smith sees "the bond among women [as] the essential knot" ("Women's Work," p. 179). Cynthia Sutherland regards the reference to knotting as "a subdued, ironic, and grisly reminder of the manner in which a stifled wife has enacted her desperate retaliation" ("American Women Playwrights," p. 323). And Elaine Hedges argues that the reference has three meanings: the rope that Minnie knotted around her husband's neck; the bond among the women; and the fact that the women have tied the men in knots ("Small Things Reconsidered," p. 107).

Miller's early plays won prizes at the University of Michigan, and he went on after graduation to write plays for radio and work for the Federal Theater Project. After failing with *The Man Who Had All the Luck* in 1944, Miller had his first successful play in 1947 with *All My Sons*.

In Boston during the pre-Broadway preview of this play, Miller had a chance meeting outside the Colonial Theater with his uncle Manny Newman, a traveling salesman. Their encounter suggested the idea of *Death of a Salesman* to Miller a short time later. Miller recalled, "I could see his grim hotel room behind him, the long trip up from New York in his little car, the hopeless hope of the day's business. Without so much as acknowledging my greeting, he said, 'Buddy is doing very well.'" Miller understood that his uncle was a competitor at all times, and that he had taken the Colonial Theater marquee advertising Miller's new play as an irresistible challenge to assert that his own son, Buddy, was also a success. To Miller, his uncle was an absurd yet unforgettable figure, "so completely isolated from the ordinary laws of gravity, so elaborate in his fantastic inventions, and despite his ugliness so lyrically in love with fame and fortune and their inevitable descent on his family, that he possessed my imagination until I knew more or less precisely how he would react to any sign or word or idea."

Yet Miller was also aware that his uncle's unexpected appearance outside the Boston theater had another effect on him, cutting "through time like a knife through a layer cake." In the encounter Miller had felt himself reduced from an accomplished thirty-year-old playwright (*All My Sons* went on to win the year's Pulitzer Prize and a Drama Critics Circle Award) to an emotionally vulnerable adolescent. He decided to write a play about his uncle "without any transitions at all, dialogue that would simply leap from bone to bone of a skeleton that would not for an instant cease being added to, an organism as strictly economic as a leaf, as trim as an ant."

In six weeks during the spring of 1948, Miller wrote the first draft of *Death of a Salesman*. He credits a production of Tennessee Williams's *A Streetcar Named Desire* the previous November as another important influence that shaped his play: Williams's "words and their liberation, the joy of the writer in writing them, the radiant eloquence of its composition." The theater historian Brenda Murphy sees a link between Williams's poetic language in that play and "the poetry of the mundane that infuses *Salesman*." Elia Kazan, who directed both *Streetcar* and *Salesman*, recalled that Miller was also greatly impressed with the staging of Williams's play, appearing to be "full of wonder at the theatre's expressive possibilities. [Miller] told me he was amazed at how simply and successfully the non-realistic elements in the play . . . blended with the realistic ones."

Collaborating with Kazan and set designer Jo Mielziner, Miller extensively revised his preproduction script of *Death of a Salesman*. It was the hit of the 1948–49 Broadway season, running for 742 performances and winning the Pulitzer Prize, the Drama Critics Circle Award, the Donaldson Award, and Tony Awards for best play, best direction, best scene design, and best supporting actor. Published as a script, the play became a best-seller, and it was the only play ever to be a Book-of-the-Month Club selection. Perhaps the drama critic Brooks Atkinson summarized its appeal for audiences in his *New York Times* review after the premier of the play: "Mr. Miller has looked with compassion into the hearts of some ordinary Americans and quietly transferred their hope and anguish to the theatre." In the essay "Tragedy and the Common Man," Miller interpreted Willy Loman's tragedy as that of Everyman: "The Chinese reaction to my Beijing production of *Salesman* would confirm what had become more and more obvious over the decades in the play's hundreds of productions throughout the world: Willy was representative everywhere, in every kind of system, of ourselves in this time."

Miller continued to write plays, most notably *The Crucible* (1953) and *A View from the Bridge* (1956). He also wrote the screenplay of the film *The Misfits* for his second wife, Marilyn Monroe, from whom he was divorced in 1961. Among his later plays are *After the Fall* (1964), *The Archbishop's Ceiling* (1977), *Danger: Memory!* (1986), and *The Last Yankee* (1993). Miller also wrote a memoir, *Timebends* (1987), and excellent essays on the theater and the craft of playwriting, many of them collected in 1978 in *The Theatre Essays of Arthur Miller*, edited by Robert A. Martin.

WEB Research Arthur Miller at bedfordstmartins.com/rewritinglit.

Death of a Salesman 1949

Certain Private Conversations in Two Acts and a Requiem

CAST

WILLY LOMAN	UNCLE BEN
LINDA	HOWARD WAGNER
BIFF	JENNY
HAPPY	STANLEY
BERNARD	MISS FORSYTHE
THE WOMAN	LETTA
CHARLEY	

SCENE: *The action takes place in Willy Loman's house and yard and in various places he visits in the New York and Boston of today.*

Throughout the play, in the stage directions, left and right mean stage left and stage right.

ACT I

A melody is heard, played upon a flute. It is small and fine, telling of grass and trees and the horizon. The curtain rises.

Before us is the Salesman's house. We are aware of towering, angular shapes behind it, surrounding it on all sides. Only the blue light of the sky falls upon the house and forestage; the surrounding area shows an angry glow of orange. As more light appears, we see a solid vault of apartment houses around the small, fragile-seeming home. An air of the dream clings to the place, a dream rising out of reality. The kitchen at center seems actual enough, for there is a kitchen table with three chairs, and a refrigerator. But no other fixtures are seen. At the back of the kitchen there is a draped entrance, which leads to the living-room. To the right of the kitchen, on a level raised two feet, is a bedroom furnished only with a brass bedstead and a straight chair. On a shelf over the bed a silver athletic trophy stands. A window opens onto the apartment house at the side.

Behind the kitchen, on a level raised six and a half feet, is the boys' bedroom, at present barely visible. Two beds are dimly seen, and at the back of the room a dormer window. (This bedroom is above the unseen living-room.) At the left a stairway curves up to it from the kitchen.

The entire setting is wholly or, in some places, partially transparent. The roof-line of the house is one-dimensional; under and over it we see the apartment buildings. Before the house lies an apron, curving beyond the forestage into the orchestra. This forward area serves as the back yard as well as the locale of all Willy's imaginings and of his city scenes. Whenever the action is in the present the actors observe the imaginary wall-lines, entering the house only through its door at the left. But in the scenes of the past these boundaries are broken, and characters enter or leave a room by stepping "through" a wall onto the forestage.

From the right, Willy Loman, the Salesman, enters, carrying two large sample cases. The flute plays on. He hears but is not aware of it. He is past sixty years of age, dressed quietly. Even as he crosses the stage to the doorway of the house, his exhaustion is apparent. He unlocks the door, comes into the kitchen, and thankfully lets his burden down, feeling the soreness of his palms. A word-sigh escapes his lips—it might be "Oh, boy, oh, boy." He closes the door, then carries his cases out into the living-room, through the draped kitchen doorway.

Linda, his wife, has stirred in her bed at the right. She gets out and puts on a robe, listening. Most often jovial, she has developed an iron repression of her exceptions to Willy's behavior—she more than loves him, she admires him, as though his mercurial nature, his temper, his massive dreams and little cruelties, served her only as sharp reminders of the turbulent longings within him, longings which she shares but lacks the temperament to utter and follow to their end.

LINDA (*hearing Willy outside the bedroom, calls with some trepidation*): Willy!

WILLY: It's all right. I came back.

LINDA: Why? What happened? (*Slight pause.*) Did something happen, Willy?

WILLY: No, nothing happened.

LINDA: You didn't smash the car, did you?

WILLY (*with casual irritation*): I said nothing happened. Didn't you hear me?

LINDA: Don't you feel well?

WILLY: I'm tired to the death. (*The flute has faded away. He sits on the bed beside her, a little numb.*) I couldn't make it. I just couldn't make it, Linda.

LINDA (*very carefully, delicately*): Where were you all day? You look terrible.

WILLY: I got as far as a little above Yonkers. I stopped for a cup of coffee. Maybe it was the coffee.

LINDA: What?

WILLY (*after a pause*): I suddenly couldn't drive any more. The car kept going off onto the shoulder, y'know?

LINDA (*helpfully*): Oh. Maybe it was the steering again. I don't think Angelo knows the Studebaker.

WILLY: No, it's me, it's me. Suddenly I realize I'm goin' sixty miles an hour and I don't remember the last five minutes. I'm—I can't seem to—keep my mind to it.

LINDA: Maybe it's your glasses. You never went for your new glasses.

WILLY: No, I see everything. I came back ten miles an hour. It took me nearly four hours from Yonkers.

LINDA (*resigned*): Well, you'll just have to take a rest, Willy, you can't continue this way.

WILLY: I just got back from Florida.

LINDA: But you didn't rest your mind. Your mind is overactive, and the mind is what counts, dear.

WILLY: I'll start out in the morning. Maybe I'll feel better in the morning. (*She is taking off his shoes.*) These goddam arch supports are killing me.

LINDA: Take an aspirin. Should I get you an aspirin? It'll soothe you.

WILLY (*with wonder*): I was driving along, you understand? And I was fine. I was even observing the scenery. You can imagine, me looking at scenery, on the road every week of my life. But it's so beautiful up there, Linda, the trees are so thick, and the sun is warm. I opened the windshield and just let the warm air bathe over me. And then all of a sudden I'm goin' off the road! I'm tellin' ya, I absolutely forgot I was driving. If I'd've gone the other way over the white line I might've killed somebody. So I went on again—and five minutes later I'm dreamin' again, and I nearly—(*He presses two fingers against his eyes.*) I have such thoughts, I have such strange thoughts.

LINDA: Willy, dear. Talk to them again. There's no reason why you can't work in New York.

WILLY: They don't need me in New York. I'm the New England man. I'm vital in New England.

LINDA: But you're sixty years old. They can't expect you to keep traveling every week.

WILLY: I'll have to send a wire to Portland. I'm supposed to see Brown and Morrison tomorrow morning at ten o'clock to show the line. Goddammit, I could sell them! (*He starts putting on his jacket.*)

LINDA (*taking the jacket from him*): Why don't you go down to the place tomorrow and tell Howard you've simply got to work in New York? You're too accommodating, dear.

WILLY: If old man Wagner was alive I'd a been in charge of New York now! That man was a prince, he was a masterful man. But that boy of his, that Howard, he don't appreciate. When I went north the first time, the Wagner Company didn't know where New England was!

LINDA: Why don't you tell those things to Howard, dear?

WILLY (*encouraged*): I will, I definitely will. Is there any cheese?

LINDA: I'll make you a sandwich.

WILLY: No, go to sleep. I'll take some milk. I'll be up right away. The boys in?

LINDA: They're sleeping. Happy took Biff on a date tonight.

WILLY (*interested*): That so?

LINDA: It was so nice to see them shaving together, one behind the other, in the bathroom. And going out together. You notice? The whole house smells of shaving lotion.

WILLY: Figure it out. Work a lifetime to pay off a house. You finally own it, and there's nobody to live in it.

LINDA: Well, dear, life is a casting off. It's always that way.

WILLY: No, no, some people—some people accomplish something. Did Biff say anything after I went this morning?

LINDA: You shouldn't have criticized him, Willy, especially after he just got off the train. You mustn't lose your temper with him.

WILLY: When the hell did I lose my temper? I simply asked him if he was making any money. Is that a criticism?

LINDA: But, dear, how could he make any money?

WILLY (*worried and angered*): There's such an undercurrent in him. He became a moody man. Did he apologize when I left this morning?

LINDA: He was crestfallen, Willy. You know how he admires you. I think if he finds himself, then you'll both be happier and not fight any more.

WILLY: How can he find himself on a farm? Is that a life? A farmhand? In the beginning, when he was young, I thought, well, a young man, it's good for him to tramp around, take a lot of different jobs. But it's more than ten years now and he has yet to make thirty-five dollars a week!

LINDA: He's finding himself, Willy.

WILLY: Not finding yourself at the age of thirty-four is a disgrace!

LINDA: Shh!

WILLY: The trouble is he's lazy, goddammit!

LINDA: Willy, please!

WILLY: Biff is a lazy bum!

LINDA: They're sleeping. Get something to eat. Go on down.

WILLY: Why did he come home? I would like to know what brought him home.

LINDA: I don't know. I think he's still lost, Willy. I think he's very lost.

WILLY: Biff Loman is lost. In the greatest country in the world a young man with such—personal attractiveness, gets lost. And such a hard worker. There's one thing about Biff—he's not lazy.

LINDA: Never.

WILLY (*with pity and resolve*): I'll see him in the morning; I'll have a nice talk with him. I'll get him a job selling. He could be big in no time. My God! Remember how they used to follow him around in high school? When he smiled at one of them their faces lit up. When he walked down the street . . . (*He loses himself in reminiscences.*)

LINDA (*trying to bring him out of it*): Willy, dear, I got a new kind of American-type cheese today. It's whipped.

WILLY: Why do you get American when I like Swiss?

LINDA: I just thought you'd like a change—

WILLY: I don't want a change! I want Swiss cheese. Why am I always being contradicted?

LINDA (*with a covering laugh*): I thought it would be a surprise.

WILLY: Why don't you open a window in here, for God's sake?

LINDA (*with infinite patience*): They're all open, dear.

WILLY: The way they boxed us in here. Bricks and windows, windows and bricks.

LINDA: We should've bought the land next door.

WILLY: The street is lined with cars. There's not a breath of fresh air in the neighborhood. The grass don't grow any more, you can't raise a carrot in the back yard. They should've had a law against apartment houses. Remember those two beautiful elm trees out there? When I and Biff hung the swing between them?

LINDA: Yeah, like being a million miles from the city.

WILLY: They should've arrested the builder for cutting those down. They massacred the neighborhood. (*Lost.*) More and more I think of those days, Linda. This time of year it was lilac and wisteria. And then the peonies would come out, and the daffodils. What fragrance in this room!

LINDA: Well, after all, people had to move somewhere.

WILLY: No, there's more people now.

LINDA: I don't think there's more people. I think—

WILLY: There's more people! That's what's ruining this country! Population is getting out of control. The competition is maddening! Smell the stink from that apartment house! And another one on the other side . . . How can they whip cheese?

On Willy's last line, Biff and Happy raise themselves up in their beds, listening.

LINDA: Go down, try it. And be quiet.

WILLY (*turning to Linda, guiltily*): You're not worried about me, are you, sweetheart?

BIFF: What's the matter?

HAPPY: Listen!

LINDA: You've got too much on the ball to worry about.

WILLY: You're my foundation and my support, Linda.

LINDA: Just try to relax, dear. You make mountains out of molehills.

WILLY: I won't fight with him any more. If he wants to go back to Texas, let him go.

LINDA: He'll find his way.

WILLY: Sure. Certain men just don't get started till later in life. Like Thomas Edison, I think. Or B. F. Goodrich. One of them was deaf. (*He starts for the bedroom doorway.*) I'll put my money on Biff.

LINDA: And Willy—if it's warm Sunday we'll drive in the country. And we'll open the windshield, and take lunch.

WILLY: No, the windshields don't open on the new cars.

LINDA: But you opened it today.

WILLY: Me? I didn't. (*He stops.*) Now isn't that peculiar! Isn't that a remarkable—(*He breaks off in amazement and fright as the flute is heard distantly.*)

LINDA: What, darling?

WILLY: That is the most remarkable thing.

LINDA: What, dear?

WILLY: I was thinking of the Chevy. (*Slight pause.*) Nineteen twenty-eight . . . when I had that red Chevy—(*Breaks off.*) That funny? I coulda sworn I was driving that Chevy today.

LINDA: Well, that's nothing. Something must've reminded you.

WILLY: Remarkable. Ts. Remember those days? The way Biff used to simonize that car? The dealer refused to believe there was eighty thousand miles on it. (*He shakes his head.*) Heh! (*To Linda.*) Close your eyes, I'll be right up. (*He walks out of the bedroom.*)

HAPPY (*to Biff*): Jesus, maybe he smashed up the car again!

LINDA (*calling after Willy*): Be careful on the stairs, dear! The cheese is on the middle shelf! (*She turns, goes over to the bed, takes his jacket, and goes out of the bedroom.*)

Light has risen on the boys' room. Unseen, Willy is heard talking to himself, "Eighty thousand miles," and a little laugh. Biff gets out of bed, comes downstage a bit, and stands attentively. Biff is two years older than his brother Happy, well built, but in these days bears a worn air and seems less self-assured. He has succeeded less, and his dreams are stronger and less acceptable than Happy's. Happy is tall, powerfully made. Sexuality is like a visible color on him, or a scent that many women have discovered. He, like his brother, is lost, but in a different way, for he has never allowed himself to turn his face toward defeat and is thus more confused and hard-skinned, although seemingly more content.

HAPPY (*getting out of bed*): He's going to get his license taken away if he keeps that up. I'm getting nervous about him, y'know, Biff?

BIFF: His eyes are going.

HAPPY: No, I've driven with him. He sees all right. He just doesn't keep his mind on it. I drove into the city with him last week. He stops at a green light and then it turns red and he goes. (*He laughs.*)

BIFF: Maybe he's color-blind.

HAPPY: Pop? Why he's got the finest eye for color in the business. You know that.

BIFF (*sitting down on his bed*): I'm going to sleep.

HAPPY: You're not still sour on Dad, are you, Biff?

BIFF: He's all right, I guess.

WILLY (*underneath them, in the living-room*): Yes, sir, eighty thousand miles—eighty-two thousand!

BIFF: You smoking?

HAPPY (*holding out a pack of cigarettes*): Want one?

BIFF (*taking a cigarette*): I can never sleep when I smell it.

WILLY: What a simonizing job, heh!

HAPPY (*with deep sentiment*): Funny, Biff, y'know? Us sleeping in here again? The old beds. (*He pats his bed affectionately.*) All the talk that went across those two beds, huh? Our whole lives.

BIFF: Yeah. Lotta dreams and plans.

HAPPY (*with a deep and masculine laugh*): About five hundred women would like to know what was said in this room.

They share a soft laugh.

BIFF: Remember that big Betsy something—what the hell was her name—over on Bushwick Avenue?

HAPPY (*combing his hair*): With the collie dog!

BIFF: That's the one. I got you in there, remember?

HAPPY: Yeah, that was my first time — I think. Boy, there was a pig! (*They laugh, almost crudely.*) You taught me everything I know about women. Don't forget that.

BIFF: I bet you forgot how bashful you used to be. Especially with girls.

HAPPY: Oh, I still am, Biff.

BIFF: Oh, go on.

HAPPY: I just control it, that's all. I think I got less bashful and you got more so. What happened, Biff? Where's the old humor, the old confidence? (*He shakes Biff's knee. Biff gets up and moves restlessly about the room.*) What's the matter?

BIFF: Why does Dad mock me all the time?

HAPPY: He's not mocking you, he —

BIFF: Everything I say there's a twist of mockery on his face. I can't get near him.

HAPPY: He just wants you to make good, that's all. I wanted to talk to you about Dad for a long time, Biff. Something's — happening to him. He — talks to himself.

BIFF: I noticed that this morning. But he always mumbled.

HAPPY: But not so noticeable. It got so embarrassing I sent him to Florida. And you know something? Most of the time he's talking to you.

BIFF: What's he say about me?

HAPPY: I can't make it out.

BIFF: What's he say about me?

HAPPY: I think the fact that you're not settled, that you're still kind of up in the air . . .

BIFF: There's one or two other things depressing him, Happy.

HAPPY: What do you mean?

BIFF: Never mind. Just don't lay it all to me.

HAPPY: But I think if you just got started — I mean — is there any future for you out there?

BIFF: I tell ya, Hap, I don't know what the future is. I don't know — what I'm supposed to want.

HAPPY: What do you mean?

BIFF: Well, I spent six or seven years after high school trying to work myself up. Shipping clerk, salesman, business of one kind or another. And it's a measly manner of existence. To get on that subway on the hot mornings in summer. To devote your whole life to keeping stock, or making phone calls, or selling or buying. To suffer fifty weeks of the year for the sake of a two-week vacation, when all you really desire is to be outdoors, with your shirt off. And always to have to get ahead of the next fella. And still — that's how you build a future.

HAPPY: Well, you really enjoy it on a farm? Are you content out there?

BIFF (*with rising agitation*): Hap, I've had twenty or thirty different kinds of jobs since I left home before the war, and it always turns out the same. I just realized it lately. In Nebraska when I herded cattle, and the Dakotas, and Arizona, and now in Texas. It's why I came home now, I guess, because I realized it. This farm I work on, it's spring there now, see? And they've got about fifteen new colts. There's nothing more inspiring or—beautiful than the sight of a mare and a new colt. And it's cool there now, see? Texas is cool now, and it's spring. And whenever spring comes to where I am, I suddenly get the feeling, my God, I'm not gettin' anywhere! What the hell am I doing, playing around with horses, twenty-eight dollars a week! I'm thirty-four years old, I oughta be makin' my future. That's when I come running home. And now, I get here, and I don't know what to do with myself. (*After a pause.*) I've always made a point of not wasting my life, and everytime I come back here I know that all I've done is to waste my life.

HAPPY: You're a poet, you know that, Biff? You're a—you're an idealist!

BIFF: No, I'm mixed up very bad. Maybe I oughta get married. Maybe I oughta get stuck into something. Maybe that's my trouble. I'm like a boy. I'm not married. I'm not in business, I just—I'm like a boy. Are you content, Hap? You're a success, aren't you? Are you content?

HAPPY: Hell, no!

BIFF: Why? You're making money, aren't you?

HAPPY (*moving about with energy, expressiveness*): All I can do now is wait for the merchandise manager to die. And suppose I get to be merchandise manager? He's a good friend of mine, and he just built a terrific estate on Long Island. And he lived there about two months and sold it, and now he's building another one. He can't enjoy it once it's finished. And I know that's just what I would do. I don't know what the hell I'm workin' for. Sometimes I sit in my apartment—all alone. And I think of the rent I'm paying. And it's crazy. But then, it's what I always wanted. My own apartment, a car, and plenty of women. And still, goddammit, I'm lonely.

BIFF (*with enthusiasm*): Listen, why don't you come out West with me?

HAPPY: You and I, heh?

BIFF: Sure, maybe we could buy a ranch. Raise cattle, use our muscles. Men built like we are should be working out in the open.

HAPPY (*avidly*): The Loman Brothers, heh?

BIFF (*with vast affection*): Sure, we'd be known all over the counties!

HAPPY (*enthralled*): That's what I dream about, Biff. Sometimes I want to just rip my clothes off in the middle of the store and outbox that goddam merchandise manager. I mean I can outbox, outrun, and outlift anybody in that store, and I have to take orders from those common, petty sons-of-bitches till I can't stand it any more.

BIFF: I'm tellin' you, kid, if you were with me I'd be happy out there.

HAPPY (*enthused*): See, Biff, everybody around me is so false that I'm constantly lowering my ideals . . .

BIFF: Baby, together we'd stand up for one another, we'd have someone to trust.

HAPPY: If I were around you—

BIFF: Hap, the trouble is we weren't brought up to grub for money. I don't know how to do it.

HAPPY: Neither can I!

BIFF: Then let's go!

HAPPY: The only thing is—what can you make out there?

BIFF: But look at your friend. Builds an estate and then hasn't the peace of mind to live in it.

HAPPY: Yeah, but when he walks into the store the waves part in front of him. That's fifty-two thousand dollars a year coming through the revolving door, and I got more in my pinky finger than he's got in his head.

BIFF: Yeah, but you just said—

HAPPY: I gotta show some of those pompous, self-important executives over there that Hap Loman can make the grade. I want to walk into the store the way he walks in. Then I'll go with you, Biff. We'll be together yet, I swear. But take those two we had tonight. Now weren't they gorgeous creatures?

BIFF: Yeah, yeah, most gorgeous I've had in years.

HAPPY: I get that any time I want, Biff. Whenever I feel disgusted. The trouble is, it gets like bowling or something. I just keep knockin' them over and it doesn't mean anything. You still run around a lot?

BIFF: Naa. I'd like to find a girl—steady, somebody with substance.

HAPPY: That's what I long for.

BIFF: Go on! You'd never come home.

HAPPY: I would! Somebody with character, with resistance! Like Mom, y'know? You're gonna call me a bastard when I tell you this. That girl Charlotte I was with tonight is engaged to be married in five weeks. (*He tries on his new hat.*)

BIFF: No kiddin'!

HAPPY: Sure, the guy's in line for the vice-presidency of the store. I don't know what gets into me, maybe I just have an overdeveloped sense of competition or something, but I went and ruined her, and furthermore I can't get rid of her. And he's the third executive I've done that to. Isn't that a crummy characteristic? And to top it all, I go to their weddings! (*Indignantly, but laughing.*) Like I'm not supposed to take bribes. Manufacturers offer me a hundred-dollar bill now and then to throw an order their way. You know how honest I am, but it's like this girl, see. I hate myself for it. Because I don't want the girl, and, still, I take it and—I love it!

BIFF: Let's go to sleep.

HAPPY: I guess we didn't settle anything, heh?

BIFF: I just got one idea that I think I'm going to try.

HAPPY: What's that?

BIFF: Remember Bill Oliver?

HAPPY: Sure, Oliver is very big now. You want to work for him again?

BIFF: No, but when I quit he said something to me. He put his arm on my shoulder, and he said, "Biff, if you ever need anything, come to me."

HAPPY: I remember that. That sounds good.

BIFF: I think I'll go to see him. If I could get ten thousand or even seven or eight thousand dollars I could buy a beautiful ranch.

HAPPY: I bet he'd back you. 'Cause he thought highly of you, Biff. I mean, they all do. You're well liked, Biff. That's why I say to come back here, and we both have the apartment. And I'm tellin' you, Biff, any babe you want . . .

BIFF: No, with a ranch I could do the work I like and still be something. I just wonder though. I wonder if Oliver still thinks I stole that carton of basketballs.

HAPPY: Oh, he probably forgot that long ago. It's almost ten years. You're too sensitive. Anyway, he didn't really fire you.

BIFF: Well, I think he was going to. I think that's why I quit. I was never sure whether he knew or not. I know he thought the world of me, though. I was the only one he'd let lock up the place.

WILLY (*below*): You gonna wash the engine, Biff?

HAPPY: Shh!

Biff looks at Happy, who is gazing down, listening. Willy is mumbling in the parlor.

HAPPY: You hear that?

They listen. Willy laughs warmly.

BIFF (*growing angry*): Doesn't he know Mom can hear that?

WILLY: Don't get your sweater dirty, Biff!

A look of pain crosses Biff's face.

HAPPY: Isn't that terrible? Don't leave again, will you? You'll find a job here. You gotta stick around. I don't know what to do about him, it's getting embarrassing.

WILLY: What a simonizing job!

BIFF: Mom's hearing that!

WILLY: No kiddin', Biff, you got a date? Wonderful!

HAPPY: Go on to sleep. But talk to him in the morning, will you?

BIFF (*reluctantly getting into bed*): With her in the house. Brother!

HAPPY (*getting into bed*): I wish you'd have a good talk with him.

The light on their room begins to fade.

BIFF (*to himself in bed*): That selfish, stupid . . .

HAPPY: Sh . . . Sleep, Biff.

Their light is out. Well before they have finished speaking, Willy's form is dimly seen below in the darkened kitchen. He opens the refrigerator, searches in there, and takes out a bottle of milk. The apartment houses are fading out, and the entire house and surroundings become covered with leaves. Music insinuates itself as the leaves appear.

WILLY: Just wanna be careful with those girls, Biff, that's all. Don't make any promises. No promises of any kind. Because a girl, y'know, they always believe what you tell 'em, and you're very young, Biff, you're too young to be talking seriously to girls.

Light rises on the kitchen. Willy, talking, shuts the refrigerator door and comes downstage to the kitchen table. He pours milk into a glass. He is totally immersed in himself, smiling faintly.

WILLY: Too young entirely, Biff. You want to watch your schooling first. Then when you're all set, there'll be plenty of girls for a boy like you. (*He smiles broadly at a kitchen chair.*) That so? The girls pay for you? (*He laughs.*) Boy, you must really be makin' a hit.

Willy is gradually addressing—physically—a point offstage, speaking through the wall of the kitchen, and his voice has been rising in volume to that of a normal conversation.

WILLY: I been wondering why you polish the car so careful. Ha! Don't leave the hubcaps, boys. Get the chamois to the hubcaps. Happy, use newspaper on the windows, it's the easiest thing. Show him how to do it, Biff! You see, Happy? Pad it up, use it like a pad. That's it, that's it, good work. You're doin' all right, Hap. (*He pauses, then nods in approbation for a few seconds, then looks upward.*) Biff, first thing we gotta do when we get time is clip that big branch over the house. Afraid it's gonna fall in a storm and hit the roof. Tell you what. We get a rope and sling her around, and then we climb up there with a couple of saws and take her down. Soon as you finish the car, boys, I wanna see ya. I got a surprise for you, boys.

BIFF (*offstage*): Whatta ya got, Dad?

WILLY: No, you finish first. Never leave a job till you're finished—remember that. (*Looking toward the "big trees."*) Biff, up in Albany I saw a beautiful hammock. I think I'll buy it next trip, and we'll hang it right between those two elms. Wouldn't that be something? Just swingin' there under those branches. Boy, that would be . . .

Young Biff and Young Happy appear from the direction Willy was addressing. Happy carries rags and a pail of water. Biff, wearing a sweater with a block "S," carries a football.

BIFF (*pointing in the direction of the car offstage*): How's that, Pop, professional?

WILLY: Terrific. Terrific job, boys. Good work, Biff.

HAPPY: Where's the surprise, Pop?

WILLY: In the back seat of the car.

HAPPY: Boy! (*He runs off.*)

BIFF: What is it, Dad? Tell me, what'd you buy?

WILLY (*laughing, cuffs him*): Never mind, something I want you to have.

BIFF (*turns and starts off*): What is it, Hap?

HAPPY (*offstage*): It's a punching bag!

BIFF: Oh, Pop!

WILLY: It's got Gene Tunney's signature on it!

Happy runs onstage with a punching bag.

BIFF: Gee, how'd you know we wanted a punching bag?

WILLY: Well, it's the finest thing for the timing.

HAPPY (*lies down on his back and pedals with his feet*): I'm losing weight, you notice, Pop?

WILLY (*to Happy*): Jumping rope is good too.

BIFF: Did you see the new football I got?

WILLY (*examining the ball*): Where'd you get a new ball?

BIFF: The coach told me to practice my passing.

WILLY: That so? And he gave you the ball, heh?

BIFF: Well, I borrowed it from the locker room. (*He laughs confidentially.*)

WILLY (*laughing with him at the theft*): I want you to return that.

HAPPY: I told you he wouldn't like it!

BIFF (*angrily*): Well, I'm bringing it back!

WILLY (*stopping the incipient argument, to Happy*): Sure, he's gotta practice with a regulation ball, doesn't he? (*To Biff.*) Coach'll probably congratulate you on your initiative!

BIFF: Oh, he keeps congratulating my initiative all the time, Pop.

WILLY: That's because he likes you. If somebody else took that ball there'd be an uproar. So what's the report, boys, what's the report?

BIFF: Where'd you go this time, Dad? Gee we were lonesome for you.

WILLY (*pleased, puts an arm around each boy and they come down to the apron*): Lonesome, heh?

BIFF: Missed you every minute.

WILLY: Don't say? Tell you a secret, boys. Don't breathe it to a soul. Someday I'll have my own business, and I'll never have to leave home any more.

HAPPY: Like Uncle Charley, heh?

WILLY: Bigger than Uncle Charley! Because Charley is not—liked. He's liked, but he's not—well liked.

BIFF: Where'd you go this time, Dad?

WILLY: Well, I got on the road, and I went north to Providence. Met the Mayor.

BIFF: The Mayor of Providence!

WILLY: He was sitting in the hotel lobby.

BIFF: What'd he say?

WILLY: He said, "Morning!" And I said, "You got a fine city here, Mayor." And then he had coffee with me. And then I went to Waterbury. Waterbury is a fine city. Big clock city, the famous Waterbury clock. Sold a nice bill there. And then Boston—Boston is the cradle of the Revolution. A fine city. And a couple of other towns in Mass., and on to Portland and Bangor and straight home!

BIFF: Gee, I'd love to go with you sometime, Dad.

WILLY: Soon as summer comes.

HAPPY: Promise?

WILLY: You and Hap and I, and I'll show you all the towns. America is full of beautiful towns and fine, upstanding people. And they know me, boys, they know me up and down New England. The finest people. And when I bring you fellas up, there'll be open sesame for all of us, 'cause one thing, boys: I have friends. I can park my car in any street in New England, and the cops protect it like their own. This summer, heh?

BIFF AND HAPPY (*together*): Yeah! You bet!

WILLY: We'll take our bathing suits.

HAPPY: We'll carry your bags, Pop!

WILLY: Oh, won't that be something! Me comin' into the Boston stores with you boys carryin' my bags. What a sensation!

Biff is prancing around, practicing passing the ball.

WILLY: You nervous, Biff, about the game?

BIFF: Not if you're gonna be there.

WILLY: What do they say about you in school, now that they made you captain?

HAPPY: There's a crowd of girls behind him everytime the classes change.

BIFF (*taking Willy's hand*): This Saturday, Pop, this Saturday—just for you, I'm going to break through for a touchdown.

HAPPY: You're supposed to pass.

BIFF: I'm takin' one play for Pop. You watch me, Pop, and when I take off my helmet, that means I'm breakin' out. Then you watch me crash through that line!

WILLY (*kisses Biff*): Oh, wait'll I tell this in Boston!

Bernard enters in knickers. He is younger than Biff, earnest and loyal, a worried boy.

BERNARD: Biff, where are you? You're supposed to study with me today.

WILLY: Hey, looka Bernard. What're you lookin' so anemic about, Bernard?

BERNARD: He's gotta study, Uncle Willy. He's got Regents next week.

HAPPY (*tauntingly, spinning Bernard around*): Let's box, Bernard!

BERNARD: Biff! (*He gets away from Happy.*) Listen, Biff, I heard Mr. Birnbaum say that if you don't start studyin' math, he's gonna flunk you, and you won't graduate. I heard him!

WILLY: You better study with him, Biff. Go ahead now.

BERNARD: I heard him!

BIFF: Oh, Pop, you didn't see my sneakers! (*He holds up a foot for Willy to look at.*)

WILLY: Hey, that's a beautiful job of printing!

BERNARD (*wiping his glasses*): Just because he printed University of Virginia on his sneakers doesn't mean they've got to graduate him, Uncle Willy!

WILLY (*angrily*): What're you talking about? With scholarships to three universities they're gonna flunk him?

BERNARD: But I heard Mr. Birnbaum say—

WILLY: Don't be a pest, Bernard! (*To his boys.*) What an anemic!

BERNARD: Okay, I'm waiting for you in my house, Biff.

Bernard goes off. The Lomans laugh.

WILLY: Bernard is not well liked, is he?

BIFF: He's liked, but he's not well liked.

HAPPY: That's right, Pop.

WILLY: That's just what I mean. Bernard can get the best marks in school, y'understand, but when he gets out in the business world, y'understand, you are going to be five times ahead of him. That's why I thank Almighty God you're both built like Adonises.° Because the man who makes an appearance in the business world, the man who creates personal interest, is the man who gets ahead. Be liked and you will never want. You take me, for instance. I never have to wait in line to see a buyer. "Willy Loman is here!" That's all they have to know, and I go right through.

BIFF: Did you knock them dead, Pop?

Adonises: In Greek mythology Adonis is a youth known for his good looks and favored by Aphrodite, the goddess of love and beauty.

WILLY: Knocked 'em cold in Providence, slaughtered 'em in Boston.
HAPPY (*on his back, pedaling again*): I'm losing weight, you notice, Pop?

Linda enters, as of old, a ribbon in her hair, carrying a basket of washing.

LINDA (*with youthful energy*): Hello, dear!
WILLY: Sweetheart!
LINDA: How'd the Chevy run?
WILLY: Chevrolet, Linda, is the greatest car ever built. (*To the boys.*) Since when do you let your mother carry wash up the stairs?
BIFF: Grab hold there, boy!
HAPPY: Where to, Mom?
LINDA: Hang them up on the line. And you better go down to your friends, Biff. The cellar is full of boys. They don't know what to do with themselves.
BIFF: Ah, when Pop comes home they can wait!
WILLY (*laughs appreciatively*): You better go down and tell them what to do, Biff.
BIFF: I think I'll have them sweep out the furnace room.
WILLY: Good work, Biff.
BIFF (*goes through wall-line of kitchen to doorway at back and calls down*): Fellas! Everybody sweep out the furnace room! I'll be right down!
VOICES: All right! Okay, Biff.
BIFF: George and Sam and Frank, come out back! We're hangin' up the wash! Come on, Hap, on the double! (*He and Happy carry out the basket.*)
LINDA: The way they obey him!
WILLY: Well, that's training, the training. I'm tellin' you, I was sellin' thousands and thousands, but I had to come home.
LINDA: Oh, the whole block'll be at that game. Did you sell anything?
WILLY: I did five hundred gross in Providence and seven hundred gross in Boston.
LINDA: No! Wait a minute, I've got a pencil. (*She pulls pencil and paper out of her apron pocket.*) That makes your commission . . . Two hundred—my God! Two hundred and twelve dollars!
WILLY: Well, I didn't figure it yet, but . . .
LINDA: How much did you do?
WILLY: Well, I—I did—about a hundred and eighty gross in Providence. Well, no—it came to—roughly two hundred gross on the whole trip.
LINDA (*without hesitation*): Two hundred gross. That's . . . (*She figures.*)
WILLY: The trouble was that three of the stores were half closed for inventory in Boston. Otherwise I woulda broke records.
LINDA: Well, it makes seventy dollars and some pennies. That's very good.
WILLY: What do we owe?
LINDA: Well, on the first there's sixteen dollars on the refrigerator—
WILLY: Why sixteen?
LINDA: Well, the fan belt broke, so it was a dollar eighty.
WILLY: But it's brand new.
LINDA: Well, the man said that's the way it is. Till they work themselves in, y'know.

They move through the wall-line into the kitchen.

WILLY: I hope we didn't get stuck on that machine.

LINDA: They got the biggest ads of any of them!

WILLY: I know, it's a fine machine. What else?

LINDA: Well, there's nine-sixty for the washing machine. And for the vacuum cleaner there's three and a half due on the fifteenth. Then the roof, you got twenty-one dollars remaining.

WILLY: It don't leak, does it?

LINDA: No, they did a wonderful job. Then you owe Frank for the carburetor.

WILLY: I'm not going to pay that man! That goddam Chevrolet, they ought to prohibit the manufacture of that car!

LINDA: Well, you owe him three and a half. And odds and ends, comes to around a hundred and twenty dollars by the fifteenth.

WILLY: A hundred and twenty dollars! My God, if business don't pick up I don't know what I'm gonna do!

LINDA: Well, next week you'll do better.

WILLY: Oh, I'll knock 'em dead next week. I'll go to Hartford. I'm very well liked in Hartford. You know, the trouble is, Linda, people don't seem to take to me.

They move onto the forestage.

LINDA: Oh, don't be foolish.

WILLY: I know it when I walk in. They seem to laugh at me.

LINDA: Why? Why would they laugh at you? Don't talk that way, Willy.

Willy moves to the edge of the stage. Linda goes into the kitchen and starts to darn stockings.

WILLY: I don't know the reason for it, but they just pass me by. I'm not noticed.

LINDA: But you're doing wonderful, dear. You're making seventy to a hundred dollars a week.

WILLY: But I gotta be at it ten, twelve hours a day. Other men—I don't know—they do it easier. I don't know why—I can't stop myself—I talk too much. A man oughta come in with a few words. One thing about Charley. He's a man of few words, and they respect him.

LINDA: You don't talk too much, you're just lively.

WILLY (*smiling*): Well, I figure, what the hell, life is short, a couple of jokes. (*To himself.*) I joke too much! (*The smile goes.*)

LINDA: Why? You're—

WILLY: I'm fat. I'm very—foolish to look at, Linda. I didn't tell you, but Christmas time I happened to be calling on F. H. Stewarts, and a salesman I know, as I was going in to see the buyer I heard him say something about—walrus. And I—I cracked him right across the face. I won't take that. I simply will not take that. But they do laugh at me. I know that.

LINDA: Darling . . .

WILLY: I gotta overcome it. I know I gotta overcome it. I'm not dressing to advantage, maybe.

LINDA: Willy, darling, you're the handsomest man in the world—

WILLY: Oh, no, Linda.

LINDA: To me you are. (*Slight pause.*) The handsomest.

From the darkness is heard the laughter of a woman. Willy doesn't turn to it, but it continues through Linda's lines.

LINDA: And the boys, Willy. Few men are idolized by their children the way you are.

Music is heard as behind a scrim, to the left of the house, The Woman, dimly seen, is dressing.

WILLY (*with great feeling*): You're the best there is, Linda, you're a pal, you know that? On the road—on the road I want to grab you sometimes and just kiss the life outa you.

The laughter is loud now, and he moves into a brightening area at the left, where The Woman has come from behind the scrim and is standing, putting on her hat, looking into a "mirror" and laughing.

WILLY: 'Cause I get so lonely—especially when business is bad and there's nobody to talk to. I get the feeling that I'll never sell anything again, that I won't make a living for you, or a business, a business for the boys. (*He talks through The Woman's subsiding laughter; The Woman primps at the "mirror."*) There's so much I want to make for—

THE WOMAN: Me? You didn't make me, Willy. I picked you.

WILLY (*pleased*): You picked me?

THE WOMAN (*who is quite proper-looking, Willy's age*): I did. I've been sitting at that desk watching all the salesmen go by, day in, day out. But you've got such a sense of humor, and we do have such a good time together, don't we?

WILLY: Sure, sure. (*He takes her in his arms.*) Why do you have to go now?

THE WOMAN: It's two o'clock . . .

WILLY: No, come on in! (*He pulls her.*)

THE WOMAN:. . . my sisters'll be scandalized. When'll you be back?

WILLY: Oh, two weeks about. Will you come up again?

THE WOMAN: Sure thing. You do make me laugh. It's good for me. (*She squeezes his arm, kisses him.*) And I think you're a wonderful man.

WILLY: You picked me, heh?

THE WOMAN: Sure. Because you're so sweet. And such a kidder.

WILLY: Well, I'll see you next time I'm in Boston.

THE WOMAN: I'll put you right through to the buyers.

WILLY (*slapping her bottom*): Right. Well, bottoms up!

THE WOMAN (*slaps him gently and laughs*): You just kill me, Willy. (*He suddenly grabs her and kisses her roughly.*) You kill me. And thanks for the stockings. I love a lot of stockings. Well, good night.

WILLY: Good night. And keep your pores open!

THE WOMAN: Oh, Willy!

The Woman bursts out laughing, and Linda's laughter blends in. The Woman disappears into the dark. Now the area at the kitchen table brightens. Linda is sitting where she was at the kitchen table, but now is mending a pair of her silk stockings.

LINDA: You are, Willy. The handsomest man. You've got no reason to feel that—

WILLY (*coming out of The Woman's dimming area and going over to Linda*): I'll make it all up to you, Linda, I'll—

LINDA: There's nothing to make up, dear. You're doing fine, better than—

WILLY (*noticing her mending*): What's that?

LINDA: Just mending my stockings. They're so expensive—

WILLY (*angrily, taking them from her*): I won't have you mending stockings in this house! Now throw them out!

Linda puts the stockings in her pocket.

BERNARD (*entering on the run*): Where is he? If he doesn't study!

WILLY (*moving to the forestage, with great agitation*): You'll give him the answers!

BERNARD: I do, but I can't on a Regents! That's a state exam! They're liable to arrest me!

WILLY: Where is he? I'll whip him, I'll whip him!

LINDA: And he'd better give back that football, Willy, it's not nice.

WILLY: Biff! Where is he? Why is he taking everything?

LINDA: He's too rough with the girls, Willy. All the mothers are afraid of him!

WILLY: I'll whip him!

BERNARD: He's driving the car without a license!

The Woman's laugh is heard.

WILLY: Shut up!

LINDA: All the mothers—

WILLY: Shut up!

BERNARD (*backing quietly away and out*): Mr. Birnbaum says he's stuck up.

WILLY: Get outa here!

BERNARD: If he doesn't buckle down he'll flunk math! (*He goes off.*)

LINDA: He's right, Willy, you've gotta—

WILLY (*exploding at her*): There's nothing the matter with him! You want him to be a worm like Bernard? He's got spirit, personality . . .

As he speaks, Linda, almost in tears, exits into the living-room. Willy is alone in the kitchen, wilting and staring. The leaves are gone. It is night again, and the apartment houses look down from behind.

WILLY: Loaded with it. Loaded! What is he stealing? He's giving it back, isn't he? Why is he stealing? What did I tell him? I never in my life told him anything but decent things.

Happy in pajamas has come down the stairs; Willy suddenly becomes aware of Happy's presence.

HAPPY: Let's go now, come on.

WILLY (*sitting down at the kitchen table*): Huh! Why did she have to wax the floors herself? Everytime she waxes the floors she keels over. She knows that!

HAPPY: Shh! Take it easy. What brought you back tonight?

WILLY: I got an awful scare. Nearly hit a kid in Yonkers. God! Why didn't I go to Alaska with my brother Ben that time! Ben! That man was a genius, that man was success incarnate! What a mistake! He begged me to go.

HAPPY: Well, there's no use in—

WILLY: You guys! There was a man started with the clothes on his back and ended up with diamond mines!

HAPPY: Boy, someday I'd like to know how he did it.

WILLY: What's the mystery? The man knew what he wanted and went out and got it! Walked into a jungle, and comes out, the age of twenty-one, and he's rich! The world is an oyster, but you don't crack it open on a mattress!

HAPPY: Pop, I told you I'm gonna retire you for life.

WILLY: You'll retire me for life on seventy goddam dollars a week? And your women and your car and your apartment, and you'll retire me for life! Christ's sake, I couldn't get past Yonkers today! Where are you guys, where are you? The woods are burning! I can't drive a car!

Charley has appeared in the doorway. He is a large man, slow of speech, laconic, immovable. In all he says, despite what he says, there is pity, and, now, trepidation. He has a robe over pajamas, slippers on his feet. He enters the kitchen.

CHARLEY: Everything all right?

HAPPY: Yeah, Charley, everything's . . .

WILLY: What's the matter?

CHARLEY: I heard some noise. I thought something happened. Can't we do something about the walls? You sneeze in here, and in my house hats blow off.

HAPPY: Let's go to bed, Dad. Come on.

Charley signals to Happy to go.

WILLY: You go ahead, I'm not tired at the moment.

HAPPY (*to Willy*): Take it easy, huh? (*He exits.*)

WILLY: What're you doin' up?

CHARLEY (*sitting down at the kitchen table opposite Willy*): Couldn't sleep good. I had a heartburn.

WILLY: Well, you don't know how to eat.

CHARLEY: I eat with my mouth.

WILLY: No, you're ignorant. You gotta know about vitamins and things like that.

CHARLEY: Come on, let's shoot. Tire you out a little.

WILLY (*hesitantly*): All right. You got cards?

CHARLEY (*taking a deck from his pocket*): Yeah, I got them. Someplace. What is it with those vitamins?

WILLY (*dealing*): They build up your bones. Chemistry.

CHARLEY: Yeah, but there's no bones in a heartburn.

WILLY: What are you talkin' about? Do you know the first thing about it?

CHARLEY: Don't get insulted.

WILLY: Don't talk about something you don't know anything about.

They are playing. Pause.

CHARLEY: What're you doin' home?

WILLY: A little trouble with the car.

CHARLEY: Oh. (*Pause.*) I'd like to take a trip to California.

WILLY: Don't say.

CHARLEY: You want a job?

WILLY: I got a job, I told you that. (*After a slight pause.*) What the hell are you offering me a job for?

CHARLEY: Don't get insulted.

WILLY: Don't insult me.

CHARLEY: I don't see no sense in it. You don't have to go on this way.

WILLY: I got a good job. (*Slight pause.*) What do you keep comin' in here for?

CHARLEY: You want me to go?

WILLY (*after a pause, withering*): I can't understand it. He's going back to Texas again. What the hell is that?

CHARLEY: Let him go.

WILLY: I got nothin' to give him, Charley, I'm clean, I'm clean.

CHARLEY: He won't starve. None a them starve. Forget about him.

WILLY: Then what have I got to remember?

CHARLEY: You take it too hard. To hell with it. When a deposit bottle is broken you don't get your nickel back.

WILLY: That's easy enough for you to say.

CHARLEY: That ain't easy for me to say.

WILLY: Did you see the ceiling I put up in the living-room?

CHARLEY: Yeah, that's a piece of work. To put up a ceiling is a mystery to me. How do you do it?

WILLY: What's the difference?

CHARLEY: Well, talk about it.

WILLY: You gonna put up a ceiling?

CHARLEY: How could I put up a ceiling?

WILLY: Then what the hell are you bothering me for?

CHARLEY: You're insulted again.

WILLY: A man who can't handle tools is not a man. You're disgusting.

CHARLEY: Don't call me disgusting, Willy.

Uncle Ben, carrying a valise and an umbrella, enters the forestage from around the right corner of the house. He is a stolid man, in his sixties, with a mustache and an authoritative air. He is utterly certain of his destiny, and there is an aura of far places about him. He enters exactly as Willy speaks.

WILLY: I'm getting awfully tired, Ben.

Ben's music is heard. Ben looks around at everything.

CHARLEY: Good, keep playing; you'll sleep better. Did you call me Ben?

Ben looks at his watch.

WILLY: That's funny. For a second there you reminded me of my brother Ben.

BEN: I only have a few minutes. (*He strolls, inspecting the place. Willy and Charley continue playing.*)

CHARLEY: You never heard from him again, heh? Since that time?

WILLY: Didn't Linda tell you? Couple of weeks ago we got a letter from his wife in Africa. He died.

CHARLEY: That so.

BEN (*chuckling*): So this is Brooklyn, eh?

CHARLEY: Maybe you're in for some of his money.

WILLY: Naa, he had seven sons. There's just one opportunity I had with that man . . .

BEN: I must make a train, William. There are several properties I'm looking at in Alaska.

WILLY: Sure, sure! If I'd gone with him to Alaska that time, everything would've been totally different.

CHARLEY: Go on, you'd froze to death up there.

WILLY: What're you talking about?

BEN: Opportunity is tremendous in Alaska, William. Surprised you're not up there.

WILLY: Sure, tremendous.

CHARLEY: Heh?

WILLY: There was the only man I ever met who knew the answers.

CHARLEY: Who?

BEN: How are you all?

WILLY (*taking a pot, smiling*): Fine, fine.

CHARLEY: Pretty sharp tonight.

BEN: Is mother living with you?

WILLY: No, she died a long time ago.

CHARLEY: Who?

BEN: That's too bad. Fine specimen of a lady, Mother.

WILLY (*to Charley*): Heh?

BEN: I'd hoped to see the old girl.

CHARLEY: Who died?

BEN: Heard anything from Father, have you?

WILLY (*unnerved*): What do you mean, who died?

CHARLEY (*taking a pot*): What're you talkin' about?

BEN (*looking at his watch*): William, it's half-past eight!

WILLY (*as though to dispel his confusion he angrily stops Charley's hand*): That's my build!

CHARLEY: I put the ace—

WILLY: If you don't know how to play the game I'm not gonna throw my money away on you!

CHARLEY (*rising*): It was my ace, for God's sake!

WILLY: I'm through, I'm through!

BEN: When did Mother die?

WILLY: Long ago. Since the beginning you never knew how to play cards.

CHARLEY (*picks up the cards and goes to the door*): All right! Next time I'll bring a deck with five aces.

WILLY: I don't play that kind of game!

CHARLEY (*turning to him*): You ought to be ashamed of yourself!

WILLY: Yeah?

CHARLEY: Yeah! (*He goes out.*)

WILLY (*slamming the door after him*): Ignoramus!

BEN (*as Willy comes toward him through the wall-line of the kitchen*): So you're William.

WILLY (*shaking Ben's hand*): Ben! I've been waiting for you so long! What's the answer? How did you do it?

BEN: Oh, there's a story in that.

Linda enters the forestage, as of old, carrying the wash basket.

LINDA: Is this Ben?

BEN (*gallantly*): How do you do, my dear.

LINDA: Where've you been all these years? Willy's always wondered why you—

WILLY (*pulling Ben away from her impatiently*): Where is Dad? Didn't you follow him? How did you get started?

BEN: Well, I don't know how much you remember.

WILLY: Well, I was just a baby, of course, only three or four years old—

BEN: Three years and eleven months.

WILLY: What a memory, Ben!

BEN: I have many enterprises, William, and I have never kept books.

WILLY: I remember I was sitting under the wagon in—was it Nebraska?

BEN: It was South Dakota, and I gave you a bunch of wild flowers.

WILLY: I remember you walking away down some open road.

BEN (*laughing*): I was going to find Father in Alaska.

WILLY: Where is he?

BEN: At that age I had a very faulty view of geography, William. I discovered after a few days that I was heading due south, so instead of Alaska, I ended up in Africa.

LINDA: Africa!

WILLY: The Gold Coast!

BEN: Principally diamond mines.

LINDA: Diamond mines!

BEN: Yes, my dear. But I've only a few minutes—

WILLY: No! Boys! Boys! (*Young Biff and Happy appear.*) Listen to this. This is your Uncle Ben, a great man! Tell my boys, Ben!

BEN: Why, boys, when I was seventeen I walked into the jungle, and when I was twenty-one I walked out. (*He laughs.*) And by God I was rich.

WILLY (*to the boys*): You see what I been talking about? The greatest things can happen!

BEN (*glancing at his watch*): I have an appointment in Ketchikan Tuesday week.

WILLY: No, Ben! Please tell about Dad. I want my boys to hear. I want them to know the kind of stock they spring from. All I remember is a man with a big beard, and I was in Mamma's lap, sitting around a fire, and some kind of high music.

BEN: His flute. He played the flute.

WILLY: Sure, the flute, that's right!

New music is heard, a high, rollicking tune.

BEN: Father was a very great and a very wild-hearted man. We would start in Boston, and he'd toss the whole family into the wagon, and then he'd drive the team right across the country; through Ohio, and Indiana, Michigan, Illinois, and all the Western states. And we'd stop in the towns and sell the flutes that he'd made on the way. Great inventor, Father.

With one gadget he made more in a week than a man like you could make in a lifetime.

WILLY: That's just the way I'm bringing them up, Ben—rugged, well liked, all-around.

BEN: Yeah? (*To Biff.*) Hit that, boy—hard as you can. (*He pounds his stomach.*)

BIFF: Oh, no, sir!

BEN (*taking boxing stance*): Come on, get to me. (*He laughs.*)

WILLY: Go to it, Biff! Go ahead, show him!

BIFF: Okay! (*He cocks his fists and starts in.*)

LINDA (*to Willy*): Why must he fight, dear?

BEN (*sparring with Biff*): Good boy! Good boy!

WILLY: How's that, Ben, heh?

HAPPY: Give him the left, Biff!

LINDA: Why are you fighting?

BEN: Good boy! (*Suddenly comes in, trips Biff, and stands over him, the point of his umbrella poised over Biff's eye.*)

LINDA: Look out, Biff!

BIFF: Gee!

BEN (*patting Biff's knee*): Never fight fair with a stranger, boy. You'll never get out of the jungle that way. (*Taking Linda's hand and bowing*): It was an honor and a pleasure to meet you, Linda.

LINDA (*withdrawing her hand coldly, frightened*): Have a nice—trip.

BEN (*to Willy*): And good luck with your—what do you do?

WILLY: Selling.

BEN: Yes. Well . . . (*He raises his hand in farewell to all.*)

WILLY: No, Ben, I don't want you to think . . . (*He takes Ben's arm to show him.*) It's Brooklyn, I know, but we hunt too.

BEN: Really, now.

WILLY: Oh, sure, there's snakes and rabbits and—that's why I moved out here. Why, Biff can fell any one of these trees in no time! Boys! Go right over to where they're building the apartment house and get some sand. We're gonna rebuild the entire front stoop now! Watch this, Ben!

BIFF: Yes, sir! On the double, Hap!

HAPPY (*as he and Biff run off*): I lost weight, Pop, you notice?

Charley enters in knickers, even before the boys are gone.

CHARLEY: Listen, if they steal any more from that building the watchman'll put the cops on them!

LINDA (*to Willy*): Don't let Biff . . .

Ben laughs lustily.

WILLY: You shoulda seen the lumber they brought home last week. At least a dozen six-by-tens worth all kinds a money.

CHARLEY: Listen, if that watchman—

WILLY: I gave them hell, understand. But I got a couple of fearless characters there.

CHARLEY: Willy, the jails are full of fearless characters.

BEN (*clapping Willy on the back, with a laugh at Charley*): And the stock exchange, friend!

WILLY (*joining in Ben's laughter*): Where are the rest of your pants?

CHARLEY: My wife bought them.

WILLY: Now all you need is a golf club and you can go upstairs and go to sleep. (*To Ben*). Great athlete! Between him and his son Bernard they can't hammer a nail!

BERNARD (*rushing in*): The watchman's chasing Biff!

WILLY (*angrily*): Shut up! He's not stealing anything!

LINDA (*alarmed, hurrying off left*): Where is he? Biff, dear! (*She exits.*)

WILLY (*moving toward the left, away from Ben*): There's nothing wrong. What's the matter with you?

BEN: Nervy boy. Good!

WILLY (*laughing*): Oh, nerves of iron, that Biff!

CHARLEY: Don't know what it is. My New England man comes back and he's bleedin', they murdered him up there.

WILLY: It's contacts, Charley, I got important contacts!

CHARLEY (*sarcastically*): Glad to hear it, Willy. Come in later, we'll shoot a little casino. I'll take some of your Portland money. (*He laughs at Willy and exits.*)

WILLY (*turning to Ben*): Business is bad, it's murderous. But not for me, of course.

BEN: I'll stop by on my way back to Africa.

WILLY (*longingly*): Can't you stay a few days? You're just what I need, Ben, because I—I have a fine position here, but I—well, Dad left when I was such a baby and I never had a chance to talk to him and I still feel—kind of temporary about myself.

BEN: I'll be late for my train.

They are at opposite ends of the stage.

WILLY: Ben, my boys—can't we talk? They'd go into the jaws of hell for me, see, but I—

BEN: William, you're being first-rate with your boys. Outstanding, manly chaps!

WILLY (*hanging on to his words*): Oh, Ben, that's good to hear! Because sometimes I'm afraid that I'm not teaching them the right kind of—Ben, how should I teach them?

BEN (*giving great weight to each word, and with a certain vicious audacity*): William, when I walked into the jungle, I was seventeen. When I walked out I was twenty-one. And, by God, I was rich! (*He goes off into darkness around the right corner of the house.*)

WILLY: . . . was rich! That's just the spirit I want to imbue them with! To walk into a jungle! I was right! I was right! I was right!

Ben is gone, but Willy is still speaking to him as Linda, in nightgown and robe, enters the kitchen, glances around for Willy, then goes to the door of the house, looks out, and sees him. Comes down to his left. He looks at her.

LINDA: Willy, dear? Willy?

WILLY: I was right!

LINDA: Did you have some cheese? (*He can't answer.*) It's very late, darling. Come to bed, heh?

WILLY (*looking straight up*): Gotta break your neck to see a star in this yard.

LINDA: You coming in?

WILLY: Whatever happened to that diamond watch fob? Remember? When Ben came from Africa that time? Didn't he give me a watch fob with a diamond in it?

LINDA: You pawned it, dear. Twelve, thirteen years ago. For Biff's radio correspondence course.

WILLY: Gee, that was a beautiful thing. I'll take a walk.

LINDA: But you're in your slippers.

WILLY (*starting to go around the house at the left*): I was right! I was! (*Half to Linda, as he goes, shaking his head.*) What a man! There was a man worth talking to. I was right!

LINDA (*calling after Willy*): But in your slippers, Willy!

Willy is almost gone when Biff, in his pajamas, comes down the stairs and enters the kitchen.

BIFF: What is he doing out there?

LINDA: Sh!

BIFF: God Almighty, Mom, how long has he been doing this?

LINDA: Don't, he'll hear you.

BIFF: What the hell is the matter with him?

LINDA: It'll pass by morning.

BIFF: Shouldn't we do anything?

LINDA: Oh, my dear, you should do a lot of things, but there's nothing to do, so go to sleep.

Happy comes down the stairs and sits on the steps.

HAPPY: I never heard him so loud, Mom.

LINDA: Well, come around more often; you'll hear him. (*She sits down at the table and mends the lining of Willy's jacket.*)

BIFF: Why didn't you ever write me about this, Mom?

LINDA: How would I write to you? For over three months you had no address.

BIFF: I was on the move. But you know I thought of you all the time. You know that, don't you, pal?

LINDA: I know, dear, I know. But he likes to have a letter. Just to know that there's still a possibility for better things.

BIFF: He's not like this all the time, is he?

LINDA: It's when you come home he's always the worst.

BIFF: When I come home?

LINDA: When you write you're coming, he's all smiles, and talks about the future, and—he's just wonderful. And then the closer you seem to come, the more shaky he gets, and then, by the time you get here, he's arguing, and he seems angry at you. I think it's just that maybe he can't bring himself to—to open up to you. Why are you so hateful to each other? Why is that?

BIFF (*evasively*): I'm not hateful, Mom.

LINDA: But you no sooner come in the door than you're fighting!

BIFF: I don't know why. I mean to change. I'm tryin', Mom, you understand?

LINDA: Are you home to stay now?

BIFF: I don't know. I want to look around, see what's doin'.

LINDA: Biff, you can't look around all your life, can you?

BIFF: I just can't take hold, Mom. I can't take hold of some kind of a life.

LINDA: Biff, a man is not a bird, to come and go with the springtime.

BIFF: Your hair . . . (*He touches her hair.*) Your hair got so gray.

LINDA: Oh, it's been gray since you were in high school. I just stopped dyeing it, that's all.

BIFF: Dye it again, will ya? I don't want my pal looking old. (*He smiles.*)

LINDA: You're such a boy! You think you can go away for a year and . . . You've got to get it into your head now that one day you'll knock on this door and there'll be strange people here—

BIFF: What are you talking about? You're not even sixty, Mom.

LINDA: But what about your father?

BIFF (*lamely*): Well, I meant him too.

HAPPY: He admires Pop.

LINDA: Biff, dear, if you don't have any feeling for him, then you can't have any feeling for me.

BIFF: Sure I can, Mom.

LINDA: No. You can't just come to see me, because I love him. (*With a threat, but only a threat, of tears.*) He's the dearest man in the world to me, and I won't have anyone making him feel unwanted and low and blue. You've got to make up your mind now, darling, there's no leeway any more. Either he's your father and you pay him that respect, or else you're not to come here. I know he's not easy to get along with—nobody knows that better than me—but . . .

WILLY (*from the left, with a laugh*): Hey, hey, Biffo!

BIFF (*starting to go out after Willy*): What the hell is the matter with him? (*Happy stops him.*)

LINDA: Don't—don't go near him!

BIFF: Stop making excuses for him! He always, always wiped the floor with you. Never had an ounce of respect for you.

HAPPY: He's always had respect for—

BIFF: What the hell do you know about it?

HAPPY (*surlily*): Just don't call him crazy!

BIFF: He's got no character—Charley wouldn't do this. Not in his own house—spewing out that vomit from his mind.

HAPPY: Charley never had to cope with what he's got to.

BIFF: People are worse off than Willy Loman. Believe me, I've seen them!

LINDA: Then make Charley your father, Biff. You can't do that, can you? I don't say he's a great man. Willy Loman never made a lot of money. His name was never in the paper. He's not the finest character that ever lived. But he's a human being, and a terrible thing is happening to him. So attention must be paid. He's not to be allowed to fall into his grave like an old dog. Attention, attention must be finally paid to such a person. You called him crazy—

BIFF: I didn't mean—

LINDA: No, a lot of people think he's lost his—balance. But you don't have to be very smart to know what his trouble is. The man is exhausted.

HAPPY: Sure!

LINDA: A small man can be just as exhausted as a great man. He works for a company thirty-six years this March, opens up unheard-of territories to their trademark, and now in his old age they take his salary away.

HAPPY (*indignantly*): I didn't know that, Mom.

LINDA: You never asked, my dear! Now that you get your spending money someplace else you don't trouble your mind with him.

HAPPY: But I gave you money last—

LINDA: Christmas time, fifty dollars! To fix the hot water it cost ninety-seven fifty! For five weeks he's been on straight commission, like a beginner, an unknown!

BIFF: Those ungrateful bastards!

LINDA: Are they any worse than his sons? When he brought them business, when he was young, they were glad to see him. But now his old friends, the old buyers that loved him so and always found some order to hand him in a pinch—they're all dead, retired. He used to be able to make six, seven calls a day in Boston. Now he takes his valises out of the car and puts them back and takes them out again and he's exhausted. Instead of walking he talks now. He drives seven hundred miles, and when he gets there no one knows him any more, no one welcomes him. And what goes through a man's mind, driving seven hundred miles home without having earned a cent? Why shouldn't he talk to himself? Why? When he has to go to Charley and borrow fifty dollars a week and pretend to me that it's his pay? How long can that go on? How long? You see what I'm sitting here and waiting for? And you tell me he has no character? The man who never worked a day but for your benefit? When does he get the medal for that? Is this his reward—to turn around at the age of sixty-three and find his sons, who he loved better than his life, one a philandering bum—

HAPPY: Mom!

LINDA: That's all you are, my baby! (*To Biff.*) And you! What happened to the love you had for him? You were such pals! How you used to talk to him on the phone every night! How lonely he was till he could come home to you!

BIFF: All right, Mom. I'll live here in my room, and I'll get a job. I'll keep away from him, that's all.

LINDA: No, Biff. You can't stay here and fight all the time.

BIFF: He threw me out of this house, remember that.

LINDA: Why did he do that? I never knew why.

BIFF: Because I know he's a fake and he doesn't like anybody around who knows!

LINDA: Why a fake? In what way? What do you mean?

BIFF: Just don't lay it all at my feet. It's between me and him — that's all I have to say. I'll chip in from now on. He'll settle for half my pay check. He'll be all right. I'm going to bed. (*He starts for the stairs.*)

LINDA: He won't be all right.

BIFF (*turning on the stairs, furiously*): I hate this city and I'll stay here. Now what do you want?

LINDA: He's dying, Biff.

Happy turns quickly to her, shocked.

BIFF (*after a pause*): Why is he dying?

LINDA: He's been trying to kill himself.

BIFF (*with great horror*): How?

LINDA: I live from day to day.

BIFF: What're you talking about?

LINDA: Remember I wrote you that he smashed up the car again? In February?

BIFF: Well?

LINDA: The insurance inspector came. He said that they have evidence. That all these accidents in the last year — weren't — weren't — accidents.

HAPPY: How can they tell that? That's a lie.

LINDA: It seems there's a woman . . . (*She takes a breath as*):

BIFF (*sharply but contained*): What woman?

LINDA (*simultaneously*): . . . and this woman . . .

LINDA: What?

BIFF: Nothing. Go ahead.

LINDA: What did you say?

BIFF: Nothing. I just said what woman?

HAPPY: What about her?

LINDA: Well, it seems she was walking down the road and saw his car. She says that he wasn't driving fast at all, and that he didn't skid. She says he came to that little bridge, and then deliberately smashed into the railing, and it was only the shallowness of the water that saved him.

BIFF: Oh, no, he probably just fell asleep again.

LINDA: I don't think he fell asleep.

BIFF: Why not?

LINDA: Last month . . . (*With great difficulty.*) Oh, boys, it's so hard to say a thing like this! He's just a big stupid man to you, but I tell you there's more good in him than in many other people. (*She chokes, wipes her eyes.*) I was looking for a fuse. The lights blew out, and I went down the cellar. And behind the fuse box — it happened to fall out — was a length of rubber pipe — just short.

HAPPY: No kidding?

LINDA: There's a little attachment on the end of it. I knew right away. And sure enough, on the bottom of the water heater there's a new little nipple on the gas pipe.

HAPPY (*angrily*): That—jerk.

BIFF: Did you have it taken off?

LINDA: I'm—I'm ashamed to. How can I mention it to him? Every day I go down and take away that little rubber pipe. But, when he comes home, I put it back where it was. How can I insult him that way? I don't know what to do. I live from day to day, boys. I tell you, I know every thought in his mind. It sounds so old-fashioned and silly, but I tell you he put his whole life into you and you've turned your backs on him. (*She is bent over in chair, weeping, her face in her hands.*) Biff, I swear to God! Biff, his life is in your hands!

HAPPY (*to Biff*): How do you like that damned fool!

BIFF (*kissing her*): All right, pal, all right. It's all settled now. I've been remiss. I know that, Mom. But now I'll stay, and I swear to you, I'll apply myself. (*Kneeling in front of her, in a fever of self-reproach.*) It's just—you see, Mom, I don't fit in business. Not that I won't try. I'll try, and I'll make good.

HAPPY: Sure you will. The trouble with you in business was you never tried to please people.

BIFF: I know, I—

HAPPY: Like when you worked for Harrison's. Bob Harrison said you were tops, and then you go and do some damn fool thing like whistling whole songs in the elevator like a comedian.

BIFF (*against Happy*): So what? I like to whistle sometimes.

HAPPY: You don't raise a guy to a responsible job who whistles in the elevator!

LINDA: Well, don't argue about it now.

HAPPY: Like when you'd go off and swim in the middle of the day instead of taking the line around.

BIFF (*his resentment rising*): Well, don't you run off? You take off sometimes, don't you? On a nice summer day?

HAPPY: Yeah, but I cover myself!

LINDA: Boys!

HAPPY: If I'm going to take a fade the boss can call any number where I'm supposed to be and they'll swear to him that I just left. I'll tell you something that I hate to say, Biff, but in the business world some of them think you're crazy.

BIFF (*angered*): Screw the business world!

HAPPY: All right, screw it! Great, but cover yourself!

LINDA: Hap, Hap!

BIFF: I don't care what they think! They've laughed at Dad for years, and you know why? Because we don't belong in this nuthouse of a city! We should be mixing cement on some open plain, or—or carpenters. A carpenter is allowed to whistle!

Willy walks in from the entrance of the house, at left.

WILLY: Even your grandfather was better than a carpenter. (*Pause. They watch him.*) You never grew up. Bernard does not whistle in the elevator, I assure you.

BIFF (*as though to laugh Willy out of it*): Yeah, but you do, Pop.

WILLY: I never in my life whistled in an elevator! And who in the business world thinks I'm crazy?

BIFF: I didn't mean it like that, Pop. Now don't make a whole thing out of it, will ya?

WILLY: Go back to the West! Be a carpenter, a cowboy, enjoy yourself!

LINDA: Willy, he was just saying—

WILLY: I heard what he said!

HAPPY (*trying to quiet Willy*): Hey, Pop, come on now . . .

WILLY (*continuing over Happy's line*): They laugh at me, heh? Go to Filene's, go to the Hub, go to Slattery's, Boston. Call out the name Willy Loman and see what happens! Big shot!

BIFF: All right, Pop.

WILLY: Big!

BIFF: All right!

WILLY: Why do you always insult me?

BIFF: I didn't say a word. (*To Linda.*) Did I say a word?

LINDA: He didn't say anything, Willy.

WILLY (*going to the doorway of the living-room*): All right, good night, good night.

LINDA: Willy, dear, he just decided . . .

WILLY (*to Biff*): If you get tired hanging around tomorrow, paint the ceiling I put up in the living-room.

BIFF: I'm leaving early tomorrow.

HAPPY: He's going to see Bill Oliver, Pop.

WILLY (*interestedly*): Oliver? For what?

BIFF (*with reserve, but trying, trying*): He always said he'd stake me. I'd like to go into business, so maybe I can take him up on it.

LINDA: Isn't that wonderful?

WILLY: Don't interrupt. What's wonderful about it? There's fifty men in the City of New York who'd stake him. (*To Biff.*) Sporting goods?

BIFF: I guess so. I know something about it and—

WILLY: He knows something about it! You know sporting goods better than Spalding, for God's sake! How much is he giving you?

BIFF: I don't know, I didn't even see him yet, but—

WILLY: Then what're you talkin' about?

BIFF (*getting angry*): Well, all I said was I'm gonna see him, that's all!

WILLY (*turning away*): Ah, you're counting your chickens again.

BIFF (*starting left for the stairs*): Oh, Jesus, I'm going to sleep!

WILLY (*calling after him*): Don't curse in this house!

BIFF (*turning*): Since when did you get so clean?

HAPPY (*trying to stop them*): Wait a . . .

WILLY: Don't use that language to me! I won't have it!

HAPPY (*grabbing Biff, shouts*): Wait a minute! I got an idea. I got a feasible idea. Come here, Biff, let's talk this over now, let's talk some sense here. When I was down in Florida last time, I thought of a great idea to sell sporting goods. It just came back to me. You and I, Biff—we have a line, the

Loman Line. We train a couple of weeks, and put on a couple of exhibitions, see?

WILLY: That's an idea!

HAPPY: Wait! We form two basketball teams, see? Two water-polo teams. We play each other. It's a million dollars' worth of publicity. Two brothers, see? The Loman Brothers. Displays in the Royal Palms—all the hotels. And banners over the ring and the basketball court: "Loman Brothers." Baby, we could sell sporting goods!

WILLY: That is a one-million-dollar idea!

LINDA: Marvelous!

BIFF: I'm in great shape as far as that's concerned.

HAPPY: And the beauty of it is, Biff, it wouldn't be like a business. We'd be out playin' ball again . . .

BIFF (*enthused*): Yeah, that's . . .

WILLY: Million-dollar . . .

HAPPY: And you wouldn't get fed up with it, Biff. It'd be the family again. There'd be the old honor, and comradeship, and if you wanted to go off for a swim or somethin'—well, you'd do it! Without some smart cooky gettin' up ahead of you!

WILLY: Lick the world! You guys together could absolutely lick the civilized world.

BIFF: I'll see Oliver tomorrow. Hap, if we could work that out . . .

LINDA: Maybe things are beginning to—

WILLY (*wildly enthused, to Linda*): Stop interrupting! (*To Biff.*) But don't wear sport jacket and slacks when you see Oliver.

BIFF: No, I'll—

WILLY: A business suit, and talk as little as possible, and don't crack any jokes.

BIFF: He did like me. Always liked me.

LINDA: He loved you!

WILLY (*to Linda*): Will you stop! (*To Biff.*) Walk in very serious. You are not applying for a boy's job. Money is to pass. Be quiet, fine, and serious. Everybody likes a kidder, but nobody lends him money.

HAPPY: I'll try to get some myself, Biff. I'm sure I can.

WILLY: I see great things for you kids, I think your troubles are over. But remember, start big and you'll end big. Ask for fifteen. How much you gonna ask for?

BIFF: Gee, I don't know—

WILLY: And don't say "Gee." "Gee" is a boy's word. A man walking in for fifteen thousand dollars does not say "Gee!"

BIFF: Ten, I think, would be top though.

WILLY: Don't be so modest. You always started too low. Walk in with a big laugh. Don't look worried. Start off with a couple of your good stories to lighten things up. It's not what you say, it's how you say it—because personality always wins the day.

LINDA: Oliver always thought the highest of him—

WILLY: Will you let me talk?

BIFF: Don't yell at her, Pop, will ya?

WILLY (*angrily*): I was talking, wasn't I?

BIFF: I don't like you yelling at her all the time, and I'm tellin' you, that's all.

WILLY: What're you, takin' over this house?

LINDA: Willy—

WILLY (*turning on her*): Don't take his side all the time, goddammit!

BIFF (*furiously*): Stop yelling at her!

WILLY (*suddenly pulling on his cheek, beaten down, guilt ridden*): Give my best to Bill Oliver—he may remember me. (*He exits through the living-room doorway.*)

LINDA (*her voice subdued*): What'd you have to start that for? (*Biff turns away.*) You see how sweet he was as soon as you talked hopefully? (*She goes over to Biff.*) Come up and say good night to him. Don't let him go to bed that way.

HAPPY: Come on, Biff, let's buck him up.

LINDA: Please, dear. Just say good night. It takes so little to make him happy. Come. (*She goes through the living-room doorway, calling upstairs from within the living-room.*) Your pajamas are hanging in the bathroom, Willy!

HAPPY (*looking toward where Linda went out*): What a woman! They broke the mold when they made her. You know that, Biff?

BIFF: He's off salary. My God, working on commission!

HAPPY: Well, let's face it: he's no hot-shot selling man. Except that sometimes, you have to admit, he's a sweet personality.

BIFF (*deciding*): Lend me ten bucks, will ya? I want to buy some new ties.

HAPPY: I'll take you to a place I know. Beautiful stuff. Wear one of my striped shirts tomorrow.

BIFF: She got gray. Mom got awful old. Gee, I'm gonna go in to Oliver tomorrow and knock him for a—

HAPPY: Come on up. Tell that to Dad. Let's give him a whirl. Come on.

BIFF (*steamed up*): You know, with ten thousand bucks, boy!

HAPPY (*as they go into the living-room*): That's the talk, Biff, that's the first time I've heard the old confidence out of you! (*From within the living-room, fading off.*) You're gonna live with me, kid, and any babe you want just say the word . . . (*The last lines are hardly heard. They are mounting the stairs to their parents' bedroom.*)

LINDA (*entering her bedroom and addressing Willy, who is in the bathroom. She is straightening the bed for him*): Can you do anything about the shower? It drips.

WILLY (*from the bathroom*): All of a sudden everything falls to pieces! Goddam plumbing, oughta be sued, those people. I hardly finished putting it in and the thing . . . (*His words rumble off.*)

LINDA: I'm just wondering if Oliver will remember him. You think he might?

WILLY (*coming out of the bathroom in his pajamas*): Remember him? What's the matter with you, you crazy? If he'd've stayed with Oliver he'd be on top by now! Wait'll Oliver gets a look at him. You don't know the average caliber any more. The average young man today—(*he is getting into bed*)—is got a caliber of zero. Greatest thing in the world for him was to bum around.

Biff and Happy enter the bedroom. Slight pause.

WILLY (*stops short, looking at Biff*): Glad to hear it, boy.

HAPPY: He wanted to say good night to you, sport.

WILLY (*to Biff*): Yeah. Knock him dead, boy. What'd you want to tell me?

BIFF: Just take it easy, Pop. Good night. (*He turns to go.*)

WILLY (*unable to resist*): And if anything falls off the desk while you're talking to him—like a package or something—don't you pick it up. They have office boys for that.

LINDA: I'll make a big breakfast—

WILLY: Will you let me finish? (*To Biff.*) Tell him you were in the business in the West. Not farm work.

BIFF: All right, Dad.

LINDA: I think everything—

WILLY (*going right through her speech*): And don't undersell yourself. No less than fifteen thousand dollars.

BIFF (*unable to bear him*): Okay. Good night, Mom. (*He starts moving.*)

WILLY: Because you got a greatness in you, Biff, remember that. You got all kinds a greatness . . . (*He lies back, exhausted. Biff walks out.*)

LINDA (*calling after Biff*): Sleep well, darling!

HAPPY: I'm gonna get married, Mom. I wanted to tell you.

LINDA: Go to sleep, dear.

HAPPY (*going*): I just wanted to tell you.

WILLY: Keep up the good work. (*Happy exits.*) God . . . remember that Ebbets Field game? The championship of the city?

LINDA: Just rest. Should I sing to you?

WILLY: Yeah. Sing to me. (*Linda hums a soft lullaby.*) When that team came out—he was the tallest, remember?

LINDA: Oh, yes. And in gold.

Biff enters the darkened kitchen, takes a cigarette, and leaves the house. He comes downstage into a golden pool of light. He smokes, staring at the night.

WILLY: Like a young god. Hercules—something like that. And the sun, the sun all around him. Remember how he waved to me? Right up from the field, with the representatives of three colleges standing by? And the buyers I brought, and the cheers when he came out—Loman, Loman, Loman! God Almighty, he'll be great yet. A star like that, magnificent, can never really fade away!

The light on Willy is fading. The gas heater begins to glow through the kitchen wall, near the stairs, a blue flame beneath red coils.

LINDA (timidly): Willy dear, what has he got against you?

WILLY: I'm so tired. Don't talk any more.

Biff slowly returns to the kitchen. He stops, stares toward the heater.

LINDA: Will you ask Howard to let you work in New York?

WILLY: First thing in the morning. Everything'll be all right.

Biff reaches behind the heater and draws out a length of rubber tubing. He is horrified and turns his head toward Willy's room, still dimly lit, from which the strains of Linda's desperate but monotonous humming rise.

WILLY (*staring through the window into the moonlight*): Gee, look at the moon moving between the buildings!

Biff wraps the tubing around his hand and quickly goes up the stairs.

Curtain

ACT II

Music is heard, gay and bright. The curtain rises as the music fades away. Willy, in shirt sleeves, is sitting at the kitchen table, sipping coffee, his hat in his lap. Linda is filling his cup when she can.

WILLY: Wonderful coffee. Meal in itself.

LINDA: Can I make you some eggs?

WILLY: No. Take a breath.

LINDA: You look so rested, dear.

WILLY: I slept like a dead one. First time in months. Imagine, sleeping till ten on a Tuesday morning. Boys left nice and early, heh?

LINDA: They were out of here by eight o'clock.

WILLY: Good work!

LINDA: It was so thrilling to see them leaving together. I can't get over the shaving lotion in this house!

WILLY (*smiling*): Mmm—

LINDA: Biff was very changed this morning. His whole attitude seemed to be hopeful. He couldn't wait to get downtown to see Oliver.

WILLY: He's heading for a change. There's no question, there simply are certain men that take longer to get—solidified. How did he dress?

LINDA: His blue suit. He's so handsome in that suit. He could be a—anything in that suit!

Willy gets up from the table. Linda holds his jacket for him.

WILLY: There's no question, no question at all. Gee, on the way home tonight I'd like to buy some seeds.

LINDA (*laughing*): That'd be wonderful. But not enough sun gets back there. Nothing'll grow any more.

WILLY: You wait, kid, before it's all over we're gonna get a little place out in the country, and I'll raise some vegetables, a couple of chickens . . .

LINDA: You'll do it yet, dear.

Willy walks out of his jacket. Linda follows him.

WILLY: And they'll get married, and come for a weekend. I'd build a little guest house. 'Cause I got so many fine tools, all I'd need would be a little lumber and some peace of mind.

LINDA (*joyfully*): I sewed the lining . . .

WILLY: I could build two guest houses, so they'd both come. Did he decide how much he's going to ask Oliver for?

LINDA (*getting him into the jacket*): He didn't mention it, but I imagine ten or fifteen thousand. You going to talk to Howard today?

WILLY: Yeah. I'll put it to him straight and simple. He'll just have to take me off the road.

LINDA: And Willy, don't forget to ask for a little advance, because we've got the insurance premium. It's the grace period now.

WILLY: That's a hundred . . . ?

LINDA: A hundred and eight, sixty-eight. Because we're a little short again.

WILLY: Why are we short?

LINDA: Well, you had the motor job on the car . . .

WILLY: That goddam Studebaker!

LINDA: And you got one more payment on the refrigerator . . .

WILLY: But it just broke again!

LINDA: Well, it's old, dear.

WILLY: I told you we should've bought a well-advertised machine. Charley bought a General Electric and it's twenty years old and it's still good, that son-of-a-bitch.

LINDA: But, Willy—

WILLY: Whoever heard of a Hastings refrigerator? Once in my life I would like to own something outright before it's broken! I'm always in a race with the junkyard! I just finished paying for the car and it's on its last legs. The refrigerator consumes belts like a goddam maniac. They time those things. They time them so when you finally paid for them, they're used up.

LINDA (*buttoning up his jacket as he unbuttons it*): All told, about two hundred dollars would carry us, dear. But that includes the last payment on the mortgage. After this payment, Willy, the house belongs to us.

WILLY: It's twenty-five years!

LINDA: Biff was nine years old when we bought it.

WILLY: Well, that's a great thing. To weather a twenty-five year mortgage is—

LINDA: It's an accomplishment.

WILLY: All the cement, the lumber, the reconstruction I put in this house! There ain't a crack to be found in it any more.

LINDA: Well, it served its purpose.

WILLY: What purpose? Some stranger'll come along, move in, and that's that. If only Biff would take this house, and raise a family . . . (*He starts to go.*) Good-by, I'm late.

LINDA (*suddenly remembering*): Oh, I forgot! You're supposed to meet them for dinner.

WILLY: Me?

LINDA: At Frank's Chop House on Forty-eighth near Sixth Avenue.

WILLY: Is that so! How about you?

LINDA: No, just the three of you. They're gonna blow you to a big meal!

WILLY: Don't say! Who thought of that?

LINDA: Biff came to me this morning, Willy, and he said, "Tell Dad, we want to blow him to a big meal." Be there six o'clock. You and your two boys are going to have dinner.

WILLY: Gee whiz! That's really somethin'. I'm gonna knock Howard for a loop, kid. I'll get an advance, and I'll come home with a New York job. Goddammit, now I'm gonna do it!

LINDA: Oh, that's the spirit, Willy!

WILLY: I will never get behind a wheel the rest of my life!

LINDA: It's changing, Willy, I can feel it changing!

WILLY: Beyond a question. G'by, I'm late. (*He starts to go again.*)

LINDA (*calling after him as she runs to the kitchen table for a handkerchief*): You got your glasses?

WILLY (*feels for them, then comes back in*): Yeah, yeah, got my glasses.

LINDA (*giving him the handkerchief*): And a handkerchief.

WILLY: Yeah, handkerchief.

LINDA: And your saccharine?

WILLY: Yeah, my saccharine.

LINDA: Be careful on the subway stairs.

She kisses him, and a silk stocking is seen hanging from her hand. Willy notices it.

WILLY: Will you stop mending stockings? At least while I'm in the house. It gets me nervous. I can't tell you. Please.

Linda hides the stocking in her hand as she follows Willy across the forestage in front of the house.

LINDA: Remember, Frank's Chop House.

WILLY (*passing the apron*): Maybe beets would grow out there.

LINDA (*laughing*): But you tried so many times.

WILLY: Yeah. Well, don't work hard today. (*He disappears around the right corner of the house.*)

LINDA: Be careful!

As Willy vanishes, Linda waves to him. Suddenly the phone rings. She runs across the stage and into the kitchen and lifts it.

LINDA: Hello? Oh, Biff! I'm so glad you called, I just . . . Yes, sure, I just told him. Yes, he'll be there for dinner at six o'clock, I didn't forget. Listen, I was just dying to tell you. You know that little rubber pipe I told you about? That he connected to the gas heater? I finally decided to go down the cellar this morning and take it away and destroy it. But it's gone! Imagine? He took it away himself, it isn't there! (*She listens.*) When? Oh, then you took it. Oh—nothing, it's just that I'd hoped he'd taken it away himself. Oh, I'm not worried, darling, because this morning he left in such high spirits, it was like the old days! I'm not afraid any more. Did Mr. Oliver see you? . . . Well, you wait there then. And make a nice impression on him, darling. Just don't perspire too much before you see him. And have a nice time with Dad. He may have big news too! . . . That's right, a New York job. And be sweet to him tonight, dear. Be loving to him. Because he's only a little boat looking for a harbor. (*She is trembling with sorrow and joy.*) Oh, that's wonderful, Biff, you'll save his life. Thanks, darling. Just put your arm around him when he comes into the restaurant. Give him a smile. That's the boy . . .

Good-by, dear . . . You got your comb? . . . That's fine. Good-by, Biff dear.

In the middle of her speech, Howard Wagner, thirty-six, wheels in a small typewriter table on which is a wire-recording machine and proceeds to plug it in. This is on the left forestage. Light slowly fades on Linda as it rises on Howard. Howard is intent on threading the machine and only glances over his shoulder as Willy appears.

WILLY: Pst! Pst!

HOWARD: Hello, Willy, come in.

WILLY: Like to have a little talk with you, Howard.

HOWARD: Sorry to keep you waiting. I'll be with you in a minute.

WILLY: What's that, Howard?

HOWARD: Didn't you ever see one of these? Wire recorder.

WILLY: Oh. Can we talk a minute?

HOWARD: Records things. Just got delivery yesterday. Been driving me crazy, the most terrific machine I ever saw in my life. I was up all night with it.

WILLY: What do you do with it?

HOWARD: I bought it for dictation, but you can do anything with it. Listen to this. I had it home last night. Listen to what I picked up. The first one is my daughter. Get this. (*He flicks the switch and "Roll Out the Barrel" is heard being whistled.*) Listen to that kid whistle.

WILLY: That is lifelike, isn't it?

HOWARD: Seven years old. Get that tone.

WILLY: Ts, ts. Like to ask a little favor if you . . .

The whistling breaks off, and the voice of Howard's daughter is heard.

HIS DAUGHTER: "Now you, Daddy."

HOWARD: She's crazy for me! (*Again the same song is whistled.*) That's me! Ha! (*He winks.*)

WILLY: You're very good!

The whistling breaks off again. The machine runs silent for a moment.

HOWARD: Sh! Get this now, this is my son.

HIS SON: "The capital of Alabama is Montgomery; the capital of Arizona is Phoenix; the capital of Arkansas is Little Rock; the capital of California is Sacramento . . ." (*and on, and on*).

HOWARD (*holding up five fingers*): Five years old, Willy!

WILLY: He'll make an announcer some day!

HIS SON (*continuing*): "The capital . . ."

HOWARD: Get that—alphabetical order! (*The machine breaks off suddenly.*) Wait a minute. The maid kicked the plug out.

WILLY: It certainly is a—

HOWARD: Sh, for God's sake!

HIS SON: "It's nine o'clock, Bulova watch time. So I have to go to sleep."

WILLY: That really is—

HOWARD: Wait a minute! The next is my wife.

They wait.

HOWARD'S VOICE: "Go on, say something." (*Pause.*) "Well, you gonna talk?"

HIS WIFE: "I can't think of anything."

HOWARD'S VOICE: "Well, talk — it's turning."

HIS WIFE (*shyly, beaten*): "Hello." (*Silence.*) "Oh, Howard, I can't talk into this . . ."

HOWARD (*snapping the machine off*): That was my wife.

WILLY: That is a wonderful machine. Can we —

HOWARD: I tell you, Willy, I'm gonna take my camera, and my bandsaw, and all my hobbies, and out they go. This is the most fascinating relaxation I ever found.

WILLY: I think I'll get one myself.

HOWARD: Sure, they're only a hundred and a half. You can't do without it. Supposing you wanna hear Jack Benny, see? But you can't be at home at that hour. So you tell the maid to turn the radio on when Jack Benny comes on, and this automatically goes on with the radio . . .

WILLY: And when you come home you . . .

HOWARD: You can come home twelve o'clock, one o'clock, any time you like, and you get yourself a Coke and sit yourself down, throw the switch, and there's Jack Benny's program in the middle of the night!

WILLY: I'm definitely going to get one. Because lots of time I'm on the road, and I think to myself, what I must be missing on the radio!

HOWARD: Don't you have a radio in the car?

WILLY: Well, yeah, but who ever thinks of turning it on?

HOWARD: Say, aren't you supposed to be in Boston?

WILLY: That's what I want to talk to you about, Howard. You got a minute? (*He draws a chair in from the wing.*)

HOWARD: What happened? What're you doing here?

WILLY: Well . . .

HOWARD: You didn't crack up again, did you?

WILLY: Oh, no. No . . .

HOWARD: Geez, you had me worried there for a minute. What's the trouble?

WILLY: Well, tell you the truth, Howard. I've come to the decision that I'd rather not travel any more.

HOWARD: Not travel! Well, what'll you do?

WILLY: Remember, Christmas time, when you had the party here? You said you'd try to think of some spot for me here in town.

HOWARD: With us?

WILLY: Well, sure.

HOWARD: Oh, yeah, yeah. I remember. Well, I couldn't think of anything for you, Willy.

WILLY: I tell ya, Howard. The kids are all grown up, y'know. I don't need much any more. If I could take home — well, sixty-five dollars a week, I could swing it.

HOWARD: Yeah, but Willy, see I —

WILLY: I tell ya why, Howard. Speaking frankly and between the two of us, y'know — I'm just a little tired.

HOWARD: Oh, I could understand that, Willy. But you're a road man, Willy, and we do a road business. We've only got a half-dozen salesmen on the floor here.

WILLY: God knows, Howard, I never asked a favor of any man. But I was with the firm when your father used to carry you in here in his arms.

HOWARD: I know that, Willy, but—

WILLY: Your father came to me the day you were born and asked me what I thought of the name of Howard, may he rest in peace.

HOWARD: I appreciate that, Willy, but there just is no spot here for you. If I had a spot I'd slam you right in, but I just don't have a single solitary spot.

He looks for his lighter. Willy has picked it up and gives it to him. Pause.

WILLY (*with increasing anger*): Howard, all I need to set my table is fifty dollars a week.

HOWARD: But where am I going to put you, kid?

WILLY: Look, it isn't a question of whether I can sell merchandise, is it?

HOWARD: No, but it's a business, kid, and everybody's gotta pull his own weight.

WILLY (*desperately*): Just let me tell you a story, Howard—

HOWARD: 'Cause you gotta admit, business is business.

WILLY (*angrily*): Business is definitely business, but just listen for a minute. You don't understand this. When I was a boy—eighteen, nineteen—I was already on the road. And there was a question in my mind as to whether selling had a future for me. Because in those days I had a yearning to go to Alaska. See, there were three gold strikes in one month in Alaska, and I felt like going out. Just for the ride, you might say.

HOWARD (*barely interested*): Don't say.

WILLY: Oh, yeah, my father lived many years in Alaska. He was an adventurous man. We've got quite a little streak of self-reliance in our family. I thought I'd go out with my older brother and try to locate him, and maybe settle in the North with the old man. And I was almost decided to go, when I met a salesman in the Parker House. His name was Dave Singleman. And he was eighty-four years old, and he'd drummed merchandise in thirty-one states. And old Dave, he'd go up to his room, y'understand, put on his green velvet slippers—I'll never forget—and pick up his phone and call the buyers, and without ever leaving his room, at the age of eighty-four, he made his living. And when I saw that, I realized that selling was the greatest career a man could want. 'Cause what could be more satisfying than to be able to go, at the age of eighty-four, into twenty or thirty different cities, and pick up a phone, and be remembered and loved and helped by so many different people? Do you know? when he died—and by the way he died the death of a salesman, in his green velvet slippers in the smoker of the New York, New Haven, and Hartford, going into Boston—when he died, hundreds of salesmen and buyers were at his funeral. Things were sad on a lotta trains for months after that. (*He stands up. Howard has not looked at him.*) In those days there was personality in it, Howard. There was respect, and comradeship, and gratitude in it. Today, it's all cut and dried, and there's no chance for bringing friendship to bear—or personality. You see what I mean? They don't know me any more.

HOWARD (*moving away, to the right*): That's just the thing, Willy.

WILLY: If I had forty dollars a week—that's all I'd need. Forty dollars, Howard.

HOWARD: Kid, I can't take blood from a stone, I—

WILLY (*desperation is on him now*): Howard, the year Al Smith° was nominated, your father came to me and—

HOWARD (*starting to go off*): I've got to see some people, kid.

WILLY (*stopping him*): I'm talking about your father! There were promises made across this desk! You mustn't tell me you've got people to see—I put thirty-four years into this firm, Howard, and now I can't pay my insurance! You can't eat the orange and throw the peel away—a man is not a piece of fruit! (*After a pause.*) Now pay attention. Your father—in 1928 I had a big year. I averaged a hundred and seventy dollars a week in commissions.

HOWARD (*impatiently*): Now, Willy, you never averaged—

WILLY (*banging his hand on the desk*): I averaged a hundred and seventy dollars a week in the year of 1928! And your father came to me—or rather, I was in the office here—it was right over this desk—and he put his hand on my shoulder—

HOWARD (*getting up*): You'll have to excuse me, Willy, I gotta see some people. Pull yourself together. (*Going out.*) I'll be back in a little while.

On Howard's exit, the light on his chair grows very bright and strange.

WILLY: Pull myself together! What the hell did I say to him? My God, I was yelling at him! How could I! (*Willy breaks off, staring at the light, which occupies the chair, animating it. He approaches this chair, standing across the desk from it.*) Frank, Frank, don't you remember what you told me that time? How you put your hand on my shoulder, and Frank . . . (*He leans on the desk and as he speaks the dead man's name he accidentally switches on the recorder, and instantly:*)

HOWARD'S SON: ". . . of New York is Albany. The capital of Ohio is Cincinnati, the capital of Rhode Island is . . ." (*The recitation continues.*)

WILLY (*leaping away with fright, shouting*): Ha! Howard! Howard! Howard!

HOWARD (*rushing in*): What happened?

WILLY (*pointing at the machine, which continues nasally, childishly, with the capital cities*): Shut it off! Shut it off!

HOWARD (*pulling the plug out*): Look, Willy . . .

WILLY (*pressing his hands to his eyes*): I gotta get myself some coffee. I'll get some coffee . . .

Willy starts to walk out. Howard stops him.

HOWARD (*rolling up the cord*): Willy, look . . .

WILLY: I'll go to Boston.

Al Smith: The Democratic candidate for president of the United States in 1928, Smith lost the election to Herbert Hoover.

HOWARD: Willy, you can't go to Boston for us.

WILLY: Why can't I go?

HOWARD: I don't want you to represent us. I've been meaning to tell you for a long time now.

WILLY: Howard, are you firing me?

HOWARD: I think you need a good long rest, Willy.

WILLY: Howard—

HOWARD: And when you feel better, come back, and we'll see if we can work something out.

WILLY: But I gotta earn money, Howard. I'm in no position to—

HOWARD: Where are your sons? Why don't your sons give you a hand?

WILLY: They're working on a very big deal.

HOWARD: This is no time for false pride, Willy. You go to your sons and you tell them that you're tired. You've got two great boys, haven't you?

WILLY: Oh, no question, no question, but in the meantime . . .

HOWARD: Then that's that, heh?

WILLY: All right, I'll go to Boston tomorrow.

HOWARD: No, no.

WILLY: I can't throw myself on my sons. I'm not a cripple!

HOWARD: Look, kid, I'm busy this morning.

WILLY (*grasping Howard's arm*): Howard, you've got to let me go to Boston!

HOWARD (*hard, keeping himself under control*): I've got a line of people to see this morning. Sit down, take five minutes, and pull yourself together, and then go home, will ya? I need the office, Willy. (*He starts to go, turns, remembering the recorder, starts to push off the table holding the recorder.*) Oh, yeah. Whenever you can this week, stop by and drop off the samples. You'll feel better, Willy, and then come back and we'll talk. Pull yourself together, kid, there's people outside.

Howard exits, pushing the table off left. Willy stares into space, exhausted. Now the music is heard—Ben's music—first distantly, then closer, closer. As Willy speaks, Ben enters from the right. He carries valise and umbrella.

WILLY: Oh, Ben, how did you do it? What is the answer? Did you wind up the Alaska deal already?

BEN: Doesn't take much time if you know what you're doing. Just a short business trip. Boarding ship in an hour. Wanted to say good-by.

WILLY: Ben, I've got to talk to you.

BEN (*glancing at his watch*): Haven't the time, William.

WILLY (*crossing the apron to Ben*): Ben, nothing's working out. I don't know what to do.

BEN: Now, look here, William. I've bought timberland in Alaska and I need a man to look after things for me.

WILLY: God, timberland! Me and my boys in those grand outdoors!

BEN: You've a new continent at your doorstep, William. Get out of these cities, they're full of talk and time payments and courts of law. Screw on your fists and you can fight for a fortune up there.

WILLY: Yes, yes! Linda, Linda!

Linda enters as of old, with the wash.

LINDA: Oh, you're back?
BEN: I haven't much time.
WILLY: No, wait! Linda, he's got a proposition for me in Alaska.
LINDA: But you've got—(*To Ben.*) He's got a beautiful job here.
WILLY: But in Alaska, kid, I could—
LINDA: You're doing well enough, Willy!
BEN (*to Linda*): Enough for what, my dear?
LINDA (*frightened of Ben and angry at him*): Don't say those things to him! Enough to be happy right here, right now. (*To Willy, while Ben laughs.*) Why must everybody conquer the world? You're well liked, and the boys love you, and someday—(*to Ben*)—why, old man Wagner told him just the other day that if he keeps it up he'll be a member of the firm, didn't he, Willy?
WILLY: Sure, sure. I am building something with this firm, Ben, and if a man is building something he must be on the right track, mustn't he?
BEN: What are you building? Lay your hand on it. Where is it?
WILLY (*hesitantly*): That's true, Linda, there's nothing.
LINDA: Why? (*To Ben.*) There's a man eighty-four years old—
WILLY: That's right, Ben, that's right. When I look at that man I say, what is there to worry about?
BEN: Bah!
WILLY: It's true, Ben. All he has to do is go into any city, pick up the phone, and he's making his living and you know why?
BEN (*picking up his valise*): I've got to go.
WILLY (*holding Ben back*): Look at this boy!

Biff, in his high school sweater, enters carrying suitcase. Happy carries Biff's shoulder guards, gold helmet, and football pants.

WILLY: Without a penny to his name, three great universities are begging for him, and from there the sky's the limit, because it's not what you do, Ben. It's who you know and the smile on your face! It's contacts, Ben, contacts! The whole wealth of Alaska passes over the lunch table at the Commodore Hotel, and that's the wonder, the wonder of this country, that a man can end with diamonds here on the basis of being liked! (*He turns to Biff.*) And that's why when you get out on that field today it's important. Because thousands of people will be rooting for you and loving you. (*To Ben, who has again begun to leave.*) And Ben! when he walks into a business office his name will sound out like a bell and all the doors will open to him! I've seen it, Ben, I've seen it a thousand times! You can't feel it with your hand like timber, but it's there!
BEN: Good-by, William.
WILLY: Ben, am I right? Don't you think I'm right? I value your advice.
BEN: There's a new continent at your doorstep, William. You could walk out rich. Rich! (*He is gone.*)

WILLY: We'll do it here, Ben! You hear me? We're gonna do it here!

Young Bernard rushes in. The gay music of the Boys is heard.

BERNARD: Oh, gee, I was afraid you left already!
WILLY: Why? What time is it?
BERNARD: It's half-past one!
WILLY: Well, come on, everybody! Ebbets Field next stop! Where's the pennants? (*He rushes through the wall-line of the kitchen and out into the living-room.*)
LINDA (*to Biff*): Did you pack fresh underwear?
BIFF (*who has been limbering up*): I want to go!
BERNARD: Biff, I'm carrying your helmet, ain't I?
HAPPY: I'm carrying the helmet.
BERNARD: How am I going to get in the locker room?
LINDA: Let him carry the shoulder guards. (*She puts her coat and hat on in the kitchen.*)
BERNARD: Can I, Biff? 'Cause I told everybody I'm going to be in the locker room.
HAPPY: In Ebbets Field it's the clubhouse.
BERNARD: I meant the clubhouse. Biff!
HAPPY: Biff!
BIFF (*grandly, after a slight pause*): Let him carry the shoulder guards.
HAPPY (*as he gives Bernard the shoulder guards*): Stay close to us now.

Willy rushes in with the pennants.

WILLY (*handing them out*): Everybody wave when Biff comes out on the field. (*Happy and Bernard run off.*) You set now, boy?

The music has died away.

BIFF: Ready to go, Pop. Every muscle is ready.
WILLY (*at the edge of the apron*): You realize what this means?
BIFF: That's right, Pop.
WILLY (*feeling Biff's muscles*): You're comin' home this afternoon captain of the All-Scholastic Championship Team of the City of New York.
BIFF: I got it, Pop. And remember, pal, when I take off my helmet, that touchdown is for you.
WILLY: Let's go! (*He is starting out, with his arm around Biff, when Charley enters, as of old, in knickers.*) I got no room for you, Charley.
CHARLEY: Room? For what?
WILLY: In the car.
CHARLEY: You goin' for a ride? I wanted to shoot some casino.
WILLY (*furiously*): Casino! (*Incredulously.*) Don't you realize what today is?
LINDA: Oh, he knows, Willy. He's just kidding you.
WILLY: That's nothing to kid about!
CHARLEY: No, Linda, what's goin' on?
LINDA: He's playing in Ebbets Field.
CHARLEY: Baseball in this weather?
WILLY: Don't talk to him. Come on, come on! (*He is pushing them out.*)

CHARLEY: Wait a minute, didn't you hear the news?

WILLY: What?

CHARLEY: Don't you listen to the radio? Ebbets Field just blew up.

WILLY: You go to hell! (*Charley laughs. Pushing them out.*) Come on, come on! We're late.

CHARLEY (*as they go*): Knock a homer, Biff, knock a homer!

WILLY (*the last to leave, turning to Charley*): I don't think that was funny, Charley. This is the greatest day of his life.

CHARLEY: Willy, when are you going to grow up?

WILLY: Yeah, heh? When this game is over, Charley, you'll be laughing out of the other side of your face. They'll be calling him another Red Grange. Twenty-five thousand a year.

CHARLEY (*kidding*): Is that so?

WILLY: Yeah, that's so.

CHARLEY: Well, then, I'm sorry, Willy. But tell me something.

WILLY: What?

CHARLEY: Who is Red Grange?

WILLY: Put up your hands. Goddam you, put up your hands!

Charley, chuckling, shakes his head and walks away, around the left corner of the stage. Willy follows him. The music rises to a mocking frenzy.

WILLY: Who the hell do you think you are, better than everybody else? You don't know everything, you big, ignorant, stupid . . . Put up your hands!

Light rises, on the right side of the forestage, on a small table in the reception room of Charley's office. Traffic sounds are heard. Bernard, now mature, sits whistling to himself. A pair of tennis rackets and an overnight bag are on the floor beside him.

WILLY (*offstage*): What are you walking away for? Don't walk away! If you're going to say something say it to my face! I know you laugh at me behind my back. You'll laugh out of the other side of your goddam face after this game. Touchdown! Touchdown! Eighty thousand people! Touchdown! Right between the goal posts.

Bernard is a quiet, earnest, but self-assured young man. Willy's voice is coming from right upstage now. Bernard lowers his feet off the table and listens. Jenny, his father's secretary, enters.

JENNY (*distressed*): Say, Bernard, will you go out in the hall?

BERNARD: What is that noise? Who is it?

JENNY: Mr. Loman. He just got off the elevator.

BERNARD (*getting up*): Who's he arguing with?

JENNY: Nobody. There's nobody with him. I can't deal with him any more, and your father gets all upset everytime he comes. I've got a lot of typing to do, and your father's waiting to sign it. Will you see him?

WILLY (*entering*): Touchdown! Touch—(*He sees Jenny.*) Jenny, Jenny, good to see you. How're ya? Workin'? Or still honest?

JENNY: Fine. How've you been feeling?

WILLY: Not much any more, Jenny. Ha, ha! (He is surprised to see the rackets.)

BERNARD: Hello, Uncle Willy.

WILLY (*almost shocked*): Bernard! Well, look who's here! (*He comes quickly, guiltily, to Bernard and warmly shakes his hand.*)

BERNARD: How are you? Good to see you.

WILLY: What are you doing here?

BERNARD: Oh, just stopped by to see Pop. Get off my feet till my train leaves. I'm going to Washington in a few minutes.

WILLY: Is he in?

BERNARD: Yes, he's in his office with the accountant. Sit down.

WILLY (*sitting down*): What're you going to do in Washington?

BERNARD: Oh, just a case I've got there, Willy.

WILLY: That so? (*Indicating the rackets.*) You going to play tennis there?

BERNARD: I'm staying with a friend who's got a court.

WILLY: Don't say. His own tennis court. Must be fine people, I bet.

BERNARD: They are, very nice. Dad tells me Biff's in town.

WILLY (*with a big smile*): Yeah, Biff's in. Working on a very big deal, Bernard.

BERNARD: What's Biff doing?

WILLY: Well, he's been doing very big things in the West. But he decided to establish himself here. Very big. We're having dinner. Did I hear your wife had a boy?

BERNARD: That's right. Our second.

WILLY: Two boys! What do you know!

BERNARD: What kind of a deal has Biff got?

WILLY: Well, Bill Oliver — very big sporting-goods man — he wants Biff very badly. Called him in from the West. Long distance, carte blanche, special deliveries. Your friends have their own private tennis court?

BERNARD: You still with the old firm, Willy?

WILLY (*after a pause*): I'm — I'm overjoyed to see how you made the grade, Bernard, overjoyed. It's an encouraging thing to see a young man really — really — Looks very good for Biff — very — (*He breaks off, then.*) Bernard — (*He is so full of emotion, he breaks off again.*)

BERNARD: What is it, Willy?

WILLY (*small and alone*): What — what's the secret?

BERNARD: What secret?

WILLY: How — how did you? Why didn't he ever catch on?

BERNARD: I wouldn't know that, Willy.

WILLY (*confidentially, desperately*): You were his friend, his boyhood friend. There's something I don't understand about it. His life ended after that Ebbets Field game. From the age of seventeen nothing good ever happened to him.

BERNARD: He never trained himself for anything.

WILLY: But he did, he did. After high school he took so many correspondence courses. Radio mechanics; television; God knows what, and never made the slightest mark.

BERNARD (*taking off his glasses*): Willy, do you want to talk candidly?

WILLY (*rising, faces Bernard*): I regard you as a very brilliant man, Bernard. I value your advice.

BERNARD: Oh, the hell with the advice, Willy. I couldn't advise you. There's just one thing I've always wanted to ask you. When he was supposed to graduate, and the math teacher flunked him—

WILLY: Oh, that son-of-a-bitch ruined his life.

BERNARD: Yeah, but, Willy, all he had to do was go to summer school and make up that subject.

WILLY: That's right, that's right.

BERNARD: Did you tell him not to go to summer school?

WILLY: Me? I begged him to go. I ordered him to go!

BERNARD: Then why wouldn't he go?

WILLY: Why? Why! Bernard, that question has been trailing me like a ghost for the last fifteen years. He flunked the subject, and laid down and died like a hammer hit him!

BERNARD: Take it easy, kid.

WILLY: Let me talk to you—I got nobody to talk to. Bernard, Bernard, was it my fault? Y'see? It keeps going around in my mind, maybe I did something to him. I got nothing to give him.

BERNARD: Don't take it so hard.

WILLY: Why did he lay down? What is the story there? You were his friend!

BERNARD: Willy, I remember, it was June, and our grades came out. And he'd flunked math.

WILLY: That son-of-a-bitch!

BERNARD: No, it wasn't right then. Biff just got very angry, I remember, and he was ready to enroll in summer school.

WILLY (*surprised*): He was?

BERNARD: He wasn't beaten by it at all. But then, Willy, he disappeared from the block for almost a month. And I got the idea that he'd gone up to New England to see you. Did he have a talk with you then?

Willy stares in silence.

BERNARD: Willy?

WILLY (*with a strong edge of resentment in his voice*): Yeah, he came to Boston. What about it?

BERNARD: Well, just that when he came back—I'll never forget this, it always mystifies me. Because I'd thought so well of Biff, even though he'd always taken advantage of me. I loved him, Willy, y'know? And he came back after that month and took his sneakers—remember those sneakers with "University of Virginia" printed on them? He was so proud of those, wore them every day. And he took them down in the cellar, and burned them up in the furnace. We had a fist fight. It lasted at least half an hour. Just the two of us, punching each other down the cellar, and crying right through it. I've often thought of how strange it was that I knew he'd given up his life. What happened in Boston, Willy?

Willy looks at him as at an intruder.

BERNARD: I just bring it up because you asked me.

WILLY (*angrily*): Nothing. What do you mean, "What happened?" What's that got to do with anything?

BERNARD: Well, don't get sore.

WILLY: What are you trying to do, blame it on me? If a boy lays down is that my fault?

BERNARD: Now, Willy, don't get—

WILLY: Well, don't—don't talk to me that way! What does that mean, "What happened?"

Charley enters. He is in his vest, and he carries a bottle of bourbon.

CHARLEY: Hey, you're going to miss that train. (*He waves the bottle.*)

BERNARD: Yeah, I'm going. (*He takes the bottle.*) Thanks, Pop. (*He picks up his rackets and bag.*) Good-by, Willy, and don't worry about it. You know. "If at first you don't succeed . . ."

WILLY: Yes, I believe in that.

BERNARD: But sometimes, Willy, it's better for a man just to walk away.

WILLY: Walk away?

BERNARD: That's right.

WILLY: But if you can't walk away?

BERNARD (*after a slight pause*): I guess that's when it's tough. (Extending his hand.) Good-by, Willy.

WILLY (*shaking Bernard's hand*): Good-by, boy.

CHARLEY (*an arm on Bernard's shoulder*): How do you like this kid? Gonna argue a case in front of the Supreme Court.

BERNARD (*protesting*): Pop!

WILLY (*genuinely shocked, pained, and happy*): No! The Supreme Court!

BERNARD: I gotta run. 'By, Dad!

CHARLEY: Knock 'em dead, Bernard!

Bernard goes off.

WILLY (*as Charley takes out his wallet*): The Supreme Court! And he didn't even mention it!

CHARLEY (*counting out money on the desk*): He don't have to—he's gonna do it.

WILLY: And you never told him what to do, did you? You never took any interest in him.

CHARLEY: My salvation is that I never took any interest in any thing. There's some money—fifty dollars. I got an accountant inside.

WILLY: Charley, look . . . (*With difficulty.*) I got my insurance to pay. If you can manage it—I need a hundred and ten dollars.

Charley doesn't reply for a moment; merely stops moving.

WILLY: I'd draw it from my bank but Linda would know, and I . . .

CHARLEY: Sit down, Willy.

WILLY (*moving toward the chair*): I'm keeping an account of everything, remember. I'll pay every penny back. (*He sits.*)

CHARLEY: Now listen to me, Willy.

WILLY: I want you to know I appreciate . . .

CHARLEY (*sitting down on the table*): Willy, what're you doin'? What the hell is goin' on in your head?

WILLY: Why? I'm simply . . .

CHARLEY: I offered you a job. You can make fifty dollars a week. And I won't send you on the road.

WILLY: I've got a job.

CHARLEY: Without pay? What kind of a job is a job without pay? (*He rises.*) Now, look, kid, enough is enough. I'm no genius but I know when I'm being insulted.

WILLY: Insulted!

CHARLEY: Why don't you want to work for me?

WILLY: What's the matter with you? I've got a job.

CHARLEY: Then what're you walkin' in here every week for?

WILLY (*getting up*): Well, if you don't want me to walk in here—

CHARLEY: I am offering you a job.

WILLY: I don't want your goddam job!

CHARLEY: When the hell are you going to grow up?

WILLY (*furiously*): You big ignoramus, if you say that to me again I'll rap you one! I don't care how big you are! (*He's ready to fight.*)

Pause.

CHARLEY (*kindly, going to him*): How much do you need, Willy?

WILLY: Charley, I'm strapped. I'm strapped. I don't know what to do. I was just fired.

CHARLEY: Howard fired you?

WILLY: That snotnose. Imagine that? I named him. I named him Howard.

CHARLEY: Willy, when're you gonna realize that them things don't mean anything? You named him Howard, but you can't sell that. The only thing you got in this world is what you can sell. And the funny thing is that you're a salesman, and you don't know that.

WILLY: I've always tried to think otherwise, I guess. I always felt that if a man was impressive, and well liked, that nothing—

CHARLEY: Why must everybody like you? Who liked J. P. Morgan? Was he impressive? In a Turkish bath he'd look like a butcher. But with his pockets on he was very well liked. Now listen, Willy, I know you don't like me, and nobody can say I'm in love with you, but I'll give you a job because—just for the hell of it, put it that way. Now what do you say?

WILLY: I—I just can't work for you, Charley.

CHARLEY: What're you, jealous of me?

WILLY: I can't work for you, that's all, don't ask me why.

CHARLEY (*angered, takes out more bills*): You been jealous of me all your life, you damned fool! Here, pay your insurance. (*He puts the money in Willy's hand.*)

WILLY: I'm keeping strict accounts.

CHARLEY: I've got some work to do. Take care of yourself. And pay your insurance.

WILLY (*moving to the right*): Funny, y'know? After all the highways, and the trains, and the appointments, and the years, you end up worth more dead than alive.

CHARLEY: Willy, nobody's worth nothin' dead. (*After a slight pause.*) Did you hear what I said?

Willy stands still, dreaming.

CHARLEY: Willy!

WILLY: Apologize to Bernard for me when you see him. I didn't mean to argue with him. He's a fine boy. They're all fine boys, and they'll end up big — all of them. Someday they'll all play tennis together. Wish me luck, Charley. He saw Bill Oliver today.

CHARLEY: Good luck.

WILLY (*on the verge of tears*): Charley, you're the only friend I got. Isn't that a remarkable thing? (*He goes out.*)

CHARLEY: Jesus!

Charley stares after him a moment and follows. All light blacks out. Suddenly raucous music is heard, and a red glow rises behind the screen at right. Stanley, a young waiter, appears, carrying a table, followed by Happy, who is carrying two chairs.

STANLEY (*putting the table down*): That's all right, Mr. Loman, I can handle it myself. (*He turns and takes the chairs from Happy and places them at the table.*)

HAPPY (*glancing around*): Oh, this is better.

STANLEY: Sure, in the front there you're in the middle of all kinds a noise. Whenever you got a party, Mr. Loman, you just tell me and I'll put you back here. Y'know, there's a lotta people they don't like it private, because when they go out they like to see a lotta action around them because they're sick and tired to stay in the house by theirself. But I know you, you ain't from Hackensack. You know what I mean?

HAPPY (*sitting down*): So how's it coming, Stanley?

STANLEY: Ah, it's a dog's life. I only wish during the war they'd a took me in the Army. I coulda been dead by now.

HAPPY: My brother's back, Stanley.

STANLEY: Oh, he come back, heh? From the Far West.

HAPPY: Yeah, big cattle man, my brother, so treat him right. And my father's coming too.

STANLEY: Oh, your father too!

HAPPY: You got a couple of nice lobsters?

STANLEY: Hundred per cent, big.

HAPPY: I want them with the claws.

STANLEY: Don't worry, I don't give you no mice. (*Happy laughs.*) How about some wine? It'll put a head on the meal.

HAPPY: No. You remember, Stanley, that recipe I brought you from overseas? With the champagne in it?

STANLEY: Oh, yeah, sure. I still got it tacked up yet in the kitchen. But that'll have to cost a buck apiece anyways.

HAPPY: That's all right.

STANLEY: What'd you, hit a number or somethin'?

HAPPY: No, it's a little celebration. My brother is — I think he pulled off a big deal today. I think we're going into business together.

STANLEY: Great! That's the best for you. Because a family business, you know what I mean?—that's the best.

HAPPY: That's what I think.

STANLEY: 'Cause what's the difference? Somebody steals? It's in the family. Know what I mean? (*Sotto voce.*°) Like this bartender here. The boss is goin' crazy what kinda leak he's got in the cash register. You put it in but it don't come out.

HAPPY (*raising his head*): Sh!

STANLEY: What?

HAPPY: You notice I wasn't lookin' right or left, was I?

STANLEY: No.

HAPPY: And my eyes are closed.

STANLEY: So what's the—?

HAPPY: Strudel's comin'.

STANLEY (*catching on, looks around*): Ah, no, there's no—

He breaks off as a furred, lavishly dressed girl enters and sits at the next table. Both follow her with their eyes.

STANLEY: Geez, how'd ya know?

HAPPY: I got radar or something. (*Staring directly at her profile.*) Oooooooo . . . Stanley.

STANLEY: I think that's for you, Mr. Loman.

HAPPY: Look at that mouth. Oh, God. And the binoculars.

STANLEY: Geez, you got a life, Mr. Loman.

HAPPY: Wait on her.

STANLEY (*going to the girl's table*): Would you like a menu, ma'am?

GIRL: I'm expecting someone, but I'd like a—

HAPPY: Why don't you bring her—excuse me, miss, do you mind? I sell champagne, and I'd like you to try my brand. Bring her a champagne, Stanley.

GIRL: That's awfully nice of you.

HAPPY: Don't mention it. It's all company money. (*He laughs.*)

GIRL: That's a charming product to be selling, isn't it?

HAPPY: Oh, gets to be like everything else. Selling is selling, y'know.

GIRL: I suppose.

HAPPY: You don't happen to sell, do you?

GIRL: No, I don't sell.

HAPPY: Would you object to a compliment from a stranger? You ought to be on a magazine cover.

GIRL (*looking at him a little archly*): I have been.

Stanley comes in with a glass of champagne.

HAPPY: What'd I say before, Stanley? You see? She's a cover girl.

STANLEY: Oh, I could see, I could see.

HAPPY (*to the Girl*): What magazine?

Sotto voce: Softly, "under the breath" (Italian).

GIRL: Oh, a lot of them. (*She takes the drink.*) Thank you.

HAPPY: You know what they say in France, don't you? "Champagne is the drink of the complexion"—Hya, Biff!

Biff has entered and sits with Happy.

BIFF: Hello, kid. Sorry I'm late.

HAPPY: I just got here. Uh, Miss—?

GIRL: Forsythe.

HAPPY: Miss Forsythe, this is my brother.

BIFF: Is Dad here?

HAPPY: His name is Biff. You might've heard of him. Great football player.

GIRL: Really? What team?

HAPPY: Are you familiar with football?

GIRL: No, I'm afraid I'm not.

HAPPY: Biff is quarterback with the New York Giants.

GIRL: Well, that is nice, isn't it? (*She drinks.*)

HAPPY: Good health.

GIRL: I'm happy to meet you.

HAPPY: That's my name. Hap. It's really Harold, but at West Point they called me Happy.

GIRL (*now really impressed*): Oh, I see. How do you do? (*She turns her profile.*)

BIFF: Isn't Dad coming?

HAPPY: You want her?

BIFF: Oh, I could never make that.

HAPPY: I remember the time that idea would never come into your head. Where's the old confidence, Biff?

BIFF: I just saw Oliver—

HAPPY: Wait a minute. I've got to see that old confidence again. Do you want her? She's on call.

BIFF: Oh, no. (*He turns to look at the Girl.*)

HAPPY: I'm telling you. Watch this. (*Turning to the Girl.*) Honey? (*She turns to him.*) Are you busy?

GIRL: Well, I am . . . but I could make a phone call.

HAPPY: Do that, will you, honey? And see if you can get a friend. We'll be here for a while. Biff is one of the greatest football players in the country.

GIRL (*standing up*): Well, I'm certainly happy to meet you.

HAPPY: Come back soon.

GIRL: I'll try.

HAPPY: Don't try, honey, try hard.

The Girl exits. Stanley follows, shaking his head in bewildered admiration.

HAPPY: Isn't that a shame now? A beautiful girl like that? That's why I can't get married. There's not a good woman in a thousand. New York is loaded with them, kid!

BIFF: Hap, look—

HAPPY: I told you she was on call!

BIFF (*strangely unnerved*): Cut it out, will ya? I want to say something to you.

HAPPY: Did you see Oliver?

BIFF: I saw him all right. Now look, I want to tell Dad a couple of things and I want you to help me.

HAPPY: What? Is he going to back you?

BIFF: Are you crazy? You're out of your goddam head, you know that?

HAPPY: Why? What happened?

BIFF (*breathlessly*): I did a terrible thing today, Hap. It's been the strangest day I ever went through. I'm all numb, I swear.

HAPPY: You mean he wouldn't see you?

BIFF: Well, I waited six hours for him, see? All day. Kept sending my name in. Even tried to date his secretary so she'd get me to him, but no soap.

HAPPY: Because you're not showin' the old confidence, Biff. He remembered you, didn't he?

BIFF (*stopping Happy with a gesture*): Finally, about five o'clock, he comes out. Didn't remember who I was or anything. I felt like such an idiot, Hap.

HAPPY: Did you tell him my Florida idea?

BIFF: He walked away. I saw him for one minute. I got so mad I could've torn the walls down! How the hell did I ever get the idea I was a salesman there? I even believed myself that I'd been a salesman for him! And then he gave me one look and—I realized what a ridiculous lie my whole life has been! We've been talking in a dream for fifteen years. I was a shipping clerk.

HAPPY: What'd you do?

BIFF (*with great tension and wonder*): Well, he left, see. And the secretary went out. I was all alone in the waiting-room. I don't know what came over me, Hap. The next thing I know I'm in his office—paneled walls, everything. I can't explain it. I—Hap, I took his fountain pen.

HAPPY: Geez, did he catch you?

BIFF: I ran out. I ran down all eleven flights. I ran and ran and ran.

HAPPY: That was an awful dumb—what'd you do that for?

BIFF (*agonized*): I don't know, I just—wanted to take something, I don't know. You gotta help me, Hap, I'm gonna tell Pop.

HAPPY: You crazy? What for?

BIFF: Hap, he's got to understand that I'm not the man somebody lends that kind of money to. He thinks I've been spiting him all these years and it's eating him up.

HAPPY: That's just it. You tell him something nice.

BIFF: I can't.

HAPPY: Say you got a lunch date with Oliver tomorrow.

BIFF: So what do I do tomorrow?

HAPPY: You leave the house tomorrow and come back at night and say Oliver is thinking it over. And he thinks it over for a couple of weeks, and gradually it fades away and nobody's the worse.

BIFF: But it'll go on forever!

HAPPY: Dad is never so happy as when he's looking forward to something!

Willy enters.

HAPPY: Hello, scout!
WILLY: Gee, I haven't been here in years!

Stanley has followed Willy in and sets a chair for him. Stanley starts off but Happy stops him.

HAPPY: Stanley!

Stanley stands by, waiting for an order.

BIFF (*going to Willy with guilt, as to an invalid*): Sit down, Pop. You want a drink?
WILLY: Sure, I don't mind.
BIFF: Let's get a load on.
WILLY: You look worried.
BIFF: N-no. (*To Stanley.*) Scotch all around. Make it doubles.
STANLEY: Doubles, right. (*He goes.*)
WILLY: You had a couple already, didn't you?
BIFF: Just a couple, yeah.
WILLY: Well, what happened, boy? (*Nodding affirmatively, with a smile.*) Everything go all right?
BIFF (*takes a breath, then reaches out and grasps Willy's hand.*): Pal . . . (*He is smiling bravely, and Willy is smiling too.*) I had an experience today.
HAPPY: Terrific, Pop.
WILLY: That so? What happened?
BIFF (*high, slightly alcoholic, above the earth*): I'm going to tell you everything from first to last. It's been a strange day. (*Silence. He looks around, composes himself as best he can, but his breath keeps breaking the rhythm of his voice.*) I had to wait quite a while for him, and—
WILLY: Oliver.
BIFF: Yeah, Oliver. All day, as a matter of cold fact. And a lot of—instances—facts, Pop, facts about my life came back to me. Who was it, Pop? Who ever said I was a salesman with Oliver?
WILLY: Well, you were.
BIFF: No, Dad, I was a shipping clerk.
WILLY: But you were practically—
BIFF (*with determination*): Dad, I don't know who said it first, but I was never a salesman for Bill Oliver.
WILLY: What're you talking about?
BIFF: Let's hold on to the facts tonight, Pop. We're not going to get anywhere bullin' around. I was a shipping clerk.
WILLY (*angrily*): All right, now listen to me—
BIFF: Why don't you let me finish?
WILLY: I'm not interested in stories about the past or any crap of that kind because the woods are burning, boys, you understand? There's a big blaze going on all around. I was fired today.
BIFF (*shocked*): How could you be?
WILLY: I was fired, and I'm looking for a little good news to tell your mother, because the woman has waited and the woman has suffered. The gist of

it is that I haven't got a story left in my head, Biff. So don't give me a lecture about facts and aspects. I am not interested. Now what've you got to say to me?

Stanley enters with three drinks. They wait until he leaves.

WILLY: Did you see Oliver?

BIFF: Jesus, Dad!

WILLY: You mean you didn't go up there?

HAPPY: Sure he went up there.

BIFF: I did. I—saw him. How could they fire you?

WILLY (*on the edge of his chair*): What kind of a welcome did he give you?

BIFF: He won't even let you work on commission?

WILLY: I'm out! (*Driving.*) So tell me, he gave you a warm welcome?

HAPPY: Sure, Pop, sure!

BIFF (*driven*): Well, it was kind of—

WILLY: I was wondering if he'd remember you. (*To Happy.*) Imagine, man doesn't see him for ten, twelve years and gives him that kind of a welcome!

HAPPY: Damn right!

BIFF (*trying to return to the offensive*): Pop, look—

WILLY: You know why he remembered you, don't you? Because you impressed him in those days.

BIFF: Let's talk quietly and get this down to the facts, huh?

WILLY (*as though Biff had been interrupting*): Well, what happened? It's great news, Biff. Did he take you into his office or'd you talk in the waiting-room?

BIFF: Well, he came in, see, and—

WILLY (*with a big smile*): What'd he say? Betcha he threw his arm around you.

BIFF: Well, he kinda—

WILLY: He's a fine man. (*To Happy.*) Very hard man to see, y'know.

HAPPY (*agreeing*): Oh, I know.

WILLY (*to Biff*): Is that where you had the drinks?

BIFF: Yeah, he gave me a couple of—no, no!

HAPPY (*cutting in*): He told him my Florida idea.

WILLY: Don't interrupt. (*To Biff.*) How'd he react to the Florida idea?

BIFF: Dad, will you give me a minute to explain?

WILLY: I've been waiting for you to explain since I sat down here! What happened? He took you into his office and what?

BIFF: Well—I talked. And—and he listened, see.

WILLY: Famous for the way he listens, y'know. What was his answer?

BIFF: His answer was—(*He breaks off, suddenly angry.*) Dad, you're not letting me tell you what I want to tell you!

WILLY (*accusing, angered*): You didn't see him, did you?

BIFF: I did see him!

WILLY: What'd you insult him or something? You insulted him, didn't you?

BIFF: Listen, will you let me out of it, will you just let me out of it!

HAPPY: What the hell!
WILLY: Tell me what happened!
BIFF (*to Happy*): I can't talk to him!

A single trumpet note jars the ear. The light of green leaves stains the house, which holds the air of night and a dream. Young Bernard enters and knocks on the door of the house.

YOUNG BERNARD (*frantically*): Mrs. Loman, Mrs. Loman!
HAPPY: Tell him what happened!
BIFF (*to Happy*): Shut up and leave me alone!
WILLY: No, no! You had to go and flunk math!
BIFF: What math? What're you talking about?
YOUNG BERNARD: Mrs. Loman, Mrs. Loman!

Linda appears in the house, as of old.

WILLY (*wildly*): Math, math, math!
BIFF: Take it easy, Pop!
YOUNG BERNARD: Mrs. Loman!
WILLY (*furiously*): If you hadn't flunked you'd've been set by now!
BIFF: Now, look, I'm gonna tell you what happened, and you're going to listen to me.
YOUNG BERNARD: Mrs. Loman!
BIFF: I waited six hours—
HAPPY: What the hell are you saying?
BIFF: I kept sending in my name but he wouldn't see me. So finally he . . . (*He continues unheard as light fades low on the restaurant.*)
YOUNG BERNARD: Biff flunked math!
LINDA: No!
YOUNG BERNARD: Birnbaum flunked him! They won't graduate him!
LINDA: But they have to. He's gotta go to the university. Where is he? Biff! Biff!
YOUNG BERNARD: No, he left. He went to Grand Central.
LINDA: Grand—You mean he went to Boston!
YOUNG BERNARD: Is Uncle Willy in Boston?
LINDA: Oh, maybe Willy can talk to the teacher. Oh, the poor, poor boy!

Light on house area snaps out.

BIFF (*at the table, now audible, holding up a gold fountain pen*): . . . so I'm washed up with Oliver, you understand? Are you listening to me?
WILLY (*at a loss*): Yeah, sure. If you hadn't flunked—
BIFF: Flunked what? What're you talking about?
WILLY: Don't blame everything on me! I didn't flunk math—you did! What pen?
HAPPY: That was awful dumb, Biff, a pen like that is worth—
WILLY (*seeing the pen for the first time*): You took Oliver's pen?
BIFF (*weakening*): Dad, I just explained it to you.
WILLY: You stole Bill Oliver's fountain pen!
BIFF: I didn't exactly steal it! That's just what I've been explaining to you!

HAPPY: He had it in his hand and just then Oliver walked in, so he got nervous and stuck it in his pocket!

WILLY: My God, Biff!

BIFF: I never intended to do it, Dad!

OPERATOR'S VOICE: Standish Arms, good evening!

WILLY (*shouting*): I'm not in my room!

BIFF (*frightened*): Dad, what's the matter? (*He and Happy stand up.*)

OPERATOR: Ringing Mr. Loman for you!

WILLY: I'm not there, stop it!

BIFF (*horrified, gets down on one knee before Willy*): Dad, I'll make good, I'll make good. (*Willy tries to get to his feet. Biff holds him down.*) Sit down now.

WILLY: No, you're no good, you're no good for anything.

BIFF: I am, Dad, I'll find something else, you understand? Now don't worry about anything. (*He holds up Willy's face.*) Talk to me, Dad.

OPERATOR: Mr. Loman does not answer. Shall I page him?

WILLY (*attempting to stand, as though to rush and silence the Operator*): No, no, no!

HAPPY: He'll strike something, Pop.

WILLY: No, no . . .

BIFF (*desperately, standing over Willy*): Pop, listen! Listen to me! I'm telling you something good. Oliver talked to his partner about the Florida idea. You listening? He—he talked to his partner, and he came to me . . . I'm going to be all right, you hear? Dad, listen to me, he said it was just a question of the amount!

WILLY: Then you . . . got it?

HAPPY: He's gonna be terrific, Pop!

WILLY (*trying to stand*): Then you got it, haven't you? You got it! You got it!

BIFF (*agonized, holds Willy down*): No, no. Look, Pop. I'm supposed to have lunch with them tomorrow. I'm just telling you this so you'll know that I can still make an impression, Pop. And I'll make good somewhere, but I can't go tomorrow, see?

WILLY: Why not? You simply—

BIFF: But the pen, Pop!

WILLY: You give it to him and tell him it was an oversight!

HAPPY: Sure, have lunch tomorrow!

BIFF: I can't say that—

WILLY: You were doing a crossword puzzle and accidentally used his pen!

BIFF: Listen, kid, I took those balls years ago, now I walk in with his fountain pen? That clinches it, don't you see? I can't face him like that! I'll try elsewhere.

PAGE'S VOICE: Paging Mr. Loman!

WILLY: Don't you want to be anything?

BIFF: Pop, how can I go back?

WILLY: You don't want to be anything, is that what's behind it?

BIFF (*now angry at Willy for not crediting his sympathy*): Don't take it that way! You think it was easy walking into that office after what I'd done to him? A team of horses couldn't have dragged me back to Bill Oliver!

WILLY: Then why'd you go?

BIFF: Why did I go? Why did I go! Look at you! Look at what's become of you!

Off left, The Woman laughs.

WILLY: Biff, you're going to lunch tomorrow, or—

BIFF: I can't go. I've got no appointment!

HAPPY: Biff, for . . . !

WILLY: Are you spiting me?

BIFF: Don't take it that way! Goddammit!

WILLY (*strikes Biff and falters away from the table*): You rotten little louse! Are you spiting me?

THE WOMAN: Someone's at the door, Willy!

BIFF: I'm no good, can't you see what I am?

HAPPY (*separating them*): Hey, you're in a restaurant! Now cut it out, both of you! (*The girls enter.*) Hello, girls, sit down.

The Woman laughs, off left.

MISS FORSYTHE: I guess we might as well. This is Letta.

THE WOMAN: Willy, are you going to wake up?

BIFF (*ignoring Willy*): How're ya, miss, sit down. What do you drink?

MISS FORSYTHE: Letta might not be able to stay long.

LETTA: I gotta get up very early tomorrow. I got jury duty. I'm so excited! Were you fellows ever on a jury?

BIFF: No, but I been in front of them! (*The girls laugh.*) This is my father.

LETTA: Isn't he cute? Sit down with us, Pop.

HAPPY: Sit him down, Biff!

BIFF (*going to him*): Come on, slugger, drink us under the table. To hell with it! Come on, sit down, pal.

On Biff's last insistence, Willy is about to sit.

THE WOMAN (*now urgently*): Willy, are you going to answer the door!

The Woman's call pulls Willy back. He starts right, befuddled.

BIFF: Hey, where are you going?

WILLY: Open the door.

BIFF: The door?

WILLY: The washroom . . . the door . . . where's the door?

BIFF (*leading Willy to the left*): Just go straight down.

Willy moves left.

THE WOMAN: Willy, Willy, are you going to get up, get up, get up, get up?

Willy exits left.

LETTA: I think it's sweet you bring your daddy along.

MISS FORSYTHE: Oh, he isn't really your father!

BIFF (*at left, turning to her resentfully*): Miss Forsythe, you've just seen a prince walk by. A fine, troubled prince. A hard-working, unappreciated prince. A pal, you understand? A good companion. Always for his boys.

LETTA: That's so sweet.

HAPPY: Well, girls, what's the program? We're wasting time. Come on, Biff. Gather round. Where would you like to go?

BIFF: Why don't you do something for him?

HAPPY: Me!

BIFF: Don't you give a damn for him, Hap?

HAPPY: What're you talking about? I'm the one who—

BIFF: I sense it, you don't give a good goddamn about him. (*He takes the rolled-up hose from his pocket and puts it on the table in front of Happy.*) Look what I found in the cellar, for Christ's sake. How can you bear to let it go on?

HAPPY: Me? Who goes away? Who runs off and—

BIFF: Yeah, but he doesn't mean anything to you. You could help him—I can't! Don't you understand what I'm talking about? He's going to kill himself, don't you know that?

HAPPY: Don't I know it! Me!

BIFF: Hap, help him! Jesus . . . help him . . . Help me, help me, I can't bear to look at his face! (*Ready to weep, he hurries out, up right.*)

HAPPY (*starting after him*): Where are you going?

MISS FORSYTHE: What's he so mad about?

HAPPY: Come on, girls, we'll catch up with him.

MISS FORSYTHE (*as Happy pushes her out*): Say, I don't like that temper of his!

HAPPY: He's just a little overstrung, he'll be all right!

WILLY (*off left, as The Woman laughs*): Don't answer! Don't answer!

LETTA: Don't you want to tell your father—

HAPPY: No, that's not my father. He's just a guy. Come on, we'll catch Biff, and, honey, we're going to paint this town! Stanley, where's the check! Hey, Stanley!

They exit. Stanley looks toward left.

STANLEY (*calling to Happy indignantly*): Mr. Loman! Mr. Loman!

Stanley picks up a chair and follows them off. Knocking is heard off left. The Woman enters, laughing. Willy follows her. She is in a black slip; he is buttoning his shirt. Raw, sensuous music accompanies their speech.

WILLY: Will you stop laughing? Will you stop?

THE WOMAN: Aren't you going to answer the door? He'll wake the whole hotel.

WILLY: I'm not expecting anybody.

THE WOMAN: Whyn't you have another drink, honey, and stop being so damn self-centered?

WILLY: I'm so lonely.

THE WOMAN: You know you ruined me, Willy? From now on, whenever you come to the office, I'll see that you go right through to the buyers. No waiting at my desk any more, Willy. You ruined me.

WILLY: That's nice of you to say that.

THE WOMAN: Gee, you are self-centered! Why so sad? You are the saddest, self-centeredest soul I ever did see-saw. (*She laughs. He kisses her.*) Come on inside, drummer boy. It's silly to be dressing in the middle of the night. (*As knocking is heard.*) Aren't you going to answer the door?

WILLY: They're knocking on the wrong door.

THE WOMAN: But I felt the knocking. And he heard us talking in here. Maybe the hotel's on fire!

WILLY (*his terror rising*): It's a mistake.

THE WOMAN: Then tell him to go away!

WILLY: There's nobody there.

THE WOMAN: It's getting on my nerves, Willy. There's somebody standing out there and it's getting on my nerves!

WILLY (*pushing her away from him*): All right, stay in the bathroom here, and don't come out. I think there's a law in Massachusetts about it, so don't come out. It may be that new room clerk. He looked very mean. So don't come out. It's a mistake, there's no fire.

The knocking is heard again. He takes a few steps away from her, and she vanishes into the wing. The light follows him, and now he is facing Young Biff, who carries a suitcase. Biff steps toward him. The music is gone.

BIFF: Why didn't you answer?

WILLY: Biff! What are you doing in Boston?

BIFF: Why didn't you answer? I've been knocking for five minutes, I called you on the phone—

WILLY: I just heard you. I was in the bathroom and had the door shut. Did anything happen home?

BIFF: Dad—I let you down.

WILLY: What do you mean?

BIFF: Dad . . .

WILLY: Biffo, what's this about? (*Putting his arm around Biff.*) Come on, let's go downstairs and get you a malted.

BIFF: Dad, I flunked math.

WILLY: Not for the term?

BIFF: The term. I haven't got enough credits to graduate.

WILLY: You mean to say Bernard wouldn't give you the answers?

BIFF: He did, he tried, but I only got a sixty-one.

WILLY: And they wouldn't give you four points?

BIFF: Birnbaum refused absolutely. I begged him, Pop, but he won't give me those points. You gotta talk to him before they close the school. Because if he saw the kind of man you are, and you just talked to him in your way, I'm sure he'd come through for me. The class came right before practice, see, and I didn't go enough. Would you talk to him? He'd like you, Pop. You know the way you could talk.

WILLY: You're on. We'll drive right back.

BIFF: Oh, Dad, good work! I'm sure he'll change it for you!

WILLY: Go downstairs and tell the clerk I'm checkin' out. Go right down.

BIFF: Yes, sir! See, the reason he hates me, Pop—one day he was late for class so I got up at the blackboard and imitated him. I crossed my eyes and talked with a lithp.

WILLY (*laughing*): You did? The kids like it?

BIFF: They nearly died laughing!

WILLY: Yeah? What'd you do?

BIFF: The thquare root of thixthy twee is . . . (*Willy bursts out laughing; Biff joins him.*) And in the middle of it he walked in!

Willy laughs and The Woman joins in offstage.

WILLY (*without hesitation*): Hurry downstairs and—

BIFF: Somebody in there?

WILLY: No, that was next door.

The Woman laughs offstage.

BIFF: Somebody got in your bathroom!

WILLY: No, it's the next room, there's a party—

THE WOMAN (*enters, laughing. She lisps this*): Can I come in? There's something in the bathtub, Willy, and it's moving!

Willy looks at Biff, who is staring open-mouthed and horrified at The Woman.

WILLY: Ah—you better go back to your room. They must be finished painting by now. They're painting her room so I let her take a shower here. Go back, go back . . . (*He pushes her.*)

THE WOMAN (*resisting*): But I've got to get dressed, Willy, I can't—

WILLY: Get out of here! Go back, go back . . . (*Suddenly striving for the ordinary*): This is Miss Francis, Biff, she's a buyer. They're painting her room. Go back, Miss Francis, go back . . .

THE WOMAN: But my clothes, I can't go out naked in the hall!

WILLY (*pushing her offstage*): Get outa here! Go back, go back!

Biff slowly sits down on his suitcase as the argument continues offstage.

THE WOMAN: Where's my stockings? You promised me stockings, Willy!

WILLY: I have no stockings here!

THE WOMAN: You had two boxes of size nine sheers for me, and I want them!

WILLY: Here, for God's sake, will you get outa here!

THE WOMAN (*enters holding a box of stockings*): I just hope there's nobody in the hall. That's all I hope. (*To Biff.*) Are you football or baseball?

BIFF: Football.

THE WOMAN (*angry, humiliated*): That's me too. G'night. (*She snatches her clothes from Willy, and walks out.*)

WILLY (*after a pause*): Well, better get going. I want to get to the school first thing in the morning. Get my suits out of the closet. I'll get my valise. (*Biff doesn't move.*) What's the matter? (*Biff remains motionless, tears falling.*) She's a buyer. Buys for J. H. Simmons. She lives down the hall—they're painting. You don't imagine—(*He breaks off. After a pause.*) Now listen, pal, she's just a buyer. She sees merchandise in her room and they have to keep it looking just so . . . (*Pause. Assuming command.*) All right, get my suits. (*Biff doesn't move.*) Now stop crying and do as I say. I gave you an order. Biff, I gave you an order! Is that what you do when I give you an order? How dare you cry! (*Putting his arm around Biff.*) Now look, Biff, when you grow up you'll understand about these things. You mustn't—you mustn't overemphasize a thing like this. I'll see Birnbaum first thing in the morning.

BIFF: Never mind.

WILLY (*getting down beside Biff*): Never mind! He's going to give you those points. I'll see to it.

BIFF: He wouldn't listen to you.

WILLY: He certainly will listen to me. You need those points for the U. of Virginia.

BIFF: I'm not going there.

WILLY: Heh? If I can't get him to change that mark you'll make it up in summer school. You've got all summer to—

BIFF (*his weeping breaking from him*): Dad . . .

WILLY (*infected by it*): Oh, my boy . . .

BIFF: Dad . . .

WILLY: She's nothing to me, Biff. I was lonely, I was terribly lonely.

BIFF: You—you gave her Mama's stockings! (*His tears break through and he rises to go.*)

WILLY (*grabbing for Biff*): I gave you an order!

BIFF: Don't touch me, you—liar!

WILLY: Apologize for that!

BIFF: You fake! You phony little fake! You fake! (*Overcome, he turns quickly and weeping fully goes out with his suitcase. Willy is left on the floor on his knees.*)

WILLY: I gave you an order! Biff, come back here or I'll beat you! Come back here! I'll whip you!

Stanley comes quickly in from the right and stands in front of Willy.

WILLY (*shouts at Stanley*): I gave you an order . . .

STANLEY: Hey, let's pick it up, pick it up, Mr. Loman. (*He helps Willy to his feet.*) Your boys left with the chippies. They said they'll see you home.

A second waiter watches some distance away.

WILLY: But we were supposed to have dinner together.

Music is heard, Willy's theme.

STANLEY: Can you make it?

WILLY: I'll—sure, I can make it. (*Suddenly concerned about his clothes.*) Do I—I look all right?

STANLEY: Sure, you look all right. (*He flicks a speck off Willy's lapel.*)

WILLY: Here—here's a dollar.

STANLEY: Oh, your son paid me. It's all right.

WILLY (*putting it in Stanley's hand*): No, take it. You're a good boy.

STANLEY: Oh, no, you don't have to . . .

WILLY: Here—here's some more, I don't need it any more. (*After a slight pause.*) Tell me—is there a seed store in the neighborhood?

STANLEY: Seeds? You mean like to plant?

As Willy turns, Stanley slips the money back into his jacket pocket.

WILLY: Yes. Carrots, peas . . .

STANLEY: Well, there's hardware stores on Sixth Avenue, but it may be too late now.

WILLY (*anxiously*): Oh, I'd better hurry. I've got to get some seeds. (*He starts off to the right.*) I've got to get some seeds, right away. Nothing's planted. I don't have a thing in the ground.

Willy hurries out as the light goes down. Stanley moves over to the right after him, watches him off. The other waiter has been staring at Willy.

STANLEY (*to the waiter*): Well, whatta you looking at?

The waiter picks up the chairs and moves off right. Stanley takes the table and follows him. The light fades on this area. There is a long pause, the sound of the flute coming over. The light gradually rises on the kitchen, which is empty. Happy appears at the door of the house, followed by Biff. Happy is carrying a large bunch of long-stemmed roses. He enters the kitchen, looks around for Linda. Not seeing her, he turns to Biff, who is just outside the house door, and makes a gesture with his hands, indicating "Not here, I guess." He looks into the living-room and freezes. Inside, Linda, unseen, is seated, Willy's coat on her lap. She rises ominously and quietly and moves toward Happy, who backs up into the kitchen, afraid.

HAPPY: Hey, what're you doing up? (*Linda says nothing but moves toward him implacably.*) Where's Pop? (*He keeps backing to the right, and now Linda is in full view in the doorway to the living-room.*) Is he sleeping?

LINDA: Where were you?

HAPPY (*trying to laugh it off*): We met two girls, Mom, very fine types. Here, we brought you some flowers. (*Offering them to her.*) Put them in your room, Ma.

She knocks them to the floor at Biff's feet. He has now come inside and closed the door behind him. She stares at Biff, silent.

HAPPY: Now what'd you do that for? Mom, I want you to have some flowers—

LINDA (*cutting Happy off, violently to Biff*): Don't you care whether he lives or dies?

HAPPY (*going to the stairs*): Come upstairs, Biff.

BIFF (*with a flare of disgust, to Happy*): Go away from me! (*To Linda.*) What do you mean, lives or dies? Nobody's dying around here, pal.

LINDA: Get out of my sight! Get out of here!

BIFF: I wanna see the boss.

LINDA: You're not going near him!

BIFF: Where is he? (*He moves into the living-room and Linda follows.*)

LINDA (*shouting after Biff*): You invite him for dinner. He looks forward to it all day—(*Biff appears in his parents' bedroom, looks around, and exits.*)—and then you desert him there. There's no stranger you'd do that to!

HAPPY: Why? He had a swell time with us. Listen, when I—(*Linda comes back into the kitchen*)—desert him I hope I don't outlive the day!

LINDA: Get out of here!

HAPPY: Now look, Mom . . .

LINDA: Did you have to go to women tonight? You and your lousy rotten whores!

Biff re-enters the kitchen.

HAPPY: Mom, all we did was follow Biff around trying to cheer him up! (*To Biff.*) Boy, what a night you gave me!

LINDA: Get out of here, both of you, and don't come back! I don't want you tormenting him any more. Go on now, get your things together! (*To Biff.*) You can sleep in his apartment. (*She starts to pick up the flowers and stops herself.*) Pick up this stuff, I'm not your maid any more. Pick it up, you bum, you!

Happy turns his back to her in refusal. Biff slowly moves over and gets down on his knees, picking up the flowers.

LINDA: You're a pair of animals! Not one, not another living soul would have had the cruelty to walk out on that man in a restaurant!

BIFF (*not looking at her*): Is that what he said?

LINDA: He didn't have to say anything. He was so humiliated he nearly limped when he came in.

HAPPY: But, Mom, he had a great time with us—

BIFF (*cutting him off violently*): Shut up!

Without another word, Happy goes upstairs.

LINDA: You! You didn't even go in to see if he was all right!

BIFF (*still on the floor in front of Linda, the flowers in his hand; with self-loathing*): No. Didn't. Didn't do a damned thing. How do you like that, heh? Left him babbling in a toilet.

LINDA: You louse. You . . .

BIFF: Now you hit it on the nose! (*He gets up, throws the flowers in the waste-basket.*) The scum of the earth, and you're looking at him!

LINDA: Get out of here!

BIFF: I gotta talk to the boss, Mom. Where is he?

LINDA: You're not going near him. Get out of this house!

BIFF (*with absolute assurance, determination*): No. We're gonna have an abrupt conversation, him and me.

LINDA: You're not talking to him!

Hammering is heard from outside the house, off right. Biff turns toward the noise.

LINDA (*suddenly pleading*): Will you please leave him alone?

BIFF: What's he doing out there?

LINDA: He's planting the garden!

BIFF (*quietly*): Now? Oh, my God!

Biff moves outside, Linda following. The light dies down on them and comes up on the center of the apron as Willy walks into it. He is carrying a flashlight, a hoe, and handful of seed packets. He raps the top of the hoe sharply to fix it firmly, and then moves to the left, measuring off the distance with his foot. He holds the flashlight to look at the seed packets, reading off the instructions. He is in the blue of night.

WILLY: Carrots . . . quarter-inch apart. Rows . . . one-foot rows. (*He measures it off.*) One foot. (*He puts down a package and measures off.*) Beets. (*He puts down another package and measures again.*) Lettuce. (*He reads the package, puts it down.*) One foot—(*He breaks off as Ben appears at the right and moves slowly down to him.*) What a proposition, ts, ts. Terrific, terrific. 'Cause she's suffered, Ben, the woman has suffered. You understand me? A man can't go out the way he came in, Ben, a man has got to add up to something. You can't, you can't—(*Ben moves toward him as though to interrupt.*) You gotta consider, now. Don't answer so quick. Remember, it's a guaranteed twenty-thousand-dollar proposition. Now look, Ben, I want you to go through the ins and outs of this thing with me. I've got nobody to talk to, Ben, and the woman has suffered, you hear me?

BEN (*standing still, considering*): What's the proposition?

WILLY: It's twenty thousand dollars on the barrelhead. Guaranteed, gilt-edged, you understand?

BEN: You don't want to make a fool of yourself. They might not honor the policy.

WILLY: How can they dare refuse? Didn't I work like a coolie to meet every premium on the nose? And now they don't pay off? Impossible!

BEN: It's called a cowardly thing, William.

WILLY: Why? Does it take more guts to stand here the rest of my life ringing up a zero?

BEN (*yielding*): That's a point, William. (*He moves, thinking, turns.*) And twenty thousand—that is something one can feel with the hand, it is there.

WILLY (*now assured, with rising power*): Oh, Ben, that's the whole beauty of it! I see it like a diamond, shining in the dark, hard and rough, that I can pick up and touch in my hand. Not like—like an appointment! This would not be another damned-fool appointment, Ben, and it changes all the aspects. Because he thinks I'm nothing, see, and so he spites me. But the funeral—(*Straightening up.*) Ben, that funeral will be massive! They'll come from Maine, Massachusetts, Vermont, New Hampshire! All the old-timers with the strange license plates—that boy will be thunderstruck, Ben, because he never realized—I am known! Rhode Island, New York, New Jersey—I am known, Ben, and he'll see it with his eyes once and for all. He'll see what I am, Ben! He's in for a shock, that boy!

BEN (*coming to the edge of the garden*): He'll call you a coward.

WILLY (*suddenly fearful*): No, that would be terrible.

BEN: Yes. And a damned fool.

WILLY: No, no, he mustn't, I won't have that! (*He is broken and desperate.*)

BEN: He'll hate you William.

The gay music of the Boys is heard.

WILLY: Oh, Ben, how do we get back to all the great times? Used to be so full of light, and comradeship, the sleigh-riding in winter, and the ruddiness on his cheeks. And always some kind of good news coming up, always something nice coming up ahead. And never even let me carry the valises in the house, and simonizing, simonizing that little red car! Why, why can't I give him something and not have him hate me?

BEN: Let me think about it. (*He glances at his watch.*) I still have a little time. Remarkable proposition, but you've got to be sure you're not making a fool of yourself.

Ben drifts off upstage and goes out of sight. Biff comes down from the left.

WILLY (*suddenly conscious of Biff, turns and looks up at him, then begins picking up the packages of seeds in confusion*): Where the hell is that seed? (*Indignantly.*) You can't see nothing out here! They boxed in the whole goddamn neighborhood!

BIFF: There are people all around here. Don't you realize that?

WILLY: I'm busy. Don't bother me.

BIFF (*taking the hoe from Willy*): I'm saying good-by to you, Pop. (*Willy looks at him, silent, unable to move.*) I'm not coming back any more.

WILLY: You're not going to see Oliver tomorrow?

BIFF: I've got no appointment, Dad.

WILLY: He put his arm around you, and you've got no appointment?

BIFF: Pop, get this now, will you? Everytime I've left it's been a fight that sent me out of here. Today I realized something about myself and I tried to explain it to you and I—I think I'm just not smart enough to make any sense out of it for you. To hell with whose fault it is or anything like that. (*He takes Willy's arm.*) Let's just wrap it up, heh? Come on in, we'll tell Mom. (*He gently tries to pull Willy to left.*)

WILLY (*frozen, immobile, with guilt in his voice*): No, I don't want to see her.

BIFF: Come on! (*He pulls again, and Willy tries to pull away.*)

WILLY (*highly nervous*): No, no, I don't want to see her.

BIFF (*tries to look into Willy's face, as if to find the answer there*): Why don't you want to see her?

WILLY (*more harshly now*): Don't bother me, will you?

BIFF: What do you mean, you don't want to see her? You don't want them calling you yellow, do you? This isn't your fault; it's me, I'm a bum. Now come inside! (*Willy strains to get away.*) Did you hear what I said to you?

Willy pulls away and quickly goes by himself into the house. Biff follows.

LINDA (*to Willy*): Did you plant, dear?

BIFF (*at the door, to Linda*): All right, we had it out. I'm going and I'm not writing any more.

LINDA (*going to Willy in the kitchen*): I think that's the best way, dear. 'Cause there's no use drawing it out, you'll just never get along.

Willy doesn't respond.

BIFF: People ask where I am and what I'm doing, you don't know, and you don't care. That way it'll be off your mind and you can start brightening up again. All right? That clears it, doesn't it? (*Willy is silent, and Biff goes to him.*) You gonna wish me luck, scout? (*He extends his hand.*) What do you say?

LINDA: Shake his hand, Willy.

WILLY (*turning to her, seething with hurt*): There's no necessity to mention the pen at all, y'know.

BIFF (*gently*): I've got no appointment, Dad.

WILLY (*erupting fiercely*): He put his arm around . . . ?

BIFF: Dad, you're never going to see what I am, so what's the use of arguing? If I strike oil I'll send you a check. Meantime forget I'm alive.

WILLY (*to Linda*): Spite, see?
BIFF: Shake hands, Dad.
WILLY: Not my hand.
BIFF: I was hoping not to go this way.
WILLY: Well, this is the way you're going. Good-by.

Biff looks at him a moment, then turns sharply and goes to the stairs.

WILLY (*stops him with*): May you rot in hell if you leave this house!
BIFF (*turning*): Exactly what is it that you want from me?
WILLY: I want you to know, on the train, in the mountains, in the valleys, wherever you go, that you cut down your life for spite!
BIFF: No, no.
WILLY: Spite, spite, is the word of your undoing! And when you're down and out, remember what did it. When you're rotting somewhere beside the railroad tracks, remember, and don't you dare blame it on me!
BIFF: I'm not blaming it on you!
WILLY: I won't take the rap for this, you hear?

Happy comes down the stairs and stands on the bottom step, watching.

BIFF: That's just what I'm telling you!
WILLY (*sinking into a chair at the table, with full accusation*): You're trying to put a knife in me — don't think I don't know what you're doing!
BIFF: All right, phony! Then let's lay it on the line. (*He whips the rubber tube out of his pocket and puts it on the table.*)
HAPPY: You crazy —
LINDA: Biff! (*She moves to grab the hose, but Biff holds it down with his hand.*)
BIFF: Leave it there! Don't move it!
WILLY (*not looking at it*): What is that?
BIFF: You know goddam well what that is.
WILLY (*caged, wanting to escape*): I never saw that.
BIFF: You saw it. The mice didn't bring it into the cellar! What is this supposed to do, make a hero out of you? This supposed to make me sorry for you?
WILLY: Never heard of it.
BIFF: There'll be no pity for you, you hear it? No pity!
WILLY (*to Linda*): You hear the spite!
BIFF: No, you're going to hear the truth — what you are and what I am!
LINDA: Stop it!
WILLY: Spite!
HAPPY (*coming down toward Biff*): You cut it now!
BIFF (*to Happy*): The man don't know who we are! The man is gonna know! (*To Willy.*) We never told the truth for ten minutes in this house!
HAPPY: We always told the truth!
BIFF (*turning on him*): You big blow, are you the assistant buyer? You're one of the two assistants to the assistant, aren't you?
HAPPY: Well, I'm practically —
BIFF: You're practically full of it! We all are! And I'm through with it. (*To Willy.*) Now hear this, Willy, this is me.

WILLY: I know you!

BIFF: You know why I had no address for three months? I stole a suit in Kansas City and I was in jail. (*To Linda, who is sobbing.*) Stop crying. I'm through with it.

Linda turns away from them, her hands covering her face.

WILLY: I suppose that's my fault!

BIFF: I stole myself out of every good job since high school!

WILLY: And whose fault is that?

BIFF: And I never got anywhere because you blew me so full of hot air I could never stand taking orders from anybody! That's whose fault it is!

WILLY: I hear that!

LINDA: Don't, Biff!

BIFF: It's goddam time you heard that! I had to be boss big shot in two weeks, and I'm through with it!

WILLY: Then hang yourself! For spite, hang yourself!

BIFF: No! Nobody's hanging himself, Willy! I ran down eleven flights with a pen in my hand today. And suddenly I stopped, you hear me? And in the middle of that office building, do you hear this? I stopped in the middle of that building and I saw—the sky. I saw the things that I love in this world. The work and the food and time to sit and smoke. And I looked at the pen and said to myself, what the hell am I grabbing this for? Why am I trying to become what I don't want to be? What am I doing in an office, making a contemptuous, begging fool of myself, when all I want is out there, waiting for me the minute I say I know who I am! Why can't I say that, Willy? (*He tries to make Willy face him, but Willy pulls away and moves to the left.*)

WILLY (*with hatred, threateningly*): The door of your life is wide open!

BIFF: Pop! I'm a dime a dozen, and so are you!

WILLY (*turning on him now in an uncontrolled outburst*): I am not a dime a dozen! I am Willy Loman, and you are Biff Loman!

Biff starts for Willy, but is blocked by Happy. In his fury, Biff seems on the verge of attacking his father.

BIFF: I am not a leader of men, Willy, and neither are you. You were never anything but a hard-working drummer who landed in the ash can like all the rest of them! I'm one dollar an hour, Willy! I tried seven states and couldn't raise it. A buck an hour! Do you gather my meaning? I'm not bringing home any prizes any more, and you're going to stop waiting for me to bring them home!

WILLY (*directly to Biff*): You vengeful, spiteful mutt!

Biff breaks from Happy. Willy, in fright, starts up the stairs. Biff grabs him.

BIFF (*at the peak of his fury*): Pop, I'm nothing! I'm nothing, Pop. Can't you understand that? There's no spite in it any more. I'm just what I am, that's all.

Biff's fury has spent itself, and he breaks down, sobbing, holding on to Willy, who dumbly fumbles for Biff's face.

WILLY (*astonished*): What're you doing? What're you doing? (*To Linda.*) Why is he crying?

BIFF (*crying, broken*): Will you let me go, for Christ's sake? Will you take that phony dream and burn it before something happens? (*Struggling to contain himself, he pulls away and moves to the stairs.*) I'll go in the morning. Put him—put him to bed. (*Exhausted, Biff moves up the stairs to his room.*)

WILLY (*after a long pause, astonished, elevated*): Isn't that—isn't that remarkable? Biff—he likes me!

LINDA: He loves you, Willy!

HAPPY (*deeply moved*): Always did, Pop.

WILLY: Oh, Biff! (*Staring wildly.*) He cried! Cried to me. (*He is choking with his love, and now cries out his promise.*) That boy—that boy is going to be magnificent!

Ben appears in the light just outside the kitchen.

BEN: Yes, outstanding, with twenty thousand behind him.

LINDA (*sensing the racing of his mind, fearfully, carefully*): Now come to bed, Willy. It's all settled now.

WILLY (*finding it difficult not to rush out of the house*): Yes, we'll sleep. Come on. Go to sleep, Hap.

BEN: And it does take a great kind of a man to crack the jungle.

In accents of dread, Ben's idyllic music starts up.

HAPPY (*his arm around Linda*): I'm getting married, Pop, don't forget it. I'm changing everything. I'm gonna run that department before the year is up. You'll see, Mom. (*He kisses her.*)

BEN: The jungle is dark but full of diamonds, Willy.

Willy turns, moves, listening to Ben.

LINDA: Be good. You're both good boys, just act that way, that's all.

HAPPY: 'Night, Pop. (*He goes upstairs.*)

LINDA (*to Willy*): Come, dear.

BEN (*with greater force*): One must go in to fetch a diamond out.

WILLY (*to Linda, as he moves slowly along the edge of the kitchen, toward the door*): I just want to get settled down, Linda. Let me sit alone for a little.

LINDA (*almost uttering her fear*): I want you upstairs.

WILLY (*taking her in his arms*): In a few minutes, Linda. I couldn't sleep right now. Go on, you look awful tired. (*He kisses her.*)

BEN: Not like an appointment at all. A diamond is rough and hard to the touch.

WILLY: Go on now. I'll be right up.

LINDA: I think this is the only way, Willy.

WILLY: Sure, it's the best thing.

BEN: Best thing!

WILLY: The only way. Everything is gonna be—go on, kid, get to bed. You look so tired.

LINDA: Come right up.

WILLY: Two minutes.

Linda goes into the living-room, then reappears in her bedroom. Willy moves just outside the kitchen door.

WILLY: Loves me. (*Wonderingly.*) Always loved me. Isn't that a remarkable thing? Ben, he'll worship me for it!

BEN (*with promise*): It's dark there, but full of diamonds.

WILLY: Can you imagine that magnificence with twenty thousand dollars in his pocket?

LINDA (*calling from her room*): Willy! Come up!

WILLY (*calling into the kitchen*): Yes! Yes. Coming! It's very smart, you realize that, don't you, sweetheart? Even Ben sees it. I gotta go, baby. 'By! 'By! (*Going over to Ben, almost dancing.*) Imagine? When the mail comes he'll be ahead of Bernard again!

BEN: A perfect proposition all around.

WILLY: Did you see how he cried to me? Oh, if I could kiss him, Ben!

BEN: Time, William, time!

WILLY: Oh, Ben, I always knew one way or another we were gonna make it, Biff and I!

BEN (*looking at his watch*): The boat. We'll be late. (*He moves slowly off into the darkness.*)

WILLY (*elegiacally, turning to the house*): Now when you kick off, boy, I want a seventy-yard boot, and get right down the field under the ball, and when you hit, hit low and hit hard, because it's important, boy. (*He swings around and faces the audience.*) There's all kinds of important people in the stands, and the first thing you know . . . (*Suddenly realizing he is alone.*) Ben! Ben, where do I . . . ? (*He makes a sudden movement of search.*) Ben, how do I . . . ?

LINDA (*calling*): Willy, you coming up?

WILLY (*uttering a gasp of fear, whirling about as if to quiet her*): Sh! (*He turns around as if to find his way; sounds, faces, voices, seem to be swarming in upon him and he flicks at them, crying.*) Sh! Sh! (*Suddenly music, faint and high, stops him. It rises in intensity, almost to an unbearable scream. He goes up and down on his toes, and rushes off around the house.*) Shhh!

LINDA: Willy?

There is no answer. Linda waits. Biff gets up off his bed. He is still in his clothes. Happy sits up. Biff stands listening.

LINDA (*with real fear*): Willy, answer me! Willy!

There is the sound of a car starting and moving away at full speed.

LINDA: No!

BIFF (*rushing down the stairs*): Pop!

As the car speeds off, the music crashes down in a frenzy of sound, which becomes the soft pulsation of a single cello string. Biff slowly returns to his bedroom. He and Happy gravely don their jackets. Linda slowly walks out of her room. The music has developed into a dead march. The leaves of day are appearing over everything. Charley and Bernard, somberly dressed, appear and knock on the kitchen door. Biff and Happy slowly descend the stairs to the kitchen as Charley and Bernard enter. All stop a moment when Linda, in clothes of mourning, bearing a little bunch of roses, comes through the draped doorway into the kitchen. She goes to Charley and takes his arm. Now all move toward the audience, through the wall-line of the kitchen. At the limit of the apron, Linda lays down the flowers, kneels, and sits back on her heels. All stare down at the grave.

REQUIEM

CHARLEY: It's getting dark, Linda.

Linda doesn't react. She stares at the grave.

BIFF: How about it, Mom? Better get some rest, heh? They'll be closing the gate soon.

Linda makes no move. Pause.

HAPPY (*deeply angered*): He had no right to do that. There was no necessity for it. We would've helped him.

CHARLEY (*grunting*): Hmmm.

BIFF: Come along, Mom.

LINDA: Why didn't anybody come?

CHARLEY: It was a very nice funeral.

LINDA: But where are all the people he knew? Maybe they blame him.

CHARLEY: Naa. It's a rough world, Linda. They wouldn't blame him.

LINDA: I can't understand it. At this time especially. First time in thirty-five years we were just about free and clear. He only needed a little salary. He was even finished with the dentist.

CHARLEY: No man only needs a little salary.

LINDA: I can't understand it.

BIFF: There were a lot of nice days. When he'd come home from a trip; or on Sundays, making the stoop; finishing the cellar; putting on the new porch; when he built the extra bathroom; and put up the garage. You know something, Charley, there's more of him in that front stoop than in all the sales he ever made.

CHARLEY: Yeah. He was a happy man with a batch of cement.

LINDA: He was so wonderful with his hands.

BIFF: He had the wrong dreams. All, all, wrong.

HAPPY (*almost ready to fight Biff*): Don't say that!

BIFF: He never knew who he was.

CHARLEY (*stopping Happy's movement and reply. To Biff*): Nobody dast blame this man. You don't understand: Willy was a salesman. And for a salesman, there is no rock bottom to the life. He don't put a bolt to a nut, he don't tell you the law or give you medicine. He's a man way out there in the blue, riding on a smile and a shoeshine. And when they start not smiling back—that's an earthquake. And then you get yourself a couple of spots on your hat, and you're finished. Nobody dast blame this man. A salesman is got to dream, boy. It comes with the territory.

BIFF: Charley, the man didn't know who he was.

HAPPY (*infuriated*): Don't say that!

BIFF: Why don't you come with me, Happy?

HAPPY: I'm not licked that easily. I'm staying right in this city, and I'm gonna beat this racket! (*He looks at Biff, his chin set.*) The Loman Brothers!

BIFF: I know who I am, kid.

HAPPY: All right, boy. I'm gonna show you and everybody else that Willy Loman did not die in vain. He had a good dream. It's the only dream you can have—to come out number-one man. He fought it out here, and this is where I'm gonna win it for him.

BIFF (*with a hopeless glance at Happy, bends toward his mother*): Let's go, Mom.

LINDA: I'll be with you in a minute. Go on, Charley. (*He hesitates.*) I want to, just for a minute. I never had a chance to say good-by.

Charley moves away, followed by Happy. Biff remains a slight distance up and left of Linda. She sits there, summoning herself. The flute begins, not far away, playing behind her speech.

LINDA: Forgive me, dear. I can't cry. I don't know what it is, but I can't cry. I don't understand it. Why did you ever do that? Help me, Willy, I can't cry. It seems to me that you're just on another trip. I keep expecting you. Willy, dear, I can't cry. Why did you do it? I search and search and I search, and I can't understand it, Willy. I made the last payment on the house today. Today, dear. And there'll be nobody home. (*A sob rises in her throat.*) We're free and clear. (*Sobbing more fully, released.*) We're free. (*Biff comes slowly toward her.*) We're free . . . We're free . . .

Biff lifts her to her feet and moves out up right with her in his arms. Linda sobs quietly. Bernard and Charley come together and follow them, followed by Happy. Only the music of the flute is left on the darkening stage as over the house the hard towers of the apartment buildings rise into sharp focus, and

The Curtain Falls

COMMENTARIES

ARTHUR MILLER

Arthur Miller analyzed what he considered the tragic dimension in Willy Loman's character when *Death of a Salesman* was published by Viking Press in 1957. In his introduction to the play, Miller discussed how his view of a tragic hero differed from Aristotle's formulation in the *Poetics*. Miller then went on to describe his dramatic method of calling Willy Loman's values into question by presenting what Miller called "an opposing system" of love within the family to counter American society's false ideals of power and success. As Miller remarked during a symposium on his play the following year, "The trouble with Willy Loman is that he has tremendously powerful ideas. . . . [If] Willy Loman, for instance, had not had a very profound sense that his life as lived had left him hollow, he would have died contentedly polishing his car on some Sunday afternoon at a ripe old age. The fact is he has values. The fact that they cannot be realized is what is driving him mad."

On *Death of a Salesman* as an American Tragedy 1957

I set out not to "write a tragedy" in this play, but to show the truth as I saw it. However, some of the attacks upon it as a pseudo-tragedy contain ideas so misleading, and in some cases so laughable, that it might be in place here to deal with a few of them.

Aristotle having spoken of a fall from the heights, it goes without saying that someone of the common mold cannot be a fit tragic hero. It is now many centuries since Aristotle lived. There is no more reason for falling down in a faint before his *Poetics* than before Euclid's geometry, which has been amended numerous times by men with new insights; nor, for that matter, would I choose to have my illness diagnosed by Hippocrates rather than the most ordinary graduate of an American medical school, despite the Greek's genius. Things do change, and even a genius is limited by his time and the nature of his society.

I would deny, on grounds of simple logic, this one of Aristotle's contentions if only because he lived in a slave society. When a vast number of people are divested of alternatives, as slaves are, it is rather inevitable that one will not be able to imagine drama, let alone tragedy, as being possible for any but the higher ranks of society. There is a legitimate question of stature here, but none of rank, which is so often confused with it. So long as the hero may be said to have had alternatives of a magnitude to have materially changed the course of his life, it seems to me that in this respect at least, he cannot be debarred from the heroic role.

The question of rank is significant to me only as it reflects the question of the social application of the hero's career. There is no doubt that if a character is shown on the stage who goes through the most ordinary actions, and is suddenly revealed to be the President of the United States, his actions immediately assume a much greater magnitude, and pose the possibilities of much greater meaning, than if he is the corner grocer. But at the same time, his stature as a hero is not so utterly dependent upon his rank that the corner grocer cannot outdistance him as a tragic figure—providing, of course, that the grocer's career engages the issues of, for instance, the survival of the race, the relationships of man to God—the questions, in short, whose answers define humanity and the right way to live so that the world is a home, instead of a battleground or a fog in which disembodied spirits pass each other in an endless twilight.

In this respect *Death of a Salesman* is a slippery play to categorize because nobody in it stops to make a speech objectively stating the great issues which I believe it embodies. If it were a worse play, less closely articulating its meanings with its actions, I think it would have more quickly satisfied a certain kind of criticism. But it was meant to be less a play than a fact; it refused admission to its author's opinions and opened itself to a revelation of process and the operations of an ethic, of social laws of action no less powerful in their effects upon individuals than any tribal law administered by gods with names. I need not claim that this play is a genuine solid gold tragedy for my opinions on tragedy to be held valid. My purpose here is simply to point out a historical fact which must be taken into account in any consideration of tragedy, and it is the sharp alteration in the meaning of rank in society between the present time and the distant past. More important to me is the fact that this particular kind of argument obscures much more relevant considerations.

One of these is the question of intensity. It matters not at all whether a modern play concerns itself with a grocer or a president if the intensity of the hero's commitment to his course is less than the maximum possible. It matters not at all whether the hero falls from a great height or a small one, whether he is highly conscious or only dimly aware of what is happening, whether his pride brings the fall or an unseen pattern written behind clouds; if the intensity, the human passion to surpass his given bounds, the fanatic insistence upon his self-conceived role—if these are not present there can only be an outline of tragedy but no living thing. I believe, for myself, that the lasting appeal of tragedy is due to our need to face the fact of death in order to strengthen ourselves for life, and that over and above this function of the tragic viewpoint there are and will be a great number of formal variations which no single definition will ever embrace.

Another issue worth considering is the so-called tragic victory, a question closely related to the consciousness of the hero. One makes nonsense of this if a "victory" means that the hero makes us feel some certain joy when, for instance, he sacrifices himself for a "cause," and unhappy and morose because he dies without one. To begin at the bottom, a man's death is and ought to be an essentially terrifying thing and ought to make nobody happy. But in a great variety of ways even death, the ultimate negative, can be, and appear to be, an assertion of bravery, and can serve to separate the death of man from the death of animals; and I think it is this distinction which underlies any conceptions of a victory in death. For a society of faith, the nature of the death can prove the existence of the spirit, and posit its immortality. For a secular society it is perhaps more difficult for such a victory to document itself and to make itself felt, but, conversely, the need to offer greater proofs of the humanity of man can make that victory more real. It goes without saying that in a society where there is basic disagreement as to the right way to live, there can hardly be agreement as to the right way to die, and both life and death must be heavily weighted with meaningless futility.

It was not out of any deference to a tragic definition that Willy Loman is filled with a joy, however broken-hearted, as he approaches his end, but simply that my sense of his character dictated his joy, and even what I felt was an exultation. In terms of his character, he has achieved a very powerful piece of knowledge, which is that he is loved by his son and has been embraced by him and forgiven. In this he is given his existence, so to speak—his fatherhood, for which he has always striven and which until now he could not achieve. That he is unable to take this victory thoroughly to his heart, that it closes the circle for him and propels him to his death, is the wage of his sin, which was to have committed himself so completely to the counterfeits of dignity and the false coinage embodied in his idea of success that he can prove his existence only by bestowing "power" on his posterity, a power deriving from the sale of his last asset, himself, for the price of his insurance policy.

I must confess here to a miscalculation, however. I did not realize while writing the play that so many people in the world do not see as clearly, or would not admit, as I thought they must, how futile most lives are; so there could be no hope of consoling the audience for the death of this man. I did not realize either how few would be impressed by the fact that this man is actually a very brave spirit who cannot settle for half but must pursue his dream of himself to the end. Finally, I thought it must be clear, even obvious, that this was no dumb brute heading mindlessly to his catastrophe.

I have no need to be Willy's advocate before the jury which decides who is and who is not a tragic hero. I am merely noting that the lingering ponderousness of so many ancient definitions has blinded students and critics to the facts before them, and not only in regard to this play. Had Willy been unaware of his separation from values that endure he would have died contentedly while polishing his car, probably on a Sunday afternoon with the ball game coming over the radio. But he was agonized by his awareness of being in a false position, so constantly haunted by the hollowness of all he had placed his faith in, so aware, in short, that he must somehow be filled in his spirit or fly apart, that he staked his very life on the ultimate assertion. That he had not the intellectual fluency to verbalize his situation is not the same thing as saying that he lacked awareness, even an overly intensified consciousness that the life he had made was without form and inner meaning.

To be sure, had he been able to know that he was as much the victim of his beliefs as their defeated exemplar, had he known how much of guilt he ought to bear and how much to shed from his soul, he would be more conscious. But it seems to me that there is of necessity a severe limitation of self-awareness in any character, even the most knowing, which serves to define him as a character, and more, that this very limit serves to complete the tragedy and, indeed, to make it at all possible. Complete consciousness is possible only in a play about forces, like *Prometheus,*° but not in a play about people. I think that the point is whether there is a sufficient awareness in the hero's career to make the audience supply the rest. Had Oedipus, for instance, been more conscious and more aware of the forces at work upon him he must surely have said that he was not really to blame for having cohabited with his mother since neither he nor anyone else knew she was his mother. He must surely decide to divorce her, provide for their children, firmly resolve to investigate the family background of his next wife, and thus deprive us of a very fine play and the name for a famous neurosis. But he is conscious only up to a point, the point at which guilt begins. Now he is inconsolable and must tear out his eyes. What is tragic about this? Why is it not even ridiculous? How can we respect a man who goes to such extremities over something he could in no way help or prevent? The answer, I think, is not that we respect the man, but that we respect the Law he has so completely broken, wittingly or not, for it is that Law which, we believe, defines us as men. The confusion of some critics viewing *Death of a Salesman* in this regard is that they do not see that Willy Loman has broken a law without whose protection life is insupportable if not incomprehensible to him and to many others; it is the law which says that a failure in society and in

---

Prometheus: *Prometheus Bound* by the Greek tragedian Aeschylus (c. 525–456 B.C.).

business has no right to live. Unlike the law against incest, the law of success is not administered by statute or church, but it is very nearly as powerful in its grip upon men. The confusion increases because, while it is a law, it is by no means a wholly agreeable one even as it is slavishly obeyed, for to fail is no longer to belong to society, in his estimate. Therefore, the path is opened for those who wish to call Willy merely a foolish man even as they themselves are living in obedience to the same law that killed him. Equally, the fact that Willy's law—the belief, in other words, which administers guilt to him—is not a civilizing statute whose destruction menaces us all; it is, rather, a deeply believed and deeply suspect "good" which, when questioned as to its value, as it is in this play, serves more to raise our anxieties than to reassure us of the existence of an unseen but humane metaphysical system in the world. My attempt in the play was to counter this anxiety with an opposing system which, so to speak, is in a race for Willy's faith, and it is the system of love which is the opposite of the law of success. It is embodied in Biff Loman, but by the time Willy can perceive his love it can serve only as an ironic comment upon the life he sacrificed for power and for success and its tokens.

HELGE NORMANN NILSEN

Helge Normann Nilsen examines the influence of Marxist theory on Miller's *Death of a Salesman.* This commentary is excerpted from an essay that appeared in the journal *English Studies.*

Marxism and the Early Plays of Arthur Miller 1994

During the period from the nineteen-thirties through the forties Marxism exercised a controlling influence on Arthur Miller's work. This is evident in several of his earliest, unpublished plays, propaganda pieces advocating the overthrow of capitalism and the establishment of a socialist system.[1] The political tendency of these plays is too obvious to be ignored, but it has escaped the attention of most readers that the same message is embodied in the first three plays that Miller published. These are *The Man Who Had All the Luck* (1944), *All My Sons* (1947), and *Death of a Salesman* (1949), his most famous work.

If one compares the unpublished plays with the published ones, the common features emerge. American capitalism is criticized and rejected, and an alternative, socialist community and system of values are pointed to. The message is implicit rather than explicit in the printed works, but the political agenda remains the same. The most important reason behind Miller's commitment to radicalism is that the Great Depression created in him a lasting and

[1]Miller has described his own and his friends' early adoption of Marxism in his autobiography: "We enjoyed a certain unity within ourselves by virtue of a higher consciousness bestowed by our expectation of a socialist evolution of the planet," *Timebends: A Life* (New York, 1987), p. 70.

traumatic impression of the devastating power of economic forces in the shaping of people's lives. This also meant that, in the early plays, he portrayed and analyzed his major characters as products of the American capitalist society and its influence.[2] At the same time he managed to give them individuality and persuasiveness as characters.

Miller's political attitudes at the time emerge mainly in the plays in question, but are also described in his autobiography. They fall within the tradition of analysis and criticism of capitalism established by Marx and the movements building on his theories. Miller's critique can be summed up as follows: capitalism is inhuman in its glorification of private property and its exclusive orientation toward profitmaking. Human beings are sacrificed to economic interests in ways that are not only immoral, but even criminal in nature. In business, ruthless competition is the norm. People's moral character is threatened. They may become scoundrels, or rendered insane and suicidal. Egocentric individualism reigns supreme, and society fosters no sense of responsibility to anyone beyond self and family. There is an unjust concentration of financial power into a few hands, making all others powerless and bereft of economic security. The capitalists also control most of the cultural life of society and the media, spreading their conservative political views. No institution or aspect of society can escape this influence. The false values of materialism and the cult of success threaten to extinguish human love and caring. Conformism rules, turning people into mere cogs in the machine of production, and genuine individualism and even enjoyment of life become hard to obtain. The coming socialist society, on the other hand, will be built on solidarity, human brotherhood, and the ownership of the workers and citizens of the means of production.[3] . . .

Death of a Salesman is . . . rooted in the playwright's early, agonized reactions to the Depression. Marxism had taught him that this disaster was one of the vagaries of capitalism, and his early, militant stance is suggested in an observation recorded in a notebook containing an early version of the play: "The restrictions, like all tyrannies, exist by default of revolutionary resistance."[4] The reference is to formal conventions in drama, but the choice of words reveals a political radicalism also.

As in the other plays, victimization by the free play of economic forces is the main theme of *Death of a Salesman*. It is suggested in the initial stage

---

[2]In the early forties Miller attended a Marxist study group and was proposed for membership in the American Communist Party. In the *New York Times*, May 25, 1947, his name appeared on a list of sponsors of the World Youth Festival, organized by the communist World Federation of Democratic Youth. See J. Schlueter and J. K. Flanagan, *Arthur Miller* (New York, 1987), pp. 6, 146.

[3]Interpreting Marx, R. W. Miller states that: "under socialism and communism, most people are less dominated, more in possession of their lives, since they are better able to develop their capacities in light of their own assessments of their needs. Moreover, their interactions will be governed to a greater extent than now by mutual well-wishing and concern," "Marx and Morality," in *Marxism*, ed. J. R. Pennock and J. W. Chapman (New York, 1983), p. 60.

[4]Notebook, in longhand, undated, in the Harry Ransom Humanities Research Center.

direction: "A melody is heard, played upon a flute. It is small and fine, telling of grass and trees and the horizon. Before us is the salesman's house. We are aware of towering, angular shapes behind it, surrounding it on all sides." The people in the house are threatened and overwhelmed by the tall buildings, symbols of the crushing power of those who win out in a capitalist struggle that has no room for failures and losers.

Willy Loman, the aging salesman, is worn out to the point of breakdown by his many years on the road. But he remains a firm believer in capitalist values and has transferred his hope of success to his son Biff. Willy is a dreamer, and the play contrasts his dreams with the harsh realities of failure and mediocrity that he tries to shut out of his mind. Corrupted, or brainwashed by the system, Willy is blind to its destructiveness and is obsessed by his plans for Biff.

Biff, however, has begun to rebel against his father's ideas and to feel his way towards different standards, meaning those that Miller associates with the socialist society. Unlike his brother Happy, he has "allowed himself to turn his face toward defeat," and even this becomes a possible source of strength for him. His lack of conventional success is slowly teaching him, not that he is worthless, but that he may not be cut out for a business career and may actually be better off without it. He is trying to understand himself and discover his real identity, this also being an aim of socialism as Miller understood it. But Biff is not yet sure of himself, in the first part of the play, and still feels guilty for not being a success. He has returned to his parents in a last attempt to fulfill his father's dreams.

Happy, who has a good job and wants to get further ahead, also has doubts about his own careerism but cannot find anything to put in its place. Biff struggles with this issue, searching for and finally finding another path for himself. However, his father remains a man whose self-respect depends entirely on his role as a breadwinner and useful cog in the production machine. He worships the memory of Ben, the youth who walked into the jungle of Africa at the age of seventeen and came out rich at twenty-one, a powerful *entrepreneur*. What Willy fails to realize is that only a very few can hope to be that successful. His greatest illusion is his belief in the capitalist myth that every man can succeed in business if he only uses his opportunities. Willy is also haunted by the equally superhuman success ideal embodied in his grandfather, a heroic pioneer figure who drove across America with his family, supporting them all by selling flutes that he made himself.

The scene in which Willy is fired by his young boss Howard is a perfect illustration of the logic of the capitalist economic mechanism. Willy has been with the firm since before Howard was born, but the almost familiar relationship between these two still counts for nothing. Mortally afraid of ruin, like Keller, Willy appeals to Howard's conscience, reminding him how long and faithfully he has worked for the company, but to no avail. Howard is not evil, however; he is even able to sympathize with Willy's plight, but this in no way interferes with his decision to fire an aging employee who can no longer ring up any sales. Howard, like Ben or Charley, a businessman who is Willy's friend and neighbor, abides by the law of profitability first that is supreme in the world of capitalist business. He is impersonal about it, again like Charley or Ben, regarding it as a law of nature.[5]

Wanting to help Willy, Charley offers him a job, but the former refuses to take it, feeling that it would be a kind of charity and would violate the image he has of himself as a self-reliant, honorable individual who does not depend on others. Rugged individualism is the ideology of the *laissez-faire* capitalism that he believes in so deeply. But the facts are that Willy's failure is destroying him and that Biff's similar fate makes his father reject him. The all-important success ideal prevents Willy from perceiving Biff as a person and an individual. Capitalist values distort and destroy what should have been a rewarding human relationship between father and son.

The horrifying consequences of a blind adherence to these values emerge in Willy's decision to commit suicide so that his life insurance payment will enable Biff to rise in the world. But Biff, like Chris Keller, instead becomes the vehicle through which Miller subtly introduces his alternative socialist perceptions and values into his work. Biff thus becomes the only character in the drama who really understands the destructive nature of capitalist priorities and feels pity and concern for his father, exclaiming: "I can't bear to look at his face!" He tries to make Willy understand the realities of their situation, which is that their lives have been dominated by a dream that is no better than a lie. Biff has realized that the whole family are victims, in various ways and like most people, of capitalist oppression and false standards. They are basically downtrodden people, "a dime a dozen." But this, of course, is the very thing that Willy refuses to admit, and he denies it furiously. Biff tries to impress upon him that they ought to lower their expectations and rely on the comforts of love and human caring. Willy, however, is not willing to correct his capitalist hierarchy of values and accuses Biff of betrayal. His son, he says, is "vengeful" and "spiteful." But Biff continues his attempt to break through to his father's feelings and establish a genuine connection and respect between them. Hence his plaintive cry: "Pop, I'm nothing . . . I'm just what I am, that's all."

In this central scene, Willy does perceive that his son wants to show him his love, but is unable to respond to this in a simple way. Instead, and in keeping with his blinkered vision, he grotesquely interprets Biff's love as yet another sign of his potentially glorious future, or as a part of the fine personality that will help make him rich: "That boy—that boy is going to be magnificent!" The insurance money will yet secure Biff's success, he thinks, and is deluded enough to assume that his son will be thankful for the sacrifice he is making.

But at Willy Loman's grave it is capitalism and the dreams it is responsible for that are indicted. Looking back on his father's life, Biff firmly declares: "He had the wrong dreams. All, all wrong." *Death of a Salesman* suggests that

[5]Brian Parker argues that because Howard and Charley, both capitalists, are ordinary men and not evil, *Death of a Salesman* cannot be an anti-capitalist play. But the fact that these are not bad men does not change the workings of the system that they represent. See "Point of View in Arthur Miller's *Death of a Salesman*," *Arthur Miller: A Collection of Critical Essays* (Englewood Cliffs, 1969), p. 99.

the right dreams are opposed to rapacious capitalism and that they are about justice, love, and genuine selfhood as envisaged by Marxism.

. . . In *Death of a Salesman* the jobless Willy Loman has become mentally disturbed, his suicide for the sake of money an eloquent testimony to the corrosive effects of the tyrannical success ideal extolled by his society. Willy is a victim, both directly and indirectly, of the logic of a capitalism which says that human worth is proportional to economic achievement. Taken as a whole, these dramas build a powerful indictment against the American capitalist system that Miller knew, but they do not stop at that point. Whether openly or more discreetly, they suggest the possibility of another, just and humane society. This new, socialist world will be built on the principles of love, mutual concern, and sharing rather than competition.

LORRAINE HANSBERRY

Lorraine Hansberry (1930–1965) was born in Chicago, the youngest of four children of Carl Hansberry, a successful real estate agent who founded one of the first African American banks in that city. Despite her parents' wealth, the family was forced by Chicago law to live in the ghetto on the South Side. When Hansberry was eight years old, her father bought a home in a white neighborhood. After the family moved into their new house, a mob threw a brick through the window, barely missing her. Carl Hansberry decided to stay in the house, although he had not been given clear title to it, and he began a civil rights suit to test the restrictive law. After he lost his case in the Illinois courts, he was supported by the National Association for the Advancement of Colored People (NAACP) to appeal the decision in the United States Supreme Court. The ruling was reversed, and the family continued to live in the house.

In *To Be Young, Gifted and Black* (1971), a posthumous collection of Hansberry's writing, she described how she became involved in a race riot in high school that radicalized her still further when she was seventeen. She attended officially integrated Englewood High School, but in 1947 the white students went on a strike against the blacks. Hansberry described how "the well-dressed, colored students like herself had stood amusedly around the parapet, staring, simply staring at the mob of several hundred striking whites, trading taunts and insults – but showing not the least inclination to further assert racial pride." Word about the riot at the high school spread from the affluent neighborhood to the South Side ghetto schools: "The ofays [whites] are out on strike and beating up and raping colored girls under the viaduct." Carloads of poor black students, "waving baseball bats and shouting slogans of the charge," drove up to Englewood High School. Hansberry watched them "come, pouring out of the bowels of the ghetto, the children of the unqualified oppressed: the black working class in their costumes of pegged pants and conked heads and tight skirts and almost knee-length sweaters and – worst of all – *colored* anklets, held up by rubber bands! Yes, they had come and they had fought . . . She never could forget one thing: *They had fought back!*"

Hansberry's ambition in high school was to become a journalist. After two years at the University of Wisconsin, she transferred to the New School for Social Research in New York City. In New York she began working as a reporter and editor for *Freedom*, a monthly magazine owned by the black actor Paul Robeson. After her marriage to the playwright Robert Nemiroff in 1953, she began to write plays full-time. *A Raisin in the Sun*, her first completed work, was produced on Broadway in 1959 with money raised by her friends. Starring the then little-known Sidney Poitier as Walter Lee Younger, the play was immediately successful. Hansberry became the first black playwright to win the New York Drama Critics Circle Award, a landmark achievement in American theater in view of both her gender and race.

Hansberry took the title of *A Raisin in the Sun* from a poem by Langston Hughes, "Harlem (A Dream Deferred)." In her play she looked beneath what Hughes called "the *surface* of Negro color" to dramatize the human situation of her characters, fulfilling Hughes's vision in his essay "Writers: Black and White" that an African American writer would succeed by becoming a "*writer* first, *colored* second. This means losing nothing of your racial identity. It is just that in the great sense of the word, anytime, any place, good art transcends land, race, or nationality, and color drops away. If you are a good writer, in the end neither blackness nor whiteness makes a difference to readers."

In the early 1960s Hansberry used her prominence as a successful playwright to champion civil rights causes, as in *The Movement: Documentary of a Struggle for Equality* (1964), a book of photographs in support of the Student Nonviolent Coordinating Committee (SNCC). Suffering from cancer, she completed only one other full-length play, *The Sign in Sidney Brustein's Window*, produced in 1964, three months before her death. In 1972 Nemiroff edited a volume of her short plays, *Les Blancs: The Collected Last Plays of Lorraine Hansberry*, and produced a musical version of *A Raisin in the Sun* that won a Tony Award.

WEB Research Lorraine Hansberry at bedfordstmartins.com/rewritinglit.

A Raisin in the Sun 1959

Harlem (A Dream Deferred)

What happens to a dream deferred?

Does it dry up
Like a raisin in the sun?
Or fester like a sore —
And then run?
Does it stink like rotten meat?
Or crust and sugar over —
Like a syrupy sweet?

Maybe it just sags
Like a heavy load.

Or does it explode?

– LANGSTON HUGHES

CHARACTERS (IN ORDER OF APPEARANCE)

RUTH YOUNGER
TRAVIS YOUNGER
WALTER LEE YOUNGER, brother
BENEATHA YOUNGER
LENA YOUNGER, Mama
JOSEPH ASAGAI
GEORGE MURCHISON
MRS. JOHNSON
KARL LINDNER
BOBO
MOVING MEN

The action of the play is set in Chicago's Southside, sometime between World War II and the present.

ACT I

SCENE I. [*Friday morning.*]

The Younger living room would be a comfortable and well-ordered room if it were not for a number of indestructible contradictions to this state of being. Its furnishings are typical and undistinguished and their primary feature now is that they have clearly had to accommodate the living of too many people for too many years—and they are tired. Still, we can see that at some time, a time probably no longer remembered by the family (except perhaps for Mama), the furnishings of this room were actually selected with care and love and even hope—and brought to this apartment and arranged with taste and pride.

That was a long time ago. Now the once-loved pattern of the couch upholstery has to fight to show itself from under acres of crocheted doilies and couch covers which have themselves finally come to be more important than the upholstery. And here a table or a chair has been moved to disguise the worn places in the carpet; but the carpet has fought back by showing its weariness, with depressing uniformity, elsewhere on its surface.

Weariness has, in fact, won in this room. Everything has been polished, washed, sat on, used, scrubbed too often. All pretenses but living itself have long since vanished from the very atmosphere of this room.

Moreover, a section of this room, for it is not really a room unto itself, though the landlord's lease would make it seem so, slopes backward to provide a small kitchen area, where the family prepares the meals that are eaten in the living room proper, which must also serve as dining room. The single window that has been provided for these "two" rooms is located in this kitchen area. The sole natural light the family may enjoy in the course of a day is only that which fights its way through this little window.

At left, a door leads to a bedroom which is shared by Mama and her daughter, Beneatha. At right, opposite, is a second room (which in the beginning of the life of this apartment was probably a breakfast room) which serves as a bedroom for Walter and his wife, Ruth.

Time: Sometime between World War II and the present.

Place: Chicago's Southside.

At Rise: It is morning dark in the living room. Travis is asleep on the make-down bed at center. An alarm clock sounds from within the bedroom at right, and presently Ruth enters from that room and closes the door behind her. She crosses sleepily toward the window. As she passes her sleeping son she reaches down and shakes him a little. At the window she raises the shade and a dusky Southside morning light comes in feebly. She fills a pot with water and puts it on to boil. She calls to the boy, between yawns, in a slightly muffled voice.

Ruth is about thirty. We can see that she was a pretty girl, even exceptionally so, but now it is apparent that life has been little that she expected, and disappointment has already begun to hang in her face. In a few years, before thirty-five even, she will be known among her people as a "settled woman."

She crosses to her son and gives him a good, final, rousing shake.

RUTH: Come on now, boy, it's seven thirty! (*Her son sits up at last, in a stupor of sleepiness.*) I say hurry up, Travis! You ain't the only person in the world got to use a bathroom! (*The child, a sturdy, handsome little boy of ten or eleven, drags himself out of the bed and almost blindly takes his towels and "today's clothes" from drawers and a closet and goes out to the bathroom, which is in an outside hall and which is shared by another family or families on the same floor. Ruth crosses to the bedroom door at right and opens it and calls in to her husband.*) Walter Lee! . . . It's after seven thirty! Lemme see you do some waking up in there now! (*She waits.*) You better get up from there, man! It's after seven thirty I tell you. (*She waits again.*) All right, you just go ahead and lay there and next thing you know Travis be finished and Mr. Johnson'll be in there and you'll be fussing and cussing round here like a madman! And be late too! (*She waits, at the end of patience.*) Walter Lee—it's time for you to GET UP!

She waits another second and then starts to go into the bedroom, but is apparently satisfied that her husband has begun to get up. She stops, pulls the door to, and returns to the kitchen area. She wipes her face with a moist cloth and runs her fingers through her sleep-disheveled hair in a vain effort and ties an apron around her housecoat. The bedroom door at right opens and her husband stands in the doorway in his pajamas, which are rumpled and mismated. He is a lean, intense young man in his middle thirties, inclined to quick nervous movements and erratic speech habits—and always in his voice there is a quality of indictment.

WALTER: Is he out yet?

RUTH: What you mean *out*? He ain't hardly got in there good yet.

WALTER (*wandering in, still more oriented to sleep than to a new day*): Well, what was you doing all that yelling for if I can't even get in there yet? (*Stopping and thinking.*) Check coming today?

RUTH: They *said* Saturday and this is just Friday and I hopes to God you ain't going to get up here first thing this morning and start talking to me 'bout no money—'cause I 'bout don't want to hear it.

WALTER: Something the matter with you this morning?

RUTH: No—I'm just sleepy as the devil. What kind of eggs you want?

WALTER: Not scrambled. (*Ruth starts to scramble eggs.*) Paper come? (*Ruth points impatiently to the rolled up* Tribune *on the table, and he gets it and spreads it out and vaguely reads the front page.*) Set off another bomb yesterday.

RUTH (*maximum indifference*): Did they?

WALTER (*looking up*): What's the matter with you?

RUTH: Ain't nothing the matter with me. And don't keep asking me that this morning.

WALTER: Ain't nobody bothering you. (*Reading the news of the day absently again.*) Say Colonel McCormick is sick.

RUTH (*affecting tea-party interest*): Is he now? Poor thing.

WALTER (*sighing and looking at his watch*): Oh, me. (*He waits.*) Now what is that boy doing in that bathroom all this time? He just going to have to start getting up earlier. I can't be being late to work on account of him fooling around in there.

RUTH (*turning on him*): Oh, no he ain't going to be getting up no earlier no such thing! It ain't his fault that he can't get to bed no earlier nights 'cause he got a bunch of crazy good-for-nothing clowns sitting up running their mouths in what is supposed to be his bedroom after ten o'clock at night . . .

WALTER: That's what you mad about, ain't it? The things I want to talk about with my friends just couldn't be important in your mind, could they?

He rises and finds a cigarette in her handbag on the table and crosses to the little window and looks out, smoking and deeply enjoying this first one.

RUTH (*almost matter of factly, a complaint too automatic to deserve emphasis*): Why you always got to smoke before you eat in the morning?

WALTER (*at the window*): Just look at 'em down there . . . Running and racing to work . . . (*He turns and faces his wife and watches her a moment at the stove, and then, suddenly.*) You look young this morning, baby.

RUTH (*indifferently*): Yeah?

WALTER: Just for a second—stirring them eggs. Just for a second it was—you looked real young again. (*He reaches for her; she crosses away. Then, drily.*) It's gone now—you look like yourself again!

RUTH: Man, if you don't shut up and leave me alone.

WALTER (*looking out to the street again*): First thing a man ought to learn in life is not to make love to no colored woman first thing in the morning. You all some eeeevil people at eight o'clock in the morning.

Travis appears in the hall doorway, almost fully dressed and quite wide awake now, his towels and pajamas across his shoulders. He opens the door and signals for his father to make the bathroom in a hurry.

TRAVIS (*watching the bathroom*): Daddy, come on!

Walter gets his bathroom utensils and flies out to the bathroom.

RUTH: Sit down and have your breakfast, Travis.

TRAVIS: Mama, this is Friday. (*Gleefully.*) Check coming tomorrow, huh?

RUTH: You get your mind off money and eat your breakfast.

TRAVIS (*eating*): This is the morning we supposed to bring the fifty cents to school.

RUTH: Well, I ain't got no fifty cents this morning.

TRAVIS: Teacher say we have to.

RUTH: I don't care what teacher say. I ain't got it. Eat your breakfast, Travis.

TRAVIS: I *am* eating.

RUTH: Hush up now and just eat!

The boy gives her an exasperated look for her lack of understanding, and eats grudgingly.

TRAVIS: You think Grandmama would have it?

RUTH: No! And I want you to stop asking your grandmother for money, you hear me?

TRAVIS (*outraged*): Gaaaleee! I don't ask her, she just gimme it sometimes!

RUTH: Travis Willard Younger—I got too much on me this morning to be—

TRAVIS: Maybe Daddy—

RUTH: *Travis!*

The boy hushes abruptly. They are both quiet and tense for several seconds.

TRAVIS (*presently*): Could I maybe go carry some groceries in front of the supermarket for a little while after school then?

RUTH: Just hush, I said. (*Travis jabs his spoon into his cereal bowl viciously, and rests his head in anger upon his fists.*) If you through eating, you can get over there and make up your bed.

The boy obeys stiffly and crosses the room, almost mechanically, to the bed and more or less folds the bedding into a heap, then angrily gets his books and cap.

TRAVIS (*sulking and standing apart from her unnaturally*): I'm gone.

RUTH (*looking up from the stove to inspect him automatically*): Come here. (*He crosses to her and she studies his head.*) If you don't take this comb and fix this here head, you better! (*Travis puts down his books with a great sigh of oppression, and crosses to the mirror. His mother mutters under her breath about his "slubbornness."*) 'Bout to march out of here with that head looking just like chickens slept in it! I just don't know where you get your slubborn ways . . . And get your jacket, too. Looks chilly out this morning.

TRAVIS (*with conspicuously brushed hair and jacket*): I'm gone.

RUTH: Get carfare and milk money—(*Waving one finger.*)—and not a single penny for no caps, you hear me?

TRAVIS (*with sullen politeness*): Yes'm.

He turns in outrage to leave. His mother watches after him as in his frustration he approaches the door almost comically. When she speaks to him, her voice has become a very gentle tease.

RUTH (*mocking; as she thinks he would say it*): Oh, Mama makes me so mad sometimes, I don't know what to do! (*She waits and continues to his back as he stands stock-still in front of the door.*) I wouldn't kiss that woman good-bye for nothing in this world this morning! (*The boy finally turns around and rolls his eyes at her, knowing the mood has changed and he is vindicated; he does not, however, move toward her yet.*) Not for nothing in this world! (*She finally laughs aloud at him and holds out her arms to him and we see that it is a way between them, very old and practiced. He crosses to her and allows her to embrace him warmly but keeps his face fixed with masculine rigidity. She holds him back from her presently and looks at him and runs her fingers over the features of his face. With utter gentleness—.*) Now—whose little old angry man are you?

TRAVIS (*the masculinity and gruffness start to fade at last*): Aw gaalee—Mama . . .

RUTH (*mimicking*): Aw—gaaaaalleeeee, Mama! (*She pushes him, with rough playfulness and finality, toward the door.*) Get on out of here or you going to be late.

TRAVIS (*in the face of love, new aggressiveness*): Mama, could I *please* go carry groceries?

RUTH: Honey, it's starting to get so cold evenings.

WALTER (*coming in from the bathroom and drawing a make-believe gun from a make-believe holster and shooting at his son*): What is it he wants to do?

RUTH: Go carry groceries after school at the supermarket.

WALTER: Well, let him go . . .

TRAVIS (*quickly, to the ally*): I *have* to—she won't gimme the fifty cents . . .

WALTER (*to his wife only*): Why not?

RUTH (*simply, and with flavor*): 'Cause we don't have it.

WALTER (*to Ruth only*): What you tell the boy things like that for? (*Reaching down into his pants with a rather important gesture.*) Here, son—

He hands the boy the coin, but his eyes are directed to his wife's. Travis takes the money happily.

TRAVIS: Thanks, Daddy.

He starts out. Ruth watches both of them with murder in her eyes. Walter stands and stares back at her with defiance, and suddenly reaches into his pocket again on an afterthought.

WALTER (*without even looking at his son, still staring hard at his wife*): In fact, here's another fifty cents . . . Buy yourself some fruit today—or take a taxicab to school or something!

TRAVIS: Whoopee—

He leaps up and clasps his father around the middle with his legs, and they face each other in mutual appreciation; slowly Walter Lee peeks around the boy to catch the violent rays from his wife's eyes and draws his head back as if shot.

WALTER: You better get down now—and get to school, man.

TRAVIS (*at the door*): O.K. Good-bye.

He exits.

WALTER (*after him, pointing with pride*): That's *my* boy. (*She looks at him in disgust and turns back to her work.*) You know what I was thinking 'bout in the bathroom this morning?

RUTH: No.

WALTER: How come you always try to be so pleasant!

RUTH: What is there to be pleasant 'bout!

WALTER: You want to know what I was thinking 'bout in the bathroom or not!

RUTH: I know what you thinking 'bout.

WALTER (*ignoring her*): 'Bout what me and Willy Harris was talking about last night.

RUTH (*immediately—a refrain*): Willy Harris is a good-for-nothing loud-mouth.

WALTER: Anybody who talks to me has got to be a good-for-nothing loudmouth, ain't he? And what you know about who is just a good-for-nothing loudmouth? Charlie Atkins was just a "good-for-nothing loudmouth" too, wasn't he! When he wanted me to go in the dry-cleaning business with him. And now—he's grossing a hundred thousand a year. A hundred thousand dollars a year! You still call *him* a loudmouth!

RUTH (*bitterly*): Oh, Walter Lee . . .

She folds her head on her arms over the table.

WALTER (*rising and coming to her and standing over her*): You tired, ain't you? Tired of everything. Me, the boy, the way we live—this beat-up hole—everything. Ain't you? (*She doesn't look up, doesn't answer.*) So tired—moaning and groaning all the time, but you wouldn't do nothing to help, would you? You couldn't be on my side that long for nothing, could you?

RUTH: Walter, please leave me alone.

WALTER: A man needs for a woman to back him up . . .

RUTH: Walter—

WALTER: Mama would listen to you. You know she listen to you more than she do me and Bennie. She think more of you. All you have to do is just sit down with her when you drinking your coffee one morning and talking 'bout things like you do and—(*He sits down beside her and demonstrates graphically what he thinks her methods and tone should be.*)—you just sip your coffee, see, and say easy like that you been thinking 'bout that deal Walter Lee is so interested in, 'bout the store and all, and sip some more coffee, like what you saying ain't really that important to you—And the next thing you know, she be listening good and asking you questions and when I come home—I can tell her the details. This ain't no fly-by-night proposition, baby. I mean we figured it out, me and Willy and Bobo.

RUTH (*with a frown*): Bobo?

WALTER: Yeah. You see, this little liquor store we got in mind cost seventy-five thousand and we figured the initial investment on the place be 'bout thirty thousand, see. That be ten thousand each. Course, there's a couple of hundred you got to pay so's you don't spend your life just waiting for them clowns to let your license get approved—

RUTH: You mean graft?

WALTER (*frowning impatiently*): Don't call it that. See there, that just goes to show you what women understand about the world. Baby, don't *nothing* happen for you in the world 'less you pay *somebody* off!

RUTH: Walter, leave me alone! (*She raises her head and stares at him vigorously—then says, more quietly.*) Eat your eggs, they gonna be cold.

WALTER (*straightening up from her and looking off*): That's it. There you are. Man say to his woman: I got me a dream. His woman say: Eat your eggs. (*Sadly, but gaining in power.*) Man say: I got to take hold of this here world, baby! And a woman will say: Eat your eggs and go to work. (*Passionately now.*) Man say: I got to change my life, I'm choking to death, baby! And his woman say—(*In utter anguish as he brings his fists down on his thighs.*)—Your eggs is getting cold!

RUTH (*softly*): Walter, that ain't none of our money.

WALTER (*not listening at all or even looking at her*): This morning, I was lookin' in the mirror and thinking about it . . . I'm thirty-five years old; I been married eleven years and I got a boy who sleeps in the living room—(*Very, very quietly.*)—and all I got to give him is stories about how rich white people live . . .

RUTH: Eat your eggs, Walter.

WALTER (*slams the table and jumps up*): —DAMN MY EGGS—DAMN ALL THE EGGS THAT EVER WAS!

RUTH: Then go to work.

WALTER (*looking up at her*): See—I'm trying to talk to you 'bout myself—(*Shaking his head with the repetition.*)—and all you can say is eat them eggs and go to work.

RUTH (*wearily*): Honey, you never say nothing new. I listen to you every day, every night and every morning, and you never say nothing new. (*Shrugging.*) So you would rather *be* Mr. Arnold than be his chauffeur. So—I would *rather* be living in Buckingham Palace.

WALTER: That is just what is wrong with the colored woman in this world . . . Don't understand about building their men up and making 'em feel like they somebody. Like they can do something.

RUTH (*drily, but to hurt*): There *are* colored men who do things.

WALTER: No thanks to the colored woman.

RUTH: Well, being a colored woman, I guess I can't help myself none.

She rises and gets the ironing board and sets it up and attacks a huge pile of rough-dried clothes, sprinkling them in preparation for the ironing and then rolling them into tight fat balls.

WALTER (*mumbling*): We one group of men tied to a race of women with small minds!

His sister Beneatha enters. She is about twenty, as slim and intense as her brother. She is not as pretty as her sister-in-law, but her lean, almost intellectual face has a handsomeness of its own. She wears a bright-red flannel nightie, and her thick hair stands wildly about her head. Her speech is a mixture of many things; it is different from the rest of the family's insofar as education has permeated her sense of English—and perhaps the Midwest rather than the South has finally—at last—won out in her inflection; but not altogether, because over all of it is a soft slurring and transformed use of vowels which is the decided influence of the Southside. She passes through the room without looking at either Ruth or Walter and goes to the outside door and looks, a little blindly, out to the bathroom. She sees that it has been lost to the Johnsons. She closes the door with a sleepy vengeance and crosses to the table and sits down a little defeated.

BENEATHA: I am going to start timing those people.

WALTER: You should get up earlier.

BENEATHA (*her face in her hands. She is still fighting the urge to go back to bed*): Really—would you suggest dawn? Where's the paper?

WALTER (*pushing the paper across the table to her as he studies her almost clinically, as though he has never seen her before*): You a horrible-looking chick at this hour.

BENEATHA (*drily*): Good morning, everybody.

WALTER (*senselessly*): How is school coming?

BENEATHA (*in the same spirit*): Lovely. Lovely. And you know, biology is the greatest. (*Looking up at him.*) I dissected something that looked just like you yesterday.

WALTER: I just wondered if you've made up your mind and everything.

BENEATHA (*gaining in sharpness and impatience*): And what did I answer yesterday morning—and the day before that?

RUTH (*from the ironing board, like someone disinterested and old*): Don't be so nasty, Bennie.

BENEATHA (*still to her brother*): And the day before that and the day before that!

WALTER (*defensively*): I'm interested in you. Something wrong with that? Ain't many girls who decide—

WALTER AND BENEATHA (*in unison*): —"to be a doctor."

Silence.

WALTER: Have we figured out yet just exactly how much medical school is going to cost?

RUTH: Walter Lee, why don't you leave that girl alone and get out of here to work?

BENEATHA (*exits to the bathroom and bangs on the door*): Come on out of there, please!

She comes back into the room.

WALTER (*looking at his sister intently*): You know the check is coming tomorrow.

BENEATHA (*turning on him with a sharpness all her own*): That money belongs to Mama, Walter, and it's for her to decide how she wants to use it. I don't care if she wants to buy a house or a rocket ship or just nail it up somewhere and look at it. It's hers. Not ours—*hers.*

WALTER (*bitterly*): Now ain't that fine! You just got your mother's interest at heart, ain't you, girl? You such a nice girl—but if Mama got that money she can always take a few thousand and help you through school too—can't she?

BENEATHA: I have never asked anyone around here to do anything for me!

WALTER: No! And the line between asking and just accepting when the time comes is big and wide—ain't it!

BENEATHA (*with fury*): What do you want from me, Brother—that I quit school or just drop dead, which!

WALTER: I don't want nothing but for you to stop acting holy 'round here. Me and Ruth done made some sacrifices for you—why can't you do something for the family?

RUTH: Walter, don't be dragging me in it.

WALTER: You are in it—Don't you get up and go work in somebody's kitchen for the last three years to help put clothes on her back?

RUTH: Oh, Walter—that's not fair . . .

WALTER: It ain't that nobody expects you to get on your knees and say thank you, Brother; thank you, Ruth; thank you, Mama—and thank you, Travis, for wearing the same pair of shoes for two semesters—

BENEATHA (*dropping to her knees*): Well—I do—all right?—thank everybody! And forgive me for ever wanting to be anything at all! (*Pursuing him on her knees across the floor.*) FORGIVE ME, FORGIVE ME, FORGIVE ME!

RUTH: Please stop it! Your mama'll hear you.

WALTER: Who the hell told you you had to be a doctor? If you so crazy 'bout messing 'round with sick people—then go be a nurse like other women—or just get married and be quiet . . .

BENEATHA: Well—you finally got it said . . . It took you three years but you finally got it said. Walter, give up; leave me alone—it's Mama's money.

WALTER: *He was my father, too!*

BENEATHA: So what? He was mine, too—and Travis' grandfather—but the insurance money belongs to Mama. Picking on me is not going to make her give it to you to invest in any liquor stores—(*Under breath, dropping into a chair.*)—and I for one say, God bless Mama for that!

WALTER (*to Ruth*): See—did you hear? Did you hear!

RUTH: Honey, please go to work.

WALTER: Nobody in this house is ever going to understand me.

BENEATHA: Because you're a nut.

WALTER: Who's a nut?

BENEATHA: You—you are a nut. Thee is mad, boy.

WALTER (*looking at his wife and his sister from the door, very sadly*): The world's most backward race of people, and that's a fact.

BENEATHA (*turning slowly in her chair*): And then there are all those prophets who would lead us out of the wilderness—(*Walter slams out of the house.*)—into the swamps!

RUTH: Bennie, why you always gotta be pickin' on your brother? Can't you be a little sweeter sometimes? (*Door opens. Walter walks in. He fumbles with his cap, starts to speak, clears throat, looks everywhere but at Ruth. Finally:*)

WALTER (*to Ruth*): I need some money for carfare.

RUTH (*looks at him, then warms; teasing, but tenderly*): Fifty cents? (*She goes to her bag and gets money.*) Here—take a taxi!

Walter exits. Mama enters. She is a woman in her early sixties, full-bodied and strong. She is one of those women of a certain grace and beauty who wear it so unobtrusively that it takes a while to notice. Her dark-brown face is surrounded by the total whiteness of her hair, and, being a woman who has adjusted to many things in life and overcome many more, her face is full of strength. She has, we can see, wit and faith of a kind that keep her eyes lit and full of interest and expectancy. She is, in a word, a beautiful woman. Her bearing is perhaps most like the noble bearing of the women of the Hereros of Southwest Africa—rather as if she imagines that as she walks she still bears a basket or a vessel upon her head. Her speech, on the other hand, is as careless as her carriage is precise—she is inclined to slur everything—but her voice is perhaps not so much quiet as simply soft.

MAMA: Who that 'round here slamming doors at this hour?

She crosses through the room, goes to the window, opens it, and brings in a feeble little plant growing doggedly in a small pot on the window sill. She feels the dirt and puts it back out.

RUTH: That was Walter Lee. He and Bennie was at it again.

MAMA: My children and they tempers. Lord, if this little old plant don't get more sun than it's been getting it ain't never going to see spring again. (*She turns from the window.*) What's the matter with you this morning, Ruth? You looks right peaked. You aiming to iron all them things? Leave some for me. I'll get to 'em this afternoon. Bennie honey, it's too drafty for you to be sitting 'round half dressed. Where's your robe?

BENEATHA: In the cleaners.

MAMA: Well, go get mine and put it on.

BENEATHA: I'm not cold, Mama, honest.

MAMA: I know—but you so thin . . .

BENEATHA (*irritably*): Mama, I'm not cold.

MAMA (*seeing the make-down bed as Travis has left it*): Lord have mercy, look at that poor bed. Bless his heart—he tries, don't he?

She moves to the bed Travis has sloppily made up.

RUTH: No—he don't half try at all 'cause he knows you going to come along behind him and fix everything. That's just how come he don't know how to do nothing right now—you done spoiled that boy so.

MAMA (*folding bedding*): Well—he's a little boy. Ain't supposed to know 'bout housekeeping. My baby, that's what he is. What you fix for his breakfast this morning?

RUTH (*angrily*): I feed my son, Lena!

MAMA: I ain't meddling—(*Under breath; busy-bodyish.*) I just noticed all last week he had cold cereal, and when it starts getting this chilly in the fall a child ought to have some hot grits or something when he goes out in the cold—

RUTH (*furious*): I gave him hot oats—is that all right!

MAMA: I ain't meddling. (*Pause.*) Put a lot of nice butter on it? (*Ruth shoots her an angry look and does not reply.*) He likes lots of butter.

RUTH (*exasperated*): Lena—

MAMA (*to Beneatha. Mama is inclined to wander conversationally sometimes*): What was you and your brother fussing 'bout this morning?

BENEATHA: It's not important, Mama.

She gets up and goes to look out at the bathroom, which is apparently free, and she picks up her towels and rushes out.

MAMA: What was they fighting about?

RUTH: Now you know as well as I do.

MAMA (*shaking her head*): Brother still worrying hisself sick about that money?

RUTH: You know he is.

MAMA: You had breakfast?

RUTH: Some coffee.

MAMA: Girl, you better start eating and looking after yourself better. You almost thin as Travis.

RUTH: Lena—

MAMA: Un-hunh?

RUTH: What are you going to do with it?

MAMA: Now don't you start, child. It's too early in the morning to be talking about money. It ain't Christian.

RUTH: It's just that he got his heart set on that store—

MAMA: You mean that liquor store that Willy Harris want him to invest in?

RUTH: Yes—

MAMA: We ain't no business people, Ruth. We just plain working folks.

RUTH: Ain't nobody business people till they go into business. Walter Lee say colored people ain't never going to start getting ahead till they start gambling on some different kinds of things in the world—investments and things.

MAMA: What done got into you, girl? Walter Lee done finally sold you on investing.

RUTH: No. Mama, something is happening between Walter and me. I don't know what it is—but he needs something—something I can't give him any more. He needs this chance, Lena.

MAMA (*frowning deeply*): But liquor, honey—

RUTH: Well—like Walter say—I spec people going to always be drinking themselves some liquor.

MAMA: Well—whether they drinks it or not ain't none of my business. But whether I go into business selling it to 'em *is*, and I don't want that on my ledger this late in life. (*Stopping suddenly and studying her daughter-in-law.*) Ruth Younger, what's the matter with you today? You look like you could fall over right there.

RUTH: I'm tired.

MAMA: Then you better stay home from work today.

RUTH: I can't stay home. She'd be calling up the agency and screaming at them, "My girl didn't come in today—send me somebody! My girl didn't come in!" Oh, she just have a fit . . .

MAMA: Well, let her have it. I'll just call her up and say you got the flu—

RUTH (*laughing*): Why the flu?

MAMA: 'Cause it sounds respectable to 'em. Something white people get, too. They know 'bout the flu. Otherwise they think you been cut up or something when you tell 'em you sick.

RUTH: I got to go in. We need the money.

MAMA: Somebody would of thought my children done all but starved to death the way they talk about money here late. Child, we got a great big old check coming tomorrow.

RUTH (*sincerely, but also self-righteously*): Now that's your money. It ain't got nothing to do with me. We all feel like that—Walter and Bennie and me—even Travis.

MAMA (*thoughtfully, and suddenly very far away*): Ten thousand dollars—

RUTH: Sure is wonderful.

MAMA: Ten thousand dollars.

RUTH: You know what you should do, Miss Lena? You should take yourself a trip somewhere. To Europe or South America or someplace—

MAMA (*throwing up her hands at the thought*): Oh, child!

RUTH: I'm serious. Just pack up and leave! Go on away and enjoy yourself some. Forget about the family and have yourself a ball for once in your life—

MAMA (*drily*): You sound like I'm just about ready to die. Who'd go with me? What I look like wandering 'round Europe by myself?

RUTH: Shoot—these here rich white women do it all the time. They don't think nothing of packing up they suitcases and piling on one of them big steamships and—swoosh!—they gone, child.

MAMA: Something always told me I wasn't no rich white woman.

RUTH: Well—what are you going to do with it then?

MAMA: I ain't rightly decided. (*Thinking. She speaks now with emphasis.*) Some of it got to be put away for Beneatha and her schoolin'—and ain't nothing going to touch that part of it. Nothing. (*She waits several seconds, trying to make up her mind about something, and looks at Ruth a little tentatively before going on.*) Been thinking that we maybe could meet the notes on a little old two-story somewhere, with a yard where Travis could play in the summertime, if we use part of the insurance for a down payment and everybody kind of pitch in. I could maybe take on a little day work again, few days a week—

RUTH (*studying her mother-in-law furtively and concentrating on her ironing, anxious to encourage without seeming to*): Well, Lord knows, we've put enough rent into this here rat trap to pay for four houses by now . . .

MAMA (*looking up at the words "rat trap" and then looking around and leaning back and sighing—in a suddenly reflective mood—*): "Rat trap"—yes, that's all it is. (*Smiling.*) I remember just as well the day me and Big Walter moved in here. Hadn't been married but two weeks and wasn't planning on living here no more than a year. (*She shakes her head at the dissolved dream.*) We was going to set away, little by little, don't you know, and buy a little place out in Morgan Park. We had even picked out the house. (*Chuckling a little.*) Looks right dumpy today. But Lord, child, you should know all the dreams I had 'bout buying that house and fixing it up and making me a little garden in the back—(*She waits and stops smiling.*) And didn't none of it happen.

Dropping her hands in a futile gesture.

RUTH (*keeps her head down, ironing*): Yes, life can be a barrel of disappointments, sometimes.

MAMA: Honey, Big Walter would come in here some nights back then and slump down on that couch there and just look at the rug, and look at me and look at the rug and then back at me—and I'd know he was down then . . . really down. (*After a second very long and thoughtful pause; she is seeing back to times that only she can see.*) And then, Lord, when I lost that baby—little Claude—I almost thought I was going to lose Big Walter too. Oh, that man grieved hisself! He was one man to love his children.

RUTH: Ain't nothin' can tear at you like losin' your baby.

MAMA: I guess that's how come that man finally worked hisself to death like he done. Like he was fighting his own war with this here world that took his baby from him.

RUTH: He sure was a fine man, all right. I always liked Mr. Younger.

MAMA: Crazy 'bout his children! God knows there was plenty wrong with Walter Younger—hard-headed, mean, kind of wild with women—plenty wrong with him. But he sure loved his children. Always wanted them to have something—be something. That's where Brother gets all these notions, I reckon. Big Walter used to say, he'd get right wet in the eyes sometimes, lean his head back with the water standing in his eyes and say, "Seem like God didn't see fit to give the black man nothing but dreams—but He did give us children to make them dreams seem worthwhile." (*She smiles.*) He could talk like that, don't you know.

RUTH: Yes, he sure could. He was a good man, Mr. Younger.

MAMA: Yes, a fine man—just couldn't never catch up with his dreams, that's all.

Beneatha comes in, brushing her hair and looking up to the ceiling, where the sound of a vacuum cleaner has started up.

BENEATHA: What could be so dirty on that woman's rugs that she has to vacuum them every single day?

RUTH: I wish certain young women 'round here who I could name would take inspiration about certain rugs in a certain apartment I could also mention.

BENEATHA (*shrugging*): How much cleaning can a house need, for Christ's sakes.

MAMA (*not liking the Lord's name used thus*): Bennie!

RUTH: Just listen to her—just listen!

BENEATHA: Oh, God!

MAMA: If you use the Lord's name just one more time—

BENEATHA (*a bit of a whine*): Oh, Mama—

RUTH: Fresh—just fresh as salt, this girl!

BENEATHA (*drily*): Well—if the salt loses its savor—

MAMA: Now that will do. I just ain't going to have you 'round here reciting the scriptures in vain—you hear me?

BENEATHA: How did I manage to get on everybody's wrong side by just walking into a room?

RUTH: If you weren't so fresh—

BENEATHA: Ruth, I'm twenty years old.

MAMA: What time you be home from school today?

BENEATHA: Kind of late. (*With enthusiasm.*) Madeline is going to start my guitar lessons today.

Mama and Ruth look up with the same expression.

MAMA: Your *what* kind of lessons?

BENEATHA: Guitar.

RUTH: Oh, Father!

MAMA: How come you done taken it in your mind to learn to play the guitar?

BENEATHA: I just want to, that's all.

MAMA (*smiling*): Lord, child, don't you know what to do with yourself? How long it going to be before you get tired of this now—like you got tired of that little play-acting group you joined last year? (*Looking at Ruth.*) And what was it the year before that?

RUTH: The horseback-riding club for which she bought that fifty-five-dollar riding habit that's been hanging in the closet ever since!

MAMA (*to Beneatha*): Why you got to flit so from one thing to another, baby?

BENEATHA (*sharply*): I just want to learn to play the guitar. Is there anything wrong with that?

MAMA: Ain't nobody trying to stop you. I just wonders sometimes why you has to flit so from one thing to another all the time. You ain't never done nothing with all that camera equipment you brought home—

BENEATHA: I don't flit! I—I experiment with different forms of expression—

RUTH: Like riding a horse?

BENEATHA: —People have to express themselves one way or another.

MAMA: What is it you want to express?

BENEATHA (*angrily*): Me! (*Mama and Ruth look at each other and burst into raucous laughter.*) Don't worry—I don't expect you to understand.

MAMA (*to change the subject*): Who you going out with tomorrow night?

BENEATHA (*with displeasure*): George Murchison again.

MAMA (*pleased*): Oh—you getting a little sweet on him?

RUTH: You ask me, this child ain't sweet on nobody but herself—(*Under breath.*) Express herself!

They laugh.

BENEATHA: Oh—I like George all right, Mama. I mean I like him enough to go out with him and stuff, but—

RUTH (*for devilment*): What does and *stuff* mean?

BENEATHA: Mind your own business.

MAMA: Stop picking at her now, Ruth. (*She chuckles—then a suspicious sudden look at her daughter as she turns in her chair for emphasis.*) What DOES it mean?

BENEATHA (*wearily*): Oh, I just mean I couldn't ever really be serious about George. He's—he's so shallow.

RUTH: Shallow—what do you mean he's shallow? He's *Rich!*

MAMA: Hush, Ruth.

BENEATHA: I know he's rich. He knows he's rich, too.

RUTH: Well—what other qualities a man got to have to satisfy you, little girl?

BENEATHA: You wouldn't even begin to understand. Anybody who married Walter could not possibly understand.

MAMA (*outraged*): What kind of way is that to talk about your brother?

BENEATHA: Brother is a flip—let's face it.

MAMA (*to Ruth, helplessly*): What's a flip?

RUTH (*glad to add kindling*): She's saying he's crazy.

BENEATHA: Not crazy. Brother isn't really crazy yet—he—he's an elaborate neurotic.

MAMA: Hush your mouth!

BENEATHA: As for George. Well. George looks good—he's got a beautiful car and he takes me to nice places and, as my sister-in-law says, he is probably the richest boy I will ever get to know and I even like him sometimes—but if the Youngers are sitting around waiting to see if their little Bennie is going to tie up the family with the Murchisons, they are wasting their time.

RUTH: You mean you wouldn't marry George Murchison if he asked you someday? That pretty, rich thing? Honey, I knew you was odd—

BENEATHA: No I would not marry him if all I felt for him was what I feel now. Besides, George's family wouldn't really like it.

MAMA: Why not?

BENEATHA: Oh, Mama—The Murchisons are honest-to-God-real-*live*-rich colored people, and the only people in the world who are more snobbish than rich white people are rich colored people. I thought everybody knew that. I've met Mrs. Murchison. She's a scene!

MAMA: You must not dislike people 'cause they well off, honey.

BENEATHA: Why not? It makes just as much sense as disliking people 'cause they are poor, and lots of people do that.

RUTH (*a wisdom-of-the-ages manner. To Mama*): Well, she'll get over some of this—

BENEATHA: Get over it? What are you talking about, Ruth? Listen, I'm going to be a doctor. I'm not worried about who I'm going to marry yet—if I ever get married.

MAMA AND RUTH: *If!*

MAMA: Now, Bennie—

BENEATHA: Oh, I probably will . . . but first I'm going to be a doctor, and George, for one, still thinks that's pretty funny. I couldn't be bothered with that. I am going to be a doctor and everybody around here better understand that!

MAMA (*kindly*): 'Course you going to be a doctor, honey, God willing.

BENEATHA (*drily*): God hasn't got a thing to do with it.

MAMA: Beneatha—that just wasn't necessary.

BENEATHA: Well—neither is God. I get sick of hearing about God.

MAMA: Beneatha!

BENEATHA: I mean it! I'm just tired of hearing about God all the time. What has He got to do with anything? Does He pay tuition?

MAMA: You 'bout to get your fresh little jaw slapped!

RUTH: That's just what she needs, all right!

BENEATHA: Why? Why can't I say what I want to around here, like everybody else?

MAMA: It don't sound nice for a young girl to say things like that—you wasn't brought up that way. Me and your father went to trouble to get you and Brother to church every Sunday.

BENEATHA: Mama, you don't understand. It's all a matter of ideas, and God is just one idea I don't accept. It's not important. I am not going out and be immoral or commit crimes because I don't believe in God. I don't even think about it. It's just that I get tired of Him getting credit for all the things the human race achieves through its own stubborn effort. There simply is no blasted God—there is only man and it is *He* who makes miracles!

Mama absorbs this speech, studies her daughter, and rises slowly and crosses to Beneatha and slaps her powerfully across the face. After, there is only silence and the daughter drops her eyes from her mother's face, and Mama is very tall before her.

MAMA: Now—you say after me, in my mother's house there is still God. (*There is a long pause and Beneatha stares at the floor wordlessly. Mama repeats the phrase with precision and cool emotion.*) In my mother's house there is still God.

BENEATHA: In my mother's house there is still God.

A long pause.

MAMA (*walking away from Beneatha, too disturbed for triumphant posture. Stopping and turning back to her daughter*): There are some ideas we ain't going to have in this house. Not long as I am at the head of this family.

BENEATHA: Yes, ma'am.

Mama walks out of the room.

RUTH (*almost gently, with profound understanding*): You think you a woman, Bennie—but you still a little girl. What you did was childish—so you got treated like a child.

BENEATHA: I see. (*Quietly.*) I also see that everybody thinks it's all right for Mama to be a tyrant. But all the tyranny in the world will never put a God in the heavens!

She picks up her books and goes out. Pause.

RUTH (*goes to Mama's door*): She said she was sorry.

MAMA (*coming out, going to her plant*): They frightens me, Ruth. My children.

RUTH: You got good children, Lena. They just a little off sometimes—but they're good.

MAMA: No—there's something come down between me and them that don't let us understand each other and I don't know what it is. One done almost lost his mind thinking 'bout money all the time and the other done commence to talk about things I can't seem to understand in no form or fashion. What is it that's changing, Ruth.

RUTH (*soothingly, older than her years*): Now . . . you taking it all too seriously. You just got strong-willed children and it takes a strong woman like you to keep 'em in hand.

MAMA (*looking at her plant and sprinkling a little water on it*): They spirited all right, my children. Got to admit they got spirit—Bennie and Walter. Like this little old plant that ain't never had enough sunshine or nothing—and look at it . . .

She has her back to Ruth, who has had to stop ironing and lean against something and put the back of her hand to her forehead.

RUTH (*trying to keep Mama from noticing*): You . . . sure . . . loves that little old thing, don't you? . . .

MAMA: Well, I always wanted me a garden like I used to see sometimes at the back of the houses down home. This plant is close as I ever got to having one. (*She looks out of the window as she replaces the plant.*) Lord, ain't nothing as dreary as the view from this window on a dreary day, is there? Why ain't you singing this morning, Ruth? Sing that "No Ways Tired." That song always lifts me up so—(*She turns at last to see that Ruth has slipped quietly to the floor, in a state of semiconsciousness.*) Ruth! Ruth honey—what's the matter with you . . . Ruth!

Curtain.

SCENE II: [*The following morning.*]

It is the following morning; a Saturday morning, and house cleaning is in progress at the Youngers'. Furniture has been shoved hither and yon and Mama is giving the kitchen-area walls a washing down. Beneatha, in dungarees, with a handkerchief tied around her face, is spraying insecticide into the cracks in the walls. As they work, the radio is on and a Southside disk-jockey program is inappropriately filling the house with a rather exotic saxophone blues. Travis, the sole idle one, is leaning on his arms, looking out of the window.

TRAVIS: Grandmama, that stuff Bennie is using smells awful. Can I go downstairs, please?

MAMA: Did you get all them chores done already? I ain't seen you doing much.

TRAVIS: Yes'm—finished early. Where did Mama go this morning?

MAMA (*looking at Beneatha*): She had to go on a little errand.

The phone rings. Beneatha runs to answer it and reaches it before Walter, who has entered from bedroom.

TRAVIS: Where?

MAMA: To tend to her business.

BENEATHA: Haylo . . . (*Disappointed.*) Yes, he is. (*She tosses the phone to Walter, who barely catches it.*) It's Willie Harris again.

WALTER (*as privately as possible under Mama's gaze*): Hello, Willie. Did you get the papers from the lawyer? . . . No, not yet. I told you the mailman doesn't get here till ten-thirty . . . No, I'll come there . . . Yeah! Right away. (*He hangs up and goes for his coat.*)

BENEATHA: Brother, where did Ruth go?

WALTER (*as he exits*): How should I know!

TRAVIS: Aw come on, Grandma. Can I go outside?

MAMA: Oh, I guess so. You stay right in front of the house, though, and keep a good lookout for the postman.

TRAVIS: Yes'm. (*He darts into bedroom for stickball and bat, reenters, and sees Beneatha on her knees spraying under sofa with behind upraised. He edges closer to the target, takes aim, and lets her have it. She screams.*) Leave them poor little cockroaches alone, they ain't bothering you none! (*He runs as she swings the spraygun at him viciously and playfully.*) Grandma! Grandma!

MAMA: Look out there, girl, before you be spilling some of that stuff on that child!

TRAVIS (*safely behind the bastion of Mama*): That's right—look out, now! (He exits.)

BENEATHA (*drily*): I can't imagine that it would hurt him—it has never hurt the roaches.

MAMA: Well, little boys' hides ain't as tough as Southside roaches. You better get over there behind the bureau. I seen one marching out of there like Napoleon yesterday.

BENEATHA: There's really only one way to get rid of them, Mama—

MAMA: How?

BENEATHA: Set fire to this building! Mama, where did Ruth go?

MAMA (*looking at her with meaning*): To the doctor, I think.

BENEATHA: The doctor? What's the matter? (*They exchange glances.*) You don't think—

MAMA (*with her sense of drama*): Now I ain't saying what I think. But I ain't never been wrong 'bout a woman neither.

The phone rings.

BENEATHA (*at the phone*): Hay-lo . . . (*Pause, and a moment of recognition.*) Well—when did you get back! . . . And how was it? . . . Of course I've missed you—in my way . . . This morning? No . . . house cleaning and all that and Mama hates it if I let people come over when the house is like this . . . You *have?* Well, that's different . . . What is it—Oh, what the hell, come on over . . . Right, see you then. *Arrividerci.*

She hangs up.

MAMA (*who has listened vigorously, as is her habit*): Who is that you inviting over here with this house looking like this? You ain't got the pride you was born with!

BENEATHA: Asagai doesn't care how houses look, Mama—he's an intellectual.

MAMA: *Who?*

BENEATHA: Asagai—Joseph Asagai. He's an African boy I met on campus. He's been studying in Canada all summer.

MAMA: What's his name?

BENEATHA: Asagai, Joseph. Ah-sah-guy . . . He's from Nigeria.

MAMA: Oh, that's the little country that was founded by slaves way back . . .

BENEATHA: No, Mama—that's Liberia.

MAMA: I don't think I never met no African before.

BENEATHA: Well, do me a favor and don't ask him a whole lot of ignorant questions about Africans. I mean, do they wear clothes and all that—

MAMA: Well, now, I guess if you think we so ignorant 'round here maybe you shouldn't bring your friends here—

BENEATHA: It's just that people ask such crazy things. All anyone seems to know about when it comes to Africa is Tarzan—

MAMA (*indignantly*): Why should I know anything about Africa?

BENEATHA: Why do you give money at church for the missionary work?

MAMA: Well, that's to help save people.

BENEATHA: You mean save them from *heathenism*—

MAMA (*innocently*): Yes.

BENEATHA: I'm afraid they need more salvation from the British and the French.

Ruth comes in forlornly and pulls off her coat with dejection. They both turn to look at her.

RUTH (*dispiritedly*): Well, I guess from all the happy faces—everybody knows.

BENEATHA: You pregnant?

MAMA: Lord have mercy, I sure hope it's a little old girl. Travis ought to have a sister.

Beneatha and Ruth give her a hopeless look for this grandmotherly enthusiasm.

BENEATHA: How far along are you?

RUTH: Two months.

BENEATHA: Did you mean to? I mean did you plan it or was it an accident?

MAMA: What do you know about planning or not planning?

BENEATHA: Oh, Mama.

RUTH (*wearily*): She's twenty years old, Lena.

BENEATHA: Did you plan it, Ruth?

RUTH: Mind your own business.

BENEATHA: It is my business—where is he going to live, on the *roof*? (*There is silence following the remark as the three women react to the sense of it.*) Gee—I didn't mean that, Ruth, honest. Gee, I don't feel like that at all. I—I think it is wonderful.

RUTH (*dully*): Wonderful.

BENEATHA: Yes—really.

MAMA (*looking at Ruth, worried*): Doctor say everything going to be all right?

RUTH (*far away*): Yes—she says everything is going to be fine . . .

MAMA (*immediately suspicious*): "She"—What doctor you went to?

Ruth folds over, near hysteria.

MAMA (*worriedly hovering over Ruth*): Ruth honey—what's the matter with you—you sick?

Ruth has her fists clenched on her thighs and is fighting hard to suppress a scream that seems to be rising in her.

BENEATHA: What's the matter with her, Mama?

MAMA (*working her fingers in Ruth's shoulders to relax her*): She be all right. Women gets right depressed sometimes when they get her way. (*Speaking softly, expertly, rapidly.*) Now you just relax. That's right . . . just lean back, don't think 'bout nothing at all . . . nothing at all—

RUTH: I'm all right . . .

The glassy-eyed look melts and then she collapses into a fit of heavy sobbing. The bell rings.

BENEATHA: Oh, my God—that must be Asagai.

MAMA (*to Ruth*): Come on now, honey. You need to lie down and rest awhile . . . then have some nice hot food.

They exit, Ruth's weight on her mother-in-law. Beneatha, herself profoundly disturbed, opens the door to admit a rather dramatic-looking young man with a large package.

ASAGAI: Hello, Alaiyo—

BENEATHA (*holding the door open and regarding him with pleasure*): Hello . . . (*Long pause.*) Well—come in. And please excuse everything. My mother was very upset about my letting anyone come here with the place like this.

ASAGAI (*coming into the room*): You look disturbed too . . . Is something wrong?

BENEATHA (*still at the door, absently*): Yes . . . we've all got acute ghetto-itus. (*She smiles and comes toward him, finding a cigarette and sitting.*) So—sit down! No! Wait! (*She whips the spraygun off sofa where she had left it and puts the cushions back. At last perches on arm of sofa. He sits.*) So, how was Canada?

ASAGAI (*a sophisticate*): Canadian.

BENEATHA (*looking at him*): Asagai, I'm very glad you are back.

ASAGAI (*looking back at her in turn*): Are you really?

BENEATHA: Yes—very.

ASAGAI: Why?—you were quite glad when I went away. What happened?

BENEATHA: You went away.

ASAGAI: Ahhhhhhhh.

BENEATHA: Before—you wanted to be so serious before there was time.

ASAGAI: How much time must there be before one knows what one feels?

BENEATHA (*stalling this particular conversation. Her hands pressed together, in a deliberately childish gesture*): What did you bring me?

ASAGAI (*handing her the package*): Open it and see.

BENEATHA (*eagerly opening the package and drawing out some records and the colorful robes of a Nigerian woman*): Oh Asagai! . . . You got them for me! . . . How beautiful . . . and the records too! (*She lifts out the robes and runs to the mirror with them and holds the drapery up in front of herself.*)

ASAGAI (*coming to her at the mirror*): I shall have to teach you how to drape it properly. (*He flings the material about her for the moment and stands back to look at her.*) Ah—*Oh-pay-gay-day, oh-gbah-mu-shay.* (*A Yoruba exclamation for admiration.*) You wear it well . . . very well . . . mutilated hair and all.

BENEATHA (*turning suddenly*): My hair—what's wrong with my hair?

ASAGAI (*shrugging*): Were you born with it like that?

BENEATHA (*reaching up to touch it*): No . . . of course not.

She looks back to the mirror, disturbed.

ASAGAI (*smiling*): How then?

BENEATHA: You know perfectly well how . . . as crinkly as yours . . . that's how.

ASAGAI: And it is ugly to you that way?

BENEATHA (*quickly*): Oh, no—not ugly . . . (*More slowly, apologetically.*) But it's so hard to manage when it's, well—raw.

ASAGAI: And so to accommodate that—you mutilate it every week?

BENEATHA: It's not mutilation!

ASAGAI (*laughing aloud at her seriousness*): Oh . . . please! I am only teasing you because you are so very serious about these things. (*He stands back from her and folds his arms across his chest as he watches her pulling at her hair and frowning in the mirror.*) Do you remember the first time you met me at school? . . . (*He laughs.*) You came up to me and you said—and I thought you were the most serious little thing I had ever seen—you said: (*He imitates her.*) "Mr. Asagai—I want very much to talk with you. About Africa. You see, Mr. Asagai, I am looking for my *identity!*"

He laughs.

BENEATHA (*turning to him, not laughing*): Yes—

Her face is quizzical, profoundly disturbed.

ASAGAI (*still teasing and reaching out and taking her face in his hands and turning her profile to him*): Well . . . it is true that this is not so much a profile of a Hollywood queen as perhaps a queen of the Nile—(*A mock dismissal of the importance of the question.*) But what does it matter? Assimilationism is so popular in your country.

BENEATHA (*wheeling, passionately, sharply*): I am not an assimilationist!

ASAGAI (*the protest hangs in the room for a moment and Asagai studies her, his laughter fading*): Such a serious one. (*There is a pause.*) So—you like the robes? You must take excellent care of them—they are from my sister's personal wardrobe.

BENEATHA (*with incredulity*): You—you sent all the way home—for me?

ASAGAI (*with charm*): For you—I would do much more . . . Well, that is what I came for. I must go.

BENEATHA: Will you call me Monday?

ASAGAI: Yes . . . We have a great deal to talk about. I mean about identity and time and all that.

BENEATHA: Time?

ASAGAI: Yes. About how much time one needs to know what one feels.

BENEATHA: You see! You never understood that there is more than one kind of feeling which can exist between a man and a woman—or, at least, there should be.

ASAGAI (*shaking his head negatively but gently*): No. Between a man and a woman there need be only one kind of feeling. I have that for you . . . Now even . . . right this moment . . .

BENEATHA: I know—and by itself—it won't do. I can find that anywhere.

ASAGAI: For a woman it should be enough.

BENEATHA: I know—because that's what it says in all the novels that men write. But it isn't. Go ahead and laugh—but I'm not interested in being someone's little episode in America or—(*With feminine vengeance.*)—one of them! (*Asagai has burst into laughter again.*) That's funny as hell, huh!

ASAGAI: It's just that every American girl I have known has said that to me. White—black—in this you are all the same. And the same speech, too!

BENEATHA (*angrily*): Yuk, yuk, yuk!

ASAGAI: It's how you can be sure that the world's most liberated women are not liberated at all. You all talk about it too much!

Mama enters and is immediately all social charm because of the presence of a guest.

BENEATHA: Oh—Mama—this is Mr. Asagai.

MAMA: How do you do?

ASAGAI (*total politeness to an elder*): How do you do, Mrs. Younger. Please forgive me for coming at such an outrageous hour on a Saturday.

MAMA: Well, you are quite welcome. I just hope you understand that our house don't always look like this. (*Chatterish.*) You must come again. I would love to hear all about—(*Not sure of the name.*)—your country. I think it's so sad the way our American Negroes don't know nothing about Africa 'cept Tarzan and all that. And all that money they pour into these churches when they ought to be helping you people over there drive out them French and Englishmen done taken away your land.

The mother flashes a slightly superior look at her daughter upon completion of the recitation.

ASAGAI (*taken aback by this sudden and acutely unrelated expression of sympathy*): Yes . . . yes . . .

MAMA (*smiling at him suddenly and relaxing and looking him over*): How many miles is it from here to where you come from?

ASAGAI: Many thousands.

MAMA (*looking at him as she would Walter*): I bet you don't half look after yourself, being away from your mama either. I spec you better come 'round here from time to time to get yourself some decent homecooked meals . . .

ASAGAI (*moved*): Thank you. Thank you very much. (*They are all quiet, then*—) Well . . . I must go. I will call you Monday, Alaiyo.

MAMA: What's that he call you?

ASAGAI: Oh—"Alaiyo." I hope you don't mind. It is what you would call a nickname, I think. It is a Yoruba word. I am a Yoruba.

MAMA (*looking at Beneatha*): I—I thought he was from—(*Uncertain.*)

ASAGAI (*understanding*): Nigeria is my country. Yoruba is my tribal origin—

BENEATHA: You didn't tell us what Alaiyo means . . . for all I know, you might be calling me Little Idiot or something . . .

ASAGAI: Well . . . let me see . . . I do not know how just to explain it . . . The sense of a thing can be so different when it changes languages.

BENEATHA: You're evading.

ASAGAI: No—really it is difficult . . . (*Thinking.*) It means . . . it means One for Whom Bread—Food—Is Not Enough. (*He looks at her.*) Is that all right?

BENEATHA (*understanding, softly*): Thank you.

MAMA (*looking from one to the other and not understanding any of it*): Well . . . that's nice . . . You must come see us again—Mr.—

ASAGAI: Ah-sah-guy . . .

MAMA: Yes . . . Do come again.

ASAGAI: Good-bye.

He exits.

MAMA (*after him*): Lord, that's a pretty thing just went out here! (*Insinuatingly, to her daughter.*) Yes, I guess I see why we done commence to get so interested in Africa 'round here. Missionaries my aunt Jenny!

She exits.

BENEATHA: Oh, Mama! . . .

She picks up the Nigerian dress and holds it up to her in front of the mirror again. She sets the headdress on haphazardly and then notices her hair again and clutches at it and then replaces the headdress and frowns at herself. Then she starts to wriggle in front of the mirror as she thinks a Nigerian woman might. Travis enters and stands regarding her.

TRAVIS: What's the matter, girl, you cracking up?

BENEATHA: Shut up.

She pulls the headdress off and looks at herself in the mirror and clutches at her hair again and squinches her eyes as if trying to imagine something. Then, suddenly, she gets her raincoat and kerchief and hurriedly prepares for going out.

MAMA (*coming back into the room*): She's resting now. Travis, baby, run next door and ask Miss Johnson to please let me have a little kitchen cleanser. This here can is empty as Jacob's kettle.

TRAVIS: I just came in.

MAMA: Do as you told. (*He exits and she looks at her daughter.*) Where you going?

BENEATHA (*halting at the door*): To become a queen of the Nile!

She exits in a breathless blaze of glory. Ruth appears in the bedroom doorway.

MAMA: Who told you to get up?

RUTH: Ain't nothing wrong with me to be lying in no bed for. Where did Bennie go?

MAMA (*drumming her fingers*): Far as I could make out—to Egypt. (*Ruth just looks at her.*) What time is it getting to?

RUTH: Ten twenty. And the mailman going to ring that bell this morning just like he done every morning for the last umpteen years.

Travis comes in with the cleanser can.

TRAVIS: She say to tell you that she don't have much.

MAMA (*angrily*): Lord, some people I could name sure is tight-fisted! (*Directing her grandson.*) Mark two cans of cleanser on the list there. If she that hard up for kitchen cleanser, I sure don't want to forget to get her none!

RUTH: Lena—maybe the woman is just short on cleanser—

MAMA (*not listening*): —Much baking powder as she done borrowed from me all these years, she could of done gone into the baking business!

The bell sounds suddenly and sharply and all three are stunned—serious and silent—midspeech. In spite of all the other conversations and distractions of the morning, this is what they have been waiting for, even Travis, who looks helplessly from his mother to his grandmother. Ruth is the first to come to life again.

RUTH (*to Travis*): Get down them steps, boy!

Travis snaps to life and flies out to get the mail.

MAMA (*her eyes wide, her hand to her breast*): You mean it done really come?

RUTH (*excited*): Oh, Miss Lena!

MAMA (*collecting herself*): Well . . . I don't know what we all so excited about 'round here for. We known it was coming for months.

RUTH: That's a whole lot different from having it come and being able to hold it in your hands . . . a piece of paper worth ten thousand dollars . . . (*Travis bursts back into the room. He holds the envelope high above his head, like a little dancer, his face is radiant and he is breathless. He moves to his grandmother with sudden slow ceremony and puts the envelope into her hands. She accepts it, and then merely holds it and looks at it.*) Come on! Open it . . . Lord have mercy, I wish Walter Lee was here!

TRAVIS: Open it, Grandmama!

MAMA (*staring at it*): Now you all be quiet. It's just a check.

RUTH: Open it . . .

MAMA (*still staring at it*): Now don't act silly . . . We ain't never been no people to act silly 'bout no money—

RUTH (*swiftly*): We ain't never had none before—OPEN IT!

Mama finally makes a good strong tear and pulls out the thin blue slice of paper and inspects it closely. The boy and his mother study it raptly over Mama's shoulders.

MAMA: Travis! (*She is counting off with doubt.*) Is that the right number of zeros?

TRAVIS: Yes'm . . . ten thousand dollars. Gaalee, grandmama, you rich.

MAMA (*She holds the check away from her, still looking at it. Slowly her face sobers into a mask of unhappiness*): Ten thousand dollars. (*She hands it to Ruth.*) Put it away somewhere, Ruth. (*She does not look at Ruth; her eyes seem to be seeing something somewhere very far off.*) Ten thousand dollars they give you. Ten thousand dollars.

TRAVIS (*to his mother, sincerely*): What's the matter with Grandmama—don't she want to be rich?

RUTH (*distractedly*): You go on out and play now, baby. (*Travis exits. Mama starts wiping dishes absently, humming intently to herself. Ruth turns to her, with kind exasperation.*) You've gone and got yourself upset.

MAMA (*not looking at her*): I spec if it wasn't for you all . . . I would just put that money away or give it to the church or something.

RUTH: Now what kind of talk is that. Mr. Younger would just be plain mad if he could hear you talking foolish like that.

MAMA (*stopping and staring off*): Yes . . . he sure would. (*Sighing.*) We got enough to do with that money, all right. (*She halts then, and turns and looks at her daughter-in-law hard; Ruth avoids her eyes and Mama wipes her hands with finality and starts to speak firmly to Ruth.*) Where did you go today, girl?

RUTH: To the doctor.

MAMA (*impatiently*): Now, Ruth . . . you know better than that. Old Doctor Jones is strange enough in his way but there ain't nothing 'bout him make somebody slip and call him "she"—like you done this morning.

RUTH: Well, that's what happened—my tongue slipped.
MAMA: You went to see that woman, didn't you?
RUTH (*defensively, giving herself away*): What woman you talking about?
MAMA (*angrily*): That woman who—

Walter enters in great excitement.

WALTER: Did it come?
MAMA (*quietly*): Can't you give people a Christian greeting before you start asking about money?
WALTER (*to Ruth*): Did it come? (*Ruth unfolds the check and lays it quietly before him, watching him intently with thoughts of her own. Walter sits down and grasps it close and counts off the zeros.*) Ten thousand dollars—(*He turns suddenly, frantically to his mother and draws some papers out of his breast pocket.*) Mama—look. Old Willy Harris put everything on paper—
MAMA: Son—I think you ought to talk to your wife . . . I'll go on out and leave you alone if you want—
WALTER: I can talk to her later—Mama, look—
MAMA: Son—
WALTER: WILL SOMEBODY PLEASE LISTEN TO ME TODAY!
MAMA (*quietly*): I don't 'low no yellin' in this house, Walter Lee, and you know it—(*Walter stares at them in frustration and starts to speak several times.*) And there ain't going to be no investing in no liquor stores.
WALTER: But, Mama, you ain't even looked at it.
MAMA: I don't aim to have to speak on that again.

A long pause.

WALTER: You ain't looked at it and you don't aim to have to speak on that again? You ain't even looked at it and *you* have decided—(*Crumpling his papers.*) Well, *you* tell that to my boy tonight when you put him to sleep on the living-room couch . . . (*Turning to Mama and speaking directly to her.*) Yeah—and tell it to my wife, Mama, tomorrow when she has to go out of here to look after somebody else's kids. And tell it to *me*, Mama, every time we need a new pair of curtains and I have to watch *you* go out and work in somebody's kitchen. Yeah, you tell me then!

Walter starts out.

RUTH: Where you going?
WALTER: I'm going out!
RUTH: Where?
WALTER: Just out of this house somewhere—
RUTH (*getting her coat*): I'll come too.
WALTER: I don't want you to come!
RUTH: I got something to talk to you about, Walter.
WALTER: That's too bad.
MAMA (*still quietly*): Walter Lee—(*She waits and he finally turns and looks at her.*) Sit down.
WALTER: I'm a grown man, Mama.

MAMA: Ain't nobody said you wasn't grown. But you still in my house and my presence. And as long as you are—you'll talk to your wife civil. Now sit down.

RUTH (*suddenly*): Oh, let him go on out and drink himself to death! He makes me sick to my stomach! (*She flings her coat against him and exits to bedroom.*)

WALTER (*violently flinging the coat after her*): And you turn mine too, baby! (*The door slams behind her.*) That was my biggest mistake—

MAMA (*still quietly*): Walter, what is the matter with you?

WALTER: Matter with me? Ain't nothing the matter with *me!*

MAMA: Yes there is. Something eating you up like a crazy man. Something more than me not giving you this money. The past few years I been watching it happen to you. You get all nervous acting and kind of wild in the eyes—(*Walter jumps up impatiently at her words.*) I said sit there now, I'm talking to you!

WALTER: Mama—I don't need no nagging at me today.

MAMA: Seem like you getting to a place where you always tied up in some kind of knot about something. But if anybody ask you 'bout it you just yell at 'em and bust out the house and go out and drink somewheres. Walter Lee, people can't live with that. Ruth's a good, patient girl in her way—but you getting to be too much. Boy, don't make the mistake of driving that girl away from you.

WALTER: Why—what she do for me?

MAMA: She loves you.

WALTER: Mama—I'm going out. I want to go off somewhere and be by myself for a while.

MAMA: I'm sorry 'bout your liquor store, son. It just wasn't the thing for us to do. That's what I want to tell you about—

WALTER: I got to go out, Mama—

He rises.

MAMA: It's dangerous, son.

WALTER: What's dangerous?

MAMA: When a man goes outside his home to look for peace.

WALTER (*beseechingly*): Then why can't there never be no peace in this house then?

MAMA: You done found it in some other house?

WALTER: No—there ain't no woman! Why do women always think there's a woman somewhere when a man gets restless. (*Picks up the check.*) Do you know what this money means to me? Do you know what this money can do for us? (*Puts it back.*) Mama—Mama—I want so many things . . .

MAMA: Yes, son—

WALTER: I want so many things that they are driving me kind of crazy . . . Mama—look at me.

MAMA: I'm looking at you. You a good-looking boy. You got a job, a nice wife, a fine boy, and—

WALTER: A job. (*Looks at her.*) Mama, a job? I open and close car doors all day long. I drive a man around in his limousine and I say, "Yes, sir; no, sir; very good, sir; shall I take the Drive, sir?" Mama, that ain't no kind of job . . . that ain't nothing at all. (*Very quietly.*) Mama, I don't know if I can make you understand.

MAMA: Understand what, baby?

WALTER (*quietly*): Sometimes it's like I can see the future stretched out in front of me—just plain as day. The future, Mama. Hanging over there at the edge of my days. Just waiting for me—a big, looming blank space—full of *nothing*. Just waiting for *me*. But it don't have to be. (*Pause. Kneeling beside her chair.*) Mama—sometimes when I'm downtown and I pass them cool, quiet-looking restaurants where them white boys are sitting back and talking 'bout things . . . sitting there turning deals worth millions of dollars . . . sometimes I see guys don't look much older than me—

MAMA: Son—how come you talk so much 'bout money?

WALTER (*with immense passion*): Because it is life, Mama!

MAMA (*quietly*): Oh—(*Very quietly.*) So now it's life. Money is life. Once upon a time freedom used to be life—now it's money. I guess the world really do change . . .

WALTER: No—it was always money, Mama. We just didn't know about it.

MAMA: No . . . something has changed. (*She looks at him.*) You something new, boy. In my time we was worried about not being lynched and getting to the North if we could and how to stay alive and still have a pinch of dignity too . . . Now here come you and Beneatha—talking 'bout things we ain't never even thought about hardly, me and your daddy. You ain't satisfied or proud of nothing we done. I mean that you had a home; that we kept you out of trouble till you was grown; that you don't have to ride to work on the back of nobody's streetcar—You my children—but how different we done become.

WALTER (*a long beat. He pats her hand and gets up*): You just don't understand, Mama, you just don't understand.

MAMA: Son—do you know your wife is expecting another baby? (*Walter stands, stunned, and absorbs what his mother has said.*) That's what she wanted to talk to you about. (*Walter sinks down into a chair.*) This ain't for me to be telling—but you ought to know. (*She waits.*) I think Ruth is thinking 'bout getting rid of that child.

WALTER (*slowly understanding*): —No—no—Ruth wouldn't do that.

MAMA: When the world gets ugly enough—a woman will do anything for her family. *The part that's already living.*

WALTER: You don't know Ruth, Mama, if you think she would do that.

Ruth opens the bedroom door and stands there a little limp.

RUTH (*beaten*): Yes I would too, Walter. (*Pause.*) I gave her a five-dollar down payment.

There is total silence as the man stares at his wife and the mother stares at her son.

MAMA (*presently*): Well—(*Tightly.*) Well—son, I'm waiting to hear you say something . . . (*She waits.*) I'm waiting to hear how you be your father's son. Be the man he was . . . (*Pause. The silence shouts.*) Your wife say she going to destroy your child. And I'm waiting to hear you talk like him and say we a people who give children life, not who destroys them—(*She rises.*) I'm waiting to see you stand up and look like your daddy and say we done give up one baby to poverty and that we ain't going to give up nary another one . . . I'm waiting.

WALTER: Ruth—(*He can say nothing.*)

MAMA: If you a son of mine, tell her! (*Walter picks up his keys and his coat and walks out. She continues, bitterly.*) You . . . you are a disgrace to your father's memory. Somebody get me my hat!

Curtain.

ACT II

SCENE I

Time: Later the same day.

At rise: Ruth is ironing again. She has the radio going. Presently Beneatha's bedroom door opens and Ruth's mouth falls and she puts down the iron in fascination.

RUTH: What have we got on tonight!

BENEATHA (*emerging grandly from the doorway so that we can see her thoroughly robed in the costume Asagai brought*): You are looking at what a well-dressed Nigerian woman wears—(*She parades for Ruth, her hair completely hidden by the headdress; she is coquettishly fanning herself with an ornate oriental fan, mistakenly more like Butterfly than any Nigerian that ever was.*) Isn't it beautiful? (*She promenades to the radio and, with an arrogant flourish, turns off the good loud blues that is playing.*) Enough of this assimilationist junk! (*Ruth follows her with her eyes as she goes to the phonograph and puts on a record and turns and waits ceremoniously for the music to come up. Then, with a shout*—) OCOMOGOSIAY!

Ruth jumps. The music comes up, a lovely Nigerian melody. Beneatha listens, enraptured, her eyes far away— "back to the past." She begins to dance. Ruth is dumfounded.

RUTH: What kind of dance is that?

BENEATHA: A folk dance.

RUTH (*Pearl Bailey*°): What kind of folks do that, honey?

BENEATHA: It's from Nigeria. It's a dance of welcome.

RUTH: Who you welcoming?

BENEATHA: The men back to the village.

RUTH: Where they been?

BENEATHA: How should I know—out hunting or something. Anyway, they are coming back now . . .

RUTH: Well, that's good.

Pearl Bailey: A popular African American singer (1918–1990).

BENEATHA (*with the record*):

Alundi, alundi
Alundi alunya
Jop pu a jeepua
Ang gu soooooooooo
Ai yai yae . . .
Ayehaye—alundi . . .

Walter comes in during this performance; he has obviously been drinking. He leans against the door heavily and watches his sister, at first with distaste. Then his eyes look off— "back to the past"—as he lifts both his fists to the roof, screaming.

WALTER: YEAH . . . AND ETHIOPIA STRETCH FORTH HER HANDS AGAIN! . . .

RUTH (*drily, looking at him*): Yes—and Africa sure is claiming her own tonight. (*She gives them both up and starts ironing again.*)

WALTER (*all in a drunken, dramatic shout*): Shut up! . . . I'm diggin them drums . . . them drums move me! . . . (*He makes his weaving way to his wife's face and leans in close to her.*) In my heart of hearts—(*He thumps his chest.*)—I am much warrior!

RUTH (*without even looking up*): In your heart of hearts you are much drunkard.

WALTER (*coming away from her and starting to wander around the room, shouting*): Me and Jomo . . . (*Intently, in his sister's face. She has stopped dancing to watch him in this unknown mood.*) That's my man, Kenyatta.° (*Shouting and thumping his chest.*) FLAMING SPEAR! HOT DAMN! (*He is suddenly in possession of an imaginary spear and actively spearing enemies all over the room.*) OCOMOGOSIAY . . .

BENEATHA (*to encourage Walter, thoroughly caught up with this side of him*): *OCOMOGOSIAY*, FLAMING SPEAR!

WALTER: THE LION IS WAKING . . . OWIMOWEH!

He pulls his shirt open and leaps up on the table and gestures with his spear.

BENEATHA: OWIMOWEH!

WALTER (*on the table, very far gone, his eyes pure glass sheets. He sees what we cannot, that he is a leader of his people, a great chief, a descendant of Chaka,°* and that the hour to march has come): Listen, my black brothers—

BENEATHA: OCOMOGOSIAY!

WALTER: —Do you hear the waters rushing against the shores of the coastlands—

BENEATHA: OCOMOGOSIAY!

WALTER: —Do you hear the screeching of the cocks in yonder hills beyond where the chiefs meet in council for the coming of the mighty war—

BENEATHA: OCOMOGOSIAY!

Kenyatta: Jomo Kenyatta (c. 1894–1978), a Kenyan politician involved in the country's nationalist movement.

Chaka: Also spelled Shaka (c. 1787–1828), he became chief of the Zulu clan in 1816 and founded the great Zulu empire by conquering most of southern Africa.

And now the lighting shifts subtly to suggest the world of Walter's imagination, and the mood shifts from pure comedy. It is the inner Walter speaking: the Southside chauffeur has assumed an unexpected majesty.

WALTER: — Do you hear the beating of the wings of the birds flying low over the mountains and the low places of our land —

BENEATHA: OCOMOGOSIAY!

WALTER: — Do you hear the singing of the women, singing the war songs of our fathers to the babies in the great houses? Singing the sweet war songs! (*The doorbell rings.*) OH, DO YOU HEAR, MY *BLACK* BROTHERS!

BENEATHA (*completely gone*): We hear you, Flaming Spear —

Ruth shuts off the phonograph and opens the door. George Murchison enters.

WALTER: Telling us to prepare for the GREATNESS OF THE TIME! (*Lights back to normal. He turns and sees George.*) Black Brother!

He extends his hand for the fraternal clasp.

GEORGE: Black Brother, hell!

RUTH (*having had enough, and embarrassed for the family*): Beneatha, you got company — what's the matter with you? Walter Lee Younger, get down off that table and stop acting like a fool . . .

Walter comes down off the table suddenly and makes a quick exit to the bathroom.

RUTH: He's had a little to drink . . . I don't know what her excuse is.

GEORGE (*to Beneatha*): Look honey, we're going to the theater — we're not going to be *in* it . . . so go change, huh?

Beneatha looks at him and slowly, ceremoniously, lifts her hands and pulls off the headdress. Her hair is close-cropped and unstraightened. George freezes mid-sentence and Ruth's eyes all but fall out of her head.

GEORGE: What in the name of —

RUTH (*touching Beneatha's hair*): Girl, you done lost your natural mind? Look at your head!

GEORGE: What have you done to your head — I mean your hair!

BENEATHA: Nothing — except cut it off.

RUTH: Now that's the truth — it's what ain't been done to it! You expect this boy to go out with you with your head all nappy like that?

BENEATHA (*looking at George*): That's up to George. If he's ashamed of his heritage —

GEORGE: Oh, don't be so proud of yourself, Bennie — just because you look eccentric.

BENEATHA: How can something that's natural be eccentric?

GEORGE: That's what being eccentric means — being natural. Get dressed.

BENEATHA: I don't like that, George.

RUTH: Why must you and your brother make an argument out of everything people say?

BENEATHA: Because I hate assimilationist Negroes!

RUTH: Will somebody please tell me what assimila-whoever means!

GEORGE: Oh, it's just a college girl's way of calling people Uncle Toms—but that isn't what it means at all.

RUTH: Well, what does it mean?

BENEATHA (*cutting George off and staring at him as she replies to Ruth*): It means someone who is willing to give up his own culture and submerge himself completely in the dominant, and in this case *oppressive* culture!

GEORGE: Oh, dear, dear, dear! Here we go! A lecture on the African past! On our Great West African Heritage! In one second we will hear all about the great Ashanti empires; the great Songhay civilizations; and the great sculpture of Bénin—and then some poetry in the Bantu—and the whole monologue will end with the word *heritage!* (*Nastily.*) Let's face it, baby, your heritage is nothing but a bunch of raggedy-assed spirituals and some grass huts!

BENEATHA: GRASS HUTS! (*Ruth crosses to her and forcibly pushes her toward the bedroom.*) See there . . . you are standing there in your splendid ignorance talking about people who were the first to smelt iron on the face of the earth! (*Ruth is pushing her through the door.*) The Ashanti were performing surgical operations when the English—(*Ruth pulls the door to, with Beneatha on the other side, and smiles graciously at George. Beneatha opens the door and shouts the end of the sentence defiantly at George.*)—were still tatooing themselves with blue dragons! (*She goes back inside.*)

RUTH: Have a seat, George. (*They both sit. Ruth folds her hands rather primly on her lap, determined to demonstrate the civilization of the family.*) Warm, ain't it? I mean for September. (*Pause.*) Just like they always say about Chicago weather: if it's too hot or cold for you, just wait a minute and it'll change. (*She smiles happily at this cliché of clichés.*) Everybody say it's got to do with them bombs and things they keep setting off. (*Pause.*) Would you like a nice cold beer?

GEORGE: No, thank you. I don't care for beer. (*He looks at his watch.*) I hope she hurries up.

RUTH: What time is the show?

GEORGE: It's an eight-thirty curtain. That's just Chicago, though. In New York standard curtain time is eight forty.

He is rather proud of this knowledge.

RUTH (*properly appreciating it*): You get to New York a lot?

GEORGE (*offhand*): Few times a year.

RUTH: Oh—that's nice. I've never been to New York.

Walter enters. We feel he has relieved himself, but the edge of unreality is still with him.

WALTER: New York ain't got nothing Chicago ain't. Just a bunch of hustling people all squeezed up together—being "Eastern."

He turns his face into a screw of displeasure.

GEORGE: Oh—you've been?

WALTER: *Plenty* of times.

RUTH (*shocked at the lie*): Walter Lee Younger!

WALTER (*staring her down*): Plenty! (*Pause.*) What we got to drink in this house? Why don't you offer this man some refreshment. (*To George.*) They don't know how to entertain people in this house, man.

GEORGE: Thank you—I don't really care for anything.

WALTER (*feeling his head; sobriety coming*): Where's Mama?

RUTH: She ain't come back yet.

WALTER (*looking Murchison over from head to toe, scrutinizing his carefully casual tweed sports jacket over cashmere V-neck sweater over soft eyelet shirt and tie, and soft slacks, finished off with white buckskin shoes*): Why all you college boys wear them faggoty-looking white shoes?

RUTH: Walter Lee!

George Murchison ignores the remark.

WALTER (*to Ruth*): Well, they look crazy as hell—white shoes, cold as it is.

RUTH (*crushed*): You have to excuse him—

WALTER: No he don't! Excuse me for what? What you always excusing me for! I'll excuse myself when I needs to be excused! (*A pause.*) They look as funny as them black knee socks Beneatha wears out of here all the time.

RUTH: It's the college *style*, Walter.

WALTER: Style, hell. She looks like she got burnt legs or something!

RUTH: Oh, Walter—

WALTER (*an irritable mimic*): Oh, Walter! Oh, Walter! (*To Murchison.*) How's your old man making out? I understand you all going to buy that big hotel on the Drive? (*He finds a beer in the refrigerator, wanders over to Murchison, sipping and wiping his lips with the back of his hand, and straddling a chair backwards to talk to the other man.*) Shrewd move. Your old man is all right, man. (*Tapping his head and half winking for emphasis.*) I mean he knows how to operate. I mean he thinks *big*, you know what I mean, I mean for a *home*, you know? But I think he's kind of running out of ideas now. I'd like to talk to him. Listen, man, I got some plans that could turn this city upside down. I mean think like he does. *Big.* Invest big, gamble big, hell, lose *big* if you have to, you know what I mean. It's hard to find a man on this whole Southside who understands my kind of thinking—you dig? (*He scrutinizes Murchison again, drinks his beer, squints his eyes and leans in close, confidential, man to man.*) Me and you ought to sit down and talk sometimes, man. Man, I got me some ideas . . .

MURCHISON (*with boredom*): Yeah—sometimes we'll have to do that, Walter.

WALTER (*understanding the indifference, and offended*): Yeah—well, when you get the time, man. I know you a busy little boy.

RUTH: Walter, please—

WALTER (*bitterly, hurt*): I know ain't nothing in this world as busy as you colored college boys with your fraternity pins and white shoes . . .

RUTH (*covering her face with humiliation*): Oh, Walter Lee—

WALTER: I see you all all the time—with the books tucked under your arms—going to your (*British A—a mimic.*) "clahsses." And for what! What the hell you learning over there? Filling up your heads—(*Counting off on his fingers.*)—with the sociology and the psychology—but they teaching you how to be a man? How to take over and run the world? They teaching you how to run a rubber plantation or a steel mill? Naw—just to talk proper and read books and wear them faggoty-looking white shoes . . .

GEORGE (*looking at him with distaste, a little above it all*): You're all wacked up with bitterness, man.

WALTER (*intently, almost quietly, between the teeth, glaring at the boy*): And you—ain't you bitter, man? Ain't you just about had it yet? Don't you see no stars gleaming that you can't reach out and grab? You happy?—You contented son-of-a-bitch—you happy? You got it made? Bitter? Man, I'm a volcano. Bitter? Here I am a giant—surrounded by ants! Ants who can't even understand what it is the giant is talking about.

RUTH (*passionately and suddenly*): Oh, Walter—ain't you with nobody!

WALTER (*violently*): No! 'Cause ain't nobody with me! Not even my own mother!

RUTH: Walter, that's a terrible thing to say!

Beneatha enters, dressed for the evening in a cocktail dress and earrings, hair natural.

GEORGE: Well—hey—(*Crosses to Beneatha; thoughtful, with emphasis, since this is a reversal.*) You look great!

WALTER (*seeing his sister's hair for the first time*): What's the matter with your head?

BENEATHA (*tired of the jokes now*): I cut it off, Brother.

WALTER (*coming close to inspect it and walking around her*): Well, I'll be damned. So that's what they mean by the African bush . . .

BENEATHA: Ha ha. Let's go, George.

GEORGE (*looking at her*): You know something? I like it. It's sharp. I mean it really is. (*Helps her into her wrap.*)

RUTH: Yes—I think so, too. (*She goes to the mirror and starts to clutch at her hair.*)

WALTER: Oh no! You leave yours alone, baby. You might turn out to have a pin-shaped head or something!

BENEATHA: See you all later.

RUTH: Have a nice time.

GEORGE: Thanks. Good night. (*Half out the door, he reopens it. To Walter.*) Good night, Prometheus!°

Beneatha and George exit.

WALTER (*to Ruth*): Who is Prometheus?

RUTH: I don't know. Don't worry about it.

WALTER (*in fury, pointing after George*): See there—they get to a point where they can't insult you man to man—they got to go talk about something ain't nobody never heard of!

RUTH: How do you know it was an insult? (*To humor him.*) Maybe Prometheus is a nice fellow.

Prometheus: In Greek myth, a Titan who was punished by Zeus for stealing fire from the gods and giving it to humankind.

WALTER: Prometheus! I bet there ain't even no such thing! I bet that simple-minded clown—

RUTH: Walter—

She stops what she is doing and looks at him.

WALTER (*yelling*): Don't start!

RUTH: Start what?

WALTER: Your nagging! Where was I? Who was I with? How much money did I spend?

RUTH (*plaintively*): Walter Lee—why don't we just try to talk about it . . .

WALTER (*not listening*): I been out talking with people who understand me. People who care about the things I got on my mind.

RUTH (*wearily*): I guess that means people like Willy Harris.

WALTER: Yes, people like Willy Harris.

RUTH (*with a sudden flash of impatience*): Why don't you all just hurry up and go into the banking business and stop talking about it!

WALTER: Why? You want to know why? 'Cause we all tied up in a race of people that don't know how to do nothing but moan, pray, and have babies!

The line is too bitter even for him and he looks at her and sits down.

RUTH: Oh, Walter . . . (*Softly.*) Honey, why can't you stop fighting me?

WALTER (*without thinking*): Who's fighting you? Who even cares about you?

This line begins the retardation of his mood.

RUTH: Well—(*She waits a long time, and then with resignation starts to put away her things.*) I guess I might as well go on to bed . . . (*More or less to herself.*) I don't know where we lost it . . . but we have . . . (*Then, to him.*) I—I'm sorry about this new baby, Walter. I guess maybe I better go on and do what I started . . . I guess I just didn't realize how bad things was with us . . . I guess I just didn't really realize—(*She starts out to the bedroom and stops.*) You want some hot milk?

WALTER: Hot milk?

RUTH: Yes—hot milk.

WALTER: Why hot milk?

RUTH: 'Cause after all that liquor you come home with you ought to have something hot in your stomach.

WALTER: I don't want no milk.

RUTH: You want some coffee then?

WALTER: No, I don't want no coffee. I don't want nothing hot to drink. (*Almost plaintively.*) Why you always trying to give me something to eat?

RUTH (*standing and looking at him helplessly*): What *else* can I give you, Walter Lee Younger?

She stands and looks at him and presently turns to go out again. He lifts his head and watches her going away from him in a new mood which began to emerge when he asked her "Who cares about you?"

WALTER: It's been rough, ain't it, baby? (*She hears and stops but does not turn around and he continues to her back.*) I guess between two people there ain't never as much understood as folks generally thinks there is. I mean like between me and you—(*She turns to face him.*) How we gets to the place where we scared to talk softness to each other. (*He waits, thinking hard himself.*) Why you think it got to be like that? (*He is thoughtful, almost as a child would be.*) Ruth, what is it gets into people ought to be close?

RUTH: I don't know, honey. I think about it a lot.

WALTER: On account of you and me, you mean? The way things are with us. The way something done come down between us.

RUTH: There ain't so much between us, Walter . . . Not when you come to me and try to talk to me. Try to be with me . . . a little even.

WALTER (*total honesty*): Sometimes . . . sometimes . . . I don't even know how to try.

RUTH: Walter—

WALTER: Yes?

RUTH (*coming to him, gently and with misgiving, but coming to him*): Honey . . . life don't have to be like this. I mean sometimes people can do things so that things are better . . . You remember how we used to talk when Travis was born . . . about the way we were going to live . . . the kind of house . . . (*She is stroking his head.*) Well, it's all starting to slip away from us . . .

He turns her to him and they look at each other and kiss, tenderly and hungrily. The door opens and Mama enters—Walter breaks away and jumps up. A beat.

WALTER: Mama, where have you been?

MAMA: My—them steps is longer than they used to be. Whew! (*She sits down and ignores him.*) How you feeling this evening, Ruth?

Ruth shrugs, disturbed at having been interrupted and watching her husband knowingly.

WALTER: Mama, where have you been all day?

MAMA (*still ignoring him and leaning on the table and changing to more comfortable shoes*): Where's Travis?

RUTH: I let him go out earlier and he ain't come back yet. Boy, is he going to get it!

WALTER: Mama!

MAMA (*as if she has heard him for the first time*): Yes, son?

WALTER: Where did you go this afternoon?

MAMA: I went downtown to tend to some business that I had to tend to.

WALTER: What kind of business?

MAMA: You know better than to question me like a child, Brother.

WALTER (*rising and bending over the table*): Where were you, Mama? (*Bringing his fists down and shouting.*) Mama, you didn't go do something with that insurance money, something crazy?

The front door opens slowly, interrupting him, and Travis peeks his head in, less than hopefully.

TRAVIS (*to his mother*): Mama, I—

RUTH: "Mama I" nothing! You're going to get it, boy! Get on in that bedroom and get yourself ready!

TRAVIS: But I—
MAMA: Why don't you all never let the child explain hisself.
RUTH: Keep out of it now, Lena.

Mama clamps her lips together, and Ruth advances toward her son menacingly.

RUTH: A thousand times I have told you not to go off like that—
MAMA (*holding out her arms to her grandson*): Well—at least let me tell him something. I want him to be the first one to hear . . . Come here, Travis (*The boy obeys, gladly.*) Travis—(*She takes him by the shoulder and looks into his face.*)—you know that money we got in the mail this morning?
TRAVIS: Yes'm—
MAMA: Well—what you think your grandmama gone and done with that money?
TRAVIS: I don't know, Grandmama.
MAMA (*putting her finger on his nose for emphasis*): She went out and she bought you a house! (*The explosion comes from Walter at the end of the revelation and he jumps up and turns away from all of them in a fury. Mama continues, to Travis.*) You glad about the house? It's going to be yours when you get to be a man.
TRAVIS: Yeah—I always wanted to live in a house.
MAMA: All right, gimme some sugar then—(*Travis puts his arms around her neck as she watches her son over the boy's shoulder. Then, to Travis, after the embrace.*) Now when you say your prayers tonight, you thank God and your grandfather—'cause it was him who give you the house—in his way.
RUTH (*taking the boy from Mama and pushing him toward the bedroom*): Now you get out of here and get ready for your beating.
TRAVIS: Aw, Mama—
RUTH: Get on in there—(*Closing the door behind him and turning radiantly to her mother-in-law.*) So you went and did it!
MAMA (*quietly, looking at her son with pain*): Yes, I did.
RUTH (*raising both arms classically*): PRAISE GOD! (*Looks at Walter a moment, who says nothing. She crosses rapidly to her husband.*) Please, honey—let me be glad . . . you be glad too. (*She has laid her hands on his shoulders, but he shakes himself free of her roughly, without turning to face her.*) Oh, Walter . . . a home . . . *a home*. (*She comes back to Mama.*) Well—where is it? How big is it? How much it going to cost?
MAMA: Well—
RUTH: When we moving?
MAMA (*smiling at her*): First of the month.
RUTH (*throwing back her head with jubilance*): Praise God!
MAMA (*tentatively, still looking at her son's back turned against her and Ruth*): It's—it's a nice house too . . . (*She cannot help speaking directly to him. An imploring quality in her voice, her manner, makes her almost like a girl now.*) Three bedrooms—nice big one for you and Ruth . . . Me and Beneatha still have to share our room, but Travis have one of his own—and (*With difficulty.*) I figure if the—new baby—is a boy, we could get

one of them double-decker outfits . . . And there's a yard with a little patch of dirt where I could maybe get to grow me a few flowers . . . And a nice big basement . . .

RUTH: Walter honey, be glad—

MAMA (*still to his back, fingering things on the table*): 'Course I don't want to make it sound fancier than it is . . . It's just a plain little old house—but it's made good and solid—and it will be *ours*. Walter Lee—it makes a difference in a man when he can walk on floors that belong to *him* . . .

RUTH: Where is it?

MAMA (*frightened at this telling*): Well—well—it's out there in Clybourne Park—

Ruth's radiance fades abruptly, and Walter finally turns slowly to face his mother with incredulity and hostility.

RUTH: Where?

MAMA (*matter-of-factly*): Four o six Clybourne Street, Clybourne Park.

RUTH: Clybourne Park? Mama, there ain't no colored people living in Clybourne Park.

MAMA (*almost idiotically*): Well, I guess there's going to be some now.

WALTER (*bitterly*): So that's the peace and comfort you went out and bought for us today!

MAMA (*raising her eyes to meet his finally*): Son—I just tried to find the nicest place for the least amount of money for my family.

RUTH (*trying to recover from the shock*): Well—well—'course I ain't one never been 'fraid of no crackers, mind you—but—well, wasn't there no other houses nowhere?

MAMA: Them houses they put up for colored in them areas way out all seem to cost twice as much as other houses. I did the best I could.

RUTH (*struck senseless with the news, in its various degrees of goodness and trouble, she sits a moment, her fists propping her chin in thought, and then she starts to rise, bringing her fists down with vigor, the radiance spreading from cheek to cheek again*): Well—well—All I can say is—if this is my time in life—*MY TIME*—to say good-bye—(*And she builds with momentum as she starts to circle the room with an exuberant, almost tearfully happy release.*)—to these Goddamned cracking walls!—(*She pounds the walls.*)—and these marching roaches!—(*She wipes at an imaginary army of marching roaches.*)—and this cramped little closet which ain't now or never was no kitchen! . . . then I say it loud and good, HALLELUJAH! AND GOOD-BYE MISERY . . . I DON'T NEVER WANT TO SEE YOUR UGLY FACE AGAIN! (*She laughs joyously, having practically destroyed the apartment, and flings her arms up and lets them come down happily, slowly, reflectively, over her abdomen, aware for the first time perhaps that the life therein pulses with happiness and not despair.*) Lena?

MAMA (*moved, watching her happiness*): Yes, honey?

RUTH (*looking off*): Is there—is there a whole lot of sunlight?

MAMA (*understanding*): Yes, child, there's a whole lot of sunlight.

Long pause.

RUTH (*collecting herself and going to the door of the room Travis is in*): Well—I guess I better see 'bout Travis. (*To Mama.*) Lord, I sure don't feel like whipping nobody today!

She exits.

MAMA (*the mother and son are left alone now and the mother waits a long time, considering deeply, before she speaks*): Son—you—you understand what I done, don't you? (*Walter is silent and sullen.*) I—I just seen my family falling apart today . . . just falling to pieces in front of my eyes . . . We couldn't of gone on like we was today. We was going backwards 'stead of forwards—talking 'bout killing babies and wishing each other was dead . . . When it gets like that in life—you just got to do something different, push on out and do something bigger . . . (*She waits.*) I wish you say something, son . . . I wish you'd say how deep inside you you think I done the right thing—

WALTER (*crossing slowly to his bedroom door and finally turning there and speaking measuredly*): What you need me to say you done right for? *You* the head of this family. You run our lives like you want to. It was your money and you did what you wanted with it. So what you need for me to say it was all right for? (*Bitterly, to hurt her as deeply as he knows is possible.*) So you butchered up a dream of mine—you—who always talking 'bout your children's dreams . . .

MAMA: Walter Lee—

He just closes the door behind him. Mama sits alone, thinking heavily.

Curtain.

SCENE II

Time: Friday night, a few weeks later.

At rise: Packing crates mark the intention of the family to move. Beneatha and George come in, presumably from an evening out again.

GEORGE: O.K. . . . O.K., whatever you say . . . (*They both sit on the couch. He tries to kiss her. She moves away.*) Look, we've had a nice evening; let's not spoil it, huh? . . .

He again turns her head and tries to nuzzle in and she turns away from him, not with distaste but with momentary lack of interest; in a mood to pursue what they were talking about.

BENEATHA: I'm *trying* to talk to you.

GEORGE: We always talk.

BENEATHA: Yes—and I love to talk.

GEORGE (*exasperated; rising*): I know it and I don't mind it sometimes . . . I want you to cut it out, see—The moody stuff, I mean. I don't like it. You're a nice-looking girl . . . all over. That's all you need, honey, forget the atmosphere. Guys aren't going to go for the atmosphere—they're going to go for what they see. Be glad for that. Drop the Garbo routine. It doesn't go with you. As for myself, I want a nice—(*Groping.*)—simple (*Thoughtfully.*)—sophisticated girl . . . not a poet—O.K.?

He starts to kiss her, she rebuffs him again and he jumps up.

BENEATHA: Why are you angry, George?

GEORGE: Because this is stupid! I don't go out with you to discuss the nature of "quiet desperation" or to hear all about your thoughts—because the world will go on thinking what it thinks regardless—

BENEATHA: Then why read books? Why go to school?

GEORGE (*with artificial patience, counting on his fingers*): It's simple. You read books—to learn facts—to get grades—to pass the course—to get a degree. That's all—it has nothing to do with thoughts.

A long pause.

BENEATHA: I see. (*He starts to sit.*) Good night, George.

George looks at her a little oddly, and starts to exit. He meets Mama coming in.

GEORGE: Oh—hello, Mrs. Younger.

MAMA: Hello, George, how you feeling?

GEORGE: Fine—fine, how are you?

MAMA: Oh, a little tired. You know them steps can get you after a day's work. You all have a nice time tonight?

GEORGE: Yes—a fine time. A fine time.

MAMA: Well, good night.

GEORGE: Good night. (*He exits. Mama closes the door behind her.*)

MAMA: Hello, honey. What you sitting like that for?

BENEATHA: I'm just sitting.

MAMA: Didn't you have a nice time?

BENEATHA: No.

MAMA: No? What's the matter?

BENEATHA: Mama, George is a fool—honest. (*She rises.*)

MAMA (*hustling around unloading the packages she has entered with. She stops*): Is he, baby?

BENEATHA: Yes.

Beneatha makes up Travis's bed as she talks.

MAMA: You sure?

BENEATHA: Yes.

MAMA: Well—I guess you better not waste your time with no fools.

Beneatha looks up at her mother, watching her put groceries in the refrigerator. Finally she gathers up her things and starts into the bedroom. At the door she stops and looks back at her mother.

BENEATHA: Mama—

MAMA: Yes, baby—

BENEATHA: Thank you.

MAMA: For what?

BENEATHA: For understanding me this time.

She exits quickly and the mother stands, smiling a little, looking at the place where Beneatha just stood. Ruth enters.

RUTH: Now don't you fool with any of this stuff, Lena—

MAMA: Oh, I just thought I'd sort a few things out. Is Brother here?

RUTH: Yes.

MAMA (*with concern*): Is he—

RUTH (*reading her eyes*): Yes.

Mama is silent and someone knocks on the door. Mama and Ruth exchange weary and knowing glances and Ruth opens it to admit the neighbor, Mrs. Johnson, ° *who is a rather squeaky wide-eyed lady of no particular age, with a newspaper under her arm.*

MAMA (*changing her expression to acute delight and a ringing cheerful greeting*): Oh—hello there, Johnson.

JOHNSON (*this is a woman who decided long ago to be enthusiastic about EVERYTHING in life and she is inclined to wave her wrist vigorously at the height of her exclamatory comments*): Hello there, yourself! H'you this evening, Ruth?

RUTH (*not much of a deceptive type*): Fine, Mis' Johnson, h'you?

JOHNSON: Fine. (*Reaching out quickly, playfully, and patting Ruth's stomach.*) Ain't you starting to poke out none yet! (*She mugs with delight at the over familiar remark and her eyes dart around looking at the crates and packing preparation; Mama's face is a cold sheet of endurance.*) Oh, ain't we getting ready round here, though! Yessir! Lookathere! I'm telling you the Youngers is really getting ready to "move on up a little higher!"—Bless God!

MAMA (*a little drily, doubting the total sincerity of the Blesser*): Bless God.

JOHNSON: He's good, ain't He?

MAMA: Oh yes, He's good.

JOHNSON: I mean sometimes He works in mysterious ways . . . but He works, don't He!

MAMA (*the same*): Yes, He does.

JOHNSON: I'm just soooooo happy for y'all. And this here child—(*about Ruth*) looks like she could just pop open with happiness, don't she. Where's all the rest of the family?

MAMA: Bennie's gone to bed—

JOHNSON: Ain't no . . . (*the implication is pregnancy*) sickness done hit you—I hope . . . ?

MAMA: No—she just tired. She was out this evening.

JOHNSON (*all is a coo, an emphatic coo*): Aw—ain't that lovely. She still going out with the little Murchison boy?

MAMA (*drily*): Ummmm huh.

JOHNSON: That's lovely. You sure got lovely children, Younger. Me and Isaiah talks all the time 'bout what fine children you was blessed with. We sure do.

MAMA: Ruth, give Mis' Johnson a piece of sweet potato pie and some milk.

Mrs. Johnson: This character and the scene of her visit were cut from the original production and early editions of the play.

JOHNSON: Oh honey, I can't stay hardly a minute—I just dropped in to see if there was anything I could do. (*Accepting the food easily.*) I guess y'all seen the news what's all over the colored paper this week . . .

MAMA: No—didn't get mine yet this week.

JOHNSON (*lifting her head and blinking with the spirit of catastrophe*): You mean you ain't read 'bout them colored people that was bombed out their place out there?

Ruth straightens with concern and takes the paper and reads it. Johnson notices her and feeds commentary.

JOHNSON: Ain't it something how bad these here white folks is getting here in Chicago! Lord, getting so you think you right down in Mississippi! (*With a tremendous and rather insincere sense of melodrama.*) 'Course I thinks it's wonderful how our folk keeps on pushing out. You hear some of these Negroes round here talking 'bout how they don't go where they ain't wanted and all that—but not me, honey! (*This is a lie.*) Wilhemenia Othella Johnson goes anywhere, any time she feels like it! (*With head movement for emphasis.*) Yes I do! Why if we left it up to these here crackers, the poor niggers wouldn't have nothing—(*She clasps her hand over her mouth.*) Oh, I always forgets you don't 'low that word in your house.

MAMA (*quietly, looking at her*): No—I don't 'low it.

JOHNSON (*vigorously again*): Me neither! I was just telling Isaiah yesterday when he come using it in front of me—I said, "Isaiah, it's just like Mis' Younger says all the time—"

MAMA: Don't you want some more pie?

JOHNSON: No—no thank you; this was lovely. I got to get on over home and have my midnight coffee. I hear some people say it don't let them sleep but I finds I can't close my eyes right lessen I done had that laaaast cup of coffee . . . (*She waits. A beat. Undaunted.*) My Goodnight coffee, I calls it!

MAMA (*with much eye-rolling and communication between herself and Ruth*): Ruth, why don't you give Mis' Johnson some coffee.

Ruth gives Mama an unpleasant look for her kindness.

JOHNSON (*accepting the coffee*): Where's Brother tonight?

MAMA: He's lying down.

JOHNSON: Mmmmmmm, he sure gets his beauty rest, don't he? Good-looking man. Sure is a good-looking man! (*Reaching out to pat Ruth's stomach again.*) I guess that's how come we keep on having babies around here. (*She winks at Mama.*) One thing 'bout Brother, he always know how to have a *good* time. And soooooo ambitious! I bet it was his idea y'all moving out to Clybourne Park. Lord—I bet this time next month y'all's names will have been in the papers plenty—(*Holding up her hands to mark off each word of the headline she can see in front of her.*) "NEGROES INVADE CLYBOURNE PARK—BOMBED!"

MAMA (*she and Ruth look at the woman in amazement*): We ain't exactly moving out there to get bombed.

JOHNSON: Oh honey—you know I'm praying to God every day that don't nothing like that happen! But you have to think of life like it is—and these here Chicago peckerwoods is some baaaad peckerwoods.

MAMA (*wearily*): We done thought about all that Mis' Johnson.

Beneatha comes out of the bedroom in her robe and passes through to the bathroom. Mrs. Johnson turns.

JOHNSON: Hello there, Bennie!

BENEATHA (*crisply*): Hello, Mrs. Johnson.

JOHNSON: How is school?

BENEATHA (*crisply*): Fine, thank you. (*She goes out.*)

JOHNSON (*insulted*): Getting so she don't have much to say to nobody.

MAMA: The child was on her way to the bathroom.

JOHNSON: I know—but sometimes she act like she ain't got time to pass the time of day with nobody ain't been to college. Oh—I ain't criticizing her none. It's just—you know how some of our young people gets when they get a little education. (*Mama and Ruth say nothing, just look at her.*) Yes—well. Well, I guess I better get on home. (*Unmoving.*) 'Course I can understand how she must be proud and everything—being the only one in the family to make something of herself. I know just being a chauffeur ain't never satisfied Brother none. He shouldn't feel like that, though. Ain't nothing wrong with being a chauffeur.

MAMA: There's plenty wrong with it.

JOHNSON: What?

MAMA: Plenty. My husband always said being any kind of a servant wasn't a fit thing for a man to have to be. He always said a man's hands was made to make things, or to turn the earth with—not to drive nobody's car for 'em—or—(*she looks at her own hands*) carry they slop jars. And my boy is just like him—he wasn't meant to wait on nobody.

JOHNSON (*rising, somewhat offended*): Mmmmmmmmm. The Youngers is too much for me! (*She looks around.*) You sure one proud-acting bunch of colored folks. Well—I always thinks like Booker T. Washington said that time—"Education has spoiled many a good plow hand"—

MAMA: Is that what old Booker T. said?

JOHNSON: He sure did.

MAMA: Well, it sounds just like him. The fool.

JOHNSON (*indignantly*): Well—he was one of our great men.

MAMA: Who said so?

JOHNSON (*nonplussed*): You know, me and you ain't never agreed about some things, Lena Younger. I guess I better be going—

RUTH (*quickly*): Good night.

JOHNSON: Good night. Oh—(*Thrusting it at her.*) You can keep the paper! (*With a trill.*) 'Night.

MAMA: Good night, Mis' Johnson.

Mrs. Johnson exits.

RUTH: If ignorance was gold . . .

MAMA: Shush. Don't talk about folks behind their backs.

RUTH: You do.

MAMA: I'm old and corrupted. (*Beneatha enters.*) You was rude to Mis' Johnson, Beneatha, and I don't like it at all.

BENEATHA (*at her door*): Mama, if there are two things we, as a people, have got to overcome, one is the Klu Klux Klan—and the other is Mrs. Johnson. (*She exits.*)

MAMA: Smart aleck.

The phone rings.

RUTH: I'll get it.

MAMA: Lord, ain't this a popular place tonight.

RUTH (*at the phone*): Hello—Just a minute. (*Goes to door.*) Walter, it's Mrs. Arnold. (*Waits. Goes back to the phone. Tense.*) Hello. Yes, this is his wife speaking . . . He's lying down now. Yes . . . well, he'll be in tomorrow. He's been very sick. Yes—I know we should have called, but we were so sure he'd be able to come in today. Yes—yes, I'm very sorry. Yes . . . Thank you very much. (*She hangs up. Walter is standing in the doorway of the bedroom behind her.*) That was Mrs. Arnold.

WALTER (*indifferently*): Was it?

RUTH: She said if you don't come in tomorrow that they are getting a new man . . .

WALTER: Ain't that sad—ain't that crying sad.

RUTH: She said Mr. Arnold has had to take a cab for three days . . . Walter, you ain't been to work for three days! (*This is a revelation to her.*) Where you been, Walter Lee Younger? (*Walter looks at her and starts to laugh.*) You're going to lose your job.

WALTER: That's right . . . (*He turns on the radio.*)

RUTH: Oh, Walter, and with your mother working like a dog every day—

A steamy, deep blues pours into the room.

WALTER: That's sad too—Everything is sad.

MAMA: What you been doing for these three days, son?

WALTER: Mama—you don't know all the things a man what got leisure can find to do in this city . . . What's this—Friday night? Well—Wednesday I borrowed Willy Harris' car and I went for a drive . . . just me and myself and I drove and drove . . . Way out . . . way past South Chicago, and I parked the car and I sat and looked at the steel mills all day long. I just sat in the car and looked at them big black chimneys for hours. Then I drove back and I went to the Green Hat. (*Pause.*) And Thursday—Thursday I borrowed the car again and I got in it and I pointed it the other way and I drove the other way—for hours—way, way up to Wisconsin, and I looked at the farms. I just drove and looked at the farms. Then I drove back and I went to the Green Hat. (*Pause.*) And today—today I didn't get the car. Today I just walked. All over the Southside. And I looked at the Negroes and they looked at me and finally I just sat down on the curb at Thirty-ninth and South Parkway and I just sat there and watched the

Negroes go by. And then I went to the Green Hat. You all sad? You all depressed? And you know where I am going right now—

Ruth goes out quietly.

MAMA: Oh, Big Walter, is this the harvest of our days?

WALTER: You know what I like about the Green Hat? I like this little cat they got there who blows a sax . . . He blows. He talks to me. He ain't but 'bout five feet tall and he's got a conked head and his eyes is always closed and he's all music—

MAMA (*rising and getting some papers out of her handbag*): Walter—

WALTER: And there's this other guy who plays the piano . . . and they got a sound. I mean they can work on some music . . . They got the best little combo in the world in the Green Hat . . . You can just sit there and drink and listen to them three men play and you realize that don't nothing matter worth a damn, but just being there—

MAMA: I've helped do it to you, haven't I, son? Walter, I been wrong.

WALTER: Naw—you ain't never been wrong about nothing, Mama.

MAMA: Listen to me, now. I say I been wrong, son. That I been doing to you what the rest of the world been doing to you. (*She turns off the radio.*) Walter—(*She stops and he looks up slowly at her and she meets his eyes pleadingly.*) What you ain't never understood is that I ain't got nothing, don't own nothing, ain't never really wanted nothing that wasn't for you. There ain't nothing as precious to me . . . There ain't nothing worth holding on to, money, dreams, nothing else—if it means—if it means it's going to destroy my boy. (*She takes an envelope out of her handbag and puts it in front of him and he watches her without speaking or moving.*) I paid the man thirty-five hundred dollars down on the house. That leaves sixty-five hundred dollars. Monday morning I want you to take this money and take three thousand dollars and put it in a savings account for Beneatha's medical schooling. The rest you put in a checking account—with your name on it. And from now on any penny that come out of it or that go in it is for you to look after. For you to decide. (*She drops her hands a little helplessly.*) It ain't much, but it's all I got in the world and I'm putting it in your hands. I'm telling you to be the head of this family from now on like you supposed to be.

WALTER (*stares at the money*): You trust me like that, Mama?

MAMA: I ain't never stop trusting you. Like I ain't never stop loving you.

She goes out, and Walter sits looking at the money on the table. Finally, in a decisive gesture, he gets up, and, in mingled joy and desperation, picks up the money. At the same moment, Travis enters for bed.

TRAVIS: What's the matter, Daddy? You drunk?

WALTER (*sweetly, more sweetly than we have ever known him*): No, Daddy ain't drunk. Daddy ain't going to never be drunk again . . .

TRAVIS: Well, good night, Daddy.

The father has come from behind the couch and leans over, embracing his son.

WALTER: Son, I feel like talking to you tonight.

TRAVIS: About what?

WALTER: Oh, about a lot of things. About you and what kind of man you going to be when you grow up . . . Son—son, what do you want to be when you grow up?

TRAVIS: A bus driver.

WALTER (*laughing a little*): A what? Man, that ain't nothing to want to be!

TRAVIS: Why not?

WALTER: 'Cause, man—it ain't big enough—you know what I mean.

TRAVIS: I don't know then. I can't make up my mind. Sometimes Mama asks me that too. And sometimes when I tell her I just want to be like you—she says she don't want me to be like that and sometimes she says she does. . . .

WALTER (*gathering him up in his arms*): You know what, Travis? In seven years you going to be seventeen years old. And things is going to be very different with us in seven years, Travis. . . . One day when you are seventeen I'll come home—home from my office downtown somewhere—

TRAVIS: You don't work in no office, Daddy.

WALTER: No—but after tonight. After what your daddy gonna do tonight, there's going to be offices—a whole lot of offices. . . .

TRAVIS: What you gonna do tonight, Daddy?

WALTER: You wouldn't understand yet, son, but your daddy's gonna make a transaction . . . a business transaction that's going to change our lives. . . . That's how come one day when you 'bout seventeen years old I'll come home and I'll be pretty tired, you know what I mean, after a day of conferences and secretaries getting things wrong the way they do . . . 'cause an executive's life is hell, man—(*The more he talks the farther away he gets.*) And I'll pull the car up on the driveway . . . just a plain black Chrysler, I think, with white walls—no—black tires. More elegant. Rich people don't have to be flashy . . . though I'll have to get something a little sportier for Ruth—maybe a Cadillac convertible to do her shopping in. . . . And I'll come up the steps to the house and the gardener will be clipping away at the hedges and he'll say, "Good evening, Mr. Younger." And I'll say, "Hello, Jefferson, how are you this evening?" And I'll go inside and Ruth will come downstairs and meet me at the door and we'll kiss each other and she'll take my arm and we'll go up to your room to see you sitting on the floor with the catalogues of all the great schools in America around you. . . . All the great schools in the world! And—and I'll say, all right son—it's your seventeenth birthday, what is it you've decided? . . . Just tell me where you want to go to school and you'll *go*. Just tell me, what it is you want to be—and you'll *be* it. . . . Whatever you want to be—Yessir! (*He holds his arms open for Travis.*) You just name it, son . . . (*Travis leaps into them.*) and I hand you the world!

Walter's voice has risen in pitch and hysterical promise and on the last line he lifts Travis high.

Blackout.

SCENE III

Time: Saturday, moving day, one week later.

Before the curtain rises, Ruth's voice, a strident, dramatic church alto, cuts through the silence.

It is, in the darkness, a triumphant surge, a penetrating statement of expectation: "Oh, Lord, I don't feel no ways tired! Children, oh, glory hallelujah!"

As the curtain rises we see that Ruth is alone in the living room, finishing up the family's packing. It is moving day. She is nailing crates and tying cartons. Beneatha enters, carrying a guitar case, and watches her exuberant sister-in-law.

RUTH: Hey!

BENEATHA (*putting away the case*): Hi.

RUTH (*pointing at a package*): Honey—look in that package there and see what I found on sale this morning at the South Center. (*Ruth gets up and moves to the package and draws out some curtains.*) Lookahere—hand-turned hems!

BENEATHA: How do you know the window size out there?

RUTH (*who hadn't thought of that*): Oh—Well, they bound to fit something in the whole house. Anyhow, they was too good a bargain to pass up. (*Ruth slaps her head, suddenly remembering something.*) Oh, Bennie—I meant to put a special note on that carton over there. That's your mama's good china and she wants 'em to be very careful with it.

BENEATHA: I'll do it.

Beneatha finds a piece of paper and starts to draw large letters on it.

RUTH: You know what I'm going to do soon as I get in that new house?

BENEATHA: What?

RUTH: Honey—I'm going to run me a tub of water up to here . . . (*With her fingers practically up to her nostrils.*) And I'm going to get in it—and I am going to sit . . . and sit . . . and sit in that hot water and the first person who knocks to tell *me* to hurry up and come out—

BENEATHA: Gets shot at sunrise.

RUTH (*laughing happily*): You said it, sister! (*Noticing how large Beneatha is absent-mindedly making the note*): Honey, they ain't going to read that from no airplane.

BENEATHA (*laughing herself*): I guess I always think things have more emphasis if they are big, somehow.

RUTH (*looking up at her and smiling*): You and your brother seem to have that as a philosophy of life. Lord, that man—done changed so 'round here. You know—you know what we did last night? Me and Walter Lee?

BENEATHA: What?

RUTH (*smiling to herself*): We went to the movies. (*Looking at Beneatha to see if she understands.*) We went to the movies. You know the last time me and Walter went to the movies together?

BENEATHA: No.

RUTH: Me neither. That's how long it been. (*Smiling again.*) But we went last night. The picture wasn't much good, but that didn't seem to matter. We went—and we held hands.

BENEATHA: Oh, Lord!

RUTH: We held hands—and you know what?

BENEATHA: What?

RUTH: When we come out of the show it was late and dark and all the stores and things was closed up . . . and it was kind of chilly and there wasn't many people on the streets . . . and we was still holding hands, me and Walter.

BENEATHA: You're killing me.

Walter enters with a large package. His happiness is deep in him; he cannot keep still with his newfound exuberance. He is singing and wiggling and snapping his fingers. He puts his package in a corner and puts a phonograph record, which he has brought in with him, on the record player. As the music, soulful and sensuous, comes up he dances over to Ruth and tries to get her to dance with him. She gives in at last to his raunchiness and in a fit of giggling allows herself to be drawn into his mood. They dip and she melts into his arms in a classic, body-melting "slow drag."

BENEATHA (*regarding them a long time as they dance, then drawing in her breath for a deeply exaggerated comment which she does not particularly mean*): Talk about—olddddddddd-fashionedddddd—Negroes!

WALTER (*stopping momentarily*): What kind of Negroes?

He says this in fun. He is not angry with her today, nor with anyone. He starts to dance with his wife again.

BENEATHA: Old-fashioned.

WALTER (*as he dances with Ruth*): You know, when these New Negroes have their convention—(*Pointing at his sister.*)—that is going to be the chairman of the Committee on Unending Agitation. (*He goes on dancing, then stops.*) Race, race, race! . . . Girl, I do believe you are the first person in the history of the entire human race to successfully brainwash yourself. (*Beneatha breaks up and he goes on dancing. He stops again, enjoying his tease.*) Damn, even the N double A C P takes a holiday sometimes! (*Beneatha and Ruth laugh. He dances with Ruth some more and starts to laugh and stops and pantomimes someone over an operating table.*) I can just see that chick someday looking down at some poor cat on an operating table and before she starts to slice him, she says . . . (*Pulling his sleeves back maliciously.*) "By the way, what are your views on civil rights down there? . . ."

He laughs at her again and starts to dance happily. The bell sounds.

BENEATHA: Sticks and stones may break my bones but . . . words will never hurt me!

Beneatha goes to the door and opens it as Walter and Ruth go on with the clowning. Beneatha is somewhat surprised to see a quiet-looking middle-aged white man in a business suit holding his hat and a briefcase in his hand and consulting a small piece of paper.

MAN: Uh—how do you do, miss. I am looking for a Mrs.—(*He looks at the slip of paper.*) Mrs. Lena Younger? (*He stops short, struck dumb at the sight of the oblivious Walter and Ruth.*)

BENEATHA (*smoothing her hair with slight embarrassment*): Oh—yes, that's my mother. Excuse me. (*She closes the door and turns to quiet the other two.*) Ruth! Brother! (*Enunciating precisely but soundlessly: "There's a white man at the door!" They stop dancing, Ruth cuts off the phonograph, Beneatha opens the door. The man casts a curious quick glance at all of them.*) Uh—come in please.

MAN (*coming in*): Thank you.

BENEATHA: My mother isn't here just now. Is it business?

MAN: Yes . . . well, of a sort.

WALTER (*freely, the Man of the House*): Have a seat. I'm Mrs. Younger's son. I look after most of her business matters.

Ruth and Beneatha exchange amused glances.

MAN (*regarding Walter, and sitting*): Well—My name is Karl Lindner . . .

WALTER (*stretching out his hand*): Walter Younger. This is my wife—(*Ruth nods politely.*)—and my sister.

LINDNER: How do you do.

WALTER (*amiably, as he sits himself easily on a chair, leaning forward on his knees with interest and looking expectantly into the newcomer's face*): What can we do for you, Mr. Lindner!

LINDNER (*some minor shuffling of the hat and briefcase on his knees*): Well—I am a representative of the Clybourne Park Improvement Association—

WALTER (*pointing*): Why don't you sit your things on the floor?

LINDNER: Oh—yes. Thank you. (*He slides the briefcase and hat under the chair.*) And as I was saying—I am from the Clybourne Park Improvement Association and we have had it brought to our attention at the last meeting that you people—or at least your mother—has bought a piece of residential property at—(*He digs for the slip of paper again.*)—four o six Clybourne Street . . .

WALTER: That's right. Care for something to drink? Ruth, get Mr. Lindner a beer.

LINDNER (*upset for some reason*): Oh—no, really. I mean thank you very much, but no thank you.

RUTH (*innocently*): Some coffee?

LINDNER: Thank you, nothing at all.

Beneatha is watching the man carefully.

LINDNER: Well, I don't know how much you folks know about our organization. (*He is a gentle man; thoughtful and somewhat labored in his manner.*) It is one of these community organizations set up to look after—oh, you know, things like block upkeep and special projects and we also have what we call our New Neighbors Orientation Committee . . .

BENEATHA (*drily*): Yes—and what do they do?

LINDNER (*turning a little to her and then returning the main force to Walter*): Well—it's what you might call a sort of welcoming committee, I guess. I mean they, we—I'm the chairman of the committee—go around and see the new people who move into the neighborhood and sort of give them the lowdown on the way we do things out in Clybourne Park.

BENEATHA (*with appreciation of the two meanings, which escape Ruth and Walter*): Un-huh.

LINDNER: And we also have the category of what the association calls—(*he looks elsewhere*)—uh—special community problems . . .

BENEATHA: Yes—and what are some of those?

WALTER: Girl, let the man talk.

LINDNER (*with understated relief*): Thank you. I would sort of like to explain this thing in my own way. I mean I want to explain to you in a certain way.

WALTER: Go ahead.

LINDNER: Yes. Well. I'm going to try to get right to the point. I'm sure we'll all appreciate that in the long run.

BENEATHA: Yes.

WALTER: Be still now!

LINDNER: Well—

RUTH (*still innocently*): Would you like another chair—you don't look comfortable.

LINDNER (*more frustrated than annoyed*): No, thank you very much. Please. Well—to get right to the point, I—(*A great breath, and he is off at last.*) I am sure you people must be aware of some of the incidents which have happened in various parts of the city when colored people have moved into certain areas—(*Beneatha exhales heavily and starts tossing a piece of fruit up and down in the air.*) Well—because we have what I think is going to be a unique type of organization in American community life—not only do we deplore that kind of thing—but we are trying to do something about it. (*Beneatha stops tossing and turns with a new and quizzical interest to the man.*) We feel—(*gaining confidence in his mission because of the interest in the faces of the people he is talking to*)—we feel that most of the trouble in this world, when you come right down to it—(*he hits his knee for emphasis*)—most of the trouble exists because people just don't sit down and talk to each other.

RUTH (*nodding as she might in church, pleased with the remark*): You can say that again, mister.

LINDNER (*more encouraged by such affirmation*): That we don't try hard enough in this world to understand the other fellow's problem. The other guy's point of view.

RUTH: Now that's right.

Beneatha and Walter merely watch and listen with genuine interest.

LINDNER: Yes—that's the way we feel out in Clybourne Park. And that's why I was elected to come here this afternoon and talk to you people. Friendly like, you know, the way people should talk to each other and see if we couldn't find some way to work this thing out. As I say, the whole business is a matter of *caring* about the other fellow. Anybody can see that you are a nice family of folks, hard working and honest I'm sure. (*Beneatha frowns slightly, quizzically, her head tilted regarding him.*) Today everybody knows what it means to be on the outside of *something*. And of course, there is always somebody who is out to take advantage of people who don't always understand.

WALTER: What do you mean?

LINDNER: Well—you see our community is made up of people who've worked hard as the dickens for years to build up that little community. They're not rich and fancy people; just hard-working, honest people who don't really have much but those little homes and a dream of the kind of community they want to raise their children in. Now, I don't say we are perfect and there is a lot wrong in some of the things they want. But you've got to admit that a man, right or wrong, has the right to want to have the neighborhood he lives in a certain kind of way. And at the moment the overwhelming majority of our people out there feel that people get along better, take more of a common interest in the life of the community, when they share a common background. I want you to believe me when I tell you that race prejudice simply doesn't enter into it. It is a matter of the people of Clybourne Park believing, rightly or wrongly, as I say, that for the happiness of all concerned that our Negro families are happier when they live in their *own* communities.

BENEATHA (*with a grand and bitter gesture*): This, friends, is the Welcoming Committee!

WALTER (*dumfounded, looking at Lindner*): Is this what you came marching all the way over here to tell us?

LINDNER: Well, now we've been having a fine conversation. I hope you'll hear me all the way through.

WALTER (*tightly*): Go ahead, man.

LINDNER: You see—in the face of all the things I have said, we are prepared to make your family a very generous offer . . .

BENEATHA: Thirty pieces and not a coin less!

WALTER: Yeah?

LINDNER (*putting on his glasses and drawing a form out of the briefcase*): Our association is prepared, through the collective effort of our people, to buy the house from you at a financial gain to your family.

RUTH: Lord have mercy, ain't this the living gall!

WALTER: All right, you through?

LINDNER: Well, I want to give you the exact terms of the financial arrangement—

WALTER: We don't want to hear no exact terms of no arrangements. I want to know if you got any more to tell us 'bout getting together?

LINDNER (*taking off his glasses*): Well—I don't suppose that you feel . . .

WALTER: Never mind how I feel—you got any more to say 'bout how people ought to sit down and talk to each other? . . . Get out of my house, man.

He turns his back and walks to the door.

LINDNER (*looking around at the hostile faces and reaching and assembling his hat and briefcase*): Well—I don't understand why you people are reacting this way. What do you think you are going to gain by moving into a neighborhood where you just aren't wanted and where some elements—

well—people can get awful worked up when they feel that their whole way of life and everything they've ever worked for is threatened.

WALTER: Get out.

LINDNER (*at the door, holding a small card*): Well—I'm sorry it went like this.

WALTER: Get out.

LINDNER (*almost sadly regarding Walter*): You just can't force people to change their hearts, son.

He turns and puts his card on a table and exits. Walter pushes the door to with stinging hatred, and stands looking at it. Ruth just sits and Beneatha just stands. They say nothing. Mama and Travis enter.

MAMA: Well—this all the packing got done since I left out of here this morning. I testify before God that my children got all the energy of the *dead*! What time the moving men due?

BENEATHA: Four o'clock. You had a caller, Mama.

She is smiling, teasingly.

MAMA: Sure enough—who?

BENEATHA (*her arms folded saucily*): The Welcoming Committee.

Walter and Ruth giggle.

MAMA (*innocently*): Who?

BENEATHA: The Welcoming Committee. They said they're sure going to be glad to see you when you get there.

WALTER (*devilishly*): Yeah, they said they can't hardly wait to see your face.

Laughter.

MAMA (*sensing their facetiousness*): What's the matter with you all?

WALTER: Ain't nothing the matter with us. We just telling you 'bout the gentleman who came to see you this afternoon. From the Clybourne Park Improvement Association.

MAMA: What he want?

RUTH (*in the same mood as Beneatha and Walter*): To welcome you, honey.

WALTER: He said they can't hardly wait. He said the one thing they don't have, that they just *dying* to have out there is a fine family of fine colored people! (*To Ruth and Beneatha.*) Ain't that right!

RUTH (*mockingly*): Yeah! He left his card—

BENEATHA (*handing card to Mama*): In case.

Mama reads and throws it on the floor—understanding and looking off as she draws her chair up to the table on which she has put her plant and some sticks and some cord.

MAMA: Father, give us strength. (*Knowingly—and without fun.*) Did he threaten us?

BENEATHA: Oh—Mama—they don't do it like that any more. He talked Brotherhood. He said everybody ought to learn how to sit down and hate each other with good Christian fellowship.

She and Walter shake hands to ridicule the remark.

MAMA (*sadly*): Lord, protect us . . .

RUTH: You should hear the money those folks raised to buy the house from us. All we paid and then some.

BENEATHA: What they think we going to do—eat 'em?

RUTH: No, honey, marry 'em.

MAMA (*shaking her head*): Lord, Lord, Lord . . .

RUTH: Well—that's the way the crackers crumble. (*A beat.*) Joke.

BENEATHA (*laughingly noticing what her mother is doing*): Mama, what are you doing?

MAMA: Fixing my plant so it won't get hurt none on the way . . .

BENEATHA: Mama, you going to take *that* to the new house?

MAMA: Un-huh—

BENEATHA: That raggedy-looking old thing?

MAMA (*stopping and looking at her*): It expresses ME!

RUTH (*with delight, to Beneatha*): So there, Miss Thing!

Walter comes to Mama suddenly and bends down behind her and squeezes her in his arms with all his strength. She is overwhelmed by the suddenness of it and, though delighted, her manner is like that of Ruth and Travis.

MAMA: Look out now, boy! You make me mess up my thing here!

WALTER (*his face lit, he slips down on his knees beside her, his arms still about her*): Mama . . . you know what it means to climb up in the chariot?

MAMA (*gruffly, very happy*): Get on away from me now . . .

RUTH (*near the gift-wrapped package, trying to catch Walter's eye*): Psst—

WALTER: What the old song say, Mama . . .

RUTH: Walter—Now?

She is pointing at the package.

WALTER (*speaking the lines, sweetly, playfully, in his mother's face*):

I got wings . . . you got wings . . .
All God's Children got wings . . .

MAMA: Boy—get out of my face and do some work . . .

WALTER:

When I get to heaven gonna put on my wings,
Gonna fly all over God's heaven . . .

BENEATHA (*teasingly, from across the room*): Everybody talking 'bout heaven ain't going there!

WALTER (*to Ruth, who is carrying the box across to them*): I don't know, you think we ought to give her that . . . Seems to me she ain't been very appreciative around here.

MAMA (*eying the box, which is obviously a gift*): What is that?

WALTER (*taking it from Ruth and putting it on the table in front of Mama*): Well—what you all think? Should we give it to her?

RUTH: Oh—she was pretty good today.

MAMA: I'll good you—

She turns her eyes to the box again.

BENEATHA: Open it, Mama.

She stands up, looks at it, turns and looks at all of them, and then presses her hands together and does not open the package.

WALTER (*sweetly*): Open it, Mama. It's for you. (*Mama looks in his eyes. It is the first present in her life without its being Christmas. Slowly she opens her package and lifts out, one by one, a brand-new sparkling set of gardening tools. Walter continues, prodding.*) Ruth made up the note—read it . . .

MAMA (*picking up the card and adjusting her glasses*): "To our own Mrs. Miniver°—Love from Brother, Ruth, and Beneatha." Ain't that lovely . . .

TRAVIS (*tugging at his father's sleeve*): Daddy, can I give her mine now?

WALTER: All right, son. (*Travis flies to get his gift.*)

MAMA: Now I don't have to use my knives and forks no more . . .

WALTER: Travis didn't want to go in with the rest of us, Mama. He got his own. (*Somewhat amused.*) We don't know what it is . . .

TRAVIS (*racing back in the room with a large hatbox and putting it in front of his grandmother*): Here!

MAMA: Lord have mercy, baby. You done gone and bought your grandmother a hat?

TRAVIS (*very proud*): Open it!

She does and lifts out an elaborate, but very elaborate, wide gardening hat, and all the adults break up at the sight of it.

RUTH: Travis, honey, what is that?

TRAVIS (*who thinks it is beautiful and appropriate*): It's a gardening hat! Like the ladies always have on in the magazines when they work in their gardens.

BENEATHA (*giggling fiercely*): Travis—we were trying to make Mama Mrs. Miniver—not Scarlett O'Hara!

MAMA (*indignantly*): What's the matter with you all! This here is a beautiful hat! (*Absurdly.*) I always wanted me one just like it!

She pops it on her head to prove it to her grandson, and the hat is ludicrous and considerably oversized.

RUTH: Hot dog! Go, Mama!

WALTER (*doubled over with laughter*): I'm sorry, Mama—but you look like you ready to go out and chop you some cotton sure enough!

They all laugh except Mama, out of deference to Travis's feelings.

MAMA (*gathering the boy up to her*): Bless your heart—this is the prettiest hat I ever owned—(*Walter, Ruth, and Beneatha chime in—noisily, festively, and insincerely congratulating Travis on his gift.*) What are we all standing around here for? We ain't finished packin' yet. Bennie, you ain't packed one book.

The bell rings.

BENEATHA: That couldn't be the movers . . . it's not hardly two good yet—

Mrs. Miniver: Title character of the 1942 film about a middle-class family's struggle to survive in wartorn Britain.

Beneatha goes into her room. Mama starts for door.

WALTER (*turning, stiffening*): Wait—wait—I'll get it.

He stands and looks at the door.

MAMA: You expecting company, son?

WALTER (*just looking at the door*): Yeah—yeah . . .

Mama looks at Ruth, and they exchange innocent and unfrightened glances.

MAMA (*not understanding*): Well, let them in, son.

BENEATHA (*from her room*): We need some more string.

MAMA: Travis—you run to the hardware and get me some string cord.

Mama goes out and Walter turns and looks at Ruth. Travis goes to a dish for money.

RUTH: Why don't you answer the door, man?

WALTER (*suddenly bounding across the floor to embrace her*): 'Cause sometimes it hard to let the future begin! (*Stooping down in her face.*)

I got wings! You got wings!
All God's children got wings!

He crosses to the door and throws it open. Standing there is a very slight little man in a not-too-prosperous business suit and with haunted frightened eyes and a hat pulled down tightly, brim up, around his forehead. Travis passes between the men and exits. Walter leans deep in the man's face, still in his jubilance.

When I get to heaven gonna put on my wings,
Gonna fly all over God's heaven . . .

The little man just stares at him.

Heaven—

Suddenly he stops and looks past the little man into the empty hallway.

Where's Willy, man?

BOBO: He ain't with me.

WALTER (*not disturbed*): Oh—come on in. You know my wife.

BOBO (*dumbly, taking off his hat*): Yes—h'you, Miss Ruth.

RUTH (*quietly, a mood apart from her husband already, seeing Bobo*): Hello, Bobo.

WALTER: You right on time today . . . Right on time. That's the way! (*He slaps Bobo on his back.*) Sit down . . . lemme hear.

Ruth stands stiffly and quietly in back of them, as though somehow she senses death, her eyes fixed on her husband.

BOBO (*his frightened eyes on the floor, his hat in his hands*): Could I please get a drink of water, before I tell you about it, Walter Lee?

Walter does not take his eyes off the man. Ruth goes blindly to the tap and gets a glass of water and brings it to Bobo.

WALTER: There ain't nothing wrong, is there?

BOBO: Lemme tell you—

WALTER: Man—didn't nothing go wrong?

BOBO: Lemme tell you—Walter Lee. (*Looking at Ruth and talking to her more than to Walter.*) You know how it was. I got to tell you how it was. I mean first I got to tell you how it was all the way . . . I mean about the money I put in, Walter Lee . . .

WALTER (*with taut agitation now*): What about the money you put in?

BOBO: Well—it wasn't much as we told you—me and Willy—(*He stops.*) I'm sorry, Walter. I got a bad feeling about it. I got a real bad feeling about it . . .

WALTER: Man, what you telling me about all this for? . . . Tell me what happened in Springfield . . .

BOBO: Springfield.

RUTH (*like a dead woman*): What was supposed to happen in Springfield?

BOBO (*to her*): This deal that me and Walter went into with Willy—Me and Willy was going to go down to Springfield and spread some money 'round so's we wouldn't have to wait so long for the liquor license . . . That's what we were going to do. Everybody said that was the way you had to do, you understand, Miss Ruth?

WALTER: Man—what happened down there?

BOBO (*a pitiful man, near tears*): I'm trying to tell you, Walter.

WALTER (*screaming at him suddenly*): THEN TELL ME, GODDAMMIT . . . WHAT'S THE MATTER WITH YOU?

BOBO: Man . . . I didn't go to no Springfield, yesterday.

WALTER (*halted, life hanging in the moment*): Why not?

BOBO (*the long way, the hard way to tell*): 'Cause I didn't have no reasons to . . .

WALTER: Man, what are you talking about!

BOBO: I'm talking about the fact that when I got to the train station yesterday morning—eight o'clock like we planned . . . Man—*Willy didn't never show up.*

WALTER: Why . . . where was he . . . where is he?

BOBO: That's what I'm trying to tell you . . . I don't know . . . I waited six hours . . . I called his house . . . and I waited . . . six hours . . . I waited in that train station six hours . . . (*Breaking into tears.*) That was all the extra money I had in the world . . . (*Looking up at Walter with the tears running down his face.*) Man, *Willy is gone.*

WALTER: Gone, what you mean Willy is gone? Gone where? You mean he went by himself. You mean he went off to Springfield by himself—to take care of getting the license—(*Turns and looks anxiously at Ruth.*) You mean maybe he didn't want too many people in on the business down there? (*Looks to Ruth again, as before.*) You know Willy got his own ways. (*Looks back to Bobo.*) Maybe you was late yesterday and he just went on down there without you. Maybe—maybe—he's been callin' you at home tryin' to tell you what happened or something. Maybe—maybe—he just got sick. He's somewhere—he's got to be somewhere. We just got to find him—me and you got to find him. (*Grabs Bobo senselessly by the collar and starts to shake him.*) We got to!

BOBO (*in sudden angry, frightened agony*): What's the matter with you, Walter! *When a cat take off with your money he don't leave you no road maps!*

WALTER (*turning madly, as though he is looking for Willy in the very room*): Willy! . . . Willy . . . don't do it . . . Please don't do it . . . Man, not with that money . . . Man, please, not with that money . . . Oh, God . . . Don't let it be true . . . (*He is wandering around, crying out for Willy and looking for him or perhaps for help from God.*) Man . . . I trusted you . . . Man, I put my life in your hands . . . (*He starts to crumple down on the floor as Ruth just covers her face in horror. Mama opens the door and comes into the room, with Beneatha behind her.*) Man . . . (*He starts to pound the floor with his fists, sobbing wildly.*) THAT MONEY IS MADE OUT OF MY FATHER'S FLESH—

BOBO (*standing over him helplessly*): I'm sorry, Walter . . . (*Only Walter's sobs reply. Bobo puts on his hat.*) I had my life staked on this deal, too . . .

He exits.

MAMA (*to Walter*): Son—(*She goes to him, bends down to him, talks to his bent head.*) Son . . . Is it gone? Son, I gave you sixty-five hundred dollars. Is it gone? All of it? Beneatha's money too?

WALTER (*lifting his head slowly*): Mama . . . I never . . . went to the bank at all . . .

MAMA (*not wanting to believe him*): You mean . . . your sister's school money . . . you used that too . . . Walter? . . .

WALTER: Yessss! All of it . . . It's all gone . . .

There is total silence. Ruth stands with her face covered with her hands; Beneatha leans forlornly against a wall, fingering a piece of red ribbon from the mother's gift. Mama stops and looks at her son without recognition and then, quite without thinking about it, starts to beat him senselessly in the face. Beneatha goes to them and stops it.

BENEATHA: Mama!

Mama stops and looks at both of her children and rises slowly and wanders vaguely, aimlessly away from them.

MAMA: I seen . . . him . . . night after night . . . come in . . . and look at that rug . . . and then look at me . . . the red showing in his eyes . . . the veins moving in his head . . . I seen him grow thin and old before he was forty . . . working and working and working like somebody's old horse . . . killing himself . . . and you—you give it all away in a day—(*She raises her arms to strike him again.*)

BENEATHA: Mama—

MAMA: Oh, God . . . (*She looks up to Him.*) Look down here—and show me the strength.

BENEATHA: Mama—

MAMA (*folding over*): Strength . . .

BENEATHA (*plaintively*): Mama . . .

MAMA: Strength!

Curtain.

ACT III

Time: An hour later.

At curtain, there is a sullen light of gloom in the living room, gray light not unlike that which began the first scene of Act I. At left we can see Walter within his room, alone with himself. He is stretched out on the bed, his shirt out and open, his arms under his head. He does not smoke, he does not cry out, he merely lies there, looking up at the ceiling, much as if he were alone in the world.

In the living room Beneatha sits at the table, still surrounded by the now almost ominous packing crates. She sits looking off. We feel that this is a mood struck perhaps an hour before, and it lingers now, full of the empty sound of profound disappointment. We see on a line from her brother's bedroom the sameness of their attitudes. Presently the bell rings and Beneatha rises without ambition or interest in answering. It is Asagai, smiling broadly, striding into the room with energy and happy expectation and conversation.

ASAGAI: I came over . . . I had some free time. I thought I might help with the packing. Ah, I like the look of packing crates! A household in preparation for a journey! It depresses some people . . . but for me . . . it is another feeling. Something full of the flow of life, do you understand? Movement, progress . . . It makes me think of Africa.

BENEATHA: Africa!

ASAGAI: What kind of a mood is this? Have I told you how deeply you move me?

BENEATHA: He gave away the money, Asagai . . .

ASAGAI: Who gave away what money?

BENEATHA: The insurance money. My brother gave it away.

ASAGAI: Gave it away?

BENEATHA: He made an investment! With a man even Travis wouldn't have trusted with his most worn-out marbles.

ASAGAI: And it's gone?

BENEATHA: Gone!

ASAGAI: I'm very sorry . . . And you, now?

BENEATHA: Me? . . . Me? . . . Me, I'm nothing . . . Me. When I was very small . . . we used to take our sleds out in the wintertime and the only hills we had were the ice-covered stone steps of some houses down the street. And we used to fill them in with snow and make them smooth and slide down them all day . . . and it was very dangerous, you know . . . far too steep . . . and sure enough one day a kid named Rufus came down too fast and hit the sidewalk and we saw his face just split open right there in front of us . . . And I remember standing there looking at his bloody open face thinking that was the end of Rufus. But the ambulance came and they took him to the hospital and they fixed the broken bones and they sewed it all up . . . and the next time I saw Rufus he just had a little line down the middle of his face . . . I never got over that . . .

ASAGAI: What?

BENEATHA: That that was what one person could do for another, fix him up—sew up the problem, make him all right again. That was the most marvelous thing in the world . . . I wanted to do that. I always thought it was the one concrete thing in the world that a human being could do. Fix up the sick, you know—and make them whole again. This was truly being God . . .

ASAGAI: You wanted to be God?

BENEATHA: No—I wanted to cure. It used to be so important to me. I wanted to cure. It used to matter. I used to care. I mean about people and how their bodies hurt . . .

ASAGAI: And you've stopped caring?

BENEATHA: Yes—I think so.

ASAGAI: Why?

BENEATHA (*bitterly*): Because it doesn't seem deep enough, close enough to what ails mankind! It was a child's way of seeing things—or an idealist's.

ASAGAI: Children see things very well sometimes—and idealists even better.

BENEATHA: I know that's what you think. Because you are still where I left off. You with all your talk and dreams about Africa! You still think you can patch up the world. Cure the Great Sore of Colonialism—(*loftily, mocking it*) with the Penicillin of Independence—!

ASAGAI: Yes!

BENEATHA: Independence *and then what?* What about all the crooks and thieves and just plain idiots who will come into power and steal and plunder the same as before—only now they will be black and do it in the name of the new Independence—WHAT ABOUT THEM?!

ASAGAI: That will be the problem for another time. First we must get there.

BENEATHA: And where does it end?

ASAGAI: End? Who even spoke of an end? To life? To living?

BENEATHA: An end to misery! To stupidity! Don't you see there isn't any real progress, Asagai, there is only one large circle that we march in, around and around, each of us with our own little picture in front of us—our own little mirage that we think is the future.

ASAGAI: That is the mistake.

BENEATHA: What?

ASAGAI: What you just said—about the circle. It isn't a circle—it is simply a long line—as in geometry, you know, one that reaches into infinity. And because we cannot see the end—we also cannot see how it changes. And it is very odd but those who see the changes—who dream, who will not give up—are called idealists . . . and those who see only the circle—we call them the "realists"!

BENEATHA: Asagai, while I was sleeping in that bed in there, people went out and took the future right out of my hands! And nobody asked me, nobody consulted me—they just went out and changed my life!

ASAGAI: Was it your money?

BENEATHA: What?

ASAGAI: Was it your money he gave away?

BENEATHA: It belonged to all of us.

ASAGAI: But did you earn it? Would you have had it at all if your father had not died?

BENEATHA: No.

ASAGAI: Then isn't there something wrong in a house—in a world—where all dreams, good or bad, must depend on the death of a man? I never thought to see *you* like this, Alaiyo. You! Your brother made a mistake and you are grateful to him so that now you can give up the ailing human race on account of it! You talk about what good is struggle, what good is anything! Where are we all going and why are we bothering!

BENEATHA: AND YOU CANNOT ANSWER IT!

ASAGAI (*shouting over her*): I LIVE THE ANSWER! (*Pause.*) In my village at home it is the exceptional man who can even read a newspaper . . . or who ever sees a book at all. I will go home and much of what I will have to say will seem strange to the people of my village. But I will teach and work and things will happen, slowly and swiftly. At times it will seem that nothing changes at all . . . and then again the sudden dramatic events which make history leap into the future. And then quiet again. Retrogression even. Guns, murder, revolution. And I even will have moments when I wonder if the quiet was not better than all that death and hatred. But I will look about my village at the illiteracy and disease and ignorance and I will not wonder long. And perhaps . . . perhaps I will be a great man . . . I mean perhaps I will hold on to the substance of truth and find my way always with the right course . . . and perhaps for it I will be butchered in my bed some night by the servants of empire . . .

BENEATHA: *The martyr!*

ASAGAI (*he smiles*): . . . or perhaps I shall live to be a very old man, respected and esteemed in my new nation . . . And perhaps I shall hold office and this is what I'm trying to tell you, Alaiyo: perhaps the things I believe now for my country will be wrong and outmoded, and I will not understand and do terrible things to have things my way or merely to keep my power. Don't you see that there will be young men and women—not British soldiers then, but my own black countrymen—to step out of the shadows some evening and slit my then useless throat? Don't you see they have always been there . . . that they always will be. And that such a thing as my own death will be an advance? They who might kill me even . . . actually replenish all that I was.

BENEATHA: Oh, Asagai, I know all that.

ASAGAI: Good! Then stop moaning and groaning and tell me what you plan to do.

BENEATHA: Do?

ASAGAI: I have a bit of a suggestion.

BENEATHA: What?

ASAGAI (*rather quietly for him*): That when it is all over—that you come home with me—

BENEATHA (*staring at him and crossing away with exasperation*): Oh—Asagai—at this moment you decide to be romantic!

ASAGAI (*quickly understanding the misunderstanding*): My dear, young creature of the New World—I do not mean across the city—I mean across the ocean: home—to Africa.

BENEATHA (*slowly understanding and turning to him with murmured amazement*): To Africa?

ASAGAI: Yes! . . . (*Smiling and lifting his arms playfully.*) Three hundred years later the African Prince rose up out of the seas and swept the maiden back across the middle passage over which her ancestors had come—

BENEATHA (*unable to play*): To—to Nigeria?

ASAGAI: Nigeria. Home. (*Coming to her with genuine romantic flippancy.*) I will show you our mountains and our stars; and give you cool drinks from gourds and teach you the old songs and the ways of our people—and, in time, we will pretend that—(*very softly*)—you have only been away for a day. Say that you'll come—(*He swings her around and takes her full in his arms in a kiss which proceeds to passion.*)

BENEATHA (*pulling away suddenly*): You're getting me all mixed up—

ASAGAI: Why?

BENEATHA: Too many things—too many things have happened today. I must sit down and think. I don't know what I feel about anything right this minute.

She promptly sits down and props her chin on her fist.

ASAGAI (*charmed*): All right, I shall leave you. No—don't get up. (*Touching her, gently, sweetly.*) Just sit awhile and think . . . Never be afraid to sit awhile and think. (*He goes to door and looks at her.*) How often I have looked at you and said, "Ah—so this is what the New World hath finally wrought . . ."

He exits. Beneatha sits on alone. Presently Walter enters from his room and starts to rummage through things, feverishly looking for something. She looks up and turns in her seat.

BENEATHA (*hissingly*): Yes—just look at what the New World hath wrought! . . . Just look! (*She gestures with bitter disgust.*) There he is! *Monsieur le petit bourgeois noir*—himself! There he is—Symbol of a Rising Class! Entrepreneur! Titan of the system! (*Walter ignores her completely and continues frantically and destructively looking for something and hurling things to floor and tearing things out of their place in his search. Beneatha ignores the eccentricity of his actions and goes on with the monologue of insult.*) Did you dream of yachts on Lake Michigan, Brother? Did you see yourself on that Great Day sitting down at the Conference Table, surrounded by all the mighty bald-headed men in America? All halted, waiting, breathless, waiting for your pronouncements on industry? Waiting for you—Chairman of the Board! (*Walter finds what he is looking for—a small piece of white paper—and pushes it in his pocket and puts on his coat and rushes out without ever having looked at her. She shouts after him.*) I look at you and I see the final triumph of stupidity in the world!

The door slams and she returns to just sitting again. Ruth comes quickly out of Mama's room.

RUTH: Who was that?

BENEATHA: Your husband.

RUTH: Where did he go?

BENEATHA: Who knows—maybe he has an appointment at U.S. Steel.

RUTH (*anxiously, with frightened eyes*): You didn't say nothing bad to him, did you?

BENEATHA: Bad? Say anything bad to him? No—I told him he was a sweet boy and full of dreams and everything is strictly peachy keen, as the ofay kids say!

Mama enters from her bedroom. She is lost, vague, trying to catch hold, to make some sense of her former command of the world, but it still eludes her. A sense of waste overwhelms her gait; a measure of apology rides on her shoulders. She goes to her plant, which has remained on the table, looks at it, picks it up and takes it to the window sill and sits it outside, and she stands and looks at it a long moment. Then she closes the window, straightens her body with effort and turns around to her children.

MAMA: Well—ain't it a mess in here, though? (*A false cheerfulness, a beginning of something.*) I guess we all better stop moping around and get some work done. All this unpacking and everything we got to do. (*Ruth raises her head slowly in response to the sense of the line; and Beneatha in similar manner turns very slowly to look at her mother.*) One of you all better call the moving people and tell 'em not to come.

RUTH: Tell 'em not to come?

MAMA: Of course, baby. Ain't no need in 'em coming all the way here and having to go back. They charges for that too. (*She sits down, fingers to her brow, thinking.*) Lord, ever since I was a little girl, I always remembers people saying, "Lena—Lena Eggleston, you aims too high all the time. You needs to slow down and see life a little more like it is. Just slow down some." That's what they always used to say down home—"Lord, that Lena Eggleston is a high-minded thing. She'll get her due one day!"

RUTH: No, Lena . . .

MAMA: Me and Big Walter just didn't never learn right.

RUTH: Lena, no! We gotta go. Bennie—tell her . . .

She rises and crosses to Beneatha with her arms outstretched. Beneatha doesn't respond.

Tell her we can still move . . . the notes ain't but a hundred and twenty-five a month. We got four grown people in this house—we can work . . .

MAMA (*to herself*): Just aimed too high all the time—

RUTH (*turning and going to Mama fast—the words pouring out with urgency and desperation*): Lena—I'll work . . . I'll work twenty hours a day in all the kitchens in Chicago . . . I'll strap my baby on my back if I have to and scrub all the floors in America and wash all the sheets in America if I have to—but we got to MOVE! We got to get OUT OF HERE!!

Mama reaches out absently and pats Ruth's hand.

MAMA: No—I sees things differently now. Been thinking 'bout some of the things we could do to fix this place up some. I seen a second-hand bureau over on Maxwell Street just the other day that could fit right there. (*She points to where the new furniture might go. Ruth wanders away from her.*) Would need some new handles on it and then a little varnish and it look like something brand-new. And—we can put up them new curtains in the kitchen . . . Why this place be looking fine. Cheer us all up so that we forget trouble ever come . . . (*To Ruth.*) And you could get some nice screens to put up in your room round the baby's bassinet . . . (*She looks at both of them pleadingly.*) Sometimes you just got to know when to give up some things . . . and hold on to what you got . . .

Walter enters from the outside, looking spent and leaning against the door, his coat hanging from him.

MAMA: Where you been, son?

WALTER (*breathing hard*): Made a call.

MAMA: To who, son?

WALTER: To The Man. (*He heads for his room.*)

MAMA: What man, baby?

WALTER (*stops in the door*): The Man, Mama. Don't you know who The Man is?

RUTH: Walter Lee?

WALTER: *The Man.* Like the guys in the streets say—The Man. Captain Boss—Mistuh Charley . . . Old Cap'n Please Mr. Bossman . . .

BENEATHA (*suddenly*): Lindner!

WALTER: That's right! That's good. I told him to come right over.

BENEATHA (*fiercely, understanding*): For what? What do you want to see him for!

WALTER (*looking at his sister*): We going to do business with him.

MAMA: What you talking 'bout, son?

WALTER: Talking 'bout life, Mama. You all always telling me to see life like it is. Well—I laid in there on my back today . . . and I figured it out. Life just like it is. Who gets and who don't get. (*He sits down with his coat on and laughs.*) Mama, you know it's all divided up. Life is. Sure enough. Between the takers and the "tooken." (*He laughs.*) I've figured it out finally. (*He looks around at them.*) Yeah. Some of us always getting "tooken." (*He laughs.*) People like Willy Harris, they don't never get "tooken." And you know why the rest of us do? 'Cause we all mixed up. Mixed up bad. We get to looking 'round for the right and the wrong; and we worry about it and cry about it and stay up nights trying to figure out 'bout the wrong and the right of things all the time . . . And all the time, man, them takers is out there operating, just taking and taking. Willy Harris? Shoot—Willy Harris don't even count. He don't even count in the big scheme of things. But I'll say one thing for old Willy Harris . . . he's taught me something. He's taught me to keep my eye on what counts in this world. Yeah—(*Shouting out a little.*) Thanks, Willy!

RUTH: What did you call that man for, Walter Lee?

WALTER: Called him to tell him to come on over to the show. Gonna put on a show for the man. Just what he wants to see. You see, Mama, the man came here today and he told us that them people out there where you want us to move—well they so upset they willing to pay us *not* to move! (*He laughs again.*) And—and oh, Mama—you would of been proud of the way me and Ruth and Bennie acted. We told him to get out . . . Lord have mercy! We told the man to get out! Oh, we was some proud folks this afternoon, yeah. (*He lights a cigarette.*) We were still full of that old-time stuff . . .

RUTH (*coming toward him slowly*): You talking 'bout taking them people's money to keep us from moving in that house?

WALTER: I ain't just talking 'bout it, baby—I'm telling you that's what's going to happen!

BENEATHA: Oh, God! Where is the bottom! Where is the real honest-to-God bottom so he can't go any farther!

WALTER: See—that's the old stuff. You and that boy that was here today. You all want everybody to carry a flag and a spear and sing some marching songs, huh? You wanna spend your life looking into things and trying to find the right and the wrong part, huh? Yeah. You know what's going to happen to that boy someday—he'll find himself sitting in a dungeon, locked in forever—and the takers will have the key! Forget it, baby! There ain't no causes—there ain't nothing but taking in this world, and he who takes most is smartest—and it don't make a damn bit of difference *how*.

MAMA: You making something inside me cry, son. Some awful pain inside me.

WALTER: Don't cry, Mama. Understand. That white man is going to walk in that door able to write checks for more money than we ever had. It's important to him and I'm going to help him . . . I'm going to put on the show, Mama.

MAMA: Son—I come from five generations of people who was slaves and sharecroppers—but ain't nobody in my family never let nobody pay 'em no money that was a way of telling us we wasn't fit to walk the earth. We ain't never been that poor. (*Raising her eyes and looking at him.*) We ain't never been that—dead inside.

BENEATHA: Well—we are dead now. All the talk about dreams and sunlight that goes on in this house. It's all dead now.

WALTER: What's the matter with you all! I didn't make this world! It was give to me this way! Hell, yes, I want me some yachts someday! Yes, I want to hang some real pearls 'round my wife's neck. Ain't she supposed to wear no pearls? Somebody tell me—tell me, who decides which women is suppose to wear pearls in this world. I tell you I am a *man*—and I think my wife should wear some pearls in this world!

This last line hangs a good while and Walter begins to move about the room. The word "Man" has penetrated his consciousness; he mumbles it to himself repeatedly between strange agitated pauses as he moves about.

MAMA: Baby, how you going to feel on the inside?

WALTER: Fine! . . . Going to feel fine . . . a man . . .

MAMA: You won't have nothing left then, Walter Lee.

WALTER (*coming to her*): I'm going to feel fine, Mama. I'm going to look that son-of-a-bitch in the eyes and say—(*he falters*)—and say, "All right, Mr. Lindner—(*he falters even more*)—that's *your* neighborhood out there! You got the right to keep it like you want! You got the right to have it like you want! Just write the check and—the house is yours." And—and I am going to say—(*his voice almost breaks*) "And you—you people just put the money in my hand and you won't have to live next to this bunch of stinking niggers! . . ." (*He straightens up and moves away from his mother, walking around the room.*) And maybe—maybe I'll just get down on my black knees . . . (*He does so; Ruth and Bennie and Mama watch him in frozen horror.*) "Captain, Mistuh, Bossman—(*Groveling and grinning and wringing his hands in profoundly anguished imitation of the slow-witted movie stereotype.*) A-hee-hee-hee! Oh, yassuh boss! Yasssssuh! Great white—(*voice breaking, he forces himself to go on*)—Father, just gi' ussen de money, fo' God's sake, and we's—we's ain't gwine come out deh and dirty up yo' white folks neighborhood . . ." (*He breaks down completely.*) And I'll feel fine! Fine! FINE! (*He gets up and goes into the bedroom.*)

BENEATHA: That is not a man. That is nothing but a toothless rat.

MAMA: Yes—death done come in this here house. (*She is nodding, slowly, reflectively.*) Done come walking in my house on the lips of my children. You what supposed to be my beginning again. You—what supposed to be my harvest. (*To Beneatha.*) You—you mourning your brother?

BENEATHA: He's no brother of mine.

MAMA: What you say?

BENEATHA: I said that that individual in that room is no brother of mine.

MAMA: That's what I thought you said. You feeling like you better than he is today? (*Beneatha does not answer.*) Yes? What you tell him a minute ago? That he wasn't a man? Yes? You give him up for me? You done wrote his epitaph too—like the rest of the world? Well, who give you the privilege?

BENEATHA: Be on my side for once! You saw what he just did, Mama! You saw him—down on his knees. Wasn't it you who taught me to despise any man who would do that? Do what he's going to do?

MAMA: Yes—I taught you that. Me and your daddy. But I thought I taught you something else too . . . I thought I taught you to love him.

BENEATHA: Love him? There is nothing left to love.

MAMA: There is *always* something left to love. And if you ain't learned that, you ain't learned nothing. (*Looking at her.*) Have you cried for that boy today? I don't mean for yourself and for the family 'cause we lost the money. I mean for him: what he been through and what it done to him. Child, when do you think is the time to love somebody the most? When they done good and made things easy for everybody? Well then, you ain't through learning—because that ain't the time at all. It's when he's at his lowest and can't believe in hisself 'cause the world done whipped him so! When you starts measuring somebody, measure him right, child, measure him right. Make sure you done taken into account what hills and valleys he come through before he got to wherever he is.

Travis bursts into the room at the end of the speech, leaving the door open.

TRAVIS: Grandmama—the moving men are downstairs! The truck just pulled up.

MAMA (*turning and looking at him*): Are they, baby? They downstairs?

She sighs and sits. Lindner appears in the doorway. He peers in and knocks lightly, to gain attention, and comes in. All turn to look at him.

LINDNER (*hat and briefcase in hand*): Uh—hello . . .

Ruth crosses mechanically to the bedroom door and opens it and lets it swing open freely and slowly as the lights come up on Walter within, still in his coat, sitting at the far corner of the room. He looks up and out through the room to Lindner.

RUTH: He's here.

A long minute passes and Walter slowly gets up.

LINDNER (*coming to the table with efficiency, putting his briefcase on the table and starting to unfold papers and unscrew fountain pens*): Well, I certainly was glad to hear from you people. (*Walter has begun the trek out of the room, slowly and awkwardly, rather like a small boy, passing the back of his sleeve across his mouth from time to time.*) Life can really be so much simpler than people let it be most of the time. Well—with whom do I negotiate? You, Mrs. Younger, or your son here? (*Mama sits with her hands folded on her lap and her eyes closed as Walter advances. Travis goes closer to Lindner and looks at the papers curiously.*) Just some official papers, sonny.

RUTH: Travis, you go downstairs—

MAMA (*opening her eyes and looking into Walter's*): No. Travis, you stay right here. And you make him understand what you doing, Walter Lee. You teach him good. Like Willy Harris taught you. You show where our five generations done come to. (*Walter looks from her to the boy, who grins at him innocently.*) Go ahead, son—(*She folds her hands and closes her eyes.*) Go ahead.

WALTER (*at last crosses to Lindner, who is reviewing the contract*): Well, Mr. Lindner. (*Beneatha turns away.*) We called you—(*there is a profound, simple groping quality in his speech*)—because, well, me and my family (*He looks around and shifts from one foot to the other.*) Well—we are very plain people . . .

LINDNER: Yes—

WALTER: I mean—I have worked as a chauffeur most of my life—and my wife here, she does domestic work in people's kitchens. So does my mother. I mean—we are plain people . . .

LINDNER: Yes, Mr. Younger—

WALTER (*really like a small boy, looking down at his shoes and then up at the man*): And—uh—well, my father, well, he was a laborer most of his life. . . .

LINDNER (*absolutely confused*): Uh, yes—yes, I understand. (*He turns back to the contract.*)

WALTER (*a beat; staring at him*): And my father—(*With sudden intensity.*) My father almost *beat a man to death* once because this man called him a bad name or something, you know what I mean?

LINDNER (*looking up, frozen*): No, no, I'm afraid I don't—

WALTER (*a beat. The tension hangs; then Walter steps back from it*): Yeah. Well—what I mean is that we come from people who had a lot of *pride*. I mean—we are very proud people. And that's my sister over there and she's going to be a doctor—and we are very proud—

LINDNER: Well—I am sure that is very nice, but—

WALTER: What I am telling you is that we called you over here to tell you that we are very proud and that this—(*Signaling to Travis.*) Travis, come here. (*Travis crosses and Walter draws him before him facing the man.*) This is my son, and he makes the sixth generation of our family in this country. And we have all thought about your offer—

LINDNER: Well, good . . . good—

WALTER: And we have decided to move into our house because my father—my father—he earned it for us brick by brick. (*Mama has her eyes closed and is rocking back and forth as though she were in church, with her head nodding the Amen yes.*) We don't want to make no trouble for nobody or fight no causes, and we will try to be good neighbors. And that's *all* we got to say about that. (*He looks the man absolutely in the eyes.*) We don't want your money. (*He turns and walks away.*)

LINDNER (*looking around at all of them*): I take it then—that you have decided to occupy . . .

BENEATHA: That's what the man said.

LINDNER (*to Mama in her reverie*): Then I would like to appeal to you, Mrs. Younger. You are older and wiser and understand things better I am sure . . .

MAMA: I am afraid you don't understand. My son said we was going to move and there ain't nothing left for me to say. (*Briskly.*) You know how these young folks is nowadays, mister. Can't do a thing with 'em! (*As he opens his mouth, she rises.*) Good-bye.

LINDNER (*folding up his materials*): Well—if you are that final about it . . . there is nothing left for me to say. (*He finishes, almost ignored by the family, who are concentrating on Walter Lee. At the door Lindner halts and looks around.*) I sure hope you people know what you're getting into.

He shakes his head and exits.

RUTH (*looking around and coming to life*): Well, for God's sake—if the moving men are here—LET'S GET THE HELL OUT OF HERE!

MAMA (*into action*): Ain't it the truth! Look at all this here mess. Ruth, put Travis' good jacket on him . . . Walter Lee, fix your tie and tuck your shirt in, you look like somebody's hoodlum! Lord have mercy, where is my plant? (*She flies to get it amid the general bustling of the family, who are deliberately trying to ignore the nobility of the past moment.*) You all start on down . . . Travis child, don't go empty-handed . . . Ruth, where did I put that box with my skillets in it? I want to be in charge of it myself . . .

I'm going to make us the biggest dinner we ever ate tonight . . . Beneatha, what's the matter with them stockings? Pull them things up, girl . . .

The family starts to file out as two moving men appear and begin to carry out the heavier pieces of furniture, bumping into the family as they move about.

BENEATHA: Mama, Asagai asked me to marry him today and go to Africa—

MAMA (*in the middle of her getting-ready activity*): He did? You ain't old enough to marry nobody—(*Seeing the moving men lifting one of her chairs precariously.*) Darling, that ain't no bale of cotton, please handle it so we can sit in it again! I had that chair twenty-five years . . .

The movers sigh with exasperation and go on with their work.

BENEATHA (*girlishly and unreasonably trying to pursue the conversation*): To go to Africa, Mama—be a doctor in Africa . . .

MAMA (*distracted*): Yes, baby—

WALTER: *Africa!* What he want you to go to Africa for?

BENEATHA: To practice there . . .

WALTER: Girl, if you don't get all them silly ideas out your head! You better marry yourself a man with some loot . . .

BENEATHA (*angrily, precisely as in the first scene of the play*): What have you got to do with who I marry!

WALTER: Plenty. Now I think George Murchison—

BENEATHA: *George Murchison!* I wouldn't marry him if he was Adam and I was Eve!

Walter and Beneatha go out yelling at each other vigorously and the anger is loud and real till their voices diminish. Ruth stands at the door and turns to Mama and smiles knowingly.

MAMA (*fixing her hat at last*): Yeah—they something all right, my children . . .

RUTH: Yeah—they're something. Let's go, Lena.

MAMA (*stalling, starting to look around at the house*): Yes—I'm coming. Ruth—

RUTH: Yes?

MAMA (*quietly, woman to woman*): He finally come into his manhood today, didn't he? Kind of like a rainbow after the rain . . .

RUTH (*biting her lip lest her own pride explode in front of Mama*): Yes, Lena.

Walter's voice calls for them raucously.

WALTER (*off stage*): Y'all come on! These people charges by the hour, you know!

MAMA (*waving Ruth out vaguely*): All right, honey—go on down. I be down directly.

Ruth hesitates, then exits. Mama stands, at last alone in the living room, her plant on the table before her as the lights start to come down. She looks around at all the walls and ceilings and suddenly, despite herself, while the children call below, a great heaving thing rises in her and she puts her fist to her mouth to stifle it, takes a final desperate look, pulls her coat about her, pats her hat, and goes out. The lights dim down. The door opens and she comes back in, grabs her plant, and goes out for the last time.

Curtain.

COMMENTARIES

LORRAINE HANSBERRY

Lorraine Hansberry reflected on the relationship between Walter Lee Younger in *A Raisin in the Sun* and Willy Loman in *Death of a Salesman* in an article published in *The Village Voice Reader* in 1962.

An Author's Reflections: Willy Loman, Walter Younger, and He Who Must Live 1962

> A man can't go out the way he came in . . . Ben, that funeral will be massive!
>
> –WILLY LOMAN, 1946

> We have all thought about your offer and we have decided to move into our house.
>
> –WALTER LEE YOUNGER, 1958

Some of the acute partisanship revolving around *A Raisin in the Sun* is amusing. Those who announce that they find the piece less than fine are regarded in some quarters with dramatic hostility, as though such admission automatically implied the meanest of racist reservations. On the other hand, the ultra-sophisticates have hardly acquitted themselves less ludicrously, gazing coolly down their noses at those who are moved by the play, and going on at length about "melodrama" and/or "soap opera" as if these were not completely definable terms which cannot simply be tacked onto any play and all plays we do not like.

Personally, I find no pain whatever—at least of the traditional ego type—in saying that *Raisin* is a play which contains dramaturgical incompletions. Fine plays tend to utilize one big fat character who runs right through the middle of the structure, by action or implication, with whom we rise or fall. A central character as such is certainly lacking from *Raisin*. I should be delighted to pretend that it was *inventiveness*, as some suggest for me, but it is, also, craft inadequacy and creative indecision. The result is that neither Walter Lee nor Mama Younger loom large enough to monumentally command the play. I consider it an enormous dramatic fault if no one else does. (Nor am I less critical of the production which, by and large, performance and direction alike, is splendid. Yet I should have preferred that the second-act curtain, for instance, be performed with quiet assertion rather than the apparently popular declamatory opulence which prevails.)

All in all, however, I believe that, for the most part, the play has been magnificently understood. In some cases it was not only thematically absorbed but attention was actually paid to the tender treacherousness of its craft-imposed "simplicity." Some, it is true, quite missed that part of the overt intent and went on to harangue the bones of the play with rather useless observations of the terribly clear fact that they are old bones indeed. More meaningful discussions tended to delve into the flesh which hangs from those bones and its implications in mid-century American drama and life.

In that connection it is interesting to note that while the names of Chekhov, O'Casey, and the early Odets were introduced for comparative purposes in some of the reviews, almost no one—with the exception of Gerald Weales in *Commentary*—discovered a simple line of descent between Walter Lee Younger and the last great hero in American drama to also *accept* the values of his culture, Willy Loman. I am sure that the already mentioned primary fault of the play must account in part for this. The family so overwhelms the play that Walter Lee necessarily fails as the true symbol he should be, even though *his* ambitions, *his* frustrations, and *his* decisions are those which decisively drive the play on. But however recognizable he proves to be, he fails to dominate our imagination and finally emerges as a reasonably interesting study, but not, like Arthur Miller's great character—and like Hamlet, of course—a summation of an immense (though not crucial) portion of his culture.

Then too, in fairness to the author and to Sidney Poitier's basically brilliant portrayal of Walter Lee, we must not completely omit reference to some of the prior attitudes which were brought into the theatre from the world outside. For in the minds of many, Walter remains, despite the play, despite performance, what American radical traditions *wish* him to be: an exotic. Some writers have been astonishingly incapable of discussing his purely *class* aspirations and have persistently confounded them with what they consider to be an exotic being's longing to "wheel and deal" in what they further consider to be (and what Walter never can) "the white man's world." Very few people today must consider the ownership of a liquor store as an expression of extraordinary affluence, and yet, as joined to a dream of Walter Younger, it takes on, for some, aspects of the fantastic. We have grown accustomed to the dynamics of "Negro" personality as expressed by white authors. Thus, de Emperor, de Lawd, and, of course, Porgy still haunt our frame of reference when a new character emerges. We have become romantically jealous of the great image of a prototype whom we believe is summarized by the wishfulness of a self-assumed opposite. Presumably there is a quality in human beings that makes us *wish* that we *were* capable of primitive contentments; the *universality* of ambition and its anguish can escape us only if we construct elaborate legends about the rudimentary simplicity of *other* men.

America, for this reason, long ago fell in love with the image of the simple, lovable, and glandular "Negro." We all know that Catfish Row was never intended to slander anyone; it was intended as a mental haven for readers and audiences who could bask in the unleashed passions of those "lucky ones" for whom abandonment was apparently permissible. In an almost paradoxical fashion, it disturbs the soul of man to truly understand what he invariably senses: that *nobody* really finds oppression and/or poverty tolerable. If we ever destroy the image of the black people who supposedly do find those things tolerable in America, then that much-touted "guilt" which allegedly haunts most middle-class white Americans with regard to the Negro question would really become unendurable. It would also mean the death of a dubious literary tradition, but it would undoubtedly and more significantly help toward the more rapid transformation of the status of a people who have never found their imposed misery very charming.

My colleagues and I were reduced to mirth and tears by that gentleman writing his review of our play in a Connecticut paper who remarked of his pleasure at seeing how "our dusky brethren" could "come up with a song and hum their troubles away." It did not disturb the writer in the least that there is no such implication in the entire three acts. He did not need it in the play; he had it in his head.

For all these reasons, then, I imagine that the ordinary impulse to compare Willy Loman and Walter Younger was remote. Walter Lee Younger jumped out at us from a play about a largely unknown world. We knew who Willy Loman was instantaneously; we recognized his milieu. We also knew at once that he represented that curious paradox in what the *English* character in that *English* play could call, though dismally, "The American Age." Willy Loman was a product of a nation of great military strength, indescribable material wealth, and incredible mastery of the physical realm, which nonetheless was unable, in 1946, to produce a *typical* hero who was capable of an affirmative view of life.

I believe it is a testament to Miller's brilliance that it is hardly a misstatement of the case, as some preferred to believe. Something has indeed gone wrong with at least part of the American dream, and Willy Loman is the victim of the detour. Willy had to be overwhelmed on the stage as, in fact, his prototypes are in everyday life. Coming out of his section of our great sprawling middle class, preoccupied with its own restlessness and displaying its obsession for the possession of trivia, Willy was indeed trapped. His predicament in a New World where there just aren't any more forests to clear or virgin railroads to lay or native American empires to first steal and then build upon left him with nothing but some left-over values which had forgotten how to prize industriousness over cunning, usefulness over mere acquisition, and, above all, humanism over "success." The potency of the great tale of a salesman's death was in our familiar recognition of his entrapment which, suicide or no, is *deathly*.

What then of this new figure who appears in American drama in 1958; from what source is he drawn so that, upon inspection, and despite class differences, so much of his encirclement must still remind us of that of Willy Loman? Why, finally, is it possible that when his third-act will is brought to bear, *his* typicality is capable of a choice which *affirms* life? After all, Walter Younger is an American more than he is anything else. His ordeal, give or take his personal expression of it, is not extraordinary but intensely familiar like Willy's. The two of them have virtually no values which have not come out of their culture, and to a significant point, no view of the possible solutions to their problems which do not also come out of the self-same culture. Walter can find no peace with that part of society which seems to permit him entry and no entry into that which has willfully excluded him. He shares with Willy Loman the acute awareness that *something* is obstructing some abstract progress that he feels he *should* be making; that *something* is in the way of his ascendancy. It does not occur to either of them to question the nature of this desired "ascendancy." Walter accepts, he believes in the "world" as it has been presented to him. When we first meet him, he does not wish to alter *it*; merely to change *his* position in it. His mentors and his associates all take the view that the institutions which frustrate him are somehow impeccable, or, at best, "unfortunate." "Things being as they are," he must look to *himself* as the only source of any rewards he may expect. Within himself, he is encouraged to believe, are the only seeds of defeat or victory within the universe. And Walter believes this and when opportunity, haphazard and rooted in death, prevails, he acts.

But the obstacles which are introduced are gigantic; the weight of the loss of the money is in fact the weight of death. In Walter Lee Younger's life, somebody *has* to die for ten thousand bucks to pile up—if then. Elsewhere in the world, in the face of catastrophe, he might be tempted to don the saffron robes of acceptance and sit on a mountain top all day contemplating the divine justice of his misery. Or, history being what it is turning out to be, he might wander down to his first Communist Party meeting. But here in the dynamic and confusing post-war years on the South Side of Chicago, his choices of action are equal to those gestures only in symbolic terms. The American ghetto hero may give up and contemplate his misery in rose-colored bars to the melodies of hypnotic saxophones, but revolution seems alien to him in his circumstances (America), and it is easier to dream of personal wealth than of a communal state wherein universal dignity is supposed to be a corollary. Yet his position in time and space does allow for one other alternative: he may take his place on any one of a number of frontiers of challenge. Challenges (such as helping to break down restricted neighborhoods) which are admittedly limited because they most certainly do not threaten the basic social order.

But why is even this final choice possible, considering the ever-present (and ever-so-popular) vogue of despair? Well, that is where Walter departs from Willy Loman; there is a second pulse in his still dual culture. His people have had "somewhere" they have been trying to get for so long that more sophisticated confusions do not yet bind them. *Thus the weight and power of their current social temperament intrudes and affects him, and it is, at the moment, at least, gloriously and rigidly affirmative.* In the course of *their* brutally difficult ascent, they have dismissed the ostrich and still sing, *"Went to the rock to hide my face, but the rock cried out: 'No hidin' place down here!'"* Walter is, despite his lack of consciousness of it, inextricably as much wedded to his special mass as Willy was to his, and the moods of each are able to decisively determine the dramatic typicality. Furthermore, the very nature of the situation of American Negroes can force their representative hero to recognize that for his *true* ascendancy he must ultimately be at cross-purposes with at least certain of his culture's values. It is to the pathos of Willy Loman that his section of American life seems to have momentarily lost that urgency; that he cannot, like Walter, draw on the strength of an incredible people who, historically, have simply refused to give up.

In other words, the symbolism of moving into the new house is quite as small as it seems and quite as significant. For if there are no waving flags and marching songs at the barricades as Walter marches out with his little battalion, it is not because the battle lacks nobility. On the contrary, he has picked up in his way, still imperfect and wobbly in his small view of human destiny, what I believe Arthur Miller once called "the golden thread of history." He becomes, in spite of those who are too intrigued with despair and hatred of man to see it, King Oedipus refusing to tear out his eyes, but attacking the Oracle instead. He is that last Jewish patriot manning his rifle in the burning ghetto at Warsaw; he is that young girl who swam into sharks to save a friend a few weeks ago; he is Anne Frank,° still believing in people; he is the nine small heroes of Little Rock;° he is Michelangelo creating David and Beethoven bursting forth with the Ninth Symphony. He is all those things because he has finally reached out in his tiny moment and caught that sweet essence which is human dignity, and it shines like the old star-touched dream that it is in his eyes. We see, in the moment, I think, what becomes, and not for Negroes alone, but for Willy and all of us, entirely an American responsibility.

Out in the darkness where we watch, most of us are not afraid to cry.

•

Lorraine Hansberry wrote about her "Shakespearean Experience" in high school in *To Be Young, Gifted and Black*, which was published four years after her death in 1965. In this piece, Hansberry began to shape her memoir of her high school English teacher nicknamed "Pale Hecate" as an essay, but within a few paragraphs she was so deeply involved in her memories of adolescence that she dramatized them in dialogue form as a series of imaginary exchanges between the teacher and her students.

My Shakespearean Experience 1969

1

My High School Yearbook bears the dedication: "Englewood High trains for citizenship in a world of many different peoples. Who could better appreciate this wonderful country than our forefathers who traveled hundreds of miles from every known nation, seeking a land of freedom from discrimination of race, color, or creed." And in illustration, there is this:

> *The Great Branches of Man at Englewood High:* in front, Mangolia Ali of East Indian Mohammedan descent; second couple, Nancy Diagre and Harold Bradley, Negroid; middle couple, Rosalind Sherr and William

---

Anne Frank: A German Jewish teenager (1929–1945) who, during World War II, hid from the Nazis with her family for twenty-five months in an annex of rooms in Amsterdam. She recorded the experience in her diary which was published in 1947, two years after her death from typhus in a Nazi concentration camp.

nine small heroes of Little Rock: Following the U.S. Supreme Court's ruling that racial segregation in U.S. schools was unconstitutional, nine black teenagers defied white mobs and a hostile governor and marched into Central High School in Little Rock, Arkansas, on September 25, 1957. They were supported by the federal government.

Krugman, Jewish religion, not a racial stock; next, Eleanor Trester and Theodore Flood, Caucasoid; extreme right, Lois Lee and Barbara Nomura, Mongoloid; rear, left, Mr. Thompson, principal.

2

I was reminded of Englewood by a questionnaire which came from *Show* magazine the other day. . . .

THE SHAKESPEAREAN EXPERIENCE
SHOW POLL #5, February 1964

Some Questions Answered by: Robert Bolt, Jean Cocteau, T. S. Eliot, Tyrone Guthrie, Lorraine Hansberry, Joan Littlewood, Harold Pinter, Alain Robbe-Grillet, Igor Stravinsky, Harry S Truman

QUESTION: *What was your first contact with Shakespeare?*

High School. English literature classwork. We had to read and memorize speeches from *Macbeth* and *Julius Caesar* all under the auspices of a strange and bewigged teacher who we, after this induction, naturally and cruelly christened "Pale Hecate"—God rest her gentle, enraptured, and igniting soul!

Pale Hecate enters, ruler in hand, and takes her place in the classroom. She surveys the class. They come to attention as her eye falls on each in turn.

PALE HECATE: Y'do not read, nor speak, nor write the English language! I suspect that y'do not even *think* in it! God only knows in what language y'do think, or if you think at all. 'Tis true the *English* have done little enough with the tongue, but being the English I expect it was the best they could do. (*They giggle.*) In any case, I'll have it learned properly before a living one of y'll pass out of this class. That I will! (*Waving a composition book and indicating the grade marked in red at the top.*) As for *you*, Miss—as for you, indeed, surely you will recognize the third letter of the alphabet when y'have seen it?

STUDENT: "C."

PALE HECATE: Aye, a "C" it 'tis! You're a bright and clever one now after all, aren't y'lass? (*The class snickers.*) And now, my brilliance, would you also be informing us as to what a grade signifies when it is thus put upon the page?

STUDENT: Average.

PALE HECATE: "Average." Yes, yes—and what else in your case, my iridescence? Well then, I'll be tellin' you in fine order. It stands for "cheat," my luminous one! (*The class sobers.*) For them that will do *half* when *all* is called for; for them that will slip and slide through life at the edge of their minds, never once pushing into the interior to see what wonders are hiding there—content to drift along on whatever gets them by, *cheating* themselves, *cheating* the world, *cheating* Nature! That is what the "C" means, my dear child—(*she smiles*)—my pet (*they giggle; in rapid order she raps each on the head with her ruler*)—my laziest *Queen of the Ethiopes!*

She exits or dims out.

QUESTION: *Which is your favorite Shakespeare play and why?*

Favorite? It is like choosing the "superiority" of autumn days; mingling titles permits a reply: *Othello* and *Hamlet*. Why? There is a sweetness in the former that lingers long after the tragedy is done. A kind of possibility that we suspect in man wherein even its flaw is a tribute. The latter because there remains a depth in the Prince that, as we all know, constantly re-engages as we mature. And it does seem that the wit remains the brightest and most instructive in all dramatic literature.

QUESTION: *What is the most important result of your familiarity with Shakespeare? What has he given you?*

Comfort and agitation so bound together that they are inseparable. Man, as set down in the plays, is large. Enormous. Capable of anything at all. And yet fragile, too, this view of the human spirit; one feels it ought to be respected and protected and loved rather fiercely.

Rollicking times, Shakespeare has given me. I love to laugh and his humor is that of everyday; of every man's foible at no man's expense. Language. At thirteen a difficult and alien tedium, those Elizabethan cadences; but soon a balm, a thrilling source of contact with life.

LYNN NOTTAGE

Lynn Nottage (b. 1964) was born and raised in Brooklyn and attended the High School of Music and Art in Harlem. After graduation from Brown University, she studied at the Yale School of Drama. She then worked at Amnesty International as a press officer until her plays began to be produced on the stage.

POOF! is an early play that was premiered at Actors Theatre of Louisville, Kentucky, in 1993. It was followed by *Por'knockers* (1994), *Crumbs from the Table of Joy* (1998), *Mud, River, Stone* (1999), and *Side Streets* (1999), a film produced by Merchant Ivory and directed by Tony Gerber, for which Nottage coauthored the script. She spent more than a year doing research in the New York Public Library for her play *Intimate Apparel* (2003), exploring the subjects of race and class in a story set in 1905 about a seamstress who sews lingerie for a varied clientele of New Yorkers including prostitutes and society ladies. In the process of writing this play, Nottage discovered that some of the historical material she had incorporated was unnecessary. She told an interviewer that her play existed "as a literary form until the first moment you sit down in a rehearsal room and allow a group of actors to read it. Then it becomes a dramatic form. . . . [T]here are things that work beautifully on a page as literature but have no dramatic life." Nottage was the recipient of a Guggenheim

Fellowship in 2005 and a MacArthur Grant in 2007. In 2009 her play *Ruined* won a Pulitzer Prize.

As a playwright, Nottage believes that the voices of African American women are very important because they are part of the American voice:

> But you would not know that by looking at TV or films. You would think that we do not exist. And part of my mission as a writer is to say, "I do exist. My mother existed, and my grandmother existed, and my great-grandmother existed, and they had stories that are rich, complicated, funny, that are beautiful and essential." And their stories have become the myth of America. There are folk tales brought over from Africa that find, many years later, they are on television as Bugs Bunny. I want people to know that my story, that of the African-American woman, is also the American story.

CONNECTION Susan Glaspell, *Trifles*, page 1410.

POOF! 1993

CHARACTERS

SAMUEL, Loureen's husband
LOUREEN, a demure housewife, early thirties
FLORENCE, Loureen's best friend, early thirties

TIME: *The present*

PLACE: *Kitchen*

A NOTE: *Nearly half the women on death row in the United States were convicted of killing abusive husbands. Spontaneous combustion is not recognized as a capital crime.*

Darkness.

SAMUEL (*In the darkness*): WHEN I COUNT TO TEN I DON' WANT TO SEE YA! I DON' WANT TO HEAR YA! ONE, TWO, THREE, FOUR—

LOUREEN (*In the darkness*): DAMN YOU TO HELL, SAMUEL!

A bright flash.

Lights rise. A huge pile of smoking ashes rests in the middle of the kitchen. Loureen, a demure housewife in her early thirties, stares down at the ashes incredulously. She bends and lifts a pair of spectacles from the remains. She ever so slowly backs away.

Samuel? Uh! (*Places the spectacles on the kitchen table*) Uh! . . . Samuel? (*Looks around*) Don't fool with me now. I'm not in the mood. (*Whispers*) Samuel? I didn't mean it really. I'll be good if you come back . . . Come on now, dinner's waiting. (*Chuckles, then stops abruptly*) Now stop your foolishness . . . And let's sit down. (*Examines the spectacles*) Uh! (*Softly*) Don't be cross with me. Sure I forgot to pick up your shirt for tomorrow. I can wash another, I'll do it right now. Right now! Sam? . . . (*Cautiously*) You hear me! (*Awaits a response*) Maybe I didn't ever intend to wash your shirt. (*Pulls back as though about to receive a blow; a moment*) Uh! (*Sits down and dials the telephone*) Florence, honey, could you come on down for a moment. There's been a . . . little . . . accident . . . Quickly please. Uh!

Loureen hangs up the phone. She gets a broom and a dust pan. She hesitantly approaches the pile of ashes. She gets down on her hands and knees and takes a closer look. A fatuous grin spreads across her face. She is startled by a sudden knock on the door. She slowly walks across the room like a possessed child. Loureen lets in Florence, her best friend and upstairs neighbor. Florence, also a housewife in her early thirties, wears a floral housecoat and a pair of oversized slippers. Without acknowledgment Loureen proceeds to saunter back across the room.

FLORENCE: HEY!

LOUREEN (*Pointing at the ashes*): Uh! . . . (*She struggles to formulate words, which press at the inside of her mouth, not quite realized*) Uh! . . .

FLORENCE: You all right? What happened? (*Sniffs the air*) Smells like you burned something? (*Stares at the huge pile of ashes*) What the devil is that?

LOUREEN (*Hushed*): Samuel . . . It's Samuel, I think.

FLORENCE: What's he done now?

LOUREEN: It's him. It's him. (*Nods her head repeatedly*)

FLORENCE: Chile, what's wrong with you? Did he finally drive you out your mind? I knew something was going to happen sooner or later.

LOUREEN: Dial 911, Florence!

FLORENCE: Why? You're scaring me!

LOUREEN: Dial 911!

Florence picks up the telephone and quickly dials.

I think I killed him.

Florence hangs up the telephone.

FLORENCE: What?

LOUREEN (*Whimpers*): I killed him! I killed Samuel!

FLORENCE: Come again? . . . He's dead dead?

Loureen wrings her hands and nods her head twice, mouthing "dead dead." Florence backs away.

No, stop it, I don't have time for this. I'm going back upstairs. You know how Samuel hates to find me here when he gets home. You're not going to get me this time. (*Louder*) Y'all can have your little joke, I'm not part of it! (*A moment. She takes a hard look into Loureen's eyes; she squints*) Did you really do it this time?

LOUREEN (*Hushed*): I don't know how or why it happened, it just did.

FLORENCE: Why are you whispering?

LOUREEN: I don't want to talk too loud—something else is liable to disappear.

FLORENCE: Where's his body?

LOUREEN (*Points to the pile of ashes*): There! . . .

FLORENCE: You burned him?

LOUREEN: I DON'T KNOW! (*Covers her mouth as if to muffle her words; hushed*) I think so.

FLORENCE: Either you did or you didn't, what you mean you don't know? We're talking murder, Loureen, not oven settings.

LOUREEN: You think I'm playing?

FLORENCE: How many times have I heard you talk about being rid of him. How many times have we sat at this very table and laughed about the many ways we could do it and how many times have you done it? None.

LOUREEN (*Lifting the spectacles*): A pair of cheap spectacles, that's all that's left. And you know how much I hate these. You ever seen him without them, no! . . . He counted to four and disappeared. I swear to God!

FLORENCE: Don't bring the Lord into this just yet! Sit down now . . . What you got to sip on?

LOUREEN: I don't know whether to have a stiff shot of scotch or a glass of champagne.

Florence takes a bottle of sherry out of the cupboard and pours them each a glass. Loureen downs hers, then holds out her glass for more.

He was . . .

FLORENCE: Take your time.

LOUREEN: Standing there.

FLORENCE: And?

LOUREEN: He exploded.

FLORENCE: Did that muthafucka hit you again?

LOUREEN: No . . . he exploded. Boom! Right in front of me. He was shouting like he does, being all colored, then he raised up that big crusty hand to hit me, and poof, he was gone . . . I barely got words out and I'm looking down at a pile of ash.

Florence belts back her sherry. She wipes her forehead and pours them both another.

FLORENCE: Chile, I'll give you this, in terms of color you've matched my husband Edgar, the story king. He came in at six Sunday morning, talking about he'd hit someone with his car, and had spent all night trying to outrun the police. I felt sorry for him. It turns out he was playing poker with his paycheck no less. You don't want to know how I found out . . . But I did.

LOUREEN: You think I'm lying?

FLORENCE: I certainly hope so, Loureen. For your sake and my heart's.

LOUREEN: Samuel always said if I raised my voice something horrible would happen. And it did. I'm a witch . . . the devil spawn!

FLORENCE: You've been watching too much television.

LOUREEN: Never seen anything like this on television. Wish I had, then I'd know what to do . . . There's no question, I'm a witch. (*Looks at her hands with disgust*)

FLORENCE: Chile, don't tell me you've been messing with them mojo women again? What did I tell ya.

Loureen, agitated, stands and sits back down.

LOUREEN: He's not coming back. Oh no, how could he? It would be a miracle! Two in one day . . . I could be canonized. Worse yet, he could be . . . All that needs to happen now is for my palms to bleed and I'll be eternally remembered as Saint Loureen, the patron of battered wives. Women from across the country will make pilgrimages to me, laying pies and pot roast at my feet and asking the good saint to make their husbands turn to dust. How often does a man like Samuel get damned to hell, and go?

She breaks down. Florence moves to console her friend, then realizes that Loureen is actually laughing hysterically.

FLORENCE: You smoking crack?

LOUREEN: Do I look like I am?

FLORENCE: Hell, I've seen old biddies creeping out of crack houses, talking about they were doing church work.

LOUREEN: Florence, please be helpful, I'm very close to the edge! . . . I don't know what to do next! Do I sweep him up? Do I call the police? Do I . . .

The phone rings.

Oh God.

FLORENCE: You gonna let it ring?

Loureen reaches for the telephone slowly.

LOUREEN: NO! (*Holds the receiver without picking it up, paralyzed*) What if it's his mother? . . . She knows!

The phone continues to ring. They sit until it stops. They both breathe a sigh of relief.

I should be mourning, I should be praying, I should be thinking of the burial, but all that keeps popping into my mind is what will I wear on television when I share my horrible and wonderful story with a studio audience . . . (*Whimpers*) He's made me a killer, Florence, and you remember what a gentle child I was. (*Whispers*) I'm a killer, I'm a killer, I'm a killer.

FLORENCE: I wouldn't throw that word about too lightly even in jest. Talk like that gets around.

LOUREEN: You think they'll lock me up? A few misplaced words and I'll probably get the death penalty, isn't that what they do with women like me, murderesses?

FLORENCE: Folks have done time for less.

LOUREEN: Thank you, just what I needed to hear!

FLORENCE: What did you expect, that I was going to throw up my arms and congratulate you? Why'd you have to go and lose your mind at this time of day, while I got a pot of rice on the stove and Edgar's about to walk in the door and wonder where his goddamn food is. (*Losing her cool*) And he's going to start in on me about all the nothing I've been doing during the day and why I can't work and then he'll mention how clean you keep your home. And I don't know how I'm going to look him in the eye without . . .

LOUREEN: I'm sorry, Florence. Really. It's out of my hands now.

She takes Florence's hand and squeezes it.

FLORENCE (*Regaining her composure*): You swear on your right tit?

LOUREEN (*Clutching both breasts*): I swear on both of them!

FLORENCE: Both your breasts, Loureen! You know what will happen if you're lying. (*Loureen nods; hushed*) Both your breasts Loureen?

LOUREEN: Yeah!

FLORENCE (*Examines the pile of ashes, then shakes her head*): Oh sweet, sweet Jesus. He must have done something truly terrible.

LOUREEN: No more than usual. I just couldn't take being hit one more time.

FLORENCE: You've taken a thousand blows from that man, couldn't you've turned the cheek and waited? I'd have helped you pack. Like we talked about.

A moment.

LOUREEN: Uh! . . . I could blow on him and he'd disappear across the linoleum. (*Snaps her fingers*) Just like that. Should I be feeling remorse or regret or some other "R" word? I'm strangely jubilant, like on prom night when Samuel and I first made love. That's the feeling! (*The women lock eyes*) Uh!

FLORENCE: Is it . . .

LOUREEN: Like a ton of bricks been lifted from my shoulders, yeah.

FLORENCE: Really?

LOUREEN: Yeah!

Florence walks to the other side of the room.

FLORENCE: You bitch!

LOUREEN: What?

FLORENCE: We made a pact.

LOUREEN: I know.

FLORENCE: You've broken it . . . We agreed that when things got real bad for both of us we'd . . . you know . . . together . . . Do I have to go back upstairs to that? . . . What next?

LOUREEN: I thought you'd tell me! . . . I don't know!

FLORENCE: I don't know!

LOUREEN: I don't know!

Florence begins to walk around the room, nervously touching objects. Loureen sits, wringing her hands and mumbling softly to herself.

FLORENCE: Now you got me, Loureen, I'm truly at a loss for words.

LOUREEN: Everybody always told me, "Keep your place, Loureen." My place, the silent spot on the couch with a wine cooler in my hand and a pleasant smile that warmed the heart. All this time I didn't know why he was so afraid for me to say anything, to speak up. Poof! . . . I've never been by myself, except for them two weeks when he won the office pool and went to Reno with his cousin Mitchell. He wouldn't tell me where he was going until I got that postcard with the cowboy smoking a hundred cigarettes . . . Didn't Sonny Larkin look good last week at Caroline's? He looked good, didn't he . . .

Florence nods. She nervously picks up Samuel's jacket, which is hanging on the back of the chair. She clutches it unconsciously.

NO! No! Don't wrinkle that, that's his favorite jacket. He'll kill me. Put it back!

Florence returns the jacket to its perch. Loureen begins to quiver.

I'm sorry. (*She grabs the jacket and wrinkles it up*) There! (*She then digs into the coat pockets and pulls out his wallet and a movie stub*) Look at that, he said he didn't go to the movies last night. Working late. (*Frantically thumbs through his wallet*) Picture of his motorcycle, Social Security card, driver's license, and look at that from our wedding. (*Smiling*) I looked good, didn't I? (*She puts the pictures back in the wallet and holds the jacket up to her face*) There were some good things. (*She then sweeps her hand over the jacket to remove the wrinkles, and folds it ever so carefully, and finally throws it in the garbage*) And out of my mouth those words made him disappear. All these years and just words, Florence. That's all they were.

FLORENCE: I'm afraid I won't ever get those words out. I'll start resenting you, honey. I'm afraid won't anything change for me.

LOUREEN: I been to that place.

FLORENCE: Yeah? But now I wish I could relax these old lines (*Touches her forehead*) for a minute maybe. Edgar has never done me the way Samuel did you, but he sure did take the better part of my life.

LOUREEN: Not yet, Florence.

FLORENCE (*Nods*): I have the children to think of . . . right?

LOUREEN: You can think up a hundred things before . . .

FLORENCE: Then come upstairs with me . . . we'll wait together for Edgar and then you can spit out your words and . . .

LOUREEN: I can't do that.

FLORENCE: Yes you can. Come on now.

Loureen shakes her head no.

Well, I guess my mornings are not going to be any different.

LOUREEN: If you can say for certain, then I guess they won't be. I couldn't say that.

FLORENCE: But you got a broom and a dust pan, you don't need anything more than that . . . He was a bastard and nobody will care that he's gone.

LOUREEN: Phone's gonna start ringing soon, people are gonna start asking soon, and they'll care.

FLORENCE: What's your crime? Speaking your mind?

LOUREEN: Maybe I should mail him to his mother. I owe her that. I feel bad for her, she didn't understand how it was. I can't just throw him away and pretend like it didn't happen. Can I?

FLORENCE: I didn't see anything but a pile of ash. As far as I know you got a little careless and burned a chicken.

LOUREEN: He was always threatening not to come back.

FLORENCE: I heard him.

LOUREEN: It would've been me eventually.

FLORENCE: Yes.

LOUREEN: I should call the police, or someone.

FLORENCE: Why? What are you gonna tell them? About all those times they refused to help, about all those nights you slept in my bed 'cause you were afraid to stay down here? About the time he nearly took out your eye 'cause you flipped the television channel?

LOUREEN: No.

FLORENCE: You've got it, girl!

LOUREEN: Good-bye to the fatty meats and the salty food. Good-bye to the bourbon and the bologna sandwiches. Good-bye to the smell of his feet, his breath and his bowel movements . . . (*A moment. She closes her eyes and, reliving a horrible memory, she shudders*) Good-bye. (*Walks over to the pile of ashes*) Samuel? . . . Just checking.

FLORENCE: Good-bye Samuel.

They both smile.

LOUREEN: I'll let the police know that he's missing tomorrow . . .

FLORENCE: Why not the next day?

LOUREEN: Chicken's warming in the oven, you're welcome to stay.

FLORENCE: Chile, I got a pot of rice on the stove, kids are probably acting out . . . and Edgar, well . . . Listen, I'll stop in tomorrow.

LOUREEN: For dinner?

FLORENCE: Edgar wouldn't stand for that. Cards maybe.

LOUREEN: Cards.

The women hug for a long moment. Florence exits. Loureen stands over the ashes for a few moments contemplating what to do. She finally decides to sweep them under the carpet, and then proceeds to set the table and sit down to eat her dinner.

END OF PLAY

COMMENTARY

LYNN NOTTAGE

Lynn Nottage was interviewed for the Web site *American Shorts* about how she became a playwright.

On Writing *POOF!*

Interviewer: How did you begin writing?

Nottage: I think a lot about the question of why I write. I think for me the journey begins downstairs at the kitchen table of my house. Down there was a gathering place for so many women. To come home from school, and my grandmother would be sitting at the table, and my mother would be sitting at the table. The woman from across the street would be sitting at the table. And they all had stories to tell. They were nurses, teachers; they were activists; they were artists. And I think that is where I got all of my inspiration as a writer.

Interviewer: When did you know you were going to be a writer?

Nottage: I don't think I made a commitment to being a writer until I finished *POOF!* I had gone to graduate school, written plays in my journal since I was a teenager. I worked for a newspaper. But I don't think until I put the last punctuation mark on the last sentence in *POOF!* that I decided that this is what I am going to do. I really like doing this. Somehow I can communicate things I am feeling, the issues that are of interest to me.

Interviewer: When you wrote *POOF!*, you had not written for a while . . .

Nottage: Well, immediately after graduate school, I found myself hungering for a different thing. I had been in academia for—what? Twelve, fourteen years. I wanted to work in the real world and to work at Amnesty International as the national press officer. I sold my computer and committed to writing press releases, op-eds, and speeches for four years of my life.

POOF! was the first play that I had written in years. It came very quickly. I literally sat down at my computer and wrote it in one sitting. I sent it to Actors Theater in Louisville for their short play competition and suddenly found myself the winner of the Heideman Award. The play wrote itself, and it was a joy to rediscover this creativity that was inside of me.

It was produced at the Humana Festival. It was done very simply, with two actresses and a pile of ash. And it somehow captured the imagination of the audience. Subsequently it has been done literally all around the world. I have photographs of the production in Japan. I got a check for the German translation of the play. My agent called me once and said it had been translated into Welsh. I was shocked by the power of this story—that somehow women around the world are connecting with the issues and have found some resonance for their lives. *POOF!* has been done in Austria, in Japan, in Singapore. It's been done in Mexico, in Spain. It's been done in Wales.

Interviewer: Why do you feel it's struck such a chord?

Nottage: I think it's because it is dealing with something universal, which is abuse against women. I think that's one of the things we continue to struggle with. We talk about the notion of human rights, but there is no one watching what's going on in the household. There is no one who's there to protect a woman from being abused. That is why I think it is important for us, as women, to discuss it—to put the issue out there. To discover that we have a voice. We have the power to say, "We will not tolerate this." And I also think there is a role that the governments can play in this. Very often the police turn a blind eye—that when they get a domestic violence call, they think, "We won't go this time. We will go the next time." The next time is too late.

A good friend of mine was a victim of domestic abuse. One of the things she said has stuck with me. She felt alone, embarrassed, trapped. As a result, she said nothing for years. I would encourage women who find themselves in that situation to find a close friend and discuss it. And if you do not have that friend, leave immediately.

EDWIN SANCHEZ

Edwin Sanchez (b. 1976) was born in Colombia. He graduated from the Yale Drama School in 1994. The following year his play *Clean*, supported by the Kennedy Center's Fund for New American Plays, was nominated by the American Theater Critics Association as the best new play of the year. In 1998 he participated in the Eugene O'Neill Playwrights Conference with his play *Barefoot Boy with Shoes On*, which was produced at the Schelykovo Playwrights Seminar in Russia in 1999. His other productions include *Unmerciful Good Fortune* at the Hyde Park Theater in Austin, Texas; *Trafficking in Broken Hearts* at the Celebration Theatre in Los Angeles; *Dona Sol and Her Trained Dog* at Latino Chicago; and *Fatty Tissue*, produced by Theater by Design of Chicago.

Sanchez is the recipient of many fellowships and awards, beginning in 1989 with the Artists Fellowship in Playwriting presented by the New York State Arts Council, and including the 1993 Eugene O'Neill Scholarship, the 1994 ASCAP Cole Porter Award, and the 1995 Berrilla Kerr Foundation Award. *Pops* was originally performed at Primary Stages in 2003. A year later the monologue featured Ivan Davila in the role of Tomás at Town Hall in New York City as part of a program commemorating the terrorist attack on the United States on 9/11.

Theater critics have noted that the most important change in theater during the last quarter century has been a movement away from formal plays and toward performance art. As Richard Gilman remarked in *The Making of Modern Drama*, this form of theater "places at the center of attention the *self* or *selves* of what we confidently used to call actors." Creating monologues such as *Pops*, Sanchez is a representative figure in this new wave of theater. He has commented, "I don't consider my work as art. I believe they are just projects and immediate actions that generate strong meanings. . . . I don't follow a specific methodology. I just let the action go on and let it define its own way. What I'm really interested in is an initial idea that can talk about a specific context and the conditions in which it is developed."

Pops

2003

The theme to I Love Lucy *plays in the background. The volume comes up, then disappears. Tomás, sixteen, stands center stage.*

TOMÁS: Can I just say, I hated Lucy. I used to have to watch it all the time with my Pops. He would call her La Colora, the Redhead. He thought she was so funny. He'd come home late at night from work, sneak me out of bed, and we'd watch *I Love Lucy* reruns. Now, that was kinda cute when I was a kid, but the older I got, the more tired it got, you know what I'm saying? When my father wanted to be funny he'd walk around the house saying (*Thick Desi accent.*), "Lucy, 'splain." My father's English was pretty bad as it is. "Lucy, 'splain." Funnee, Pops. Laugh riot. Parents should never be allowed to try to be funny. So one night he drags me out of bed again, and I'm so not in the mood, I don't even remember why, and we're sitting there watching Lucy and my father is laughing as loud as Ricky would. You know, almost like he's pronouncing "Ha-ha-ha." And I couldn't take it anymore and I snapped, "Man, why do you think that's still so funny? You've only seen it, like, a hundred times." My father got real quiet after that and I felt terrible. So I started laughing really hard, trying to make it up to him, you know. But he didn't dare laugh anymore. I think my father thought I was smarter than him, so if I told him he shouldn't laugh, then he shouldn't laugh. He went to bed early that night. He was a busboy and he had a breakfast shift the next day at the restaurant where he worked. Windows on the World at the World Trade Center. He didn't come home the next day. Or ever. I had to go with my mother to all these agencies to translate for her, but no one could help us. "He was a busboy, not a citizen." I tried to explain to my mother in Spanish, but she would just look at them and say, "Please 'splain." And people would roll their eyes, or try to be nice or get impatient and try to get us out of whatever office we were in. "Busboy, not a citizen." We had the wake in our apartment. We didn't have a body, of course, just a picture of my Pops. He was smiling in it. All our relatives and neighbors were there, and the priest came by. I stood in a corner, facing away from his picture. From the laugh I had silenced, I could see my mother on the sofa, crying quietly, people trying to comfort her. I turned then and walked up to my father's picture, and outta nowhere, it started. (*In perfect Lucy.*) "Are you tired, run-down, listless? Do you poop out at parties?" The room fell to a dead hush. (*Lucy-like.*) "The answer to all your problems are in this biddle lottle." (*Quickly corrects himself as Lucy did.*) "Little bottle!" My cousins started to scream with laughter, my uncle looked like he wanted to kill me, and my mother just stared at me. But I couldn't stop. I was by Lucy possessed. I started doing all her bits, I was, like, "Lucy's Greatest Hits." Lucy trapped in the icebox, Lucy as a showgirl with a heavy headdress, Lucy in the chocolate factory. Pretty soon everybody is laughing so loud you can barely hear me. The priest calls out "Do Lucy in the wine vat!" Like now I'm getting requests? I look at my mother and she is laughing so hard tears are flowing down her cheeks. And when I finally break, when I can't take anymore, I cry like Lucy did when Ricky caught her doing something she shouldn't have. (*Lucy-like.*) "Wah!!!!!!!" (*Changing to real pain. Silence.*) My mother now has to work two jobs, she wanted us to stay in the U.S. because that's what my father wanted. The busboy, not the citizen. He never got a plaque and no one mentions him or nothing, so I like to think that every time there's an *I Love Lucy* rerun on, it's a tribute to my father. And baby, that Colora, she is on twenty-four hours a day.

Theme to I Love Lucy *returns.*

END OF PLAY

25.

Conversation on *Hamlet* as Text and Performance

This Conversation on Shakespeare's *Hamlet* contains several items to help you understand the play. The section begins with a commentary by Geoffrey Bullough, who discusses two early treatments of this basic plot closer to Shakespeare's time, one by the French historian François de Belleforest (1530–1583) and the other by the Elizabethan playwright Thomas Kyd (1558–1594), whose play *The Spanish Tragedy* was the most popular revenge tragedy in the London theater before Shakespeare's *Hamlet.* Bullough speculates that one of the plays Kyd wrote shortly before Shakespeare created his version of the popular story might have been the original *Hamlet.* The text of this play (nicknamed "the *Ur-Hamlet*" by modern historians) unfortunately has not survived.

Next, the excerpt from the letter by the English Romantic poet John Keats to his brothers on December 21, 1817, contains his comments on what he calls Shakespeare's "negative capability." This term has been widely discussed by generations of critics since the publication of Keats's letter. Some interpret it as Shakespeare's ability as a dramatist to lose his identity in the creation of a wide range of characters. Others believe that Keats meant that as a poet Shakespeare was able to deal with uncertainty, that he did not adhere (as did Milton in *Paradise Lost,* for example) to the strict tenets of religion or moral philosophy, trusting his "sense of Beauty" instead.

The biographical critic Stephen Greenblatt discussed "The Ghost in *Hamlet*" in his book *Will in the World: How Shakespeare Became Shakespeare* (2004). The final commentaries by a contemporary playwright, two actors, and a theater critic are some responses to *Hamlet* inspired by the idea of the play in performance. Photographs of actual performances accompany them. In 1979, the English playwright Tom Stoppard wrote a two-part play, *Dogg's Hamlet, Cahoot's Macbeth,* in which *Dogg's Hamlet* was meant to be a farcical version

An image of William Shakespeare included on the First Folio, a collected edition of Shakespeare plays published seven years after his death. (Reprinted by permission of The Folger Shakespeare Library.)

of Shakespeare's play. Stoppard intended it as an encore to a performance of *Hamlet* enacted on top of a double-decker London bus. The eminent English actor John Gielgud describes in his autobiography, *Early Stages* (1939), how he prepared for the demanding role of Hamlet on the stage. The American theater critic John Lahr reviews the performance of actor Ralph Fiennes as Hamlet in a landmark 1995 production of the play that created what Lahr describes as a melodramatic and highly effective "climate of delirium" on Broadway. Lahr also discusses the costumes and stage settings of the production, which the play's director, Jonathan Kent, set in Edwardian England. The actor Michael Pennington's summary of the play as "an image of entrapment sustained by a series of beautiful gestures" concludes the Conversation.

COMMENTARIES

GEOFFREY BULLOUGH

Sources of Shakespeare's *Hamlet* 1973

There was no Ghost in Saxo [Grammaticus] or [François de] Belleforest, but it was the feature of the *Ur-Hamlet* which most affected spectators and lingered on in public memory, so that in 1596 Thomas Lodge (in *Wits Miserie*) described a devil looking "as pale as the Visard of the ghost which cried so miserably at the Theatre, like an oister-wife, Hamlet, revenge."

When [Thomas] Kyd, or whoever else wrote it, adapted Belleforest's tale in terms of Senecan drama,° he dealt only with the first part of Amleth's life until his triumph over Feng, and changed the climax of that to make it tragic and (no doubt) easier to stage. The main factors shaping the altered plot were the secrecy of Amleth's father's murder and the introduction of his Ghost to incite the hero to revenge. Whereas in *The Spanish Tragedy* the Ghost of Andrea (killed before the play opens) accompanies Revenge to watch the action and "serve for Chorus in this tragedie," taking no part in the action save to express impatience at the slowness with which punishment falls on the wicked, in the *Ur-Hamlet* the father's Ghost really had some reason for demanding vengeance, and presumably started off the action by revealing it. This was a new departure in ghostly behaviour,[1] and it makes me believe that *Hamlet* was written after *The Spanish Tragedy*.

Seneca's dramas lacked the religious attitude of Greek tragedy and the theme of personal revenge superseded divine retribution; horror became a dominant effect, and the Senecan Chorus contributed to this.[2] Thus at the beginning of *Agamemnon*, Thyestes' Ghost rises from Hell to describe his own adultery with his brother Atreus' wife, and how Atreus took revenge by feasting him on the flesh of his own son; tells too how he raped his own daughter Pelopea (who later married Atreus) and had by her a son, Aegysthus, who is now Clytemnestra's paramour and will shortly help her murder Thyestes' nephew, her husband Agamemnon. The Ghost does not interfere in the action; it expounds the past and prepares the atmosphere of horror. The *Agamemnon* also has a scene in which Electra accuses her mother of adultery and murder—a striking anticipation of the closet-scene in *Hamlet*. The Amleth saga was in

Senecan drama: Tragedies by the Roman playwright and Stoic philosopher Seneca (4 B.C.–A.D. 65).

[1]Cf. F. T. Bowers, *Elizabethan Revenge Tragedy*, Gloucester, Mass., 1940; E. Prosser, *Hamlet and Revenge*, Stanford, 1967.

[2]H. B. Charlton, *The Senecan Tradition in Renaissance Tragedy*, 1946.

this tradition of fraternal hate and incest; hence no doubt its appeal to Elizabethan Senecan playwrights.

In *Troades* Talthybius tells how the Ghost of Achilles demanded the sacrifice of Polyxena (whom he had loved while living) before the Greek fleet could sail from Troy. In the Latin play this ghost did not appear in person, but Jasper Heywood introduced it in Act II of his translation, craving revenge on the Trojans.[3] Ignoring this proof of survival after death, Seneca's Chorus later doubts whether the soul lives on. There is a resemblance here to the apparent inconsistency in *Hamlet* where, soon after accepting the Ghost as his "father's spirit," the hero speaks of "the undiscover'd country from whose bourn / No traveller returns."

Professor Eleanor Prosser's study of the ghosts in Elizabethan drama shows that many act as Chorus or Prologue, or as the retributory voices of conscience, and that these are almost all pagan ghosts risen from Hades.[4] Few ghosts show Christian characteristics. After *Hamlet* three or four mingle Christian and pagan qualities. Only Andrugio in *Antonio's Revenge* (probably derived from the *Ur-Hamlet*) and the Ghost in *Hamlet* "appear to a protagonist to command blood revenge." (This occasionally occurred in Italian Senecan tragedies.) Andrugio's Ghost comes from his coffin to demand that his son

> Invent some stratagem of vengeance
> Which, but to think on, may like lightning glide
> With horror through thy breast.

He combines delight in the most awful tortures with assurances that he is in league with Heaven. But the play is so confused in tone that some critics have regarded it as a parody. Old Hamlet's Ghost is unique in the problems it posits, and "Shakespeare may well have intended to jolt his audience into a fresh response to what had become a hackneyed convention."[5] It is extremely unlikely that the inventor of Andrea in *The Spanish Tragedy* also created a spirit so complex as that in *Hamlet* Q2.

This is not a suitable place in which to enter the debate about the nature of this ghost. W. W. Greg's suggestion that it is a figment of Hamlet's imagination was countered by E. Stoll who thought it an objectivation of Elizabethan popular lore. For J. D. Wilson it was an occasion for Shakespeare to present three different attitudes to ghosts: the Catholic view (of Marcellus and Bernardo) that a soul could come from Purgatory; the sceptical view of Horatio (like Reginald Scot's) but soon changed to belief; and Hamlet's Protestant view (held by L. Lavater and James VI) that ghosts were probably devils but might be angels, never the souls of men. Another school of thought, including Roy W. Battenhouse and Miss Prosser, argues that the Ghost is a damned spirit come to mislead Hamlet into offending against the divine injunction against revenge.

---

[3]Cf. G. Ll. Evans, "Shakespeare, Seneca and the Kingdom of Violence," in *Roman Drama*, ed. T. A. Dorey and D. R. Dudley, 1965.
[4]E. Prosser, *op. cit.* Appendix A.
[5]Prosser, *op. cit.* pp. 101–102.

My own view is nearer to that of I. J. Semper who saw the Ghost as a visitant from Purgatory and that of Sister Miriam who sees Hamlet as justifiably doubting and testing it. But we should not exaggerate the doctrinal strictness of Shakespeare's approach or assume that he was a Catholic because he used the idea of Purgatory. P. N. Siegel was right to insist: "The Hamlet Ghost is a compound of the Senecan revenge ghost, the Catholic purgatorial spirit and the popular graveyard spook, created for an audience prepared by theatrical tradition, by what Cardinal Newman called "floating religious opinions" (as against official dogma) and by current folklore to give it dramatic credence."[6] The pagan element appears in the Ghost's insistence on quasi-physical horrors unspeakable and the reference to "Lethe wharf"; its purgatorial quality in [act 1, scene 5]. It has an almost Miltonic apprehension of virtue and vice; it loves the Sacraments and deeply regrets having died. "Unhousel'd, disappointed, unaneal'd." Its folklore features include the hour when it walks and when it disappears, and its knocking underground.

JOHN KEATS
From a Letter to George and Thomas Keats, 21 December 1817

Hampstead Sunday

My dear Brothers,

I must crave your pardon for not having written ere this. . . .

. . . Brown and Dilke walked with me and back from the Christmas pantomime. I had not a dispute but a disquisition, with Dilke on various subjects; several things dove-tailed in my mind, and at once it struck me what quality went to form a Man of Achievement, especially in Literature and which Shakespeare possessed so enormously—I mean *Negative Capability,* that is, when a man is capable of being in uncertainties, mysteries, doubts, without any irritable reaching after fact and reason—[Samuel Taylor] Coleridge, for instance, would let go by a fine isolated verisimilitude caught from the Penetralium of mystery, from being incapable of remaining content with half-knowledge. This pursued through volumes would perhaps take us no further than this, that with a great poet the sense of Beauty overcomes every other consideration, or rather obliterates all consideration.

[Percy Bysshe] Shelley's poem is out, and there are words about its being objected to as much as "Queen Mab" was. Poor Shelley, I think he has his Quota of good qualities, in sooth la!! Write soon to your most sincere friend and affectionate Brother

John.

[6]P. N. Siegel, "Discerning the Ghost in *Hamlet,*" *PMLA*, lxxviii, 1963, p. 148.

STEPHEN GREENBLATT

Stephen Greenblatt, University Professor of the Humanities at Harvard University, argued in his book *Will in the World: How Shakespeare Became Shakespeare* (2004) that the text of *Hamlet* was "intensely alert to the social and political realities" of its time, mirroring the theological controversy in England as the official religion changed from Catholic to Protestant. As a biographical critic, Greenblatt also noted that Shakespeare wrote this play shortly after the death of his son Hamnet and during the impending death of his father. This was a time of "psychic disturbance that may help to explain the explosive power and inwardness of *Hamlet*" as the tragic hero's "paralyzing doubts and anxieties displace revenge as the center of the play's interest."

On the Ghost in *Hamlet* 2004

The official Protestant line in Shakespeare's time was that there were no ghosts at all. The apparitions that men and women encountered from time to time—apparitions that uncannily bore the appearance of loved ones or friends—were mere delusions, or, still worse, they were devils in disguise, come to tempt their victims to sin. Hamlet at first declares that he has seen an "honest ghost" (1.5.142), but his initial confidence gives way to uncertainty:

The spirit that I have seen
May be the devil, and the devil hath power
T'assume a pleasing shape; yea, and perhaps,
Out of my weakness and my melancholy—
As he is very potent with such spirits—
Abuses me to damn me. (2.2.575–80)

Such thoughts lead to a cycle of delay, self-reproach, continued failure to act, and renewed self-reproach. They account for the play-within-the-play—Hamlet's device to get some independent confirmation of the ghost's claims—and for the hero's queasy sense of groping in the dark. And they are linked to a broader sense of doubt and disorientation in a play where the whole ritual structure that helped men and women deal with loss has been fatally damaged.

Shakespeare would have experienced the consequences of this damage as he stood by the grave of his son or tried to cope with his father's pleas for help in the afterlife. The Protestant authorities had attacked the beliefs and outlawed the practices that the Catholic Church had offered as a way to negotiate with the dead. They said that the whole concept of purgatory was a lie and that all one needed was robust faith in the saving power of Christ's sacrifice. There were those who firmly possessed such faith, but nothing in Shakespeare's works suggests that he was among them. He was instead part of a very large group, probably the bulk of the population, who found themselves still grappling with longings and fears that the old resources of the Catholic Church had served to address. It was because of those longings and fears that people like John Shakespeare secretly signed "spiritual testaments."

All funerals invite those who stand by the grave to think about what, if anything, they believe in. But the funeral of one's own child does more than this: it compels parents to ask questions of God and to interrogate their own faith. Shakespeare must have attended the regular services in his Protestant parish; otherwise his name would have turned up on lists of recusants. But did he believe what he heard and recited? His works suggest that he did have faith, of a sort, but it was not a faith securely bound either by the Catholic Church or by the Church of England. By the late 1590s, insofar as his faith could be situated in any institution at all, that institution was the theater, and not only in the sense that his profoundest energies and expectations were all focused there.

Shakespeare grasped that crucial death rituals in his culture had been gutted. He may have felt this with enormous pain at his son's graveside. But he also believed that the theater—and his theatrical art in particular—could tap into the great reservoir of passionate feelings that, for him and for thousands of his contemporaries, no longer had a satisfactory outlet.

The Reformation was in effect offering him an extraordinary gift—the broken fragments of what had been a rich, complex edifice—and he knew exactly how to accept and use this gift. He was hardly indifferent to the success he could achieve, but it was not a matter of profit alone. Shakespeare drew upon the pity, confusion, and dread of death in a world of damaged rituals (the world in which most of us continue to live) because he himself experienced those same emotions at the core of his being. He experienced them in 1596, at the funeral of his child, and he experienced them with redoubled force in anticipation of his father's death. He responded not with prayers but with the deepest expression of his being: *Hamlet*.

In the early eighteenth century, the editor and biographer Nicholas Rowe, trying to find out something about Shakespeare's career as an actor, made inquiries, but memories had faded. "I could never meet with any further account of him this way," Rowe noted, "than that the top of his performance was the Ghost in his own *Hamlet*." Enacting the purgatorial spirit who demands that the living listen carefully to his words—"lend thy serious hearing / To what I shall unfold" (1.5.5–6)—Shakespeare must have conjured up within himself the voice of his dead son, the voice of his dying father, and perhaps too his own voice, as it would sound when it came from the grave. Small wonder that it would have been his best role.

TOM STOPPARD

Dogg's Hamlet: The Encore 1979

SCENE: *Staging the play on a double-decker London bus, Stoppard gave directions for two folding screens to be placed left and right at the back of the playing area. The screen on the left had a bolt through the top for a cut-out sun, moon, and crown on hinges to be swung in and out of sight. The other screen had a two-dimensional grave for Ophelia.*

Flourish of trumpets, crown hinges up. Enter Claudius and Gertrude.

CLAUDIUS: Our sometime sister, now our Queen,
(*Enter Hamlet.*)
Have we taken to wife.
(*Crown hinges down.*)

HAMLET: That it should come to this!
(*Exit Claudius and Gertrude. Wind noise. Moon hinges up. Enter Horatio above.*)

HORATIO: My lord, I saw him yesternight—
The King, your father.

HAMLET: Angels and ministers of grace defend us!
(*Exit, running, through rest of speech.*)
Something is rotten in the state of Denmark.
(*Enter Ghost above.*)

GHOST: I am thy father's spirit.
The serpent that did sting thy father's life
(*Enter Hamlet above.*)
Now wears his crown.

HAMLET: O my prophetic soul!
Hereafter I shall think meet
To put an antic disposition on.
(*Moon hinges down. Exeunt. Short flourish of trumpets. Enter Polonius below, running. Crown hinges up.*)

POLONIUS: Look where sadly the poor wretch comes.
(*Exit Polonius, running, Enter Hamlet.*)

HAMLET: I have heard that guilty creatures sitting at a play
Have by the very cunning of the scene been struck.
(*Enter Claudius, Gertrude, Ophelia, Marcellus, and Horatio joking. All sit to watch imaginary play, puppets appear above screen.*)
If he but blench, I know my course.
(*Masque music. Claudius rises.*)
The King rises!

ALL: Give o'er the play!
(*Exeunt all except Gertrude and Hamlet. Crown hinges down.*)

HAMLET: I'll take the ghost's word for a thousand pounds.
(*Enter Polonius, goes behind arras. Short flourish of trumpets.*)
Mother, you have my father much offended.

GERTRUDE: Help!

POLONIUS: Help, Ho!

HAMLET: (*Stabs Polonius.*) Dead for a ducat, dead!
(*Polonius falls dead offstage. Exit Gertrude and Hamlet. Short flourish of trumpets. Enter Claudius followed by Hamlet.*)

CLAUDIUS: Hamlet, this deed must send thee hence.
(*Exit Hamlet.*)
Do it, England.
(*Exit Claudius. Enter Ophelia, falls to ground. Rises and pulls gravestone to cover herself. Bell tolls twice. Enter Gravedigger and Hamlet.*)

HAMLET: A pirate gave us chase. I alone became their prisoner.
(*Takes skull from Gravedigger.*)
Alas poor Yorick—but soft (*Returns skull to Gravedigger.*)
—This is I,
Hamlet the Dane!
(*Exit Gravedigger. Enter Laertes.*)
LAERTES: The devil take thy soul!
(*They grapple, then break. Enter Osric between them with swords. They draw. Crown hinges up. Enter Claudius and Gertrude with goblets.*)
HAMLET: Come on, Sir!
(*Laertes and Hamlet fight.*)
OSRIC: A hit, a very palpable hit!
CLAUDIUS: Give him the cup. Gertrude, do not drink!
GERTRUDE: I am poisoned! (*Dies.*)
LAERTES: Hamlet, thou art slain! (*Dies.*)
HAMLET: Then venom to thy work! (*Kills Claudius. Crown hinges down.*)
The rest is silence. (Dies.)

(*Two shots offstage. End.*)

SIR JOHN GIELGUD

On Playing Hamlet

1939

The last production of my first Old Vic season was *Hamlet*. It was exciting to have the chance of playing it after all, but I did not think it likely that I should give an interesting performance. I had not made a success of Romeo, though I had played the part before, and I considered Richard and Macbeth, in which I had done better work, were both character parts. From my childhood I had had some sort of picture in my mind of these two personages. I could imagine myself at once dressed in their clothes and I tried, in rehearsing and acting them, to forget myself completely, to keep the imagined image fresh and vivid, and to some extent I had succeeded. Hamlet was different. How could I seem great enough, simple enough to say those hackneyed, wonderful lines as if I was thinking of them for the first time? How could I avoid certain passages in the manner of other actors I had seen, how could I put into the part my own personal feelings—many of which fitted the feelings of Hamlet—and yet lift them to a high classical style worthy of the character?

We began to rehearse. Some of the scenes came to me more easily than others; the first appearance of Hamlet particularly—one of my favorite scenes of all the plays I have ever read or acted—sincerity, real emotion, and marvellously simple words to express them in. The second scene, when Hamlet first sees the Ghost, difficult, sudden, technically hard to speak, the following Ghost scene terribly difficult, intensely tiring to act, nothing to say, then, after the Ghost disappears, too many words. Impossible to convey, even with Shakespeare's help, the horror and madness of the situation, the changing tenderness and weary resignation.

The mad scenes. How mad should Hamlet be? So easy to score off Polonius, to get laughs, so important not to clown, to keep the story true—then the intricate scene with Rosencrantz and Guildenstern, and my favorite prose speech in the play, "What a piece of work is a man! . . ." The arrival of the players, easier again, natural, true feeling, but the big soliloquy is coming in a minute, one must concentrate, take care not to anticipate, not begin worrying beforehand how one is going to say it, take time, but don't lose time, don't break the verse up, don't succumb to the temptation of a big melodramatic effect for the sake of gaining applause at the curtain—Nunnery scene. Shall it be a love scene? How much emotion? When should Hamlet see the King? I feel so much that I convey nothing. This scene never ceases to baffle me.

Interval—The Advice to the Players. Dreadful little pill to open the second part, all the people coming back to their seats, slamming them down, somehow try to connect the speech with the rest of the play, not just a set piece—Tender for the tiny scene with Horatio, a moment's relief—then into the Play Scene. Relax if possible, enjoy the scene, watch the Gonzago Play, watch the King, forget that this is the most famous of famous scenes, remember that Hamlet is not yet sure of Claudius, delay the climax, then carry it (and it needs all the control and breath in the world to keep the pitch at the right level). No pause before the Recorders scene begins, and this cannot make the effect it should unless Rosencrantz and Guildenstern pull their weight and share the scene with Hamlet. Half a minute to collect oneself, and on again to the praying King, such a difficult unsatisfactory scene, and how important to the play—but the closet scene is more grateful, and a woman's voice helps to make a contrast in tone and pitch. The scene starts at terrific emotional tension, though, and only slows up for a minute in the middle for the beautiful passage with the Ghost. The "hiding of Polonius's body" scene . . . and then grab a cloak and hat in the wings and rush on to speak the Fortinbras soliloquy as if it wasn't the last hundred yards in a relay race.

Now the one long interval for Hamlet, while Ophelia is doing her mad scene, and Claudius and Laertes are laying their plot, and the Queen is saying her willow speech. Last lap. Graveyard scene, with the lovely philosophizing, and the lines about Yorick, and that hellish shouting fight and the "Ossa" speech at the end, which takes the last ounce of remaining breath. Now for Osric, and a struggle to hold one's own with the scene-shifters banging about behind the front cloth, and a careful ear for the first coughs and fidgets in the audience, which must somehow be silenced before the "fall of a sparrow" (I remember one night a gentleman in the front row took out a large watch in this scene, and wound it resignedly). And so to the apology to Laertes, with half one's mind occupied trying to remember the fight, which has been so carefully rehearsed but always goes wrong at least once a week, and on to the poisoning of the Queen and Claudius's death, and, if all has gone well, a still, attentive audience to the very end. . . .

. . . In rehearsing Hamlet I found it at first impossible to characterize. I could not "imagine" the part, and live in it, forgetting myself in the words and adventures of the character, as I had tried to do in other plays. This difficulty surprised and alarmed me. Although I knew the theatrical effect that should be produced by each scene, I could only act the part if I felt that I really experienced every word of it as I spoke. The need to "make an effort" or "force a climax" paralyzed my imagination immediately, and destroyed any reality which I had begun to feel. I knew that I must act in a broad style, that I must be grander, more dignified and noble, more tender and gracious, more bitter and scathing, than was absolutely natural—that I must not be as slow as I should be if I were really thinking aloud, that I must drive the dialogue along at a regular moving pace, and, above all, that every shade of thought must be arranged, behind the lines, so that nothing should be left to chance in presenting them to the audience correctly and clearly in the pattern which I had conceived. All through rehearsals I was dismayed by my utter inability to forget myself while I was acting. It was not until I stood before an audience that I seemed to find the breadth and voice which enabled me suddenly to shake off my self-consciousness and live the part in my imagination, while I executed the technical difficulties with another part of my consciousness at the same time.

Photographs of *Hamlet* in Performance

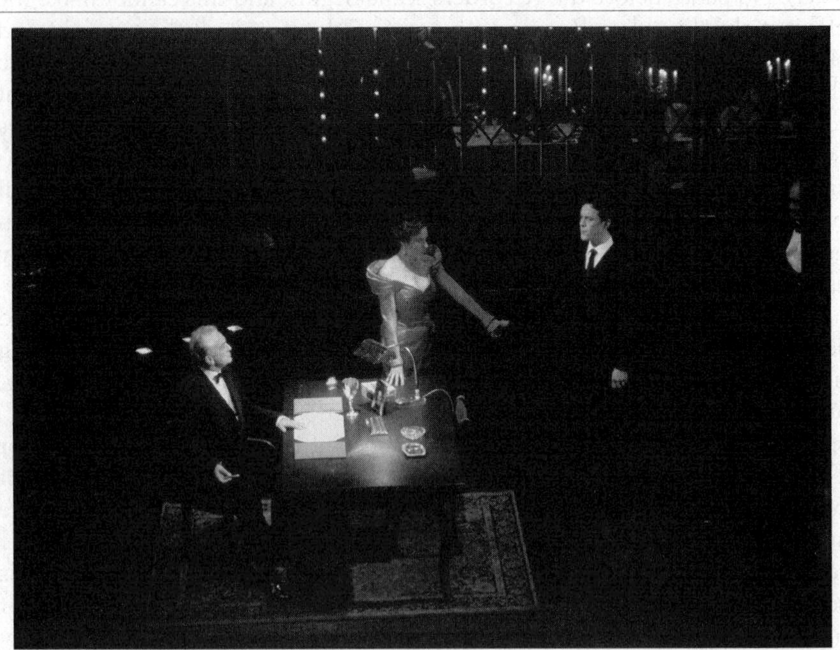

Paul Freeman as Claudius, Diana Quick as Gertrude, and Alex Jennings as Hamlet in the Royal Shakespeare Company's 1997 production in Stratford, directed by Matthew Warchus. (Photo: Clive Barda/PAL)

Foreground: Yoshisada Sakaguchi as Polonius and Hiroyuki Sanada as Hamlet in the Ninagawa Theatre Company's August 1998 production at the Barbican Theatre, London, directed by Yukio Ninagawa. (Photo: Colin Willoughby/ArenaPAL)

Ralph Fiennes as Hamlet and Tara Fitzgerald as Ophelia in the Almeida Theatre/Hackney Empire's 1995 performance. (Photo: Ben Christopher/ArenaPAL)

Tim Woodward as Claudius and Mark Rylance as Hamlet in a March 2000 performance directed by Giles Block at the restored Globe Theatre in London. (Photo: Colin Willoughby/ArenaPAL)

JOHN LAHR

Review of *Hamlet*

1994

Hamlet is a play that tests the best actors of each generation, and also each generation's sense of itself. Over the last thirty years, in England, no fewer than three *Hamlets* have served as such cultural bellwethers. In 1965, during the Vietnam War, David Warner gave us an untidy undergraduate Hamlet who was frustrated by Denmark's military-industrial complex. In 1980, as Britain's economy went into a weird free fall, Jonathan Pryce's Hamlet was possessed by the ghost of his father, who spoke through him in a frightening supernatural flirtation with madness. And now, in the neutral, post-Thatcher nineties, Ralph Fiennes has pitched his drop-dead matinee-idol profile and the modesty of his sensitive soul into a postmodern *Hamlet* whose refusal to risk interpretation reflects Britain's current bland and winded times.

Fiennes, an intelligent, reticent player, seems almost as unwilling to enter the vortex of Hamlet's torment as Hamlet himself is to take action. Fiennes radiates an elegance of spirit that rivets the audience with its sense of unspoken mystery. His performance is a stylish event, much more the "mould of form" than the "glass of fashion." He has a mellow, reedy voice that filters Shakespeare's gorgeous complexity and gives the language an accessible colloquial ring. Fiennes is not one for grand histrionic gestures. His personality doesn't take up a lot of space. He compels attention by his decency, not by his declaiming. Fiennes, who has limpid green eyes and tousled chestnut hair, and who is a laid-back, brooding, romantic star, is catnip to the public and oxygen at the box office. (The Almeida Theatre Company's production, which began its much ballyhooed life at the Hackney Empire, the wonderful old music-hall venue in London's East End, has arrived at the Belasco for a fourteen-week Broadway engagement.) This *Hamlet* has been designed to be a people's *Hamlet*, which is to say a *Hamlet* in which the plot, not the psychology, is complicated, and in which the cast works the room instead of working for meaning. Inevitably, therefore, Fiennes's Hamlet is not a navel-gazing scholar or an alienated adolescent or a demented psychological case study. His Hamlet turns out to be the guy Horatio always said he was: a "sweet prince," a sort of rogue and *pleasant* slave.

The director, Jonathan Kent, who last year transferred the Almeida's *Medea*, with Diana Rigg, to Broadway with great success, has set the play in Edwardian England and has lopped an hour off the playing time. The speed favors breadth over depth; the streamlining suits the cut of Fiennes's jib, and he wears James Acheson's period clothes well. What we have here is a ripping Shakespearean yarn that shows off the thrills and chills of the story's melodramatic elements: the ghost of a murdered king, a mother's hasty marriage to her husband's murderer, a prince driven to near-madness and revenge, a lovelorn suicide, a lot of ghoulish high jinks around graves, a terrific sword fight, and a quadruple poisoning. The result is lucid without being moving: a kind of aerobic *Hamlet*, which works hard to keep up the pace while going nowhere.

The lights come up on a bare, raked stage, and the sound of crashing waves fills the auditorium. In the background, the environs of Elsinore are suggested by faint, blurred beams of light projected through a murky scrim on which the outlines of rocks are just visible. A sentinel climbs up through a trapdoor—more for effect than for sense, it seems, like many things in this production. "Who's there?" he calls. That's the play; the whole existential ball of wax. Hamlet's entire dramatic journey is foreshadowed in these first words. He, too, must penetrate the surrounding darkness and tease out the reality of his parents, of the corrupt court, and of himself. By finally taking action—which means accepting loss, including the loss of his own life, Hamlet sees clear into the heart of things and achieves his adulthood. In this sense, *Hamlet* is both a detective story and a metaphysical investigation. The practical and the philosophical aspects of the tale need time to build properly, as the saying goes, "No delay, no play." But here, with the proceedings speeded up, the text is not so much examined as *done*. It's significant that Fiennes attacks the "To be, or not to be" soliloquy, which sets out Hamlet's spiritual quandary, by coming toward us in manic stutter steps and turning the famous meditation into yapping thought. He skirts the issue of interpretation by turning talk into behavior. The image is novel but little nuance comes across the footlights. In this ranting mode, dissembling a madness that is really giddy grief, the barefoot Fiennes grabs Ophelia's crotch and insolently shoves Claudius's shoulder. But Fiennes can't really get up a convincingly antic head of steam. He is slow to kindle and never really burns. He's not so much tormented as pissed off.

Fiennes has his best moment with the grave-digger (the excellent grizzled Terence Rigby, who also plays Hamlet's father's ghost and the Player King). Listening to the Gravedigger expound matter-of-factly on how a body decomposes, and learning that a skull he has unearthed belonged to Yorick, the former King's jester, Hamlet gently takes this relic of his old acquaintance from the grave-digger. "This?" Fiennes says, uttering the word with a huge sense of recognition, wonder, and sadness. His sensitivity and the mournfulness of the moment coalesce. "Where be your gibes now? your gambols? your songs? your flashes of merriment, that were wont to set the table on a roar?" Fiennes says, with a delicacy that delivers Shakespeare's observations about mortality like a punch to the heart.

The production's obsession with surface has its most effective expression in Peter J. Davison's sets. He creates a dark, lugubrious officialdom of behemoth ceilings, heavy brown-stained doors, and large shuttered windows that turn the actors into scuttling Lilliputians. Hamlet is first seen framed by one of these gigantic windows, standing upstage with his back turned away from the bustle of power, whose aggrandizement is reflected in the monumentality that surrounds it. Still, Davison, too, succumbs to the production's impulse to startle rather than compel. The ghost is conjured up on a high platform behind the scrim. There, lit from above by the white glare of a halogen lamp and announced by a jolt of electronic sound, Hamlet's dead father appears twice, in his carapace of armor: a "Star Wars" effect that is a projection of commercial instincts more than of Hamlet's unconscious. Similarly, Jonathan Kent's eye for business is sometimes shrewder than his eye for detail. When Laertes and

Hamlet take turns leaping into Ophelia's grave and embracing her body, each trying to outdo the remorse of the other, the poor dead girl bobs up and down like a hand puppet. And at the finale, when Fortinbras (Rupert Penry-Jones, who is also Fiennes's understudy) arrives to take over the kingdom that Hamlet has died to save, his Aryan good looks and the gray capes of his lieutenants make it seem as if the Luftwaffe had invaded Denmark.

In American theatrical circles, the definition of a genius is anybody from England. But the prestige of this production can't hide the unevenness of its seasoned supporting cast, who prove the adage that British actors are either tours de force or forced to tour. Besides Terence Rigby, only the lanky, bearded Peter Eyre, as Polonius, breathes distinctive life into his role. Eyre plays the meddling bureaucrat as a long drink of cold water: cleaning his pince-nez as he counsels his hotheaded son to "neither a borrower, nor a lender be," and withholding his hand from Laertes when he goes, Eyre misses no opportunity to have fun with the old blowhard's pedantry. Polonius rushes to the Queen with a letter that Hamlet has sent his daughter, and reads it to her as a presenting symptom of Hamlet's lunacy. Reciting "To the celestial and my soul's idol, the most beautified Ophelia," Eyre's Polonius bristles with dopey patrician disdain. "That's an ill phrase, a vile phrase, 'beautified' is a vile phrase," he says, and gets one of the evening's best laughs.

Others are not so much at home in Shakespeare's climate of delirium. Tara Fitzgerald, a talented young actress with a bright future, flounders as Ophelia. There is nothing fractured or vulnerable about her, and when Ophelia goes mad Fitzgerald won't let her rip. Fitzgerald's behavior—the compulsive walking back and forth, the sexual taunts directed at Claudius—feels tame and glib: a trick of the mind, not a journey of the heart. Often, when English actors are nowhere near the center of their parts they rely on the power of their articulate voices; James Laurenson's Claudius falls into the trap of such posturing. Claudius is John Gotti with a pedigree—carnal, vicious, power-hungry, ruthless—but Laurenson gives us chicanery on the half shell. He does a lot of Urgent Shakespeare Acting. A few wheeling turns upstage, some nips at the top of his hand, a little booming oratory, and—presto!—you have a villain. This stock rep stuff is also dished up by the beautiful Francesca Annis, as a Gertrude who can't manage much grief at the sight of Ophelia's dementia but does manage a long, lingering kiss with Hamlet. It's a bit of business that has become the theatrical baggage of the role in this century, but the incestuous overtone seems inappropriate, especially in such an unanalytic production.

A word about Hamlet's duel. Jonathan Kent and the fight director, William Hobbs, have built up this face-off between idealism and treachery into a scintillating contest that takes excellent advantage of the story's melodrama. A cream-colored tarp is rolled downstage for the match, and the court sits watching upstage right, in gray upholstered chairs. Hamlet fights with graceful, playful enthusiasm, unaware that he's up against the double whammy of Laertes' poisoned sword and Claudius's poisoned chalice. Hamlet gets the first couple of touches; then Laertes' temper flares, and he cuts Hamlet. They scuffle, and in the hurly-burly their swords get mixed up. Hamlet chases Laertes around the room, sending chairs flying and courtiers scurrying for safety. It's exciting and well-staged hokum, in which Laertes ends up hoist with his own petard. At that point, the Queen, who has drunk from the chalice, collapses; then the Grand Guignol of Shakespeare's ending quickly plays itself out. At the finale, Fortinbras's men lift Hamlet's corpse on their shoulders and, swaying, carry him slowly upstage and toward the light beyond. Fiennes's head falls back, giving the audience one last glimpse of the star. Even backward, upside down, and dead, Fiennes exits looking good.

MICHAEL PENNINGTON

Michael Pennington, an English actor who performed the role of Hamlet so many times that he felt he's had "a small lifetime of Hamlets," eloquently described the way Shakespeare's play actually works on the stage in *Hamlet: A User's Guide* published by Nick Hern Books in London.

Hamlet's Madness 1996

The play's most pathologically interesting feature is also its cheapest effect: Hamlet's madness, a highly negotiable term upon which air of all heats has been expended. Apart from its dubious tactical value—assuming an "antic disposition" is more likely to draw attention to him than give him an alibi—this "madness" almost makes the play unplayable, since it makes fools of the rest of the cast, many of whom are not supposed to be fools. It also sets the central actor on an unrewarding search for eccentric dress and funny voices. In fact, aside from a few moments of calculated gibberish, Hamlet speaks nothing but searing good sense throughout the play—a lucidity that drives everyone else to distraction, rage and sorrow—and drops liberal hints about his pretence to all the wrong people. Gertrude keeps changing her mind about his condition, eager to believe that he is mad only "in craft" but becoming ever more lyrical in her descriptions of his insanity. Polonius, the arch-politician, at first thinks Hamlet *is* mad, and then changes his mind when he finds himself mocked. The only person who sees through Hamlet without effort is Claudius, himself a dissembler. He is the most sceptical—but also the most inconsistent, using terms for madness and assumed madness interchangeably. The most damaging case is that of Ophelia, with whom Hamlet is extremely explicit, rejecting and denouncing her in a *tour de force* of sexual rhetoric which she then describes as the ravings of a noble mind o'erthrown. This makes her stupid or vain—and her lack of vision leaves the part almost unintelligible, depending on a virtuoso performance of the Mad Scene. In fact, Hamlet's "distraction" is really a fascinating effect, drawn from the sources to make him attractive to an audience who, lacking our sober apprehensions of mental illness, loved this sort of thing, and got very excited by images of melancholia and bedlam. Even in these terms, it is unevenly delivered: as voyeurs, the Elizabethans might have preferred the twelfth-century source in which the Hamlet figure comes to his mother flapping his arms and crowing like a cock, stomps Polonius to death under a mattress, chops up his body and boils the pieces, finally feeding them to the palace pigs. That's what I call madness: Shakespeare replaces it with perhaps the most intelligent man ever written—otherwise we wouldn't have been listening to him all these years.

There is nothing either good or bad, but thinking makes it so; and listing the deficiencies of the play has the effect of drawing attention to the extraordinary hold it has exercised on the imagination, everywhere, for four centuries and continuing. Every reservation above contains the seed of the play's strengths: it is, in practice, a triumph. Believing we should be held by the spiritual conundrums of *Hamlet*, we respond, time after time, to the energetic storytelling, its loose ends raised to the status of enigma, and the haunting, inexplicable hologram of the Prince. Drawing on archetypes as old as the *Oresteia* at one end and passing them forward to Disney's *The Lion King* (which even has a paternal Ghost intoning "Remember!") at the other, the play has galvanic force in the theatre, an ability, for all its despair, to heal, and an effect on an audience of any age quite unlike any other I know. It is an image of entrapment sustained by a series of beautiful gestures—a son with his father's ghost, a theatre within a theatre, a man with a sword over a praying murderer, a skull and a spade, a wounded duellist—crystallised by a remarkable narrative to which they are locked like barnacles: all except To Be Or Not To Be, which hovers over the play like a great wing, its greatness lying in its very detachment.

◆ Topics for Writing about Drama ◆

1. The critic Daniel Mendelsohn wrote that Sophocles's *Oedipus* "derives its horrible excitement from a relentless exposition of its protagonist's fall from grace—and from the fact that his confidence and his talents are what prevented him from seeing the looming disaster." Write an essay in which you compare and contrast the "relentless exposition of its protagonist's fall from grace" in *Oedipus* and *Hamlet*.
2. John Keats's intriguing idea about what he called "Negative Capability" (p. 1596) in writers of genius such as Shakespeare has fascinated literary researchers ever since his 1817 letter to his brothers was first published. Research the different interpretations of Keats's phrase "negative capability" in the past century and present them in an essay along with your own explanation of Keats's insight.
3. In *Dogg's Hamlet:* The Encore (p. 1598), Tom Stoppard didn't include a speaking role for Ophelia, yet she is clearly an important character since her grave figures prominently in his stage properties. Write an essay in which you analyze Ophelia's importance in Stoppard's version of *Hamlet*.
4. In *Hamlet: A User's Guide* (1996), the English actor Michael Pennington quoted a criticism of the play by Voltaire (1694–1778):

> In the tragedy of *Hamlet*, the ghost of a king appears on the stage; Hamlet goes crazy in the second act, and his mistress in the third; the Prince slays

> his mistress's father under the pretense of killing a rat, and the heroine throws herself into the river. Meantime another of the actors conquers Poland. Hamlet, his mother, and his father-in-law [*sic*] carouse on the stage, songs are sung at table, there's quarrelling, fighting, killing; it is a vulgar and barbarous drama which would not be tolerated by the vilest populace of France or Italy.

Pennington also stated that *A Midsummer Night's Dream* "is funnier than *Hamlet*, and in many ways more metaphysical as well." Write an essay in which you agree or disagree with Voltaire's and Pennington's criticisms of Shakespeare's plays.

5. Choose any one of the major characters in a play that you have read in this anthology, and write an essay analyzing this character from the point of view of an actor preparing to play this character on the stage.

PART FOUR

Writing about Literature

. . . a combination of the artistic and scientific [temperament]. The enthusiastic artist alone is apt to be too subjective in his attitude toward a book, and so a scientific coolness of judgment will temper the intuitive heat.

—VLADIMIR NABOKOV (on the qualities of the ideal reader)

A story writer is more than happy to be read by students; the fact that these serious readers think and feel something in response to his work he finds life-giving.

—EUDORA WELTY (on her readers' response to "A Worn Path")

I now know and trust completely that writing happens long before I ever type a word; that my best thinking and writing will happen before and after the first draft but not necessarily during it.

—ALEX JOHNSON

26.

Critical Reading and Literary Theory

> Literary criticism should arise out of a debt of love. In a manner evident and yet mysterious, the poem or the drama or the novel seizes upon our imaginings. We are not the same when we put down the work as we were when we took it up. To borrow an image from another domain: he who has truly apprehended a painting by Cézanne will thereafter see an apple or a chair as he had not seen them before. Great works of art pass through us like storm-winds, flinging open the doors of perception, pressing upon the architecture of our beliefs with their transforming powers. We seek to record their impact, to put our shaken house in its new order. Through some primary instinct of communion we seek to convey to others the quality and force of our experience. We would persuade them to lay themselves open to it. In this attempt at persuasion originate the truest insights criticism can afford.
>
> –GEORGE STEINER, *Tolstoy or Dostoevsky*

The effort to communicate "the quality and force of our experience" after reading a story, poem, or play that has moved us is behind all of our attempts to write papers about literature. Initially all readers bring their different experiences of life to what they find on the page, but after you begin to read a text critically in order to write about it, you can choose different approaches that can help you to organize your response to what you have read. You can decide (or you are told) to concentrate on the text, on the author, on the wider historical or cultural context of the writing, or on you yourself as the reader. In recent years these different critical perspectives have given rise to different literary theories. Learning about these theories can offer you more choices in deciding how to organize your insights when you are given the assignment to write about literature.

In the opening pages of his book *Literary Theory*, the contemporary English critic Terry Eagleton wrote that "hostility to theory usually means an opposition to other people's theories and an oblivion of one's own." Initially you may feel that literary theory is formidable, but as you begin to explore the various commentaries by short story writers, poets, dramatists, and critics in this anthology, you will discover they make available several different approaches that can help you to write your own papers. For example, Sandra M. Gilbert and Susan Gubar give a feminist reading of Gilman's "The Yellow

Wallpaper" (p. 239) and Cleanth Brooks and Robert Penn Warren develop a formalist or new critical analysis of Poe's "The Fall of the House of Usher" (p. 656). You can read a student essay adapting a reader-response perspective in the paper on Eudora Welty's "A Worn Path" in Chapter 27 (p. 1634). Becoming conscious of a critic's perspective may also make you become more aware of the assumptions that underlie your own thoughts about literature.

Literary theory is the term used in academic criticism to characterize particular methods of inquiry into the nature and value of literature. Formulating general critical principles—rather than analyzing particular literary texts—is the job of theorists like Terry Eagleton, whereas your assignment is usually to analyze a specific story, poem, or play. The following ten critical approaches to literary texts are the ones you will encounter most frequently in your reading of the commentaries. They offer some useful perspectives to consider in your critical thinking and writing about literature.

FORMALIST CRITICISM

Formalist criticism is probably the most common approach to the analysis of literature. Along with other theoretical perspectives, critics often use it to develop their interpretation of literary texts. René Wellek and Austin Warren, the pioneering practitioners of formalism in the United States, wrote in their *Theory of Literature* (1942) that "the natural and sensible starting point for work in literary scholarship is the interpretation and analysis of the works of literature themselves."

Formalists regard a work of fiction, poetry, or drama as a world in itself that can be understood by its intrinsic nature—focusing on form over content. The organization of this textbook—into chapters featuring discussions of the elements of the short story, the poem, and the play—is implicitly formalist. However, a pure formalist approach would not include headnotes about the authors, considering facts about the author's life and historical times irrelevant to the appreciation of a text. Instead, a formalist would concentrate on analyzing how the various elements of a story, poem, or play are integrated into the complex and unique structure of a self-contained aesthetic work.

For example, the academic critic Cleanth Brooks and the poet Robert Penn Warren give a formalist analysis of T. S. Eliot's "The Love Song of J. Alfred Prufrock" on page 965. Their discussion was included in *Understanding Poetry* (1938), a college textbook that introduced generations of teachers and students to the formalist techniques of what was then called "New Criticism" based on a close reading of the text. In Brooks and Warren's discussion of Eliot's poem, they emphasize the irony implicit in its tone. They compare Prufrock's character to that of Hamlet but for the most part their references remain inside the text, explicating the poem line by line to unravel the complexity of Eliot's linguistic and cultural erudition.

BIOGRAPHICAL CRITICISM

In "The Formalist Critic," Cleanth Brooks stated that

> the formalist critic is concerned primarily with the work itself. Speculation on the mental processes of the author takes the critic away from the work into biography and psychology. There is no reason, of course, why he should not turn away into biography and psychology. Such explorations are very much worth making. But they should not be confused with an account of the work. Such studies describe the process of composition, not the structure of the thing composed. . . .

Unlike formalist criticism, **biographical criticism** starts with the premise that stories, poems, and plays are written by human beings, and that important facts about the life of an author often can shed light on literary texts. Usually this kind of critical approach develops the thesis of a paper by suggesting the connection of *cause and effect.* That is, you maintain that the imaginative world of the text has characteristics that originate from causes or sources in the author's background.

You have probably written papers about literature in a biographical context. A favorite high-school English term paper project is to assign an author as a topic, requiring research into the details about his or her life. If you ever wrote this kind of paper, you may have organized your material chronologically, tracing the life of your author and listing his or her most important literary works, often with no clearly defined thesis in mind. In writing papers for college English classes based on a unified central idea, on the other hand, you must ask yourself how knowing the facts of an author's life can help you to understand a specific text. Usually you do not attempt to survey an author's complete works in a short paper.

A biographical approach to literature requires at least as much care as formalist criticism—care in presenting only the relevant facts of an author's life and in using a sensitive interpretation of them to show clear connections between the writer's experience or personality and the work. Brett C. Millier's discussion of Elizabeth Bishop's poem "One Art" (p. 932) is an exemplary use of the biographical approach to literature. Millier has focused this account of Bishop's revision of the poem through a careful examination of the seventeen drafts of the manuscript. In the long middle paragraph of the analysis, Millier introduces Bishop's biographical information, a summary of the poet's losses beginning with the disappearance and death of her parents when she was still a child. The biographical critic then concludes that the list of these personal losses encoded into the poem is an example of Bishop's method of "reticence" as a confessional poet, part of her lifelong process of acquiring self-discipline.

PSYCHOLOGICAL CRITICISM

Psychological criticism is indebted to modern psychology, which began with the psychoanalytic theories of its founder, the Austrian psychoanalyst Sigmund Freud (1856–1939). Freud wrote that he learned nearly as much about psychology from reading authors such as Sophocles and Shakespeare as he did from his clinical work with his patients in Vienna as an analyst and physician. Freud's writing about psychology, along with books by his disciples including Carl Jung, Marie Bonaparte, and Bruno Bettelheim, modified our understanding of human behavior, introducing such concepts as the unconscious forces of the id and the superego active within every individual.

Three approaches are most often taken by critics interested in exploring the psychological aspect of literature. First is the investigation of the creative process and the nature of literary genius. This field of investigation can also include other forms of genius—musical, mathematical, and so forth. The second is the study of an individual writer (or artist or musician or scientist), particularly appropriate if, like the American poets Anne Sexton, Sylvia Plath, and Robert Lowell, the individual was deeply involved in psychological therapy or analysis. The third is the analysis of fictional characters, which began with Freud's study of the character of Oedipus when he analyzed Sophocles' play in his book *The Interpretation of Dreams* (1900).

An excerpt from Freud's discussion of "The Oedipus Complex" is on page 1179 of this anthology. Freud begins his analysis by referring to the childhood of his neurotic patients, many of whom he observed obsessing on "a magnified scale feelings of love and hatred to their parents." The psychoanalyst then summarizes the plot of *Oedipus the King,* observing that Sophocles has dramatized "a legend whose profound and universal power to move can only be understood if the hypothesis I have put forward in regard to the psychology of children has an equally universal validity." Freud argues that the destiny of the fictional king of Thebes "moves us only because it might have been ours—because the oracle laid the same curse upon us before our birth as upon him." Moving from literary analysis to psychological generalizations, Freud used literature to formulate universal theories about human psychology that have continued to influence our ideas for over a century.

MYTHOLOGICAL CRITICISM

Mythological criticism developed out of psychoanalytic theory in the work of Freud's younger disciple, the Swiss psychiatrist Carl G. Jung. A man of vast reading in anthropology and comparative religion as well as literature, Jung formulated the theory of the archetype. Derived from the experience of the human race in different cultures, **archetypes** consist of images present in the unconscious mind of every individual, which Jung called the "collective unconscious." Archetypal images of the sun, for example, are inherent in every culture and give rise to storytelling that results in tribal myths. The critic Northrop Frye defined the archetype in strictly literary terms as "a symbol, usually an image, which recurs often enough in literature to be recognizable as an element of one's literary experience as a whole."

When critics characterize archetypal images in specific works of literature, they usually refer to several texts beyond the one being scrutinized in order to establish an underlying pattern of similarity. You can try your hand at the mythological critical approach by comparing and contrasting Leslie Marmon

Silko's story "Yellow Woman" (p. 572) with the Native American myth told by Paula Gunn Allen in "Whirlwind Man Steals Yellow Woman" (p. 579).

HISTORICAL CRITICISM

Historical criticism approaches a literary work through its historical context, the events that were occurring in the world during the time the author wrote a particular story, poem, or play. This method is often combined with the biographical approach, if the historical events contributed to the author's thought process and resulted in the creation of a work of literature. Historical critics may also explain the meaning that the work had for its original readers, especially if the text includes words that had different connotations in the past.

The critic Sally Fitzgerald, who was a close friend of the writer Flannery O'Connor, takes a historical approach in her discussion of the 1953 short story "A Good Man Is Hard to Find" (p. 647). During the years of their friendship, O'Connor sent Fitzgerald clippings of articles with "lurid headlines" from local newspapers of her hometown, Milledgeville, Georgia. Although O'Connor was merely trying to amuse Fitzgerald, the critic saved the clippings and used them in an article about O'Connor titled "Happy Endings," published in *Image* in 1997. The newspaper clippings from the early 1950s included accounts of a prize-winning child singer "decked out in ribbons and tutu and sausage curls," whose winning song was titled "A Good Man Is Hard to Find," as well as a series of articles about a criminal "aloose" in the region who totaled up a record of twenty-six kidnappings and ten car thefts, among other high jinks, in what Fitzgerald described in her essay as "two fun-filled weeks." The critic suggests how these documents may have influenced O'Connor when she created the fictional character of The Misfit. Fitzgerald concludes by using the newspaper articles to shed light on the theme of redemption dramatized in the story.

SOCIOLOGICAL CRITICISM

Sociological criticism is written by critics interested in exploring the economic, racial, and political context in which works of literature are created and read. Examining the relationships between writers and their society, these critics focus on the ideological aspects inherent in stories, poems, and plays. As the critic Wilbur Scott understood, "Art is not created in a vacuum; it is the work not simply of a person, but of an author fixed in time and space, answering a community of which he is an important, because articulate, part." The novelist Joseph Conrad went even further in making a connection between literature and society when he wrote in *Notes on Life and Letters*:

> Fiction is history, human history, or it is nothing. But it is also more than that; it stands on firmer ground, being based on the reality of forms and the observation of social phenomena, whereas history is based on documents, and the reading of print and handwriting—on second-hand impression. Thus fiction is nearer truth.

Perhaps the most controversial type of sociological criticism is **Marxist criticism**. Marxist critics, including the Hungarian philosopher Georg Lukács, believe that all art is political. This approach can become highly theoretical, as in Mikhail Bakhtin and V. N. Voloshinov's 1929 study *Marxism and the Philosophy of Language*, which argues that language is fundamentally "dialogic," a focus of social struggle and contradiction. As Eagleton explained in *Literary Theory*, for these critics, "it was not simply a matter of asking 'what the sign [word] meant,' but of investigating its varied history, as conflicting social groups, classes, individuals, and discourses sought to appropriate it and imbue it with their own meanings. Language, in short, was a field of ideological contention, not a monolithic system."

In this anthology, Helge Normann Nilsen examines the influence of Marxist theory on *Death of a Salesman* in her essay "Marxism and the Early Plays of Arthur Miller" on page 1502. Nilsen bases her analysis of Miller's political attitudes on his statements about the destructive aspects of capitalism in his autobiography, bolstering her argument with footnotes from the playwright's *Timebends: A Life* (1987).

READER-RESPONSE CRITICISM

For much of the twentieth century, the formalist approach to "close reading" of stories, poems, and plays was the most popular method of analysis in American college classrooms. After the turbulent social changes of the 1960s, literary critics in the United States became receptive to many new approaches to the text. The critic Ross Murfin has summarized the reaction against the "New Critical" practices:

> About 1970, the New Criticism came under attack by reader-response critics (who believe that the meaning of a work is not inherent in its internal form but rather is cooperatively produced by the reader and the text) and poststructuralists (who, following the philosophy of Jacques Derrida, argue that texts are inevitably self-contradictory and that we can find form in them only by ignoring or suppressing conflicting details or elements). In retrospect it is clear that, in their outspoken opposition to the New Criticism notwithstanding, the reader-response critics and poststructuralists of the 1970s were very much like their formalist predecessors in two important respects: for the most part, they ignored the world beyond the text and its reader, and, for the most part, they ignored the historical contexts within which literary works are written and read.

Reader-response criticism postulates that reading is as much a creative act as the writing of a text, because both involve the play of imagination and intelligence. Some reader-response critics even go so far as to say that a literary text has no existence outside of a reader's mind. Recognizing that different readers can find different meaning in works of literature, reader-response critics also emphasize the fact that the same reader can, at different periods of his or her life, find the experience of reading a book changes with maturity. If you keep the notes you take on reading *Hamlet* as a college freshman, for example, you will probably find that in twenty years or so, your interpretation of the play will change if you read it again or see a new production in the theater. On page

1107 of this anthology you will find a reader's response to the opening lines of Strindberg's *The Stronger*.

POSTSTRUCTURALIST AND DECONSTRUCTIONIST CRITICISM

Poststructuralist and **deconstructionist criticism** are two modern approaches to critical theory that, like reader-response criticism, focus on the multiple, sometimes self-contradictory meanings that exist in a literary work—meanings that resist a final interpretation. Critics who practice these approaches believe in a basic logical syllogism:

A. Human language is fundamentally unstable, as its meaning is dependent on changing but omnipresent social and historical factors.
B. Literary texts are composed of human language.
C. Therefore, literary texts are fundamentally unstable. Q.E.D.

Arguing that the literary text is unstable, deconstructionist critics like the French authorities Roland Barthes and Michel Foucault have called for "the death of literature" and "the death of the author." In 1968 Barthes explained in his essay "The Death of the Author":

> Once the Author is removed, the claim to decipher a text becomes quite futile. To give a text an Author is to impose a limit on that text, to furnish it with a final signified, to close the writing. Such a conception suits criticism very well, the latter then allotting itself the important task of discovering the Author (or its hypostases: society, history, psyche, liberty) beneath the work: when the Author has been found, the text is "explained"—victory to the critic. . . . In the multiplicity of writing, everything is to be *disentangled*, nothing *deciphered;* the structure can be followed, "run" (like the thread of a stocking) at every point and at every level, but there is nothing beneath. . . . writing ceaselessly posits meaning ceaselessly to evaporate it, carrying out a systematic exemption of meaning.

While formalists find coherence in the different elements of a text, deconstructionists show how the author's language can be broken or "deconstructed" into irreconcilable meanings. Their efforts have influenced many contemporary critics, and their theories are worth investigating if you continue your study of literature in upper-division courses and graduate school.

You can sample their approach in the list of books at the end of this section, as well as in J. Gerald Kennedy's deconstructive reading of Poe's "The Fall of the House of Usher" on page 658 of this anthology.

GENDER CRITICISM

Gender criticism emerged in the wake of the development of feminist criticism on American college campuses in the 1970s, gradually evolving into gender criticism with the inclusion of gay and lesbian critics. This branch of critical theory is indebted to early works such as the French critic Simone de Beauvoir's *The Second Sex* (1949) as well as the American feminists Betty

Friedan's *The Feminine Mystique* (1963) and Kate Millett's *Sexual Politics* (1970).

Gender critics are concerned with the gender and sexual orientation of both writers and readers of literature. They argue that our patriarchal culture is so imbued with assumptions of heterosexual male superiority that we must continuously correct the imbalance by identifying and analyzing its components and negative influences. Explaining how gender has influenced both an author's work and a reader's response to a literary text, this approach often contains aspects of reader-response criticism.

On page 239 of this anthology you can read the feminist commentary of the eminent critics Sandra M. Gilbert and Susan Gubar on Charlotte Perkins Gilman's "The Yellow Wallpaper." This excerpt is taken from their book *The Madwoman in the Attic: The Woman Writer and the Nineteenth-Century Literary Imagination* (1979). Gilbert and Gubar place the story within the context of what they call the "literature of confinement," where a woman trapped by the patriarchal society attempts to free herself "through strategic re-definitions of self, art, and society."

CULTURAL CRITICISM

Cultural criticism, like gender criticism, can be viewed as an important contemporary development in literary studies erected upon the sturdy but limited foundation of formalist practice. Cultural critics, including New Historicists, do not advocate any one particular approach to literary study. Frequently they participate in interdisciplinary approaches, combining more than one field of academic study due to their assumption that individual works of literature should be approached as part of a larger cultural context. For example, if you investigated the changes in 1960s popular music as reflected in Joyce Carol Oates's "Where Are You Going, Where Have You Been?" (p. 452), incorporating musical history into your paper, you have been practicing cultural criticism. Sydney Plum's reading of "The Veil" by Marjane Satrapi is an example of cultural criticism (p. 570). As the poet X. J. Kennedy realizes,

> In theory, a cultural studies critic might employ any methodology. In practice, however, he or she will most often borrow concepts from deconstruction, Marxism analysis, gender criticism, race theory, and psychology. . . . Whereas traditional critical approaches often sought to demonstrate the unity of a literary work, cultural studies often seeks to portray social, political, and psychological conflicts it masks.

SELECTED BIBLIOGRAPHY

GENERAL OVERVIEW

Eagleton, Terry. *Literary Theory: An Introduction.* 2nd ed. Minneapolis: U of Minnesota P, 1996. Print.

Selden, Raman, ed. *Theory of Criticism.* New York: Addison Wesley, 1988. Print.

THE CHANGING LITERARY CANON

Lauter, Paul. *Canons and Contexts.* New York: Oxford UP, 1991. Print.

FORMALIST CRITICISM

Brooks, Cleanth. *The Well Wrought Urn: Studies in the Structure of Poetry.* New York: Reynal and Hitchcock, 1947. Print.

Eliot, T. S. *The Sacred Wood: Essays in Poetry and Criticism.* London: Methuen, 1920. Print.

Ransom, John Crowe. *The New Criticism.* Norfolk, CT: New Directions, 1941. Print.

Wellek, René, and Austin Warren. *Theory of Literature.* New York: Harcourt, Brace and World, 1949. Print.

BIOGRAPHICAL AND PSYCHOLOGICAL CRITICISM

Bloom, Harold. *The Anxiety of Influence.* 2nd ed. New York: Oxford UP, 1997. Print.

Crews, Frederick. *Out of My System: Psychoanalysis, Ideology, and Critical Method.* New York: Oxford UP, 1975. Print.

Freud, Sigmund. *The Standard Edition of the Complete Psychological Works.* 24 vols. Ed. James Strachey. London: Hogarth Press and the Institute of Psychoanalysis, 1940–68. Print.

Lesser, Simon O. *Fiction and the Unconscious.* Boston: Beacon Press, 1957. Print.

Skura, Meredith Anne. *The Literary Use of the Psychoanalytic Process.* New Haven: Yale UP, 1981. Print.

MYTHOLOGICAL CRITICISM

Bodkin, Maud. *Archetypal Patterns in Poetry.* London: Oxford UP, 1934. Print.

Frye, Northrop. *Anatomy of Criticism: Four Essays.* Princeton: Princeton UP, 1957. Print.

Jung, Carl Gustav. *Collected Works.* Ed. Herbert Read, Michael Fordham, and Gerhard Adler. 17 vols. New York: Pantheon, 1953. Print.

HISTORICAL AND SOCIOLOGICAL CRITICISM

Escarpit, Robert. *Sociology of Literature.* Painesville, OH: Lake Erie College P, 1965. Print.

Frow, John. *Marxism and Literary History.* Cambridge: Harvard UP, 1986. Print.

Lindenberger, Herbert. *Historical Drama: The Relation of Literature and Reality.* Chicago: U of Chicago P, 1975. Print.

Williams, Raymond. *Marxism and Literature.* Oxford: Oxford UP, 1977. Print.

READER-RESPONSE CRITICISM

Booth, Wayne C. *The Rhetoric of Fiction.* 2nd ed. Chicago: U of Chicago P, 1983. Print.

Eco, Umberto. *The Role of the Reader: Explorations in the Semiotics of Texts.* Bloomington: Indiana UP, 1979. Print.

Fish, Stanley. *Is There a Text in This Class? The Authority of Interpretive Communities.* Cambridge: Harvard UP, 1980. Print.

Freund, Elizabeth. *The Return of the Reader: Reader-Response Criticism.* London: Methuen, 1987. Print.

Tompkins, Jane P., ed. *Reader-Response Criticism: From Formalism to Post-Structuralism.* Baltimore: Johns Hopkins UP, 1980. Print.

POSTSTRUCTURALIST AND DECONSTRUCTIONIST CRITICISM

Barthes, Roland. *The Rustle of Language.* Trans. Richard Howard. New York: Hill and Wang, 1986. Print.

Culler, Jonathan. *On Deconstruction: Theory and Criticism after Structuralism.* Ithaca: Cornell UP, 1982. Print.

Derrida, Jacques. *Of Grammatology.* Trans. Gayatri Chakravorty Spivak. Baltimore: Johns Hopkins UP, 1976. Print.

Foucault, Michel. *Language, Counter-Memory, Practice.* Ed. Donald F. Bouchard. Trans. Donald F. Bouchard and Sherry Simon. Ithaca: Cornell UP, 1977. Print.

Smith, Barbara Herrnstein. *On the Margins of Discourse: The Relation of Literature to Language.* Chicago: U of Chicago P, 1979. Print.

GENDER CRITICISM

Baym, Nina. *Feminism and American Literary History.* New Brunswick: Rutgers UP, 1992. Print.

Edelman, Lee. *Homographesis: Essays in Gay Literary and Cultural Theory.* New York: Routledge, 1994. Print.

Fetterley, Judith. *The Resisting Reader: A Feminist Approach to American Fiction.* Bloomington: Indiana UP, 1978. Print.

Jagose, Annamarie. *Queer Theory.* Victoria: Melbourne UP, 1996. Print.

Sedgwick, Eve Kosofsky. *Between Men: English Literature and Male Homosocial Desire.* New York: Columbia UP, 1985. Print.

Showalter, Elaine. *A Literature of Their Own.* Princeton: Princeton UP, 1977. Print.

Smith, Barbara. *Toward a Black Feminist Criticism.* New York: Out and Out, 1977. Print.

CULTURAL CRITICISM

Clayton, Jay, and Eric Rothstein, eds. *Influence and Intertextuality in Literary History.* Madison: U of Wisconsin P, 1991. Print.

Cox, Jeffrey N., and Larry J. Reynolds, eds. *New Historical Literary Study: Essays on Reproducing Texts, Representing History.* Princeton: Princeton UP, 1993. Print.

Eagleton, Terry. *After Theory.* New York: Basic Books, 2003. Print.

Storey, John, ed. *What Is Cultural Studies?* New York: St. Martin's, 1996. Print.

White, Hayden. *Tropics of Discourse: Essays in Cultural Criticism.* Baltimore: Johns Hopkins UP, 1978. Print.

WEB Learn more about literary criticism through VirtuaLit and LitGloss at bedfordstmartins.com/rewritinglit.

27. Using the Writing Process to Develop Your Paper

> Literature is our conversation between the past and present out of which we articulate ourselves.
>
> –DANA GIOIA, "Fallen Star," *Hungry Mind Review* 52

Read literature for the pleasure of it, Ernest Hemingway once told an interviewer, adding that "whatever else you find will be the measure of what you brought to the reading." Literature expands your view of the world, by inviting you to share the perspective of gifted storytellers, poets, and dramatists who can entertain, instruct, and perhaps enchant you. An assignment to write a paper about literature gives you the opportunity to explain how you have been affected by what you have read. There you explore your connection with the text and clarify your ideas about its significance. The writing process begins as soon as you ask the smallest question about the meaning or the structure of a literary work.

Good ideas are essential to a successful paper. How do you develop your initial emotional response to a story, poem, or play into ideas for a paper? There is no magic formula that guarantees a good result, since all writers must find their own way and learn to do it for themselves. If you understand the various steps involved, the writing process can become much easier. As the essayist Alex Johnson has observed, writing is always a challenge, but it does not always have to be a chore. In "Having a Bad Morning," she confessed uncertainty as to "how to get the thinking out."

> It took me years of trial and error to learn the obvious: writing is best and most satisfying done in stages. . . . I now know and trust completely that writing happens long before I ever type a word; that my best thinking and writing will happen before and after the first draft but not necessarily during it; that by seeing writing as a process, I now know the pleasure of making connections: ruminating on a subject, seeing patterns emerge, watching an argument evolve, evidence cohere. In short, that glorious territoriality of staking and claiming a subject as my own.

The best way to write a paper about literature is to proceed in stages, understanding that good writing is as much a process as it is an end result. When you are fully engaged in this endeavor, you will discover that the process also turns you into a better reader. Both as a reader and a writer, you will exercise your sensitivity and intelligence if you work conscientiously through the various stages toward the final draft of your paper.

Assume, for example, that your first writing assignment will be a two-to-three-page paper (500 to 750 words) on Eudora Welty's literary style in "A Worn Path" (p. 619) developing a formalist approach or a close reading of the text. You have one week to turn in your paper. Everyone works differently, but here is a description of how you might budget your time most efficiently during the week by taking the writing process in stages. This process is a lot easier than procrastinating until the day before your paper is due and then pulling a hectic all-nighter in a desperate effort to get the work finished on time.

First, before you start to write, you must read the story carefully at least twice. In "Good Readers and Good Writers," Vladimir Nabokov suggested that the ideal reader should develop "a combination of the artistic and the scientific [temperament]. The enthusiastic artist alone is apt to be too subjective in his attitude toward a book, and so a scientific coolness of judgment will temper the intuitive heat." Read Welty's story the first time for pleasure; bring out your "scientific coolness" when you study it the second time.

KEEPING A JOURNAL OR NOTEBOOK TO RECORD YOUR INITIAL RESPONSES TO THE TEXT

Often the earliest stage in responding to a literary work occurs as you read the text and feel the impulse to underline words or phrases that instinctively strike you as significant. It's relatively easy to give in to this impulse. Using a pen as a highlighter is a step in the right direction, but there's a better way that will get you started on your paper. Keeping a journal or a notebook in which you record your responses to your reading will help you to generate ideas about what you find there.

In her essay "Keeping a Notebook," the writer Joan Didion said the main reason writers keep a record of their experience is that "we forget all too soon the things we thought we could never forget. . . . Keeping in touch is what notebooks are all about." Recording your impressions right after reading the assignment helps you to remember what you thought about it.

For most students, a journal of responses to literature is an important stage in the journey of transforming themselves from readers into writers. Once you become aware of how you are reading a text, you have begun the process of using your own words to describe what you find significant about a story, play, or poem. This is the beginning of your discovery of "the measure of what you brought to the reading."

In your journal, you should note your responses after your first (or second) reading of Welty's story. Jot down short quotations from the story if they strike you as significant. Your notes might look something like this:

JOURNAL ENTRY

Eudora Welty's "A Worn Path" . . . starts right in on the story introducing a very old woman named Phoenix Jackson, who's taking a long walk by herself on a December afternoon in the country. Author knows the setting very well—lots of specific details of trees, bushes, hills, and creek—Phoenix talks to herself but she's a feisty old thing. Has trouble seeing, but she picks up and hides a nickel belonging to a hunter she meets on the trail—the old lady's conscience bothers her, but she doesn't let on—he speaks so condescendingly to her that I think she's entitled to take his money—it's just a nickel—wait—did he drop the nickel or did she just see it on the ground? yes, Welty says it fell out of his pocket—so she could have given it back to him. The old lady gets tired but she keeps going and finally arrives at Natchez. Then she goes into a building in town where "she walked up and around and around until her feet knew to stop." So she's been there often before. It seems to be a nurses' office—and she's so old and tired she forgets why she's there—then remembers that she's come to get medicine for her grandson. Horrible—the little boy swallowed lye. He lives with Phoenix, and she makes the long walk to town for his sake every year. The nurse likes Phoenix—gives her a nickel as a Christmas present. Phoenix really loves her grandson—she tells the nurse she's going to buy him a present before she starts the long walk home. I wonder, is this grandson alive or dead? Is the old woman senile? Can we trust her?

You will notice that in your journal you began by summarizing the plot in your own words. That is the first response of most students when given the assignment of writing about literature. You need not regard it as a wasted effort because you can use your notes later to review the story when studying for an exam. But your instructor has asked you to write a paper. How can your notes help you find an idea to develop into a paper?

Notice that summarizing the events of the story has led you to ask a question about the main character's actions: Can we trust Phoenix Jackson, or is she so old that she's really senile and doesn't know whether her grandson is alive or dead? If you are an insecure reader, you may think that your question is foolish, but it isn't. Often getting the answer to a simple question that arises as you read the text will lead you to more complex ideas about its significance that you can develop in your paper.

You can bring your question about "A Worn Path" to your instructor in class. Or, working by yourself, you can find commentaries by authors and critics in this anthology that shed light on your reading. So many students asked this question about the story that Welty wrote a commentary titled "Is Phoenix Jackson's Grandson Really Dead?" (p. 625). Reading her commentary will not only show you that you have asked a good question, but it will also help you generate ideas about the story for your paper. The important thing is *your* response to the story—what makes it significant for you. Reading commentaries, such as Welty's on "A Worn Path," will help you become a more informed reader and may stimulate your critical thinking about the story.

A number of commentaries on the stories, poems, and plays in this anthology are included throughout *Literature and Its Writers* because reading commentaries can help you feel more confident when you begin to think critically about literature. While commentaries by authors and critics often clear up specific questions about a text, they always introduce you to important aspects of the significance of a story, poem, or play that you might have missed on your own. You may agree or disagree with the commentaries, but they will usually stimulate your critical thinking.

USING THE COMMENTARIES TO ASK NEW QUESTIONS ABOUT WHAT YOU HAVE READ

Reading Welty's commentary answered your first question about the story: The author tells you that the grandson is alive. After Welty answers the question, you might be struck by how seriously she takes what she calls the "fiction writer's responsibility" in the second part of her essay. Welty says that a good writer never uses tricks in order to mislead the reader; the words in a story must always "mean what they say."

Welty's commentary has caused you to look at "A Worn Path" in a new way. How does an author make her words "mean what they say"? Now you might feel a flicker of excitement as you begin to think about how Welty has selected particular words to make up her story about a solitary old woman she glimpsed walking in a country landscape. Welty states that she wanted her story to illustrate an idea she had about this woman's journey: She wanted to dramatize what she imagined as "the deep-grained habit of love."

Thinking about the commentary, you might be impressed by Welty's sympathy for her central character, Phoenix Jackson. When you scan the opening paragraphs of "A Worn Path" again, you find that this sympathy is conveyed by the words Welty has chosen to tell her story. You ask yourself, how does the author keep her subject from becoming sentimental? What words in the text suggest Welty's feelings for the woman she writes about in the story without going overboard? You remember a line from the story that you jotted down in your journal: "she walked up and around and around until her feet knew to stop." Suddenly it's clear to you that Welty has chosen words that Phoenix Jackson would use. Now your mind is full of questions about the story. You are ready for the next stage in the writing process.

GENERATING IDEAS BY BRAINSTORMING, FREEWRITING, AND LISTING

Generating ideas for the assignment can be done in a variety of ways, either as a solitary process of jotting down ideas on paper or as a communal process of talking over your ideas with a friend or classmate who has also read the story. If you follow the latter course, be sure to take notes as your conversation progresses so that your ideas do not evaporate in the general glow of good company.

Usually sufficient ideas for your paper will evolve during one of these exercises of brainstorming, freewriting, and listing. Initially you might try them all to find out which one works best for you.

Brainstorming for Ideas

Perhaps the notion that Welty has written her story in words that Phoenix Jackson might use intrigues you so much that you decide to brainstorm by yourself. Record the thoughts that occur to you while you look over the story again. Begin with Welty's first sentence and free associate about whatever comes to your mind:

> Simple language, telling the month and day and time. Welty's so logical—large (month) to small (morning) time units.

Now try to think more specifically about Welty's choice of words. Brainstorm further by finding adjectives to describe your impressions of the words she uses to introduce Phoenix Jackson:

> respectful, warm, sympathetic, humane, compassionate, a little funny but gently so—Welty never makes a joke at Phoenix's expense. She's "neat and tidy," but still human—her shoelaces drag and she hasn't bothered to lace her shoes. Is it because she's too old to bend down to lace them? Or maybe her feet hurt and she can't buy another pair.

At this point you might discover that brainstorming has put your imagination to work on the story. Your brief vision of the figure of Phoenix Jackson so frail with age that she is unable to bend over to tie her own shoes has made her become almost as real to you as your own grandmother. This might amuse you and cause you to realize that you have learned something about the magic of literature: Writing about it can make you a more active participant in it.

This might be a good time to review your notes. Can you find a pattern in the details Welty has given you about Phoenix Jackson? If you have been as conscious of your thoughts about the story as Phoenix was aware of the path she was following through the woods, you might begin to sense Welty building something in her careful choice of descriptive details. She seems to suggest one thing and then to continue on to its opposite. Phoenix is "an old Negro woman" (respectable), but "her head tied in a red rag" (poor, shabby). She is "neat and tidy," but her shoelaces drag. And so on. Why does Welty do this?

As you think about it, you realize that while Welty sometimes chooses words that Phoenix Jackson might use, the author is clearly in control, selecting details about her character very carefully. How do you develop this new idea? You might try another technique to help you focus your thoughts, an exercise called freewriting.

Freewriting

Like brainstorming, focused freewriting can help you develop an idea when you begin to think critically about literature. In a freewriting session, you state everything that comes to mind when you try to answer a question relating to the subject of your paper. Do not stop to think of forming complete sentences or using correct grammar or spelling. Give yourself a set time—perhaps ten or fifteen minutes or even longer if you feel inspired—to spill out all your associations about the topic. You can use a scratch pad, a notebook, or a computer—whatever you have at hand. Keep the story beside you as you write, so that you can refer to it as necessary. Then go back and underline ideas in your writing that you think could be organized into a coherent outline and developed further in your paper. Here is an example of freewriting about "A Worn Path" on the topic of Welty's style or choice of words as a storyteller.

> What does she do that makes me want to read on, one word following the next, until I'm hooked and want to know "what happens next"? First of all, her words make Phoenix into a complicated character. Simple to begin with, but more there than obviously meets the eye. Not a lot of dramatic action but a soft tone, almost as if she wanted to make you bend closer to her to hear her better. Serious, simple tone to begin the story. Then that business about the red rag. Does that do it? Or is it the choice of words, so simple and down-to-earth. Just like the character Welty's trying to describe. She's like anybody's granny in the country—even if it's Mississippi by the end of the story. Think about it. The way Welty uses alliteration, "red rag" and "path through the pinewoods," so her voice sounds good—it's very musical and rhythmic prose. Perhaps she's creating the rhythm of Phoenix's walk, "the balanced heaviness and lightness."

Focused freewriting can make you conscious of ideas you did not know you had, like the thought that Welty's prose is so musical and rhythmic that it suggests the pace of Phoenix's physical movements as she makes her slow way along the worn, familiar path to town. Brainstorming ideas and freewriting can often help you to think critically about a literary work. At this point you might want to make a list of all the things you have discovered about the story so far.

Listing

Another useful technique in the preliminary stage of the writing process is making lists. You are probably experienced at doing this whenever you try to keep several things in mind at once, especially if you are planning to use the list later on, as for grocery shopping or organizing "things to do" over the course of a busy weekend. Listing also can become a way to help you develop your thoughts about literature. Making a list is more focused than brainstorming or freewriting; first you must be clear about what you want to list.

For example, if you would like to develop the idea that what attracts you about Welty's storytelling voice is its musical quality, you could comb "A Worn Path" for more instances of memorable alliteration (like "red rag") in the words describing the protagonist. You will probably find that—strangely enough—once your brain starts to go to work analyzing literature, one idea seems to stimulate another during the writing process.

As you scan the story again, you suddenly notice the beautiful simile that Welty uses in the second paragraph to describe Phoenix's wrinkled face: "as though a whole little tree stood in the middle of her forehead." You see that Welty emphasizes the vitality and beauty of Phoenix's skin color—"golden." And this detail is followed at the end of the paragraph by another compliment, that her hair falls "in the frailest of ringlets, still black, and with an odor like copper." What is "an odor like copper"? you ask yourself. Is it a good smell or a bad one? This makes you remember an early idea when you started thinking about the assignment, that Welty blends positive and negative attributes into her description of Phoenix Jackson. Could that be how she keeps her story about the old woman from becoming sentimental?

You may feel that you have gotten a little sidetracked, but that is no matter, because your thoughts about the second paragraph have carried you further along on your idea about Welty's method of drawing you into the story by her poetic description of Phoenix Jackson's face. Return to the story to find the examples that you started looking for, of musical alliteration. They are as easy to find in the opening paragraph as ripe red strawberries in summer:

red rag
side to side in her steps
sugar sacks

When you begin to notice examples of assonance, like the sound of the *o*'s in "odor of copper," you could start to make another list. You could also jot down a third list of examples of inverted word order that Welty has used in her sentences to achieve musical effect, such as "On she went." And you could create a fourth list for examples of the regular rhythm of sentences she (or Phoenix) chants using the melody of parallel structure: "Up through pines. . . . Now down through oaks."

ORGANIZING YOUR NOTES INTO A PRELIMINARY THESIS SENTENCE AND OUTLINE

After you have given yourself sufficient time to think critically about the story, you are ready to organize your thoughts about what you intend to write. *This is the most crucial step in the process of creating your paper.* Many students make the mistake of beginning to write the first draft of their paper too soon, before they have taken the time to stimulate new ideas and create a strong **thesis sentence**. They string together sentences about a topic, rather than develop a clearly focused response to their assignment. If you work on a strong thesis sentence first, before you start writing your paper, you will save yourself considerable anxiety and several false starts, or—even worse—an unfocused paper that doesn't communicate clearly to your reader.

Whether you are writing only a few paragraphs or a research paper of several thousand words, the basic requirement is always the same. A paper on any subject is a type of expository writing, and *expository* means "serving to clarify, set forth, or explain in detail" a central idea about your topic. Do not start until you are able to express a strong idea in a well-crafted sentence.

An effective paper always requires two things: first, a good thesis sentence or central idea about your topic to start your paper, and second, an adequate development of your thesis sentence. Often it helps you get started if you concentrate on stating your thesis as clearly as you can in your rough draft. When you revise, you can make sure that you have presented sufficient evidence to support your main idea. Some useful ways of organizing longer papers about literature—by explication, analysis, and comparison and contrast—are discussed in Chapter 28. Regardless of your paper's length, you should always begin by trying to express your central idea about the topic so that it can evolve and develop in the writing process.

Which of your notes about Welty's story is the best candidate to serve as a thesis sentence? It should express the main point of your paper. Consider it a *preliminary* thesis at this point, subject to revision when you rewrite your rough draft. After some thought, you might come up with the following thesis sentences:

1. *Welty's way of telling her story is interesting.* This is a common, quick, and facile solution to the problem of formulating a thesis sentence. It is totally inadequate because it is too general. A moment's reflection will reveal that a topic is not the same as a thesis. A topic is a general subject ("*Welty's way of telling her story*"); a thesis makes a statement about a topic ("*is interesting*" is not much of a statement).
2. *Welty's way of telling her story draws the reader into "A Worn Path."* This is a much more useful thesis sentence. You have thought about the topic and narrowed it down to focus on the relationship of the topic to a specific idea. The test of a thesis sentence is whether your general subject ("*Welty's way of telling her story*") is followed by a clearly focused predicate ("*draws the reader into 'A Worn Path'*").
3. *Welty uses language as a storyteller the way that Phoenix Jackson would use words to express her thoughts.* This was your first insight into Welty's way of telling her story. It could serve as a useful preliminary thesis. You have narrowed the topic even further. Your general subject ("*Welty uses language as a storyteller*") is followed by a very specific predicate ("*the way that Phoenix Jackson would use words to express her thoughts*"). This thesis sentence unmistakably points the way to how you could begin to develop your rough draft. You might suspect that this idea is too narrowly focused for your entire paper, but you will discover whether this is true as you write.
4. *Welty uses language the way a poet does to keep readers interested in her story.* This idea came out of the listing exercise, where you found examples

of Welty's use of alliteration, assonance, and rhetorical structure. Like the previous two ideas, this could also serve as a useful preliminary thesis sentence to get you started on your rough draft.

Assume you take the third choice, because this was your original insight about the story and you like the idea best. Working on a paper is always more enjoyable when you are enthusiastic about the assignment. Before you sit down at the computer, you will find that making a brief outline will help you see the direction to take more clearly. It does not have to be a traditional outline. Shape it in any way that will help you remember the points you intend to make if you are interrupted. Start by writing down your preliminary thesis sentence. Then assemble the evidence you have found to support it.

As a storyteller, Welty uses language the way that Phoenix Jackson uses words to express her thoughts.

1. Simple, down-to-earth vocabulary.
2. Poetic and musical phrases.

Because your assignment is a short paper, this initial thesis sentence and outline will get you started on your first draft. Don't worry about making the thesis perfect at this stage. You will bring your thesis into even sharper focus as you develop what you have to say about your topic. As Alex Johnson understood, the object of a first draft is to shape the thesis sentence into what she called a "controlling idea":

> The most common misconception is that the first draft is about writing *per se*. It's not. It's about thinking. If you've managed to turn out felicitous phrasing, I always tell students, it's icing on the cake. The real concern is how your idea evolves and sharpens, how its deeper structure emerges. To help this process along, don't agonize over word choice. Underline a word or simply leave a space and go back in the revision stage to get it right. Use momentum. Gag your internal critic and perfectionist when they report, correctly, that the draft seems sketchy. That's why it's called a first draft.

WRITING THE FIRST DRAFT

If you include a strong thesis sentence in the first paragraph of your first draft, it can often jumpstart further ideas. The effort of writing itself, the act of finding the right words to express your thoughts, can suggest new ways to develop your preliminary thesis. That is the reason you should allow plenty of time to complete an assignment. It is an unusual first draft in which the central idea is developed coherently and fully enough to be turned in as the finished paper. Revision usually stimulates further thought, sharpening and refining your argument.

You will probably discover that, like most people, you are better at rewriting than you are at writing. More often than not, the 500 or 750 words you might think are perfect when you turn in your final paper will be the end result—if you took enough time and care in writing—of winnowing many more words from your rough drafts. In your revision you can support your thesis by editing your sentences and paragraphs so that each one relates coherently to your central idea. Then your paper will express your insights about the story so clearly that they can be understood by your reader as you intended.

SAMPLE FIRST DRAFT OF A PAPER ON EUDORA WELTY'S "A WORN PATH"

An author's voice a point to consider about
^~~A storyteller's style~~ is^ key ~~to understanding~~^ the way she

From 's choice of words, we can hear that
tells her story.^ Eudora Welty^ ~~is a warm and sympathetic~~

she is a warm and sympathetic
^narrator in "A Worn Path." She uses language so simply

interests us
and concretely that she^ ~~makes us interested~~ immediately

named Phoenix Jackson
in the journey of an old woman^ as she walks through the

pinewoods to Natchez to get medicine for her grandson.

In fact, often
^Welty^ uses language the way Phoenix uses it to express

, because when she comes to the city
her thoughts/^ ~~At the end of the story~~ we are told that "she

walked up and around and around until her feet knew to

stop" (623).

captures the reader's attention
This simple, down-to-earth vocabulary^ ~~grounds us~~.

Welty
It is as if ~~the author~~^ could read the mind of the character

is creating
she^ ~~has created~~ on the page. We all would like to be able

mind and
to get inside the ~~thoughts~~^ of another person, ~~to~~^ share their

thoughts
most private^ ~~interior world,~~ so we want to read further.

This could be considered a trick, since Welty's own voice

(and mind) could not be exactly the same as the uneducated

Begin with broad generalization about the story.

Narrow your topic into a thesis sentence.

New insight in second paragraph develops out of writing the rough draft.

fictional
Phoenix, but Welty's ~~sincere~~ feeling for her ^ character
shines through the story. Her voice is sincere.

use of words as a storyteller
Welty's ^ ~~voice~~ interests us for another reason. She chooses words the way a poet would. She's writing
a prose story, *her*
^ ~~a short story,~~ but she chooses ^ words like a poet. There are many examples of alliteration and assonance in
opening *first*
the ^ ~~first~~ paragraph of her story, when she must ^ capture
, like "red rag" and "path through the pinewoods" (619).
our interest ^ In the second paragraph, she ~~gives~~
compares the pattern of wrinkles on
^ Phoenix's ~~wrinkled~~ face to a "whole little tree" (619). This
and poetic
is a fresh ^ image to help us visualize the old woman's appearance. The plot and characterization of Phoenix later in the story show us how resourceful and loving she is as a person. As a storyteller, Welty speaks of her heroine with great affection. She blends telling and showing in "A Worn Path."

Final paragraph needs further revision: repetitious vocabulary, ideas scattered, conclusion unfocused.

REVISING YOUR PAPER

Usually your first draft will be shorter than your final draft, but at this point you shouldn't worry about length. Instead, savor the feeling of satisfaction that you have made a good start on your paper. If you have the time, you should put your rough draft away for a day or so, and then read it again with fresh eyes. Before you return to it, you might want to reread the literature you are writing about, looking for more details to develop your thesis statement. In your revision, you could also try to incorporate relevant material you might be discussing in class, like the concept of an author's voice as an aspect of literary style.

Revision means exactly what it says—the opportunity to revisit your paper and take another look at it. This is the writing stage where you get the chance to do your best work. You can refine your argument by strengthening your evidence and tying together loose ends. Most students are surprised to find how rough and unfinished their first drafts appear after time away. Always go over your work with a pen or a pencil in hand so that you can continue to clarify what you have written for your reader.

If you compare the first draft of the paper on "A Worn Path" with the revised draft, you can see how the paper became more fully developed and more coherent. Two additional middle paragraphs give specific examples from the story, evidence that supports the thesis sentence. This sentence now concludes the opening paragraph, putting more emphasis on this central idea and pointing the way to its development in the following paragraphs. In the final version, the paper begins with a general sentence based on information from class discussions of short fiction about an author's voice as an aspect of literary style. This concept ties together several ideas about the story that had emerged from brainstorming, freewriting, and listing and also provides a title for the paper. The argument is further strengthened by the specific reference to Welty's commentary "Is Phoenix Jackson's Grandson Really Dead?"

SAMPLE REVISED DRAFT

The Voice of the Storyteller
in Eudora Welty's "A Worn Path"

An author's voice is a key point to consider about the effect of literary style on a reader. From Eudora Welty's choice of words in "A Worn Path," we can tell she's a warm and sympathetic narrator. She uses language so simply and concretely that she makes us interested in the journey of an old woman named Phoenix Jackson as she walks through the pinewoods to Natchez to get medicine for her grandson. In fact, Welty often uses language the way that Phoenix would use it to express her thoughts.

At the beginning of the story, Welty introduces Phoenix by describing her as "an old Negro woman with her head tied in a red rag" (619). This description, so clear and direct, gives us a vivid image of the central character. In the second paragraph, Welty tells us what Phoenix is wearing, a dark dress covered by a "long apron of bleached sugar sacks" (619). This old woman may be poor, but she is also clean and thrifty. We respect her even before we learn that she cares enough about her sick grandson to walk many miles along a rugged country path from her home to the clinic for a bottle of medicine.

When the old woman comes to the city sidewalks, we are told that "she walked up and around and around until her feet knew to stop" (623). Phoenix has gotten tired after her long trek through the woods, over the hills, across a creek, through a field of dead cornstalks, along a wagon track, and across a swamp on her way to Natchez. These are the words that she herself would use, and the sentence is structured the way she would talk.

This lively colloquial vocabulary captures the reader's attention. It is as if the author could read the mind of her character. We all would like to be able to get inside the mind of another person, to share his or her private thoughts and feelings, so we want to read further. Welty has revealed in her commentary on "A Worn Path" that "the story is told through Phoenix's mind" (626). This could be considered a trick, since Welty's own voice (and mind) could not be exactly the same as uneducated, unsophisticated Phoenix. But Welty shows her deep respect for what she calls "the deep-grained habit of love" in Phoenix's actions (627). The sound of the author's voice is sincere, so we trust her.

Welty's voice attracts us for another reason. She is writing prose, but she chooses words like a poet. There are many examples of alliteration and assonance in the opening paragraph of her story, like "red rag" and "path through the pinewoods" (619), when the author must first capture our interest. In the second paragraph, Welty uses a poetic simile to compare the pattern of wrinkles on Phoenix's face to a "whole little tree" (619). This comparison helps us visualize the old woman's appearance. It is also so down-to-earth that it could even have occurred to Phoenix herself if we imagine her seeing her reflection in the water of a stream or in a Natchez shop window. We are irresistibly drawn into the story by the skillful voice of the storyteller in "A Worn Path."

MAKING A FINAL CHECK OF YOUR FINISHED PAPER

Before you turn in your paper, you should check the quotations you have used to make sure that you have copied them accurately. If you have used a computer, you should also run a spell-check. The following guide can help you in the final preparation of your paper:

1. Be sure to include your name, date, and class section on the paper.
2. Check your title. Ideally, it should suggest an idea of your approach to the assigned topic. If you include the author's name or title of the work here, be sure you have spelled it correctly and have used quotation marks or underlining appropriately.
3. Include the name of the author and title of the work you are writing about in your opening paragraph so that the reader knows what you plan to discuss. Often, at least in short papers, the reader expects you to state your thesis sentence in the first paragraph.
4. Review your organization. Does your paper offer solid evidence to support your thesis statement? Does it develop ideas clearly and coherently? For effective emphasis, do your paragraphs proceed from the least important to the most important point? Can some of the longer paragraphs be divided into shorter units to clarify your main points? Are your short paragraphs adequately developed? Does each sentence relate to the one before? Have you supplied transitional sentences between paragraphs? Do you need to write shorter sentences so that your ideas come through more clearly?
5. Include quotations from the work you are discussing to add variety to the vocabulary you customarily use. Such a practice also offers a change of pace to the reader of your paper, as well as a reminder of the pleasures of the original text.
6. Check that your punctuation and grammar are correct throughout your paper, and that you have written varied and complete sentences, not sentence fragments. If you spot unintentional verbal repetitions, find fresh words to replace them or revise the sentence to eliminate wordiness.
7. Look for the conclusion to your paper. If it is a short paper, you can phrase your conclusion as a sentence or two in the final paragraph. In a longer paper, you could devote at least an entire final paragraph to a statement of your conclusion.

Peer Review

Before turning in the assignment, you could exchange papers with another student to check each other's work. Your instructor might also include a peer review of rough drafts or finished papers during class time, allowing you to benefit from other readers' suggestions for improvement. This could help you clarify your ideas and strengthen your argument. If you are given another student's paper, read it twice. The first time, read it straight through for enjoyment and illumination; the second time, read it critically.

If you think your classmate can improve the paper, put a question mark in the margin close to any places where the sentences are unclear or you don't understand what the writer is trying to say. Put a check mark in the margin where you would like to see a quotation from the text to illustrate and strengthen the writer's interpretation of the material. Can you identify the thesis statement? Would it be more effective if placed earlier in the essay? Underline it and, if necessary, suggest how it could be repositioned or rewritten more clearly and forcefully. Does the writer adequately discuss the specific quotations from the text so that you understand why they are in the paper? Finally, comment on the writer's conclusion: Have you learned something from the paper? Does the conclusion relate back to the thesis statement and sum up the central idea?

COMMON PROBLEMS IN WRITING ABOUT LITERATURE

Interpret, don't summarize. Summarizing the contents of a story, poem, or play is not the same as giving insights into the work's pattern and meaning. Occasionally you can summarize the plot in a sentence if you are making a transition from one part of your paper to another, but keep in mind that the reader of your paper is usually your instructor, who has already read the work and will get the impression that you do not know much about what you are doing if you merely summarize it.

Write about how you read the story, poem, or play. Try to express your own ideas through the text. If you find yourself summarizing it in more than a couple of sentences, it is probably because you did not organize your paper around a strong thesis. Your impressions and ideas are the measure of your encounter with literature. Writing encourages your clarification of these ideas. Be sure to state your central idea in a sentence in your paper. It does not matter where it appears, although if you include it in your opening paragraph it will help you keep your discussion focused.

Avoid long personal anecdotes. Writing on the basis of your personal experience can result in a fine memoir, but such an approach is usually not about the literature you were asked to discuss. You may want to introduce an analysis of D. H. Lawrence's "The Rocking-Horse Winner" (p. 375) with a short anecdote about a relevant experience you had as a child with a rocking horse, but make sure your anecdote goes on for only a few sentences before you connect it explicitly with your central idea about Lawrence's story.

Use the text to check your interpretation. Opinions about literature can be wrong. Do not insist on ideas that will not fit the details of the work. You may stumble on a central idea for your paper with an intuitive leap or a hunch about a text's meaning, but be sure the specific details support your interpretation. "Whatever I discover in the work is right for me," you may say, but that will not take you very far when writing a paper for an English class. Works of literature are tough, tangible constructions of language, not shifting tea leaves in the bottom of an empty cup onto which you can project whatever meaning you like.

Make good use of quotations. You must quote from the text to give evidence of your interpretation. Usually a sentence should introduce and follow each quotation, linking it to the idea being developed in your paper. Never drop quotations into the body of your essay without a comment.

Be careful not to quote too much. Use only those passages that are relevant to your discussion. Overquoting can weaken an essay, easily turning it into a string of short quotations choppily connected by a few insufficient words from you. Be sure to make it clear to the reader why the passage you are quoting is important.

When the quotation is short (four lines or less), it should be enclosed in quotation marks and included within the regular text, as you have seen in the sample papers. When typing a quotation longer than four lines, separate it from the preceding typewritten line with double space. Then indent ten spaces, *omit quotation marks*, and type with a double spacing (unless your instructor tells you differently). If you include the opening paragraph of "Young Goodman Brown" (p. 261) in a research paper, for example, you would indent it like this:

> Young Goodman Brown came forth at sunset into the street at Salem village; but put his head back, after crossing the threshold, to exchange a parting kiss with his young wife. And Faith, as the wife was aptly named, thrust her own pretty head into the street, letting the wind play with the pink ribbons of her cap while she called to Goodman Brown.

In a shorter passage in which you use a quotation within a quotation, such as a line of dialogue inside an excerpt from a story, use double and single quotation marks: "The echoes of the forest mocked him, crying, 'Faith! Faith!' as if bewildered wretches were seeking her all through the wilderness."

If you wish to leave out words in a quoted passage, use ellipsis points, that is, three periods (or four periods if the omitted material includes the end of a sentence): "And Faith . . . thrust her own pretty head into the street. . . ."

Always quote the exact wording, punctuation, and capitalization of the original text. If you underline words in a quotation for emphasis, say that you have done so.

If you find an error, for example a misspelled word in a quotation, indicate that the error is in the original by inserting [*sic*], a Latin word meaning "thus," in brackets after the error itself.

Last but not least, punctuate sentences that appear in quotation marks correctly. Commas and periods always belong *inside* the quotation marks, whether or not they appeared in the original text. Semicolons, question marks, colons, and exclamation points, however, belong *outside* the quotation marks, unless they are part of the quoted material.

Avoid plagiarism. Any material you borrow from other sources and include in your paper must be documented. If you present someone else's material (other than factual information) as if it were your own, you may be open to the charge of plagiarism. Even with factual information, if you use the exact wording of a source, you must indicate that it is a quotation. To be on the safe side, it is always better to footnote your original source, or give credit by working into your paper the name of the author and the title of the work in which you found the material you cited.

The one exception to this principle is information that is considered *common knowledge.* Common knowledge is material that is repeated in a number of sources, so that it is difficult to tell what the original source might have been. Such items as the basic biographical facts about an author or information about the publication of literary works do not need footnoting, unless you quote someone's exact words at length in your essay.

Know when and how to document the sources in your bibliography. Include the name of the author and the page number in a parenthetical citation or in the text itself when you use references other than this textbook:

In Richard J. Jacobson's study, we learn that Hawthorne feared the artist might become "insulated from the common business of life" (27).

If you cite from more than one book by an author, mention the title in the text or include a shortened form of the title in the citation:

We learn that Hawthorne feared the artist might become "insulated from the common business of life" (Jacobson, *Hawthorne's Conception* 27).

If your instructor asks you to use footnotes or endnotes, instead of parenthetical citation, you may place notes at the bottom of the page on which the reference appears, or they may be gathered together on a separate *notes* page at the end of your paper. When you footnote a source, indent the first line of each footnote five spaces before listing the author's first and last name; the title of the book; the city of publication, publisher, and date in parentheses; and the page number cited:

[1]Richard J. Jacobson, *Hawthorne's Conception of the Creative Process* (Cambridge, MA: Harvard UP, 1965) 27.

A separate bibliography of sources is handled differently than a list of notes or footnotes. When you gather several sources together on a separate page at the end of your paper as a bibliography, you list them alphabetically, starting with the *last* name of the author.

Welty, Eudora. "Is Phoenix Jackson's Grandson Really Dead?" *Literature and Its Writers.* 6th ed. Ed. Ann Charters and Samuel Charters. Boston: Bedford, 2013. Print. 625-27.

Instructions for basic documentation form for different sources—books, magazines, encyclopedias, and so on—appear in every handbook and guide to writing college papers. They may also be found in various manuals of style and style sheets that should be available in the reference section of your college library. You will find a guide to the most frequently used types of citation in the chapter on the research paper that concludes this textbook.

GUIDELINES FOR WRITING A PAPER ABOUT LITERATURE

1. *Do not wait until the last minute to start.* Allow plenty of time to write and revise.
2. *Be sure you have a clear idea of what you want to say about the work.* Can you state this idea as a sharply focused thesis sentence? Remember that all expository writing serves to clarify, set forth, or explain in detail an idea about a topic.
3. *Read the work over again.* Check the notes in your journal and take notes that will help you amplify your central idea. If necessary, try to generate ideas by brainstorming, freewriting, and listing. Use the commentaries to ask new questions about the text. It might help at this point to assemble a short outline, to stake out the ground you intend your paper to cover. Look for an approach that is distinctive enough to be worth your time and effort yet manageable enough to be handled in a paper of the length you are assigned.
4. *Develop a strong thesis sentence.* It should express your central idea about your topic.
5. *Write a first draft of your paper.* Be sure to state your central idea as a thesis sentence somewhere—preferably at the beginning of your work. If you are using an outline, try to follow it, but allow yourself the possibility of discovering something new that you did not know you had to say while you are writing. If you have taken notes or jotted down quotations from your reading, try to introduce such material smoothly into your discussion. Remember that the heart of literary criticism is good quotation. Brief, accurate examples from the text that illustrate the points you are trying to make about your thesis are essential in writing about literature.
6. *Allow some time to pass before you look over your rough draft—at least a day. Then make at least one thorough revision before you copy or type a finished draft of your paper.* Some students find they need several revisions before they are satisfied with what they have written. When you review your rough draft, concentrate and read critically. Let your words stimulate a flow of ideas about your topic; this will lead you to find more ways to develop your train of thought. Fill out paragraphs that seem thin. Be sure transitions between paragraphs are smooth and quotations are integrated into the discussion. If you

sense that your sentences are wordy, try to be more concise. Eliminate repetition. Be sure your general organization is coherent and your discussion proceeds in a clear, logical order.

7. *Check over your paper one last time.* Make sure you have always used complete sentences and correct spelling and punctuation. Avoid sentence fragments and exclamation points, unless they are part of a quotation.
8. *Type the paper or write it neatly in its final form.* If your instructor requires some particular style for class papers, such as extra-wide margins or triple spacing, follow those instructions. Use 8½-by-11-inch paper. Type if you can, double spacing between lines. If you write by hand, use ink and write on only one side of each piece of paper. Leave generous margins at the top, bottom, and sides. Number the pages, beginning with the number 2 (not the word *two*) in the upper-right-hand corner of the second page. (Your title on the first page will indicate that it is the first page.) Clip or staple your pages together in the upper-left-hand corner. Be sure your name, your instructor's name, your class and section number, and the date appear on your paper.
9. *Read your paper over one last time for typographical errors.* Make legible corrections in ink. Have you put quotation marks around titles of short stories ("A Rose for Emily") and used italics for the titles of books (*A Room of One's Own*)? Have you placed commas and periods *within* quotation marks in the titles and quotations that appear in your paper? Have you inadvertently left out any words or sentences when you went from the rough draft to the final version?
10. *Finally, make a copy of your paper.* If you have written the paper by hand, make a photocopy of it before handing it in; if you wrote it on a computer, be sure to save a copy of it. It is a good idea to save your notes and rough drafts as well, in case the accuracy of a quotation or the originality of your work is called into question.

What do you do after you hand in your paper? You have probably spent so much time on it—thinking, organizing, writing, and rewriting—that you feel you may never want to look at it again. The act of writing will have clarified your thinking and brought you closer to the literary work, so you carry with you the intangible benefit of something learned in the process. Returning to your paper in the future might have one final benefit: It will refresh your memory, reminding you of what you did not know you knew, about both yourself and literature.

WEB For more information on writing your paper, visit bedfordstmartins.com/rewritinglit.

28. Basic Types of Literary Papers

Regardless of the critical perspective that you choose to formulate your ideas about literature, you will probably be using one of the three basic ways to develop your thinking in your papers. Here are examples of these useful rhetorical strategies along with student papers incorporating them.

EXPLICATION

The word **explication** is derived from a Latin word that means "unfolding." When you explicate a text, you unfold its meaning, proceeding carefully to interpret it passage by passage, sometimes even line by line or word by word. A good explication concentrates on details, quoting the text of the story, poem, or play to bring the details to the attention of a reader who might have missed them approaching the text from a different perspective.

An entire story, poem, or play is usually too long to explicate completely—the explication would be far longer than the original work. You usually select a short passage or section that relates to the idea you are developing. If a poem is brief, you can explicate all of it, as in the following student paper on Langston Hughes's poem "The Negro Speaks of Rivers" (p. 893). In a play, you could choose to explicate a key scene or some lines of crucial dialogue. In a story, you could concentrate on the opening or closing paragraph, where you might suggest the implications of the text to develop your central idea.

Explication does not usually concern itself with the author's life or times, but his or her historical period may determine the definitions of words or the meaning of concepts that appear in the passage you are interpreting. If the literary work is a century or more old, the meanings of some words may have changed. The explication is supposed to reveal what the author might have meant when he or she wrote the poem, story, or play (not assuming conscious intentions but explicating possibilities).

For older literature, you will have to do a little research if the passage you choose for explication contains words whose meanings have changed. *The Oxford English Dictionary,* available in the reference section of your college library, will give you the meaning of a word in a particular era. The philosophical, religious, scientific, or political beliefs of the author or of his or her historical time may also enter into your interpretation of the text. The main emphasis in explication, however, is on the meaning of the words—both *denotative* and *connotative*—and the way those words affect you.

SAMPLE PAPER

An Interpretation of Langston Hughes's
"The Negro Speaks of Rivers"

In the poem "The Negro Speaks of Rivers," Langston Hughes uses elements of the blues to suggest the history of blacks from ancient Egypt to the twentieth century through the extended metaphor of the river. He explores the cultural identity and endurance of his people, emphasizing his racial uniqueness by his rejection of traditional European writing styles.

At the beginning of "The Negro Speaks of Rivers," Hughes is searching for his cultural identity. The poem is written in plain-spoken free verse, with an emphasis on spoken rhythm and an intimate, blues-like tone as opposed to a structured rhyme and formal rhythmic scheme. A statement of his situation in the first line ("I've known rivers") is repeated in the second, as in a blues lyric, but extended so it can be followed with a third line that stands alone as well as comments on the first two. With this third line ("My soul has grown deep like the rivers"), Hughes begins a brief historical account as the voice of the African American race.

This history celebrates the transition from slavery to freedom, suggesting the strength of Hughes's race by connecting it to the image of the river. The representation of rivers and pyramids in the next lines of the poem suggests the endurance of the human spirit through time, mystically connecting the poet's heritage to something "older than the flow of human blood in human veins." As the rivers continue to flow, so do his people continue to thrive through the changing times and the slow acceptance of racial differences.

Hughes then moves from this portrayal of his race in the bondage of slavery from the old world to the new, where Abraham Lincoln symbolizes the progressive movement from slavery to freedom. Hughes's pride and love for his race can be seen as the water of the Mississippi turns "all golden in the sunset." The last three lines of the poem suggest the sadness and complexity of the racial situation in Hughes's somber conclusion. As in a blues lyric, he ends by repeating the line that introduced his historical panorama of African American history: "My soul has grown deep like the rivers."

ANALYSIS

An analysis of a literary work is the result of the process of separating it into its parts in order to study the whole. Analysis is commonly applied in thinking about almost any complex subject. When you are asked to analyze literature, you must break it down into various parts and then usually select a single aspect for close study. Often what you are analyzing is one of the elements of fiction, poetry, or drama—characterization, setting, dialogue, or an aspect of style such as tone or symbolism, for example.

Whereas explication deals with a specific section of the text, analysis can range further, discussing details through the story, poem, or play that are related to your thesis. You cannot possibly analyze every word of a literary work any more than you would attempt to explicate all of it. You might begin with a general idea, or arrive at one by thinking about some smaller detail that catches your attention, as the student did by analyzing the storyteller's voice as an aspect of literary style in Eudora Welty's "A Worn Path" (see pp. 1634–1635).

Most students find that when they are asked to write a paper analyzing a poem, they can come closer to the poem by copying it out double-spaced into a computer or writing it in longhand on paper. Then you can scribble your observations about the poem in the margins of your paper, brainstorming alongside the text itself. To analyze Robert Frost's poem "Mending Wall" (p. 870), for example, you could write a list of adjectives and uses for a wall—*to hide, block out, a barrier, protection, a blockade, safety, security, separation,* and so on—to familiarize yourself with the "walled" metaphor of the poem. You could also annotate Frost's use of language and the technical means of poetry. You could consider the title, weighing its various connotations in your mind after you've studied the poem. When one student tried freewriting about her response to the poem, she was reminded of a photograph of Ireland on a travel poster. This memory inspired her opening paragraph in the following paper, "Nature and Neighbors in Robert Frost's 'Mending Wall.'"

SAMPLE PAPER

Nature and Neighbors
in Robert Frost's "Mending Wall"

Funnel paragraph, narrows down to focus on assigned topic of paper.

Ireland is known for its rolling green countryside. Without forests, the land appears to be a sea of green stretching to a sea of blue. The land, however, is not uninterrupted; there are a few roads and homes floating in that green sea, and they are even further outnumbered by Ireland's stone walls. They streak across every grazing field, surround the family farmhouses, and never seem to be in need of repair. The reason these walls remain has little to do with the skill of their original builders. Years of maintenance keep them strong. Why the walls are maintained, despite the fact that few sheep graze within their boundaries, can be explained by examining Robert Frost's poem "Mending Wall."

Summary of poem's subject.

The wall is in need of repair as the narrator and his neighbor meet to fill in the gaps a cold winter has made. As the two walk along the wall at "spring mending time" one on each side, they replace the fallen stones and rebuild the tumbled-down boundaries. As the stones are restored to their places in the wall, the chaos of nature is replaced by a man-made sense of order.

Summary of poem's theme.

The neighbors "set the wall between [them] once again," and in doing so, they strengthen the order a year of freedom has weakened. As they repair the wall, they are restoring order to the natural world in which they live and work and to their emotional worlds, where the relationships they have with one another reside. In both cases, the wall symbolizes the control the two men wish to possess over unpredictable forces in their lives.

Beginning of analysis—ritual as a sense of control over nature.

As a control over nature, the wall has many weaknesses. When nature does not work against the wall in New England, sending "the frozen ground swell under it," hunters come through, leaving "not one stone on a stone." Each year in an annual ritual, the two neighbors must meet again to repair the damage not because they enjoy the endless process of rebuilding the wall, but because the wall's presence gives them some sense of control over the chaos of nature. The wall divides the wilderness into manageable segments that are far easier to maintain than an endless expanse of farmland. In a visible and tangible way, the wall reminds the two that, despite nature's awesome power, they can in some, though impermanent, way check that power.

Ritual as a statement of the neighbors' relationship—use of quotations.

The borders the wall forms also indicate where the responsibility of one person ends and the duty of another begins. It is in this way that the wall crosses from control over nature to a controlling factor in the neighbors' relationship. Despite the fact that the wall separates two plots of trees, and the "apple trees will never get across and eat the cones under [the] pines," the wall is necessary in maintaining their friendly and mutually beneficial relationship. As the neighbor states, in the most memorable line of the poem, "Good fences make good neighbors." And in answer to the narrator's question of "Why do they make good neighbors?," one can look to the final image of the poem, a comparison of the neighbor to "an old stone savage armed."

Analysis of poetic imagery as it relates to the theme of the poem.

In addition to illustrating the idea of ancient property rights, this image turns the neighbor into a threatening creature; revealing anything to him could prove dangerous. "He moves in darkness"—not the darkness caused by the shade a tree casts on a sunny day but a deeper darkness that holds the power to damage emotions that the wall symbolically protects. Therefore, the wall is a wise protection against a potentially hostile invader. It is for this reason that a wall, in this case a mental wall or symbolic sense of limits, is essential in the relationship.

Below the surface of any human being is the potential to do harm, just as in the distance, on a clear day, a storm may be brewing. Though it is not the trusting thing to do, both neighbors understand the necessity of the wall in separating their properties and respecting personal space. The narrator begins to question his faith in the wall and the distrust it perpetuates, but in the end, as is evident by his repetition of the line "Good fences make good neighbors," he realizes the truth in such a motto. For the symbolic protection it affords and its ability to give some order to chaos, the wall has become a part of their lives.

Fresh comparison to a natural phenomenon.

Beginning of conclusion.

In Ireland, as in New England, the old stone walls remain, climbing to the tops of mountains and disappearing over the ridge. They seem to hold the green sea of grasses down as a row of stones might hold down a blanket on a breezy day. In the walls the neighbors find a sense of control over their wild land, restraining the endless landscape in manageable squares and rectangles, keeping each neighbor's overgrown field of nettles within the walls and allowing responsibility to begin and end with the stone borders. In a way the good relations between neighbors are maintained with as much devotion as the walls have been maintained over the years.

Conclusion refers back to opening paragraph and restates thesis sentence.

COMPARISON AND CONTRAST

If you were to write about two works of literature in this anthology, you would probably use the technique of comparison and contrast. When making a comparison, you place the two works side by side and comment on their similarities. When contrasting them, you point out their differences. It is always more meaningful to compare and contrast two literary works that have something in common than two that are unrelated. As you work on your paper you will find that if there are not important similarities between the two works, your discussion will be as strained and pointless as an attempt to link closely any two dissimilar objects, like elephants and oranges.

If you decide to use the method of comparison and contrast to develop the ideas in your essay, it is usually smoother to mingle them as you go along, rather than using contrast in the first half of your paper and comparison in the second half. The result of such a fifty-fifty split is rarely a unified essay. Rather, it tends to give the impression of two separate analyses linked together at the last minute.

Here is an example of a student paper comparing works in two literary genres. After reading Susan Glaspell's *Trifles* (p. 1410) and Leonard Mustazza's commentary on Glaspell's transformation of the play into a story (p. 1420), the student decided to present his own ideas about why the author might have chosen to rewrite the play a year later as "A Jury of Her Peers" (p. 243).

SAMPLE PAPER

On the Differences between Susan Glaspell's *Trifles* and "A Jury of Her Peers"

What is the difference between a play and a short story? Why should an author choose to write one over the other? An essential difference between a short story and a play lies in how each expresses emotion and thought to the audience. A short story allows the reader to enter a character's thoughts much more easily than a play would. In drama, a thought that could be said in a sentence in a short story requires a soliloquy or dialogue with another character that the audience can trust. On the other hand, a simple action or gesture in drama could require a great amount of narration in a short story. Each type of literature has its strengths and weaknesses.

Given the differences between the two genres, why did Susan Glaspell choose to turn her play *Trifles* into the short story "A Jury of Her Peers," instead of reworking the play? The answer to this question lies in what her goal with each work was, and how she wanted to achieve that goal. Both works have exactly the same dialogue, but "A Jury of Her Peers" is much longer, and has a different and more complex theme. It is the variances in theme, and the manner in which those variances are achieved, that illustrate why Glaspell might have been tempted to change genres when she transformed *Trifles* into a short story.

Transforming *Trifles* means narrating the story from the point of view of one of the main characters, even though by doing so Glaspell loses two of the themes she developed in her play. One of those is the diminution of wives by their husbands over "trifles." Another theme is the importance of the little things or "trifles" in life. The main theme in "A Jury of Her Peers," however, is much more complex. As the title suggests, the theme of the story is based on how two women, Mrs. Hale and Mrs. Peters, come to one opinion in judging another woman, Mrs. Wright. Illustrating their coming together necessitates a change in the point of view of the narratives. *Trifles* is presented, as most drama is, in the third-person objective while "A Jury of Her Peers" is presented in the third-person limited: The reader sees into the mind of Mrs. Hale.

In "A Jury of Her Peers," dramatizing the difference in the minds of the two women and watching them reach a consensus is the main action of the story. Glaspell makes it evident early in the narrative that Mrs. Hale and Mrs. Peters think differently. Mrs. Hale says, "I'd hate to have men comin' into my kitchen, . . . snoopin' round and criticizin' " (249). Here Mrs. Hale is testing Mrs. Peters's response to see if Mrs. Peters will follow the letter of the law. Initially, Mrs. Peters believes in the letter of the law: " 'Of course it's no more than their duty,' said the sheriff's wife, in her manner of timid acquiescence" (249). Mrs. Peters's "acquiescence" refers to the fact that she feels she must remind Mrs. Hale of the law. But her manner is "timid," suggesting that there might be room for change in Mrs. Peters's mind.

The evolution of Mrs. Peters's attitude is evident when she says, "A person gets discouraged—and loses heart" (251). Here Mrs. Peters shows that she understands why Mrs. Wright might have murdered her husband, given that she now knows that Mr. Wright was not the kind of person who made life enjoyable for his wife. Nevertheless, as the sheriff's wife, Mrs. Peters still struggles with the concept that "the law is the law" (251).

Mrs. Peters's real transformation comes when Mrs. Hale starts to restitch the bad sewing. When Mrs. Peters says, "I don't think that we ought to touch things," the narrator describes her comment as being said "a little helplessly" (252). At this point she realizes that she has lost the battle to follow the letter of the law; she starts to see things as Mrs. Hale does, in the spirit of the law. Then, when the topic of how still the house was after the death of the bird arises, Mrs. Peters remembers the death of her baby in Dakota. She now understands the life that Mrs. Wright led and feels compassion for her. Mrs. Peters now discerns the position of Mrs. Hale. They come to an unspoken agreement to tamper with the evidence in the kitchen.

On the stage in *Trifles*, there is no need for the women to come to agreement over the issue of withholding evidence. When the bad sewing and the bird are found in the play, it is almost as if both women know that it must be hidden. Both seem to realize that the other knows as well. This mutual sharing of each other's feelings shows an underdevelopment of characterization in *Trifles*, making it seem flat in comparison to "A Jury of Her Peers." The use of a narrator to develop characterization is what gives the story a more complex theme.

Character revelation aside, the conclusion of both the play and the story is the same. The women come to agree that even though Mrs. Wright is guilty of murder, she does not deserve the punishment that the county attorney seeks. Both women feel compassion for Mrs. Wright because they can relate to her. Mrs. Hale relates the unfinished work in the Wright house to the unfinished work in her own house. Mrs. Peters relates to the stillness that was in the house. The understanding that both women have of Mrs. Wright causes them to tamper with the evidence.

Changes in the theme reflect the genre change, but they don't explain why Glaspell changed genres. A little biographical background is relevant here. Writing in the early twentieth century, Glaspell often emphasized feminist issues. *Trifles* tells men that women are capable of noticing details and that they have sharp minds. "A Jury of Her Peers" tells men that one of the strengths of women is their compassion. While both works tell about compassion, only the story shows men the path to feeling compassion for others.

"A Jury of Her Peers" argues that in the case of Mrs. Wright, the full weight of the law is not a just punishment for murder, because Mrs. Wright's personality and lifestyle were adversely altered by her husband. Before her marriage, she was Minnie Foster. As Mrs. Hale says, "She used to wear pretty clothes and be lively—when she was Minnie Foster, one of the town girls, singing in the choir" (250). The key word in that passage is "when." It means that Mrs. Wright *used to be* like that, before her marriage. Mr. Wright is described as "a hard man.... Just to pass the time of day with him—.... Like a raw wind that gets to the bone" (254). Mr. Wright liked none of the "trifles" that make life enjoyable. Mrs. Wright lived with him for twenty years, meaning that she did not enjoy life for twenty years. From this perspective, she could have committed murder to save her own sanity. If this was the case, then the harsh punishment that the county attorney seeks would be excessive. Though murder is wrong, seeking an excessive punishment is worse. It is akin to the saying "two wrongs don't make a right." Compassionately paying attention to the spirit of the law is what men can learn from women.

Teaching men what women have to offer society seems to be one of the reasons that Glaspell changed *Trifles* from a play into a short story in "A Jury of Her Peers." The story illustrates a change from thinking to feeling compassion, a transition particularly necessary for men at a time when women were still denied the right to vote or serve on juries. The evolution of the characters gives "A Jury of Her Peers" a feeling of completeness lacking in *Trifles*. New themes, descriptions, and lessons to be taught are all aspects of "A Jury of Her Peers." Together they form an answer to the question of why Susan Glaspell chose to change her play *Trifles* into a short story.

This student began to think critically about Glaspell's play and short story after reading a commentary. The method of comparison and contrast works especially well when you are thinking about two or more works by a single writer. You can also use this method when you analyze two works by different authors that are closely related.

WRITING ABOUT THE CONTEXT OF LITERATURE

In addition to developing an idea by explication, analysis, or comparison and contrast—all methods primarily involving a close reading of the text—there are other ways to write about literature. The *context* of stories, poems, and plays is important to our understanding and appreciation of the text, as you have learned from reading the headnotes to each author's work in this anthology. The context of literature is usually defined as the biographical and historical background of the work. Literature does not exist in a vacuum. Created by a human being at some particular time in history, it is intended to speak to other human beings about ideas that have human relevance. Any critical method that clarifies the meaning and the pattern of literature is valuable, and often literary critics use more than one method in their approach to a text.

A paper on the context of literature is also an expository essay based on the development of a central idea or thesis statement. A critic creating this kind of paper, as for example in biographical criticism, develops the thesis of the paper by suggesting the connection of *cause and effect*. That is, you maintain that the story, poem, or play has characteristics that originate from causes or sources in the author's background—personal life, historical period, or literary influences. For example, you can use Kate Chopin's statement on her discovery of Maupassant's stories (p. 176) to show something about her own method of writing short fiction. To establish this connection between the life and work of a writer, you could also analyze or explicate a Chopin story, or compare one of her stories with one of Maupassant's.

Material from other classes can also be used in papers about literature. If you major in history or psychology, for example, you can investigate the way stories, poems, or plays are sometimes read to give valuable historical or psychological information about the world they describe. You are not limited to writing about remote times when you take this approach. Joyce Carol Oates's story "Where Are You Going, Where Have You Been?" (p. 452) is about modern teenage life. A paper about it could investigate the connection between Oates's fantasy and psychological theories about adolescence in contemporary America. Characters in literature are often used in psychological and sociological textbooks to illustrate pathological symptoms or complexes. Sociology textbooks, for example, cite Oates's fictional characters as representing current tendencies toward *anomie*, a condition in which normative standards of conduct have weakened or disappeared. It is possible in writing about literature to illustrate philosophical, historical, sociological, or psychological material you are familiar with through your work in other college courses.

At times the background of the author can suggest an ideological approach: Richard Wright was a communist, Tillie Olsen was a feminist, Flannery O'Connor was a Catholic, and so forth. At other times an ideology held by the student but not necessarily by the author can lead to a fresh reading of a story. Depending on what you as a reader bring to "The Metamorphosis" (p. 340), for example, there is a "Freudian Kafka, an existentialist Kafka, a Catholic

Kafka, a Marxist Kafka, a Zionist Kafka," and so forth, as suggested by the critic Hans Eichner.

Proceed with your literary analysis according to your ideology with great care, realizing that you might become insensitive to nuances of meaning other than those you are predisposed to find in a doctrinaire interpretation of the text. At the same time an ideological approach can illuminate aspects of literature that are particularly valid and relevant for contemporary readers. A feminist interpretation of "Young Goodman Brown" (p. 261), for example, must not take the story literally, because Hawthorne wrote it as a moral allegory, but a feminist could use the story to argue provocatively about implied sexual stereotyping in Hawthorne's characterization of women.

You misread literature if you think of it as absolute, perfect, final statements far removed from the commonplaces of life. It needs the reader's involvement to come alive. Through their aesthetic patterns, stories, poems, and plays show us what life is like. What they are ultimately saying, in their affirmation of life and human creativity, is—in the words of Henry James—"Live! Live!"

29. Writing Research Papers

THREE KEYS TO LITERARY RESEARCH

The first key to doing good research is to understand its purpose. In a literature class using this anthology, research writing is really an extension of the other sorts of writing you will do, such as explication, analysis, or comparison and contrast. As with these other sorts of writing, the purpose is for you to learn more about one or more pieces of literature, and perhaps about the context in which it was written, and to pass what you learn on to a reader.

The second key to doing effective literary research is understanding that a good research paper is not a dull collection of facts and quotations. Rather, a research paper is a type of essay. It should have a strong and compelling thesis, maintain a focus on a particular question or issue, and clearly be a product of serious, original thinking on the part of its author.

The third key to literary research is simple and practical: Do not wait. Get moving with the process of your paper as soon as you get the assignment, and never put off working on it under the assumption that you'll have plenty of time later. Sometimes the best research materials may be difficult to find, and they may take longer to read and understand than you anticipate. Organizing thoughts provoked by many sources and presenting them in a clear manner may take quite a bit of time too. Finally, you will probably need extra editing and proofreading time to make sure you get the details of citation and documentation just right.

FINDING AND FOCUSING A TOPIC

The topic of your research paper may be assigned by your teacher, or you may have free choice as to what you will write about. Either way, you will need to do some thinking and focusing before you dive into the research. Regardless of the form of your assignment, try to bring something of yourself, your personality and interests, to your research.

Once you have chosen a topic or found an approach to an assigned topic, try to stick with it. It can be tempting to drop your topic or change directions if the first stages of the research don't go as smoothly as you had hoped. Students cause themselves many wasted hours and a great deal of anguish by changing topics before giving their original ideas the real chance they deserve.

Assigned Topics

Even if the topic is assigned, it is still your job to make it your own and to find an angle which will allow you to write an original essay on the subject. Consider for example the two following topics:

1. What is the function of the literary allusions in Eliot's "The Love Song of J. Alfred Prufrock"?
2. The nineteenth century was a time of great upheaval in norms regarding marriage and family. How does Ibsen's *A Doll House* reflect this upheaval?

In both of these topics, the questions are broad, and given enough time and energy you would probably end up with far more to say than you could comfortably fit into a single, well-focused paper. In other words, you need to narrow and focus the topics so that your paper takes on a clear purpose and you have the chance to develop fully whatever ideas you choose to pursue.

For the first question, you would probably need to begin by doing some library research in literary criticism and history in order to develop a sense of what the possibilities are and how these might fit in with your own initial response to Eliot's poem. Only after this stage could you proceed to narrowing the topic and focusing your research on those aspects of the poem most interesting to you. For the second question, you might be able to find an initial direction for your research right away and frame some questions you would like to answer. You could then proceed with your research knowing from the start what to look for.

Choosing Your Own Topic

If you are given free, or relatively free, choice of a topic for your paper, your initial job is both harder and easier than if you are given a specific assignment. It can be difficult, when faced with the almost limitless possibilities of such a project, to focus your thoughts and get down to work. Still, you have the opportunity to begin with a writer or a piece of literature that you find especially exciting and choose to investigate an issue in which you have some personal investment.

The best place to begin finding your topic is by choosing a piece of literature which had a strong effect on you. Read through the work and its headnote again, making note of those things you find most worth thinking more about, especially any unanswered questions you may have.

Then take some time to brainstorm a list of questions about the work, the author, and the context. Write down all your questions, even those which you think you won't be pursuing. Try to move quickly beyond the sorts of questions which can be answered with a *yes* or *no* or which can be answered by a simple piece of information—*who, when,* and *where* questions. Think instead of meaty *how, what,* and *why* questions. What are the major themes and issues in the literature? How does the literature relate to other writings (by the same author or others)? What impact did the author's life have on his or her work? How did social and historical conditions shape the literature? What did previous critics and researchers—experts on this author, perhaps—have to say about the work?

Once you have a substantial list, check it for the two or three questions that most interest you. Would one of these make a good focus for your paper? If you can find enough information about the issues the question raises, could you write a paper of the appropriate length and type? Is the question narrow enough in its scope that you can investigate it thoroughly? If so, you are just about ready to begin researching. If not, look over your list again and try talking to your instructor or fellow students to see if they can offer some further refinements of your ideas. If you are concerned that the information you need will not be out there, have a backup question ready. In any case, it's important to be flexible in the early stages of your research and allow your questions to evolve and grow more complex as you become more of an expert on the topic you have chosen.

FINDING AND USING SOURCES

There are as many ways of proceeding with research as there are researchers. In working on previous projects, you may have developed your own perfect method for keeping track of sources, taking notes, and organizing your ideas. If, on the other hand, you haven't done a great deal of research (or if you have had less than satisfactory experiences with research), you might benefit from trying out the method outlined in the next section, which has worked for many researchers over the years. The system involves taking two different kinds of notes: bibliographic notes to find and acknowledge your sources, and content notes to keep track of the information you find in these sources. As you become a more practiced researcher, you will probably find yourself adapting the method to fit your own working style. The only solid rule is to be precise with your notes and references. Nothing is more frustrating than finding a gap or mistake in your notes and having to go back to the library to check a page number or the spelling of a name.

Begin your research by thinking about what sources you will need to complete your project. Plan a strategy to find those sources—the section on library research will suggest some approaches—and start a working bibliography of the books, articles, and other resources that will help you answer your research questions.

Library Research

Once you have reread the primary source (the literature about which you are writing), the headnote on the writer, and any related information in the commentaries or conversations sections of this textbook, continue your search in the college or university library. How you proceed will depend upon your topic and focus, so consider some questions before you start your search. Is your topic primarily literary, leading you to books and articles that focus on a writer's life and works? Or will you be delving into questions about history or religion or philosophy or other fields outside literary criticism? Are you researching a well-established author or one who has recently emerged and hasn't yet attracted much attention? Do you have some specific questions in mind at this point, or do you want to browse around and see how other researchers have approached your primary source? At any time during your research, you can ask a reference librarian for help, either while using one of the tools described below or simply to discuss where to look next.

The most complete listing of publications in the field of literature is the Modern Language Association's *MLA International Bibliography.* Published annually and available in some libraries in electronic format, this bibliography can provide the most thorough list of sources if what you are looking for is scholarly books and articles about writers and their work. It also covers linguistics, folklore, and to some extent, film criticism.

The print version of this bibliography covers a year at a time and is in two volumes, one that lists works by nationality, period, author, and work and another volume that is an alphabetical subject index. If, for example, you wanted to see what had been published recently on D. H. Lawrence's story "The Rocking-Horse Winner" you could look in the first volume of the most recent year, find the section for English literature, then the subsection for the twentieth century (labeled *1900–99*), and then the listing for Lawrence, which would be further subdivided for general studies and for each of his major works. If you are using an electronic version, which may be available through your library's Web site or at a CD-ROM station in the library, you can type in the name of an author or the title of a work to see what has been published on that topic. You can also search by a theme or subject or combine a topic and author (such as *Lawrence and childhood*). As with all unfamiliar electronic databases, spending ten minutes skimming through the help screens or asking a librarian how to get started is a wise investment of time.

The *MLA International Bibliography* is a good place to get a sense of how literary scholars have approached a primary source. However, because it strives for completeness, it can provide an overwhelming amount of sources when the work is well known and frequently analyzed by critics. On the other hand, you may not find enough information. If you are researching a contemporary writer, you may find few sources because there usually is a time lag before a writer gains scholarly attention. And the *MLA International Bibliography* doesn't cover publications in other fields, such as history.

For these needs, most libraries provide access to an interdisciplinary database of articles covering the major journals in various fields, including history, urban affairs, and ethnic studies. Many also index some popular publications that may include book reviews of contemporary fiction or interviews with writers. Ask your reference librarians which interdisciplinary databases are available locally and whether they might work for your topic.

Your library's online catalog is another resource. An excellent first step is to find a basic critical study of a writer and his or her works. Look for recently published, general studies that will give you background knowledge of your author's life and work to ground your research. As with all scholarly writing, these texts will provide useful bibliographies that will point you to the most significant books and articles about your topic.

The reference section of your library is a rich source of background and factual information. A series such as *Contemporary Literary Criticism* or *American Writers* can provide a quick and thorough overview of a writer's life and work. The *Encyclopedia of the American Religious Experience* might give you insight into the spiritual world of Emily Dickinson; the *Encyclopedia of African American History and Culture* may answer questions raised in reading a play by Lorraine Hansberry. The reference section is full of such specialized resources. A librarian will be able to take you straight to the sources that will provide answers.

Finally, don't expect to gather all of your sources in one or two visits to the library. As you find resources, scan through them to evaluate how they might be useful, what issues they raise, and what publications they cite as critical evidence. Read as you research and let that reading help you refine the questions you are asking.

Using the Web for Research

The World Wide Web is an increasingly popular place to conduct research. For some topics, such as public affairs, politics, and popular culture, it is an excellent source of information; for others, including many topics in literature, it is less useful. Most literary scholars are more likely to publish their work in the form of journal articles and books than they are to put it on the Web to mingle indiscriminately with a sixth grader's term paper or a hobbyist's fan page. However, you might find interesting sites devoted to the culture of a period or digitized primary-source collections at sites such as the *Electronic Text Center* at the University of Virginia or the *American Memory* project at the Library of Congress, where you can find old film clips, recordings of speeches, and such treasures as Orson Welles's hand-annotated working script for a production of *Macbeth* that he directed in Harlem in 1936.

General search engines are of limited use for the literary scholar. Search engines work by mining the Web mechanically, pulling together sites based on words used on pages and in URLs, regardless of quality or depth. Relevance ratings are assigned not by actually reading the sites but by counting the number of uses of a word or by some other automated mechanism. And even the most thorough search engines currently index less than 20 percent of the Web. If you use a search engine, try to focus your search. For example, a search for "Shakespeare" will retrieve tens of thousands of sites, many of them of limited usefulness. But a search that uses the terms *Hamlet, Branagh,* and *film* will narrow your search to sites about the 1996 Kenneth Branagh film version of *Hamlet*. An alternative to using general search engines is to use subject-oriented selective Web directories such as the Argus Clearinghouse or Scout Signpost. These have been compiled by researchers who have attempted to find and organize by subject the best sites on the Web. Another option is to seek out valuable digital collections such as the *American Memory* project and use the search capabilities of that site to find useful resources. Finally, reference librarians pay attention to quality Web sites and may be able to point you to helpful sites. If you are researching a particular author or literary period, be sure to visit the companion Web site for this book at bedfordstmartins.com where LitLinks provides clear, concise annotations and links to over 500 literature sites. Each critical annotation will help you choose the best Web sources for your research.

In addition to sites available to anyone on the Web, many subscription information sources are now available from libraries through the Web. Library catalogs and indexes are frequently accessible through Web browsers. If your library has an electronic version of the *MLA International Bibliography,* it may be Web-based. Your library may also subscribe to full-text journal collections such as Project Muse or JSTOR, which reproduce the contents of hundreds of scholarly journals in Web format. And they may have access to general resources such as Lexis/Nexis Universe, which provides newspaper and magazine coverage as well as political and legal information. These sites are not part of the "free" Web and are not indexed by general search engines. They are generally available to a campus community either through the campus network or by modem, but may not be accessible if you connect to the Internet through a service provider other than your college or university.

Your research will most likely require you to use a combination of electronic and print resources. Above all, bear in mind that you want to find the best sources you can, regardless of how they are packaged.

Evaluating Print and Online Sources

Not all information is created equal, and just because an item has found its way into print (or has a place on a flashy Web site), you should not necessarily believe it. You should evaluate every potential source you identify in at least two ways before you include it in your paper, first to determine if the source is respectable (that is, likely to be accurate) and second to find out if it is really appropriate to your purpose.

The first and most obvious question to ask is, *Who wrote and published the information?* For an academic paper, the best and most reliable sources are usually scholarly journals and books published by university presses. This is not to say that a paperback book, an article from a popular magazine, or a Web site can never be an appropriate source in an academic paper. Depending on the topic of your paper, these may prove to be valuable and even vital sources. But don't forget in compiling your bibliography that in general your paper will carry more weight if it derives its substance from scholarly sources.

Dates are also worth being aware of. Not all literary research needs to be absolutely up to date; sometimes historical research is the key to a successful paper. But if you have a choice between two critical studies, one written in 1954 and one written in 1994, use the more recent one unless you have a compelling reason to choose the other. Not only will the recent work be based on more up-to-date theories and utilize recently discovered information, but it is also likely to incorporate the ideas of earlier researchers as well.

Special caution is needed when evaluating online sources. The Internet is a vast and largely uncensored place, and much of the information available on it is incomplete, misleading, or just plain wrong. If you can't tell whether a Robert Frost Web page was posted by a professor of American literature or a middle-school student doing a project for English class, be sure to confirm any doubtful information. Sometimes the author of a Web site will include a link to a personal home page at the bottom of the page, where you might learn more about the author's credentials. If an organization has sponsored a Web project, look for links to information about the purpose and nature of the organization. URLs can offer clues as to whether the site is running on a university server (*.edu*), a commercial server (*.com*), a federal government server (*.gov*), a school (*.k12*), or the site of an organization (*.org*). Country abbreviations such as *.ca* for Canada or *.uk* for United Kingdom may also be useful clues. If you delete the part of the URL after the first slash, you can sometimes learn something useful. It may reveal that your author has posted a page at a particular university (which doesn't necessarily tell you about its academic quality—most universities allow the members of its community to post just about anything on their sites) or at a federal government agency such as the Library of Congress (which is particular about its content). Apply to Web sites the same criteria of accuracy and relevance that you use in evaluating printed information.

Once you have established the general respectability of your sources, you need to be sure that they are actually pertinent to your research question. Including information tangential to your point just because it is interesting or comes from a strong source will not improve your paper. Your first priority should be to make the paper as sharp and well focused as possible, even if it means leaving out some fascinating ideas or facts you encounter.

Your Working Bibliography

Each time you identify a potential source of information, you will add a reference to your working bibliography. More and more these days, researchers keep bibliographies as computer files that can later be adapted into a list of works cited. If you like to work on a computer, and especially if you have a laptop model you can take to the library with you, by all means keep your working bibliography this way. The traditional way of keeping bibliographic notes, however, is on 3-by-5-inch note cards, one reference to a card, and even many computer-savvy researchers still prefer this method because they can take notes anywhere without worrying about booting up a computer.

Complete instructions on the information you will need to turn your working bibliography into a list of works cited can be found in the section on

MLA format (p. 1669). The rule of thumb: If you think there is any chance the information may be needed, write it down. Copy source information from the title and copyright pages of a book (or the pages of an article or other short work).

It will save you time and trouble in preparing your list of works cited if you put the correct format for capitalization and punctuation in your bibliographic references. All titles and publication information should appear in capital and lowercase letters, even when the original is in all capitals. Subtitles are separated from titles by a colon. The titles of long works should be italicized; these works include books, plays, newspapers, magazines, journals, CDs, films, and radio and television programs. Titles of short works are put in quotation marks, not italicized; these works include stories, poems, essays, articles, chapters of books, songs, and single episodes of radio or television programs.

For a book, your bibliographic references should always present the full name of the author or editor; the full title of the book (italicized); the city, publisher, date of publication, and medium (Print). In addition, if the book is an edition other than the first, a volume in a series, a translation, or a work in more than one volume, provide that information too. The example shows a useful format for writing down this information and one easily adaptable for your list of works cited.

BIBLIOGRAPHY ENTRY FOR A BOOK

Danticat, Edwidge. *Breath, Eyes, Memory*. New York: Random, 1998. Print.

If your source is an article in a journal, magazine, or newspaper, the information will be slightly different. You will still begin with the name of the author and the title of the article (in quotation marks), followed by the title of the periodical in which the article appeared (italicized). For an academic journal, next come the volume and issue numbers and year of publication. For a magazine or newspaper, note the date (or month for a monthly publication) and year and the edition if one is given. For all types of periodicals, be sure to note the inclusive pages on which the article appeared, and include the medium at the end.

BIBLIOGRAPHY ENTRY FOR A PERIODICAL

Thompson, Deborah. "Keeping Up with the Joneses: The Naming of Radical Identities in the Autobiographical Writings of LeRoi Jones/Amiri Baraka, Hetti Jones and Lisa Jones." *College Literature* 29.1 (2002): 83-101. Print.

Many academic books are collections of short works or essays written by a number of different authors on a certain topic. If you include such sources, make note of the author of the essay or chapter, the title of the chapter, the title and editor of the book, and the same publication information as for a book by a single author. The same format is used for works (including poems, stories, plays, and nonfiction essays and articles) in anthologies.

WORK IN A COLLECTION OR AN ANTHOLOGY

Davis, Tracy C. "Shotgun Wedlock: Annie Oakley's Power Politics in the Wild West." *Gender in Performance: The Presentation of Difference in the Performing Arts*. Ed. Laurence Senelick. Hanover: UP of New England, 1992. 141-57. Print.

If you intend to use online or other electronic sources, you will need to collect bibliographic information similar to that for traditional print sources, with a few notable additions. Full citation formats to use in your list of works cited are shown in the section on MLA format (p. 1669), but the following brief guidelines should help you proceed at the information-gathering stage of your research. It is not always possible to find all of the information called for, especially for Internet sources. If any of the information you need from any source—electronic or traditional—is missing, simply skip it and keep the format of the rest of your citation exactly the same.

For full-text articles published in both print and electronic formats, give the print source followed by the medium and your date of access. Use the abbreviation "N. pag." if the source has no page numbers.

Harper, Michael S. "Mary Kinzie's Talk on Milton." *Callaloo* 24.1 (2001): 1033-34. Web. Oct. 2002.

For articles retrieved through a database, provide the name of the database, publication information for the article, the medium (Web), and your date of access.

Vonnegut, Kurt. "Despite Tough Guys, Life Is Not the Only School for Real Novelists." *New York Times* 24 May 1999: E1. *LexisNexis Universe*. Web. 14 Nov. 1999.

There are several kinds of Internet sources you might use in your research beyond the Web-accessible databases your library provides. These include Web sites, e-mail messages, and postings to newsgroups and e-mail lists. Full documentation styles for each may be found in the section on MLA format. For Web sites, give as much of the following information as you can find: author, title of the section of the site (in quotation marks), title of the site itself (italicized), sponsor (an institution or organization associated with the site), the date of publication or last update, the medium (Web), and your date of access. If the source has no sponsor, use the abbreviation "n.p."; if it has no update date, use "n.d." If your instructor requires a URL, add it in angle brackets after your date of access.

"The New Deal Stage: Selections from the Federal Theatre Project, 1935-1939." *American Memory*. Lib. of Cong. Web. 14 Nov. 2000.

When citing communications through e-mail, newsgroups, or e-mail discussion lists, include the subject line in quotation marks (use the description "Online Posting" if there is no subject line); the title of the Web site; the sponsor of the site; the date of publication; the medium (Web); and your date of access.

Downs, Jerry. "Re: Joseph Pequigney's 'Such Is My Love—A Study of Shakespeare's Sonnets." Shakespeare Electronic Conference. Bowie State University. 3 Oct. 2002. Web. 4 Oct. 2002.

When is your working bibliography complete? There is no easy answer to that question because the number and types of sources you need will depend upon the sort of paper you are writing. Also, as your research proceeds, you will likely come across additional references you will want to follow up, so in theory the bibliography is in flux until the paper is completed. Realistically, though, at some point you need to stop looking for leads and begin working with the sources themselves.

WORKING WITH SOURCES AND TAKING NOTES

So far, we have discussed how to find the information sources you will need for your research. This detective work is what many people think of when they hear the word "research." But it is only now—when the sources are in your hands—that the real research begins, as you start the intellectual work of reading, assimilating, and working with your sources.

Careful note taking is crucial to this phase of the process. No matter how sharp your memory or your organizational skills, as you work with a growing number of sources, it is easy to forget who wrote what, or even if an idea was original to you or came from another author. So it is especially important to keep yourself well organized at this point. You should have a stack of cards or a computer file with your bibliographic notes, but now you will begin to take the second kind of notes for your project—content notes. Most researchers prefer to take content notes on larger (generally 4-by-6-inch) cards, that serve the dual purpose of making them instantly distinguishable from bibliographic cards and allow more room to make comments on the notes. Once again, if you work with a computer, you can take notes directly into a word-processing file.

As you begin to read each source, start a new note card with a heading indicating the author's last name and perhaps a shortened version of the source's title. If you are using more than one source by the same author, noting the source on each card will save you a lot of trouble should your cards get shuffled later on. Also be sure to include on all notes the page numbers from which the note is taken. When the time comes to write your paper and document your sources, you will need to provide page references for every fact, opinion, or idea you get from an outside source, whether you use the author's words or your own to record the idea.

A good way to begin note taking is with a brief summary (perhaps a few sentences) of the author's main point or idea. Try to phrase this summary in your own words. This will not only help you to be sure that you have understood your reading, it will also help you compose your essay later on because you will already have had to think through the ideas and produce some prose of your own. Remember that just changing the order of the author's words or substituting a few words of your own is not the same as writing notes in your own voice.

After you have the main idea down, your notes can grow more specific, homing in on those elements of your reading that most relate to the research question you have set for yourself. If a section of one of your sources seems especially important or speaks directly to your question, devote a separate card to it. Remember that you might disagree with an author and still find his or her ideas important, if only as points to argue against in your paper. When you are comfortably familiar with your authors and their arguments, you will almost certainly want to pull out some direct quotations from your sources. It is best to reserve quoting for times when the author has written something in memorable and effective language or when he or she expresses an idea so succinctly and clearly that you really can't imagine saying it any better. If you find yourself wanting to note more than a few short quotations from each source, you may not be focusing on what's important. When you transcribe a quotation, put the material in quotation marks; always double check to make sure that your transcription is scrupulously accurate. Remember to note the page number from which the quotation was taken. If the quotation spans two pages in the original, mark the spot in your note at which the new page begins.

Imagine, for example, you were focusing your research on the ways gender roles are portrayed in Charlotte Perkins Gilman's "The Yellow Wallpaper." Sandra M. Gilbert and Susan Gubar's commentary on the story, reprinted in this anthology (see p. 239), directly relates to this issue and would be a good place to start your research. Here are examples of how you might write three note cards—a summary, a paraphrase, and a quotation—from this source. The numbers in parentheses are page numbers in the original. These cards, of course, would be keyed to bibliographic cards giving the authors' full names, the article's complete title, and the necessary publication information.

SUMMARY

The authors focus on the ways in which women—in literature and in real life—are made to feel trapped and imprisoned, in actual rooms and houses as well as in social roles. The wallpaper symbolically imprisons the narrator, and her madness allows her a sort of freedom.

PARAPHRASE

The woman trapped behind the wallpaper represents how the narrator herself is trapped in circumstances beyond her control. In freeing the woman, she frees herself through her madness (241-42).

QUOTATION

". . . even when a supposedly 'mad' woman has been sentenced to imprisonment in the 'infected' house of her own body, she may discover that, as Sylvia Plath was to put it seventy years later, she has 'a self to recover, a queen' " (242).

Of course, as you work with your sources and take notes from them, don't let yourself be so swept up in other people's words and arguments that you forget your own purpose and ideas in writing the paper. Write your own responses and opinions directly on your note cards—but be sure to distinguish them from the author's ideas, perhaps by using a different color ink. If your reading sparks any major new ideas from you (which ideally it will), make note of these on separate cards, indicating your own name as a heading and treating these cards for now as you would the material from outside sources.

DRAFTING YOUR RESEARCH PAPER

By the time you have read and assimilated your preliminary research materials, you should basically know the direction of your paper and what you want it to say. Now is the time to write a tentative thesis statement and to begin drafting your paper. A thesis statement does not just name your topic or state a fact; it asserts what the rest of your paper will argue. It should be clearly focused and guide the reader as to the general direction of your paper. Consider these two potential theses:

1. Kate Chopin's writing was very controversial in its day.
2. By developing characters like Mrs. Mallard in "The Story of an Hour," Kate Chopin showed that she was interested more in portraying emotional truth than in the social norms of her day.

The first of these is too vague, merely stating a fact that can be easily verified. The second is more specific, more interesting, and gives its writer a real assertion to defend. The tentative thesis as you initially draft it may or may not find its way into your final paper, but it should help you set a single, manageable task for yourself and keep you on track as you begin organizing your notes and ideas.

After you have drafted your tentative thesis, you must impose some order on the pile of notes and ideas you have amassed. (If you have taken your notes on a computer, this is a good time to print out a hard copy. You may wish to cut the printout into individual notes so that you can shuffle them around.) Whatever method you normally use to begin writing can probably be adapted to deal with including outside sources as well. But if you are having trouble getting all your thoughts in order, one way to start is by arranging smaller stacks of related notes on subtopics. Don't worry if the stacks are very uneven or if some notes seem to be unrelated to the others; you can deal with these anomalies later. And don't forget to include the notes that contain your own original ideas; they are the most important notes you have.

Now look over the cards again and put aside any that no longer seem relevant to your thesis. At this point you may discover that ideas are represented in your research about which you do not have enough information, and you will want to follow these up with more reading. You can continue with your research now, or you can proceed with writing the paper, leaving a space to be filled in later.

Start drafting your paper by whatever process has worked for you in the past for other types of writing. Some students find it helpful to begin with an outline (formal or not) or a list of key points. Others prefer to jump right into the writing itself, knowing that they will probably have to substantially reorganize the draft work at a later stage. Chapter 27 of this anthology provides several ideas, beginning on page 1623, for how to use brainstorming, freewriting, listing, and questioning to start the writing process.

The following sections suggest how to develop your research materials as you write. Don't forget, though, that this is *your* paper, not a mere presentation of other people's ideas, however compelling they may be. Each time you mention an idea from an outside source, comment on it thoroughly. You may agree, dispute, analyze, or explain, but never let a quote or thought from someone else stand on its own.

Summarizing, Paraphrasing, and Quoting

You can integrate the material you have found in your research sources into your paper in three ways—as summaries, paraphrases, or quotations. Each of these techniques is useful, and you will probably end up using all three in your paper. Each time you write from a source, consider your purpose in using this source.

Integrating summaries. To help your readers understand the background and the important questions within your topic, you will sometimes want to provide a quick overview of an author's main ideas or major contributions to scholarship. In these cases, rather than give an exhaustive account of all an author has to say, you should provide brief summaries. In some cases, the summary may be as simple as rephrasing a part of your summary note card for a source. For instance, the example of a summary note from the feminist reading of "The Yellow Wallpaper" (p. 239) might appear in your paper as follows.

> Gilbert and Gubar focus on the ways in which women—in literature and in real life—are made to feel trapped and imprisoned, in actual rooms and houses as well as in social roles.

Note that such a summary gives direct credit to the authors whose ideas you are discussing and presents those ideas succinctly, without getting bogged down in the article's supporting details.

Integrating paraphrases. You will sometimes want to focus on a more specific point made by one of your sources, and in these cases you will need either to paraphrase or to quote. As a general rule, think about paraphrasing first and save quoting for especially important points. As it did at the note-taking stage, paraphrasing makes clear that you understand the material with which you are working. It also keeps the ideas in your own words so that they fit in better with your own prose style. The example shows a paraphrase of part of the Gilbert and Gubar essay just summarized.

> Gilbert and Gubar consider the narrator's madness—and women's madness in general—a sort of triumph which allows her to be free of her oppressive surroundings.

Although the words of this paraphrase do not appear in the original essay, the idea it expresses is Gilbert and Gubar's. A paraphrase of this sort acknowledges the source of the idea while setting up the expectation that you will offer further comment on the critics' reading.

Integrating quotations. When you want your readers to pay special attention to the material you are using, the time has come for quoting. Many students worry about how to integrate quotations into their research papers, but with practice it eventually becomes much easier and more natural. Keep in mind a few formatting features and helpful tips as you begin working with quotations from both primary and secondary sources. First, quotations should be short, using as few words as you can while conveying what you need to. Long quotations are distracting, can be difficult to integrate with your own prose, and may suggest (unjustifiably or not) that you are trying to pad your paper.

Quotations of four lines of prose (from a literary or a critical source) or three lines of poetry should be integrated into your paragraph and enclosed within quotation marks. For longer quotations, set off the quoted material from your paragraph by beginning a new line and indenting an inch from the left margin only. It will be clear to your readers that any material thus set off is a quotation, so do not use quotation marks and do not switch to single spacing. The examples show the formats for integrating a short and a long quotation.

> Melville begins "Bartleby, the Scrivener" with the narrator's description of his qualifications as a storyteller. Melville's narrator begins by telling us the following information about himself:
>
> > I am a rather elderly man. The nature of my avocations, for the last thirty years, has brought me into more than ordinary contact with what would seem an interesting and somewhat singular set of men, of whom, as yet, nothing, that I know of, has ever been written—I mean, the law-copyists, or scriveners. (406)

Indicate deletions with an ellipsis. A few special situations deserve note. In some cases, you might wish to change a quotation slightly to make it fit the grammar of your sentence, or you may choose to delete part of a quotation in the interest of being succinct. Any additions or changes in wording that you make should be placed within brackets. Short deletions that you make should be indicated with an ellipsis. For deletions of more than a sentence, use four periods for the ellipsis (the first period is closed up; a space then follows each one). The example shows changes and a short deletion from the Melville passage quoted.

> The narrator says that "[t]he nature of [his] avocations . . . has brought [him] into more than ordinary contact with what would seem an interesting and somewhat singular set of men" (406).

Of course, it is dishonest to put words into someone else's mouth, so it is important that any changes you make do not affect the basic content or meaning of the passage you quote.

Indicate line breaks in a short quotation from a poem. When a short quotation is from a poem, you need to indicate any line breaks that occur within the quotation. This is done with a slash mark, with single spaces before and after.

> Langston Hughes declares, "They'll see how beautiful I am / And be ashamed—I, too, am America" (16-18).

Indicate a quotation within a quotation. When part of the material you need to put in quotation marks is already in quotation marks in the original, use single quotation marks to indicate the marks that appear in the original and double quotation marks to indicate what you are quoting.

> The narrator calls, " 'Bartleby! quick, I am waiting' " (412).

In addition to understanding the correct format for presenting and punctuating quotations, you will need to integrate them smoothly into your paper so that they do not interrupt or distract from your original prose. Three ways of integrating quotations are explained, from the least to the most effective.

Avoid the floating quotation. First, try to avoid the *floating quotation*, which is simply a sentence or phrase lifted out of the original and put in quotation marks with the attribution of the source and any commentary coming in another sentence (if at all).

> "Rage, rage against the dying of the light" (3). These words show Dylan Thomas's passionate sorrow at his father's impending death.

This method creates two problems. First, because the quotation is self-contained, it leaves a reader (albeit momentarily) to ponder its source and wonder why it has been presented at this point. Also, it makes for choppy reading; it presents an awkward transition from the poet's voice to that of the commentator.

Use an attributed quotation. When possible, then, you should always use at least an *attributed quotation*, which identifies the author with a lead-in to the quotation.

> Thomas writes, "Rage, rage against the dying of the light" (3). In doing so he demonstrates his passionate sorrow at his father's impending death.

With this type of quotation, the reader sees immediately where the quoted text comes from and knows (or at least expects) that your commentary will follow.

Use an integrated quotation. Even more effective is the *integrated quotation;* it not only attributes the quoted material to its author but smoothly makes the quotation a part of your own sentence.

> Thomas demonstrates his passionate sorrow when he begs his father to "rage against the dying of the light" (3).

This is the hardest sort of integration to achieve because you have to make the quotation fit in grammatically with your own sentence. Usually, though, the payoff in sharp prose is well worth a little time spent in revising.

DOCUMENTING YOUR SOURCES

Beginning researchers often find frustrating the precise format they must follow in giving credit to sources. Once again, understanding why documentation format exists as it does will help you to learn how to do it right. Documentation serves two purposes: It protects you from charges of plagiarism, and it allows your readers to find the source of any quoted or cited material.

Nearly all students know that copying the words of an author and turning them in as their own work is plagiarism. What many do not realize, however, is that plagiarism can take more subtle forms. In fact, because they don't fully understand the concept, students often plagiarize unintentionally. Plagiarism occurs any time a writer uses another person's words or ideas without giving full credit to the original source. So even if you paraphrase another writer's thoughts entirely in your own words, you must document fully where those thoughts originated. Your readers will assume that everything not credited in your paper is either your original idea or that you are trying to take credit for it. The only exception to the rule on crediting sources is that you need not document common knowledge, which might be defined as anything that a reasonably well-educated person should be expected to know. The name of the U.S. president or the fact that William Shakespeare was an English playwright, for instance, would not need to be attributed. If you are unsure whether something counts as common knowledge, document it.

MLA Format

Several systems of documentation are used in academic disciplines, and while these systems vary, they all serve the same purpose. For papers in literature and some of the humanities, the format is the one developed by the Modern Language Association, or MLA. The system breaks down into two parts. First are brief in-text parenthetical citations that occur in the body of a paper to indicate an author and page number for each summary, paraphrase, or quotation. Second is a works cited list (a bibliography) that provides complete information about the sources for those citations. When readers come across a reference to an author in the body of your paper, they can then turn to the list of works cited, look up the name, and find out more about the source. Check the *MLA Handbook* for complete instructions on citing all types of sources.

In-Text or Parenthetical Citations

MLA style presents two types of in-text citations: when the author's name appears in a signal phrase, or when the name is not included or there is no signal phrase. In the first, you signal the author's name in the lead-in to your citation (see instructions for attributed and integrated quotations, pp. 1668–1669) and provide a page reference in parentheses following the citation. The examples demonstrate the method using both a short and long quotation from literature.

SHORT QUOTATION WITH AUTHOR'S NAME IN TEXT

In Lorraine Hansberry's *A Raisin in the Sun*, Walter says, "Rich people don't have to be flashy" (1552).

LONG QUOTATION WITH AUTHOR'S NAME IN TEXT

In his poem "Mexicans Begin Jogging," Gary Soto asks,

> What could I do but yell *vivas*
> To baseball, milkshakes, and those sociologists
> Who would clock me
> As I jog into the next century
> On the power of a great, silly grin. (17-21)

For circumstances such as works by more than one author, multiple works by the same author, anonymous works, and works by corporate authors, the system for in-text citations is essentially the same, with a few notable differences.

WORK WITH TWO OR THREE AUTHORS

According to Gates and Appiah, . . .

WORK WITH MORE THAN THREE AUTHORS

Berger et al. claim . . .

If your paper refers to more than one work by the same author or to an anonymous work, it is especially important to include the name of the work in your signal phrase.

MORE THAN ONE WORK BY THE SAME AUTHOR

In "Technique in Writing the Short Story," Chekhov argues . . .

ANONYMOUS WORK

A *US News and World Report* article titled "Barbour Gets a Comeuppance" states that . . .

If the author is an organization rather than an individual, use the organization name.

ORGANIZATION AS AUTHOR

The American Psychological Association reports that . . .

The second type of MLA in-text citation is used when the author is not named in a signal phrase. In this case, both the author's last name and the page number appear in the parentheses.

CITATION WITH AUTHOR'S NAME IN REFERENCE

The authors explain that "a setting may be either a simple backdrop to the action or it may be crucial in itself" (DeMarr and Bekerman 109).

The citation consists of only the last name (or names) and page number with no additional punctuation or information. The exception to this is when your paper cites more than one work by the same author; in this case your citation should include the author's name followed by a comma, the title (or a shortened version of it) of the work being cited, and the page number.

CITATION WITH AUTHOR'S NAME AND TITLE OF WORK IN REFERENCE

The author feels that words must mean what they say (Welty, "Is Phoenix" 626).

List of Works Cited

Start your list of works cited on a new page in your paper, with the words "Works Cited" centered at the top. Continue double-spacing throughout, but do not add additional spaces between entries. Use hanging indentation in your list of works cited; this means that all lines *except* the first of each entry are indented. All entries are alphabetized by author's last name (or in the event of an anonymous work, by the first word of the title, disregarding *a, an,* or *the*).

Citing information from books. An entry for a book should contain as much of the following information as is applicable, in the following order and format, with periods between groups of elements. For most books you will use, details on editor, translator, volume, or series will not be needed.

1. The name of the author (or editor, if no author is listed), last name first
2. The title (in italics), including any subtitle (separate the title from subtitle by a colon)

3. The name of the editor (for a book with both author and editor), translator, or compiler (with the abbreviation "ed.," "trans.," or "comp.")
4. The edition, if it is not the first
5. Volume used if the book is part of a multivolume set
6. Series name if the book is part of a series
7. City of publication (followed by a colon), name of the publisher (comma), and year of publication
8. The medium (Print)

The most basic entry would be for a book by a single author or editor.

BOOK BY A SINGLE AUTHOR OR EDITOR

Moody, Anthony David. *Thomas Stearns Eliot, Poet.* 2nd ed. Cambridge: Cambridge UP, 1994. Print.

Adams, Hazard, ed. *Critical Essays on William Blake.* Boston: Hall, 1991. Print.

Citing works in anthologies. When you are citing an article, story, poem, or other shorter work that appears as a part of a book, include as much of the following information as you can.

1. The name of the author of the short work
2. The title of the short work, enclosed in quotation marks
3. The title of the anthology, in italics
4. The name of the anthology's editor or editors (preceded by "Ed.")
5. The edition of the anthology, if beyond the first
6. Relevant publication information as it would appear in a book citation
7. The inclusive page numbers for the shorter work
8. The medium

WORK IN AN ANTHOLOGY

Ellison, Ralph. "Battle Royal." *Literature and Its Writers: An Introduction to Fiction, Poetry, and Drama.* Ed. Ann Charters and Samuel Charters. 6th ed. Boston: Bedford, 2013. 204-14. Print.

Citing works in periodicals. When you cite sources from journals, magazines, or newspapers, include the following information.

1. The name of the author of the short work
2. The title of the short work, enclosed in quotation marks
3. The title of the periodical, italicized
4. All relevant publication information (specified in the examples)
5. The inclusive page numbers for the shorter work
6. The medium

For a work in a scholarly journal, publication information should include the volume number and the year of publication (in parentheses), followed by a colon and the page numbers.

ARTICLE IN A SCHOLARLY JOURNAL

Montgomery, Thomas. "The Presence of a Text: *The Poema de Cid.*" *MLN* 108.2 (1993): 199-213. Print.

Citing newspaper articles. To cite an article in a newspaper, include the date (day, month, then year) and an edition if one is listed on the masthead, followed by a colon and the page number. Remember that many papers paginate each section separately, so you may need to include a section number or letter as part of the page number.

ARTICLE IN A NEWSPAPER

Swarns, Rachel. "Zimbabwe's Novels of Reckoning." *New York Times* 7 Oct. 2002: B1. Print.

Citing other sources. You may want to cite a review, a television or radio program, a video or sound recording, a letter, e-mail communication, or interview. The following models demonstrate the basic format to follow.

REVIEW

Brantley, Ben. "A Pedophile Even a Mother Could Love." Rev. of *How I Learned to Drive*, by Paula Vogel. *New York Times* 17 Mar. 1997, late ed.: C11. Print.

TELEVISION OR RADIO PROGRAM

Elie Wiesel: First Person Singular. PBS. WGBH, Boston, 25 Oct. 2002. Television.

VIDEO OR SOUND RECORDING

William Shakespeare's King Lear. Dir. Peter Brook. Orion, 1970. DVD.

Kinnell, Galway. "In the Hotel of Lost Light." *The Poetry and Voice of Galway Kinnell.* Caedmon, 1971. CD.

E-MAIL COMMUNICATION, INTERVIEW, OR LETTER

Higgins, Andrew J. Message to the author. 4 June 2008. E-mail.

Charters, Ann. Personal interview [or Telephone interview]. 12 Apr. 2009.

Crane, Carolyn. Letter to the author. 8 Feb. 2008. TS.

("TS" indicates "typescript"; for example, a typed letter.)

Citing CD-ROMs, the Internet, and other electronic sources. Cite information from such electronic sources using these formats. If any of the required information is missing from an electronic source, skip it and keep the format for the rest of the citation exactly the same.

NONPERIODICAL PUBLICATION ON CD-ROM

"Eliot, George." *Discovering Authors.* Vers. 1.0. Detroit: Gale, 1992. CD-ROM.

PERIODICALLY PUBLISHED DATABASE ON CD-ROM

Gauch, Patricia Lee. "A Quest for the Heart of Fantasy." *New Advocate* 7.3 (1994): 159-67. Abstract. CD-ROM. *ERIC.* SilverPlatter. 1999.

ONLINE POSTING

Merrian, Joanne. "Spinoff: Monsterpiece Theatre." *SHAKESPER: The Global Electronic Shakespeare Conference.* University of Toronto, 30 Apr. 1994. Web. 2 Feb. 2009.

WEB SITE

Groden, Michael, Martin Kreiswirth, and Imre Szeman, eds. *The Johns Hopkins Guide to Literary Theory and Criticism.* Johns Hopkins UP, 2005. Web. 7 May 2009.

The instructions and examples above will cover the vast majority of the sources you encounter. Complete information for how to cite these and any other types of sources as well as additional information on conducting research and the mechanics of writing and formatting a research paper can be found in:

Modern Language Association, *MLA Handbook for Writers of Research Papers.* 7th ed. New York: MLA, 2009.

Footnotes and Endnotes

You will have noticed that the MLA format, with its in-text citations and list of works cited, does not require footnotes or endnotes to refer to sources. However, the format does allow for the use of notes in two specific circumstances. The first instance is for *bibliographic notes* in which the writer of the research paper, in addition to referring the reader to one or more sources, makes specific comment on the sources themselves. The second is for *content notes,* in which the writer makes a comment that is related to the research topic but does not fit easily within the text of the paper itself. Both types of notes should be used only when you cannot find another way to integrate the information, and for most research papers such notes will probably not be necessary.

Unless your instructor specifically asks for footnotes, always use endnotes instead. As the name implies, endnotes appear at the end of the paper—on a separate page, after the text but before the works cited list. To signal a note in your paper, use a superscript numeral in the text matching the numeral that precedes the note. Notes should be in the same type font and size as the rest of your paper and should maintain double spacing. For examples of both sorts of notes, see the sample research paper that begins on page 1677.

REVISING YOUR RESEARCH PAPER

Once your research paper is completely drafted, with all sources fully integrated and documented, the time has come to revise it, just as you would any other paper. The following six-part checklist provides a systematic method for approaching revision. You might also ask a classmate, or even your instructor, to look over the draft and offer advice.

1. First, look again at your tentative thesis statement. Now that you have written the paper, does the thesis still seem exactly right? It is possible, even likely, that in the process of writing you may have refined or changed your ideas about your topic. If so, reword the thesis to accurately reflect your new thinking.
2. Now look again at the supporting evidence you offer in each body paragraph. Do all of the ideas directly relate to and uphold the thesis? If any of them do not, you should cut these sections from your paper, regardless of the intrinsic interest of the ideas or the strength of the writing.
3. Are there any portions of the paper where you worry that the argument may be thin or underdeveloped or where the connection to your thesis may not be entirely clear? If so, you should try to explain your ideas more fully. You may even need to do some additional research to fill in the gaps.
4. After any necessary cuts and additions have been made, you may need to slightly reorganize the paper. Is your argument presented in the most logical order and are all related ideas kept together? Rearrange and revise any awkwardly placed paragraphs or sentences.
5. Does the style and voice sound at all like your usual writing? It is easy when reading the thoughts and words of other authors to begin adopting the style of these authors and losing your own voice. Check to make sure that the vocabulary and tone reflect your personality and your attitude toward the subject. By writing in your own voice, you make the material and the project your own.
6. Finally, carefully review the assignment and make sure that your paper conforms to your instructor's guidelines in all respects. In the event of disagreement, his or her guidelines should always take precedence over those offered here or anywhere else.

Your paper should now be ready for the final polish before you turn it in. Print out a clean copy and review it twice more. The first time, edit and proofread for word choice, grammar, spelling, and punctuation as well as any other small changes that will improve style and readability. If you are in doubt about anything, look it up. Even small mistakes can have a large negative effect on a reader. The second time, go over the format of all quotations, parenthetical references, and your works cited page to make sure that they are consistent and conform exactly to guidelines. You are now ready to make your last changes, print out a final copy, and turn in a research paper you can be proud of.

WEB For more information on writing a research paper, visit bedfordstmartins.com/rewritinglit.

STUDENT RESEARCH PAPER

The student research paper that follows puts into practice the instructions and suggestions we have been discussing. You can also use it as a guide to proper manuscript format. Unless your teacher calls for some other format (such as a cover page), you should begin in the upper left corner of page 1 with your name, your instructor's name, the course for which you are writing the paper, and the date you turn it in. Double-space and center the title of your paper in capitals and lowercase letters without underlining or quotation marks (unless, of course, a quotation or title appears within your own title). Then begin the paper itself, with regular one-inch margins and double-spacing throughout (including for quotations and the list of works cited). A running head with your last name and the page number should appear in the upper right corner of each page. All word-processing programs make it easy to include such headings.

Silva 1

Writer's name typed before page number.

Jennifer Silva

Professor Gardner

English 102

7 November ----

Format for paper without a title page.

Emily Dickinson and Religion

Title centered and double-spaced.

Upon a cursory examination of her biography, it could be easy to dismiss religion as playing an insignificant role in Emily Dickinson's life and work. At the time of the Second Great Awakening, when most of New England was swept along by the fervent religious revival movement, Dickinson resisted. Even after the rest of her family formally joined the church, she refused since she just could not accept all aspects of church doctrine (Benet 19). Even in her poems, because "most have predictable rhyme schemes" and are "easy to memorize," it is easy to overlook the religious value (Schmidt 31). Many readers and critics have, in fact, drawn attention to her unconventional views, claiming that "she was deprived of an orthodox and steady religious faith" (Wilbur 859). But according to poet and critic Alicia Ostriker: "Her relationship with God, or the failure of a relationship, became an obsessive theme for Dickinson." In overlooking or dismissing the important role that religion played in her life, we miss an important element of Emily Dickinson's poetry.

In-text citation for paraphrase.

In-text citation for Internet source; no page number.

Even though she never felt able to fully accept all aspects of Christian doctrine, it would be wrong to assume that religion did not influence Dickinson's life and work. In fact, religion and her faith in God seem to have played a large role. Emily Dickinson was raised in a deeply religious household. As a child, she was discouraged from reading anything except the Bible (Higginson 856). In her childhood, adolescence, and early twenties, she attended church with her family twice every Sunday, hearing at least 1,500 sermons during this period. From the letters she wrote, it is clear

Silva 2

that she was "capable of being transported by a good sermon" and "the effect on her of these weekly . . . invasions of her spirit . . . was profound" (Doriani 45). While she still didn't accept all of the conventions of the church, Dickinson wrote to her brother Austin that the preachings of Professor Edwards Amasa Park of Andover Theological Seminary, Reverend Edward S. Dwight, and especially Reverend Charles Wadsworth, among others, greatly inspired her (Doriani 46).

The influence of religion on her life spills over into her poetry, which reveals her strong belief in God and heaven. Dickinson discloses her great faith, her ability to believe without the assurance of concrete proof, in the poem "I never saw a Moor—." She writes,

> I never spoke with God
> Nor visited in Heaven—
> Yet certain am I of the spot
> As if the Checks were given— (5–8)

Indent quotation of three or more lines of poetry, four or more lines of prose.

She does not have to see God or heaven to know that they exist, just as she has never seen "a Moor" or "the Sea" but still knows "how the Heather looks / And what a Billow be" (3-4). For her, the existence of heaven is as real and certain as the existence of the heather and billow. How can she be so sure of the existence of these things she cannot see? Presumably, she has learned about the heather and billows through the written and spoken accounts of others. In the same way, she accepts the existence of God and heaven probably as a result of the influence of the Bible, the words of the many preachers she has heard in her life, and the teachings of her family. Surrounded by these testimonies since early childhood, Dickinson feels she can faithfully commit herself to believing in God and heaven's existence.

Line numbers only; author cited in text.

Her faith and religion are such a significant part of her life that words with religious connotations even appear in her poems about other subjects, as if her immersion in religion is so great that she cannot separate it from other parts of her life. Even in her poetry about secular subjects, Dickinson's "Puritan heritage persistently provided her with a vocabulary, with metaphors, for experience that she and her world understood" (Juhasz 124). In poems about love and death (such as "Love—thou art high—," "If you were coming in the Fall," and "Because I could not stop for Death—") appear the words "eternity" and "Eden," words with significant religious meaning and implications which affect the connotations of the poems. "I taste a liquor never brewed—" includes the religious words "seraphs" and "saints": " . . . Seraphs swing their snowy Hats— / And Saints—to windows run—" (13-14). Religion has a place in all parts of her life, and consequently in all of her poetry. We can read these poems without focusing on their religious content, but to do so deprives us of an important layer of their meaning.

Slash indicates line break in poetry.

Even the formal style of Dickinson's poetry reflects the influence of religion, for the hymns she learned in church and psalms she read in the Bible shaped her work. Many of her poems, written in simple quatrains, generally in iambic tetrameter with only the second and fourth lines rhyming, follow the same basic pattern as conventional, ordinary church hymns.[1] Poems written in this hymn-like form—with approximate rhyme of the second and fourth lines, written in primarily iambic tetrameter and trimeter in simple quatrains—include "Because I could not stop for Death—," "If you were coming in the Fall," and "I heard a Fly buzz—when I died—." Once again, while these poems do not focus on explicitly religious subjects, the impact of religion on their form and content is evident.

Superscript numeral for endnote.

Because of the hymn-like quality of Dickinson's poetry, readers can be swept along quickly by the rhythm and miss some of the meaning of a poem. To alleviate this problem, Dickinson uses dashes as pauses to slow fast-moving lines, similar to the pausing technique she observed preachers using to emphasize a thought or hold the audience's attention (Doriani 48). For example, to place emphasis on the word "Nobody" in line 2 of the poem "I'm Nobody! Who are you?," she surrounds the word with dashes: "Are you—Nobody—Too?" Similarly, in "I died for Beauty—but was scarce" Dickinson uses dashes to slow down the reading of line 7 and emphasize the word "Truth": "And I—for Truth—Themself are One—." By adopting a convention used by the preachers who impressed her, Dickinson not only indicates the influence of religion in her life but also enhances the quality of her poetry for readers.

Another preaching technique that Dickinson adopted for her poetry concerns the use of natural speech. In addition to pausing for emphasis, "the practice of the preachers of the Puritan legacy . . . [was] to reject an affected style or an eloquence not characteristic of ordinary speech" (Doriani 16). This style is mirrored in much of Dickinson's poetry. Even when attempting to capture a complex concept like hope in her poetry, she skillfully expresses her thoughts with refreshingly simple, yet elegant language without compromising the elevated content. In "'Hope' is the thing with feathers—" she describes the complicated feeling of hope with very simple words and metaphors: "the thing with feathers— / That perches in the soul— / . . . sweetest—in the Gale . . ." (1-2, 5). At times, Dickinson even seems to be conversing with the reader through her poems. The poem "I'm Nobody! Who are you?" addresses the reader directly in a conversational tone. The many preachers that she heard using this type of language in speeches and sermons must surely have influenced her poetry style.

Brackets for addition or change to citation.

Much has been made of the fact that the young Emily Dickinson "found that she must refuse to become a professing Christian" (Wilbur 859).[2] But even though Dickinson's religion has no church, her faith in God should not be doubted. A distinction must be made between nonconformist religious views and an outright rejection of God or religious values. Throughout her life, Dickinson strongly believed, "God's residence is next to mine, / His furniture is love" ("Who has" 197). Her God resides with her always—a guiding force touching all aspects of her life. Her faith is strong and unwavering. And if we read her work carefully and with an open mind, we can see that Dickinson's religious faith did not die with her in her Amherst house in 1886. Its fervor and vitality are still alive in her elegant poetry, preserved in simple verse to inspire generations for all time.

Silva 6

Notes

[1] A number of interesting studies—including Morris and Wolosky—discuss the ways in which Dickinson adapted and reshaped the hymn form in her poems.

Bibliographic endnote commenting on sources.

[2] Nearly all biographies of the poet stress her resistance to the doctrine preached during her brief time at Mount Holyoke Seminary.

Content endnote.

Silva 7

Works Cited

Benet, Laura. *The Mystery of Emily Dickinson.* New York: Dodd, 1974. Print.

Book by a single author.

Charters, Ann, and Samuel Charters, eds. *Literature and Its Writers: An Introduction to Fiction, Poetry, and Drama.* 6th ed. Boston: Bedford, 2013. Print.

Anthology cited by editors' names.

Dickinson, Emily. "'Hope' is the thing with feathers—." Charters and Charters 846.

———. "I died for Beauty—but was scarce." Charters and Charters 848.

More than one work by an author.

———. "I'm Nobody! Who are you?" Charters and Charters 847.

———. "I never saw a Moor—." *The Complete Poems of Emily Dickinson.* Boston: Little, Brown, 1960. 480. Print.

———. "I taste a liquor never brewed—." Charters and Charters 846.

———. "Who has not found the heaven below." *Selected Poems and Letters of Emily Dickinson.* Ed. Robert N. Linscott. Garden City: Anchor, 1959. 197. Print.

Doriani, Beth Maclay. *Emily Dickinson, Daughter of Prophecy.* Amherst: U of Massachusetts P, 1996. Print.

Higginson, Thomas Wentworth. "Emily Dickinson's Letters." Charters and Charters 851-57.

Cross-reference to another citation in an anthology.

Juhasz, Suzanne. *The Undiscovered Continent: Emily Dickinson and the Space of the Mind.* Bloomington: Indiana UP, 1983. Print.

Morris, Timothy. "The Development of Dickinson's Style." *American Literature* 60.1 (1988): 26-41. JSTOR. Web. 14 Nov. 2002.

Article in a scholarly journal.

Ostriker, Alicia. "When I Was Growing Up Our Teachers Told Us." Titanic Operas. Dickinson Electronic Archives. 10 Mar. 2008. Web.

Internet source.

Schmidt, Elizabeth. "Imagining Emily." *New York Times Book Review* 2 Mar. 1997: 31. Print.

Wilbur, Richard. "On Emily Dickinson." Charters and Charters 859-61.

Wolosky, Shira. "Rhetoric or Not: Hymnal Tropes in Emily Dickinson and Isaac Watts." *New England Quarterly* 61.2 (1988): 214-32. Print.

Article in a newspaper.

Glossary of Literary Terms

The boldfaced page references indicate where a key term is highlighted in the text.

Abstraction Language that describes ideas or qualities rather than tangible, observable people, places, and things, which are described in concrete language. **732**

Accent The strong syllable, or syllables, in a word; the emphasis, or stress, given a syllable in pronunciation. All words with more than one syllable will have at least one *strong* accent. The other syllables are called *weak* accents. **700**, **714**–715

Action At its simplest, the events or things that happen in a PLOT — what the CHARACTERS do and what is done to them. See also FALLING ACTION. 1093

Alexandrine A line of poetry with six stressed accents.

Allegory A NARRATIVE usually restricted to a single meaning or general truth, in which characters, places, things, and events represent abstract qualities. Such characters, places, things, and events thus often function as SYMBOLS of the concepts or ideas referred to. See also PARABLE. **45**

Alliteration The repetition of the same consonant sounds beginning each word in a sequence of words. **694**

Allusion An implied or indirect reference to something with which the reader is supposed to be familiar. **828**

Anacrusis An unstressed syllable at the beginning of a line that does not affect the overall poetic meter. **719**

Anapest See FOOT.

Anapestic meter See FOOT.

Antagonist The character in a short story or play who is in real or imagined opposition to the PROTAGONIST. The conflict between these characters makes up the action, or plot, of the story. It is usually resolved in some way, but it need not be. **41, 1116**

Aphorism A short, concise statement of a principle or a sentiment. **778**

Apostrophe A figure of speech in which the poet addresses something that is inanimate or abstract as a personified thing. **726, 739, 744**

Archetypes The characters, images, and themes that symbolically embody universal human meanings and experiences. **1616**

Assonance The repetition of internal vowel sounds without the repetition of consonant sounds used as an alternative to rhyme in verse to create an aural unity within a poetic line or sequence of lines. **694**

Ballad A narrative poem, often a song, that tells a story. **748**

Biographical criticism A critical approach that uses important facts about the life of an author to shed light on literary texts. **1615**

Blank verse Unrhymed iambic pentameter. It was used by Shakespeare and other Elizabethan dramatists because iambic meter was closest to the natural rhythms of English speech. **720**

Blocking The actors' movement onstage during the duration of the play. **1120**

Caesura A break or pause within a line of poetry that contributes to the rhythm of the line. **719**

Character Any person who plays a part in a narrative work. Characters may be *flat* — simple and one-dimensional; or *static* — unsurprising and unchanging; or *round* — complex, full, described in detail; or *dynamic* — often contradictory and changing in some way during the story. The main character can usually be labeled the PROTAGONIST or hero; he or she is often in conflict with some other character, an ANTAGONIST. Other characters who affect the ACTION slightly or only indirectly are called *minor* characters; but, depending on the intention or the skill of the author, the main characters need not be round, nor the minor characters flat. **40**, 1104, **1116**–1118

Climax The turning point or point of highest interest in a narrative; the point at which the most important part of the ACTION takes place and the final outcome or RESOLUTION of the PLOT becomes inevitable. Leading up to the climax is the RISING ACTION of the story; after the climax, the FALLING ACTION takes the reader to the *denouement*, in which the resolution or the outcome of the conflict is presented. **26, 1113**

Close reading Reading works of literature analytically in order to understand the author's creation of design and pattern in the text. **4**

Closed form Traditional verse forms, as opposed to OPEN FORM or FREE VERSE. **746**

Comedy A literary work, often written in a light and amusing style, in which the plot ends happily. See also TRAGEDY. **1094**

Connotative meaning The associated meanings that have built up around a word, or what a word connotes. These implications go beyond the literal meaning of a word. See also DENOTATIVE MEANING. **731**

Convention A traditional or commonly accepted technique of writing or device used in writing, sometimes an unbelievable device that the reader agrees to believe — such as, for example, the fact that a FIRST-PERSON NARRATOR is addressing the reader in a friendly and intimate manner.

Couplet Two consecutive lines of poetry with the same meter that end in a perfect rhyme. See also RHYME. **747**

Cultural criticism A critical method that advocates an interdisciplinary approach, often using history, sociology, or philosophy, to study literary works in a cultural context. **1620**

Dactyl See FOOT.

Dactylic meter See FOOT.

Deconstructionist criticism An approach to literature that emphasizes a close reading guided not so much by a search for surface meaning as by an exploration of the text's internal contradictions, the places where meaning does not remain stable. **1619**

Denotative meaning The direct, specific meaning of a word, as distinct from an implied or associated meaning. See also CONNOTATIVE MEANING. **731**

Dialogue The exchange of words between characters in a story, poem, or play. Do not confuse with *dialect,* which is a type of nonstandard English diction spoken by people from a particular geographic region, economic group, or social class. 27, 1104, **1117**–1118

Diction A writer's choice of language — including words, phrases, and sentence structure. A writer's diction is an important element of STYLE. The same idea will leave a different impression on the reader when it is narrated in street slang, in the precise language of an old schoolteacher, or in the professional jargon of a social worker. **Poetic diction** refers to the way poets can employ an elevated diction that is different from common speech, using so-called poetic language. **57, 931**

Didactic Literature that attempts to instruct or teach a lesson, convey a moral, or inspire and provide a model for proper behavior. 747, **1124**

Drama Originating in the Greek verb *dran,* "to perform," drama may refer to a single play or to a group of plays ("Elizabethan drama"). Usually drama is designed to be performed in a theater where actors take on the roles of the characters. A *play* is the general term for a work of dramatic literature; it is created by a *playwright,* a writer who makes plays. **1093**

Dramatic monologue A poem written in the form of a speech or extended narration that the person who is the speaker in the poem delivers to someone else. This kind of lyric poetry often describes a dramatic situation while also indirectly suggesting an important aspect of the speaker's personality. **773**

Dramatic poetry The use of poetry in the writing of drama. 772

Dynamic character See CHARACTER.

Elegy A serious, contemplative lyric poem written to lament someone's death and memorialize his or her life. See also LYRIC POETRY. **758**

End orientation The suggestion of the outcome of the action or the conclusion of the plot contained in the opening paragraphs of a short story. **26**

End rhyme See RHYME.

End-stopped line A poetic line that comes to a definite stop or pause at the end. **701**

Enjambed/enjambment A poetic line whose meaning is not complete at the end but continues on without pause to the next line. This is also called a *run-on line.* **701**

Epic The oldest form of narrative poetry, usually written in an elevated style, that chronicles important heroic deeds and events in a nation's history. See also NARRATIVE POETRY. **748**

Epigram Short poems, often rhymed, that are usually funny or wryly satirical. They are intended to make a sharp comment or witty observation. **778**

Epiphany A "showing forth" or sudden revelation of the true nature of a CHARACTER or situation through a specific event — a word, gesture, or other action — that causes the reader to see the significance of that character or situation in a new light. The term was first associated with modern literature in the writing of James Joyce. 15

Explication The act of explaining or interpreting the meaning of a text. **1642**

Exposition The presentation of background information, usually early in a story, that a reader or a theatrical audience must be aware of, especially about situations that exist and events that have occurred before the ACTION of a NARRATIVE begins. **26, 1112**

Eye rhyme See RHYME.

Falling action The events of a NARRATIVE that follow the CLIMAX and lead to the resolution of the conflict before the story is brought to its conclusion. **26, 1112**

Falling meter See METER.

Feminine rhyme See RHYME.

Feminist criticism See GENDER CRITICISM.

Figurative language The use of a word or a group of words that is literally inaccurate but is used to describe or define a person, event, or thing more vividly by calling forth the sensations or responses that person, event, or thing evokes. Such language often takes the form of METAPHORS, in which one thing is equated with another, or of SIMILES, in which one thing is compared to another by using *like, as,* or some other such connecting word. **57, 726, 734**

First-person narration The telling of a story by a person who was involved in or directly observed the action narrated. Such a narrator refers to himself as *I* and becomes a CHARACTER in the story, with his or her understanding shaping the reader's perception of the events and the other characters. The first-person narrator can be either a major or a minor character in the story. **32**

Flat character See CHARACTER.

Foot The unit of the rhythmic pattern that makes up the meter, usually consisting of one stressed and one or two unstressed syllables. An *iambic foot* or *iambic meter* consists of one unstressed syllable followed by one stressed syllable ("invok'd"). A *trochaic foot* consists of one stressed syllable followed by an unstressed syllable ("wonder"). An *anapestic foot* is two unstressed syllables followed by one stressed syllable ("by the sea"). A *dactylic foot* is one stressed syllable followed by two unstressed syllables ("beautiful"). A *spondee* is a foot consisting of two stressed syllables ("drop dead"). A *pyrrhus* is a foot with two unstressed syllables. **715–720**

Foreshadowing The introduction of specific words into a NARRATIVE to suggest or anticipate later events that are central to the ACTION and its RESOLUTION. **27**

Formalist criticism An approach to literature that focuses on the formal elements of the work. Formalist critics concentrate on analyzing how the various elements of a literary work — especially such aspects of style as irony, metaphor, and symbol — are integrated into the unique structure of a literary work. Anything outside of the work, such as biographical information or the work's historical context, is usually not discussed. See also NEW CRITICISM. **1614**

Free verse Poetry written by poets who felt that they had to break free of traditional poetic forms. Often free verse uses colloquial speech patterns and breath pauses to shape the poetic line, and it usually is unrhymed. See also OPEN FORM. **747**

Gender criticism An approach to literature that considers the gender and sexual orientation of both writers and readers of literature. Gender criticism developed from *feminist criticism,* which sought to correct or supplement a predominantly male-dominated critical perspective with a woman's point of view, often showing how women's writing strategies were related to their social conditions. **1619**–1620

Genre A type of literary work, such as SHORT STORY, novel, essay, play, or poem. The term may also be used to classify literature within a type, such as science-fiction stories or detective novels. In film, the term refers to a recognizable type of movie, such as a western or a thriller, that follows familiar NARRATIVE or visual conventions.

Graphic novels Substantial single volumes of pictorial images arranged in a sequence to narrate a story with or without words.

Haiku A short lyric poetic form found in Japanese poetry that suggests a world of allusion and response. The traditional haiku form is three lines, with five syllables in the two outer lines and seven syllables in the middle line. 803–**804**

Historical criticism An approach to literature that investigates the historical background of the text. Historical critics may also explain the meaning that the work had for its original readers, especially if the text includes words that had different connotations in the past. **1617**

Hyperbole Exaggerated statements that are not intended to be taken for the truth. Often called *overstatement*, hyperbole is often used for comic or ironic effect. **742**

Iamb See FOOT.

Iambic meter See FOOT.

Iambic pentameter A metrical pattern in poetry that consists of five iambic feet per line, each foot consisting of one unstressed syllable followed by a stressed syllable. See also BLANK VERSE. **720**

Imagery A word, phrase, or figure of speech such as a simile or a metaphor that suggests mental pictures of sensory impressions, such as *visual images* (things we see), *aural images* (things we hear), and *tactile images* (things we touch). **732**

Imagism A term invented by the American poet Ezra Pound as the name for a group of poets experimenting with the language of common speech before World War I. As an imagist poet, Pound believed that poems should "present an image. Poetry should render particulars exactly, and not deal in vague generalities, however magnificent and sonorous." **793**–795

Initial alliteration Repetition of the same sounding letters; when the first letter of a word is repeated and the letter is a consonant, it is called initial alliteration.

Internal rhyme See RHYME.

Irony A literary device that uses words to express something other than what is meant by the speaker. *Verbal irony* is a figure of speech that occurs when the speaker says one thing but means the opposite. If the intention of the speaker is to hurt someone else, then this form of verbal irony verges on *sarcasm. Dramatic irony* occurs when the reader (or the audience of a play) knows more about a situation than the imaginary characters. **63**, 1105

Limerick A short, humorous poem consisting of five lines with the rhyme scheme *aabba*. Since the characteristic anapestic meter of limericks makes them easy to remember, they are one of the most widespread types of folk poetry. **779**

Line A sequence of words printed on the page. Poetic lines are often measured by the number of feet they contain, such as:

monometer: one foot	*pentameter*: five feet
dimeter: two feet	*hexameter*: six feet
trimeter: three feet	*heptameter*: seven feet
tetrameter: four feet	*octameter*: eight feet

The number of feet in a line, along with the name of the foot, describes the metrical qualities of that line. See also END-STOPPED LINE, ENJAMBMENT, FOOT, METER.

Literal language Words used in their denotative sense, the opposite of FIGURATIVE LANGUAGE. **734**

Literary theory The term used by academic critics to characterize a method of inquiry into the nature and value of literature. **1614**

Lyric poetry The word *lyric* comes from *lyre,* the small harp played by the Greek poets to accompany their songs. A lyric is a type of poem that is highly suggestive, deeply personal, and often intensely emotional. Among the types of lyric poetry are the ELEGY, the ODE, and the SONNET. **808**

Lyrics The text of a song.

Marxist criticism An approach to literature based on the writings of Karl Marx that emphasizes the political and socioeconomic aspects and contexts of literary works. See also SOCIOLOGICAL CRITICISM. **1618**

Masculine rhyme See RHYME.

Metaphor A figure of speech or type of FIGURATIVE SPEECH in which one thing is equated with another in an indirect comparison without using the word *like* or *as*. Writers use metaphors in order not to define the first terms mentioned, but to attribute certain qualities to the thing being discussed, such as "Love is a rose" or "The exam was a killer." See also METONYMY, PERSONIFICATION, SYNECDOCHE. **735**

Meter The pattern set up by the regular rhythm of words in a poem. *Rising meter* refers to metrical feet moving from unstressed to stressed sounds, such as the iambic foot. *Falling meter* refers to metrical feet moving from stressed to unstressed sounds, such as the dactylic foot. See also ACCENT, FOOT, LINE. 713–716

Metonymy A type of metaphor in which the writer uses the name of one thing in place of the name of something closely related to it, such as saying "I knew him in his cradle" to mean "I knew him when he was young." See also METAPHOR. **726, 741**

Minimalism A literary style exemplifying economy and restraint, as seen in the early stories of Raymond Carver. Some of Ernest Hemingway's stories, such as "Hills Like White Elephants," are considered pioneering works of minimalism.

Monologue A play meant to be spoken or performed by one actor appearing alone on stage. **1110**

Mythological criticism An approach to literature that developed out of Jungian psychoanalytic theory about the importance of archetypal human behavior. Mythological critics attempt to identify and analyze the psychological elements of recurrent patterns in literary works that create deep universal responses in readers. See also ARCHETYPES. **1616**

Narrative An example of discourse designed to represent a connected succession of events or happenings, usually involving CHARACTERS, PLOT, and SETTING. **10, 33**

Narrative poetry A long or short poem that tells a story. See also EPIC. **748**

Narrator The dramatic voice of the person telling the story, not to be confused with the author's voice. With FIRST-PERSON NARRATION, the *I* in the story presents the viewpoint of only one character, who may play either a major or a minor role in the action. An UNRELIABLE NARRATOR gives an interpretation of events that the reader cannot trust to represent the view of the author. A *naive narrator* is usually too innocent or inexperienced to understand the deeper meaning of the action. An OMNISCIENT NARRATOR is an all-knowing narrator, usually the author, who is not a character in the story. *Limited omniscience* occurs when the author restricts a story in THIRD-PERSON NARRATION to the single perspective of either a major or a minor character. See also OBJECTIVE NARRATION, PERSONA, POINT OF VIEW. **32**–34

Near rhyme See RHYME.

New criticism An approach to literature developed after World War II that evolved out of FORMALIST CRITICISM. New critics emphasize close reading of literary texts rather than inquiring into their biographical or historical backgrounds. **1614**

Objective narration A way of telling a story from a third-person point of view without revealing the thoughts or feelings of any character. The detached and impersonal narrator reports action and dialogue directly, without analysis or interpretation, relying on the dialogue, actions, and physical descriptions to reveal the meaning of the story to the reader. See also NARRATOR, POINT OF VIEW, THIRD-PERSON NARRATION. 34

Octave A poetic stanza of eight lines, often forming one part of a SONNET. **747**

Ode One of the oldest forms of poetry, a lyric that serves as a formal, serious poem of praise, often presenting philosophic ideas and moral concerns. See also LYRIC POETRY. **753**–754

Omniscient narrator Literally "all-knowingness"; the ability of an author or narrator (usually in THIRD-PERSON NARRATION) to tell the reader directly about any events that have occurred, are occurring, or will occur in the PLOT of a story, and about the thoughts and feelings of any CHARACTER. See also NARRATOR. **34**

Onomatopoeia A term referring to the use of a word that resembles the sound it denotes, for example, *buzz*. Writers may also create lines or entire paragraphs using onomatopoeia, where the sound of the words helps to convey the meaning of the passage. **695**

Open form Earlier called FREE VERSE, open form poetry breaks from traditional use of METER and RHYME. Instead, the poet depends upon the arrangement of words on the printed page, or grammatical structure, or other means to produce the concentration and technical virtuosity of poetry written in closed forms. **747, 808**

Ottava rima An eight-line stanza with a rhyme scheme of *ABABABCC*.

Oxymoron A statement that contradicts itself, such as "jumbo shrimp." **742**

Parable A short narrative used to answer a difficult moral question or teach a moral truth. Often a form of ALLEGORY, because each person, event, or thing in the parable represents a literally unrelated person, event, thing, or quality that is involved in the moral dilemma being examined. **10**

Paradox A statement that on the surface seems that it cannot possibly be true, but that turns out to be true after all. To solve a paradox, the reader must uncover a meaning that is not evident at first sight. Poets often use paradox to capture a reader's attention by suggesting an idea that appears to be nonsense, as in John Donne's statement "Death, thou shalt die." **741**–742

Paraphrase A device used by poets as a response to poetic tradition, where writers find their own words to express their sense of an earlier literary work they consider important. **764, 827**

Parody A humorous imitation of another, usually serious, work or type of work, in which the parodist adopts the quirks of STYLE or the CONVENTIONS of the work or works being imitated and uses them in extreme and ridiculous ways, or applies them to a comically inappropriate subject matter. **830**

Pattern poem (also called "shaped poem") The oldest of the poetic forms used in many classic Greek poems; in this style the physical placing of letters and words creates a picture. **775**

Perfect rhyme See RHYME.

Persona An imaginary person through whom the poet can speak. Literally, a persona is a mask, behind which an author speaks or narrates a story. A persona is always a separate self, neither a character in the narrative, nor the author's personal voice. **808**

Personification A form of metaphor in which human characteristics are given to something inanimate, animal, or abstract. For example, in Keats's "Ode on a Grecian Urn," the urn is called an "unravished bride of quietness." See also METAPHOR. **737**

Plot The sequence of events in a short story or a play and their relation to one another. Authors select and arrange the incidents to give their stories a particular focus or emphasis. The series of events in the narrative form the ACTION, in which a CHARACTER or characters face an internal or external conflict that propels the plot to a CLIMAX and an ultimate RESOLUTION. The conclusion of the plot may have a *closed ending,* in which the major issues are resolved, or an *open ending,* in which the future actions of the characters are undetermined. Literary works concluding with the death of the protagonist are considered to have *closed endings.* See also WELL-MADE PLAY. **25**–28, 1104, **1112**

Poetic diction See DICTION.

Point of view The author's choice of a narrator for the story to shape what the reader knows and how the reader feels about the events of a story. See also FIRST-PERSON NARRATION, NARRATOR, OBJECTIVE NARRATION, THIRD-PERSON NARRATION. **32**–34

Poststructuralist criticism Similar to DECONSTRUCTIONIST CRITICISM, this is a modern approach to critical theory that focuses on the multiple, sometimes self-contradictory meanings that exist in a literary work. **1619**

Prose poem A lyric poem that has all the characteristics of a lyric but is written in densely compact prose. It presents one image or, like a lyric poem in open form, a response to a single emotion. See also LYRIC POETRY. **812**

Protagonist The main CHARACTER of a narrative, who engages the reader's interest and empathy. The ACTION of a story is usually the presentation and RESOLUTION of some internal or external conflict of the protagonist; if the conflict is with another major character, that character may be called the ANTAGONIST. **41, 1116**

Psychological criticism An approach to literature indebted to modern psychological theories, including those of Sigmund Freud, that explores the unconscious motivations of characters and the symbolic meaning of events, as well as the reader's personal responses to the text. **1615**

Pyrrhus See FOOT.

Quatrain A four-line stanza, usually rhymed, that for centuries has continued to be one of the most widely used poetic means in English and American poetry. **747**

Reader-response criticism An approach to literature that suggests that reading is as much a creative act as the writing of a text, because both involve the play of imagination and intelligence. The consciousness of the reader as he or she reads the literary work is the subject of this type of criticism, investigating the possibility of multiple readings and analyzing what our readings tell us about ourselves. **1618**

Realism The telling of a story or a drama in a manner that is faithful to the reader's experience of real life, limiting events in the PLOT to things that might actually happen and CHARACTERS to people who might actually exist.

Refrain The repeated line that ends the verses in a BALLAD. **748**

Resolution The outcome of a plot's conflicts and complications. The resolution follows the CLIMAX and the FALLING ACTION and leads to the conclusion of the story or play. 26, **1113**

Revenge tragedies Plays in which the plot typically centers on a spectacular attempt to avenge the murder of a family member. **1186**

Rhyme The repetition of similar or identical terminal sounds of concluding syllables in different words, usually at the ends of lines. *Eye rhyme* is when two words look as though they would sound alike, but their sound, if spoken aloud, is different, such as *bough* and *cough.* Words can rhyme even if they aren't spelled the same way or look as if they rhyme, such as *day, weigh,* and *bouquet. End rhyme* is when the words at the end of the line rhyme. The *rhyme scheme* of a poem is the pattern of end rhymes. *Internal rhyme* places at least one of the rhymed words in the middle of the line. *Masculine rhyme* means that the accent on the rhyming words is on a final stressed syllable (*betray* and *away*) or the rhyming consists of one-syllable words (*milk* and *silk*). *Feminine rhyme* consists of a rhymed stressed syllable followed by one or more identical unstressed syllables (*season* and *reason*). *Exact* or *perfect rhymes* (such as the examples above) exist between words that share the same stressed vowel sounds as well as the sounds that follow the vowel. In *near rhyme* or *slant rhyme,* the sound of the rhyming words is close but not exact, such as *read* and *red, ball* and *bell. Consonance* is a common form of near rhyme, in which identical consonant sounds are preceded by different vowel sounds, such as *home* and *same, worth* and *breath.* **693**, 696–701

Rhyme royal A seven-line stanza in iambic pentameter with a rhyme scheme of *ABABBCC.* **701**

Rhythm A term used to refer to the recurrence of stressed and unstressed sounds in poetry. The pattern of words in LINES and STANZAS, and the repetitions of sounds within the poem create different rhythmic effects that add to the pleasure of reading, reciting, and listening to poetry. 714–716

Rising action See PLOT.

Rising meter See METER.

Romanticism, romantic movement A literary movement that flourished in the nineteenth century, valuing individuality, imagination, and the truth revealed in nature. **1013**

Round (characters) See CHARACTER.

Satire A work that ridicules some aspect of human behavior by portraying it at its most extreme; distinguished from PARODY, which burlesques the STYLE or content of a work.

Scansion The reader's analysis of the arrangement of ACCENTS or STRESSED SYLLABLES in a LINE of poetry in an attempt to understand its pattern. **715**

Sentimentality A negative term in literary criticism, suggesting that the author of a literary work has engaged in emotional overindulgence, trying to force emotional responses in the reader that are not justified by the situation or characters' behavior.

Sestet A six-line stanza. See also STANZA. **747**

Sestina A verse form composed of six stanzas, each six lines long, with a concluding verse of three lines called the *envoy.* **769**–770

Setting The physical details of the place, the time, and the social context that influence the actions of the CHARACTERS. Often setting also evokes a mood or atmosphere, FORESHADOWING events to come for the attentive reader. **45**, 50–51

Shaped poem See PATTERN POEM.

Short story A short fictional prose narrative, usually consisting of one unified episode or a sequence of related events. Fables, sketches, and tales are included in this genre. The term is often applied to any work of narrative prose fiction shorter than a novel. Edgar Allan Poe said the tale or story's distinguishing feature was that it was a prose form possessing aesthetic unity that could be read in one sitting. The trouble with that definition, as writer William Saroyan later pointed out, is that some people can sit longer than others. **10, 25**

Simile A figure of speech that makes an explicit comparison between two things by using words such as *like* or *as.* "My love is like a red, red rose" is a simile. "My love is a red rose" is a metaphor. "My love smells like a red rose because she is wearing perfume tonight" is a sentence that uses *like,* but it is not a simile; it is a statement of fact. 734–**735**

Sketch A relaxed, predominantly descriptive prose composition that usually includes some action. Typically, however, a sketch doesn't develop characterization or dramatize complex, causally related actions that resolve a conflict.

Slant rhyme See RHYME.

Sociological criticism An approach to literature by critics interested in exploring the economic, racial, and political context in which fiction, poetry, and drama are created and read. Sociological critics treat literature as either a document reflecting social conditions, or a literary work produced by those conditions. MARXIST CRITICISM and *feminist criticism* are two forms of sociological criticism. See also GENDER CRITICISM. **1617**

Soliloquy A dramatic convention by means of which a character speaks his or her thoughts aloud when alone onstage, conveniently informing the audience about his or her state of mind so that we can understand the character's motivation for subsequent acts. Hamlet's soliloquy beginning "To be or not to be" is the most famous soliloquy in English. **1119**

Sonnet A fourteen-line lyric poem written in a regular rhyme sequence, often in iambic pentameter. The two basic types are the *Italian sonnet,* perfected in Italy in the early fourteenth century, and the *English sonnet.* The Italian sonnet, also known as the Petrarchan sonnet, is divided into an OCTAVE and a SESTET. The English sonnet is organized into three QUATRAINS and a concluding COUPLET, typically rhyming *ABAB-CDCD-EFEF-GG.* This rhyme scheme is more suited to the English language, which has fewer rhyming words than Italian. **763**

Spenserian stanza Eight lines of iambic pentameter and a last line of six stressed feet (an ALEXANDRINE). This nine-line stanza is named after the English poet Edmund Spenser, who used it for his epic poem *The Faerie Queen,* written at the end of the sixteenth century.

Spondee See FOOT.

Stanza A grouping of lines, set off by a space on the page, that usually has a set pattern of METER and RHYME. **721, 747**

Static character See CHARACTER.

Stock characters Characters who are oversimplified and generalized into stock types in a literary work, whose thoughts and actions are easily predictable because they are used so frequently that they have become conventional. 40

Stressed syllables Syllables given heavier emphasis when reading a line of poetry. See also ACCENT. **715**

Style The distinctive and recognizable way an author uses language to create a work of literature. This can involve the writer's DICTION, sentence length and SYNTAX, TONE, use of figures of speech, IRONY, and THEME. **57**

Subplot A minor PLOT, often involving one or more secondary CHARACTERS, that may add a complication to the ACTION of a SHORT STORY or DRAMA. A subplot may also reinforce the major plot or provide an enlightening contrast to it or a welcome relief from its tension. **1115**

Symbol A word (or person, object, image, or event) that evokes a range of additional meanings that are usually more abstract than its literal significance. *Conventional symbols* such as the American flag have so much meaning attached to them that we cannot see them without immediately thinking about something else at the same time. Writers use conventional symbols to reinforce meanings or suggest FORESHADOWING, as when Edgar Allan Poe mentions the mound of bones in the crypt into which Montresor has lured Fortunato to suggest Fortunato's imminent death. *Literary* or *contextual symbols* are settings, characters, actions, or things in a work of fiction, poetry, or drama that keep their literal significance but also suggest symbolic interpretation. **63, 741**

Synecdoche A type of metaphor in which the writer uses part of something to stand for the whole thing, such as saying "He has a heavy bat" to mean "He hits the ball well." See also METAPHOR. **726, 741**

Syntax A reference to the order of the words in writing of any kind. Syntax usually implies a word order that results in meaningful verbal patterns in the author's choice of words, phrases, and sentence structure. These verbal choices allow authors to emphasize any word of their choice as they manipulate syntax. **57, 732**

Tale An early form of the SHORT STORY, usually involving remote places and times, and often events that lead to a dramatic, conclusive ending. Early tales were told in either poetry or prose. 9

Tercet A three-line STANZA. **747**

Terza rima A TERCET in IAMBIC PENTAMETER with an interlocking three-line rhyme scheme: *ABA, BCB, CDC, DED,* etc. **756**

Theme A generalization about the meaning of a story, poem, or play. It is an abstract concept that is made concrete through the other means available to the writer, such as PLOT, CHARACTERIZATION, and SYMBOL. This underlying central idea serves as a unifying point around which the literary work is created and/or understood. **68,** 1105, **1121**

Thesis sentence The central idea of an essay expressed in a complete sentence (or group of sentences, if the central idea to be developed in the essay is a complex one). **1629**

Third-person narration A way of telling a story using the third person "he" or "she," in which the narrator is a nonparticipant in the story. There are many varieties of third-person narration, including OMNISCIENT, limited omniscient, and OBJECTIVE. See also NARRATOR and POINT OF VIEW. **32**

Tone The way authors convey their unstated attitudes toward their subjects as revealed in their literary STYLE. Tone can be described as serious or comic, ironic or naive, angry or funny, or any other emotional states that human beings can experience and find words to express. **62**, **726**–727

Tragedy A drama typically describing the downfall of a human being, often a conflict between the PROTAGONIST and a superior force (such as fate or a powerful ANTAGONIST), leading to a disastrous conclusion that excites pity or terror. A *tragic flaw* is a defect in the tragic hero that precipitates his or her downfall, such as ambition or pride. **1094**

Tragicomedy A mixture of sad and happy events in a DRAMA. Often the PLOT of a tragicomedy is fast moving, dealing with love, jealousy, intrigue, and surprises, but at the end of the story the audience usually experiences the play as a positive statement, an affirmation of life. **1094**

Triplet A TERCET in which all three lines rhyme.

Trochaic meter See FOOT.

Trochee See FOOT.

Understatement Describing something, often for comic effect, in terms that suggest it is much smaller or less important than we know it really is. Understatement is the opposite of HYPERBOLE. **742**

Unity The relation of all parts of a work to one central or organizing principle that forms them into a complete and coherent whole. 648–651

Unreliable narrator A fictional CHARACTER telling the story whose knowledge or judgment about events and other characters is so flawed or so limited as to make him or her a misleading guide to the reader. **33**

Unstressed syllables Syllables given less emphasis when reading a line of poetry. See also ACCENT. **715**

Verse A term used generically to mean poetry or a specific unit within a poem. The term can also be used to describe metrical writing distinguished from poetry by its lower level of intensity. **747**

Villanelle A fixed form of poetry in nineteen lines composed of five TERCETS and a final QUATRAIN, written in IAMBIC PENTAMETER. The rhyme scheme for the tercets is *ABA*, and the quatrain repeats the final rhyme, *ABAA*. Like the SESTINA, the villanelle is an elaborate word game in which entire lines appear again and again. Dylan Thomas's "Do not go gentle into that good night" is a villanelle. **769**, 771

Voice A term referring to the specific manner chosen by the author to create a story or poem. Voice encompasses elements of literary STYLE such as TONE and DICTION. It is usually difficult to get a sense of the original author's voice in a text that has been translated from a foreign language into English. **62**

Well-made play A nineteenth-century realistic play that was so carefully and logically constructed that its plot led unfailingly to a final scene resolving and concluding all the dramatic conflicts. Henrik Ibsen challenged the *closed ending* convention of a well-made play when *A Doll House* culminated in an *open ending* without a clear resolution of the complex moral and gender issues dramatized onstage. See also PLOT. 1349

Acknowledgments (continued from p. viii)

Diane Ackerman. "The Work of the Poet Is to Name What Is Holy" from *Origami Bridges: Poems of Psychoanalysis and Fire* by Diane Ackerman. Copyright © 2002 by Diane Ackerman. Reprinted by permission of HarperCollins Publishers.

Rolf Aggestam. "Fragment I–IV" by Rolf Aggestam. Translated by Samuel Charters. Reprinted by permission.

Claribel Alegría. "Carmen Bomba: Poet" from *Poetry Like Bread: Poets of the Political Imagination* from Curbstone Press, edited by Martín Espada. Reprinted by permission of Northwestern University Press.

Sherman Alexie. "The Lone Ranger and Tonto Fistfight in Heaven" from *The Lone Ranger and Tonto Fistfight in Heaven*, copyright © 1993, 2005 by Sherman Alexie. Used by permission of Grove/Atlantic, Inc. "Superman and Me." Copyright © 1997 by Sherman Alexie. All rights reserved. Reprinted by permission of Nancy Stauffer Associates.

Paula Gunn Allen. "Whirlwind Man Steals Yellow Woman" from *Spider Woman's Granddaughters* by Paula Gunn Allen (Beacon Press). Copyright © 1984. Reprinted by permission of Beacon Press.

Dorothy Allison. "Jason Who Will Be Famous." Copyright © 2009 by Dorothy Allison. Reprinted by permission of The Frances Goldin Literary Agency.

Guillaume Apollinaire. "Hail World" and "It's Raining" from *Calligrammes: Poems of Peace and War (1913–1916)* by Guillaume Apollinaire, translated by Anne Hyde Greet, © 1980 by the Regents of the University of California. Published by the University of California Press.

Aristotle. Excerpt from *Poetics* by Aristotle, translated by Gerald Else (Ann Arbor: The University of Michigan Press, 1967). Copyright © 1967 Gerald F. Else. Reprinted by permission of the University of Michigan Press.

Margaret Atwood. "Happy Endings" from *Good Bones and Simple Murders* by Margaret Atwood, copyright © 1983, 1992, 1994, by O. W. Toad Ltd. A Nan A. Talese Book. Used by permission of Doubleday, a division of Random House, Inc. Also published by McClelland & Stewart. Used with permission of the author and the publisher. All rights reserved.

W. H. Auden. "Musée des Beaux Arts," copyright 1940 and renewed 1968 by W. H. Auden, and "Stop All the Clocks," copyright 1940 and renewed 1968 by W. H. Auden, from *Collected Poems of W. H. Auden* by W. H. Auden. Used by permission of Random House, Inc. "Lay Your Sleeping Head, My Love," copyright © 1937 by W. H. Auden. Reprinted by permission of Curtis Brown, Ltd.

Ronald Baatz. "as though the whole earth," "our beautiful old love," and "The Oldest Songs." Reprinted by permission of the author.

James Baldwin. "Sonny's Blues" by James Baldwin was originally published in *Partisan Review*. Copyright renewed. Collected in *Going to Meet the Man*, published by Vintage Books. Reprinted by arrangement with the James Baldwin Estate. Excerpt from *Notes of a Native Son* by James Baldwin. Copyright © 1955, renewed 1983 by James Baldwin. Reprinted by permission of Beacon Press, Boston.

Toni Cade Bambara. "The Lesson," copyright © 1972 by Toni Cade Bambara, from *Gorilla, My Love* by Toni Cade Bambara. Used by permission of Random House, Inc.

Bernard Bergonzi. Excerpt from "Nearly Hard Poems' King" in *Gerard Manley Hopkins* by Bernard Bergonzi (Macmillan, 1977). Reprinted by permission of Bernard Bergonzi.

Sven Birkerts. "James Wright's 'Hammock': A Sounding." Reprinted by permission of the author.

Elizabeth Bishop. "The Bight," "Sestina," "Manners — for a child of 1918," "Sandpiper," "One Art," and "The Fish" from *The Complete Poems 1927–1979*. Copyright © 1979, 1983 by Alice Helen Methfessel. Reprinted by permission of Farrar, Straus and Giroux, LLC.

Robert Bly. "On Tomas Tranströmer." Reprinted by permission of the author.

Louise Bogan. Excerpt from "Song for the Last Act" from *The Blue Estuaries* by Louise Bogan. Copyright © 1968 by Louise Bogan. Copyright renewed 1996 by Ruth Limmer. Reprinted by permission of Farrar, Straus and Giroux, LLC.

Roberto Bolaño. "Jim" by Roberto Bolaño, translated by Chris Andrews, from *The Insufferable Gaucho*, copyright © 2003 by The Heirs of Roberto Bolaño, translation copyright © 2010 by Chris Andrews. Reprinted by permission of New Directions Publishing Corp.

Jenny Bornholdt. "The Boyfriends." Reprinted by permission of the author.

Bonnie Bremser. "A First Meeting with the Beats" excerpted from *Poets and Odd Fellows*. Reprinted by permission of the author.

Ray Bremser. "Blues for Bonnie — Take 1, January 1960." Permission granted by Jeffrey H. Weinberg, Water Row Books. "Blues for Bonnie — Take 1, January 1960" © 1960 Ray Bremser.

Cleanth Brooks and Robert Penn Warren. "A New Critical Reading of 'The Fall of the House of Usher'" excerpted from *Understanding Fiction*, 3rd edition, by Cleanth Brooks and Robert Penn Warren, © 1979, pp. 202–205. Reprinted by permission of Pearson Education, Inc., Upper Saddle River, NJ. "On Eliot's 'The Love Song of J. Alfred Prufrock,'" excerpted from *Understanding Poetry*, 4th edition, by Cleanth Brooks and Robert Penn Warren, © 1976 Heinle/Arts & Sciences, a part of Cengage Learning, Inc. Reproduced by permission. www.cengage.com/permissions.

Gwendolyn Brooks. "Rites for Cousin Vit," "We Real Cool," "The Mother," and "The Bean Eaters" from *Blacks* by Gwendolyn Brooks. Copyright © 1991 by Gwendolyn Brooks. Reprinted by consent of Brooks Permissions.

Geoffrey Bullough. "Sources of Shakespeare's *Hamlet*" from *Narrative and Dramatic Sources of Shakespeare*, 8 vols. Copyright © 1964 and renewed 1992 by Geoffrey Bullough. Reprinted by permission of Columbia University Press.

José Antonio Burciaga. "La Puerta." Reprinted with permission from C. P. Burciaga.

Nick Carbó. "American Adobo" from *El Grupo McDonald's* by Nick Carbó. Published by Tia Chucha Press. Copyright © 2004 by Nick Carbó. Also published in *Asian American Poetry: The New Generation* (University of Illinois Press). Reprinted by permission of the author.

John Carley. "buoyed up on the rising tide" by John Carley (*Magma*, no. 19, 2001). Reprinted by permission of the author.

Raymond Carver. "Cathedral" from *Cathedral* by Raymond Carver, copyright © 1981, 1982, 1983 by Raymond Carver. Used by permission of Alfred A. Knopf, a division of Random House, Inc. "Creative Writing 101." All pages [pp. xi–xix] from Foreword (as it appears in *On Being a Novelist* by John Gardner) by Raymond Carver. Foreword copyright © 1983 by Raymond Carver. Reprinted by permission of HarperCollins Publishers. "Popular Mechanics" from *What We Talk About When We Talk About Love* by Raymond Carver, copyright © 1974, 1976, 1978, 1980, 1981 by Raymond Carver. Used by permission of Alfred A. Knopf, a division of Random House, Inc. "On Writing" from *Fires: Essays, Poems, Stories* by Raymond Carver. Copyright © 1968, 1969, 1970, 1971, 1972, 1973, 1974, 1975, 1976, 1977, 1978, 1979, 1980, 1981, 1982, 1983 by Raymond Carver. Copyright © 1983, 1984 by the Estate of Raymond Carver, used by permission of The Wylie Agency LLC.

John Casteen. "Night Hunting" first appeared in *Ploughshares* and in *The Best American Poetry 2008*. Reprinted with permission.

Anton Chekhov. "The Lady with the Pet Dog," translated by Avrahm Yarmolinsky, from *The Portable Chekhov* by Anton Chekhov, edited by Avrahm Yarmolinsky, copyright 1947, © 1968 by Viking Penguin, Inc., renewed © 1975 by Avrahm Yarmolinsky. Used by permission of Viking Penguin, a division of Penguin Group (USA) Inc.

Marilyn Chin. "On the Canon" by Marilyn Chin from *June Jordan's Poetry for the People*, edited by Lauren Mullen and the Blueprint Collective. Copyright © 1995 by Routledge. Reprinted by permission of Taylor & Francis, Inc. Permission conveyed through Copyright Clearance Center, Inc. "How I Got That Name" and "Sad Guitar" in *The Phoenix Gone, The Terrace Empty* (Minneapolis: Milkweed Editions, 1994). Copyright © 1994 by Marilyn Chin. Reprinted with permission from Milkweed Editions. www.milkweed.org.

Lucille Clifton. "to ms. ann" from *Collected Poems of Lucille Clifton*. Copyright © 1987 by Lucille Clifton. Reprinted with the permission of The Permissions Company, Inc., on behalf of BOA Editions, Ltd. www.boaeditions.org.

Judith Ortiz Cofer. "Quinceañera" is reprinted with permission from the publisher of *Terms of Survival* by Judith Ortiz Cofer. © 1987 Arte Público Press–University of Houston.

Billy Collins. "The Only Day in Existence" and "Today" from *Nine Horses* by Billy Collins, copyright © 2002 by Billy Collins. Used by permission of Random House, Inc. "Memento Mori" from *Questions About Angels* by Billy Collins, © 1991. Reprinted by permission of the University of Pittsburgh Press.

Gregory Corso. "I am 25" from *Gasoline* by Gregory Corso. Copyright © 1981 by City Lights Books. Reprinted by permission of the publisher.

Countee Cullen. "Yet Do I Marvel," "Heritage," and "Color" from *Color*. Copyrights held by Amistad Research Center Tulane University. Administered by Thompson and Thompson, Brooklyn, NY. Reprinted by permission.

e. e. cummings. "when god lets my body be." Copyright 1923, 1951, ©1991 by the Trustees for the E. E. Cummings Trust. Copyright © 1976 by George James Firmage. "somewhere I have never travelled, gladly beyond." Copyright 1931, © 1959, 1991 by the Trustees for the E. E. Cummings Trust. Copyright © 1979 by George James Firmage. "Buffalo Bill 's." Copyright 1923, 1951, © 1991 by the Trustees for the E. E. Cummings Trust. Copyright © 1976 by George James Firmage. "goodby Betty, don't remember me." Copyright 1923, 1951, © 1991 by the Trustees for the E. E. Cummings Trust. Copyright © 1976 by George James Firmage. "in Just-." Copyright 1923, 1951, © 1991 by the Trustees for the E. E. Cummings Trust. Copyright © 1976 by George James Firmage from *Complete Poems: 1904–1962* by E. E. Cummings, edited by George James Firmage. "since feeling is first." Copyright 1926, 1954, © 1991 by the Trustees for the E. E. Cummings Trust. Copyright © 1985 by George James Firmage. Used by permission of Liveright Publishing Corporation.

Lydia Davis. "Blind Date" from *The Collected Stories of Lydia Davis* by Lydia Davis. Copyright © 2009 by Lydia Davis. Reprinted by permission of Farrar, Straus and Giroux, LLC.

Junot Díaz. "How to Date a Browngirl, Blackgirl, Whitegirl, or Halfie" from *Drown* by Junot Díaz, copyright © 1996 by Junot Díaz. Used by permission of Riverhead Books, an imprint of Penguin Group (USA) Inc.

Emily Dickinson. "A word is dead," "I think I was enchanted," "You love me—you are sure—," "I'm 'wife'—I've finished that—," "I taste a liquor never brewed—," "Wild Nights—Wild Nights!," "'Hope' is the thing with feathers—," "There's a certain Slant of light," "I'm Nobody! Who are you?" "After great pain, a formal feeling comes—," "Much Madness is divinest Sense," "I died for Beauty—but was scarce," "I heard a Fly buzz—when I died—," "Because I could not stop for Death—," "A narrow Fellow in the Grass," and excerpt from "I never saw a Moor—." Reprinted by permission of the publishers and the Trustees of Amherst College from *The Poems of Emily Dickinson*, edited by Thomas H. Johnson (Cambridge, Mass.: The Belknap Press of Harvard University Press). Copyright © 1951, 1955, 1979, 1983 by the President and Fellows of Harvard College.

Diane di Prima. "Revolutionary Letter #3" from *Revolutionary Letters* by Diane di Prima. Fifth edition published by Last Gasp. © 1971, 1974, 1979, 2007 Diane di Prima. All Rights Reserved. Reprinted with permission.

Rita Dove. "The Pond, Porch-View: Six P.M., Early Spring" and "Singsong" from *On the Bus with Rosa Parks* by Rita Dove. Copyright © 1999 by Rita Dove. Used by permission of W. W. Norton & Company, Inc. "An Intact World" from *Mother Love* by Rita Dove. Copyright © 1995 by Rita Dove. Used by permission of W. W. Norton & Company, Inc.

W. E. B. Du Bois. *The Souls of Black Folk* by W. E. B. Du Bois (Chicago: A. C. McClurg & Co., 1903). Reproduced by permission of Penguin Books Ltd.

Robert Duncan. "A Poem Beginning with a Line from Pindar" from *The Opening of the Field*, copyright © 1960 by Robert Duncan. Reprinted by permission of New Directions Publishing Corp.

Bob Dylan. "Blowin' in the Wind." Written by Bob Dylan. Published by Special Rider Music. Reprinted with permission.

T. S. Eliot. "The Love Song of J. Alfred Prufrock" from *Collected Poems 1909–1962* by T. S. Eliot (Faber & Faber Ltd.). "The Journey of the Magi" taken from *Collected Poems 1909–1962* © Estate of T. S. Eliot. Copyright 1936 by Houghton Mifflin Harcourt Publishing Company. Copyright © renewed 1964 by T. S. Eliot. Reprinted by permission of Houghton Mifflin Harcourt Publishing Company and Faber and Faber Ltd. All rights reserved.

Ralph Ellison. "Battle Royal," copyright 1948 and renewed 1976 by Ralph Ellison, from *Invisible Man* by Ralph Ellison. Used by permission of Random House, Inc. "The Influence of Folklore on 'Battle Royal'" from *Shadow and Act* by Ralph Ellison, copyright 1953, 1964 and renewed 1981, 1992 by Ralph Ellison. Used by permission of Random House, Inc.

William Faulkner. "A Rose for Emily" copyright 1930 and renewed 1958 by William Faulkner from *Collected Stories of William Faulkner* by William Faulkner. Used by permission of Random House, Inc. "The Meaning of 'A Rose for Emily'" from *Faulkner in the University*, edited by Frederick L. Gwynn and Joseph L. Blotner, © 1995 by the Rector and Visitors of the University of Virginia. Reprinted by permission of the University of Virginia Press.

Jessie Fauset. "Meeting Langston Hughes." The authors and publishers wish to thank the Crisis Publishing Co., Inc., the publisher of the magazine of the National Association for the Advancement of Colored People, for the use of this material first published in the March 1926 issue of *Crisis* Magazine.

Lawrence Ferlinghetti. "Dog" from *A Coney Island of the Mind* by Lawrence Ferlinghetti, copyright ©1958 by Lawrence Ferlinghetti. Reprinted by permission of New Directions Publishing Corp.

Sally Fitzgerald. "Southern Sources of 'A Good Man Is Hard to Find'" from *Happy Endings* by Sally Fitzgerald in *Image* (Summer 1997). Reprinted by permission of Ughetta Fitzgerald Lubin.

Carolyn Forché. All pages from "The Colonel" from *The Country Between Us* by Carolyn Forché. Copyright © 1981 by Carolyn Forché. Originally appeared in Women's International Resource Exchange. Reprinted by permission of HarperCollins Publishers.

Sigmund Freud. "The Oedipus Complex." Copyright © 1955 Sigmund Freud. Reprinted by permission of Basic Books, a member of the Perseus Books Group. From *The Standard Edition of The Complete Psychological Words of Sigmund Freud,* translated and edited by James Strachey, published by Vintage Books. Reprinted by permission of The Random House Group Ltd.

Robert Frost. "The Pasture" and "Mending Wall." Copyright 1930, 1939, 1969 by Henry Holt and Company, Copyright © 1958 by Robert Frost, Copyright © 1967 by Lesley Frost Ballantine from *The Poetry of Robert Frost,* edited by Edward Connery Lathem. "To Earthward" and "Stopping by Woods on a Snowy Evening" from *The Poetry of Robert Frost,* edited by Edward Connery Lathem (Henry Holt and Company). Copyright 1923, 1969 by Henry Holt and Company, Copyright © 1951 by Robert Frost. "Home Burial," "Birches," "The Road Not Taken," "After Apple-Picking." "Stars" from *The Poetry of Robert Frost,* edited by Edward Connery Lathem. Copyright © 1934, 1969 by Henry Holt and Company, copyright © 1962 by Robert Frost. Reprinted by permission of Henry Holt and Company, LLC.

Gabriel García Márquez. All pages from "A Very Old Man with Enormous Wings" from *Leaf Storm and Other Stories* by Gabriel García Márquez, translated by Gregory Rabassa. Copyright © 1971 by Gabriel García Márquez. Reprinted by permission of HarperCollins Publishers.

Philip L. Gerber. "On Frost's 'After Apple-Picking'" from *Robert Frost,* revised edition, 1st edition. © 1982 Gale, a part of Cengage Learning, Inc. Reproduced by permission. www.cengage.com/permissions.

Sir John Gielgud. "On Playing Hamlet" from *Early Stages* by Sir John Gielgud. Copyright © 1939 by Sir John Gielgud. Reprinted by permission of the Trustees of the Sir John Gielgud Charitable Trust.

Dagoberto Gilb. "Love in L.A." from *The Magic of Blood* by Dagoberto Gilb. Reprinted by permission of the author.

Sandra Gilbert and Susan Gubar. "A Feminist Reading of Gilman's 'The Yellow Wallpaper'" from *Madwoman in the Attic* by Sandra Gilbert and Susan Gubar. Copyright © 1979 by Yale University. Reprinted by permission of Yale University Press.

Charlotte Perkins Gilman. "Undergoing the Cure for Nervous Prostration" from *The Living of Charlotte Perkins Gilman* by Charlotte Perkins Gilman. © 1987 by the Board of Regents of the University of Wisconsin System. Reprinted by permission of The University of Wisconsin Press.

Allen Ginsberg. All lines from "A Supermarket in California" and all (55) lines from "Sunflower Sutra" from *Collected Poems 1947–1980* by Allen Ginsberg. Copyright © 1955 by Allen Ginsberg. Reprinted by permission of HarperCollins Publishers.

Dana Gioia. "Summer Storm," © 2001 by Dana Gioia. Reprinted with permission of the author.

Nikki Giovanni. "Adulthood" from *Selected Poems* by Nikki Giovanni is reprinted by permission of the author.

Kate Gleason. "After Fighting for Hours." First appeared in *Green Mountains Review* (Fall/Winter 1995–1996).

Louise Glück. "The Wild Iris" from *The Wild Iris* by Louise Glück. Copyright © 1992 by Louise Glück. Reprinted by permission of HarperCollins Publishers. "First Memory" from *Ararat* by Louise Glück. Copyright © 1990 by Louise Glück. Reprinted by permission of HarperCollins Publishers. "Happiness" from *Descending Figure* from *The First Four Books of Poems* by Louise Glück. Copyright 1968, 1971, 1972, 1973, 1974, 1975, 1976, 1977, 1978, 1979, 1980, 1985, 1995 by Louise Glück. Reprinted by permission of HarperCollins Publishers. "Gratitude" from *The First Four Books of Poems* by Louise Glück. Copyright © 1968, 1971, 1972, 1973, 1974, 1975, 1976, 1977, 1978, 1979, 1980, 1985, 1995 by Louise Glück. Reprinted by permission of HarperCollins Publishers.

Alasdair Gray. "Pillow Talk." Copyright © Alasdair Gray. Reproduced by permission of the author c/o Rogers, Coleridge & White Ltd., 20 Powis Mews, London W11 1JN.

Stephen Greenblatt. "On the Ghost in Hamlet" (editor's title) excerpted from *Will in the World* by Stephen Greenblatt. Copyright © 2004 by Stephen Greenblatt. Used by permission of W. W. Norton & Company, Inc.

Richard Leighton Greene. "Apropos Coleridge's 'Kubla Khan.'" Reprinted by permission.

Angelina Weld Grimké. "Black Finger" and "Tenebris" from the Grimké Papers. Reprinted by permission of the Moorland-Spingarn Research Center, Howard University.

Susan Grimm. "Things I Can Know" from *Lake Erie Blue* by Susan Grimm (BkMk Press, University of Missouri–Kansas City). Reprinted by permission.

Marilyn Hacker. "Rondeau after a Transatlantic Telephone Call" from *Taking Notice* by Marilyn Hacker. Copyright © 1976, 1978, 1979, 1980 by Marilyn Hacker. Reprinted by permission of Frances Collin, Literary Agent.

Forrest Hamer. "My Father's Viet Nam Tour Near Over." Copyright 2000, *Middle Ear* (Roundhouse), Berkeley, CA.

Lorraine Hansberry. *A Raisin in the Sun* by Lorraine Hansberry, copyright © 1958 by Robert Nemiroff, as an unpublished work. Copyright © 1959, 1966, 1984 by Robert Nemiroff. Copyright renewed 1986, 1987 by Robert Nemiroff. Used by permission of Random House, Inc. "My Shakespearean Experience." Reprinted with the permission of Simon & Schuster, Inc., from *To Be Young, Gifted and Black: Lorraine Hansberry in Her Own Words* by Lorraine Hansberry. Copyright © 1969 by Robert Nemiroff and Robert Nemiroff as Executor of the Estate of Lorraine Hansberry. All rights reserved. "An Author's Reflections: Willy Loman, Walter Younger, and He Who Must Live" by Lorraine Hansberry from *The Village Voice Reader*, edited by Daniel Wolf and Edwin Fancher. Copyright © 1962 by Daniel Wolf and Edwin Fancher. Reprinted by permission of the William Morris Agency, LLC, on behalf of the Author.

Robert Hass. "Tranströmer's Style," © Robert Hass. Reprinted by permission of the author.

Robert Hayden. "On Negro Poetry" from *Kaleidoscope: Poems by American Negro Poets*, copyright © 1967 by Harcourt, Inc. and renewed 1995 by Maia Patillo. Reprinted by permission of Houghton Mifflin Harcourt Publishing Company. "Those Winter Sundays." Copyright © 1966 by Robert Hayden, from *Collected Poems of Robert Hayden* by Robert Hayden, edited by Frederick Glaysher. Used by permission of Liveright Publishing Corporation.

Seamus Heaney. "Digging" and "Mid-Term Break" from *Opened Ground: Selected Poems 1966–1996* by Seamus Heaney. Copyright © 1998 by Seamus Heaney. Reprinted by permission of Farrar, Straus and Giroux, LLC, and Faber and Faber Limited.

Ernest Hemingway. "Hills Like White Elephants" from *The Short Stories of Ernest Hemingway* by Ernest Hemingway. Copyright © 1927 by Charles Scribner's Sons. Copyright renewed © 1955 by Ernest Hemingway. All rights reserved. Reprinted with the permission of Scribner, a division of Simon & Schuster, Inc.

Victor Hernández Cruz. "today is a day of great joy." © Victor Hernández Cruz 1969–2011.

Tobey Hiller. "the closing of the south park road." Reprinted by permission of the author.

Sara Holbrook. "Canvassing." Reprinted by permission of the author.

John Clellon Holmes. "This Is the Beat Generation." Reprinted by permission of Liz Von Vogt.

Langston Hughes. "The Negro Speaks of Rivers," "Mother to Son," "Negro," "Love Again Blues," "I, Too," "Song for a Dark Girl," "House in the World," and excerpt from "Harlem (2)" from *The Collected Poems of Langston Hughes* by Langston Hughes, edited by Arnold Rampersad with David Roessel, Associate Editor, copyright © 1994 by the Estate of Langston Hughes. Used by permission of Alfred A. Knopf, a division of Random House, Inc. "A Toast to Harlem" from *The Best of Simple* by Langston Hughes. Copyright © 1961 by Langston Hughes. Copyright renewed 1989 by George Houston Bass. Reprinted by permission of Hill and Wang, a division of Farrar, Straus and Giroux, LLC.

Zora Neale Hurston. "Sweat" by Zora Neale Hurston (Wall, Cheryl A., ed.). Copyright © 1997 by Rutgers, the State University. Reprinted by permission of Rutgers University Press. "How It Feels to Be Colored Me." Used with permission from the Zora Neale Hurston Trust and Victoria Sanders & Associates, LLC.

Shirley Jackson. "Biography of a Story (The Morning of June 28, 1948, and 'The Lottery')," copyright © 1960 by Shirley Jackson, from *Come Along with Me* by Shirley Jackson. Used by permission of Viking Penguin, a division of Penguin Group (USA) Inc. "The Lottery" from *The Lottery* by Shirley Jackson. Copyright © 1948, 1949 by Shirley Jackson. Copyright renewed © 1976, 1977 by Lawrence Hyman, Barry Hyman, Mrs. Sarah Webster, and Mrs. Joanne Schnurer. Reprinted by permission of Farrar, Straus and Giroux, LLC.

Gustav Janouch. "Kafka's View of 'The Metamorphosis'" by Gustav Janouch, translated by Goronwy Rees, from *Conversations with Kafka,* copyright © 1968 by S. Fischer Verlag GMBH, translation copyright © 1971 S. Fischer Verlag GMBH. Reprinted by permission of New Directions Publishing Corp.

Randall Jarrell. "The Death of the Ball Turret Gunner" from *The Complete Poems* by Randall Jarrell. Copyright © 1969, renewed 1997 by Mary von S. Jarrell. Reprinted by permission of Farrar, Straus and Giroux, LLC.

Ha Jin. "Saboteur" from *The Bridegroom* by Ha Jin, copyright © 2000 by Ha Jin. Used by permission of Pantheon Books, a division of Random House, Inc.

Erica Jong. "Devouring Time: Shakespeare's Sonnets" from *Touchstones: American Poets on a Favorite Poem,* edited by Robert Pack and Jay Parini. Copyright © 1996 by the President and Fellows of Middlebury College. Reprinted by permission of the University Press of New England.

June Jordan. "Something Like a Sonnet for Phillis Miracle Wheatley." © June M. Jordan Literary Trust 2005. Reprinted by permission of The June M. Jordan Literary Trust, www.junejordan.com.

Yasunari Kawabata. "The Grasshopper and the Bell Cricket" from *Palm-of-the-Hand Stories* by Yasunari Kawabata, translated by Lane Dunlop and J. Martin Holman. Translation copyright © 1988 by Lane Dunlop and J. Martin Holman. Reprinted by permission of North Point Press, a division of Farrar, Straus and Giroux, LLC.

J. Gerald Kennedy. "On 'The Fall of the House of Usher'" from *Death and the Life of Writing.* Copyright © 1987 by Yale University. Reprinted by permission of Yale University Press.

T. S. Kerrigan. "Elvis Kissed Me" from *Another Bloomsday at Molly Malone's Pub* (Laguna Poets Series). The Inevitable Press. Copyright © 1999 by T. S. Kerrigan. Reprinted by permission of the author.

Jamaica Kincaid. "Girl" from *At the Bottom of the River* by Jamaica Kincaid. Copyright © 1983 by Jamaica Kincaid. Reprinted by permission of Farrar, Straus and Giroux, LLC.

Etheridge Knight. "The Idea of Ancestry" from *The Essential Etheridge Knight* by Etheridge Knight, © 1986. Reprinted by permission of the University of Pittsburgh Press.

Tom Kryss. "Things Thrown Away" by Tom Kryss, originally published in *The Search for the Reason Why—New and Selected Poems* (Bottom Dog Press, 2006).

John Lahr. "Review of *Hamlet*" excerpted from *Light Fantastic* by John Lahr, copyright © 1996 by John Lahr. Used by permission of The Dial Press/Dell Publishing, a division of Random House, Inc.

Philip Larkin. "This Be the Verse" from *Collected Poems* by Philip Larkin. Copyright © 1988, 2003 by the Estate of Philip Larkin. Reprinted by permission of Farrar, Straus and Giroux, LLC, and Faber and Faber Ltd.

D. H. Lawrence. "The Rocking-Horse Winner," copyright 1933 by the Estate of D. H. Lawrence, renewed © 1961 by Angelo Ravagli and C. M. Weekley, Executors of the Estate of Frieda Lawrence, from *Complete Short Stories of D. H. Lawrence* by D. H. Lawrence. Used by permission of Viking Penguin, a division of Penguin Group (USA) Inc. "The White Horse" from *The Complete Poems of D. H. Lawrence* by D. H. Lawrence, edited by V. de Sola Pinto & F. W. Roberts, copyright © 1964, 1971 by Angelo Ravagli and C. M. Weekley, Executors of the Estate of Frieda Lawrence Ravagli. Used by permission of Viking Penguin, a division of Penguin Group (USA) Inc.

Li-Young Lee. "Eating Alone" from *Rose*. Copyright © 1986 by Li-Young Lee. Reprinted with the permission of The Permissions Company, Inc. on behalf of BOA Editions Ltd. www.boaeditions.org.

Philip Levine. "The Lost Angel" from *Not This Pig* © 1968 by Philip Levine. Reprinted by permission of Wesleyan University Press.

Li T'ai Po. "A Song of Changgan" from *The Jade Mountain*, translated by Witter Bynner, translation copyright 1929 and renewed 1957 by Alfred A. Knopf, a division of Random House, Inc. Used by permission of Alfred A. Knopf, a division of Random House, Inc.

Alain Locke. Reprinted with the permission of Scribner, a Division of Simon & Schuster, Inc., from *The New Negro* by Alain Locke. Copyright © 1925 by Albert & Charles Boni, Inc. Introduction copyright © 1992 by Macmillan Publishing Company. All rights reserved.

Gerald Locklin. "The Small Presses and Little Magazines: A Few Reflections" and "So It Goes." Reprinted by permission of the author. "Friday Night Lights" from *Modest Aspirations: New Poems* by Gerald Locklin (Lummox Press, 2010). Copyright © by Gerald Locklin. By permission of the author.

Audre Lorde. "Hanging Fire" from *The Black Unicorn* by Audre Lorde. Copyright © 1978 by Audre Lorde. Used by permission of W. W. Norton & Company, Inc.

Amy Lowell. "Evelyn Ray" from *What's O'Clock* by Amy Lowell. Copyright © 1925 by Houghton Mifflin Company, renewed 1953 by Harvey H. Bundy and G. d'Andelot Belin Jr., Trustees of the Estate of Amy Lowell. Reprinted by permission of Houghton Mifflin Harcourt Publishing Company. All rights reserved.

Robert Lowell. "For the Union Dead," "Skunk Hour," "An Explication of Skunk Hour," and "Epilogue" from *Collected Poems* by Robert Lowell. Copyright © 2003 by Harriet Lowell and Sheridan Lowell. Reprinted by permission of Farrar, Straus and Giroux, LLC.

Archibald MacLeish. "Ars Poetica" from *Collected Poems 1917–1982* by Archibald MacLeish. Copyright © 1985 by The Estate of Archibald MacLeish. Reprinted by permission of Houghton Mifflin Harcourt Publishing Company. All rights reserved.

Naguib Mahfouz. "Half a Day," translated by Denys Johnson-Davis, copyright © 1991 by American University in Cairo Press, from *The Time and the Place & Other Stories* by Naguib Mahfouz. Used by permission of Doubleday, a division of Random House, Inc.

Bobbie Ann Mason. "On Tim O'Brien's 'The Things They Carried.'" Copyright © 1986 by Bobbie Ann Mason. Reprinted by permission of International Creative Management, Inc.

Country Joe McDonald. "I-Feel-Like-I'm-Fixin'-to-Die Rag." Words and music by Joe McDonald. © 1965 renewed 1993 by Alkatraz Corner Music Co. Used by permission.

Robert E. McDonough. "Résumé." *Minnesota Review* (nos. 63–64, Spring/Summer 2005). Reprinted by permission.

Ann Menebroker. "A Mere Glimpse" and "Repossessed." Reprinted by permission of the author.

James Merrill. "Coda: The Higher Keys" from *The Changing Light at Sandover* by James Merrill, copyright © 1980, 1982 by James Merrill. Used by permission of Alfred A. Knopf, a division of Random House, Inc.

Edna St. Vincent Millay. "What lips my lips have kissed, and where, and why" © 1923, 1951 by Edna St. Vincent Millay and Norma Millay Ellis. Reprinted by permission of Holly Peppe, Literary Executor, The Millay Society. Excerpt from "The Buck in the Snow" from *Collected Poems.* Copyright 1928, © 1955 by Edna St. Vincent Millay and Norma Millay Ellis. Reprinted with the permission of The Permissions Company, Inc., on behalf of Holly Peppe, Literary Executor, The Millay Society, www.millay.org.

Arthur Miller. *Death of a Salesman* by Arthur Miller, copyright 1949, renewed © 1977 by Arthur Miller. "Introduction" from *Arthur Miller's Collected Plays* by Arthur Miller, copyright © 1957 by Arthur Miller. Used by permission of Viking Penguin, a division of Penguin Group (USA) Inc.

Brett C. Millier. "On Elizabeth Bishop's 'One Art'" from *Elizabeth Bishop: Life and the Memory of It* by Brett C. Millier. Copyright © 1992 by Brett C. Millier. Reprinted by permission of The University of California Press, via Copyright Clearance Center.

Lorrie Moore. "How to Become a Writer" copyright © 1985 by M. L. Moore, from *Self-Help* by Lorrie Moore. Used by permission of Alfred A. Knopf, a division of Random House, Inc.

Marianne Moore. "Poetry" from *The Collected Poems of Marianne Moore* by Marianne Moore. Copyright © 1935 by Marianne Moore, renewed 1963 by Marianne Moore and T. S. Eliot. All rights reserved. Reprinted with the permission of Scribner, a Division of Simon & Schuster, Inc. "The Student" from *The Collected Poems of Marianne Moore* by Marianne Moore. Copyright © 1941 by Marianne Moore; renewed 1969 by Marianne Moore. All rights reserved. Reprinted with the permission of Scribner, a Division of Simon & Schuster, Inc.

Pat Mora. "Elena" is reprinted with permission from the publisher of *My Own True Name* by Pat Mora (© 2000 Arte Público Press–University of Houston).

Rosario Morales. "The Day It Happened." *Callaloo* 15.4 (1992), 970–972. © 1992 Charles H. Rowell. Reprinted with permission of The Johns Hopkins University Press.

Herta Müller. "Workday" from *Nadirs* by Herta Müller, translated by Sieglinde Lug. Copyright 1988 Rotbuch Verlag, Berlin. Translation copyright 1999 by the University of Nebraska Press. Reprinted by permission of the University of Nebraska Press.

Les Murray. "The Cows on Killing Day" from *Learning Human* by Les Murray. Copyright © 1998 by Les Murray. Reprinted by permission of Farrar, Straus and Giroux, LLC.

Leonard Mustazza. "Generic Translation and Thematic Shift in Glaspell's *Trifles* and 'A Jury of Her Peers.'" *Studies in Short Fiction* 26.4 (Fall 1989): 489–96. Copyright 1989 by Studies in Short Fiction, Inc.

Pablo Neruda. "Poetry." Reprinted by permission of Farrar, Straus and Giroux, LLC.

Helge Normann Nilsen. "Marxism and the Early Plays of Arthur Miller" from "*Honors at Dawn* to *Death of a Salesman*: Marxism and the Early Plays of Arthur Miller" in *English Studies* 75.2. Copyright © 1994 by Taylor & Francis Ltd. Reprinted by permission of Taylor & Francis Group, http://www.informaworld.com.

Lynn Nottage. *POOF!* by Lynn Nottage. Copyright © 1993, 2004 by Lynn Nottage. Published by Theatre Communications Group. Used by permission of Theatre Communications Group. Interview with Lynn Nottage for American Shorts (from www.ket.org/americanshorts/poof/nottage.htm) reprinted by permission of Kentucky Educational Television and Lynn Nottage. KET Foundation, Inc.

Joyce Carol Oates. "Where Are You Going, Where Have You Been?" from *The Wheel of Love and Other Stories* by Joyce Carol Oates. Copyright © 1970 The Ontario Review. "The Lady with the Pet Dog" from *Marriages and Infidelities* by Joyce Carol Oates. Copyright © 1968, 1969, 1970, 1971, 1972 by Joyce Carol Oates. "Where Are You Going, Where Have You Been?: *Smooth Talk*: Short Story into Film" from *Woman Writer: Occasions and Opportunities* by Joyce Carol Oates, copyright © 1988 by The Ontario Review. Reprinted by permission of Dutton, a division of Penguin Group (USA) Inc.

Tim O'Brien. "The Things They Carried" from *The Things They Carried* by Tim O'Brien. Copyright © 1990 by Tim O'Brien. Reprinted by permission of Houghton Mifflin Harcourt Publishing Company. All rights reserved.

Flannery O'Connor. "Writing Short Stories" and "The Element of Suspense in 'A Good Man Is Hard to Find.'" Excerpted from "On Her Own Work" from *Mystery and Manners: Occasional Prose,* selected and edited by Sally and Robert Fitzgerald. Copyright © 1969 by the Estate of Mary Flannery O'Connor. All reprinted by permission of Farrar, Straus and Giroux, LLC. Letters of 26 December 1954, 15 January 1955, 22 January 1955, 26 February 1955, and 7 March 1955 from *The Habit of Being: Letters of Flannery O'Connor,* edited by Sally Fitzgerald. Copyright © 1979 by Regina O'Connor. Reprinted by permission of Farrar, Straus and Giroux, LLC. "Good Country People" copyright © 1955 by Flannery O'Connor and renewed 1983 by Regina O'Connor and "A Good Man Is Hard to Find" copyright © 1953 by Flannery O'Connor and renewed 1981 by Regina O'Connor. Both from *A Good Man Is Hard to Find and Other Stories.* Reprinted by permission of Houghton Mifflin Harcourt Publishing Company.

Sharon Olds. "Parents' Day" from *The Wellspring* by Sharon Olds, copyright © 1996 by Sharon Olds. Used by permission of Alfred A. Knopf, a division of Random House, Inc. "I Go Back to May 1937" from *The Gold Cell* by Sharon Olds, copyright © 1987 by Sharon Olds. Used by permission of Alfred A. Knopf, a division of Random House, Inc. "Sex without Love" from *The Dead and the Living* by Sharon Olds, copyright © 1987 by Sharon Olds. Used by permission of Alfred A. Knopf, a division of Random House, Inc.

Mary Oliver. "Sleeping in the Forest" from *Twelve Moons* by Mary Oliver. Copyright © 1978 by Mary Oliver. By permission of Little, Brown and Company. All rights reserved.

Tillie Olsen. "I Stand Here Ironing" from *Tell Me a Riddle* by Tillie Olsen. Copyright © 1956, 1957, 1960, 1961 by Tillie Olsen. Reprinted by permission of Elaine Markson Agency.

Charles Olson. "I, Maximus of Gloucester, to You." © 1983 by the Regents of the University of California. Reprinted by permission of the University of California Press.

Daniel Orozco. "Orientation" from *The Seattle Review*. Reprinted by permission.

Alicia Suskin Ostriker. "The Change" from *The Little Space: Poems Selected and New, 1968–1998* by Alicia Suskin Ostriker, © 1998. Reprinted by permission of the University of Pittsburgh Press.

ZZ Packer. "Brownies," from *Drinking Coffee Elsewhere* by ZZ Packer, copyright © 2003 by ZZ Packer. Used by permission of Riverhead Books, an imprint of Penguin Group (USA) Inc.

Grace Paley. "A Conversation with Ann Charters." Reprinted by permission. "A Conversation with My Father" and "Samuel" from *Enormous Changes at the Last Minute* by Grace Paley. Copyright © 1971, 1974 by Grace Paley. Reprinted by permission of Farrar, Straus and Giroux, LLC.

Dorothy Parker. "A Pig's-Eye View of Literature: The Lives and Times of John Keats, Percy Bysshe Shelley, and George Gordon Noel, Lord Byron" from *The Portable Dorothy Parker* by Dorothy Parker, edited by Marion Meade, copyright 1928, renewed © 1956 by Dorothy Parker; copyright © 1973, 2006 by The National Association for the Advancement of Colored People. Used by permission of Viking Penguin, a division of Penguin Group (USA) Inc.

Linda Pastan. "To a Daughter Leaving Home" from *The Imperfect Paradise* by Linda Pastan. Copyright © 1988 by Linda Pastan. Used by permission of W. W. Norton & Company, Inc.

Michael Pennington. "On Hamlet's Madness" reprinted from *Hamlet in Pieces,* copyright © 2001 by Andy Lavender, published by Nick Hern Books, www.nickhernbooks.co.uk.

Sylvia Plath. All lines from "Metaphors" from *Crossing the Water* by Sylvia Plath. Copyright © 1960 by Ted Hughes. Reprinted by permission of HarperCollins Publishers and Faber and Faber Ltd. "Morning Song" and "Daddy" from *Ariel: Poems* by Sylvia Plath. Copyright © 1961, 1962, 1963, 1964, 1965, 1966 by Ted Hughes. Reprinted by permission of HarperCollins Publishers and Faber and Faber Ltd.

Sydney Plum. "Reading 'The Veil' by Marjane Satrapi" by Sydney Plum. Reprinted by permission of the author.

Allen Polite. "Song" by Allen Polite. Used by permission of Helene Polite.

Ezra Pound. "In a Station of the Metro" and "The River Merchant's Wife: A Letter" (original by Rihaku) by Ezra Pound, from *Personae,* copyright © 1926 by Ezra Pound. Reprinted by permission of New Directions Publishing Corp. "On the Principles of Imagism" by Ezra Pound, from *The Literary Essays of Ezra Pound,* copyright © 1935 by Ezra Pound. Reprinted by permission of New Directions Publishing Corp. "What I Feel about Walt Whitman" by Ezra Pound, from *Selected Prose 1909–1965,* copyright © 1973 by The Estate of Ezra Pound. Reprinted by permission of New Directions Publishing Corp.

Arnold Rampersad. "Langston Hughes as Folk Poet" from *The Collected Poems of Langston Hughes* by Langston Hughes, edited by Arnold Rampersad with David Roessel, Associate Editor, copyright © 1994 by the Estate of Langston Hughes. Used by permission of Alfred A. Knopf, a division of Random House, Inc.

Dudley Randall. "Ballad of Birmingham" from *Cities Burning*. Reprinted with the permission of the Estate of Dudley Randall.

Lou Reed. "Chelsea Girls," written by Lou Reed and Sterling Morrison. Reprinted by permission of Garnant Music c/o Christopher R. Whent, and Oakfield Avenue Music. Copyright © Oakfield Avenue Music, Ltd. U.S. and Canadian Rights for Oakfield Avenue Music, Ltd. Administered and Controlled by Spirit One Music (BMI). World excluding U.S. and Canadian Rights Administered and Controlled by EMI Music Publishing, Ltd. International Copyright Secured. Used by Permission. All Rights Reserved.

David S. Reynolds. "Poe's Art of Transformation in 'The Cask of Amontillado'" by David S. Reynolds, excerpted from *New Essays on Poe's Major Tales,* edited by Kenneth Silverman. Copyright © 1993. Reprinted with the permission of Cambridge University Press.

Adrienne Rich. "Aunt Jennifer's Tigers" and "Diving into the Wreck." Copyright © 2002, 1951 by Adrienne Rich. Copyright © 2002 by Adrienne Rich. Copyright © 1973 by W. W. Norton & Company, Inc, from *The Fact of a Doorframe: Selected Poems 1950–2001* by Adrienne Rich. Used by permission of the author and W. W. Norton & Company, Inc.

James Richardson. #4, 24, 54, 179, 248, 251, and 488 from *Vectors: Five Hundred Aphorisms and Ten-Second Essays*. Copyright © 2001 by James Richardson. Reprinted with the permission of The Permissions Company, Inc. on behalf of Copper Canyon Press, www.coppercanyonpress.org.

Luis J. Rodríguez. "Carrying My Tools" from *Poetry Like Bread: Poets of the Political Imagination* (Curbstone Press), edited by Martín Espada. Reprinted by permission of Northwestern University Press.

Theodore Roethke. "My Papa's Waltz," copyright 1942 by Hearst Magazines, Inc. and "Elegy for Jane," copyright © 1950 by Theodore Roethke from *Collected Poems of Theodore Roethke* by Theodore Roethke. Used by permission of Doubleday, a division of Random House, Inc.

Alexis Rotella. "just friends" from *The Haiku Anthology*, edited by Cor van den Heuvel (W. W. Norton). Reprinted by permission of the author.

Carol Rumens. "This Be the Verse." Copyright © Carol Rumens. Reproduced by permission of the author c/o Rogers, Coleridge & White Ltd., 20 Powis Mews, London W11 1JN.

Willy Russell. Excerpt from act 1, scene 6 of *Educating Rita*, copyright © 1981 by Willy Russell. Reprinted by permission of Methuen Drama, an imprint of A&C Black Publishers.

Edwin Sanchez. *Pops*. Reprinted by permission of the author.

Sonia Sanchez. "a/coltrane/poem" Reprinted by permission.

Carl Sandburg. "Grass" from *The Complete Poems of Carl Sandburg, Revised and Expanded Edition*. Copyright © 1969, 1970 by Lilian Steichen Sandburg, Trustee. Reprinted by permission of Houghton Mifflin Harcourt Publishing Company. All rights reserved.

Edward Sanders. "After a Year of Isolation" from *Hymn to the Rebel Café* by Edward Sanders. Copyright © by Edward Sanders. Reprinted by permission of Black Sparrow Books, an imprint of David R. Godine, Publisher, Inc.

Marisa de los Santos. "Because I Love You" from *From the Bones Out* by Marisa de los Santos. Copyright © 2000 by Marisa de los Santos. Reprinted with permission of the University of South Carolina Press.

Marjane Satrapi. "The Veil" from *Persepolis: The Story of a Childhood* by Marjane Satrapi, translated by Mattias Ripa and Blake Ferris, translation copyright © 2003 by L'Association, Paris, France. Used by permission of Pantheon Books, a division of Random House, Inc.

Anne Sexton. "An Obsessive Combination of Ontological Inscape, Trickery and Love" from *Selected Poems of Anne Sexton*. Copyright © 1988 by Linda G. Sexton. Reprinted by permission of Houghton Mifflin Harcourt Publishing Company. All rights reserved. "And One for My Dame" and "Pain for a Daughter" from *Live or Die* by Anne Sexton. Copyright © 1966 by Anne Sexton, renewed 1994 by Linda G. Sexton. Reprinted by permission of Houghton Mifflin Harcourt Publishing Company. All rights reserved. "The Fortress" and "To a Friend Whose Work Has Come to Triumph" from *All My Pretty Ones* by Anne Sexton. Copyright © 1962 by Anne Sexton, renewed 1990 by Linda G. Sexton. Reprinted by permission of Houghton Mifflin Harcourt Publishing Company. All rights reserved.

William Shakespeare. Notes to *Hamlet, Prince of Denmark* and notes to *A Midsummer Night's Dream* from *An Introduction to Shakespeare, Revised Edition* by Hardin Craig and David Bevington. © 1975. Reprinted by permission of Pearson Education, Inc., Upper Saddle River, NJ.

Elaine Showalter. "On Glaspell's 'A Jury of Her Peers'" excerpted from *A Jury of her Peers: American Women Writers from Anne Bradstreet to Annie Proulx* by Elaine Showalter, copyright © 2009 by Elaine Showalter. Used by permission of Alfred A. Knopf, a division of Random House, Inc.

Leslie Marmon Silko. "Yellow Woman" from *Storyteller* by Leslie Marmon Silko. Copyright © 1981 by Leslie Marmon Silko. Used by permission of The Wylie Agency LLC.

Joan Jobe Smith. "Feminist Arm Candy for the Mafia and Sinatra" from *Nerve Cowboy*, 2006. Reprinted by permission of the author. "The Carol Burnett Show" originally appeared in *Wormwood Review* circa 1990. Reprinted by permission of the author.

Stevie Smith. "Not Waving but Drowning" by Stevie Smith, from *Collected Poems of Stevie Smith*, copyright ©1957 by Stevie Smith. Reprinted by permission of New Directions Publishing Corp.

Sophocles. "Oedipus the King" from *Three Theban Plays* by Sophocles, translated by Robert Fagles, copyright © 1982 by Robert Fagles. Used by permission of Viking Penguin, a division of Penguin Group (USA) Inc.

Gary Soto. "Mexicans Begin Jogging" and "Oranges" from *New and Selected Poems* © 1995 by Gary Soto. Used with permission of Chronicle Books LLC, San Francisco. Visit ChronicleBooks.com. "Waiting at the Curb: Lynwood, California, 1967." Copyright © 2006 by Gary Soto. Reprinted by permission of the author.

Marcia Southwick. "A Star Is Born in the Eagle Nebula" from *The Best American Poetry 1999*. Reprinted by permission of the author.

Robert Spiess. "an aging willow." Reprinted by permission of Lee Gurga on behalf of the Estate of Robert Spiess.

John Steinbeck. "The Chrysanthemums" copyright 1937, renewed © 1965 by John Steinbeck, from *The Long Valley* by John Steinbeck. Used by permission of Viking Penguin, a division of Penguin Group (USA) Inc.

Wallace Stevens. "Thirteen Ways of Looking at a Blackbird" from *The Collected Poems of Wallace Stevens* by Wallace Stevens, copyright 1954 by Wallace Stevens and renewed 1982 by Holly Stevens. Used by permission of Alfred A. Knopf, a division of Random House, Inc.

Tom Stoppard. "*Dogg's Hamlet*: The Encore" copyright © 1980 by Tom Stoppard. Used by permission of Grove/Atlantic, Inc.

August Strindberg. *The Stronger* by August Strindberg, translated by Ann Charters. Reprinted by permission of the translator.

Adrienne Su. Excerpt from "The English Canon" by Adrienne Su © 2006. Published by Manic D Press. Reprinted by permission of publisher and author.

Amy Tan. "Two Kinds" from *The Joy Luck Club* by Amy Tan, copyright © 1989 by Amy Tan. Used by permission of G. P. Putnam's Sons, a division of Penguin Group (USA) Inc.

James Tate. "Like It or Not We Are Part of Our Time." First appeared in *Best American Poetry 1997*, edited by David Lehman. Reprinted by permission.

Joan Templeton. Excerpt from "The *Doll House* Backlash: Criticism, Feminism, and Ibsen," *PMLA* (1989): 28–40. Reprinted by permission of the Modern Language Association.

Dylan Thomas. "Do Not Go Gentle into That Good Night" by Dylan Thomas from *The Poems of Dylan Thomas*, copyright © 1952 by Dylan Thomas. Reprinted by permission of New Directions Publishing Corp. "The Last Time I Slept with the Queen" from *The Silver Treasury of Light Verse* by Dylan Thomas. Copyright © 1956 by New Directions. Reprinted by permission of Harold Ober Associates, Inc.

Jean Toomer. "Storm Ending," "Reapers," and "Kabnis" from *Cane* by Jean Toomer. Copyright 1923 by Boni & Liveright, renewed 1951 by Jean Toomer. Used by permission of Liveright Publishing Corporation.

Tomas Tranströmer. "Tranströmer on Poetry" by Tomas Tranströmer. © Tomas Tranströmer. "Romanesque Arches," "Allegro," "Beginning of the Late Autumn Night's

Novel," "Schubertiana," and "March '79" by Tomas Tranströmer, translated by Samuel Charters. Copyright © Tomas Tranströmer. Reprinted by permission.

Liv Ullmann. "On Performing Nora in *A Doll House*" from *Changing* by Liv Ullmann. Copyright © 1976, 1977 by Liv Ullmann. Used by permission of Alfred A. Knopf, a division of Random House, Inc.

Louis Untermeyer. "A 'book of people' " A contemporary review of Robert Frost's *North of Boston* (1915). Reprinted by permission.

John Updike. "A & P" from *Pigeon Feathers and Other Stories* by John Updike, copyright © 1962 and renewed 1990 by John Updike. Used by permission of Alfred A. Knopf, a division of Random House, Inc.

Helen Vendler. "Tranströmer and the 'Other Side' of Consciousness." Reprinted by permission of the author.

Kurt Vonnegut Jr. "Harrison Bergeron" from *Welcome to the Monkey House* by Kurt Vonnegut Jr., copyright © 1961 by Kurt Vonnegut Jr. Used by permission of Dell Publishing, a division of Random House, Inc.

Fred Voss. "How Many Times Can We Follow Dante Down Into Hell?" Reprinted by permission of the author. "I Once Needed a Chance Too" from *In the Teatime at the Bouquet Morale*. Reprinted by permission.

Anne Waldman. "stereo" from *Marriage: A Sentence* by Anne Waldman, copyright © 2000 by Anne Waldman. Used by permission of Penguin, a division of Penguin Group (USA) Inc.

Alice Walker. "Everyday Use" from *In Love & Trouble: Stories of Black Women*, copyright © 1973 by Alice Walker, reprinted by permission of Houghton Mifflin Harcourt Publishing Company. Foreword by Alice Walker to *Zora Neale Hurston: A Literary Biography* by Robert E. Hemenway. Copyright 1977 by the Board of Trustees of the University of Illinois. Used with permission of the author and the University of Illinois Press. "I Said to Poetry" from *Horses Make a Landscape Look More Beautiful: Poems* by Alice Walker, copyright © 1984 by Alice Walker. Reprinted by permission of Houghton Mifflin Harcourt Publishing Company. All rights reserved.

David Foster Wallace. "Everything Is Green" from *The Girl with Curious Hair* by David Foster Wallace. Copyright © 1989 by David Foster Wallace. Used by permission of W. W. Norton & Company, Inc.

Ed Webster. "i. After Mail Call" and "ii. Juvenilia" from *San Joaquin Valley Poems: 1969*. Appeared in *Western Humanities Review*. Reprinted by permission of the publisher.

Eudora Welty. "A Worn Path" from *A Curtain of Green and Other Stories*, copyright 1941 and renewed 1969 by Eudora Welty. Reprinted by permission of Houghton Mifflin Harcourt Publishing Company. "Is Phoenix Jackson's Grandson Really Dead?" from *The Eye of the Story* by Eudora Welty, copyright © 1978 by Eudora Welty. Used by permission of Random House, Inc.

William Carlos Williams. "The Use of Force" by William Carlos Williams, from *The Collected Stories of William Carlos Williams*, copyright © 1938 by William Carlos Williams. Reprinted by permission of New Directions Publishing Corp. "To Waken an Old Lady," "The Red Wheelbarrow," "Spring and All: Section I," "Danse Russe," "from *March*," and "The Widow's Lament in Springtime" from *The Collected Poems: Volume I, 1909–1939*, copyright © 1938 by New Directions Publishing Corp. Reprinted by permission of New Directions Publishing Corp. "Spirit of '76, the poet writes to a publisher" by William Carlos Williams, from New Directions Pub. Acting as agent, copyright © 1920 by William Carlos Williams. Reprinted by permission of New Directions Publishing Corp.

David C. Wojahn. Excerpt from "Maggie's Farm No More: The Fate of Political Poetry" from *The Writer's Chronicle* May/Summer 2007. Reprinted by permission of the author.

Tobias Wolff. "Say Yes" from *Back in the World* by Tobias Wolff. Copyright © 1985 by Tobias Wolff. Reprinted by permission of International Creative Management, Inc.

Eve Wood. "Recognition." Originally published in *Santa Monica Review*. Reprinted by permission.

Charles Wright. "After Reading Tu Fu, I Go Outside to the Dwarf Orchard" from *Negative Blue: Selected Later Poems* by Charles Wright. Copyright © 2000 by Charles Wright. Reprinted by permission of Farrar, Straus and Giroux, LLC.

James Wright. "Evening," "A Blessing," and "Lying in a Hammock at William Duffy's Farm in Pine Island, Minnesota" from *Collected Poems* © 1971 by James Wright. Reprinted by permission of Wesleyan University Press.

Judith Wright. Excerpt from "Brevity" in *A Human Pattern: Selected Poems* (ETT Imprint, Sydney 2010). Reprinted by permission.

Daisy Zamora. "Precisely" from *Clean Slate: New & Selected Poems* by Daisy Zamora, translated by Margaret Randall and Elinor Randall (Curbstone Press, 1993). Reprinted by permission of Northwestern University Press.

Index of First Lines

19-year-old Hector, 1057

A born salesman, 706
Abortions will not let you forget, 942
About suffering they were never wrong, 926
A chair missing only two rungs, 1084
A crust of bread and a corner to sleep in, 721
A dented spider like a snow drop white, 870
After great pain, a formal feeling comes—, 847
After my father died and I had to, 1087
A lake, 1032
A lightning bolt, 739
All me are standing on feed. The sky is shining, 740
All things within this fading world hath end, 940
A man and a woman lie on a white bed, 969
Among twenty snowy mountains, 798
an aging willow—, 806
An angst-ridden amorist, Fred, 780
A narrow Fellow in the Grass, 850
And God stepped out on space, 893
And it was at that age . . . Poetry arrived, 670
an icicle the moon drifting through it, 807
Any good craftsman carries his tools, 817
A poem should be palpable and mute, 672
Are you alive?, 793
A shaded lamp and a waving blind, 866
A silver flash from the sinking sun, 1046
As I went through the marshes, 1034
as though the whole earth, 807
As virtuous men pass mildly away, 956
A thawed pond, 806
At low tide like this how sheer the water is, 733
At the end of my suffering, 742
At the factory I worked, 1000
Aunt Jennifer's tigers prance across a screen, 994
A word is dead, 693

Bananas ripe and green, and gingerroot, 896
Batter my heart, three-personed God; for You, 959
Because I could not stop for Death—, 849
Because we wanted things the way they were, 1035
Bent double, like old beggards under sacks, 1064
Between my finger and my thumb, 970
Bits of song—what else?, 803

Black reapers with the sound of steel on stones, 897
Blind immigrant, 946
Blind with love, my daughter, 998
Bright star, would I were steadfast as thou art—, 976
Buffalo Bill 's, 954
buoyed up on the rising tide, 807
Burly, dozing, humble-bee, 717
Busy, with an idea for a code, I write, 998
Busy old fool, unruly sun, 957
Byron and Shelley and Keats, 778
By the road to the contagious hospital, 1009

Carried her unprotesting out the door, 769
Children's imitations of cormorants, 806
Come on all of you big strong men, 1059
Consider Icarus, pasting those sticky wings on, 998

Death, be not proud, though some have callèd thee, 766
Did Ophelia ask Hamlet to bed?, 780
Do not go gentle into that good night, 771
Do not weep, maiden, for war is kind, 1063
Down this road, 805

Early one morning in May I set out, 869
Earth has not anything to show more fair, 766
East of me, west of me, full summer, 803
"Elvis kissed me once," she swears, 831
Eyes, what are they? Coloured glass, 723

Farewel dear babe, my hearts too much content, 941
Farewell, thou child of my right hand, and joy, 703
"Father, father, where are you going?, 936
First having read the book of myths, 994
First there was me. Then there was Ray and me. It happened like this. I, 1071
Four little children, 809
From my mother's sleep I fell into the state, 1065
From the west, wind blowing, 805

Gather ye rosebuds while ye may, 703
Girl from the realm of birds florid and fleet, 769
Glory be to God for dappled things—, 973
Go-go girl Sindy, who changed the first letter of her name, 1056
goodby Betty, don't remember me, 954

H, 776
"Had he and I but met, 1064
Had we but world enough, and time, 780
Happening now! it is happening, 1038
Hear the voice of the Bard!, 936
Here's Room 506, 708
He saw her from the bottom of the stairs, 872
His body moves to a solemn measure, 829
"Hope" is the thing with feathers—, 846
How do I love thee? Let me count the ways, 767
How do they do it, the ones who make love, 988
How many roads must a man walk down, 1059

I, too, dislike it, 669
I, too, sing America, 901
I am a Negro, 900
I am fourteen, 1050
I am hungering, 1080
I am Marilyn Mei Ling Chin, 944
I breathed shallow as I looked for her, 987
I called him to come in, 1023
I cannot tell you that last night in the exhaust-, 817
I caught a tremendous fish, 930
I caught this morning morning's minion, king-, 972
I celebrate myself, and sing myself, 1004
I died for Beauty—but was scarce, 848
I doubt not God is good, well-meaning, kind, 768
I dug and dug amongst the snow, 842
If ever there were a spring day so perfect, 952
If ever two were one, then surely we, 940
I find no peace, and all my war is done, 765
If I when my wife is sleeping, 1010
If we must die, let it not be like hogs, 896
I had found the secret of a garret-room, 1036
I have just seen a beautiful thing, 895

I heard a Fly buzz—when I died—, 848
I know what the caged bird feels, alas!, 1046
I'm a riddle in nine syllables, 742
I met a traveler from an antique land, 767
I 'm going out to clean the pasture spring, 870
I'm looking for a house, 902
I'm Nobody! Who are you?, 847
I must be mad, or very tired, 797
I'm "wife"—I've finished that—, 845
I need not go, 723
in Just-, 955
In the evening darkness at a place outside New York, an outlook, 913
In the winter snow, 807
In Xanadu did Kubla Khan, 948
I play Haydn after a black day, 912
I remember the neckcurls, limp and damp as tendrils, 762
I said to Poetry: "I'm finished, 677
I sat all morning in the college sick bay, 971
I see them standing at the formal gates of their colleges, 988
I sit, and sit, and will my thoughts, 960
I still have moments when I look around and wonder what I'm doing, 676
I taste a liquor never brewed—, 846
I think I was enchanted, 840
I thought the earth, 1034
It is 12:20 in New York a Friday, 1077
It little profits an idle king, 783
it's raining women's voices as if they were dead even in memory, 777
It's spring, 805
It was in and about the Martinmas time, 750
i usta wonder who i'd be, 1053
I've known rivers, 893
I've pulled the last of the year's young onions, 815
I walked on the banks of the tincan banana dock and sat down under, 1073
I wandered lonely as a cloud, 782
I wander through each chartered street, 938
I want to die while you love me, 697
I was angry with my friend, 938
I went to the dances at Chandlerville, 869
I went to the Garden of Love, 939
I will arise and go now, and go to Innisfree, 1027
i will have to forget, 1051
"I wish," he says, "it was the opposite, 1089
I write. My mother was a Florentine, 720

Jenny kiss'd me when we met, 831
Just friends, 807
Just off the highway to Rochester, Minnesota, 1024

Lay your sleeping head, my love, 927
Let's contend no more, Love, 704
Little Lamb, who made thee?, 935
Long ago, I was wounded. I lived, 969
Lord, who createdst man in wealth and store, 775
Love at the lips was touch, 878
Loveliest of trees, the cherry now, 696
Love set you going like a fat gold watch, 991
Luisa always felt refreshed when she remembered Carmen Bomba, the, 814

Mark but this flea, and mark in this, 958
Marriage marriage is like you say everything everything in stereo stereo, 1039
Miniver Cheevy, child of scorn, 728
"Mother dear, may I go downtown, 1048
Much have I travell'd in the realms of gold, 824
Much Madness is divinest Sense—, 848
My dolls have been put away like dead, 814
My grandfather said to me, 927
My heart aches, and a drowsy numbness pains, 977
My heart is like a singing bird, 782
My life ain't nothin', 902
My long two-pointed ladder's sticking through a tree, 875
My mother, when young, scrubbed laundry in a tub, 1037
My Spanish isn't enough, 1056

Nautilus Island's hermit, 981
Night and again, 806
Nobody heard him, the dead man, 699

No coward soul is mine, 841
No decent man will cross a field, 751
Not everybody's, 832

Of all the ways to avoid living perfect discipline is the most admired, 779
Ohoo, Slidin' Delta done been here and gone, 710
Old age is, 737
Old houses were scaffolding once, 795
Old pond, 805
Old pond—frog jumped in—sound of water, 805
Once riding in old Baltimore, 899
One more Unfortunate, 722
On the beach at night alone, 1033
O Rose, thou art sick!, 937
Over my head, I see the bronze butterfly, 1025
"O where have you been, my long, long love, 748
O wild West Wind, thou breath of Autumn's being, 756
O world, I cannot hold thee close enough!, 1033

Pile the bodies high at Austerlitz and Waterloo, 728
Piping down the valleys wild, 934
Precisely because I do not have, 1041

Remember me when I am gone away, 842
rock a-by baby . . . , 897

Season of mists and mellow fruitfulness, 738
Seeds in a dry pod, tick, tick, tick, 714
September rain falls on the house, 770
She fears him, and will always ask, 867
She showed up on the doorstep of my apartment, 815
Should you ask me, whence these stories?, 718
since feeling is first, 684
S'io credesse che mia risposta fosse, 961
Sitting with my father, 806
Skimming lightly, wheeling still, 1062
Something there is that doesn't love a wall, 870
somewhere i have never travelled, gladly beyond, 953
so much depends, 798
Sorrow is my own yard, 1011
Stop all the clocks, cut off the telephone, 926
store water; make a point of filling your bathtub, 1078
Success is counted sweetest, 844
Sundays too my father got up early, 1047

Taped to the wall of my cell are 47 pictures: 47 black, 1047
That's my last Duchess painted on the wall, 773
That time of year thou mayst in me behold, 763
The apparition of these faces in the crowd, 795
The art of losing isn't hard to master, 932
The boyfriends all love you but they don't really know how, 1040
the bright sunlight against the snows, 1088
The Child is Father of the Man, 1013
The curfew tolls the knell of parting day, 758
The dog trots freely in the street, 1075
The fine English poet, John Donne, 780
The first time I walked, 1001
The Frost performs its secret ministry, 949
The last time I slept with the Queen, 779
The little boy lost in the lonely fen, 936
The morning sun is so pale, 951
The nightingale is singing, 683
The old South Boston Aquarium stands, 982
The passenger boat smells of oil and something rattles all the time like, 913
The poem begins—, 675
There is a heaven, for ever, day by day, 1045
There is a tree, by day, 896
There is no need for me to keep a skull on my desk, 952
There's a certain Slant of light, 847
The roaring alongside he takes for granted, 927
The rolls and harrows lie at rest beside, 1032
These are the front doors made of steel, 1058
"these blues broke out in a gallery, 1072
The sparrow chirps—, 806
The summer grass—, 805
the sun was shining, 1085
The tourists are crowded into the enormous Romanesque church, 912

The trees are in their autumn beauty, 1028
The whiskey on your breath, 706
The woman on the subway touches my hand by mistake, and in that instant an, 813
The world is charged with the grandeur of God, 973
The world is too much with us; late and soon, 1019
The year my parents met, an earthquake rocked, 1086
They eat beans mostly, this old yellow pair, 943
They flee from me, that sometime did me seek, 702
They fuck you up, your mum and dad, 832
The young dead soldier was younger, 1067
The youth walks up to the white horse, to put its halter on, 796
They've finally admitted that trying to save oil-soaked, 812
This is what I do: I teach, 1086
Those blessed structures, plot and rhyme—, 984
Thou art indeed just, Lord, if I contend, 973
Thou still unravished bride of quietness, 754
Through the ample open door of the peaceful country barn, 695
Thunder blossoms gorgeously above our heads, 897
Tired of everyone who comes with words words but, 915
Tomorrow, and tomorrow, and tomorrow, 772
Turning and turning in the widening gyre, 1028
'Twas brillig, and the slithy toves, 730
'Twas mercy brought me from my *Pagan* land, 1045
'Twas on a Holy Thursday, their innocent faces clean, 935
Two roads diverged in a yellow wood, 877
Tyger! Tyger! burning bright, 937

Under the pink quilted covers, 810

Way Down South in Dixie, 902
We are moving to this house out in the country, 1083
Well, son, I'll tell you, 901
We real cool. We, 942
Western wind, when wilt thou blow, 683
We stood on the rented patio, 707
What a great life I've had—, 1089
What are heavy? sea-sand and sorrow, 719
What is Africa to me, 898
What lips my lips have kissed, and where, and why, 768
What thoughts I have of you tonight, Walt Whitman, for I walked down, 833
What you heard is true. I was in his house. His wife carried a tray of, 1055
When all else fails, 743
When approached by a person from Porlock, 780
Whenever Richard Cory went down town, 729
when god lets my body be, 705
When I have fears that I may cease to be, 979
When I see birches bend to left and right, 876
When I sing this song without accompaniment, 1049
When I taught you, 686
When I was young, the moon spoke in riddles, 960
When last I saw thee, I did not thee see, 765
When my father wrote from the Tonkin Gulf about coyotes—, 1066
When our two souls stand up erect and strong, 841
When the porch light snaps on, 1002
When they stop poems, 679
While my hair was still cut straight across my forehead, 802
Whirl up, sea—, 796
Whose woods these are I think I know, 879
Wild Nights—Wild Nights!, 846
Winter is long in this climate, 1011
with a love a madness for Shelley, 1079

You do not do, you do not do, 991
You love me—you are sure—, 845
Your red blossoms amid green leaves, 868
You thought I had the strength of men, 716

Index of Authors and Titles

Adulthood, 1053
After a great pain, a formal feeling comes—, 847
After Apple-Picking, 875
After a Year of Isolation, 1080
After Fighting for Hours, 743
After Reading Tu Fu, I Go Outside to the Dwarf Orchard, 803
Aggestam, Rolf
  Lightning Bolt, 738
aging willow—, an, 806
Aldrich, Thomas Bailey
  In *Re Emily Dickinson*, 857
Alegría, Claribel
  Carmen Bomba: Poet, 814
Alexie, Sherman
  The Lone Ranger and Tonto Fistfight in Heaven, 80
  Superman and Me, 85
Allard, Matsuo
  an icicle the moon, 807
Allegro, 912
Allen, Paula Gunn
  Whirlwind Man Steals Yellow Woman, 579
Allison, Dorothy
  Jason Who Will Be Famous, 88
American Adobo, 815
And One for My Dame, 706
A & P, 599
Apollinaire, Guillaume
  Hail World, 776
  It's Raining, 777
Apropos Coleridge's "Kubla Khan," 780
Araby, 317
Aristotle
  On the Elements and General Principles of Tragedy, 1173
Ars Poetica, 672
as though the whole earth, 807
Atwood, Margaret
  Happy Endings, 95
Auden, W. H.
  Lay your sleeping head, my love, 927
  Musée des Beaux Arts, 926
  Stop All the Clocks, 926
August Midnight, An, 866
Aunt Jennifer's Tigers, 994
Author's Reflections, An: Willy Loman, Walter Younger, and He Who Must Live, 1575
Autobiographical Notes, 121

Baatz, Ronald
  as though the whole earth, 807
  The Oldest Songs, 1088

Baldwin, James
Autobiographical Notes, 121
Sonny's Blues, 99
Ballad of Birmingham, 1048
Bambara, Toni Cade
The Lesson, 126
Barbara Allan, 750
Bartleby, the Scrivener, 406
Bashō, Matsuo
Down this road, 805
It's spring, 805
Old pond, 805
The summer grass, 805
Batter my heart, three-personed God, 959
Battle Royal, 204
Bean Eaters, The, 943
Because I could not stop for Death—, 849
Because I Love You, 817
Beddoes, Thomas Lovell
A Lake, 1032
Before the Birth of One of Her Children, 940
Beginning of the Late Autumn Night's Novel, 913
Bergonzi, Bernard
On Hopkins's "The Windhover," 974
Bight, The, 733
Birches, 876
Birkerts, Sven
James Wright's "Hammock": A Sounding, 1025
Birthday, A, 782
Bishop, Elizabeth
The Bight, 733
The Fish, 930
Manners, 929
One Art, 932
Sandpiper, 929
Sestina, 770
Bits of song, 803
Black Finger, The, 895
Blackness in Hawthorne's "Young Goodman Brown," 271
Blake, William
The Garden of Love, 939
Holy Thursday, 935
The Lamb, 935
The Little Boy Found, 936
The Little Boy Lost, 936
London, 938
A Poison Tree, 938
The Sick Rose, 937
"Songs of Experience," Introduction from, 936
"Songs of Innocence," Introduction from, 934
The Tyger, 937
Blessing, A, 1024
Blind Date, 59
Blowin' in the Wind, 1059
Blues for Bonnie—Take 1, January 1960, 1072
Bly, Robert
On Tomas Tranströmer, 916
Bolaño, Roberto
Jim, 42
"book of people," A, 866
Books, books, books!, 1036
Bornholdt, Jenny
The Boyfriends, 1040
Boyfriends, The, 1040
Bradstreet, Anne
Before the Birth of One of Her Children, 940
In Memory of My Dear Grand-Child Elizabeth Bradstreet, Who Deceased August, 1665, Being a Year and a Half Old, 941
To My Dear and Loving Husband, 940
Bremser, Bonnie
A First Meeting with the Beats, 1071
Bremser, Ray
Blues for Bonnie—Take 1, January 1960, 1072
"Bridge of Sighs, The" from, 722
Bright Star, 976
Brontë, Emily
Last Lines, 841
Brooks, Cleanth
A New Critical Reading of "The Fall of the House of Usher," 656
On Eliot's "The Love Song of J. Alfred Prufrock," 965
Brooks, Gwendolyn
The Bean Eaters, 943
The Mother, 942
The Rites for Cousin Vit, 769
We Real Cool, 942
Brownies, 516

Browning, Elizabeth Barrett
- Books, books, books!, 1036
- How Do I Love Thee?, 767
- I write, 720
- When our two souls stand up erect and strong, 841

Browning, Robert
- My Last Duchess, 773
- A Woman's Last Word, 704

Buffalo Bill 's, 954
Bullough, Geoffrey
- Sources of Shakespeare's *Hamlet*, 1594

buoyed up on the rising tide, 807
Burciaga, José Antonio
- La Puerta, 132

Buson, Taniguchi
- The nightingale is singing, 683
- On the anniversary of Bashō's death, 805
- The sparrow chirps, 806

Cane, lyrics from, 897
Canvassing, 1058
Carbó, Nick
- American Adobo, 815

Carley, John
- buoyed up on the rising tide, 807

Carmen Bomba: Poet, 814
Carol Burnett Show, The, 1087
Carroll, Lewis
- Jabberwocky, 730

Carrying My Tools, 817
Carver, Raymond
- Cathedral, 137
- Creative Writing 101, 151
- On Writing, 148
- Popular Mechanics, 28

Cask of Amontillado, The, 543
Casteen, John
- Night Hunting, 1035

Cathedral, 137
Change, The, 1038
Charters, Ann
- The Woman in the Long, Dark Raincoat: A Poetry Reading with Sharon Olds, 989

Charters, Samuel
- A Man Dancing Alone on an Island in Greece, 829
- On Translating Tomas Tranströmer, 919

Chekhov, Anton
- The Lady with the Pet Dog, 156
- Technique in Writing the Short Story, 168

Chelsea Girls, 708
Children's imitations of cormorants, 806
Chin, Marilyn
- How I Got That Name, 944
- On the Canon, 834
- Sad Guitar, 946

Chopin, Kate
- Désirée's Baby, 170
- How I Stumbled upon Maupassant, 176
- The Story of an Hour, 174

Chrysanthemums, The, 581
Cinna, A.
- On *Hamlet*, 780

Clare, John
- The Sky Lark, 1032

Clever Woman, A, 716
Clifton, Lucille
- to ms. ann, 1051

Cofer, Judith Ortiz
- Quinceañera, 814

Coleridge, Mary
- A Clever Woman, 716
- Eyes, 723

Coleridge, Samuel Taylor
- Frost at Midnight, 949
- Kubla Khan: or, a Vision in a Dream, 948

Collins, Billy
- Memento Mori, 952
- The Only Day in Existence, 951
- Today, 952

Colonel, The, 1055
Conversation with Ann Charters, A, 536
Conversation with My Father, A, 532
Cope, Wendy
- The fine English poet, John Donne, 780

Corso, Gregory
- I am 25, 1079

Cows on Killing Day, The, 740
Crane, Stephen
- The Open Boat, 178
- *The Red Badge of Courage*, from, 1062
- The Sinking of the *Commodore*, 196
- War Is Kind, 1063

Creation, The, 893
Creative Writing 101, 151
Crumb, R.
A Hunger Artist, 330
Cullen, Countee
"Heritage," from, 898
Incident, 899
Yet Do I Marvel, 768
cummings, e. e.
Buffalo Bill 's, 954
goodby Betty, don't remember me, 954
in Just-, 955
since feeling is first, 684
somewhere i have never travelled, 953
when god lets my body be, 705

Daddy, 991
Daemon Lover, The, 748
Danse Russe, 1010
Davis, Lydia
Blind Date, 59
Day It Happened, The, 73
Day Lady Died, The, 1077
Death, be not proud, 766
Death of a Salesman, 1429
Death of the Ball Turret Gunner, The, 1065
"Defence of Poetry, A," from, 787
de los Santos, Marisa
Because I Love You, 817
Department of Labor Haiku, 807
Désirée's Baby, 170
Devouring Time: Shakespeare's Sonnets, 785
Díaz, Junot
How to Date a Browngirl, Blackgirl, Whitegirl, or Halfie, 200
Dickinson, Emily
Because I could not stop for Death—, 849
After a great pain, a formal feeling comes—, 847
"Hope" is the thing with feathers—, 846
I died for Beauty—but was scarce, 848
I heard a Fly buzz—when I died—, 848
I'm Nobody! Who are you?, 847
I'm "wife"—I've finished that—, 845
I taste a liquor never brewed—, 846
I think I was enchanted, 840
Much Madness is divinest Sense—, 848
A narrow Fellow in the Grass, 850
Success is counted sweetest, 842
There's a certain Slant of light, 847
Wild Nights—Wild Nights!, 846
A Word is dead, 693
You love me—you are sure—, 845
Digging, 970
di Prima, Diane
Revolutionary Letter #3, 1078
Diving into the Wreck, 994
Doe at Evening, A, 1034
Dog, 1075
Dogg's Hamlet: The Encore, 1598
Doll House, A, 1349
Donne, John
Batter my heart, three-personed God, 959
Death, be not proud, 766
The Flea, 958
The Sun Rising, 957
A Valediction: Forbidding Mourning, 956
Do Not Go Gentle into That Good Night, 771
Doolittle, Hilda
Oread, 796
The Pool, 793
Dove, Rita
The Pond, Porch-View: Six p.m., Early Spring, 960
Singsong, 960
Down this road, 805
Du Bois, W. E. B.
"The Souls of Black Folk," from, 890
Dulce et Decorum Est, 1064
Dunbar, Paul Laurence
Life, 721
Sympathy, 1046
Theology, 1045
Dylan, Bob
Blowin' in the Wind, 1059

Early One Morning, 869
Easter Wings, 775
Eating Alone, 815
Educating Rita, from, 1122

Elegy for Jane, 762
Elegy Written in a Country Churchyard, 758
Element of Suspense in "A Good Man Is Hard to Find," The, 644
Elena, 1056
Eliot, T. S.
The Love Song of J. Alfred Prufrock, 961
Ellison, Ralph
Battle Royal, 204
The Influence of Folklore on "Battle Royal," 214
Elvis Kissed Me, 831
Emerson, Ralph Waldo
"The Humble Bee," from, 717
"Emily Dickinson's Letters," from, 851
Epilogue, 984
Eros Tyrannos, 867
Evelyn Ray, 750
Evening, 1023
Everyday Use, 610
Everything Is Green, 58
Explication of "Skunk Hour," An, 984
Eyes, 723

Fall of the House of Usher, The, 548
Farm Picture, A, 695
Faulkner, William
The Meaning of "A Rose for Emily," 224
A Rose for Emily, 217
Fauset, Jessie
Meeting Langston Hughes, 904
Feld, Rose C.
An Interview with Robert Frost, 879
Feminist Arm Candy for the Mafia and Sinatra, 1056
Feminist Reading of Gilman's "The Yellow Wallpaper," A, 240
Ferlinghetti, Lawrence
Dog, 1075
fine English poet, John Donne, The, 780
First Meeting with the Beats, A, 1071
First Memory, 969
Fish, The, 930
Fitzgerald, Sally
Southern Sources of "A Good Man Is Hard to Find," 647
Flea, The, 958
Forché, Carolyn
The Colonel, 1055
For the Union Dead, 982
Fortress, The, 810
Freud, Sigmund
The Oedipus Complex, 1179
Friday Night Lights, 1089
Frost, Carol
"Sincerity and Inventions: On Robert Frost," from, 882
Frost, Robert
After Apple-Picking, 875
Birches, 876
Home Burial, 872
In White, 870
Mending Wall, 870
The Pasture, 870
The Road Not Taken, 877
Stopping by Woods on a Snowy Evening, 879
To Earthward, 878
Frost at Midnight, 949

García Márquez, Gabriel
A Very Old Man with Enormous Wings, 51
Garden of Love, The, 939
Generic Translation and Thematic Shift in Glaspell's *Trifles* and "A Jury of Her Peers," 1420
Gerber, Philip L.
On Frost's "After Apple-Picking," 883
Gielgud, John
On Playing Hamlet, 1600
Gilb, Dagoberto
Love in L.A., 35
Gilbert, Sandra M.
A Feminist Reading of Gilman's "The Yellow Wallpaper," 240
Gilman, Charlotte Perkins
Undergoing the Cure for Nervous Prostration, 238
The Yellow Wallpaper, 226
Ginsberg, Allen
Sunflower Sutra, 1073
A Supermarket in California, 833
Gioia, Dana
Summer Storm, 707
Giovanni, Nikki
Adulthood, 1053

Girl, 44
Glaspell, Susan
  A Jury of Her Peers, 243
  Trifles, 1410
Gleason, Kate
  After Fighting for Hours, 743
Glück, Louise
  First Memory, 969
  Happiness, 969
  The Wild Iris, 742
God's Grandeur, 973
God's World, 1033
goodby Betty, don't remember me, 954
Good Country People, 483
Good Man Is Hard to Find, A, 497
Grass, 728
Grasshopper and the Bell Cricket, The, 65
Gray, Alasdair
  Pillow Talk, 30
Gray, Thomas
  Elegy Written in a Country Churchyard, 758
Greene, Richard Leighton
  Apropos Coleridge's "Kubla Khan," 780
Greenblatt, Stephen
  On the Ghost in *Hamlet*, 1597
Grimké, Angelina Weld
  The Black Finger, 895
  Tenebris, 896
Grimm, Susan
  Things I Can Know, 1086
Gubar, Susan
  A Feminist Reading of Gilman's "The Yellow Wallpaper," 240

H. D. *See* Doolittle, Hilda
Hail World, 776
Half a Day, 71
Hamer, Forrest
  My Father's Viet Nam Tour Near Over, 1067
Hamlet, Prince of Denmark, 1244
Hamlet's Madness, 1608
Hanging Fire, 1050
Hansberry, Lorraine
  An Author's Reflections: Willy Loman, Walter Younger, and He Who Must Live, 1575
  My Shakespearean Experience, 1579
  A Raisin in the Sun, 1507
Happiness, 969
Happy Endings, 95
Hardy, Thomas
  An August Midnight, 866
  I need not go, 723
  The Man He Killed, 1064
Harrison Bergeron, 604
Hass, Robert
  Tranströmer's Style, 917
Hawthorne, Nathaniel
  Young Goodman Brown, 261
Hayden, Robert
  On Negro Poetry, 1042
  Those Winter Sundays, 1047
Heaney, Seamus
  Digging, 970
  Mid-Term Break, 971
Hearn, Lafcadio
  Old pond, 805
Hemingway, Ernest
  Hills Like White Elephants, 273
Herbert, George
  Easter Wings, 775
"Heritage," from, 898
Hernández Cruz, Victor
  today is a day of great joy, 679
Herrick, Robert
  To the Virgins, to Make Much of Time, 703
Higginson, Thomas Wentworth
  "Emily Dickinson's Letters," from, 851
Hills Like White Elephants, 273
Holbrook, Sara
  Canvassing, 1058
Holmes, John Clellon
  "This Is the Beat Generation," from, 1069
Holy Thursday, 935
Home Burial, 872
Hood, Thomas
  "The Bridge of Sighs," from, 722
"Hope" is the thing with feathers—, 846
Hopkins, Gerard Manley
  God's Grandeur, 973
  Pied Beauty, 973
  Thou Art Indeed Just, Lord, 973
  The Windhover, 972

House in the World, 902
Housman, A. E.
  Loveliest of trees, the cherry now, 696
How Do I Love Thee?, 767
How I Got That Name, 944
How I Stumbled upon Maupassant, 176
How It Feels to Be Colored Me, 286
How Many Times Can We Follow Dante Down Into Hell?, 676
How to Become a Writer, 433
How to Date a Browngirl, Blackgirl, Whitegirl, or Halfie, 200
Hughes, Langston
  House in the World, 902
  I, Too, 901
  Love Again Blues, 902
  Mother to Son, 901
  Negro, 900
  The Negro Speaks of Rivers, 893
  Song for a Dark Girl, 902
  A Toast to Harlem, 903
Hulme, T. E.
  Images, 795
"Humble Bee, The," from, 717
Hunger Artist, A (Crumb and Zane), 330
Hunger Artist, A (Kafka), 322
Hunt, Leigh
  Jenny Kiss'd Me, 831
Hurston, Zora Neale
  How It Feels to Be Colored Me, 286
  Sweat, 278

I, Too, 901
I am 25, 1079
Ibsen, Henrik
  A Doll House, 1349
  Notes for *A Doll House*, 1403
icicle the moon, an, 807
Idea of Ancestry, The, 1047
I died for Beauty—but was scarce, 848
I-Feel-Like-I'm-Fixin'-to-Die Rag, 1059
If We Must Die, 896
I Go Back to May 1937, 988
I heard a Fly buzz—when I died—, 848
Images, 795
I'm Nobody! Who are you?, 847
Importance of the Single Effect in a Prose Tale, The, 650
I'm "wife"—I've finished that—, 845
In an Iridescent Time, 1037
In a Station of the Metro, 795
Incident, 899
I need not go, 723
Influence of Folklore on "Battle Royal," The, 214
in Just-, 955
In Memory of My Dear Grand-Child Elizabeth Bradstreet, Who Deceased August, 1665, Being a Year and a Half Old, 941
In *Re Emily Dickinson*, 857
Interview with Robert Frost, An, 879
In White, 870
I Once Needed a Chance Too, 1057
Is *A Doll House* a Feminist Text?, 1405
I Said to Poetry, 677
Is Phoenix Jackson's Grandson Really Dead?, 625
Issa, Kobayashi
  Children's imitations of cormorants, 806
  Sitting with my father, 806
I Stand Here Ironing, 509
I taste a liquor never brewed—, 846
I think I was enchanted, 840
"It is difficult to begin without borrowing . . . ," 1031
It's Raining, 777
It's spring, 805
I Wandered Lonely as a Cloud, 782
I Want to Die While You Love Me, 697
I Wish I Were a Red Indian, 64
I write, 720

Jabberwocky, 730
Jackson, Shirley
  The Lottery, 290
  The Morning of June 28, 1948, and "The Lottery," 297
James Wright's "Hammock": A Sounding, 1025
Janouch, Gustav
  Kafka's View of "The Metamorphosis," 373
Jarrell, Randall
  The Death of the Ball Turret Gunner, 1065
Jason Who Will Be Famous, 88
Jenny Kiss'd Me, 831

Jewett, Sarah Orne
A White Heron, 300
Jim, 42
Jin, Ha
Saboteur, 308
Johnson, Georgia Douglas
I Want to Die While You Love Me, 697
Johnson, James Weldon
The Creation, 893
Sunset in the Tropics, 1046
Jong, Erica
Devouring Time: Shakespeare's Sonnets, 785
Jonson, Ben
On My First Son, 703
Jordan, June
Something Like a Sonnet for Phillis Miracle Wheatley, 769
Joyce, James
Araby, 317
Judgment of King Solomon, The, 9
Jury of Her Peers, A, 243
Just friends, 807

Kafka, Franz
A Hunger Artist, 322
I Wish I Were a Red Indian, 64
The Metamorphosis, 340
Kafka's View of "The Metamorphosis," 373
Kawabata, Yasunari
The Grasshopper and the Bell Cricket, 65
Keats, John
Bright Star, 976
Letter to George and Thomas Keats, 21 December 1817, from a, 1596
Ode on a Grecian Urn, 754
Ode to a Nightingale, 977
On First Looking into Chapman's Homer, 824
To Autumn, 738
When I have fears, 979
Kennedy, J. Gerald
On "The Fall of the House of Usher," 659
Kerrigan, T. S.
Elvis Kissed Me, 831
Kincaid, Jamaica
Girl, 44
Knight, Etheridge
The Idea of Ancestry, 1047
Kryss, Tom
Things Thrown Away, 1084
Kubla Khan: or, a Vision in a Dream, 948

Lady with the Pet Dog, The (Chekhov), 156
Lady with the Pet Dog, The (Oates), 439
Lahr, John
Review of *Hamlet*, 1605
Lake, A, 1032
Lake Isle of Innisfree, The, 1027
Lamb, The, 935
Langston Hughes as Folk Poet, 906
La Puerta, 132
Larkin, Philip
This Be the Verse, 832
Last Lines, 841
last time I slept with the Queen, The, 779
Lawrence, D. H.
A Doe at Evening, 1034
On "The Fall of the House of Usher" and "The Cask of Amontillado," 653
The Rocking-Horse Winner, 375
The White Horse, 796
Lay your sleeping head, my love, 927
Lee, Li-Young
Eating Alone, 815
Lesson, The, 126
Letters, 1954–55, from, 636
Letter to George and Thomas Keats, 21 December 1817, from a, 1596
Levine, Philip
The Lost Angel, 809
levy, d. a.
perhaps (#5), 1085
Life, 721
Lightning Bolt, 738
Like It or Not, We Are a Part of Our Time, 679
Li T'ai Po
A Song of Changgan, 801
Little Boy Found, The, 936
Little Boy Lost, The, 936
Locke, Alain
"The New Negro," from, 891

Locklin, Gerald
Friday Night Lights, 1089
The Small Presses and Little Magazines: A Few Reflections, 1082
So It Goes, 1089
London, 938
London, Jack
To Build a Fire, 387
Lone Ranger and Tonto Fistfight in Heaven, The, 80
Longfellow, Henry Wadsworth
"The Song of Hiawatha," from, 718
Lorde, Audre
Hanging Fire, 1050
Lost Angel, The, 809
Lottery, The, 290
Love Again Blues, 902
Love in L.A., 35
Loveliest of trees, the cherry now, 696
Love's Inconsistency, 765
Love Song of J. Alfred Prufrock, The, 961
Lowell, Amy
Evelyn Ray, 750
Meeting-House Hill, 797
On the Definition of Free Verse, 821
Lowell, Robert
An Explication of "Skunk Hour," 984
Epilogue, 984
For the Union Dead, 982
Skunk Hour, 981
Lucinda Matlock, 869
Lying in a Hammock at William Duffy's Farm in Pine Island, Minnesota, 1025
Lyrical Ballads, from the Introduction to, 1019

Mabel Osborne, 868
MacLeish, Archibald
Ars Poetica, 672
Mahfouz, Naguib
Half a Day, 71
Mairowitz, David Zane
A Hunger Artist, 330
Man Dancing Alone on an Island in Greece, A, 829
Man He Killed, The, 1064
Manners, 929
March '79, 915
"March," from, 1011
Marvell, Andrew
To His Coy Mistress, 780
Marxism and the Early Plays of Arthur Miller, 1502
Mason, Bobbie Ann
On Tim O'Brien's "The Things They Carried," 481
Masters, Edgar Lee
Lucinda Matlock, 869
Mabel Osborne, 868
Petit, the Poet, 714
Maupassant, Guy de
The Necklace, 399
McDonald, Country Joe
I-Feel-Like-I'm-Fixin'-to-Die Rag, 1059
McDonough, Robert E.
Résumé, 1086
McKay, Claude
If We Must Die, 896
The Tropics in New York, 896
Meaning of "A Rose for Emily," The, 224
Meeting-House Hill, 797
Meeting Langston Hughes, 904
Melville, Herman
Bartleby, the Scrivener, 406
Blackness in Hawthorne's "Young Goodman Brown," 271
Shiloh, 1062
Memento Mori, 952
Mending Wall, 870
Menebroker, Ann
A Mere Glimpse, 675
Repossessed, 1083
Mere Glimpse, A, 675
Metamorphosis, The, 340
Metaphors, 742
Mexicans Begin Jogging, 1000
Midsummer Night's Dream, A, 1187
Mid-Term Break, 971
Millay, Edna St. Vincent
God's World, 1033
What lips my lips have kissed, and where, and why, 768
Miller, Arthur
Death of a Salesman, 1429
On *Death of a Salesman* as an American Tragedy, 1499

Millier, Brett C.
On Elizabeth Bishop's "One Art," 932
Miniver Cheevy, 728
Moore, Lorrie
How to Become a Writer, 433
Moore, Marianne
Poetry, 669
Mora, Pat
Elena, 1056
Morales, Rosario
The Day It Happened, 73
Morning of June 28, 1948, and "The Lottery," The, 297
Morning Song, 991
Mother, The, 942
Mother to Son, 901
Much Madness is divinest Sense—, 848
Müller, Herta
Workday, 32
Murray, Les
The Cows on Killing Day, 740
Musée des Beaux Arts, 926
Music of Robert Frost's "Stopping by Woods on a Snowy Evening," The, 885
Mustazza, Leonard
Generic Translation and Thematic Shift in Glaspell's *Trifles* and "A Jury of Her Peers," 1420
My Father's Viet Nam Tour Near Over, 1067
My Last Duchess, 773
My Papa's Waltz, 706
My Shakespearean Experience, 1579

narrow Fellow in the Grass, A, 850
Necklace, The, 399
Negro, 900
Negro Speaks of Rivers, The, 893
Neruda, Pablo
Poetry, 670
New Critical Reading of "The Fall of the House of Usher," A, 656
"New Negro, The" from, 891
Night and again, 806
Night Hunting, 1035
nightingale is singing, The, 683
Nilsen, Helge Normann
Marxism and the Early Plays of Arthur Miller, 1502
Noguchi, Yone
Bits of song, 803
Notes for *A Doll House*, 1403
Nottage, Lynn
POOF!, 1582
On Writing *POOF!*, 1588
Not Waving but Drowning, 699

Oates, Joyce Carol
The Lady with the Pet Dog, 439
Smooth Talk: Short Story into Film, 464
Where Are You Going, Where Have You Been?, 452
O'Brien, Tim
The Things They Carried, 468
Obsessive Combination of Ontological Inscape, Trickery and Love, An, 998
O'Connor, Flannery
The Element of Suspense in "A Good Man Is Hard to Find," 644
Good Country People, 483
A Good Man Is Hard to Find, 497
Letters, 1954–55, from, 636
Writing Short Stories, 639
Ode, 1013
Ode on a Grecian Urn, 754
Ode to a Nightingale, 977
Ode to the West Wind, 756
Oedipus Complex, The, 1179
Oedipus the King, 1129
O'Hara, Frank
The Day Lady Died, 1077
Oldest Songs, The, 1088
Old pond (Bashō), 805
Old pond (Hearn), 805
Olds, Sharon
I Go Back to May 1937, 988
Parents' Day, 987
Sex without Love, 988
Old Testament
The Judgment of King Solomon, 9
Oliver, Mary
Sleeping in the Forest, 1034
Olsen, Tillie
I Stand Here Ironing, 509
On *A Doll House*, 1403
On Being Brought from Africa to America, 1045

On *Death of a Salesman* as an American Tragedy, 1499
One Art, 932
On Eliot's "The Love Song of J. Alfred Prufrock," 965
On Elizabeth Bishop's "One Art," 932
On Emily Dickinson, 859
On First Looking into Chapman's Homer, 824
On Frost's "After Apple-Picking," 883
On Glaspell's "A Jury of Her Peers," 258
On *Hamlet*, 780
On Hopkins's "The Windhover," 974
Only Day in Existence, The, 951
On My First Son, 703
On Negro Poetry, 1042
On Performing Nora in Ibsen's *A Doll House*, 1407
On Playing Hamlet, 1600
On Poetry, 915
On Political Poetry, 1053
On T. S. Eliot's "Prufrock," 780
On the anniversary of Bashō's death, 805
On the Beach at Night Alone, 1033
On the Canon, 834
On the Definition of Free Verse, 821
On the Elements and General Principles of Tragedy, 1173
On "The Fall of the House of Usher," 659
On "The Fall of the House of Usher" and "The Cask of Amontillado," 653
On the Ghost in *Hamlet*, 1597
On the Principles of Imagism, 818
On Tim O'Brien's "The Things They Carried," 481
On Tomas Tranströmer, 916
On Translating Tomas Tranströmer, 919
On Writing, 148
On Writing *POOF!*, 1588
Open Boat, The, 178
Oranges, 101
Oread, 796
Orientation, 46
Orozco, Daniel
  Orientation, 46
Ostriker, Alicia Suskin
  The Change, 1038
Owen, Wilfred
  Dulce et Decorum Est, 1064
Ozymandias, 767
Packer, ZZ
  Brownies, 516
Pain for a Daughter, 998
Paley, Grace
  A Conversation with Ann Charters, 536
  A Conversation with My Father, 532
  Samuel, 11, 17
Parents' Day, 987
Parker, Dorothy
  "A Pig's-Eye View of Literature," from, 778
Pastan, Linda
  To a Daughter Leaving Home, 686
Pasture, The, 870
Pennington, Michael
  Hamlet's Madness, 1608
perhaps (#5), 1085
Petit, the Poet, 714
Petrarca, Francesco
  Love's Inconsistency, 765
Pied Beauty, 973
"Pig's-Eye View of Literature, A," from, 778
Pillow Talk, 30
Pirandello, Luigi
  War, 538
Plath, Sylvia
  Daddy, 991
  Metaphors, 742
  Morning Song, 991
Plum, Sydney
  Reading "The Veil" by Marjane Satrapi, 570
Poe, Edgar Allan
  The Cask of Amontillado, 543
  The Fall of the House of Usher, 548
  The Importance of the Single Effect in a Prose Tale, 650
Poe's Art of Transformation in "The Cask of Amontillado," 662
Poetry (Moore), 669
Poetry (Neruda), 670
Poison Tree, A, 938
Polite, Allen
  Song, 1049
Pond, Porch-View, The: Six P.M., Early Spring, 960
POOF!, 1582
Pool, The, 793

Pops, 1590
Popular Mechanics, 28
Pound, Ezra
In a Station of the Metro, 795
On the Principles of Imagism, 818
The River-Merchant's Wife: A Letter, 802
What I Feel about Walt Whitman, 1007
Precisely, 1041

Quinceañera, 814

Raisin in the Sun, A, 1507
Rampersad, Arnold
Langston Hughes as Folk Poet, 906
Randall, Dudley
Ballad of Birmingham, 1048
Reading "The Veil" by Marjane Satrapi, 570
Recognition, 813
Red Badge of Courage, The, from, 1062
Red Wheelbarrow, The, 798
Reed, Lou
Chelsea Girls, 708
Remember, 842
Repossessed, 1083
Résumé, 1086
Review of *Hamlet*, 1605
Review of "Leaves of Grass," A, 1006
Revolutionary Letter #3, 1078
Reynolds, David S.
Poe's Art of Transformation in "The Cask of Amontillado," 662
Rich, Adrienne
Aunt Jennifer's Tigers, 994
Diving into the Wreck, 994
Richard Cory, 729
Richardson, James
"Vectors: Five Hundred Aphorisms and Ten-Second Essays," from, 779
Rites for Cousin Vit, The, 769
River-Merchant's Wife, The: A Letter, 802
Road Not Taken, The, 877
Robinson, Edwin Arlington
Eros Tyrannos, 867
Miniver Cheevy, 728
Richard Cory, 729
Rocking-Horse Winner, The, 375
Rodríguez, Luis J.
Carrying My Tools, 817
Roethke, Theodore
Elegy for Jane, 762
My Papa's Waltz, 706
Romanesque Arches, 912
Rose for Emily, A, 217
Rossetti, Christina
A Birthday, 782
Remember, 842
"Sing-Song," from, 842
What are heavy? sea-sand and sorrow, 719
Rotella, Alexis
Just friends, 807
Rumens, Carol
This Be the Verse, 832
Russell, Willy
Educating Rita, from, 1122

Saboteur, 308
Sad Guitar, 946
Samuel, 11, 17
Sanchez, Edwin
Pops, 1590
Sandburg, Carl
Grass, 728
Sanders, Edward
After a Year of Isolation, 1080
Sandpiper, 929
San Joaquin Valley Poems: 1969, from, 1066
Satrapi, Marjane
The Veil, from *Persepolis*, 563
Savageau, Cheryl
Department of Labor Haiku, 807
Say Yes, 632
Schubertiana, 913
Second Coming, The, 1028
Sestina, 770
Sexton, Anne
The Fortress, 810
An Obsessive Combination of Ontological Inscape, Trickery and Love, 998
And One for My Dame, 706
Pain for a Daughter, 998
To a Friend Whose Work Has Come to Triumph, 998
Sex without Love, 988

Shakespeare, William
Hamlet, Prince of Denmark, 1244
A Midsummer Night's Dream, 1187
That time of year thou mayst in me behold, 763
Tomorrow, and tomorrow, and tomorrow, 772
Shaw, George Bernard
On *A Doll House,* 1403
Shelley, Percy Bysshe
"A Defence of Poetry," from, 787
Ode to the West Wind, 756
Ozymandias, 767
Shiki, Masaoka
Night and again, 806
A thawed pond, 806
Shiloh, 1062
Short, J. D.
Slidin' Delta, 710
Showalter, Elaine
On Glaspell's "A Jury of Her Peers," 258
Sick Rose, The, 937
Silko, Leslie Marmon
Yellow Woman, 572
since feeling is first, 684
"Sincerity and Inventions: On Robert Frost," from, 882
Singsong, 960
"Sing-Song," from, 842
Sinking of the *Commodore,* The, 196
Sitting with my father, 806
Skunk Hour, 981
Sky Lark, The, 1032
Sleeping in the Forest, 1034
Slidin' Delta, 710
Small Presses and Little Magazines, The: A Few Reflections, 1082
Smith, Joan Jobe
The Carol Burnett Show, 1087
Feminist Arm Candy for the Mafia and Sinatra, 1056
Smith, Stevie
Not Waving but Drowning, 699
Smooth Talk: Short Story into Film, 464
So It Goes, 1089
Something Like a Sonnet for Phillis Miracle Wheatley, 769
somewhere i have never travelled, 953
Song, 1049
Song for a Dark Girl, 902
Song of Changgan, A, 801
"Song of Hiawatha, The," from, 718
"Song of Myself," from, 1004
"Songs of Experience," Introduction from, 936
"Songs of Innocence," Introduction from, 934
Sonny's Blues, 99
Sophocles
Oedipus the King, 1129
Soto, Gary
Mexicans Begin Jogging, 1000
Oranges, 101
Waiting at the Curb: Lynwood, California, 1967, 1002
"Souls of Black Folk, The," from, 890
Sources of Shakespeare's *Hamlet,* 1594
Southern Sources of "A Good Man Is Hard to Find," 647
Southwick, Marcia
A Star Is Born in the Eagle Nebula, 812
sparrow chirps, The, 806
Spiess, Robert
an aging willow—, 806
Spirit of '76, 1012
Spring and All, 1009
Star Is Born in the Eagle Nebula, A, 812
Steinbeck, John
The Chrysanthemums, 581
stereo, 1039
Stevens, Wallace
Thirteen Ways of Looking at a Blackbird, 798
Stone, Ruth
In an Iridescent Time, 1037
Stop All the Clocks, 926
Stoppard, Tom
Dogg's Hamlet: The Encore, 1598
Stopping by Woods on a Snowy Evening, 879
Story of an Hour, The, 174
Strindberg, August
The Stronger, 1096, 1103
Stronger, The, 1096, 1103
Success is counted sweetest, 842
summer grass, The, 805
Summer Storm, 707
Sunflower Sutra, 1073

Sun Rising, The, 957
Sunset in the Tropics, 1046
Superman and Me, 85
Supermarket in California, A, 833
Sweat, 278
Sympathy, 1046

Tan, Amy
  Two Kinds, 590
Tate, James
  Like It or Not, We Are a Part of Our Time, 679
Technique in Writing the Short Story, 168
Templeton, Joan
  Is *A Doll House* a Feminist Text?, 1405
Tenebris, 896
Tennyson, Alfred, Lord
  Ulysses, 783
That time of year thou mayst in me behold, 763
thawed pond, A, 806
Theology, 1045
There's a certain Slant of light, 847
They Flee from Me, 702
Things I Can Know, 1086
Things They Carried, The, 468
Things Thrown Away, 1084
Thirteen Ways of Looking at a Blackbird, 798
This Be the Verse (Larkin), 832
This Be the Verse (Rumens), 832
"This Is the Beat Generation," from, 1069
Thomas, Dylan
  Do Not Go Gentle into That Good Night, 771
  The last time I slept with the Queen, 779
Thomas, Edward
  Early One Morning, 869
Thoreau, Henry David
  "It is difficult to begin without borrowing . . . ," 1031
Those Winter Sundays, 1047
Thou Art Indeed Just, Lord, 973
To a Daughter Leaving Home, 686
To a Friend Whose Work Has Come to Triumph, 998
Toast to Harlem, A, 903
To Autumn, 738
To Build a Fire, 387
Today, 952
today is a day of great joy, 679
To Earthward, 878
To His Coy Mistress, 780
Tomorrow, and tomorrow, and tomorrow, 772
to ms. ann, 1051
To My Dear and Loving Husband, 940
Toomer, Jean
  Cane, lyrics from, 897
To the Virgins, to Make Much of Time, 703
To Waken an Old Lady, 737
Tranströmer, Tomas
  Allegro, 912
  Beginning of the Late Autumn Night's Novel, 913
  March '79, 915
  On Poetry, 915
  Romanesque Arches, 912
  Schubertiana, 913
Tranströmer and the "Other Side" of Consciousness, 918
Tranströmer's Style, 917
Trifles, 1410
Tropics in New York, The, 896
Two Kinds, 590
Tyger, The, 937

Ullmann, Liv
  On Performing Nora in Ibsen's *A Doll House*, 1407
Ulysses, 783
Undergoing the Cure for Nervous Prostration, 238
Untermeyer, Louis
  A "book of people," 866
Updike, John
  A & P, 599
Upon Westminster Bridge, Sept. 3, 1802, 766
Use of Force, The, 628

Valediction: Forbidding Mourning, A, 956
"Vectors: Five Hundred Aphorisms and Ten-Second Essays," from, 779
Veil, The, from *Persepolis*, 563
Vendler, Helen
  Tranströmer and the "Other Side" of Consciousness, 918

Very Old Man with Enormous Wings, A, 51
Vonnegut, Kurt, Jr.
  Harrison Bergeron, 604
Voss, Fred
  How Many Times Can We Follow Dante Down Into Hell?, 676
  I Once Needed a Chance Too, 1057

Waiting at the Curb: Lynwood, California, 1967, 1002
Waldman, Anne
  stereo, 1039
Walker, Alice
  Everyday Use, 610
  I Said to Poetry, 677
  Zora Neale Hurston: A Cautionary Tale and a Partisan View, 616
Walker, J.
  On T. S. Eliot's "Prufrock," 780
Wallace, David Foster
  Everything Is Green, 58
War, 538
War Is Kind, 1063
Warren, Robert Penn
  A New Critical Reading of "The Fall of the House of Usher," 656
  On Eliot's "The Love Song of J. Alfred Prufrock," 965
Webster, Ed
  San Joaquin Valley Poems: 1969, from, 1066
Welty, Eudora
  Is Phoenix Jackson's Grandson Really Dead?, 625
  A Worn Path, 619
We Real Cool, 942
Western wind, when wilt thou blow, 683
What are heavy? sea-sand and sorrow, 719
What I Feel about Walt Whitman, 1007
What lips my lips have kissed, and where, and why, 768
Wheatley, Phillis
  On Being Brought from Africa to America, 1045
when god lets my body be, 705
When I have fears, 979
When last I saw thee, I did not thee see, 765
When our two souls stand up erect and strong, 841
Where Are You Going, Where Have You Been?, 452
Whirlwind Man Steals Yellow Woman, 579
White Heron, A, 300
White Horse, The, 796
Whitman, Walt
  A Farm Picture, 695
  On the Beach at Night Alone, 1033
  A Review of *Leaves of Grass*, 1006
  "Song of Myself," from, 1004
Widow's Lament in Springtime, The, 1011
Wilbur, Richard
  On Emily Dickinson, 859
Wild Iris, The, 742
Wild Nights—Wild Nights!, 846
Wild Swans at Coole, The, 1028
Williams, William Carlos
  Danse Russe, 1010
  "March," from, 1011
  The Red Wheelbarrow, 798
  Spirit of '76, 1012
  Spring and All, 1009
  To Waken an Old Lady, 737
  The Use of Force, 628
  The Widow's Lament in Springtime, 1011
Windhover, The, 972
Wojahn, David
  On Political Poetry, 1053
Wolff, Tobias
  Say Yes, 632
Woman in the Long, Dark Raincoat, The: A Poetry Reading with Sharon Olds, 989
Woman's Last Word, A, 704
Wood, Eve
  Recognition, 813
word is dead, A, 693
Wordsworth, William
  I Wandered Lonely as a Cloud, 782
  Lyrical Ballads, from the Introduction to, 1019
  Ode, 1013
  Upon Westminster Bridge, Sept. 3, 1802, 766
  The world is too much with us, 1019
Workday, 32

world is too much with us, The, 1019
Worn Path, A, 619
Wright, Charles
After Reading Tu Fu, I Go Outside to the Dwarf Orchard, 803
Wright, James
A Blessing, 1024
Evening, 1023
Lying in a Hammock at William Duffy's Farm in Pine Island, Minnesota, 1025
The Music of Robert Frost's "Stopping by Woods on a Snowy Evening," 885
Writing Short Stories, 639
Wroth, Mary
When last I saw thee, I did not thee see, 765
Wyatt, Thomas
They Flee from Me, 702

Yeats, William Butler
The Lake Isle of Innisfree, 1027
The Second Coming, 1028
The Wild Swans at Coole, 1028
Yellow Wallpaper, The, 226
Yellow Woman, 572
Yet Do I Marvel, 768
You love me—you are sure—, 845
Young Goodman Brown, 261

Zamora, Daisy
Precisely, 1041
Zora Neale Hurston: A Cautionary Tale and a Partisan View, 616

RESOURCES FOR READING AND

CHAPTERS ON READING AND WRITING

Introduction: Connecting with Literature p. 1

2. Reading, Thinking, and Writing about Short Fiction p. 14
9. Reading, Thinking, and Writing about Poetry p. 681
22. Reading, Thinking, and Writing about Drama p. 1101
26. Critical Reading and Literary Theory p. 1613
27. Using the Writing Process to Develop Your Paper p. 1623
28. Basic Types of Literary Papers p. 1642
29. Writing Research Papers p. 1654

GUIDELINES FOR READING AND WRITING

Guidelines for Reading Fiction p. 16

Guidelines for Reading Poetry p. 686

Guidelines for Reading Drama p. 1102

Guidelines for Writing a Paper about Literature p. 1640

SAMPLE CLOSE READING

FICTION

Sample Close Reading: Grace Paley, "Samuel" p. 17

POETRY

Sample Close Reading: Linda Pastan, "To a Daughter Leaving Home" p. 686

DRAMA

Sample Close Reading: August Strindberg, *The Stronger* p. 1103

QUESTIONS FOR CRITICAL THINKING

Questions for Critical Thinking about Plot p. 29

Questions for Critical Thinking about Point of View p. 37

Questions for Critical Thinking about Character p. 43

Questions for Critical Thinking about Setting p. 50

Questions for Critical Thinking about Style p. 68

Questions for Critical Thinking about Theme p. 76

Questions for Critical Thinking about Drama p. 1124

SAMPLE PAPERS

SAMPLE RESPONSE PAPERS

Raymond Carver's "Creative Writing 101" p. 2

"Every Pane Stays Whole": The Sustaining Power of Art in Tranströmer's Poetry p. 922

A Reader's Response to the Opening Lines of Strindberg's *The Stronger* p. 1107